British Companies Legislation

COMPANIES ACT 1985

INSOLVENCY ACT 1986

COMPANIES ACT 1989

and Related Legislation

5th Edition

Volume

CCH Editions Limited
TAX, BUSINESS AND LAW PUBLISHERS
Telford Road, Bicester
Oxfordshire OX6 0XD
Phone: Bicester (0869) 253300
Facsimile No.: Bicester (0869) 245814
DX: 40162 Bicester

About the Publisher

CCH Editions Limited is part of a world-wide group of companies that specialises in tax and business law publishing. The group produces a wide range of books and reporting services for the accounting, business and legal professions. The Oxfordshire premises are the centre for all UK and European operations.

All CCH publications are designed to provide practical, authoritative reference works and useful guides, and are written by CCH's highly qualified and experienced editorial team and specialist outside authors.

CCH Editions Limited publishes bound books and loose-leaf reporting services for the UK and other European countries, as well as distributing the publications of its overseas affiliate companies.

Disclaimer

This publication is designed to provide accurate and authoritative information in regard to the subject matter covered. It is sold with the understanding that the publisher is not engaged in rendering legal or other professional service. If legal advice or other expert assistance is required, the services of a competent professional person should be sought.

The publisher advises that the legislation in this publication is not the authorised official version. In its preparation, however, the greatest care has been taken to ensure exact conformity with the law as enacted.

While copyright in all the legislation resides in the Crown, copyright in any indexes, annotations and tables of destinations relating to that legislation and in the table to the Companies Act 1989 is vested in the publisher.

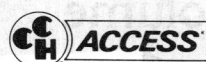 
ISBN 0 86325 247 8
ISSN 0268-9588

First Edition, July 1985
  Revised impression, August 1985
Second Edition, June 1986

Third Edition, April 1987
Fourth Edition, August 1988
Fifth Edition, September 1990

Introduction

The fifth edition of *British Companies Legislation* comprises two volumes. It contains the full text of the following eight main statutes:

the *Companies Act* 1985;

the *Business Names Act* 1985;

the *Company Securities (Insider Dealing) Act* 1985;

the *Companies Consolidation (Consequential Provisions) Act* 1985;

the *Insolvency Act* 1986;

the *Company Directors Disqualification Act* 1986;

the *Financial Services Act* 1986; and

the *Companies Act* 1989.

The first four of the above statutes represent the consolidation of the Companies Acts 1948 to 1983 and operate from 1 July 1985. Tables of derivations for each of the 1985 statutes appear at pages 36,501, 40,002, 43,004 and 44,704 respectively. At page 36,623 there is a detailed CCH table of destinations relating each provision of the former legislation to the corresponding provision in the consolidated legislation. The *Companies Act* 1985 has been significantly amended by the *Companies Act* 1989 (see below).

The *Insolvency Act* 1986 and the *Company Directors Disqualification Act* 1986 are the consolidation of the *Insolvency Act* 1985 with over two hundred sections of the *Companies Act* 1985 relating to receivership and companies winding up. The *Insolvency Act* 1985 represented the most comprehensive review of corporate and individual insolvency in more than a century. Provisions in that Act relating to disqualification and personal liability of directors and others came into force on 28 April 1986 — the only substantive provisions of the 1985 Act ever to come into force.

The *Insolvency Act* 1986 and the *Company Directors Disqualification Act* 1986 received Royal Assent on 25 July 1986 and came into force, together with a number of rules and regulations (see below), on 29 December 1986. All the substantive provisions on insolvency — including the disqualification and personal liability provisions referred to above — are now to be found in these two 1986 statutes.

However, although the *Insolvency Act* 1985 has been superseded by the 1986 statutes, it made many amendments to other legislation. These commenced operation throughout 1986, the last of them immediately before the 1986 consolidated legislation which itself included still more amendments. All such amendments to legislation in this publication have been included where relevant as have the five commencement orders to the *Insolvency Act* 1985 (see pages 83,562, 83,572, 83,593, 83,633 and 84,472). It is to be noted that the commencement date of the two 1986 Acts is tied to the last available commencement date for the *Insolvency Act* 1985 (see IA 1986, sec. 443, CDDA 1986, sec. 25 and S.I. 1986 No. 1924 (C. 71)).

Tables of derivations for the two 1986 Acts appear at pages 58,001 and 59,802 while a CCH table of destinations, linking relevant provisions of the *Companies Act* 1985 and the *Insolvency Act* 1985 to these current two 1986 Acts is at page 58,201.

The *Financial Services Act* 1986 received Royal Assent on 7 November 1986 and set up the new system of self-regulation intended to give greater protection to both private and professional investors. The Act's key provision is sec. 3 which came into force on 29 April 1988 (the so-called "A-Day") and makes it an offence to carry on investment business without authorisation or exemption. The Financial Services Act has made a large number of amendments to companies legislation. Because of this close relationship with much of the legislation in this book it has been included in full text together with commencement orders in a separate division. Operative amendments from the Act are included throughout the publication. There are also many amendments to the Act by the *Companies Act* 1989 (see below).

As at the time of writing 12 commencement orders to the Financial Services Act have appeared. However there remain a number of provisions not yet (fully) in force. On 12 July 1990 the Department of Trade and Industry published proposals for new regulations governing offers of unlisted securities. These proposals, if enacted, would implement Pt. V of the Financial Services Act and EC Directive 89/298 concerning the prospectus to be published when transferable securities are offered to the public. The proposals would also make some changes to the arrangements governing offers of listed securities. Part V will ultimately replace the existing provisions of Pt. III of the *Companies Act* 1985 relating to prospectuses. Since February 1987 offers of listed securities have been governed by Pt. IV of the 1986 Act and the International Stock Exchange's Yellow Book. The Department is seeking comments on the draft proposals by mid-September 1990 and the new provisions may well come into force in 1991.

The last statute in the above list, the *Companies Act* 1989, is reproduced in an appendix in Volume 2. It is a most significant statute, being the first non-consolidating Act devoted primarily to company law for over eight years. It could be described as the most reforming Companies Act for over 40 years.

The *Companies Act* 1989 received Royal Assent on 16 November 1989 after a protracted passage through Parliament. It has 216 sections and 24 Schedules and contains provisions amending the law in regard to company accounts, regulation of auditors, investigations and powers to obtain information, registration of company charges, mergers, financial markets and insolvency and the transfer of securities. There are also many provisions which effect miscellaneous amendments to company law, including the reform of the ultra vires rule, and numerous amendments to the *Financial Services Act* 1986.

Only a small number of provisions of the 1989 Act came into force on Royal Assent (see sec. 215 for details). Since then there have been five commencement orders which have brought into force a great range of provisions, including many of those making amendments to the *Companies Act* 1985 and the *Financial Services Act* 1986. These orders contain relevant transitional and saving provisions. See pages 86,134, 86,171, 86,193 and 86,423 where the orders are reproduced in full. At the time of writing, publication of a sixth commencement order is imminent and further commencement orders are anticipated to bring provisions into force well into 1991. Many of the new provisions of the 1989 Act require supporting regulations and some of these have been issued to date (see below). The text of the 1989 Act is reproduced in full in an appendix as it is not yet fully in force and included with it are a separate index (see page 90,101) and a useful CCH table relating provisions in the new Act to the provisions of relevant statutues it affects (see page 90,151).

The last division in Volume 1 contains relevant provisions of ancillary acts — see page 65,001ff. Included amongst these are various Finance Act provisions, the *Partnership Act* 1890, the *Limited Partnership Act* 1907, the Stock Transfer Acts and provisions of such statutes as the *Theft Act* 1968, the *Fair Trading Act* 1973, the *Employment Protection (Consolidation) Act* 1978 and the *Criminal Justice Act* 1987 (relating to the Serious Fraud Office).

Volume 2 of the fifth edition contains the *Insolvency Rules* 1986 and other subordinate legislation as well as the appendix already referred to with the *Companies Act* 1989, its index and table.

The *Insolvency Rules* 1986 are reproduced in full text at page 75,001ff. They are the most significant piece of subordinate legislation under the *Insolvency Act* 1986 as they provide the procedural gloss to the framework of the Act. Like the Act, they operate from 29 December 1986. There have been two sets of amendments to the Rules and these amendments have been included at appropriate places.

The "Rules and Regulations" division in Volume 2 contains a variety of other subordinate legislation including that remade in light of the 1985 companies legislation and like it operative from 1 July 1985. Amongst these are the *Companies (Tables A to F) Regulations* 1985 which include the revised form of Table A articles of association. The former Table A (as contained in the First Schedule to the now repealed *Companies Act* 1948) is reproduced after the 1985 Regulations as it is still relevant for many companies incorporated before 1 July 1985.

The "Rules and Regulations" division also contains subordinate legislation other than the Insolvency Rules (see above) which is relevant for the *Insolvency Act* 1986 and the *Company Directors Disqualification Act* 1986, including that relating specifically to Scotland. The division has two sets of regulations relating to European Economic Interest Groupings, three recent orders under the *Company Securities (Insider Dealing) Act* 1985, important 1990 statutory instruments including several made in light of amended provisions from the *Companies Act* 1989 and amendments to four statutory instruments prescribing fees (see pages 83,552, 84,933, 85,872 and 86,091). As already noted, the first five commencement orders to the *Companies Act* 1989 are reproduced here.

Throughout the statutes and the various rules and regulations, repealed or revoked provisions and some amending provisions have been omitted. In the case of certain more recent repeals and amendments history notes have been inserted to indicate the previous wording. Additional notes have also been included referring to other relevant provisions, and to incidental matters.

The publisher advises that the legislation in this fifth edition is not the authorised version. In its preparation, however, the greatest care has been taken to ensure exact conformity with the law as enacted. Some changes in printing style have been adopted for convenience and to improve readability. For example, marginal notes appearing in the official statutes have been reproduced in bold type above the section to which they relate. CCH has also added its own subsection notes in square brackets, thus [   ].

A number of indexes are included in Volume 1. A comprehensive Index to Statutes commences at page 1,101. The index references are to provisions of the *Companies Act* 1985 except where they show prefix letters as explained on page 1,003. The Index to Statutes is followed on page 2,101 by an Index to Regulations. There is a separate Index to *Insolvency Rules* 1986 at page 2,201.

CCH Editions Limited
August 1990

Important: Stop Press

Just as the fifth edition of *British Companies Legislation* was going to press four important relevant statutory instruments were published:

- the *Companies Act 1989 (Commencement No. 6 and Transitional and Saving Provisions) Order* 1990 (S.I. 1990 No. 1392 (C. 41));
- the *Companies (Fair Dealing by Directors) (Increase in Financial Limits) Order* 1990 (S.I. 1990 No. 1393);
- the *Companies (Unregistered Companies) (Amendment No. 2) Regulations* 1990 (S.I. 1990 No. 1394); and
- the *Financial Services Act 1986 (Restriction of Scope of Act and Meaning of Collective Investment Scheme) (No. 2) Order* 1990 (S.I. 1990 No. 1493).

The statutory instruments are reproduced below. Note that they are not covered or referred to in the main body of the publication — they will be covered in a subsequent edition.

THE COMPANIES ACT 1989 (COMMENCEMENT NO. 6 AND TRANSITIONAL AND SAVING PROVISIONS) ORDER 1990

(S.I. 1990 No. 1392 (C. 41))

Made on 9 July 1990 by the Secretary of State for Trade and Industry under sec. 215(2), (3) and (4) of the Companies Act 1989.

CITATION

1 This Order may be cited as the Companies Act 1989 (Commencement No. 6 and Transitional and Saving Provisions) Order 1990.

PROVISIONS OF THE COMPANIES ACT 1989 COMMENCED BY THIS ORDER

2 In Part V of the Companies Act 1989:—

    (a) section 129 shall come into force on 1st November 1990;

    (b) section 130 and Schedule 17 shall come into force on 31st July 1990;

    (c) section 138 shall come into force on 31st July 1990 subject to the saving provision set out in article 5 below; and

    (d) section 144 and Schedule 18 shall come into force on 1st November 1990, subject to the transitional provisions set out in article 6 below.

3 Part IX of the Companies Act 1989 shall come into force on 1st November 1990.

4 Part X of the Companies Act 1989:—

    (a) section 211(2), subject to the saving provision set out in article 7 below, and section 211(3) shall come into force on 31st July 1990; and

    (b) the repeals effected by Schedule 24 in or of:

        (i) section 651(1) and Schedule 22 (in so far as Schedule 24 effects a repeal of the entry relating to section 36(4)) of the Companies Act 1985; and

        (ii) Schedules 15 and 18 to the Building Societies Act 1986.

    together with section 212 so far as relating to those repeals, shall come into force on 31st July 1990.

SAVING PROVISION RELATING TO SECTION 138 OF THE COMPANIES ACT 1989

5 For the avoidance of doubt, section 345(3) of the Companies Act 1985 shall apply to section 138 of the Companies Act 1989 as it applies to an order made under section 345 of the Companies Act 1985.

TRANSITIONAL PROVISIONS RELATING TO SECTION 144 OF THE COMPANIES ACT 1989

6(1) The new section 736 of the Companies Act 1985, inserted by section 144(1) of the Companies Act 1989 shall not have effect for the purposes of the provisions of the unamended Companies Act 1985 continued in force by paragraph 13 of Part II of Schedule 2 and paragraph 3 of Schedule 3 to the Companies Act 1989 (Commencement No. 4 and Transitional and Saving Provisions) Order 1990 and section 736 of the unamended Companies Act 1985 shall continue to apply for the purposes of those provisions.

6(2) The new section 736 of the Companies Act 1985, inserted by section 144(1) of the Companies Act 1989 shall not have effect, and section 736 of the unamended Companies Act 1985 shall continue to apply, for the purposes of the statutory provisions amended by paragraphs 26 to 30 and 33 of Schedule 10 to the Companies Act 1989, if the new section 736 would otherwise apply to those provisions as a consequence of paragraph 1 of Schedule 3 to the Companies Act 1989 (Commencement No. 4 and Transitional and Saving Provisions) Order 1990.

6(3) The new section 736, inserted by section 144(l) of the Companies Act 1989 shall, until 1st January 1993, not have effect for the purposes of Part VIII of the Building Societies Act 1986 and the provisions of that Part shall have effect, until that date, as if section 144 of the Companies Act 1989 had not been passed.

6(4) For the purposes of this paragraph **"the unamended Companies Act 1985"** means that Act prior to its amendment by the provisions of the Companies Act 1989.

SAVING PROVISION RELATING TO SECTION 211 OF THE COMPANIES ACT 1989

7 Where an individual was appointed to act as an insolvency practitioner in relation to a building society within the meaning of the Building Societies Act 1986 before the commencement of subsection 211(2)(a) of the Companies Act 1989, the application of subsections (2) and (3) of section 390 of the Insolvency Act 1986 effected by the amendments made by subsection 211(2)(a) shall not prevent that individual from being qualified to act as an insolvency practitioner pursuant to that appointment for the purposes of Part XIII of the Insolvency Act 1986.

AMENDMENT OF THE COMPANIES ACT 1985

8 The section 23 inserted by section 129 of the Companies Act 1989 into the Companies Act 1985 shall be amended, with effect from 1st November 1990, as follows:

(a) in sub-section (4)(b), the words "1st November 1990" shall be substituted for the words "the commencement of section 129 of the Companies Act 1989"; and

(b) in sub-sections (4) and (5), the words "1st November 1990" shall be substituted for the words "the commencement of that section" where they appear in those subsections.

EXPLANATORY NOTE

(This Note is not part of the Order)

This Order brings into force certain of the provisions of the Companies Act 1989.

Article 2 of this Order commences, in Part V of the 1989 Act, sections 129 (Membership of holding company), 130 together with Schedule 17 (Company contracts and execution of documents by companies), 138 (Increase of limits on certain exemptions in Part X of the Companies Act 1985) and section 144 together with Schedule 18 (new definitions of "subsidiary", "holding company" and "wholly-owned subsidiary"). Sections 129 and 144, together with Schedule 18, come into force on 1st November 1990 whilst sections 130 and 138 and Schedule 17 come into force on 31st July 1990.

Section 138 is commenced subject to a saving provision with respect to past events, which is set out in article 5 of the Order.

Section 144 and Schedule 18 are commenced subject to transitional provisions set out in article 6 of the Order. Those provisions, in outline, preserve the pre-existing definitions of "subsidiary", "holding company" and "wholly-owned subsidiary" for the purposes of the accounts of companies and certain other bodies for financial years commencing prior to 23rd December 1989 (in relation to which the Companies Act 1989 (Commencement No. 4 and Transitional and Saving Provisions) Order 1990 largely preserves the pre-1989 Act law on the content of accounts).

Article 3 of this Order brings into force Part IX of the Companies Act 1989 on 1st November 1990. Part IX enables provision to be made by Regulations for title to securities to be evidenced and transferred without a written instrument.

Article 4 of this Order brings into force on 31st July 1990 section 211(2) and (3) (Building Societies: miscellaneous amendments) and certain repeals effected by Schedule 24 and section 212. Section 211(2) and (3) are commenced subject to a saving provision set out in article 7 of the Order.

Article 8 of this Order inserts a reference to the actual date of commencement of section 129 of the 1989 Act into the new section 23 of the Companies Act 1985 inserted by that former section.

NOTE AS TO EARLIER COMMENCEMENT ORDERS

(*This Note is not part of the Order*)

The following provisions of the Companies Act 1989 have been brought into force by commencement order made before the date of this Order:

Provision	Date of Commencement	S.I. No.
Ss. 1 and 15 but only for the purpose of inserting a new section 251 into the Companies Act 1985 (subject to certain transitional and saving provisions)	1.3.1990	S.I. 1990/142
The remaining provisions of Part I (subject to important transitional and saving provisions) other than section 7 (in so far as it inserts a new section 233(5) into the Companies Act 1985), 11 (in so far as it inserts a new section 242A into the Companies Act 1985), 12 and 23 (in part).	1.4.1990 (save paragraph 19 of Schedule 10 which is commenced on 1.8.1990)	S.I. 1990/355
S.24 but only for the purposes of any provision brought into force by article 3 of S.I. 1990/142	1.3.1990	S.I. 1990/142
S. 30	1.3.1990	S.I. 1990/142
S. 31 but only for purposes relating to the recognition of supervisory bodies under Schedule 11 to the Companies Act 1989 ("the 1989 Act") and for the purpose of enabling the Secretary of State to approve a qualification under section 31(4) and (5) of the 1989 Act	1.3.1990	S.I. 1990/142
Ss. 32 and 33	1.3.1990	S.I. 1990/142
Ss. 37 to 40	1.3.1990	S.I. 1990/142
S. 41(1) and (4) but only for the purposes of an application under any provision brought into force by article 3 of S.I. 1990/142 or of any requirement imposed under any such provision	1.3.1990	S.I. 1990/142
S. 41(3)	1.3.1990	S.I. 1990/142
S. 41(5) and (6) but only for the purposes of S. 41(3) of the 1989 Act	1.3.1990	S.I. 1990/142
Ss. 42 to 44 but only for the purposes of any provision brought into force by article 3 of S.I. 1990/142	1.3.1990	S.I. 1990/142
S. 45	1.3.1990	S.I. 1990/142
S.47(1)	1.3.1990	S.I. 1990/142
S. 48(1) and (2)	1.3.1990	S.I. 1990/142
S. 49 but only for the purposes of any provision brought into force by article 3 of S.I. 1990/142	1.3.1990	S.I. 1990/142
Ss. 50 and 51	1.3.1990	S.I. 1990/142
Ss. 52 to 54 but only for the purposes of any provision brought into force by article 3 of S.I. 1990/142	1.3.1990	S.I. 1990/142

Provision	Date of Commencement	S.I. No.
Ss. 55 to 64	21.2.1990	S.I. 1990/142
S. 65(1)	21.2.1990	S.I. 1990/142
S. 65(2) except to the extent that it refers to Part VII of the 1989 Act and except, in the case of s. 65(2)(g), to the extent that the said paragraph refers to a body established under s. 46 of the 1989 Act	21.2.1990	S.I. 1990/142
S. 65(3) to (7)	21.2.1990	S.I. 1990/142
S. 66 to 74	21.2.1990	S.I. 1990/142
S. 75(1)	21.2.1990	S.I. 1990/142
S. 75(2)	25.1.1990	S.I. 1990/98
S. 75(3), insofar as it provides for the insertion in s. 180(1) of the Financial Services Act 1986 of a new paragraph (00)	25.1.1990	S.I. 1990/98
S. 75(3) except insofar as brought into force as referred to above, except to the extent that it refers to Part VII of the 1989 Act and except, in the case of s. 75(3)(c), to the extent that it refers to a body established by order under s. 46 of the 1989 Act.	21.2.1990	S.I. 1990/142
S. 75(4) insofar as it provides a definition of "public servant" for the purposes of the new s. 180(1) (00) of the Financial Services Act 1986	25.1.1990	S.I. 1990/98
S. 75(4) except insofar as brought into force as referred to above	21.2.1990	S.I. 1990/142
S. 75(6)	21.2.1990	S.I. 1990/142
S. 75(7)	25.1.1990	S.I. 1990/98
Ss. 76 to 79	21.2.1990	S.I. 1990/142
S. 80 except to the extent that it refers to Part VII of the 1989 Act	21.2.1990	S.I. 1990/142
S. 81(1)	21.2.1990	S.I. 1990/142
S. 81(2) except to the extent that it refers to Part VII of the 1989 Act	21.2.1990	S.I. 1990/142
S. 81(3) and (4)	21.2.1990	S.I. 1990/142
S. 81(5) except to the extent that it refers to Part VII of the 1989 Act	21.2.1990	S.I. 1990/142
Ss. 82 to 86	21.2.1990	S.I. 1990/142
S. 87(1) to (3)	21.2.1990	S.I. 1990/142
S. 87(4) except to the extent that it refers to Part VII of the 1989 Act	21.2.1990	S.I. 1990/142
S. 87(5) and (6)	21.2.1990	S.I. 1990/142
Ss. 88 to 91	21.2.1990	S.I. 1990/142

Provision	Date of Commencement	S.I. No.
Sections 113 to 124 (subject to transitional and saving provisions)	1.4.1990	S.I. 1990/355
Sections 131 and 132 (subject, in the case of the former, a saving provision)	1.4.1990	S.I. 1990/355
Section 134(1) to (3), (5) and (6) (subject to certain provisions)	31.5.1990	S.I. 1990/713
Section 136 (subject to a transitional provision)	1.4.1990	S.I. 1990/355
Section 137(1); section 137(2) in part (subject to a transitional provision)	1.4.1990	S.I. 1990/355
S. 145 but only insofar as it relates to paragraphs 1, 8, 9, 12, 19 and 21 of Schedule 19 to the 1989 Act	1.3.1990	S.I. 1990/142
S. 145 but only insofar as it relates to paragraphs 15 to 18 of Schedule 19 to the 1989 Act	1.4.1990	S.I. 1990/355
S. 146	1.4.1990	S.I. 1990/142
S. 151	1.4.1990	S.I. 1990/142
S. 152	1.3.1990	S.I. 1990/142
S. 153 but only insofar as it relates to paragraphs 1, 13, 17, 21 and 26 of Schedule 20 to the 1989 Act	1.4.1990	S.I. 1990/142
S. 192 insofar as it inserts section 47A into the Financial Services Act 1986 (subject to transitional and saving provisions)	15.3.1990	S.I. 1990/354
S. 193 insofar as is necessary in order to enable regulations to be made under section 62A of, and paragraph 22A of Schedule 11 to, the Financial Services Act 1986 (subject to transitional and saving provisions)	15.3.1990	S.I. 1990/354
Sections 194 to 200 (subject to transitional and saving provisions)	15.3.1990	S.I. 1990/354
Sections 203 to 205 (subject to transitional and saving provisions)	15.3.1990	S.I. 1990/354
S. 206(1) except in so far as it relates to the insertion by paragraph 32 of Schedule 23 to the 1989 Act of paragraph 13B into Schedule 11 of the Financial Services Act 1986 (subject to transitional and saving provisions)	15.3.1990	S.I. 1990/354
S. 206(2) to (4) (subject to transitional and saving provisions)	15.3.1990	S.I. 1990/354
S. 208	1.3.1990	S.I. 1990/142
S. 209	21.2.1990	S.I. 1990/142
S. 210	1.4.1990	S.I. 1990/142

Provision	Date of Commencement	S.I. No.
S. 212 insofar as it relates to the repeals effected by Schedule 24 to the 1989 Act referred to below	On the dates referred to below in connection with Schedule 24	In the SIs listed below in connection with Schedule 24
Schedule 24 insofar as it relates to repeals in or of ss. 435, 440, 443, 446, 447, 449, 452 and 735A of the Companies Act 1985, ss. 94, 105, 179, 180, 198(1) and 199(9) of the Financial Services Act 1986 and s. 84(1) of the Banking Act 1987	21.2.1990	S.I. 1990/142
Schedule 24 insofar as it relates to the repeal in s. 21(2) of the Company Directors Disqualification Act 1986	1.3.1990	S.I. 1990/142
Schedule 24 insofar as it relates to the repeals in, or of, sections 48, 55, 119, 159 and 160 of, and paragraphs 4, 10 and 14 of Schedule 11 to the Financial Services Act 1986	15.3.1990	S.I. 1990/354
Schedule 24 insofar as it relates to repeals in or of ss. 46(3) and 85 of the Fair Trading Act 1973	1.4.1990	S.I. 1990/142
Schedule 24 insofar as it relates to repeals in or of section 42(6) of the Harbours Act 1964; sections 716, 717, 744 (in part) and 746 of, and Schedules 2, 4, 9, 11, 22 (in part) and 24 (in part) to, the Companies Act 1985: paragraphs 23 and 45 of Schedule 6 to the Insolvency Act 1985: and the entries in Part 1 of Schedule 13 to the Insolvency Act 1986 relating to sections 222(4) and 225	1.4.1990	S.I. 1990/355
Schedule 24 insofar as it relates to repeals in or of section 199(9) of, and paragraph 22 of Schedule 16 to, the Financial Services Act 1986	1.4.1990	S.I. 1990/355
Schedule 24 insofar as it relates to repeals in or of sections 201, 202(1) and 209(1)(j) of the Companies Act 1985	31.5.1990	S.I. 1990/713
Ss. 213 to 215 insofar as they were not already in force at the time of the making of S.I. 1990/142	2.2.1990	S.I. 1990/142
S. 216	25.1.1990	S.I. 1990/98

THE COMPANIES (FAIR DEALING BY DIRECTORS) (INCREASE IN FINANCIAL LIMITS) ORDER 1990

(S.I. 1990 No. 1393)

Made on 9 July 1990 by the Secretary of State for Trade and Industry under sec. 345(1) of the Companies Act 1985. Operative from 31 July 1990.

CITATION AND COMMENCEMENT

1 This Order may be cited as the Companies (Fair Dealing by Directors) (Increase in Financial Limits) Order 1990 and shall come into force on 31st July 1990.

INCREASE IN FINANCIAL LIMITS

2 Part X of the Companies Act 1985 (enforcement of fair dealing by directors) shall be amended as follows:

(a) in section 320(2) (substantial property transactions involving directors, etc.) for "£1,000" substitute "£2,000" and for "£50,000" substitute "£100,000";

(b) in section 335(1) (minor and business transactions) for "£5,000" substitute "£10,000";

(c) in section 337(3) (funding of director's expenditure on duty to company) for "£10,000" substitute "£20,000";

(d) in section 340(7) ("value" of transactions and arrangements) for "£50,000" substitute "£100,000"; and

(e) in section 344(1) (exceptions from section 343) for "£1,000 substitute "£2,000".

EXPLANATORY NOTE
(*This Note is not part of the Order*)

This Order increases certain of the financial limits specified in Part X of the Companies Act 1985 (enforcement of fair dealing by directors). The limits in question are the sums specified in sections 320(2), 335(1), 337(3), 340(7), and 344(1). In each case, the sum specified is doubled. Section 138 of the Companies Act 1989 (c.40) provides for increases in the other financial limits (relating to loans etc. to directors) specified in Part X of the Companies Act 1985.

THE COMPANIES (UNREGISTERED COMPANIES) (AMENDMENT NO. 2) REGULATIONS 1990

(S.I. 1990 No. 1394)

Made on 9 July 1990 by the Secretary of State for Trade and Industry under sec. 718 of and Sch. 22 to the Companies Act 1985. Operative from 31 July 1990.

1 These Regulations may be cited as the Companies (Unregistered Companies) (Amendment No. 2) Regulations 1990 and shall come into force on 31st July 1990.

2 The Companies (Unregistered Companies) Regulations 1985 are hereby amended as follows:

(a) in Regulation 6(d), the words "36 to 36B," shall be inserted before the words "40 and 186"; and

(b) in the entry in the Schedule relating to Part I of the Companies Act 1985, for the entry relating to section 36(4) there shall be substituted the following entry:

"sections 36 to 36C . . . Company contracts and execution of documents by companies."

EXPLANATORY NOTE

(This Note is not part of the Order)

These Regulations amend the Companies (Unregistered Companies) Regulations 1985, which apply certain provisions of the Companies Act 1985 to unregistered companies. The amendments have the effect of applying to such companies the new provisions relating to company contracts and execution of documents inserted into the Companies Act 1985 by the Companies Act 1989. These provisions include the abolition of the requirement to have a corporate seal.

THE FINANCIAL SERVICES 1986 (RESTRICTION OF SCOPE OF ACT AND MEANING OF COLLECTIVE INVESTMENT SCHEME) (NO. 2) ORDER 1990

(S.I. 1990 No. 1493)

Made on 24 July 1990 by the Secretary of State for Trade and Industry under sec. 2 and 75(9) of the Financial Services Act 1986. Operative from 25 July 1990.

CITATION, COMMENCEMENT AND INTERPRETATION

1(1) This Order may be cited as the Financial Services Act 1986 (Restriction of Scope of Act and Meaning of Collective Investment Scheme) (No. 2) Order 1990 and shall come into force on 25th July 1990.

1(2) In this Order, **"the Act"** means the Financial Services Act 1986.

EMPLOYEE SHARE SCHEMES IN THE ELECTRICITY INDUSTRY

2 In paragraph 35 of Schedule 1 to the Act after paragraph (e) there shall be added the following paragraph—

"(f) arrangements where—

(i) each of the participants is a bona fide employee or former employee (or the wife, husband, widow, widower, or child (including, in Northern Ireland, adopted child) or step-child under the age of eighteen of such an employee or former employee) of any of the following bodies corporate, that is to say, The National Grid Company plc, Electricity Association Services Limited or any other body corporate in the same group as either of them and which is operated by any of those bodies corporate; and

(ii) the property to which the arrangements relate consists of shares or debentures (as defined in paragraph 20(4) above) in or of a body corporate which is an electricity successor company for the purposes of Part II of the Electricity Act 1989 or a body corporate which would be regarded as connected with such an electricity successor company for the purposes of paragraph 20 above.

and for the purposes of this paragraph references to former employees shall have the same meaning as in the Financial Services Act 1986 (Electricity Industry Exemptions) Order 1990."

SALE OF GOODS AND SUPPLY OF SERVICES

3 Paragraph 19 of Schedule 1 to the Act shall be amended by the substitution, in paragraph 19(3)(a), of the figure "5" for the figure "6".

REVOCATION

4 Article 4 of the Financial Services Act 1986 (Restriction of Scope of Act and Meaning of Collective Investment Scheme) Order 1990 is hereby revoked.

EXPLANATORY NOTE

(*This Note is not part of the Order*)

This Order excludes the employee share schemes described in article 2 of the Order from the scope of the provisions of the Financial Services Act 1986 relating to collective investment schemes.

Article 3 of the Order corrects an error contained in article 4 of the Financial Services Act 1986 (Restriction of Scope of Act and Meaning of Collective Investment Scheme) Order 1990. Article 4 is consequential upon the provisions of article 3.

Table of Contents

Volume 1

Table of Contents

Table of Contents

Table of Contents

Table of Contents

Table of Contents

INDEX

Table of Contents

[The next page is 1,003]

Key to Statute Index Codes

References in this Index are to sections and Schedules of the Companies Act 1985 unless they show prefixes as follows:

[The next page is 1,101]

INDEX TO STATUTES

See Key to Statute Index Codes at p. 1,003

Ass

Boo

Codes of practice — continued   **Provision**

. . Director General of Fair
    Trading .... FS 122(1)–(4)
. . Fair Trading Act 1973 ...... FS 124(1), (3)
. Secretary of State's powers ..... FS 205A, 206
. self-regulating organisations, recognition
    requirements .... FS Sch. 2, para. 4

Cold calling — see **Unsolicited calls**

Collective investment schemes .... FS 75
. authorised unit trust schemes
. . alteration of schemes .... FS 82
. . applications for authorisation .... FS 77
. . authorisation orders .... FS 78
. . avoidance of exclusion clauses .... FS 84
. . changes of manager or trustee .... FS 82
. . constitution and management .... FS 81
. . publication of scheme particulars .... FS 85
. . representations against refusal
    or revocation .... FS 80
. . restrictions on activities of manager ... FS 83
. . revocation of authorisation .... FS 79
. body corporate .... FS 75(7)
. contraventions .... FS 95
. definition .... FS 75(1), 207(1)
. investigations .... FS 94
. investment business ...... FS Sch. 1, para. 16
. open-ended investment company .... FS 75(8)
. operators and trustees, authorised
    persons .... FS 24
. overseas — see Overseas collective
    investment schemes
. powers of Secretary of State
. . applications to the court .... FS 93
. . directions .... FS 91
. . notice of directions .... FS 92
. promotion of, restriction on .... FS 76
. transitional
    provisions .... FS Sch. 15, para. 10, 11
. units in .... FS Sch. 1, para. 6
. unit trust scheme .... FS 75(8)

Colonial stock
. forged transfers FT91 5

Colonies
. extent of provisions .... IA 442

Commencement date
. definition .... CP 31(1)

Commencement of business
. notice of .... FS Sch. 15, para. 7

**Commencement of the winding up of
the company**
. definition .... IA 185(3)

Commissioners
. winding up, taking evidence .... IA 197(2)

Commissions   **Provision**
. allotment of shares, power of
    company to pay 97
. . prohibition 98
. debentures, registration of charges .... 397(2)
. . Scotland 413

Committee of creditors
. administrative receiver, summoning . IA 49(2)
. administrator summoned .... IA 26(2)
. control of trustee .... IA 301
. . exercise by Secretary of State
    of functions .... IA 302
. establishment .... IA 26(1), 49(1)
. receivers, Scotland .... IA 68

Common control
. definition .... FTR 65(2)
. enterprise .... FTR 65(2)
. . control .... FTR 65(4)

Companies Acts
. companies formed and registered under 675
. companies not formed under, but
    authorised to register 680
. . certificate 688
. . change of name 682
. . effect of registration 689
. . joint stock company — see Joint
    stock company
. . memorandum/articles substituted for
    deed of settlement 690
. . name 687
. . procedural requirements 681
. . requirements 686
. companies registered/not formed under 676
. companies re-registered with altered
    status under former 677
. definition .... 744; CDDA 22(7); IA 436

Companies legislation
. definition .... CDDA 22(7)
. interaction with Insolvency Act .... CDDA 21

Company
. definition ..... 289(4), 410(5), 425(6), 427(6),
    427A(8), 459(3), 486(1), 735(1),
    736(6), Sch. 1, para. 2(2); CDDA 22(2);
    FS Sch. 1, para. 1, 28(4); IA70(1), 111,
    216(8), 217(6), 388(4), 435(11); ID11;
    FT91 2; FTR 75(4K)

Company ownership
. investigation, provisions 443

Company Directors Disqualification Act 1986
. admissibility of statements in
    evidence .... CDDA 20
. disqualification orders — see
    Disqualification orders
. interaction with Insolvency
    Act 1986 .... CDDA 21

Col

	Provision
. behalf of company	36(1)
. debentures	195
. directors	
.. disclosure of interests	317
.. employment for more than 5 years	319
.. service, open to inspection	318
. form of	36
. pre-incorporation	36(4)
. prospectus	
.. particulars	Sch. 3, para. 11
.. requirements where foreign language	65(3)
. receiver's liability	IA 37
.. Scotland	IA 57
. redeemable shares, contingent purchase	165
. rescission by the court, winding up	IA 186
. Scotland, execution of deed	36(3)

Contracts for differences
. insider dealing	FS 176
. investments	FS Sch. 1, para. 9

Contracts of insurance — see **Insurance business**

Contributories
. meaning	IA 79
. meeting to ascertain wishes	IA 195
. petition for winding up	IA 124(2)
. winding up	IA 74–83
.. bankruptcy of contributory	IA 82
.. companies registered under Companies Act, Part XXII, Chapter II	IA 83
.. death of a member	IA 81
.. liability of present and past members	IA 74
.. nature of liability	IA 80
.. unregistered companies	IA 226
. winding up by the court	
.. adjustment of rights	IA 154
.. debts due from contributory to company	IA 149
.. meeting to choose liquidator	IA 139
.. order on contributory to be conclusive evidence	IA 152
.. orders for calls on contributories, Scotland	IA 161
.. power to arrest absconding contributory	IA 158
.. settlement of list of contributories and application of assets	IA 148

Control
. definition	FTR 77(5)

Control contract
. meaning	Sch. 10A, para. 4(2)

Convertible securities
. takeover offers	430F

	Provision
Conveyance	
. definition	IA 190(3)
Copyrights	
. registration of charges	306
.. Scotland	410(4)
. transitional provisions and savings	IA Sch. 11, para. 15
Corporate interests	
. shares, notification	203(2)
Corporation	
. definition	740
. meetings, representation	375
Correspondence	
. company name to appear	349
. company particulars to appear	351
Cost-book companies	
. partnership property, procedure against for partner's separate judgment debt	P 23(4)
. repeal of obsolete provisions	CP 28
Costs	
. directors, removal	304(5)
. investigation into company affairs	439
. restricted shares, sale by court order	457(3)
Council of Stock Exchange	FS 142(9), 157
. competent authority	FS 142(6)
Country	
. definition	FS 40(5)
County courts	
. failure to pay under county court administration order	CDDA 12
. jurisdiction	
.. insolvent individuals	IA 373
.. winding up	IA 117
Court — see also **Powers of the court**	
. alteration of memorandum, application for cancellation	5
. change of company name, application to set aside direction	32(3)
. company insolvency rules, provisions capable of inclusion	IA Sch. 8, para. 1, 2
. co-operation between courts exercising jurisdiction in relation to insolvency	IA 426
. definition	744; CDDA 2(1), 3(4), 4(2), 6(3), 8(3), 11(2); IA216(5), 385, 423(4); P 45
. dissolution of company, power to declare void	651
. individual insolvency rules, provisions capable of inclusion	IA Sch. 9, para. 1–4
. interim orders — see Interim orders	

Cou

	Provision
Custody	
. inquiry into company's dealings	IA 236(6)
Customs and Excise	
. debts due	IA Sch. 6, para. 3–5

D

	Provision
Damages	
. actions for	FS 62
. auditors	
. . loss of office, annual appointment	
dispensed with	386(4)
. . removal	391(2)
. . termination of appointment	393(7)
. exemptions from	FS 187
. members' rights to	111A
Data protection	FS 190
Daughter	
. definition	327(2)
Day of Stock Exchange reforms	
. definition	FA86 66(5)
Dealing in investments	
. investment business	FS Sch. 1, para. 12
Dealing in securities	
. definition	ID 13
Death	
. dissolution of partnership	P 33
. shareholders, pre-emption offers	90(4)
Debenture holders	
. accounts/reports copies, right to	
. . demand	239
. . receive	238
. charge on land	396(3)
. compromise with creditors and	
members	426(4)
. debts, payment out of assets	
subject to floating charge	196
. register	190
. . right to inspect	191
Debentures — see also **Debenture holders**	
. accounts, particulars to	
be shown	Sch. 4, para. 38–41
. allotment — see Allotment of shares	
. alteration of company's objects	5(8)
. charge for securing an issue,	
registration	396
. contract to subscribe	195
. debts, payment out of assets	
subject to floating charge	196
. definition	744; FS Sch. 1, para. 28(4);
	ID 16(1); ST82 Sch. 1, para. 6(2)

	Provision
. investigation into ownership,	
Secretary of State's power	444
. investments	FS Sch. 1, para. 2
. offers	
. . public, rules governing	59
. . short-dated	FS 195
. . without prospectus, prohibition	56
. perpetual	193
. redeemed, power to re-issue	194
. registration of charges	397
. . endorsement of certificate	402
. . Scotland	413
. re-issue, saving of rights	
of mortgagees	CP 13
. Scotland	197
. subsidiary undertakings, group accounts	
. . companies not required to	
prepare	Sch. 5, para. 6
. . companies required to	
prepare	Sch. 5, para. 20
. transfer	
. . certification	184
. . conditions	183
. . issue of certificates, duty of company	185
. . registration	183
. trustees, liability	192
Debenture warrants	
. definition	FS Sch. 1, para. 28(4)
Debt avoidance	
. transaction defrauding creditors	IA 423
. . application for court order	IA 424
. . provision which may be made	
by court order	IA 425
Debtor	
. definition	IA 385, 386(2), 423(5)
Debtor's petition	
. bankruptcy order	
. . action on report of insolvency	
practitioner	IA 274
. . appointment of insolvency practitioner	
by the court	IA 273
. . grounds	IA 272
. . summary administration	IA 275
. definition	IA 385
Debts — see also **Creditors**	
. bankruptcy, avoidance of general	
assignment of book debts	IA 344
. debt defined	IA 385
. director's personal liability	IA 217
. effect of memorandum/articles	14(2)
. inability to pay	
. . definition	IA 123
. . unregistered company	IA 222–224, 417
. old, priority in winding up	CP 21

Cus

Def

Provision	Provision
. regulatory functions .... FS 180(1A)	. share warrant .. 188(2); FS Sch. 1, para. 28(4)
. related company ....ID 11; FS 105(9)	. sheriff .... IA 183(4), 184(6)
. related person .... FS 138(4)	. short lease ....Sch. 4, para. 83,
. related quoted options .... FA86 89(1A)	Sch. 9, Pt. I, para. 34
. relative .... FTR 77(6)	. significant .... FS 147(2), 164(2)
. relevant accounting reference	. six month period .... IA Sch. 6, para. 3
period .... 244(6), 702(6)	. small bankruptcies level ....IA 273(1)
. relevant amounts 339	. social security costs ....Sch. 4, para. 94
. relevant balance sheet ....43(4)	. solicitor ....716(3)
. relevant benefits ..... Sch. 2, para. 5(2), 9(4)	. son ....327(2)
. relevant body corporate .... IND 13(5)	. special resolution ....378(2)
. relevant class .... FS 130(2)	. specified ....IA 197(1)
. relevant company ....331(6)	. specified securities ....ST82 2(1)
. relevant country or territory ......IA 426(11)	. Standard Industrial
. relevant date ... 196(4), Sch. 15B, para. 6(1);	Classification .... IND 37(1)
IA 131(6), 387	. statutory maximum ....BN 8(1);
. relevant day .... IA 166(6), 372(1)	IA Sch. 10; ID 16(1)
. relevant debentures ....323(3)	. stock exchange ....ST63 4(1)
. relevant employee shares ....94(4)	. stock exchange nominee .... 185(4);
. relevant event .... IND 12(2)	FA76 127(5); FA89 175(3)
. relevant member .... Sch. 15A, para. 2(1)	. stock exchange transaction ....ST63 4(1)
. relevant period ...146(3), 265(5); IND 19(3);	. subordinate legislation .... IA 436
IA 95(7), 98(5)	. subsidiary . 736; FTR 75(4K), 75E; IND 37(1)
. relevant property ....IA 43(7)	. subsidiary undertaking ....258, 742(1)
. relevant regulatory authority .....FS 128B(1)	. summary offence .... CDDA 5(4)
. relevant report ....FT Sch. 8, para. 10(3)	. surname ....289(2), 290(3), 305(4),
. relevant securities ....80(2)	Sch. 1, para. 4; BN 8(1)
. relevant share capital ....198, 220(1)	. take-over offer for a company .... ID 14
. relevant shares .... 94(5), 323(3)	. takeover offers ....428(1)
. relevant supervisory authority ...... FS 33(6)	. telecommunications
. relevant time .... IA 240, 341	services .... IA 233(5), 372(5)
. remuneration .... 390A(4); EP 123(4)	. teletext transmission .... FS Sch. 1,
. residual interest ...... Sch. 2, para. 1(2), 6(2)	para. 25A(2)
. resolution for voluntary winding up .IA 84(2)	. terms and conditions
. responsible person .... FS 138(4)	of employment ......FT Sch. 8, para. 3(4)
. retention of title agreement .... IA 251	. transaction .... IA 436
. rules .... IA 251, 384; FS 207(1)	. transfer ....185(2)
. scheme .... 427A(8)	. transferee body .... FS 207(1)
. Scots land tenure ....Sch. 4, para. 93,	. transferee company .... FS 427A(8)
Sch. 9, Pt. I, para. 36	. transferor company .... FS 427A(8)
. secretary 698	. transfer order .... FS 207(1)
. section 28 fund or funds ....FS 136(1)	. Tribunal .... FS 207(1); IA 396
. secured ....IA 383, 385	. true and fair view 262
. secured creditor .... IA 67(9), 248	. trustee ....FS 75(8), 207(1); IA 385
. secured debenture ....IA 70(1)	. turnover 262
. securities ....228(6); ID 12; FS 142(7),	. uncalled share capital ....737(2)
158(3); FA87 50(3); ST63 4(1)	. undertaking 259
. security .... BC 4(1); IA 248, 425(4)	. undistributable reserves ....264(3), 744
. self-regulating organisation .... FS 8(1)	. unit .... FS 75(8), 207(1);
. self-regulating organisation for	BC 4(1); FA90 108(4)
friendly societies ....FS Sch. 11, para. 1	. unit trust scheme .... FS 75(8), 207(1);
. series of secured debentures ....IA 70(1)	BC 4(1); FA86 99; FA90 108(4)
. services ....331(8)	. unlisted investment .... Sch. 9, Pt. I, para. 33
. shadow director ... 741; CDDA 22(5); IA 251	. unpublished price sensitive
. share ....744; FS Sch. 1, para. 28(4);	information .... ID 10
IA 428(2); ID 16(1); BC 4(1);	. unquoted company ....389(2)
FTR 75(4K)	. unregistered company ..... IA 220; ID 16(1)

Del

	Provision
Fine	
. definition	IA 281(8)
Firm — see also **Partnerships**	
. definition	P4 (1); LP 3
. liability for wrongs	P 10
. misapplication of money or property	P 11
. name	P 4(1)
. partners	
.. acts of; notice not to be bound by	P 8
.. bound by acts on behalf of	P 6
.. credit used for private purposes	P 7
.. duty not to compete with	P 30
.. notice to acting	P 16
.. power to bind	P 5
. revocation of continuing guaranty	
by change	P 18
Firm name	
. definition	LP 3
Fixed assets	
. accounting rules	Sch. 4, para. 17–21
. accounts, information to	
be given	Sch. 4, para. 42–44
. definition	262, 742(1)
Fixed security	
. definition	486(1); IA 70(1)
Floating charge	
. avoidance	IA 245
. debts out of assets subject to,	
payment	196
. definition	744; IA 251
. holder's appointment of receiver,	
Scotland	IA 51(1)
.. mode of appointment	IA 53
.. precedence among receivers	IA 56
. Industrial and Provident Societies	
Act 1967	CP 26
. interpretation of references	IA 70(3)
. payment of debts out of assets	
subject to charge	IA 40
. registration	396
.. Scotland	410(4)
. Scotland	
.. alteration by execution of instrument	466
.. creation by execution of instrument	462(2)
.. execution by attorney	462(3)
.. heritable property	462(5)
.. incorporated company, power to make	462
.. ranking	464
.. registration	410(4)
.. securing of debt	462(1)
.. subsisting before 17 November 1972	465
.. winding up	463
.. winding up, effect	CP 18

	Provision
Foreign companies	
. bearer instrument,	
stamp duty	FA88 143(5), (6)
Foreign Jurisdiction Act 1890	
. overseas branch register	362
Forged transfers	
. building societies	FT91 3
. Colonial Stock Act 1877	FT91 5
. compensation	
.. borrowings to meet	FT91 1(3)
.. cash payment	FT91 1(1)
.. fees for fund	FT91 1(2)
.. losses from	FT91 1
.. remedies	FT91 1(5)
. conservancy authorities	FT91 4
. friendly benefit societies	FT91 3
. harbour authorities	FT91 4
. industrial provident societies	FT91 3
. loan societies	FT91 3
. transfer of shares, restrictions	FT91 1(4)
Formation of companies	
. incorporated company	1
Former Companies Acts	
. definition	735(1)
Former enactments	
. definition	IA Sch. 11, para. 22
Former law	
. definition	IA Sch. 11, para. 2(2), 3, 4(2)
Fraud	
. anticipation of winding up	IA 206
. bankruptcy offences	
.. fraudulent dealing with property	
obtained on credit	IA 359
.. fraudulent disposal of property	IA 357
. discharge from bankruptcy	IA 281(3)
. dissolution of partnership,	
rights of partners	P 41
. Serious Fraud Office	CJ 1
. transactions in fraud of creditors	IA 207
. winding up, disqualification	
orders	CDDA 4
Fraudulent trading	IA 213
. criminal liability	458
Friendly benefit societies	
. forged transfers	FT91 3
Friendly societies	FS 140
. authorised persons	FS 23
. indemnity schemes	FS 141
. registrar's powers	
.. conduct of investment	
business	FS Sch. 11, para. 14–22
.. exercise under enactments relating to	
friendly societies	FS Sch. 11, para. 26, 27
.. information	FS Sch. 11, para. 23–25

	Provision
Government stock	
. redemption	ST82 4
. warrants to purchase, stamp duty	FA87 50
Grant of probate	
. evidence	187
Grants	
. Secretary of State's power to make, accounting standards	256(3)
Gratuitous alienations	
. Scotland	IA 242
Gross	
. meaning	249(4)
Group	
. definition	262, Sch. 5, para. 14; FS 207(1)
. excluded activities	FS Sch. 1, para. 18
. small/medium-sized companies exemptions, ineligible	246(4)
Group accounts — see also **Accounts**	
. accounts publication	240(2)
. acquisition and merger accounting	Sch. 4A, para. 7–16
. banking groups	255A
. . associated undertakings	Sch. 9, Pt. II, para. 4
. . balance sheet	Sch. 9, Pt. I, para. 2–13
. . disclosure requirements, modification	255B
. . exemptions	Sch. 9, Pt. II, para. 5
. . individual accounts provisions, application	Sch. 9, Pt. II, para. 2
. . minority interests	Sch. 9, Pt. II, para. 4
. . profit and loss account	Sch. 9, Pt. I, para. 14–18
. . undertakings	Sch. 9, Pt. II, para. 1, 6, Pt. II
. defective, laying and delivering	245(2)
. form and content	Sch. 4A
. group transaction, elimination	Sch. 4A, para. 6
. individual profit and loss account	230
. insurance groups	255A
. . associated undertakings	Sch. 9, Pt. II, para. 4
. . balance sheet	Sch. 9, Pt. I, para. 2–13
. . disclosure requirements, modification	255B
. . exemptions	Sch. 9, Pt. II, para. 5
. . individual accounts provisions, application	Sch. 9, Pt. II, para. 2
. . minority interests	Sch. 9, Pt. II, para. 4
. . profit and loss account	Sch. 9, Pt. I, para. 14–18
. . undertakings	Sch. 9, Pt. II, para. 1

	Provision
. interests	
. . minority	Sch. 4A, para. 17
. . subsidiary undertaking excluded from consolidation	Sch. 4A, para. 18
. joint ventures	Sch. 4A, para. 19
. medium sized groups, exemptions	248(1), Sch. 8, para. 18, 19
. parent company's exemption	228
. small group, exemptions	248(1), Sch. 8, para. 13–17
. undertakings	
. . companies not required to prepare	Sch. 5, Pt. I
. . companies required to prepare	Sch. 5, Pt. II
Group reconstruction	
. share premiums, relief	132
Groups	
. inter-company loans	333
Group undertaking	
. accounts, parent company/subsidiary undertaking	Sch. 4, para. 59, 59A
. meaning	259(5)
Guarantees	
. accounts	
. . group undertakings	Sch. 4, para. 59A
. . information to be given	Sch. 4, para. 50
. borrowing	BC 4(4)
. definition	331(2), Sch. 6, para. 27(1), 30
Guidance	
. definition	FS 207(1)

H

Harbour authority	
. definition	FT91 4(2)
. forged transfers	FT91 4
Health and safety	
. employees, directors' report	Sch. 7, para. 10
Heritable property	
. Scotland, floating charge	462(5)
High Court	
. enforcement of orders	728
. jurisdiction	
. . competent authority	FS 188
. . designated agency	FS 188
. . insolvent individuals	IA 373
. . self-regulating organisation	FS 188
. . transferee body	FS 188
. . winding up	IA 117
Hire-purchase agreements	
. administration orders, effect of application	IA 10(4)
. definition	744; IA 436
. Scotland, administrator's power to deal with charged property	IA 16

Gov

Lim

Per

	Provision

Probate
. evidence of 187

Probate Judge of the High Court of Northern Ireland
. exempted person .... FS 45(1)(b)

Professional bodies — see Recognised professional bodies

Profit and loss account
. banking companies/
.. groups ....Sch. 9, Pt. I para. 14–18
. form and content ....Sch. 4, Pt. I
.. group accounts ....Sch. 4A
. individual, group accounts prepared 230
. insurance companies/
.. groups ....Sch. 9, Pt. I para. 14–18
. meaning ....742(1)
. medium-sized companies ......Sch.8, para. 5
. medium sized groups ....Sch. 8, para. 18
. small companies ....Sch. 8, para. 2
. small groups ....Sch. 8, para. 14

Profits
. distribution
.. accounts — see Accounts
.. banking/insurance companies 279
.. investment companies 265
.. prohibition 263
.. provisions before Act of 1980 278
.. restraints 281
.. Secretary of State, extension of
... provisions 267
.. unlawful 277
. insurance company, realised 268
. private companies, redemption/purchase
.. of own shares from 172

Prohibited persons ....FS 59

Prohibition orders
. contravention, remedies ....IND 17
. dispute, submitted to Tribunal ....IND 20(2)
. important manufacturing undertaking,
.. change of control ....IND 13(1)
.. Parliament, approval by ....IND 15(1)
. territorial scope of ....IND 18

Promissory notes 37

Proper address
. definition ....IND 36(3)

Property
. administrator's duties ....IA 17(1)
. bankruptcy offences
.. concealment ....IA 354
.. fraudulent dealing with property
... obtained on credit ....IA 359
.. fraudulent disposal ....IA 357

	Provision

. bankrupt's estate — see Bankrupt's estate
. bankrupts, seizure of property ....IA 365
. companies not formed under companies
.. legislation, vesting of
.. property ....Sch. 21, para. 2
. definition ....427(6);
.............FS Sch. 1, para. 28(1); IA 436
. directors' substantial transactions ...320, 321
.. liabilities 322
. dissolved companies, bona vacantia 654
.. Crown, power to disclaim
... title ....656, 657, Sch. 20, para. 5–9
. disposition of interest 655
. England and Wales, charges created
.. elsewhere 409
. heritable, Scotland ....462(5)
. Northern Ireland, registration of
.. charge ....398(4)
. partnerships ....P 20
. bought with partnership money ....P 21
.. conversion into personal estate
... of land held ....P 22
.. co-owner of land ....P 20(3)
.. devolution of legal estate or
... interest in land ....P 20(2)
.. interest and duties subject to
... special agreement ....P 24
.. misapplication ....P 11
. partner's separate judgment debt,
.. procedure against ....P 23
.. rights on dissolution ....P 39
. receiver's disposal of interest,
.. Scotland ....IA 61
. registration of charges, Scotland ..398(4), 411
.. charges existing on property acquired ...416
. situated outside UK, verification
.. of charge 398
. transfer
.. associated companies relief from
... transfer stamp duty FA30 42
.. compromise/arrangement with
... creditors/members, company
... reconstruction or amalgamation .....427(4)
.. directors, disclosure and approval
... of payments 313
. winding up by the court
.. avoidance of dispositions ....IA 127
.. liquidator's custody of company
... property ....IA 144
.. vesting of company property in
... liquidator ....IA 145

Proposals
. voluntary arrangements — see
.. Voluntary arrangements

Prosecuting authority
. definition ....IA 218(2)

Provision

Prosecutions ....FS 201

Prospectus
. accountant's report to be
   set out ....Sch. 3, para. 17
. allotment of shares/debentures ....82(1)
. . returns 87
. . sale offer ....82(6)
. auditors
. . names and addresses
   to be stated ....Sch. 3, para. 12
. . report to be set out ....Sch. 2, para. 16
. company incorporated outside
   Great Britain
. . criminal offences 78
. . deemed issue 79
. . registration before issue 77
. . requirements 73
. . restrictions on allotment to be secured ...75
. . share offer without, prohibition 72
. . statement by expert 74
. . stock exchange certificate exemption 76
. compensation for subscribers mislead
   by statement 67
. contracts, full particulars to
   be given ....Sch. 3, para. 11
. criminal liability for untrue statements 70
. date 63
. definition 744
. directors
. . indemnity, where innocent/expert 69
. . interests, nature and
   extent ....Sch. 3, para. 13
. . liability, exemption 66
. documents offering shares/debentures
   for sale deemed 58
. exemption for those acting
   with propriety 68
. matters to be stated ....Sch. 3
. offers of unlisted securities
. . admission to approved exchange .....FS 159
. . compensation for false or misleading .FS 166
. . exemption from liability to pay
   compensation ....FS 167
. . exemptions from disclosure ....FS 165
. . form and content ....FS 162
. . general duty of disclosure ....FS 163
. . persons responsible for ....FS 168
. . primary or secondary offer ....FS 160
. . supplementary ....FS 164
. offer to the public, rules governing 59
. . exceptions 60
. registration 64
. . additional requirements when
   issued generally 65
. . contract in foreign language ....65(3)
. requirements 57

Provision

. share offers without, prohibition 56
. shares offered to public ....Sch. 3, para. 2
. statement by expert 61
. . meaning of expert 62
. untrue/misleading 71

Prospectus issued generally
. definition 744

Provident societies — see also **Industrial
   and provident societies**
. statement, publication 720

Provisional liquidator
. acting as insolvency practitioner ....IA 230(4)
. appointment to office of two
   or more persons ....IA 231
. company insolvency rules, provisions
   capable of inclusion .... IA Sch. 8, para. 7
. getting in the company's property ....IA 234
. supplies of gas, water, electricity .....IA 233
. validity of office-holder's acts ....IA 232

Proxy vote
. meetings 372

Public bodies
. insider dealing ....FS 173

Public company — see also **Old public
   company**
. accounting records, preservation ......222(5)
. allotment of share capital, issue
   not fully subscribed 84
. allotment of shares
. . non-cash asset, transfer 104
. . one-quarter paid up ....101(1)
. certificate of registration,
   statement ....13(6)
. company not formed under Companies
   Acts but authorised to register
. . joint stock company registration as 685
. . name ....687(2)
. definition ....1(3), 735(2)
. directors, number required 282
. disclosure of interests in shares 198
. distribution of assets, restriction 264
. mergers — see Mergers
. minimum authorised capital, statement
   in memorandum 11
. name as stated in memorandum ....25(1)
. offence, false impression of trading
   as private ....33(2)
. . penalty ....33(3)
. private company re-registered as 43
. . elective resolution, effect on ......379A(4)
. purchase of own shares, returns ......169(2)
. redeemable shares, authority for
   off-market purchase ....164(4)
. register of interest in shares ....211(1)

Reg

Rel

© **1990 CCH Editions Limited**

BCL BCL$$$$ISS

Sec

Sha

Provision

. pension and employees' share schemes,
   held on trust .... Sch. 2
. premiums — see Share premiums
. private companies, redemption/purchase
   out of capital — see Private company
. prospectus — see Prospectus
. purchase of own — see Purchase of
   own shares
. redeemable — see Redeemable shares
. restrictions on
. . court may order sale of
   shares ....456(4), 457
. . effect 454
. . evasion, punishment for 455
. . relaxation and removal 456
. subsidiary undertakings, group accounts
. . companies not required to
   prepare ....Sch. 5, para. 6
. . companies required to
   prepare ....Sch. 5, para. 20
. taken over by company FT92 4
. takeover offers — see Takeovers
. transfers — see Transfer of shares
. warrants — see Share warrants

Share schemes
. employees' financial assistance ....FS 196

Share warrants
. definition ..... 188(2); FS Sch. 1, para. 28(4)
. director's share qualification .... 291(2)
. issue/effect to bearer 188
. offences, Scotland 189
. register of members 355

Sheriff
. bankruptcy, enforcement
   procedures ....IA 346(4)
. definition .... IA 183(4), 184(6)
. duties, England and Wales .... IA 184

Sheriff clerk
. exempted person .... FS 45(1)(i)

Sheriff principal
. winding up, examination
   of witnesses ....IA 197(1)
. . Scotland .... IA 198

Sheriff court
. winding up, jurisdiction .... IA 120

Ships
. registration of charges 396
. . Scotland ....410(4)

Short lease
. definition ....Sch. 4, para. 83,
   Sch. 9, Pt. I, para. 34

Signatures
. articles of association .... 7(3)

Provision

. certificate, registration of charges ..... 401(2)
. memorandum of association ....2(6)
. prospectus ....64(2)
. re-registration private company
   as public ....43(3)
. statement of directors and secretary .... 10(3)

Six-month period
. definition .... IA Sch. 6, para. 3

Small bankruptcies level
. definition ....IA 273(1)

Small companies
. accounts, exemptions ...246, Sch. 8, Pt. I, III
. qualification ....248(7)

Small groups
. accounts, exemptions 248, Sch. 8, para. 13–17
. . ineligible ....248(2)
. qualification 249

Social security contributions
. debts due .... IA Sch. 6, para. 6–7

Social security costs
. definition ....Sch. 4, para. 94

Solicitors
. meaning ....716(3)
. partnerships, prohibitions 716
. privileged information 452
. Serious Fraud Office membership ....CJ 1

Solvency
. statutory declaration, voluntary
   winding up .... IA 89

Son
. definition ....327(2)

Sound broadcasting
. advice ....FS Sch. 1, para. 25A

Speciality debt 14

Special manager
. bankruptcy, power of court to appoint ..IA 370
. winding up, appointment and powers .. IA 177

Special resolutions
. alteration, conditions in memorandum
   which could have been in articles 17
. articles/memorandum substituted for
   deed of settlement, companies not
   formed under Companies Acts but
   authorised to register 690
. articles of association, alteration 9
. change of company name ....28(1)
. definition ....378(2)
. dormant companies, not to appoint
   auditors 250
. limited company
. . directors' unlimited liability 307

	Provision

Unfair preferences
. Scotland .... IA 243

Unfair prejudice — see also **Minority shareholders**
. court orders 461
. members' application to court .... 459(1)
. Secretary of State, order on
    application 460

Unincorporated association
. application for authorisation ....FS 26
. . grant or refusal ....FS 27
. offences ....FS 202
. recognised clearing house, application ..FS 39
. recognised investment exchange,
    application for recognition as ..... FS 37(1)

Unincorporated bodies
. criminal proceedings 734

Unit
. definition .... FS 75(8), 207(1);
    BC 4(1); FA90 108(4)

United Kingdom
. charges on property outside
. . Scotland 411
. . verification of charge 398

Unit trusts
. stamp duty reserve tax FA86 90
. . public issue, exemptions FA86 89A

Unit trust schemes — see also **Authorised unit trust schemes**
. borrowing .... BC 1(2)
. definition .... BC 4(1); FS 75(8), 207(1);
    FA86 99(9); FA90 108(4)

Unlimited company
. articles of association, amount of
    share capital ....7(2)
. delivery of accounts/reports, exemption ...254
. formerly limited, winding up .... IA 78
. holding company membership ....23(5)
. limited company re-registered as 49
. re-registration as limited 51
. . certificates 52
. re-registration private company as public,
    modification for 48
. share capital
. . amount ....7(2)
. . reserve 124

Unlisted investment
. definition .... Sch. 9, Pt. I, para. 33

Unlisted securities ....FS 158
. advertisements
. . exceptions ....FS 161

. . exemptions ....FS 160A
. . offering, on admission to approved
    exchange ....FS 159
. . primary or secondary offer ....FS 160
. . contraventions ....FS 171
. private companies, advertisements by .FS 170
. prospectus
. . compensation for false or misleading .FS 166
. . exemption from liability to
    pay compensation ....FS 167
. . exemptions from disclosure ....FS 165
. . form and content ....FS 162
. . general duty of disclosure ....FS 163
. . persons responsible for ....FS 168
. . supplementary ....FS 164
. public companies, advertisements by ..FS 170
. terms and implementation of offer ....FS 169

Unpublished price sensitive information
. definition .... ID 10

Unquoted company
. auditors ....389(2)
. definition ....389(2)

Unregistered companies ....718, Sch. 22
. definition .... IA 220; ID 16(1)
. winding up .... IA 221
. . actions stayed .... IA 228
. . contributories .... IA 226
. . inability to pay debts .... IA 224
. . inability to pay debts: debt remaining
    after action brought .... IA 223
. . inability to pay debts: increase or
    reduction of money sum .... IA 417
. . inability to pay debts: unpaid
    creditor for £750 or more .... IA 222
. . oversea company .... IA 225
. . power of court to stay, sist or
    restrain proceedings .... IA 227
. . provisions to be cumulative .... IA 229

Unsolicited calls ....FS 56
. definition ....FS 56(8)

V

Valuable security
. definition .... TA 20(3)

Valuation
. allotment of shares
. . communication to registrar 111
. . entitlement of values to full disclosure ..110
. . non-cash consideration 108
. assets in mergers ....FTR 67

Vesting of assets
. trustee ....FS 67

Ves

[The next page is 2,003]

Key to Regulation Index Codes

References in this Index are to orders, regulations and rules, with prefixes as follows:

[The next page is 2,101]

INDEX TO REGULATIONS

For Insolvency Rules 1986, see Index at p. 2,201
See Key to Regulation Index Codes at p. 2,003

	Provision
Creditors' meeting	
. winding up by the court,	
Scotland	IS 4.12–4.14
Creditors voluntary winding up	
. Scotland	IS 5, Sch. 1

D

	Provision
Debenture holders	
. registers	
. . kept otherwise than in legible form	RR 4
. . place of inspection, notice of	RR 5
. ECSC levy debts	EC
Deceased persons	
. administration of insolvent estates	IE
. . death after presentation of	
bankruptcy petition	IE Sch. 2
. . death before presentation of	
bankruptcy petition	IE Sch. 1
Definitions and meanings	
. Accountant in Bankruptcy	IP 1
. acquired enterprise	RTP 2
. an exempt transfer	GSC
. applicant	PT 1
. articles	AT Table A, 1
. associate	IP 1
. authorisation	IP 1
. Bank	GSC; GSE85; GSE87; GSE88; GSE89; GSE90
. business	IP 1; RTP 2
. certified translation	EEIG 2
. CGO	GSC; GSE85; GSE87; GSE88; GSE89; GSE90
. CGO Service	GSC; GSE85; GSE87; GSE88; GSE89; GSE90
. CGO Service member	GSC; GSE85; GSE87; GSE88; GSE89
. clear days	AT Table A, 1
. company	RTP 2
. contract	EEIG 2
. contract of employment	RTP 2
. Crown employment	IP 1
. director	MP 1
. EC Regulation	EEIG 2; EEIG(F)
. EEIG	EEIG 2
. executed	AT Table A, 1
. full accounts and reports	SF 2
. goods	RTP 2
. group	RT 2
. holder	AT Table A, 1
. insolvency practice	IP 1
. insolvency practitioner	IP 1
. insolvency proceedings	IP 1
. insolvency work experience	IP 1

	Provision
. interim trustee	IP 1
. listed public company	SF 2
. member of issuing company	RTP 2
. office	AT Table A, 1
. office-holder	IP 1
. officer	EEIG 2
. permanent trustee	IP 1
. place for inspection	RR 1(2)
. proxy	IS 7.14
. public servant	PS
. purchaser	RTP 2
. register	RR 1(2)
. register of directors' interests	RR 1(2)
. registrar	EEIG 2
. relevant Community obligations	EEIG(F)
. relevant restriction	RTP 2
. relevant time	IP 1
. Scottish case	PT 1
. seal	AT Table A, 1
. secretary	AT Table A, 1
. securities	GSC
. services	RTP 2
. stock exchange nominee	AF 4
. Treasury Solicitor	PT 1
. trust deed for creditors	IP 1
. United Kingdom	AT Table A, 1
. working day	MP 1
Department of Trade and Industry (DTI)	
. fees	DT Sch. 1; DT88; EEIG(F)
. Insolvency Service address	RG 2(4); RGA88
Deposit Protection Board	
. administration proceedings	BA
. voting rights	IS Sch. 3
Designated Authorities	
. disclosure of information	ID
Director General of Fair Trading	
. information disclosure, designated	
authorities	ID
. merger prenotification	MP 7
Directors	
. companies limited by shares	
. . alternate directors	AT Table A, 65–69
. . appointment and	
retirement	AT Table A, 73–80
. . appointments and	
interests	AT Table A, 84–86
. . delegation of powers	AT Table A, 72
. . disqualification and	
removal	AT Table A, 81
. . expenses	AT Table A, 83
. . gratuities and pensions	AT Table A, 87
. . indemnity	AT Table A, 118
. . number required	AT Table A, 64

24-8-90
Index to Regulations
For Insolvency Rules 1986, see Index at p. 2,201
See Key to Regulation Index Codes at p. 2,003

2,105

24-8-90

Index to Regulations   *For Insolvency Rules 1986, see Index at p. 2,201*   **2,107**
See Key to Regulation Index Codes at p. 2,003

24-8-90

Index to Regulations
For Insolvency Rules 1986, see Index at p. 2,201
See Key to Regulation Index Codes at p. 2,003

2,109

	Provision
Office	
. definition	AT Table A, 1
Officers — see also **Directors**	
. definition	EEIG 2
. indemnity, companies limited by	
shares	AT Table A, 118
. public examination	IS 4.74, 4.75
Official receiver	
. administrative records	RGA88
. disqualification of unfit directors,	
application for order	UD 1(3)
. remuneration	RG 19–22; RGA
OM London Ltd.	
. recognised stock exchange	SE 90
Oversea companies	
. accounts and related documents	OC

P

Partnerships	
. insolvency — see Insolvent partnerships	
Penalties	
. insolvency proceedings, punishment	
of offences	IS 7.29, Sch. 4
. punishable extent	EEIG 21
Pensions	
. directors, companies limited	
by shares	AT Table A, 87
Personal representatives	
. directors, disclosure of interest	DI
Place for inspection	
. definition	RR 1(2)
Preferential debts	
. levies on coal and steel production	EC
Private companies	
. limited by guarantee and having share	
capital, memorandum of	
association	AT Table D, Pt. III
. limited by shares, memorandum of	
association	AT Table B
Professional bodies	
. insolvency practitioners	PB
Profits	
. capitalisation, companies	
limited by shares	AT Table A, 110
Proposals	
. voluntary arrangements in Scotland — see	
Voluntary arrangements in Scotland	

	Provision
Provisional liquidator	
. winding up by the court, Scotland —	
see Winding up by the court	
Proxy	
. insolvency proceedings	
. . definition of proxy	IS 7.14
. . form of proxy	IS 7.15
. . proxy-holder with financial	
interest	IS 7.19
. . retention of proxy	IS 7.17
. . right of inspection	IS 7.18
. . use at meetings	IS 7.16
Public companies	
. disclosure of interests in shares,	
investment management exclusion	IM
. limited by guarantee and having	
share capital, memorandum	
of association	AT Table D, Pt. I
. listed — see Listed public companies	
. mergers and divisions	MD
Public servant	
. definition	PS
Purchaser	
. meaning	RTP 2

R

Receivers	RS; SS 15–17
. abstract of receipts and payments	IS 3.9
. appointment	IS 3.1
. . applications	SA 214, 216
. . intimation, service and advertisement	
of petition	SA 215
. bad debt relief, issue of	
certificate of insolvency	IS 3.12
. creditors' committee	
. . application of provisions relating to	
liquidation committee	IS 3.6
. . constitution	IS 3.4
. . functions	IS 3.5
. information from receiver	IS 3.7
. . members' dealings with the	
company	IS 3.8
. deceased	IS 3.10
. statement of affairs	
. . expenses	IS 3.3
. . notice requiring statement	IS 3.2
. vacation of office	IS 3.11
Recognised professional bodies	
. insolvency practitioners	PB
Recognised stock exchange	
. NASDAQ	SE 89
. OM London Ltd	SE 90

Off

© **1990 CCH Editions Limited**

24-8-90

Index to Regulations *For Insolvency Rules 1986, see Index at p. 2,201*
See Key to Regulation Index Codes at p. 2,003

2,111

Sea

[The next page is 2,201]

INDEX TO INSOLVENCY RULES 1986

The entries in the provision column are rules of the Insolvency Rules 1986 (as amended) unless otherwise stated

COMPANIES ACT 1985

Table of Contents

[The next page is 3,051]

COMPANIES ACT 1985

(1985 Chapter 6)

ARRANGEMENT OF SECTIONS

PART I — FORMATION AND REGISTRATION OF COMPANIES; JURIDICAL STATUS AND MEMBERSHIP

CHAPTER I — COMPANY FORMATION

CHAPTER II — COMPANY NAMES

[The next page is 3,071]

CHAPTER VIII — MISCELLANEOUS PROVISIONS ABOUT SHARES AND DEBENTURES

Share and debenture certificates, transfers and warrants

Debentures

PART VI — DISCLOSURE OF INTERESTS IN SHARES

Individual and group acquisitions

PART VII — ACCOUNTS AND AUDIT

CHAPTER I — PROVISIONS APPLYING TO COMPANIES GENERALLY

[The next page is 3,091]

SECTION

CHAPTER II — EXEMPTIONS, EXCEPTIONS AND SPECIAL PROVISIONS

Small and medium-sized companies and groups

Dormant companies

Listed public companies

PART IX — A COMPANY'S MANAGEMENT; DIRECTORS AND SECRETARIES; THEIR QUALIFICATIONS, DUTIES AND RESPONSIBILITIES

[The next page is 3,111]

CCH Editions Limited

SECTION

PART XII — REGISTRATION OF CHARGES

CHAPTER I — REGISTRATION OF CHARGES (ENGLAND AND WALES)

CHAPTER II — REGISTRATION OF CHARGES (SCOTLAND)

[The next page is 3,151]

SCHEDULES

[The next page is 3,201]

CCH Editions Limited

COMPANIES ACT 1985

(1985 Chapter 6)

An Act to consolidate the greater part of the Companies Acts.

[*11th March 1985*]

PART I — FORMATION AND REGISTRATION OF COMPANIES; JURIDICAL STATUS AND MEMBERSHIP

Chapter I — Company Formation

MEMORANDUM OF ASSOCIATION

SEC. 1   Mode of forming incorporated company

1(1)   [Formation]   Any two or more persons associated for a lawful purpose may, by subscribing their names to a memorandum of association and otherwise complying with the requirements of this Act in respect of registration, form an incorporated company, with or without limited liability.

1(2)   [Types of company]   A company so formed may be either—

(a)   a company having the liability of its members limited by the memorandum to the amount, if any, unpaid on the shares respectively held by them ("a company limited by shares");

(b)   a company having the liability of its members limited by the memorandum to such amount as the members may respectively thereby undertake to contribute to the assets of the company in the event of its being wound up ("a company limited by guarantee"); or

(c)   a company not having any limit on the liability of its members ("an unlimited company").

1(3)   [Classification as public or private]   A "public company" is a company limited by shares or limited by guarantee and having a share capital, being a company—

(a)   the memorandum of which states that it is to be a public company, and

(b)   in relation to which the provisions of this Act or the former Companies Acts as to the registration or re-registration of a company as a public company have been complied with on or after 22nd December 1980;

and a "private company" is a company that is not a public company.

1(4)   [Restriction on types]   With effect from 22nd December 1980, a company cannot be formed as, or become, a company limited by guarantee with a share capital.

SEC. 2   Requirements with respect to memorandum

2(1)   [Contents of memorandum]   The memorandum of every company must state—

(a) the name of the company;

(b) whether the registered office of the company is to be situated in England and Wales, or in Scotland;

(c) the objects of the company.

Note
S. 2(1)(a): see s. 25 ff. re company names.

2(2)   [Registered office in Wales]   Alternatively to subsection (1)(b), the memorandum may contain a statement that the company's registered office is to be situated in Wales; and a company whose registered office is situated in Wales may by special resolution alter its memorandum so as to provide that its registered office is to be so situated.

2(3)   [Limited liability]   The memorandum of a company limited by shares or by guarantee must also state that the liability of its members is limited.

2(4)   [Limited by guarantee]   The memorandum of a company limited by guarantee must also state that each member undertakes to contribute to the assets of the company if it should be wound up while he is a member, or within one year after he ceases to be a member, for payment of the debts and liabilities of the company contracted before he ceases to be a member, and of the costs, charges and expenses of winding up, and for adjustment of the rights of the contributories among themselves, such amount as may be required, not exceeding a specified amount.

2(5)   [Company having a share capital]   In the case of a company having a share capital—

(a) the memorandum must also (unless it is an unlimited company) state the amount of the share capital with which the company proposes to be registered and the division of the share capital into shares of a fixed amount;

(b) no subscriber of the memorandum may take less than one share; and

(c) there must be shown in the memorandum against the name of each subscriber the number of shares he takes.

2(6)   [Signing and attestation]   The memorandum must be signed by each subscriber in the presence of at least one witness, who must attest the signature; and that attestation is sufficient in Scotland as well as in England and Wales.

2(7)   [Restriction on alteration]   A company may not alter the conditions contained in its memorandum except in the cases, in the mode and to the extent, for which express provision is made by this Act.

SEC. 3   Forms of memorandum

3(1)   [Form]   Subject to the provisions of sections 1 and 2, the form of the memorandum of association of—

(a) a public company, being a company limited by shares,

(b) a public company, being a company limited by guarantee and having a share capital,

(c) a private company limited by shares,

(d) a private company limited by guarantee and not having a share capital,

(e) a private company limited by guarantee and having a share capital, and

(f) an unlimited company having a share capital,

shall be as specified respectively for such companies by regulations made by the Secretary of State, or as near to that form as circumstances admit.

3(2) **[Regulations]** Regulations under this section shall be made by statutory instrument subject to annulment in pursuance of a resolution of either House of Parliament.

SEC. 4 Resolution to alter objects

4 A company may by special resolution alter its memorandum with respect to the objects of the company, so far as may be required to enable it—

(a) to carry on its business more economically or more efficiently; or

(b) to attain its main purpose by new or improved means; or

(c) to enlarge or change the local area of its operations; or

(d) to carry on some business which under existing circumstances may conveniently or advantageously be combined with the business of the company; or

(e) to restrict or abandon any of the objects specified in the memorandum; or

(f) to sell or dispose of the whole or any part of the undertaking of the company; or

(g) to amalgamate with any other company or body of persons;

but if an application is made under the following section, the alteration does not have effect except in so far as it is confirmed by the court.

SEC. 5 Procedure for objecting to alteration

5(1) **[Application to court]** Where a company's memorandum has been altered by special resolution under section 4, application may be made to the court for the alteration to be cancelled.

5(2) **[Applicants]** Such an application may be made—

(a) by the holders of not less in the aggregate than 15 per cent in nominal value of the company's issued share capital or any class of it or, if the company is not limited by shares, not less than 15 per cent of the company's members; or

(b) by the holders of not less than 15 per cent of the company's debentures entitling the holders to object to an alteration of its objects;

but an application shall not be made by any person who has consented to or voted in favour of the alteration.

5(3) **[Time for application]** The application must be made within 21 days after the date on which the resolution altering the company's objects was passed, and may be made on behalf of the persons entitled to make the application by such one or more of their number as they may appoint in writing for the purpose.

5(4) **[Orders by court]** The court may on such an application make an order confirming the alteration either wholly or in part and on such terms and conditions as it thinks fit, and may—

    (a) if it thinks fit, adjourn the proceedings in order that an arrangement may be made to its satisfaction for the purchase of the interests of dissentient members, and

    (b) give such directions and make such orders as it thinks expedient for facilitating or carrying into effect any such arrangement.

5(5) **[Order for purchase of shares]** The court's order may (if the court thinks fit) provide for the purchase by the company of the shares of any members of the company, and for the reduction accordingly of its capital, and may make such alterations in the company's memorandum and articles as may be required in consequence of that provision.

5(6) **[Order for no alteration]** If the court's order requires the company not to make any, or any specified, alteration in its memorandum or articles, the company does not then have power without the leave of the court to make any such alteration in breach of that requirement.

5(7) **[Effect of alteration by order]** An alteration in the memorandum or articles of a company made by virtue of an order under this section, other than one made by resolution of the Company, is of the same effect as if duly made by resolution; and this Act applies accordingly to the memorandum or articles as so altered.

5(8) **[Debentures entitling holders to object]** The debentures entitling the holders to object to an alteration of a company's objects are any debentures secured by a floating charge which were issued or first issued before 1st December 1947 or form part of the same series as any debentures so issued; and a special resolution altering a company's objects requires the same notice to the holders of any such debentures as to members of the company.

In the absence of provisions regulating the giving of notice to any such debenture holders, the provisions of the company's articles regulating the giving of notice to members apply.

SEC. 6 Provisions supplementing sec. 4, 5

6(1) **[Requirements made where resolution altering objects]** Where a company passes a resolution altering its objects, then—

    (a) if with respect to the resolution no application is made under section 5, the company shall within 15 days from the end of the period for making such an application deliver to the registrar of companies a printed copy of its memorandum as altered; and

    (b) if such an application is made, the company shall—

        (i) forthwith give notice (in the prescribed form) of that fact to the registrar, and

        (ii) within 15 days from the date of any order cancelling or confirming the alteration, deliver to the registrar an office copy of the order and, in the case of an order confirming the alteration, a printed copy of the memorandum as altered.

6(2) **[Extension of time for delivery of documents]** The court may by order at any time extend the time for the delivery of documents to the registrar under subsection (1)(b) for such period as the court may think proper.

6(3) **[Penalty in default]** If a company makes default in giving notice or delivering any document to the registrar of companies as required by sub-section (1), the company and every officer of it who is in default is liable to a fine and, for continued contravention, to a daily default fine.

6(4) **[Validity of alteration of objects]** The validity of an alteration of a company's memorandum with respect to the objects of the company shall not be questioned on the ground that it was not authorised by section 4, except in proceedings taken for the purpose (whether under section 5 or otherwise) before the expiration of 21 days after the date of the resolution in that behalf.

6(5) **[Where proceedings otherwise than under sec. 5]** Where such proceedings are taken otherwise than under section 5, subsections (1) to (3) above apply in relation to the proceedings as if they had been taken under that section, and as if an order declaring the alteration invalid were an order cancelling it, and as if an order dismissing the proceedings were an order confirming the alteration.

ARTICLES OF ASSOCIATION

SEC. 7   Articles prescribing regulations for companies

7(1) **[Articles signed by subscribers]** There may in the case of a company limited by shares, and there shall in the case of a company limited by guarantee or unlimited, be registered with the memorandum articles of association signed by the subscribers to the memorandum and prescribing regulations for the company.

7(2) **[Articles of unlimited company]** In the case of an unlimited company having a share capital, the articles must state the amount of share capital with which the company proposes to be registered.

7(3) **[Printing, numbering and signing]** Articles must—

   (a)   be printed,

   (b)   be divided into paragraphs numbered consecutively, and

   (c)   be signed by each subscriber to the memorandum in the presence of at least one witness who must attest the signature (which attestation is sufficient in Scotland as well as in England and Wales).

SEC. 8   Tables A, C, D and E

8(1) **[Table A]** Table A is as prescribed by regulations made by the Secretary of State; and a company may for its articles adopt the whole or any part of that Table.

8(2) **[Articles not registered]** In the case of a company limited by shares, if articles are not registered or, if articles are registered, in so far as they do not exclude or modify Table A, that Table (so far as applicable, and as in force at the date of the company's registration) constitutes the company's articles, in the same manner and to the same extent as if articles in the form of that Table had been duly registered.

8(3) **[If Table A altered]** If in consequence of regulations under this section Table A is altered, the alteration does not affect a company registered before the alteration takes effect, or repeal as respects that company any portion of the Table.

8(4)   **[Tables C, D and E]**   The form of the articles of association of—

   (a)   a company limited by guarantee and not having a share capital,

   (b)   a company limited by guarantee and having a share capital, and

   (c)   an unlimited company having a share capital,

shall be respectively in accordance with Table C, D or E prescribed by regulations made by the Secretary of State, or as near to that form as circumstances admit.

8(5)   **[Regulations]**   Regulations under this section shall be made by statutory instrument subject to annulment in pursuance of a resolution of either House of Parliament.

Note
See The Companies (Tables A to F) Regulations 1985 (S.I. 1985 No. 805).

SEC. 9   Alteration of articles by special resolution

9(1)   **[Special resolution]**   Subject to the provisions of this Act and to the conditions contained in its memorandum, a company may by special resolution alter its articles.

9(2)   **[Effect of alteration]**   Alterations so made in the articles are (subject to this Act) as valid as if originally contained in them, and are subject in like manner to alteration by special resolution.

REGISTRATION AND ITS CONSEQUENCES

SEC. 10   Documents to be sent to registrar

10(1)   **[Memorandum and articles]**   The company's memorandum and articles (if any) shall be delivered—

   (a)   to the registrar of companies for England and Wales, if the memorandum states that the registered office of the company is to be situated in England and Wales, or that it is to be situated in Wales; and

   (b)   to the registrar of companies for Scotland, if the memorandum states that the registered office of the company is to be situated in Scotland.

10(2)   **[Statement of directors and secretary]**   With the memorandum there shall be delivered a statement in the prescribed form containing the names and requisite particulars of—

   (a)   the person who is, or the persons who are, to be the first director or directors of the company; and

   (b)   the person who is, or the persons who are, to be the first secretary or joint secretaries of the company;

and the requisite particulars in each case are those set out in Schedule 1.

10(3)   **[Signing of sec. 10(2) statement]**   The statement shall be signed by or on behalf of the subscribers of the memorandum and shall contain a consent signed by each of the persons named in it as a director, as secretary or as one of joint secretaries, to act in the relevant capacity.

10(4)   **[Where statement delivered by agent]**   Where a memorandum is delivered by a person as agent for the subscribers, the statement shall specify that fact and the person's name and address.

10(5) **[Appointment by articles also to be in statement]** An appointment by any articles delivered with the memorandum of a person as director or secretary of the company is void unless he is named as a director or secretary in the statement.

10(6) **[Registered office]** There shall in the statement be specified the intended situation of the company's registered office on incorporation.

SEC. 11 Minimum authorised capital (public companies)

11 When a memorandum delivered to the registrar of companies under section 10 states that the association to be registered is to be a public company, the amount of the share capital stated in the memorandum to be that with which the company proposes to be registered must not be less than the authorised minimum (defined in section 118).

SEC. 12 Duty of registrar

12(1) **[Registrar to be satisfied re requirements]** The registrar of companies shall not register a company's memorandum delivered under section 10 unless he is satisfied that all the requirements of this Act in respect of registration and of matters precedent and incidental to it have been complied with.

12(2) **[Registration]** Subject to this, the registrar shall retain and register the memorandum and articles (if any) delivered to him under that section.

12(3) **[Statutory declaration of compliance]** A statutory declaration in the prescribed form by—

(a) a solicitor engaged in the formation of a company, or

(b) a person named as a director or secretary of the company in the statement delivered under section 10(2),

that those requirements have been complied with shall be delivered to the registrar of companies, and the registrar may accept such a declaration as sufficient evidence of compliance.

SEC. 13 Effect of registration

13(1) **[Certification registration]** On the registration of a company's memorandum, the registrar of companies shall give a certificate that the company is incorporated and, in the case of a limited company, that it is limited.

13(2) **[Certificate to be signed or sealed]** The certificate may be signed by the registrar, or authenticated by his official seal.

13(3) **[Effect]** From the date of incorporation mentioned in the certificate, the subscribers of the memorandum, together with such other persons as may from time to time become members of the company, shall be a body corporate by the name contained in the memorandum.

13(4) **[Capability of body corporate]** That body corporate is then capable forthwith of exercising all the functions of an incorporated company, but with such liability on the part of its members to contribute to its assets in the event of its being wound up as is provided by this Act and the Insolvency Act.

This is subject, in the case of a public company, to section 117 (additional certificate as to amount of allotted share capital).

History
In s. 13(4) the words "and the Insolvency Act" added by   29 December 1986 (see IA 1986, s. 443 and S.I. 1986
Insolvency Act 1986, s. 439(1) and Sch. 13 as from   No. 1924 (C. 71)).

13(5)   [First directors and secretary]   The persons named in the statement under section 10 as directors, secretary or joint secretaries are, on the company's incorporation, deemed to have been respectively appointed as its first directors, secretary or joint secretaries.

13(6)   [Statement in certificate re public company]   Where the registrar registers an association's memorandum which states that the association is to be a public company, the certificate of incorporation shall contain a statement that the company is a public company.

13(7)   [Effect of certificate of incorporation]   A certificate of incorporation given in respect of an association is conclusive evidence—

(a) that the requirements of this Act in respect of registration and of matters precedent and incidental to it have been complied with, and that the association is a company authorised to be registered, and is duly registered, under this Act, and

(b) if the certificate contains a statement that the company is a public company, that the company is such a company.

SEC. 14   Effect of memorandum and articles

14(1)   [Company and members bound]   Subject to the provisions of this Act, the memorandum and articles, when registered, bind the company and its members to the same extent as if they respectively had been signed and sealed by each member, and contained covenants on the part of each member to observe all the provisions of the memorandum and of the articles.

14(2)   [Debt by member]   Money payable by a member to the company under the memorandum or articles is a debt due from him to the company, and in England and Wales is of the nature of a specialty debt.

SEC. 15   Memorandum and articles of company limited by guarantee

15(1)   [Provision re right to profits void]   In the case of a company limited by guarantee and not having a share capital, every provision in the memorandum or articles, or in any resolution of the company purporting to give any person a right to participate in the divisible profits of the company otherwise than as a member, is void.

15(2)   [Provisions dividing into shares]   For purposes of provisions of this Act relating to the memorandum of a company limited by guarantee, and for those of section 1(4) and this section, every provision in the memorandum or articles, or in any resolution, of a company so limited purporting to divide the company's undertaking into shares or interests is to be treated as a provision for a share capital, notwithstanding that the nominal amount or number of the shares or interests is not specified by the provision.

SEC. 16 Effect of alteration on company's members

16(1) [Alterations not binding on members] A member of a company is not bound by an alteration made in the memorandum or articles after the date on which he became a member, if and so far as the alteration—

    (a) requires him to take or subscribe for more shares than the number held by him at the date on which the alteration is made; or

    (b) in any way increases his liability as at that date to contribute to the company's share capital or otherwise to pay money to the company.

16(2) [Exception] Subsection (1) operates notwithstanding anything in the memorandum or articles; but it does not apply in a case where the member agrees in writing, either before or after the alteration is made, to be bound by the alteration.

SEC. 17 Conditions in memorandum which could have been in articles

17(1) [Alteration by special resolution] A condition contained in a company's memorandum which could lawfully have been contained in articles of association instead of in the memorandum may be altered by the company by special resolution; but if an application is made to the court for the alteration to be cancelled, the alteration does not have effect except in so far as it is confirmed by the court.

17(2) [Application of section] This section—

    (a) is subject to section 16, and also to Part XVII (court order protecting minority), and

    (b) does not apply where the memorandum itself provides for or prohibits the alteration of all or any of the conditions above referred to, and does not authorise any variation or abrogation of the special rights of any class of members.

17(3) [Application of parts of sec. 5, 6] Section 5 (except subsections (2)(b) and (8)) and section 6(1) to (3) apply in relation to any alteration and to any application made under this section as they apply in relation to alterations and applications under sections 4 to 6.

SEC. 18 Amendments of memorandum or articles to be registered

18(1) [Printed copy to registrar] Where an alteration is made in a company's memorandum or articles by any statutory provision, whether contained in an Act of Parliament or in an instrument made under an Act, a printed copy of the Act or instrument shall, not later than 15 days after that provision comes into force, be forwarded to the registrar of companies and recorded by him.

18(2) [Also printed copy of memorandum or articles as altered] Where a company is required (by this section or otherwise) to send to the registrar any document making or evidencing an alteration in the company's memorandum or articles (other than a special resolution under section 4), the company shall send with it a printed copy of the memorandum or articles as altered.

18(3) [Penalty on default] If a company fails to comply with this section, the company and any officer of it who is in default is liable to a fine and, for continued contravention, to a daily default fine.

SEC. 19   Copies of memorandum and articles to be given to members

19(1)   [Copies to member on request]   A company shall, on being so required by any member, send to him a copy of the memorandum and of the articles (if any), and a copy of any Act of Parliament which alters the memorandum, subject to payment—

> (a)   in the case of a copy of the memorandum and of the articles, of 5 pence or such less sum as the company may prescribe, and

> (b)   in the case of a copy of an Act, of such sum not exceeding its published price as the company may require.

19(2)   [Penalty on default]   If a company makes default in complying with this section, the company and every officer of it who is in default is liable for each offence to a fine.

SEC. 20   Issued copy of memorandum to embody alterations

20(1)   [Copies in accordance with alteration]   Where an alteration is made in a company's memorandum, every copy of the memorandum issued after the date of the alteration shall be in accordance with the alteration.

20(2)   [Penalty on default]   If, where any such alteration has been made, the company at any time after the date of the alteration issues any copies of the memorandum which are not in accordance with the alteration, it is liable to a fine, and so too is every officer of the company who is in default.

SEC. 21   Registered documentation of Welsh companies

21(1)   [Documents may be in Welsh, but with English translation]   Where a company is to be registered with a memorandum stating that its registered office is to be situated in Wales, the memorandum and articles to be delivered for registration under section 10 may be in Welsh; but, if they are, they shall be accompanied by a certified translation into English.

21(2)   [Where memorandum altered]   Where a company whose registered office is situated in Wales has altered its memorandum as allowed by section 2(2), it may deliver to the registrar of companies for registration a certified translation into Welsh of its memorandum and articles.

21(3)   [Other documents delivered to registrar]   A company whose memorandum states that its registered office is to be situated in Wales may comply with any provision of this Act requiring it to deliver any document to the registrar of companies by delivering to him that document in Welsh (or, if it consists of a prescribed form, completed in Welsh), together with a certified translation into English.

But any document making or evidencing an alteration in the company's memorandum or articles, and any copy of a company's memorandum or articles as altered, shall be in the same language as the memorandum and articles originally registered and, if that language is Welsh, shall be accompanied by a certified translation into English.

21(4)   [Document making or evidencing alteration]   Where a company has under subsection (2) delivered a translation into Welsh of its memorandum and articles, it may, when delivering to the registrar of companies a document making or evidencing an alteration in the memorandum or articles or a copy of the memorandum or articles as altered, deliver with it a certified translation into Welsh.

21(5) [**"Certified translation"**] In this section **"certified translation"** means a translation certified in the prescribed manner to be a correct translation; and a reference to delivering a document includes sending, forwarding, producing or (in the case of a notice) giving it.

A COMPANY'S MEMBERSHIP

SEC. 22 Definition of "member"

22(1) [**Subscribers**] The subscribers of a company's memorandum are deemed to have agreed to become members of the company, and on its registration shall be entered as such in its register of members.

22(2) [**Other persons**] Every other person who agrees to become a member of a company, and whose name is entered in its register of members, is a member of the company.

SEC. 23 Membership of holding company

23(1) [**Body corporate not to be member of its holding company**] Except in the cases mentioned below in this section, a body corporate cannot be a member of a company which is its holding company; and any allotment or transfer of shares in a company to its subsidiary is void.

23(2) [**Pre 1 July 1948**] This does not prevent a subsidiary which was, on 1st July 1948, a member of its holding company, from continuing to be a member; but (subject to subsection(4)) the subsidiary has no right to vote at meetings of the holding company or any class of its members.

23(3) [**Nominee for subsidiary body corporate**] Subject as follows, subsections (1) and (2) apply in relation to a nominee for a body corporate which is a subsidiary, as if references to such a body corporate included a nominee for it.

23(4) [**Where subsidiary trustee etc.**] Nothing in this section applies where the subsidiary is concerned as personal representative, or where it is concerned as trustee, unless the holding company or a subsidiary of it is beneficially interested under the trust and is not so interested only by way of security for the purposes of a transaction entered into by it in the ordinary course of a business which includes the lending of money.

Schedule 2 has effect for the interpretation of the reference in this subsection to a company or its subsidiary being beneficially interested.

23(5) [**Company limited by guarantee, unlimited company**] In relation to a company limited by guarantee or unlimited which is a holding company, the reference in subsection (1) to shares (whether or not the company has a share capital) includes the interest of its members as such, whatever the form of that interest.

SEC. 24   Minimum membership for carrying on business

24   If a company carries on business without having at least two members and does so for more than 6 months, a person who, for the whole or any part of the period that it so carries on business after those 6 months—

    (a)   is a member of the company, and

    (b)   knows that it is carrying on business with only one member,

is liable (jointly and severally with the company) for the payment of the company's debts contracted during the period or, as the case may be, that part of it.

Chapter II — Company Names

SEC. 25   Name as stated in memorandum

25(1)   **[End of name of public company]**   The name of a public company must end with the words "public limited company" or, if the memorandum states that the company's registered office is to be situated in Wales, those words or their equivalent in Welsh ("cwmni cyfyngedig cyhoeddus"); and those words or that equivalent may not be preceded by the word "limited" or its equivalent in Welsh ("cyfyngedig").

25(2)   **[End of name of company limited by shares or guarantee — not public]**   In the case of a company limited by shares or by guarantee (not being a public company), the name must have "limited" as its last word, except that—

    (a)   this is subject to section 30 (exempting, in certain circumstances, a company from the requirement to have "limited" as part of the name), and

    (b)   if the company is to be registered with a memorandum stating that its registered office is to be situated in Wales, the name may have "cyfyngedig" as its last word.

SEC. 26   Prohibition on registration of certain names

26(1)   **[Names not to be registered]**   A company shall not be registered under this Act by a name—

    (a)   which includes, otherwise than at the end of the name, any of the following words or expressions, that is to say, "limited", "unlimited" or "public limited company" or their Welsh equivalents ("cyfyngedig", "anghyfyngedig" and "cwmni cyfyngedig cyhoeddus" respectively);

    (b)   which includes, otherwise than at the end of the name, an abbreviation of any of those words or expressions;

    (c)   which is the same as a name appearing in the registrar's index of company names;

    (d)   the use of which by the company would in the opinion of the Secretary of State constitute a criminal offence; or

    (e)   which in the opinion of the Secretary of State is offensive.

Note
For the registrar's index of company names see s. 714.

26(2) **[Further names not to be registered — except with approval]** Except with the approval of the Secretary of State, a company shall not be registered under this Act by a name which—

(a) in the opinion of the Secretary of State would be likely to give the impression that the company is connected in any way with Her Majesty's Government or with any local authority; or

(b) includes any word or expression for the time being specified in regulations under section 29.

"Local authority" means any local authority within the meaning of the Local Government Act 1972 or the Local Government (Scotland) Act 1973, the Common Council of the City of London or the Council of the Isles of Scilly.

26(3) **[Determination of same name]** In determining for purposes of subsection (1)(c) whether one name is the same as another, there are to be disregarded—

(a) the definite article, where it is the first word of the name;

(b) the following words and expressions where they appear at the end of the name, that is to say—

"company" or its Welsh equivalent ("cwmni"),

"and company" or its Welsh equivalent ("a'r cwmni"),

"company limited" or its Welsh equivalent ("cwmni cyfyngedig"),

"and company limited" or its Welsh equivalent ("a'r cwmni cyfyngedig"),

"limited" or its Welsh equivalent ("cyfyngedig"),

"unlimited" or its Welsh equivalent ("anghyfyngedig"), and

"public limited company" or its Welsh equivalent ("cwmni cyfyngedig cyhoeddus");

(c) abbreviations of any of those words or expressions where they appear at the end of the name; and

(d) type and case of letters, accents, spaces between letters and punctuation marks;

and "and" and "&" are to be taken as the same.

SEC. 27 Alternatives of statutory designations

27(1) **[Specified alternative abbreviations]** A company which by any provision of this Act is either required or entitled to include in its name, as its last part, any of the words specified in subsection (4) below may, instead of those words, include as the last part of the name the abbreviations there specified as alternatives in relation to those words.

27(2) **[Reference to name of company]** A reference in this Act to the name of a company or to the inclusion of any of those words in a company's name includes a reference to the name including (in place of any of the words so specified) the appropriate alternative, or to the inclusion of the appropriate alternative, as the case may be.

27(3) **[Reference to company not including words in name]**   A provision of this Act requiring a company not to include any of those words in its name also requires it not to include the abbreviated alternative specified in subsection (4).

27(4) **[Abbreviations]**   For the purposes of this section—

(a) the alternative of "limited" is "ltd.";

(b) the alternative of "public limited company" is "p.l.c.";

(c) the alternative of "cyfyngedig" is "cyf."; and

(d) the alternative of "cwmni cyfyngedig cyhoeddus" is "c.c.c.".

SEC. 28   Change of name

28(1) **[Change by special resolution]**   A company may by special resolution change its name (but subject to section 31 in the case of a company which has received a direction under subsection (2) of that section from the Secretary of State).

28(2) **[Direction to change same or similar name]**   Where a company has been registered by a name which—

(a) is the same as or, in the opinion of the Secretary of State, too like a name appearing at the time of the registration in the registrar's index of company names, or

(b) is the same as or, in the opinion of the secretary of State, too like a name which should have appeared in that index at that time,

the Secretary of State may within 12 months of that time, in writing, direct the company to change its name within such period as he may specify.

Section 26(3) applies in determining under this subsection whether a name is the same as or too like another.

28(3) **[Direction where misleading information given]**   If it appears to the Secretary of State that misleading information has been given for the purpose of a company's registration with a particular name, or that undertakings or assurances have been given for that purpose and have not been fulfilled, he may within 5 years of the date of its registration with that name in writing direct the company to change its name within such period as he may specify.

28(4) **[Extension of time for direction under sec. 28(2), (3)]**   Where a direction has been given under subsection (2) or (3), the Secretary of State may by a further direction in writing extend the period within which the company is to change its name, at any time before the end of that period.

28(5) **[Daily default]**   A company which fails to comply with a direction under this section, and any officer of it who is in default, is liable to a fine and, for continued contravention, to a daily default fine.

28(6) **[New company name]**   Where a company changes its name under this section, the registrar of companies shall (subject to section 26) enter the new name on the register in place of the former name, and shall issue a certificate of incorporation altered to meet the circumstances of the case; and the change of name has effect from the date on which the altered certificate is issued.

28(7) **[Effect of change of name]**   A change of name by a company under this section does not affect any rights or obligations of the company or render defective any legal proceedings by or against it; and any legal proceedings that might have been continued or commenced against it by its former name may be continued or commenced against it by its new name.

SEC. 29 Regulations about names

29(1) [Regulations by Secretary of State] The Secretary of State may by regulations—

(a) specify words or expressions for the registration of which as or as part of a company's corporate name his approval is required under section 26(2)(b), and

(b) in relation to any such word or expression, specify a Government department or other body as the relevant body for purposes of the following subsection.

29(2) [Request to relevant body under sec. 29(1)(b)] Where a company proposes to have as, or as part of, its corporate name any such word or expression and a Government department or other body is specified under subsection (1)(b) in relation to that word or expression, a request shall be made (in writing) to the relevant body to indicate whether (and if so why) it has any objections to the proposal; and the person to make the request is—

(a) in the case of a company seeking to be registered under this Part, the person making the statutory declaration required by section 12(3),

(b) in the case of a company seeking to be registered under section 680, the persons making the statutory declaration required by section 686(2), and

(c) in any other case, a director or secretary of the company concerned.

29(3) [Statement re request in sec. 29(2) to registrar] The person who has made that request to the relevant body shall submit to the registrar of companies a statement that it has been made and a copy of any response received from that body, together with—

(a) the requisite statutory declaration, or

(b) a copy of the special resolution changing the company's name,

according as the case is one or other of those mentioned in subsection (2).

29(4) [Non-application of sec. 709, 710] Sections 709 and 710 (public rights of inspection of documents kept by registrar of companies) do not apply to documents sent under subsection (3) of this section.

29(5) [Transitional provisions etc.] Regulations under this section may contain such transitional provisions and savings as the Secretary of State thinks appropriate and may make different provision for different cases or classes of case.

29(6) [Approval of regulations etc.] The regulations shall be made by statutory instrument, to be laid before Parliament after it is made; and the regulations shall cease to have effect at the end of 28 days beginning with the day on which the regulations were made (but without prejudice to anything previously done by virtue of them or to the making of new regulations), unless during that period they are approved by resolution of each House. In reckoning that period, no account is to be taken of any time during which Parliament is dissolved or prorogued or during which both Houses are adjourned for more than 4 days.

SEC. 30   Exemption from requirement of "limited" as part of the name

30(1)   [Certain companies exempt]   Certain companies are exempt from requirements of this Act relating to the use of "limited" as part of the company name.

30(2)   [Exempt companies]   A private company limited by guarantee is exempt from those requirements, and so too is a company which on 25th February 1982 was a private company limited by shares with a name which, by virtue of a licence under section 19 of the Companies Act 1948, did not include "limited"; but in either case the company must, to have the exemption, comply with the requirements of the following subsection.

30(3)   [Requirements for exemption]   Those requirements are that—

(a)   the objects of the company are (or, in the case of a company about to be registered, are to be) the promotion of commerce, art, science, education, religion, charity or any profession, and anything incidental or conducive to any of those objects; and

(b)   the company's memorandum or articles—

  (i)   require its profits (if any) or other income to be applied in promoting its objects,

  (ii)   prohibit the payment of dividends to its members, and

  (iii)   require all the assets which would otherwise be available to its members generally to be transferred on its winding up either to another body with objects similar to its own or to another body the objects of which are the promotion of charity and anything incidental or conducive thereto (whether or not the body is a member of the company).

30(4)   [Statutory declaration to registrar]   A statutory declaration that a company complies with the requirements of subsection (3), may be delivered to the registrar of companies, who may accept the declaration as sufficient evidence of the matters stated in it; and the registrar may refuse to register a company by a name which does not include the word "limited" unless such a declaration has been delivered to him.

30(5)   [Requirements for statutory declaration in sec. 30(4)]   The statutory declaration must be in the prescribed form and be made—

(a)   in the case of a company to be formed, by a solicitor engaged in its formation or by a person named as director or secretary in the statement delivered under section 10(2);

(b)   in the case of a company to be registered in pursuance of section 680, by two or more directors or other principal officers of the company; and

(c)   in the case of a company proposing to change its name so that it ceases to have the word "limited" as part of its name, by a director or secretary of the company.

30(6)   [References to "limited"]   References in this section to the word "limited" include (in an appropriate case) its Welsh equivalent ("cyfyngedig"), and the appropriate alternative ("ltd." or "cyf.", as the case may be).

30(7)   [Additional exemption]   A company which is exempt from requirements relating to the use of "limited" and does not include that word as part of its name, is also exempt from the requirements of this Act relating to the publication of its name and the sending of lists of members to the registrar of companies.

SEC. 31 Provisions applying to company exempt under sec. 30

31(1) **[Memorandum and articles of exempt company not to be altered]** A company which is exempt under section 30 and whose name does not include "limited" shall not alter its memorandum or articles of association so that it ceases to comply with the requirements of subsection (3) of that section.

31(2) **[Exempt company contravening requirements]** If it appears to the Secretary of State that such a company—

> (a) has carried on any business other than the promotion of any of the objects mentioned in that subsection, or
>
> (b) has applied any of its profits or other income otherwise than in promoting such objects, or
>
> (c) has paid a dividend to any of its members,

he may, in writing, direct the company to change its name by resolution of the directors within such period as may be specified in the direction, so that its name ends with "limited".

A resolution passed by the directors in compliance with a direction under this subsection is subject to section 380 of this Act (copy to be forwarded to the registrar of companies within 15 days).

31(3) **[Company directed under sec. 31(2)]** A company which has received a direction under subsection (2) shall not thereafter be registered by a name which does not include "limited", without the approval of the Secretary of State.

31(4) **[References to "limited"]** References in this section to the word "limited" include (in an appropriate case) its Welsh equivalent ("cyfyngedig"), and the appropriate alternative ("ltd." or "cyf.", as the case may be).

31(5) **[Penalty for contravention of sec. 31(1)]** A company which contravenes subsection (1), and any officer of it who is in default, is liable to a fine and, for continued contravention, to a daily default fine.

31(6) **[Failure to comply with sec. 31(2) direction]** A company which fails to comply with a direction by the Secretary of State under subsection (2), and any officer of the company who is in default, is liable to a fine and, for continued contravention, to a daily default fine.

SEC. 32 Power to require company to abandon misleading name

32(1) **[Direction to change name]** If in the Secretary of State's opinion the name by which a company is registered gives so misleading an indication of the nature of its activities as to be likely to cause harm to the public, he may direct it to change its name.

32(2) **[Time for compliance with direction]** The direction must, if not duly made the subject of an application to the court under the following subsection, be complied with within a period of 6 weeks from the date of the direction or such longer period as the Secretary of State may think fit to allow.

32(3) **[Application to court to set aside direction]** The company may, within a period of 3 weeks from the date of the direction, apply to the court to set it aside; and the court may set the direction aside or confirm it and, if it confirms the direction, shall specify a period within which it must be complied with.

32(4) **[Penalty for non-compliance with direction]** If a company makes default in complying with a direction under this section, it is liable to a fine and, for continued contravention, to a daily default fine.

32(5) **[New certificate of incorporation on change of name]** Where a company changes its name under this section, the registrar shall (subject to section 26) enter the new name on the register in place of the former name, and shall issue a certificate of incorporation altered to meet the circumstances of the case; and the change of name has effect from the date on which the altered certificate is issued.

32(6) **[Effect of change of name]** A change of name by a company under this section does not affect any of the rights or obligations of the company, or render defective any legal proceedings by or against it; and any legal proceedings that might have been continued or commended against it by its former name may be continued or commenced against it by its new name.

SEC. 33   Prohibition on trading under misleading name

33(1) **[Non-public company using misleading title]** A person who is not a public company is guilty of an offence if he carries on any trade, profession or business under a name which includes, as its last part, the words "public limited company" or their equivalent in Welsh ("cwmni cyfyngedig cyhoeddus").

33(2) **[Public company giving false impression]** A public company is guilty of an offence if, in circumstances in which the fact that it is a public company is likely to be material to any person, it uses a name which may reasonably be expected to give the impression that it is a private company.

33(3) **[Penalty]** A person guilty of an offence under subsection (1) or (2) and, if that person is a company, any officer of the company who is in default, is liable to a fine and, for continued contravention, to a daily default fine.

SEC. 34   Penalty for improper use of "limited" or "cyfyngedig"

34 If any person trades or carries on business under a name or title of which "limited" or "cyfyngedig", or any contraction or imitation of either of those words, is the last word, that person, unless duly incorporated with limited liability, is liable to a fine and, for continued contravention, to a daily default fine.

Chapter III — A Company's Capacity; Formalities of Carrying on Business

SEC. 35   Company's capacity: power of directors to bind it

35(1) **[Third party dealing with company]** In favour of a person dealing with a company in good faith, any transaction decided on by the directors is deemed to be one which it is within the capacity of the company to enter into, and the power of the directors to bind the company is deemed to be free of any limitation under the memorandum or articles.

35(2)   [Presumption of good faith of third party]   A party to a transaction so decided on is not bound to enquire as to the capacity of the company to enter into it or as to any such limitation on the powers of the directors, and is presumed to have acted in good faith unless the contrary is proved.

SEC. 36   Form of company contracts

36(1)   [Contracts on behalf of company]   Contracts on behalf of a company may be made as follows—

   (a)   a contract which if made between private persons would be by law required to be in writing, and if made according to the law of England and Wales to be under seal, may be made on behalf of the company in writing under the company's common seal;

   (b)   a contract which if made between private persons would be by law required to be in writing, signed by the parties to be charged therewith, may be made on behalf of the company in writing signed by any person acting under its authority, express or implied;

   (c)   a contract which if made between private persons would by law be valid although made by parol only, and not reduced into writing, may be made by parol on behalf of the company by any person acting under its authority, express or implied.

36(2)   [Effect of contract and variation]   A contract made according to this section—

   (a)   is effectual in law, and binds the company and its successors and all other parties to it;

   (b)   may be varied or discharged in the same manner in which it is authorised by this section to be made.

36(3)   [Execution of deed in Scotland]   A deed to which a company is a party is held to be validly executed according to the law of Scotland on behalf of the company if it is executed in accordance with this Act or is sealed with the company's common seal and subscribed on behalf of the company by two of the directors, or by a director and the secretary; and such subscription on behalf of the company is binding whether attested by witnesses or not.

36(4)   [Pre-incorporation contracts]   Where a contract purports to be made by a company, or by a person as agent for a company, at a time when the company has not been formed, then subject to any agreement to the contrary the contract has effect as one entered into by the person purporting to act for the company or as agent for it, and he is personally liable on the contract accordingly.

SEC. 37   Bills of exchange and promissory notes

37   A bill of exchange or promissory note is deemed to have been made, accepted or endorsed on behalf of a company if made, accepted or endorsed in the name of, or by or on behalf or on account of, the company by a person acting under its authority.

SEC. 38   Execution of deeds abroad

38(1)   [Execution by attorney]   A company may, by writing under its common seal, empower any person, either generally or in respect of any specified matters, as its attorney, to execute deeds on its behalf in any place elsewhere than in the United Kingdom.

38(2)   [Effect]   A deed signed by such an attorney on behalf of the company and under his seal binds the company and has the same effect as if it were under the company's common seal.

SEC. 39   Power of company to have official seal for use abroad

39(1)   [Official seal]   A company whose objects require or comprise the transaction of business in foreign countries may, if authorised by its articles, have for use in any territory, district, or place elsewhere than in the United Kingdom, an official seal, which shall be a facsimile of the common seal of the company, with the addition on its face of the name of every territory, district or place where it is to be used.

39(2)   [Deed etc. with official seal]   A deed or other document to which the official seal is duly affixed binds the company as if it had been sealed with the company's common seal.

39(3)   [Authority to agent to affix official seal]   A company having an official seal for use in any such territory, district or place may, by writing under its common seal, authorise any person appointed for the purpose in that territory, district or place to affix the official seal to any deed or other document to which the company is party in that territory, district or place.

39(4)   [Duration of agent's authority]   As between the company and a person dealing with such an agent, the agent's authority continues during the period (if any) mentioned in the instrument conferring the authority, or if no period is there mentioned, then until notice of the revocation or determination of the agent's authority has been given to the person dealing with him.

39(5)   [Certificate or deed etc.]   The person affixing the official seal shall certify in writing on the deed or other instrument to which the seal is affixed the date on which and the place at which it is affixed.

SEC. 40   Official seal for share certificates, etc.

40   A company may have, for use for sealing securities issued by the company and for sealing documents creating or evidencing securities so issued, an official seal which is a facsimile of the company's common seal with the addition on its face of the word "Securities".

SEC. 41   Authentication of documents

41   A document or proceeding requiring authentication by a company may be signed by a director, secretary or other authorised officer of the company, and need not be under the company's common seal.

SEC. 42   Events affecting a company's status

42(1) [Official notification etc.] A company is not entitled to rely against other persons on the happening of any of the following events—

    (a) the making of a winding-up order in respect of the company, or the appointment of a liquidator in a voluntary winding up of the company, or

    (b) any alteration of the company's memorandum or articles, or

    (c) any change among the company's directors, or

    (d) (as regards service of any document on the company) any change in the situation of the company's registered office,

if the event had not been officially notified at the material time and is not shown by the company to have been known at that time to the person concerned, or if the material time fell on or before the 15th day after the date of official notification (or, where the 15th day was a non-business day, on or before the next day that was not) and it is shown that the person concerned was unavoidably prevented from knowing of the event at that time.

42(2) [Definitions] In subsection (1)—

    (a) **"official notification"** and **"officially notified"** have the meanings given by section 711(2) (registrar of companies to give public notice of the issue or receipt by him of certain documents), and

    (b) **"non-business day"** means a Saturday or Sunday, Christmas Day, Good Friday and any other day which is a bank holiday in the part of Great Britain where the company is registered.

PART II — RE-REGISTRATION AS A MEANS OF ALTERING A COMPANY'S STATUS

PRIVATE COMPANY BECOMING PUBLIC

SEC. 43   Re-registration of private company as public

43(1) [Requirements for re-registration] Subject to this and the following five sections, a private company (other than a company not having a share capital) may be re-registered as a public company if—

    (a) a special resolution that it should be so re-registered is passed; and

    (b) an application for re-registration is delivered to the registrar of companies, together with the necessary documents.

A company cannot be re-registered under this section if it has previously been re-registered as unlimited.

43(2) [Special resolution] The special resolution must—

    (a) alter the company's memorandum so that it states that the company is to be a public company; and

    (b) make such other alterations in the memorandum as are necessary to bring it (in substance and in form) into conformity with the requirements of this

Act with respect to the memorandum of a public company (the alterations to include compliance with section 25(1) as regards the company's name); and

(c) make such alterations in the company's articles as are requisite in the circumstances.

43(3) **[Requirements for application under sec. 43(1)(b)]** The application must be in the prescribed form and be signed by a director or secretary of the company; and the documents to be delivered with it are the following—

(a) a printed copy of the memorandum and articles as altered in pursuance of the resolution;

(b) a copy of a written statement by the company's auditors that in their opinion the relevant balance sheet shows that at the balance sheet date the amount of the company's net assets (within the meaning given to that expression by section 264(2)) was not less than the aggregate of its called-up share capital and undistributable reserves;

(c) a copy of the relevant balance sheet, together with a copy of an unqualified report (defined in section 46) by the company's auditors in relation to that balance sheet;

(d) if section 44 applies, a copy of the valuation report under subsection (2)(b) of that section; and

(e) a statutory declaration in the prescribed form by a director or secretary of the company—

(i) that the special resolution required by this section has been passed and that the conditions of the following two sections (so far as applicable have been satisfied, and

(ii) that, between the balance sheet date and the application for re-registration, there has been no change in the company's financial position that has resulted in the amount of its net assets becoming less than the aggregate of its called-up share capital and undistributable reserves.

43(4) **["Relevant balance sheet"]** "Relevant balance sheet" means a balance sheet prepared as at a date not more than 7 months before the company's application under this section.

43(5) **[Change of company name]** A resolution that a company be re-registered as a public company may change the company name by deleting the word "company" or the words "and company", or its or their equivalent in Welsh ("cwmni", "a'r cwmni"), including any abbreviation of them.

SEC. 44 Consideration for shares recently allotted to be valued

44(1) **[Application of section]** The following applies if shares have been allotted by the company between the date as at which the relevant balance sheet was prepared and the passing of the special resolution under section 43, and those shares were allotted as fully or partly paid up as to their nominal value or any premium on them otherwise than in cash.

44(2) **[Conditions for sec. 43 application]** Subject to the following provisions, the registrar of companies shall not entertain an application by the company under section 43 unless beforehand—

(a) the consideration for the allotment has been valued in accordance with section 108, and

(b) a report with respect to the value of the consideration has been made to the company (in accordance with that section) during the 6 months immediately preceding the allotment of the shares.

44(3) **[Consideration for the allotment]** Where an amount standing to the credit of any of the company's reserve accounts, or of its profit and loss account, has been applied in paying up (to any extent) any of the shares allotted or any premium on those shares, the amount applied does not count as consideration for the allotment, and accordingly subsection (2) does not apply to it.

44(4) **[Non-application of sec. 44(2)]** Subsection (2) does not apply if the allotment is in connection with an arrangement providing for it to be on terms that the whole or part of the consideration for the shares allotted is to be provided by the transfer to the company or the cancellation of all or some of the shares, or of all or some of the shares of a particular class, in another company (with or without the issue to the company applying under section 43 of shares, or of shares of any particular class, in that other company).

44(5) **[Qualification to sec. 44(4)]** But subsection (4) does not exclude the application of sub-section (2), unless under the arrangement it is open to all the holders of the shares of the other company in question (or, where the arrangement applies only to shares of a particular class, all the holders of the other company's shares of that class) to take part in the arrangement.

In determining whether that is the case, shares held by or by a nominee of the company allotting shares in connection with the arrangement, or by a nominee of a company which is that company's holding company or subsidiary or a company which is a subsidiary of its holding company, are to be disregarded.

44(6) **[Allotment in connection with merger]** Subsection (2) does not apply to preclude an application under section 43, if the allotment of the company's shares is in connection with its proposed merger with another company; that is, where one of the companies concerned proposes to acquire all the assets and liabilities of the other in exchange for the issue of shares or other securities of that one to shareholders of the other, with or without any cash payment to shareholders.

44(7) **[Definitions]** In this section—

(a) **"arrangement"** means any agreement, scheme or arrangement, including an arrangement sanctioned in accordance with section 425 (company compromise with creditors and members) or section 110 of the Insolvency Act (liquidator in winding up accepting shares as consideration for sale of company's property), and

(b) **"another company"** includes any body corporate and any body to which letters patent have been issued under the Chartered Companies Act 1837.

History
In s. 44(7)(a) the words "section 110 of the Insolvency Act" substituted for the former words "section 582" by Insolvency Act 1986, s. 439(1) and Sch. 13 as from 29 December 1986 (see IA 1986, s. 443 and S.I. 1986 No. 1924 (C. 71)).

SEC. 45   Additional requirements relating to share capital

45(1)   [Conditions re share capital]   For a private company to be re-registered under section 43 as a public company, the following conditions with respect to its share capital must be satisfied at the time the special resolution under that section is passed.

45(2)   [Nominal value requirements]   Subject to subsections (5) to (7) below—

(a) the nominal value of the company's allotted share capital must be not less than the authorised minimum, and

(b) each of the company's allotted shares must be paid up at least as to one-quarter of the nominal value of that share and the whole of any premium on it.

45(3)   [Undertaking for work or services]   Subject to subsection (5), if any shares in the company or any premium on them have been fully or partly paid up by an undertaking given by any person that he or another should do work or perform services (whether for the company or any other person), the undertaking must have been performed or otherwise discharged.

45(4)   [Undertaking — where paid up otherwise than in cash]   Subject to subsection (5), if shares have been allotted as fully or partly paid up as to their nominal value or any premium on them otherwise than in cash, and the consideration for the allotment consists of or includes an undertaking to the company (other than one to which subsection (3) applies), then either—

(a) the undertaking must have been performed or otherwise discharged, or

(b) there must be a contract between the company and some person pursuant to which the undertaking is to be performed within 5 years from the time the resolution under section 43 is passed.

45(5)   [Determination of compliance with sec. 45(2)(b), (3), (4)]   For the purpose of determining whether subsections (2)(b), (3) and (4) are complied with, certain shares in the company may be disregarded; and these are—

(a) subject to the next subsection, any share which was allotted before 22nd June 1982, and

(b) any share which was allotted in pursuance of an employees' share scheme and by reason of which the company would, but for this subsection, be precluded under subsection (2)(b) (but not otherwise) from being re-registered as a public company.

45(6)   [Share not disregarded under sec. 45(5)(a)]   A share is not to be disregarded under subsection (5)(a) if the aggregate in nominal value of that share and other shares proposed to be so disregarded is more than one-tenth of the nominal value of the company's allotted share capital; but for this purpose the allotted share capital is treated as not including any shares disregarded under subsection (5)(b).

45(7)   [Shares disregarded under sec. 45(5)]   Any shares disregarded under subsection (5) are treated as not forming part of the allotted share capital for the purposes of subsection (2)(a).

SEC. 46 Meaning of "unqualified report" in sec. 43(3)

46(1) **[Reference to auditors' unqualified report]** The following subsections explain the reference in section 43(3)(c) to an unqualified report of the company's auditors on the relevant balance sheet.

46(2) **[Where balance sheet prepared re financial year]** If the balance sheet was prepared for a financial year of the company, the reference is to an auditors' report stating without material qualification the auditors' opinion that the balance sheet has been properly prepared in accordance with this Act.

46(3) **[Where balance sheet not prepared re financial year]** If the balance sheet was not prepared for a financial year of the company, the reference is to an auditors' report stating without material qualification the auditors' opinion that the balance sheet has been properly prepared in accordance with the provisions of this Act which would have applied if it had been so prepared.

For the purposes of an auditors' report under this subsection the provisions of this Act shall be deemed to apply with such modifications as are necessary by reason of the fact that the balance sheet is not prepared for a financial year of the company.

46(4) **[Where qualification material]** A qualification shall be regarded as material unless the auditors state in their report that the matter giving rise to the qualification is not material for the purpose of determining (by reference to the company's balance sheet) whether at the balance sheet date the amount of the company's net assets was not less than the aggregate of its called up share capital and undistributable reserves.

In this subsection **"net assets"** and **"undistributable reserves"** have the meaning given by section 264(2) and (3).

History

S. 46(2)–(4) substituted for the former s. 46(2)–(6) by CA 1989, s. 23 and Sch. 10, para. 1 as from 1 April 1990 subject to transitional and saving provisions (see S.I. 1990 No. 355 (C. 13), art. 3, Sch. 1, and also art. 6–9); the former s. 46(2)–(6) read as follows:

"**46(2)** If the balance sheet was prepared in respect of an accounting reference period of the company, that reference is to a report made by the auditors and stating without material qualification, that in their opinion the balance sheet—

(a) has been properly prepared in accordance with this Act, and

(b) gives a true and fair view of the state of the company's affairs as at the balance sheet date.

(3) In any other case the reference is to a report by the auditors stating without material qualification that in their opinion the balance sheet—

(a) complies with the applicable accounting provisions, and

(b) without prejudice to that (but subject to subsection (4) below), gives a true and fair view of the state of the company's affairs as at the balance sheet date;

and the accounting provisions referred to in paragraph (a) are sections 228 and 238(1) in Chapter I of Part VII and (where applicable) section 258 in Chapter II of that Part.

(4) Where the balance sheet is prepared under Chapter II of Part VII (special category companies), and the company is entitled to avail itself, and has availed itself, of any of the provisions of Part III of Schedule 9, the auditors' report is not required to state that the balance sheet gives a true and fair view of the company's state of affairs as at the balance sheet date.

(5) For purposes of references in this section to the auditors' report, a qualification is not material if, but only if, the auditors in their report state that the thing giving rise to the qualification is not material for the purpose of determining (by reference to the balance sheet) whether at the balance sheet date the amount of the company's net assets was not less than the agregate of its called up share capital and undistributable reserves.

(6) For the purposes of a report of the auditors falling within subsection (3)—

(a) section 228 in Chapter I of Part VII, and Schedule 4 (form and content of company accounts), and

(b) (where applicable) section 258 in Chapter II of that Part, and Schedule 9 (the same, in relation to special category companies),

are deemed to have effect in relation to the balance sheet with such modifications as are necessary by reason of the fact that the balance sheet is prepared otherwise than as at the end of an accounting reference period."

SEC. 47   Certificate of re-registration under sec. 43

47(1)   **[Obligations of registrar on receipt of application]**   If the registrar of companies is satisfied, on an application under section 43, that a company may be re-registered under that section as a public company, he shall—

(a) retain the application and other documents delivered to him under the section; and

(b) issue the company with a certificate of incorporation stating that the company is a public company.

47(2)   **[Statutory declaration under sec. 43(3)(e) sufficient evidence]**   The registrar may accept a declaration under section 43(3)(e) as sufficient evidence that the special resolution required by that section has been passed and the other conditions of re-registration satisfied.

47(3)   **[No certificate if nominal value below authorised minimum]**   The registrar shall not issue the certificate if it appears to him that the court has made an order confirming a reduction of the company's capital which has the effect of bringing the nominal value of the company's allotted share capital below the authorised minimum.

47(4)   **[Effect of issue of certificate]**   Upon the issue to a company of a certificate of incorporation under this section—

(a) the company by virtue of the issue of that certificate becomes a public company; and

(b) any alterations in the memorandum and articles set out in the resolution take effect accordingly.

47(5)   **[Certificate conclusive evidence]**   The certificate is conclusive evidence—

(a) that the requirements of this Act in respect of re-registration and of matters precedent and incidental thereto have been complied with; and

(b) that the company is a public company.

SEC. 48   Modification for unlimited company re-registering

48(1)   **[Modification of sec. 43 to 47]**   In their application to unlimited companies, sections 43 to 47 are modified as follows.

48(2)   **[Extra matters in sec. 43(1) resolution]**   The special resolution required by section 43(1) must, in addition to the matters mentioned in subsection (2) of that section—

(a) state that the liability of the members is to be limited by shares, and what the company's share capital is to be; and

(b) make such alterations in the company's memorandum as are necessary to bring it in substance and in form into conformity with the requirements of this Act with respect to the memorandum of a company limited by shares.

48(3)   **[Extra matters in sec. 47(1) certificate]**   The certificate of incorporation issued under section 47(1) shall, in addition to containing the statement required by paragraph (b) of that subsection, state that the company has been incorporated as a company limited by shares; and—

CA 1985, sec. 47(1)

(a) the company by virtue of the issue of the certificate becomes a public company so limited; and

(b) the certificate is conclusive evidence of the fact that it is such a company.

LIMITED COMPANY BECOMING UNLIMITED

SEC. 49   Re-registration of limited company as unlimited

49(1)   [Application]   Subject as follows, a company which is registered as limited may be re-registered as unlimited in pursuance of an application in that behalf complying with the requirements of this section.

49(2)   [Exclusion from section]   A company is excluded from re-registering under this section if it is limited by virtue of re-registration under section 44 of the Companies Act 1967 or section 51 of this Act.

49(3)   [Further exclusion]   A public company cannot be re-registered under this section; nor can a company which has previously been re-registered as unlimited.

49(4)   [Requirements for application]   An application under this section must be in the prescribed form and be signed by a director or the secretary of the company, and be lodged with the registrar of companies, together with the documents specified in subsection (8) below.

49(5)   [Alterations to memorandum to be set out]   The application must set out such alterations in the company's memorandum as—

(a) if it is to have a share capital, are requisite to bring it (in substances and in form) into conformity with the requirements of this Act with respect to the memorandum of a company to be formed as an unlimited company having a share capital; or

(b) if it is not to have a share capital, are requisite in the circumstances.

49(6)   [Alterations in articles to be set out]   If articles have been registered, the application must set out such alterations in them as—

(a) if the company is to have a share capital, are requisite to bring the articles (in substance and in form) into conformity with the requirements of this Act with respect to the articles of a company to be formed as an unlimited company having a share capital; or

(b) if the company is not to have a share capital, are requisite in the circumstances.

49(7)   [If articles not registered]   If articles have not been registered, the application must have annexed to it, and request the registration of, printed articles; and these must, if the company is to have a share capital, comply with the requirements mentioned in subsection (6)(a) and, if not, be articles appropriate to the circumstances.

49(8)   [Documents to be lodged with registrar]   The documents to be lodged with the registrar are—

(a) the prescribed form of assent to the company's being registered as unlimited, subscribed by or on behalf of all the members of the company;

(b) a statutory declaration made by the directors of the company—

(i) that the persons by whom or on whose behalf the form of assent is subscribed constitute the whole membership of the company, and

(ii) if any of the members have not subscribed that form themselves, that the directors have taken all reasonable steps to satisfy themselves that each person who subscribed it on behalf of a member was lawfully empowered to do so;

(c) a printed copy of the memorandum incorporating the alterations in it set out in the application; and

(d) if articles have been registered, a printed copy of them incorporating the alterations set out in the application.

49(9)   [Interpretation]   For purposes of this section—

(a) subscription to a form of assent by the legal personal representative of a deceased member of a company is deemed subscription by him; and

(b) a trustee in bankruptcy of a member of a company is, to the exclusion of the latter, deemed a member of the company.

SEC. 50   Certificate of re-registration under sec. 49

50(1)   [Registration, issue of certificate]   The registrar of companies shall retain the application and other documents lodged with him under section 49 and shall—

(a) if articles are annexed to the application, register them; and

(b) issue to the company a certificate of incorporation appropriate to the status to be assumed by it by virtue of that section.

50(2)   [Effect of issue of certificate]   On the issue of the certificate—

(a) the status of the company, by virtue of the issue, is changed from limited to unlimited; and

(b) the alterations in the memorandum set out in the application and (if articles have been previously registered) any alterations to the articles so set out take effect as if duly made by resolution of the company; and

(c) the provisions of this Act apply accordingly to the memorandum and articles as altered.

50(3)   [Certificate conclusive evidence]   The certificate is conclusive evidence that the requirements of section 49 in respect of re-registration and of matters precedent and incidental to it have been complied with, and that the company was authorised to be re-registered under this Act in pursuance of that section and was duly so re-registered.

UNLIMITED COMPANY BECOMING LIMITED

SEC. 51   Re-registration of unlimited company as limited

51(1)   [Re-registration — special resolution etc.]   Subject as follows, a company which is registered as unlimited may be re-registered as limited if a special resolution that it should be so re-registered is passed, and the requirements of this section are complied with in respect of the resolution and otherwise.

51(2) **[Limitations]** A company cannot under this section be re-registered as a public company; and a company is excluded from registering under it if it is unlimited by virtue of re-registration under section 43 of the Companies Act 1967 or section 49 of this Act.

51(3) **[Requirements for special resolution]** The special resolution must state whether the company is to be limited by shares or by guarantee and—

(a) if it is to be limited by shares, must state what the share capital is to be and provide for the making of such alterations in the memorandum as are necessary to bring it (in substance and in form) into conformity with the requirements of this Act with respect to the memorandum of a company so limited, and such alterations in the articles as are requisite in the circumstances;

(b) if it is to be limited by guarantee, must provide for the making of such alterations in its memorandum and articles as are necessary to bring them (in substance and in form) into conformity with the requirements of this Act with respect to the memorandum and articles of a company so limited.

51(4) **[Time limit for documents to registrar]** The special resolution is subject to section 380 of this Act (copy to be forwarded to registrar within 15 days); and an application for the company to be re-registered as limited, framed in the prescribed form and signed by a director or by the secretary of the company, must be lodged with the registrar of companies, together with the necessary documents, not earlier than the day on which the copy of the resolution forwarded under section 380 is received by him.

51(5) **[Documents to be lodged with registrar]** The documents to be lodged with the registrar are—

(a) a printed copy of the memorandum as altered in pursuance of the resolution; and

(b) a printed copy of the articles as so altered.

51(6) **[Non-application of section]** This section does not apply in relation to the re-registration of an unlimited company as a public company under section 43.

SEC. 52 Certification of re-registration under sec. 51

52(1) **[Certificate from registrar]** The registrar shall retain the application and other documents lodged with him under section 51, and shall issue to the company a certificate of incorporation appropriate to the status to be assumed by the company by virtue of that section.

52(2) **[Effect of issue of certificate]** On the issue of the certificate—

(a) the status of the company is, by virtue of the issue, changed from unlimited to limited; and

(b) the alterations in the memorandum specified in the resolution and the alterations in, and additions to, the articles so specified take effect.

52(3) **[Certificate conclusive evidence]** The certificate is conclusive evidence that the requirements of section 51 in respect of re-registration and of matters precedent and incidental to it have been complied with, and that the company was authorised to be re-registered in pursuance of that section and was duly so re-registered.

PUBLIC COMPANY BECOMING PRIVATE

SEC. 53   Re-registration of public company as private

53(1)   [Requirements for re-registration]   A public company may be re-registered as a private company if—

(a) a special resolution complying with subsection (2) below that it should be so re-registered is passed and has not been cancelled by the court under the following section;

(b) an application for the purpose in the prescribed form and signed by a director or the secretary of the company is delivered to the registrar of companies, together with a printed copy of the memorandum and articles of the company as altered by the resolution; and

(c) the period during which an application for the cancellation of the resolution under the following section may be made has expired without any such application having been made; or

(d) where such an application has been made, the application has been withdrawn or an order has been made under section 54(5) confirming the resolution and a copy of that order has been delivered to the registrar.

53(2)   [Alteration to memorandum etc.]   The special resolution must alter the company's memorandum so that it no longer states that the company is to be a public company and must make such other alterations in the company's memorandum and articles as are requisite in the circumstances.

53(3)   [Extent of section]   A company cannot under this section be re-registered otherwise than as a company limited by shares or by guarantee.

SEC. 54   Litigated objection to resolution under sec. 53

54(1)   [Application for cancellation of resolution]   Where a special resolution by a public company to be re-registered under section 53 as a private company has been passed, an application may be made to the court for the cancellation of that resolution.

54(2)   [Applicants]   The application may be made—

(a) by the holders of not less in the aggregate than 5 per cent in nominal value of the company's issued share capital or any class thereof;

(b) if the company is not limited by shares, by not less than 5 per cent of its members; or

(c) by not less than 50 of the company's members;

but not by a person who has consented to or voted in favour of the resolution.

54(3)   [Time limit etc. for application]   The application must be made within 28 days after the passing of the resolution and may be made on behalf of the persons entitled to make the application by such one or more of their number as they may appoint in writing for the purpose.

54(4) [**Notice to registrar**] If such an application is made, the company shall forthwith give notice in the prescribed form of that fact to the registrar of companies.

54(5) [**Court order**] On the hearing of the application, the court shall make an order either cancelling or confirming the resolution and—

(a) may make that order on such terms and conditions as it thinks fit, and may (if it thinks fit) adjourn the proceedings in order that an arrangement may be made to the satisfaction of the court for the purchase of the interests of dissentient members; and

(b) may give such directions and make such orders as it thinks expedient for facilitating or carrying into effect any such arrangement.

54(6) [**Extent of court order**] The court's order may, if the court thinks fit, provide for the purchase by the company of the shares of any of its members and for the reduction accordingly of the company's capital, and may make such alterations in the company's memorandum and articles as may be required in consequence of that provision.

54(7) [**Office copy of order to registrar**] The company shall, within 15 days from the making of the court's order, or within such longer period as the court may at any time by order direct, deliver to the registrar of companies an office copy of the order.

54(8) [**If order requires no alteration to memorandum or articles**] If the court's order requires the company not to make any, or any specified, alteration in its memorandum or articles, the company has not then power without the leave of the court to make any such alteration in breach of the requirement.

54(9) [**Alteration by virtue of order**] An alteration in the memorandum or articles made by virtue of an order under this section, if not made by resolution of the company, is of the same effect as if duly made by resolution; and this Act applies accordingly to the memorandum or articles as so altered.

54(10) [**Penalty on default**] A company which fails to comply with subsection (4) or subsection (7), and any officer of it who is in default, is liable to a fine and, for continued contravention, to a daily default fine.

SEC. 55   Certificate of re-registration under sec. 53

55(1) [**Obligations of registrar**] If the registrar of companies is satisfied that a company may be re-registered under section 53, he shall—

(a) retain the application and other documents delivered to him under that section; and

(b) issue the company with a certificate of incorporation appropriate to a private company.

55(2) [**Effect of issue of certificate**] On the issue of the certificate—

(a) the company by virtue of the issue becomes a private company; and

(b) the alterations in the memorandum and articles set out in the resolution under section 53 take effect accordingly.

55(3)   **[Certificate conclusive evidence]**   The certificate is conclusive evidence—

(a) that the requirements of section 53 in respect of re-registration and of matters precedent and incidental to it have been complied with; and

(b) that the company is a private company.

PART III — CAPITAL ISSUES

Chapter I — Issues by Companies Registered, or to be Registered, in Great Britain

THE PROSPECTUS

SEC. 56   Matters to be stated, and reports to be set out, in prospectus

56(1)   **[Matters and reports in prospectus]**   Every prospectus issued by or on behalf of a company, or by or on behalf of any person who is or has been engaged or interested in the formation of the company, must comply—

(a) with Part I of Schedule 3 to this Act, as respects the matters to be stated in the prospectus, and

(b) with Part II of that Schedule, as respects the reports to be set out.

56(2)   **[Requirement for prospectus]**   It is unlawful to issue any form of application for shares in or debentures of a company unless the form is issued with a prospectus which complies with the requirements of this section.

56(3)   **[Exceptions to sec. 56(2)]**   Subsection (2) does not apply if it is shown that the form of application was issued either—

(a) in connection with a bona fide invitation to a person to enter into an underwriting agreement with respect to the shares or debentures, or

(b) in relation to shares or debentures which were not offered to the public.

56(4)   **[Penalty for contravention]**   If a person acts in contravention of subsection (2), he is liable to a fine.

56(5)   **[Exceptions to sec. 56]**   This section does not apply—

(a) to the issue to existing members or debenture holders of a company of a prospectus or form of application relating to shares in or debentures of the company, whether an applicant for shares or debentures will or will not have the right to renounce in favour of other persons, or

(b) to the issue of a prospectus or form of application relating to shares or debentures which are or are to be in all respects uniform with shares or debentures previously issued and for the time being listed on a prescribed stock exchange;

but subject to this, it applies to a prospectus or a form of application whether issued on or with reference to the formation of a company or subsequently.

Note
See note after s. 79.

SEC. 57 Attempted evasion of sec. 56 to be void

57 A condition requiring or binding an applicant for shares in or debentures of a company to waive compliance with any requirement of section 56, or purporting to affect him with notice of any contract, document or matter not specifically referred to in the prospectus, is void.

Note
See note after s. 79.

SEC. 58 Document offering shares etc. for sale deemed a prospectus

58(1) [Deemed prospectus] If a company allots or agrees to allot its shares or debentures with a view to all or any of them being offered for sale to the public, any document by which the offer for sale to the public is made is deemed for all purposes a prospectus issued by the company.

58(2) [Application of prospectus rules] All enactments and rules of law as to the contents of prospectuses, and to liability in respect of statements in and omissions from prospectuses, or otherwise relating to prospectuses, apply and have effect accordingly, as if the shares or debentures had been offered to the public for subscription and as if persons accepting the offer in respect of any shares or debentures were subscribers for those shares or debentures.

This is without prejudice to the liability (if any) of the persons by whom the offer is made, in respect of mis-statements in the document or otherwise in respect of it.

58(3) [Allotment with view to offer to public] For purposes of this Act it is evidence (unless the contrary is proved) that an allotment of, or an agreement to allot, shares or debentures was made with a view to their being offered for sale to the public if it is shown—

(a) than an offer of the shares or debentures (or of any of them) for sale to the public was made within 6 months after the allotment or agreement to allot, or

(b) that at the date when the offer was made the whole consideration to be received by the company in respect of the shares or debentures had not been so received.

58(4) [Effect of sec. 56] Section 56 as applied by this section has effect as if it required a prospectus to state, in addition to the matters required by that section—

(a) the net amount of the consideration received or to be received by the company in respect of the shares or debentures to which the offer relates, and

(b) the place and time at which the contract under which those shares or debentures have been or are to be allotted may be inspected.

Note
See note after s. 79.

SEC. 59 Rule governing what is an "offer to the public"

59(1) [Offering shares or debentures to public] Subject to the next section, any reference in this Act to offering shares or debentures to the public is to be read (subject to any provision to the contrary) as including a reference to offering them to any section of the public, whether selected as members or debenture holders of the company concerned, or as clients of the person issuing the prospectus, or in any other manner.

59(2)   [Invitation to public to subscribe]   The same applies to any reference in this Act, or in a company's articles, to an invitation to the public to subscribe for shares or debentures.

Note
See note after s. 79.

SEC. 60   Exceptions from rule in sec. 59

60(1)   [Offers not treated as made to public]   Section 59 does not require an offer or invitation to be treated as made to the public if it can properly be regarded, in all the circumstances, as not being calculated to result, directly or indirectly, in the shares or debentures becoming available for subscription or purchase by persons other than those receiving the offer or invitation, or otherwise as being a domestic concern of the persons receiving and making it.

60(2)   [Provision in articles]   In particular, a provision in a company's articles prohibiting invitations to the public to subscribe for shares or debentures is not to be taken as prohibiting the making to members or debenture holders of an invitation which can properly be regarded as falling within the preceding subsection.

60(3)   [Offer a domestic concern]   For purposes of that subsection, an offer of shares in or debentures of a private company, or an invitation to subscribe for such shares or debentures, is to be regarded (unless the contrary is proved) as being a domestic concern of the persons making and receiving the offer or invitation if it falls within any of the following descriptions.

60(4)   [Where offer is domestic concern]   It is to be so regarded if it is made to—

   (a) an existing member of the company making the offer or invitation,

   (b) an existing employee of that company,

   (c) a member of the family of such a member or employee, or

   (d) an existing debenture holder.

60(5)   [Members of family under sec. 60(4)(c)]   For purposes of subsection (4)(c), the members of a person's family are—

   (a) the person's husband or wife, widow or widower and children (including stepchildren) and their descendants, and

   (b) any trustee (acting in his capacity as such) of a trust the principal beneficiary of which is the person him or herself, or any of those relatives.

60(6)   [Employees' share scheme]   The offer or invitation is also to be so regarded if it is to subscribe for shares or debentures to be held under an employees' share scheme.

60(7)   [Renounceable rights]   The offer or invitation is also to be so regarded if it falls within subsection (4) or (6) and it is made on terms which permit the person to whom it is made to renounce his right to the allotment of shares or issue of debentures, but only in favour—

CA 1985, sec. 59(2)

(a) of such a person as is mentioned in any of the paragraphs of subsection (4), or

(b) of such a person as is mentioned in any of the paragraphs of subsection (4), or

60(8) **[Where application to Stock Exchange]** Where application has been made to the Council of The Stock Exchange for admission of any securities to the Official List of the Stock Exchange, then an offer of those securities for subscription or sale to a person whose ordinary business it is to buy or sell shares or debentures (whether as principal or agent) is not deemed an offer to the public for purposes of this Part.
Note
See note after s. 79.

SEC. 61 Prospectus containing statement by expert

61(1) **[Conditions for issue]** A prospectus inviting persons to subscribe for a company's shares or debentures and including a statement purporting to be made by an expert shall not be issued unless—

(a) he (the expert) has given and has not, before delivery of a copy of the prospectus for registration, withdrawn his written consent to its issue with the statement included in the form and context in which it is in fact included; and

(b) a statement that he has given and not withdrawn that consent appears in the prospectus.

61(2) **[Penalty]** If a prospectus is issued in contravention of this section, the company and every person who is knowingly a party to the issue of the prospectus is liable to a fine.
Note
See note after s. 79.

SEC. 62 Meaning of "expert"

62 The expression **"expert"**, in both Chapters of this Part, includes engineer, valuer, accountant and any other person whose profession gives authority to a statement made by him.
Note
See note after s. 79.

SEC. 63 Prospectus to be dated

63 A prospectus issued by or on behalf of a company, or in relation to an intended company, shall be dated; and that date shall, unless the contrary is proved, be taken as its date of publication.
Note
See note after s. 79.

REGISTRATION OF PROSPECTUS

SEC. 64 Registration requirement applicable in all cases

64(1) **[Prospectus not to be issued until registered]** No prospectus shall be issued by or on behalf of a company, or in relation to an intended company, unless on or before the date of its publication there has been delivered to the registrar of companies for registration a copy of the prospectus—

   (a) signed by every person who is named in it as a director or proposed director of the company, or by his agent authorised in writing, and

   (b) having endorsed on or attached to it any consent to its issue required by section 61 from any person as an expert.

64(2) [Signing of prospectus] Where the prospectus is such a document as is referred to in section 58, the signatures required by subsection (1) above include those of every person making the offer, or his agent authorised in writing.

    Where the offer is made by a company or a firm, it is sufficient for the purposes of this subsection if the document is signed on its behalf by two directors or (as the case may be) not less than half of the partners; and a director or partner may sign by his agent authorised in writing.

64(3) [Statements in prospectus] Every prospectus shall on its face—

   (a) state that a copy has been delivered for registration as required by this section, and

   (b) specify, or refer to statements in the prospectus specifying, any documents required by this or the following section to be endorsed on or attached to the copy delivered.

64(4) [Requirements before registered] The registrar shall not register a prospectus unless it is dated and the copy of it signed as required by this section and unless it has endorsed on or attached to it the documents (if any) specified in subsection (3)(b).

64(5) [Penalty] If a prospectus is issued without a copy of it being delivered to the registrar as required by this section, or without the copy so delivered having the required documents endorsed on or attached to it, the company and every person who is knowingly a party to the issue of the prospectus is liable to a fine and, for continued contravention, to a daily default fine.

Note
See note after s. 79.

SEC. 65   Additional requirements in case of prospectus issued generally

65(1) [Extra provisions] In the case of a prospectus issued generally (that is, to persons who are not existing members or debenture holders of the company), the following provisions apply in addition to those of section 64.

65(2) [Copy of contract memorandum to be attached] The copy of the prospectus delivered to the registrar of companies must also have endorsed on or attached to it a copy of any contract required by paragraph 11 of Schedule 3 to be stated in the prospectus or, in the case of a contract not reduced into writing, a memorandum giving full particulars of it.

65(3) [Where contract in foreign language] In the case of a contract wholly or partly in a foreign language—

   (a) the copy required by subsection (2) to be endorsed on or attached to the prospectus must be a copy of a translation of the contract into English or (as the case may be) a copy embodying a translation into English of the parts in a foreign language, and

(b) the translation must be certified in the prescribed manner to be a correct translation.

65(4) **[Statement re adjustments]** If the persons making any report required by Part II of Schedule 3 have made in the report, or have (without giving reasons) indicated in it, any such adjustments as are mentioned in paragraph 21 of the Schedule (profits, losses, assets, liabilities), the copy of the prospectus delivered to the registrar must have endorsed on or attached to it a written statement signed by those persons setting out the adjustments and giving the reasons for them.

Note
See note after s. 79.

LIABILITIES AND OFFENCES IN CONNECTION WITH PROSPECTUS

SEC. 66 Directors, etc. exempt from liability in certain cases

66(1) **[Exemption re non-compliance with sec. 56]** In the event of non-compliance with or contravention of section 56, a director or other person responsible for the prospectus does not incur any liability by reason of that non-compliance or contravention if—

(a) as regards any matter not disclosed, he proves that he was not cognisant of it, or

(b) he proves that the non-compliance or contravention arose from an honest mistake of fact on his part, or

(c) the non-compliance or contravention was in respect of matters which, in the opinion of the court dealing with the case, were immaterial or was otherwise such as ought (in the court's opinion, having regard to all the circumstances of the case) reasonably to be excused.

66(2) **[Exemption re failure to disclose interests]** In the event of failure to include in a prospectus a statement with respect to the matters specified in paragraph 13 of Schedule 3 (disclosure of directors' interests), no director or other person incurs any liability in respect of the failure unless it is proved that he had knowledge of the matters not disclosed.

66(3) **[Liability under general law]** Nothing in section 56 or 57 or this section limits or diminishes any liability which a person may incur under the general law or this Act apart from those provisions.

Note
See note after s. 79.

SEC. 67 Compensation for subscribers misled by statement in prospectus

67(1) **[Compensation for loss or damage]** Where a prospectus invites persons to subscribe for a company's shares or debentures, compensation is payable to all those who subscribe for any shares or debentures on the faith of the prospectus for the loss or damage which they may have sustained by reason of any untrue statement included in it.

67(2) **[Persons liable to pay compensation]** The persons liable to pay the compensation are—

(a) every person who is a director of the company at the time of the issue of the prospectus,

(b) every person who authorised himself to be named, and is named, in the prospectus as a director or as having agreed to become a director (either immediately or after an interval of time),

(c) every person being a promoter of the company, and

(d) every person who has authorised the issue of the prospectus.

67(3) **[''Promoter'' in sec. 67, 68, 69]** The above has effect subject to the two sections next following; and here and in those sections **"promoter"** means a promoter who was party to the preparation of the prospectus, or of the portion of it containing the untrue statement, but does not include any person by reason of his acting in a professional capacity for persons engaged in procuring the formation of the company.

Note
See note after s. 79.

SEC. 68   Exemption from sec. 67 for those acting with propriety

68(1) **[Conditions for exemption]** A person is not liable under section 67 if he proves—

(a) that, having consented to become a director of the company, he withdrew his consent before the issue of the prospectus, and that it was issued without his authority or consent, or

(b) that the prospectus was issued without his knowledge or consent, and that on becoming aware of its issue he forthwith gave reasonable public notice that it was issued without his knowledge or consent, or

(c) that after issue of the prospectus and before allotment under it he, on becoming aware of any untrue statement in it, withdrew his consent to its issue and gave reasonable public notice of the withdrawal and of the reason for it.

68(2) **[Further conditions]** A person is not liable under that section if he proves that—

(a) as regards every untrue statement not purporting to be made on the authority of an expert or of a public official document or statement, he had reasonable ground to believe, and did up to the time of the allotment of the shares or debentures (as the case may be) believe, that the statement was true; and

(b) as regards every untrue statement purporting to be a statement by an expert or contained in what purports to be a copy of or extract from a report or valuation of an expert, it fairly represented the statement, or was a correct and fair copy of or extract from the report or valuation, and he had reasonable ground to believe and did up to the time of issue of the prospectus believe that the person making the statement was competent to make it and that person had given the consent required by section 61 to the issue of the prospectus and had not withdrawn that consent before delivery of a copy of the prospectus for registration or, to the defendant's knowledge, before allotment under it; and

(c) as regards every untrue statement purporting to be made by an official person or contained in what purports to be a copy of or extract from a public official document, it was a correct and fair representation of the statement or copy of or extract from the document.

68(3) **[Non-application of sec. 68(1),(2)]** Subsections (1) and (2) of this section do not apply in the case of a person liable, by reason of his having given a consent required of him by section 61, as a person who has authorised the issue of the prospectus in respect of an untrue statement purporting to be made by him as an expert.

68(4) **[Person giving consent under sec. 61]** Where under section 61 the consent of a person is required to the issue of a prospectus and he has given that consent, he is not by reason of his having given it liable under section 67 as a person who has authorised the issue of the prospectus except in respect of an untrue statement purporting to be made by him as an expert.

68(5) **[Exemption for person usually liable under sec. 67]** A person who, apart from this subsection, would under section 67 be liable, by reason of his having given a consent required of him by section 61, as a person who has authorised the issue of a prospectus in respect of an untrue statement purporting to be made by him as an expert is not so liable if he proves—

(a) that, having given his consent under the section to the issue of the prospectus, he withdrew it in writing before the delivery of a copy of the prospectus for registration; or

(b) that, after delivery of a copy of the prospectus for registration and before allotment under it, he, on becoming aware of the untrue statement, withdrew his consent in writing and gave reasonable public notice of the withdrawal and of the reason for it; or

(c) that he was competent to make the statement and that he had reasonable ground to believe, and did up to the time of the allotment of the shares or debentures (as the case may be) believe, that the statement was true.

Note
See note after s. 79.

SEC. 69 Indemnity for innocent director or expert

69(1) **[Application of section]** This section applies where—

(a) the prospectus contains the name of a person as a director of the company, or as having agreed to become a director of it, and he has not consented to become a director, or has withdrawn his consent before the issue of the prospectus, and has not authorised or consented to its issue, or

(b) the consent of a person is required under section 61 to the issue of the prospectus and he either has not given that consent or has withdrawn it before the issue of the prospectus.

69(2) **[Indemnity against damages, costs and expenses]** The directors of the company (except any without whose knowledge or consent the prospectus was issued) and any other person who authorised its issue are liable to indemnify the person named, or whose consent was required under section 61 (as the case may be), against all damages, costs and expenses to which he may be liable by reason of his name having been inserted in the prospectus or of the inclusion in it of a statement purporting to be made by him as an expert (as the case may be), or in defending himself against any action or legal proceeding brought against him in respect of it.

69(3)   [Interpretation]   A person is not deemed for purposes of this section to have authorised the issue of a prospectus by reason only of his having given the consent required by section 61 to the inclusion of a statement purporting to be made by him as an expert.

Note
See note after s. 79.

SEC. 70   Criminal liability for untrue statements

70(1)   [Penalty]   If a prospectus is issued with an untrue statement included in it, any person who authorised the issue of the prospectus is guilty of an offence and liable to imprisonment or a fine, or both, unless he proves either—

   (a) that the statement was immaterial, or

   (b) that he had reasonable ground to believe and did, up to the time of the issue of the prospectus, believe that the statement was true.

70(2)   [Interpretation]   A person is not deemed for purposes of this section to have authorised the issue of a prospectus by reason only of his having given the consent required by section 61 to the inclusion in it of a statement purporting to be made by him as an expert.

Note
See note after s. 79.

SUPPLEMENTARY

SEC. 71   Interpretation for sec. 56 to 70

71   For purposes of sections 56 to 70—

   (a) a statement included in a prospectus is deemed to be untrue if it is misleading in the form and context in which it is included, and

   (b) a statement is deemed to be included in a prospectus if it is contained in it, or in any report or memorandum appearing on its face, or by reference incorporated in, or issued with, the prospectus.

Note
See note after s. 79.

Chapter II — Issues by Companies Incorporated, or to be Incorporated, Outside Great Britain

SEC. 72   Prospectus of oversea company

72(1)   [Requirement for compliance with sec. 72(2), (3)]   It is unlawful for a person to issue, circulate or distribute in Great Britain any prospectus offering for subscription shares in or debentures of a company incorporated or to be incorporated outside

Great Britain (whether the company has or has not established, or when formed will or will not establish, a place of business in Great Britain) unless the prospectus complies with the requirement of the next two subsections.

72(2) **[Particulars in prospectus]** The prospectus must be dated and contain particulars with respect to the following matters—

    (a) the instrument constituting or defining the constitution of the company;

    (b) the enactments, or provisions having the force of an enactment, by or under which the incorporation of the company was effected;

    (c) an address in Great Britain where that instrument, and those enactments or provisions, or copies of them (and, if they are in a foreign language, a translation of them certified in the prescribed manner), can be inspected;

    (d) the date on which, and the country in which, the company was incorporated; and

    (e) whether the company has established a place of business in Great Britain and, if so, the address of its principal office in Great Britain.

72(3) **[Compliance with Sch. 3]** Subject to the following provisions, the prospectus must comply—

    (a) with Part I of Schedule 3, as respects the matters to be stated in the prospectus, and

    (b) with Part II of that Schedule, as respects the reports to be set out.

72(4) **[Non-application of sec. 72(2)(a) to (c)]** Paragraphs (a) to (c) of subsection (2) do not apply in the case of a prospectus issued more than 2 years after the company is entitled to commence business.

72(5) **[Prospectus must accompany form of application]** It is unlawful for a person to issue to any person in Great Britain a form of application for shares in or debentures of such a company or intended company as is mentioned in subsection (1) unless the form is issued with a prospectus which complies with this Chapter and the issue of which in Great Britain does not contravene section 74 or 75 below.

This subsection does not apply if it is shown that the form of application was issued in connection with a bona fide invitation to a person to enter into an underwriting agreement with respect to the shares or debentures.

72(6) **[Exceptions]** This section—

    (a) does not apply to the issue to a company's existing members or debenture holders of a prospectus or form of application relating to shares in or debentures of the company, whether an applicant for shares or debentures will or will not have the right to renounce in favour of other persons; and

    (b) except in so far as it requires a prospectus to be dated, does not apply to the issue of a prospectus relating to shares or debentures which are or are to be in all respects uniform with shares or debentures previously issued and for the time being listed on a prescribed stock exchange;

but subject to this, it applies to a prospectus or form of application whether issued or on with reference to the formation of a company or subsequently.

Note
See note after s. 79.

SEC. 73   Attempted evasion of sec. 72 to be void

73   A condition requiring or binding an applicant for shares or debentures to waive compliance with any requirement imposed—

    (a)   by subsection (2) of section 72, as regards the particulars to be contained in the prospectus, or

    (b)   by subsection (3) of that section, as regards compliance with Schedule 3,

or purporting to affect an applicant with notice of any contract, document or matter not specifically referred to in the prospectus, is void.

Note
See note after s. 79.

SEC. 74   Prospectus containing statement by expert

74(1)   [Application]   This section applies in the case of a prospectus offering for subscription shares in or debentures of a company incorporated or to be incorporated outside Great Britain (whether it has or has not established, or when formed will or will not establish, a place of business in Great Britain), if the prospectus includes a statement purporting to be made by an expert.

74(2)   [Requirements for such prospectus]   It is unlawful for any person to issue, circulate or distribute in Great Britain such a prospectus if—

    (a)   the expert has not given, or has before delivery of the prospectus for registration withdrawn, his written consent to the issue of the prospectus with the statement included in the form and context in which it is included, or

    (b)   there does not appear in the prospectus a statement that he has given and has not withdrawn his consent as above mentioned.

74(3)   [Interpretation]   For purposes of this section, a statement is deemed to be included in a prospectus if it is contained in it, or in any report or memorandum appearing on its face, or by reference incorporated in, or issued with, the prospectus.

Note
See note after s. 79.

SEC. 75   Restrictions on allotment to be secured in prospectus

75(1)   [Application]   It is unlawful for a person to issue, circulate or distribute in Great Britain a prospectus offering for subscription shares in or debentures of a company incorporated or to be incorporated outside Great Britain (whether the company has or has not established, or when formed will or will not establish, a place of business in Great Britain), unless the prospectus complies with the following condition.

75(2)   [Prospectus must make all persons bound by sec. 82, 86, 87]   The prospectus must have the effect, where an application is made in pursuance of it, of rendering all persons concerned bound by all the provisions (other than penal provisions) of sections 82, 86 and 87 (restrictions on allotment), so far as applicable.

Note
See note after s. 79.

SEC. 76 Stock exchange certificate exempting from compliance with Sch. 3

76(1) **[Application]** The following applies where—

(a) it is proposed to offer to the public by a prospectus issued generally any shares in or debentures of a company incorporated or to be incorporated outside Great Britain (whether the company has or has not established, or when formed will or will not establish, a place of business in Great Britain), and

(b) application is made to a prescribed stock exchange for permission for those shares or debentures to be listed on that stock exchange.

"**Issued generally**" means issued to persons who are not existing members or debenture holders of the company.

76(2) **[Issue of certificate]** There may on the applicant's request be given by or on behalf of that stock exchange a certificate that, having regard to the proposals (as stated in the request) as to the size and other circumstances of the issue of shares or debentures and as to any limitation on the number and class of persons to whom the offer is to be made, compliance with Schedule 3 would be unduly burdensome.

76(3) **[Where certificate given]** If a certificate is given under subsection (2), and if the proposals above mentioned are adhered to and the particulars and information required to be published in connection with the application for permission to the stock exchange are so published, then—

(a) a prospectus giving the particulars and information in the form in which they are so required to be published is deemed to comply with Schedule 3, and

(b) except as respects the requirement for the prospectus to be dated, section 72 does not apply to any issue, after the permission applied for is given, of a prospectus or form of application relating to the shares or debentures.

Note
See note after s. 79.

SEC. 77 Registration of oversea prospectus before issue

77(1) **[Requirement of registration]** It is unlawful for a person to issue, circulate or distribute in Great Britain a prospectus offering for subscription shares in or debentures of a company incorporated or to be incorporated outside Great Britain (whether the company has or has not established, or when formed will or will not establish, a place of business in Great Britain), unless before the issue, circulation or distribution the requirements of this section have been complied with.

77(2) **[Certified copy of prospectus to registrar]** A copy of the prospectus, certified by the chairman and two other directors of the company as having been approved by resolution of the managing body, must have been delivered for registration to the registrar of companies.

77(3) **[Endorsements or attachments to prospectus]** The prospectus must state on the face of it that a copy has been so delivered to the registrar of companies; and the following must be endorsed on or attached to that copy of the prospectus—

  (a) any consent to the issue of the prospectus which is required by section 74;

  (b) a copy of any contract required by paragraph 11 of Schedule 3 to be stated in the prospectus or, in the case of a contract not reduced into writing, a memorandum giving full particulars of it; and

  (c) where the persons making any report required by Part II of Schedule 3 have made in it or have, without giving the reasons, indicated in it any such adjustments as are mentioned in paragraph 21 of the Schedule, a written statement signed by those persons setting out the adjustments and giving the reasons for them.

77(4) [Requirements for prospectus certified under sec. 76] If in the case of a prospectus deemed by virtue of a certificate under section 76 to comply with Schedule 3, a contract or a copy of it, or a memorandum of a contract, is required to be available for inspection in connection with application under that section to the stock exchange, a copy or (as the case may be) a memorandum of the contract must be endorsed on or attached to the copy of the prospectus delivered to the registrar for registration.

77(5) [Reference to copy of a contract in sec. 77(3)(b),(4)] References in subsections (3)(b) and (4) to the copy of a contract are, in the case of a contract wholly or partly in a foreign language, to a copy of a translation of the contract into English, or a copy embodying a translation into English of the parts in a foreign language (as the case may be); and—

  (a) the translation must in either case be certified in the prescribed manner to be a correct translation, and

  (b) the reference in subsection (4) to a copy of a contract required to be available for inspection includes a copy of a translation of it or a copy embodying a translation of parts of it.

Note
See note after s. 79.

SEC. 78 Consequences (criminal and civil) of non-compliance with sec. 72–77

78(1) [Penalty for non-compliance] A person who is knowingly responsible for the issue, circulation or distribution of a prospectus, or for the issue of a form of application for shares or debentures, in contravention of any sections 72 to 77 is liable to a fine.

78(2) [Extension of sec. 67, 68, 69] Sections 67, 68 and 69 extend to every prospectus offering for subscription shares in or debentures of a company incorporated or to be incorporated outside Great Britain (whether the company has or has not established, or when formed will or will not establish, a place of business in Great Britain), substituting for any reference to section 61 a reference to section 74.

78(3) [Exception to liability re non-compliance of sec. 72(2), (3)] In the event of non-compliance with or contravention of any of the requirements of section 72(2) as regards the particulars to be contained in the prospectus, or section 72(3) as regards compliance with Schedule 3, a director or other person responsible for the prospectus incurs no liability by reason of the non-compliance or contravention if—

(a) as regards any matter not disclosed, he proves that he was not cognisant of it, or

(b) he proves that the non-compliance or contravention arose from an honest mistake of fact on his part, or

(c) the non-compliance or contravention was in respect of matters which, in the opinion of the court dealing with the case, were immaterial or were otherwise such as ought, in the court's opinion, having regard to all the circumstances of the case, reasonably to be excused.

78(4) **[Exception to liability for not including Sch. 3 para. 13 statement]** In the event of failure to include in a prospectus to which this Chapter applies a statement with respect to the matters contained in paragraph 13 of Schedule 3, no director or other person incurs any liability in respect of the failure unless it is proved that he had knowledge of the matters not disclosed.

78(5) **[Liability under general law]** Nothing in section 72 or 73 or this section, limits or diminishes any liability which a person may incur under the general law or this Act, apart from those provisions.

Note
See note after s. 79.

SEC. 79 Supplementary

79(1) **[Deeming of foreign prospectus]** Where a document by which the shares or debentures of a company incorporated outside Great Britain are offered for sale to the public would, if the company had been a company incorporated under this Act, have been deemed by virtue of section 58 to be a prospectus issued by the company, that document is deemed, for the purposes of this Chapter, a prospectus so issued.

79(2) **[Ordinary buyer or seller of shares]** An offer of shares or debentures for subscription or sale to a person whose ordinary business it is to buy or sell shares or debentures (whether as principal or agent) is not deemed an offer to the public for those purposes.

79(3) **["Shares", "debentures"]** In this Chapter **"shares"** and **"debentures"** have the same meaning as when those expressions are used, elsewhere in this Act, in relation to a company incorporated under this Act.

Note
S. 56–79 (Pt. III) repealed by Financial Services Act 1986, s. 212(3) and Sch. 17, Pt. I to the extent that those sections would apply re any investment listed or the subject of a listing application under Financial Services Act 1986, Pt. IV and commencing:

- on 12 January 1987 for all purposes relating to the admission of securities offered by or on behalf of a Minister of the Crown or a body corporate controlled by a Minister of the Crown or a subsidiary of such a body corporate to the Official List in respect of which an application is made after that date;

- on 16 February 1987 for purposes relating to the admission of securities in respect of which an application is made

after that date other than those referred to in the preceding paragraph and otherwise for all purposes.

(See S.I. 1986 No. 2246 (C. 88).)

Pt. III also repealed by Financial Services Act 1986, s. 212(3) and Sch. 17, Pt. I as from 29 April 1988 as far as it would apply to a prospectus offering for subscription, or to any form of application for units in a body corporate which is a recognised scheme; and as from 1 July 1988 as far as it would apply to a prospectus offering for subscription, or to any application form for, units in a body corporate which is an open-ended investment company (see S.I. 1988 No. 740 (C. 22)).

PART IV — ALLOTMENT OF SHARES AND DEBENTURES

GENERAL PROVISIONS AS TO ALLOTMENT

SEC. 80   Authority of company required for certain allotments

80(1)   [Limit on directors' powers]   The directors of a company shall not exercise any power of the company to allot relevant securities, unless they are, in accordance with this section or section 80A, authorised to do so by—

(a) the company in general meeting; or

(b) the company's articles.

History
In s. 80(1) the words "or section 80A" inserted by CA 1989, s. 115(1) as from 1 April 1990 subject to transitional and saving provisions (see S.I. 1990 No. 355 (C. 13), art. 4(a) and also art. 10).

80(2)   ["Relevant securities"]   In this section **"relevant securities"** means—

(a) shares in the company other than shares shown in the memorandum to have been taken by the subscribers to it or shares allotted in pursuance of an employees' share scheme, and

(b) any right to subscribe for, or to convert any security into, shares in the company (other than shares so allotted);

and a reference to the allotment of relevant securities includes the grant of such a right but (subject to subsection (6) below), not the allotment of shares pursuant to such a right.

80(3)   [Extent of authority given]   Authority under this section may be given for a particular exercise of the power or for its exercise generally, and may be unconditional or subject to conditions.

80(4)   [Content of authority]   The authority must state the maximum amount of relevant securities that may be allotted under it and the date on which it will expire, which must be not more than 5 years from whichever is relevant of the following dates—

(a) in the case of an authority contained in the company's articles at the time of its original incorporation, the date of that incorporation; and

(b) in any other case, the date on which the resolution is passed by virtue of which the authority is given;

but such an authority (including an authority contained in the articles) may be previously revoked or varied by the company in general meeting.

80(5)   [Renewal of authority]   The authority may be renewed or further renewed by the company in general meeting for a further period not exceeding 5 years; but the resolution must state (or restate) the amount of relevant securities which may be allotted under the authority or, as the case may be, the amount remaining to be allotted under it, and must specify the date on which the renewed authority will expire.

80(6)   [Reference in sec. 80(4),(5) to maximum amount of relevant securities]   In relation to authority under this section for the grant of such rights as are mentioned in subsection (2)(b), the reference in subsection (4) (as also the corresponding reference in subsection (5)) to the maximum amount of relevant securities that may be allotted under the authority is to the maximum amount of shares which may be allotted pursuant to the rights.

80(7) **[Allotment after expiration of authority]** The directors may allot relevant securities, notwithstanding that authority under this section has expired, if they are allotted in pursuance of an offer or agreement made by the company before the authority expired and the authority allowed it to make an offer or agreement which would or might require relevant securities to be allotted after the authority expired.

80(8) **[Variation, revocation etc. of authority]** A resolution of a company to give, vary, revoke or renew such an authority may, notwithstanding that it alters the company's articles, be an ordinary resolution; but it is in any case subject to section 380 of this Act (copy to be forwarded to registrar within 15 days).

80(9) **[Penalty]** A director who knowingly and wilfully contravenes, or permits or authorises a contravention of, this section is liable to a fine.

80(10) **[Validity of allotment]** Nothing in this section affects the validity of any allotment.

80(11) **[Non-application of section]** This section does not apply to any allotment of relevant securities by a company, other than a public company registered as such on its original incorporation, if it is made in pursuance of an offer or agreement made before the earlier of the following two dates—

(a) the date of the holding of the first general meeting of the company after its registration or re-registration as a public company, and

(b) 22nd June 1982;

but any resolution to give, vary or revoke an authority for the purposes of section 14 of the Companies Act 1980 or this section has effect for those purposes if passed at any time after the end of April 1980.

SEC. 80A   Election by private company as to duration of authority

80A(1) **[Power of private company re authority]** A private company may elect (by elective resolution in accordance with section 379A) that the provisions of this section shall apply, instead of the provisions of section 80(4) and (5), in relation to the giving or renewal, after the election, of an authority under that section.

80A(2) **[Authority]** The authority must state the maximum amount of relevant securities that may be allotted under it and may be given—

(a) for an indefinite period, or

(b) for a fixed period, in which case it must state the date on which it will expire.

80A(3) **[Revocation or variation of authority]** In either case an authority (including an authority contained in the articles) may be revoked or varied by the company in general meeting.

80A(4) **[Renewal of authority]** An authority given for a fixed period may be renewed or further renewed by the company in general meeting.

80A(5) **[Resolution renewing authority]** A resolution renewing an authority—

(a) must state, or re-state, the amount of relevant securities which may be allotted under the authority or, as the case may be, the amount remaining to be allotted under it, and

(b) must state whether the authority is renewed for an indefinite period or for a fixed period, in which case it must state the date on which the renewed authority will expire.

80A(6)   [Maximum amount of relevant securities allotted]   The references in this section to the maximum amount of relevant securities that may be allotted shall be construed in accordance with section 80(6).

80A(7)   [If election ceases to have effect]   If an election under this section ceases to have effect, an authority then in force which was given for an indefinite period or for a fixed period of more than five years—

(a) if given five years or more before the election ceases to have effect, shall expire forthwith, and

(b) otherwise, shall have effect as if it had been given for a fixed period of five years.

History
S. 80A inserted by CA 1989, s. 115(1) as from 1 April 1990
subject to transitional and saving provisions (see S.I. 1990
No. 355 (C. 13), art. 4(a) and also art. 10).

SEC. 81   Restriction on public offers by private company

81(1)   [Offence by private company]   A private limited company (other than a company limited by guarantee and not having a share capital) commits an offence if it—

(a) offers to the public (whether for cash or otherwise) any shares in or debentures of the company; or

(b) allots or agrees to allot (whether for cash or otherwise) any shares in or debentures of the company with a view to all or any of those shares or debentures being offered for sale to the public (within the meaning given to that expression by sections 58 to 60).

81(2)   [Penalty]   A company guilty of an offence under this section, and any officer of it who is in default, is liable to a fine.

81(3)   [Validity of allotment]   Nothing in this section affects the validity of any allotment or sale of shares or debentures, or of any agreement to allot or sell shares or debentures.

Note
See note after s. 83.

SEC. 82   Application for, and allotment of, shares and debentures

82(1)   [Allotment re prospectus issued generally]   No allotment shall be made of a company's shares or debentures in pursuance of a prospectus issued generally, and no proceedings shall be taken on applications made in pursuance of a prospectus so issued, until the beginning of the third day after than on which the prospectus is first so issued or such later time (if any) as may be specified in the prospectus.

82(2) **[Definition]** The beginning of that third day, or that later time, is "the time of the opening of the subscription lists".

82(3) **[First issue of prospectus in sec. 82(1)]** In subsection (1), the reference to the day on which the prospectus is first issued generally is to the day when it is first so issued as a newspaper advertisement; and if it is not so issued as a newspaper advertisement before the third day after that on which it is first so issued in any other manner, the reference is to the day on which it is first so issued in any manner.

82(4) **[Interpretation]** In reckoning for this purpose the third day after another day—

(a) any intervening day which is a Saturday or Sunday, or is a bank holiday in any part of Great Britain, is to be disregarded; and

(b) if the third day (as so reckoned) is itself a Saturday or Sunday, or a bank holiday, there is to be substituted the first day after that which is none of them.

82(5) **[Validity of allotment, penalty]** The validity of an allotment is not affected by any contravention of subsections (1) to (4); but in the event of contravention, the company and every officer of it who is in default is liable to a fine.

82(6) **[Prospectus offering shares etc. for sale]** As applying to a prospectus offering shares or debentures for sale, the above provisions are modified as follows—

(a) for references to allotment, substitute references to sale; and

(b) for the reference to the company and every officer of it who is in default, substitute a reference to any person by or through whom the offer is made and who knowingly and wilfully authorises or permits the contravention.

82(7) **[Revocation of application re prospectus issued generally]** An application for shares in or debentures of a company which is made in pursuance of a prospectus issued generally is not revocable until after the expiration of the third day after the time of the opening of the subcription lists, or the giving before the expiration of that day of the appropriate public notice; and that notice is one given by some person responsible under sections 67 to 69 for the prospectus and having the effect under those sections of excluding or limiting the responsibility of the giver.

Note
See note after s. 83.

SEC. 83   No allotment unless minimum subscription received

83(1) **[Minimum share subscription]** No allotment shall be made of any share capital of a company offered to the public for subscription unless—

(a) there has been subscribed the amount stated in the prospectus as the minimum amount which, in the opinion of the directors, must be raised by the issue of share capital in order to provide for the matters specified in paragraph 2 of Schedule 3 (preliminary expenses, purchase of property, working capital, etc.); and

(b) the sum payable on application for the amount so stated has been paid to and received by the company.

83(2) **[Sum paid to the company under sec. 83(1)(b)]** For purposes of subsection (1)(b), a sum is deemed paid to the company, and received by it, if a cheque for that sum has been received in good faith by the company and the directors have no reason for suspecting that the cheque will not be paid.

83(3) **["The minimum subscription"]** The amount so stated in the prospectus is to be reckoned exclusively of any amount payable otherwise than in cash and is known as "the minimum subscription".

83(4) **[Repayment to applicants if conditions not satisfied]** If the above conditions have not been complied with on the expiration of 40 days after the first issue of the prospectus, all money received from applicants for shares shall be forthwith repaid to them without interest.

83(5) **[Where no repayment under sec. 83(4) within 48 days]** If any of the money is not repaid within 48 days after the issue of the prospectus, the directors of the company are jointly and severally liable to repay it with interest at the rate of 5 per cent per annum from the expiration of the 48th day; except that a director is not so liable if he proves that the default in the repayment of the money was not due to any misconduct or negligence on his part.

83(6) **[Conditions re waiver etc. void]** Any condition requiring or binding an applicant for shares to waive compliance with any requirement of this section is void.

83(7) **[Non-application of section]** This section does not apply to an allotment of shares subsequent to the first allotment of shares offered to the public for subscription.

Note
S. 81–83 repealed by Financial Services Act 1986, s. 212(3) and Sch. 17, Pt. I to the extent to which they would apply re any investment listed as the subject of a listing application under Financial Services Act 1986, Pt. IV and commencing:

• on 12 January 1987 for all purposes relating to the admission of securities offered by or on behalf of a Minister of the Crown or a body corporate controlled by a Minister of the Crown or a subsidiary of such a body corporate to the Official List in respect of which an application is made after that date;

• on 16 February 1987 for purposes relating to the admission of securities in respect of which an application is made

after that date other than those referred to in the preceding paragraph and otherwise for all purposes.

(See S.I. 1986 No. 2246 (C. 88).)

The above sections also repealed by Financial Services Act 1986, s. 212(3) and Sch. 17, Pt. I as from 29 April 1988 as far as they would apply to a prospectus offering for subscription, or to any form of application for units in a body corporate which is a recognised scheme (see S.I. 1988 No. 740 (C. 22)).

SEC. 84   Allotment where issue not fully subscribed

84(1) **[Conditions for allotment of share capital in public company]** No allotment shall be made of any share capital of a public company offered for subscription unless—

    (a) that capital is subscribed for in full; or

    (b) the offer states that, even if the capital is not subscribed for in full, the amount of that capital subscribed for may be allotted in any event or in the event of the conditions specified in the offer being satisfied;

and, where conditions are so specified, no allotment of the capital shall be made by virtue of paragraph (b) unless those conditions are satisfied.

    This is without prejudice to section 83.

Note
In s. 84(1) the words "This is without prejudice to section 83" repealed by Financial Services Act 1986, s. 212(3) and Sch. 17, Pt. I to the extent applicable re any investment listed or the subject of a listing application under Financial

Services Act 1986, Pt. IV and commencing on 12 January, 16 February 1987 (see note after s. 83 and S.I. 1986 No. 2246 (C. 88)).

The words also repealed by Financial Services Act 1986, s. 212(3) and Sch. 17, Pt. I as from 29 April 1988 as far as they would apply to a prospectus offering for subscription, or to any form of application for units in a body corporate which is a body corporate which is a recognised scheme (see S.I. 1988 No. 740 (C. 22)).

84(2)　[Repayment to applicants if share not allotted due to sec. 84(1)]　If shares are prohibited from being allotted by subsection (1) and 40 days have elapsed after the first issue of the prospectus, all money received from applicants for shares shall be forthwith repaid to them without interest.

84(3)　[Where no repayment within 48 days]　If any of the money is not repaid within 48 days after the issue of the prospectus, the directors of the company are jointly and severally liable to repay it with interest at the rate of 5 per cent per annum from the expiration of the 48th day; except that a director is not so liable if he proves that the default in repayment was not due to any misconduct or negligence on his part.

84(4)　[Application of shares]　This section applies in the case of shares offered as wholly or partly payable otherwise than in cash as it applies in the case of shares offered for subscription (the word "subscribed" in subsection (1) being construed accordingly).

84(5)　[Interpretation of sec. 84(2), (3)]　In subsections (2) and (3) as they apply to the case of shares offered as wholly or partly payable otherwise than in cash, references to the repayment of money received from applicants for shares include—

(a)　the return of any other consideration so received (including, if the case so requires, the release of the applicant from any undertaking), or

(b)　if it is not reasonably practicable to return the consideration, the payment of money equal to its value at the time it was so received,

and references to interest apply accordingly.

84(6)　[Condition re waiver etc. void]　Any condition requiring or binding an applicant for shares to waive compliance with any requirement of this section is void.

SEC. 85　Effect of irregular allotment

85(1)　[Allotment under sec. 83, 84 voidable]　An allotment made by a company to an applicant in contravention of section 83 or 84 is voidable at the instance of the applicant within one month after the date of the allotment, and not later, and is so voidable notwithstanding that the company is in the course of being wound up.

Note

In s. 85(1) the words "83 or" repealed by Financial Services Act 1986, s. 212(3) and Sch. 17, Pt. I to the extent applicable re any investment listed or the subject of a listing application under Financial Services Act 1986, Pt. IV and commencing on 12 January, 16 February 1987 (see note after s.83 and S.I. 1986 No. 2246 (C. 88)).

The words also repealed by Financial Services Act 1986, s. 212(3) and Sch. 17, Pt. I as from 29 April 1988 as far as they would apply to a prospectus offering for subscription, or to any form of application for units in a body corporate which is a body corporate which is a recognised scheme (see S.I. 1988 No. 740 (C. 22)).

85(2)　[Directors liable to compensate for contravention]　If a director of a company knowingly contravenes, or permits or authorises the contravention of, any provision of either of those sections with respect to allotment, he is liable to compensate the company and the allottee respectively for any loss, damages or costs which the company or the allottee may have sustained or incurred by the contravention.

85(3)　[Time limit for compensation proceedings]　But proceedings to recover any such loss, damages or costs shall not be commenced after the expiration of 2 years from the date of the allotment.

SEC. 86 Allotment of shares etc. to be dealt in on stock exchange

86(1) [**Application of section**]   The following applies where a prospectus, whether issued generally or not, states that application has been or will be made for permission for the shares or debentures offered by it to be listed on any stock exchange.

86(2) [**Allotment void if permission not applied for or refused**]   An allotment made on an application in pursuance of the prospectus is, whenever made, void if the permission has not been applied for before the third day after the first issue of the prospectus or, if the permission has been refused, before the expiration of 3 weeks from the date of the closing of the subscription lists or such longer period (not exceeding 6 weeks) as may, within those 3 weeks, be notified to the applicant for permission by or on behalf of the stock exchange.

86(3) [**Interpretation**]   In reckoning for this purpose the third day after another day—

  (a)   any intervening day which is a Saturday or Sunday, or is a bank holiday in any part of Great Britain, is to be disregarded; and

  (b)   if the third day (as so reckoned) is itself a Saturday or Sunday, or a bank holiday, there is to be substituted the first day after that which is none of them.

86(4) [**Repayment if permission was applied for or refused**]   Where permission has not been applied for as above, or has been refused as above, the company shall forthwith repay (without interest) all money received from applicants in pursuance of the prospectus.

86(5) [**If money not repaid within 8 days**]   If any of the money is not repaid within 8 days after the company becomes liable to repay it, the directors of the company are jointly and severally liable to repay the money with interest at the rate of 5 per cent per annum from the expiration of the 8th day, except that a director is not liable if he proves that the default in the repayment of the money was not due to any misconduct or negligence on his part.

86(6) [**Money from applicants to be in separate bank account**]   All money received from applicants in pursuance of the prospectus shall be kept in a separate bank account so long as the company may become liable to repay it under subsection (4); and if default is made in complying with this subsection, the company and every officer of it who is in default is liable to a fine.

86(7) [**Condition re waiver void**]   Any condition requiring or binding an applicant for shares or debentures to waive compliance with any requirement of this section is void.

86(8) [**Where permission not deemed refused**]   For purposes of this section, permission is not deemed to be refused if it is intimated that the application for it, though not at present granted, will be given further consideration.

86(9) [**Shares etc. agreed to be taken**]   This section has effect in relation to shares or debentures agreed to be taken by a person underwriting an offer of them by a prospectus as if he had applied for them in pursuance of the prospectus.

Note
See note after s. 87.

SEC. 87　Operation of sec. 86 where prospectus offers shares for sale

87(1)　[Application]　The following has effect as regards the operation of section 86 in relation to a prospectus offering shares for sale.

87(2)　[Application of sec. 86(1), (2)]　Subsections (1) and (2) of that section apply, but with the substitution for the reference in subsection (2) to allotment of a reference to sale.

87(3)　[Non-application of sec. 86(4), (5)]　Subsections (4) and (5) of that section do not apply; but—

(a) if the permission referred to in section 86(2) has not been applied for as there mentioned, or has been refused as there mentioned, the offeror of the shares shall forthwith repay (without interest) all money received from applicants in pursuance of the prospectus, and

(b) if any such money is not repaid within 8 days after the offeror becomes liable to repay it, he becomes liable to pay interest on the money due, at the rate of 5 per cent per annum from the end of the 8th day.

87(4)　[Application of sec. 86(6) to (9)]　Subsections (6) to (9) apply, except that in subsection (6)—

(a) for the first reference to the company there is substituted a reference to the offeror, and

(b) for the reference to the company and every officer of the company who is in default there is substituted a reference to any person by or through whom the offer is made and who knowingly and wilfully authorises or permits the default.

Note

S. 86 and 87 repealed by Financial Services Act 1986, s. 212(3) and Sch. 17, Pt. I to the extent they apply re any investment listed or the subject of a listing application under Financial Services Act 1986, Pt. IV and commencing on 12 January, 16 February 1987 (see note after s. 83 and S.I. 1986 No. 2246 (C. 88)).

These sections also repealed by Financial Services Act 1986, s. 212(3) and Sch. 17, Pt. I as from 29 April 1988 as far as they would apply to a prospectus offering for subscription, or to any form of application for units in a body corporate which is a body corporate which is a recognised scheme (see S.I. 1988 No. 740 (C. 22)).

SEC. 88　Return as to allotments, etc.

88(1)　[Application]　This section applies to a company limited by shares and to a company limited by guarantee and having a share capital.

88(2)　[Documents to registrar]　When such a company makes an allotment of its shares, the company shall within one month thereafter deliver to the registrar of companies for registration—

(a) a return of the allotments (in the prescribed form) stating the number and nominal amount of the shares comprised in the allotment, the names and addresses of the allottees, and the amount (if any) paid or due and payable on each share, whether on account of the nominal value of the share or by way of premium; and

[The next page is 6,551]

(b) in the case of shares allotted as fully or partly paid up otherwise than in cash—

    (i) a contract in writing constituting the title of the allottee to the allotment together with any contract of sale, or for services or other consideration in respect of which that allotment was made (such contracts being duly stamped), and

    (ii) a return stating the number and nominal amount of shares so allotted, the extent to which they are to be treated as paid up, and the consideration for which they have been allotted.

88(3) **[Where contract in sec. 88(2)(b)(i) not in writing]** Where such a contract as above mentioned is not reduced to writing, the company shall within one month after the allotment deliver to the registrar of companies for registration the prescribed particulars of the contract stamped with the same stamp duty as would have been payable if the contract had been reduced to writing.

88(4) **[Particulars in sec. 88(3) deemed an instrument for stamping]** Those particulars are deemed an instrument within the meaning of the Stamp Act 1891; and the registrar may, as a condition of filing the particulars, require that the duty payable on them be adjudicated under section 12 of that Act.

88(5) **[Penalty on default]** If default is made in complying with this section, every officer of the company who is in default is liable to a fine and, for continued contravention, to a daily default fine, but subject as follows.

88(6) **[Relief re default in delivering documents to registrar]** In the case of default in delivering to the registrar within one month after the allotment any document required by this section to be delivered, the company, or any officer liable for the default, may apply to the court for relief; and the court, if satisfied that the omission to deliver the document was accidental or due to inadvertence, or that it is just and equitable to grant relief, may make an order extending the time for the delivery of the document for such period as the court thinks proper.

PRE-EMPTION RIGHTS

SEC. 89   Offers to shareholders to be on pre-emptive basis

89(1) **[Requirements for company allotting equity securities]** Subject to the provisions of this section and the seven sections next following, a company proposing to allot equity securities (defined in section 94)—

(a) shall not allot any of them on any terms to a person unless it has made an offer to each person who holds relevant shares or relevant employee shares to allot to him on the same or more favourable terms a proportion of those securities which is as nearly as practicable equal to the proportion in nominal value held by him of the aggregate of relevant shares and relevant employee shares, and

(b) shall not allot any of those securities to a person unless the period during which any such offer may be accepted has expired or the company has received notice of the acceptance or refusal of every offer so made.

89(2) **[Application of sec. 89(3)]** Subsection (3) below applies to any provision of a company's memorandum or articles which requires the company, when proposing to allot equity securities consisting of relevant shares of any particular class, not to allot those securities on any terms unless it has complied with the condition that it makes such an offer as is described in subsection (1) to each person who holds relevant shares or relevant employee shares of that class.

89(3)   [Exception to sec. 89(1)]   If in accordance with a provision to which this subsection applies—

    (a)   a company makes an offer to allot securities to such a holder, and

    (b)   he or anyone in whose favour he has renounced his right to their allotment accepts the offer.

subsection (1) does not apply to the allotment of those securities, and the company may allot them accordingly; but this is without prejudice to the application of subsection (1) in any other case.

89(4)   [Non-application of sec. 89(1)]   Subsection (1) does not apply to a particular allotment of equity securities if these are, or are to be, wholly or partly paid up otherwise than in cash; and securities which a company has offered to allot to a holder of relevant shares or relevant employee shares may be allotted to him, or anyone in whose favour he has renounced his right to their allotment, without contravening subsection (1)(b).

89(5)   [Further non-application]   Subsection (1) does not apply to the allotment of securities which would, apart from a renunciation or assignment of the right to their allotment, be held under an employees' share scheme.

SEC. 90   Communication of pre-emption offers to shareholders

90(1)   [Application]   This section has effect as to the manner in which offers required by section 89(1), or by a provision to which section 89(3) applies, are to be made to holders of a company's shares.

90(2)   [Mode of making offers]   Subject to the following subsections, an offer shall be in writing and shall be made to a holder of shares either personally or by sending it by post (that is to say, prepaying and posting a letter containing the offer) to him or to his registered address or, if he has no registered address in the United Kingdom, to the address in the United Kingdom supplied by him to the company for the giving of notice to him.

    If sent by post, the offer is deemed to be made at the time at which the letter would be delivered in the ordinary course of post.

90(3)   [Where shares held jointly]   Where shares are held by two or more persons jointly, the offer may be made to the joint holder first named in the register of members in respect of the shares.

90(4)   [Where holder dead or bankrupt]   In the case of a holder's death or bankruptcy, the offer may be made—

    (a)   by sending it by post in a prepaid letter addressed to the persons claiming to be entitled to the shares in consequence of the death or bankruptcy by name, or by the title of representatives of the deceased, or trustee of the bankrupt, or by any like description, at the address in the United Kingdom supplied for the purpose by those so claiming, or

(b) (until such an address has been so supplied) by giving the notice in any manner in which it might have been given if the death or bankruptcy had not occurred.

90(5) **[Publication in Gazette]** If the holder—

(a) has no registered address in the United Kingdom and has not given to the company an address in the United Kingdom for the service of notices on him, or

(b) is the holder of a share warrant,

the offer may be made by causing it, or a notice specifying where a copy of it can be obtained or inspected, to be published in the Gazette.

90(6) **[Period for acceptance]** The offer must state a period of not less than 21 days during which it may be accepted; and the offer shall not be withdrawn before the end of that period.

90(7) **[Effect on provision to which sec. 89(3) applies]** This section does not invalidate a provision to which section 89(3) applies by reason that that provision requires or authorises an offer under it to be made in contravention of any of subsections (1) to (6) above; but, to the extent that the provision requires or authorises such an offer to be so made, it is of no effect.

SEC. 91 Exclusion of sec. 89, 90 by private company

91(1) **[Exclusion by memorandum or articles]** Section 89(1), section 90(1) to (5) or section 90(6) may, as applying to allotments by a private company of equity securities or to such allotments of a particular description, be excluded by a provision contained in the memorandum or articles of that company.

91(2) **[Effect of inconsistent requirement in memorandum or articles]** A requirement or authority contained in the memorandum or articles of a private company, if it is inconsistent with any of those subsections, has effect as a provision excluding that sub-section; but a provision to which section 89(3) applies is not to be treated as inconsistent with section 89(1).

SEC. 92 Consequences of contravening sec. 89, 90

92(1) **[Liability for compensation]** If there is a contravention of section 89(1), or of section 90(1) to (5) or section 90(6), or of a provision to which section 89(3) applies, the company, and every officer of it who knowingly authorised or permitted the contravention, are jointly and severally liable to compensate any person to whom an offer should have been made under the subsection or provision contravened for any loss, damage, costs or expenses which the person has sustained or incurred by reason of the contravention.

92(2) **[Time limit for compensation proceedings]** However, no proceedings to recover any such loss, damage, costs or expenses shall be commenced after the expiration of 2 years from the delivery to the registrar of companies of the return of allotments in question or, where equity securities other than shares are granted, from the date of the grant.

SEC. 93   Saving for other restrictions as to offers

93(1)   [Enactments forbidding allotments of equity securities]   Sections 89 to 92 are without prejudice to any enactment by virtue of which a company is prohibited (whether generally or in specified circumstances) from offering or allotting equity securities to any person.

93(2)   [Effect of sec. 89 to 92]   Where a company cannot by virtue of such an enactment offer or allot equity securities to a holder of relevant shares or relevant employee shares, those sections have effect as if the shares held by that holder were not relevant shares or relevant employee shares.

SEC. 94   Definitions for sec. 89–96

94(1)   [Application]   The following subsections apply for the interpretation of sections 89 to 96.

94(2)   ["Equity security"]   "Equity security", in relation to a company, means a relevant share in the company (other than a share shown in the memorandum to have been taken by a subscriber to the memorandum or a bonus share), or a right to subscribe for, or to convert securities into, relevant shares in the company.

94(3)   [Reference to allotment of equity securities etc.]   A reference to the allotment of equity securities or of equity securities consisting of relevant shares of a particular class includes the grant of a right to subscribe for, or to convert any securities into, relevant shares in the company or (as the case may be) relevant shares of a particular class; but such a reference does not include the allotment of any relevant shares pursuant to such a right.

94(4)   ["Relevant employee shares"]   "Relevant employee shares", in relation to a company, means shares of the company which would be relevant shares in it but for the fact that they are held by a person who acquired them in pursuance of an employees' share scheme.

94(5)   ["Relevant shares"]   "Relevant shares", in relation to a company, means shares in the company other than—

   (a) shares which as respects dividends and capital carry a right to participate only up to a specified amount in a distribution, and

   (b) shares which are held by a person who acquired them in pursuance of an employees' share scheme or, in the case of shares which have not been allotted, are to be allotted in pursuance of a such a scheme.

94(6)   [Reference to a class of shares]   A reference to a class of shares is to shares to which the same rights are attached as to voting and as to participation, both as respects dividends and as respects capital, in a distribution.

94(7)   [Interpretation]   In relation to an offer to allot securities required by section 89(1) or by any provision to which section 89(3) applies, a reference in sections 89 to 94 (however expressed) to the holder of shares of any description is to whoever was at the close of business on a date, to be specified in the offer and to fall in the period of 28 days immediately before the date of the offer, the holder of shares of that description.

SEC. 95 Disapplication of pre-emption rights

95(1) [Allotment contrary to or varying sec. 89(1)] Where the directors of a company are generally authorised for purposes of section 80, they may be given power by the articles, or by a special resolution of the company, to allot equity securities pursuant to that authority as if—

(a) section 89(1) did not apply to the allotment, or

(b) that subsection applied to the allotment with such modifications as the directors may determine;

and where the directors make an allotment under this subsection, sections 89 to 94 have effect accordingly.

95(2) [Resolution contrary to or varying sec. 89(1)] Where the directors of a company are authorised for purposes of section 80 (whether generally or otherwise), the company may by special resolution resolve either—

(a) that section 89(1) shall not apply to a specified allotment of equity securities to be made pursuant to that authority, or

(b) that that subsection shall apply to the allotment with such modifications as may be specified in the resolution;

and where such a resolution is passed, sections 89 to 94 have effect accordingly.

95(3) [Revocation, expiration, rewewal of authority] The power conferred by subsection (1) or a special resolution under subsection (2) ceases to have effect when the authority to which it relates is revoked or would (if not renewed) expire; but if the authority is renewed, the power or (as the case may be) the resolution may also be renewed, for a period not longer than that for which the authority is renewed, by a special resolution of the company.

95(4) [Allotment after expiration of power or resolution] Notwithstanding that any such power or resolution has expired, the directors may allot equity securities in pursuance of an offer or agreement previously made by the company, if the power or resolution enabled the company to make an offer or agreement which would or might require equity securities to be allotted after it expired.

95(5) [Requirements for sec. 95(2) special resolution] A special resolution under subsection (2), or a special resolution to renew such a resolution, shall not be proposed unless it is recommended by the directors and there has been circulated, with the notice of the meeting at which the resolution is proposed, to the members entitled to have that notice a written statement by the directors setting out—

(a) their reasons for making the recommendation,

(b) the amount to be paid to the company in respect of the equity securities to be allotted, and

(c) the directors' justification of that amount.

95(6) [Penalty re inclusion of misleading matter etc.] A person who knowingly or recklessly authorises or permits the inclusion in a statement circulated under subsection (5) of any matter which is misleading, false or deceptive in a material particular is liable to imprisonment or a fine, or both.

SEC. 96   Saving for company's pre-emption procedure operative before 1982

96(1)   [Non-application of sec. 89 to 95]   Where a company which is re-registered or registered as a public company is or, but for the provisions of the Companies Act 1980 and the enactments replacing it, would be subject at the time of re-registration or (as the case may be) registration to a pre-1982 pre-emption requirement, sections 89 to 95 do not apply to an allotment of the equity securities which are subject to that requirement.

96(2)   ["Pre-1982 pre-emption requirement"]   A "pre-1982 pre-emption requirement" is a requirement imposed (whether by the company's memorandum or articles, or otherwise) before the relevant date in 1982 by virtue of which the company must, when making an allotment of equity securities, make an offer to allot those securities or some of them in a manner which (otherwise than because involving a contravention of section 90(1) to (5) or 90(6)) is inconsistent with sections 89 to 94; and "the relevant date in 1982" is—

   (a) except in a case falling within the following paragraph, 22nd June in that year, and

   (b) in the case of a company which was re-registered or registered as a public company on an application made before that date, the date on which the application was made.

96(3)   [Effect of certain requirements in private company]   A requirement which—

   (a) is imposed on a private company (having been so imposed before the relevant date in 1982) otherwise than by the company's memorandum or articles, and

   (b) if contained in the company's memorandum or articles, would have effect under section 91 to the exclusion of any provisions of sections 89 to 94,

has effect, so long as the company remains a private company, as if it were contained in the memorandum or articles.

96(4)   [Treatment of company subject to requirement in sec. 89(2)]   If on the relevant date in 1982 a company, other than a public company registered as such on its original incorporation, was subject to such a requirement as is mentioned in section 89(2) imposed otherwise than by the memorandum or articles, the requirement is to be treated for purposes of sections 89 to 94 as if it were contained in the memorandum or articles.

COMMISSIONS AND DISCOUNTS

SEC. 97   Power of company to pay commissions

97(1)   [Commission lawful subject to conditions]   It is lawful for a company to pay a commission to any person in consideration of his subscribing or agreeing to subscribe (whether absolutely or conditionally) for any shares in the company, or procuring or agreeing to procure subscriptions (whether absolute or conditional) for any shares in the company, if the following conditions are satisfied.

Note
Prospective amendment to s. 97(1) by Financial Services
Act 1986, s. 212(2) and Sch. 16, para. 16(a) from a day to
be appointed.

97(2) **[Conditions]** The payment of the commission must be authorised by the company's articles; and—

    (a) the commission paid or agreed to be paid must not exceed 10 per cent of the price at which the shares are issued or the amount or rate authorised by the articles, whichever is the less; and

    (b) the amount or rate per cent of commission paid or agreed to be paid, and the number of shares which persons have agreed for a commission to subscribe absolutely, must be disclosed in the manner required by the following subsection.

Note

Prospective amendment to s. 97(2)(a) by Financial Services Act 1986, s. 212(2) and Sch. 16, para. 16(b) from a day to be appointed.

S. 97(2)(b) together with the word "and" immediately preceding it repealed by Financial Services Act 1986, s. 212(3) and Sch. 17, Pt. I to the extent applying re any instrument listed or the subject of a listing application under Financial Services Act 1986, Pt. IV and commencing:

● on 12 January 1987 for all purposes relating to the admission of securities offered by or on behalf of a Minister of the Crown or a body corporate controlled by a Minister of the Crown or a subsidiary of such a body corporate to the Official List in respect of which an application is made after that date;

● on 16 February 1987 for purposes relating to the admission of securities in respect of which an application is made after that date other than those referred to in the preceding paragraph and otherwise for all purposes.

(See S.I. 1986 No. 2246 (C. 88).)

S. 97(2)(b) and the word "and" also repealed by Financial Services Act 1986, s. 212(3) and Sch. 17, Pt. I as from 29 April 1988 as far as they would apply to a prospectus offering for subscription, or to any form of application for units in a body corporate which is a recognised scheme (see S.I. 1988 No. 740 (C. 22)).

97(3) **[Disclosure of matters]** Those matters must, in the case of shares offered to the public for subscription, be disclosed in the prospectus; and in the case of shares not so offered—

    (a) they must be disclosed in a statement in the prescribed form signed by every director of the company or by his agent authorised in writing, and delivered (before payment of the commission) to the registrar of companies for registration; and

    (b) where a circular or notice (not being a prospectus) inviting subscription for the shares is issued, they must also be disclosed in that circular or notice.

97(4) **[Penalty for non-compliance with sec. 97(3)(a)]** If default is made in complying with subsection (3)(a) as regards delivery to the registrar of the statement in prescribed form, the company and every officer of it who is in default is liable to a fine.

Note

S. 97(3), (4) repealed by Financial Services Act 1986, s. 212(3) and Sch. 17, Pt. I to the extent that they apply re any instrument listed or the subject of a listing application under Financial Services Act 1986, Pt. IV and commencing on 12 January, 16 February 1987 (see note to s. 97(2) above and S.I. 1986 No. 2246 (C. 88)).

S. 97(3), (4) also repealed by Financial Services Act 1986, s. 212(3) and Sch. 17, Pt. I as from 29 April 1988 as far as they would apply to a prospectus offering for subscription, or to any form of application for units in a body corporate which is a recognised scheme (see S.I. 1988, No. 740 (C. 22)).

SEC. 98   Apart from sec. 97, commissions and discounts barred

98(1) **[Prohibition]** Except as permitted by section 97, no company shall apply any of its shares or capital money either directly or indirectly in payment of any commission, discount or allowance to any person in consideration of his subscribing or agreeing to subscribe (whether absolutely or conditionally) for any shares in the company, or procuring or agreeing to procure subscriptions (whether absolute or conditional) for any shares in the company.

98(2) **[Type of commission covered]** This applies whether the shares or money be so applied by being added to the purchase money of any property acquired by the company or to the contract price of any work to be executed for the company, or the money be paid out of the nominal purchase money or contract price, or otherwise.

98(3)   **[Continuation of lawful brokerage]**   Nothing in section 97 or this section affects the power of a company to pay such brokerage as has previously been lawful.

98(4)   **[Vendors, promoters etc.]**   A vendor to, or promoter of, or other person who receives payment in money or shares from, a company has, and is deemed always to have had, power to apply any part of the money or shares so received in payment of any commission, the payment of which, if made directly by the company, would have been lawful under section 97 and this section.

AMOUNT TO BE PAID FOR SHARES; THE MEANS OF PAYMENT

SEC. 99   General rules as to payment for shares on allotment

99(1)   **[Payment in money or money's worth]**   Subject to the following provisions of this Part, shares allotted by a company, and any premium on them, may be paid up in money or money's worth (including goodwill and know-how).

99(2)   **[No undertaking re work or services]**   A public company shall not accept at any time, in payment up of its shares or any premium on them, an undertaking given by any person that he or another should do work or perform services for the company or any other person.

99(3)   **[Where public company accepts undertaking as in sec. 99(2)]**   If a public company accepts such an undertaking in payment up of its shares or any premium on them, the holder of the shares when they or the premium are treated as paid up (in whole or in part) by the undertaking is liable—

   (a)   to pay the company in respect of those shares an amount equal to their nominal value, together with the whole of any premium or, if the case so requires, such proportion of that amount as is treated as paid up by the undertaking; and

   (b)   to pay interest at the appropriate rate on the amount payable under paragraph (a) above.

99(4)   **[Bonus shares etc.]**   This section does not prevent a company from allotting bonus shares to its members or from paying up, with sums available for the purpose, any amounts for the time being unpaid on any of its shares (whether on account of the nominal value of the shares or by way of premium).

99(5)   **[Reference to holder of shares in sec. 99(3)]**   The reference in subsection (3) to the holder of shares includes any person who has an unconditional right to be included in the company's register of members in respect of those shares or to have an instrument of transfer of them executed in his favour.

SEC. 100   Prohibition on allotment of shares at a discount

100(1)   **[Prohibition]**   A company's shares shall not be allotted at a discount.

100(2)   **[If shares allotted in contravention]**   If shares are allotted in contravention of this section, the allottee is liable to pay the company an amount equal to the amount of the discount, with interest at the appropriate rate.

SEC. 101   Shares to be allotted as at least one quarter paid-up

101(1)   [Condition for allotment by public company]   A public company shall not allot a share except as paid up at least as to one-quarter of its nominal value and the whole of any premium on it.

[The next page is 7,051]

101(2) **[Exception for employees' share scheme]** Subsection (1) does not apply to shares allotted in pursuance of an employees' share scheme.

101(3) **[Where shares allotted in contravention]** If a company allots a share in contravention of sub-section (1), the share is to be treated as if one-quarter of its nominal value, together with the whole of any premium on it, had been received.

101(4) **[Payment by allottee]** But the allottee is liable to pay the company the minimum amount which should have been received in respect of the share under subsection (1) (less the value of any consideration actually applied in payment up, to any extent, of the share and any premium on it), with interest at the appropriate rate.

101(5) **[Non-application of sec. 101(3), (4)]** Subsections (3) and (4) do not apply to the allotment of bonus shares, unless the allottee knew or ought to have known the shares were allotted in contravention of subsection (1).

SEC. 102 Restriction on payment by long-term undertaking

102(1) **[Certain shares not to be allotted as paid up]** A public company shall not allot shares as fully or partly paid up (as to their nominal value or any premium on them) otherwise than in cash if the consideration for the allotment is or includes an undertaking which is to be, or may be, performed more than 5 years after the date of the allotment.

102(2) **[Shares allotted in contravention of sec. 102(1)]** If a company allots shares in contravention of subsection (1), the allottee is liable to pay the company an amount equal to the aggregate of their nominal value and the whole of any premium (or, if the case so requires, so much of that aggregate as is treated as paid up by the undertaking), with interest at the appropriate rate.

102(3) **[Void variations of contract]** Where a contract for the allotment of shares does not contravene subsection (1), any variation of the contract which has the effect that the contract would have contravened the subsection, if the terms of the contract as varied had been its original terms, is void.

102(4) **[Application of sec. 102(3)]** Subsection (3) applies also to the variation by a public company of the terms of a contract entered into before the company was re-registered as a public company.

102(5) **[Sec. 102(1) undertaking not performed within five years]** The following subsection applies where a public company allots shares for a consideration which consists of or includes (in accordance with subsection (1)) an undertaking which is to be performed within 5 years of the allotment, but the undertaking is not performed within the period allowed by the contract for the allotment of the shares.

102(6) **[Liability of allottee in sec. 102(5) situation]** The allottee is then liable to pay the company, at the end of the period so allowed, an amount equal to the aggregate of the nominal value of the shares and the whole of any premium (or, if the case so requires, so much of that aggregate as is treated as paid up by the undertaking), with interest at the appropriate rate.

102(7) **[Interpretation]** A reference in this section to a contract for the allotment of shares includes an ancillary contract relating to payment in respect of them.

SEC. 103   Non-cash consideration to be valued before allotment

103(1)   [Conditions for allotment otherwise than in cash]   A public company shall not allot shares as fully or partly paid up (as to their nominal value or any premium on them) otherwise than in cash unless—

(a)   the consideration for the allotment has been independently valued under section 108; and

(b)   a report with respect to its value has been made to the company by a person appointed by the company (in accordance with that section) during the 6 months immediately preceding the allotment of the shares; and

(c)   a copy of the report has been sent to the proposed allottee.

103(2)   [Amounts not included as consideration under sec. 103(1)]   Where an amount standing to the credit of any of a company's reserve accounts, or of its profit and loss account, is applied in paying up (to any extent) any shares allotted to members of the company or any premiums on shares so allotted, the amount applied does not count as consideration for the allotment, and accordingly subsection (1) does not apply in that case.

103(3)   [Non-application of sec. 103(1) re certain transfers]   Subsection (1) does not apply to the allotment of shares by a company in connection with an arrangement providing for the allotment of shares in that company on terms that the whole or part of the consideration for the shares allotted is to be provided by the transfer to that company (or the cancellation) of all or some of the shares, or of all or some of the shares of a particular class, in another company (with or without the issue to that company of shares, or of shares of any particular class, in that other company).

103(4)   [Qualification to sec. 103(3)]   But subsection (3) does not exclude the application of subsection (1) unless under the arrangement it is open to all the holders of the shares in the other company in question (or, where the arrangement applies only to shares of a particular class, to all the holders of shares in that other company, being holders of shares of that class) to take part in the arrangement.

In determining whether that is the case, shares held by or by a nominee of the company proposing to allot the shares in connection with the arrangement, or by or by a nominee of a company which is that company's holding company or subsidiary or a company which is a subsidiary of its holding company, shall be disregarded.

103(5)   [Non-application of sec. 103(1) re proposed mergers]   Subsection (1) also does not apply to the allotment of shares by a company in connection with its proposed merger with another company; that is, where one of the companies proposes to acquire all the assets and liabilities of the other in exchange for the issue of shares or other securities of that one to shareholders of the other, with or without any cash payment to shareholders.

103(6)   [Where allotment in contravention of sec. 103(1) etc.]   If a company allots shares in contravention of subsection (1) and either—

(a)   the allottee has not received the valuer's report required by that subsection to be sent to him; or

(b)   there has been some other contravention of this section or section 108 which the allottee knew or ought to have known amounted to a contravention, the allottee is liable to pay the company an amount equal to the aggregate of the nominal value of the shares and the whole of any premium (or, if the case so requires, so much of that aggregate as is treated as paid up by the consideration), with interest at the appropriate rate.

103(7) **[Interpretation]** In this section—

   (a) **"arrangement"** means any agreement, scheme or arrangement (including an arrangement sanctioned in accordance with section 425 (company compromise with creditors and members) or section 110 of the Insolvency Act (liquidator in winding up accepting shares as consideration for sale of company property)), and

   (b) any reference to a company, except where it is or is to be construed as a reference to a public company, includes any body corporate and any body to which letters patent have been issued under the Chartered Companies Act 1837.

History
In s. 103(7)(a) the words "section 110 of the Insolvency Act" substituted for the former words "section 582" by Insolvency Act 1986, s. 439(1) and Sch. 13 as from 29 December 1986 (see IA 1986, s. 443, S.I. 1986 No. 1924 (C. 71)).

SEC. 104 Transfer to public company of non-cash asset in initial period

104(1) **[General prohibition]** A public company formed as such shall not, unless the conditions of this section have been complied with, enter into an agreement with a person for the transfer by him during the initial period of one or more non-cash assets to the company or another, if—

   (a) that person is a subscriber to the company's memorandum, and

   (b) the consideration for the transfer to be given by the company is equal in value at the time of the agreement to one-tenth or more of the company's nominal share capital issued at that time.

104(2) **["Initial period"]** The "initial period" for this purpose is 2 years beginning with the date of the company being issued with a certificate under section 117 (or the previous corresponding provision) that it was entitled to do business.

104(3) **[Application to company re-registered as public]** This section applies also to a company re-registered as a public company (except one re-registered under section 8 of the Companies Act 1980 or section 2 of the Consequential Provisions Act), or registered under section 685 (joint stock company) or the previous corresponding provision; but in that case—

   (a) there is substituted a reference in subsection (1)(a) to a person who is a member of the company on the date of registration or re-registration, and

   (b) the initial period is then 2 years beginning with that date.

In this subsection the reference to a company re-registered as a public company includes a private company so re-registered which was a public company before it was a private company.

104(4)   [Conditions for transfer]   The conditions of this section are as follows—

(a) the consideration to be received by the company, and any consideration other than cash to be given by the company, must have been independently valued under section 109;

(b) a report with respect to the consideration to be so received and given must have been made to the company in accordance with that section during the 6 months immediately preceding the date of the agreement;

(c) the terms of the agreement must have been approved by an ordinary resolution of the company; and

(d) not later than the giving of the notice of the meeting at which the resolution is proposed, copies of the resolution and report must have been circulated to the members of the company entitled to receive the notice and, if the person with whom the agreement in question is proposed to be made is not then a member of the company so entitled, to that person.

104(5)   [Interpretation of sec. 104(4)(a)]   In subsection (4)(a)—

(a) the reference to the consideration to be received by the company is to the asset to be transferred to it or the advantage to the company of the asset's transfer to another person; and

(b) the specified condition is without prejudice to any requirement to value any consideration for purposes of section 103.

104(6)   [Non-application of section to certain agreements]   In the case of the following agreements, this section does not apply—

(a) where it is part of the company's ordinary business to acquire, or arrange for other persons to acquire, assets of a particular description, an agreement entered into by the company in the ordinary course of its business for the transfer of an asset of that description to it or to such a person, as the case may be;

(b) an agreement entered into by the company under the supervision of the court, or of an officer authorised by the court for the purpose, for the transfer of an asset to the company or to another.

SEC. 105   Agreements contravening sec. 104

105(1)   [Application]   The following subsection applies if a public company enters into an agreement contravening section 104, the agreement being made with the person referred to in subsection (1)(a) or (as the case may be) subsection (3) of that section, and either—

(a) that person has not received the valuer's report required for compliance with the conditions of the section, or

(b) there has been some other contravention of the section or of section 108(1), (2) or (5) or section 109, which he knew or ought to have known amounted to a contravention.

105(2)   [Where there is sec. 105(1) situation]   The company is then entitled to recover from that person any consideration given by it under the agreement, or an amount equal to the value of the consideration at the time of the agreement; and the agreement, so far as not carried out, is void.

105(3) **[If agreement for allotment of shares]** However, if the agreement is or includes an agreement for the allotment of shares in the company, then—

> (a) whether or not the agreement also contravenes section 103, subsection (2) above does not apply to it in so far as it is for the allotment of shares; and
>
> (b) the allottee is liable to pay the company an amount equal to the aggregate of the nominal value of the shares and the whole of any premium (or, if the case so requires, so much of that aggregate as is treated as paid up by the consideration), with interest at the appropriate rate.

SEC. 106 Shares issued to subscribers of memorandum

106 Shares taken by a subscriber to the memorandum of a public company in pursuance of an undertaking of his in the memorandum, and any premium on the shares, shall be paid up in cash.

SEC. 107 Meaning of "the appropriate rate"

107 In sections 99 to 105 **"the appropriate rate"**, in relation to interest, means 5 per cent per annum or such other rate as may be specified by order made by the Secretary of State by statutory instrument subject to annulment in pursuance of a resolution of either House of Parliament.

VALUATION PROVISIONS

SEC. 108 Valuation and report (sec. 103)

108(1) **[Independent person to make valuation and report]** The valuation and report required by section 103 (or, where applicable, section 44) shall be made by an independent person, that is to say a person qualified at the time of the report to be appointed, or continue to be, an auditor of the company.

108(2) **["Valuer" may accept valuation by another person]** However, where it appears to the independent person (from here on referred to as "the valuer") to be reasonable for the valuation of the consideration, or part of it, to be made (or for him to accept such a valuation) by another person who—

> (a) appears to him to have the requisite knowledge and experience to value the consideration or that part of it; and
>
> (b) is not an officer or servant of the company or any other body corporate which is that company's subsidiary or holding company or a subsidiary of that company's holding company or a partner or employee of such an officer or servant,

he may arrange for or accept such a valuation, together with a report which will enable him to make his own report under this section and provide the note required by subsection (6) below.

108(3) **[Officer or servant in sec. 108(2)(b)]** The reference in subsection (2)(b) to an officer or servant does not include an auditor.

108(4)   [Contents of valuer's report]   The valuer's report shall state—

   (a) the nominal value of the shares to be wholly or partly paid for by the consideration in question;

   (b) the amount of any premium payable on the shares;

   (c) the description of the consideration and, as respects so much of the consideration as he himself has valued, a description of that part of the consideration, the method used to value it and the date of the valuation;

   (d) the extent to which the nominal value of the shares and any premium are to be treated as paid up—

     (i) by the consideration;

     (ii) in cash.

108(5)   [Where consideration valued by person other than valuer]   Where the consideration or part of it is valued by a person other than the valuer himself, the latter's report shall state that fact and shall also—

   (a) state the former's name and what knowledge and experience he has to carry out the valuation, and

   (b) describe so much of the consideration as was valued by the other person, and the method used to value it, and specify the date of the valuation.

108(6)   [Note to accompany valuer's report]   The valuer's report shall contain or be accompanied by a note by him—

   (a) in the case of a valuation made by a person other than himself that it appeared to himself reasonable to arrange for it to be so made or to accept a valuation so made;

   (b) whoever made the valuation, that the method of valuation was reasonable in all the circumstances;

   (c) that it appears to the valuer that there has been no material change in the value of the consideration in question since the valuation; and

   (d) that on the basis of the valuation the value of the consideration, together with any cash by which the nominal value of the shares or any premium payable on them is to be paid up, is not less than so much of the aggregate of the nominal value and the whole of any such premium as is treated as paid up by the consideration and any such cash.

108(7)   [Where consideration part paid up nominal value etc. and part something else]   Where the consideration to be valued is accepted partly in payment up of the nominal value of the shares and any premium and partly for some other consideration given by the company, section 103 (and, where applicable, section 44) and the foregoing provisions of this section apply as if references to the consideration accepted by the company included the proportion of that consideration which is properly attributable to the payment up of that value and any premium; and—

   (a) the valuer shall carry out, or arrange for, such other valuations as will enable him to determine that proportion; and

   (b) his report shall state what valuations have been made under this subsection and also the reason for, and method and date of, any such valuation and any other matters which may be relevant to that determination.

CA 1985, sec. 108(4)

SEC. 109 Valuation and report (sec. 104)

109(1) [Further application of sec. 108(1), (3), (5)] Subsections (1) to (3) and (5) of section 108 apply also respects the valuation and report of for the purposes of section 104.

109(2) [Contents of valuer's report] The valuer's report for those purposes shall—

(a) state the consideration to be received by the company, describing the asset in question (specifying the amount to be received in cash) and the consideration to be given by the company (specifying the amount to be given in cash);

(b) state the method and date of valuation;

(c) contain or be accompanied by a note as to the matters mentioned in section 108(6)(a) to (c); and

(d) contain or be accompanied by a note that on the basis of the valuation the value of the consideration to be received by the company is not less than the value of the consideration to be given by it.

109(3) [Reference to consideration] A reference in section 104 or this section to consideration given for the transfer of an asset includes consideration given partly for its transfer; but—

(a) the value of any consideration partly so given is to be taken as the proportion of the consideration properly attributable to its transfer;

(b) the valuer shall carry out or arrange for such valuations of anything else as will enable him to determine that proportion; and

(c) his report for purposes of section 104 shall state what valuation has been made under this subsection and also the reason for and method and date of any such valuation and any other matters which may be relevant to that determination.

SEC. 110 Entitlement of valuer to full disclosure

110(1) [Information from company officers] A person carrying out a valuation or making a report under section 103 or 104, with respect to any consideration proposed to be accepted or given by a company, is entitled to require from the officers of the company such information and explanation as he thinks necessary to enable him to carry out the valuation or make the report and provide a note under section 108(6) or (as the case may be) section 109(2)(c).

110(2) [Penalty for misleading statement etc.] A person who knowingly or recklessly makes a statement which—

(a) is misleading, false or deceptive in a material particular, and

(b) is a statement to which this subsection applies,

is guilty of an offence and liable to imprisonment or a fine, or both.

110(3) [Application of sec. 110(2)] Subsection (2) applies to any statement made (whether orally or in writing) to a person carrying out a valuation or making a report under section 108 or 109, being a statement which conveys or purports to convey any information or explanation which that person requires, or is entitled to require, under subsection (1) of this section.

SEC. 111   Matters to be communicated to registrar

111(1)   **[Report under sec. 108 to registrar]**   A company to which a report is made under section 108 as to the value of any consideration for which, or partly for which, it proposes to allot shares shall deliver a copy of the report to the registrar of companies for registration at the same time that it files the return of the allotments of those shares under section 88.

111(2)   **[Resolution under sec. 104 to registrar]**   A company which has passed a resolution under section 104 with respect to the transfer of an asset shall, within 15 days of so doing, deliver to the registrar of companies a copy of the resolution together with the valuer's report required by that section.

111(3)   **[Penalty for contravening sec. 111(1)]**   If default is made in complying with subsection (1), every officer of the company who is in default is liable to a fine and, for continued contravention, to a daily default fine; but this is subject to the same exception as is made by section 88(6) (relief on application to the court) in the case of default in complying with that section.

111(4)   **[Penalty for contravening sec. 111(2)]**   If a company fails to comply with subsection (2), it and every officer of it who is in default is liable to a fine and, for continued contravention, to a daily default fine.

OTHER MATTERS ARISING OUT OF ALLOTMENT ETC.

SEC. 111A   Right to damages, etc. not affected

111A   A person is not debarred from obtaining damages or other compensation from a company by reason only of his holding or having held shares in the company or any right to apply or subscribe for shares or to be included in the company's register in respect of shares.

History
S. 111A inserted by CA 1989, s. 131(1) as from 1 April
1990 subject to a saving provision (see S.I. 1990 No. 355
(C. 13), art. 4(b) and also art. 11).

SEC. 112   Liability of subsequent holders of shares allotted

112(1)   **[Subsequent holder of shares liable]**   If a person becomes a holder of shares in respect of which—

     (a)   there has been a contravention of section 99, 100, 101 or 103; and

     (b)   by virtue of that contravention, another is liable to pay any amount under the section contravened,

that person is also liable to pay that amount (jointly and severally with any other person so liable), unless he is exempted from liability by subsection (3) below.

112(2)   **[Where agreement in contravention of sec. 104]**   If a company enters into an agreement in contravention of section 104 and—

     (a)   the agreement is or includes an agreement for the allotment of shares in the company; and

CA 1985, sec. 111(1)   [The next page is 7,551]

   (b) a person becomes a holder of shares allotted under the agreement; and

   (c) by virtue of the agreement and allotment under it, another person is liable to pay any amount under section 105,

the person who becomes the holder of the shares is also liable to pay that amount (jointly and severally with any other person so liable), unless he is exempted from liability by the following subsection; and this applies whether or not the agreement also contravenes section 103.

112(3) **[Exemption from liability under sec. 112(1), (2)]** A person otherwise liable under subsection (1) or (2) is exempted from that liability if either—

   (a) he is a purchaser for value and, at the time of the purchase, he did not have actual notice of the contravention concerned; or

   (b) he derived title to the shares (directly or indirectly) from a person who became a holder of them after the contravention and was not liable under subsection (1) or (as the case may be) subsection (2).

112(4) **[References to holder]** References in this section to a holder, in relation to shares in a company, include any person who has an unconditional right to be included in the company's register of members in respect of those shares or to have an instrument of transfer of the shares executed in his favour.

112(5) **[Further application of sec. 112(1), (3)]** As subsections (1) and (3) apply in relation to the contraventions there mentioned, they also apply—

   (a) to a contravention of section 102; and

   (b) to a failure to carry out a term of a contract as mentioned in subsections (5) and (6) of that section.

SEC. 113   Relief in respect of certain liabilities under sec. 99 ff.

113(1) **[Application for exemption from liability]** Where a person is liable to a company under—

   (a) section 99, 102, 103 or 105;

   (b) section 112(1) by reference to a contravention of section 99 or 103; or

   (c) section 112(2) or (5),

in relation to payment in respect of any shares in the company, or is liable by virtue of an undertaking given to it in, or in connection with, payment for any such shares, the person so liable may make an application to the court to be exempted in whole or in part from the liability.

113(2) **[Limitation on court's power to exempt]** If the liability mentioned in subsection (1) arises in relation to payment in respect of any shares, the court may, on an application under that subsection, exempt the applicant from the liability only—

   (a) if and to the extent that it appears to the court just and equitable to do so having regard to the matters mentioned in the following subsection,

   (b) if and to the extent that it appears to the court just and equitable to do so in respect of any interest which he is liable to pay the company under any of the relevant sections.

113(3)   [Matters to be considered under sec. 113(2)(a)]   The matters to be taken into account by the court under subsection (2)(a) are—

(a) whether the applicant has paid, or is liable to pay, any amount in respect of any other liability arising in relation to those shares under any of the relevant sections, or of any liability arising by virtue of any undertaking given in or in connection with payment for those shares;

(b) whether any person other than the applicant has paid or is likely to pay (whether in pursuance of an order of the court or otherwise) any such amount; and

(c) whether the applicant or any other person has peformed, in whole or in part, or is likely so to perform any such undertaking, or has done or is likely to do any other thing in payment or part payment for the shares.

113(4)   [Further limitation]   Where the liability arises by virtue of an undertaking given to the company in, or in connection with, payment for shares in it, the court may, on an application under subsection (1), exempt the applicant from the liability only if and to the extent that it appears to the court just and equitable to do so having regard to—

(a) whether the applicant has paid or is liable to pay any amount in respect of liability arising in relation to the shares under any of the provisions mentioned in that subsection; and

(b) whether any person other than the applicant has paid or is likely to pay (whether in pursuance of an order of the court or otherwise) any such amount.

113(5)   [Overriding principles for court]   In determining whether it should exempt the applicant in whole or in part from any liability, the court shall have regard to the following overriding principles, namely—

(a) that a company which has allotted shares should receive money or money's worth at least equal in value to the aggregate of the nominal value of those shares and the whole of any premium or, if the case so requires, so much of that aggregate as is treated as paid up; and

(b) subject to this, that where such a company would, if the court did not grant the exemption, have more than one remedy against a particular person, it should be for the company to decide which remedy it should remain entitled to pursue.

113(6)   [Proceedings against contributor]   If a person brings proceedings against another ("the contributor") for a contribution in respect of liability to a company arising under any of sections 99 to 105 or 112, and it appears to the court that the contributor is liable to make such a contribution, the court may exercise the powers of the following subsection.

113(7)   [Powers of court in sec. 113(6) situation]   The court may, if and to the extent that it appears to it, having regard to the respective culpability (in respect of the liability to the company) of the contributor and the person bringing the proceedings, that it is just and equitable to do so—

(a) exempt the contributor in whole or in part from his liability to make such a contribution; or

CCH Editions Limited
BCL BCL6$$$20A

(b) order the contributor to make a larger contribution than, but for this subsection, he would be liable to make.

113(8) **[Power of court to exempt person liable under sec. 105(2)]** Where a person is liable to a company under section 105(2), the court may, on application, exempt him in whole or in part from that liability if and to the extent that it appears to the court just and equitable to do so having regard to any benefit accruing to the company by virtue of anything done by him towards the carrying out of the agreement mentioned in that subsection.

SEC. 114 Penalty for contravention

114 If a company contravenes any of the provisions of sections 99 to 104 and 106 the company and any officer of it who is in default is liable to a fine.

SEC. 115 Undertakings to do work, etc.

115(1) **[Undertaking enforceable]** Subject to section 113, an undertaking given by any person, in or in connection with payment for shares in a company, to do work or perform services or to do any other thing, if it is enforceable by the company apart from this Act, is so enforceable notwithstanding that there has been a contravention in relation to it of section 99, 102 or 103.

115(2) **[Where sec. 104 contravened]** Where such an undertaking is given in contravention of section 104 in respect of the allotment of shares, it is so enforceable notwithstanding the contravention.

SEC. 116 Application of sec. 99 ff. to special cases

116 Except as provided by section 9 of the Consequential Provisions Act (transitional cases dealt with by section 31 of the Companies Act 1980), sections 99, 101 to 103, 106, 108, 110, 111 and 112 to 115 apply—

(a) to a company which has passed and not revoked a resolution to be re-registered under section 43 as a public company, and

(b) to a joint stock company which has passed, and not revoked, a resolution that the company be a public company,

as those sections apply to a public company.

History
In s. 116 the words "110, 111 and 112 to 115" substituted for the former words "and 110 to 115" by CA 1989, s. 131(2) as from 1 April 1990 subject to a saving provision (see S.I. 1990 No. 355 (C. 13), art. 4(c) and also art. 11).

PART V — SHARE CAPITAL, ITS INCREASE, MAINTENANCE AND REDUCTION

Chapter I — General Provisions About Share Capital

SEC. 117 Public company share capital requirements

117(1) **[No business until certificate or re-registered]** A company registered as a public company on its original incorporation shall not do business or exercise any borrowing powers unless the registrar of companies has issued it with a certificate under this section or the company is re-registered as a private company.

117(2)   **[Issue of certificate by registrar]**   The registrar shall issue a company with such a certificate if, on an application made to him by the company in the prescribed form, he is satisfied that the nominal value of the company's allotted share capital is not less than the authorised minimum, and there is delivered to him a statutory declaration complying with the following subsection.

117(3)   **[Statutory declaration]**   The statutory declaration must be in the prescribed form and be signed by a director or secretary of the company; and it must—

    (a) state that the nominal value of the company's allotted share capital is not less than the authorised minimum;

    (b) specify the amount paid up, at the time of the application, on the allotted share capital of the company;

    (c) specify the amount, or estimated amount, of the company's preliminary expenses and the persons by whom any of those expenses have been paid or are payable; and

    (d) specify any amount or benefit paid or given, or intended to be paid or given, to any promoter of the company, and the consideration for the payment or benefit.

117(4)   **[Share under employees' share scheme]**   For the purposes of subsection (2), a share allotted in pursuance of an employees' share scheme may not be taken into account in determining the nominal value of the company's allotted share capital unless it is paid up at least as to one-quarter of the nominal value of the share and the whole of any premium on the share.

117(5)   **[Statutory declaration as sufficient evidence]**   The registrar may accept a statutory declaration delivered to him under this section as sufficient evidence of the matters stated in it.

117(6)   **[Certificate conclusive evidence]**   A certificate under this section in respect of a company is conclusive evidence that the company is entitled to do business and exercise any borrowing powers.

117(7)   **[Penalty]**   If a company does business or exercises borrowing powers in contravention of this section, the company and any officer of it who is in default is liable to a fine.

117(8)   **[Failure to comply with obligations]**   Nothing in this section affects the validity of any transaction entered into by a company; but, if a company enters into a transaction in contravention of this section and fails to comply with its obligations in that connection within 21 days from being called upon to do so, the directors of the company are jointly and severally liable to indemnify the other party to the transaction in respect of any loss or damage suffered by him by reason of the company's failure to comply with those obligations.

SEC. 118   The authorised minimum

118(1)   **[Definition]**   In this Act, **"the authorised minimum"** means £50,000, or such other sum as the Secretary of State may by order made by statutory instrument specify instead.

118(2) **[Order increasing authorised minimum]** An order under this section which increases the authorised minimum may—

    (a) require any public company having an allotted share capital of which the nominal value is less than the amount specified in the order as the authorised minimum to increase that value to not less than that amount or make application to be re-registered as a private company;

    (b) make, in connection with any such requirement, provision for any of the matters for which provision is made by this Act relating to a company's registration, re-registration or change of name, to payment for any share comprised in a company's capital and to offers of shares in or debentures of a company to the public, including provision as to the consequences

[The next page is 7,801]

(whether in criminal law or otherwise) of a failure to comply with any requirement of the order; and

(c) contain such supplemental and transitional provisions as the Secretary of State thinks appropriate, make different provision for different cases and, in particular, provide for any provision of the order to come into operation on different days for different purposes.

118(3) **[Approval of order]** An order shall not be made under this section unless a draft of it has been laid before Parliament and approved by resolution of each House.

SEC. 119 Provision for different amounts to be paid on shares

119 A company, if so authorised by its articles, may do any one or more of the following things—

(a) make arrangements on the issue of shares for a difference between the shareholders in the amounts and times of payment of calls on their shares;

(b) accept from any member the whole or a part of the amount remaining unpaid on any shares held by him, although no part of that amount has been called up;

(c) pay dividend in proportion to the amount paid up on each share where a larger amount is paid up on some shares than on others.

SEC. 120 Reserve liability of limited company

120 A limited company may by special resolution determine that any portion of its share capital which has not been already called up shall not be capable of being called up except in the event and for the purposes of the company being wound up; and that portion of its share capital is then not capable of being called up except in that event and for those purposes.

SEC. 121 Alteration of share capital (limited companies)

121(1) **[Power to alter memorandum]** A company limited by shares or a company limited by guarantee and having a share capital, if so authorised by its articles, may alter the conditions of its memorandum in any of the following ways.

121(2) **[Extent of power]** The company may—

(a) increase its share capital by new shares of such amount as it thinks expedient;

(b) consolidate and divide all or any of its share capital into shares of larger amount than its existing shares;

(c) convert all or any of its paid-up shares into stock, and re-convert that stock into paid-up shares of any denomination;

(d) sub-divide its shares, or any of them, into shares of smaller amount than is fixed by the memorandum (but subject to the following subsection);

(e) cancel shares which, at the date of the passing of the resolution to cancel them, have not been taken or agreed to be taken by any person, and diminish the amount of the company's share capital by the amount of the shares so cancelled.

121(3) **[Requirement for any division under sec. 121(2)(d)]** In any sub-division under subsection (2)(d) the proportion between the amount paid and the amount, if any, unpaid on each reduced share must be the same as it was in the case of the share from which the reduced share is derived.

121(4) **[Exercise of powers]** The powers conferred by this section must be exercised by the company in general meeting.

121(5) **[Cancellation of shares]** A cancellation of shares under this section does not for purposes of this Act constitute a reduction of share capital.

SEC. 122   Notice to registrar of alteration

122(1) **[Notice re consolidation, division etc.]** If a company having a share capital has—

(a) consolidated and divided its share capital into shares of larger amount than its existing shares; or

(b) converted any shares into stock; or

(c) re-converted stock into shares; or

(d) sub-divided its shares or any of them; or

(e) redeemed any redeemable shares; or

(f) cancelled any shares (otherwise than in connection with a reduction of share capital under section 135),

it shall within one month after so doing give notice in the prescribed form to the registrar of companies, specifying (as the case may be) the shares consolidated, divided, converted, sub-divided, redeemed or cancelled, or the stock re-converted.

122(2) **[Penalty on default]** If default is made in complying with this section, the company and every officer of it who is in default is liable to a fine and, for continued contravention, to a daily default fine.

SEC. 123   Notice to registrar of increased share capital

123(1) **[Notice to registrar]** If a company having a share capital (whether or not its shares have been converted into stock) increases its share capital beyond the registered capital, it shall within 15 days after the passing of the resolution authorising the increase, give to the registrar of companies notice of the increase, and the registrar shall record the increase.

123(2) **[Particulars in notice]** The notice must include such particulars as may be prescribed with respect to the classes of shares affected and the conditions subject to which the new shares have been or are to be issued.

123(3) **[Copy of resolution with notice]** There shall be forwarded to the registrar together with the notice a printed copy of the resolution authorising the increase, or a copy of the resolution in some other form approved by the registrar.

123(4) **[Penalty on default]** If default is made in complying with this section, the company and every officer of it who is in default is liable to a fine and, for continued contravention, to a daily default fine.

SEC. 124   Reserve capital of unlimited company

124   An unlimited company having a share capital may by its resolution for re-registration as a public company under section 43, or as a limited company under section 51—

(a) increase the nominal amount of its share capital by increasing the nominal amount of each of its shares (but subject to the condition that no part of the increased capital is to be capable of being called up except in the event and for the purpose of the company being wound up), and

(b) alternatively or in addition, provide that a specified portion of its uncalled share capital is not to be capable of being called up except in that event and for that purpose.

Chapter II — Class Rights

SEC. 125   Variation of class rights

125(1)   [Subject of section]   This section is concerned with the variation of the rights attached to any class of shares in a company whose share capital is divided into shares of different classes.

125(2)   [Conditions for variation of rights]   Where the rights are attached to a class of shares otherwise than by the company's memorandum, and the company's articles do not contain provision with respect to the variation of the rights, those rights may be varied if, but only if—

(a) the holders of three-quarters in nominal value of the issued shares of that class consent in writing to the variation; or

(b) an extraordinary resolution passed at a separate general meeting of the holders of that class sanctions the variation;

and any requirement (howsoever imposed) in relation to the variation of those rights is complied with to the extent that it is not comprised in paragraphs (a) and (b) above.

125(3)   [Non-variation of rights]   Where—

(a) the rights are attached to a class of shares by the memorandum or otherwise;

(b) the memorandum or articles contain provision for the variation of those rights; and

(c) the variation of those rights is connected with the giving, variation, revocation or renewal of an authority for allotment under section 80 or with a reduction of the company's share capital under section 135;

those rights shall not be varied unless—

(i) the condition mentioned in subsection (2)(a) or (b) above is satisfied; and

(ii) any requirement of the memorandum or articles in relation to the variation of rights of that class is complied with to the extent that it is not comprised in that condition.

125(4) [Variation only in accordance with articles] If the rights are attached to a class of shares in the company by the memorandum or otherwise and—

(a) where they are so attached by the memorandum, the articles contain provision with respect to their variation which had been included in the articles at the time of the company's original incorporation; or

(b) where they are so attached otherwise, the articles contain such provision (whenever first so included),

and in either case the variation is not connected as mentioned in subsection (3)(c), those rights may only be varied in accordance with that provision of the articles.

125(5) [Variation if all members agree] If the rights are attached to a class of shares by the memorandum, and the memorandum and articles do not contain provision with respect to the variation of those rights, those rights may be varied if all the members of the company agree to the variation.

125(6) [Application of sec. 369, 370, 376, 377 etc.] The provisions of section 369 (length of notice for calling company meetings), section 370 (general provisions as to meetings and votes), and sections 376 and 377 (circulation of members' resolutions) and the provisions of the articles relating to general meetings shall, so far as applicable, apply in relation to any meeting of shareholders required by this section or otherwise to take place in connection with the variation of the rights attached to a class of shares, and shall so apply with the necessary modifications and subject to the following provisions, namely—

(a) the necessary quorum at any such meeting other than an adjourned meeting shall be two persons holding or representing by proxy at least one-third in nominal value of the issued shares of the class in question and at an adjourned meeting one person holding shares of the class in question or his proxy;

(b) any holder of shares of the class in question present in person or by proxy may demand a poll.

125(7) [Alteration of provision in articles] Any alteration of a provision contained in a company's articles for the variation of the rights attached to a class of shares, or the insertion of any such provision into the articles, is itself to be treated as a variation of those rights.

125(8) [Reference to variation to include abrogation] In this section and (except where the context otherwise requires) in any provision for the variation of the rights attached to a class of shares contained in a company's memorandum or articles, references to the variation of those rights are to be read as including references to their abrogation.

SEC. 126 Saving for court's powers under other provisions

126 Nothing in subsections (2) and (5) of section 125 derogates from the powers of the court under the following sections of this Act, namely—

sections 4 to 6 (company resolution to alter objects),

section 54 (litigated objection to public company becoming private by re-registration),

CA 1985, sec. 125(4)   [The next page is 8,051]   **CCH Editions Limited**

section 425 (court control of company compromising with members and creditors),

section 427 (company reconstruction or amalgamation),

sections 459 to 461 (protection of minorities).

SEC. 127 Shareholders' right to object to variation

127(1) **[Application of section]** This section applies if, in the case of a company whose share capital is divided into different classes of shares—

(a) provision is made by the memorandum or articles for authorising the variation of the rights attached to any class of shares in the company, subject to—

    (i) the consent of any specified proportion of the holders of the issued shares of that class, or

    (ii) the sanction of a resolution passed at a separate meeting of the holders of those shares,

and in pursuance of that provision the rights attached to any such class of shares are at any time varied; or

(b) the rights attached to any class of shares in the company are varied under section 125(2).

127(2) **[Application to court for cancellation of variation]** The holders of not less in the aggregate than 15 per cent of the issued shares of the class in question (being persons who did not consent to or vote in favour of the resolution for the variation), may apply to the court to have the variation cancelled; and if such an application is made, the variation has no effect unless and until it is confirmed by the court.

127(3) **[Time for application to the court]** Application to the court must be made within 21 days after the date on which the consent was given or the resolution was passed (as the case may be), and may be made on behalf of the shareholders entitled to make the application by such one or more of their number as they may appoint in writing for the purpose.

127(4) **[Disallowance or confirmation of variation by court]** The court, after hearing the applicant and any other persons who apply to the court to be heard and appear to the court to be interested in the application, may, if satisfied having regard to all the circumstances of the case, that the variation would unfairly prejudice the shareholders of the class represented by the applicant, disallow the variation and shall, if not so satisfied, confirm it.

The decision of the court on any such application is final.

127(5) **[Copy of order to registrar, penalty on default]** The company shall within 15 days after the making of an order by the court on such an application forward a copy of the order to the registrar of companies; and, if default is made in complying with this provision, the company and every officer of it who is in default is liable to a fine and, for continued contravention, to a daily default fine.

127(6) **["Variation", "varied"]** "Variation", in this section, includes abrogation; and "varied" is to be construed accordingly.

SEC. 128   Registration of particulars of special rights

128(1)   [Statement of special rights to registrar]   If a company allots shares with rights which are not stated in its memorandum or articles, or in any resolution or agreement which is required by section 380 to be sent to the registrar of companies, the company shall deliver to the registrar of companies, within one month from allotting the shares, a statement in the prescribed form containing particulars of those rights.

128(2)   [Special shares — interpretation]   This does not apply if the shares are in all respects uniform with shares previously allotted; and shares are not for this purpose to be treated as different from shares previously allotted by reason only that the former do not carry the same rights to dividends as the latter during the 12 months immediately following the former's allotment.

128(3)   [Statement of variation to registrar]   Where the rights attached to any shares of a company are varied otherwise than by an amendment of the company's memorandum or articles or by a resolution or agreement subject to section 380, the company shall within one month from the date on which the variation is made deliver to the registrar of companies a statement in the prescribed form containing particulars of the variation.

128(4)   [Notice of name of new class to registrar]   Where a company (otherwise than by any such amendment, resolution or agreement as is mentioned above) assigns a name or other designation, or a new name or other designation, to any class of its shares, it shall within one month from doing so deliver to the registrar of companies a notice in the prescribed form giving particulars of the name or designation so assigned.

128(5)   [Penalty]   If a company fails to comply with this section, the company and every officer of it who is in default is liable to a fine and, for continued contravention, to a daily default fine.

SEC. 129   Registration of newly created class rights

129(1)   [Statement by company not having share capital]   If a company not having a share capital creates a class of members with rights which are not stated in its memorandum or articles or in a resolution or agreement to which section 380 applies, the company shall deliver to the registrar of companies within one month from the date on which the new class is created a statement in the prescribed form containing particulars of the rights attached to that class.

129(2)   [Statement of variation to registrar]   If the rights of any class of members of the company are varied otherwise than by an amendment of the memorandum or articles or by a resolution or agreement subject to section 380, the company shall within one month from the date on which the variation is made deliver to the registrar a statement in the prescribed form containing particulars of the variation.

129(3)   [Notice of name of class to registrar]   If a company (otherwise than by such an amendment, resolution or agreement as is mentioned above) assigns a name or other designation, or a new name or other designation, to any class of its members, it shall within one month from doing so deliver to the registrar a notice in the prescribed form giving particulars of the name or designation so assigned.

129(4) **[Penalty]** If a company fails to comply with this section, the company and every officer who is in default is liable to a fine and, for continued contravention, to a daily default fine.

Chapter III — Share Premiums

SEC. 130 Application of share premiums

130(1) **[Transfer to "the share premium account"]** If a company issues shares at a premium, whether for cash or otherwise, a sum equal to the aggregate amount or value of the premiums on those shares shall be transferred to an account called "the share premium account".

130(2) **[Application of account]** The share premium account may be applied by the company in paying up unissued shares to be allotted to members as fully paid bonus shares, or in writing off—

(a) the company's preliminary expenses; or

(b) the expenses of, or the commission paid or discount allowed on, any issue of shares or debentures of the company,

or in providing for the premium payable on redemption of debentures of the company.

130(3) **[Provisions re reduction of capital]** Subject to this, the provisions of this Act relating to the reduction of a company's share capital apply as if the share premium account were part of its paid up share capital.

130(4) **[Relief under sec. 131, 132]** Sections 131 and 132 below give relief from the requirements of this section, and in those sections references to the issuing company are to the company issuing shares as above mentioned.

SEC. 131 Merger relief

131(1) **[Application]** With the exception made by section 132(8) (group reconstruction) this section applies where the issuing company has secured at least a 90 per cent equity holding in another company in pursuance of an arrangement providing for the allotment of equity shares in the issuing company on terms that the consideration for the shares allotted is to be provided—

(a) by the issue or transfer to the issuing company of equity shares in the other company, or

(b) by the cancellation of any such shares not held by the issuing company.

History
In s. 131(1) the words "section 132(8)" substituted for the former words "section 132(4)" by CA 1989, s. 145 and Sch. 19, para. 1 as from 1 March 1990 (see S.I. 1990 No. 142 (C. 5), art. 5) but note that this amendment is deemed always to have had effect.

131(2) **[Shares issued at a premium]** If the equity shares in the issuing company allotted in pursuance of the arrangement in consideration for the acquisition or cancellation of equity shares in the other company are issued at a premium, section 130 does not apply to the premiums on those shares.

131(3) **[Consideration by issue or transfer of non-equity shares]** Where the arrangement also provides for the allotment of any shares in the issuing company on terms that the consideration for those shares is to be provided by the issue or transfer to the issuing company of non-equity shares in the other company or by the cancellation of any such shares in that company not held by the issuing comany, relief under subsection (2) extends to any shares in the issuing company allotted on those terms in pursuance of the arrangement.

131(4)   **[90 per cent equity holding in sec. 131(1)]**   Subject to the next subsection, the issuing company is to be regarded for purposes of this section as having secured at least a 90 per cent equity holding in another company in pursuance of such an arrangement as is mentioned in subsection (1) if in consequence of an acquisition or cancellation of equity shares in that company (in pursuance of that arrangement) it holds equity shares in that company (whether all or any of those shares were acquired in pursuance of that arrangement, or not) of an aggregate nominal value equal to 90 per cent or more of the nominal value of that company's equity share capital.

131(5)   **[Where equity share capital in other company in different classes]**   Where the equity share capital of the other company is divided into different classes of shares, this section does not apply unless the requirements of subsection (1) are satisfied in relation to each of those classes of shares taken separately.

131(6)   **[Shares held by holding company or subsidiary]**   Shares held by a company which is the issuing company's holding company or subsidiary, or a subsidiary of the issuing company's holding company, or by its or their nominees, are to be regarded for purposes of this section as held by the issuing company.

131(7)   **[Definitions]**   In relation to a company and its shares and capital, the following definitions apply for purposes of this section—

    (a) **"equity shares"** means shares comprised in the company's equity share capital; and

    (b) **"non-equity shares"** means shares (of any class) not so comprised;

and **"arrangement"** means any agreement, scheme or arrangement (including an arrangement sanctioned under section 425 (company compromise with members and creditors) or section 110 of the Insolvency Act (liquidator accepting shares etc. as consideration for sale of company property).

History
In s. 131(7) the words "section 110 of the Insolvency Act" substituted for the former words "section 582" by Insolvency   Act 1986, s. 439(1) and Sch. 13 as from 29 December 1986 (see IA 1986, s. 443 and S.I. 1986 No. 1924 (C. 71)).

131(8)   **[Non-application of relief]**   The relief allowed by this section does not apply if the issue of shares took place before 4th February 1981.

SEC. 132   Relief in respect of group reconstructions

132(1)   **[Application]**   This section applies where the issuing company—

    (a) is a wholly-owned subsidiary of another company ("the holding company"), and

    (b) allots shares to the holding company or to another wholly-owned subsidiary of the holding company in consideration for the transfer to the issuing company of assets other than cash, being assets of any company ("the transferor company") which is a member of the group of companies which comprises the holding company and all its wholly-owned subsidiaries.

132(2)   **[Relief from sec. 130]**   Where the shares in the issuing company allotted in consideration for the transfer are issued at a premium, the issuing company is not required by section 130 to transfer any amount in excess of the minimum premium value to the share premium account.

132(3) [Interpretation of sec. 132(2)] In subsection (2), **"the minimum premium value"** means the amount (if any) by which the base value of the consideration for the shares alloted exceeds the aggregate nominal value of those shares.

132(4) [Interpretation of sec. 132(3)] For the purposes of subsection (3), the base value of the consideration for the shares allotted is the amount by which the base value of the assets transferred exceeds the base value of any liabilities of the transferor company assumed by the issuing company as part of the consideration for the assets transferred.

132(5) [Interpretation of sec. 132(4)] For the purposes of subsection (4)—

  (a) the base value of the assets transferred is to be taken as—

    (i) the cost of those assets to the transferor company, or

    (ii) the amount at which those assets are stated in the transferor company's accounting records immediately before the transfer,

  whichever is the less; and

  (b) the base value of the liabilities assumed is to be taken as the amount at which they are stated in the transferor company's accounting records immediately before the transfer.

132(6) [Non-application of relief] The relief allowed by this section does not apply (subject to the next subsection) if the issue of shares took place before the date of the coming into force of the Companies (Share Premium Account) Regulations 1984 (which were made on 21st December 1984).

132(7) [Qualification to sec. 132(6)] To the extent that the relief allowed by this section would have been allowed by section 38 of the Companies Act 1981 as originally enacted (the text of which section is set out in Schedule 25 to this Act), the relief applies where the issue of shares took place before the date of the coming into force of those Regulations, but not if the issue took place before 4th February 1981.

132(8) [Non-application of sec. 131] Section 131 does not apply in a case falling within this section.

SEC. 133 Provisions supplementing sec. 131,132

133(1) [Inclusion of shares or other consideration in company's balance sheet] An amount corresponding to one representing the premiums or part of the premiums on shares issued by a company which by virtue of sections 131 or 132 of this Act, or section 12 of the Consequential Provisions Act, is not included in the company's share premium account may also be disregarded in determining the amount at which any shares or other consideration provided for the shares issued is to be included in the company's balance sheet.

133(2) [References in Ch. III] References in this Chapter (however expressed) to—

  (a) the acquisition by a company of shares in another company; and

  (b) the issue or allotment of shares to, or the transfer of shares to or by, a company, include (respectively) the acquisition of any of those shares by, and the issue or allotment or (as the case may be) the transfer of any of those shares to or by, nominees of that company; and the reference in section 132 to the company transferring the shares is to be construed accordingly.

133(3)   **[Further references]**   References in this Chapter to the transfer of shares in a company include the transfer of a right to be included in the company's register of members in respect of those shares.

133(4)   **["Company" in sec. 131 to 133]**   In sections 131 to 133 "company", except in references to the issuing company, includes any body corporate.

SEC. 134   Provision for extending or restricting relief from sec. 130

134(1)   **[Regulations for relief etc.]**   The Secretary of State may by regulations in a statutory instrument make such provision as appears to him to be appropriate—

    (a)   for relieving companies from the requirements of section 130 in relation to premiums other than cash premiums, or

    (b)   for restricting or otherwise modifying any relief from those requirements provided by this Chapter.

134(2)   **[Incidental provisions under regulations]**   Regulations under this section may make different provision for different cases or classes of case and may contain such incidental and supplementary provisions as the Secretary of State thinks fit.

134(3)   **[Approval of regulations]**   No such regulations shall be made unless a draft of the instrument containing them has been laid before Parliament and approved by a resolution of each House.

Chapter IV — Reduction of Share Capital

SEC. 135   Special resolution for reduction of share capital

135(1)   **[Reduction by special resolution]**   Subject to confirmation by the court, a company limited by shares or a company limited by guarantee and having a share capital may, if so authorised by its articles, by special resolution reduce its share capital in any way.

135(2)   **[Types of reduction]**   In particular, and without prejudice to subsection (1), the company may—

    (a)   extinguish or reduce the liability on any of its shares in respect of share capital not paid up; or

    (b)   either with or without extinguishing or reducing liability on any of its shares, cancel any paid-up share capital which is lost or unrepresented by available assets; or

    (c)   either with or without extinguishing or reducing liability on any of its shares, pay off any paid-up share capital which is in excess of the company's wants;

and the company may, if and so far as is necessary, alter its memorandum by reducing the amount of its share capital and of its shares accordingly.

135(3) [**"A resolution for reducing share capital"**]   A special resolution under this section is in this Act referred to as "a resolution for reducing share capital".

SEC. 136   Application to court for order of confirmation

136(1) [**Application to court**]   Where a company has passed a resolution for reducing share capital, it may apply to the court for an order confirming the reduction.

136(2) [**Application of sec. 136 (3), (4), (5)**]   If the proposed reduction of share capital involves either—

(a) diminution of liability in respect of unpaid share capital; or

(b) the payment to a shareholder of any paid-up share capital,

and in any other case if the court so directs, the next three subsections have effect, but subject throughout to subsection (6).

136(3) [**Creditor entitled to object to reduction**]   Every creditor of the company who at the date fixed by the court is entitled to any debt or claim which, if that date were the commencement of the winding up of the company, would be admissible in proof against the company is entitled to object to the reduction of capital.

136(4) [**List of creditors entitled to object**]   The court shall settle a list of creditors entitled to object, and for that purpose—

(a) shall ascertain, as far as possible without requiring an application from any creditor, the names of those creditors and the nature and amount of their debts or claims; and

(b) may publish notices fixing a day or days within which creditors not entered on the list are to claim to be so entered or are to be excluded from the right of objecting to the reduction of capital.

136(5) [**Court may dispense with consent of creditor**]   If a creditor entered on the list whose debt or claim is not discharged or has not determined does not consent to the reduction, the court may, if it thinks fit, dispense with the consent of that creditor, on the company securing payment of his debt or claim by appropriating (as the court may direct) the following amount—

(a) if the company admits the full amount of the debt or claim or, though not admitting it, is willing to provide for it, then the full amount of the debt or claim;

(b) if the company does not admit, and is not willing to provide for, the full amount of the debt or claim, or if the amount is contingent or not ascertained, then an amount fixed by the court after the like enquiry and adjudication as if the company were being wound up by the court.

136(6) [**Direction by court that sec. 136(3)–(5) not apply**]   If a proposed reduction of share capital involves either the diminution of any liability in respect of unpaid share capital or the payment to any shareholder of any paid-up share capital, the court may, if having regard to any special circumstances of the case it thinks proper to do so, direct that subsections (3) to (5) of this section shall not apply as regards any class or any classes of creditors.

SEC. 137   Court order confirming reduction

137(1)   [Order by court]   The court, if satisfied with respect to every creditor of the company who under section 136 is entitled to object to the reduction of capital that either—

(a) his consent to the reduction has been obtained; or

(b) his debt or claim has been discharged or has determined, or has been secured,

may make an order confirming the reduction on such terms and conditions as it thinks fit.

137(2)   [Directions under order]   Where the court so orders, it may also—

(a) if for any special reason it thinks proper to do so, make an order directing that the company shall, during such period (commencing on or at any time after the date of the order) as is specified in the order, add to its name as its last words the words "and reduced"; and

(b) make an order requiring the company to publish (as the court directs) the reasons for reduction of capital or such other information in regard to it as the court thinks expedient with a view to giving proper information to the public and (if the court thinks fit) the causes which led to the reduction.

137(3)   ["And reduced"]   Where a company is ordered to add to its name the words "and reduced", those words are, until the expiration of the period specified in the order, deemed to be part of the company's name.

SEC. 138   Registration of order and minute of reduction

138(1)   [Conditions for registration]   The registrar of companies, on production to him of an order of the court confirming the reduction of a company's share capital, and the delivery to him of a copy of the order and of a minute (approved by the court) showing, with respect to the company's share capital as altered by the order—

(a) the amount of the share capital;

(b) the number of shares into which it is to be divided, and the amount of each share; and

(c) the amount (if any) at the date of the registration deemed to be paid up on each share,

shall register the order and minute (but subject to section 139).

138(2)   [Resolution takes effect on registration]   On the registration of the order and minute, and not before, the resolution for reducing share capital as confirmed by the order so registered takes effect.

138(3)   [Publication of notice of registration]   Notice of the registration shall be published in such manner as the court may direct.

138(4)   [Certification of registration etc.]   The registrar shall certify the registration of the order and minute; and the certificate—

(a) may be either signed by the registrar, or authenticated by his official seal;

(b) is conclusive evidence that all the requirements of this Act with respect to the reduction of share capital have been complied with, and that the company's share capital is as stated in the minute.

138(5) **[Effect of registration of minute]** The minute when registered is deemed to be substituted for the corresponding part of the company's memorandum, and is valid and alterable as if it had been originally contained therein.

138(6) **[Alteration within sec. 20]** The substitution of such a minute for part of the company's memorandum is deemed an alteration of the memorandum for purposes of section 20.

SEC. 139 Public company reducing capital below authorised minimum

139(1) **[Application]** This section applies where the court makes an order confirming a reduction of a public company's capital which has the effect of bringing the nominal value of its allotted share capital below the authorised minimum.

139(2) **[Registrar not to register order under sec. 138]** The registrar of companies shall not register the order under section 138 unless the court otherwise directs, or the company is first re-registered as a private company.

139(3) **[Re-registration without sec. 53 special resolution]** The court may authorise the company to be so re-registered without its having passed the special resolution required by section 53; and where that authority is given, the court shall specify in the order the alterations in the company's memorandum and articles to be made in connection with that re-registration.

139(4) **[Re-registration as private company]** The company may then be re-registered as a private company, if an application in the prescribed form and signed by a director or secretary of the company is delivered to the registrar, together with a printed copy of the memorandum and articles as altered by the court's order.

139(5) **[Issue of certificate etc.]** On receipt of such an application, the registrar shall retain it and the other documents delivered with it and issue the company with a certificate of incorporation appropriate to a company that is not a public company; and—

    (a) the company by virtue of the issue of the certificate becomes a private company, and the alterations in the memorandum and articles set out in the court's order take effect; and

    (b) the certificate is conclusive evidence that the requirements of this section in respect of re-registration and of matters precedent and incidental thereto have been complied with, and that the company is a private company.

SEC. 140 Liability of members on reduced shares

140(1) **[Limitation of liability]** Where a company's share capital is reduced, a member of the company (past or present) is not liable in respect of any share to any call or contribution exceeding in amount the difference (if any) between the amount of the share as fixed by the minute and the amount paid on the share or the reduced amount (if any), which is deemed to have been paid on it, as the case may be.

140(2) **[Application of sec. 140(2), (3)]** But the following two subsections apply if—

    (a) a creditor, entitled in respect of a debt or claim to object to the reduction of share capital, by reason of his ignorance of the proceedings for reduction of share capital, or of their nature and effect with respect to his claim, is not entered on the list of creditors; and

(b) after the reduction of capital, the company is unable (within the meaning of section 123 of the Insolvency Act) to pay the amount of his debt or claim.

History
In s. 140(2)(b) the words "section 123 of the Insolvency Act" substituted for the former words "section 518" by   Insolvency Act 1986, s. 439(1) and Sch. 13 as from 29 December 1986 (see IA 1986, s. 443 and S.I. 1986 No. 1924 (C. 71)).

140(3)   **[Payment to creditor]**   Every person who was a member of the company at the date of the registration of the order for reduction and minute is then liable to contribute for the payment of the debt or claim in question an amount not exceeding that which he would have been liable to contribute if the company had commenced to be wound up on the day before that date.

140(4)   **[Where company wound up]**   If the company is wound up, the court, on the application of the creditor in question and proof of ignorance referred to in subsection (2)(a), may (if it thinks fit) settle accordingly a list of persons so liable to contribute, and make and enforce calls and orders on the contributories settled on the list, as if they were ordinary contributories in a winding up.

140(5)   **[Rights of contributories]**   Nothing in this section affects the rights of the contributories among themselves.

SEC. 141   Penalty for concealing name of creditor, etc.

141   If an officer of the company—

(a) wilfully conceals the name of a creditor entitled to object to the reduction of capital; or

(b) wilfully misrepresents the nature or amount of the debt or claim of any creditor; or

(c) aids, abets or is privy to any such concealment or misrepresentation as is mentioned above,

he is guilty of an offence and liable to a fine.

Chapter V — Maintenance of Capital

SEC. 142   Duty of directors on serious loss of capital

142(1)   **[Extraordinary general meeting]**   Where the net assets of a public company are half or less of its called-up share capital, the directors shall, not later than 28 days from the earliest day on which that fact is known to a director of the company, duly convene an extraordinary general meeting of the company for a date not later than 56 days from that day for the purpose of considering whether any, and if so what, steps should be taken to deal with the situation.

142(2)   **[Penalty]**   If there is a failure to convene an extraordinary general meeting as required by subsection (1), each of the directors of the company who—

(a) knowingly and wilfully authorises or permits the failure, or

(b) after the expiry of the period during which that meeting should have been convened, knowingly and wilfully authorises or permits the failure to continue,

is liable to a fine.

142(3) **[Other matters at meeting]** Nothing in this section authorises the consideration, at a meeting convened in pursuance of subsection (1), of any matter which could not have been considered at that meeting apart from this section.

SEC. 143 General rule against company acquiring own shares

143(1) **[General prohibition]** Subject to the following provisions, a company limited by shares or limited by guarantee and having a share capital shall not acquire its own shares, whether by purchase, subscription or otherwise.

143(2) **[Penalty]** If a company purports to act in contravention of this section, the company is liable to a fine, and every officer of the company who is in default is liable to imprisonment or a fine, or both; and the purported acquisition is void.

143(3) **[Non-application of sec. 143(1)]** A company limited by shares may acquire any of its own fully paid shares otherwise than for valuable consideration; and subsection (1) does not apply in relation to—

(a) the redemption or purchase of shares in accordance with Chapter VII of this Part,

(b) the acquisition of shares in a reduction of capital duly made,

(c) the purchase of shares in pursuance of an order of the court under section 5 (alteration of objects), section 54 (litigated objection to resolution for company to be re-registered as private) or Part XVII (relief to members unfairly prejudiced), or

(d) the forfeiture of shares, or the acceptance of shares surrendered in lieu, in pursuance of the articles, for failure to pay any sum payable in respect of the shares.

SEC. 144 Acquisition of shares by company's nominee

144(1) **[Where shares are issued to nominee]** Subject to section 145, where shares are issued to a nominee of a company mentioned in section 143(1), or are acquired by a nominee of such a company from a third person as partly paid up, then, for all purposes—

(a) the shares are to be treated as held by the nominee on his own account; and

(b) the company is to be regarded as having no beneficial interest in them.

144(2) **[Failure by nominee to pay up]** Subject to that section, if a person is called on to pay any amount for the purpose of paying up, or paying any premium on, any shares in such a company which were issued to him, or which he otherwise acquired, as the company's nominee and he fails to pay that amount within 21 days from being called on to do so, then—

(a) if the shares were issued to him as subscriber to the memorandum by virtue of an undertaking of his in the memorandum, the other subscribers to the memorandum, or

(b) if the shares were otherwise issued to or acquired by him, the directors of the company at the time of the issue or acquisition,

are jointly and severally liable with him to pay that amount.

144(3)   **[Relief of nominee from liability]**   If in proceedings for the recovery of any such amount from any such subscriber or director under this section it appears to the court—

    (a)   that he is or may be liable to pay that amount, but

    (b)   that he has acted honestly and reasonably and, having regard to all the circumstances of the case, he ought fairly to be excused from liability,

the court may relieve him, either wholly or partly, from his liability on such terms as the court thinks fit.

144(4)   **[Relief for subscriber or director]**   Where any such subscriber or director has reason to apprehend that a claim will or might be made for the recovery of any such amount from him, he may apply to the court for relief; and the court has the same power to relieve him as it would have had in proceedings for the recovery of that amount.

SEC. 145   Exceptions from sec. 144

145(1)   **[Non-application of sec. 144(1)]**   Section 144(1) does not apply to shares acquired otherwise than by subscription by a nominee of a public company, where a person acquires shares in the company with financial assistance given to him directly or indirectly by the company for the purpose of or in connection with the acquisition, and the company has a beneficial interest in the shares.

145(2)   **[Non-application of sec. 144(1), (2)]**   Section 144(1) and (2) do not apply—

    (a)   to shares acquired by a nominee of a company when the company has no beneficial interest in those shares, or

    (b)   to shares issued in consequence of an application made before 22nd December 1980, or transferred in pursuance of an agreement to acquire them made before that date.

145(3)   **[Effect of Sch. 2]**   Schedule 2 to this Act has effect for the interpretation of references in this section to a company having, or not having, a beneficial interest in shares.

SEC. 146   Treatment of shares held by or for public company

146(1)   **[Application]**   Except as provided by section 148, the following applies to a public company—

    (a)   where shares in the company are forfeited, or surrendered to the company in lieu, in pursuance of the articles, for failure to pay any sum payable in respect of the shares;

    (b)   where shares in the company are acquired by it (otherwise than by any of the methods mentioned in section 143(3)(a) to (d)) and the company has a beneficial interest in the shares;

    (c)   where the nominee of the company acquires shares in the company from a third person without financial assistance being given directly or indirectly by the company and the company has a beneficial interest in the shares; or

(d) where a person acquires shares in the company with financial assistance given to him directly or indirectly by the company for the purpose of or in connection with the acquisition, and the company has a beneficial interest in the shares.

Schedule 2 to this Act has effect for the interpretation of references in this subsection to the company having a beneficial interest in shares.

146(2) **[Shares or any interest in company not previously disposed of]** Unless the shares or any interest of the company in them are previously disposed of, the company must not later than the end of the relevant period from their forfeiture or surrender or, in a case within subsection (1)(b), (c) or (d), their acquisition—

(a) cancel them and diminish the amount of the share capital by the nominal value of the shares cancelled, and

(b) where the effect of cancelling the shares will be that the nominal value of the company's allotted share capital is brought below the authorised minimum, apply for re-registration as a private company, stating the effect of the cancellation.

146(3) **["The relevant period"]** For this purpose "the relevant period" is—

(a) 3 years in the case of shares forfeited or surrendered to the company in lieu of forfeiture, or acquired as mentioned in subsection (1)(b) or (c);

(b) one year in the case of shares acquired as mentioned in subsection (1)(d).

146(4) **[Prohibition on voting rights]** The company and, in a case within subsection (1)(c) or (d), the company's nominee or (as the case may be) the other shareholder must not exercise any voting rights in respect of the shares; and any purported exercise of those rights is void.

SEC. 147 Matters arising out of compliance with sec. 146(2)

147(1) **[Not necessary to comply with sec. 135, 136]** The directors may take such steps as are requisite to enable the company to carry out its obligations under section 146(2) without complying with sections 135 and 136 (resolution to reduce share capital; application to court for approval).

147(2) **[Alterations in resolution]** The steps taken may include the passing of a resolution to alter the company's memorandum so that it no longer states that the company is to be a public company; and the resolution may make such other alterations in the memorandum as are requisite in the circumstances.

Such a resolution is subject to section 380 (copy to be forwarded to registrar within 15 days).

147(3) **[Sec. 146(2)(b) application for re-registration]** The application for re-registration required by section 146(2)(b) must be in the prescribed form and be signed by a director or secretary of the company, and must be delivered to the registrar of companies together with a printed copy of the memorandum and articles of the company as altered by the resolution.

147(4) **[Issue of appropriate certificate of incorporation]** If the registrar is satisfied that the company may be re-registered under section 146, he shall retain the application and other documents delivered with it and issue the company with a certificate of incorporation appropriate to a company that is not a public company; and—

(a) the company by virtue of the issue of the certificate becomes a private company, and the alterations in the memorandum and articles set out in the resolution take effect accordingly, and

(b) the certificate is conclusive evidence that the requirements of sections 146 to 148 in respect of re-registration and of matters precedent and incidental to it have been complied with, and that the company is a private company.

SEC. 148   Further provisions supplementing sec. 146, 147

148(1)   [Private company re-registering as public company]   Where, after shares in a private company—

(a) are forfeited in pursuance of the company's articles or are surrendered to the company in lieu of forfeiture, or

(b) are acquired by the company (otherwise than by such surrender or forfeiture, and otherwise than by any of the methods mentioned in section 143(3)), the company having a beneficial interest in the shares, or

(c) are acquired by the nominee of a company in the circumstances mentioned in section 146(1)(c), or

(d) are acquired by any person in the circumstances mentioned in section 146(1)(d),

the company is re-registered as a public company, sections 146 and 147, and also section 149, apply to the company as if it had been a public company at the time of the forfeiture, surrender or acquisition, but with the modification required by the following subsection.

148(2)   [Modification to sec. 148(1)]   That modification is to treat any reference to the relevant period from the forfeiture, surrender or acquisition as referring to the relevant period from the re-registration of the company as a public company.

148(3)   [Effect of Sch. 2]   Schedule 2 to this Act has effect for the interpretation of the reference in subsection (1)(b) to the company having a beneficial interest in shares.

148(4)   [Shares or interest shown as asset in balance sheet]   Where a public company or a nominee of a public company acquires shares in the company or an interest in such shares, and those shares are (or that interest is) shown in a balance sheet of the company as an asset, an amount equal to the value of the shares or (as the case may be) the value to the company of its interest in them shall be transferred out of profits available for dividend to a reserve fund and are not then available for distribution.

SEC. 149   Sanctions for non-compliance

149(1)   [Failure to re-register as private company within relevant period]   If a public company required by section 146(2) to apply to be re-registered as a private company fails to do so before the end of the relevant period referred to in that subsection, section 81 (restriction on public offers) applies to it as if it were a private company such as is mentioned in that section; but, subject to this, the company continues to be treated for the purpose of this Act as a public company until it is so re-registered.

149(2)   [Failure to comply with sec. 146(2)]   If a company when required to do so by section 146(2) (including that subsection as applied by section 148(1)) fails to cancel any shares in accordance with paragraph (a) of that subsection or to make an application for re-registration in accordance with paragraph (b) of it, the company and every officer of it who is in default is liable to a fine and, for continued contravention, to a daily default fine.

SEC. 150   Charges of public companies on own shares

150(1)   [Charge on own shares void]   A lien or other charge of a public company on its own shares (whether taken expressly or otherwise), except a charge permitted by any of the following subsections, is void.

This is subject to section 6 of the Consequential Provisions Act (saving for charges of old public companies on their own shares).

150(2)   [Exception if shares not fully paid]   In the case of any description of company, a charge on its own shares is permitted if the shares are not fully paid and the charge is for any amount payable in respect of the shares.

150(3)   [Exception for money lending or credit companies]   In the case of a company whose ordinary business—

(a) includes the lending of money, or

(b) consists of the provision of credit or the bailment (in Scotland, hiring) of goods under a hire purchase agreement, or both,

a charge of the company on its own shares is permitted (whether the shares are fully paid or not) if it arises in connection with a transaction entered into by the company in the ordinary course of its business.

150(4)   [Exception where charge prior to registration/re-registration]   In the case of a company which is re-registered or is registered under section 680 as a public company, a charge on its own shares is permitted if the charge was in existence immediately before the company's application for re-registration or (as the case may be) registration.

This subsection does not apply in the case of such a company as is referred to in section 6(3) of the Consequential Provisions Act (old public company remaining such after 22nd March 1982, not having applied to be re-registered as public company).

Chapter VI — Financial Assistance by a Company for Acquisition of its Own Shares

PROVISIONS APPLYING TO BOTH PUBLIC AND PRIVATE COMPANIES

SEC. 151   Financial assistance generally prohibited

151(1)   [No direct or indirect financial assistance]   Subject to the following provisions of this Chapter, where a person is acquiring or is proposing to acquire shares in a company, it is not lawful for the company or any of its subsidiaries to give financial assistance directly or indirectly for the purpose of that acquisition before or at the same time as the acquisition takes place.

151(2) **[No financial assistance to reduce or discharge liability]** Subject to those provisions, where a person has acquired shares in a company and any liability has been incurred (by that or any other person), for the purpose of that acquisition, it is not lawful for the company or any of its subsidiaries to give financial assistance directly or indirectly for the purpose of reducing or discharging the liability so incurred.

151(3) **[Penalty]** If a company acts in contravention of this section, it is liable to a fine, and every officer of it who is in default is liable to imprisonment or a fine, or both.

SEC. 152   Definitions for this Chapter

152(1) **[''Financial assistance'', ''distributable profits'', ''distribution'']** In this Chapter—

   (a) **''financial assistance''** means—

     (i) financial assistance given by way of gift,

     (ii) financial assistance given by way of guarantee, security or indemnity, other than an indemnity in respect of the indemnifier's own neglect or default, or by way of release or waiver,

     (iii) financial assistance given by way of a loan or any other agreement under which any of the obligations of the person giving the assistance are to be fulfilled at a time when in accordance with the agreement any obligation of another party to the agreement remains unfulfilled, or by way of the novation of, or the assignment of rights arising under, a loan or such other agreement, or

     (iv) any other financial assistance given by a company the net assets of which are thereby reduced to a material extent or which has no net assets;

   (b) **''distributable profits''**, in relation to the giving of any financial assistance—

     (i) means those profits out of which the company could lawfully make a distribution equal in value to that assistance, and

     (ii) includes, in a case where the financial assistance is or includes a non-cash asset, any profit which, if the company were to make a distribution of that asset, would under section 276 (distributions in kind) be available for that purpose,

     and

   (c) **''distribution''** has the meaning given by section 263(2).

152(2) **[''Net assets'', ''liabilities'']** In subsection (1)(a)(iv), **''net assets''** means the aggregate of the company's assets, less the aggregate of its liabilities (''liabilities'' to include any provision for liabilities or charges within paragraph 89 of Schedule 4).

152(3) **[Interpretation]** In this Chapter—

(a) a reference to a person incurring a liability includes his changing his financial position by making an agreement or arrangement (whether enforceable or unenforceable, and whether made on his own account or with any other person) or by any other means, and

(b) a reference to a company giving financial assistance for the purpose of reducing or discharging a liability incurred by a person for the purpose of the acquisition of shares includes its giving such assistance for the purpose of wholly or partly restoring his financial position to what it was before the acquisition took place.

SEC. 153   Transactions not prohibited by sec. 151

153(1) **[Exception to sec. 151(1) prohibition]** Section 151(1) does not prohibit a company from giving financial assistance for the purpose of an acquisition of shares in it or its holding company if—

(a) the company's principal purpose in giving that assistance is not to give it for the purpose of any such acquisition, or the giving of the assistance for that purpose is but an incidental part of some larger purpose of the company, and

(b) the assistance is given in good faith in the interests of the company.

153(2) **[Exception to sec. 151(2) prohibition]** Section 151(2) does not prohibit a company from giving financial assistance if—

(a) the company's principal purpose in giving the assistance is not to reduce or discharge any liability incurred by a person for the purpose of the acquisition of shares in the company or its holding company, or the reduction or discharge of any such liability is but an incidental part of some larger purpose of the company, and

(b) the assistance is given in good faith in the interests of the company.

153(3) **[Various exceptions to sec. 151]** Section 151 does not prohibit—

(a) a distribution of a company's assets by way of dividend lawfully made or a distribution made in the course of the company's winding up,

(b) the allotment of bonus shares,

(c) a reduction of capital confirmed by order of the court under section 137,

(d) a redemption or purchase of shares made in accordance with Chapter VII of this Part,

(e) anything done in pursuance of an order of the court under section 425 (compromises and arrangements with creditors and members),

(f) anything done under an arrangement made in pursuance of section 110 of the Insolvency Act (acceptance of shares by liquidator in winding up as consideration for sale of property), or

(g) anything done under an arrangement made between a company and its creditors which is binding on the creditors by virtue of Part I of the Insolvency Act.

History
In s. 153(3):
- in para. (f) the words "section 110 of the Insolvency Act" substituted for the former words "section 582" by Insolvency Act 1986, s. 439(1) and Sch. 13 as from 29 December 1986 (see IA 1986, s. 443 and S.I. 1986 No. 1924 (C. 71));
- in para. (g) the words "Part I of the Insolvency Act" substituted for the former words "Chapter II of Part II of the Insolvency Act 1985" by Insolvency Act 1986, s. 439(1) and Sch. 13 as from 29 December 1986 as above (those former words themselves previously substituted for "section 601 (winding up imminent or in progress)" by Insolvency Act 1985, s. 109 and Sch. 6, para. 8: see S.I. 1986 No. 1924 (C. 71)).

153(4)   **[Further exceptions to sec. 151]**   Section 151 does not prohibit—

    (a)   where the lending of money is part of the ordinary business of the company, the lending of money by the company in the ordinary course of its business,

    (b)   the provision by a company, in good faith in the interests of the company, of financial assistance for the purposes of an employees' share scheme.

    (bb)   without prejudice to paragraph (b), the provision of financial assistance by a company or any of its subsidiaries for the purposes of or in connection with anything done by the company (or a company connected with it) for the purpose of enabling or facilitating transactions in shares in the first-mentioned company between, and involving the acquisition of beneficial ownership of those shares by, any of the following persons—

        (i)   the bona fide employees or former employees of that company or of another company in the same group; or

        (ii)   the wives, husbands, widows, widowers, children or step-children under the age of eighteen of any such employees or former employees,

    (c)   the making by a company of loans to persons (other than directors) employed in good faith by the company with a view to enabling those persons to acquire fully paid shares in the company or its holding company to be held by them by way of beneficial ownership.

History
S. 153(4)(b) substituted by CA 1989, s. 132 as from 1 April 1990 (see S.I. 1990 No. 355 (C. 13), art. 4(c)); s. 153(4)(b) formerly read as follows:

  ."(b)   the provision by a company in accordance with an employees' share scheme of money for the acquisition of fully paid shares in the company or its holding company,".

S. 153(4)(bb) inserted by Financial Services Act 1986, s. 196(2) as from 1 December 1987 (see S.I. 1987 No. 1997 (C. 59)).

153(5)   **[Connected company in sec. 153(4)(bb)]**   For the purposes of subsection (4)(bb) a company is connected with another company if—

    (a)   they are in the same group; or

    (b)   one is entitled, either alone or with any other company in the same group, to exercise or control the exercise of a majority of the voting rights attributable to the share capital which are exercisable in all circumstances at any general meeting of the other company or of its holding company;

and in this section **"group"** in relation to a company, means that company, any other company which is its holding company or subsidiary and any other company which is a subsidiary of that holding company.

History
S. 153(5) inserted by Financial Services Act 1986, s. 196(3) as from 1 December 1987 (see S.I. 1987 No. 1997 (C. 59)).

SEC. 154   Special restriction for public companies

154(1)   **[Limitations on financial assistance by public company]**   In the case of a public company, section 153(4) authorises the giving of financial assistance only if the company has net assets which are not thereby reduced or, to the extent that those assets are thereby reduced, if the assistance is provided out of distributable profits.

154(2) **["Net assets", "liabilities"]** For this purpose the following definitions apply—

  (a) **"net assets"** means the amount by which the aggregate of the company's assets exceeds the aggregate of its liabilities (taking the amount of both assets and liabilities to be as stated in the company's accounting records immediately before the financial assistance is given);

  (b) **"liabilities"** includes any amount retained as reasonably necessary for the purpose of providing for any liability or loss which is either likely to be incurred, or certain to be incurred but uncertain as to amount or as to the date on which it will arise.

PRIVATE COMPANIES

SEC. 155 Relaxation of sec. 151 for private companies

155(1) **[Exception to sec. 151]** Section 151 does not prohibit a private company from giving financial assistance in a case where the acquisition of shares in question is or was an acquisition of shares in the company or, if it is a subsidiary of another private company, in that other company if the following provisons of this section, and sections 156 to 158, are complied with as respects the giving of that assistance.

155(2) **[Assistance to come from distributable profits]** The financial assistance may only be given if the company has net assets which are not thereby reduced or, to the extent that they are reduced, if the assistance is provided out of distributable profits.

Section 154(2) applies for the interpretation of this subsection.

155(3) **[No financial assistance where acquisition in holding company]** This section does not permit financial assistance to be given by a subsidiary, in a case where the acquisition of shares in question is or was an acquisition of shares in its holding company, if it is also a subsidiary of a public company which is itself a subsidiary of that holding company.

155(4) **[Approval by special resolution in general meeting]** Unless the company proposing to give the financial assistance is a wholly-owned subsidiary, the giving of assistance under this section must be approved by special resolution of the company in general meeting.

155(5) **[Approval in sec. 155(3) situation]** Where the financial assistance is to be given by the company in a case where the acquisition of shares in question is or was an acquisition of shares in its holding company, that holding company and any other company which is both the company's holding company and a subsidiary of that other holding company (except, in any case, a company which is a wholly-owned subsidiary) shall also approve by special resolution in general meeting the giving of the financial assistance.

155(6) **[Statutory declaration by directors under sec. 156]** The directors of the company proposing to give the financial assistance and, where the shares acquired or to be acquired are shares in its holding company, the directors of that company and of any other company which is both the company's holding company and a subsidiary of that other holding company shall before the financial assistance is given make a statutory declaration in the prescribed form complying with the section next following.

SEC. 156   Statutory declaration under sec. 155

156(1)   **[Statutory declaration referred to in sec. 155(6)]**   A statutory declaration made by a company's directors under section 155(6) shall contain such particulars of the financial assistance to be given, and of the business of the company of which they are directors, as may be prescribed and shall identify the person to whom the assistance is to be given.

156(2)   **[Contents of statutory declaration]**   The declaration shall state that the directors have formed the opinion, as regards the company's initial situation immediately following the date on which the assistance is proposed to be given, that there will be no ground on which it could then be found to be unable to pay its debts; and either—

   (a)   if it is intended to commence the winding up of the company within 12 months of that date, that the company will be able to pay its debts in full within 12 months of the commencement of the winding up, or

   (b)   in any other case, that the company will be able to pay its debts as they fall due during the year immediately following that date.

156(3)   **[Matters for directors' opinion under sec. 156(2)]**   In forming their opinion for purposes of subsection (2), the directors shall take into account the same liabilities (including contingent and prospective liabilities) as would be relevant under section 122 of the Insolvency Act (winding up by the court) to the question whether the company is unable to pay its debts.

History
In s. 156(3) the words "section 122 of the Insolvency Act"   Act 1986, s. 439(1) and Sch. 13 as from 29 December 1986
substituted for the former words "section 517" by Insolvency   (see IA 1986, s. 443 and S.I. 1986 No. 1924 (C. 71)).

156(4)   **[Auditors' report to be annexed]**   The directors' statutory declaration shall have annexed to it a report addressed to them by their company's auditors stating that—

   (a)   they have enquired into the state of affairs of the company, and

   (b)   they are not aware of anything to indicate that the opinion expressed by the directors in the declaration as to any of the matters mentioned in subsection (2) of this section is unreasonable in all the circumstances.

156(5)   **[Delivery of documents to registrar]**   The statutory declaration and auditors' report shall be delivered to the registrar of companies—

   (a)   together with a copy of any special resolution passed by the company under section 155 and delivered to the registrar in compliance with section 380, or

   (b)   where no such resolution is required to be passed, within 15 days after the making of the declaration.

156(6)   **[Failure to comply with sec. 156(5)]**   If a company fails to comply with subsection (5), the company and every officer of it who is in default is liable to a fine and, for continued contravention, to a daily default fine.

156(7)   **[Making sec. 155 statutory declaration without reasonable grounds]**   A director of a company who makes a statutory declaration under section 155 without having reasonable grounds for the opinion expressed in it is liable to imprisonment or a fine, or both.

SEC. 157   Special resolution under sec. 155

157(1)   [Timing of special resolution and statutory declaration]   A special resolution required by section 155 to be passed by a company approving the giving of financial assistance must be passed on the date on which the directors of that company make the statutory declaration required by that section in connection with the giving of that assistance, or within the week immediately following that date.

157(2)   [Application for cancellation of special resolution]   Where such a resolution has been passed, an application may be made to the court for the cancellation of the resolution—

   (a) by the holders of not less in the aggregate than 10 per cent in nominal value of the company's issued share capital or any class of it, or

   (b) if the company is not limited by shares, by not less than 10 per cent of the company's members;

but the application shall not be made by a person who has consented to or voted in favour of the resolution.

157(3)   [Application of sec. 54(3) to (10)]   Subsections (3) to (10) of section 54 (litigation to cancel resolution under section 53) apply to applications under this section as to applications under section 54.

157(4)   [Requirements to be effective]   A special resolution passed by a company is not effective for purposes of section 155—

   (a) unless the declaration made in compliance with subsection (6) of that section by the directors of the company, together with the auditors' report annexed to it, is available for inspection by members of the company at the meeting at which the resolution is passed,

   (b) if it is cancelled by the court on an application under this section.

SEC. 158   Time for giving financial assistance under sec. 155

158(1)   [Application]   This section applies as to the time before and after which financial assistance may not be given by a company in pursuance of section 155.

158(2)   [Earliest time for assistance]   Where a special resolution is required by that section to be passed approving the giving of the assistance, the assistance shall not be given before the expiry of the period of 4 weeks beginning with—

   (a) the date on which the special resolution is passed, or

   (b) where more than one such resolution is passed, the date on which the last of them is passed,

unless, as respects that resolution (or, if more than one, each of them), every member of the company which passed the resolution who is entitled to vote at general meetings of the company voted in favour of the resolution.

158(3)   [Where application for cancellation made under sec. 157]   If application for the cancellation of any such resolution is made under section 157, the financial assistance shall not be given before the final determination of the application unless the court otherwise orders.

158(4)   [Latest time for assistance]   The assistance shall not be given after the expiry of the period of 8 weeks beginning with—

    (a) the date on which the directors of the company proposing to give the assistance made their statutory declaration under section 155, or

    (b) where that company is a subsidiary and both its directors and the directors of any of its holding companies made such a declaration, the date on which the earliest of the declarations is made,

unless the court, on an application under section 157, otherwise orders.

Chapter VII — Redeemable Shares;
Purchase by a Company of its Own Shares

REDEMPTION AND PURCHASE GENERALLY

SEC. 159   Power to issue redeemable shares

159(1)   [Power]   Subject to the provisions of this Chapter, a company limited by shares or limited by guarantee and having a share capital may, if authorised to do so by its articles, issue shares which are to be redeemed or are liable to be redeemed at the option of the company or the shareholder.

159(2)   [Must be issued shares]   No redeemable shares may be issued at a time when there are no issued shares of the company which are not redeemable.

159(3)   [Shares must be fully paid]   Redeemable shares may not be redeemed unless they are fully paid; and the terms of redemption must provide for payment on redemption.

SEC. 160   Financing, etc. of redemption

160(1)   [From distributable profits of company]   Subject to the next subsection and to sections 171 (private companies redeeming or purchasing own shares out of capital) and 178(4) (terms of redemption or purchase enforceable in a winding up)—

    (a) redeemable shares may only be redeemed out of distributable profits of the company or out of the proceeds of a fresh issue of shares made for the purposes of the redemption; and

    (b) any premium payable on redemption must be paid out of distributable profits of the company.

160(2)   [Premiums payable on redemption]   If the redeemable shares were issued at a premium, any premium payable on their redemption may be paid out of the proceeds of a fresh issue of shares made for the purposes of the redemption, up to an amount equal to—

    (a) the aggregate of the premiums received by the company on the issue of the shares redeemed, or

    (b)   the current amount of the company's share premium account (including any sum transferred to that account in respect of premiums on the new shares),

whichever is the less; and in that case the amount of the company's share premium account shall be reduced by a sum corresponding (or by sums in the aggregate corresponding) to the amount of any payment made by virtue of this subsection out of the proceeds of the issue of the new shares.

160(3) **[Redemption in accordance with articles]** Subject to the following provisions of this Chapter, redemption of shares may be effected on such terms and in such manner as may be provided by the company's articles.

160(4) **[Shares redeemed treated as cancelled]** Shares redeemed under this section shall be treated as cancelled on redemption, and the amount of the company's issued share capital shall be diminished by the nominal value of those shares accordingly; but the redemption of shares by a company is not to be taken as reducing the amount of the company's authorised share capital.

160(5) **[Extent of power to issue shares]** Without prejudice to subsection (4), where a company is about to redeem shares, it has power to issue shares up to the nominal value of the shares to be redeemed as if those shares had never been issued.

SEC. 161 Stamp duty on redemption of shares

161 (Repealed by Finance Act 1988, sec. 148 and Sch. 14, Pt. XI as from 22 March 1988.)

History
S. 161 formerly read as follows:

"**161(1)** For the purposes of section 47 of the Finance Act 1973, the issue of shares by a company in place of shares redeemed under section 160 constitutes a chargeable transaction if, and only if, the actual value of the shares so issued exceeds the value of the shares redeemed at the date of their redemption.

(2) Where the issue of the shares does constitute a chargeable transaction for those purposes, the amount on which stamp duty on the relevant document relating to that transaction is chargeable under section 47(5) of the Finance Act 1973 is the difference between—

    (a) the amount on which that duty would be so chargeable if the shares had not been issued in place of shares redeemed under section 160; and

    (b) the value of the shares redeemed at the date of their redemption.

(3) Subject to the following subsection, for the purposes of subsections (1) and (2) shares issued by a company—

    (a) up to the nominal amount of any shares which the company has redeemed under section 160; or

    (b) in pursuance of section 160(5) before the redemption of shares which the company is about to redeem under that section,

are to be regarded as issued in place of the shares redeemed or (as the case may be) about to be redeemed.

(4) Shares issued in pursuance of section 160(5) are not to be regarded for purposes of subsections (1) and (2) of this section as issued in place of the shares about to be redeemed, unless those shares are redeemed within one month after the issue of the new shares."

SEC. 162 Power of company to purchase own shares

162(1) **[Power]** Subject to the following provisions of this Chapter, a company limited by shares or limited by guarantee and having a share capital may, if authorised to do so by its articles, purchase its own shares (including any redeemable shares).

162(2) **[Application of sec. 159 to 161]** Sections 159 to 161 apply to the purchase by a company under this section of its own shares as they apply to the redemption of redeemable shares, save that the terms and manner of purchase need not be determined by the articles as required by section 160(3).

162(3) [Limitation on purchase] A company may not under this section purchase its shares if as a result of the purchase there would no longer be any member of the company holding shares other than redeemable shares.

SEC. 163 Definitions of "off-market" and "market" purchase

163(1) ["Off-market" purchase] A purchase by a company of its own shares is "off-market" if the shares either—

(a) are purchased otherwise than on a recognised investment exchange, or

(b) are purchased on a recognised investment exchange but are not subject to a marketing arrangement on that investment exchange.

History
In s. 163(1) the words "a recognised investment exchange" substituted for the former words "a recognised stock exchange" in both places where they appear and the words "that investment exchange" substituted for the former words "that stock exchange" by Financial Services Act 1986, s. 212(2) and Sch. 16, para. 17(a), (b) as from 29 April 1988 (see S.I. 1988 No. 740 (C. 22)).

163(2) [Interpretation of sec. 163(1)] For this purpose, a company's shares are subject to a marketing arrangement on a recognised investment exchange if either—

(a) they are listed under Part IV of the Financial Services Act 1986; or

(b) the company has been afforded facilities for dealings in those shares to take place on that investment exchange without prior permission for individual transactions from the authority governing that investment exchange and without limit as to the time during which those facilities are to be available.

History
In s. 163(2) the words "a recognised investment exchange" substituted for the former words "a recognised stock exchange" by Financial Services Act 1986, s. 212(2) and Sch. 16, para. 17(a) as from 29 April 1988 (see S.I. 1988 No. 740 (C. 22)), in para. (a) the words "under Part IV of the Financial Services Act 1986" substituted for the former words "on that stock exchange" by Financial Services Act 1986, s. 212(2) and Sch. 16, para. 17(c) as from 12 January 1987 (see S.I. 1986 No. 2246 (C. 88)), and in para. (b) the words "that investment exchange" substituted for the former words "that stock exchange" in both places where they occur by Financial Services Act 1986, s. 212(2) and Sch. 16, para. 17(a), (c) as from 29 April 1988 (see S.I. 1988 No. 740 (C. 22)).

163(3) ["Market" purchase] A purchase by a company of its own shares is a "market purchase" if it is a purchase made on a recognised investment exchange, other than a purchase which is an off-market purchase by virtue of subsection (1)(b).

History
In s. 163(3) the words "a recognised investment exchange" substituted for the former words "a recognised stock exchange" by Financial Services Act 1986, s. 212(2) and Sch. 16, para. 17(a) as from 29 April 1988 (see S.I. 1988 No. 740 (C. 22)).

163(4) ["Recognised investment exchange"] In this section **"recognised investment exchange"** means a recognised investment exchange other than an overseas investment exchange within the meaning of the Financial Services Act 1986.

History
S. 163(4) inserted by Financial Services Act 1986, s. 212(2) and Sch. 16, para. 17(d) as from 29 April 1988 (see S.I. 1988 No. 740 (C. 22)).

SEC. 164 Authority for off-market purchase

164(1) [Limitation on off-market purchase] A company may only make an off-market purchase of its own shares in pursuance of a contract approved in advance in accordance with this section or under section 165 below.

164(2) [Authority for proposed contract] The terms of the proposed contract must be authorised by a special resolution of the company before the contract is entered into; and the following subsections apply with respect to that authority and to resolutions conferring it.

164(3)   [Variation etc. of authority]   Subject to the next subsection, the authority may be varied, revoked or from time to time renewed by special resolution of the company.

164(4)   [Authority for public company]   In the case of a public company, the authority conferred by the resolution must specify a date on which the authority is to expire; and in a resolution conferring or renewing authority that date must not be later than 18 months after that on which the resolution is passed.

164(5)   [Special resolution not effective in certain cases]   A special resolution to confer, vary, revoke or renew authority is not effective if any member of the company holding shares to which the resolution relates exercises the voting rights carried by any of those shares in voting on the resolution and the resolution would not have been passed if he had not done so.

For this purpose—

(a) a member who holds shares to which the resolution relates is regarded as exercising the voting rights carried by those shares not only if he votes in respect of them on a poll on the question whether the resolution shall be passed, but also if he votes on the resolution otherwise than on a poll;

(b) notwithstanding anything in the company's articles, any member of the company may demand a poll on that question; and

(c) a vote and a demand for a poll by a person as proxy for a member are the same respectively as a vote and a demand by the member.

[The next page is 9,551]

164(6) **[Copy of contract or terms to be available for inspection]** Such a resolution is not effective for the purposes of this section unless (if the proposed contract is in writing) a copy of the contract or (if not) a written memorandum of its terms is available for inspection by members of the company both—

(a) at the company's registered office for not less than 15 days ending with the date of the meeting at which the resolution is passed, and

(b) at the meeting itself.

A memorandum of contract terms so made available must include the names of any members holding shares to which the contract relates; and a copy of the contract so made available must have annexed to it a written memorandum specifying any such names which do not appear in the contract itself.

164(7) **[Limitation on variation of existing contract]** A company may agree to a variation of an existing contract so approved, but only if the variation is authorised by a special resolution of the company before it is agreed to; and subsections (3) to (6) above apply to the authority for a proposed variation as they apply to the authority for a proposed contract, save that a copy of the original contract or (as the case may require) a memorandum of its terms, together with any variations previously made, must also be available for inspection in accordance with subsection (6).

SEC. 165 Authority for contingent purchase contract

165(1) **[Contingent purchase contract]** A contingent purchase contract is a contract entered into by a company and relating to any of its shares—

(a) which does not amount to a contract to purchase those shares, but

(b) under which the company may (subject to any conditions) become entitled or obliged to purchase those shares.

165(2) **[Approval in advance]** A company may only make a purchase of its own shares in pursuance of a contingent purchase contract if the contract is approved in advance by a special resolution of the company before the contract is entered into; and subsections (3) to (7) of section 164 apply to the contract and its terms.

SEC. 166 Authority for market purchase

166(1) **[Authority by company in general meeting]** A company shall not make a market purchase of its own shares unless the purchase has first been authorised by the company in general meeting.

166(2) **[Types of authority]** That authority—

(a) may be general for that purpose, or limited to the purchase of shares of any particular class of description, and

(b) may be unconditional or subject to conditions.

166(3) **[Requirements of authority]** The authority must—

(a) specify the maximum number of shares authorised to be acquired,

(b) determine both the maximum and the minimum prices which may be paid for the shares, and

(c) specify a date on which it is to expire.

166(4)   **[Variation, revocation, renewal of authority]**   The authority may be varied, revoked or from time to time renewed by the company in general meeting, but this is subject to subsection (3) above; and in a resolution to confer or renew authority, the date on which the authority is to expire must not be later than 18 months after that on which the resolution is passed.

166(5)   **[Company's purchase of own shares]**   A company may under this section make a purchase of its own shares after the expiry of the time limit imposed to comply with subsection (3)(c), if the contract of purchase was concluded before the authority expired and the terms of the authority permitted the company to make a contract of purchase which would or might be executed wholly or partly after its expiration.

166(6)   **[Resolution conferring or varying authority]**   A resolution to confer or vary authority under this section may determine either or both the maximum and minimum prices for purchase by—

    (a)   specifying a particular sum, or

    (b)   providing a basis or formula for calculating the amount of the price in question without reference to any person's discretion or opinion.

166(7)   **[Application of sec. 380]**   A resolution of a company conferring, varying, revoking or renewing authority under this section is subject to section 380 (resolution to be sent to registrar of companies within 15 days).

SEC. 167   Assignment or release of company's right to purchase own shares

167(1)   **[Prohibition of assignment]**   The rights of a company under a contract approved under section 164 or 165, or under a contract for a purchase authorised under section 166, are not capable of being assigned.

167(2)   **[Release of rights — conditions]**   An agreement by a company to release its rights under a contract approved under section 164 or 165 is void unless the terms of the release agreement are approved in advance by a special resolution of the company before the agreement is entered into; and subsections (3) to (7) of section 164 apply to approval for a proposed release agreement as to authority for a proposed variation of an existing contract.

SEC. 168   Payments apart from purchase price to be made out of distributable profits

168(1)   **[Types of payment]**   A payment made by a company in consideration of—

    (a)   acquiring any right with respect to the purchase of its own shares in pursuance of a contract approved under section 165, or

    (b)   the variation of a contract approved under section 164 or 165, or

    (c)   the release of any of the company's obligations with respect to the purchase any of its own shares under a contract approved under section 164 or 165 or under a contract for a purchase authorised under section 166,

must be made out of the company's distributable profits.

168(2) **[Effect of not satisfying sec. 168(2) requirements]** If the requirements of subsection (1) are not satisfied in relation to a contract—

    (a) in a case within paragraph (a) of the subsection, no purchase by the company of its own shares in pursuance of that contract is lawful under this Chapter,

    (b) in a case within paragraph (b), no such purchase following the variation is lawful under this Chapter, and

    (c) in a case within paragraph (c), the purported release is void.

SEC. 169 Disclosure by company of purchase of own shares

169(1) **[Return to registrar]** Within the period of 28 days beginning with the date on which any shares purchased by a company under this Chapter are delivered to it, the company shall deliver to the registrar of companies for registration a return in the prescribed form stating with respect to shares of each class purchased the number and nominal value of those shares and the date on which they were delivered to the company.

169(2) **[Return for public company]** In the case of a public company, the return shall also state—

    (a) the aggregate amount paid by the company for the shares; and

    (b) the maximum and minimum prices paid in respect of shares of each class purchased.

169(3) **[Inclusion in single return]** Particulars of shares delivered to the company on different dates and under different contracts may be included in a single return to the registrar; and in such a case the amount required to be stated under subsection (2)(a) is the aggregate amount paid by the company for all the shares to which the return relates.

169(4) **[Particulars of authorised contracts to be kept at registered office]** Where a company enters into a contract approved under section 164 or 165, or a contract for a purchase authorised under section 166, the company shall keep at its registered office—

    (a) if the contract is in writing, a copy of it; and

    (b) if not, a memorandum of its terms,

from the conclusion of the contract until the end of the period of 10 years beginning with the date on which the purchase of all the shares in pursuance of the contract is completed or (as the case may be) the date on which the contract otherwise determines.

169(5) **[Sec. 169(4) particulars open for inspection]** Every copy and memorandum so required to be kept shall, during business hours (subject to such reasonable restrictions as the company may in general meeting impose, provided that not less than 2 hours in each day are allowed for inspection) be open to inspection without charge—

    (a) by any member of the company, and

    (b) if it is a public company, by any other person.

169(6) **[Penalty for non-delivery of return]** If default is made in delivering to the registrar any return required by this section, every officer of the company who is in default is liable to a fine and, for continued contravention, to a daily default fine.

169(7)　[Penalty for contravention of sec. 169(4), (5)]　If default is made in complying with subsection (4), or if an inspection required under subsection (5) is refused, the company and every officer of it who is in default is liable to a fine and, for continued contravention, to a daily default fine.

169(8)　[Power of court to compel sec. 169(4) inspection]　In the case of a refusal of an inspection required under subsection (5) of a copy or memorandum, the court may by order compel an immediate inspection of it.

169(9)　[Application of sec. 169(4)]　The obligation of a company under subsection (4) to keep a copy of any contract or (as the case may be) a memorandum of its terms applies to any variation of the contract so long as it applies to the contract.

SEC. 170　The capital redemption reserve

170(1)　["Capital redemption reserve"]　Where under this Chapter shares of a company are redeemed or purchased wholly out of the company's profits, the amount by which the company's issued share capital is diminished in accordance with section 160(4) on cancellation of the shares redeemed or purchased shall be transferred to a reserve, called "the capital redemption reserve".

170(2)　[Transfer to capital redemption reserve]　If the shares are redeemed or purchased wholly or partly out of the proceeds of a fresh issue and the aggregate amount of those proceeds is less than the aggregate nominal value of the shares redeemed or purchased, the amount of the difference shall be transferred to the capital redemption reserve.

170(3)　[Exception to application of sec. 170(2)]　But subsection (2) does not apply if the proceeds of the fresh issue are applied by the company in making a redemption or purchase of its own shares in addition to a payment out of capital under section 171.

170(4)　[Reduction of share capital provisions]　The provisions of this Act relating to the reduction of a company's share capital apply as if the capital redemption reserve were paid-up share capital of the company, except that the reserve may be applied by the company in paying up its unissued shares to be allotted to members of the company as fully paid bonus shares.

REDEMPTION OR PURCHASE OF OWN SHARES OUT OF CAPITAL (PRIVATE COMPANIES ONLY)

SEC. 171　Power of private companies to redeem or purchase own shares out of capital

171(1)　[Source of payment]　Subject to the following provisions of this Chapter, a private company limited by shares or limited by guarantee and having a share capital may, if so authorised by its articles, make a payment in respect of the redemption or purchase under section 160 or (as the case may be) section 162, of its own shares otherwise than out of its distributable profits or the proceeds of a fresh issue of shares.

171(2)　[References to payment out of capital]　References below in this Chapter to payment out of capital are (subject to subsection (6)) to any payment so made, whether or not it would be regarded apart from this section as a payment out of capital.

171(3) **[Amount of payment]** The payment which may (if authorised in accordance with the following provisions of this Chapter) be made by a company out of capital in respect of the redemption or purchase of its own shares is such an amount as, taken together with—

> (a) any available profits of the company, and
>
> (b) the proceeds of any fresh issue of shares made for the purposes of the redemption or purchase,

is equal to the price of redemption or purchase; and the payment permissible under this subsection is referred to below in this Chapter as the permissible capital payment for the shares.

171(4) **[Transfer to capital redemption reserve]** Subject to subsection (6), if the permissible capital payment for shares redeemed or purchased is less than their nominal amount, the amount of the difference shall be transferred to the company's capital redemption reserve.

171(5) **[Permissible capital payment exceeding nominal amount of shares]** Subject to subsection (6), if the permissible capital payment is greater than the nominal amount of the shares redeemed or purchased—

> (a) the amount of any capital redemption reserve, share premium account or fully paid share capital of the company, and
>
> (b) any amount representing unrealised profits of the company for the time being standing to the credit of any reserve maintained by the company in accordance with paragraph 34 of Schedule 4 (revaluation reserve),

may be reduced by a sum not exceeding (or by sums not in the aggregate exceeding) the amount by which the permissible capital payment exceeds the nominal amount of the shares.

171(6) **[Proceeds of fresh issue]** Where the proceeds of a fresh issue are applied by a company in making any redemption or purchase of its own shares in addition to a payment out of capital under this section, the references in subsections (4) and (5) to the permissible capital payment are to be read as referring to the aggregate of that payment and those proceeds.

SEC. 172 Availability of profits for purposes of sec. 171

172(1) **[Reference to available profits of the company]** The reference in section 171(3)(a) to available profits of the company is to the company's profits which are available for distribution (within the meaning of Part VIII); but the question whether a company has any profits so available and the amount of any such profits are to be determined for purposes of that section in accordance with the following subsections, instead of sections 270 to 275 in that Part.

172(2) **[Determination of amount of profits]** Subject to the next subsection, that question is to be determined by reference to—

> (a) profits, losses, assets and liabilities,
>
> (b) provisions of any of the kinds mentioned in paragraphs 88 and 89 of Schedule 4 (depreciation, diminution in value of assets, retentions to meet liabilities, etc.), and

(c) share capital and reserves (including undistributable reserves),

as stated in the relevant accounts for determining the permissible capital payment for shares.

172(3) [The relevant accounts in sec. 172(2)] The relevant accounts for this purpose are such accounts, prepared as at any date within the period for determining the amount of the permissible capital payment, as are necessary to enable a reasonable judgment to be made as to the amounts of any of the items mentioned in subsection (2)(a) to (c) above.

172(4) [Determination of amount of permissible capital payment] For purposes of determining the amount of the permissible capital payment for shares, the amount of the company's available profits (if any) determined in accordance with subsections (2) and (3) is treated as reduced by the amount of any distributions lawfully made by the company after the date of the relevant accounts and before the end of the period for determining the amount of that payment.

172(5) [Lawful distributions in sec. 172(4)] The reference in subsection (4) to distributions lawfully made by the company includes—

(a) financial assistance lawfully given out of distributable profits in a case falling within section 154 or 155,

(b) any payment lawfully made by the company in respect of the purchase by it of any shares in the company (except a payment lawfully made otherwise than out of distributable profits), and

(c) a payment of any description specified in section 168(1) lawfully made by the company.

172(6) [Period for determining the amount of permissible capital payment] References in this section to the period for determining the amount of the permissible capital payment for shares are to the period of 3 months ending with the date on which the statutory declaration of the directors purporting to specify the amount of that payment is made in accordance with subsection (3) of the section next following.

SEC. 173   Conditions for payment out of capital

173(1) [Requirements for payment by private company] Subject to any order of the court under section 177, a payment out of capital by a private company for the redemption or purchase of its own shares is not lawful unless the requirements of this and the next two sections are satisfied.

173(2) [Approval by special resolution] The payment out of capital must be approved by a special resolution of the company.

173(3) [Statutory declaration by directors] The company's directors must make a statutory declaration specifying the amount of the permissible capital payment for the shares in question and stating that, having made full inquiry into the affairs and prospects of the company, they have formed the opinion—

(a) as regards its initial situation immediately following the date on which the payment out of capital is proposed to be made, that there will be no grounds on which the company could then be found unable to pay its debts, and

(b) as regards its prospects for the year immediately following that date, that, having regard to their intentions with respect to the management of the company's business during that year and to the amount and character of the financial resources which will in their view be available to the company during that year, the company will be able to continue to carry on business as a going concern (and will accordingly be able to pay its debts as they fall due) throughout that year.

173(4)   [Directors' opinion in sec. 173(3)(a)]   In forming their opinion for purposes of subsection (3)(a), the directors shall take into account the same liabilities (including prospective and contingent liabilities) as would be relevant under section 122 of the Insolvency Act (winding up by the court) to the question whether a company is unable to pay its debts.

History
In s. 173(4) the words "section 122 of the Insolvency Act"   Act 1986, s. 439(1) and Sch. 13 as from 29 December 1986
substituted for the former words "section 517" by Insolvency   (see IA 1986, s. 443 and S.I. 1986 No. 1924 (C. 71)).

173(5)   [Form and content of statutory declaration, auditors' report]   The directors' statutory declaration must be in the prescribed form and contain such information with respect to the nature of the company's business as may be prescribed, and must in addition have annexed to it a report addressed to the directors by the company's auditors stating that—

(a) they have inquired into the company's state of affairs; and

(b) the amount specified in the declaration as the permissible capital payment for the shares in question is in their view properly determined in accordance with sections 171 and 172; and

(c) they are not aware of anything to indicate that the opinion expressed by the directors in the declaration as to any of the matters mentioned in subsection (3) is unreasonable in all the circumstances.

173(6)   [Penalty for unreasonable declaration]   A director who makes a declaration under this section without having reasonable grounds for the opinion expressed in the declaration is liable to imprisonment or a fine, or both.

SEC. 174   Procedure for special resolution under sec. 173

174(1)   [Dates for special resolution and payment out of capital]   The resolution required by section 173 must be passed on, or within the week immediately following, the date on which the directors make the statutory declaration required by that section; and the payment out of capital must be made no earlier than 5 nor more than 7 weeks after the date of the resolution.

174(2)   [Limitation on approval by special resolution]   The resolution is ineffective if any member of the company holding shares to which the resolution relates exercises the voting rights carried by any of those shares in voting on the resolution and the resolution would not have been passed if he had not done so.

174(3)   [Interpretation of sec. 174(2)]   For purposes of subsection (2), a member who holds such shares is to be regarded as exercising the voting rights carried by them in voting on the resolution not only if he votes in respect of them on a poll on the question whether the resolution shall be passed, but also if he votes on the resolution otherwise than on a poll; and, notwithstanding anything in a company's articles, any member of the company may demand a poll on that question.

174(4)   **[Inspection of statutory declaration and auditors' report]**   The resolution is ineffective unless the statutory declaration and auditors' report required by the section are available for inspection by members of the company at the meeting at which the resolution is passed.

174(5)   **[Vote and demand for poll by person as proxy]**   For purposes of this section a vote and a demand for a poll by a person as proxy for a member are the same (respectively) as a vote and demand by the member.

SEC. 175   Publicity for proposed payment out of capital

175(1)   **[Notice in Gazette]**   Within the week immediately following the date of the resolution for payment out of capital the company must cause to be published in the Gazette a notice—

- (a) stating that the company has approved a payment out of capital for the purpose of acquiring its own shares by redemption or purchase or both (as the case may be);
- (b) specifying the amount of the permissible capital payment for the shares in question and the date of the resolution under section 173;
- (c) stating that the statutory declaration of the directors and the auditors' report required by that section are available for inspection at the company's registered office; and
- (d) stating that any creditor of the company may at any time within the 5 weeks immediately following the date of the resolution for payment out of capital apply to the court under section 176 for an order prohibiting the payment.

175(2)   **[Notice in appropriate national newspapers]**   Within the week immediately following the date of the resolution the company must also either cause a notice to the same effect as that required by subsection (1) to be published in an appropriate national newspaper or give notice in writing to that effect to each of its creditors.

175(3)   **["An appropriate national newspaper"]**   "An appropriate national newspaper" means a newspaper circulating throughout England and Wales (in the case of a company registered in England and Wales), and a newspaper circulating throughout Scotland (in the case of a company registered in Scotland).

175(4)   **[References to first notice date]**   References below in this section to the first notice date are to the day on which the company first publishes the notice required by subsection (1) or first publishes or gives the notice required by subsection (2) (whichever is the earlier).

175(5)   **[Statutory declaration and auditors' report to register]**   Not later than the first notice date the company must deliver to the registrar of companies a copy of the statutory declaration of the directors and of the auditors' report required by section 173.

175(6)   **[Statutory declaration and auditors' report available for inspection]**   The statutory declaration and auditors' report—

- (a) shall be kept at the company's registered office throughout the period beginning with the first notice date and ending 5 weeks after the date of the resolution for payment out of capital, and

    (b) shall during business hours on any day during that period be open to the inspection of any member or creditor of the company without charge.

175(7)   **[Penalty on refusal of sec. 175(6) inspection]**   If an inspection required under subsection (6) is refused, the company and every officer of it who is in default is liable to a fine and, for continued contravention, to a daily default fine.

175(8)   **[Power of court to compel inspection]**   In the case of refusal of an inspection required under subsection (6) of a declaration or report, the court may by order compel an immediate inspection of that declaration or report.

SEC. 176   Objections by company's members or creditors

176(1)   **[Application for cancellation]**   Where a private company passes a special resolution approving for purposes of this Chapter any payment out of capital for the redemption or purchase of any of its shares—

    (a) any member of the company other than one who consented to or voted in favour of the resolution; and

    (b) any creditor of the company,

may within 5 weeks of the date on which the resolution was passed apply to the court for cancellation of the resolution.

176(2)   **[Maker of application]**   The application may be made on behalf of the persons entitled to make it by such one or more of their number as they may appoint in writing for the purpose.

176(3)   **[Obligations of company]**   If an application is made, the company shall—

    (a) forthwith give notice in the prescribed form of that fact to the registrar of companies; and

    (b) within 15 days from the making of any order of the court on the hearing of the application, or such longer period as the court may by order direct, deliver an office copy of the order to the registrar.

176(4)   **[Penalty]**   A company which fails to comply with subsection (3), and any officer of it who is in default, is liable to a fine and for continued contravention, to a daily default fine.

SEC. 177   Powers of court on application under sec. 176

177(1)   **[Adjournment, directions and orders by court]**   On the hearing of an application under section 176 the court may, if it thinks fit, adjourn the proceedings in order that an arrangement may be made to the court's satisfaction for the purchase of the interests of dissentient members or for the protection of dissentient creditors (as the case may be); and the court may give such directions and make such orders as it thinks expedient for facilitating or carrying into effect any such arrangement.

177(2)   **[Terms of court order etc.]**   Without prejudice to its powers under subsection (1), the court shall make an order on such terms and conditions as it thinks fit either confirming or cancelling the resolution; and, if the court confirms the resolution, it may in particular by order alter or extend any date or period of time specified in the resolution or in any provision in this Chapter which applies to the redemption or purchase of shares to which the resolution refers.

177(3)   [Further scope of court order]   The court's order may, if the court thinks fit, provide for the purchase by the company of the shares of any of its members and for the reduction accordingly of the company's capital, and may make such alterations in the company's memorandum and articles as may be required in consequence of that provision.

177(4)   [Where order requires no alteration in memorandum or articles]   If the court's order requires the company not to make any, or any specified, alteration in its memorandum or articles, the company has not then power without leave of the court to make any such alteration in breach of the requirement.

177(5)   [Effect of sec. 177(4) alteration]   An alteration in the memorandum or articles made by virtue of an order under this section, if not made by resolution of the company, is of the same effect as if duly made by resolution; and this Act applies accordingly to the memorandum or articles as so altered.

SUPPLEMENTARY

SEC. 178   Effect of company's failure to redeem or purchase

178(1)   [Effect]   This section has effect where a company has, on or after 15th June 1982,—

(a) issued shares on terms that they are or are liable to be redeemed, or

(b) agreed to purchase any of its own shares.

178(2)   [Company not liable in damages]   The company is not liable in damages in respect of any failure on its part to redeem or purchase any of the shares.

178(3)   [Qualification to sec. 178(2)]   Subsection (2) is without prejudice to any right of the holder of the shares other than his right to sue the company for damages in respect of its failure; but the court shall not grant an order for specific performance of the terms of redemption or purchase if the company shows that it is unable to meet the costs of redeeming or purchasing the shares in question out of distributable profits.

178(4)   [Enforcement of terms of redemption or purchase]   If the company is wound up and at the commencement of the winding up any of the shares have not been redeemed or purchased, the terms of redemption or purchase may be enforced against the company; and when shares are redeemed or purchased under this subsection, they are treated as cancelled.

178(5)   [Non-application of sec. 178(4)]   However, subsection (4) does not apply if—

(a) the terms provided for the redemption or purchase to take place at a date later than that of the commencement of the winding up, or

(b) during the period beginning with the date on which the redemption or purchase was to have taken place and ending with the commencement of the winding up the company could not at any time have lawfully made a distribution equal in value to the price at which the shares were to have been redeemed or purchased.

178(6) **[Priority payments]** There shall be paid in priority to any amount which the company is liable under subsection (4) to pay in respect of any shares—

(a) all other debts and liabilities of the company (other than any due to members in their character as such),

(b) if other shares carry rights (whether as to capital or as to income) which are preferred to the rights as to capital attaching to the first-mentioned shares, any amount due in satisfaction of those preferred rights;

but, subject to that, any such amount shall be paid in priority to any amounts due to members in satisfaction of their rights (whether as to capital or income) as members.

178(7) (Repealed by Insolvency Act 1985, sec. 235 and Sch. 10, Pt. II as from 29 December 1986.)

History

In regard to the date of the above repeal, see S.I. 1986 No. 1924 (C. 71). S. 178(7) formerly read as follows:

"**178(7)** Where by virtue of section 66 of the Bankruptcy Act 1914 (payment of interest on debts) as applied by section 612 (application of bankruptcy rules to insolvent companies in England and Wales) a creditor of a company is entitled to payment of any interest only after payment of all other debts of the company, the company's debts and liabilities for purposes of subsection (6) of this section include the liability to pay that interest."

SEC. 179 Power for Secretary of State to modify this Chapter

179(1) **[Regulations modifying provisions of Ch. VII]** The Secretary of State may by regulations made by statutory instrument modify the provisions of this Chapter with respect to any of the following matters—

(a) the authority required for a purchase by a company of its own shares,

(b) the authority required for the release by a company or its rights under a contract for the purchase of its own shares or a contract under which the company may (subject to any conditions) become entitled or obliged to purchase its own shares,

(c) the information to be included in a return delivered by a company to the registrar of companies in accordance with section 169(1),

(d) the matters to be dealt with in the statutory declaration of the directors under section 173 with a view to indicating their opinion of their company's ability to make a proposed payment out of capital with due regard to its financial situation and prospects, and

(e) the contents of the auditors' report required by that section to be annexed to that declaration.

179(2) **[Further regulations]** The Secretary of State may also by regulations so made make such provision (including modification of the provisions of this Chapter) as appears to him to be appropriate—

(a) for wholly or partly relieving companies from the requirement of section 171(3)(a) that any available profits must be taken into account in determining the amount of the permissible capital payment for shares under that section, or

(b) for permitting a company's share premium account to be applied, to any extent appearing to the Secretary of State to be appropriate, in providing for the premiums payable on the redemption or purchase by the company of any of its own shares.

179(3) **[Content of regulations]** Regulations under this section—

(a) may make such further modification of any provisions of this Chapter as appears to the Secretary of State to be reasonably necessary in consequence of any provision made under such regulations by virtue of subsection (1) or (2),

(b) may make different provision for different cases or classes of case, and

(c) may contain such further consequential provisions, and such incidental and supplementary provisions, as the Secretary of State thinks fit.

179(4) **[Approval of regulations]** No regulations shall be made under this section unless a draft of the instrument containing them has been laid before Parliament and approved by resolution of each House.

SEC. 180   Transitional cases arising under this Chapter; and savings

180(1) **[Certain preference shares issued before 15 June 1982]** Any preference shares issued by a company before 15th June 1982 which could but for the repeal by the Companies Act 1981 of section 58 of the Companies Act 1948 (power to issue redeemable preference shares) have been redeemed under that section are subject to redemption in accordance with the provisions of this Chapter.

180(2) **[Where sec. 159, 160 apply]** In a case to which sections 159 and 160 apply by virtue of this section, any premium payable on redemption may, notwithstanding the repeal by the 1981 Act of any provision of the 1948 Act, be paid out of the share premium account instead of out of profits, or partly out of that account and partly out of profits (but subject to the provisions of this Chapter so far as payment is out of profits).

180(3) **[Capital redemption reserve fund before 15 June 1982]** Any capital redemption reserve fund established before 15th June 1982 by a company for the purposes of section 58 of the Act of 1948 is to be known as the company's capital redemption reserve and be treated as if it had been established for the purposes of section 170 of this Act; and accordingly, a reference in any enactment or in the articles of any company, or in any other instrument, to a company's capital redemption reserve fund is to be construed as a reference to the company's capital redemption reserve.

SEC. 181   Definitions for Chapter VII

181 In this Chapter—

(a) **"distributable profits"**, in relation to the making of any payment by a company, means those profits out of which it could lawfully make a distribution (within the meaning given by section 263(2)) equal in value to the payment, and

(b) **"permissible capital payment"** means the payment permitted by section 171;

and references to payment out of capital are to be construed in accordance with section 171.

Chapter VIII — Miscellaneous Provisions about Shares and Debentures

SHARE AND DEBENTURE CERTIFICATES, TRANSFERS AND WARRANTS

SEC. 182 Nature, transfer and numbering of shares

182(1) **[Nature, transfer]** The shares or other interest of any member in a company—

(a) are personal estate or, in Scotland, moveable property and are not in the nature of real estate or heritage,

(b) are transferable in manner provided by the company's articles, but subject to the Stock Transfer Act 1963 (which enables securities of certain descriptions to be transferred by a simplified process).

182(2) **[Numbering]** Each share in a company having a share capital shall be distinguished by its appropriate number; except that, if at any time all the issued shares in a company, or all the issued shares in it of a particular class, are fully paid up and rank pari passu for all purposes, none of those shares need thereafter have a distinguishing number so long as it remains fully paid up and ranks pari passu for all purposes with all shares of the same class for the time being issued and fully paid up.

SEC. 183 Transfer and registration

183(1) **[Conditions for registration of transfer]** It is not lawful for a company to register a transfer of shares in or debentures of the company unless a proper instrument of transfer has been delivered to it, or the transfer is an exempt transfer within the Stock Transfer Act 1982.

This applies notwithstanding anything in the company's articles.

183(2) **[Where shares transmitted by operation of law]** Subsection (1) does not prejudice any power of the company to register as shareholder or debenture holder a person to whom the right to any shares in or debentures of the company has been transmitted by operation of law.

183(3) **[Transfer by personal representative]** A transfer of the share or other interest of a deceased member of a company made by his personal representative, although the personal representative is not himself a member of the company, is as valid as if he had been such a member at the time of the execution of the instrument of transfer.

183(4) **[Registration of transfer at request of transferor]** On the application of the transferor of any share or interest in a company, the company shall enter in its register of members the name of the transferee in the same manner and subject to the same conditions as if the application for the entry were made by the transferee.

183(5) **[Notice of refusal to register transfer]** If a company refuses to register a transfer of shares or debentures, the company shall, within 2 months after the date on which the transfer was lodged with it, send to the transferee notice of the refusal.

183(6)   **[Penalty re sec. 183(5)]**   If default is made in complying with subsection (5), the company and every officer of it who is in default is liable to a fine and, for continued contravention, to a daily default fine.

SEC. 184   Certification of transfers

184(1)   **[Effect of certification by company]**   The certification by a company of any instrument of transfer of any shares in, or debentures of, the company is to be taken as a representation by the company to any person acting on the faith of the certification that there have been produced to the company such documents as on their face show a prima facie title to the shares or debentures in the transferor named in the instrument.

However, the certification is not to be taken as a representation that the transferor has any title to the shares or debentures.

184(2)   **[Liability of company for negligently made false certification]**   Where a person acts on the faith of a false certification by a company made negligently, the company is under the same liability to him as if the certification had been made fraudulently.

184(3)   **[Interpretation]**   For purposes of this section—

    (a)   an instrument of transfer is deemed certificated if it bears the words "certificate lodged" (or words to the like effect);

    (b)   the certification of an instrument of transfer is deemed made by a company if—

        (i)   the person issuing the instrument is a person authorised to issue certificated instruments of transfer on the company's behalf, and

        (ii)   the certification is signed by a person authorised to certificate transfers on the company's behalf or by an officer or servant either of the company or of a body corporate so authorised;

    (c)   a certification is deemed signed by a person if—

        (i)   it purports to be authenticated by his signature or initials (whether handwritten or not), and

        (ii)   it is not shown that the signature or initials was or were placed there neither by himself nor by a person authorised to use the signature or initials for the purpose of certificating transfers on the company's behalf.

SEC. 185   Duty of company as to issue of certificates

185(1)   **[General obligations of company]**   Subject to the following provisions, every company shall—

    (a)   within 2 months after the allotment of any of its shares, debentures or debenture stock, and

    (b)   within 2 months after the date on which a transfer of any such shares, debentures or debenture stock is lodged with the company,

complete and have ready for delivery the certificates of all shares, the debentures and the certificates of all debenture stock allotted or transferred (unless the conditions of issue of the shares, debentures or debenture stock otherwise provide).

185(2) **["Transfer"]** For this purpose, **"transfer"** means a transfer duly stamped and otherwise valid, or an exempt transfer within the Stock Transfer Act 1982, and does not include such a transfer as the company is for any reason entitled to refuse to register and does not register.

185(3) **[Non-application of sec. 185(1)]** Subsection (1) does not apply in the case of a transfer to any person where, by virtue of regulations under section 3 of the Stock Transfer Act 1982, he is not entitled to a certificate or other document of or evidencing title in respect of the securities transferred; but if in such a case the transferee—

(a) subsequently becomes entitled to such a certificate or other document by virtue of any provision of those regulations, and

(b) gives notice in writing of that fact to the company,

this section has effect as if the reference in subsection (1)(b) to the date of the lodging of the transfer were a reference to the date of the notice.

185(4) **[Exception to sec. 185(1) for clearing house or nominee]** A company of which shares or debentures are allotted or debenture stock is allotted to a recognised clearing house or a nominee of a recognised clearing house or of a recognised investment exchange, or with which a transfer is lodged for transferring any shares, debentures or debenture stock of the company to such a clearing house or nominee, is not required, in consequence of the allotment or the lodging of the transfer, to comply with subsection (1); but no person shall be a nominee for the purposes of this section unless he is a person designated for the purposes of this section in the rules of the recognised investment exchange in question.

"Recognised clearing house" means a recognised clearing house within the meaning of the Financial Services Act 1986 acting in relation to a recognised investment exchange and **"recognised investment exchange"** has the same meaning as in that Act.

Note
In s. 185(4):

- the words "a recognised clearing house or a nominee of a recognised clearing house or of a recognised investment exchange" substituted for the former words "a stock exchange nominee";

- the words "such a clearing house or nominee" substituted for the former words "a stock exchange nominee";

- the words from "; but no person shall be a nominee" to the end of the paragraph inserted; and

- the second paragraph substituted for the former words "'**stock exchange nominee'** means any person whom the Secretary of State designates, by order in a statutory instrument, as a nominee of The Stock Exchange for the purposes of this section"

by Financial Services Act, s. 195(5) as from 29 April 1988 (see S.I. 1988 No. 740 (C. 22)).

185(5) **[Penalty re sec. 185(1)]** If default is made in complying with subsection (1), the company and every officer of it who is in default is liable to a fine and, for continued contravention, to a daily default fine.

185(6) **[Application to court on continuing default]** If a company on which a notice has been served requiring it to make good any default in complying with subsection (1) fails to make good the default within 10 days after service of the notice, the court may, on the application of the person entitled to have the certificates or the debentures delivered to him, exercise the power of the following subsection.

185(7) **[Court order re default]** The court may make an order directing the company and any officer of it to make good the default within such time as may be specified in the order; and the order may provide that all costs of and incidental to the application shall be borne by the company or by an officer of it responsible for the default.

SEC. 186   Certificate to be evidence of title

186   A certificate, under the common seal of the company or the seal kept by the company by virtue of section 40, specifying any shares held by a member, is prima facie evidence of his title to the shares.

SEC. 187   Evidence of grant of probate or confirmation as executor

187   The production to a company of any document which is by law sufficient evidence of probate of the will, or letters of administration of the estate, or confirmation as executor, of a deceased person having been granted to some person shall be accepted by the company as sufficient evidence of the grant.

This has effect notwithstanding anything in the company's articles.

SEC. 188   Issue and effect of share warrant to bearer

188(1)   **[Issue of warrant]**   A company limited by shares, if so authorised by its articles, may, with respect to any fully paid-up shares, issue under its common seal a warrant stating that the bearer of the warrant is entitled to the shares specified in it, and may provide (by coupons or otherwise) for the payment of the future dividends on the shares included in the warrant.

188(2)   **["Share warrant", effect]**   Such a warrant is termed a "share warrant" and entitles the bearer to the shares specified in it: and the shares may be transferred by delivery of the warrant.

SEC. 189   Offences in connection with share warrants (Scotland)

189(1)   **[Offence re defrauding warrant etc., penalty]**   If in Scotland a person—

    (a)   with intent to defraud, forges or alters, or offers, utters, disposes of, or puts off, knowing the same to be forged or altered, any share warrant or coupon, or any document purporting to be a share warrant or coupon, issued in pursuance of this Act; or

    (b)   by means of any such forged or altered share warrant, coupon, or document, purporting as aforesaid, demands or endeavours to obtain or receive any share or interest in any company under this Act, or to receive any dividend or money payable in respect thereof, knowing the warrant, coupon, or document to be forged or altered;

he is on conviction thereof liable to imprisonment or a fine, or both.

189(2)   **[Offence re making warrants, penalty]**   If in Scotland a person without lawful authority or excuse (proof whereof lies on him)—

    (a)   engraves or makes on any plate, wood, stone, or other material, any share warrant or coupon purporting to be—

        (i)   a share warrant or coupon issued or made by any particular company in pursuance of this Act; or

    (ii) a blank share warrant or coupon so issued or made; or

    (iii) a part of such a share warrant or coupon; or

  (b) uses any such plate, wood, stone, or other material, for the making or printing of any such share warrant or coupon, or of any such blank share warrant or coupon, or any part thereof respectively; or

  (c) knowingly has in his custody or possession any such plate, wood, stone, or other material;

he is on conviction thereof liable to imprisonment or a fine, or both.

[The next page is 10,551]

DEBENTURES

SEC. 190 Register of debenture holders

190(1) [Scottish register not needed for English or Welsh companies] A company registered in England and Wales shall not keep in Scotland any register of holders of debentures of the company or any duplicate of any such register or part of any such register which is kept outside Great Britain.

190(2) [English or Welsh register not needed for Scottish companies] A company registered in Scotland shall not keep in England and Wales any such register as above-mentioned.

190(3) [Location of register] Neither a register of holders of debentures of a company nor a duplicate of any such register or part of any such register which is kept outside Great Britian shall be kept in England and Wales (in the case of a company registered in England and Wales) or in Scotland (in the case of a company registered in Scotland) elsewhere than—

   (a) at the company's registered office; or

   (b) at any office of the company at which the work of making it up is done; or

   (c) if the company arranges with some other person for the making up of the register or duplicate to be undertaken on its behalf by that other person, at the office of that other person at which the work is done.

190(4) [Register and duplicate to be at same place] Where a company keeps (in England and Wales or in Scotland, as the case may be) both such a register and such a duplicate, it shall keep them at the same place.

190(5) [Notice to registrar] Every company which keeps any such register or duplicate in England and Wales or Scotland shall send to the registrar of companies notice (in the prescribed form) of the place where the register or duplicate is kept and of any change in that place.

190(6) [No sec. 190(5) notice if always at registered office] But a company is not bound to send notice under sub-section (5) where the register or duplicate has, at all times since it came into existence, been kept at the company's registered office.

SEC. 191 Right to inspect register

191(1) [Inspection of register] Every register of holders of debentures of a company shall, except when duly closed (but subject to such reasonable restrictions as the company may impose in general meeting, so that not less than 2 hours in each day shall be allowed for inspection), be open to the inspection—

   (a) of the registered holder of any such debentures or any holder of shares in the company without fee; and

   (b) of any other person on payment of a fee of 5 pence or such less sum as may be prescribed by the company.

191(2) [Copy of register] Any such registered holder of debentures or holder of shares, or any other person, may require a copy of the register of the holders of debentures of the company or any part of it, on payment of 10 pence (or such less sum as may be prescribed by the company) for every 100 words, or fractional part of 100 words, required to be copied.

191(3)   **[Copy on request of trust deed securing issue of debentures]**   A copy of any trust deed for securing an issue of debentures shall be forwarded to every holder of any such debentures at his request on payment—

     (a)   in the case of a printed trust deed, of 20 pence (or such less sum as may be prescribed by the company), or

     (b)   where the trust deed has not been printed, of 10 pence (or such less sum as may be so prescribed), for every 100 words, or fractional part of 100 words, required to be copied.

191(4)   **[Penalty re refusal of inspection]**   If inspection is refused, or a copy is refused or not forwarded, the company and every officer of it who is in default is liable to a fine and, for continued contravention, to a daily default fine.

191(5)   **[Court may compel inspection]**   Where a company is in default as above-mentioned, the court may by order compel an immediate inspection of the register or direct that the copies required be sent to the person requiring them.

191(6)   **[Closure of register]**   For purposes of this section, a register is deemed to be duly closed if closed in accordance with provisions contained in the articles or in the debentures or, in the case of debenture stock, in the stock certificates, or in the trust deed or other document securing the debentures or debenture stock, during such period or periods, not exceeding in the whole 30 days in any year, as may be therein specified.

191(7)   **[Time limit re liability for deletion etc.]**   Liability incurred by a company from the making or deletion of an entry in its register of debenture holders, or from a failure to make or delete any such entry, is not enforceable more than 20 years after the date on which the entry was made or deleted or, in the case of any such failure, the failure first occurred.

     This is without prejudice to any lesser period of limitation.

SEC. 192   Liability of trustees of debentures

192(1)   **[Certain provisions in trust deed exempting trustees void]**   Subject to this section, any provision contained—

     (a)   in a trust deed for securing an issue of debentures, or

     (b)   in any contract with the holders of debentures secured by a trust deed,

is void in so far as it would have the effect of exempting a trustee of the deed from, or indemnifying him against, liability for breach of trust where he fails to show the degree of care and diligence required of him as trustee, having regard to the provisions of the trust deed conferring on him any powers, authorities or discretions.

192(2)   **[Releases etc.]**   Subsection (1) does not invalidate—

     (a)   a release otherwise validly given in respect of anything done or omitted to be done by a trustee before the giving of the release; or

(b)   any provision enabling such a release to be given—

    (i)   on the agreement thereto of a majority of not less than three-fourths in value of the debenture holders present and voting in person or, where proxies are permitted, by proxy at a meeting summoned for the purpose, and

    (ii)   either with respect to specific acts or omissions or on the trustee dying or ceasing to act.

192(3)   [Exceptions to sec. 192(1)]   Subsection (1) does not operate—

(a)   to invalidate any provision in force on 1st July 1948 so long as any person then entitled to the benefit of that provision or afterwards given the benefit of that provision under the following subsection remains a trustee of the deed in question; or

(b)   to deprive any person of any exemption or right to be indemnified in respect of anything done or omitted to be done by him while any such provision was in force.

192(4)   [Benefits of sec. 192(3)]   While any trustee of a trust deed remains entitled to the benefit of a provision save by subsection (3), the benefit of that provision may be given either—

(a)   to all trustees of the deed, present and future; or

(b)   to any named trustees or proposed trustees of it,

by a resolution passed by a majority of not less than three-fourths in value of the debenture holders present in person or, where proxies are permitted, by proxy at a meeting summoned for the purpose in accordance with the provisions of the deed or, if the deed makes no provision for summoning meetings, a meeting summoned for the purpose in any manner approved by the court.

SEC. 193   Perpetual debentures

193   A condition contained in debentures, or in a deed for securing debentures, is not invalid by reason only that the debentures are thereby made irredeemable or redeemable only on the happening of a contingency (however remote), or on the expiration of a period (however long), any rule of equity to the contrary notwithstanding.

This applies to debentures whenever issued, and to deeds whenever executed.

SEC. 194   Power to re-issue redeemed debentures

194(1)   [Power to re-issue]   Where (at any time) a company has redeemed debentures previously issued, then—

(a)   unless provision to the contrary, whether express or implied, is contained in the articles or in any contract entered into by the company; or

(b)   unless the company has, by passing a resolution to that effect or by some other act, manifested its intention that the debentures shall be cancelled,

the company has, and is deemed always to have had, power to re-issue the debentures, either by re-issuing the same debentures or by issuing other debentures in their place.

194(2)   [Priorities of re-issued debentures]   On a re-issue of redeemed debentures, the person entitled to the debentures has, and is deemed always to have had, the same priorities as if the debentures had never been redeemed.

194(3)   [Current account, debentures not redeemed]   Where a company has (at any time) deposited any of its debentures to secure advances from time to time on current account or otherwise, the debentures are not deemed to have been redeemed by reason only of the company's account having ceased to be in debit while the debentures remained so deposited.

194(4)   [Treatment of re-issue for stamp duty purposes]   The re-issue of a debenture or the issue of another debenture in its place under the power which by this section is given to or deemed to be possessed by a company is to be treated as the issue of a new debenture for purposes of stamp duty; but it is not to be so treated for the purposes of any provision limiting the amount or number of debentures to be issued.

This applies whenever the issue or re-issue was made.

194(5)   [Liability for non-payment of stamp duty]   A person lending money on the security of a debenture re-issued under this section which appears to be duly stamped may give the debenture in evidence in any proceedings for enforcing his security without payment of the stamp duty or any penalty in respect of it, unless he had notice (or, but for his negligence, might have discovered) that the debenture was not duly stamped: but in that case the company is liable to pay the proper stamp duty and penalty.

SEC. 195   Contract to subscribe for debentures

195   A contract with a company to take up and pay for debentures of the company may be enforced by an order for specific performance.

SEC. 196   Payment of debts out of assets subject to floating charge (England and Wales)

196(1)   [Application]   The following applies, in the case of a company registered in England and Wales, where debentures of the company are secured by a charge which, as created, was a floating charge.

196(2)   [If company not being wound up]   If possession is taken, by or on behalf of the holders of any of the debentures, of any property comprised in or subject to the charge, and the company is not at that time in course of being wound up, the company's preferential debts shall be paid out of assets coming to the hands of the person taking possession in priority to any claims for principal or interest in respect of the debentures.

196(3)   [Definitions]   "Preferential debts" means the categories of debts listed in Schedule 6 to the Insolvency Act; and for the purposes of that Schedule "the relevant date" is the date of possession being taken as above mentioned.

196(4)   [Recoupment of assets]   Payments made under this section shall be recouped, as far as may be, out of the assets of the company available for payment of general creditors.

History
S. 196 substituted by Insolvency Act 1986, s. 439(1) and Sch. 13 as from 29 December 1986 (see IA 1986, s. 443 and S.I. 1986 No. 1924 (C. 71)).

The section formerly read (as amended by Insolvency Act 1985, s. 109 and Sch. 6, para. 15: see S.I. 1986 No. 1924 (C. 71)) as follows:

"**196(1)** The following applies, in the case of a company registered in England and Wales, where either a receiver is appointed on behalf of the holders of any debentures of the company secured by a charge which, as created, was a floating charge, or possession is taken by or on behalf of those debenture-holders of any property comprised in or subject to the charge.

(2) If the company is not at the time in course of being wound up, the debts which in a winding up are, under section 89 of the Insolvency Act 1985 and Schedule 4 to that Act (read with Schedule 3 to the Social Security Pensions Act 1975), to be paid in priority to all other debts shall be paid out of assets coming to the hands of the receiver or other person taking possession, in priority to any claim for principal or interest in respect of the debentures.

(3) For the purposes of this section Schedule 4 to the said Act of 1985 and Schedule 3 to the said Act of 1975 shall each have effect as if—

    (a) references to the relevant date were references to the date of the appointment of the receiver or the taking of possession as mentioned in subsection (1) above; and

    (b) references to the company going into liquidation were references to the appointment of the receiver or the taking of possession as so mentioned.

(5) Payments made under this section shall be recouped as far as may be out of the assets of the company available for payment of general creditors."

Prior to the Insolvency Act 1985 amendments, s. 196 read as follows:

"**196(1)** The following applies, in the case of a company registered in England and Wales, where either a receiver is appointed on behalf of the holders of any debentures of the company secured by a floating charge, or possession is taken by or on behalf of those debenture-holders of any property comprised in or subject to the charge.

(2) If the company is not at the time in course of being wound up, the debts which in a winding up are, under the relevant provisions of Chapter V of Part XX relating to the preferential payments, to be paid in priority to all other debts shall be paid out of assets coming to the hands of the receiver or other person taking possession, in priority to any claims for principal or interest in respect of the debentures.

(3) In the application of those provisions of Part XX, section 614 and Schedule 19 are to be read as if the provision for payment of accrued holiday remuneration becoming payable on the termination of employment before or by the effect of the winding-up order or resolution were a provision for payment of such remuneration becoming payable on the termination of employment before or by the effect of the appointment of the receiver or possession being taken as mentioned in subsection (1) of this section.

(4) The periods of time mentioned in those provisions of Part XX are to be reckoned from the date of the appointment of the receiver or possession being taken as above mentioned, as the case may be; and in Schedule 19 as it applies for the purposes of this section '**the relevant date**' means that date.

(5) Payments made under this section shall be recouped as far as may be out of the assets of the company available for payment of general creditors."

(It should be noted that the amendment to s. 196(1) by Insolvency Act 1985 was in operation from 28 April 1986: see S.I. 1986 No. 463 (C. 14).)

SEC. 197 Debentures to bearer (Scotland)

197 Notwithstanding anything in the statute of the Scots Parliament of 1696, chapter 25, debentures to bearer issued in Scotland are valid and binding according to their terms.

PART VI — DISCLOSURE OF INTERESTS IN SHARES

INDIVIDUAL AND GROUP ACQUISITIONS

SEC. 198 Obligation of disclosure: the cases in which it may arise and "the relevant time"

198(1) **[Obligation to notify]** Where a person either—

    (a) to his knowledge acquires an interest in shares comprised in a public company's relevant share capital, or ceases to be interested in shares so comprised (whether or not retaining an interest in other shares so comprised), or

    (b) becomes aware that he has acquired an interest in shares so comprised or that he has ceased to be interested in shares so comprised in which he was previously interested, then in certain circumstances he comes under an obligation ("the obligation of disclosure") to make notification to the company of the interests which he has, or had, in its shares.

198(2)   ["Relevant share capital"]   In relation to a public company, **"relevant share capital"** means the company's issued share capital of a class carrying rights to vote in all circumstances at general meetings of the company; and it is hereby declared for the avoidance of doubt that—

(a)   where a company's share capital is divided into different classes of shares, references in this Part to a percentage of the nominal value of its relevant share capital are to a percentage of the nominal value of the issued shares comprised in each of the classes taken separately, and

(b)   the temporary suspension of voting rights in respect of shares comprised in issued share capital of a company of any such class does not affect the application of this Part in relation to interests in those or any other shares comprised in that class.

198(3)   [Further requirement for notification]   Where, otherwise than in circumstances within subsection (1), a person—

(a)   is aware at the time when it occurs of any change of circumstances affecting facts relevant to the application of the next following section to an existing interest of his in shares comprised in a company's share capital of any description, or

(b)   otherwise becomes aware of any such facts (whether or not arising from any such change of circumstances),

then in certain circumstances he comes under the obligation of disclosure.

198(4)   [Circumstances leading to obligation to notify]   The existence of the obligation in a particular case depends (in part) on circumstances obtaining before and after whatever is in that case the relevant time; and that is—

(a)   in a case within subsection (1)(a) or (3)(a), the time of the event or change of circumstances there mentioned, and

(b)   in a case within subsection (1)(b) or (3)(b), the time at which the person became aware of the facts in question.

SEC. 199   Interests to be disclosed

199(1)   [Interests in relevant share capital]   For purposes of the obligation of disclosure, the interests to be taken into account are those in relevant share capital of the company concerned.

199(2)   [Notifiable interest]   A person has a notifiable interest at any time when he is interested in shares comprised in that share capital of an aggregate nominal value equal to or more than 3 per cent of the nominal value of that share capital.

History

In s. 199(2) the words from "3 per cent" to the end substituted for the former words "the percentage of the nominal value of that share capital which is for the time being the notifiable percentage" by CA 1989, s. 134(1), (2) as from 31 May 1990 (see S.I. 1990 No. 713 (C. 22), art. 3(i)).

Note

S.I. 1990 No. 713 (C. 22), art. 4:

"**4(1)**   Where in consequence of the coming into force of section 134(2) of the 1989 Act a person's interest in the shares of a company becomes notifiable, and he is or becomes aware that he has such an interest,

(a) then he comes under an obligation to make notification to the company in respect of it, and

(b) the obligation must be performed within the period of 2 days next following the day on which he is or becomes so aware,

and the provisions of Part VI of the 1985 Act apply as if that obligation arose under section 198 of the 1985 Act.

(2) Any day that is a Saturday or Sunday or a bank holiday (as defined in s. 744 of the 1985 Act) in any part of Great Britain is to be disregarded in reckoning the period of 2 days referred to in paragraph (1)(b) of this article.''

199(3) [Relevant facts] All facts relevant to determining whether a person has a notifiable interest at any time (or the percentage level of his interest) are taken to be what he knows the facts to be at that time.

199(4) [When sec. 198(1), (3) obligation arises] The obligation of disclosure arises under section 198(1) or (3) where the person has a notifiable interest immediately after the relevant time, but did not have such an interest immediately before that time.

199(5) [Further case where sec. 198(1) obligation arises] The obligation also arises under section 198(1) where—

(a) the person had a notifiable interest immediately before the relevant time, but does not have such an interest immediately after it, or

(b) he had a notifiable interest immediately before that time, and has such an interest immediately after it, but the percentage levels of his interest immediately before and immediately after that time are not the same.

SEC. 200 "Percentage level" in relation to notifiable interests

200(1) ["Percentage level"] Subject to the qualification mentioned below, "**percentage level**", in section 199(5)(b), means the percentage figure found by expressing the aggregate nominal value of all the shares comprised in the share capital concerned in which the person is interested immediately before or (as the case may be) immediately after the relevant time as a percentage of the nominal value of that share capital and rounding that figure down, if it is not a whole number, to the next whole number.

200(2) [Further interpretation] Where the nominal value of the share capital is greater immediately after the relevant time than it was immediately before, the percentage level of the person's interest immediately before (as well as immediately after) that time is determined by reference to the larger amount.

SEC. 201 The notifiable percentage

201 (Repealed by Companies Act 1989, sec. 212 and Sch. 24 as from 31 May 1990.)

History

In regard to the date of the above repeal see S.I. 1990 No. 713 (C. 22), art. 3(ii); s. 201 formerly read as follows:

"**201(1)** The reference in section 199(2) to the notifiable percentage is to 5 per cent or such other percentage as may be prescribed by regulations under this section.

(2) The Secretary of State may by regulations in a statutory instrument from time to time prescribe the percentage to apply in determining whether a person's interest in a company's shares is notifiable under section 198; and different percentages may be prescribed in relation to companies of different classes or descriptions.

No regulations shall be made under this section unless a draft of the instrument containing them has been laid before Parliament and approved by a resolution of each House.

(3) Where in consequence of a reduction in the percentage made by such regulations a person's interest in a company's shares becomes notifiable, he then comes under the obligation of disclosure in respect of it; and the obligation must be performed within the period of 10 days next following the day on which it arises."

SEC. 202   Particulars to be contained in notification

202(1)   **[Time for notification]**   Where notification is required by section 198 with respect to a person's interest (if any) in shares comprised in relevant share capital of a public company, the obligation to make the notification must be performed within the period of 2 days next following the day on which that obligation arises; and the notification must be in writing to the company.

History

In s. 202(1) the words "(except where section 201(3) applies)" formerly appearing before the words "be performed" repealed and the words "2 days" substituted for the former words "5 days" by CA 1989, s. 134(1), (3),

212 and Sch. 24 as from 31 May 1990 (see S.I. 1990 No. 713 (C. 22), art. 3).

Note

See note after s. 202(4).

202(2)   **[Contents of notification]**   The notification must specify the share capital to which it relates, and must also—

    (a)   state the number of shares comprised in that share capital in which the person making the notification knows he was interested immediately after the time when the obligation arose, or

    (b)   in a case where the person no longer has a notifiable interest in shares comprised in that share capital, state that he no longer has that interest.

202(3)   **[Also particulars re shareholders]**   A notification with respect to a person's interest in a company's relevant share capital (other than one stating that he no longer has a notifiable interest in shares comprised in that share capital) shall include particulars of—

    (a)   the identity of each registered holder of shares to which the notification relates, and

    (b)   the number of those shares held by each such registered holder,

so far as known to the person making the notification at the date when the notification is made.

202(4)   **[Changes in particulars]**   A person who has an interest in shares comprised in a company's relevant share capital, that interest being notifiable, is under obligation to notify the company in writing—

    (a)   of any particulars in relation to those shares which are specified in subsection (3), and

    (b)   of any change in those particulars,

of which in either case he becomes aware at any time after any interest notification date and before the first occasion following that date on which he comes under any further obligation of disclosure with respect to his interest in shares comprised in that share capital.

    An obligation arising under this subsection must be performed within the period of 2 days next following the day on which it arises.

History

In s. 202(4) the words "2 days" substituted for the former words "5 days" by CA 1989, s. 134(1), (3) as from 31 May 1990 (see S.I. 1990 No. 713 (C. 22), art. 3(i)).

Note

In regard to s. 202(1), (4) the coming into force of CA 1989, s. 134(3) (which amends those provisions) does not affect the time for fulfilling any obligation arising before 31 May 1990: see S.I. 1990 No. 713 (C. 22), art. 5.

202(5)   **[Interest notification date]**   The reference in subsection (4) to a interest notification date, in relation to a person's interest in shares comprised in a public company's relevant share capital, is to either of the following—

(a) the date of any notification made by him with respect to his interest under this Part, and

(b) where he has failed to make a notification, the date on which the period allowed for making it came to an end.

202(6) **[Continuing notifiable interest]** A person who at any time has an interest in shares which is notifiable to be regarded under subsection (4) as continuing to have a notifiable interest in them unless and until he comes under obligation to make a notification stating that he no longer has such an interest in those shares.

SEC. 203 Notification of family and corporate interests

203(1) **[Family interests]** For purposes of sections 198 to 202, a person is taken to be interested in any shares in which his spouse or any infant child or step-child of his is interested; and **"infant"** means, in relation to Scotland, pupil or minor.

203(2) **[Corporate interests]** For those purposes, a person is taken to be interested in shares if a body corporate is interested in them and—

(a) that body or its directors are accustomed to act in accordance with his directions or instructions, or

(b) he is entitled to exercise or control the exercise of one-third or more of the voting power at general meetings of that body corporate.

203(3) **[Voting power in sec. 203(2)(b)]** Where a person is entitled to exercise or control the exercise of one-third or more of the voting power at general meetings of a body corporate and that body corporate is entitled to exercise or control the exercise of any of the voting power at general meetings of another body corporate ("the effective voting power") then, for purposes of subsection (2)(b), the effective voting power is taken as exercisable by that person.

203(4) **[Entitlement to exercise voting power]** For purposes of subsections (2) and (3), a person is entitled to exercise or control the exercise of voting power if—

(a) he has a right (whether subject to conditions or not) the exercise of which would make him so entitled, or

(b) he is under an obligation (whether or not so subject) the fulfilment of which would make him so entitled.

SEC. 204 Agreement to acquire interests in a particular company

204(1) **[Agreement between two or more persons]** In certain circumstances the obligation of disclosure may arise from an agreement between two or more persons which includes provision for the acquisition by any one or more of them of interests in shares of a particular public company ("the target company"), being shares comprised in the relevant share capital of that company.

204(2) **[Application of section to sec. 204(1) agreement]** This section applies to such an agreement if—

(a) the agreement also includes provisions imposing obligations or restrictions on any one or more of the parties to it with respect to their use, retention or disposal of their interests in that company's shares acquired in pursuance of the agreement (whether or not together with any other interests of theirs in the company's shares to which the agreement relates), and

(b) any interest in the company's shares is in fact acquired by any of the parties in pursuance of the agreement;

and in relation to such an agreement references below in this section, and in sections 205 and 206, to the target company are to the company which is the target company for that agreement in accordance with this and the previous subsection.

204(3)   **[Use of interest in shares in target company in sec. 204(2)(a)]**   The reference in subsection (2)(a) to the use of interests in shares in the target company is to the exercise of any rights or of any control or influence arising from those interests (including the right to enter into any agreement for the exercise, or for control of the exercise, of any of those rights by another person).

204(4)   **[Continuation of application of section]**   Once any interest in shares in the target company has been acquired in pursuance of such an agreement as is mentioned above, this section continues to apply to that agreement irrespective of—

(a) whether or not any further acquisitions of interests in the company's shares take place in pursuance of the agreement, and

(b) any change in the persons who are for the time being parties to it, and

(c) any variation of the agreement,

so long as the agreement continues to include provisions of any description mentioned in subsection (2)(a).

References in this subsection to the agreement include any agreement having effect (whether directly or indirectly) in substitution for the original agreement.

204(5)   **["Agreement" in Pt. VI]**   In this section, and also in references elsewhere in this Part to an agreement to which this section applies, **"agreement"** includes any agreement or arrangement; and references in this section to provisions of an agreement—

(a) accordingly include undertakings, expectations or understandings operative under any arrangement, and

(b) (without prejudice to the above) also include any provisions, whether express or implied and whether absolute or not.

204(6)   **[Exception to application of section]**   However, this section does not apply to an agreement which is not legally binding unless it involves mutuality in the undertakings, expectations or understandings of the parties to it; nor does the section apply to an agreement to underwrite or sub-underwrite any offer of shares in a company, provided the agreement is confined to that purpose and any matters incidental to it.

SEC. 205   Obligation of disclosure arising under sec. 204

205(1)   **[Each party to agreement interested in all shares of target company]**   In the case of an agreement to which section 204 applies, each party to the agreement is taken (for purposes of the obligation of disclosure) to be interested in all shares in the target company in which any other party to it is interested apart from the agreement (whether or not the interest of the other party in question was acquired, or includes any interest which was acquired, in pursuance of the agreement).

205(2) [Interest of party to agreement in shares in target company] For those purposes, and also for those of the next section, an interest of a party to such an agreement in shares in the target company is an interest apart from the agreement if he is interested in those shares otherwise than by virtue of the application of section 204 and this section in relation to the agreement.

205(3) [Interpretation additional to sec. 205(2)] Accordingly, any such interest of the person (apart from the agreement) includes for those purposes any interest treated as his under section 203 or by the application of section 204 and this section in relation to any other agreement with respect to shares in the target company to which he is a party.

205(4) [Notification of interest in shares of target company] A notification with respect to his interest in shares in the target company made to that company under this Part by a person who is for the time being a party to an agreement to which section 204 applies shall—

    (a) state that the person making the notification is a party to such an agreement,

    (b) include the names and (so far as known to him) the addresses of the other parties to the agreement, identifying them as such, and

    (c) state whether or not any of the shares to which the notification relates are shares in which he is interested by virtue of section 204 and this section and, if so, the number of those shares.

205(5) [Contents of notification] Where a person makes a notification to a company under this Part in consequence of ceasing to be interested in any shares of that company by virtue of the fact that he or any other person has ceased to be a party to an agreement to which section 204 applies, the notification shall include a statement that he or that other person has ceased to be a party to the agreement (as the case may require) and also (in the latter case) the name and (if known to him) the address of that other.

SEC. 206 Obligation of persons acting together to keep each other informed

206(1) [Application] A person who is a party to an agreement to which section 204 applies is subject to the requirements of this section at any time when—

    (a) the target company is a public company, and he knows it to be so, and

    (b) the shares in that company to which the agreement relates consist of or include shares comprised in relevant share capital of the company, and he knows that to be the case; and

    (c) he knows the facts which make the agreement one to which section 204 applies.

206(2) [Obligation to notify other parties to agreement] Such a person is under obligation to notify every other party to the agreement, in writing, of the relevant particulars of his interest (if any) apart from the agreement in shares comprised in relevant share capital of the target company—

   (a)　on his first becoming subject to the requirements of this section, and

   (b)　on each occurrence after that time while he is still subject to those requirements of any event or circumstances within section 198(1) (as it applies to his case otherwise than by reference to interests treated as his under section 205 as applying to that agreement).

206(3)　[Relevant particulars of interest in sec. 206(2)]　The relevant particulars to be notified under subsection (2) are—

   (a)　the number of shares (if any) comprised in the target company's relevant share capital in which the person giving the notice would be required to state his interest if he were under the obligation of disclosure with respect to that interest (apart from the agreement) immediately after the time when the obligation to give notice under subsection (2) arose, and

   (b)　the relevant particulars with respect to the registered ownership of those shares, so far as known to him at the date of the notice.

206(4)　[Further obligation to notify other parties to agreement]　A person who is for the time being subject to the requirements of this section is also under obligation to notify every other party to the agreement, in writing—

   (a)　of any relevant particulars with respect to the registered ownership of any shares comprised in relevant share capital of the target company in which he is interested apart from the agreement, and

   (b)　of any change in those particulars,

of which in either case he becomes aware at any time after any interest notification date and before the first occasion following that date on which he becomes subject to any further obligation to give notice under subsection (2) with respect to his interest in shares comprised in that share capital.

206(5)　[Interest notification date in sec. 206(4)]　The reference in subsection (4) to an interest notification date, in relation to a person's interest in shares comprised in the target company's relevant share capital, is to either of the following—

   (a)　the date of any notice given by him with respect to his interest under subsection (2), and

   (b)　where he has failed to give that notice, the date on which the period allowed by this section for giving the notice came to an end.

206(6)　[Notification of current address]　A person who is a party to an agreement to which section 204 applies is under an obligation to notify each other party to the agreement, in writing, of his current address—

   (a)　on his first becoming subject to the requirements of this section, and

   (b)　on any change in his address occurring after that time and while he is still subject to those requirements.

206(7)　[Relevant particulars re registered ownership]　A reference to the relevant particulars with respect to the registered ownership of shares is to such particulars in relation to those shares as are mentioned in section 202(3)(a) or (b).

206(8)　[Time for notification]　A person's obligation to give any notice required by this section to any other person must be performed within the period of 2 days next following the day on which that obligation arose.

CA 1985, sec. 206(3)　　　[The next page is 11,201]　　　　　**CCH Editions Limited**

History
In s. 206(8) the words "2 days" substituted for the former words "5 days" by CA 1989, s. 134(1), (3) as from 31 May 1990 (see S.I. 1990 No. 713 (C. 22), art. 3(i)).

Note
In regard to s. 206(8) the coming into force of CA 1989, s. 134(3) (which amends that provision) does not affect the time for fulfilling any obligation arising before 31 May 1990: see S.I. 1990 No. 713 (C. 22), art. 5.

SEC. 207 Interests in shares by attribution

207(1) [Interest by other person's interest] Where section 198 or 199 refers to a person acquiring an interest in shares or ceasing to be interested in shares, that reference in certain cases includes his becoming or ceasing to be interested in those shares by virtue of another person's interest.

207(2) [Becoming or ceasing to be interested] Such is the case where he becomes or ceases to be interested by virtue of section 203 or (as the case may be) section 205 whether—

  (a) by virtue of the fact that the person who is interested in the shares becomes or ceases to be a person whose interests (if any) fall by virtue of either section to be treated as his, or

  (b) in consequence of the fact that such a person has become or ceased to be interested in the shares, or

  (c) in consequence of the fact that he himself becomes or ceases to be a party to an agreement to which section 204 applies to which the person interested in the shares is for the time being a party, or

  (d) in consequence of the fact that an agreement to which both he and that person are parties becomes or ceases to be one to which that section applies.

207(3) [Knowledge of acquisition of or cessation of interest] The person is then to be treated as knowing he has acquired an interest in the shares or (as the case may be) that he has ceased to be interested in them, if and when he knows both—

  (a) the relevant facts with respect to the other person's interest in the shares, and

  (b) the relevant facts by virtue of which he himself has become or ceased to be interested in them in accordance with section 203 or 205.

207(4) [Knowledge in sec. 207(3)(a)] He has the knowledge referred to in subsection (3)(a) if he knows (whether contemporaneously or not) either of the subsistence of the other person's interest at any material time or of the fact that the other has become or ceased to be interested in the shares at any such time; and "material time" is any time at which the other's interests (if any) fall or fell to be treated as his under section 203 or 205.

207(5) [Knowledge of subsistence of other person's interest] A person is to be regarded as knowing of the subsistence of another's interest in shares or (as the case may be) that another has become or ceased to be interested in shares if he has been notified under section 206 of facts with respect to the other's interest which indicate that he is or has become or ceased to be interested in the shares (whether on his own account or by virtue of a third party's interest in them).

SEC. 208   Interests in shares which are to be notified

208(1)   **[Application]**   This section applies, subject to the section next following, in determining for purposes of sections 198 to 202 whether a person has a notifiable interest in shares.

208(2)   **[Reference to interest in shares]**   A reference to an interest in shares is to be read as including an interest of any kind whatsoever in the shares; and accordingly there are to be disregarded any restraints or restrictions to which the exercise of any right attached to the interest is or may be subject.

208(3)   **[Interest in shares in trust property]**   Where property is held on trust and an interest in shares is comprised in the property, a beneficiary of the trust who apart from this subsection does not have an interest in the shares is to be taken as having such an interest.

208(4)   **[Deemed interest in shares]**   A person is taken to have an interest in shares if—

   (a)   he enters into a contract for their purchase by him (whether for cash or other consideration), or

   (b)   not being the registered holder, he is entitled to exercise any right conferred by the holding of the shares or is entitled to control the exercise of any such right.

208(5)   **[Further deemed interest]**   A person is taken to have an interest in shares if, otherwise than by virtue of having an interest under a trust—

   (a)   he has a right to call for delivery of the shares to himself or to his order, or

   (b)   he has a right to acquire an interest in shares or is under an obligation to take an interest in shares,

whether in any case the right or obligation is conditional or absolute.

208(6)   **[Entitlement to exercise or control exercise of any right]**   For purposes of subsection (4)(b), a person is entitled to exercise or control the exercise of any right conferred by the holding of shares if he—

   (a)   has a right (whether subject to conditions or not) the exercise of which would make him so entitled, or

   (b)   is under an obligation (whether so subject or not) the fulfilment of which would make him so entitled.

208(7)   **[Joint interests]**   Persons having a joint interest are taken each of them to have that interest.

208(8)   **[Unidentifiable shares]**   It is immaterial that shares in which a person has an interest are unidentifiable.

SEC. 209   Interests to be disregarded

209(1)   **[Interests disregarded for sec. 198 to 202]**   The following interests in shares are disregarded for purposes of sections 198 to 202—

   (a)   where property is held on trust according to the law of England and Wales and an interest in shares is comprised in that property, an interest in reversion or remainder or of a bare trustee or a custodian trustee, and any discretionary interest;

(b) where property is held on trust according to the law of Scotland and an interest in shares is comprised in that property, an interest in fee or of a simple trustee and any discretionary interest;

(c) an interest which subsists by virtue of an authorised unit trust scheme within the meaning of the Financial Services Act 1986, a scheme made under section 22 of the Charities Act 1960, section 11 of the Trustee Investments Act 1961 or section 1 of the Administration of Justice Act 1965 or the scheme set out in the Schedule to the Church Funds Investment Measure 1958;

(d) an interest of the Church of Scotland General Trustees or of the Church of Scotland Trust in shares held by them or of any other person in shares held by those Trustees or that Trust otherwise than as simple trustees;

(e) an interest for the life of himself or another of a person under a settlement in the case of which the property comprised in the settlement consists of or includes shares, and the conditions mentioned in subsection (3) below are satisfied;

(f) an exempt interest held by a recognised jobber or market maker;

(g) an exempt security interest;

(h) an interest of the President of the Family Division of the High Court subsisting by virtue of section 9 of the Administration of Estates Act 1925;

(i) an interest of the Accountant General of the Supreme Court in shares held by him.

History
In s. 209(1)(c) the words "the Financial Services Act 1986" substituted for the former words "the Prevention of Fraud (Investments) Act 1958" by Financial Services Act 1986, s. 212(2) and Sch. 16, para. 18, in s. 209(1)(f) the words "or market maker" inserted by Financial Services Act 1986, s. 197(1)(a) as from 29 April 1988 (see S.I. 1988 No. 740 (C. 22)) and s. 209(1)(j) formerly appearing at the end repealed by CA 1989, s. 212 and Sch. 24 as from 31 May 1990 (see S.I. 1990 No. 713 (C. 22), art. 3(ii)); s. 209(1)(j) formerly read as follows:

"(j) such interests, or interests of such a class, as may be prescribed for purposes of this paragraph by regulations made by the Secretary of State by statutory instrument."

209(2) [Proxy not person interested in shares]   A person is not by virtue of section 208(4)(b) taken to be interested in shares by reason only that he has been appointed a proxy to vote at a specified meeting of a company or of any class of its members and at any adjournment of that meeting, or has been appointed by a corporation to act as its representative at any meeting of a company or of any class of its members.

209(3) [Conditions in sec. 209(1)(e)]   The conditions referred to in subsection (1)(e) are, in relation to a settlement—

(a) that it is irrevocable, and

(b) that the settlor (within the meaning of section 670 of the Income and Corporation Taxes Act 1988) has no interest in any income arising under, or property comprised in, the settlement.

History
In s. 209(3)(b) the words "670 of the Income and Corporation Taxes Act" substituted for the former words "444 of the Income and Corporation Taxes Act 1970" by Income and Corporation Taxes Act 1988, s. 844 and Sch. 29, para. 32 for companies' accounting periods ending after 5 April 1988 (see s. 843(1)).

209(4) [Recognised jobber] A person is a recognised jobber for purposes of subsection (1)(f) if he is a member of The Stock Exchange recognised by the Council of The Stock Exchange as carrying on the business of a jobber; and an interest of such a person in shares is an exempt interest for those purposes if—

   (a) he carries on that business in the United Kingdom, and

   (b) he holds the interest for the purposes of that business.

209(4A) [Market maker] A person is a market maker for the purposes of subsection (1)(f) if—

   (a) he holds himself out at all normal times in compliance with the rules of a recognised investment exchange other than an overseas investment exchange (within the meaning of the Financial Services Act 1986) as willing to buy and sell securities at prices specified by him; and

   (b) is recognised as doing so by that investment exchange;

and an interest of such a person in shares is an exempt interest if he carries on business as a market maker in the United Kingdom, is subject to such rules in the carrying on of that business and holds the interest for the purposes of that business.

History
S. 209(4A) inserted by Financial Services Act 1986, s. 197(1)(b) as from 29 April 1988 (see S.I. 1988 No. 740 (C. 22)).

209(5) [Exempt security interest] An interest in shares is an exempt security interest for purposes of subsection (1)(g) if—

   (a) it is held by a person who is—

     (i) a banking company or an insurance company to which Part II of the Insurance Companies Act 1982 applies, or

     (ii) a trustee savings bank (within the Trustee Savings Banks Act 1981), or

     (iii) a member of The Stock Exchange carrying on business in the United Kingdom as a stock broker,

    and

   (b) it is held by way of security only for the purposes of a transaction entered into in the ordinary course of his business as such a person,

or if it is held by way of security only either by the Bank of England or by the Post Office for the purposes of a transaction entered into in the ordinary course of that part of the business of the Post Office which consists of the provision of banking services.

History
In s. 209(5)(a) the words "a banking company" substituted for the former words "an authorised institution" by CA 1989, s. 23 and Sch. 10, para. 2 as from 1 April 1990 subject to transitional and saving provisions (see S.I. 1990 No. 355 (C. 13), art. 3, Sch. 1 and also see art. 6–9); previously the words "an authorised institution" substituted for the original words "a recognised bank or licensed institution within the meaning of the Banking Act 1979" by Banking Act 1987, s. 108(1) and Sch. 6, para. 18(1) as from 1 October 1987 (see S.I. 1987 No. 1664 (C. 50)).

SEC. 210   Other provisions about notification under this Part

210(1) [Notification by agent of shares acquired or disposed of] Where a person authorises another ("the agent") to acquire or dispose of, on his behalf, interests in shares comprised in relevant share capital of a public company, he shall secure that the agent notifies him immediately of acquisitions or disposals effected by the agent which will or may give rise to any obligation of disclosure imposed on him by this Part with respect to his interest in that share capital.

210(2) **[Particulars of person making notification]** An obligation of disclosure imposed on a person by any provision of sections 198 to 202 is treated as not being fulfilled unless the notice by means of which it purports to be fulfilled identifies him and gives his address and, in a case where he is a director of the company, is expressed to be given in fulfilment of that obligation.

210(3) **[Offences]** A person who—

    (a) fails to fulfil, within the proper period, an obligation of disclosure imposed on him by this Part, or

    (b) in purported fulfilment of any such obligation makes to a company a statement which he knows to be false, or recklessly makes to a company a statement which is false, or

    (c) fails to fulfil, within the proper period, an obligation to give another person a notice required by section 206, or

    (d) fails without reasonable excuse to comply with subsection (1) of this section,

is guilty of an offence and liable to imprisonment or a fine, or both.

210(4) **[Defence to sec. 210(3) offences]** It is a defence for a person charged with an offence under subsection (3)(c) to prove that it was not possible for him to give the notice to the other person required by section 206 within the proper period, and either—

    (a) that it has not since become possible for him to give the notice so required, or

    (b) that he gave the notice as soon after the end of that period as it became possible for him to do so.

210(5) **[Directions by Secretary of State where person convicted of offence]** Where a person is convicted of an offence under this section (other than an offence relating to his ceasing to be interested in a company's shares), the Secretary of State may by order direct that the shares in relation to which the offence was committed shall, until further order, be subject to the restrictions of Part XV of this Act; and such an order may be made notwithstanding any power in the company's memorandum or articles enabling the company to impose similar restrictions on those shares.

210(6) **[Application of sec. 732, 733(2), (3)]** Sections 732 (restriction on prosecutions) and 733(2) and (3) (liability of directors, etc.) apply to offences under this section.

SEC. 210A(1) Power to make further provision by regulations

210A(1) **[Scope of regulations]** The Secretary of State may by regulations amend—

    (a) the definition of "relevant share capital" (section 198(2)),

    (b) the percentage giving rise to a "notifiable interest" (section 199(2)),

    (c) the periods within which an obligation of disclosure must be fulfilled or a notice must be given (sections 202(1) and (4) and 206(8)),

(d) the provisions as to what is taken to be an interest in shares (section 208) and what interests are to be disregarded (section 209), and

(e) the provisions as to company investigations (section 212);

and the regulations may amend, replace or repeal the provisions referred to above and make such other consequential amendments or repeals of provisions of this Part as appear to the Secretary of State to be appropriate.

Note
Under CA 1989, s. 134(6) any regulations under the former s. 209(1)(j) in force immediately before the repeal of that provision have effect as if made under s. 210A(1)(d) — see the Public Companies (Disclosure of Interests in Shares) (Investment Management Exclusion) Regulations 1988 (S.I. 1988 No. 706) in the "Rules and Regulations" division.

210A(2)   [Different provisions for different descriptions]   The regulations may in any case make different provision for different descriptions of company; and regulations under subsection (1)(b), (c) or (d) may make different provision for different descriptions of person, interest or share capital.

210A(3)   [Transitional, supplementary and incidental provisions]   The regulations may contain such transitional and other supplementary and incidental provisions as appear to the Secretary of State to be appropriate, and may in particular make provision as to the obligations of a person whose interest in a company's shares becomes or ceases to be notifiable by virtue of the regulations.

210A(4)   [Statutory instrument]   Regulations under this section shall be made by statutory instrument.

210A(5)   [Approval by Parliament]   No regulations shall be made under this section unless a draft of the regulations has been laid before and approved by a resolution of each House of Parliament.

History
S. 210A inserted by CA 1989, s. 134(1), (5) as from 31 May 1990 (see S.I. 1990 No. 713 (C. 22), art. 3(i)).

REGISTRATION AND INVESTIGATION OF SHARE ACQUISITIONS AND DISPOSALS

SEC. 211   Register of interests in shares

211(1)   [Public company to keep register]   Every public company shall keep a register for purposes of sections 198 to 202, and whenever the company receives information from a person in consequence of the fulfilment of an obligation imposed on him by any of those sections, it is under obligation to inscribe in the register, against that person's name, that information and the date of the inscription.

211(2)   [Recording of notification by company]   Without prejudice to subsection (1), where a company receives a notification under this Part which includes a statement that the person making the notification, or any other person, has ceased to be a party to an agreement to which section 204 applies, the company is under obligation to record that information against the name of that person in every place where his name appears in the register as a party to that agreement (including any entry relating to him made against another person's name).

211(3)   [Time for fulfilling sec. 211(1), (2) obligations]   An obligation imposed by subsection (1) or (2) must be fulfilled within the period of 3 days next following the day on which it arises.

CA 1985, sec. 210A(2)

211(4) **[Company not on notice or inquiry]** The company is not, by virtue of anything done for the purposes of this section, affected with notice of, or put upon enquiry as to, the rights of any person in relation to any shares.

211(5) **[Chronological order of entries]** The register must be so made up that the entries against the several names entered in it appear in chronological order.

211(6) **[Index of names in register]** Unless the register is in such form as to constitute in itself an index, the company shall keep an index of the names entered in the register which shall in respect of each name contain a sufficient indication to enable the information entered against it to be readily found; and the company shall, within 10 days after the date on which a name is entered in the register, make any necessary alteration in the index.

211(7) **[Company ceasing to be public company]** If the company ceases to be a public company it shall continue to keep the register and any associated index until the end of the period of 6 years beginning with the day next following that on which it ceases to be such a company.

211(8) **[Location and inspection of register and index]** The register and any associated index—

(a) shall be kept at the place at which the register required to be kept by the company by section 325 (register of directors' interests) is kept, and

(b) subject to the next subsection, shall be available for inspection in accordance with section 219 below.

211(9) **[Limitation on inspection]** Neither the register nor any associated index shall be available for inspection in accordance with that section in so far as it contains information with respect to a company for the time being entitled to avail itself of the benefit conferred by section 231(3) (disclosure of shareholdings not required if it would be harmful to company's business).

History
In s. 211(9) the words "section 231(3)" substituted for the former words "paragraph 3 or 10 of Schedule 5" by CA 1989, s. 23 and Sch. 10, para. 3 as from 1 April 1990 subject to transitional and saving provisions (see S.I. 1990 No. 355 (C. 13), art. 3, Sch. 1 and also art. 6–9).

211(10) **[Penalty for non-compliance]** If default is made in complying with subsection (1) or (2), or with any of subsections (5) to (7), the company and every officer of it who is in default is liable to a fine and, for continued contravention, to a daily default fine.

211(11) **[Continuation of register under previous legislation]** Any register kept by a company immediately before 15th June 1982 under section 34 of the Companies Act 1967 shall continue to be kept by the company under and for the purposes of this section.

SEC. 212 Company investigations

212(1) **[Notice by company requiring information]** A public company may by notice in writing require a person whom the company knows or has reasonable cause to believe to be or, at any time during the 3 years immediately preceding the date on which the notice is issued, to have been interested in shares comprised in the company's relevant share capital—

   (a) to confirm that fact or (as the case may be) to indicate whether or not it is the case, and

   (b) where he holds or has during that time held an interest in shares so comprised, to give such further information as may be required in accordance with the following subsection.

212(2)   **[Contents of notice]**   A notice under this section may require the person to whom it is addressed—

   (a) to give particulars of his own past or present interest in shares comprised in relevant share capital of the company (held by him at any time during the 3-year period mentioned in subsection (1)),

   (b) where the interest is a present interest and any other interest in the shares subsists or, in any case, where another interest in the shares subsisted during that 3-year period at any time when his own interest subsisted, to give (so far as lies within his knowledge) such particulars with respect to that other interest as may be required by the notice,

   (c) where his interest is a past interest, to give (so far as lies within his knowledge) particulars of the identity of the person who held that interest immediately upon his ceasing to hold it.

212(3)   **[Particulars in sec. 212(2)(a), (b)]**   The particulars referred to in subsection (2)(a) and (b) include particulars of the identity of persons interested in the shares in question and of whether persons interested in the same shares are or were parties to any agreement to which section 204 applies or to any agreement or arrangement relating to the exercise of any rights conferred by the holding of the shares.

212(4)   **[Information in response to notice]**   A notice under this section shall require any information given in response to the notice to be given in writing within such reasonable time as may be specified in the notice.

212(5)   **[Construction]**   Sections 203 to 205 and 208 apply for the purpose of construing references in this section to persons interested in shares and to interests in shares respectively, as they apply in relation to sections 198 to 201 (but with the omission of any reference to section 209).

212(6)   **[Further application of section]**   This section applies in relation to a person who has or previously had, or is or was entitled to acquire, a right to subscribe for shares in a public company which would on issue be comprised in relevant share capital of that company as it applies in relation to a person who is or was interested in shares so comprised; and references above in this section to an interest in shares so comprised and to shares so comprised are to be read accordingly in any such case as including respectively any such right and shares which would on issue be so comprised.

SEC. 213   Registration of interests disclosed under sec. 212

213(1)   **[Obligation to enter information in register]**   Whenever in pursuance of a requirement imposed on a person under section 212 a company receives information to which this section applies relating to shares comprised in its relevant share capital, it is under obligation to enter against the name of the registered holder of those shares, in a separate part of its register of interests in shares—

(a) the fact that the requirement was imposed and the date on which it was imposed, and

(b) any information to which this section applies received in pursuance of the requirement.

213(2) **[Application of section]** This section applies to any information received in pursuance of a requirement imposed by section 212 which relates to the present interests held by any persons in shares comprised in relevant share capital of the company in question.

213(3) **[Application of sec. 211(3) to (10)]** Subsections (3) to (10) of section 211 apply in relation to any part of the register maintained in accordance with subsection (1) of this section as they apply in relation to the remainder of the register, reading references to subsection (1) of that section to include subsection (1) of this.

213(4) **[Continuation of register under previous legislation]** In the case of a register kept by a company immediately before 15th June 1982 under section 34 of the Companies Act 1967, any part of the register so kept for the purposes of section 27 of the Companies Act 1976 shall continue to be kept by the company under and for the purposes of this section.

SEC. 214 Company investigation on requisition by members

214(1) **[Requisition of members]** A company may be required to exercise its powers under section 212 on the requisition of members of the company holding at the date of the deposit of the requisition not less than one-tenth of such of the paid-up capital of the company as carries at that date the right of voting at general meetings of the company.

214(2) **[Contents of requisition]** The requisition must—

(a) state that the requisitionists are requiring the company to exercise its powers under section 212,

(b) specify the manner in which they require those powers to be exercised, and

(c) give reasonable grounds for requiring the company to exercise those powers in the manner specified,

and must be signed by the requisitionists and deposited at the company's registered office.

214(3) **[May contain several documents]** The requisition may consist of several documents in like form each signed by one or more requisitionists.

214(4) **[Duty of company]** On the deposit of a requisition complying with this section it is the company's duty to exercise its powers under section 212 in the manner specified in the requisition.

214(5) **[Penalty on default]** If default is made in complying with subsection (4), the company and every officer of it who is in default is liable to a fine.

SEC. 215 Company report to members

215(1) **[Report on conclusion of sec. 214 investigation]** On the conclusion of an investigation carried out by a company in pursuance of a requisition under section 214, it is the company's duty to cause a report of the information received in pursuance of that investigation to be prepared, and the report shall be made available at the company's registered office within a reasonable period after the conclusion of that investigation.

215(2)   [Interim reports]   Where—

(a) a company undertakes an investigation in pursuance of a requisition under section 214, and

(b) the investigation is not concluded before the end of 3 months beginning with the date immediately following the date of the deposit of the requisition,

it is the duty of the company to cause to be prepared, in respect of that period and each successive period of 3 months ending before the conclusion of the investigation, and interim report of the information received during that period in pursuance of the investigation. Each such report shall be made available at the company's registered office within a reasonable period after the end of the period to which it relates.

215(3)   [Period for making report]   The period for making any report prepared under this section available as required by subsection (1) or (2) shall not exceed 15 days.

215(4)   [Information not to be included]   Such a report shall not include any information with respect to a company entitled to avail itself of the benefit conferred by section 231(3) (disclosure of shareholdings not required if it would be harmful to company's business); but where any such information is omitted, that fact shall be stated in the report.

History
In s. 215(4) the words "section 231(3)" substituted for the former words "paragraph 3 or 10 of Schedule 5" by CA 1989, s. 23 and Sch. 10, para. 3 as from 1 April 1990 subject to transitional and saving provisions (see S.I. 1990 No. 355 (C. 13), art. 3, Sch. 1 and also art. 6–9).

215(5)   [Notification that report available]   The company shall, within 3 days of making any report prepared under this section available at its registered office, notify the requisitionists that the report is so available.

215(6)   [Conclusion of investigation]   An investigation carried out by a company in pursuance of a requisition under section 214 is regarded for purposes of this section as concluded when the company has made all such inquiries as are necessary or expedient for the purposes of the requisition and in the case of each such inquiry, either a response has been received by the company or the time allowed for a response has elapsed.

215(7)   [Location and inspection of report]   A report prepared under this section—

(a) shall be kept at the company's registered office from the day on which it is first available there in accordance with subsection (1) or (2) until the expiration of 6 years beginning with the day next following that day, and

(b) shall be available for inspection in accordance with section 219 below so long as it is so kept.

215(8)   [Penalty on default]   If default is made in complying with subsection (1), (2), (5) or (7)(a), the company and every officer of it who is in default is liable to a fine.

SEC. 216   Penalty for failure to provide information

216(1)   [Application to court by company]   Where notice is served by a company under section 212 on a person who is or was interested in shares of the company and that person fails to give the company any information required by the notice within the time specified in it, the company may apply to the court for an order directing that the shares in question be subject to the restrictions of Part XV of this Act.

216(2) **[Order by court]** Such an order may be made by the court notwithstanding any power contained in the applicant company's memorandum or articles enabling the company itself to impose similar restrictions on the shares in question.

216(3) **[Penalty for non-compliance with sec. 212 notice, untrue statement etc.]** Subject to the following subsections, a person who fails to comply with a notice under section 212 or who, in purported compliance with such a notice, makes any statement which he knows to be false in a material particular or recklessly makes any statement which is false in a material particular is guilty of an offence and liable to imprisonment or a fine, or both.

Section 733(2) and (3) of this Act (liability of individuals for corporate default) apply to offences under this subsection.

216(4) **[Exception to offence in sec. 216(3)]** A person is not guilty of an offence by virtue of failing to comply with a notice under section 212 if he proves that the requirement to give the information was frivolous or vexatious.

216(5) **[Exemptions from compliance with sec. 212]** A person is not obliged to comply with a notice under section 212 if he is for the time being exempted by the Secretary of State from the operation of that section; but the Secretary of State shall not grant any such exemption unless—

   (a) he has consulted with the Governor of the Bank of England, and

   (b) he (the Secretary of State) is satisfied that, having regard to any undertaking given by the person in question with respect to any interest held or to be held by him in any shares, there are special reasons why that person should not be subject to the obligations imposed by that section.

SEC. 217   Removal of entries from register

217(1) **[Removal from register]** A company may remove an entry against a person's name from its register of interests in shares if more than 6 years have elapsed since the date of the entry being made, and either—

   (a) that entry recorded the fact that the person in question had ceased to have an interest notifiable under this Part in relevant share capital of the company, or

   (b) it has been superseded by a later entry made under section 211 against the same person's name;

and in a case within paragraph (a) the company may also remove that person's name from the register.

217(2) **[Notification by company to person named as having interest]** If a person in pursuance of an obligation imposed on him by any provision of this Part gives to a company the name and address of another person as being interested in shares in the company, the company shall, within 15 days of the date on which it was given that information, notify the other person that he has been so named and shall include in that notification—

   (a) particulars of any entry relating to him made, in consequence of its being given that information, by the company in its register of interests in shares, and

   (b) a statement informing him of his right to apply to have the entry removed in accordance with the following provisions of this section.

217(3) [Application for removal of name by person notified] A person who has been notified by a company in pursuance of subsection (2) that an entry relating to him has been made in the company's register of interests in shares may apply in writing to the company for the removal of that entry from the register; and the company shall remove the entry if satisfied that the information in pursuance of which the entry was made was incorrect.

217(4) [Application where no longer party to agreement] If a person who is identified in a company's register of interests in shares as being a party to an agreement to which section 204 applies (whether by an entry against his own name or by an entry relating to him made against another person's name as mentioned in subsection (2)(a)) ceases to be a party to that agreement, he may apply in writing to the company for the inclusion of that information in the register; and if the company is satisfied that he has ceased to be a party to the agreement, it shall record that information (if not already recorded) in every place where his name appears as a party to that agreement in the register.

217(5) [Application to court] If an application under subsection (3) or (4) is refused (in a case within subsection (4), otherwise than on the ground that the information has already been recorded) the applicant may apply to the court for an order directing the company to remove the entry in question from the register or (as the case may be) to include the information in question in the register; and the court may, if it thinks fit, make such an order.

217(6) [Time for alteration of register etc.] Where a name is removed from a company's register of interests in shares in pursuance of subsection (1) or (3) or an order under subsection (5), the company shall within 14 days of the date of that removal make any necessary alteration in any associated index.

217(7) [Penalty on default] If default is made in complying with subsection (2) or (6), the company and every officer of it who is in default is liable to a fine and, for continued contravention, to a daily default fine.

SEC. 218   Otherwise, entries not to be removed

218(1) [Deletion of names] Entries in a company's register of interests in shares shall not be deleted except in accordance with section 217.

218(2) [Restoring of deleted name] If an entry is deleted from a company's register of interests in shares in contravention of subsection (1), the company shall restore that entry to the register as soon as is reasonably practicable.

218(3) [Penalty] If default is made in complying with subsection (1) or (2), the company and every officer of it who is in default is liable to a fine and, for continued contravention of subsection (2), to a daily default fine.

SEC. 219　Inspection of register and reports

219(1)　**[Inspection]**　Any register of interests in shares and any report which is required by section 215(7) to be available for inspection in accordance with this section shall, during business hours (subject to such reasonable restrictions as the company may in general meeting impose, but so that not less than 2 hours in each day are allowed for inspection) be open to the inspection of any member of the company or of any other person without charge.

219(2)　**[Copy of register or report]**　Any such member or other person may require a copy of any such register or report, or any part of it, on payment of 10 pence or such less sum as the company may prescribe, for every 100 words or fractional part of 100 words required to be copied; and the company shall cause any copy so required by a person to be sent to him before the expiration of the period of 10 days beginning with the day next following that on which the requirement is received by the company.

219(3)　**[Penalty]**　If an inspection required under this section is refused or a copy so required is not sent within the proper period, the company and every officer of it who is in default is liable to a fine and, for continued contravention, to a daily default fine.

219(4)　**[Power of court to compel inspection or copy]**　In the case of a refusal of an inspection required under this section of any register or report, the court may by order compel an immediate inspection of it; and in the case of failure to send a copy required under this section, the court may by order direct that the copy required shall be sent to the person requiring it.

219(5)　**[Regulations]**　The Secretary of State may by regulations made by statutory instrument substitute a sum specified in the regulations for the sum for the time being mentioned in subsection (2).

SUPPLEMENTARY

SEC. 220　Definitions for Part VI

220(1)　**[Definitions]**　In this Part of this Act—

　　"associated index", in relation to a register, means the index kept in relation to that register in pursuance of section 211(6),

　　"register of interests in shares" means the register kept in pursuance of section 211 including, except where the context otherwise requires, that part of the register kept in pursuance of section 213, and

　　"relevant share capital" has the meaning given by section 198(2).

220(2)　**[Calculation of time]**　Where the period allowed by any provision of this Part for fulfilling an obligation is expressed as a number of days, any day that is a Saturday or Sunday or a bank holiday in any part of Great Britain is to be disregarded in reckoning that period.

PART VII — ACCOUNTS AND AUDIT

Chapter I — Provisions Applying to Companies Generally

ACCOUNTING RECORDS

SEC. 221   Duty to keep accounting records

221(1)   [Duty of company]   Every company shall keep accounting records which are sufficient to show and explain the company's transactions and are such as to—

   (a)   disclose with reasonable accuracy, at any time, the financial position of the company at that time, and

   (b)   enable the directors to ensure that any balance sheet and profit and loss account prepared under this Part complies with the requirements of this Act.

221(2)   [Contents]   The accounting records shall in particular contain—

   (a)   entries from day to day of all sums of money received and expended by the company, and the matters in respect of which the receipt and expenditure takes place, and

   (b)   a record of the assets and liabilities of the company.

221(3)   [Where business re goods]   If the company's business involves dealing in goods, the accounting records shall contain—

   (a)   statements of stock held by the company at the end of each financial year of the company,

   (b)   all statements of stocktakings from which any such statement of stock as is mentioned in paragraph (a) has been or is to be prepared, and

   (c)   except in the case of goods sold by way of ordinary retail trade, statements of all goods sold and purchased, showing the goods and the buyers and sellers in sufficient detail to enable all these to be identified.

221(4)   [Duty of parent company]   A parent company which has a subsidiary undertaking in relation to which the above requirements do not apply shall take reasonable steps to secure that the undertaking keeps such accounting records as to enable the directors of the parent company to ensure that any balance sheet and profit and loss account prepared under this Part complies with the requirements of this Act.

221(5)   [Offence]   If a company fails to comply with any provision of this section, every officer of the company who is in default is guilty of an offence unless he shows that he acted honestly and that in the circumstances in which the company's business was carried on the default was excusable.

221(6)   [Penalty]   A person guilty of an offence under this section is liable to imprisonment or a fine, or both.

History
See history note after s. 262A.

SEC. 222 Where and for how long records to be kept

222(1) [Location, inspection] A company's accounting records shall be kept at its registered office or such other place as the directors think fit, and shall at all times be open to inspection by the company's officers.

222(2) [If records outside Great Britain] If accounting records are kept at a place outside Great Britain, accounts and returns with respect to the business dealt with in the accounting records so kept shall be sent to, and kept at, a place in Great Britain, and shall at all times be open to such inspection.

222(3) [Accounts and records sent to Great Britain] The accounts and returns to be sent to Great Britain shall be such as to—

    (a) disclose with reasonable accuracy the financial position of the business in question at intervals of not more than six months, and

    (b) enable the directors to ensure that the company's balance sheet and profit and loss account comply with the requirements of this Act.

222(4) [Offence] If a company fails to comply with any provision of subsections (1) to (3), every officer of the company who is in default is guilty of an offence, and liable to imprisonment or a fine or both, unless he shows that he acted honestly and that in the circumstances in which the company's business was carried on the default was excusable.

222(5) [Preservation of records] Accounting records which a company is required by section 221 to keep shall be preserved by it—

    (a) in the case of a private company, for three years from the date on which they are made, and

    (b) in the case of a public company, for six years from the date on which they are made.

    This is subject to any provision contained in rules made under section 411 of the Insolvency Act 1986 (company insolvency rules).

222(6) [Offence, penalty re sec. 222(5)] An officer of a company is guilty of an offence, and liable to imprisonment or a fine or both, if he fails to take all reasonable steps for securing compliance by the company with subsection (5) or intentionally causes any default by the company under that subsection.

History
See history note after s. 262A.

A COMPANY'S FINANCIAL YEAR AND ACCOUNTING REFERENCE PERIODS

SEC. 223 A company's financial year

223(1) ["Financial year"] A company's "financial year" is determined as follows.

223(2) [First financial year] Its first financial year begins with the first day of its first accounting reference period and ends with the last day of that period or such other date, not more than seven days before or after the end of that period, as the directors may determine.

223(3) [Subsequent financial years] Subsequent financial years begin with the day immediately following the end of the company's previous financial year and end with the last day of its next accounting reference period or such other date, not more than seven days before or after the end of that period, as the directors may determine.

223(4)   [Undertaking not a company]   In relation to an undertaking which is not a company, references in this Act to its financial year are to any period in respect of which a profit and loss account of the undertaking is required to be made up (by its constitution or by the law under which it is established), whether that period is a year or not.

223(5)   [Subsidiary undertakings]   The directors of a parent company shall secure that, except where in their opinion there are good reasons against it, the financial year of each of its subsidiary undertakings coincides with the company's own financial year.

History
See history note after s. 262A.

SEC. 224   Accounting reference periods and accounting reference date

224(1)   [Determination of periods]   A company's accounting reference periods are determined according to its accounting reference date.

224(2)   [Notice by company]   A company may, at any time before the end of the period of nine months beginning with the date of its incorporation, by notice in the prescribed form given to the registrar specify its accounting reference date, that is, the date on which its accounting reference period ends in each calendar year.

224(3)   [Where no sec. 224(2) notice]   Failing such notice, a company's accounting reference date is—

  (a) in the case of a company incorporated before 1st April 1990, 31st March;

  (b) in the case of a company incorporated after 1st April 1990, the last day of the month in which the anniversary of its incorporation falls.

History
In s. 224(3) the words "1st April 1990" (appearing twice) substituted for the former words "the commencement of section 3 of the Companies Act 1989" and "the commencement of that section" respectively by S.I. 1990 No. 355 (C. 13), art. 15 as from 1 April 1990.

224(4)   [First accounting reference period]   A company's first accounting reference period is the period of more than six months, but not more than 18 months, beginning with the date of its incorporation and ending with its accounting reference date.

224(5)   [Subsequent periods]   Its subsequent accounting reference periods are successive periods of twelve months beginning immediately after the end of the previous accounting reference period and ending with its accounting reference date.

224(6)   [Effect of sec. 225]   This section has effect subject to the provisions of section 225 relating to the alteration of accounting reference dates and the consequences of such alteration.

History
See history note after s. 262A.

SEC. 225   Alteration of accounting reference date

225(1)   [Notice by company re current and subsequent periods]   A company may by notice in the prescribed form given to the registrar specify a new accounting reference date having effect in relation to the company's current accounting reference period and subsequent periods.

225(2) **[Notice re previous periods]** A company may by notice in the prescribed form given to the registrar specify a new accounting reference date having effect in relation to the company's previous accounting reference period and subsequent periods if—

(a) the company is a subsidiary undertaking or parent undertaking of another company and the new accounting reference date coincides with the accounting reference date of that other company, or

(b) an administration order under Part II of the Insolvency Act 1986 is in force.

A company's **"previous accounting reference period"** means that immediately preceding its current accounting reference period.

225(3) **[Contents of sec. 225(1), (2) notice]** The notice shall state whether the current or previous accounting reference period—

(a) is to be shortened, so as to come to an end on the first occasion on which the new accounting reference date falls or fell after the beginning of the period, or

(b) is to be extended, so as to come to an end on the second occasion on which that date falls or fell after the beginning of the period.

225(4) **[Time for sec. 225(1) notice]** A notice under subsection (1) stating that the current accounting reference period is to be extended is ineffective, except as mentioned below, if given less than five years after the end of an earlier accounting reference period of the company which was extended by virtue of this section.

This subsection does not apply—

(a) to a notice given by a company which is a subsidiary undertaking or parent undertaking of another company and the new accounting reference date coincides with that of the other company, or

(b) where an administration order is in force under Part II of the Insolvency Act 1986,

or where the Secretary of State directs that it should not apply, which he may do with respect to a notice which has been given or which may be given.

225(5) **[Where no sec. 225(2)(a) notice]** A notice under subsection (2)(a) may not be given if the period allowed for laying and delivering accounts and reports in relation to the previous accounting reference period has already expired.

225(6) **[Limit on extension of accounting reference period]** An accounting reference period may not in any case, unless an administration order is in force under Part II of the Insolvency Act 1986, be extended so as to exceed 18 months and a notice under this section is ineffective if the current or previous accounting reference period as extended in accordance with the notice would exceed that limit.

History
See history note after s. 262A.

ANNUAL ACCOUNTS

* **SEC. 226** **Duty to prepare individual company accounts**

226(1) **[Duty of directors]** The directors of every company shall prepare for each financial year of the company—

(a) a balance sheet as at the last day of the year, and

(b) a profit and loss account.

Those accounts are referred to in this Part as the company's "individual accounts".

226(2)   [Requirements for true and fair view]   The balance sheet shall give a true and fair view of the state of affairs of the company as at the end of the financial year; and the profit and loss account shall give a true and fair view of the profit or loss of the company for the financial year.

226(3)   [Compliance with Sch. 4]   A company's individual accounts shall comply with the provisions of Schedule 4 as to the form and content of the balance sheet and profit and loss account and additional information to be provided by way of notes to the accounts.

226(4)   [Additional information]   Where compliance with the provisions of that Schedule, and the other provisions of this Act as to the matters to be included in a company's individual accounts or in notes to those accounts, would not be sufficient to give a true and fair view, the necessary additional information shall be given in the accounts or in a note to them.

226(5)   [Special circumstances]   If in special circumstances compliance with any of those provisions is inconsistent with the requirement to give a true and fair view, the directors shall depart from that provision to the extent necessary to give a true and fair view.

Particulars of any such departure, the reasons for it and its effect shall be given in a note to the accounts.

History
See history note after s. 262A.

SEC. 227   Duty to prepare group accounts

227(1)   [Directors' duty]   If at the end of a financial year a company is a parent company the directors shall, as well as preparing individual accounts for the year, prepare group accounts.

227(2)   [Contents of group accounts]   Group accounts shall be consolidated accounts comprising—

(a) a consolidated balance sheet dealing with the state of affairs of the parent company and its subsidiary undertakings, and

(b) a consolidated profit and loss account dealing with the profit or loss of the parent company and its subsidiary undertakings.

227(3)   [Requirements for true and fair view]   The accounts shall give a true and fair view of the state of affairs as at the end of the financial year, and the profit or loss for the financial year, of the undertakings included in the consolidation as a whole, so far as concerns members of the company.

227(4)   [Compliance with Sch. 4A]   A company's group accounts shall comply with the provisions of Schedule 4A as to the form and content of the consolidated balance sheet and consolidated profit and loss account and additional information to be provided by way of notes to the accounts.

227(5)   [Additional information]   Where compliance with the provisions of that Schedule, and the other provisions of this Act, as to the matters to be included in a company's group accounts or in notes to those accounts, would not be sufficient to give a true and fair view, the necessary additional information shall be given in the accounts or in a note to them.

227(6) [Special circumstances] If in special circumstances compliance with any of those provisions is inconsistent with the requirement to give a true and fair view, the directors shall depart from that provision to the extent necessary to give a true and fair view.

Particulars of any such departure, the reasons for it and its effect shall be given in a note to the accounts.

History
See history note after s. 262A.

SEC. 228 Exemption for parent companies included in accounts of larger group

228(1) [Exemption from requirement to prepare group accounts] A company is exempt from the requirement to prepare group accounts if it is itself a subsidiary undertaking and its immediate parent undertaking is established under the law of a member State of the European Economic Community, in the following cases—

(a) where the company is a wholly-owned subsidiary of that parent undertaking;

(b) where that parent undertaking holds more than 50 per cent of the shares in the company and notice requesting the preparation of group accounts has not been served on the company by shareholders holding in aggregate—

(i) more than half of the remaining shares in the company, or

(ii) 5 per cent of the total shares in the company.

Such notice must be served not later than six months after the end of the financial year before that to which it relates.

228(2) [Conditions for exemption] Exemption is conditional upon compliance with all of the following conditions—

(a) that the company is included in consolidated accounts for a larger group drawn up to the same date, or to an earlier date in the same financial year, by a parent undertaking established under the law of a member State of the European Economic Community;

(b) that those accounts are drawn up and audited, and that parent undertaking's annual report is drawn up, according to that law, in accordance with the provisions of the Seventh Directive (83/349/EEC);

(c) that the company discloses in its individual accounts that it is exempt from the obligation to prepare and deliver group accounts;

(d) that the company states in its individual accounts the name of the parent undertaking which draws up the group accounts referred to above and—

(i) if it is incorporated outside Great Britain, the country in which it is incorporated,

(ii) if it is incorporated in Great Britain, whether it is registered in England and Wales or in Scotland, and

(iii) if it is unincorporated, the address of its principal place of business;

    (e) that the company delivers to the registrar, within the period allowed for delivering its individual accounts, copies of those group accounts and of the parent undertaking's annual report, together with the auditors' report on them; and

    (f) that if any document comprised in accounts and reports delivered in accordance with paragraph (e) is in a language other than English, there is annexed to the copy of that document delivered a translation of it into English, certified in the prescribed manner to be a correct translation.

228(3)   **[No exemption for certain listed companies]**   The exemption does not apply to a company any of whose securities are listed on a stock exchange in any member State of the European Economic Community.

228(4)   **[Interpretation re sec. 228(1)(a)]**   Shares held by directors of a company for the purpose of complying with any share qualification requirement shall be disregarded in determining for the purposes of subsection (1)(a) whether the company is a wholly-owned subsidiary.

228(5)   **[Interpretation re sec. 228(1)(b)]**   For the purposes of subsection (1)(b) shares held by a wholly-owned subsidiary of the parent undertaking, or held on behalf of the parent undertaking or a wholly-owned subsidiary, shall be attributed to the parent undertaking.

228(6)   **["Securities" in sec. 228(3)]**   In subsection (3) "securities" includes—

    (a) shares and stock,

    (b) debentures, including debenture stock, loan stock, bonds, certificates of deposit and other instruments creating or acknowledging indebtedness,

    (c) warrants or other instruments entitling the holder to subscribe for securities falling within paragraph (a) or (b), and

    (d) certificates or other instruments which confer—

        (i) property rights in respect of a security falling within paragraph (a), (b) or (c),

        (ii) any right to acquire, dispose of, underwrite or convert a security, being a right to which the holder would be entitled if he held any such security to which the certificate or other instrument relates, or

        (iii) a contractual right (other than an option) to acquire any such security otherwise than by subscription.

History
See history note after s. 262A.

SEC. 229   Subsidiary undertakings included in the consolidation

229(1)   **[All subsidiaries to be in consolidation]**   Subject to the exceptions authorised or required by this section, all the subsidiary undertakings of the parent company shall be included in the consolidation.

229(2)   **[Exclusion if not material]**   A subsidiary undertaking may be excluded from consolidation if its inclusion is not material for the purpose of giving a true and fair view; but two or more undertakings may be excluded only if they are not material taken together.

229(3) **[Further grounds for exclusion]** In addition, a subsidiary undertaking may be excluded from consolidation where—

(a) severe long-term restrictions substantially hinder the exercise of the rights of the parent company over the assets or management of that undertaking, or

(b) the information necessary for the preparation of group accounts cannot be obtained without disproportionate expense or undue delay, or

(c) the interest of the parent company is held exclusively with a view to subsequent resale and the undertaking has not previously been included in consolidated group accounts prepared by the parent company.

The reference in paragraph (a) to the rights of the parent company and the reference in paragraph (c) to the interest of the parent company are, respectively, to rights and interests held by or attributed to the company for the purposes of section 258 (definition of "parent undertaking") in the absence of which it would not be the parent company.

229(4) **[Where subsidiaries' activities so different]** Where the activities of one or more subsidiary undertakings are so different from those of other undertakings to be included in the consolidation that their inclusion would be incompatible with the obligation to give a true and fair view, those undertakings shall be excluded from consolidation.

This subsection does not apply merely because some of the undertakings are industrial, some commercial and some provide services, or because they carry on industrial or commercial activities involving different products or provide different services.

229(5) **[Where all subsidiaries within exclusions]** Where all the subsidiary undertakings of a parent company fall within the above exclusions, no group accounts are required.

History
See history note after s. 262A.

SEC. 230   Treatment of individual profit and loss account where group accounts prepared

230(1) **[Application]** The following provisions apply with respect to the individual profit and loss account of a parent company where—

(a) the company is required to prepare and does prepare group accounts in accordance with this Act, and

(b) the notes to the company's individual balance sheet show the company's profit or loss for the financial year determined in accordance with this Act.

230(2) **[Profit and loss accent need not have certain information]** The profit and loss account need not contain the information specified in paragraphs 52 to 57 of Schedule 4 (information supplementing the profit and loss account).

230(3) **[Approval, omission]** The profit and loss account must be approved in accordance with section 233(1) (approval by board of directors) but may be omitted from the company's annual accounts for the purposes of the other provisions below in this Chapter.

230(4) **[Disclosure re exemption]** The exemption conferred by this section is conditional upon its being disclosed in the company's annual accounts that the exemption applies.

History
See history note after s. 262A.

SEC. 231 Disclosure required in notes to accounts: related undertakings

231(1) **[Information in Sch. 5]** The information specified in Schedule 5 shall be given in notes to a company's annual accounts.

231(2) **[Sch. 5, Pt. I, II]** Where the company is not required to prepare group accounts, the information specified in Part I of that Schedule shall be given; and where the company is required to prepare group accounts, the information specified in Part II of that Schedule shall be given.

231(3) **[Information need not be disclosed re certain foreign undertakings]** The information required by Schedule 5 need not be disclosed with respect to an undertaking which—

    (a) is established under the law of a country outside the United Kingdom, or

    (b) carries on business outside the United Kingdom,

if in the opinion of the directors of the company the disclosure would be seriously prejudicial to the business of that undertaking, or to the business of the company or any of its subsidiary undertakings, and the Secretary of State agrees that the information need not be disclosed.

This subsection does not apply in relation to the information required under paragraph 5(2), 6 or 20 of that Schedule.

231(4) **[Where advantage taken of sec. 231(3)]** Where advantage is taken of subsection (3), that fact shall be stated in a note to the company's annual accounts.

231(5) **[Where information of excessive length]** If the directors of the company are of the opinion that the number of undertakings in respect of which the company is required to disclose information under any provision of Schedule 5 to this Act is such that compliance with that provision would result in information of excessive length being given, the information need only be given in respect of—

    (a) the undertakings whose results or financial position, in the opinion of the directors, principally affected the figures shown in the company's annual accounts, and

    (b) undertakings excluded from consolidation under section 229(3) or (4).

This subsection does not apply in relation to the information required under paragraph 10 or 29 of that Schedule.

231(6) **[Where advantage taken of sec. 231(5)]** If advantage is taken of subsection (5)—

    (a) there shall be included in the notes to the company's annual accounts a statement that the information is given only with respect to such undertakings as are mentioned in that subsection, and

(b) the full information (both that which is disclosed in the notes to the accounts and that which is not) shall be annexed to the company's next annual return.

For this purpose the **"next annual return"** means that next delivered to the registrar after the accounts in question have been approved under section 233.

231(7)   [Penalty re non-compliance with sec. 231(6)(b)]   If a company fails to comply with subsection (6)(b), the company and every officer of it who is in default is liable to a fine and, for continued contravention, to a daily default fine.

History
See history note after s. 262A.

SEC. 232   Disclosure required in notes to accounts: emoluments and other benefits of directors and others

232(1)   [Information in Sch. 6]   The information specified in Schedule 6 shall be given in notes to a company's annual accounts.

232(2)   [Sch. 6, Pt. I–III]   In that Schedule—

Part I relates to the emoluments of directors (including emoluments waived), pensions of directors and past directors, compensation for loss of office to directors and past directors and sums paid to third parties in respect of directors' services,

Part II relates to loans, quasi-loans and other dealings in favour of directors and connected persons, and

Part III relates to transactions, arrangements and agreements made by the company or a subsidiary undertaking for officers of the company other than directors.

232(3)   [Notice by directors and others]   It is the duty of any director of a company, and any person who is or has at any time in the preceding five years been an officer of the company, to give notice to the company of such matters relating to himself as may be necessary for the purposes of Part I of Schedule 6.

232(4)   [Offence re sec. 232(3)]   A person who makes default in complying with subsection (3) commits an offence and is liable to a fine.

History
See history note after s. 262A.

APPROVAL AND SIGNING OF ACCOUNTS

SEC. 233   Approval and signing of accounts

233(1)   [Approval, signing]   A company's annual accounts shall be approved by the board of directors and signed on behalf of the board by a director of the company.

233(2)   [Signature on balance sheet]   The signature shall be on the company's balance sheet.

233(3)   [Every balance sheet to state name of signatory]   Every copy of the balance sheet which is laid before the company in general meeting, or which is otherwise circulated, published or issued, shall state the name of the person who signed the balance sheet on behalf of the board.

233(4) [Signatory of balance sheet delivered to registrar] The copy of the company's balance sheet which is delivered to the registrar shall be signed on behalf of the board by a director of the company.

233(5) [Offence, penalty re non-compliance] If annual accounts are approved which do not comply with the requirements of this Act, every director of the company who is party to their approval and who knows that they do not comply or is reckless as to whether they comply is guilty of an offence and liable to a fine.

For this purpose every director of the company at the time the accounts are approved shall be taken to be a party to their approval unless he shows that he took all reasonable steps to prevent their being approved.

Note
S. 233(5) not in force with rest of section — see S.I. 1990
No. 355 (C. 13), art. 3, Sch. 1.

233(6) [Further offence, penalty] If a copy of the balance sheet—

(a) is laid before the company, or otherwise circulated, published or issued, without the balance sheet having been signed as required by this section or without the required statement of the signatory's name being included, or

(b) is delivered to the registrar without being signed as required by this section,

the company and every officer of it who is in default is guilty of an offence and liable to a fine.

History
See history note after s. 262A but note that s. 233(5) not in
force at same time as rest of section.

DIRECTORS' REPORT

SEC. 234 Duty to prepare directors' report

234(1) [Duty of directors] The directors of a company shall for each financial year prepare a report—

(a) containing a fair review of the development of the business of the company and its subsidiary undertakings during the financial year and of their position at the end of it, and

(b) stating the amount (if any) which they recommend should be paid as dividend and the amount (if any) which they propose to carry to reserves.

234(2) [Contents of report] The report shall state the names of the persons who, at any time during the financial year, were directors of the company, and the principal activities of the company and its subsidiary undertakings in the course of the year and any significant change in those activities in the year.

234(3) [Compliance with Sch. 7] The report shall also comply with Schedule 7 as regards the disclosure of the matters mentioned there.

234(4) [Sch. 7, Pt. I–V] In Schedule 7—

Part I relates to matters of a general nature, including changes in asset values, directors' shareholdings and other interests and contributions for political and charitable purposes,

Part II relates to the acquisition by a company of its own shares or a charge on them,

Part III relates to the <u>employment, training and advancement of disabled persons,</u>

Part IV relates to the <u>health, safety and welfare at work of the company's employees</u>, and

Part V relates to the involvement of employees in the affairs, policy and performance of the company.

234(5) **[Offence, penalty]** In the case of <u>any failure to comply with the provisions of this Part as to the preparation of a directors' report and the contents of the report,</u> every person who was a director of the company immediately before the end of the period for laying and delivering accounts and reports for the financial year in question is guilty of an offence and liable to a fine.

234(6) **[Defence]** In proceedings against a person for an offence under this section it is a defence for him to prove that he took all reasonable steps for securing compliance with the requirements in question.

History
See history note after s. 262A.

SEC. 234A Approval and signing of directors' report

234A(1) **[Approval, signing]** <u>The directors' report shall be approved by the board of directors and signed on behalf of the board by a director or the secretary of the company.</u>

234A(2) **[Every report to state name of signatory]** <u>Every copy of the directors' report which is laid before the company in general meeting, or which is otherwise circulated, published or issued, shall state the name of the person who signed it on behalf of the board.</u>

234A(3) **[Signatory of report sent to registrar]** <u>The copy of the directors' report which is delivered to the registrar shall be signed on behalf of the board by a director or the secretary of the company.</u>

234A(4) **[Offence, penalty]** If a copy of the directors' report—

(a) is laid before the company, or otherwise circulated, published or issued, without the report having been signed as required by this section or without the required statement of the signatory's name being included, or

(b) is delivered to the registrar without being signed as required by this section,

the company and every officer of it who is in default is guilty of an offence and liable to a fine.

History
See history note after s. 262A.

AUDITORS' REPORT

SEC. 235 Auditors' report

235(1) **[Duty of auditors]** <u>A company's auditors shall make a report to the company's members on all annual accounts of the company of which copies are to be laid before the company in general meeting during their tenure of office.</u>

235(2)   [Contents of report]   The auditors' report shall state whether in the auditors' opinion the annual accounts have been properly prepared in accordance with this Act, and in particular whether a true and fair view is given—

(a) in the case of an individual balance sheet, of the state of affairs of the company as at the end of the financial year,

(b) in the case of an individual profit and loss account, of the profit or loss of the company for the financial year,

(c) in the case of group accounts, of the state of affairs as at the end of the financial year, and the profit or loss for the financial year, of the undertakings included in the consolidation as a whole, so far as concerns members of the company.

235(3)   [Consideration of whether directors' report consistent with accounts]   The auditors shall consider whether the information given in the directors' report for the financial year for which the annual accounts are prepared is consistent with those accounts; and if they are of opinion that it is not they shall state that fact in their report.

History
See history note after s. 262A.

SEC. 236   Signature of auditors' report

236(1)   [Report to state names and be signed]   The auditors' report shall state the names of the auditors and be signed by them.

236(2)   [Every copy to state names]   Every copy of the auditors' report which is laid before the company in general meeting, or which is otherwise circulated, published or issued, shall state the names of the auditors.

236(3)   [Copy to registrar]   The copy of the auditors' report which is delivered to the registrar shall state the names of the auditors and be signed by them.

236(4)   [Offence, penalty]   If a copy of the auditors' report—

(a) is laid before the company, or otherwise circulated, published or issued, without the required statement of the auditors' names, or

(b) is delivered to the registrar without the required statement of the auditors' names or without being signed as required by this section,

the company and every officer of it who is in default is guilty of an offence and liable to a fine.

236(5)   [Interpretation]   References in this section to signature by the auditors are, where the office of auditor is held by a body corporate or partnership, to signature in the name of the body corporate or partnership by a person authorised to sign on its behalf.

History
See history note after s. 262A.

SEC. 237   Duties of auditors

237(1)   [Investigations]   A company's auditors shall, in preparing their report, carry out such investigations as will enable them to form an opinion as to—

(a) whether proper accounting records have been kept by the company and proper returns adequate for their audit have been received from branches not visited by them, and

(b) whether the company's individual accounts are in agreement with the accounting records and returns.

237(2) [Statement re improper returns etc.] If the auditors are of opinion that proper accounting records have not been kept, or that proper returns adequate for their audit have not been received from branches not visited by them, or if the company's individual accounts are not in agreement with the accounting records and returns, the auditors shall state that fact in their report.

237(3) [Statement re failure to obtain information] If the auditors fail to obtain all the information and explanations which, to the best of their knowledge and belief, are necessary for the purposes of their audit, they shall state that fact in their report.

237(4) [Statement giving Sch. 6 particulars] If the requirements of Schedule 6 (disclosure of information: emoluments and other benefits of directors and others) are not complied with in the annual accounts, the auditors shall include in their report, so far as they are reasonably able to do so, a statement giving the required particulars.

History
See history note after s. 262A.

PUBLICATION OF ACCOUNTS AND REPORTS

SEC. 238   Persons entitled to receive copies of accounts and reports

238(1) [Who must receive copies] A copy of the company's annual accounts, together with a copy of the directors' report for that financial year and of the auditors' report on those accounts, shall be sent to—

(a) every member of the company,

(b) every holder of the company's debentures, and

(c) every person who is entitled to receive notice of general meetings,

not less than 21 days before the date of the meeting at which copies of those documents are to be laid in accordance with section 241.

238(2) [Who need not receive copies] Copies need not be sent—

(a) to a person who is not entitled to receive notices of general meetings and of whose address the company is unaware, or

(b) to more than one of the joint holders of shares or debentures none of whom is entitled to receive such notices, or

(c) in the case of joint holders of shares or debentures some of whom are, and some not, entitled to receive such notices, to those who are not so entitled.

238(3) [Companies not having a share capital] In the case of a company not having a share capital, copies need not be sent to anyone who is not entitled to receive notices of general meetings of the company.

238(4) [Where copies sent outside time limit] If copies are sent less than 21 days before the date of the meeting, they shall, notwithstanding that fact, be deemed to have been duly sent if it is so agreed by all the members entitled to attend and vote at the meeting.

238(5)   [Offence, penalty]   If default is made in complying with this section, the company and every officer of it who is in default is guilty of an offence and liable to a fine.

238(6)   [Where copies sent over period]   Where copies are sent out under this section over a period of days, references elsewhere in this Act to the day on which copies are sent out shall be construed as references to the last day of that period.

History
See history note after s. 262A.

SEC. 239   Right to demand copies of accounts and reports

239(1)   [Those entitled]   Any member of a company and any holder of a company's debentures is entitled to be furnished, on demand and without charge, with a copy of the company's last annual accounts and directors' report and a copy of the auditors' report on those accounts.

239(2)   [Entitlement]   The entitlement under this section is to a single copy of those documents, but that is in addition to any copy to which a person may be entitled under section 238.

239(3)   [Offence, penalty]   If a demand under this section is not complied with within seven days, the company and every officer of it who is in default is guilty of an offence and liable to a fine and, for continued contravention, to a daily default fine.

239(4)   [Onus of proof re receiving document]   If in proceedings for such an offence the issue arises whether a person had already been furnished with a copy of the relevant document under this section, it is for the defendant to prove that he had.

History
See history note after s. 262A.

SEC. 240   Requirements in connection with publication of accounts

240(1)   [Auditors' report to accompany accounts]   If a company publishes any of its statutory accounts, they must be accompanied by the relevant auditors' report under section 235.

240(2)   [Group accounts to accompany individual accounts]   A company which is required to prepare group accounts for a financial year shall not publish its statutory individual accounts for that year without also publishing with them its statutory group accounts.

240(3)   [Where non-statutory account published]   If a company publishes non-statutory accounts, it shall publish with them a statement indicating—

    (a)   that they are not the company's statutory accounts,

    (b)   whether statutory accounts dealing with any financial year with which the non-statutory accounts purport to deal have been delivered to the registrar,

    (c)   whether the company's auditors have made a report under section 235 on the statutory accounts for any such financial year, and

    (d)   whether any report so made was qualified or contained a statement under section 237(2) or (3) (accounting records or returns inadequate, accounts not agreeing with records and returns or failure to obtain necessary information and explanations);

CA 1985, sec. 238(5)

and it shall not publish with the non-statutory accounts any auditors' report under section 235.

240(4) **[Publication of document]** For the purposes of this section a company shall be regarded as publishing a document if it publishes, issues or circulates it or otherwise makes it available for public inspection in a manner calculated to invite members of the public generally, or any class of members of the public, to read it.

240(5) **[Interpretation]** References in this section to a company's statutory accounts are to its individual or group accounts for a financial year as required to be delivered to the registrar under section 242; and references to the publication by a company of "non-statutory accounts" are to the publication of—

(a) any balance sheet or profit and loss account relating to, or purporting to deal with, a financial year of the company, or

(b) an account in any form purporting to be a balance sheet or profit and loss account for the group consisting of the company and its subsidiary undertakings relating to, or purporting to deal with, a financial year of the company,

otherwise than as part of the company's statutory accounts.

240(6) **[Offence, penalty]** A company which contravenes any provision of this section, and any officer of it who is in default, is guilty of an offence and liable to a fine.

History
See history note after s. 262A.

LAYING AND DELIVERING OF ACCOUNTS AND REPORTS

SEC. 241 Accounts and reports to be laid before company in general meeting

241(1) **[Duty of directors]** The directors of a company shall in respect of each financial year lay before the company in general meeting copies of the company's annual accounts, the directors' report and the auditors' report on those accounts.

241(2) **[Offence, penalty]** If the requirements of subsection (1) are not complied with before the end of the period allowed for laying and delivering accounts and reports, every person who immediately before the end of that period was a director of the company is guilty of an offence and liable to a fine and, for continued contravention, to a daily default fine.

241(3) **[Defence]** It is a defence for a person charged with such an offence to prove that he took all reasonable steps for securing that those requirements would be complied with before the end of that period.

241(4) **[Not a defence]** It is not a defence to prove that the documents in question were not in fact prepared as required by this Part.

History
See history note after s. 262A.

SEC. 242 Accounts and reports to be delivered to the registrar

242(1) **[Duty of directors]** The directors of a company shall in respect of each financial year deliver to the registrar a copy of the company's annual accounts together with a copy of the directors' report for that year and a copy of the auditors' report on those accounts.

If any document comprised in those accounts or reports is in a language other than English, the directors shall annex to the copy of that document delivered a translation of it into English, certified in the prescribed manner to be a correct translation.

242(2)   [Offence, penalty re sec. 242(1)]   If the requirements of subsection (1) are not complied with before the end of the period allowed for laying and delivering accounts and reports, every person who immediately before the end of that period was a director of the company is guilty of an offence and liable to a fine and, for continued contravention, to a daily default fine.

242(3)   [Power of court re default]   Further, if the directors of the company fail to make good the default within 14 days after the service of a notice on them requiring compliance, the court may on the application of any member or creditor of the company or of the registrar, make an order directing the directors (or any of them) to make good the default within such time as may be specified in the order.

The court's order may provide that all costs of and incidental to the application shall be borne by the directors.

242(4)   [Defence]   It is a defence for a person charged with an offence under this section to prove that he took all reasonable steps for securing that the requirements of subsection (1) would be complied with before the end of the period allowed for laying and delivering accounts and reports.

242(5)   [Not a defence]   It is not a defence in any proceedings under this section to prove that the documents in question were not in fact prepared as required by this Part.

History
See history note after s. 262A but note that there is a
s. 242A ultimately also to be inserted by CA 1989, s. 11.

SEC. 243   Accounts of subsidiary undertakings to be appended in certain cases

243(1)   [Application]   The following provisions apply where at the end of the financial year a parent company has as a subsidiary undertaking—

    (a) a body corporate incorporated outside Great Britain which does not have an established place of business in Great Britain, or

    (b) an unincorporated undertaking,

which is excluded from consolidation in accordance with section 229(4) (undertaking with activities different from the undertakings included in the consolidation).

243(2)   [Documents to be appended]   There shall be appended to the copy of the company's annual accounts delivered to the registrar in accordance with section 242 a copy of the undertaking's latest individual accounts and, if it is a parent undertaking, its latest group accounts.

If the accounts appended are required by law to be audited, a copy of the auditors' report shall also be appended.

243(3) **[Period for accounts]** The accounts must be for a period ending not more than twelve months before the end of the financial year for which the parent company's accounts are made up.

243(4) **[Documents not in English]** If any document required to be appended is in a language other than English, the directors shall annex to the copy of that document delivered a translation of it into English, certified in the prescribed manner to be a correct translation.

243(5) **[Qualifications]** The above requirements are subject to the following qualifications—

(a) an undertaking is not required to prepare for the purposes of this section accounts which would not otherwise be prepared, and if no accounts satisfying the above requirements are prepared none need be appended;

(b) a document need not be appended if it would not otherwise be required to be published, or made available for public inspection, anywhere in the world, but in that case the reason for not appending it shall be stated in a note to the company's accounts;

(c) where an undertaking and all its subsidiary undertakings are excluded from consolidation in accordance with section 229(4), the accounts of such of the subsidiary undertakings of that undertaking as are included in its consolidated group accounts need not be appended.

243(6) **[Application of sec. 242(2)–(4)]** Subsections (2) to (4) of section 242 (penalties, etc. in case of default) apply in relation to the requirements of this section as they apply in relation to the requirements of subsection (1) of that section.
History
See history note after s. 262A.

SEC. 244 Period allowed for laying and delivering accounts and reports

244(1) **[Usual relevant period]** The period allowed for laying and delivering accounts and reports is—

(a) for a private company, 10 months after the end of the relevant accounting reference period, and

(b) for a public company, 7 months after the end of that period.

This is subject to the following provisions of this section.

244(2) **[If first accounting reference period is more than 12 months]** If the relevant accounting reference period is the company's first and is a period of more than 12 months, the period allowed is—

(a) 10 months or 7 months, as the case may be, from the first anniversary of the incorporation of the company, or

(b) 3 months from the end of the accounting reference period,

whichever last expires.

244(3) **[Notice where foreign business]** Where a company carries on business, or has interests, outside the United Kingdom, the Channel Islands and the Isle of Man, the directors may, in respect of any financial year, give to the registrar before the end of the period allowed by subsection (1) or (2) a notice in the prescribed form—

    (a) stating that the company so carries on business or has such interests, and

    (b) claiming a 3 month extension of the period allowed for laying and delivering accounts and reports;

and upon such a notice being given the period is extended accordingly.

244(4)   **[Where accounting reference period shortened by sec. 225]**   If the relevant accounting period is treated as shortened by virtue of a notice given by the company under section 225 (alteration of accounting reference date), the period allowed for laying and delivering accounts is that applicable in accordance with the above provisions or 3 months from the date of the notice under that section, whichever last expires.

244(5)   **[Power to extend period]**   If for any special reason the Secretary of State thinks fit he may, on an application made before the expiry of the period otherwise allowed, by notice in writing to a company extend that period by such further period as may be specified in the notice.

244(6)   **[''The relevant accounting reference period'']**   In this section **''the relevant accounting reference period''** means the accounting reference period by reference to which the financial year for the accounts in question was determined.

History
See history note after s. 262A.

SEC. 245   Penalty for laying or delivering defective accounts

245(1)   **[Offence for directors]**   If any accounts of a company of which a copy is laid before the company in general meeting or delivered to the registrar of companies do not comply with the requirements of this Act as to the matters to be included in, or in a note to, those accounts, every person who at the time when the copy is so laid or delivered is a director of the company is guilty of an offence and, in respect of each offence, liable to a fine.

This subsection does not apply to a company's group accounts.

245(2)   **[Offence by directors re group accounts]**   If any group accounts of which a copy is laid before a company in general meeting or delivered to the registrar of companies do not comply with section 229(5) to (7) or section 230, and with the other requirements of this Act as to the matters to be included in or in a note to those accounts, every person who at the time when the copy was so laid or delivered was a director of the company is guilty of an offence and liable to a fine.

245(3)   **[Defence]**   In proceedings against a person for an offence under this section, it is a defence for him to prove that he took all reasonable steps for securing compliance with the requirements in question.

Note
Prospective amendment by CA 1989, s. 1, 12: insertion of
new s. 245–245C.

Chapter II — Exemptions, Exceptions and Special Provisions

SMALL AND MEDIUM-SIZED COMPANIES AND GROUPS

SEC. 246 Exemptions for small and medium-sized companies

246(1) **[Exemptions]** A company which qualifies as a small or medium-sized company in relation to a financial year—

(a) is exempt from the requirements of paragraph 36A of Schedule 4 (disclosure with respect to compliance with accounting standards), and

(b) is entitled to the exemptions provided by Schedule 8 with respect to the delivery to the registrar under section 242 of individual accounts and other documents for that financial year.

246(2) **[Sch. 8, Pt. I–III]** In that Schedule—

Part I relates to small companies,

Part II relates to medium-sized companies, and

Part III contains supplementary provisions.

246(3) **[Company not entitled]** A company is not entitled to the exemptions mentioned in subsection (1) if it is, or was at any time within the financial year to which the accounts relate—

(a) a public company,

(b) a banking or insurance company, or

(c) an authorised person under the Financial Services Act 1986,

or if it is or was at any time during that year a member of an ineligible group.

246(4) **[Ineligible group]** A group is ineligible if any of its members is—

(a) a public company or a body corporate which (not being a company) has power under its constitution to offer its shares or debentures to the public and may lawfully exercise that power,

(b) an authorised institution under the Banking Act 1987,

(c) an insurance company to which Part II of the Insurance Companies Act 1982 applies, or

(d) an authorised person under the Financial Services Act 1986.

246(5) **[Parent company as small company]** A parent company shall not be treated as qualifying as a small company in relation to a financial year unless the group headed by it qualifies as a small group, and shall not be treated as qualifying as a medium-sized company in relation to a financial year unless that group qualifies as a medium-sized group (see section 249).

History
See history note after s. 262A.

SEC. 247 Qualification of company as small or medium-sized

247(1) **[Time for meeting qualifying conditions]** A company qualifies as small or medium-sized in relation to a financial year if the qualifying conditions are met—

(a) in the case of the company's first financial year, in that year, and

(b) in the case of any subsequent financial year, in that year and the preceding year.

247(2)   [Relevant financial year for qualification]   A company shall be treated as qualifying as small or medium-sized in relation to a financial year—

(a) if it so qualified in relation to the previous financial year under subsection (1); or

(b) if it was treated as so qualifying in relation to the previous year by virtue of paragraph (a) and the qualifying conditions are met in the year in question.

247(3)   [Qualification requirements]   The qualifying conditions are met by a company in a year in which it satisfies two or more of the following requirements—

Small company

1. Turnover	Not more than £2 million
2. Balance sheet total	Not more than £975,000
3. Number of employees	Not more than 50

Medium-sized company

1. Turnover	Not more than £8 million
2. Balance sheet total	Not more than £3.9 million
3. Number of employees	Not more than 250.

247(4)   [Where financial year not a year]   For a period which is a company's financial year but not in fact a year the maximum figures for turnover shall be proportionately adjusted.

247(5)   [Balance sheet total]   The balance sheet total means—

(a) where in the company's accounts Format 1 of the balance sheet formats set out in Part I of Schedule 4 is adopted, the aggregate of the amounts shown in the balance sheet under the headings corresponding to items A to D in that Format, and

(b) where Format 2 is adopted, the aggregate of the amounts shown under the general heading "Assets".

247(6)   [Number of employees]   The number of employees means the average number of persons employed by the company in the year (determined on a weekly basis).

That number shall be determined by applying the method of calculation prescribed by paragraph 56(2) and (3) of Schedule 4 for determining the corresponding number required to be stated in a note to the company's accounts.

History
See history note after s. 262A.

SEC. 248   Exemption for small and medium-sized groups

248(1)   [Where parent need not prepare groups accounts]   A parent company need not prepare group accounts for a financial year in relation to which the group headed by that company qualifies as a small or medium-sized group and is not an ineligible group.

248(2) **[Ineligible group]** A group is ineligible if any of its members is—

(a) a public company or a body corporate which (not being a company) has power under its constitution to offer its shares or debentures to the public and may lawfully exercise that power,

(b) an authorised institution under the Banking Act 1987,

(c) an insurance company to which Part II of the Insurance Companies Act 1982 applies, or

(d) an authorised person under the Financial Services Act 1986.

248(3) **[Report by auditors to directors]** If the directors of a company propose to take advantage of the exemption conferred by this section, it is the auditors' duty to provide them with a report stating whether in their opinion the company is entitled to the exemption.

248(4) **[Conditions for exemptions]** The exemption does not apply unless—

(a) the auditors' report states that in their opinion the company is so entitled, and

(b) that report is attached to the individual accounts of the company.

History
See history note after s. 262A.

SEC. 249 Qualification of group as small or medium-sized

249(1) **[Time for meeting qualifying conditions]** A group qualifies as small or medium-sized in relation to a financial year if the qualifying conditions are met—

(a) in the case of the parent company's first financial year, in that year, and

(b) in the case of any subsequent financial year, in that year and the preceding year.

249(2) **[Relevant financial year for qualification]** A group shall be treated as qualifying as small or medium-sized in relation to a financial year—

(a) if it so qualified in relation to the previous financial year under subsection (1); or

(b) if it was treated as so qualifying in relation to the previous year by virtue of paragraph (a) and the qualifying conditions are met in the year in question.

249(3) **[Qualification requirements]** The qualifying conditions are met by a group in a year in which it satisfies two or more of the following requirements—

Small group

1. Aggregate turnover	Not more than £2 million net (or £2.4 million gross)
2. Aggregate balance sheet total	Not more than £1 million net (or £1.2 million gross)
3. Aggregate number of employees	Not more than 50

Medium-sized group

1. Aggregate turnover	Not more than £8 million net (or £9.6 million gross)
2. Aggregate balance sheet total	Not more than £3.9 million net (or £4.7 million gross)
3. Aggregate number of employees	Not more than 250. P.T.O.

249(4)   **[Aggregate figures]**   The aggregate figures shall be ascertained by aggregating the relevant figures determined in accordance with section 247 for each member of the group.

In relation to the aggregate figures for turnover and balance sheet total, **"net"** means with the set-offs and other adjustments required by Schedule 4A in the case of group accounts and **"gross"** means without those set-offs and other adjustments; and a company may satisfy the relevant requirement on the basis of either the net or the gross figure.

249(5)   **[Figures for each subsidiary]**   The figures for each subsidiary undertaking shall be those included in its accounts for the relevant financial year, that is—

(a) if its financial year ends with that of the parent company, that financial year, and

(b) if not, its financial year ending last before the end of the financial year of the parent company.

249(6)   **[Expense, delay re figures]**   If those figures cannot be obtained without disproportionate expense or undue delay, the latest available figures shall be taken.

History
See history note after s. 262A.

DORMANT COMPANIES

SEC. 250   Resolution not to appoint auditors

250(1)   **[Cases where special resolution possible]**   A company may by special resolution make itself exempt from the provisions of this Part relating to the audit of accounts in the following cases—

(a) if the company has been dormant from the time of its formation, by a special resolution passed before the first general meeting of the company at which annual accounts are laid;

(b) if the company has been dormant since the end of the previous financial year and—

(i) is entitled in respect of its individual accounts for that year to the exemptions conferred by section 246 on a small company, or would be so entitled but for being a member of an ineligible group, and

(ii) is not required to prepare group accounts for that year,

by a special resolution passed at a general meeting of the company at which the annual accounts for that year are laid.

250(2)   **[Where resolution not permitted]**   A company may not pass such a resolution if it is—

(a) a public company,

(b) a banking or insurance company, or

(c) an authorised person under the Financial Services Act 1986.

250(3)   **["Dormant"]**   A company is **"dormant"** during a period in which no significant accounting transaction occurs, that is, no transaction which is required by section 221 to be entered in the company's accounting records; and a company ceases to be dormant on the occurrence of such a transaction.

For this purpose there shall be disregarded any transaction arising from the taking of shares in the company by a subscriber to the memorandum in pursuance of an undertaking of his in the memorandum.

250(4) **[Consequences of exemption]** Where a company is, at the end of a financial year, exempt by virtue of this section from the provisions of this Part relating to the audit of accounts—

    (a) sections 238 and 239 (right to receive or demand copies of accounts and reports) have effect with the omission of references to the auditors' report;

    (b) no copies of an auditors' report need be laid before the company in general meeting;

    (c) no copy of an auditors' report need be delivered to the registrar, and if none is delivered, the copy of the balance sheet so delivered shall contain a statement by the directors, in a position immediately above the signature required by section 233(4), that the company was dormant throughout the financial year; and

    (d) the company shall be treated as entitled in respect of its individual accounts for that year to the exemptions conferred by section 246 on a small company notwithstanding that it is a member of an ineligible group.

250(5) **[Cessation of exemption]** Where a company which is exempt by virtue of this section from the provisions of this Part relating to the audit of accounts—

    (a) ceases to be dormant, or

    (b) would no longer qualify (for any other reason) to make itself exempt by passing a resolution under this section,

it shall thereupon cease to be so exempt.

History
See history note after s. 262A.

LISTED PUBLIC COMPANIES

SEC. 251 Provision of summary financial statement to shareholders

251(1) **[Statement instead of sec. 238(1) statement]** A public company whose shares, or any class of whose shares, are listed need not, in such cases as may be specified by regulations made by the Secretary of State, and provided any conditions so specified are complied with, send copies of the documents referred to in section 238(1) to members of the company, but may instead send them a summary financial statement.

In this subsection **"listed"** means admitted to the Official List of The International Stock Exchange of the United Kingdom and the Republic of Ireland Limited.

251(2) **[Right of members to require sec. 238(1) documents]** Copies of the documents referred to in section 238(1) shall, however, be sent to any member of the company who wishes to receive them; and the Secretary of State may by regulations make provision as to the manner in which it is to be ascertained whether a member of the company wishes to receive them.

251(3) **[Form and derivation of statement]** The summary financial statement shall be derived from the company's annual accounts and the directors' report and shall be in such form and contain such information as may be specified by regulations made by the Secretary of State.

Note
See the Companies (Summary Financial Statement) Regulations 1990 (S.I. 1990 No. 515).

251(4)   [Requirements for statement]   Every summary financial statement shall—

   (a) state that it is only a summary of information in the company's annual accounts and the directors' report;

   (b) contain a statement by the company's auditors of their opinion as to whether the summary financial statement is consistent with those accounts and that report and complies with the requirements of this section and regulations made under it;

   (c) state whether the auditors' report on the annual accounts was unqualified or qualified, and if it was qualified set out the report in full together with any further material needed to understand the qualification;

   (d) state whether the auditors' report on the annual accounts contained a statement under—

      (i) section 237(2) (accounting records or returns inadequate or accounts not agreeing with records and returns), or

     (ii) section 237(3) (failure to obtain necessary information and explanations),

     and if so, set out the statement in full.

251(5)   [Regulations]   Regulations under this section shall be made by statutory instrument which shall be subject to annulment in pursuance of a resolution of either House of Parliament.

251(6)   [Penalty on default]   If default is made in complying with this section or regulations made under it, the company and every officer of it who is in default is guilty of an offence and liable to a fine.

251(7)   [Non-application of sec. 240]   Section 240 (requirements in connection with publication of accounts) does not apply in relation to the provision to members of a company of a summary financial statement in accordance with this section.

History
S. 251 inserted by CA 1989, s. 1, 15 as from 1 March 1990 (see S.I. 1990 No. 142 (C. 5), art. 2); for former s. 251 see history note after s. 262A.

PRIVATE COMPANIES

SEC. 252   Election to dispense with laying of accounts and reports before general meeting

252(1)   [Right of private company]   A private company may elect (by elective resolution in accordance with section 379A) to dispense with the laying of accounts and reports before the company in general meeting.

252(2)   [Effect of election]   An election has effect in relation to the accounts and reports in respect of the financial year in which the election is made and subsequent financial years.

252(3) [**Operation of other provisions**] Whilst an election is in force, the references in the following provisions of this Act to the laying of accounts before the company in general meeting shall be read as references to the sending of copies of the accounts to members and others under section 238(1)—

(a) section 235(1) (accounts on which auditors are to report),

(b) section 270(3) and (4) (accounts by reference to which distributions are justified), and

(c) section 320(2) (accounts relevant for determining company's net assets for purposes of ascertaining whether approval required for certain transactions);

and the requirement in section 271(4) that the auditors' statement under that provision be laid before the company in general meeting shall be read as a requirement that it be sent to members and others along with the copies of the accounts sent to them under section 238(1).

252(4) [**If election ceases to have effect**] If an election under this section ceases to have effect, section 241 applies in relation to the accounts and reports in respect of the financial year in which the election ceases to have effect and subsequent financial years.

History
See history note after s. 262A.

SEC. 253 Right of shareholder to require laying of accounts

253(1) [**Sending of copies of accounts and reports**] Where an election under section 252 is in force, the copies of the accounts and reports sent out in accordance with section 238(1)—

(a) shall be sent not less than 28 days before the end of the period allowed for laying and delivering accounts and reports, and

(b) shall be accompanied, in the case of a member of the company, by a notice informing him of his right to require the laying of the accounts and reports before a general meeting;

and section 238(5) (penalty for default) applies in relation to the above requirements as to the requirements contained in that section.

253(2) [**Right of member or auditor to require meeting**] Before the end of the period of 28 days beginning with the day on which the accounts and reports are sent out in accordance with section 238(1), any member or auditor of the company may by notice in writing deposited at the registered office of the company require that a general meeting be held for the purpose of laying the accounts and reports before the company.

253(3) [**If no meeting held**] If the directors do not within 21 days from the date of the deposit of such a notice proceed duly to convene a meeting, the person who deposited the notice may do so himself.

253(4) [**Holding of meeting**] A meeting so convened shall not be held more than three months from that date and shall be convened in the same manner, as nearly as possible, as that in which meetings are to be convened by directors.

253(5) [**Expenses where directors do not convene meeting**] Where the directors do not duly convene a meeting, any reasonable expenses incurred by reason of that failure by the person who deposited the notice shall be made good to him by the company, and shall be recouped by the company out of any fees, or other remuneration in respect of their services, due or to become due to such of the directors as were in default.

253(6) **[If meeting out of time]** The directors shall be deemed not to have duly convened a meeting if they convene a meeting for a date more than 28 days after the date of the notice convening it.

History
See history note after s. 262A.

UNLIMITED COMPANIES

SEC. 254 Exemption from requirement to deliver accounts and reports

254(1) **[Exemption for directors of unlimited company]** The directors of an unlimited company are not required to deliver accounts and reports to the registrar in respect of a financial year if the following conditions are met.

254(2) **[Conditions for exemption]** The conditions are that at no time during the relevant accounting reference period—

    (a) has the company been, to its knowledge, a subsidiary undertaking of an undertaking which was then limited, or

    (b) have there been, to its knowledge, exercisable by or on behalf of two or more undertakings which were then limited, rights which if exercisable by one of them would have made the company a subsidiary undertaking of it, or

    (c) has the company been a parent company of an undertaking which was then limited.

The references above to an undertaking being limited at a particular time are to an undertaking (under whatever law established) the liability of whose members is at that time limited.

254(3) **[Where company promoter of trading stamp scheme]** The exemption conferred by this section does not apply if at any time during the relevant accounting period the company carried on business as the promoter of a trading stamp scheme within the Trading Stamps Act 1964.

254(4) **[Effects of sec. 240]** Where a company is exempt by virtue of this section from the obligation to deliver accounts, section 240 (requirements in connection with publication of accounts) has effect with the following modifications—

    (a) in subsection (3)(b) for the words from "whether statutory accounts" to "have been delivered to the registrar" substitute "that the company is exempt from the requirement to deliver statutory accounts", and

    (b) in subsection (5) for "as required to be delivered to the registrar under section 242" substitute "as prepared in accordance with this Part and approved by the board of directors".

History
See history note after s. 262A.

BANKING AND INSURANCE COMPANIES AND GROUPS

SEC. 255 Special provisions for banking and insurance companies

255(1) **[Individual accounts under Sch. 9, Pt. I]** A banking or insurance company may prepare its individual accounts in accordance with Part I of Schedule 9 rather than Schedule 4.

255(2) **[Statement in such accounts]** Accounts so prepared shall contain a statement that they are prepared in accordance with the special provisions of this Part relating to banking companies or insurance companies, as the case may be.

255(3) **[References to Sch. 4]** In relation to the preparation of individual accounts in accordance with the special provisions of this Part relating to banking or insurance companies, the references to the provisions of Schedule 4 in section 226(4) and (5) (relationship between specific requirements and duty to give true and fair view) shall be read as references to the provisions of Part I of Schedule 9.

255(4) **[Modification of requirements]** The Secretary of State may, on the application or with the consent of the directors of a company which prepares individual accounts in accordance with the special provisions of this Part relating to banking or insurance companies, modify in relation to the company any of the requirements of this Part for the purpose of adapting them to the circumstances of the company.

This does not affect the duty to give a true and fair view.

History
See history note after s. 262A.

SEC. 255A Special provisions for banking and insurance groups

255A(1) **[Group accounts under Sch. 9, Pt. II]** The parent company of a banking or insurance group may prepare group accounts in accordance with the provisions of this Part as modified by Part II of Schedule 9.

255A(2) **[Statement in such accounts]** Accounts so prepared shall contain a statement that they are prepared in accordance with the special provisions of this Part relating to banking groups or insurance groups, as the case may be.

255A(3) **[References to a banking group]** References in this Part to a banking group are to a group where—

(a) the parent company is a banking company, or

(b) at least one of the undertakings in the group is an authorised institution under the Banking Act 1987 and the predominant activities of the group are such as to make it inappropriate to prepare group accounts in accordance with the formats in Part I of Schedule 4.

255A(4) **[References to an insurance group]** References in this Part to an insurance group are to a group where—

(a) the parent company is an insurance company, or

(b) the predominant activity of the group is insurance business and activities which are a direct extension of or ancillary to insurance business.

255A(5) **[References to Sch. 4A]** In relation to the preparation of group accounts in accordance with the special provisions of this Part relating to banking or insurance groups, the references to the provisions of Schedule 4A in section 227(5) and (6) (relationship between specific requirements and duty to give true and fair view) shall be read as references to those provisions as modified by Part II of Schedule 9.

255A(6)   [Modification of requirements]   The Secretary of State may, on the application or with the consent of the directors of a company which prepares group accounts in accordance with the special provisions of this Part relating to banking or insurance groups, modify in relation to the company any of the requirements of this Part for the purpose of adapting them to the circumstances of the company.

History
See history note after s. 262A.

SEC. 255B   Modification of disclosure requirements in relation to banking company or group

255B(1)   [Sch. 5]   In relation to a company which prepares accounts in accordance with the special provisions of this Part relating to banking companies or groups, the provisions of Schedule 5 (additional disclosure: related undertakings) have effect subject to Part III of Schedule 9.

255B(2)   [Sch. 6]   In relation to a banking company, or the parent company of a banking company, the provisions of Schedule 6 (disclosure: emoluments and other benefits of directors and others) have effect subject to Part IV of Schedule 9.

History
See history note after s. 262A.

SEC. 255C   Directors' report where accounts prepared in accordance with special provisions

255C(1)   [Application]   The following provisions apply in relation to the directors' report of a company for a financial year in respect of which it prepares accounts in accordance with the special provisions of this Part relating to banking or insurance companies or groups.

255C(2)   [Information in report instead of annexed to accounts]   The information required to be given by paragraph 6, 8 or 13 of Part I of Schedule 9 (which is allowed to be given in a statement or report annexed to the accounts), may be given in the directors' report instead.

Information so given shall be treated for the purposes of audit as forming part of the accounts.

255C(3)   [Amount to be carried to reserves]   The reference in section 234(1)(b) to the amount proposed to be carried to reserves shall be construed as a reference to the amount proposed to be carried to reserves within the meaning of Part I of Schedule 9.

255C(4)   [If certain exemptions used]   If the company takes advantage, in relation to its individual or group accounts, of the exemptions conferred by paragraph 27 or 28 of Part I of Schedule 9, paragraph 1 of Schedule 7 (disclosure of asset values) does not apply.

255C(5)   [Compliance with Sch. 10]   The directors' report shall, in addition to complying with Schedule 7, also comply with Schedule 10 (which specifies additional matters to be disclosed).

History
See history note after s. 262A.

SEC. 255D   Power to apply provisions to banking partnerships

255D(1)   [**Power to make regulations**]   The Secretary of State may by regulations apply to banking partnerships, subject to such exceptions, adaptations and modifications as he considers appropriate, the provisions of this Part applying to banking companies.

255D(2)   [**"Banking partnership"**]   A **"banking partnership"** means a partnership which is an authorised institution under the Banking Act 1987.

255D(3)   [**Regulations by statutory instrument**]   Regulations under this section shall be made by statutory instrument.

255D(4)   [**Approval by Parliament**]   No regulations under this section shall be made unless a draft of the instrument containing the regulations has been laid before Parliament and approved by a resolution of each House.

History
See history note after s. 262A.

Chapter III — Supplementary Provisions

SEC. 256   Accounting standards

256(1)   [**"Accounting standards"**]   In this Part **"accounting standards"** means statements of standard accounting practice issued by such body or bodies as may be prescribed by regulations.

256(2)   [**Interpretation**]   References in this Part to accounting standards applicable to a company's annual accounts are to such standards as are, in accordance with their terms, relevant to the company's circumstances and to the accounts.

256(3)   [**Power of Seretary of State to make grants**]   The Secretary of State may make grants to or for the purposes of bodies concerned with—

  (a) issuing accounting standards,

  (b) overseeing and directing the issuing of such standards, or

  (c) investigating departures from such standards or from the accounting requirements of this Act and taking steps to secure compliance with them.

256(4)   [**Content of regulations**]   Regulations under this section may contain such transitional and other supplementary and incidental provisions as appear to the Secretary of State to be appropriate.

History
See history note after s. 262A.

POWER TO ALTER ACCOUNTING REQUIREMENTS

SEC. 257   Power of Secretary of State to alter accounting requirements

257(1)   [**Power to make regulations**]   The Secretary of State may by regulations made by statutory instrument modify the provisions of this Part.

257(2)   [**Certain regulations require approval by Parliament**]   Regulations which—

  (a) add to the classes of documents required to be prepared, laid before the company in general meeting or delivered to the registrar,

   (b) restrict the classes of company which have the benefit of any exemption, exception or special provision,

   (c) require additional matter to be included in a document of any class, or

   (d) otherwise render the requirements of this Part more onerous,

shall not be made unless a draft of the instrument containing the regulations has been laid before Parliament and approved by a resolution of each House.

257(3)   [Other regulations subject to annulment]   Otherwise, a statutory instrument containing regulations under this section shall be subject to annulment in pursuance of a resolution of either House of Parliament.

257(4)   [Scope of regulations]   Regulations under this section may—

   (a) make different provision for different cases or classes of case,

   (b) repeal and re-enact provisions with modifications of form or arrangement, whether or not they are modified in substance,

   (c) make consequential amendments or repeals in other provisions of this Act, or in other enactments, and

   (d) contain such transitional and other incidental and supplementary provisions as the Secretary of State thinks fit.

257(5)   [Enactments outside the Companies Acts]   Any modification by regulations under this section of section 258 or Schedule 10A (parent and subsidiary undertakings) does not apply for the purposes of enactments outside the Companies Acts unless the regulations so provide.

History
See history note after s. 262A.

PARENT AND SUBSIDIARY UNDERTAKINGS

SEC. 258   Parent and subsidiary undertakings

258(1)   [Construction]   The expressions "**parent undertaking**" and "**subsidiary undertaking**" in this Part shall be construed as follows; and a "**parent company**" means a parent undertaking which is a company.

258(2)   [Parent undertaking]   An undertaking is a parent undertaking in relation to another undertaking, a subsidiary undertaking, if—

   (a) it holds a majority of the voting rights in the undertaking, or

   (b) it is a member of the undertaking and has the right to appoint or remove a majority of its board of directors, or

   (c) it has the right to exercise a dominant influence over the undertaking—

      (i) by virtue of provisions contained in the undertaking's memorandum or articles, or

      (ii) by virtue of a control contract, or

   (d) it is a member of the undertaking and controls alone, pursuant to an agreement with other shareholders or members, a majority of the voting rights in the undertaking.

258(3)   [Member of another undertaking]   For the purposes of subsection (2) an undertaking shall be treated as a member of another undertaking—

(a) if any of its subsidiary undertakings is a member of that undertaking, or

(b) if any shares in that other undertaking are held by a person acting on behalf of the undertaking or any of its subsidiary undertakings.

258(4) **[Another parent undertaking]** An undertaking is also a parent undertaking in relation to another undertaking, a subsidiary undertaking, if it has a participating interest in the undertaking and—

(a) it actually exercises a dominant influence over it, or

(b) it and the subsidiary undertaking are managed on a unified basis.

258(5) **[Treatment as parent undertaking]** A parent undertaking shall be treated as the parent undertaking of undertakings in relation to which any of its subsidiary undertakings are, or are to be treated as, parent undertakings; and references to its subsidiary undertakings shall be construed accordingly.

258(6) **[Sch. 10A]** Schedule 10A contains provisions explaining expressions used in this section and otherwise supplementing this section.

History
See history note after s. 262A.

OTHER INTERPRETATION PROVISIONS

SEC. 259 Meaning of "undertaking" and related expressions

259(1) **["Undertaking"]** In this Part **"undertaking"** means—

(a) a body corporate or partnership, or

(b) an unincorporated association carrying on a trade or business, with or without a view to profit.

259(2) **[References to shares]** In this Part references to shares—

(a) in relation to an undertaking with a share capital, are to allotted shares;

(b) in relation to an undertaking with capital but no share capital, are to rights to share in the capital of the undertaking; and

(c) in relation to an undertaking without capital, are to interests—

(i) conferring any right to share in the profits or liability to contribute to the losses of the undertaking, or

(ii) giving rise to an obligation to contribute to the debts or expenses of the undertaking in the event of a winding up.

259(3) **[Other expressions appropriate to companies]** Other expressions appropriate to companies shall be construed, in relation to an undertaking which is not a company, as references to the corresponding persons, officers, documents or organs, as the case may be, appropriate to undertakings of that description.

This is subject to provision in any specific context providing for the translation of such expressions.

259(4) **["Fellow subsidiary undertakings"]** References in this Part to "fellow subsidiary undertakings" are to undertakings which are subsidiary undertakings of the same parent undertaking but are not parent undertakings or subsidiary undertakings of each other.

259(5)   **["Group undertaking"]**   In this Part **"group undertaking"**, in relation to an undertaking, means an undertaking which is—

(a) a parent undertaking or subsidiary undertaking of that undertaking, or

(b) a subsidiary undertaking of any parent undertaking of that undertaking.

History
See history note after s. 262A.

SEC. 260   Participating interests

260(1)   **["Participating interest"]**   In this Part a **"participating interest"** means an interest held by an undertaking in the shares of another undertaking which it holds on a long-term basis for the purpose of securing a contribution to its activities by the exercise of control or influence arising from or related to that interest.

260(2)   **[Presumption]**   A holding of 20 per cent or more of the shares of an undertaking shall be presumed to be a participating interest unless the contrary is shown.

260(3)   **[Interest in shares in sec. 260(1)]**   The reference in subsection (1) to an interest in shares includes—

(a) an interest which is convertible into an interest in shares, and

(b) an option to acquire shares or any such interest;

and an interest or option falls within paragraph (a) or (b) notwithstanding that the shares to which it relates are, until the conversion or the exercise of the option, unissued.

260(4)   **[Interest held on behalf of undertaking]**   For the purposes of this section an interest held on behalf of an undertaking shall be treated as held by it.

260(5)   **["Participating interest" in sec. 258(4)]**   For the purposes of this section as it applies in relation to the expression "participating interest" in section 258(4) (definition of "subsidiary undertaking")—

(a) there shall be attributed to an undertaking any interests held by any of its subsidiary undertakings, and

(b) the references in subsection (1) to the purpose and activities of an undertaking include the purposes and activities of any of its subsidiary undertakings and of the group as a whole.

260(6)   **[In formats in Sch. 4, Pt. I]**   In the balance sheet and profit and loss formats set out in Part I of Schedule 4, "participating interest" does not include an interest in a group undertaking.

260(7)   **[In group situations]**   For the purposes of this section as it applies in relation to the expression "participating interest"—

(a) in those formats as they apply in relation to group accounts, and

(b) in paragraph 20 of Schedule 4A (group accounts: undertakings to be accounted for as associated undertakings),

the references in subsections (1) to (4) to the interest held by, and the purposes and activities of, the undertaking concerned shall be construed as references to the interest held by, and the purposes and activities of, the group (within the meaning of paragraph 1 of that Schedule).

History
See history note after s. 262A.

SEC. 261 Notes to the accounts

261(1) **[Information required to be in notes]** Information required by this Part to be given in notes to a company's annual accounts may be contained in the accounts or in a separate document annexed to the accounts.

261(2) **[Interpretation]** References in this Part to a company's annual accounts, or to a balance sheet or profit and loss account, include notes to the accounts giving information which is required by any provision of this Act, and required or allowed by any such provision to be given in a note to company accounts.

History
See history note after s. 262A.

SEC. 262 Minor definitions

262(1) **[Particular definitions]** In this Part—

"**annual accounts**" means—

(a) the individual accounts required by section 226, and

(b) any group accounts required by section 227,

(but see also section 230 (treatment of individual profit and loss account where group accounts prepared));

"**annual report**", in relation to a company, means the directors' report required by section 234;

"**balance sheet date**" means the date as at which the balance sheet was made up;

"**capitalisation**", in relation to work or costs, means treating that work or those costs as a fixed asset;

"**credit institution**" means an undertaking carrying on a deposit-taking business within the meaning of the Banking Act 1987;

"**fixed assets**" means assets of a company which are intended for use on a continuing basis in the company's activities, and "**current assets**" means assets not intended for such use;

"**group**" means a parent undertaking and its subsidiary undertakings;

"**included in the consolidation**", in relation to group accounts, or "**included in consolidated group accounts**", means that the undertaking is included in the accounts by the method of full (and not proportional) consolidation, and references to an undertaking excluded from consolidation shall be construed accordingly;

"**purchase price**", in relation to an asset of a company or any raw materials or consumables used in the production of such an asset, includes any consideration (whether in cash or otherwise) given by the company in respect of that asset or those materials or consumables, as the case may be;

"**qualified**", in relation to an auditors' report, means that the report does not state the auditors' unqualified opinion that the accounts have been properly prepared in accordance with this Act or, in the case of an undertaking not required to prepare accounts in accordance with this Act, under any corresponding legislation under which it is required to prepare accounts;

"true and fair view" refers—

(a) in the case of individual accounts, to the requirement of section 226(2), and

(b) in the case of group accounts, to the requirement of section 227(3);

"turnover", in relation to a company, means the amounts derived from the provision of goods and services falling within the company's ordinary activities, after deduction of—

(i) trade discounts,

(ii) value added tax, and

(iii) any other taxes based on the amounts so derived.

262(2) [Undertaking not trading for profit] In the case of an undertaking not trading for profit, any reference in this Part to a profit and loss account is to an income and expenditure account; and references to profit and loss and, in relation to group accounts, to a consolidated profit and loss account shall be construed accordingly.

262(3) [References to "realised profits" and "realised losses"] References in this Part to "realised profits" and "realised losses", in relation to a company's accounts, are to such profits or losses of the company as fall to be treated as realised in accordance with principles generally accepted, at the time when the accounts are prepared, with respect to the determination for accounting purposes of realised profits or losses.

This is without prejudice to—

(a) the construction of any other expression (where appropriate) by reference to accepted accounting principles or practice, or

(b) any specific provision for the treatment of profits or losses of any description as realised.

History
See history note after s. 262A.

SEC. 262A   Index of defined expressions

262A The following Table shows the provisions of this Part defining or otherwise explaining expressions used in this Part (other than expressions used only in the same section or paragraph)—

accounting reference date and accounting reference period	section 224
accounting standards and applicable accounting standards	section 256
annual accounts	
(generally)	section 262(1)
(includes notes to the accounts)	section 261(2)
annual report	section 262(1)
associated undertaking (in Schedule 4A)	paragraph 20 of that Schedule
balance sheet (includes notes)	section 261(2)
balance sheet date	section 262(1)
banking group	section 255A(3)

CA 1985, sec. 262(2)

capitalisation (in relation to work or costs)	section 262(1)
credit institution	section 262(1)
current assets	section 262(1)
fellow subsidiary undertaking	section 259(4)
financial year	section 223
fixed assets	section 262(1)
group	section 262(1)
group undertaking	section 259(5)
historical cost accounting rules (in Schedule 4)	paragraph 29 of that Schedule
included in the consolidation and related expressions	section 262(1)
individual accounts	section 262(1)
insurance group	section 255A(4)
land of freehold tenure and land of leasehold tenure (in relation to Scotland)	
— in Schedule 4	paragraph 93 of that Schedule
— in Schedule 9	paragraph 36 of that Schedule
lease, long lease and short lease	
— in Schedule 4	paragraph 83 of that Schedule
— in Schedule 9	paragraph 34 of that Schedule
listed investment	
— in Schedule 4	paragraph 84 of that Schedule
— in Schedule 9	paragraph 33 of that Schedule
notes to the accounts	section 261(1)
parent undertaking (and parent company)	section 258 and Schedule 10A
participating interest	section 260
pension costs (in Schedule 4)	paragraph 94(2) and (3) of that Schedule
period allowed for laying and delivering accounts and reports	section 244
profit and loss account	
(includes notes)	section 261(2)
(in relation to a company not trading for profit)	section 262(2)
provision	
— in Schedule 4	paragraphs 88 and 89 of that Schedule
— in Schedule 9	paragraph 32 of that Schedule
purchase price	section 262(1)

qualified	section 262(1)
realised losses and realised profits	section 262(3)
reserve (in Schedule 9)	paragraph 32 of that Schedule
shares	section 259(2)
social security costs (in Schedule 4)	paragraph 94(1) and (3) of that Schedule
special provisions for banking and insurance companies and groups	sections 255 and 255A
subsidiary undertaking	section 258 and Schedule 10A
true and fair view	section 262(1)
turnover	section 262(1)
undertaking and related expressions	section 259(1) to (3)

History

S. 221–244, 246–262A inserted by CA 1989, s. 1–11, 13–22 as from 1 April 1990 (with the exception of s. 233(5), 242A and 251 — see history notes after s. 233(5), 242 and 251) subject to transitional and saving provisions (see S.I. 1990 No. 355 (C. 13), art. 3, Sch. 1 and also art. 6–9); the former s. 221–244, 246–262 read as follows:

"ACCOUNTING RECORDS

SEC. 221   Companies to keep accounting records

221(1)   Every company shall cause accounting records to be kept in accordance with this section.

(2)   The accounting records shall be sufficient to show and explain the company's transactions, and shall be such as to—

   (a)   disclose with reasonable accuracy, at any time, the financial position of the company at that time, and

   (b)   enable the directors to ensure that any balance sheet and profit and loss account prepared under this Part comply with the requirements of this Act as to the form and content of company accounts and otherwise.

(3)   The accounting records shall in particular contain—

   (a)   entries from day to day of all sums of money received and expended by the company, and the matters in respect of which the receipt and expenditure takes place, and

   (b)   a record of the assets and liabilities of the company.

(4)   If the company's business involves dealing in goods, the accounting records shall contain—

   (a)   statements of stock held by the company at the end of each financial year of the company,

   (b)   all statements of stocktakings from which any such statement of stock as is mentioned in paragraph (a) has been or is to be prepared, and

   (c)   except in the case of goods sold by way of ordinary retail trade, statements of all goods sold and purchased, showing the goods and the buyers and sellers in sufficient detail to enable all these to be identified.

SEC. 222   Where and for how long records to be kept

222(1)   Subject as follows, a company's accounting records shall be kept at its registered office or such other place as the directors think fit, and shall at all times be open to inspection by the company's officers.

(2)   If accounting records are kept at a place outside Great Britain, accounts and returns with respect to the business dealt with in the accounting records so kept shall be sent to, and kept at, a place in Great Britain, and shall at all times be open to such inspection.

(3)   The accounts and returns to be sent to Great Britain in accordance with subsection (2) shall be such as to—

   (a)   disclose with reasonable accuracy the financial position of the business in question at intervals of not more than 6 months, and

   (b)   enable the directors to ensure that the company's balance sheet and profit and loss account comply with the requirements of this Act as to the form and content of company accounts and otherwise.

(4)   Accounting records which a company is required by section 221 to keep shall be preserved by it—

   (a)   in the case of a private company, for 3 years from the date on which they are made, and

   (b)   in the case of a public company, for 6 years from that date.

    This is subject to any provision contained in rules made under section 411 of the Insolvency Act."

(In s. 222(4) previously the words "section 411 of the Insolvency Act" substituted for the former words "section 106 of the Insolvency Act 1985" by Insolvency Act 1986, s. 439(1) and Sch. 13 as from 29 December 1986 (see IA 1986, s. 443 and S.I. 1986 No. 1924 (C. 71)) — that substitution repealed by CA 1989, s. 212 and Sch. 24 as from 1 April 1990 (see S.I. 1990 No. 355 (C. 13), art. 5(1)(d)). Immediately before this the words "provision contained in rules made under section 106 of the Insolvency Act 1985" substituted for the original words "direction with respect to the disposal of records given under winding-up rules under section 663": see S.I. 1986 No. 1924 (C. 71) — that substitution by the Insolvency Act 1985 was repealed by CA 1989, s. 212 and Sch. 24 as from 1 April 1990 (see S.I. 1990 No. 355 (C. 13), art. 5(1)(c)).)

"SEC. 223   Penalties for non-compliance with sec. 221, 222

223(1)   If a company fails to comply with any provision of section 221 or 222(1) or (2), every officer of the company who is in default is guilty of an offence unless he shows that he acted honestly and that in the circumstances in which the company's business was carried on the default was excusable.

(2)   An officer of a company is guilty of an offence if he fails to take all reasonable steps for securing compliance by the company with section 222(4), or has intentionally caused any default by the company under it.

CA 1985, sec. 262A   [The next page is 13,401]

(3) A person guilty of an offence under this section is liable to imprisonment or a fine, or both.

A COMPANY'S ACCOUNTING REFERENCE PERIODS AND FINANCIAL YEAR

SEC. 224 Accounting reference period and date

224(1) A company's accounting reference periods are determined according to its accounting reference date.

(2) A company may give notice in the prescribed form to the registrar of companies specifying a date in the calendar year as being the date on which in each successive calendar year an accounting reference period of the company is to be treated as coming to an end; and the date specified in the notice is then the company's accounting reference date.

(3) However, no such notice has effect unless it is given before the end of 6 months beginning with the date of the company's incorporation; and, failing such notice, the company's accounting reference date is 31st March.

(4) A company's first accounting reference period is such period ending with its accounting reference date as begins on the date of its incorporation and is a period of more than 6 months and not more than 18 months; and each successive period of 12 months beginning after the end of the first accounting reference period and ending with the accounting reference date is also an accounting reference period of the company.

(5) This section is subject to section 225, under which in certain circumstances a company may alter its accounting reference date and accounting reference periods.

SEC. 225 Alteration of accounting reference period

225(1) At any time during a period which is an accounting reference period of a company by virtue of section 224 or 226 the company may give notice in the prescribed form to the registrar of companies specifying a date in the calendar year ('the new accounting reference date') on which that accounting reference period ('the current accounting reference period') and each subsequent accounting reference period of the company is to be treated as coming to an end or (as the case may require) as having come to an end.

(2) At any time after the end of a period which was an accounting reference period of a company by virtue of section 224 or 226 the company may give notice in the prescribed form to the registrar of companies specifying a date in the calendar year ('the new accounting reference date') on which that accounting reference period ('the previous accounting reference period') and each subsequent accounting reference period of the company is to be treated as coming or (as the case may require) as having come to an end.

(3) But a notice under subsection (2)—

(a) has no effect unless the company is a subsidiary or holding company of another company and the new accounting reference date coincides with the accounting reference date of that other company, and

(b) has no effect if the period allowed (under section 242) for laying and delivering accounts in relation to the previous accounting reference period has already expired at the time when the notice is given.

(4) A notice under this section shall state whether the current or previous accounting reference period of the company—

(a) is to be treated as shortened, so as to come to an end or (as the case may require) be treated as having come to an end on the new accounting reference date on the first occasion on which that date falls or fell after the beginning of that accounting reference period, or

(b) is to be treated as extended, so as to come to an end or (as the case may require) be treated as having come to an end on the new accounting reference date on the second occasion on which that date falls or fell after the beginning of that accounting reference period.

(5) A notice which states that the current or previous accounting reference period is to be extended has no effect if the current or previous accounting reference period, as extended in accordance with the notice, would exceed 18 months.

(6) Subject to any direction given by the Secretary of State under the next subsection, a notice which states that the current or previous accounting reference period is to be extended has no effect unless—

(a) no earlier accounting reference period of the company has been extended by virtue of a previous notice given by the company under this section, or

(b) the notice is given not less than 5 years after the date on which any earlier accounting reference period of the company which was so extended came to an end, or

(c) the company is a subsidiary or holding company of another company and the new accounting reference date coincides with the accounting reference date of that other company.

(7) The Secretary of State may, if he thinks fit, direct that subsection (6) shall not apply to a notice already given by a company under this section or (as the case may be) in relation to a notice which may be so given.

(8) At any time when an administration order under Part II of the Insolvency Act is in force, this section has effect as if subsections (3) and (5) to (7) were omitted."

(S. 225(8) previously added by Insolvency Act 1986, s. 439(1) and Sch. 13 as from 29 December 1986 (see IA 1986, s. 443 and S.I. 1986 No. 1924 (C. 71)) — that addition repealed by CA 1989, s. 212 and Sch. 24 as from 1 April 1990 (see S.I. 1990 No. 355 (C. 13), art. 5(d)).)

"SEC. 226 Consequence of giving notice under sec. 225

226(1) Where a company has given notice with effect in accordance with section 225, and that notice has not been superseded by a subsequent notice by the company which has such effect, the new date specified in the notice is the company's accounting reference date, in substitution for that which, by virtue of section 224 or this section, was its accounting reference date at the time when the notice was given.

(2) Where by virtue of such a notice one date is substituted for another as the accounting reference date of a company—

(a) the current or previous accounting reference period, shortened or extended (as the case may be) in accordance with the notice, and

(b) each successive period of 12 months beginning after the end of that accounting reference period (as so shortened or extended) and ending with the new accounting reference date,

is or (as the case may require) is to be treated as having been an accounting reference period of the company, instead of any period which would be an accounting reference period of the company if the notice had not been given.

(3) Section 225 and this section do not affect any accounting reference period of the company which—

(a) in the case of a notice under section 225(1), is earlier than the current accounting reference period, or

(b) in the case of a notice under section 225(2), is earlier than the previous accounting reference period.

SEC. 227   Directors' duty to prepare annual accounts

227(1)   In the case of every company, the directors shall in respect of each accounting reference period of the company prepare a profit and loss account for the financial year or, if it is a company not trading for profit, an income and expenditure account.

(2)   Where it is the company's first accounting reference period, the financial year begins with the first day of that period and ends with—

(a) the date on which the accounting reference period ends, or

(b) such other date, not more than 7 days before or more than 7 days after the end of that period, as the directors may determine;

and after that the financial year begins with the day after the date to which the last preceding profit and loss account was made up and ends as mentioned in paragraphs (a) and (b) above.

(3)   The directors shall prepare a balance sheet as at the last day of the financial year.

(4)   In the case of a holding company, the directors shall secure that, except where in their opinion there are good reasons against it, the financial year of each of its subsidiaries coincides with the company's own financial year.

FORM AND CONTENT OF COMPANY INDIVIDUAL AND GROUP ACCOUNTS

SEC. 228   Form and content of individual accounts

228(1)   A company's accounts prepared under section 227 shall comply with the requirements of Schedule 4 (so far as applicable) with respect to the form and content of the balance sheet and profit and loss account and any additional information to be provided by way of notes to the accounts.

(2)   The balance sheet shall give a true and fair view of the state of affairs of the company as at the end of the financial year; and the profit and loss account shall give a true and fair view of the profit or loss of the company for the financial year.

(3)   Subsection (2) overrides—

(a) the requirements of Schedule 4, and

(b) all other requirements of this Act as to the matters to be included in a company's accounts or in notes to those accounts;

and accordingly the following two subsections have effect.

(4)   If the balance sheet or profit and loss account drawn up in accordance with those requirements would not provide sufficient information to comply with subsection (2), any necessary additional information must be provided in that balance sheet or profit and loss account, or in a note to the accounts.

(5)   If, owing to special circumstances in the case of any company, compliance with any such requirement in relation to the balance sheet or profit and loss account would prevent compliance with subsection (2) (even if additional information were provided in accordance with subsection (4)), the directors shall depart from that requirement in preparing the balance sheet or profit and loss amount (so far as necessary in order to comply with subsection (2)).

(6)   If the directors depart from any such requirement, particulars of the departure, the reasons for it and its effect shall be given in a note to the accounts.

(7)   Subsections (1) to (6) do not apply to group accounts prepared under the next section; and subsections (1) and (2) do not apply to a company's profit and loss account (or require the notes otherwise required in relation to that account) if—

(a) the company has subsidiaries, and

(b) the profit and loss account is framed as a consolidated account dealing with all or any of the company's subsidiaries as well as the company, and—

(i) complies with the requirements of this Act relating to consolidated profit and loss accounts, and

(ii) shows how much of the consolidated profit or loss for the financial year is dealt with in the company's individual accounts.

If group accounts are prepared, and advantage is taken of this subsection, that fact shall be disclosed in a note to the group accounts.

SEC. 229   Group accounts of holding company

229(1)   If at the end of its financial year a company has subsidiaries, the directors shall, as well as preparing individual accounts for that year, also prepare group accounts, being accounts or statements which deal with the state of affairs and profit or loss of the company and the subsidiaries.

(2)   This does not apply if the company is at the end of the financial year the wholly-owned subsidiary of another body corporate incorporated in Great Britain.

(3)   Group accounts need not deal with a subsidiary if the company's directors are of opinion that—

(a) it is impracticable, or would be of no real value to the company's members, in view of the insignificant amounts involved, or

(b) it would involve expense or delay out of proportion to the value to members, or

(c) the result would be misleading, or harmful to the business of the company or any of its subsidiaries, or

(d) the business of the holding company and that of the subsidiary are so different that they cannot reasonably be treated as a single undertaking;

and, if the directors are of that opinion about each of the company's subsidiaries, group accounts are not required.

(4)   However, the approval of the Secretary of State is required for not dealing in group accounts with a subsidiary on the ground that the result would be harmful or on the ground of difference between the business of the holding company and that of the subsidiary.

(5)   A holding company's group accounts shall be consolidated accounts comprising—

(a) a consolidated balance sheet dealing with the state of affairs of the company and all the subsidiaries to be dealt with in group accounts, and

(b) a consolidated profit and loss account dealing with the profit or loss of the company and those subsidiaries.

(6)   However, if the directors are of opinion that it is better for the purpose of presenting the same or equivalent information about the state of affairs and profit or loss of the company and those subsidiaries, and of so presenting it that it may be readily appreciated by the company's members, the group accounts may be prepared in other than consolidated form, and in particular may consist—

(a) of more than one set of consolidated accounts dealing respectively with the company and one group of subsidiaries and with other groups of subsidiaries, or

(b) of separate accounts dealing with each of the subsidiaries, or

CCH Editions Limited

BCL BCL6$$$28C

(c) of statements expanding the information about the subsidiaries in the company's individual accounts,

or of any combination of those forms.

(7) The group accounts may be wholly or partly incorporated in the holding company's individual balance sheet and profit and loss account.

SEC. 230   Form and content of group accounts

230(1)   A holding company's group accounts shall comply with the requirements of Schedule 4 (so far as applicable to group accounts in the form in which those accounts are prepared) with respect to the form and content of those accounts and any additional information to be provided by way of notes to those accounts.

(2)   Group accounts (together with any notes to them) shall give a true and fair view of the state of affairs and profit or loss of the company and the subsidiaries dealt with by those accounts as a whole, so far as concerns members of the company.

(3)   Subsection (2) overrides—

   (a)   the requirements of Schedule 4, and

   (b)   all other requirements of this Act as to the matters to be included in group accounts or in notes to those accounts,

and accordingly the following two subsections have effect.

(4)   If group accounts drawn up in accordance with those requirements would not provide sufficient information to comply with subsection (2), any necessary additional information must be provided in, or in a note to, the group accounts.

(5)   If, owing to special circumstances in the case of any company, compliance with any such requirement in relation to its group accounts would prevent those accounts from complying with subsection (2) (even if additional information were provided in accordance with subsection (4)), the directors shall depart from that requirement in preparing the group accounts (so far as necessary to comply with subsection (2)).

(6)   If the directors depart from any such requirement, particulars of that departure, the reason for it and its effect shall be given in a note to the group accounts.

(7)   If the financial year of a subsidiary does not coincide with that of the holding company, the group accounts shall (unless the Secretary of State, on the application or with the consent of the holding company's directors, otherwise directs) deal with the subsidiary's state of affairs as at the end of its relevant financial year, that is—

   (a)   if its financial year ends with that of the holding company, that financial year, and

   (b)   if not, the subsidiary's financial year ending last before the end of the financial year of the holding company dealt with in the group accounts,

and with the subsidiary's profit or loss for its relevant financial year.

(8)   The Secretary of State may, on the application or with the consent of a company's directors, modify the requirements of Schedule 4 as they have effect in relation to that company by virtue of subsection (1), for the purpose of adapting them to the company's circumstances; and references above in this section to the requirements of Schedule 4 are then to be read in relation to that company as references to those requirements as modified.

SEC. 231   Additional disclosure required in notes to accounts

231(1)   Schedule 5 has effect with respect to additional matters which must be disclosed in company accounts for a financial year; and in that Schedule, where a thing is required to be stated or shown, or information is required

to be given, it means that the thing is to be stated or shown, or the information is to be given, in a note to those accounts.

(2)   In Schedule 5—

   (a)   Parts I and II are concerned, respectively, with the disclosure of particulars of the company's subsidiaries and of its other shareholdings,

   (b)   Part III is concerned with the disclosure of financial information relating to subsidiaries,

   (c)   Part IV requires a company which is itself a subsidiary to disclose its ultimate holding company,

   (d)   Part V is concerned with the emoluments of directors (including emoluments waived), pensions of directors and past directors and compensation for loss of office to directors and past directors, and

   (e)   Part VI is concerned with disclosure of the number of the company's employees who are remunerated at higher rates.

(3)   Whenever it is stated in Schedule 5 that this subsection applies to certain particulars or information, it means that the particulars or information shall be annexed to the annual return first made by the company after copies of its accounts have been laid before it in general meeting; and if a company fails to satisfy an obligation thus imposed, the company and every officer of it who is in default is liable to a fine and, for continued contravention, to a daily default fine.

(4)   It is the duty of any director of a company to give notice to the company of such matters relating to himself as may be necessary for purposes of Part V of Schedule 5; and this applies to persons who are or have at any time in the preceding 5 years been directors, as it applies to directors.

A person who makes default in complying with this subsection is liable to a fine.

SEC. 232   Loans in favour of directors and connected persons

232(1)   A holding company's group accounts for a financial year shall comply with Part I of Schedule 6 (so far as applicable) as regards the disclosure of transactions, arrangements and agreements there mentioned (loans, quasi-loans and other dealings in favour of directors).

(2)   In the case of a company other than a holding company, its individual accounts shall comply with Part I of Schedule 6 (so far as applicable) as regards disclosure of those matters.

(3)   Particulars which are required by Part I of Schedule 6 to be contained in any accounts shall be given by way of notes to the accounts, and are required in respect of shadow directors as well as directors.

(4)   Where by virtue of section 229(2) or (3) a company does not prepare group accounts for a financial year, subsection (1) of this section requires disclosure of such matters in its individual accounts as would have been disclosed in group accounts.

(5)   The requirements of this section apply with such exceptions as are mentioned in Part I of Schedule 6 (including in particular exceptions for and in respect of authorised institutions)."

(In s. 232(5) previously the words "authorised institutions" substituted for the former words "recognised banks" by Banking Act 1987, s. 108(1) and Sch. 6, para. 18(2) as from 1 October 1987 (see S.I. 1987 No. 1664 (C. 50)).)

"SEC. 233   Loans etc. to company's officers; statement of amounts outstanding

233(1)   A holding company's group accounts for a financial year shall comply with Part II of Schedule 6 (so far as applicable) as regards transactions, arrangements and agreements made by the company or a subsidiary of it for persons who at any time during that financial year were officers of the company (but not directors).

(2) In the case of a company other than a holding company, its individual accounts shall comply with Part II of Schedule 6 (so far as applicable) as regards those matters.

(3) Subsections (1) and (2) do not apply in relation to any transaction, arrangement or agreement made by an authorised institution for any officer of the institution or for any officer of its holding company unless the officer is a chief executive or manager within the meaning of the Banking Act 1987; and references to officers in Part II of Schedule 6 shall be construed accordingly."

(S. 233(3) previously substituted by Banking Act 1987, s. 90(1) as from 1 October 1987 (see S.I. 1987 No. 1664 (C. 50)); s. 233(3) formerly read as follows:

> "**(3)** Subsections (1) and (2) do not apply in relation to any transaction, arrangement or agreement made by a recognised bank for any of its officers or for any of the officers of its holding company.")

"**(4)** Particulars required by Part II of Schedule 6 to be contained in any accounts shall be given by way of notes to the accounts.

(5) Where by virtue of section 229(2) or (3) a company does not prepare group accounts for a financial year, subsection (1) of this section requires such matters to be stated in its individual accounts as would have been stated in group accounts.

SEC. 234 Authorised institutions: disclosure of dealings with and for directors

234(1) The group accounts of a company which is, or is the holding company of, an authorised institution, and the individual accounts of any other company which is an authorised institution, shall comply with Part III of Schedule 6 (so far as applicable) as regards transactions, arrangements and agreements made by the company preparing the accounts (if it is an authorised institution) and, in the case of a holding company, by any of its subsidiaries which is an authorised institution, for persons who at any time during the financial year were directors of the company or connected with a director of it."

(In s. 234(1) previously the words "an authorised institution", wherever they occurred, substituted for the former words "a recognised bank" by Banking Act 1987, s. 108(1) and Sch. 6, para. 18(3) as from 1 October 1987 (see S.I. No. 1664 (C. 50). Also in heading to s. 234 the words "authorised institutions" substituted for the words "Recognised banks" by CCH to reflect the amendment by the Banking Act 1987 noted above.)

"**(2)** Particulars required by Part III of Schedule 6 to be contained in any accounts shall be given by way of notes to those accounts, and are required in respect of shadow directors as well as directors.

(3) Where by virtue of section 229(2) or (3) a company does not prepare group accounts for a financial year, subsection (1) of this section requires such matters to be stated in its individual accounts as would have been stated in group accounts.

DIRECTORS' AND AUDITORS' REPORTS

SEC. 235 Directors' report

235(1) In the case of every company there shall for each financial year be prepared a report by the directors—

    (a) containing a fair review of the development of the business of the company and its subsidiaries during the financial year and of their position at the end of it, and

    (b) stating the amount (if any) which they recommend

should be paid as dividend and the amount (if any) which they propose to carry to reserves.

(2) The directors' report shall state the names of the persons who, at any time during the financial year, were directors of the company, and the principal activities of the company and its subsidiaries in the course of the year and any significant change in those activities in the year.

(3) The report shall also state the matters, and give the particulars, required by Part I of Schedule 7 (changes in asset values, directors' shareholdings and other interests, contributions for political and charitable purposes, etc.).

(4) Part II of Schedule 7 applies as regards the matters to be stated in the directors' report in the circumstances there specified (company acquiring its own shares or a permitted charge on them).

(5) Parts III, IV and V of Schedule 7 apply respectively as regards the matters to be stated in the directors' report relative to the employment, training and advancement of disabled persons; the health, safety and welfare at work of the company's employees; and the involvement of employees in the affairs, policy and performance of the company.

(6) If the company's individual accounts are accompanied by group accounts which are special category, the directors' report shall, in addition to complying with Schedule 7, also comply with paragraphs 2 to 6 of Schedule 10 (turnover and profitability; size of labour force and wages paid).

(7) In respect of any failure to comply with the requirements of this Act as to the matters to be stated, and the particulars to be given, in the directors' report, every person who was a director of the company immediately before the end of the relevant period (meaning whatever is under section 242 the period for laying and delivering accounts) is guilty of an offence and liable to a fine.

In proceedings for an offence under this subsection, it is a defence for the person to prove that he took all reasonable steps for securing compliance with the requirements in question.

SEC. 236 Auditors' report

236(1) A company's auditors shall make a report to its members on the accounts examined by them, and on every balance sheet and profit and loss account, and on all group accounts, copies of which are to be laid before the company in general meeting during the auditors' tenure of office.

(2) The auditors' report shall state—

    (a) whether in the auditors' opinion the balance sheet and profit and loss account and (if it is a holding company submitting group accounts) the group accounts have been properly prepared in accordance with this Act; and

    (b) without prejudice to the foregoing, whether in their opinion a true and fair view is given—

        (i) in the balance sheet, of the state of the company's affairs at the end of the financial year,

        (ii) in the profit and loss account (if not framed as a consolidated account), of the company's profit or loss for the financial year, and

        (iii) in the case of group accounts, of the state of affairs and profit or loss of the company and its subsidiaries dealt with by those accounts, so far as concerns members of the company.

SEC. 237 Auditors' duties and powers

237(1) It is the duty of the company's auditors, in preparing their report, to carry out such investigations as will enable them to form an opinion as to the following matters—

    (a) whether proper accounting records have been kept

by the company and proper returns adequate for their audit have been received from branches not visited by them,

(b) whether the company's balance sheet and (if not consolidated) its profit and loss account are in agreement with the accounting records and returns.

(2) If the auditors are of opinion that proper accounting records have not been kept, or that proper returns adequate for their audit have not been received from branches not visited by them, or if the balance sheet and (if not consolidated) the profit and loss account are not in agreement with the accounting records and returns, the auditors shall state that fact in their report.

(3) Every auditor of a company has a right of access at all times to the company's books, accounts and vouchers, and is entitled to require from the company's officers such information and explanations as he thinks necessary for the performance of the auditor's duties.

(4) If the auditors fail to obtain all the information and explanations which, to the best of their knowledge and belief, are necessary for the purposes of their audit, they shall state that fact in their report.

(5) If the requirements of Parts V and VI of Schedule 5 and Parts I to III of Schedule 6 are not complied with in the accounts, it is the auditors' duty to include in their report, so far as they are reasonably able to do so, a statement giving the required particulars.

(6) It is the auditors' duty to consider whether the information given in the directors' report for the financial year for which the accounts are prepared is consistent with those accounts; and if they are of opinion that it is not, they shall state that fact in their report.

PROCEDURE ON COMPLETION OF ACCOUNTS

SEC. 238 Signing of balance sheet; documents to be annexed

238(1) A company's balance sheet, and every copy of it which is laid before the company in general meeting or delivered to the registrar of companies, shall be signed on behalf of the board by two of the directors of the company or, if there is only one director, by that one.

(2) If a copy of the balance sheet—

(a) is laid before the company or delivered to the registrar without being signed as required by this section, or

(b) not being a copy so laid or delivered, is issued, circulated or published in a case where the balance sheet has not been signed as so required or where (the balance sheet having been so signed) the copy does not include a copy of the signatures or signature, as the case may be,

the company and every officer of it who is in default is liable to a fine.

(3) A company's profit and loss account and, so far as not incorporated in its individual balance sheet or profit and loss account, any group accounts of a holding company shall be annexed to the balance sheet, and the auditors' report shall be attached to it.

(4) Any accounts so annexed shall be approved by the board of directors before the balance sheet is signed on their behalf.

SEC. 239 Documents to be included in company's accounts

239 For the purposes of this Part, a company's accounts for a financial year are to be taken as comprising the following documents—

(a) the company's profit and loss account and balance sheet,

(b) the directors' report,

(c) the auditors' report, and

(d) where the company has subsidiaries and section 229 applies, the company's group accounts.

SEC. 240 Persons entitled to receive accounts as of right

240(1) In the case of every company, a copy of the company's accounts for the financial year shall, not less than 21 days before the date of the meeting at which they are to be laid in accordance with the next section, be sent to each of the following persons—

(a) every member of the company (whether or not entitled to receive notice of general meetings),

(b) every holder of the company's debentures (whether or not so entitled), and

(c) all persons other than members and debenture holders, being persons so entitled.

(2) In the case of a company not having a share capital, subsection (1) does not require a copy of the accounts to be sent to a member of the company who is not entitled to receive notices of general meetings of the company, or to a holder of the company's debentures who is not so entitled.

(3) Subsection (1) does not require copies of the accounts to be sent—

(a) to a member of the company or a debenture holder, being in either case a person who is not entitled to receive notices of general meetings, and of whose address the company is unaware, or

(b) to more than one of the joint holders of any shares or debentures none of whom are entitled to receive such notices, or

(c) in the case of joint holders of shares or debentures some of whom are, and some not, entitled to receive such notices, to those who are not so entitled.

(4) If copies of the accounts are sent less than 21 days before the date of the meeting, they are, notwithstanding that fact, deemed to have been duly sent if it is so agreed by all the members entitled to attend and vote at the meeting.

(5) If default is made in complying with subsection (1), the company and every officer of it who is in default is liable to a fine.

SEC. 241 Directors' duty to lay and deliver accounts

241(1) In respect of each financial year of a company the directors shall lay before the company in general meeting copies of the accounts of the company for that year.

(2) The auditors' report shall be read before the company in general meeting, and be open to the inspection of any member of the company.

(3) In respect of each financial year the directors—

(a) shall deliver to the registrar of companies a copy of the accounts for the year, and

(b) if any document comprised in the accounts is in a language other than English, shall annex to the copy of that document delivered a translation of it into English, certified in the prescribed manner to be a correct translation.

(4) In the case of an unlimited company, the directors are not required by subsection (3) to deliver a copy of the accounts if—

(a) at no time during the accounting reference period has the company been, to its knowledge, the subsidiary of a company that was then limited and at no such time, to its knowledge, have there been held or been exercisable, by or on behalf of two or more companies that were then limited, shares or powers which, if they had been held or been exercisable by one of them, would have made the company its subsidiary, and

(b) at no such time has the company been the holding company of a company which was then limited, and

(c) at no such time has the company been carrying on business as the promoter of a trading stamp scheme within the Trading Stamps Act 1964.

References here to a company that was limited at a particular time are to a body corporate (under whatever law incorporated) the liability of whose members was at that time limited.

SEC. 242   Period allowed for laying and delivery

242(1)   The period allowed for laying and delivering a company's accounts for a financial year is as follows in this section, being determined by reference to the end of the relevant accounting reference period (that is, the accounting reference period in respect of which the financial year of the company is ascertained).

(2)   Subject to the following subsections, the period allowed is—

(a) for a private company, 10 months after the end of the relevant accounting reference period, and

(b) for a public company, 7 months after the end of that period.

(3)   If a company carries on business, or has interests, outside the United Kingdom, the Channel Islands and the Isle of Man and in respect of a financial year the directors (before the end of the period allowed by subsection (2)) give to the registrar of companies notice in the prescribed form—

(a) stating that the company so carries on business or has such interests, and

(b) claiming an extension of the period so allowed by a further 3 months,

the period allowed in relation to that financial year is then so extended.

(4)   Where a company's first accounting reference period—

(a) begins on the date of its incorporation, and

(b) is a period of more than 12 months,

the period otherwise allowed for laying and delivering accounts is reduced by the number of days by which the relevant accounting reference period is longer than 12 months.

However, the period allowed is not by this provision reduced to less than 3 months after the end of that accounting reference period.

(5)   Where a company's relevant accounting reference period has been shortened under section 226 (in consequence of notice by the company under section 225), the period allowed for laying and delivering accounts is—

(a) the period allowed in accordance with subsections (2) to (4) above, or

(b) the period of 3 months beginning with the date of the notice under section 225,

whichever of those periods last expires.

(6)   If for any special reason the Secretary of State thinks fit to do so, he may by notice in writing to a company extend, by such further period as may be specified in the notice, the period otherwise allowed for laying and delivering accounts for any financial year of the company.

SEC. 243   Penalty for non-compliance with sec. 241

243(1)   If for a financial year of a company any of the requirements of section 241(1) or (3) is not complied with before the end of the period allowed for laying and delivering

accounts, every person who immediately before the end of that period was a director of the company is, in respect of each of those subsections which is not so complied with, guilty of an offence and liable to a fine and, for continued contravention, to a daily default fine.

(2)   If a person is charged with that offence in respect of any of the requirements of section 241(1) or (3), it is a defence for him to prove that he took all reasonable steps for securing that those requirements would be complied with before the end of the period allowed for laying and delivering accounts.

(3)   If in respect of the company's financial year any of the requirements of section 241(3) is not complied with before the end of the period allowed for laying and delivering accounts, the company is liable to a penalty, recoverable in civil proceedings by the Secretary of State.

(4)   The amount of the penalty is determined by reference to the length of the period between the end of the accounting reference period and the earliest day by which all those requirements have been complied with, and is—

(a) £20 where the period is not more than one month,

(b) £50 where the period is more than 1 month but not more than 3 months,

(c) £100 where the period is more than 3 months but not more than 6 months,

(d) £200 where the period is more than 6 months but not more than 12 months, and

(e) £450 where the period is more than 12 months.

(5)   In proceedings under this section with respect to a requirement to lay a copy of a document before a company in general meeting, or to deliver a copy of a document to the registrar of companies, it is not a defence to prove that the document in question was not in fact prepared as required by this Part.

(6)   Subsections (3) and (4) of this section do not come into force unless and until made to do so by an order of the Secretary of State in a statutory instrument."

(There appear to have been no statutory instruments under s. 243(6).)

"SEC. 244   Default order in case of non-compliance

244(1)   If—

(a) in respect of a company's financial year any of the requirements of section 241(3) has not been complied with before the end of the period allowed for laying and delivering accounts, and

(b) the directors of the company fail to make good the default within 14 days after the service of a notice on them requiring compliance,

the court may, on application by any member or creditor of the company, or by the registrar of companies, make an order directing the directors (or any of them) to make good the default within such time as may be specified in the order.

(2)   The court's order may provide that all costs of and incidental to the application shall be borne by the directors.

(3)   Nothing in this section prejudices section 243.

SEC. 246   Shareholders' right to obtain copies of accounts

246(1)   Any member of a company, whether or not he is entitled to have sent to him copies of the company's accounts, and any holder of the company's debentures (whether or not so entitled) is entitled to be furnished (on demand and without charge) with a copy of its last accounts.

(2)   If, when a person makes a demand for a document with which he is entitled by this section to be furnished, default is made in complying with the demand within 7 days after its making, the company and every officer of it who is in default is liable to a fine and, for continued contravention, to a daily default fine (unless it is proved that the person has already made a demand for, and been furnished with, a copy of the document).

MODIFIED ACCOUNTS

SEC. 247 Entitlement to deliver accounts in modified form

247(1) In certain cases a company's directors may, in accordance with Part I of Schedule 8, deliver modified accounts in respect of a financial year; and whether they may do so depends on the company qualifying, in particular financial years, as small or medium-sized.

(2) Modified accounts for a financial year may not be delivered in the case of a company which is, or was at any time in that year—

(a) a public company,

(b) a special category company (Chapter II of this Part), or

(c) subject to the next-but-one subsection, a member of a group which is ineligible for this purpose.

(3) 'Group' here means a holding company and its subsidiaries together; and a group is ineligible if any of its members is—

(a) a public company or a special category company, or

(b) a body corporate (other than a company) which has power under its constitution to offer its shares or debentures to the public and may lawfully exercise that power, or

(c) a body corporate (other than a company) which is either an authorised institution or an insurance company to which Part II of the Insurance Companies Act 1982 applies."

(In s. 247(3)(c) previously the words "an authorised institution" substituted for the former words "a recognised bank or licensed institution within the Banking Act 1979" by Banking Act 1987, s. 108(2) and Sch. 6, para. 18(4) as from 1 October 1987 (see S.I. 1987 No. 1664 (C. 50)).)

"(4) Notwithstanding subsection (2)(c), modified accounts for a financial year may be delivered if the company is exempt under section 252 (dormant companies) from the obligation to appoint auditors and either—

(a) was so exempt throughout that year, or

(b) became so exempt by virtue of a special resolution under that section passed during that year.

(5) For purposes of sections 247 to 250 and Schedule 8, 'deliver' means deliver to the registrar of companies under this Chapter; and for purposes of subsection (3)(b), 'shares' and 'debentures' have the same meaning as when used in relation to a company.

SEC. 248 Qualification of company as small or medium-sized

248(1) A company qualifies as small in a financial year if for that year two or more of the following conditions are satisfied—

(a) the amount of its turnover for the year is not more than £2 million;

(b) its balance sheet total is not more than £975,000;

(c) the average number of persons employed by the company in the year (determined on a weekly basis) does not exceed 50."

(In s. 248(1) previously the figure "£2 million" substituted for the former figure "£1.4 million", and the figure "£975,000" substituted for the former figure "£700,000" by the Companies (Modified Accounts) Amendment

Regulations 1986 (S.I. 1986 No. 1865), reg. 2 as from 30 November 1986.)

"(2) A company qualifies as medium-sized in a financial year if for that year two or more of the following conditions are satisfied—

(a) the amount of its turnover for the year is not more than £8 million;

(b) its balance sheet total is not more than £3.9 million;

(c) the average number of persons employed by the company (determined on a weekly basis) does not exceed 250."

(In s. 248(2) previously the figure "£8 million" substituted for the former figure "£5.75 million", and the figure "£3.9 million" substituted for the former figure "£2.8 million" by the Companies (Modified Accounts) Amendment Regulations 1986 (S.I. 1986 No. 1865), reg. 3 as from 30 November 1986.)

"(3) In subsections (1) and (2), 'balance sheet total' means, in relation to a company's financial year—

(a) where in the company's accounts Format 1 of the balance sheet formats set out in Part I of Schedule 4 is adopted, the aggregate of the amounts shown in the balance sheet under the headings corresponding to items A to D in that Format, and

(b) where Format 2 is adopted, the aggregate of the amounts shown under the general heading 'Assets'.

(4) The average number of persons employed as mentioned in subsections (1)(c) and (2)(c) is determined by applying the method of calculation prescribed by paragraph 56(2) and (3) of Schedule 4 for determining the number required by sub-paragraph (1)(a) of that paragraph to be stated in a note to the company's accounts.

(5) In applying subsections (1) and (2) to a period which is a company's financial year but not in fact a year, the maximum figures for turnover in paragraph (a) of each subsection are to be proportionately adjusted.

SEC. 249 Modified individual accounts

249(1) This section specifies the cases in which a company's directors may (subject to section 250, where the company has subsidiaries) deliver individual accounts modified as for a small or a medium-sized company; and Part I of Schedule 8 applies with respect to the delivery of accounts so modified.

(2) In respect of the company's first financial year the directors may—

(a) deliver accounts modified as for a small company, if in that year it qualifies as small,

(b) deliver accounts modified as for a medium-sized company, if in that year it qualifies as medium-sized.

(3) The next three subsections are concerned only with a company's financial year subsequent to the first.

(4) The directors may in respect of a financial year—

(a) deliver accounts modified as for a small company if in that year the company qualifies as small and it also so qualified in the preceding year,

(b) deliver accounts modified as for a medium-sized company if in that year the company qualifies as medium-sized and it also so qualified in the preceding year.

(5) The directors may in respect of a financial year—

(a) deliver accounts modified as for a small company (although not qualifying in that year as small), if in the preceding year it so qualified and the directors were entitled to deliver accounts so modified in respect of that year, and

(b) deliver accounts modified as for a medium-sized company (although not qualifying in that year as medium-sized), if in the preceding year it so qualified and the directors were entitled to deliver accounts so modified in respect of that year.

(6) The directors may in respect of a financial year—

(a) deliver accounts modified as for a small company, if in that year the company qualifies as small and the directors were entitled under subsection (5)(a) to deliver accounts so modified for the preceding year (although the company did not in that year qualify as small), and

(b) deliver accounts modified as for a medium-sized company if in that year the company qualifies as medium-sized and the directors were entitled under subsection (5)(b) to deliver accounts so modified for the preceding year (although the company did not in that year qualify as medium-sized).

SEC. 250   Modified accounts of holding company

250(1)   This section applies to a company ('the holding company') where in respect of a financial year section 229 requires the preparation of group accounts for the company and its subsidiaries.

(2)   The directors of the holding company may not under section 249—

(a) deliver accounts modified as for a small company, unless the group (meaning the holding company and its subsidiaries together) is in that year a small group,

(b) deliver accounts modified as for a medium-sized company, unless in that year the group is medium-sized;

and the group is small or medium-sized if it would so qualify under section 248 (applying that section as directed by sub-sections (3) and (4) below), if it were all one company.

(3)   The figures to be taken into account in determining whether the group is small or medium-sized (or neither) are the group account figures, that is—

(a) where the group accounts are prepared as consolidated accounts, the figures for turnover, balance sheet total and numbers employed which are shown in those accounts, and

(b) where not, the corresponding figures given in the group accounts, with such adjustment as would have been made if the accounts had been prepared in consolidated form,

aggregated in either case with the relevant figures for the subsidiaries (if any) omitted from the group accounts (excepting those for any subsidiary omitted under section 229(3)(a) on the ground of impracticability).

(4)   In the case of each subsidiary omitted from the group accounts, the figures relevant as regards turnover, balance sheet total and numbers employed are those which are included in the accounts of that subsidiary prepared in respect of its relevant financial year (with such adjustment as would have been made if those figures had been included in group accounts prepared in consolidated form).

(5)   For the purposes of subsection (4), the relevant financial year of the subsidiary is—

(a) if its financial year ends with that of the holding company to which the group accounts relate, that financial year, and

(b) if not, the subsidiary's financial year ending last before the end of the financial year of the holding company.

(6)   If the directors are entitled to deliver modified accounts (whether as for a small or a medium-sized company), they

may also deliver modified group accounts; and this means that the group accounts—

(a) if consolidated, may be in accordance with Part II of Schedule 8 (while otherwise comprising or corresponding with group accounts prepared under section 229), and

(b) if not consolidated, may be such as (together with any notes) give the same or equivalent information as required by paragraph (a) above;

and Part III of the Schedule applies to modified group accounts, whether consolidated or not.

SEC. 251   Power of Secretary of State to modify sec. 247–250 and Sch. 8

251(1)   The Secretary of State may by regulations in a statutory instrument modify the provisions of section 247(1) to (3), 248 to 250 and Schedule 8; and those provisions then apply as modified by regulations for the time being in force.

(2)   Regulations under this section reducing the classes of companies which have the benefit of those provisions, or rendering the requirements of those provisions more onerous, shall not be made unless a draft of the instrument containing the regulations has been laid before Parliament and approved by a resolution of each House.

(3)   Otherwise, a statutory instrument containing such regulations is subject to annulment in pursuance of a resolution of either House.

DORMANT COMPANIES

SEC. 252   Company resolution not to appoint auditors

252(1)   In certain circumstances a company may, with a view to the subsequent laying and delivery of unaudited accounts, pass a special resolution making itself exempt from the obligation to appoint auditors as otherwise required by section 384.

(2)   Such a resolution may be passed at a general meeting of the company at which its accounts for a financial year are laid as required by section 241 (if it is not a year for which the directors are required to lay group accounts); but the following conditions must be satisfied—

(a) the directors must be entitled under section 249 to deliver, in respect of that financial year, accounts modified as for a small company (or would be so entitled but for the company being, or having at any time in the financial year been, a member of an ineligible group within section 247(3)), and

(b) the company must have been dormant since the end of the financial year.

(3)   A company may by such a resolution make itself exempt from the obligation to appoint auditors if the resolution is passed at some time before the first general meeting of the company at which accounts are laid as required by section 241, provided that the company has been dormant from the time of its formation until the resolution is passed.

(4)   A company may not under subsection (3) pass such a resolution if it is a public company or a special category company.

(5)   For purposes of this and the next section, a company is **'dormant'** during any period in which no transaction occurs which is for the company a significant accounting transaction; and—

(a) this means a transaction which is required by section 221 to be entered in the company's accounting records (disregarding any which arises from the taking of shares in the company by a subscriber to the memorandum in pursuance of an undertaking of his in the memorandum), and

(b) a company which has been dormant for any period

ceases to be so on the occurrence of any such transaction.

(6) A company which has under this section made itself exempt from the obligation to appoint auditors loses that exemption if—

(a) it ceases to be dormant, or

(b) it would no longer qualify (for any other reason) to exclude that obligation by passing a resolution under this section.

(7) Where the exemption is lost, the directors may, at any time before the next meeting of the company at which accounts are to be laid, appoint an auditor or auditors, to hold office until the conclusion of that meeting; and if they fail to exercise that power, the company in general meeting may exercise it.

SEC. 253 Laying and delivery of unaudited accounts

253(1) The following applies in respect of a company's accounts for a financial year if the company is exempt under section 252 from the obligation to appoint auditors and either—

(a) was so exempt throughout that year, or

(b) became so exempt by virtue of a special resolution passed during that year, and retained the exemption until the end of that year.

(2) A report by the company's auditors need not be included (as otherwise required by preceding provisions of this Chapter) with the accounts laid before the company in general meeting and delivered to the registrar of companies.

(3) If the auditors' report is omitted from the accounts so delivered, then—

(a) the balance sheet shall contain a statement by the directors (in a position immediately above their signatures to the balance sheet) that the company was dormant throughout the financial year, and

(b) if the accounts delivered to the registrar are modified as permitted by sections 247 to 249—

(i) the modified balance sheet need not contain the statement otherwise required by paragraph 9 of Schedule 8, and

(ii) the modified accounts need not include the special report of the auditors otherwise required by paragraph 10 of that Schedule.

PUBLICATION OF ACCOUNTS

SEC. 254 Publication of full company accounts

254(1) This section applies to the publication by a company of full individual or group accounts, that is to say the accounts required by section 241 to be laid before the company in general meeting and delivered to the registrar of companies (including the directors' report, unless dispensed with under paragraph 3 of Schedule 8).

(2) If a company publishes individual accounts (modified or other) for a financial year, it shall publish with them the relevant auditors' report.

(3) If a company required by section 229 to prepare group accounts for a financial year publishes individual accounts for that year, it shall also publish with them its group accounts (modified or other).

(4) If a company publishes group accounts (modified or other), otherwise than together with its individual accounts, it shall publish with them the relevant auditors' report.

(5) References above to the relevant auditors' report are to the auditors' report under section 236 or, in the case of modified accounts (individual or group), the auditors' special report under paragraph 10 of Schedule 8.

(6) A company which contravenes any provision of this section, and any officer of it who is in default, is liable to a fine.

SEC. 255 Publication of abridged accounts

255(1) This section applies to the publication by a company of abridged accounts, that is to say any balance sheet or profit and loss account relating to a financial year of the company or purporting to deal with any such financial year, otherwise than as part of full accounts (individual or group) to which section 254 applies.

(2) The reference above to a balance sheet or profit and loss account, in relation to accounts published by a holding company, includes an account in any form purporting to be a balance sheet or profit and loss account for the group consisting of the holding company and its subsidiaries.

(3) If the company publishes abridged accounts, it shall publish with those accounts a statement indicating—

(a) that the accounts are not full accounts,

(b) whether full individual or full group accounts (according as the abridged accounts deal solely with the company's own affairs or with the affairs of the company and any subsidiaries) have been delivered to the registrar of companies or, in the case of an unlimited company exempt under section 241(4) from the requirement to deliver accounts, that the company is so exempt,

(c) whether the company's auditors have made a report under section 236 on the company's accounts for any financial year with which the abridged accounts purport to deal, and

(d) whether any report so made was unqualified (meaning that it was a report, without qualification, to the effect that in the opinion of the person making it the company's accounts had been properly prepared).

(4) Where a company publishes abridged accounts, it shall not publish with those accounts any such report of the auditors as is mentioned in subsection (3)(c).

(5) A company which contravenes any provision of this section, and any officer of it who is in default, is liable to a fine.

SUPPLEMENTARY

SEC. 256 Power of Secretary of State to alter accounting requirements

256(1) The Secretary of State may by regulations in a statutory instrument—

(a) add to the classes of documents—

(i) to be comprised in a company's accounts for a financial year to be laid before the company in general meeting as required by section 241, or

(ii) to be delivered to the registrar of companies under that section,

and make provision as to the matters to be included in any document to be added to either class;

(b) modify the requirements of this Act as to the matters to be stated in a document of any such class;

(c) reduce the classes of documents to be delivered to the registrar of companies under section 241.

(2) In particular, the Secretary of State may by such regulations alter or add to the requirements of Schedule 4 and Schedule 9 (special category companies); and any reference in this Act to a provision of it then refers to that provision as it has effect subject to regulations in force under this section.

(3) Where regulations made under subsection (1)(a) add to either class of documents there mentioned documents dealing with the state of affairs and profit or loss of a company and other bodies, the regulations may also—

(a) extend the provisions of this Act relating to group accounts (or such of those provisions as may be specified) to such documents,

(b) exempt that company from the requirement to prepare group accounts in respect of any period for which it has prepared such a document.

(4) Regulations under this section may make different provision for different cases or classes of case, and may contain such incidental and supplementary provisions as the Secretary of State thinks fit.

(5) Regulations under subsection (1)(a), or extending the classes of company to which any requirement mentioned in sub-section (1)(b) applies or rendering those requirements more onerous, shall not be made unless a draft of the instrument containing them has been laid before Parliament and approved by a resolution of each House.

(6) Otherwise, a statutory instrument containing such regulations is subject to annulment in pursuance of a resolution of either House.

Chapter II — Accounts of Banking, Shipping and Insurance Companies

SEC. 257   Special category companies and their accounts

257(1) For purposes of this Act, **'special category companies'** are banking companies, shipping companies and insurance companies; and—

(a) **'banking company'** means a company which is an authorised insitution;

(b) **'insurance company'** means an insurance company to which Part II of the Insurance Companies Act 1982 applies; and

(c) **'shipping company'** means a company which, or a subsidiary of which, owns ships or includes among its activities the management or operation of ships and which satisfies the Secretary of State that it ought in the national interest to be treated under this Part of this Act as a shipping company.''

(In s. 257(1) previously para. (a) substituted by Banking Act 1987, s. 108(1) and Sch. 6, para. 18(5) as from 1 October 1987 (see S.I. 1987 No. 1664 (C. 50)); the former para. (a) read as follows:

    "(a)   **'banking company'** means a company which is a recognised bank for the purposes of the Banking Act 1979 or is a licensed institution within that Act;")

''(2) Except as otherwise provided below, Chapter I of this Part applies to a special category company and its accounts as it applies to, and to the accounts of, any other company.

(3) The individual accounts of a special category company, and the group accounts of a holding company which is, or has as its subsidiary, a special category company, may be prepared under this Chapter and not under Chapter I, and contain a statement that they are so prepared; and a reference in this Act to a company's accounts (individual or group) being 'special category' is to their being so prepared and containing that statement.

(4) Subject as follows, a reference in any enactment or other document to section 228 or 230 of this Act or to Schedule 4 is, in relation to special category accounts, to be read as a reference to section 258 or 259 or Schedule 9 (as the case may require); but this is subject to any contrary context.

SEC. 258   Special category individual accounts

258(1) Where a company's individual accounts are special category, section 228 and Schedule 4 do not apply, but—

(a) the balance sheet shall give a true and fair view of the state of affairs of the company as at the end of the financial year, and

(b) the profit and loss account shall give a true and fair view of the company's profit or loss for the financial year.

(2) The balance sheet and profit and loss account shall comply with the requirements of Schedule 9, so far as applicable.

(3) Except as expressly provided by this section or Part III of Schedule 9, the requirements of subsection (2) and that Schedule are without prejudice to the general requirements of sub-section (1) or to any other requirements of this Act.

(4) The Secretary of State may, on the application or with the consent of the company's directors, modify in relation to that company any of the requirements of this Chapter as to the matters to be stated in a company's balance sheet or profit and loss account (except the requirements of subsection (1) above), for the purpose of adapting them to the circumstances of the company.

(5) So much of subsections (1) and (2) as relates to the profit and loss account does not apply if—

(a) the company has subsidiaries, and

(b) the profit and loss account is framed as a consolidated account dealing with all or any of the company's subsidiaries as well as the company and—

(i) complies with the requirements of this Act relating to consolidated profit and loss accounts (as those requirements apply in the case of special category companies), and

(ii) shows how much of the consolidated profit or loss for the financial year is dealt with in the company's accounts.

SEC. 259   Special category group accounts

259(1) Where a holding company's group accounts are special category, those accounts shall give a true and fair view of the state of affairs and profit or loss of the company and the subsidiaries dealt with by those accounts as a whole, so far as concerns members of the company.

(2) Where the financial year of a subsidiary does not coincide with that of the holding company, the group accounts shall (unless the Secretary of State on the application or with the consent of the holding company's directors otherwise directs) deal with the subsidiary's state of affairs as at the end of its relevant financial year, that is—

(a) if its financial year ends with that of the holding company, that financial year, and

(b) if not, the subsidiary's financial year ending last before the end of the financial year of the holding company dealt with in the group accounts,

and with the subsidiary's profit or loss for its relevant financial year.

(3) Without prejudice to subsection (1), the group accounts, if prepared as consolidated accounts, shall comply with the requirements of Schedule 9 (so far as applicable), and if not so prepared shall give the same or equivalent information.

(4) However, the Secretary of State may, on the application or with the consent of the holding company's directors, modify the requirements of Schedule 9 in relation to that company for the purpose of adapting them to the company's circumstances.

SEC. 260   Notes to special category accounts

260(1) In Schedule 5 (matters to be dealt with in notes to accounts—

(a) paragraph 8 in Part II (disclosure of shareholdings in other bodies corporate, not being subsidiaries), and

(b) Part III (financial information about subsidiaries),

do not apply in the case of special category accounts.

(2) Where an item is given in a note to special category accounts, to comply with Part V or VI of Schedule 5 (directors' emoluments, pensions etc.; emoluments of higher-paid employees), the corresponding amount for the immediately preceding financial year shall be included in the note.

(3) If a person, being a director of a company preparing special category accounts, fails to take all reasonable steps to secure compliance with subsection (2), he is in respect of each offence liable to a fine; but in proceedings against a person for that offence it is a defence to prove that he had reasonable ground to believe, and did believe, that a competent and reliable person was charged with the duty of seeing that subsection (2) was complied with and was in a position to discharge that duty.

SEC. 261   Directors' report

261(1) Where a company's individual accounts are special category, the following applies with respect to the directors' report accompanying the accounts.

(2) Paragraphs (a) and (b) of section 235(1) do not apply as regards the contents of the report; but the report shall deal with the company's state of affairs, the amount (if any) which the directors recommend should be paid as dividend, and the amount (if any) which they propose to carry to reserves (within the meaning of Schedule 9).

(3) Information which is otherwise required to be given in the accounts, and allowed to be given in a statement annexed, may be given in the directors' report instead of in the accounts.

If any information is so given, the report is treated as forming part of the accounts for the purposes of audit,

except that the auditors shall report on it only so far as it gives that information.

(4) Where advantage is taken of subsection (3) to show an item in the directors' report instead of in the accounts, the report shall also show the corresponding amount for (or, as the case may require, as at the end of) the immediately preceding financial year of that item, except where the amount would not have had to be shown had the item been shown in the accounts.

(5) Schedule 7 applies to the directors' report only in respect of the matters to be stated, and the information to be given, under paragraphs 1 to 5 (but excluding paragraph 2(3)) and 9, 10 and 11; and paragraph 1 of the Schedule does not apply if the company has the benefit of any provision of Part III of Schedule 9.

(6) The report shall, in addition to complying with those paragraphs of Schedule 7, also comply with Schedule 10, where and so far as applicable (disclosure of recent share and debenture issues; turnover and profitability; size of labour force and wages paid; and other general matters); but in that Schedule paragraphs 2 to 4 and 6 do not apply to a directors' report attached to any accounts unless the documents required to be comprised in those accounts include group accounts which are special category.

(7) Section 237(6) does not apply.

SEC. 262   Auditors' report

262(1) The following applies where a company is entitled to avail itself, and has availed itself, of the benefit of any of the provisions of Part III of Schedule 9.

(2) In that case section 236(2) does not apply; and the auditors' report shall state whether in their opinion the company's balance sheet and profit and loss account and (if it is a holding company submitting group accounts) the group accounts have been properly prepared in accordance with this Act.''

PART VIII — DISTRIBUTION OF PROFITS AND ASSETS

LIMITS OF COMPANY'S POWER OF DISTRIBUTION

SEC. 263   Certain distributions prohibited

263(1)   [Distribution only out of profits]   A company shall not make a distribution except out of profits available for the purpose.

263(2)   [''Distribution'']   In this Part, **''distribution''** means every description of distribution of a company's assets to its members, whether in cash or otherwise, except distribution by way of—

(a) an issue of shares as fully or partly paid bonus shares,

(b) the redemption or purchase of any of the company's own shares out of capital (including the proceeds of any fresh issue of shares) or out of unrealised profits in accordance with Chapter VII of Part V,

(c) the reduction of share capital by extinguishing or reducing the liability of any of the members on any of the company's shares in respect of share capital not paid up, or by paying off paid up share capital, and

(d) a distribution of assets to members of the company on its winding-up.

263(3)   [Profits available for distribution]   For purposes of this Part, a company's profits available for distribution are its accumulated, realised profits, so far as not previously utilised by distribution or capitalisation, less its accumulated, realised losses, so far as not previously written off in a reduction or reorganisation of capital duly made.

This is subject to the provision made by sections 265 and 266 for investment and other companies.

263(4)   [Unrealised profits not to be applied etc.]   A company shall not apply an unrealised profit in paying up debentures, or any amounts unpaid on its issued shares.

263(5)   [Some profits treated as realised]   Where the directors of a company are, after making all reasonable enquiries, unable to determine whether a particular profit made before 22nd December 1980 is realised or unrealised, they may treat the profit as realised; and where after making such enquiries they are unable to determine whether a particular loss so made is realised or unrealised, they may treat the loss as unrealised.

SEC. 264   Restriction on distribution of assets

264(1)   [Distribution by public company]   A public company may only make a distribution at any time—

    (a) if at that time the amount of its net assets is not less than the aggregate of its called-up share capital and undistributable reserves, and

    (b) if, and to the extent that, the distribution does not reduce the amount of those assets to less than that aggregate.

This is subject to the provision made by sections 265 and 266 for investment and other companies.

264(2)   ["Net assets" in sec. 264(1)]   In subsection (1), **"net assets"** means the aggregate of the company's assets less the aggregate of its liabilities ("liabilities" to include any provision for liabilities or charges within paragraph 89 of Schedule 4).

264(3)   [Company's undistributable reserves]   A company's undistributable reserves are—

    (a) the share premium account,

    (b) the capital redemption reserve,

    (c) the amount by which the company's accumulated, unrealised profits, so far as not previously utilised by capitalisation of a description to which this paragraph applies, exceed its accumulated, unrealised losses (so far as not previously written off in a reduction or reorganisation of capital duly made), and

    (d) any other reserve which the company is prohibited from distributing by any enactment (other than one contained in this Part) or by its memorandum or articles;

and paragraph (c) applies to every description of capitalisation except a transfer of profits of the company to its capital redemption reserve on or after 22nd December 1980.

264(4)   [Uncalled share capital not to be asset]   A public company shall not include any uncalled share capital as an asset in any accounts relevant for purposes of this section.

SEC. 265   Other distributions by investment companies

265(1)   **[Distribution out of profits]**   Subject to the following provisions of this section, an investment company (defined in section 266) may also make a distribution at any time out of its accumulated, realised revenue profits, so far as not previously utilised by distribution or capitalisation, less its accumulated revenue losses (whether realised or unrealised), so far as not previously written off in a reduction or reorganisation of capital duly made—

   (a) if at that time the amount of its assets is at least equal to one and a half times the aggregate of its liabilities, and

   (b) if, and to the extent that, the distribution does not reduce that amount to less than one and a half times that aggregate.

265(2)   **["Liabilities" in sec. 265(1)(a)]**   In subsection (1)(a), **"liabilities"** includes any provision for liabilities or charges (within the meaning of paragraph 89 of Schedule 4).

265(3)   **[Uncalled share capital not to be asset]**   The company shall not include any uncalled share capital as an asset in any accounts relevant for purposes of this section.

265(4)   **[Conditions for sec. 265(1) distribution]**   An investment company may not make a distribution by virtue of subsection (1) unless—

   (a) its shares are listed on a recognised investment exchange other than an overseas investment exchange within the meaning of the Financial Services Act 1986, and

   (b) during the relevant period it has not—

     (i) distributed any of its capital profits, or

     (ii) applied any unrealised profits or any capital profits (realised or unrealised) in paying up debentures or amounts unpaid on its issued shares.

History
In s. 265(4)(a) the words "recognised investment exchange other than an overseas investment exchange within the meaning of the Financial Services Act 1986" substituted for the former words "recognised stock exchange" by Financial Services Act 1986, s. 212(2) and Sch. 16, para. 19 as from 29 April 1988 (see S.I. 1988 No. 740 (C. 22)).

265(5)   **["Relevant period" under sec. 265(4)]**   The "relevant period" under subsection (4) is the period beginning with—

   (a) the first day of the accounting reference period immediately preceding that in which the proposed distribution is to be made, or

   (b) where the distribution is to be made in the company's first accounting reference period, the first day of that period,

and ending with the date of the distribution.

265(6)   **[Requisite notice to registrar before sec. 265(1) distribution]**   An investment company may not make a distribution by virtue of subsection (1) unless the company gave to the registrar of companies the requisite notice (that is, notice under section 266(1)) of the company's intention to carry on business as an investment company—

   (a) before the beginning of the relevant period under subsection (4), or

   (b) in the case of a company incorporated on or after 22nd December 1980, as soon as may have been reasonably practicable after the date of its incorporation.

SEC. 266   Meaning of "investment company"

266(1)   ["Investment company" in sec. 265]   In section 265 "investment company" means a public company which has given notice in the prescribed form (which has not been revoked) to the registrar of companies of its intention to carry on business as an investment company, and has since the date of that notice complied with the requirements specified below.

266(2)   [Requirements in sec. 266(1)]   Those requirements are—

- (a) that the business of the company consists of investing its funds mainly in securities, with the aim of spreading investment risk and giving members of the company the benefit of the results of the management of its funds,

- (b) that none of the company's holdings in companies (other than those which are for the time being investment companies) represents more than 15 per cent by value of the investing company's investments,

- (c) that distribution of the company's capital profits is prohibited by its memorandum or articles of association,

- (d) that the company has not retained, otherwise than in compliance with this Part, in respect of any accounting reference period more than 15 per cent of the income it derives from securities.

266(3)   [Revocation of sec. 266(1) notice]   Notice to the registrar of companies under subsection (1) may be revoked at any time by the company on giving notice in the prescribed form to the registrar that it no longer wishes to be an investment company within the meaning of this section; and, on giving such notice, the company ceases to be such a company.

266(4)   [Application of tax legislation]   Subsections (1A) to (3) of section 842 of the Income and Corporation Taxes Act 1988 apply for the purposes of subsection (2)(b) above as for those of subsection (1)(b) of that section.

History
S. 266(4) substituted by Finance Act 1988, s. 117(3), (4) for companies' accounting periods ending after 5 April 1988: s. 266(4) formerly read as follows:

"Section 359(2) and (3) of the Income and Corporation Taxes Act 1970 and section 93(6)(b) of the Finance Act 1972 apply for purposes of subsection (2)(b) as for those of section 359(1)(b) of the Act first mentioned."

There were also some amendments by Income and Corporation Taxes Act 1988, s. 844 and Sch. 29, para. 32 which did not take effect.

SEC. 267   Extension of sec. 265, 266 to other companies

267(1)   [Regulations]   The Secretary of State may by regulations in a statutory instrument extend the provisions of sections 265 and 266 (with or without modifications) to companies whose principal business consists of investing their funds in securities, land or other assets with the aim of spreading investment risk and giving their members the benefit of the results of the management of the assets.

267(2)   [Scope and approval of regulations]   Regulations under this section—

- (a) may make different provision for different classes of companies and may contain such transitional and supplemental provisions as the Secretary of State considers necessary, and

- (b) shall not be made unless a draft of the statutory instrument containing them has been laid before Parliament and approved by a resolution of each House.

CA 1985, sec. 266(1)

SEC. 268 Realised profits of insurance company with long term business

268(1) **[Realised profits and losses]** Where an insurance company to which Part II of the Insurance Companies Act 1982 applies carries on long term business—

- (a) any amount properly transferred to the profit and loss account of the company from a surplus in the fund or funds maintained by it in respect of that business, and

- (b) any deficit in that fund or those funds,

are to be (respectively) treated, for purposes of this Part, as a realised profit and a realised loss; and, subject to this, any profit or loss arising in that business is to be left out of account for those purposes.

268(2) **[Surplus and deficit in sec. 268(1)]** In subsection (1)—

- (a) the reference to a surplus in any fund or funds of an insurance company is to an excess of the assets representing that fund or those funds over the liabilities of the company attributable to its long term business, as shown by an actuarial investigation, and

- (b) the reference to a deficit in any such fund or funds is to the excess of those liabilities over those assets, as so shown.

268(3) **[Definitions]** In this section—

- (a) **"actuarial investigation"** means an investigation to which section 18 of the Insurance Companies Act 1982 (periodic actuarial investigation of company with long term business) applies or which is made in pursuance of a requirement imposed by section 42 of that Act (actuarial investigation required by Secretary of State); and

- (b) **"long term business"** has the same meaning as in that Act.

SEC. 269 Treatment of development costs

269(1) **[Realised loss, realised revenue loss]** Subject as follows, where development costs are shown as an asset in a company's accounts, any amount shown in respect of those costs is to be treated—

- (a) under section 263, as a realised loss, and

- (b) under section 265, as a realised revenue loss.

269(2) **[Non-application]** This does not apply to any part of that amount representing an unrealised profit made on revaluation of those costs; nor does it apply if—

- (a) there are special circumstances in the company's case justifying the directors in deciding that the amount there mentioned is not to be treated as required by subsection (1), and

- (b) the note to the accounts required by paragraph 20 of Schedule 4 (reasons for showing development costs as an asset) states that the amount is not to be so treated and explains the circumstances relied upon to justify the decision of the directors to that effect.

RELEVANT ACCOUNTS

SEC. 270   Distribution to be justified by reference to company's accounts

270(1)   [Distribution without contravening sec. 263 to 265]   This section and sections 271 to 276 below are for determining the question whether a distribution may be made by a company without contravening section 263, 264 or 265.

270(2)   [Determination of amount of distribution]   The amount of a distribution which may be made is determined by reference to the following items as stated in the company's accounts—

(a) profits, losses, assets and liabilities,

(b) provisions of any of the kinds mentioned in paragraphs 88 and 89 of Schedule 4 (depreciation, diminution in value of assets, retentions to meet liabilities, etc.), and

(c) share capital and reserves (including undistributable reserves).

270(3)   [Relevant accounts]   Except in a case falling within the next subsection, the company's accounts which are relevant for this purpose are its last annual accounts, that is to say those prepared under Part VII which were laid in respect of the last preceding accounting reference period in respect of which accounts so prepared were laid; and for this purpose accounts are laid if section 241(1) has been complied with in relation to them.

270(4)   [Exception — interim and initial accounts]   In the following two cases—

(a) where the distribution would be found to contravene the relevant section if reference were made only to the company's last annual accounts, or

(b) where the distribution is proposed to be declared during the company's first accounting reference period, or before any accounts are laid in respect of that period,

the accounts relevant under this section (called "interim accounts" in the first case, and "initial accounts" in the second) are those necessary to enable a reasonable judgment to be made as to the amounts of the items mentioned in subsection (2) above.

270(5)   [Contravention]   The relevant section is treated as contravened in the case of a distribution unless the statutory requirements about the relevant accounts (that is, the requirements of this and the following three sections, as and where applicable) are complied with in relation to that distribution.

SEC. 271   Requirements for last annual accounts

271(1)   [If last annual accounts only relevant accounts]   If the company's last annual accounts constitute the only accounts relevant under section 270, the statutory requirements in respect of them are as follows.

     CCH Editions Limited
BCL BCL6$$$28C

271(2) **[Requirements for last annual accounts]** The accounts must have been properly prepared in accordance with this Act, or have been so prepared subject only to matters which are not material for determining, by reference to items mentioned in section 270(2), whether the distribution would contravene the relevant section; and, without prejudice to the foregoing—

    (a) so much of the accounts as consists of a balance sheet must give a true and fair view of the state of the company's affairs as at the balance sheet date, and

    (b) so much of the accounts as consists of a profit and loss account must give a true and fair view of the company's profit or loss for the period in respect of which the accounts were prepared.

271(3) **[Auditors must have made report]** The auditors must have made their report on the accounts under section 235; and the following subsection applies if the report is a qualified report, that is to say, it is not a report without qualification to the effect that in the auditors' opinion the accounts have been properly prepared in accordance with this Act.

History
In s. 271(3) the words "section 235" substituted for the former words "section 236" by CA 1989, s. 23 and Sch. 10, para. 4 as from 1 April 1990 subject to transitional and saving provisions (see S.I. 1990 No. 355 (C. 13), art. 3, Sch. 1 and also art. 6–9).

271(4) **[Statement if qualified auditors' report]** The auditors must in that case also have stated in writing (either at the time of their report or subsequently) whether, in their opinion, the matter in respect of which their report is qualified is material for determining, by reference to items mentioned in section 270(2), whether the distribution would contravene the relevant section; and a copy of the statement must have been laid before the company in general meeting.

271(5) **[Sec. 271(4) statement]** A statement under subsection (4) suffices for purposes of a particular distribution not only if it relates to a distribution which has been proposed but also if it relates to distributions of any description which includes that particular distribution, notwithstanding that at the time of the statement it has not been proposed.

SEC. 272 Requirements for interim accounts

272(1) **[Statutory requirements]** The following are the statutory requirements in respect of interim accounts prepared for a proposed distribution by a public company.

272(2) **[Accounts to have been properly prepared]** The accounts must have been properly prepared, or have been so prepared subject only to matters which are not material for determining, by reference to items mentioned in section 270(2), whether the proposed distribution would contravene the relevant section.

272(3) **["Properly prepared"]** "Properly prepared" means that the accounts must comply with section 226 (applying that section and Schedule 4 with such modifications as are necessary because the accounts are prepared otherwise than in respect of an accounting reference period) and any balance sheet comprised in the accounts must have been signed in accordance with section 233; and, without prejudice to the foregoing—

(a) so much of the accounts as consists of a balance sheet must give a true and fair view of the state of the company's affairs as at the balance sheet date, and

(b) so much of the accounts as consists of a profit and loss account must give a true and fair view of the company's profit or loss for the period in respect of which the accounts were prepared.

History
In s. 272(3) the words "section 226" and "section 233" substituted for the former words "section 228" and "section 238" respectively by CA 1989, s. 23 and Sch. 10, para. 5 as from 1 April 1990 subject to transitional and saving provisions (see S.I. 1990 No. 355 (C. 13), art. 3, Sch. 1 and also art. 6–9).

272(4) [Copy of accounts to registrar]   A copy of the accounts must have been delivered to the registrar of companies.

272(5) [Certified translation of accounts etc.]   If the accounts are in a language other than English and the second sentence of section 242(1) (translation) does not apply, a translation into English of the accounts, certified in the prescribed manner to be a correct translation, must also have been delivered to the registrar.

History
In s. 272(5) the words "the second sentence of section 242(1)" substituted for the former words "section 241(3)(b)" by CA 1989, s. 23 and Sch. 10, para. 6 as from 1 April 1990 subject to transitional and saving provisions (see S.I. 1990 No. 355 (C. 13), art. 3, Sch. 1 and also art. 6–9).

SEC. 273   Requirements for initial accounts

273(1) [Statutory requirements]   The following are the statutory requirements in respect of initial accounts prepared for a proposed distribution by a public company.

273(2) [Accounts to have been properly prepared]   The accounts must have been properly prepared, or they must have been so prepared subject only to matters which are not material for determining, by reference to items mentioned in section 270(2), whether the proposed distribution would contravene the relevant section.

273(3) ["Properly prepared"]   Section 272(3) applies as respects the meaning of "properly prepared".

273(4) [Auditors must have made report]   The company's auditors must have made a report stating whether in their opinion the accounts have been properly prepared; and the following subsection applies if their report is a qualified report, that is to say it is not a report without qualification to the effect that in the auditors' opinion the accounts have been so prepared.

273(5) [Statement if qualified report]   The auditors must in that case also have stated in writing whether, in their opinion, the matter in respect of which their report is qualified is material for determining, by reference to items mentioned in section 270(2), whether the distribution would contravene the relevant section.

273(6) [Copies of accounts, auditors report, statement to registrar]   A copy of the accounts, of the auditors' report under subsection (4) and of the auditors' statement (if any) under subsection (5) must have been delivered to the registrar of companies.

273(7) [Certified translation of accounts etc.]   If the accounts are, or the auditors' report under subsection (4) or their statement (if any) under subsection (5) is, in a language other than English and the second sentence of section 242(1) (translation) does not apply, a translation into English of the accounts, the report or the statement (as the case may be), certified in the prescribed manner to be a correct translation, must also have been delivered to the registrar.

History
In s. 273(7) the words "the second sentence of section 242(1)" substituted for the former words "section 241(3)(b)" by CA 1989, s. 23 and Sch. 10, para. 6 as from 1 April 1990

subject to transitional and saving provisions (see S.I. 1990 No. 355 (C. 13), art. 3, Sch. 1 and also art. 6–9).

SEC. 274   Method of applying sec. 270 to successive distributions

274(1)   **[Effect of sec. 270]**   For the purpose of determining by reference to particular accounts whether a proposed distribution may be made by a company, section 270 has effect, in a case where one or more distributions have already been made in pursuance of determinations made by reference to those same accounts, as if the amount of the proposed distribution was increased by the amount of the distributions so made.

274(2)   **[Application of sec. 274(1)]**   Subsection (1) of this section applies (if it would not otherwise do so) to—

(a)   financial assistance lawfully given by a public company out of its distributable profits in a case where the assistance is required to be so given by section 154,

(b)   financial assistance lawfully given by a private company out of its distributable profits in a case where the assistance is required to be so given by section 155(2),

(c)   financial assistance given by a company in contravention of section 151, in a case where the giving of that assistance reduces the company's net assets or increases its net liabilities,

(d)   a payment made by a company in respect of the purchase by it of shares in the company (except a payment lawfully made otherwise than out of distributable profits), and

(e)   a payment of any description specified in section 168 (company's purchase of right to acquire its own shares, etc.),

being financial assistance given or payment made since the relevant accounts were prepared, as if any such financial assistance or payment were a distribution already made in pursuance of a determination made by reference to those accounts.

274(3)   **[Definitions]**   In this section the following definitions apply—

"**financial assistance**" means the same as in Chapter VI of Part V;

"**net assets**" has the meaning given by section 154(2)(a); and

"**net liabilities**", in relation to the giving of financial assistance by a company, means the amount by which the aggregate amount of the company's liabilities (within the meaning of section 154(2)(b)) exceeds the aggregate amount of its assets, taking the amount of the assets and liabilities to be as stated in the company's accounting records immediately before the financial assistance is given.

274(4)   **[Regulations]**   Subsections (2) and (3) of this section are deemed to be included in Chapter VII of Part V for purposes of the Secretary of State's power to make regulations under section 179.

SEC. 275 Treatment of assets in the relevant accounts

275(1)   [Certain provisions treated as realised loss]   For purposes of sections 263 and 264, a provision of any kind mentioned in paragraphs 88 and 89 of Schedule 4, other than one in respect of a diminution in value of a fixed asset appearing on a revaluation of all the fixed assets of the company, or of all of its fixed assets other than goodwill, is treated as a realised loss.

275(2)   [Realised profit on revaluation]   If, on the revaluation of a fixed asset, an unrealised profit is shown to have been made and, on or after the revaluation, a sum is written off or retained for depreciation of that asset over a period, then an amount equal to the amount by which that sum exceeds the sum which would have been so written off or retained for the depreciation of that asset over that period, if that profit had not been made, is treated for purposes of sections 263 and 264 as a realised profit made over that period.

275(3)   [Where no record of original cost of asset]   Where there is no record of the original cost of an asset, or a record cannot be obtained without unreasonable expense or delay, then for the purpose of determining whether the company has made a profit or loss in respect of that asset, its cost is taken to the value ascribed to it in the earliest available record of its value made on or after its acquisition by the company.

275(4)   [Consideration by directors of value of fixed asset]   Subject to subsection (6), any consideration by the directors of the value at a particular time of a fixed asset is treated as a revaluation of the asset for the purposes of determining whether any such revaluation of the company's fixed assets as is required for purposes of the exception from subsection (1) has taken place at that time.

275(5)   [Application of sec. 275(4) exception]   But where any such assets which have not actually been revalued are treated as revalued for those purposes under subsection (4), that exception applies only if the directors are satisfied that their aggregate value at that time in question is not less than the aggregate amount at which they are for the time being stated in the company's accounts.

275(6)   [Non-application of sec. 275(4), (5)]   Where section 271(2), 272(2) or 273(2) applies to the relevant accounts, subsections (4) and (5) above do not apply for the purpose of determining whether a revaluation of the company's fixed assets affecting the amount of the relevant items (that is, the items mentioned in section 270(2)) as stated in those accounts has taken place, unless it is stated in a note to the accounts—

(a) that the directors have considered the value at any time of any fixed assets of the company, without actually revaluing those assets,

(b) that they are satisfied that the aggregate value of those assets at the time in question is or was not less than the aggregate amount at which they are or were for the time being stated in the company's accounts, and

(c) that the relevant items in question are accordingly stated in the relevant accounts on the basis that a revaluation of the company's fixed assets which by virtue of subsections (4) and (5) included the assets in question took place at that time.

SEC. 276 Distributions in kind

276   Where a company makes a distribution of or including a non-cash asset, and any part of the amount at which that asset is stated in the accounts relevant for the purposes of the distribution in accordance with sections 270 to 275 represents an unrealised profit, that profit is to be treated as a realised profit—

    (a) for the purpose of determining the lawfulness of the distribution in accordance with this Part (whether before or after the distribution takes place), and

    (b) for the purpose of the application of paragraphs 12(a) and 34(3)(a) of Schedule 4 (only realised profits to be included in or transferred to the profit and loss account) in relation to anything done with a view to or in connection with the making of that distribution.

History
In s. 276(b) "34(3)(a)" substituted for the former "34(4)(b)" by CA 1989, s. 23 and Sch. 10, para. 7 as from 1 April 1990   subject to transitional and saving provisions (see S.I. 1990 No. 355 (C. 13), art. 3, Sch. 1 and also art. 6–9).

SUPPLEMENTARY

SEC. 277   Consequences of unlawful distribution

277(1)   **[Penalty etc.]**   Where a distribution, or part of one, made by a company to one of its members is made in contravention of this Part and, at the time of the distribution, he knows or has reasonable grounds for believing that it is so made, he is liable to repay it (or that part of it, as the case may be) to the company or (in the case of a distribution made otherwise than in cash) to pay the company a sum equal to the value of the distribution (or part) at that time.

277(2)   **[Without prejudice to general repayment obligation]**   The above is without prejudice to any obligation imposed apart from this section on a member of a company to repay a distribution unlawfully made to him; but this section does not apply in relation to—

    (a) financial assistance given by a company in contravention of section 151, or

    (b) any payment made by a company in respect of the redemption or purchase by the company of shares in itself.

277(3)   Subsection (2) of this section is deemed included in Chapter VII of Part V for purposes of the Secretary of State's power to make regulations under section 179.

SEC. 278   Saving for provision in articles operative before Act of 1980

278   Where immediately before 22nd December 1980 a company was authorised by a provision of its articles to apply its unrealised profits in paying up in full or in part unissued shares to be allotted to members of the company as fully or partly paid bonus shares, that provision continues (subject to any alteration of the articles) as authority for those profits to be so applied after that date.

SEC. 279   Distributions by banking or insurance companies

279   Where a company's accounts relevant for the purposes of this Part are prepared in accordance with the special provisions of Part VII relating to banking or insurance companies, sections 264 to 275 apply with the modifications shown in Schedule 11.

History
S. 279 substituted by CA 1989, s. 23 and Sch. 10, para. 8 as from 1 April 1990 subject to transitional and saving provisions (see S.I. 1990 No. 355 (C. 13), art. 3, Sch. 1 and also art. 6–9); s. 279 formerly read as follows:

"**SEC. 279 Distributions by special category companies**
279 Where a company's accounts relevant for the purposes of this Part are special category, sections 265 to 275 apply with the modifications shown in Schedule 11."

SEC. 280   Definitions for Part VIII

280(1) [Interpretation] The following has effect for the interpretation of this Part.

280(2) ["Capitalisation"] **"Capitalisation"**, in relation to a company's profits, means any of the following operations (whenever carried out)—

    (a) applying the profits in wholly or partly paying up unissued shares in the company to be allotted to members of the company as fully or partly paid bonus shares, or

    (b) transferring the profits to capital redemption reserve.

280(3) [References to profits and losses etc.] References to profits and losses of any description are (respectively) to profits and losses of that description made at any time and, except where the context otherwise requires, are (respectively) to revenue and capital profits and revenue and capital losses.

SEC. 281   Saving for other restraints on distribution

281 The provisions of this Part are without prejudice to any enactment or rule of law, or any provision of a company's memorandum or articles, restricting the sums out of which, or the cases in which, a distribution may be made.

PART IX — A COMPANY'S MANAGEMENT; DIRECTORS AND SECRETARIES; THEIR QUALIFICATIONS, DUTIES AND RESPONSIBILITIES

OFFICERS AND REGISTERED OFFICE

SEC. 282   Directors

282(1) [Public company on or after 1 November 1929] Every company registered on or after 1st November 1929 (other than a private company) shall have at least two directors.

282(2) [Public company before 1 November 1929] Every company registered before that date (other than a private company) shall have at least one director.

282(3) [Private company] Every private company shall have at least one director.

SEC. 283   Secretary

283(1) [Obligation] Every company shall have a secretary.

283(2) [Not sole director] A sole director shall not also be secretary.

283(3) [If office vacant] Anything required or authorised to be done by or to the secretary may, if the office is vacant or there is for any other reason no secretary capable of acting, be done by or to any assistant or deputy secretary or, if there is no assistant or deputy secretary capable of acting, by or to any officer of the company authorised generally or specially in that behalf by the directors.

283(4)   [Certain persons not to be sole director or secretary]   No company shall—

  (a) have as secretary to the company a corporation the sole director of which is a sole director of the company;

  (b) have as sole director of the company a corporation the sole director of which is secretary to the company.

SEC. 284   Acts done by person in dual capacity

284   A provision requiring or authorising a thing to be done by or to a director and the secretary is not satisfied by its being done by or to the same person acting both as director and as, or in place of, the secretary.

SEC. 285   Validity of acts of directors

285   The acts of a director or manager are valid notwithstanding any defect that may afterwards be discovered in his appointment or qualification; and this provision is not excluded by section 292(2) (void resolution to appoint).

SEC. 286   Qualifications of company secretaries

286(1)   [Duty of directors to secure appropriate secretary]   It is the duty of the directors of a public company to take all reasonable steps to secure that the secretary (or each joint secretary) of the company is a person who appears to them to have the requisite knowledge and experience to discharge the functions of secretary of the company and who—

  (a) on 22nd December 1980 held the office of secretary or assistant or deputy secretary of the company; or

  (b) for at least 3 of the 5 years immediately preceding his appointment as secretary held the office of secretary of a company other than a private company; or

  (c) is a member of any of the bodies specified in the following subsection; or

  (d) is a barrister, advocate or solicitor called or admitted in any part of the United Kingdom; or

  (e) is a person who, by virtue of his holding or having held any other position or his being a member of any other body, appears to the directors to be capable of discharging those functions.

286(2)   [Bodies specified in sec. 286(1)(c)]   The bodies referred to in subsection (1)(c) are—

  (a) the Institute of Chartered Accountants in England and Wales;

  (b) the Institute of Chartered Accountants of Scotland;

  (c) the Chartered Association of Certified Accountants;

  (d) the Institute of Chartered Accountants in Ireland;

  (e) the Institute of Chartered Secretaries and Administrators;

(f) the Institute of Cost and Management Accountants;

(g) the Chartered Institute of Public Finance and Accountancy.

SEC. 287   Registered office

287(1)   [Duty to have registered office]   A company shall at all times have a registered office to which all communications and notices may be addressed.

287(2)   [Situation on incorporation]   On incorporation the situation of the company's registered office is that specified in the statement sent to the registrar under section 10.

287(3)   [Change of registered office]   The company may change the situation of its registered office from time to time by giving notice in the prescribed form to the registrar.

287(4)   [Effective date of change]   The change takes effect upon the notice being registered by the registrar, but until the end of the period of 14 days beginning with the date on which it is registered a person may validly serve any document on the company at its previous registered office.

287(5)   [Date of change re company's duties]   For the purposes of any duty of a company—

(a) to keep at its registered office, or make available for public inspection there, any register, index or other document, or

(b) to mention the address of its registered office in any document,

a company which has given notice to the registrar of a change in the situation of its registered office may act on the change as from such date, not more than 14 days after the notice is given, as it may determine.

287(6)   [Where no failure to comply with sec. 287(5) duty]   Where a company unavoidably ceases to perform at its registered office any such duty as is mentioned in subsection (5)(a) in circumstances in which it was not practicable to give prior notice to the registrar of a change in the situation of its registered office, but—

(a) resumes performance of that duty at other premises as soon as practicable, and

(b) gives notice accordingly to the registrar of a change in the situation of its registered office within 14 days of doing so,

it shall not be treated as having failed to comply with that duty.

287(7)   [Onus in proceedings for failure to comply]   In proceedings for an offence of failing to comply with any such duty as is mentioned in subsection (5), it is for the person charged to show that by reason of the matters referred to in that subsection or subsection (6) no offence was committed.

History

S. 287 substituted by CA 1989, s. 136 as from 1 April 1990 subject to a transitional and saving provision (see S.I. 1990 No. 355 (C. 13), art. 4(d) and also art. 12); s. 287 formerly read as follows:

"SEC. 287   Registered office

287(1) A company shall at all times have a registered office to which all communications and notices may be addressed.

(2) Notice (in the prescribed form) of any change in the situation of a company's registered office shall be given within 14 days of the change to the registrar of companies, who shall record the new situation.

(3) If default is made in complying with subsection (1) or (2), the company and every officer of it who is in default is liable to a fine and, for continued contravention, to a daily default fine."

CA 1985, sec. 287(1)   [The next page is 14,401]

CCH Editions Limited
BCL BCL6$$$34A

SEC. 288 Register of directors and secretaries

288(1) [Obligation to keep register] Every company shall keep at its registered office a register of its directors and secretaries; and the register shall, with respect to the particulars to be contained in it of those persons, comply with sections 289 and 290 below.

288(2) [Notification of change etc. to registrar] The company shall, within the period of 14 days from the occurrence of—

(a) any change among its directors or in its secretary, or

(b) any change in the particulars contained in the register,

send to the registrar of companies a notification in the prescribed form of the change and of the date on which it occurred; and a notification of a person having become a director or secretary, or one of joint secretaries, of the company shall contain a consent, signed by that person, to act in the relevant capacity.

288(3) [Inspection of register] The register shall during business hours (subject to such reasonable restrictions as the company may by its articles or in general meeting impose, so that not less than 2 hours in each day be allowed for inspection) be open to the inspection of any member of the company without charge and of any other person on payment of 5 pence or such less sum as the company may prescribe, for each inspection.

288(4) [Penalty for refusal of inspection] If an inspection required under this section is refused, or if default is made in complying with subsection (1) or (2), the company and every officer of it who is in default is liable to a fine and, for continued contravention, to a daily default fine.

288(5) [Compelling inspection] In the case of a refusal of inspection of the register, the court may by order compel an immediate inspection of it.

288(6) [Shadow director] For purposes of this and the next section, a shadow director of a company is deemed a director and officer of it.

SEC. 289 Particulars of directors to be registered under sec. 288

289(1) [Particulars] Subject to the provisions of this section, the register kept by a company under section 288 shall contain the following particulars with respect to each director—

(a) in the case of an individual—

(i) his present Christian name and surname,

(ii) any former Christian name or surname,

(iii) his usual residential address,

(iv) his nationality,

(v) his business occupation (if any),

(vi) particulars of any other directorships held by him or which have been held by him, and

(vii) in the case of a company subject to section 293 (age-limit), the date of his birth;

   (b) in the case of a corporation, its corporate name and registered or principal office.

289(2) **[Interpretation of sec. 289(1)]** In subsection (1)—

   (a) **"Christian name"** includes a forename,

   (b) **"surname"**, in the case of a peer or a person usually known by a title different from his surname, means that title, and

   (c) the reference to a former Christian name or surname does not include—

     (i) in the case of a peer or a person usually known by a British title different from his surname, the name by which he was known previous to the adoption of or succession to the title, or

    (ii) in the case of any person, a former Christian name or surname where that name or surname was changed or disused before the person bearing the name attained the age of 18, or has been changed or disused for a period of not less than 20 years, or

   (iii) in the case of a married woman, the name or surname by which she was known previous to the marriage.

289(3) **[Particulars not required to be registered]** It is not necessary for the register to contain on any day particulars of a directorship—

   (a) which has not been held by a director at any time during the 5 years preceding that day,

   (b) which is held by a director in a company which—

     (i) is dormant or grouped with the company keeping the register, and

    (ii) if he also held that directorship for any period during those 5 years, was for the whole of that period either dormant or so grouped,

   (c) which was held by a director for any period during those 5 years in a company which for the whole of that period was either dormant or grouped with the company keeping the register.

289(4) **["Company" in sec. 289(3)]** For purposes of subsection (3), **"company"** includes any body corporate incorporated in Great Britain; and—

   (a) section 250(3) applies as regards whether and when a company is or has been dormant, and

   (b) a company is to be regarded as being, or having been, grouped with another at any time if at that time it is or was a company of which the other is or was a wholly-owned subsidiary, or if it is or was a wholly-owned subsidiary of the other or of another company of which that other is or was a wholly-owned subsidiary.

History

In s. 289(4) the words "section 250(3)" substituted for the former words "section 252(5)" by CA 1989, s. 23 and Sch. 10, para. 9 as from 1 April 1990 subject to transitional and saving provisions (see S.I. 1990 No. 355 (C. 13), art. 3, Sch. I and also art. 6–9).

SEC. 290   Particulars of secretaries to be registered under sec. 288

290(1) **[Particulars]** The register to be kept by a company under section 288 shall contain the following particulars with respect to the secretary or, where there are joint secretaries, with respect to each of them—

(a) in the case of an individual, his present Christian name and surname, any former Christian name or surname and his usual residential address, and

(b) in the case of a corporation or a Scottish firm, its corporate or firm name and registered or principal office.

290(2) **[Partners joint secretaries]** Where all the partners in a firm are joint secretaries, the name and principal office of the firm may be stated instead of the particulars specified above.

290(3) **[Interpretation]** Section 289(2) applies as regards the meaning of "**Christian name**", "**surname**" and "**former Christian name or surname**".

PROVISIONS GOVERNING APPOINTMENT OF DIRECTORS

SEC. 291 Share qualification of directors

291(1) **[Director to obtain required share qualification]** It is the duty of every director who is by the company's articles required to hold a specified share qualification, and who is not already qualified, to obtain his qualification within 2 months after his appointment, or such shorter time as may be fixed by the articles.

291(2) **[Bearer of share warrant not holder of shares]** For the purpose of any provision of the articles requiring a director or manager to hold any specified share qualification, the bearer of a share warrant is not deemed the holder of the shares specified in the warrant.

291(3) **[Vacation of office of director]** The office of director of a company is vacated if the director does not within 2 months from the date of his appointment (or within such shorter time as may be fixed by the articles) obtain his qualification, or if after the expiration of that period or shorter time he ceases at any time to hold his qualification.

291(4) **[No re-appointment unless has share qualification]** A person vacating office under this section is incapable of being reappointed to be a director of the company until he has obtained his qualification.

291(5) **[Penalty]** If after the expiration of that period or shorter time any unqualified person acts as a director of the company, he is liable to a fine and, for continued contravention, to a daily default fine.

SEC. 292 Appointment of directors to be voted on individually

292(1) **[Directors appointed by single resolution]** At a general meeting of a public company, a motion for the appointment of two or more persons as directors of the company by a single resolution shall not be made, unless a resolution that it shall be so made has first been agreed to by the meeting without any vote being given against it.

292(2) **[Resolution in contravention of sec. 292]** A resolution moved in contravention of this section is void, whether or not its being so moved was objected to at the time; but where a resolution so moved is passed, no provision for the automatic reappointment of retiring directors in default of another appointment applies.

292(3) **[Interpretation]** For purposes of this section, a motion for approving a person's appointment, or for nominating a person for appointment, is to be treated as a motion for his appointment.

292(4)   [Non-application of section]   Nothing in this section applies to a resolution altering the company's articles.

SEC. 293   Age limit for directors

293(1)   [Application]   A company is subject to this section if—

(a) it is a public company, or

(b) being a private company, it is a subsidiary of a public company or of a body corporate registered under the law relating to companies for the time being in force in Northern Ireland as a public company.

293(2)   [Age limit of 70]   No person is capable of being appointed a director of a company which is subject to this section if at the time of his appointment he has attained the age of 70.

293(3)   [Vacation of office at next annual general meeting after turning 70]   A director of such a company shall vacate his office at the conclusion of the annual general meeting commencing next after he attains the age of 70; but acts done by a person as director are valid notwithstanding that it is afterwards discovered that his appointment had terminated under this subsection.

293(4)   [Vacancy of retiring director under sec. 293(3) may be filled casually]   Where a person retires under subsection (3), no provision for the automatic reappointment of retiring directors in default of another appointment applies; and if at the meeting at which he retires the vacancy is not filled, it may be filled as a casual vacancy.

293(5)   [No age limit if approval by general meeting etc.]   Nothing in subsections (2) to (4) prevents the appointment of a director at any age, or requires a director to retire at any time, if his appointment is or was made or approved by the company in general meeting; but special notice is required of a resolution appointing or approving the appointment of a director for it to have effect under this subsection, and the notice of the resolution given to the company, and by the company to its members, must state, or have stated, the age of the person to whom it relates.

293(6)   [Commencement of re-appointed director]   A person reappointed director on retiring under subsection (3), or appointed in place of a director so retiring, is to be treated, for the purpose of determining the time at which he or any other director is to retire, as if he had become director on the day on which the retiring director was last appointed before his retirement.

Subject to this, the retirement of a director out of turn under subsection (3) is to be disregarded in determining when any other directors are to retire.

293(7)   [Extent of effect of section]   In the case of a company first registered after the beginning of 1947, this section has effect subject to the provisions of the company's articles; and in the case of a company first registered before the beginning of that year—

(a) this section has effect subject to any alterations of the company's articles made after the beginning of that year; and

(b) if at the beginning of that year the company's articles contained provision for retirement of directors under an age limit, or for preventing or restricting appointments of directors over a given age, this section does not apply to directors to whom that provision applies.

SEC. 294 Duty of director to disclose his age

294(1) **[Notice of age]** A person who is appointed or to his knowledge proposed to be appointed director of a company subject to section 293 at a time when he has attained any retiring age applicable to him under that section or under the company's articles shall give notice of his age to the company.

294(2) **[Companies deemed subject to sec. 293]** For purposes of this section, a company is deemed subject to section 293 notwithstanding that all or any of the section's provisions are excluded or modified by the company's articles.

294(3) **[Non-application of sec. 294(1)]** Subsection (1) does not apply in relation to a person's reappointment on the termination of a previous appointment as director of the company.

294(4) **[Penalty]** A person who—

(a) fails to give notice of his age as required by this section; or

(b) acts as director under any appointment which is invalid or has terminated by reason of his age,

is liable to a fine and, for continued contravention, to a daily default fine.

294(5) **[Interpretation of sec. 294(4)]** For purposes of subsection (4), a person who has acted as director under an appointment which is invalid or has terminated is deemed to have continued so to act throughout the period from the invalid appointment or the date on which the appointment terminated (as the case may be), until the last day on which he is shown to have acted thereunder.

DISQUALIFICATION

295–299 (Repealed by Company Directors Disqualification Act 1986, sec. 23(2) and Sch. 4 as from 29 December 1986.)

History
In regard to the date of the above repeal, see Company Directors Disqualification Act 1986, s. 25, Insolvency Act 1986, s. 443 and S.I. 1986 No. 1924 (C. 71). S. 295 had previously been amended by Insolvency Act 1985, s. 109 and Sch. 6, para. 1 as from 28 April 1986: see S.I. 1986 No. 463 (C. 14). S. 295–299 (including these Insolvency Act 1985 amendments) formerly read as follows:

"**SEC. 295 Disqualification orders: introductory**

295(1) In the circumstances specified in sections 296 to 299, a court may make against a person a disqualification order, that is to say an order that he shall not, without leave of the court—

(a) be a director of a company, or

(b) be a liquidator or administrator of a company, or

(c) be a receiver or manager of a company's property, or

(d) in any way, whether directly or indirectly, be concerned or take part in the promotion, formation or management of a company,

for a specified period beginning with the date of the order.

(2) The maximum period to be so specified is—

(a) in the case of an order made under section 297 or made by a court of summary jurisdiction, 5 years, and

(b) in any other case, 15 years; and where a disqualification order is made against a person who is already subject to such an order the periods specified in those orders shall run concurrently.

(3) In this section and sections 296 to 299, '**company**' includes any company which may be wound up under Part XXI.

(4) A disqualification order may be made on grounds which are or include matters other than criminal convictions, notwithstanding that the person in respect of whom it is to be made may be criminally liable in respect of those matters.

(5) In sections 296 to 299, any reference to provisions, or to a particular provision, of this Act or the Consequential Provisions Act includes the corresponding provision or provisions of the former Companies Acts.

(6) Part I of Schedule 12 has effect with regard to the procedure for obtaining a disqualification order, and to applications for leave under such an order; and Part III of that Schedule has effect—

(a) in connection with certain transitional cases arising under sections 93 and 94 of the Companies Act 1981, so as to limit the power to make a disqualification order, or to restrict the duration of an order, by reference to events occurring or things done before those sections came into force, and

(b) to preserve orders made under section 28 of the Companies Act 1976 (repealed by the Act of 1981).

(7) If a person acts in contravention of a disqualification order, he is in respect of each offence liable to imprisonment or a fine, or both.

SEC. 296 Disqualification on conviction of indictable offence

296(1) The court may make a disqualification order against a person where he is convicted of an indictable offence (whether on indictment or summarily) in connection with the promotion, formation, management or liquidation of a company, or with the receivership or management of a company's property.

(2) **'The court'** for this purpose means—

(a) any court having jurisdiction to wind up the company in relation to which the offence was committed, or

(b) the court by or before which the person is convicted of the offence, or

(c) in the case of a summary conviction in England and Wales, any other magistrates' court acting for the same petty sessions area;

and for purposes of this section the definition of **'indictable offence'** in Schedule 1 to the Interpretation Act 1978 applies in relation to Scotland as it does in relation to England and Wales.

SEC. 297   Disqualification for persistent default under Companies Acts

297(1) The court may make a disqualification order against a person where it appears to it that he has been persistently in default in relation to provisions of this Act or the Consequential Provisions Act requiring any return, account or other document to be filed with, delivered or sent, or notice of any matter to be given, to the registrar of companies.

(2) On an application to the court for an order to be made under this section, the fact that a person has been persistently in default in relation to such provisions as are mentioned above may (without prejudice to its proof in any other manner) be conclusively proved by showing that in the 5 years ending with the date of the application he has been adjudged guilty (whether or not on the same occasion) of three or more defaults in relation to those provisions.

(3) A person is treated under subsection (2) as being adjudged guilty of a default in relation to any such provision if—

(a) he is convicted (whether on indictment or summarily) of an offence consisting in a contravention of or failure to comply with that provision (whether on his own part or on the part of any company), or

(b) a default order is made against him, that is to say an order under—

(i) section 244 (order requiring delivery of company accounts), or

(ii) section 499 (enforcement of receiver's or manager's duty to make returns), or

(iii) section 636 (corresponding provision for liquidator in winding-up), or

(iv) section 713 (enforcement of company's duty to make returns),

in respect of any such contravention of or failure

to comply with that provision (whether on his own part or on the part of any company).

(4) In this section **'the court'** means any court having jurisdiction to wind up any of the companies in relation to which the offence or other default has been or is alleged to have been committed.

SEC. 298   Disqualification for fraud, etc. in winding-up

298(1) The court may make a disqualification order against a person if, in the course of the winding-up of a company, it appears that he—

(a) has been guilty of an offence for which he is liable (whether he has been convicted or not) under section 458 (fraudulent trading), or

(b) has otherwise been guilty, while an officer or liquidator of the company or receiver or manager of its property, of any fraud in relation to the company or of any breach of his duty as such officer, liquidator, receiver or manager.

(2) In this section **'the court'** means the same as in section 297; and **'officer'** includes a shadow director.

SEC. 299   Disqualification on summary conviction

299(1) An offence counting for the purposes of this section is one of which a person is convicted (either on indictment or summarily) in consequence of a contravention of, or failure to comply with, any provision of this Act or the Consequential Provisions Act requiring a return, account or other document to be filed with, delivered or sent, or notice of any matter to be given, to the registrar of companies (whether the contravention or failure is on the person's own part or on the part of any company).

(2) Where a person is convicted of a summary offence counting for those purposes, the court by which he is convicted (or, in England and Wales, any other magistrates' court acting for the same petty sessions area) may make a disqualification order against him if the circumstances specified in the next subsection are present.

(3) Those circumstances are that, during the 5 years ending with the date of the conviction, the person has had made against him, or has been convicted of, in total not less than 3 default orders and offences counting for the purposes of this section; and those offences may include that of which he is convicted as mentioned in subsection (2) and any other offence of which he is convicted on the same occasion.

(4) For the purposes of this section—

(a) the definition of **'summary offence'** in Schedule 1 to the Interpretation Act 1978 applies for Scotland as for England and Wales, and

(b) **'default order'** means the same as in section 297(3)(b)."

Note
See table of destinations at p. 58,201, for the corresponding current provisions in the Company Directors Disqualification Act 1986.

SEC. 300   Disqualification by reference to association with insolvent companies

300   (Repealed by Insolvency Act 1985, sec. 235 and Sch. 10, Pt. II as from 28 April 1986.)

History
The above date is referred to in S.I. 1986 No. 463 (C. 14). S. 300 formerly read as follows:

"**300(1)** The court may make a disqualification order against a person where, on an application under this section, it appears to it that he—

(a) is or has been a director of a company which has at any time gone into liquidation (whether while he

was a director or subsequently) and was insolvent at that time, and

(b) is or has been a director of another such company which has gone into liquidation within 5 years of the date on which the first-mentioned company went into liquidation,

CCH Editions Limited
BCL BCL6$$$34B

and that his conduct as director of any of those companies makes him unfit to be concerned in the management of a company.

(2) In the case of a person who is or has been a director of a company which has gone into liquidation as abovementioned and is being wound up by the court, **'the court'** in subsection (1) means the court by which the company is being wound up; and in any other case it means the High Court or, in Scotland, the Court of Session.

(3) The Secretary of State may require the liquidator or former liquidator of a company—

    (a) to furnish him with such information with respect to the company's affairs, and

    (b) to produce and permit inspection of such books or documents of or relevant to the company,

as the Secretary of State may reasonably require for the purpose of determining whether to make an application

under this section in respect of a person who is or has been a director of that company; and if a person makes default in complying with such a requirement, the court may, on the Secretary of State's application, make an order requiring that person to make good the default within such time as may be specified.

(4) For purposes of this section, a shadow director of a company is deemed a director of it; and a company goes into liquidation—

    (a) if it is wound up by the court, on the date of the winding-up order, and

    (b) in any other case, on the date of the passing of the resolution for voluntary winding-up.''

Note
For current provisions see Company Directors Disqualification Act 1986, s. 6–8 and Insolvency Act 1986, s. 214, 215. See also S.I. 1986 No. 463 (C.14).

SEC. 301   Register of disqualification orders

301 (Repealed by Company Directors Disqualification Act 1986, sec. 23(2) and Sch. 4 as from 29 December 1986.)

History
In regard to the date of the above repeal see Company Directors Disqualification Act 1986, s. 25, Insolvency Act 1986, s. 443 and S.I. 1986 No. 1924 (C. 71).

S. 301 (as previously amended by Insolvency Act 1985, s. 109 and Sch. 6, para. 2 as from 28 April 1986: see S.I. 1986 No. 463 (C. 14)) formerly read as follows:

"**301(1)** The Secretary of State may make regulations requiring officers of courts to furnish him with such particulars as the regulations may specify of cases in which—

    (a) a disqualification order is made under any of sections 296 to 299, or

    (b) any action is taken by a court in consequence of which such an order is varied or ceases to be in force, or

    (c) leave is granted by a court for a person subject to such an order to do any thing which otherwise the order prohibits him from doing;

and the regulations may specify the time within which, and the form and manner in which, such particulars are to be furnished.

(2) The Secretary of State shall, from the particulars so furnished, continue to maintain the register of orders, and of cases in which leave has been granted as mentioned in subsection (1)(c), which was set up by him under section 29 of the Companies Act 1976.

(3) When an order of which entry is made in the register ceases to be in force, the Secretary of State shall delete the entry from the register and all particulars relating to it which have been furnished to him under this section.

(4) The register shall be open to inspection on payment of such fee as may be specified by the Secretary of State in regulations.

(5) Regulations under this section shall be made by statutory instrument subject to annulment in pursuance of a resolution of either House of Parliament.''

Note
For current provision, see Company Directors Disqualification Act 1986, s. 18.

SEC. 302   Provision against undischarged bankrupt acting as director etc.

302 (Repealed by Company Directors Disqualification Act 1986, sec. 23(2) and Sch. 4 as from 29 December 1986.)

History
In regard to the date of the above repeal see Company Directors Disqualification Act 1986, s. 25, Insolvency Act 1986, s. 443 and S.I. 1986 No. 1924 (C. 71). Immediately prior to the repeal there was an amendment by Insolvency Act 1985, s. 235 and Sch. 10. S. 302 originally read as follows:

"**302(1)** If any person being an undischarged bankrupt acts as director or liquidator of, or directly or indirectly takes part in or is concerned in the promotion, formation or management of, a company except with the leave of the court, he is liable to imprisonment or a fine, or both.

(2) 'the court' for this purpose is the court by which the person was adjudged bankrupt or, in Scotland, sequestration of his estates was awarded.

(3) In England and Wales, the leave of the court shall not be given unless notice of intention to apply for it has been served on the official receiver in bankruptcy; and it is the latter's duty, if he is of opinion that it is contrary to the public interest that the application should be granted, to attend on the hearing of the application and oppose it.

(4) In this section **'company'** includes an unregistered company and a company incorporated outside Great Britain which has an established place of business in Great Britain.''

Note
For current provisions, see Company Directors Disqualification Act 1986, s. 11, 13, 22(2)(a).

REMOVAL OF DIRECTORS

SEC. 303   Resolution to remove director

303(1)   [Removal by ordinary resolution]   A company may by ordinary resolution remove a director before the expiration of his period of office, notwithstanding anything in its articles or in any agreement between it and him.

303(2)   [Special notice]   Special notice is required of a resolution to remove a director under this section or to appoint somebody instead of a director so removed at the meeting at which he is removed.

303(3)   [Filling of vacancy]   A vacancy created by the removal of a director under this section, if not filled at the meeting at which he is removed, may be filled as a casual vacancy.

303(4)   [Person appointed director in place of removed director]   A person appointed director in place of a person removed under this section is treated, for the purpose of determining the time at which he or any other director is to retire, as if he had become director on the day on which the person in whose place he is appointed was last appointed a director.

303(5)   [Compensation, damages for termination etc.]   This section is not to be taken as depriving a person removed under it of compensation or damages payable to him in respect of the termination of his appointment as director or of any appointment terminating with that as director, or as derogating from any power to remove a director which may exist apart from this section.

SEC. 304   Director's right to protest removal

304(1)   [Copy of removal notice under sec. 303 to director]   On receipt of notice of an intended resolution to remove a director under section 303, the company shall forthwith send a copy of the notice to the director concerned; and he (whether or not a member of the company) is entitled to be heard on the resolution at the meeting.

304(2)   [Company to circulate director's representations]   Where notice is given of an intended resolution to remove a director under that section, and the director concerned makes with respect to it representations in writing to the company (not exceeding a reasonable length) and requests their notification to members of the company, the company shall, unless the representations are received by it too late for it to do so—

(a) in any notice of the resolution given to members of the company state the fact of the representations having been made; and

(b) send a copy of the representations to every member of the company to whom notice of the meeting is sent (whether before or after receipt of the representations by the company).

304(3)   [If representations not sent as in sec. 304(2)]   If a copy of the representations is not sent as required by subsection (2) because received too late or because of the company's default, the director may (without prejudice to his right to be heard orally) require that the representations shall be read out at the meeting.

304(4)   [Exception where court satisfied there is abuse of rights]   But copies of the representations need not be sent out and the representations need not be read out at the meeting if, on the application either of the company or of any other person who claims to be aggrieved, the court is satisfied that the rights conferred by this section are being abused to secure needless publicity for defamatory matter.

304(5) **[Company's costs]** The court may order the company's costs on an application under this section to be paid in whole or in part by the director, notwithstanding that he is not a party to the application.

OTHER PROVISIONS ABOUT DIRECTORS AND OFFICERS

SEC. 305 Directors' names on company correspondence, etc.

305(1) **[Reference to directors]** A company to which this section applies shall not state, in any form, the name of any of its directors (otherwise than in the text or as a signatory) on any business letter on which the company's name appears unless it states on the letter in legible characters the Christian name (or its initials) and surname of every director of the company who is an individual and the corporate name of every corporate director.

305(2) **[Application]** This section applies to—

(a) every company registered under this Act or under the former Companies Acts (except a company registered before 23rd November 1916); and

(b) every company incorporated outside Great Britain which has an established place of business within Great Britain, unless it had established such a place of business before that date.

305(3) **[Penalty on default]** If a company makes default in complying with this section, every officer of the company who is in default is liable for each offence to a fine; and for this purpose, where a corporation is an officer of the company, any officer of the corporation is deemed an officer of the company.

305(4) **[Interpretation]** For purposes of this section—

(a) **"director"** includes shadow director, and **"officer"** is to be construed accordingly;

(b) **"Christian name"** includes a forename;

(c) **"initials"** includes a recognised abbreviation of a Christian name; and

(d) in the case of a peer or a person usually known by a title different from his surname, **"surname"** means that title.

SEC. 306 Limited company may have directors with unlimited liability

306(1) **[Liability of directors etc. may be limited]** In the case of a limited company the liability of the directors or managers, or of the managing director, may, if so provided by the memorandum, be unlimited.

306(2) **[Statement re liability for proposed director etc.]** In the case of a limited company in which the liability of a director or manager is unlimited, the directors and any managers of the company and the member who proposes any person for election or appointment to the office of director or manager, shall add to that proposal a statement that the liability of the person holding that office will be unlimited.

306(3)   [Notice re liability to proposed director]   Before the person accepts the office or acts in it, notice in writing that his liability will be unlimited shall be given to him by the following or one of the following persons, namely—

   (a) the promoters of the company,

   (b) the directors of the company,

   (c) any managers of the company,

   (d) the company secretary.

306(4)   [Penalty on default]   If a director, manager or proposer makes default in adding such a statement, or if a promoter, director, manager or secretary makes default in giving the notice required by subsection (3), then—

   (a) he is liable to a fine, and

   (b) he is also liable for any damage which the person so elected or appointed may sustain from the default;

but the liability of the person elected or appointed is not affected by the default.

SEC. 307   Special resolution making liability of directors unlimited

307(1)   [Special resolution]   A limited company, if so authorised by its articles, may by special resolution alter its memorandum so as to render unlimited the liability of its directors or managers, or of any managing director.

307(2)   [Effect of special resolution]   When such a special resolution is passed, its provisions are as valid as if they had been originally contained in the memorandum.

SEC. 308   Assignment of office by directors

308   If provision is made by a company's articles, or by any agreement entered into between any person and the company, for empowering a director or manager of the company to assign his office as such to another person, any assignment of office made in pursuance of that provision is (notwithstanding anything to the contrary contained in the provision) of no effect unless and until it is approved by a special resolution of the company.

SEC. 309   Directors to have regard to interests of employees

309(1)   [Interests of company's employees in general]   The matters to which the directors of a company are to have regard in the performance of their functions include the interests of the company's employees in general, as well as the interests of its members.

309(2)   [Duty owed to company]   Accordingly, the duty imposed by this section on the directors is owed by them to the company (and the company alone) and is enforceable in the same way as any other fiduciary duty owed to a company by its directors.

309(3)   [Shadow directors]   This section applies to shadow directors as it does to directors.

CCH Editions Limited
BCL BCL6$$$34B

SEC. 310 Provisions exempting officers and auditors from liability

310(1) **[Application]** This section applies to any provision, whether contained in a company's articles or in any contract with the company or otherwise, for exempting any officer of the company or any person (whether an officer or not) employed by the company as auditor from, or indemnifying him against, any liability which by virtue of any rule of law would otherwise attach to him in respect of any negligence, default, breach of duty or breach of trust of which he may be guilty in relation to the company.

310(2) **[Provisions as in sec. 310(1) void]** Except as provided by the following subsection, any such provision is void.

310(3) **[Insurance, indemnity by company]** This section does not prevent a company—

   (a) from purchasing and maintaining for any such officer or auditor insurance against any such liability, or

   (b) from indemnifying any such officer or auditor against any liability incurred by him—

   (i) in defending any proceedings (whether civil or criminal) in which judgment is given in his favour or he is acquitted, or

   (ii) in connection with any application under section 144(3) or (4) (acquisition of shares by innocent nominee) or section 727 (general power to grant relief in case of honest and reasonable conduct) in which relief is granted to him by the court.

History
S. 310(3) substituted by CA 1989, s. 137(1) as from 1 April 1990 (see S.I. 1990 No. 355 (C. 13), art. 4(e)(i)); s. 310(3) formerly read as follows:

"**310(3)** A company may, in pursuance of such a provision, indemnify any such officer or auditor against any liability incurred by him in defending any proceedings (whether civil or criminal) in which judgment is given in his favour or he is acquitted, or in connection with any application under section 144(3) or (4) (acquisition of shares by innocent nominee) or section 727 (director in default, but not dishonest or unreasonable), in which relief is granted to him by the court."

PART X — ENFORCEMENT OF FAIR DEALING BY DIRECTORS

RESTRICTIONS ON DIRECTORS TAKING FINANCIAL ADVANTAGE

SEC. 311 Prohibition on tax-free payments to directors

311(1) **[No tax-free remuneration]** It is not lawful for a company to pay a director remuneration (whether as director or otherwise) free of income tax, or otherwise calculated by reference to or varying with the amount of his income tax, or to or with any rate of income tax.

311(2) **[Effect of certain provisions in articles and contracts]** Any provision contained in a company's articles, or in any contract, or in any resolution of a company or a company's directors, for payment to a director of remuneration as above mentioned has effect as if it provided for payment, as a gross sum subject to income tax, of the net sum for which it actually provides.

SEC. 312   Payment to director for loss of office etc.

312   It is not lawful for a company to make to a director of the company any payment by way of compensation for loss of office, or as consideration for or in connection with his retirement from office, without particulars of the proposed payment (including its amount) being disclosed to members of the company and the proposal being approved by the company.

SEC. 313   Company approval for property transfer

313(1)   **[Disclosure and approval]**   It is not lawful, in connection with the transfer of the whole or any part of the undertaking or property of a company, for any payment to be made to a director of the company by way of compensation for loss of office, or as consideration for or in connection with his retirement from office, unless particulars of the proposed payment (including its amount) have been disclosed to members of the company and the proposal approved by the company.

313(2)   **[Unlawful payment deemed on trust for company]**   Where a payment unlawful under this section is made to a director, the amount received is deemed to be received by him in trust for the company.

SEC. 314   Director's duty of disclosure on takeover, etc.

314(1)   **[Application]**   This section applies where, in connection with the transfer to any persons of all or any of the shares in a company, being a transfer resulting from—

    (a)   an offer made to the general body of shareholders; or

    (b)   an offer made by or on behalf of some other body corporate with a view to the company becoming its subsidiary or a subsidiary of its holding company; or

    (c)   an offer made by or on behalf of an individual with a view to his obtaining the right to exercise or control the exercise of not less than one-third of the voting power at any general meeting of the company; or

    (d)   any other offer which is conditional on acceptance to a given extent,

a payment is to be made to a director of the company by way of compensation for loss of office, or as consideration for or in connection with his retirement from office.

314(2)   **[Director to give full particulars re sec. 314(1) payment in notice of offer]**   It is in those circumstances the director's duty to take all reasonable steps to secure that particulars of the proposed payment (including its amount) are included in or sent with any notice of the offer made for their shares which is given to any shareholders.

314(3)   **[Penalty on default]**   If—

    (a)   the director fails to take those steps, or

    (b)   any person who has been properly required by the director to include those particulars in or send them with the notice required by subsection (2) fails to do so,

he is liable to a fine.

CCH Editions Limited

BCL BCL6$$$34B

SEC. 315   Consequences of non-compliance with sec. 314

315(1)   [Deemed trust for shareholders]   If in the case of any such payment to a director as is mentioned in section 314(1)—

(a) his duty under that section is not complied with, or

(b) the making of the proposed payment is not, before the transfer of any shares in pursuance of the offer, approved by a meeting (summoned for the purpose) of the holders of the shares to which the offer relates and of other holders of shares of the same class as any of those shares,

any sum received by the director on account of the payment is deemed to have been received by him in trust for persons who have sold their shares as a result of the offer made; and the expenses incurred by him in distributing that sum amongst those persons shall be borne by him and not retained out of that sum.

315(2)   [Where shareholders in sec. 315(1)(b) not all members]   Where—

(a) the shareholders referred to in subsection (1)(b) are not all the members of the company, and

(b) no provision is made by the articles for summoning or regulating the meeting referred to in that paragraph,

the provisions of this Act and of the company's articles relating to general meetings of the company apply (for that purpose) to the meeting either without modification or with such modifications as the Secretary of State on the application of any person concerned may direct for the purpose of adapting them to the circumstances of the meeting.

315(3)   [Where no quorum at meeting]   If at a meeting summoned for the purpose of approving any payment as required by subsection (1)(b) a quorum is not present and, after the meeting has been adjourned to a later date, a quorum is again not present, the payment is deemed for the purposes of that subsection to have been approved.

SEC. 316   Provisions supplementing sec. 312 to 315

316(1)   [Payments deemed in trust]   Where in proceedings for the recovery of any payment as having, by virtue of section 313(2) or 315(1) been received by any person in trust, it is shown that—

(a) the payment was made in pursuance of any arrangement entered into as part of the agreement for the transfer in question, or within one year before or two years after that agreement or the offer leading to it; and

(b) the company or any person to whom the transfer was made was privy to that arrangement,

the payment is deemed, except in so far as the contrary is shown, to be one to which the provisions mentioned above in this subsection apply.

316(2)   [Excess consideration]   If in connection with any such transfer as is mentioned in any of sections 313 to 315—

(a) the price to be paid to a director of the company whose office is to be abolished or who is to retire from office for any shares in the company held by him is in excess of the price which could at the time have been obtained by other holders of the like shares; or

(b) any valuable consideration is given to any such director,

the excess or the money value of the consideration (as the case may be) is deemed for the purposes of that section to have been a payment made to him by way of compensation for loss of office or as consideration for or in connection with his retirement from office.

316(3)   [Interpretation]   References in sections 312 to 315 to payments made to a director by way of compensation for loss of office or as consideration for or in connection with his retirement from office, do not include any bona fide payment by way of damages for breach of contract or by way of pension in respect of past services.

"**Pension**" here includes any superannuation allowance, superannuation gratuity or similar payment.

316(4)   [Rules of law re disclosure etc.]   Nothing in sections 313 to 315 prejudices the operation of any rule of law requiring disclosure to be made with respect to such payments as are there mentioned, or with respect to any other like payments made or to be made to a company's directors.

SEC. 317   Directors to disclose interest in contracts

317(1)   [Duty to declare interest at directors' meeting]   It is the duty of a director of a company who is in any way, whether directly or indirectly, interested in a contract or proposed contract with the company to declare the nature of his interest at a meeting of the directors of the company.

317(2)   [Declaration of interest re proposed contract]   In the case of a proposed contract, the declaration shall be made—

(a) at the meeting of the directors at which the question of entering into the contract is first taken into consideration; or

(b) if the director was not at the date of that meeting interested in the proposed contract, at the next meeting of the directors held after he became so interested;

and, in a case where the director becomes interested in a contract after it is made, the declaration shall be made at the first meeting of the directors held after he becomes so interested.

317(3)   [General notice deemed sufficient declaration of interest re contracts]   For purposes of this section, a general notice given to the directors of a company by a director to the effect that—

(a) he is a member of a specified company or firm and is to be regarded as interested in any contract which may, after the date of the notice, be made with that company or firm; or

(b) he is to be regarded as interested in any contract which may after the date of the notice be made with a specified person who is connected with him (within the meaning of section 346 below),

is deemed a sufficient declaration of interest in relation to any such contract.

317(4) **[Requirements for sec. 317(3) notice to be of effect]** However, no such notice is of effect unless either it is given at a meeting of the directors or the director takes reasonable steps to secure that it is brought up and read at the next meeting of the directors after it is given.

317(5) **[Interpretation]** A reference in this section to a contract includes any transaction or arrangement (whether or not constituting a contract) made or entered into on or after 22nd December 1980.

317(6) **[Further interpretation]** For purposes of this section, a transaction or arrangement of a kind described in section 330 (prohibition of loans, quasi-loans etc. to directors) made by a company for a director of the company or a person connected with such a director is treated (if it would not otherwise be so treated, and whether or not it is prohibited by that section) as a transaction or arrangment in which that director is interested.

317(7) **[Penalty on default]** A director who fails to comply with this section is liable to a fine.

317(8) **[Application to shadow director]** This section applies to a shadow director as it applies to a director, except that a shadow director shall declare his interest, not at a meeting of the directors, but by a notice in writing to the directors which is either—

    (a) a specific notice given before the date of the meeting at which, if he had been a director, the declaration would be required by subsection (2) to be made; or

    (b) a notice which under subsection (3) falls to be treated as a sufficient declaration of that interest (or would fall to be so treated apart from subsection (4)).

317(9) **[Rules of law etc.]** Nothing in this section prejudices the operation of any rule of law restricting directors of a company from having an interest in contracts with the company.

SEC. 318 Directors' service contracts to be open to inspection

318(1) **[Particulars of contracts etc. to be kept at appropriate place]** Subject to the following provisions, every company shall keep at an appropriate place—

    (a) in the case of each director whose contract of service with the company is in writing, a copy of that contract;

    (b) in the case of each director whose contract of service with the company is not in writing, a written memorandum setting out its terms; and

    (c) in the case of each director who is employed under a contract of service with a subsidiary of the company, a copy of that contract or, if it is not in writing, a written memorandum setting out its terms.

318(2) **[Copies etc. at same place]** All copies and memoranda kept by a company in pursuance of subsection (1) shall be kept at the same place.

318(3) **[Appropriate places for sec. 318(1)]** The following are appropriate places for the purposes of subsection (1)—

    (a) the company's registered office;

    (b) the place where its register of members is kept (if other than its registered office);

    (c) its principal place of business, provided that is situated in that part of Great Britain in which the company is registered.

318(4)   [Notice to registrar re place under sec. 318(1), changes etc.]   Every company shall send notice in the prescribed form to the registrar of companies of the place where copies and memoranda are kept in compliance with subsection (1), and of any change in that place, save in a case in which they have at all times been kept at the company's registered office.

318(5)   [Where director working outside UK]   Subsection (1) does not apply to a director's contract of service with the company or with a subsidiary of it if that contract required him to work wholly or mainly outside the United Kingdom; but the company shall keep a memorandum—

    (a) in the case of a contract of service with the company, giving the director's name and setting out the provisions of the contract relating to its duration;

    (b) in the case of a contract of service with a subsidiary, giving the director's name and the name and place of incorporation of the subsidiary, and setting out the provisions of the contract relating to its duration,

at the same place as copies and memoranda are kept by the company in pursuance of subsection (1).

318(6)   [Shadow director]   A shadow director is treated for purposes of this section as a director.

318(7)   [Inspection]   Every copy and memorandum required by subsection (1) or (5) to be kept shall, during business hours (subject to such reasonable restrictions as the company may in general meeting impose, so that not less than 2 hours in each day be allowed for inspection), be open to inspection of any member of the company without charge.

318(8)   [Offence, penalty]   If—

    (a) default is made in complying with subsection (1) or (5), or

    (b) an inspection required under subsection (7) is refused, or

    (c) default is made for 14 days in complying with subsection (4),

the company and every officer of it who is in default is liable to a fine and, for continued contravention, to a daily default fine.

318(9)   [Compelling inspection]   In the case of a refusal of an inspection required under subsection (7) of a copy or memorandum, the court may by order compel an immediate inspection of it.

318(10)   [Variation of director's contract]   Subsections (1) and (5) apply to a variation of a director's contract of service as they apply to the contract.

318(11)   [Exception]   This section does not require that there be kept a copy of, or memorandum setting out the terms of, a contract (or its variation) at a time when the unexpired portion of the term for which the contract is to be in force is less than 12 months, or at a time at which the contract can, within the next ensuing 12 months, be terminated by the company without payment of compensation.

CA 1985, sec. 318(4)   [The next page is 15,201]

SEC. 319 Director's contract of employment for more than 5 years

319(1) **[Application]** This section applies in respect of any term of an agreement whereby a director's employment with the company of which he is a director or, where he is the director of a holding company, his employment within the group is to continue, or may be continued, otherwise than at the instance of the company (whether under the original agreement or under a new agreement entered into in pursuance of it), for a period of more than 5 years during which the employment—

(a) cannot be terminated by the company by notice; or

(b) can be so terminated only in specified circumstances.

319(2) **[Further application]** In any case where—

(a) a person is or is to be employed with a company under an agreement which cannot be terminated by the company by notice or can be so terminated only in specified circumstances; and

(b) more than 6 months before the expiration of the period for which he is or is to be so employed, the company enters into a further agreement (otherwise than in pursuance of a right conferred by or under the original agreement on the other party to it) under which he is to be employed with the company or, where he is a director of a holding company, within the group,

this section applies as if to the period for which he is to be employed under that further agreement there were added a further period equal to the unexpired period of the original agreement.

319(3) **[Approval by general meeting]** A company shall not incorporate in an agreement such a term as is mentioned in subsection (1), unless the term is first approved by a resolution of the company in general meeting and, in the case of a director of a holding company, by a resolution of that company in general meeting.

319(4) **[Bodies corporate covered by section]** No approval is required to be given under this section by any body corporate unless it is a company within the meaning of this Act, or is registered under section 680, or if it is a wholly-owned subsidiary of any body corporate, wherever incorporated.

319(5) **[Memorandum re agreement to be available at meeting]** A resolution of a company approving such a term as is mentioned in subsection (1) shall not be passed at a general meeting of the company unless a written memorandum setting out the proposed agreement incorporating the term is available for inspection by members of the company both—

(a) at the company's registered office for not less than 15 days ending with the date of the meeting; and

(b) at the meeting itself.

319(6) **[Contravening term in agreement void]** A term incorporated in an agreement in contravention of this section is, to the extent that it contravenes the section, void; and that agreement and, in a case where subsection (2) applies, the original agreement are deemed to contain a term entitling the company to terminate it at any time by the giving of reasonable notice.

319(7)   **[Interpretation]**   In this section—

    (a)   **"employment"** includes employment under a contract for services; and

    (b)   **"group"**, in relation to a director of a holding company, means the group which consists of that company and its subsidiaries;

and for purposes of this section a shadow director is treated as a director.

SEC. 320   Substantial property transactions involving directors, etc.

320(1)   **[Prohibition unless approved by general meeting]**   With the exceptions provided by the section next following, a company shall not enter into an arrangement—

    (a)   whereby a director of the company or its holding company, or a person connected with such a director, acquires or is to acquire one or more non-cash assets of the requisite value from the company; or

    (b)   whereby the company acquires or is to acquire one or more non-cash assets of the requisite value from such a director or a person so connected,

unless the arrangement is first approved by a resolution of the company in general meeting and, if the director or connected person is a director of its holding company or a person connected with such a director, by a resolution in general meeting of the holding company.

320(2)   **[Non-cash asset of requisite value in sec. 320(1)]**   For this purpose a non-cash asset is of the requisite value if at the time the arrangement in question is entered into its value is not less than £1,000 but (subject to that) exceeds £50,000 or 10 per cent of the company's asset value, that is—

    (a)   except in a case falling within paragraph (b) below, the value of the company's net assets determined by reference to the accounts prepared and laid under Part VII in respect of the last preceding financial year in respect of which such accounts were so laid; and

    (b)   where no accounts have been so prepared and laid before that time, the amount of the company's called-up share capital.

320(3)   **[Shadow director]**   For purposes of this section and sections 321 and 322, a shadow director is treated as a director.

SEC. 321   Exceptions from sec. 320

321(1)   **[Bodies corporate covered by sec. 320]**   No approval is required to be given under section 320 by any body corporate unless it is a company within the meaning of this Act or registered under section 680 or, if it is a wholly-owned subsidiary of any body corporate, wherever incorporated.

321(2)   **[Exception to sec. 320(1)]**   Section 320(1) does not apply to an arrangement for the acquisition of a non-cash asset—

    (a)   if the asset is to be acquired by a holding company from any of its wholly-owned subsidiaries or from a holding company by any of its wholly-owned subsidiaries, or by one wholly-owned subsidiary of a holding company from another wholly-owned subsidiary of that same holding company, or

(b) if the arrangement is entered into by a company which is being wound up, unless the winding-up is a members' voluntary winding-up.

321(3) **[Exception to sec. 320(1)(a)]** Section 320(1)(a) does not apply to an arrangement whereby a person is to acquire an asset from a company of which he is a member, if the arrangement is made with that person in his character as a member.

321(4) **[Exception to sec. 321(1) re independent brokers]** Section 320(1) does not apply to a transaction on a recognised investment exchange which is effected by a director, or a person connected with him, through the agency of a person who in relation to the transaction acts as an independent broker.

For this purpose an "**independent broker**" means—

(a) in relation to a transaction on behalf of a director, a person who independently of the director selects the person with whom the transaction is to be effected, and

(b) in relation to a transaction on behalf of a person connected with a director, a person who independently of that person or the director selects the person with whom the transaction is to be effected;

and "**recognised**", in relation to an investment exchange, means recognised under the Financial Services Act 1986.

History
S. 321(4) inserted by CA 1989, s. 145 and Sch. 19, para. 8
as from 1 March 1990 (see S.I. 1990 No. 142 (C. 5), art. 5).

SEC. 322   Liabilities arising from contravention of sec. 320

322(1) **[Arrangement in contravention of sec. 320 voidable]** An arrangement entered into by a company in contravention of section 320, and any transaction entered into in pursuance of the arrangement (whether by the company or any other person) is voidable at the instance of the company unless one or more of the conditions specified in the next subsection is satisfied.

322(2) **[Conditions for exemption to sec. 322(1)]** Those conditions are that—

(a) restitution of any money or other asset which is the subject-matter of the arrangement or transaction is no longer possible or the company has been indemnified in pursuance of this section by any other person for the loss or damage suffered by it; or

(b) any rights acquired bona fide for value and without actual notice of the contravention by any person who is not a party to the arrangement or transaction would be afffected by its avoidance; or

(c) the arrangement is, within a reasonable period, affirmed by the company in general meeting and, if it is an arrangement for the transfer of an asset to or by a director of its holding company or a person who is connected with such a director, is so affirmed with the approval of the holding company given by a resolution in general meeting.

322(3) **[Directors liable to account to or indemnify company]** If an arrangement is entered into with a company by a director of the company or its holding company or a person connected with him in contravention of section 320, that director and the person so connected, and any other director of the company who authorised the arrangement or any transaction entered into in pursuance of such an arrangement, is liable—

    (a) to account to the company for any gain which he has made directly or indirectly by the arrangement or transaction, and

    (b) (jointly and severally with any other person liable under this subsection) to indemnify the company for any loss or damage resulting from the arrangement or transaction.

322(4)   [Extent of sec. 322(3)]   Subsection (3) is without prejudice to any liability imposed otherwise than by that subsection, and is subject to the following two subsections; and the liability under subsection (3) arises whether or not the arrangement or transaction entered into has been avoided in pursuance of subsection (1).

322(5)   [Exception to sec. 322(3) — all reasonable steps taken etc.]   If an arrangement is entered into by a company and person connected with a director of the company or its holding company in contravention of section 320, that director is not liable under subsection (3) if he shows that he took all reasonable steps to secure the company's compliance with that section.

322(6)   [Exception to sec. 322(3) — no knowledge]   In any case, a person so connected and any such other director as is mentioned in subsection (3) is not so liable if he shows that, at the time the arrangement was entered into, he did not know the relevant circumstances constituting the contravention.

SHARE DEALINGS BY DIRECTORS AND THEIR FAMILIES

SEC. 323   Prohibition on directors dealing in share options

323(1)   [Offence]   It is an offence for a director of a company to buy—

    (a) a right to call for delivery at a specified price and within a specified time of a specified number of relevant shares or a specified amount of relevant debentures; or

    (b) a right to make delivery at a specified price and within a specified time of a specified number of relevant shares or a specified amount of relevant debentures; or

    (c) a right (as he may elect) to call for delivery at a specified price and within a specified time or to make delivery at a specified price and within a specified time of a specified number of relevant shares or a specified amount of relevant debentures.

323(2)   [Penalty]   A person guilty of an offence under subsection (1) is liable to imprisonment or a fine, or both.

323(3)   [Definitions]   In subsection (1)—

    (a) "relevant shares", in relation to a director of a company, means shares in the company or in any other body corporate, being the company's subsidiary or holding company, or a subsidiary of the company's holding company, being shares as respects which there has been granted a listing on a stock exchange (whether in Great Britain or elsewhere);

(b) **"relevant debentures"**, in relation to a director of a company, means debentures of the company or of any other body corporate, being the company's subsidiary or holding company or a subsidiary of the company's holding company, being debentures as respects which there has been granted such a listing; and

(c) **"price"** includes any consideration other than money.

323(4) **[Shadow director]** This section applies to a shadow director as to a director.

323(5) **[Extent of section]** This section is not to be taken as penalising a person who buys a right to subscribe for shares in, or debentures of, a body corporate or buys debentures of a body corporate that confer upon the holder of them a right to subscribe for, or to convert the debentures (in whole or in part) into, shares of that body.

SEC. 324 Duty of director to disclose shareholdings in own company

324(1) **[Duty to notify re certain interests etc.]** A person who becomes a director of a company and at the time when he does so is interested in shares in, or debentures of, the company or any other body corporate, being the company's subsidiary or holding company or a subsidiary of the company's holding company, is under obligation to notify the company in writing—

(a) of the subsistence of his interests at that time; and

(b) of the number of shares of each class in, and the amount of debentures of each class of, the company or other such body corporate in which each interest of his subsists at that time.

324(2) **[Duty to notify re certain events]** A director of a company is under obligation to notify the company in writing of the occurrence, while he is a director, of any of the following events—

(a) any event in consequence of whose occurrence he becomes, or ceases to be, interested in shares in, or debentures of, the company or any other body corporate, being the company's subsidiary or holding company or a subsidiary of the company's holding company;

(b) the entering into by him of a contract to sell any such shares or debentures;

(c) the assignment by him of a right granted to him by the company to subscribe for shares in, or debentures of, the company; and

(d) the grant to him by another body corporate, being the company's subsidiary or holding company or a subsidiary of the company's holding company, of a right to subscribe for shares in, or debentures of, that other body corporate, the exercise of such a right granted to him and the assignment by him of such a right so granted;

and notification to the company must state the number or amount, and class, of shares or debentures involved.

324(3) **[Effect of Sch. 13, Pt. I, II, III; exceptions to sec. 324(1), (2)]** Schedule 13 has effect in connection with subsections (1) and (2) above; and of that Schedule—

   (a) Part I contains rules for the interpretation of, and otherwise in relation to, those subsections and applies in determining, for purposes of those subsections, whether a person has an interest in shares or debentures;

   (b) Part II applies with respect to the periods within which obligations imposed by the subsections must be fulfilled; and

   (c) Part III specifies certain circumstances in which obligations arising from subsection (2) are to be treated as not discharged;

and subsections (1) and (2) are subject to any exceptions for which provision may be made by regulations made by the Secretary of State by statutory instrument.

324(4)   **[Qualification to sec. 324(2)]**   Subsection (2) does not require the notification by a person of the occurrence of an event whose occurrence comes to his knowledge after he has ceased to be a director.

324(5)   **[Notice must refer to obligation]**   An obligation imposed by this section is treated as not discharged unless the notice by means of which it purports to be discharged is expressed to be given in fulfilment of that obligation.

324(6)   **[Shadow directors, wholly-owned subsidiary]**   This section applies to shadow directors as to directors; but nothing in it operates so as to impose an obligation with

[The next page is 15,801]

CCH Editions Limited
BCL BCL6$$$$36

respect to shares in a body corporate which is the wholly-owned subsidiary of another body corporate.

324(7) **[Offence, penalty]** A person who—

(a) fails to discharge, within the proper period, an obligation to which he is subject under subsection (1) or (2), or

(b) in purported discharge of an obligation to which he is so subject, makes to the company a statement which he knows to be false, or recklessly makes to it a statement which is false,

is guilty of an offence and liable to imprisonment or a fine, or both.

324(8) **[Application of sec. 732]** Section 732 (restriction on prosecutions) applies to an offence under this section.

SEC. 325 Register of directors' interests notified under sec. 324

325(1) **[Register for sec. 324 purposes]** Every company shall keep a register for the purposes of section 324.

325(2) **[Particulars to be entered in register]** Whenever a company receives information from a director given in fulfilment of an obligation imposed on him by that section, it is under obligation to enter in the register, against the director's name, the information received and the date of the entry.

325(3) **[Rights of directors to be entered]** The company is also under obligation, whenever it grants to a director a right to subscribe for shares in, or debentures of, the company to enter in the register against his name—

(a) the date on which the right is granted,

(b) the period during which, or time at which, it is exercisable,

(c) the consideration for the grant (or, if there is no consideration, that fact), and

(d) the description of shares or debentures involved and the number or amount of them, and the price to be paid for them (or the consideration, if otherwise than in money).

325(4) **[Further details re sec. 325(3)]** Whenever such a right as is mentioned above is exercised by a director, the company is under obligation to enter in the register against his name that fact (identifying the right), the number or amount of shares or debentures in respect of which it is exercised and, if they were registered in his name, that fact and, if not, the name or names of the person or persons in whose name or names they were registered, together (if they were registered in the names of two persons or more) with the number or amount of the shares or debentures registered in the name of each of them.

325(5) **[Effect of Sch. 13, Pt. IV, inspection etc.]** Part IV of Schedule 13 has effect with respect to the register to be kept under this section, to the way in which entries in it are to be made, to the right of inspection, and generally.

325(6) **[Shadow director]** For purposes of this section, a shadow director is deemed a director.

SEC. 326   Sanctions for non-compliance

326(1)   [Application]   The following applies with respect to defaults in complying with, and to contraventions of, section 325 and Part IV of Schedule 13.

326(2)   [Default re sec. 325(1), (2), (3), (4); Sch. 13, para. 21, 22, 28]   If default is made in complying with any of the following provisions—

(a)   section 325(1), (2), (3) or (4), or

(b)   Schedule 13, paragraph 21, 22 or 28,

the company and every officer of it who is in default is liable to a fine and, for continued contravention, to a daily default fine.

326(3)   [Refusal of inspection of register etc.]   If an inspection of the register required under paragraph 25 of the Schedule is refused, or a copy required under paragraph 26 is not sent within the proper period, the company and every officer of it who is in default is liable to a fine and, for contined contravention, to a daily default fine.

326(4)   [Default re notice of where register kept]   If default is made for 14 days in complying with paragraph 27 of the Schedule (notice to registrar of where register is kept), the company and every officer of it who is in default is liable to a fine and, for continued contravention, to a daily default fine.

326(5)   [Default re producing register]   If default is made in complying with paragraph 29 of the Schedule (register to be produced at annual general meeting), the company and every officer of it who is in default is liable to a fine.

326(6)   [Compelling inspection of register etc.]   In the case of a refusal of an inspection of the register required under paragraph 25 of the Schedule, the court may by order compel an immediate inspection of it; and in the case of failure to send within the proper period a copy required under paragraph 26, the court may by order direct that the copy be sent to the person requiring it.

SEC. 327   Extension of sec. 323 to spouses and children

327(1)   [Application to spouse etc; defence]   Section 323 applies to—

(a)   the wife or husband of a director of a company (not being herself or himself a director of it), and

(b)   an infant son or infant daughter of a director (not being himself or herself a director of the company),

as it applies to the director; but it is a defence for a person charged by virtue of this section with an offence under section 323 to prove that he (she) had no reason to believe that his (her) spouse or, as the case may be, parent was a director of the company in question.

327(2)   [Interpretation]   For purposes of this section—

(a)   "**son**" includes step-son, and "**daughter**" includes step-daughter ("parent" being construed accordingly),

(b)   "**infant**" means, in relation to Scotland, pupil or minor, and

(c)   a shadow director of a company is deemed a director of it.

CA 1985, sec. 326(1)

SEC. 328 Extension of sec. 324 to spouses and children

328(1) **[Interest of spouse, children treated as director's interest]** For the purposes of section 324—

    (a) an interest of the wife or husband of a director of a company (not being herself or himself a director of it) in shares or debentures is to be treated as the director's interest; and

    (b) the same applies to an interest of an infant son or infant daughter of a director of a company (not being himself or herself a director of it) in shares or debentures.

328(2) **[Contract etc. of spouse, children treated as that of director]** For those purposes—

    (a) a contract, assignment or right of subscription entered into, exercised or made by, or a grant made to, the wife or husband of a director of a company (not being herself or himself a director of it) is to be treated as having been entered into, exercised or made by, or (as the case may be) as having been made to, the director; and

    (b) the same applies to a contract, assignment or right of subscription entered into, exercised or made by, or grant made to, an infant son or infant daughter of a director of a company (not being himself or herself a director of it).

328(3) **[Directors to notify company re certain events]** A director of a company is under obligation to notify the company in writing of the occurrence while he or she is a director, of either of the following events, namely—

    (a) the grant by the company to his (her) spouse, or to his or her infant son or infant daughter, of a right to subscribe for shares in, or debentures of, the company; and

    (b) the exercise by his (her) spouse or by his or her infant son or infant daughter of such a right granted by the company to the wife, husband, son or daughter.

328(4) **[Contents of sec. 328(3) notice]** In a notice given to the company under subsection (3) there shall be stated—

    (a) in the case of the grant of a right, the like information as is required by section 324 to be stated by the director on the grant to him by another body corporate of a right to subscribe for shares in, or debentures of, that other body corporate; and

    (b) in the case of the exercise of a right, the like information as is required by that section to be stated by the director on the exercise of a right granted to him by another body corporate to subscribe for shares in, or debentures of, that other body corporate.

328(5) **[Time for fulfillment of sec. 328(3) obligation]** An obligation imposed by subsection (3) on a director must be fulfilled by him before the end of 5 days beginning with the day following that on which the occurrence of the event giving rise to it comes to his knowledge; but in reckoning that period of days there is disregarded any Saturday or Sunday, and any day which is a bank holiday in any part of Great Britain.

328(6)   [Offence, penalty]   A person who—

   (a)   fails to fulfil, within the proper period, an obligation to which he is subject under subsection (3), or

   (b)   in purported fulfilment of such an obligation, makes to a company a statement which he knows to be false, or recklessly makes to a company a statement which is false,

is guilty of an offence and liable to imprisonment or a fine, or both.

328(7)   [Interpretation]   The rules set out in Part I of Schedule 13 have effect for the interpretation of, and otherwise in relation to, subsections (1) and (2); and subsections (5), (6) and (8) of section 324 apply with any requisite modification.

328(8)   [Definitions]   ]   In this section, **"son"** includes step-son, **"daughter"** includes step-daughter, and **"infant"** means, in relation to Scotland, pupil or minor.

328(9)   [Obligation treated as under sec. 324]   For purposes of section 325, an obligation imposed on a director by this section is to be treated as if imposed by section 324.

SEC. 329   Duty to notify stock exchange of matters notified under preceding sections

329(1)   [Obligation for company to notify]   Whenever a company whose shares or debentures are listed on a recognised investment exchange other than an overseas investment exchange within the meaning of the Financial Services Act 1986 is notified of any matter by a director in consequence of the fulfilment of an obligation imposed by section 324 or 328, and that matter relates to shares or debentures so listed, the company is under obligation to notify that investment exchange of that matter; and the investment exchange may publish, in such manner as it may determine, any information received by it under this subsection.

History
In s. 329(1) the words "recognised investment exchange other than an overseas investment exchange within the meaning of the Financial Services Act 1986", "that investment exchange" and "the investment exchange" substituted respectively for the former words "recognised stock exchange", "that stock exchange" and "the stock exchange" by Financial Services Act 1986, s. 212 and Sch. 16, para. 20 as from 29 April 1988 (see S.I. 1988 No. 740 (C. 22)).

329(2)   [Time for fulfilling sec. 329(1) obligation]   An obligation imposed by subsection (1) must be fulfilled before the end of the day next following that on which it arises; but there is disregarded for this purpose a day which is a Saturday or a Sunday or a bank holiday in any part of Great Britain.

329(3)   [Penalty on default]   If default is made in complying with this section, the company and every officer of it who is in default is guilty of an offence and liable to a fine and, for continued contravention, to a daily default fine.

   Section 732 (restriction on prosecutions) applies to an offence under this section.

RESTRICTIONS ON A COMPANY'S POWER TO MAKE LOANS ETC. TO DIRECTORS AND PERSONS CONNECTED WITH THEM

SEC. 330   General restrictions on loans etc. to directors and persons connected with them

330(1)   [Prohibitions, exceptions]   The prohibitions listed below in this section are subject to the exceptions in sections 332 to 338.

330(2) [**Loans etc.**] A company shall not—

    (a) make a loan to a director of the company or of its holding company;

    (b) enter into any guarantee or provide any security in connection with a loan made by any person to such a director.

330(3) [**Quasi-loans etc.**] A relevant company shall not—

    (a) make a quasi-loan to a director of the company or of its holding company;

    (b) make a loan or a quasi-loan to a person connected with such a director;

    (c) enter into a guarantee or provide any security in connection with a loan or quasi-loan made by any other person for such a director or a person so connected.

330(4) [**Credit transactions etc.**] A relevant company shall not—

    (a) enter into a credit transaction as creditor for such a director or a person so connected;

    (b) enter into any guarantee or provide any security in connection with a credit transaction made by any other person for such a director or a person so connected.

330(5) [**Shadow director**] For purposes of sections 330 to 346, a shadow director is treated as a director.

330(6) [**Prohibition of certain assignments**] A company shall not arrange for the assignment to it, or the assumption by it, of any rights, obligations or liabilities under a transaction which, if it had been entered into by the company, would have contravened subsection (2), (3) or (4); but for the purposes of sections 330 to 347 the transaction is to be treated as having been entered into on the date of the arrangement.

330(7) [**Prohibition of further arrangements**] A company shall not take part in any arrangement whereby—

    (a) another person enters into a transaction which, if it had been entered into by the company, would have contravened any of subsections (2), (3), (4) or (6); and

    (b) that other person, in pursuance of the arrangement, has obtained or is to obtain any benefit from the company or its holding company or a subsidiary of the company or its holding company.

SEC. 331   Definitions for sec. 330 ff.

331(1) [**Interpretation of sec. 330 to 346**] The following subsections apply for the interpretation of sections 330 to 346.

331(2) [**"Guarantee"**] "Guarantee" includes indemnity, and cognate expressions are to be construed accordingly.

331(3) [**Quasi-loans**] A quasi-loan is a transaction under which one party ("the creditor") agrees to pay, or pays otherwise than in pursuance of an agreement, a sum for another ("the borrower") or agrees to reimburse, or reimburses otherwise than in pursuance of an agreement, expenditure incurred by another party for another ("the borrower")—

(a) on terms that the borrower (or a person on his behalf) will reimburse the creditor; or

(b) in circumstances giving rise to a liability on the borrower to reimburse the creditor.

331(4)   **[Borrower under quasi-loan]**   Any reference to the person to whom a quasi-loan is made is a reference to the borrower; and the liabilities of a borrower under a quasi-loan include the liabilities of any person who has agreed to reimburse the creditor on behalf of the borrower.

331(5)   (Repealed by Banking Act 1987, sec. 108(2) and Sch. 7, Pt. I as from 1 October 1987)

History
In regard to the date of the above repeal, see S.I. 1987 No. 1664 (C. 50): s. 331(5) formerly read as follows:

"**331(5) 'Recognised bank'** means a company which is recognised as a bank for the purposes of the Banking Act 1979."

331(6)   **["Relevant company"]**   **"Relevant company"** means a company which—

(a) is a public company, or

(b) is a subsidiary of a public company, or

(c) is a subsidiary of a company which has as another subsidiary a public company, or

(d) has a subsidiary which is a public company.

331(7)   **[Credit transactions]**   A credit transaction is a transaction under which one party ("the creditor")—

(a) supplies any goods or sells any land under a hire-purchase agreement or a conditional sale agreement;

(b) leases or hires any land or goods in return for periodical payments;

(c) otherwise disposes of land or supplies goods or services on the understanding that payment (whether in a lump sum or instalments or by way of periodical payments or otherwise) is to be deferred.

331(8)   **["Services"]**   **"Services"** means anything other than goods or land.

331(9)   **[Transactions etc. for a person]**   A transaction or arrangement is made "for" a person if—

(a) in the case of a loan or quasi-loan, it is made to him;

(b) in the case of a credit transaction, he is the person to whom goods or services are supplied, or land is sold or otherwise disposed of, under the transaction;

(c) in the case of a guarantee or security, it is entered into or provided in connection with a loan or quasi-loan made to him or a credit transaction made for him;

(d) in the case of an arrangement within subsection (6) or (7) of section 330, the transaction to which the arrangement relates was made for him; and

(e) in the case of any other transaction or arrangement for the supply or transfer of, or of any interest in, goods, land or services, he is the person to whom the goods, land or services (or the interest) are supplied or transferred.

331(10) **["Conditional sale agreement"]** "Conditional sale agreement" means the same as in the Consumer Credit Act 1974.

SEC. 332 Short-term quasi-loans

332(1) **[Certain quasi-loans possible to directors]** Subsection (3) of section 330 does not prohibit a company ("the creditor") from making a quasi-loan to one of its directors or to a director of its holding company if—

    (a) the quasi-loan contains a term requiring the director or a person on his behalf to reimburse the creditor his expenditure within 2 months of its being incurred; and

    (b) the aggregate of the amount of that quasi-loan and of the amount outstanding under each relevant quasi-loan does not exceed £1,000.

332(2) **[Quasi-loan relevant for sec. 332(1)]** A quasi-loan is relevant for this purpose if it was made to the director by virtue of this section by the creditor or its subsidiary or, where the director is a director of the creditor's holding company, any other subsidiary of that company; and **"the amount outstanding"** is the amount of the outstanding liabilities of the person to whom the quasi-loan was made.

SEC. 333 Inter-company loans in same group

333 In the case of a relevant company which is a member of a group of companies (meaning a holding company and its subsidiaries), paragraphs (b) and (c) of section 330(3) do not prohibit the company from—

    (a) making a loan or quasi-loan to another member of that group; or

    (b) entering into a guarantee or providing any security in connection with a loan or quasi-loan made by any person to another member of the group,

by reason only that a director of one member of the group is associated with another.

SEC. 334 Loans of small amounts

334 Without prejudice to any other provision of sections 332 to 338, paragraph (a) of section 330(2) does not prohibit a company from making a loan to a director of the company or of its holding company if the aggregate of the relevant amounts does not exceed £2,500.

SEC. 335 Minor and business transactions

335(1) **[Exception to sec. 330(4)]** Section 330(4) does not prohibit a company from entering into a transaction for a person if the aggregate of the relevant amounts does not exceed £5,000.

335(2) **[Conditions for exception]** Section 330(4) does not prohibit a company from entering into a transaction for a person if—

    (a) the transaction is entered into by the company in the ordinary course of its business; and

(b) the value of the transaction is not greater, and the terms on which it is entered into are no more favourable, in respect of the person for whom the transaction is made, than that or those which it is reasonable to expect the company to have offered to or in respect of a person of the same financial standing but unconnected with the company.

SEC. 336   Transactions at behest of holding company

336   The following transactions are excepted from the prohibitions of section 330—

(a) a loan or quasi-loan by a company to its holding company, or a company entering into a guarantee or providing any security in connection with a loan or quasi-loan made by any person to its holding company;

(b) a company entering into a credit transaction as creditor for its holding company, or entering into a guarantee or providing any security in connection with a credit transaction made by any other person for its holding company.

SEC. 337   Funding of director's expenditure on duty to company

337(1)   **[Exception to sec. 330]**   A company is not prohibited by section 330 from doing anything to provide a director with funds to meet expenditure incurred or to be incurred by him for the purposes of the company or for the purpose of enabling him properly to perform his duties as an officer of the company.

337(2)   **[Extension of sec. 337(1)]**   Nor does the section prohibit a company from doing anything to enable a director to avoid incurring such expenditure.

337(3)   **[Conditions for sec. 337(1),(2)]**   Subsections (1) and (2) apply only if one of the following conditions is satisfied—

(a) the thing in question is done with prior approval of the company given at a general meeting at which there are disclosed all the matters mentioned in the next subsection;

(b) that thing is done on condition that, if the approval of the company is not so given at or before the next annual general meeting, the loan is to be repaid, or any other liability arising under any such transaction discharged, within 6 months from the conclusion of that meeting;

but those subsections do not authorise a relevant company to enter into any transaction if the aggregate of the relevant amounts exceeds £10,000.

337(4)   **[Matters to be disclosed under sec. 337(3)(a)]**   The matters to be disclosed under subsection (3)(a) are—

(a) the purpose of the expenditure incurred or to be incurred, or which would otherwise be incurred, by the director,

(b) the amount of the funds to be provided by the company, and

(c) the extent of the company's liability under any transaction which is or is connected with the thing in question.

SEC. 338 Loan or quasi-loan by money-lending company

338(1) **[Exception to sec. 330]** There is excepted from the prohibitions in section 330—

(a) a loan or quasi-loan made by a money-lending company to any person; or

(b) a money-lending company entering into a guarantee in connection with any other loan or quasi-loan.

338(2) **["Money-lending company"]** "Money-lending company" means a company whose ordinary business includes the making of loans or quasi-loans, or the giving of guarantees in connection with loans or quasi-loans.

338(3) **[Conditions for sec. 338(1)]** Subsection (1) applies only if both the following conditions are satisfied—

(a) the loan or quasi-loan in question is made by the company, or it enters into the guarantee, in the ordinary course of the company's business; and

(b) the amount of the loan or quasi-loan, or the amount guaranteed, is not greater, and the terms of the loan, quasi-loan or guarantee are not more favourable, in the case of the person to whom the loan or quasi-loan is made or in respect of whom the guarantee is entered into, than that or those which it is reasonable to expect that company to have offered to or in respect of a person of the same financial standing but unconnected with the company.

338(4) **[No authorisation in sec. 338(1) if amounts over £50,000]** But subsection (1) does not authorise a relevant company (unless it is a banking company) to enter into any transaction if the aggregate of the relevant amounts exceeds £50,000.

History

In s. 338(4) the words "a banking company" substituted for the former words "an authorised institution" by CA 1989, s. 23 and Sch. 10, para. 10 as from 1 April 1990 subject to transitional and saving provisions (see S.I. 1990 No. 355 (C. 13), art. 3, Sch. 1 and also art. 6–9); previously the words "an authorised institution" substituted for the original words "a recognised bank" by Banking Act 1987, s. 108(2) and Sch. 6, para. 18(6) as from 1 October 1987 (see S.I. 1987 No. 1664 (C. 50).

338(5) **[Determination of sec. 338(4) aggregate]** In determining that aggregate, a company which a director does not control is deemed not to be connected with him.

338(6) **[Extent of condition in sec. 338(3)(b)]** The condition specified in subsection (3)(b) does not of itself prevent a company from making a loan to one of its directors or a director of its holding company—

(a) for the purpose of facilitating the purchase, for use as that director's only or main residence, of the whole or part of any dwelling-house together with any land to be occupied and enjoyed with it;

(b) for the purpose of improving a dwelling-house or part of a dwelling-house so used or any land occupied and enjoyed with it;

(c) in substitution for any loan made by any person and falling within paragraph (a) or (b) of this subsection,

if loans of that description are ordinarily made by the company to its employees and on terms no less favourable than those on which the transaction in question is made, and the aggregate of the relevant amounts does not exceed £50,000.

SEC. 339   "Relevant amounts" for purposes of sec. 334 ff.

339(1)   [Defining relevant amount for exceptions]   This section has effect for defining the "relevant amounts" to be aggregated under sections 334, 335(1), 337(3) and 338(4); and in relation to any proposed transaction or arrangement and the question whether it falls within one or other of the exceptions provided by those sections, **"the relevant exception"** is that exception; but where the relevant exception is the one provided by section 334 (loan of small amount), references in this section to a person connected with a director are to be disregarded.

339(2)   [Relevant amounts for proposed transaction or arrangement]   Subject as follows, the relevant amounts in relation to a proposed transaction or arrangement are—

    (a) the value of the proposed transaction or arrangement,

    (b) the value of any existing arrangement which—

        (i) falls within subsection (6) or (7) of section 330, and

        (ii) also falls within subsection (3) of this section, and

        (iii) was entered into by virtue of the relevant exception by the company or by a subsidiary of the company or, where the proposed transaction or arrangement is to be made for a director of its holding company or a person connected with such a director, by that holding company or any of its subsidiaries;

    (c) the amount outstanding under any other transaction—

        (i) falling within subsection (3) below, and

        (ii) made by virtue of the relevant exception, and

        (iii) made by the company or by a subsidiary of the company or, where the proposed transaction or arrangement is to be made for a director of its holding company or a person connected with such a director by that holding company or any of its subsidiaries.

339(3)   [Transactions under sec. 339(2)]   A transaction falls within this subsection if it was made—

    (a) for the director for whom the proposed transaction or arrangement is to be made, or for any person connected with that director; or

    (b) where the proposed transaction or arrangement is to be made for a person connected with a director of a company, for that director or any person connected with him;

and an arrangement also falls within this subsection if it relates to a transaction which does so.

339(4)   [Sec. 338 transaction — banking company]   But where the proposed transaction falls within section 338 and is one which a banking company proposes to enter into under subsection (6) of that section (housing loans, etc.), any other transaction or arrangement which apart from this subsection would fall within subsection (3) of this section does not do so unless it was entered into in pursuance of section 338(6).

CA 1985, sec. 339(1)

CCH Editions Limited
BCL BCL6$$$$38

History
In s. 339(4) the words "a banking company" substituted for the former words "an authorised institution" by CA 1989, s. 23 and Sch. 10, para. 10 as from 1 April 1990 subject to transitional and saving provisions (see S.I. 1990 No. 355 (C. 13), art. 3, Sch. 1, and also art. 6–9); previously

the words "an authorised institution" substituted for the original words "a recognised bank" by Banking Act 1987, s. 108(1) and Sch. 6, para. 18(6) as from 1 October 1987 (see S.I. 1987 No. 1664 (C. 50)).

339(5)   [Exception to sec. 339(3) re certain subsidiaries etc.]   A transaction entered into by a company which is (at the time of that transaction being entered into) a subsidiary of the company which is to make the proposed transaction, or is a subsidiary of that company's holding company, does not fall within subsection (3) if at the time when the question arises (that is to say, the question whether the proposed transaction or arrangement falls within any relevant exception), it no longer is such a subsidiary.

339(6)   [Values under sec. 339(2)]   Values for purposes of subsection (2) of this section are to be determined in accordance with the section next following; and **"the amount outstanding"** for purposes of subsection (2)(c) above is the value of the transaction less any amount by which that value has been reduced.

SEC. 340   "Value" of transactions and arrangements

340(1)   [Application]   This section has effect for determining the value of a transaction or arrangement for purposes of sections 330 to 339.

340(2)   [Loan]   The value of a loan is the amount of its principal.

340(3)   [Quasi-loan]   The value of a quasi-loan is the amount, or maximum amount, which the person to whom the quasi-loan is made is liable to reimburse the creditor.

340(4)   [Guarantee or security]   The value of a guarantee or security is the amount guaranteed or secured.

340(5)   [Sec. 330(6) or (7) arrangement]   The value of an arrangement to which section 330(6) or (7) applies is the value of the transaction to which the arrangement relates less any amount by which the liabilities under the arrangement or transaction of the person for whom the transaction was made have been reduced.

340(6)   [Arrangement not under sec. 340(2) to (5)]   The value of a transaction or arrangement not falling within subsections (2) to (5) above is the price which it is reasonable to expect could be obtained for the goods, land or services to which the transaction or arrangement relates if they had been supplied (at the time the transaction or arrangement is entered into) in the ordinary course of business and on the same terms (apart from price) as they have been supplied, or are to be supplied, under the transaction or arrangement in question.

340(7)   [Where value not able to be expressed as specific sum]   For purposes of this section, the value of a transaction or arrangement which is not capable of being expressed as a specific sum of money (because the amount of any liability arising under the transaction or arrangement is unascertainable, or for any other reason), whether or not any liability under the transaction or arrangement has been reduced, is deemed to exceed £50,000.

SEC. 341   Civil remedies for breach of sec. 330

341(1)   [Contravening provision voidable]   If a company enters into a transaction or arrangement in contravention of section 330, the transaction or arrangement is voidable at the instance of the company unless—

(a) restitution of any money or any other asset which is the subject matter of the arrangement or transaction is no longer possible, or the company has been indemnified in pursuance of subsection (2)(b) below for the loss or damage suffered by it, or

(b) any rights acquired bona fide for value and without actual notice of the contravention by a person other than the person for whom the transaction or arrangement was made would be affected by its avoidance.

341(2)   **[Liability of director and connected person to account or indemnify]**   Where an arrangement or transaction is made by a company for a director of the company or its holding company or a person connected with such a director in contravention of section 330, that director and the person so connected and any other director of the company who authorised the transaction or arrangement (whether or not it has been avoided in pursuance of subsection (1)) is liable—

(a) to account to the company for any gain which he has made directly or indirectly by the arrangement or transaction; and

(b) (jointly and severally with any other person liable under this subsection) to indemnify the company for any loss or damage resulting from the arrangement or transaction.

341(3)   **[Extent of sec. 341(2)]**   Subsection (2) is without prejudice to any liability imposed otherwise than by that subsection, but is subject to the next two subsections.

341(4)   **[Exception to sec. 341(2) — all reasonable steps taken etc.]**   Where an arrangement or transaction is entered into by a company and a person connected with a director of the company or its holding company in contravention of section 330, that director is not liable under subsection (2) of this section if he shows that he took all reasonable steps to secure the company's compliance with that section.

341(5)   **[Exception to sec. 341(2) — no knowledge]**   In any case, a person so connected and any such other director as is mentioned in subsection (2) is not so liable if he shows that, at the time the arrangement or transaction was entered into, he did not know the relevant circumstances constituting the contravention.

SEC. 342   Criminal penalties for breach of sec. 330

342(1)   **[Offence by director]**   A director of a relevant company who authorises or permits the company to enter into a transaction or arrangement knowing or having reasonable cause to believe that the company was thereby contravening section 330 is guilty of an offence.

342(2)   **[Offence by relevant company]**   A relevant company which enters into a transaction or arrangement for one of its directors or for a director of its holding company in contravention of section 330 is guilty of an offence.

342(3)   **[Offence of procuring contravention by relevant company]**   A person who procures a relevant company to enter into a transaction or arrangement knowing or having reasonable cause to believe that the company was thereby contravening section 330 is guilty of an offence.

342(4)   **[Penalty]**   A person guilty of an offence under this section is liable to imprisonment or a fine, or both.

342(5)   **[Exception for relevant company]**   A relevant company is not guilty of an offence under subsection (2) if it shows that, at the time the transaction or arrangement was entered into, it did not know the relevant circumstances.

SEC. 343 Record of transactions not disclosed in company accounts

343(1) **[Application re banking companies and sec. 344 exceptions]** The following provisions of this section—

(a) apply in the case of a company which is, or is the holding company of, a banking company, and

(b) are subject to the exceptions provided by section 344.

History
In s. 343(1)(a) the words "a banking company" substituted for the former words "an authorised institution" by CA 1989, s. 23 and Sch. 10, para. 10 as from 1 April 1990 subject to transitional and saving provisions (see S.I. 1990 No. 355 (C. 13), art. 3, Sch. 1 and also art. 6–9); previously the words "an authorised institution" substituted for the original words "a recognised bank" by Banking Act 1987, s. 108(1) and Sch. 6, para. 18(6) as from 1 October 1987 (see S.I. 1987 No. 1664 (C. 50)).

343(2) **[Register of transactions etc. to be kept]** Such a company shall maintain a register containing a copy of every transaction, arrangement or agreement of which particulars would, but for paragraph 2 of Part IV of Schedule 9, be required to be disclosed in the company's accounts or group accounts for the current financial year and for each of the preceding 10 financial years.

History
In s. 343(2) the words "paragraph 2 of Part IV of Schedule 9, be required" substituted for the former words "paragraph 4 of Schedule 6, be required by section 232" by CA 1989, s. 23 and Sch. 10, para. 11 as from 1 April 1990 subject to transitional and saving provisions (see S.I. 1990 No. 355 (C. 13), art. 3, Sch. 1 and also art. 6–9).

343(3) **[Transactions etc. not in writing]** In the case of a transaction, arrangement or agreement which is not in writing, there shall be contained in the register a written memorandum setting out its terms.

343(4) **[Statement re transactions etc. to be available at registered office]** Such a company shall before its annual general meeting make available at its registered office for not less than 15 days ending with the date of the meeting a statement containing the particulars of transactions, arrangements and agreements which the company would, but for paragraph 2 of Part IV of Schedule 9, be required to disclose in its accounts or group accounts for the last complete financial year preceding that meeting.

History
In s. 343(4) the words "paragraph 2 of Part IV of Schedule 9, be required" substituted for the former words "paragraph 4 of Schedule 6, be required by section 232" by CA 1989, s. 23 and Sch. 10, para. 11 as from 1 April 1990 subject to transitional and saving provisions (see S.I. 1990 No. 355 (C. 13), art. 3, Sch. 1 and also art. 6–9).

343(5) **[Inspection by members]** The statement shall be so made available for inspection by members of the company; and such a statement shall also be made available for their inspection at the annual general meeting.

343(6) **[Auditors' report on statement]** It is the duty of the company's auditors to examine the statement before it is made available to members of the company and to make a report to the members on it; and the report shall be annexed to the statement before it is made so available.

343(7) **[Statement in auditors' report etc.]** The auditors' report shall state whether in their opinion the statement contains the particulars required by subsection (4); and, where their opinion is that it does not, they shall include in the report, so far as they are reasonably able to do so, a statement giving the required particulars.

343(8)   [Offence, penalty, defence: shadow director]   If a company fails to comply with any provision of subsections (2) to (5), every person who at the time of the failure is a director of it is guilty of an offence and liable to a fine; but—

(a) it is a defence in proceedings against a person for this offence to prove that he took all reasonable steps for securing compliance with the subsection concerned, and

(b) a person is not guilty of the offence by virtue only of being a shadow director of the company.

343(9)   [Application to certain loans and quasi-loans]   For purposes of the application of this section to loans and quasi-loans made by a company to persons connected with a person who at any time is a director of the company or of its holding company, a company which a person does not control is not connected with him.

SEC. 344   Exceptions from sec. 343

344(1)   [Certain transactions etc. less than £1,000]   Section 343 does not apply in relation to—

(a) transactions or arrangements made or subsisting during a financial year by a company or by a subsidiary of a company for a person who was at any time during that year a director of the company or of its holding company or was connected with such a director, or

(b) an agreement made or subsisting during that year to enter into such a transaction or arrangement,

if the aggregate of the values of each transaction or arrangement made for that person, and of each agreement for such a transaction or arrangement, less the amount (if any) by which the value of those transactions, arrangements and agreements has been reduced, did not exceed £1,000 at any time during the financial year.

For purposes of this subsection, values are to be determined as under section 340.

344(2)   [Certain UK subsidiary banking companies]   Section 343(4) and (5) do not apply to a banking company which is the wholly-owned subsidiary of a company incorporated in the United Kingdom.

History
In s. 344(2) the words "a banking company" substituted for the former words "an authorised institution" by CA 1989, s. 23 and Sch. 10, para. 10 as from 1 April 1990 subject to transitional and saving provisions (see S.I. 1990 No. 355 (C. 13), art. 3, Sch. 1 and also art. 6–9); previously the words "an authorised institution" substituted for the original words "a recognised bank" by Banking Act 1987, s. 108(1) and Sch. 6, para. 18(6) as from 1 October 1987 (see S.I. 1987 No. 1664 (C. 50)).

SUPPLEMENTARY

SEC. 345   Power to increase financial limits

345(1)   [Larger sum]   The Secretary of State may by order in a statutory instrument substitute for any sum of money specified in this Part a larger sum specified in the order.

345(2)   [Annulment of order]   An order under this section is subject to annulment in pursuance of a resolution of either House of Parliament.

345(3)　**[No effect on things done before]**　Such an order does not have effect in relation to anything done or not done before its coming into force; and accordingly, proceedings in respect of any liability (whether civil or criminal) incurred before that time may be continued or instituted as if the order had not been made.

SEC. 346　"Connected persons", etc.

346(1)　**[Application]**　This section has effect with respect to references in this Part to a person being "connected" with a director of a company, and to a director being "associated with" or "controlling" a body corporate.

346(2)　**[Persons connected with director]**　A person is connected with a director of a company if, but only if, he (not being himself a director of it) is—

  (a)　that director's spouse, child or step-child; or

  (b)　except where the context otherwise requires, a body corporate with which the director is associated; or

  (c)　a person acting in his capacity as trustee of any trust the beneficiaries of which include—

    (i)　the director, his spouse or any children or step-children of his, or

    (ii)　a body corporate with which he is associated, or of a trust whose terms confer a power on the trustees that may be exercised for the benefit of the director, his spouse, or any children or step-children of his, or any such body corporate; or

  (d)　a person acting in his capacity as partner of that director or of any person who, by virtue of paragraph (a), (b) or (c) of this subsection, is connected with that director; or

  (e)　a Scottish firm in which—

    (i)　that director is a partner,

    (ii)　a partner is a person who, by virtue of paragraph (a), (b) or (c) above, is connected with that director, or

    (iii)　a partner is a Scottish firm in which that director is a partner or in which there is a partner who, by virtue of paragraph (a), (b) or (c) above, is connected with that director.

346(3)　**[Interpretation of sec. 346(2)]**　In subsection (2)—

  (a)　a reference to the child or step-child of any person includes an illegitimate child of his, but does not include any person who has attained the age of 18; and

  (b)　paragraph (c) does not apply to a person acting in his capacity as trustee under an employees' share scheme or a pension scheme.

346(4)　**[Where director associated with body corporate]**　A director of a company is associated with a body corporate if, but only if, he and the persons connected with him, together—

  (a)　are interested in shares comprised in the equity share capital of that body corporate of a nominal value equal to at least one-fifth of that share capital; or

(b) are entitled to exercise or control the exercise of more than one-fifth of the voting power at any general meeting of that body.

346(5)   **[Where director deemed to control body corporate]**   A director of a company is deemed to control a body corporate if, but only if—

(a) he or any person connected with him is interested in any part of the equity share capital of that body or is entitled to exercise or control the exercise of any part of the voting power at any general meeting of that body; and

(b) that director, the persons connected with him and the other directors of that company, together, are interested in more than one-half of that share capital or are entitled to exercise or control the exercise of more than one-half of that voting power.

346(6)   **[Supplementary to sec. 346(4),(5)]**   For purposes of subsections (4) and (5)—

(a) a body corporate with which a director is associated is not to be treated as connected with that director unless it is also connected with him by virtue of subsection (2)(c) or (d); and

(b) a trustee of a trust the beneficiaries of which include (or may include) a body corporate with which a director is associated is not to be treated as connected with a director by reason only of that fact.

346(7)   **[Rules in Sch. 13, Pt. I]**   The rules set out in Part I of Schedule 13 apply for the purposes of subsections (4) and (5).

346(8)   **[Interpretation of sec. 346(4),(5)]**   References in those subsections to voting power the exercise of which is controlled by a director include voting power whose exercise is controlled by a body corporate controlled by him; but this is without prejudice to other provisions of subsections (4) and (5).

SEC. 347   Transactions under foreign law

347   For purposes of sections 319 to 322 and 330 to 343, it is immaterial whether the law which (apart from this Act) governs any arrangement or transaction is the law of the United Kingdom, or of a part of it, or not.

PART XI — COMPANY ADMINISTRATION AND PROCEDURE

Chapter I — Company Identification

SEC. 348   Company name to appear outside place of business

348(1)   **[Name to be painted, affixed etc.]**   Every company shall paint or affix, and keep painted or affixed, its name on the outside of every office or place in which its business is carried on, in a conspicuous position and in letters easily legible.

348(2)   **[Penalty on default]**   If a company does not paint or affix its name as required above, the company and every officer of it who is in default is liable to a fine; and if a company does not keep its name painted or affixed as so required, the company and every officer of it who is in default is liable to a fine and, for continued contravention, to a daily default fine.

SEC. 349 Company's name to appear in its correspondence, etc.

349(1) **[Name in business letters, notices etc.]** Every company shall have its name mentioned in legible characters—

  (a) in all busines letters of the company,

  (b) in all its notices and other official publications,

  (c) in all bills of exchange, promissory notes, endorsements, cheques and orders for money or goods purporting to be signed by or on behalf of the company, and

  (d) in all its bills of parcels, invoices, receipts and letters of credit.

349(2) **[Penalty on default]** If a company fails to comply with subsection (1) it is liable to a fine.

349(3) **[Officer issuing letter etc. without name as required by sec. 349(1)]** If an officer of a company or a person on its behalf—

  (a) issues or authorises the issue of any business letter of the company, or any notice or other official publication of the company, in which the company's name is not mentioned as required by subsection (1), or

  (b) issues or authorises the issue of any bill of parcels, invoice, receipt or letter of credit of the company in which its name is not so mentioned,

he is liable to a fine.

349(4) **[Liability of officer, other person et al.]** If an officer of a company or a person on its behalf signs or authorises to be signed on behalf of the company any bill of exchange, promissory note, endorsement, cheque or order for money or goods in which the company's name is not mentioned as required by subsection (1), he is liable to a fine; and he is further personally liable to the holder of the bill of exchange, promissory note, cheque or order for money or goods for the amount of it (unless it is duly paid by the company).

SEC. 350 Company seal

350(1) **[Name on seal; penalty on default]** Every company shall have its name engraved in legible characters on its seal; and if a company fails to comply with this subsection, it is liable to a fine.

350(2) **[Officer using seal without name]** If an officer of a company or a person on its behalf uses or authorises the use of any seal purporting to be a seal of the company on which its name is not engraved as required by subsection (1), he is liable to a fine.

SEC. 351 Particulars in correspondence, etc.

351(1) **[Particulars in business letters and order forms]** Every company shall have the following particulars mentioned in legible characters in all business letters and order forms of the company, that is to say—

[The next page is 16,801]

(a) the company's place of registration and the number with which it is registered,

(b) the address of its registered office,

(c) in the case of an investment company (as defined in section 266), the fact that it is such a company, and

(d) in the case of a limited company exempt from the obligation to use the word "limited" as part of its name, the fact that it is a limited company.

351(2) **[Reference to share capital]** If in the case of a company having a share capital there is on the stationery used for any such letters, or on the company's order forms, a reference to the amount of share capital, the reference must be to paid-up share capital.

351(3) **[Welsh public limited company]** Where the name of a public company includes, as its last part, the equivalent in Welsh of the words "public limited company" ("cwmni cyfyngedig cyhoeddus"), the fact that the company is a public limited company shall be stated in English and in legible characters—

(a) in all prospectuses, bill-heads, letter paper, notices and other official publications of the company, and

(b) in a notice conspicuously displayed in every place in which the company's business is carried on.

351(4) **[Welsh limited company]** Where the name of a limited company has "cyfyngedig" as the last word, the fact that the company is a limited company shall be stated in English and in legible characters—

(a) in all prospectuses, bill-heads, letter paper, notices and other official publications of the company, and

(b) in a notice conspicuously displayed in every place in which the company's business is carried on.

351(5) **[Contraventions]** As to contraventions of this section, the following applies—

(a) if a company fails to comply with subsection (1) or (2), it is liable to a fine,

(b) if an officer of a company or a person on its behalf issues or authorises the issue of any business letter or order form not complying with those subsections, he is liable to a fine, and

(c) if subsection (3) or (4) is contravened, the company and every officer of it who is in default is liable to a fine and, in the case of subsection (3), to a daily default fine for continued contravention.

Chapter II — Register of Members

SEC. 352 Obligation to keep and enter up register

352(1) **[Obligation on every company]** Every company shall keep a register of its members and enter in it the particulars required by this section.

352(2)   [Matters to be entered]   There shall be entered in the register—

    (a) the names and addresses of the members;

    (b) the date on which each person was registered as a member; and

    (c) the date at which any person ceased to be a member.

352(3)   [Company with share capital]   The following applies in the case of a company having a share capital—

    (a) with the names and addresses of the members there shall be entered a statement—

        (i) of the shares held by each member, distinguishing each share by its number (so long as the share has a number) and, where the company has more than one class of issued shares, by its class, and

        (ii) of the amount paid or agreed to be considered as paid on the shares of each member;

    (b) where the company has converted any of its shares into stock and given notice of the conversion to the registrar of companies, the register shall show the amount and class of stock held by each member, instead of the amount of shares and the particulars relating to shares specified in paragraph (a).

352(4)   [Company not having share capital]   In the case of a company which does not have a share capital but has more than one class of members, there shall be entered in the register, with the names and addresses of the members, the class to which each member belongs.

352(5)   [Penalty on default]   If a company makes default in complying with this section, the company and every officer of it who is in default is liable to a fine and, for continued contravention, to a daily default fine.

352(6)   [Removal of entries re former member]   An entry relating to a former member of the company may be removed from the register after the expiration of 20 years from the date on which he ceased to be a member.

352(7)   [Liability of company re deletions]   Liability incurred by a company from the making or deletion of an entry in its register of members, or from a failure to make or delete any such entry, is not enforceable more than 20 years after the date on which the entry was made or deleted or, in the case of any such failure, the failure first occurred.

    This is without prejudice to any lesser period of limitation.

SEC. 353   Location of register

353(1)   [Usually at registered office]   A company's register of members shall be kept at its registered office, except that—

    (a) if the work of making it up is done at another office of the company, it may be kept there; and

    (b) if the company arranges with some other person for the making up of the register to be undertaken on its behalf by that other, it may be kept at the office of the other at which the work is done;

but it must not be kept, in the case of a company registered in England and Wales, at any place elsewhere than in England and Wales or, in the case of a company registered in Scotland, at any place elsewhere than in Scotland.

353(2) **[Notice to registrar re location and change]** Subject as follows, every company shall send notice in the prescribed form to the registrar of companies of the place where its register of members is kept, and of any change in that place.

353(3) **[Notice not necessary if always at registered office]** The notice need not be sent if the register has, at all times since it came into existence (or, in the case of a register in existence on 1st July 1948, at all times since then) been kept at the company's registered office.

353(4) **[Penalty on default]** If a company makes default for 14 days in complying with subsection (2), the company and every officer of it who is in default is liable to a fine and, for continued contravention, to a daily default fine.

SEC. 354   Index of members

354(1) **[Index if more than 50 members]** Every company having more than 50 members shall, unless the register of members is in such a form as to constitute in itself an index, keep an index of the names of the members of the company and shall, within 14 days after the date on which any alteration is made in the register of members, make any necessary alteration in the index.

354(2) **[Requirement for entry]** The index shall in respect of each member contain a sufficient indication to enable the account of that member in the register to be readily found.

354(3) **[Location of index]** The index shall be at all times kept at the same place as the register of members.

354(4) **[Penalty on default]** If default is made in complying with this section, the company and every officer of it who is in default is liable to a fine and, for continued contravention, to a daily default fine.

SEC. 355   Entries in register in relation to share warrants

355(1) **[Amendment of register on issue of share warrant]** On the issue of a share warrant the company shall strike out of its register of members the name of the member then entered in it as holding the shares specified in the warrant as if he had ceased to be a member, and shall enter in the register the following particulars, namely—

  (a) the fact of the issue of the warrant;

  (b) a statement of the shares included in the warrant, distinguishing each share by its number so long as the share has a number; and

  (c) the date of the issue of the warrant.

355(2) **[Entitlement to re-entry on cancellation of share warrant]** Subject to the company's articles, the bearer of a share warrant is entitled, on surrendering it for cancellation, to have his name entered as a member in the register of members.

355(3)   [Company responsible for loss]   The company is responsible for any loss incurred by any person by reason of the company entering in the register the name of a bearer of a share warrant in respect of the shares specified in it without the warrant being surrendered and cancelled.

355(4)   [Sec. 355(1) particulars sufficient until surrender]   Until the warrant is surrendered, the particulars specified in subsection (1) are deemed to be those required by this Act to be entered in the register of members; and, on the surrender, the date of the surrender must be entered.

355(5)   [Status of bearer of share warrant]   Except as provided by section 291(2) (director's share qualification), the bearer of a share warrant may, if the articles of the company so provide, be deemed a member of the company within the meaning of this Act, either to the full extent or for any purposes defined in the articles.

SEC. 356   Inspection of register and index

356(1)   [Open for inspection]   Except when the register of members is closed under the provisions of this Act, the register and the index of members' names shall during business hours be open to the inspection of any member of the company without charge, and of any other person on payment of the appropriate charge.

356(2)   [Business hours]   The reference to business hours is subject to such reasonable restrictions as the company in general meeting may impose, but so that not less than 2 hours in each day is to be allowed for inspection.

356(3)   [Copies of register for charge etc.]   Any member of the company or other person may require a copy of the register, or of any part of it, on payment of the appropriate charge; and the company shall cause any copy so required by a person to be sent to him within 10 days beginning with the day next following that on which the requirement is received by the company.

356(4)   [Appropriate charges]   The appropriate charge is—

    (a) under subsection (1), 5 pence or such less sum as the company may prescribe, for each inspection; and

    (b) under subsection (3), 10 pence or such less sum as the company may prescribe, for every 100 words (or fraction of 100 words) required to be copied.

356(5)   [Penalty for refusal of inspection etc.]   If an inspection required under this section is refused, or if a copy so required is not sent within the proper period, the company and every officer of it who is in default is liable in respect of each offence to a fine.

356(6)   [Compelling of inspection etc.]   In the case of such refusal or default, the court may by order compel an immediate inspection of the register and index, or direct that the copies required be sent to the persons requiring them.

SEC. 357   Non-compliance with sec. 353, 354, 356; agent's default

357   Where under section 353(1)(b), the register of members is kept at the office of some person other than the company, and by reason of any default of his the company fails to comply with—

section 353(2) (notice to registrar),

section 354(3) (index to be kept with register), or

section 356 (inspection),

or with any requirement of this Act as to the production of the register, that other person is liable to the same penalties as if he were an officer of the company who was in default, and the power of the court under section 356(6) extends to the making of orders against that other and his officers and servants.

SEC. 358 Power to close register

358 A company may, on giving notice by advertisement in a newspaper circulating in the district in which the company's registered office is situated, close the register of members for any time or times not exceeding in the whole 30 days in each year.

SEC. 359 Power of court to rectify register

359(1) [Application for rectification] If—

(a) the name of any person is, without sufficient cause, entered in or omitted from a company's register of members, or

(b) default is made or unnecessary delay takes place in entering on the register the fact of any person having ceased to be a member,

the person aggrieved, or any member of the company, or the company, may apply to the court for rectification of the register.

359(2) [Court may refuse application or grant rectification] The court may either refuse the application or may order rectification of the register and payment by the company of any damages sustained by any party aggrieved.

359(3) [Court may decide on other matters] On such an application the court may decide any question relating to the title of a person who is a party to the application to have his name entered in or omitted from the register, whether the question arises between members or alleged members, or between members or alleged members on the one hand and the company on the other hand, and generally may decide any question necessary or expedient to be decided for rectification of the register.

359(4) [Notice to be given of rectification to registrar] In the case of a company required by this Act to send a list of its members to the registrar of companies, the court, when making an order for rectification of the register, shall by its order direct notice of the rectification to be given to the registrar.

SEC. 360 Trusts not to be entered on register in England and Wales

360 No notice of any trust, expressed, implied or contructive, shall be entered on the register, or be receivable by the registrar, in the case of companies registered in England and Wales.

SEC. 361 Register to be evidence

361 The register of members is prima facie evidence of any matters which are by this Act directed or authorised to be inserted in it.

SEC. 362   Overseas branch registers

362(1) **[Branch register]**   A company having a share capital whose objects comprise the transaction of business in any of the countries or territories specified in Part I of Schedule 14 to this Act may cause to be kept in any such country or territory in which it transacts business a branch register of members resident in that country or territory.

362(2) **["Overseas branch register", references to dominion register etc.]**   Such a branch register is to be known as an **"overseas branch register"**; and—

(a) any dominion register kept by a company under section 119 of the Companies Act 1948 is to become known as an overseas branch register of the company;

(b) where any Act or instrument (including in particular a company's articles) refers to a company's dominion register, that reference is to be read (unless the context otherwise requires) as being to an overseas branch register kept under this section; and

(c) references to a colonial register occurring in articles registered before 1st November 1929 are to be read as referring to an overseas branch register.

362(3) **[Sch. 14, Pt. II, III]**   Part II of Schedule 14 has effect with respect to overseas branch registers kept under this section; and Part III of the Schedule enables corresponding facilities in Great Britain to be accorded to companies incorporated in other parts of the world.

362(4) **[Foreign Jurisdiction Act]**   The Foreign Jurisdiction Act 1890 has effect as if subsection (1) of this section, and Part II of Schedule 14, were included among the enactments which by virtue of section 5 of that Act may be applied by Order in Council to foreign countries in which for the time being Her Majesty has jurisdiction.

362(5) **[Possible extension]**   Her Majesty may by Order in Council direct that subsection (1) above and Part II of Schedule 14 shall extend, with such exceptions, modifications or adaptations (if any) as may be specified in the Order, to any territories under Her Majesty's protection to which those provisions cannot be extended under the Foreign Jurisdiction Act 1890.

Chapter III — Annual Return

SEC. 363   Annual return (company having a share capital)

363(1) **[Return once every year etc.]**   Subject to the provisions of this section, every company having a share capital shall, at least once in every year, make a return containing with respect to the company's registered office, registers of members and debenture holders, shares and debentures, indebtedness, past and present members and directors and secretary, the matters specified in Schedule 15.

363(2) **[Form]**   The annual return shall be in the prescribed form.

363(3) **[Qualification to sec. 363(1)]**   A company need not make a return under subsection (1) either in the year of its incorporation or, if it is not required by this Act to hold an annual general meeting during the following year, in that year.

363(4) **[Where shares converted to stock and registrar notified]** Where the company has converted any of its shares into stock and given notice of the conversion to the registrar of companies, the list referred to in paragraph 5 of Schedule 15 must state the amount of stock held by each of the existing members instead of the amount of shares and the particulars relating to shares required by that paragraph.

363(5) **[Abbreviated particulars in certain cases]** The return may, in any year, if the return for either of the two immediately preceding years has given (as at the date of that return) the full particulars required by that paragraph of the Schedule, give only such of those particulars as relate to persons ceasing to be or becoming members since the date of the last return and to shares transferred since that date or to changes as compared with that date in the amount of stock held by a member.

363(6) **[Company keeping overseas branch register]** The following applies to a company keeping an overseas branch register—

  (a) references in subsection (5) to the particulars required by paragraph 5 are to be taken as not including any such particulars contained in the overseas branch register, in so far as copies of the entries containing those particulars are not received at the company's registered office before the date when the return in question is made;

  (b) if an annual return is made between the date when entries are made in the overseas branch register and the date when copies of those entries are received at the company's registered office, the particulars contained in those entries (so far as relevant to an annual return) shall be included in the next or a subsequent annual return, as may be appropriate having regard to the particulars included in that return with respect to the company's register of members.

363(7) **[Penalty on default]** If a company fails to comply with this section, the company and every officer of it who is in default is liable to a fine and, for continued contravention, to a daily default fine.

363(8) **[Shadow director]** For purposes of this section and Schedule 15, a shadow director is deemed a director and officer.

SEC. 364 Annual return (company not having a share capital)

364(1) **[Return once every calendar year etc.]** Every company not having a share capital shall once at least in every calendar year make a return in the prescribed form stating—

  (a) the address of the company's registered office;

  (b) if the register of members is under provisions of this Act kept elsewhere than at that office, the address of the place where it is kept;

  (c) if any register of holders of debentures of the company or any duplicate of any such register or part of it is under provisions of this Act kept elsewhere than at the company's registered office, the address of the place where it is kept;

  (d) all such particulars with respect to the persons who at the date of the return are the directors of the company, and any person who at that date is its secretary, as are by this Act required to be contained (with respect to directors and the secretary respectively) in the company's register of directors and secretaries.

364(2)   [Qualification to sec. 364(1)]   A company need not make a return under subsection (1) either in the year of its incorporation or, if it is not required by this Act to hold an annual general meeting during the following year, in that year.

364(3)   [Statement of indebtedness]   There shall be included in the return a statement containing particulars of the total amount of the company's indebtedness in respect of all mortgages and charges (whenever created) of any description specified in section 396(1) or, in the case of a company registered in Scotland, section 410(4).

364(4)   [Penalty on default]   If a company fails to comply with this section, the company and every officer of it who is in default is liable to a fine and, for continued contravention, to a daily default fine.

364(5)   [Shadow director]   For purposes of this section, a shadow director is deemed a director and officer.

SEC. 365   Time for completion of annual return

365(1)   [Within 42 days of annual general meeting]   A company's annual return must be completed within 42 days after the annual general meeting for the year, whether or not that meeting is the first or only ordinary general meeting, or the first or only general meeting of the company in that year.

365(2)   [Copy of signed return to registrar]   The company must forthwith forward to the registrar of companies a copy of the return signed both by a director and by the secretary of the company.

365(3)   [Penalty on default, shadow director]   If a company fails to comply with this section, the company and every officer of it who is in default is liable to a fine and, for continued contravention, to a daily default fine; and for this purpose a shadow director is deemed an officer.

Chapter IV — Meetings and Resolutions

MEETINGS

SEC. 366   Annual general meeting

366(1)   [Annual general meeting each year]   Every company shall in each year hold a general meeting as its annual general meeting in addition to any other meetings in that year, and shall specify the meetings as such in the notices calling it.

366(2)   [Qualification to sec. 366(1)]   However, so long as a company holds its first annual general meeting within 18 months of its incorporation, it need not hold it in the year of its incorporation or in the following year.

366(3)   [Time between annual general meetings]   Not more than 15 months shall elapse between the date of one annual general meeting of a company and that of the next.

366(4)   [Penalty on default]   If default is made in holding a meeting in accordance with this section, the company and every officer of it who is in default is liable to a fine.

[The next page is 17,151]

SEC. 366A Election by private company to dispense with annual general meetings

366A(1) **[Power of private company]** A private company may elect (by elective resolution in accordance with section 379A) to dispense with the holding of annual general meetings.

366A(2) **[Effect of election]** An election has effect for the year in which it is made and subsequent years, but does not affect any liability already incurred by reason of default in holding an annual general meeting.

366A(3) **[Power of member to require meeting]** In any year in which an annual general meeting would be required to be held but for the election, and in which no such meeting has been held, any member of the company may, by notice to the company not later than three months before the end of the year, require the holding of an annual general meeting in that year.

366A(4) **[If sec. 366A(3) notice given]** If such a notice is given, the provisions of section 366(1) and (4) apply with respect to the calling of the meeting and the consequences of default.

366A(5) **[If election ceases to have effect]** If the election ceases to have effect, the company is not obliged under section 366 to hold an annual general meeting in that year if, when the election ceases to have effect, less than three months of the year remains.

This does not affect any obligation of the company to hold an annual general meeting in that year in pursuance of a notice given under subsection (3).

History
S. 366A inserted by CA 1989, s. 115(2) as from 1 April 1990 subject to transitional and saving provisions (see S.I. 1990 No. 355 (C. 13), art. 4(a) and also art. 10).

SEC. 367 Secretary of State's power to call meeting in default

367(1) **[Power of Secretary of State on application by member]** If default is made in holding a meeting in accordance with section 366, the Secretary of State may, on the application of any member of the company, call, or direct the calling of, a general meeting of the company and give such ancillary or consequential directions as he thinks expedient, including directions modifying or supplementing, in relation to the calling, holding and conduct of the meeting, the operation of the company's articles.

367(2) **[Sec. 367(1) directions]** The directions that may be given under subsection (1) include a direction that one member of the company present in person or by proxy shall be deemed to constitute a meeting.

367(3) **[Penalty for not complying with directions]** If default is made in complying with directions of the Secretary of State under subsection (1), the company and every officer of it who is in default is liable to a fine.

367(4) **[Status of general meeting under section]** A general meeting held under this section shall, subject to any directions of the Secretary of State, be deemed to be an annual general meeting of the company; but, where a meeting so held is not held in the year in which the default in holding the company's annual general meeting occurred, the meeting so held shall not be treated as the annual general meeting for the year in which it is held unless at that meeting the company resolves that it be so treated.

367(5)   [Copy of resolution to registrar]   Where a company so resolves, a copy of the resolution shall, within 15 days after its passing, be forwarded to the registrar of companies and recorded by him; and if default is made in complying with this subsection, the company and every officer of it who is in default is liable to a fine and, for continued contravention, to a daily default fine.

SEC. 368   Extraordinary general meeting on members' requisition

368(1)   [Directors to convene meeting]   The directors of a company shall, on a members' requisition, forthwith proceed duly to convene an extraordinary general meeting of the company.

This applies notwithstanding anything in the company's articles.

368(2)   [Members' requisition]   A members' requisition is a requisition of—

(a) members of the company holding at the date of the deposit of the requisition not less than one-tenth of such of the paid-up capital of the company as at that date carries the right of voting at general meetings of the company; or

(b) in the case of a company not having a share capital, members of it representing not less than one-tenth of the total voting rights of all the members having at the date of deposit of the requisition a right to vote at general meetings.

368(3)   [Requirements of requisition]   The requisition must state the objects of the meeting, and must be signed by the requisitionists and deposited at the registered office of the company, and may consist of several documents in like form each signed by one or more requisitionists.

368(4)   [Where directors fail to convene meeting within 21 days]   If the directors do not within 21 days from the date of the deposit of the requisition proceed duly to convene a meeting, the requisitionists, or any of them representing more than one half of the total voting rights of all of them, may themselves convene a meeting, but any meeting so convened shall not be held after the expiration of 3 months from that date.

368(5)   [Convening of meeting]   A meeting convened under this section by requisitionists shall be convened in the same manner, as nearly as possible, as that in which meetings are to be convened by directors.

368(6)   [Reasonable expenses to be repaid by company]   Any reasonable expenses incurred by the requisitionists by reason of the failure of the directors duly to convene a meeting shall be repaid to the requisitionists by the company, and any sum so repaid shall be retained by the company out of any sums due or to become due from the company by way of fees or other remuneration in respect of their services to such of the directors as were in default.

368(7)   [Where sec. 378(2) notice not given]   In the case of a meeting at which a resolution is to be proposed as a special resolution, the directors are deemed not to have duly convened the meeting if they do not give the notice required for special resolutions by section 378(2).

368(8)   **[Where meeting not duly convened]**   The directors are deemed not to have duly convened a meeting if they convene a meeting for a date more than 28 days after the date of the notice convening the meeting.

History
S. 368(8) added by CA 1989, s. 145 and Sch. 19, para. 9 as from 1 March 1990 (see S.I. 1990 No. 142 (C. 5), art. 5).

SEC. 369   Length of notice for calling meetings

369(1)   **[Minimum notice for meetings]**   A provision of a company's articles is void in so far as it provides for the calling of a meeting of the company (other than an adjourned meeting) by a shorter notice than—

> (a)   in the case of the annual general meeting, 21 days' notice in writing; and
>
> (b)   in the case of a meeting other than an annual general meeting or a meeting for the passing of a special resolution—
>
> > (i)   7 days' notice in writing in the case of an unlimited company, and
> >
> > (ii)   otherwise, 14 days' notice in writing.

369(2)   **[Usual notice]**   Save in so far as the articles of a company make other provision in that behalf (not being a provision avoided by subsection (1)), a meeting of the company (other than an adjourned meeting) may be called—

> (a)   in the case of the annual general meeting, by 21 days' notice in writing; and
>
> (b)   in the case of a meeting other than an annual general meeting or a meeting for the passing of a special resolution—
>
> > (i)   by 7 days' notice in writing in the case of an unlimited company, and
> >
> > (ii)   otherwise, 14 days' notice in writing.

369(3)   **[Agreement to short notice]**   Notwithstanding that a meeting is called by shorter notice than that specified in subsection (2) or in the company's articles (as the case may be), it is deemed to have been duly called if it is so agreed—

> (a)   in the case of a meeting called as the annual general meeting, by all the members entitled to attend and vote at it; and
>
> (b)   otherwise, by the requisite majority.

369(4)   **[Requisite majority in sec. 369(3)(b)]**   The requisite majority for this purpose is a majority in number of the members having a right to attend and vote at the meeting, being a majority—

> (a)   together holding not less than 95 per cent in nominal value of the shares giving a right to attend and vote at the meeting; or
>
> (b)   in the case of a company not having a share capital, together representing not less than 95 per cent of the total voting rights at that meeting of all the members.

A private company may elect (by elective resolution in accordance with section 379A) that the above provisions shall have effect in relation to the company as if for the references to 95 per cent there were substituted references to such lesser percentage, but not less than 90 per cent, as may be specified in the resolution or subsequently determined by the company in general meeting.

History
In s. 369(4) the words from "A private company may elect" to the end inserted by CA 1989, s. 115(3) as from 1 April 1990 subject to transitional and saving provisions (see S.I. 1990 No. 355 (C. 13), art. 4(a) and also art. 10).

SEC. 370   General provisions as to meetings and votes

370(1)   [If articles do not provide otherwise]   The following provisions have effect in so far as the articles of the company do not make other provision in that behalf.

370(2)   [Service of notice of meeting]   Notice of the meeting of a company shall be served on every member of it in the manner in which notices are required to be served by Table A (as for the time being in force).

370(3)   [Members calling meeting]   Two or more members holding not less than one-tenth of the issued share capital or, if the company does not have a share capital, not less than 5 per cent in number of the members of the company may call a meeting.

370(4)   [Quorum]   Two members personally present are a quorum.

370(5)   [Chairman]   Any member elected by the members present at a meeting may be chairman of it.

370(6)   [Votes]   In the case of a company originally having a share capital, every member has one vote in respect of each share or each £10 of stock held by him; and in any other case every member has one vote.

SEC. 371   Power of court to order meeting

371(1)   [Impracticable to call meeting in accordance with Act]   If for any reason it is impracticable to call a meeting of a company in any manner in which meetings of that company may be called, or to conduct the meeting in manner prescribed by the articles or this Act, the court may, either of its own motion or on the application—

(a) of any director of the company, or

(b) of any member of the company who would be entitled to vote at the meeting,

order a meeting to be called, held and conducted in any manner the court thinks fit.

371(2)   [Ancillary directions]   Where such an order is made, the court may give such ancillary or consequential directions as it thinks expedient; and these may include a direction that one member of the company present in person or by proxy be deemed to constitute a meeting.

371(3)   [Status of meeting]   A meeting called, held and conducted in accordance with an order under subsection (1) is deemed for all purposes a meeting of the company duly called, held and conducted.

SEC. 372   Proxies

372(1)   [Entitlement to appoint proxy]   Any member of a company entitled to attend and vote at a meeting of it is entitled to appoint another person (whether a member or not) as his proxy to attend and vote instead of him; and in the case of a private company a proxy appointed to attend and vote instead of a member has also the same right as the member to speak at the meeting.

372(2)   [Limitations re proxy]   But, unless the articles otherwise provide—

(a) subsection (1) does not apply in the case of a company not having a share capital; and

(b) a member of a private company is not entitled to appoint more than one proxy to attend on the same occasion; and

(c) a proxy is not entitled to vote except on a poll.

372(3) **[Statement re proxy in notice re meeting]** In the case of a company having a share capital, in every notice calling a meeting of the company there shall appear with reasonable prominence a statement that a member entitled to attend and vote is entitled to appoint a proxy or, where that is allowed, one or more proxies to attend and vote instead of him, and that a proxy need not also be a member.

372(4) **[Penalty on default re sec. 372(3)]** If default is made in complying with subsection (3) as respects any meeting, every officer of the company who is in default is liable to a fine.

372(5) **[Certain provisions in articles void]** A provision contained in a company's articles is void in so far as it would have the effect of requiring the instrument appointing a proxy, or any other document necessary to show the validity of, or otherwise relating to, the appointment of a proxy, to be received by the company or any other person more than 48 hours before a meeting or adjourned meeting in order that the appointment may be effective.

372(6) **[Issue of invitations to appoint proxy to some members only]** If for the purpose of any meeting of a company invitations to appoint as proxy a person or one of a number of persons specified in the invitations are issued at the company's expense to some only of the members entitled to be sent a notice of the meeting and to vote at it by proxy, then every officer of the company who knowingly and wilfully authorises or permits their issue in that manner is liable to a fine.

However, an officer is not so liable by reason only of the issue to a member at his request in writing of a form of appointment naming the proxy, or of a list of persons willing to act as proxy, if the form or list is available on request in writing to every member entitled to vote at the meeting by proxy.

372(7) **[Application]** This section applies to meetings of any class of members of a company as it applies to general meetings of the company.

SEC. 373 Right to demand a poll

373(1) **[Certain provisions in articles re excluding poll etc. void]** A provision contained in a company's articles is void in so far as it would have the effect either—

(a) of excluding the right to demand a poll at a general meeting on any question other than the election of the chairman of the meeting or the adjournment of the meeting; or

(b) of making ineffective a demand for a poll on any such question which is made either—

(i) by not less than 5 members having the right to vote at the meeting; or

(ii) by a member or members representing not less than one-tenth of the total voting rights of all the members having the right to vote at the meeting; or

    (iii) by a member or members holding shares in the company conferring a right to vote at the meeting, being shares on which an aggregate sum has been paid up equal to not less than one-tenth of the total sum paid up on all the shares conferring that right.

373(2) **[Proxy may demand poll]** The instrument appointing a proxy to vote at a meeting of a company is deemed also to confer authority to demand or join in demanding a poll; and for the purposes of subsection (1) a demand by a person as proxy for a member is the same as a demand by the member.

SEC. 374   Voting on a poll

374 On a poll taken at a meeting of a company or a meeting of any class of members of a company, a member entitled to more than one vote need not, if he votes, use all his votes or cast all the votes he uses in the same way.

SEC. 375   Representation of corporations at meetings

375(1) **[Corporation as member or creditor]** A corporation, whether or not a company within the meaning of this Act, may—

    (a) if it is a member of another corporation, being such a company, by resolution of its directors or other governing body authorise such person as it thinks fit to act as its representative at any meeting of the company or at any meeting of any class of members of the company;

    (b) if it is a creditor (including a holder of debentures) of another corporation, being such a company, by resolution of its directors or other governing body authorise such person as it thinks fit to act as its representative at any meeting of creditors of the company held in pursuance of this Act or of rules made under it, or in pursuance of the provisions contained in any debenture or trust deed, as the case may be.

375(2) **[Person authorised under sec. 375(1)]** A person so authorised is entitled to exercise the same powers on behalf of the corporation which he represents as that corporation could exercise if it were an individual shareholder, creditor or debenture-holder of the other company.

RESOLUTIONS

SEC. 376   Circulation of members' resolutions

376(1) **[Company to supply details of proposed resolutions etc.]** Subject to the section next following, it is the duty of a company, on the requisition in writing of such number of members as is specified below and (unless the company otherwise resolves) at the expense of the requisitionists—

    (a) to give to members of the company entitled to receive notice of the next annual general meeting notice of any resolution which may properly be moved and is intended to be moved at that meeting;

    (b) to circulate to members entitled to have notice of any general meeting sent to them any statement of not more than 1,000 words with respect to the matter referred to in any proposed resolution or the business to be dealt with at that meeting.

376(2) **[Number of members for sec. 376(1) requisition]** The number of members necessary for a requisition under subsection (1) is—

(a) any number representing not less than one-twentieth of the total voting rights of all the members having at the date of the requisition a right to vote at the meeting to which the requisition relates; or

(b) not less than 100 members holding shares in the company on which there has been paid up an average sum, per member, of not less than £100.

376(3) **[Service of notice re resolution to members entitled to notice]** Notice of any such resolution shall be given, and any such statement shall be circulated, to members of the company entitled to have notice of the meeting sent to them, by serving a copy of the resolution or statement on each such member in any manner permitted for service of notice of the meeting.

376(4) **[Notice to other members]** Notice of any such resolution shall be given to any other member of the company by giving notice of the general effect of the resolution in any manner permitted for giving him notice of meetings of the company.

376(5) **[Compliance with sec. 376(3), (4)]** For compliance with subsections (3) and (4), the copy must be served, or notice of the effect of the resolution be given (as the case may be), in the same manner and (so far as practicable) at the same time as notice of the meeting; and, where it is not practicable for it to be served or given at the same time, it must be served or given as soon as practicable thereafter.

376(6) **[Business at annual general meeting]** The business which may be dealt with at an annual general meeting includes any resolution of which notice is given in accordance with this section; and for purposes of this subsection notice is deemed to have been so given notwithstanding the accidental omission, in giving it, of one or more members. This has effect notwithstanding anything in the company's articles.

376(7) **[Penalty on default]** In the event of default in complying with this section, every officer of the company who is in default is liable to a fine.

SEC. 377 In certain cases, compliance with sec. 376 not required

377(1) **[Situations where company bound under sec. 376]** A company is not bound under section 376 to give notice of a resolution or to circulate a statement unless—

(a) a copy of the requisition signed by the requisitionists (or two or more copies which between them contain the signatures of all the requisitionists) is deposited at the registered office of the company—

  (i) in the case of a requisition requiring notice of a resolution, not less than 6 weeks before the meeting, and

  (ii) otherwise, not less than one week before the meeting; and

(b) there is deposited or tendered with the requisition a sum reasonably sufficient to meet the company's expenses in giving effect to it.

377(2) **[Extension of sec. 377(1)]** But if, after a copy of a requisition requiring notice of a resolution has been deposited at the company's registered office, an annual general meeting is called for a date 6 weeks or less after the copy has been deposited, the copy (though not deposited within the time required by subsection (1)) is deemed properly deposited for the purposes of that subsection.

377(3)   [Exception to sec. 376 where rights abused to secure publicity etc.]   The company is also not bound under section 376 to circulate a statement if, on the application either of the company or of any other person who claims to be aggrieved, the court is satisfied that the rights conferred by that section are being abused to secure needless publicity for defamatory matter; and the court may order the company's costs on such an application to be paid in whole or in part by the requisitionists, notwithstanding that they are not parties to the application.

SEC. 378   Extraordinary and special resolutions

378(1)   [Extraordinary resolution]   A resolution is an extraordinary resolution when it has been passed by a majority of not less than three-fourths of such members as (being entitled to do so) vote in person or, where proxies are allowed, by proxy, at a general meeting of which notice specifying the intention to propose the resolution as an extraordinary resolution has been duly given.

378(2)   [Special resolution]   A resolution is a special resolution when it has been passed by such a majority as is required for the passing of an extraordinary resolution and at a general meeting of which not less than 21 days' notice, specifying the intention to propose the resolution as a special resolution, has been duly given.

378(3)   [Agreement to short notice re special resolution]   If it is so agreed by a majority in number of the members having the right to attend and vote at such a meeting, being a majority—

   (a) together holding not less than 95 per cent in nominal value of the shares giving that right; or

   (b) in the case of a company not having a share capital, together representing not less than 95 per cent of the total voting rights at that meeting of all the members,

a resolution may be proposed and passed as a special resolution at a meeting of which less than 21 days' notice has been given.

   A private company may elect (by elective resolution in accordance with section 379A) that the above provisions shall have effect in relation to the company as if for the references to 95 per cent there were substituted references to such lesser percentage, but not less than 90 per cent, as may be specified in the resolution or subsequently determined by the company in general meeting.

History
In s. 378(3) the words from "A private company may elect" to the end inserted by CA 1989, s. 115(3) as from 1 April 1990 subject to transitional and saving provisions (see S.I. 1990 No. 355 (C. 13), art. 4(a) and also art. 10).

378(4)   [Declaration of chairman conclusive evidence]   At any meeting at which an extraordinary resolution or a special resolution is submitted to be passed, a declaration by the chairman that the resolution is carried is, unless a poll is demanded, conclusive evidence of the fact without proof of the number or proportion of the votes recorded in favour of or against the resolution.

378(5)   [Majority on poll]   In computing the majority on a poll demanded on the question that an extraordinary resolution or a special resolution be passed, reference is to be had to the number of votes cast for and against the resolution.

378(6) **[Notice of meeting]** For purposes of this section, notice of a meeting is deemed duly given, and the meeting duly held, when the notice is given and the meeting held in the manner provided by this Act or the company's articles.

SEC. 379 Resolution requiring special notice

379(1) **[28 days notice of intention to move]** Where by any provision of this Act special notice is required of a resolution, the resolution is not effective unless notice of the intention to move it has been given to the company at least 28 days before the meeting at which it is moved.

379(2) **[Notice to members of resolution]** The company shall give its members notice of any such resolution at the same time and in the same manner as it gives notice of the meeting or, if that is not practicable, shall give them notice either by advertisement in a newspaper having an appropriate circulation or in any other mode allowed by the company's articles, at least 21 days before the meeting.

379(3) **[Where notice deemed properly given]** If, after notice of the intention to move such a resolution has been given to the company, a meeting is called for a date 28 days or less after the notice has been given, the notice is deemed properly given, though not given within the time required.

SEC. 379A Elective resolution of private company

379A(1) **["Elective resolution"]** An election by a private company for the purposes of—

(a) section 80A (election as to duration of authority to allot shares),

(b) section 252 (election to dispense with laying of accounts and reports before general meeting),

(c) section 366A (election to dispense with holding of annual general meeting),

(d) section 369(4) or 378(3) (election as to majority required to authorise short notice of meeting), or

(e) section 386 (election to dispense with appointment of auditors annually),

shall be made by resolution of the company in general meeting in accordance with this section.

Such a resolution is referred to in this Act as an "elective resolution".

379A(2) **[Conditions for resolution to be effective]** An elective resolution is not effective unless—

(a) at least 21 days' notice in writing is given of the meeting, stating that an elective resolution is to be proposed and stating the terms of the resolution, and

(b) the resolution is agreed to at the meeting, in person or by proxy, by all the members entitled to attend and vote at the meeting.

379A(3) **[Revocation of resolution]** The company may revoke an elective resolution by passing an ordinary resolution to that effect.

379A(4) **[Effect of re-registration as public company]** An elective resolution shall cease to have effect if the company is re-registered as a public company.

379A(5)   [Contrary provision in memorandum or articles]   An elective resolution may be passed or revoked in accordance with this section, and the provisions referred to in subsection (1) have effect, notwithstanding any contrary provision in the company's articles of association.

History
S. 379A inserted by CA 1989, s. 116(1), (2) as from 1 April 1990 (see S.I. 1990 No. 355 (C. 13), art. 4(a)).

Note
See CA 1989, s. 117 for Secretary of State's power to make further provision by regulations.

SEC. 380   Registration, etc. of resolutions and agreements

380(1)   [Copies of resolutions etc. to registrar within 15 days]   A copy of every resolution or agreement to which this section applies shall, within 15 days after it is passed or made, be forwarded to the registrar of companies and recorded by him; and it must be either a printed copy or else a copy in some other form approved by the registrar.

380(2)   [Copies of resolution etc. to be attached to articles]   Where articles have been registered, a copy of every such resolution or agreement for the time being in force shall be embodied in or annexed to every copy of the articles issued after the passing of the resolution or the making of the agreement.

380(3)   [Where articles in sec. 380(2) not registered]   Where articles have not been registered, a printed copy of every such resolution or agreement shall be forwarded to any member at his request on payment of 5 pence or such less sum as the company may direct.

380(4)   [Application]   This section applies to—

(a) special resolutions;

(b) extraordinary resolutions;

(bb) an elective resolution or a resolution revoking such a resolution;

(c) resolutions or agreements which have been agreed to by all the members of a company but which, if not so agreed to, would not have been effective for their purpose unless (as the case may be) they had been passed as special resolutions or as extraordinary resolutions;

(d) resolutions or agreements which have been agreed to by all the members of some class of shareholders but which, if not so agreed to, would not have been effective for their purpose unless they had been passed by some particular majority or otherwise in some particular manner, and all resolutions or agreements which effectively bind all the members of any class of shareholders though not agreed to by all those members;

(e) a resolution passed by the directors of a company in compliance with a direction under section 31(2) (change of name on Secretary of State's direction);

(f) a resolution of a company to give, vary, revoke or renew an authority to the directors for the purposes of section 80 (allotment of relevant securities);

(g) a resolution of the directors passed under section 147(2) (alteration of memorandum on company ceasing to be a public company, following acquisition of its own shares);

(h) a resolution conferring, varying, revoking or renewing authority under section 166 (market purchase of company's own shares);

(j) a resolution for voluntary winding up, passed under section 84(1)(a) of the Insolvency Act;

(k) a resolution passed by the directors of an old public company, under section 2(1) of the Consequential Provisions Act, that the company should be re-registered as a public company.

History
S. 380(4)(bb) inserted by CA 1989, s. 116(1), (3) as from 1 April 1990 (see S.I. 1990 No. 355 (C. 13), art. 4(a)) and in s. 380(4)(j) the words "section 84(1)(a) of the Insolvency Act" substituted for the former words "section 572(1)(a)" by Insolvency Act 1986, s. 439(1) and Sch. 13 as from 29 December 1986 (see IA 1986, s. 443 and S.I. 1986 No. 1924 (C. 71)).

380(5) **[Penalty on default re sec. 380(1)]** If a company fails to comply with subsection (1), the company and every officer of it who is in default is liable to a fine and, for continued contravention, to a daily default fine.

380(6) **[Penalty on default re sec. 380(2), (3)]** If a company fails to comply with subsection (2) or (3), the company and every officer of it who is in default is liable to a fine.

380(7) **[Liquidator officer]** For purposes of subsections (5) and (6), a liquidator of a company is deemed an officer of it.

SEC. 381 Resolution passed at adjourned meeting

381 Where a resolution is passed at an adjourned meeting of—

(a) a company;

(b) the holders of any class of shares in a company;

(c) the directors of a company;

the resolution is for all purposes to be treated as having been passed on the date on which it was in fact passed, and is not to be deemed passed on any earlier date.

WRITTEN RESOLUTIONS OF PRIVATE COMPANIES

SEC. 381A Written resolutions of private companies

381A(1) **[Matters may be done by written resolution]** Anything which in the case of a private company may be done—

(a) by resolution of the company in general meeting, or

(b) by resolution of a meeting of any class of members of the company,

may be done, without a meeting and without any previous notice being required, by resolution in writing signed by or on behalf of all the members of the company who at the date of the resolution would be entitled to attend and vote at such meeting.

381A(2) **[Signatures]** The signatures need not be on a single document provided each is on a document which accurately states the terms of the resolution.

381A(3) **[Date of resolution]** The date of the resolution means when the resolution is signed by or on behalf of the last member to sign.

381A(4) **[Effect of resolution]** A resolution agreed to in accordance with this section has effect as if passed—

(a) by the company in general meeting, or

(b) by a meeting of the relevant class of members of the company, as the case may be; and any reference in any enactment to a meeting at which a resolution is passed or to members voting in favour of a resolution shall be construed accordingly.

381A(5)   [Reference to date of passing of resolution]   Any reference in any enactment to the date of passing of a resolution is, in relation to a resolution agreed to in accordance with this section, a reference to the date of the resolution, unless section 381B(4) applies in which case it shall be construed as a reference to the date from which the resolution has effect.

381A(6)   [Types of resolutions otherwise required]   A resolution may be agreed to in accordance with this section which would otherwise be required to be passed as a special, extraordinary or elective resolution; and any reference in any enactment to a special, extraordinary or elective resolution includes such a resolution.

381A(7)   [Sch. 15A: exceptions, procedure]   This section has effect subject to the exceptions specified in Part I of Schedule 15A; and in relation to certain descriptions of resolution under this section the procedural requirements of this Act have effect with the adaptations specified in Part II of that Schedule.

History
See history note after s. 381C.

SEC. 381B   Right of auditors in relation to written resolution

381B(1)   [Copy of proposed resolution to auditors]   A copy of any written resolution proposed to be agreed to in accordance with section 381A shall be sent to the company's auditors.

381B(2)   [Right of auditors if resolution concerns them]   If the resolution concerns the auditors as auditors, they may within seven days from the day on which they receive the copy give notice to the company stating their opinion that the resolution should be considered by the company in general meeting or, as the case may be, by a meeting of the relevant class of members of the company.

381B(3)   [Conditions for resolution to have effect]   A written resolution shall not have effect unless—

    (a) the auditors notify the company that in their opinion the resolution—

        (i) does not concern them as auditors, or

        (ii) does so concern them but need not be considered by the company in general meeting or, as the case may be, by a meeting of the relevant class of members of the company, or

    (b) the period for giving a notice under subsection (2) expires without any notice having been given in accordance with that subsection.

381B(4)   [Further condition]   A written resolution previously agreed to in accordance with section 381A shall not have effect until that notification is given or, as the case may be, that period expires.

History
See history note after s. 381C.

SEC. 381C   Written resolutions: supplementary provisions

381C(1)   [Provision in memorandum or articles]   Sections 381A and 381B have effect notwithstanding any provision of the company's memorandum or articles.

381C(2) **[Things not affected by sec. 381A, 381B]** Nothing in those sections affects any enactment or rule of law as to—

(a) things done otherwise than by passing a resolution, or

(b) cases in which a resolution is treated as having been passed, or a person is precluded from alleging that a resolution has not been duly passed.

History
S. 381A–381C inserted by CA 1989, s. 113(1), (2) as from
1 April 1990 (see S.I. 1990 No. 355 (C. 13), art. 4(a)).

RECORDS OF PROCEEDINGS

SEC. 382 Minutes of meetings

382(1) **[Minutes to be entered in books]** Every company shall cause minutes of all proceedings of general meetings, all proceedings at meetings of its directors and, where there are managers, all proceedings at meetings of its managers to be entered in books kept for that purpose.

382(2) **[Minutes signed by chairman evidence]** Any such minute, if purporting to be signed by the chairman of the meeting at which the proceedings were had, or by the chairman of the next succeeding meeting, is evidence of the proceedings.

382(3) **[Where shadow director declaring interest by sec. 317(8)]** Where a shadow director by means of a notice required by section 317(8) declares an interest in a contract or proposed contract, this section applies—

(a) if it is a specific notice under paragraph (a) of that subsection, as if the declaration had been made at the meeting there referred to, and

(b) otherwise, as if it had been made at the meeting of the directors next following the giving of the notice;

and the making of the declaration is in either case deemed to form part of the proceedings at the meeting.

382(4) **[Where minutes kept meeting deemed held, etc.]** Where minutes have been made in accordance with this section of the proceedings at any general meeting of the company or meeting of directors or managers, then, until the contrary is proved, the meeting is deemed duly held and convened, and all proceedings had at the meeting to have been duly had; and all appointments of directors, managers or liquidators are deemed valid.

382(5) **[Penalty on default re sec. 382(1)]** If a company fails to comply with subsection (1), the company and every officer of it who is in default is liable to a fine and, for continued contravention, to a daily default fine.

SEC. 382A Recording of written resolutions

382A(1) **[Duty of company to make record]** Where a written resolution is agreed to in accordance with section 381A which has effect as if agreed by the company in general meeting, the company shall cause a record of the resolution (and of the signatures) to be entered in a book in the same way as minutes of proceedings of a general meeting of the company.

382A(2) **[Record evidence, deemed compliance]** Any such record, if purporting to be signed by a director of the company or by the company secretary, is evidence of the proceedings in agreeing to the resolution; and where a record is made in accordance with this section, then, until the contrary is proved, the requirements of this Act with respect to those proceedings shall be deemed to be complied with.

382A(3)   **[Penalty, inspection]**   Section 382(5) (penalties) applies in relation to a failure to comply with subsection (1) above as it applies in relation to a failure to comply with subsection (1) of that section; and section 383 (inspection of minute books) applies in relation to a record made in accordance with this section as it applies in relation to the minutes of a general meeting.

History
S. 382A inserted by CA 1989, s. 113(1), (3) as from 1 April
1990 (see S.I. 1990 No. 355 (C. 13), art. 4(a)).

SEC. 383   Inspection of minute books

383(1)   **[Books at registered office and open to inspection]**   The books containing the minutes of proceedings of any general meeting of a company held on or after 1st November 1929 shall be kept at the company's registered office, and shall during business hours be open to the inspection of any member without charge.

383(2)   **[Business hours in sec. 383(1)]**   The reference to business hours is subject to such reasonable restrictions as the company may by its articles or in general meeting impose, but so that not less than 2 hours in each day be allowed for inspection.

383(3)   **[Copy of minutes]**   Any member shall be entitled to be furnished, within 7 days after he has made a request in that behalf to the company, with a copy of any such minutes as are referred to above, at a charge of not more than $2\frac{1}{2}$ pence for every 100 words.

383(4)   **[Penalty re refusal of inspection etc.]**   If an inspection required under this section is refused or if a copy required under this section is not sent within the proper time, the company and every officer of it who is in default is liable in respect of each offence to a fine.

383(5)   **[Court may compel inspection etc.]**   In the case of any such refusal or default, the court may by order compel an immediate inspection of the books in respect of all proceedings of general meetings, or direct that the copies required be sent to the persons requiring them.

Chapter V — Auditors

APPOINTMENT OF AUDITORS

SEC. 384   Duty to appoint auditors

384(1)   **[Every company to have auditor(s)]**   Every company shall appoint an auditor or auditors in accordance with this Chapter.

This is subject to section 388A (dormant company exempt from obligation to appoint auditors).

384(2)   **[Appointment]**   Auditors shall be appointed in accordance with section 385 (appointment at general meeting at which accounts are laid), except in the case of a private company which has elected to dispense with the laying of accounts in which case the appointment shall be made in accordance with section 385A.

384(3) [End of time for appointing auditors] References in this Chapter to the end of the time for appointing auditors are to the end of the time within which an appointment must be made under section 385(2) or 385A(2), according to whichever of those sections applies.

384(4) [Private companies may dispense with auditors] Sections 385 and 385A have effect subject to section 386 under which a private company may elect to dispense with the obligation to appoint auditors annually.

History
See history note after s. 394A.

SEC. 385 Appointment at general meeting at which accounts laid

385(1) [Application] This section applies to every public company and to a private company which has not elected to dispense with the laying of accounts.

385(2) [Duty of company] The company shall, at each general meeting at which accounts are laid, appoint an auditor or auditors to hold office from the conclusion of that meeting until the conclusion of the next general meeting at which accounts are laid.

385(3) [First auditors] The first auditors of the company may be appointed by the directors at any time before the first general meeting of the company at which accounts are laid; and auditors so appointed shall hold office until the conclusion of that meeting.

385(4) [If directors fail to exercise powers] If the directors fail to exercise their powers under subsection (3), the powers may be exercised by the company in general meeting.

History
See history note after s. 394A.

SEC. 385A Appointment by private company which is not obliged to lay accounts

385A(1) [Application] This section applies to a private company which has elected in accordance with section 252 to dispense with the laying of accounts before the company in general meeting.

385A(2) [Appointment] Auditors shall be appointed by the company in general meeting before the end of the period of 28 days beginning with the day on which copies of the company's annual accounts for the previous financial year are sent to members under section 238 or, if notice is given under section 253(2) requiring the laying of the accounts before the company in general meeting, the conclusion of that meeting.

Auditors so appointed shall hold office from the end of that period or, as the case may be, the conclusion of that meeting until the end of the time for appointing auditors for the next financial year.

385A(3) [First auditors] The first auditors of the company may be appointed by the directors at any time before—

(a) the end of the period of 28 days beginning with the day on which copies of the company's first annual accounts are sent to members under section 238, or

(b) if notice is given under section 253(2) requiring the laying of the accounts before the company in general meeting, the beginning of that meeting;

and auditors so appointed shall hold office until the end of that period or, as the case may be, the conclusion of that meeting.

385A(4) **[If directors fail to exercise powers]** If the directors fail to exercise their powers under subsection (3), the powers may be exercised by the company in general meeting.

385A(5) **[Continuation of office]** Auditors holding office when the election is made shall, unless the company in general meeting determines otherwise, continue to hold office until the end of the time for appointing auditors for the next financial year; and auditors holding office when an election ceases to have effect shall continue to hold office until the conclusion of the next general meeting of the company at which accounts are laid.

History
See history note after s. 394A.

SEC. 386   Election by private company to dispense with annual appointment

386(1) **[Power of private company]** A private company may elect (by elective resolution in accordance with section 379A) to dispense with the obligation to appoint auditors annually.

386(2) **[Deemed re-appointment]** When such an election is in force the company's auditors shall be deemed to be re-appointed for each succeeding financial year on the expiry of the time for appointing auditors for that year, unless—

(a) a resolution has been passed under section 250 by virtue of which the company is exempt from the obligation to appoint auditors, or

(b) a resolution has been passed under section 393 to the effect that their appointment should be brought to an end.

386(3) **[If election ceases]** If the election ceases to be in force, the auditors then holding office shall continue to hold office—

(a) where section 385 then applies, until the conclusion of the next general meeting of the company at which accounts are laid;

(b) where section 385A then applies, until the end of the time for appointing auditors for the next financial year under that section.

386(4) **[Compensation or damages for loss of office]** No account shall be taken of any loss of the opportunity of further deemed re-appointment under this section in ascertaining the amount of any compensation or damages payable to an auditor on his ceasing to hold office for any reason.

History
See history note after s. 394A.

SEC. 387   Appointment by Secretary of State in default of appointment by company

387(1) **[Power of Secretary of State]** If in any case no auditors are appointed, re-appointed or deemed to be re-appointed before the end of the time for appointing auditors, the Secretary of State may appoint a person to fill the vacancy.

387(2) [Notice by company – offence, penalty] In such a case the company shall within one week of the end of the time for appointing auditors give notice to the Secretary of State of his power having become exercisable.

If a company fails to give the notice required by this subsection, the company and every officer of it who is in default is guilty of an offence and liable to a fine and, for continued contravention, to a daily default fine.

History
See history note after s. 394A.

SEC. 388 Filling of casual vacancies

388(1) [Power of directors, general meeting] The directors, or the company in general meeting, may fill a casual vacancy in the office of auditor.

388(2) [Continuation to act in vacancy] While such a vacancy continues, any surviving or continuing auditor or auditors may continue to act.

388(3) [Special notice for certain resolutions] Special notice is required for a resolution at a general meeting of a company—

   (a) filling a casual vacancy in the office of auditor, or

   (b) re-appointing as auditor a retiring auditor who was appointed by the directors to fill a casual vacancy.

388(4) [Duty of company on receipt of notice] On receipt of notice of such an intended resolution the company shall forthwith send a copy of it—

   (a) to the person proposed to be appointed, and

   (b) if the casual vacancy was caused by the resignation of an auditor, to the auditor who resigned.

History
See history note after s. 394A.

SEC. 388A Dormant company exempt from obligation to appoint auditors

388A(1) [Extended exemption] A company which by virtue of section 250 (dormant companies: exemption from provisions as to audit of accounts) is exempt from the provisions of Part VII relating to the audit of accounts is also exempt from the obligation to appoint auditors.

388A(2) [If exemption ceases] The following provisions apply if the exemption ceases.

388A(3) [Where sec. 385 applies] Where section 385 applies (appointment at general meeting at which accounts are laid), the directors may appoint auditors at any time before the next meeting of the company at which accounts are to be laid; and auditors so appointed shall hold office until the conclusion of that meeting.

388A(4) [Where sec. 385A applies] Where section 385A applies (appointment by private company not obliged to lay accounts), the directors may appoint auditors at any time before—

   (a) the end of the period of 28 days beginning with the day on which copies of the company's annual accounts are next sent to members under section 238, or

(b) if notice is given under section 253(2) requiring the laying of the accounts before the company in general meeting, the beginning of that meeting;

and auditors so appointed shall hold office until the end of that period or, as the case may be, the conclusion of that meeting.

388A(5) [If directors fail to exercise sec. 388A(3), (4) powers]   If the directors fail to exercise their powers under subsection (3) or (4), the powers may be exercised by the company in general meeting.

History
See history note after s. 394A.

SEC. 389   Qualification for appointment as auditor

389(1) [Required qualifications]   Subject to the next subsection, a person is not qualified for appointment as auditor of a company unless either—

(a) he is a member of a body of accountants established in the United Kingdom and for the time being recognised for the purposes of this provision by the Secretary of State; or

(b) he is for the time being authorised by the Secretary of State to be so appointed, as having similar qualifications obtained outside the United Kingdom or else he retains an authorisation formerly granted by the Board of Trade or the Secretary of State under section 161(1)(b) of the Companies Act 1948 (adequate knowledge and experience, or pre-1947 practice).

389(2) [Auditor of unquoted company]   Subject to subsections (6) to (8) below, a person is qualified for appointment as auditor of an unquoted company if he retains an authorisation granted by the Board of Trade or the Secretary of State under section 13(1) of the Companies Act 1967.

In this subsection—

(a) **"unquoted company"** means a company in the case of which, at the time of the person's appointment, the following condition is satisfied, namely, that no shares or debentures of the company, or of a body corporate of which it is the subsidiary, have been quoted on a stock exchange (whether in Great Britain or elsewhere) to the public for subscription or purchase, and

(b) **"company"** does not include a company that carries on business as the promoter of a trading stamp scheme within the meaning of the Trading Stamps Act 1964.

389(3) [Bodies of accountants for sec. 389(1)(a)]   Subject to the next subsection, the bodies of accountants recognised for the purposes of subsection (1)(a) are—

(a) the Institute of Chartered Accountants in England and Wales,

(b) the Institute of Chartered Accountants of Scotland,

(c) the Chartered Association of Certified Accountants, and

(d) the Institute of Chartered Accountants in Ireland.

389(4) [Regulations amending sec. 389(3)]   The Secretary of State may by regulations in a statutory instrument amend subsection (3) by adding or deleting any body, but shall not make regulations—

(a) adding any body, or

(b) deleting any body which has not consented in writing to its deletion,

unless he has published notice of his intention to do so in the London and Edinburgh Gazettes at least 4 months before making the regulations.

389(5) **[Refusal of sec. 389(1)(b) authorisation if no reciprocal recognition]** The Secretary of State may refuse an authorisation under subsection (1)(b) to a person as having qualifications obtained outside the United Kingdom if it appears to him that the country in which the qualifications were obtained does not confer on persons qualified in the United Kingdom privileges corresponding to those conferred by that subsection.

389(6) **[Persons not to be auditors]** None of the following persons is qualified for appointment as auditor of a company—

(a) an officer or servant of the company;

(b) a person who is a partner of or in the employment of an officer or servant of the company;

(c) a body corporate;

and for this purpose an auditor of a company is not to be regarded as either officer or servant of it.

389(7) **[Disqualified from being auditor of related company]** A person is also not qualified for appointment as auditor of a company if he is, under subsection (6), disqualified for appointment as auditor of any other body corporate which is that company's subsidiary or holding company or a subsidiary of that company's holding company, or would be so disqualified if the body corporate were a company.

389(8) **[Scottish firm]** Notwithstanding subsections (1), (6) and (7), a Scottish firm is qualified for appointment as auditor of a company if, but only if, all the partners are qualified for appointment as auditor of it.

389(9) **[No person to be auditor if knows disqualified]** No person shall act as auditor of a company at a time when he knows that he is disqualified for appointment to that office; and if an auditor of a company to his knowledge becomes so disqualified during his term of office he shall thereupon vacate his office and give notice in writing to the company that he has vacated it by reason of that disqualification.

389(10) **[Penalty for contravention re sec. 389(9)]** A person who acts as auditor in contravention of subsection (9), or fails without reasonable excuse to give notice of vacating his office as required by that subsection, is guilty of an offence and liable to a fine and, for continued contravention, to a daily default fine.

Note
Prospective repeal of s. 389 by CA 1989, s. 212 and Sch. 24
and replacement by provisions in CA 1989, Pt. II.

RIGHTS OF AUDITORS

SEC. 389A   Rights to information

389A(1) **[Auditors' right of access]** The auditors of a company have a right of access at all times to the company's books, accounts and vouchers, and are entitled to require from the company's officers such information and explanations as they think necessary for the performance of their duties as auditors.

389A(2)   [Offence, penalty]   An officer of a company commits an offence if he knowingly or recklessly makes to the company's auditors a statement (whether written or oral) which—

(a) conveys or purports to convey any information or explanations which the auditors require, or are entitled to require, as auditors of the company, and

(b) is misleading, false or deceptive in a material particular.

A person guilty of an offence under this subsection is liable to imprisonment or a fine, or both.

389A(3)   [Duty of subsidiary undertaking, offence and penalty]   A subsidiary undertaking which is a body corporate incorporated in Great Britain, and the auditors of such an undertaking, shall give to the auditors of any parent company of the undertaking such information and explanations as they may reasonably require for the purposes of their duties as auditors of that company.

If a subsidiary undertaking fails to comply with this subsection, the undertaking and every officer of it who is in default is guilty of an offence and liable to a fine; and if an auditor fails without reasonable excuse to comply with this subsection he is guilty of an offence and liable to a fine.

389A(4)   [Duty of parent where subsidiary not GB body corporate, offence and penalty]   A parent company having a subsidiary undertaking which is not a body corporate incorporated in Great Britain shall, if required by its auditors to do so, take all such steps as are reasonably open to it to obtain from the subsidiary undertaking such information and explanations as they may reasonably require for the purposes of their duties as auditors of that company.

If a parent company fails to comply with this subsection, the company and every officer of it who is in default is guilty of an offence and liable to a fine.

389A(5)   [Application of sec. 734]   Section 734 (criminal proceedings against unincorporated bodies) applies to an offence under subsection (3).

History
See history note after s. 394A.

SEC. 390   Right to attend company meetings, etc.

390(1)   [Auditors' rights of attendance, etc.]   A company's auditors are entitled—

(a) to receive all notices of, and other communications relating to, any general meeting which a member of the company is entitled to receive;

(b) to attend any general meeting of the company; and

(c) to be heard at any general meeting which they attend on any part of the business of the meeting which concerns them as auditors.

390(2)   [Rights re sec. 381A written resolution]   In relation to a written resolution proposed to be agreed to by a private company in accordance with section 381A, the company's auditors are entitled—

(a) to receive all such communications relating to the resolution as, by virtue of any provision of Schedule 15A, are required to be supplied to a member of the company,

CA 1985, sec. 389A(2)   [The next page is 17,851]   **CCH Editions Limited**

(b) to give notice in accordance with section 381B of their opinion that the resolution concerns them as auditors and should be considered by the company in general meeting or, as the case may be, by a meeting of the relevant class of members of the company,

(c) to attend any such meeting, and

(d) to be heard at any such meeting which they attend on any part of the business of the meeting which concerns them as auditors.

390(3)   [Exercise of rights by corporate or partnership auditors]   The right to attend or be heard at a meeting is exercisable in the case of a body corporate or partnership by an individual authorised by it in writing to act as its representative at the meeting.

History
See history note after s. 394A.

REMUNERATION OF AUDITORS

SEC. 390A   Remuneration of auditors

390A(1)   [Auditors appointed by general meeting]   The remuneration of auditors appointed by the company in general meeting shall be fixed by the company in general meeting or in such manner as the company in general meeting may determine.

390A(2)   [Auditors appointed by directors, Secretary of State]   The remuneration of auditors appointed by the directors or the Secretary of State shall be fixed by the directors or the Secretary of State, as the case may be.

390A(3)   [Note to accounts re remuneration]   There shall be stated in a note to the company's annual accounts the amount of the remuneration of the company's auditors in their capacity as such.

390A(4)   ["Remuneration"]   For the purposes of this section "remuneration" includes sums paid in respect of expenses.

390A(5)   [Application]   This section applies in relation to benefits in kind as to payments in cash, and in relation to any such benefit references to its amount are to its estimated money value.

The nature of any such benefit shall also be disclosed.

History
See history note after s. 394A.

SEC. 390B   Remuneration of auditors or their associates for non-audit work

390B(1)   [Power of Secretary of State to make regulations]   The Secretary of State may make provision by regulations for securing the disclosure of the amount of any remuneration received or receivable by a company's auditors or their associates in respect of services other than those of auditors in their capacity as such.

390B(2)   [Scope of regulations]   The regulations may—

(a) provide that "remuneration" includes sums paid in respect of expenses,

(b) apply in relation to benefits in kind as to payments in cash, and in relation to any such benefit require disclosure of its nature and its estimated money value,

(c) define "associate" in relation to an auditor,

(d) require the disclosure of remuneration in respect of services rendered to associated undertakings of the company, and

(e) define "associated undertaking" for that purpose.

390B(3)   [Regulations may require disclosure of certain information]   The regulations may require the auditors to disclose the relevant information in their report or require the relevant information to be disclosed in a note to the company's accounts and require the auditors to supply the directors of the company with such information as is necessary to enable that disclosure to be made.

390B(4)   [Different provision for different cases]   The regulations may make different provision for different cases.

390B(5)   [Annulment by Parliament]   Regulations under this section shall be made by statutory instrument which shall be subject to annulment in pursuance of a resolution of either House of Parliament.

History
See history note after s. 394A.

REMOVAL, RESIGNATION, ETC. OF AUDITORS

SEC. 391   Removal of auditors

391(1)   [Power of company]   A company may by ordinary resolution at any time remove an auditor from office, notwithstanding anything in any agreement between it and him.

391(2)   [Notice of resolution removing auditors, offence and penalty]   Where a resolution removing an auditor is passed at a general meeting of a company, the company shall within 14 days give notice of that fact in the prescribed form to the registrar.

If a company fails to give the notice required by this subsection, the company and every officer of it who is in default is guilty of an offence and liable to a fine and, for continued contravention, to a daily default fine.

391(3)   [Compensation or damages]   Nothing in this section shall be taken as depriving a person removed under it of compensation or damages payable to him in respect of the termination of his appointment as auditor or of any appointment terminating with that as auditor.

391(4)   [Removed auditor still has sec. 390 rights]   An auditor of a company who has been removed has, notwithstanding his removal, the rights conferred by section 390 in relation to any general meeting of the company—

(a) at which his term of office would otherwise have expired, or

(b) at which it is proposed to fill the vacancy caused by his removal.

In such a case the references in that section to matters concerning the auditors as auditors shall be construed as references to matters concerning him as a former auditor.

History
See history note after s. 394A.

CCH Editions Limited
BCL BCL6$$$$42

SEC. 391A Rights of auditors who are removed or not re-appointed

391A(1) [Special notice] Special notice is required for a resolution at a general meeting of a company—

(a) removing an auditor before the expiration of his term of office, or

(b) appointing as auditor a person other than a retiring auditor.

391A(2) [Copy of notice to relevant persons] On receipt of notice of such an intended resolution the company shall forthwith send a copy of it to the person proposed to be removed or, as the case may be, to the person proposed to be appointed and to the retiring auditor.

391A(3) [Representations by relevant persons] The auditor proposed to be removed or (as the case may be) the retiring auditor may make with respect to the intended resolution representations in writing to the company (not exceeding a reasonable length) and request their notification to members of the company.

391A(4) [Duty of company] The company shall (unless the representations are received by it too late for it to do so)—

(a) in any notice of the resolution given to members of the company, state the fact of the representations having been made, and

(b) send a copy of the representations to every member of the company to whom notice of the meeting is or has been sent.

391A(5) [Where copies of representations not sent or sent too late] If a copy of any such representations is not sent out as required because received too late or because of the company's default, the auditor may (without prejudice to his right to be heard orally) require that the representations be read out at the meeting.

391A(6) [Power of court on application] Copies of the representations need not be sent out and the representations need not be read at the meeting if, on the application either of the company or of any other person claiming to be aggrieved, the court is satisfied that the rights conferred by this section are being abused to secure needless publicity for defamatory matter; and the court may order the company's costs on the application to be paid in whole or in part by the auditor, notwithstanding that he is not a party to the application.

History
See history note after s. 394A.

SEC. 392 Resignation of auditors

392(1) [Resignation by notice] An auditor of a company may resign his office by depositing a notice in writing to that effect at the company's registered office.

The notice is not effective unless it is accompanied by the statement required by section 394.

392(2) [Effect of notice] An effective notice of resignation operates to bring the auditor's term of office to an end as of the date on which the notice is deposited or on such later date as may be specified in it.

392(3) [Copy of notice to registrar, offence and penalty] The company shall within 14 days of the deposit of a notice of resignation send a copy of the notice to the registrar of companies.

If default is made in complying with this subsection, the company and every officer of it who is in default is guilty of an offence and liable to a fine and, for continued contravention, a daily default fine.

History
See history note after s. 394A.

SEC. 392A   Rights of resigning auditors

392A(1)   [Application]   This section applies where an auditor's notice of resignation is accompanied by a statement of circumstances which he considers should be brought to the attention of members or creditors of the company.

392A(2)   [Signed requisition may accompany notice]   He may deposit with the notice a signed requisition calling on the directors of the company forthwith duly to convene an extraordinary general meeting of the company for the purpose of receiving and considering such explanation of the circumstances connected with his resignation as he may wish to place before the meeting.

392A(3)   [Right of auditor to request circulation of statement]   He may request the company to circulate to its members—

(a) before the meeting convened on his requisition, or

(b) before any general meeting at which his term of office would otherwise have expired or at which it is proposed to fill the vacancy caused by his resignation,

a statement in writing (not exceeding a reasonable length) of the circumstances connected with his resignation.

392A(4)   [Duty of company re statement]   The company shall (unless the statement is received too late for it to comply)—

(a) in any notice of the meeting given to members of the company, state the fact of the statement having been made, and

(b) send a copy of the statement to every member of the company to whom notice of the meeting is or has been sent.

392A(5)   [Offence, penalty]   If the directors do not within 21 days from the date of the deposit of a requisition under this section proceed duly to convene a meeting for a day not more than 28 days after the date on which the notice convening the meeting is given, every director who failed to take all reasonable steps to secure that a meeting was convened as mentioned above is guilty of an offence and liable to a fine.

392A(6)   [Right of auditor where statement not sent]   If a copy of the statement mentioned above is not sent out as required because received too late or because of the company's default, the auditor may (without prejudice to his right to be heard orally) require that the statement be read out at the meeting.

392A(7)   [Power of court on application]   Copies of a statement need not be sent out and the statement need not be read out at the meeting if, on the application either of the company or of any other person who claims to be aggrieved, the court is satisfied that the rights conferred by this section are being abused to secure needless publicity for defamatory matter; and the court may order the company's costs on such an application to be paid in whole or in part by the auditor, notwithstanding that he is not a party to the application.

CA 1985, sec. 392A(1)   [The next page is 18,101]   **CCH Editions Limited**

392A(8) **[Resigning auditor still has sec. 390 rights]** An auditor who has resigned has, notwithstanding his resignation, the rights conferred by section 390 in relation to any such general meeting of the company as is mentioned in subsection (3)(a) or (b).

In such a case the references in that section to matters concerning the auditors as auditors shall be construed as references to matters concerning him as a former auditor.

History
See history note after s. 394A.

SEC. 393 Termination of appointment of auditors not appointed annually

393(1) **[Notice by member]** When an election is in force under section 386 (election by private company to dispense with annual appointment), any member of the company may deposit notice in writing at the company's registered office proposing that the appointment of the company's auditors be brought to an end.

No member may deposit more than one such notice in any financial year of the company.

393(2) **[Duty of directors]** If such a notice is deposited it is the duty of the directors—

(a) to convene a general meeting of the company for a date not more than 28 days after the date on which the notice was given, and

(b) to propose at the meeting a resolution in a form enabling the company to decide whether the appointment of the company's auditors should be brought to an end.

393(3) **[If general meeting decided auditors' appointment ended]** If the decision of the company at the meeting is that the appointment of the auditors should be brought to an end, the auditors shall not be deemed to be re-appointed when next they would be and, if the notice was deposited within the period immediately following the distribution of accounts, any deemed re-appointment for the financial year following that to which those accounts relate which has already occurred shall cease to have effect.

The period immediately following the distribution of accounts means the period beginning with the day on which copies of the company's annual accounts are sent to members of the company under section 238 and ending 14 days after that day.

393(4) **[Where directors do not call meeting]** If the directors do not within 14 days from the date of the deposit of the notice proceed duly to convene a meeting, the member who deposited the notice (or, if there was more than one, any of them) may himself convene the meeting; but any meeting so convened shall not be held after the expiration of three months from that date.

393(5) **[Meeting called by member]** A meeting convened under this section by a member shall be convened in the same manner, as nearly as possible, as that in which meetings are to be convened by directors.

393(6) **[Reasonable expenses re member calling meeting]** Any reasonable expenses incurred by a member by reason of the failure of the directors duly to convene a meeting shall be made good to him by the company; and any such sums shall be recouped by the company from such of the directors as were in default out of any sums payable, or to become payable, by the company by way of fees or other remuneration in respect of their services.

393(7)   [Provision in agreement, compensation or damages]   This section has effect notwithstanding anything in any agreement between the company and its auditors; and no compensation or damages shall be payable by reason of the auditors' appointment being terminated under this section.

History
See history note after s. 394A.

SEC. 394   Statement by person ceasing to hold office as auditor

394(1)   [Duty of auditor to deposit statement]   Where an auditor ceases for any reason to hold office, he shall deposit at the company's registered office a statement of any circumstances connected with his ceasing to hold office which he considers should be brought to the attention of the members or creditors of the company or, if he considers that there are no such circumstances, a statement that there are none.

394(2)   [Time for depositing statement]   In the case of resignation, the statement shall be deposited along with the notice of resignation; in the case of failure to seek re-appointment, the statement shall be deposited not less than 14 days before the end of the time allowed for next appointing auditors; in any other case, the statement shall be deposited not later than the end of the period of 14 days beginning with the date on which he ceases to hold office.

394(3)   [Duty of company if there are certain circumstances]   If the statement is of circumstances which the auditor considers should be brought to the attention of the members or creditors of the company, the company shall within 14 days of the deposit of the statement either—

(a)   send a copy of it to every person who under section 238 is entitled to be sent copies of the accounts, or

(b)   apply to the court.

394(4)   [Notice to auditor re application to court]   The company shall if it applies to the court notify the auditor of the application.

394(5)   [If no notice of application auditors must send copy of statement to registrar]   Unless the auditor receives notice of such an application before the end of the period of 21 days beginning with the day on which he deposited the statement, he shall within a further seven days send a copy of the statement to the registrar.

394(6)   [Power of court where statement used for publicity]   If the court is satisfied that the auditor is using the statement to secure needless publicity for defamatory matter—

(a)   it shall direct that copies of the statement need not be sent out, and

(b)   it may further order the company's costs on the application to be paid in whole or in part by the auditor, notwithstanding that he is not a party to the application;

and the company shall within 14 days of the court's decision send to the persons mentioned in subsection (3)(a) a statement setting out the effect of the order.

394(7) **[Power of court where statement not so used]** If the court is not so satisfied, the company shall within 14 days of the court's decision—

(a) send copies of the statement to the persons mentioned in subsection (3)(a), and

(b) notify the auditor of the court's decision;

and the auditor shall within seven days of receiving such notice send a copy of the statement to the registrar.

History
See history note after s. 394A.

SEC. 394A   Offences of failing to comply with sec. 394

394A(1) **[Offence, penalty]** If a person ceasing to hold office as auditor fails to comply with section 394 he is guilty of an offence and liable to a fine.

394A(2) **[Defence]** In proceedings for an offence under subsection (1) it is a defence for the person charged to show that he took all reasonable steps and exercised all due diligence to avoid the commission of the offence.

394A(3) **[Application of sec. 733, 734]** Sections 733 (liability of individuals for corporate default) and 734 (criminal proceedings against unincorporated bodies) apply to an offence under subsection (1).

394A(4) **[Offence re company, penalty]** If a company makes default in complying with section 394, the company and every officer of it who is in default is guilty of an offence and liable to a fine and, for continued contravention, to a daily default fine.

History
S. 384–388A, 389A–394A inserted by CA 1989, s. 118, 119–124 as from 1 April 1990 subject to transitional and saving provisions (see S.I. 1990 No. 355 (C. 13), art. 4(a) and also art. 10) — see also note to s. 389; the former s. 384–388, 390–394 read as follows:

"SEC. 384 Annual appointment of auditors

384(1) Every company shall, at each general meeting of the company at which accounts are laid in accordance with section 241, appoint an auditor or auditors to hold office from the conclusion of that meeting until the conclusion of the next general meeting at which the requirements of section 241 are complied with.

This is subject to section 252 (exemption for dormant companies).

(2) The first auditors of a company may be appointed by the directors at any time before the first general meeting of the company at which accounts are laid; and auditors so appointed shall hold office until the conclusion of that meeting.

(3) If the directors fail to exercise their powers under subsection (2), those powers may be exercised by the company in general meeting.

(4) The directors, or the company in general meeting, may fill any casual vacancy in the office of auditor; but while any such vacancy continues, the surviving or continuing auditor or auditors (if any) may act.

(5) If at any general meeting of a company at which accounts are laid as required by section 241 no auditors are appointed or reappointed, the Secretary of State may appoint a person to fill the vacancy; and the company shall, within one week of that power of the Secretary of State becoming exercisable, give to him notice of that fact.

If a company fails to give the notice required by this subsection, the company and every officer of it who is in default is guilty of an offence and liable to a fine and, for continued contravention, to a daily default fine.

SEC. 385 Remuneration of auditors

385(1) The remuneration of a company's auditors shall be fixed by the company in general meeting, or in such manner as the company in general meeting may determine.

(2) This does not apply in the case of auditors appointed by the directors or by the Secretary of State; and in that case their remuneration may be fixed by the directors or by the Secretary of State (as the case may be).

(3) For the purpose of this section, **"remuneration"** includes any sums paid by the company in respect of the auditor's expenses.

SEC. 386 Removal of auditors

386(1) A company may by ordinary resolution remove an auditor before the expiration of his term of office, notwithstanding anything in any agreement between it and him.

(2) Where a resolution removing an auditor is passed at a general meeting of a company, the company shall within 14 days give notice of that fact in the prescribed form to the registrar of companies.

If a company fails to give the notice required by this subsection, the company and every officer of it who is in default is guilty of an offence and liable to a fine and, for continued contravention, to a daily default fine.

(3) Nothing in this section is to be taken as depriving a person removed under it of compensation or damages payable to him in respect of the termination of his appointment as auditor or of any appointment terminating with that as auditor.

SEC. 387 Auditors' right to attend company meetings

387(1) A company's auditors are entitled to attend any general meeting of the company and to receive all notices of, and other communications relating to, any general meeting which a member of the company is entitled to receive, and to be heard at any general meeting which they attend on any part of the business of the meeting which concerns them as auditors.

(2) An auditor of a company who has been removed is entitled to attend—

  (a) the general meeting at which his term of office would otherwise have expired, and

  (b) any general meeting at which it is proposed to fill the vacancy caused by his removal,

and to receive all notices of, and other communications relating to, any such meeting which any member of the company is entitled to receive, and to be heard at any such meeting which he attends on any part of the business of the meeting which concerns him as former auditor of the company.

SEC. 388 Supplementary provisions as to auditors

388(1) Special notice is required for a resolution at a general meeting of a company—

  (a) appointing as auditor a person other than a retiring auditor; or

  (b) filling a casual vacancy in the office of auditor; or

  (c) reappointing as auditor a retiring auditor who was appointed by the directors to fill a casual vacancy; or

  (d) removing an auditor before the expiration of his term of office.

(2) On receipt of notice of such an intended resolution as is mentioned above the company shall forthwith send a copy of it—

  (a) to the person proposed to be appointed or removed, as the case may be;

  (b) in a case within subsection (1)(a), to the retiring auditor; and

  (c) where, in a case within subsection (1) (b) or (c), the casual vacancy was caused by the resignation of an auditor, to the auditor who resigned.

(3) Where notice is given of such a resolution as is mentioned in subsection (1)(a) or (d), and the retiring auditor or (as the case may be) the auditor proposed to be removed makes with respect to the intended resolution representations in writing to the company (not exceeding a reasonable length) and requests their notification to members of the company, the company shall (unless the representations are received by it too late for it to do so)—

  (a) in any notice of the resolution given to members of the company state the fact of the representations having been made, and

  (b) send a copy of the representations to every member of the company to whom notice of the meeting is or has been sent.

(4) If a copy of any such representations is not sent out as required by subsection (3) because received too late or because of the company's default, the auditor may (without prejudice to his right to be heard orally) require that the representations shall be read out at the meeting.

(5) Copies of the representations need not be sent out and the representations need not be read out at the meeting if, on the application either of the company or of any other person claiming to be aggrieved, the court is satisfied that the rights conferred by this section are being abused to secure needless publicity for defamatory matter; and the court may order the company's costs on the application to be paid in whole or in part by the auditor, notwithstanding that he is not a party to the application.

SEC. 390 Resignation of auditors

390(1) An auditor of a company may resign his office by depositing a notice in writing to that effect at the company's registered office; and any such notice operates to bring his term of office to an end on the date on which the notice is deposited, or on such later date as may be specified in it.

(2) An auditor's notice of resignation is not effective unless it contains either—

  (a) a statement to the effect that there are no circumstances connected with his resignation which he considers should be brought to the notice of the members or creditors of the company; or

  (b) a statement of any such circumstances as are mentioned above.

(3) Where a notice under this section is deposited at a company's registered office, the company shall within 14 days send a copy of the notice—

  (a) to the registrar of companies; and

  (b) if the notice contained a statement under subsection (2)(b), to every person who under section 240 is entitled to be sent copies of the accounts.

(4) The company or any person claiming to be aggrieved may, within 14 days of the receipt by the company of a notice containing a statement under subsection (2)(b), apply to the court for an order under the next subsection.

(5) If on such an application the court is satisfied that the auditor is using the notice to secure needless publicity for defamatory matter, it may by order direct that copies of the notice need not be sent out; and the court may further order the company's costs on the application to be paid in whole or in part by the auditor, notwithstanding that he is not a party to the application.

(6) The company shall, within 14 days of the court's decision, send to the persons mentioned in subsection (3)—

  (a) if the court makes an order under subsection (5), a statement setting out the effect of the order;

  (b) if not, a copy of the notice containing the statement under subsection (2)(b).

(7) If default is made in complying with subsection (3) or (6), the company and every officer of it who is in default is liable to a fine and, for continued contravention, to a daily default fine.

SEC. 391 Right of resigning auditor to requisition company meeting

391(1) Where an auditor's notice of resignation contains a statement under section 390(2)(b) there may be deposited with the notice a requisition signed by the auditor calling on the directors of the company forthwith duly to convene an extraordinary general meeting of the company for the purpose of receiving and considering such explanation of the circumstances connected with his resignation as he may wish to place before the meeting.

(2) Where an auditor's notice of resignation contains such a statement, the auditor may request the company to circulate to its members—

  (a) before the general meeting at which his term of office would otherwise have expired; or

  (b) before any general meeting at which it is proposed

to fill the vacancy caused by his resignation or convened on his requisition,

a statement in writing (not exceeding a reasonable length) of the circumstances connected with his resignation.

(3) The company shall in that case (unless the statement is received by it too late for it to comply)—

(a) in any notice of the meeting given to members of the company state the fact of the statement having been made, and

(b) send a copy of the statement to every member of the company to whom notice of the meeting is or has been sent.

(4) If the directors do not within 21 days from the date of the deposit of a requisition under this section proceed duly to convene a meeting for a day not more than 28 days after the date on which the notice convening the meeting is given, every director who failed to take all reasonable steps to secure that a meeting was convened as mentioned above is guilty of an offence and liable to a fine.

(5) If a copy of the statement mentioned in subsection (2) is not sent out as required by subsection (3) because received too late or because of the company's default, the auditor may (without prejudice to his right to be heard orally) require that the statement shall be read out at the meeting.

(6) Copies of a statement need not be sent out and the statement need not be read out at the meeting if, on the application either of the company or of any other person who claims to be aggrieved, the court is satisfied that the rights conferred by this section are being abused to secure needless publicity for defamatory matter; and the court may order the company's costs on such an application to be paid in whole or in part by the auditor, notwithstanding that he is not a party to the application.

(7) An auditor who has resigned his office is entitled to attend any such meeting as is mentioned in subsection (2)(a) or (b) and to receive all notices of, and other communications relating to, any such meeting which any member of the company is entitled to receive, and to be heard at any such meeting which he attends on any part of the business of the meeting which concerns him as former auditor of the company.

SEC. 392 Powers of auditors in relation to subsidiaries

392(1) Where a company ("the holding company") has a subsidiary, then—

(a) if the subsidiary is a body corporate incorporated in Great Britain, it is the duty of the subsidiary and its auditors to give to the auditors of the holding company such information and explanation as those auditors may reasonably require for the purposes of their duties as auditors of the holding company;

(b) in any other case, it is the duty of the holding company, if required by its auditors to do so, to take all such steps as are reasonably open to it to obtain from the subsidiary such information and explanation as are mentioned above.

(2) If a subsidiary or holding company fails to comply with subsection (1), the subsidiary or holding company and every officer of it who is in default is guilty of an offence and liable to a fine; and if an auditor fails without reasonable excuse to comply with paragraph (a) of the subsection, he is guilty of an offence and so liable.

SEC. 393 False statements to auditors

393 An officer of a company commits an offence if he knowingly or recklessly makes to a company's auditors a statement (whether written or oral) which—

(a) conveys or purports to convey any information or explanation which the auditors require, or are entitled to require, as auditors of the company, and

(b) is misleading, false or deceptive in a material particular.

A person guilty of an offence under this section is liable to imprisonment or a fine, or both.

SEC. 394 Auditors of trade unions

394(1) Subject as follows, this section applies to every body which is both a company and a trade union or an employers' association to which section 11 of the Trade Union and Labour Relations Act 1974 applies.

(2) Section 11(3) of the Act of 1974 and paragraphs 6 to 15 of Schedule 2 to that Act (qualifications, appointment and removal of auditors) do not have effect in relation to bodies to which this section applies.

(3) The rights and powers conferred, and the duties imposed, by paragraphs 16 to 21 of that Schedule on the auditors of a body to which this section applies belong to the auditors from time to time appointed by or on behalf of that body under section 384 of this Act."

PART XII — REGISTRATION OF CHARGES

Chapter 1 — Registration of Charges (England and Wales)

SEC. 395 Certain charges void if not registered

395(1) [Void against liquidator or administrator and creditors] Subject to the provisions of this Chapter, a charge created by a company registered in England and Wales and being a charge to which this section applies is, so far as any security on the company's property or undertaking is conferred by the charge, void against the liquidator or administrator and any creditor of the company, unless the prescribed particulars of the charge together with the instrument (if any) by which the charge is created or evidenced, are delivered to or received by the registrar of companies for registration in the manner required by this Chapter within 21 days after the date of the charge's creation.

History
In s. 395(1) the words "or administrator" appearing after the word "liquidator" inserted by Insolvency Act 1985, s. 109 and Sch. 6, para. 10 as from 29 December 1986 (see S.I. 1986 No. 1924 (C. 71)).

395(2)   [Contracts for repayment etc.]   Subsection (1) is without prejudice to any contract or obligation for repayment of the money secured by the charge; and when a charge becomes void under this section, the money secured by it immediately becomes payable.

SEC. 396   Charges which have to be registered

396(1)   [Application of sec. 395]   Section 395 applies to the following charges—

   (a) a charge for the purpose of securing any issue of debentures,

   (b) a charge on uncalled share capital of the company,

   (c) a charge created or evidenced by an instrument which, if executed by an individual, would require registration as a bill of sale,

   (d) a charge on land (wherever situated) or any interest in it, but not including a charge for any rent or other periodical sum issuing out of the land,

   (e) a charge on book debts of the company,

   (f) a floating charge on the company's undertaking or property,

   (g) a charge on calls made but not paid,

   (h) a charge on a ship or aircraft, or any share in a ship,

   (j) a charge on goodwill, on a patent or a licence under a patent, on a trademark or on a copyright or a licence under a copyright.

396(2)   [Negotiable instrument securing payment of book debts]   Where a negotiable instrument has been given to secure the payment of any book debts of a company, the deposit of the instrument for the purpose of securing an advance to the company is not, for purposes of section 395, to be treated as a charge on those book debts.

396(3)   [Holding of debentures entitling holder to charge on land]   The holding of debentures entitling the holder to a charge on land is not for purposes of this section deemed to be an interest in land.

396(4)   ["Charge"]   In this Chapter, **"charge"** includes mortgage.

SEC. 397   Formalities of registration (debentures)

397(1)   [Required particulars re series of debentures]   Where a series of debentures containing, or giving by reference to another instrument, any charge to the benefit of which the debenture holders of that series are entitled pari passu is created by a company, it is for purposes of section 395 sufficient if there are delivered to or received by the registrar, within 21 days after the execution of the deed containing the charge (or, if there is no such deed, after the execution of any debentures of the series), the following particulars in the prescribed form—

   (a) the total amount secured by the whole series, and

   (b) the dates of the resolutions authorising the issue of the series and the date of the covering deed (if any) by which the security is created or defined, and

CA 1985, sec. 395(2)

(c) a general description of the property charged, and

(d) the names of the trustees (if any) for the debenture holders,

together with the deed containing the charge or, if there is no such deed, one of the debentures of the series:

Provided that there shall be sent to the registrar of companies, for entry in the register, particulars in the prescribed form of the date and amount of each issue of debentures of the series, but any omission to do this does not affect the validity of any of those debentures.

397(2) [Required particulars where commission etc. paid] Where any commission, allowance or discount has been paid or made either directly or indirectly by a company to a person in consideration of his—

(a) subscribing or agreeing to subscribe, whether absolutely or conditionally, for debentures of the company, or

(b) procuring or agreeing to procure subscriptions, whether absolute or conditional, for such debentures,

the particulars required to be sent for registration under section 395 shall include particulars as to the amount or rate per cent of the commission, discount or allowance so paid or made, but omission to do this does not affect the validity of the debentures issued.

397(3) [Interpretation in sec. 397(2)] The deposit of debentures as security for a debt of the company is not, for the purposes of subsection (2), treated as the issue of the debentures at a discount.

SEC. 398 Verification of charge on property outside United Kingdom

398(1) [Charge created outside UK re property within UK] In the case of a charge created out of the United Kingdom comprising property situated outside the United Kingdom, the delivery to and the receipt by the registrar of companies of a copy (verified in the prescribed manner) of the instrument by which the charge is created or evidenced has the same effect for purposes of sections 395 to 398 as the delivery and receipt of the instrument itself.

398(2) [Timing] In that case, 21 days after the date on which the instrument or copy could, in due course of post (and if despatched with due diligence), have been received in the United Kingdom are substituted for the 21 days mentioned in section 395(1) (or as the case may be, section 397(1)) as the time within which the particulars and instrument or copy are to be delivered to the registrar.

398(3) [Charge created in UK re property outside UK] Where a charge is created in the United Kingdom but comprises property outside the United Kingdom, the instrument creating or purporting to create the charge may be sent for registration under section 395 notwithstanding that further proceedings may be necessary to make the charge valid or effectual according to the law of the country in which the property is situated.

398(4)   [Charge re property in Scotland or Northern Ireland]   Where a charge comprises property situated in Scotland or Northern Ireland and registration in the country where the property is situated is necessary to make the charge valid or effectual according to the law of that country, the delivery to and the receipt by the registrar of a copy (verified in the prescribed manner) of the instrument by which the charge is created or evidenced, together with a certificate in the prescribed form stating that the charge was presented for registration in Scotland or Northern Ireland (as the case may be) on the date on which it was so presented has, for purposes of sections 395 to 398, the same effect as the delivery and receipt of the instrument itself.

SEC. 399   Company's duty to register charges it creates

399(1)   [Company's obligation]   It is a company's duty to send to the registrar of companies for registration the particulars of every charge created by the company and of the issues of debentures of a series requiring registration under sections 395 to 398; but registration of any such charge may be effected on the application of any person interested in it.

399(2)   [Where registration by person other than company]   Where registration is effected on the application of some person other than the company, that person is entitled to recover from the company the amount of any fees properly paid by him to the registrar on the registration.

399(3)   [Penalty on default re sec. 399(1)]   If a company fails to comply with subsection (1), then, unless the registration has been effected on the application of some other person, the company and every officer of it who is in default is liable to a fine and, for continued contravention, to a daily default fine.

SEC. 400   Charges existing on property acquired

400(1)   [Application]   This section applies where a company registered in England and Wales acquires property which is subject to a charge of any such kind as would, if it had been created by the company after the acquisition of the property, have been required to be registered under this Chapter.

400(2)   [Particulars and copy of instrument to registrar within 21 days]   The company shall cause the prescribed particulars of the charge, together with a copy (certified in the prescribed manner to be a correct copy) of the instrument (if any) by which the charge was created or is evidenced, to be delivered to the registrar of companies for registration in manner required by this Chapter within 21 days after the date on which the acquisition is completed.

400(3)   [If property and charge outside Great Britain]   However, if the property is situated and the charge was created outside Great Britain, 21 days after the date on which the copy of the instrument could in due course of post, and if despatched with due diligence, have been received in the United Kingdom is substituted for the 21 days above-mentioned as the time within which the particulars and copy of the instrument are to be delivered to the registrar.

400(4)   [Penalty on default]   If default is made in complying with this section, the company and every officer of it who is in default is liable to a fine and, for continued contravention, to a daily default fine.

SEC. 401 Register of charges to be kept by registrar of companies

401(1) [Matters to be entered in register] The registrar of companies shall keep, with respect to each company, a register in the prescribed form of all the charges requiring registration under this Chapter; and he shall enter in the register with respect to such charges the following particulars—

    (a) in the case of a charge to the benefit of which the holders of a series of debentures are entitled, the particulars specified in section 397(1),

    (b) in the case of any other charge—

      (i) if it is a charge created by the company, the date of its creation, and if it is a charge which was existing on property acquired by the company, the date of the acquisition of the property, and

     (ii) the amount secured by the charge, and

    (iii) short particulars of the property charged, and

    (iv) the persons entitled to the charge.

401(2) [Issue of certificate by registrar] The registrar shall give a certificate of the registration of any charge registered in pursuance of this Chapter, stating the amount secured by the charge.

    The certificate—

    (a) shall be either signed by the registrar, or authenticated by his official seal, and

    (b) is conclusive evidence that the requirements of this Chapter as to registration have been satisfied.

401(3) [Inspection of register] The register kept in pursuance of this section shall be open to inspection by any person.

SEC. 402 Endorsement of certificate on debentures

402(1) [Company to endorse debenture etc.] The company shall cause a copy of every certificate of registration given under section 401 to be endorsed on every debenture or certificate of debenture stock which is issued by the company and the payment of which is secured by the charge so registered.

402(2) [No endorsement before charge created] But this does not require a company to cause a certificate or registration of any charge so given to be endorsed on any debenture or certificate of debenture stock issued by the company before the charge was created.

402(3) [Offence, penalty] If a person knowingly and wilfully authorises or permits the delivery of a debenture or certificate of debenture stock which under this section is required to have endorsed on it a copy of a certificate of registration without the copy being so endorsed upon it, he is liable (without prejudice to any other liability) to a fine.

SEC. 403   Entries of satisfaction and release

403(1)   [Entry by registrar] The registrar of companies, on receipt of a statutory declaration in the prescribed form verifying, with respect to a registered charge,—

    (a) that the debt for which the charge was given has been paid or satisfied in whole or in part, or

    (b) that part of the property or undertaking charged has been released from the charge or has ceased to form part of the company's property or undertaking,

may enter on the register a memorandum of satisfaction in whole or in part, or of the fact that part of the property or undertaking has been released from the charge or has ceased to form part of the company's property or undertaking (as the case may be).

403(2)   [Copy of memorandum of satisfaction in whole] Where the registrar enters a memorandum of satisfaction in whole, he shall if required furnish the company with a copy of it.

SEC. 404   Rectification of register of charges

404(1)   [Application] The following applies if the court is satisfied that the omission to register a charge within the time required by this Chapter or that the omission or mis-statement of any particular with respect to any such charge or in a memorandum of satisfaction was accidental, or due to inadvertence or to some other sufficient cause, or is not of a nature to prejudice the position of creditors or shareholders of the company, or that on other grounds it is just and equitable to grant relief.

404(2)   [Order by court] The court may, on the application of the company or a person interested, and on such terms and conditions as seem to the court just and expedient, order that the time for registration shall be extended or, as the case may be, that the omission or mis-statement shall be rectified.

SEC. 405   Registration of enforcement of security

405(1)   [Notice to registrar re appointment of receiver etc.] If a person obtains an order for the appointment of a receiver or manager of a company's property, or appoints such a receiver or manager under powers contained in an instrument, he shall within 7 days of the order or of the appointment under those powers, give notice of the fact to the registrar of companies; and the registrar shall enter the fact in the register of charges.

405(2)   [Receiver to notify registrar of ceasing to act] Where a person appointed receiver or manager of a company's property under powers contained in an instrument ceases to act as such receiver or manager, he shall, on so ceasing, give the registrar notice to that effect, and the registrar shall enter the fact in the register of charges.

405(3)   [Form of notice] A notice under this section shall be in the prescribed form.

405(4)   [Penalty on default] If a person makes default in complying with the requirements of this section, he is liable to a fine and, for continued contravention, to a daily default fine.

SEC. 406 Companies to keep copies of instruments creating charges

406(1) **[Copies to be kept at registered office]** Every company shall cause a copy of every instrument creating a charge requiring registration under this Chapter to be kept at its registered office.

406(2) **[Series of uniform debentures]** In the case of a series of uniform debentures, a copy of one debenture of the series is sufficient.

SEC. 407 Company's register of charges

407(1) **[Register at registered office]** Every limited company shall keep at its registered office a register of charges and enter in it all charges specifically affecting property of the company and all floating charges on the company's undertaking or any of its property.

407(2) **[Details of entries]** The entry shall in each case give a short description of the property charged, the amount of the charge and, except in the case of securities to bearer, the names of the persons entitled to it.

407(3) **[Offence, penalty]** If an officer of the company knowingly and wilfully authorises or permits the omission of an entry required to be made in pursuance of this section, he is liable to a fine.

SEC. 408 Right to inspect instruments which create charges, etc.

408(1) **[Open to inspection free to creditor or member]** The copies of instruments creating any charge requiring registration under this Chapter with the registrar of companies, and the register of charges kept in pursuance of section 407, shall be open during business hours (but subject to such reasonable restrictions as the company in general meeting may impose, so that not less than 2 hours in each day be allowed for inspection) to the inspection of any creditor or member of the company without fee.

408(2) **[Open to inspection to others for fee]** The register of charges shall also be open to the inspection of any other person on payment of such fee, not exceeding 5 pence, for each inspection, as the company may prescribe.

408(3) **[Penalty re refusal of inspection]** If inspection of the copies referred to, or of the register, is refused, every officer of the company who is in default is liable to a fine and, for continued contravention, to a daily default fine.

408(4) **[Court may compel inspection]** If such a refusal occurs in relation to a company registered in England and Wales, the court may by order compel an immediate inspection of the copies or register.

SEC. 409 Charges on property in England and Wales created elsewhere

409(1) **[Extent of Chapter I]** This Chapter extends to charges on property in England and Wales which are created, and to charges on property in England and Wales which is acquired, by a company (whether a company within the meaning of this Act or not) incorporated outside Great Britain which has an established place of business in England and Wales.

409(2) **[Application of sec. 406, 407]** In relation to such a company, sections 406 and 407 apply with the substitution, for the reference to the company's registered office, of a reference to its principal place of business in England and Wales.

Chapter II — Registration of Charges (Scotland)

SEC. 410   Charges void unless registered

410(1) **[Application]** The following provisions of this Chapter have effect for the purpose of securing the registration in Scotland of charges created by companies.

410(2) **[Particulars etc. to registrar within 21 days]** Every charge created by a company, being a charge to which this section applies, is, so far as any security on the company's property or any part of it is conferred by the charge, void against the liquidator or administrator and any creditor of the company unless the prescribed particulars of the charge, together with a copy (certified in the prescribed manner to be a correct copy) of the instrument (if any) by which the charge is created or evidenced, are delivered to or received by the registrar of companies for registration in the manner required by this Chapter within 21 days after the date of the creation of the charge.

History
In s. 410(2) the words "or administrator" appearing after   s. 109 and Sch. 6, para. 10 as from 29 December 1986 (see
the word "liquidator" inserted by Insolvency Act 1985,   S.I. 1986 No. 1924 (C. 71)).

410(3) **[Extent of sec. 410(2)]** Subsection (2) is without prejudice to any contract or obligation for repayment of the money secured by the charge; and when a charge becomes void under this section the money secured by it immediately becomes payable.

410(4) **[Charges covered]** This section applies to the following charges—

    (a) a charge on land wherever situated, or any interest in such land (not including a charge for any rent, ground annual or other periodical sum payable in respect of the land, but including a charge created by a heritable security within the meaning of section 9(8) of the Conveyancing and Feudal Reform (Scotland) Act 1970),

    (b) a security over the uncalled share capital of the company,

    (c) a security over incorporeal moveable property of any of the following categories—

        (i) the book debts of the company,

        (ii) calls made but not paid,

        (iii) goodwill,

        (iv) a patent or a licence under a patent,

        (v) a trademark,

        (vi) a copyright or a licence under a copyright,

    (d) a security over a ship or aircraft or any share in a ship, and

    (e) a floating charge.

410(5) [**"Company"**] In this Chapter **"company"** (except in section 424) means an incorporated company registered in Scotland; "registrar of companies" means the registrar or other officer performing under this Act the duty of registration of companies in Scotland; and references to the date of creation of a charge are—

(a) in the case of a floating charge, the date on which the instrument creating the floating charge was executed by the company creating the charge, and

(b) in any other case, the date on which the right of the person entitled to the benefit of the charge was constituted as a real right.

SEC. 411 Charges on property outside United Kingdom

411(1) [**Charge created outside United Kingdom**] In the case of a charge created out of the United Kingdom comprising property situated outside the United Kingdom, the period of 21 days after the date on which the copy of the instrument creating it could (in due course of post, and if despatched with due diligence) have been received in the United Kingdom is substituted for the period of 21 days after the date of the creation of the charge as the time within which, under section 410(2), the particulars and copy are to be delivered to the registrar.

411(2) [**Charge created in United Kingdom**] Where a charge is created in the United Kingdom but comprises property outside the United Kingdom, the copy of the instrument creating or purporting to create the charge may be sent for registration under section 410 notwithstanding that further proceedings may be necessary to make the charge valid or effectual according to the law of the country in which the property is situated.

SEC. 412 Negotiable instrument to secure book debts

412 Where a negotiable instrument has been given to secure the payment of any book debts of a company, the deposit of the instrument for the purpose of securing an advance to the company is not, for purposes of section 410, to be treated as a charge on those book debts.

SEC. 413 Charges associated with debentures

413(1) [**Holding of debentures entitling holder to charge on land**] The holding of debentures entitling the holder to a charge on land is not, for the purposes of section 410, deemed to be an interest in land.

413(2) [**Required particulars re series of debentures**] Where a series of debentures containing, or giving by reference to any other instrument, any charge to the benefit of which the debenture-holders of that series are entitled pari passu, is created by a company, it is sufficient for purposes of section 410 if there are delivered to or received by the registrar of companies within 21 days after the execution of the deed containing the charge or, if there is no such deed, after the execution of any debentures of the series, the following particulars in the prescribed form—

(a) the total amount secured by the whole series,

(b) the date of the resolutions authorising the issue of the series and the date of the covering deed (if any) by which the security is created or defined,

(c) a general description of the property charged,

(d) the names of the trustees (if any) for the debenture holders, and

(e) in the case of a floating charge, a statement of any provisions of the charge and of any instrument relating to it which prohibit or restrict or regulate the power of the company to grant further securities ranking in priority to, or pari passu with, the floating charge, or which vary or otherwise regulate the order of ranking of the floating charge in relation to subsisting securities,

together with a copy of the deed containing the charge or, if there is no such deed, of one of the debentures of the series:

Provided that, where more than one issue is made of debentures in the series, there shall be sent to the registrar of companies for entry in the register particulars (in the prescribed form) of the date and amount of each issue of debentures of the series, but any omission to do this does not affect the validity of any of those debentures.

413(3)   [Required particulars where commission paid for subscription]   Where any commission, allowance or discount has been paid or made, either directly or indirectly, by a company to any person in consideration of his subscribing or agreeing to subscribe, whether absolutely or conditionally, for any debentures of the company, or procuring or agreeing to procure subscriptions (whether absolute or conditional) for any such debentures, the particulars required to be sent for registration under section 410 include particulars as to the amount or rate per cent of the commission, discount or allowance so paid or made; but any omission to do this does not affect the validity of the debentures issued.

The deposit of any debentures as security for any debt of the company is not, for purposes of this subsection, treated as the issue of the debentures at a discount.

SEC. 414   Charge by way of ex facie absolute disposition, etc.

414(1)   [Effect of compliance with sec. 410(2)]   For the avoidance of doubt, it is hereby declared that, in the case of a charge created by way of an ex facie absolute disposition or assignation qualified by a back letter or other agreement, or by a standard security qualified by an agreement, compliance with section 410(2) does not of itself render the charge unavailable as security for indebtedness incurred after the date of compliance.

414(2)   [Increase of charge]   Where the amount secured by a charge so created is purported to be increased by a further back letter or agreement, a further charge is held to have been created by the ex facie absolute disposition or assignation or (as the case may be) by the standard security, as qualified by the further back letter or agreement; and the provisions of this Chapter apply to the further charge as if—

(a) references in this Chapter (other than in this section) to the charge were references to the further charge, and

(b) references to the date of the creation of the charge were references to the date on which the further back letter or agreement was executed.

SEC. 415 Company's duty to register charges created by it

415(1) [Company to send details of charge] It is a company's duty to send to the registrar of companies for registration the particulars of every charge created by the company and of the issues of debentures of a series requiring registration under sections 410 to 414; but registration of any such charge may be effected on the application of any person interested in it.

415(2) [Fees recoverable by other persons effecting registration] Where registration is effected on the application of some person other than the company, that person is entitled to recover from the company the amount of any fees properly paid by him to the registrar on the registration.

415(3) [Penalty on default] If a company makes default in sending to the registrar for registration the particulars of any charge created by the company or of the issues of debentures of a series requiring registration as above mentioned, then, unless the registration has been effected on the application of some other person, the company and every officer of it who is in default is liable to a fine and, for continued contravention, to a daily default fine.

SEC. 416 Duty to register charges existing on property acquired

416(1) [Particulars etc. to registrar within 21 days] Where a company acquires any property which is subject to a charge of any kind as would, if it had been created by the company after the acquisition of the property, have been required to be registered under this Chapter, the company shall cause the prescribed particulars of the charge, together with a copy (certified in the prescribed manner to be a correct copy) of the instrument (if any) by which the charge was created or is evidenced, to be delivered to the registrar of companies for registration in the manner required by this Chapter within 21 days after the date on which the transaction was settled.

416(2) [If property and charge outside Great Britain] If, however, the property is situated and the charge was created outside Great Britain, 21 days after the date on which the copy of the instrument could (in due course of post, and if despatched with due diligence) have been received in the United Kingdom are substituted for 21 days after the settlement of the transaction as the time within which the particulars and the copy of the instrument are to be delivered to the registrar.

416(3) [Penalty on default] If default is made in complying with this section, the company and every officer of it who is in default is liable to a fine and, for continued contravention, to a daily default fine.

SEC. 417 Register of charges to be kept by registrar of companies

417(1) [Register to be kept] The registrar of companies shall keep, with respect to each company, a register in the prescribed form of all the charges requiring registration under this Chapter, and shall enter in the register with respect to such charges the particulars specified below.

417(2) [Charge re holders of series of debentures] In the case of a charge to the benefit of which the holders of a series of debentures are entitled, there shall be entered in the register the particulars specified in section 413(2).

417(3) **[Details of entries]** In the case of any other charge, there shall be entered—

(a) if it is a charge created by the company, the date of its creation, and if it was a charge existing on property acquired by the company, the date of the acquisition of the property,

(b) the amount secured by the charge,

(c) short particulars of the property charged,

(d) the persons entitled to the charge, and

(e) in the case of a floating charge, a statement of any of the provisions of the charge and of any instrument relating to it which prohibit or restrict or regulate the company's power to grant further securities ranking in priority to, or pari passu with, the floating charge, or which vary or otherwise regulate the order of ranking of the floating charge in relation to subsisting securities.

417(4) **[Inspection of register]** The register kept in pursuance of this section shall be open to inspection by any person.

SEC. 418 Certificate of registration to be issued

418(1) **[Registrar to give certificate]** The registrar of companies shall give a certificate of the registration of any charge registered in pursuance of this Chapter.

418(2) **[Details re certificate; conclusive evidence]** The certificate—

(a) shall be either signed by the registrar, or authenticated by his official seal,

(b) shall state the name of the company and the person first-named in the charge among those entitled to the benefit of the charge (or, in the case of a series of debentures, the name of the holder of the first such debenture to be issued) and the amount secured by the charge, and

(c) is conclusive evidence that the requirements of this Chapter as to registration have been complied with.

SEC. 419 Entries of satisfaction and relief

419(1) **[Memorandum of satisfaction may be entered on register]** The registrar of companies, on application being made to him in the prescribed form, and on receipt of a statutory declaration in the prescribed form verifying, with respect to any registered charge—

(a) that the debt for which the charge was given has been paid or satisfied in whole or in part, or

(b) that part of the property charged has been released from the charge or has ceased to form part of the company's property,

may enter on the register a memorandum of satisfaction (in whole or in part) regarding that fact.

419(2) **[Copy to registrar]** Where the registrar enters a memorandum of satisfaction in whole, he shall, if required, furnish the company with a copy of the memorandum.

419(3) **[Requirements for registrar to be satisfied]** Without prejudice to the registrar's duty under this section to require to be satisfied as above mentioned, he shall not be so satisfied unless—

(a) the creditor entitled to the benefit of the floating charge, or a person authorised to do so on his behalf, certifies as correct the particulars submitted to the registrar with respect to the entry on the register or a memorandum under this section, or

(b) the court, on being satisfied that such certification cannot readily be obtained, directs him accordingly.

419(4) **[Extent of company's obligation]** Nothing in this section requires the company to submit particulars with respect to the entry in the register of a memorandum of satisfaction where the company, having created a floating charge over all or any part of its property, disposes of part of the property subject to the floating charge.

419(5) **[Form]** A memorandum or certification required for the purposes of this section shall be in such form as may be prescribed.

SEC. 420 Rectification of register

420 The court, on being satisfied that the omission to register a charge within the time required by this Act or that the omission or mis-statement of any particular with respect to any such charge or in a memorandum of satisfaction was accidental, or due to inadvertence or to some other sufficient cause, or is not of a nature to prejudice the position of creditors or shareholders of the company, or that it is one other grounds just and equitable to grant relief, may, on the application of the company or any person interested, and on such terms and conditions as seem to the court just and expedient, order that the time for registration shall be extended or (as the case may be) that the omission or mis-statement shall be rectified.

SEC. 421 Copies of instruments creating charges to be kept by company

421(1) **[Copies to be kept at registered office]** Every company shall cause a copy of every instrument creating a charge requiring registration under this Chapter to be kept at the company's registered office.

421(2) **[Series of uniform debentures]** In the case of a series of uniform debentures, a copy of one debenture of the series is sufficient.

SEC. 422 Company's register of charges

422(1) **[Register to be kept at registered office]** Every company shall keep at its registered office a register of charges and enter in it all charges specifically affecting property of the company, and all floating charges on any property of the company.

422(2) **[Details re each charge]** There shall be given in each case a short description of the property charged, the amount of the charge and, except in the case of securities to bearer, the names of the persons entitled to it.

422(3) **[Offence, penalty]** If an officer of the company knowingly and wilfully authorises or permits the omission of an entry required to be made in pursuance of this section, he is liable to a fine.

SEC. 423   Right to inspect copies of instruments, and company's register

423(1)   [Inspection by creditors and members]   The copies of instruments creating charges requiring registration under this Chapter with the registrar of companies, and the register of charges kept in pursuance of section 422, shall be open during business hours (but subject to such reasonable restrictions as the company in general meeting may impose, so that not less than 2 hours in each day be allowed for inspection) to the inspection of any creditor or member of the company without fee.

423(2)   [Inspection by others]   The register of charges shall be open to the inspection of any other person on payment of such fee, not exceeding 5 pence for each inspection, as the company may prescribe.

423(3)   [Penalty re refusal of inspection]   If inspection of the copies or register is refused, every officer of the company who is in default is liable to a fine and, for continued contravention, to a daily default fine.

423(4)   [Court may compel inspection re company]   If such a refusal occurs in relation to a company, the court may by order compel an immediate inspection of the copies or register.

SEC. 424   Extension of Chapter II

424(1)   [Companies incorporated outside Great Britain]   This Chapter extends to charges on property in Scotland which are created, and to charges on property in Scotland which is acquired, by a company incorporated outside Great Britain which has a place of business in Scotland.

424(2)   [Application of sec. 421, 422]   In relation to such a company, sections 421 and 422 apply with the substitution, for the reference to the company's registered office, of a reference to its principal place of business in Scotland.

PART XIII — ARRANGEMENTS AND RECONSTRUCTIONS

SEC. 425   Power of company to compromise with creditors and members

425(1)   [Court may order meeting]   Where a compromise or arrangement is proposed between a company and its creditors, or any class of them, or between the company and its members, or any class of them, the court may on the application of the company or any creditor or member of it or, in the case of a company being wound up, or an administration order being in force in relation to a company, of the liquidator or administrator, order a meeting of the creditors or class of creditors, or of the members of the company or class of members (as the case may be), to be summoned in such manner as the court directs.

History
In s. 425(1) the words "or an administration order being in force in relation to a company, of the liquidator or administrator" substituted for the former words "of the liquidator" by Insolvency Act 1985, s. 109 and Sch. 6, para. 11 as from 29 December 1986 (see S.I. 1986 No. 1924 (C. 71)).

Note
For details of the modifications to Pt. XIII where a statutory water company under the Water Act 1989 makes an application under s. 425(1), see the Companies Act 1985 (Modifications for Statutory Water Companies) Regulations 1989 (S.I. 1989 No. 1461).

425(2) [Three-fourths majority binding] If a majority in number representing three-fourths in value of the creditors or class of creditors or members or class of members (as the case may be), present and voting either in person or by proxy at the meeting, agree to any compromise or arrangement, the compromise or arrangement, if sanctioned by the court, is binding on all the creditors or the class of creditors, or on the members or class of members (as the case may be), and also on the company or, in the case of a company in the course of being wound up, on the liquidator and contributories of the company.

425(3) [Sec. 425(2) order of no effect until copy to registrar etc.] The court's order under subsection (2) has no effect until an office copy of it has been delivered to the registrar of companies for registration; and a copy of every such order shall be annexed to every copy of the company's memorandum issued after the order has been made or, in the case of a company not having a memorandum, of every copy so issued of the instrument constituting the company or defining its constitution.

425(4) [Penalty on default re sec. 425(3)] If a company makes default in complying with subsection (3), the company and every officer of it who is in default is liable to a fine.

425(5) [Sec. 425(1) order in Scotland] An order under subsection (1) pronounced in Scotland by the judge acting as vacation judge is not subject to review, reduction, suspension or stay of execution.

History
In s. 425(5) the former words "in pursuance of section 4 of the Administration of Justice (Scotland) Act 1933" (which appeared after the words "vacation judge") repealed by Court of Session Act 1988, s. 52(2) and Sch. 2, Pt. I and III as from 29 September 1988.

425(6) [Definitions] In this section and the next—

(a) **"company"** means any company liable to be wound up under this Act, and

(b) **"arrangement"** includes a reorganisation of the company's share capital by the consolidation of shares of different classes or by the division of shares into shares of different classes, or by both of those methods.

SEC. 426   Information as to compromise to be circulated

426(1) [Application] The following applies where a meeting of creditors or any class of creditors, or of members or any class of members, is summoned under section 425.

426(2) [Explanatory statement with notice summoning meeting] With every notice summoning the meeting which is sent to a creditor or member there shall be sent also a statement explaining the effect of the compromise or arrangement and in particular stating any material interests of the directors of the company (whether as directors or as members or as creditors of the company or otherwise) and the effect on those interests of the compromise or arrangement, in so far as it is different from the effect on the like interests of other persons.

426(3)   [Where notice given by way of advertisement]   In every notice summoning the meeting which is given by advertisement there shall be included either such a statement as above-mentioned or a notification of the place at which, and the manner in which, creditors or members entitled to attend the meeting may obtain copies of the statement.

426(4)   [Where compromise affects debenture holders' rights]   Where the compromise or arrangement affects the rights of debenture holders of the company, the statement shall give the like explanation as respects the trustees of any deed for securing the issue of the debentures as it is required to give as respects the company's directors.

426(5)   [In sec. 426(3) situation applicants to get free copy of statement]   Where a notice given by advertisement includes a notification that copies of a statement explaining the effect of the compromise or arrangement proposed can be obtained by creditors or members entitled to attend the meeting, every such creditor or member shall, on making application in the manner indicated by the notice, be furnished by the company free of charge with a copy of the statement.

426(6)   [Penalty on default by company, defence]   If a company makes default in complying with any requirement of this section, the company and every officer of it who is in default is liable to a fine; and for this purpose a liquidator or administrator of the company and a trustee of a deed for securing the issue of debentures of the company is deemed an officer of it.

However, a person is not liable under this subsection if he shows that the default was due to the refusal of another person, being a director or trustee for debenture holders, to supply the necessary particulars of his interests.

History
In s. 426(6) the words "or administrator" inserted by Insolvency Act 1985, s. 109 and Sch. 6, para. 12 as from 29 December 1986 (see S.I. 1986 No. 1924 (C. 71)).

426(7)   [Notice by director and trustee for debenture holders]   It is the duty of any director of the company, and of any trustee for its debenture holders, to give notice to the company of such matters relating to himself as may be necessary for purposes of this section; and any person who makes default in complying with this subsection is liable to a fine.

SEC. 427   Provisions for facilitating company reconstruction or amalgamation

427(1)   [Application]   The following applies where application is made to the court under section 425 for the sanctioning of a compromise or arrangement proposed between a company and any such persons as are mentioned in that section.

427(2)   [Court order]   If it is shown—

(a) that the compromise or arrangement has been proposed for the purposes of, or in connection with, a scheme for the reconstruction of any company or companies, or the amalgamation of any two or more companies, and

(b) that under the scheme the whole or any part of the undertaking or the property of any company concerned in the scheme ("a transferor company") is to be transferred to another company ("the transferee company"), the court may, either by the order sanctioning the compromise or arrangement or by any subsequent order, make provision for all or any of the following matters.

427(3) **[Provisions in court order]** The matters for which the court's order may make provision are—

(a) the transfer to the transferee company of the whole or any part of the undertaking and of the property or liabilities of any transferor company,

(b) the allotting or appropriation by the transferee company of any shares, debentures, policies or other like interests in that company which under the compromise or arrangement are to be allotted or appropriated by that company to or for any person,

(c) the continuation by or against the transferee company of any legal proceedings pending by or against any transferor company,

(d) the dissolution, without winding-up, of any transferor company,

(e) the provision to be made for any persons who, within such time and in such manner as the court directs, dissent from the compromise or arrangement,

(f) such incidental, consequential and supplemental matters as are necessary to secure that the reconstruction or amalgamation is fully and effectively carried out.

427(4) **[Effect of order for transfer of property or liabilities]** If an order under this section provides for the transfer of property or liabilities, then—

(a) that property is by virtue of the order transferred to, and vests in, the transferee company, and

(b) those liabilities are, by virtue of the order, transferred to and become liabilities of that company;

and property (if the order so directs), vests freed from any charge which is by virtue of the compromise or arrangement to cease to have effect.

427(5) **[Company to send copy of order to registrar, penalty on default]** Where an order is made under this section, every company in relation to which the order is made shall cause an office copy of the order to be delivered to the registrar of companies for registration within 7 days after its making; and if default is made in complying with this subsection, the company and every officer of it who is in default is liable to a fine and, for continued contravention, to a daily default fine.

427(6) **[Interpretation]** In this section the expression **"property"** includes property, rights and powers of every description; the expression **"liabilities"** includes duties and **"company"** includes only a company as defined in section 735(1).

SEC. 427A Application of sec. 425–427 to mergers and divisions of public companies

427A(1) **[Operation of sec. 425–427]** Where—

(a) a compromise or arrangement is proposed between a public company and any such persons as are mentioned in section 425(1) for the purposes of, or in connection with, a scheme for the reconstruction of any company or companies or the amalgamation of any two or more companies,

SEC. 427A. Application of secs. 425–427 to mergers and divisions of public companies.

   (b) the circumstances are as specified in any of the Cases described in subsection (2), and

   (c) the consideration for the transfer or each of the transfers envisaged in the Case in question is to be shares in the transferee company or any of the transferee companies receivable by members of the transferor company or transferor companies, with or without any cash payment to members,

sections 425 to 427 shall, as regards that compromise or arrangement, have effect subject to the provisions of this section and Schedule 15B.

History
In s. 427A(1) "15B" substituted for the former "15A" by
CA 1989, s. 114(2) as from 1 April 1990 (see S.I. 1990 No.
355 CC. 13), art. 4(a)).

427A(2) [Cases referred to in sec. 427A(1)] The Cases referred to in subsection (1) are as follows—

Case 1

Where under the scheme the undertaking, property and liabilities of the company in respect of which the compromise or arrangement in question is proposed are to be transferred to another public company, other than one formed for the purpose of, or in connection with, the scheme.

Case 2

Where under the scheme the undertaking, property and liabilities of each of two or more public companies concerned in the scheme, including the company in respect of which the compromise or arrangement in question is proposed, are to be transferred to a company (whether or not a public company) formed for the purpose of, or in connection with, the scheme.

Case 3

Where under the scheme the undertaking, property and liabilities of the company in respect of which the compromise or arrangement in question is proposed are to be divided among and transferred to two or more companies each of which is either—

   (a) a public company, or

   (b) a company (whether or not a public company) formed for the purposes of, or in connection with, the scheme.

427A(3) [Application to court for meeting] Before sanctioning any compromise or arrangement under section 425(2) the court may, on the application of any pre-existing transferee company or any member or creditor of it or, an administration order being in force in relation to the company, the administrator, order a meeting of the members of the company or any class of them or of the creditors of the company or any class of them to be summoned in such manner as the court directs.

427A(4) [Exception if company is winding-up] This section does not apply where the company in respect of which the compromise or arrangement is proposed is being wound up.

427A(5) [Exception if application under sec. 425(1)] This section does not apply to compromises or arrangements in respect of which an application has been made to the court for an order under section 425(1) before 1 January 1988.

427A(6)   [Application if transferee is Northern Ireland company]   Where section 427 would apply in the case of a scheme but for the fact that the transferee company or any of the transferee companies is a company within the meaning of Article 3 of the Companies (Northern Ireland) Order 1986 (and thus not within the definition of "company" in subsection (6) of section 427), section 427 shall apply notwithstanding that fact.

427A(7)   [Registrar of Companies, Northern Ireland]   In the case of a scheme mentioned in subsection (1), for a company within the meaning of Article 3 of the Companies (Northern Ireland) Order 1986, the reference in section 427(5) to the registrar of companies shall have effect as a reference to the registrar as defined in Article 2 of that Order.

427A(8)   [Definitions]   In this section and Schedule 15B—

> **"transferor company"** means a company whose undertaking, property and liabilities are to be transferred by means of a transfer envisaged in any of the Cases specified in subsection (2);
>
> **"transferee company"** means a company to which a transfer envisaged in any of those Cases is to be made;
>
> **"pre-existing transferee company"** means a transferee company other than one formed for the purpose of, or in connection with, the scheme;
>
> **"compromise or arrangement"** means a compromise or arrangement to which subsection (1) applies;
>
> **"the scheme"** means the scheme mentioned in subsection (1)(a);
>
> **"company"** includes only a company as defined in section 735(1) except that, in the case of a transferee company, it also includes a company as defined in Article 3 of the Companies (Northern Ireland) Order 1986 (referred to in these definitions as a **"Northern Ireland company"**);
>
> **"public company"** means, in relation to a transferee company which is a Northern Ireland company, a public company within the meaning of Article 12 of the Companies (Northern Ireland) Order 1986;
>
> **"the registrar of companies"** means, in relation to a transferee company which is a Northern Ireland company, the registrar as defined in Article 2 of the Companies (Northern Ireland) Order 1986;
>
> **"the Gazette"** means, in relation to a transferee company which is a Northern Ireland company, the Belfast Gazette;
>
> **"Case 1 Scheme"**, **"Case 2 Scheme"** and **"Case 3 Scheme"** mean a scheme of a kind described in Cases 1, 2 and 3 of subsection (2) respectively;
>
> **"property"** and **"liabilities"** have the same meaning as in section 427.

History

In s. 427A(8) "15B" substituted for the former "15A" by CA 1989, s. 114(2) as from 1 April 1990 (see S.I. 1990 No. 355 (C. 13), art. 4(a)).

S. 427A inserted by the Companies (Mergers and Divisions) Regulations 1987 (S.I. 1987 No. 1991), reg. 2(a) and Sch., Pt. I, as from 1 January 1988.

PART XIIIA — TAKEOVER OFFERS

SEC. 428 "Takeover offers"

428(1) ["A takeover offer"] In this Part of this Act "**a takeover offer**" means an offer to acquire all the shares, or all the shares of any class or classes, in a company (other than shares which at the date of the offer are already held by the offeror), being an offer on terms which are the same in relation to all the shares to which the offer relates or, where those shares include shares of different classes, in relation to all the shares of each class.

428(2) ["Shares" in sec. 428(1)] In subsection (1) "**shares**" means shares which have been allotted on the date of the offer but a takeover offer may include among the shares to which it relates all or any shares that are subsequently allotted before a date specified in or determined in accordance with the terms of the offer.

428(3) [Terms re shares] The terms offered in relation to any shares shall for the purposes of this section be treated as being the same in relation to all the shares or, as the case may be, all the shares of a class to which the offer relates notwithstanding any variation permitted by subsection (4).

428(4) [Where variation permitted] A variation is permitted by this subsection where—

    (a) the law of a country or territory outside the United Kingdom precludes an offer of consideration in the form or any of the forms specified in the terms in question or precludes it except after compliance by the offeror with conditions with which he is unable to comply or which he regards as unduly onerous; and

    (b) the variation is such that the persons to whom an offer of consideration in that form is precluded are able to receive consideration otherwise than in that form but of substantially equivalent value.

428(5) [Shares already held by offeror in sec. 428(1)] The reference in subsection (1) to shares already held by the offeror includes a reference to shares which he has contracted to acquire but that shall not be construed as including shares which are the subject of a contract binding the holder to accept the offer when it is made, being a contract entered into by the holder either for no consideration and under seal or for no consideration other than a promise by the offeror to make the offer.

428(6) [Application of sec. 428(5) to Scotland] In the application of subsection (5) to Scotland, the words "and under seal" shall be omitted.

428(7) [Revision of terms of offer] Where the terms of an offer make provision for their revision and for acceptances on the previous terms to be treated as acceptances on the revised terms, the revision shall not be regarded for the purposes of this Part of this Act as the making of a fresh offer and references in this Part of this Act to the date of the offer shall accordingly be construed as references to the date on which the original offer was made.

428(8) ["The offeror"] In this Part of this Act "**the offeror**" means, subject to section 430D, the person making a takeover offer and "**the company**" means the company whose shares are the subject of the offer.

Note
See history note after s. 430F.

SEC. 429 Right of offeror to buy out minority shareholders

429(1) [Notice to shareholders] If, in a case in which a takeover offer does not relate to shares of different classes, the offeror has by virtue of acceptances of the offer acquired or contracted to acquire not less than nine-tenths in value of the shares to which the offer relates he may give notice to the holder of any shares to which the offer relates which the offeror has not acquired or contracted to acquire that he desires to acquire those shares.

429(2) [Notice where shares of different classes] If, in a case in which a takeover offer relates to shares of different classes, the offeror has by virtue of acceptances of the offer acquired or contracted to acquire not less than nine-tenths in value of the shares of any class to which the offer relates, he may give notice to the holder of any

[The next page is 19,501]

shares of that class which the offeror has not acquired or contracted to acquire that he desires to acquire those shares.

429(3) **[Condition for sec. 429(1), (2) notice]** No notice shall be given under subsection (1) or (2) unless the offeror has acquired or contracted to acquire the shares necessary to satisfy the minimum specified in that subsection before the end of the period of four months beginning with the date of the offer; and no such notice shall be given after the end of the period of two months beginning with the date on which he has acquired or contracted to acquire shares which satisfy that minimum.

429(4) **[Form of notice]** Any notice under this section shall be given in the prescribed manner; and when the offeror gives the first notice in relation to an offer he shall send a copy of it to the company together with a statutory declaration by him in the prescribed form stating that the conditions for the giving of the notice are satisfied.

Note
See also reg. 4 of The Companies (Forms) (Amendment)
Regulations 1987 (S.I. 1987 No. 752).

429(5) **[Statutory declaration where offeror company]** Where the offeror is a company (whether or not a company within the meaning of this Act) the statutory declaration shall be signed by a director.

429(6) **[Penalty for non-compliance]** Any person who fails to send a copy of a notice or a statutory declaration as required by subsection (4) or makes such a declaration for the purposes of that subsection knowing it to be false or without having reasonable grounds for believing it to be true shall be liable to imprisonment or a fine, or both, and for continued failure to send the copy or declaration, to a daily default fine.

429(7) **[Defence re sec. 429(4) offence]** If any person is charged with an offence for failing to send a copy of a notice as required by subsection (4) it is a defence for him to prove that he took reasonable steps for securing compliance with that subsection.

429(8) **[Acquisition other than by acceptances of offer]** Where during the period within which a takeover offer can be accepted the offeror acquires or contracts to acquire any of the shares to which the offer relates but otherwise than by virtue of acceptances of the offer, then, if—

(a) the value of the consideration for which they are acquired or contracted to be acquired ("the acquisition consideration") does not at that time exceed the value of the consideration specified in the terms of the offer; or

(b) those terms are subsequently revised so that when the revision is announced the value of the acquisition consideration, at the time mentioned in paragraph (a) above, no longer exceeds the value of the consideration specified in those terms,

the offeror shall be treated for the purposes of this section as having acquired or contracted to acquire those shares by virtue of acceptances of the offer; but in any other case those shares shall be treated as excluded from those to which the offer relates.

History
See history note after s. 430F.

SEC. 430 Effect of notice under sec. 429

430(1) **[Application]** The following provisions shall, subject to section 430C, have effect where a notice is given in respect of any shares under section 429.

430(2)   **[Right and duty of offeror]**   The offeror shall be entitled and bound to acquire those shares on the terms of the offer.

430(3)   **[Notice to include details re choice of consideration]**   Where the terms of an offer are such as to give the holder of any shares a choice of consideration the notice shall give particulars of the choice and state—

  (a)   that the holder of the shares may within six weeks from the date of the notice indicate his choice by a written communication sent to the offeror at an address specified in the notice; and

  (b)   which consideration specified in the offer is to be taken as applying in default of his indicating a choice as aforesaid;

and the terms of the offer mentioned in subsection (2) shall be determined accordingly.

430(4)   **[Application of sec. 430(3)]**   Subsection (3) applies whether or not any time-limit or other conditions applicable to the choice under the terms of the offer can still be complied with; and if the consideration chosen by the holder of the shares—

  (a)   is not cash and the offeror is no longer able to provide it; or

  (b)   was to have been provided by a third party who is no longer bound or able to provide it,

the consideration shall be taken to consist of an amount of cash payable by the offeror which at the date of the notice is equivalent to the chosen consideration.

430(5)   **[Copy of notice to company etc.]**   At the end of six weeks from the date of the notice the offeror shall forthwith—

  (a)   send a copy of the notice to the company; and

  (b)   pay or transfer to the company the consideration for the shares to which the notice relates.

430(6)   **[If shares registered]**   If the shares to which the notice relates are registered the copy of the notice sent to the company under subsection (5)(a) shall be accompanied by an instrument of transfer executed on behalf of the shareholder by a person appointed by the offeror; and on receipt of that instrument the company shall register the offeror as the holder of those shares.

430(7)   **[If shares transferable by delivery of warrants]**   If the shares to which the notice relates are transferable by the delivery of warrants or other instruments the copy of the notice sent to the company under subsection (5)(a) shall be accompanied by a statement to that effect; and the company shall on receipt of the statement issue the offeror with warrants or other instruments in respect of the shares and those already in issue in respect of the shares shall become void.

430(8)   **[Sec. 430(5) consideration]**   Where the consideration referred to in paragraph (b) of subsection (5) consists of shares or securities to be allotted by the offeror the reference in that paragraph to the transfer of the consideration shall be construed as a reference to the allotment of the shares or securities to the company.

430(9)   **[Sums under sec. 430(5) to be held on trust]**   Any sum received by a company under paragraph (b) of subsection (5) and any other consideration received under that paragraph shall be held by the company on trust for the person entitled to the shares in respect of which the sum or other consideration was received.

CA 1985, sec. 430(2)

430(10) **[Sec. 430(5) sums to be paid into separate bank account]** Any sum received by a company under paragraph (b) of subsection (5), and any dividend or other sum accruing from any other consideration received by a company under that paragraph, shall be paid into a separate bank account, being an account the balance on which bears interest at an appropriate rate and can be withdrawn by such notice (if any) as is appropriate.

430(11) **[Where person entitled to consideration unable to be found]** Where after reasonable enquiry made at such intervals as are reasonable the person entitled to any consideration held on trust by virtue of subsection (9) cannot be found and twelve years have elapsed since the consideration was received or the company is wound up the consideration (together with any interest, dividend or other benefit that has accrued from it) shall be paid into court.

430(12) **[Company registered in Scotland]** In relation to a company registered in Scotland, subsections (13) and (14) shall apply in place of subsection (11).

430(13) **[Termination of trust etc. re sec. 430(11)]** Where after reasonable enquiry made at such intervals as are reasonable the person entitled to any consideration held on trust by virtue of subsection (9) cannot be found and twelve years have elapsed since the consideration was received or the company is wound up—

    (a)   the trust shall terminate;

    (b)   the company or, as the case may be, the liquidator shall sell any consideration other than cash and any benefit other than cash that has accrued from the consideration; and

    (c)   a sum representing—

        (i)   the consideration so far as it is cash;

        (ii)   the proceeds of any sale under paragraph (b) above; and

        (iii)   any interest, dividend or other benefit that has accrued from the consideration,

        shall be deposited in the name of the Accountant of Court in a bank account such as is referred to in subsection (10) and the receipt for the deposit shall be transmitted to the Accountant of Court.

430(14) **[Application of Bankruptcy (Scotland) Act 1985]** Section 58 of the Bankruptcy (Scotland) Act 1985 (so far as consistent with this Act) shall apply with any necessary modifications to sums deposited under subsection (13) as that section applies to sums deposited under section 57(1)(a) of that Act.

430(15) **[Expenses of sec. 430(11), (13) enquiry]** The expenses of any such enquiry as is mentioned in subsection (11) or (13) may be defrayed out of the money or other property held on trust for the person or persons to whom the enquiry relates.

History
See history note after s. 430F.

SEC. 430A Right of minority shareholder to be bought out by offeror

430A(1) **[Shareholder may require acquisition]** If a takeover offer relates to all the shares in a company and at any time before the end of the period within which the offer can be accepted—

    (a)   the offeror has by virtue of acceptances of the offer acquired or contracted to acquire some (but not all) of the shares to which the offer relates; and

    (b)   those shares, with or without any other shares in the company which he has acquired or contracted to acquire, amount to not less than nine-tenths in value of all the shares in the company,

the holder of any shares to which the offer relates who has not accepted the offer may by a written communication addressed to the offeror require him to acquire those shares.

430A(2)   **[Right re classes of shares]**   If a takeover offer relates to shares of any class or classes and at any time before the end of the period within which the offer can be accepted—

    (a)   the offeror has by virtue of acceptances of the offer acquired or contracted to acquire some (but not all) of the shares of any class to which the offer relates; and

    (b)   those shares, with or without any other shares of that class which he has acquired or contracted to acquire, amount to not less than nine-tenths in value of all the shares of that class,

the holder of any shares of that class who has not accepted the offer may by a written communication addressed to the offeror require him to acquire those shares.

430A(3)   **[Notice within one month of sec. 430A(1), (2) time]**   Within one month of the time specified in subsection (1) or, as the case may be, subsection (2) the offeror shall give any shareholder who has not accepted the offer notice in the prescribed manner of the rights that are exercisable by him under that subsection; and if the notice is given before the end of the period mentioned in that subsection it shall state that the offer is still open for acceptance.

Note
See also reg. 4 of The Companies (Forms) (Amendment)
Regulations 1987 (S.I. 1987 No. 752).

430A(4)   **[Sec. 430A(3) may specify period]**   A notice under subsection (3) may specify a period for the exercise of the rights conferred by this section and in that event the rights shall not be exercisable after the end of that period; but no such period shall end less than three months after the end of the period within which the offer can be accepted.

430A(5)   **[Non-application of sec. 430A(3)]**   Subsection (3) does not apply if the offeror has given the shareholder a notice in respect of the shares in question under section 429.

430A(6)   **[Penalty on default]**   If the offeror fails to comply with subsection (3) he and, if the offeror is a company, every officer of the company who is in default or to whose neglect the failure is attributable, shall be liable to a fine and, for continued contravention, to a daily default fine.

430A(7)   **[Defence]**   If an offeror other than a company is charged with an offence for failing to comply with subsection (3) it is a defence for him to prove that he took all reasonable steps for securing compliance with that subsection.

History
See history note after s. 430F.

SEC. 430B   Effect of requirement under sec. 430A

430B(1)   **[Application]**   The following provisions shall, subject to section 430C, have effect where a shareholder exercises his rights in respect of any shares under section 430A.

430B(2) **[Right and duty re aquisition of shares]** The offeror shall be entitled and bound to acquire those shares on the terms of the offer or on such other terms as may be agreed.

430B(3) **[Indication of choice re consideration]** Where the terms of an offer are such as to give the holder of shares a choice of consideration the holder of the shares may indicate his choice when requiring the offeror to acquire them and the notice given to the holder under section 430A(3)—

(a) shall give particulars of the choice and of the rights conferred by this subsection; and

(b) may state which consideration specified in the offer is to be taken as applying in default of his indicating a choice;

and the terms of the offer mentioned in subsection (2) shall be determined accordingly.

430B(4) **[Application of sec. 430B(3)]** Subsection (3) applies whether or not any time-limit or other conditions applicable to the choice under the terms of the offer can still be complied with; and if the consideration chosen by the holder of the shares—

(a) is not cash and the offeror is no longer able to provide it; or

(b) was to have been provided by a third party who is no longer bound or able to provide it,

the consideration shall be taken to consist of an amount of cash payable by the offeror which at the date when the holder of the shares requires the offeror to acquire them is equivalent to the chosen consideration.

History
See history note after s. 430F.

SEC. 430C Applications to the court

430C(1) **[Order by court]** Where a notice is given under section 429 to the holder of any shares the court may, on an application made by him within six weeks from the date on which the notice was given—

(a) order that the offeror shall not be entitled and bound to acquire the shares; or

(b) specify terms of acquisition different from those of the offer.

430C(2) **[Where sec. 430C application pending]** If an application to the court under subsection (1) is pending at the end of the period mentioned in subsection (5) of section 430 that subsection shall not have effect until the application has been disposed of.

430C(3) **[Where sec. 430A rights exercised]** Where the holder of any shares exercises his rights under section 430A the court may, on an application made by him or the offeror, order that the terms on which the offeror is entitled and bound to acquire the shares shall be such as the court thinks fit.

430C(4) **[Order for costs, expenses]** No order for costs or expenses shall be made against a shareholder making an application under subsection (1) or (3) unless the court considers—

(a) that the application was unnecessary, improper or vexatious; or

(b) that there has been unreasonable delay in making the application or unreasonable conduct on his part in conducting the proceedings on the application.

430C(5) [Where not sufficient acceptance for sec. 429 notices] Where a takeover offer has not been accepted to the extent necessary for entitling the offeror to give notices under subsection (1) or (2) of section 429 the court may, on the application of the offeror, make an order authorising him to give notices under that subsection if satisfied—

(a) that the offeror has after reasonable enquiry been unable to trace one or more of the persons holding shares to which the offer relates;

(b) that the shares which the offeror has acquired or contracted to acquire by virtue of acceptances of the offer, together with the shares held by the person or persons mentioned in paragraph (a), amount to not less than the minimum specified in that subsection; and

(c) that the consideration offered is fair and reasonable;

but the court shall not make an order under this subsection unless it considers that it is just and equitable to do so having regard, in particular, to the number of shareholders who have been traced but who have not accepted the offer.

History
See history note after s. 430F.

SEC. 430D   Joint offers

430D(1) [Making of joint offers] A takeover offer may be made by two or more persons jointly and in that event this Part of this Act has effect with the following modifications.

430D(2) [Satisfaction of sec. 429, 430A conditions] The conditions for the exercise of the rights conferred by sections 429 and 430A shall be satisfied by the joint offerors acquiring or contracting to acquire the necessary shares jointly (as respects acquisitions by virtue of acceptances of the offer) and either jointly or separately (in other cases); and, subject to the following provisions, the rights and obligations of the offeror under those sections and sections 430 and 430B shall be respectively joint rights and joint and several obligations of the joint offerors.

430D(3) [Sufficient compliance with sec. 429, 430A] It shall be a sufficient compliance with any provision of those sections requiring or authorising a notice or other document to be given or sent by or to the joint offerors that it is given or sent by or to any of them; but the statutory declaration required by section 429(4) shall be made by all of them and, in the case of a joint offeror being a company, signed by a director of that company.

430D(4) [References to offeror in sec. 428, 430(8), 430E] In sections 428, 430(8) and 430E references to the offeror shall be construed as references to the joint offerors or any of them.

430D(5) [References to offeror in sec. 430(6), (7)] In section 430(6) and (7) references to the offeror shall be construed as references to the joint offerors or such of them as they may determine.

CA 1985, sec. 430C(5)   [The next page is 19,801]   **CCH Editions Limited**

430D(6) **[References in sec. 430(4)(a), 430B(4)(a)]** In sections 430(4)(a) and 430B(4)(a) references to the offeror being no longer able to provide the relevant consideration shall be construed as references to none of the joint offerors being able to do so.

430D(7) **[References to offeror in sec. 430C]** In section 430C references to the offeror shall be construed as references to the joint offerors except that any application under subsection (3) or (5) may be made by any of them and the reference in subsection (5)(a) to the offeror having been unable to trace one or more of the persons holding shares shall be construed as a reference to none of the offerors having been able to do so.

History
See history note after s. 430F.

SEC. 430E Associates

430E(1) **[Satisfaction re sec. 428(1) requirement]** The requirement in section 428(1) that a takeover offer must extend to all the shares, or all the shares of any class or classes, in a company shall be regarded as satisfied notwithstanding that the offer does not extend to shares which associates of the offeror hold or have contracted to acquire; but, subject to subsection (2), shares which any such associate holds or has contracted to acquire, whether at the time when the offer is made or subsequently, shall be disregarded for the purposes of any reference in this Part of this Act to the shares to which a takeover offer relates.

430E(2) **[Acquisition by associate of offeror]** Where during the period within which a takeover offer can be accepted any associate of the offeror acquires or contracts to acquire any of the shares to which the offer relates, then, if the condition specified in subsection (8)(a) or (b) of section 429 is satisfied as respects those shares they shall be treated for the purposes of that section as shares to which the offer relates.

430E(3) **[Interpretation re sec. 430A(1)(b), (2)(b)]** In section 430A(1)(b) and (2)(b) the reference to shares which the offeror has acquired or contracted to acquire shall include a reference to shares which any associate of his has acquired or contracted to acquire.

430E(4) **["Associate"]** In this section "**associate**", in relation to an offeror means—

(a) a nominee of the offeror;

(b) a holding company, subsidiary or fellow subsidiary of the offeror or a nominee of such a holding company, subsidiary or fellow subsidiary;

(c) a body corporate in which the offeror is substantially interested; or

(d) any person who is, or is a nominee of, a party to an agreement with the offeror for the acquisition of, or of an interest in, the shares which are the subject of the takeover offer, being an agreement which includes provisions imposing obligations or restrictions such as are mentioned in section 204(2)(a).

430E(5) **[Interpretation re sec. 430E(4)(b)]** For the purposes of subsection (4)(b) a company is a fellow subsidiary of another body corporate if both are subsidiaries of the same body corporate but neither is a subsidiary of the other.

430E(6) **[Interpretation re sec. 430E(4)(c)]** For the purposes of subsection (4)(c) an offeror has a substantial interest in a body corporate if—

    (a) that body or its directors are accustomed to act in accordance with his directions or instructions; or

    (b) he is entitled to exercise or control the exercise of one-third or more of the voting power at general meetings of that body.

430E(7) **[Application of other sections to sec. 430E(4)(d), (6)]** Subsections (5) and (6) of section 204 shall apply to subsection (4)(d) above as they apply to that section and subsections (3) and (4) of section 203 shall apply for the purposes of subsection (6) above as they apply for the purposes of subsection (2)(b) of that section.

430E(8) **[Spouse et al. of offeror]** Where the offeror is an individual his associates shall also include his spouse and any minor child or step-child of his.

SEC. 430F Convertible securities

430F(1) **[Securities to be treated as shares]** For the purposes of this Part of this Act securities of a company shall be treated as shares in the company if they are convertible into or entitle the holder to subscribe for such shares; and references to the holder of shares or a shareholder shall be construed accordingly.

430F(2) **[Qualification to sec. 430F(1)]** Subsection (1) shall not be construed as requiring any securities to be treated—

    (a) as shares of the same class as those into which they are convertible or for which the holder is entitled to subscribe; or

    (b) as shares of the same class as other securities by reason only that the shares into which they are convertible or for which the holder is entitled to subscribe are of the same class.

History

S. 428–430F (Pt. XIIIA) substituted by Financial Services Act 1986, s. 172 and Sch. 12 as from 30 April 1987 (see S.I. 1986 No. 2246 (C. 88)); but note the exception in s. 172(2) for offers made before that date. The former s. 428–430 read as follows:

"SEC. 428 Power to acquire shares of dissenting minority

428(1) This section applies where a scheme or contract involving the transfer of shares or any class of shares in a company ("the transferor company") to another company, whether or not a company as defined in section 735(1) ("the transferee company") has, within 4 months after the making of the offer in that behalf by the transferee company, been approved by the holders of not less than nine-tenths in value of the shares whose transfer is involved (other than shares already held at the date of the offer by, or by a nominee for, the transferee company or its subsidiary).

(2) In those circumstances, the transferee company may, at any time within 2 months after the expiration of the 4 months mentioned above, give notice in the prescribed manner to any dissenting shareholder that it desires to acquire his shares.

(3) The expression "dissenting shareholder" includes a shareholder who has not assented to the scheme or contract, and any shareholder who has failed or refused to transfer his shares to the transferee company in accordance with the scheme or contract.

(4) If such a notice is given, the transferee company is then (unless on an application made by the dissenting shareholder within one month from the date on which the notice was given, the court thinks fit to order otherwise) entitled and bound to acquire those shares on the terms on which, under the scheme or contract, the shares of the approving shareholders are to be transferred to the transferee company.

(5) But where shares in the transferor company of the same class or classes as the shares whose transfer is involved are already held (at the date of the offer) by, or by a nominee for, the transferee company or its subsidiary to a value greater than one-tenth of the aggregate of their value and that of the shares (other than those already so held) whose transfer is involved, subsections (2) and (4) do not apply unless—

    (a) the transferee company offers the same terms to all holders of the shares (other than those already so held) whose transfer is involved or, where those shares include shares of different classes, of each class of them, and

    (b) the holders who approve the scheme or contract, besides holding not less than nine-tenths in value of the shares (other than those so held) whose transfer is involved, are not less than three-fourths in number of the holders of those shares.

SEC. 429 Dissentient's right to compel acquisition of his shares

429(1) This section applies where, in pursuance of such a scheme or contract as is mentioned in section 428(1), shares in a company are transferred to another company or its nominee, and those shares (together with any other shares in the first-mentioned company held by, or by a nominee for, the transferee company or its subsidiary at the date of the transfer) comprise or include nine-tenths in value of the shares in the first-mentioned company or of any class of those shares.

(2) The transferee company shall within one month from the date of the transfer (unless on a previous transfer in pursuance of the scheme or contract it has already complied with this requirement) give notice of that fact in the prescribed manner to the holders of the remaining shares or of the remaining shares of that class (as the case may be) who have not assented to the scheme or contract.

(3) Any such holder may, within 3 months from the giving of that notice to him, himself give notice (in the prescribed form) requiring the transferee company to acquire the shares in question.

(4) If a shareholder gives notice under subsection (3) with respect to any shares, the transferee company is then entitled and bound to acquire those shares on the terms on which under the scheme or contract the shares of the approving shareholders were transferred to it, or on such other terms as may be agreed or as the court on the application of either the transferee company or the shareholder thinks fit to order.

SEC. 430 Provisions supplementing sec. 428, 429

430(1) Where notice has been given by the transferee company under section 428(2) and the court has not, on an application made by the dissenting shareholder, ordered to the contrary, the two following subsections apply.

(2) The transferee company shall, on expiration of one month from the date on which the notice has been given (or, if an application to the court by the dissenting shareholder is then pending, after that application has been disposed of) transmit a copy of the notice to the transferor company together with an instrument of transfer executed on behalf of the shareholder by any person appointed by the transferee company and on its own behalf by the transferee company.

An instrument of transfer is not required for any share for which a share warrant is for the time being outstanding.

(3) The transferee company shall also pay or transfer to the transferor company the amount or other consideration representing the price payable by the transferee company for the shares which by virtue of section 428(4) that company is entitled to acquire; and the transferor company shall thereupon register the transferee company as the holder of those shares.

(4) Any sums received by the transferor company under this section shall be paid into a separate bank account, and any such sums and any other consideration so received shall be held by that company on trust for the several persons entitled to the shares in respect of which those sums, or that other consideration, were respectively received.''

PART XIV — INVESTIGATION OF COMPANIES AND THEIR AFFAIRS; REQUISITION OF DOCUMENTS

APPOINTMENT AND FUNCTIONS OF INSPECTORS

SEC. 431 Investigation of a company on its own application or that of its members

431(1) [**Appointment of inspectors**] The Secretary of State may appoint one or more competent inspectors to investigate the affairs of a company and to report on them in such manner as he may direct.

431(2) [**Appointment made on application**] The appointment may be made—

(a) in the case of a company having a share capital, on the application either of not less than 200 members or of members holding not less than one-tenth of the shares issued,

(b) in the case of a company not having a share capital, on the application of not less than one-fifth in number of the persons on the company's register of members, and

(c) in any case, on application of the company.

431(3) [**Supporting evidence to application**] The application shall be supported by such evidence as the Secretary of State may require for the purpose of showing that the applicant or applicants have good reason for requiring the investigation.

431(4) [**Applicants may be required to give security etc.**] The Secretary of State may, before appointing inspectors, require the applicant or applicants to give security, to an amount not exceeding £5,000, or such other sum as he may by order specify, for payment of the costs of the investigation.

An order under this subsection shall be made by statutory instrument subject to annulment in pursuance of a resolution of either House of Parliament.

SEC. 432   Other company investigations

432(1)   [Appointment of inspectors]   The Secretary of State shall appoint one or more competent inspectors to investigate the affairs of a company and report on them in such manner as he directs, if the court by order declares that its affairs ought to be so investigated.

432(2)   [Circumstances when appointment may be made]   The Secretary of State may make such an appointment if it appears to him that there are circumstances suggesting—

   (a) that the company's affairs are being or have been conducted with intent to defraud its creditors or the creditors of any other person, or otherwise for a fraudulent or unlawful purpose, or in a manner which is unfairly prejudicial to some part of its members, or

   (b) that any actual or proposed act or omission of the company (including an act or omission on its behalf) is or would be so prejudicial, or that the company was formed for any fraudulent or unlawful purpose, or

   (c) that persons concerned with the company's formation or the management of its affairs have in connection therewith been guilty of fraud, misfeasance or other misconduct towards it or towards its members, or

   (d) that the company's members have not been given all the information with respect to its affairs which they might reasonably expect.

432(2A)   [Terms of appointment]   Inspectors may be appointed under subsection (2) on terms that any report they may make is not for publication; and in such a case, the provisions of section 437(3)(availability and publication of inspectors' reports) do not apply.

History
S. 432(2A) inserted by CA 1989, s. 55 as from 21 February
1990 (see S.I. 1990 No. 142 (C. 5), art. 4).

432(3)   [Extent of powers under sec. 432(1), (2)]   Subsections (1) and (2) are without prejudice to the powers of the Secretary of State under section 431; and the power conferred by subsection (2) is exercisable with respect to a body corporate notwithstanding that it is in course of being voluntarily wound up.

432(4)   [Interpretation of sec. 432(2)(a)]   The reference in subsection (2)(a) to a company's members includes any person who is not a member but to whom shares in the company have been transferred or transmitted by operation of law.

SEC. 433   Inspectors' powers during investigation

433(1)   [Investigation of connected body corporate]   If inspectors appointed under section 431 or 432 to investigate the affairs of a company think it necessary for the purposes of their investigation to investigate also the affairs of another body corporate which is or at any relevant time has been the company's subsidiary or holding company, or a subsidiary of its holding company or a holding company of its subsidiary, they have power to do so; and they shall report on the affairs of the other body corporate so far as they think that the results of their investigation of its affairs are relevant to the investigation of the affairs of the company first mentioned above.

433(2) (Omitted by Financial Services Act 1986, sec. 182 and Sch. 13, para. 7 as from 15, 27 November 1986 and repealed by sec. 212(3) and Sch. 17 as from 27 November 1986.)

History
In regard to the dates of the above omission and repeal see S.I. 1986 No. 1940 (C. 69) and S.I. 1986 No. 2031 (C. 76). The subsection formerly read as follows:

"Inspectors appointed under either section may at any time in the course of their investigation, without the necessity of making an interim report, inform the Secretary of State of matters coming to their knowledge as a result of the investigation tending to show that an offence has been committed."

SEC. 434 Production of documents and evidence to inspectors

434(1) [**Duty of company officers et al.**] When inspectors are appointed under section 431 or 432, it is the duty of all officers and agents of the company, and of all officers and agents of any other body corporate whose affairs are investigated under section 433(1)—

(a) to produce to the inspectors all documents of or relating to the company or, as the case may be, the other body corporate which are in their custody or power,

(b) to attend before the inspectors when required to do so, and

(c) otherwise to give the inspectors all assistance in connection with the investigation which they are reasonably able to give.

History
In s. 434(1) the word "documents" substituted for the former words "books and documents" by CA 1989, s. 56(1), (2) as from 21 February 1990 (see S.I. 1990 No. 142 (C. 5), art. 4).

434(2) [**Power of inspectors re production etc.**] If the inspectors consider that an officer or agent of the company or other body corporate, or any other person, is or may be in possession of information relating to a matter which they believe to be relevant to the investigation, they may require him—

(a) to produce to them any documents in his custody or power relating to that matter,

(b) to attend before them, and

(c) otherwise to give them all assistance in connection with the investigation which he is reasonably able to give;

and it is that person's duty to comply with the requirement.

History
S. 434(2) substituted by CA 1989, s. 56(1), (3) as from 21 February 1990 (see S.I. 1990 No. 142(C. 5), art. 4); s. 434(2) formerly read as follows:

"If the inspectors consider that a person other than an officer or agent of the company or other body corporate is or may be in possession of information concerning its affairs, they may require that person to produce to them any books or documents in his custody or power relating to the company or other body corporate, to attend before them and otherwise to give them all assistance in connection with the investigation which he is reasonably able to give; and it is that person's duty to comply with the requirement."

434(3) [**Examination an oath**] An inspector may for the purposes of the investigation examine any person on oath, and may administer an oath accordingly.

History
S. 434(3) substituted by CA 1989, s. 56(1), (4) as from 21 February 1990 (see S.I. 1990 No. 142 (C. 5), art. 4); s. 434(3) formerly read as follows:

"An inspector may examine on oath the officers and agents of the company or other body corporate, and any such person as is mentioned in subsection (2), in relation to the affairs of the company or other body, and may administer an oath accordingly."

434(4)   [Interpretation]   In this section a reference to officers or to agents includes past, as well as present, officers or agents (as the case may be); and **"agents"**, in relation to a company or other body corporate, includes its bankers and solicitors and persons employed by it as auditors, whether these persons are or are not officers of the company or other body corporate.

434(5)   [Answer can be used in evidence]   An answer given by a person to a question put to him in exercise of powers conferred by this section (whether as it has effect in relation to an investigation under any of sections 431 to 433, or as applied by any other section in this Part) may be used in evidence against him.

434(6)   ["Documents"]   In this section **"documents"** includes information recorded in any form; and, in relation to information recorded otherwise than in legible form, the power to require its production includes power to require the production of a copy of the information in legible form.

History
S. 434(6) inserted by CA 1989, s. 56(1), (5) as from 21 February 1990 (see S.I. 1990 No. 142 (C. 5), art. 4).

SEC. 435   Power of inspector to call for directors' bank accounts

435   (Repealed by Companies Act 1989, sec. 212 and Sch. 24 as from 21 February 1990.)

History
In regard to the date of the above repeal see S.I. 1990 No. 142 (C. 5), art. 7(d); s. 435 formerly read as follows:

"**435(1)**   If an inspector has reasonable grounds for believing that a director, or past director, of the company or other body corporate whose affairs he is investigating maintains or has maintained a bank account of any description (whether alone or jointly with another person and whether in Great Britain or elsewhere), into or out of which there has been paid—

(a)   the emoluments or part of the emoluments of his office as such director particulars of which have not been disclosed in the accounts of the company or other body corporate for any financial year, contrary to paragraphs 24 to 26 of Schedule 5, or

(b)   any money which has resulted from or been used in the financing of an undisclosed transaction, arrangement or agreement, or

(c)   any money which has been in any way connected with an act or omission, or series of acts or omissions, which on the part of that director constituted misconduct (whether fraudulent or not)

towards the company or body corporate or its members,

the inspector may require the director to produce to him all documents in the director's possession, or under his control, relating to that bank account.

(2)   For purposes of subsection (1)(b), an '**undisclosed**' transaction, arrangement or agreement is one—

(a)   particulars of which have not been disclosed in the notes to the accounts of any company for any financial year, contrary to section 232 and Part I of Schedule 6 (disclosure of contracts between companies and their directors, etc.), or

(b)   in respect of which an amount outstanding was not included in the aggregate amounts required to be disclosed in the notes to the accounts of any company for any financial year by section 234 and Part III of Schedule 6, contrary to that section (transactions between banks and their directors), or

(c)   particulars of which were not included in the register of transactions, arrangements and agreements required to be maintained by section 343, contrary to that section."

SEC. 436   Obstruction of inspectors treated as contempt of court

436(1)   [Inspectors' certificate re refusal]   If any person—

(a)   fails to comply with section 434(1)(a) or (c),

(b)   refuses to comply with a requirement under section 434(1)(b) or (2), or

(c)   refuses to answer any question put to him by the inspectors for the purposes of the investigation, the inspectors may certify that fact in writing to the court.

History
S. 436(1) substituted for the former s. 436(1), (2) by CA 1989, s. 56(6) as from 21 February 1990 (see S.I. 1990 No. 142 (C. 5), art. 4); the former s. 436(1), (2) read as follows:

"**436(1)** When inspectors are appointed under section 431 or 432 to investigate the affairs of a company, the following applies in the case of—

(a) any officer or agent of the company,

(b) any officer or agent of another body corporate whose affairs are investigated under section 433, and

(c) any such person as is mentioned in section 434(2).

Section 434(4) applies with regard to references in this subsection to an officer or agent.

(2) If that person—

(a) refuses to produce any book or document which it is his duty under section 434 or 435 to produce, or

(b) refuses to attend before the inspectors when required to do so, or

(c) refuses to answer any question put to him by the inspectors with respect to the affairs of the company or other body corporate (as the case may be),

the inspectors may certify the refusal in writing to the court."

436(3)   [Enquiry by court, punishment]   The court may thereupon enquire into the case; and, after hearing any witnesses who may be produced against or on behalf of the alleged offender and after hearing any statement which may be offered in defence, the court may punish the offender in like manner as if he had been guilty of contempt of the court.

SEC. 437   Inspectors' reports

437(1)   [Interim and final reports]   The inspectors may, and if so directed by the Secretary of State shall, make interim reports to the Secretary of State, and on the conclusion of their investigation shall make a final report to him.

Any such report shall be written or printed, as the Secretary of State directs.

437(1A)   [Power, duty to inform Secretary of State]   Any persons who have been appointed under section 431 or 432 may at any time and, if the Secretary of State directs them to do so, shall inform him of any matters coming to their knowledge as a result of their investigations.

History
S. 437(1A) inserted by Financial Services Act 1986, s. 182 and Sch. 13, para. 7 as from 15 November 1986 for certain purposes (see S.I. 1986 No. 1940 (C. 69)) and as from

27 November 1986 for remaining purposes (see S.I. 1986 No. 2031 (C. 76)).

437(1B)   [Where possible criminal offence]   If it appears to the Secretary of State that matters have come to light in the course of the inspectors' investigation which suggest that a criminal offence has been committed, and those matters have been referred to the appropriate prosecuting authority, he may direct the inspectors to take no further steps in the investigation or to take only such further steps as are specified in the direction.

History
See history note after s. 437(1C).

437(1C)   [Where sec. 437(1B) direction]   Where an investigation is the subject of a direction under subsection (1B), the inspectors shall make a final report to the Secretary of State only where—

(a) they were appointed under section 432(1) (appointment in pursuance of an order of the court), or

(b) the Secretary of State directs them to do so.

History
S. 437(1B), (1C) inserted by CA 1989, s. 57 as from 21 February 1990 (see S.I. 1990 No. 142 (C. 5), art. 4).

437(2)   [Copy of report to court]   If the inspectors were appointed under section 432 in pursuance of an order of the court, the Secretary of State shall furnish a copy of any report of theirs to the court.

437(3)   [Powers of Secretary of State re reports]   In any case the Secretary of State may, if he thinks fit—

(a) forward a copy of any report made by the inspectors to the company's registered office,

(b) furnish a copy on request and on payment of the prescribed fee to—

   (i)   any member of the company or other body corporate which is the subject of the report,

   (ii) any person whose conduct is referred to in the report,

   (iii) the auditors of that company or body corporate,

   (iv) the applicants for the investigation,

   (v)   any other person whose financial interests appear to the Secretary of State to be affected by the matters dealt with in the report, whether as a creditor of the company or body corporate, or otherwise, and

(c) cause any such report to be printed and published.

Note
For provision re disqualification of directors see Company
Directors Disqualification Act 1986, s. 8.

SEC. 438   Power to bring civil proceedings on company's behalf

438(1)   [Proceedings by Secretary of State]   If from any report made or information obtained under this Part it appears to the Secretary of State that any civil proceedings ought in the public interest to be brought by any body corporate, he may himself bring such proceedings in the name and on behalf of the body corporate.

History
In s. 438(1) the opening words down to "it appears to the Secretary of State" substituted for the former words "If, from any report made under section 437 or from information or documents obtained under section 447 or 448 below, it appears to the Secretary of State" by CA 1989, s. 58 as from 21 February 1990 (see S.I. 1990 No. 142 (C. 5), art. 4).

438(2)   [Indemnity re costs and expenses]   The Secretary of State shall indemnify the body corporate against any costs or expenses incurred by it in or in connection with proceedings brought under this section.

SEC. 439   Expenses of investigating a company's affairs

439(1)   [Defraying of expenses]   The expenses of an investigation under any of the powers conferred by this Part shall be defrayed in the first instance by the Secretary of State, but he may recover those expenses from the persons liable in accordance with this section.

There shall be treated as expenses of the investigation, in particular, such reasonable sums as the Secretary of State may determine in respect of general staff costs and overheads.

History
S. 439(1) substituted by CA 1989, s. 59(1), (2) as from 21 February 1990 (see S.I. 1990 No. 142 (C. 5), art. 4); s. 439(1) formerly read as follows:

"**439(1)**   The expenses of and incidental to an investigation by inspectors appointed by the Secretary of State shall be defrayed in the first instance by him; but the persons mentioned in the following 4 subsections are, to the extent there specified, liable to make repayment to the Secretary of State."

439(2)   [Person convicted on prosecution re investigation]   A person who is convicted on a prosecution instituted as a result of the investigation, or is ordered to pay the whole or any part of the costs of proceedings brought under section 438, may in the same proceedings be ordered to pay those expenses to such extent as may be specified in the order.

439(3) **[Body corporate in whose name proceedings brought]** A body corporate in whose name proceedings are brought under that section is liable to the amount or value of any sums or property recovered by it as a result of those proceedings; and any amount for which a body corporate is liable under this subsection is a first charge on the sums or property recovered.

439(4) **[Other bodies corporate]** A body corporate dealt with by an inspectors' report, where the inspectors were appointed otherwise than of the Secretary of State's own motion, is liable except where it was the applicant for the investigation, and except so far as the Secretary of State otherwise directs.

History
In s. 439(4) the words "an inspectors' report" substituted
for the former words "the inspectors' report" by CA 1989,
s. 59(1), (3) as from 21 February 1990 (see S.I. 1990 No.
142 (C. 5), art. 4).

439(5) **[Liability of sec. 431, 442(3) applicants]** Where inspectors were appointed—

   (a) under section 431, or

   (b) on an application under section 442(3).

the applicant or applicants for the investigation is or are liable to such extent (if any) as the Secretary of State may direct.

History
S. 439(5) substituted by CA 1989, s. 59(1), (4) as from 21   "The applicant or applicants for the investigation, where
February 1990 (see S.I. 1990 No. 142 (C. 5), art. 4); s.   the inspectors were appointed under section 431, is or are
439(5) formerly read as follows: liable to such extent (if any) as the Secretary of State may
                                                          direct."

439(6) **[Recommendation in report re sec. 439(4), (5) directors]** The report of inspectors appointed otherwise than of the Secretary of State's own motion may, if they think fit, and shall if the Secretary of State so directs, include a recommendation as to the directions (if any) which they think appropriate, in the light of their investigation, to be given under subsection (4) or (5) of this section.

439(7) **[Costs re proceedings under sec. 438]** For purposes of this section, any costs or expenses incurred by the Secretary of State in or in connection with proceedings brought under section 438 (including expenses incurred under subsection (2) of it) are to be treated as expenses of the investigation giving rise to the proceedings.

439(8) **[Indemnities]** Any liability to repay the Secretary of State imposed by subsections (2) and (3) above is (subject to satisfaction of his right to repayment) a liability also to indemnify all persons against liability under subsections (4) and (5); and any such liability imposed by subsection (2) is (subject as mentioned above) a liability also to indemnify all persons against liability under subsection (3).

439(9) **[Contribution between persons liable]** A person liable under any one of those subsections is entitled to contribution from any other person liable under the same subsection, according to the amount of their respective liabilities under it.

439(10) **[Expenses defrayed by Secretary of State]** Expenses to be defrayed by the Secretary of State under this section shall, so far as not recovered under it, be paid out of money provided by Parliament.

SEC. 440   Power of Secretary of State to present winding-up petition

440   (Repealed by Companies Act 1989, sec. 60(1), 212 and Sch. 24 as from 21 February 1990.)

History

In regard to the date of the above repeal see S.I. 1990 No. 142 (C. 5), art. 4 and 7(d); s. 440 formerly read as follows:

"If in the case of a body corporate liable to be wound up under this Act it appears to the Secretary of State from a report made by inspectors under section 437 above or section 94 of the Financial Services Act 1986, or from information or documents obtained under section 447 or 448 below or section 105 of that Act or section 2 of the Criminal Justice Act 1987 or section 52 of the Criminal Justice (Scotland) Act 1987, that it is expedient in the public interest that the body should be wound up, he may (unless the body is already being wound up by the court) present a petition for it to be so wound up if the court thinks it just and equitable for it to be so."

There had previously been a number of amendments to s. 440: the words "above or section 94 of the Financial Services Act 1986" inserted by Financial Services Act 1986, s. 198(1)(a) as from 29 April 1988 (see S.I. 1988 No. 740 (C. 22)) and the words "or section 105 of that Act" inserted by Financial Services Act 1986, s. 198(1)(b) as from 18 December 1986 (see S.I. 1988 No. 2246 (C. 88)); the words "or section 52 of the Criminal Justice (Scotland) Act 1987" inserted by Criminal Justice (Scotland) Act 1987, s. 55(a) as from 1 January 1988 (see S.I. 1987 No. 2119 (C. 62) (S. 143)); and the words or "or section 2 of the Criminal Justice Act 1987" inserted by Criminal Justice Act 1988, s. 145(a) as from 12 October 1988 (see S.I. 1988 No. 1676 (C.60)).

Note

For re-enactment of s. 440 (with modifications), see Insolvency Act 1986, s. 124A.

SEC. 441   Inspectors' report to be evidence

441(1)   [Evidence of inspectors' opinion]   A copy of any report of inspectors appointed under this Part, certified by the Secretary of State to be a true copy, is admissible in any legal proceedings as evidence of the opinion of the inspectors in relation to any matter contained in the report and, in proceedings on an application under section 8 of the Company Directors Disqualification Act 1986, as evidence of any fact stated therein.

History

In s. 441(1) the words "and, in proceedings on an application" to the end inserted by Insolvency Act 1985, s. 109 and Sch. 6, para. 3 as from 28 April 1986. In addition the words "section 8 of the Company Directors Disqualification Act 1986" substituted for the former words "section 13 of the Insolvency Act 1985" by Insolvency Act 1986, s. 439(1) and Sch. 13 as from 29 December 1986 (see IA 1986, s. 443 and S.I. 1986 No. 1924 (C. 71)). Also the words "this Part" substituted for the former words "section 431 or 432" by CA 1989, s. 61 as from 21 February 1990 (see S.I. 1990 No. 142 (C. 5), art. 4).

441(2)   [Admissibility of certificate]   A document purporting to be such a certificate as is mentioned above shall be received in evidence and be deemed to be such a certificate, unless the contrary is proved.

OTHER POWERS OF INVESTIGATION AVAILABLE TO SECRETARY OF STATE

SEC. 442   Power to investigate company ownership

442(1)   [Secretary of State may appoint inspectors re ownership etc.]   Where it appears to the Secretary of State that there is good reason to do so, he may appoint one or more competent inspectors to investigate and report on the membership of any company, and otherwise with respect to the company, for the purpose of determining the true persons who are or have been financially interested in the success or failure (real or apparent) of the company or able to control or materially to influence its policy.

442(2)   [Scope and limit of investigation]   The appointment of inspectors under this section may define the scope of their investigation (whether as respects the matter or the period to which it is to extend or otherwise) and in particular may limit the investigation to matters connected with particular shares or debentures.

442(3) **[Application for investigation]** If an application for investigation under this section with respect to particular shares or debentures of a company is made to the Secretary of State by members of the company, and the number of applicants or the amount of shares held by them is not less than that required for an application for the appointment of inspectors under section 431(2)(a) or (b), then, subject to the following provisions, the Secretary of State shall appoint inspectors to conduct the investigation applied for.

442(3A) **[Vexatious application, unreasonable matter]** The Secretary of State shall not appoint inspectors if he is satisfied that the application is vexatious; and where inspectors are appointed their terms of appointment shall exclude any matter in so far as the Secretary of State is satisfied that it is unreasonable for it to be investigated.

442(3B) **[Order for security by applicant]** The Secretary of State may, before appointing inspectors, require the applicant or applicants to give security, to an amount not exceeding £5,000, or such other sum as he may by order specify, for payment of the costs of the investigation.

An order under this subsection shall be made by statutory instrument which shall be subject to annulment in pursuance of a resolution of either House of Parliament.

442(3C) **[Alternative investigation under sec. 440]** If on an application under subsection (3) it appears to the Secretary of State that the powers conferred by section 444 are sufficient for the purposes of investigating the matters which inspectors would be appointed to investigate, he may instead conduct the investigation under that section.

History
S. 442(3)–(3C) substituted for the former s. 442(3) by CA 1989, s. 62 as from 21 February 1990 (see S.I. 1990 No. 142 (C. 5), art. 4); the former s. 442(3) read as follows:

"If application for an investigation under this section with respect to particular shares or debentures of a company is made to the Secretary of State by members of the company, and the number of applicants or the amount of the shares held by them is not less than that required for an application for the appointment of inspectors under section 431(2)(a) and (b)—

(a) the Secretary of State shall appoint inspectors to conduct the investigation (unless he is satisfied that the application is vexatious), and

(b) the inspectors' appointment shall not exclude from the scope of their investigation any matter which the application seeks to have included, except in so far as the Secretary of State is satisfied that it is unreasonable for that matter to be investigated."

442(4) **[Powers of inspectors]** Subject to the terms of their appointment, the inspectors' powers extend to the investigation of any circumstances suggesting the existence of an arrangement or understanding which, though not legally binding, is or was observed or likely to be observed in practice and which is relevant to the purposes of the investigation.

SEC. 443 Provisions applicable on investigation under sec. 442

443(1) **[Application of sec. 433(1), 434, 436, 437]** For purposes of an investigation under section 442, sections 433(1), 434, 436 and 437 apply with the necessary modifications of references to the affairs of the company or to those of any other body corporate, subject however to the following subsections.

443(2) **[How those sections apply]** Those sections apply to—

(a) all persons who are or have been, or whom the inspector has reasonable cause to believe to be or have been, financially interested in the success or failure or the apparent success or failure of the company or any other body corporate whose membership is investigated with that of the company, or able to control or materially influence its policy (including persons concerned only on behalf of others), and

(b) any other person whom the inspector has reasonable cause to believe possesses information relevant to the investigation,

as they apply in relation to officers and agents of the company or the other body corporate (as the case may be).

443(3)   [Parts of report need not be disclosed]   If the Secretary of State is of opinion that there is good reason for not divulging any part of a report made by virtue of section 442 and this section, he may under section 437 disclose the report with the omission of that part; and he may cause to be kept by the registrar of companies a copy of the report with that part omitted or, in the case of any other such report, a copy of the whole report.

443(4)   (Repealed by Companies Act 1989, sec. 212 and Sch. 24 as from 21 February 1990.)

History
In regard to the date of the above repeal see S.I. 1990 No. 142 (C. 5), art. 7(d); s. 443(4) formerly read as follows: "The expenses of an investigation under section 442 shall be defrayed by the Secretary of State out of money provided by Parliament."

SEC. 444   Power to obtain information as to those interested in shares, etc.

444(1)   [Secretary of State may require persons to produce information]   If it appears to the Secretary of State that there is good reason to investigate the ownership of any shares in or debentures of a company and that it is unnecessary to appoint inspectors for the purpose, he may require any person whom he has reasonable cause to believe to have or to be able to obtain any information as to the present and past interests in those shares or debentures and the names and addresses of the persons interested and of any persons who act or have acted on their behalf in relation to the shares or debentures to give any such information to the Secretary of State.

444(2)   [Interpretation]   For this purpose a person is deemed to have an interest in shares or debentures if he has any right to acquire or dispose of them or of any interest in them, or to vote in respect of them, or if his consent is necessary for the exercise of any of the rights of other persons interested in them, or if other persons interested in them can be required, or are accustomed, to exercise their rights in accordance with his instructions.

444(3)   [Failure to give information etc.]   A person who fails to give information required of him under this section, or who in giving such information makes any statement which he knows to be false in a material particular, or recklessly makes any statement which is false in a material particular, is liable to imprisonment or a fine, or both.

SEC. 445   Power to impose restrictions on shares and debentures

445(1)   [Secretary may impose restrictions]   If in connection with an investigation under either section 442 or 444 it appears to the Secretary of State that there is difficulty in finding out the relevant facts about any shares (whether issued or to be issued), he may by order direct that the shares shall until further order be subject to the restrictions of Part XV of this Act.

445(2) **[Application of sec. 445 and Pt. XV re debentures]** This section, and Part XV in its application to orders under it, apply in relation to debentures as in relation to shares.

SEC. 446   Investigation of share dealings

446(1) **[Inspectors may be appointed by Secretary of State]** If it appears to the Secretary of State that there are circumstances suggesting that contraventions may have occurred, in relation to a company's shares or debentures, of section 323 or 324 (taken with Schedule 13), or of subsections (3) to (5) of section 328 (restrictions on share dealings by directors and their families; obligation of director to disclose shareholding in his own company), he may appoint one or more competent inspectors to carry out such investigations as are requisite to establish whether or not such contraventions have occurred and to report the result of their investigations to him.

446(2) **[Limits of investigation]** The appointment of inspectors under this section may limit the period to which their investigation is to extend or confine it to shares or debentures of a particular class, or both.

446(3) **[Application of sec. 434 to 437]** For purposes of an investigation under this section, sections 434 to 437 apply—

   (a) with the substitution, for references to any other body corporate whose affairs are investigated under section 433(1), of a reference to any other body corporate which is, or has at any relevant time been, the company's subsidiary or holding company, or a subsidiary of its holding company.

History
In s. 446(3) the words "to 437" substituted for the former words "to 436" by Financial Services Act 1986, s. 182 and Sch. 7, para. 8 as from 27 November 1986 — see S.I. 1986 No. 2031 (C. 76). Also para. (b) and the word "and" preceding it repealed by CA 1989, s. 212 and Sch. 24 as from 21 February 1990 (see S.I. 1990 No. 142 (C. 5), art. 7(d)); the former para. (b) read as follows:

   "(b) with the necessary modification of references in section 436 to the affairs of the company or other body corporate."

446(4) **[How sec. 434 to 436 apply]** Sections 434 to 436 apply under the preceding subsection—

   (a) to any individual who is an authorised person within the meaning of the Financial Services Act 1986;

   (b) to any individual who holds a permission granted under paragraph 23 of Schedule 1 to that Act;

   (c) to any officer (whether past or present) of a body corporate which is such an authorised person or holds such a permission;

   (d) to any partner (whether past or present) in a partnership which is such an authorised person or holds such a permission;

   (e) to any member of the governing body or officer (in either case whether past or present) of an unincorporated association which is such an authorised person or holds such a permission

as they apply to officers of the company or of the other body corporate.

History
In s. 446(4), para. (a) to (e) substituted for former para. (a) to (c) by Financial Services Act 1986, s. 212(2) and Sch. 16, para. 21 as from 29 April 1988 (see S.I. 1988 No. 740 (C. 22)): the former para. (a) to (c) read as follows:

"(a) to members of a recognised stock exchange or of a recognised association of dealers in securities who are individuals and to officers (past as well as present) of members of such an exchange or association being bodies corporate,

(b) to holders of licences granted under section 3 of the Prevention of Fraud (Investments) Act 1958 who are individuals and to officers (past as well as present) of holders of licences so granted being bodies corporate, and

(c) to any individual declared by an order of the Secretary of State for the time being in force to be an exempted dealer for purposes of that Act and to officers (past as well as present) of any body corporate declared by an order of the Secretary of State for the time being in force to be such a dealer,".

446(5)   (Omitted and repealed by Financial Services Act 1986, sec. 182, 212(3), Sch. 13, para. 8 and Sch. 17, Pt. I as from 27 November 1986.)

History
In regard to the date of the above repeal see S.I. 1986 No. 2031 (C. 76). The subsection formerly read as follows:

"The inspectors may, and if so directed by the Secretary of State shall, make interim reports to him; and, on conclusion of the investigation, they shall make to him a final report.

Any such report shall be written or printed, as the Secretary of State may direct; and he may cause it to be published."

446(6)   (Repealed by Financial Services Act 1986, sec. 212(3) and Sch. 17, Pt. I as from 29 April 1988.)

History
In regard to the date of the above repeal see S.I. 1988 No. 740 (C. 22): the subsection formerly read as follows:

"'**Recognised association of dealers in securities**' means any body of persons which is for the time being such an association for purposes of the Prevention of Fraud (Investments) Act 1958."

446(7)   (Repealed by Companies Act 1989, sec. 212 and Sch. 24 as from 21 February 1990.)

History
In regard to the date of the above repeal, see S.I. 1990 No. 142 (C. 5), art. 7(d); s. 446(7) formerly read as follows:

"The expenses of an investigation under this section shall be defrayed by the Secretary of State out of money provided by Parliament."

REQUISITION AND SEIZURE OF BOOKS AND PAPERS

SEC. 447   Secretary of State's power to require production of documents

447(1)   (Omitted and repealed by Companies Act 1989, sec. 63(1), (2), 212 and Sch. 24 as from 21 February 1990.)

History
In regard to the date of the above repeal, see S.I. 1990 No. 142 (C. 5), art. 4, 7(d); s. 447(1) formerly read as follows:

"The powers of this section are exercisable in relation to the following bodies—

(a) a company, as defined by section 735(1);

(b) a company to which this Act applies by virtue of section 676 or which is registered under section 680;

(c) a body corporate incorporated in, and having a principal place of business in, Great Britain, being a body to which any of the provisions of this Act with respect to prospectuses and allotments apply by virtue of section 718 (unregistered companies); and

(d) a body corporate incorporated outside Great Britain which is carrying on business in Great Britain or has at any time carried on business there."

447(2)   **[Directions to produce]**   The Secretary of State may at any time, if he thinks there is good reason to do so, give directions to a company requiring it, at such time and place as may be specified in the directions, to produce such documents as may be so specified.

History
In s. 447(2) the words "a company" substituted for the former words "any such body" and the word "documents" substituted for the former words "books or papers" by CA 1989, s. 63(1), (2)(a), (3) as from 21 February 1990 (see S.I. 1990 No. 142 (C. 5), art. 4).

447(3) **[Secretary of State may authorise officer to produce etc.]** The Secretary of State may at any time, if he thinks there is good reason to do so, authorise an officer of his or any other competent person, on producing (if so required) evidence of his authority, to require a company to produce to him (the officer or other person) forthwith any documents which he (the officer or other person) may specify.

History
In s. 447(3) the words "a company" substituted for the former words "any such body" and the word "documents" substituted for the former words "books or papers" by CA 1989, s. 63(1), (2)(a), (3) and the words "or any other competent person" and "or other person" inserted and the | words "he (the officer or other person)" substituted for the former words "the officer" by CA 1989, s. 63(1), (4) as from 21 February 1990 (see S.I. 1990 No. 142(C. 5), art. 4).

447(4) **[Production from other persons]** Where by virtue of subsection (2) or (3) the Secretary of State or an officer of his or other person has power to require the production of documents from a company, he or the officer or other person has the like power to require production of those documents from any person who appears to him or the officer or other person to be in possession of them; but where any such person claims a lien on documents produced by him, the production is without prejudice to the lien.

History
In s. 447(4) the words "a company" substituted for the former words "any body", the words "or other person" (appearing three times) inserted and the word "documents" (appearing three times) substituted for the former words | "books or papers" by CA 1989, s. 63(1), (2)(b), (3), (5) as from 21 February 1990 (see S.I. 1990 No. 142 (C. 5), art. 4).

447(5) **[Powers included]** The power under this section to require a company or other person to produce documents includes power—

    (a) if the documents are produced—

        (i) to take copies of them or extracts from them, and

        (ii) to require that person, or any other person who is a present or past officer of, or is or was at any time employed by, the company in question, to provide an explanation of any of them;

    (b) if the documents are not produced, to require the person who was required to produce them to state, to the best of his knowledge and belief, where they are.

History
In s. 447(5) the words "a company" substituted for the former words "a body", the words "the company" substituted for the former words "the body" and the word "documents" (appearing three times) substituted for the | former words "books and papers" by CA 1989, s. 63(1), 2(b), (c), (3) as from 21 February 1990 (see S.I. 1990 No. 142 (C. 5), art. 4).

447(6) **[Offence re non-production, penalty]** If the requirement to produce documents or provide an explanation or make a statement is not complied with, the company or other person on whom the requirement was so imposed is guilty of an offence and liable to a fine.

    Sections 732 (restriction on prosecutions), 733 (liability of individuals for corporate default) and 734 (criminal proceedings against unincorporated bodies) apply to this offence.

History
In s. 447(6) the words "the company" substituted for the former words "the body", the word "documents" substituted for the former words "books and papers" and the second sentence substituted by CA 1989, s. 63(1), (2)(c), (3), (6) as from 21 February 1990 (see S.I. 1990 | No. 142 (C. 5), art. 4); the second sentence formerly read as follows:

"Sections 732 (restriction on prosecutions) and 733(2) and (4) (liability of individuals for corporate default) apply to this offence."

447(7) **[Defence]** However, where a person is charged with an offence under subsection (6) in respect of a requirement to produce any documents, it is a defence to prove that they were not in his possession or under his control and that it was not reasonably practicable for him to comply with the requirement.

History
In s. 447(7) the word "documents" substituted for the former words "books or papers" by CA 1989, s. 63(3) as from 21 February 1990 (see S.I. 1990 No. 142 (C. 5), art. 4).

447(8) **[Evidence]** A statement made by a person in compliance with such a requirement may be used in evidence against him.

447(9) **["Documents"]** In this section **"documents"** includes information recorded in any form; and, in relation to information recorded otherwise than in legible form, the power to require its production includes power to require the production of a copy of it in legible form.

History
S. 447(9) inserted by CA 1989, s. 63(1), (7) as from 21 February 1990 (see S.I. 1990 No. 142 (C. 5), art. 4).

Note
For provision re disqualification of directors see Company Directors Disqualification Act 1986, s. 8.

SEC. 448   Entry and search of premises

448(1) **[Power of JP to issue warrant]** A justice of the peace may issue a warrant under this section if satisfied on information on oath given by or on behalf of the Secretary of State, or by a person appointed or authorised to exercise powers under this Part, that there are reasonable grounds for believing that there are on any premises documents whose production has been required under this Part and which have not been produced in compliance with the requirement.

448(2) **[Further warrant power]** A justice of the peace may also issue a warrant under this section if satisfied on information on oath given by or on behalf of the Secretary of State, or by a person appointed or authorised to exercise powers under this Part—

(a) that there are reasonable grounds for believing that an offence has been committed for which the penalty on conviction on indictment is imprisonment for a term of not less than two years and that there are on any premises documents relating to whether the offence has been committed,

(b) that the Secretary of State, or the person so appointed or authorised, has power to require the production of the documents under this Part, and

(c) that there are reasonable grounds for believing that if production was so required the documents would not be produced but would be removed from the premises, hidden, tampered with or destroyed.

448(3) **[Extent of warrant]** A warrant under this section shall authorise a constable, together with any other person named in it and any other constables—

(a) to enter the premises specified in the information, using such force as is reasonably necessary for the purpose;

(b) to search the premises and take possession of any documents appearing to be such documents as are mentioned in subsection (1) or (2), as the case may be, or to take, in relation to any such documents, any other steps which may appear to be necessary for preserving them or preventing interference with them;

(c) to take copies of any such documents; and

(d) to require any person named in the warrant to provide an explanation of them or to state where they may be found.

448(4) [Where re sec. 448(2) warrant — other documents] If in the case of a warrant under subsection (2) the justice of the peace is satisfied on information on oath that there are reasonable grounds for believing that there are also on the premises other documents relevant to the investigation, the warrant shall also authorise the actions mentioned in subsection (3) to be taken in relation to such documents.

448(5) [Duration of warrant] A warrant under this section shall continue in force until the end of the period of one month beginning with the day on which it is issued.

448(6) [Retention of documents] Any documents of which possession is taken under this section may be retained—

(a) for a period of three months; or

(b) if within that period proceedings to which the documents are relevant are commenced against any person for any criminal offence, until the conclusion of those proceedings.

448(7) [Offence] Any person who intentionally obstructs the exercise of any rights conferred by a warrant issued under this section or fails without reasonable excuse to comply with any requirement imposed in accordance with subsection (3)(d) is guilty of an offence and liable to a fine.

Sections 732 (restriction on prosecutions), 733 (liability of individuals for corporate default) and 734 (criminal proceedings against unincorporated bodies) apply to this offence.

448(8) [Interpretation re sec. 449, 451A] For the purposes of sections 449 and 451A (provision for security of information) documents obtained under this section shall be treated as if they had been obtained under the provision of this Part under which their production was or, as the case may be, could have been required.

448(9) [Application to Scotland] In the application of this section to Scotland for the references to a justice of the peace substitute references to a justice of the peace or a sheriff, and for the references to information on oath substitute references to evidence on oath.

448(10) ["Document"] In this section **"document"** includes information recorded in any form.

History

S. 448 substituted by CA 1989, s. 64(1) as from 21 February 1990 (see S.I. 1990 No. 142 (C. 5), art. 4); s.448 formerly read as follows:

"**SEC. 448 Entry and search of premises**

448(1) The following applies if a justice of the peace is satisfied on information on oath laid by an officer of the Secretary of State, or laid under the Secretary of State's authority, that there are reasonable grounds for suspecting that there are on any premises any books or papers of which production has been required under section 447 and which have not been produced in compliance with that requirement.

(2) The justice may issue a warrant authorising any constable, together with any other persons named in the warrant and any other constables, to enter the premises specified in the information (using such force as is reasonably necessary for the purpose) and to search the premises and take possession of any books or papers appearing to be such books or papers as are mentioned above, or to take, in relation to any books or papers so appearing, any other steps which may appear to be necessary for preserving them and preventing interference with them.

(3) A warrant so issued continues in force until the end of one month after the date on which it is issued.

(4) Any books or papers of which possession is taken under this section may be retained—

(a) for a period of 3 months, or

(b) if within that period there are commenced any

such criminal proceedings as are mentioned in subsection (1)(a) or (b) of the next following section (being proceedings to which the books or papers are relevant), until the conclusion of those proceedings.

(5) A person who obstructs the exercise of a right of entry or search conferred by a warrant issued under this section, or who obstructs the exercise of a right so conferred to take possession of any books or papers, is guilty of an offence and liable to a fine.

Sections 732 (restriction on prosecutions) and 733(2) and (4) (liability of individuals for corporate default) apply to this offence.

(6) In the application of this section to Scotland, the reference to a justice of the peace includes the sheriff and a magistrate.''

Note
For provision re disqualification of directors see Company Directors Disqualification Act 1986, s. 8.

SEC. 449 Provision for security of information obtained

449(1) [Limitation on publication or disclosure of information] No information or document relating to a company which has been obtained under section 447 shall, without the previous consent in writing of that company, be published or disclosed, except to a competent authority, unless the publication or disclosure is required—

(a) with a view to the institution of or otherwise for the purposes of criminal proceedings,

(ba) with a view to the institution of, or otherwise for the purposes of any proceedings on an application under section 6, 7 or 8 of the Company Directors Disqualification Act 1986,

(c) for the purposes of enabling or assisting any inspector appointed under this Part, or under section 94 or 177 of the Financial Services Act 1986, to discharge his functions,

(cc) for the purpose of enabling or assisting any person authorised to exercise powers under section 44 of the Insurance Companies Act 1982, section 447 of this Act, section 106 of the Financial Services Act 1986 or section 84 of the Companies Act 1989 to discharge his functions,

(d) for the purpose of enabling or assisting the Secretary of State to exercise any of his functions under this Act, the Insider Dealing Act, the Prevention of Fraud (Investments) Act 1958, the Insurance Companies Act 1982, the Insolvency Act 1986, the Company Directors Disqualification Act 1986, the Financial Services Act 1986 or Part II, III or VII of the Companies Act 1989,

(dd) for the purpose of enabling or assisting the Department of Economic Development for Northern Ireland to exercise any powers conferred on it by the enactments relating to companies or insolvency or for the purpose of enabling or assisting any inspector appointed by it under the enactments relating to companies to discharge his functions,

(e) (Omitted and repealed by Companies Act 1989, sec. 65(1), (2)(e), 212 and Sch. 24 as from 21 February 1990),

(f) for the purpose of enabling or assisting the Bank of England to discharge its functions under the Banking Act 1987 or any other functions,

(g) for the purpose of enabling or assisting the Deposit Protection Board to discharge its functions under that Act,

(h) for any purpose mentioned in section 180(1)(b), (e), (h) or (n) of the Financial Services Act 1986,

(hh) for the purpose of enabling or assisting a body established by order under section 46 of the Companies Act 1989 to discharge its functions under Part II of that Act, or of enabling or assisting a recognised supervisory or qualifying body within the meaning of that Part to discharge its functions as such,

(i) for the purpose of enabling or assisting the Industrial Assurance Commissioner or the Industrial Assurance Commissioner for Northern Ireland to discharge his functions under the enactments relating to industrial assurance,

(j) for the purpose of enabling or assisting the Insurance Brokers Registration Council to discharge its functions under the Insurance Brokers (Registration) Act 1977,

(k) for the purpose of enabling or assisting an official receiver to discharge his functions under the enactments relating to insolvency or for the purpose of enabling or assisting a body which is for the time being a recognised professional body for the purposes of section 391 of the Insolvency Act 1986 to discharge its functions as such,

(l) with a view to the institution of, or otherwise for the purposes of, any disciplinary proceedings relating to the exercise by a solicitor, auditor, accountant, valuer or actuary of his professional duties,

(ll) with a view to the institution of, or otherwise for the purposes of, any disciplinary proceedings relating to the discharge by a public servant of his duties,

(m) for the purpose of enabling or assisting an overseas regulatory authority to exercise its regulatory functions.

History

In s. 449(1):

- in the opening words "company" (appearing twice) substituted for the former word "body" and the words "or 448" repealed by CA 1989, s. 65(1), (2), 212 and Sch. 24 as from 21 February 1990 (see S.I. 1990 No. 142 (C. 5), art. 4),

- para. (a) substituted for the former para. (a) and (b) by Financial Services Act 1986, s. 182 and Sch. 13, para. 9(1)(a) as from 15 November 1986 for certain purposes (see S.I. 1986 No. 1940 (C. 69)) and as from 27 November 1986 for remaining purposes (see S.I. 1986 No. 2031 (C. 76)); the former para. (a) and (b) read as follows:

"(a) with a view to the institution of, or otherwise for the purposes of, any criminal proceedings pursuant to, or arising out of, this Act, the Insider Dealing Act or the Insurance Companies Act 1982, or any criminal proceedings for an offence entailing misconduct in connection with the management of the body's affairs or misapplication or wrongful retainer of its property;

(b) with a view to the institution of, or otherwise for the purposes of, any criminal proceedings pursuant to, or arising out of, the Exchange Control Act 1947,",

- para. (ba) inserted by Insolvency Act 1985, s. 109 and Sch. 6, para. 4 as from 28 April 1986 (see S.I. 1986 No. 463 (C. 14)). In that paragraph the words "section 6, 7 or 8 of the Company Directors Disqualification Act 1986" substituted for the former words "section 12 or 13 of the Insolvency Act 1985" by Insolvency Act 1986,

s. 439(1) and Sch. 13 as from 29 December 1986 (see IA 1986, s. 443 and S.I. 1986 No. 1924 (C. 71)),

- para. (c) substituted and para. (cc) inserted by CA 1989, s. 65(1), (2)(b), (c) as from 21 February 1990 (see S.I. 1990 No. 142 (C. 5), art. 4); para. (c) formerly read as follows:

"(c) for the purposes of the examination of any person by inspectors appointed under section 431, 432, 442 or 446 in the course of their investigation,",

- in para. (d) the words ", the Financial Services Act 1986 or Part II, III or VII of the Companies Act 1989," substituted for the former words "or the Financial Services Act 1986" by CA 1989, s. 65(1), (2)(d) as from 21 February 1990 except in regard to the reference to Pt. VII of the 1989 Act (see S.I. 1990 No. 142 (C. 5), art. 4(b)); para. (d) and (dd) previously substituted for the original para. (d) by Financial Services Act 1986, s. 182 and Sch. 13, para. 9(1)(b) as from 15 November 1986 for certain purposes (see S.I. 1986 No. 1940 (C. 69)) and as from 27 November 1986 for remaining purposes (see S.I. 1986 No. 2031 (C. 76)); the original para. (d) read as follows:

"(d) for the purpose of enabling the Secretary of State to exercise, in relation to that or any other body, any of his functions under this Act, the Insider Dealing Act, the Prevention of Fraud (Investments) Act 1958 and the Insurance Companies Act 1982,",

- in regard to the date of the omission and repeal of para. (e) see S.I. 1990 No. 142 (C. 5), art. 4,

- para. (f)–(m) (not including (hh) and (ll) originally inserted by Financial Services Act 1986, s. 182 and Sch. 13, para. 9(1)(c) as from 15 November 1986 for certain purposes (see S.I. 1986 No. 1940 (C. 69)) and as from 27 November 1986 for remaining purposes (see S.I. 1986 No. 2031 (C. 76)),
- in para. (f) the words "the Banking Act 1987" substituted for the former words "the Banking Act 1979" by Banking Act 1987, s. 108(1) and Sch. 6, para. 18(7) as from 1 October 1987 (see S.I. 1987 No. 1664 (C. 50)),
- in para. (h) the words "or (n)" substituted for the former words "(n) or (p)" by CA 1989, s. 63(1), (2)(f) as from 21 February 1990 (see S.I. 1990 No. 142 (C. 5), art. 4),
- para. (hh) inserted by CA 1989, s. 65(1), (2)(g) as from 21 February 1990 except in regard to the reference to a body established by order under CA 1989, s. 46 (see S.I. 1990 No. 142 (C. 5), art. 4(a)),

- para. (ll) inserted by CA 1989, s. 65(1), (2)(b) as from 21 February 1990 (see S.I. 1990 No. 142 (C. 5), art. 4),
- para. (m) substituted by CA 1989, s. 65(1), (2)(i) as from 21 February 1990 (see S.I. 1990 No. 142 (C. 5), art. 4); para (m) formerly read as follows:

"(m) for the purpose of enabling or assisting an authority in a country or territory outside the United Kingdom to exercise corresponding supervisory functions."

Note
In s. 449(1)(d) the words "the Prevention of Fraud (Investments) Act 1958" repealed by Financial Services Act 1986, s. 212(3) and Sch. 17, Pt. I as from 29 April 1988 as far as they would apply to a prospectus offering for subscription, or to any form of application for units in a body corporate which is a recognised scheme (see S.I. 1988 No. 740 (C. 22)).

449(1A)   [Definitions]   In subsection (1)—

(a) in paragraph (ll) **"public servant"** means an officer or servant of the Crown or of any public or other authority for the time being designated for the purposes of that paragraph by the Secretary of State by order made by statutory instrument; and

(b) in paragraph (m) **"overseas regulatory authority"** and **"regulatory functions"** have the same meaning as in section 82 of the Companies Act 1989.

History
S. 65(1A) substituted by CA 1989, s. 65(1), (3) as from 21 February 1990 (see S.I. 1990 No. 142 (C. 5), art. 4); s. 449(1A) formerly read as follows:

"In subsection (1) above 'corresponding supervisory functions' means functions corresponding to those of the Secretary of State or the competent authority under the Financial Services Act 1986 or to those of the Secretary of State under the Insurance Companies Act 1982 or to those of the Bank of England under the Banking Act 1987 or any

other functions in connection with rules of law corresponding to the provisions of the Insider Dealing Act or Part VII of the Financial Services Act 1986."

In that former s. 449(1A) the words "the Banking Act 1987" substituted for the original words "the Banking Act 1979" by Banking Act 1987, s. 108(1) and Sch. 6, para. 18(7) as from 1 October 1987 (see S.I. 1987 No. 1664 (C. 50)).

449(1B)   [Exception to sec. 449(1) limitation]   Subject to subsection (1C), subsection (1) shall not preclude publication or disclosure for the purpose of enabling or assisting any public or other authority for the time being designated for the purposes of this subsection by the Secretary of State by an order in a statutory instrument to discharge any functions which are specified in the order.

History
In s. 449(1B) the words "designated for the purposes of this subsection" substituted for the former words "designated for the purposes of this section" by CA 1989,

s. 65(1), (4) as from 21 February 1990 (see S.I. 1990 No. 142 (C. 5), art. 4).
Note
See note after s. 449(1C).

449(1C)   [Qualification to sec. 449(1B)]   An order under subsection (1B) designating an authority for the purpose of that subsection may—

(a) impose conditions subject to which the publication or disclosure of any information or document is permitted by that subsection; and

(b) otherwise restrict the circumstances in which that subsection permits publication or disclosure.

Note
The following orders have been made under s. 449(1B), (1C): the Financial Services (Disclosure of Information) (Designated Authorities) Order 1986 (S.I. 1986 No. 2046) in operation from 28 November 1986; the Financial Services (Disclosure of Information) (Designated Authorities No. 2) Order 1987 (S.I. 1987 No. 859) in operation from 13 May 1987; the Financial Services (Disclosure of Information) (Designated Authorities) (No. 3) Order 1987 (S.I. 1987 No. 1141) in operation from 4 July 1987; the Financial Services (Disclosure of Information) (Designated

Authorities) (No. 4) Order 1988 (S.I. 1988 No. 1058) in operation from 17 June 1988, the Companies (Disclosure of Information) (Designated Authorities) Order 1988 (S.I. 1988 No. 1334) in operation from 19 August 1988, the Financial Services (Disclosure of Information) (Designated Authorities) (No. 5) Order 1989 (S.I. 1989 No. 940) in operation from 7 June 1989 and the Financial Services (Disclosure of Information) (Designated Authorities) (No. 6) Order 1989 (S.I. 1989 No. 2009) in operation from 28 November 1989.

449(1D) **[Further exception to sec. 449(1) limitation]** Subsection (1) shall not preclude the publication or disclosure of any such information as is mentioned in section 180(5) of the Financial Services Act 1986 by any person who by virtue of that section is not precluded by section 179 of that Act from disclosing it.

History
S. 449(1A)–(1D) inserted by Financial Services Act 1986, s. 182 and Sch. 13, para. 9(2) as from 15 November 1986 for certain purposes (see S.I. 1986 No. 1940 (C. 69)) and as from 27 November 1986 for remaining purposes (see S.I. 1986 No. 2031 (C. 76)).

449(2) **[Offence, penalty]** A person who publishes or discloses any information or document in contravention of this section is guilty of an offence and liable to imprisonment or a fine, or both.

Sections 732 (restrictions on prosecutions), 733 (liability of individuals for corporate default) and 734 (criminal proceedings against unincorporated bodies) apply to this offence.

History
In s. 449(2) second sentence substituted by CA 1989, s. 65(1), (5) as from 21 February 1990 (see S.I. 1990 No. 142 (C. 5), art. 4); the second sentence formerly read as follows: "Sections 732 (restriction on prosecutions) and 733(2) and (4) (liability of individuals for corporate default) apply to this offence."

449(3) **[Competent authorities]** For the purposes of this section each of the following is a competent authority—

   (a) the Secretary of State,

   (b) an inspector appointed under this Part or under section 94 or 177 of the Financial Services Act 1986,

   (c) any person authorised to exercise powers under section 44 of the Insurance Companies Act 1982, section 447 of this Act, section 106 of the Financial Services Act 1986 or section 84 of the Companies Act 1989,

   (d) the Department of Economic Development in Northern Ireland,

   (e) the Treasury,

   (f) the Bank of England,

   (g) the Lord Advocate,

   (h) the Director of Public Prosecutions, and the Director of Public Prosecutions for Northern Ireland,

   (i) any designated agency or transferee body within the meaning of the Financial Services Act 1986, and any body administering a scheme under section 54 of or paragraph 18 of Schedule 11 to that Act (schemes for compensation of investors),

   (j) the Chief Registrar of friendly societies and the Registrar of Friendly Societies for Northern Ireland,

   (k) the Industrial Assurance Commissioner and the Industrial Assurance Commissioner for Northern Ireland,

   (l) any constable,

   (m) any procurator fiscal.

History
See history note after s. 449(3A).

449(3A)   [Disclosure to officers or servants]   Any information which may by virtue of this section be disclosed to a competent authority may be disclosed to any officer or servant of the authority.

History

S. 449(3), (3A) substituted for the former s. 449(3) by CA 1989, s. 65(1), (6) as from 21 February 1990 (see S.I. 1990 No. 142 (C. 5), art. 4); the former s. 449(3) read as follows:

"For the purposes of this section each of the following is a competent authority—

(a)   the Secretary of State,

(b)   the Department of Economic Development for Northern Ireland and any officer of that Department,

(c)   an inspector appointed under this Part by the Secretary of State,

(d)   the Treasury and any officer of the Treasury,

(e)   the Bank of England and any officer or servant of the Bank,

(f)   the Lord Advocate,

(g)   the Director of Public Prosecutions, and the Director of Public Prosecutions for Northern Ireland,

(h)   any designated agency or transferee body within the meaning of the Financial Services Act 1986 and any officer or servant of such an agency or body,

(i)   any person appointed or authorised to exercise any powers under section 94, 106 or 177 of the Financial Services Act 1986 and any officer or servant of such a person,

(j)   the body administering a scheme under section 54 of or paragraph 18 of Schedule 11 to that Act and any officer or servant of such a body,

(k)   the Chief Registrar of friendly societies and the Registrar of Friendly Societies for Northern Ireland and any officer or servant of either of them,

(l)   the Industrial Assurance Commissioner and the

Industrial Assurance Commissioner for Northern Ireland and any officer of either of them,

(m)   any constable,

(n)   any procurator fiscal."

Previously s. 449(3), (4) substituted for the original s. 449(3) by Financial Services Act 1986, s. 182 and Sch. 13, para. 9(3) as from 15 November 1986 for certain purposes (see S.I. 1986 No. 1940 (C. 69)) and as from 27 November 1986 for remaining purposes (see S.I. 1986 No. 2031 (C. 76)); the original s. 449(3) read as follows:

"For purposes of this section—

(a)   in relation to information or a document relating to a body other than one carrying on industrial assurance business (as defined by section 1(2) of the Industrial Assurance Act 1923), each of the following is a competent authority—

(i)   the Secretary of State for Trade and Industry, and any officer of his,

(ii)   an inspector appointed under this Part by the Secretary of State,

(iii)   the Treasury, and any officer of the Treasury,

(iv)   the Lord Advocate,

(v)   the Director of Public Prosecutions,

(vi)   any constable, and

(vii)   any procurator fiscal;

(b)   in relation to information or a document relating to a body carrying on industrial assurance business (as so defined), all the same persons as above specified are competent authorities, and also the Industrial Assurance Commissioner and any officer of his."

449(4)   [Order under sec. 449(1B)]   A statutory instrument containing an order under subsection (1A)(a) or (1B) is subject to annulment in pursuance of a resolution of either House of Parliament.

History

In s. 449(4) the words "subsection (1A)(a) or (1B)" substituted for the former words "subsection (1B)" by CA 1989 s. 65(1), (7) as from 21 February 1990 (see S.I. 1990 No. 142 (C. 5), art. 4); originally s. 449(4) was substituted, with s. 449(3), for the original s. 449(3) — see history note to s. 449(3) above.

Note

Re s. 449(4) see Financial Services (Disclosure of Information) (Designated Authorities) Order 1986 (S.I. 1986 No. 2046) in operation from 28 November 1986.

SEC. 450   Punishment for destroying, mutilating etc. company documents

450(1)   [Offence of destruction etc.]   An officer of the company, or an insurance company to which Part II of the Insurance Companies Act 1982 applies, who—

(a)   destroys, mutilates or falsifies, or is privy to the destruction, mutilation or falsification of a document affecting or relating to the company's property or affairs, or

(b)   makes, or is privy to the making of, a false entry in such a document,

is guilty of an offence, unless he proves that he had no intention to conceal the state of affairs of the company or to defeat the law.

CA 1985, sec. 449(3A)   **CCH Editions Limited**

History
In s. 450(1) the words "An officer of the company, or an insurance company" substituted for the former words "A person, being an officer of any such body as is mentioned in paragraphs (a) to (d) of section 447(1) or a body other than as there mentioned, being an insurance company",

the word "company's" substituted for the former word "body's" and the word "the company" substituted for the former word "the body" by CA 1989, s. 66(1), (2) as from 21 February 1990 (see S.I. 1990 No. 142 (C. 5), art. 4).

450(2) **[Offence re fraudulent omissions etc.]** Such a person as above mentioned who fraudulently either parts with, alters or makes an omission in any such document or is privy to fraudulent parting with, fraudulent altering or fraudulent making of an omission in, any such document, is guilty of an offence.

450(3) **[Penalty]** A person guilty of an offence under this section is liable to imprisonment or a fine, or both.

450(4) **[Application of sec. 732–734]** Sections 732 (restriction on prosecutions), 733 (liability of individuals for corporate default) and 734 (criminal proceedings against unincorporated bodies) apply to an offence under this section.

History
S. 450(4) substituted by CA 1989, s. 66(1), (3) as from 21 February 1990 (see S.I. 1990 No. 142 (C. 5), art. 4); s. 450(4) formerly read as follows:

"Sections 732 (restriction on prosecutions) and 733(2) and (4) (liability of individuals for corporate default) apply to an offence under this section."

450(5) **["Document"]** In this section "document" includes information recorded in any form.

History
S. 450(5) inserted by CA 1989, s. 66(1), (4) as from 21 February 1990 (see S.I. 1990 No. 142 (C. 5), art. 4).

SEC. 451 Punishment for furnishing false information

451 A person who, in purported compliance with a requirement imposed under section 447 to provide an explanation or make a statement, provides or makes an explanation or statement which he knows to be false in a material particular or recklessly provides or makes an explanation or statement which is so false, is guilty of an offence and liable to imprisonment or a fine, or both.

Sections 732 (restriction on prosecutions) and 733 (liability of individuals for corporate default) and 734 (criminal proceedings against unincorporated bodies) apply to this offence.

History
In s. 451 second sentence substituted by CA 1989, s. 67 as from 21 February 1990 (see S.I. 1990 No. 142 (C. 5), art. 4); the second sentence formerly read as follows:

"Sections 732 (restriction on prosecutions) and 733(2) and (4) (liability of individuals for corporate default) apply to this offence."

SEC. 451A Disclosure of information by Secretary of State or inspector

451A(1) **[Application]** This section applies to information obtained under sections 434 to 446.

451A(2) **[Power of Secretary of State]** The Secretary of State may, if he thinks fit—

(a) disclose any information to which this section applies to any person to whom, or for any purpose for which, disclosure is permitted under section 449, or

(b) authorise or require an inspector appointed under this Part to disclose such information to any such person or for any such purpose.

451A(3)   **[Limit on disclosure]**   Information to which this section applies may also be disclosed by an inspector appointed under this Part to—

(a) another inspector appointed under this Part or an inspector appointed under section 94 or 177 of the Financial Services Act 1986, or

(b) a person authorised to exercise powers under section 44 of the Insurance Companies Act 1982, section 447 of this Act, section 106 of the Financial Services Act 1986 or section 84 of the Companies Act 1989.

451A(4)   **[Disclosure to officer or servant]**   Any information which may by virtue of subsection (3) be disclosed to any person may be disclosed to any officer or servant of that person.

451A(5)   **[Further power of Secretary of State]**   The Secretary of State may, if he thinks fit, disclose any information obtained under section 444 to—

(a) the company whose ownership was the subject of the investigation,

(b) any member of the company,

(c) any person whose conduct was investigated in the course of the investigation,

(d) the auditors of the company, or

(e) any person whose financial interests appear to the Secretary of State to be affected by matters covered by the investigation.

History
S. 451A substituted by CA 1989, s. 68 as from 21 February 1990 (see S.I. 1990 No. 142 (C. 5), art. 4); s. 451 formerly read as follows:

"**SEC. 451A Disclosure of information by Secretary of State**

451A The Secretary of State may, if he thinks fit, disclose any information obtained under this Part of this Act—

   (a) to any person who is a competent authority for the purposes of section 449, or

(b) in any circumstances in which or for any purpose for which that section does not preclude the disclosure of the information to which it applies."

S. 451A originally inserted by Financial Services Act 1986, s. 182 and Sch. 13, para. 10 as from 15 November 1986 for certain purposes (see S.I. 1986 No. 1940 (C. 69)) and as from 27 November 1986 for remaining purposes (see S.I. 1986 No. 2031 (C. 76)).

SUPPLEMENTARY

SEC. 452   Privileged information

452(1)   **[Privilege re legal proceedings, bankers — sec. 431 to 446]**   Nothing in sections 431 to 446 requires the disclosure to the Secretary of State or to an inspector appointed by him—

(a) by any person of information which he would in an action in the High Court or the Court of Session be entitled to refuse to disclose on grounds of legal professional privilege except, if he is a lawyer, the name and address of his client,

(b) (omitted and repealed by Companies Act 1989, sec. 69(1), (2), 212 and Sch. 24 as from 21 February 1990).

History
In regard to the date of the above omission and repeal see S.I. 1990 No. 142 (C. 5); para. (b) formerly read as follows:

"(b) by a company's bankers (as such) of information as to the affairs of any of their customers other than the company."

452(1A)   **[Qualification re privilege]**   Nothing in section 434, 443 or 446 requires a person (except as mentioned in subsection (1B) below) to disclose information or produce documents in respect of which he owes an obligation of confidence by virtue of carrying on the business of banking unless—

CA 1985, sec. 451A(3)   [The next page is 20,901]

(a) the person to whom the obligation of confidence is owed is the company or other body corporate under investigation,

(b) the person to whom the obligation of confidence is owed consents to the disclosure or production, or

(c) the making of the requirement is authorised by the Secretary of State.

History
See history note after s. 452(1B).

452(1B) **[Non application of sec. 452(1A)** Subsection (1A) does not apply where the person owing the obligation of confidence is the company or other body corporate under investigation under section 431, 432 or 433.

History
S. 452(1A), (1B) inserted by CA 1989, s. 69(1), (3) as from
21 February 1990 (see S.I. 1990 No. 142 (C. 5), art. 4).

452(2) **[Legal proceedings — sec. 447 to 451]** Nothing in sections 447 to 451 compels the production by any person of a document which he would in an action in the High Court or the Court of Session be entitled to refuse to produce on grounds of legal professional privilege, or authorises the taking of possession of any such document which is in the person's possession.

452(3) **[Bankers — sec. 447]** The Secretary of State shall not under section 447 require, or authorise an officer of his or other person to require, the production by a person carrying on the business of banking of a document relating to the affairs of a customer of his unless either it appears to the Secretary of State that it is necessary to do so for the purpose of investigating the affairs of the first-mentioned person or the customer is a person on whom a requirement has been imposed under that section, or under section 44(2) to (4) of the Insurance Companies Act 1982 (provision corresponding to section 447).

History
In s. 452(3) the words "or other person" inserted by CA
1989, s. 69(1), (4) as from 21 February 1990 (see S.I. 1990
No. 142 (C. 5), art. 4).

SEC. 453 Investigation of oversea companies

453(1) **[Companies covered by Pt. XIV]** The provisions of this Part apply to bodies corporate incorporated outside Great Britain which are carrying on business in Great Britain, or have at any time carried on business there, as they apply to companies under this Act; but subject to the following exceptions, adaptations and modifications.

453(1A) **[Provisions not applying to sec. 453(1A) bodies]** The following provisions do not apply to such bodies—

(a) section 431 (investigation on application of company or its members),

(b) section 438 (power to bring civil proceedings on the company's behalf),

(c) sections 442 to 445 (investigation of company ownership and power to obtain information as to those interested in shares, etc.), and

(d) section 446 (investigation of share dealings).

453(1B) **[Other provisions of Pt. XIV]** The other provisions of this Part apply to such bodies subject to such adaptations and modifications as may be specified by regulations made by the Secretary of State.

History
S. 453(1)–(1B) substituted for the former s. 453(1) by CA 1989, s. 70 as from 21 February 1990; the former s. 453(1) read as follows:

"**453(1)** Sections 432 to 437, 439, 441 and 452(1) apply to all bodies corporate incorporated outside Great Britain which are carrying on business in Great Britain or have at any time carried on business there as if they were companies under this Act, but subject to such (if any) adaptations and modifications as may be specified by regulations made by the Secretary of State."

453(2)   **[Regulations]**   Regulations under this section shall be made by statutory instrument subject to annulment in pursuance of a resolution of either House of Parliament.

PART XV — ORDERS IMPOSING RESTRICTIONS ON SHARES (SECTIONS 210, 216, 445)

SEC. 454   Consequence of order imposing restrictions

454(1)   **[Effect of restrictions]**   So long as any shares are directed to be subject to the restrictions of this Part—

    (a) any transfer of those shares or, in the case of unissued shares, any transfer of the right to be issued with them, and any issue of them, is void;

    (b) no voting rights are exercisable in respect of the shares;

    (c) no further shares shall be issued in right of them or in pursuance of any offer made to their holder; and

    (d) except in a liquidation, no payment shall be made of any sums due from the company on the shares, whether in respect of capital or otherwise.

454(2)   **[Effect of sec. 454(1)(a) restriction]**   Where shares are subject to the restrictions of subsection (1)(a), any agreement to transfer the shares or, in the case of unissued shares, the right to be issued with them is void (except an agreement to sell the shares on the making of an order under section 456(3)(b) below).

454(3)   **[Effect of sec. 454(1)(c), (d)]**   Where shares are subject to the restrictions of subsection (1)(c) or (d), an agreement to transfer any right to be issued with other shares in right of those shares, or to receive any payment on them (otherwise than in a liquidation) is void (except an agreement to transfer any such right on the sale of the shares on the making of an order under section 456(3)(b) below).

SEC. 455   Punishment for attempted evasion of restrictions

455(1)   **[Offence by person]**   A person is liable to a fine if he—

    (a) exercises or purports to exercise any right to dispose of any shares which, to his knowledge, are for the time being subject to the restrictions of this Part or of any right to be issued with any such shares, or

    (b) votes in respect of any such shares (whether as holder or proxy), or appoints a proxy to vote in respect of them, or

    (c) being the holder of any such shares, fails to notify of their being subject to those restrictions any person whom he does not know to be aware of that fact but does know to be entitled (apart from the restrictions) to vote in respect of those shares whether as holder or as proxy, or

    (d) being the holder of any such shares, or being entitled to any right to be issued with other shares in right of them, or to receive any payment on them (otherwise than in a liquidation), enters into any agreement which is void under section 454(2) or (3).

455(2) **[Offence by company]** If shares in a company are issued in contravention of the restrictions, the company and every officer of it who is in default is liable to a fine.

455(3) **[Application of sec. 732]** Section 732 (restriction on prosecutions) applies to an offence under this section.

SEC. 456   Relaxation and removal of restrictions

456(1) **[Application to court]** Where shares in a company are by order made subject to the restrictions of this Part, application may be made to the court for an order directing that the shares be no longer so subject.

456(2) **[Persons entitled to make application]** If the order applying the restrictions was made by the Secretary of State, or he has refused to make an order disapplying them, the application may be made by any person aggrieved; and if the order was made by the court under section 216 (non-disclosure of share holding), it may be made by any such person or by the company.

456(3) **[Conditions for order by court or Secretary of State]** Subject as follows, an order of the court or the Secretary of State directing that shares shall cease to be subject to the restrictions may be made only if—

(a) the court or (as the case may be) the Secretary of State is satisfied that the relevant facts about the shares have been disclosed to the company and no unfair advantage has accrued to any person as a result of the earlier failure to make that disclosure, or

(b) the shares are to be sold and the court (in any case) or the Secretary of State (if the order was made under section 210 or 445) approves the sale.

[The next page is 21,051]

456(4) **[Order re sale of shares etc.]** Where shares in a company are subject to the restrictions, the court may on application order the shares to be sold, subject to the court's approval as to the sale, and may also direct that the shares shall cease to be subject to the restrictions.

An application to the court under this subsection may be made by the Secretary of State (unless the restrictions were imposed by court order under section 216), or by the company.

456(5) **[Further order when order made under sec. 456(4)]** Where an order has been made under subsection (4), the court may on application make such further order relating to the sale or transfer of the shares as it thinks fit.

An application to the court under this subsection may be made—

(a) by the Secretary of State (unless the restrictions on the shares were imposed by court order under section 216), or

(b) by the company, or

(c) by the person appointed by or in pursuance of the order to effect the sale, or

(d) by any person interested in the shares.

456(6) **[Continuation of certain restrictions]** An order (whether of the Secretary of State or the court) directing that shares shall cease to be subject to the restrictions of this Part, if it is—

(a) expressed to be made with a view to permitting a transfer of the shares, or

(b) made under subsection (4) of this section,

may continue the restrictions mentioned in paragraphs (c) and (d) of section 454(1), either in whole or in part, so far as they relate to any right acquired or offer made before the transfer.

456(7) **[Non-application of sec. 456(3)]** Subsection (3) does not apply to an order directing that shares shall cease to be subject to any restrictions which have been continued in force in relation to those shares under subsection (6).

SEC. 457 Further provisions on sale by court order of restricted shares

457(1) **[Proceeds of sale of shares under sec. 456(4)]** Where shares are sold in pursuance of an order of the court under section 456(4) the proceeds of sale, less the costs of the sale, shall be paid into court for the benefit of the persons who are beneficially interested in the shares; and any such person may apply to the court for the whole or part of those proceeds to be paid to him.

457(2) **[Application under sec. 457(1) for payment of proceeds etc.]** On application under subsection (1) the court shall (subject as provided below) order the payment to the applicant of the whole of the proceeds of sale together with any interest thereon or, if any other person had a beneficial interest in the shares at the time of their sale, such proportion of those proceeds and interest as is equal to the proportion which the value of the applicant's interest in the shares bears to the total value of the shares.

457(3) **[Order re applicant's costs]** On granting an application for an order under section 456(4) or (5) the court may order that the applicant's costs be paid out of the proceeds of sale; and if that order is made, the applicant is entitled to payment of his costs out of those proceeds before any person interested in the shares in question receives any part of those proceeds.

PART XVI — FRAUDULENT TRADING BY A COMPANY

SEC. 458   Punishment for fraudulent trading

458   If any business of a company is carried on with intent to defraud creditors of the company or creditors of any other person, or for any fraudulent purpose, every person who was knowingly a party to the carrying on of the business in that manner is liable to imprisonment or a fine, or both.

This applies whether or not the company has been, or is in the course of being, wound up.

PART XVII — PROTECTION OF COMPANY'S MEMBERS AGAINST UNFAIR PREJUDICE

SEC. 459   Order on application of company member

459(1)   **[Application for order that affairs conducted in unfairly prejudicial way]**   A member of a company may apply to the court by petition for an order under this Part on the ground that the company's affairs are being or have been conducted in a manner which is unfairly prejudicial to the interests of some part of the members (including at least himself) or that any actual or proposed act or omission of the company (including an act or omission on its behalf) is or would be so prejudicial.

459(2)   **[Application to certain non-members]**   The provisions of this Part apply to a person who is not a member of a company but to whom shares in the company have been transferred or transmitted by operation of law, as those provisions apply to a member of the company; and references to a member or members are to be construed accordingly.

459(3)   **["Company" to include statutory water company]**   In this section (and so far as applicable for the purposes of this section, in section 461(2)) **"company"** means any company within the meaning of this Act or any company which is not such a company but is a statutory water company within the meaning of the Water Act 1989.

History
S. 459(3) inserted by Water Act 1989, s. 190(1) and Sch. 25, para. 71(3) as from 1 September 1989 (see Water Act 1989, s. 4,194(4) and S.I. 1989 No. 1146 (C. 37) — see also S.I. 1989 No. 1530 (C. 51)).

SEC. 460   Order on application of Secretary of State

460(1)   **[Secretary of State may apply for order]**   If in the case of any company—

   (a) the Secretary of State has received a report under section 437, or exercised his powers under section 447 or 448 of this Act or section 44(2) to (6) of the Insurance Companies Act 1982 (inspection of company's books and papers), and

(b) it appears to him that the company's affairs are being or have been conducted in a manner which is unfairly prejudicial to the interests of some part of the members, or that any actual or proposed act or omission of the company (including an act or omission on its behalf) is or would be so prejudicial,

he may himself (in addition to or instead of presenting a petition under section 440 for the winding up of the company) apply to the court by petition for an order under this Part.

460(2) **["Company"]** In this section (and, so far as applicable for its purposes, in the section next following) "**company**" means any body corporate which is liable to be wound up under this Act.

SEC. 461 Provisions as to petitions and orders under this Part

461(1) **[Order by court]** If the court is satisfied that a petition under this Part is well founded, it may make such order as it thinks fit for giving relief in respect of the matters complained of.

461(2) **[Scope of order]** Without prejudice to the generality of subsection (1), the court's order may—

(a) regulate the conduct of the company's affairs in the future,

(b) require the company to refrain from doing or continuing an act complained of by the petitioner or to do an act which the petitioner has complained it has omitted to do,

(c) authorise civil proceedings to be brought in the name and on behalf of the company by such person or persons and on such terms as the court may direct,

(d) provide for the purchase of the shares of any members of the company by other members or by the company itself and, in the case of a purchase by the company itself, the reduction of the company's capital accordingly.

461(3) **[Order forbidding alteration of memorandum or articles]** If an order under this Part requires the company not to make any, or any specified, alteration in the memorandum or articles, the company does not then have power without leave of the court to make any such alteration in breach of that requirement.

461(4) **[Effect of alteration by court order]** Any alteration in the company's memorandum or articles made by virtue of an order under this Part is of the same effect as if duly made by resolution of the company, and the provisions of this Act apply to the memorandum or articles as so altered accordingly.

461(5) **[Copy of order re alteration etc. to registrar, penalty on default]** An office copy of an order under this Part altering, or giving leave to alter, a company's memorandum or articles shall, within 14 days from the making of the order or such longer period as the court may allow, be delivered by the company to the registrar of companies for registration; and if a company makes default in complying with this subsection, the company and every officer of it who is in default is liable to a fine and, for continued contravention, to a daily default fine.

461(6)   [Power under Insolvency Act, sec. 411]   The power under section 411 of the Insolvency Act to make rules shall, so far as it relates to a winding-up petition, apply for the purposes of a petition under this Part.

History
In s. 461(6) the words "section 411 of the Insolvency Act" substituted for the former words "section 106 of the Insolvency Act 1985" by Insolvency Act 1986, s. 439(1) and Sch. 13 as from 29 December 1986 (see IA 1986, s. 443 and S.I. 1986 No. 1924 (C. 71)), in addition the subsection was previously substituted by Insolvency Act 1985, s. 109 and Sch. 6, para. 24 — it originally read as follows:

"**461(6)**   Section 663 (winding-up rules) applies in relation to a petition under this Part as in relation to a winding-up petition."

It should be noted that the amendment by the Insolvency Act 1985 was in force as from 1 March 1986 in regard to the making of rules under s. 106 of Insolvency Act 1985 — see S.I. 1986 No. 185 (C. 7).

PART XVIII — FLOATING CHARGES AND RECEIVERS (SCOTLAND)

Chapter I — Floating Charges

SEC. 462   Power of incorporated company to create floating charge

462(1)   [Securing of debt by floating charge]   It is competent under the law of Scotland for an incorporated company (whether a company within the meaning of this Act or not), for the purpose of securing any debt or other obligation (including a cautionary obligation) incurred or to be incurred by, or binding upon, the company or any other person, to create in favour of the creditor in the debt or obligation a charge, in this Part referred to as a floating charge, over all or any part of the property (including uncalled capital) which may from time to time be comprised in its property and undertaking.

462(2)   [Creation by execution of instrument etc.]   A floating charge may be created, in the case of a company which the Court of Session has jurisdiction to wind up, only by the execution, under the seal of the company, of an instrument or bond or other written acknowledgment of debt or obligation which purports to create such a charge.

462(3)   [Execution by attorney]   Execution in accordance with this section includes execution by an attorney authorised for such purpose by the company by writing under its common seal; and any such execution on behalf of the company binds the company.

462(4)   [Interpretation]   References in this Part to the instrument by which a floating charge was created are, in the case of a floating charge created by words in a bond or other written acknowledgment, references to the bond or, as the case may be, the other written acknowledgment.

462(5)   [Effect re heritable property in Scotland]   Subject to this Act, a floating charge has effect in accordance with this Part and Part III of the Insolvency Act 1986 in relation to any heritable property in Scotland to which it relates, notwithstanding that the instrument creating it is not recorded in the Register of Sasines or, as appropriate, registered in accordance with the Land Registration (Scotland) Act 1979.

History
In s. 462(5) the words "and Part III of the Insolvency Act 1986" inserted by Insolvency Act 1986, s. 439(1) and Sch. 13 as from 29 December 1986 (see IA 1986, s. 443 and S.I. 1986 No. 1924 (C. 71)).

SEC. 463   Effect of floating charge on winding up

463(1)   [Attachment on winding up]   On the commencement of the winding up of a company, a floating charge created by the company attaches to the property then

[The next page is 21,301]

comprised in the company's property and undertaking or, as the case may be, in part of that property and undertaking, but does so subject to the rights of any person who—

(a) has effectually executed diligence on the property or any part of it; or

(b) holds a fixed security over the property or any part of it ranking in priority to the floating charge; or

(c) holds over the property or any part of it another floating charge so ranking.

463(2) **[Application of Pt. XX to floating charge]** The provisions of Part IV of the Insolvency Act (except section 185) have effect in relation to a floating charge, subject to subsection (1), as if the charge were a fixed security over the property to which it has attached in respect of the principal of the debt or obligation to which it relates and any interest due or to become due thereon.

History
In s. 463(2) the words "Part IV of the Insolvency Act (except section 185)" substituted for the former words "Part XX (except section 623(4))" by Insolvency Act 1986, s. 439(1) and Sch. 13 as from 29 December 1986 (see IA 1986, s. 443 and S.I. 1986 No. 1924 (C. 71)).

463(3) **[Operation of Insolvency Act]** Nothing in this section derogates from the provisions of sections 53(7) and 54(6) of the Insolvency Act (attachment of floating charge on appointment of receiver), or prejudices the operation of sections 175 and 176 of that Act (payment of preferential debts in winding up).

History
S. 463(3) substituted by Insolvency Act 1986, s. 439(1) and Sch. 13 as from 29 December 1986 (see IA 1986, s. 443 and S.I. 1986 No. 1924 (C. 71)); s. 463(3) (as previously amended by Insolvency Act 1985, s. 109 and Sch. 6, para. 18) read as follows:

"**463(3)** Nothing in this section—

(a) prejudices the operation of section 89 of the Insolvency Act 1985;

(b) derogates from the provisions of sections 469(7) and 470(6) in this Part."

The original wording of s. 463(3)(a) was: "prejudices the operation of section 614(2)".

463(4) **[Accrual of interest]** Interest accrues, in respect of a floating charge which after 16th November 1972 attaches to the property of the company, until payment of the sum due under the charge is made.

History
In s. 463(4) the words "Subject to section 617", formerly appearing at the beginning repealed by Insolvency Act 1986, s. 438 and Sch. 12 as from 29 December 1986 (see IA 1986, s. 443 and S.I. 1986 No. 1924 (C. 71)).

SEC. 464 Ranking of floating charges

464(1) **[Contents of instrument creating floating charge]** Subject to subsection (2), the instrument creating a floating charge over all or any part of the company's property under section 462 may contain—

(a) provisions prohibiting or restricting the creation of any fixed security or any other floating charge having priority over, or ranking pari passu with, the floating charge; or

(b) provisions regulating the order in which the floating charge shall rank with any other subsisting or future floating charges or fixed securities over that property or any part of it.

464(2) **[Priority of fixed security by operation of law]** Where all or any part of the property of a company is subject both to a floating charge and to a fixed security arising by operation of law, the fixed security has priority over the floating charge.

464(3) **[Priority with other floating charges and fixed securities]** Where the order of ranking of the floating charge with any other subsisting or future floating charges or fixed securities over all or any part of the company's property is not regulated by provisions contained in the instrument creating the floating charge, the order of ranking is determined in accordance with the following provisions of this section.

464(4)   [Rules of priority]   Subject to the provisions of this section—

   (a) a fixed security, the right to which has been constituted as a real right before a floating charge has attached to all or any part of the property of the company, has priority of ranking over the floating charge;

   (b) floating charges rank with one another according to the time of registration in accordance with Chapter II of Part XII;

   (c) floating charges which have been received by the registrar for registration by the same postal delivery rank with one another equally.

464(5)   [Restriction of priority of one floating charge over another]   Where the holder of a floating charge over all or any part of the company's property which has been registered in accordance with Chapter II of Part XII has received intimation in writing of the subsequent registration in accordance with that Chapter of another floating charge over the same property or any part thereof, the preference in ranking of the first-mentioned floating charge is restricted to security for—

   (a) the holder's present advances;

   (b) future advances which he may be required to make under the instrument creating the floating charge or under any ancillary document;

   (c) interest due or to become due on all such advances; and

   (d) any expenses or outlays which may reasonably be incurred by the holder.

464(6)   [Sec. 175, 176 of Insolvency Act]   This section is subject to sections 175 and 176 of the Insolvency Act.

History
In s. 464(6) the words "sections 175 and 176 of the Insolvency Act" substituted by Insolvency Act 1986, s. 439(1) and Sch. 13 as from 29 December 1986 (see IA 1986, s. 443 and S.I. 1986 No. 1924 (C. 71)). The former words were "section 89 of the Insolvency Act 1985", themselves substituted briefly by Insolvency Act 1985, s. 109 and Sch. 6, para. 19 for the original words "section 614(2) (preferential debts in winding up)" (see S.I. 1986 No. 1924 (C. 71)).

SEC. 465   Continued effect of certain charges validated by Act of 1972

465(1)   [Subsisting floating charges]   Any floating charge which—

   (a) purported to subsist as a floating charge on 17th November 1972, and

   (b) if it had been created on or after that date, would have been validly created by virtue of the Companies (Floating Charges and Receivers) (Scotland) Act 1972,

is deemed to have subsisted as a valid floating charge as from the date of its creation.

465(2)   [Subsisting provisions]   Any provision which—

   (a) is contained in an instrument creating a floating charge or in any ancillary document executed prior to, and still subsisting at, the commencement of that Act,

   (b) relates to the ranking of charges, and

   (c) if it had been made after the commencement of that Act, would have been a valid provision,

is deemed to have been a valid provision as from the date of its making.

SEC. 466 Alteration of floating charges

466(1) **[Alteration by execution of instrument of alteration by company et al.]** The instrument creating a floating charge under section 462 or any ancillary document may be altered by the execution of an instrument of alteration by the company, the holder of the charge and the holder of any other charge (including a fixed security) which would be adversely affected by the alteration.

466(2) **[Valid execution of instrument of alteration]** Such an instrument of alteration is validly executed if it is executed—

(a) in the case of a company, under its common seal or by an attorney authorised for such purpose by the company by a writing under its common seal;

(b) where trustees for debenture-holders are acting under and in accordance with a trust deed, by those trustees;

(c) where, in the case of a series of secured debentures, no such trustees are acting, by or on behalf of—

(i) a majority in nominal value of those present or represented by proxy and voting at a meeting of debenture-holders at which the holders of at least one-third in nominal value of the outstanding debentures of the series are present or so represented; or

(ii) where no such meeting is held, the holders of at least one-half in nominal value of the outstanding debentures of the series; or

(d) in such manner as may be provided for in the instrument creating the floating charge or any ancillary document.

466(3) **[Application of sec. 464]** Section 464 applies to an instrument of alteration under this section as it applies to an instrument creating a floating charge.

466(4) **[Application of sec. 410(2), (3), 420]** Subject to the next subsection, section 410(2) and (3) and section 420 apply to an instrument of alteration under this section which—

(a) prohibits or restricts the creation of any fixed security or any other floating charge having priority over, or ranking pari passu with, the floating charge; or

(b) varies, or otherwise regulates the order of, the ranking of the floating charge in relation to fixed securities or to other floating charges; or

(c) releases property from the floating charge; or

(d) increases the amount secured by the floating charge.

466(5) **[Interpretation re sec. 466(4)]** Section 410(2) and (3) and section 420 apply to an instrument of alteration falling under subsection (4) of this section as if references in the said sections to a charge were references to an alteration to a floating charge, and as if in section 410(2) and (3)—

(a) references to the creation of a charge were references to the execution of such alteration; and

(b) for the words from the beginning of subsection (2) to the word "applies" there were substituted the words "Every alteration to a floating charge created by a company".

466(6)   [Reference to floating charge includes reference to floating charge as altered]
Any reference (however expressed) in any enactment, including this Act, to a floating charge is, for the purposes of this section and unless the context otherwise requires, to be construed as including a reference to the floating charge as altered by an instrument of alteration falling under subsection (4) of this section.

Chapter II — Receivers

467–485   (Repealed by Insolvency Act 1986, sec. 438 and Sch. 12 as from 29 December 1986.)

Note
For the corresponding new provisions of the 1986 consolidation, see the CCH table of destinations at page 58,201.

History
In regard to the date of the above repeal, see IA 1986, s. 443 and S.I. 1986 No. 1924 (C. 71). These were some previous amendments and repeals by Insolvency Act 1985 which only came into force briefly — see IA 1985, Sch. 6, 10 and the above S.I. (note in particular art. 4(b)). The sections originally read as follows:

"**SEC. 467 Power to appoint receiver**

467(1)   It is competent under the law of Scotland for the holder of a floating charge over all or any part of the property (including uncalled capital), which may from time to time be comprised in the property and undertaking of an incorporated company (whether a company within the meaning of this Act or not) which the Court of Session has jurisdiction to wind up, to appoint a receiver of such part of the property of the company as is subject to the charge.

(2)   It is competent under the law of Scotland for the court, on the application of the holder of such a floating charge, to appoint a receiver of such part of the property of the company as is subject to the charge.

(3)   The following are disqualified from being appointed as receiver—

(a) a body corporate;

(b) an undischarged bankrupt; and

(c) a firm according to the law of Scotland.

(4)   A body corporate or a firm according to the law of Scotland which acts as a receiver is liable to a fine.

(5)   An undischarged bankrupt who so acts is liable to imprisonment or a fine, or both.

(6)   In this section, '**receiver**' includes joint receivers.

SEC. 468 Circumstances justifying appointment

468(1)   A receiver may be appointed under section 467(1) by the holder of the floating charge on the occurrence of any event which, by the provisions of the instrument creating the charge, entitles the holder of the charge to make that appointment and, in so far as not otherwise provided for by the instrument, on the occurrence of any of the following events, namely—

(a) the expiry of a period of 21 days after the making of a demand for payment of the whole or any part of the principal sum secured by the charge, without payment having been made;

(b) the expiry of a period of two months during the whole of which interest due and payable under the charge has been in arrears;

(c) the making of an order or the passing of a resolution to wind up the company;

(d) the appointment of a receiver by virtue of any other floating charge created by the company.

(2)   A receiver may be appointed by the court under section 467(2) on the occurrence of any event which, by the provisions of the instrument creating the floating charge, entitles the holder of the charge to make that appointment and, in so far as not otherwise provided for by the instrument, on the occurrence of any of the following events, namely—

(a) where the court, on the application of the holder of the charge, pronounces itself satisfied that the position of the holder of the charge is likely to be prejudiced if no such appointment is made;

(b) any of the events referred to in paragraphs (a) to (c) of subsection (1) above.

SEC. 469 Mode of appointment by holder of charge

469(1)   The appointment of a receiver by the holder of the floating charge under section 467(1) shall be by means of a validly executed instrument in writing (referred to as the 'instrument of appointment'), a copy (certified in the prescribed manner to be a correct copy) whereof shall be delivered by or on behalf of the person making the appointment to the registrar of companies for registration within 7 days of its execution and shall be accompanied by a notice in the prescribed form.

(2)   If any person without reasonable excuse makes default in complying with the requirements of subsection (1), he is liable to a fine and, for continued contravention, to a daily default fine.

(3)   The instrument of appointment is validly executed—

(a) by a company, if it is executed in accordance with the provisions of section 36 of this Act as if it were a contract; and

(b) by any other person, if it is executed in the manner required or permitted by the law of Scotland in the case of an attested deed.

(4)   The instrument may be executed on behalf of the holder of the floating charge by virtue of which the receiver is to be appointed—

(a) by any person duly authorised in writing by the holder to execute the instrument; and

(b) in the case of an appointment of a receiver by the holders of a series of secured debentures, by any person authorised by resolution of the debenture-holders to execute the instrument.

(5)   On receipt of the certified copy of the instrument of appointment in accordance with subsection (1) of this section, the registrar shall, on payment of the prescribed fee, enter the particulars of the appointment in the register of charges.

(6) The receiver is to be regarded as having been appointed on the date of the execution of the instrument of his appointment.

(7) On the appointment of a receiver under this section, the floating charge by virtue of which he was appointed attaches to the property then subject to the charge; and such attachment has effect as if the charge was a fixed security over the property to which it has attached.

SEC. 470 Appointment by court

470(1) Application for the appointment of a receiver by the court under section 467(2) shall be by petition to the court, which shall be served on the company.

(2) On such application, the court shall, if it thinks fit, issue an interlocutor making the appointment of the receiver on such terms as to caution as it may think fit.

(3) A copy (certified by the clerk of the court to be a correct copy) of the court's interlocutor making the appointment shall be delivered by or on behalf of the petitioner to the registrar of companies for registration, accompanied by a notice in the prescribed form, within 7 days of the date of the interlocutor or such longer period as the court may allow.

If any person without reasonable excuse makes default in complying with the requirements of this subsection he is liable to a fine and, for continued contravention, to a daily default fine.

(4) On receipt of the certified copy interlocutor in accordance with subsection (3), and on receipt of a certificate by the appropriate officer of the court that caution as ordered by the court has been found, the registrar shall, on payment of the prescribed fee, enter the particulars of the appointment in the register of charges.

(5) The receiver is to be regarded as having been appointed on the date of his being appointed by the court.

(6) On the appointment of a receiver under this section, the floating charge by virtue of which he was appointed attaches to the property then subject to the charge; and such attachment has effect as if the charge were a fixed security over the property to which it has attached.

(7) In making rules of court for the purposes of this section, the Court of Session shall have regard to the need for special provision for cases which appear to the court to require to be dealt with as a matter of urgency.

SEC. 471 Powers of receiver

471(1) Subject to subsection (2) below, a receiver has in relation to such part of the property of the company as is attached by the floating charge by virtue of which he was appointed, the powers, if any, given to him by the instrument creating that charge and, in addition, he has under this Part the following powers as respects that property, in so far as these are not inconsistent with any provision contained in that instrument, namely—

(a) power to take possession of, collect and get in the property from the company or a liquidator thereof or any other person, and for that purpose, to take such proceedings as may seem to him expedient;

(b) power to sell, feu, hire out or otherwise dispose of the property by public roup or private bargain and with or without advertisement;

(c) power to borrow money and grant security therefor over the property;

(d) power to appoint a solicitor or accountant or other professionally qualified person to assist him in the performance of his functions;

(e) power to apply to the court for directions in connection with the performance of his functions;

(f) power to bring or defend any action or other legal proceedings in the name and on behalf of the company;

(g) power to refer to arbitration all questions affecting the company;

(h) power to effect and maintain insurances in respect of the business and property of the company;

(i) power to use the company's seal;

(j) power to do all acts and to execute in the name and on behalf of the company any deed, receipt or other document;

(k) power to draw, accept, make and endorse any bill of exchange or promissory note in the name and on behalf of the company;

(l) power to appoint any agent to do any business which he is unable to do himself or which can more conveniently be done by an agent and power to employ and discharge servants;

(m) power to have carried out to the best advantage any work on the property of the company and in general to do all such other things as may be necessary for the realisation of the property;

(n) power to make any payment which is necessary or incidental to the performance of his functions;

(o) power to carry on the business of the company so far as he thinks it desirable to do so;

(p) power to grant any lease of the property, and to input and output tenants, and to take on lease any property required or convenient for the business of the company;

(q) power to rank and claim in the bankruptcy, insolvency, sequestration or liquidation of any person or company indebted to the company and to receive dividends, and to accede to trust deeds for creditors of any such person;

(r) power to present or defend a petition for the winding up of the company; and

(s) power to do all other things incidental to the exercise of the powers mentioned in this subsection.

(2) Subsection (1) applies—

(a) subject to the rights of any person who has effectually executed diligence on all or any part of the property of the company prior to the appointment of the receiver; and

(b) subject to the rights of any person who holds over all or any part of the property of the company a fixed security or floating charge having priority over, or ranking pari passu with, the floating charge by virtue of which the receiver was appointed.

(3) A person transacting with a receiver shall not be concerned to inquire whether any event has happened to authorise the receiver to act.

SEC. 472 Precedence among receivers

472(1) Where there are two or more floating charges subsisting over all or any part of the property of the company, a receiver may be appointed under this Chapter by virtue of each such charge, but a receiver appointed by, or on the application of, the holder of a floating charge having priority of ranking over any other floating charge by virtue of which a receiver has been appointed has the powers given to a receiver by section 471 to the exclusion of any other receiver.

(2) Where two or more floating charges rank with one another equally, and two or more receivers have been appointed by virtue of such charges, the receivers so appointed are deemed to have been appointed as joint receivers.

(3) Receivers appointed, or deemed to have been appointed, as joint receivers shall act jointly unless the instrument of appointment or respective instruments of appointment otherwise provide.

(4) Subject to subsection (5) below, the powers of a receiver appointed by, or on the application of, the holder of a floating charge are suspended by, and as from the date of, the appointment of a receiver by, or on the application of, the holder of a floating charge having priority of ranking over that charge to such extent as may be necessary to enable the receiver second mentioned to exercise his powers under section 471; and any powers so suspended take effect again when the floating charge having priority of ranking ceases to attach to the property then subject to the charge, whether such cessation is by virtue of section 478(6) or otherwise.

(5) The suspension of the powers of a receiver under subsection (4) does not have the effect of requiring him to release any part of the property (including any letters or documents) of the company from his control until he receives from the receiver superseding him a valid indemnity (subject to the limit of the value of such part of the property of the company as is subject to the charge by virtue of which he was appointed) in respect of any expenses, charges and liabilities he may have incurred in the performance of his functions as receiver.

(6) The suspension of the powers of a receiver under subsection (4) does not cause the floating charge by virtue of which he was appointed to cease to attach to the property to which it attached by virtue of section 469(7) or 470(6).

(7) Nothing in this section prevents the same receiver being appointed by virtue of two or more floating charges.

SEC. 473 Agency and liability of receiver for contracts

473(1) A receiver is deemed to be the agent of the company in relation to such property of the company as is attached by the floating charge by virtue of which he was appointed.

(2) Subject to subsection (1), a receiver (including a receiver whose powers are subsequently suspended under section 472) is personally liable on any contract entered into by him in the performance of his functions, except in so far as the contract otherwise provides.

(3) A receiver who is personally liable by virtue of subsection (2) is entitled to be indemnified out of the property in respect of which he was appointed.

(4) Any contract entered into by or on behalf of the company prior to the appointment of a receiver continues in force (subject to its terms) notwithstanding that appointment, but the receiver does not by virtue only of his appointment incur any personal liability on any such contract.

(5) Any contract entered into by a receiver in the performance of his functions continues in force (subject to its terms) although the powers of the receiver are subsequently suspended under section 472.

SEC. 474 Remuneration of receiver

474(1) The remuneration to be paid to a receiver is to be determined by agreement between the receiver and the holder of the floating charge by virtue of which he was appointed.

(2) Where the remuneration to be paid to the receiver has not been determined under subsection (1) or where it has been so determined but is disputed by any of the persons mentioned in paragraphs (a) to (d), it may be fixed instead by the Auditor of the Court of Session on application made to him by—

(a) the receiver;

(b) the holder of any floating charge or fixed security over all or any part of the property of the company;

(c) the company; or

(d) the liquidator of the company.

(3) Application to the Auditor of the Court of Session under subsection (2) shall be made in writing not later than one month after the sending of the abstract of receipts and payments of the receiver mentioned in this Chapter which discloses the remuneration, if any, payable to the receiver.

(4) Where the receiver has been paid or has retained for his remuneration for any period before the remuneration has been fixed by the Auditor of the Court of Session under subsection (2) any amount in excess of the remuneration so fixed for that period, the receiver or his personal representatives shall account for the excess.

SEC. 475 Priority of debts

475(1) Where a receiver is appointed and the company is not at the time of the appointment in course of being wound up, the debts which fall under subsection (2) of this section shall be paid out of any assets coming to the hands of the receiver in priority to any claim for principal or interest by the holder of the floating charge by virtue of which the receiver was appointed.

(2) Debts falling under this subsection are debts which satisfy the conditions of this subsection, that is to say, they are debts—

(a) which in every winding up are, under the provisions of Part XX relating to preferential payments, to be paid in priority to all other debts; and

(b) which, by the end of a period of six months after advertisement by the receiver for claims in the Edinburgh Gazette and in a newspaper circulating in the district where the company carries on business, either—

    (i) have been intimated to him; or

    (ii) have become known to him.

(3) In the application of Part XX, section 614 and Schedule 19 are to be read as if the provision for payment of accrued holiday remuneration becoming payable on the termination of employment before or by the effect of the winding-up order or resolution were a provision for payment of such remuneration becoming payable on the termination of employment before or by the effect of the appointment of the receiver.

(4) The periods of time mentioned in Schedule 19 are to be reckoned from the date of the appointment of the receiver under section 469(6) or 470(5).

(5) Any payments made under this section shall be recouped as far as may be out of the assets of the company available for payment of ordinary creditors.

SEC. 476 Distribution of monies

476(1) Subject to section 477, and to the rights of any of the following categories of persons, namely—

(a) the holder of any fixed security which is over property subject to the floating charge and which ranks prior to, or pari passu with, the floating charge;

(b) all persons who have effectually executed diligence on any part of the property of the company which is subject to the charge by virtue of which the receiver was appointed;

(c) creditors in respect of all liabilities, charges and expenses incurred by or on behalf of the receiver;

(d) the receiver in respect of his liabilities, expenses and remuneration; and

(e) the preferential creditors entitled to payment under section 475,

the receiver shall pay monies received by him to the holder of the floating charge by virtue of which the receiver was appointed in or towards satisfaction of the debt secured by the floating charge.

(2) Any balance of monies remaining after the provisions of subsection (1) of this section and section 477 have been satisfied shall be paid in accordance with their respective rights and interests to the following persons, as the case may require, namely—

(a) any other receiver;

(b) the holder of a fixed security which is over property subject to the floating charge;

(c) the company or its liquidator, as the case may be.

(3) Where any question arises as to the person entitled to a payment under this section, or where a receipt or a discharge of a security cannot be obtained in respect of any such payment, the receiver shall consign the amount of such payment in any joint stock bank of issue in Scotland in name of the Accountant of Court for behoof of the person or persons entitled thereto.

SEC. 477 Disposal of interest in property

477(1) Where the receiver sells or disposes, or is desirous of selling or disposing, of any property or interest in property of the company which is subject to the floating charge by virtue of which the receiver was appointed and which is—

(a) subject to any security or interest of, or burden or encumbrance in favour of, a creditor the ranking of which is prior to, pari passu with, or postponed to the floating charge; or

(b) property or an interest in property affected or attached by effectual diligence executed by any person;

and the receiver is unable to obtain the consent of such creditor or, as the case may be, such person to such a sale or disposal, the receiver may apply to the court for authority to sell or dispose of the property or interest in property free of such security, interest, burden, encumbrance or diligence.

(2) On such an application, the court may, if it thinks fit, authorise the sale or disposal of the property or interest in question free of such security, interest, burden, encumbrance or diligence, and such authorisation may be on such terms or conditions as the court thinks fit:

But that authorisation shall not be given where a fixed security over the property or interest in question which ranks prior to the floating charge has not been met or provided for in full.

(3) Where any sale or disposal is effected in accordance with the authorisation of the court under subsection (2) of this section, the receiver shall grant to the purchaser or disponee an appropriate document of transfer or conveyance of the property or interest in question, and that document has the effect, or, where recording, intimation or registration of that document is a legal requirement for completion of title to the property or interest, then that recording, intimation or registration, as the case may be, has the effect, of—

(a) disencumbering the property or interest of the security, interest, burden or encumbrance affecting it; and

(b) freeing the property or interest from the diligence executed upon it.

(4) Nothing in this section prejudices the right of any creditor of the company to rank for his debt in the winding up of the company.

SEC. 478 Cessation of appointment of receiver

478(1) A receiver appointed by the holder of a floating charge under section 467(1) may resign on giving one month's notice thereof to—

(a) the holders of floating charges over all or any part of the property of the company;

(b) the company or its liquidator; and

(c) the holders of any fixed security over property of the company which is subject to the floating charge by virtue of which the receiver was appointed.

(2) A receiver appointed by the court under section 467(2) may resign only with the authority of the court and on such terms and conditions, if any, as may be laid down by the court.

(3) Subject to subsection (4) below, a receiver may, on application to the court by the holder of the floating charge by virtue of which he was appointed, be removed by the court on cause shown.

(4) Where a receiver ceases to act as such, then, in respect of any expenses, charges or other liabilities he may have incurred in the performance of his functions as receiver, he is entitled to be indemnified out of the property which is subject to the floating charge by virtue of which he was appointed.

(5) When a receiver ceases to act as such otherwise than by death he shall, and, when a receiver is removed by the court, the holder of the floating charge by virtue of which he was appointed shall, within 7 days of the cessation or removal, as the case may be, give the registrar of companies notice to that effect, and the registrar shall enter the notice in the register of charges.

If the receiver or the holder of the floating charge, as the case may require, makes default in complying with the requirements of this subsection, he is liable to a fine and, for continued contravention, to a daily default fine.

(6) If by the expiry of a period of one month following upon the removal of the receiver or his ceasing to act as such no other receiver has been appointed, the floating charge by virtue of which the receiver was appointed—

(a) thereupon ceases to attach to the property then subject to the charge; and

(b) again subsists as a floating charge.

SEC. 479 Powers of court

479(1) A holder of a floating charge by virtue of which a receiver was appointed may apply to the court for directions in any matter arising in connection with the performance by the receiver of his functions.

(2) Where a floating charge by virtue of which a person is purported to have been appointed receiver is discovered to be invalid, the court may, if it thinks fit, in whole or in part relieve that person from personal liability in respect of anything done or omitted to be done which, had he been validly appointed, would have been properly done or omitted.

(3) The court may, if it thinks fit, make the person by whom the invalid appointment was made personally liable in respect of anything done or omitted to be done to the extent to which the person purported to have been appointed receiver has been relieved of personal liability.

SEC. 480 Notification that receiver appointed

480(1) Where a receiver has been appointed, every invoice, order for goods or business letter issued by or on behalf of the company or the receiver or the liquidator of the company, being a document on or in which the name of the company appears, shall contain a statement that a receiver has been appointed.

(2) If default is made in complying with the requirements of this section, the company and any of the following persons who knowingly and wilfully authorises or permits the default, namely, any officer of the company, any liquidator of the company and any receiver, is liable to a fine.

SEC. 481 Provisions as to information where receiver appointed

481(1) Where a receiver is appointed then, subject to the provisions of this section and the section next following—

(a) he shall forthwith send notice to the company of his appointment; and

(b) there shall, within 14 days after receipt of the notice, or such longer period as may be allowed by the court or in writing by the receiver, be made out and submitted to the receiver in accordance with section 482 a statement in the prescribed form as to the affairs of the company; and

(c) the receiver shall, within 2 months after receipt of the statement, send—

   (i) to the registrar of companies and to the court, a copy of the statement and of any comments he sees fit to make thereon and, in the case of the registrar of companies, also a summary of the statement and of his comments (if any) thereon; and

   (ii) to the company, a copy of any such comments or, if he does not see fit to make any comment, a notice to that effect; and

   (iii) to the holder of the floating charge by virtue of which he was appointed, to any trustees for the debenture-holders on whose behalf he was appointed and, so far as he is aware of their addresses, to all such debenture-holders, a copy of the said summary.

(2) The receiver shall, within two months, or such longer period as the court may allow, after the expiration of the period of 12 months from the date of his appointment and of every subsequent period of twelve months, and within two months, or such longer period as the court may allow, after he ceases to act as receiver, send to—

(a) the registrar of companies;

(b) the company;

(c) the holder of the floating charge by virtue of which he was appointed;

(d) any trustees for the debenture-holders of the company on whose behalf he was appointed;

(e) all such debenture-holders (so far as he is aware of their addresses); and

(f) the holders of all other floating charges or fixed securities over property of the company,

an abstract in the prescribed form showing his receipts and payments during that period of twelve months, or, where he ceases to act as receiver, during the period from the end of the period to which the last preceding abstract related (or, if no preceding abstract has been sent under this section, from the date of his appointment) up to the date of his so ceasing, and the aggregate amounts of his receipts and of his payments during all preceding periods since his appointment.

(3) Where the receiver is appointed by the holder of the floating charge under section 467, this section has effect—

(a) with the omission of the references to the court in subsection (1); and

(b) with the substitution for the references to the court in subsection (2) of references to the Secretary of State;

and, in any other case, references to the court shall be taken as referring to the court by which the receiver was appointed.

(4) Subsection (1) does not apply in relation to the appointment of a receiver to act with an existing receiver or in place of a receiver dying or ceasing to act, except that, where that subsection applies to a receiver who dies or ceases to act before it has been fully complied with, the references in paragraphs (b) and (c) of the subsection include (subject to subsection (5)) reference to his successor and to any continuing receiver.

Nothing in this subsection shall be taken as limiting the meaning of the expression 'the receiver' where used in, or in relation to, subsection (2).

(5) Where the company is being wound up, this section and section 482 shall apply notwithstanding that the receiver and the liquidator are the same person, but with any necessary modifications arising from that fact.

(6) Nothing in subsection (2) above prejudices the duty of the receiver to render proper accounts of his receipts and payments to the persons to whom, and at the times at which, he may be required to do so apart from that subsection.

(7) If the receiver makes default in complying with the requirements of this section, he is liable to a fine and, for continued contravention, to a daily default fine.

SEC. 482 Special provisions as to statement submitted to receiver

482(1) The statement as to the affairs of a company required by section 481 to be submitted to the receiver (or his successor) shall show as at the date of the receiver's appointment the particulars of the company's assets, debts and liabilities, the names, residences and occupations of its creditors, the securities held by them respectively, the dates when the securities were respectively given and such further or other information as may be prescribed.

(2) The statement shall be submitted by, and be verified by the statutory declaration of, one or more of the persons who are at the date of the receiver's appointment the directors, and by the person who is at that date the secretary, of the company, or by such of the persons mentioned below in this subsection as the receiver (or his successor), subject to the direction of the court, may require to submit and verify the statement, that is to say, persons—

(a) who are or have been officers of the company;

(b) who have taken part in the formation of the company at any time within one year before the date of the receiver's appointment;

(c) who are in the employment of the company, or have been in its employment within that year, and are, in the opinion of the receiver, capable of giving the information required;

(d) who are, or have been within that year, officers of, or in the employment of, a company which is, or within that year was, an officer of the company to which the statement relates.

(3) Any person making the statement and statutory declaration shall be allowed, and shall be paid by the receiver (or his successor) out of his receipts, such costs and expenses incurred in the preparation and making of the statement and statutory declaration as the receiver (or his successor) may consider reasonable, subject to an appeal to the court.

(4) Where the receiver is appointed by the holder of the floating charge under section 467(1), this section has effect with the substitution for the references to the court in subsections (2) and (3) of references to the Secretary of State; and in any other case references to the court are to be taken as referring to the court by which the receiver was appointed.

(5) If any person without reasonable excuse makes default in complying with the requirements of this section, he is liable to a fine and, for continued contravention, to a daily default fine.

(6) References in this section to the receiver's successor include a continuing receiver.

SEC. 483 Enforcement of receiver's duty to make returns, etc.

483(1) If any receiver—

(a) having made default in filing, delivering or making any return, account or other document, or in giving any notice, which a receiver is by law required to file, deliver, make or give, fails to make good the default within 14 days after the service on him of a notice requiring him to do so; or

(b) has, after being required at any time by the liquidator of the company so to do, failed to render proper accounts of his receipts and payments and to vouch the same and to pay over to the liquidator the amount properly payable to him,

the court may, on an application made for the purpose, make an order directing the receiver to make good the default within such time as may be specified in the order.

(2) In the case of any such default as is mentioned in subsection (1)(a), an application for the purposes of this section may be made by any member or creditor of the company or by the registrar of companies, and, in the case of any such default as is mentioned in subsection (1)(b) the application shall be made by the liquidator, and, in either case, the order may provide that all expenses of and incidental to the application shall be borne by the receiver.

(3) Nothing in this section prejudices the operation of any enactments imposing penalties on receivers in respect of any such default as is mentioned in subsection (1).

SEC. 484 Interpretation for Chapter II

484(1) In this Chapter, unless the contrary intention appears, the following expressions have the following meanings respectively assigned to them, that is to say—

'company' means an incorporated company (whether a company within the meaning of this Act or not) which the Court of Session has jurisdiction to wind up;

'secured debenture' means a bond, debenture, debenture stock or other security which, either itself or by reference to any other instrument, creates a floating charge over all or any part of the property of the company, but does not include a security which creates no charge other than a fixed security;

'series of secured debentures' means two or more secured debentures created as a series by the company in such a manner that the holders thereof are entitled pari passu to the benefit of the floating charge.

(2) Where a floating charge, secured debenture or series of secured debentures has been created by the company, then, except where the context otherwise requires, any reference in this Chapter to the holder of the floating charge shall—

(a) where the floating charge, secured debenture or series of secured debentures provides for a receiver to be appointed by any person or body, be construed as a reference to that person or body;

(b) where, in the case of a series of secured debentures, no such provision has been made therein but—

(i) there are trustees acting for the debenture-holders under and in accordance with a trust deed, be construed as a reference to those trustees; and

(ii) where no such trustees are acting, be construed as a reference to—

(aa) a majority in nominal value of those present or represented by proxy and voting at a meeting of debenture-holders at which the holders of at least one-third in nominal value of the outstanding debentures of the series are present or so represented; or

(bb) where no such meeting is held, the holders of at least one-half in nominal value of the outstanding debentures of the series.

(3) Any reference in this Chapter to a floating charge, secured debenture, series of secured debentures or instrument creating a charge includes, except where the context otherwise requires, a reference to that floating charge, debenture, series of debentures or instrument as varied by any instrument.

SEC. 485 Prescription of forms etc., and regulations

485(1) The notice referred to in section 478(5) and the notice referred to in section 481(1)(a) and the statutory declaration referred to in section 482(2) shall be in such form as may be prescribed.

(2) Any power conferred by this Part on the Secretary of State to make regulations is exercisable by statutory instrument; and a statutory instrument made in the exercise of any power so conferred to prescribe a fee is subject to annulment in pursuance of a resolution of either House of Parliament.''

Chapter III — General

SEC. 486 Interpretation for Part XVIII generally

486(1) [Definitions] In this Part, unless the context otherwise requires, the following expressions have the following meanings respectively assigned to them, that is to say—

''ancillary document'' means—

(a) a document which relates to the floating charge and which was executed by the debtor or creditor in the charge before the registration of the charge in accordance with Chapter II of Part XII; or

(b) an instrument of alteration such as is mentioned in section 466 in this Part;

"**company**" means an incorporated company (whether a company within the meaning of this Act or not);

"**fixed security**" in relation to any property of a company, means any security, other than a floating charge or a charge having the nature of a floating charge, which on the winding up of the company in Scotland would be treated as an effective security over that property, and (without prejudice to that generality) includes a security over that property, being a heritable security within the meaning of section 9(8) of the Conveyancing and Feudal Reform (Scotland) Act 1970;

"**Register of Sasines**" means the appropriate division of the General Register of Sasines.

History
In s. 486(1):

- in the definition of "company" the words "other than in Chapter II of this part" formerly appearing before the word "means" repealed by Insolvency Act 1986, s. 438 and Sch. 12 as from 29 December 1986;

- the definitions of "instrument of appointment", "prescribed", "receiver"; and "register of changes" formerly appearing after the definition of "fixed security" repealed by Insolvency Act 1986, s. 438 and Sch. 12 as from 29 December 1986; these definitions formerly read as follows:

"'instrument of appointment' has the meaning given by section 469(1);

'prescribed' means prescribed by regulations made under this Part by the Secretary of State;

'receiver' means a receiver of such part of the property of the company as is subject to the floating charge by virtue of which he has been appointed under section 467;

'register of charges' means the register kept by the registrar of companies for the purposes of Chapter II of Part XII;" ·

In regard to the date of the above repeals, see IA 1986, s. 443 and S.I. 1986 No. 1924 (C. 71).

SEC. 487   Extent of Part XVIII

487   This Part extends to Scotland only.

PART XIX — RECEIVERS AND MANAGERS (ENGLAND AND WALES)

488–500   (Repealed by Insolvency Act 1986, sec. 438 and Sch. 12 as from 29 December 1986.)

Note
For the corresponding new provisions of the 1986 consolidation, see the CCH table of destinations at page 58,201.

History
In regard to the date of the above repeal, see Insolvency Act 1986, s. 443 and S.I. 1986 No. 1924 (C. 71). There were some amendments and repeals by Insolvency Act 1985 which very briefly came into force — see Insolvency Act 1985, Sch. 6,10 and S.I. 1986 No. 1924 (C. 71). The sections originally read as follows:

"**SEC. 488   Extent of this Part**

488   This Part does not apply to receivers under Part XVIII.

SEC. 489   Disqualification of body corporate from acting as receiver

489   A body corporate is not qualified for appointment as receiver of the property of a company, and any body corporate which acts as such a receiver is liable to a fine.

SEC. 490   Disqualification of undischarged bankrupt

490   If a person being an undischarged bankrupt acts as receiver or manager of the property of a company on behalf of debenture holders, he is liable to imprisonment or a fine, or both.

This does not apply to a receiver or manager acting under an appointment made by the court.

SEC. 491   Power for court to appoint official receiver

491   Where application is made to the court to appoint a receiver on behalf of the debenture holders or other creditors of a company which is being wound up by the court, the official receiver may be appointed.

SEC. 492   Receivers and managers appointed out of court

492(1)   A receiver or manager of the property of a company appointed under powers contained in an instrument may apply to the court for directions in relation to any particular matter arising in connection with the performance of his functions.

(2) On such an application, the court may give such directions, or may make such order declaring the rights of persons before the court or otherwise, as it thinks just.

(3) A receiver or manager so appointed is, to the same extent as if he had been appointed by order of a court—

    (a) personally liable on any contract entered into by him in the performance of his functions (except in so far as the contract otherwise provides), and

    (b) entitled in respect of that liability to indemnity out of the assets;

but this subsection does not limit any right to indemnity which the receiver or manager would have apart from it, nor limit his liability on contracts entered into without authority, nor confer any right to indemnity in respect of that liability.

SEC. 493 Notification that receiver or manager appointed

493(1) When a receiver or manager of the property of a company has been appointed, every invoice, order for goods or business letter issued by or on behalf of the company or the receiver or manager or the liquidator of the company, being a document on or in which the company's name appears, shall contain a statement that a receiver or manager has been appointed.

(2) If default is made in complying with this section, the company and any of the following persons, who knowingly and wilfully authorises or permits the default, namely, any officer of the company, any liquidator of the company and any receiver or manager, is liable to a fine.

SEC. 494 Court's power to fix remuneration of receiver or manager

494(1) The court may, on an application made by the liquidator of a company, by order fix the amount to be paid by way of remuneration to a person who, under powers contained in an instrument, has been appointed receiver or manager of the company's property.

(2) The court's power under subsection (1), where no previous order has been made with respect thereto under the subsection—

    (a) extends to fixing the remuneration for any period before the making of the order or the application for it, and

    (b) is exercisable notwithstanding that the receiver or manager has died or ceased to act before the making of the order or the application, and

    (c) where the receiver or manager has been paid or has retained for his remuneration for any period before the making of the order any amount in excess of that so fixed for that period, extends to requiring him or his personal representative to account for the excess or such part of it as may be specified in the order.

But the power conferred by paragraph (c) shall not be exercised as respects any period before the making of the application for the order under this section, unless in the court's opinion there are special circumstances making it proper for the power to be exercised.

(3) The court may from time to time on an application made either by the liquidator or by the receiver or manager, vary or amend an order made under subsection (1).

SEC. 495 Information to be given by and to receiver on appointment

495(1) The following applies where, in the case of a company registered in England and Wales, a receiver or manager of the whole (or substantially the whole) of the company's property is appointed on behalf of the holders of any debentures of the company secured by a floating charge.

In this and the following two sections, he is referred to as 'the receiver'.

(2) Subject to the following provisions of this section, and to sections 496 and 497—

    (a) the receiver shall forthwith send to the company notice of his appointment in the prescribed form, and

    (b) there shall within 14 days after receipt of the notice (or such longer period as may be allowed by the court or by the receiver) be made out and submitted to the receiver in accordance with section 496 a statement in the prescribed form as to the affairs of the company.

(3) The receiver shall, within 2 months after receipt of the statement, send—

    (a) to the registrar of companies and to the court, a copy of the statement and of any comments he sees fit to make on it and, in the case of the registrar of companies, also a summary of the statement and of his comments (if any) on it; and

    (b) to the company, a copy of any such comments as above-mentioned or, if he does not see fit to make any comments, a notice to that effect; and

    (c) to any trustees for the debenture holders on whose behalf he was appointed and, so far as he is aware of their addresses, to all such debenture holders a copy of the summary.

(4) If the receiver is appointed under powers contained in an instrument, subsections (2) and (3) have effect with the omission of references to the court; and in any other case references to the court are to the court by which the receiver was appointed.

(5) This section does not apply in relation to the appointment of a receiver or manager to act—

    (a) with an existing receiver or manager, or

    (b) in place of a receiver or manager dying or ceasing to act,

except that, where it applies to a receiver or manager who dies or ceases to act before it has been fully complied with, the references in subsection (2)(b) and (3) to the receiver include (subject to the next subsection) his successor and any continuing receiver or manager.

(6) If the company is being wound up, this section and section 496 apply notwithstanding that the receiver or manager and the liquidator are the same person, but with any necessary modifications arising from that fact.

(7) If the receiver makes default in complying with this section, he is liable to a fine and, for continued contravention, to a daily default fine.

SEC. 496 Company's statement of affairs

496(1) The company's statement of affairs required by section 495 to be submitted to the receiver (or his successor) shall show as at the date of the receiver's appointment—

    (a) the particulars of the company's assets, debts and liabilities,

    (b) the names, residences and occupations of its creditors,

    (c) the securities held by them respectively,

    (d) the dates when the securities were respectively given, and

    (e) such further or other information as may be prescribed.

(2) The statement shall be submitted by, and be verified by affidavit of, one or more of the persons who are at the date of the receiver's appointment the directors and by the person who is at that date the secretary of the company, or by such of the persons mentioned in the next subsection as the receiver (or his successor), subject to the direction of the court, may require to submit and verify the statement.

(3) The persons referred to above are those—

(a) who are or have been officers of the company,

(b) who have taken part in the company's formation at any time within one year before the date of the receiver's appointment,

(c) who are in the company's employment, or have been in its employment during that year and are in the receiver's opinion capable of giving the information required,

(d) who are or have been during that year officers of or in the employment of a company which is, or within that year was, an officer of the company to which the statement relates.

(4) A person making the statement and affidavit shall be allowed, and shall be paid by the receiver (or his successor) out of his receipts, such costs and expenses incurred in and about the preparation and making of the statement and affidavit as the receiver (or his successor) may consider reasonable, subject to an appeal to the court.

(5) Where the receiver is appointed under powers contained in an instrument, this section applies with the substitution for references to the court of references to the Secretary of State, and for references to an affidavit of references to a statutory declaration; and in any other case references to the court are to the court by which the receiver was appointed.

(6) If a person without reasonable excuse makes default in complying with the requirements of this section, he is liable to a fine and, for continued contravention, to a daily default fine.

(7) References in this section to the receiver's successor include a continuing receiver or manager.

SEC. 497 Subsequent returns by receiver

497(1) In the case mentioned in section 495(1), the receiver shall—

(a) within 2 months (or such longer period as the court may allow) after the expiration of 12 months from the date of his appointment and of every subsequent period of 12 months, and

(b) within 2 months (or such longer period as the court may allow) after he ceases to act as receiver or manager of the company's property,

send the requisite accounts of his receipts and payments to the registrar of companies, to any trustees for the debenture holders on whose behalf he was appointed, to the company and (so far as he is aware of their addresses) to all such debenture holders.

(2) The requisite accounts shall be an abstract in the prescribed form showing—

(a) receipts and payments during the relevant period of 12 months, or

(b) where the receiver ceases to act, receipts and payments during the period from the end of the period of 12 months to which the last preceding abstract related (or, if no preceding abstract has been sent under this section, from the date of his appointment) up to the date of his so ceasing, and the aggregate amount of receipts and payments during all preceding periods since his appointment.

(3) Nothing in section 495(5) is to be taken as limiting the meaning of the expression 'the receiver' where used in, or in relation to, subsection (1) or (2) above.

(4) Where the receiver is appointed under powers contained in an instrument, this section has effect with the substitution of the Secretary of State for the court; and in any other case references to the court are to the court by which the receiver was appointed.

(5) This section applies, where the company is being wound up, notwithstanding that the receiver or manager and the liquidator are the same person, but with any necessary modifications arising from that fact.

(6) This section does not prejudice the receiver's duty to render proper accounts of his receipts and payments to the persons to whom, and at the times at which, he may be required to do so apart from this section.

(7) If the receiver makes default in complying with the requirements of this section, he is liable to a fine and, for continued contravention, to a daily default fine.

SEC. 498 Receivership accounts to be delivered to registrar

498(1) Except where section 497 applies, every receiver or manager of a company's property who has been appointed under powers contained in an instrument shall deliver to the registrar of companies for registration the requisite accounts of his receipts and payments.

(2) The accounts shall be delivered within one month (or such longer period as the registrar may allow) after the expiration of 6 months from the date of his appointment and of every subsequent period of 6 months, and also within one month after he ceases to act as receiver or manager.

(3) The requisite accounts shall be an abstract in the prescribed form showing—

(a) receipts and payments during the relevant period of 6 months, or

(b) where the receiver or manager ceases to act, receipts and payments during the period from the end of the period of 6 months to which the last preceding abstract related (or, if no preceding abstract has been delivered under this section, from the date of his appointment) up to the date of his so ceasing, and the aggregate amount of receipts and payments during all preceding periods since his appointment.

(4) A receiver or manager who makes default in complying with this section is liable to a fine and, for continued contravention, to a daily default fine.

SEC. 499 Enforcement of duty of receivers to make returns

499(1) If a receiver or manager of a company's property—

(a) having made default in filing, delivering or making any return, account or other document, or in giving any notice, which a receiver or manager is by law required to file, deliver, make or give, fails to make good the default within 14 days after the service on him of a notice requiring him to do so, or

(b) having been appointed under powers contained in an instrument, has, after being required at any time by the liquidator of the company to do so, failed to render proper accounts of his receipts and payments and to vouch them and pay over to the liquidator the amount properly payable to him,

the court may, on an application made for the purpose, make an order directing the receiver or manager (as the case may be) to make good the default within such time as may be specified in the order.

(2) In the case of the default mentioned in subsection (1)(a), application to the court may be made by any member or creditor of the company or by the registrar of companies;

and in the case of the default mentioned in subsection (1)(b), the application shall be made by the liquidator.

In either case the court's order may provide that all costs of and incidental to the application shall be borne by the receiver or manager, as the case may be.

(3) Nothing in this section prejudices the operation of any enactment imposing penalties on receivers in respect of any such default as is mentioned in subsection (1).

SEC. 500 Construction of references to receivers and managers

500 It is hereby declared that, except where the context

otherwise requires—

(a) any reference in this Act to a receiver or manager of the property of a company, or to a receiver of it, includes a reference to a receiver or manager, or (as the case may be) to a receiver of part only of that property and to a receiver only of the income arising from the property or from part of it, and

(b) any reference in this Act to the appointment of a receiver or manager under powers contained in an instrument includes a reference to an appointment made under powers which, by virtue of any enactment, are implied in and have effect as if contained in an instrument."

PART XX — WINDING UP OF COMPANIES REGISTERED UNDER THIS ACT OR THE FORMER COMPANIES ACTS

501–650 (Repealed by Insolvency Act 1986, sec. 438 and Sch. 12 as from 29 December 1986.)

Note
For the corresponding new provisions of the 1986 consolidation, see the CCH table of destinations at page 58,201.

History
In regard to the date of the above repeal, see Insolvency Act 1986, s. 443 and S.I. 1986 No. 1924 (C. 71). There were some amendments and repeals by Insolvency Act 1985 — some of which came into force (see S.I. 1986 No. 185 (C. 7), S.I. 1986 No. 463 (C. 14)) and some of which came into force only briefly — for complete details see Insolvency Act 1985, Sch. 6, 10 and S.I. 1986 No. 1924 (C. 71). Similarly s. 613, 615A, 615B, 623, 643 had been effected by Bankruptcy (Scotland) Act 1985 (see also S.I. 1985 No. 1924) and s. 638 by Finance Act 1985. Immediately before the Insolvency Act 1986 repeals the sections read as follows:

"**Chapter I — Preliminary**

MODES OF WINDING UP

SEC. 501 The three modes in which a company may be wound up

501(1) The winding up of a company may be either—

(a) by the court, or

(b) voluntary, or

(c) subject to the supervision of the court.

(2) This Part applies, unless the contrary appears, to the winding up of a company in any of those modes.

CONTRIBUTORIES

SEC. 502 Liability as contributories of present and past members

502(1) When a company is wound up, every present and past member is liable to contribute to its assets to any amount sufficient for payment of its debts and liabilities, and the costs, charges and expenses of the winding up, and for the adjustment of the rights of the contributories among themselves.

(2) This is subject as follows—

(a) a past member is not liable to contribute if he has

ceased to be a member for one year or more before the commencement of the winding up;

(b) a past member is not liable to contribute in respect of any debt or liability of the company contracted after he ceased to be a member;

(c) a past member is not liable to contribute unless it appears to the court that the existing members are unable to satisfy the contributions required to be made by them in pursuance of this Act;

(d) in the case of a company limited by shares, no contribution is required from any member exceeding the amount (if any) unpaid on the shares in respect of which he is liable as a present or past member;

(e) nothing in this Act invalidates any provision contained in a policy of insurance or other contract whereby the liability of individual members on the policy or contract is restricted, or whereby the funds of the company are alone made liable in respect of the policy or contract;

(f) a sum due to any member of the company (in his character of a member) by way of dividends, profits or otherwise is not deemed to be a debt of the company, payable to that member in a case of competition between himself and any other creditor not a member of the company, but any such sum may be taken into account for the purpose of the final adjustment of the rights of the contributories among themselves.

(3) In the case of a company limited by guarantee, no contribution is required from any member exceeding the amount undertaken to be contributed by him to the company's assets in the event of its being wound up; but if it is a company with a share capital, every member of it is liable (in addition to the amount so undertaken to be contributed to the assets), to contribute to the extent of any sums unpaid on shares held by him.

SEC. 503 Directors, etc., with unlimited liability

503(1) In the winding up of a limited company, any director or manager (whether past or present) whose liability is under this Act unlimited, is liable, in addition to his liability (if any) to contribute as an ordinary member, to make a further contribution as if he were at the commencement of the winding up a member of an unlimited company.

(2) However—

(a) a past director or manager is not liable to make such further contribution if he has ceased to hold office for a year or more before the commencement of the winding up;

(b) a past director or manager is not liable to make such further contribution in respect of any debt or liability of the company contracted after he ceased to hold office;

(c) subject to the company's articles, a director or manager is not liable to make such further contribution unless the court deems it necessary to require that contribution in order to satisfy the company's debts and liabilities and the costs, charges and expenses of the winding up.

SEC. 504 Liability of past directors and shareholders

504(1) This section applies where a company is being wound up and—

(a) it has under Chapter VII of Part V made a payment out of capital in respect of the redemption or purchase of any of its own shares (the payment being referred to below as 'the relevant payment'), and

(b) the aggregate amount of the company's assets and the amounts paid by way of contribution to its assets (apart from this section) is not sufficient for payment of its debts and liabilities and the costs, charges and expenses of the winding up.

(2) If the winding up commenced within one year of the date on which the relevant payment was made, then—

(a) the person from whom the shares were redeemed or purchased, and

(b) the directors who signed the statutory declaration made in accordance with section 173(3) for purposes of the redemption or purchase (except a director who shows that he had reasonable grounds for forming the opinion set out in the declaration),

are, so as to enable that insufficiency to be met, liable to contribute to the following extent to the company's assets.

(3) A person from whom any of the shares were redeemed or purchased is liable to contribute an amount not exceeding so much of the relevant payment as was made by the company in respect of his shares; and the directors are jointly and severally liable with that person to contribute that amount.

(4) A person who has contributed any amount to the assets in pursuance of this section may apply to the court for an order directing any other person jointly and severally liable in respect of that amount to pay him such amount as the court thinks just and equitable.

(5) Sections 502 and 503 above do not apply in relation to liability accruing by virtue of this section.

(6) This section is deemed included in Chapter VII of Part V for the purposes of the Secretary of State's power to make regulations under section 179.

SEC. 505 Limited company formerly unlimited

505(1) This section applies in the case of a company being wound up which was at some former time registered as unlimited but has re-registered—

(a) as a public company under section 43 of this Act (or the former corresponding provision, section 5 of the Companies Act 1980), or

(b) as a limited company under section 51 of this Act

(or the former corresponding provision, section 44 of the Companies Act 1967).

(2) Notwithstanding section 502(2)(a) above, a past member of the company who was a member of it at the time of re-registration, if the winding up commences within the period of 3 years beginning with the day on which the company was re-registered, is liable to contribute to the assets of the company in respect of debts and liabilities contracted before that time.

(3) If no persons who were members of the company at that time are existing members of it, a person who at that time was a present or past member is liable to contribute as above notwithstanding that the existing members have satisfied the contributions required to be made by them under this Act.

This applies subject to section 502(2)(a) above and to subsection (2) of this section, but notwithstanding section 502(2)(c).

(4) Notwithstanding section 502(2)(d) and (3), there is no limit on the amount which a person who, at that time, was a past or present member of the company is liable to contribute as above.

SEC. 506 Unlimited company formerly limited

506(1) This section applies in the case of a company being wound up which was at some former time registered as limited but has been re-registered as unlimited under section 49 (or the former corresponding provision, section 43 of the Companies Act 1967).

(2) A person who, at the time when the application for the company to be re-registered was lodged, was a past member of the company and did not after that again become a member of it is not liable to contribute to the assets of the company more than he would have been liable to contribute had the company not been re-registered.

SEC. 507 Meaning of 'contributory'

507(1) In this Act, the expression "contributory" means every person liable to contribute to the assets of a company in the event of its being wound up (other than a person so liable by virtue of a declaration under section 630 below or section 15 of the Insolvency Act 1985), and for the purposes of all proceedings for determining, and all proceedings prior to the final determination of, the persons who are to be deemed contributories, includes any person alleged to be a contributory.

(2) A reference in a company's articles to a contributory does not (unless the context requires) include a person who is a contributory only by virtue of section 504.

This subsection is deemed included in Chapter VII of Part V for the purposes of the Secretary of State's power to make regulations under section 179.

SEC. 508 Nature of contributory's liability

508 The liability of a contributory creates a debt (in England and Wales in the nature of a specialty) accruing due from him at the time when his liability commenced, but payable at the times when calls are made for enforcing the liability.

SEC. 509 Contributories in case of death of a member

509(1) If a contributory dies either before or after he has been placed on the list of contributories, his personal representatives, and the heirs and legatees of heritage of his heritable estate in Scotland, are liable in a due course of administration to contribute to the assets of the company in discharge of his liability and are contributories accordingly.

(2) Where the personal representatives are placed on the list of contributories, the heirs or legatees of heritage need

not be added, but they may be added as and when the court thinks fit.

(3) If in England and Wales the personal representatives make default in paying any money ordered to be paid by them, proceedings may be taken for administering the estate of the deceased contributory and for compelling payment out of it of the money due.

SEC. 510 Effect of contributory's bankruptcy

510(1) The following applies if a contributory becomes bankrupt, either before or after he has been placed on the list of contributories.

(2) His trustee in bankruptcy represents him for all purposes of the winding up, and is a contributory accordingly.

(3) The trustee may be called on to admit to proof against the bankrupt's estate, or otherwise allow to be paid out of the bankrupt's assets in due course of law, any money due from the bankrupt in respect of his liability to contribute to the company's assets.

(4) There may be proved against the bankrupt's estate the estimated value of his liability to future calls as well as calls already made.

SEC. 511 Companies registered under Part XXII, Chapter II

511(1) The following applies in the event of a company being wound up which has been registered under section 680 (or the previous corresponding provision).

(2) Every person is a contributory, in respect of the company's debts and liabilities contracted before registration, who is liable—

    (a) to pay or contribute to the payment of any debt or liability so contracted, or

    (b) to pay or contribute to the payment of any sum for the adjustment of the rights of the members among themselves in respect of any such debt or liability, or

    (c) to pay or contribute to the payment of the costs and expenses of winding up the company, so far as relates to the debts or liabilities above-mentioned.

(3) Every contributory is liable to contribute to the assets of the company, in the course of the winding up, all sums due from him in respect of any such liability.

(4) In the event of the death, bankruptcy or insolvency of any contributory, provisions of this Act with respect to the personal representatives, to the heirs and legatees of heritage of the heritable estate in Scotland of deceased contributories and to the trustees of bankrupt or insolvent contributories respectively, apply.

Chapter II — Winding up by the Court

JURISDICTION (ENGLAND AND WALES)

SEC. 512 High Court and county court jurisdiction

512(1) The High Court has jurisdiction to wind up any company registered in England and Wales.

(2) Where the amount of a company's share capital paid up or credited as paid up does not exceed £120,000, then (subject to the provisions of this section) the county court of the district in which the company's registered office is situated has concurrent jurisdiction with the High Court to wind up the company.

(3) The money sum for the time being specified in subsection (2) is subject to increase or reduction by regulations under section 664; but no reduction of it affects any case in which proceedings were begun before the coming into force of the reduction.

(4) The Lord Chancellor may by order in a statutory instrument exclude a county court from having winding-up jurisdiction, and for the purposes of that jurisdiction may attach its district, or any part thereof, to any other county court, and may by statutory instrument revoke or vary any such order.

In exercising the powers of this section, the Lord Chancellor shall provide that a county court is not to have winding-up jurisdiction unless it has for the time being jurisdiction in bankruptcy.

(5) Every court in England and Wales having winding-up jurisdiction has for the purposes of that jurisdiction all the powers of the High Court; and every prescribed officer of the court shall perform any duties which an officer of the High Court may discharge by order of a judge of that court or otherwise in relation to winding-up.

(6) For purposes of this section, a company's **'registered office'** is the place which has longest been its registered office during the 6 months immediately preceding the presentation of the petition for winding up.

SEC. 513 Proceedings taken in wrong court

513(1) Nothing in section 512 invalidates a proceeding by reason of its being taken in the wrong court.

(2) The winding up of a company by the court in England and Wales, or any proceedings in the winding up, may be retained in the court in which the proceedings were commenced, although it may not be the court in which they ought to have been commenced.

SEC. 514 Proceedings in county court: case stated for High Court

514 If any question arises in any winding up proceedings in a county court which all the parties to the proceeding, or which one of them and the judge of the court, desire to have determined in the first instance in the High Court, the judge shall state the facts in the form of a special case for the opinion of the High Court; and thereupon the special case and the proceedings (or such of them as may be required) shall be transmitted to the High Court for the purposes of the determination.

JURISDICTION (SCOTLAND)

SEC. 515 Court of Session and sheriff's court jurisdiction

515(1) The Court of Session has jurisdiction to wind up any company registered in Scotland.

(2) When the Court of Session is in vacation, the jurisdiction conferred on that court by this section may (subject to the provisions of this Part) be exercised by the judge acting as vacation judge in pursuance of section 4 of the Administration of Justice (Scotland) Act 1933.

(3) Where the amount of a company's share capital paid up or credited as paid up does not exceed £120,000, the sheriff court of the sheriffdom in which the company's registered office is situated has concurrent jurisdiction with the Court of Session to wind up the company; but—

    (a) the Court of Session may, if it thinks expedient having regard to the amount of the company's assets to do so—

        (i) remit to a sheriff court any petition presented to the Court of Session for winding up such a company, or

        (ii) require such a petition presented to a sheriff court to be remitted to the Court of Session; and

    (b) the Court of Session may require any such petition as above-mentioned presented to one sheriff court to be remitted to another sheriff court; and

    (c) in a winding up in the sheriff court it is lawful for

the sheriff to submit a stated case for the opinion of the Court of Session on any question of law arising in that winding up.

(4) For the purposes of this section, the expression 'registered office' means the place which has longest been the company's registered office during the 6 months immediately preceding the presentation of the petition for winding up.

(5) The money sum for the time being specified in subsection (3) is subject to increase or reduction by regulations under section 664; but no reduction of it affects any case in which proceedings were begun before the coming into force of the reduction.

SEC. 516 Power to remit winding up to Lord Ordinary

516(1) The Court of Session may, by Act of Sederunt, make provision for the taking of proceedings in a winding up before one of the Lords Ordinary; and, where provision is so made, the Lord Ordinary has, for the purposes of the winding up, all the powers and jurisdiction of the court.

(2) However, the Lord Ordinary may report to the Inner House any matter which may arise in the course of a winding up.

GROUNDS AND EFFECT OF WINDING-UP PETITION

SEC. 517 Circumstances in which company may be wound up by the court

517(1) A company may be wound up by the court if—

(a) the company has by special resolution resolved that the company be wound up by the court,

(b) being a public company which was registered as such on its original incorporation, the company has not been issued with a certificate under section 117 (public company share capital requirements) and more than a year has expired since it was so registered,

(c) it is an old public company, within the meaning of section 1 of the Consequential Provisions Act,

(d) the company does not commence its business within a year from its incorporation or suspends its business for a whole year,

(e) the number of members is reduced below 2,

(f) the company is unable to pay its debts,

(g) the court is of the opinion that it is just and equitable that the company should be wound up.

(2) In Scotland, a company which the Court of Session has jurisdiction to wind up may be wound up by the Court if there is subsisting a floating charge over property comprised in the company's property and undertaking, and the court is satisfied that the security of the creditor entitled to the benefit of the floating charge is in jeopardy.

For this purpose a creditor's security is deemed to be in jeopardy if the Court is satisfied that events have occurred or are about to occur which render it unreasonable in the creditor's interests that the company should retain power to dispose of the property which is subject to the floating charge.

SEC. 518 Definition of inability to pay debts

518(1) A company is deemed unable to pay its debts—

(a) if a creditor (by assignment or otherwise) to whom the company is indebted in a sum exceeding £750 then due has served on the company, by leaving it at the company's registered office, a written demand requiring the company to pay the sum so due and the company has for 3 weeks thereafter neglected

to pay the sum or to secure or compound for it to the reasonable satisfaction of the creditor, or

(b) if, in England and Wales, execution or other process issued on a judgment, decree or order of any court in favour of a creditor of the company is returned unsatisfied in whole or in part, or

(c) if, in Scotland, the induciae of a charge for payment on an extract decree, or an extract registered bond, or an extract registered protest, have expired without payment being made, or

(d) if, in Northern Ireland, a certificate of unenforceability has been granted in respect of a judgment against the company, or

(e) if it is proved to the satisfaction of the court that the company is unable to pay its debts (and, in determining that question, the court shall take into account the company's contingent and prospective liabilities).

(2) The money sum for the time being specified in subsection (1)(a) is subject to increase or reduction by regulations under section 664; but no increase of it affects any case in which the winding-up petition was presented before the coming into force of the increase.

SEC. 519 Application for winding up

519(1) Subject to the provisions of this section, an application to the court for the winding up of a company shall be by petition presented either by the company or by any creditor or creditors (including any contingent or prospective creditor or creditors), contributory or contributories, or by all or any of those parties, together or separately.

(2) Except as mentioned below, a contributory is not entitled to present a winding-up petition unless either—

(a) the number of members is reduced below 2, or

(b) the shares in respect of which he is a contributory, or some of them, either were originally allotted to him, or have been held by him, and registered in his name, for at least 6 months during the 18 months before the commencement of the winding up, or have devolved on him through the death of a former holder.

(3) A person who is liable under section 504 to contribute to a company's assets in the event of its being wound up may petition on either of the grounds set out in section 517(1)(f) and (g), and subsection (2) above does not then apply; but unless the person is a contributory otherwise than under section 504 he may not in his character as contributory petition on any other ground.

This subsection is deemed included in Chapter VII of Part V for the purposes of the Secretary of State's power to make regulations under section 179.

(4) If the ground of the petition is that in section 517(1)(b) or (c), a winding-up petition may be presented by the Secretary of State.

(5) The court shall not hear a petition presented by a contingent or prospective creditor until such security for costs has been given as the court thinks reasonable (or until caution is found, if so ordered by a Scottish court) and until a prima facie case for winding up has been established to the satisfaction of the court.

(6) In a case falling within section 440 (expedient in the public interest, following report of inspectors, etc.) a winding-up petition may be presented by the Secretary of State.

(7) Where a company is being wound up voluntarily or subject to supervision in England and Wales, a winding-up petition may be presented by the official receiver attached to the court as well as by any other person authorised in

that behalf under the other provisions of this section; but the court shall not make a winding-up order on the petition unless it is satisfied that the voluntary winding up or winding up subject to supervision cannot be continued with due regard to the interests of the creditors or contributories.

SEC. 520 Powers of court on hearing of petition

520(1) On hearing a winding-up petition the court may dismiss it, or adjourn the hearing conditionally or unconditionally, or make an interim order, or any other order that it thinks fit; but the court shall not refuse to make a winding-up order on the ground only that the company's assets have been mortgaged to an amount equal to or in excess of those assets or that the company has no assets.

(2) If the petition is presented by members of the company as contributories on the ground that it is just and equitable that the company should be wound up, the court, if it is of opinion—

    (a) that the petitioners are entitled to relief either by winding up the company or by some other means, and

    (b) that in the absence of any other remedy it would be just and equitable that the company should be wound up,

shall make a winding-up order; but this does not apply if the court is also of the opinion both that some other remedy is available to the petitioners and that they are acting unreasonably in seeking to have the company wound up instead of pursuing that other remedy.

SEC. 521 Power to stay or restrain proceedings against company

521(1) At any time after the presentation of a winding-up petition and before a winding-up order has been made, the company, or any creditor or contributory, may—

    (a) where any action or proceeding against the company is pending in the High Court or Court of Appeal in England and Wales or Northern Ireland, apply to the court in which the action or proceeding is pending for a stay of proceedings therein, and

    (b) where any other action or proceeding is pending against the company, apply to the court having jurisdiction to wind up the company to restrain further proceedings in the action or proceeding,

and the court to which application is so made may (as the case may be) stay, sist or restrain the proceedings accordingly on such terms as it thinks fit.

(2) In the case of a company registered under section 680, where the application to stay, sist or restrain is by a creditor, this section extends to actions and proceedings against any contributory of the company.

SEC. 522 Avoidance of property dispositions, etc.

522 In a winding up by the court, any disposition of the company's property, and any transfer of shares, or alteration in the status of the company's members, made after the commencement of the winding up is, unless the court otherwise orders, void.

SEC. 523 Avoidance of attachments, etc.

523(1) Where a company registered in England and Wales is being wound up by the court, any attachment, sequestration, distress or execution put in force against the estate or effects of the company after the commencement of the winding up is void.

(2) This section, so far as relates to any estate or effects of the company situated in England and Wales, applies in the case of a company registered in Scotland as it applies in the case of a company registered in England and Wales.

COMMENCEMENT OF WINDING UP

SEC. 524 Commencement of winding up

524(1) If, before the presentation of a petition for the winding up of a company by the court, a resolution has been passed by the company for voluntary winding up, the winding up of the company is deemed to have commenced at the time of the passing of the resolution; and unless the court, on proof of fraud or mistake, directs otherwise, all proceedings taken in the voluntary winding up are deemed to have been validly taken.

(2) In any other case, the winding up of a company by the court is deemed to commence at the time of the presentation of the petition for winding up.

SEC. 525 Consequences of winding-up order

525(1) On the making of a winding-up order, a copy of the order must forthwith be forwarded by the company (or otherwise as may be prescribed) to the registrar of companies, who shall enter it in his records relating to the company.

(2) When a winding-up order has been made or a provisional liquidator has been appointed, no action or proceeding shall be proceeded with or commenced against the company except by leave of the court and subject to such terms as the court may impose.

(3) When an order has been made for winding up a company registered under section 680, no action or proceeding shall be commenced or proceeded with against the company or any contributory of the company, in respect of any debt of the company, except by leave of the court, and subject to such terms as the court may impose.

(4) An order for winding up a company operates in favour of all the creditors and of all contributories of the company as if made on the joint petition of a creditor and of a contributory.

THE OFFICIAL RECEIVER
(ENGLAND AND WALES ONLY)

SEC. 526 The official receiver

526(1) For the purposes of this Act as it relates to the winding up of companies by the court in England and Wales, the term **'official receiver'** means the official receiver (if any) attached to the court for bankruptcy purposes or, if there is more than one such official receiver, then such one of them as the Secretary of State may appoint or, if there is no such official receiver, then an officer appointed for the purpose by the Secretary of State.

(2) Any such officer shall, for the purpose of his duties under this Act, be styled 'the official receiver'.

SEC. 527 Appointment of official receiver by court in certain cases

527(1) If in the case of the winding up of a company by the court in England and Wales it appears to the court desirable, with a view to securing the more convenient and economical conduct of the winding up, that some officer other than the person who would under section 526 be the official receiver should be the official receiver for the purposes of that winding up, the court may appoint that other officer to act.

(2) The officer so appointed is then deemed, for all purposes of this Act, to be the official receiver in that winding up.

SEC. 528 Statement of company's affairs

528(1) Where the court in England and Wales has made a winding-up order or appointed a provisional liquidator, there shall (unless the court otherwise orders) be made out and submitted to the official receiver a statement as to the affairs of the company in the prescribed form.

(2)   The statement shall be verified by affidavit and show particulars of the company's assets, its debts and liabilities, the names, residences and occupations of its creditors, the securities held by them respectively, the dates when the securities were respectively given, and such further or other information as may be prescribed or as the official receiver may require.

(3)   The statement shall be submitted and verified by one or more of the persons who are at the relevant date the directors and by the person who at that date is the secretary of the company, or by such of the persons mentioned in the following subsection as the official receiver (subject to the direction of the court) may require to submit and verify the statement.

(4)   The persons referred to above are—

  (a)   those who are or have been officers of the company,

  (b)   those who have taken part in the formation of the company at any time within one year before the relevant date,

  (c)   those who are in the employment of the company, or have been in its employment within the year just mentioned, and are in the opinion of the official receiver capable of giving the information required, and

  (d)   those who are or have been within that year officers of or in the employment of a company which is, or within that year was, an officer of the company to which the statement relates.

(5)   For purposes of this section, 'the relevant date' is—

  (a)   in a case where a provisional liquidator is appointed, the date of his appointment, and

  (b)   in a case where no such appointment is made, the date of the winding-up order.

(6)   The statement of affairs required by this section shall be submitted within 14 days from the relevant date, or within such extended time as the official receiver or the court may for special reasons appoint.

(7)   If a person, without reasonable excuse, makes default in complying with the requirements of this section, he is liable to a fine and, for continued contravention, to a daily default fine.

SEC. 529 Further provisions as to statement etc. under sec. 528

529(1)   A person making or concurring in the making of the statement and affidavit required by section 528 shall be allowed, and shall be paid by the official receiver or provisional liquidator (as the case may be) out of the company's assets such costs and expenses incurred in and about the preparation and making of the statement and affidavit as the official receiver may consider reasonable, subject to an appeal to the court.

(2)   A person stating himself in writing to be a creditor or contributory of the company is entitled by himself or by his agent at all reasonable times, on payment of the prescribed fee, to inspect the statement submitted under section 528, and to a copy of or extract from it.

(3)   A person untruthfully so stating himself to be a creditor or contributory is guilty of a contempt of court and, on the application of the official receiver or the liquidator, punishable accordingly.

(4)   The statement required by section 528 may be used in evidence against any person making or concurring in making it.

SEC. 530 Report by official receiver

530(1)   When a winding-up order is made, the official receiver shall, as soon as practicable after the receipt of the statement to be submitted under section 528 (or, in a case where the court orders that no statement shall be submitted, as soon as practicable after the date of the order) submit a preliminary report to the court—

  (a)   as to the amount of capital issued, subscribed and paid up, and the estimated amount of assets and liabilities, and

  (b)   if the company has failed, as to the causes of the failure, and

  (c)   whether in his opinion further enquiry is desirable as to any matter relating to the promotion, formation or failure of the company or the conduct of its business.

(2)   The official receiver may also, if he thinks fit, make further reports (one or more) stating the manner in which the company was formed and whether in his opinion any fraud has been committed by any person in its promotion or formation, or by any officer of the company in relation to it since its formation, and any other matter which in his opinion it is desirable to bring to the notice of the court.

(3)   If the official receiver states in any such further report that in his opinion a fraud has been committed as above-mentioned, the court has the further powers provided in sections 563 and 564 (public examination of promoters and officers).

LIQUIDATORS

SEC. 531 Power of court to appoint liquidators

531   For the purpose of conducting the proceedings in winding up a company and performing such duties in reference thereto as the court may impose, the court may appoint a liquidator or liquidators.

SEC. 532 Appointment and powers of provisional liquidator

532(1)   Subject to the provisions of this section, the court may, at any time after the presentation of a winding-up petition, appoint a liquidator provisionally.

(2)   In England and Wales, the appointment of a provisional liquidator may be made at any time before the making of a winding-up order, and either the official receiver or any other fit person may be appointed.

(3)   In Scotland, such an appointment may be made at any time before the first appointment of liquidators.

(4)   When a liquidator is provisionally appointed by the court, his powers may be limited by the order appointing him.

SEC. 533 Appointment, style, etc., of liquidators in England and Wales

533(1)   The following provisions with respect to liquidators have effect on a winding-up order being made in England and Wales.

(2)   The official receiver by virtue of his office becomes the provisional liquidator and shall continue to act as such until he or another person becomes liquidator and is capable of acting as such.

(3)   The official receiver shall summon separate meetings of the company's creditors and contributories for the purpose of determining whether or not an application is to be made to the court for appointing a liquidator in the place of the official receiver.

(4)   The court may make any appointment and order required to give effect to that determination; and, if there is a difference between the determinations of the meetings

of the creditors and contributories in respect of the matter in question, the court shall decide the difference and make such order thereon as it may think fit.

(5) If a liquidator is not appointed by the court, the official receiver shall be the liquidator of the company.

(6) The official receiver is, ex officio, the liquidator during any vacancy.

(7) A liquidator shall be described, where a person other than the official receiver is liquidator, by the style of 'the liquidator' and, where the official receiver is liquidator, by the style of 'the official receiver and liquidator', of the particular company in respect of which he is appointed (and not by his individual name).

SEC. 534 Liquidator other than official receiver

534 If in the winding up of a company by the court in England and Wales a person other than the official receiver is appointed liquidator, that person—

    (a) cannot act as liquidator until he has notified his appointment to the registrar of companies and given security in the prescribed manner to the satisfaction of the Secretary of State,

    (b) shall give the official receiver such information, and such access to and facilities for inspecting the company's books and documents, and generally such aid as may be requisite for enabling that officer to perform his duties under this Act.

SEC. 535 Liquidators in Scotland

535(1) The following provisions with respect to liquidators have effect in a winding up by the court in Scotland.

(2) The court may determine whether any and what caution is to be found by a liquidator on his appointment.

(3) A liquidator shall be described by the style of 'the official liquidator' of the particular company in respect of which he is appointed (and not by his individual name).

(4) Where an order has been made for winding up a company subject to supervision and an order is afterwards made for winding up by the court, the court may by the last-mentioned or by a subsequent order appoint any person who is then liquidator, either provisionally or permanently, and either with or without any other person, to be liquidator in the winding up by the court.

SEC. 536 General provisions as to liquidators

536(1) A liquidator appointed by the court may resign or, on cause shown, be removed by the court.

(2) Where a person other than the official receiver is appointed liquidator, he shall receive such salary or remuneration by way of percentage or otherwise as the court may direct; and, if more such persons than one are appointed liquidators, their remuneration shall be distributed among them in such proportions as the court directs.

(3) A vacancy in the office of a liquidator appointed by the court shall be filled by the court.

(4) If more than one liquidator is appointed by the court, the court shall declare whether any act required or authorised by this Act to be done by the liquidator is to be done by all or any one or more of the persons appointed.

(5) Subject to section 634 (disqualification of bodies corporate for appointment as liquidator), the acts of a liquidator are valid notwithstanding any defects that may afterwards be discovered in his appointment or qualification.

SEC. 537 Custody of company's property

537(1) When a winding-up order has been made, or where a provisional liquidator has been appointed, the liquidator or the provisional liquidator (as the case may be) shall take into his custody or under his control all the property and things in action to which the company is or appears to be entitled.

(2) In a winding up by the court in Scotland, if and so long as there is no liquidator, all the property of the company is deemed to be in the custody of the court.

SEC. 538 Vesting of company property in liquidator

538(1) When a company is being wound up by the court, the court may on the application of the liquidator by order direct that all or any part of the property of whatsoever description belonging to the company or held by trustees on its behalf shall vest in the liquidator by his official name; and thereupon the property to which the order relates vests accordingly.

(2) The liquidator may, after giving such indemnity (if any) as the court may direct, bring or defend in his official name any action or other legal proceeding which relates to that property or which it is necessary to bring or defend for the purpose of effectually winding up the company and recovering its property.

SEC. 539 Powers of liquidator

539(1) The liquidator in a winding up by the court has power, with the sanction either of the court or of the committee of inspection—

    (a) to bring or defend any action or other legal proceeding in the name and on behalf of the company,

    (b) to carry on the business of the company so far as may be necessary for its beneficial winding up,

    (c) to appoint a solicitor to assist him in the performance of his duties,

    (d) to pay any class of creditors in full,

    (e) to make any compromise or arrangement with creditors or persons claiming to be creditors, or having or alleging themselves to have any claim (present or future, certain or contingent, ascertained or sounding only in damages) against the company, or whereby the company may be rendered liable,

    (f) to compromise all calls and liabilities to calls, debts and liabilities capable of resulting in debts, and all claims (present or future, certain or contingent, ascertained or sounding only in damages) subsisting or supposed to subsist between the company and a contributory or alleged contributory or other debtor or person apprehending liability to the company, and all questions in any way relating to or affecting the assets or the winding up of the company, on such terms as may be agreed, and take any security for the discharge of any such call, debt, liability or claim and give a complete discharge in respect of it.

(2) The liquidator in a winding up by the court has the power—

    (a) to sell any of the company's property by public auction or private contract, with power to transfer the whole thereof to any person or to sell the same in parcels,

    (b) to do all acts and to execute, in the name and on behalf of the company, all deeds, receipts and other documents and for that purpose to use, when necessary, the company's seal,

    (c) to prove, rank and claim in the bankruptcy, insolvency or sequestration of any contributory for any balance against his estate, and to receive dividends in the bankruptcy, insolvency or sequestration in respect of that balance, as a separate debt due from the bankrupt or insolvent, and rateably with the other separate creditors,

(d) to draw, accept, make and indorse any bill of exchange or promissory note in the name and on behalf of the company, with the same effect with respect to the company's liability as if the bill or note had been drawn, accepted, made or indorsed by or on behalf of the company in the course of its business,

(e) to raise on the security of the assets of the company any money requisite,

(f) to take out in his official name letters of administration to any deceased contributory, and to do in his official name any other act necessary for obtaining payment of any money due from a contributory or his estate which cannot conveniently be done in the name of the company (and in all such cases the money due is deemed, for the purpose of enabling the liquidator to take out the letters of administration or recover the money, to be due to the liquidator himself),

(g) to appoint an agent to do any business which the liquidator is unable to do himself,

(h) to do all such other things as may be necessary for winding up the company's affairs and distributing its assets.

(3) The exercise by the liquidator in a winding up by the court of the powers conferred by this section is subject to the control of the court, and any creditor or contributory may apply to the court with respect to any exercise or proposed exercise of any of those powers.

(4) In the case of a winding up in Scotland, the court may provide by order that the liquidator may, where there is no committee of inspection, exercise any of the powers mentioned in subsection (1)(a) or (b) without the sanction or intervention of the court.

(5) In a winding up by the court in Scotland, the liquidator has (subject to general rules), the same powers as a trustee on a bankrupt estate.

PROVISIONS ABOUT LIQUIDATORS APPLYING IN ENGLAND AND WALES ONLY

SEC. 540 Exercise and control of liquidator's powers

540(1) Subject to the provisions of this Act, the liquidator of a company which is being wound up by the court in England and Wales shall, in the administration of the company's assets and their distribution among its creditors, have regard to any directions that may be given by resolution of the creditors or contributories at any general meeting or by the committee of inspection.

(2) Directions given by the creditors or contributories at any general meeting are, in case of conflict, deemed to override any directions given by the committee of inspection.

(3) The liquidator may summon general meetings of the creditors or contributories for the purpose of ascertaining their wishes; and it is his duty to summon meetings at such times as the creditors or contributories by resolution (either at the meeting appointing the liquidator or otherwise) may direct, or whenever requested in writing to do so by one tenth in value of the creditors or contributories (as the case may be).

(4) The liquidator may apply to the court (in the prescribed manner) for directions in relation to any particular matter arising in the winding up.

(5) Subject to the provisions of this Act, the liquidator shall use his own discretion in the management of the estate and its distribution among the creditors.

(6) If any person is aggrieved by any act or decision of the liquidator, that person may apply to the court; and the court may confirm, reverse or modify the act or decision complained of, and make such order in the case as it thinks just.

SEC. 541 Books to be kept by liquidator

541(1) Every liquidator of a company which is being wound up by the court in England and Wales shall keep, in the prescribed manner, proper books in which he shall cause to be made entries or minutes of proceedings at meetings, and of such other matters as may be prescribed.

(2) Any creditor or contributory may, subject to the control of the court, personally or by his agent inspect any such books.

SEC. 542 Payments by liquidator into bank

542(1) The following applies to a liquidator of a company which is being wound up by the court in England and Wales.

(2) Subject to the next subsection, the liquidator shall, in such manner and at such times as the Secretary of State (with the concurrence of the Treasury) directs, pay the money received by him to the Insolvency Services Account at the Bank of England; and the Secretary of State shall furnish him with a certificate of receipt of the money so paid.

(3) However, if the committee of inspection satisfies the Secretary of State that for the purpose of carrying on the company's business or of obtaining advances, or for any other reason, it is for the advantage of the creditors or contributories that the liquidator should have an account at any other bank, the Secretary of State shall, on the application of the committee of inspection, authorise the liquidator to make his payments into and out of such other bank as the committee may select, and thereupon those payments shall be made in the prescribed manner.

(4) If the liquidator at any time retains for more than 10 days a sum exceeding £100 or such other amount as the Secretary of State in any particular case authorises him to retain, then unless he explains the retention to the Secretary of State's satisfaction, he shall pay interest on the amount so retained in excess at the rate of 20 per cent per annum, and is liable to disallowance of all or such part of his remuneration as the Secretary of State thinks just, and to be removed from his office by the Secretary of State, and is liable to pay any expenses occasioned by reason of his default.

(5) The liquidator shall not pay any sums received by him as liquidator into his private banking account.

(6) The money sum for the time being specified in subsection (4) is subject to increase or reduction by regulations under section 664.

SEC. 543 Submission of liquidator's accounts for audit

543(1) The following applies in the case of a company which is being wound up by the court in England and Wales.

(2) The liquidator shall, at such times as may be prescribed but not less than twice in each year during his tenure of office, send to the Secretary of State (or as he directs) an account of his receipts and payments as liquidator.

(3) The account shall be in the prescribed form, shall be made in duplicate, and shall be verified by a statutory declaration in the prescribed form; and the Secretary of State may cause the account to be audited.

(4) The liquidator shall furnish the Secretary of State with such vouchers and information as he requires, and the Secretary of State may at any time require the production of, and inspect, any books or accounts kept by the liquidator.

This applies whether or not the Secretary of State decides to cause the account to be audited, and extends to production and inspection at the liquidator's premises.

(5) After the account has been audited (or, as the case may be, forthwith if the Secretary of State decides not to have an audit) one copy of the account shall be filed by the Secretary of State, to be retained by him, and the other copy shall be delivered to the court for filing, each copy when filed to be open to inspection by any person on payment of the prescribed fee.

(6) The liquidator shall, when the account has been audited (alternatively, when he has been notified of the Secretary of State's decision not to have an audit), cause the account, or a summary of it, to be printed, and shall send a printed copy by post to every creditor or contributory.

The Secretary of State may in any case dispense with compliance with this subsection.

SEC. 544 Control of liquidators by Secretary of State

544(1) The Secretary of State shall take cognizance of the conduct of liquidators of companies which are being wound up by the court in England and Wales; and—

  (a)   if a liquidator does not faithfully perform his duties and duly observe all the requirements imposed on him by statute, rules or otherwise with respect to the performance of his duties, or

  (b)   if any complaint is made to the Secretary of State by any creditor or contributory in regard thereto,

the Secretary of State shall inquire into the matter, and take such action on it as he thinks expedient.

(2) The Secretary of State may at any time require the liquidator to answer any inquiry in relation to a winding up in which he is engaged and may, if the Secretary of State thinks fit, apply to the court to examine him or any other person on oath concerning the winding up.

(3) The Secretary of State may also direct a local investigation to be made of the liquidator's books and vouchers.

SEC. 545 Release of liquidators

545(1) The following applies to the liquidator of a company which is being wound up by the court in England and Wales.

(2) When the liquidator has realised all the company's property, or so much of it as can (in his opinion) be realised without needlessly protracting the liquidation, and has distributed a final dividend (if any) to the creditors, and adjusted the rights of the contributories among themselves, and made a final return (if any) to the contributories, or has resigned, or has been removed from his office, the following subsection has effect.

(3) The Secretary of State shall, on the liquidator's application, cause a report on the latter's accounts to be prepared and, on his complying with all the Secretary of State's requirements, shall take into consideration the report and any objection which may be urged by any creditor or contributory or person interested against the release of the liquidator, and shall either grant or withhold the release accordingly, subject nevertheless to an appeal to the High Court.

(4) If the release of the liquidator is withheld, the court may, on the application of any creditor or contributory or person interested, make such order as it thinks just, charging the liquidator with the consequences of any act or default which he may have done or made contrary to his duty.

(5) An order of the Secretary of State releasing the liquidator discharges him from all liability in respect of any act done or default made by him in the administration of the company's affairs or otherwise in relation to his conduct

as liquidator; but any such order may be revoked on proof that it was obtained by fraud or by suppression or concealment of any material fact.

(6) If the liquidator has not previously resigned or been removed, his release operates as removal of him from his office.

COMMITTEES OF INSPECTION

SEC. 546 Decision whether committee of inspection to be appointed

546(1) When a winding-up order has been made by the court in England and Wales, and separate meetings of creditors and contributories have been summoned for the purpose of determining whether an application should be made to the court for the appointment of a liquidator in place of the official receiver, it is the business of those meetings to determine further whether or not an application is to be made to the court for the appointment of a committee of inspection to act with the liquidator, and who are to be members of the committee if appointed.

(2) In Scotland, when a winding-up order has been made by the court, the liquidator shall summon separate meetings of the company's creditors and contributories for the purpose of determining whether or not an application is to be made to the court for the appointment of a committee of inspection and who are to be the members of the committee if appointed.

However, if the winding-up order has been made on the ground that the company is unable to pay its debts, it is not necessary for the liquidator to summon a meeting of the contributories.

(3) The court may make the appointment and order required to give effect to such determination; and if there is a difference between the determinations of the meetings of the creditors and contributories in respect of the matters referred to above, the court shall decide the difference and make such order on those matters as the court may think fit.

SEC. 547 Constitution and proceedings of committee of inspection

547(1) Subject as follows, the committee of inspection (if appointed) shall consist of creditors and contributories of the company or persons holding general powers of attorney from creditors and contributories in such proportions as may be agreed on by the meetings of creditors and contributories or as, in case of difference, may be determined by the court.

(2) In Scotland—

  (a)   if a winding-up order has been made on the ground that the company is unable to pay its debts, the committee shall consist of creditors or persons holding general powers of attorney from creditors, and

  (b)   the committee has, in addition to the powers and duties conferred and imposed on it by this Act, such of the powers and duties of commissioners on a bankrupt estate as may be conferred and imposed on committees of inspection by general rules.

(3) Schedule 17 has effect with respect to the committee of inspection and its proceedings.

SEC. 548 Power of Secretary of State to in place of committee

548 If in the case of a winding up in England and Wales there is no committee of inspection, the Secretary of State may, on the application of the liquidator, do any act or thing or give any direction or permission which is by this Act authorised or required to be done or given by the committee.

GENERAL POWERS OF COURT IN CASE OF WINDING UP BY THE COURT

SEC. 549 Power to stay or sist winding up

549(1) The court may at any time after an order for winding up, on the application either of the liquidator or the official receiver or any creditor or contributory, and on proof to the satisfaction of the court that all proceedings in the winding up ought to be stayed or sisted, make an order staying or sisting the proceedings, either altogether or for a limited time, on such terms and conditions as the court thinks fit.

(2) The court may, before making an order, require the official receiver to furnish to the court a report with respect to any facts or matters which are in his opinion relevant to the application.

(3) A copy of every order made under this section shall forthwith be forwarded by the company, or otherwise as may be prescribed, to the registrar of companies, who shall enter it in his records relating to the company.

SEC. 550 Settlement of list of contributories and application of assets

550(1) As soon as may be after making a winding-up order, the court shall settle a list of contributories, with power to rectify the register of members in all cases where rectification is required in pursuance of this Act, and shall cause the company's assets to be collected, and applied in discharge of its liabilities.

(2) If it appears to the court that it will not be necessary to make calls on or adjust the rights of contributories, the court may dispense with the settlement of a list of contributories.

(3) In settling the list, the court shall distinguish between persons who are contributories in their own right and persons who are contributories as being representatives of or liable for the debts of others.

SEC. 551 Delivery of property to liquidator

551 The court may, at any time after making a winding-up order, require any contributory for the time being on the list of contributories and any trustee, receiver, banker, agent or officer of the company to pay, deliver, convey, surrender or transfer forthwith (or within such time as the court directs) to the liquidator any money, property or books and papers in his hands to which the company is prima facie entitled.

SEC. 552 Debts due from contributory to company

552(1) The court may, at any time after making a winding-up order, make an order on any contributory for the time being on the list of contributories to pay, in manner directed by the order, any money due from him (or from the estate of the person whom he represents) to the company, exclusive of any money payable by him or the estate by virtue of any call in pursuance of this Act.

(2) The court in making such an order may—

(a) in the case of an unlimited company, allow to the contributory by way of set-off any money due to him or the estate which he represents from the company on any independent dealing or contract with the company, but not any money due to him as a member of the company in respect of any dividend or profit, and

(b) in the case of a limited company, make to any director or manager whose liability is unlimited or to his estate the like allowance.

(3) In the case of any company, whether limited or unlimited, when all the creditors are paid in full, any money due on any account whatever to a contributory from the company may be allowed to him by way of set-off against any subsequent call.

SEC. 553 Power to make calls

553(1) The court may, at any time after making a winding-up order, and either before or after it has ascertained the sufficiency of the company's assets, make calls on all or any of the contributories for the time being settled on the list of the contributories to the extent of their liability, for payment of any money which the court considers necessary to satisfy the company's debts and liabilities, and the costs, charges and expenses of winding up, and for the adjustment of the rights of the contributories among themselves, and make an order for payment of any calls so made.

(2) In making a call the court may take into consideration the probability that some of the contributories may partly or wholly fail to pay it.

SEC. 554 Payment into bank of money due to company

554(1) The court may order any contributory, purchaser or other person from whom money is due to the company to pay the amount due into the Bank of England (or any branch of it) to the account of the liquidator instead of to the liquidator, and any such order may be enforced in the same manner as if it had directed payment to the liquidator.

(2) All money and securities paid or delivered into the Bank of England (or branch) in the event of a winding up by the court are subject in all respects to the orders of the court.

SEC. 555 Order on contributory to be conclusive evidence

555(1) An order made by the court on a contributory is conclusive evidence that the money (if any) thereby appearing to be due or ordered to be paid is due, but subject to any right of appeal.

(2) All other pertinent matters stated in the order are to be taken as truly stated as against all persons and in all proceedings, except proceedings in Scotland against the heritable estate of a deceased contributory; and in that case the order is only prima facie evidence for the purpose of charging his heritable estate, unless his heirs or legatees of heritage were on the list of contributories at the time of the order being made.

SEC. 556 Appointment of special manager (England and Wales)

556(1) Where in proceedings in England and Wales the official receiver becomes the liquidator of a company, whether provisionally or otherwise, he may, if satisfied that the nature of the company's estate or business, or the interests of the creditors of contributories generally, require the appointment of a special manager of the estate or business other than himself, apply to the court.

(2) The court may on the application appoint a special manager of the company's estate or business to act during such time as the court may direct, with such powers (including any of the powers of a receiver or manager) as may be entrusted to him by the court.

(3) The special manager shall give such security and account in such manner as the Secretary of State directs, and shall receive such remuneration as may be fixed by the court.

SEC. 557 Power to exclude creditors not proving in time

557 The court may fix a time or times within which creditors are to prove their debts or claims or to be excluded from the benefit of any distribution made before those debts are proved.

SEC. 558 Adjustment of rights of contributories

558 The court shall adjust the rights of the contributories among themselves and distribute any surplus among the persons entitled to it.

SEC. 559 Inspection of books by creditors and contributories

559(1) The court may, at any time after making a winding-up order, make such order for inspection of the company's books and papers by creditors and contributories as the court thinks just; and any books and papers in the company's possession may be inspected by creditors and contributories accordingly, but not further or otherwise.

(2) Nothing in this section excludes or restricts any statutory rights of a government department or person acting under the authority of a government department.

SEC. 560 Costs of winding up may be made payable out of assets

560 The court may, in the event of the assets being insufficient to satisfy the liabilities, make an order as to the payment out of the assets of the costs, charges and expenses incurred in the winding up in such order of priority as the court thinks just.

SEC. 561 Summoning of persons suspected of having company property, etc.

561(1) The court may, at any time after the appointment of a provisional liquidator or the making of a winding-up order, summon before it any officer of the company or any person known or suspected to have in his possession any property of the company or supposed to be indebted to the company, or any person whom the court deems capable of giving information concerning the promotion, formation, trade, dealings, affairs or property of the company.

(2) The court may examine the officer or other person summoned on oath concerning those matters either by word of mouth or on written interrogatories, and may reduce his answers to writing and require him to sign them.

(3) The court may require him to produce any books and papers in his custody or power relating to the company; but if he claims any lien on books or papers produced by him, the production is without prejudice to that lien, and the court has jurisdiction in the winding up to determine all questions relating to that lien.

(4) If a person so summoned, after being tendered a reasonable sum for his expenses, refuses to come before the court at the time appointed, not having a lawful impediment (made known to the court at the time of its sitting and allowed by it), the court may cause him to be apprehended and brought before the court for examination.

SEC. 562 Attendance at company meetings (Scotland)

562 In the winding up by the court of a company registered in Scotland, the court has power to require the attendance of any officer of the company at any meeting of creditors or of contributories, or of a committee of inspection, for the purpose of giving information as to the trade, dealings, affairs or property of the company.

SEC. 563 Public examination of promoters and officers (England and Wales)

563(1) Where an order has been made in England and Wales for winding up a company by the court, and the official receiver has made a further report under this Act stating that in his opinion a fraud has been committed by any person in the promotion or formation of the company, or by any officer of the company in relation to it since its formation, the following applies.

(2) The court may, after consideration of the report, direct that that person or officer shall attend before the court on a day appointed by the court for that purpose and be publicly examined as to the promotion or formation of the company, or the conduct of its business, or as to the conduct or dealings of that person as an officer of it.

(3) The official receiver shall take part in the examination and for that purpose may, if specially authorised by the Secretary of State in that behalf, employ a solicitor with or without counsel.

(4) The liquidator (where the official receiver is not the liquidator) and any creditor or contributory may also take part in the examination either personally or by solicitor or counsel.

SEC. 564 Procedure under sec. 563

564(1) On a public examination ordered by the court under section 563, the court may put such questions to the person examined as it thinks fit.

(2) The person examined shall be examined on oath and shall answer all such questions as the court may put or allow to be put to him.

(3) The person shall at his own cost, before his examination, be furnished with a copy of the official receiver's report, and may at his own cost employ a solicitor with or without counsel, who is at liberty to put to him such questions as the court may deem just for the purpose of enabling him to explain or qualify any answers given by him.

(4) If the person applies to the court to be exculpated from any charges made or suggested against him, it is the duty of the official receiver to appear on the hearing of the application and call the court's attention to any matters which appear to him to be relevant; and if the court, after hearing evidence given or witnesses called by the official receiver, grants the application, the court may allow the applicant such costs as in its discretion it thinks fit.

(5) Notes of a person's public examination shall be taken down in writing, and shall be read over to or by, and signed by, him and may thereafter be used in evidence against him, and shall be open to the inspection of any creditor or contributory at all reasonable times.

(6) The court may, if it thinks fit, adjourn the examination from time to time.

(7) The examination may, if the court so directs (and subject to general rules) be held before any Circuit judge, or before any officer of the Supreme Court being an official referee, master or registrar in bankruptcy, or before a district registrar of the High Court named for the purpose by the Lord Chancellor; and the powers of the court under this section may be exercised by the person before whom the examination is held.

SEC. 565 Power to arrest absconding contributory

565 The court, at any time either before or after making a winding-up order, on proof of probable cause for believing that a contributory is about to quit the United Kingdom or otherwise to abscond or to remove or conceal any of his property for the purpose of evading payment of calls or of avoiding examination respecting the company's affairs, may cause the contributory to be arrested and his books and papers and movable personal property to be seized and him and them to be kept safely until such time as the court may order.

SEC. 566 Powers of court to be cumulative

566 Powers conferred by this Act on the court are in addition to and not in restriction of any existing powers of instituting proceedings against a contributory or debtor of the company, or the estate of any contributory or debtor, for the recovery of any call or other sums.

SEC. 567 Delegation of powers to liquidator (England and Wales)

567(1) Provision may be made by general rules for enabling or requiring all or any of the powers and duties conferred and imposed on the court in England and Wales by this Act in respect of the following matters—

(a) the holding and conducting of meetings to ascertain the wishes of creditors and contributories,

(b) the settling of lists of contributories and the rectifying of the register of members where required, and the collection and application of the assets,

(c) the payment, delivery, conveyance, surrender or transfer of money, property, books or papers to the liquidator,

(d) the making of calls,

(e) the fixing of a time within which debts and claims must be proved,

to be exercised or performed by the liquidator as an officer of the court, and subject to the court's control.

(2) But the liquidator shall not, without the special leave of the court, rectify the register of members, and shall not make any call without either that special leave or the sanction of the committee of inspection.

SEC. 568 Dissolution of company

568(1) When the company's affairs have been completely wound up, the court (if the liquidator makes an application in that behalf) shall make an order that the company be dissolved from the date of the order, and the company is then dissolved accordingly.

(2) A copy of the order shall within 14 days from its date be forwarded by the liquidator to the registrar of companies who shall record the company's dissolution.

(3) If the liquidator makes default in complying with the requirements of subsection (2), he is liable to a fine and, for continued contravention, to a daily default fine.

ENFORCEMENT OF, AND APPEAL FROM, ORDERS

SEC. 569 Orders for calls on contributories (Scotland)

569(1) In Scotland, where an order, interlocutor or decree has been made for winding up a company by the court, it is competent to the court, on production by the liquidators of a list certified by them of the names of the contributories liable in payment of any calls, and of the amount due by each contributory, and of the date when that amount became due, to pronounce forthwith a decree against those contributories for payment of the sums so certified to be due, with interest from that date until payment (at 5 per cent per annum) in the same way and to the same effect as if they had severally consented to registration for execution, on a charge of 6 days, of a legal obligation to pay those calls and interest.

(2) The decree may be extracted immediately, and no suspension of it is competent, except on caution or consignation, unless with special leave of the court.

SEC. 570 Enforcement throughout United Kingdom of orders made in winding up

570 (Repealed by Insolvency Act 1985, sec. 235 and Sch. 10, Pt. IV as from 1 April 1986.)

SEC. 571 Appeals from orders in Scotland

571(1) Subject to the provisions of this section and to rules of court, an appeal from any order or decision made or given in the winding up of a company by the court in Scotland under this Act lies in the same manner and subject to the same conditions as an appeal from an order or decision of the court in cases within its ordinary jurisdiction.

(2) In regard to orders or judgments pronounced by the judge acting as vacation judge in pursuance of section 4 of the Administration of Justice (Scotland) Act 1933—

(a) none of the orders specified in Part I of Schedule

16 to this Act are subject to review, reduction, suspension or stay of execution, and

(b) every other order or judgment (except as mentioned below) may be submitted to review by the Inner House by reclaiming motion enrolled within 14 days from the date of the order or judgment.

(3) However, an order being one of those specified in Part II of the Schedule shall, from the date of the order and notwithstanding that it has been submitted to review as above, be carried out and receive effect until the Inner House have disposed of the matter.

(4) In regard to orders or judgments pronounced in Scotland by a Lord Ordinary before whom proceedings in a winding up are being taken, any such order or judgment may be submitted to review by the Inner House by reclaiming motion enrolled within 14 days from its date; but should it not be so submitted to review during session, the provisions of this section in regard to orders or judgments pronounced by the judge acting as vacation judge apply.

(5) Nothing in this section affects provisions of this Act in reference to decrees in Scotland for payment of calls in the winding up of companies, whether voluntary or by, or subject to the supervision of, the court.

Chapter III — Voluntary Winding Up

RESOLUTIONS FOR, AND COMMENCEMENT OF, VOLUNTARY WINDING UP

SEC. 572 Circumstances in which company may be wound up voluntarily

572(1) A company may be wound up voluntarily—

(a) when the period (if any) fixed for the duration of the company by the articles expires, or the event (if any) occurs, on the occurrence of which the articles provide that the company is to be dissolved, and the company in general meeting has passed a resolution requiring it to be wound up voluntarily;

(b) if the company resolves by special resolution that it be wound up voluntarily;

(c) if the company resolves by extraordinary resolution to the effect that it cannot by reason of its liabilities continue its business, and that it is advisable to wind up.

(2) In this Act the expression 'a resolution for voluntary winding up' means a resolution passed under any of the paragraphs of subsection (1).

(3) A resolution passed under paragraph (a) of subsection (1), as well as a special resolution under paragraph (b) and an extraordinary resolution under paragraph (c), is subject to section 380 (copy of resolution to be forwarded to registrar of companies within 15 days).

SEC. 573 Notice of resolution to wind up voluntarily

573(1) When a company has passed a resolution for voluntary winding up, it shall, within 14 days after the passing of the resolution, give notice of the resolution by advertisement in the Gazette.

(2) If default is made in complying with this section, the company and every officer of it who is in default is liable to a fine and, for continued contravention, to a daily default fine.

For purposes of this subsection the liquidator is deemed an officer of the company.

SEC. 574 Commencement of voluntary winding up

574 A voluntary wnding up is deemed to commence at the time of the passing of the resolution for voluntary winding up.

CONSEQUENCES OF VOLUNTARY WINDING UP

SEC. 575 Effect on business and status of company

575(1) In case of a voluntary winding up, the company shall from the commencement of the winding up cease to carry on its business, except so far as may be required for its beneficial winding up.

(2) However, the corporate state and corporate powers of the company, notwithstanding anything to the contrary in its articles, continue until the company is dissolved.

SEC. 576 Avoidance of share transfers etc., other winding up resolution

576 Any transfer of shares, not being a transfer made to or with the sanction of the liquidator, and any alteration in the status of the company's members, made after the commencement of a voluntary winding up is void.

DECLARATION OF SOLVENCY

SEC. 577 Statutory declaration of solvency

577(1) Where it is proposed to wind up a company voluntarily, the directors (or, in the case of a company having more than two directors, the majority of them) may at a directors' meeting make a statutory declaration to the effect that they have made a full inquiry into the company's affairs and that, having done so, they have formed the opinion that the company will be able to pay its debts in full within such period, not exceeding 12 months from the commencement of the winding up, as may be specified in the declaration.

(2) Such a declaration by the directors has no effect for purposes of this Act unless—

(a) it is made within the 5 weeks immediately preceding the date of the passing of the resolution for winding up, or on that date but before the passing of the resolution, and

(b) it embodies a statement of the company's assets and liabilities as at the latest practicable date before the making of the declaration.

(3) The declaration shall be delivered to the registrar of companies before the expiration of 15 days immediately following the date on which the resolution for winding up is passed.

(4) A director making a declaration under this section without having reasonable grounds for the opinion that the company will be able to pay its debts in full within the period specified is liable to imprisonment or a fine, or both.

(5) If the company is wound up in pursuance of a resolution passed within 5 weeks after the making of the declaration, and its debts are not paid or provided for in full within the period specified, it is to be presumed (unless the contrary is shown) that the director did not have reasonable grounds for his opinion.

(6) If a declaration required by subsection (3) to be delivered to the registrar is not so delivered within the time prescribed by that subsection, the company and every officer in default is liable to a fine and, for continued contravention, to a daily default fine.

SEC. 578 Distinction between 'members' and 'creditors' voluntary winding up

578 A winding up in the case of which a directors' statutory declaration under section 577 has been made is a 'members' voluntary winding up'; and a winding up in the case of which such a declaration has not been made is a 'creditors' voluntary winding up'.

PROVISIONS APPLICABLE TO A MEMBERS' VOLUNTARY WINDING UP

SEC. 579 Introduction to next 7 sections

579 The provisions contained in sections 580 to 586 apply in relation to a members' voluntary winding up.

SEC. 580 Company's power to appoint and fix remuneration of liquidator

580(1) The company in general meeting shall appoint one or more liquidators for the purpose of winding up the company's affairs and distributing its assets, and may fix the remuneration to be paid to him or them.

(2) On the appointment of a liquidator all the powers of the directors cease, except so far as the company in general meeting or the liquidator sanctions their continuance.

SEC. 581 Power to fill vacancy in office of liquidator

581(1) If a vacancy occurs by death, resignation or otherwise in the office of liquidator appointed by the company, the company in general meeting may, subject to any arrangement with its creditors, fill the vacancy.

(2) For that purpose a general meeting may be convened by any contributory or, if there were more liquidators than one, by the continuing liquidators.

(3) The meeting shall be held in manner provided by this Act or by the articles, or in such manner as may, on application by any contributory or by the continuing liquidators, be determined by the court.

SEC. 582 Liquidator accepting shares as consideration for sale of company property

582(1) The following applies where a company is proposed to be, or is being, wound up altogether voluntarily, and the whole or part of its business or property is proposed to be transferred or sold to another company ('the transferee company'), whether or not this latter is a company within the meaning of this Act.

(2) The liquidator of the company to be, or being, wound up ('the transferor company') may, with the sanction of a special resolution of that company, conferring either a general authority on himself or an authority in respect of any particular arrangement, receive, in compensation or part compensation for the transfer or sale, shares, policies or other like interests in the transferee company for distribution among the members of the transferor company.

(3) Alternatively, the liquidator may (with that sanction) enter into any other arrangement whereby the members of the transferor company may, in lieu of receiving cash, shares, policies or other like interests (or in addition thereto) participate in the profits of, or receive any other benefit from, the transferee company.

(4) A sale or arrangement in pursuance of this section is binding on members of the transferor company.

(5) If a member of the transferor company who did not vote in favour of the special resolution expresses his dissent from it in writing addressed to the liquidator, and left at the company's registered office within 7 days after the passing of the resolution, he may require the liquidator either to abstain from carrying the resolution into effect or to purchase his interest at a price to be determined by agreement or by arbitration in manner provided by this section.

(6) If the liquidator elects to purchase the member's interest, the purchase money must be paid before the company is dissolved and be raised by the liquidator in such manner as may be determined by special resolution.

(7) A special resolution is not invalid for purposes of this section by reason that it is passed before or concurrently with a resolution for voluntary winding up or for appointing

liquidators; but, if an order is made within a year for winding up the company by or subject to the supervision of the court, the special resolution is not valid unless sanctioned by the court.

(8) For purposes of an arbitration under this section, the provisions of the Companies Clauses Consolidation Act 1845 or, in the case of a winding up in Scotland, the Companies Clauses Consolidation (Scotland) Act 1845 with respect to the settlement of disputes by arbitration are incorporated with this Act, and—

    (a)   in the construction of those provisions this Act is deemed the special Act and **'the company'** means the transferor company, and

    (b)   any appointment by the incorporated provisions directed to be made under the hand of the secretary or any two of the directors may be made in writing by the liquidator (or, if there is more than one liquidator, then any two or more of them).

SEC. 583 Creditors' meeting in case of insolvency

583(1) If the liquidator is at any time of opinion that the company will not be able to pay its debts in full within the period stated in the directors' declaration under section 577, he shall forthwith summon a meeting of the creditors, and shall lay before the meeting a statement of the company's assets and liabilities.

(2) If the liquidator fails to comply with this section, he is liable to a fine.

SEC. 584 General company meeting at each year's end

584(1) Subject to section 586, in the event of the winding up continuing for more than one year, the liquidator shall summon a general meeting of the company at the end of the first year from the commencement of the winding up, and of each succeeding year, or at the first convenient date within 3 months from the end of the year or such longer period as the Secretary of State may allow, and shall lay before the meeting an account of his acts and dealings and of the conduct of the winding up during the preceding year.

(2) If the liquidator fails to comply with this section, he is liable to a fine.

SEC. 585 Final meeting and dissolution

585(1) As soon as the company's affairs are fully wound up, the liquidator shall make up an account of the winding up, showing how it has been conducted and the company's property has been disposed of, and thereupon shall call a general meeting of the company for the purpose of laying before it the account, and giving an explanation of it.

(2) The meeting shall be called by advertisement in the Gazette, specifying its time, place and object and published at least one month before the meeting.

(3) Within one week after the meeting, the liquidator shall send to the registrar of companies a copy of the account, and shall make a return to him of the holding of the meeting and of its date; and if the copy is not sent or the return is not made in accordance with this subsection the liquidator is liable to a fine and, for continued contravention, to a daily default fine.

(4) If a quorum is not present at the meeting, the liquidator shall, in lieu of the return mentioned above, make a return that the meeting was duly summoned and that no quorum was present; and upon such a return being made, the provisions of subsection (3) as to the making of the return and deemed complied with.

(5) The registrar on receiving the account and either of these returns shall forthwith register them, and on the expiration of 3 months from the registration of the return the company is deemed to be dissolved; but the court may, on the application of the liquidator or of any other person

who appears to the court to be interested, make an order deferring the date at which the dissolution of the company is to take effect for such time as the court thinks fit.

(6) It is the duty of the person on whose application an order of the court under this section is made within 7 days after the making of the order to deliver to the registrar an office copy of the order for registration; and if that person fails to do so he is liable to a fine and, for continued contravention, to a daily default fine.

(7) If the liquidator fails to call a general meeting of the company as required by subsection (1), he is liable to a fine.

SEC. 586 Alternative provision as to company meetings in case of insolvency

586(1) Where section 583 has effect, sections 594 and 595 apply to the winding up to the exclusion of sections 584 and 585, as if the winding up were a creditors' voluntary winding up and not a members' voluntary winding up.

(2) However, the liquidator is not required to summon a meeting of creditors under seciton 594 at the end of the first year from the commencement of the winding up, unless the meeting held under section 583 is held more than 3 months before the end of that year.

PROVISIONS APPLICABLE TO A CREDITORS' VOLUNTARY WINDING UP

SEC. 587 Introduction to next 8 sections

587 The provisions contained in sections 588 to 595 apply in relation to a creditors' voluntary winding up.

SEC. 588 Meeting of creditors

588(1) The company shall give at least 7 days' notice of the company meeting at which the resolution for voluntary winding up is to be proposed.

This applies notwithstanding any power of the members, or of any particular majority of the members, to exclude or waive any other requirement of this Act or the company's articles with respect to the period of notice to be given of any company meeting.

(2) The company shall in addition—

    (a)   cause a meeting of its creditors to be summoned for the day, or the day next following the day, on which the company meeting is to be held,

    (b)   cause the notices of the creditors' meeting to be sent by post to the creditors simultaneously with the sending of the notices of the company meeting, and

    (c)   cause notice of the creditors' meeting to be advertised once in the Gazette and once at least in two local newspapers circulating in the district in which the company's registered office or its principal place of business is situated.

(3) The directors of the company shall—

    (a)   cause a full statement of the position of the company's affairs, together with a list of its creditors and the estimated amount of their claims, to be laid before the creditors' meeting, and

    (b)   appoint one of their number to preside at the meeting;

and it is the duty of the director so appointed to attend the meeting and preside at it.

(4) If the company meeting at which the resolution for voluntary winding up is to be proposed is adjourned and the resolution is passed at an adjourned meeting, any resolution passed at the creditors' meeting held under subsection (2) has effect as if it had been passed immediately after the passing of the resolution for voluntary winding up.

(5) If default is made—

   (a) by the company in complying with subsections (1) and (2),

   (b) by the directors in complying with subsection (3),

   (c) by any director in complying with that subsection, so far as requiring him to attend and preside at the creditors' meeting,

the company, the directors or the director (as the case may be) is or are liable to a fine; and, in the case of default by the company, every officer of the company who is in default is also so liable.

(6) Failure to give notice of the company meeting as required by subsection (1) does not affect the validity of any resolution passed or other thing done at that meeting which would be valid apart from that subsection.

SEC. 589 Appointment of liquidator

589(1) The creditors and the company at their respective meetings mentioned in section 588 may nominate a person to be liquidator for the purpose of winding up the company's affairs and distributing its assets.

(2) If the creditors and the company nominate different persons, the person nominated by the creditors shall be liquidator; and if no person is nominated by the creditors the person (if any) nominated by the company shall be liquidator.

(3) In the case of different persons being nominated, any director, member or creditor of the company may, within 7 days after the date on which the nomination was made by the creditors, apply to the court for an order either—

   (a) directing that the person nominated as liquidator by the company shall be liquidator instead of or jointly with the person nominated by the creditors, or

   (b) appointing some other person to be liquidator instead of the person nominated by the creditors.

SEC. 590 Appointment of committee of inspection

590(1) The creditors at the meeting to be held under section 588 or at any subsequent meeting may, if they think fit, appoint a committee of inspection consisting of not more than 5 persons.

(2) If such a committee is appointed, the company may, either at the meeting at which the resolution for voluntary winding up is passed or at any time subsequently in general meeting, appoint such number of persons as they think fit to act as members of the committee, not exceeding 5.

(3) However, the creditors may, if they think fit, resolve that all or any of the persons so appointed by the company ought not to be members of the committee of inspection; and if the creditors so resolve—

   (a) the persons mentioned in the resolution are not then, unless the court otherwise directs, qualified to act as members of the committee, and

   (b) on any application to the court under this provision the court may, if it thinks fit, appoint other persons to act as such members in place of the persons mentioned in the resolution.

(4) Schedule 17 has effect with respect to a committee of inspection appointed under this section and its proceedings.

(5) In Scotland, such a committee has, in addition to the powers and duties conferred and imposed on it by this Act, such of the powers and duties of commissioners on a bankrupt estate as may be conferred and imposed on committees of inspection by general rules.

SEC. 591 Remuneration of liquidator; cesser of directors' powers

591(1) The committee of inspection or, if there is no such committee, the creditors may fix the remuneration to be paid to the liquidator or liquidators.

(2) On the appointment of a liquidator, all the powers of the directors cease, except so far as the committee of inspection (or, if there is no such committee, the creditors) sanction their continuance.

SEC. 592 Vacancy in office of liquidator

592 If a vacancy occurs, by death, resignation or otherwise, in the office of a liquidator (other than a liquidator appointed by, or by the direction of, the court), the creditors may fill the vacancy.

SEC. 593 Application of sec. 582 to creditors' voluntary winding up

593 Section 582 applies in the case of a creditors' voluntary winding up as in the case of a members' voluntary winding up, with the modification that the liquidator's powers under that section are not to be exercised except with the sanction either of the court or of the committee of inspection.

SEC. 594 Meetings of company and creditors at end of each year

594(1) If the winding up continues for more than one year, the liquidator shall summon a general meeting of the company and a meeting of the creditors at the end of the first year from the commencement of the winding up, and of each succeeding year, or at the first convenient date within 3 months from the end of the year or such longer period as the Secretary of State may allow, and shall lay before the meetings an account of his acts and dealings and of the conduct of the winding up during the preceding year.

(2) If the liquidator fails to comply with this section, he is liable to a fine.

SEC. 595 Final meeting and dissolution

595(1) As soon as the company's affairs are fully wound up, the liquidator shall make up an account of the winding up, showing how it has been conducted and the company's property has been disposed of, and thereupon shall call a general meeting of the company and a meeting of the creditors for the purpose of laying the account before the meetings and giving an explanation of it.

(2) Each such meeting shall be called by advertisement in the Gazette specifying the time, place and object of the meeting, and published at least one month before it.

(3) Within one week after the date of the meetings (or, if they are not held on the same date, after the date of the later one) the liquidator shall send to the registrar of companies a copy of the account, and shall make a return to him of the holding of the meetings and of their dates.

(4) If the copy is not sent or the return is not made in accordance with subsection (3), the liquidator is liable to a fine and, for continued contravention, to a daily default fine.

(5) However, if a quorum is not present at either such meeting, the liquidator shall, in lieu of the return required by subsection (3), make a return that the meeting was duly summoned and that no quorum was present; and upon such return being made the provisions of that subsection as to the making of the return are, in respect of that meeting, deemed complied with.

(6) The registrar on receiving the account and, in respect of each such meeting, either of the returns mentioned above, shall forthwith register them, and on the expiration of 3 months from their registration the company is deemed to be dissolved; but the court may, on the application of the liquidator or of any other person who appears to the court to be interested, make an order deferring the date at which the dissolution of the company is to take effect for such time as the court thinks fit.

(7) It is the duty of the person on whose application an order of the court under this section is made, within 7 days after the making of the order, to deliver to the registrar an office copy of the order for registration; and if that person fails to do so he is liable to a fine and, for continued contravention, to a daily default fine.

(8) If the liquidator fails to call a general meeting of the company or a meeting of the creditors as required by this section, he is liable to a fine.

PROVISIONS APPLICABLE TO EVERY
VOLUNTARY WINDING UP

SEC. 596 Introduction to next 9 sections

596 The provisions of sections 597 to 605 apply to every voluntary winding up, whether a members' or a creditors' winding up.

SEC. 597 Distribution of company's property

597 Subject to the provisions of this Act as to preferential payments, the company's property shall on the winding up be applied in satisfaction of the company's liabilities pari passu and, subject to that application, shall (unless the articles otherwise provide) be distributed among the members according to their rights and interests in the company.

SEC. 598 Powers and duties of liquidator in voluntary winding up

598(1) The liquidator may —

   (a) in the case of a members' voluntary winding up, with the sanction of an extraordinary resolution of the company, and

   (b) in the case of a creditors' voluntary winding up, with the sanction of the court or the committee of inspection (or, if there is no such committee, a meeting of the creditors),

exercise any of the powers given by paragraphs (d), (e) and (f) of section 539(1) to a liquidator in a winding up by the court.

(2) The liquidator may, without sanction, exercise any of the other powers given by this Act to the liquidator in a winding up by the court.

(3) The liquidator may —

   (a) exercise the court's power of settling a list of contributories (and the list of contributories is prima facie evidence of the liability of the persons named in it to be contributories),

   (b) exercise the court's power of making calls,

   (c) summon general meetings of the company for the purpose of obtaining its sanction by special or extraordinary resolution or for any other purpose he may think fit.

(4) The liquidator shall pay the company's debts and adjust the rights of the contributories among themselves.

(5) When several liquidators are appointed, any power given by this Act may be exercised by such one or more of them as may be determined at the time of their appointment or, in default of such determination, by any number not less than two.

SEC. 599 Appointment or removal of liquidator by the court

599(1) If from any cause whatever there is no liquidator acting, the court may appoint a liquidator.

(2) The court may, on cause shown, remove a liquidator and appoint another.

SEC. 600 Notice by liquidator of his appointment

600(1) The liquidator shall, within 14 days after his appointment, publish in the Gazette and deliver to the registrar of companies for registration a notice of his appointment in the prescribed form.

(2) If the liquidator fails to comply with this section he is liable to a fine and, for continued contravention, to a daily default fine.

SEC. 601 Arrangement when binding on creditors

601(1) Any arrangement entered into between a company about to be, or in the course of being, wound up and its creditors is (subject to the right of appeal under this section) binding —

   (a) on the company, if sanctioned by an extraordinary resolution, and

   (b) on the creditors, if acceded to by three-fourths in number and value of them.

(2) Any creditor or contributory may, within 3 weeks from the completion of the arrangement, appeal to the court against it; and the court may thereupon, as it thinks just, amend, vary or confirm the arrangement.

SEC. 602 Reference of questions and powers to court

602(1) The liquidator or any contributory or creditor may apply to the court to determine any question arising in the winding up of a company, or to exercise, as respects the enforcing of calls or any other matter, all or any of the powers which the court might exercise if the company were being wound up by the court.

(2) The court, if satisfied that the determination of the question or the required exercise of power will be just and beneficial, may accede wholly or partially to the application on such terms and conditions as it thinks fit or may make such other order on the application as it thinks just.

(3) A copy of an order made by virtue of this section staying the proceedings in the winding up shall forthwith be forwarded by the company, or otherwise as may be prescribed, to the registrar of companies, who shall enter it in his records relating to the company.

SEC. 603 Court's power to control proceedings (Scotland)

603 If the court, on the application of the liquidator in the winding up of a company registered in Scotland, so directs, no action or proceeding shall be proceeded with or commenced against the company except by leave of the court and subject to such terms as the court may impose.

SEC. 604 Costs of voluntary winding up

604 All costs, charges and expenses properly incurred in the winding up, including the remuneration of the liquidator, are payable out of the company's assets in priority to all other claims.

SEC. 605 Saving for rights of creditors and contributories

605 The winding up of a company under this Chapter does not bar the right of any creditor or contributory to have it wound up by the court; but in the case of an application by a contributory the court must be satisfied that the rights of the contributories will be prejudiced by a voluntary winding up.

Chapter IV — Winding Up
Subject to Supervision of Court

SEC. 606 Power to order winding up under supervision

606 When a company has passed a resolution for voluntary winding up, the court may make an order that the voluntary winding up shall continue but subject to such supervision of the court, and with such liberty for creditors, contributories or others to apply to the court, and generally on such terms and conditions, as the court thinks just.

SEC. 607 Effect of petition for court supervision

607 A petition for the continuance of a voluntary winding up subject to the supervision of the court is deemed, for the purpose of giving jurisdiction to the court over actions, to be a petition for winding up by the court.

SEC. 608 Application of sec. 522, 523

608 A winding up subject to the supervision of the court is deemed for the purposes of sections 522 and 523 (avoidance of dispositions of property, etc.) to be a winding up by the court.

SEC. 609 Appointment and removal of liquidators

609(1) Where an order is made for a winding up subject to supervision, the court may by that or any subsequent order appoint an additional liquidator.

(2) A liquidator so appointed has the same powers, is subject to the same obligations, and in all respects stands in the same position, as if he had been duly appointed in accordance with provisions of this Act with respect to the appointment of liquidators in a voluntary winding up.

(3) The court may remove a liquidator so appointed by the court, or any liquidator continued under the supervision order, and fill any vacancy occasioned by the removal, or by death or resignation.

SEC. 610 Effect of supervision order

610(1) Where an order is made for a winding up subject to supervision, the liquidator may (subject to any restrictions imposed by the court) exercise all his powers, without the court's sanction or intervention, in the same manner as if the company were being wound up altogether voluntarily.

(2) However, the powers specified in paragraphs (d), (e) and (f) of section 539(1) shall not be exercised by the liquidator except with the sanction of the court or, in a case where before the order the winding up was a creditors' voluntary winding up, with the sanction of the court or the committee of inspection or (if there is no such committee) a meeting of the creditors.

(3) A winding up subject to the supervision of the court is not a winding up by the court for the purposes of the provisions of this Act specified in Schedule 18, nor for those of section 491 (power in England and Wales to appoint official receiver as receiver for debenture holders or creditors); but, subject to this, an order for a winding up subject to supervision is deemed to be for all purposes an order for winding up by the court.

(4) But where the order for winding up subject to supervision was in relation to a creditors' voluntary winding up in which a committee of inspection had been appointed, the order is deemed an order for winding up by the court for the purposes of section 547(2)(b) and Schedule 17, except in so far as the operation of those provisions is excluded in a voluntary winding up by general rules.

Chapter V — Provisions Applicable to Every Mode of Winding Up

PROOF AND RANKING OF CLAIMS

SEC. 611 Debts of all descriptions may be proved

611(1) In every winding up (subject, in the case of insolvent companies, to the application in accordance with this Act of the law of bankruptcy) all debts payable on a contingency, and all claims against the company, present or future, certain or contingent, ascertained or sounding only in damages, are admissible to proof against the company.

(2) A just estimate is to be made (so far as possible) of the value of such debts or claims as may be subject to any contingency or sound only in damages, or for some other reason do not bear a certain value.

SEC. 612 Application of bankruptcy rules (England and Wales)

612(1) In the winding up of an insolvent company registered in England and Wales the same rules prevail and are to be observed with regard to the respective rights of secured and unsecured creditors, and to debts provable and to the valuation of annuities and future and contingent liabilities, as are in force for the time being under the law of bankruptcy in England and Wales with respect to the estates of persons adjudged bankrupt.

(2) All those who in any such case would be entitled to prove for and receive dividends out of the company's assets may come in under the winding up and make such claims against the company as they respectively are entitled to by virtue of this section.

SEC. 613 Ranking of claims (Scotland)

613(1) In the winding up of a company registered in Scotland, the following enactments—

(a) sections 22 (except subsection (8)), 23(1) and (2), 48 (except in so far as it relates to the application of section 22(8)), 49 and 50 of, and Schedule 1 to, the Bankruptcy (Scotland) Act 1985 (claims by creditors for voting and payment of dividends);

(b) paragraphs 11 and 13 of Schedule 6 to that Act (voting at meetings);

(c) section 60 of that Act (liabilities and rights of co-obligants); and

(d) sections 8(5) and 22(8) of that Act (including section 22(8) as applied by section 48(7) of that Act);

apply, so far as is consistent with this Act, in like manner as they apply in the sequestration of a bankrupt's estate, with the substitutions specified below, and with any other necessary modifications.

(2) The substitutions to be made in those sections of the Act of 1985 are as follows—

(a) for references to sequestration, substitute references to winding up,

(b) for references to the sheriff, substitute references to the court,

(c) for references to the interim or permanent trustee, substitute references to the liquidator, and

(d) for references to the debtor, substitute references to the company.

SEC. 614 Preferential payments

614(1) In a winding up the preferential debts listed in Schedule 19 shall be paid in priority to all other debts, but with the exceptions and reservations specified in that Schedule.

(2) The preferential debts shall—

(a) rank equally among themselves and be paid in full, unless the assets are insufficient to meet them, in which case they shall abate in equal proportions, and

(b) so far as the assets of the company available for payment of general creditors are insufficient to meet them, have priority over the claims of holders of debentures under any floating charge created by the company, and be paid accordingly out of any property comprised in or subject to that charge.

(3) Subject to the retention of such sums as may be necessary for the costs and expenses of the winding up, the preferential debts shall be discharged forthwith so far as the assets are sufficient to meet them; and in the case of the debts to which priority is given by paragraph 8 of Schedule 19 (social security payments), formal proof of them is not required except in so far as is otherwise provided by general rules.

(4) In the event of a landlord or other person distraining or having distrained on any goods or effects of the company within 3 months next before the date of a winding-up order, the preferential debts are a first charge on the goods or effects so distrained on, or the proceeds of their sale; but in respect of any money paid under such a charge, the landlord or other person has the same rights of priority as the person to whom the payment is made.

EFFECT OF WINDING UP ON ANTECEDENT AND OTHER TRANSACTIONS

SEC. 615 Fraudulent preference

615(1) Any conveyance, mortgage, delivery of goods, payment, execution or other act relating to property made or done by or against a company within 6 months before the commencement of its winding up which, had it been made or done by or against an individual within 6 months before the presentation of a bankruptcy petition on which he is adjudged bankrupt, would be deemed in his bankruptcy a fraudulent preference, is in the event of the company being wound up deemed a fraudulent preference of its creditors and invalid accordingly.

(2) Any conveyance or assignment by a company of all its property to trustees for the benefit of all its creditors is void to all intents.

(3) In the application of this section to Scotland, **'bankruptcy petition'** means petition for sequestration.

SEC. 615A Gratuitous alienations

615A(1) Where this subsection applies and—

  (a) the winding up of a company has commenced, an alienation by the company is challengeable by—

    (i) any creditor who is a creditor by virtue of a debt incurred on or before the date of such commencement; or

    (ii) the liquidator;

  (b) an administration order is in force in relation to a company, an alienation by the company is challengeable by the administrator.

(2) Subsection (1) applies where—

  (a) by the alienation, whether before or after the coming into force of section 75 of the Bankruptcy (Scotland) Act 1985, any part of the company's property is transferred or any claim or right of the company is discharged or renounced; and

  (b) the alienation takes place on a relevant day.

(3) For the purposes of subsection (2)(b), the day on which an alienation takes place is the day on which it becomes completely effectual; and in that subsection **'relevant day'** means, if the alienation has the effect of favouring—

  (a) a person who is an associate (within the meaning of the Bankruptcy (Scotland) Act 1985) of the company, a day not earlier than 5 years before the date on which—

    (i) the winding up of the company commences; or

    (ii) as the case may be, the administration order is made; or

  (b) any other person, a day not earlier than 2 years before such date.

(4) Subsections (4) to (6) and (8) of section 34 of the Bankruptcy (Scotland) Act 1985 (challenge of gratuitous alienation) apply for the purposes of this section as they apply for the purposes of that section but as if—

  (a) for any reference to the debtor there is substituted a reference to the company; and

  (b) in subsection (8) for the words from the beginning to '1889' there are substituted the words

    'A liquidator and, after the coming into force of Chapter III of Part II of the Insolvency Act 1985, an administrator appointed thereunder.'

(5) In subsections (1) to (3) above, any reference to an administrator or to an administration order—

  (a) shall be construed in accordance with Chapter III of Part II of the Insolvency Act 1985; and

  (b) shall be of no effect until the coming into force of that Chapter.

(6) This section extends to Scotland only.

SEC. 615B Unfair preferences

615B(1) Section 36 of the Bankruptcy (Scotland) Act 1985 (unfair preferences) applies for the purposes of this Act as it applies for the purposes of that Act but as if—

  (a) for any reference to a debtor there is substituted a reference to a company;

  (b) in subsection (1), for paragraphs (a) to (c) there are substituted the words 'the commencement of the winding up of the company or the making of an administration order in relation to the company.';

  (c) in subsection (4) for paragraphs (a) and (b) there are substituted the following paragraphs—

    '(a) in the case of a winding up—

      (i) any creditor who is a creditor by virtue of a debt incurred on or before the date of commencement of the winding up; or

      (ii) the liquidator; and

    (b) in the case of an administration order, the administrator.';

  (d) in subsection (6), for the words from the beginning to '1889' there are substituted the words 'A liquidator and an administrator'; and

  (e) for subsection (7) there is substituted the following subsection—

    '(7) This section shall be construed as one with Part XX of the Companies Act 1985; and subsection (5) of section 615A of that Act shall apply in relation to the foregoing provisions of this section as it applies in relation to subsections (1) to (3) of that section.'.

(2) This section applies to Scotland only.

SEC. 616 Liabilities and rights of those fraudulently preferred (England and Wales)

616(1) Where in the case of a company wound up in England and Wales anything made or done is void under section 615 as a fraudulent preference of a person interested in property mortgaged or charged to secure the company's debt, then (without prejudice to any rights or liabilities arising apart from this provision) the person preferred is subject to the same liabilities, and has the same rights, as if he had undertaken to be personally liable as surety for the debt to the extent of the charge on the property or the value of his interest, whichever is the less.

(2) The value of the person's interest is determined as at the date of the transaction constituting the fraudulent preference, and as if the interest were free of all incumbrances other than those to which the charge for the company's debt was then subject.

(3) On an application made to the court with respect to any payment on the ground that the payment was a fraudulent preference of a surety or guarantor, the court has jurisdiction to determine any question with respect to the payment arising between the person to whom the payment was made and the surety or guarantor, and to grant relief in respect of it.

(4) The court's jurisdiction under subsection (3) is exercisable notwithstanding that the determination of the question is not necessary for the purposes of the winding up; and the court may for the purposes of that subsection give leave to bring in the surety or guarantor as a third party as in the case of an action for the recovery of the sum paid.

(5) Subsections (3) and (4) apply, with the necessary modifications, in relation to transactions other than the payment of money as they apply in relation to payments.

SEC. 617 Effect of floating charge

617(1) Where a company is being wound up, a floating charge on its undertaking or property created within 12 months of the commencement of the winding up is invalid (unless it is proved that the company immediately after the creation of the charge was solvent), except to the amount of any cash paid to the company at the time of or subsequently to the creation of, and in consideration for, the charge, together with interest on that amount.

(2) Interest under this section is at the rate of 5 per cent per annum or such other rate as may for the time being be prescribed by order of the Treasury in a statutory instrument subject to annulment in pursuance of a resolution of either House of Parliament.

(3) Where a company is being wound up in Scotland, a floating charge over all or any part of its property is not to be held an alienation or preference voidable by statute (other than by the provisions of this section) or at common law on the ground of insolvency or notour bankruptcy.

SEC. 618 Disclaimer of onerous property (England and Wales)

618(1) Where any part of the property of a company which is being wound up consists of land (of any tenure) burdened with onerous covenants, of shares or stock in companies, of unprofitable contracts, or of any other property that is unsaleable, or not readily saleable, by reason of its binding its possessor to the performance of any onerous act or to the payment of any sum of money, the liquidator may, with the leave of the court and subject to the provisions of this section and the next, disclaim the property.

(2) The power to disclaim is exercisable notwithstanding that the liquidator has endeavoured to sell or has taken possession of the property or exercised any act of ownership in relation to it; and the disclaimer must be in writing signed by him.

(3) The power is exercisable at any time within 12 months after the commencement of the winding up or such extended period as may be allowed by the court; but where any such property has not come to the liquidator's knowledge within one month after the commencement of the winding up, he may disclaim at any time within 12 months after he has become aware of it or such extended period as may be so allowed.

(4) The disclaimer operates to determine, as from the date of disclaimer, the rights, interests and liabilities of the company, and the company's property, in or in respect of the property disclaimed; but it does not (except so far as is necessary for the purpose of releasing the company and its property from liability) affect the rights or liabilities of any other person.

(5) This section does not apply in the case of a winding up in Scotland.

SEC. 619 Further provisions about disclaimer under sec. 618

619(1) The court, before or on granting leave to disclaim under section 618, may require such notices to be given to persons interested, and impose such terms as a condition of granting leave, and make such other order in the matter, as the court thinks just.

(2) The liquidator is not entitled to disclaim property under section 618 in a case where application in writing has been made to him by persons interested in the property requiring him to decide whether he will or will not disclaim and he has not within 28 days after the receipt of the application (or such further period as may be allowed by the court) given notice to the applicant that he intends to apply to the court for leave to disclaim.

(3) In the case of a contract, if the liquidator after such an application does not within that period or further period disclaim the contract, the company is deemed to have adopted it.

(4) The court may, on the application of a person who is, as against the liquidator, entitled to the benefit or subject to the burden of a contract made with the company, make an order rescinding the contract on such terms as to payment by or to either party of damages for the non-performance of the contract, or otherwise as the court thinks just; and any damages payable under the order to such a person may be proved by him as a debt in the winding up.

(5) The court may, on an application by a person who either claims an interest in disclaimed property or is under a liability not discharged by this Act in respect of disclaimed property, and on hearing any such persons as it thinks fit, make an order for the vesting of the property in or its delivery to any persons entitled to it, or to whom it may seem just that the property should be delivered by way of compensation for such liability, or a trustee for him, and on such terms as the court thinks just.

(6) On such a vesting order being made, the property comprised in it vests accordingly in the person named in that behalf in the order, without conveyance or assignment for that purpose.

(7) Part I of Schedule 20 has effect for the protection of third parties where the property disclaimed is of a leasehold nature.

(8) A person injured by the operation of a disclaimer under section 618 and this section is deemed a creditor of the company to the amount of the injury, and may accordingly prove the debt in the winding up.

SEC. 620 Liability for rentchange on company's land after disclaimer

620(1) Where on a disclaimer under section 618 land in England and Wales vests subject to a rentcharge in the Crown or any other person, that does not impose on the Crown or that other person, or on its or his successors in title, any personal liability in respect of the rentcharge.

(2) But this section does not affect any liability in respect of sums accruing due after the Crown or other person, or some person claiming through or under it or him, has taken possession or control of the land or has entered into occupation of it.

(3) This section applies to land whenever vesting, and to sums whenever accrued.

SEC. 621 Effect of execution or attachment (England and Wales)

621(1) Where a creditor has issued execution against the goods or land of a company or has attached any debt due to it, and the company is subsequently wound up, he is not entitled to retain the benefit of the execution or attachment against the liquidator in the winding up unless he has completed the execution or attachment before the commencement of the winding up.

(2) However —

(a) if a creditor has had notice of a meeting having been called at which a resolution for voluntary winding up is to be proposed, the date on which he had notice is substituted, for the purpose of subsection (1), for the date of commencement of the winding up,

(b) a person who purchases in good faith under a sale by the sheriff any goods of a company on which execution has been levied in all cases acquires a good title to them against the liquidator, and

(c) the rights conferred by subsection (1) on the liquidator may be set aside by the court in favour of the creditor to such extent and subject to such terms as the court thinks fit.

(3) For purposes of this Act —

(a) an execution against goods is completed by seizure and sale, or by the making of a charging order under section 1 of the Charging Orders Act 1979,

(b) an attachment of a debt is completed by receipt of the debt; and

(c) an execution against land is completed by seizure, by the appointment of a receiver, or by the making of a charging order under section 1 of the Act above-mentioned.

(4) In this section, 'goods' includes all chattels personal; and 'the sheriff' includes any officer charged with the execution of a writ or other process.

(5) This section does not apply in the case of a winding up in Scotland.

SEC. 622 Duties of sheriff where goods seized in execution (England and Wales)

622(1) The following applies where a company's goods are taken in execution and, before their sale or the completion of the execution (by the receipt or recovery of the full amount of the levy), notice is served on the sheriff that a provisional liquidator has been appointed or that a winding-up order has been made, or that a resolution for voluntary winding up has been passed.

(2) The sheriff shall, on being so required, deliver the goods and any money seized or received in part satisfaction of the execution to the liquidator; but the costs of execution are a first charge on the goods or money so delivered, and the liquidator may sell the goods, or a sufficient part of them, for the purpose of satisfying the charge.

(3) If under an execution in respect of a judgment for a sum exceeding £250 a company's goods are sold or money is paid in order to avoid sale, the sheriff shall deduct the costs of the execution from the proceeds of sale or the money paid and retain the balance for 14 days.

(4) If within that time notice is served on the sheriff of a petition for the winding up of the company having been presented, or of a meeting having been called at which there is to be proposed a resolution for voluntary winding up, and an order is made or a resolution passed (as the case may be), the sheriff shall pay the balance to the liquidator, who is entitled to retain it as against the execution creditor.

(5) The rights conferred by this section on the liquidator may be set aside by the court in favour of the creditor to such extent and subject to such terms as the court thinks fit.

(6) In this section, 'goods' includes all chattels personal; and 'the sheriff' includes any officer charged with the execution of a writ or other process.

(7) The money sum for the time being specified in subsection (3) is subject to increase or reduction by regulations under section 664; but no increase or reduction of its affects any case where the goods are sold, or the payment to avoid sale is made, before the coming into force of the increase or reduction.

(8) This section does not apply in the case of a winding up in Scotland.

SEC. 623 Effect of diligence within 60 days of winding up

623(1) In the winding up of a company registered in Scotland, the following provisions of the Bankruptcy (Scotland) Act 1985—

(a) subsections (1) to (6) of section 37 (effect of sequestration on diligence); and

(b) subsections (3), (4), (7) and (8) of section 39 (realisation of estate),

apply, so far as is consistent with this Act, in like manner as they apply in the sequestration of a debtor's estate, with the substitutions specified below and with any other necessary modifications.

(2) The substitutions to be made in those sections of the Act of 1985 are as follows—

(a) for references to the debtor, substitute references to the company,

(b) for references to the sequestration, substitute references to the winding up,

(c) for references to the date of sequestration, substitute references to the commencement of the winding up of the company, and

(d) for references to the permanent trustee, substitute references to the liquidator.

(3) In this section, 'the commencement of the winding up of the company' means, where it is being wound up by the court, the day on which the winding up order is made.

(4), (5) (Sec. 623(1)–(3) substituted for former 623(1)–(5) by Bankruptcy (Scotland) Act 1985, s. 75(1) and Sch. 7 as from 1 April 1986 (see S.I. 1985 No. 1924).

(6) This section, so far as relating to any estate or effects of the company situated in Scotland, applies in the case of a company registered in England as in the case of one registered in Scotland.

OFFENCES OF FRAUD, DECEPTION, ETC. BEFORE AND IN COURSE OF WINDING UP: FRAUDULENT TRADING AND ITS CONSEQUENCES

SEC. 624 Fraud, etc. in anticipation of winding up

624(1) When a company is ordered to be wound up by the court, or passes a resolution for voluntary winding up, any person, being a past or present officer of the company, is deemed to have committed an offence if, within the 12 months immediately preceding the commencement of the winding up, he has—

(a) concealed any part of the company's property to the value of £120 or more, or concealed any debt due to or from the company,

(b) fraudulently removed any part of the company's property to the value of £120 or more, or

(c) concealed, destroyed, mutilated or falsified any book or paper affecting or relating to the company's property or affairs, or

(d) made any false entry in any book or paper affecting or relating to the company's property or affairs, or

(e) fraudulently parted with, altered or made any omission in any document affecting or relating to the company's property or affairs, or

(f) pawned, pledged or disposed of any property of the company which has been obtained on credit and has not been paid for (unless the pawning, pledging or disposal was in the ordinary way of the company's business).

(2) Such a person is deemed to have committed an offence if within the period above mentioned he has been privy to the doing by others of any of the things mentioned in paragraphs (c), (d) and (e) of subsection (1); and he commits an offence if, at any time after the commencement of the winding up, he does any of the things mentioned in paragraphs (a) to (f) of that subsection, or is privy to the doing by others of any of the things mentioned in paragraphs (c) to (e) of it.

(3) For purposes of this section, **'officer'** includes a shadow director.

(4) It is a defence —

    (a) for a person charged under paragraph (a) or (f) of subsection (1) (or under subsection (2) in respect of the things mentioned in either of those paragraphs) to prove that he had no intent to defraud, and

    (b) for a person charged under paragraph (c) or (d) of subsection (1) (or under subsection (2) in respect of the things mentioned in either of those two paragraphs) to prove that he had no intent to conceal the state of affairs of the company or to defeat the law.

(5) Where a person pawns, pledges or disposes of any property in circumstances which amount to an offence under subsection (1)(f), every person who takes in pawn or pledge, or otherwise receives the property knowing it to be pawned, pledged or disposed of in such circumstances, is guilty of an offence.

(6) A person guilty of an offence under this section is liable to imprisonment or a fine, or both.

(7) The money sums specified in paragraphs (a) and (b) of subsection (1) are subject to increase or reduction by regulations under section 664.

SEC. 625 Transactions in fraud of creditors

625(1) When a company is ordered to be wound up by the court or passes a resolution for voluntary winding up, a person is deemed to have committed an offence if he, being at the time an officer of the company —

    (a) with intent to defraud creditors of the company, has made or caused to be made any gift or transfer of, or charge on, or has caused or connived at the levying of any execution against, the company's property, or

    (b) with that intent, has concealed or removed any part of the company's property since, or within 2 months before, the date of any unsatisfied judgment or order for the payment of money obtained against the company.

(2) A person guilty of an offence under this section is liable to imprisonment or a fine, or both.

SEC. 626 Misconduct in course of winding up

626(1) When a company is being wound up, whether by or under the supervision of the court or voluntarily, any person, being a past or present officer of the company, commits an offence if he —

    (a) does not to the best of his knowledge and belief fully and truly discover to the liquidator all the company's property, and how and to whom and

for what consideration and when the company disposed of any part of that property (except such part as has been disposed of in the ordinary way of the company's business), or

(b) does not deliver up to the liquidator (or as he directs) all such part of the company's property as is in his custody or under his control, and which he is required by law to deliver up, or

(c) does not deliver up to the liquidator (or as he directs) all books and papers in his custody or under his control belonging to the company and which he is required by law to deliver up, or

(d) knowing or believing that a false debt has been proved by any person in the winding up, fails for the period of a month to inform the liquidator of it, or

(e) after the commencement of the winding up, prevents the production of any book or paper affecting or relating to the company's property or affairs.

(2) Such a person commits an offence if after the commencement of the winding up he attempts to account for any part of the company's property by fictitious losses or expenses; and he is deemed to have committed that offence if he has so attempted at any meeting of the company's creditors within the 12 months immediately preceding the commencement of the winding up.

(3) For purposes of this section, **'officer'** includes a shadow director.

(4) It is a defence —

    (a) for a person charged under paragraph (a), (b) or (c) of subsection (1) to prove that he had no intent to defraud, and

    (b) for a person charged under paragraph (e) of that subsection to prove that he had no intent to conceal the state of affairs of the company or to defeat the law.

(5) A person guilty of an offence under this section is liable to imprisonment or a fine, or both.

SEC. 627 Falsification of company's books

627(1) When a company is being wound up, an officer or contributory of the company commits an offence if he destroys, mutilates, alters or falsifies any books, papers or securities, or makes or is privy to the making of any false or fraudulent entry in any register, book or account or document belonging to the company with intent to defraud or deceive any person.

(2) A person guilty of an offence under this section is liable to imprisonment or a fine, or both.

SEC. 628 Material omissions from statements relating to company affairs

628(1) When a company is being wound up, whether by or under the supervision of the court or voluntarily, any person, being a past or present officer of the company, commits an offence if he makes any material omission in any statement relating to the company's affairs.

(2) When a company has been ordered to be wound up by the court, or has passed a resolution for voluntary winding up, any such person is deemed to have committed that offence if, prior to the winding up, he has made any material omission in any such statement.

(3) For purposes of this section, **'officer'** includes a shadow director.

(4) It is a defence for a person charged under this section to prove that he had no intent to defraud.

(5) A person guilty of an offence under this section is liable to imprisonment or a fine, or both.

SEC. 629 False representations to creditors

629(1) When a company is being wound up, whether by or under the supervision of the court or voluntarily, any person, being a past or present officer of the company —

(a) commits an offence if he makes any false representation or commits any other fraud for the purpose of obtaining the consent of the company's creditors or any of them to an agreement with reference to the company's affairs or to the winding up, and

(b) is deemed to have committed that offence if, prior to the winding up, he has made any false representation, or committed any other fraud, for that purpose.

(2) For purposes of this section, **'officer'** includes a shadow director.

(3) A person guilty of an offence under this section is liable to imprisonment or a fine, or both.

SEC. 630 Responsibility of individuals for company's fraudulent trading

630(1) If in the course of the winding up of a company it appears that any business of the company has been carried on with intent to defraud creditors of the company or creditors of any other person, or for any fraudulent purpose, the following has effect.

(2) The court, on the application of the liquidator, may declare that any persons who were knowingly parties to the carrying on of the business in the manner above mentioned are to be liable to make such contributions (if any) to the company's assets as the court thinks proper.

(3) On the hearing of the application, the liquidator may himself give evidence or call witnesses.

(4) Where the court makes such a declaration, it may give such further directions as it thinks proper for giving effect to the declaration; and in particular, the court may —

(a) provide for the liability of any person under the declaration to be a charge on any debt or obligation due from the company to him, or on any mortgage or charge or any interest in a mortgage or charge on assets of the company held by or vested in him, or any person on his behalf, or any person claiming as assignee from or through the person liable or any person acting on his behalf, and

(b) from time to time make such further order as may be necessary for enforcing any charge imposed under this subsection.

(5) For purposes of subsection (4), **'assignee'** —

(a) includes a person to whom or in whose favour, by the directions of the person made liable, the debt, obligation, mortgage or charge was created, issued or transferred or the interest created, but

(b) does not include an assignee for valuable consideration (not including consideration by way of marriage) given in good faith and without notice of any of the matters on the ground of which the declaration is made.

(5A) Where the court makes a declaration under subsection (2) above in relation to a person who is a creditor of the company, it may direct that the whole or any part of any debt owed by the company to that person and any interest thereon shall rank in priority after all other debts owed by the company and after any interest on those debts.

(6) This section has effect notwithstanding that the person concerned may be criminally liable in respect of matters on the ground of which the declaration under subsection (2) is to be made: and where the declaration is made in the case of a winding up in England and Wales, it is deemed a final judgment within section 1(1)(g) of the Bankruptcy Act 1914.

SEC. 631 Assessment of damages against delinquent directors, etc.

631(1) The following applies if in the course of winding up a company it appears that a person who has taken part in its formation or promotion, or any past or present director, manager or liquidator, or an officer of the company, has misapplied or retained or become liable or accountable for any money or property of the company, or been guilty of any misfeasance or breach of trust in relation to the company.

(2) The court may, on the application of the official receiver or the liquidator, or of any creditor or contributory, examine into the conduct of the promoter, director, manager, liquidator or officer and compel him—

(a) to repay or restore the money or property, or any part of it, respectively with interest at such rate as the court thinks just, or

(b) to contribute such sum to the company's assets by way of compensation in respect of the misapplication, retainer, misfeasance or breach of trust as the court thinks just.

(3) This section has effect notwithstanding that the offence is one for which the offencer may be criminally liable.

(4) If in the case of a winding up in England and Wales an order for payment of money is made under this section, the order is deemed a final judgment within section 1(1)(g) of the Bankruptcy Act 1914.

SEC. 632 Prosecution of delinquent officers and members of company

632(1) If it appears to the court in the course of a winding up by, or subject to the supervision of, the court that any past or present officer, or any member, of the company has been guilty of any offence in relation to the company for which he is criminally liable, the court may (either on the application of a person interested in the winding up or of its own motion) direct the liquidator to refer the matter to the prosecuting authority.

(2) **'The prosecuting authority'** means —

(a) in the case of a winding up in England and Wales, the Director of Public Prosecutions, and

(b) in the case of a winding up in Scotland, the Lord Advocate.

(3) If it appears to the liquidator in the course of a voluntary winding up that any past or present officer of the company, or any member of it, has been guilty of any offence in relation to the company for which he is criminally liable, he shall —

(a) forthwith report the matter to the prosecuting authority, and

(b) furnish to that authority such information and give to him such access to and facilities for inspecting and taking copies of documents (being information or documents in the possession or under the control of the liquidator and relating to the matter in question) as the authority requires.

(4) Where a report is made to him under subsection (3), the prosecuting authority may, if he thinks fit, refer the matter to the Secretary of State for further enquiry; and the Secretary of State —

(a) shall thereupon investigate the matter, and

(b) for the purpose of his investigation may exercise any of the powers which are exercisable by inspectors appointed under section 431 or 432 to investigate a company's affairs.

(5) If it appears to the court in the course of a voluntary winding up that any past or present officer of the company, or any member of it, has been guilty as above-mentioned, and that no report with respect to the matter has been made by the liquidator to the prosecuting authority under subsection (3), the court may (on the application of any person interested in the winding up or of its own motion) direct the liquidator to make such a report; and on a report being made accordingly this section has effect as though the report had been made in pursuance of subsection (3).

SEC. 633 Obligations arising under sec. 632

633(1) For the purpose of an investigation by the Secretary of State under section 632(4), any obligation imposed on a person by any provision of this Act to produce documents or give information to, or otherwise to assist, inspectors appointed as mentioned in that subsection is to be regarded as an obligation similarly to assist the Secretary of State in his investigation.

(2) An answer given by a person to a question put to him in exercise of the powers conferred by section 632(4) may be used in evidence against him.

(3) Where criminal proceedings are instituted by the prosecuting authority or the Secretary of State following any report or reference under section 632, it is the duty of the liquidator and every officer and agent of the company past and present (other than the defendant or defender) to give to that authority or the Secretary of State (as the case may be) all assistance in connection with the prosecution which he is reasonably able to give.

For this purpose 'agent' includes any banker or solicitor of the company and any person employed by the company as auditor, whether that person is or is not an officer of the company.

(4) If a person fails or neglects to give assistance in the manner required by subsection (3), the court may, on the application of the prosecuting authority or the Secretary of State (as the case may be) direct the person to comply with that subsection; and if the application is made with respect to a liquidator, the court may (unless it appears that the failure or neglect to comply was due to the liquidator not having in his hands sufficient assets of the company to enable him to do so) direct that the costs shall be borne by the liquidator personally.

SUPPLEMENTARY PROVISIONS AS TO WINDING UP

SEC. 634 Disqualification for appointment as liquidator

634(1) A body corporate is not qualified for appointment as liquidator of a company, whether in a winding up by or under the supervision of the court or in a voluntary winding up.

(2) Any appointment made in contravention of this section is void; and a body corporate which acts as liquidator of a company is liable to a fine.

SEC. 635 Corrupt inducement affecting appointment as liquidator

635 A person who gives or agrees or offers to give to any member or creditor of a company any valuable consideration with a view to securing his own appointment or nomination, or to securing or preventing the appointment or nomination of some person other than himself, as the company's liquidator is liable to a fine.

SEC. 636 Enforcement of liquidator's duty to make returns, etc.

636(1) If a liquidator who has made any default —

(a) in filing, delivering or making any return, account or other document, or

(b) in giving any notice which he is by law required to file, deliver, make or give,

fails to make good the default within 14 days after the service on him of a notice requiring him to do so, the court has the following powers.

(2) On an application made by any creditor or contributory of the company, or by the registrar of companies, the court may make an order directing the liquidator to make good the default within such time as may be specified in the order.

(3) The court's order may provide that all costs of and incidental to the application shall be borne by the liquidator.

(4) Nothing in this section prejudices the operation of any enactment imposing penalties on a liquidator in respect of any such default as is mentioned above.

SEC. 637 Notification that company is in liquidation

637(1) When a company is being wound up, whether by or under supervision of the court or voluntarily, every invoice, order for goods or business letter issued by or on behalf of the company, or a liquidator of the company, or a receiver or manager of the company's property, being a document on or in which the name of the company appears, shall contain a statement that the company is being wound up.

(2) If default is made in complying with this section, the company and any of the following persons who knowingly and wilfully authorises or permits the default, namely, any officer of the company, any liquidator of the company and any receiver or manager, is liable to a fine.

SEC. 638 In a winding up, certain documents exempt from stamp duty

638(1) In the case of a winding up by the court, or of a creditors' voluntary winding up, the following has effect as regards exemption from duties chargeable under the enactments relating to stamp duties.

(2) If the company is registered in England and Wales, the following documents are exempt from stamp duty —

(a) every assurance relating solely to freehold or leasehold property, or to any estate, right or interest in, any real or personal property, which forms part of the company's assets and which, after the execution of the assurance, either at law or in equity, is or remains part of those assets, and

(b) every writ, order, certificate, or other instrument or writing relating solely to the property of any company which is being wound up as mentioned in subsection (1), or to any proceeding under such a winding up.

'Assurance' here includes deed, conveyance, assignment and surrender.

(3) If the company is registered in Scotland, the following documents are exempt from stamp duty —

(a) every conveyance relating solely to property which forms part of the company's assets and which, after the execution of the conveyance, is or remains the company's property for the benefit of its creditors,

(b) every articles of roup or sale, submission and every other instrument and writing whatsoever relating solely to the company's property, and

(c) every deed or writing forming part of the proceedings in the winding up.

'Conveyance' here includes assignation, instrument, discharge, writing and deed.

SEC. 639 Company's books to be evidence

639 Where a company is being wound up, all books and papers of the company and of the liquidators are, as between

the contributories of the company, prima facie evidence of the truth of all matters purporting to be recorded in them.

SEC. 640 Disposal of books and papers

640(1) When a company has been wound up and is about to be dissolved, its books and papers and those of the liquidators may be disposed of as follows —

   (a) in the case of a winding up by or subject to the supervision of the court, in such way as the court directs;

   (b) in the case of a members' voluntary winding up, in such way as the company by extraordinary resolution directs, and

   (c) in the case of a creditors' voluntary winding up, in such way as the committee of inspection or, if there is no such committee, the company's creditors may direct.

(2) After 5 years from the company's dissolution no responsibility rests on the company, the liquidators, or any person to whom the custody of the books and papers has been committed, by reason of any book or paper not being forthcoming to a person claiming to be interested in it.

(3) Provision may be made by general rules —

   (a) for enabling the Secretary of State to prevent, for such period as he thinks proper (but not exceeding 5 years from the company's dissolution), the destruction of the books and papers of a company which has been wound up, and

   (b) for enabling any creditor or contributory of the company to make representations to the Secretary of State and to appeal to the court from any direction which may be given by the Secretary of State in the matter.

(4) If a person acts in contravention of general rules made for the purposes of this section, or of any direction of the Secretary of State under them, he is liable to a fine.

SEC. 641 Information as to pending liquidations

641(1) If the winding up of a company is not concluded within one year after its commencement, the liquidator shall, at such intervals as may be prescribed, until the winding up is concluded, send to the registrar of companies a statement in the prescribed form and containing the prescribed particulars with respect to the proceedings in, and position of, the liquidation.

(2) If a liquidator fails to comply with this section, he is liable to a fine and, for continued contravention, to a daily default fine.

SEC. 642 Unclaimed assets (England and Wales)

642(1) This section applies if, where a company is being wound up in England and Wales, it appears (either from any statement sent to the registrar under section 641 or otherwise) that a liquidator has in his hands or under his control any money —

   (a) representing unclaimed or undistributed assets of the company which have remained unclaimed or undistributed for 6 months after the date of their receipt, or

   (b) held by the company in trust in respect of dividends or other sums due to any person as a member of the company.

(2) The liquidator shall forthwith pay the money in question to the Insolvency Services Account at the Bank of England, and is entitled to the prescribed certificate of receipt for the money so paid, and that certificate is an effectual discharge to him in respect of it.

(3) For the purpose of ascertaining and getting in any money payable into the Bank of England in pursuance of this section, the like powers may be exercised, and by the like authority, as are exercisable under section 153 of the Bankruptcy Act 1914 for the purpose of ascertaining and getting in the sums, funds and dividends referred to in that section.

(4) Any person claiming to be entitled to money paid into the Bank of England under this section may apply to the Secretary of State for payment; and the Secretary of State may, on a certificate by the liquidator that the person claiming is entitled, make an order for payment to that person of the sum due.

(5) Any person dissatisfied with a decision of the Secretary of State in respect of a claim made under this section may appeal to the High Court.

SEC. 643 Unclaimed dividends, etc. (Scotland)

643(1) The following applies where a company registered in Scotland has been wound up, and is about to be dissolved.

(2) The liquidator shall lodge in an appropriate bank or institution as defined in section 73(1) (interpretation) of the Bankruptcy (Scotland) Act 1985 (not being a bank or institution in or of which the liquidator is acting partner, manager, agent or cashier) in the name of the Accountant of Court the whole unclaimed dividends and unapplied or undistributable balances, and the deposit receipts shall be transmitted to the Accountant of Court.

(3) The provisions of section 58 of the Bankruptcy (Scotland) Act 1985 (so far as consistent with this Act) apply with any necessary modifications to sums lodged in a bank or institution under this section as they apply to sums deposited under that section.

SEC. 644 Resolutions passed at adjourned meetings

644 Where a resolution is passed at an adjourned meeting of a company's creditors or contributories, the resolution is treated for all purposes as having been passed on the date on which it was in fact passed, and not as having been passed on any earlier date.

SUPPLEMENTARY POWERS OF COURT

SEC. 645 Meetings to ascertain wishes of creditors or contributories

645(1) The court may —

   (a) as to all matters relating to the winding up of a company, have regard to the wishes of the creditors or contributories (as proved to it by any sufficient evidence), and

   (b) if it thinks fit, for the purpose of ascertaining those wishes, direct meetings of the creditors or contributories to be called, held and conducted in such manner as the court directs, and appoint a person to act as chairman of any such meeting and report the result of it to the court.

(2) In the case of creditors, regard shall be had to the value of each creditor's debt.

(3) In the case of contributories, regard shall be had to the number of votes conferred on each contributory by this Act or the articles.

SEC. 646 Judicial notice of signature of court officers

646 In all proceedings under this Part, all courts, judges and persons judicially acting, and all officers, judicial or ministerial, of any court, or employed in enforcing the process of any court shall take judicial notice —

   (a) of the signature of any officer of the High Court or of a county court in England and Wales, or of the Court of Session or a sheriff court in Scotland, or of the High Court in Northern Ireland, and also

(b) of the official seal or stamp of the several offices of the High Court in England and Wales or Northern Ireland, or of the Court of Session, appended to or impressed on any document made, issued or signed under the provisions of this Act, or any official copy of such a document.

SEC. 647 Commission for receiving evidence

647(1) When a company is wound up in England and Wales or in Scotland, the court may refer the whole or any part of the examination of witnesses —

(a) to a specified county court in England and Wales, or

(b) to the sheriff principal for a specified sheriffdom in Scotland, or

(c) to the High Court in Northern Ireland or a specified Northern Ireland County Court,

(**'specified'** meaning specified in the order of the winding-up court).

(2) Any person exercising jurisdiction as a judge of the court to which the reference is made (or, in Scotland, the sheriff principal to whom it is made) shall then, by virtue of this section, be a commissioner for the purpose of taking the evidence of those witnesses.

(3) The judge or sheriff principal has in the matter referred the same power of summoning and examining witnesses, of requiring the production and delivery of documents, of punishing defaults by witnesses, and of allowing costs and expenses to witnesses, as the court which made the winding-up order.

These powers are in addition to any which the judge or sheriff principal might lawfully exercise apart from this section.

(4) The examination so taken shall be returned or reported to the court which made the order in such manner as that court requests.

(5) This section extends to Northern Ireland.

SEC. 648 Court order for examination of persons in Scotland

648(1) The court may direct the examination in Scotland of any person for the time being in Scotland (whether a contributory of the company or not), in regard to the trade, dealings, affairs or property of any company in course of being wound up, or of any person being a contributory of the company, so far as the company may be interested by reason of his being a contributory.

(2) The order or commission to take the examination shall be directed to the sheriff principal of the sheriffdom in which the person to be examined is residing or happens to be for the time; and the sheriff principal shall summon the person to appear before him at a time and place to be specified in the summons for examination on oath as a witness or as a haver, and to produce any books or papers called for which are in his possession or power.

(3) The sheriff principal may take the examination either orally or on written interrogatories, and shall report the same in writing in the usual form to the court, and shall transmit with the report the books and papers produced, if the originals are required and specified by the order or commission, or otherwise copies or extracts authenticated by the sheriff.

(4) If a person so summoned fails to appear at the time and place specified, or refuses to be examined or to make the production required, the sheriff principal shall proceed against him as a witness or haver duly cited; and failing to appear or refusing to give evidence or make production may be proceeded against by the law of Scotland.

(5) The sheriff principal is entitled to such fees, and the witness is entitled to such allowances, as sheriffs principal when acting as commissioners under appointment from the Court of Session and as witnesses and havers are entitled to in the like cases according to the law and practice of Scotland.

(6) If any objection is stated to the sheriff principal by the witness, either on the ground of his incompetency as a witness, or as to the production required, or on any other ground, the sheriff principal may, if he thinks fit, report the objection to the court, and suspend the examination of the witness until it has been disposed of by the court.

SEC. 649 Costs of application for leave to proceed (Scottish companies)

649 Where a petition or application for leave to proceed with an action or proceeding against a company which is being wound up in Scotland is unopposed and is granted by the court, the costs of the petition or application shall, unless the court otherwise directs, be added to the amount of the petitioner's or applicant's claim against the company.

SEC. 650 Affidavits, etc., in United Kingdom and overseas

650(1) An affidavit required to be sworn under or for the purposes of this Part may be sworn in the United Kingdom or elsewhere in Her Majesty's dominions, before any court, judge or person lawfully authorised to take and receive affidavits, or before any of Her Majesty's consuls or vice-consuls in any place outside Her dominions.

(2) All courts, judges, justices, commissioners and persons acting judicially shall take judicial notice of the seal or stamp or signature (as the case may be) of any such court, judge, person, consul or vice-consul attached, appended or subscribed to any such affidavit, or to any other document to be used for the purposes of this Part.''

Chapter VI — Matters Arising Subsequent to Winding Up

SEC. 651 Power of court to declare dissolution of company void

651(1) [Declaration by court, on application] Where a company has been dissolved, the court may, on an application made for the purpose by the liquidator of the company or by any other person appearing to the court to be interested, make an order, on such terms as the court thinks fit, declaring the dissolution to have been void.

History
In s. 651(1) the words "at any time within 2 years of the date of the dissolution" formerly appearing after the words "the court may" omitted by CA 1989, s. 141(2) as from 16 November 1989 (see CA 1989, s. 215(1)(a)). Previously the words "12 years" were to have been substituted for the words "2 years" by Insolvency Act 1985, s. 109 and Sch. 6, para. 45 from a day to be appointed (see S.I. 1986 No. 1924 (C. 71), art. 4(a)) but such day was never appointed and from 1 April 1990 Insolvency Act 1986, Sch. 6, para. 45 repealed by CA 1989, s. 212 and Sch. 24 (see S.I. 1990 No. 355 (C. 13), art. 5(1)(c)).

651(2) [Proceedings] Thereupon such proceedings may be taken as might have been taken if the company had not been dissolved.

651(3) [Copy of order to registrar, penalty on default] It is the duty of the person on whose application the order was made, within 7 days after its making (or such further time as the court may allow), to deliver to the registrar of companies for registration an office copy of the order.

If the person fails to do so, he is liable to a fine and, for continued contravention, to a daily default fine.

651(4) [Timing of application] Subject to the following provisions, an application under this section may not be made after the end of the period of two years from the date of the dissolution of the company.

651(5) [Applications for damages] An application for the purpose of bringing proceedings against the company—

(a) for damages in respect of personal injuries (including any sum claimed by virtue of section 1(2)(c) of the Law Reform (Miscellaneous Provisions) Act 1934 (funeral expenses)), or

(b) for damages under the Fatal Accidents Act 1976 or the Damages (Scotland) Act 1976,

may be made at any time; but no order shall be made on such an application if it appears to the court that the proceedings would fail by virtue of any enactment as to the time within which proceedings must be brought.

651(6) [Qualification to sec. 651(5)] Nothing in subsection (5) affects the power of the court on making an order under this section to direct that the period between the dissolution of the company and the making of the order shall not count for the purposes of any such enactment.

651(7) ["Personal injuries" in sec. 651(5)(a)] In subsection (5)(a) **"personal injuries"** includes any disease and any impairment of a person's physical or mental condition.

History
S. 651(4)–(7) added by CA 1989, s. 141(3) as from 16 November 1989 (see CA 1989, s. 215(1)(a)).

Note
Re s. 651 and matters before commencement of CA 1989 amendments, see CA 1989, s. 141(4), (5).

SEC. 652   Registrar may strike defunct companies off register

652(1) [Registrar's letter] If the registrar of companies has reasonable cause to believe that a company is not carrying on business or in operation, he may send to the company by post a letter inquiring whether the company is carrying on business or in operation.

652(2) [Where no answer to registrar's letter] If the registrar does not within one month of sending the letter receive any answer to it, he shall within 14 days after the expiration of that month send to the company by post a registered letter referring to the first letter, and stating that no answer to it has been received, and that if an answer is not received to the second letter within one month from its date, a notice will be published in the Gazette with a view to striking the company's name off the register.

652(3) [Notice of proposed dissolution] If the registrar either receives an answer to the effect that the company is not carrying on business or in operation, or does not within one month after sending the second letter receive any answer, he may publish in the Gazette, and send to the company by post, a notice that at the expiration of 3 months from the date of that notice the name of the company mentioned in it will, unless cause is shown to the contrary, be struck off the register and the company will be dissolved.

652(4)   [Notice if no liquidator etc.]   If, in a case where a company is being wound up, the registrar has reasonable cause to believe either that no liquidator is acting, or that the affairs of the company are fully wound up, and the returns required to be made by the liquidator have not been made for a period of 6 consecutive months, the registrar shall publish in the Gazette and send to the company or the liquidator (if any) a like notice as is provided in subsection (3).

652(5)   [Striking name off register, notice in Gazette]   At the expiration of the time mentioned in the notice the registrar may, unless cause to the contrary is previously shown by the company, strike its name off the register, and shall publish notice of this in the Gazette; and on the publication of that notice in the Gazette the company is dissolved.

652(6)   [Qualification to sec. 652(5)]   However —

   (a) the liability (if any) of every director, managing officer and member of the company continues and may be enforced as if the company had not been dissolved, and

   (b) nothing in subsection (5) affects the power of the court to wind up a company the name of which has been struck off the register.

652(7)   [Addresses for notices]   A notice to be sent to a liquidator under this section may be addressed to him at his last known place of business; and a letter or notice to be sent under this section to a company may be addressed to the company at its registered office or, if no office has been registered, to the care of some officer of the company.

If there is no officer of the company whose name and address are known to the registrar of companies, the letter or notice may be sent to each of the persons who subscribed the memorandum, addressed to him at the address mentioned in the memorandum.

SEC. 653   Objection to striking off by person aggrieved

653(1)   [Application]   The following applies if a company or any member or creditor of it feels aggrieved by the company having been struck off the register.

653(2)   [On application court may order restoration of name to register]   The court, on an application by the company or the member or creditor made before the expiration of 20 years from publication in the Gazette of notice under section 652, may, if satisfied that the company was at the time of the striking off carrying on business or in operation, or otherwise that it is just that the company be restored to the register, order the company's name to be restored.

653(3)   [Effect of order etc.]   On an office copy of the order being delivered to the registrar of companies for registration the company is deemed to have continued in existence as if its name had not been struck off; and the court may by the order give such directions and make such provisions as seem just for placing the company and all other persons in the same position (as nearly as may be) as if the company's name had not been struck off.

SEC. 654   Property of dissolved company to be bona vacantia

654(1)   **[All property and rights vested in Crown etc.]**   When a company is dissolved, all property and rights whatsoever vested in or held on trust for the company immediately before its dissolution (including leasehold property, but not including property held by the company on trust for any other person) are deemed to be bona vacantia and—

(a) accordingly belong to the Crown, or to the Duchy of Lancaster or to the Duke of Cornwall for the time being (as the case may be), and

(b) vest and may be dealt with in the same manner as other bona vacantia accruing to the Crown, to the Duchy of Lancaster or to the Duke of Cornwall.

654(2)   **[Orders under sec. 651, 653]**   Except as provided by the section next following, the above has effect subject and without prejudice to any order made by the court under section 651 or 653.

SEC. 655   Effect on sec. 654 of company's revival after dissolution

655(1)   **[Disposition of interest once sec. 654 order made]**   The person in whom any property or right is vested by section 654 may dispose of, or of an interest in, that property or right notwithstanding that an order may be made under section 651 or 653.

655(2)   **[Effect of sec. 654 order]**   Where such an order is made—

(a) it does not affect the disposition (but without prejudice to the order so far as it relates to any other property or right previously vested in or held on trust for the company) and

(b) the Crown or, as the case may be, the Duke of Cornwall shall pay to the company an amount equal to—

   (i) the amount of any consideration received for the property or right, or interest therein, or

   (ii) the value of any such consideration at the time of the disposition,

or, if no consideration was received, an amount equal to the value of the property, right or interest disposed of, as at the date of the disposition.

655(3)   **[Where liability accrued to Duchy of Lancaster before order under sec. 651, 653]**   Where a liability accrues under subsection (2) in respect of any property or right which, before the order under section 651 or 653 was made, had accrued as bona vacantia to the Duchy of Lancaster, the Attorney General of the Duchy shall represent Her Majesty in any proceedings arising in connection with that liability.

655(4)   **[Where liability accrued to Duchy of Cornwall before order under sec. 651, 653]**   Where a liability accrues under subsection (2) in respect of any property or right which, before the order under section 651 or 653 was made, had accrued as bona vacantia to the Duchy of Cornwall, such persons as the Duke of Cornwall (or other possessor for the time being of the Duchy) may appoint shall represent the Duke (or other possessor) in any proceedings arising out of that liability.

655(5) **[Application]** This section applies in relation to the disposition of any property, right or interest on or after 22nd December 1981, whether the company concerned was dissolved before, on or after that day.

SEC. 656 Crown disclaimer of property vesting as bona vacantia

656(1) **[Disclaimer by notice]** Where property vests in the Crown under section 654, the Crown's title to it under that section may be disclaimed by a notice signed by the Crown representative, that is to say the Treasury Solicitor, or, in relation to property in Scotland, the Queen's and Lord Treasurer's Remembrancer.

656(2) **[Waiver of right to execute notice]** The right to execute a notice of disclaimer under this section may be waived by or on behalf of the Crown either expressly or by taking possession or other act envincing that intention.

656(3) **[Requirements for notice of disclaimer to be of effect]** A notice of disclaimer under this section is of no effect unless it is executed —

(a) within 12 months of the date on which the vesting of the property under section 654 came to the notice of the Crown representative, or

(b) if an application in writing is made to the Crown representative by any person interested in the property requiring him to decide whether he will or will not disclaim, within a period of 3 months after the receipt of the application or such further period as may be allowed by the court which would have had jurisdiction to wind up the company if it had not been dissolved.

[The next page is 23,801]

656(4) **[Statements in notice sufficient evidence]** A statement in a notice of disclaimer of any property under this section that the vesting of it came to the notice of the Crown representative on a specified date, or that no such application as above mentioned was received by him with respect to the property before a specified date, is sufficient evidence of the fact stated, until the contrary is proved.

656(5) **[Notice to registrar, publication in Gazette, distribution]** A notice of disclaimer under this section shall be delivered to the registrar of companies and retained and registered by him; and copies of it shall be published in the Gazette and sent to any persons who have given the Crown representative notice that they claim to be interested in the property.

656(6) **[Application]** This section applies to property vested in the Duchy of Lancaster or the Duke of Cornwall under section 654 as if for references to the Crown and the Crown representative there were respectively substituted references to the Duchy of Lancaster and to the Solicitor to that Duchy, or to the Duke of Cornwall and to the Solicitor to the Duchy of Cornwall, as the case may be.

SEC. 657   Effect of Crown disclaimer under sec. 656

657(1) **[Effect of disclaimer]** Where notice of disclaimer is executed under section 656 as respects any property, that property is deemed not to have vested in the Crown under section 654.

657(2) **[Property in England and Wales]** As regards property in England and Wales, section 178(4) and sections 179 to 182 of the Insolvency Act shall apply as if the property had been disclaimed by the liquidator under the said section 91 immediately before the dissolution of the company.

History
S. 657(2) substituted by Insolvency Act 1985, s. 109(1) and Sch. 6, para. 46 and further amended by Insolvency Act 1986, s. 439(1) and Sch. 13, Pt. I as from 29 December 1986 (see S.I. 1986 No. 1924 (C. 71)).

Note
The reference to s. 91 should be to s. 178 to 180.

657(3) **[Re property in Scotland]** As regards property in Scotland, the following 4 subsections apply.

657(4) **[Operation in Scotland]** The Crown's disclaimer operates to determine, as from the date of the disclaimer, the rights, interests and liabilities of the company, and the property of the company, in or in respect of the property disclaimed; but it does not (except so far as is necessary for the purpose of releasing the company and its property from liability) affect the rights or liabilities of any other person.

657(5) **[Scotland — court order on application]** The court may, on application by a person who either claims an interest in disclaimed property or is under a liability not discharged by this Act in respect of disclaimed property, and on hearing such persons as it thinks fit, make an order for the vesting of the property in or its delivery to any persons entitled to it, or to whom it may seem just that the property should be delivered by way of compensation for such liability, or a trustee for him, and on such terms as the court thinks just.

657(6) **[Effect of sec. 657(5) order]** On such a vesting order being made, the property comprised in it vests accordingly in the person named in that behalf in the order, without conveyance or assignation for that purpose.

657(7)   [Protection of third parties re lease in Scotland]   Part II of Schedule 20 has effect for the protection of third parties where the property disclaimed is held under a lease.

SEC. 658   Liability for rentcharge on company's land after dissolution

658(1)   [Application of IA, sec. 180]   Section 180 of the Insolvency Act shall apply to land in England and Wales which by operation of law vests subject to a rentcharge in the crown or any other person on the dissolution of a company as it applies to land so vesting on a disclaimer under that section.

History
S. 658(1) substituted by Insolvency 1985, s. 109(1) and Sch. 6, para. 47 and further amended by Insolvency Act 1986, s. 439(1) and Sch. 13, Pt. I as from 29 December 1986 (see S.I. 1986 No. 1924 (C. 71)).

658(2)   ["Company"]   In this section **"company"** includes any body corporate.

Chapter VII — Miscellaneous Provisions About Winding Up

659–664   (Repealed by Insolvency Act 1986, sec. 438 and Sch. 12 as from 29 December 1986.)

Note
For the corresponding new provisions of the 1986 consolidation, see the CCH table of destinations at page 58,201.

History
In regard to the date of the above repeal, see Insolvency Act 1986, s. 443 and S.I. 1986 No. 1924 (C. 71). There were some amendments and repeals by Insolvency Act 1985 which very briefly came into force (see S.I. 1986 No. 1924 (C. 71)) — except the repeal of s. 663 for England and Wales from 1 March 1986 (see S.I. 1986 No. 185 (C. 7)). See Insolvency Act 1985, Sch. 6, 10 for details. The sections originally read as follows:

"SEC. 659 Power to make over assets to employees

659(1) On the winding up of a company (whether by the court or voluntarily), the liquidator may, subject to the following provisions of this section, make any payment which the company has, before the commencement of the winding up, decided to make under section 719 (power to provide for employees or former employees on cessation or transfer of business).

(2) The power which a company may exercise by virtue only of that section may be exercised by the liquidator after the winding up has commenced if, after the company's liabilities have been fully satisfied and provision has been made for the costs of the winding up, the exercise of that power has been sanctioned by such a resolution of the company as would be required of the company itself by section 719(3) before that commencement, if paragraph (b) of that subsection were omitted and any other requirement applicable to its exercise by the company had been met.

(3) Any payment which may be made by a company under this section (that is, a payment after the commencement of its winding up) may be made out of the company's assets which are available to the members on the winding up.

(4) On a winding up by the court, the exercise by the liquidator of his powers under this section is subject to the court's control, and any creditor or contributory may apply to the court with respect to any exercise or proposed exercise of the power.

(5) Subsections (1) and (2) above have effect notwithstanding anything in any rule of law or in section 597 of this Act (property of company after satisfaction of liabilities to be distributed among members).

SEC. 660 Separate accounts of particular estates (England and Wales)

660(1) An account shall be kept by the Secretary of State of the receipts and payments in the winding up of each company in England and Wales.

(2) When the cash balance standing to the credit of the account of any company is in excess of the amount which, in the opinion of the committee of inspection, is required for the time being to answer demands in respect of the company's estate, the Secretary of State shall on the request of the committee invest the amount not so required in Government securities, to be placed to the credit of that account for the company's benefit.

(3) When any part of the money so invested is, in the opinion of the committee of inspection, required to answer any demands in respect of the company's estate, the Secretary of State shall, on the committee's request, raise such sum as may be required by the sale of such part of those securities as may be necessary.

(4) The dividends on investments under this section shall be paid to the credit of the company.

(5) When the balance at the credit of a company's account in the hands of the Secretary of State exceeds £2,000, and the liquidator gives notice to him that the excess is not required for the purposes of the liquidation, the company is entitled to interest on the excess at such rate as may for the time being be prescribed by order of the Treasury.

(6) The Treasury's power to make orders under this section is exercisable by statutory instrument subject to annulment in pursuance of a resolution of either House of Parliament.

SEC. 661 Officers and remuneration (England and Wales)

661(1) The Secretary of State may, with the approval of the Treasury, appoint such additional officers as may be required by him for the execution of this Part as respects England and Wales, and may remove any person so appointed.

(2) The Secretary of State, with the concurrence of the Treasury, shall direct whether any and what remuneration is to be allowed to any officer of, or person attached to, his department performing any duties under this Part in relation to the winding up of companies in England and Wales, and may vary, increase or diminish that remuneration as he (the Secretary of State) thinks fit.

SEC. 662 Returns by officers in winding up (England and Wales)

662 The officers of the courts acting in the winding up of companies in England and Wales shall make to the Secretary of State such returns of the business of their respective courts and offices at such times, and in such manner and form, as may be prescribed; and from these returns the Secretary of State shall cause books to be prepared which shall (under regulations made by him) be open for public information and searches.

SEC. 663 Rules and fees

663(1) The Lord Chancellor may, with the concurrence of the Secretary of State, make general rules for carrying into effect the objects of this Act so far as relates to the winding up of companies in England and Wales.

(2) The Court of Session may by Act of Sederunt make general rules for carrying into effect the objects of this Act so far as relates to the winding up of companies in Scotland.

(3) An answer given by a person to a question put to him in exercise of powers conferred by general rules may be used in evidence against him.

(4) There shall be paid in respect of proceedings under this Act in relation to the winding up of companies in England and Wales such fees as the Lord Chancellor may, with the sanction of the Treasury, direct; and the Treasury may direct by whom and in what manner the fees are to be collected and accounted for.

(5) The powers conferred by this section on the Lord Chancellor, the Court of Session and the Treasury are exercisable by statutory instrument; and a statutory instrument containing general rules shall be laid before Parliament after being made.

(6) Fees in respect of proceedings under this Act in relation to the winding up of companies shall be paid into the Consolidated Fund.

SEC. 664 Power to increase monetary limits

664(1) The Secretary of State may by regulations in a statutory instrument increase or reduce any of the money sums for the time being specified in the following provisions of this Part —

> section 512(2),
> section 515(3),
> section 518(1)(a),
> section 542(4),
> section 622(3),
> section 624(1)(a) and (b), and paragraph 12 of Schedule 19.

(2) Regulations shall not be made under this section unless a draft of the statutory instrument containing them has been approved by resolution of each House of Parliament."

PART XXI — WINDING UP OF UNREGISTERED COMPANIES

665–674 (Repealed by Insolvency Act 1986, sec. 438 and Sch. 12 as from 29 December 1986.)

Note

For the corresponding new provisions of the 1986 consolidation, see the CCH table of destinations at page 58,201.

History

In regard to the date of the above repeal, see Insolvency Act 1986, s. 443 and S.I. 1986 No. 1924 (C. 71).

There were some previous repeals to s. 665 by Bankruptcy (Scotland) Act 1985, s. 75(2) and Sch. 8 as from 1 April 1986 (see S.I. 1985 No. 1924 (C. 71)) and to s. 665 and 666(6) by Trustee Savings Bank Act 1985, s. 4(3), 7(3) and Sch. 4 as from 21 July 1986 (see S.I. 1986 No. 1223 (C. 36)). There were other amendments and repeals by Insolvency Act 1985 which were very briefly in force — see Insolvency Act 1985, Sch. 6, 10 and S.I. 1986 No. 1924 (C. 71) for details. Prior to the Insolvency Act 1986 repeals the sections read as follows:

"SEC. 665 Meaning of 'unregistered company'

665 For the purposes of this Part, the expression **'unregistered company'** includes any partnership, any association and any company, with the following exceptions —

> (a) a railway company incorporated by Act of Parliament,

> (b) a company registered in any part of the United Kingdom under the Joint Stock Companies Acts or under the legislation (past or present) relating to companies in Great Britain,

> (c) a partnership, association or company which consists of less than 8 members and is not a foreign partnership, association or company,

> (d) a limited partnership.

SEC. 666 Winding up of unregistered companies

666(1) Subject to the provisions of this Part, any unregistered company may be wound up under this Act; and all the provisions of this Act about winding up apply to an unregistered company, with the exceptions and additions mentioned in the following subsections.

(2) If an unregistered company has a principal place of business situated in Northern Ireland, it shall not be wound up under this Part unless it has a principal place of business situated in England and Wales or Scotland, or in both England and Wales and Scotland.

(3) For the purpose of determining a court's winding-up jurisdiction, an unregistered company is deemed —

> (a) to be registered in England and Wales or Scotland, according as its principal place of business is situated in England and Wales or Scotland, or

(b) if it has a principal place of business situated in both countries, to be registered in both countries;

and the principal place of business situated in that part of Great Britain in which proceedings are being instituted is, for all purposes of the winding up, deemed to be the registered office of the company.

(4) No unregistered company shall be wound up under this Act voluntarily or subject to supervision.

(5) The circumstances in which an unregistered company may be wound up are as follows —

(a) if the company is dissolved, or has ceased to carry on business, or is carrying on business only for the purpose of winding up its affairs;

(b) if the company is unable to pay its debts;

(c) if the court is of opinion that it is just and equitable that the company should be wound up.

(6) (Repealed by Trustee Savings Bank Act 1985, s. 4(3), 7(3) and Sch. 4 from 21 July 1986 (see S.I. 1986 No. 1223 (C. 36)).

(7) In the case of a limited partnership, the provisions of this Act about winding up apply with such modifications (if any) as may be provided by rules made by statutory instrument by the Lord Chancellor with the concurrence of the Secretary of State, and with the substitution of general partners for directors.

(8) In Scotland, an unregistered company which the Court of Session has jurisdiction to wind up may be wound up by the court if there is subsisting a floating charge over property comprised in the company's property and undertaking, and the court is satisfied that the security of the creditor entitled to the benefit of the floating charge is in jeopardy.

For this purpose a creditor's security is deemed to be in jeopardy if the court is satisfied that events have occurred or are about to occur which render it unreasonable in the creditor's interests that the company should retain power to dispose of the property which is subject to the floating charge.

SEC. 667 Inability to pay debts: unpaid creditor for £750 or more

667(1) An unregistered company is deemed (for purposes of section 666) unable to pay its debts if there is a creditor, by assignment or otherwise, to whom the company is indebted in a sum exceeding £750 then due and —

(a) the creditor has served on the company, by leaving at its principal place of business, or by delivering to the secretary or some director, manager or principal officer of the company, or by otherwise serving in such manner as the court may approve or direct, a written demand requiring the company to pay the sum due, and

(b) the company has for 3 weeks after the service of the demand neglected to pay the sum or to secure or compound for it to the creditor's satisfaction.

(2) The Secretary of State may by regulations in a statutory instrument increase or reduce the money sum for the time being specified in subsection (1); but —

(a) such regulations shall not be made unless a draft of the statutory instrument containing them has been approved by resolution of each House of Parliament, and

(b) no increase in the sum so specified affects any case in which the winding-up petition was presented before the coming into force of the increase.

SEC. 668 Inability to pay debts: debt remaining unsatisfied after action brought

668 An unregistered company is deemed (for purposes of section 666) unable to pay its debts if an action or other proceeding has been instituted against any member for any debt or demand due, or claimed to be due, from the company, or from him in his character of member, and —

(a) notice in writing of the institution of the action or proceeding has been served on the company by leaving it at the company's principal place of business (or by delivering it to the secretary, or some director, manager or principal officer of the company, or by otherwise serving it in such manner as the court may approve or direct), and

(b) the company has not within 10 days after service of the notice paid, secured or compounded for the debt or demand, or procured the action or proceeding to be stayed or sisted, or indemnified the defendant or defender to his reasonable satisfaction against the action or proceeding, and against all costs, damages and expenses to be incurred by him because of it.

SEC. 669 Inability to pay debts: other cases

669 An unregistered company is deemed (for purposes of section 666) unable to pay its debts —

(a) if in England and Wales execution or other process issued on a judgment, decree or order obtained in any court in favour of a creditor against the company, or any member of it as such, or any person authorised to be sued as nominal defendant on behalf of the company, is returned unsatisfied;

(b) if in Scotland the induciae of a charge for payment on an extract decree, or an extract registered bond, or an extract registered protest, have expired without payment being made;

(c) if in Northern Ireland a certificate of unenforceability has been granted in respect of any judgment, decree or order obtained as mentioned in paragraph (a);

(d) if it is otherwise proved to the satisfaction of the court that the company is unable to pay its debts.

SEC. 670 Oversea company may be wound up, though dissolved

670 Where a company incorporated outside Great Britain which has been carrying on business in Great Britain ceases to carry on business in Great Britain, it may be wound up as an unregistered company under this Act, notwithstanding that it has been dissolved or otherwise ceased to exist as a company under or by virtue of the laws of the country under which it was incorporated.

SEC. 671 Contributories in winding up of unregistered company

671(1) In the event of an unregistered company being wound up, every person is deemed a contributory who is liable to pay or contribute to the payment of any debt or liability of the company, or to pay or contribute to the payment of any sum for the adjustment of the rights of members among themselves, or to pay or contribute to the payment of the costs and expenses of winding up the company.

(2) Every contributory is liable to contribute to the company's assets all sums due from him in respect of any such liability as is mentioned above.

(3) In the case of an unregistered company engaged in or formed for working mines within the stannaries, a past member is not liable to contribute to the assets if he has ceased to be a member for 2 years or more either before the mine ceased to be worked or before the date of the winding up order.

(4) In the event of the death, bankruptcy or insolvency of any contributory, the provisions of this Act with respect to the personal representatives, to the heirs and legatees of heritable of the heritable estate in Scotland of deceased contributories, and to the trustees of bankrupt or insolvent contributories, respectively apply.

SEC. 672 Power of court to stay, sist or restrain proceedings

672 The provisions of this Part with respect to staying, sisting or restraining actions and proceedings against a company at any time after the presentation of a petition for winding up and before the making of a winding up order extend, in the case of an unregistered company, where the application to stay, sist or restrain is presented by a creditor, to actions and proceedings against any contributory of the company.

SEC. 673 Actions stayed on winding up order

673 Where an order has been made for winding up an unregistered company, no action or proceeding shall be proceeded with or commenced against any contributory of the company in respect of any debt of the company, except by leave of the court, and subject to such terms as the court may impose.

SEC. 674 Provisions of this Part to be cumulative

674(1) The provisions of this Part with respect to unregistered companies are in addition to and not in restriction of any provisions in Part XX with respect to winding up companies by the court; and the court or liquidator may exercise any powers or do any act in the case of unregistered companies which might be exercised or done by it or him in winding up companies formed and registered under this Act.

(2) However, an unregistered company is not, except in the event of its being wound up, deemed to be a company under this Act, and then only to the extent provided by this Part."

PART XXII — BODIES CORPORATE SUBJECT, OR BECOMING SUBJECT, TO THIS ACT (OTHERWISE THAN BY ORIGINAL FORMATION UNDER PART I)

Chapter I — Companies Formed or Registered under Former Companies Acts

SEC. 675 Companies formed and registered under former Companies Acts

675(1) **[Application to existing companies]** In its application to existing companies, this Act applies in the same manner —

(a) in the case of a limited company (other than a company limited by guarantee) as if the company had been formed and registered under Part I of this Act as a company limited by shares,

(b) in the case of a company limited by guarantee, as if the company had been formed and registered under that Part as a company limited by guarantee, and

(c) in the case of a company other than a limited company, as if the company had been formed and registered under that Part as an unlimited company.

675(2) **[Reference to date of registration]** But reference, express or implied, to the date of registration is to be read as the date at which the company was registered under the Joint Stock Companies Acts, the Companies Act 1862, the Companies (Consolidation) Act 1908, the Companies Act 1929, or the Companies Act 1948.

SEC. 676   Companies registered but not formed under former Companies Acts

676(1)   **[Application of this Act]**   This Act applies to every company registered but not formed under the Joint Stock Companies Acts, the Companies Act 1862, the Companies (Consolidation) Act 1908, the Companies Act 1929, or the Companies Act 1948, in the same manner as it is in Chapter II of this Part declared to apply to companies registered but not formed under this Act.

676(2)   **[Reference to date of registration]**   But reference, express or implied, to the date of registration is to be read as referring to the date at which the company was registered under the Joint Stock Companies Acts, the Companies Act 1862, the Companies (Consolidation) Act 1908, the Companies Act 1929, or the Companies Act 1948.

SEC. 677   Companies re-registered with altered status under former Companies Acts

677(1)   **[Application of this Act]**   This Act applies to every unlimited company registered or re-registered as limited in pursuance of the Companies Act 1879, section 57 of the Companies (Consolidation) Act 1908, section 16 of the Companies Act 1929, section 16 of the Companies Act 1948 or section 44 of the Companies Act 1967 as it (this Act) applies to an unlimited company re-registered as limited in pursuance of Part II of this Act.

677(2)   **[Reference to date of registration]**   But reference, express or implied, to the date of registration or re-registration is to be read as referring to the date at which the company was registered or re-registered as a limited company under the relevant enactment.

SEC. 678   Companies registered under Joint Stock Companies Acts

678(1)   **[Transfer of shares]**   A company registered under the Joint Stock Companies Acts may cause its shares to be transferred in manner hitherto in use, or in such other manner as the company may direct.

678(2)   **[Power of altering articles under sec. 9]**   The power of altering articles under section 9 of this Act extends, in the case of an unlimited company formed and registered under the Joint Stock Companies Acts, to altering any regulations relating to the amount of capital or to its distribution into shares, notwithstanding that those regulations are contained in the memorandum.

SEC. 679   Northern Ireland and Irish companies

679   Nothing in sections 675 to 678 applies to companies registered in Northern Ireland or the Republic of Ireland.

Chapter II — Companies not Formed under Companies Legislation, but Authorised to Register

SEC. 680 Companies capable of being registered under this Chapter

680(1) **[Application in prescribed form]** With the exceptions and subject to the provisions contained in this section and the next —

    (a) any company consisting of two or more members, which was in existence on 2nd November 1862, including any company registered under the Joint Stock Companies Acts, and

    (b) any company formed after that date (whether before or after the commencement of this Act), in pursuance of any Act of Parliament (other than this Act), or of letters patent, or being otherwise duly constituted according to law, and consisting of two or more members,

may at any time, on making application in the prescribed form, register under this Act as an unlimited company, or as a company limited by shares, or as a company limited by guarantee; and the registration is not invalid by reason that it has taken place with a view to the company's being wound up.

680(2) **[Companies registered in UK]** A company registered in any part of the United Kingdom under the Companies Act 1862, the Companies (Consolidation) Act 1908, the Companies Act 1929 or the Companies Act 1948 shall not register under this section.

680(3) **[Limited companies]** A company having the liability of its members limited by Act of Parliament or letters patent, and not being a joint stock company, shall not register under this section.

680(4) **[Limited companies becoming unlimited or limited by guarantee]** A company having the liability of its members limited by Act of Parliament or letters patent shall not register in pursuance of this section as an unlimited company or as a company limited by guarantee.

680(5) **[Joint stock companies]** A company that is not a joint stock company shall not register under this section as a company limited by shares.

SEC. 681 Procedural requirements for registration

681(1) **[Assent of general meeting]** A company shall not register under section 680 without the assent of a majority of such of its members as are present in person or by proxy (in cases where proxies are allowed) at a general meeting summoned for the purpose.

681(2) **[Company reregistering as limited]** Where a company not having the liability of its members limited by Act of Parliament or letters patent is about to register as a limited company, the majority required to assent as required by subsection (1) shall consist of not less than three-fourths of the members present in person or by proxy at the meeting.

681(3) **[Computation of majority]** In computing any majority under this section when a poll is demanded, regard is to be had to the number of votes to which each member is entitled according to the company's regulations.

681(4) **[Resolution to accompany assent]** Where a company is about to register (under section 680) as a company limited by guarantee, the assent to its being so registered shall be accompanied by a resolution declaring that each member undertakes to contribute to the company's assets, in the event of its being wound up while he is a member, or within one year after he ceases to be a member, for payment of the company's debts and liabilities contracted before he ceased to be a member, and of the costs and expenses of winding up and for the adjustment of the rights of the contributories among themselves, such amount as may be required, not exceeding a specified amount.

681(5) **[Documents to registrar]** Before a company is registered under section 680, it shall deliver to the registrar of companies —

    (a) a statement that the registered office of the company is to be situated in England, or in Wales, or in Scotland (as the case may be),

    (b) a statement specifying the intended situation of the company's registered office after registration, and

    (c) in an appropriate case, if the company wishes to be registered with the Welsh equivalent of "public limited company" or, as the case may be, "limited" as the last words or word of its name, a statement to that effect.

681(6) **[Sec. 681(5) statements]** Any statement delivered to the registrar under subsection (5) shall be made in the prescribed form.

SEC. 682 Change of name on registration

682(1) **[If existing name precluded etc.]** Where the name of a company seeking registration under section 680 is a name by which it is precluded from registration by section 26 of this Act, either because it falls within subsection (1) of that section or, if it falls within subsection (2), because the Secretary of State would not approve the company's being registered with that name, the company may change its name with effect from the date on which it is registered under this Chapter.

682(2) **[Assent as in sec. 681]** A change of name under this section requires the like assent of the company's members as is required by section 681 for registration.

SEC. 683 Definition of "joint stock company"

683(1) **["Joint stock company"]** For purposes of this Chapter, as far as relates to registration of companies as companies limited by shares, **"joint stock company"** means a company —

    (a) having a permanent paid-up or nominal share capital of fixed amount divided into shares, also of fixed amount, or held and transferable as stock, or divided and held partly in one way and partly in the other, and

    (b) formed on the principle of having for its members the holders of those shares or that stock, and no other persons.

683(2) **[Deemed company limited by shares]** Such a company when registered with limited liability under this Act is deemed a company limited by shares.

SEC. 684 Requirements for registration by joint stock companies

684(1)   [Documents to registrar]   Before the registration under section 680 of a joint stock company, there shall be delivered to the registrar of companies the following documents —

(a)   a statement in the prescribed form specifying the name with which the company is proposed to be registered,

(b)   a list in the prescribed form showing the names and addresses of all persons who on a day named in the list (not more than 28 clear days before the day of registration) were members of the company, with the addition of the shares or stock held by them respectively (distinguishing, in cases where the shares are numbered, each share by its number), and

(c)   a copy of any Act of Parliament, royal charter, letters patent, deed of settlement, contract of copartnery or other instrument constituting or regulating the company.

History
In s. 684(1)(b) the words "(not more than 28 clear days before the day of registration)" substituted for the former words "(not more than 6 clear days before the day of registration)" by CA 1989, s. 145 and Sch. 19, para. 12 as from 1 March 1990 (see S.I. 1990 No. 142 (C. 5), art. 5).

684(2)   [Statements to be registered as limited]   If the company is intended to be registered as a limited company, there shall also be delivered to the registrar of companies a statement in the prescribed form specifying the following particulars —

(a)   the nominal share capital of the company and the number of shares into which it is divided, or the amount of stock of which it consists, and

(b)   the number of shares taken and the amount paid on each share.

SEC. 685 Registration of joint stock company as public company

685(1)   [Application for registration]   A joint stock company applying to be registered under section 680 as a company limited by shares may, subject to —

(a)   satisfying the conditions set out in section 44(2)(a) and (b) (where applicable) and section 45(2) to (4) as applied by this section, and

(b)   complying with subsection (4) below,

apply to be so registered as a public company.

685(2)   [Application of sec. 44, 45]   Sections 44 and 45 apply for this purpose as in the case of a private company applying to be re-registered under section 43, but as if a reference to the special resolution required by section 43 were to the joint stock company's resolution that it be a public company.

685(3)   [Change of name]   The resolution may change the company's name by deleting the word "company" or the words "and company", or its or their equivalent in Welsh ("cwmni", "a'r cwmni"), including any abbreviation of them.

685(4)   [Documents to registrar]   The joint stock company's application shall be made in the form prescribed for the purpose, and shall be delivered to the registrar of companies together with the following documents (as well as those required by section 684), namely —

(a) a copy of the resolution that the company be a public company,

(b) a copy of a written statement by an accountant with the appropriate qualifications that in his opinion a relevant balance sheet shows that at the balance sheet date the amount of the company's net assets was not less than the aggregate of its called up share capital and undistributable reserves,

(c) a copy of the relevant balance sheet, together with a copy of an unqualified report (by an accountant with such qualifications) in relation to that balance sheet,

(d) a copy of any valuation report prepared under section 44(2)(b) as applied by this section, and

(e) a statutory declaration in the prescribed form by a director or secretary of the company —

   (i) that the conditions set out in section 44(2)(a) and (b) (where applicable) and section 45(2) to (4) have been satisfied, and

  (ii) that, between the balance sheet date referred to in paragraph (b) of this subsection and the joint stock company's application, there has been no change in the company's financial position that has resulted in the amount of its net assets becoming less than the aggregate of its called up share capital and undistributable reserves.

685(5)   [Section 685(4)(e) declaration sufficient evidence]   The registrar may accept a declaration under subsection (4)(e) as sufficient evidence that the conditions referred to in that paragraph have been satisfied.

685(6)   [Definitions]   In this section —

    ''**accountant with the appropriate qualifications**'' means a person who would be qualified under section 389(1) for appointment as the company's auditor, if it were a company registered under this Act,

    ''**relevant balance sheet**'' means a balance sheet prepared as at a date not more than 7 months before the joint stock company's application to be registered as a public company limited by shares, and

    ''**undistributable reserves**'' has the meaning given by section 264(3);

and section 46 applies (with necessary modifications) for the interpretation of the reference in subsection (4)(c) above to an unqualified report by the accountant.

SEC. 686   Other requirements for registration

686(1)   [Documents to registrar]   Before the registration in pursuance of this Chapter of any company (not being a joint stock company), there shall be delivered to the registrar of companies —

(a) a statement in the prescribed form specifying the name with which the company is proposed to be registered,

(b) a list showing the names, addresses and occupations of the directors or other managers (if any) of the company,

(c) a copy of any Act of Parliament, letters patent, deed of settlement, contract of copartnery or other instrument constituting or regulating the company, and

(d) in the case of a company intended to be registered as a company limited by guarantee, a copy of the resolution declaring the amount of the guarantee.

686(2) [Verification by statutory declaration] The lists of members and directors and any other particulars relating to the company which are required by this Chapter to be delivered to the registrar shall be verified by a statutory declaration in the prescribed form made by any two or more directors or other principal officers of the company.

686(3) [Evidence re whether joint stock company] The registrar may require such evidence as he thinks necessary for the purpose of satisfying himself whether a company proposing to be registered is or is not a joint stock company as defined by section 683).

SEC. 687 Name of company registering

687(1) [Applications] The following applies with respect to the name of a company registering under this Chapter (whether a joint stock company or not).

687(2) [Public company] If the company is to be registered as a public company, its name must end with the words "public limited company" or, if it is stated that the company's registered office is to be situated in Wales, with those words or their equivalent in Welsh ("cwmni cyfyngedig cyhoeddus"); and those words or that equivalent may not be preceded by the word "limited" or its equivalent in Welsh ("cyfyngedig").

687(3) [Company limited by shares or guarantee] In the case of a company limited by shares or by guarantee (not being a public company), the name must have "limited" as its last word (or, if the company's registered office is to be situated in Wales, "cyfyngedig"); but this is subject to section 30 (exempting a company, in certain circumstances, from having "limited" as part of the name).

687(4) [Addition to name of company with limited liability] If the company is registered with limited liability, then any additions to the company's name set out in the statements delivered under section 684(1)(a) or 686(1)(a) shall form and be registered as the last part of the company's name.

SEC. 688 Certificate of registration under this Chapter

688(1) [Issue of certificate] On compliance with the requirements of this Chapter with respect to registration, the registrar of companies shall give a certificate (which may be signed by him, or authenticated by his official seal) that the company applying for registration is incorporated as a company under this Act and, in the case of a limited company, that it is limited.

688(2) [Effect of issue] On the issue of the certificate, the company shall be so incorporated; and a banking company in Scotland so incorporated is deemed a bank incorporated, constituted or established by or under Act of Parliament.

688(3) [Certificate conclusive evidence] The certificate is conclusive evidence that the requirements of this Chapter in respect of registration, and of matters precedent and incidental to it, have been complied with.

688(4) [Joint stock company registered as public limited company] Where on an application by a joint stock company to register as a public company limited by shares the registrar of companies is satisfied that the company may be registered as a public company so limited, the certificate of incorporation given under this section shall state that the company is a public company; and that statement is conclusive evidence that the requirement of section 685 have been complied with and that the company is a public company so limited.

SEC. 689   Effect of registration

689   Schedule 21 to this Act has effect with respect to the consequences of registration under this Chapter, the vesting of property, savings for existing liabilities, continuation of existing actions, status of the company following registration, and other connected matters.

SEC. 690   Power to substitute memorandum and articles for deed of settlement

690(1)   [Alteration of constitution by special resolution]   Subject as follows, a company registered in pursuance of this Chapter may by special resolution alter the form of its constitution by substituting a memorandum and articles for a deed of settlement.

690(2)   [Application of sec. 4–6]   The provisions of sections 4 to 6 of this Act with respect to applications to the court for cancellation of alterations of the objects of a company and matters consequential on the passing of resolutions for such alterations (so far as applicable) apply, but with the following modifications —

    (a) there is substituted for the printed copy of the altered memorandum required to be delivered to the registrar of companies a printed copy of the substituted memorandum and articles, and

    (b) on the delivery to the registrar of the substituted memorandum and articles or the date when the alteration is no longer liable to be cancelled by order of the court (whichever is the later) —

        (i) the substituted memorandum and articles apply to the company in the same manner as if it were a company registered under Part I with that memorandum and those articles, and

        (ii) the company's deed of settlement ceases to apply to the company.

690(3)   [Alteration of objects]   An alteration under this section may be made either with or without alteration of the company's objects.

690(4)   ["Deed of settlement"]   In this section "deed of settlement" includes any contract of copartnery or other instrument constituting or regulating the company, not being an Act of Parliament, a royal charter or letters patent.

PART XXIII — OVERSEA COMPANIES

Chapter I — Registration, etc.

SEC. 691   Documents to be delivered to registrar

691(1)   [Documents to registrar]   When a company incorporated outside Great Britain establishes a place of business in Great Britain, it shall within one month of doing so deliver to the registrar of companies for registration —

(a) a certified copy of the charter, statutes or memorandum and articles of the company or other instrument constituting or defining the company's constitution, and, if the instrument is not written in the English language, a certified translation of it; and

(b) a return in the prescribed form containing —

    (i) a list of the company's directors and secretary, containing the particulars specified in the next subsection,

    (ii) a list of the names and addresses of some one or more persons resident in Great Britain authorised to accept on the company's behalf service of process and any notices required to be served on it,

    (iii) a list of the documents delivered in compliance with paragraph (a) of this subsection, and

    (iv) a statutory declaration (made by a director or secretary of the company or by any person whose name and address are given in the list required by sub-paragraph (ii)), stating the date on which the company's place of business in Great Britain was established.

691(2) **[Particulars in list in sec. 691(1)(b)(i)]** The list referred to in subsection (1)(b)(i) shall contain the following particulars —

(a) with respect to each director—

    (i) in the case of an individual, his present Christian name and surname and any former Christian name or surname, his usual residential address, his nationality and his business occupation (if any), or, if he has no business occupation but holds other directorships, particulars of any of them,

    (ii) in the case of a corporation, its corporate name and registered or principal office;

(b) with respect to the secretary (or, where there are joint secretaries, with respect to each of them)—

    (i) in the case of an individual, his present Christian name and surname, any former Christian name and surname and his usual residential address,

    (ii) in the case of a corporation or a Scottish firm, its corporate or firm name and registered or principal office.

Where all the partners in a firm are joint secretaries of the company, the name and principal office of the firm may be stated instead of the particulars mentioned in paragraph (b).

Section 289(2) applies for the purposes of the construction of references above to present and former Christian names and surnames.

SEC. 692   Registration of altered particulars

692(1) **[Return re alterations]** If any alteration is made in —

(a) the charter, statutes, or memorandum and articles of an oversea company or any such instrument as is mentioned above, or

(b) the directors or secretary of an oversea company or the particulars contained in the list of the directors and secretary, or

(c) the names or addresses of the persons authorised to accept service on behalf of an oversea company, the company shall, within the time specified below, deliver to the registrar of companies for registration a return containing the prescribed particulars of the alteration.

692(2)   [Return re change of name]   If any change is made in the corporate name of an oversea company, the company shall, within the time specified below, deliver to the registrar of companies for registration a return containing the prescribed particulars of the change.

692(3)   [Time for delivery of returns]   The time for delivery of the returns required by subsections (1) and (2) is —

(a) in the case of an alteration to which subsection (1)(c) applies, 21 days after the making of the alteration, and

(b) otherwise, 21 days after the date on which notice of the alteration or change in question could have been received in Great Britain in due course of post (if despatched with due diligence).

SEC. 693   Obligation to state name and particulars

693   Every oversea company shall —

(a) in every prospectus inviting subscriptions for its shares or debentures in Great Britain, state the country in which the company is incorporated,

(b) conspicuously exhibit on every place where it carries on business in Great Britain the company's name and the country in which it is incorporated,

(c) cause the company's name and the country in which it is incorporated to be stated in legible characters in all bill-heads and letter paper, and in all notices and other official publications of the company, and

(d) if the liability of the members of the company is limited, cause notice of that fact to be stated in legible characters in every such prospectus as above mentioned and in all bill-heads, letter paper, notices and other official publications of the company in Great Britain, and to be affixed on every place where it carries on its business.

Note

In s. 693, para. (a) and in para. (d) the words "in every such prospectus as above mentioned" repealed by Financial Services Act 1986, s. 212(3) and Sch. 17 Pt. I to the extent to which they would apply re any investment listed as the subject of a listing application under Financial Services Act 1986, Pt. IV and commencing:

- on 12 January 1987 for all purposes relating to the admission of securities offered by or on behalf of a Minister of the Crown or a body corporate controlled by a Minister of the Crown or a subsidiary of such a body corporate to the Official List in respect of which an application is made after that date;

- on 16 February 1987 for the purposes relating to the admission of securities in respect of which an application

is made after that date other than those referred to in the preceding paragraph and otherwise for all purposes.

(See S.I. 1986 No. 2246 (C. 88).)

Para. (a) and the above words in para. (a) also repealed by Financial Services Act 1986, s. 212(3) and Sch. 17, Pt. I as from 29 April 1988 as far as they would apply to a prospectus offering for subscription, or to any form of application for units in a body corporate which is a recognised scheme; and as from 1 July 1988 as far as they would apply to a prospectus offering for subscription, or to any application form for, units in a body corporate which is an open-ended investment company (see S.I. 1988 No. 740 (C. 22)).

SEC. 694   Regulation of oversea companies in respect of their names

694(1)   [Notice re non-registration of name]   If it appears to the Secretary of State that the corporate name of an oversea company is a name by which the company, had it been formed under this Act, would on the relevant date (defined below in subsection (3)) have been precluded from being registered by section 26 either—

(a) because it falls within subsection (1) of that section, or

(b) if it falls within subsection (2) of that section, because the Secretary of State would not approve the company's being registered with that name,

the Secretary of State may serve a notice on the company, stating why the name would not have been registered.

694(2) [Name too similar] If the corporate name of an oversea company is in the Secretary of State's opinion too like a name appearing on the relevant date in the index of names kept by the registrar of companies under section 714 or which should have appeared in that index on that date, or is the same as a name which should have so appeared, the Secretary of State may serve a notice on the company specifying the name in the index which the company's name is too like or which is the same as the company's name.

694(3) [Time for notice under sec. 694(1), (2)] No notice shall be served on a company under subsection (1) or (2) later than 12 months after the relevant date, being the date on which the company has complied with —

(a) section 691 in this Part, or

(b) if there has been a change in the company's corporate name, section 692(2).

694(4) [Statement by oversea company re alternative name] An oversea company on which a notice is served under subsection (1) or (2) —

(a) may deliver to the registrar of companies for registration a statement in the prescribed form specifying a name approved by the Secretary of State other than its corporate name under which it proposes to carry on business in Great Britain, and

(b) may, after that name has been registered, at any time deliver to the registrar for registration a statement in the prescribed form specifying a name approved by the Secretary of State (other than its corporate name) in substitution for the name previously registered.

694(5) [Name under sec. 694(4)] The name by which an oversea company is for the time being registered under subsection (4) is, for all purposes of the law applying in Great Britain (including this Act and the Business Names Act 1985), deemed to be the company's corporate name; but —

(a) this does not affect references to the corporate name in this section, or any rights or obligations of the company, or render defective any legal proceedings by or against the company, and

(b) any legal proceedings that might have been continued or commenced against the company by its corporate name or its name previously registered under this section may be continued or commenced against it by its name for the time being so registered.

694(6) [Prohibition of carrying on business] An oversea company on which a notice is served under subsection (1) or (2) shall not at any time after the expiration of 2 months from the service of that notice (or such longer period as may be specified in that notice) carry on business in Great Britain under its corporate name.

Nothing in this subsection, or in section 697(2) (which imposes penalties for its contravention) invalidates any transaction entered into by the company.

694(7)   [Withdrawal of sec. 694(1), (2) notice]   The Secretary of State may withdraw a notice served under subsection (1) or (2) at any time before the end of the period mentioned in subsection (6); and that subsection does not apply to a company served with a notice which has been withdrawn.

SEC. 695   Service of documents on oversea company

695(1)   [Usual service]   Any process or notice required to be served on an oversea company is sufficiently served if addressed to any person whose name has been delivered to the registrar under preceding sections in this Part and left at or sent by post to the address which has been so delivered.

695(2)   [Other service]   However —

  (a) where such a company makes default in delivering to the registrar the name and address of a person resident in Great Britain who is authorised to accept on behalf of the company service of process or notices, or

  (b) if at any time all the persons whose names and addresses have been so delivered are dead or have ceased so to reside, or refuse to accept service on the company's behalf, or for any reason cannot be served,

a document may be served on the company by leaving it at, or sending it by post to, any place of business established by the company in Great Britain.

SEC. 696   Office where documents to be filed

696(1)   [Delivery to registrar]   Any document which an oversea company is required to deliver to the registrar of companies shall be delivered to the registrar at the registration office in England and Wales or Scotland, according to where the company has established a place of business.

696(2)   [If places of business in England and Wales and in Scotland]   If the company has established a place of business both in England and Wales and in Scotland, the document shall be delivered at the registration office both in England and Wales and in Scotland.

696(3)   [Interpretation]   References in this Part to the registrar of companies are to be construed in accordance with the above subsections.

696(4)   [Notice re cessation of place of business in Great Britain]   If an oversea company ceases to have a place of business in either part of Great Britain, it shall forthwith give notice of that fact to the registrar of companies for that part; and as from the date on which notice is so given the obligation of the company to deliver any document to the registrar ceases.

SEC. 697   Penalties for non-compliance

697(1)   [Non-compliance with sec. 691 to 693, 696]   If an oversea company fails to comply with any of sections 691 to 693 and 696, the company, and every officer or agent of the company who knowingly and wilfully authorises or permits the default, is liable to a fine and, in the case of a continuing offence, to a daily default fine for continued contravention.

697(2) **[Contravention of sec. 694(6)]** If an oversea company contravenes section 694(6), the company and every officer or agent of it who knowingly and wilfully authorises or permits the contravention is guilty of an offence and liable to a fine and, for continued contravention, to a daily default fine.

SEC. 698 Definitions for this Chapter

698 For purposes of this Chapter —

"**certified**" means certified in the prescribed manner to be a true copy or a correct translation;

"**director**", in relation to an oversea company, includes shadow director; and

"**secretary**" includes any person occupying the position of secretary by whatever name called.

SEC. 699 Channel Islands and Isle of Man companies

699(1) **[Application of other provisions]** With the exceptions specified in subsection (3) below, the provisions of this Act requiring documents to be forwarded or delivered to or filed with the registrar of companies and applying to companies formed and registered under Part I apply also (if they would not otherwise) to an oversea company incorporated in the Channel Islands or the Isle of Man.

699(2) **[Where such provisions apply]** Those provisions apply to such a company —

(a) if it has established a place of business in England and Wales, as if it were registered in England and Wales,

(b) if it has established a place of business in Scotland, as if it were registered in Scotland, and

(c) if it has established a place of business both in England and Wales and in Scotland, as if it were registered in both England and Wales and Scotland,

with such modifications as may be necessary and, in particular, apply in a similar way to documents relating to things done outside Great Britain as if they had been done in Great Britain.

699(3) **[Exceptions]** The exceptions are —

section 6(1) (resolution altering company's objects),

section 18 (alteration of memorandum or articles by statute or statutory instrument),

section 242(1) (directors' duty to file accounts),

section 288(2) (notice to registrar of change of directors or secretary), and

section 380 (copies of certain resolutions and agreements to be sent to registrar within 15 days), so far as applicable to a resolution altering a company's memorandum or articles.

History
In s. 699(3) the words "section 242(1)" substituted for the former words "section 24(3)" by CA 1989, s. 213 and Sch. 10, para. 12 as from 1 April 1990 subject to transitional and saving provisions (see S.I. 1990 No. 355 (C. 13), art. 3, Sch. 1 and also art. 6–9.)

Chapter II — Delivery of Accounts and Reports

SEC. 700   Preparation of accounts and reports by oversea companies

700(1)   [Same duties as other companies]   Every oversea company shall in respect of each financial year of the company prepare the like accounts and directors' report, and cause to be prepared such an auditors' report, as would be required if the company were formed and registered under this Act.

700(2)   [Order by Secretary of State]   The Secretary of State may by order—

    (a) modify the requirements referred to in subsection (1) for the purpose of their application to oversea companies;

    (b) exempt an oversea company from those requirements or from such of them as may be specified in the order.

700(3)   [Scope of order]   An order may make different provision for different cases or classes of case and may contain such incidental and supplementary provisions as the Secretary of State thinks fit.

Note
Re s. 700(2), (3) see the Oversea Companies (Accounts) (Modifications and Exemptions) Order 1990 (S.I. 1990 No. 440).

700(4)   [Annulment of order]   An order under this section shall be made by statutory instrument which shall be subject to annulment in pursuance of a resolution of either House of Parliament.

History
See history note after s. 703.

SEC. 701   Oversea company's financial year and accounting reference periods

701(1)   [Application of sec. 223–225]   Sections 223 to 225 (financial year and accounting reference periods) apply to an oversea company, subject to the following modifications.

701(2)   [Interpretation]   For the references to the incorporation of the company substitute references to the company establishing a place of business in Great Britain.

701(3)   [Omission of sec. 225(4)]   Omit section 225(4) (restriction on frequency with which current accounting reference period may be extended).

History
See history note after s. 703.

SEC. 702   Delivery to registrar of accounts and reports of oversea company

702(1)   [Duty of oversea company]   An oversea company shall in respect of each financial year of the company deliver to the registrar copies of the accounts and reports prepared in accordance with section 700.

If any document comprised in those accounts or reports is in a language other than English, the directors shall annex to the copy delivered a translation of it into English, certified in the prescribed manner to be a correct translation.

702(2) **[Period for delivering accounts and reports]** In relation to an oversea company the period allowed for delivering accounts and reports is 13 months after the end of the relevant accounting reference period.

This is subject to the following provisions of this section.

702(3) **[If accounting reference period first]** If the relevant accounting reference period is the company's first and is a period of more than 12 months, the period allowed is 13 months from the first anniversary of the company's establishing a place of business in Great Britain.

702(4) **[If accounting reference period shortened]** If the relevant accounting period is treated as shortened by virtue of a notice given by the company under section 225 (alteration of accounting reference date), the period allowed is that applicable in accordance with the above provisions or three months from the date of the notice under that section, whichever last expires.

702(5) **[Power of Secretary of State to extend period]** If for any special reason the Secretary of State thinks fit he may, on an application made before the expiry of the period otherwise allowed, by notice in writing to an oversea company extend that period by such further period as may be specified in the notice.

702(6) **["The relevant accounting reference period"]** In this section **"the relevant accounting reference period"** means the accounting reference period by reference to which the financial year for the accounts in question was determined.

History
See history note after s. 703.

SEC. 703 Penalty for non-compliance

703(1) **[Offence, penalty]** If the requirements of section 702(1) are not complied with before the end of the period allowed for delivering accounts and reports, or if the accounts and reports delivered do not comply with the requirements of this Act, the company and every person who immediately before the end of that period was a director of the company is guilty of an offence and liable to a fine and, for continued contravention, to a daily default fine.

703(2) **[Defence]** It is a defence for a person charged with such an offence to prove that he took all reasonable steps for securing that the requirements in question would be complied with.

703(3) **[Not a defence]** It is not a defence in relation to a failure to deliver copies to the registrar to prove that the documents in question were not in fact prepared as required by this Act.

History
Ch. II (s. 700–703) substituted by CA 1989, s. 23 and Sch. 10, para. 13 as from 1 April 1990 subject to transitional and saving provisions (see S.I. 1990 No. 355 (C. 13), art. 3, Sch. 1 and also art. 6–9); Ch. II formerly read as follows:

"Chapter II — Delivery of Accounts

SEC. 700 Preparation and delivery of accounts by oversea companies

700(1) Every oversea company shall in respect of each accounting reference period of the company prepare such accounts, made up by reference to such date or dates, and in such form, containing such particulars and having annexed to them such documents, as would have been required if it were a company formed and registered under this Act.

(2) An oversea company shall, in respect of each accounting reference period of the company, deliver to the registrar of companies copies of the accounts and other documents required by subsection (1); and, if such an account or other document is in a language other than English, there shall be annexed to the copy so delivered a translation of it into English certified in the prescribed manner to be a correct translation.

(3) If in relation to an accounting reference period the company's directors would be exempt under section 241(4) from compliance with subsection (3) of that section (independent company with unlimited liability), if the company were otherwise subject to that section, compliance with this section is not required in respect of that accounting reference period.

(4) The Secretary of State may by order in a statutory instrument—

(a) modify the requirements referred to in subsection (1) for the purpose of their application to oversea companies,

(b) exempt an oversea company from those requirements or from such of them as may be specified in the order.

(5) An order under subsection (4) may make different provision in relation to different cases or classes of case and may contain such incidental and supplementary provisions as the Secretary of State thinks fit; and a statutory instrument containing an order so made is subject to annulment in pursuance of a resolution of either House of Parliament.

SEC. 701   Oversea company's accounting reference period and date

701(1) An oversea company's accounting reference periods are determined according to its accounting reference date.

(2) The company may give notice in the prescribed form to the registrar of companies specifying a date in the calendar year as being the date on which in each successive calendar year an accounting reference period of the company is to be treated as coming to an end; and the date specified in the notice is then the company's accounting reference date.

(3) No such notice has effect unless it is given before the end of 6 months beginning with the date on which a place of business in Great Britain is or was established by the company; and, failing such a notice, the company's accounting reference date is 31st March.

(4) The company's first accounting reference period is such period ending with its accounting reference date as—

(a) begins or began on a date determined by the company, but not later than that on which a place of business is or was established in Great Britain, and

(b) is a period exceeding 6 months and not exceeding 18 months.

(5) Each successive period of 12 months beginning after the end of the first accounting reference period and ending with the company's accounting reference date is also an accounting reference period of the company.

(6) Subsections (2) to (5) are subject to section 225 of this Act, under which in certain circumstances a company's accounting reference period may be altered, and which applies to oversea companies as well as to companies subject to Part VII, but omitting subsections (6) and (7).

SEC. 702   Period allowed for delivering accounts

702(1) In the case of an oversea company, the period allowed for delivering accounts in relation to an accounting reference period is 13 months after the end of the period.

(2) Where the company's first accounting reference period—

(a) begins or began on the date determined by the company for the purposes of section 701(4)(a) and

(b) is or was a period of more than 12 months,

the period which would otherwise be allowed for delivering accounts in relation to that accounting reference period is treated as reduced by the number of days by which the accounting reference period is or was longer than 12 months.

(3) But the period allowed in relation to a company's first accounting reference period is not by subsection (2) reduced to less than 3 months after the end of that accounting reference period.

(4) In relation to an accounting reference period of an oversea company as respects which notice is given by the company under section 225 (as applied) and which by virtue of that section is treated as shortened in accordance with the notice, the period allowed for delivering accounts is—

(a) the period allowed in relation to that accounting reference period in accordance with the preceding subsections, or

(b) the period of 3 months beginning with the date of the notice,

whichever of those periods last expires.

(5) If for any special reason the Secretary of State thinks fit to do so, he may by notice in writing to an oversea company extend, by such further period as may be specified in the notice, the period which in accordance with the preceding subsections is the period allowed for delivering accounts in relation to any accounting reference period of the company.

SEC. 703   Penalty for non-compliance

703(1) If in respect of an accounting reference period of an oversea company any of the requirements of section 700(2) is not complied with before the end of the period allowed for delivering accounts, the company and every officer or agent of it who knowingly and wilfully authorises or permits the default is, in respect of the company's failure to comply with the requirements in question, guilty of an offence and liable to a fine and, for continued contravention, to a daily default fine.

(2) For purposes of any proceedings under this section with respect to a requirement to deliver a copy of a document to the registrar of companies, it is not a defence to prove that the document in question was not in fact prepared as required by section 700.''

PART XXIV — THE REGISTRAR OF COMPANIES, HIS FUNCTIONS AND OFFICES

SEC. 704   Registration offices

704(1)   [Offices in England, Wales and Scotland]   For the purposes of the registration of companies under the Companies Acts, there shall continue to be offices in England and Wales and in Scotland, at such places as the Secretary of State thinks fit.

704(2)   [Officers appointed]   The Secretary of State may appoint such registrars, assistant registrars, clerks and servants as he thinks necessary for that purpose, and may make regulations with respect to their duties, and may remove any persons so appointed.

704(3) **[Salaries of officers]** The salaries of the persons so appointed continue to be fixed by the Secretary of State, with the concurrence of the Treasury, and shall be paid out of money provided by Parliament.

704(4) **[Seal for authentication of documents]** The Secretary of State may direct a seal or seals to be prepared for the authentication of documents required for or in connection with the registration of companies; and any seal so prepared is referred to in this Act as the registrar's official seal.

704(5) **[Things to be done by registrar]** Wherever any act is by the Companies Acts directed to be done to or by the registrar of companies, it shall (until the Secretary of State otherwise directs) be done to or by the existing registrar of companies in England and Wales or in Scotland (as the case may be), or to or by such person as the Secretary of State may for the time being authorise.

704(6) **[Alteration of constitution of offices]** In the event of the Secretary of State altering the constitution of the existing registration offices or any of them, any such act shall be done to or by such officer and at such place with reference to the local situation of the registered offices of the companies to be registered as the Secretary of State may appoint.

SEC. 705   Companies' registered numbers

705(1) **[Allocation of numbers and letters]** The registrar of companies shall allocate to every company a number, which shall be known as the company's registered number; and he may in addition allocate to any such company a letter, which is then deemed for all purposes to be part of the registered number.

705(2) **["Company"]** "Company" here includes —

    (a) an oversea company which has complied with section 691 (delivery of statutes to registrar of companies, etc.) and which does not appear to the registrar not to have a place of business in Great Britain, and

    (b) any incorporated or unincorporated body to which any provision of this Act applies by virtue of section 718 (unregistered companies).

SEC. 706   Size, durability, etc. of documents delivered to registrar

706(1) **[Regulations re documents]** For the purpose of securing that documents delivered to the registrar of companies under the Companies Acts are of standard size, durable and easily legible, regulations made by the Secretary of State by statutory instrument may prescribe such requirements (whether as to size, weight, quality or colour of paper, size, type or colouring of lettering, or otherwise) as he may consider appropriate; and different requirements may be so prescribed for different documents or classes of documents.

706(2) **[Notice re non-compliance with requirements]** If under any such provision there is delivered to the registrar a document (whether an original document or a copy) which in the registrar's opinion does not comply with such requirements prescribed under this section as are applicable to it, the registrar may serve on any person by whom under that provision the document was required to be delivered (or, if there are two or more such persons, may serve on any of them) a notice stating his opinion to that effect and indicating the requirements so prescribed with which in his opinion the document does not comply.

706(3)   **[Effect of service of sec. 706(2) notice]**   Where the registrar serves such a notice with respect to a document delivered under any such provision, then, for the purposes of any enactment which enables a penalty to be imposed in respect of any omission to deliver to the registrar of companies a document required to be delivered under that provision (and, in particular, for the purposes of any such enactment whereby such a penalty may be imposed by reference to each day during which the omission continues) —

(a) any duty imposed by that provision to deliver such a document to the registrar is to be treated as not having been discharged by the delivery of that document, but

(b) no account is to be taken of any days falling within the period mentioned in the following subsection.

706(4)   **[Period in sec. 706(3)(b)]**   That period begins with the day on which the document was delivered to the registrar as mentioned in subsection (2) and ends with the 14th day after the date of service of the notice under subsection (2) by virtue of which subsection (3) applies.

706(5)   **[Interpretation]**   In this section any reference to delivering a document includes sending, forwarding, producing or (in the case of a notice) giving it.

SEC. 707   Power of registrar to accept information on microfilm, etc.

707(1)   **[Material other than document]**   The registrar of companies may, if he thinks fit, accept under any provision of the Companies Acts requiring a document to be delivered to him any material other than a document which contains the information in question and is of a kind approved by him.

707(2)   **[Sufficient compliance]**   The delivery to the registrar of material so accepted is sufficient compliance with the provision in question.

707(3)   **[Interpretation]**   In this section any reference to delivering a document includes sending, forwarding, producing or (in the case of a notice) giving it.

SEC. 708   Fees payable to registrar

708(1)   **[Regulations re fees]**   The Secretary of State may by regulations made by statutory instrument require the payment to the registrar of companies of such fees as may be specified in the regulations in respect of —

(a) the performance by the registrar of such functions under the Companies Acts as may be so specified, including the receipt by him of any notice or other document which under those Acts is required to be given, delivered, sent or forwarded to him.

(b) the inspection of documents or other material kept by him under those Acts.

708(2) **[Approval of certain regulations]** A statutory instrument containing regulations under this section requiring the payment of a fee in respect of a matter for which no fee was previously payable, or increasing a fee, shall be laid before Parliament after being made and shall cease to have effect at the end of the period of 28 days beginning with the day on which the regulations were made (but without prejudice to anything previously done under the regulations or to the making of further regulations) unless in that period the regulations are approved by resolution of each House of Parliament.

In reckoning that period of 28 days no account is to be taken of any time during which Parliament is dissolved or prorogued or during which both Houses are adjourned for more than 4 days.

708(3) **[Annulment]** A statutory instrument containing regulations under this section, where subsection (2) does not apply, is subject to annulment in pursuance of a resolution of either House of Parliament.

708(4) **[Fees into Consolidated Fund]** Fees paid to the registrar under the Companies Acts shall be paid into the Consolidated Fund.

708(5) **[Fees for other services]** It is hereby declared that the registrar may charge a fee for any services provided by him otherwise than in pursuance of an obligation imposed on him by law.

SEC. 709 Inspection of documents kept by registrar

709(1) **[Inspection, requirement of certificate of incorporation, etc.]** Subject to the provisions of this section, any person may —

(a) inspect a copy of any document kept by the registrar of companies or, if the copy is illegible or unavailable, the document itself,

(b) require a certificate of the incorporation of any company, or a certified copy or extract of any other document or any part of any other document.

A certificate given under paragraph (b) may be signed by the registrar, or authenticated by his official seal.

709(2) **[Documents delivered to registrar with prospectus under sec. 65(2)]** In relation to documents delivered to the registrar with a prospectus in pursuance of section 65(2), the rights conferred by subsection (1) of this section are exercisable only during the 14 days beginning with the date of publication of the prospectus, or with the permission of the Secretary of State.

709(3) **[Documents delivered under sec. 77(3)(b), (4)]** In relation to documents so delivered in pursuance of section 77(3)(b) and (4) (prospectus of oversea company), those rights are exercisable only during the 14 days beginning with the date of the prospectus, or with that permission.

Note
S. 709(2), (3) repealed by Financial Services Act 1986, s. 212(3) and Sch. 17, Pt. I to the extent to which they would apply re any investment listed or the subject of a listing application under Financial Services Act 1986, Pt. IV commencing:

- on 12 January 1987 for all purposes relating to the admission of securities offered by or on behalf of a Minister of the Crown or a body corporate controlled by a Minister of the Crown or a subsidiary of such a body corporate to the Official List in respect of which an application is made after that date;

- on 16 February 1987 for purposes relating to the admission of securities in respect of which an application is made after that date other than those referred to in the preceding paragraph and otherwise for all purposes.

(See S.I. 1986 No. 2246 (C. 88).)

S. 709(2), (3) also repealed by Financial Services Act 1986, s. 212(3) and Sch. 17, Pt. I as from 29 April 1988 as far as they would apply to a prospectus offering for subscription, or to any form of application for units in a body corporate which is a recognised scheme (see S.I. 1988 No. 740 (C.22)).

709(4) (Repealed by Insolvency Act 1986, sec. 438 and Sch. 12 as from 29 December 1986.)

History
In regard to the date of the above repeal, see Insolvency Act 1986, s. 443 and S.I. 1986 No. 1924 (C. 71); s. 709(4) formerly read as follows:

"The right conferred by subsection (1)(a) of this section does not extend to any copy sent to the registrar under section 495 (information to be given by receiver or manager following his appointment) of a statement as to the affairs of a company, or of any comments of the

receiver or his successor, or a continuing receiver or manager, on the statement, but only to the summary of it, except where the person claiming the right either is or is the agent of a person stating himself in writing to be a member or creditor of the company to which the statement relates.

The rights conferred by subsection (1)(b) are similarly limited."

SEC. 710   Additional provisions about inspection

710(1) **[Compelling production by registrar with leave of court]**   No process for compelling the production of any document kept by the registrar shall issue from any court except with the leave of that court; and any such process if issued shall bear on it a statement that it is issued with leave of the court.

710(2) **[Certified copies as evidence]**   A copy of, or extract from, any document kept and registered at any of the offices for the registration of companies in England and Wales or Scotland, certified in writing by the registrar (whose official position it is unnecessary to prove) to be a true copy, is in all legal proceedings admissible in evidence as of equal validity with the original document.

710(3) **[Sealed copies]**   Copies or extracts of documents or parts of documents furnished by the registrar under section 709 may, instead of being certified by him in writing to be true copies, be sealed with his official seal.

710(4) (Repealed by Insolvency Act 1986, sec. 438 and Sch. 12 as from 29 December 1986.)

History
In regard to the date of the above repeal, see Insolvency Act 1986, s. 443 and S.I. 1986 No. 1924 (C. 71); s. 710(4) formerly read as follows:

"Any person untruthfully stating himself in writing for the purposes of section 709(4) to be a member or creditor of a company is liable to a fine."

710(5) **[Copy may include copy of copy]**   For purposes of section 709 and this section, a copy is to be taken to be the copy of a document notwithstanding that it is taken from a copy or other reproduction of the original; and in both sections "**document**" includes any material which contains information kept by the registrar of companies for purposes of the Companies Acts.

SEC. 711   Public notice by registrar of receipt and issue of certain documents

711(1) **[Relevant documents]**   The registrar of companies shall cause to be published in the Gazette notice of the issue or receipt by him of documents of any of the following descriptions (stating in the notice the name of the company, the description of document and the date of issue or receipt) —

(a) any certificate of incorporation of a company,

(b) any document making or evidencing an alteration in a company's memorandum or articles,

(c) any notification of a change among the directors of a company,

(d) any copy of a resolution of a public company which gives, varies, revokes or renews an authority for the purposes of section 80 (allotment of relevant securities),

(e) any copy of a special resolution of a public company passed under section 95(1), (2) or (3) (disapplication of pre-emption rights),

(f) any report under section 103 or 104 as to the value of a non-cash asset,

(g) any statutory declaration delivered under section 117 (public company share capital requirements),

(h) any notification (given under section 122) of the redemption of shares,

(j) any statement or notice delivered by a public company under section 128 (registration of particulars of special rights),

(k) any documents delivered by a company under section 242(1) (accounts and reports),

(l) a copy of any resolution or agreement to which section 380 applies and which —

    (i) states the rights attached to any shares in a public company, other than shares which are in all respects uniform (for purposes of section 128) with shares previously allotted, or

    (ii) varies rights attached to any shares in a public company, or

    (iii) assigns a name or other designation, or a new name or designation, to any class of shares in a public company,

(m) any return of allotments of a public company,

(n) any notice of a change in the situation of a company's registered office,

(p) any copy of a winding-up order in respect of a company,

(q) any order for the dissolution of a company on a winding up,

(r) any return by a liquidator of the final meeting of a company on a winding up,

(s) any copy of a draft of the terms of a scheme delivered to the registrar of companies under paragraph 2(1) of Schedule 15B,

(t) any copy of an order under section 425(2) or section 427 in respect of a compromise or arrangement to which section 427A(1) applies.

History

In s. 711(1)(k) the words "section 242(1) (accounts and reports)" substituted for the former words "section 241 (annual accounts)" by CA 1989, s. 23 and Sch. 10, para. 14 as from 1 April 1990 subject to transitional and saving provisions (see S.I. 1990 No. 355 (C. 13), art. 3, Sch. 1 and also art. 6–9). S. 711(1)(s), (t) added by the Companies (Mergers and Divisions) Regulations 1987 (S.I. 1987 No. 1991), reg. 2(b) as from 1 January 1988.

Note

In s. 711(1)(s) CCH has altered the previous reference from "Schedule 15A" to "Schedule 15B" because of the amendment made by CA 1989, s. 114(2).

711(2) [**"Official notification"**] In section 42 **"official notification"** means—

(a) in relation to anything stated in a document of any of the above descriptions, the notification of that document in the Gazette under this section, and

(b) in relation to the appointment of a liquidator in a voluntary winding up, the notification of it in the Gazette under section 109 of the Insolvency Act;

and **"officially notified"** is to be construed accordingly.

History
In s. 711(2)(b) the words "section 109 of The Insolvency Act" substituted for the words "section 600" by Insolvency Act 1986, s. 439(1) and Sch. 13 as from 29 December 1986 (see S.I. 1986 No. 1924 (C. 71)).

SEC. 712 Removal of documents to Public Record Office

712(1) [**Where company dissolved**] Where a company has been dissolved, whether under this Act or otherwise, the registrar may, at any time after the expiration of 2 years from the date of the dissolution, direct that any documents in his custody relating to that company may be removed to the Public Record Office; and documents in respect of which such a direction is given shall be disposed of in accordance with the enactments relating to that Office and the rules made under them.

712(2) [**"Company"**] In this section "company" includes a company provisionally or completely registered under the Joint Stock Companies Act 1844.

712(3) [**Scotland**] This section does not extend to Scotland.

SEC. 713 Enforcement of company's duty to make returns

713(1) [**Order by court on application**] If a company, having made default in complying with any provision of the Companies Acts which requires it to file with, deliver or send to the registrar of companies any return, account or other document, or to give notice to him of any matter, fails to make good the default within 14 days after the service of a notice on the company requiring it to do so, the court may, on an application made to it by any member or creditor of the company or by the registrar of companies, make an order directing the company and any officer of it to make good the default within such time as may be specified in the order.

713(2) [**Costs**] The court's order may provide that all costs of and incidental to the application shall be borne by the company or by any officers of it responsible for the default.

713(3) [**Other enactments imposing penalties**] Nothing in this section prejudices the operation of any enactment imposing penalties on a company or its officers in respect of any such default as is mentioned above.

SEC. 714 Registrar's index of company and corporate names

714(1) [**Index to be kept re certain bodies**] The registrar of companies shall keep an index of the names of the following bodies —

(a) companies as defined by this Act,

(b) companies incorporated outside Great Britain which have complied with section 691 and which do not appear to the registrar of companies not to have a place of business in Great Britain,

  (c) incorporated and unincorporated bodies to which any provision of this Act applies by virtue of section 718 (unregistered companies),

  (d) limited partnerships registered under the Limited Partnerships Act 1907,

  (e) companies within the meaning of the Companies Act (Northern Ireland) 1960,

  (f) companies incorporated outside Northern Ireland which have complied with section 356 of that Act (which corresponds with section 691 of this Act), and which do not appear to the registrar not to have a place of business in Northern Ireland, and

  (g) societies registered under the Industrial and Provident Societies Act 1965 or the Industrial and Provident Societies Act (Northern Ireland) 1969.

714(2) [Variation or deletion re sec. 714(1)]   The Secretary of State may by order in a statutory instrument vary subsection (1) by the addition or deletion of any class of body, except any within paragraph (a) or (b) of the subsection, whether incorporated or unincorporated; and any such statutory instrument is subject to annulment in pursuance of a resolution of either House of Parliament.

SEC. 715   Destruction of old records

715(1) [Documents which may be destroyed]   The registrar of companies may destroy any documents or other material which he has kept for over 10 years and which were, or were comprised in or annexed or attached to, the accounts or annual returns of any company.

715(2) [Copies to be kept]   The registrar shall retain a copy of any document or other material destroyed in pursuance of subsection (1); and sections 709 and 710 apply in relation to any such copy as if it were the original.

PART XXV — MISCELLANEOUS AND SUPPLEMENTARY PROVISIONS

SEC. 716   Prohibition of partnerships with more than 20 members

716(1) [Requirement of registration]   No company, association or partnership consisting of more than 20 persons shall be formed for the purpose of carrying on any business that has for its object the acquisition of gain by the company, association or partnership, or by its individual members, unless it is registered as a company under this Act, or is formed in pursuance of some other Act of Parliament, or of letters patent.

716(2) [Qualification to sec. 716(1)]   However, this does not prohibit the formation—

  (a) for the purpose of carrying on practice as solicitors, of a partnership consisting of persons each of whom is a solicitor;

  (b) for the purpose of carrying on practice as accountants, of a partnership consisting of persons each of whom falls within either paragraph (a) or (b) of section 389(1) (qualifications of company auditors);

  (c) for the purpose of carrying on business as members of a recognised stock exchange, of a partnership consisting of persons each of whom is a member of that stock exchange;

(d) for any purpose prescribed by regulations (which may include a purpose mentioned above), of a partnership of a description so prescribed.

History
In s. 716(2), para. (d) inserted and words formerly appearing at the end omitted and repealed by CA 1989, s. 145, 212, Sch. 19, para. 15(1),(2) and Sch. 24 as from 1 April 1990 (see S.I. 1990 No. 355 (C. 13), art. 4(f), 5(1)(b), (2) and also relevant transitional or saving provisions in that S.I.); the former words were originally inserted by Financial Services Act 1986, s. 212(2) and Sch. 16, para. 22 as from 29 April 1988 (see S.I. 1988 No. 740 (C. 22)) (but now

repealed by CA 1989, s. 212 and Sch. 24 — see S.I. 1990 No. 355 (C. 13), art. 5(1)(e)) and read as follows:

"and in this subsection **"recognised stock exchange"** means The Stock Exchange and any other stock exchange which is declared to be a recognised stock exchange for the purposes of this section by an order in a statutory instrument made by the Secretary of State which is for the time being in force."

716(3)   ["Solicitor"]   In subsection (2)(a) **"solicitor"**—

(a) in relation to England and Wales, means solicitor of the Supreme Court, and

(b) in relation to Scotland, means a person enrolled or deemed enrolled as a solicitor in pursuance of the Solicitors (Scotland) Act 1980.

History
See history note after s. 716(4).

716(4)   ["Recognised stock exchange"]   In subsection (2)(c) **"recognised stock exchange"** means—

(a) The International Stock Exchange of the United Kingdom and the Republic of Ireland Limited, and

(b) any other stock exchange for the time being recognised for the purposes of this section by the Secretary of State by order made by statutory instrument.

History
S. 716(3), (4) substituted by CA 1989, s. 145 and Sch. 19, para. 15(1), (3) as from 1 April 1990 (see S.I. 1990 No. 355 (C. 13), art. 4(f)); s. 716(3), (4) formerly read as follows:

"716(3)   The Secretary of State may by regulations in a statutory instrument provide that subsection (1) shall not apply to the formation (otherwise than as permitted by subsection (2)), for a purpose specified in the regulations, of a partnership of a description so specified.

(4)   In this section "solicitor"—

(a) in relation to England and Wales, means solicitor of the Supreme Court, and

(b) in relation to Scotland, means a person enrolled or deemed enrolled as a solicitor in pursuance of the Solicitors (Scotland) Act 1980."

716(5)   [Non-application of sec. 716(1)]   Subsection (1) does not apply in relation to any body of persons for the time being approved for the purposes of the Marine and Aviation Insurance (War Risks) Act 1952 by the Secretary of State, being a body the objects of which are or include the carrying on of business by way of the re-insurance of risks which may be re-insured under any agreement for the purpose mentioned in section 1(1)(b) of that Act.

SEC. 717   Limited partnerships: limit on number of members

717(1)   [Exceptions to Limited Partnerships Act 1907]   So much of the Limited Partnerships Act 1907 as provides that a limited partnership shall not consist of more than 20 persons does not apply—

(a) to a partnership carrying on practice as solicitors and consisting of persons each of whom is a solicitor,

(b) to a partnership carrying on practice as accountants and consisting of persons each of whom falls within either paragraph (a) or (b) of section 389(1) of this Act (qualification of company auditors),

(c) to a partnership carrying on business as members of a recognised stock exchange and consisting of persons each of whom is a member of that exchange;

(d) to a partnership carrying on business of any description prescribed by regulations (which may include a business of any description mentioned above), of a partnership of a description so prescribed.

History

In s. 717(1), para. (d) inserted and words formerly appearing at the end omitted and repealed as from 1 April 1990 by CA 1989, s. 145, 212, Sch. 19, para. 16(1), (2) and Sch. 24 as from 1 April 1990 (see S.I. 1990 No. 355 (C. 13), art. 4(f), 5(1)(b), (2) and also relevant transitional or saving provisions in that S.I.); the former words were originally inserted by Financial; Services Act 1986, s. 212(2) and Sch. 16, para. 22 as from 29 April 1988 (see S.I. 1988 No. 740 (C. 22)) (but now repealed by CA 1989, s. 212 and Sch. 24.

— see S.I. 1990 No. 355 (C. 13), art. 5(1)(e) read as follows:

"and in this subsection **'recognised stock exchange'** means The Stock Exchange and any other stock exchange which is declared to be a recognised stock exchange for the purposes of this section by an order in a statutory instrument made by the Secretary of State which is for the time being in force."

717(2) **[Regulations]** The Secretary of State may by regulations in a statutory instrument provide that so much of section 4(2) of the Act of 1907 as provides that a limited partnership shall not consist of more than 20 persons shall not apply to a partnership (other than one permitted by subsection (1) of this section) carrying on business of a description specified in the regulations, being a partnership of a description so specified.

717(3) **["Solicitor"]** In this section **"solicitor"** means the same as in section 716.

SEC. 718 Unregistered companies

718(1) **[Application of provisions to certain unregistered companies]** The provisions of this Act specified in the first column of Schedule 22 (relating respectively to the matters specified in the second column of the Schedule) apply to all bodies corporate incorporated in and having a principal place of business in Great Britain, other than those mentioned in subsection (2) below, as if they were companies registered under this Act, but subject to any limitations mentioned in relation to those provisions respectively in the third column and to such adaptations and modifications (if any) as may be specified by regulations made by the Secretary of State.

718(2) **[Exception to application of sec. 718(1)]** Those provisions of this Act do not apply by virtue of this section to any of the following—

(a) any body incorporated by or registered under any public general Act of Parliament,

(b) any body not formed for the purpose of carrying on a business which has for its object the acquisition of gain by the body or its individual members,

(c) any body for the time being exempted by direction of the Secretary of State (or before him by the Board of Trade).

718(3) **[Application by regulations]** Where against any provision of this Act specified in the first column of Schedule 22 there appears in the third column the entry **"Subject to section 718(3)"**, it means that the provision is to apply by virtue of this section so far only as may be specified by regulations made by the Secretary of State and to such bodies corporate as may be so specified.

718(4) **[Certain unincorporated bodies, etc.]** The provisions specified in the first column of the Schedule also apply in like manner in relation to any unincorporated body of persons entitled by virtue of letters patent to any of the privileges conferred by the Chartered Companies Act 1837 and not registered under any other public general Act of Parliament, but subject to the like exceptions as are provided for in the case of bodies corporate by paragraphs (b) and (c) of subsection (2).

718(5)   [Operation of section]   This section does not repeal or revoke in whole or in part any enactment, royal charter or other instrument constituting or regulating any body in relation to which those provisions are applied by virtue of this section, or restrict the power of Her Majesty to grant a charter in lieu of or supplementary to any such charter as above mentioned; but, in relation to any such body, the operation of any such enactment, charter or instrument is suspended in so far as it is inconsistent with any of those provisions as they apply for the time being to that body.

718(6)   [Regulations]   The power to make regulations conferred by this section (whether regulations under subsection (1) or subsection (3)) is exercisable by statutory instrument subject to annulment in pursuance of a resolution of either House of Parliament.

Note
Re s. 718 see the Companies (Unregistered Companies) Regulations 1985 (S.I. 1985 No. 680), as amended.

SEC. 719   Power of company to provide for employees on cessation or transfer of business

719(1)   [For benefit of employees]   The powers of a company include (if they would not otherwise do so apart from this section) power to make the following provision for the benefit of persons employed or formerly employed by the company or any of its subsidiaries, that is to say, provision in connection with the cessation or the transfer to any person of the whole or part of the undertaking of the company or that subsidiary.

719(2)   [Exercise of sec. 719(1) power]   The power conferred by subsection (1) is exercisable notwithstanding that its exercise is not in the best interests of the company.

719(3)   [Sanctions for exercise of power]   The power which a company may exercise by virtue only of subsection (1) shall only be exercised by the company if sanctioned —

   (a) in a case not falling within paragraph (b) or (c) below, by an ordinary resolution of the company, or

   (b) if so authorised by the memorandum or articles, a resolution of the directors, or

   (c) if the memorandum or articles require the exercise of the power to be sanctioned by a resolution of the company of some other description for which more than a simple majority of the members voting is necessary, with the sanction of a resolution of that description;

and in any case after compliance with any other requirements of the memorandum or articles applicable to its exercise.

719(4)   [Source of payment]   Any payment which may be made by a company under this section may, if made before the commencement of any winding up of the company, be made out of profits of the company which are available for dividend.

SEC. 720 Certain companies to publish periodical statement

720(1) [Statement in form of Sch. 23] Every company, being an insurance company or a deposit, provident or benefit society, shall before it commences business, and also on the first Monday in February and the first Tuesday in August in every year during which it carries on business, make a statement in the form set out in Schedule 23, or as near to it as circumstances admit.

720(2) [Copy of statement in registered office, etc.] A copy of the statement shall be put up in a conspicuous place in the company's registered office, and in every branch office or place where the business of the company is carried on.

720(3) [Entitlement to copy] Every member and every creditor of the company is entitled to a copy of the statement, on payment of a sum not exceeding $2\frac{1}{2}$ pence.

720(4) [Penalty on default] If default is made in complying with this section, the company and every officer of it who is in default is liable to a fine and, for continued contravention, to a daily default fine.

720(5) [Deemed insurance company] For purposes of this Act, a company which carries on the business of insurance in common with any other business or businesses is deemed an insurance company.

720(6) [Exception re certain insurance companies] In the case of an insurance company to which Part II of the Insurance Companies Act 1982 applies, this section does not apply if the company complies with provisions of that Act as to the accounts and balance sheet to be prepared annually and deposited by such a company.

720(7) [Regulations] The Secretary of State may, by regulations in a statutory instrument (subject to annulment in pursuance of a resolution of either House of Parliament), alter the form in Schedule 23.

SEC. 721 Production and inspection of books where offence suspected

721(1) [Application re possible offence in company management, etc.] The following applies if on an application made—

(a) in England and Wales, to a judge of the High Court by the Director of Public Prosecutions, the Secretary of State or a chief officer of police, or

(b) in Scotland, to one of the Lords Commissioners of Justiciary by the Lord Advocate,

there is shown to be reasonable cause to believe that any person has, while an officer of a company, committed an offence in connection with the management of the company's affairs and that evidence of the commission of the offence is to be found in any books or papers of or under the control of the company.

721(2) [Court order for inspection or production] An order may be made—

(a) authorising any person named in it to inspect the books or papers in question, or any of them, for the purpose of investigating and obtaining evidence of the offence, or

(b) requiring the secretary of the company or such other officer of it as may be named in the order to produce the books or papers (or any of them) to a person named in the order at a place so named.

721(3)   [Application of sec. 721(1), (2) to bankers]   The above applies also in relation to any books or papers of a person carrying on the business of banking so far as they relate to the company's affairs, as it applies to any books or papers of or under the control of the company, except that no such order as is referred to in subsection (2)(b) shall be made by virtue of this subsection.

721(4)   [No appeal from court decision]   The decision of a judge of the High Court or of any of the Lords Commissioners of Justiciary on an application under this section is not appealable.

SEC. 722   Form of company registers, etc.

722(1)   [Form]   Any register, index, minute book or accounting records required by the Companies Acts to be kept by a company may be kept either by making entries in bound books or by recording the matters in question in any other manner.

722(2)   [Precautions against falsification, etc.]   Where any such register, index, minute book or accounting record is not kept by making entries in a bound book, but by some other means, adequate precautions shall be taken for guarding against falsification and facilitating its discovery.

722(3)   [Penalty on default re sec. 722(2)]   If default is made in complying with subsection (2), the company and every officer of it who is in default is liable to a fine and, for continued contravention, to a daily default fine.

SEC. 723   Use of computers for company records

723(1)   [Records otherwise than in legible form]   The power conferred on a company by section 722(1) to keep a register or other record by recording the matters in question otherwise than by making entries in bound books includes power to keep the register or other record by recording those matters otherwise than in a legible form, so long as the recording is capable of being reproduced in a legible form.

723(2)   [Certain provisions in instrument before 12 February 1979]   Any provision of an instrument made by a company before 12th February 1979 which requires a register of holders of the company's debentures to be kept in a legible form is to be read as requiring the register to be kept in a legible or non-legible form.

723(3)   [Extension of duty re inspection, etc.]   If any such register or other record of a company as is mentioned in section 722(1), or a register of holders of a company's debentures, is kept by the company by recording the matters in question otherwise than in a legible form, any duty imposed on the company by this Act to allow inspection of, or to furnish a copy of, the register or other record or any part of it is to be treated as a duty to allow inspection of, or to furnish, a reproduction of the recording or of the relevant part of it in a legible form.

723(4)   [Additional provisions in regulations]   The Secretary of State may by regulations in a statutory instrument make such provision in addition to subsection (3) as he considers appropriate in connection with such registers or other records as are mentioned in that subsection, and are kept as so mentioned; and the regulations may make modifications of provisions of this Act relating to such registers or other records.

723(5) **[Annulment of sec. 723(4) statutory instrument]** A statutory instrument under subsection (4) is subject to annulment in pursuance of a resolution of either House of Parliament.

SEC. 724 Cross-border operation of receivership provisions

724 (Repealed by Insolvency Act 1986, sec. 438 and Sch. 12 as from 29 December 1986.)

History

In regard to the date of the above repeal see Insolvency Act 1986, s. 443 and S.I. 1986 No. 1924 (C. 71). S. 724 formerly read as follows:

"**724(1)** A receiver appointed under the law of either part of Great Britain in respect of the whole or any part of any property or undertaking of a company and in consequence of the company having created a charge which, as created, was a floating charge may exercise his powers in the other part of Great Britain so far as their exercise is not inconsistent with the law applicable there.

(2) In subsection (1) '**receiver**' includes a manager and a person who is appointed both receiver and manager."

SEC. 725 Service of documents

725(1) **[Usual service]** A document may be served on a company by leaving it at, or sending it by post to, the company's registered office.

725(2) **[Scottish registered company carrying on business in England]** Where a company registered in Scotland carries on business in England and Wales, the process of any court in England and Wales may be served on the company by leaving it at, or sending it by post to, the company's principal place of business in England and Wales, addressed to the manager or other head officer in England and Wales of the company.

725(3) **[Copy to registered office if sec. 725(2) service]** Where process is served on a company under subsection (2), the person issuing out the process shall send a copy of it by post to the company's registered office.

SEC. 726 Costs and expenses in actions by certain limited companies

726(1) **[Security for costs — England and Wales]** Where in England and Wales a limited company is plaintiff in an action or other legal proceeding, the court having jurisdiction in the matter may, if it appears by credible testimony that there is reason to believe that the company will be unable to pay the defendant's costs if successful in his defence, require sufficient security to be given for those costs, and may stay all proceedings until the security is given.

726(2) **[Caution for costs — Scotland]** Where in Scotland a limited company is pursuer in an action or other legal proceeding, the court having jurisdiction in the matter may, if it appears by credible testimony that there is reason to believe that the company will be unable to pay the defender's expenses if successful in his defence, order the company to find caution and sist the proceedings until caution is found.

SEC. 727 Power of court to grant relief in certain cases

727(1) **[Relief of officers from liability]** If in any proceedings for negligence, default, breach of duty or breach of trust against an officer of a company or a person employed by a company as auditor (whether he is or is not an officer of the company) it appears to the court hearing the case that that officer or person is or may be liable in respect of the negligence, default, breach of duty or breach of trust, but that he has acted honestly and reasonably, and that having regard to all the circumstances of the case (including those connected with his appointment) he ought fairly to be excused for the negligence, default, breach of duty or breach of trust, that court may relieve him, either wholly or partly, from his liability on such terms as it thinks fit.

727(2)   [Application by officer for relief]   If any such officer or person as above-mentioned has reason to apprehend that any claim will or might be made against him in respect of any negligence, default, breach of duty or breach of trust, he may apply to the court for relief; and the court on the application has the same power to relieve him as under this section it would have had if it had been a court before which proceedings against that person for negligence, default, breach of duty or breach of trust had been brought.

727(3)   [Withdrawal of case from jury]   Where a case to which subsection (1) applies is being tried by a judge with a jury, the judge, after hearing the evidence, may, if he is satisfied that the defendant or defender ought in pursuance of that subsection to be relieved either in whole or in part from the liability sought to be enforced against him, withdraw the case in whole or in part from the jury and forthwith direct judgment to be entered for the defendant or defender on such terms as to costs or otherwise as the judge may think proper.

SEC. 728   Enforcement of High Court orders

728   Orders made by the High Court under this Act may be enforced in the same manner as orders made in an action pending in that court.

SEC. 729   Annual report by Secretary of State

729   The Secretary of State shall cause a general annual report of matters within the Companies Acts to be prepared and laid before both Houses of Parliament.

SEC. 730   Punishment of offences

730(1)   [Sch. 24]   Schedule 24 to this Act has effect with respect to the way in which offences under this Act are punishable on conviction.

730(2)   [First, second and third columns of Schedule]   In relation to an offence under a provision of this Act specified in the first column of the Schedule (the general nature of the offence being described in the second column), the third column shows whether the offence is punishable on conviction on indictment, or on summary conviction, or either in the one way or the other.

730(3)   [Fourth column]   The fourth column of the Schedule shows, in relation to an offence, the maximum punishment by way of fine or imprisonment under this Act which may be imposed on a person convicted of the offence in the way specified in relation to it in the third column (that is to say, on indictment or summarily), a reference to a period of years or months being to a term of imprisonment of that duration.

730(4)   [Fifth column]   The fifth column shows (in relation to an offence for which there is an entry in that column) that a person convicted of the offence after continued contravention is liable to a daily default fine; that is to say, he is liable on a second or subsequent summary conviction of the offence to the fine specified in that column for each day on which the contravention is continued (instead of the penalty specified for the offence in the fourth column of the Schedule).

730(5) **["Officer who is in default"]** For the purpose of any enactment in the Companies Acts which provides that an officer of a company or other body who is in default is liable to a fine or penalty, the expression **"officer who is in default"** means any officer of the company or other body who knowingly and wilfully authorises or permits the default, refusal or contravention mentioned in the enactment.

History
In s. 730(5) the words "or other body" (appearing twice)
inserted by CA 1989, s. 145 and Sch. 19, para. 17 as from
1 April 1990 (see S.I. 1990 No. 355 (C. 13), art. 4(f)).

SEC. 731 Summary proceedings

731(1) **[Taking of summary proceedings]** Summary proceedings for any offence under the Companies Acts may (without prejudice to any jurisdiction exercisable apart from this subsection) be taken against a body corporate at any place at which the body has a place of business, and against any other person at any place at which he is for the time being.

731(2) **[Time for laying information]** Notwithstanding anything in section 127(1) of the Magistrates' Courts Act 1980, an information relating to an offence under the Companies Acts which is triable by a magistrates' court in England and Wales may be so tried if it is laid at any time within 3 years after the commission of the offence and within 12 months after the date on which evidence sufficient in the opinion of the Director of Public Prosecutions or the Secretary of State (as the case may be) to justify the proceedings comes to his knowledge.

731(3) **[Time for commencement of summary proceedings in Scotland]** Summary proceedings in Scotland for an offence under the Companies Acts shall not be commenced after the expiration of 3 years from the commission of the offence.

Subject to this (and notwithstanding anything in section 331 of the Criminal Procedure (Scotland) Act 1975), such proceedings may (in Scotland) be commenced at any time within 12 months after the date on which evidence sufficient in the Lord Advocate's opinion to justify the proceedings came to his knowledge or, where such evidence was reported to him by the Secretary of State, within 12 months after the date on which it came to the knowledge of the latter; and subsection (3) of that section applies for the purpose of this subsection as it applies for the purpose of that section.

731(4) **[Certificate by DPP et al. conclusive evidence]** For purposes of this section, a certificate of the Director of Public Prosecutions, the Lord Advocate or the Secretary of State (as the case may be) as to the date on which such evidence as is referred to above came to his knowledge is conclusive evidence.

SEC. 732 Prosecution by public authorities

732(1) **[Institution of proceedings only with consent]** In respect of an offence under any of sections 210, 324, 329, 447 to 451 and 455, proceedings shall not, in England and Wales, be instituted except by or with the consent of the appropriate authority.

732(2)   [Authority under sec. 732(1)]   That authority is—

(a) for an offence under any of sections 210, 324 and 329, the Secretary of State or the Director of Public Prosecutions,

(b) for an offence under any of sections 447 to 451, either one of those two persons or the Industrial Assurance Commissioner, and

(c) for an offence under section 455, the Secretary of State.

732(3)   [Legal professional privilege]   Where proceedings are instituted under the Companies Acts against any person by the Director of Public Prosecutions or by or on behalf of the Secretary of State or the Lord Advocate, nothing in those Acts is to be taken to require any person to disclose any information which he is entitled to refuse to disclose on grounds of legal professional privilege.

SEC. 733   Offences by bodies corporate

733(1)   [Application]   The following applies to offences under any of sections 210, 216(3), 394A(1) and 447 to 451.

History
In s. 733(1) "295(7)" inserted by Insolvency Act 1985, s. 109 and Sch. 6, para. 7(2) as from 28 April 1986; and omitted by Insolvency Act 1986, s. 439(1) and Sch. 13 as from 29 December 1986 (see IA 1986, s. 443 and S.I. 1986 No. 1924 (C. 71)). Also in s. 733(1) ", 394A(1)" inserted by CA 1989, s. 123(3) as from 1 April 1990 subject to transitional and saving provisions (see S.I. 1990 No. 355 (C. 13), art. 4(a) and also art. 10).

733(2)   [Offence re officer]   Where a body corporate is guilty of such an offence and it is proved that the offence occurred with the consent or connivance of, or was attributable to any neglect on the part of any director, manager, secretary or other similar officer of the body, or any person who was purporting to act in any such capacity, he as well as the body corporate is guilty of that offence and is liable to be proceeded against and punished accordingly.

733(3)   [Where managers are members]   Where the affairs of a body corporate are managed by its members, then in the case of an offence under section 210, or 216(3), subsection (2) above applies in relation to the acts and defaults of a member in connection with his functions of management as if he were a director of the body corporate.

History
In s. 733(3) the words "210, 216(3) or 295(7)" substituted for the former words "210 or 216(3)" by Insolvency Act 1985, s. 109 and Sch. 6, para. 7(3) as from 28 April 1986. In addition the words "or 216(3)" substituted for the former words "216(3) or 295(7)" by Insolvency Act 1986, s. 439(1) and Sch. 13 as from 29 December 1986 (see IA 1986, s. 443 and S.I. 1986 No. 1924 (C. 71)).

733(4)   ["Director"]   In this section **"director"**, in relation to an offence under any of sections 447 to 451, includes a shadow director.

SEC. 734   Criminal proceedings against unincorporated bodies

734(1)   [Offences by unincorporated body]   Proceedings for an offence alleged to have been committed under section 389A(3) or section 394A(1) or any of sections 447 to 451 by an unincorporated body shall be brought in the name of that body (and not in that of any of its members), and for the purposes of any such proceedings, any rules of court relating to the service of documents apply as if that body were a corporation.

History
In s. 734(1) the words "section 389A(3) or" and "section 394A(1) or" inserted by CA 1989, s. 120(2), 123(4) as from 1 April 1990 subject to transitional and saving provisions (see S.I. 1990 No. 355 (C. 13), art. 4(a) and also art. 10).

734(2) **[Payment of fine]** A fine imposed on an unincorporated body on its conviction of such an offence shall be paid out of the funds of that body.

734(3) **[Application of Criminal Justice Act, etc.]** In a case in which an unincorporated body is charged in England and Wales with such an offence, section 33 of the Criminal Justice Act 1925 and Schedule 3 to the Magistrates' Courts Act 1980 (procedure on charge of an offence against a corporation) have effect in like manner as in the case of a corporation so charged.

734(4) **[Scotland: application of Criminal Procedure (Scotland) Act]** In relation to proceedings on indictment in Scotland for such an offence alleged to have been committed by an unincorporated body, section 74 of the Criminal Procedure (Scotland) Act 1975 (proceedings on indictment against bodies corporate) has effect as if that body were a body corporate.

734(5) **[Offence by partner]** Where such an offence committed by a partnership is proved to have been committed with the consent or connivance of, or to be attributable to any neglect on the part of, a partner, he as well as the partnership is guilty of the offence and liable to be proceeded against and punished accordingly.

734(6) **[Offence by member of unincorporated body]** Where such an offence committed by an unincorporated body (other than a partnership) is proved to have been committed with the consent or connivance of, or to be attributable to any neglect on the part of, any officer of the body or any member of its governing body, he as well as the body is guilty of the offence and liable to be proceeded against and punished accordingly.

History
S. 734(5), (6) added by CA 1989, s. 145 and Sch. 19, para. 18 as from 1 April 1990 (see S.I. 1990 No. 355 (C. 13), art. 4(f)).

PART XXVI — INTERPRETATION

SEC. 735 "Company", etc.

735(1) **["Company", "existing company", etc.]** In this Act—

(a) **"company"** means a company formed and registered under this Act, or an existing company;

(b) **"existing company"** means a company formed and registered under the former Companies Acts, but does not include a company registered under the Joint Stock Companies Acts, the Companies Act 1862 or the Companies (Consolidation) Act 1908 in what was then Ireland;

(c) **"the former Companies Acts"** means the Joint Stock Companies Acts, the Companies Act 1862, the Companies (Consolidation) Act 1908, the Companies Act 1929 and the Companies Acts 1948 to 1983.

735(2) **["Public company", "private company"]** "Public company" and "private company" have the meanings given by section 1(3).

735(3) **["The Joint Stock Companies Acts"]**   **"The Joint Stock Companies Acts"** means the Joint Stock Companies Act 1856, the Joint Stock Companies Acts 1856, 1857, the Joint Stock Banking Companies Act 1857 and the Act to enable Joint Stock Banking Companies to be formed on the principle of limited liability, or any one or more of those Acts (as the case may require), but does not include the Joint Stock Companies Act 1844.

735(4) **[Application of definitions]**   The definitions in this section apply unless the contrary intention appears.

SEC. 735A   Relationship of this Act to Insolvency Act

735A(1) **["The Insolvency Act"]**   In this Act **"the Insolvency Act"** means the Insolvency Act 1986; and in the following provisions of this Act, namely, sections 375(1)(b), 425(6)(a), 460(2), 675, 676, 677, 699(1), 728 and Schedule 21, paragraph 6(1), the words "this Act" are to be read as including Parts I to VII of that Act, sections 411, 413, 414, 416 and 417 in Part XV of that Act, and also the Company Directors Disqualification Act 1986.

History
In s. 735A(1) the words "440, 449(1)(a) and (d)" formerly appearing after "425(6)(a)", repealed by CA 1989, sec.   212 and Sch. 24 as from 21 February 1990 (see S.I. 1990 No. 142 (C. 5), art. 7(d)).

735A(2) **[Interpretation]**   In sections 704(5), 706(1), 707(1), 708(1)(a) and (4), 710(5), 713(1), 729 and 732(3) references to the Companies Acts include Parts I to VII of the Insolvency Act, sections 411, 413, 414, 416 and 417 in Part XV of that Act, and also the Company Directors Disqualification Act 1986.

735A(3) **[Application of sec. 735A(1), (2)]**   Subsections (1) and (2) apply unless the contrary intention appears.

History
S. 735A inserted by Insolvency Act 1986, s. 439(1) and Sch. 13, Pt. II as from 29 December 1986 (see IA 1986, s. 443 and S.I. 1986 No. 1924 (C. 71)).

SEC. 736   "Holding company", "subsidiary" and "wholly-owned subsidiary"

736(1) **[Where company subsidiary of another]**   For the purposes of this Act, a company is deemed to be a subsidiary of another if (but only if) —

   (a) that other either —

     (i) is a member of it and controls the composition of its board of directors, or

     (ii) holds more than half in nominal value of its equity share capital, or

   (b) the first-mentioned company is a subsidiary of any company which is that other's subsidiary.

   The above is subject to subsection (4) below in this section.

736(2) **[Where board controlled by another company]**   For purposes of subsection (1), the composition of a company's board of directors is deemed to be controlled by another company if (but only if) that other company by the exercise of some power exercisable by it without the consent or concurrence of any other person can appoint or remove the holders of all or a majority of the directorships.

736(3) [**Conditions re power to appoint to directorship under sec. 736(2)**] For purposes of this last provision, the other company is deemed to have power to appoint to a directorship with respect to which any of the following conditions is satisfied —

    (a) that a person cannot be appointed to it without the exercise in his favour by the other company of such a power as is mentioned above, or

    (b) that a person's appointment to the directorship follows necessarily from his appointment as director of the other company, or

    (c) that the directorship is held by the other company itself or by a subsidiary of it.

736(4) [**Determination of whether one company subsidiary of another**] In determining whether one company is a subsidiary of another —

    (a) any shares held or power exercisable by the other in a fiduciary capacity are to be treated as not held or exercisable by it,

    (b) subject to the two following paragraphs, any shares held or power exercisable—

      (i) by any person as nominee for the other (except where the other is concerned only in a fiduciary capacity), or

      (ii) by, or by a nominee for, a subsidiary of the other (not being a subsidiary which is concerned only in a fiduciary capacity),

      are to be treated as held or exercisable by the other,

    (c) any shares held or power exercisable by any person by virtue of the provisions of any debentures of the first-mentioned company or of a trust deed for securing any issue of such debentures are to be disregarded,

    (d) any shares held or power exercisable by, or by a nominee for, the other or its subsidiary (not being held or exercisable as mentioned in paragraph (c)) are to be treated as not held or exercisable by the other if the ordinary business of the other or its subsidiary (as the case may be) includes the lending of money and the shares are held or the power is exercisable as above mentioned by way of security only for the purposes of a transaction entered into in the ordinary course of that business.

736(5) [**Holding company and wholly-owned subsidiary**] For purposes of this Act—

    (a) a company is deemed to be another's holding company if (but only if) the other is its subsidiary, and

    (b) a body corporate is deemed the wholly-owned subsidiary of another if it has no members except that other and that other's wholly-owned subsidiaries and its or their nominees.

736(6) [**"Company"**] In this section **"company"** includes any body corporate.

SEC. 737   "Called-up share capital"

737(1) [**"Called-up share capital"**] In this Act, **"called-up share capital"** in relation to a company, means so much of its share capital as equals the aggregate amount of the calls made on its shares (whether or not those calls have been paid), together with any share capital paid up without being called and any share capital to be paid on a specified future date under the articles, the terms of allotment of the relevant shares or any other arrangements for payment of those shares.

737(2)   **["Uncalled share capital"]**   "Uncalled share capital" is to be construed accordingly.

737(3)   **[Application of definitions]**   The definitions in this section apply unless the contrary intention appears.

SEC. 738   "Allotment" and "paid up"

738(1)   **[Where share allotted]**   In relation to an allotment of shares in a company, the shares are to be taken for the purposes of this Act to be allotted when a person acquires the unconditional right to be included in the company's register of members in respect of those shares.

738(2)   **[Where share paid up in cash, or allotted in cash]**   For purposes of this Act, a share in a company is deemed paid up (as to its nominal value or any premium on it) in cash, or allotted for cash, if the consideration for the allotment or payment up is cash received by the company, or is a cheque received by it in good faith which the directors have no reason for suspecting will not be paid, or is a release of a liability of the company for a liquidated sum, or is an undertaking to pay cash to the company at a future date.

738(3)   **[References to consideration other than cash, etc.]**   In relation to the allotment or payment up of any shares in a company, references in this Act (except sections 89 to 94) to consideration other than cash and to the payment up of shares and premiums on shares otherwise than in cash include the payment of, or any undertaking to pay, cash to any person other than the company.

738(4)   **["Cash"]**   For the purpose of determining whether a share is or is to be allotted for cash, or paid up in cash, "**cash**" includes foreign currency.

SEC. 739   "Non-cash asset"

739(1)   **["Non-cash asset"]**   In this Act "**non-cash asset**" means any property or interest in property other than cash; and for this purpose "**cash**" includes foreign currency.

739(2)   **[Reference to transfer of non-cash asset, etc.]**   A reference to the transfer or acquisition of a non-cash asset includes the creation or extinction of an estate or interest in, or a right over, any property and also the discharge of any person's liability, other than a liability for a liquidated sum.

SEC. 740   "Body corporate" and "corporation"

740   References in this Act to a body corporate or to a corporation do not include a corporation sole, but include a company incorporated elsewhere than in Great Britain.

     Such references to a body corporate do not include a Scottish firm.

SEC. 741   "Director" and "shadow director"

741(1)   **["Director"]**   In this Act, "**director**" includes any person occupying the position of director, by whatever name called.

741(2) ["**Shadow director**"]   In relation to a company, "**shadow director**" means a person in accordance with whose directions or instructions the directors of the company are accustomed to act.

However, a person is not deemed a shadow director by reason only that the directors act on advice given by him in a professional capacity.

741(3) [**Where body corporate not shadow director of subsidiary**]   For the purposes of the following provisions of this Act, namely —

section 309 (directors' duty to have regard to interests of employees),

section 319 (directors' long-term contracts of employment),

sections 320 to 322 (substantial property transactions involving directors), and

sections 330 to 346 (general restrictions on power of companies to make loans, etc., to directors and others connected with them),

(being provisions under which shadow directors are treated as directors), a body corporate is not to be treated as a shadow director of any of its subsidiary companies by reason only that the directors of the subsidiary are accustomed to act in accordance with its directions or instructions.

SEC. 742   Expressions used in connection with accounts

742(1) [**Definitions**]   In this Act, unless a contrary intention appears, the following expressions have the same meaning as in Part VII (accounts)—

"**annual accounts**",

"**accounting reference date**" and "**accounting reference period**",

"**balance sheet**" and "**balance sheet date**",

"**current assets**",

"**financial year**", in relation to a company,

"**fixed assets**",

"**parent company**" and "**parent undertaking**",

"**profit and loss account**", and

"**subsidiary undertaking**".

742(2) [**References to "realised profits", "realised losses"**]   References in this Act to "realised profits" and "realised losses", in relation to a company's accounts, shall be construed in accordance with section 262(3).

History
S. 742 substituted by CA 1989, s. 23 and Sch. 10, para. 15 as from 1 April 1990 subject to transitional and saving provisions (see S.I. 1990 No. 355 (C. 13), art. 3, Sch. 1 and also art. 6–9); s. 742 formerly read as follows:

"**SEC. 742**   Expressions used in connection with accounts

742(1)   In this Act, unless the contrary intention appears—

(a)   '**accounting reference period**' has the meaning given by sections 224 to 226;

(b)   '**accounts**' includes a company's group accounts (within the meaning of section 229), whether prepared in the form of accounts or not;

(c)   '**balance sheet date**', in relation to a balance sheet, means the date as at which the balance sheet was prepared;

(d)   '**financial year**' —

(i)   in relation to a body corporate to which Part VII applies, means a period in respect of which a profit and loss account under section 227 in that Part is made up, and

(ii)   in relation to any other body corporate, means a period in respect of which a profit and loss account of the body laid before it in general meeting is made up,

(whether, in either case, that period is a year or not);

(e)   any reference to a profit and loss account, in the case of a company not trading for profit, is to its income and expenditure account, and references to profit or loss and, if the company has subsidiaries, references to a consolidated profit and loss account are to be construed accordingly.

(2) Except in relation to special category accounts, any reference to a balance sheet or profit and loss account includes any notes to the account in question giving information which is required by any provision of this Act, and required or allowed by any such provision to be given in a note to company accounts.

(3) In relation to special category accounts, any reference to a balance sheet or profit and loss account includes any notes thereon or document annexed thereto giving information which is required by this Act and is thereby allowed to be so given.

(4) References to special category companies and special category accounts are to be construed in accordance with Chapter II of Part VII.

(5) For the purposes of Part VII, a body corporate is to be regarded as publishing any balance sheet or other account if it publishes, issues or circulates it or otherwise makes it available for public inspection in a manner calculated to invite members of the public generally, or any class of members of the public, to read it.

(6) Expressions which, when used in Schedule 4, fall to be construed in accordance with any provision of Part VII of that Schedule have the same meaning (unless the contrary intention appears) when used in any provision of this Act.''

SEC. 743   "Employees' share scheme"

743 For purposes of this Act, an employees' share scheme is a scheme for encouraging or facilitating the holding of shares or debentures in a company by or for the benefit of—

    (a) the bona fide employees or former employees of the company, the company's subsidiary or holding company or a subsidiary of the company's holding company, or

    (b) the wives, husbands, widows, widowers or children or step-children under the age of 18 of such employees or former employees.

SEC. 743A   Meaning of "office copy" in Scotland

743A References in this Act to an office copy of a court order shall be construed, as respects Scotland, as references to a certified copy interlocutor.

History
S. 743A inserted by CA 1989, s. 145 and Sch. 19, para. 19 as from 1 March 1990 (see S.I. 1990 No. 142 (C. 5), art. 5).

SEC. 744   Expressions used generally in this Act

744 In this Act, unless the contrary intention appears, the following definitions apply—

    "agent" does not include a person's counsel acting as such;

    "annual return" means the return to be made by a company under section 363 or 364 (as the case may be);

    "articles" means, in relation to a company, its articles of association, as originally framed or as altered by resolution, including (so far as applicable to the company) regulations contained in or annexed to any enactment relating to companies passed before this Act, as altered by or under any such enactment;

    "authorised minimum" has the meaning given by section 118;

    "bank holiday" means a holiday under the Banking and Financial Dealings Act 1971;

    "banking company" means a company which is authorised under the Banking Act 1987;

    "books and papers" and **"books or papers"** include accounts, deeds, writings and documents;

"the Companies Acts" means this Act, the Insider Dealing Act and the Consequential Provisions Act;

"the Consequential Provisions Act" means the Companies Consolidation (Consequential Provisions) Act 1985;

"the court", in relation to a company, means the court having jurisdiction to wind up the company;

"debenture" includes debenture stock, bonds and any other securities of a company, whether constituting a charge on the assets of the company or not;

"document" includes summons, notice, order, and other legal process, and registers;

"equity share capital" means, in relation to a company, its issued share capital excluding any part of that capital which, neither as respects dividends nor as respects capital, carries any right to participate beyond a specified amount in a distribution;

"expert" has the meaning given by section 62;

"floating charge" includes a floating charge within the meaning given by section 462;

"the Gazette" means, as respects companies registered in England and Wales, the London Gazette and, as respects companies registered in Scotland, the Edinburgh Gazette;

"hire-purchase agreement" has the same meaning as in the Consumer Credit Act 1974;

"the Insider Dealing Act" means the Company Securities (Insider Dealing) Act 1985;

"insurance company" means the same as in the Insurance Companies Act 1982;

"joint stock company" has the meaning given by section 683;

"memorandum", in relation to a company, means its memorandum of association, as originally framed or as altered in pursuance of any enactment;

"number", in relation to shares, includes amount, where the context admits of the reference to shares being construed to include stock;

"officer", in relation to a body corporate, includes a director, manager or secretary;

"official seal", in relation to the registrar of companies, means a seal prepared under section 704(4) for the authentication of documents required for or in connection with the registration of companies;

"oversea company" means —

(a) a company incorporated elsewhere than in Great Britain which, after the commencement of this Act, establishes a place of business in Great Britain, and

(b) a company so incorporated which has, before that commencement, established a place of business and continues to have an established place of business in Great Britain at that commencement;

"place of business" includes a share transfer or share registration office;

"prescribed" means—

(a) as respects provisions of this Act relating to winding up, prescribed by general rules, and

(b) otherwise, prescribed by statutory instrument made by the Secretary of State;

"prospectus" means any prospectus, notice, circular, advertisement, or other invitation, offering to the public for subscription or purchase any shares in or debentures of a company;

"prospectus issued generally" means a prospectus issued to persons who are not existing members of the company or holders of its debentures;

"the registrar of companies" and **"the registrar"** mean the registrar or other officer performing under this Act the duty of registration of companies in England and Wales or in Scotland, as the case may require;

"share" means share in the share capital of a company, and includes stock (except where a distinction between shares and stock is express or implied); and

"undistributable reserves" has the meaning given by section 264(3).

History
In s. 744

● the definition of "banking company" inserted and the definition of "authorised institution" formerly appearing omitted by CA 1989, s. 23, 212, Sch. 10, para. 16 and Sch. 24 as from 1 April 1990 subject to transitional and saving provisions (see S.I. 1990 No. 355 (C. 13), art 3, 5(1)(b), (2), Sch. 1 and also art. 6–9); the former definition of "authorised institution" read as follows:

"**'authorised institution'** means a company which is an institution authorised under the Banking Act 1987;"

Previously the definition of "authorised institution" inserted and the definition of "recognised bank" formerly appearing omitted by Banking Act 1987, s. 108(1) and Sch. 6, para. 18(8) as from 1 October 1987 (the latter definition also repealed by s. 108(2) and Sch. 7, Pt. I of that Act from the same date) (see S.I. 1987 No. 1664 (C. 50)); the former definition of "recognised bank" read as follows:

"**'recognised bank'** means a company which is recognised as a bank for the purposes of the Banking Act 1979;"

● the definition "**'general rules'** means general rules made under section 663, and includes forms;", and in the

definition "prescribed" the words "under section 663" formerly appearing after the words "general rules" repealed by Insolvency Act 1985, s. 235 and Sch. 10, Pt. II as from 1 March 1986 as far as they relate to the meaning of general rules in relation to England and Wales (see S.I. 1986 No. 185 (C. 7)), and otherwise from 29 December 1986 (see IA 1986, s. 443 and S.I. 1986 No. 1924 (C. 71)).

● the definition of "recognised stock exchange" formerly appearing repealed by Financial Services Act 1986, s. 212(3) and Sch. 17, Pt. I as from 29 April 1986 (see S.I. 1988 No. 740 (C. 22)): the former definition read as follows:

"**'recognised stock exchange'** means any body of persons which is for the time being a recognised stock exchange for the purposes of the Prevention of Fraud (Investments) Act 1958;"

Note
In s. 744 the definition of "prospectus issued generally" repealed by Financial Services Act 1986, s. 212(3) and Sch. 17, Pt. I as from 29 April 1988 as far as they would apply to a prospectus offering for subscription, or to any form of application for units in a body corporate which is a recognised scheme (see S.I. 1988 No. 740 (C. 22)).

PART XXVII — FINAL PROVISIONS

SEC. 745   Northern Ireland

745(1) [Application only when expressly provided] Except where otherwise expressly provided, nothing in this Act (except provisions relating expressly to companies registered or incorporated in Northern Ireland or outside Great Britain) applies to or in relation to companies so registered or incorporated.

745(2) **[Not usually applicable]** Subject to any such provision, and to any express provision as to extent, this Act does not extend to Northern Ireland.

SEC. 746 Commencement

746 This Act comes into force on 1st July 1985.

History
In s. 746 the words "Except as provided by section 243(6)," formerly appearing at the beginning repealed by CA 1989, s. 212 and Sch. 24 as from 1 April 1990 subject to any relevant transitional or saving provisions (see S.I. 1990 No. 355 (C. 13), art. 5(1)(b), (2)).

SEC. 747 Citation

747 This Act may be cited as the Companies Act 1985.

SCHEDULES

Schedule 1 — Particulars of Directors etc. to be Contained in Statement Under Section 10

Section 10

DIRECTORS

1 Subject as provided below, the statement under section 10(2) shall contain the following particulars with respect to each person named as director —

   (a) in the case of an individual, his present Christian name and surname, any former Christian name or surname, his usual residential address, his nationality, his business occupation (if any), particulars of any other directorships held by him, or which have been held by him and, in the case of a company subject to section 293, the date of his birth;

   (b) in the case of a corporation, its corporate name and registered or principal office.

2(1) It is not necessary for the statement to contain particulars of a directorship —

   (a) which has not been held by a director at any time during the 5 years preceding the date on which the statement is delivered to the registrar,

   (b) which is held by a director in a company which —

      (i) is dormant or grouped with the company delivering the statement, and

      (ii) if he also held that directorship for any period during those 5 years, was for the whole of that period either dormant or so grouped,

   (c) which was held by a director for any period during those 5 years in a company which for the whole of that period was either dormant or grouped with the company delivering the statement.

2(2) For these purposes, **"company"** includes any body corporate incorporated in Great Britain; and —

   (a) section 250(3) applies as regards whether and when a company is or has been "dormant", and

   (b) a company is treated as being or having been at any time grouped with another company if at that time it is or was a company of which that other is or was a wholly-owned subsidiary, or if it is or was a wholly-owned subsidiary of the other or of another company of which that other is or was a wholly-owned subsidiary.

History
In para. 2(2)(a) the words "section 250(3)" substituted for the former words "section 252(5)" by CA 1989, s. 23 and Sch. 10, para. 17 as from 1 April 1990 subject to transitional

and saving provisions (see S.I. 1990 No. 355 (C. 13), art. 3, Sch. 1 and also art. 6–9).

SECRETARIES

3(1)   The statement shall contain the following particulars with respect to the person named as secretary or, where there are to be joint secretaries, with respect to each person named as one of them —

(a) in the case of an individual, his present Christian name and surname, any former Christian name or surname and his usual residential address,

(b) in the case of a corporation or a Scottish firm, its corporate or firm name and registered or principal office.

3(2)   However, if all the partners in a firm are joint secretaries, the name and principal office of the firm may be stated instead of the particulars otherwise required by this paragraph.

INTERPRETATION

4   In paragraphs 1 and 3 above —

(a) **"Christian name"** includes a forename,

(b) **"surname"**, in the case of a peer or a person usually known by a title different from his surname, means that title,

(c) the reference to a former Christian name or surname does not include —

(i) in the case of a peer or a person usually known by a British title different from his surname, the name by which he was known previous to the adoption of or succession to the title, or

(ii) in the case of any person, a former Christian name or surname where that name or surname was changed or disused before the person bearing the name attained the age of 18 or has been changed or disused for a period of not less than 20 years, or

(iii) in the case of a married woman, the name or surname by which she was known previous to the marriage.

Schedule 2 — Interpretation of References to "Beneficial Interest"

Sections 23, 145, 146, 148

Part I — References in Sections 23, 145, 146 and 148

History
The heading "Part I — References in Sections 23, 145, 146 and 148" inserted by CA 1989, s. 23 and Sch. 10, para. 18(1), (2), as from 1 April 1990 subject to transitional and

saving provisions (see S.I. 1990 No. 355 (C. 13), art. 3, Sch. 1 and also art. 6–9).

RESIDUAL INTERESTS UNDER PENSION AND EMPLOYEES' SHARE SCHEMES

1(1)   Where shares in a company are held on trust for the purposes of a pension scheme or an employees' share scheme, there is to be disregarded any residual

CA 1985, Sch. 2, para. 1(1)

interest which has not vested in possession, being an interest of the company or, as respects—

section 23(4),

of any subsidiary of the company.

History
In para. 1(1) the words "paragraph 60(2) of Schedule 4, or paragraph 19(3) of Schedule 9," formerly appearing after the words "section 23(4)," omitted and repealed by CA 1989, s. 23, 212, Sch. 10, para. 18(1), (3)(a) and Sch. 24 as

from 1 April 1990 subject to transitional and saving provisions (see S.I. 1990 No. 355 (C. 13), art. 3, 5(1)(a), (2), Sch. 1 and also art. 6–9).

1(2) In this paragraph, **"a residual interest"** means a right of the company or subsidiary in question ("the residual beneficiary") to receive any of the trust property in the event of—

    (a) all the liabilities arising under the scheme having been satisfied or provided for, or

    (b) the residual beneficiary ceasing to participate in the scheme, or

    (c) the trust property at any time exceeding what is necessary for satisfying the liabilities arising or expected to arise under the scheme.

1(3) In sub-paragraph (2), references to a right include a right dependent on the exercise of a discretion vested by the scheme in the trustee or any other person; and references to liabilities arising under a scheme include liabilities that have resulted or may result from the exercise of any such discretion.

1(4) For purposes of this paragraph, a residual interest vests in possession—

    (a) in a case within (a) of sub-paragraph (2), on the occurrence of the event there mentioned, whether or not the amount of the property receivable pursuant to the right mentioned in that sub-paragraph is then ascertained, and

    (b) in a case within (b) or (c) of that sub-paragraph, when the residual beneficiary becomes entitled to require the trustee to transfer to that beneficiary any of the property receivable pursuant to that right.

1(5) (Omitted and repealed by Companies Act 1989, sec. 23, 212, Sch. 10, para. 18(1), (3)(b) and Sch. 24 as from 1 April 1990.)

History
In regard to the date of the above omission and repeal see S.I. 1990 No. 355 (C. 13), art. 3, 5(1)(b), (2), Sch. 1 and also note transitional and saving provisions in art. 6–9; para. 1(5) formerly read as follows:

"As respects paragraph 60(2) of Schedule 4 and paragraph 19(3) of Schedule 9, sub-paragraph (1) has effect as if references to shares included debentures."

2(1) The following has effect as regards the operation of sections 144, 145 and 146 to 149 in cases where a residual interest vests in possession.

History
In para. 2(1) "23," formerly appearing before "144, 145" repealed by CA 1989, s. 212 and Sch. 24 as from 1 April

1990 subject to transitional and saving provisions (see S.I. 1990 No. 355 (C. 13), art. 4, 5(1)(b), (2) and also art. 6–9).

2(2) (Repealed by Companies Act 1989, sec. 212 and Sch. 24 as from 1 April 1990.)

History
In regard to the date of the above repeal see S.I. 1990 No. 355 (C. 13), art. 5(1)(b), (2) and also note transitional and saving provisions in art. 6–9; para. 2(2) formerly read as follows:

"Where by virtue of the vesting in possession of a residual interest a subsidiary ceases to be exempt from

section 23, that section does not prevent the subsidiary from continuing to be a member of its holding company; but subject to subsection (4) of that section, the subsidiary has no right from the date of vesting to vote at meetings of the holding company or any class of its members."

2(3) Where by virtue of paragraph 1 of this Schedule any shares are exempt from section 144 or 145 at the time when they are issued or acquired but the residual interest in question vests in possession before they are disposed of or fully paid up, those sections apply to the shares as if they had been issued or acquired on the date on which that interest vests in possession.

2(4) Where by virtue of paragraph 1 any shares are exempt from sections 146 to 149 at the time when they are acquired but the residual interest in question vests in possession before they are disposed of, those sections apply to the shares as if they had been acquired on the date on which that interest vests in possession.

2(5) The above sub-paragraphs apply irrespective of the date on which the residual interest vests or vested in possession; but where the date on which it vested was before 26th July 1983 (the passing of the Companies (Beneficial Interests) Act 1983), they have effect as if the vesting had occurred on that date.

EMPLOYER'S CHARGES AND OTHER RIGHTS OF RECOVERY

3(1) Where shares in a company are held on trust, there are to be disregarded —

  (a) if the trust is for the purposes of a pension scheme, any such rights as are mentioned in the following sub-paragraph, and

  (b) if the trust is for the purposes of an employees' share scheme, any such rights as are mentioned in (a) of the sub-paragraph,

being rights of the company or, as respects section 23(4) of any subsidiary of the company.

History
In para. 3(1) the words ", paragraph 60(2) of Schedule 4 or paragraph 19(3) of Schedule 9" formerly appearing after the words "section 23(4)," omitted and repealed by CA 1989, s. 23, 212, Sch. 10, para. 18(1), (4)(a) and Sch. 24 as from 1 April 1990 subject to transitional and saving provisions (see S.I. 1990 No. 355 (C. 13), art. 3, 5(1)(a), (2), Sch. 1 and also art. 6–9).

3(2) The rights referred to are —

  (a) any charge or lien on, or set-off against, any benefit or other right or interest under the scheme for the purpose of enabling the employer or former employer of a member of the scheme to obtain the discharge of a monetary obligation due to him from the member, and

  (b) any right to receive from the trustee of the scheme, or as trustee of the scheme to retain, an amount that can be recovered or retained under section 47 of the Social Security Pensions Act 1975 (deduction of premium from refund of contributions) or otherwise as reimbursement or partial reimbursement for any state scheme premium paid in connection with the scheme under Part III of that Act.

3(3) (Omitted and repealed by Companies Act 1989, s. 23, 212, Sch. 10, para. 18(1), (4)(b) and Sch. 24 as from 1 April 1990.)

History
In regard to the date of the above omission and repeal see S.I. 1990 No. 355 (C. 13), art. 3, 5(1)(b), (2), Sch. 1 and also note transitional and saving provisions in art. 6–9; para. 3(3) formerly read as follows:

"As respects paragraph 60(2) of Schedule 4 and paragraph 19(3) of Schedule 9, sub-paragraph (1) has effect as if references to shares included debentures."

TRUSTEE'S RIGHT TO EXPENSES, REMUNERATION, INDEMNITY, ETC.

4(1) Where a company is a trustee, there are to be disregarded any rights which the company has in its capacity as trustee including, in particular, any right to recover its expenses or be remunerated out of the trust property and any right to be indemnified out of that property for any liability incurred by reason of any act or omission of the company in the performance of its duties as trustee.

History
In para. 4(1) the words "(whether as personal representative or otherwise)" formerly appearing after the words "is a trustee" omitted and repealed by CA 1989, s. 23, 212, Sch. 10, para. 18(1), (5)(a) and Sch. 24 as from 1 April 1990 subject to transitional and saving provisions (see S.I. 1990 No. 355 (C. 13), art. 3, 5(1)(b), (2), Sch. 1 and also art. 6–9).

4(2) As respects section 23(4), sub-paragraph (1) has effect as if references to a company included any body corporate which is a subsidiary of a company.

History
In para. 4(2) the words ", paragraph 60(2) of Schedule 4 and paragraph 19(3) of Schedule 9" formerly appearing after the words "section 23(4)" omitted and repealed by CA 1989, s. 23, 212, Sch. 10, para. 18(1), (5)(b) and Sch. 24 as from 1 April 1990 subject to transitional and saving provisions (see S.I. 1990 No. 355 (C. 13), art. 3, 5(1)(a), (2), Sch. 1 and also art. 6–9).

4(3) As respects sections 145, 146 and 148, sub-paragraph (1) above applies where a company is a personal representative as it applies where a company is a trustee.

History
Para. 4(3) added by CA 1989, s. 23 and Sch. 10, para. 18(1), (5) as from 1 April 1990 subject to transitional and saving provisions (see S.I. 1990 No. 355 (C. 13), art. 3, Sch. 1 and also art. 6–9).

SUPPLEMENTARY

5(1) The following applies for the interpretation of this Part of this Schedule.

History
In para. 5(1) the words "this Part of this Schedule" substituted for the former words "this Schedule" by CA 1989, s. 23 and Sch. 10, para. 18(1), (6) as from 1 April 1990 subject to transitional and saving provisions (see S.I. 1990 No. 355 (C. 13), art. 3, Sch. 1 and also art. 6–9).

5(2) **"Pension scheme"** means any scheme for the provision of benefits consisting of or including relevant benefits for or in respect of employees or former employees; and **"relevant benefits"** means any pension, lump sum, gratuity or other like benefit given or to be given on retirement or on death or in anticipation of retirement or, in connection with past service, after retirement or death.

5(3) In sub-paragraph (2) of this paragraph, and in paragraph 3(2)(a), "employer" and "employee" are to be read as if a director of a company were employed by it.

Part II — References in Schedule 5

RESIDUAL INTERESTS UNDER PENSION AND EMPLOYEES' SHARE SCHEMES

6(1) Where shares in an undertaking are held on trust for the purposes of a pension scheme or an employees' share scheme, there shall be disregarded any residual interest which has not vested in possession, being an interest of the undertaking or any of its subsidiary undertakings.

6(2) In this paragraph a **"residual interest"** means a right of the undertaking in question (the "residual beneficiary") to receive any of the trust property in the event of—

(a) all the liabilities arising under the scheme having been satisfied or provided for, or

(b) the residual beneficiary ceasing to participate in the scheme, or

    (c) the trust property at any time exceeding what is necessary for satisfying the liabilities arising or expected to arise under the scheme.

6(3) In sub-paragraph (2) references to a right include a right dependent on the exercise of a discretion vested by the scheme in the trustee or any other person; and references to liabilities arising under a scheme include liabilities that have resulted or may result from the exercise of any such discretion.

6(4) For the purposes of this paragraph a residual interest vests in possession —

    (a) in a case within sub-paragraph (2)(a), on the occurrence of the event there mentioned, whether or not the amount of the property receivable pursuant to the right mentioned in that sub-paragraph is then ascertained;

    (b) in a case within sub-paragraph (2)(b) or (c), when the residual beneficiary becomes entitled to require the trustee to transfer to that beneficiary any of the property receivable pursuant to that right.

EMPLOYER'S CHARGES AND OTHER RIGHTS OF RECOVERY

7(1) Where shares in an undertaking are held on trust, there shall be disregarded —

    (a) if the trust is for the purposes of a pension scheme, any such rights as are mentioned in sub-paragraph (2) below;

    (b) if the trust is for the purposes of an employees' share scheme, any such rights as are mentioned in paragraph (a) of that sub- paragraph,

being rights of the undertaking or any of its subsidiary undertakings.

7(2) The rights referred to are—

    (a) any charge or lien on, or set-off against, any benefit or other right or interest under the scheme for the purpose of enabling the employer or former employer of a member of the scheme to obtain the discharge of a monetary obligation due to him from the member, and

    (b) any right to receive from the trustee of the scheme, or as trustee of the scheme to retain, an amount that can be recovered or retained under section 47 of the Social Security Pensions Act 1975 (deduction of premium from refund of pension contributions) or otherwise as reimbursement or partial reimbursement for any state scheme premium paid in connection with the scheme under Part III of that Act.

TRUSTEE'S RIGHT TO EXPENSES, REMUNERATION, INDEMNITY, ETC.

8 Where an undertaking is a trustee, there shall be disregarded any rights which the undertaking has in its capacity as trustee including, in particular, any right to recover its expenses or be remunerated out of the trust property and any right to be indemnified out of that property for any liability incurred by reason of any act or omission of the undertaking in the performance of its duties as trustee.

SUPPLEMENTARY

9(1) The following applies for the interpretation of this Part of this Schedule.

9(2) "Undertaking", and "shares" in relation to an undertaking, have the same meaning as in Part VII.

CA 1985, Sch. 2, para. 6(3)

9(3) This Part of this Schedule applies in relation to debentures as it applies in relation to shares.

9(4) **"Pension scheme"** means any scheme for the provision of benefits consisting of or including relevant benefits for or in respect of employees or former employees; and **"relevant benefits"** means any pension, lump sum, gratuity or other like benefit given or to be given on retirement or on death or in anticipation of retirement or, in connection with past service, after retirement or death.

9(5) In sub-paragraph (4) of this paragraph and in paragraph 7(2) "employee" and "employer" shall be read as if a director of an undertaking were employed by it.

History
Pt. II (para. 6–9) inserted by CA 1989, s. 23 and Sch. 10, para. 18(1), (7) as from 1 April 1990 subject to transitional and saving provisions (see S.I. 1990 No. 355 (C. 13), art. 3, Sch. 1 and also art. 6–9).

Schedule 3 — Mandatory Contents of Prospectus

Section 57, et passim in Part III

Part I — Matters to be Stated

THE COMPANY'S PROPRIETORSHIP, MANAGEMENT AND ITS CAPITAL REQUIREMENT

1(1) The prospectus must state —

- (a) the number of founders or management or deferred shares (if any) and the nature and extent of the interest of the holders in the property and profits of the company;

- (b) the number of shares (if any) fixed by the company's articles as the qualification of a director, and any provision in the articles as to the remuneration of directors; and

- (c) the names, descriptions and addresses of the directors or proposed directors.

1(2) As this paragraph applies for the purposes of section 72(3), sub-paragraph (1)(b) is to be read with the substitution for the reference to the company's articles of a reference to its constitution.

1(3) Sub-paragraphs (1)(b) and (1)(c) do not apply in the case of a prospectus issued more than 2 years after the date at which the company is entitled to commence business.

2 Where shares are offered to the public for subscription, the prospectus must give particulars as to —

- (a) the minimum amount which, in the opinion of the directors, must be raised by the issue of those shares in order to provide the sums (or, if any part of them is to be defrayed in any other manner, the balance of the sums) required to be provided in respect of each of the following —

  - (i) the purchase price of any property purchased or to be purchased which is to be defrayed in whole or in part out of the proceeds of the issue,

  - (ii) any preliminary expenses payable by the company, and any commission so payable to any person in consideration of his agreeing to subscribe

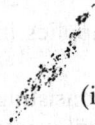

for, or of his procuring or agreeing to procure subscriptions for, any shares in the company,

(iii) the repayment of any money borrowed by the company in respect of any of the foregoing matters,

(iv) working capital, and

(b) the amounts to be provided in respect of the matters above mentioned otherwise than out of the proceeds of the issue and the sources out of which those amounts are to be provided.

DETAILS RELATING TO THE OFFER

3(1)   The prospectus must state —

(a) the time of the opening of the subscription lists, and

(b) the amount payable on application and allotment on each share (including the amount, if any, payable by way of premium).

3(2)   In the case of a second or subsequent offer of shares, there must also be stated the amount offered for subscription on each previous allotment made within the 2 preceding years, the amount actually allotted and the amount (if any) paid on the shares so allotted, including the amount (if any) paid by way of premium.

4(1)   There must be stated the number, description and amount of any shares in or debentures of the company which any person has, or is entitled to be given, an option to subscribe for.

4(2)   The following particulars of the option must be given —

(a) the period during which it is exercisable,

(b) the price to be paid for shares or debentures subscribed for under it,

(c) the consideration (if any) given or to be given for it or the right to it,

(d) the names and addresses of the persons to whom it or the right to it was given or, if given to existing shareholders or debenture holders as such, the relevant shares or debentures.

4(3)   References in this paragraph to subscribing for shares or debentures include acquiring them from a person to whom they have been allotted or agreed to be allotted with a view to his offering them for sale.

5   The prospectus must state the number and amount of shares and debentures which within the 2 preceding years have been issued, or agreed to be issued, as fully or partly paid up otherwise than in cash; and —

(a) in the latter case the extent to which they are so paid up, and

(b) in either case the consideration for which those shares or debentures have been issued or are proposed or intended to be issued.

PROPERTY ACQUIRED OR TO BE ACQUIRED BY THE COMPANY

6(1)   For purposes of the following two paragraphs, **"relevant property"** is property purchased or acquired by the company, or proposed so to be purchased or acquired,

(a) which is to be paid for wholly or partly out of the proceeds of the issue offered for subscription by the prospectus, or

(b) the purchase or acquisition of which has not been completed at the date of the issue of the prospectus.

6(2) But those two paragraphs do not apply to property —

(a) the contract for whose purchase or acquisition was entered into in the ordinary course of the company's business, the contract not being made in contemplation of the issue nor the issue in consequence of the contract, or

(b) as respects which the amount of the purchase money is not material.

7 As respects any relevant property, the prospectus must state —

(a) the names and addresses of the vendors,

(b) the amount payable in cash, shares or debentures to the vendor and, where there is more than one separate vendor, or the company is a sub-purchaser, the amount so payable to each vendor,

(c) short particulars of any transaction relating to the property completed within the 2 preceding years in which any vendor of the property to the company or any person who is, or was at the time of the transaction, a promoter or a director or proposed director of the company had any interest direct or indirect.

8 There must be stated the amount (if any) paid or payable as purchase money in cash, shares or debentures for any relevant property, specifying the amount (if any) payable for goodwill.

9(1) The following applies for the interpretation of paragraphs 6, 7 and 8.

9(2) Every person is deemed a vendor who has entered into any contract (absolute or conditional) for the sale or purchase, or for any option of purchase, of any property to be acquired by the company, in any case where —

(a) the purchase money is not fully paid at the date of the issue of the prospectus,

(b) the purchase money is to be paid or satisfied wholly or in part out of the proceeds of the issue offered for subscription by the prospectus,

(c) the contract depends for its validity or fulfilment on the result of that issue.

9(3) Where any property to be acquired by the company is to be taken on lease, paragraphs 6, 7 and 8 apply as if "vendor" included the lessor, "purchase money" included the consideration for the lease, and "sub-purchaser" included a sub-lessee.

9(4) For purposes of paragraph 7, where the vendors or any of them are a firm, the members of the firm are not to be treated as separate vendors.

COMMISSIONS, PRELIMINARY EXPENSES, ETC.

10(1) The prospectus must state —

(a) the amount (if any) paid within the 2 preceding years, or payable, as commission (but not including commission to sub-underwriters) for subscribing or agreeing to subscribe, or procuring or agreeing to procure subscriptions, for any shares in or debentures of the company, or the rate of any such commission,

(b) the amount or estimated amount of any preliminary expenses and the persons by whom any of those expenses have been paid or are payable, and the amount or estimated amount of the expenses of the issue and the persons by whom any of those expenses have been paid or are payable,

   (c) any amount or benefit paid or given within the 2 preceding years or intended to be paid or given to any promoter, and the consideration for the payment or the giving of the benefit.

10(2) Sub-paragraph (1)(b) above, so far as it relates to preliminary expenses, does not apply in the case of a prospectus issued more than 2 years after the date at which the company is entitled to commence business.

CONTRACTS

11(1) The prospectus must give the dates of, parties to and general nature of every material contract.

11(2) This does not apply to a contract entered into in the ordinary course of the business carried on or intended to be carried on by the company, or a contract entered into more than 2 years before the date of issue of the prospectus.

AUDITORS

12 The prospectus must state the names and addresses of the company's auditors (if any).

INTERESTS OF DIRECTORS

13(1) The prospectus must give full particulars of —

   (a) the nature and extent of the interest (if any) of every director in the promotion of, or in the property proposed to be acquired by, the company, or

   (b) where the interest of such a director consists in being a partner in a firm, the nature and extent of the interest of the firm.

13(2) With the particulars under sub-paragraph (1)(b) must be provided a statement of all sums paid or agreed to be paid to the director or the firm in cash or shares or otherwise by any person either to induce him to become, or to qualify him as, a director, or otherwise for services rendered by him or the firm in connection with the promotion or formation of the company.

13(3) This paragraph does not apply in the case of a prospectus issued more than 2 years after the date at which the company is entitled to commence business.

OTHER MATTERS

14 If the prospectus invites the public to subscribe for shares in the company and the company's share capital is divided into different classes of shares, the prospectus must state the right of voting at meetings of the company conferred by, and the rights in respect of capital and dividends attached to, the several classes of shares respectively.

15 In the case of a company which has been carrying on business, or of a business which has been carried on for less than 3 years, the prospectus must state the length of time during which the business of the company (or the business to be acquired, as the case may be) has been carried on.

Part II — Auditors' and Accountants' Reports to be Set Out in Prospectus

AUDITORS' REPORT

16(1) The prospectus shall set out a report by the company's auditors with respect to —

(a) profits and losses and assets and liabilities, in accordance with sub-paragraphs (2) and (3) below, as the case requires, and

(b) the rates of the dividends (if any) paid by the company in respect of each class of shares in respect of each of the 5 financial years immediately preceding the issue of the prospectus, giving particulars of each such class of shares on which such dividends have been paid and particulars of the cases in which no dividends have been paid in respect of any class of shares in respect of any of those years.

If no accounts have been made up in respect of any part of the 5 years ending on a date 3 months before the issue of the prospectus, the report shall contain a statement of that fact.

16(2) If the company has no subsidiary undertakings, the report shall—

(a) deal with profits and losses of the company in respect of each of the 5 financial years immediately preceding the issue of the prospectus, and

(b) deal with the assets and liabilities of the company at the last date to which the company's accounts were made up.

History
In para. 16(2) the words "subsidiary undertakings" substituted for the former words "subsidiaries" by CA 1989, s. 23 and Sch. 10, para. 19(1), (2) as from 1 August   1990 subject to transitional and saving provisions (see S.I. 1990 No. 355 (C. 13), art. 3, Sch. 1 and also art. 6–9).

16(3) If the company has subsidiary undertakings, the report shall —

(a) deal separately with the company's profits or losses as provided by sub-paragraph (2), and in addition deal either —

    (i) as a whole with the combined profits or losses of its subsidiary undertakings, so far as they concern members of the company, or

    (ii) individually with the profits or losses of each of its subsidiary undertakings, so far as they concern members of the company,

or, instead of dealing separately with the company's profits or losses, deal as a whole with the profits or losses of the company and (so far as they concern members of the company) with the combined profits and losses of its subsidiary undertakings; and

(b) deal separately with the company's assets and liabilities as provided by sub-paragraph (2), and in addition deal either —

    (i) as a whole with the combined assets and liabilities of its subsidiary undertakings, with or without the company's assets and liabilities, or

    (ii) individually with the assets and liabilities of each of its subsidiary undertakings, indicating, as respects the assets and liabilities of its subsidiary undertakings, the allowance to be made for persons other than members of the company.

History

Para. 16(3) substituted by CA 1989, s. 23 and Sch. 10, para. 19(1), (2) as from 1 August 1990 subject to transitional and saving provisions (see S.I. 1990 No. 355 (C. 13), art. 3, Sch. 1 and also art. 6–9); para. 16(3) formerly read as follows:

"If the company has subsidiaries, the report shall—

  (a) deal separately with the company's profits or losses as provided by sub-paragraph (2), and in addition deal either—

    (i) as a whole with the combined profits or losses of its subsidiaries, so far as they concern members of the company, or

    (ii) individually with the profits or losses of each subsidiary, so far as they concern members of the company,

or, instead of dealing separately with the company's

profits or losses, deal as a whole with the profits or losses of the company and (so far as they concern members of the company) with the combined profits and losses of its subsidiaries; and

  (b) deal separately with the company's assets and liabilities as provided by sub-paragraph (2), and in addition deal either—

    (i) as a whole with the combined assets and liabilities of its subsidiaries, with or without the company's assets and liabilities, or

    (ii) individually with the assets and liabilities of each subsidiary,

indicating, as respects the assets and liabilities of the subsidiaries, the allowance to be made for persons other than members of the company."

ACCOUNTANTS' REPORTS

17   If the proceeds of the issue of the shares or debentures are to be applied directly or indirectly in the purchase of any business, or any part of the proceeds of the issue is to be so applied, there shall be set out in the prospectus a report made by accountants upon—

  (a) the profits or losses of the business in respect of each of the 5 financial years immediately preceding the issue of the prospectus, and

  (b) the assets and liabilities of the business at the last date to which the accounts of the business were made up.

18(1)   The following provisions apply if—

  (a) the proceeds of the issue are to be applied directly or indirectly in any manner resulting in the acquisition by the company of shares in any other undertaking, or any part of the proceeds is to be so applied, and

  (b) by reason of that acquisition or anything to be done in consequence of or in connection with it, that undertaking will become a subsidiary undertaking of the company.

18(2)   There shall be set out in the prospectus a report made by accountants upon—

  (a) the profits or losses of the other undertaking in respect of each of the five financial years immediately preceding the issue of the prospectus, and

  (b) the assets and liabilities of the other undertaking at the last date to which its accounts were made up.

18(3)   The report shall—

  (a) indicate how the profits or losses of the other undertaking would in respect of the shares to be acquired have concerned members of the company and what allowance would have fallen to be made, in relation to assets and liabilities so dealt with, for holders of other shares, if the company had at all material times held the shares to be acquired, and

  (b) where the other undertaking is a parent undertaking, deal with the profits or losses and the assets and liabilities of the undertaking and its subsidiary

CA 1985, Sch. 3, para. 17   [The next page is 26,801]   **CCH Editions Limited**

undertakings in the manner provided by paragraph 16(3) above in relation to the company and its subsidiary undertakings.

18(4) In this paragraph **"undertaking"** and **"shares"**, in relation to an undertaking, have the same meaning as in Part VII.

History
Para. 18 substituted by CA 1989, s. 23 and Sch. 10, para. 19(1), (3) as from 1 August 1990 subject to transitional and saving provisions (see S.I. 1990 No. 355 (C. 13), art. 3, Sch. 1 and also art. 6–9); para. 18 formerly read as follows:

"**18(1)** The following applies if—

(a) the proceeds of the issue are to be applied directly or indirectly in any manner resulting in the acquisition by the company of shares in any other body corporate, or any part of the proceeds is to be so applied, and

(b) by reason of that acquisition or anything to be done in consequence of or in connection with it, that body corporate will become a subsidiary of the company.

(2) There shall be set out in the prospectus a report made by accountants upon—

(a) the profits or losses of the other body corporate in respect of each of the 5 financial years immediately preceding the issue of the prospectus, and

(b) the assets and liabilities of the other body corporate at the last date to which its accounts were made up.

(3) The accountants' report required by this paragraph shall—

(a) indicate how the profits of losses of the other body corporate dealt with by the report would, in respect of the shares to be acquired, have concerned members of the company and what allowance would have fallen to be made, in relation to assets and liabilities so dealt with, for holders of other shares, if the company had at all material times held the shares to be acquired, and

(b) where the other body corporate has subsidiaries, deal with the profits or losses and the assets and liabilities of the body corporate and its subsidiaries in the manner provided by paragraph 16(3) above in relation to the company and its subsidiaries."

PROVISIONS INTERPRETING PRECEDING PARAGRAPHS, AND MODIFYING THEM IN CERTAIN CASES

19 If in the case of a company which has been carrying on business, or of a business which has been carried on for less than 5 years, the accounts of the company or business have only been made up in respect of 4 years, 3 years, 2 years or one year, the preceding paragraphs of this Part have effect as if references to 4 years, 3 years, 2 years or one year (as the case may be) were substituted for references to 5 years.

20 The expression **"financial year"** in this Part means the year in respect of which the accounts of the company or of the business (as the case may be) are made up; and where by reason of any alteration of the date on which the financial year of the company or business terminates the accounts have been made up for a period greater or less than one year, that greater or less period is for purposes of this Part deemed to be a financial year.

21 Any report required by this Part shall either indicate by way of note any adjustments as respects the figures of any profits or losses or assets and liabilities dealt with by the report which appear to the persons making the report necessary, or shall make those adjustments and indicate that adjustments have been made.

22(1) A report required by paragraph 17 or 18 shall be made by accountants qualified under this Act for appointment as auditors of a company.

22(2) Such a report shall not be made by an accountant who is an officer or servant, or a partner of or in the employment of an officer or servant, of—

(a) the company or any of its subsidiary undertakings,

(b) a parent undertaking of the company or any subsidiary undertaking of such an undertaking.

History
Para. 22(2) substituted by CA 1989, s. 23 and Sch. 10, para. 19(1), (4) as from 1 August 1990 subject to transitional and saving provisions (see S.I. 1990 No. 355 (C. 13), art. 3, Sch. 1 and also art. 6–9); para. 22(2) formerly read as follows:

"Such a report shall not be made by any accountant who is an officer or servant, or a partner of or in the employment of an officer or servant, of the company or the company's subsidiary or holding company or of a subsidiary of the company's holding company.
In this paragraph, **'officer'** includes a proposed director, but not an auditor."

22(3) The accountants making any report required for purposes of paragraph 17 or 18 shall be named in the prospectus.

Note

Sch. 3 repealed by Financial Services Act 1986, s. 212(3) and Sch. 17, Pt. I to the extent to which Sch. 3 would apply re any investment listed or the subject of a listing application under Financial Services Act 1986, Pt. IV and commencing:

- on 12 January 1987 for all purposes relating to the admission of securities offered by or on behalf of a Minister of the Crown or a body corporate controlled by a Minister of the Crown or a subsidiary of such a body corporate to the Official List in respect of which an application is made after that date;

- on 16 February 1987 for purposes relating to the admission of securities in respect of which an application is made

after that date other than those referred to in the preceding paragraph and otherwise for all purposes.

(See S.I. 1986 No. 2246 (C. 88)).

Sch. 3 also repealed by Financial Services Act 1986, s. 212(3) and Sch. 17, Pt. I as from 29 April 1988 as far as it would apply to a prospectus offering for subscription, or to any form of application for units in a body corporate which is a recognised scheme; and as from 1 July 1988 as far as it would apply to a prospectus offering for subscription, or to any application form for, units in a body corporate which is an open-ended investment company (see S.I. 1988 No. 740 (C. 22)).

Schedule 4 — Form and Content of Company Accounts

[Companies Act 1985, sec. 226;
Companies Act 1989, sec. 1, 4(2), Sch. 1]

Part I — General Rules and Formats

SECTION A — GENERAL RULES

1(1) Subject to the following provisions of this Schedule—

   (a) every balance sheet of a company shall show the items listed in either of the balance sheet formats set out below in section B of this Part; and

   (b) every profit and loss account of a company shall show the items listed in any one of the profit and loss account formats so set out;

in either case in the order and under the headings and sub-headings given in the format adopted.

1(2) Sub-paragraph (1) above is not to be read as requiring the heading or sub-heading for any item to be distinguished by any letter or number assigned to that item in the format adopted.

2(1) Where in accordance with paragraph 1 a company's balance sheet or profit and loss account for any financial year has been prepared by reference to one of the formats set out in section B below, the directors of the company shall adopt the same format in preparing the accounts for subsequent financial years of the company unless in their opinion there are special reasons for a change.

2(2) Particulars of any change in the format adopted in preparing a company's balance sheet or profit and loss account in accordance with paragraph 1 shall be disclosed, and the reasons for the change shall be explained, in a note to the accounts in which the new format is first adopted.

3(1) Any item required in accordance with paragraph 1 to be shown in a company's balance sheet or profit and loss account may be shown in greater detail than required by the format adopted.

3(2) A company's balance sheet or profit and loss account may include an item representing or covering the amount of any asset or liability, income or expenditure not otherwise covered by any of the items listed in the format adopted, but the following shall not be treated as assets in any company's balance sheet—

    (a) preliminary expenses;

    (b) expenses of and commission on any issue of shares or debentures; and

    (c) costs of research.

3(3) In preparing a company's balance sheet or profit and loss account the directors of the company shall adapt the arrangement and headings and sub-headings otherwise required by paragraph 1 in respect of items to which an Arabic number is assigned in the format adopted, in any case where the special nature of the company's business requires such adaptation.

3(4) Items to which Arabic numbers are assigned in any of the formats set out in section B below may be combined in a company's accounts for any financial year if either—

    (a) their individual amounts are not material to assessing the state of affairs or profit or loss of the company for that year; or

    (b) the combination facilitates that assessment;

but in a case within paragraph (b) the individual amounts of any items so combined shall be disclosed in a note to the accounts.

3(5) Subject to paragraph 4(3) below, a heading or sub-heading corresponding to an item listed in the format adopted in preparing a company's balance sheet or profit and loss account shall not be included if there is no amount to be shown for that item in respect of the financial year to which the balance sheet or profit and loss account relates.

3(6) Every profit and loss account of a company shall show the amount of the company's profit or loss on ordinary activities before taxation.

3(7) Every profit and loss account of a company shall show separately as additional items—

    (a) any amount set aside or proposed to be set aside to, or withdrawn or proposed to be withdrawn from, reserves; and

    (b) the aggregate amount of any dividends paid and proposed.

4(1) In respect of every item shown in a company's balance sheet or profit and loss account the corresponding amount for the financial year immediately preceding that to which the balance sheet or profit and loss account relates shall also be shown.

4(2) Where that corresponding amount is not comparable with the amount to be shown for the item in question in respect of the financial year to which the balance sheet or profit and loss account relates, the former amount shall be adjusted and particulars of the adjustment and the reasons for it shall be disclosed in a note to the accounts.

4(3) Paragraph 3(5) does not apply in any case where an amount can be shown for the item in question in respect of the financial year immediately preceding that to which the balance sheet or profit and loss account relates, and that amount shall be shown under the heading or sub-heading required by paragraph 1 for that item.

5 Amounts in respect of items representing assets or income may not be set off against amounts in respect of items representing liabilities or expenditure (as the case may be), or vice versa.

SECTION B — THE REQUIRED FORMATS FOR ACCOUNTS

Preliminary

6 References in this Part of this Schedule to the items listed in any of the formats set out below are to those items read together with any of the notes following the formats which apply to any of those items, and the requirement imposed by paragraph 1 to show the items listed in any such format in the order adopted in the format is subject to any provision in those notes for alternative positions for any particular items.

7 A number in brackets following any item in any of the formats set out below is a reference to the note of that number in the notes following the formats.

8 In the notes following the formats—

    (a) the heading of each note gives the required heading or sub-heading for the item to which it applies and a reference to any letters and numbers assigned to that item in the formats set out below (taking a reference in the case of Format 2 of the balance sheet formats to the item listed under "Assets" or under "Liabilities" as the case may require); and

    (b) references to a numbered format are to the balance sheet format or (as the case may require) to the profit and loss account format of that number set out below.

Balance Sheet Formats

Format 1

A.   Called up share capital not paid *(1)*

B.   Fixed assets

  I Intangible assets
    1. Development costs
    2. Concessions, patents, licences, trade marks and similar rights and assets *(2)*
    3. Goodwill *(3)*
    4. Payments on account

  II Tangible assets
    1. Land and buildings
    2. Plant and machinery
    3. Fixtures, fittings, tools and equipment
    4. Payments on account and assets in course of construction

  III Investments
    1. Shares in group undertakings
    2. Loans to group undertakings
    3. Participating interests
    4. Loans to undertakings in which the company has a participating interest
    5. Other investments other than loans

CA 1985, Sch. 4, para. 5   [The next page is 27,101]

　　　6.　Other loans
　　　7.　Own shares *(4)*

C.　Current assets

　I　Stocks
　　　1.　Raw materials and consumables
　　　2.　Work in progress
　　　3.　Finished goods and goods for resale
　　　4.　Payments on account

　II　Debtors *(5)*
　　　1.　Trade debtors
　　　2.　Amounts owed by group undertakings
　　　3.　Amounts owed by undertakings in which the company has a
　　　　　participating interest
　　　4.　Other debtors
　　　5.　Called up share capital not paid *(1)*
　　　6.　Prepayments and accrued income *(6)* ✷

　III　Investments
　　　1.　Shares in group undertakings
　　　2.　Own shares *(4)*
　　　3.　Other investments

　IV　Cash at bank and in hand

D.　Prepayments and accrued income *(6)* ✷

E.　Creditors: amounts falling due within one year
　　　1.　Debenture loans *(7)*
　　　2.　Bank loans and overdrafts
　　　3.　Payments received on account *(8)*
　　　4.　Trade creditors
　　　5.　Bills of exchange payable
　　　6.　Amounts owed to group undertakings
　　　7.　Amounts owed to undertakings in which the company has a
　　　　　participating interest
　　　8.　Other creditors including taxation and social security *(9)*
　　　9.　Accruals and deferred income *(10)* ✷

F.　Net current assets (liabilities) *(11)*

G.　Total assets less current liabilities

H.　Creditors: amounts falling due after more than one year
　　　1.　Debenture loans *(7)*
　　　2.　Bank loans and overdrafts
　　　3.　Payments received on account *(8)*
　　　4.　Trade creditors
　　　5.　Bills of exchange payable
　　　6.　Amounts owed to group undertakings
　　　7.　Amounts owed to undertakings in which the company has a
　　　　　participating interest
　　　8.　Other creditors including taxation and social security *(9)*

    9. Accruals and deferred income *(10)* *

I. Provisions for liabilities and charges

    1. Pensions and similar obligations
    2. Taxation, including deferred taxation
    3. Other provisions

J. Accruals and deferred income *(10)* *

K. Capital and reserves

   I Called up share capital *(12)*
   II Share premium account
   III Revaluation reserve
   IV Other reserves
    1. Capital redemption reserve
    2. Reserve for own shares
    3. Reserves provided for by the articles of association
    4. Other reserves
   V Profit and loss account

Note
See history note at end of Pt. I.

Balance Sheet Formats

Format 2

ASSETS

A. Called up share capital not paid *(1)*

B. Fixed assets

   I Intangible assets
    1. Development costs
    2. Concessions, patents, licences, trade marks and similar rights and assets *(2)*
    3. Goodwill *(3)*
    4. Payments on account

   II Tangible assets
    1. Land and buildings
    2. Plant and machinery
    3. Fixtures, fittings, tools and equipment
    4. Payments on account and assets in course of construction

   III Investments
    1. Shares in group undertakings
    2. Loans to group undertakings
    3. Participating interests
    4. Loans to undertakings in which the company has a participating interest
    5. Other investments other than loans
    6. Other loans
    7. Own shares *(4)*

C.   Current assets

  I   Stocks
    1.   Raw materials and consumables
    2.   Work in progress
    3.   Finished goods and goods for resale
    4.   Payments on account

  II   Debtors *(5)*
    1.   Trade debtors
    2.   Amounts owed by group undertakings
    3.   Amounts owed by undertakings in which the company has a
          participating interest
    4.   Other debtors
    5.   Called up share capital not paid *(1)*
    6.   Prepayments and accrued income *(6)*

  III   Investments
    1.   Shares in group undertakings
    2.   Own shares *(4)*
    3.   Other investments

  IV   Cash at bank and in hand

D.   Prepayments and accrued income *(6)*

LIABILITIES

A.   Capital and reserves

  I   Called up share capital *(12)*
  II   Share premium account
  III   Revaluation reserve
  IV   Other reserves
    1.   Capital redemption reserve
    2.   Reserve for own shares
    3.   Reserves provided for by the articles of association
    4.   Other reserves
  V   Profit and loss account

B.   Provisions for liabilities and charges

    1.   Pensions and similar obligations
    2.   Taxation including deferred taxation
    3.   Other provisions

C.   Creditors *(13)*

    1.   Debenture loans *(7)*
    2.   Bank loans and overdrafts
    3.   Payments received on account *(8)*
    4.   Trade creditors
    5.   Bills of exchange payable
    6.   Amounts owed to group undertakings

7. Amounts owed to undertakings in which the company has a participating interest
8. Other creditors including taxation and social security *(9)*
9. Accruals and deferred income *(10)*

D.   Accruals and deferred income *(10)*

Note
See history note at end of Pt. I.

Notes on the balance sheet formats

(1) Called up share capital not paid — (Formats 1 and 2, items A and C.II.5.)

This item may be shown in either of the two positions given in Formats 1 and 2.

(2) Concessions, patents, licences, trade marks and similar rights and assets — (Formats 1 and 2, item B.I.2.)

Amounts in respect of assets shall only be included in a company's balance sheet under this item if either—

(a) the assets were acquired for valuable consideration and are not required to be shown under goodwill; or

(b) the assets in question were created by the company itself.

(3) Goodwill — (Formats 1 and 2, item B.I.3.)

Amounts representing goodwill shall only be included to the extent that the goodwill was acquired for valuable consideration.

(4) Own shares — (Formats 1 and 2, items B.III.7 and C.III.2.)

The nominal value of the shares held shall be shown separately.

(5) Debtors — (Formats 1 and 2, items C.II.1 to 6.)

The amount falling due after more than one year shall be shown separately for each item included under debtors.

(6) Prepayments and accrued income — (Formats 1 and 2, items C.II.6 and D.)

This item may be shown in either of the two positions given in Formats 1 and 2.

(7) Debenture loans — (Format 1, items E.1 and H.1 and Format 2, item C.1.)

The amount of any convertible loans shall be shown separately.

(8) Payments received on account — (Format 1, items E.3 and H.3 and Format 2, item C.3.)

Payments received on account of orders shall be shown for each of these items in so far as they are not shown as deductions from stocks.

(9) Other creditors including taxation and social security — (Format 1, items E.8 and H.8 and Format 2, item C.8.)

The amount for creditors in respect of taxation and social security shall be shown separately from the amount for other creditors.

(10) Accruals and deferred income — (Format 1, items E.9, H.9 and J and Format 2, items C.9 and D.)

The two positions given for this item in Format 1 at E.9 and H.9 are an alternative to the position at J, but if the item is not shown in a position corresponding to that at J it may be shown in either or both of the other two positions (as the case may require).

The two positions given for this item in Format 2 are alternatives.

(11) Net current assets (liabilities) — (Format 1, item F.)

In determining the amount to be shown for this item any amounts shown under "prepayments and accrued income" shall be taken into account wherever shown.

(12) Called up share capital — (Format 1, item K.I and Format 2, item A.I.)

The amount of allotted share capital and the amount of called up share capital which has been paid up shall be shown separately.

(13) Creditors — (Format 2, items C.1 to 9.)

Amounts falling due within one year and after one year shall be shown separately for each of these items and their aggregate shall be shown separately for all of these items.

<u>**Profit and loss account formats**</u>

Format 1

(see note *(17)* below)

1. Turnover
2. Cost of sales *(14)*
3. Gross profit or loss
4. Distribution costs *(14)*
5. Administrative expenses *(14)*
6. Other operating income
7. Income from shares in group undertakings
8. Income from participating interests
9. Income from other fixed asset investments *(15)*
10. Other interest receivable and similar income *(15)*
11. Amounts written off investments
12. Interest payable and similar charges *(16)*
13. Tax on profit or loss on ordinary activities
14. Profit or loss on ordinary activities after taxation
15. Extraordinary income
16. Extraordinary charges
17. Extraordinary profit or loss
18. Tax on extraordinary profit or loss
19. Other taxes not shown under the above items
20. Profit or loss for the financial year

Note
See history note at end of Pt. I.

British Companies Legislation **CA 1985, Sch. 4**

Profit and loss account formats

Format 2

1. Turnover
2. Change in stocks of finished goods and in work in progress
3. Own work capitalised
4. Other operating income
5. (a) Raw materials and consumables
   (b) Other external charges
6. Staff costs:
   (a) wages and salaries
   (b) social security costs
   (c) other pension costs
7. (a) Depreciation and other amounts written off tangible and intangible fixed assets
   (b) Exceptional amounts written off current assets
8. Other operating charges
9. Income from shares in group undertakings
10. Income from participating interests
11. Income from other fixed asset investments *(15)*
12. Other interest receivable and similar income *(15)*
13. Amounts written off investments
14. Interest payable and similar charges *(16)*
15. Tax on profit or loss on ordinary activities
16. Profit or loss on ordinary activities after taxation
17. Extraordinary income
18. Extraordinary charges
19. Extraordinary profit or loss
20. Tax on extraordinary profit or loss
21. Other taxes not shown under the above items
22. Profit or loss for the financial year

Note
See history note at end of Pt. I.

Profit and loss account formats

Format 3

(see note *(17)* below)

A. Charges
   1. Cost of sales*(14)*
   2. Distribution costs *(14)*
   3. Administrative expenses *(14)*
   4. Amounts written off investments
   5. Interest payable and similar charges *(16)*
   6. Tax on profit or loss on ordinary activities
   7. Profit or loss on ordinary activities after taxation
   8. Extraordinary charges

9.   Tax on extraordinary profit or loss
10. Other taxes not shown under the above items
11. Profit or loss for the financial year

B.   Income
1.   Turnover
2.   Other operating income
3.   Income from shares in group undertakings
4.   Income from participating interests
5.   Income from other fixed asset investments *(15)*
6.   Other interest receivable and similar income *(15)*
7.   Profit or loss on ordinary activities after taxation
8.   Extraordinary income
9.   Profit or loss for the financial year

Note
See history note at end of Pt. I.

Profit and loss account formats

Format 4

A.   Charges
1.   Reduction in stocks of finished goods and in work in progress
2.   (a) Raw materials and consumables
     (b) Other external charges
3.   Staff costs:
     (a) wages and salaries
     (b) social security costs
     (c) other pension costs
4.   (a) Depreciation and other amounts written off tangible and intangible fixed assets
     (b) Exceptional amounts written off current assets
5.   Other operating charges
6.   Amounts written off investments
7.   Interest payable and similar charges *(16)*
8.   Tax on profit or loss on ordinary activities
9.   Profit or loss on ordinary activities after taxation
10. Extraordinary charges
11. Tax on extraordinary profit or loss
12. Other taxes not shown under the above items
13. Profit or loss for the financial year

B.   Income
1.   Turnover
2.   Increase in stocks of finished goods and in work in progress
3.   Own work capitalised
4.   Other operating income
5.   Income from shares in group undertakings
6.   Income from participating interests
7.   Income from other fixed asset investments *(15)*
8.   Other interest receivable and similar income *(15)*

9. Profit or loss on ordinary activities after taxation
10. Extraordinary income
11. Profit or loss for the financial year

Note
See history note at end of Pt. I.

Notes on the profit and loss account formats

(14) Cost of sales: distribution costs: administrative expenses — (Format 1, items 2, 4 and 5 and Format 3, items A.1, 2 and 3.)

These items shall be stated after taking into account any necessary provisions for depreciation or diminution in value of assets.

(15) Income from other fixed asset investments: other interest receivable and similar income — (Format 1, items 9 and 10: Format 2, items 11 and 12: Format 3, items B.5 and 6: Format 4, items B.7 and 8.)

Income and interest derived from group undertakings shall be shown separately from income and interest derived from other sources.

(16) Interest payable and similar charges — (Format 1, item 12: Format 2, item 14: Format 3, item A.5: Format 4, item A.7.)

The amount payable to group undertakings shall be shown separately.

(17) Formats 1 and 3

The amount of any provisions for depreciation and diminution in value of tangible and intangible fixed assets falling to be shown under items 7(a) and A.4(a) respectively in Formats 2 and 4 shall be disclosed in a note to the accounts in any case where the profit and loss account is prepared by reference to Format 1 or Format 3.

History
In the balance sheet formats, profit and loss account formats and notes (15) and (16) to the latter, the words "group undertakings", "participating interests" and "undertakings in which the company has a participating interest" wherever they occur, substituted for the former words "group companies", "shares in related companies" and "related companies" respectively by CA 1989, s. 1, 4(2) and Sch. 1, para. 1–4 as from 1 April 1990 subject to transitional and saving provisions (see S.I. 1990 No. 355 (C. 13), art. 3, Sch. 1 and also art. 6–9).

Part II — Accounting Principles and Rules

SECTION A — ACCOUNTING PRINCIPLES

Preliminary

9 Subject to paragraph 15 below, the amounts to be included in respect of all items shown in a company's accounts shall be determined in accordance with the principles set out in paragraphs 10 to 14.

Accounting principles

10 The company shall be presumed to be carrying on business as a going concern.

11 Accounting policies shall be applied consistently within the same accounts and from one financial year to the next.

History
Para. 11 substituted by CA 1989, s. 1, 4(2) and Sch. 1, para. 1, 5 as from 1 April 1990 subject to transitional and saving provisions (see S.I. 1990 No. 355 (C. 13), art. 3, Sch. 1 and also art. 6–9); para. 11 formerly read as follows:

"Accounting policies shall be applied consistently from one financial year to the next."

12 The amount of any item shall be determined on a prudent basis, and in particular—

    (a) only profits realised at the balance sheet date shall be included in the profit and loss account; and

    (b) all liabilities and losses which have arisen or are likely to arise in respect of the financial year to which the accounts relate or a previous financial year shall be taken into account, including those which only become apparent between the balance sheet date and the date on which it is signed on behalf of the board of directors in pursuance of section 233 of this Act.

History
In para. 12(b) the words "section 233" substituted for the former words "section 238" by CA 1989, s. 23 and Sch. 10, para. 20 as from 1 April 1990 subject to transitional and saving provisions (see S.I. 1990 No. 355 (C. 13), art. 3, Sch. 1 and also art. 6–9).

13 All income and charges relating to the financial year to which the accounts relate shall be taken into account, without regard to the date of receipt or payment.

14 In determining the aggregate amount of any item the amount of each individual asset or liability that falls to be taken into account shall be determined separately.

Departure from the accounting principles

15 If it appears to the directors of a company that there are special reasons for departing from any of the principles stated above in preparing the company's accounts in respect of any financial year they may do so, but particulars of the departure, the reasons for it and its effect shall be given in a note to the accounts.

SECTION B — HISTORICAL COST ACCOUNTING RULES

Preliminary

16 Subject to section C of this Part of this Schedule, the amounts to be included in respect of all items shown in a company's accounts shall be determined in accordance with the rules set out in paragraphs 17 to 28.

Fixed assets

General rules

17 Subject to any provision for depreciation or diminution in value made in accordance with paragraph 18 or 19 the amount to be included in respect of any fixed asset shall be its purchase price or production cost.

18 In the case of any fixed asset which has a limited useful economic life, the amount of—

    (a) its purchase price or production cost; or

    (b) where it is estimated that any such asset will have a residual value at the end of the period of its useful economic life, its purchase price or production cost less that estimated residual value;

shall be reduced by provisions for depreciation calculated to write off that amount systematically over the period of the asset's useful economic life.

19(1)   Where a fixed asset investment of a description falling to be included under item B.III of either of the balance sheet formats set out in Part I of this Schedule has diminished in value provisions for diminution in value may be made in respect of it and the amount to be included in respect of it may be reduced accordingly; and any such provisions which are not shown in the profit and loss account shall be disclosed (either separately or in aggregate) in a note to the accounts.

19(2)   Provisions for diminution in value shall be made in respect of any fixed asset which has diminished in value if the reduction in its value is expected to be permanent (whether its useful economic life is limited or not), and the amount to be included in respect of it shall be reduced accordingly; and any such provisions which are not shown in the profit and loss account shall be disclosed (either separately or in aggregate) in a note to the accounts.

19(3)   Where the reasons for which any provision was made in accordance with sub-paragraph (1) or (2) have ceased to apply to any extent, that provision shall be written back to the extent that it is no longer necessary; and any amounts written back in accordance with this sub-paragraph which are not shown in the profit and loss account shall be disclosed (either separately or in aggregate) in a note to the accounts.

Rules for determining particular fixed asset items

20(1)   Notwithstanding that an item in respect of "development costs" is included under "fixed assets" in the balance sheet formats set out in Part I of this Schedule, an amount may only be included in a company's balance sheet in respect of development costs in special circumstances.

20(2)   If any amount is included in a company's balance sheet in respect of development costs the following information shall be given in a note to the accounts—

  (a) the period over which the amount of those costs originally capitalised is being or is to be written off; and

  (b) the reasons for capitalising the development costs in question.

21(1)   The application of paragraphs 17 to 19 in relation to goodwill (in any case where goodwill is treated as an asset) is subject to the following provisions of this paragraph.

21(2)   Subject to sub-paragraph (3) below, the amount of the consideration for any goodwill acquired by a company shall be reduced by provisions for depreciation calculated to write off that amount systematically over a period chosen by the directors of the company.

21(3)   The period chosen shall not exceed the useful economic life of the goodwill in question.

21(4)   In any case where any goodwill acquired by a company is shown or included as an asset in the company's balance sheet the period chosen for writing off the consideration for that goodwill and the reasons for choosing that period shall be disclosed in a note to the accounts.

Current assets

22   Subject to paragraph 23, the amount to be included in respect of any current asset shall be its purchase price or production cost.

23(1) If the net realisable value of any current asset is lower than its purchase price or production cost the amount to be included in respect of that asset shall be the net realisable value.

23(2) Where the reasons for which any provision for diminution in value was made in accordance with sub-paragraph (1) have ceased to apply to any extent, that provision shall be written back to the extent that it is no longer necessary.

Miscellaneous and supplementary provisions

Excess of money owed over value received as an asset item

24(1) Where the amount repayable on any debt owed by a company is greater than the value of the consideration received in the transaction giving rise to the debt, the amount of the difference may be treated as an asset.

24(2) Where any such amount is so treated—

(a) it shall be written off by reasonable amounts each year and must be completely written off before repayment of the debt; and

(b) if the current amount is not shown as a separate item in the company's balance sheet it must be disclosed in a note to the accounts.

Assets included at a fixed amount

25(1) Subject to the following sub-paragraph, assets which fall to be included—

(a) amongst the fixed assets of a company under the item "tangible assets"; or

(b) amongst the current assets of a company under the item "raw materials and consumables";

may be included at a fixed quantity and value.

25(2) Sub-paragraph (1) applies to assets of a kind which are constantly being replaced, where—

(a) their overall value is not material to assessing the company's state of affairs; and

(b) their quantity, value and composition are not subject to material variation.

Determination of purchase price or production cost

26(1) The purchase price of an asset shall be determined by adding to the actual price paid any expenses incidental to its acquisition.

26(2) The production cost of an asset shall be determined by adding to the purchase price of the raw materials and consumables used the amount of the costs incurred by the company which are directly attributable to the production of that asset.

26(3) In addition, there may be included in the production cost of an asset—

(a) a reasonable proportion of the costs incurred by the company which are only indirectly attributable to the production of that asset, but only to the extent that they relate to the period of production; and

(b) interest on capital borrowed to finance the production of that asset, to the extent that it accrues in respect of the period of production;

provided, however, in a case within paragraph (b) above, that the inclusion of the interest in determining the cost of that asset and the amount of the interest so included is disclosed in a note to the accounts.

26(4)   In the case of current assets distribution costs may not be included in production costs.

27(1)   Subject to the qualification mentioned below, the purchase price or production cost of—

   (a) any assets which fall to be included under any item shown in a company's balance sheet under the general item "stocks"; and

   (b) any assets which are fungible assets (including investments);

may be determined by the application of any of the methods mentioned in sub-paragraph (2) below in relation to any such assets of the same class.

   The method chosen must be one which appears to the directors to be appropriate in the circumstances of the company.

27(2)   Those methods are—

   (a) the method known as "first in, first out" (FIFO);

   (b) the method known as "last in, first out" (LIFO);

   (c) a weighted average price; and

   (d) any other method similar to any of the methods mentioned above.

27(3)   Where in the case of any company—

   (a) the purchase price or production cost of assets falling to be included under any item shown in the company's balance sheet has been determined by the application of any method permitted by this paragraph; and

   (b) the amount shown in respect of that item differs materially from the relevant alternative amount given below in this paragraph;

the amount of that difference shall be disclosed in a note to the accounts.

27(4)   Subject to sub-paragraph (5) below, for the purposes of sub-paragraph (3)(b) above, the relevant alternative amount, in relation to any item shown in a company's balance sheet, is the amount which would have been shown in respect of that item if assets of any class included under that item at an amount determined by any method permitted by this paragraph had instead been included at their replacement cost as at the balance sheet date.

27(5)   The relevant alternative amount may be determined by reference to the most recent actual purchase price or production cost before the balance sheet date of assets of any class included under the item in question instead of by reference to their replacement cost as at that date, but only if the former appears to the directors of the company to constitute the more appropriate standard of comparison in the case of assets of that class.

27(6)   For the purposes of this paragraph, assets of any description shall be regarded as fungible if assets of that description are substantially indistinguishable one from another.

Substitution of original stated amount where price or cost unknown

28 Where there is no record of the purchase price or production cost of any asset of a company or of any price, expenses or costs relevant for determining its purchase price or production cost in accordance with paragraph 26, or any such record cannot be obtained without unreasonable expense or delay, its purchase price or production cost shall be taken for the purposes of paragraphs 17 to 23 to be the value ascribed to it in the earliest available record of its value made on or after its acquisition or production by the company.

SECTION C — ALTERNATIVE ACCOUNTING RULES

Preliminary

29(1) The rules set out in section B are referred to below in this Schedule as the historical cost accounting rules.

29(2) Those rules, with the omission of paragraphs 16, 21 and 25 to 28, are referred to below in this Part of this Schedule as the depreciation rules; and references below in this Schedule to the historical cost accounting rules do not include the depreciation rules as they apply by virtue of paragraph 32.

30 Subject to paragraphs 32 to 34, the amounts to be included in respect of assets of any description mentioned in paragraph 31 may be determined on any basis so mentioned.

Alternative accounting rules

31(1) Intangible fixed assets, other than goodwill, may be included at their current cost.

31(2) Tangible fixed assets may be included at a market value determined as at the date of their last valuation or at their current cost.

31(3) Investments of any description falling to be included under item B.III of either of the balance sheet formats set out in Part I of this Schedule may be included either—

    (a) at a market value determined as at the date of their last valuation; or

    (b) at a value determined on any basis which appears to the directors to be appropriate in the circumstances of the company;

but in the latter case particulars of the method of valuation adopted and of the reasons for adopting it shall be disclosed in a note to the accounts.

31(4) Investments of any description falling to be included under item C.III of either of the balance sheet formats set out in Part I of this Schedule may be included at their current cost.

31(5) Stocks may be included at their current cost.

Application of the depreciation rules

32(1) Where the value of any asset of a company is determined on any basis mentioned in paragraph 31, that value shall be, or (as the case may require) be the starting point for determining, the amount to be included in respect of that asset in the company's accounts, instead of its purchase price or production cost or any value previously so determined for that asset; and the depreciation rules shall apply accordingly in relation to any such asset with the substitution for any reference to its purchase price or production cost of a reference to the value most recently determined for that asset on any basis mentioned in paragraph 31.

32(2)   The amount of any provision for depreciation required in the case of any fixed asset by paragraph 18 or 19 as it applies by virtue of sub-paragraph (1) is referred to below in this paragraph as the adjusted amount, and the amount of any provision which would be required by that paragraph in the case of that asset according to the historical cost accounting rules is referred to as the historical cost amount.

32(3)   Where sub-paragraph (1) applies in the case of any fixed asset the amount of any provision for depreciation in respect of that asset—

(a) included in any item shown in the profit and loss account in respect of amounts written off assets of the description in question; or

(b) taken into account in stating any item so shown which is required by note (14) of the notes on the profit and loss account formats set out in Part I of this Schedule to be stated after taking into account any necessary provisions for depreciation or diminution in value of assets included under it;

may be the historical cost amount instead of the adjusted amount, provided that the amount of any difference between the two is shown separately in the profit and loss account or in a note to the accounts.

Additional information to be provided in case of departure from historical cost accounting rules

33(1)   This paragraph applies where the amounts to be included in respect of assets covered by any items shown in a company's accounts have been determined on any basis mentioned in paragraph 31.

33(2)   The items affected and the basis of valuation adopted in determining the amounts of the assets in question in the case of each such item shall be disclosed in a note to the accounts.

33(3)   In the case of each balance sheet item affected (except stocks) either—

(a) the comparable amounts determined according to the historical cost accounting rules; or

(b) the differences between those amounts and the corresponding amounts actually shown in the balance sheet in respect of that item;

shall be shown separately in the balance sheet or in a note to the accounts.

33(4)   In sub-paragraph (3) above, references in relation to any item to the comparable amounts determined as there mentioned are references to—

(a) the aggregate amount which would be required to be shown in respect of that item if the amounts to be included in respect of all the assets covered by that item were determined according to the historical cost accounting rules; and

(b) the aggregate amount of the cumulative provisions for depreciation or diminution in value which would be permitted or required in determining those amounts according to those rules.

Revaluation reserve

34(1) With respect to any determination of the value of an asset of a company on any basis mentioned in paragraph 31, the amount of any profit or loss arising from that determination (after allowing, where appropriate, for any provisions for depreciation or diminution in value made otherwise than by reference to the value so determined and any adjustments of any such provisions made in the light of that determination) shall be credited or (as the case may be) debited to a separate reserve ("the revaluation reserve").

34(2) The amount of the revaluation reserve shall be shown in the company's balance sheet under a separate sub-heading in the position given for the item "revaluation reserve" in Format 1 or 2 of the balance sheet formats set out in Part I of this Schedule, but need not be shown under that name.

34(3) An amount may be transferred from the revaluation reserve—

> (a) to the profit and loss account, if the amount was previously charged to that account or represents realised profit, or
>
> (b) on capitalisation;

and the revaluation reserve shall be reduced to the extent that the amounts transferred to it are no longer necessary for the purposes of the valuation method used.

34(3A) In sub-paragraph (3)(b) **"capitalisation"**, in relation to an amount standing to the credit of the revaluation reserve, means applying it in wholly or partly paying up unissued shares in the company to be allotted to members of the company as fully or partly paid shares.

34(3B) The revaluation reserve shall not be reduced except as mentioned in this paragraph.

History
Para. 34(3), (3A) and (3B) substituted for the former para. 34(3) by CA 1989, s. 1, 4(2) and Sch. 1, para. 6 as from 1 April 1990 subject to transitional and saving provisions (see S.I. 1990 No. 355 (C. 13), art. 3, Sch. 1 and also art. 6–9); former para. 34(3) read as follows:

"The revaluation reserve shall be reduced to the extent that the amounts standing to the credit of the reserve are in the opinion of the directors of the company no longer necessary for the purpose of the accounting policies adopted by the company; but an amount may only be transferred from the reserve to the profit and loss account if either—

> (a) the amount in question was previously charged to that account; or
>
> (b) it represents realised profit."

34(4) The treatment for taxation purposes of amounts credited or debited to the revaluation reserve shall be disclosed in a note to the accounts.

Part III — Notes to the Accounts

Preliminary

35 Any information required in the case of any company by the following provisions of this Part of this Schedule shall (if not given in the company's accounts) be given by way of a note to those accounts.

Disclosure of accounting policies

36 The accounting policies adopted by the company in determining the amounts to be included in respect of items shown in the balance sheet and in determining the profit or loss of the company shall be stated (including such policies with respect to the depreciation and diminution in value of assets). *eg. Acc'ng Convention - H.C.*

36A   It shall be stated whether the accounts have been prepared in accordance with applicable accounting standards and particulars of any material departure from those standards and the reasons for it shall be given.

History
Para. 36A inserted by CA 1989, s. 1, 4(2) and Sch. 1, para. 1, 7 as from 1 April 1990 subject to transitional and saving provisons (see S.I. 1990 No. 355 (C. 13), art. 3, Sch. 1 and also art. 6–9).

Information supplementing the balance sheet

37   Paragraphs 38 to 51 require information which either supplements the information given with respect to any particular items shown in the balance sheet or is otherwise relevant to assessing the company's state of affairs in the light of the information so given.

Share capital and debentures

38(1)   The following information shall be given with respect to the company's share capital—

    (a) the authorised share capital; and

    (b) where shares of more than one class have been allotted, the number and aggregate nominal value of shares of each class allotted.

38(2)   In the case of any part of the allotted share capital that consists of redeemable shares, the following information shall be given—

    (a) the earliest and latest dates on which the company has power to redeem those shares;

    (b) whether those shares must be redeemed in any event or are liable to be redeemed at the option of the company or of the shareholder; and

    (c) whether any (and, if so, what) premium is payable on redemption.

39   If the company has allotted any shares during the financial year, the following information shall be given—

    (a) the reason for making the allotment;

    (b) the classes of shares allotted; and

    (c) as respects each class of shares, the number allotted, their aggregate nominal value, and the consideration received by the company for the allotment.

40(1)   With respect to any contingent right to the allotment of shares in the company the following particulars shall be given—

    (a) the number, description and amount of the shares in relation to which the right is exercisable;

    (b) the period during which it is exercisable; and

    (c) the price to be paid for the shares allotted.

40(2)   In sub-paragraph (1) above **"contingent right to the allotment of shares"** means any option to subscribe for shares and any other right to require the allotment of shares to any person whether arising on the conversion into shares of securities of any other description or otherwise.

CA 1985, Sch. 4, para. 36A   [The next page is 27,901]   **CCH Editions Limited**

41(1) If the company has issued any debentures during the financial year to which the accounts relate, the following information shall be given—

    (a) the reason for making the issue;

    (b) the classes of debentures issued; and

    (c) as respects each class of debentures, the amount issued and the consideration received by the company for the issue.

41(2) Particulars of any redeemed debentures which the company has power to reissue shall also be given.

41(3) Where any of the company's debentures are held by a nominee of or trustee for the company, the nominal amount of the debentures and the amount at which they are stated in the accounting records kept by the company in accordance with section 221 of this Act shall be stated.

Fixed assets

42(1) In respect of each item which is or would but for paragraph 3(4)(b) be shown under the general item "fixed assets" in the company's balance sheet the following information shall be given—

    (a) the appropriate amounts in respect of that item as at the date of the beginning of the financial year and as at the balance sheet date respectively;

    (b) the effect on any amount shown in the balance sheet in respect of that item of—

        (i) any revision of the amount in respect of any assets included under that item made during that year on any basis mentioned in paragraph 31;

        (ii) acquisitions during that year of any assets;

        (iii) disposals during that year of any assets; and

        (iv) any transfers of assets of the company to and from that item during that year.

42(2) The reference in sub-paragraph (1)(a) to the appropriate amounts in respect of any item as at any date there mentioned is a reference to amounts representing the aggregate amounts determined, as at that date, in respect of assets falling to be included under that item on either of the following bases, that is to say—

    (a) on the basis of purchase price or production cost (determined in accordance with paragraphs 26 and 27); or

    (b) on any basis mentioned in paragraph 31,

(leaving out of account in either case any provisions for depreciation or diminution in value).

42(3) In respect of each item within sub-paragraph (1)—

    (a) the cumulative amount of provisions for depreciation or diminution in value of assets included under that item as at each date mentioned in sub-paragraph (1)(a);

    (b) the amount of any such provisions made in respect of the financial year;

    (c) the amount of any adjustments made in respect of any such provisions during that year in consequence of the disposal of any assets; and

    (d) the amount of any other adjustments made in respect of any such provisions during that year;

shall also be stated.

43 Where any fixed assets of the company (other than listed investments) are included under any item shown in the company's balance sheet at an amount determined on any basis mentioned in paragraph 31, the following information shall be given—

    (a) the years (so far as they are known to the directors) in which the assets were severally valued and the several values; and

    (b) in the case of assets that have been valued during the financial year, the names of the persons who valued them or particulars of their qualifications for doing so and (whichever is stated) the bases of valuation used by them.

44 In relation to any amount which is or would but for paragraph 3(4)(b) be shown in respect of the item "land and buildings" in the company's balance sheet there shall be stated—

    (a) how much of that amount is ascribable to land of freehold tenure and how much to land of leasehold tenure; and

    (b) how much of the amount ascribable to land of leasehold tenure is ascribable to land held on long lease and how much to land held on short lease.

Investments

45(1) In respect of the amount of each item which is or would but for paragraph 3(4)(b) be shown in the company's balance sheet under the general item "investments" (whether as fixed assets or as current assets) there shall be stated—

    (a) how much of that amount is ascribable to listed investments; and

    (b) how much of any amount so ascribable is ascribable to investments as respects which there has been granted a listing on a recognised investment exchange other than an overseas investment exchange within the meaning of the Financial Services Act 1986 and how much to other listed investments.

History
In para. 45(1) the words "recognised investment exchange other than an overseas investment exchange within the meaning of the Financial Services Act 1986" substituted for the former words "recognised stock exchange" by Financial Services Act 1986, s. 212(2) and Sch. 16, para. 23(a) as from 29 April 1988 (see S.I. 1988 No. 740 (C. 22)).

45(2) Where the amount of any listed investments is stated for any item in accordance with sub-paragraph (1)(a), the following amounts shall also be stated—

    (a) the aggregate market value of those investments where it differs from the amount so stated; and

    (b) both the market value and the stock exchange value of any investments of which the former value is, for the purposes of the accounts, taken as being higher than the latter.

Reserves and provisions

46(1) Where any amount is transferred—

    (a) to or from any reserves; or

    (b) to any provisions for liabilities and charges; or

CA 1985, Sch. 4, para. 43

    (c) from any provision for liabilities and charges otherwise than for the purpose for which the provision was established;

and the reserves or provisions are or would but for paragraph 3(4)(b) be shown as separate items in the company's balance sheet, the information mentioned in the following sub-paragraph shall be given in respect of the aggregate of reserves or provisions included in the same item.

46(2) That information is—

    (a) the amount of the reserves or provisions as at the date of the beginning of the financial year and as at the balance sheet date respectively;

    (b) any amounts transferred to or from the reserves or provisions during that year; and

    (c) the source and application respectively of any amounts so transferred.

46(3) Particulars shall be given of each provision included in the item "other provisions" in the company's balance sheet in any case where the amount of that provision is material.

Provision for taxation

47 The amount of any provision for deferred taxation shall be stated separately from the amount of any provision for other taxation.

History
Para. 47 substituted by CA 1989, s. 1, 4(2) and Sch. 1, para. 1, 8 as from 1 April 1990 subject to transitional and saving provisions (see S.I. 1990 No. 355 (C. 13), art. 3, Sch. 1 and also art. 6–9); para. 47 formerly read as follows:

"The amount of any provisions for taxation other than deferred taxation shall be stated."

Details of indebtedness

48(1) In respect of each item shown under "creditors" in the company's balance sheet there shall be stated—

    (a) the aggregate amount of any debts included under that item which are payable or repayable otherwise than by instalments and fall due for payment or repayment after the end of the period of five years beginning with the day next following the end of the financial year; and

    (b) the aggregate amount of any debts so included which are payable or repayable by instalments any of which fall due for payment after the end of that period;

and in the case of debts within paragraph (b) above the aggregate amount of instalments falling due after the end of that period shall also be disclosed for each such item.

48(2) Subject to sub-paragraph (3), in relation to each debt falling to be taken into account under sub-paragraph (1), the terms of payment or repayment and the rate of any interest payable on the debt shall be stated.

48(3) If the number of debts is such that, in the opinion of the directors, compliance with sub-paragraph (2) would result in a statement of excessive length, it shall be sufficient to give a general indication of the terms of payment or repayment and the rates of any interest payable on the debts.

48(4)　In respect of each item shown under "creditors" in the company's balance sheet there shall be stated—

  (a)　the aggregate amount of any debts included under that item in respect of which any security has been given by the company; and

  (b)　an indication of the nature of the securities so given.

48(5)　References above in this paragraph to an item shown under "creditors" in the company's balance sheet include references, where amounts falling due to creditors within one year and after more than one year are distinguished in the balance sheet—

  (a)　in a case within sub-paragraph (1), to an item shown under the latter of those categories; and

  (b)　in a case within sub-paragraph (4), to an item shown under either of those categories;

and references to items shown under "creditors" include references to items which would but for paragraph 3(4)(b) be shown under that heading.

49　If any fixed cumulative dividends on the company's shares are in arrear, there shall be stated—

  (a)　the amount of the arrears; and

  (b)　the period for which the dividends or, if there is more than one class, each class of them are in arrear.

Guarantees and other financial commitments

50(1)　Particulars shall be given of any charge on the assets of the company to secure the liabilities of any other person, including, where practicable, the amount secured.

50(2)　The following information shall be given with respect to any other contingent liability not provided for—

  (a)　the amount or estimated amount of that liability;

  (b)　its legal nature; and

  (c)　whether any valuable security has been provided by the company in connection with that liability and if so, what.

50(3)　There shall be stated, where practicable—

  (a)　the aggregate amount or estimated amount of contracts for capital expenditure, so far as not provided for; and

  (b)　the aggregate amount or estimated amount of capital expenditure authorised by the directors which has not been contracted for.

50(4)　Particulars shall be given of—

  (a)　any pension commitments included under any provision shown in the company's balance sheet; and

  (b)　any such commitments for which no provision has been made;

and where any such commitment relates wholly or partly to pensions payable to past directors of the company separate particulars shall be given of that commitment so far as it relates to such pensions.

50(5) Particulars shall also be given of any other financial commitments which—

(a) have not been provided for; and

(b) are relevant to assessing the company's state of affairs.

50(6) (Repealed by Companies Act 1989, sec. 221 and Sch. 24 as from 1 April 1990.)

History
In regard to the date of the above repeal see S.I. 1990 No. 355 (C. 13), art. 5(1)(b), (2) and art. 6–9 for transitional and saving provisions; para. 50(6) formerly read as follows:

"Commitments within any of the preceding sub-paragraphs undertaken on behalf of or for the benefit of—

(a) any holding company or fellow subsidiary of the company; or

(b) any subsidiary of the company;

shall be stated separately from the other commitments within that sub-paragraph (and commitments within paragraph (a) shall also be stated separately from those within paragraph (b))."

Miscellaneous matters

51(1) Particulars shall be given of any case where the purchase price or production cost of any asset is for the first time determined under paragraph 28.

51(2) Where any outstanding loans made under the authority of section 153(4)(b), (bb) or (c) or section 155 of this Act (various cases of financial assistance by a company for purchase of its own shares) are included under any item shown in the company's balance sheet, the aggregate amount of those loans shall be disclosed for each item in question.

History
In para. 51(2) ", (bb)" inserted after "153(4)(b)" by CA 1989, s. 1, 4(2) and Sch. 1, para. 1, 9 as from 1 April 1990 subject to transitional and saving provisions (see S.I. 1990 No. 355 (C. 13), art. 3, Sch. 1 and also art. 6–9).

51(3) The aggregate amount which is recommended for distribution by way of dividend shall be stated.

Information supplementing the profit and loss account

52 Paragraphs 53 to 57 require information which either supplements the information given with respect to any particular items shown in the profit and loss account or otherwise provides particulars of income or expenditure of the company or of circumstances affecting the items shown in the profit and loss account.

Separate statement of certain items of income and expenditure

53(1) Subject to the following provisions of this paragraph, each of the amounts mentioned below shall be stated.

53(2) The amount of the interest on or any similar charges in respect of—

(a) bank loans and overdrafts, and loans made to the company (other than bank loans and overdrafts) which—

(i) are repayable otherwise than by instalments and fall due for repayment before the end of the period of five years beginning with the day next following the end of the financial year; or

(ii) are repayable by instalments the last of which falls due for payment before the end of that period; and

(b) loans of any other kind made to the company.

This sub-paragraph does not apply to interest or charges on loans to the company from group undertakings, but, with that exception, it applies to interest or charges on all loans, whether made on the security of debentures or not.

History
In para. 53(2) the words "group undertakings" substituted for the former words "group companies" by CA 1989, s. 1, 4(2) and Sch. 1, para. 1, 2(1)(e) as from 1 April 1990   subject to transitional and saving provisions (see S.I. 1990 No. 355 (C. 13), art. 3, Sch. 1 and also art. 6–9).

53(3)   The amounts respectively set aside for redemption of share capital and for redemption of loans.

53(4)   The amount of income from listed investments.

53(5)   The amount of rents from land (after deduction of ground rents, rates and other outgoings).

This amount need only be stated if a substantial part of the company's revenue for the financial year consists of rents from land.

53(6)   The amount charged to revenue in respect of sums payable in respect of the hire of plant and machinery.

53(7)   (Repealed by Companies Act 1989, sec. 212 and Sch. 24 as from 1 April 1990.)

History
In regard to the date of the above repeal see S.I. No. 355 (C. 13), art. 5(1)(b), (2) and art. 6–9 for transitional and saving provisions; para. 53(7) formerly read as follows: "The amount of the remuneration of the auditors (taking **'remuneration'**, for the purposes of this sub-paragraph, as including any sums paid by the company in respect of the auditors' expenses)."

Particulars of tax

54(1)   The basis on which the charge for United Kingdom corporation tax and United Kingdom income tax is computed shall be stated.

54(2)   Particulars shall be given of any special circumstances which affect liability in respect of taxation of profits, income or capital gains for the financial year or liability in respect of taxation of profits, income or capital gains for succeeding financial years.

54(3)   The following amounts shall be stated—

  (a) the amount of the charge for United Kingdom corporation tax;

  (b) if that amount would have been greater but for relief from double taxation, the amount which it would have been but for such relief;

  (c) the amount of the charge for United Kingdom income tax; and

  (d) the amount of the charge for taxation imposed outside the United Kingdom of profits, income and (so far as charged to revenue) capital gains.

These amounts shall be stated separately in respect of each of the amounts which is or would but for paragraph 3(4)(b) be shown under the following items in the profit and loss account, that is to say "tax on profit or loss on ordinary activities" and "tax on extraordinary profit or loss".

Particulars of turnover

55(1)   If in the course of the financial year the company has carried on business of two or more classes that, in the opinion of the directors, differ substantially from each other, there shall be stated in respect of each class (describing it)—

  (a) the amount of the turnover attributable to that class; and

  (b) the amount of the profit or loss of the company before taxation which is in the opinion of the directors attributable to that class.

55(2) If in the course of the financial year the company has supplied markets that, in the opinion of the directors, differ substantially from each other, the amount of the turnover attributable to each such market shall also be stated.

In this paragraph **"market"** means a market delimited by geographical bounds.

55(3) In analysing for the purposes of this paragraph the source (in terms of business or in terms of market) of turnover or (as the case may be) of profit or loss, the directors of the company shall have regard to the manner in which the company's activities are organised.

55(4) For the purposes of this paragraph—

    (a) classes of business which, in the opinion of the directors, do not differ substantially from each other shall be treated as one class; and

    (b) markets which, in the opinion of the directors, do not differ substantially from each other shall be treated as one market;

and any amounts properly attributable to one class of business or (as the case may be) to one market which are not material may be included in the amount stated in respect of another.

55(5) Where in the opinion of the directors the disclosure of any information required by this paragraph would be seriously prejudicial to the interests of the company, that information need not be disclosed, but the fact that any such information has not been disclosed must be stated.

Particulars of staff

56(1) The following information shall be given with respect to the employees of the company—

    (a) the average number of persons employed by the company in the financial year; and

    (b) the average number of persons so employed within each category of persons employed by the company.

56(2) The average number required by sub-paragraph (1)(a) or (b) shall be determined by dividing the relevant annual number by the number of weeks in the financial year.

56(3) The relevant annual number shall be determined by ascertaining for each week in the financial year—

    (a) for the purposes of sub-paragraph (1)(a), the number of persons employed under contracts of service by the company in that week (whether throughout the week or not);

    (b) for the purposes of sub-paragraph (1)(b), the number of persons in the category in question of persons so employed;

and, in either case, adding together all the weekly numbers.

56(4) In respect of all persons employed by the company during the financial year who are taken into account in determining the relevant annual number for the purposes of sub-paragraph (1)(a) there shall also be stated the aggregate amounts respectively of—

    (a) wages and salaries paid or payable in respect of that year to those persons;

(b) social security costs incurred by the company on their behalf; and

(c) other pension costs so incurred;

save in so far as those amounts or any of them are stated in the profit and loss account.

56(5) The categories of persons employed by the company by reference to which the number required to be disclosed of sub-paragraph (1)(b) is to be determined shall be such as the directors may select, having regard to the manner in which the company's activities are organised.

Miscellaneous matters

57(1) Where any amount relating to any preceding financial year is included in any item in the profit and loss account, the effect shall be stated.

57(2) Particulars shall be given of any extraordinary income or charges arising in the financial year.

57(3) The effect shall be stated of any transactions that are exceptional by virtue of size or incidence though they fall within the ordinary activities of the company.

General

58(1) Where sums originally denominated in foreign currencies have been brought into account under any items shown in the balance sheet or profit and loss account, the basis on which those sums have been translated into sterling shall be stated.

58(2) Subject to the following sub-paragraph, in respect of every item stated in a note to the accounts the corresponding amount for the financial year immediately preceding that to which the accounts relate shall also be stated and where the corresponding amount is not comparable, it shall be adjusted and particulars of the adjustment and the reasons for it shall be given.

58(3) Sub-paragraph (2) does not apply in relation to any amounts stated by virtue of any of the following provisions of this Act—

(a) paragraph 13 of Schedule 4A (details of accounting treatment of acquisitions),

(b) paragraphs 2, 8(3), 16, 21(1)(d), 22(4) and (5), 24(3) and (4) and 27(3) and (4) of Schedule 5 (shareholdings in other undertakings),

(c) Parts II and III of Schedule 6 (loans and other dealings in favour of directors and others), and

(d) paragraphs 42 and 46 above (fixed assets and reserves and provisions).

History
Para. 58(3)(a)–(d) substituted for former para. 58(3)(a)–(c) by CA 1989, s. 1, 4(2) and Sch. 1, para. 1, 10 as from 1 April 1990 subject to transitional and saving provisions (see S.I. 1990 No. 355 (C. 13), art. 3, Sch. 1 and also art. 6–9); the former para. 58(3)(a)–(c) read as follows:

"(a) section 231 as applying Parts I and II of Schedule 5 (proportion of share capital of subsidiaries and other bodies corporate held by the company, etc.),

(b) sections 232 to 234 and Schedule 6 (particulars of loans to directors, etc.), and

(c) paragraphs 42 and 46 above."

[The next page is 28,301]

CA 1985, Sch. 4, para. 56(5)

Part IV — Special Provisions Where Company is a Parent or Subsidiary Undertaking

History
The heading to Pt. IV substituted by CA 1989, s. 1, 4(2) and Sch. 1, para. 1, 11(1) as from 1 April 1990 subject to transitional and saving provisions (see S.I. 1990 No. 355 (C. 13), art. 3, Sch. 1 and also art. 6–9); heading formerly read as follows:

"Part IV — Special Provisions Where the Company is a Holding or Subsidiary Company".

Company's own accounts

Dealings with or interests in group undertakings

59 Where a company is a parent company or a subsidiary undertaking and any item required by Part I of this Schedule to be shown in the company's balance sheet in relation to group undertakings includes—

(a) amounts attributable to dealings with or interests in any parent undertaking or fellow subsidiary undertaking, or

(b) amounts attributable to dealings with or interests in any subsidiary undertaking of the company,

the aggregate amounts within paragraphs (a) and (b) respectively shall be shown as separate items, either by way of subdivision of the relevant item in the balance sheet or in a note to the company's accounts.

History
Para. 59 substituted by CA 1989, s. 1, 4(2) and Sch. 1, para. 1, 11(2) as from 1 April 1990 subject to transitional and saving provisions (see S.I. 1990 No. 355 (C. 13), art. 3, Sch. 1 and also art. 6–9); para. 59 formerly read as follows:

"Where a company is a holding company or a subsidiary of another body corporate and any item required by Part I of this Schedule to be shown in the company's balance sheet in relation to group companies includes—

(a) amounts attributable to dealings with or interests in any holding company or fellow subsidiary of the company; or

(b) amounts attributable to dealings with or interests in any subsidiary of the company;

the aggregate amounts within paragraphs (a) and (b) respectively shall be shown as separate items, either by way of subdivision of the relevant item in the balance sheet or in a note to the company's accounts."

Guarantees and other financial commitments in favour of group undertakings

59A Commitments within any of sub-paragraphs (1) to (5) of paragraph 50 (guarantees and other financial commitments) which are undertaken on behalf of or for the benefit of—

(a) any parent undertaking or fellow subsidiary undertaking, or

(b) any subsidiary undertaking of the company,

shall be stated separately from the other commitments within that sub-paragraph, and commitments within paragraph (a) shall also be stated separately from those within paragraph (b).

History
Para. 59A inserted by CA 1989, s. 1, 4(2) and Sch. 1, para. 1, 11(3) as from 1 April 1990 subject to transitional and saving provisions (see S.I. 1990 No. 355 (C. 13), art. 3, Sch. 1 and also art. 6–9).

60–70 (Repealed by Companies Act 1989, sec. 212 and Sch. 24 as from 1 April 1990.)

History
In regard to the date of the above repeal see S.I. 1990 No. 355 (C. 13), art. 5(1)(b), (2) and art. 6–9 for transitional and saving provisions; para. 60–70 formerly read as follows:

"60(1) Subject to the following sub-paragraph, where the company is a holding company, the number, description and amount of the shares in and debentures of the company held by its subsidiaries or their nominees shall be disclosed in a note to the company's accounts.

(2) Sub-paragraph (1) does not apply in relation to any shares or debentures—

(a) in the case of which the subsidiary is concerned as personal representative; or

(b)   in the case of which it is concerned as trustee;

provided that in the latter case neither the company nor any subsidiary of the company is beneficially interested under the trust, otherwise than by way of security only for the purposes of a transaction entered into by it in the ordinary course of a business which includes the lending of money.

Schedule 2 to this Act has effect for the interpretation of the reference in this sub-paragraph to a beneficial interest under a trust.

Consolidated accounts of holding company and subsidiaries

61   Subject to paragraphs 63 and 66, the consolidated balance sheet and profit and loss account shall combine the information contained in the separate balance sheets and profit and loss accounts of the holding company and of the subsidiaries dealt with by the consolidated accounts, but with such adjustments (if any) as the directors of the holding company think necessary.

62   Subject to paragraphs 63 to 66, and to Part V of this Schedule, the consolidated accounts shall, in giving the information required by paragraph 61, comply so far as practicable with the requirements of this Schedule and with the other requirements of this Act as if they were the accounts of an actual company.

63   The following provisions of this Act, namely—

(a)   section 231 as applying Schedule 5, but only Parts II, III, V and VI of that Schedule, and

(b)   sections 232 to 234 and Schedule 6, so far as relating to accounts other than group accounts,

do not, by virtue of paragraphs 61 and 62, apply for the purposes of the consolidated accounts.

64   Paragraph 62 is without prejudice to any requirement of this Act which applies (otherwise than by virtue of paragraph 61 or 62) to group accounts.

65(1)   Notwithstanding paragraph 62, the consolidated accounts prepared by a holding company may deal with an investment of any member of the group in the shares of any other body corporate by way of the equity method of accounting in any case where it appears to the directors of the holding company that that body corporate is so closely associated with any member of the group as to justify the use of that method in dealing with investments by that or any other member of the group in the shares of that body corporate.

(2)   In this paragraph, references to the group, in relation to consolidated accounts prepared by a holding company, are references to the holding company and the subsidiaries dealt with by the accounts.

66   Notwithstanding paragraphs 61 and 62, paragraphs 17 to 19 and 21 do not apply to any amount shown in the consolidated balance sheet in respect of goodwill arising on consolidation.

67   In relation to any subsidiaries of the holding company not dealt with by the consolidated accounts paragraphs 59 and 60 apply for the purpose of those accounts as if those accounts were the accounts of an actual company of which they were subsidiaries.

Group accounts not prepared as consolidated accounts

68   Group accounts which are not prepared as consolidated accounts, together with any notes to those accounts, shall give the same or equivalent information as that required to be given by consolidated accounts by virtue of paragraphs 61 to 67.

Provisions of general application

69(1)   This paragraph applies where the company is a holding company and either—

(a)   does not prepare group accounts; or

(b)   prepares group accounts which do not deal with one or more of its subsidiaries;

and references below in this paragraph to the company's subsidiaries shall be read in a case within paragraph (b) as references to such of the company's subsidiaries as are excluded from the group accounts.

(2)   Subject to the following provisions of this paragraph—

(a)   the reasons why the subsidiaries are not dealt with in group accounts; and

(b)   a statement showing any qualifications contained in the reports of the auditors of the subsidiaries on their accounts for their respective financial years ending with or during the financial year of the company, and any note or saving contained in those accounts to call attention to a matter which, apart from the note or saving, would properly have been referred to in such a qualification, in so far as the matter which is the subject of the qualification or note is not covered by the company's own accounts and is material from the point of view of its members,

shall be given in a note to the company's accounts.

(3)   Subject to the following provisions of this paragraph, the aggregate amount of the total investment of the holding company in the shares of the subsidiaries shall be stated in a note to the company's accounts by way of the equity method of valuation.

(4)   Sub-paragraph (3) does not apply where the company is a wholly owned subsidiary of another body corporate incorporated in Great Britain if there is included in a note to the company's accounts a statement that in the opinion of the directors of the company the aggregate value of the assets of the company consisting of shares in, or amounts owing (whether on account of a loan or otherwise) from, the company's subsidiaries is not less than the aggregate of the amounts at which those assets are stated or included in the company's balance sheet.

(5)   In so far as information required by any of the preceding provisions of this paragraph to be stated in a note to the company's accounts is not obtainable, a statement to that effect shall be given instead in a note to those accounts.

(6)   The Secretary of State may, on the application or with the consent of the company's directors, direct that in relation to any subsidiary sub-paragraphs (2) and (3) shall not apply, or shall apply only to such extent as may be provided by the direction.

(7)   Where in any case within sub-paragraph (1)(b) the group accounts are consolidated accounts, references above in this paragraph to the company's accounts and the company's balance sheet respectively shall be read as references to the consolidated accounts and the consolidated balance sheet.

70   Where a company has subsidiaries whose financial years did not end with that of the company, the following information shall be given in relation to each such subsidiary (whether or not dealt with in any group accounts prepared by the company) by way of a note to the company's accounts or (where group accounts are prepared) to the group accounts, that is to say—

(a)   the reasons why the company's directors consider that the subsidiaries' financial years should not end with that of the company; and

(b)   the dates on which the subsidiaries' financial years ending last before that of the company respectively ended or the earliest and latest of those dates.''

Part V — Special Provisions where the Company is an Investment Company

71(1) Paragraph 34 does not apply to the amount of any profit or loss arising from a determination of the value of any investments of an investment company on any basis mentioned in paragraph 31(3).

71(2) Any provisions made by virtue of paragraph 19(1) or (2) in the case of an investment company in respect of any fixed asset investments need not be charged to the company's profit and loss account provided they are either—

(a) charged against any reserve account to which any amount excluded by subparagraph (1) from the requirements of paragraph 34 has been credited; or

(b) shown as a separate item in the company's balance sheet under the subheading "other reserves".

71(3) For the purposes of this paragraph, as it applies in relation to any company, **"fixed asset investment"** means any asset falling to be included under any item shown in the company's balance sheet under the subdivision "investments" under the general item "fixed assets".

72(1) Any distribution made by an investment company which reduces the amount of its net assets to less than the aggregate of its called-up share capital and undistributable reserves shall be disclosed in a note to the company's accounts.

72(2) For purposes of this paragraph, a company's net assets are the aggregate of its assets less the aggregate of its liabilities (including any provision for liabilities or charges within paragraph 89); and **"undistributable reserves"** has the meaning given by section 264(3) of this Act.

73 A company shall be treated as an investment company for the purposes of this Part of this Schedule in relation to any financial year of the company if—

(a) during the whole of that year it was an investment company as defined by section 266 of this Act, and

(b) it was not at any time during that year prohibited under section 265(4) of this Act (no distribution where capital profits have been distributed, etc.) from making a distribution by virtue of that section.

74 (Repealed by Companies Act 1989, see 212 and Sch. 24 as from 1 April 1990.)

History
In regard to the date of the above repeal see S.I. 1990 No. 355 (C. 13), art. 5(1)(b), (2) and art. 6–9 for transitional and saving provisions; para. 74 formerly read as follows:

"Where a company entitled to the benefit of any provision contained in this Part of this Schedule is a holding company, the reference in paragraph 62 to consolidated accounts complying with the requirements of this Act shall, in relation to consolidated accounts of that company, be construed as referring to those requirements in so far only—

(a) as they apply to the individual accounts of that company; and

(b) as they apply otherwise than by virtue of paragraphs 61 and 62 to any group accounts prepared by that company."

Part VI — Special Provisions Where the Company has Entered into Arrangements Subject to Merger Relief

75   (Repealed by Companies Act 1989, sec. 212 and Sch. 24 as from 1 April 1990.)

History
In regard to the date of the above repeal see S.I. 1990 No. 355 (C. 13), art. 5(1)(b), (2) and art. 6–9 for transitional and saving provisons; para. 75 formerly read as follows:

"**75(1)**   Where during the financial year the company has allotted shares in consideration for the issue, transfer or cancellation of shares in another body corporate ('the other company') in circumstances where by virtue of section 131(2) of this Act (merger relief) section 130 did not apply to the premiums on those shares, the following information shall be given by way of a note to the company's accounts—

  (a)   the name of the other company;

  (b)   the number, nominal value and class of shares so allotted;

  (c)   the number, nominal value and class of shares in the other company so issued, transferred or cancelled;

  (d)   particulars of the accounting treatment adopted in the company's accounts (including any group accounts) in respect of such issue, transfer or cancellation; and

  (e)   where the company prepares group accounts, particulars of the extent to which and manner in which the profit or loss for the year of the group which appears in those accounts is affected by any profit or loss of the other company or any of its subsidiaries which arose at any time before the allotment.

(2)   Where the company has during the financial year or during either of the two financial years immediately preceding it made such an allotment of shares as is mentioned in sub-paragraph (1) above and there is included in the company's consolidated profit and loss account or, if it has no such account, in its individual profit and loss account, any profit or loss (or part thereof) to which this sub-paragraph applies then the net amount of any such profit or loss (or part thereof) shall be shown in a note to the accounts together with an explanation of the transactions to which that information relates.

(3)   Sub-paragraph (2) applies—

  (a)   to any profit or loss realised during the financial year by the company, or any of its subsidiaries, on the disposal of any shares in the other company or of any assets which were fixed assets of the other company, or of any of its subsidiaries, at the time of the allotment; and

  (b)   to any part of any profit or loss realised during the financial year by the company, or any of its subsidiaries, on the disposal of any shares (not being shares in the other company), which was attributable to the fact that at the time of the disposal there were amongst the assets of the company which issued those shares, or any of its subsidiaries, such shares or assets as are described in sub-paragraph (a) above.

(4)   Where in pursuance of the arrangement in question shares are allotted on different dates, the time of allotment for the purposes of sub-paragraphs (1)(e) and (3)(a) above is taken to be—

  (a)   if the other company becomes a subsidiary of the company as a result of the arrangement—

    (i)   if the arrangement becomes binding only upon the fulfilment of a condition, the date on which that condition is fulfilled, and

    (ii)   in any other case, the date on which the other company becomes a subsidiary of the company;

  (b)   if the other company is a subsidiary of the company when the arrangement is proposed, the date of the first allotment pursuant to that arrangement."

Part VII — Interpretation of Schedule

76   The following paragraphs apply for the purposes of this Schedule and its interpretation.

77–81   (Repealed by Companies Act 1989, sec. 212 and Sch. 24 as from 1 April 1990.)

History
In regard to the date of the above repeal see S.I. 1990 No. 355 (C. 13), art. 5(1)(b), (2) and art. 6–9 for transitional and saving provisions; para. 77–81 formerly read as follows:

"*Assets: fixed or current*

77   Assets of a company are taken to be fixed assets if they are intended for use on a continuing basis in the company's activities, and any assets not intended for such use shall be taken to be current assets.

Balance sheet date

78   'Balance sheet date', in relation to a balance sheet, means the date as at which the balance sheet was prepared.

Capitalisation

79   References to capitalising any work or costs are to treating that work or those costs as a fixed asset.

Fellow subsidiary

80   A body corporate is treated as a fellow subsidiary of another body corporate if both are subsidiaries of the same body corporate but neither is the other's.

Group companies

81   'Group company', in relation to any company, means any body corporate which is that company's subsidiary or holding company, or a subsidiary of that company's holding company."

[The next page is 28,501]

Historical cost accounting rules

82   References to the historical cost accounting rules shall be read in accordance with paragraph 29.

Leases

83(1)   **"Long lease"** means a lease in the case of which the portion of the term for which it was granted remaining unexpired at the end of the financial year is not less than 50 years.

83(2)   **"Short lease"** means a lease which is not a long lease.

83(3)   **"Lease"** includes an agreement for a lease.

Listed investments

84   **"Listed investment"** means an investment as respects which there has been granted a listing on a recognised investment exchange other than an overseas investment exchange within the meaning of the Financial Services Act 1986 or on any stock exchange of repute outside Great Britain.

History
In para. 84 the words from "on a recognised investment exchange" to the end substituted for the former words "on a recognised stock exchange, or on any stock exchange of repute (other than a recognised stock exchange) outside Great Britain " by Financial Services Act 1986, s. 212(2) and Sch. 16, para. 23(b) as from 29 April 1988 (see S.I. 1988 No. 740 (C. 22)).

Loans

85   A loan is treated as falling due for repayment, and an instalment of a loan is treated as falling due for payment, on the earliest date on which the lender could require repayment or (as the case may be) payment, if he exercised all options and rights available to him.

Materiality

86   Amounts which in the particular context of any provision of this Schedule are not material may be disregarded for the purposes of that provision.

87   (Repealed by Companies Act 1989, sec. 212 and Sch. 24 as from 1 April 1990.)

History
In regard to the date of the above repeal see S.I. 1990 No. 355 (C. 13), art. 5(1)(b), (2) and art. 6–9 for transitional and saving provisions; para. 87 formerly read as follows:

"Notes to the accounts
87   Notes to a company's accounts may be contained in the accounts or in a separate document annexed to the accounts."

Provisions

88(1)   References to provisions for depreciation or diminution in value of assets are to any amount written off by way of providing for depreciation or diminution in value of assets.

88(2)   Any reference in the profit and loss account formats set out in Part I of this Schedule to the depreciation of, or amounts written off, assets of any description is to any provision for depreciation or diminution in value of assets of that description.

89   References to provisions for liabilities or charges are to any amount retained as reasonably necessary for the purpose of providing for any liability or loss which is either likely to be incurred, or certain to be incurred but uncertain as to amount or as to the date on which it will arise.

90–92   (Repealed by Companies Act 1989, sec. 212 and Sch. 24 as from 1 April 1990.)

History

In regard to the date of the above repeal see S.I. 1990 No. 355 (C. 13), art. 5(1)(b), (2) and art. 6–9 for transitional and saving provisions; para. 90–92 formerly read as follows:

"Purchase price

90 References (however expressed) to the purchase price of any asset of a company or of any raw materials or consumables used in the production of any such asset include any consideration (whether in cash or otherwise) given by the company in respect of that asset or in respect of those materials or consumables (as the case may require).

Realised profits

91 Without prejudice to—

(a) the construction of any other expression (where appropriate) by reference to accepted accounting principles or practice, or

(b) any specific provision for the treatment of profits of any description as realised,

it is hereby declared for the avoidance of doubt that references in this Schedule to realised profits, in relation to a company's accounts, are to such profits of the company as fall to be treated as realised profits for the purposes of those accounts in accordance with principles generally accepted with respect to the determination for accounting purposes of realised profits at the time when those accounts are prepared.

Related companies

92(1) **'Related company'**, in relation to any company, means any body corporate (other than one which is a group company in relation to that company) in which that company holds on a long-term basis a qualifying capital interest for the purpose of securing a contribution to that company's own activities by the exercise of any control or influence arising from that interest.

(2) In this paragraph **'qualifying capital interest'** means, in relation to any body corporate, an interest in shares comprised in the equity share capital of that body corporate of a class carrying rights to vote in all circumstances at general meetings of that body corporate.

(3) Where—

(a) a company holds a qualifying capital interest in a body corporate; and

(b) the nominal value of any relevant shares in that body corporate held by that company is equal to twenty per cent. or more of the nominal value of all relevant shares in that body corporate;

it shall be presumed to hold that interest on the basis and for the purpose mentioned in sub-paragraph (1), unless the contrary is shown.

In this sub-paragraph **'relevant shares'** means, in relation to any body corporate, any such shares in that body corporate as are mentioned in sub-paragraph (2)."

Scots land tenure

93 In the application of this Schedule to Scotland, **"land of freehold tenure"** means land in respect of which the company is the proprietor of the *dominium utile* or, in the case of land not held on feudal tenure, is the owner; **"land of leasehold tenure"** means land of which the company is the tenant under a lease; and the reference to ground-rents, rates and other outgoings includes feu-duty and ground annual.

Staff costs

94(1) **"Social security costs"** means any contributions by the company to any state social security or pension scheme, fund or arrangement.

94(2) **"Pension costs"** includes any other contributions by the company for the purposes of any pension scheme established for the purpose of providing pensions for persons employed by the company, any sums set aside for that purpose and any amounts paid by the company in respect of pensions without first being so set aside.

94(3) Any amount stated in respect of either of the above items or in respect of the item "wages and salaries" in the company's profit and loss account shall be determined by reference to payments made or costs incurred in respect of all persons employed by the company during the financial year who are taken into account in determining the relevant annual number for the purposes of paragraph 56(1)(a).

95 (Repealed by Companies Act 1989, sec. 212 and Sch. 24 as from 1 April 1990.)

History

In regard to the date of the above repeal see S.I. 1990 No. 355 (C. 13), art. 5(1)(b), (2) and art. 6–9 for transitional and saving provisions; para. 95 formerly read as follows:

"Turnover

95 **'Turnover'**, in relation to a company, means the amounts derived from the provision of goods and services

falling within the company's ordinary activities, after deduction of—

(a) trade discounts,

(b) value added tax, and

(c) any other taxes based on the amounts so derived."

Schedule 4A — Form and Content of Group Accounts

[Companies Act 1985, sec. 227;
Companies Act 1989, sec. 1, 5(2)]

GENERAL RULES

1(1) Group accounts shall comply so far as practicable with the provisions of Schedule 4 as if the undertakings included in the consolidation ("the group") were a single company.

1(2) In particular, for the purposes of paragraph 59 of that Schedule (dealings with or interests in group undertakings) as it applies to group accounts—

    (a) any subsidiary undertakings of the parent company not included in the consolidation shall be treated as subsidiary undertakings of the group, and

    (b) if the parent company is itself a subsidiary undertaking, the group shall be treated as a subsidiary undertaking of any parent undertaking of that company, and the reference to fellow-subsidiary undertakings shall be construed accordingly.

1(3) Where the parent company is treated as an investment company for the purposes of Part V of that Schedule (special provisions for investment companies) the group shall be similarly treated.

2(1) The consolidated balance sheet and profit and loss account shall incorporate in full the information contained in the individual accounts of the undertakings included in the consolidation, subject to the adjustments authorised or required by the following provisions of this Schedule and to such other adjustments (if any) as may be appropriate in accordance with generally accepted accounting principles or practice.

2(2) If the financial year of a subsidiary undertaking included in the consolidation differs from that of the parent company, the group accounts shall be made up—

    (a) from the accounts of the subsidiary undertaking for its financial year last ending before the end of the parent company's financial year, provided that year ended no more than three months before that of the parent company, or

    (b) from interim accounts prepared by the subsidiary undertaking as at the end of the parent company's financial year.

3(1) Where assets and liabilities to be included in the group accounts have been valued or otherwise determined by undertakings according to accounting rules differing from those used for the group accounts, the values or amounts shall be adjusted so as to accord with the rules used for the group accounts.

3(2) If it appears to the directors of the parent company that there are special reasons for departing from sub-paragraph (1) they may do so, but particulars of any such departure, the reasons for it and its effect shall be given in a note to the accounts.

3(3) The adjustments referred to in this paragraph need not be made if they are not material for the purpose of giving a true and fair view.

4 Any differences of accounting rules as between a parent company's individual accounts for a financial year and its group accounts shall be disclosed in a note to the latter accounts and the reasons for the difference given.

5   Amounts which in the particular context of any provision of this Schedule are not material may be disregarded for the purposes of that provision.

ELIMINATION OF GROUP TRANSACTIONS

6(1)   Debts and claims between undertakings included in the consolidation, and income and expenditure relating to transactions between such undertakings, shall be eliminated in preparing the group accounts.

6(2)   Where profits and losses resulting from transactions between undertakings included in the consolidation are included in the book value of assets, they shall be eliminated in preparing the group accounts.

6(3)   The elimination required by sub-paragraph (2) may be effected in proportion to the group's interest in the shares of the undertakings.

6(4)   Sub-paragraphs (1) and (2) need not be complied with if the amounts concerned are not material for the purpose of giving a true and fair view.

ACQUISITION AND MERGER ACCOUNTING

7(1)   The following provisions apply where an undertaking becomes a subsidiary undertaking of the parent company.

7(2)   That event is referred to in those provisions as an "acquisition", and references to the "undertaking acquired" shall be construed accordingly.

8   An acquisition shall be accounted for by the acquisition method of accounting unless the conditions for accounting for it as a merger are met and the merger method of accounting is adopted.

9(1)   The acquisition method of accounting is as follows.

9(2)   The identifiable assets and liabilities of the undertaking acquired shall be included in the consolidated balance sheet at their fair values as at the date of acquisition.

In this paragraph the **"identifiable"** assets or liabilities of the undertaking acquired means the assets or liabilities which are capable of being disposed of or discharged separately, without disposing of a business of the undertaking.

9(3)   The income and expenditure of the undertaking acquired shall be brought into the group accounts only as from the date of the acquisition.

9(4)   There shall be set off against the acquisition cost of the interest in the shares of the undertaking held by the parent company and its subsidiary undertakings the interest of the parent company and its subsidiary undertakings in the adjusted capital and reserves of the undertaking acquired.

For this purpose—

> **"the acquisition cost"** means the amount of any cash consideration and the fair value of any other consideration, together with such amount (if any) in respect of fees and other expenses of the acquisition as the company may determine, and

> **"the adjusted capital and reserves"** of the undertaking acquired means its capital and reserves at the date of the acquisition after adjusting the

identifiable assets and liabilities of the undertaking to fair values as at that date.

9(5)   The resulting amount if positive shall be treated as goodwill, and if negative as a negative consolidation difference.

10(1)   The conditions for accounting for an acquisition as a merger are—

   (a)   that at least 90 per cent of the nominal value of the relevant shares in the undertaking acquired is held by or on behalf of the parent company and its subsidiary undertakings,

   (b)   that the proportion referred to in paragraph (a) was attained pursuant to an arrangement providing for the issue of equity shares by the parent company or one or more of its subsidiary undertakings,

   (c)   that the fair value of any consideration other than the issue of equity shares given pursuant to the arrangement by the parent company and its subsidiary undertakings did not exceed 10 per cent of the nominal value of the equity shares issued, and

   (d)   that adoption of the merger method of accounting accords with generally accepted accounting principles or practice.

10(2)   The reference in sub-paragraph (1)(a) to the "relevant shares" in an undertaking acquired is to those carrying unrestricted rights to participate both in distributions and in the assets of the undertaking upon liquidation.

11(1)   The merger method of accounting is as follows.

11(2)   The assets and liabilities of the undertaking acquired shall be brought into the group accounts at the figures at which they stand in the undertaking's accounts, subject to any adjustment authorised or required by this Schedule.

11(3)   The income and expenditure of the undertaking acquired shall be included in the group accounts for the entire financial year, including the period before the acquisition.

11(4)   The group accounts shall show corresponding amounts relating to the previous financial year as if the undertaking acquired had been included in the consolidation throughout that year.

11(5)   There shall be set off against the aggregate of—

   (a)   the appropriate amount in respect of qualifying shares issued by the parent company or its subsidiary undertakings in consideration for the acquisition of shares in the undertaking acquired, and

   (b)   the fair value of any other consideration for the acquisition of shares in the undertaking acquired, determined as at the date when those shares were acquired,

the nominal value of the issued share capital of the undertaking acquired held by the parent company and its subsidiary undertakings.

11(6)   The resulting amount shall be shown as an adjustment to the consolidated reserves.

11(7)   In sub-paragraph (5)(a) **"qualifying shares"** means—

   (a)   shares in relation to which section 131 (merger relief) applies, in respect of which the appropriate amount is the nominal value; or

(b) shares in relation to which section 132 (relief in respect of group reconstructions) applies, in respect of which the appropriate amount is the nominal value together with any minimum premium value within the meaning of that section.

12(1)   Where a group is acquired, paragraphs 9 to 11 apply with the following adaptations.

12(2)   References to shares of the undertaking acquired shall be construed as references to shares of the parent undertaking of the group.

12(3)   Other references to the undertaking acquired shall be construed as references to the group; and references to the assets and liabilities, income and expenditure and capital and reserves of the undertaking acquired shall be construed as references to the assets and liabilities, income and expenditure and capital and reserves of the group after making the set-offs and other adjustments required by this Schedule in the case of group accounts.

13(1)   The following information with respect to acquisitions taking place in the financial year shall be given in a note to the accounts.

13(2)   There shall be stated—

(a) the name of the undertaking acquired or, where a group was acquired, the name of the parent undertaking of that group, and

(b) whether the acquisition has been accounted for by the acquisition or the merger method of accounting;

and in relation to an acquisition which significantly affects the figures shown in the group accounts, the following further information shall be given.

13(3)   The composition and fair value of the consideration for the acquisition given by the parent company and its subsidiary undertakings shall be stated.

13(4)   The profit or loss of the undertaking or group acquired shall be stated—

(a) for the period from the beginning of the financial year of the undertaking or, as the case may be, of the parent undertaking of the group, up to the date of the acquisition, and

(b) for the previous financial year of that undertaking or parent undertaking;

and there shall also be stated the date on which the financial year referred to in paragraph (a) began.

13(5)   Where the acquisition method of accounting has been adopted, the book values immediately prior to the acquisition, and the fair values at the date of acquisition, of each class of assets and liabilities of the undertaking or group acquired shall be stated in tabular form, including a statement of the amount of any goodwill or negative consolidation difference arising on the acquisition, together with an explanation of any significant adjustments made.

13(6)   Where the merger method of accounting has been adopted, an explanation shall be given of any significant adjustments made in relation to the amounts of the assets and liabilities of the undertaking or group acquired, together with a statement of any resulting adjustment to the consolidated reserves (including the re-statement of opening consolidated reserves).

CA 1985, Sch. 4A, para. 12(1)

13(7)   In ascertaining for the purposes of sub-paragraph (4), (5) or (6) the profit or loss of a group, the book values and fair values of assets and liabilities of a group or the amount of the assets and liabilities of a group, the set-offs and other adjustments required by this Schedule in the case of group accounts shall be made.

14(1)   There shall also be stated in a note to the accounts the cumulative amount of goodwill resulting from acquisitions in that and earlier financial years which has been written off.

14(2)   That figure shall be shown net of any goodwill attributable to subsidiary undertakings or businesses disposed of prior to the balance sheet date.

15   Where during the financial year there has been a disposal of an undertaking or group which significantly affects the figures shown in the group accounts, there shall be stated in a note to the accounts—

  (a) the name of that undertaking or, as the case may be, of the parent undertaking of that group, and

  (b) the extent to which the profit or loss shown in the group accounts is attributable to profit or loss of that undertaking or group.

16   The information required by paragraph 13, 14 or 15 above need not be disclosed with respect to an undertaking which—

  (a) is established under the law of a country outside the United Kingdom, or

  (b) carries on business outside the United Kingdom,

if in the opinion of the directors of the parent company the disclosure would be seriously prejudicial to the business of that undertaking or to the business of the parent company or any of its subsidiary undertakings and the Secretary of State agrees that the information should not be disclosed.

MINORITY INTERESTS

17(1)   The formats set out in Schedule 4 have effect in relation to group accounts with the following additions.

17(2)   In the Balance Sheet Formats a further item headed "Minority interests" shall be added—

  (a) in Format 1, either after item J or at the end (after item K), and

  (b) in Format 2, under the general heading "LIABILITIES", between items A and B;

and under that item shall be shown the amount of capital and reserves attributable to shares in subsidiary undertakings included in the consolidation held by or on behalf of persons other than the parent company and its subsidiary undertakings.

17(3)   In the Profit and Loss Account Formats a further item headed "Minority interests" shall be added—

  (a) in Format 1, between items 14 and 15,

  (b) in Format 2, between items 16 and 17,

  (c) in Format 3, between items 7 and 8 in both sections A and B, and

  (d) in Format 4, between items 9 and 10 in both sections A and B;

and under that item shall be shown the amount of any profit or loss on ordinary activities attributable to shares in subsidiary undertakings included in the consolidation held by or on behalf of persons other than the parent company and its subsidiary undertakings.

17(4)   In the Profit and Loss Account Formats a further item headed "Minority interests" shall be added—

    (a) in Format 1, between items 18 and 19,

    (b) in Format 2, between items 20 and 21,

    (c) in Format 3, between items 9 and 10 in section A and between items 8 and 9 in section B, and

    (d) in Format 4, between items 11 and 12 in section A and between items 10 and 11 in section B;

and under that item shall be shown the amount of any profit or loss on extraordinary activities attributable to shares in subsidiary undertakings included in the consolidation held by or on behalf of persons other than the parent company and its subsidiary undertakings.

17(5)   For the purposes of paragraph 3(3) and (4) of Schedule 4 (power to adapt or combine items)—

    (a) the additional item required by sub-paragraph (2) above shall be treated as one to which a letter is assigned, and

    (b) the additional items required by sub-paragraphs (3) and (4) above shall be treated as ones to which an Arabic number is assigned.

INTERESTS IN SUBSIDIARY UNDERTAKINGS EXCLUDED FROM CONSOLIDATION

18   The interest of the group in subsidiary undertakings excluded from consolidation under section 229(4) (undertakings with activities different from those of undertakings included in the consolidation), and the amount of profit or loss attributable to such an interest, shall be shown in the consolidated balance sheet or, as the case may be, in the consolidated profit and loss account by the equity method of accounting (including dealing with any goodwill arising in accordance with paragraphs 17 to 19 and 21 of Schedule 4).

JOINT VENTURES

19(1)   Where an undertaking included in the consolidation manages another undertaking jointly with one or more undertakings not included in the consolidation, that other undertaking ("the joint venture") may, if it is not—

    (a) a body corporate, or

    (b) a subsidiary undertaking of the parent company,

be dealt with in the group accounts by the method of proportional consolidation.

19(2)   The provisions of this Part relating to the preparation of consolidated accounts apply, with any necessary modifications, to proportional consolidation under this paragraph.

ASSOCIATED UNDERTAKINGS

20(1) An **"associated undertaking"** means an undertaking in which an undertaking included in the consolidation has a participating interest and over whose operating and financial policy it exercises a significant influence, and which is not—

(a) a subsidiary undertaking of the parent company, or

(b) a joint venture dealt with in accordance with paragraph 19.

20(2) Where an undertaking holds 20 per cent or more of the voting rights in another undertaking, it shall be presumed to exercise such an influence over it unless the contrary is shown.

20(3) The voting rights in an undertaking means the rights conferred on shareholders in respect of their shares or, in the case of an undertaking not having a share capital, on members, to vote at general meetings of the undertaking on all, or substantially all, matters.

20(4) The provisions of paragraphs 5 to 11 of Schedule 10A (rights to be taken into account and attribution of rights) apply in determining for the purposes of this paragraph whether an undertaking holds 20 per cent or more of the voting rights in another undertaking.

21(1) The formats set out in Schedule 4 have effect in relation to group accounts with the following modifications.

21(2) In the Balance Sheet Formats the items headed "Participating interests", that is—

(a) in Format 1, item B.III.3, and

(b) In Format 2, item B.III.3 under the heading "ASSETS",

shall be replaced by two items, "Interests in associated undertakings" and "Other participating interests".

21(3) In the Profit and Loss Account Formats, the items headed "Income from participating interests", that is—

(a) in Format 1, item 8,

(b) in Format 2, item 10,

(c) in Format 3, item B.4, and

(d) in Format 4, item B.6,

shall be replaced by two items, "Income from interests in associated undertakings" and "Income from other participating interests".

22(1) The interest of an undertaking in an associated undertaking, and the amount of profit or loss attributable to such an interest, shall be shown by the equity method of accounting (including dealing with any goodwill arising in accordance with paragraphs 17 to 19 and 21 of Schedule 4).

22(2) Where the associated undertaking is itself a parent undertaking, the net assets and profits or losses to be taken into account are those of the parent and its subsidiary undertakings (after making any consolidation adjustments).

22(3) The equity method of accounting need not be applied if the amounts in question are not material for the purpose of giving a true and fair view.

History
Sch. 4A inserted by CA 1989, s. 1, 5(2) and Sch. 2 as from 1 April 1990 subject to transitional and saving provisions (see S.I. 1990 No. 355 (C. 13), art. 3, Sch. 1 and also art. 6–9).

Schedule 5 — Disclosure of Information: Related Undertakings

[Companies Act 1985, sec. 231;
Companies Act 1989, sec. 1, 6(2), Sch. 3]

Part I — Companies not Required to Prepare Group Accounts

SUBSIDIARY UNDERTAKINGS

1(1) The following information shall be given where at the end of the financial year the company has subsidiary undertakings.

1(2) The name of each subsidiary undertaking shall be stated.

1(3) There shall be stated with respect to each subsidiary undertaking—

(a) if it is incorporated outside Great Britain, the country in which it is incorporated;

(b) if it is incorporated in Great Britain, whether it is registered in England and Wales or in Scotland;

(c) if it is unincorporated, the address of its principal place of business.

1(4) The reason why the company is not required to prepare group accounts shall be stated.

1(5) If the reason is that all the subsidiary undertakings of the company fall within the exclusions provided for in section 229, it shall be stated with respect to each subsidiary undertaking which of those exclusions applies.

HOLDINGS IN SUBSIDIARY UNDERTAKINGS

2(1) There shall be stated in relation to shares of each class held by the company in a subsidiary undertaking—

(a) the identity of the class, and

(b) the proportion of the nominal value of the shares of that class represented by those shares.

2(2) The shares held by or on behalf of the company itself shall be distinguished from those attributed to the company which are held by or on behalf of a subsidiary undertaking.

FINANCIAL INFORMATION ABOUT SUBSIDIARY UNDERTAKINGS

3(1) There shall be disclosed with respect to each subsidiary undertaking—

(a) the aggregate amount of its capital and reserves as at the end of its relevant financial year, and

(b) its profit or loss for that year.

3(2) That information need not be given if the company is exempt by virtue of section 228 from the requirement to prepare group accounts (parent company included in accounts of larger group).

3(3) That information need not be given if—

(a) the subsidiary undertaking is not required by any provision of this Act to deliver a copy of its balance sheet for its relevant financial year and does not otherwise publish that balance sheet in Great Britain or elsewhere, and

(b) the company's holding is less than 50 per cent of the nominal value of the shares in the undertaking.

3(4) Information otherwise required by this paragraph need not be given if it is not material.

3(5) For the purposes of this paragraph the "relevant financial year" of a subsidiary undertaking is—

(a) if its financial year ends with that of the company, that year, and

(b) if not, its financial year ending last before the end of the company's financial year.

FINANCIAL YEARS OF SUBSIDIARY UNDERTAKINGS

4 Where the financial year of one or more subsidiary undertakings did not end with that of the company, there shall be stated in relation to each such undertaking—

(a) the reasons why the company's directors consider that its financial year should not end with that of the company, and

(b) the date on which its last financial year ended (last before the end of the company's financial year).

Instead of the dates required by paragraph (b) being given for each subsidiary undertaking the earliest and latest of those dates may be given.

FURTHER INFORMATION ABOUT SUBSIDIARY UNDERTAKINGS

5(1) There shall be disclosed—

(a) any qualifications contained in the auditors' reports on the accounts of subsidiary undertakings for financial years ending with or during the financial year of the company, and

(b) any note or saving contained in such accounts to call attention to a matter which, apart from the note or saving, would properly have been referred to in such a qualification,

in so far as the matter which is the subject of the qualification or note is not covered by the company's own accounts and is material from the point of view of its members.

5(2) The aggregate amount of the total investment of the company in the shares of subsidiary undertakings shall be stated by way of the equity method of valuation, unless—

(a) the company is exempt from the requirement to prepare group accounts by virtue of section 228 (parent company included in accounts of larger group), and

(b) the directors state their opinion that the aggregate value of the assets of the company consisting of shares in, or amounts owing (whether on account of a loan or otherwise) from, the company's subsidiary undertakings is not less than the aggregate of the amounts at which those assets are stated or included in the company's balance sheet.

5(3) In so far as information required by this paragraph is not obtainable, a statement to that effect shall be given instead.

SHARES AND DEBENTURES OF COMPANY HELD BY SUBSIDIARY UNDERTAKINGS

6(1) The number, description and amount of the shares in and debentures of the company held by or on behalf of its subsidiary undertakings shall be disclosed.

6(2) Sub-paragraph (1) does not apply in relation to shares or debentures in the case of which the subsidiary undertaking is concerned as personal representative or, subject as follows, as trustee.

6(3) The exception for shares or debentures in relation to which the subsidiary undertaking is concerned as trustee does not apply if the company, or any subsidiary undertaking of the company, is beneficially interested under the trust, otherwise than by way of security only for the purposes of a transaction entered into by it in the ordinary course of a business which includes the lending of money.

6(4) Schedule 2 to this Act has effect for the interpretation of the reference in sub-paragraph (3) to a beneficial interest under a trust.

SIGNIFICANT HOLDINGS IN UNDERTAKINGS OTHER THAN SUBSIDIARY UNDERTAKINGS

7(1) The information required by paragraphs 8 and 9 shall be given where at the end of the financial year the company has a significant holding in an undertaking which is not a subsidiary undertaking of the company.

7(2) A holding is significant for this purpose if—

(a) it amounts to 10 per cent or more of the nominal value of any class of shares in the undertaking, or

(b) the amount of the holding (as stated or included in the company's accounts) exceeds one-tenth of the amount (as so stated) of the company's assets.

8(1) The name of the undertaking shall be stated.

8(2) There shall be stated—

(a) if the undertaking is incorporated outside Great Britain, the country in which it is incorporated;

(b) if it is incorporated in Great Britain, whether it is registered in England and Wales or in Scotland;

(c) if it is unincorporated, the address of its principal place of business.

8(3) There shall also be stated—

(a) the identity of each class of shares in the undertaking held by the company, and

(b) the proportion of the nominal value of the shares of that class represented by those shares.

9(1)   Where the company has a significant holding in an undertaking amounting to 20 per cent or more of the nominal value of the shares in the undertaking, there shall also be stated—

  (a) the aggregate amount of the capital and reserves of the undertaking as at the end of its relevant financial year, and

  (b) its profit or loss for that year.

9(2)   That information need not be given if—

  (a) the company is exempt by virtue of section 228 from the requirement to prepare group accounts (parent company included in accounts of larger group), and

  (b) the investment of the company in all undertakings in which it has such a holding as is mentioned in sub-paragraph (1) is shown, in aggregate, in the notes to the accounts by way of the equity method of valuation.

9(3)   That information need not be given in respect of an undertaking if—

  (a) the undertaking is not required by any provision of this Act to deliver a copy of its balance sheet for its relevant financial year and does not otherwise publish that balance sheet in Great Britain or elsewhere, and

  (b) the company's holding is less than 50 per cent of the nominal value of the shares in the undertaking.

9(4)   Information otherwise required by this paragraph need not be given if it is not material.

9(5)   For the purposes of this paragraph the "relevant financial year" of an undertaking is—

  (a) if its financial year ends with that of the company, that year, and

  (b) if not, its financial year ending last before the end of the company's financial year.

ARRANGEMENTS ATTRACTING MERGER RELIEF

10(1)   This paragraph applies to arrangements attracting merger relief, that is, where a company allots shares in consideration for the issue, transfer or cancellation of shares in another body corporate ("the other company") in circumstances such that section 130 of this Act (share premium account) does not, by virtue of section 131(2) (merger relief), apply to the premiums on the shares.

10(2)   If the company makes such an arrangement during the financial year, the following information shall be given—

  (a) the name of the other company,

  (b) the number, nominal value and class of shares allotted,

  (c) the number, nominal value and class of shares in the other company issued, transferred or cancelled, and

  (d) particulars of the accounting treatment adopted in the company's accounts in respect of the issue, transfer or cancellation.

10(3)   Where the company made such an arrangement during the financial year, or during either of the two preceding financial years, and there is included in the company's profit and loss account—

(a) any profit or loss realised during the financial year by the company on the disposal of—

  (i) any shares in the other company, or

  (ii) any assets which were fixed assets of the other company or any of its subsidiary undertakings at the time of the arrangement, or

(b) any part of any profit or loss realised during the financial year by the company on the disposal of any shares (other than shares in the other company) which was attributable to the fact that there were at the time of the disposal amongst the assets of the company which issued the shares, or any of its subsidiary undertakings, such shares or assets as are described in paragraph (a) above,

then, the net amount of that profit or loss or, as the case may be, the part so attributable shall be shown, together with an explanation of the transactions to which the information relates.

10(4)   For the purposes of this paragraph the time of the arrangement shall be taken to be—

(a) where as a result of the arrangement the other company becomes a subsidiary undertaking of the company, the date on which it does so or, if the arrangement in question becomes binding only on the fulfilment of a condition, the date on which that condition is fulfilled;

(b) if the other company is already a subsidiary undertaking of the company, the date on which the shares are allotted or, if they are allotted on different days, the first day.

PARENT UNDERTAKING DRAWING UP ACCOUNTS FOR LARGER GROUP

11(1)   Where the company is a subsidiary undertaking, the following information shall be given with respect to the parent undertaking of—

(a) the largest group of undertakings for which group accounts are drawn up and of which the company is a member, and

(b) the smallest such group of undertakings.

11(2)   The name of the parent undertaking shall be stated.

11(3)   There shall be stated—

(a) if the undertaking is incorporated outside Great Britain, the country in which it is incorporated;

(b) if it is incorporated in Great Britain, whether it is registered in England and Wales or in Scotland;

(c) if it is unincorporated, the address of its principal place of business.

11(4)   If copies of the group accounts referred to in sub-paragraph (1) are available to the public, there shall also be stated the addresses from which copies of the accounts can be obtained.

CA 1985, Sch. 5, para. 10(4)

IDENTIFICATION OF ULTIMATE PARENT COMPANY

12(1) Where the company is a subsidiary undertaking, the following information shall be given with respect to the company (if any) regarded by the directors as being the company's ultimate parent company.

12(2) The name of that company shall be stated.

12(3) If known to the directors, there shall be stated—

> (a) if that company is incorporated outside Great Britain, the country in which it is incorporated;

> (b) if it is incorporated in Great Britain, whether it is registered in England and Wales or in Scotland.

12(4) In this paragraph "company" includes any body corporate.

CONSTRUCTIONS OF REFERENCES TO SHARES HELD BY COMPANY

13(1) References in this Part of this Schedule to shares held by a company shall be construed as follows.

13(2) For the purposes of paragraphs 2 to 5 (information about subsidiary undertakings)—

> (a) there shall be attributed to the company any shares held by a subsidiary undertaking, or by a person acting on behalf of the company or a subsidiary undertaking; but

> (b) there shall be treated as not held by the company any shares held on behalf of a person other than the company or a subsidiary undertaking.

13(3) For the purposes of paragraphs 7 to 9 (information about undertakings other than subsidiary undertakings)—

> (a) there shall be attributed to the company shares held on its behalf by any person; but

> (b) there shall be treated as not held by a company shares held on behalf of a person other than the company.

13(4) For the purposes of any of those provisions, shares held by way of security shall be treated as held by the person providing the security—

> (a) where apart from the right to exercise them for the purpose of preserving the value of the security, or of realising it, the rights attached to the shares are exercisable only in accordance with his instructions, and

> (b) where the shares are held in connection with the granting of loans as part of normal business activities and apart from the right to exercise them for the purpose of preserving the value of the security, or of realising it, the rights attached to the shares are exercisable only in his interests.

Part II — Companies Required to Prepare Group Accounts

INTRODUCTORY

14 In this Part of this Schedule **"the group"** means the group consisting of the parent company and its subsidiary undertakings.

SUBSIDIARY UNDERTAKINGS

15(1) The following information shall be given with respect to the undertakings which are subsidiary undertakings of the parent company at the end of the financial year.

15(2) The name of each undertaking shall be stated.

15(3) There shall be stated—

(a) if the undertaking is incorporated outside Great Britain, the country in which it is incorporated;

(b) if it is incorporated in Great Britain, whether it is registered in England and Wales or in Scotland;

(c) if it is unincorporated, the address of its principal place of business.

15(4) It shall also be stated whether the subsidiary undertaking is included in the consolidation and, if it is not, the reasons for excluding it from consolidation shall be given.

15(5) It shall be stated with respect to each subsidiary undertaking by virtue of which of the conditions specified in section 258(2) or (4) it is a subsidiary undertaking of its immediate parent undertaking.

That information need not be given if the relevant condition is that specified in subsection (2)(a) of that section (holding of a majority of the voting rights) and the immediate parent undertaking holds the same proportion of the shares in the undertaking as it holds voting rights.

HOLDINGS IN SUBSIDIARY UNDERTAKINGS

16(1) The following information shall be given with respect to the shares of a subsidiary undertaking held—

(a) by the parent company, and

(b) by the group;

and the information under paragraphs (a) and (b) shall (if different) be shown separately.

16(2) There shall be stated—

(a) the identity of each class of shares held, and

(b) the proportion of the nominal value of the shares of that class represented by those shares.

FINANCIAL INFORMATION ABOUT SUBSIDIARY UNDERTAKINGS NOT INCLUDED IN THE CONSOLIDATION

17(1) There shall be shown with respect to each subsidiary undertaking not included in the consolidation—

(a) the aggregate amount of its capital and reserves as at the end of its relevant financial year, and

(b) its profit or loss for that year.

17(2) That information need not be given if the group's investment in the undertaking is included in the accounts by way of the equity method of valuation or if—

CA 1985, Sch. 5, para. 15(1) [The next page is 29,251] **CCH Editions Limited**

(a) the undertaking is not required by any provision of this Act to deliver a copy of its balance sheet for its relevant financial year and does not otherwise publish that balance sheet in Great Britain or elsewhere, and

(b) the holding of the group is less than 50 per cent of the nominal value of the shares in the undertaking.

17(3) Information otherwise required by this paragraph need not be given if it is not material.

17(4) For the purposes of this paragraph the "relevant financial year" of a subsidiary undertaking is—

(a) if its financial year ends with that of the company, that year, and

(b) if not, its financial year ending last before the end of the company's financial year.

FURTHER INFORMATION ABOUT SUBSIDIARY UNDERTAKINGS EXCLUDED FROM CONSOLIDATION

18(1) The following information shall be given with respect to subsidiary undertakings excluded from consolidation.

18(2) There shall be disclosed—

(a) any qualifications contained in the auditors' reports on the accounts of the undertaking for financial years ending with or during the financial year of the company, and

(b) any note or saving contained in such accounts to call attention to a matter which, apart from the note or saving, would properly have been referred to in such a qualification,

in so far as the matter which is the subject of the qualification or note is not covered by the consolidated accounts and is material from the point of view of the members of the parent company.

18(3) In so far as information required by this paragraph is not obtainable, a statement to that effect shall be given instead.

FINANCIAL YEARS OF SUBSIDIARY UNDERTAKINGS

19 Where the financial year of one or more subsidiary undertakings did not end with that of the company, there shall be stated in relation to each such undertaking—

(a) the reasons why the company's directors consider that its financial year should not end with that of the company, and

(b) the date on which its last financial year ended (last before the end of the company's financial year).

Instead of the dates required by paragraph (b) being given for each subsidiary undertaking the earliest and latest of those dates may be given.

SHARES AND DEBENTURES OF COMPANY HELD BY SUBSIDIARY UNDERTAKINGS

20(1) The number, description and amount of the shares in and debentures of the company held by or on behalf of its subsidiary undertakings shall be disclosed.

20(2)   Sub-paragraph (1) does not apply in relation to shares or debentures in the case of which the subsidiary undertaking is concerned as personal representative or, subject as follows, as trustee.

20(3)   The exception for shares or debentures in relation to which the subsidiary undertaking is concerned as trustee does not apply if the company or any of its subsidiary undertakings is beneficially interested under the trust, otherwise than by way of security only for the purposes of a transaction entered into by it in the ordinary course of a business which includes the lending of money.

20(4)   Schedule 2 to this Act has effect for the interpretation of the reference in sub-paragraph (3) to a beneficial interest under a trust.

JOINT VENTURES

21(1)   The following information shall be given where an undertaking is dealt with in the consolidated accounts by the method of proportional consolidation in accordance with paragraph 19 of Schedule 4A (joint ventures)—

   (a) the name of the undertaking;

   (b) the address of the principal place of business of the undertaking;

   (c) the factors on which joint management of the undertaking is based; and

   (d) the proportion of the capital of the undertaking held by undertakings included in the consolidation.

21(2)   Where the financial year of the undertaking did not end with that of the company, there shall be stated the date on which a financial year of the undertaking last ended before that date.

ASSOCIATED UNDERTAKINGS

22(1)   The following information shall be given where an undertaking included in the consolidation has an interest in an associated undertaking.

22(2)   The name of the associated undertaking shall be stated.

22(3)   There shall be stated—

   (a) if the undertaking is incorporated outside Great Britain, the country in which it is incorporated;

   (b) if it is incorporated in Great Britain, whether it is registered in England and Wales or in Scotland;

   (c) if it is unincorporated, the address of its principal place of business.

22(4)   The following information shall be given with respect to the shares of the undertaking held—

   (a) by the parent company, and

   (b) by the group;

and the information under paragraphs (a) and (b) shall be shown separately.

22(5)   There shall be stated—

   (a) the identity of each class of shares held, and

   (b) the proportion of the nominal value of the shares of that class represented by those shares.

CCH Editions Limited
BCL BCL6$$$74A

22(6) In this paragraph **"associated undertaking"** has the meaning given by paragraph 20 of Schedule 4A; and the information required by this paragraph shall be given notwithstanding that paragraph 22(3) of that Schedule (materiality) applies in relation to the accounts themselves.

OTHER SIGNIFICANT HOLDINGS OF PARENT COMPANY OR GROUP

23(1) The information required by paragraphs 24 and 25 shall be given where at the end of the financial year the parent company has a significant holding in an undertaking which is not one of its subsidiary undertakings and does not fall within paragraph 21 (joint ventures) or paragraph 22 (associated undertakings).

23(2) A holding is significant for this purpose if—

(a) it amounts to 10 per cent or more of the nominal value of any class of shares in the undertaking, or

(b) the amount of the holding (as stated or included in the company's individual accounts) exceeds one-tenth of the amount of its assets (as so stated).

24(1) The name of the undertaking shall be stated.

24(2) There shall be stated—

(a) if the undertaking is incorporated outside Great Britain, the country in which it is incorporated;

(b) if it is incorporated in Great Britain, whether it is registered in England and Wales or in Scotland;

(c) if it is unincorporated, the address of its principal place of business.

24(3) The following information shall be given with respect to the shares of the undertaking held by the parent company.

24(4) There shall be stated—

(a) the identity of each class of shares held, and

(b) the proportion of the nominal value of the shares of that class represented by those shares.

25(1) Where the company has a significant holding in an undertaking amounting to 20 per cent or more of the nominal value of the shares in the undertaking, there shall also be stated—

(a) the aggregate amount of the capital and reserves of the undertaking as at the end of its relevant financial year, and

(b) its profit or loss for that year.

25(2) That information need not be given in respect of an undertaking if—

(a) the undertaking is not required by any provision of this Act to deliver a copy of its balance sheet for its relevant financial year and does not otherwise publish that balance sheet in Great Britain or elsewhere, and

(b) the company's holding is less than 50 per cent of the nominal value of the shares in the undertaking.

25(3) Information otherwise required by this paragraph need not be given if it is not material.

25(4)   For the purposes of this paragraph the "relevant financial year" of an undertaking is—

(a) if its financial year ends with that of the company, that year, and

(b) if not, its financial year ending last before the end of the company's financial year.

26(1)   The information required by paragraphs 27 and 28 shall be given where at the end of the financial year the group has a significant holding in an undertaking which is not a subsidiary undertaking of the parent company and does not fall within paragraph 21 (joint ventures) or paragraph 22 (associated undertakings).

26(2)   A holding is significant for this purpose if—

(a) it amounts to 10 per cent or more of the nominal value of any class of shares in the undertaking, or

(b) the amount of the holding (as stated or included in the group accounts) exceeds one-tenth of the amount of the group's assets (as so stated).

27(1)   The name of the undertaking shall be stated.

27(2)   There shall be stated—

(a) if the undertaking is incorporated outside Great Britain, the country in which it is incorporated;

(b) if it is incorporated in Great Britain, whether it is registered in England and Wales or in Scotland;

(c) if it is unincorporated, the address of its principal place of business.

27(3)   The following information shall be given with respect to the shares of the undertaking held by the group.

27(4)   There shall be stated—

(a) the identity of each class of shares held, and

(b) the proportion of the nominal value of the shares of that class represented by those shares.

28(1)   Where the holding of the group amounts to 20 per cent or more of the nominal value of the shares in the undertaking, there shall also be stated—

(a) the aggregate amount of the capital and reserves of the undertaking as at the end of its relevant financial year, and

(b) its profit or loss for that year.

28(2)   That information need not be given if—

(a) the undertaking is not required by any provision of this Act to deliver a copy of its balance sheet for its relevant financial year and does not otherwise publish that balance sheet in Great Britain or elsewhere, and

(b) the holding of the group is less than 50 per cent of the nominal value of the shares in the undertaking.

28(3)   Information otherwise required by this paragraph need not be given if it is not material.

28(4)   For the purposes of this paragraph the "relevant financial year" of an outside undertaking is—

(a) if its financial year ends with that of the parent company, that year, and

(b) if not, its financial year ending last before the end of the parent company's financial year.

ARRANGEMENTS ATTRACTING MERGER RELIEF

29(1) This paragraph applies to arrangements attracting merger relief, that is, where a company allots shares in consideration for the issue, transfer or cancellation of shares in another body corporate ("the other company") in circumstances such that section 130 of this Act (share premium account) does not, by virtue of section 131(2) (merger relief), apply to the premiums on the shares.

29(2) If the parent company made such an arrangement during the financial year, the following information shall be given—

(a) the name of the other company,

(b) the number, nominal value and class of shares allotted,

(c) the number, nominal value and class of shares in the other company issued, transferred or cancelled, and

(d) particulars of the accounting treatment adopted in the parent company's individual and group accounts in respect of the issue, transfer or cancellation, and

(e) particulars of the extent to which and manner in which the profit or loss for the financial year shown in the group accounts is affected by any profit or loss of the other company, or any of its subsidiary undertakings, which arose before the time of the arrangement.

29(3) Where the parent company made such an arrangement during the financial year, or during either of the two preceding financial years, and there is included in the consolidated profit and loss account—

(a) any profit or loss realised during the financial year on the disposal of—

(i) any shares in the other company, or

(ii) any assets which were fixed assets of the other company or any of its subsidiary undertakings at the time of the arrangement, or

(b) any part of any profit or loss realised during the financial year on the disposal of any shares (other than shares in the other company) which was attributable to the fact that there were at the time of the disposal amongst the assets of the company which issued the shares, or any of its subsidiary undertakings, such shares or assets as are described in paragraph (a) above,

then, the net amount of that profit or loss or, as the case may be, the part so attributable shall be shown, together with an explanation of the transactions to which the information relates.

29(4) For the purposes of this paragraph the time of the arrangement shall be taken to be—

(a) where as a result of the arrangement the other company becomes a subsidiary undertaking of the company in question, the date on which it does so or, if the arrangement in question becomes binding only on the fulfilment of a condition, the date on which that condition is fulfilled;

(b) if the other company is already a subsidiary undertaking of that company, the date on which the shares are allotted or, if they are allotted on different days, the first day.

PARENT UNDERTAKING DRAWING UP ACCOUNTS FOR LARGER GROUP

30(1)   Where the parent company is itself a subsidiary undertaking, the following information shall be given with respect to that parent undertaking of the company which heads—

(a) the largest group of undertakings for which group accounts are drawn up and of which that company is a member, and

(b) the smallest such group of undertakings.

30(2)   The name of the parent undertaking shall be stated.

30(3)   There shall be stated—

(a) if the undertaking is incorporated outside Great Britain, the country in which it is incorporated;

(b) if it is incorporated in Great Britain, whether it is registered in England and Wales or in Scotland;

(c) if it is unincorporated, the address of its principal place of business.

30(4)   If copies of the group accounts referred to in sub-paragraph (1) are available to the public, there shall also be stated the addresses from which copies of the accounts can be obtained.

IDENTIFICATION OF ULTIMATE PARENT COMPANY

31(1)   Where the parent company is itself a subsidiary undertaking, the following information shall be given with respect to the company (if any) regarded by the directors as being that company's ultimate parent company.

31(2)   The name of that company shall be stated.

31(3)   If known to the directors, there shall be stated—

(a) if that company is incorporated outside Great Britain, the country in which it is incorporated;

(b) if it is incorporated in Great Britain, whether it is registered in England and Wales or in Scotland.

31(4)   In this paragraph "company" includes any body corporate.

CONSTRUCTION OF REFERENCES TO SHARES HELD BY PARENT COMPANY OR GROUP

32(1)   References in this Part of this Schedule to shares held by the parent company or the group shall be construed as follows.

32(2)   For the purposes of paragraphs 16, 22(4) and (5) and 23 to 25 (information about holdings in subsidiary and other undertakings)—

(a) there shall be attributed to the parent company shares held on its behalf by any person; but

(b) there shall be treated as not held by the parent company shares held on behalf of a person other than the company.

32(3) References to shares held by the group are to any shares held by or on behalf of the parent company or any of its subsidiary undertakings; but there shall be treated as not held by the group any shares held on behalf of a person other than the parent company or any of its subsidiary undertakings.

32(4) Shares held by way of security shall be treated as held by the person providing the security—

(a) where apart from the right to exercise them for the purpose of preserving the value of the security, or of realising it, the rights attached to the shares are exercisable only in accordance with his instructions, and

(b) where the shares are held in connection with the granting of loans as part of normal business activities and apart from the right to exercise them for the purpose of preserving the value of the security, or of realising it, the rights attached to the shares are exercisable only in his interests.

History
Sch. 5 substituted by CA 1989, s. 6(2) and Sch. 3 as from 1 April 1990 subject to transitional and saving provisions (see S.I. 1990 No. 355 (C. 13), art. 3, Sch. 1 and also art. 6–9); Sch. 5 formerly read as follows:

"**Schedule 5 — Miscellaneous Matters to be Disclosed in Notes to Company Accounts**

Section 231

Part I — Particulars of Subsidiaries

1 If at the end of the financial year the company has subsidiaries, there shall in the case of each subsidiary be stated—

(a) the name of the subsidiary and—

   (i) if it is incorporated in Great Britain and if it is registered in England and Wales and the company is registered in Scotland (or vice versa), the part of Great Britain in which it is registered, and

   (ii) if it is incorporated outside Great Britain, the country in which it is incorporated; and

(b) in relation to shares of each class of the subsidiary held by the company, the identity of the class and the proportion of the nominal value of the allotted shares of that class represented by the shares held.

2 The particulars required by paragraph 1 include, with reference to the proportion of the nominal value of the allotted shares of a class represented by shares held by the company, a statement of the extent (if any) to which it consists in shares held by, or by a nominee for, a subsidiary of the company and the extent (if any) to which it consists in shares held by, or by a nominee for, the company itself.

3 Paragraph 1 does not require the disclosure of information with respect to a body corporate which is the subsidiary of another and is incorporated outside the United Kingdom or, being incorporated in the United Kingdom, carries on business outside it if the disclosure would, in the opinion of the directors of that other, be harmful to the business of that other or of any of its subsidiaries and the Secretary of State agrees that the information need not be disclosed.

4 If at the end of its financial year the company has subsidiaries and the directors are of the opinion that the number of them is such that compliance with paragraph 1 would result in particulars of excessive length being given, compliance with that paragraph is required only in the case of the subsidiaries carrying on the businesses the results of the carrying on of which (in the opinion of the directors) principally affected the amount of the profit or loss of the company and its subsidiaries or the amount of the assets of the company and its subsidiaries.

5 If advantage is taken of paragraph 4, there must be included in the statement required by this Part the information that it deals only with the subsidiaries carrying on such businesses as are referred to in that paragraph; and in that case section 231(3) (subsequent disclosure with annual return) applies to the particulars given in compliance with paragraph 1, together with those which (but for the fact that advantage is so taken) would have to be so given.

6 For purposes of this Part, shares of a body corporate are treated as held, or not held, by another such body if they would, by virtue of section 736(4) of this Act, be treated as being held or (as the case may be) not held by that other body for the purpose of determining whether the first-mentioned body is its subsidiary.

Part II — Shareholdings in Companies etc. Other than Subsidiaries

7 If at the end of its financial year the company holds shares of any class comprised in the equity share capital of another body corporate (not being its subsidiary) exceeding in nominal value one-tenth of the nominal value of the allotted shares of that class, there shall be stated—

(a) the name of that other body corporate and—

   (i) if it is incorporated in Great Britain and if it is registered in England and Wales and the company is registered in Scotland (or vice versa), the part of Great Britain in which it is registered, and

   (ii) if it is incorporated outside Great Britain, the country in which it is incorporated;

(b) the identity of the class and the proportion of the nominal value of the allotted shares of that class represented by the shares held; and

(c) if the company also holds shares in that other body corporate of another class (whether or not comprised in its equity share capital), or of other classes (whether or not so comprised), the like particulars as respects that other class or (as the case may be) those other classes.

8 If at the end of its financial year the company holds shares comprised in the share capital of another body corporate (not being its subsidiary) exceeding in nominal value one-tenth of the allotted share capital of that other body, there shall be stated—

  (a) with respect to that other body corporate, the same information as is required by paragraph 7(a), and

  (b) the identity of each class of such shares held and the proportion of the nominal value of the allotted shares of that class represented by the shares of that class held by the company.

9 If at the end of its financial year the company holds shares in another body corporate (not being its subsidiary) and the amount of all the shares in it which the company holds (as stated or included in the company's accounts) exceeds one-tenth of the amount of the company's assets (as so stated), there shall be stated—

  (a) with respect to the other body corporate, the same information as is required by paragraph 7(a), and

  (b) in relation to shares in that other body corporate of each class held, the identity of the class and the proportion of the nominal value of the allotted shares of that class represented by the shares held.

10 None of the foregoing provisions of this Part requires the disclosure by a company of information with respect to another body corporate if that other is incorporated outside the United Kingdom or, being incorporated in the United Kingdom, carries on business outside it if the disclosure would, in the opinion of the company's directors, be harmful to the business of the company or of that other body and the Secretary of State agrees that the information need not be disclosed.

11 If at the end of its financial year the company falls within paragraph 7 or 8 in relation to more bodies corporate than one, and the number of them is such that, in the directors' opinion, compliance with either or both of those paragraphs would result in particulars of excessive length being given, compliance with paragraph 7 or (as the case may be) paragraph 8 is not required except in the case of the bodies carrying on the businesses the results of the carrying on of which (in the directors' opinion) principally affected the amount of the profit or loss of the company or the amount of its assets.

12 If advantage is taken of paragraph 11, there must be included in the statement dealing with the bodies last mentioned in that paragraph the information that it deals only with them; and section 231(3) of this Act (subsequent disclosure in annual return) applies to the particulars given in compliance with paragraph 7 or 8 (as the case may be), together with those which, but for the fact that advantage is so taken, would have to be so given.

13 For purposes of this Part, shares of a body corporate are treated as held, or not held, by another such body if they would, by virtue of section 736(4) of this Act (but on the assumption that paragraph (b)(ii) were omitted from that subsection) be treated as being held or (as the case may be), not held by that other body for the purpose of determining whether the first-mentioned body is its subsidiary.

Part III — Financial Information About Subsidiaries

14 If—

  (a) at the end of its financial year the company has subsidiaries, and

  (b) it is required by paragraph 1 in Part I above to disclose particulars with respect to any of those subsidiaries,

the additional information specified below shall be given with respect to each subsidiary to which the requirement under paragraph 1 applies.

15 If—

  (a) at the end of the financial year the company holds shares in another body corporate, and

  (b) it is required by paragraph 8 in Part II above to disclose particulars with respect to that body corporate, and

  (c) the shares held by the company in that body corporate exceed in nominal value one-fifth of the allotted share capital of that body,

the additional information specified below shall be given with respect to that body corporate.

16 The information required by paragraphs 14 and 15 is, in relation to any body corporate (whether a subsidiary of the company or not) the aggregate amount of the capital and reserves of that body corporate as at the end of its relevant financial year, and its profit or loss for that year; and for this purpose the relevant financial year is—

  (a) if the financial year of the body corporate ends with that of the company giving the information in a note to its accounts, that financial year, and

  (b) if not, the body corporate's financial year ending last before the end of the financial year of the company giving that information.

  This is subject to the exceptions and other provisions in the next paragraph.

17(1) The information otherwise required by paragraph 16 need not be given in respect of a subsidiary of a company if either—

  (a) the company is exempt under this Act from the requirement to prepare group accounts, as being at the end of its financial year the wholly-owned subsidiary of another body corporate incorporated in Great Britain, or

  (b) the company prepares group accounts and—

    (i) the accounts of the subsidiary are included in the group accounts, or

    (ii) the investment of the company in the shares of the subsidiary is included in, or in a note to, the company's accounts by way of the equity method of valuation.

(2) That information need not be given in respect of another body corporate in which the company holds shares if the company's investment in those shares is included in or in a note to the accounts by way of the equity method of valuation.

(3) That information need not be given in respect of any body corporate if—

  (a) that body is not required by any provision of this Act to deliver a copy of its balance sheet for its relevant financial year mentioned in paragraph 16, and does not otherwise publish that balance sheet in Great Britain or elsewhere, and

  (b) the shares held by the company in that body do not amount to at least one half in nominal value of the body's allotted share capital.

(4) Information otherwise required by paragraph 16 need not be given if it is not material.

18 Where with respect to any subsidiary of the company or any other body corporate particulars which would otherwise be required by paragraph 1 in Part I or paragraph 8 in Part II of this Schedule to be stated in a note to the company's accounts are omitted by virtue of paragraph 4 or (as the case may be) paragraph 11, section 231(3) of this Act (subsequent disclosure in next annual return) applies—

  (a) to any information with respect to any other subsidiary or body corporate which is given in or in a note to the company's accounts in accordance with this Part, and

(b) to any information which would have been required by this Part to be given in relation to a subsidiary or other body corporate but for the exemption under paragraph 4 or 11.

19 For purposes of this Part, shares of a body corporate are treated as held, or not held, by the company if they would, by virtue of section 736(4) of this Act (but on the assumption that paragraph (b)(ii) were omitted from that subsection), be treated as being held or (as the case may be) not held by the company for the purpose of determining whether that body corporate is the company's subsidiary.

Part IV — Identification of Ultimate Holding Company

20 If at the end of its financial year the company is the subsidiary of another body corporate, there shall be stated the name of the body corporate regarded by the directors as being the company's ultimate holding company and, if known to them, the country in which it is incorporated.

21 Paragraph 20 does not require the disclosure by a company which carries on business outside the United Kingdom of information with respect to the body corporate regarded by the directors as being its ultimate holding company if the disclosure would, in their opinion, be harmful to the business of that holding company or of the first-mentioned company, or any other of that holding company's subsidiaries, and the Secretary of State agrees that the information need not be disclosed.

Part V — Chairman's and Directors' Emoluments, Pensions and Compensation for Loss of Office

EMOLUMENTS

22(1) There shall be shown the aggregate amount of the directors' emoluments.

(2) This amount—

(a) includes any emoluments paid to or receivable by a person in respect of his services as director of the company or in respect of his services, while director of the company, as director of any subsidiary of it or otherwise in connection with the management of the affairs of the company or any subsidiary of it; and

(b) shall distinguish between emoluments in respect of services as director, whether of the company or its subsidiary, and other emoluments.

(3) For purposes of this paragraph **'emoluments'**, in relation to a director, includes fees and percentages, any sums paid by way of expenses allowance (in so far as those sums are charged to United Kingdom income tax), any contributions paid in respect of him under any pension scheme and the estimated money value of any other benefits received by him otherwise than in cash.

23 A company which is neither a holding company nor a subsidiary of another body corporate need not comply with paragraphs 24 to 27 below as respects a financial year in the case of which the amount shown in compliance with paragraph 22 above does not exceed £60,000.

24(1) The following applies as respects the emoluments of the company's chairman; and for this purpose **'chairman'** means the person elected by the directors to be chairman of their meetings and includes a person who, though not so elected, holds any office (however designated) which in accordance with the company's constitution carries with it functions substantially similar to those discharged by a person so elected.

(2) If one person has been chairman throughout the financial year, there shall be shown his emoluments, unless his duties as chairman were wholly or mainly discharged outside the United Kingdom.

(3) Otherwise, there shall be shown with respect to each person who has been chairman during the year his emoluments so far as attributable to the period during which he was chairman, unless his duties as chairman were wholly or mainly discharged outside the United Kingdom.

25(1) The following applies as respects the emoluments of directors.

(2) With respect to all the directors (other than any who discharged their duties as such wholly or mainly outside the United Kingdom), there shall be shown—

(a) the number (if any) who had no emoluments or whose several emoluments amounted to not more than £5,000; and

(b) by reference to each pair of adjacent points on a scale whereon the lowest point is £5,000 and the succeeding ones are successive integral multiples of £5,000, the number (if any) whose several emoluments exceeded the lower point but did not exceed the higher.

(3) If, of the directors (other than any who discharged their duties as such wholly or mainly outside the United Kingdom), the emoluments of one only exceed the relevant amount, his emoluments (so far as so ascertainable) shall also be shown.

(4) If, of the directors (other than any who discharged their duties as such wholly or mainly outside the United Kingdom), the emoluments of each of two or more exceed the relevant amount, the emoluments of him (or them, in the case of equality) who had the greater or, as the case may be, the greatest shall also be shown.

(5) **'The relevant amount'**—

(a) if one person has been chairman throughout the year, means the amount of his emoluments; and

(b) otherwise, means an amount equal to the aggregate of the emoluments, so far as attributable to the period during which he was chairman, of each person who has been chairman during the year.

26 There shall under paragraphs 24 and 25 be brought into account as emoluments of a person all such amounts (other than contributions paid in respect of him under a pension scheme) as in his case are to be included in the amount shown under paragraph 22.

EMOLUMENTS WAIVED

27(1) There shall be shown—

(a) the number of directors who have waived rights to receive emoluments which, but for the waiver, would have fallen to be included in the amount shown under paragraph 22, and

(b) the aggregate amount of those emoluments.

(2) For these purposes—

(a) it is assumed that a sum not receivable in respect of a period would have been paid at the time at which it was due to be paid,

(b) a sum not so receivable that was payable only on demand, being a sum the right to receive which has been waived, is deemed to have been due to be paid at the time of the waiver.

PENSIONS OF DIRECTORS AND PAST DIRECTORS

28(1) There shall be shown the aggregate amount of directors' or past directors' pensions.

(2) This amount does not include any pension paid or receivable under a pension scheme if the scheme is such that the contributions under it are substantially adequate for the maintenance of the scheme; but, subject to this, it includes any pension paid or receivable in respect of any such services of a director or past director as are mentioned in paragraph 22(2), whether to or by him or, on his nomination or by virtue of dependence on or other connection with him, to or by any other person.

(3)   The amount shown shall distinguish between pensions in respect of services as director, whether of the company or its subsidiary, and other pensions.

COMPENSATION TO DIRECTORS FOR LOSS OF OFFICE

29(1)   There shall be shown the aggregate amount of any compensation to directors or past directors in respect of loss of office.

(2)   This amount—

(a)   includes any sums paid to or receivable by a director or past director by way of compensation for the loss of office as director of the company or for the loss, while director of the company or on or in connection with his ceasing to be a director of it, of any other office in connection with the management of the company's affairs or of any office as director or otherwise in connection with the management of the affairs of any subsidiary of the company; and

(b)   shall distinguish between compensation in respect of the office of director, whether of the company or its subsidiary, and compensation in respect of other offices.

(3)   References to compensation for loss of office include sums paid as consideration for or in connection with a person's retirement from office.

SUPPLEMENTARY

30(1)   The following applies with respect to the amounts to be shown under paragraphs 22, 28 and 29.

(2)   The amount in each case includes all relevant sums paid by or receivable from—

(a)   the company; and

(b)   the company's subsidiaries; and

(c)   any other person,

except sums to be accounted for to the company or any of its subsidiaries or, by virtue of sections 314 and 315 of this Act (duty of directors to make disclosure on company takeover; consequence of non-compliance), to past or present members of the company or any of its subsidiaries or any class of those members.

(3)   The amount to be shown under paragraph 29 shall distinguish between the sums respectively paid by or receivable from the company, the company's subsidiaries and persons other than the company and its subsidiaries.

31(1)   The amounts to be shown for any financial year under paragraphs 22, 28 and 29 are the sums receivable in respect of that year (whenever paid) or, in the case of sums not receivable in respect of a period, the sums paid during that year.

(2)   But where—

(a)   any sums are not shown in a note to the accounts for the relevant financial year on the ground that the person receiving them is liable to account for them as mentioned in paragraph 30(2), but the liability is thereafter wholly or partly released or is not enforced within a period of 2 years; or

(b)   any sums paid by way of express allowances are charged to United Kingdom income tax after the end of the relevant financial year,

those sums shall, to the extent to which the liability is released or not enforced or they are charged as mentioned above (as the case may be), be shown in a note to the first accounts in which it is practicable to show them and shall be distinguished from the amounts to be shown apart from this provision.

32   Where it is necessary to do so for the purpose of making any distinction required by the preceding paragraphs in an amount to be shown in compliance with this Part, the directors may apportion any payments between the matters in respect of which these have been paid or are receivable in such manner as they think appropriate.

INTERPRETATION

33(1)   The following applies for the interpretation of paragraphs 22 to 32.

(2)   A reference to the company's subsidiary—

(a)   in relation to a person who is or was, while a director of the company, a director also, by virtue of the company's nomination (direct or indirect) of any other body corporate, includes (subject to the following sub-paragraph) that body corporate, whether or not it is or was in fact the company's subsidiary, and

(b)   for purposes of paragraphs 22 to 28 (including any provision of this Part referring to paragraph 22) is to a subsidiary at the time the services were rendered, and for purposes of paragraph 29 to a subsidiary immediately before the loss of office as director.

(3)   The following definitions apply—

(a)   'pension' includes any superannuation allowance, superannuation gratuity or similar payment,

(b)   'pension scheme' means a scheme for the provision of pensions in respect of services as director or otherwise which is maintained in whole or in part by means of contributions, and

(c)   'contribution', in relation to a pension scheme, means any payment (including an insurance premium) paid for the purposes of the scheme by or in respect of persons rendering services in respect of which pensions will or may become payable under the scheme, except that it does not include any payment in respect of two or more persons if the amount paid in respect of each of them is not ascertainable.

SUPPLEMENTARY

34   This Part of this Schedule requires information to be given only so far as it is contained in the company's books and papers or the company has the right to obtain it from the persons concerned.

Part VI — Particulars Relating to Number of Employees Remunerated at Higher Rates

35(1)   There shall be shown by reference to each pair of adjacent points on a scale where the lowest point is £30,000 and the succeeding ones are successive integral multiples of £5,000 beginning with that in the case of which the multiplier is 7, the number (if any) of persons in the company's employment whose several emoluments exceeded the lower point but did not exceed the higher.

(2)   The persons whose emoluments are to be taken into account for this purpose do not include—

(a)   directors of the company; or

(b)   persons (other than directors of the company) who—

(i)   if employed by the company throughout the financial year, worked wholly or mainly during that year outside the United Kingdom, or

(ii)   if employed by the company for part only of that year, worked wholly or mainly during that part outside the United Kingdom.

36(1)   For these purposes, a person's emoluments include any paid to or receivable by him from the company, the company's subsidiaries and any other person in respect of his services as a person in the employment of the company or a subsidiary of it or as a director of a subsidiary of the company (except sums to be accounted for to the company or any of its subsidiaries).

(2)   'Emoluments' here includes fees and percentages, any sums paid by way of expenses allowance in so far as those sums are charged to United Kingdom income tax, and the estimated money value of any other benefits received by a person otherwise than in cash.

(3) The amounts to be brought into account for the purpose of complying with paragraph 35 are the sums receivable in respect of the financial year (whenever paid) or, in the case of sums not receivable in respect of a period, the sums paid during that year.

(4) But where—

(a) any sums are not brought into account for the financial year on the ground that the person receiving them is liable to account for them as mentioned in sub-paragraph (1), but the liability is wholly or partly released or is not enforced within a period of 2 years; or

(b) any sums paid to a person by way of expenses allowance are charged to United Kingdom income tax after the end of the financial year,

those sums shall, to the extent to which the liability is released or not enforced or they are charged as above mentioned (as the case may be), be brought into account for the purpose of complying with paragraph 35 on the first occasion on which it is practicable to do so.

37 References in paragraph 36 to a company's subsidiary—

(a) in relation to a person who is or was, while employed by the company a director, by virtue of the company's nomination (direct or indirect), of any other body corporate, include that body corporate (but subject to the following sub-paragraph), whether or not it is or was in fact the company's subsidiary; and

(b) are to be taken as referring to a subsidiary at the time the services are rendered.''

Schedule 6 — Disclosure of Information: Emoluments and Other Benefits of Directors and Others

[Companies Act 1988, sec. 232; Companies Act 1989, sec. 1, 6 and Sch. 4]

History
Heading substituted by CA 1989, s. 1, 6(4) and Sch. 4, para. 1, 2 as from 1 April 1990 subject to transitional and saving provisions (see S.I. 1990 No. 355 (C. 13), art. 3 and also art. 6–9); former heading read as follows:

"Particulars in Company Accounts of Loan and Other Transactions Favouring Directors and Officers".

Part I — Chairman's and Directors' Emoluments, Pensions and Compensation for Loss of Office

AGGREGATE AMOUNT OF DIRECTORS' EMOLUMENTS

1(1) The aggregate amount of directors' emoluments shall be shown.

1(2) This means the emoluments paid to or receivable by any person in respect of—

(a) his services as a director of the company, or

(b) his services while director of the company—

(i) as director of any of its subsidiary undertakings, or

(ii) otherwise in connection with the management of the affairs of the company or any of its subsidiary undertakings.

1(3) There shall also be shown, separately, the aggregate amount within sub-paragraph (2)(a) and (b)(i) and the aggregate amount within sub-paragraph (2)(b)(ii).

1(4) For the purposes of this paragraph the "emoluments" of a person include—

(a) fees and percentages,

(b) sums paid by way of expenses allowance (so far as those sums are chargeable to United Kingdom income tax),

(c) contributions paid in respect of him under any pension scheme, and

(d) the estimated money value of any other benefits received by him otherwise than in cash,

and emoluments in respect of a person's accepting office as director shall be treated as emoluments in respect of his services as director.

DETAILS OF CHAIRMAN'S AND DIRECTORS' EMOLUMENTS

2   Where the company is a parent company or a subsidiary undertaking, or where the amount shown in compliance with paragraph 1(1) is £60,000 or more, the information required by paragraphs 3 to 6 shall be given with respect to the emoluments of the chairman and directors, and emoluments waived.

3(1)   The emoluments of the chairman shall be shown.

3(2)   The "**chairman**" means the person elected by the directors to be chairman of their meetings, and includes a person who, though not so elected, holds an office (however designated) which in accordance with the company's constitution carries with it functions substantially similar to those discharged by a person so elected.

3(3)   Where there has been more than one chairman during the year, the emoluments of each shall be stated so far as attributable to the period during which he was chairman.

3(4)   The emoluments of a person need not be shown if his duties as chairman were wholly or mainly discharged outside the United Kingdom.

4(1)   The following information shall be given with respect to the emoluments of directors.

4(2)   There shall be shown the number of directors whose emoluments fell within each of the following bands—

> not more than £5,000,
>
> more than £5,000 but not more than £10,000,
>
> more than £10,000 but not more than £15,000,
>
> and so on.

4(3)   If the emoluments of any of the directors exceeded that of the chairman, there shall be shown the greatest amount of emoluments of any director.

4(4)   Where more than one person has been chairman during the year, the reference in sub-paragraph (3) to the emoluments of the chairman is to the aggregate of the emoluments of each person who has been chairman, so far as attributable to the period during which he was chairman.

4(5)   The information required by sub-paragraph (2) need not be given in respect of a director who discharged his duties as such wholly or mainly outside the United Kingdom; and any such director shall be left out of account for the purposes of sub-paragraph (3).

5   In paragraphs 3 and 4 "emoluments" has the same meaning as in paragraph 1, except that it does not include contributions paid in respect of a person under a pension scheme.

EMOLUMENTS WAIVED

6(1)   There shall be shown—

   (a) the number of directors who have waived rights to receive emoluments which, but for the waiver, would have fallen to be included in the amount shown under paragraph 1(1), and

   (b) the aggregate amount of those emoluments.

6(2) For the purposes of this paragraph it shall be assumed that a sum not receivable in respect of a period would have been paid at the time at which it was due, and if such a sum was payable only on demand, it shall be deemed to have been due at the time of the waiver.

PENSIONS OF DIRECTORS AND PAST DIRECTORS

7(1) There shall be shown the aggregate amount of directors' or past directors' pensions.

7(2) This amount does not include any pension paid or receivable under a pension scheme if the scheme is such that the contributions under it are substantially adequate for the maintenance of the scheme; but, subject to this, it includes any pension paid or receivable in respect of any such services of a director or past director as are mentioned in paragraph 1(2), whether to or by him or, on his nomination or by virtue of dependence on or other connection with him, to or by any other person.

7(3) The amount shown shall distinguish between pensions in respect of services as director, whether of the company or any of its subsidiary undertakings, and other pensions.

7(4) References to pensions include benefits otherwise than in cash and in relation to so much of a pension as consists of such a benefit references to its amount are to the estimated money value of the benefit.

The nature of any such benefit shall also be disclosed.

COMPENSATION TO DIRECTORS FOR LOSS OF OFFICE

8(1) There shall be shown the aggregate amount of any compensation to directors or past directors in respect of loss of office.

8(2) This amount includes compensation received or receivable by a director or past director for—

    (a) loss of office as director of the company, or

    (b) loss, while director of the company or on or in connection with his ceasing to be a director of it, of—

        (i) any other office in connection with the management of the company's affairs, or

        (ii) any office as director or otherwise in connection with the management of the affairs of any subsidiary undertaking of the company;

and shall distinguish between compensation in respect of the office of director, whether of the company or any of its subsidiary undertakings, and compensation in respect of other offices.

8(3) References to compensation include benefits otherwise than in cash; and in relation to such compensation references to its amount are to the estimated money value of the benefit.

The nature of any such compensation shall be disclosed.

8(4) References to compensation for loss of office include compensation in consideration for, or in connection with, a person's retirement from office.

SUMS PAID TO THIRD PARTIES IN RESPECT OF DIRECTORS' SERVICES

9(1)   There shall be shown the aggregate amount of any consideration paid to or receivable by third parties for making available the services of any person—

  (a)   as a director of the company, or

  (b)   while director of the company—

     (i)   as director of any of its subsidiary undertakings, or

     (ii)   otherwise in connection with the management of the affairs of the company or any of its subsidiary undertakings.

9(2)   The reference to consideration includes benefits otherwise than in cash; and in relation to such consideration the reference to its amount is to the estimated money value of the benefit.

  The nature of any such consideration shall be disclosed.

9(3)   The reference to third parties is to persons other than—

  (a)   the director himself or a person connected with him or body corporate controlled by him, and

  (b)   the company or any of its subsidiary undertakings.

SUPPLEMENTARY

10(1)   The following applies with respect to the amounts to be shown under paragraphs 1, 7, 8 and 9.

10(2)   The amount in each case includes all relevant sums paid by or receivable from—

  (a)   the company; and

  (b)   the company's subsidiary undertakings; and

  (c)   any other person,

except sums to be accounted for to the company or any of its subsidiary undertakings or, by virtue of sections 314 and 315 of this Act (duty of directors to make disclosure on company takeover; consequence of non-compliance), to past or present members of the company or any of its subsidiaries or any class of those members.

10(3)   The amount to be shown under paragraph 8 shall distinguish between the sums respectively paid by or receivable from the company, the company's subsidiary undertakings and persons other than the company and its subsidiary undertakings.

10(4)   References to amounts paid to or receivable by a person include amounts paid to or receivable by a person connected with him or a body corporate controlled by him (but not so as to require an amount to be counted twice).

11(1)   The amounts to be shown for any financial year under paragraphs 1, 7, 8 and 9 are the sums receivable in respect of that year (whenever paid) or, in the case of sums not receivable in respect of a period, the sums paid during that year.

11(2)   But where—

  (a)   any sums are not shown in a note to the accounts for the relevant financial year on the ground that the person receiving them is liable to account for them as mentioned in paragraph 10(2), but the liability is thereafter wholly or partly released or is not enforced within a period of 2 years; or

(b) any sums paid by way of expenses allowance are charged to United Kingdom income tax after the end of the relevant financial year,

those sums shall, to the extent to which the liability is released or not enforced or they are charged as mentioned above (as the case may be), be shown in a note to the first accounts in which it is practicable to show them and shall be distinguished from the amounts to be shown apart from this provision.

12 Where it is necessary to do so for the purpose of making any distinction required by the preceding paragraphs in an amount to be shown in compliance with this Part of this Schedule, the directors may apportion any payments between the matters in respect of which these have been paid or are receivable in such manner as they think appropriate.

INTERPRETATION

13(1) The following applies for the interpretation of this Part of this Schedule.

13(2) A reference to a subsidiary undertaking of the company—

(a) in relation to a person who is or was, while a director of the company, a director also, by virtue of the company's nomination (direct or indirect) of any other undertaking, includes (subject to the following sub-paragraph) that undertaking, whether or not it is or was in fact a subsidiary undertaking of the company, and

(b) for the purposes of paragraphs 1 to 7 (including any provision of this Part of this Schedule referring to paragraph 1) is to an undertaking which is a subsidiary undertaking at the time the services were rendered, and for the purposes of paragraph 8 to a subsidiary undertaking immediately before the loss of office as director.

13(3) The following definitions apply—

(a) **"pension"** includes any superannuation allowance, superannuation gratuity or similar payment,

(b) **"pension scheme"** means a scheme for the provision of pensions in respect of services as director or otherwise which is maintained in whole or in part by means of contributions, and

(c) **"contribution"**, in relation to a pension scheme, means any payment (including an insurance premium) paid for the purposes of the scheme by or in respect of persons rendering services in respect of which pensions will or may become payable under the scheme except that it does not include any payment in respect of two or more persons if the amount paid in respect of each of them is not ascertainable.

13(4) References in this Part of this Schedule to a person being "connected" with a director, and to a director "controlling" a body corporate, shall be construed in accordance with section 346.

SUPPLEMENTARY

14   This Part of this Schedule requires information to be given only so far as it is contained in the company's books and papers or the company has the right to obtain it from the persons concerned.

History
Pt. I inserted by CA 1989, s. 6(4) and Sch. 4, para. 1, 3 as from 1 April 1990 subject to transitional and saving provisions (see S.I. 1990 No. 385 (C. 13), art. 3, Sch. 1 and also art. 6–9).

Part II — Loans, Quasi-Loans and Other Dealings in Favour of Directors

History
Heading substituted for former heading of Pt. I by CA 1989, s. 1, 6(4) and Sch. 4, para. 1, 4(1) as from 1 April 1990 subject to transitional and saving provisions (see S.I. 1990 No. 355 (C. 13), art. 3, Sch. 1 and also art. 6–9); former Pt. I heading read as follows: "Part I — Matters to be Disclosed Under Section 232".

15   The group accounts of a holding company, or if it is not required to prepare group accounts its individual accounts, shall contain the particulars required by this Schedule of—

(a)   any transaction or arrangement of a kind described in section 330 entered into by the company or by a subsidiary of the company for a person who at any time during the financial year was a director of the company or its holding company, or was connected with such a director;

(b)   an agreement by the company or by a subsidiary of the company to enter into any such transaction or arrangement for a person who was at any time during the financial year a director of the company or its holding company, or was connected with such a director; and

(c)   any other transaction or arrangement with the company or a subsidiary of it in which a person who at any time during the financial year was a director of the company or its holding company had, directly or indirectly, a material interest.

History
In para. 15 (formerly numbered 1 — in regard to renumbering of paragraphs in this Part see history note after para. 27) the words "The group accounts of" to "its individual accounts" substituted for the former words "Group accounts" by CA 1989, s. 1, 6(4) and Sch. 4, para. 1, 4(4) as from 1 April 1990 subject to transitional and saving provisions (see S.I. 1990 No. 355 (C. 13), art. 3, Sch. 1 and also art. 6–9).

16   The accounts prepared by a company other than a holding company shall contain the particulars required by this Schedule of—

(a)   any transaction or arrangement of a kind described in section 330 entered into by the company for a person who at any time during the financial year was a director of it or of its holding company or was connected with such a director;

(b)   an agreement by the company to enter into any such transaction or arrangement for a person who at any time during the financial year was a director of the company or its holding company or was connected with such a director; and

(c)   any other transaction or arrangement with the company in which a person who at any time during the financial year was a director of the company or of its holding company had, directly or indirectly, a material interest.

17(1) For purposes of paragraphs 15(c) and 16(c), a transaction or arrangement between a company and a director of it or of its holding company, or a person connected with such a director, is to be treated (if it would not otherwise be so) as a transaction, arrangement or agreement in which that director is interested.

17(2) An interest in such a transaction or arrangement is not **"material"** for purposes of those sub-paragraphs if in the board's opinion it is not so; but this is without prejudice to the question whether or not such an interest is material in a case where the board have not considered the matter.

"The board" here means the directors of the company preparing the accounts, or a majority of those directors, but excluding in either case the director whose interest it is.

History

Formerly appearing here was a paragraph (numbered 4 — in regard to renumbering of paragraphs in this Part see history note after para. 27) omitted by CA 1989, s. 1, 6(4) and Sch. 4, para. 1, 4(3) as from 1 April 1990 subject to transitional and saving provisions (see S.I. 1990 No. 355 (C. 13), art. 3, Sch. 1 and also art. 6–9); former para. 4 read as follows:

"Paragraphs 1 and 2 do not apply, for the purposes of accounts prepared by a company which is, or is the holding company of, an authorised institution, in relation to a transaction or arrangement of a kind described in section 330 or an agreement to enter into such a transaction or arrangement, to which that authorised institution is a party." In former para. 4 the words "an authorised institution" and "that authorised institution" substituted respectively for the original words "a recognised bank" and "that recognised bank" by Banking Act 1987, s. 108(1) and Sch. 6, para. 18(9) as from 1 October 1987 (see S.I. 1987 No. 1664 (C. 50)).

18 Paragraphs 15 and 16 do not apply in relation to the following transactions, arrangements and agreements—

   (a) a transaction, arrangement or agreement between one company and another in which a director of the former or of its subsidiary or holding company is interested only by virtue of his being a director of the latter;

   (b) a contract of service between a company and one of its directors or a director of its holding company, or between a director of a company and any of that company's subsidiaries:

   (c) a transaction, arrangement or agreement which was not entered into during the financial year and which did not subsist at any time during that year.

19 Paragraphs 15 and 16 apply whether or not—

   (a) the transaction or arrangement was prohibited by section 330;

   (b) the person for whom it was made was a director of the company or was connected with a director of it at the time it was made;

   (c) in the case of a transaction or arrangement made by a company which at any time during a financial year is a subsidiary of another company, it was a subsidiary of that other company at the time the transaction or arrangement was made.

20 Neither paragraph 15(c) nor paragraph 16(c) applies in relation to any transaction or arrangement if—

   (a) each party to the transaction or arrangement which is a member of the same group of companies (meaning a holding company and its subsidiaries) as the company entered into the transaction or arrangment in the ordinary course of business, and

   (b) the terms of the transaction or arrangement are not less favourable to any such party than it would be reasonable to expect if the interest mentioned in that sub-paragraph had not been an interest of a person who was a director of the company or of its holding company.

21   Neither paragraph 15(c) nor paragraph 16(c) applies in relation to any transaction or arrangement if—

(a) the company is a member of a group of companies (meaning a holding company and its subsidiaries), and

(b) either the company is a wholly-owned subsidiary or no body corporate (other than the company or a subsidiary of the company) which is a member of the group of companies which includes the company's ultimate holding company was a party to the transaction or arrangement, and

(c) the director in question was at some time during the relevant period associated with the company, and

(d) the material interest of the director in question in the transaction or arrangement would not have arisen if he had not been associated with the company at any time during the relevant period.

THE PARTICULARS REQUIRED BY THIS PART

22(1)   Subject to the next paragraph, the particulars required by this Part are those of the principal terms of the transaction, arrangement or agreement.

22(2)   Without prejudice to the generality of sub-paragraph (1), the following particulars are required—

(a) a statement of the fact either that the transaction, arrangement or agreement was made or subsisted (as the case may be) during the financial year;

(b) the name of the person for whom it was made and, where that person is or was connected with a director of the company or of its holding company, the name of that director;

(c) in a case where paragraph 15(c) or 16(c) applies, the name of the director with the material interest and the nature of that interest;

(d) in the case of a loan or an agreement for a loan or an arrangement within section 330(6) or (7) of this Act relating to a loan—

 (i) the amount of the liability of the person to whom the loan was or was agreed to be made, in respect of principal and interest, at the beginning and at the end of the financial year;

 (ii) the maximum amount of that liability during that year;

 (iii) the amount of any interest which, having fallen due, has not been paid; and

 (iv) the amount of any provision (within the meaning of Schedule 4 to this Act) made in respect of any failure or anticipated failure by the borrower to repay the whole or part of the loan or to pay the whole or part of any interest on it;

(e) in the case of a guarantee or security or an arrangement within section 330(6) relating to a guarantee or security—

 (i) the amount for which the company (or its subsidiary) was liable under the guarantee or in respect of the security both at the beginning and at the end of the financial year;

CA 1985, Sch. 6, para. 21

(ii) the maximum amount for which the company (or its subsidiary) may become so liable; and

(iii) any amount paid and any liability incurred by the company (or its subsidiary) for the purpose of fulfilling the guarantee or discharging the security (including any loss incurred by reason of the enforcement of the guarantee or security); and

(f) in the case of any transaction, arrangement or agreement other than those mentioned in sub-paragraphs (d) and (e), the value of the transaction or arrangement or (as the case may be) the value of the transaction or arrangement to which the agreement relates.

23   In paragraph 22(2) above, sub-paragraphs (c) to (f) do not apply in the case of a loan or quasi-loan made or agreed to be made by a company to or for a body corporate which is either—

(a) a body corporate of which that company is a wholly-owned subsidiary, or

(b) a wholly-owned subsidiary of a body corporate of which that company is a wholly-owned subsidiary, or

(c) a wholly-owned subsidiary of that company,

if particulars of that loan, quasi-loan or agreement for it would not have been required to be included in that company's annual accounts if the first-mentioned body corporate had not been associated with a director of that company at any time during the relevant period.

EXCLUDED TRANSACTIONS

History
Heading before para. 24 (formerly numbered 11 — in regard to renumbering of paragraphs in this Part see history note to Pt. II, after para. 27) substituted by CA 1989, s. 16(4) and Sch. 4, para. 1, 4(5) as from 1 April 1990   subject to transitional and saving provisons (see S.I. 1990 No. 355(C. 13), art. 3, Sch. 1 and also art. 6–9); former heading read as follows:
   "TRANSACTIONS EXCLUDED FROM SECTION 232".

24(1)   In relation to a company's accounts for a financial year, compliance with this Part is not required in the case of transactions of a kind mentioned in the following sub-paragraph which are made by the company or a subsidiary of it for a person who at any time during that financial year was a director of the company or of its holding company, or was connected with such a director, if the aggregate of the values of each transaction, arrangement or agreement so made for that director or any person connected with him, less the amount (if any) by which the liabilities of the person for whom the transaction or arrangement was made has been reduced, did not at any time during the financial year exceed £5,000.

24(2)   The transactions in question are—

(a) credit transactions,

(b) guarantees provided or securities entered into in connection with credit transactions,

(c) arrangements within subsection (6) or (7) of section 330 relating to credit transactions,

(d) agreements to enter into credit transactions.

25   In relation to a company's accounts for a financial year, compliance with this Part is not required by virtue of paragraph 15(c) or 16(c) in the case of any transaction or arrangement with a company or any of its subsidiaries in which a director of the company or its holding company had, directly or indirectly, a material interest if—

   (a) the value of each transaction or arrangement within paragraph 15(c) or 16(c) (as the case may be) in which that director had (directly or indirectly) a material interest and which was made after the commencement of the financial year with the company or any of its subsidiaries, and

   (b) the value of each such transaction or arrangement which was made before the commencement of the financial year less the amount (if any) by which the liabilities of the person for whom the transaction or arrangement was made have been reduced,

did not at any time during the financial year exceed in the aggregate £1,000 or, if more, did not exceed £5,000 or 1 per cent of the value of the net assets of the company preparing the accounts in question as at the end of the financial year, whichever is the less.

   For this purpose a company's net assets are the aggregate of its assets, less the aggregate of its liabilities (**"liabilities"** to include any provision for liabilities or charges within paragraph 89 of Schedule 4).

26   Section 345 of this Act (power of Secretary of State to alter sums by statutory instrument subject to negative resolution in Parliament) applies as if the money sums specified in paragraph 21 or 22 above were specified in Part X.

INTERPRETATION

27(1)   The following provisions of this Act apply for purposes of this Part of this Schedule—

   (a) section 331(2), and (7), as regards the meaning of **"guarantee"**, and **"credit transaction"**;

   (b) section 331(9), as to the interpretation of references to a transaction or arrangement being made **"for"** a person;

   (c) section 340, in assigning values to transactions and arrangements, and

   (d) section 346, as to the interpretation of references to a person being **"connected with"** a director of a company.

27(2)   In this Part of this Schedule **"director"** includes a shadow director.

History
Para. 27(2) inserted and existing provision (para. 14, renumbered 27 — in regard to renumbering of paragraphs in Pt. II see history note below) made sub-paragraph (1) by CA 1989, s. 16,(4) and Sch. 4, para. 1, 5 as from 1 April 1990 subject to transitional and saving provisions (see S.I. 1990 No. 355 (C. 13), art. 3, Sch. 1 and also art. 6–9).

In para. 14(a), renumbered 27(1)(a), the figure "(5)" formerly appearing after the figure "331(2)" and the words "**'recognised bank'**" formerly appearing after the word "**guarantee,**'" repealed by Banking Act 1987, s. 108(2) and Sch. 7, Pt. I as from 1 October 1987 (see S.I. 1987 No. 1664 (C. 50)).

History note to Pt. II
In Pt. II (in regard to its renumbering as Pt. II see history note above para. 15), para. 15–27 renumbered as such and internal cross-references renumbered accordingly by CA 1989, s. 1, 6,(4) and Sch. 4, para. 1, 4(2) as from 1 April 1990 subject to transitional and saving provisions (see S.I. 1990 No. 355 (C. 13), art. 3, Sch. 1 and also art. 6–9); formerly the paragraphs were numbered 1–3 and 5–14 (in regard to omission of former para. 4 see history note above para. 18).

[The next page is 30,101]

Part III — Other Transactions, Arrangements and Agreements

History

Heading substituted for former heading of Pt. II by CA 1989, s. 1, 6(4) and Sch. 4, para. 1, 6(1) as from 1 April 1990 subject to transitional and saving provisons (see S.I.

1990 No. 355 (C. 13), art. 3, Sch. 1 and also art. 6–9); former Pt. II heading read as follows:

"Part II — Matters to be Disclosed under Section 233".

28 This Part of this Schedule applies in relation to the following classes of transactions, arrangements and agreements—

(a) loans, guarantees and securities relating to loans, arrangements of a kind described in subsection (6) or (7) of section 330 of this Act relating to loans and agreements to enter into any of the foregoing transactions and arrangements;

(b) quasi-loans, guarantees and securities relating to quasi-loans arrangements of a kind described in either of those subsections relating to quasi-loans and agreements to enter into any of the foregoing transactions and arrangements;

(c) credit transactions, guarantees and securities relating to credit transactions, arrangements of a kind described in either of those subsections relating to credit transactions and agreements to enter into any of the foregoing transactions and arrangements.

29(1) To comply with this Part of this Schedule, the accounts must contain a statement, in relation to transactions, arrangements and agreements made by the company or a subsidiary of it for persons who at any time during the financial year were officers of the company (but not directors or shadow directors), of—

(a) the aggregate amounts outstanding at the end of the financial year under transactions, arrangements and agreements within sub-paragraphs (a), (b) and (c) respectively of paragraph 28 above, and

(b) the numbers of officers for whom the transactions, arrangements and agreements falling within each of those sub-paragraphs were made.

History

In para. 29(1) (formerly numbered 16(1) — in regard to renumbering of paragraphs in this Part see history note after para. 30) the words "made by the company or a subsidiary of it for persons who at any time during the financial year were officers of the company (but not directors

or shadow directors)" substituted for the former words "made as mentioned in section 233(1)" by CA 1989, s. 16(4) and Sch. 4, para. 1, 6(3) as from 1 April 1990 subject to transactions and saving provisions (see S.I. 1990 No. 355 (C. 13), art. 3, Sch. 1 and also art. 6–9).

29(2) This paragraph does not apply to transactions, arrangements and agreements made by the company or any of its subsidiaries for an officer of the company if the aggregate amount outstanding at the end of the financial year under the transactions, arrangements and agreements so made for that officer does not exceed £2,500.

29(3) Section 345 of this Act (power of Secretary of State to alter money sums by statutory instrument subject to negative resolution in Parliament) applies as if the money sum specified above in this paragraph were specified in Part X.

30 The following provisions of this Act apply for purposes of this Part—

(a) section 331(2), (3), and (7), as regards the meaning of **"guarantee"**, **"quasi-loan"**, and **"credit transaction"**, and

(b) section 331(9), as to the interpretation of references to a transaction or arrangement being made **"for"** a person;

and **"amount outstanding"** means the amount of the outstanding liabilities of the person for whom the transaction, arrangement or agreement was made or, in the case of a guarantee or security, the amount guaranteed or secured.

History
In para. 30(a) (previously numbered 17(a)), the figure "(5)" formerly appearing after the figure "(3)" and the words "recognised bank" formerly appearing after the word "quasi-loan," repealed by Banking Act 1987, s. 108(2) and Sch. 7, Pt. I as from 1 October 1987 (see S.I. 1987 No. 1664 (C. 50)).

History note to Pt. III
In Pt. III (in regard to its renumbering as Pt. III see history note above para. 28), para. 28–30 renumbered as such and internal cross-references renumbered accordingly by CA 1989, s. 6(4) and Sch. 4, para. 1, 6(2) as from 1 April 1990 subject to transitional and saving provisions (see S.I. 1990 No. 355 (C. 13), art. 3, Sch. 1 and also art. 6–9); formerly the paragraphs were numbered 15–17.

History note to former Pt. III
Former Pt. III ("Part III — Matters to be Disclosed under Section 234 (Authorised Institutions)") omitted by CA 1989, s. 1, 6(4) and Sch. 4, para. 1, 7 as from 1 April 1990 subject to transitional and saving provisions (see S.I. 1990 No. 355 (C. 13), art. 3, Sch. 1 and also art. 6–9). In the heading to former Pt. III the words "Authorised Institutions" substituted for the previous words "Recognised Banks" by Banking Act 1987, s. 108(1) and Sch. 6, para. 18(9) as from 1 October 1987 (see S.I. 1987 No. 1664 (C. 50)); former Pt. III read as follows:

"**18** This Part of this Schedule applies in relation to the same classes of transactions, arrangements and agreements as does Part II.

19 To comply with this Part, the accounts must contain a statement, in relation to such transactions, arrangements and agreements made as mentioned in section 234(1), of—

(a) the aggregate amounts outstanding at the end of the financial year under transactions, arrangements and agreements within sub-paragraphs (a), (b) and (c) respectively of paragraph 15 of this Schedule, and

(b) the numbers of persons for whom the transactions, arrangements and agreements falling within each of those sub-paragraphs were made.

20 For the purposes of the application of paragraph 16 in relation to loans and quasi-loans made by a company to persons connected with a person who at any time is a director of the company or of its holding company, a company which a person does not control is not connected with him.

21 The following provisions of this Act apply for purposes of this Part—

(a) section 331(3), as regards the meaning of '**quasi-loan**';

(b) section 331(9), as to the interpretation of references to a transaction or arrrangement being made '**for**' a person; and

(c) section 346, as to the interpretation of references to a person being connected with a director, or to a director controlling a company;

and '**amount outstanding**' means the amount of the outstanding liabilities of the person for whom the transaction, arrangement or agreement was made or, in the case of a guarantee or security, the amount guaranteed or secured."

Schedule 7 — Matters to be Dealt With in Directors' Report

⊛ **[Section 234(3), (4)]**

Part I — Matters of a General Nature

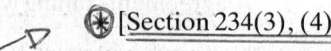
(1) ACTIVITIES +(2)BUSINESS REVIEW
(3) ASSET VALUES

1(1) If significant changes in the fixed assets of the company or of any of its subsidiary undertakings have occurred in the financial year, the report shall contain particulars of the changes.

History
In para. 1(1) the words "subsidiary undertakings" substituted for the former words "subsidiaries" by CA 1989, s. 1, 8(2) and Sch. 7, para. 1, (2)(1) as from 1 April 1990 subject to transitional and saving provisions (see S.I. 1990 No. 355 (C. 13), art. 3, Sch. 1 and also art. 6–9).

1(2) If, in the case of such of those assets as consist in interests in land, their market value (as at the end of the financial year) differs substantially from the amount at which they are included in the balance sheet, and the difference is, in the directors' opinion, of such significance as to require that the attention of members of the company or of holders of its debentures should be drawn to it, the report shall indicate the difference with such degree of precision as is practicable.

(4) DIRECTORS' INTERESTS

2(1) The information required by paragraphs 2A and 2B shall be given in the directors' report, or by way of notes to the company's annual accounts, with respect to each person who at the end of the financial year was a director of the company.

2(2) In those paragraphs—

(a) **"the register"** means the register of directors' interests kept by the company under section 325; and

(b) references to a body corporate being in the same group as the company are to its being a subsidiary or holding company, or another subsidiary of a holding company, of the company.

2A(1) It shall be stated with respect to each director whether, according to the register, he was at the end of the financial year interested in shares in or debentures of the company or any other body corporate in the same group.

2A(2) If he was so interested, there shall be stated the number of shares in and amount of debentures of each body (specifying it) in which, according to the register, he was then interested.

2A(3) If a director was interested at the end of the financial year in shares in or debentures of the company or any other body corporate in the same group—

(a) it shall also be stated whether, according to the register, he was at the beginning of the financial year (or, if he was not then a director, when he became one) interested in shares in or debentures of the company or any other body corporate in the same group, and

(b) if he was so interested, there shall be stated the number of shares in and amount of debentures of each body (specifying it) in which, according to the register, he was then interested.

2A(4) In this paragraph references to an interest in shares or debentures have the same meaning as in section 324; and references to the interest of a director include any interest falling to be treated as his for the purposes of that section.

2A(5) The reference above to the time when a person became a director is, in the case of a person who became a director on more than one occasion, to the time when he first became a director.

2B(1) It shall be stated with respect to each director whether, according to the register, any right to subscribe for shares in or debentures of the company or another body corporate in the same group was during the financial year granted to, or exercised by, the director or a member of his immediate family.

2B(2) If any such right was granted to, or exercised by, any such person during the financial year, there shall be stated the number of shares in and amount of debentures of each body (specifying it) in respect of which, according to the register, the right was granted or exercised.

2B(3) A director's **"immediate family"** means his or her spouse and infant children; and for this purpose "children" includes step-children, and **"infant"**, in relation to Scotland, means pupil or minor.

2B(4) The reference above to a member of the director's immediate family does not include a person who is himself or herself a director of the company.

History

Para. 2, 2A and 2B substituted for former para. 2 by CA 1989, s. 8(2) and Sch. 5, para. 1, 3 as from 1 April 1990 subject to transitional and saving provisions (see S.I. 1990 No. 355 (C. 13), art. 3, Sch. 1 and also art. 6–9); former para. 2 read as follows:

"2(1) The report shall state the following, with respect to each person who, at the end of the financial year, was a director of the company—

  (a) whether or not, according to the register kept by the company for the purposes of sections 324 to 328 of this Act (director's obligation to notify his interests in the company and companies in the same group), he was at the end of that year interested in shares in, or debentures of, the company or any other body corporate, being the company's subsidiary or holding company or a subsidiary of the company's holding company;

  (b) if he was so interested—

    (i) the number and amount of shares in, and debentures of each body (specifying it) in which, according to that register, he was then interested,

    (ii) whether or not (according to that register) he was, at the beginning of that year (or, if he was not then a director, when he became one), interested in shares in, or debentures of, the company or any other such body corporate, and

    (iii) if he was, the number and amount of shares in, and debentures of, each body (specifying it) in which, according to that register, he was interested at the beginning of the financial year or (as the case may be) when he became a director.

(2) An interest in shares or debentures which, under sections 324 to 328, falls to be treated as being the interest of a director is so treated for the purposes of this paragraph; and the references above to the time when a person became a director, in the case of a person who became a director on more than one occasion, is to the time when he first became a director.

(3) The particulars required by this paragraph may be given by way of notes to the company's accounts in respect of the financial year, instead of being stated in the directors' report."

(5) NAMES OF ALL DIRECTORS   (6) POST-B/SHEET EVENTS

(7) POLITICAL AND CHARITABLE GIFTS

3(1)   The following applies if the company (not being the wholly-owned subsidiary of a company incorporated in Great Britain) has in the financial year given money for political purposes or charitable purposes or both.

3(2)   If the money given exceeded £200 in amount, there shall be contained in the directors' report for the year—

  (a) in the case of each of the purposes for which money has been given, a statement of the amount of money given for that purpose, and

  (b) in the case of political purposes for which money has been given, the following particulars (so far as applicable)—

    (i) the name of each person to whom money has been given for those purposes exceeding £200 in amount and the amount of money given.

    (ii) if money exceeding £200 in amount has been given by way of donation or subscription to a political party, the identity of the party and the amount of money given.

4(1)   Paragraph 3 does not apply to a company which, at the end of the financial year, has subsidiaries which have, in that year, given money as mentioned above, but is not itself the wholly-owned subsidiary of a company incorporated in Great Britain.

4(2)   But in such a case there shall (if the amount of money so given in that year by the company and the subsidiaries between them exceeds £200) be contained in the directors' report for the year—

  (a) in the case of each of the purposes for which money has been given by the company and the subsidiaries between them, a statement of the amount of money given for that purpose, and

  (b) in the case of political purposes for which money has been given, the like particulars (so far as applicable) as are required by paragraph 3.

5(1)   The following applies for the interpretation of paragraphs 3 and 4.

CA 1985, Sch. 7, para. 3(1)   [The next page is 30,251]   **CCH Editions Limited**

5(2) A company is to be treated as giving money for political purposes if, directly or indirectly—

  (a) it gives a donation or subscription to a political party of the United Kingdom or any part of it; or

  (b) it gives a donation or subscription to a person who, to the company's knowledge, is carrying on, or proposing to carry on, any activities which can, at the time at which the donation or subscription was given, reasonably be regarded as likely to affect public support for such a political party as is mentioned above.

5(3) Money given for charitable purposes to a person who, when it was given, was ordinarily resident outside the United Kingdom is to be left out of account.

5(4) **"Charitable purposes"** means purposes which are exclusively charitable; and, as respects Scotland, **"charitable"** is to be construed as if it were contained in the Income Tax Acts.

INSURANCE EFFECTED FOR OFFICERS OR AUDITORS

5A Where in the financial year the company has purchased or maintained any such insurance as is mentioned in section 310(3)(a) (insurance of officers or auditors against liabilities in relation to the company), that fact shall be stated in the report.

✷ **History** ✦
Para. 5A inserted by CA 1989, s. 137(2) as from 1 April 1990 for the purposes of a directors' report of a company (within the meaning of CA 1985, s. 735) but subject to a transitional provision (see S.I. 1990 No. 355 (C. 13), art. 4(e)(ii) and also art. 13).

✳ MISCELLANEOUS

6 The directors' report shall contain—

  (a) particulars of any important events affecting the company or any of its subsidiary undertakings which have occurred since the end of the financial year,

  (b) an indication of likely future developments in the business of the company and of its subsidiary undertakings, and

  (c) an indication of the activities (if any) of the company and its subsidiary undertakings in the field of research and development.

History
In para. 6 the words "subsidiary undertakings" (occurring three times) substituted for the former word "subsidiary" by CA 1989, s. 1, 8(2) and Sch. 5, para. 1, 2(2) as from 1 April 1990 subject to transitional and saving provisions (see S.I. 1990 No. 355 (C. 13), art. 3, Sch. 1 and also art. 6–9).

Part II — Disclosure Required by Company Acquiring its Own Shares, etc.

7 This Part of this Schedule applies where shares in a company—

  (a) are purchased by the company or are acquired by it by forfeiture or surrender in lieu of forfeiture, or in pursuance of section 143(3) of this Act (acquisition of own shares by company limited by shares), or

   (b) are acquired by another person in circumstances where paragraph (c) or (d) of section 146(1) applies (acquisition by company's nominee, or by another with company financial assistance, the company having a beneficial interest), or

   (c) are made subject to a lien or other charge taken (whether expressly or otherwise) by the company and permitted by section 150(2) or (4), or section 6(3) of the Consequential Provisions Act (exceptions from general rule against a company having a lien or charge on its own shares).

8 The directors' report with respect to a financial year shall state—

   (a) the number and nominal value of the shares so purchased, the aggregate amount of the consideration paid by the company for such shares and the reasons for their purchase;

   (b) the number and nominal value of the shares so acquired by the company, acquired by another person in such circumstances and so charged respectively during the financial year;

   (c) the maximum number and nominal value of shares which, having been so acquired by the company, acquired by another person in such circumstances or so charged (whether or not during that year) are held at any time by the company or that other person during that year;

   (d) the number and nominal value of the shares so acquired by the company, acquired by another person in such circumstances or so charged (whether or not during that year) which are disposed of by the company or that other person or cancelled by the company during that year;

   (e) where the number and nominal value of the shares of any particular description are stated in pursuance of any of the preceding sub-paragraphs, the percentage of the called-up share capital which shares of that description represent;

   (f) where any of the shares have been so charged the amount of the charge in each case; and

   (g) where any of the shares have been disposed of by the company or the person who acquired them in such circumstances for money or money's worth the amount or value of the consideration in each case.

Part III — Disclosure Concerning Employment, etc., of Disabled Persons

9(1) This Part of this Schedule applies to the directors' report where the average number of persons employed by the company in each week during the financial year exceeded 250.

9(2) That average number is the quotient derived by dividing, by the number of weeks in the financial year, the number derived by ascertaining, in relation to each of those weeks, the number of persons who, under contracts of service, were employed in the week (whether throughout it or not) by the company, and adding up the numbers ascertained.

CA 1985, Sch. 7, para. 8

9(3)   The directors' report shall in that case contain a statement describing such policy as the company has applied during the financial year—

   (a)   for giving full and fair consideration to applications for employment by the company made by disabled persons, having regard to their particular aptitude and abilities,

   (b)   for continuing the employment of, and for arranging appropriate training for, employees of the company who have become disabled persons during the period when they were employed by the company, and

   (c)   otherwise for the training, career development and promotion of disabled persons employed by the company.

9(4)   In this Part—

   (a)   **"employment"** means employment other than employment to work wholly or mainly outside the United Kingdom, and **"employed"** and **"employee"** shall be construed accordingly; and

   (b)   **"disabled person"** means the same as in the Disabled Persons (Employment) Act 1944.

Part IV — Health, Safety and Welfare at Work of Company's Employees

10(1)   In the case of companies of such classes as may be prescribed by regulations made by the Secretary of State, the directors' report shall contain such information as may be so prescribed about the arrangements in force in the financial year for securing the health, safety and welfare at work of employees of the company and its subsidiaries, and for protecting other persons against risks to health or safety arising out of or in connection with the activities at work of those employees.

10(2)   Regulations under this Part may—

   (a)   make different provision in relation to companies of different classes,

   (b)   enable any requirements of the regulations to be dispensed with or modified in particular cases by any specified person or by any person authorised in that behalf by a specified authority,

   (c)   contain such transitional provisions as the Secretary of State thinks necessary or expedient in connection with any provision made by the regulations.

10(3)   The power to make regulations under this paragraph is exercisable by statutory instrument subject to annulment in pursuance of a resolution of either House of Parliament.

10(4)   Any expression used in sub-paragraph (1) above and in Part I of the Health and Safety at Work etc. Act 1974 has the same meaning here as it has in that Part of that Act; section 1(3) of that Act applies for interpreting that sub-paragraph; and in sub-paragraph (2) **"specified"** means specified in regulations made under that sub-paragraph.

Part V — Employee Involvement

11(1) This Part of this Schedule applies to the directors' report where the average number of persons employed by the company in each week during the financial year exceeded 250.

11(2) That average number is the quotient derived by dividing by the number of weeks in the financial year the number derived by ascertaining, in relation to each of those weeks, the number of persons who, under contracts of service, were employed in the week (whether throughout it or not) by the company, and adding up the numbers ascertained.

11(3) The directors' report shall in that case contain a statement describing the action that has been taken during the financial year to introduce, maintain or develop arrangements aimed at—

   (a) providing employees systematically with information on matters of concern to them as employees,

   (b) consulting employees or their representatives on a regular basis so that the views of employees can be taken into account in making decisions which are likely to affect their interests,

   (c) encouraging the involvement of employees in the company's performance through an employee's share scheme or by some other means,

   (d) achieving a common awareness on the part of all employees of the financial and economic factors affecting the performance of the company.

11(4) In sub-paragraph (3) **"employee"** does not include a person employed to work wholly or mainly outside the United Kingdom; and for the purposes of sub-paragraph (2) no regard is to be had to such a person.

Schedule 8 — Exemptions for Small and Medium-sized Companies

[Companies Act 1985, sec. 246;
Companies Act 1989, sec. 1, 13(2) and Sch. 6]

Part I — Small Companies

BALANCE SHEET

1(1) The company may deliver a copy of an abbreviated version of the full balance sheet, showing only those items to which a letter or Roman number is assigned in the balance sheet format adopted under Part I of Schedule 4, but in other respects corresponding to the full balance sheet.

1(2) If a copy of an abbreviated balance sheet is delivered, there shall be disclosed in it or in a note to the company's accounts delivered—

   (a) the aggregate of the amounts required by note (5) of the notes on the balance sheet formats set out in Part I of Schedule 4 to be shown separately for each item included under debtors (amounts falling due after one year), and

(b) the aggregate of the amounts required by note (13) of those notes to be shown separately for each item included under creditors in Format 2 (amounts falling due within one year or after more than one year).

1(3) The provisions of section 233 as to the signing of the copy of the balance sheet delivered to the registrar apply to a copy of an abbreviated balance sheet delivered in accordance with this paragraph.

PROFIT AND LOSS ACCOUNT

✱ 2 A copy of the company's profit and loss account need not be delivered.

DISCLOSURE OF INFORMATION IN NOTES TO ACCOUNTS

3(1) Of the information required by Part III of Schedule 4 (information to be given in notes to accounts if not given in the accounts themselves) only the information required by the following provisions need be given—

paragraph 36 (accounting policies),

paragraph 38 (share capital),

paragraph 39 (particulars of allotments),

paragraph 42 (fixed assets), so far as it relates to those items to which a letter or Roman number is assigned in the balance sheet format adopted,

paragraph 48(1) and (4) (particulars of debts),

paragraph 58(1) (basis of conversion of foreign currency amounts into sterling),

paragraph 58(2) (corresponding amounts for previous financial year), so far as it relates to amounts stated in a note to the company's accounts by virtue of a requirement of Schedule 4 or under any other provision of this Act.

3(2) Of the information required by Schedule 5 to be given in notes to the accounts, the information required by the following provisions need not be given—

paragraph 4 (financial years of subsidiary undertakings),

paragraph 5 (additional information about subsidiary undertakings),

paragraph 6 (shares and debentures of company held by subsidiary undertakings),

paragraph 10 (arrangements attracting merger relief).

3(3) Of the information required by Schedule 6 to be given in notes to the accounts, the information required by Part I (directors' and chairman's emoluments, pensions and compensation for loss of office) need not be given.

DIRECTORS' REPORT

✱ 4 A copy of the directors' report need not be delivered.

Part II — Medium-sized Companies

PROFIT AND LOSS ACCOUNT

5 The company may deliver a profit and loss account in which the following items listed in the profit and loss account formats set out in Part I of Schedule 4 are combined as one item under the heading "gross profit or loss"—

Items 1, 2, 3 and 6 in Format 1;

Items 1 to 5 in Format 2;

Items A.1, B.1 and B.2 in Format 3;

Items A.1, A.2 and B.1 to B.4 in Format 4.

DISCLOSURE OF INFORMATION IN NOTES TO ACCOUNTS

6   The information required by paragraph 55 of Schedule 4 (particulars of turnover) need not be given.

Part III — Supplementary Provisions

STATEMENT THAT ADVANTAGE TAKEN OF EXEMPTIONS

7(1)   Where the directors of a company take advantage of the exemptions conferred by Part I or Part II of this Schedule, the company's balance sheet shall contain—

(a) a statement that advantage is taken of the exemptions conferred by Part I or, as the case may be, Part II of this Schedule, and

(b) a statement of the grounds on which, in the directors' opinion, the company is entitled to those exemptions.

7(2)   The statements shall appear in the balance sheet immediately above the signature required by section 233.

SPECIAL AUDITORS' REPORT

8(1)   If the directors of a company propose to take advantage of the exemptions conferred by Part I or II of this Schedule, it is the auditors' duty to provide them with a report stating whether in their opinion the company is entitled to those exemptions and whether the documents to be proposed to be delivered in accordance with this Schedule are properly prepared.

8(2)   The accounts delivered shall be accompanied by a special report of the auditors stating that in their opinion—

(a) the company is entitled to the exemptions claimed in the directors' statement, and

(b) the accounts to be delivered are properly prepared in accordance with this Schedule.

8(3)   In such a case a copy of the auditors' report under section 235 need not be delivered separately, but the full text of it shall be reproduced in the special report; and if the report under section 235 is qualified there shall be included in the special report any further material necessary to understand the qualification.

8(4)   Section 236 (signature of auditors' report) applies to a special report under this paragraph as it applies to a report under section 235.

DORMANT COMPANIES

9   Paragraphs 7 and 8 above do not apply where the company is exempt by virtue of section 250 (dormant companies) from the obligation to appoint auditors.

REQUIREMENTS IN CONNECTION WITH PUBLICATION OF ACCOUNTS

10(1) Where advantage is taken of the exemptions conferred by Part I or II of this Schedule, section 240 (requirements in connection with publication of accounts) has effect with the following adaptations.

10(2) Accounts delivered in accordance with this Schedule and accounts in the form in which they would be required to be delivered apart from this Schedule are both "statutory accounts" for the purposes of that section.

10(3) References in that section to the auditors' report under section 235 shall be read, in relation to accounts delivered in accordance with this Schedule, as references to the special report under paragraph 8 above.

History

Sch. 8 substituted by CA 1989, s. 1, 13(2) and Sch. 6 as from 1 April 1990 subject to transitional and saving provisions (see S.I. 1990 No. 355 (C. 13), art. 3,Sch. 1 and also art. 6–9); Sch. 8 formerly read as follows:

"**Schedule 8 — Modified Accounts of Companies Qualifying as Small or Medium Sized**

Sections 247, 249, 250, 253, 254

Part I — Modified Individual Accounts

INTRODUCTORY

1 In this Part of this Schedule—

(a) paragraphs 2 to 6 relate to a company's individual accounts modified as for a small company,

(b) paragraphs 7 and 8 relate to a company's individual accounts modified as for a medium-sized company, and

(c) paragraphs 9 to 11 relate to both cases.

ACCOUNTS MODIFIED AS FOR A SMALL COMPANY

2(1) In respect of the relevant financial year, there may be delivered a copy of a modified balance sheet, instead of the full balance sheet.

(2) The modified balance sheet shall be an abbreviated version of the full balance sheet, showing only those items to which a letter or Roman number is assigned in the balance sheet format adopted under Schedule 4, Part I, but in other respects corresponding to the full balance sheet.

(3) The copy of the modified balance sheet shall be signed as required by section 238.

3 A copy of the company's profit and loss account need not be delivered, nor a copy of the directors' report otherwise required by section 241.

4 The information required by Parts V and VI of Schedule 5 need not be given.

5 The information required by Schedule 4 to be given in notes to the accounts need not be given, with the exception of any information required by the following provisions of that Schedule—

    paragraph 36 (accounting policies),
    paragraph 38 (share capital),
    paragraph 39 (particulars of allotments),
    paragraph 48(1) and (4) (particulars of debts),
    paragraph 58(1) (basis of translation of foreign currency amounts into sterling), and
    paragraph 58(2) (corresponding amounts for preceding financial year);

and the reference here to paragraph 58(2) includes that sub-paragraph as applied to any item stated in a note to the

company's accounts, whether by virtue of a requirement of Schedule 4 or under any other provision of this Act.

6 If a modified balance sheet is delivered, there shall be disclosed in it (or in a note to the company's accounts delivered)—

(a) the aggregate of the amounts required by note (5) of the notes on the balance sheet formats set out in Schedule 4 Part I to be shown separately for each item included under debtors (amounts falling due after one year), and

(b) the aggregate of the amounts required by note (13) of those notes to be shown separately for each item included under creditors in Format 2 (amounts falling due within one year or after more than one year).

ACCOUNTS MODIFIED AS FOR A MEDIUM-SIZED COMPANY

7(1) There may be delivered a copy of a modified profit and loss account, instead of the company's full profit and loss account (that is, the profit and loss account prepared as under section 227).

(2) The modified profit and loss account shall, save for one exception, correspond to the full profit and loss account; and that exception is the combination as one item, under the heading 'gross profit or loss', of the following items listed in the profit and loss account formats set out in Schedule 4 Part I—

    Items 1, 2, 3 and 6 in Format 1;
    Items 1 to 5 in Format 2;
    Items A.1, B.1 and B.2 in Format 3; and
    Items A.1, A.2 and B.1 to B.4 in Format 4.

8 The information required by paragraph 55 of Schedule 4 (particulars of turnover) need not be given.

BOTH CASES

9 The company's balance sheet shall contain a statement by the directors that—

(a) they rely on sections 247 to 249 of this Act as entitling them to deliver modified accounts, and

(b) they do so on the ground that the company is entitled to the benefit of those sections as a small or (as the case may be) a medium-sized company;

and the statement shall appear in the balance sheet immediately above the signatures of the directors.

10(1) The accounts delivered shall be accompanied by a special report of the auditors stating that in their opinion—

(a) the directors are entitled to deliver modified accounts in respect of the financial year, as claimed in the directors' statement, and

(b) any accounts comprised in the documents delivered as modified accounts are properly prepared as such in accordance with this Schedule.

(2) A copy of the auditors' report under section 236 need not be delivered; but the full text of it shall be reproduced in the special report under this paragraph.

(3) If the directors propose to rely on sections 247 to 249 as entitling them to deliver modified accounts, it is the auditors' duty to provide them with a report stating whether in their opinion the directors are so entitled, and whether the documents to be delivered as modified accounts are properly prepared in accordance with this Act.

11 Subject as above, where the directors rely on sections 247 to 249 in delivering any documents, and—

(a) the company is entitled to the benefit of those sections on the ground claimed by the directors in their statement under paragraph 9, and

(b) the accounts comprised in the documents delivered as modified accounts are properly prepared in accordance with this Schedule,

then section 241(3) has effect as if any document which by virtue of this Part of this Schedule is included in or omitted from the document delivered as modified accounts were (or, as the case may be, were not) required by this Act to be comprised in the company's accounts in respect of the financial year.

Part II — Modified Group Accounts
(in Consolidated Form)

INTRODUCTORY

12 In this Part of this Schedule—

(a) paragraphs 13 to 17 relate to modified accounts for a small group, and

(b) paragraphs 18 and 19 relate to modified accounts for a medium-sized group.

SMALL GROUPS

13(1) In respect of the relevant financial year, there may be delivered a copy of a modified balance sheet, instead of the full consolidated balance sheet.

(2) The modified balance sheet shall be an abbreviated version of the full consolidated balance sheet, showing only those items to which a letter or Roman numeral is assigned in the balance sheet format adopted under Schedule 4 Part I, but in other respects corresponding to the full consolidated balance sheet.

14 A copy of the profit and loss account need not be delivered, nor a copy of the directors' report otherwise required by section 241.

15 The information required by Schedule 4 to be given in notes to group accounts need not be given, with the exception of any information required by provisions of that Schedule listed in paragraph 5 above.

16 There shall be disclosed in the modified balance sheet, or in a note to the group accounts delivered, aggregate amounts corresponding to those specified in paragraph 6 above.

17 The information required by Parts V and VI of Schedule 5 need not be given.

MEDIUM-SIZED GROUPS

18(1) There may be delivered a copy of a modified profit and loss account, instead of a full consolidated profit and loss account prepared as under section 229.

(2) The modified profit and loss account shall, save for one exception, correspond to the full consolidated profit and loss account; and that exception is the combination as one item, under the heading 'gross profit or loss', of the items listed in the profit and loss account formats set out in Schedule 4 Part I which are specified in paragraph 7(2) above.

19 The information required by paragraph 55 of Schedule 4 (particulars of turnover) need not be given.

Part III — Modified Group Accounts
(Consolidated or Other)

20 If modified group accounts are delivered, the following paragraphs apply.

21 The directors' statement required by paragraph 9 to be contained in the balance sheet shall include a statement that the documents delivered include modified group accounts, in reliance on section 250.

22(1) The auditors' special report under paragraph 10 shall include a statement that in their opinion—

(a) the directors are entitled to deliver modified group accounts, as claimed in their statement in the balance sheet, and

(b) any accounts comprised in the documents delivered as modified group accounts are properly prepared as such in accordance with this Schedule.

(2) A copy of the auditors' report under section 236 need not be delivered; but the full text of it shall be reproduced in the special report under paragraph 10.

(3) If the directors propose to rely on section 250 as entitling them to deliver modified group accounts, it is the auditors' duty to provide them with a report stating whether in their opinion the directors are so entitled, and whether the documents to be delivered as modified group accounts are properly prepared in accordance with this Schedule.

23 Subject as above, where the directors rely on section 250 in delivering any documents, and

(a) the company is entitled to the benefit of that section on the ground claimed by the directors in their statement in the balance sheet, and

(b) the accounts comprised in the documents delivered as modified accounts are properly prepared in accordance with this Schedule,

then section 241(3) has effect as if any document which by virtue of this Part of this Schedule is included in or omitted from the documents delivered as modified group accounts were (or, as the case may be, were not) required by this Act to be comprised in the company's accounts in respect of the financial year.''

[The next page is 30,551]

Schedule 9 — Special Provisions for Banking and Insurance Companies and Groups

Section 258

History
Heading to Sch. 9 substituted by CA 1989, s. 18(3) and Sch. 7, preliminary para. (a) as from 1 April 1990 subject to transitional and saving provisions (see S.I. 1990 No. 355 (C. 13), art. 3, Sch. 1 and also art. 6–9); former heading read "Form and Content of Special Category Accounts".

Also introductory paragraph and its heading formerly following the heading omitted and repealed by CA 1989, s. 18(3), 212, Sch. 7, preliminary para. (b) and Sch. 24 as from 1 April 1990 subject to transitional and saving provisions (see S.I. 1990 No. 355 (C. 13), art. 3, 5(1)(b), (2), Sch. 1 and also art. 6–9); the former paragraph and heading read as follows:

"PRELIMINARY

1 Paragraphs 2 to 13 of this Schedule apply to the balance sheet and 14 to 18 to the profit and loss account, and are subject to the exceptions and modifications provided for by Part II of this Schedule in the case of a holding or subsidiary company and by Part III thereof in the case of companies of the classes there mentioned."

Part I — Form and Content of Accounts

History
Heading for Pt. I substituted by CA 1989, s. 18(3) and Sch. 7, preliminary para. (c)(i) as from 1 April 1990 subject to transitional and saving provisions (see S.I. 1990 No. 355 (C. 13), art. 3, Sch. 1 and also art. 6–9); former heading

read "General Provisions as to Balance Sheet and Profit and Loss Account". Note that former Part headings before para. 19, 27, 31 and 32 also omitted.

BALANCE SHEET

2 The authorised share capital, issued share capital, liabilities and assets shall be summarised, with such particulars as are necessary to disclose the general nature of the assets and liabilities, and there shall be specified—

(a) any part of the issued capital that consists of redeemable shares, the earliest and latest dates on which the company has power to redeem those shares, whether those shares must be redeemed in any event or are liable to be redeemed at the option of the company or of the shareholder and whether any (and, if so, what) premium is payable on redemption;

(b) so far as the information is not given in the profit and loss account, any share capital on which interest has been paid out of capital during the financial year, and the rate at which interest has been so paid;

(c) the amount of the share premium account;

(d) particulars of any redeemed debentures which the company has power to re-issue.

3 There shall be stated under separate headings, so far as they are not written off,—

(a) the preliminary expenses;

(b) any expenses incurred in connection with any issue of share capital or debentures;

(c) any sums paid by way of commission in respect of any shares or debentures;

(d) any sums allowed by way of discount in respect of any debentures; and

(e) the amount of the discount allowed on any issue of shares at a discount.

4(1) The reserves, provisions, liabilities and assets shall be classified under headings appropriate to the company's business:

Provided that—

(a) where the amount of any class is not material, it may be included under the same heading as some other class; and

(b) where any assets of one class are not separable from assets of another class, those assets may be included under the same heading.

4(2) Fixed assets, current assets and assets that are neither fixed nor current shall be separately identified.

4(3) The method or methods used to arrive at the amount of the fixed assets under each heading shall be stated.

5(1) The method of arriving at the amount of any fixed asset shall, subject to the next following sub-paragraph, be to take the difference between—

(a) its cost or, if it stands in the company's books at a valuation, the amount of the valuation; and

(b) the aggregate amount provided or written off since the date of acquisition or valuation, as the case may be, for depreciation or diminution in value;

and for the purposes of this paragraph the net amount at which any assets stood in the company's books on 1st July 1948 (after deduction of the amounts previously provided or written off for depreciation or diminution in value) shall, if the figures relating to the period before that date cannot be obtained without unreasonable expense or delay, be treated as if it were the amount of a valuation of those assets made at that date and, where any of those assets are sold, the said net amount less the amount of the sales shall be treated as if it were the amount of a valuation so made of the remaining assets.

5(2) The foregoing sub-paragraph shall not apply—

(a) to assets for which the figures relating to the period beginning with 1st July 1948 cannot be obtained without unreasonable expense or delay; or

(b) to assets the replacement of which is provided for wholly or partly—

    (i) by making provision for renewals and charging the cost of replacement against the provision so made; or

    (ii) by charging the cost of replacement direct to revenue; or

(c) to any listed investments or to any unlisted investments of which the value as estimated by the directors is shown either as the amount of the investments or by way of note; or

(d) to goodwill, patents or trade marks.

5(3) For the assets under each heading whose amount is arrived at in accordance with sub-paragraph (1) of this paragraph, there shall be shown—

(a) the aggregate of the amounts referred to in paragraph (a) of that sub-paragraph; and

(b) the aggregate of the amounts referred to in paragraph (b) thereof.

5(4) As respects the assets under each heading whose amount is not arrived at in accordance with the said sub-paragraph (1) because their replacement is provided for as mentioned in sub-paragraph (2)(b) of this paragraph, there shall be stated—

(a) the means by which their replacement is provided for; and

     CCH Editions Limited

BCL BCL6$$$76A

(b) the aggregate amount of the provision (if any) made for renewals and not used.

6 In the case of unlisted investments consisting in equity share capital of other bodies corporate (other than any whose values as estimated by the directors are separately shown, either individually or collectively or as to some individually and as to the rest collectively, and are so shown either as the amount thereof, or by way of note), the matters referred to in the following heads shall, if not otherwise shown, be stated by way of note or in a statement or report annexed:—

(a) the aggregate amount of the company's income for the financial year that is ascribable to the investments;

(b) the amount of the company's share before taxation, and the amount of that share after taxation, of the net aggregate amount of the profits of the bodies in which the investments are held, being profits for the several periods to which accounts sent by them during the financial year to the company related, after deducting those bodies' losses for those periods (or vice versa);

(c) the amount of the company's share of the net aggregate amount of the undistributed profits accumulated by the bodies in which the investments are held since the time when the investments were acquired after deducting the losses accumulated by them since that time (or vice versa);

(d) the manner in which any losses incurred by the said bodies have been dealt with in the company's accounts.

7 The aggregate amounts respectively of reserves and provisions (other than provisions for depreciation, renewals or diminution in value of assets) shall be stated under separate headings;

Provided that—

(a) this paragraph shall not require a separate statement of either of the said amounts which is not material; and

(b) the Secretary of State may direct that a separate statement shall not be required of the amount of provisions where he is satisfied that that is not required in the public interest and would prejudice the company, but subject to the condition that any heading stating an amount arrived at after taking into account a provision (other than as aforesaid) shall be so framed or marked as to indicate that fact.

8(1) There shall also be shown (unless it is shown in the profit and loss account or a statement or report annexed thereto, or the amount involved is not material)—

(a) where the amount of the reserves or of the provisions (other than provisions for depreciation, renewals or diminution in value of assets) shows an increase as compared with the amount at the end of the immediately preceding financial year, the source from which the amount of the increase has been derived; and

(b) where—

(i) the amount of the reserves shows a decrease as compared with the amount at the end of the immediately preceding financial year; or

(ii) the amount at the end of the immediately preceding financial year of the provisions (other than provisions for depreciation, renewals or diminution in value of assets) exceeded the aggregate of the sums since applied and amounts still retained for the purposes thereof;

the application of the amounts derived from the difference.

8(2)   Where the heading showing the reserves or any of the provisions aforesaid is divided into sub-headings, this paragraph shall apply to each of the separate amounts shown in the sub-headings instead of applying to the aggregate amount thereof.

9   If an amount is set aside for the purpose of its being used to prevent undue fluctuations in charges for taxation, it shall be stated.

10(1)   There shall be shown under separate headings—

(a) the aggregate amounts respectively of the company's listed investments and unlisted investments;

(b) if the amount of the goodwill and of any patents and trade marks or part of that amount is shown as a separate item in or is otherwise ascertainable from the books of the company, or from any contract for the sale or purchase of any property to be acquired by the company, or from any documents in the possession of the company relating to the stamp duty payable in respect of any such contract or the conveyance of any such property, the said amount so shown or ascertained as far as not written off or, as the case may be, the said amount so far as it is so shown or ascertainable and as so shown or ascertained, as the case may be;

(c) the aggregate amount of any outstanding loans made under the authority of section 153(4)(b), (bb) or (c) or 155 of this Act;

(d) the aggregate amount of bank loans and overdrafts and the aggregate amount of loans made to the company which—

(i) are repayable otherwise than by instalments and fall due for repayment after the expiration of the period of five years beginning with the day next following the expiration of the financial year; or

(ii) are repayable by instalments any of which fall due for payment after the expiration of that period;

not being, in either case, bank loans or overdrafts;

(e) the aggregate amount which is recommended for distribution by way of dividend.

History
In para. 10(1)(c) ", (bb)" inserted by CA 1989, s. 18(3) and Sch. 7, Pt. I, para. 1 as from 1 April 1990 subject   to transitional and saving provisions (see S.I. 1990 No. 355 (C. 13), art. 3, Sch. 1 and also art. 6–9).

10(2)   Nothing in head (b) of the foregoing sub-paragraph shall be taken as requiring the amount of the goodwill, patents and trade marks to be stated otherwise than as a single item.

10(3)   The heading showing the amount of the listed investments shall be subdivided, where necessary, to distinguish the investments as respects which there has, and those as respects which there has not, been granted a listing on a recognised investment exchange other than an overseas investment exchange within the meaning of the Financial Services Act 1986.

History
In para. 10(3) the words from "recognised investment exchange" to the end substituted for the former words "recognised stock exchange" by Financial Services Act 1986, s. 212(2) and Sch. 16, para. 24 as from 29 April 1988 (see S.I. 1988 No. 740 (C. 22)).

10(4) In relation to each loan falling within head (d) of sub-paragraph (1) of this paragraph (other than a bank loan or overdraft), there shall be stated by way of note (if not otherwise stated) the terms on which it is repayable and the rate at which interest is payable thereon:

Provided that if the number of loans is such that, in the opinion of the directors, compliance with the foregoing requirement would result in a statement of excessive length, it shall be sufficient to give a general indication of the terms on which the loans are repayable and the rates at which interest is payable thereon.

11 Where any liability of the company is secured otherwise than by operation of law on any assets of the company, the fact that that liability is so secured shall be stated, but it shall not be necessary to specify the assets on which the liability is secured.

12 Where any of the company's debentures are held by a nominee of or trustee for the company, the nominal amount of the debentures and the amount at which they are stated in the books of the company shall be stated.

13(1) The matters referred to in the following sub-paragraphs shall be stated by way of note, or in a statement or report annexed, if not otherwise shown.

13(2) The number, description and amount of any shares in the company which any person has an option to subscribe for, together with the following particulars of the option, that is to say—

    (a) the period during which it is exercisable;

    (b) the price to be paid for shares subscribed for under it.

13(3) (Omitted and repealed by Companies Act 1989, sec. 18(3), 212 and Sch. 7, Pt. I, para. 2 and Sch. 24 as from 1 April 1990.)

History
In regard to the date of the above omission and repeal see S.I. 1990 No. 355 (C. 13), art. 3, 5(1)(b), (2), Sch. 1 and art. 6–9) for transitional and saving provisions; para. 13(3) formerly read as follows:

"Where shares in a public company (other than an old public company within the meaning of section 1 of the Consequential Provisions Act) are purchased or are acquired by the company by forfeiture or surrender in lieu of forfeiture, or as expressly permitted by section 143(3) of this Act, or are acquired by another person in circumstances where paragraph (c) or (d) of section 146(1) applies or are made subject to a lien or charge taken (whether expressly or otherwise) by the company and permitted by section 150(2) or (4), or section 6(3) of the Consequential Provisions Act—

    (a) the number and nominal value of the shares so purchased, the aggregate amount of the consideration paid by the company for such shares and the reasons for their purchase;

    (b) the number and nominal value of the shares so acquired by the company, acquired by another person in such circumstances and so charged respectively during the financial year;

    (c) the maximum number and nominal value of shares which, having been so acquired by the company, acquired by another person in such circumstances or so charged (whether or not during the financial year) are held at any time by the company or that other person during that year;

    (d) the number and nominal value of shares so acquired by the company, acquired by another person in such circumstances or so charged (whether or not during that year) which are disposed of by the company or that other person or cancelled by the company during that year;

    (e) where the number and nominal value of the shares of any particular description are stated in pursuance of any of the preceding paragraphs, the percentage of the called-up share capital which shares of that description represent;

    (f) where any of the shares have been so charged, the amount of the charge in each case;

    (g) where any of the shares have been disposed of by the company or the person who acquired them in such circumstances for money or money's worth, the amount or value of the consideration in each case."

13(4)   Any distribution made by an investment company within the meaning of Part VIII of this Act which reduces the amount of its net assets to less than the aggregate of its called-up share capital and undistributable reserves.

For purposes of this sub-paragraph, a company's net assets are the aggregate of its assets less the aggregate of its liabilities; and **"undistributable reserves"** has the meaning given by section 264(3).

13(5)   The amount of any arrears of fixed cumulative dividends on the company's shares and the period for which the dividends or, if there is more than one class, each class of them are in arrear.

13(6)   Particulars of any charge on the assets of the company to secure the liabilities of any other person, including, where practicable, the amount secured.

13(7)   The general nature of any other contingent liabilities not provided for and, where practicable, the aggregate amount or estimated amount of those liabilities, if it is material.

13(8)   Where practicable the aggregate amount or estimated amount, if it is material, of contracts for capital expenditure, so far as not provided for and, where practicable, the aggregate amount or estimated amount, if it is material, of capital expenditure authorised by the directors which has not been contracted for.

13(9)   In the case of fixed assets under any heading whose amount is required to be arrived at in accordance with paragraph 5(1) of this Schedule (other than unlisted investments) and is so arrived at by reference to a valuation, the years (so far as they are known to the directors) in which the assets were severally valued and the several values, and, in the case of assets that have been valued during the financial year, the names of the persons who valued them or particulars of their qualifications for doing so and (whichever is stated) the bases of valuation used by them.

13(10)   If there are included amongst fixed assets under any heading (other than investments) assets that have been acquired during the financial year, the aggregate amount of the assets acquired as determined for the purpose of making up the balance sheet, and if during that year any fixed assets included under a heading in the balance sheet made up with respect to the immediately preceding financial year (other than investments) have been disposed of or destroyed, the aggregate amount thereof as determined for the purpose of making up that balance sheet.

13(11)   Of the amount of fixed assets consisting of land, how much is ascribable to land of freehold tenure and how much to land of leasehold tenure, and, of the latter, how much is ascribable to land held on long lease and how much to land held on short lease.

13(12)   If in the opinion of the directors any of the current assets have not a value, on realisation in the ordinary course of the company's business, at least equal to the amount at which they are stated, the fact that the directors are of that opinion.

13(13)   The aggregate market value of the company's listed investments where it differs from the amount of the investments as stated and the stock exchange value of any investments of which the market value is shown (whether separately or not) and is taken as being higher than their stock exchange value.

13(14)   If a sum set aside for the purpose of its being used to prevent undue fluctuations in charges for taxation has been used during the financial year for another purpose, the amount thereof and the fact that it has been so used.

13(15)   If the amount carried forward for stock in trade or work in progress is material for the appreciation by its members of the company's state of affairs or of its profit or loss for the financial year, the manner in which that amount has been computed.

13(16)   The basis on which foreign currencies have been converted into sterling, where the amount of the assets or liabilities affected is material.

13(17)   The basis on which the amount, if any, set aside for United Kingdom corporation tax is computed.

13(18)   (Repealed by Companies Act 1989, sec. 212 and Sch. 24 as from 1 April 1990.)

History
In regard to the date of the above repeal see S.I. 1990 No. 355 (C. 13), art. 5(1)(b), (2) and art. 6–9 for transitional and saving provisions; para. 13(8) formerly read as follows:

"The corresponding amounts at the end of the immediately the balance sheet other than any item the amount for which is shown—

    (a) in pursuance of sub-paragraph (10) of this paragraph, or

    (b) as an amount the source or application of which is required by paragraph 8 to be shown."

PROFIT AND LOSS ACCOUNT

14(1)   There shall be shown—

    (a) the amount charged to revenue by way of provision for depreciation, renewals or diminution in value of fixed assets;

    (b) the amount of the interest on loans of the following kinds made to the company (whether on the security of debentures or not), namely, bank loans, overdrafts and loans which, not being bank loans or overdrafts,—

        (i) are repayable otherwise than by instalments and fall due for repayment before the expiration of the period of five years beginning with the day next following the expiration of the financial year; or

        (ii) are repayable by instalments the last of which falls due for payment before the expiration of that period;

      and the amount of the interest on loans of other kinds so made (whether on the security of debentures or not);

    (c) the amount of the charge to revenue for United Kingdom corporation tax and, if that amount would have been greater but for relief from double taxation, the amount which it would have been but for such relief, the amount of the charge for United Kingdom income tax, and the amount of the charge for taxation imposed outside the United Kingdom of profits, income and (so far as charged to revenue) capital gains;

    (d) the amounts respectively set aside for redemption of share capital and for redemption of loans;

    (e) the amount, if material, set aside or proposed to be set aside to, or withdrawn from, reserves;

    (f) subject to sub-paragraph (2) of this paragraph, the amount, if material, set aside to provisions other than provisions for depreciation, renewals, or diminution in value of assets or, as the case may be, the amount, if material, withdrawn from such provisions and not applied for the purposes thereof;

    (g) the amounts respectively of income from listed investments and income from unlisted investments;

    (h) if a substantial part of the company's revenue for the financial year consists in rents from land, the amount thereof (after deduction of ground-rents, rates and other outgoings);

    (j) the amount, if material, charged to revenue in respect of sums payable in respect of the hire of plant and machinery;

    (k) the aggregate amount of the dividends paid and proposed.

14(2) The Secretary of State may direct that a company shall not be obliged to show an amount set aside to provisions in accordance with sub-paragraph (1)(f) of this paragraph, if he is satisfied that that is not required in the public interest and would prejudice the company, but subject to the condition that any heading stating an amount arrived at after taking into account the amount set aside as aforesaid shall be so framed or marked as to indicate that fact.

14(3) If, in the case of any assets in whose case an amount is charged to revenue by way of provision for depreciation or diminution in value, an amount is also so charged by way of provision for renewal thereof, the last-mentioned amount shall be shown separately.

14(4) If the amount charged to revenue by way of provision for depreciation or diminution in value of any fixed assets (other than investments) has been determined otherwise than by reference to the amount of those assets as determined for the purpose of making up the balance sheet, that fact shall be stated.

15 The amount of any charge arising in consequence of the occurrence of an event in a preceding financial year and of any credit so arising shall, if not included in a heading relating to other matters, be stated under a separate heading.

16 (Repealed by Companies Act 1989. sec. 212 and Sch. 24 as from 1 April 1990.)

History
In regard to the date of the above repeal see S.I. 1990 No. 355 (C. 13), art. 5(1)(b), (2) and art. 6–9 for transitional and saving provisions; para. 16 formerly read as follows:

"The amount of the remuneration of the auditors shall be purposes of this paragraph, any sums paid by the company in respect of the auditors' expenses shall be deemed to be included in the expression 'remuneration'."

17(1) The following matters shall be stated by way of note, if not otherwise shown.

17(2) The turnover for the financial year, except in so far as it is attributable to the business of banking or discounting or to business of such other class as may be prescribed for the purposes of this sub-paragraph.

17(3) If some or all of the turnover is omitted by reason of its being attributable as aforesaid, the fact that it is so omitted.

17(4) The method by which turnover stated is arrived at.

17(5) A company shall not be subject to the requirements of this paragraph if it is neither a parent company nor a subsidiary undertaking and the turnover which, apart from this sub-paragraph, would be required to be stated does not exceed £1 million.

History
In para. 17(5) the words "neither a parent company nor a subsidiary undertaking" substituted for the former words "neither a holding company nor a subsidiary of another body corporate" by CA 1989, s. 18(3) and Sch. 7, Pt. I, para. 3 as from 1 April 1990 (see S.I. 1990 No. 355 (C. 13), art. 3, Sch. 1 and also art. 6–9).

18(1)   The following matters shall be stated by way of note, if not otherwise shown.

18(2)   If depreciation or replacement of fixed assets is provided for by some method other than a depreciation charge or provision for renewals, or is not provided for, the method by which it is provided for or the fact that it is not provided for, as the case may be.

18(3)   The basis on which the charge for United Kingdom corporation tax and United Kingdom income tax is computed.

18(4)   Any special circumstances which affect liability in respect of taxation of profits, income or capital gains for the financial year or liability in respect of taxation of profits, income or capital gains for succeeding financial years.

18(5)   (Repealed by Companies Act 1989, sec. 212 and Sch. 24 as from 1 April 1990.)

History
In regard to the date of the above repeal see S.I. 1990 No. 355 (C. 13), art. 5(1)(b), (2) and art. 6–9 for transitional and saving provisions; para. 18(5) formerly read as follows: "The corresponding amounts for the immediately preceding financial year for all items shown in the profit and loss account."

18(6)   Any material respects in which items shown in the profit and loss account are affected—

> (a) by transactions of a sort not usually undertaken by the company or otherwise by circumstances of an exceptional or non-recurrent nature; or

> (b) by any change in the basis of accounting.

SUPPLEMENTARY PROVISIONS

18A(1)   Accounting policies shall be applied consistently within the same accounts and from one financial year to the next.

18A(2)   If it appears to the directors of a company that there are special reasons for departing from the principle stated in sub-paragraph (1) in preparing the company's accounts in respect of any financial year, they may do so; but particulars of the departure, the reasons for it and its effect shall be given in a note to the accounts.

18B   It shall be stated whether the accounts have been prepared in accordance with applicable accounting standards, and particulars of any material departure from those standards and the reasons for it shall be given.

18C(1)   In respect of every item shown in the balance sheet or profit and loss account, or stated in a note to the accounts, there shall be shown or stated the corresponding amount for the financial year immediately preceding that to which the accounts relate, subject to sub-paragraph (3).

18C(2)   Where the corresponding amount is not comparable, it shall be adjusted and particulars of the adjustment and the reasons for it shall be given in a note to the accounts.

18C(3)   Sub-paragraph (1) does not apply in relation to an amount shown—

(a) as an amount the source or application of which is required by paragraph 8 above (reserves and provisions),

(b) in pursuance of paragraph 13(10) above (acquisitions and disposals of fixed assets),

(c) by virtue of paragraph 13 of Schedule 4A (details of accounting treatment of acquisitions),

(d) by virtue of paragraph 2, 8(3), 16, 21(1)(d), 22(4) or (5), 24(3) or (4) or 27(3) or (4) of Schedule 5 (shareholdings in other undertakings), or

(e) by virtue of Part II or III of Schedule 6 (loans and other dealings in favour of directors and others).

History
Para. 18A–18C inserted by CA 1989, s. 18(3) and Sch. 7, Pt. I, para. 4 as from 1 April 1990 subject to transitional and saving provisions (see S.I. 1990 No. 355 (C. 13), art. 3, Sch. 1 and also art. 6–9).

PROVISIONS WHERE COMPANY IS PARENT COMPANY OR SUBSIDIARY UNDERTAKING

History
Former Part heading before para. 19 omitted by CA 1989, s. 18(3) and Sch. 7, preliminary para. c(ii) and new heading inserted by CA 1989, s. 18(3) and Sch. 7, Pt. I, para. 5(1) as from 1 April 1990 subject to transitional and saving provisions (see S.I. 1990 No. 355 (C. 13), art. 3, Sch. 1 and also art. 6–9); former heading read "Part II — Special Provisions where the Company is a Holding or Subsidiary Company". It seems that the heading (appearing below in square brackets) was never actually omitted.

[MODIFICATIONS OF AND ADDITIONS TO REQUIREMENTS AS TO COMPANY'S OWN ACCOUNTS]

19(1)   This paragraph applies where the company is a parent company.

History
In para. 19(1) the words "is a parent company" substituted for the former words "is a holding company, whether or not it is itself a subsidiary of another body corporate" by CA 1989, s. 18(3) and Sch. 7, Pt. I, para. 5(1), (2) as from 1 April 1990 subject to transitional and saving provisions (see S.I. 1990 No. 355 (C. 13), art. 3, Sch. 1 and also art. 6–9).

19(2)   The aggregate amount of assets consisting of shares in, or amounts owing (whether on account of a loan or otherwise) from, the company's subsidiary undertakings, distinguishing shares from indebtedness, shall be set out in the balance sheet separately from all the other assets of the company, and the aggregate amount of indebtedness (whether on account of a loan or otherwise) to the company's subsidiary undertakings shall be so set out separately from all its other liabilities and—

(a) the references in paragraphs 5, 6, 10, 13 and 14 of this Schedule to the company's investments (except those in paragraphs 13(10) and 14(4)) shall not include investments in its subsidiary undertakings required by this paragraph to be separately set out; and

(b) paragraph 5, sub-paragraph (1)(a) of paragraph 14, and sub-paragraph (2) of paragraph 18 of this Schedule shall not apply in relation to fixed assets consisting of interests in the company's subsidiary undertakings.

History
In para. 19(2) the words "subsidiary undertakings" (appearing four times) substituted for the former words "subsidiaries" and (in para. 19(2)(a)) the words "paragraphs 5, 6, 10, 13 and 14" substituted for the former words "Part I" by CA 1989, s. 18(3) and Sch. 7, Pt. I, para. 5(1), (3) as from 1 April 1990 subject to transitional and saving provisions (see S.I. 1990 No. 355 (C. 13), art. 3, Sch. 1 and also art. 6–9).

19(3)–(7) (Omitted and repealed by Companies Act 1989, sec. 18(3), 212, Sch. 7, Pt. I, para. 5(1), (4) and Sch. 24 as from 1 April 1990.)

History

In regard to the date of the above omission and repeal see S.I. 1990 No. 355 (C. 13), art. 3, 5(1)(b), (2), Sch. 1. See art. 6–9 for transitional and saving provisions; para. 19(3–(7) formerly read as follows:

"**19(3)** There shall be shown by way of note on the balance sheet or in a statement or report annexed thereto the number, description and amount of the shares in and debentures of the company held by its subsidiaries or their nominees, but excluding any of those shares or debentures in the case of which the subsidiary is concerned as personal representative or in the case of which it is concerned as trustee and neither the company nor any subsidiary thereof is beneficially interested under the trust, otherwise than by way of security only for the purposes of a transaction entered into by it in the ordinary course of a business which includes the lending of money.

Schedule 2 has effect for the interpretation of the reference in this sub-paragraph to a beneficial interest under a trust.

(4) Where group accounts are not submitted, there shall be annexed to the balance sheet a statement showing—

(a) the reasons why subsidiaries are not dealt with in group accounts;

(b) the net aggregate amount, so far as it concerns members of the holding company and is not dealt with in the company's accounts, of the subsidiaries' profits after deducting the subsidiaries' losses (or vice versa)—

(i) for the respective financial years of the subsidiaries ending with or during the financial year of the company; and

(ii) for their previous financial years since they respectively became the holding company's subsidiary;

(c) the net aggregate amount of the subsidiaries' profits after deducting the subsidiaries' losses (or vice versa)—

(i) for the respective financial years of the subsidiaries ending with or during the financial year of the company; and

(ii) for their other financial years since they respectively became the holding company's subsidiary;

so far as those profits are dealt with, or provision is made for those losses, in the company's accounts;

(d) any qualifications contained in the report of the auditors of the subsidiaries on their accounts for their respective financial years ending as aforesaid, and any note or saving contained in those accounts to call attention to a matter which, apart from the note or saving, would properly have been referred to in such a qualification, in so far as the matter which is the subject of the qualification or note is not covered by the company's own accounts and is material from the point of view of its members;

or, in so far as the information required by this sub-paragraph is not obtainable, a statement that it is not obtainable:

Provided that the Secretary of State may, on the application or with the consent of the company's directors, direct that in relation to any subsidiary this sub-paragraph shall not apply or shall apply only to such extent as may be provided by the direction.

(5) Paragraphs (b) and (c) of the last foregoing sub-paragraph shall apply only to profits and losses of a subsidiary which may properly be treated in the holding company's accounts as revenue profits or losses, and the profits or losses attributable to any shares in a subsidiary for the time being held by the holding company or any other of its subsidiaries shall not (for the purposes of those paragraphs) be treated as aforesaid so far as they are profits or losses for the period before the date on or as from which the shares were acquired by the company or any of its subsidiaries, except that they may in a proper case be so treated where—

(a) the company is itself the subsidiary of another body corporate; and

(b) the shares were acquired from that body corporate or a subsidiary of it;

and for the purpose of determining whether any profits or losses are to be treated as profits or losses for the said period the profit or loss for any financial year of the subsidiary may, if it is not practicable to apportion it with reasonable accuracy by reference to the facts, be treated as accruing from day to day during that year and be apportioned accordingly.

The amendment of the previous corresponding provision by section 40(3) of the Companies Act 1981 (substituting '(for the purposes of those paragraphs)' for '(for that or any other purpose)') is without prejudice to any other restriction with respect to the manner in which a holding company may treat pre-acquisition profits or losses of a subsidiary in its accounts.

(6) Paragraphs (b) and (c) of sub-paragraph (4) above shall not apply where the company is a wholly-owned subsidiary of another body corporate incorporated in Great Britain if there is annexed to the balance sheet a statement that in the opinion of the directors of the company the aggregate value of the assets of the company consisting of shares in, or amounts owing (whether on account of a loan or otherwise) from, the company's subsidiaries is not less than the aggregate of the amounts at which those assets are stated or included in the balance sheet.

(7) Where group accounts are not submitted, there shall be annexed to the balance sheet a statement showing, in relation to the subsidiaries (if any) whose financial years did not end with that of the company—

(a) the reasons why the company's directors consider that the subsidiaries' financial years should not end with that of the company; and

(b) the dates on which the subsidiaries' financial years ending last before that of the company respectively ended or the earliest and latest of those dates."

20(1) This paragraph applies where the company is a subsidiary undertaking.

20(2) The balance sheet of the company shall show —

(a) the aggregate amount of its indebtedness to undertakings of which it is a subsidiary undertaking or which are fellow subsidiary undertakings, and

(b) the aggregate amount of the indebtedness of all such undertakings, to it, distinguishing in each case between indebtedness in respect of debentures and otherwise.

20(3)   The balance sheet shall also show the aggregate amount of assets consisting of shares in fellow subsidiary undertakings.

History

Para. 20 substituted by CA 1989, s. 18(3) and Sch. 7, Pt. I, para. 6 as from 1 April 1990 subject to transitional and saving provisions (see S.I. 1990 No. 355 (C. 13), art. 3, Sch. 1 and also art. 6–9); para. 20 formerly read as follows:

"**20(1)** The balance sheet of a company which is a subsidiary of another body corporate, whether or not it is itself a holding company, shall show the aggregate amount of its indebtedness to all bodies corporate of which it is a subsidiary or a fellow subsidiary and the aggregate amount of indebtedness of all such bodies corporate to it, distinguishing in each case between indebtedness in respect of debentures and otherwise, and the aggregate amount of assets consisting of shares in fellow subsidiaries.

(2) For the purposes of this paragraph a company shall be deemed to be a fellow subsidiary of another body corporate if both are subsidiaries of the same body corporate but neither is the other's."

CONSOLIDATED ACCOUNTS OF HOLDING COMPANY AND SUBSIDIARIES

21–26   (Omitted and repealed by Companies Act 1989, sec. 18(3), 212, Sch. 7, Pt. I, para. 7 and Sch. 24 as from 1 April 1990.)

History

In regard to the date of the above repeal see S.I. 1990 No. 355 (C. 13), art. 3, 5(1)(b), (2), Sch. 1 and art. 6–9 for transitional and saving provisions; para. 21–26 formerly read as follows:

"**21** Subject to the following paragraphs of this Part of this Schedule the consolidated balance sheet and profit and loss account shall combine the information contained in the separate balance sheets and profit and loss accounts of the holding company and of the subsidiaries dealt with by the consolidated accounts, but with such adjustments (if any) as the directors of the holding company think necessary.

22 Subject as aforesaid and to Part III of this Schedule, the consolidated accounts shall, in giving the said information, comply so far as practicable, with the requirements of this Act as if they were the accounts of an actual company.

23 The following provisions of this Act, namely—

   (a)   section 231 as applying Schedule 5, but only Parts II, V and VI of that Schedule, and

   (b)   sections 232 to 234 and Schedule 6, so far as relating to accounts other than group accounts,

do not by virtue of the two last foregoing paragraphs apply for the purpose of the consolidated accounts.

24 Paragraph 22 above is without prejudice to any requirement of this Act which applies (otherwise than by virtue of paragraph 21 or 22) to group accounts.

25 In relation to any subsidiaries of the holding company not dealt with by the consolidated accounts—

   (a)   sub-paragraphs (2) and (3) of paragraph 19 of this Schedule shall apply for the purpose of those accounts as if those accounts were the accounts of an actual company of which they were subsidiaries; and

   (b)   there shall be annexed the like statement as is required by sub-paragraph (4) of that paragraph where there are no group accounts, but as if references therein to the holding company's accounts were references to the consolidated accounts.

26 In relation to any subsidiary (whether or not dealt with by the consolidated accounts), whose financial year did not end with that of the company, there shall be annexed the like statement as is required by sub-paragraph (7) of paragraph 19 of this Schedule where there are no group accounts."

EXCEPTIONS FOR CERTAIN COMPANIES

History

Former Part heading before para. 27 omitted by CA 1989, s. 18(3) and Sch. 7, preliminary para. c(ii) and new heading inserted by CA 1989, s. 18(3) and Sch. 7, Pt. I, para. 8(1) as from 1 April 1990 subject to transitional and saving provisions (see S.I. 1990 No. 355 (C. 13), art. 3, Sch. 1 and also art. 6–9); former heading read "Part III — Exceptions for Certain Special Category Companies".

27(1)   The following applies to a banking company which satisfies the Secretary of State that it ought to have the benefit of this paragraph.

27(2)   The company shall not be subject to the requirements of paragraphs 2 to 18 of this Schedule other than—

   (a)   as respects its balance sheet, those of paragraphs 2 and 3, paragraph 4 (so far as it relates to assets), paragraph 10 (except sub-paragraphs (1)(d)and (4)), paragraphs 11 and 12 and paragraph 13 (except sub-paragraphs (9), (10), (11), (13) and (14)); and

(b) as respects its profit and loss account, those of sub-paragraph (1)(h) and (k) of paragraph 14, and paragraph 15.

History

In para. 27(2) the words "paragraphs 2 to 18 of this Schedule" substituted for the former words "Part I of this Schedule" and in para. 27(2)(b) the words "and paragraph 15" substituted for the former words "paragraphs 15 and 16 and sub-paragraphs (1) and (15) of paragraph 18" by CA 1989, s. 18(3) and Sch. 7, Pt. I, para. 8(1), (2) as from 1 April 1990 subject to transitional and saving provisions (see S.I. 1990 No. 355 (C. 13), art. 3, Sch. 1 and also art. 6–9.)

27(3) But, where in the company's balance sheet reserves or provisions (other than provisions for depreciation, renewals or diminution in value of assets) are not stated separately, any heading stating an amount arrived at after taking into account a reserve or such a provision shall be so framed or marked as to indicate that fact, and its profit and loss account shall indicate by appropriate words the manner in which the amount stated for the company's profit or loss has been arrived at.

27(4) The company's accounts shall not be deemed, by reason only of the fact that they do not comply with any requirements from which the company is exempt by virtue of this paragraph, not to give the true and fair view required by this Act.

History

In para. 27(4) the words "of the said Part I" formerly appearing after the words "any requirements" omitted and repealed by CA 1989, s. 18(3), 212 and Sch. 7, Pt. I, para. 8(1), (3) and Sch. 24 as from 1 April 1990 subject to transitional and saving provisions (see S.I. 1990 No. 355 (C. 13), art. 3, 5(1)(b), (2), Sch. 1 and also art. 6–9).

28(1) An insurance company to which Part II of the Insurance Companies Act 1982 applies shall not be subject to the following requirements of paragraphs 2 to 18 of this Schedule, that is to say—

(a) as respects its balance sheet, those of paragraphs 4 to 8 (both inclusive), sub-paragraphs (1)(a) and (3) of paragraph 10 and sub-paragraphs (6), (7) and (9) to (13) (both inclusive) of paragraph 13;

(b) as respects its profit and loss account, those of paragraph 14 (except sub-paragraph (1)(b), (c), (d) and (k)) and paragraph 18(2);

but, where in its balance sheet reserves or provisions (other than provisions for depreciation, renewals or diminution in value of assets) are not stated separately, any heading stating an amount arrived at after taking into account a reserve or such a provision shall be so framed or marked as to indicate that fact, and its profit and loss account shall indicate by appropriate words the manner in which the amount stated for the company's profit or loss has been arrived at:

Provided that the Secretary of State may direct that any such insurance company whose business includes to a substantial extent business other than insurance business shall comply with all the requirements of the said paragraphs 2 to 18 or such of them as may be specified in the direction and shall comply therewith as respects either the whole of its business or such part thereof as may be so specified.

History

In para. 28(1) the words "paragraphs 2 to 18" (appearing twice) substituted for the former words "Part I" by CA 1989, s. 18(3) and Sch. 7, Pt. I, para. 9 as from 1 April 1990 subject to transitional and saving provisions (see S.I. 1990 No. 355 (C. 13), art. 3, Sch. 1 and also art. 6–9).

28(2) The accounts of a company shall not be deemed, by reason only of the fact that they do not comply with any requirement of paragraphs 2 to 18 of this Schedule from which the company is exempt by virtue of this paragraph, not to give the true and fair view required by this Act.

History

In para. 28(2) the words "paragraphs 2 to 18" substituted for the former words "Part I" by CA 1989, s. 18(3) and Sch. 7, Pt. I, para. 9 as from 1 April 1990 subject to transitional and saving provisions (see S.I. 1990 No. 355 (C. 13), art. 3, Sch. 1 and also art. 6–9) — the new reference must be to para. 2–18 of Part I. There appears to be a contradictory repeal from the same date by CA 1989, s. 212 and Sch. 24 of the words "of Part I of this Schedule" (see S.I. 1990 No. 355 (C. 13), art. 5(1)(b), (2)).

28A   Where a company is entitled to, and has availed itself of, any of the provisons of paragraph 27 or 28 of this Schedule, section 235(2) only requires the auditors to state whether in their opinion the accounts have been properly prepared in accordance with this Act.

History

Para. 28A inserted by CA 1989, s. 18(3) and Sch. 7, Pt. I, para. 10 as from 1 April 1990 subject to transitional and saving provisions (see S.I. 1990 No. 355 (C. 13), art. 3, Sch. 1 and also art. 6–9).

29–31   (Omitted and repealed by Companies Act 1989, sec. 18(3), 212, Sch. 7, Pt. I, para. 11 and Sch. 24 as from 1 April 1990.)

History

In regard to the date of the above omission and repeal see S.I. 1990 No. 355 (C. 13), art. 3, 5, Sch. 1 and art. 6–9 for transitional and saving provisions; also the Part heading before para. 31 omitted by CA 1989, s. 18(3) and Sch. 7, preliminary para. (c)(ii) as from the same date and subject to the same provisions; para. 29–31 (including the Part heading) formerly read as follows:

"**29(1)**   A shipping company shall not be subject to the following requirements of Part I of this Schedule, that is to say—

(a)   as respects its balance sheet, those of paragraph 4 (except so far as it relates to assets), paragraphs 5, 7 and 8 and sub-paragraphs (9) and (10) of paragraph 13;

(b)   as respects its profit and loss account, those of sub-paragraph (1)(a), (e) and (f) and sub-paragraphs (3) and (4) of paragraph 14 and paragraph 17.

(2)   The accounts of a company shall not be deemed, by reason only of the fact that they do not comply with any requirements of Part I of this Schedule from which the company is exempt by virtue of this paragraph, not to give the true and fair view required by this Act.

30   Where a company entitled to the benefit of any provision contained in this Part of this Schedule is a holding company, the reference in Part II of this Schedule to consolidated accounts complying with the requirements of this Act shall, in relation to consolidated accounts of that company, be construed as referring to those requirements in so far only—

(a)   as they apply to the individual accounts of that company, and

(b)   as they apply (otherwise than by virtue of paragraphs 21 and 22) to the group accounts prepared by that company.

Part IV — Special Provisions Where the Company Has Entered into Arrangements Subject to Merger Relief

31(1)   Where during the financial year the company has allotted shares in consideration for the issue, transfer or cancellation of shares in another body corporate ('the other company') in circumstances where by virtue of section 131(2) (merger relief) section 130 did not apply to the premiums on those shares, the following information shall be given by way of a note to the company's accounts—

(a)   the name of the other company;

(b)   the number, nominal value and class of shares so allotted;

(c)   the number, nominal value and class of shares in the other company so issued, transferred or cancelled;

(d)   particulars of the accounting treatment adopted in the company's accounts (including any group accounts) in respect of such issue, transfer or cancellation; and

(e)   where the company prepares group accounts, particulars of the extent to which and manner in which the profit or loss for the year of the group which appears in those accounts is affected by any profit or loss of the other company or any of its subsidiaries which arose at any time before the allotment.

(2)   Where the company has during the financial year or during either of the two financial years immediately preceding it made such an allotment of shares as is mentioned in sub-paragraph (1) above and there is included in the company's consolidated profit and loss account, or if it has no such account, in its individual profit and loss account, any profit or loss (or part thereof) to which this sub-paragraph applies then the net amount of any such profit or loss (or part thereof) shall be shown in a note to the accounts together with an explanation of the transactions to which that information relates.

(3)   Sub-paragraph (2) applies—

(a)   to any profit or loss realised during the financial year by the company, or any of its subsidiaries, on the disposal of any shares in the other company or of any assets which were fixed assets of the other company, or of any of its subsidiaries, at the time of the allotment; and

(b)   to any part of any profit or loss realised during the financial year by the company, or any of its subsidiaries, on the disposal of any shares (not being shares in the other company), which was attributable to the fact that at the time of the disposal there were amongst the assets of the company which issued those shares, or any of its subsidiaries, such shares or assets as are described in paragraph (a) above.

(4)   Where in pursuance of the arrangement in question shares are allotted on different dates, the time of allotment for the purposes of sub-paragraphs (1)(e) and (3)(a) above is taken to be—

(a)   if the other company becomes a subsidiary of the company as a result of the arrangement—

(i)   if the arrangement becomes binding only upon the fulfilment of a condition, the date on which that condition is fulfilled, and

(ii)   in any other case, the date on which the other company becomes a subsidiary of the company;

(b)   if the other company is a subsidiary of the company when the arrangement is proposed, the date of the first allotment pursuant to that arrangement."

INTERPRETATION

History
Former Part heading before para. 32 omitted by CA 1989, s. 18(3) and Sch. 7, preliminary para. (c)(ii) and new heading inserted by CA 1989, s. 18(3) and Sch. 7, Pt. I, para. 12 as from 1 April 1990 subject to transitional and saving provisions (see S.I. 1990 No. 355 (C. 13), art. 3, Sch. 1 and also art. 6–9); former heading read "Part V — Interpretation of Schedule".

32(1) For the purposes of this Part of this Schedule, unless the context otherwise requires,—

(a) the expression **"provision"** shall, subject to sub-paragraph (2) of this paragraph, mean any amount written off or retained by way of providing for depreciation, renewals or diminution in value of assets or retained by way of providing for any known liability of which the amount cannot be determined with substantial accuracy;

(b) the expression "reserve" shall not, subject as aforesaid, include any amount written off or retained by way of providing for depreciation, renewals or diminution in value of assets or retained by way of providing for any known liability or any sum set aside for the purpose of its being used to prevent undue fluctuations in charges for taxation;

and in this paragraph the expression "liability" shall include all liabilities in respect of expenditure contracted for and all disputed or contingent liabilities.

History
In para. 32(1) the words "this Part of this Schedule" substituted for the former words "this Schedule" by CA 1989, s. 18(3) and Sch. 7, Pt. I, para. 12 as from 1 April 1990 (see S.I. 1990 No. 355 (C. 13), art. 3, Sch. 1 and also art. 6–9).

32(2) Where—

(a) any amount written off or retained by way of providing for depreciation, renewals or diminution in value of assets; or

(b) any amount retained by way of providing for any known liability;

is in excess of that which in the opinion of the directors is reasonably necessary for the purpose, the excess shall be treated for the purposes of this Part of this Schedule as a reserve and not as a provision.

History
In para. 32(2) the words "this Part of this Schedule" substituted for the former words "this Schedule" by CA 1989, s. 18(3) and Sch. 7, Pt. I, para. 12 as from 1 April 1990 (see S.I. 1990 No. 355 (C. 13), art. 3, Sch. 1 and also art. 6–9).

33 For the purposes aforesaid, the expression **"listed investment"** means an investment as respects which there has been granted a listing on a recognised investment exchange other than an overseas investment exchange within the meaning of the Financial Services Act 1986, or on any stock exchange of repute outside Great Britain and the expression **"unlisted investment"** shall be construed accordingly.

History
In para. 33 the words from "recognised investment exchange" to "Financial Services Act 1986" substituted for the former words "recognised stock exchange" by Financial Services Act 1986, s. 212(2) and Sch. 16, para. 24 as from 29 April 1988 (see S.I. 1988 No. 740 (C. 22)).

34 For the purposes aforesaid, the expression **"long lease"** means a lease in the case of which the portion of the term for which it was granted remaining unexpired at the end of the financial year is not less than fifty years, the expression **"short lease"** means a lease which is not a long lease and the expression "lease" includes an agreement for a lease.

35　For the purposes aforesaid, a loan shall be deemed to fall due for repayment, and an instalment of a loan shall be deemed to fall due for payment, on the earliest date on which the lender could require repayment or, as the case may be, payment if he exercised all options and rights available to him.

36　In the application of this Part of this Schedule to Scotland, **"land of freehold tenure"** means land in respect of which the company is the proprietor of the *dominium utile* or, in the case of land not held on feudal tenure, is the owner; **"land of leasehold tenure"** means land of which the company is the tenant under a lease; and the reference to ground-rents, rates and other outgoings includes a reference to feu-duty and ground annual.

History
In para. 36 the words "this Part of this Schedule" substituted for the former words "this Schedule" by CA 1989, s. 18(3) and Sch. 7, Pt. I, para. 12 as from 1 April 1990 (see S.I. 1990 No. 355 (C. 13), art. 3, Sch. 1 and also art. 6–9).

Part II — Accounts of Banking or Insurance Group

UNDERTAKINGS TO BE INCLUDED IN CONSOLIDATION

1　The following descriptions of undertaking shall not be excluded from consolidation under section 229(4) (exclusion of undertakings whose activities are different from those of the undertakings consolidated)—

(a) in the case of a banking group, an undertaking (other than a credit institution) whose activities are a direct extension of or ancillary to banking business;

(b) in the case of an insurance group, an undertaking (other than one carrying on insurance business) whose activities are a direct extension of or ancillary to insurance business.

For the purposes of paragraph (a) **"banking"** means the carrying on of a deposit-taking business within the meaning of the Banking Act 1987.

History
See history note after Pt. IV.

GENERAL APPLICATION OF PROVISIONS APPLICABLE TO INDIVIDUAL ACCOUNTS

2(1)　In paragraph 1 of Schedule 4A (application to group accounts of provisions applicable to individual accounts), the reference in sub-paragraph (1) to the provisions of Schedule 4 shall be construed as a reference to the provisions of Part I of this Schedule; and accordingly —

(a) the reference in sub-paragraph (2) to paragraph 59 of Schedule 4 shall be construed as a reference to paragraphs 19(2) and 20 of Part I of this Schedule; and

(b) sub-paragraph (3) shall be omitted.

2(2)　The general application of the provisions of Part I of this Schedule in place of those of Schedule 4 is subject to the following provisions.

History
See history note after Pt. IV.

TREATMENT OF GOODWILL

3(1) The rules in paragraph 21 of Schedule 4 relating to the treatment of goodwill, and the rules in paragraphs 17 to 19 of that Schedule (valuation of fixed assets) so far as they relate to goodwill, apply for the purpose of dealing with any goodwill arising on consolidation.

3(2) Goodwill shall be shown as a separate item in the balance sheet under an appropriate heading; and this applies notwithstanding anything in paragraph 10(1)(b) or (2) of Part I of this Schedule (under which goodwill, patents and trade marks may be stated in the company's individual accounts as a single item).

History
See history note after Pt. IV.

MINORITY INTERESTS AND ASSOCIATED UNDERTAKINGS

4 The information required by paragraphs 17 and 20 to 22 of Schedule 4A (minority interests and associated undertakings) to be shown under separate items in the formats set out in Part I of Schedule 4 shall be shown separately in the balance sheet and profit and loss account under appropriate headings.

History
See history note after Pt. IV.

COMPANIES ENTITLED TO BENEFIT OF EXEMPTIONS

5(1) Where a banking or insurance company is entitled to the exemptions conferred by paragraph 27 or 28 of Part I of this Schedule, a group headed by that company is similarly entitled.

5(2) Paragraphs 27(4), 28(2) and 28A (accounts not to be taken to be other than true and fair; duty of auditors) apply accordingly where advantage is taken of those exemptions in relation to group accounts.

History
See history note after Pt. IV.

INFORMATION AS TO UNDERTAKING IN WHICH SHARES HELD AS RESULT OF FINANCIAL ASSISTANCE OPERATION

6(1) The following provisions apply where the parent company of a banking group has a subsidiary undertaking which —

(a) is a credit institution of which shares are held as a result of a financial assistance operation with a view to its reorganisation or rescue, and

(b) is excluded from consolidation under section 229(3)(c) (interest held with a view to resale).

6(2) Information as to the nature and terms of the operation shall be given in a note to the group accounts and there shall be appended to the copy of the group accounts delivered to the registrar in accordance with section 242 a copy of the undertaking's latest individual accounts and, if it is a parent undertaking, its latest group accounts.

If the accounts appended are required by law to be audited, a copy of the auditors' report shall also be appended.

6(3) If any document required to be appended is in a language other than English, the directors shall annex to the copy of that document delivered a translation of it into English, certified in the prescribed manner to be a correct translation.

6(4)   The above requirements are subject to the following qualifications —

  (a) an undertaking is not required to prepare for the purposes of this paragraph accounts which would not otherwise be prepared, and if no accounts satisfying the above requirements are prepared none need be appended;

  (b) the accounts of an undertaking need not be appended if they would not otherwise be required to be published, or made available for public inspection, anywhere in the world, but in that case the reason for not appending the accounts shall be stated in a note to the consolidated accounts.

6(5)   Where a copy of an undertaking's accounts is required to be appended to the copy of the group accounts delivered to the registrar, that fact shall be stated in a note to the group accounts.

6(6)   Subsections (2) to (4) of section 242 (penalties, etc. in case of default) apply in relation to the requirements of this paragraph as regards the delivery of documents to the registrar as they apply in relation to the requirements of subsection (1) of that section.

History
See history note after Pt. IV.

Part III — Additional Disclosure: Related Undertakings

1   Where accounts are prepared in accordance with the special provisions of this Part relating to banking companies or groups, there shall be disregarded for the purposes of —

  (a) paragraphs 7(2)(a), 23(2)(a) and 26(2)(a) of Schedule 5 (information about significant holdings in undertakings other than subsidiary undertakings: definition of 10 per cent holding), and

  (b) paragraphs 9(1), 25(1) and 28(1) of that Schedule (additional information in case of 20 per cent holding),

any holding of shares not comprised in the equity share capital of the undertaking in question.

History
See history note after Pt. IV.

Part IV — Additional Disclosure: Emoluments and Other Benefits of Directors and Others

1   The provisions of this Part of this Schedule have effect with respect to the application of Schedule 6 (additional disclosure: emoluments and other benefits of directors and others) to a banking company or the holding company of such a company.

History
See history note after para. 3.

LOANS, QUASI-LOANS AND OTHER DEALINGS

2   Part II of Schedule 6 (loans, quasi-loans and other dealings) does not apply for the purposes of accounts prepared by a banking company, or a company which is the holding company of a banking company, in relation to a transaction or arrangement of a kind mentioned in section 330, or an agreement to enter into such a transaction or arrangement, to which that banking company is a party.

History
See history note after para. 3.

OTHER TRANSACTIONS, ARRANGEMENTS AND AGREEMENTS

3(1) Part III of Schedule 6 (other transactions, arrangements and agreements) applies for the purposes of accounts prepared by a banking company, or a company which is the holding company of a banking company, only in relation to a transaction, arrangement or agreement made by that banking company for —

    (a) a person who was a director of the company preparing the accounts, or who was connected with such a director, or

    (b) a person who was a chief executive or manager (within the meaning of the Banking Act 1987) of that company or its holding company.

3(2) References in that Part to officers of the company shall be construed accordingly as including references to such persons.

3(3) In this paragraph "director" includes a shadow director.

3(4) For the purposes of that Part as it applies by virtue of this paragraph, a company which a person does not control shall not be treated as connected with him.

3(5) Section 346 of this Act applies for the purposes of this paragraph as regards the interpretation of references to a person being connected with a director or controlling a company.

History
Pt. II–IV inserted — see CA 1989, s. 18(3), (4), Sch. 7, preliminary para. (d) and Pt. II–IV — as from 1 April 1990   subject to transitional and saving provisions (see S.I. 1990 No. 355 (C. 13), art. 3, Sch. 1 and also art. 6–9).

Schedule 10 — Directors' Report where Accounts Prepared in Accordance with Special Provisions for Banking or Insurance Companies or Groups

[Companies Act 1985, sec. 255–255C;
Companies Act 1989, sec. 1, 18(5) and Sch. 8]

RECENT ISSUES

1(1) This paragraph applies where a company prepares individual accounts in accordance with the special provisions of this Part relating to banking or insurance companies.

1(2) If in the financial year to which the accounts relate the company has issued any shares or debentures, the directors' report shall state the reason for making the issue, the classes of shares or debentures issued and, as respects each class, the number of shares or amount of debentures issued and the consideration received by the company for the issue.

TURNOVER AND PROFITABILITY

2(1) This paragraph applies where a company prepares group accounts in accordance with the special provisions of this Part relating to banking or insurance groups.

31,354   Sch. 10 — Directors' Report where Accounts Prepared in
Accordance with Special Provisions for Banking
or Insurance Companies or Groups

2(2)   If in the course of the financial year to which the accounts relate the group carried on business of two or more classes (other than banking or discounting or a class prescribed for the purposes of paragraph 17(2) of Part I of Schedule 9) that in the opinion of the directors differ substantially from each other, there shall be contained in the directors' report a statement of —

(a) the proportions in which the turnover for the financial year (so far as stated in the consolidated accounts) is divided amongst those classes (describing them), and

(b) as regards business of each class, the extent or approximate extent (expressed in money terms) to which, in the opinion of the directors, the carrying on of business of that class contributed to or restricted the profit or loss of the group for that year (before taxation).

2(3)   In ·ub-paragraph (2) "**the group**" means the undertakings included in the consolidation.

2(4)   For the purposes of this paragraph classes of business which in the opinion of the directors do not differ substantially from each other shall be treated as one class.

LABOUR FORCE AND WAGES PAID

3(1)   This paragraph applies where a company prepares individual or group accounts in accordance with the special provisions of this Part relating to banking or insurance companies or groups.

3(2)   There shall be stated in the directors' report —

(a) the average number of persons employed by the company or, if the company prepares group accounts, by the company and its subsidiary undertakings, and

(b) the aggregate amount of the remuneration paid or payable to persons so employed.

3(3)   The average number of persons employed shall be determined by adding together the number of persons employed (whether throughout the week or not) in each week of the financial year and dividing that total by the number of weeks in the financial year.

3(4)   The aggregate amount of the remuneration paid or payable means the total amount of remuneration paid or payable in respect of the financial year; and for this purpose remuneration means gross remuneration and includes bonuses, whether payable under contract or not.

3(5)   The information required by this paragraph need not be given if the average number of persons employed is less than 100.

3(6)   No account shall be taken for the purposes of this paragraph of persons who worked wholly or mainly outside the United Kingdom.

3(7)   This paragraph does not apply to a company which is a wholly-owned subsidiary of a company incorporated in Great Britain.

[The next page is 31,501]

History

Sch. 10 substituted by CA 1989, s. 1, 18(5) and Sch. 8 as from 1 April 1990 subject to transitional and saving provisions (see S.I. 1990 No. 355 (C. 13), art. 3, Sch. 1 and also art. 6–9); Sch. 10 formerly read as follows:

"Schedule 10 — Additional Matters to be Dealt with in Directors' Report Attached to Special Category Accounts

RECENT ISSUES

1(1) If in the financial year to which the accounts relate the company has issued any shares, the directors' report shall state the reason for making the issue, the classes of shares issued and, as respects each class of shares, the number issued and the consideration received by the company for the issue.

(2) If in that year the company has issued any debentures, the report shall state the reason for making the issue, the classes of debentures issued, and, as respects each class of debentures, the amount issued and the consideration received by the company for the issue.

TURNOVER AND PROFITABILITY

2 If in the course of the financial year the company (being one subject to the requirements of paragraph 17 of Schedule 9, but not one that has subsidiaries at the end of the year and submits in respect of that year group accounts prepared as consolidated accounts) has carried on business of two or more classes (other than banking or discounting or a class prescribed for the purpose of paragraph 17(2) of that Schedule) that, in the opinion of the directors, differ substantially from each other, there shall be contained in the directors' report a statement of—

(a) the proportions in which the turnover for the year (so far as stated in the accounts in respect of the year in pursuance of that Schedule) is divided amongst those classes (describing them), and

(b) as regards business of each class, the extent or approximate extent (expressed, in either case, in monetary terms) to which, in the opinion of the directors, the carrying on of business of that class contributed to, or restricted, the profit or loss of the company for that year before taxation.

3(1) This paragraph applies if—

(a) the company has subsidiaries at the end of the financial year and submits in respect of that year group accounts prepared as consolidated accounts, and

(b) the company and the subsidiaries dealt with by the accounts carried on between them in the course of the year business of two or more classes (other than banking or discounting or a class prescribed for the purposes of paragraph 17(2) of Schedule 9) that, in the opinion of the directors, differ substantially from each other.

(2) There shall be contained in the directors' report a statement of—

(a) the proportions in which the turnover for the financial year (so far as stated in the accounts for that year in pursuance of Schedule 9) is divided amongst those classes (describing them), and

(b) as regards business of each class, the extent or approximate extent (expressed, in either case, in monetary terms) to which, in the opinion of the directors of the company, the carrying on of business of that class contributed to, or restricted, the profit or loss for that year (before taxation) of the company and the subsidiaries dealt with by the accounts.

4 For the purposes of the preceding two paragraphs, classes of business which, in the opinion of the directors, do not differ substantially from each other, are to be treated as one class.

LABOUR FORCE AND WAGES PAID

5(1) If at the end of the financial year the company does not have subsidiaries, there shall be contained in the directors' report a statement of—

(a) the average number of persons employed by the company in each week in the year, and

(b) the aggregate remuneration paid or payable in respect of the year to the persons by reference to whom the number stated under sub-paragraph (a) is ascertained.

(2) The number to be stated under that sub-paragraph is the quotient derived by dividing, by the number of weeks in the financial year, the number derived by ascertaining, in relation to each of those weeks, the number of persons who, under contracts of service, were employed in the week (whether throughout it or not) by the company and adding up the numbers ascertained.

6(1) If at the end of the financial year the company has subsidiaries, there shall be contained in the directors' report a statement of—

(a) the average number of persons employed between them in each week in that year by the company and the subsidiaries, and

(b) the aggregate remuneration paid or payable in respect of that year to the persons by reference to whom the number stated under sub-paragraph (a) is ascertained.

(2) The number to be stated under that sub-paragraph is the quotient derived by dividing, by the number of weeks in the financial year, the number derived by ascertaining, in relation to each of those weeks, the number of persons who, under contracts of service, were employed between them in the week (whether throughout it or not) by the company and its subsidiaries and adding up the numbers ascertained.

7 The remuneration to be taken into account under sub-paragraphs 5(1)(b) and 6(1)(b) is the gross remuneration paid or payable in respect of the financial year; and for this purpose **'remuneration'** includes bonuses (whether payable under contract or not).

8(1) Paragraphs 5 and 6 are qualified as follows.

(2) Neither paragraph applies if the number that, apart from this sub-paragraph, would fall to be stated under paragraph 5(1)(a) or 6(1)(a) is less than 100.

(3) Neither paragraph applies to a company which is a wholly-owned subsidiary of a company incorporated in Great Britain.

(4) For purposes of both paragraphs, no regard is to be had to any person who worked wholly or mainly outside the United Kingdom.

GENERAL MATTERS

9 The directors' report shall contain particulars of any matters (other than those required to be dealt with in it by section 261(5) and the preceding provisions of this Schedule) so far as they are material for the appreciation of the state of the company's affairs by its members, being matters the disclosure of which will not, in the opinion of the directors, be harmful to the business of the company or of any of its subsidiaries."

Schedule 10A — Parent and Subsidiary Undertakings: Supplementary Provisions

[Companies Act 1985, sec. 258;
Companies Act 1989, sec. 1, 21(2) and Sch. 9]

INTRODUCTION

1 The provisions of this Schedule explain expressions used in section 258 (parent and subsidiary undertakings) and otherwise supplement that section.

VOTING RIGHTS IN AN UNDERTAKING

2(1) In section 258(2)(a) and (d) the references to the voting rights in an undertaking are to the rights conferred on shareholders in respect of their shares or, in the case of an undertaking not having a share capital, on members, to vote at general meetings of the undertaking on all, or substantially all, matters.

2(2) In relation to an undertaking which does not have general meetings at which matters are decided by the exercise of voting rights, the references to holding a majority of the voting rights in the undertaking shall be construed as references to having the right under the constitution of the undertaking to direct the overall policy of the undertaking or to alter the terms of its constitution.

RIGHT TO APPOINT OR REMOVE A MAJORITY OF THE DIRECTORS

3(1) In section 258(2)(b) the reference to the right to appoint or remove a majority of the board of directors is to the right to appoint or remove directors holding a majority of the voting rights at meetings of the board on all, or substantially all, matters.

3(2) An undertaking shall be treated as having the right to appoint to a directorship if —

    (a) a person's appointment to it follows necessarily from his appointment as director of the undertaking, or

    (b) the directorship is held by the undertaking itself.

3(3) A right to appoint or remove which is exercisable only with the consent or concurrence of another person shall be left out of account unless no other person has a right to appoint or, as the case may be, remove in relation to that directorship.

RIGHT TO EXERCISE DOMINANT INFLUENCE

4(1) For the purposes of section 258(2)(c) an undertaking shall not be regarded as having the right to exercise a dominant influence over another undertaking unless it has a right to give directions with respect to the operating and financial policies of that other undertaking which its directors are obliged to comply with whether or not they are for the benefit of that other undertaking.

4(2) A "**control contract**" means a contract in writing conferring such a right which —

    (a) is of a kind authorised by the memorandum or articles of the undertaking in relation to which the right is exercisable, and

CA 1985, Sch. 10A, para. 1

(b) is permitted by the law under which that undertaking is established.

4(3) This paragraph shall not be read as affecting the construction of the expression "actually exercises a dominant influence" in section 258(4)(a).

RIGHTS EXERCISABLE ONLY IN CERTAIN CIRCUMSTANCES OR TEMPORARILY INCAPABLE OF EXERCISE

5(1) Rights which are exercisable only in certain circumstances shall be taken into account only —

(a) when the circumstances have arisen, and for so long as they continue to obtain, or

(b) when the circumstances are within the control of the person having the rights.

5(2) Rights which are normally exercisable but are temporarily incapable of exercise shall continue to be taken into account.

RIGHTS HELD BY ONE PERSON ON BEHALF OF ANOTHER

6 Rights held by a person in a fiduciary capacity shall be treated as not held by him.

7(1) Rights held by a person as nominee for another shall be treated as held by the other.

7(2) Rights shall be regarded as held as nominee for another if they are exercisable only on his instructions or with his consent or concurrence.

RIGHTS ATTACHED TO SHARES HELD BY WAY OF SECURITY

8 Rights attached to shares held by way of security shall be treated as held by the person providing the security —

(a) where apart from the right to exercise them for the purpose of preserving the value of the security, or of realising it, the rights are exercisable only in accordance with his instructions, and

(b) where the shares are held in connection with the granting of loans as part of normal business activities and apart from the right to exercise them for the purpose of preserving the value of the security, or of realising it, the rights are exercisable only in his interests.

RIGHTS ATTRIBUTED TO PARENT UNDERTAKING

9(1) Rights shall be treated as held by a parent undertaking if they are held by any of its subsidiary undertakings.

9(2) Nothing in paragraph 7 or 8 shall be construed as requiring rights held by a parent undertaking to be treated as held by any of its subsidiary undertakings.

9(3) For the purposes of paragraph 8 rights shall be treated as being exercisable in accordance with the instructions or in the interests of an undertaking if they are exercisable in accordance with the instructions of or, as the case may be, in the interests of any group undertaking.

DISREGARD FOR CERTAIN RIGHTS

10 The voting rights in an undertaking shall be reduced by any rights held by the undertaking itself.

SUPPLEMENTARY

11 References in any provision of paragraphs 6 to 10 to rights held by a person include rights falling to be treated as held by him by virtue of any other provision of those paragraphs but not rights which by virtue of any such provision are to be treated as not held by him.

History

Sch. 10A inserted by CA 1989, s. 1, 21(2) and Sch. 9 as from 1 April 1990 subject to transitional and saving provisions (see S.I. 1990 No. 355 (C. 13), art. 3, Sch. 1 and also art. 6–9).

Schedule 11 — Modifications of Part VIII where Company's Accounts Prepared in Accordance with Special Provisions for Banking or Insurance Companies

Section 279

History

Heading substituted for former heading "Modifications of Part VIII where Company's Relevant Accounts are Special Category" by CA 1989, s. 23 and Sch. 10, para. 21(1), (2) as from 1 April 1990 subject to transitional and saving provisions (see S.I. 1990 No. 355 (C. 13), art. 3, Sch. 1 and also art. 6–9).

1 Section 264 applies as if in subsection (2) for the words following "the aggregate of its liabilities" there were substituted "("liabilities" to include any provision within the meaning of Part I of Schedule 9, except to the extent that that provision is taken into account in calculating the value of any asset of the company)".

History

In para. 1 the words "Part I of Schedule 9" substituted for the former words "Schedule 9" by CA 1989, s. 23 and Sch. 10, para. 21(1), (3) as from 1 April 1990 subject to transitional and saving provisions (see S.I. 1990 No. 355 (C. 13), art. 3, Sch. 1 and also art. 6–9).

2 Section 265 applies as if—

    (a) for subsection (2) there were substituted—

        "(2) In subsection (1)(a), "liabilities" includes any provision (within the meaning of Part I of Schedule 9) except to the extent that that provision is taken into account for the purposes of that subsection in calculating the value of any asset of the company", and

    (b) there were added at the end of the section—

        "(7) In determining capital and revenue profits and losses, an asset which is not a fixed asset or a current asset is treated as a fixed asset".

History

In para. 2(a) the words "Part I of Schedule 9" substituted for the former words "Schedule 9" by CA 1989, s. 23 and Sch. 10, para. 21(1), (3) as from 1 April 1990 subject to transitional and saving provisions (see S.I. 1990 No. 355 (C. 13), art. 3, Sch. 1 and also art. 6–9).

3 Section 269 does not apply.

4 Section 270 applies as if—

    (a) in subsection (2) the following were substituted for paragraph (b)—

        "(b) provisions (within the meaning of Part I of Schedule 9)".

History
In para. 4(a) the words "Part I of Schedule 9" substituted for the former words "Schedule 9" and para. 4(b), (c) omitted and repealed by CA 1989, s. 23, 212, Sch. 10, para. 21(1), (4) and Sch. 24 as from 1 April 1990 subject to transitional and saving provisions (see S.I. 1990 No. 355 (C. 13), art. 3, 5(1)(b), (2), Sch. 1 and also art. 6–9); para. 4(b), (c) formerly read as follows:

"(b)   in subsection (3), for the words from 'which were laid' onwards there were substituted—

'which were laid or filed in respect of the last preceding accounting reference period in respect of which accounts so prepared were laid or filed; and for this purpose accounts are laid or filed if section 241(1) or (as the case may be) (3) has been complied with in relation to them'; and

(c)   in subsection (4)(b) the words 'or filed' were inserted after 'laid'."

5   Section 271 applies as if—

(a)   in subsection (2), immediately before paragraph (a) there were inserted "except where the company is entitled to avail itself, and has availed itself, of any of the provisions of paragraph 27 or 28 of Schedule 9".

History
In para. 5(a) the words "paragraph 27 or 28 of Schedule 9" substituted for the former words "Part III of Schedule 9" and para. 5(b) omitted and repealed by CA 1989, s. 23, 212, Sch. 10, para. 21(1), (5) and Sch. 24 as from 1 April 1990 subject to transitional and saving provisions (see S.I. 1990 No. 355 (C. 13), art. 3, 5(1)(b), (2), Sch. 1 and also art. 6–9); para. 5(b) formerly read as follows:

"(b)   at the end of subsection (4) there were added the words 'or delivered to the registrar of companies according as those accounts have been laid or filed'."

6   Sections 272 and 273 apply as if in section 272(3)—

(a)   for the references to section 226 and Schedule 4 there were substituted references to section 255 and Part I of Schedule 9, and

(b)   immediately before paragraph (a) there were inserted "except where the company is entitled to avail itself, and has availed itself, of any of the provisions of paragraph 27 or 28 of Schedule 9".

History
In para. 6(a) the words "section 226" and "section 255 and Part I of Schedule 9" substituted for the former words "section 228" and "section 258 and Schedule 9" respectively and in para. 6(b) the words "paragraph 27 or 28 of Schedule 9" substituted for the former words "Part III of Schedule 9" by CA 1989, s. 23 and Sch. 10, para. 21(1), (6) as from 1 April 1990 subject to transitional and saving provisions (see S.I. 1990 No. 355 (C. 13), art. 3, Sch. 1 and also art. 6–9).

7   Section 275 applies as if—

(a)   for subsection (1) there were substituted—

"(1) For purposes of section 263, any provision (within the meaning of Part I of Schedule 9), other than one in respect of any diminution of value of a fixed asset appearing on a revaluation of all the fixed assets of the company, or of all its fixed assets other than goodwill, is to be treated as a realised loss"; and

(b)   **"fixed assets"** were defined to include any other asset which is not a current asset.

History
In para. 7(a) the words "Part I of Schedule 9" substituted for the former words "Schedule 9" by CA 1989, s. 23 and Sch. 10, para. 21(1), (7) as from 1 April 1990 subject to transitional and saving provisions (see S.I. 1990 No. 355 (C. 13), art. 3, Sch. 1 and also art. 6–9).

Schedule 12 — Supplementary Provisions in Connection with Disqualification Orders

Section 295

(Repealed by Company Directors Disqualification Act 1986, sec. 23(2) and Sch. 4 as from 29 December 1986.)

History

In regard to the date of the above repeal, see Company Directors Disqualification Act 1986, s. 25, Insolvency Act 1986, s. 443 and S.I. 1986 No. 1924 (C. 71). The previous form of the schedule appears below (see IA 1985, Sch. 6, para. 14 for a small amendment to para. 4(3)):

"Part I — Orders under Sections 296 to 299

APPLICATION FOR ORDER

1 A person intending to apply for the making of an order under any of sections 296 to 299 by the court having jurisdiction to wind up a company shall give not less than 10 days' notice of his intention to the person against whom the order is sought; and on the hearing of the application the last-mentioned person may appear and himself give evidence or call witnesses.

2 An application to a court with jurisdiction to wind up companies for the making of such an order against any person may be made by the Secretary of State or the official receiver, or by the liquidator or any past or present member or creditor of any company in relation to which that person has committed or is alleged to have committed an offence or other default.

HEARING OF APPLICATION

3 On the hearing of an application made by the Secretary of State or the official receiver or the liquidator the applicant shall appear and call the attention of the court to any matters which seem to him to be relevant, and may himself give evidence or call witnesses.

APPLICATION FOR LEAVE UNDER AN ORDER

4(1) As regards the court to which application must be made for leave under a disqualification order made under any of sections 296 to 299, the following applies.

(2) Where the application is for leave to promote or form a company, it is any court with jurisdiction to wind up companies.

(3) Where the application is for leave to be a liquidator or director of, or otherwise to take part in the management of a company, or to be a receiver or manager of a company's property, it is any court having jurisdiction to wind up that company.

5 On the hearing of an application for leave made by a person against whom a disqualification order has been made on the application of the Secretary of State, the official receiver or the liquidator, the Secretary of State, official receiver or liquidator shall appear and call the attention of the court to any matters which seem to him to be relevant, and may himself give evidence or call witnesses.

Part II — Orders under Section 300

6–8 (Repealed by Insolvency Act 1985, sec. 235 and Sch. 10, Pt. II as from 28 April 1986.)

Part III — Transitional Provisions and Savings from Companies Act 1981, sec. 93, 94

9 Sections 296 and 298(1)(b) do not apply in relation to anything done before 15th June 1982 by a person in his capacity as liquidator of a company or as receiver or manager of a company's property.

10 Subject to paragraph 9—

    (a) section 296 applies in a case where a person is convicted on indictment of an offence which he committed (and, in the case of a continuing offence, has ceased to commit) before 15th June 1982; but

[The next page is 31,801]

CA 1985, former Sch. 12

in such a case a disqualification order under that section shall not be made for a period in excess of 5 years;

(b) that section does not apply in a case where a person is convicted summarily—

    (i) in England and Wales, if he had consented so to be tried before that date, or

    (ii) in Scotland, if the summary proceedings commenced before that date.

11 Subject to paragraph 9, section 298 applies in relation to an offence committed or other thing done before 15th June 1982; but a disqualification order made on the grounds of such an offence or other thing done shall not be made for a period in excess of 5 years.

12 The powers of a court under section 299 are not exercisable in a case where a person is convicted of an offence which he committed (and, in the case of a continuing offence, had ceased to commit) before 15th June 1982.

13 For purposes of section 297(1) and section 299, no account is to be taken of any offence which was committed, or any default order which was made, before 1st June 1977.

14 An order made under section 28 of the Companies Act 1976 has effect as if made under section 297 of this Act; and an application made before 15th June 1982 for such an order is to be treated as an application for an order under the section last mentioned.

15, 16 (Repealed by Insolvency Act 1985, sec. 235 and Sch. 10, Pt. II as from 28 April 1986.)"

Note

For current provisions, see Company Directors Disqualification Act 1986, s. 16, 17 and Sch. 2.

Schedule 13 — Provisions Supplementing and Interpreting Sections 324 to 328

Sections 324, 325, 326, 328 and 346

Part I — Rules for Interpretation of the Sections and also Section 346(4) and (5)

1(1) A reference to an interest in shares or debentures is to be read as including any interest of any kind whatsoever in shares or debentures.

1(2) Accordingly, there are to be disregarded any restraints or restrictions to which the exercise of any right attached to the interest is or may be subject.

2 Where property is held on trust and any interest in shares or debentures is comprised in the property, any beneficiary of the trust who (apart from this paragraph) does not have an interest in the shares or debentures is to be taken as having such an interest; but this paragraph is without prejudice to the following provisions of this Part of this Schedule.

3(1) A person is taken to have an interest in shares or debentures if—

(a) he enters into a contract for their purchase by him (whether for cash or other consideration), or

(b) not being the registered holder, he is entitled to exercise any right conferred by the holding of the shares or debentures, or is entitled to control the exercise of any such right.

3(2) For purposes of sub-paragraph (1)(b), a person is taken to be entitled to exercise or control the exercise of a right conferred by the holding of shares or debentures if he—

(a) has a right (whether subject to conditions or not) the exercise of which would make him so entitled, or

(b) is under an obligation (whether or not so subject) the fulfilment of which would make him so entitled.

3(3) A person is not by virtue of sub-paragraph (1)(b) taken to be interested in shares or debentures by reason only that he—

   (a) has been appointed a proxy to vote at a specified meeting of a company or of any class of its members and at any adjournment of that meeting, or

   (b) has been appointed by a corporation to act as its representative at any meeting of a company or of any class of its members.

4   A person is taken to be interested in shares or debentures if a body corporate is interested in them and—

   (a) that body corporate or its directors are accustomed to act in accordance with his directions or instructions, or

   (b) he is entitled to exercise or control the exercise of one-third or more of the voting power at general meetings of that body corporate.

   As this paragraph applies for the purposes of section 346(4) and (5), "more than one-half" is substituted for "one-third or more".

5   Where a person is entitled to exercise or control the exercise of one-third or more of the voting power at general meetings of a body corporate, and that body corporate is entitled to exercise or control the exercise of any of the voting power at general meetings of another body corporate ("the effective voting power"), then, for purposes of paragraph 4(b), the effective voting power is taken to be exercisable by that person.

   As this paragraph applies for the purposes of section 346(4) and (5), "more than one-half" is substituted for "one-third or more".

6(1)   A person is taken to have an interest in shares or debentures if, otherwise than by virtue of having an interest under a trust—

   (a) he has a right to call for delivery of the shares or debentures to himself or to his order, or

   (b) he has a right to acquire an interest in shares or debentures or is under an obligation to take an interest in shares or debentures;

whether in any case the right or obligation is conditional or absolute.

6(2)   Rights or obligations to subscribe for shares or debentures are not to be taken, for purposes of sub-paragraph (1), to be rights to acquire, or obligations to take, an interest in shares or debentures.

   This is without prejudice to paragraph 1.

7   Persons having a joint interest are deemed each of them to have that interest.

8   It is immaterial that shares or debentures in which a person has an interest are unidentifiable.

9   So long as a person is entitled to receive, during the lifetime of himself or another, income from trust property comprising shares or debentures, an interest in the shares or debentures in reversion or remainder or (as regards Scotland) in fee, are to be disregarded.

10   A person is to be treated as uninterested in shares or debentures if, and so long as, he holds them under the law in force in England and Wales as a bare trustee or as a custodian trustee, or under the law in force in Scotland, as a simple trustee.

CA 1985, Sch. 13, para. 4

11 There is to be disregarded an interest of a person subsisting by virtue of—

   (a) any unit trust scheme which is an authorised unit trust scheme within the meaning of the Financial Services Act 1986;

   (b) a scheme made under section 22 of the Charities Act 1960, section 11 of the Trustee Investments Act 1961 or section 1 of the Administration of Justice Act 1965; or

   (c) the scheme set out in the Schedule to the Church Funds Investment Measure 1958.

History
Para. 11(a) substituted by Financial Services Act 1986, s. 212(2) and Sch. 16, para. 25 as from 29 April 1988 (see S.I. 1988 No. 740 (C. 22)): para. 11(a) formerly read as follows:
  "(a) any unit trust scheme declared by an order of the Secretary of State (or any predecessor of his) for the time being in force under the Prevention of Fraud (Investments) Act 1958 to be an authorised unit trust scheme for the purposes of that Act".

12 There is to be disregarded any interest—

   (a) of the Church of Scotland General Trustees or of the Church of Scotland Trust in shares or debentures held by them;

   (b) of any other person in shares or debentures held by those Trustees or that Trust otherwise than as simple trustees.

"The Church of Scotland General Trustees" are the body incorporated by the order confirmed by the Church of Scotland (General Trustees) Order Confirmation Act 1921; and **"the Church of Scotland Trust"** is the body incorporated by the order confirmed by the Church of Scotland Trust Order Confirmation Act 1932.

13 Delivery to a person's order of shares or debentures in fulfilment of a contract for the purchase of them by him or in satisfaction of a right of his to call for their delivery, or failure to deliver shares or debentures in accordance with the terms of such a contract or on which such a right falls to be satisfied, is deemed to constitute an event in consequence of the occurrence of which he ceases to be interested in them, and so is the lapse of a person's right to call for delivery of shares or debentures.

Part II — Periods Within Which Obligations Imposed By Section 324 Must Be Fulfilled

14(1) An obligation imposed on a person by section 324(1) to notify an interest must, if he knows of the existence of the interest on the day on which he becomes a director, be fulfilled before the expiration of the period of 5 days beginning with the day following that day.

14(2) Otherwise, the obligation must be fulfilled before the expiration of the period of 5 days beginning with the day following that on which the existence of the interest comes to his knowledge.

15(1) An obligation imposed on a person by section 324(2) to notify the occurrence of an event must, if at the time at which the event occurs he knows of its occurrence and of the fact that its occurrence gives rise to the obligation, be fulfilled before the expiration of the period of 5 days beginning with the day following that on which the event occurs.

15(2) Otherwise, the obligation must be fufilled before the expiration of a period of 5 days beginning with the day following that on which the fact that the occurrence of the event gives rise to the obligation comes to his knowledge.

16   In reckoning, for purposes of paragraphs 14 and 15, any period of days, a day that is a Saturday or Sunday, or a bank holiday in any part of Great Britain, is to be disregarded.

Part III — Circumstances in Which Obligation Imposed by Section 324 is not Discharged

17(1)   Where an event of whose occurrence a director is, by virtue of section 324(2)(a), under obligation to notify a company consists of his entering into a contract for the purchase by him of shares or debentures, the obligation is not discharged in the absence of inclusion in the notice of a statement of the price to be paid by him under the contract.

17(2)   An obligation imposed on a director by section 324(2)(b) is not discharged in the absence of inclusion in the notice of the price to be received by him under the contract.

18(1)   An obligation imposed on a director by virtue of section 324(2)(c) to notify a company is not discharged in the absence of inclusion in the notice of a statement of the consideration for the assignment (or, if it be the case that there is no consideration, that fact).

18(2)   Where an event of whose occurrence a director is, by virtue of section 324(2)(d), under obligation to notify a company consists in his assigning a right, the obligation is not discharged in the absence of inclusion in the notice of a similar statement.

19(1)   Where an event of whose occurrence a director is, by virtue of section 324(2)(d), under obligation to notify a company consists in the grant to him of a right to subscribe for shares or debentures, the obligation is not discharged in the absence of inclusion in the notice of a statement of—

    (a)   the date on which the right was granted,

    (b)   the period during which or the time at which the right is exercisable,

    (c)   the consideration for the grant (or, if it be the case that there is no consideration, that fact), and

    (d)   the price to be paid for the shares or debentures.

19(2)   Where an event of whose occurrence a director is, by section 324(2)(d), under obligation to notify a company consists in the exercise of a right granted to him to subscribe for shares or debentures, the obligation is not discharged in the absence of inclusion in the notice of a statement of—

    (a)   the number of shares or amount of debentures in respect of which the right was exercised, and

    (b)   if it be the case that they were registered in his name, that fact, and, if not, the name or names of the person or persons in whose name or names they were registered, together (if they were registered in the names of 2 persons or more) with the number or amount registered in the name of each of them.

20 In this Part, a reference to price paid or received includes any consideration other than money.

Part IV — Provisions with Respect to Register of Directors' Interests to be Kept Under Section 325

21 The register must be so made up that the entries in it against the several names appear in chronological order.

22 An obligation imposed by section 325(2) to (4) must be fulfilled before the expiration of the period of 3 days beginning with the day after that on which the obligation arises; but in reckoning that period, a day which is a Saturday or Sunday or a bank holiday in any part of Great Britain is to be disregarded.

23 The nature and extent of an interest recorded in the register of a director in any shares or debentures shall, if he so requires, be recorded in the register.

24 The company is not, by virtue of anything done for the purposes of section 325 or this Part of this Schedule, affected with notice of, or put upon enquiry as to, the rights of any person in relation to any shares or debentures.

25 The register shall—

(a) if the company's register of members is kept at its registered office, be kept there;

(b) if the company's register of members is not so kept, be kept at the company's registered office or at the place where its register of members is kept;

and shall during business hours (subject to such reasonable restrictions as the company in general meeting may impose, so that not less than 2 hours in each day be allowed for inspection) be open to the inspection of any member of the company without charge and of any other person on payment of 5 pence, or such less sum as the company may prescribe, for each inspection.

26(1) Any member of the company or other person may require a copy of the register, or of any part of it, on payment of 10 pence, or such less sum as the company may prescribe, for every 100 words or fractional part of 100 words required to be copied.

26(2) The company shall cause any copy so required by a person to be sent to him within the period of 10 days beginning with the day after that on which the requirement is received by the company.

27 The company shall send notice in the prescribed form to the registrar of companies of the place where the register is kept and of any change in that place, save in a case in which it has at all times been kept at its registered office.

28 Unless the register is in such a form as to constitute in itself an index, the company shall keep an index of the names inscribed in it, which shall—

(a) in respect of each name, contain a sufficient indication to enable the information entered against it to be readily found; and

(b) be kept at the same place as the register;

and the company shall, within 14 days after the date on which a name is entered in the register, make any necessary alteration in the index.

29   The register shall be produced at the commencement of the company's annual general meeting and remain open and accessible during the continuance of the meeting to any person attending the meeting.

Schedule 14 — Overseas Branch Registers

Section 362

Part I — Countries and Territories in Which Overseas Branch Register May be Kept

Northern Ireland

Any part of Her Majesty's dominions outside the United Kingdom, the Channel Islands or the Isle of Man

> Bangladesh
> Cyprus
> Dominica
> The Gambia
> Ghana
> Guyana
> India
> Kenya
> Kiribati
> Lesotho
> Malawi
> Malaysia
> Malta
> Nigeria
> Pakistan
> Republic of Ireland
> Seychelles
> Sierra Leone
> Singapore
> South Africa
> Sri Lanka
> Swaziland
> Trinidad and Tobago
> Uganda
> Zimbabwe

Part II — General Provisions With Respect to Overseas Branch Registers

1(1)   A company keeping an overseas branch register shall give to the registrar of companies notice in the prescribed form of the situation of the office where any overseas branch register is kept and of any change in its situation, and, if it is discontinued, of its discontinuance.

1(2) Any such notice shall be given within 14 days of the opening of the office or of the change or discontinuance, as the case may be.

1(3) If default is made in complying with this paragraph, the company and every officer of it who is in default is liable to a fine and, for continued contravention, to a daily default fine.

2(1) An overseas branch register is deemed to be part of the company's register of members ("the principal register").

2(2) It shall be kept in the same manner in which the principal register is by this Act required to be kept, except that the advertisement before closing the register shall be inserted in a newspaper circulating in the district where the overseas branch register is kept.

3(1) A competent court in a country or territory where an overseas branch register is kept may exercise the same jurisdiction of rectifying the register as is under this Act exercisable by the court in Great Britain; and the offences of refusing inspection or copies of the register, and of authorising or permitting the refusal, may be prosecuted summarily before any tribunal having summary criminal jurisdiction.

3(2) This paragraph extends only to those countries and territories where, immediately before the coming into force of this Act, provision to the same effect made by section 120(2) of the Companies Act 1948 had effect as part of the local law.

4(1) The company shall—

    (a) transmit to its registered office a copy of every entry in its overseas branch register as soon as may be after the entry is made, and

    (b) cause to be kept at the place where the company's principal register is kept a duplicate of its overseas branch register duly entered up from time to time.

Every such duplicate is deemed for all purposes of this Act to be part of the principal register.

4(2) If default is made in complying with sub-paragraph (1), the company and every officer of it who is in default is liable to a fine and, for continued contravention, to a daily default fine.

4(3) Where, by virtue of section 353(1)(b), the principal register is kept at the office of some person other than the company, and by reason of any default of his the company fails to comply with sub-paragraph (1)(b) above he is liable to the same penalty as if he were an officer of the company who was in default.

5 Subject to the above provisions with respect to the duplicate register, the shares registered in an overseas branch register shall be distinguished from those registered in the principal register; and no transaction with respect to any shares registered in an overseas branch register shall, during the continuance of that registration, be registered in any other register.

6 A company may discontinue to keep an overseas branch register, and thereupon all entries in that register shall be transferred to some other overseas branch register kept by the company in the same country or territory, or to the principal register.

7   Subject to the provisions of this Act, any company may, by its articles, make such provisions as it thinks fit respecting the keeping of overseas branch registers.

8   An instrument of transfer of a share registered in an overseas branch register (other than such a register kept in Northern Ireland) is deemed a transfer of property situated outside the United Kingdom and, unless executed in a part of the United Kingdom, is exempt from stamp duty chargeable in Great Britain.

Note

In para. 8 prospective repeal of the words "and, unless executed in a part of the United Kingdom, is exempt from stamp duty chargeable in Great Britain" by Finance Act 1990, s. 132 and Sch. 19, Pt. VI in accordance with s. 107, 108 of that Act and from a day to be appointed under s. 111(1).

Part III — Provisions for Branch Registers of Oversea Companies to be Kept in Great Britain

9(1)   If by virtue of the law in force in any country or territory to which this paragraph applies companies incorporated under that law have power to keep in Great Britain branch registers of their members resident in Great Britain, Her Majesty may by Order in Council direct that—

(a) so much of section 353 as requires a company's register of members to be kept at its registered office,

(b) section 356 (register to be open to inspection by members), and

(c) section 359 (power of court to rectify),

shall, subject to any modifications and adaptations specified in the Order, apply to and in relation to any such branch registers kept in Great Britain as they apply to and in relation to the registers of companies subject to those sections.

9(2)   The countries and territories to which this paragraph applies are—

(a) all those specified in Part I of this Schedule, plus the Channel Islands and the Isle of Man,

(b) Botswana, Zambia and Tonga, and

(c) any territory for the time being under Her Majesty's protection or administered by the Government of the United Kingdom under the Trusteeship System of the United Nations.

Schedule 15 — Contents of Annual Return of a Company having a Share Capital

Section 363

1   The address of the registered office of the company.

2(1)   If the register of members is, under the provisions of this Act, kept elsewhere than at the registered office of the company, the address of the place where it is kept.

2(2)   If any register of holders of debentures of the company or any duplicate of any such register or part of any such register is, under the provisions of this Act, kept, in England and Wales in the case of a company registered in England and Wales or in Scotland in the case of a company registered in Scotland, elsewhere than at the registered office of the company, the address of the place where it is kept.

3   A summary, distinguishing between shares issued for cash and shares issued as fully or partly paid up otherwise than in cash, specifying the following particulars—

(a) the amount of the share capital of the company and the number of shares into which it is divided;

(b) the number of shares taken from the commencement of the company up to the date of the return;

(c) the amount called up on each share;

(d) the total amount of calls received;

(e) the total amount of calls unpaid;

(f) the total amount of the sums (if any) paid by way of commission in respect of any shares or debentures;

(g) the discount allowed on the issue of any shares issued at a discount or so much of that discount as has not been written off at the date on which the return is made;

(h) the total amount of the sums (if any) allowed by way of discount in respect of any debentures since the date of the last return;

(i) the total number of shares forfeited;

(j) the total number of shares for which share warrants are outstanding at the date of the return and of share warrants issued and surrendered respectively since the date of the last return, and the number of shares comprised in each warrant.

4 Particulars of the total amount of the company's indebtedness in respect of all mortgages and charges (whenever created) of any description specified in section 396(1) or, in the case of a company registered in Scotland, section 410(4).

5 A list—

(a) containing the names and addresses of all persons who, on the fourteenth day after the company's annual general meeting for the year, are members of the company, and of persons who have ceased to be members since the date of the last return or, in the case of the first return, since the incorporation of the company;

(b) stating the number of shares held by each of the existing members at the date of the return, specifying shares transferred since the date of the last return (or, in the case of the first return, since the incorporation of the company) by persons who are still members and have ceased to be members respectively and the dates of registration of the transfers;

(c) if the names are not arranged in alphabetical order, having annexed to it an index sufficient to enable the name of any person in the list to be easily found.

6 All such particulars with respect to the persons who at the date of the return are the directors of the company and any person who at that date is the secretary of the company as are by this Act required to be contained with respect to directors and the secretary respectively in the register of the directors and secretaries of a company.

Schedule 15A — Written Resolutions of Private Companies

Part I — Exceptions

1   Section 381A does not apply to—

    (a) a resolution under section 303 removing a director before the expiration of his period of office, or

    (b) a resolution under section 391 removing an auditor before the expiration of his term of office.

Part II — Adaptation of Procedural Requirements
INTRODUCTORY

2(1)   In this Part of this Schedule (which adapts certain requirements of this Act in relation to proceedings under section 381A)—

    (a) a **"written resolution"** means a resolution agreed to, or proposed to be agreed to, in accordance with that section, and

    (b) a **"relevant member"** means a member by whom, or on whose behalf, the resolution is required to be signed in accordance with that section.

2(2)   A written resolution is not effective if any of the requirements of this Part of this Schedule is not complied with.

SECTION 95 (DISAPPLICATION OF PRE-EMPTION RIGHTS)

3(1)   The following adaptations have effect in relation to a written resolution under section 95(2) (disapplication of pre-emption rights), or renewing a resolution under that provision.

3(2)   So much of section 95(5) as requires the circulation of a written statement by the directors with a notice of meeting does not apply, but such a statement must be supplied to each relevant member at or before the time at which the resolution is supplied to him for signature.

3(3)   Section 95(6) (offences) applies in relation to the inclusion in any such statement of matter which is misleading, false or deceptive in a material particular.

SECTION 155 (FINANCIAL ASSISTANCE FOR PURCHASE OF COMPANY'S OWN SHARES OR THOSE OF HOLDING COMPANY)

4   In relation to a written resolution giving approval under section 155(4) or (5) (financial assistance for purchase of company's own shares or those of holding company), section 157(4)(a) (documents to be available at meeting) does not apply, but the documents referred to in that provision must be supplied to each relevant member at or before the time at which the resolution is supplied to him for signature.

SECTIONS 164, 165 AND 167 (AUTHORITY FOR OFF-MARKET PURCHASE OR CONTINGENT PURCHASE CONTRACT OF COMPANY'S OWN SHARES)

5(1)   The following adaptations have effect in relation to a written resolution—

    (a) conferring authority to make an off-market purchase of the company's own shares under section 164(2),

(b) conferring authority to vary a contract for an off-market purchase of the company's own shares under section 164(7), or

(c) varying, revoking or renewing any such authority under section 164(3).

5(2) Section 164(5) (resolution ineffective if passed by exercise of voting rights by member holding shares to which the resolution relates) does not apply; but for the purposes of section 381A(1) a member holding shares to which the resolution relates shall not be regarded as a member who would be entitled to attend and vote.

5(3) Section 164(6) (documents to be available at company's registered office and at meeting) does not apply, but the documents referred to in that provision and, where that provision applies by virtue of section 164(7), the further documents referred to in that provision must be supplied to each relevant member at or before the time at which the resolution is supplied to him for signature.

5(4) The above adaptations also have effect in relation to a written resolution in relation to which the provisions of section 164(3) to (7) apply by virtue of—

(a) section 165(2) (authority for contingent purchase contract), or

(b) section 167(2) (approval of release of rights under contract approved under section 164 or 165).

SECTION 173 (APPROVAL FOR PAYMENT OUT OF CAPITAL)

6(1) The following adaptations have effect in relation to a written resolution giving approval under section 173(2) (redemption or purchase of company's own shares out of capital).

6(2) Section 174(2) (resolution ineffective if passed by exercise of voting rights by member holding shares to which the resolution relates) does not apply; but for the purposes of section 381A(1) a member holding shares to which the resolution relates shall not be regarded as a member who would be entitled to attend and vote.

6(3) Section 174(4) (documents to be available at meeting) does not apply, but the documents referred to in that provision must be supplied to each relevant member at or before the time at which the resolution is supplied to him for signature.

SECTION 319 (APPROVAL OF DIRECTOR'S SERVICE CONTRACT)

7 In relation to a written resolution approving any such term as is mentioned in section 319(1) (director's contract of employment for more than five years), section 319(5) (documents to be available at company's registered office and at meeting) does not apply, but the documents referred to in that provision must be supplied to each relevant member at or before the time at which the resolution is supplied to him for signature.

SECTION 337 (FUNDING OF DIRECTOR'S EXPENDITURE IN PERFORMING HIS DUTIES)

8 In relation to a written resolution giving approval under section 337(3)(a) (funding a director's expenditure in performing his duties), the requirement of that provision that certain matters be disclosed at the meeting at which the resolution is passed does not apply, but those matters must be disclosed to each relevant member at or before the time at which the resolution is supplied to him for signature.".

History
Sch. 15A inserted by CA 1989, s. 114(1) as from 1 April
1990 (see S.I. 1990 No. 355 (C.13), art. 4(a)).

Schedule 15B — Provisions Subject to which Sections 425–427 have effect in their Application to Mergers and Divisions of Public Companies

Section 427A

MEETING OF TRANSFEREE COMPANY

1 Subject to paragraphs 10(1), 12(4) and 14(2), the court shall not sanction a compromise or arrangement under section 425(2) unless a majority in number representing three-fourths in value of each class of members of every pre-existing transferee company concerned in the scheme, present and voting either in person or by proxy at a meeting, agree to the scheme.

DRAFT TERMS OF MERGER

2(1) The court shall not sanction the compromise or arrangement under section 425(2) unless—

(a) a draft of the proposed terms of the scheme (from here on referred to as the "draft terms") has been drawn up and adopted by the directors of all the transferor and pre-existing transferee companies concerned in the scheme,

(b) subject to paragraph 11(3), in the case of each of those companies the directors have delivered a copy of the draft terms to the registrar of companies and the registrar has published in the Gazette notice of receipt by him of a copy of the draft terms from that company, and

(c) subject to paragraphs 10 to 14, that notice was so published at least one month before the date of any meeting of that company summoned under section 425(1) or for the purposes of paragraph 1.

2(2) Subject to paragraph 12(2), the draft terms shall give particulars of at least the following matters—

(a) in respect of each transferor company and transferee company concerned in the scheme, its name, the address of its registered office and whether it is a company limited by shares or a company limited by guarantee and having a share capital;

(b) the number of shares in any transferee company to be allotted to members of any transferor company for a given number of their shares (from here on referred to as the "share exchange ratio") and the amount of any cash payment;

(c) the terms relating to the allotment of shares in any transferee company;

(d) the date from which the holding of shares in a transferee company will entitle the holders to participate in profits, and any special conditions affecting that entitlement;

(e) the date from which the transactions of any transferor company are to be treated for accounting purposes as being those of any transferee company;

(f) any rights or restrictions attaching to shares or other securities in any transferee company to be allotted under the scheme to the holders of shares to which any special rights or restrictions attach, or of other securities, in any transferor company, or the measures proposed concerning them;

   (g) any amount or benefit paid or given or intended to be paid or given to any of the experts referred to in paragraph 5 or to any director of a transferor company or pre-existing transferee company, and the consideration for the payment of benefit.

2(3) Where the scheme is a Case 3 Scheme the draft terms shall also—

   (a) give particulars of the property and liabilities to be transferred (to the extent these are known to the transferor company) and their allocation among the transferee companies;

   (b) make provision for the allocation among and transfer to the transferee companies of any other property and liabilities which the transferor company has or may subsequently acquire; and

   (c) specify the allocation to members of the transferor company of shares in the transferee companies and the criteria upon which that allocation is based.

DOCUMENTS AND INFORMATION TO BE MADE AVAILABLE

3 Subject to paragraphs 10 to 14, the court shall not sanction the compromise or arrangement under section 425(2) unless—

   (a) in the case of each transferor company and each pre-existing transferee company the directors have drawn up and adopted a report complying with paragraph 4 (from here on referred to as a "directors' report");

   (b) where the scheme is a Case 3 Scheme, the directors of the transferor company have reported to every meeting of the members or any class of members of that company summoned under section 425(1), and to the directors of each transferee company, any material changes in the property and liabilities of the transferor company between the date when the draft terms were adopted and the date of the meeting in question;

   (c) where the directors of a transferor company have reported to the directors of a transferee company such a change as is mentioned in sub-paragraph (b) above, the latter have reported that change to every meeting of the members or any class of members of that transferee company summoned for the purposes of paragraph 1, or have sent a report of that change to every member who would have been entitled to receive a notice of such a meeting;

   (d) a report complying with paragraph 5 has been drawn up on behalf of each transferor company and pre-existing transferee company (from here on referred to as an "expert's report");

   (e) the members of any transferor company or transferee company were able to inspect at the registered office of that company copies of the documents listed in paragraph 6(1) in relation to every transferor company and pre-existing transferee company concerned in the scheme during a period beginning one month before, and ending on, the date of the first meeting of the members or any class of members of the first-mentioned transferor or transferee company summoned either under section 425(1) or for the purposes of paragraph 1 and those members were able to obtain copies of those documents or any part of them on request during that period free of charge; and

(f) the memorandum and articles of association of any transferee company which is not a pre-existing transferee company, or a draft thereof, has been approved by ordinary resolution of every transferor company concerned in the scheme.

DIRECTOR'S REPORT

4(1)   The directors' report shall consist of—

(a) the statement required by section 426, and

(b) insofar as that statement does not contain the following matters, a further statement—

    (i) setting out the legal and economic grounds for the draft terms, and in particular for the share exchange ratio, and, where the scheme is a Case 3 Scheme, for the criteria upon which the allocation to the members of the transferor company of shares in the transferee companies was based, and

    (ii) specifying any special valuation difficulties.

4(2)   Where the scheme is a Case 3 Scheme the directors' report shall also state whether a report has been made to the transferee company under section 103 (non-cash consideration to be valued before allotment) and, if so, whether that report has been delivered to the registrar of companies.

EXPERT'S REPORT

5(1)   Except where a joint expert is appointed under sub-paragraph (2) below, an expert's report shall consist of a separate written report on the draft terms to the members of one transferor company or pre-existing transferee company concerned in the scheme drawn up by a separate expert appointed on behalf of that company.

5(2)   The court may, on the joint application of all the transferor companies and pre-existing transferee companies concerned in the scheme, approve the appointment of a joint expert to draw up a single report on behalf of all those companies.

5(3)   An expert shall be independent of any of the companies concerned in the scheme, that is to say a person qualified at the time of the report to be appointed, or to continue to be, an auditor of those companies.

5(4)   However, where it appears to an expert that a valuation is reasonably necessary to enable him to draw up the report, and it appears to him to be reasonable for that valuation, or part of it, to be made (or for him to accept such a valuation) by another person who—

(a) appears to him to have the requisite knowledge and experience to make the valuation or that part of it; and

(b) is not an officer or servant of any of the companies concerned in the scheme or any other body corporate which is one of those companies' subsidiary or holding company or a subsidiary of one of those companies' holding company or a partner or employee of such an officer or servant, he may arrange for or accept such a valuation, together with a report which will enable him to make his own report under this paragraph.

5(5)   The reference in sub-paragraph (4) above to an officer or servant does not include an auditor.

5(6)   Where any valuation is made by a person other than the expert himself, the latter's report shall state that fact and shall also—

(a) state the former's name and what knowledge and experience he has to carry out the valuation, and

(b) describe so much of the undertaking, property and liabilities as were valued by the other person, and the method used to value them, and specify the date of the valuation.

5(7)   An expert's report shall—

(a) indicate the method or methods used to arrive at the share exchange ratio proposed;

(b) give an opinion as to whether the method or methods used are reasonable in all the circumstances of the case, indicate the values arrived at using each such method and (if there is more than one method) give an opinion on the relative importance attributed to such methods in arriving at the value decided on;

(c) describe any special valuation difficulties which have arisen;

(d) state whether in the expert's opinion the share exchange ratio is reasonable; and

(e) in the case of a valuation made by a person other than himself, state that it appeared to himself reasonable to arrange for it to be so made or to accept a valuation so made.

5(8)   Each expert has the right of access to all such documents of all the transferor companies and pre-existing transferee companies concerned in the scheme, and the right to require from the companies' officers all such information, as he thinks necessary for the purpose of making his report.

INSPECTION OF DOCUMENTS

6(1)   The documents referred to in paragraph 3(e) are, in relation to any company—

(a) the draft terms;

(b) the directors' report referred to in paragraph 4 above;

(c) the expert's report;

(d) the company's annual accounts, together with the relevant directors' report and auditors' report, for the last three financial years ending on or before the relevant date; and

(e) if the last of those financial years ended more than six months before the relevant date, an accounting statement in the form described in the following provisions.

   In paragraphs (d) and (e) **"the relevant date"** means one month before the first meeting of the company summoned under section 425(1) or for the purposes of paragraph 1.

History

In para. 6(1)(b) the words "referred to in paragraph 4 above" inserted, para. 6(1)(d), (e) substituted and the words after para. 6(1)(e) added by CA 1989, s. 23 and Sch. 10, para. 22(1)–(4) as from 1 April 1990 subject to transitional and saving provisions (see S.I. 1990 No. 355 (C.13), art. 3, Sch. 1 and also art. 6–9); para. 6(1)(d), (e) formerly read as follows:

"(d) the company's accounts within the meaning of section 239 for the last three complete financial

years ending on or before a date one month earlier than the first meeting of the company summoned either under section 425(1) or for the purposes of paragraph 1 (in this paragraph referred to as the 'relevant date');

(e) if the last complete financial year in respect of which accounts were prepared for the company ended more than 6 months before the relevant date, an accounting statement in the form described in the following sub-paragraph."

6(2)   The accounting statement shall consist of—

    (a) a balance sheet dealing with the state of the affairs of the company as at a date not more than three months before the draft terms were adopted by the directors, and

    (b) where the company would be required to prepare group accounts if that date were the last day of a financial year, a consolidated balance sheet dealing with the state of affairs of the company and its subsidiary undertakings as at that date.

History

See history note after para. 6(5).

6(3)   The requirements of this Act as to balance sheets forming part of a company's annual accounts, and the matters to be included in notes thereto, apply to any balance sheet required for the accounting statement, with such modifications as are necessary by reason of its being prepared otherwise than as at the last day of a financial year.

History

See history note after para. 6(5).

6(4)   Any balance sheet required for the accounting statement shall be approved by the board of directors and signed on behalf of the board by a director of the company.

History

See history note after para. 6(5).

6(5)   In relation to a company within the meaning of Article 3 of the Companies (Northern Ireland) Order 1986, the references in this paragraph to the requirements of this Act shall be construed as reference to the corresponding requirements of that Order.

History

Para. 6(2)–(5) substituted by CA 1989, s. 23 and Sch. 10, para. 22(1), (5) as from 1 April 1990 subject to transitional and saving provisions (see S.I. 1990 No. 355 (C.13), art. 3, Sch. 1 and also art. 6–9); para. 6(2)–(5) formerly read as follows:

"**6(2)**   The accounting statement shall consist of—

  (a) a balance sheet dealing with the state of affairs of the company, and;

  (b) where the company has subsidiaries and section 229 would apply if the relevant date were the end of the company's financial year, a further balance sheet or balance sheets dealing with the state of affairs of the company and the subsidiaries.

(3)   Subject to sub-paragraph (4) below, any balance sheet required by sub-paragraph (2)(a) or (b) above shall comply with section 228 or section 230 (as appropriate) and with all other requirements of this Act as to the matters to be included in a company's balance sheet or in notes thereto (applying those sections and Schedule 4 and those other requirements with such modifications as are necessary

because the balance sheet is prepared otherwise than as at the last day of the financial year) and must be signed in accordance with section 238.

(4)   Notwithstanding sub-paragraph (3) above, any balance sheet required by sub-paragraph (2)(a) or (b) above shall deal with the state of affairs of the company or subsidiaries as at a date not earlier than the first day of the third month preceding the date when the draft terms were adopted by the directors, and the requirement in section 228 to give a true and fair view shall for the purposes of this paragraph have effect as a requirement to give a true and fair view of the state of affairs of the company as at the first-mentioned date.

(5)   In sub-paragraphs (1) to (4) above, references to section 228, 229, 230, 238 and 239 and Schedule 4 shall, in the case of a company within the meaning of Article 3 of the Companies (Northern Ireland) Order 1986, have effect as references to Articles 236, 237, 238, 246 and 247 and Schedule 4 of that Order respectively, and references to the requirements of this Act shall have effect as references to the requirements of that Order."

[The next page is 32,701]

TRANSFEROR COMPANY HOLDING ITS OWN SHARES

7 The court shall not sanction under section 425(2) a compromise or arrangement under which any shares in a transferee company are to be allotted to a transferor company or its nominee in respect of shares in that transferor company held by it or its nominee.

SECURITIES OTHER THAN SHARES TO WHICH SPECIAL RIGHTS ARE ATTACHED

8(1) Where any security of a transferor company to which special rights are attached is held by a person other than as a member or creditor of the company, the court shall not sanction a compromise or arrangement under section 425(2) unless under the scheme that person is to receive rights in a transferee company of equivalent value.

8(2) Sub-paragraph (1) above shall not apply in the case of any such security where—

    (a) the holder has agreed otherwise; or

    (b) the holder is, or under the scheme is to be, entitled to have the security purchased by a transferee company involved in the scheme on terms which the court considers reasonable.

DATE AND CONSEQUENCES OF THE COMPROMISE OR ARRANGEMENT

9(1) The following provisions of this paragraph shall apply where the court sanctions a compromise or arrangement.

9(2) The court shall in the order sanctioning the compromise or arrangement or in a subsequent order under section 427 fix a date on which the transfer or transfers to the transferee company or transferee companies of the undertaking, property and liabilities of the transferor company shall take place; and any such order which provide for the dissolution of the transferor company shall fix the same date for the dissolution.

9(3) If it is necessary for the transferor company to take any steps to ensure that the undertaking, property and liabilities are fully transferred, the court shall fix a date, not later than six months after the date fixed under sub-paragraph (2) above, by which such steps must be taken and for that purpose may postpone the dissolution of the transferor company until that date.

9(4) The court may postpone or further postpone the date fixed under sub-paragraph (3) above if it is satisfied that the steps there mentioned cannot be completed by the date (or latest date) fixed under that sub-paragraph.

EXCEPTIONS

10(1) The court may sanction a compromise or arrangement under section 425(2) notwithstanding that—

    (a) any meeting otherwise required by paragraph 1 has not been summoned by a pre-existing transferee company ("the relevant company"), and

    (b) paragraphs 2(1)(c) and 3(e) have not been complied with in respect of that company,

if the court is satisfied that the conditions specified in sub-paragraph (2) below have been complied with.

10(2)   Subject to paragraphs 11(3) and 12(3), the conditions mentioned in sub-paragraph (1) above are—

(a) that the publication of notice of receipt of the draft terms by the registrar of companies referred to in paragraph 2(1)(b) took place in respect of the relevant company at least one month before the date of any meeting of members of any transferor company concerned in the scheme summoned under section 425(1);

(b) that the members of the relevant company were able to inspect at the registered office of that company the documents listed in paragraph 6(1) in relation to every transferor company and transferee company concerned in the scheme during a period ("the relevant period") beginning one month before, and ending on, the date of any such meeting, and that they were able to obtain copies of those documents or any part of them on request during that period free of charge; and

(c) that one or more members of the relevant company, who together held not less than five per cent of the paid-up capital of that company which carried the right to vote at general meetings of the company, would have been able during the relevant period to require that a meeting of each class of members be called for the purpose of deciding whether or not to agree to the scheme but that no such requisition had been made.

11(1)   The following sub-paragraphs apply where the scheme is a Case 3 Scheme.

11(2)   Sub-paragraphs (a) to (d) of paragraph 3 shall not apply and sub-paragraph (e) of that paragraph shall not apply as regards the documents listed in paragraph 6(1)(b), (c) and (e), if all members holding shares in, and all persons holding other securities of, any of the transferor companies and pre-existing transferee companies concerned in the scheme on the date of the application to the court under section 425(1), being shares or securities which as at that date carry the right to vote in general meetings of the company, so agree.

11(3)   The court may by order direct in respect of any transferor company or pre-existing transferee company that the requirements relating to—

(a) delivering copies of the draft terms and publication of notice of receipt of the draft terms under paragraph 2(1)(b) and (c), or

(b) inspection under paragraph 3(e),

shall not apply, and may by order direct that paragraph 10 shall apply to any pre-existing transferee company with the omission of sub-paragraph (2)(a) and (b) of that paragraph.

11(4)   The court shall not make any order under sub-paragraph (3) above unless it is satisfied that the following conditions will be fulfilled—

(a) that the members of the company will have received or will have been able to obtain free of charge copies of the documents listed in paragraph 6(1) in time to examine them before the date of the first meeting of the members or any class of members of the company summoned under section 425(1) or for the purposes of paragraph 1;

(b) in the case of a pre-existing transferee company, where in the circumstances described in paragraph 10 no meeting is held, that the members of that company will have received or will have been able to obtain free of charge copies of those documents in time to require a meeting under paragraph 10(2)(c);

(c) that the creditors of the company will have received or will have been able to obtain free of charge copies of the draft terms in time to examine them before the date of the meeting of the members or any class of members of the company, or, in the circumstances referred to in paragraph (b) above, at the same time as the members of the company; and

(d) that no prejudice would be caused to the members or creditors of any transferor company or transferee company concerned in the scheme by making the order in question.

TRANSFEREE COMPANY OR COMPANIES HOLDING SHARES IN THE TRANSFEROR COMPANY

12(1) Where the scheme is a Case 1 Scheme and in the case of every transferor company concerned—

(a) the shares in that company, and

(b) such securities of that company (other than shares) as carry the right to vote at general meetings of that company,

are all held by or on behalf of the transferee company, section 427A and this Schedule shall apply subject to the following sub-paragraphs.

12(2) The draft terms need not give particulars of the matters mentioned in paragraph 2(2)(b), (c) or (d).

12(3) Section 426 and sub-paragraphs (a) and (d) of paragraph 3 shall not apply, and sub-paragraph (e) of that paragraph shall not apply as regards the documents listed in paragraph 6(1)(b) and (c).

12(4) The court may sanction the compromise or arrangement under section 425(2) notwithstanding that—

(a) any meeting otherwise required by section 425 or paragraph 1 has not been summoned by any company concerned in the scheme, and

(b) paragraphs 2(1)(c) and 3(e) have not been complied with in respect of that company,

if it is satisfied that the conditions specified in the following sub-paragraphs have been complied with.

12(5) The conditions mentioned in the previous sub-paragraph are—

(a) that the publication of notice of receipt of the draft terms by the registrar of companies referred to in paragraph 2(1)(b) took place in respect of every transferor company and transferee company concerned in the scheme at least one month before the date of the order under section 425(2) ("the relevant date");

(b) that the members of the transferee company were able to inspect at the registered office of that company copies of the documents listed in paragraphs 6(1)(a), (d) and (e) in relation to every transferor company or transferee company concerned in the scheme during a period ("the relevant period") beginning one month before, and ending on, the relevant date and that they were able to obtain copies of those documents or any part of them on request during that period free of charge; and

(c) that one or more members of the transferee company who together held not less than five per cent of the paid-up capital of the company which carried the right to vote at general meetings of the company would have been able during the relevant period to require that a meeting of each class of members be called for the purpose of deciding whether or not to agree to the scheme but that no such requisition has been made.

13(1)   Where the scheme is a Case 3 Scheme and—

(a) the shares in the transferor company, and

(b) such securities of that company (other than shares) as carry the right to vote at general meetings of that company,

are all held by or on behalf of one or more transferee companies, section 427A and this Schedule shall apply subject to the following sub-paragraphs.

13(2)   The court may sanction a compromise or arrangement under section 425(2) notwithstanding that—

(a) any meeting otherwise required by section 425 has not been summoned by the transferor company, and

(b) paragraphs 2(1)(c) and 3(b) and (e) have not been complied with in respect of that company,

if it is satisfied that the conditions specified in the following sub-paragraph have been complied with.

13(3)   The conditions referred to in the previous sub-paragraph are—

(a) the conditions set out in paragraph 12(5)(a) and (c);

(b) that the members of the transferor company and every transferee company concerned in the scheme were able to inspect at the registered office of the company of which they were members copies of the documents listed in paragraph 6(1) in relation to every such company during a period beginning one month before, and ending on, the date of the order under section 425(2) ("the relevant date"), and that they were able to obtain copies of those documents or any part of them on request during that period free of charge; and

(c) that the directors of the transferor company have sent to every member who would have been entitled to receive a notice of the meeting (had it been called), and to the directors of each transferee company, a report of any material changes in the property and liabilities of the transferor company between the date when the draft terms were adopted and a date one month before the relevant date.

14(1)   Where the scheme is a Case 1 Scheme and in the case of every transferor company concerned ninety per cent or more (but not all) of—

(a) the shares in that company, and

(b) such securities of that company (other than shares) as carry the right to vote at general meetings of that company,

CA 1985, Sch. 15B, para. 13(1)   [The next page is 32,901]

are held by or on behalf of the transferee company, section 427A and this Schedule shall apply subject to the following sub-paragraphs.

14(2) The court may sanction a compromise or arrangement under section 425(2) notwithstanding that—

(a) any meeting otherwise required by paragraph 1 has not been summoned by the transferee company, and

(b) paragraphs 2(1)(c) and 3(e) have not been complied with in respect of that company,

if the court is satisfied that the conditions specified in the following sub-paragraph have been complied with.

14(3) The conditions referred to in the previous sub-paragraph are the same conditions as those specified in paragraph 10(2), save that for this purpose the condition contained in paragraph 10(2)(b) shall be treated as referring only to the documents listed in paragraph 6(1)(a), (d) and (e).

LIABILITY OF TRANSFEREE COMPANIES FOR THE DEFAULT OF ANOTHER

15(1) Where the scheme is a Case 3 Scheme, each transferee company shall be jointly and severally liable, subject to sub-paragraph (2) below, for any liability transferred to any other transferee company under the scheme to the extent that that other company has made default in satisfying that liability, but so that no transferee company shall be so liable for an amount greater than the amount arrived at by calculating the value at the time of the transfer of the property transferred to it under the scheme less the amount at that date of the liabilities so transferred.

15(2) If a majority in number representing three-fourths in value of the creditors or any class of creditors of the transferor company present and voting either in person or by proxy at a meeting summoned under section 425(1) so agree, sub-paragraph (1) above shall not apply in respect of the liabilities of the creditors or that class of creditors.

History
Sch. 15B renumbered as such by CA 1989, s. 114(2) as from 1 April 1990 (see S.I. 1990 No. 355 (C.13), art. 4(a)) — the schedule was previously Sch. 15A and was inserted by the Companies (Mergers and Divisions) Regulations 1987 (S.I. 1987 No. 1991), reg. 2(c) and Sch., Pt. II as from 1 January 1988.

Schedule 16 — Orders in Course of Winding Up Pronounced in Vacation (Scotland)

Section 571

(Repealed by Insolvency Act 1986, sec. 438 and Sch. 12 as from 29 December 1986.)

History
In regard to the date of the above repeal, see Insolvency Act 1986, s. 443 and S.I. 1986 No. 1924 (C. 71); Sch. 16 formerly read as follows:

"Part I — Orders Which are to be Final

Order under section 557, as to the time for proving debts and claims.

Orders under section 561, as to the attendance of, and production of documents by, persons indebted to, or having property of, or information as to the affairs or property of, a company.

Orders under section 645 as to meetings for ascertaining wishes of creditors or contributories.

Orders under section 648, as to the examination of witnesses in regard to the property or affairs of a company.

Part II — Orders Which are to take Effect Until Matter Disposed of by Inner House

Orders under section 521(1), 525(2) or (3), 549, 672 or 673, restraining or permitting the commencement or the continuance of legal proceedings.

Orders under section 532(4), limiting the powers of provisional liquidators.

Orders under section 536, 599 or 609, appointing a liquidator to fill a vacancy, or appointing (except to fill a vacancy caused by the removal of a liquidator by the court) a liquidator for a winding up voluntarily or subject to supervision.

Orders under section 539, sanctioning the exercise of any power by a liquidator, other than the powers specified in paragraphs (c), (d), (e) and (f) of subsection (1).

Orders under section 551, requiring the delivery of property or documents to the liquidator.

Orders under section 565, as to the arrest and detention of an absconding contributory and his property.

Orders under section 606, for continuance of winding up subject to supervision."

Schedule 17 — Proceedings of Committee of Inspection

Sections 547, 590

(Repealed by Insolvency Act 1985, sec. 235 and Sch. 10, Pt. II as from 29 December 1986.)

History

In regard to the date of the above repeal, see S.I. 1986 No. 1924 (C. 71); Sch. 17 formerly read as follows:

"**1** The committee shall meet at such times as it may from time to time appoint and, failing such appointment, at least once a month; and the liquidator or any member of the committee may also call a meeting of the committee as and when he thinks necessary.

2 The committee may act by a majority of its members present at a meeting, but shall not act unless a majority of the committee are present.

3 A member of the committee may resign by notice in writing signed by him and delivered to the liquidator.

4 If a member of the committee becomes bankrupt or compounds or arranges with his creditors or is absent from five consecutive meetings of the committee without leave of those members who together with himself represent the creditors or contributories (as the case may be), his office thereupon becomes vacant.

5 A member of the committee may be removed by an ordinary resolution at a meeting of creditors (if he represents creditors) or of contributories (if he represents contributories) of which 7 days' notice has been given, stating the object of the meeting.

6(1) On a vacancy occurring in the committee the liquidator shall forthwith summon a meeting of creditors or of contributories (as the case may require) to fill the vacancy; and the meeting may, by resolution, reappoint the same or appoint another creditor or contributory to fill the vacancy.

6(2) However, if the liquidator, having regard to the position in the winding up, is of the opinion that it is unnecessary for the vacancy to be filled, he may apply to the court; and the court may make an order that the vacancy be not filled, or be not filled except in circumstances specified by the order.

6(3) The continuing members of the committee, if not less than two, may act notwithstanding any vacancy in the committee."

Schedule 18 — Provisions of Part XX Not Applicable in Winding Up Subject to Supervision of the Court

Section 610

(Repealed by Insolvency Act 1985, sec. 235 and Sch. 10, Pt. II as from 29 December 1986.)

History

In regard to the date of the above repeal, see S.I. 1986 No. 1924 (C. 71). Sch. 18 formerly read as follows:

Section	Subject matter
528	Statement of company's affairs to be submitted to official receiver.
529	
530	Report by official receiver.
531	Power of court to appoint liquidators.
532	Appointment and powers of provisional liquidator.
533	Appointment, style, etc. of liquidators in England and Wales.
534	Provisions where person other than official receiver is appointed liquidator.
535	Provision as to liquidators in Scotland.
536 (except subs. (5)).	General provisions as to liquidators.
540	Exercise and control of liquidator's powers in England and Wales.
541	Books to be kept by liquidator (England and Wales).

542		Payments of liquidator into bank (England and Wales).
543		Audit of liquidator's accounts (England and Wales).
544		Control of Secretary of State over liquidators in England and Wales.
545		Release of liquidators (England and Wales).
546		Meetings of creditors and contributories to determine whether committee of inspection shall be appointed.
547 548	(with Sch. 17)	Constitution, proceedings, etc. of committee of inspection; powers of Secretary of State where no committee.
556		Appointment of special manager (England and Wales).
563 564		Power to order public examination of promoters and officers (England and Wales).
567		Delegation to liquidator of certain powers of the court (England and Wales)."

Schedule 19 — Preference Among Creditors in Company Winding Up

Section 614

(Repealed by Insolvency Act 1985, sec. 235 and Sch. 10, Pt. II as from 29 December 1986.)

History
In regard to the date of the above repeal, see S.I. 1986 No. 1924 (C. 71); Sch. 19 formerly read as follows:

"'THE RELEVANT DATE'

1 For the purposes of this Schedule, **'the relevant date'** is—

   (a) in the case of a company ordered to be wound up compulsorily, the date of the appointment (or first appointment) of a provisional liquidator or, if no such appointment has been made, the date of the winding-up order, unless in either case the company had commenced to be wound up voluntarily before that date, and

   (b) otherwise, the date of the passing of the resolution for winding up the company.

DEBTS TO INLAND REVENUE

2 All income tax, corporation tax, capital gains tax and other assessed taxes, assessed on the company up to 5th April next before the relevant date, and not exceeding in the whole one year's assessment.

3 Any sums due at the relevant date from the company on account of tax deductions for the 12 months next before that date.

The sums here referred to—

   (a) are those due by way of deduction of income tax from emoluments during the relevant period, which the company was liable to make under section 204 of the Income and Corporation Taxes Act 1970, less the amount of the repayments of income tax which the company was liable to make during the same period, and

   (b) include amounts due from the company in respect of deductions required to be made by it under section 69 of the Finance (No. 2) Act 1975 (construction industry contract workers).

DEBTS DUE TO CUSTOMS & EXCISE

4 Any value added tax due at the relevant date from the company and having become due within the 12 months next before that date.

For purposes of this paragraph, the tax having become due within those 12 months in respect of any prescribed accounting period falling partly within and partly outside those 12 months is taken to be such part of the tax due for the whole of that accounting reference period as is proportionate to the part of the period falling within the 12 months.

5 The amount of any car tax due at the relevant date from the company and having become due within the 12 months next before that date.

6 Any amount due—

   (a) by way of general betting duty or bingo duty, or

   (b) under section 12(1) of the Betting and Gaming Duties Act 1981 (general betting duty and pool betting duty recoverable from agent collecting stakes), or

   (c) under section 14 of, or Schedule 2 to, that Act (gaming licence duty),

from the company at the relevant date and which became due within the 12 months next before that date.

LOCAL RATES

7 All local rates due from the company at the relevant date and having become due and payable within 12 months next before that date.

SOCIAL SECURITY DEBTS

8 All the debts specified in section 153(2) of the Social Security Act 1975, Schedule 3 to the Social Security Pensions Act 1975, and any corresponding provisions in force in Northern Ireland.

(This does not apply if the company is being wound up voluntarily merely for the purposes of reconstruction or amalgamation with another company.)

DEBTS TO AND IN RESPECT OF COMPANY'S EMPLOYEES

9 All wages or salary (whether or not earned wholly or in part by way of commission) of any clerk or servant in respect of services rendered to the company during 4 months next before the relevant date, and all wages (whether payable for time or for piece work) of any workman or labourer in respect of services so rendered.

10 All accrued holiday remuneration becoming payable to any clerk, servant, workman or labourer (or in the case of his death to any other person in his right) on the termination of his employment before or by the effect of the winding-up order or resolution.

This includes, in relation to any person, all sums which, by virtue either of his contract of employment or of any enactment (including any order made or direction given under an Act), are payable on account of the remuneration which would, in the ordinary course, have become payable to him in respect of a period of holiday had his employment with the company continued until he became entitled to be allowed the holiday.

11 The following amounts owed by the company to an employee are treated as wages payable by it to him in respect of the period for which they are payable—

  (a) a guarantee payment under section 12(1) of the Employment Protection (Consolidation) Act 1978 (employee without work to do for a day or part of a day),

  (b) remuneration on suspension on medical grounds under section 19 of that Act,

  (c) any payment for time off under section 27(3) (trade union duties), 31(3) (looking for work, etc.) or 31A(4) (ante-natal care) of that Act,

  (d) statutory sick pay under Part I of the Social Security and Housing Benefits Act 1982, and

  (e) remuneration under a protective award made by an industrial tribunal under section 101 of the Employment Protection Act 1975 (redundancy dismissal with compensation).

12(1) The remuneration to which priority is to be given under paragraph 9 shall not, in the case of any claimant, exceed £800:

Provided that where a claimant under paragraph 9 is a labourer in husbandry who has entered into a contract for the payment of a portion of his wages in a lump sum at the end of the year of hiring, he had priority in respect of the whole of that sum, or a part of it, as the court may decide to be due under the contract, proportionate to the time of service up to the relevant date.

12(2) No increase or reduction of the money sum specified above in this paragraph affects any case where the relevant date (or, where provisions of this Schedule apply by virtue of section 196, the date referred to in subsection (4) of that section) occurred before the coming into force of the increase or reduction.

PRIORITY FOR THIRD PARTY ADVANCING FUNDS FOR WAGE-PAYMENTS, ETC.

13 Where any payment has been made—

  (a) to any clerk, servant, workman or labourer in the employment of the company on account of wages or salary, or

  (b) to any such clerk, servant, workman or labourer or, in case of his death, to any other person in his right, on account of accrued holiday remuneration,

out of money advanced by some person for that purpose, the person by whom the money was advanced has in the winding-up a right of priority in respect of the money so advanced and paid up to the amount by which the sum in respect of which the clerk, servant, workman or labourer, or other person in his right, would have been entitled to priority in the winding-up has been diminished by reason of the payment having been made.

INTERPRETATION FOR THE ABOVE PARAGRAPHS

14 For purposes of this Schedule—

  (a) any remuneration in respect of a period of holiday or of absence from work through sickness or other good cause is deemed to be wages in respect of services rendered to the company in that period; and

  (b) references to remuneration in respect of a period of holiday include any sums which, if they had been paid, would have been treated for purposes of the enactments relating to social security as earnings in respect of that period.''

Schedule 20 — Vesting of Disclaimed Property; Protection of Third Parties

Section 619

Part I — Disclaimer by Liquidator under sections 618, 619; Crown Disclaimer under section 656

(England and Wales Only)

(Repealed by Insolvency Act 1985, sec. 235 and Sch. 10, Pt. II as from 29 December 1986.)

History

In regard to the date of the above repeal see S.I. 1986 No. 1924 (C. 71); Sch. 20, Pt. I formerly read as follows:

''**1** The court shall not under section 619 (including that section as applied by section 657(2)) make a vesting order, where the property disclaimed is of a leasehold nature, in favour of a person claiming under the company, except on the following terms.

2 The person must by the order be made subject—

  (a) to the same liabilities and obligations as those to which the company was subject under the lease in respect of the property at the commencement of the winding up, or

  (b) (if the court thinks fit) only to the same liabilities and obligations as if the lease had been assigned to him at that date;

and in either event (if the case so requires) the liabilities and obligations must be as if the lease had comprised only the property comprised in the vesting order.

3 A mortgagee or under-lessee declining to accept a vesting order on such terms is excluded from all interest in and security on the property.

4 If there is no person claiming under the company who is willing to accept an order on such terms, the court has power to vest the company's estate and interest in the property in any person liable (either personally or in a representative character, and either alone or jointly with the company) to perform the lessee's covenants in the lease, freed and discharged from all estates, incumbrances and interests created therein by the company."

Part II — Crown Disclaimer under section 656
(Scotland Only)

5 The court shall not under section 657 make a vesting order, where the property disclaimed is held under a lease, in favour of a person claiming under the company (whether as sub-lessee or as creditor in a duly registered or, as appropriate, recorded heritable security over a lease), except on the following terms.

6 The person must by the order be made subject—

(a) to the same liabilities and obligations as those to which the company was subject under the lease in respect of the property at the commencement of the winding up, or

(b) (if the court thinks fit) only to the same liabilities and obligations as if the lease had been assigned to him at that date;

and in either event (if the case so requires) the liabilities and obligations must be as if the lease had comprised only the property comprised in the vesting order.

7 A creditor or sub-lessee declining to accept a vesting order on such terms is excluded from all interest in and security over the property.

8 If there is no person claiming under the company who is willing to accept an order on such terms, the court has power to vest the company's estate and interest in the property in any person liable (either personally or in a representative character, and either alone or jointly with the company) to perform the lessee's obligations under the lease, freed and discharged from all interests, rights and obligations created by the company in the lease or in relation to the lease.

9 For the purposes of paragraph 5 above, a heritable security is duly recorded if it is recorded in the Register of Sasines and is duly registered if registered in accordance with the Land Registration (Scotland) Act 1979.

Schedule 21 — Effect of Registration under section 680

Section 689

INTERPRETATION

1 In this Schedule—

"**registration**" means registration in pursuance of section 680 in Chapter II of Part XXII of this Act, and "**registered**" has the corresponding meaning, and

"**instrument**" includes deed of settlement, contract of copartnery and letters patent.

VESTING OF PROPERTY

2   All property belonging to or vested in the company at the date of its registration passes to and vests in the company on registration for all the estate and interest of the company in the property.

EXISTING LIABILITIES

3   Registration does not affect the company's rights or liabilities in respect of any debt or obligation incurred, or contract entered into, by, to, with or on behalf of the company before registration.

PENDING ACTIONS AT LAW

4(1)   All actions and other legal proceedings which at the time of the company's registration are pending by or against the company, or the public officer or any member of it, may be continued in the same manner as if the registration had not taken place.

4(2)   However, execution shall not issue against the effects of any individual member of the company on any judgment, decree or order obtained in such an action or proceeding; but in the event of the company's property and effects being insufficient to satisfy the judgment, decree or order, an order may be obtained for winding up the company.

THE COMPANY'S CONSTITUTION

5(1)   All provisions contained in any Act of Parliament or other instrument constituting or regulating the company are deemed to be conditions and regulations of the company, in the same manner and with the same incidents as if so much of them as would, if the company had been formed under this Act, have been required to be inserted in the memorandum, were contained in a registered memorandum, and the residue were contained in registered articles.

5(2)   The provisions brought in under this paragraph include, in the case of a company registered as a company limited by guarantee, those of the resolution declaring the amount of the guarantee; and they include also the statement under section 681(5)(a), and any statement under section 684(2).

6(1)   All the provisions of this Act apply to the company, and to its members, contributories and creditors, in the same manner in all respects as if it had been formed under this Act, subject as follows.

6(2)   Table A does not apply unless adopted by special resolution.

6(3)   Provisions relating to the numbering of shares do not apply to any joint stock company whose shares are not numbered.

6(4)   Subject to the provisions of this Schedule, the company does not have power—

    (a) to alter any provision contained in an Act of Parliament relating to the company,

    (b) without the sanction of the Secretary of State, to alter any provision contained in letters patent relating to the company.

6(5)   The company does not have power to alter any provision contained in a royal charter or letters patent with respect to the company's objects.

CAPITAL STRUCTURE

7 Provisions of this Act with respect to—

(a) the registration of an unlimited company as limited,

(b) the powers of an unlimited company on registration as a limited company to increase the nominal amount of its share capital and to provide that a portion of its share capital shall not be capable of being called up except in the event of winding up, and

(c) the power of a limited company to determine that a portion of its share capital shall not be capable of being called up except in that event,

apply, notwithstanding any provisions contained in an Act of Parliament, royal charter or other instrument constituting or regulating the company.

SUPPLEMENTARY

8 Nothing in paragraphs 5 to 7 authorises a company to alter any such provisions contained in an instrument constituting or regulating the company as would, if the company had originally been formed under this Act, have been required to be contained in the memorandum and are not authorised to be altered by this Act.

9 None of the provisions of this Act (except section 461(3)) derogate from any power of altering the company's constitution or regulations which may, by virtue of any Act of Parliament or other instrument constituting or regulating it, be vested in the company.

Schedule 22 — Provisions of this Act applying to Unregistered Companies

Section 718

Provisions of this Act applied	Subject matter	Limitations and exceptions (if any)
In Part I —		
section 18 … … … …	Statutory and other amendments of memorandum and articles to be registered.	Subject to section 718(3).
section 35 … … …	Company's capacity; power of directors to bind it.	Subject to section 718(3).
section 36(4) … … …	Binding effect of contract made for company before its formation.	Subject to section 718(3).
section 40 … … …	Official seal for share certificates, etc.	Subject to section 718(3).
section 42 … … …	Events affecting a company's status to be officially notified.	Subject to section 718(3).
In Part III, Chapter I (with Schedule 3)	Prospectus and requirements in connection with it.	Subject to section 718(3)
In Part IV, sections 82, 86 and 87 …	Allotments.	Subject to section 718(3).
In Part V —		
section 185(4) … … … …	Exemption from duty to prepare certificates where shares etc. issued to clearing house or nominee.	Subject to section 718(3).
section 186 … … … …	Certificate as evidence of title.	Subject to section 718(3).
Part VII, with — Schedules 4 to 8 … … … Schedule 9 (except sub-paragraphs (a) to (d) of paragraph 2, sub-paragraphs (c), (d) and (e) of paragraph 3 and sub-paragraph (1)(c) of paragraph 10), and Schedule 10 and 10A … …	Accounts and audit.	Subject to section 718(3).
In Part IX —		
section 287 … … …	Registered office.	Subject to section 718(3).
sections 288 to 290 … … …	Register of directors and secretaries.	—

Provisions of this Act applied	Subject matter	Limitations and exceptions (if any)
In Part X, sections 343 to 347	Register to be kept of certain transactions not disclosed in accounts; other related matters.	Subject to section 718(3).
In Part XI — section 351(1), (2) and (5)(a)	Particulars of company to be given in correspondence.	Subject to section 718(3).
sections 363 (with Schedule 15) to 365	Annual return.	Subject to section 718(3).
sections 384 to 394A	Appointment, etc., of auditors.	Subject to section 718(3).
Part XIV (except section 446)	Investigation of companies and their affairs; requisition of documents.	—
Part XV	Effect of order imposing restrictions on shares.	To apply so far only as relates to orders under section 445.
Part XVI	Fraudulent trading by a company.	—
In Part XXIV — sections 706, 708 to 710, 712 and 713	Miscellaneous provisions about registration.	—
section 711	Public notice by registrar of companies with respect to certain documents.	Subject to section 718(3).
In Part XXV — section 720	Companies to publish periodical statement.	Subject to section 718(3).
section 721	Production and inspection of company's books.	To apply so far only as these provisions have effect in relation to provisions applying by virtue of the foregoing provisions of this Schedule.
section 722	Form of company registers, etc.	
section 723	Use of computers for company records.	
section 725	Service of documents.	
section 730, with Schedule 24	Punishment of offences; meaning of "officer in default".	
section 731	Summary proceedings.	
section 732	Prosecution by public authorities.	
Part XXVI	Interpretation.	To apply so far as requisite for the interpretation of other provisions applied by section 718 and this Schedule.

History

In the second column of the entry in Sch. 22 relating to s. 185(4) the words "clearing house or" substituted for the former words "stock exchange" by Financial Services Act 1986, s. 212(2) and Sch. 16, para. 26 as from 29 April 1988 (see S.I. 1988 No. 740 (C. 22)).

In Sch. 22 in the entry relating to Pt. VII, in column 1 the words "Schedules 10 and 10A" substituted for the former word "Schedule 10" by CA 1989, s. 23 and Sch. 10, para. 23 as from 1 April 1990 subject to transitional and saving provisions (see S.I. 1990 No. 355 (C. 13), art. 3, Sch. 1 and also art. 6–9).

In Sch. 22 in the entry relating to Pt. XI, sections 384 to 394A in column 1 "394A" substituted for the former "393" and in column 2 the word "qualifications" formerly appearing after "Appointment" repealed by CA 1989, s. 123(5), 212 and Sch. 24 as from 1 April 1990 subject to transitional and saving provisions (see S.I. 1990 No. 355 (C. 13), art. 4(a), 5(1)(b), (2) and also art. 6–10).

In Sch. 22 the entry relating to Pt. XIV substituted by CA 1989, s. 71 as from 21 February 1990 (see S.I. 1990 No. 142 (C. 5), art. 4); the entry formerly read as follows:

Provisions of this Act applied	Subject matter	Limitations and exceptions (if any)
"In Part XIV, sections 431 to 445 and 452(1)	Investigation of companies and their affairs.	—."

In Sch. 22 the entry relating to Pt. XVI inserted by CA 1989, s. 145 and Sch. 19, para. 21 as from 1 March 1990 (see S.I. 1990 No. 142 (C. 5), art. 5).

Note
Entries in Sch. 22 relating to Pt. III and IV repealed by Financial Services Act 1986, s. 212(3) and Sch. 17 to the extent to which those entries would apply re any investment listed or the subject of a listing application under Financial Services Act 1986, Pt. IV and commencing:

- on 12 January 1987 for all purposes relating to the admission of securities offered by or on behalf of a Minister of the Crown or a body corporate controlled by a Minister of the Crown or a subsidiary of such a

body corporate to the Official List in respect of which an application is made after that date;

- on 16 February 1987 for purposes relating to the admission of securities in respect of which an applciation is made after that date other than those referred to in the preceding paragraph and otherwise for all purposes.

(See S.I. 1986 No. 2246 (C. 88).)

The same entries repealed by Financial Services Act 1986, s. 212(3) and Sch. 17 as far as they would apply to a prospectus offering for subscription, or to any form of application for units in a body corporate which is a recognised scheme (see S.I. 1988 No. 740 (C. 22)).

Schedule 23 — Form of Statement to be Published by Certain Companies Under Section 720

Section 720

* The share capital of the company is   , divided into   shares of   each.

The number of shares issued is

Calls to the amount of   pounds per share have been made, under which the sum of   pounds has been received.

The liabilities of the company on the first day of January (*or* July) were —

   Debts owing to sundry persons by the company.

   On judgment (in Scotland, in respect of which decree has been granted), £

   On specialty, £

   On notes or bills, £

   On simple contracts, £

   On estimated liabilities, £

   The assets of the company on that day were —

   Government securities [*stating them*]

   Bills of exchange and promissory notes, £

   Cash at the bankers, £

   Other securities, £

---

   * If the company has no share capital the portion of the statement relating to capital and shares must be omitted.

CA 1985, Sch. 23

Section 730

Schedule 24 — Punishment of Offences Under this Act

Note: In the fourth and fifth columns of this Schedule, "**the statutory maximum**" means —

(a) in England and Wales, the prescribed sum under section 32 of the Magistrates' Courts Act 1980 (c. 43), and

(b) in Scotland, the prescribed sum under section 289B of the Criminal Procedure (Scotland) Act 1975 (c. 21).

Section of Act creating offence	General nature of offence	Mode of prosecution	Punishment	Daily default fine (where applicable)
6(3) ...	Company failing to deliver to register notice or other document, following alteration of its objects.	Summary.	One-fifth of the statutory maximum.	One-fiftieth of the statutory maximum.
18(3) ...	Company failing to register change in memorandum or articles.	Summary.	One-fifth of the statutory maximum.	One-fiftieth of the statutory maximum.
19(2) ...	Company failing to send to one of its members a copy of the memorandum or articles, when so required by the member.	Summary.	One-fifth of the statutory maximum.	
20(2) ...	Where company's memorandum altered, company issuing copy of the memorandum without the alteration.	Summary.	One-fifth of the statutory maximum for each occasion on which copies are so issued after the date of the alteration.	
28(5) ...	Company failing to change name on direction of Secretary of State.	Summary.	One-fifth of the statutory maximum.	One-fiftieth of the statutory maximum.
31(5) ...	Company altering its memorandum or articles, so ceasing to be exempt from having "limited" as part of its name.	Summary.	The statutory maximum.	One-tenth of the statutory maximum.
31(6) ...	Company failing to change name, on Secretary of State's direction, so as to have "limited" (or Welsh equivalent) at the end.	Summary.	One-fifth of the statutory maximum.	One-fiftieth of the statutory maximum.

Section of Act creating offence	General nature of offence	Mode of prosecution	Punishment	Daily default fine (where applicable)
32(4) ...	Company failing to comply with Secretary of State's direction to change its name, on grounds that the name is misleading.	Summary.	One-fifth of the statutory maximum.	One-fiftieth of the statutory maximum.
33 ...	Trading under misleading name (use of "public limited company" or Welsh equivalent when not so entitled); purporting to be a private company.	Summary.	One-fifth of the statutory maximum.	One-fiftieth of the statutory maximum.
34 ...	Trading or carrying on business with improper use of "limited" or "cyfyngedig".	Summary.	One-fifth of the statutory maximum.	One-fiftieth of the statutory maximum.
54(10) ...	Public company failing to give notice, or copy of court order, to registrar, concerning application to re-register as private company.	Summary.	One-fifth of the statutory maximum.	One-fiftieth of the statutory maximum.
56(4) ...	Issuing form of application for shares or debentures without accompanying prospectus.	1. On indictment. 2. Summary.	A fine. The statutory maximum.	
61 ...	Issuing prospectus with expert's statement in it, he not having given his consent; omission to state in prospectus that expert has consented.	1. On indictment. 2. Summary.	A fine. The statutory maximum.	
64(5) ...	Issuing company prospectus without copy being delivered to registrar of companies, or without requisite documents endorsed or attached.	Summary.	One-fifth of the statutory maximum.	One-fiftieth of the statutory maximum.
70(1) ...	Authorising issue of prospectus with untrue statement.	1. On indictment. 2. Summary.	2 years or a fine; or both. 6 months or the statutory maximum, or both.	
78(1) ...	Being responsible for issue, circulation of prospectus, etc. contrary to Part III, Chapter II (oversea companies).	1. On indictment. 2. Summary.	A fine. The statutory maximum.	

Section of Act creating offence	General nature of offence	Mode of prosecution	Punishment	Daily default fine (where applicable)
80(9)	Directors exercising company's power of allotment without the authority required by section 80(1).	1. On indictment. 2. Summary.	A fine. The statutory maximum.	
81(2)	Private limited company offering shares to the public, or allotting shares with a view to their being so offered.	1. On indictment. 2. Summary.	A fine. The statutory maximum.	
82(5)	Allotting shares or debentures before third day after issue of prospectus.	1. On indictment. 2. Summary.	A fine. The statutory maximum.	
86(6)	Company failing to keep money in separate bank account, where received in pursuance of prospectus stating that stock exchange listing is to be applied for.	1. On indictment. 2. Summary.	A fine. The statutory maximum.	
87(4)	Offeror of shares for sale failing to keep proceeds in separate bank account.	1. On indictment. 2. Summary.	A fine. The statutory maximum.	
88(5)	Officer of company failing to deliver return of allotments, etc., to registrar.	1. On indictment. 2. Summary.	A fine. The statutory maximum.	One-tenth of the statutory maximum.
95(6)	Knowingly or recklessly authorising or permitting misleading, false or deceptive material in statement by directors under section 95(5).	1. On indictment. 2. Summary.	2 years or a fine; or both. 6 months or the statutory maximum; or both.	
97(4)	Company failing to deliver to registrar the prescribed form disclosing amount or rate of share commission.	Summary.	One-fifth of the statutory maximum.	
110(2)	Making misleading, false or deceptive statement in connection with valuation under section 103 or 104.	1. On indictment. 2. Summary.	2 years or a fine; or both. 6 months or the statutory maximum; or both.	

Section of Act creating offence	General nature of offence	Mode of prosecution	Punishment	Daily default fine (where applicable)
111(3) ...	Officer of company failing to deliver copy of asset valuation report to registrar.	1. On indictment. 2. Summary.	A fine. The statutory maximum.	One-tenth of the statutory maximum.
111(4) ...	Company failing to deliver to registrar copy of resolution under section 104(4), with respect to transfer of an asset as consideration for allotment.	Summary.	One-fifth of the statutory maximum.	One-fiftieth of the statutory maximum.
114 ...	Contravention of any of the provisions of sections 99 to 104, 106.	1. On indictment. 2. Summary.	A fine. The statutory maximum.	
117(7) ...	Company doing business or exercising borrowing powers contrary to section 117.	1. On indictment. 2. Summary.	A fine. The statutory maximum.	
122(2) ...	Company failing to give notice to registrar of re-organisation of share capital.	Summary.	One-fifth of the statutory maximum.	One-fiftieth of the statutory maximum.
123(4) ...	Company failing to give notice to registrar of increase of share capital.	Summary.	One-fifth of the statutory maximum.	One-fiftieth of the statutory maximum.
127(5) ...	Company failing to forward to registrar copy of court order, when application made to cancel resolution varying shareholders' rights.	Summary.	One-fifth of the statutory maximum.	One-fiftieth of the statutory maximum.
128(5) ...	Company failing to send to registrar statement or notice required by section 128 (particulars of shares carrying special rights).	Summary.	One-fifth of the statutory maximum.	One-fiftieth of the statutory maximum.
129(4) ...	Company failing to deliver to registrar statement or notice required by section 129 (registration of newly created class rights).	Summary.	One-fifth of the statutory maximum.	One-fiftieth of the statutory maximum.

Section of Act creating offence	General nature of offence	Mode of prosecution	Punishment	Daily default fine (where applicable)
141	Officer of company concealing name of creditor entitled to object to reduction of capital, or wilfully misrepresenting nature or amount of debt or claim, etc.	1. On indictment. 2. Summary.	A fine. The statutory maximum.	
142(2) ...	Director authorising or permitting non-compliance with section 142 (requirement to convene company meeting to consider serious loss of capital).	1. On indictment. 2. Summary.	A fine. The statutory maximum.	
143(2) ...	Company acquiring its own shares in breach of section 143.	1. On indictment. 2. Summary.	In the case of the company, a fine. In the case of an officer of the company who is in default, 2 years or a fine; or both. In the case of the company, the statutory maximum. In the case of an officer of the company who is in default, 6 months or the statutory maximum; or both.	
149(2) ...	Company failing to cancel its own shares, acquired by itself, as required by section 146(2); or failing to apply for re-registration as private company as so required in the case there mentioned.	Summary.	One-fifth of the statutory maximum.	One-fiftieth of the statutory maximum.

Section of Act creating offence	General nature of offence	Mode of prosecution	Punishment	Daily default fine (where applicable)
151(3) ...	Company giving financial assistance towards acquisition of its own shares.	1. On indictment.	Where the company is convicted, a fine. Where an officer of the company is convicted, 2 years or a fine; or both.	
		2. Summary.	Where the company is convicted, the statutory maximum. Where an officer of the company is convicted, 6 months or the statutory maximum; or both.	
156(6) ...	Company failing to register statutory declaration under section 155.	Summary.	The statutory maximum.	One-fiftieth of the statutory maximum.
156(7) ...	Director making statutory declaration under section 155, without having reasonable grounds for opinion expressed in it.	1. On indictment. 2. Summary.	2 years or a fine; or both. 6 months or the statutory maximum; or both.	
169(6) ...	Default by company's officer in delivering to registrar the return required by section 169 (disclosure by company of purchase of own shares).	1. On indictment. 2. Summary.	A fine. The statutory maximum.	One-tenth of the statutory maximum.
169(7) ...	Company failing to keep copy of contract, etc., at registered office; refusal of inspection to person demanding it.	Summary.	One-fifth of the statutory maximum.	One-fiftieth of the statutory maximum.
173(6) ...	Director making statutory declaration under section 173 without having reasonable grounds for the opinion expressed in the declaration.	1. On indictment. 2. Summary.	2 years or a fine; or both. 6 months or the statutory maximum; or both.	
175(7) ...	Refusal of inspection of statutory declaration and auditors' report under section 173, etc.	Summary.	One-fifth of the statutory maximum.	One-fiftieth of the statutory maximum.

Section of Act creating offence	General nature of offence	Mode of prosecution	Punishment	Daily default fine (where applicable)
176(4) …	Company failing to give notice to registrar of application to court under section 176, or to register court order.	Summary.	One-fifth of the statutory maximum.	One-fiftieth of the statutory maximum.
183(6) …	Company failing to send notice of refusal to register a transfer of shares or debentures.	Summary.	One-fifth of the statutory maximum.	One-fiftieth of the statutory maximum.
185(5) …	Company default in compliance with section 185(1) (certificates to be made ready following allotment or transfer of shares, etc.).	Summary.	One-fifth of the statutory maximum.	One-fiftieth of the statutory maximum.
189(1) …	Offences of fraud and forgery in connection with share warrants in Scotland.	1. On indictment. 2. Summary.	7 years or a fine; or both. 6 months or the statutory maximum; or both.	
189(2) …	Unauthorised making of, or using or possessing apparatus for making, share warrants in Scotland.	1. On indictment. 2. Summary.	7 years or a fine; or both. 6 months or the statutory maximum; or both.	
191(4) …	Refusal of inspection or copy of register of debenture-holders, etc.	Summary.	One-fifth of the statutory maximum.	One-fiftieth of the statutory maximum.
210(3) …	Failure to discharge obligation of disclosure under Part VI; other forms of non-compliance with that Part.	1. On indictment. 2. Summary.	2 years or a fine; or both. 6 months or the statutory maximum; or both.	
211(10) …	Company failing to keep register of interests disclosed under Part VI; other contraventions of section 211.	Summary.	One-fifth of the statutory maximum.	One-fiftieth of the statutory maximum.
214(5) …	Company failing to exercise powers under section 212, when so required by the members.	1. On indictment. 2. Summary.	A fine. The statutory maximum.	
215(8) …	Company default in compliance with section 215 (company report of investigation of shareholdings on members' requisition).	1. On indictment. 2. Summary.	A fine. The statutory maximum.	

Section of Act creating offence	General nature of offence	Mode of prosecution	Punishment	Daily default fine (where applicable)
216(3)	Failure to comply with company notice under section 212; making false statement in response, etc.	1. On indictment. 2. Summary.	2 years or a fine; or both 6 months or the statutory maximum; or both.	
217(7)	Company failing to notify a person that he has been named as a shareholder; on removal of name from register, failing to alter associated index.	Summary.	One-fifth of the statutory maximum.	One-fiftieth of the statutory maximum.
218(3)	Improper removal of entry from register of interests disclosed; company failing to restore entry improperly removed.	Summary.	One-fifth of the statutory maximum.	For continued contravention of section 218(2) one-fiftieth of the statutory maximum.
219(3)	Refusal of inspection of register or report under Part VI; failure to send copy when required.	Summary.	One-fifth of the statutory maximum.	One-fiftieth of the statutory maximum.
221(5) or 222(4)	Company failing to keep accounting records (liability of officers).	1. On indictment. 2. Summary.	2 years or a fine; or both 6 months or the statutory maximum; or both.	
222(6)	Officer of company failing to secure compliance with, or intentionally causing default under section 222(5) (preservation of accounting records for requisite number of years).	1. On indictment. 2. Summary.	2 years or a fine; or both. 6 months or the statutory maximum; or both.	
231(6)	Company failing to annex to its annual return certain particulars required by Schedule 5 and not included in annual accounts.	Summary.	One-fifth of the statutory maximum.	One-fiftieth of the statutory maximum.
232(4)	Default by director or officer of a company in giving notice of matters relating to himself for purposes of Schedule 6 Part I.	Summary.	One-fifth of the statutory maximum.	

Section of Act creating offence	General nature of offence	Mode of prosecution	Punishment	Daily default fine (where applicable)
233(6) ...	Laying or delivering of unsigned balance sheet; circulating copies of balance sheet without signatures.	Summary.	One-fifth of the statutory maximum.	
234(5) ...	Non-compliance with Part VII, as to directors' report and its content; directors individually liable.	1. On indictment. 2. Summary.	A fine. The statutory maximum.	
234A(4) ...	Laying, circulating or delivering directors' report without required signature.	Summary.	One-fifth of the statutory maximum.	
236(4) ...	Laying, circulating or delivering auditors' report without required signature.	Summary.	One-fifth of the statutory maximum.	
238(5) ...	Failing to send company's annual accounts, directors' report and auditors' report to those entitled to receive them.	1. On indictment. 2. Summary.	A fine. The statutory maximum.	
239(3) ...	Company failing to supply copy of accounts and reports to shareholder on his demand.	Summary.	One-fifth of the statutory maximum.	One-fiftieth of the statutory maximum.
240(6) ...	Failure to comply with requirements in connection with publication of accounts.	Summary.	One-fifth of the statutory maximum.	
241(2) or 242(2) ...	Director in default as regards duty to lay and deliver company's annual accounts, directors' report and auditors' report.	Summary.	The statutory maximum.	One-tenth of the statutory maximum.
245(1) ...	Company's individual accounts not in conformity with requirements of this Act; directors individually liable.	1. On indictment. 2. Summary.	A fine. The statutory maximum.	
245(2) ...	Holding company's group accounts not in conformity with sections 229 and 230 and other requirements of this Act; directors individually liable.	1. On indictment. 2. Summary.	A fine. The statutory maximum.	
251(6) ...	Failure to comply with requirements in relation to summary financial statements.	Summary.	One-fifth of the statutory maximum.	

Section of Act creating offence	General nature of offence	Mode of prosecution	Punishment	Daily default fine (where applicable)
288(4) ...	Default in complying with section 288 (keeping register of directors and secretaries, refusal of inspection).	Summary.	The statutory maximum.	One-tenth of the statutory maximum.
291(5) ...	Acting as director of a company without having the requisite share qualification.	Summary.	One-fifth of the statutory maximum.	One-fiftieth of the statutory maximum.
294(4) ...	Director failing to give notice of his attaining retirement age; acting as director under appointment invalid due to his attaining it.	Summary.	One-fifth of the statutory maximum.	One-fiftieth of the statutory maximum.
305(3) ...	Company default in complying with section 305 (directors' names to appear on company correspondence, etc.).	Summary.	One-fifth of the statutory maximum.	
306(4) ...	Failure to state that liability of proposed director or manager is unlimited; failure to give notice of that fact to person accepting office.	1. On indictment. 2. Summary.	A fine. The statutory maximum.	
314(3) ...	Director failing to comply with section 314 (duty to disclose compensation payable on takeover, etc.); a person's failure to include required particulars in a notice he has to give of such matters.	Summary.	One-fifth of the statutory maximum.	
317(7) ...	Director failing to disclose interest in contract.	1. On indictment. 2. Summary.	A fine. The statutory maximum.	
318(8) ...	Company default in complying with section 318(1) or (5) (directors' service contracts to be open to inspection); 14 days' default in complying with section 318(4) (notice to registrar as to where copies of contracts and memoranda are kept); refusal of inspection required under section 318(7).	Summary.	One-fifth of the statutory maximum.	One-fiftieth of the statutory maximum.

Section of Act creating offence	General nature of offence	Mode of prosecution	Punishment	Daily default fine (where applicable)
323(2) …	Director dealing in options to buy or sell company's listed shares or debentures.	1. On indictment. 2. Summary.	2 years or a fine; or both. 6 months or the statutory maximum; or both.	
324(7) …	Director failing to notify interest in company's shares; making false statement in purported notification.	1. On indictment. 2. Summary.	2 years or a fine; or both. 6 months or the statutory maximum; or both.	
326(2), (3), (4), (5) …	Various defaults in connection with company register of directors' interests.	Summary.	One-fifth of the statutory maximum.	Except in the case of section 326(5), one-fiftieth of the statutory maximum.
328(6) …	Director failing to notify company that members of his family have, or have exercised, options to buy shares or debentures; making false statement in purported notification.	1. On indictment. 2. Summary.	2 years or a fine; or both. 6 months or the statutory maximum; or both.	
329(3) …	Company failing to notify investment exchange of acquisition of its securities by a director.	Summary.	One-fifth of the statutory maximum.	One-fiftieth of the statutory maximum.
342(1) …	Director of relevant company authorising or permitting company to enter into transaction or arrangement, knowing or suspecting it to contravene section 330.	1. On indictment. 2. Summary.	2 years or a fine; or both. 6 months or the statutory maximum; or both.	
342(2) …	Relevant company entering into transaction or arrangement for a director in contravention of section 330.	1. On indictment. 2. Summary.	2 years or a fine; or both. 6 months or the statutory maximum; or both.	
342(3) …	Procuring a relevant company to enter into transaction or arrangement known to be contrary to section 330.	1. On indictment. 2. Summary.	2 years or a fine; or both. 6 months or the statutory maximum; or both.	

Section of Act creating offence	General nature of offence	Mode of prosecution	Punishment	Daily default fine (where applicable)
343(8) ...	Company failing to maintain register of transactions, etc., made with and for directors and not disclosed in company accounts; failing to make register available at registered office or at company meeting.	1. On indictment. 2. Summary.	A fine. The statutory maximum.	
348(2) ...	Company failing to paint or affix name; failing to keep it painted or affixed.	Summary.	One-fifth of the statutory maximum.	In the case of failure to keep the name painted or affixed, one-fiftieth of the statutory maximum.
349(2) ...	Company failing to have name on business correspondence, invoices, etc.	Summary.	One-fifth of the statutory maximum.	
349(3) ...	Officer of company issuing business letter or document not bearing company's name.	Summary.	One-fifth of the statutory maximum.	
349(4) ...	Officer of company signing cheque, bill of exchange, etc. on which company's name not mentioned.	Summary.	One-fifth of the statutory maximum.	
350(1) ...	Company failing to have its name engraved on company seal.	Summary.	One-fifth of the statutory maximum.	
350(2) ...	Officer of company, etc., using company seal without name engraved on it.	Summary.	One-fifth of the statutory maximum.	
351(5)(a) ...	Company failing to comply with section 351(1) or (2) (matters to be stated on business correspondence, etc.).	Summary.	One-fifth of the statutory maximum.	
351(5)(b) ...	Officer or agent of company issuing or authorising issue of, business document not complying with those subsections.	Summary.	One-fifth of the statutory maximum.	

Section of Act creating offence	General nature of offence	Mode of prosecution	Punishment	Daily default fine (where applicable)
351(5)(c) ...	Contravention of section 351(3) or (4) (information in English to be stated on Welsh Company's business correspondence, etc.).	Summary	One-fifth of the statutory maximum.	For contravention of section 351(3), one-fiftieth of the statutory maximum.
352(5) ...	Company default in complying with section 352 (requirement to keep register of members and their particulars).	Summary.	One-fifth of the statutory maximum.	One-fiftieth of the statutory maximum.
353(4) ...	Company failing to send notice to registrar as to place where register of members is kept.	Summary.	One-fifth of the statutory maximum.	One-fiftieth of the statutory maximum.
354(4) ...	Company failing to keep index of members.	Summary.	One-fifth of the statutory maximum.	One-fiftieth of the statutory maximum.
356(5) ...	Refusal of inspection of members' register; failure to send copy on requisition.	Summary.	One-fifth of the statutory maximum.	One-fiftieth of the statutory maximum.
363(7) ...	Company with share capital failing to make annual return.	Summary.	The statutory maximum.	One-tenth of the statutory maximum.
364(4) ...	Company without share capital failing to complete and register annual return in due time.	Summary.	The statutory maximum.	One-tenth of the statutory maximum.
365(3) ...	Company failing to complete and send annual return to registrar in due time.	Summary.	The statutory maximum.	One-tenth of the statutory maximum.
366(4) ...	Company default in holding annual general meeting.	1. On indictment. 2. Summary.	A fine. The statutory maximum.	
367(3) ...	Company default in complying with Secretary of State's direction to hold company meeting.	1. On indictment. 2. Summary.	A fine. The statutory maximum.	
367(5) ...	Company failing to register resolution that meeting held under section 367 is to be its annual general meeting.	Summary.	One-fifth of the statutory maximum.	One-fiftieth of the statutory maximum.

Section of Act creating offence	General nature of offence	Mode of prosecution	Punishment	Daily default fine (where applicable)
372(4) ...	Failure to give notice, to member entitled to vote at company meeting, that he may do so by proxy.	Summary.	One-fifth of the statutory maximum.	
372(6) ...	Officer of company authorising or permitting issue of irregular invitations to appoint proxies.	Summary.	One-fifth of the statutory maximum.	
376(7) ...	Officer of company in default as to circulation of members' resolutions for company meeting.	1. On indictment. 2. Summary.	A fine. The statutory maximum.	
380(5) ...	Company failing to comply with section 380 (copies of certain resolutions etc. to be sent to registrar of companies).	Summary.	One-fifth of the statutory maximum.	One-fiftieth of the statutory maximum.
380(6) ...	Company failing to include copy of resolution to which section 380 applies in articles; failing to forward copy to member on request.	Summary.	One-fifth of the statutory maximum for each occasion on which copies are issued or, as the case may be, requested.	
382(5) ...	Company failing to keep minutes of proceedings at company and board meetings, etc.	Summary.	One-fifth of the statutory maximum.	One-fiftieth of the statutory maximum.
383(4) ...	Refusal of inspection of minutes of general meeting; failure to send copy of minutes on member's request.	Summary.	One-fifth of the statutory maximum.	One-fiftieth of the statutory maximum.
387(2) ...	Company failing to give Secretary of State notice of non-appointment of auditors.	Summary.	One-fifth of the statutory maximum.	One-fiftieth of the statutory maximum.
389(10) ...	Person acting as company auditor knowing himself to be disqualified; failing to give notice vacating office when he becomes disqualified.	1. On indictment. 2. Summary.	A fine. The statutory maximum.	One-tenth of the statutory maximum.

Section of Act creating offence	General nature of offence	Mode of prosecution	Punishment	Daily default fine (where applicable)
389A(2) ...	Officer of company making false, misleading or deceptive statement to auditors.	1. On indictment. 2. Summary.	2 years or a fine; or both. 6 months or the statutory maximum; or both.	
389A(3) ...	Subsidiary undertaking or its auditor failing to give information to auditors of parent company.	Summary.	One-fifth of the statutory maximum.	
389A(4) ...	Parent company failing to obtain from subsidiary undertaking information for purposes of audit.	Summary.	One-fifth of the statutory maximum.	
391(2) ...	Failing to give notice to registrar of removal of auditor.	Summary.	One-fifth of the statutory maximum.	One-fiftieth of the statutory maximum.
392(3) ...	Company failing to forward notice of auditor's resignation to registrar.	1. On indictment. 2. Summary.	A fine. The statutory maximum.	One-tenth of the statutory maximum.
392A(5) ...	Directors failing to convene meeting requisitioned by resigning auditor.	1. On indictment. 2. Summary.	A fine. The statutory maximum.	
394A(1) ...	Person ceasing to hold office as auditor failing to deposit statement as to circumstances.	1. On indictment. 2. Summary.	A fine. The statutory maximum.	
394A(4) ...	Company failing to comply with requirements as to statement of person ceasing to hold office as auditor.	1. On indictment. 2. Summary.	A fine. The statutory maximum.	One-tenth of the statutory maximum.
399(3) ...	Company failing to send to registrar particulars of charge created by it, or of issue of debentures which requires registration.	1. On indictment. 2. Summary.	A fine. The statutory maximum.	One-tenth of the statutory maximum.
400(4) ...	Company failing to send to registrar particulars of charge on property acquired.	1. On indictment. 2. Summary.	A fine. The statutory maximum.	One-tenth of the statutory maximum.

Section of Act creating offence	General nature of offence	Mode of prosecution	Punishment	Daily default fine (where applicable)
402(3)	Authorising or permitting delivery of debenture or certificate of debenture stock, without endorsement on it of certificate of registration of charge.	Summary.	One-fifth of the statutory maximum.	
405(4)	Failure to give notice to registrar of appointment of receiver or manager, or of his ceasing to act.	Summary.	One-fifth of the statutory maximum.	One fiftieth of the statutory maximum.
407(3)	Authorising or permitting omission from company register of charges.	1. On indictment. 2. Summary	1. A fine. 2. The statutory maximum.	
408(3)	Officer of company refusing inspection of charging instrument, or of register of charges.	Summary.	One-fifth of the statutory maximum.	One fiftieth of the statutory charges.
415(3)	Scottish company failing to send to registrar particulars of charge created by it, or of issue of debentures which requires registration.	1. On indictment. 2. Summary.	1. A fine. 2. The statutory maximum.	One-tenth of the statutory maximum.
416(3)	Scottish company failing to send to registrar particulars of charge on property acquired by it.	1. On indictment. 2. Summary.	1. A fine. 2. The statutory maximum.	One-tenth of the statutory maximum.
422(3)	Scottish company authorising or permitting omission from its register of charges.	1. On indictment. 2. Summary.	1. A fine. 2. The statutory maximum.	
423(3)	Officer of Scottish company refusing inspection of charging instrument, or of register of charges.	Summary.	One-fifth of the statutory maximum.	One-fiftieth of the statutory maximum.
425(4)	Company failing to annex to memorandum court order sanctioning compromise or arrangement with creditors.	Summary.	One-fifth of the statutory maximum.	
426(6)	Company failing to comply with requirements of section 426 (information to members and creditors about compromise or arrangement.)	1. On indictment. 2. Summary.	1. A fine. 2. The statutory maximum.	
426(7)	Director or trustee for debenture holders failing to give notice to company of matters necessary for purposes of section 426.	Summary.	One-fifth of the statutory maximum.	

Section of Act creating offence	General nature of offence	Mode of prosecution	Punishment	Daily default fine (where applicable)
427(5) ...	Failure to deliver to registrar office copy of court order under section 427 (company reconstruction or amalgamation).	Summary.	One-fifth of the statutory maximum.	One-fiftieth of the statutory maximum.
429(6) ...	Offeror failing to send copy of notice or making statutory declaration knowing it to be false, etc.	1. On indictment. 2. Summary.	2 years or a fine; or both. 6 months or the statutory maximum; or both.	One-fiftieth of the statutory maximum.
430A(6) ...	Offeror failing to give notice of rights to minority shareholder.	1. On indictment. 2. Summary.	A fine. The statutory maximum.	One-fiftieth of the statutory maximum.
444(3) ...	Failing to give Secretary of State, when required to do so, information about interests in shares, etc.; giving false information.	1. On indictment. 2. Summary.	2 years or a fine; or both. 6 months or the statutory maximum; or both.	
447(6) ...	Failure to comply with requirement to produce documents imposed by Secretary of State under section 447.	1. On indictment. 2. Summary.	A fine. The statutory maximum.	
448(7) ...	Obstructing the exercise of any rights conferred by a warrant or failing to comply with a requirement imposed under subsection (3)(d).	1. On indictment. 2. Summary.	A fine. The statutory maximum.	
449(2) ...	Wrongful disclosure of information or document obtained under section 447 or 448.	1. On indictment. 2. Summary.	2 years or a fine; or both. 6 months or the statutory maximum; or both.	
450 ...	Destroying or mutilating company documents; falsifying such documents or making false entries; parting with such documents or altering them or making omissions.	1. On indictment. 2. Summary.	7 years or a fine; or both. 6 months or the statutory maximum; or both.	
451 ...	Making false statement or explanation in purported compliance with section 447.	1. On indictment. 2. Summary.	2 years or a fine; or both. 6 months or the statutory maximum; or both.	

Section of Act creating offence	General nature of offence	Mode of prosecution	Punishment	Daily default fine (where applicable)
455(1) ...	Exercising a right to dispose of, or vote in respect of, shares which are subject to restrictions under Part XV; failing to give notice in respect of shares so subject; entering into agreement void under section 454(2). (3).	1. On indictment. 2. Summary.	A fine. The statutory maximum.	
455(2) ...	Issuing shares in contravention of restrictions of Part XV.	1. On indictment. 2. Summary.	A fine. The statutory maximum.	
458 ...	Being a party to carrying on company's business with intent to defraud creditors, or for any fraudulent purpose.	1. On indictment. 2. Summary.	7 years or a fine; or both. 6 months or the statutory maximum; or both.	
461(5) ...	Failure to register office copy of court order under Part XVII altering, or giving leave to alter, company's memorandum.	Summary.	One-fifth of the statutory maximum.	One-fiftieth of the statutory maximum.
651(3) ...	Person obtaining court order to declare company's dissolution void, then failing to register the order.	Summary.	One-fifth of the statutory maximum.	One-fiftieth of the statutory maximum.
697(1) ...	Oversea company failing to comply with any of sections 691 to 693 or 696.	Summary.	For an offence which is not a continuing offence, one-fifth of the statutory maximum. For an offence which is a continuing offence, one-fifth of the statutory maximum.	One-fiftieth of the statutory maximum.
697(2) ...	Oversea company contravening section 694(6) (carrying on business under its corporate name after Secretary of State's direction).	1. On indictment. 2. Summary.	A fine. The statutory maximum.	One-tenth of the statutory maximum.
703(1) ...	Oversea company failing to comply with requirements as to accounts and reports.	1. On indictment. 2. Summary.	A fine. The statutory maximum.	One-tenth of the statutory maximum.

Section of Act creating offence	General nature of offence	Mode of prosecution	Punishment	Daily default fine (where applicable)
720(4) ...	Insurance company etc. failing to send twice-yearly statement in form of Schedule 23.	Summary.	One-fifth of the statutory maximum.	One-fiftieth of the statutory maximum.
722(3) ...	Company failing to comply with section 722(2), as regards the manner of keeping registers, minute books and accounting records.	Summary.	One-fifth of the statutory maximum.	One-fiftieth of the statutory maximum.
Sch. 14, Pt. II, para. 1(3)	Company failing to give notice of location of overseas branch register, etc.	Summary.	One-fifth of the statutory maximum.	One-fiftieth of the statutory maximum.
Sch. 14, Pt. II, para. 4(2)	Company failing to transmit to its registered office in Great Britain copies of entries in overseas branch register, or to keep a duplicate of overseas branch register.	Summary.	One-fifth of the statutory maximum.	One-fiftieth of the statutory maximum.

Note
Entries in Sch. 24 relating to s. 56(4), 61, 64(5), 70(1), 78(1), 81(2), 82(5), 86(6), 87(4) and 97(4) repealed by Financial Services Act 1986, s. 212(3) and Sch. 17 to the extent to which those entries would apply to any investment listed or the subject of a listing application under Financial Services Act 1986, Pt. IV and commencing:

- on 12 January 1987 for all purposes relating to the admission of securities offered by or on behalf of a Minister of the Crown or a body corporate controlled by a Minister of the Crown or a subsidiary of such a body corporate to the Official List in respect of which an application is made after that date;

- on 16 February 1987 for purposes relating to the admission of securities in respect of which an application is made after that date other than those referred to in the preceding paragraph and otherwise for all purposes.

(See S.I. 1986 No. 2246 (C. 88).)

Those same entries repealed by Financial Services Act 1986, s. 212(3) and Sch. 17 as from 29 April 1988 as far as they would apply to a prospectus offering for subscription, or to any form of application for, units in a body corporate which is a recognised scheme (see S.I. 1988 No. 740 (C. 22)).

History
(1) In Sch. 24 entries relating to s. 221(5)–251(6) amended as a result of CA 1989, s. 23, 212, Sch. 10, para. 24(1)–(3) and Sch. 24 as from 1 April 1990 subject to transitional and saving provisions (see S.I. 1990 No. 355 (C. 13), art. 3, 5(1)(b), 2, and also art. 6–9); prior to the amendments the entries read as follows:

Section of Act creating offence	General nature of offence	Mode of prosecution	Punishment	Daily default fine (where applicable)
"223(1) ...	Company failing to keep accounting records (liability of officers).	1. On indictment. 2. Summary.	2 years or a fine; or both 6 months or the statutory maximum; or both.	

Section of Act creating offence	General nature of offence	Mode of prosecution	Punishment	Daily default fine (where applicable)
223(2)	Officer of company failing to secure compliance with, or intentionally causing default under section 222(4) (preservation of accounting records for requisite number of years).	1. On indictment. 2. Summary.	2 years or a fine; or both. 6 months or the statutory maximum; or both.	
231(3)	Company failing to annex to its annual return certain particulars required by Schedule 5 and not included in annual accounts.	Summary.	One-fifth of the statutory maximum.	One-fiftieth of the statutory maximum.
231(4)	Default by director or officer of a company in giving notice of matters relating to himself for purposes of Schedule 5 Part V.	Summary.	One-fifth of the statutory maximum.	
235(7)	Non-compliance with the section, as to directors' report and its content; directors individually liable.	1. On indictment. 2. Summary.	A fine. The statutory maximum.	
238(2)	Laying or delivery of unsigned balance sheet; circulating copies of balance sheet without signatures.	Summary.	One-fifth of the statutory maximum.	
240(5)	Failing to send company balance sheet, directors' report and auditors' report to those entitled to receive them.	1. On indictment. 2. Summary.	A fine. The statutory maximum.	One-tenth of the statutory maximum.
243(1)	Director in default as regards duty to lay and deliver company accounts.	Summary.	The statutory maximum.	
245(1)	Company's individual accounts not in conformity with requirements of this Act; directors individually liable.	1. On indictment. 2. Summary.	A fine. The statutory maximum.	
245(2)	Holding company's group accounts not in conformity with sections 229 and 230 and other requirements of this Act; directors individually liable.	1. On indictment. 2. Summary.	A fine. The statutory maximum.	
246(2)	Company failing to supply copy of accounts to shareholder on his demand.	Summary.	One-fifth of the statutory maximum.	One-fiftieth of the statutory maximum.
254(6)	Company or officer in default contravening section 254 as regards publication of full individual or group accounts.	Summary.	One-fifth of the statutory maximum.	
255(5)	Company or officer in default contravening section 255 as regards publication of abridged accounts.	Summary.	One-fifth of the statutory maximum.	
260(3)	Director of special category company failing to secure compliance with special disclosure provision.	1. On indictment. 2. Summary.	A fine. The statutory maximum.	One-fiftieth of the statutory maximum.

Section of Act creating offence	General nature of offence	Mode of prosecution	Punishment	Daily default fine (where applicable)
287(3) ...	Company failing to have registered office; failing to notify change in its situation.	Summary.	One-fifth of the statutory maximum.	One-fiftieth of the statutory maximum."

(2) In Sch. 24 entries relating to s. 295(7) and 302(1) repealed by Company Directors Disqualification Act 1986, s. 23(2) and Sch. 4 as from 29 December 1986 (in regard to the date of the repeal, see CDDA 1986, s. 25, IA 1986, s. 443 and S.I. 1986 No. 1924 (C. 71)); the former wording of those entries was as follows:

Section of Act creating offence	General nature of offence	Mode of prosecution	Punishment	Daily default fine (where applicable)
"295(7) ...	Acting in contravention of a disqualification order under sections 295 to 300.	1. On indictment. 2. Summary.	2 years or a fine; or both. 6 months or the statutory maximum; or both.	
302(1) ...	Undischarged bankrupt acting as director, etc.	1. On indictment. 2. Summary.	2 years or a fine; or both. 6 months or the statutory maximum; or both."	

(3) Also in Sch. 24 entries relating to s. 467–641(2), and the entry relating to s. 710(4) 497(7), 528(7), 568(3), 583(2), 588(5) and 640(4) previously repealed by Insolvency repealed by Insolvency Act 1986, s. 438 and Sch. 12 as from 29 December 1986 (see IA Act 1985, s. 235 and Sch. 10, Pt. II immediately before that date (see S.I. 1986 No. 1924 1986, s. 443 and S.I. 1986 No. 1924 (C. 71)). The entries relating to s. 495(7), 496(6), (C. 71)); the former wording of all the above entries was as follows:

Section of Act creating offence	General nature of offence	Mode of prosecution	Punishment	Daily default fine (where applicable)
"467(4) ...	Body corporate or Scottish firm acting as receiver.	1. On indictment. 2. Summary.	A fine. The statutory maximum.	
467(5) ...	Undischarged bankrupt acting as receiver.	1. On indictment. 2. Summary.	2 years or a fine; or both. 6 months or the statutory maximum; or both.	
469(2) ...	Failing to deliver to registrar copy instrument of appointment of receiver.	Summary.	One-fifth of the statutory maximum.	One-fiftieth of the statutory maximum.
470(3) ...	Failing to deliver to registrar the court's interlocuter making the appointment of a receiver.	Summary.	One-fifth of the statutory maximum.	One-fiftieth of the statutory maximum.
478(5) ...	Failing to give notice to registrar of cessation or removal of receiver.	Summary.	One-fifth of the statutory maximum.	One-fiftieth of the statutory maximum.
480(2) ...	Not stating on company documents that receiver has been appointed.	Summary.	One-fifth of the statutory maximum.	One-fiftieth of the statutory maximum.

Section of Act creating offence	General nature of offence	Mode of prosecution	Punishment	Daily default fine (where applicable)
481(7)	Receiver making default in complying with provisions as to information where receiver appointed.	Summary.	One-fifth of the statutory maximum.	One-fiftieth of the statutory maximum.
482(5)	Default in relation to provisions as to statement to be submitted to receiver.	Summary.	One-fifth of the statutory maximum.	One-fiftieth of the statutory maximum.
489	Body corporate acting as receiver.	1. On indictment. 2. Summary.	A fine. The statutory maximum.	
490	Undischarged bankrupt acting as receiver or manager.	1. On indictment. 2. Summary.	2 years or a fine; or both. 6 months or the statutory maximum; or both.	
493(2)	Company failing to state in its correspondence, etc. that a receiver has been appointed.	Summary.	One-fifth of the statutory maximum.	One-fiftieth of the statutory maximum.
495(7)	Receiver failing to notify his appointment to the company; failing to send company's statement of affairs to registrar and others concerned.	Summary.	One-fifth of the statutory maximum.	One-fiftieth of the statutory maximum.
496(6)	Default in relation to statement of affairs to be given to receiver.	Summary.	One-fifth of the statutory maximum.	One-fiftieth of the statutory maximum.
497(7)	Receiver failing to send accounts of his receipts and payments to registrar and others concerned.	Summary.	One-fifth of the statutory maximum.	One-fiftieth of the statutory maximum.
498(4)	Receiver failing to send accounts to registrar for registration.	Summary.	One-fifth of the statutory maximum.	One-fiftieth of the statutory maximum.
528(7)	Default in compliance with section 528 (submission of statement of company's affairs to official receiver).	1. On indictment. 2. Summary.	A fine. The statutory maximum.	One-tenth of the statutory maximum.
568(3)	Liquidator failing to send to registrar of companies copy of court order dissolving company.	Summary.	One-fifth of the statutory maximum.	One-fiftieth of the statutory maximum.
573(2)	Company failing to give notice in Gazette of resolution for voluntary winding up.	Summary.	One-fifth of the statutory maximum.	One-fiftieth of the statutory maximum.
577(4)	Director making statutory declaration of company's solvency without reasonable grounds for his opinion.	1. On indictment. 2. Summary.	2 years or a fine; or both. 6 months or the statutory maximum; or both.	
577(6)	Declaration under section 577 not delivered to registrar of companies within prescribed time.	Summary.	One-fifth of the statutory maximum.	One-fiftieth of the statutory maximum.
583(2)	Liquidator failing to summon creditors' meeting in case of insolvency.	Summary.	One-fifth of the statutory maximum.	One-fiftieth of the statutory maximum.
584(2)	Liquidator failing to summon general meeting of company at end of each year from commencement of winding up.	Summary.	One-fifth of the statutory maximum.	One-fiftieth of the statutory maximum.
585(3)	Liquidator failing to send to registrar a copy of the account of a winding up and return of final general meeting.	Summary.	One-fifth of the statutory maximum.	One-fiftieth of the statutory maximum.

24-8-90

Section of Act creating offence	General nature of offence	Mode of prosecution	Punishment	Daily default fine (where applicable)
585(6)	Failing to deliver to registrar office copy of court order for registration made under the section.	Summary.	One-fifth of the statutory maximum.	One-fiftieth of the statutory maximum.
585(7)	Liquidator failing to summon final meeting of company prior to dissolution.	Summary.	One-fifth of the statutory maximum.	
588(5)	Company or its directors or officers failing to comply with the section in relation to summoning or advertisement of creditors' meeting.	1. On indictment. 2. Summary.	A fine. The statutory maximum.	
594(2)	Liquidator failing to summon general meeting of company, and meeting of creditors, at end of each year.	Summary.	One-fifth of the statutory maximum.	
595(4)	Liquidator failing to send to registrar account of winding up and return of final company and creditors' meetings.	Summary.	One-fifth of the statutory maximum.	One-fiftieth of the statutory maximum.
595(7)	Failing to deliver to registrar office copy of court order for registration made under the section.	Summary.	One-fifth of the statutory maximum.	One-fiftieth of the statutory maximum.
595(8)	Liquidator failing to call final meeting of company or creditors.	Summary.	One-fifth of the statutory maximum.	One-fiftieth of the statutory maximum.
600(2)	Liquidator failing to publish notice of his appointment.	Summary.	One-fifth of the statutory maximum.	One-fiftieth of the statutory maximum.
624(2)	Fraud, etc., in anticipation of winding up (offence under subsection (1) or (2) of the section).	1. On indictment. 2. Summary.	7 years or a fine; or both. 6 months or the statutory maximum; or both.	
624(5)	Knowingly taking in pawn or pledge, or otherwise receiving, company property.	1. On indictment. 2. Summary.	7 years or a fine; or both. 6 months or the statutory maximum; or both.	
625	Officer of company entering into transactions in fraud of company's creditors.	1. On indictment. 2. Summary.	2 years or a fine; or both. 6 months or the statutory maximum; or both.	
626	Officer of company misconducting himself in course of winding up.	1. On indictment. 2. Summary.	7 years or a fine; or both. 6 months or the statutory maximum; or both.	
627	Officer or contributory destroying, falsifying, etc., company's books.	1. On indictment. 2. Summary.	7 years or a fine; or both. 6 months or the statutory maximum; or both.	
628	Officer of company making material omission from statement relating to company's affairs.	1. On indictment. 2. Summary.	7 years or a fine; or both. 6 months or the statutory maximum; or both.	
629	False representation or fraud for purpose of obtaining creditors' consent to an agreement in connection with winding up.	1. On indictment. 2. Summary.	7 years or a fine; or both. 6 months or the statutory maximum; or both.	
634	Body corporate acting as liquidator.	1. On indictment. 2. Summary.	A fine. The statutory maximum.	

Section of Act creating offence	General nature of offence	Mode of prosecution	Punishment	Daily default fine (where applicable)
635 …	Giving, offering, etc., corrupt inducement affecting appointment of liquidator.	1. On indictment. 2. Summary.	A fine. The statutory maximum.	
637(2) …	Default in compliance with the section, as to notification that company is being wound up.	Summary.	One-fifth of the statutory maximum.	One-fiftieth of the statutory maximum.
640(4) …	Contravention of general rules as to disposal of company books and papers after winding up.	Summary.	One-fifth of the statutory maximum.	
641(2) …	Liquidator failing to notify registrar as to progress of winding up.	Summary.	One-fifth of the statutory maximum.	
710(4) …	Person untruthfully stating himself to be a member or creditor of company, for purpose of obtaining or inspecting company documents."	Summary.	One-fifth of the statutory maximum."	

(4) Also in Sch. 24 in second column of entry relating to s. 329(3) the words "investment exchange" substituted for the former words "stock exchange" by Financial Services Act 1986, s. 212(2) and Sch. 16, para. 27(a) as from 29 April 1988 (see S.I. 1988 No. 740 (C. 22)) and entries relating to s. 429(6) and s. 430A(6) inserted by Financial Services Act 1986, s. 212(2) and Sch. 16, para. 27(b) as from 4 June 1987 (see S.I. 1987 No. 907 (C. 24)).

(5) Also in Sch. 24 former entries relating to s. 384(5), 386(2), 390(7), 391(4), 392(2) and 393 repealed by CA 1989, s. 212 and Sch. 24 and entries relating to s. 387(2), 389A(2)–(4), 391(2), (3), 392A(5), 394A(1), (4) inserted by CA 1989, s. 119(2), 120(3), 122(2), 123(2) as from 1 April 1990 subject to transitional and saving provisions (see S.I. 1990 No. 355 (C. 13), art. 4(a), 5(1)(b), (2) and also art. 6–10); the former entries read as follows:

Section of Act creating offence	General nature of offence	Mode of prosecution	Punishment	Daily default fine (where applicable)
"384(5) …	Company failing to give Secretary of State notice of non-appointment of auditors.	Summary.	One-fifth of the statutory maximum.	One-fiftieth of the statutory maximum.
386(2) …	Failing to give notice to registrar of removal of auditor.	Summary.	One-fifth of the statutory maximum.	One-fiftieth of the statutory maximum.
390(7) …	Company failing to forward notice of auditor's resignation to registrar or persons entitled under section 240 in Part VII; failing to send to persons so entitled statement as to effect of court order or, if no such order, the auditor's resignation statement.	1. On indictment. 2. Summary.	A fine. The statutory maximum.	One-tenth of the statutory maximum.
391(4) …	Directors failing to convene meeting requisitioned by resigning auditors.	1. On indictment. 2. Summary.	A fine. The statutory maximum.	

Section of Act creating offence	General nature of offence	Mode of prosecution	Punishment	Daily default fine (where applicable)
392(2) ...	Failure of subsidiary to give its holding company, and failure of holding company to obtain from its subsidiary, information needed for purposes of audit; failure of subsidiary's auditors to give information and explanation to holding company's auditors.	Summary	One-fifth of the statutory maximum.	
393 ...	Company officer making misleading, false or deceptive statement to auditors.	1. On indictment. 2. Summary.	2 years or a fine; or both. 6 months or the statutory maximum; or both."	

(6) Also in Sch. 24 in entry relating to s. 447(6) the word "documents" substituted for the former words "books or papers" by CA 1989, s. 63(1), (8) as from 21 February 1990 (see S.I. 1990 No. 142 (C. 5), art. 4).

(7) Also in Sch. 24 in entry relating to s. 448(7) in the first column "448(7)" substituted for "448(5)" and in the second column the words substituted by CA 1989, s. 64(2) as from 21 February 1990 (see S.I. 1990 No. 142 (C. 5), art. 4); the words in the second column formerly read as follows:

"Obstructing the exercise of a right of entry or search, or a right to take possession of books or papers."

(8) Also in Sch. 24 in entry relating to s. 703(1) in column 2 the words "requirements as to accounts and reports" substituted for the former words "s. 700 as respects delivery of annual accounts" by CA 1989, s. 23 and Sch. 10, para. 24(1), (4) as from 1 April 1990 subject to transitional and saving provisions (see S.I. 1990 No. 355 (C. 13), art. 3, Sch. 1 and also art. 6–9).

Schedule 25 — Companies Act 1981, Section 38, as Originally Enacted

SEC. 38   Relief from section 56 in respect of group reconstructions

38(1)   This section applies where the issuing company—

   (a) is a wholly-owned subsidiary of another company ("the holding company"); and

   (b) allots shares to the holding company or to another wholly-owned subsidiary of the holding company in consideration for the transfer to it of shares in another subsidiary (whether wholly-owned or not) of the holding company.

38(2)   Where the shares in the issuing company allotted in consideration for the transfer are issued at a premium, the issuing company shall not be required by section 56 of the 1948 Act to transfer any amount in excess of the minimum premium value to the share premium account.

38(3)   In subsection (2) above **"the minimum premium value"** means the amount (if any) by which the base value of the shares transferred exceeds the aggregate nominal value of the shares allotted in consideration for the transfer.

38(4)   For the purposes of subsection (3) above, the base value of the shares transferred shall be taken as—

   (a) the cost of those shares to the company transferring them; or

   (b) the amount at which those shares are stated in that company's accounting records immediately before the transfer; whichever is the less.

38(5)   Section 37 of this Act shall not apply in a case to which this section applies.

[The next page is 36,501]

    CCH Editions Limited

TABLE OF DERIVATIONS
[This table has no official status]

The following abbreviations are used in this Table:—

"1948" = Companies Act 1948 (c. 38).
"1967" = Companies Act 1967 (c. 81).
"1972 Sc." = Companies (Floating Charges and Receivers) (Scotland) Act 1972 (c. 67).
"ECA 1972" = European Communities Act 1972 (c. 68).
"SECOBA" = Stock Exchange (Completion of Bargains) Act 1976 (c. 47).
"1976 c. 60" = Insolvency Act 1976 (c. 60).
"1976" = Companies Act 1976 (c. 69).
"1980" = Companies Act 1980 (c. 22).
"1981" = Companies Act 1981 (c. 62).
"STA 1982" = Stock Transfer Act 1982 (c. 41).
"1983 (BI)" = Companies (Beneficial Interests) Act 1983 (c. 50).
"OinC–1" = Companies Acts (Pre-Consolidation Amendments) Order 1984 (S.I. 1984/134).
"OinC–2" = Companies Acts (Pre-Consolidation Amendments) (No. 2) Order 1984 (S.I. 1984/1169).

Provision	Derivation
1	1948 s. 1; 1980 ss. 1(1), (2), 2(1), Sch. 3 para. 2.
2	1948 ss. 2, 3, 4; 1976 s. 30(1), (2); OinC–1 No. 1.
3	1948 ss. 11(a)–(d), 454(2); 1980 s. 2(4), Sch. 3 para. 34.
4	1948 s. 5(1).
5	1948 s. 5(2)–(5); 1980 Sch. 3 para. 4.
6	1948 s. 5(7)–(9); 1976 Sch. 1.
7	1948 ss. 6, 7, 9; OinC–1 No. 2.
8	1948 ss. 8, 11(b)–(d), 454(2).
9	1948 s. 10; 1980 Sch. 3 para. 2.
10	1948 s. 12; 1976 ss. 21(1)–(5), 23(2), Sch. 2.
11	1980 s. 3(2).
12	1948 s. 12; 1980 s. 3(1), (5).
13	1948 s. 13; 1976 ss. 21(5), 38(2), Sch. 2; 1980 s. 3(3), (4); 1981 s. 99.
14	1948 s. 20.
15	1948 s. 21; 1980 s. 1(3).
16	1948 s. 22.
17	1948 s. 23; 1980 Sch. 3 para. 6.
18	ECA 1972 s. 9(5).
19	1948 s. 24.
20	1948 s. 25.
21	1976 s. 30(6)–(9).
22	1948 s. 26.
23	1948 s. 27; 1983 (BI) s. 2.

Provision	Derivation
24	1948 s. 31; 1980 Sch. 3 para. 7.
25	1948 s. 2(1)(a); 1976 s. 30(3); 1980 ss. 2(2), 78(4)(a), (d), Sch. 3 para. 3.
26	1980 s. 78(4)(a)–(e); 1981 ss. 22, 34, Sch. 3 para. 60.
27	1980 s. 78(1)–(3).
28	1981 s. 24; OinC–1 No. 53.
29	1981 ss. 31(1), (2), (4), (5), 32; OinC–1 No. 55.
30	1981 s. 25(1)–(4), (8).
31	1981 s. 25(5)–(10).
32	1967 s. 46; 1981 Sch. 3 para. 31; OinC–1 No. 33.
33	1980 s. 76(1), (2), (4).
34	1948 s. 439; 1976 Sch. 2.
35	ECA 1972 s. 9(1).
36	1948 s. 32; ECA 1972 s. 9(2).
37	1948 s. 33.
38	1948 s. 34.
39	1948 s. 35.
40	SECOBA s. 2(1).
41	1948 s. 36.
42	ECA 1972 s. 9(3) (in part), (4).
43	1980 ss. 2(3), 5(1)–(3), (10) (in part), 78(4); OinC–1 No. 39.
44	1980 s. 5(5), as applying s. 24(2), (2A), (3), (11A), (12) (in part); 1980 s. 87(1); 1981 Sch. 3 para. 42; OinC–1 No. 40.
45	1980 s. 6.
46	1980 s. 5(10) (in part), (11), (12); 1981 Sch. 2 para. 6(1).
47	1980 s. 5(4), (6)–(9).
48	1980 s. 7(1)–(3).
49	1967 s. 43(1)–(3), (7); 1980 Sch. 3 para. 43; OinC–1 No. 31.
50	1967 s. 43(4), (5).
51	1967 s. 44(1)–(3); 1980 s. 7(4), Sch. 3 para. 44; OinC–1 No. 32.
52	1967 s. 44(4), (5).
53	1980 s. 10(1), (2); OinC–1 No. 41.
54	1980 s. 11.
55	1980 s. 10(3)–(5).
56	1948 s. 38(1), (3), (5); 1976 Sch. 2.
57	1948 s. 38(2).
58	1948 s. 45.
59	1948 s. 55(1).
60	1948 s. 55(2)–(4); 1980 Sch. 3 para. 11; S.I. 1984 No. 716. Art. 7(2).
61	1948 s. 40(1), (2).

Provision	Derivation
62	1948 s. 40(3).
63	1948 s. 37.
64	1948 ss. 41(1)(a), (2)–(4), 45(3), (4).
65	1948 ss. 41(1)(b), etc., 455(1).
66	1948 s. 38(4), (6).
67	1948 s. 43(1), (5).
68	1948 s. 43(1) proviso, (2), (3).
69	1948 s. 43(4).
70	1948 s. 44.
71	1948 s. 46.
72	1948 s. 417(1), (3), (5); 1976 Sch. 2.
73	1948 s. 417(2).
74	1948 s. 419(1) (excl. para. (b)), (2).
75	1948 s. 419(1) (excl. para. (a)), (2).
76	1948 ss. 418, 455(1); 1976 Sch. 2.
77	1948 s. 420.
78	1948 ss. 417(4), (6), 421, 422.
79	1948 s. 423.
80	1980 s. 14; OinC–1 No. 42.
81	1980 s. 15(1), (3), (4).
82	1948 s. 50(1)–(6).
83	1948 s. 47.
84	1980 s. 16 (applying 1948 s. 47(4), (5)).
85	1948 s. 49; 1980 s. 16(2), Sch. 3 para. 8.
86	1948 ss. 50(6), 51(1)–(5), (6)(a); 1976 Sch. 2; OinC–1 No. 3.
87	1948 s. 51(7), inserted by OinC–1 No. 3.
88	1948 s. 52; 1976 Schs. 1, 2; OinC–1 No. 4.
89	1980 s. 17(1)–(5).
90	1980 s. 17(6)–(8); Table A Regs. 131–134.
91	1980 s. 17(9).
92	1980 s. 17(10).
93	1980 s. 17(12).
94	1980 s. 17(11), (13); 1981 Sch. 3 para. 40; OinC–1 No. 43.
95	1980 s. 18.
96	1980 s. 19(1)(b), (2)–(5).
97	1948 ss. 53(1), (5); 1980 Sch. 3 para. 9.
98	1948 s. 53(2)–(4).
99	1980 s. 20(1)–(3), (5), (6).

Provision	Derivation
100	1980 s. 21(1), (2); 1981 Sch. 3 para. 41.
101	1980 s. 22(1)–(4).
102	1980 s. 23(1)–(5), (7).
103	1980 s. 24(1)–(3), (8), (9), (11A), (12)(aa), (a); 1981 Sch. 3 para. 42; OinC–1 No. 44.
104	1980 s. 26(1)–(4).
105	1980 s. 26(7), (8) (in part).
106	1980 s. 29.
107	1980 s. 87(1), (6).
108	1980 s. 24(4)–(7), (11), (12)(b).
109	1980 ss. 26(5), (6), 27(3).
110	1980 ss. 25(1), (3)–(5), 27(1).
111	1980 s. 25(2) (with 1948 s. 52(3) as applied); 1980 s. 27(2).
112	1980 ss. 20(4), (6), 21(3), 22(5), 23(6), 24(10), 26(8).
(2)	1980 s. 26(8)(b), applying s. 20(4).
(3)	1980 s. 20(4), as applied.
(4)	1980 s. 20(6).
(5)	1980 s. 23(6), applying s. 20(4).
113	1980 s. 28.
114	1980 s. 30(1).
115	1980 s. 30(2).
116	1980 s. 31 (in part).
117	1980 s. 4.
118	1980 s. 85.
119	1948 s. 59.
120	1948 s. 60.
121	1948 s. 61.
122	1948 s. 62; 1976 Sch. 1.
123	1948 s. 63; 1967 s. 51(1).
124	1948 s. 64; 1967 s. 44(6); 1980 s. 7(4).
125	1980 s. 32(1)–(7) (excl. (6)(a), (b)), (9).
126	1980 s. 32(10).
127	1948 s. 72; 1980 s. 32(8).
128	1980 s. 33(1)–(4), (6).
129	1981 s. 102(1)–(3), (5).
130	1948 s. 56(1), (2); 1980 Sch. 3 para. 12; 1981 s. 36.
131	1981 ss. 37, 40(6).
132	1981 s. 38; S.I. 1984/2007.
133	1981 s. 40(1), (4), (5), (7).

[The next page is 36,521]

Provision	Derivation
134	1981 s. 41.
135	1948 s. 66.
136	1948 s. 67.
137	1948 s. 68.
138	1948 s. 69; 1976 s. 38(2); 1981 s. 99.
139	1980 s. 12, with modified application of s. 10.
140	1948 s. 70.
141	1948 s. 71.
142	1980 s. 34.
143	1980 s. 35; 1981 Sch. 3 para. 43.
144	1980 s. 36(1)–(4).
145	1980 s. 36(5) (with s. 37(1)(d)), s. 36(6); 1983 (BI).
146	1980 s. 37(1)–(3), (11); 1981 Sch. 3, para. 44; 1983 (BI).
147	1980 s. 37(2) (in part), (4), (5), (8).
148	1980 s. 37(9), (10); 1983 (BI); OinC–1 Nos. 45, 59.
149	1980 s. 37(6), (7).
150	1980 s. 38.
151	1981 s. 42(1), (2), (12).
152	1981 ss. 42(8)–(10), 62(1).
153	1981 s. 42(3)–(6), (11).
154	1981 s. 42(7), (11).
155	1981 ss. 43(1)–(6), 44(8), 62(1); OinC–1 No. 57.
156	1981 ss. 43(7), (8), 44(5)–(7).
157	1981 s. 44(1)–(4).
158	1981 s. 43(9).
159	1981 s. 45(1)–(4).
160	1981 s. 45(5)–(9).
161	1981 s. 45(10)–(12).
162	1981 s. 46.
163	1981 ss. 47(2), (3), 49(2).
164	1981 s. 47(4)–(12).
165	1981 s. 48.
166	1981 s. 49(3)–(10).
167	1981 s. 50.
168	1981 s. 51.
169	1981 s. 52.
170	1981 ss. 53, 54(6)(b).
171	1981 s. 54(1)–(6).

Provision	Derivation
172	1981 s. 54(7)–(10).
173	1981 s. 55(1)–(5), (9).
174	1981 s. 55(6)–(8), (10).
175	1981 s. 56.
176	1981 s. 57(1)–(3), (7).
177	1981 s. 57(4)–(6); 1980 s. 11(7)–(9) (as applied).
178	1981 s. 59.
179	1981 s. 61.
180	1981 s. 62(2)–(4).
181	1981 s. 62(1).
182	1948 ss. 73, 74.
183	1948 ss. 75–78; STA 1982 Sch. 2.
184	1948 s. 79.
185	1948 s. 80; SECOBA ss. 1, 7(2); STA 1982 Sch. 2.
186	1948 s. 81; SECOBA s. 2(3).
187	1948 s. 82.
188	1948 s. 83.
189	1948 s. 85.
190	1948 s. 86; 1976 Sch. 1.
191	1948 ss. 87, 110(6); 1967 s. 52(1); 1981 s. 101(2).
192	1948 s. 88.
193	1948 s. 89.
194	1948 s. 90.
195	1948 s. 92.
196	1948 s. 94; F.A. 1952 s. 30(3).
197	1948 s. 93.
198	1981 ss. 63(1), (4), (9), (10), 82(2).
199	1981 s. 63(2), (3), (5), (6).
200	1981 s. 63(7).
201	1981 ss. 63(8), 64.
202	1981 s. 65.
203	1981 s. 66.
204	1981 s. 67(1)–(5), (10).
205	1981 s. 67(6)–(9).
206	1981 s. 68.
207	1981 s. 69.
208	1981 s. 70.
209	1981 s. 71.

Provision	Derivation
210	1981 ss. 72(1)–(7), (9), 81.
211	1981 s. 73.
212	1981 s. 74.
213	1981 ss. 75, 83(8).
214	1981 s. 76(1)–(4), (12).
215	1981 s. 76(5)–(12).
216	1981 ss. 77(1), (2), (5)–(7); OinC–1 No. 58.
217	1981 s. 78.
218	1981 s. 79.
219	1981 s. 80.
220	1981 s. 82(1), (3).
221	1976 s. 12(1)–(5).
222	1976 s. 12(6)–(9).
223	1976 s. 12(10), (11).
224	1976 s. 2(1), (2), (4), (5).
225	1976 s. 3(1)–(7).
226	1976 s. 3(8)–(10).
227	1948 ss. 149(8)(b), 153(1); 1976 s. 1(1)–(4); 1981 s. 1.
228	1948 s. 149(1)–(6) (inserted, 1981 s. 1(1)).
229	1948 ss. 150(1) (as substituted, 1976 s. 8(1)), 150(2), 151(1) (as am. 1976 Sch. 2), (2), (3).
230	1948 s. 152 (as inserted, 1981 s. 2); OinC–1 No. 12.
231	1948 s. 196(1); 1967 ss. 3(1), 4(1), 5(1), 6(1), 7(1), (2), 8(1); 1981 s. 4, Sch. 3 paras. 10, 23, 25, 26.
(3)	1967 ss. 3(5)(b), (6), 4(5)(b), (6); 1980 Sch. 3 para. 41; 1981 s. 4(8), (9).
(4)	1948 s. 198; 1967 ss. 6(5), 7(3).
232	1980 ss. 54(1), (2), (2A), (3), 63(1); 1981 Sch. 3 para. 51.
233	1980 s. 56(2), (3), (6); 1981 Sch. 3 para. 52.
234	1980 ss. 56(4), (4A), (6), 63(1); 1981 Sch. 3 para. 52.
235	1948 s. 157(1); 1967 ss. 16(1), 16A(1), 19(1), 23; 1976 Sch. 2; 1980 Sch. 3; 1981 ss. 13(1), 14, Sch. 3 para. 6.
(6)	1981 s. 16(1) (partially excluding 1967 ss. 17, 18).
236	1967 s. 14(1), (3)(a); 1976 Sch. 2; 1980 Sch. 3 para. 41(3); 1981 Sch. 3 para. 27.
237	1948 s. 196(8); 1967 ss. 6(4), 7(3), 8(4), 14(4)–(6), 23A; 1976 Sch. 2; 1980 s. 59; 1981 s. 15.
238	1948 ss. 155, 156, 1976 Sch. 2.
239	1948 s. 150(1) (as substituted, 1976 s. 8(1); 1976 s. 1(5)).
240	1948 s. 158(1), (3); 1967 s. 24; 1976 Sch. 2.
241	1967 s. 14(2); 1976 s. 1(6)–(8).

Provision	Derivation
242	1976 s. 6.
243	1976 ss. 4(1)–(5), 45(3).
244	1976 s. 5.
245	1948 ss. 149(5), (7) (as inserted, 1981 s. 1(1)), 149A(6), 150(3); 1976 s. 8; 1980 Sch. 3 para. 20; 1981 Sch. 3 para. 5.
246	1948 s. 158(2), (3); 1967 s. 24.
247	1981 ss. 5(1)–(5), 6(1), 12(7), (9).
248	1981 s. 8(1)–(3), (9)–(11).
249	1981 s. 8(1), (5), (6), (7).
250	1981 ss. 9(1)–(6), 10(1)–(3); OinC–2 No. 10.
251	1981 s. 5(7)–(9).
252	1981 s. 12(1)–(6), (12), (13); OinC–1 No. 52.
253	1981 s. 12(7), (8), (10), (11) (including s. 7(2) as applied).
254	1981 s. 11(1)–(5), (9), (10).
255	1980 s. 43(8); 1981 s. 11(6)–(8), (10).
256	1948 s. 454(1), (1A), (2A), (3), (4); 1981 s. 18.
257	1981 Sch. 2 paras. 1–3, 5(7), 8.
258	1948 s. 149A(1)–(5), (7)(a); 1981 s. 1(1), Sch. 2 para. 4(1).
259	1948 s. 152A; 1976 Sch. 2; 1981 s. 2, Sch. 2 para. 4(1); OinC–2 No. 1.
260	1967 s. 11; 1981 Sch. 2 paras. 5(1), (2), 7(1).
261(2)	1948 s. 157(1); 1981 Sch. 2 para. 4(2).
(3)	1948 s. 163, proviso; 1981 Sch. 2 para. 4(3).
(4)	1967 s. 22; 1981 Sch. 2 para. 5(6).
(5)	1967 s. 16; 1981 Sch. 2 para. 5(4), (5).
(6)	1967 ss. 17, 18.
(7)	1981 Sch. 2 para. 5(5) (excluding 1967 s. 23A).
262	1967 s. 14(3)(b); 1980 Sch. 3 para. 41(3)(b).
263	1980 ss. 39(1)–(3), 45(2); 1981 Sch. 3 para. 48(a).
264	1980 ss. 40, 87(4).
265	1980 s. 41(1), (2), (5), (6); 1981 Sch. 3 para. 46.
266	1980 s. 41(3), (4), (7), (8).
267	1980 s. 41(9), (10).
268	1980 s. 42.
269	1980 s. 42A; 1981 s. 84.
270	1980 s. 43(1), (2), (8); 1981 Sch. 3 para. 47.
271	1980 s. 43(3), (4), (8).
272	1980 s. 43(5), (8), (9).
273	1980 s. 43(6), (8), (9).
274	1980 s. 43(7); 1981 ss. 60(1), (3), 61.

[The next page is 36,541]

Provision	Derivation
275	1980 ss. 39(4), (4A), (5)–(7), 40(4), 43(7A); 1981 Sch. 3 paras. 45(1), (2), 47.
276	1980 s. 43A; 1981 s. 85.
277	1980 s. 44; 1981 ss. 60(2), 61.
278	1980 s. 45(1).
279	1981 Sch. 2 para. 6.
280	1980 s. 45(3), (4); 1981 Sch. 3 para. 48(b).
281	1980 s. 45(5).
282	1948 s. 176.
283	1948 ss. 177, 178.
284	1948 s. 179.
285	1948 ss. 180, 183(2)(a).
286	1980 s. 79.
287	1976 s. 23(1), (3), (4).
288	1948 s. 200(1), (4), (6)–(8), (9)(a); 1976 s. 22(1); 1981 s. 95(1)–(3).
289	1948 s. 200(2), (9)(b)–(d); 1981 s. 95(2).
290	1948 s. 200(3), (9)(b)–(d).
291	1948 s. 182.
292	1948 s. 183; 1980 Sch. 3 para. 22.
293	1948 s. 185; 1980 Sch. 3 para. 23.
294	1948 s. 186.
295	1948 s. 188(1B), (2D), (2F), (6), (7); 1976 c. 60 s. 9(1), (1A), (2), (5), (7A); 1981 ss. 93, 94.
296	1948 s. 188(1)(a), (2D), (2E); 1981 s. 93.
297	1948 s. 188(1)(b), (2C), (2D); 1981 s. 93.
298	1948 s. 188(1)(c), (2D); 1981 s. 93.
299	1948 s. 188(1A), (2D), (2E); 1981 s. 93.
300	1976 c. 60 s. 9(1), (2), (6), (7A); 1981 s. 94.
301	1976 s. 29; 1981 Sch. 3 para. 36; OinC–1 No. 38.
302	1948 s. 187; 1981 Sch. 3 para. 9; OinC–2 No. 2.
303	1948 s. 184(1), (2), (4)–(6).
304	1948 s. 184(2), (3).
305	1948 s. 201; 1981 Sch. 3 para. 11.
306	1948 s. 202.
307	1948 s. 203.
308	1948 s. 204.
309	1980 ss. 46, 63(1).
310	1948 s. 205; 1980 Sch. 3 para. 26.
311	1948 s. 189.

Provision	Derivation
312	1948 s. 191.
313	1948 s. 192.
314	1948 s. 193(1), (2).
315	1948 s. 193(3)–(5).
316	1948 s. 194.
317	1948 s. 199; 1980 ss. 60, 63(3), Sch. 3 para. 25.
318	1967 s. 26; 1976 Sch. 1; 1980 ss. 61, 63(4).
319	1980 ss. 47, 63(1).
320	1980 ss. 48(1), (2), 63(1); 1981 s. 110(2); OinC–1 No. 46.
321	1980 s. 48(6)–(8); 1981 s. 110(3).
322	1980 s. 48(3), (4), (5); OinC–1 No. 47.
323	1967 s. 25; 1976 Sch. 2; 1981 Sch. 3 para. 28.
324	1967 s. 27(1), (2), (4), (8)–(11), (13); 1976 Sch. 2.
325	1967 s. 29(1), (2), (14); 1981 Sch. 3 para. 28.
326	1967 s. 29(12), (13).
327	1967 s. 30.
328	1967 s. 31; 1976 s. 24.
329	1976 s. 25.
330	1980 ss. 49, 63(1).
331	1980 ss. 65(1), (2), (3), (6), 87(1); 1981 Sch. 3 para. 56.
332	1980 s. 50(2).
333	1980 s. 50(1); 1981 Sch. 3 para. 49.
334	1980 s. 50(2A); 1981 s. 111(1).
335	1980 s. 50(3)(a), (b).
336	1980 s. 50(4)(a), (b).
337	1980 s. 50(4)(c), (5).
338	1980 ss. 50(4)(d), (6), (7), 65(1).
339	1980 s. 51; 1981 s. 11(2), Sch. 3 para. 50.
340	1980 s. 65(4), (5).
341	1980 s. 52.
342	1980 s. 53; OinC–2 No. 6.
343	1980 ss. 57(1)–(4), (6), (7), (8), 63(2); OinC–1 No. 49.
344	1980 ss. 57(5), 58(4).
345	1980 s. 62.
346	1980 s. 64; 1981 Sch. 3 paras. 54, 55; OinC–2 No. 7.
347	1980 s. 65(8).
348	1948 s. 108(1)(a), (2).
349	1948 s. 108(1)(c), (3), (4)(b), (c).

Provision	Derivation
350	1948 s. 108(1)(b), (3), (4)(a).
351	ECA 1972 s. 9(7) (as am. 1980 Sch. 3 para. 45(2)); 1976 s. 30(5); 1980 s. 77.
352	1948 s. 110(1), (4)–(6); 1981 s. 101(1), (2).
353	1948 s. 110(2)–(4); 1976 Sch. 1.
354	1948 s. 111.
355	1948 s. 112.
356	1948 s. 113; 1967 s. 52(2).
357	1948 s. 114.
358	1948 s. 115.
359	1948 s. 116.
360	1948 s. 117.
361	1948 s. 118.
362	1948 ss. 119(1), (4), 122.
363	1948 s. 124; 1981 Sch. 3 para. 4; OinC–1 No. 7.
364	1948 s. 125(1)–(4); 1976 Sch. 1; 1981 Sch. 3 para. 4; OinC–1 Nos. 8, 9.
365	1948 s. 126; OinC–1 No. 10.
366	1948 s. 131(1), (5).
367	1948 s. 131(2)–(4), (5).
368	1948 s. 132.
369	1948 s. 133.
370	1948 s. 134; 1980 Sch. 3 para. 16.
371	1948 s. 135.
372	1948 s. 136.
373	1948 s. 137.
374	1948 s. 138.
375	1948 s. 139.
376	1948 s. 140(1)–(3), (6), (7).
377	1948 s. 140(4), (5).
378	1948 s. 141.
379	1948 s. 142.
380	1948 s. 143; 1967 s. 51(2); 1980 s. 14(6), Sch. 3 para. 17; 1981 ss. 25(6), 49(10); OinC–1 No. 11.
381	1948 s. 144.
382	1948 s. 145; 1980 s. 63(3); OinC–1 No. 50.
383	1948 s. 146.
384	1976 s. 14(1)–(5), (7).
385	1976 s. 14(8).
386	1976 s. 14(6), (7), (10).
387	1967 s. 14(7); 1976 s. 15(6).

Provision	Derivation
388	1976 s. 15(1)–(5).
389	1948 s. 161; 1967 s. 13(1), (6); 1976 s. 13.
390	1976 s. 16(1)–(7).
391	1976 s. 17.
392	1976 s. 18.
393	1976 s. 19(1), (2).
394	1976 s. 20.
395	1948 s. 95(1).
396	1948 s. 95(2), (6), (7), (10)(a), (b); S.I. 1972/1268, Art. 16(2).
397	1948 s. 95(8), (9); 1976 Sch. 1; 1980 Sch. 3 paras. 15, 52.
398	1948 s. 95(3)–(5).
399	1948 s. 96.
400	1948 s. 97.
401	1948 s. 98; 1976 s. 38(2); 1981 s. 99.
402	1948 s. 99.
403	1948 s. 100; 1976 Sch. 1.
404	1948 s. 101.
405	1948 s. 102; 1976 Sch. 1.
406	1948 s. 103.
407	1948 s. 104.
408	1948 s. 105.
409	1948 s. 106; 1981 Sch. 3 para. 3; OinC–1 No. 5.
410	1948 s. 106A(1), (2), (10); 1972 Sc. ss. 6, 32(2), Sch.; S.I. 1972/1268; OinC–2 No. 5.
411	1948 s. 106A(3), (4).
412	1948 s. 106A(5).
413	1948 s. 106A(6), (7), (8); 1976 Sch. 1; 1980 Sch. 3 paras. 15, 52.
414	1948 s. 106A(9).
415	1948 s. 106B.
416	1948 s. 106C.
417	1948 s. 106D.
418	1948 s. 106E; 1976 s. 38(2); 1981 s. 99.
419	1948 s. 106F; 1976 Sch. 1.
420	1948 s. 106G.
421	1948 s. 106H.
422	1948 s. 106I.
423	1948 s. 106J.
424	1948 s. 106K; OinC–1 No. 6.
425	1948 s. 206.

Provision	Derivation
426	1948 s. 207.
427	1948 s. 208.
428	1948 s. 209(1), (5).
429	1948 s. 209(2); 1976 Sch. 1.
430	1948 s. 209(3), (4).
431	1948 s. 164; 1981 s. 86(1), (2).
432	1948 s. 165; 1980 Sch. 3 para. 21; 1981 s. 86(3).
433	1948 s. 166; 1967 s. 41.
434	1948 s. 167(1), (1A), (2), (5); 1967 ss. 39(a), (b), 50; 1981 s. 87, Sch. 3 para. 32; OinC–1 No. 13.
435	1948 s. 167(1B); 1981 s. 87(1).
436	1948 s. 167(3); 1967 s. 39; 1981 s. 87(2).
437	1948 s. 168; 1981 s. 88(1).
438	1967 s. 37(1), (2).
439	1948 s. 170; 1967 ss. 37(3), 40(1)–(4); 1981 Sch. 3 para. 7.
440	1967 s. 35(1).
441	1948 s. 171; 1981 s. 88(2).
442	1948 s. 172(1)–(4); 1981 Sch. 3 para. 8.
443	1948 s. 172(5), (6); 1981 s. 89.
444	1948 s. 173; 1981 s. 90.
445	1948 s. 174(1), (8).
446	1967 s. 32.
447	1967 s. 109.
448	1967 s. 110.
449	1967 s. 111; 1973 c. 58 Sch. 1 para. 16; 1976 s. 39(2); 1980 s. 84(3); 1981 s. 104(1)–(3); OinC–1 No. 34.
450	1967 s. 113; 1974 c. 49 Sch. 1; 1982 c. 50.
451	1967 s. 114.
452	1948 s. 175; 1967 ss. 32(6), 116 (as am. 1974 c. 49 Sch. 1, 1982 c. 50 Sch. 5 para. 6); 1981 s. 103(1), (3).
453	1967 s. 42.
454	1948 s. 174(2), (2A), (2B).
455	1948 s. 174(5)–(7); 1981 ss. 72(8), 77(4), 91(7).
456	1948 s. 174(3), (3A), (3B), (3C), (4), (4A); 1981 ss. 72(8), 77(3), (4), 91(4)–(6).
457	1948 s. 174(3D), (3E), (3F); 1981 ss. 72(8), 77(4), 91(4).
458	1948 s. 332(3); 1981 s. 96.
459	1980 s. 75(1), (9).
460	1980 s. 75(2), (10).

Provision	Derivation
461	1980 s. 75(3)–(8).
462	1972 Sc. ss. 1(1), 2, 3; 1979 c. 33 s. 29(2).
463	1972 Sc. s. 1(2)–(4).
464	1972 Sc. s. 5.
465	1972 Sc. s. 30(2), (3).
466	1972 Sc. ss. 5(1), 7.
467	1972 Sc. s. 11; OinC–2 No. 4.
468	1972 Sc. s. 12.
469	1972 Sc. s. 13.
470	1972 Sc. s. 14(1)–(6), (8).
471	1972 Sc. s. 15.
472	1972 Sc. s. 16.
473	1972 Sc. s. 17.
474	1972 Sc. s. 18.
475	1972 Sc. s. 19.
476	1972 Sc. s. 20.
477	1972 Sc. s. 21.
478	1972 Sc. s. 22.
479	1972 Sc. s. 23.
480	1972 Sc. s. 24.
481	1972 Sc. s. 25; OinC–1 No. 35.
482	1972 Sc. s. 26.
483	1972 Sc. s. 27.
484	1972 Sc. s. 28.
485	1972 Sc. s. 29.
486	1972 Sc. s. 31.
487	1972 Sc. s. 32.
488	1972 Sc. s. 31(5).
489	1948 s. 366.
490	1948 s. 367.
491	1948 s. 368.
492	1948 s. 369.
493	1948 s. 370.
494	1948 s. 371.
495	1948 s. 372(1), (3)–(5), (7); 1976 Sch. 1.
496	1948 s. 373.
497	1948 s. 372(2), (3), (4), (5)–(7); OinC–1 No. 18.
498	1948 s. 374; OinC–1 No. 19.

Provision	Derivation
499	1948 s. 375.
500	1948 s. 376.
501	1948 s. 211.
502	1948 s. 212(1), (3).
503	1948 s. 212(2); 1981 s. 58(5).
504	1981 ss. 58(1)–(5), 61.
505	1967 s. 44(7); 1980 s. 7(4).
506	1967 s. 43(6).
507	1948 s. 213; 1981 ss. 58(6), 61.
508	1948 s. 214.
509	1948 s. 215.
510	1948 s. 216.
511	1948 s. 394(3)(f), (g).
512	1948 s. 218(1), (3), (5), (6), (8); 1976 c. 60 s. 1(1), Sch. 1 Parts I, II.
513	1948 ss. 218(7), 219(1).
514	1948 s. 219(3).
515	1948 s. 220; 1976 c. 60 s. 1(1), (2), Sch. 1 Pts. I, II.
516	1948 s. 221.
517	1948 s. 222; 1972 Sc. s. 4; 1980 Sch. 3 para. 27.
518	1948 s. 223; 1976 c. 60 s. 1(1), (2), Sch. 1 Pts. I, II; S.I. 1984/1199.
519	1948 s. 224; 1980 Sch. 3 para. 28; 1981 s. 58(7).
520	1948 s. 225.
521	1948 ss. 226, 396.
522	1948 s. 227.
523	1948 s. 228.
524	1948 s. 229.
525	1948 ss. 230, 231, 232, 397.
526	1948 s. 233.
527	1948 s. 234.
528	1948 s. 235(1)–(3), (5), (8).
529	1948 s. 235(4), (6), (7); 1967 s. 50.
530	1948 s. 236.
531	1948 s. 237.
532	1948 s. 238.
533	1948 s. 239.
534	1948 s. 240.
535	1948 s. 241.
536	1948 s. 242.

Provision	Derivation
537	1948 s. 243.
538	1948 s. 244.
539	1948 s. 245.
540	1948 s. 246.
541	1948 s. 247.
542	1948 s. 248; 1976 c. 60 ss. 1(1), (2), 3, Sch. 2 para. 3.
543	1948 s. 249; 1976 c. 60 s. 2; OinC–1 No. 14.
544	1948 s. 250.
545	1948 s. 251.
546	1948 s. 252.
547	1948 ss. 253(1), 255.
548	1948 s. 254.
549	1948 s. 256.
550	1948 s. 257.
551	1948 s. 258.
552	1948 s. 259.
553	1948 s. 260.
554	1948 s. 261.
555	1948 s. 262.
556	1948 s. 263.
557	1948 s. 264.
558	1948 s. 265.
559	1948 s. 266.
560	1948 s. 267.
561	1948 s. 268.
562	1948 s. 269.
563	1948 s. 270(1)–(3).
564	1948 s. 270(4)–(9).
565	1948 s. 271.
566	1948 s. 272.
567	1948 s. 273.
568	1948 s. 274.
569	1948 s. 275.
570	1948 s. 276.
571	1948 s. 277.
572	1948 ss. 143(4)(e), 278.
573	1948 s. 279.
574	1948 s. 280.

[The next page is 36,581]

Provision	Derivation
575	1948 s. 281.
576	1948 s. 282.
577	1948 s. 283(1)–(3); 1981 s. 105(1).
578	1948 s. 283(4).
579	1948 s. 284.
580	1948 s. 285.
581	1948 s. 286.
582	1948 s. 287.
583	1948 s. 288.
584	1948 s. 289.
585	1948 s. 290.
586	1948 s. 291.
587	1948 s. 292.
588	1948 s. 293; 1981 s. 106.
589	1948 s. 294.
590	1948 s. 295.
591	1948 s. 296.
592	1948 s. 297.
593	1948 s. 298.
594	1948 s. 299.
595	1948 s. 300.
596	1948 s. 301.
597	1948 s. 302.
598	1948 s. 303.
599	1948 s. 304.
600	1948 s. 305.
601	1948 s. 306.
602	1948 s. 307.
603	1948 s. 308(1).
604	1948 s. 309.
605	1948 s. 310.
606	1948 s. 311.
607	1948 s. 312.
608	1948 s. 313.
609	1948 s. 314.
610	1948 s. 315.
611	1948 s. 316.
612	1948 s. 317.

Provision	Derivation
613	1948 s. 318.
614	1948 s. 319.
615	1948 s. 320; OinC–1 No. 15.
616	1948 s. 321.
617	1948 s. 322; 1972 Sc. s. 8; OinC–1 No. 16.
618	1948 s. 323(1), (2), (8).
619	1948 s. 323(3)–(7).
620	1948 s. 324.
621	1948 s. 325; Charging Orders Act 1979 s. 4.
622	1948 s. 326; 1976 c. 60 s. 1(1), (2), Sch. 1 Pts. I, II.
623	1948 s. 327.
624	1948 s. 328(1)(d), (e), (i), (j), (k), (o), s. 328(2), (3); 1976 c. 60 s. 1, Sch. 1 Pt. I; OinC–2 No. 3.
625	1948 s. 330.
626	1948 s. 328(1)(a)–(c), (g), (h), (l), proviso, (3).
627	1948 s. 329.
628	1948 s. 328(1)(f), proviso, (3).
629	1948 s. 328(1)(p), (3).
630	1948 s. 332(1), (2), (4).
631	1948 s. 333.
632	1948 s. 334(1)–(3), (4); 1981 s. 92(1).
633	1948 s. 334(5), (6); 1981 s. 92(1)–(4).
634	1948 s. 335.
635	1948 s. 336.
636	1948 s. 337.
637	1948 s. 338.
638	1948 s. 339.
639	1948 s. 340.
640	1948 s. 341.
641	1948 s. 342.
642	1948 s. 343; 1976 c. 60 Sch. 2.
643	1948 s. 344.
644	1948 s. 345.
645	1948 s. 346.
646	1948 s. 347.
647	1948 s. 348; OinC–1 No. 17.
648	1948 s. 349.
649	1948 s. 350.
650	1948 s. 351.

Provision	Derivation
651	1948 s. 352.
652	1948 s. 353(1)–(5), (7).
653	1948 s. 353(6).
654	1948 s. 354; 1981 s. 108(5).
655	1981 s. 108(1)–(4).
656	1948 s. 355.
657	1948 s. 355(2), (9).
658	1948 s. 356.
659	1980 s. 74(4), (5), (6)(b), (7), (8).
660	1948 s. 362.
661	1948 s. 363.
662	1948 s. 364.
663	1948 s. 365(1), (3), (5); 1967 s. 50; 1970 c. 8 s. 1(3)(c).
664	1976 c. 60 s. 1(2), (4).
665	1948 s. 398; 1981 c. 65 Sch. 6.
666	1948 s. 399(1)–(5), (8), (9); 1972 Sc. s. 4; 1981 c. 65 Sch. 6.
667	1948 s. 399(6)(a); 1976 c. 60 s. 1(2), (4), Sch. 1 Pts. I, II; S.I. 1984/1199.
668	1948 s. 399(6)(b).
669	1948 s. 399(6)(c), (d), (e).
670	1948 s. 400.
671	1948 ss. 401, 455(1).
672	1948 s. 402.
673	1948 s. 403.
674	1948 s. 404.
675	1948 s. 377.
676	1948 s. 378.
677	1948 s. 379; 1967 s. 53(2).
678	1948 s. 380.
679	1948 s. 381.
680	1948 s. 382(1), excl. proviso (v)–(vii); 1976 Sch. 1; 1980 Sch. 3 para. 29.
681	1948 s. 382(1) proviso (v)–(vii), (2)–(4); 1980 Sch. 3 para. 29; 1981 Sch. 3 para. 13.
682	1981 s. 26(1), (2).
683	1948 s. 383.
684	1948 s. 384; 1976 Sch. 1; 1981 Sch. 3 para. 14; OinC–1 Nos. 20, 21, 24.
685	1980 ss. 2(3), 13(1)–(5), (7).
686	1948 ss. 385, 386, 387; 1976 Sch. 1; OinC-1 No. 22.
687	1981 s. 26(3); OinC–1 Nos. 23, 54.
688	1948 s. 390; 1976 s. 38(2), Sch. 2; 1980 s. 13(6), Sch. 3 para. 31; 1981 s. 99.

Provision	Derivation
689	1948 ss. 391, 392, 393, 394.
690	1948 s. 395.
691	1948 s. 407(1), (2); 1976 Sch. 1; 1981 Sch. 3 para. 15; OinC-1 No. 25.
692	1948 s. 409(1), (2); 1976 Sch. 2; OinC–1 No. 26.
693	1948 s. 411.
694	1976 s. 31; 1981 s. 27.
695	1948 s. 412.
696	1948 s. 413.
697	1948 s. 414; 1976 s. 31(5).
698	1948 s. 415.
699	1948 s. 416; 1981 s. 109.
700	1976 s. 9(1)–(3), (3A), (3B); 1980 Sch. 3 para. 49; 1981 s. 19; OinC–1 No. 37.
701	1976 ss. 2, 3 (as applied by s. 10).
702	1976 s. 6 (as applied by s. 11(2), (3)).
703	1976 s. 11(1), (4).
704	1948 s. 424; 1981 Sch. 3 para. 16.
705	1981 ss. 23(2), 97.
706	1976 s. 35.
707	1976 s. 36.
708	1948 s. 452(2); 1976 s. 37; 1981 Sch. 3 para. 37.
709	1948 s. 426(1); 1976 Sch. 2; 1981 ss. 98(1), 99.
710	1948 s. 426(2)–(6); 1976 s. 38(3); 1981 ss. 98(2), 99.
711	ECA 1972 s. 9(3); 1976 ss. 1(10), 22(3), 23(6); 1980 Sch. 3 para. 45(1); 1981 Sch. 3 para. 34.
712	1948 s. 427.
713	1948 s. 428; 1976 s. 16(8); 1980 s. 84(1); 1981 s. 115(1).
714	1981 s. 23; S.I. 1982/1654.
715	981 s. 100.
716	1948 s. 434(1); 1967 s. 120; 1979 c. 37 Sch. 7.
717	1967 s. 121.
718	1948 s. 435.
719	1980 s. 74(1)–(3), (6)(a).
720	1948 ss. 433, 454(2)(a).
721	1948 s. 441.
722	1948 s. 436; 1967 s. 56(6), Sch. 4; 1976 Sch. 2.
723	SECOBA s. 3 1976 Sch. 2; 1980 Sch. 3 para. 48.
724	1977 c. 38 s. 7.
725	1948 s. 437.

[The next page is 36,601]

Provision	Derivation
726	1948 s. 447.
727	1948 s. 448.
728	1948 s. 449.
729	1948 s. 451; 1976 s. 38(1); 1980 Sch. 3 para. 33; 1981 Sch. 3 para. 18.
730(4)	1980 s. 80(2).
(5)	1948 s. 440(2).
731	1967 ss. 49(2)–(5), 115(1); 1972 Sc. s. 28(4); 1980 s. 84(2); 1981 s. 115(2).
732	1948 ss. 174(7), 446; 1967 s. 27(10); 1967 s. 91, as applied ibid. s. 115(2); 1976 s. 25(4); 1981 s. 72(9).
733	1967 ss. 89, as applied ibid. s. 115(2), 102(3); 1981 s. 81.
734	1967 s. 88, as applied ibid. s. 115(2).
735	1948 s. 455.
736	1948 ss. 150(4), 154.
737	1980 s. 87(1).
738	1980 s. 87(2), (3).
739	1980 s. 87(1), (4)(b).
740	1948 s. 455(3).
741	1948 s. 455(1), (2); 1980 s. 63(1), (5).
742	1948 ss. 149(8)(a), (b), 149A(7)(a), 455(1); 1967 s. 56(2); 1976 s. 1(9); 1980 s. 87(1); 1981 ss. 1, 21(1), (3), Sch. 2 para. 5(7), Sch. 3 para. 33.
743	1980 s. 87(1).
744	1948 ss. 154(5), 406, 455(1); 1976 s. 1(9); 1980 s. 87(1), Sch. 3 para. 35; OinC–1 No. 27.
745	(Northern Ireland).
746	(Commencement).
747	(Citation).
Sch. 1	1948 s. 200(2), (3); 1976 s. 21(1), (2); 1981 s. 95(2).
Sch. 2	1983 (BI) ss. 2–5, Sch.
Sch. 3	1948 s. 417(1)(b), Sch. 4: 1976 s. 33.
para. 1	1948 Sch. 4 paras. 1–3, 22.
2	1948 Sch. 4 para. 4.
3	1948 Sch. 4 paras. 5, 6; 1976 s. 33.
4	1948 Sch. 4 paras. 7, 25.
5	1948 Sch. 4 para. 8.
6	1948 Sch. 4 para. 9(2).
7	1948 Sch. 4 para. 9(1).
8	1948 Sch. 4 para. 10.
9	1948 Sch. 4 paras. 23, 24, 26.
10	1948 Sch. 4 paras. 11–13, 22.
11	1948 Sch. 4 para. 14.
12	1948 Sch. 4 para. 15.
13	1948 Sch. 4 paras. 16, 22.

Provision	Derivation
14	1948 Sch. 4 para. 17.
15	1948 Sch. 4 para. 18.
16	1948 Sch. 4 para. 19.
17	1948 Sch. 4 para. 20.
18	1948 Sch. 4 para. 21.
19	1948 Sch. 4 para. 27.
20	1948 Sch. 4 para. 28.
21	1948 Sch. 4 para. 29.
22(1)	1948 Sch. 4 para. 30.
(3)	1948 Sch. 4 paras. 20, 21(1).
Sch. 4	1948 Sch. 8 substituted by 1981 s. 1.
para. 38(2)	OinC–1 No. 29.
60	1983 (BI) s. 2.
75(4)	S.I. 1984/1859.
Part VI	1948 Sch. 8 Part VA, inserted by S.I. 1982/1092.
Sch. 5	
para. 1	1967 s. 3(1); 1980 Sch. 3 para. 41; 1981 Sch. 3 paras. 23, 24.
2	1967 s. 3(2); 1981 Sch. 3 para. 24.
3	1967 s. 3(3).
4	1967 s. 3(4).
5	1967 s. 3(5).
6	1967 s. 3(2).
7	1967 s. 4(1); 1981 Sch. 3 paras. 23, 24.
8	1967 s. 4(1A); 1981 s. 3(1).
9	1967 s. 4(2); 1980 Sch. 3 para. 41; 1981 Sch. 3 para. 24.
10	1967 s. 4(3); 1981 s. 3(2)(a).
11	1967 s. 4(4); 1981 s. 3(2)(b).
12	1967 s. 4(5); 1981 s. 3(2)(c).
13	1967 s. 4(7).
14	1981 s. 4(1).
15	1981 s. 4(2).
16	1981 s. 4(3); OinC–2 No. 8.
17	1981 s. 4(4)–(7); OinC–2 No. 9.
18	1981 s. 4(8).
19	1981 s. 4(10).
20	1967 s. 5(1); 1980 Sch. 3 para. 41; 1981 Sch. 3 para. 23.
21	1967 s. 5(2).
22	1948 s. 196(1)(a), (2); 1981 Sch. 3 para. 10.
23	1967 s. 6(6); S.I. 1982/1698.
24	1967 s. 6(1)(a), (7)(a).
25	1967 s. 6(1)(b), (2), (7)(b); S.I. 1979/1618 para. 3; 1981 Sch. 3 para. 6.
26	1967 s. 6(3).
27	1967 s. 7(1)–(3); 1981 Sch. 3 para. 26.
28	1948 s. 196(1)(b), (3).
29	1948 s. 196(1)(c), (4).
30	1948 s. 196(5).
31	1948 s. 196(6); 1981 Sch. 3 para. 10.
32	1948 s. 196(7).
33	1948 s. 196(3), (9).

Provision	Derivation
34	1948 s. 196(1); 1967 ss. 6(1), 7(1).
35	1967 s. 8(1); 1981 Sch. 3 para. 26; S.I. 1982/1698.
36	1967 s. 8(2), (3).
37	1967 s. 8(5).
Sch. 6	
para. 1	1980 s. 54(1); 1981 Sch. 3 para. 51
2	1980 s. 54(2).
3	1980 s. 54(4).
4	1980 s. 54(5).
5	1980 s. 54(6); 1981 Sch. 3 para. 51.
6	1980 s. 54(7).
7	S.I. 1984/1860.
8	S.I. 1984/1860.
9	1980 s. 55; OinC–1 No. 48.
10	S.I. 1984/1860.
11	1980 s. 58(1), (2).
12	1980 ss. 58(3), 87(4); 1981 Sch. 3 paras. 53, 62.
13	1980 s. 62.
14	1980 ss. 64, 65(1), (3), (4), (6).
15	1980 s. 56(1).
16	1980 ss. 56(2), (2A), (3), 62; 1981 Sch. 3 para. 52.
17	1980 ss. 56(8), 64, 65(1), (2), (3).
18	1980 s. 56(1), (4).
19	1980 s. 56(4).
20	1980 s. 56(5).
21	1980 ss. 56(8), 64, 65(2), (6).
Sch. 7	
para. 1	1967 s. 16(1)(a).
2	1967 s. 16(1)(e), (4), (4A); 1981 s. 13(4).
3	1967 s. 19(1); S.I. 1980/1055.
4	1967 s. 19(2); S.I. 1980/1055.
5	1967 s. 19(3)–(5).
6	1967 s. 16(1)(f); 1981 s. 13(3).
7	1967 s. 16A(1), inserted 1981 s. 14.
8	1967 s. 16A(2), inserted 1981 s. 14.
9	S.I. 1980/1160.
10	1967 s. 16(1)(g), (5)–(7); 1974 c. 37 s. 79(3).
11	1967 s. 16(1)(h), (1A), (8); 1982 c. 46 s. 1.
Sch. 8	
Part I	
para. 1	1981 ss. (6)–(8), 7(1)–(8).
2	1981 ss. 6(2)(a), (3), 7(1).
3	1981 s. 6(2)(b), (6).
4	1981 s. 6(2)(d).
5	1981 s. 6(2)(c), (5).
6	1981 s. 6(4).
7	1981 s. 6(7)(a), (8).
8	1981 s. 6(7)(b).
9	1981 s. 7(2), (3).

Provision	Derivation
10	1981 s. 7(4)–(6), (8).
11	1981 s. 7(7).
Part II	1981 s. 10(4), (5).
Part III	1981 s. 10(3)–(5).
Sch. 9	1948 Sch. 8A (formerly Sch. 8, renumbered 8A by 1981 s. 1(2)), as amended by 1967 s. 9, Sch. 2.
para. 2	1948 Sch. 8A para. 2(a), as modified by 1981 Sch. 2 para. 4(4); OinC–1 No. 30.
5(2)	1948 Sch. 8A para. 5(2)(c), as amended by 1976 Sch. 2.
6	1948 Sch. 8A para. 5A, as amended by 1976 Sch. 2.
10	1948 Sch. 8A para. 8(1), (3), as amended by 1976 Sch. 2, and modified by 1981 Sch. 2 para. 4(4).
13	1948 Sch. 8A para. 11, with insertions by 1980 Sch. 3 para. 39(2), amendments by S.I. 1970/1333, 1976 Sch. 2 and 1980 Sch. 3 para. 39(2), and modification by 1981 Sch. 2 para. 4(4).
14	1948 Sch. 8A para. 12, with amendment by 1976 Sch. 2 and modification by 1981 Sch. 2 para. 4(4).
17	1948 Sch. 8A para. 13A(5), as amended by S.I. 1979/1618.
19	1948 Sch. 8A para. 15, with amendments by S.I. 1973/1150 and 1981 s. 40(3); 1983 (BI).
22	1948 Sch. 8A para. 18, as modified by 1981 Sch. 2 para. 4(4).
23	1948 Sch. 8A para. 19, as modified by 1981 Sch. 2 para. 4(4)(f).
24	1948 Sch. 8A para. 19A, inserted by 1981 Sch. 2 para. 4(4).
27	1948 Sch. 8A para. 23, as modified by 1981 Sch. 2 para. 4(5); S.I. 1970/327.
28	1948 Sch. 8A para. 24, as modified by 1981 Sch. 2 para. 4(5).
30	1948 Sch. 8A para. 26, as modified by 1981 Sch. 2 para. 4(4).
Part IV	1948 Sch. 8A Part IIIA, inserted by S.I. 1982/1092; as amended by S.I. 1984/1859.
para. 33	1948 Sch. 8A para. 28, as amended by 1976 Sch. 2.
Sch. 10	
para. 1	1967 s. 16(1)(b); 1981 Sch. 2 para. 5(4).
2	1967 s. 17(1); 1981 Sch. 2 para. 5(4).
3	1967 s. 17(2); 1981 Sch. 2 para. 5(4).
4	1967 s. 17(3).
5	1967 s. 18(1), (3).
6	1967 s. 18(2), (3).
7	1967 s. 18(4).
8	1967 s. 18(5), (6).
9	1967 s. 16(1)(f).
Sch. 11	1981 Sch. 2 para. 6(1)–(4).
Sch. 12	
Part I	1948 s. 188(2D), (3), (4); 1981 s. 93.
Part II	1976 c. 60 s. 9(2), (3), (4).
Part III	1948 s. 188(1C), (2)(a), (b), (2A), (2B); 1976 c. 60 s. 9(1A), (9); 1981 s. 93(5).
Sch. 13	1967 ss. 27–29; 1981 Sch. 3 paras. 28, 29.
Sch. 14	
Part I	1948 s. 119(1).

[The next page is 36,621]   **CCH Editions Limited**

Provision	Derivation
Part II	1948 ss. 119(2), (3), 120, 121; 1976 Sch. 1.
Part III	1948 s. 123.
Sch. 15	1948 Sch. 6 Part I.
para. 4	1948 Sch. 6 para. 4, OinC–1 No. 28.
Sch. 16	1948 Sch. 10.
Sch. 17	1948 ss. 253(2)–(8), 295(2).
Sch. 18	1948 Sch. 11.
Sch. 19	
para. 1	1948 s. 319(8)(d).
2	1948 s. 319(1)(a)(ii); F.A. 1966 Sch. 6 para. 14.
3	F.A. 1952 s. 30(2), (4), (5); F.A. (No. 2) 1975 s. 69.
4	V.A.T. Act 1983 (c. 55) Sch. 7 para. 12(1)(c).
5	Car Tax Act 1983 (c. 53) Sch. 1 para. 4(1)(c).
6	1981 c. 63 s. 30(1), (2).
7	1948 s. 319(1)(a)(i).
8	1948 s. 319(1)(e), as amended by Social Security Act 1973 (c. 38) and Social Security Pensions Act 1975 (c. 60).
9	1948 s. 319(1)(b).
10	1948 s. 319(1)(b), (d), (8)(b).
11	1978 c. 44 s. 121(1)(c), (2); 1980 c. 42 Sch. 1 para. 15; 1982 c. 24 Sch. 2 para. 12.
12	1948 s. 319(1)(c).
13	1948 s. 319(2); 1976 c. 60 s. 1, Sch. 1 Parts I, II.
14	1948 s. 319(4).
15	1948 s. 319(8)(a), (c).
Sch. 20	
Part I	1948 s. 323(6) proviso.
Part II	1948 s. 355(9).
Sch. 21	
para. 1	1948 s. 394(7).
2	1948 s. 391.
3	1948 s. 392.
4	1948 s. 393.
5	1948 s. 394(2); 1980 Sch. 3 para. 32(a).
6	1948 s. 394(3)(a)–(e).
7	1948 s. 394(4).
8	1948 s. 394(5).
9	1948 s. 394(6).
Sch. 22	1948 Sch. 14, as amended by 1967 s. 54, ECA 1972 s. 9(8), 1976 s. 41, SECOBA s. 4, 1980 s. 67, 1981 s. 20; OinC–1 No. 36.
Sch. 23	1948 Sch. 13.

Provision	Derivation
Sch. 24	The derivation of any entry in this Schedule is the cumulative effect of the original provision of the Act of 1948, 1967, 1972 Sc., 1976, 1980 or 1981 in so far as it provided a penalty for contravention, with the effect (in certain cases) of section 80 of, and Schedule 2 to, the Act of 1980. The derivation may also include provisions of the general law relating to the trial and punishment of statutory offences of greater or lesser gravity. 1980 Sch. 2 was amended by OinC–1 No. 51. OinC–2 Nos. 2, 3 and 4 amended 1948 ss. 187 and 328 and 1972 Sc. s. 11 in respect of punishment of contraventions of those sections in Scotland.
Sch. 25	1981 s. 38.

TABLE OF DESTINATIONS

The table below, prepared by CCH editorial staff, relates the provisions of the former legislation (in the left-hand column) to the corresponding provisions of the consolidated legislation (in the right-hand column), namely:

> The Companies Act 1985
> The Business Names Act 1985
> The Company Securities (Insider Dealing) Act 1985
> The Companies Consolidation (Consequential Provisions) Act 1985

Note: The left-hand column does not include provisions of the former legislation which were transitional or later superseded, were amending provisions or had otherwise become no longer relevant through the passage of time.

The following abbreviations are used in this table:—

"CA 1985"	= Companies Act 1985.
"BNA 1985"	= Business Names Act 1985.
"CS (ID)A 1985"	= Company Securities (Insider Dealing) Act 1985.
"CC (CP)A 1985"	= Companies Consolidation (Consequential Provisions) Act 1985.
"OinC–1"	= Companies Acts (Pre-Consolidation Amendments) Order 1984 (S.I. 1984/134).
"OinC–2"	= Companies Acts (Pre-Consolidation Amendments) (No. 2) Order 1984 (S.I. 1984/1169).

Provision of former Acts	Destination
Companies Act 1948	
1	CA 1985, s. 1.
2 (except 2(1)(a)), 3, 4	s. 2.
2(1)(a)	s. 25(2).
5(1)	s. 4.
5(2)–(5)	s. 5.
5(7)–(9)	s. 6.
6	s. 7(1).
7 (as amended by OinC–1)	s. 7(2).
8	s. 8(1), (2).
9	s. 7(3).
10	s. 9.
11	s. 3(1), 8(4).
12	s. 10(1), 12(2).
13	s. 13(1)–(4).
20	s. 14.
21	s. 15, CC(CP)A 1985, s. 10.
22	s. 16.
23	s. 17.
24	s. 19.

Provision of former Acts	Destination
Companies Act 1948	
25	CA 1985, s. 20.
26	s. 22.
27	s. 23(1), (2), (3), (4)(part), (5).
31	s. 24.
32	s. 36(1)–(3).
33	s. 37.
34	s. 38.
35	s. 39.
36	s. 41.
37	s. 63.
38(1)	s. 56(1).
38(2)	s. 57.
38(3)	s. 56(2)–(4).
38(4)	s. 66(1), (2).
38(5)	s. 56(5).
38(6)	s. 66(3).
40(1), (2)	s. 61.
40(3)	s. 62.
41(1)(a), (2)–(4)	s. 64(1), (3), (4), (5).
41(1)(b) etc.	s. 65.
43(1) except proviso	s. 67(1), (2).
43(1) proviso, (2), (3)	s. 68.
43(4)	s. 69.
43(5)	s. 67(3).
44	s. 70.
45(1)–(3)	s. 58.
45(4)	s. 64(2).
46	s. 71.
47	s. 83.
49	s. 85.
50	s. 82 (and s. 86(2)).
51(1)–(5), 6(a)	
(51(6)(b) omitted by OinC-1)	s. 86.
51(7) (inserted by OinC-1)	s. 87.
52	s. 88.
53(1), (5)	s. 97.
53(2)–(4)	s. 98.
55(1)	s. 59.

Provision of former Acts	Destination
Companies Act 1948	
55(2)–(4)	CA 1985, s. 60(1)–(7).
56(1), (2)	s. 130(1)–(3).
59	s. 119.
60	s. 120.
61	s. 121.
62	s. 122.
63	s. 123.
64	s. 124.
66	s. 135.
67	s. 136.
68	s. 137.
69	s. 138.
70	s. 140.
71	s. 141.
72	s. 127.
73	s. 182(1).
74	s. 182(2).
75	s. 183(1), (2).
76	s. 183(3).
77	s. 183(4).
78	s. 183(5), (6).
79	s. 184.
80	s. 185(1)–(3), (5)–(7).
81	s. 186.
82	s. 187.
83	s. 188.
85	s. 189.
86	s. 190.
87	s. 191.
88	s. 192.
89	s. 193.
90	s. 194.
91	CC(CP)A 1985, s. 13.
92	CA 1985, s. 195.
93	s. 197.
94	s. 196.
95(1)	s. 395.
95(2)	s. 396(1).

Provision of former Acts	Destination
Companies Act 1948	
95(3)–(5)	CA 1985, s. 398.
95(6)	s. 396(2).
95(7)	s. 396(3).
95(8)	s. 397(1).
95(9)	s. 397(2), (3).
95(10)(a)	s. 396(4).
96	s. 399.
97	s. 400.
98	s. 401.
99	s. 402.
100	s. 403.
101	s. 404.
102	s. 405.
103	s. 406.
104	s. 407.
105	s. 408.
106(1)	s. 409(1).
106(2) (inserted by OinC-1)	s. 409(2).
106A(1)	s. 410(2), (3).
106A(2)	s. 410(4).
106A(3), (4)	s. 411.
106A(5)	s. 412.
106A(6)–(8)	s. 413.
106A(9)	s. 414.
106A(10)	s. 410(5).
106B	s. 415.
106C	s. 416.
106D	s. 417.
106E	s. 418.
106F	s. 419.
106G	s. 420.
106H	s. 421.
106I	s. 422.
106J	s. 423.
106K(1)	s. 424(1).
106K(2) (inserted by OinC–1)	s. 424(2).
108(1)(a)	s. 348(1).
108(1)(b)	s. 350(1) (part).

Provision of former Acts	Destination
Companies Act 1948	
108(1)(c)	CA 1985, s. 349(1).
108(2)	s. 348(2).
108(3)	s. 349(2), 350(1) (part).
108(4)(a)	s. 350(2).
108(4)(b)	s. 349(4) (part).
108(4)(c)	s. 349(3)(b).
108(4) balance	s. 349(4) (part).
110(1)	s. 352(1)–(3).
110(2)	s. 353(1).
110(3)	s. 353(2), (3).
110(4)	s. 352(5), 353(4).
110(5)	s. 352(6).
110(6)	s. 191(7), 352(7).
111	s. 354.
112	s. 355.
113(1)	s. 356(1), (2), 4(a).
113(2)	s. 356(3), 4(b).
113(3)	s. 356(5).
113(4)	s. 356(6).
114	s. 357.
115	s. 358.
116	s. 359.
117	s. 360.
118	s. 361.
119(1)	s. 362(1), Sch. 14, Pt. I.
119(2)	Sch. 14, Pt. II, para. 1(1).
119(3)	Sch. 14, Pt. II, para. 1(3).
119(4)	s. 362(2)(c).
120(1)	Sch. 14, Pt. II, para. 2(1).
120(2)	Sch. 14, Pt. II, para. 2(2), 3(1).
120(3)	Sch. 14, Pt. II, para. 4(1).
120(4)	Sch. 14, Pt. II, para. 5.
120(5)	Sch. 14, Pt. II, para. 6.
120(6)	Sch. 14, Pt. II, para. 7.
120(7)	Sch. 14, Pt. II, para. 4(2), (3).
121	Sch. 14, Pt. II, para. 8.
122	s. 362(4), (5).
123	Sch. 14, Pt. III.

Provision of former Acts	Destination
Companies Act 1948	
124(1) (as amended by OinC-1)	CA 1985, s. 363(1)–(5).
124(2)	s. 363(6).
124(3)	s. 363(7).
124(4)	s. 363(8).
125(1)	s. 364(1), (2).
125(2) (as amended by OinC-1)	s. 364(3).
125(3)	s. 364(4).
125(4)	s. 364(5).
126(1)	s. 365(1), (2).
126(2) (as amended by OinC-1)	s. 365(3).
131(1)	s. 366(1)–(3).
131(2)	s. 367(1), (2).
131(3)	s. 367(4).
131(4)	s. 367(5) (part).
131(5)	s. 366(4), 367(3), (5) (part).
132(1)	s. 368(1), (2).
132(2)	s. 368(3).
132(3)	s. 368(4).
132(4)	s. 368(5).
132(5)	s. 368(6).
132(6)	s. 368(7).
133(1)	s. 369(1).
133(2)	s. 369(2).
133(3)	s. 369(3), (4).
134	s. 370.
135(1)	s. 371(1), (2).
135(2)	s. 371(3).
136(1)	s. 372(1), (2).
136(2)	s. 372(3), (4).
136(3)	s. 372(5).
136(4)	s. 372(6).
136(5)	s. 372(7).
137	s. 373.
138	s. 374.
139	s. 375.
140(1)	s. 376(1).
140(2)	s. 376(2).
140(3)	s. 376(3)–(5).

Provision of former Acts	Destination
Companies Act 1948	
140(4)	CA 1985, s. 377(1), (2).
140(5)	s. 377(3).
140(6)	s. 376(6).
140(7)	s. 376(7).
141(1)	s. 378(1).
141(2)	s. 378(2), (3).
141(3)	s. 378(4).
141(4)	s. 378(5).
141(5)	s. 378(6).
142	s. 379.
143(1) (and CA 1967, s. 51(2))	s. 380(1).
143(2)	s. 380(2).
143(3)	s. 380(3).
143(4) (as amended by OinC-1)	s. 380(4).
143(4)(e)	s. 572(3).
143(5)	s. 380(5).
143(6)	s. 380(6).
143(7)	s. 380(7).
144	s. 381.
145(1)	s. 382(1).
145(2)	s. 382(2).
145(3)	s. 382(4).
145(4)	s. 382(5).
146(1)	s. 383(1), (2).
146(2)	s. 383(3).
146(3)	s. 383(4).
146(4)	s. 383(5).
149(1)	s. 228(1).
149(2)	s. 228(2).
149(3)	s. 228(3)–(5).
149(4)	s. 228(6).
149(5), (6)	s. 228(7), s. 245(1).
149(7)	s. 245(1), (3).
149(8)(a)	s. 742(2).
149(8)(b)	s. 227(1), s. 742(1)(e).
149A(1)–(5)	s. 258.
149A(6)	s. 245(1), (3).
149A(7)(a)	s. 742(2).

Provision of former Acts	Destination
Companies Act 1948	
149A(7)(b)	CA 1985, s. 227(1), s. 742(1)(e).
150(1)	s. 229(1).
150(2)(a)	s. 229(2).
150(2)(b)	s. 229(3).
150(2) proviso	s. 229(4).
150(3)	s. 245(2), (3).
150(4)	s. 736(5)(b).
151(1)	s. 229(5).
151(2)	s. 229(6).
151(3)	s. 229(7).
152(1)	s. 230(1).
152(2)	s. 230(2).
152(3)	s. 230(3)–(6).
152(4) (as amended by OinC-1)	s. 230(7).
152(5)	s. 230 (8).
152A(1)	s. 259(1).
152A(2) (as amended by OinC-2)	s. 259(2).
152A(3)	s. 259(3), (4).
153(1)	s. 227(4).
154(1)	s. 736(1).
154(2)	s. 736(2), (3).
154(3)	s. 736(4).
154(4)	s. 736(5)(a).
154(5)	s. 736(6), 744.
155(1)	s. 238(1).
155(3)	s. 238(2).
156(1)	s. 238(3).
156(2)	s. 238(4).
157(1)	s. 235(1), 261(2).
158(1)	s. 240(1)–(4).
158(2)	s. 246(1).
158(3) part	s. 240(5).
158(3) part	s. 246(2).
161(1)	s. 389(1).
161(2)	s. 389(6).
161(3)	s. 389(7).
161(4)	s. 389(8).
163 saving re provisio	see s. 261(3).

Provision of former Acts	Destination
Companies Act 1948	
164(1)	CA 1985, s. 431(1), (2).
164(2)	s. 431(3), (4).
165(1)	s. 432(1), (2).
165(2)	s. 432(3), (4).
166	s. 433(1).
167(1)	s. 434(1).
167(1A)	s. 434(2).
167(1B)	s. 435.
167(2) (as amended by OinC-1)	s. 434(3).
167(3)	s. 436.
167(5)	s. 434(4).
168(1)	s. 437(1).
168(2)	s. 437(2), (3).
170(1)	s. 439(1)–(5).
170(2)	s. 439(6).
170(3)	s. 439(7).
170(4)	s. 439(8), (9).
170(5)	s. 439(10).
171	s. 441.
172(1)–(4)	s. 442.
172(5)	s. 443(1)–(3).
172(6)	s. 443(4).
173	s. 444.
174(1)	s. 445(1).
174(2)–(2B)	s. 454.
174(3)	s. 456(1), (2).
174(3A)–(3C)	s. 456(3)–(5).
174(3D)–(3F)	s. 457.
174(4), (4A)	s. 456(6), (7).
174(5), (6)	s. 455(1), (2).
174(7)	s. 455(3), s. 732(1).
174(8)	s. 445(2).
175	s. 452(1).
176	s. 282.
177	s. 283(1)–(3).
178	s. 283(4).
179	s. 284.
180	s. 285 (part).

Provision of former Acts	Destination
Companies Act 1948	
182	CA 1985, s. 291.
183(1)	s. 292(1).
183(2)	s. 285 (part), s. 292(2).
183(3), (4)	s. 292(3), (4).
184(1) part	s. 303(1).
proviso	CC(CP)A 1985, s. 14.
184(2)	CA 1985, s. 303(2), 304(1).
184(3)	s. 304(2)–(5).
184(4)–(6)	s. 303(3)–(5).
185(1)–(3)	s. 293(2)–(4).
185(5)–(7)	s. 293(5)–(7).
185(8)	s. 293(1).
186(1)	s. 294(1), (3).
186(2), (3)	s. 294(4), (5).
187(1)	s. 302(1).
187(2)	s. 302(3).
187(3)	s. 302(4).
187(4)	s. 302(2).
187(5) (inserted by OinC-2) see	s. 302(1), Sch. 24.
188(1)(a)	s. 296(1).
(b)	s. 297(1).
(c)	s. 298(1).
188(1A)	s. 299(2), (3).
188(1B)	s. 295(1).
188(1C)	Sch. 12, Pt. III, para. 10.
188(2)	Sch. 12, Pt. III, para. 11.
188(2A)	Sch. 12, Pt. III, para. 12.
188(2B)	Sch. 12, Pt. III, para. 12.
188(2C)	s. 297(2), (3).
188(2D)	s. 295(2), (3), s. 296(2), 297(3), (4), 298(2), 299(4)(b).
188(2E)	s. 296(2), 299(4)(a).
(2F)	s. 295(4).
(3)	Sch. 12, Pt. I, para. 1.
(4)	Sch. 12, Pt. I, para. 2, 3
(6), (7)	s. 295(7).
189(1)	s. 311(1), CC(CP)A 1985, s. 15.
189(2)	s. 311(2).
191	s. 312.

Provision of former Acts	Destination
Companies Act 1948	
192	CA 1985, s. 313.
193(1)	s. 314(1), (2).
193(2)	s. 314(3).
193(3)–(5)	s. 315.
194	s. 316.
196(1)	s. 231; Sch. 5, Pt. V, para. 34, 22(1), 28(1), 29(1).
196(2)	Sch. 5, Pt. V, para. 22(2), (3).
196(3)	Sch. 5, Pt. V, para. 28(2), (3), 33(3).
196(4)	Sch. 5, Pt. V, para. 29(2), (3).
196(5)–(7)	Sch. 5, Pt. V, para. 30–32.
196(8)	s. 237(5).
196(9)	Sch. 5, Pt. V, para 33(1).
198	s. 231(4).
199(1), (2)	s. 317(1), (2).
199(3)	s. 317(3), (4).
199(4)	s. 317(7).
199(5)	s. 317(9).
200(1)	s. 288(1).
200(2)	s. 289(1), (3), (4), Sch. 1.
200(3)	s. 290(1), (2), Sch. 1.
200(4)	s. 288(2).
200(6)–(8)	s. 288(3)–(5).
200(9)	s. 288(6), 289(2), 290(3).
201	s. 305.
202(1)	s. 306(1).
202(2)	s. 306(2), (3).
202(3)	s. 306(4).
203	s. 307.
204	s. 308.
205	s. 310.
206	s. 425.
207(1)	s. 426(1)–(3).
207(2)–(5)	s. 426(4)–(7).
208(1)	s. 427(1)–(3).
208(2), (3)	s. 427(4), (5).
208(4), (5)	s. 427(6).
209(1)	s. 428(1), (2), (4), (5).
209(2)	s. 429.

Provision of former Acts	Destination
Companies Act 1948	
209(3)	CA 1985, s. 430(1)–(3).
209(4)	s. 430(4).
209(5)	s. 428(3).
211	s. 501.
212(1)	s. 502(1), (2), (3) (part).
212(2)	s. 503.
212(3)	s. 502(3) (part).
213	s. 507(1).
214	s. 508.
215	s. 509.
216	s. 510.
218(1), (3)	s. 512(1), (2).
218(4)	cease to have effect by CC(CP)A 1985, s. 28
218(5) (as amended by CC(CP)A 1985, s. 28)	CA 1985, s. 512(4).
218(6)	s. 512(5).
218(7)	s. 513(1).
218(8)	s. 512(6).
219(1)	s. 513(2).
219(3)	s. 514.
220	s. 515(1)–(4).
221	s. 516.
222	s. 517(1).
223	s. 518(1).
224(1)	s. 519(1), (2), (4)–(6).
224(2)	s. 519(7).
225	s. 520.
226	s. 521(1).
227	s. 522.
228	s. 523.
229	s. 524.
230	s. 525(1).
231	s. 525(2).
232	s. 525(4).
233	s. 526.
234	s. 527.
235(1)	s. 528(1), (2).
235(2)	s. 528(3), (4).
235(3)	s. 528(6).

Provision of former Acts	Destination
Companies Act 1948	
235(4)	CA 1985, s. 529(1).
235(5)	s. 528(7).
235(6), (7)	s. 529(2), (3).
235(8)	s. 528(5).
236	s. 530.
237	s. 531.
238	s. 532.
239	s. 533.
240	s. 534.
241	s. 535.
242	s. 536.
243	s. 537.
244	s. 538.
245	s. 539.
246(1)	s. 540(1), (2).
246(2)–(5)	s. 540(3)–(6).
247	s. 541.
248(1)	s. 542(1)–(3).
248(2), (3)	s. 542(4), (5).
249(1)	s. 543(1), (2).
249(2), (3)	s. 543(3), (4).
249(4), (5) (as amended by OinC-1)	s. 543(5), (6).
250	s. 544.
251(1)	s. 545(1)–(3).
251(2)–(4)	s. 545(4)–(6).
252	s. 546.
253(1)	s. 547(1), (2)(a).
253(2)–(6)	Sch. 17, para. 1–5.
253(7)	Sch. 17, para. 6(1), (2).
253(8)	Sch. 17, para. 6(3).
254	s. 548.
255	s. 547(2)(b).
256	s. 549.
257(1)	s. 550(1), (2).
257(2)	s. 550(3).
258	s. 551.
259	s. 552.
260	s. 553.

Provision of former Acts	Destination
Companies Act 1948	
261	CA 1985, s. 554.
262	s. 555.
263(1)	s. 556(1), (2).
263(2), (3)	s. 556(3).
264	s. 557.
265	s. 558.
266	s. 559.
267	s. 560.
268	s. 561.
269	s. 562.
270(1)	s. 563(1), (2).
270(2), (3)	s. 563(3), (4).
270(4), (5)	s. 564(1), (2).
270(6)	s. 564(3), (4).
270(7)–(9)	s. 564(5)–(7).
271	s. 565.
272	s. 566.
273	s. 567.
274	s. 568.
275	s. 569.
276	s. 570(1)–(4).
277(1)	s. 571(1).
277(2)	s. 571(2), (3).
277(3), (4)	s. 571(4), (5).
278(1), (2)	s. 572(1), (2).
279	s. 573.
280	s. 574.
281	s. 575.
282	s. 576.
283(1)–(2A)	s. 577(1)–(3).
283(3)	s. 577(4), (5).
283(4)	s. 578.
283(4A)	s. 577(6).
284	s. 579.
285	s. 580.
286	s. 581.
287(1)	s. 582(1)–(3).
287(2)–(6)	s. 582(4)–(8).

Provision of former Acts	Destination
Companies Act 1948	
316	CA 1985, s. 611.
317	s. 612.
318	s. 613.
319(1)	s. 614(1);
(1)(a)	Sch. 19, para. 7, 2.
(1)(b)	Sch. 19, para. 9.
(1)(c)	Sch. 19, para. 9ff.
(1)(d)	Sch. 19, para. 10.
(1)(e)	Sch. 19, para. 8.
(1)(f), (g)	Sch. 19, para. 9ff.
319(2)	Sch. 19, para. 12(1).
319(3)	Sch. 19, para. 9ff.
319(4)	Sch. 19, para. 13.
319(5)–(7)	s. 614(2)–(4).
319(8)(a)	Sch. 19, para. 14(a).
319(8)(b)	Sch. 19, para. 10.
(8)(c)	Sch. 19, para. 14(b).
(8)(d)	Sch. 19, para. 1.
320(1)	s. 615(1).
320(2)	s. 615(2).
320(3) (as amended by OinC-1)	s. 615(3).
321(1), (2)	s. 616(1), (2).
321(3)	s. 616(3)–(5).
322(1), (2)	s. 617(1), (2).
322(1) proviso	CC(CP)A 1985, s. 18.
322(3) (as amended by OinC-1)	CA 1985, s. 617(3).
323(1)	s. 618(1)–(3).
323(2)	s. 618(4).
323(3)	s. 619(1).
323(4)	s. 619(2), (3).
323(5)	s. 619(4).
323(6)	s. 619(5)–(7): Sch. 20, Pt. I.
323(7)	s. 619(8).
323(8)	s. 618(5).
324	s. 620.
325(1)	s. 621(1), (2).
325(2)–(4)	s. 621(3)–(5).
326(1)	s. 622(1), (2).

Provision of former Acts	Destination
Companies Act 1948	
288	CA 1985, s. 583.
289	s. 584.
290(1), (2)	s. 585(1), (2).
290(3)	s. 585(3), (4).
290(4)–(6)	s. 585(5)–(7).
291	s. 586.
292	s. 587.
293(1)	s. 588(1), (2)(a), (b).
293(2)	s. 588(2)(c).
293(3), (4)	s. 588(3).
293(5)–(7)	s. 588(4)–(6).
294	s. 589.
295(1)	s. 590(1)–(3).
295(2)	Sch. 17.
296	s. 591.
297	s. 592.
298	s. 593.
299	s. 594.
300(1), (2)	s. 595(1), (2).
300(3)	s. 595(3)–(5).
300(4)–(6)	s. 595(6)–(8).
301	s. 596.
302	s. 597.
303(1)	s. 598(1)–(3).
303(2), (3)	s. 598(4), (5).
304	s. 599.
305	s. 600.
306	s. 601.
307	s. 602.
308	s. 603.
309	s. 604.
310	s. 605.
311	s. 606.
312	s. 607.
313	s. 608.
314	s. 609.
315(1)	s. 610(1), (2).
315(2)	s. 610(3), (4).

Provision of former Acts	Destination
Companies Act 1948	
326(2)	CA 1985, s. 622(3), (4).
326(3), (4)	s. 622(5), (6).
326(5)	s. 622(8).
327(1)	s. 623(1)–(5).
327(2)	s. 623(6).
328(1)(a)-(c)	s. 626(1)(a)–(c).
(1)(d), (e)	s. 624(1)(a), (b).
(1)(f)	s. 628(1).
(1)(g), (h)	s. 626(1)(d), (e).
(1)(i)-(k)	s. 624(1)(c)-(e).
(1)(l)	s. 626(2).
(1)(o)	s. 624(1)(f).
(1)(p)	s. 629(1).
(1) proviso	s. 626(4), 628(4).
328(2)	s. 624(5), (6).
328(3)	s. 624(3), 626(3).
328(4) (as inserted by OinC-2) see	s. 624(6) (part), Sch. 24.
329	s. 627.
330	s. 625.
332(1)	s. 630(1)–(3).
332(2)	s. 630(4), (5).
332(3)	s. 458.
332(4)	s. 630(6).
333(1)	s. 631(1), (2).
333(2), (3)	s. 631(3), (4).
334(1)	s. 632(1), (2).
334(2)	s. 632(3).
334(3)	s. 632(4); 633(1).
334(3A)	s. 633(2).
334(4)	s. 632(5).
334(5), (6)	s. 633(3), (4).
335	s. 634.
336	s. 635.
337(1)	s. 636(1), (2).
337(2), (3)	s. 636(3), (4).
338	s. 637.
339(1)	s. 638(1), (2).
339(2)	s. 638(3) (part).

Provision of former Acts	Destination
Companies Act 1948	
339(3)	CA 1985, s. 638(2), (3) (part).
340	s. 639.
341	s. 640.
342	s. 641.
343(1)	s. 642(1), (2).
343(2)–(4)	s. 642(3)–(5).
344	s. 643.
345	s. 644.
346	s. 645.
347	s. 646.
348 (as substituted by OinC-1)	s. 647.
349	s. 648.
350(1)	s. 649.
350(2)	CC(CP)A 1985, s. 19.
351	CA 1985, s. 650.
352(1)	s. 651(1), (2).
352(2)	s. 651(3).
353(1)–(4)	s. 652(1)–(4).
353(5)	s. 652(5), (6).
353(6)	s. 653.
353(7)	s. 652(7).
354	s. 654.
355(1)	s. 656(1).
355(2)	s. 657(1), (2).
355(3)–(6)	s. 656(2)–(5).
355(8)	s. 656(6).
355(9)	s. 657(3)–(7), Sch. 20, Pt. II.
356	s. 658.
357–359	ceased to have effect by CC(CP)A 1985, s. 28.
362(1)	CA 1985, s. 660(1), (2).
362(2)–(5)	s. 660(3)–(6).
363	s. 661.
364	s. 662.
365(1)	s. 663(1), (2).
365(2)	see s. 663(3).
365(3), (5)	s. 663(4), (5).
366	s. 489.
367	s. 490.

Provision of former Acts	Destination
Companies Act 1948	
368	CA 1985, s. 491.
369(1)	s. 492(1), (2).
369(2)	s. 492(3).
370	s. 493.
371(1)–(3)	s. 494.
372(1)	s. 495(1)–(3).
372(2)	s. 497(1), (2).
372(3)	s. 495(4), 497(4).
372(4)	s. 495(5), 497(3).
372(5)	s. 495(6), 497(5).
372(6)	s. 497(6).
372(7)	s. 495(7), 497(7).
373(1)	s. 496(1).
373(2)	s. 496(2), (3).
373(3)–(6)	s. 496(4)–(7).
374(1) (as amended by OinC-1)	s. 498(1)–(3).
374(2)	s. 498(4).
375	s. 499.
376	s. 500.
377	s. 675.
378	s. 676.
379	s. 677.
380	s. 678.
381	s. 679.
382(1) (part) (as amended by CC(CP)A 1985, s. 28) + proviso (i)-(iv)	s. 680.
382(1) proviso (v)-(vii)	s. 681(1), (2), (4).
382(2)	s. 681(3).
382(3)	s. 681(5).
382(4)	s. 681(6).
383	s. 683.
384 (as amended by OinC-1 and CC(CP)A 1985, s. 28)	s. 684, 687.
385 (as amended by OinC-1 and CC(CP)A 1985, s. 28)	s. 686(1).
386	s. 686(2).
387	s. 686(3).
387A (inserted by OinC-2)	s. 687(1)–(3).

Provision of former Acts	Destination
Companies Act 1948	
390(1)	CA 1985, s. 688(1), (2).
390(2)	s. 688(3).
391	s. 689, Sch. 21, para. 2.
392	Sch. 21, para. 3.
393	Sch. 21, para. 4.
394(1), (2)	s. 689, Sch. 21, para. 5.
394(3)(a)-(e)	Sch. 21, para. 6.
394(3)(f), (g)	s. 511.
394(4)–(6)	Sch. 21, para. 7–9.
394(7) (as amended by CC(CP)A 1985, s. 28)	Sch. 21, para. 1.
395	s. 690.
396	s. 521.
397	s. 525(3).
398	s. 665.
399(1)–(5)	s. 666(1)–(5).
399(6)(a)	s. 667(1).
399(6)(b)	s. 668.
399(6)(c)-(e)	s. 669.
399(8), (9)	s. 666(6), (7).
400	s. 670.
401(1)	s. 671(1), (2).
401(2)	s. 671(4).
402	s. 672.
403	s. 673.
404	s. 674.
405	see CC(CP)A 1985, s. 31(8)(c).
406	CA 1985, s. 744.
407(1) (as substituted by OinC-1)	s. 691(1).
407(2) (as amended by OinC-1)	s. 691(2).
407(2A)	ceased to have effect by OinC-1.
409(1), (2) (as amended by OinC-1)	CA 1985, s. 692(1), (2).
409(3) (as inserted by OinC-1)	s. 692(3).
411	s. 693.
412	s. 695.
413(1)	s. 696(1)–(3).
413(2)	s. 696(4).
414	s. 697(1).
415	s. 698, 744.

Provision of former Acts	Destination
Companies Act 1948	
416	CA 1985, s. 699(1)–(3).
417(1)	s. 72(1)–(4), Sch. 3.
417(2)	s. 73.
417(3)	s. 72(5).
417(4)	s. 78(3), (4).
417(5)	s. 72(6).
418(1)	s. 76(1) (except for definition — see s. 455(1)) 76(2).
418(2)	s. 76(3).
419(1) (excluding para. (a))	s. 75.
419(1) (excluding para. (b))	s. 74(1), (2).
419(2)	s. 62, 74(3).
420(1)	s. 77(1)–(4).
420(2)	s. 77(5).
421	s. 78(1).
422	s. 78(2).
423(1), (2)	s. 79(1), (2).
423(3)	see s. 744.
424(1)–(3)	s. 704(1)–(3).
424(4)	ceased to have effect by CC(CP)A 1985, s. 28.
424(5)	CA 1985, s. 704(4).
424(6)	s. 704(5), (6).
425(2)	s. 708(4).
426(1)	s. 709.
426(2)–(4)	s. 710(1), (2), (4).
426(5), (6)	s. 710(5).
427	s. 712.
428	s. 713.
433	s. 720(1)–(6).
434(1) (as amended by CC(CP)A 1985, s. 28)	s. 716(1).
435(1), (2)	s. 718(1), (2), Sch. 22.
435(3)–(5)	s. 718(4)–(6).
436(1)	s. 722(1).
436(2)	s. 722(2), (3).
437	s. 725.
439	s. 34.
440(2)	s.730(5).
441(1)	s. 721(1), (2).

Provision of former Acts	Destination
Companies Act 1948	
441(2), (3)	CA 1985, s. 721(3), (4).
441(4)	
446	s. 732(3).
447	s. 726.
448	s. 727.
449	s. 728.
450	ceased to have effect by CC(CP)A 1985, s. 28.
451	CA 1985, s. 729.
454(1)	s. 256(1), (2).
454(1A)	s. 256(3).
454(2)	s. 3, 8, 720(7).
454(2A)–(4)	s. 256(4)–(6).
455(1) (as amended by OinC-1 and CC(CP)A 1985, s. 28)	s. 735, 741(1), (2), (part), 742(1), 744, CS(ID)A 1985, s. 16(1), (2).
455(2)	s. 741(2) (part).
455(3)	s. 740.
459	see CC(CP)A 1985, s. 31(9).
460	CC(CP)A 1985, s. 22.
461	CA 1985, s. 745.
Sch. 1	now in regulations under CA 1985, s. 3, 8.
Sch. 4	CA 1985, Sch. 3.
para. 1–3	para. 1(1).
para. 4	para. 2.
para. 5, 6	para. 3.
para. 7	para. 4(1), (2).
para. 8	para. 5.
para. 9(1)	para. 7.
para. 9(2)	para. 6.
para. 10	para. 8.
para. 11–13	para. 10.
para. 14–21	para. 11–18, 22(3).
para. 22	para. 1(3), 10(2), 13(3).
para. 23	para. 9(2).
para. 24	para. 9(3).
para. 25	para. 4(3).
para. 26	para. 9(4).
para. 27–29	para. 19–21.
para. 30	para. 22(1), (2).
Sch. 6, Pt. I (para. 4 amended by OinC-1)	Sch. 15

Provision of former Acts	Destination
Companies Act 1948	
Sch. 6, Pt. II	see S.I. 1985 No. 854.
Sch. 8 (para. 38(2) amended by OinC-1)	CA 1985, Sch. 4.
Sch. 8A (para. 2(a) amended by OinC-1)	Sch. 9.
Sch. 10	Sch. 16.
Sch. 11	Sch. 18.
Sch. 13	Sch. 23.
Sch. 14 (as amended by OinC-1)	Sch. 22
Companies Act 1967	
3(1)	s. 231(1).
3(1)–(5)	Sch. 5, Pt. I.
3(5)(b)	s. 231(3).
3(6)	s. 231(3).
4(1)	s. 231(1); Sch. 5, para. 7.
4(1A)	Sch. 5, para. 8.
4(1B)	
4(2)–(5)	Sch. 5, para. 9–12.
4(5)(b)	s. 231(3).
4(6)	s. 231(3).
4(7)	Sch. 5, para. 13.
4(8)	s. 744.
5(1)	s. 231(1); Sch. 5, para. 20.
5(2)	Sch. 5, para. 21.
6(1)	s. 231(1).
6(1)(a)	Sch. 5, para. 24(2), (3).
(b)	Sch. 5, para. 25(2).
6(2)	Sch. 5, para. 25(3), (4).
6(3)	Sch. 5, para. 26.
6(4)	s. 237(5).
6(5)	s. 231(4).
6(6)	Sch. 5, para. 23.
6(7)(a)	Sch. 5, para. 24(1).
(b)	Sch. 5, para. 25(5).
7(1), (2)	s. 231(1); Sch. 5, para. 27.
7(3)	s. 231(4).
8(1)	s. 231(1); Sch. 5, para. 35.
8(2)	Sch. 5, para. 36(1), (2).

British Companies Legislation

Provision of former Acts	Destination
Companies Act 1967	
8(3)	CA 1985, Sch. 5, para. 36(3), (4).
8(4)	s. 235(5).
8(5)	Sch. 5, para. 37.
11	s. 260(2), (3).
13(1), (6)	s. 389(2).
14(1)	s. 236(1).
14(2)	s. 241(2)
14(3)(a)	s. 236(2).
(b)	s. 262.
14(4)	s. 237(1), (2).
14(5), (6)	s. 237(3), (4).
14(7)	s. 387(1).
15	
16	s. 261(5).
16(1)	s. 235(2).
16(1)(a)	Sch. 7, para. 1.
(b)	Sch. 10, para. 1.
(e)	Sch. 7, para. 2(1).
(f)	Sch. 7, para. 6; Sch. 10, para. 9.
(g)	Sch. 7, para. 10(1).
(h)	Sch. 7, para. 11(3).
16(1A)	Sch. 7, para. 11(1), (2).
16(4), (4A)	Sch. 7, para. 2(2), (3).
16(5)–(7)	Sch. 7, para. 10(2)–(4).
16(8)	Sch. 7, para. 11(4).
16A	Sch. 7, Pt. II.
17	s. 261(6), Sch. 10, para. 2–4.
18(1)	s. 261(6), Sch. 10, para. 5(1).
18(2)	Sch. 10, para. 6(1).
18(3)	Sch. 10, para. 5(2), 6(2).
18(4)	Sch. 10, para. 7.
18(5)	Sch. 10, para. 8(2), (3).
18(6)	Sch. 10, para. 8(4).
18(7)	s. 736(5)(b).
19(1), (2)	s. 235(3), Sch. 7, para. 3, 4.
19(3)–(5)	Sch. 7, para. 5.
22	*see* s. 261(4).
23	s. 235(7).
23A	s. 237(6).

Provision of former Acts	Destination
Companies Act 1967	
24	see CA 1985, s. 240, 246.
25(1)	CA 1985, s. 323(1), (2).
25(2)–(4)	s. 323(3)–(5).
26(1)	s. 318(1), (2).
26(2)–(3A)	s. 318(3)–(5).
26(4)–(8)	s. 318(7)–(11).
27(1)	s. 324(1), (2).
27(2)	Sch. 13, Pt. I.
27(3)(a)	Sch. 13, para. 14.
(b)	Sch. 13, para. 15.
27(4)	s. 324(4).
27(5)–(7)	Sch. 13, para. 17–19.
27(8)	s. 324(7).
27(9)	s. 324(5).
27(10)	s. 324(8), 732.
27(11)	s. 324(6).
27(12)	Sch. 13, para. 16.
27(13)	s. 324(6).
28(1)	s. 324(3)(a).
28(2), (3)	Sch. 13, para. 1, 2.
28(4)	Sch. 13, para. 3(1).
28(4A)–(4C)	Sch. 13, para. 4–6.
28(4D), (4E)	Sch. 13, para. 3(2), (3).
28(4F)	Sch. 13, para. 6(2).
28(5)–(11)	Sch. 13, para. 7–13.
29(1)	s. 325(1), (2).
29(2)	s. 325(3), (4).
29(3)–(7)	Sch. 13, para. 21–25.
29(8), (9)	Sch. 13, para. 27, 28.
29(10)	Sch. 13, para. 26.
29(11)	Sch. 13, para. 29.
29(12)	s. 326(2)–(5).
29(13)	s. 326(6).
29(14)	s. 325(6).
30	s. 327.
31(1)	s. 328(1), (2).
31(2)	s. 328(3)–(5).
31(3)–(6)	s. 328(6)–(9).

Provision of former Acts		Destination
Companies Act 1967		
32(1), (2)		CA 1985, s. 446(1), (2).
32(3)		s. 446(3), (4).
32(4), (5)		s. 446(5).
32(6)		s. 452(1).
32(7)		s. 446(7).
32(8)		s. 446(6).
35(1)		s. 440.
37(1), (2)		s. 438(1), (2).
37(3)		s. 439(2), (7).
41		s. 433(2).
42		s. 453.
43(1), (1A) (1A inserted by OinC-1)		s. 49(1)–(4).
43(2)		s. 49(5)–(7).
43(3)		s. 49(8).
43(4)		s. 50(1), (2).
43(5)		s. 50(3).
43(6)		s. 506.
43(7)		s. 49(9).
43(8)		s. 744.
44(1), (1A) ((1A) inserted by OinC-1)		s. 51(1), (2), (4), (6).
44(2)		s. 51(3).
44(3)		s. 51(5).
44(4)		s. 52(1), (2).
44(5)		s. 52(3).
44(6)		s. 124.
44(7)		s. 505(2)–(4).
44(9)		s. 744.
46(1)–(3)		s. 32(1)–(3).
46(3A) (inserted by OinC-1)		s. 32(5).
46(4)		s. 32(4).
46(5)		s. 32(5), (6).
49(2)–(5)		s. 731.
50		s. 434(5); s. 663(3).
51(1)		s. 123(3).
51(2)		s. 380(1).
53		s. 677.
54 (supplementary provisions)	see	s. 718, Sch. 22.

Provision of former Acts	Destination
Companies Act 1967	
56	see CA 1985, s. 722, 742.
109(1)	CA 1985, s. 447(1)–(3).
109(2), (3)	s. 447(4), (5).
109(4)	s. 447(6), (7).
109(5)	s. 447(8).
110(1)	s. 448(1), (2).
110(2)–(5)	s. 448(3)–(6).
111 (as amended by OinC-1)	s. 449, see also CC(CP)A 1985, s. 25.
113(1), (2)	s. 450(1), (2).
113(3)	s. 450(3), (4).
114	s. 451.
116(1)	s. 452(1), (2).
116(2)	s. 452(3).
120(1), (2)	s. 716(2), (3).
120(3)	s. 716(4); 744.
121	s. 717, 744.
Companies (Floating Charges and Receivers) (Scotland) Act 1972	
1(1)	s. 462(1).
1(2)	s. 463(1), (2), (3)(a).
1(3)	s. 463(3)(b).
1(4)	s. 463(4).
2(1)	s. 462(2).
2(2)	s. 462(3), (4).
3	s. 462(5).
4	s. 517(2); 666(8).
5	s. 464, 466(3).
6	s. 410(1).
7(1), (2)	s. 466(1), (2).
7(3)–(5)	s. 466(4)–(6).
10	see CC(CP)A 1985, s. 26.
11(1)–(3)	CA 1985, s. 467(1)–(3).
11(4)	s. 467(4), (5).
11(5)	s. 467(6).
11(7) (added by OinC-2)	see　s. 467(5), Sch. 24.
12	s. 468.
13	s. 469.
14(1), (2)	s. 470(1), (2).

British Companies Legislation

Provision of former Acts	Destination
Companies (Floating Charges and Receivers) (Scotland) Act 1972	
14(3), (4)	CA 1985, s. 470(3).
14(5)–(8)	s. 470(4)–(7).
15(1)–(3)	s. 471.
16	s. 472.
17	s. 473.
18	s. 474.
19	s. 475.
20	s. 476.
21	s. 477.
22	s. 478.
23(1)	s. 479(1).
23(2)	s. 479(2), (3).
24	s. 480.
25(1)	s. 481(1).
25(2) (as amended by OinC-1)	s. 481(2).
25(3)–(7)	s. 481(3)–(7).
26	s. 482.
27	s. 483.
28(1)–(3)	s. 484.
28(4)	see s. 731.
29	s. 485.
30	s. 465.
31(1)	s. 486.
31(5)	s. 488.
32	s. 487.
European Communities Act 1972 (sec. 9).	
9(1)	s. 35.
9(2)	s. 36(4).
9(3)	s. 42(2)(a), 711.
9(4)	s. 42(1), 2(b).
9(5)	s. 18.
9(7)	s. 351(1), (2), (5)(a), (b).
9(8) (as amended by OinC-1)	Sch. 22.

Provision of former Acts	Destination
Stock Exchange (Completion of Bargains) Act 1976 (sec. 1 to 4).	
1	CA 1985, s. 185(4).
2(1)	s. 40.
2(2)	CC(CP)A 1985, s. 11.
3	CA 1985, s. 723.
4	s. 718, Sch. 22.
Insolvency Act 1976 (sec. 9).	
9(1)	s. 295(1), s. 300(1).
9(1A)	s. 295(2), Sch. 12, para. 15.
9(2)	s. 300(2), Sch. 12, para. 6.
9(3)	Sch. 12, para. 7, 8(b).
9(4)	Sch. 12, para. 8(a).
9(5)	s. 295(7).
9(6)	s. 300(3).
9(7)	s. 295(3), 300(4).
9(7A)	s. 295(4).
9(9)	Sch. 12, para. 16.
Companies Act 1976	
1(1)	s. 227(1).
1(2), (3)	s. 227(2).
1(4)	s. 227(3).
1(5)	s. 239.
1(6)	s. 241(1).
1(7)	s. 241(3).
1(8)	s. 241(4).
1(11)	s. 227(1).
2(1)	s. 224(1), (2).
2(2)	s. 224(3).
2(4), (5)	s. 224(4), (5).
3(1)–(7)	s. 225.
3(8)–(10)	s. 226.
4	s. 243(1)–(5).
5	s. 244.
6(1)–(3)	s. 242(1)–(3).
6(4), (5)	s. 242(4).
6(6), (7)	s. 242(5), (6).
9(1)	s. 700(1).

Provision of former Acts	Destination
Companies Act 1976	
9(2) (as amended by OinC-1)	CA 1985, s. 700(2).
9(3)–(3B)	s. 700(3)–(5).
10 (applying s. 2, 3)	s. 701.
11(1)	s. 703(1).
11(2), (3) (applying s. 6)	s. 702.
11(4)	s. 703(2).
12(1)	s. 221(1).
12(2), (3)	s. 221(2).
12(4), (5)	s. 221(3), (4).
12(6)–(9)	s. 222.
12(10)	s. 223(1), (2).
12(11)	s. 223(3).
13(1)–(3)	s. 389(3)–(5).
13(4)	s. 389(2).
13(5), (6)	s. 389(9), (10).
14(1)	s. 384(1).
14(2)	s. 384(5).
14(3)–(5)	s. 384(2)–(4).
14(6)	s. 386(1), (2).
14(7)	s. 384(5).
14(8)	s. 385.
14(10)	s. 386(3).
15(1)–(5)	s. 388.
15(6)	s. 387(2).
16(1)–(7)	s. 390.
16(8)	see s. 713.
17(1)	s. 391(1).
17(2)	s. 391(2), (3).
17(3)	s. 391(4), (5).
17(4), (5)	s. 391(6), (7).
18(1)	s. 392(1).
18(2), (3)	s. 392(2).
19	s. 393.
20(1)	s. 394(1).
20(3), (4)	s. 394(2), (3).
21(1)	s. 10(2).
21(2)	Sch. 1.
21(3)–(5) (part)	s. 10(3)–(5).

Provision of former Acts		Destination
Companies Act 1976		
21(5) (part)		CA 1985, s. 13(5).
23(1)		s. 287(1).
23(2)		s. 10(6).
23(3), (4)		s. 287(2), (3).
25(1), (2)		s. 329(1), (2).
25(3), (4)		s. 329(3) (see also s. 732).
29 (as substituted by OinC-1)		s. 301.
30(1), (2)		s. 2(2).
30(3)		s. 25(2).
30(5)		s. 351(4), (5)(c).
30(6)		s. 21(1), (2).
30(7)–(9)		s. 21(3)–(5).
31(1), (1A)		s. 694(1), (2).
31(2)–(6)		s. 694(3)–(7), 697(2).
35		s. 706.
36(1), (2)		s. 707(1), (2).
36(4)		s. 707(3).
37(1)–(3)		s. 708(1)–(3).
37(5), (6)		s. 708(4), (5).
38(2)		s. 688; 704(4).
38(3)		s. 710(3).
39		s. 449.
41	see	s. 718, Sch. 22.
Companies Act 1980		
1(1), (2)		s. 1(3), (4).
1(3)		s. 15(2).
2(1)	see	s. 1(1).
2(2)		s. 25(1).
2(3)		s. 43(2)(b), (5), 685.
2(4)		s. 3.
3(1)		s. 12(1).
3(2)		s. 11.
3(3)		s. 13(6).
3(4)		s. 13(7).
3(5)		s. 12(3).
4		s. 117.
5(1), (1A) ((1A) inserted by OinC-1)		s. 43(1).

British Companies Legislation

Provision of former Acts	Destination
Companies Act 1980	
5(2), (3)	CA 1985, s. 43(2), (3).
5(4)	s. 47(2).
5(5)	s. 44(1), (2).
5(6)	s. 47(1).
5(7)–(9)	s. 47(3)–(5).
5(10)	s. 43(4), 46(1)–(4), 264(3).
5(11), (12)	s. 46(5), (6).
6(1)	s. 45(1)–(4).
6(2)	s. 45(5), (7).
6(3)	s. 45(6).
7(1)–(3)	s. 48.
7(4)	s. 51(6), see also s. 124, 505.
8(1), (2)	CC(CP)A 1985, s. 1.
8(3), (4)	s. 2(1), (2).
8(5)–(7)	s. 2(4)–(6).
8(8)	s. 4(2).
8(9), (10)	s. 4(4), (5).
8(11)	s. 3.
8(12)	s. 4(3).
9	s. 5.
10(1), (2)	CA 1985, s. 53(1), (2).
10(1A) (inserted by OinC-1)	s. 53(3).
10(3)–(5)	s. 55.
11(1), (2)	s. 54(1); CC(CP)A 1985, s. 4(1).
11(3), (4)	s. 54(2), (3).
11(5)(a)	s. 54(4).
(b)	s. 54(7).
11(6), (7)	s. 54(5), (6).
11(8)–(10)	s. 54(8)–(10).
12(1)	s. 139(1), (2).
12(2)	s. 139(3).
12(3) (applying s. 10)	s. 139(4), (5).
13(1), (2)	s. 685(1), (2).
13(4), (5)	s. 685(4), (5).
13(6)	s. 688(4).
13(7)	s. 685(6) (part).
14(1)	s. 80(1).
14(2)–(4)	s. 80(3)–(5).

Provision of former Acts	Destination
Companies Act 1980	
14(5)–(9)	CA 1985, s. 80(7)–(11), see also s. 380.
14(10) (amended by OinC-1)	s. 80(2).
14(11) (inserted by OinC-1)	s. 80(6).
15(1)	s. 81(1), CC(CP)A 1985, s. 7.
15(3), (4)	s. 81(2), (3).
16 (applying CA 1948,	
s. 47(4), (5))	s. 84, 85.
17(1)–(5)	s. 89.
17(6)–(8)	s. 90(5)–(7).
17(9)	s. 91.
17(10)	s. 92.
17(11)	s. 94(1)–(6).
17(12)	s. 93.
17(13) (as amended by OinC-1)	s. 94(7).
18	s. 95.
19(1)(b), (2)–(5)	s. 96.
20(1)–(3)	s. 99(1)–(3).
20(4)	s. 112(1).
20(5)	s. 99(4).
20(6)	s. 99(5); 112(4).
21(1), (2)	s. 100.
21(3)	s. 112.
22(1)	s. 101(1).
22(2)	s. 101(3), (4).
22(3)	s. 101(5).
22(4)	s. 101(2).
22(5)	s. 112.
23(1)–(4)	s. 102(1)–(4).
23(5)	s. 102(5), (6).
23(6)	s. 112.
23(7)	s. 102(7).
24(1)	s. 103(1).
24(2)	s. 103(3), (5) (part).
24(2A) (as amended by OinC-1)	s. 103(4).
24(3)	s. 103(5) (part).
24(4)	s. 108(1), (2).
24(5)–(7)	s. 108(4)–(6).
24(8), (9)	s. 103(6).
24(10)	s. 112.

Provision of former Acts	Destination
Companies Act 1980	
24(11)	CA 1985, s. 108(7).
24(11A)	s. 103(2).
24(12)(a), (aa)	s. 103(7).
24(12)(b)	s. 108(3).
25(1)	s. 110(1), (3).
25(2)	s. 111(1), (3).
25(3)	s. 110(2) (part).
25(4)	s. 110(3).
25(5)	s. 110(2) (part).
26(1), (2)	s. 104(1)–(3).
26(3)	s. 104(4), (5).
26(4)	s. 104(6).
26(5), (6)	s. 109(1), (2).
26(7)	s. 105(1), (2).
26(8)	s. 105(3), 112(2).
27(1)	s. 110(1), (3).
27(2)	s. 111(2), (4).
27(3)	s. 109(3).
28(1)	s. 113(1).
28(2)	s. 113(2), (3).
28(3), (4)	s. 113(4), (5).
28(5)	s. 113(6), (7).
28(6)	s. 113(8).
29	s. 106.
30(1)	s. 114.
30(2)	s. 115.
31(1)(a), (c)	s. 116.
31(1)(b), (2)	CC(CP)A 1985, s. 9.
32(1)–(7)	CA 1985, s. 125(1)–(7).
32(8)	s. 127(1).
32(9)	s. 125(8).
32(10)	s. 126.
33(1)–(4)	s. 128(1)–(4).
33(6)	s. 128(5).
34(1)–(3)	s. 142(1)–(3).
35(1)	s. 143(1).
35(2)	s. 143(3) (part).
35(3)	s. 143(2).

Provision of former Acts	Destination
Companies Act 1980	
35(4)	CA 1985, s. 143(3) (part).
36(1)–(4)	s. 144.
36(5)	s. 145(1) (part).
36(6)	s. 145(2).
37(1)	s. 146(1) (part).
37(2)	s. 146(2); 147(1).
37(3)	s. 146(4).
37(4), (5)	s. 147(2), (3).
37(6), (7)	s. 149.
37(8) (applying s. 10(3)–(5))	s. 147(4).
37(9)	s. 148(1) (for most part).
37(10)	s. 148(4).
37(11)	s. 146(3).
37(12)	CC(CP)A 1985, s. 6(2).
38(1)	CA 1985, s. 150(1), see also CC(CP)A 1985, s. 6.
38(2)	s. 150(2)–(4).
39(1)	s. 263(1).
39(2), (3)	s. 263(3), (4).
39(4)	s. 275(1).
39(4A)	s. 275(4), (5).
39(5), (6)	s. 275(2), (3).
39(7)	s. 263(5).
40(1)	s. 264(1).
40(2), (3)	s. 264(3).
40(4)	s. 275.
40(5)	s. 264(4).
41(1), (2)	s. 265(1), (2).
41(3), (4)	s. 266(1), (2).
41(5)	s. 265(4), (5)
41(6)	s. 265(6).
41(7), (8)	s. 266(3), (4).
41(9), (10)	s. 267.
42	s. 268.
42A(1)	s. 269(1).
42A(2), (3)	s. 269(2).
43(1)	s. 270(1), (2) (part), (5) (part).
43(2)	s. 270(3), (4).
43(3)	s. 271(1), (2) (part), (3) (part), (4).

Provision of former Acts	Destination
Companies Act 1980	
43(4)	CA 1985, s. 271(5).
43(5)	s. 272(1), (2), (4), (5).
43(6)	s. 273(1), (2), (4) (part), (5)–(7).
43(7)	s. 274(1).
43(7A)	s. 275(6).
43(8)	s. 255, s. 270(2) (part), 271(2) (part), 271(3) (part), 272(3) (part), 273(3), 273(4) (part).
43(9)	s. 272(3) (part), 273(3).
43A	s. 276.
44(1)	s. 277(1).
44(2)	s. 277(2) (part).
45(1)	s. 278.
45(2)	s. 263(2).
45(3), (4)	s. 280(2), (3).
45(5)	s. 281.
46	s. 309(1), (2).
47(1)	s. 319(3).
47(2), (3)	s. 319(1), (2).
47(4), (5)	s. 319(5), (6).
47(6)	s. 319(4).
47(7)	s. 319(7) (part).
48(1) (as amended by OinC-1)	s. 320(1).
48(2)	s. 320(2).
48(3) (as amended by OinC-1)	s. 322(1), (2).
48(4)	s. 322(3), (4).
48(5)	s. 322(5), (6).
48(6)–(8)	s. 321.
49(1)	s. 330(2), (3).
49(2)	s. 330(4).
49(3), (4)	s. 330(6), (7).
50(1)	s. 333.
50(2)	s. 332.
50(2A)	s. 334.
50(3)	s. 335.
50(4)(a), (b)	s. 336.
50(4)(c)	s. 337(1), (2).
50(4)(d)	s. 338(1).
50(5)	s. 337(3).

Provision of former Acts	Destination
Companies Act 1980	
50(6)	CA 1985, s. 338(3)–(5).
50(7)	s. 338(6).
51(1), (2)	s. 339(1), (2).
51(2A)	s. 339(4).
51(3)	s. 339(3).
51(4), (5)	s. 339(5), (6).
52(1)	s. 341(1).
52(2)	s. 341(2), (3).
52(3)	s. 341(4), (5).
53(1)–(3)	s. 342(1)–(3).
53(4) (as amended by OinC-2)	s. 342(5).
53(5)	s. 342(4).
54(1)	s. 232(1), (2), Sch. 6, para. 1.
54(2)	Sch. 6, para. 2.
54(2A)	s. 232(3) (part).
54(3)	s. 232(4).
54(4)–(7)	Sch. 6, para. 3–6.
54(8), (9)	Sch. 6, para. 7, 8.
55(1) (as amended by OinC-1)	Sch. 6, para. 9.
55(2)	Sch. 6, para. 10.
56(1)	Sch. 6, para. 15.
56(2)	s. 233(1), (2), Sch. 6, para. 16(1).
56(2A)	Sch. 6, para. 16(2).
56(3)	s. 233(3), Sch. 6, para. 16.
56(4)	s. 234(1), (2), Sch. 6, para. 16.
56(4A)	s. 234(2) (part).
56(5)	s. 234(2) (part), Sch. 6, para. 20.
56(6)	s. 234(3), Sch. 6, para. 16.
56(8)	Sch. 6, para. 21 (part).
57(1) (as amended by OinC-1)	s. 343(1)–(3).
57(2)	s. 343(4).
57(3), (4)	s. 343(6), (7).
57(5)	s. 344(2).
57(6), (7)	s. 343(8) (except (b)).
57(8)	s. 343(9).
58(1), (2)	Sch. 6, para. 11.
58(3)	Sch. 6, para. 12 (part).
58(4)	s. 344(1).

Provision of former Acts		Destination
Companies Act 1980		
59		CA 1985, s. 237(5).
60		s. 317(5), (6).
61(3)	see	s. 318(7)–(11).
62		s. 345, Sch. 6, para. 13.
63(1)		s. 232(3) (part), 234(2) (part), 319(7) (part), 320(3), 330(5), 741(2).
63(2)		s. 343(8)(b).
63(3)		s. 317(8).
63(4)		s. 318(6).
63(5)		s. 232(3) (part), 234(2) (part).
64	see	Sch. 6, para. 14, 17, 21.
64(1) (para. (e) inserted by (OinC-2)		s. 346(2).
64(2)		s. 346(3).
64(3)		s. 346(4)–(6), Sch. 13, Pt. I.
64(4)		s. 346(7), (8).
65(1)		s. 331(2), (5), (6), 338(2), Sch. 6, para. 14(a), 17(a).
65(2)		s. 331(3), (4), Sch. 6, para. 17(a), 21(a).
65(3)		s. 331(7), Sch. 6, para. 14(a).
65(4)		s. 340(2)–(6), Sch. 6, para. 14(c).
65(5)		s. 340(7).
65(6)		s. 331(9), Sch. 6, para. 14(b), 21(b).
65(8)		s. 347.
67	see	s. 718, Sch. 22.
68(1), (2)		CS(ID)A 1985, s. 1(1), (2).
68(3)		s. 1(3), (4).
68(4)–(7)		s. 1(5)–(8).
68(8), (9)		s. 3(1).
68(10)		s. 3(2).
68(11)		s. 7.
69(1)–(3)		s. 2.
69(4)		s. 3(1), 7.
69(5)		s. 3(2).
70(1), (2)		s. 4, 5, 7.
70(3)		s. 12(c), 13(3).
70(4)		s. 13(4)(a).
70(5)		s. 13(5).
71(1), (1A)		s. 6(1), (2).

Provision of former Acts	Destination
Companies Act 1980	
71(2)	CS(ID)A 1985, s. 15(1).
71(3)(a)–(c)	s. 15(2).
(d), (e)	s. 6(3).
71(4)	s. 15(4).
71(5)	s. 6(4).
72	s. 8.
73(1), (2)	s. 9, 10.
73(3)	s. 13(1).
73(4)	s. 13(4)(b).
73(5)	s. 11, 12(a), (b), 13(2), 14, 16(1), (3).
74(1)–(3)	CA 1985, s. 719(1)–(3).
74(4), (5)	s. 659(1), (2).
74(6)(a)	s. 719(4).
(b)	s. 659(3).
74(7), (8)	s. 659(4), (5).
75(1)	s. 459(1).
75(2)	s. 460(1).
75(3)–(8)	s. 461(1)–(6).
75(9)	s. 459(2).
75(10)	s. 460(2).
76(1)	s. 33(1), CC(CP)A 1985, s. 8(1).
76(2)	s. 33(2).
76(3)	see CC(CP)A 1985, s. 1(2).
76(4)	CA 1985, s. 33(3), CC(CP)A 1985, 8(2).
77	s. 351(3), 5(c) (part).
78(1)	s. 27(1), (2).
78(2), (3)	s. 27(3), (4).
78(4)	s. 25(1), 26(1), (3), 43(5).
79	s. 286.
80	s. 730, Sch. 24, BNA 1985, s. 7.
83	CC(CP)A 1985, s. 20.
84(1)	see CA 1985, s. 713.
84(2)	see s. 731.
84(3)	see s. 449.
85	s. 118.
87(1)	s. 107, 737, 739(1), 742, 743, 744.
87(2)	s. 738(1).
87(3)	s. 738(2)–(4).

Provision of former Acts	Destination
Companies Act 1980	
87(4)(b)	CA 1985, s. 739(2).
(c)	s. 264(2).
Sch. 1.	now in regulations under CA 1985, s. 3, 8.
Sch. 2 (as amended by OinC-1)	CA 1985, Sch. 24.
Companies Act 1981	
4	s. 231.
4(1), (2)	Sch. 5, para. 14, 15.
4(3) (as amended by OinC-2)	Sch. 5, para. 16.
4(4), (5)	Sch. 5, para. 17(1), (2).
4(6) (as amended by OinC-2)	Sch. 5, para. 17(3).
4(7)	Sch. 5, para. 17(4).
4(8)	Sch. 5, para. 18.
4(9)	s. 231(3) (part).
4(10)	Sch. 5, para. 19.
5(1)	s. 247(1) (part).
5(3)	s. 247(2).
5(4), (5)	s. 247(3).
5(7)–(9)	s. 251.
6(1)	s. 247(1) (part).
6(2)(a)	Sch. 8, para. 2(1).
(b)	Sch. 8, para. 3 (part).
(c)	Sch. 8, para. 5 (part).
(d)	Sch. 8, para. 4.
6(3)	Sch. 8, para. 2(2).
6(4)	Sch. 8, para. 6.
6(5)	Sch. 8, para. 5 (part).
6(6)	Sch. 8, para. 3 (part).
6(7)(a)	Sch. 8, para. 7(1).
(b)	Sch. 8, para. 8.
6(8)	Sch. 8, para. 7(2).
7(1)–(3)	Sch. 8, para. 9.
7(4)–(6)	Sch. 8, para. 10.
7(7)	Sch. 8, para. 11.
7(8)	Sch. 8, para. 10.
8(1)	s. 248(1) (part), 249(1) (part).
8(2)	s. 248(1) (part).
8(3)	s. 248(2).
8(4)	s. 249(1) (part).

Provision of former Acts	Destination
Companies Act 1981	
8(5)–(7)	CA 1985, s. 249(3)–(6).
8(9)–(11)	s. 248(3)–(5).
9(1)–(6) (s. 9(6) amended by OinC-2)	s. 250(1)–(4).
9(7) (added by OinC-2)	s. 250(5).
10	s. 250(6), Sch. 8, Pt. II, III.
11(1)	s. 254(2).
11(2)	s. 254(1) (part).
11(3), (4)	s. 254(3), (4).
11(5)	s. 254(1) (part).
11(6), (7)	s. 255(3), (4).
11(8)	s. 255(1), (2).
11(9)	s. 254(5).
11(10)	s. 254(6), 255(5).
12(1)	s. 252(1).
12(2)–(4)	s. 252(2).
12(5) (as amended by OinC-1)	s. 252(3), (4).
12(6)	s. 252(5).
12(7), (8), (9).	s. 247(4), 253(1), (2).
12(10), (11)	s. 253(3).
12(12)	s. 252(6), (7) (part).
12(13)	s. 252(7) (part).
16(1)	s. 235(6).
17	s. 257–262, Sch. 9–11.
20	see s. 718, Sch. 22.
21(1)	s. 742(6).
21(2)	s. 742(1).
21(3)	s. 742(5).
22	s. 26.
23(1)	s. 714(1).
23(2)	s. 705(2).
23(3)	s. 714(2).
24(1), (2)	s. 28(1), (2).
24(3) (as substituted by OinC-1)	s. 28(3).
24(4)–(7)	s. 28(4)–(7).
25(1)	s. 30(1), (2).
25(2)	s. 30(3).
25(3)	s. 30(7).
25(4)	s. 30(4), (5).

Provision of former Acts	Destination
Companies Act 1981	
25(5)–(10)	CA 1985, s. 31, see also s. 380.
26(1), (2)	s. 682.
26(3) (as amended by OinC-1)	s. 687(4).
28(1)	BNA 1985, s. 1(1).
28(2)	s. 2(1).
28(3)	s. 1(2).
28(4), (5)	s. 2(2), (3).
28(6)	s. 8(1) (part).
28(7)	s. 2(4), 7(1)–(3).
28(8), (9)	s. 7(4), (5).
29(1)–(5)	s. 4(1)–(5).
29(6)	s. 4(6), 7(1)–(3).
29(7)	s. 4(7), 7(1), (2).
29(8)	s. 7(4), (5).
30	s. 5.
31(1)	s. 3(1); CA 1985, s. 29(1).
31(2) (as amended by OinC-1)	CA 1985, s. 29(2) (except (c)).
31(3) (as amended by OinC-1)	BNA 1985, s. 3(2).
31(4)	CA 1985, s. 29(2)(c).
31(5)	s. 29(4).
32	s. 29(6), BNA 1985, s. 6.
34	s. 26(2), BNA 1985, s. 8(1) (part).
36(1)	s. 130(4), CC(CP)A 1985, s. 12.
36(2), (3)	s. 131(8).
37(1)–(6)	s. 131(1)–(6).
37(7)	s. 131(7) (part).
38	s. 132(1)–(5), (8).
39	CC(CP)A 1985, s. 12.
40(1)	CA 1985, s. 133(1).
40(4), (5)	s. 133(2), (3), CC(CP)A 1985, s. 12.
40(6)	s. 131(7) (part).
40(7)	s. 133(4).
41	s. 134, CC(CP)A 1985, s. 12.
42(1), (2)	s. 151(1), (2).
42(3)–(6)	s. 153.
42(7)	s. 154(1).
42(8)	s. 152(1)(a).
42(9), (10)	s. 152(3).

Provision of former Acts	Destination
Companies Act 1981	
42(11)	CA 1985, s. 154(2).
42(12)	s. 151(3).
43(1)–(5)	s. 155(1)–(5).
43(6) (as amended by OinC-1)	s. 155(6).
43(7)	s. 156(1)–(3).
43(8)	s. 156(4).
43(9)	s. 158.
44(1)–(4)	s. 157.
44(5)–(7)	s. 156(5)–(7).
44(8)	s. 155(2) (part).
45(1), (2)	s. 159(1), (2).
45(3), (4)	s. 159(3).
45(5)–(9)	s. 160.
45(10)	s. 161(1), (2).
45(11), (12)	s. 161(3), (4).
46	s. 162.
47(2), (3)	s. 163(1), (2).
47(4)–(6)	s. 164(1)–(3).
47(7), (8)	s. 164(4).
47(9)	s. 164(5) (except (c)).
47(10), (11)	s. 164(6), (7).
47(12)	s. 164(5)(c).
48(1)	s. 165(1).
48(2), (3)	s. 165(2).
49(1)	s. 166(1) (part).
49(2)	s. 163(3).
49(3)–(5)	s. 166(1)–(3).
49(6), (7)	s. 166(4).
49(8)–(10)	s. 166(5)–(7), see also s. 380.
50(1)	s. 167(1).
50(2), (3)	s. 167(2).
51	s. 168.
52	s. 169.
53(1), (2)	s. 170(1), (2).
53(3)	s. 170(4).
54(1)	s. 171(1), (2).
54(2), (3)	s. 171(3).
54(4), (5)	s. 171(4), (5).

Provision of former Acts	Destination
Companies Act 1981	
54(6) (except (b))	CA 1985, s. 171(6).
54(6)(b)	s. 170(3).
54(7)	s. 172(1).
54(8)	s. 172(2), (3).
54(9)	s. 172(4), (5).
54(10)	s. 172(6).
55(1)–(5)	s. 173(1)–(5).
55(6)	s. 174(1).
55(7)	s. 174(2), (3).
55(8)	s. 174(4).
55(9)	s. 173(6).
55(10)	s. 174(5).
56(1)	s. 175(1).
56(2)	s. 175(2), (3).
56(3)–(7)	s. 175(4)–(8).
57(1)–(3)	s. 176(1)–(3).
57(4), (5)	s. 177(1), (2).
57(6) (applying s. 11(7)–(9) of 1980 Act)	s. 177(3)–(5).
57(7)	s. 176(4).
58(1)	s. 504(1)(a).
58(2)	s. 504(1)(b), (2).
58(3)–(5)	s. 504(3)–(5), see also s. 503.
58(6)	s. 507(2) (part).
58(7)	s. 519(3) (part).
59	s. 178.
60(1)	s. 274(1), (2).
60(2)	s. 277(2).
60(3)	s. 274(3).
61	s. 179, 274(4), 277(3), 504(6), 507(2).
62(1)	s. 181, see also s. 155.
62(2)–(4)	s. 180.
63(1)	s. 198(1).
63(2)	s. 199(4), (5).
63(3)	s. 199(1)–(3).
63(4)	s. 198(3).
63(5)	s. 202(1) (part), (2).
63(6)	s. 202(1) (part).
63(7)	s. 200.

Provision of former Acts	Destination
Companies Act 1981	
63(8)	CA 1985, s. 201(1).
63(9)	s. 198(4).
63(10)	s. 198(2).
64(1)	s. 201(2) (part).
64(2), (3)	s. 201(3).
64(4)	s. 201(2) (part).
65(1)	s. 202(3).
65(2)	s. 202(4) (part).
65(3), (4)	s. 202(5), (6).
65(5)	s. 202(4) (part).
66(1)	s. 203(1) (part).
66(2)–(4)	s. 203(2)–(4).
66(5)	s. 203(1) (part).
67(1)	s. 204(1), (2).
67(2)–(4)	s. 204(3)–(5).
67(5)	s. 204(6) (part).
67(6)	s. 205(1).
67(7)	s. 205(2), (3).
67(8), (9)	s. 205(4), (5).
67(10)	s. 204(6) (part).
68	s. 206.
69	s. 207.
70	s. 208.
71	s. 209.
72(1), (2)	s. 210(1), (2).
72(3), (4)	s. 210(3), see also s. 455.
72(5)	s. 210(4).
72(6), (7)	s. 210(5).
72(8)	s. 456(3), see also s. 457.
72(9)	s. 210(6) (part).
73	s. 211(1)–(10).
74	s. 212.
75	s. 213(1)–(3).
76(1)–(4)	s. 214(1)–(4).
76(5)–(11)	s. 215(1)–(7).
76(12)	s. 214(5), 215(8).
77(1), (2)	s. 216(1), (2), see also s. 457.
77(3), (4)	s. 456(1), (2).

Provision of former Acts	Destination
Companies Act 1981	
77(5), (6)	CA 1985, s. 216(3), (4), see also s. 455.
77(7) (as amended by OinC-1)	s. 216(5).
78	s. 217.
79	s. 218.
80	s. 219.
81	s. 210(6) (part), 216, 733.
82(1)	s. 220(1), 198(2) (part).
82(2)	s. 198(2)(a).
82(3)	s. 220(2).
91(8) (saving)	CC(CP)A 1985, s. 23.
97	CA 1985, s. 705.
100	s. 715.
102(1)–(3)	s. 129(1)–(3).
102(5)	s. 129(4).
103(3), 104(1)–(3)	see CC(CP)A 1985, s. 25.
107 (saving)	s. 24(1).
108(1)–(4)	CA 1985, s. 654(2), 655.
113	CC(CP)A 1985, s. 1(2).
115	CA 1985, s. 713, 731.
116	see S.I. 1984/134; S.I. 1984/1169 ("OinC-1", "OinC-2").
Sch. 1	see CA 1985, Sch. 4.
Companies (Beneficial Interests) Act 1983	
1(1)(a)	see s. 23(4).
1(1)(b)	Sch. 4, para. 60(2) (part); Sch. 9, para. 19(3) (part).
1(1)(c)	s. 145(1) (part), (3).
1(1)(d)	s. 146(1) (part).
1(1)(e) (as inserted by OinC-1)	s. 148(1)(b), (3).
2(1)–(3)	Sch. 2, para. 1(1)–(3).
2(4)	Sch. 2, para. 2(1).
2(5), (6)	Sch. 2, para. 1(4), (5).
3	Sch. 2, para. 3.
4(1), (2)	Sch. 2, para. 4.
5(2), (3)	Sch. 2, para. 5(2), (3).
5(4)	see s. 743.
Sch.	Sch. 2, para. 2(2)–(5).

BUSINESS NAMES ACT 1985

Table of Contents

For a CCH Table of Destinations (indicating references in the former legislation and the corresponding references in the new legislation) see p. 36,623 ff.

[The next page is 39,051]

BUSINESS NAMES ACT 1985

(1985 Chapter 7)

ARRANGEMENT OF SECTIONS

[The next page is 39,101]

BUSINESS NAMES ACT 1985

(1985 Chapter 7)

An Act to consolidate certain enactments relating to the names under which persons may carry on business in Great Britain.

[11th March 1985]

SEC. 1   Persons subject to this Act

1(1)   [Application]   This Act applies to any person who has a place of business in Great Britain and who carries on business in Great Britain under a name which—

(a) in the case of a partnership, does not consist of the surnames of all partners who are individuals and the corporate names of all partners who are bodies corporate without any addition other than an addition permitted by this Act;

(b) in the case of an individual, does not consist of his surname without any addition other than one so permitted;

(c) in the case of a company, being a company which is capable of being wound up under the Companies Act 1985, does not consist of its corporate name without any addition other than one so permitted.

1(2)   [Permitted additions for sec. 1(1)]   The following are permitted additions for the purposes of subsection (1)—

(a) in the case of a partnership, the forenames of individual partners or the initials of those forenames or, where two or more individual partners have the same surname, the addition of "s" at the end of that surname; or

(b) in the case of an individual, his forename or its initial;

(c) in any case, any addition merely indicating that the business is carried on in succession to a former owner of the business.

SEC. 2   Prohibition of use of certain business names

2(1)   [Exclusion of certain names]   Subject to the following subsections, a person to whom this Act applies shall not, without the written approval of the Secretary of State, carry on business in Great Britain under a name which—

(a) would be likely to give the impression that the business is connected with Her Majesty's Government or with any local authority; or

(b) includes any word or expression for the time being specified in regulations made under this Act.

2(2)   [Non-application of sec. 2(1)]   Subsection (1) does not apply to the carrying on of a business by a person—

(a) to whom the business has been transferred on or after 26th February 1982; and

(b) who carries on the business under the name which was its lawful business name immediately before that transfer,

during the period of 12 months beginning with the date of that transfer.

2(3)   **[Further non-application of sec. 2(1)]**   Subsection (1) does not apply to the carrying on of a business by a person who—

(a) carried on that business immediately before 26th February 1982; and

(b) continues to carry it on under the name which immediately before that date was its lawful business name.

2(4)   **[Offence]**   A person who contravenes subsection (1) is guilty of an offence.

SEC. 3   Words and expressions requiring Secretary of State's approval

3(1)   **[Regulations]**   The Secretary of State may by regulations—

(a) specify words or expressions for the use of which as or as part of a business name his approval is required by section 2(1)(b); and

(b) in relation to any such word or expression, specify a Government department or other body as the relevant body for purposes of the following subsection.

3(2)   **[Request for use of certain names]**   Where a person to whom this Act applies proposes to carry on a business under a name which is or includes any such word or expression, and a Government department or other body is specified under subsection (1)(b) in relation to that word or expression, that person shall—

(a) request (in writing) the relevant body to indicate whether (and if so why) it has any objections to the proposal; and

(b) submit to the Secretary of State a statement that such a request has been made and a copy of any response received from the relevant body.

SEC. 4   Disclosure required of persons using business names

4(1)   **[Disclosure of names and addresses]**   A person to whom this Act applies shall—

(a) subject to subsection (3), state in legible characters on all business letters, written orders for goods or services to be supplied to the business, invoices and receipts issued in the course of the business and written demands for payment of debts arising in the course of the business—

   (i) in the case of a partnership, the name of each partner,

  (ii) in the case of an individual, his name,

 (iii) in the case of a company, its corporate name, and

 (iv) in relation to each person so named, an address in Great Britain at which service of any document relating in any way to the business will be effective; and

(b) in any premises where the business is carried on and to which the customers of the business or suppliers of any goods or services to the business have access, display in a prominent position so that it may easily be read by such customers or suppliers a notice containing such names and addresses.

4(2) **[Names and addresses to be supplied on request]** A person to whom this Act applies shall secure that the names and addresses required by subsection (1)(a) to be stated on his business letters, or which would have been so required but for the subsection next following, are immediately given, by written notice to any person with whom anything is done or discussed in the course of the business and who asks for such names and addresses.

4(3) **[Sec. 4(1)(a) not to apply to certain partnerships]** Subsection (1)(a) does not apply in relation to any document issued by a partnership of more than 20 persons which maintains at its principal place of business a list of the names of all the partners if—

(a) none of the names of the partners appears in the document otherwise than in the text or as a signatory; and

(b) the document states in legible characters the address of the partnership's principal place of business and that the list of the partners' names is open to inspection at that place.

4(4) **[Inspection of list of partners' names]** Where a partnership maintains a list of the partners' names for purposes of subsection (3), any person may inspect the list during office hours.

4(5) **[Regulations]** The Secretary of State may by regulations require notices under subsection (1)(b) or (2) to be displayed or given in a specified form.

4(6) **[Offence]** A person who without reasonable excuse contravenes subsection (1) or (2), or any regulations made under subsection (5), is guilty of an offence.

4(7) **[Refusal of sec. 4(4) inspection an offence]** Where an inspection required by a person in accordance with subsection (4) is refused, any partner of the partnership concerned who without reasonable excuse refused that inspection, or permitted it to be refused, is guilty of an offence.

SEC. 5   Civil remedies for breach of sec. 4

5(1) **[Dismissal of certain legal proceedings]** Any legal proceedings brought by a person to whom this Act applies to enforce a right arising out of a contract made in the course of a business in respect of which he was, at the time the contract was made, in breach of subsection (1) or (2) of section 4 shall be dismissed if the defendant (or, in Scotland, the defender) to the proceedings shows—

(a) that he has a claim against the plaintiff (pursuer) arising out of that contract which he has been unable to pursue by reason of the latter's breach of section 4(1) or (2), or

(b) that he has suffered some financial loss in connection with the contract by reason of the plaintiff's (pursuer's) breach of section 4(1) or (2),

unless the court before which the proceedings are brought is satisfied that it is just and equitable to permit the proceedings to continue.

5(2) **[Without prejudice]** This section is without prejudice to the right of any person to enforce such rights as he may have against another person in any proceedings brought by that person.

SEC. 6   Regulations

6(1)   **[Regulations by statutory instrument]**   Regulations under this Act shall be made by statutory instrument and may contain such transitional provisions and savings as the Secretary of State thinks appropriate, and may make different provision for different cases or classes of case.

6(2)   **[Regulations under sec. 3]**   In the case of regulations made under section 3, the statutory instrument containing them shall be laid before Parliament after the regulations are made and shall cease to have effect at the end of the period of 28 days beginning with the day on which they were made (but without prejudice to anything previously done by virtue of them or to the making of new regulations) unless during that period they are approved by a resolution of each House of Parliament.

     In reckoning this period of 28 days, no account is to be taken of any time during which Parliament is dissolved or prorogued, or during which both Houses are adjourned for more than 4 days.

6(3)   **[Regulations under sec. 4]**   In the case of regulations made under section 4, the statutory instrument containing them is subject to annulment in pursuance of a resolution of either House of Parliament.

SEC. 7   Offences

7(1)   **[Summary conviction]**   Offences under this Act are punishable on summary conviction.

7(2)   **[Fine]**   A person guilty of an offence under this Act is liable to a fine not exceeding one-fifth of the statutory maximum.

7(3)   **[Fine for continued contravention]**   If after a person has been convicted summarily of an offence under section 2 or 4(6) the original contravention is continued, he is liable on a second or subsequent summary conviction of the offence to a fine not exceeding one-fiftieth of the statutory maximum for each day on which the contravention is continued (instead of to the penalty which may be imposed on the first conviction of the offence).

7(4)   **[Penalty relating to officers of body corporate]**   Where an offence under section 2 or 4(6) or (7) committed by a body corporate is proved to have been committed with the consent or connivance of, or to be attributable to any neglect on the part of, any director, manager, secretary or other similar officer of the body corporate, or any person who was purporting to act in any such capacity, he as well as the body corporate is guilty of the offence and liable to be proceeded against and punished accordingly.

7(5)   **[Where body corporate managed by members]**   Where the affairs of a body corporate are managed by its members, subsection (4) applies in relation to the acts and defaults of a member in connection with his functions of management as if he were a director of the body corporate.

7(6)   **[Sec. 731, 732(3) of Companies Act 1985]**   For purposes of the following provisions of the Companies Act 1985—

     (a)   section 731 (summary proceedings under the Companies Acts), and

     (b)   section 732(3) (legal professional privilege),

this Act is to be treated as included in those Acts.

SEC. 8   Interpretation

8(1)   **[Definitions]**   The following definitions apply for purposes of this Act—

"**business**" includes a profession;

"**initial**" includes any recognised abbreviation of a name;

"**lawful business name**", in relation to a business, means a name under which the business was carried on without contravening section 2(1) of this Act or section 2 of the Registration of Business Names Act 1916;

"**local authority**" means any local authority within the meaning of the Local Government Act 1972 or the Local Government (Scotland) Act 1973, the Common Council of the City of London or the Council of the Isles of Scilly;

"**partnership**" includes a foreign partnership;

"**statutory maximum**" means—

    (a) in England and Wales the prescribed sum under section 32 of the Magistrates' Courts Act 1980, and

    (b) in Scotland, the prescribed sum under section 289B of the Criminal Procedure (Scotland) Act 1975;

and "**surname**", in relation to a peer or person usually known by a British title different from his surname, means the title by which he is known.

8(2)   **[Expressions also in Companies Act 1985]**   Any expression used in this Act and also in the Companies Act 1985 has the same meaning in this Act as in that.

SEC. 9   Northern Ireland

9   This Act does not extend to Northern Ireland.

SEC. 10   Commencement

10   This Act comes into force on 1st July 1985.

SEC. 11   Citation

11   This Act may be cited as the Business Names Act 1985.

TABLE OF DERIVATIONS

[This table has no official status]

The following abbreviations are used in this Table:—

"1980"   = Companies Act 1980 (c. 22).
"1981"   = Companies Act 1981 (c. 62).
"OinC–1" = Companies Acts (Pre-Consolidation Amendments) Order 1984
             (S.I. 1984 No. 134).

Provision	Derivation
1	1981 s. 28(1), (3).
2	1981 s. 28(2), (4), (5), (7).
3	1981 s. 31(1), (3); OinC–1 No. 56.
4	1981 ss. 29(1)–(7).
5	1981 s. 30.
6	1981 s. 32.
7	1980 s. 80(2); 1981 ss. 28(7)–(9), 29(6)–(8).
8	1981 ss. 28(6), 34; Sch. 3 para. 19.
9	(Northern Ireland).
10	(Commencement).
11	(Citation).

COMPANY SECURITIES (INSIDER DEALING) ACT 1985

Table of Contents

For a CCH Table of Destinations (indicating references in the former legislation and the corresponding references in the new legislation) see p. 36,623 ff.

[The next page is 41,051]

COMPANY SECURITIES (INSIDER DEALING) ACT 1985

Table of Contents

For a full Table of Derivations (including references to the former legislation and the corresponding references in the new legislation) see p. 141,901.

COMPANY SECURITIES (INSIDER DEALING) ACT 1985

(1985 Chapter 8)

ARRANGEMENT OF SECTIONS

[The next page is 41,101]

COMPANY SECURITIES (INSIDER DEALING) ACT 1985

(1985 Chapter 8)

An Act to consolidate the enactments relating to insider dealing in company securities.

[*11th March 1985*]

REGULATION OF INSIDER DEALING

SEC. 1 Prohibition on stock exchange deals by insiders, etc.

1(1) **[Prohibition on dealing in company's securities]** Subject to section 3, an individual who is, or at any time in the preceding 6 months has been, knowingly connected with a company shall not deal on a recognised stock exchange in securities of that company if he has information which—

(a) he holds by virtue of being connected with the company,

(b) it would be reasonable to expect a person so connected, and in the position by virtue of which he is so connected, not to disclose except for the proper performance of the functions attaching to that position, and

(c) he knows is unpublished price sensitive information in relation to those securities.

1(2) **[Prohibition on dealing in connected company's securities]** Subject to section 3, an individual who is, or at any time in the preceding 6 months has been, knowingly connected with a company shall not deal on a recognised stock exchange in securities of any other company if he has information which—

(a) he holds by virtue of being connected with the first company,

(b) it would be reasonable to expect a person so connected, and in the position by virtue of which he is so connected, not to disclose except for the proper performance of the functions attaching to that position,

(c) he knows is unpublished price sensitive information in relation to those securities of that other company, and

(d) relates to any transaction (actual or contemplated) involving both the first company and that other company, or involving one of them and securities of the other, or to the fact that any such transaction is no longer contemplated.

1(3) **[Application of sec. 1(4)]** The next subsection applies where—

(a) an individual has information which he knowingly obtained (directly or indirectly) from another individual who—

(i) is connected with a particular company, or was at any time in the 6 months preceding the obtaining of the information so connected, and

(ii) the former individual knows or has reasonable cause to believe held the information by virtue of being so connected, and

(b) the former individual knows or has reasonable cause to believe that, because of the latter's connection and position, it would be reasonable to expect him not to disclose the information except for the proper performance of the functions attaching to that position.

1(4)   [Individual with information from person connected with company]   Subject to section 3, the former individual in that case—

(a) shall not himself deal on a recognised stock exchange in securities of that company if he knows that the information is unpublished price sensitive information in relation to those securities, and

(b) shall not himself deal on a recognised stock exchange in securities of any other company if he knows that the information is unpublished price sensitive information in relation to those securities and it relates to any transaction (actual or contemplated) involving the first company and the other company, or involving one of them and securities of the other, or to the fact that any such transaction is no longer contemplated.

1(5)   [Individual contemplating take-over offer]   Subject to section 3, where an individual is contemplating, or has contemplated, making (whether with or without another person) a take-over offer for a company in a particular capacity, that individual shall not deal on a recognised stock exchange in securities of that company in another capacity if he knows that information that the offer is contemplated, or is no longer contemplated, is unpublished price sensitive information in relation to those securities.

1(6)   [Individual with information from individual in sec. 1(5)]   Subject to section 3, where an individual has knowingly obtained (directly or indirectly), from an individual to whom subsection (5) applies, information that the offer referred to in that subsection is being contemplated or is no longer contemplated, the former individual shall not himself deal on a recognised stock exchange in securities of that company if he knows that the information is unpublished price sensitive information in relation to those securities.

1(7)   [Individual covered by sec. 1 shall not counsel another person]   Subject to section 3, an individual who is for the time being prohibited by any provision of this section from dealing on a recognised stock exchange in any securities shall not counsel or procure any other person to deal in those securities, knowing or having reasonable cause to believe that that person would deal in them on a recognised stock exchange.

1(8)   [Individual covered by sec. 1 shall not communicate information]   Subject to section 3, an individual who is for the time being prohibited as above mentioned from dealing on a recognised stock exchange in any securities by reason of his having any information, shall not communicate that information to any other person if he knows or has reasonable cause to believe that that or some other person will make use of the information for the purpose of dealing, or of counselling or procuring any other person to deal, on a recognised stock exchange in those securities.

Note
Re powers of entry re offence under s. 1, see Financial
Services Act 1986, s. 199.

SEC. 2   Abuse of information obtained in official capacity

2(1)   [Application]   This section applies to any information which—

(a)   is held by a public servant or former public servant by virtue of his position or former position as a public servant, or is knowingly obtained by an individual (directly or indirectly) from a public servant or former public servant who he knows or has reasonable cause to believe held the information by virtue of any such position,

(b)   it would be reasonable to expect an individual in the position of the public servant or former position of the former public servant not to disclose except for the proper performance of the functions attaching to that position, and

(c)   the individual holding it knows is unpublished price sensitive information in relation to securities of a particular company ("relevant securities").

2(2)   [Public servant and individual acquiring information from him]   This section applies to a public servant or former public servant holding information to which this section applies and to any individual who knowingly obtained any such information (directly or indirectly) from a public servant or former public servant who that individual knows or has reasonable cause to believe held the information by virtue of his position or former position as a public servant.

History
In s. 2(1), (2) the word "public" wherever appearing substituted for the former word "Crown" by Financial Services Act 1986, s. 173(1) as from 12 January 1987 (see S.I. 1986 No. 2246 (C. 88)).

2(3)   [Prohibition]   Subject to section 3, an individual to whom this section applies—

(a)   shall not deal on a recognised stock exchange in any relevant securities,

(b)   shall not counsel or procure any other person to deal in any such securities, knowing or having reasonable cause to believe that that other person would deal in them on a recognised stock exchange, and

(c)   shall not communicate to any other person the information held or (as the case may be) obtained by him as mentioned in subsection (2) if he knows or has reasonable cause to believe that that or some other person will make use of the information for the purpose of dealing, or of counselling or procuring any other person to deal, on a recognised stock exchange in any such securities.

2(4)   ["Public servant"]   "Public servant" means—

(a)   a Crown servant;

(b)   a member, officer or servant of a designated agency, competent authority or transferee body (within the meaning of the Financial Services Act 1986);

(c)   an officer or servant of a recognised self-regulating organisation, recognised investment exchange or recognised clearing house (within the meaning of that Act);

(d)   any person declared by an order for the time being in force under subsection (5) to be a public servant for the purposes of this section.

2(5)   [Order by Secretary of State]   If it appears to the Secretary of State that the members, officers or employees of or persons otherwise connected with any body appearing to him to exercise public functions may have access to unpublished price sensitive information relating to securities, he may by order declare that those persons are to be public servants for the purposes of this section.

Note
See the Insider Dealing (Public Servants) Order 1989 (S.I. 1989 No. 2164).

2(6) **[Exercise of sec. 2(5) power]** The power to make an order under subsection (5) shall be exercisable by statutory instrument and an instrument containing such an order shall be subject to annulment in pursuance of a resolution of either House of Parliament.

History
S. 2(4)–(6) added by Financial Services Act 1986, s. 173(2) as from 12 January 1987 (see S.I. 1986 No. 2246 (C. 88)).

Note
For powers of entry re offence under s. 2, see Financial Services Act 1986, s. 199.

SEC. 3   Actions not prohibited by sec. 1, 2

3(1) **[Exceptions to prohibitions in sec. 1, 2]** Sections 1 and 2 do not prohibit an individual by reason of his having any information from—

(a) doing any particular thing otherwise than with a view to the making of a profit or the avoidance of a loss (whether for himself or another person) by the use of that information;

(b) entering into a transaction in the course of the exercise in good faith of his functions as liquidator, receiver or trustee in bankruptcy;

(c) doing any particular thing if the information—

(i) was obtained by him in the course of a business of a jobber in which he was engaged or employed, and

(ii) was of a description which it would be reasonable to expect him to obtain in the ordinary course of that business,

and he does that thing in good faith in the course of that business; or

(d) doing any particular thing in relation to any particular securities if the information—

(i) was obtained by him in the course of a business of a market maker in those securities in which he was engaged or employed, and

(ii) was of a description which it would be reasonable to expect him to obtain in the ordinary course of that business,

and he does that thing in good faith in the course of that business.

"**Jobber**" means an individual, partnership or company dealing in securities on a recognised stock exchange and recognised by the Council of The Stock Exchange as carrying on the business of a jobber.

"**Market maker**" means a person (whether an individual, partnership or company) who—

(a) holds himself out at all normal times in compliance with the rules of a recognised stock exchange as willing to buy and sell securities at prices specified by him; and

(b) is recognised as doing so by that recognised stock exchange.

History
In s. 3(1) the word "; or", para. (d) and the definition
of "market maker" inserted by Financial Services Act
1986, s. 174(1), (2) as from 18 December 1986 (see S.I.
1986 No. 2246 (C. 88)). The word "or" formerly appearing
immediately preceding para. (c) repealed by Financial
Services Act 1986, s. 212(3) and Sch. 17 as from 12 January
1987 (see S.I. 1986 No. 2246 (C. 88)).

3(2)   [Qualifications to prohibitions]   An individual is not, by reason only of his having information relating to any particular transaction, prohibited—

(a) by section 1(2), (4)(b), (5) or (6) from dealing on a recognised stock exchange in any securities, or

(b) by section 1(7) or (8) from doing any other thing in relation to securities which he is prohibited from dealing in by any of the provisions mentioned in paragraph (a), or

(c) by section 2 from doing anything,

if he does that thing in order to facilitate the completion or carrying out of the transaction.

SEC. 4   Off-market deals in advertised securities

4(1)   [Application of sec. 1–3]   Subject to section 6, sections 1 to 3 apply in relation to—

(a) dealing otherwise than on a recognised stock exchange in the advertised securities of any company—

(i) through an off-market dealer who is making a market in those securities, in the knowledge that he is an off-market dealer, that he is making a market in those securities and that the securities are advertised securities, or

(ii) as an off-market dealer who is making a market in those securities or as an officer, employee or agent of such a dealer acting in the course of the dealer's business;

(b) counselling or procuring a person to deal in advertised securities in the knowledge or with reasonable cause to believe that he would deal in them as mentioned in paragraph (a);

(c) communicating any information in the knowledge or with reasonable cause to believe that it would be used for such dealing or for such counselling or procuring,

as they apply in relation to dealing in securities on a recognised stock exchange and to counselling or procuring or communicating any information in connection with such dealing.

4(2)   [Application of "market maker" definition]   In its application by virtue of this section the definition of "market maker" in section 3(1) shall have effect as if the references to a recognised stock exchange were references to a recognised investment exchange (other than an overseas investment exchange) within the meaning of the Financial Services Act 1986.

History
S. 4(1) renumbered as such and s. 4(2) inserted by Financial
Services Act, s. 174(3) as from 29 April 1988 (see S.I. 1988
No. 740 (C. 22)).

SEC. 5   Restriction on promoting off-market deals abroad

5(1)   [Prohibition]   An individual who, by reason of his having information, is for the time being prohibited by any provision of section 1 or 2 from dealing in any securities shall not—

(a) counsel or procure any other person to deal in those securities in the knowledge or with reasonable cause to believe that that person would deal in the securities outside Great Britain on any stock exchange other than a recognised stock exchange, or

(b) communicate that information to any other person in the knowledge or with reasonable cause to believe that that or some other person will make use of the information for the purpose of dealing or of counselling or procuring any other person to deal in the securities outside Great Britain on any stock exchange other than a recognised stock exchange.

5(2)   [Qualifications to sec. 5(1) prohibition]   Subsection (1) does not prohibit an individual by reason of his having any information from acting as mentioned in any of paragraphs (a) to (c) of section 3(1).

5(3)   [Further qualification]   An individual is not, by reason only of having information relating to a particular transaction, prohibited by any provision of this section from doing anything if he does that thing in order to facilitate the completion or carrying out of the transaction.

Note
For powers of entry re offence under s. 5, see Financial Services Act 1986, s. 199.

SEC. 6   Price stabilisation

6(1)   [Limit on sec. 1, 2, 4 or 5 prohibition]   No provision of section 1, 2, 4 or 5 prohibits an individual from doing anything for the purpose of stabilising the price of securities if it is done in conformity with rules made under section 48 of the Financial Services Act 1986 and—

(a) in respect of securities which fall within any of paragraphs 1 to 5 of Schedule 1 to that Act and are specified by the rules; and

(b) during such period before or after the issue of those securities as is specified by the rules.

6(2)   [Application of order under sec. 48(8) of Financial Services Act]   Any order under subsection (8) of section 48 of that Act shall apply also in relation to subsection (1) of this section.

History
S. 6 substituted by Financial Services Act 1986, s. 175 as from 29 April 1988 (see S.I. 1988 No. 740 (C. 22)): s. 6 formerly read as follows:

"SEC. 6 International bonds

6(1) Section 1 does not by virtue of section 4 or 5 prohibit an individual from doing anything in relation to a debenture, or a right to subscribe for, call for or make delivery of a debenture, if—

(a) that thing is done by him in good faith in connection with an international bond issue—

(i) not later than 3 months after the issue date, or

(ii) in a case where the international bond issue is

not proceeded with, before the decision is taken not to proceed with the issue,

and he is an issue manager for that issue or is an officer, employee or agent of an issue manager for that issue, or

(b) he is or was an issue manager for an international bond issue who is making a market in that debenture or right, or is an officer, employee or agent of such an issue manager, and that thing is done by him in good faith as a person making a market in that debenture or right or as an officer, employee or agent of such a person, and in either case the unpublished price sensitive information by virtue of which section 1 would (but for this section) apply in relation to that thing is information which he holds by virtue of his being (or having been) such an issue manager or an officer, employee or agent of such an issue manager, and is information which it would be reasonable to expect him to have obtained as an issue manager, or as such officer, employee or agent.

6(2) Where an individual holds unpublished price sensitive information in relation to any securities but by virtue of subsection (1) of this section he is not prohibited by section 1 from doing anything in relation to those securities, he is also not prohibited (by virtue of his holding that information) by section 5 from doing any other thing in relation to those securities.

6(3) The Secretary of State may by regulations made by statutory instrument make provision—

(a) extending the exemptions conferred by subsection (1) or (2) (or both) for things done in relation to other advertised securities or other advertised securities of any specified class;

(b) amending or disapplying sub-paragraph (i) or (ii) (or both) of subsection (1)(a) in relation to an international bond issue or an international bond issue of a specified class.

6(4) Regulations under subsection (3)—

(a) may make different provision for different cases or classes of case and may contain such incidental and supplementary provisions as the Secretary of State may think fit,

(b) shall not be made unless a draft of the instrument containing them has been laid before Parliament and approved by a resolution of each House.''

SEC. 7 Trustees and personal representatives

7(1) **[Actions of trustees, etc.]**   Where a trustee or personal representative or, where a trustee or personal representative is a body corporate, an individual acting on behalf of that trustee or personal representative who, apart from paragraph (a) of section 3(1) or, as the case may be, subsection (2) of section 5, would be prohibited by any of sections 1 to 5 from dealing, or counselling or procuring any other person to deal, in any securities deals in those securities or counsels or procures any other person to deal in them, he is presumed to have acted with propriety if he acted on the advice of a person who—

(a) appeared to him to be an appropriate person from whom to seek such advice, and

(b) did not appear to him to be prohibited by section 1, 2, 4 or 5 from dealing in those securities.

7(2) **[Interpretation]**   ''**With propriety**'' means otherwise than with a view to the making of a profit or the avoidance of a loss (whether for himself or another person) by the use of the information in question.

SEC. 8 Punishment of contraventions

8(1) **[Penalty]**   An individual who contravenes section 1, 2, 4 or 5 is liable—

(a) on conviction on indictment to imprisonment for a term not exceeding 7 years or a fine, or both, and

(b) on summary conviction to imprisonment for a term not exceeding 6 months or a fine not exceeding the statutory maximum, or both.

History
In s. 8(1)(a) the figure ''7'' substituted for the former figure ''2'' by Criminal Justice Act 1988, s. 48(1) and 171(6) as from 29 September 1988.

8(2) **[Institution of proceedings]**   Proceedings for an offence under this section shall not be instituted in England and Wales except by, or with the consent of, the Secretary of State or the Director of Public Prosecutions.

History
In s. 8(2) the words ''by, or with the consent of the Secretary of State or the Director of Public Prosecutions'' substituted for the former words ''by the Secretary of State or by, or with the consent of, the Director of Public Prosecutions'' by CA 1989, s. 209 as from 21 February 1990 (see S.I. 1990 No. 142 (C. 5), art. 7(b)).

8(3) **[Effect of contravention]**   No transaction is void or voidable by reason only that it was entered into in contravention of section 1, 2, 4 or 5.

INTERPRETATION FOR SEC. 1–8

SEC. 9 "Connected with a company"

9 For purposes of this Act, an individual is connected with a company if, but only if—

  (a) he is a director of that company or a related company, or

  (b) he occupies a position as an officer (other than a director) or employee of that company or a related company or a position involving a professional or business relationship between himself (or his employer or a company of which he is a director) and the first company or a related company which in either case may reasonably be expected to give him access to information which, in relation to securities of either company, is unpublished price sensitive information, and which it would be reasonable to expect a person in his position not to disclose except for the proper performance of his functions.

SEC. 10 "Unpublished price sensitive information"

10 Any reference in this Act to unpublished price sensitive information in relation to any securities of a company is a reference to information which—

  (a) relates to specific matters relating or of concern (directly or indirectly) to that company, that is to say, is not of a general nature relating or of concern to that company, and

  (b) is not generally known to those persons who are accustomed or would be likely to deal in those securities but which would if it were generally known to them be likely materially to affect the price of those securities.

SEC. 11 "Company"; "related company"

11 In this Act—

  (a) **"company"** means any company, whether or not a company within the meaning of the Companies Act 1985, and

  (b) **"related company"**, in relation to a company, means any body corporate which is that company's subsidiary or holding company, or a subsidiary of that company's holding company.

SEC. 12 "Securities", etc.

12 In this Act—

  (a) **"securities"** means listed securities and, in the case of a company within the meaning of the Companies Act 1985, or a company registered under Chapter II of Part XXII of that Act or an unregistered company, the following securities (whether or not listed), that is to say, any shares, any debentures, or any right to subscribe for, call for or make delivery of a share or debenture;

  (b) **"listed securities"**, in relation to a company, means any securities of the company listed on a recognised stock exchange; and

  (c) **"advertised securities"**, in relation to a particular occurrence, means listed securities or securities in respect of which, not more than 6 months before that occurrence, information indicating the prices at which persons have dealt or were willing to deal in those securities has been published for the purpose of facilitating deals in those securities.

SEC. **13** "Deal in securities"; "off-market dealer", etc.

13(1) **[Dealing in securities]** For purposes of this Act, a person deals in securities if (whether as principal or agent) he buys or sells or agrees to buy or sell any securities; and references to dealing in securities on a recognised stock exchange include dealing in securities through an investment exchange.

Note
Prospective omission and repeal in s. 13(1) by Financial Services Act 1986, s. 174(4)(a) and s. 212(3) and Sch. 17, Pt. I from day(s) to be appointed.

13(1A) **[Buying and selling investments]** For the purposes of this Act a person who (whether as principal or agent) buys or sells or agrees to buy or sell investments within paragraph 9 of Schedule 1 to the Financial Services Act 1986 (contracts for differences etc.) where the purpose or pretended purpose mentioned in that paragraph is to secure a profit or avoid a loss wholly or partly by reference to fluctuations in the value or price of securities shall be treated as if he were dealing in those securities.

History
S. 13(1A) inserted by Financial Services Act 1986, s. 176 as from 12 January 1987 (see S.I. 1986 No. 2246 (C. 88)).

13(2) **["Investment exchange"]** "Investment exchange" means an organisation maintaining a system whereby an offer to deal in securities made by a subscriber to the organisation is communicated, without his identity being revealed, to other subscribers to the organisation, and whereby any acceptance of that offer by any of those other subscribers is recorded and confirmed.

Note
Prospective repeal of s. 13(2) by Financial Services Act 1986, s. 212(3) and Sch. 17, Pt. I from a day to be appointed.

13(3) **["Off-market dealer"]** "Off-market dealer" means a person who is an authorised person within the meaning of the Financial Services Act 1986.

History
S. 13(3) substituted by Financial Services Act 1986, s. 174(4)(b) as from 29 April 1988 (see S.I. 1988 No. 740 (C. 22)): s. 13(3) formerly read as follows:

"**13(3)** 'Off-market dealer' means a person who—

  (a) holds a licence under section 3 of the Prevention of Fraud (Investments) Act 1958 (principals' and

representatives' licences for dealers in securities), or

  (b) is a member of a recognised stock exchange or recognised association of dealers in securities within the meaning of that Act, or

  (c) is an exempted dealer within the meaning of that Act."

13(4) **[Activities of off-market dealer]** An off-market dealer is taken—

  (a) to deal in advertised securities, if he deals in such securities or acts as an intermediary in connection with deals made by other persons in such securities (references to such a dealer's officer, employee or agent dealing in such securities to be construed accordingly), and

  (b) to make a market in any securities, if in the course of his business as an off-market dealer he holds himself out both to prospective buyers and to prospective sellers of those securities (other than particular buyers or sellers) as willing to deal in them otherwise than on a recognised stock exchange.

13(5)   **[Individual dealing through off-market dealer]**   For purposes of section 4, an individual is taken to deal through an off-market dealer if the latter is a party to the transaction, is an agent for either party to the transaction or is acting as an intermediary in connection with the transaction.

SEC. 14   "Take-over offer"

14   In this Act, **"take-over offer for a company"** means an offer made to all the holders (or all the holders other than the person making the offer and his nominees) of the shares in the company to acquire those shares or a specified proportion of them, or to all the holders (or all the holders other than the person making the offer and his nominees) of a particular class of those shares to acquire the shares of that class or a specified proportion of them.

SEC. 15   (Repealed by Financial Services Act 1986, sec. 212(3) and Sch. 17, Pt. I as from 29 April 1988)

History

In regard to the date of the above repeal see S.I. 1988 No. 740 (C. 22): s. 15 formerly read as follows (in s. 15(3) the words ", British National (Overseas)," having been inserted by S.I. 1986 No. 948):

"**SEC. 15 Expressions used in sec. 6**

15(1) For purposes of section 6, the following definitions apply—

(a) **'international bond issue'** means an issue of debentures of a company ("the issuing company")—

  (i) all of which are offered or to be offered by an off-market dealer to persons (whether principals or agents) whose ordinary business includes the buying or selling of debentures, and

  (ii) where the debentures are denominated in sterling, not less than 50 per cent in nominal value of the debentures are or are to be so offered to persons who have not the requisite connection with the United Kingdom;

(b) **'issue date'** means the date on which the first of those debentures is issued by the issuing company; and

(c) **'issue manager'** means—

  (i) an off-market dealer acting as an agent of the issuing company for the purposes of an international bond issue, or

  (ii) where the issuing company issues or proposes to issue the debentures to an off-market dealer under an arrangement in pursuance of which

he is to sell them to other persons, that off-market dealer.

15(2) The Secretary of State may by regulations in a statutory instrument provide—

(a) for permitting persons of any specified class to be treated as issue managers for purposes of subsection (1) or (2) (or both) of section 6,

(b) for permitting persons of any specified class to be treated as off-market dealers for those purposes,

(c) for permitting an issue of international securities of any specified class to be treated as an international bond issue for those purposes.

15(3) The reference in subsection (1)(a)(ii) of this section to persons who have not the requisite connection with the United Kingdom is to persons who are neither—

(a) British citizens, British Dependent Territories citizens, British National (Overseas), or British Overseas citizens, nor

(b) companies incorporated or otherwise formed under the law of any part of the United Kingdom.

15(4) The reference in subsection (2)(c) to international securities is to any securities (whether listed, advertised or other) which are in any way connected with a country outside Great Britain for example—

(a) securities issued by a body incorporated or resident outside Great Britain, or

(b) securities which are denominated in a currency other than sterling, or dealt in by bodies incorporated or resident outside Great Britain or by individuals so resident."

SEC. 16   General interpretation provisions

16(1)   **[Definitions]**   In this Act—

  "Crown servant" means an individual who holds office under, or is employed by, the Crown;

  "debenture" has the same meaning in relation to companies not incorporated under the Companies Act 1985 as it has in relation to companies so incorporated;

  "recognised stock exchange" means The Stock Exchange and any other investment exchange which is declared by an order of the Secretary of State for the time being in force to be a recognised stock exchange for the purposes of this Act;

"share" has the same meaning in relation to companies not incorporated under the Companies Act 1985 as it has in relation to companies so incorporated;

"statutory maximum" means—

(a) in England and Wales, the prescribed sum within section 32 of the Magistrates' Courts Act 1980, and

(b) in Scotland, the prescribed sum within section 289B of the Criminal Procedure (Scotland) Act 1975;

"unregistered company" means any body corporate to which the provisions of the Companies Act 1985 specified in Schedule 22 to that Act apply by virtue of section 718 of that Act.

History
In s. 16(1) the definition of "recognised stock exchange" substituted by Financial Services Act 1986, s. 212(2) and Sch. 16, para. 28(a) as from 12 January 1987 (see S.I. 1986 No. 2246 (C. 88); the former definition read as follows:
"'**recognised stock exchange**' means any body of persons which is for the time being a recognised stock exchange for the purposes of the Prevention of Fraud (Investments) Act 1958;".

Note
See note to s. 16(1A) below.

16(1A)　[Exercise of sec. 16(1) power]　The power to make an order under subsection (1) above shall be exercisable by statutory instrument.

History
S. 16(1A) inserted by Financial Services Act 1986, s. 212(2) and Sch. 16, para. 28(b) as from 12 January 1987 (see S.I. 1986 No. 2246 (C. 88)).

Note
See the Insider Dealing (Recognised Stock Exchange) Order 1989 (S.I. 1989 No. 2165) and the Insider Dealing (Recognised Stock Exchange) (No. 2) Order 1990 (S.I. 1990 No. 47) made under sec. 16(1) and (1A).

16(2)　[Expressions in Companies Act 1985]　Subject to sections 9 to 14 and this section, expressions used in this Act and the Companies Act 1985 have the same meaning in this Act as in that.

History
In s. 16(2) the word "14" substituted for the former word "15" by Financial Services Act 1986, s. 212(2) and Sch. 16, para. 28(c) as from 29 April 1988 (see S.I. 1988 No. 740 (C. 22)).

16(3)　[Application of definitions]　The definitions in sections 11, 12(a) and (b), 13(2) and 14, and in subsection (1) above, apply except where the context otherwise requires.

GENERAL

SEC. 17　Northern Ireland

17　This Act does not extend to Northern Ireland.

SEC. 18　Commencement

18　This Act comes into force on 1st July 1985.

SEC. 19　Citation

19　This Act may be cited as the Company Securities (Insider Dealing) Act 1985.

TABLE OF DERIVATIONS

[This table has no official status]

The following abbreviations are used in this Table:—

"1948" = Companies Act 1948 (c. 38).
"1980" = Companies Act 1980 (c. 22).
"1981" = Companies Act 1981 (c. 62).

Provision	Derivation
1	1980 s. 68(1)–(7).
2	1980 s. 69(1)–(3).
3	1980 ss. 68(8), (10), 69(4) (in part), (5).
4	1980 s. 70(1).
5	1980 s. 70(2).
6	1980 s. 71(1), (1A), (3), (d), (e), (5); 1981 s. 112.
7	1980 ss. 68(11), 69(4), 70(2) (end piece).
8	1980 s. 72; 1981 Sch. 3, para. 59.
9	1980 s. 73(1).
10	1980 s. 73(2).
11	1980 s. 73(5).
12	1980 ss. 70(3), 73(5).
13	1980 ss. 70(3)–(5), 73(3), (5).
14	1980 s. 73(5).
15	1980 s. 71(2), (3)(a)–(c), (4).
16	1948 s. 455(1); 1980 ss. 68(9), 73(5), 87(1).
17	(Northern Ireland).
18	(Commencement).
19	(Citation).

44,001

COMPANIES CONSOLIDATION (CONSEQUENTIAL PROVISIONS) ACT 1985

Table of Contents

> For a CCH Table of Destinations (indicating references in the former legislation and the corresponding references in the new legislation) see p. 36,623 ff.

[The next page is 44,051]

COMPANIES CONSOLIDATION (CONSEQUENTIAL PROVISIONS) ACT 1985

Table of Contents

For a CCH Table of Destination (indicating references to the former legislation and the corresponding references to the new legislation) see p. 31,121.

[Title tax page follows]

COMPANIES CONSOLIDATION (CONSEQUENTIAL PROVISIONS) ACT 1985

(1985 Chapter 9)

ARRANGEMENT OF SECTIONS

[The next page is 44,101]

COMPANIES CONSOLIDATION (CONSEQUENTIAL PROVISIONS) ACT 1985

(1985 Chapter 9)

An Act to make, in connection with the consolidation of the Companies Acts 1948 to 1983 and other enactments relating to companies, provision for transitional matters and savings, repeals (including the repeal, in accordance with recommendations of the Law Commission, of certain provisions of the Companies Act 1948 which are no longer of practical utility) and consequential amendments of other Acts.

[*11th March 1985*]

OLD PUBLIC COMPANIES

SEC. 1   Meaning of "old public company"

1(1)   [Definitions]   For the purposes of the Companies Act 1985 ("the principal Act") and this Act, an "old public company" is a company limited by shares or by guarantee and having a share capital in respect of which the following conditions are satisfied—

(a) the company either existed on 22nd December 1980 or was incorporated after that date pursuant to an application made before that date,

(b) on that date or, if later, on the day of the company's incorporation the company was not or (as the case may be) would not have been a private company within section 28 of the Companies Act 1948, and

(c) the company has not since that date or the day of the company's incorporation (as the case may be) either been re-registered as a public company or become a private company.

1(2)   [References to public company, etc.]   References in the principal Act (other than so much of it as is derived from Part I of the Companies Act 1980, and other than section 33 (penalty for trading under misleading name)) to a public company or a company other than a private company are to be read as including (unless the context otherwise requires) references to an old public company, and references in that Act to a private company are to be read accordingly.

SEC. 2   Re-registration as public company

2(1)   [Re-registration as public company]   An old public company may be re-registered as a public company if—

(a) the directors pass a resolution, complying with the following subsection, that it should be so re-registered, and

(b) an application for the purpose in the prescribed form and signed by a director or secretary of the company is delivered to the registrar of companies together with the documents mentioned in subsection (4) below; and

(c) at the time of the resolution, the conditions specified in section 3 below are satisfied.

2(2)   **[Resolution in sec. 2(1)]**   The resolution must alter the company's memorandum so that it states that the company is to be a public company and make such other alterations in it as are necessary to bring it in substance and in form into conformity with the requirements of the principal Act with respect to the memorandum of a public company.

2(3)   **[Copy of resolution to registrar]**   A resolution of the directors under this section is subject to section 380 of the principal Act (copy of resolution to be forwarded to registrar of companies within 15 days).

2(4)   **[Documents in sec. 2(1)(b)]**   The documents referred to in subsection (1)(b) are—

(a) a printed copy of the memorandum as altered in pursuance of the resolution, and

(b) a statutory declaration in the prescribed form by a director or secretary of the company that the resolution has been passed and that the conditions specified in section 3 of this Act were satisfied at the time of the resolution.

2(5)   **[Sec. 2(4)(b) declaration sufficient evidence]**   The registrar may accept a declaration under subsection (4)(b) as sufficient evidence that the resolution has been passed and the necessary conditions were satisfied.

2(6)   **[Application of sec. 47(1), (3) to (5) of principal Act]**   Section 47(1) and (3) to (5) of the principal Act apply on an application for re-registration under this section as they apply on an application under section 43 of that Act.

SEC. 3   Conditions for re-registering under sec. 2

3(1)   **[Conditions for sec. 2(1)(c), 4]**   The following are the conditions referred to in section 2(1)(c) (being conditions also relevant under section 4).

3(2)   **[Nominal value of allotted share capital]**   At the time concerned, the nominal value of the company's allotted share capital must not be less than the authorised minimum (defined in section 118 of the principal Act).

3(3)   **[Shares-requirements]**   In the case of all the shares of the company, or of all those of its shares which are comprised in a portion of the share capital which satisfies the condition in subsection (2)—

(a) each share must be paid up at least as to one-quarter of the nominal value of that share and the whole of any premium on it;

(b) where any of the shares in question or any premium payable on them has been fully or partly paid up by an undertaking given by any person that he or another should do work or perform services for the company or another, the undertaking must have been performed or otherwise discharged; and

(c) where any of the shares in question has been allotted as fully or partly paid up as to its nominal value or any premium payable on it otherwise than in cash, and the consideration for the allotment consists of or includes an undertaking (other than one to which paragraph (b) applies) to the company, then either—

(i) that undertaking must have been either performed or otherwise discharged, or

(ii) there must be a contract between the company and some person pursuant to which the undertaking is to be performed within 5 years from the time of the resolution.

SEC. 4 Old public company becoming private

4(1) [Non-registration as public company — resolution] An old public company may pass a special resolution not to be re-registered under section 2 as a public company; and section 54 of the principal Act (litigated objection by shareholders) applies to the resolution as it would apply to a special resolution by a public company to be re-registered as private.

4(2) [Certificate from registrar] If either—

(a) 28 days from the passing of the resolution elapse without an application being made under section 54 of the principal Act (as applied), or

(b) such an application is made and proceedings are concluded on the application without the court making an order for the cancellation of the resolution,

the registrar of companies shall issue the company with a certificate stating that it is a private company; and the company then becomes a private company by virtue of the issue of the certificate.

4(3) [Conclusion of proceedings on application] For the purposes of subsection (2)(b), proceedings on the application are concluded—

(a) except in a case within the following paragraph, when the period mentioned in section 54(7) of the principal Act (as applied) for delivering an office copy of the court's order under that section to the registrar of companies has expired, or

(b) when the company has been notified that the application has been withdrawn.

4(4) [Certificate from registrar] If an old public company delivers to the registrar of companies a statutory declaration in the prescribed form by a director or secretary of the company that the company does not at the time of the declaration satisfy the conditions specified in section 3 for the company to be re-registered as public, the registrar shall issue the company with a certificate stating that it is a private company; and the company then becomes a private company by virtue of the issue of the certificate.

4(5) [Certificate under sec. 4(2), (4) conclusive evidence] A certificate issued to a company under subsection (2) or (4) is conclusive evidence that the requirements of that subsection have been complied with and that the company is a private company.

SEC. 5 Failure by old public company to obtain new classification

5(1) [Offence] If at any time a company which is an old public company has not delivered to the registrar of companies a declaration under section 4(4), the company and any officer of it who is in default is guilty of an offence unless at that time the company—

(a) has applied to be re-registered under section 2, and the application has not been refused or withdrawn, or

(b) has passed a special resolution not to be re-registered under that section, and the resolution has not been revoked, and has not been cancelled under section 54 of the principal Act as applied by section 4 above.

5(2) **[Penalty]** A person guilty of an offence under subsection (1) is liable on summary conviction to a fine not exceeding one-fifth of the statutory maximum or, on conviction after continued contravention, to a daily default fine not exceeding one-fiftieth of the statutory maximum for every day on which the subsection is contravened.

SEC. 6 Shares of old public company held by itself; charges on own shares

6(1) **[Effect of section]** The following has effect notwithstanding section 1(2).

6(2) **[References in sec. 146 to 149 of principal Act]** References to a public company in sections 146 to 149 of the principal Act (treatment of a company's shares when acquired by itself) do not include an old public company; and references in those sections to a private company are to be read accordingly.

6(3) **[Permitted charge]** In the case of a company which after 22nd March 1982 remained an old public company and did not before that date apply to be re-registered under section 8 of the Act of 1980 as a public company, any charge on its own shares which was in existence on or immediately before that date is a permitted charge for the purposes of Chapter V of Part V of the principal Act and accordingly not void under section 150 of that Act.

SEC. 7 (Repealed by Financial Services Act 1986, sec. 212(3) and Sch. 17, Pt. I as from 29 April 1988.)

History
In regard to the date of the above repeal see S.I. 1988 No. 740 (C. 22): s. 7 formerly read as follows:

"**SEC. 7 Offers of shares and debentures by old public company**
7 Section 81 of the principal Act applies to an old public company as if it were a private company such as is mentioned in subsection (1) of that section."

SEC. 8 Trading under misleading name

8(1) **[Offence]** An old public company is guilty of an offence if it carries on any trade, profession or business under a name which includes, as its last part, the words "public limited company" or "cwmni cyfyngedig cyhoeddus".

8(2) **[Penalty]** A company guilty of an offence under this section, and any officer of the company who is in default, is liable on summary conviction as for an offence under section 33 of the principal Act.

SEC. 9 Payment for share capital

9(1) **[Application of sections of principal Act]** Subject as follows, sections 99, 101 to 103, 106, 108 and 110 to 115 in Part IV of the principal Act apply to a company whose directors have passed and not revoked a resolution to be re-registered under section 2 of this Act, as those sections apply to a public company.

9(2) **[Non-application of sections of principal Act]** Sections 99, 101 to 103, 108 and 112 of the principal Act do not apply to the allotment of shares by a company, other than a public company registered as such on its original incorporation, where the contract for the allotment was entered into—

> (a) except in a case falling within the following paragraph, on or before 22nd June 1982;
>
> (b) in the case of a company re-registered or registered as a public company in pursuance of—
>
>> (i) a resolution to be re-registered under section 43 of the principal Act,
>>
>> (ii) a resolution to be re-registered under section 2 of this Act, or
>>
>> (iii) a resolution by a joint stock company that the company be a public company,
>>
>> being a resolution that was passed on or before 22nd June 1982, before the date on which the resolution was passed.

MISCELLANEOUS SAVINGS

SEC. 10   Pre-1901 companies limited by guarantee

10 Section 15 of the principal Act does not apply in the case of companies registered before 1st January 1901.

SEC. 11   Company official seal

11(1) **[Seal mentioned in sec. 40 of principal Act]** A company which was incorporated before 12th February 1979 and which has such an official seal as is mentioned in section 40 of the principal Act may use the seal for sealing such securities and documents as are there mentioned, notwithstanding anything in any instrument constituting or regulating the company or in any instrument made before that date which relates to any securities issued by the company.

11(2) **[Application of instruments]** Any provision of such an instrument which requires any such securities or documents to be signed shall not apply to the securities or documents if they are sealed with that seal.

SEC. 12   Share premiums: retrospective relief

12(1) **[Application of section]** The relief given by this section (being a replacement of section 39 of the Companies Act 1981) applies only where a company has issued shares in circumstances to which this section applies before 4th February 1981.

12(2) **[Shares issued at a premium]** Subject as follows, this section applies where the issuing company (that is, the company issuing shares as mentioned in section 130 of the principal Act) has issued at a premium shares which were allotted in pursuance of any arrangement providing for the allotment of shares in the issuing company on terms that the consideration for the shares allotted was to be provided by the issue or transfer to the issuing company of shares in another company or by the cancellation of any shares in that other company not held by the issuing company.

12(3)   **[Other company]**   The other company in question must either have been at the time of the arrangement a subsidiary of the issuing company or of any company which was then the issuing company's holding company or have become such a subsidiary on the acquisition or cancellation of its shares in pursuance of the arrangement.

12(4)   **[Premiums not transferred to account]**   Any part of the premiums on the shares so issued which was not transferred to the company's share premium account in accordance with section 56 of the Act of 1948 shall be treated as if that section had never applied to those premiums (and may accordingly be disregarded in determining the sum to be included in the company's share premium account).

12(5)   **[Interpretation]**   Section 133(2) and (3) of the principal Act apply for the interpretation of this section; and for the purposes of this section—

    (a) "company" (except in references to the issuing company) includes any body corporate, and

    (b) the definition of "arrangement" in section 131(7) of the principal Act applies.

12(6)   **[Regulations re relief from sec. 130 of principal Act]**   This section is deemed included in Chapter III of Part V of the principal Act for the purpose of the Secretary of State's power under section 134 of that Act to make regulations in respect of relief from the requirements of section 130 of that Act.

SEC. 13   Saving, in case of re-issued debentures, of rights of certain mortgagees

13   Whereas by section 104 of the Companies (Consolidation) Act 1908 it was provided that, upon the re-issue of redeemed debentures, the person entitled to the debentures should have the same rights and priorities as if the debentures had not previously been issued:

And whereas section 45 of the Companies Act 1928 amended section 104 of the Act of 1908 so as to provide (among other things) that the said person should have the same priorities as if the debentures had never been redeemed, but saved, in the case of debentures redeemed before, but re-issued after, 1st November 1929, the rights and priorities of persons under mortgages and charges created before that date:

Now, therefore, where any debentures which were redeemed before the date last mentioned have been re-issued after that date and before the commencement of the Act of 1948 (1st July 1948), or are or have been re-issued after that commencement, the re-issue of the debentures does not prejudice, and is deemed never to have prejudiced, any right or priority which any person would have had under or by virtue of any such mortgage or charge as above referred to if section 104 of the Act of 1908, as originally enacted, had been enacted in the Act of 1948 instead of section 90 of that Act, and in the principal Act instead of section 194 of that Act.

SEC. 14   Removal of directors appointed for life pre-1945

14   Section 303(1) of the principal Act does not, in the case of a private company, authorise the removal of a director holding office for life on 18th July 1945, whether or not subject to retirement under an age limit by virtue of the articles or otherwise.

SEC. 15   Tax-free payments to directors

15   Section 311(1) of the principal Act does not apply to remuneration under a contract which was in force on 18th July 1945 and provides expressly (and not by reference to the articles) for payment of remuneration as mentioned in that subsection; and section 311(2) does not apply to any provision contained in such a contract.

SEC. 16   Statutory declaration of solvency in voluntary winding up

16   In relation to a winding up commenced before 22nd December 1981, section 577 of the principal Act applies in the form of section 283 of the Act of 1948, without the amendment of that section made by section 105 of the Act of 1981.

SEC. 17   Court's power to control proceedings

17   Nothing in section 603 of the principal Act affects the practice or powers of the court as existing immediately before 1st November 1929, with respect to the staying of proceedings against a company registered in England and Wales and in course of being wound up.

SEC. 18   Effect of floating charge in winding up

18   In relation to a charge created before 31st December 1947, section 617(1) of the principal Act has effect with the substitution of "6 months" for "12 months".

SEC. 19   Saving from sec. 649 of principal Act

19   Nothing in section 649 of the principal Act affects the practice or powers of the court as existing immediately before 1st November 1929, with respect to the costs of an application for leave to proceed with an action or proceeding against a company which is being wound up in England and Wales.

SEC. 20   (Repealed by Banking Act 1987, sec. 108(2) and Sch. 7, Pt. I as from 1 October 1987.)

History
In regard to the date of the above repeal see S.I. 1987 No. 1664 (C. 50): s. 20 formerly read as follows:

"**SEC. 20 Continued application of certain provisions of 1963 c. 16**

20(1) The repeal by the Banking Act 1979 ("the 1979 Act") of the Protection of Depositors Act 1963 ("the 1963 Act") shall not affect, and shall be deemed never to have affected, the application of the following provisions of the 1963 Act to unexempted companies on and after the commencement of Parts I and III of the 1979 Act, that is to say—

(a)   sections 6 to 17, and

(b)   so far as relevant to the operation of those sections, sections 5 and 22 to 27.

20(2) In this section '**unexempted company**' means any company within the meaning of the 1963 Act which is not excepted by section 2(1) of the 1979 Act from the prohibition on the acceptance of deposits imposed by section 1 of the latter Act."

SEC. 21   Priority of old debts in winding up

21   Nothing in this Act affects the priority to which any person may have been entitled under section 319 of the 1948 Act in respect of a debt of any of the descriptions specified in paragraph (a)(ii) of subsection (1) of that section (which included references to profits tax and excess profits tax), or in paragraph (f) or (g) of that subsection (old workmen's compensation cases).

SEC. 22 Saving as to certain old liquidations

22(1) [Winding up provisions not to apply] The provisions of the principal Act with respect to winding up (other than sections 635, 658 and 620 as applied for the purposes of section 620 and subsection (2) below) shall not apply to any company of which the winding up commenced before 1st November 1929; but every such company shall be wound up in the same manner and with the same incidents as if the Companies Act 1929, the Act of 1948 and the principal Act (apart from the sections above-mentioned) had not passed; and, for the purposes of the winding up, the Act or Acts under which the winding up commenced shall be deemed to remain in full force.

22(2) [Copy of staying order to registrar] A copy of every order staying or sisting the proceedings in a winding up commenced as above shall forthwith be forwarded by the company, or otherwise as may be prescribed, to the registrar of companies, who shall enter the order in his records relating to the company.

SEC. 23 Restrictions on shares imposed pre-1982

23 Where before 3rd December 1981 shares in a company were directed by order of the Secretary of State to be subject to the restrictions imposed by section 174 of the Act of 1948, and the order remains in force at the commencement date, nothing in this Act prevents the continued application of the order with such effect as it had immediately before the repeal of section 174 took effect.

SEC. 24 Saving for conversion of winding up under 1981 sec. 107

24(1) [Effect of repeal of sec. 107] The repeal of section 107 of the 1981 Act (conversion of creditors' winding up into members' voluntary winding up, due to circumstances arising in the period April to August 1981) does not affect the enablement for such a conversion by means of a statutory declaration (complying with subsection (2) of the section) delivered to the registrar of companies after the commencement date.

24(2) [For purposes of sec. 577(4), 583 of principal Act] For the purposes of sections 577(4) and 583 of the principal Act (consequences of actual or prospective failure to pay debts in full within the period stated by the directors in the declaration of solvency), the period stated in the declaration in the case of a winding up converted under section 107 is taken to have been 12 months from the commencement of the winding up, unless the contrary is shown.

MISCELLANEOUS AMENDMENTS

SEC. 25 Security of information obtained for official purposes; privilege from disclosure

25 In the Insurance Companies Act 1982, after section 47 the following sections are inserted—

"Security of information

47A(1) No information or document relating to a body which has been obtained under section 44(2) to (4) above shall, without the previous consent in writing of that body, be published or disclosed, except to a competent authority, unless the publication or disclosure is required for any of the purposes specified in section 449(1)(a) to (e) of the Companies Act.

47A(2)   The competent authorities for the purposes of this section are the same as those specified in section 449 of that Act.

47(A)3   This section does not extend to Northern Ireland.

Privilege from disclosure

47B(1)   A requirement imposed under section 44(2) to (4) above shall not compel the production by any person of a document which he would in an action in the High Court or, in Scotland, in the Court of Session be entitled to refuse to produce on grounds of legal professional privilege or authorise the taking of possession of any such document which is in his possession.

47B(2)   This section does not extend to Northern Ireland."

SEC. 26   Industrial and Provident Societies Act 1967

26(1)   **[Effect of section]**   The following provisions of this section have effect with regard to the Industrial and Provident Societies Act 1967 (of which certain provisions were amended by section 10 of the Companies (Floating Charges and Receivers) (Scotland) Act 1972).

26(2)   **[Substitution of sec. 3 of 1967 Act]**   For section 3 of the Act of 1967 the following shall be substituted—

"Application to registered societies
of provisions relating to floating charges

3(1)   Subject to the following provisions of this section, the following provisions of the Companies Act 1985 relating to floating charges, namely Chapter I of Part XVIII together with sections 517(2) and 617(3) (which provisions are in this Part referred to as 'the relevant provisions') shall apply to a registered society as they apply to an incorporated company.

3(2)   Accordingly (subject as aforesaid) the relevant provisions shall, so far as applicable, apply as if—

(a) references to a company or an incorporated company were references to a registered society;

(b) references to the registrar and the registrar of companies were references to the registrar under this Act; and

(c) references, however expressed, to registration of a floating charge, or registration in accordance with Chapter II of Part XII of the Act of 1985, or delivery to or receipt by the registrar of particulars for registration, were references to the delivery to the registrar of any document required by section 4(1) of this Act to be so delivered.

3(3)   Where, in the case of a registered society, there are in existence—

(a) a floating charge created by the society under the relevant provisions as applied by this section, and

(b)   an agricultural charge created by the society under Part II of the Agricultural Credits (Scotland) Act 1929,

and any assets of the society are subject to both charges, sections 463(1)(c) and 464(4)(b) of the Act of 1985, shall have effect for the purpose of determining the ranking with one another of those charges as if the agricultural charge were a floating charge created under the relevant provisions and registered under that Act at the same time as it was registered under Part II of the Act of 1929.

3(4)   In this section, and in the following provisions of this Part of this Act, 'registered society' does not include a registered society whose registered office is situated in England and Wales.

3(5)   In their application to a registered society, the relevant provisions shall have effect with the following modifications—

(a)   in sections 462(2) and 517(2), the references to the Court of Session shall be read as references to any sheriff court;

(b)   section 462(5) shall be subject only to such provisions of the Act of 1985 as apply (by virtue of section 55 of the principal Act) to registered societies; and

(c)   in section 466, subsections (4) and (5) and the words 'subsection (4) of' in subsection (6) shall be omitted.''

26(3)   **[Continuation of sec. 4(1), (2)(a) of 1967 Act]**   Subsections (1) and (2)(a) of section 4 of the Act of 1967 continue in force as amended by paragraph (iv) of section 10 of the Companies (Floating Charges and Receivers) (Scotland) Act 1972.

26(4)   **[Substitution]**   In sections 4 and 5 of the Act of 1967, for the words "Part I of the Act of 1972" there shall be substituted the words "the relevant provisions of the Companies Act 1985".

SEC. 27   Amendment of Table A

27   In Table A scheduled to the Companies (Alteration of Table A etc.) Regulations 1984, for the words "the Acts", wherever they occur, there shall be substituted the words "the Act"; and in regulation 1 of the Table (definitions) for "Companies Acts 1948 to 1983" there shall be substituted "Companies Act 1985".

Note
Now see The Companies (Tables A to F) Regulations 1985
(S.I. 1985 No. 805).

REPEAL OF OBSOLETE PROVISIONS

SEC. 28   Stannaries and cost-book companies

28   In the Act of 1948, the following enactments shall cease to have effect—

in section 218 (courts' winding-up jurisdiction), subsection (4) and, in subsection (5), the words from "An order made under this provision" to "1896";

section 357 (attachment of debt due to contributory in stannaries court winding-up);

section 358 (preferential payments in stannaries cases);

section 359 (provisions as to mine-club funds);

in section 382 (companies not formed under 1948 Act or its predecessors, but authorised to register), in subsection (1)(b), the words "or being a company within the stannaries";

in section 384(b) and section 385(b) (documents required for registration), the words "cost-book regulations" in each paragraph;

in section 394(7) (definition of "instrument"), the words "cost-book regulations";

in section 424 (registration offices), subsection (4);

in section 434 (prohibition of partnerships with more than 20 members), in subsection (1), the words from "or is a company" to the end of the subsection;

section 450 (jurisdiction of stannaries court); and

in section 455(1) (interpretation), the definition of "the court exercising the stannaries jurisdiction" and, in the definition of "the registrar of companies", the words "or in the stannaries".

REPEALS, ETC. CONSEQUENTIAL ON COMPANIES ACTS CONSOLIDATION; CONTINUITY OF LAW

SEC. 29　Repeals

29　The enactments specified in the second column of Schedule 1 to this Act are repealed to the extent specified in the third column of the Schedule.

SEC. 30　Amendment of post-1948 statutes

30　The enactments specified in the first column of Schedule 2 to this Act (being enactments passed after the Act of 1948 and containing references to that Act or others of the Companies Acts 1948 to 1983) are amended as shown in the second column of the Schedule.

SEC. 31　Continuity of law

31(1)　**[Definitions]**　In this section—

　(a) **"the new Acts"** means the principal Act, the Company Securities (Insider Dealing) Act 1985, the Business Names Act 1985 and this Act;

　(b) **"the old Acts"** means the Companies Acts 1948 to 1983 and any other enactment which is repealed by this Act and replaced by a corresponding provision in the new Acts; and

　(c) **"the commencement date"** means 1st July 1985.

31(2)　**[Anything done or treated as done under old Acts]**　So far as anything done or treated as done under or for the purposes of any provision of the old Acts could have been done under or for the purposes of the corresponding provision of the new Acts, it is not invalidated by the repeal of that provision but has effect as if done under or for the purposes of the corresponding provision; and any order, regulation or other instrument made or having effect under any provision of the old Acts shall, in so far as its effect is preserved by this subsection, be treated for all purposes as made and having effect under the corresponding provision.

31(3) [Periods of time in old Acts] Where any period of time specified in a provision of the old Acts is current immediately before the commencement date, the new Acts have effect as if the corresponding provision had been in force when the period began to run; and (without prejudice to the foregoing) any period of time so specified and current is deemed for the purposes of the new Acts—

(a) to run from the date or event from which it was running immediately before the commencement date, and

(b) to expire (subject to any provision of the new Acts for its extension) whenever it would have expired if the new Acts had not been passed;

and any rights, priorities, liabilities, reliefs, obligations, requirements, powers, duties or exemptions dependent on the beginning, duration or end of such a period as above mentioned shall be under the new Acts as they were or would have been under the old.

31(4) [References to provisions of new Acts] Where in any provision of the new Acts there is a reference to another provision of those Acts, and the first-mentioned provision operates, or is capable of operating, in relation to things done or omitted, or events occurring or not occurring, in the past (including in particular past acts of compliance with any enactment, failures of compliance, contraventions, offences and convictions of offences), the reference to that other provision is to be read as including a reference to the corresponding provision of the old Acts.

31(5) [Effect of contravention of old Acts before commencement date] A contravention of any provision of the old Acts committed before the commencement date shall not be visited with any severer punishment under or by virtue of the new Acts than would have been applicable under that provision at the time of the contravention; but—

(a) where an offence for the continuance of which a penalty was provided has been committed under any provision of the old Acts, proceedings may be taken under the new Acts in respect of the continuance of the offence after the commencement date in the like manner as if the offence had been committed under the corresponding provision of the new Acts; and

(b) the repeal of any transitory provision of the old Acts (not replaced by any corresponding provision of the new Acts) requiring a thing to be done within a certain time does not affect a person's continued liability to be prosecuted and punished in respect of the failure, or continued failure, to do that thing.

31(6) [Interpretation of references to old provisions] A reference in any enactment, instrument or document (whether express or implied, and in whatever phraseology) to a provision (whether first in force before or after the Act of 1948 or contained in that Act) which is replaced by a corresponding provision of the new Acts is to be read, where necessary to retain for the enactment, instrument or document the same force and effect as it would have had but for the passing of the new Acts, as, or as including, a reference to that corresponding provision.

31(7) [Effect off sec. 31(6)] The generality of subsection (6) is not affected by any specific conversion of references made by this Act, nor by the inclusion in any provision of the new Acts of a reference (whether express or implied, and in whatever phraseology) to the provision of the old Acts corresponding to that provision, or to a provision of the old Acts which is replaced by a corresponding provision of the new.

31(8) [Effect of new Acts]   Nothing in the new Acts affects—

(a) the registration or re-registration of any company under the former Companies Acts, or the continued existence of any company by virtue of such registration or re-registration; or

(b) the application of—

(i) Table B in the Joint Stock Companies Act 1856, or

(ii) Table A in the Companies Act 1862, the Companies (Consolidation) Act 1908, the Companies Act 1929 or the Companies Act 1948,

to any company existing immediately before the commencement date; or

(c) the operation of any enactment providing for any partnership, association or company being wound up, or being wound up as a company or as an unregistered company under any of the former Companies Acts.

31(9)   [Savings from repeal of sec. 459 of 1948 Act]   Anything saved from repeal by section 459 of the Act of 1948 and still in force immediately before the commencement date remains in force notwithstanding the repeal of the whole of that Act.

31(10)   [Provisions of new Acts previously in statutory instruments]   Where any provision of the new Acts was, immediately before the commencement date, contained in or given effect by a statutory instrument (whether or not made under a power in any of the old Acts), then—

(a) the foregoing provisions of this section have effect as if that provision was contained in the old Acts, and

(b) insofar as the provision was, immediately before that date, subject to a power (whether or not under the old Acts) of variation or revocation, nothing in the new Acts is to be taken as prejudicing any future exercise of the power.

31(11)   [Without prejudice]   The provisions of this section are without prejudice to the operation of sections 16 and 17 of the Interpretation Act 1978 (savings from, and effect of, repeals); and for the purposes of section 17(2) of that Act (construction of references to enactments repealed and replaced; continuity of powers preserved in repealing enactment), any provision of the old Acts which is replaced by a provision of the principal Act, the Company Securities (Insider Dealing) Act 1985 or the Business Names Act 1985 is deemed to have been repealed and re-enacted by that one of the new Acts and not by this Act.

GENERAL

SEC. 32   Interpretation

32   In this Act—

"**the Act of 1948**" means the Companies Act 1948,

"**the Act of 1980**" means the Companies Act 1980,

"**the Act of 1981**" means the Companies Act 1981, and

"the principal Act" means the Companies Act 1985;

and expressions used in this Act and also in the principal Act have the same meanings in this Act as in that (the provisions of Part XXVI of that Act to apply accordingly).

SEC. 33   Northern Ireland

33   Except in so far as it has effect for maintaining the continuity of the law, or—

(a)   repeals any enactment which extends to Northern Ireland, or

(b)   amends any enactment which extends to Northern Ireland (otherwise than by the insertion of provisions expressed not so to extend),

nothing in this Act extends to Northern Ireland.

SEC. 34   Commencement

34   This Act comes into force on 1st July 1985.

SEC. 35   Citation

35   This Act may be cited as the Companies Consolidation (Consequential Provisions) Act 1985.

Schedule 1 — Enactments Repealed

Section 29

Chapter	Short title	Extent of repeal
1948 c. 38.	Companies Act 1948.	The whole Act.
1952 c. 33.	Finance Act 1952.	In section 30, subsections (2) and (3); in subsection (5) the words "(2) or (3)"; and in subsection (6) the words from "and subsection (3)" to the end.
1961 c. 46.	Companies (Floating Charges) (Scotland) Act 1961.	Section 7.
1966 c. 18.	Finance Act 1966.	In Schedule 6, in paragraph 14, the words "section 319(1)(a)(ii) of the Companies Act 1948 and in".
1966 c. 29.	Singapore Act 1966.	In the Schedule, paragraph 14.
1967 c. 81.	Companies Act 1967.	The whole Act, except so much of Part II as remains unrepealed immediately before the commencement of this Act.
1970 c. 8.	Insolvency Services (Accounting and Investment) Act 1970.	In section 1(3), paragraph (c) (with the "and" immediately preceding it).
1972 c. 67.	Companies (Floating Charges and Receivers) (Scotland) Act 1972.	The whole Act.
1972 c. 68.	European Communities Act 1972.	Section 9.
1973 c. 38.	Social Security Act 1973.	In Schedule 27, paragraph 9.
1973 c. 48.	Pakistan Act 1973.	In Schedule 3, paragraph 3(1) and (4).
1973 c. 51.	Finance Act 1973.	In Schedule 19, paragraph 14.
1974 c. 37.	Health and Safety at Work Etc. Act 1974.	Section 79.
1975 c. 18.	Social Security (Consequential Provisions) Act 1975.	In Schedule 2, paragraph 7.
1975 c. 45.	Finance (No. 2) Act 1975.	In Part IV of Schedule 12, paragraph 6(1)(e).
1975 c. 60.	Social Security Pensions Act 1975.	In Schedule 4, paragraph 3.

Chapter	Short title	Extent of repeal
1976 c. 47.	Stock Exchange (Completion of Bargains) Act 1976.	Sections 1 to 4. Section 7(3).
1976 c. 60.	Insolvency Act 1976.	In section 1(1), the words "the winding up of companies and". Section 9. Section 14(3). In section 14(6), the word "9". In Part I of Schedule 1, the heading "The Companies Act 1948" and the entries under that heading; and in Part II of that Schedule in paragraph 1, sub-paragraph (c), in paragraph 2, sub-paragraph (c), paragraph 6, and in paragraph 7, sub-paragraph (b). In Schedule 2, paragraphs 3 and 4.
1976 c. 69.	Companies Act 1976.	The whole Act.
1979 c. 53.	Charging Orders Act 1979.	In section 4, the words "and in section 325 of the Companies Act 1948", and the words "in each case".
1980 c. 22.	Companies Act 1980.	The whole Act.
1981 c. 54.	Supreme Court Act 1981.	In Schedule 5, the entry relating to the Companies Act 1948.
1981 c. 62.	Companies Act 1981.	The whole Act.
1981 c. 63.	Betting and Gaming Duties Act 1981.	In section 30(1), the word "or" at the end of paragraph (b), and paragraph (c). In section 30(2), paragraph (c).
1981 c. 65.	Trustee Savings Banks Act 1981.	In Schedule 6, the entry under "COMPANIES ACT 1948".
1982 c. 4.	Stock Transfer Act 1982.	In Schedule 2, paragraphs 4 and 5.
1982 c. 46.	Employment Act 1982.	Section 1.
1982 c. 48.	Criminal Justice Act 1982.	In section 46(4)(a) the words from "except" to "1981".
1982 c. 50.	Insurance Companies Act 1982.	In Schedule 4, paragraph 14.
1983 c. 50.	Companies (Beneficial Interests) Act 1983.	The whole Act.

Chapter	Short title	Extent of repeal
1983 c. 53.	Car Tax Act 1983.	In Schedule 1, in paragraph 4(1), the word "or" at the end of sub-paragraph (b), and sub-paragraph (c); and in that Schedule, in paragraph 4(2), sub-paragraph (c).
1983 c. 55.	Value Added Tax Act 1983.	In Schedule 7, in paragraph 12(1), the word "or" at the end of sub-paragraph (b); and sub-paragraph (c), and in that Schedule, in paragraph 12(2), sub-paragraph (c).

Schedule 2 — Amendments of Enactments Consequential on Consolidation of Companies Acts

Section 30

Enactment	Amendment
Landlord and Tenant Act 1954 (c. 56):	
Section 42(1)	For the words from "Companies Act 1948" to the end of the subsection substitute "Companies Act 1985 by section 736 of that Act".
Opticians Act 1958 (c. 32):	
Section 27(3)	For "paragraph (a) of subsection (1) of section one hundred and sixty-one of the Companies Act 1948 by the Board of Trade" substitute "section 389(1)(a) of the Companies Act 1985 by the Secretary of State".
Agricultural Marketing Act 1958 (c. 47):	
Schedule 2	(a) In paragraph 4(1) for "Part IX of the Companies Act 1948" substitute "Part XXI of the Companies Act 1985".
	(b) In paragraph 4(2), for "section three hundred and ninety-nine of the Companies Act 1948" substitute "sections 666 to 669 of the Companies Act 1985".

Enactment	Amendment
Horticultural Act 1960 (c. 22):	
Section 14(3) … … … … …	(c) For paragraph 4(3) substitute— "(3) Section 668 shall not apply, and section 669 shall apply as if in paragraph (a) of that section the words "or any member of it as such" were omitted.".
Corporate Bodies' Contracts Act 1960 (c. 46):	
Section 2 … … … … …	For "paragraph (a) of subsection (1) of section one hundred and sixty-one of the Companies Act 1948 by the Board of Trade" substitute "section 389(1)(a) of the Companies Act 1985 by the Secretary of State".
Charities Act 1960 (c. 58):	For "Companies Act 1948" substitute "Companies Act 1985".
Section 8(3) … … … … …	For "paragraph (a) of subsection (1) of section one hundred and sixty-one of the Companies Act 1948 by the Board of Trade" substitute "section 389(1)(a) of the Companies Act 1985 by the Secretary of State".
Section 30(1)	For "Companies Act 1948" substitute "Companies Act 1985".
Professions Supplementary to Medicine Act 1960 (c. 66):	
Schedule 1, Part III … … …	In paragraph 18(4), for "paragraph (a) of subsection (1) of section one hundred and sixty-one of the Companies Act 1948 by the Board of Trade" substitute "section 389(1)(a) of the Companies Act 1985 by the Secretary of State".
Transport Act 1962 (c. 46):	
Section 24(2) … … … …	For "paragraph (a) of subsection (1) of section one hundred and sixty-one of the Companies Act 1948 by the Board of Trade" substitute "section 389(1)(a) of the Companies Act 1985 by the Secretary of State".
Section 92 … … … …	In the definition of "subsidiary", for "section one hundred and fifty-four of the Companies Act 1948" substitute "section 736 of the Companies Act 1985".
Betting, Gaming and Lotteries Act 1963 (c. 2):	
Section 55(1) … … … …	In the definition of "qualified accountant", for "section 161(1)(a) of the Companies Act 1948 by the Board of Trade" substitute "section 389(1)(a) of the Companies Act 1985 by the Secretary of State".
Schedule 2 … … … …	(a) In paragraph 24(1), for "section 1 of the Companies Act 1976" substitute "section 241 of the Companies Act 1985".

Enactment	Amendment
	(b) In paragraph 24(2), for "section 14(3), (4) and (6) of the Companies Act 1967" substitute — "the following provisions of the Companies Act 1985 — section 236(2), as read with section 262 (matters to be stated in auditors' report), and section 237(1) and (4) (responsibilities of auditors in preparing their report)".
Stock Transfer Act 1963 (c. 18): Section 1(4) ... ... Section 2	In paragraph (a), for "Companies Act 1948" substitute "Companies Act 1985". (a) In subsection (2), for "section 79(1) of the Companies Act 1948" substitute "section 184 of the Companies Act 1985". (b) In subsection (3)(a), for "section 75 of the Companies Act 1948" substitute "section 183(1) and (2) of the Companies Act 1985".
Harbours Act 1964 (c. 40): Section 42	(a) In subsection (6), for "Companies Act 1948 to 1981" substitute "Companies Act 1985"; and for "those Acts" substitute "that Act". (b) In subsection (7)(a), for "Companies Acts 1948 to 1981" substitute "Companies Act 1985". (c) In subsection (9), for "section 154 of the Companies Act 1948" substitute "section 736 of the Companies Act 1985".
Trading Stamps Act 1964 (c. 71): Section 1(4)	For "Companies Act 1948" substitute "Companies Act 1985".
Hairdressers (Registration) Act 1964 (c. 89): Section 13(2)	For "section 161(1)(a) of the Companies Act 1948 by the Board of Trade" substitute "section 389(1)(a) of the Companies Act 1985 by the Secretary of State".
Industrial and Provident Societies Act 1965 (c. 12): Section 1(2) ... ... Section 52(2) ... ... Section 53	For "Companies Act 1948" substitute "Companies Act 1985". The same amendment; and for "Act of 1948" substitute "Act of 1985". (a) In subsection (1), for "section 141 of the Companies Act 1948" substitute "section 378 of the Companies Act 1985". (b) In subsection (4), for "Companies Act 1948" substitute "Companies Act 1985".

Enactment	Amendment
Section 55	For "Companies Act 1948" substitute "Companies Act 1985".
Section 74	In the definition of "Companies Acts", the same amendment.
Cereals Marketing Act 1965 (c. 14):	
Section 21(5) ...	In paragraph (b), for "section 161(1)(a) of the Companies Act 1948 by the Board of Trade" substitute "section 389(1)(a) of the Companies Act 1985 by the Secretary of State".
Teaching Council (Scotland) Act 1965 (c. 19):	
Schedule 1 ...	In paragraph 13(3), for "section 161(1)(a) of the Companies Act 1948 by the Board of Trade" substitute "section 389(1)(a) of the Companies Act 1985 by the Secretary of State".
Coal Industry Act 1965 (c. 82):	
Section 1(2)	In paragraph (d), for "section 154 of the Companies Act 1948" substitute "section 736 of the Companies Act 1985".
National Health Service Act 1966 (c. 8):	
Section 8(2)	In paragraph (e), for "section 161(1)(a) of the Companies Act 1948 by the Board of Trade" substitute "section 389(1)(a) of the Companies Act 1985 by the Secretary of State".
Universities (Scotland) Act 1966 (c. 13):	
Section 12(2)	In paragraph (e), for "section 161(1)(a) of the Companies Act 1948 by the Board of Trade" substitute "section 389(1)(a) of the Companies Act 1985 by the Secretary of State".
General Rate Act 1967 (c. 9):	
Section 32A(6)	In the definition of "subsidiary", for "section 154 of the Companies Act 1948" substitute "section 736 of the Companies Act 1985".
Agriculture Act 1967 (c. 22):	
Section 19(3)	For "section 161(1)(a) of the Companies Act 1948 by the Board of Trade" substitute "section 389(1)(a) of the Companies Act 1985 by the Secretary of State".
Development of Inventions Act 1967 (c. 32):	
Section 12(3)	For "section 161(1)(a) of the Companies Act 1948 by the Board of Trade" substitute "section 389(1)(a) of the Companies Act 1985 by the Secretary of State".
Companies Act 1967 (c. 81):	

Enactment	Amendment
Section 90	For this section substitute the following—

For this section substitute the following—

"*Summary proceedings*

90(1) Summary proceedings for an offence under this Part may (without prejudice to any jurisdiction exercisable apart from this subsection) be taken against a body corporate at any place at which the body has a place of business, and against any other person at any place at which he is for the time being.

90(2) Notwithstanding anything in section 127(1) of the Magistrates' Courts Act 1980, an information relating to an offence under this Part which is triable by a magistrates' court in England and Wales may be so tried if it is laid at any time within 3 years after the commission of the offence and within 12 months after the date on which evidence sufficient in the opinion of the Director of Public Prosecutions, the Secretary of State or the Industrial Assurance Commissioner (as the case may be) to justify the proceedings comes to his knowledge.

90(3) Summary proceedings in Scotland for an offence under this part shall not be commenced after the expiration of 3 years from the commission of the offence.

Subject to this (and notwithstanding anything in section 331 of the Criminal Procedure (Scotland) Act 1975), such proceedings may (in Scotland) be commenced at any time within 12 months after the date on which evidence sufficient in the Lord Advocate's opinion to justify the proceedings comes to his knowledge or, where such evidence was reported to him by the Secretary of State or the Industrial Assurance Commissioner, within 12 months after the date on which it came to the knowledge of the former or the latter (as the case may be); and subsection (3) of that section applies for the purpose of this subsection as it applies for the purposes of that section.

90(4) For purposes of this section, a certificate of the Director of Public Prosecutions, the Lord Advocate, the Secretary of State or the Industrial Assurance Commissioner (as the case may be) as to the date on which such evidence came to his knowledge is conclusive evidence."

Hearing Aid Council Act 1968 (c. 50):
Section 12(3)   ...   .

For "Board of Trade for the purposes of paragraph (a) of subsection (1) of section 161 of the Companies Act 1948" substitute "Secretary of State for the purposes of section 389(1)(a) of the Companies Act 1985".

Enactment	Amendment
Friendly and Industrial and Provident Societies Act 1968 (c. 55):	
Section 7(1) … … … …	For "section 161(1)(a) of the Companies Act 1948 by the Board of Trade" substitute "section 389(1)(a) of the Companies Act 1985 by the Secretary of State"; and for "by the Board of Trade under section 161(1)(b)" substitute "by the Secretary of State under section 389(1)(b)".
Section 8(2) … … …	In paragraph (b), for "section 161(2) of the Companies Act 1948" substitute "section 389(6) of the Companies Act 1985".
Transport Act 1968 (c. 73):	
Section 14(2) … … …	For "section 161(1)(a) of the Companies Act 1948 by the Board of Trade" substitute "section 389(1)(a) of the Companies Act 1985 by the Secretary of State".
Section 69(11) … … …	For "section 154(5) of the Companies Act 1948" substitute "section 744 of the Companies Act 1985".
Section 92(1) … … …	In the definition of "subsidiary", for "section 154 of the Companies Act 1948" substitute "section 736 of the Companies Act 1985".
Post Office Act 1969 (c. 48):	
Section 86(2) … … …	For "section 154 of the Companies Act 1948" substitute "section 736 of the Companies Act 1985"; and for "section 150(4)" substitute "section 736(5)(b)".
Development of Tourism Act 1969 (c. 51):	
Section 14(2) … … …	For "section 154 of the Companies Act 1948" substitute "section 736 of the Companies Act 1985".
Taxes Management Act 1970 (c. 9):	
Section 108(2) … … …	For "Companies Act 1948" substitute "Companies Act 1985".
Income and Corporation Taxes Act 1970 (c. 10):	
Section 64A … … …	For "proviso (b) to section 54(1) of the Companies Act 1948" substitute "section 153(4)(b) of the Companies Act 1985".
Section 242(1) … … …	For "Companies Act 1948" substitute "Companies Act 1985".
Section 247(7) … … …	The same amendment.
Section 265(5) … … …	For "section 244 of the Companies Act 1948" substitute "section 538 of the Companies Act 1985".
Section 272(2) … … …	For "Companies Act 1948" substitute "Companies Act 1985".

Enactment	Amendment
Section 280(3)	For "section 66 of the Companies Act 1948" substitute "section 135 of the Companies Act 1985".
Section 343(9)	For "Companies Act 1948" substitute "Companies Act 1985".
Section 482(10)	For "section 455 of the Companies Act 1948" substitute "Part XXVI of the Companies Act 1985".
Agriculture Act 1970 (c. 40):	
Section 20(2)	For "section 161(1)(a) of the Companies Act 1948 by the Board of Trade" substitute "section 389(1)(a) of the Companies Act 1985 by the Secretary of State".
Section 24(3)	For "Companies Act 1948" substitute "Companies Act 1985".
Atomic Energy Authority Act 1971 (c. 11):	
Section 14	For "Companies Acts 1948 to 1967" substitute "Companies Act 1985".
Coal Industry Act 1971 (c. 16):	
Section 10(3)	For "section 154 of the Companies Act 1948" substitute "section 736 of the Companies Act 1985"; and for "subsection (4) of section 150 of that Act" substitute "subsection (5)(b) of that section".
Redemption of Standard Securities (Scotland) Act 1971 (c. 45):	
Section 2	For "section 89 of the Companies Act 1948" substitute "section 193 of the Companies Act 1985".
Investment and Building Grants Act 1971 (c. 51):	
Section 1(7)	For "section 154 of the Companies Act 1948" substitute "section 736 of the Companies Act 1985".
Prevention of Oil Pollution Act 1971 (c. 60):	
Section 15	(a) In subsection (1), for "section 412 or section 437 of the Companies Act 1948" substitute "section 695 or section 725 of the Companies Act 1985".
	(b) In subsection (3), for "sections 412 and 437 of the Companies Act 1948" substitute "sections 695 and 725 of the Companies Act 1985".
Finance Act 1971 (c. 68):	
Section 31(4)	For "section 30 of the Finance Act 1952" substitute "section 614 of the Companies Act 1985 (with paragraph 3 of Schedule 19 to that Act)".

Enactment	Amendment
Finance Act 1972 (c. 41): Schedule 16	In paragraph 13(5), for "Companies Act 1948" substitute "Companies Act 1985".
Gas Act 1972 (c. 60): Section 23(7)	For "section 161(1)(a) of the Companies Act 1948" substitute "section 389(1)(a) of the Companies Act 1985".
Section 48(1)	(a) In the definition of "company", for "Companies Act 1948" substitute "Companies Act 1985".
	(b) In the definition of "holding company", for "section 154 of the Companies Act 1948" substitute "section 736 of the Companies Act 1985".
	(c) In the definition of "subsidiary", for "section 154 of the Companies Act 1948" substitute "section 736 of the Companies Act 1985"; and for "section 150(4) of that Act" substitute "subsection (5)(b) of that section".
Land Charges Act 1972 (c. 61): Section 3(8)	Omit "and", and insert at the end of the subsection "and sections 395 to 398 of the Companies Act 1985".
Industry Act 1972 (c. 63): Section 10	For "Companies Act 1948 by section 154" substitute "Companies Act 1985 by section 736".
Coal Industry Act 1973 (c. 8): Section 12(1)	For "section 154 of the Companies Act 1948" substitute "section 736 of the Companies Act 1985"; and for "subsection (4) of section 150 of that Act" substitute "subsection (5)(b) of that section".
Fair Trading Act 1973 (c. 41): Section 92	For subsections (2) and (3) substitute — "(2) The matters which may be so specified or described are any matters which in the case of a company registered under the Companies Act 1985 (or the previous corresponding legislation)— (a) could in accordance with sections 432 and 433 of that Act be investigated by an inspector appointed under section 432, or (b) could in accordance with section 442 of that Act, or in accordance with any provisions as applied by section 443(1), be investigated by an inspector appointed under section 442.

Enactment	Amendment
	(3) For purposes connected with any investigation made by an inspector appointed under this section —
	(a) sections 434 to 436 of the Companies Act 1985 (or those sections as applied by section 443(1)) shall have effect as they do for the purposes of any investigation under section 432 or 442 of that Act, and
	(b) the provisions of that Act referred to in this and the last preceding subsection shall be taken to extend throughout the United Kingdom.".
Section 137(5) … … … …	For "section 154 of the Companies Act 1948" substitute "section 736 of the Companies Act 1985".
Hallmarking Act 1973 (c. 43):	
Schedule 4 … … … …	In paragraph 19, sub-paragraph (2), for "section 161(1)(a) of the Companies Act 1948" substitute "section 389(1)(a) of the Companies Act 1985".
Merchant Shipping Act 1974 (c. 43):	
Section 2(9) … … … …	In the definition of "group", for "section 154 of the Companies Act 1948" substitute "section 736 of the Companies Act 1985".
Friendly Societies Act 1974 (c. 46):	
Section 36(1) … … … …	For "section 161(1)(a) of the Companies Act 1948" substitute "section 389(1)(a) of the Companies Act 1985"; and for "section 161(1)(b)" substitute "section 389(1)(b)".
Section 87(2) … … … …	For "Companies Act 1948" substitute "Companies Act 1985".
Section 111(1) … … … …	For "Companies Acts 1948 to 1967" substitute "Companies Act 1985".

Enactment	Amendment
Trade Union and Labour Relations Act 1974 (c. 52):	
Section 2(2)	For "Companies Act 1948" substitute "Companies Act 1985".
Section 3(4)	For "section 434 of the Companies Act 1948" substitute "section 716 of the Companies Act 1985".
Section 4(4)	For "section 75 or 117 of the Companies Act 1948" substitute "section 183(1) or 360 of the Companies Act 1985".
Section 30(1)	In the definition of "special register body", for "Companies Act 1948" substitute "Companies Act 1985".
Schedule 2	(a) In paragraph 6, for "section 161(1)(a) of the Companies Act 1948" substitute "section 389(1)(a) of the Companies Act 1985"; and for "section 161(1)(b)" substitute "section 389(1)(b)".
	(b) In paragaph 8, for "section 161(1)(b) of the Companies Act 1948" substitute "section 389(1)(b) of the Companies Act 1985".
Finance Act 1975 (c. 7):	
Section 48(5)	In paragraph (b), for "section 154 of the Companies Act 1948" substitute "section 736 of the Companies Act 1985".
Farriers Registration Act 1975 (c. 35):	
Schedule 1, Part I	In paragraph 12(2)(e) for "section 161(1)(a) of the Companies Act 1948" substitute "section 389(1)(a) of the Companies Act 1985".
Finance (No. 2) Act 1975 (c. 45):	
Section 36(4)	For "section 150(4) of the Companies Act 1948" substitute "section 736(5)(b) of the Companies Act 1985".
Schedule 12, Part IV	In paragraph 6(1), for "Companies Act 1948" substitute "Companies Act 1985"; and —
	(a) in sub-paragraphs (a) to (d), for "107", "124", "125" and "126" substitute respectively "287", "363", "364" and "365";
	(b) omit sub-paragraph (e);
	(c) in sub-paragraphs (f) to (h), for "200(4)", "407" and "409" substitute respectively "288(2)", "691" and "692";
	(d) in sub-paragraph (i), for "section 410" substitute "Chapter II of Part XXIII"; and
	(e) in sub-paragraphs (j) and (k), for "411" and "416" substitute respectively "693" and "699".

Enactment	Amendment
Prescription and Limitation (Scotland) Act 1975 (c. 52):	
Section 9(1)	In paragraph (b), for "section 318 of the Companies Act 1948" substitute "section 613 of the Companies Act 1985".
Industry Act 1975 (c. 68):	
Section 37(1)	In the definitions of "holding company" and "subsidiary", for "section 154 of the Companies Act 1948" (twice) substitute "section 736 of the Companies Act 1985"; and in the definition of "wholly-owned subsidiary", for "section 150(4) of the Companies Act 1948" substitute "section 736(5)(b) of the Companies Act 1985".
	In paragraph 19, for "Section 209 of the Companies Act 1948" substitute "Sections 428 to 430 of the Companies Act 1985"; and for "that section" substitute those sections".
Schedule 1	
Schedule 2	In paragraph 7(2), for "section 161(1)(a) of the Companies Act 1948" substitute "section 389(1)(a) of the Companies Act 1985".
Petroleum and Submarine Pipe-lines Act 1975 (c. 74):	
Section 10(4)	For "section 161(1)(a) of the Companies Act 1948" substitute "section 389(1)(a) of the Companies Act 1985".
Section 48	For "section 154 of the Companies Act 1948" substitute "section 736 of the Companies Act 1985"; and for "section 150(4) of the said Act of 1948" substitute "section 736(5)(b) of the said Act of 1985".
Policyholders Protection Act 1975 (c. 75):	
Section 5(1)	In paragraph (a), for "Companies Act 1948" substitute "Companies Act 1985".
Section 15(1)	For "section 238 of the Companies Act 1948" substitute "section 532 of the Companies Act 1985".
Section 16	(a) In subsection (1)(b), for "Companies Act 1948" substitute "Companies Act 1985". (b) In subsection (1)(c), for "section 206 of the Companies Act 1948" substitute "section 425 of the Companies Act 1985". (c) In subsection (6), in paragraph (c) of the definition of "the relevant time", for "section 206 of the Companies Act 1948" substitute "section 425 of the Companies Act 1985".
Section 20	For subsection (8) substitute — "(8) In subsections (3) to (7) above, "company" includes any body corporate."
Section 27	For "section 111 of the Companies Act 1967" substitute "section 449 of the Companies Act 1985".

Enactment	Amendment
Section 29	The same amendment.
Schedule 1	In paragraph 14(3), for "section 161(1)(a) of the Companies Act 1948" substitute "section 389(1)(a) of the Companies Act 1985".
Airports Authority Act 1975 (c. 78):	
Section 8(2)	For "section 161(1)(a) of the Companies Act 1948" substitute "section 389(1)(a) of the Companies Act 1985".
Development Land Tax Act 1976 (c. 24):	
Section 33(1)	For "section 244 of the Companies Act 1948" substitute "section 538 of the Companies Act 1985".
Section 42(4)	For paragraph (c) substitute —
	"(c) section 614 of the Companies Act 1985, with paragraph 2 of Schedule 19 to that Act".
Theatres Trust Act 1976 (c. 27):	
Schedule	In paragraph 14, for "paragraph (a) of subsection (1) of section 161 of the Companies Act 1948" substitute "section 389(1)(a) of the Companies Act 1985".
Restrictive Trade Practices Act 1976 (c. 34):	
Section 33	For "Companies Act 1948" (twice) substitute "Companies Act 1985".
Section 43(1)	For "section 154 of the Companies Act 1948" substitute "section 736 of the Companies Act 1985".
Resale Prices Act 1976 (c. 53):	
Section 27	In the definition of "interconnected bodies corporate", for "section 154 of the Companies Act 1948" substitute "section 736 of the Companies Act 1985".
Insolvency Act 1976 (c. 60):	
Section 3(3)	In paragraph (b), for "Companies Act 1948" substitute "Companies Act 1985".
Industrial Common Ownership Act 1976 (c. 78):	
Section 2(5)	For "section 455(1) of the Companies Act 1948" substitute "section 735 of the Companies Act 1985"; and for "Companies Act 1948" (the second time) substitute "Companies Act 1985".
Dock Work Regulation Act 1976 (c. 79):	
Schedule 1	In paragraph 11(1)(e), for "section 161(1)(a) of the Companies Act 1948" substitute "section 389(1)(a) of the Companies Act 1985".

Enactment	Amendment
Nuclear Industry (Finance) Act 1977 (c. 71): Section 3	For "Companies Act 1948" substitute "Companies Act 1985".
Patents Act 1977 (c. 37): Section 88(3)	For "Companies Act 1948" substitute "Companies Act 1985".
Section 114(2)	In paragraph (a), the same amendment.
Section 131	In paragraph (d), the same amendment.
Coal Industry Act 1977 (c. 39): Section 14(1)	For "section 150(4) of the Companies Act 1948" substitute "section 736(5)(b) of the Companies Act 1985".
Insurance Brokers (Registration) Act 1977 (c. 46): Section 11(4)	For "section 161(1)(b) of the Companies Act 1948" substitute "section 389(1)(b) of the Companies Act 1985".
Section 29(1)	In the definition of "recognised body of accountants", for "section 161(1)(a) of the Companies Act 1948" substitute "section 389(1)(a) of the Companies Act 1985".
Participation Agreements Act 1978 (c. 1): Section 1(4)	For "Sections 150(4) and 154 of the Companies Act 1948" substitute "Section 736 of the Companies Act 1985".
Commonwealth Development Corporation Act 1978 (c. 2): Section 9A(6)(b)	For "section 154 of the Companies Act 1948" substitute "section 736 of the Companies Act 1985".
Shipbuilding (Redundancy Payments) Act 1978 (c. 11): Section 1(4)	For "section 154 of the Companies Act 1948" substitute "the Companies Act 1985"; and for "section 150 of the Companies Act 1948 and section 144 of" substitute "the Companies Act 1985 and".
Co-operative Development Agency Act 1978 (c. 21): Schedule 2	In paragraph 1(2), for "section 161(1)(a) of the Companies Act 1948" substitute "section 389(21)(a) of the Companies Act 1985".

Enactment	Amendment
Capital Gains Tax Act 1979 (c. 14):	
Section 9(3)	In paragraph (b), for "section 154 of the Companies Act 1948" substitute "section 736 of the Companies Act 1985".
Section 149(7)	For "Companies Act 1948" substitute "Companies Act 1985".
Credit Unions Act 1979 (c. 34):	
Section 6(1)	For "section 222(d) of the Companies Act 1948" substitute "section 517(1)(e) of the Companies Act 1985"; and after the word "seven" insert "(or, in the case of section 517(1)(e) of the Act of 1985, for the word 'two')".
Nurses, Midwives and Health Visitors Act 1979 (c. 36):	
Schedule 4	In paragraph 3, for "section 161(1)(a) of the Companies Act 1948" substitute "section 389(1)(a) of the Companies Act 1985".
Estate Agents Act 1979 (c. 38):	
Section 14	(a) In subsection (6) —
	(i) in paragraph (a), for "section 161(1)(a) of the Companies Act 1948" substitute "section 389(1)(a) of the Companies Act 1985";
	(ii) in paragraph (b), for "section 161(1)(b) of the Companies Act 1948" substitute "section 389(1)(b) of the Companies Act 1985"; and
	(iii) in paragraph (c), for "section 13(1) of the Companies Act 1967" substitute "section 389(2) of the Companies Act 1985".
	(b) In subsection (7), for "by subsection (2), subsection (3) or subsection (4) of either section 161 of the Companies Act 1948 or" substitute "either by subsection (6), subsection (7) or subsection (8) of section 389 of the Companies Act 1985 or by subsection (2), subsection (3) or subsection (4) of".
Crown Agents Act 1979 (c. 43):	
Section 22(6)	For "section 161(1)(a) of the Companies Act 1948" substitute "section 389(1)(a) of the Companies Act 1985".
Section 31	In the definition of "subsidiary", for "section 154 of the Companies Act 1948" substitute "section 736 of the Companies Act 1985"; and in the definition of "wholly-owned subsidiary", for "section 150(4) of the Companies Act 1948" substitute "section 736(5)(b) of the Companies Act 1985".

Enactment	Amendment
Competition Act 1980 (c. 21):	
Section 11(3)	In paragraph (f), for "Companies Act 1948" substitute "Companies Act 1985".
Section 12(4)	The same amendment.
British Aerospace Act 1980 (c. 26):	
Section 3(3)	In paragraph (b), for "Companies Acts 1948 to 1980" substitute "Companies Act 1985".
Section 4	(a) In subsection (3), for "section 40(2)(d) of the Companies Act 1980" substitute "section 264(3)(d) of the Companies Act 1985"; and for "section 40(2)(c)" substitute "section 264(3)(c)".
	(b) In subsection (7), for "Companies Acts 1948 to 1980" substitute "Companies Act 1985".
Section 9(1)	In paragraph (a), for "Companies Act 1948" substitute "Companies Act 1985".
Industry Act 1980 (c. 33):	
Section 2(4)	For "section 154 of the Companies Act 1948" substitute "section 736 of the Companies Act 1985".
Section 3	(a) In subsection (5), for "Companies Acts 1948 to 1980" substitute "Companies Act 1985".

Enactment	Amendment
Transport Act 1980 (c. 34):	
Section 47	(b) In subsection (7), for "Companies Act 1948" substitute "Companies Act 1985"; and for "section 154 of the said Act of 1948" substitute "section 736 of the said Act of 1985".
Section 48(4)	(a) In subsection (2), for "section 56 of the Companies Act 1948" substitute "section 130 of the Companies Act 1985". (b) In subsection (5), the same amendment. For "section 161(1)(a) of the Companies Act 1948" substitute "section 389(1)(a) of the Companies Act 1985".
Education (Scotland) Act 1980 (c. 44):	
Section 111(3)	In paragraph (e), for "section 161(1)(a) of the Companies Act 1948" substitute "section 389(1)(a) of the Companies Act 1985".
Finance Act 1980 (c. 48):	
Schedule 10	(a) In paragraph 10(1)(b), for "section 206 of the Companies Act 1948" substitute "section 425 of the Companies Act 1985". (b) In paragraph 10(1)(c), for "section 209 of the said Act of 1948" substitute "sections 428 to 430 of the said Act of 1985".
Civil Aviation Act 1980 (c. 60):	
Section 4(3)	In paragraph (b), for "Companies Acts 1948 to 1980" substitute "Companies Act 1985".
Section 5(5)	The same amendment.
Local Government Planning and Land Act 1980 (c. 65):	
Section 100(1)	For "section 150(4) of the Companies Act 1948" substitute "section 736(5)(b) of the Companies Act 1985". The same amendment.
Section 141(7)	
Section 170	(a) In subsection (1)(d), the same amendment. (b) In subsection (2), the same amendment.
Schedule 31	In paragraph 11(2), for "section 161 of the Companies Act 1948" substitute "section 389 of the Companies Act 1985".
English Industrial Estates Corporation Act 1981 (c. 13):	

Enactment	Amendment
Section 7(3)	For "section 161(1)(a) of the Companies Act 1948" substitute "section 389(1)(a) of the Companies Act 1985".
National Film Finance Corporation Act 1981 (c. 15):	
Section 7(3)	For "section 161(1)(a) of the Companies Act 1948" substitute "section 389(1)(a) of the Companies Act 1985".
Schedule 2	In paragraph 3(3), for "Companies Act 1948" substitute "Companies Act 1985".
Film Levy Finance Act 1981 (c. 16):	
Schedule 1	In paragraph 7(3), for "section 161(1)(a) of the Companies Act 1948" substitute "section 389(1)(a) of the Companies Act 1985".
Licensing (Alcohol Education and Research) Act 1981 (c. 28):	
Section 10(2)	In paragraph (a), for "section 161(1)(a) of the Companies Act 1948" substitute "section 389(1)(a) of the Companies Act 1985".
Finance Act 1981 (c. 35):	
Section 55(4)	For "Companies Act 1948" substitute "Companies Act 1985".
British Telecommunications Act 1981 (c. 38):	
Section 85(2)	For "section 154 of the Companies Act 1948" substitute "section 736 of the Companies Act 1985"; and for "section 150(4) of that Act" substitute "subsection (5)(b) of that section".
Supreme Court Act 1981 (c. 54):	
Section 40A(2)	For "section 325 of the Companies Act 1948" substitute "section 621 of the Companies Act 1985".
Transport Act 1981 (c. 56):	
Section 11	(a) In subsection (2), for "sections 39 and 40 of the Companies Act 1980" substitute "sections 263 and 264 of the Companies Act 1985". (b) In subsection (3), for "40" substitute "264". (c) In subsection (4), for "section 157(1) of the Companies Act 1948" substitute "section 235 of the Companies Act 1985".
Section 13(6)	For "Companies Act 1948" substitute "Companies Act 1985".
Section 14(3)	In the definition of "subsidiary", for "section 154 of the Companies Act 1948" substitute "section 736 of the Companies Act 1985".

Enactment	Amendment
New Towns Act 1981 (c. 64): Section 68(2)	For "paragraph (a) of section 161(1) of the Companies Act 1948" substitute "section 389(1)(a) of the Companies Act 1985".
Trustee Savings Banks Act 1981 (c. 65): Section 24(2)	For "section 161(1)(a) of the Companies Act 1948" substitute "section 389(1)(a) of the Companies Act 1985"; and for "section 161(1)(b) of that Act of 1948" substitute "section 389(1)(b) of that Act of 1985".
Section 31	In paragraph (b), for "section 399 of the Companies Act 1948" substitute "sections 666 to 669 of the Companies Act 1985".
Section 54	(a) In subsection (1), in the definition of "subsidiary", for "section 154 of the Companies Act 1948" substitute "section 736 of the Companies Act 1985".
	(b) In subsection (2), for "section 399(8) of the Companies Act 1948" substitute "section 666(6) of the Companies Act 1985".
Schedule 2	In paragraph 16(2), for "section 161(1)(a) of the Companies Act 1948" substitute "section 389(1)(a) of the Companies Act 1985"; and for "section 161(1)(b) of that Act of 1948" substitute "section 389(1)(b) of that Act of 1985".
Broadcasting Act 1981 (c. 68): Section 12(4)	For "section 154 of the Companies Act 1948" substitute "section 736 of the Companies Act 1985".
Section 42(2)	For "section 161(1)(a) of the Companies Act 1948" substitute "section 389(1)(a) of the Companies Act 1985".
Section 63(1)	In the definition of "associate", for "section 154 of the Companies Act 1948" substitute "section 736 of the Companies Act 1985".
Schedule 7	In paragraph 8(2), for "section 161(1)(a) of the Companies Act 1948" substitute "section 389(1)(a) of the Companies Act 1985".
Agricultural Training Board Act 1982 (c. 9): Section 8(2)	In paragraph (e), for "section 161(1)(a) of the Companies Act 1948" substitute "section 389(1)(a) of the Companies Act 1985".
Industrial Training Act 1982 (c. 10): Section 8(2)	In paragraph (e), for "section 161(1)(a) of the Companies Act 1948" substitute "section 389(1)(a) of the Companies Act 1985".
Civil Aviation Act 1982 (c. 16):	

Enactment	Amendment
Section 15(2)(a)	For "section 161(1)(a) of the Companies Act 1948" substitute "section 389(1)(a) of the Companies Act 1985".
Section 23(3)	For "Companies Act 1948" substitute "Companies Act 1985"; and for "section 407(1)(c) of the said Act of 1948" substitute "section 691(1)(b)(ii) of the said Act of 1985".
Section 105(1)	In the definition of "subsidiary", for "section 154 of the Companies Act 1948" substitute "section 736 of the Companies Act 1985".
Oil and Gas (Enterprise) Act 1982 (c. 23):	
Section 2	(a) In subsection (4), for "section 56 of the Companies Act 1948" substitute "section 130 of the Companies Act 1985"; for "Part III of the Companies Act 1980" substitute "Part VIII of the Companies Act 1985"; and for "the said section 56" substitute "the said section 130".
	(b) In subsection (8), for "Companies Acts 1948 to 1981" substitute "Companies Act 1985".
Section 10	(a) In subsection (4), for "section 56 of the Companies Act 1948" substitute "section 130 of the Companies Act 1985"; for "Part III of the Companies Act 1980" substitute "Part VIII of the Companies Act 1985"; and for "the said section 56" substitute "the said section 130".
	(b) In subsection (8), for "Companies Acts 1948 to 1981" substitute "Companies Act 1985".
Iron and Steel Act 1982 (c. 25):	
Section 24	(a) In subsection (3), for "section 161(1)(a) of the Companies Act 1948" substitute "section 389(1)(a) of the Companies Act 1985".
	(b) In subsection (4)(b), for the words from "the Companies Act 1948 (as amended" to "this Act)" substitute "the Companies Act 1985".
	(c) In subsection (5), for "section 157 of the Companies Act 1948" substitute "section 235 of the Companies Act 1985".
Section 37	(a) In the definition of "company", for "Companies Act 1948" substitute "Companies Act 1985".
	(b) In the definition of "subsidiary", for "section 154 of the Companies Act 1948" substitute "section 736 of the Companies Act 1985".

Enactment	Amendment
Schedule 4	(a) Throughout the Schedule, for "the Companies Acts 1948 to 1980", "the Companies Act 1948" and "the Companies Act 1967" substitute "the Companies Act"; and at the end of paragraph 1 insert "(which in this Schedule means the Companies Act 1985)".
	(b) In paragraph 2, for "134" substitute "370".
	(c) In paragraph 3(5), for "143" substitute "380".
	(d) In paragraph 3(6), for "14(7)" substitute "387(1)".
	(e) In paragraph 5, for "section 184" substitute "sections 303 and 304 (and also section 14 of the Companies Consolidation (Consequential Provisions) Act 1985)".
	(f) In paragraph 7, for "subsection (1) of section 23" substitute "section 17(1)".
	(g) In paragraph 8, for "66" substitute "135"; and—
	(i) in sub-paragraph (a), for "69" substitute "138";
	(ii) in sub-paragraph (b), for "69(3) and (4)" substitute "138(3) and (4)", and
	(iii) in sub-paragraph (c), for "67, 68, 70 and 71" substitute "136, 137, 140 and 141".
Civil Jurisdiction and Judgments Act 1982 (c. 27):	
Schedule 5	In paragraph 1, for "Companies Act 1948" substitute "Companies Act 1985".
Local Government (Finance) Act 1982 (c. 32):	
Section 31(5)	For "section 154 of the Companies Act 1948" substitute "section 736 of the Companies Act 1985".
Finance Act 1982 (c. 39):	
Schedule 9	In paragraph 3(5), for "Part III of the Companies Act 1980" substitute "Part VIII of the Companies Act 1985".
Duchy of Cornwall Management Act 1982 (c. 47):	
Section 9(2)	For "section 161(1)(a) of the Companies Act 1948" substitute "section 389(1)(a) of the Companies Act 1985".
Transport Act 1982 (c. 49):	
Section 7	For "section 154 of the Companies Act 1948" substitute "section 736 of the Companies Act 1985"; and for "section 150(4)" substitute "section 736(5)(b)".
Section 13(2)	For "Companies Act 1948" substitute "Companies Act 1985".

Enactment	Amendment
Insurance Companies Act 1982 (c. 50):	
Section 7(1)	Throughout the Act, for "Companies Act 1948" substitute "Companies Act".
Section 10(5)	For "455" substitute "735".
Section 21(1)	The same amendment.
Section 48	For "Companies Acts 1948 to 1981" substitute "Companies Act". (a) In subsection (1), for "Section 37(1) of the Companies Act 1967" substitute "section 438(1) of the Companies Act". (b) In subsection (3), for "section 37(1) of the said Act of 1967" substitute "section 438(1) of the Companies Act".
Section 49(7)	For "206 or 208" substitute "425 or 427".
Section 50(3)	For "75" (the first time) substitute "183(1)".
Section 53	For "that Act of 1948" substitute "the Companies Act".
Section 54(1)	(a) In paragraph (a), for "222 and 223 or section 399" substitute "518 or sections 667 to 669". (b) In paragraph (c), for "section 12 of the Companies Act 1976" substitute "sections 221 and 222 of the Companies Act".
Section 55	(b) In subsection (6), for "333(1) of the said Act of 1948" substitute "631 of the Companies Act".
Section 56	(b) In subsection (7), for "245(1) of the said Act of 1948" substitute "539(1) of the Companies Act".
Section 71	After subsection (4), insert — "(4A) A person who publishes or discloses any information or document in contravention of section 47A above shall be guilty of an offence under section 449 of the Companies Act and liable accordingly."
Section 87	(a) In subsection (1), for section 406 of the Companies Act 1948" substitute "the Companies Act". (b) In subsection (2), for paragraphs (a) and (b) substitute — "(a) sections 691 to 693, 695 to 698, 700 to 703 and 708 of the Companies Act".
Section 89	(a) In subsection (1), for "434" substitute "716". (b) In subsection (2), the same amendment.
Section 96(1)	(a) After the definition of "chief executive" insert — "'the Companies Act' means the Companies Act 1985". (b) In the definition of "holding company", for "154" substitute "736".

Enactment	Amendment
Section 100	(c) At the end of the definition of "former Companies Acts" add "and the Companies Acts 1948 to 1983".
	(d) In the definition of "insolvent", for "222 and 223 or section 399" substitute "517 and 518 or section 666".
	(e) In the definition of "registrar of companies", for "meaning given in section 455 of" substitute "the same meaning as in".
	(f) In the definition of "subsidiary", for "154" substitute "736".
	In subsection (3), after "Act" insert "except sections 47A, 47B and 71(4A)".
Pilotage Act 1983 (c. 21):	
Section 4(4)	For "section 161(1)(a) of the Companies Act 1948" substitute "section 389(1)(a) of the Companies Act 1985".
Finance Act 1983 (c. 28):	
Schedule 5	(a) In paragraph 5(4), for "Companies Act 1948" substitute "Companies Act 1985".
	(b) In paragraph 10(4)(a), for "Companies Act 1980" substitute "Companies Act 1985"; and for "section 4" (twice) substitute "section 117".
	(c) In paragraph 20(2), for "section 455 of the Companies Act 1948" substitute "section 735 of the Companies Act 1985".
National Heritage Act 1983 (c. 47):	
Schedule 3	In paragraph 12(6)(a), for "section 161(1)(a) of the Companies Act 1948" substitute "section 389(1)(a) of the Companies Act 1985".
Car Tax Act 1983 (c. 53):	
Schedule 1	In paragraph 4, in both sub-paragraphs (1)(c) and (2)(c), for "section 319 of the Companies Act 1948" substitute "section 614 of the Companies Act 1985, with Schedule 19 to that Act"; and for "section 94 of the Act of 1948" substitute "section 196 of the Act of 1985".
Medical Act 1983 (c. 54):	
Schedule 1	In paragraph 18(3), for "section 161(1)(a) of the Companies Act 1948" substitute "section 389(1)(a) of the Companies Act 1985".
Value Added Tax Act 1983 (c. 55):	
Section 29(8)	For "Companies Act 1948" substitute "Companies Act 1985".

Enactment	Amendment
Schedule 7	In paragraph 12, in both sub-paragraphs (1)(c) and (2)(c), for section 319 of the Companies Act 1948" substitute "section 614 of the Companies Act 1985, with Schedule 19 to that Act"; and for "section 94 of the Act of 1948" substitute "section 196 of the Act of 1985".
Telecommunications Act 1984 (c. 12):	
Section 60(3)	For "Companies Act 1948" substitute "Companies Act 1985 or the enactments thereby replaced".
Section 61(4)	In paragraph (b), for "Companies Acts 1948 to 1981" substitute "Companies Act 1985".
Section 66	(a) In subsection (3), for "section 40(2)(d) of the Companies Act 1980" substitute "section 264(3)(d) of the Companies Act 1985"; and for "section 40(2)(c)" substitute "section 264(3)(c)".
	(b) In subsection (6), for "Companies Acts 1948 to 1981" substitute "Companies Act 1985".
Section 68	In subsection (1), for "Companies Act 1948" substitute "Companies Act 1985".
Section 70	(a) In subsection (1), for "Schedule 4 to the Companies Act 1948" substitute "Schedule 3 to the Companies Act 1985".
	(b) In subsection (3)(a), for "section 41 of the said Act of 1948" substitute "section 64(1) of the Companies Act 1985".
	(c) In subsection (5)(a), for "sections 37 to 46 of the said Act of 1948" substitute "Chapter I of Part III of the Companies Act 1985".
Section 73(1)	For "Companies Act 1948" substitute "Companies Act 1985".
Schedule 5	In paragraph 51, substitute the following for sub-paragraphs (1) and (2) —
	"(1) Where a distribution is proposed to be declared during the accounting reference period of the successor company which includes the transfer date or before any accounts are laid or filed in respect of that period, sections 270 to 274 and 275(7) of the Companies Act 1985 (accounts relevant for determining whether a distribution may be made by a company without contravening Part VIII of that Act) shall have effect as if —
	(a) the reference in section 270(2) to the company's accounts, and
	(b) references in section 273 to initial accounts,
	included references to such accounts as, on the assumptions stated in sub-paragraph (3) below, would have been prepared under Part VII of that Act in respect of the relevant year."

Enactment	Amendment
County Courts Act 1984 (c. 28):	
Section 98(3)	For "sections 325 and 326 of the Companies Act 1948" substitute "sections 621 and 622 of the Companies Act 1985".
Food Act 1984 (c. 30):	
Section 51(2)	In paragraph (a), for "1948" substitute "1985"; and for "Part IV" substitute "Part XI".
Capital Transfer Tax Act 1984 (c. 51):	
Section 13(5):	For "Companies Act 1948" substitute "Companies Act 1985".
Section 103(2)	The same amendment.
Section 234(3)	In paragraph (b), the same amendment.

History

(1) In Sch. 2 entries relating to Insolvency Services (Accounting and Investment) Act 1970, s. 4; Employment Protection (Consolidation) Act 1978, s. 122(7); Banking Act 1979, s. 28(b), 31; and Insurance Companies Act 1982, s. 55(5), 56(4), 59 repealed by Insolvency Act 1985, s. 235 and Sch. 10, Pt. II. The repeals of provisions with reference to Companies Act 1985, s. 663 (Banking Act 1979, s. 31(7)(a); Insurance Companies Act 1982, s. 59), operate from 1 March 1986 (see S.I. 1986 No. 185 (C. 7)) while the others operate from 29 December 1986 (see S.I. 1986 No. 1924 (C. 71)).

(2) Also in Sch. 2 entries relating to Social Security Act 1975; Insolvency Act 1976, s. 2, 10(1). Sch. 1; Employment Protection (Consolidation) Act 1978; and Banking Act 1979, s. 18, 19(8)(a) repealed by Insolvency Act 1985, s. 235 and Sch. 10, Pt. IV. The repeal of Insolvency Act 1976, s. 10(1)(b) operates from 1 March 1986 (see S.I. 1986 No. 185 (C. 7)) while the others operate from 29 December 1986 (see S.I. 1986 No. 1924 (C. 71)). See Insolvency Act 1986, s. 437, Sch. 11, Pt. II for transitional provisions.

The former wording of all the above entries is as follows:

Enactment	Amendment
"Insolvency Services (Accounting and Investment) Act 1970 (c. 8):	
Section 4	For 'section 362(4) of the Companies Act 1948' substitute 'section 660(5) of the Companies Act 1985 (or the previous corresponding provision of the Companies Act 1948)'.
Social Security Act 1975 (c. 14):	
Schedule 18	(a) In paragraph 2(1), for 'section 319 of the Companies Act 1948' substitute 'section 614 of the Companies Act 1985, taken with paragraph 8 of Schedule 19 to that Act'.
	(b) In paragraph 3(1), for the words 'the following' and paragraphs (a) and (b) substitute 'sections 196 and 475 of the Companies Act 1985'.
[Insolvency Act 1976 (c. 60):]	
Section 2	For this section substitute —
	'2(1) The Secretary of State may cause any accounts sent to him under section 92 of the Bankruptcy Act 1914 or section 543 of the Companies Act 1985 to be audited.
	2(2) So much of section 92(3) of the Act of 1914 and section 543(4) of the Act of 1985 as enables the Secretary of State to call for vouchers and information and to require the production of and to inspect books and accounts applies whether or not he decides to cause an account to be audited and extends to production and inspection at the premises of the trustee or liquidator.
	2(3) Where the Secretary of State decides not to cause an account to be audited, section 92(4) of the Act of 1914 and section 543(5) of the Act of 1985 apply as if the subsection in each case required copies of the accounts to be filed or delivered for filing forthwith; and the liquidator shall comply with section 543(5) when notified of the decision.

Enactment	Amendment
	2(4) Only the copy filed with the court shall be open to inspection under section 92(4) of the Act of 1914 or section 543(5) of the Act of 1985'.
Section 10(1)　　：：　：：　：：	In paragraph (b), for 'section 365 of the Companies Act 1948' substitute 'section 663 of the Companies Act 1985'.
Schedule 1, Part II	In paragraph 1, for 'bankruptcy petition or winding-up' substitute 'or bankruptcy'.
Employment Protection (Consolidation) Act 1978 (c. 44):	
Section 121(1)　　：：　：：　：：	For paragraph (c) substitute — '(c) section 614 of, and Schedule 19 to, the Companies Act 1985.'.
Section 122(7)　　：：　：：　：：	For 'section 317 of the Companies Act 1948' substitute 'section 612 of the Companies Act 1985'.
Section 125(2)　　：：　：：　：：	For paragraph (c) substitute — '(c) section 614 of the Companies Act 1985, with Schedule 19 to that Act'.
[Banking Act 1979 (c. 37):]	
Section 18　　：：　：：　：：	(a) In subsection (1), for 'Companies Act 1948' substitute 'Companies Act 1985'.
	(b) For subsection (2) substitute —
	'(2) If a petition is presented by the Bank by virtue of this section for the winding up of a recognised bank or licensed institution which, apart fom this subsection, would be excluded from being an unregistered company for the purposes of Part XXI of the Companies Act 1985 by virtue of —
	(a) paragraph (c) of section 665 of that Act (partnerships with less than 8 members), or
	(b) paragraph (d) of that section (limited partnerships),
	the court has jurisdiction, and the Companies Act 1985 has effect, as if the institution concerned were an unregistered company within the meaning of Part XXI of that Act.'
[Section 19]	(b) In subsection (8)(a), for '165', '172' and '1948' substitute respectively '432', '442' and '1985'.
[Section 28]	(b) In subsection (6), in paragraph (b)(iv), for 'Part V or Part IX of the Companies Act 1948' substitute 'Part XX or Part XXI of the Companies Act 1985'.
Section 31　　：：　：：　：：	In subsection (7), for 'section 365 of the Companies Act 1948' (twice) substitute 'section 663 of the Companies Act 1985'.
[Insurance Companies Act 1982 (c. 50):]	
[Section 55]　：：　：：　：：	(a) In subsection (5), for '(1) and (2) of section 246' substitute '(1) to (3) of section 540'.
[Section 56]　：：　：：　：：	(a) In subsection (4) —
	(i) for 'Subsections (2) and (3) of section 263' substitute 'Section 556(3)', and
	(ii) for 'section 263 of the said Act of 1948' substitute 'section 556 of the Companies Act'.
Section 59　：：　：：	(a) In subsection (1), for '365' substitute '663'.
	(b) In subsection (2), for '365 of the said Act of 1948' substitute '663 of the Companies Act'; and in paragraph (b) of the subsection, for '319 of the said Act of 1948' substitute '614 of, and Schedule 19 to, the Companies Act'.'

(3) In Sch. 2 the entry relating to the Banking Act 1979, s. 20 repealed by Financial Services Act 1986, s. 212(3) and Sch. 17 as from 27 November 1986 (see S.I. 1986 No. 2031 (C. 76). The entry formerly read as follows:

"(a) In subsection (1)—

   (i) in paragraph (a), for '109', '110', '1967' and '111' substitute respectively '447', '448', '1985' and '449'; and

   (ii) in paragraph (b), for '164', '165', '172' and '1948' substitute respectively '431', '432', '442' and '1985'.

(b) in subsection (3)—

   (i) in paragraph (a), for section 111 of the Companies Act 1967 substitute 'section 449 of the Companies Act 1985'; and

   (ii) in paragraph (b), for '111' substitute '449'."

The remaining entries relating to the Banking Act 1979 repealed by Banking Act 1987, s. 108(2) and Sch. 7, Pt. I as from 1 October 1987 (see S.I. 1987 No. 1664 (C. 50). The entries formerly read as follows:

Enactment	Amendment
"Banking Act 1979 (c. 37):	
Section 6(3)	In paragraph (b), for 'Part IX of the Companies Act 1948' substitute 'Part XXI of the Companies Act 1985'.
Section 17(6)	In paragraph (a), for 'section 154 of the Companies Act 1948' substitute 'section 736 of the Companies Act 1985'.
Section 19	(a) For subsection (5) substitute— '(5) Nothing in subsection (1) above prohibits the disclosure to the Secretary of State of information relating to a body corporate to which section 432 or 442 of the Companies Act 1985 applies, if it appears to the bank that there may be circumstances relating to the body corporate in which the Secretary of State might wish to appoint inspectors under— (a) any of paragraphs (a) to (c) of subsection (2) of the said section 432 (investigation of cases of fraud, etc.), or (b) the said section 442 (investigation of ownership of companies, etc.).'. (a) In subsection (4), in paragraph (a), for 'Part IX of the Companies Act 1948' substitute 'Part XXI of the Companies Act 1985'.
Section 28 ...	In subsection (7)(a), for 'section 150(4) of the Companies Act 1948' substitute 'section 736 of the Companies Act 1985'.
Section 36 ...	(a) In subsection (4)— (i) in paragraph (a), for 'section 407(1) of the Companies Act 1948' substitute 'section 691(1) of the Companies Act 1985'; and (ii) in paragraph (b), for '407(1)' substitute '691(1)'. (b) In subsection (5)— (i) in paragraph (a), for 'section 409 of the Companies Act 1948' substitute 'section 692 of the Companies Act 1985'; and (ii) in paragraph (b), for 'subsection (2) of section 413' substitute 'subsection (4) of section 696'. (c) In subsection (6), for 'section 407, section 409 and subsection (2) of section 413 of the Companies Act 1948' substitute 'section 691, section 692 and subsection (4) of section 696 of the Companies Act 1985'.
Section 40 ...	For 'Companies Act 1948' substitute 'Companies Act 1985'.
Section 48(1)	The same amendment.
Section 49(2)	(a) In the definition of 'debenture', for Companies Act 1948 substitute 'Companies Act 1985'.
Section 50(1)	(b) In the definition of 'subsidiary', for 'section 154 of the Companies Act 1948' substitute 'section 736 of the Companies Act 1985'.
Schedule 3 ...	In paragraph 8, for sub-paragraph (a) substitute— '(a) at the time of its application for recognition is either a company within the meaning of the Companies Act 1985 or any other body corporate having its place of central management and control in the United Kingdom (having in either case been such on 9th November 1978 and so continued since that date).'
Schedule 5 ...	In paragraph 4(4), for 'section 161(1)(a) of the Companies Act 1948' substitute 'section 389(1)(a) of the Companies Act 1985'; and for 'section 161(1)(b)' substitute 'section 389(1)(b)'."

(4) In Sch. 2 the entry relating to the Baking Industry (Hours of Work) Act 1954, s. 11 repealed by the Sex Discrimination Act 1986 as from 27 February 1987 (see S.I. 1986 No. 2313 (C. 95). The entry formerly read as follows:

"For 'Companies Act 1948' substitute 'Companies Act 1985'."

(5) In Sch. 2 the entries relating to the Housing Act 1964, Housing Subsidies Act 1967, Housing Act 1974, Housing Act 1980 and Housing and Building Control Act 1984 repealed by Housing (Consequential Provisions) Act 1985, s. 3 and Sch. 1, Pt. I. The entries formerly read as follows:

Enactment	Amendment
"Housing Act 1964 (c. 56): 　Section 10　　…　　…　　:	For 'section 161(1)(a) of the Companies Act 1948 by the Board of Trade' substitute 'section 389(1)(a) of the Companies Act 1985 by the Secretary of State'.
Housing Subsidies Act 1967 (c. 29): 　Section 32(1)　　…　　…　　:	In the definition of 'insurance company', for 'paragraph 24 of Schedule 8 to the Companies Act 1948' substitute 'paragraph 28 of Schedule 9 to the Companies Act 1985'.
Housing Act 1974 (c. 44): 　Section 12　　…　　…　　: 　Section 22(1)　　…　　…　　: 　Section 24(4)　　…　　…　　:	In the definition of 'subsidiary', for 'Companies Act 1948' substitute 'Companies Act 1985'. The same amendment. For 'section 141 of the Companies Act 1948' substitute 'section 378 of the Companies Act 1985'; and in paragraph (b) of the subsection, for 'section 143 of the Companies Act 1948' substitute 'section 380 of the Companies Act 1985'.
Section 25(1)　　…　　…　　:	For 'Companies Act 1948' substitute 'Companies Act 1985'.
Housing Act 1980 (c. 51): 　Schedule 16　　…　　…　　: 　Schedule 19　　…　　…　　:	In paragraph 3(2), for 'section 161(1)(a) of the Companies Act 1948' substitute 'section 389(1)(a) of the Companies Act 1985'; and for 'section 161(1)(b)' substitute 'section 389(1)(b)'. In paragraph 17(2), for 'section 154 of the Companies Act 1948' substitute 'section 736 of the Companies Act 1985'.
Housing and Building Control Act 1984 (c. 29): 　Schedule 4　　…　　…　　:	(a) In paragraph 11(1), for 'section 161(1)(a) of the Companies Act 1948' substitute 'section 389(1)(a) of the Companies Act 1985'; and for 'section 161(1)(b)' substitute 'section 389(1)(b)'. (b) In paragraph 11(2), for 'section 154 of the Companies Act 1948' substitute 'section 736 of the Companies Act 1985'."

(6) In Sch. 2 the entry relating to the Weights and Measures Act 1979 repealed by Weights and Measures Act 1985, s. 98(1) and Sch. 13, Pt. I. The entry formerly read as follows:

Enactment	Amendment
"Weights and Measures Act 1979 (c. 45): 　Section 10(3)　　…　　…　　:	For 'section 161(1)(a) of the Companies Act 1948' substitute 'section 389(1)(a) of the Companies Act 1985'."

(7) In Sch. 2 the entries relating to the Building Societies Act 1962 repealed by Building Societies Act 1986, s. 120(2) and Sch. 19, Pt. I as from 1 January 1987 (see S.I. 1986 No. 1560 (C. 56). The entries formerly read as follows:

Enactment	Amendment
"Building Societies Act 1962 (c. 37): 　Section 22(8)　　…　　…　　: 　Section 50(5)　　…　　…　　: 　Section 55(5)　　…　　…　　:	For 'Companies Act 1948' substitute 'Companies Act 1985'. The same amendment. The same amendment.

Enactment	Amendment
Section 86(1)(e)	For 'paragraph (a) of subsection (1) of section one hundred and sixty-one of the Companies Act 1948 by the Board of Trade' substitute 'section 389(1)(a) of the Companies Act 1985 by the Secretary of State'.
Section 86(2)	For 'paragraph (b) of subsection (1) of section one hundred and sixty-one of the Companies Act 1948' substitute 'section 389(1)(b) of the Companies Act 1985'.
Section 92(4)	For 'Section four hundred and forty-eight of the Companies Act 1948' substitute 'Section 727 of the Companies Act 1985'.
Section 103	For 'Companies Act 1948' substitute 'Companies Act 1985'.
Schedule 1	In paragraphs 5 (twice) and 6(3), for 'Companies Act 1948' substitute 'Companies Act 1985'.
Schedule 3	In paragraph 12(1)(b), for 'section 406 of the Companies Act 1948' substitute 'section 744 of the Companies Act 1985'.''

(8) In Sch. 2 the entry relating to the Finance Act 1973 repealed by Finance Act 1988, s. 148 and Sch. 14, Pt. XI as from 22 March 1988. The entry formerly read as follows:

Enactment	Amendment
''Finance Act 1973 (c. 51):	
Section 47	(a) In subsection (2)(a), for 'Companies Act 1948' substitute 'Companies Act 1985'. (b) In subsection (3), for 'section 12 of Companies Act 1948' substitute 'section 10(1) of the Companies Act 1985'; and for 'the said section 12' substitute 'section 12 of the Companies Act 1985'.
Schedule 19	In paragraph 11, for 'section 206 of the Companies Act 1948' substitute 'section 425 of the Companies Act 1985'.''

(9) In Sch. 2 2 entries relating to the Prevention of Fraud (Investments) Act 1958, the Scottish Development Agency Act 1975, Sch. 1, para. 19, the Welsh Development Agency Act 1975, Sch. 1, para. 22, the Stock Exchange (Completion of Bargains) Act 1976 and the Aircraft and Shipbuilding Industries Act 1977, s. 3(5) repealed by Financial Services Act 1986, s. 212(3) and Sch. 17, Pt. I as from 29 April 1988 (see S.I. 1988 No. 740 (C. 22)). The entries formerly read as follows:

Enactment	Amendment

''Prevention of Fraud (Investments) Act 1958 (c. 45):
Section 2 ... ...
	For subsection (2), to the end of sub-paragraph (d), substitute —
	'(2) For the purpose of determining whether or not a person has contravened any of the restrictions imposed by section 1 of this Act, no account shall be taken of his having done any of the following things (whether as a principal or as an agent), that is to say —
	(a) effecting transactions with, or through the agency of —
	  (i) such a person as is mentioned in paragraph (a), paragraph (b) or paragraph (c) of the preceding subsection, or a person acting on behalf of such a person as is so mentioned, or
	  (ii) the holder of a licence;
	(b) issuing any prospectus to which —
	  (i) section 56 of the Companies Act 1985 applies or would apply if not excluded by paragraph (b) of subsection (5) of that section, or
	  (ii) section 72 of that Act applies or would apply if not excluded by paragraph (b) of subsection (6) of that section or by section 76 of that Act;
	(c) issuing any document relating to securities of a corporation incorporated in Great Britain which is not a registered company, being a document which —
	  (i) would, if the corporation were a registered company, be a prospectus to which section 56 of the Companies Act 1985 applies or would apply if not excluded by paragraph (b) of subsection (5) of that section, and

Enactment	Amendment
	(ii) contains all the matters and is issued with the consents which, by virtue of sections 72 to 75 of that Act, it would have to contain and be issued with if the corporation were a company incorporated outside Great Britain and the document were a prospectus issued by that company; and
	(d) issuing any form of application for shares in, or debentures of, a corporation together with—
	(i) a prospectus which complies with the requirements of section 56 of the Companies Act 1985, or is not required to comply with it because excluded by paragraph (b) of subsection (5) of that section, or complies with the requirements of Chapter II of Part III of that Act relating to prospectuses and is not issued in contravention of sections 74 and 75 of that Act, or
	(ii) in the case of a corporation incorporated in Great Britain which is not a registered company, a document containing all the matters and issued with the consents mentioned in paragraph (c)(ii) of this subsection'.
Section 12	(a) For 'Board of Trade' (twice) substitute 'Secretary of State'.
	(b) For 'the Board' substitute 'the Secretary of State'.
	(c) In subsection (2)—
	(i) for the words from the beginning to 'subsection (2)' substitute 'Sections 434 to 436 of the Companies Act 1985, subsection (1) of section 437 of that Act and so much of subsection (3)'; and
	(ii) for 'section one hundred and sixty-four' substitute 'section 431'.
Section 14	(a) In subsection (2), for paragraphs (a) and (b) substitute—
	'(a) in relation to any distribution of a prospectus to which section 56 of the Companies Act 1985 applies or would apply if not excluded by paragraph (b) of subsection (5) of that section or section 72 of that Act applies or would apply if not excluded by paragraph (b) of subsection (6) of that section or by section 76 of that Act, or in relation to any distribution of a document relating to securities of a corporation incorporated in Great Britain which is not a registered company, being a document which—
	(i) would, if the corporation were a registered company, be a prospectus to which the said section 56 applies or would apply if not excluded as aforesaid, and
	(ii) contains all the matters and is issued with the consents which, by virtue of sections 72 to 75 of that Act it would have to contain and be issued with if the corporation were a company incorporated outside Great Britain and the document were a prospectus issued by that company;
	(b) in relation to any issue of a form of application for shares in, or debentures of, a corporation, together with—
	(i) a prospectus which complies with the requirements of section 56 of the Companies Act 1985, or is not required to comply therewith because excluded by paragraph (b) of subsection (5) of that section, or complies with the requirements of Chapter II of Part III of that Act relating to prospectuses and is not issued in contravention of sections 74 and 75 of that Act, or
	(ii) in the case of a corporation incorporated in Great Britain which is not a registered company, a document containing all the matters and issued with the consents mentioned in paragraph (a)(ii) of this subsection, or in connection with a bona fide invitation to a person to enter into an underwriting agreement with respect to the shares or debentures, or'.
	(c) In subsection (3)(a)(iii), for 'section one hundred and fifty-four of the Companies Act 1948' substitute 'section 736 of the Companies Act 1985'.
	In subsection (2)(a), for 'Companies Act 1948' substitute 'Companies Act 1985'.
	In subsection (1)—
Section 16	(a) in the definition of 'prospectus', for 'Companies Act 1948' substitute 'Companies Act 1985';
Section 26	(b) in the definition of 'registered company', after the words 'registered under' insert 'the Companies Act 1985', and for 'section four hundred and fifty-five of the Companies Act 1948' substitute 'section 735(3) of the Companies Act 1985';
	(c) in the definition of 'statutory corporation', for 'Companies Act 1948' substitute 'Companies Act 1985'.

Enactment	Amendment
Scottish Development Agency Act 1975 (c. 69):	
Section 25(1)	In the definitions of 'holding company' and 'subsidiary', for 'section 154 of the Companies Act 1948' substitute 'section 736 of the Companies Act 1985'; and in the definition of 'wholly-owned subsidiary' for 'section 150(4) of the Companies Act 1948' substitute 'section 736(5)(b) of the Companies Act 1985'.
Schedule 1	In paragraph 19, for 'Section 209 of the Companies Act 1948' substitute 'Sections 428 to 430 of the Companies Act 1985'; and for that section' substitute 'those sections'.
Welsh Development Agency Act 1975 (c. 70):	
Section 27(1)	In the definitions of 'holding company' and 'subsidiary', for 'section 154 of the Companies Act 1948' (twice) substitute 'section 736 of the Companies Act 1985'; and in the definition of 'wholly-owned subsidiary', for 'section 150(4) of the Companies Act 1948' substitute 'section 736(5)(b) of the Companies Act 1985'.
Schedule 1	In paragraph 22, for 'Section 209 of the Companies Act 1948' substitute 'Sections 428 to 430 of the Companies Act 1985'; and for that section' substitute 'those sections'."
Stock Exchange (Completion of Bargains) Act 1976 (c. 47):	
Section 7	For subsection (2) substitute — '(2) In this Act 'stock exchange nominee' means the person designated by the Secretary of State by order under section 185(4) of the Companies Act 1985'.
Aircraft and Shipbuilding Industries Act 1977 (c. 3):	
Section 3(5)	For 'Section 209 of the Companies Act 1948' substitute 'Sections 428 to 430 of the Companies Act 1985'.
Section 17(8)	For 'section 161(1)(a) of the Companies Act 1948' substitute 'section 389(1)(a) of the Companies Act 1985'.
Section 23(8)	For 'Companies Act 1948' substitute 'Companies Act 1985'.
Section 56(1)	(a) In the definition of 'equity share capital', for 'section 154 of the Companies Act 1948' substitute 'section 736 of the Companies Act 1985'.
	(b) In the definition of 'holding company', for 'section 154 of the Companies Act 1948' substitute 'section 736 of the Companies Act 1985'.
	(c) In the definition of 'subsidiary', for 'Companies Act 1948' substitute 'Companies Act 1985'.
	(d) In the definition of 'wholly-owned subsidiary', for 'section 150 of the Companies Act 1948' substitute 'section 736(5)(b) of the Companies Act 1985'."

(10) In Sch. 2 the entry relating to the Water Act 1973 repealed by Water Act 1989, s. 190(3) and Sch. 27, Pt. I as from 1 September 1989 (see Water Act 1989, s. 4, 194(3)(g) and S.I. 1989 No. 1146 (C. 37) — see also S.I. 1989 No.1530 (C. 51)). The entry formerly read as follows:

Enactment	Amendment
"Water Act 1973 (c. 37):	
Schedule 3	In paragraph 39(2)(a), for 'section 161(1)(a) of the Companies Act 1948' substitute 'section 389(1)(a) of the Companies Act 1985'."

Note
See Insolvency Act 1986, s. 437 and Sch. 11, Pt. II re certain relevant transitional provisions.

TABLE OF DERIVATIONS

[This table has no official status]

Notes:

The following abbreviations are used in this Table:—

"1948"	=	Companies Act 1948 (c. 38).
"1967"	=	Companies Act 1967 (c. 81).
"SECOBA"	=	Stock Exchange (Completion of Bargains) Act 1976 (c. 47).
"1980"	=	Companies Act 1980 (c. 22).
"1981"	=	Companies Act 1981 (c. 62).

1. The entry "Drafting" in the right-hand column indicates that the section in question does not reproduce any specific provision of an Act repealed by the Act, but is required for accuracy in the Act's provisions.

2. Section 28 of the Act effects certain repeals in the Companies Act 1948 in pursuance of recommendations of the Law Commission, and does not form part of the consolidation of the Companies Acts.

3. Section 31 of the Act, with the side-note "Continuity of law", contains savings and transitional provisions of the character to be found in any conventional consolidation. It does not reproduce any specific provision of an Act repealed by the Act.

4. The entry "Consequential" in the right-hand column indicates amendments of enactments (and, in the case of section 27, a statutory instrument) required to maintain their consistency with provisions of the consolidation.

Provision	Derivation
1	1980 s. 8(1), (2); 1981 s. 113.
2	1980 s. 8(3)–(7).
3	1980 s. 8(11).
4	1980 ss. 8(8)–(10), (12), 11(1).
5	1980 s. 9.
6	1980 ss. 37(12), 38(1), (2)(d).
7	1980 s. 15(5).
8	1980 s. 76(1), (4).
9	1980 s. 31(1)(b), (2).
10	1948 s. 21.
11	SECOBA s. 2(2).
12	1981 ss. 36(3), 39, 40(4)–(7), 41.
13	1948 s. 91.
14	1948 s. 184(1) proviso.
15	1948 s. 189.
16	1981 s. 105(2).
17	1948 s. 308(2).
18	1948 s. 322(1) proviso.
19	1948 s. 350(2).
20	1980 s. 83.
21	Drafting.

[The next page is 44,751]   **CCH Editions Limited**

Provision	Derivation
22	1948 s. 460.
23	1981 s. 91(8).
24	1981 s. 107.
25	1967 ss. 111, 116(1); 1974 c. 49 Sch. 1; 1981 ss. 103(3), 104(1)–(3); 1982 c. 50 Sch. 5 para. 6.
26	1967 c. 48 s. 3; 1972 c. 67 s. 10.
27	Consequential.
28	See Note 2 above.
29	—
30	Consequential.
31	See Note 3 above.
32	Drafting.
33–35	—
Sch. 1	—
Sch. 2	Consequential.

INSOLVENCY ACT 1986

Table of Contents

[The next page is 50,051]

50.001

INSOLVENCY ACT 1986

[The text begins on p. 50.201]

INSOLVENCY ACT 1986

(1986 Chapter 45)

ARRANGEMENT OF SECTIONS

THE FIRST GROUP OF PARTS

COMPANY INSOLVENCY; COMPANIES WINDING UP

PART I — COMPANY VOLUNTARY ARRANGEMENTS

PART II — ADMINISTRATION ORDERS

British Companies Legislation

PART IV — WINDING UP OF COMPANIES REGISTERED UNDER THE COMPANIES ACTS

CHAPTER I — PRELIMINARY

Modes of winding up

Contributories

PART IX — BANKRUPTCY

CHAPTER I — BANKRUPTCY PETITIONS; BANKRUPTCY ORDERS

SECTION

[The next page is 50,111]

SCHEDULE

[The next page is 50,201]

INSOLVENCY ACT 1986

(1986 Chapter 45)

An Act to consolidate the enactments relating to company insolvency and winding up (including the winding up of companies that are not insolvent, and of unregistered companies); enactments relating to the insolvency and bankruptcy of individuals; and other enactments bearing on those two subject matters, including the functions and qualification of insolvency practitioners, the public administration of insolvency, the penalisation and redress of malpractice and wrongdoing, and the avoidance of certain transactions at an undervalue. *[25th July 1986]*

THE FIRST GROUP OF PARTS
COMPANY INSOLVENCY; COMPANIES WINDING UP

PART I — COMPANY VOLUNTARY ARRANGEMENTS

THE PROPOSAL

SEC. 1   Those who may propose an arrangement

1(1) **[Directors]** The directors of a company (other than one for which an administration order is in force, or which is being wound up) may make a proposal under this Part to the company and to its creditors for a composition in satisfaction of its debts or a scheme of arrangement of its affairs (from here on referred to, in either case, as a "voluntary arrangement").

1(2) **[Interpretation]** A proposal under this part is one which provides for some person ("the nominee") to act in relation to the voluntary arrangement either as trustee or otherwise for the purpose of supervising its implementation; and the nominee must be a person who is qualified to act as an insolvency practitioner in relation to the company.

1(3) **[Administrator, liquidator]** Such a proposal may also be made—

    (a) where an administration order is in force in relation to the company, by the administrator, and

    (b) where the company is being wound up, by the liquidator.

SEC. 2   Procedure where nominee is not the liquidator or administrator

2(1) **[Application]** This section applies where the nominee under section 1 is not the liquidator or administrator of the company.

2(2)   **[Report to court]**   The nominee shall, within 28 days (or such longer period as the court may allow) after he is given notice of the proposal for a voluntary arrangement, submit a report to the court stating—

   (a)   whether, in his opinion, meetings of the company and of its creditors should be summoned to consider the proposal, and

   (b)   if in his opinion such meetings should be summoned, the date on which, and time and place at which, he proposes the meetings should be held.

2(3)   **[Information to nominee]**   For the purposes of enabling the nominee to prepare his report, the person intending to make the proposal shall submit to the nominee—

   (a)   a document setting out the terms of the proposed voluntary arrangement, and

   (b)   a statement of the company's affairs containing—

      (i)   such particulars of its creditors and of its debts and other liabilities and of its assets as may be prescribed, and

      (ii)   such other information as may be prescribed.

2(4)   **[Replacement of nominee by court]**   The court may, on an application made by the person intending to make the proposal, in a case where the nominee has failed to submit the report required by this section, direct that the nominee be replaced as such by another person qualified to act as an insolvency practitioner in relation to the company.

Note

For procedure and relevant forms prescribed for s. 2, see
The Insolvency Rules 1986, r. 1.2–1.9.

SEC. 3   Summoning of meetings

3(1)   **[Meetings in accordance with report]**   Where the nominee under section 1 is not the liquidator or administrator, and it has been reported to the court that such meetings as are mentioned in section 2(2) should be summoned, the person making the report shall (unless the court otherwise directs) summon those meetings for the time, date and place proposed in the report.

3(2)   **[Where nominee liquidator or administrator]**   Where the nominee is the liquidator or administrator, he shall summon meetings of the company and of its creditors to consider the proposal for such a time, date and place as he thinks fit.

3(3)   **[Persons summoned]**   The persons to be summoned to a creditors' meeting under this section are every creditor of the company of whose claim and address the person summoning the meeting is aware.

CONSIDERATION AND IMPLEMENTATION OF PROPOSAL

SEC. 4   Decisions of meetings

4(1)   **[Decision]**   The meetings summoned under section 3 shall decide whether to approve the proposed voluntary arrangement (with or without modifications).

4(2)   **[Modifications]**   The modifications may include one conferring the functions proposed to be conferred on the nominee on another person qualified to act as an insolvency practitioner in relation to the company.

But they shall not include any modification by virtue of which the proposal ceases to be a proposal such as is mentioned in section 1.

4(3) **[Limitation on approval]** A meeting so summoned shall not approve any proposal or modification which affects the right of a secured creditor of the company to enforce his security, except with the concurrence of the creditor concerned.

4(4) **[Further limitation]** Subject as follows, a meeting so summoned shall not approve any proposal or modification under which—

(a) any preferential debt of the company is to be paid otherwise than in priority to such of its debts as are not preferential debts, or

(b) a preferential creditor of the company is to be paid an amount in respect of a preferential debt that bears to that debt a smaller proportion than is borne to another preferential debt by the amount that is to be paid in respect of that other debt.

However, the meeting may approve such a proposal or modification with the concurrence of the preferential creditor concerned.

4(5) **[Meeting in accordance with rules]** Subject as above, each of the meetings shall be conducted in accordance with the rules.

Note
See The Insolvency Rules 1986, r. 1.13ff.

4(6) **[Report to court, notice]** After the conclusion of either meeting in accordance with the rules, the chairman of the meeting shall report the result of the meeting to the court, and, immediately after reporting to the court, shall give notice of the result of the meeting to such persons as may be prescribed.

Note
See The Insolvency Rules 1986, r. 1.14, 1.21.

4(7) **[Interpretation]** References in this section to preferential debts and preferential creditors are to be read in accordance with section 386 in Part XII of this Act.

SEC. 5 Effect of approval

5(1) **[Operation]** This section has effect where each of the meetings summoned under section 3 approves the proposed voluntary arrangement either with the same modifications or without modifications.

5(2) **[Effect of composition or scheme]** The approved voluntary arrangement—

(a) takes effect as if made by the company at the creditors' meeting, and

(b) binds every person who in accordance with the rules had notice of, and was entitled to vote at, that meeting (whether or not he was present or represented at the meeting) as if he were a party to the voluntary arrangement.

5(3) **[Court powers]** Subject as follows, if the company is being wound up or an administration order is in force, the court may do one or both of the following, namely—

(a) by order stay or sist all proceedings in the winding up or discharge the administration order;

(b) give such directions with respect to the conduct of the winding up or the administration as it thinks appropriate for facilitating the implementation of the approved voluntary arrangement.

5(4) [Limit on sec. 5(3)(a)]   The court shall not make an order under subsection (3)(a)—

(a) at any time before the end of the period of 28 days beginning with the first day on which each of the reports required by section 4(6) has been made to the court, or

(b) at any time when an application under the next section or an appeal in respect of such an application is pending, or at any time in the period within which such an appeal may be brought.

SEC. 6   Challenge of decisions

6(1) [Application to court]   Subject to this section, an application to the court may be made, by any of the persons specified below, on one or both of the following grounds, namely—

(a) that a voluntary arrangement approved at the meetings summoned under section 3 unfairly prejudices the interests of a creditor, member or contributory of the company;

(b) that there has been some material irregularity at or in relation to either of the meetings.

6(2) [Applicants]   The persons who may apply under this section are—

(a) a person entitled, in accordance with the rules, to vote at either of the meetings;

(b) the nominee or any person who has replaced him under section 2(4) or 4(2); and

(c) if the company is being wound up or an administration order is in force, the liquidator or administrator.

6(3) [Time for application]   An application under this section shall not be made after the end of the period of 28 days beginning with the first day on which each of the reports required by section 4(6) has been made to the court.

6(4) [Powers of court]   Where on such an application the court is satisfied as to either of the grounds mentioned in subsection (1), it may do one or both of the following, namely—

(a) revoke or suspend the approvals given by the meetings or, in a case falling within subsection (1)(b), any approval given by the meeting in question;

(b) give a direction to any person for the summoning of further meetings to consider any revised proposal the person who made the original proposal may make or, in a case falling within subsection (1)(b), a further company or (as the case may be) creditors' meeting to reconsider the original proposal.

6(5) [Revocation or suspension of approval]   Where at any time after giving a direction under subsection (4)(b) for the summoning of meetings to consider a revised proposal the court is satisfied that the person who made the original proposal does not intend to submit a revised proposal, the court shall revoke the direction and revoke or suspend any approval given at the previous meetings.

6(6) **[Supplemental directions]** In a case where the court, on an application under this section with respect to any meeting—

(a) gives a direction under subsection (4)(b), or

(b) revokes or suspends an approval under subsection (4)(a) or (5),

the court may give such supplemental directions as it thinks fit and, in particular, directions with respect to things done since the meeting under any voluntary arrangement approved by the meeting.

6(7) **[Effect of irregularity]** Except in pursuance of the preceding provisions of this section, an approval given at a meeting summoned under section 3 is not invalidated by any irregularity at or in relation to the meeting.

Note
For procedure on making of s. 6 order, see The Insolvency
Rules 1986, r. 1.25.

SEC. 7   Implementation of proposal

7(1) **[Application]** This section applies where a voluntary arrangement approved by the meetings summoned under section 3 has taken effect.

7(2) **[Supervisor of composition or scheme]** The person who is for the time being carrying out in relation to the voluntary arrangement the functions conferred—

(a) by virtue of the approval on the nominee, or

(b) by virtue of section 2(4) or 4(2) on a person other than the nominee,

shall be known as the supervisor of the voluntary arrangement.

7(3) **[Application to court]** If any of the company's creditors or any other person is dissatisfied by any act, omission or decision of the supervisor, he may apply to the court; and on the application the court may—

(a) confirm, reverse or modify any act or decision of the supervisor,

(b) give him directions, or

(c) make such other order as it thinks fit.

7(4) **[Application for directions by supervisor]** The supervisor—

(a) may apply to the court for directions in relation to any particular matter arising under the voluntary arrangement, and

(b) is included among the persons who may apply to the court for the winding up of the company or for an administration order to be made in relation to it.

7(5) **[Court appointment powers]** The court may, whenever—

(a) it is expedient to appoint a person to carry out the functions of the supervisor, and

(b) it is inexpedient, difficult or impracticable for an appointment to be made without the assistance of the court,

make an order appointing a person who is qualified to act as an insolvency practitioner in relation to the company, either in substitution for the existing supervisor or to fill a vacancy.

7(6) **[Limit on sec. 7(5) power]** The power conferred by subsection (5) is exercisable so as to increase the number of persons exercising the functions of supervisor or, where there is more than one person exercising those functions, so as to replace one or more of those persons.

PART II — ADMINISTRATION ORDERS

MAKING, ETC. OF ADMINISTRATION ORDER

SEC. 8 Power of court to make order

8(1) **[Administration order]** Subject to this section, if the court—

    (a) is satisfied that a company is or is likely to become unable to pay its debts (within the meaning given to that expression by section 123 of this Act), and

    (b) considers that the making of an order under this section would be likely to achieve one or more of the purposes mentioned below,

the court may make an administration order in relation to the company.

8(2) **[Definition]** An administration order is an order directing that, during the period for which the order is in force, the affairs, business and property of the company shall be managed by a person ("the administrator") appointed for the purpose by the court.

8(3) **[Purposes for order]** The purposes for whose achievement an administration order may be made are—

    (a) the survival of the company, and the whole or any part of its undertaking, as a going concern;

    (b) the approval of a voluntary arrangement under Part 1;

    (c) the sanctioning under section 425 of the Companies Act of a compromise or arrangement between the company and any such persons as are mentioned in that section; and

    (d) a more advantageous realisation of the company's assets than would be effected on a winding up;

and the order shall specify the purpose or purposes for which it is made.

8(4) **[Where order not to be made]** An administration order shall not be made in relation to a company after it has gone into liquidation, nor where it is—

    (a) an insurance company within the meaning of the Insurance Companies Act 1982, or

    (b) an authorised institution or former authorised institution within the meaning of the Banking Act 1987.

History

In s. 8(4), para. (b) substituted by Banking Act 1987, s. 108(1) and Sch. 6, para. 25(1) as from 1 October 1987 (see S.I. 1987 No. 1664 (C. 50)): the former para. (b) read as follows:

"(b) a recognised bank or licensed institution within the meaning of the Banking Act 1979, or an institution to which sections 16 and 18 of that Act apply as if it were a licensed institution."

SEC. 9 Application for order

9(1) **[Application to court]** An application to the court for an administration order shall be by petition presented either by the company or the directors, or by a creditor or creditors (including any contingent or prospective creditor or creditors), or by the clerk of a magistrates' court in the exercise of the power conferred by section 87A of the Magistrates' Courts Act 1980 (enforcement of fines imposed on companies) or by all or any of those parties, together or separately.

History
In s. 9(1) the words "or by the clerk of a magistrates' court in the exercise of the power conferred by section 87A of the Magistrates' Courts Act 1980 (enforcement of fines imposed on companies)" inserted by Criminal Justice Act 1988, s. 62(2)(a) as from 5 January 1989 (see S.I. 1988 No. 2073(C. 78)).

9(2)   [On presentation of petition to court]   Where a petition is presented to the court—

(a)   notice of the petition shall be given forthwith to any person who has appointed, or is or may be entitled to appoint, an administrative receiver of the company, and to such other persons as may be prescribed, and

(b)   the petition shall not be withdrawn except with the leave of the court.

Note
For the "other persons" in s. 9(2)(a), see The Insolvency Rules 1986, r. 2.6.

9(3)   [Duties of court]   Where the court is satisfied that there is an administrative receiver of the company, the court shall dismiss the petition unless it is also satisfied either—

(a)   that the person by whom or on whose behalf the receiver was appointed has consented to the making of the order, or

(b)   that, if an administration order were made, any security by virtue of which the receiver was appointed would—

(i)   be liable to be released or discharged under sections 238 to 240 in Part VI (transactions at an undervalue and preferences),

(ii)   be avoided under section 245 in that Part (avoidance of floating charges), or

(iii)   be challengeable under section 242 (gratuitous alienations) or 243 (unfair preferences) in that Part, or under any rule of law in Scotland.

9(4)   [Court powers on hearing petition]   Subject to subsection (3), on hearing a petition the court may dismiss it, or adjourn the hearing conditionally or unconditionally, or make an interim order or any other order that it thinks fit.

9(5)   [Extent of interim order]   Without prejudice to the generality of subsection (4), an interim order under that subsection may restrict the exercise of any powers of the directors or of the company (whether by reference to the consent of the court or of a person qualified to act as an insolvency practitioner in relation to the company, or otherwise).

SEC. 10   Effect of application

10(1)   [Limitations]   During the period beginning with the presentation of a petition for an administration order and ending with the making of such an order or the dismissal of the petition—

(a)   no resolution may be passed or order made for the winding up of the company;

(b)   no steps may be taken to enforce any security over the company's property, or to repossess goods in the company's possession under any hire-purchase agreement, except with the leave of the court and subject to such terms as the court may impose; and

(c)   no other proceedings and no execution or other legal process may be commenced or continued, and no distress may be levied, against the company or its property except with the leave of the court and subject to such terms as aforesaid.

10(2)   [Where leave not required]   Nothing in subsection (1) requires the leave of the court—

    (a) for the presentation of a petition for the winding up of the company,

    (b) for the appointment of an administrative receiver of the company, or

    (c) for the carrying out by such a receiver (whenever appointed) of any of his functions.

10(3)   [Period in sec. 10(1)]   Where—

    (a) a petition for an administration order is presented at a time when there is an administrative receiver of the company, and

    (b) the person by or on whose behalf the receiver was appointed has not consented to the making of the order,

the period mentioned in subsection (1) is deemed not to begin unless and until that person so consents.

10(4)   [Hire-purchase agreements]   References in this section and the next to hire-purchase agreements include conditional sale agreements, chattel leasing agreements and retention of title agreements.

10(5)   [Scotland]   In the application of this section and the next to Scotland, references to execution being commenced or continued include references to diligence being carried out or continued, and references to distress being levied shall be omitted.

SEC. 11   Effect of order

11(1)   [On making of administration order]   On the making of an administration order—

    (a) any petition for the winding up of the company shall be dismissed, and

    (b) any administrative receiver of the company shall vacate office.

11(2)   [Vacation of office by receiver]   Where an administration order has been made, any receiver of part of the company's property shall vacate office on being required to do so by the administrator.

11(3)   [Limitations]   During the period for which an administration order is in force—

    (a) no resolution may be passed or order made for the winding up of the company;

    (b) no administrative receiver of the company may be appointed;

    (c) no other steps may be taken to enforce any security over the company's property, or to repossess goods in the company's possession under any hire-purchase agreement, except with the consent of the administrator or the leave of the court and subject (where the court gives leave) to such terms as the court may impose; and

[The next page is 50,401]

(d) no other proceedings and no execution or other legal process may be commenced or continued, and no distress may be levied, against the company or its property except with the consent of the administrator or the leave of the court and subject (where the court gives leave) to such terms as aforesaid.

11(4) **[Where vacation of office under sec. 11(1)(b), (2)]** Where at any time an administrative receiver of the company has vacated office under subsection (1)(b), or a receiver of part of the company's property has vacated office under subsection (2)—

(a) his remuneration and any expenses properly incurred by him, and

(b) any indemnity to which he is entitled out of the assets of the company,

shall be charged on and (subject to subsection (3) above) paid out of any property of the company which was in his custody or under his control at that time in priority to any security held by the person by or on whose behalf he was appointed.

11(5) **[Sec. 40, 59]** Neither an administrative receiver who vacates office under subsection (1)(b) nor a receiver who vacates office under subsection (2) is required on or after so vacating office to take any steps for the purpose of complying with any duty imposed on him by section 40 or 59 of this Act (duty to pay preferential creditors).

SEC. 12 Notification of order

12(1) **[Information in invoices etc.]** Every invoice, order for goods or business letter which, at a time when an administration order is in force in relation to a company, is issued by or on behalf of the company or the administrator, being a document on or in which the company's name appears, shall also contain the administrator's name and a statement that the affairs, business and property of the company are being managed by the administrator.

12(2) **[Penalty on default]** If default is made in complying with this section, the company and any of the following persons who without reasonable excuse authorises or permits the default, namely, the administrator and any officer of the company, is liable to a fine.

ADMINISTRATORS

SEC. 13 Appointment of administrator

13(1) **[Appointment]** The administrator of a company shall be appointed either by the administration order or by an order under the next subsection.

13(2) **[Court may fill vacancy]** If a vacancy occurs by death, resignation or otherwise in the office of the administrator, the court may by order fill the vacancy.

13(3) **[Application for sec. 13(2) order]** An application for an order under subsection (2) may be made—

(a) by any continuing administrator of the company; or

(b) where there is no such administrator, by a creditors' committee established under section 26 below; or

    (c) where there is no such administrator and no such committee, by the company or the directors or by any creditor or creditors of the company.

SEC. **14**   General powers

14(1)   **[Powers of administrator]**   The administrator of a company—

    (a) may do all such things as may be necessary for the management of the affairs, business and property of the company, and

    (b) without prejudice to the generality of paragraph (a), has the powers specified in Schedule 1 to this Act;

and in the application of that Schedule to the administrator of a company the words "he" and "him" refer to the administrator.

14(2)   **[Extra powers]**   The administrator also has power—

    (a) to remove any director of the company and to appoint any person to be a director of it, whether to fill a vacancy or otherwise, and

    (b) to call any meeting of the members or creditors of the company.

14(3)   **[Application for directions]**   The administrator may apply to the court for directions in relation to any particular matter arising in connection with the carrying out of his functions.

14(4)   **[Conflict with other powers]**   Any power conferred on the company or its officers, whether by this Act or the Companies Act or by the memorandum or articles of association, which could be exercised in such a way as to interfere with the exercise by the administrator of his powers is not exercisable except with the consent of the administrator, which may be given either generally or in relation to particular cases.

14(5)   **[Administrator agent]**   In exercising his powers the administrator is deemed to act as the company's agent.

14(6)   **[Third party]**   A person dealing with the administrator in good faith and for value is not concerned to inquire whether the administrator is acting within his powers.

SEC. **15**   Power to deal with charged property, etc.

15(1)   **[Power of disposal etc.]**   The administrator of a company may dispose of or otherwise exercise his powers in relation to any property of the company which is subject to a security to which this subsection applies as if the property were not subject to the security.

15(2)   **[Court orders, on application by administrator]**   Where, on an application by the administrator, the court is satisfied that the disposal (with or without other assets) of—

    (a) any property of the company subject to a security to which this subsection applies, or

    (b) any goods in the possession of the company under a hire-purchase agreement,

would be likely to promote the purpose or one or more of the purposes specified in the administration order, the court may by order authorise the administrator to dispose of the property as if it were not subject to the security or to dispose of the goods as if all rights of the owner under the hire-purchase agreement were vested in the company.

15(3)   [Application of sec. 15(1), (2)]   Subsection (1) applies to any security which, as created, was a floating charge; and subsection (2) applies to any other security.

15(4)   [Effect of security where property disposed of]   Where property is disposed of under subsection (1), the holder of the security has the same priority in respect of any property of the company directly or indirectly representing the property disposed of as he would have had in respect of the property subject to the security.

15(5)   [Conditions for sec. 15(2) order]   It shall be a condition of an order under subsection (2) that—

(a) the net proceeds of the disposal, and

(b) where those proceeds are less than such amount as may be determined by the court to be the net amount which would be realised on a sale of the property or goods in the open market by a willing vendor, such sums as may be required to make good the deficiency,

shall be applied towards discharging the sums secured by the security or payable under the hire-purchase agreement.

15(6)   [Where sec. 15(5) condition re two or more securities]   Where a condition imposed in pursuance of subsection (5) relates to two or more securities, that condition requires the net proceeds of the disposal and, where paragraph (b) of that subsection applies, the sums mentioned in that paragraph to be applied towards discharging the sums secured by those securities in the order of their priorities.

15(7)   [Copy of sec. 15(2) order to registrar]   An office copy of an order under subsection (2) shall, within 14 days after the making of the order, be sent by the administrator to the registrar of companies.

15(8)   [Non-compliance with sec. 15(7)]   If the administrator without reasonable excuse fails to comply with subsection (7), he is liable to a fine and, for continued contravention, to a daily default fine.

15(9)   [Interpretation]   References in this section to hire-purchase agreements include conditional sale agreements, chattel leasing agreements and retention of title agreements.

SEC. 16   Operation of sec. 15 in Scotland

16(1)   [Administrator's duty]   Where property is disposed of under section 15 in its application to Scotland, the administrator shall grant to the disponee an appropriate document of transfer or conveyance of the property, and—

(a) that document, or

(b) where any recording, intimation or registration of the document is a legal requirement for completion of title to the property, that recording, intimation or registration,

has the effect of disencumbering the property of or, as the case may be, freeing the property from the security.

16(2)   [Disposal of goods on hire-purchase etc.]   Where goods in the possession of the company under a hire-purchase agreement, conditional sale agreement, chattel leasing agreement or retention of title agreement are disposed of under section 15 in its application to Scotland, the disposal has the effect of extinguishing, as against the disponee, all rights of the owner of the goods under the agreement.

SEC. 17   General duties

17(1)   [Control of company property]   The administrator of a company shall, on his appointment, take into his custody or under his control all the property to which the company is or appears to be entitled.

17(2)   [Management of affairs, etc.]   The administrator shall manage the affairs, business and property of the company—

(a) at any time before proposals have been approved (with or without modifications) under section 24 below, in accordance with any directions given by the court, and

(b) at any time after proposals have been so approved, in accordance with those proposals as from time to time revised, whether by him or a predecessor of his.

17(3)   [Summoning of creditors meeting]   The administrator shall summon a meeting of the company's creditors if—

(a) he is requested, in accordance with the rules, to do so by one-tenth, in value, of the company's creditors, or

(b) he is directed to do so by the court.

Note
For the rules relevant for s. 17(3), see The Insolvency Rules 1986, r. 2.21ff.

SEC. 18   Discharge or variation of administration order

18(1)   [Application to court by administrator]   The administrator of a company may at any time apply to the court for the administration order to be discharged, or to be varied so as to specify an additional purpose.

18(2)   [Duty to make application]   The administrator shall make an application under this section if—

(a) it appears to him that the purpose or each of the purposes specified in the order either has been achieved or is incapable of achievement, or

(b) he is required to do so by a meeting of the company's creditors summoned for the purpose in accordance with the rules.

18(3)   [Court order]   On the hearing of an application under this section, the court may by order discharge or vary the administration order and make such consequential provision as it thinks fit, or adjourn the hearing conditionally or unconditionally, or make an interim order or any other order it thinks fit.

18(4)   [Copy of order to registrar]   Where the administration order is discharged or varied the administrator shall, within 14 days after the making of the order effecting the discharge or variation, send an office copy of that order to the registrar of companies.

18(5) **[Non-compliance with sec. 18(4)]** If the administrator without reasonable excuse fails to comply with subsection (4), he is liable to a fine and, for continued contravention, to a daily default fine.

SEC. **19** Vacation of office

19(1) **[Removal or resignation]** The administrator of a company may at any time be removed from office by order of the court and may, in the prescribed circumstances, resign his office by giving notice of his resignation to the court.

Note
For the prescribed circumstances, see The Insolvency Rules
1986, r. 2.53.

19(2) **[Vacation of office, etc.]** The administrator shall vacate office if—

  (a) he ceases to be qualified to act as an insolvency practitioner in relation to the company, or

  (b) the administration order is discharged.

19(3) **[Ceasing to be administrator]** Where at any time a person ceases to be administrator, the next two subsections apply.

19(4) **[Remuneration and expenses]** His remuneration and any expenses properly incurred by him shall be charged on and paid out of any property of the company which is in his custody or under his control at that time in priority to any security to which section 15(1) then applies.

19(5) **[Debts or liabilities]** Any sums payable in respect of debts or liabilities incurred, while he was administrator, under contracts entered into or contracts of employment adopted by him or a predecessor of his in the carrying out of his or the predecessor's functions shall be charged on and paid out of any such property as is mentioned in subsection (4) in priority to any charge arising under that subsection.

For this purpose, the administrator is not to be taken to have adopted a contract of employment by reason of anything done or omitted to be done within 14 days after his appointment.

SEC. **20** Release of administrator

20(1) **[Time of release]** A person who has ceased to be the administrator of a company has his release with effect from the following time, that is to say—

  (a) in the case of a person who has died, the time at which notice is given to the court in accordance with the rules that he has ceased to hold office;

  (b) in any other case, such time as the court may determine.

Note
The relevant rule for s. 20(1)(a) is The Insolvency Rules
1986, r. 2.54.

20(2) **[Discharge from liability, etc.]** Where a person has his release under this section, he is, with effect from the time specified above, discharged from all liability both in respect of acts or omissions of his in the administration and otherwise in relation to his conduct as administrator.

20(3)   **[Sec. 212]**   However, nothing in this section prevents the exercise, in relation to a person who has had his release as above, of the court's powers under section 212 in Chapter X of Part IV (summary remedy against delinquent directors, liquidators, etc.).

ASCERTAINMENT AND INVESTIGATION OF COMPANY'S AFFAIRS

SEC. 21   Information to be given by administrator

21(1)   **[Duties of administrator]**   Where an administration order has been made, the administrator shall—

- (a) forthwith send to the company and publish in the prescribed manner a notice of the order, and
- (b) within 28 days after the making of the order, unless the court otherwise directs, send such a notice to all creditors of the company (so far as he is aware of their addresses).

21(2)   **[Copy of order to registrar]**   Where an administration order has been made, the administrator shall also, within 14 days after the making of the order, send an office copy of the order to the registrar of companies and to such other persons as may be prescribed.

Note
See The Insolvency Rules 1986, r. 2.10.

21(3)   **[Penalty for non-compliance]**   If the administrator without reasonable excuse fails to comply with this section, he is liable to a fine and, for continued contravention, to a daily default fine.

SEC. 22   Statement of affairs to be submitted to administrator

22(1)   **[Duty of administrator]**   Where an administration order has been made, the administrator shall forthwith require some or all of the persons mentioned below to make out and submit to him a statement in the prescribed form as to the affairs of the company.

Note
See The Insolvency Rules 1986, r. 2.11.

22(2)   **[Contents of statement]**   The statement shall be verified by affidavit by the persons required to submit it and shall show—

- (a) particulars of the company's assets, debts and liabilities;
- (b) the names and addresses of its creditors;
- (c) the securities held by them respectively;
- (d) the dates when the securities were respectively given; and
- (e) such further or other information as may be prescribed.

22(3)   **[Persons in sec. 22(1)]**   The persons referred to in subsection (1) are—

- (a) those who are or have been officers of the company;
- (b) those who have taken part in the company's formation at any time within one year before the date of the administration order;

(c) those who are in the company's employment or have been in its employment within that year, and are in the administrator's opinion capable of giving the information required;

(d) those who are or have been within that year officers of or in the employment of a company which is, or within that year was, an officer of the company.

In this subsection **"employment"** includes employment under a contract for services.

22(4) **[Time for submitting statement]** Where any persons are required under this section to submit a statement of affairs to the administrator, they shall do so (subject to the next subsection) before the end of the period of 21 days beginning with the day after that on which the prescribed notice of the requirement is given to them by the administrator.

22(5) **[Powers re release, extension of time]** The administrator, if he thinks fit, may—

(a) at any time release a person from an obligation imposed on him under subsection (1) or (2), or

(b) either when giving notice under subsection (4) or subsequently, extend the period so mentioned;

and where the administrator has refused to exercise a power conferred by this subsection, the court, if it thinks fit, may exercise it.

22(6) **[Penalty for non-compliance]** If a person without reasonable excuse fails to comply with any obligation imposed under this section, he is liable to a fine and, for continued contravention, to a daily default fine.

ADMINISTRATOR'S PROPOSALS

SEC. 23 Statement of proposals

23(1) **[Duties of administrator]** Where an administration order has been made, the administrator shall, within 3 months (or such longer period as the court may allow) after the making of the order—

(a) send to the registrar of companies and (so far as he is aware of their addresses) to all creditors a statement of his proposals for achieving the purpose or purposes specified in the order, and

(b) lay a copy of the statement before a meeting of the company's creditors summoned for the purpose on not less than 14 days' notice.

23(2) **[Copies of statement]** The administrator shall also, within 3 months (or such longer period as the court may allow) after the making of the order, either—

(a) send a copy of the statement (so far as he is aware of their addresses) to all members of the company, or

(b) publish in the prescribed manner a notice stating an address to which members of the company should write for copies of the statement to be sent to them free of charge.

Note
See The Insolvency Rules 1986, r. 2.17.

23(3) **[Penalty for non-compliance]** If the administrator without reasonable excuse fails to comply with this section, he is liable to a fine and, for continued contravention, to a daily default fine.

SEC. 24   Consideration of proposals by creditors' meeting

24(1) **[Creditors' meeting to decide]** A meeting of creditors summoned under section 23 shall decide whether to approve the administrator's proposals.

24(2) **[Approval, modifications]** The meeting may approve the proposals with modifications, but shall not do so unless the administrator consents to each modification.

24(3) **[Meeting in accordance with rules]** Subject as above, the meeting shall be conducted in accordance with the rules.

Note
See The Insolvency Rules 1986, r. 2.19ff.

24(4) **[Report and notice by administrator]** After the conclusion of the meeting in accordance with the rules, the administrator shall report the result of the meeting to the court and shall give notice of that result to the registrar of companies and to such persons as may be prescribed.

Note
See The Insolvency Rules 1986, r. 2.30.

24(5) **[If meeting does not approve]** If a report is given to the court under subsection (4) that the meeting has declined to approve the administrator's proposals (with or without modifications), the court may by order discharge the administration order and make such consequential provision as it thinks fit, or adjourn the hearing conditionally or unconditionally, or make an interim order or any other order that it thinks fit.

24(6) **[Where administration order discharged]** Where the administration order is discharged, the administrator shall, within 14 days after the making of the order effecting the discharge, send an office copy of that order to the registrar of companies.

24(7) **[Penalty for non-compliance]** If the administrator without reasonable excuse fails to comply with subsection (6), he is liable to a fine and, for continued contravention, to a daily default fine.

SEC. 25   Approval of substantial revisions

25(1) **[Application]** This section applies where—

   (a) proposals have been approved (with or without modifications) under section 24, and

   (b) the administrator proposes to make revisions of those proposals which appear to him substantial.

25(2) **[Duties of administrator]** The administrator shall—

   (a) send to all creditors of the company (so far as he is aware of their addresses) a statement in the prescribed form of his proposed revisions, and

   (b) lay a copy of the statement before a meeting of the company's creditors summoned for the purpose on not less than 14 days' notice;

and he shall not make the proposed revisions unless they are approved by the meeting.

25(3) **[Copies of statement]** The administrator shall also either—

   (a) send a copy of the statement (so far as he is aware of their addresses) to all members of the company, or

   (b) publish in the prescribed manner a notice stating an address to which members of the company should write for copies of the statement to be sent to them free of charge.

25(4) **[Approval, modifications]** The meeting of creditors may approve the proposed revisions with modifications, but shall not do so unless the administrator consents to each modification.

25(5) **[Meeting in accordance with rules]** Subject as above, the meeting shall be conducted in accordance with the rules.

25(6) **[Notification to registrar, et al.]** After the conclusion of the meeting in accordance with the rules, the administrator shall give notice of the result of the meeting to the registrar of companies and to such persons as may be prescribed.

MISCELLANEOUS

SEC. 26 Creditors' committee

26(1) **[Meeting may establish committee]** Where a meeting of creditors summoned under section 23 has approved the administrator's proposals (with or without modifications), the meeting may, if it thinks fit, establish a committee (**"the creditors' committee"**) to exercise the functions conferred on it by or under this Act.

26(2) **[Committee may summon administrator]** If such a committee is established, the committee may, on giving not less than 7 days' notice, require the administrator to attend before it at any reasonable time and furnish it with such information relating to the carrying out of his functions as it may reasonably require.

SEC. 27 Protection of interests of creditors and members

27(1) **[Application by creditor or member]** At any time when an administration order is in force, a creditor or member of the company may apply to the court by petition for an order under this section on the ground—

   (a) that the company's affairs, business and property are being or have been managed by the administrator in a manner which is unfairly prejudicial to the interests of its creditors or members generally, or of some part of its creditors or members (including at least himself), or

   (b) that any actual or proposed act or omission of the administrator is or would be so prejudicial.

27(2) **[Court order]** On an application for an order under this section the court may, subject as follows, make such order as it thinks fit for giving relief in respect of the matters complained of, or adjourn the hearing conditionally or unconditionally, or make an interim order or any other order that it thinks fit.

27(3) **[Limits of order]** An order under this section shall not prejudice or prevent—

   (a) the implementation of a voluntary arrangement approved under section 4 in Part I, or any compromise or arrangement sanctioned under section 425 of the Companies Act; or

   (b) where the application for the order was made more than 28 days after the approval of any proposals or revised proposals under section 24 or 25, the implementation of those proposals or revised proposals.

27(4) **[Contents of order]** Subject as above, an order under this section may in particular—

    (a) regulate the future management by the administrator of the company's affairs, business and property;

    (b) require the administrator to refrain from doing or continuing an act complained of by the petitioner, or to do an act which the petitioner has complained he has omitted to do;

    (c) require the summoning of a meeting of creditors or members for the purpose of considering such matters as the court may direct;

    (d) discharge the administration order and make such consequential provision as the court thinks fit.

27(5) **[Sec. 15, 16]** Nothing in sections 15 or 16 is to be taken as prejudicing applications to the court under this section.

27(6) **[Copy of discharge order to registrar]** Where the administration order is discharged, the administrator shall, within 14 days after the making of the order effecting the discharge, send an office copy of that order to the registrar of companies; and if without reasonable excuse he fails to comply with this subsection, he is liable to a fine and, for continued contravention, to a daily default fine.

PART III — RECEIVERSHIP

Chapter I — Receivers and Managers (England and Wales)

PRELIMINARY AND GENERAL PROVISIONS

SEC. 28   Extent of this Chapter

28 This Chapter does not apply to receivers appointed under Chapter II of this Part (Scotland).

SEC. 29   Definitions

29(1) **[Interpretation]** It is hereby declared that, except where the context otherwise requires—

    (a) any reference in the Companies Act or this Act to a receiver or manager of the property of a company, or to a receiver of it, includes a receiver or manager, or (as the case may be) a receiver of part only of that property and a receiver only of the income arising from the property or from part of it; and

    (b) any reference in the Companies Act or this Act to the appointment of a receiver or manager under powers contained in an instrument includes an appointment made under powers which, by virtue of any enactment, are implied in and have effect as if contained in an instrument.

29(2) **["Administrative receiver"]** In this Chapter **"administrative receiver"** means—

    (a) a receiver or manager of the whole (or substantially the whole) of a company's property appointed by or on behalf of the holders of any debentures of the company secured by a charge which, as created, was a floating charge, or by such a charge and one or more other securities; or

(b) a person who would be such a receiver or manager but for the appointment of some other person as the receiver of part of the company's property.

SEC. 30   Disqualification of body corporate from acting as receiver

30   A body corporate is not qualified for appointment as receiver of the property of a company, and any body corporate which acts as such a receiver is liable to a fine.

SEC. 31   Disqualification of undischarged bankrupt

31   If a person being an undischarged bankrupt acts as receiver or manager of the property of a company on behalf of debenture holders, he is liable to imprisonment or a fine, or both.

This does not apply to a receiver or manager acting under an appointment made by the court.

SEC. 32   Power for court to appoint official receiver

32   Where application is made to the court to appoint a receiver on behalf of the debenture holders or other creditors of a company which is being wound up by the court, the official receiver may be appointed.

RECEIVERS AND MANAGERS APPOINTED OUT OF COURT

SEC. 33   Time from which appointment is effective

33(1)   [Effect of appointment]   The appointment of a person as a receiver or manager of a company's property under powers contained in an instrument—

(a) is of no effect unless it is accepted by that person before the end of the business day next following that on which the instrument of appointment is received by him or on his behalf, and

(b) subject to this, is deemed to be made at the time at which the instrument of appointment is so received.

33(2)   [Joint receivers or managers]   This section applies to the appointment of two or more persons as joint receivers or managers of a company's property under powers contained in an instrument, subject to such modifications as may be prescribed by the rules.

Note
See The Insolvency Rules, r. 3.1.

SEC. 34   Liability for invalid appointment

34   Where the appointment of a person as the receiver or manager of a company's property under powers contained in an instrument is discovered to be invalid (whether by virtue of the invalidity of the instrument or otherwise), the court may order the person by whom or on whose behalf the appointment was made to indemnify the person appointed against any liability which arises solely by reason of the invalidity of the appointment.

SEC. 35   Application to court for directions

35(1)   **[Application]**   A receiver or manager of the property of a company appointed under powers contained in an instrument, or the persons by whom or on whose behalf a receiver or manager has been so appointed, may apply to the court for directions in relation to any particular matter arising in connection with the performance of the functions of the receiver or manager.

35(2)   **[Order, directions by court]**   On such an application, the court may give such directions, or may make such order declaring the rights of persons before the court or otherwise, as it thinks just.

SEC. 36   Court's power to fix remuneration

36(1)   **[Remuneration]**   The court may, on an application made by the liquidator of a company, by order fix the amount to be paid by way of remuneration to a person who, under powers contained in an instrument, has been appointed receiver or manager of the company's property.

36(2)   **[Extent of court's power]**   The court's power under subsection (1), where no previous order has been made with respect thereto under the subsection—

    (a) extends to fixing the remuneration for any period before the making of the order or the application for it,

    (b) is exercisable notwithstanding that the receiver or manager has died or ceased to act before the making of the order or the application, and

    (c) where the receiver or manager has been paid or has retained for his remuneration for any period before the making of the order any amount in excess of that so fixed for that period, extends to requiring him or his personal representatives to account for the excess or such part of it as may be specified in the order.

But the power conferred by paragraph (c) shall not be exercised as respects any period before the making of the application for the order under this section, unless in the court's opinion there are special circumstances making it proper for the power to be exercised.

36(3)   **[Variation, amendment of order]**   The court may from time to time on an application made either by the liquidator or by the receiver or manager, vary or amend an order made under subsection (1).

SEC. 37   Liability for contracts, etc.

37(1)   **[Personal liability, indemnity]**   A receiver or manager appointed under powers contained in an instrument (other than an administrative receiver) is, to the same extent as if he had been appointed by order of the court—

    (a) personally liable on any contract entered into by him in the performance of his functions (except in so far as the contract otherwise provides) and on any contract of employment adopted by him in the performance of those functions, and

    (b) entitled in respect of that liability to indemnity out of the assets.

37(2) [Interpretation of sec. 37(1)(a)] For the purposes of subsection (1)(a), the receiver or manager is not to be taken to have adopted a contract of employment by reason of anything done or omitted to be done within 14 days after his appointment.

37(3) [Extent of sec. 37(1)] Subsection (1) does not limit any right to indemnity which the receiver or manager would have apart from it, nor limit his liability on contracts entered into without authority, nor confer any right to indemnity in respect of that liability.

37(4) [Vacation of office] Where at any time the receiver or manager so appointed vacates office—

> (a) his remuneration and any expenses properly incurred by him, and

> (b) any indemnity to which he is entitled out of the assets of the company,

shall be charged on and paid out of any property of the company which is in his custody or under his control at that time in priority to any charge or other security held by the person by or on whose behalf he was appointed.

SEC. 38   Receivership accounts to be delivered to registrar

38(1) [Where appointment under powers in instrument] Except in the case of an administrative receiver, every receiver or manager of a company's property who has been appointed under powers contained in an instrument shall deliver to the registrar of companies for registration the requisite accounts of his receipts and payments.

38(2) [Time for delivering accounts] The accounts shall be delivered within one month (or such longer period as the registrar may allow) after the expiration of 12 months from the date of his appointment and of every subsequent period of 6 months, and also within one month after he ceases to act as receiver or manager.

38(3) [Form of accounts] The requisite accounts shall be an abstract in the prescribed form showing—

> (a) receipts and payments during the relevant period of 12 or 6 months, or

> (b) where the receiver or manager ceases to act, receipts and payments during the period from the end of the period of 12 or 6 months to which the last preceding abstract related (or, if no preceding abstract has been delivered under this section, from the date of his appointment) up to the date of his so ceasing, and the aggregate amount of receipts and payments during all preceding periods since his appointment.

38(4) ["Prescribed"] In this section **"prescribed"** means prescribed by regulations made by statutory instrument by the Secretary of State.

38(5) [Penalty on default] A receiver or manager who makes default in complying with this section is liable to a fine and, for continued contravention, to a daily default fine.

PROVISIONS APPLICABLE TO EVERY RECEIVERSHIP

SEC. 39   Notification that receiver or manager appointed

39(1) [Statement in invoices etc.] When a receiver or manager of the property of a company has been appointed, every invoice, order for goods or business letter issued by or on behalf of the company or the receiver or manager or the liquidator of the company, being a document on or in which the company's name appears, shall contain a statement that a receiver or manager has been appointed.

39(2)   [Penalty on default]   If default is made in complying with this section, the company and any of the following persons, who knowingly and wilfully authorises or permits the default, namely, any officer of the company, any liquidator of the company and any receiver or manager, is liable to a fine.

SEC. 40   Payment of debts out of assets subject to floating charge

40(1)   [Application]   The following applies, in the case of a company, where a receiver is appointed on behalf of the holders of any debentures of the company secured by a charge which, as created, was a floating charge.

40(2)   [Payment of preferential debts]   If the company is not at the time in course of being wound up, its preferential debts (within the meaning given to that expression by section 386 in Part XII) shall be paid out of the assets coming to the hands of the receiver in priority to any claims for principal or interest in respect of the debentures.

40(3)   [Recoupment of payments]   Payments made under this section shall be recouped, as far as may be, out of the assets of the company available for payment of general creditors.

SEC. 41   Enforcement of duty to make returns

41(1)   [Court order re defaults]   If a receiver or manager of a company's property—

   (a) having made default in filing, delivering or making any return, account or other document, or in giving any notice, which a receiver or manager is by law required to file, deliver, make or give, fails to make good the default within 14 days after the service on him of a notice requiring him to do so, or

   (b) having been appointed under powers contained in an instrument, has, after being required at any time by the liquidator of the company to do so, failed to render proper accounts of his receipts and payments and to vouch them and pay over to the liquidator the amount properly payable to him,

the court may, on an application made for the purpose, make an order directing the receiver or manager (as the case may be) to make good the default within such time as may be specified in the order.

41(2)   [Application for order]   In the case of the default mentioned in subsection (1)(a), application to the court may be made by any member or creditor of the company or by the registrar of companies; and in the case of the default mentioned in subsection (1)(b), the application shall be made by the liquidator.

    In either case the court's order may provide that all costs of and incidental to the application shall be borne by the receiver or manager, as the case may be.

41(3)   [Other enactments]   Nothing in this section prejudices the operation of any enactment imposing penalties on receivers in respect of any such default as is mentioned in subsection (1).

ADMINISTRATIVE RECEIVERS: GENERAL

SEC. 42   General powers

42(1)   [Powers in Sch. 1]   The powers conferred on the administrative receiver of a company by the debentures by virtue of which he was appointed are deemed to include (except in so far as they are inconsistent with any of the provisions of those debentures) the powers specified in Schedule 1 to this Act.

42(2) [Interpretation of Sch. 1]   In the application of Schedule 1 to the administrative receiver of a company—

  (a) the words "he" and "him" refer to the administrative receiver, and

  (b) references to the property of the company are to the property of which he is or, but for the appointment of some other person as the receiver of part of the company's property, would be the receiver or manager.

42(3) [Deemed capacity]   A person dealing with the administrative receiver in good faith and for value is not concerned to inquire whether the receiver is acting within his powers.

SEC. 43   Power to dispose of charged property, etc.

43(1) [Application to court]   Where, on an application by the administrative receiver, the court is satisfied that the disposal (with or without other assets) of any relevant property which is subject to a security would be likely to promote a more advantageous realisation of the company's assets than would otherwise be effected, the court may by order authorise the administrative receiver to dispose of the property as if it were not subject to the security.

43(2) [Application of sec. 43(1)]   Subsection (1) does not apply in the case of any security held by the person by or on whose behalf the administrative receiver was appointed, or of any security to which a security so held has priority.

43(3) [Conditions for order]   It shall be a condition of an order under this section that—

  (a) the net proceeds of the disposal, and

  (b) where those proceeds are less than such amount as may be determined by the court to be the net amount which would be realised on the sale of the property in the open market by a willing vendor, such sums as may be required to make good the deficiency,

shall be applied towards discharging the sums secured by the security.

43(4) [Where two or more securities]   Where a condition imposed in pursuance of subsection (3) relates to two or more securities, that condition shall require the net proceeds of the disposal and, where paragraph (b) of that subsection applies, the sums mentioned in that paragraph to be applied towards discharging the sums secured by those securities in the order of their priorities.

43(5) [Copy of order to registrar]   An office copy of an order under this section shall, within 14 days of the making of the order, be sent by the administrative receiver to the registrar of companies.

43(6) [Penalty for non-compliance]   If the administrative receiver without reasonable excuse fails to comply with subsection (5), he is liable to a fine and, for continued contravention, to a daily default fine.

43(7) ["Relevant property"]   In this section **"relevant property"**, in relation to the administrative receiver, means the property of which he is or, but for the appointment of some other person as the receiver of part of the company's property, would be the receiver or manager.

SEC. 44   Agency and liability for contracts

44(1) [Position of administrative receiver] The administrative receiver of a company—

(a) is deemed to be the company's agent, unless and until the company goes into liquidation;

(b) is personally liable on any contract entered into by him in the carrying out of his functions (except in so far as the contract otherwise provides) and on any contract of employment adopted by him in the carrying out of those functions; and

(c) is entitled in respect of that liability to an indemnity out of the assets of the company.

44(2) [Interpretation] For the purposes of subsection (1)(b) the administrative receiver is not to be taken to have adopted a contract of employment by reason of anything done or omitted to be done within 14 days after his appointment.

44(3) [Effect on other rights] This section does not limit any right to indemnity which the administrative receiver would have apart from it, nor limit his liability on contracts entered into or adopted without authority, nor confer any right to indemnity in respect of that liability.

SEC. 45   Vacation of office

45(1) [Removal by court, resignation] An administrative receiver of a company may at any time be removed from office by order of the court (but not otherwise) and may resign his office by giving notice of his resignation in the prescribed manner to such persons as may be prescribed.

45(2) [Vacation of office] An administrative receiver shall vacate office if he ceases to be qualified to act as an insolvency practitioner in relation to the company.

45(3) [Effect of vacation of office] Where at any time an administrative receiver vacates office—

(a) his remuneration and any expenses properly incurred by him, and

(b) any indemnity to which he is entitled out of the assets of the company,

shall be charged on and paid out of any property of the company which is in his custody or under his control at that time in priority to any security held by the person by or on whose behalf he was appointed.

45(4) [Notice to registrar] Where an administrative receiver vacates office otherwise than by death, he shall, within 14 days after his vacation of office, send a notice to that effect to the registrar of companies.

45(5) [Penalty for non-compliance] If an administrative receiver without reasonable excuse fails to comply with subsection (4), he is liable to a fine and, for continued contravention, to a daily default fine.

ADMINISTRATIVE RECEIVERS: ASCERTAINMENT AND
INVESTIGATION OF COMPANY'S AFFAIRS

SEC. 46 Information to be given by administrative receiver

46(1) [Notices] Where an administrative receiver is appointed, he shall—

(a) forthwith send to the company and publish in the prescribed manner a notice of his appointment, and

(b) within 28 days after his appointment, unless the court otherwise directs, send such a notice to all the creditors of the company (so far as he is aware of their addresses).

46(2) [Non-application] This section and the next do not apply in relation to the appointment of an administrative receiver to act—

(a) with an existing administrative receiver, or

(b) in place of an administrative receiver dying or ceasing to act,

except that, where they apply to an administrative receiver who dies or ceases to act before they have been fully complied with, the references in this section and the next to the administrative receiver include (subject to the next subsection) his successor and any continuing administrative receiver.

46(3) [Where company being wound up] If the company is being wound up, this section and the next apply notwithstanding that the administrative receiver and the liquidator are the same person, but with any necessary modifications arising from that fact.

46(4) [Penalty for non-compliance] If the administrative receiver without reasonable excuse fails to comply with this section, he is liable to a fine and, for continued contravention, to a daily default fine.

SEC. 47 Statement of affairs to be submitted

47(1) [Duty of administrative receiver] Where an administrative receiver is appointed, he shall forthwith require some or all of the persons mentioned below to make out and submit to him a statement in the prescribed form as to the affairs of the company.

47(2) [Contents of statement] A statement submitted under this section shall be verified by affidavit by the persons required to submit it and shall show—

(a) particulars of the company's assets, debts and liabilities;

(b) the names and addresses of its creditors;

(c) the securities held by them respectively;

(d) the dates when the securities were respectively given; and

(e) such further or other information as may be prescribed.

47(3)   [Persons in sec. 47(1)]   The persons referred to in subsection (1) are—

(a)   those who are or have been officers of the company;

(b)   those who have taken part in the company's formation at any time within one year before the date of the appointment of the administrative receiver;

(c)   those who are in the company's employment, or have been in its employment within that year, and are in the administrative receiver's opinion capable of giving the information required;

(d)   those who are or have been within that year officers of or in the employment of a company which is, or within that year was, an officer of the company.

In this subsection **"employment"** includes employment under a contract for services.

47(4)   [Time for statement]   Where any persons are required under this section to submit a statement of affairs to the administrative receiver, they shall do so (subject to the next subsection) before the end of the period of 21 days beginning with the day after that on which the prescribed notice of the requirement is given to them by the administrative receiver.

47(5)   [Release, extension of time]   The administrative receiver, if he thinks fit, may—

(a)   at any time release a person from an obligation imposed on him under subsection (1) or (2), or

(b)   either when giving notice under subsection (4) or subsequently, extend the period so mentioned;

and where the administrative receiver has refused to exercise a power conferred by this subsection, the court, if it thinks fit, may exercise it.

47(6)   [Penalty for non-compliance]   If a person without reasonable excuse fails to comply with any obligation imposed under this section, he is liable to a fine and, for continued contravention, to a daily default fine.

SEC. 48   Report by administrative receiver

48(1)   [Duty of administrative receiver]   Where an administrative receiver is appointed, he shall, within 3 months (or such longer period as the court may allow) after his appointment, send to the registrar of companies, to any trustees for secured creditors of the company and (so far as he is aware of their addresses) to all such creditors a report as to the following matters, namely—

(a)   the events leading up to his appointment, so far as he is aware of them;

(b)   the disposal or proposed disposal by him of any property of the company and the carrying on or proposed carrying on by him of any business of the company;

(c)   the amounts of principal and interest payable to the debenture holders by whom or on whose behalf he was appointed and the amounts payable to preferential creditors; and

(d)   the amount (if any) likely to be available for the payment of other creditors.

48(2) **[Copies of report]** The administrative receiver shall also, within 3 months (or such longer period as the court may allow) after his appointment, either—

(a) send a copy of the report (so far as he is aware of their addresses) to all unsecured creditors of the company; or

(b) publish in the prescribed manner a notice stating an address to which unsecured creditors of the company should write for copies of the report to be sent to them free of charge,

and (in either case), unless the court otherwise directs, lay a copy of the report before a meeting of the company's unsecured creditors summoned for the purpose on not less than 14 days' notice.

48(3) **[Conditions for sec. 48(2) direction]** The court shall not give a direction under subsection (2) unless—

(a) the report states the intention of the administrative receiver to apply for the direction, and

(b) a copy of the report is sent to the persons mentioned in paragraph (a) of that subsection, or a notice is published as mentioned in paragraph (b) of that subsection, not less than 14 days before the hearing of the application.

48(4) **[Where company in liquidation]** Where the company has gone or goes into liquidation, the administrative receiver—

(a) shall, within 7 days after his compliance with subsection (1) or, if later, the nomination or appointment of the liquidator, send a copy of the report to the liquidator, and

(b) where he does so within the time limited for compliance with subsection (2), is not required to comply with that subsection.

48(5) **[Report to include summary of statement]** A report under this section shall include a summary of the statement of affairs made out and submitted to the administrative receiver under section 47 and of his comments (if any) upon it.

48(6) **[Limit on report only]** Nothing in this section is to be taken as requiring any such report to include any information the disclosure of which would seriously prejudice the carrying out by the administrative receiver of his functions.

48(7) **[Application of sec. 46(2)]** Section 46(2) applies for the purposes of this section also.

48(8) **[Penalty for non-compliance]** If the administrative receiver without reasonable excuse fails to comply with this section, he is liable to a fine and, for continued contravention, to a daily default fine.

SEC. 49 Committee of creditors

49(1) **[Meeting may establish committee]** Where a meeting of creditors is summoned under section 48, the meeting may, if it thinks fit, establish a committee (**"the creditors' committee"**) to exercise the functions conferred on it by or under this Act.

49(2) **[Committee may summon administrative receiver]** If such a committee is established, the committee may, on giving not less than 7 days' notice, require the administrative receiver to attend before it at any reasonable time and furnish it with such information relating to the carrying out by him of his functions as it may reasonably require.

Chapter II — Receivers (Scotland)

SEC. 50   Extent of this Chapter

50   This Chapter extends to Scotland only.

Note
For Ch. II, reference should be made to The Receivers
(Scotland) Regulations 1986 (S.I. 1986 No. 1917 (S. 141)).

SEC. 51   Power to appoint receiver

51(1)   [Floating charge holder may appoint receiver]   It is competent under the law of Scotland for the holder of a floating charge over all or any part of the property (including uncalled capital), which may from time to time be comprised in the property and undertaking of an incorporated company (whether a company within the meaning of the Companies Act or not) which the Court of Session has jurisdiction to wind up, to appoint a receiver of such part of the property of the company as is subject to the charge.

51(2)   [Appointment by court on application]   It is competent under the law of Scotland for the court, on the application of the holder of such a floating charge, to appoint a receiver of such part of the property of the company as is subject to the charge.

51(3)   [Those disqualified]   The following are disqualified from being appointed as receiver—

(a) a body corporate;

(b) an undischarged bankrupt; and

(c) a firm according to the law of Scotland.

51(4)   [Scottish firm]   A body corporate or a firm according to the law of Scotland which acts as a receiver is liable to a fine.

51(5)   [Undischarged bankrupt]   An undischarged bankrupt who so acts is liable to imprisonment or a fine, or both.

51(6)   ["Receiver"]   In this section, **"receiver"** includes joint receivers.

SEC. 52   Circumstances justifying appointment

52(1)   [Events for sec. 51(1) appointment]   A receiver may be appointed under section 51(1) by the holder of the floating charge on the occurrence of any event which, by the provisions of the instrument creating the charge, entitles the holder of the charge to make that appointment and, in so far as not otherwise provided for by the instrument, on the occurrence of any of the following events, namely—

(a) the expiry of a period of 21 days after the making of a demand for payment of the whole or any part of the principal sum secured by the charge, without payment having been made;

(b) the expiry of a period of 2 months during the whole of which interest due and payable under the charge has been in arrears;

(c) the making of an order or the passing of a resolution to wind up the company;

(d) the appointment of a receiver by virtue of any other floating charge created by the company.

52(2) [Events for sec. 51(2) appointment] A receiver may be appointed by the court under section 51(2) on the occurrence of any event which, by the provisions of the instrument creating the floating charge, entitles the holder of the charge to make that appointment and, in so far as not otherwise provided for by the instrument, on the occurrence of any of the following events, namely—

(a) where the court, on the application of the holder of the charge, pronounces itself satisfied that the position of the holder of the charge is likely to be prejudiced if no such appointment is made;

(b) any of the events referred to in paragraphs (a) to (c) of subsection (1).

SEC. 53 Mode of appointment by holder of charge

53(1) [Instrument of appointment] The appointment of a receiver by the holder of the floating charge under section 51(1) shall be by means of a validly executed instrument in writing ("the instrument of appointment"), a copy (certified in the prescribed manner to be a correct copy) whereof shall be delivered by or on behalf of the person making the appointment to the registrar of companies for registration within 7 days of its execution and shall be accompanied by a notice in the prescribed form.

53(2) [Penalty on default] If any person without reasonable excuse makes default in complying with the requirements of subsection (1), he is liable to a fine and, for continued contravention, to a daily default fine.

53(3) [Execution of instrument] The instrument of appointment is validly executed—

(a) by a company, if it is executed in accordance with the provisions of section 36 of the Companies Act as if it were a contract, and

(b) by any other person, if it is executed in the manner required or permitted by the law of Scotland in the case of an attested deed.

53(4) [Execution on behalf of floating charge holder] The instrument may be executed on behalf of the holder of the floating charge by virtue of which the receiver is to be appointed—

(a) by any person duly authorised in writing by the holder to execute the instrument, and

(b) in the case of an appointment of a receiver by the holders of a series of secured debentures, by any person authorised by resolution of the debenture-holders to execute the instrument.

53(5) [Entry on register] On receipt of the certified copy of the instrument of appointment in accordance with subsection (1), the registrar shall, on payment of the prescribed fee, enter the particulars of the appointment in the register of charges.

53(6) [Effect of appointment] The appointment of a person as a receiver by an instrument of appointment in accordance with subsection (1)—

(a) is of no effect unless it is accepted by that person before the end of the business day next following that on which the instrument of appointment is received by him or on his behalf, and

(b) subject to paragraph (a), is deemed to be made on the day on and at the time at which the instrument of appointment is so received, as evidenced by a written docquet by that person or on his behalf;

and this subsection applies to the appointment of joint receivers subject to such modifications as may be prescribed.

53(7) [Attachment of charge]   On the appointment of a receiver under this section, the floating charge by virtue of which he was appointed attaches to the property then subject to the charge; and such attachment has effect as if the charge was a fixed security over the property to which it has attached.

Note
See the regulations referred to in the note to s. 50, especially
Form 1 (Scot).

SEC. 54   Appointment by court

54(1) [Petition to court]   Application for the appointment of a receiver by the court under section 51(2) shall be by petition to the court, which shall be served on the company.

54(2) [Issue of interlocutor]   On such an application, the court shall, if it thinks fit, issue an interlocutor making the appointment of the receiver.

54(3) [Copy of interlocutor to registrar, penalty on default]   A copy (certified by the clerk of the court to be a correct copy) of the court's interlocutor making the appointment shall be delivered by or on behalf of the petitioner to the registrar of companies for registration, accompanied by a notice in the prescribed form, within 7 days of the date of the interlocutor or such longer period as the court may allow.

If any person without reasonable excuse makes default in complying with the requirements of this subsection, he is liable to a fine and, for continued contravention, to a daily default fine.

54(4) [Entry on register]   On receipt of the certified copy interlocutor in accordance with subsection (3), the registrar shall, on payment of the prescribed fee, enter the particulars of the appointment in the register of charges.

54(5) [Date of appointment]   The receiver is to be regarded as having been appointed on the date of his being appointed by the court.

54(6) [Attachment of charge]   On the appointment of a receiver under this section, the floating charge by virtue of which he was appointed attaches to the property then subject to the charge; and such attachment has effect as if the charge were a fixed security over the property to which it has attached.

54(7) [Rules of court re urgent cases]   In making rules of court for the purposes of this section, the Court of Session shall have regard to the need for special provision for cases which appear to the court to require to be dealt with as a matter of urgency.

Note
See Form 2 (Scot) and note to s. 50.

SEC. 55   Powers of receiver

55(1) [Powers in instrument]   Subject to the next subsection, a receiver has in relation to such part of the property of the company as is attached by the floating charge by virtue of which he was appointed, the powers, if any, given to him by the instrument creating that charge.

55(2) **[Powers in Sch. 2]** In addition, the receiver has under this Chapter the powers as respects that property (in so far as these are not inconsistent with any provision contained in that instrument) which are specified in Schedule 2 to this Act.

55(3) **[Restriction on powers]** Subsections (1) and (2) apply—

    (a) subject to the rights of any person who has effectually executed diligence on all or any part of the property of the company prior to the appointment of the receiver, and

    (b) subject to the rights of any person who holds over all or any part of the property of the company a fixed security or floating charge having priority over, or ranking pari passu with, the floating charge by virtue of which the receiver was appointed.

55(4) **[Enquiry as to authority not necessary]** A person dealing with a receiver in good faith and for value is not concerned to enquire whether the receiver is acting within his powers.

SEC. 56 Precedence among receivers

56(1) **[Order of precedence]** Where there are two or more floating charges subsisting over all or any part of the property of the company, a receiver may be appointed under this Chapter by virtue of each such charge; but a receiver appointed by, or on the application of, the holder of a floating charge having priority of ranking over any other floating charge by virtue of which a receiver has been appointed has the powers given to a receiver by section 55 and Schedule 2 to the exclusion of any other receiver.

56(2) **[Where floating charges rank equally]** Where two or more floating charges rank with one another equally, and two or more receivers have been appointed by virtue of such charges, the receivers so appointed are deemed to have been appointed as joint receivers.

56(3) **[Receivers to act jointly]** Receivers appointed, or deemed to have been appointed, as joint receivers shall act jointly unless the instrument of appointment or respective instruments of appointment otherwise provide.

56(4) **[Suspension of receiver's powers]** Subject to subsection (5) below, the powers of a receiver appointed by, or on the application of, the holder of a floating charge are suspended by, and as from the date of, the appointment of a receiver by, or on the application of, the holder of a floating charge having priority of ranking over that charge to such extent as may be necessary to enable the receiver second mentioned to exercise his powers under section 55 and Schedule 2; and any powers so suspended take effect again when the floating charge having priority of ranking ceases to attach to the property then subject to the charge, whether such cessation is by virtue of section 62(6) or otherwise.

56(5) **[Effect of suspension]** The suspension of the powers of a receiver under subsection (4) does not have the effect of requiring him to release any part of the property (including any letters or documents) of the company from his control until he receives from the receiver superseding him a valid indemnity (subject to the limit of the value of such part of the property of the company as is subject to the charge by virtue of which he was appointed) in respect of any expenses, charges and liabilities he may have incurred in the performance of his functions as receiver.

56(6)   **[Floating charge remains attached]**   The suspension of the powers of a receiver under subsection (4) does not cause the floating charge by virtue of which he was appointed to cease to attach to the property to which it attached by virtue of section 53(7) or 54(6).

56(7)   **[Same receiver by several charges]**   Nothing in this section prevents the same receiver being appointed by virtue of two or more floating charges.

SEC. 57   Agency and liability of receiver for contracts

57(1)   **[Receiver deemed agent]**   A receiver is deemed to be the agent of the company in relation to such property of the company as is attached by the floating charge by virtue of which he was appointed.

57(2)   **[Personal liability]**   A receiver (including a receiver whose powers are subsequently suspended under section 56) is personally liable on any contract entered into by him in the performance of his functions, except in so far as the contract otherwise provides, and on any contract of employment adopted by him in the carrying out of those functions.

57(3)   **[Indemnity]**   A receiver who is personally liable by virtue of subsection (2) is entitled to be indemnified out of the property in respect of which he was appointed.

57(4)   **[Contracts before appointment]**   Any contract entered into by or on behalf of the company prior to the appointment of a receiver continues in force (subject to its terms) notwithstanding that appointment, but the receiver does not by virtue only of his appointment incur any personal liability on any such contract.

57(5)   **[Interpretation of sec. 57(2)]**   For the purposes of subsection (2), a receiver is not to be taken to have adopted a contract of employment by reason of anything done or omitted to be done within 14 days after his appointment.

57(6)   **[Effect]**   This section does not limit any right to indemnity which the receiver would have apart from it, nor limit his liability on contracts entered into or adopted without authority, nor confer any right to indemnity in respect of that liability.

57(7)   **[Continuation of contract]**   Any contract entered into by a receiver in the performance of his functions continues in force (subject to its terms) although the powers of the receiver are subsequently suspended under section 56.

SEC. 58   Remuneration of receiver

58(1)   **[Remuneration by agreement]**   The remuneration to be paid to a receiver is to be determined by agreement between the receiver and the holder of the floating charge by virtue of which he was appointed.

58(2)   **[Where remuneration not specified or disputed]**   Where the remuneration to be paid to the receiver has not been determined under subsection (1), or where it has been so determined but is disputed by any of the persons mentioned in paragraphs (a) to (d) below, it may be fixed instead by the Auditor of the Court of Session on application made to him by—

(a) the receiver;

(b) the holder of any floating charge or fixed security over all or any part of the property of the company;

(c) the company; or

(d) the liquidator of the company.

58(3) [Accounting for excess]   Where the receiver has been paid or has retained for his remuneration for any period before the remuneration has been fixed by the Auditor of the Court of Session under subsection (2) any amount in excess of the remuneration so fixed for that period, the receiver or his personal representatives shall account for the excess.

SEC. 59   Priority of debts

59(1) [Certain debts to be paid in priority out of assets]   Where a receiver is appointed and the company is not at the time of the appointment in course of being wound up, the debts which fall under subsection (2) of this section shall be paid out of any assets coming to the hands of the receiver in priority to any claim for principal or interest by the holder of the floating charge by virtue of which the receiver was appointed.

59(2) [Preferential debts]   Debts falling under this subsection are preferential debts (within the meaning given by section 386 in Part XII) which, by the end of a period of 6 months after advertisement by the receiver for claims in the Edinburgh Gazette and in a newspaper circulating in the district where the company carries on business either—

(i) have been intimated to him, or

(ii) have become known to him.

59(3) [Recoupment of payments]   Any payments made under this section shall be recouped as far as may be out of the assets of the company available for payment of ordinary creditors.

SEC. 60   Distribution of moneys

60(1) [Payment of moneys by receiver]   Subject to the next section, and to the rights of any of the following categories of persons (which rights shall, except to the extent otherwise provided in any instrument, have the following order of priority), namely—

(a) the holder of any fixed security which is over property subject to the floating charge and which ranks prior to, or pari passu with, the floating charge;

(b) all persons who have effectually executed diligence on any part of the property of the company which is subject to the charge by virtue of which the receiver was appointed;

(c) creditors in respect of all liabilities, charges and expenses incurred by or on behalf of the receiver;

(d) the receiver in respect of his liabilities, expenses and remuneration, and any indemnity to which he is entitled out of the property of the company; and

(e) the preferential creditors entitled to payment under section 59, the receiver shall pay moneys received by him to the holder of the floating charge by virtue of which the receiver was appointed in or towards satisfaction of the debt secured by the floating charge.

60(2)   [Balance of moneys]   Any balance of moneys remaining after the provisions of subsection (1) and section 61 below have been satisfied shall be paid in accordance with their respective rights and interests to the following persons, as the case may require—

    (a) any other receiver;

    (b) the holder of a fixed security which is over property subject to the floating charge;

    (c) the company or its liquidator, as the case may be.

60(3)   [Doubt as to person entitled]   Where any question arises as to the person entitled to a payment under this section, or where a receipt or a discharge of a security cannot be obtained in respect of any such payment, the receiver shall consign the amount of such payment in any joint stock bank of issue in Scotland in name of the Accountant of Court for behoof of the person or persons entitled thereto.

SEC. 61   Disposal of interest in property

61(1)   [Application to court]   Where the receiver sells or disposes, or is desirous of selling or disposing, of any property or interest in property of the company which is subject to the floating charge by virtue of which the receiver was appointed and which is—

    (a) subject to any security or interest of, or burden or encumbrance in favour of, a creditor the ranking of which is prior to, or pari passu with, or postponed to the floating charge, or

    (b) property or an interest in property affected or attached by effectual diligence executed by any person,

and the receiver is unable to obtain the consent of such creditor or, as the case may be, such person to such a sale or disposal, the receiver may apply to the court for authority to sell or dispose of the property or interest in property free of such security, interest, burden, encumbrance or diligence.

61(2)   [Authorisation by court]   Subject to the next subsection, on such an application the court may, if it thinks fit, authorise the sale or disposal of the property or interest in question free of such security, interest, burden, encumbrance or diligence, and such authorisation may be on such terms or conditions as the court thinks fit.

61(3)   [Condition for authorisation]   In the case of an application where a fixed security over the property or interest in question which ranks prior to the floating charge has not been met or provided for in full, the court shall not authorise the sale or disposal of the property or interest in question unless it is satisfied that the sale or disposal would be likely to provide a more advantageous realisation of the company's assets than would otherwise be effected.

61(4)   [Condition for sec. 61(3)]   It shall be a condition of an authorisation to which sub-section (3) applies that—

    (a) the net proceeds of the disposal, and

IA 1986, sec. 60(2)

(b) where those proceeds are less than such amount as may be determined by the court to be the net amount which would be realised on a sale of the property or interest in the open market by a willing seller, such sums as may be required to make good the deficiency,

shall be applied towards discharging the sums secured by the fixed security.

61(5) [Where sec. 61(4) condition re several securities] Where a condition imposed in pursuance of subsection (4) relates to two or more such fixed securities, that condition shall require the net proceeds of the disposal and, where paragraph (b) of that subsection applies, the sums mentioned in that paragraph to be applied towards discharging the sums secured by those fixed securities in the order of their priorities.

61(6) [Copy of authorisation to registrar] A copy of an authorisation under subsection (2) certified by the cerk of court shall, within 14 days of the granting of the authorisation, be sent by the receiver to the registrar of companies.

61(7) [Penalty for non-compliance] If the receiver without reasonable excuse fails to comply with subsection (6), he is liable to a fine and, for continued contravention, to a daily default fine.

61(8) [Receiver to give document to disponee] Where any sale or disposal is effected in accordance with the authorisation of the court under subsection (2), the receiver shall grant to the purchaser or disponee an appropriate document of transfer or conveyance of the property or interest in question, and that document has the effect, or, where recording, intimation or registration of that document is a legal requirement for completion of title to the property or interest, then that recording, intimation or registration (as the case may be) has the effect, of—

(a) disencumbering the property or interest of the security, interest, burden or encumbrance affecting it, and

(b) freeing the property or interest from the diligence executed upon it.

61(9) [Ranking of creditor in winding up] Nothing in this section prejudices the right of any creditor of the company to rank for his debt in the winding up of the company.

SEC. 62 Cessation of appointment of receiver

62(1) [Removal, resignation] A receiver may be removed from office by the court under subsection (3) below and may resign his office by giving notice of his resignation in the prescribed manner to such persons as may be prescribed.

62(2) [Cessation of qualification] A receiver shall vacate office if he ceases to be qualified to act as an insolvency practitioner in relation to the company.

62(3) [Removal on application] Subject to the next subsection, a receiver may, on application to the court by the holder of the floating charge by virtue of which he was appointed, be removed by the court on cause shown.

62(4) [On vacation of office] Where at any time a receiver vacates office—

(a) his remuneration and any expenses properly incurred by him, and

(b) any indemnity to which he is entitled out of the property of the company,

shall be paid out of the property of the company which is subject to the floating charge and shall have priority as provided for in section 60(1).

62(5)   **[Notice of cessation to registrar, penalty on default]**   When a receiver ceases to act as such otherwise than by death he shall, and, when a receiver is removed by the court, the holder of the floating charge by virtue of which he was appointed shall, within 14 days of the cessation or removal (as the case may be) give the registrar of companies notice to that effect, and the registrar shall enter the notice in the register of charges.

If the receiver or the holder of the floating charge (as the case may require) makes default in complying with the requirements of this subsection, he is liable to a fine and, for continued contravention, to a daily default fine.

Note
See Form 3 (Scot) in regulations referred to in note to
s. 50.

62(6)   **[Cessation of attachment of charge]**   If by the expiry of a period of one month following upon the removal of the receiver or his ceasing to act as such no other receiver has been appointed, the floating charge by virtue of which the receiver was appointed—

    (a)   thereupon ceases to attach to the property then subject to the charge, and

    (b)   again subsists as a floating charge;

and for the purposes of calculating the period of one month under this subsection no account shall be taken of any period during which an administration order under Part II of this Act is in force.

SEC. 63   Powers of court

63(1)   **[Directions, on application]**   The court on the application of—

    (a)   the holder of a floating charge by virtue of which a receiver was appointed, or

    (b)   a receiver appointed under section 51,

may give directions to the receiver in respect of any matter arising in connection with the performance by him of his functions.

63(2)   **[Where receiver's appointment invalid]**   Where the appointment of a person as a receiver by the holder of a floating charge is discovered to be invalid (whether by virtue of the invalidity of the instrument or otherwise), the court may order the holder of the floating charge to indemnify the person appointed against any liability which arises solely by reason of the invalidity of the appointment.

SEC. 64   Notification that receiver appointed

64(1)   **[Statement in invoices etc.]**   Where a receiver has been appointed, every invoice, order for goods or business letter issued by or on behalf of the company or the receiver or the liquidator of the company, being a document on or in which the name of the company appears, shall contain a statement that a receiver has been appointed.

64(2)   **[Penalty on default]**   If default is made in complying with the requirements of this section, the company and any of the following persons who knowingly and wilfully authorises or permits the default, namely any officer of the company, any liquidator of the company and any receiver, is liable to a fine.

SEC. 65   Information to be given by receiver

65(1)   [Notification of appointment]   Where a receiver is appointed, he shall—

- (a)   forthwith send to the company and publish notice of his appointment, and
- (b)   within 28 days after his appointment, unless the court otherwise directs, send such notice to all the creditors of the company (so far as he is aware of their addresses).

Note
See Form 4 (Scot) in regulations referred to in note to s. 50.

65(2)   [Restriction]   This section and the next do not apply in relation to the appointment of a receiver to act—

- (a)   with an existing receiver, or
- (b)   in place of a receiver who has died or ceased to act,

except that, where they apply to a receiver who dies or ceases to act before they have been fully complied with, the references in this section and the next to the receiver include (subject to subsection (3) of this section) his successor and any continuing receiver.

65(3)   [If company being wound up]   If the company is being wound up, this section and the next apply notwithstanding that the receiver and the liquidator are the same person, but with any necessary modifications arising from that fact.

65(4)   [Penalty for non-compliance]   If a person without reasonable excuse fails to comply with this section, he is liable to a fine and, for continued contravention, to a daily default fine.

SEC. 66   Company's statement of affairs

66(1)   [Duty of receiver]   Where a receiver of a company is appointed, the receiver shall forthwith require some or all of the persons mentioned in subsection (3) below to make out and submit to him a statement in the prescribed form as to the affairs of the company.

Note
See Form 5 (Scot) in regulations referred to in note to s. 50.

66(2)   [Contents of statement]   A statement submitted under this section shall be verified by affidavit by the persons required to submit it and shall show—

- (a)   particulars of the company's assets, debts and liabilities;
- (b)   the names and addresses of its creditors;
- (c)   the securities held by them respectively;
- (d)   the dates when the securities were respectively given; and
- (e)   such further or other information as may be prescribed.

66(3)   [Persons in sec. 66(1)]   The persons referred to in subsection (1) are—

- (a)   those who are or have been officers of the company;
- (b)   those who have taken part in the company's formation at any time within one year before the date of the appointment of the receiver;

(c) those who are in the company's employment or have been in its employment within that year, and are in the receiver's opinion capable of giving the information required;

(d) those who are or have been within that year officers of or in the employment of a company which is, or within that year was, an officer of the company.

In this subsection **"employment"** includes employment under a contract for services.

66(4) **[Time for statement]**   Where any persons are required under this section to submit a statement of affairs to the receiver they shall do so (subject to the next subsection) before the end of the period of 21 days beginning with the day after that on which the prescribed notice of the requirement is given to them by the receiver.

66(5) **[Release, extension re statement]**   The receiver, if he thinks fit, may—

(a) at any time release a person from an obligation imposed on him under subsection (1) or (2), or

(b) either when giving the notice mentioned in subsection (4) or subsequently extend the period so mentioned,

and where the receiver has refused to exercise a power conferred by this subsection, the court, if it thinks fit, may exercise it.

66(6) **[Penalty for non-compliance]**   If a person without reasonable excuse fails to comply with any obligation imposed under this section, he is liable to a fine and, for continued contravention, to a daily default fine.

SEC. 67   Report by receiver

67(1) **[Duty of receiver]**   Where a receiver is appointed under section 51, he shall within 3 months (or such longer period as the court may allow) after his appointment, send to the registrar of companies, to the holder of the floating charge by virtue of which he was appointed and to any trustees for secured creditors of the company and (so far as he is aware of their addresses) to all such creditors a report as to the following matters, namely—

(a) the events leading up to his appointment, so far as he is aware of them;

(b) the disposal or proposed disposal by him of any property of the company and the carrying on or proposed carrying on by him of any business of the company;

(c) the amounts of principal and interest payable to the holder of the floating charge by virtue of which he was appointed and the amounts payable to preferential creditors; and

(d) the amount (if any) likely to be available for the payment of other creditors.

67(2) **[Copies of report]**   The receiver shall also, within 3 months (or such longer period as the court may allow) after his appointment, either—

(a) send a copy of the report (so far as he is aware of their addresses) to all unsecured creditors of the company, or

(b) publish in the prescribed manner a notice stating an address to which unsecured creditors of the company should write for copies of the report to be sent to them free of charge, and (in either case), unless the court otherwise directs, lay a copy of the report before a meeting of the company's unsecured creditors summoned for the purpose on not less than 14 days' notice.

67(3) **[Condition for court direction in sec. 67(2)]** The court shall not give a direction under subsection (2) unless—

(a) the report states the intention of the receiver to apply for the direction, and

(b) a copy of the report is sent to the persons mentioned in paragraph (a) of that subsection, or a notice is published as mentioned in paragraph (b) of that subsection, not less than 14 days before the hearing of the application.

67(4) **[Where company in liquidation]** Where the company has gone or goes into liquidation, the receiver—

(a) shall, within 7 days after his compliance with subsection (1) or, if later, the nomination or appointment of the liquidator, send a copy of the report to the liquidator, and

(b) where he does so within the time limited for compliance with subsection (2), is not required to comply with that subsection.

67(5) **[Report to involve summary of statement of affairs]** A report under this section shall include a summary of the statement of affairs made out and submitted under section 66 and of his comments (if any) on it.

67(6) **[Information not to be disclosed]** Nothing in this section shall be taken as requiring any such report to include any information the disclosure of which would seriously prejudice the carrying out by the receiver of his functions.

67(7) **[Sec. 65(2)]** Section 65(2) applies for the purposes of this section also.

67(8) **[Penalty for non-compliance]** If a person without reasonable excuse fails to comply with this section, he is liable to a fine and, for continued contravention, to a daily default fine.

67(9) **["Secured creditor"]** In this section **"secured creditor"**, in relation to a company, means a creditor who holds in respect of his debt a security over property of the company, and **"unsecured creditor"** shall be construed accordingly.

SEC. 68 Committee of creditors

68(1) **[Creditors' meeting may establish committee]** Where a meeting of creditors is summoned under section 67, the meeting may, if it thinks fit, establish a committee **("the creditors' committee")** to exercise the functions conferred on it by or under this Act.

68(2) **[Powers of committee]** If such a committee is established, the committee may on giving not less than 7 days' notice require the receiver to attend before it at any reasonable time and furnish it with such information relating to the carrying out by him of his functions as it may reasonably require.

Section 69 Enforcement of receiver's duty to make returns, etc.

69(1) **[Court order re receiver's default]** If any receiver—

(a) having made default in filing, delivering or making any return, account or other document, or in giving any notice, which a receiver is by law required to file, deliver, make or give, fails to make good the default within 14 days after the service on him of a notice requiring him to do so; or

   (b)   has, after being required at any time by the liquidator of the company so to do, failed to render proper accounts of his receipts and payments and to vouch the same and to pay over to the liquidator the amount properly payable to him,

the court may, on an application made for the purpose, make an order directing the receiver to make good the default within such time as may be specified in the order.

69(2)   **[Application to court]**   In the case of any such default as is mentioned in subsection 1(a), an application for the purposes of this section may be made by any member or creditor of the company or by the registrar of companies; and, in the case of any such default as is mentioned in subsection (1)(b), the application shall be made by the liquidator; and, in either case, the order may provide that all expenses of and incidental to the application shall be borne by the receiver.

69(3)   **[Other enactments]**   Nothing in this section prejudices the operation of any enactments imposing penalties on receivers in respect of any such default as is mentioned in subsection (1).

SEC. 70   Interpretation for Chapter II

70(1)   **[Definitions]**   In this Chapter, unless the contrary intention appears, the following expressions have the following meanings respectively assigned to them—

"**company**" means an incorporated company (whether or not a company within the meaning of the Companies Act) which the Court of Session has jurisdiction to wind up;

"**fixed security**", in relation to any property of a company, means any security, other than a floating charge or a charge having the nature of a floating charge, which on the winding up of the company in Scotland would be treated as an effective security over that property, and (without prejudice to that generality) includes a security over that property, being a heritable security within the meaning of the Conveyancing and Feudal Reform (Scotland) Act 1970;

"**instrument of appointment**" has the meaning given by section 53(1);

"**prescribed**" means prescribed by regulations made under this Chapter by the Secretary of State;

"**receiver**" means a receiver of such part of the property of the company as is subject to the floating charge by virtue of which he has been appointed under section 51;

"**register of charges**" means the register kept by the registrar of companies for the purposes of Chapter II of Part XII of the Companies Act;

"**secured debenture**" means a bond, debenture, debenture stock or other security which, either itself or by reference to any other instrument, creates a floating charge over all or any part of the property of the company, but does not include a security which creates no charge other than a fixed security; and

"**series of secured debentures**" means two or more secured debentures created as a series by the company in such a manner that the holders thereof are entitled pari passu to the benefit of the floating charge.

70(2) **[Reference to holder of floating charge]** Where a floating charge, secured debenture or series of secured debentures has been created by the company, then, except where the context otherwise requires, any reference in this Chapter to the holder of the floating charge shall—

  (a) where the floating charge, secured debenture or series of secured debentures provides for a receiver to be appointed by any person or body, be construed as a reference to that person or body;

  (b) where, in the case of a series of secured debentures, no such provision has been made therein but—

     (i) there are trustees acting for the debenture-holders under and in accordance with a trust deed, be construed as a reference to those trustees, and

     (ii) where no such trustees are acting, be construed as a reference to —

        (aa) a majority in nominal value of those present or represented by proxy and voting at a meeting of debenture-holders at which the holders of at least one-third in nominal value of the outstanding debentures of the series are present or so represented, or

        (bb) where no such meeting is held, the holders of at least one-half in nominal value of the outstanding debentures of the series.

70(3) **[Reference to floating charge etc.]** Any reference in this Chapter to a floating charge, secured debenture, series of secured debentures or instument creating a charge includes, except where the context otherwise requires, a reference to that floating charge, debenture, series of debentures or instrument as varied by any instrument.

70(4) **[Reference to instrument]** References in this Chapter to the instrument by which a floating charge was created are, in the case of a floating charge created by words in a bond or other written acknowledgement, references to the bond or, as the case may be, the other written acknowledgement.

SEC. 71   Prescription of forms, etc.; regulations

71(1) **[Prescribed forms]** The notice referred to in section 62(5), and the notice referred to in section 65(1)(a) shall be in such form as may be prescribed.

71(2) **[Regulations]** Any power conferred by this Chapter on the Secretary of State to make regulations is exercisable by statutory instrument; and a statutory instrument made in the exercise of the power so conferred to prescribe a fee is subject to annulment in pursuance of a resolution of either House of Parliament.

Note
See the note to s. 50.

Chapter III — Receivers' Powers in Great Britain as a Whole

SEC. 72   Cross-border operation of receivership provisions

72(1) **[Receivers' powers]** A receiver appointed under the law of either part of Great Britain in respect of the whole or any part of any property or undertaking of a company and in consequence of the company having created a charge which, as created, was a floating charge may exercise his powers in the other part of Great Britain so far as their exercise is not inconsistent with the law applicable there.

72(2) [**"Receiver"**]   In subsection (1) **"receiver"** includes a manager and a person who is appointed both receiver and manager.

PART IV — WINDING UP OF COMPANIES REGISTERED UNDER THE COMPANIES ACTS

Chapter I — Preliminary

MODES OF WINDING UP

SEC. 73   Alternative modes of winding up

73(1) [**Voluntary, by court**]   The winding up of a company, within the meaning given to that expression by section 735 of the Companies Act, may be either voluntary (Chapters II, III, IV and V in this Part) or by the court (Chapter VI).

73(2) [**Application of Ch. I, VII–X**]   This Chapter, and Chapters VII to X, relate to winding up generally, except where otherwise stated.

CONTRIBUTORIES

SEC. 74   Liability as contributories of present and past members

74(1) [**Liability to contribute**]   When a company is wound up, every present and past member is liable to contribute to its assets to any amount sufficient for payment of its debts and liabilities, and the expenses of the winding up, and for the adjustment of the rights of the contributories among themselves.

74(2) [**Qualifications to liability**]   This is subject as follows—

(a) a past member is not liable to contribute if he has ceased to be a member for one year or more before the commencement of the winding up;

(b) a past member is not liable to contribute in respect of any debt or liability of the company contracted after he ceased to be a member;

(c) a past member is not liable to contribute, unless it appears to the court that the existing members are unable to satisfy the contributions required to be made by them in pursuance of the Companies Act and this Act;

(d) in the case of a company limited by shares, no contribution is required from any member exceeding the amount (if any) unpaid on the shares in respect of which he is liable as a present or past member;

(e) nothing in the Companies Act or this Act invalidates any provision contained in a policy of insurance or other contract whereby the liability of individual members on the policy or contract is restricted, or whereby the funds of the company are alone made liable in respect of the policy or contract;

(f) a sum due to any member of the company (in his character of a member) by way of dividends, profits or otherwise is not deemed to be a debt of the company, payable to that member in a case of competition between himself and any other creditor not a member of the company, but any such sum may be taken into account for the purpose of the final adjustment of the rights of the contributories among themselves.

74(3) **[Company limited by guarantee]** In the case of a company limited by guarantee, no contribution is required from any member exceeding the amount undertaken to be contributed by him to the company's assets in the event of its being wound up; but if it is a company with a share capital, every member of it is liable (in addition to the amount so undertaken to be contributed to the assets), to contribute to the extent of any sums unpaid on shares held by him.

SEC. 75 Directors, etc. with unlimited liability

75(1) **[Liability in winding up]** In the winding up of a limited company, any director or manager (whether past or present) whose liability is under the Companies Act unlimited is liable, in addition to his liability (if any) to contribute as an ordinary member, to make a further contribution as if he were at the commencement of the winding up a member of an unlimited company.

75(2) **[Qualifications to liability]** However—

(a) a past director or manager is not liable to make such further contribution if he has ceased to hold office for a year or more before the commencement of the winding up;

(b) a past director or manager is not liable to make such further contribution in respect of any debt or liability of the company contracted after he ceased to hold office;

(c) subject to the company's articles, a director or manager is not liable to make such further contribution unless the court deems it necessary to require that contribution in order to satisfy the company's debts and liabilities, and the expenses of the winding up.

SEC. 76 Liability of past directors and shareholders

76(1) **[Application]** This section applies where a company is being wound up and—

(a) it has under Chapter VII of Part V of the Companies Act (redeemable shares; purchase by a company of its own shares) made a payment out of capital in respect of the redemption or purchase of any of its own shares (the payment being referred to below as "the relevant payment"), and

(b) the aggregate amount of the company's assets and the amounts paid by way of contribution to its assets (apart from this section) is not sufficient for payment of its debts and liabilities, and the expenses of the winding up.

76(2) **[Contribution of past shareholders, directors]** If the winding up commenced within one year of the date on which the relevant payment was made, then—

(a) the person from whom the shares were redeemed or purchased, and

(b) the directors who signed the statutory declaration made in accordance with section 173(3) of the Companies Act for purposes of the redemption or purchase (except a director who shows that he had reasonable grounds for forming the opinion set out in the declaration),

are, so as to enable that insufficiency to be met, liable to contribute to the following extent to the company's assets.

76(3)   **[Amount payable]**   A person from whom any of the shares were redeemed or purchased is liable to contribute an amount not exceeding so much of the relevant payment as was made by the company in respect of his shares; and the directors are jointly and severally liable with that person to contribute that amount.

76(4)   **[Application to court]**   A person who has contributed any amount to the assets in pursuance of this section may apply to the court for an order directing any other person jointly and severally liable in respect of that amount to pay him such amount as the court thinks just and equitable.

76(5)   **[Non-application of sec. 74, 75]**   Sections 74 and 75 do not apply in relation to liability accruing by virtue of this section.

76(6)   **[Regulations]**   This section is deemed included in Chapter VII of Part V of the Companies Act for the purposes of the Secretary of State's power to make regulations under section 179 of that Act.

SEC. 77   Limited company formerly unlimited

77(1)   **[Application]**   This section applies in the case of a company being wound up which was at some former time registered as unlimited but has re-registered—

(a) as a public company under section 43 of the Companies Act (or the former corresponding provision, section 5 of the Companies Act 1980), or

(b) as a limited company under section 51 of the Companies Act (or the former corresponding provision, section 44 of the Companies Act 1967).

77(2)   **[Contribution by past members]**   Notwithstanding section 74(2)(a) above, a past member of the company who was a member of it at the time of re-registration, if the winding up commences within the period of 3 years beginning with the day on which the company was re-registered, is liable to contribute to the assets of the company in respect of debts and liabilities contracted before that time.

77(3)   **[If no past members existing members]**   If no persons who were members of the company at that time are existing members of it, a person who at that time was a present or past member is liable to contribute as above notwithstanding that the existing members have satisfied the contributions required to be made by them under the Companies Act and this Act.

This applies subject to section 74(2)(a) above and to subsection (2) of this section, but notwithstanding section 74(2)(c).

77(4)   **[No limitation on contribution]**   Notwithstanding section 74(2)(d) and (3), there is no limit on the amount which a person who, at that time, was a past or present member of the company is liable to contribute as above.

SEC. 78   Unlimited company formerly limited

78(1)   **[Application]**   This section applies in the case of a company being wound up which was at some former time registered as limited but has been re-registered as unlimited under section 49 of the Companies Act (or the former corresponding provision, section 43 of the Companies Act 1967).

78(2) **[Limitation on contribution]**   A person who, at the time when the application for the company to be re-registered was lodged, was a past member of the company and did not after that again become a member of it is not liable to contribute to the assets of the company more than he would have been liable to contribute had the company not been re-registered.

SEC. 79   Meaning of "contributory"

79(1) **["Contributory"]**   In this Act and the Companies Act the expression **"contributory"** means every person liable to contribute to the assets of a company in the event of its being wound up, and for the purposes of all proceedings for determining, and all proceedings prior to the final determination of, the persons who are to be deemed contributories, includes any person alleged to be a contributory.

79(2) **[Qualification]**   The reference in subsection (1) to persons liable to contribute to the assets does not include a person so liable by virtue of a declaration by the court under section 213 (imputed responsibility for company's frauduent trading) or section 214 (wrongful trading) in Chapter X of this Part.

79(3) **[Reference in articles]**   A reference in a company's articles to a contributory does not (unless the context requires) include a person who is a contributory only by virtue of section 76.

This subsection is deemed included in Chapter VII of Part V of the Companies Act for the purposes of the Secretary of State's power to make regulations under section 179 of that Act.

SEC. 80   Nature of contributory's liability

80   The liability of a contributory creates a debt (in England and Wales in the nature of a specialty) accruing due from him at the time when his liability commenced, but payable at the times when calls are made for enforcing the liability.

SEC. 81   Contributories in case of death of a member

81(1) **[Personal representative liable]**   If a contributory dies either before or after he has been placed on the list of contributories, his personal representatives, and the heirs and legatees of heritage of his heritable estate in Scotland, are liable in a due course of administration to contribute to the assets of the company in discharge of his liability and are contributories accordingly.

81(2) **[Where personal representatives on list of contributories]**   Where the personal representatives are placed on the list of contributories, the heirs or legatees of heritage need not be added, but they may be added as and when the court thinks fit.

81(3) **[Where default in payment]**   If in England and Wales the personal representatives make default in paying any money ordered to be paid by them, proceedings may be taken for administering the estate of the deceased contributory and for compelling payment out of it of the money due.

SEC. 82   Effect of contributory's bankruptcy

82(1)   [Application]   The following applies if a contributory becomes bankrupt, either before or after he has been placed on the list of contributories.

82(2)   [Trustee in bankruptcy a contributory]   His trustee in bankruptcy represents him for all purposes of the winding up, and is a contributory accordingly.

82(3)   [Trustee called on to admit to proof]   The trustee may be called on to admit to proof against the bankrupt's estate, or otherwise allow to be paid out of the bankrupt's assets in due course of law, any money due from the bankrupt in respect of his liability to contribute to the company's assets.

82(4)   [Estimated value of liability to future calls]   There may be proved against the bankrupt's estate the estimated value of his liability to future calls as well as calls already made.

SEC. 83   Companies registered under Companies Act, Part XXII, Chapter II

83(1)   [Application]   The following applies in the event of a company being wound up which has been registered under section 680 of the Companies Act (or previous corresponding provisions in the Companies Act 1948 or earlier Acts).

83(2)   [Contributories re debts and liabilities before registration]   Every person is a contributory, in respect of the company's debts and liabilities contracted before registration, who is liable—

(a) to pay, or contribute to the payment of, any debt or liability so contracted, or

(b) to pay, or contribute to the payment of, any sum for the adjustment of the rights of the members among themselves in respect of any such debt or liability, or

(c) to pay, or contribute to the amount of, the expenses of winding up the company, so far as relates to the debts or liabilities above-mentioned.

83(3)   [Amounts liable to be contributed]   Every contributory is liable to contribute to the assets of the company, in the course of the winding up, all sums due from him in respect of any such liability.

83(4)   [Death, etc. of contributory]   In the event of the death, bankruptcy or insolvency of any contributory, provisions of this Act, with respect to the personal representatives, to the heirs and legatees of the heritage of the heritable estate in Scotland of deceased contributories and to the trustees of bankrupt or insolvent contributories respectively, apply.

Chapter II — Voluntary Winding Up (Introductory and General)

RESOLUTIONS FOR, AND COMMENCEMENT OF, VOLUNTARY WINDING UP

SEC. 84   Circumstances in which company may be wound up voluntarily

84(1)   [Circumstances]   A company may be wound up voluntarily—

(a) when the period (if any) fixed for the duration of the company by the articles expires, or the event (if any) occurs, on the occurence of which the articles provide that the company is to be dissolved, and the company in general meeting has passed a resolution requiring it to be wound up voluntarily;

(b) if the company resolves by special resolution that it be wound up voluntarily;

(c) if the company resolves by extraordinary resolution to the effect that it cannot by reason of its liabilities continue its business, and that it is advisable to wind up.

84(2) [Definition] In this Act the expression "**a resolution for voluntary winding up**" means a resolution passed under any of the paragraphs of subsection (1).

84(3) [Copy of resolution to registrar] A resolution passed under paragraph (a) of subsection (1), as well as a special resolution under paragraph (b) and an extraordinary resolution under paragraph (c), is subject to section 380 of the Companies Act (copy of resolution to be forwarded to registrar of companies within 15 days).

SEC. 85   Notice of resolution to wind up

85(1) [Notice in Gazette] When a company has passed a resolution for voluntary winding up, it shall, within 14 days after the passing of the resolution, give notice of the resolution by advertisement in the Gazette.

85(2) [Penalty on default] If default is made in complying with this section, the company and every officer of it who is in default is liable to a fine and, for continued contravention, to a daily default fine.

For purposes of this subsection the liquidator is deemed an officer of the company.

SEC. 86   Commencement of winding up

86 A voluntary winding up is deemed to commence at the time of the passing of the resolution for voluntary winding up.

CONSEQUENCES OF RESOLUTION TO WIND UP

SEC. 87   Effect on business and status of company

87(1) [Cessation of business] In case of a voluntary winding up, the company shall from the commencement of the winding up cease to carry on its business, except so far as may be required for its beneficial winding up.

87(2) [Continuation of corporate state, etc.] However, the corporate state and corporate powers of the company, notwithstanding anything to the contrary in its articles, continue until the company is dissolved.

SEC. 88   Avoidance of share transfers, etc. after winding-up resolution

88 Any transfer of shares, not being a transfer made to or with the sanction of the liquidator, and any alteration in the status of the company's members, made after the commencement of a voluntary winding up, is void.

DECLARATION OF SOLVENCY

SEC. 89   Statutory declaration of solvency

89(1) [Declaration by directors] Where it is proposed to wind up a company voluntarily, the directors (or, in the case of a company having more than two directors, the majority of them) may at a directors' meeting make a statutory declaration to the effect that they have made a full inquiry into the company's affairs and that, having done so, they have formed the opinion that the company will be able to pay its debts in full, together with interest at the official rate (as defined in section 251), within such period, not exceeding 12 months from the commencement of the winding up, as may be specified in the declaration.

89(2) [Requirements for declaration] Such a declaration by the directors has no effect for purposes of this Act unless—

(a) it is made within the 5 weeks immediately preceding the date of the passing of the resolution for winding up, or on that date but before the passing of the resolution, and

(b) it embodies a statement of the company's assets and liabilities as at the latest practicable date before the making of the declaration.

89(3) [Declaration to registrar] The declaration shall be delivered to the registrar of companies before the expiration of 15 days immediately following the date on which the resolution for winding up is passed.

89(4) [Offence, penalty] A director making a declaration under this section without having reasonable grounds for the opinion that the company will be able to pay its debts in full, together with interest at the official rate, within the period specified is liable to imprisonment or a fine, or both.

89(5) [Presumption] If the company is wound up in pursuance of a resolution passed within 5 weeks after the making of the declaration, and its debts (together with interest at the official rate) are not paid or provided for in full within the period specified, it is to be presumed (unless the contrary is shown) that the director did not have reasonable grounds for his opinion.

89(6) [Penalty for non-compliance with sec. 89(3)] If a declaration required by subsection (3) to be delivered to the registrar is not so delivered within the time prescribed by that subsection, the company and every officer in default is liable to a fine and, for continued contravention, to a daily default fine.

SEC. 90   Distinction between "members'" and "creditors'" voluntary winding up

90 A winding up in the case of which a directors' statutory declaration under section 89 has been made is a "members' voluntary winding up"; and a winding up in the case of which such a declaration has not been made is a "creditors' voluntary winding up".

Chapter III — Members' Voluntary Winding Up

SEC. 91 Appointment of liquidator

91(1) [**Appointment by general meeting**] In a members' voluntary winding up, the company in general meeting shall appoint one or more liquidators for the purpose of winding up the company's affairs and distributing its assets.

91(2) [**Cessation of directors' powers**] On the appointment of a liquidator all the powers of the directors cease, except so far as the company in general meeting or the liquidator sanctions their continuance.

SEC. 92 Power to fill vacancy in office of liquidator

92(1) [**Filling of vacancy**] If a vacancy occurs by death, resignation or otherwise in the office of liquidator appointed by the company, the company in general meeting may, subject to any arrangement with its creditors, fill the vacancy.

92(2) [**Convening of general meeting**] For that purpose a general meeting may be convened by any contributory or, if there were more liquidators than one, by the continuing liquidators.

92(3) [**Manner of holding meeting**] The meeting shall be held in manner provided by this Act or by the articles, or in such manner as may, on application by any contributory or by the continuing liquidators, be determined by the court.

SEC. 93 General company meeting at each years' end

93(1) [**If winding up for more than one year**] Subject to sections 96 and 102, in the event of the winding up continuing for more than one year, the liquidator shall summon a general meeting of the company at the end of the first year from the commencement of the winding up, and of each succeeding year, or at the first convenient date within 3 months from the end of the year or such longer period as the Secretary of State may allow.

93(2) [**Account by liquidator**] The liquidator shall lay before the meeting an account of his acts and dealings, and of the conduct of the winding up, during the preceding year.

93(3) [**Penalty for non-compliance**] If the liquidator fails to comply with this section, he is liable to a fine.

SEC. 94 Final meeting prior to dissolution

94(1) [**Account of winding up, final meeting**] As soon as the company's affairs are fully wound up, the liquidator shall make up an account of the winding up showing how it has been conducted and the company's property has been disposed of, and thereupon shall call a general meeting of the company for the purpose of laying before it the account and giving an explanation of it.

94(2) [**Advertisement in Gazette**] The meeting shall be called by advertisement in the Gazette, specifying its time, place and object and published at least one month before the meeting.

94(3) **[Copy of account, etc. to registrar]** Within one week after the meeting, the liquidator shall send to the registrar of companies a copy of the account, and shall make a return to him of the holding of the meeting and of its date.

94(4) **[Penalty on default]** If the copy is not sent or the return is not made in accordance with subsection (3), the liquidator is liable to a fine and, for continued contravention, to a daily default fine.

94(5) **[If no quorum at meeting]** If a quorum is not present at the meeting, the liquidator shall, in lieu of the return mentioned above, make a return that the meeting was duly summoned and that no quorum was present; and upon such a return being made, the provisions of subsection (3) as to the making of the return are deemed complied with.

94(6) **[Penalty if no general meeting called]** If the liquidator fails to call a general meeting of the company as required by subsection (1), he is liable to a fine.

SEC. 95   Effect of company's insolvency

95(1) **[Application]** This section applies where the liquidator is of the opinion that the company will be unable to pay its debts in full (together with interest at the official rate) within the period stated in the directors' declaration under section 89.

95(2) **[Duties of liquidator]** The liquidator shall—

(a) summon a meeting of creditors for a day not later than the 28th day after the day on which he formed that opinion;

(b) send notices of the creditors' meeting to the creditors by post not less than 7 days before the day on which that meeting is to be held;

(c) cause notice of the creditors' meeting to be advertised once in the Gazette and once at least in 2 newspapers circulating in the relevant locality (that is to say the locality in which the company's principal place of business in Great Britain was situated during the relevant period); and

(d) during the period before the day on which the creditors' meeting is to be held, furnish creditors free of charge with such information concerning the affairs of the company as they may reasonably require;

and the notice of the creditors' meeting shall state the duty imposed by paragraph (d) above.

95(3) **[Duties of liquidator re statement of affairs]** The liquidator shall also—

(a) make out a statement in the prescribed form as to the affairs of the company;

(b) lay that statement before the creditors' meeting; and

(c) attend and preside at that meeting.

Note
See The Insolvency Rules 1986, r. 4.34ff., 4.49.

95(4) **[Contents of statement of affairs]** The statement as to the affairs of the company shall be verified by affidavit by the liquidator and shall show—

(a) particulars of the company's assets, debts and liabilities;

(b) the names and addresses of the company's creditors;

(c) the securities held by them respectively;

(d) the dates when the securities were respectively given; and

(e) such further or other information as may be prescribed.

95(5)   [Where principal place of business in different places]   Where the company's principal place of business in Great Britain was situated in different localities at different times during the relevant period, the duty imposed by subsection (2)(c) applies separately in relation to each of those localities.

95(6)   [Where no place of business in Great Britain]   Where the company had no place of business in Great Britain during the relevant period, references in subsections (2)(c) and (5) to the company's principal place of business in Great Britain are replaced by references to its registered office.

95(7)   ["The relevant period"]   In this section **"the relevant period"** means the period of 6 months immediately preceding the day on which were sent the notices summoning the company meeting at which it was resolved that the company be wound up voluntarily.

95(8)   [Penalty for non-compliance]   If the liquidator without reasonable excuse fails to comply with this section, he is liable to a fine.

SEC. 96   Conversion to creditors' voluntary winding up

96   As from the day on which the creditors' meeting is held under section 95, this Act has effect as if—

(a) the directors' declaration under section 89 had not been made; and

(b) the creditors' meeting and the company meeting at which it was resolved that the company be wound up voluntarily were the meetings mentioned in section 98 in the next Chapter;

and accordingly the winding up becomes a creditors' voluntary winding up.

Chapter IV — Creditors' Voluntary Winding Up

SEC. 97   Application of this Chapter

97(1)   [Application]   Subject as follows, this Chapter applies in relation to a creditors' voluntary winding up.

97(2)   [Non-application of sec. 98, 99]   Sections 98 and 99 do not apply where, under section 96 in Chapter III, a members' voluntary winding up has become a creditors' voluntary winding up.

SEC. 98   Meeting of creditors

98(1)   [Duty of company]   The company shall—

(a) cause a meeting of its creditors to be summoned for a day not later than the 14th day after the day on which there is to be held the company meeting at which the resolution for voluntary winding up is to be proposed;

(b) cause the notices of the creditors' meeting to be sent by post to the creditors not less than 7 days before the day on which that meeting is to be held; and

(c) cause notice of the creditors' meeting to be advertised once in the Gazette and once at least in two newspapers circulating in the relevant locality (that is to say the locality in which the company's principal place of business in Great Britain was situated during the relevant period).

98(2) [Contents of notice of meeting] The notice of the creditors' meeting shall state either—

(a) the name and address of a person qualified to act as an insolvency practitioner in relation to the company who, during the period before the day on which that meeting is to be held, will furnish creditors free of charge with such information concerning the company's affairs as they may reasonably require; or

(b) a place in the relevant locality where, on the two business days falling next before the day on which that meeting is to be held, a list of the names and addresses of the company's creditors will be available for inspection free of charge.

98(3) [Where principal place of business in different places, etc.] Where the company's principal place of business in Great Britain was situated in different localities at different times during the relevant period, the duties imposed by subsections (1)(c) and (2)(b) above apply separately in relation to each of those localities.

98(4) [Where no place of business in Great Britain] Where the company had no place of business in Great Britain during the relevant period, references in subsections (1)(c) and (3) to the company's principal place of business in Great Britain are replaced by references to its registered office.

98(5) ["The relevant period"] In this section **"the relevant period"** means the period of 6 months immediately preceding the day on which were sent the notices summoning the company meeting at which it was resolved that the company be wound up voluntarily.

98(6) [Penalty for non-compliance] If the company without reasonable excuse fails to comply with subsection (1) or (2), it is guilty of an offence and liable to a fine.

Note
See The Insolvency Rules 1986, r. 4.49ff.

SEC. 99   Directors to lay statement of affairs before creditors

99(1) [Duty of directors] The directors of the company shall—

(a) make out a statement in the prescribed form as to the affairs of the company;

(b) cause that statement to be laid before the creditors' meeting under section 98; and

(c) appoint one of their number to preside at that meeting;

and it is the duty of the director so appointed to attend the meeting and preside over it.

99(2) [Contents of statement] The statement as to the affairs of the company shall be verified by affidavit by some or all of the directors and shall show—

(a) particulars of the company's assets, debts and liabilities;

IA 1986, sec. 98(2)   [The next page is 51,501]

   (b) the names and addresses of the company's creditors;

   (c) the securities held by them respectively;

   (d) the dates when the securities were respectively given; and

   (e) such further or other information as may be prescribed.

99(3)   **[Penalty for non-compliance]** If—

   (a) the directors without reasonable excuse fail to comply with subsection (1) or (2); or

   (b) any director without reasonable excuse fails to comply with subsection (1), so far as requiring him to attend and preside at the creditors' meeting,

the directors are or (as the case may be) the director is guilty of an offence and liable to a fine.

Note
See The Insolvency Rules 1986, r. 4.34ff.

SEC. 100   Appointment of liquidator

100(1)   **[Nomination of liquidator at meetings]** The creditors and the company at their respective meetings mentioned in section 98 may nominate a person to be liquidator for the purpose of winding up the company's affairs and distributing its assets.

100(2)   **[Person who is liquidator]** The liquidator shall be the person nominated by the creditors or, where no person has been so nominated, the person (if any) nominated by the company.

100(3)   **[Where different persons nominated]** In the case of different persons being nominated, any director, member or creditor of the company may, within 7 days after the date on which the nomination was made by the creditors, apply to the court for an order either—

   (a) directing that the person nominated as liquidator by the company shall be liquidator instead of or jointly with the person nominated by the creditors, or

   (b) appointing some other person to be liquidator instead of the person nominated by the creditors.

SEC. 101   Appointment of liquidation committee

101(1)   **[Creditors may appoint committee]** The creditors at the meeting to be held under section 98 or at any subsequent meeting may, if they think fit, appoint a committee ("the liquidation committee") of not more than 5 persons to exercise the functions conferred on it by or under this Act.

101(2)   **[Members appointed by company]** If such a committee is appointed, the company may, either at the meeting at which the resolution for voluntary winding up is passed or at any time subsequently in general meeting, appoint such number of persons as they think fit to act as members of the committee, not exceeding 5.

101(3)   **[Creditors may object to members appointed by company]** However, the creditors may, if they think fit, resolve that all or any of the persons so appointed by the company ought not to be members of the liquidation committee; and if the creditors so resolve—

    (a) the persons mentioned in the resolution are not then, unless the court otherwise directs, qualified to act as members of the committee; and

    (b) on any application to the court under this provision the court may, if it thinks fit, appoint other persons to act as such members in place of the persons mentioned in the resolution.

101(4) **[Scotland]**   In Scotland, the liquidation committee has, in addition to the powers and duties conferred and imposed on it by this Act, such of the powers and duties of commissioners on a bankrupt estate as may be conferred and imposed on liquidation committees by the rules.

SEC. 102   Creditors' meeting where winding up converted under sec. 96

102   Where, in the case of a winding up which was, under section 96 in Chapter III, converted to a creditors' voluntary winding up, a creditors' meeting is held in accordance with section 95, any appointment made or committee established by that meeting is deemed to have been made or established by a meeting held in accordance with section 98 in this Chapter.

SEC. 103   Cesser of directors' powers

103   On the appointment of a liquidator, all the powers of the directors cease, except so far as the liquidation committee (or, if there is no such committee, the creditors) sanction their continuance.

SEC. 104   Vacancy in office of liquidator

104   If a vacancy occurs, by death, resignation or otherwise, in the office of a liquidator (other than a liquidator appointed by, or by the direction of, the court), the creditors may fill the vacancy.

SEC. 105   Meetings of company and creditors at each year's end

105(1) **[Liquidator to summon meetings]**   If the winding up continues for more than one year, the liquidator shall summon a general meeting of the company and a meeting of the creditors at the end of the first year from the commencement of the winding up, and of each succeeding year, or at the first convenient date within 3 months from the end of the year or such longer period as the Secretary of State may allow.

105(2) **[Liquidator to lay account]**   The liquidator shall lay before each of the meetings an account of his acts and dealings and of the conduct of the winding up during the preceding year.

105(3) **[Penalty for non-compliance]**   If the liquidator fails to comply with this section, he is liable to a fine.

105(4) **[Qualification to requirement]**   Where under section 96 a members' voluntary winding up has become a creditors' voluntary winding up, and the creditors' meeting under section 95 is held 3 months or less before the end of the first year from the commencement of the winding up, the liquidator is not required by this section to summon a meeting of creditors at the end of that year.

SEC. 106   Final meeting prior to dissolution

106(1)   [Account of winding up, meetings]   As soon as the company's affairs are fully wound up, the liquidator shall make up an account of the winding up, showing how it has been conducted and the company's property has been disposed of, and thereupon shall call a general meeting of the company and a meeting of the creditors for the purpose of laying the account before the meetings and giving an explanation of it.

106(2)   [Advertisement in Gazette]   Each such meeting shall be called by advertisement in the Gazette specifying the time, place and object of the meeting, and published at least one month before it.

106(3)   [Copy of account, return to registrar]   Within one week after the date of the meetings (or, if they are not held on the same date, after the date of the later one) the liquidator shall send to the registrar of companies a copy of the account, and shall make a return to him of the holding of the meetings and of their dates.

106(4)   [Penalty on default re sec. 106(3)]   If the copy is not sent or the return is not made in accordance with subsection (3), the liquidator is liable to a fine and, for continued contravention, to a daily default fine.

106(5)   [If quorum not present at either meeting]   However, if a quorum is not present at either such meeting, the liquidator shall, in lieu of the return required by subsection (3), make a return that the meeting was duly summoned and that no quorum was present; and upon such return being made the provisions of that subsection as to the making of the return are, in respect of that meeting, deemed complied with.

106(6)   [Penalty if no meetings called]   If the liquidator fails to call a general meeting of the company or a meeting of the creditors as required by this section, he is liable to a fine.

Chapter V — Provisions Applying to both kinds of Voluntary Winding Up

SEC. 107   Distribution of company's property

107   Subject to the provisions of this Act as to preferential payments, the company's property in a voluntary winding up shall on the winding up be applied in satisfaction of the company's liabilities pari passu and, subject to that application, shall (unless the articles otherwise provide) be distributed among the members according to their rights and interests in the company.

SEC. 108   Appointment or removal of liquidator by the court

108(1)   [If no liquidator acting]   If from any cause whatever there is no liquidator acting, the court may appoint a liquidator.

108(2)   [**Removal, replacement**]   The court may, on cause shown, remove a liquidator and appoint another.

SEC. 109   Notice by liquidator of his appointment

109(1)   [**Notice in Gazette and to registrar**]   The liquidator shall, within 14 days after his appointment, publish in the Gazette and deliver to the registrar of companies for registration a notice of his appointment in the form prescribed by statutory instrument made by the Secretary of State.

109(2)   [**Penalty on default**]   If the liquidator fails to comply with this section, he is liable to a fine and, for continued contravention, to a daily default fine.

SEC. 110   Acceptance of shares, etc., as consideration for sale of company property

110(1)   [**Application**]   This section applies, in the case of a company proposed to be, or being, wound up voluntarily, where the whole or part of the company's business or property is proposed to be transferred or sold to another company ("the transferee company"), whether or not the latter is a company within the meaning of the Companies Act.

110(2)   [**Shares etc. in compensation for transfer**]   With the requisite sanction, the liquidator of the company being, or proposed to be, wound up ("the transferor company") may receive, in compensation or part compensation for the transfer or sale, shares, policies or other like interests in the transferee company for distribution among the members of the transferor company.

110(3)   [**Sanction for sec. 110(2)**]   The sanction requisite under subsection (2) is—

    (a)   in the case of a members' voluntary winding up, that of a special resolution of the company, conferring either a general authority on the liquidator or an authority in respect of any particular arrangement, and

    (b)   in the case of a creditors' voluntary winding up, that of either the court or the liquidation committee.

110(4)   [**Alternative to sec. 110(2)**]   Alternatively to subsection (2), the liquidator may (with that sanction) enter into any other arrangement whereby the members of the transferor company may, in lieu of receiving cash, shares, policies or other like interests (or in addition thereto), participate in the profits of, or receive any other benefit from, the transferee company.

110(5)   [**Sale binding on transferors**]   A sale or arrangement in pursuance of this section is binding on members of the transferor company.

110(6)   [**Special resolution**]   A special resolution is not invalid for purposes of this section by reason that it is passed before or concurrently with a resolution for voluntary winding up or for appointing liquidators; but, if an order is made within a year for winding up the company by the court, the special resolution is not valid unless sanctioned by the court.

SEC. 111   Dissent from arrangement under sec. 110

111(1)   [**Application**]   This section applies in the case of a voluntary winding up where, for the purposes of section 110(2) or (4), there has been passed a special resolution of the transferor company providing the sanction requisite for the liquidator under that section.

111(2) **[Objections by members of transferor company]** If a member of the transferor company who did not vote in favour of the special resolution expresses his dissent from it in writing, addressed to the liquidator and left at the company's registered office within 7 days after the passing of the resolution, he may require the liquidator either to abstain from carrying the resolution into effect or to purchase his interest at a price to be determined by agreement or by arbitration under this section.

111(3) **[Where liquidator purchases member's interest]** If the liquidator elects to purchase the member's interest, the purchase money must be paid before the company is dissolved and be raised by the liquidator in such manner as may be determined by special resolution.

111(4) **[Arbitration]** For purposes of an arbitration under this section, the provisions of the Companies Clauses Consolidation Act 1845 or, in the case of a winding up in Scotland, the Companies Clauses Consolidation (Scotland) Act 1845 with respect to the settlement of disputes by arbitration are incorporated with this Act, and—

    (a) in the construction of those provisions this Act is deemed the special Act and **"the company"** means the transferor company, and

    (b) any appointment by the incorporated provisions directed to be made under the hand of the secretary or any two of the directors may be made in writing by the liquidator (or, if there is more than one liquidator, then any two or more of them).

SEC. 112   Reference of questions to court

112(1) **[Application to court]** The liquidator or any contributory or creditor may apply to the court to determine any question arising in the winding up of a company, or to exercise, as respects the enforcing of calls or any other matter, all or any of the powers which the court might exercise if the company were being wound up by the court.

112(2) **[Court order]** The court, if satisfied that the determination of the question or the required exercise of power will be just and beneficial, may accede wholly or partially to the application on such terms and conditions as it thinks fit, or may make such other order on the application as it thinks just.

112(3) **[Copy of order to registrar]** A copy of an order made by virtue of this section staying the proceedings in the winding up shall forthwith be forwarded by the company, or otherwise as may be prescribed, to the registrar of companies, who shall enter it in his records relating to the company.

SEC. 113   Court's power to control proceedings (Scotland)

113 If the court, on the application of the liquidator in the winding up of a company registered in Scotland, so directs, no action or proceeding shall be proceeded with or commenced against the company except by leave of the court and subject to such terms as the court may impose.

SEC. **114**   No liquidator appointed or nominated by company

114(1)   **[Application]**   This section applies where, in the case of a voluntary winding up, no liquidator has been appointed or nominated by the company.

114(2)   **[Limit on exercise of directors' powers]**   The powers of the directors shall not be exercised, except with the sanction of the court or (in the case of a creditors' voluntary winding up) so far as may be necessary to secure compliance with sections 98 (creditors' meeting) and 99 (statement of affairs), during the period before the appointment or nomination of a liquidator of the company.

114(3)   **[Non-application of sec. 114(2)]**   Subsection (2) does not apply in relation to the powers of the directors—

   (a) to dispose of perishable goods and other goods the value of which is likely to diminish if they are not immediately disposed of, and

   (b) to do all such other things as may be necessary for the protection of the company's assets.

114(4)   **[Penalty for non-compliance]**   If the directors of the company without reasonable excuse fail to comply with this section, they are liable to a fine.

SEC. **115**   Expenses of voluntary winding up

115   All expenses properly incurred in the winding up, including the remuneration of the liquidator, are payable out of the company's assets in priority to all other claims.

SEC. **116**   Saving for certain rights

116   The voluntary winding up of a company does not bar the right of any creditor or contributory to have it wound up by the court; but in the case of an application by a contributory the court must be satisfied that the rights of the contributories will be prejudiced by a voluntary winding up.

Chapter VI — Winding Up by the Court

JURISDICTION (ENGLAND AND WALES)

SEC. **117**   High Court and county court jurisdiction

117(1)   **[High Court]**   The High Court has jurisdiction to wind up any company registered in England and Wales.

117(2)   **[County court]**   Where the amount of a company's share capital paid up or credited as paid up does not exceed £120,000, then (subject to this section) the county court of the district in which the company's registered office is situated has concurrent jurisdiction with the High Court to wind up the company.

117(3)   **[Increase, reduction of sec. 117(2) sum]**   The money sum for the time being specified in subsection (2) is subject to increase or reduction by order under section 416 in Part XV.

117(4)   **[Exclusion of jurisdiction for county court]**   The Lord Chancellor may by order in a statutory instrument exclude a county court from having winding-up jurisdiction, and for the purposes of that jurisdiction may attach its district, or any part thereof, to any other county court, and may by statutory instrument revoke or vary any such order.

In exercising the powers of this section, the Lord Chancellor shall provide that a county court is not to have winding-up jurisdiction unless it has for the time being jurisdiction for the purposes of Parts VIII to XI of this Act (individual insolvency).

117(5) **[Extent of winding-up jurisdiction]** Every court in England and Wales having winding-up jurisdiction has for the purposes of that jurisdiction all the powers of the High Court; and every prescribed officer of the court shall perform any duties which an officer of the High Court may discharge by order of a judge of that court or otherwise in relation to winding up.

117(6) **["Registered office"]** For the purposes of this section, a company's **"registered office"** is the place which has longest been its registered office during the 6 months immediately preceding the presentation of the petition for winding up.

SEC. **118** Proceedings taken in wrong court

118(1) **[Wrong court]** Nothing in section 117 invalidates a proceeding by reason of its being taken in the wrong court.

118(2) **[Continuation]** The winding up of a company by the court in England and Wales, or any proceedings in the winding up, may be retained in the court in which the proceedings were commenced, although it may not be the court in which they ought to have been commenced.

SEC. **119** Proceedings in county court; case stated for High Court

119(1) **[Special case]** If any question arises in any winding-up proceedings in a county court which all the parties to the proceedings, or which one of them and the judge of the court, desire to have determined in the first instance in the High Court, the judge shall state the facts in the form of a special case for the opinion of the High Court.

119(2) **[Transmission]** Thereupon the special case and the proceedings (or such of them as may be required) shall be transmitted to the High Court for the purposes of the determination.

JURISDICTION (SCOTLAND)

SEC. **120** Court of Session and sheriff court jurisdiction

120(1) **[Court of Session]** The Court of Session has jurisdiction to wind up any company registered in Scotland.

120(2) **[Vacation judge]** When the Court of Session is in vacation, the jurisdiction conferred on that court by this section may (subject to the provisions of this Part) be exercised by the judge acting as vacation judge.

History
In s. 120(2) the former words "in pursuance of section 4 of the Administration of Justice (Scotland) Act 1933" (which appeared at the end) repealed by Court of Session Act 1988, s. 52(2) and Sch. 2, Pt. I and III as from 29 September 1988.

120(3) **[Concurrent jurisdiction of sheriff court]**   Where the amount of a company's share capital paid up or credited as paid up does not exceed £120,000, the sheriff court of the sheriffdom in which the company's registered office is situated has concurrent jurisdiction with the Court of Session to wind up the company; but—

- (a) the Court of Session may, if it thinks expedient having regard to the amount of the company's assets to do so—
  - (i) remit to a sheriff court any petition presented to the Court of Session for winding up such a company, or
  - (ii) require such a petition presented to a sheriff court to be remitted to the Court of Session; and
- (b) the Court of Session may require any such petition as above-mentioned presented to one sheriff court to be remitted to another sheriff court; and
- (c) in a winding up in the sheriff court the sheriff may submit a stated case for the opinion of the Court of Session on any question of law arising in that winding up.

120(4) **["Registered office"]**   For the purposes of this section, the expression **"registered office"** means the place which has longest been the company's registered office during the 6 months immediately preceding the presentation of the petition for winding up.

120(5) **[Increase, reduction of sec. 120(3) sum]**   The money sum for the time being specified in subsection (3) is subject to increase or reduction by order under section 416 in Part XV.

SEC. 121   Power to remit winding up to Lord Ordinary

121(1) **[Remission to Lord Ordinary]**   The Court of Session may, by Act of Sederunt, make provision for the taking of proceedings in a winding up before one of the Lords Ordinary; and, where provision is so made, the Lord Ordinary has, for the purposes of the winding up, all the powers and jurisdiction of the court.

121(2) **[Report by Lord Ordinary]**   However, the Lord Ordinary may report to the Inner House any matter which may arise in the course of a winding up.

GROUNDS AND EFFECT OF WINDING-UP PETITION

SEC. 122   Circumstances in which company may be wound up by the court

122(1) **[Circumstances]**   A company may be wound up by the court if—

- (a) the company has by special resolution resolved that the company be wound up by the court,
- (b) being a public company which was registered as such on its original incorporation, the company has not been issued with a certificate under section 117 of the Companies Act (public company share capital requirements) and more than a year has expired since it was so registered,
- (c) it is an old public company, within the meaning of the Consequential Provisions Act,
- (d) the company does not commence its business within a year from its incorporation or suspends its business for a whole year,

(e) the number of members is reduced below 2,

(f) the company is unable to pay its debts,

(g) the court is of the opinion that it is just and equitable that the company should be wound up.

122(2) **[Scotland]** In Scotland, a company which the Court of Session has jurisdiction to wind up may be wound up by the Court if there is subsisting a floating charge over property comprised in the the company's property and undertaking, and the court is satisfied that the security of the creditor entitled to the benefit of the floating charge is in jeopardy.

For this purpose a creditor's security is deemed to be in jeopardy if the Court is satisfied that events have occurred or are about to occur which render it unreasonable in the creditor's interests that the company should retain power to dispose of the property which is subject to the floating charge.

SEC. 123   Definition of inability to pay debts

123(1) **[Inability to pay debts]**   A company is deemed unable to pay its debts—

(a) if a creditor (by assignment or otherwise) to whom the company is indebted in a sum exceeding £750 then due has served on the company, by leaving it at the company's registered office, a written demand (in the prescribed form) requiring the company to pay the sum so due and the company has for 3 weeks thereafter neglected to pay the sum or to secure or compound for it to the reasonable satisfaction of the creditor, or

(b) if, in England and Wales, execution or other process issued on a judgment, decree or order of any court in favour of a creditor of the company is returned unsatisfied in whole or in part, or

(c) if, in Scotland, the induciae of a charge for payment on an extract decree, or an extract registered bond, or an extract registered protest, have expired without payment being made, or

(d) if, in Northern Ireland, a certificate of unenforceability has been granted in respect of a judgment against the company, or

(e) if it is proved to the satisfaction of the court that the company is unable to pay its debts as they fall due.

123(2) **[Proof that assets less than liabilities]**   A company is also deemed unable to pay its debts if it is proved to the satisfaction of the court that the value of the company's assets is less than the amount of its liabilities, taking into account its contingent and prospective liabilities.

123(3) **[Increase, reduction of sum in sec. 123(1)(a)]**   The money sum for the time being specified in subsection (1)(a) is subject to increase or reduction by order under section 416 in Part XV.

SEC. 124   Application for winding up

124(1) **[Application to court]**   Subject to the provisions of this section, an application to the court for the winding up of a company shall be by petition presented either by the company, or the directors, or by any creditor or creditors (including any contingent or prospective creditor or creditors), contributory or contributories or by the clerk of a magistrates' court in the exercise of the power conferred by section 87A of the Magistrates' Courts Act 1980 (enforcement of fines imposed on companies), or by all or any of those parties, together or separately.

History
In s. 124(1) the words "or by the clerk of a magistrates' court in the exercise of the power conferred by section 87A of the Magistrates' Courts Act 1980 (enforcement of fines imposed on companies)" inserted by Criminal Justice Act 1988, s. 62(2)(b) as from 5 January 1989 (see S.I. 1988 No. 2073 (C. 78)).

124(2)   [Conditions for contributory to present winding up petition]   Except as mentioned below, a contributory is not entitled to present a winding-up petition unless either—

    (a)   the number of members is reduced below 2, or

    (b)   the shares in respect of which he is a contributory, or some of them, either were originally allotted to him, or have been held by him, and registered in his name, for at least 6 months during the 18 months before the commencement of the winding up, or have devolved on him through the death of a former holder.

124(3)   [Non-application of sec. 124(2)]   A person who is liable under section 76 to contribute to a company's assets in the event of its being wound up may petition on either of the grounds set out in section 122(1)(f) and (g), and subsection (2) above does not then apply; but unless the person is a contributory otherwise than under section 76, he may not in his character as contributory petition on any other ground.

This subsection is deemed included in Chapter VII of Part V of the Companies Act (redeemable shares; purchase by a company of its own shares) for the purposes of the Secretary of State's power to make regulations under section 179 of that Act.

124(4)   [Petition by Secretary of State]   A winding-up petition may be presented by the Secretary of State—

    (a)   if the ground of the petition is that in section 122(1)(b) or (c), or

    (b)   in a case falling within section 124A below.

History
In s. 124(4), para. (b) substituted by CA 1989, s. 60(2) as from 21 February 1990 (see S.I. 1990 No. 142 (C. 5), art. 4); para. (b) formerly read as follows:

"(b)   in a case falling within section 440 of the Companies Act (expedient in the public interest, following report of inspectors, etc.)."

124(5)   [Petition by official receiver]   Where a company is being wound up voluntarily in England and Wales, a winding-up petition may be presented by the official receiver attached to the court as well as by any other person authorised in that behalf under the other provisions of this section; but the court shall not make a winding-up order on the petition unless it is satisfied that the voluntary winding up cannot be continued with due regard to the interests of the creditors or contributories.

Note
See the Insolvency Rules 1986, r. 4.7ff.

SEC. 124A   Petition for winding up on grounds of public interest

124A(1)   [Power of Secretary of State]   Where it appears to the Secretary of State from—

    (a)   any report made or information obtained under Part XIV of the Companies Act 1985 (company investigations, etc.),

(b) any report made under section 94 or 177 of the Financial Services Act 1986 or any information obtained under section 105 of that Act,

(c) any information obtained under section 2 of the Criminal Justice Act 1987 or section 52 of the Criminal Justice (Scotland) Act 1987 (fraud investigations), or

(d) any information obtained under section 83 of the Companies Act 1989 (powers exercisable for purpose of assisting overseas regulatory authorities),

that it is expedient in the public interest that a company should be wound up, he may present a petition for it to be wound up if the court thinks it just and equitable for it to be so.

124A(2) **[Non-application]** This section does not apply if the company is already being wound up by the court.

History
S. 124A inserted by CA 1989, s. 60(3) as from 21 February 1990 (see S.I. 1990 No. 142 (C. 5), art. 4).

Note
S. 124A re-enacts (with modifications) CA 1985, s. 440 which was repealed by CA 1989.

SEC. 125 Powers of court on hearing of petition

125(1) **[Extent of powers]** On hearing a winding-up petition the court may dismiss it, or adjourn the hearing conditionally or unconditionally, or make an interim order, or any other order that it thinks fit; but the court shall not refuse to make a winding-up order on the ground only that the company's assets have been mortgaged to an amount equal to or in excess of those assets, or that the company has no assets.

125(2) **[Just and equitable winding up]** If the petition is presented by members of the company as contributories on the ground that it is just and equitable that the company should be wound up, the court, if it is of opinion—

(a) that the petitioners are entitled to relief either by winding up the company or by some other means, and

(b) that in the absence of any other remedy it would be just and equitable that the company should be wound up,

shall make a winding-up order; but this does not apply if the court is also of the opinion both that some other remedy is available to the petitioners and that they are acting unreasonably in seeking to have the company wound up instead of pursuing that other remedy.

SEC. 126 Power to stay or restrain proceedings against company

126(1) **[Exercise of power]** At any time after the presentation of a winding-up petition, and before a winding-up order has been made, the company, or any creditor or contributory, may—

(a) where any action or proceeding against the company is pending in the High Court or Court of Appeal in England and Wales or Northern Ireland, apply to the court in which the action or proceeding is pending for a stay of proceedings therein, and

(b) where any other action or proceeding is pending against the company, apply to the court having jurisdiction to wind up the company to restrain further proceedings in the action or proceeding;

and the court to which application is so made may (as the case may be) stay, sist or restrain the proceedings accordingly on such terms as it thinks fit.

126(2)   **[Where company registered under CA, sec. 680]**   In the case of a company registered under section 680 of the Companies Act (pre-1862 companies; companies formed under legislation other than the Companies Acts) or the previous corresponding legislation, where the application to stay, sist or restrain is by a creditor, this section extends to actions and proceedings against any contributory of the company.

SEC. 127   Avoidance of property dispositions, etc.

127   In a winding up by the court, any disposition of the company's property, and any transfer of shares, or alteration in the status of the company's members, made after the commencement of the winding up is, unless the court otherwise orders, void.

SEC. 128   Avoidance of attachments, etc.

128(1)   **[Attachments etc. void]**   Where a company registered in England and Wales is being wound up by the court, any attachment, sequestration, distress or execution put in force against the estate or effects of the company after the commencement of the winding up is void.

128(2)   **[Application to Scotland]**   This section, so far as relates to any estate or effects of the company situated in England and Wales, applies in the case of a company registered in Scotland as it applies in the case of a company registered in England and Wales.

COMMENCEMENT OF WINDING UP

SEC. 129   Commencement of winding up by the court

129(1)   **[Time of passing of resolution]**   If, before the presentation of a petition for the winding up of a company by the court, a resolution has been passed by the company for voluntary winding up, the winding up of the company is deemed to have commenced at the time of the passing of the resolution; and unless the court, on proof of fraud or mistake, directs otherwise, all proceedings taken in the voluntary winding up are deemed to have been validly taken.

129(2)   **[Time of presentation of petition]**   In any other case, the winding up of a company by the court is deemed to commence at the time of the presentation of the petition for winding up.

SEC. 130   Consequences of winding-up order

130(1)   **[Copy of order to registrar]**   On the making of a winding-up order, a copy of the order must forthwith be forwarded by the company (or otherwise as may be prescribed) to the registrar of companies, who shall enter it in his records relating to the company.

130(2)   **[Actions stayed on winding up order]**   When a winding-up order has been made or a provisional liquidator has been appointed, no action or proceeding shall be proceeded with or commenced against the company or its property, except by leave of the court and subject to such terms as the court may impose.

130(3) **[Actions stayed re companies registered under CA, sec. 680]** When an order has been made for winding up a company registered under section 680 of the Companies Act, no action or proceeding shall be commenced or proceeded with against the company or its property or any contibutory of the company, in respect of any debt of the company, except by leave of the court, and subject to such terms as the court may impose.

130(4) **[Effect of order]** An order for winding up a company operates in favour of all the creditors and of all contributories of the company as if made on the joint petition of a creditor and of a contributory.

INVESTIGATION PROCEDURES

SEC. 131 Company's statement of affairs

131(1) **[Powers of official receiver]** Where the court has made a winding-up order or appointed a provisional liquidator, the official receiver may require some or all of the persons mentioned in subsection (3) below to make out and submit to him a statement in the prescribed form as to the affairs of the company.

131(2) **[Contents of statement]** The statement shall be verified by affidavit by the persons required to submit it and shall show—

    (a) particulars of the company's assets, debts and liabilities;

    (b) the names and addresses of the company's creditors;

    (c) the securities held by them respectively;

    (d) the dates when the securities were respectively given; and

[The next page is 51,801]

(e) such further or other information as may be prescribed or as the official receiver may require.

131(3)   [Persons in sec. 131(1)]   The persons referred to in subsection (1) are—

   (a) those who are or have been officers of the company;

   (b) those who have taken part in the formation of the company at any time within one year before the relevant date;

   (c) those who are in the company's employment, or have been in its employment within that year, and are in the official receiver's opinion capable of giving the information required;

   (d) those who are or have been within that year officers of, or in the employment of, a company which is, or within that year was, an officer of the company.

131(4)   [Time for submitting statement]   Where any persons are required under this section to submit a statement of affairs to the official receiver, they shall do so (subject to the next subsection) before the end of the period of 21 days beginning with the day after that on which the prescribed notice of the requirement is given to them by the official receiver.

131(5)   [Release, extension of time]   The official receiver, if he thinks fit, may—

   (a) at any time release a person from an obligation imposed on him under subsection (1) or (2) above; or

   (b) either when giving the notice mentioned in subsection (4) or subsequently, extend the period so mentioned;

and where the official receiver has refused to exercise a power conferred by this subsection, the court, if it thinks fit, may exercise it.

131(6)   [Definitions]   In this section—

   "**employment**" includes employment under a contract for services; and

   "**the relevant date**" means—

   (a) in a case where a provisional liquidator is appointed, the date of his appointment; and

   (b) in a case where no such appointment is made, the date of the winding-up order.

131(7)   [Penalty on default]   If a person without reasonable excuse fails to comply with any obligation imposed under this section, he is liable to a fine and, for continued contravention, to a daily default fine.

131(8)   [Scotland]   In the application of this section to Scotland references to the official receiver are to the liquidator or, in a case where a provisional liquidator is appointed, the provisional liquidator.

SEC. 132   Investigation by official receiver

132(1)   [Duty of official receiver]   Where a winding-up order is made by the court in England and Wales, it is the duty of the official receiver to investigate—

   (a) if the company has failed, the causes of the failure; and

   (b) generally, the promotion, formation, business, dealings and affairs of the company, and to make such report (if any) to the court as he thinks fit.

132(2)   [Report prima facie evidence]   The report is, in any proceedings, prima facie evidence of the facts stated in it.

SEC. 133   Public examination of officers

133(1)   [Application to court]   Where a company is being wound up by the court, the official receiver or, in Scotland, the liquidator may at any time before the dissolution of the company apply to the court for the public examination of any person who—

   (a) is or has been an officer of the company; or

   (b) has acted as liquidator or administrator of the company or as receiver or manager or, in Scotland, receiver of its property; or

   (c) not being a person falling within paragraph (a) or (b), is or has been concerned, or has taken part, in the promotion, formation or management of the company.

133(2)   [Request to make application]   Unless the court otherwise orders, the official receiver or, in Scotland, the liquidator shall make an application under subsection (1) if he is requested in accordance with the rules to do so by—

   (a) one-half, in value, of the company's creditors; or

   (b) three-quarters, in value, of the company's contributories.

133(3)   [Court's duties]   On an application under subsection (1), the court shall direct that a public examination of the person to whom the application relates shall be held on a day appointed by the court; and that person shall attend on that day and be publicly examined as to the promotion, formation or management of the company or as to the conduct of its business and affairs, or his conduct or dealings in relation to the company.

133(4)   [Persons taking part]   The following may take part in the public examination of a person under this section and may question that person concerning the matters mentioned in subsection (3), namely—

   (a) the official receiver;

   (b) the liquidator of the company;

   (c) any person who has been appointed as special manager of the company's property or business;

   (d) any creditor of the company who has tendered a proof or, in Scotland, submitted a claim in the winding up;

   (e) any contributory of the company.

Note
See The Insolvency Rules 1986, r. 4.211ff.

SEC. 134   Enforcement of sec. 133

134(1)   [Non-attendance]   If a person without reasonable excuse fails at any time to attend his public examination under section 133, he is guilty of a contempt of court and liable to be punished accordingly.

IA 1986, sec. 132(2)

134(2) [Warrant, etc. re non-attendance] In a case where a person without reasonable excuse fails at any time to attend his examination under section 133 or there are reasonable grounds for believing that a person has absconded, or is about to abscond, with a view to avoiding or delaying his examination under that section, the court may cause a warrant to be issued to a constable or prescribed officer of the court—

(a) for the arrest of that person; and

(b) for the seizure of any books, papers, records, money or goods in that person's possession.

134(3) [Consequences of warrant] In such a case the court may authorise the person arrested under the warrant to be kept in custody, and anything seized under such a warrant to be held, in accordance with the rules, until such time as the court may order.

APPOINTMENT OF LIQUIDATOR

SEC. 135 Appointment and powers of provisional liquidator

135(1) [Time of appointment] Subject to the provisions of this section, the court may, at any time after the presentation of a winding-up petition, appoint a liquidator provisionally.

135(2) [Appointment in England, Wales] In England and Wales, the appointment of a provisional liquidator may be made at any time before the making of a winding-up order; and either the official receiver or any other fit person may be appointed.

135(3) [Appointment in Scotland] In Scotland, such an appointment may be made at any time before the first appointment of liquidators.

135(4) [Provisional liquidator] The provisional liquidator shall carry out such functions as the court may confer on him.

135(5) [Powers of provisional liquidator] When a liquidator is provisionally appointed by the court, his powers may be limited by the order appointing him.

SEC. 136 Functions of official receiver in relation to office of liquidator

136(1) [Application] The following provisions of this section have effect, subject to section 140 below, on a winding-up order being made by the court in England and Wales.

136(2) [Official receiver liquidator] The official receiver, by virtue of his office, becomes the liquidator of the company and continues in office until another person becomes liquidator under the provisions of this Part.

136(3) [Vacancy] The official receiver is, by virtue of his office, the liquidator during any vacancy.

136(4) [Powers of official receiver when liquidator] At any time when he is the liquidator of the company, the official receiver may summon separate meetings of the company's creditors and contributories for the purpose of choosing a person to be liquidator of the company in place of the official receiver.

136(5)   [Duty of official receiver]   It is the duty of the official receiver—

(a) as soon as practicable in the period of 12 weeks beginning with the day on which the winding-up order was made, to decide whether to exercise his power under subsection (4) to summon meetings, and

(b) if in pursuance of paragraph (a) he decides not to exercise that power, to give notice of his decision, before the end of that period, to the court and to the company's creditors and contributories, and

(c) (whether or not he has decided to exercise that power) to exercise his power to summon meetings under subsection (4) if he is at any time requested, in accordance with the rules, to do so by one-quarter, in value, of the company's creditors;

and accordingly, where the duty imposed by paragraph (c) arises before the official receiver has performed a duty imposed by paragraph (a) or (b), he is not required to perform the latter duty.

136(6)   [Contents of sec. 136(5)(b) notice]   A notice given under subsection (5)(b) to the company's creditors shall contain an explanation of the creditors' power under subsection (5)(c) to require the official receiver to summon meetings of the company's creditors and contributories.

SEC. 137   Appointment by Secretary of State

137(1)   [Application by official receiver]   In a winding up by the court in England and Wales the official receiver may, at any time when he is the liquidator of the company, apply to the Secretary of State for the appointment of a person as liquidator in his place.

137(2)   [Decision by official receiver]   If meetings are held in pursuance of a decision under section 136(5)(a), but no person is chosen to be liquidator as a result of those meetings, it is the duty of the official receiver to decide whether to refer the need for an appointment to the Secretary of State.

137(3)   [Duty of Secretary of State]   On an application under subsection (1), or a reference made in pursuance of a decision under subsection (2), the Secretary of State shall either make an appointment or decline to make one.

137(4)   [Notice of appointment by liquidator]   Where a liquidator has been appointed by the Secretary of State under subsection (3), the liquidator shall give notice of his appointment to the company's creditors or, if the court so allows, shall advertise his appointment in accordance with the directions of the court.

137(5)   [Contents of notice or advertisement]   In that notice or advertisement the liquidator shall—

(a) state whether he proposes to summon a general meeting of the company's creditors under section 141 below for the purpose of determining (together with any meeting of contributories) whether a liquidation committee should be established under that section, and

(b) if he does not propose to summon such a meeting, set out the power of the company's creditors under that section to require him to summon one.

SEC. 138 Appointment of liquidator in Scotland

138(1) [Appointment] Where a winding-up order is made by the court in Scotland, a liquidator shall be appointed by the court at the time when the order is made.

138(2) [Period of office of interim liquidator] The liquidator so appointed (here referred to as "the interim liquidator") continues in office until another person becomes liquidator in his place under this section or the next.

138(3) [Meetings to be summoned] The interim liquidator shall (subject to the next subsection) as soon as practicable in the period of 28 days beginning with the day on which the winding-up order was made or such longer period as the court may allow, summon separate meetings of the company's creditors and contributories for the purpose of choosing a person (who may be the person who is the interim liquidator) to be liquidator of the company in place of the interim liquidator.

138(4) [Qualification to sec. 138(3)] If it appears to the interim liquidator, in any case where a company is being wound up on grounds including its inability to pay its debts, that it would be inappropriate to summon under subsection (3) a meeting of the company's contributories, he may summon only a meeting of the company's creditors for the purpose mentioned in that subsection.

138(5) [If no person appointed at meetings] If one or more meetings are held in pursuance of this section but no person is appointed or nominated by the meeting or meetings, the interim liquidator shall make a report to the court which shall appoint either the interim liquidator or some other person to be liquidator of the company.

138(6) [Notification] A person who becomes liquidator of the company in place of the interim liquidator shall, unless he is appointed by the court, forthwith notify the court of that fact.

SEC. 139 Choice of liquidator at meetings of creditors and contributories

139(1) [Application] This section applies where a company is being wound up by the court and separate meetings of the company's creditors and contributories are summoned for the purpose of choosing a person to be liquidator of the company.

139(2) [Nomination of liquidator] The creditors and the contributories at their respective meetings may nominate a person to be liquidator.

139(3) [Liquidator] The liquidator shall be the person nominated by the creditors or, where no person has been so nominated, the person (if any) nominated by the contributories.

139(4) [Where different persons nominated] In the case of different persons being nominated, any contributory or creditor may, within 7 days after the date on which the nomination was made by the creditors, apply to the court for an order either—

    (a) appointing the person nominated as liquidator by the contributories to be a liquidator instead of, or jointly with, the person nominated by the creditors; or

    (b) appointing some other person to be liquidator instead of the person nominated by the creditors.

SEC. 140   Appointment by the court following administration or voluntary arrangement

140(1)   [Appointment of administrator]   Where a winding-up order is made immediately upon the discharge of an administration order, the court may appoint as liquidator of the company the person who has ceased on the discharge of the administration order to be the administrator of the company.

140(2)   [Appointment of supervisor]   Where a winding-up order is made at a time when there is a supervisor of a voluntary arrangement approved in relation to the company under Part I, the court may appoint as liquidator of the company the person who is the supervisor at the time when the winding-up order is made.

140(3)   [Position of official receiver]   Where the court makes an appointment under this section, the official receiver does not become the liquidator as otherwise provided by section 136(2), and he has no duty under section 136(5)(a) or (b) in respect of the summoning of creditors' or contributories' meetings.

LIQUIDATION COMMITTEES

SEC. 141   Liquidation committee (England and Wales)

141(1)   [Meetings may establish committee]   Where a winding-up order has been made by the court in England and Wales and separate meetings of creditors and contributories have been summoned for the purpose of choosing a person to be liquidator, those meetings may establish a committee ("the liquidation committee") to exercise the functions conferred on it by or under this Act.

141(2)   [Separate meetings may be summoned]   The liquidator (not being the official receiver) may at any time, if he thinks fit, summon separate general meetings of the company's creditors and contributories for the purpose of determining whether such a committee should be established and, if it is so determined, of establishing it.

The liquidator (not being the official receiver) shall summon such a meeting if he is requested, in accordance with the rules, to do so by one-tenth, in value, of the company's creditors.

141(3)   [Where meetings disagree]   Where meetings are summoned under this section, or for the purpose of choosing a person to be liquidator, and either the meeting of creditors or the meeting of contributories decides that a liquidation committee should be established, but the other meeting does not so decide or decides that a committee should not be established, the committee shall be established in accordance with the rules, unless the court otherwise orders.

141(4)   [Committee not to function where official receiver liquidator]   The liquidation committee is not to be able or required to carry out its functions at any time when the official receiver is liquidator; but at any such time its functions are vested in the Secretary of State except to the extent that the rules otherwise provide.

141(5)   [Where no committee etc.]   Where there is for the time being no liquidation committee, and the liquidator is a person other than the official receiver, the functions of such a committee are vested in the Secretary of State except to the extent that the rules otherwise provide.

Note
See The Insolvency Rules 1986, r. 4.151ff.

IA 1986, sec. 140(1)

SEC. 142   Liquidation committee (Scotland)

142(1)   [Establishing committees in Scotland]   Where a winding-up order has been made by the court in Scotland and separate meetings of creditors and contributories have been summoned for the purpose of choosing a person to be liquidator or, under section 138(4), only a meeting of creditors has been summoned for that purpose, those meetings or (as the case may be) that meeting may establish a committee ("the liquidation committee") to exercise the functions conferred on it by or under this Act.

142(2)   [Separate meetings may be summoned]   The liquidator may at any time, if he thinks fit, summon separate general meetings of the company's creditors and contributories for the purpose of determining whether such a committee should be established and, if it is so determined, of establishing it.

142(3)   [Meetings to be summoned on request]   The liquidator, if appointed by the court otherwise than under section 139(4)(a), is required to summon meetings under subsection (2) if he is requested, in accordance with the rules, to do so by one-tenth, in value, of the company's creditors.

142(4)   [Where meetings disagree]   Where meetings are summoned under this section, or for the purpose of choosing a person to be liquidator, and either the meeting of creditors or the meeting of contributories decides that a liquidation committee should be established, but the other meeting does not so decide or decides that a committee should not be established, the committee shall be established in accordance with the rules, unless the court otherwise orders.

142(5)   [Where no committee etc.]   Where in the case of any winding up there is for the time being no liquidation committee, the functions of such a committee are vested in the court except to the extent that the rules otherwise provide.

142(6)   [Powers and duties of committee]   In addition to the powers and duties conferred and imposed on it by this Act, a liquidation committee has such of the powers and duties of commissioners in a sequestration as may be conferred and imposed on such committees by the rules.

THE LIQUIDATOR'S FUNCTIONS

SEC. 143   General functions in winding up by the court

143(1)   [Functions]   The functions of the liquidator of a company which is being wound up by the court are to secure that the assets of the company are got in, realised and distributed to the company's creditors and, if there is a surplus, to the persons entitled to it.

143(2)   [Duty of liquidator not official receiver]   It is the duty of the liquidator of a company which is being wound up by the court in England and Wales, if he is not the official receiver—

  (a) to furnish the official receiver with such information,

  (b) to produce to the official receiver, and permit inspection by the official receiver of, such books, papers and other records, and

  (c) to give the official receiver such other assistance,

as the official receiver may reasonably require for the purposes of carrying out his functions in relation to the winding up.

SEC. 144   Custody of company's property

144(1)   [Liquidator to take property into custody]   When a winding-up order has been made, or where a provisional liquidator has been appointed, the liquidator or the provisional liquidator (as the case may be) shall take into his custody or under his control all the property and things in action to which the company is or appears to be entitled.

144(2)   [In Scotland where no liquidator]   In a winding up by the court in Scotland, if and so long as there is no liquidator, all the property of the company is deemed to be in the custody of the court.

SEC. 145   Vesting of company property in liquidator

145(1)   [Court order]   When a company is being wound up by the court, the court may on the application of the liquidator by order direct that all or any part of the property of whatsoever description belonging to the company or held by trustees on its behalf shall vest in the liquidator by his official name; and thereupon the property to which the order relates vests accordingly.

145(2)   [Action re property by liquidator]   The liquidator may, after giving such indemnity (if any) as the court may direct, bring or defend in his official name any action or other legal proceeding which relates to that property or which it is necessary to bring or defend for the purpose of effectually winding up the company and recovering its property.

SEC. 146   Duty to summon final meeting

146(1)   [Summoning final meeting]   Subject to the next subsection, if it appears to the liquidator of a company which is being wound up by the court that the winding up of the company is for practical purposes complete and the liquidator is not the official receiver, the liquidator shall summon a final general meeting of the company's creditors which—

(a) shall receive the liquidator's report of the winding up, and

(b) shall determine whether the liquidator should have his release under section 174 in Chapter VII of this Part.

146(2)   [Time for notice]   The liquidator may, if he thinks fit, give the notice summoning the final general meeting at the same time as giving notice of any final distribution of the company's property but, if summoned for an earlier date, that meeting shall be adjourned (and, if necessary, further adjourned) until a date on which the liquidator is able to report to the meeting that the winding up of the company is for practical purposes complete.

146(3)   [Retention of sums]   In the carrying out of his functions in the winding up it is the duty of the liquidator to retain sufficient sums from the company's property to cover the expenses of summoning and holding the meeting required by this section.

GENERAL POWERS OF COURT

SEC. 147 Power to stay or sist winding up

147(1) [Court may order stay on application] The court may at any time after an order for winding up, on the application either of the liquidator or the official receiver or any creditor or contributory, and on proof to the satisfaction of the court that all proceedings in the winding up ought to be stayed or sisted, make an order staying or sisting the proceedings, either altogether or for a limited time, on such terms and conditions as the court thinks fit.

147(2) [Report by official receiver] The court may, before making an order, require the official receiver to furnish to it a report with respect to any facts or matters which are in his opinion relevant to the application.

147(3) [Copy of order to registrar] A copy of every order made under this section shall forthwith be forwarded by the company, or otherwise as may be prescribed, to the registrar of companies, who shall enter it in his records relating to the company.

SEC. 148 Settlement of list of contributories and application of assets

148(1) [Court's duties] As soon as may be after making a winding-up order, the court shall settle a list of contributories, with power to rectify the register of members in all cases where rectification is required in pursuance of the Companies Act or this Act, and shall cause the company's assets to be collected, and applied in discharge of its liabilities.

148(2) [Court may dispense with list] If it appears to the court that it will not be necessary to make calls on or adjust the rights of contributories, the court may dispense with the settlement of a list of contributories.

148(3) [Distinction between types of contributories] In settling the list, the court shall distinguish between persons who are contributories in their own right and persons who are contributories as being representatives of or liable for the debts of others.

SEC. 149 Debts due from contributory to company

149(1) [Court may order payment from contributory] The court may, at any time after making a winding-up order, make an order on any contributory for the time being on the list of contributories to pay, in manner directed by the order, any money due from him (or from the estate of the person whom he represents) to the company, exclusive of any money payable by him or the estate by virtue of any call in pursuance of the Companies Act or this Act.

149(2) [Allowances and set-offs] The court in making such an order may—

   (a) in the case of an unlimited company, allow to the contributory by way of set-off any money due to him or the estate which he represents from the company on any independent dealing or contract with the company, but not any money due to him as a member of the company in respect of any dividend or profit, and

(b) in the case of a limited company, make to any director or manager whose liability is unlimited or to his estate the like allowance.

149(3) **[Money due to contributory may be allowed when creditors paid]**   In the case of any company, whether limited or unlimited, when all the creditors are paid in full (together with interest at the official rate), any money due on any account whatever to a contributory from the company may be allowed to him by way of set-off against any subsequent call.

SEC. 150   Power to make calls

150(1) **[Court may make calls to satisfy debts]**   The court may, at any time after making a winding-up order, and either before or after it has ascertained the sufficiency of the company's assets, make calls on all or any of the contributories for the time being settled on the list of the contributories to the extent of their liability, for payment of any money which the court considers necessary to satisfy the company's debts and liabilities, and the expenses of winding up, and for the adjustment of the rights of the contributories among themselves, and make an order for payment of any calls so made.

150(2) **[Matters to be considered]**   In making a call the court may take into consideration the probability that some of the contributories may partly or wholly fail to pay it.

SEC. 151   Payment into bank of money due to company

151(1) **[Court may order payment into Bank of England]**   The court may order any contributory, purchaser or other person from whom money is due to the company to pay the amount due into the Bank of England (or any branch of it) to the account of the liquidator instead of to the liquidator, and such an order may be enforced in the same manner as if it had directed payment to the liquidator.

151(2) **[Moneys in Bank subject to court orders]**   All money and securities paid or delivered into the Bank of England (or branch) in the event of a winding up by the court are subject in all respects to the orders of the court.

SEC. 152   Order on contributory to be conclusive evidence

152(1) **[Order evidence that money due]**   An order made by the court on a contributory is conclusive evidence that the money (if any) thereby appearing to be due or ordered to be paid is due, but subject to any right of appeal.

152(2) **[Other matters stated in order]**   All other pertinent matters stated in the order are to be taken as truly stated as against all persons and in all proceedings except proceedings in Scotland against the heritable estate of a deceased contributory; and in that case the order is only prima facie evidence for the purpose of charging his heritable estate, unless his heirs or legatees of heritage were on the list of contributories at the time of the order being made.

SEC. 153   Power to exclude creditors not proving in time

153   The court may fix a time or times within which creditors are to prove their debts or claims or to be excluded from the benefit of any distribution made before those debts are proved.

SEC. 154   Adjustment of rights of contributories

154   The court shall adjust the rights of the contributories among themselves and distribute any surplus among the persons entitled to it.

SEC. 155   Inspection of books by creditors, etc.

155(1)   **[Court may make order for inspection]**   The court may, at any time after making a winding-up order make such order for inspection of the company's books and papers by creditors and contributories as the court thinks just; and any books and papers in the company's possession may be inspected by creditors and contributories accordingly, but not further or otherwise.

155(2)   **[Statutory rights of government department]**   Nothing in this section excludes or restricts any statutory rights of a government department or person acting under the authority of a government department.

SEC. 156   Payment of expenses of winding up

156   The court may, in the event of the assets being insufficient to satisfy the liabilities, make an order as to the payment out of the assets of the expenses incurred in the winding up in such order of priority as the court thinks just.

SEC. 157   Attendance at company meetings (Scotland)

157   In the winding up by the court of a company registered in Scotland, the court has power to require the attendance of any officer of the company at any meeting of creditors or of contributories, or of a liquidation committee, for the purpose of giving information as to the trade, dealings, affairs or property of the company.

SEC. 158   Power to arrest absconding contributory

158   The court, at any time either before or after making a winding-up order, on proof of probable cause for believing that a contributory is about to quit the United Kingdom or otherwise to abscond or to remove or conceal any of his property for the purpose of evading payment of calls, may cause the contributory to be arrested and his books and papers and movable personal property to be seized and him and them to be kept safely until such time as the court may order.

SEC. 159   Powers of court to be cumulative

159   Powers conferred by this Act and the Companies Act on the court are in addition to, and not in restriction of, any existing powers of instituting proceedings against a contributory or debtor of the company, or the estate of any contributory or debtor, for the recovery of any call or other sums.

SEC. 160   Delegation of powers to liquidator (England and Wales)

160(1)   **[Delegation by rules]**   Provision may be made by rules for enabling or requiring all or any of the powers and duties conferred and imposed on the court in

England and Wales by the Companies Act and this Act in respect of the following matters—

    (a) the holding and conducting of meetings to ascertain the wishes of creditors and contributories,

    (b) the settling of lists of contributories and the rectifying of the register of members where required, and the collection and application of the assets,

    (c) the payment, delivery, conveyance, surrender or transfer of money, property, books or papers to the liquidator,

    (d) the making of calls,

    (e) the fixing of a time within which debts and claims must be proved,

to be exercised or performed by the liquidator as an officer of the court, and subject to the court's control.

160(2) **[No rectifications etc. without special leave]** But the liquidator shall not, without the special leave of the court, rectify the register of members, and shall not make any call without either that special leave or the sanction of the liquidation committee.

Note
See The Insolvency Rules 1986, r. 4.54ff., 4.179ff., 4.185,
4.195ff., 4.196, 4.202ff.

ENFORCEMENT OF, AND APPEAL FROM, ORDERS

SEC. 161   Orders for calls on contributories (Scotland)

161(1) **[Court may order calls on contributories on receipt of list]** In Scotland, where an order, interlocutor or decree has been made for winding up a company by the court, it is competent to the court, on production by the liquidators of a list certified by them of the names of the contributories liable in payment of any calls, and of the amount due by each contributory, and of the date when that amount became due, to pronounce forthwith a decree against those contributories for payment of the sums so certified to be due, with interest from that date until payment (at 5 per cent per annum) in the same way and to the same effect as if they had severally consented to registration for execution, on a charge of 6 days, of a legal obligation to pay those calls and interest.

161(2) **[Extraction of decree]** The decree may be extracted immediately, and no suspension of it is competent, except on caution or consignation, unless with special leave of the court.

SEC. 162   Appeals from orders in Scotland

162(1) **[Appeal from order on winding up]** Subject to the provisions of this section and to rules of court, an appeal from any order or decision made or given in the winding up of a company by the court in Scotland under this Act lies in the same manner and subject to the same conditions as an appeal from an order or decision of the court in cases within its ordinary jurisdiction.

162(2) **[Orders by judge acting as vacation judge]** In regard to orders or judgments pronounced by the judge acting as vacation judge—

(a) none of the orders specified in Part I of Schedule 3 to this Act are subject to review, reduction, suspension or stay of execution, and

(b) every other order or judgment (except as mentioned below) may be submitted to review by the Inner House by reclaiming motion enrolled within 14 days from the the date of the order or judgment.

History
In s. 162(2) the former words "in pursuance of section 4 of the Administration of Justice (Scotland) Act 1933" (which appeared after the words "vacation judge") repealed by Court of Session Act 1988, s. 52(2) and Sch. 2, Pt. I and III as from 29 September 1988.

162(3) **[Order in Sch. 3, Pt. II]** However, an order being one of those specified in Part II of that Schedule shall, from the date of the order and notwithstanding that it has been submitted to review as above, be carried out and receive effect until the Inner House have disposed of the matter.

162(4) **[Orders by Lord Ordinary]** In regard to orders of judgments pronounced in Scotland by a Lord Ordinary before whom proceedings in a winding up are being taken, any such order or judgment may be submitted to review by the Inner House by reclaiming motion enrolled within 14 days from its date; but should it not be so submitted to review during session, the provisions of this section in regard to orders or judgments pronounced by the judge acting as vacation judge apply.

162(5) **[Decrees for payment of calls in winding up]** Nothing in this section affects provisions of the Companies Act or this Act in reference to decrees in Scotland for payment of calls in the winding up of companies, whether voluntary or by the court.

Chapter VII — Liquidators

PRELIMINARY

SEC. 163 Style and title of liquidators

163 The liquidator of a company shall be described—

(a) where a person other than the official receiver is liquidator, by the style of "the liquidator" of the particular company, or

(b) where the official receiver is liquidator, by the style of "the official receiver and liquidator" of the particular company;

and in neither case shall he be described by an individual name.

SEC. 164 Corrupt inducement affecting appointment

164 A person who gives, or agrees or offers to give, to any member or creditor of a company any valuable consideration with a view to securing his own appointment or nomination, or to securing or preventing the appointment or nomination of some person other than himself, as the company's liquidator is liable to a fine.

LIQUIDATOR'S POWERS AND DUTIES

SEC. 165 Voluntary winding up

165(1) **[Application]** This section has effect where a company is being wound up voluntarily, but subject to section 166 below in the case of a creditors' voluntary winding up.

165(2)   **[Powers in Sch. 4, Pt. I]**   The liquidator may—

(a) in the case of a members' voluntary winding up, with the sanction of an extraordinary resolution of the company, and

(b) in the case of a creditors' voluntary winding up, with the sanction of the court or the liquidation committee (or, if there is no such committee, a meeting of the company's creditors),

exercise any of the powers specified in Part I of Schedule 4 to this Act (payment of debts, compromise of claims, etc.).

165(3)   **[Powers in Sch. 4, Pt. II, III]**   The liquidator may, without sanction, exercise either of the powers specified in Part II of that Schedule (institution and defence of proceedings; carrying on the business of the company) and any of the general powers specified in Part III of that Schedule.

165(4)   **[Other powers]**   The liquidator may—

(a) exercise the court's power of settling a list of contributories (which list is prima facie evidence of the liability of the persons named in it to be contributories),

(b) exercise the court's power of making calls,

(c) summon general meetings of the company for the purpose of obtaining its sanction by special or extraordinary resolution or for any other purpose he may think fit.

165(5)   **[Duty re payment of debts]**   The liquidator shall pay the company's debts and adjust the rights of the contributories among themselves.

165(6)   **[Notice to committee re exercise of powers]**   Where the liquidator in exercise of the powers conferred on him by this Act disposes of any property of the company to a person who is connected with the company (within the meaning of section 249 in Part VII), he shall, if there is for the time being a liquidation committee, give notice to the committee of that exercise of his powers.

SEC. 166   Creditors' voluntary winding up

166(1)   **[Application]**   This section applies where, in the case of a creditors' voluntary winding up, a liquidator has been nominated by the company.

166(2)   **[Non-exercise of sec. 165 powers]**   The powers conferred on the liquidator by section 165 shall not be exercised, except with the sanction of the court, during the period before the holding of the creditors' meeting under section 98 in Chapter IV.

166(3)   **[Non-application of sec. 166(2)]**   Subsection (2) does not apply in relation to the power of the liquidator—

(a) to take into his custody or under his control all the property to which the company is or appears to be entitled;

(b) to dispose of perishable goods and other goods the value of which is likely to diminish if they are not immediately disposed of; and

(c) to do all such other things as may be necessary for the protection of the company's assets.

166(4) **[Liquidator to attend sec. 98 meeting]** The liquidator shall attend the creditors' meeting held under section 98 and shall report to the meeting on any exercise by him of his powers (whether or not under this section or under section 112 or 165).

166(5) **[Where default re sec. 98, 99]** If default is made—

(a) by the company in complying with subsection (1) or (2) of section 98, or

(b) by the directors in complying with subsection (1) or (2) of section 99,

the liquidator shall, within 7 days of the relevant day, apply to the court for directions as to the manner in which that default is to be remedied.

166(6) **["The relevant day"]** "The relevant day" means the day on which the liquidator was nominated by the company or the day on which he first became aware of the default, whichever is the later.

166(7) **[Penalty for non-compliance]** If the liquidator without reasonable excuse fails to comply with this section, he is liable to a fine.

SEC. 167 Winding up by the court

167(1) **[Powers of liquidator]** Where a company is being wound up by the court, the liquidator may—

(a) with the sanction of the court or the liquidation committee, exercise any of the powers specified in Parts I and II of Schedule 4 to this Act (payment of debts; compromise of claims, etc.; institution and defence of proceedings; carrying on of the business of the company), and

(b) with or without that sanction, exercise any of the general powers specified in Part III of that Schedule.

167(2) **[Duty of liquidator]** Where the liquidator (not being the official receiver), in exercise of the powers conferred on him by this Act—

(a) disposes of any property of the company to a person who is connected with the company (within the meaning of section 249 in Part VII), or

(b) employs a solicitor to assist him in the carrying out of his functions,

he shall, if there is for the time being a liquidation committee, give notice to the committee of that exercise of his powers.

167(3) **[Control of court]** The exercise by the liquidator in a winding up by the court of the powers conferred by this section is subject to the control of the court, and any creditor or contributory may apply to the court with respect to any exercise or proposed exercise of any of those powers.

SEC. 168 Supplementary powers (England and Wales)

168(1) **[Application]** This section applies in the case of a company which is being wound up by the court in England and Wales.

168(2) **[Liquidator may summon general meetings]** The liquidator may summon general meetings of the creditors or contributories for the purpose of ascertaining their wishes; and it is his duty to summon meetings at such times as the creditors or contributories by resolution (either at the meeting appointing the liquidator or otherwise) may direct, or whenever requested in writing to do so by one-tenth in value of the creditors or contributories (as the case may be).

168(3)   [Liquidator may apply to court for directions]   The liquidator may apply to the court (in the prescribed manner) for directions in relation to any particular matter arising in the winding up.

168(4)   [Liquidator to use own discretion]   Subject to the provisions of this Act, the liquidator shall use his own discretion in the management of the assets and their distribution among the creditors.

168(5)   [Application to court re acts of liquidator]   If any person is aggrieved by an act or decision of the liquidator, that person may apply to the court; and the court may confirm, reverse or modify the act or decision complained of, and make such order in the case as it thinks just.

SEC. 169   Supplementary powers (Scotland)

169(1)   [Where no liquidation committee]   In the case of a winding up in Scotland, the court may provide by order that the liquidator may, where there is no liquidation committee, exercise any of the following powers, namely—

- (a)   to bring or defend any action or other legal proceeding in the name and on behalf of the company, or
- (b)   to carry on the business of the company so far as may be necessary for its beneficial winding up,

without the sanction or intervention of the court.

169(2)   [Liquidator's powers]   In a winding up by the court in Scotland, the liquidator has (subject to the rules) the same powers as a trustee on a bankrupt estate.

Note
See The Insolvency (Scotland) Rules 1986 (S.I. 1986 No. 1915 (S. 139)), r. 4.68.

SEC. 170   Enforcement of liquidator's duty to make returns, etc.

170(1)   [Powers of court if liquidator fails to file returns etc.]   If a liquidator who has made any default—

- (a)   in filing, delivering or making any return, account or other document, or
- (b)   in giving any notice which he is by law required to file, deliver, make or give,

fails to make good the default within 14 days after the service on him of a notice requiring him to do so, the court has the following powers.

170(2)   [On application court may order to make good default]   On an application made by any creditor or contributory of the company, or by the registrar of companies, the court may make an order directing the liquidator to make good the default within such time as may be specified in the order.

170(3)   [Costs]   The court's order may provide that all costs of and incidental to the application shall be borne by the liquidator.

170(4)   [Penalties]   Nothing in this section prejudices the operation of any enactment imposing penalties on a liquidator in respect of any such default as is mentioned above.

REMOVAL; VACATION OF OFFICE

SEC. 171 Removal, etc. (voluntary winding up)

171(1) [Application] This section applies with respect to the removal from office and vacation of office of the liquidator of a company which is being wound up voluntarily.

171(2) [Removal from office] Subject to the next subsection, the liquidator may be removed from office only by an order of the court or—

  (a) in the case of a members' voluntary winding up, by a general meeting of the company summoned specially for that purpose, or

  (b) in the case of a creditors' voluntary winding up, by a general meeting of the company's creditors summoned specially for that purpose in accordance with the rules.

171(3) [Where liquidator appointed by court under sec. 108] Where the liquidator was appointed by the court under section 108 in Chapter V, a meeting such as is mentioned in subsection (2) above shall be summoned for the purpose of replacing him only if he thinks fit or the court so directs or the meeting is requested, in accordance with the rules—

  (a) in the case of a members' voluntary winding up, by members representing not less than one-half of the total voting rights of all the members having at the date of the request a right to vote at the meeting, or

  (b) in the case of a creditors' voluntary winding up, by not less than one-half, in value, of the company's creditors.

171(4) [Vacation of office] A liquidator shall vacate office if he ceases to be a person who is qualified to act as an insolvency practitioner in relation to the company.

171(5) [Resignation] A liquidator may, in the prescribed circumstances, resign his office by giving notice of his resignation to the registrar of companies.

171(6) [Where final meetings held] Where—

  (a) in the case of a members' voluntary winding up, a final meeting of the company has been held under section 94 in Chapter III, or

  (b) in the case of a creditors' voluntary winding up, final meetings of the company and of the creditors have been held under section 106 in Chapter IV,

the liquidator whose report was considered at the meeting or meetings shall vacate office as soon as he has complied with subsection (3) of that section and has given notice to the registrar of companies that the meeting or meetings have been held and of the decisions (if any) of the meeting or meetings.

SEC. 172 Removal, etc. (winding up by the court)

172(1) [Application] This section applies with respect to the removal from office and vacation of office of the liquidator of a company which is being wound up by the court, or of a provisional liquidator.

172(2) [Removal from office] Subject as follows, the liquidator may be removed from office only by an order of the court or by a general meeting of the company's creditors summoned specially for that purpose in accordance with the rules; and a provisional liquidator may be removed from office only by an order of the court.

172(3) [Replacing certain types of liquidator]   Where—

(a) the official receiver is liquidator otherwise than in succession under section 136(3) to a person who held office as a result of a nomination by a meeting of the company's creditors or contributories, or

(b) the liquidator was appointed by the court otherwise than under section 139(4)(a) or 140(1), or was appointed by the Secretary of State,

a general meeting of the company's creditors shall be summoned for the purpose of replacing him only if he thinks fit, or the court so directs, or the meeting is requested, in accordance with the rules, by not less that one-quarter, in value, of the creditors.

172(4) [If liquidator appointed by Secretary of State]   If appointed by the Secretary of State, the liquidator may be removed from office by a direction of the Secretary of State.

172(5) [Vacation of office]   A liquidator or provisional liquidator, not being the official receiver, shall vacate office if he ceases to be a person who is qualified to act as an insolvency practitioner in relation to the company.

172(6) [Resignation]   A liquidator may, in the prescribed circumstances, resign his office by giving notice of his resignation to the court.

172(7) [Where sec. 204 order]   Where an order is made under section 204 (early dissolution in Scotland) for the dissolution of the company, the liquidator shall vacate office when the dissolution of the company takes effect in accordance with that section.

172(8) [Where final meeting under sec. 146]   Where a final meeting has been held under section 146 (liquidator's report on completion of winding up), the liquidator whose report was considered at the meeting shall vacate office as soon as he has given notice to the court and the registrar of companies that the meeting has been held and of the decisions (if any) of the meeting.

Note
See The Insolvency Rules 1986, r. 4.119ff.

RELEASE OF LIQUIDATOR

SEC. 173   Release (voluntary winding up)

173(1) [Application]   This section applies with respect to the release of the liquidator of a company which is being wound up voluntarily.

173(2) [Time of release]   A person who has ceased to be a liquidator shall have his release with effect from the following time, that is to say—

(a) in the case of a person who has been removed from office by a general meeting of the company or by a general meeting of the company's creditors that has not resolved against his release or who has died, the time at which notice is given to the registrar of companies in accordance with the rules that that person has ceased to hold office;

(b) in the case of a person who has been removed from office by a general meeting of the company's creditors that has resolved against his release, or by the court, or who has vacated office under section 171(4) above, such time as the Secretary of State may, on the application of that person, determine;

(c) in the case of a person who has resigned, such time as may be prescribed;

(d) in the case of a person who has vacated office under subsection (6)(a) of section 171, the time at which he vacated office;

(e) in the case of a person who has vacated office under subsection (6)(b) of that section—

    (i) if the final meeting of the creditors referred to in that subsection has resolved against that person's release, such time as the Secretary of State may, on an application by that person, determine, and

    (ii) if that meeting has not resolved against that person's release, the time at which he vacated office.

173(3) [**Application to Scotland**]   In the application of subsection (2) to the winding up of a company registered in Scotland, the references to a determination by the Secretary of State as to the time from which a person who has ceased to be liquidator shall have his release are to be read as references to such a determination by the Accountant of Court.

173(4) [**Effect of release**]   Where a liquidator has his release under subsection (2), he is, with effect from the time specified in that subsection, discharged from all liability both in respect of acts or omissions of his in the winding up and otherwise in relation to his conduct as liquidator.

But nothing in this section prevents the exercise, in relation to a person who has had his release under subsection (2), of the court's powers under section 212 of this Act (summary remedy against delinquent directors, liquidators, etc.).

SEC. 174   Release (winding up by the court)

174(1) [**Application**]   This section applies with respect to the release of the liquidator of a company which is being wound up by the court, or of a provisional liquidator.

174(2) [**Where official receiver ceases to be liquidator**]   Where the official receiver has ceased to be liquidator and a person becomes liquidator in his stead, the official receiver has his release with effect from the following time, that is to say—

(a) in a case where that person was nominated by a general meeting of creditors or contributories, or was appointed by the Secretary of State, the time at which the official receiver gives notice to the court that he has been replaced;

(b) in a case where that person is appointed by the court, such time as the court may determine.

174(3) [**Where official receiver gives notice to Secretary of State**]   If the official receiver while he is a liquidator gives notice to the Secretary of State that the winding up is for practical purposes complete, he has his release with effect from such time as the Secretary of State may determine.

174(4) **[Person other than official receiver]**   A person other than the official receiver who has ceased to be a liquidator has his release with effect from the following time, that is to say—

    (a) in the case of a person who has been removed from office by a general meeting of creditors that has not resolved against his release or who has died, the time at which notice is given to the court in accordance with the rules that that person has ceased to hold office;

    (b) in the case of a person who has been removed from office by a general meeting of creditors that has resolved against his release, or by the court or the Secretary of State, or who has vacated office under section 172(5) or (7), such time as the Secretary of State may, on an application by that person, determine;

    (c) in the case of a person who has resigned, such time as may be prescribed;

    (d) in the case of a person who has vacated office under section 172(8)—

        (i) if the final meeting referred to in that subsection has resolved against that person's release, such time as the Secretary of State may, on an application by that person, determine, and

        (ii) if that meeting has not so resolved, the time at which that person vacated office.

Note
See The Insolvency Rules 1986, r. 4.121, 4.132.

174(5) **[Provisional liquidator]**   A person who has ceased to hold office as a provisional liquidator has his release with effect from such time as the court may, on an application by him, determine.

174(6) **[Effect of release]**   Where the official receiver or a liquidator or provisional liquidator has his release under this section, he is, with effect from the time specified in the preceding provisions of this section, discharged from all liability both in respect of acts or omissions of his in the winding up and otherwise in relation to his conduct as liquidator or provisional liquidator.

But nothing in this section prevents the exercise, in relation to a person who has had his release under this section, of the court's powers under section 212 (summary remedy against delinquent directors, liquidators, etc.).

174(7) **[Application to Scotland]**   In the application of this section to a case where the order for winding up has been made by the court in Scotland, the references to a determination by the Secretary of State as to the time from which a person who has ceased to be liquidator has his release are to such a determination by the Accountant of Court.

Chapter VIII — Provisions of General Application in Winding Up

PREFERENTIAL DEBTS

SEC. 175   Preferential debts (general provision)

175(1) **[Payment in priority]**   In a winding up the company's preferential debts (within the meaning given by section 386 in Part XII) shall be paid in priority to all other debts.

175(2) **[Ranking and priority]** Preferential debts—

(a) rank equally among themselves after the expenses of the winding up and shall be paid in full, unless the assets are insufficient to meet them, in which case they abate in equal proportions; and

(b) so far as the assets of the company available for payment of general creditors are insufficient to meet them, have priority over the claims of holders of debentures secured by, or holders of, any floating charge created by the company, and shall be paid accordingly out of any property comprised in or subject to that charge.

SEC. 176 Preferential charge on goods distrained

176(1) **[Application]** This section applies where a company is being wound up by the court in England and Wales, and is without prejudice to section 128 (avoidance of attachments, etc.).

176(2) **[Where distraining in previous 3 months]** Where any person (whether or not a landlord or person entitled to rent) has distrained upon the goods or effects of the company in the period of 3 months ending with the date of the winding-up order, those goods or effects, or the proceeds of their sale, shall be charged for the benefit of the company with the preferential debts of the company to the extent that the company's property is for the time being insufficient for meeting them.

176(3) **[Surrender of goods under sec. 176(2)]** Where by virtue of a charge under subsection (2) any person surrenders any goods or effects to a company or makes a payment to a company, that person ranks, in respect of the amount of the proceeds of sale of those goods or effects by the liquidator or (as the case may be) the amount of the payment, as a preferential creditor of the company, except as against so much of the company's property as is available for the payment of preferential creditors by virtue of the surrender or payment.

SPECIAL MANAGERS

SEC. 177 Power to appoint special manager

177(1) **[Power of court]** Where a company has gone into liquidation or a provisional liquidator has been appointed, the court may, on an application under this section, appoint any person to be the special manager of the business or property of the company.

177(2) **[Application to court]** The application may be made by the liquidator or provisional liquidator in any case where it appears to him that the nature of the business or property of the company, or the interests of the company's creditors or contributories or members generally, require the appointment of another person to manage the company's business or property.

177(3) **[Powers of special manager]** The special manager has such powers as may be entrusted to him by the court.

177(4) **[Extent of sec. 177(3) powers]** The court's power to entrust powers to the special manager includes power to direct that any provision of this Act that has effect in relation to the provisional liquidator or liquidator of a company shall have the like effect in relation to the special manager for the purposes of the carrying out by him of any of the functions of the provisional liquidator or liquidator.

177(5)   [Duties of special manager]   The special manager shall—

(a)   give such security or, in Scotland, caution as may be prescribed;

(b)   prepare and keep such accounts as may be prescribed; and

(c)   produce those accounts in accordance with the rules to the Secretary of State or to such other persons as may be prescribed.

DISCLAIMER (ENGLAND AND WALES ONLY)

SEC. 178   Power to disclaim onerous property

178(1)   [Application]   This and the next two sections apply to a company that is being wound up in England and Wales.

178(2)   [Disclaimer by liquidator]   Subject as follows, the liquidator may, by giving of the prescribed notice, disclaim any onerous property and may do so notwithstanding that he has taken possession of it, endeavoured to sell it, or otherwise exercised rights of ownership in relation to it.

178(3)   [Onerous property]   The following is onerous property for the purposes of this section—

(a)   any unprofitable contract, and

(b)   any other property of the company which is unsaleable or not readily saleable or is such that it may give rise to a liability to pay money or perform any other onerous act.

178(4)   [Effect of disclaimer]   A disclaimer under this section—

(a)   operates so as to determine, as from the date of the disclaimer, the rights, interests and liabilities of the company in or in respect of the property disclaimed; but

(b)   does not, except so far as is necessary for the purpose of releasing the company from any liability, affect the rights or liabilities of any other person.

178(5)   [Where notice of disclaimer not to be given]   A notice of disclaimer shall not be given under this section in respect of any property if—

(a)   a person interested in the property has applied in writing to the liquidator or one of his predecessors as liquidator requiring the liquidator or that predecessor to decide whether he will disclaim or not, and

(b)   the period of 28 days begining with the day on which that application was made, or such longer period as the court may allow, has expired without a notice of disclaimer having been given under this section in respect of that property.

178(6)   [Persons sustaining loss etc.]   Any person sustaining loss or damage in consequence of the operation of a disclaimer under this section is deemed a creditor of the company to the extent of the loss or damage and accordingly may prove for the loss or damage in the winding up.

SEC. 179 Disclaimer of leaseholds

179(1) [Requirement for disclaimer to take effect] The disclaimer under section 178 of any property of a leasehold nature does not take effect unless a copy of the disclaimer has been served (so far as the liquidator is aware of their addresses) on every person claiming under the company as underlessee or mortgagee and either—

(a) no application under section 181 below is made with respect to that property before the end of the period of 14 days beginning with the day on which the last notice served under this subsection was served; or

(b) where such an application has been made, the court directs that the disclaimer shall take effect.

179(2) [Court's directions or orders] Where the court gives a direction under subsection (1)(b) it may also, instead of or in addition to any order it makes under section 181, make such orders with respect to fixtures, tenant's improvements and other matters arising out of the lease as it thinks fit.

SEC. 180 Land subject to rentcharge

180(1) [Application] The following applies where, in consequence of the disclaimer under section 178 of any land subject to a rentcharge, that land vests by operation of law in the Crown or any other person (referred to in the next subsection as "the proprietor").

180(2) [Liability of proprietor et al.] The proprietor and the successors in title of the proprietor are not subject to any personal liability in repect of any sums becoming due under the rentcharge except sums becoming due after the proprietor, or some person claiming under or through the proprietor, has taken possession or control of the land or has entered into occupation of it.

SEC. 181 Powers of court (general)

181(1) [Application] This section and the next apply where the liquidator has disclaimed property under section 178.

181(2) [Application to court] An application under this section may be made to the court by—

(a) any person who claims an interest in the disclaimed property, or

(b) any person who is under any liability in respect of the disclaimed property, not being a liability discharged by the disclaimer.

181(3) [Powers of court] Subject as follows, the court may on the application make an order, on such terms as it thinks fit, for the vesting of the disclaimed property in, or for its delivery to—

(a) a person entitled to it or a trustee for such a person, or

(b) a person subject to such a liability as is mentioned in subsection (2)(b) or a trustee for such a person.

181(4) [Limit on court's powers] The court shall not make an order under subsection (3)(b) except where it appears to the court that it would be just to do so for the purpose of compensating the person subject to the liability in respect of the disclaimer.

181(5)   [Relationship with sec. 178(6)]   The effect of any order under this section shall be taken into account in assessing for the purpose of section 178(6) the extent of any loss or damage sustained by any person in consequence of the disclaimer.

181(6)   [Effect of vesting order]   An order under this section vesting property in any person need not be completed by conveyance, assignment or transfer.

SEC. 182   Powers of court (leaseholds)

182(1)   [Limit on court's power]   The court shall not make an order under section 181 vesting property of a leasehold nature on any person claiming under the company as underlessee or mortgagee except on terms making that person—

(a) subject to the same liabilities and obligations as the company was subject to under the lease at the commencement of the winding up, or

(b) if the court thinks fit, subject to the same liabilities and obligations as that person would be subject to if the lease had been assigned to him at the commencement of the winding up.

182(2)   [Where order re part of property in lease]   For the purposes of an order under section 181 relating to only part of any property comprised in a lease, the requirements of subsection (1) apply as if the lease comprised only the property to which the order relates.

182(3)   [Court may vest estate in someone else]   Where subsection (1) applies and no person claiming under the company as underlessee or mortagee is willing to accept an order under section 181 on the terms required by virtue of that subsection, the court may, by order under that section, vest the company's estate or interest in the property in any person who is liable (whether personally or in a representative capacity, and whether alone or jointly with the company) to perform the lessee's covenants in the lease.

The court may vest that estate and interest in such a person freed and discharged from all estates, incumbrances and interests created by the company.

182(4)   [Where sec. 182(1) applies]   Where subsection (1) applies and a person claiming under the company as underlessee or mortgagee declines to accept an order under section 181, that person is excluded from all interest in the property.

EXECUTION, ATTACHMENT AND THE SCOTTISH EQUIVALENTS

SEC. 183   Effect of execution or attachment (England and Wales)

183(1)   [Where creditor seeking benefit of execution or atttachment]   Where a creditor has issued execution against the goods or land of a company or has attached any debt due to it, and the company is subsequently wound up, he is not entitled to retain the benefit of the execution or attachment against the liquidator unless he has completed the execution or attachment before the commencement of the winding up.

183(2)   [Qualifications]   However—

(a) if a creditor has had notice of a meeting having been called at which a resolution for voluntary winding up is to be proposed, the date on which he had notice is substituted, for the purpose of subsection (1), for the date of commencement of the winding up;

(b) a person who purchases in good faith under a sale by the sheriff any goods of a company on which execution has been levied in all cases acquires a good title to them against the liquidator; and

(c) the rights conferred by subsection (1) on the liquidator may be set aside by the court in favour of the creditor to such extent and subject to such terms as the court thinks fit.

183(3) **[Execution, attachment]** For the purposes of this Act—

(a) an execution against goods is completed by seizure and sale, or by the making of a charging order under section 1 of the Charging Orders Act 1979;

(b) an attachment of a debt is completed by receipt of the debt; and

(c) an execution against land is completed by seizure, by the appointment of a receiver, or by the making of a charging order under section 1 of the Act above mentioned.

183(4) **[Definitions]** In this section **"goods"** includes all chattels personal; and **"the sheriff"** includes any officer charged with the execution of a writ or other process.

183(5) **[Scotland]** This section does not apply in the case of a winding up in Scotland.

SEC. 184 Duties of sheriff (England and Wales)

184(1) **[Application]** The following applies where a company's goods are taken in execution and, before their sale or the completion of the execution (by the receipt or recovery of the full amount of the levy), notice is served on the sheriff that a provisional liquidator has been appointed or that a winding-up order has been made, or that a resolution for voluntary winding up has been passed.

184(2) **[Sheriff to deliver goods and money to liquidator]** The sheriff shall, on being so required, deliver the goods and any money seized or received in part satisfaction of the execution to the liquidator; but the costs of execution are a first charge on the goods or money so delivered, and the liquidator may sell the goods, or a sufficient part of them, for the purpose of satisfying the charge.

184(3) **[Costs where goods sold etc.]** If under an execution in respect of a judgment for a sum exceeding £500 a company's goods are sold or money is paid in order to avoid sale, the sheriff shall deduct the costs of the execution from the proceeds of sale or the money paid and retain the balance for 14 days.

Note
The figure of £500 was increased from £250 by The Insolvency Proceedings (Monetary Limits) Order 1986 (S.I. 1986 No. 1996) as from 29 December 1986.

184(4) **[If within time notice is served]** If within that time notice is served on the sheriff of a petition for the winding up of the company having been presented, or of a meeting having been called at which there is to be proposed a resolution for voluntary winding up, and an order is made or a resolution passed (as the case may be), the sheriff shall pay the balance to the liquidator who is entitled to retain it as against the execution creditor.

184(5)   [Liquidator's rights may be set aside by court]   The rights conferred by this section on the liquidator may be set aside by the court in favour of the creditor to such extent and subject to such terms as the court thinks fit.

184(6)   [Definitions]   In this section, **"goods"** includes all chattels personal; and **"the sheriff"** includes any officer charged with the execution of a writ or other process.

184(7)   [Increase, reduction of sec. 184(3) sum]   The money sum for the time being specified in subsection (3) is subject to increase or reduction by order under section 416 in Part XV.

184(8)   [Scotland]   This section does not apply in the case of a winding up in Scotland.

SEC. 185   Effect of diligence (Scotland)

185(1)   [Application of Bankruptcy (Scotland) Act]   In the winding up of a company registered in Scotland, the following provisions of the Bankruptcy (Scotland) Act 1985—

    (a) subsections (1) to (6) of section 37 (effect of sequestration on diligence); and

    (b) subsections (3), (4), (7) and (8) of section 39 (realisation of estate),

apply, so far as consistent with this Act, in like manner as they apply in the sequestration of a debtor's estate, with the substitutions specified below and with any other necessary modifications.

185(2)   [Substitutions]   The substitutions to be made in those sections of the Act of 1985 are as follows—

    (a) for references to the debtor, substitute references to the company;

    (b) for references to the sequestration, substitute references to the winding up;

    (c) for references to the date of sequestration, substitute references to the commencement of the winding up of the company; and

    (d) for references to the permanent trustee, substitute references to the liquidator.

185(3)   [Definition]   In this section, **"the commencement of the winding up of the company"** means, where it is being wound up by the court, the day on which the winding-up order is made .

185(4)   [English company with estate in Scotland]   This section, so far as relating to any estate or effects of the company situated in Scotland, applies in the case of a company registered in England and Wales as in the case of one registered in Scotland.

MISCELLANEOUS MATTERS

SEC. 186   Rescission of contracts by the court

186(1)   [Power of court]   The court may, on the application of a person who is, as against the liquidator, entitled to the benefit or subject to the burden of a contract made with the company, make an order rescinding the contract on such terms as to payment by or to either party of damages for the non-performance of the contract, or otherwise as the court thinks just.

186(2) **[Damages]** Any damages payable under the order to such a person may be proved by him as a debt in the winding up.

SEC. 187 Power to make over assets to employees

187(1) **[CA, sec. 719 payment on winding up]** On the winding up of a company (whether by the court or voluntarily), the liquidator may, subject to the following provisions of this section, make any payment which the company has, before the commencement of the winding up, decided to make under section 719 of the Companies Act (power to provide for employees or former employees on cessation or transfer of business).

187(2) **[Power exercisable by liquidator]** The power which a company may exercise by virtue only of that section may be exercised by the liquidator after the winding up has commenced if, after the company's liabilities have been fully satisfied and provision has been made for the expenses of the winding up, the exercise of that power has been sanctioned by such a resolution of the company as would be required of the company itself by section 719(3) before that commencement, if paragraph (b) of that subsection were omitted and any other requirement applicable to its exercise by the company had been met.

187(3) **[Source of payment]** Any payment which may be made by a company under this section (that is, a payment after the commencement of its winding up) may be made out of the company's assets which are available to the members on the winding up.

187(4) **[Control by court]** On a winding up by the court, the exercise by the liquidator of his powers under this section is subject to the court's control, and any creditor or contributory may apply to the court with respect to any exercise or proposed exercise of the power.

187(5) **[Effect]** Subsections (1) and (2) above have effect notwithstanding anything in any rule of law or in section 107 of this Act (property of company after satisfaction of liabilities to be distributed among members).

SEC. 188 Notification that company is in liquidation

188(1) **[Statement in invoices etc.]** When a company is being wound up, whether by the court or voluntarily, every invoice, order for goods or business letter issued by or on behalf of the company, or a liquidator of the company, or a receiver or manager of the company's property, being a document on or in which the name of the company appears, shall contain a statement that the company is being wound up.

188(2) **[Penalty on default]** If default is made in complying with this section, the company and any of the following persons who knowingly and wilfully authorises or permits the default, namely, any officer of the company, any liquidator of the company and any receiver or manager, is liable to a fine.

SEC. 189   Interest on debts

189(1)   [Payment of interest]   In a winding up interest is payable in accordance with this section on any debt proved in the winding up, including so much of any such debt as represents interest on the remainder.

189(2)   [Surplus after payment of debts]   Any surplus remaining after the payment of the debts proved in a winding up shall, before being applied for any other purpose, be applied in paying interest on those debts in respect of the periods during which they have been outstanding since the company went into liquidation.

189(3)   [Ranking of interest]   All interest under this section ranks equally, whether or not the debts on which it is payable rank equally.

189(4)   [Rate of interest]   The rate of interest payable under this section in respect of any debt ("the official rate" for the purposes of any provision of this Act in which that expression is used) is whichever is the greater of—

(a) the rate specified in section 17 of the Judgments Act 1838 on the day on which the company went into liquidation, and

(b) the rate applicable to that debt apart from the winding up.

189(5)   [Scotland]   In the application of this section to Scotland—

(a) references to a debt proved in a winding up have effect as references to a claim accepted in a winding up, and

(b) the reference to section 17 of the Judgments Act 1838 has effect as a reference to the rules.

Note
See The Insolvency (Scotland) Rules 1986 (S.I. 1986 No. 1915 (S. 139)).

SEC. 190   Documents exempt from stamp duty

190(1)   [Application]   In the case of a winding up by the court, or of a creditors' voluntary winding up, the following has effect as regards exemption from duties chargeable under the enactments relating to stamp duties.

190(2)   [Exempt documents of company registered in England and Wales]   If the company is registered in England and Wales, the following documents are exempt from stamp duty—

(a) every assurance relating solely to freehold or leasehold property, or to any estate, right or interest in, any real or personal property, which forms part of the company's assets and which, after the execution of the assurance, either at law or in equity, is or remains part of those assets, and

(b) every writ, order, certificate, or other instrument or writing relating solely to the property of any company which is being wound up as mentioned in subsection (1), or to any proceeding under such a winding up.

"**Assurance**" here includes deed, conveyance, assignment and surrender.

190(3)   [Exempt document of company registered in Scotland]   If the company is registered in Scotland, the following documents are exempt from stamp duty—

(a) every conveyance relating solely to property, which forms part of the company's assets and which, after the execution of the conveyance, is or remains the company's property for the benefit of its creditors,

(b) any articles of roup or sale, submission and every other instrument and writing whatsoever relating solely to the company's property, and

(c) every deed or writing forming part of the proceedings in the winding up.

"Conveyance" here includes assignation, instrument, discharge, writing and deed.

SEC. 191 Company's books to be evidence

191 Where a company is being wound up, all books and papers of the company and of the liquidators are, as between the contributories of the company, prima facie evidence of the truth of all matters purporting to be recorded in them.

SEC. 192 Information as to pending liquidations

192(1) [Statement to registrar] If the winding up of a company is not concluded within one year after its commencment, the liquidator shall, at such intervals as may be prescribed, until the winding up is concluded, send to the registrar of companies a statement in the prescribed form and containing the prescribed particulars with respect to the proceedings in, and position of, the liquidation.

192(2) [Penalty on default] If a liquidator fails to comply with this section, he is liable to a fine and, for continued contravention, to a daily default fine.

SEC. 193 Unclaimed dividends (Scotland)

193(1) [Application] The following applies where a company registered in Scotland has been wound up, and is about to be dissolved.

193(2) [Liquidator to lodge unclaimed money in bank] The liquidator shall lodge in an appropriate bank or institution as defined in section 73(1) of the Bankruptcy (Scotland) Act 1985 (not being a bank or institution in or of which the liquidator is an acting partner, manager, agent or cashier) in the name of the Accountant of Court the whole unclaimed dividends and unapplied or undistributable balances, and the deposit receipts shall be transmitted to the Accountant of Court.

193(3) [Application of Bankruptcy (Scotland) Act] The provisions of section 58 of the Bankruptcy (Scotland) Act 1985 (so far as consistent with this Act and the Companies Act) apply with any necessary modifications to sums lodged in a bank or institution under this section as they apply to sums deposited under section 57 of the Act first mentioned.

SEC. 194 Resolutions passed at adjourned meetings

194 Where a resolution is passed at an adjourned meeting of a company's creditors or contributories, the resolution is treated for all purposes as having been passed on the date on which it was in fact passed, and not as having been passed on any earlier date.

SEC. 195   Meetings to ascertain wishes of creditors or contributories

195(1)   [Power of court]   The court may—

(a) as to all matters relating to the winding up of a company, have regard to the wishes of the creditors or contributories (as proved to it by any sufficient evidence), and

(b) if it thinks fit, for the purpose of ascertaining those wishes, direct meetings of the creditors or contributories to be called, held and conducted in such manner as the court directs, and appoint a person to act as chairman of any such meeting and report the result of it to the court.

195(2)   [Creditors]   In the case of creditors, regard shall be had to the value of each creditor's debt.

195(3)   [Contributories]   In the case of contributories, regard shall be had to the number of votes conferred on each contributory by the Companies Act or the articles.

SEC. 196   Judicial notice of court documents

196   In all proceedings under this Part, all courts, judges and persons judicially acting, and all officers, judicial or ministerial, of any court, or employed in enforcing the process of any court shall take judicial notice—

(a) of the signature of any officer of the High Court or of a county court in England and Wales, or of the Court of Session or a sheriff court in Scotland, or of the High Court in Northern Ireland, and also

(b) of the official seal or stamp of the several offices of the High Court in England and Wales or Northern Ireland, or of the Court of Session, appended to or impressed on any document made, issued or signed under the provisions of this Act or the Companies Act, or any official copy of such a document.

SEC. 197   Commission for receiving evidence

197(1)   [Courts for examination of witnesses]   When a company is wound up in England and Wales or in Scotland, the court may refer the whole or any part of the examination of witnesses—

(a) to a specified county court in England and Wales, or

(b) to the sheriff principal for a specified sheriffdom in Scotland, or

(c) to the High Court in Northern Ireland or a specified Northern Ireland County Court,

("**specified**" meaning specified in the order of the winding-up court).

197(2)   [Commissioners for taking evidence]   Any person exercising jurisdiction as a judge of the court to which the reference is made (or, in Scotland, the sheriff principal to whom it is made) shall then, by virtue of this section, be a commissioner for the purpose of taking the evidence of those witnesses.

197(3)   [Power of judge or sheriff principal]   The judge or sheriff principal has in the matter referred the same power of summoning and examining witnesses, of requiring the production and delivery of documents, of punishing defaults by witnesses, and of allowing costs and expenses to witnesses, as the court which made the winding-up order.

These powers are in addition to any which the judge or sheriff principal might lawfully exercise apart from this section.

197(4) **[Return or report re examination]** The examination so taken shall be returned or reported to the court which made the order in such manner as that court requests.

197(5) **[Northern Ireland]** This section extends to Northern Ireland.

SEC. 198   Court order for examination of persons in Scotland

198(1) **[Examination of any person on affairs of company]** The court may direct the examination in Scotland of any person for the time being in Scotland (whether a contributory of the company or not), in regard to the trade, dealings, affairs or property of any company in the course of being wound up, or of any person being a contributory of the company, so far as the company may be interested by reason of his being a contributory.

198(2) **[Directions to take examination]** The order or commission to take the examination shall be directed to the sheriff principal of the sheriffdom in which the person to be examined is residing or happens to be for the time; and the sheriff principal shall summon the person to appear before him at a time and place to be specified in the summons for examination on oath as a witness or as a haver, and to produce any books or papers called for which are in his possession or power.

198(3) **[Duties of sheriff principal re examination]** The sheriff principal may take the examination either orally or on written interrogatories, and shall report the same in writing in the usual form to the court, and shall transmit with the report the books and papers produced, if the originals are required and specified by the order or commission, or otherwise copies or extracts authenticated by the sheriff.

198(4) **[Where person fails to appear for examination]** If a person so summoned fails to appear at the time and place specified, or refuses to be examined or to make the production required, the sheriff principal shall proceed against him as a witness or haver duly cited; and failing to appear or refusing to give evidence or make production may be proceeded against by the law of Scotland.

198(5) **[Fees and allowances]** The sheriff principal is entitled to such fees, and the witness is entitled to such allowances, as sheriffs principal when acting as commissioners under appointment from the Court of Session and as witnesses and havers are entitled to in the like cases according to the law and practice of Scotland.

198(6) **[Objection by witness]** If any objection is stated to the sheriff principal by the witness, either on the ground of his incompetency as a witness, or as to the production required, or on any other ground, the sheriff principal may, if he thinks fit, report the objection to the court, and suspend the examination of the witness until it has been disposed of by the court.

SEC. 199   Costs of application for leave to proceed (Scottish companies)

199 Where a petition or application for leave to proceed with an action or proceeding against a company which is being wound up in Scotland is unopposed and is granted by the court, the costs of the petition or application shall, unless the court otherwise directs, be added to the amount of the petitioner's or applicant's claim against the company.

SEC. 200   Affidavits etc. in United Kingdom and overseas

200(1)   [Swearing of affidavit]   An affidavit required to be sworn under or for the purposes of this Part may be sworn in the United Kingdom, or elsewhere in Her Majesty's dominions, before any court, judge or person lawfully authorised to take and receive affidavits, or before any of Her Majesty's consuls or vice-consuls in any place outside Her dominions.

200(2)   [Judicial notice of signatures etc.]   All courts, judges, justices, commissioners and persons acting judicially shall take judicial notice of the seal or stamp or signature (as the case may be) of any such court, judge, person, consul or vice-consul attached, appended or subscribed to any such affidavit, or to any other document to be used for the purposes of this Part.

Chapter IX — Dissolution of Companies After Winding Up

SEC. 201   Dissolution (voluntary winding up)

201(1)   [Application]   This section applies, in the case of a company wound up voluntarily, where the liquidator has sent to the registrar of companies his final account and return under section 94 (members' voluntary) or section 106 (creditors' voluntary).

201(2)   [Duty of registrar]   The registrar on receiving the account and return shall forthwith register them; and on the expiration of 3 months from the registration of the return the company is deemed to be dissolved.

201(3)   [Power of court re deferring date]   However, the court may, on the application of the liquidator or any other person who appears to the court to be interested, make an order deferring the date at which the dissolution of the company is to take effect for such time as the court thinks fit.

201(4)   [Copy of order to registrar]   It is the duty of the person on whose application an order of the court under this section is made within 7 days after the making of the order to deliver to the registrar an office copy of the order for registration; and if that person fails to do so he is liable to a fine and, for continued contravention, to a daily default fine.

SEC. 202   Early dissolution (England and Wales)

202(1)   [Application]   This section applies where an order for the winding up of a company has been made by the court in England and Wales.

202(2)   [Official receiver may apply for dissolution]   The official receiver, if—

    (a) he is the liquidator of the company, and

    (b) it appears to him—

(i) that the realisable assets of the company are insufficient to cover the expenses of the winding up, and

(ii) that the affairs of the company do not require any further investigation,

may at any time apply to the registrar of companies for the early dissolution of the company.

202(3) **[Notice by official receiver]** Before making that application, the official receiver shall give not less than 28 days' notice of his intention to do so to the company's creditors and contributories and, if there is an administrative receiver of the company, to that receiver.

202(4) **[Effect of notice on official receiver]** With the giving of that notice the official receiver ceases (subject to any directions under the next section) to be required to perform any duties imposed on him in relation to the company, its creditors or contributories by virtue of any provision of this Act, apart from a duty to make an application under subsection (2) of this section.

202(5) **[Duty of registrar]** On the receipt of the official receiver's application under subsection (2) the registrar shall forthwith register it and, at the end of the period of 3 months beginning with the day of the registration of the application, the company shall be dissolved.

However, the Secretary of State may, on the application of the official receiver or any other person who appears to the Secretary of State to be interested, give directions under section 203 at any time before the end of that period.

SEC. 203 Consequence of notice under sec. 202

203(1) **[Application for directions]** Where a notice has been given under section 202(3), the official receiver or any creditor or contributory of the company, or the administrative receiver of the company (if there is one) may apply to the Secretary of State for directions under this section.

203(2) **[Grounds for application]** The grounds on which that application may be made are—

(a) that the realisable assets of the company are sufficient to cover the expenses of the winding up;

(b) that the affairs of the company do require further investigation; or

(c) that for any other reason the early dissolution of the company is inappropriate.

203(3) **[Scope of directions]** Directions under this section—

(a) are directions making such provision as the Secretary of State thinks fit for enabling the winding up of the company to proceed as if no notice had been given under section 202(3), and

(b) may, in the case of an application under section 202(5), include a direction deferring the date at which the dissolution of the company is to take effect for such period as the Secretary of State thinks fit.

203(4) **[Appeal to court]** An appeal to the court lies from any decision of the Secretary of State on an application for directions under this section.

203(5)   [Copy of directions etc. to registrar]   It is the duty of the person on whose application any directions are given under this section, or in whose favour an appeal with respect to an application for such directions is determined, within 7 days after the giving of the directions or the determination of the appeal, to deliver to the registrar of companies for registration such a copy of the directions or determination as is prescribed.

203(6)   [Penalty on default re sec. 203(5)]   If a person without reasonable excuse fails to deliver a copy as required by subsection (5), he is liable to a fine and, for continued contravention, to a daily default fine.

SEC. 204   Early dissolution (Scotland)

204(1)   [Application]   This section applies where a winding-up order has been made by the court in Scotland.

204(2)   [Application by liquidator]   If after a meeting or meetings under section 138 (appointment of liquidator in Scotland) it appears to the liquidator that the realisable assets of the company are insufficient to cover the expenses of the winding up, he may apply to the court for an order that the company be dissolved.

204(3)   [Court order]   Where the liquidator makes that application, if the court is satisfied that the realisable assets of the company are insufficient to cover the expenses of the winding up and it appears to the court appropriate to do so, the court shall make an order that the company be dissolved in accordance with this section.

204(4)   [Copy of order to registrar etc.]   A copy of the order shall within 14 days from its date be forwarded by the liquidator to the registrar of companies, who shall forthwith register it; and, at the end of the period of 3 months beginning with the day of the registration of the order, the company shall be dissolved.

204(5)   [Court may defer dissolution]   The court may, on an application by any person who appears to the court to have an interest, order that the date at which the dissolution of the company is to take effect shall be deferred for such period as the court thinks fit.

204(6)   [Copy of sec. 204(5) order to registrar]   It is the duty of the person on whose application an order is made under subsection (5), within 7 days after the making of the order, to deliver to the registrar of companies such a copy of the order as is prescribed.

204(7)   [Penalty for non-compliance with sec. 204(4)]   If the liquidator without reasonable excuse fails to comply with the requirements of subsection (4), he is liable to a fine and, for continued contravention, to a daily default fine.

204(8)   [Penalty for non-compliance with sec. 204(6)]   If a person without reasonable excuse fails to deliver a copy as required by subsection (6), he is liable to a fine and, for continued contravention, to a daily default fine.

SEC. 205   Dissolution otherwise than under sec. 202–204

205(1)   [Application]   This section applies where the registrar of companies receives—

   (a) a notice served for the purposes of section 172(8) (final meeting of creditors and vacation of office by liquidator), or

(b) a notice from the official receiver that the winding up of a company by the court is complete.

205(2) [**Duty of registrar etc.**] The registrar shall, on receipt of the notice, forthwith register it; and, subject as follows, at the end of the period of 3 months beginning with the day of the registration of the notice, the company shall be dissolved.

205(3) [**Deferral by Secretary of State**] The Secretary of State may, on the application of the official receiver or any other person who appears to the Secretary of State to be interested, give a direction deferring the date at which the dissolution of the company is to take effect for such period as the Secretary of State thinks fit.

205(4) [**Appeal to court**] An appeal to the court lies from any decision of the Secretary of State on an application for a direction under subsection (3).

205(5) [**Non-application of sec. 205(3) in Scotland**] Subsection (3) does not apply in a case where the winding-up order was made by the court in Scotland, but in such a case the court may, on an application by any person appearing to the court to have an interest, order that the date at which the dissolution of the company is to take effect shall be deferred for such period as the court thinks fit.

205(6) [**Copy of direction etc. to registrar**] It is the duty of the person—

(a) on whose application a direction is given under subsection (3);

(b) in whose favour an appeal with respect to an application for such a direction is determined; or

(c) on whose application an order is made under subsection (5),

within 7 days after the giving of the direction, the determination of the appeal or the making of the order, to deliver to the registrar for registration such a copy of the direction, determination or order as is prescribed.

205(7) [**Penalty for non-compliance with sec. 205(6)**] If a person without reasonable excuse fails to deliver a copy as required by subsection (6), he is liable to a fine and, for continued contravention, to a daily default fine.

Chapter X — Malpractice before and during Liquidation; Penalisation of Companies and Company Officers; Investigations and Prosecutions

OFFENCES OF FRAUD, DECEPTION, ETC.

SEC. 206 Fraud, etc. in anticipation of winding up

206(1) [**Offences by officers**] When a company is ordered to be wound up by the court, or passes a resolution for voluntary winding up, any person, being a past or present officer of the company, is deemed to have committed an offence if, within the 12 months immediately preceding the commencement of the winding up, he has—

   (a) concealed any part of the company's property to the value of £500 or more, or concealed any debt due to or from the company, or

   (b) fraudulently removed any part of the company's property to the value of £500 or more, or

   (c) concealed, destroyed, mutilated or falsified any book or paper affecting or relating to the company's property or affairs, or

   (d) made any false entry in any book or paper affecting or relating to the company's property or affairs, or

   (e) fraudulently parted with, altered or made any omission in any document affecting or relating to the company's property or affairs, or

   (f) pawned, pledged or disposed of any property of the company which has been obtained on credit and has not been paid for (unless the pawning, pledging or disposal was in the ordinary way of the company's business).

206(2) [Further offences] Such a person is deemed to have committed an offence if within the period above mentioned he has been privy to the doing by others of any of the things mentioned in paragraphs (c), (d) and (e) of subsection (1); and he commits an offence if, at any time after the commencement of the winding up, he does any of the things mentioned in paragraphs (a) to (f) of that subsection, or is privy to the doing by others of any of the things mentioned in paragraphs (c) to (e) of it.

206(3) ["Officer"] For purposes of this section, "officer" includes a shadow director.

206(4) [Defences] It is a defence—

   (a) for a person charged under paragraph (a) or (f) of subsection (1) (or under subsection (2) in respect of the things mentioned in either of those two paragraphs) to prove that he had no intent to defraud, and

   (b) for a person charged under paragraph (c) or (d) of subsection (1) (or under subsection (2) in respect of the things mentioned in either of those two paragraphs) to prove that he had no intent to conceal the state of affairs of the company or to defeat the law.

206(5) [Offence re person pawning property etc. as in sec. 206(1)(f)] Where a person pawns, pledges or disposes of any property in circumstances which amount to an offence under subsection (1)(f), every person who takes in pawn or pledge, or otherwise receives, the property knowing it to be pawned, pledged or disposed of in such circumstances, is guilty of an offence.

206(6) [Penalty] A person guilty of an offence under this section is liable to imprisonment or a fine, or both.

206(7) [Increase, reduction of sums in sec. 206(1)(a),(b)] The money sums specified in paragraphs (a) and (b) of subsection (1) are subject to increase or reduction by order under section 416 in Part XV.

Note
The amount in s. 206(1)(a), (b) increased from £120 by
The Insolvency Proceedings (Monetary Limits) Order 1986
(S.I. 1986 No. 1996) as from 29 December 1986.

SEC. 207 Transactions in fraud of creditors

207(1) **[Offences by officers]** When a company is ordered to be wound up by the court or passes a resolution for voluntary winding up, a person is deemed to have committed an offence if he, being at the time an officer of the company—

    (a) has made or caused to be made any gift or transfer of, or charge on, or has caused or connived at the levying of any execution against, the company's property, or

    (b) has concealed or removed any part of the company's property since, or within 2 months before, the date of any unsatisfied judgment or order for the payment of money obtained against the company.

207(2) **[Exception]** A person is not guilty of an offence under this section—

    (a) by reason of conduct constituting an offence under subsection (1)(a) which occurred more than 5 years before the commencement of the winding up, or

    (b) if he proves that, at the time of the conduct constituting the offence, he had no intent to defraud the company's creditors.

207(3) **[Penalty]** A person guilty of an offence under this section is liable to imprisonment or a fine, or both.

SEC. 208 Misconduct in course of winding up

208(1) **[Offences by officers]** When a company is being wound up, whether by the court or voluntarily, any person, being a past or present officer of the company, commits an offence if he—

    (a) does not to the best of his knowledge and belief fully and truly discover to the liquidator all the company's property, and how and to whom and for what consideration and when the company disposed of any part of that property (except such part as has been disposed of in the ordinary way of the company's business), or

    (b) does not deliver up to the liquidator (or as he directs) all such part of the company's property as is in his custody or under his control, and which he is required by law to deliver up, or

    (c) does not deliver up to the liquidator (or as he directs) all books and papers in his custody or under his control belonging to the company and which he is required by law to deliver up, or

    (d) knowing or believing that a false debt has been proved by any person in the winding up, fails to inform the liquidator as soon as practicable, or

    (e) after the commencement of the winding up, prevents the production of any book or paper affecting or relating to the company's property or affairs.

208(2) **[Further offences]** Such a person commits an offence if after the commencement of the winding up he attempts to account for any part of the company's property by fictitious losses or expenses; and he is deemed to have committed that offence if he has so attempted at any meeting of the company's creditors within the 12 months immediately preceding the commencement of the winding up.

208(3)   **["Officer"]**   For purposes of this section, **"officer"** includes a shadow director.

208(4)   **[Defences]**   It is a defence—

- (a) for a person charged under paragraph (a), (b) or (c) of subsection (1) to prove that he had no intent to defraud, and

- (b) for a person charged under paragraph (e) of that subsection to prove that he had no intent to conceal the state of affairs of the company or to defeat the law.

208(5)   **[Penalty]**   A person guilty of an offence under this section is liable to imprisonment or a fine, or both.

SEC. 209   Falsification of company's books

209(1)   **[Offence by officer or contributory]**   When a company is being wound up, an officer or contributory of the company commits an offence if he destroys, mutilates, alters or falsifies any books, papers or securities, or makes or is privy to the making of any false or fraudulent entry in any register, book of account or document belonging to the company with intent to defraud or deceive any person.

209(2)   **[Penalty]**   A person guilty of an offence under this section is liable to imprisonment or a fine, or both.

SEC. 210   Material omissions from statement relating to company's affairs

210(1)   **[Offence by past or present officer]**   When a company is being wound up, whether by the court or voluntarily, any person, being a past or present officer of the company, commits an offence if he makes any material omission in any statement relating to the company's affairs.

210(2)   **[Offence prior to winding up]**   When a company has been ordered to be wound up by the court, or has passed a resolution for voluntary winding up, any such person is deemed to have committed that offence if, prior to the winding up, he has made any material omission in any such statement.

210(3)   **["Officer"]**   For purposes of this section, **"officer"** includes a shadow director.

210(4)   **[Defence]**   It is a defence for a person charged under this section to prove that he had no intent to defraud.

210(5)   **[Penalty]**   A person guilty of an offence under this section is liable to imprisonment or a fine, or both.

SEC. 211   False representations to creditors

211(1)   **[Offences by past or present officer]**   When a company is being wound up, whether by the court or voluntarily, any person, being a past or present officer of the company—

- (a) commits an offence if he makes any false representation or commits any other fraud for the purpose of obtaining the consent of the company's creditors or any of them to an agreement with reference to the company's affairs or to the winding up, and

(b) is deemed to have committed that offence if, prior to the winding up, he has made any false representation, or committed any other fraud, for that purpose.

211(2) **["Officer"]** For purposes of this section, **"officer"** includes a shadow director.

211(3) **[Penalty]** A person guilty of an offence under this section is liable to imprisonment or a fine, or both.

PENALISATION OF DIRECTORS AND OFFICERS

SEC. 212 Summary remedy against delinquent directors, liquidators, etc.

212(1) **[Application]** This section applies if in the course of the winding up of a company it appears that a person who—

(a) is or has been an officer of the company,

(b) has acted as liquidator, administrator or administrative receiver of the company, or

(c) not being a person falling within paragraph (a) or (b), is or has been concerned, or has taken part, in the promotion, formation or management of the company,

has misapplied or retained, or become accountable for, any money or other property of the company, or been guilty of any misfeasance or breach of any fiduciary or other duty in relation to the company.

212(2) **[Interpretation]** The reference in subsection (1) to any misfeasance or breach of any fiduciary or other duty in relation to the company includes, in the case of a person who has acted as liquidator or administrator of the company, any misfeasance or breach of any fiduciary or other duty in connection with the carrying out of his functions as liquidator or administrator of the company.

212(3) **[Examination, orders]** The court may, on the application of the official receiver or the liquidator, or of any creditor or contributory, examine into the conduct of the person falling within subsection (1) and compel him—

(a) to repay, restore or account for the money or property or any part of it, with interest at such rate as the court thinks just, or

(b) to contribute such sum to the company's assets by way of compensation in respect of the misfeasance or breach of fiduciary or other duty as the court thinks just.

212(4) **[Limit on sec. 212(3) application]** The power to make an application under subsection (3) in relation to a person who has acted as liquidator or administrator of the company is not exercisable, except with the leave of the court, after that person has had his release.

212(5) **[Exercise of sec. 212(3) power]** The power of a contributory to make an application under subsection (3) is not exercisable except with the leave of the court, but is exercisable notwithstanding that he will not benefit from any order the court may make on the application.

SEC. 213   Fraudulent trading

213(1)   [Application]   If in the course of the winding up of a company it appears that any business of the company has been carried on with intent to defraud creditors of the company or creditors of any other person, or for any fraudulent purpose, the following has effect.

213(2)   [Court may hold persons liable]   The court, on the application of the liquidator may declare that any persons who were knowingly parties to the carrying on of the business in the manner above-mentioned are to be liable to make such contributions (if any) to the company's assets as the court thinks proper.

SEC. 214   Wrongful trading

214(1)   [Declaration by court, on application]   Subject to subsection (3) below, if in the course of the winding up of a company it appears that subsection (2) of this section applies in relation to a person who is or has been a director of the company, the court, on the application of the liquidator, may declare that that person is to be liable to make such contribution (if any) to the company's assets as the court thinks proper.

214(2)   [Application]   This subsection applies in relation to a person if—

    (a) the company has gone into insolvent liquidation,

    (b) at some time before the commencement of the winding up of the company, that person knew or ought to have concluded that there was no reasonable prospect that the company would avoid going into insolvent liquidation, and

    (c) that person was a director of the company at that time;

but the court shall not make a declaration under this section in any case where the time mentioned in paragraph (b) above was before 28th April 1986.

214(3)   [Limit on declaration]   The court shall not make a declaration under this section with respect to any person if it is satisfied that after the condition specified in subsection (2)(b) was first satisfied in relation to him that person took every step with a view to minimising the potential loss to the company's creditors as (assuming him to have known that there was no reasonable prospect that the company would avoid going into insolvent liquidation) he ought to have taken.

214(4)   [Interpretation of sec. 214(2),(3)]   For the purposes of subsections (2) and (3), the facts which a director of a company ought to know or ascertain, the conclusions which he ought to reach and the steps which he ought to take are those which would be known or ascertained, or reached or taken, by a reasonably diligent person having both—

    (a) the general knowledge, skill and experience that may reasonably be expected of a person carrying out the same functions as are carried out by that director in relation to the company, and

    (b) the general knowledge, skill and experience that that director has.

214(5) **[Interpretation of sec. 214(4)]** The reference in subsection (4) to the functions carried out in relation to a company by a director of the company includes any functions which he does not carry out but which have been entrusted to him.

214(6) **[Interpretation re insolvent liquidation]** For the purposes of this section a company goes into insolvent liquidation if it goes into liquidation at a time when its assets are insufficient for the payment of its debts and other liabilities and the expenses of the winding up.

214(7) **["Director"]** In this section **"director"** includes a shadow director.

214(8) **[Sec. 213]** This section is without prejudice to section 213.

SEC. 215 Proceedings under sec. 213, 214

215(1) **[Evidence by liquidator]** On the hearing of an application under section 213 or 214, the liquidator may himself give evidence or call witnesses.

215(2) **[Further court directions]** Where under either section the court makes a declaration, it may give such further directions as it thinks proper for giving effect to the declaration; and in particular, the court may—

    (a) provide for the liability of any person under the declaration to be a charge on any debt or obligation due from the company to him, or on any mortgage or charge or any interest in a mortgage or charge on assets of the company held by or vested in him, or any person on his behalf, or any person claiming as assignee from or through the person liable or any person acting on his behalf, and

    (b) from time to time make such further order as may be necessary for enforcing any charge imposed under this subsection.

215(3) **["Assignee"]** For the purposes of subsection (2), **"assignee"**—

    (a) includes a person to whom or in whose favour, by the directions of the person made liable, the debt, obligation, mortgage or charge was created, issued or transferred or the interest created, but

    (b) does not include an assignee for valuable consideration (not including consideration by way of marriage) given in good faith and without notice of any of the matters on the ground of which the declaration is made.

215(4) **[Directions re priority of debts]** Where the court makes a declaration under either section in relation to a person who is a creditor of the company, it may direct that the whole or any part of any debt owed by the company to that person and any interest thereon shall rank in priority after all other debts owed by the company and after any interest on those debts.

215(5) **[Sec. 213, 214]** Sections 213 and 214 have effect notwithstanding that the person concerned may be criminally liable in respect of matters on the ground of which the declaration under the section is to be made.

SEC. 216 Restriction on re-use of company names

216(1) **[Application]** This section applies to a person where a company ("the liquidating company") has gone into insolvent liquidation on or after the appointed day and he was a director or shadow director of the company at any time in the period of 12 months ending with the day before it went into liquidation.

216(2)   [Prohibited name]   For the purposes of this section, a name is a prohibited name in relation to such a person if—

- (a) it is a name by which the liquidating company was known at any time in that period of 12 months, or

- (b) it is a name which is so similar to a name falling within paragraph (a) as to suggest an association with that company.

216(3)   [Restriction]   Except with leave of the court or in such circumstances as may be prescribed, a person to whom this section applies shall not at any time in the period of 5 years beginning with the day on which the liquidating company went into liquidation—

- (a) be a director of any other company that is known by a prohibited name, or

- (b) in any way, whether directly or indirectly, be concerned or take part in the promotion, formation or management of any such company, or

- (c) in any way, whether directly or indirectly, be concerned or take part in the carrying on of a business carried on (otherwise than by a company) under a prohibited name.

216(4)   [Penalty]   If a person acts in contravention of this section, he is liable to imprisonment or a fine, or both.

216(5)   ["The court"]   In subsection (3) **"the court"** means any court having jurisdiction to wind up companies; and on an application for leave under that subsection, the Secretary of State or the official receiver may appear and call the attention of the court to any matters which seem to him to be relevant.

216(6)   [Interpretation re name]   References in this section, in relation to any time, to a name by which a company is known are to the name of the company at that time or to any name under which the company carries on business at that time.

216(7)   [Interpretation re insolvent liquidation]   For the purposes of this section a company goes into insolvent liquidation if it goes into liquidation at a time when its assets are insufficient for the payment of its debts and other liabilities and the expenses of the winding up.

216(8)   ["Company"]   In this section **"company"** includes a company which may be wound up under Part V of this Act.

SEC. 217   Personal liability for debts, following contravention of sec. 216

217(1)   [Personal liability]   A person is personally responsible for all the relevant debts of a company if at any time—

- (a) in a contravention of section 216, he is involved in the management of the company, or

- (b) as a person who is involved in the management of the company, he acts or is willing to act on instructions given (without the leave of the court) by a person whom he knows at that time to be in contravention in relation to the company of section 216.

217(2) **[Joint and several liability]** Where a person is personally responsible under this section for the relevant debts of a company, he is jointly and severally liable in respect of those debts with the company and any other person who, whether under this section or otherwise, is so liable.

217(3) **[Relevant debts of company]** For the purposes of this section the relevant debts of a company are—

(a) in relation to a person who is personally responsible under paragraph (a) of subsection (1), such debts and other liabilities of the company as are incurred at a time when that person was involved in the management of the company, and

(b) in relation to a person who is personally responsible under paragraph (b) of that subsection, such debts and other liabilities of the company as are incurred at a time when that person was acting or was willing to act on instructions given as mentioned in that paragraph.

217(4) **[Person involved in management]** For the purposes of this section, a person is involved in the management of a company if he is a director of the company or if he is concerned, whether directly or indirectly, or takes part, in the management of the company.

217(5) **[Interpretation]** For the purposes of this section a person who, as a person involved in the management of a company, has at any time acted on instructions given (without the leave of the court) by a person whom he knew at that time to be in contravention in relation to the company of section 216 is presumed, unless the contrary is shown, to have been willing at any time thereafter to act on any instructions given by that person.

217(6) **["Company"]** In this section **"company"** includes a company which may be wound up under Part V.

INVESTIGATION AND PROSECUTION OF MALPRACTICE

SEC. 218 Prosecution of delinquent officers and members of company

218(1) **[Court may direct matter to be referred for prosecution]** If it appears to the court in the course of a winding up by the court that any past or present officer, or any member, of the company has been guilty of any offence in relation to the company for which he is criminally liable, the court may (either on the application of a person interested in the winding up or of its own motion) direct the liquidator to refer the matter to the prosecuting authority.

218(2) **["The prosecuting authority"]** "The prosecuting authority" means—

(a) in the case of a winding up in England and Wales, the Director of Public Prosecutions, and

(b) in the case of a winding up in Scotland, the Lord Advocate.

218(3) **[Report — winding up by court]** If in the case of a winding up by the court in England and Wales it appears to the liquidator, not being the official receiver, that any past or present officer of the company, or any member of it, has been guilty of an offence in relation to the company for which he is criminally liable, the liquidator shall report the matter to the official receiver.

218(4)   [Report — voluntary winding up]   If it appears to the liquidator in the course of a voluntary winding up that any past or present officer of the company, or any member of it, has been guilty of an offence in relation to the company for which he is criminally liable, he shall—

(a)   forthwith report the matter to the prosecuting authority, and

(b)   furnish to that authority such information and give to him such access to and facilities for inspecting and taking copies of documents (being information or documents in the possession or under the control of the liquidator and relating to the matter in question) as the authority requires.

218(5)   [Reference to Secretary of State]   Where a report is made to him under subsection (4), the prosecuting authority may, if he thinks fit, refer the matter to the Secretary of State for further enquiry; and the Secretary of State—

(a)   shall thereupon investigate the matter reported to him and such other matters relating to the affairs of the company as appear to him to require investigation, and

(b)   for the purpose of his investigation may exercise any of the powers which are exercisable by inspectors appointed under section 431 or 432 of the Companies Act to investigate a company's affairs.

History
S. 218(5)(a) substituted by CA 1989, s. 78 as from 21 February 1990 (see S.I. 1990 No. 142 (C. 5), art. 4); s. 218(5)(a) formerly read as follows:
"(a) shall thereupon investigate the matter, and"

218(6)   [Court may direct liquidator to make report]   If it appears to the court in the course of a voluntary winding up that—

(a)   any past or present officer of the company, or any member of it, has been guilty as above-mentioned, and

(b)   no report with respect to the matter has been made by the liquidator to the prosecuting authority under subsection (4),

the court may (on the application of any person interested in the winding up or of its own motion) direct the liquidator to make such a report.

On a report being made accordingly, this section has effect as though the report had been made in pursuance of subsection (4).

SEC. 219   Obligations arising under sec. 218

219(1)   [Assistance to investigation by Secretary of State]   For the purpose of an investigation by the Secretary of State under section 218(5), any obligation imposed on a person by any provision of the Companies Act to produce documents or give information to, or otherwise to assist, inspectors appointed as mentioned in that subsection is to be regarded as an obligation similarly to assist the Secretary of State in his investigation.

219(2)   [Answer may be used as evidence]   An answer given by a person to a question put to him in exercise of the powers conferred by section 218(5) may be used in evidence against him.

219(3) **[Liquidator and officer to assist, where criminal proceedings instituted]** Where criminal proceedings are instituted by the prosecuting authority or the Secretary of State following any report or reference under section 218, it is the duty of the liquidator and every officer and agent of the company past and present (other than the defendant or defender) to give to that authority or the Secretary of

[The next page is 52,901]

State (as the case may be) all assistance in connection with the prosecution which he is reasonably able to give.

For this purpose **"agent"** includes any banker or solicitor of the company and any person employed by the company as auditor, whether that person is or is not an officer of the company.

219(4) **[Direction by court re assistance]** If a person fails or neglects to give assistance in the manner required by subsection (3), the court may, on the application of the prosecuting authority or the Secretary of State (as the case may be) direct the person to comply with that subsection; and if the application is made with respect to a liquidator, the court may (unless it appears that the failure or neglect to comply was due to the liquidator not having in his hands sufficient assets of the company to enable him to do so) direct that the costs shall be borne by the liquidator personally.

PART V — WINDING UP OF UNREGISTERED COMPANIES

SEC. 220   Meaning of "unregistered company"

220(1) **["Unregistered company"]** For the purposes of this Part, the expression **"unregistered company"** includes any association and any company, with the following exceptions—

  (a) a railway company incorporated by Act of Parliament,

  (b) a company registered in any part of the United Kingdom under the Joint Stock Companies Acts or under the legislation (past or present) relating to companies in Great Britain.

History
In s. 220(1) the words "any trustee savings bank certified   appearing after the word "includes" ceased to have effect
under the enactments relating to such banks" formerly   and repealed by virtue of s. 220(2).

220(2) **[Repeal of certain words]** On such day as the Treasury appoints by order under section 4(3) of the Trustee Savings Banks Act 1985, the words in subsection (1) from "any trustee" to "banks" cease to have effect and are hereby repealed.

Note
The relevant day is 5 July 1988—see S.I. 1988 No. 1168.

SEC. 221   Winding up of unregistered companies

221(1) **[Application of winding up provisions]** Subject to the provisions of this Part, any unregistered company may be wound up under this Act; and all the provisions of this Act and the Companies Act about winding up apply to an unregistered company with the exceptions and additions mentioned in the following subsections.

221(2) **[Principal place of business in Northern Ireland]** If an unregistered company has a principal place of business situated in Northern Ireland, it shall not be wound up under this Part unless it has a principal place of business situated in England and Wales or Scotland, or in both England and Wales and Scotland.

221(3) **[Deemed registration, registered office]** For the purpose of determining a court's winding-up jurisdiction, an unregistered company is deemed—

(a) to be registered in England and Wales or Scotland, according as its principal place of business is situated in England and Wales or Scotland, or

(b) if it has a principal place of business situated in both countries, to be registered in both countries;

and the principal place of business situated in that part of Great Britain in which proceedings are being instituted is, for all purposes of the winding up, deemed to be the registered office of the company.

221(4) **[No voluntary winding up]** No unregistered company shall be wound up under this Act voluntarily.

221(5) **[Circumstances for winding up]** The circumstances in which an unregistered company may be wound up are as follows—

(a) if the company is dissolved, or has ceased to carry on business, or is carrying on business only for the purpose of winding up its affairs;

(b) if the company is unable to pay its debts;

(c) if the court is of opinion that it is just and equitable that the company should be wound up.

221(6) **[Winding up trustee savings bank]** A petition for winding up a trustee savings bank may be presented by the Trustee Savings Banks Central Board or by a commissioner appointed under section 35 of the Trustee Savings Banks Act 1981 as well as by any person authorised under Part IV of this Act to present a petition for the winding up of a company.

On such day as the Treasury appoints by order under section 4(3) of the Trustee Savings Bank Act 1985, this subsection ceases to have effect and is hereby repealed.

Note
The relevant day is 21 July 1986 — see S.I. 1986 No. 1223
(C. 36).

221(7) **[Scotland]** In Scotland, an unregistered company which the Court of Session has jurisdiction to wind up may be wound up by the court if there is subsisting a floating charge over property comprised in the company's property and undertaking, and the court is satisfied that the security of the creditor entitled to the benefit of the floating charge is in jeopardy.

For this purpose a creditor's security is deemed to be in jeopardy if the court is satisfied that events have occurred or are about to occur which render it unreasonable in the creditor's interest that the company should retain power to dispose of the property which is subject to the floating charge.

SEC. 222   Inability to pay debts: unpaid creditor for £750 or more

222(1) **[Deemed inability to pay debts]** An unregistered company is deemed (for the purposes of section 221) unable to pay its debts if there is a creditor, by assignment or otherwise, to whom the company is indebted in a sum exceeding £750 then due and—

(a) the creditor has served on the company, by leaving at its principal place of business, or by delivering to the secretary or some director, manager or principal officer of the company, or by otherwise serving in such manner as the court may approve or direct, a written demand in the prescribed form requiring the company to pay the sum due, and

(b) the company has for 3 weeks after the service of the demand neglected to pay the sum or to secure or compound for it to the creditor's satisfaction.

222(2) **[Increase or reduction of sec. 222(1) sum]** The money sum for the time being specified in subsection (1) is subject to increase or reduction by regulations under section 417 in Part XV; but no increase in the sum so specified affects any case in which the winding-up petition was presented before the coming into force of the increase.

SEC. 223 Inability to pay debts: debt remaining unsatisfied after action brought

223 An unregistered company is deemed (for the purposes of section 221) unable to pay its debts if an action or other proceeding has been instituted against any member for any debt or demand due, or claimed to be due, from the company, or from him in his character of member, and—

(a) notice in writing of the institution of the action or proceeding has been served on the company by leaving it at the company's principal place of business (or by delivering it to the secretary, or some director, manager or principal officer of the company, or by otherwise serving it in such manner as the court may approve or direct), and

(b) the company has not within 3 weeks after service of the notice paid, secured or compounded for the debt or demand, or procured the action or proceeding to be stayed or sisted, or indemnified the defendant or defender to his reasonable satisfaction against the action or proceeding, and against all costs, damages and expenses to be incurred by him because of it.

SEC. 224 Inability to pay debts: other cases

224(1) **[Deemed inability to pay debts]** An unregistered company is deemed (for purposes of section 221) unable to pay its debts—

(a) if in England and Wales execution or other process issued on a judgment, decree or order obtained in any court in favour of a creditor against the company, or any member of it as such, or any person authorised to be sued as nominal defendant on behalf of the company, is returned unsatisfied;

(b) if in Scotland the induciae of a charge for payment on an extract decree, or an extract registered bond, or an extract registered protest, have expired without payment being made;

(c) if in Northern Ireland a certificate of unenforceability has been granted in respect of any judgment, decree or order obtained as mentioned in paragraph (a);

(d) it is otherwise proved to the satisfaction of the court that the company is unable to pay its debts as they fall due.

224(2) **[Deemed inability — another situation]** An unregistered company is also deemed unable to pay its debts if it is proved to the satisfaction of the court that the value of the company's assets is less than the amount of its liabilities, taking into account its contingent and prospective liabilities.

SEC. 225   Oversea company may be wound up though dissolved

225   Where a company incorporated outside Great Britain which has been carrying on business in Great Britain ceases to carry on business in Great Britain, it may be wound up as an unregistered company under this Act, notwithstanding that it has been dissolved or otherwise ceased to exist as a company under or by virtue of the laws of the country under which it was incorporated.

SEC. 226   Contributories in winding up of unregistered company

226(1)   [Deemed contributory]   In the event of an unregistered company being wound up, every person is deemed a contributory who is liable to pay or contribute to the payment of any debt or liability of the company, or to pay or contribute to the payment of any sum for the adjustment of the rights of members among themselves, or to pay or contribute to the payment of the expenses of winding up the company.

226(2)   [Liability for contribution]   Every contributory is liable to contribute to the company's assets all sums due from him in respect of any such liability as is mentioned above.

226(3)   [Unregistered company re mines in stannaries]   In the case of an unregistered company engaged in or formed for working mines within the stannaries, a past member is not liable to contribute to the assets if he has ceased to be a member for 2 years or more either before the mine ceased to be worked or before the date of the winding-up order.

226(4)   [Death, bankruptcy, insolvency of contributory]   In the event of the death, bankruptcy or insolvency of any contributory, the provisions of this Act with respect to the personal representatives, to the heirs and legatees of heritage of the heritable estate in Scotland of deceased contributories, and to the trustees of bankrupt or insolvent contributories, respectively apply.

SEC. 227   Power of court to stay, sist or restrain proceedings

227   The provisions of this Part with respect to staying, sisting or restraining actions and proceedings against a company at any time after the presentation of a petition for winding up and before the making of a winding-up order extend, in the case of an unregistered company, where the application to stay, sist or restrain is presented by a creditor, to actions and proceedings against any contributory of the company.

SEC. 228   Actions stayed on winding-up order

228   Where an order has been made for winding up an unregistered company, no action or proceeding shall be proceeded with or commenced against any contributory of the company in respect of any debt of the company , except by leave of the court, and subject to such terms as the court may impose.

SEC. 229   Provisions of this Part to be cumulative

229(1)   [Pt. V in addition to Pt. IV]   The provisions of this Part with respect to unregistered companies are in addition to and not in restriction of any provisions in

Part IV with respect to winding up companies by the court; and the court or liquidator may exercise any powers or do any act in the case of unregistered companies which might be exercised or done by it or him in winding up companies formed and registered under the Companies Act.

229(2) [Unregistered company not usually company under CA] However, an unregistered company is not, except in the event of its being wound up, deemed to be a company under the Companies Act, and then only to the extent provided by this Part of this Act.

PART VI — MISCELLANEOUS PROVISIONS APPLYING TO COMPANIES WHICH ARE INSOLVENT OR IN LIQUIDATION

OFFICE-HOLDERS

SEC. 230 Holders of office to be qualified insolvency practitioners

230(1) [Administrator] Where an administration order is made in relation to a company, the administrator must be a person who is qualified to act as an insolvency practitioner in relation to the company.

230(2) [Administrative receiver] Where an administrative receiver of a company is appointed, he must be a person who is so qualified.

230(3) [Liquidator] Where a company goes into liquidation, the liquidator must be a person who is so qualified.

230(4) [Provisional liquidator] Where a provisional liquidator is appointed, he must be a person who is so qualified.

230(5) [Official receiver] Subsections (3) and (4) are without prejudice to any enactment under which the official receiver is to be, or may be, liquidator or provisional liquidator.

SEC. 231 Appointment to office of two or more persons

231(1) [Application] This section applies if an appointment or nomination of any person to the office of administrator, administrative receiver, liquidator or provisional liquidator—

(a) relates to more than one person, or

(b) has the effect that the office is to be held by more than one person.

231(2) [Declaration in appointment or nomination] The appointment or nomination shall declare whether any act required or authorised under any enactment to be done by the administrator, administrative receiver, liquidator or provisional liquidator is to be done by all or any one or more of the persons for the time being holding the office in question.

SEC. 232   Validity of office-holder's acts

232   The acts of an individual as administrator, administrative receiver, liquidator or provisional liquidator of a company are valid notwithstanding any defect in his appointment, nomination or qualifications.

MANAGEMENT BY ADMINISTRATORS, LIQUIDATORS, ETC.

SEC. 233   Supplies of gas, water, electricity, etc.

233(1)   **[Application]**   This section applies in the case of a company where—

    (a)   an administration order is made in relation to the company, or

    (b)   an administrative receiver is appointed, or

    (c)   a voluntary arrangement under Part I, approved by meetings summoned under section 3, has taken effect, or

    (d)   the company goes into liquidation, or

    (e)   a provisional liquidator is appointed;

and **"the office-holder"** means the administrator, the administrative receiver, the supervisor of the voluntary arrangement, the liquidator or the provisional liquidator, as the case may be.

233(2)   **[If request by office-holder]**   If a request is made by or with the concurrence of the office-holder for the giving, after the effective date, of any of the supplies mentioned in the next subsection, the supplier—

    (a)   may make it a condition of the giving of the supply that the office-holder personally guarantees the payment of any charges in respect of the supply, but

    (b)   shall not make it a condition of the giving of the supply, or do anything which has the effect of making it a condition of the giving of the supply, that any outstanding charges in respect of a supply given to the company before the effective date are paid.

233(3)   **[Supplies in sec. 233(2)]**   The supplies referred to in subsection (2) are—

    (a)   a public supply of gas,

    (b)   a supply of electricity by an Electricity Board,

    (c)   a supply of water by a water undertaker or, in Scotland, a water authority,

    (d)   a supply of telecommunication services by a public telecommunications operator.

History
In s. 233(3)(c) the words "a water undertaker" substituted for the former words "statutory water undertakers" by Water Act 1989, s. 190(1) and Sch. 25, para. 78(1) as from 1 September 1989 (see Water Act 1989, s. 4, 194(4) and S.I. 1989 No. 1146 (C. 37) — see also S.I. 1989 No. 1530 (C. 51)).

233(4)   **[Effective date]**   "The effective date" for the purposes of this section is whichever is applicable of the following dates—

    (a)   the date on which the administration order was made,

(b) the date on which the administrative receiver was appointed (or, if he was appointed in succession to another administrative receiver, the date on which the first of his predecessors was appointed),

(c) the date on which the voluntary arrangement was approved by the meetings summoned under section 3,

(d) the date on which the company went into liquidation,

(e) the date on which the provisional liquidator was appointed.

233(5) **[Definitions]** The following applies to expressions used in subsection (3)—

(a) **"public supply of gas"** means a supply of gas by the British Gas Corporation or a public gas supplier within the meaning of Part I of the Gas Act 1986,

(b) **"Electricity Board"** means the same as in the Energy Act 1983,

(c) **"water authority"** means the same as in the Water (Scotland) Act 1980, and

(d) **"telecommunication services"** and **"public telecommunications operator"** mean the same as in the Telecommunications Act 1984, except that the former does not include services consisting in the conveyance of programmes included in cable programme services (within the meaning of the Cable and Broadcasting Act 1984).

SEC. 234 Getting in the company's property

234(1) **[Application]** This section applies in the case of a company where—

(a) an administration order is made in relation to the company, or

(b) an administrative receiver is appointed, or

(c) the company goes into liquidation, or

(d) a provisional liquidator is appointed;

and **"the office-holder"** means the administrator, the administrative receiver, the liquidator or the provisional liquidator, as the case may be.

234(2) **[Court's powers]** Where any person has in his possession or control any property, books, papers or records to which the company appears to be entitled, the court may require that person forthwith (or within such period as the court may direct) to pay, deliver, convey, surrender or transfer the property, books, papers or records to the office-holder.

234(3) **[Application of sec. 234(4)]** Where the office-holder—

(a) seizes or disposes of any property which is not property of the company, and

(b) at the time of seizure or disposal believes, and has reasonable grounds for believing, that he is entitled (whether in pursuance of an order of the court or otherwise) to seize or dispose of that property,

the next subsection has effect.

234(4) **[Liability of office-holder]** In that case the office-holder—

(a) is not liable to any person in respect of any loss or damage resulting from the seizure or disposal except in so far as that loss or damage is caused by the office-holder's own negligence, and

(b) has a lien on the property, or the proceeds of its sale, for such expenses as were incurred in connection with the seizure or disposal.

SEC. 235   Duty to co-operate with office-holder

235(1)   [Application]   This section applies as does section 234; and it also applies, in the case of a company in respect of which a winding-up order has been made by the court in England and Wales, as if references to the office-holder included the official receiver, whether or not he is the liquidator.

235(2)   [Duty to give information, etc.]   Each of the persons mentioned in the next subsection shall—

(a) give to the office-holder such information concerning the company and its promotion, formation, business, dealings, affairs or property as the office-holder may at any time after the effective date reasonably require, and

(b) attend on the office-holder at such times as the latter may reasonably require.

235(3)   [Persons in sec. 235(2)]   The persons referred to above are—

(a) those who are or have at any time been officers of the company,

(b) those who have taken part in the formation of the company at any time within one year before the effective date,

(c) those who are in the employment of the company, or have been in its employment (including employment under a contract for services) within that year, and are in the office-holder's opinion capable of giving information which he requires,

(d) those who are, or have within that year been, officers of, or in the employment (including employment under a contract for services) of, another company which is, or within that year was, an officer of the company in question, and

(e) in the case of a company being wound up by the court, any person who has acted as administrator, administrative receiver or liquidator of the company.

235(4)   ["The effective date"]   For the purposes of subsections (2) and (3), **"the effective date"** is whichever is applicable of the following dates—

(a) the date on which the administration order was made,

(b) the date on which the administrative receiver was appointed or, if he was appointed in succession to another administrative receiver, the date on which the first of his predecessors was appointed,

(c) the date on which the provisional liquidator was appointed, and

(d) the date on which the company went into liquidation.

235(5)   [Penalty for non-compliance]   If a person without reasonable excuse fails to comply with any obligation imposed by this section, he is liable to a fine and, for continued contravention, to a daily default fine.

IA 1986, sec. 235(1)   [The next page is 53,051]   CCH Editions Limited

SEC. 236   Inquiry into company's dealings, etc.

236(1)   [Application]   This section applies as does section 234; and it also applies in the case of a company in respect of which a winding-up order has been made by the court in England and Wales as if references to the office-holder included the official receiver, whether or not he is the liquidator.

[The next page is 53,101]

236(2) **[Court's powers]** The court may, on the application of the office-holder, summon to appear before it—

(a) any officer of the company,

(b) any person known or suspected to have in his possession any property of the company or supposed to be indebted to the company, or

(c) any person whom the court thinks capable of giving information concerning the promotion, formation, business, dealings, affairs or property of the company.

236(3) **[Powers re account, production]** The court may require any such person as is mentioned in subsection (2)(a) to (c) to submit an affidavit to the court containing an account of his dealings with the company or to produce any books, papers or other records in his possession or under his control relating to the company or the matters metioned in paragraph (c) of the subsection.

236(4) **[Application of sec. 236(5)]** The following applies in a case where—

(a) a person without reasonable excuse fails to appear before the court when he is summoned to do so under this section, or

(b) there are reasonable grounds for believing that a person has absconded, or is about to abscond, with a view to avoiding his appearance before the court under this section.

236(5) **[Court's power re warrant]** The court may, for the purpose of bringing that person and anything in his possession before the court, cause a warrant to be issued to a constable or prescribed officer of the court—

(a) for the arrest of that person, and

(b) for the seizure of any books, papers, records, money or goods in that person's possession.

236(6) **[Court authorisation re custody]** The court may authorise a person arrested under such a warrant to be kept in custody, and anything seized under such a warrant to be held, in accordance with the rules, until that person is brought before the court under the warrant or until such other time as the court may order.

SEC. 237 *Court's enforcement powers under sec. 236*

237(1) **[Order to deliver property]** If it appears to the court, on consideration of any evidence obtained under section 236 or this section, that any person has in his possession any property of the company, the court may, on the application of the office-holder, order that person to deliver the whole or any part of the property to the officer-holder at such time, in such manner and on such terms as the court thinks fit.

237(2) **[Order to pay money due]** If it appears to the court, on consideration of any evidence so obtained, that any person is indebted to the company, the court may, on the application of the office-holder, order that person to pay to the office-holder, at such time and in such manner as the court may direct, the whole or any part of the amount due, whether in full discharge of the debt or otherwise, as the court thinks fit.

237(3) **[Order re examination of persons]** The court may, if it thinks fit, order that any person who if within the jurisdiction of the court would be liable to be summoned to appear before it under section 236 or this section shall be examined in any part of the United Kingdom where he may for the time being be, or in a place outside the United Kingdom.

237(4)   [Examination on oath etc.]   Any person who appears or is brought before the court under section 236 or this section may be examined on oath, either orally or (except in Scotland) by interrogatories, concerning the company or the matters mentioned in section 236(2)(c).

ADJUSTMENT OF PRIOR TRANSACTIONS (ADMINISTRATION AND LIQUIDATION)

SEC. 238   Transactions at undervalue (England and Wales)

238(1)   [Application]   This section applies in the case of a company where—

   (a) an administration order is made in relation to the company, or

   (b) the company goes into liquidation;

and **"the office-holder"** means the administrator or the liquidator, as the case may be.

238(2)   [Application to court by office-holder]   Where the company has at a relevant time (defined in section 240) entered into a transaction with any person at an undervalue, the office-holder may apply to the court for an order under this section.

238(3)   [Court order]   Subject as follows, the court shall, on such an application, make such order as it thinks fit for restoring the position to what it would have been if the company had not entered into that transaction.

238(4)   [Interpretation]   For the purposes of this section and section 241, a company enters into a transaction with a person at an undervalue if—

   (a) the company makes a gift to that person or otherwise enters into a transaction with that person on terms that provide for the company to receive no consideration, or

   (b) the company enters into a transaction with that person for a consideration the value of which, in money or money's worth, is significantly less than the value, in money or money's worth, of the consideration provided by the company.

238(5)   [Restriction on court order]   The court shall not make an order under this section in respect of a transaction at an undervalue if it is satisfied—

   (a) that the company which entered into the transaction did so in good faith and for the purpose of carrying on its business, and

   (b) that at the time it did so there were reasonable grounds for believing that the transaction would benefit the company.

SEC. 239   Preferences (England and Wales)

239(1)   [Application]   This section applies as does section 238.

239(2)   [Application to court by office-holder]   Where the company has at a relevant time (defined in the next section) given a preference to any person, the office-holder may apply to the court for an order under this section.

239(3) [**Court order**] Subject as follows, the court shall, on such an application, make such order as it thinks fit for restoring the position to what it would have been if the company had not given that preference.

239(4) [**Interpretation**] For the purposes of this section and section 241, a company gives a preference to a person if—

(a) that person is one of the company's creditors or a surety or guarantor for any of the company's debts or other liabilities, and

(b) the company does anything or suffers anything to be done which (in either case) has the effect of putting that person into a position which, in the event of the company going into insolvent liquidation, will be better than the position he would have been in if that thing had not been done.

239(5) [**Restriction on court order**] The court shall not make an order under this section in respect of a preference given to any person unless the company which gave the preference was influenced in deciding to give it by a desire to produce in relation to that person the effect mentioned in subsection (4)(b).

239(6) [**Presumption**] A company which has given a preference to a person connected with the company (otherwise than by reason only of being its employee) at the time the preference was given is presumed, unless the contrary is shown, to have been influenced in deciding to give it by such a desire as is mentioned in subsection (5).

239(7) [**Interpretation re preference**] The fact that something has been done in pursuance of the order of a court does not, without more, prevent the doing or suffering of that thing from constituting the giving of a preference.

SEC. 240 "Relevant time" under sec. 238, 239

240(1) [**Relevant time**] Subject to the next subsection, the time at which a company enters into a transaction at an undervalue or gives a preference is a relevant time if the transaction is entered into, or the preference given—

(a) in the case of a transaction at an undervalue or of a preference which is given to a person who is connected with the company (otherwise than by reason only of being its employee), at a time in the period of 2 years ending with the onset of insolvency (which expression is defined below),

(b) in the case of a preference which is not such a transaction and is not so given, at a time in the period of 6 months ending with the onset of insolvency, and

(c) in either case, at a time between the presentation of a petition for the making of an administration order in relation to the company and the making of such an order on that petition.

240(2) [**Where not relevant time**] Where a company enters into a transaction at an undervalue or gives a preference at a time mentioned in subsection (1)(a) or (b), that time is not a relevant time for the purposes of section 238 or 239 unless the company—

(a) is at that time unable to pay its debts within the meaning of section 123 in Chapter VI of Part IV, or

(b) becomes unable to pay its debts within the meaning of that section in consequence of the transaction or preference;

but the requirements of this subsection are presumed to be satisfied, unless the contrary is shown, in relation to any transaction at an undervalue which is entered into by a company with a person who is connected with the company.

240(3) [Onset of insolvency] For the purposes of subsection (1), the onset of insolvency is—

    (a) in a case where section 238 or 239 applies by reason of the making of an administration order or of a company going into liquidation immediately upon the discharge of an administration order, the date of the presentation of the petition on which the administration order was made, and

    (b) in a case where the section applies by reason of a company going into liquidation at any other time, the date of the commencement of the winding up.

SEC. 241   Orders under sec. 238, 239

241(1) [Extent of orders] Without prejudice to the generality of sections 238(3) and 239(3), an order under either of those sections with respect to a transaction or preference entered into or given by a company may (subject to the next subsection)—

    (a) require any property transferred as part of the transaction, or in connection with the giving of the preference, to be vested in the company,

    (b) require any property to be so vested if it represents in any person's hands the application either of the proceeds of sale of property so transferred or of money so transferred,

    (c) release or discharge (in whole or in part) any security given by the company,

    (d) require any person to pay, in respect of benefits received by him from the company, such sums to the office-holder as the court may direct,

    (e) provide for any surety or guarantor whose obligations to any person were released or discharged (in whole or in part) under the transaction, or by the giving of the preference, to be under such new or revived obligations to that person as the court thinks appropriate,

    (f) provide for security to be provided for the discharge of any obligation imposed by or arising under the order, for such an obligation to be charged on any property and for the security or charge to have the same priority as a security or charge released or discharged (in whole or in part) under the transaction or by the giving of the preference, and

    (g) provide for the extent to which any person whose property is vested by the order in the company, or on whom obligations are imposed by the order, is to be able to prove in the winding up of the company for debts or other liabilities which arose from, or were released or discharged (in whole or in part) under or by, the transaction or the giving of the preference.

241(2) [Restriction on orders] An order under section 238 or 239 may affect the property of, or impose any obligation on, any person whether or not he is the person with whom the company in question entered into the transaction or (as the case may be) the person to whom the preference was given; but such an order—

(a) shall not prejudice any interest in property which was acquired from aperson other than the company and was acquired in good faith, for value and without notice of the relevant circumstances, or prejudice any interest deriving from such an interest, and

(b) shall not require a person who received a benefit from the transaction or preference in good faith, for value and without notice of the relevant circumstances to pay a sum to the office-holder, except where that person was a party to the transaction or the payment is to be in respect of a preference given to that person at a time when he was a creditor of the company.

241(3) [Relevant circumstances] For the purposes of this section the relevant circumstances, in relation to a transaction or preference, are—

(a) the circumstances by virtue of which an order under section 238 or (as the case may be) 239 could be made in respect of the transaction or preference if the company were to go into liquidation, or an administration order were made in relation to the company, within a particular period after the transaction is entered into or the preference given, and

(b) if that period has expired, the fact that the company has gone into liquidation or that such an order has been made.

241(4) [Application of sec. 238–241] The provisions of sections 238 to 241 apply without prejudice to the availability of any other remedy, even in relation to a transaction or preference which the company had no power to enter into or give.

SEC. 242   Gratuitous alienations (Scotland)

242(1) [Challenge to alienations] Where this subsection applies and—

(a) the winding up of a company has commenced, an alienation by the company is challengeable by—

  (i) any creditor who is a creditor by virtue of a debt incurred on or before the date of such commencement, or

  (ii) the liquidator;

(b) an administration order is in force in relation to a company, an alienation by the company is challengeable by the administrator.

242(2) [Application of sec. 242(1)] Subsection (1) applies where—

(a) by the alienation, whether before or after 1st April 1986 (the coming into force of section 75 of the Bankruptcy (Scotland) Act 1985), any part of the company's property is transferred or any claim or right of the company is discharged or renounced, and

(b) the alienation takes place on a relevant day.

242(3) [Interpretation of sec. 242(2)(b)] For the purposes of subsection (2)(b), the day on which an alienation takes place is the day on which it becomes completely effectual; and in that subsection **"relevant day"** means, if the alienation has the effect of favouring—

    (a) a person who is an associate (within the meaning of the Bankruptcy (Scotland) Act 1985) of the company, a day not earlier than 5 years before the date on which—

        (i) the winding up of the company commences, or

        (ii) as the case may be, the administration order is made; or

    (b) any other person, a day not earlier than 2 years before that date.

242(4)   **[Duties of court on challenge under sec. 242(1)]**   On a challenge being brought under subsection (1), the court shall grant decree of reduction or for such restoration of property to the company's assets or other redress as may be appropriate; but the court shall not grant such a decree if the person seeking to uphold the alienation establishes—

    (a) that immediately, or at any other time, after the alienation the company's assets were greater than its liabilities, or

    (b) that the alienation was made for adequate consideration, or

    (c) that the alienation—

        (i) was a birthday, Christmas or other conventional gift, or

        (ii) was a gift made, for a charitable purpose, to a person who is not an associate of the company,

    which, having regard to all the circumstances, it was reasonable for the company to make:

Provided that this subsection is without prejudice to any right or interest acquired in good faith and for value from or through the transferee in the alienation.

242(5)   **["Charitable purpose" in sec. 242(4)]**   In subsection (4) above, **"charitable purpose"** means any charitable, benevolent or philanthropic purpose, whether or not it is charitable within the meaning of any rule of law.

242(6)   **[Interpretation]**   For the purposes of the foregoing provisions of this section, an alienation in implementation of a prior obligation is deemed to be one for which there was no consideration or no adequate consideration to the extent that the prior obligation was undertaken for no consideration or no adequate consideration.

242(7)   **[Rights of challenge]**   A liquidator and an administrator have the same right as a creditor has under any rule of law to challenge an alienation of a company made for no consideration or no adequate consideration.

242(8)   **[Scotland only]**   This section applies to Scotland only.

SEC. 243   Unfair preferences (Scotland)

243(1)   **[Application of sec. 243(4)]**   Subject to subsection (2) below, subsection (4) below applies to a transaction entered into by a company, whether before or after 1st April 1986, which has the effect of creating a preference in favour of a creditor to the prejudice of the general body of creditors, being a preference created not earlier than 6 months before the commencement of the winding up of the company or the making of an administration order in relation to the company.

243(2)   **[Non-application of sec. 243(4)]**   Subsection (4) below does not apply to any of the following transactions—

(a) a transaction in the ordinary course of trade or business;

(b) a payment in cash for a debt which when it was paid had become payable, unless the transaction was collusive with the purpose of prejudicing the general body of creditors;

(c) a transaction whereby the parties to it undertake reciprocal obligations (whether the performance by the parties of their respective obligations occurs at the same time or at different times) unless the transaction was collusive as aforesaid;

(d) the granting of a mandate by a company authorising an arrestee to pay over the arrested funds or part thereof to the arrester where—

    (i) there has been a decree for payment or a warrant for summary diligence, and

    (ii) the decree or warrant has been preceded by an arrestment on the dependence of the action or followed by an arrestment in execution.

243(3)   [Interpretation of sec. 243(1)]   For the purposes of subsection (1) above, the day on which a preference was created is the day on which the preference became completely effectual.

243(4)   [Persons who may challenge]   A transaction to which this subsection applies is challengeable by—

(a) in the case of a winding up—

    (i) any creditor who is a creditor by virtue of a debt incurred on or before the date of commencement of the winding up, or

    (ii) the liquidator; and

(b) in the case of an administration order, the administrator.

243(5)   [Duties of court on sec. 243(4) challenge]   On a challenge being brought under subsection (4) above, the court, if satisfied that the transaction challenged is a transaction to which this section applies, shall grant decree of reduction or for such restoration of property to the company's assets or other redress as may be appropriate:

Provided that this subsection is without prejudice to any right or interest acquired in good faith and for value from or through the creditor in whose favour the preference was created.

243(6)   [Rights of challenge]   A liquidator and an administrator have the same right as a creditor has under any rule of law to challenge a preference created by a debtor.

243(7)   [Scotland only]   This section applies to Scotland only.

SEC. 244   Extortionate credit transactions

244(1)   [Application]   This section applies as does section 238, and where the company is, or has been, a party to a transaction for, or involving, the provision of credit to the company.

244(2)   [Court order re extortionate transaction]   The court may, on the application of the office-holder, make an order with respect to the transaction if the transaction is or was extortionate and was entered into in the period of 3 years ending with the day on which the administration order was made or (as the case may be) the company went into liquidation.

244(3) **[Extortionate transaction — interpretation]** For the purposes of this section a transaction is extortionate if, having regard to the risk accepted by the person providing the credit—

(a) the terms of it are or were such as to require grossly exorbitant payments to be made (whether unconditionally or in certain contingencies) in respect of the provision of the credit, or

(b) it otherwise grossly contravened ordinary principles of fair dealing;

and it shall be presumed, unless the contrary is proved, that a transaction with respect to which an application is made under this section is or, as the case may be, was extortionate.

244(4) **[Extent of court order]** An order under this section with respect to any transaction may contain such one or more of the following as the court thinks fit, that is to say—

(a) provision setting aside the whole or part of any obligation created by the transaction,

(b) provision otherwise varying the terms of the transaction or varying the terms on which any security for the purposes of the transaction is held,

(c) provision requiring any person who is or was a party to the transaction to pay to the office-holder any sums paid to that person, by virtue of the transaction, by the company,

(d) provision requiring any person to surrender to the office-holder any property held by him as security for the purposes of the transaction,

(e) provision directing accounts to be taken between any persons.

244(5) **[Exercise of powers]** The powers conferred by this section are exercisable in relation to any transaction concurrently with any powers exercisable in relation to that transaction as a transaction at an undervalue or under section 242 (gratuitous alienations in Scotland).

SEC. 245   Avoidance of certain floating charges

245(1) **[Application]** This section applies as does section 238, but applies to Scotland as well as to England and Wales.

245(2) **[Invalidity of floating charge]** Subject as follows, a floating charge on the company's undertaking or property created at a relevant time is invalid except to the extent of the aggregate of—

(a) the value of so much of the consideration for the creation of the charge as consists of money paid, or goods or services supplied, to the company at the same time as, or after, the creation of the charge,

(b) the value of so much of that consideration as consists of the discharge or reduction, at the same time as, or after, the creation of the charge, of any debt of the company, and

IA 1986, sec. 244(3)   [The next page is 53,301]

(c) the amount of such interest (if any) as is payable on the amount falling within paragraph (a) or (b) in pursuance of any agreement under which the money was so paid, the goods or services were so supplied or the debt was so discharged or reduced.

245(3) **[Relevant time]** Subject to the next subsection, the time at which a floating charge is created by a company is a relevant time for the purposes of this section if the charge is created—

(a) in the case of a charge which is created in favour of a person who is connected with the company, at a time in the period of 2 years ending with the onset of insolvency,

(b) in the case of a charge which is created in favour of any other person, at a time in the period of 12 months ending with the onset of insolvency, or

(c) in either case, at a time between the presentation of a petition for the making of an administration order in relation to the company and the making of such an order on that petition.

245(4) **[Qualification to sec. 245(3)(b)]** Where a company creates a floating charge at a time mentioned in subsection (3)(b) and the person in favour of whom the charge is created is not connected with the company, that time is not a relevant time for the purposes of this section unless the company—

(a) is at that time unable to pay its debts within the meaning of section 123 in Chapter VI of Part IV, or

(b) becomes unable to pay its debts within the meaning of that section in consequence of the transaction under which the charge is created.

245(5) **[Onset of insolvency in sec. 245(3)]** For the purposes of subsection (3), the onset of insolvency is—

(a) in a case where this section applies by reason of the making of an administration order, the date of the presentation of the petition on which the order was made, and

(b) in a case where this section applies by reason of a company going into liquidation, the date of the commencement of the winding up.

245(6) **[Value of goods, services etc. in sec. 245(2)(a)]** For the purposes of subsection (2)(a) the value of any goods or services supplied by way of consideration for a floating charge is the amount in money which at the time they were supplied could reasonably have been expected to be obtained for supplying the goods or services in the ordinary course of business and on the same terms (apart from the consideration) as those on which they were supplied to the company.

SEC. 246 Unenforceability of liens on books, etc.

246(1) **[Application]** This section applies in the case of a company where—

(a) an administration order is made in relation to the company, or

(b) the company goes into liquidation, or

(c) a provisional liquidator is appointed;

and **"the office-holder"** means the administrator, the liquidator or the provisional liquidator, as the case may be.

246(2)   **[Lien etc. unenforceable]**   Subject as follows, a lien or other right to retain possession of any of the books, papers or other records of the company is unenforceable to the extent that its enforcement would deny possession of any books, papers or other records to the office-holder.

246(3)   **[Non-application]**   This does not apply to a lien on documents which give a title to property and are held as such.

PART VII — INTERPRETATION FOR FIRST GROUP OF PARTS

SEC. 247   "Insolvency" and "go into liquidation"

247(1)   **["Insolvency"]**   In this Group of Parts, except in so far as the context otherwise requires, **"insolvency"**, in relation to a company, includes the approval of a voluntary arrangement under Part I, the making of an administration order or the appointment of an administrative receiver.

247(2)   **[Company in liquidation]**   For the purposes of any provision in this Group of Parts, a company goes into liquidation if it passes a resolution for voluntary winding up or an order for its winding up is made by the court at a time when it has not already gone into liquidation by passing such a resolution.

SEC. 248   "Secured creditor", etc.

248   In this Group of Parts, except in so far as the context otherwise requires—

    (a) **"secured creditor"**, in relation to a company, means a creditor of the company who holds in respect of his debt a security over property of the company, and **"unsecured creditor"** is to be read accordingly; and

    (b) **"security"** means—

        (i) in relation to England and Wales, any mortgage, charge, lien or other security, and

        (ii) in relation to Scotland, any security (whether heritable or moveable), any floating charge and any right of lien or preference and any right of retention (other than a right of compensation or set off).

SEC. 249   "Connected" with a company

249   For the purposes of any provision in this Group of Parts, a person is connected with a company if—

    (a) he is a director or shadow director of the company or an associate of such a director or shadow director, or

    (b) he is an associate of the company;

and **"associate"** has the meaning given by section 435 in Part XVIII of this Act.

SEC. 250 "Member" of a company

250 For the purposes of any provision in this Group of Parts, a person who is not a member of a company but to whom shares in the company have been transferred, or transmitted by operation of law, is to be regarded as a member of the company, and references to a member or members are to be read accordingly.

SEC. 251 Expressions used generally

251 In this Group of Parts, except in so far as the context otherwise requires—

"**administrative receiver**" means—

    (a) an administrative receiver as defined by section 29(2) in Chapter I of Part III, or

    (b) a receiver appointed under section 51 in Chapter II of that Part in a case where the whole (or substantially the whole) of the company's property is attached by the floating charge;

"**business day**" means any day other than a Saturday, a Sunday, Christmas Day, Good Friday or a day which is a bank holiday in any part of Great Britain;

"**chattel leasing agreement**" means an agreement for the bailment or, in Scotland, the hiring of goods which is capable of subsisting for more than 3 months;

"**contributory**" has the meaning given by section 79;

"**director**" includes any person occupying the position of director, by whatever name called;

"**floating charge**" means a charge which, as created, was a floating charge and includes a floating charge within section 462 of the Companies Act (Scottish floating charges);

"**office copy**", in relation to Scotland, means a copy certified by the clerk of court;

"**the official rate**", in relation to interest, means the rate payable under section 189(4);

"**prescribed**" means prescribed by the rules;

"**receiver**", in the expression "**receiver or manager**", does not include a receiver appointed under section 51 in Chapter II of Part III;

"**retention of title agreement**" means an agreement for the sale of goods to a company, being an agreement—

    (a) which does not constitute a charge on the goods, but

    (b) under which, if the seller is not paid and the company is wound up, the seller will have priority over all other creditors of the company as respects the goods or any property representing the goods;

"**the rules**" means rules under section 411 in Part XV; and

"**shadow director**", in relation to a company, means a person in accordance with whose directions or instructions the directors of the company are accustomed to act (but so that a person is not deemed a shadow director by reason only that the directors act on advice given by him in a professional capacity);

and any expression for whose interpretation provision is made by Part XXVI of the Companies Act, other than an expression defined above in this section, is to be construed in accordance with that provision.

THE SECOND GROUP OF PARTS
INSOLVENCY OF INDIVIDUALS; BANKRUPTCY

PART VIII — INDIVIDUAL VOLUNTARY ARRANGEMENTS

MORATORIUM FOR INSOLVENT DEBTOR

SEC. 252   Interim order of court

252(1)   [Power of court]   In the circumstances specified below, the court may in the case of a debtor (being an individual) make an interim order under this section.

252(2)   [Effect of interim order]   An interim order has the effect that, during the period for which it is in force—

- (a) no bankruptcy petition relating to the debtor may be presented or proceeded with, and
- (b) no other proceedings, and no execution or other legal process, may be commenced or continued against the debtor or his property except with the leave of the court.

SEC. 253   Application for interim order

253(1)   [Where application made]   Application to the court for an interim order may be made where the debtor intends to make a proposal to his creditors for a composition in satisfaction of his debts or a scheme of arrangement of his affairs (from here on referred to, in either case, as a "voluntary arrangement").

253(2)   [Nominee]   The proposal must provide for some person ("the nominee") to act in relation to the voluntary arrangement either as trustee or otherwise for the purpose of supervising its implementation.

253(3)   [Applicants]   Subject as follows, the application may be made—

- (a) if the debtor is an undischarged bankrupt, by the debtor, the trustee of his estate, or the official receiver, and
- (b) in any other case, by the debtor.

253(4)   [Notice for sec. 253(3)(a)]   An application shall not be made under subsection (3)(a) unless the debtor has given notice of his proposal (that is, the proposal to his creditors for a voluntary arrangement) to the official receiver and, if there is one, the trustee of his estate.

253(5) **[When application not to be made]** An application shall not be made while a bankruptcy petition presented by the debtor is pending, if the court has, under section 273 below, appointed an insolvency practitioner to inquire into the debtor's affairs and report.

SEC. 254 Effect of application

254(1) **[Stay pending interim order]** At any time when an application under section 253 for an interim order is pending, the court may stay any action, execution or other legal process against the property or person of the debtor.

254(2) **[Stay or continuance]** Any court in which proceedings are pending against an individual may, on proof that an application under that section has been made in respect of that individual, either stay the proceedings or allow them to continue on such terms as it thinks fit.

SEC. 255 Cases in which interim order can be made

255(1) **[Conditions for order]** The court shall not make an interim order on an application under section 253 unless it is satisfied—

(a) that the debtor intends to make such a proposal as is mentioned in that section;

(b) that on the day of the making of the application the debtor was an undischarged bankrupt or was able to petition for his own bankruptcy;

(c) that no previous application has been made by the debtor for an interim order in the period of 12 months ending with that day; and

(d) that the nominee under the debtor's proposal to his creditors is a person who is for the time being qualified to act as an insolvency practitioner in relation to the debtor, and is willing to act in relation to the proposal.

255(2) **[Order to facilitate consideration and implementation of proposal]** The court may make an order if it thinks that it would be appropriate to do so for the purpose of facilitating the consideration and implementation of the debtor's proposal.

255(3) **[Where debtor is undischarged bankrupt]** Where the debtor is an undischarged bankrupt, the interim order may contain provision as to the conduct of the bankruptcy, and the administration of the bankrupt's estate, during the period for which the order is in force.

255(4) **[Extent of sec. 255(3) provision]** Subject as follows, the provision contained in an interim order by virtue of subsection (3) may include provision staying proceedings in the bankruptcy or modifying any provision in this Group of Parts, and any provision of the rules in their application to the debtor's bankruptcy.

255(5) **[Limit to interim order]** An interim order shall not, in relation to a bankrupt, make provision relaxing or removing any of the requirements of provisions in this Group of Parts, or of the rules, unless the court is satisfied that that provision is unlikely to result in any significant diminution in, or in the value of, the debtor's estate for the purposes of the bankruptcy.

255(6) **[When order ceases to have effect]** Subject to the following provisions of this Part, an interim order made on an application under section 253 ceases to have effect at the end of the period of 14 days beginning with the day after the making of the order.

SEC. 256   Nominee's report on debtor's proposal

256(1)   **[Report to court]**   Where an interim order has been made on an application under section 253, the nominee shall, before the order ceases to have effect, submit a report to the court stating—

     (a) whether, in his opinion, a meeting of the debtor's creditors should be summoned to consider the debtor's proposal, and

     (b) if in his opinion such a meeting should be summoned, the date on which, and time and place at which, he proposes the meeting should be held.

256(2)   **[Information to nominee]**   For the purpose of enabling a nominee to prepare his report the debtor shall submit to the nominee—

     (a) a document setting out the terms of the voluntary arrangement which the debtor is proposing, and

     (b) a statement of his affairs containing—

         (i) such particulars of his creditors and of his debts and other liabilities and of his assets as may be prescribed, and

         (ii) such other information as may be prescribed.

256(3)   **[Directions by court]**   The court may, on an application made by the debtor in a case where the nominee has failed to submit the report required by this section, do one or both of the following, namely—

     (a) direct that the nominee shall be replaced as such by another person qualified to act as an insolvency practitioner in relation to the debtor;

     (b) direct that the interim order shall continue, or (if it has ceased to have effect) be renewed, for such further period as the court may specify in the direction.

256(4)   **[Extension of period of interim order]**   The court may, on the application of the nominee, extend the period for which the interim order has effect so as to enable the nominee to have more time to prepare his report.

256(5)   **[Extension for consideration by creditors]**   If the court is satisfied on receiving the nominee's report that a meeting of the debtor's creditors should be summoned to consider the debtor's proposal, the court shall direct that the period for which the interim order has effect shall be extended, for such further period as it may specify in the direction, for the purpose of enabling the debtor's proposal to be considered by his creditors in accordance with the following provisions of this Part.

256(6)   **[Discharge of interim order]**   The court may discharge the interim order if it is satisfied, on the application of the nominee—

     (a) that the debtor has failed to comply with his obligations under subsection (2), or

     (b) that for any other reason it would be inappropriate for a meeting of the debtor's creditors to be summoned to consider the debtor's proposal.

SEC. 257 Summoning of creditors' meeting

257(1) **[Meeting to be summoned]** Where it has been reported to the court under section 256 that a meeting of the debtor's creditors should be summoned, the nominee (or his replacement under section 256(3)(a)) shall, unless the court otherwise directs, summon that meeting for the time, date and place proposed in his report.

257(2) **[Persons summoned to meeting]** The persons to be summoned to the meeting are every creditor of the debtor of whose claim and address the person summoning the meeting is aware.

257(3) **[Creditors of debtor]** For this purpose the creditors of a debtor who is an undischarged bankrupt include—

(a) every person who is a creditor of the bankrupt in respect of a bankruptcy debt, and

(b) every person who would be such a creditor if the bankruptcy had commenced on the day on which notice of the meeting is given.

CONSIDERATION AND IMPLEMENTATION OF DEBTOR'S PROPOSAL

SEC. 258 Decisions of creditors' meeting

258(1) **[Decision re approval]** A creditors' meeting summoned under section 257 shall decide whether to approve the proposed voluntary arrangement.

258(2) **[Approval with modifications]** The meeting may approve the proposed voluntary arrangement with modifications, but shall not do so unless the debtor consents to each modification.

258(3) **[Extent of modifications]** The modifications subject to which the proposed voluntary arrangement may be approved may include one conferring the functions proposed to be conferred on the nominee on another person qualified to act as an insolvency practitioner in relation to the debtor.

But they shall not include any modification by virtue of which the proposal ceases to be a proposal such as is mentioned in section 253.

258(4) **[Certain modifications not to be approved]** The meeting shall not approve any proposal or modification which affects the right of a secured creditor of the debtor to enforce his security, except with the concurrence of the creditor concerned.

258(5) **[Other modifications not to be approved]** Subject as follows, the meeting shall not approve any proposal or modification under which—

(a) any preferential debt of the debtor is to be paid otherwise than in priortity to such of his debts as are not preferential debts, or

(b) a preferential creditor of the debtor is to be paid an amount in respect of a preferential debt that bears to that debt a smaller proportion than is borne to another preferential debt by the amount that is to be paid in respect of that other debt.

However, the meeting may approve such a proposal or modification with the concurrence of the preferential creditor concerned.

258(6) **[Meeting in accordance with rules]** Subject as above, the meeting shall be conducted in accordance with the rules.

258(7)   [Definitions]   In this section **"preferential debt"** has the meaning given by section 386 in Part XII; and **"preferential creditor"** is to be construed accordingly.

SEC. 259   Report of decisions to court

259(1)   [Report to court, notice]   After the conclusion in accordance with the rules of the meeting summoned under section 257, the chairman of the meeting shall report the result of it to the court and, immediately after so reporting, shall give notice of the result of the meeting to such persons as may be prescribed.

259(2)   [Discharge of interim order]   If the report is that the meeting has declined (with or without modifications) to approve the debtor's proposal, the court may discharge any interim order which is in force in relation to the debtor.

SEC. 260   Effect of approval

260(1)   [Effect]   This section has effect where the meeting summoned under section 257 approves the proposed voluntary arrangement (with or without modifications).

260(2)   [Effect of approved composition or scheme]   The approved arrangement—

   (a) takes effect as if made by the debtor at the meeting, and

   (b) binds every person who in accordance with the rules had notice of, and was entitled to vote at, the meeting (whether or not he was present or represented at it) as if he were a party to the arrangement.

260(3)   [Deeds of Arrangement Act]   The Deeds of Arrangement Act 1914 does not apply to the approved voluntary arrangement.

260(4)   [Certain interim orders to cease]   Any interim order in force in relation to the debtor immediately before the end of the period of 28 days beginning with the day on which the report with respect to the creditors' meeting was made to the court under section 259 ceases to have effect at the end of that period.

   This subsection applies except to such extent as the court may direct for the purposes of any application under section 262 below.

260(5)   [Bankruptcy petition stayed by sec. 260(4) interim order]   Where proceedings on a bankruptcy petition have been stayed by an interim order which ceases to have effect under subsection (4), that petition is deemed, unless the court otherwise orders, to have been dismissed.

SEC. 261   Effect where debtor an undischarged bankrupt

261(1)   [If debtor undischarged bankrupt]   Subject as follows, where the creditors' meeting summoned under section 257 approves the proposed voluntary arrangement (with or without modifications) and the debtor is an undischarged bankrupt, the court may do one or both of the following, namely—

   (a) annul the bankruptcy order by which he was adjudged bankrupt;

   (b) give such directions with respect to the conduct of the bankruptcy and the administration of the bankrupt's estate as it thinks appropriate for facilitating the implementation of the approved voluntary arrangement.

261(2) **[Annulment of bankruptcy order]** The court shall not annul a bankruptcy order under subsection (1)—

(a) at any time before the end of the period of 28 days beginning with the day on which the report of the creditors' meeting was made to the court under section 259, or

(b) at any time when an application under section 262 below, or an appeal in respect of such an application, is pending or at any time in the period within which such an appeal may be brought.

SEC. 262 Challenge of meeting's decision

262(1) **[Application to court]** Subject to this section, an application to the court may be made, by any of the persons specified below, on one or both of the following grounds, namely—

(a) that a voluntary arrangement approved by a creditor's meeting summoned under section 257 unfairly prejudices the interests of a creditor of the debtor;

(b) that there has been some material irregularity at or in relation to such a meeting.

262(2) **[Applicants]** The persons who may apply under this section are—

(a) the debtor;

(b) a person entitled, in accordance with the rules, to vote at the creditors' meeting;

(c) the nominee (or his replacement under section 256(3)(a) or 258(3)); and

(d) if the debtor is an undischarged bankrupt, the trustee of his estate or the official receiver.

262(3) **[Time for application]** An application under this section shall not be made after the end of the period of 28 days beginning with the day on which the report of the creditors' meeting was made to the court under section 259.

262(4) **[Court's powers]** Where on an application under this section the court is satisfied as to either of the grounds mentioned in subsection (1), it may do one or both of the following, namely—

(a) revoke or suspend any approval given by the meeting;

(b) give a direction to any person for the summoning of a further meeting of the debtor's creditors to consider any revised proposal he may make or, in a case falling within subsection (1)(b), to reconsider his original proposal.

262(5) **[Revocation of direction, approval]** Where at any time after giving a direction under subsection (4)(b) for the summoning of a meeting to consider a revised proposal the court is satisfied that the debtor does not intend to submit such a proposal, the court shall revoke the direction and revoke or suspend any approval given at the previous meeting.

262(6) **[Further direction]** Where the court gives a direction under subsection (4)(b), it may also give a direction continuing or, as the case may require, renewing, for such period as may be specified in the direction, the effect in relation to the debtor of any interim order.

262(7)   [Supplemental directions]   In any case where the court, on an application made under this section with respect to a creditors' meeting, gives a direction under subsection (4)(b) or revokes or suspends an approval under subsection (4)(a) or (5), the court may give such supplemental directions as it thinks fit, and, in particular, directions with respect to—

(a) things done since the meeting under any voluntary arrangement approved by the meeting, and

(b) such things done since the meeting as could not have been done if an interim order had been in force in relation to the debtor when they were done.

262(8)   [Effects of irregularity at meeting]   Except in pursuance of the preceding provisions of this section, an approval given at a creditors' meeting summoned under section 257 is not invalidated by any irregularity at or in relation to the meeting.

SEC. 263   Implementation and supervision of approved voluntary arrangement

263(1)   [Application]   This section applies where a voluntary arrangement approved by a creditors' meeting summoned under section 257 has taken effect.

263(2)   [Supervisor of voluntary arrangement]   The person who is for the time being carrying out, in relation to the voluntary arrangement, the functions conferred by virtue of the approval on the nominee (or his replacement under section 256(3)(a) or 258(3)) shall be known as the supervisor of the voluntary arrangement.

263(3)   [Application to court re actions of supervisor]   If the debtor, any of his creditors or any other person is dissatisfied by any act, omission or decision of the supervisor, he may apply to the court; and on such an application the court may—

(a) confirm, reverse or modify any act or decision of the supervisor,

(b) give him directions, or

(c) make such other order as it thinks fit.

263(4)   [Application for directions]   The supervisor may apply to the court for directions in relation to any particular matter arising under the voluntary arrangement.

263(5)   [Court may fill supervisor vacancy etc.]   The court may, whenever—

(a) it is expedient to appoint a person to carry out the functions of the supervisor, and

(b) it is inexpedient, difficult or impracticable for an appointment to be made without the assistance of the court,

make an order appointing a person who is qualified to act as an insolvency practitioner in relation to the debtor, either in substitution for the existing supervisor or to fill a vacancy.

This is without prejudice to section 41(2) of the Trustee Act 1925 (power of court to appoint trustees of deeds of arrangement).

263(6)   [Exercise of sec. 263(5) power]   The power conferred by subsection (5) is exercisable so as to increase the number of persons exercising the functions of the supervisor or, where there is more than one person exercising those functions, so as to replace one or more of those persons.

PART IX — BANKRUPTCY

Chapter I — Bankruptcy Petitions; Bankruptcy Orders

PRELIMINARY

SEC. 264   Who may present a bankruptcy petition

264(1)   [Presentation of petition]   A petition for a bankruptcy order to be made against an individual may be presented to the court in accordance with the following provisions of this Part—

(a)   by one of the individual's creditors or jointly by more than one of them,

(b)   by the individual himself,

(c)   by the supervisor of, or any person (other than the individual) who is for the time being bound by, a voluntary arrangement proposed by the individual and approved under Part VIII, or

(d)   where a criminal bankruptcy order has been made against the individual, by the Official Petitioner or by any person specified in the order in pursuance of section 39(3)(b) of the Powers of Criminal Courts Act 1973.

Note
S. 264(1)(d) and the word "or" immediately preceding it   repealed by Criminal Justice Act 1988, s. 170(2) and Sch. 16 as from a day to be appointed.

264(2)   [Power of court to make order]   Subject to those provisions, the court may make a bankruptcy order on any such petition.

SEC. 265   Conditions to be satisfied in respect of debtor

265(1)   [Conditions for presentation of petition]   A bankruptcy petition shall not be presented to the court under section 264(1)(a) or (b) unless the debtor—

(a)   is domiciled in England and Wales,

(b)   is personally present in England and Wales on the day on which the petition is presented, or

(c)   at any time in the period of 3 years ending with that day—

(i)   has been ordinarily resident, or has had a place of residence, in England and Wales, or

(ii)   has carried on business in England and Wales.

265(2)   [Interpretation]   The reference in subsection (1)(c) to an individual carrying on business includes—

(a)   the carrying on of business by a firm or partnership of which the individual is a member, and

(b)   the carrying on of business by an agent or manager for the individual or for such a firm or partnership.

SEC. 266   Other preliminary conditions

266(1)   [Treatment of petition]   Where a bankruptcy petition relating to an individual is presented by a person who is entitled to present a petition under two or more paragraphs of section 264(1), the petition is to be treated for the purposes of this Part as a petition under such one of those paragraphs as may be specified in the petition.

266(2) **[Limit on withdrawal of petition]** A bankruptcy petition shall not be withdrawn without the leave of the court.

266(3) **[Power of dismissal or stay]** The court has a general power, if it appears to it appropriate to do so on the grounds that there has been a contravention of rules or for any other reason, to dismiss a bankruptcy petition or to stay proceedings on such a petition; and, where it stays proceedings on a petition, it may do so on such terms and conditions as it thinks fit.

266(4) **[Where criminal bankruptcy order]** Without prejudice to subsection (3), where a petition under section 264(1)(a), (b) or (c) in respect of an individual is pending at a time when a criminal bankruptcy order is made against him, or is presented after such an order has been so made, the court may on the application of the Official Petitioner dismiss the petition if it appears to it appropriate to do so.

Note
S. 266(4) repealed by Criminal Justice Act 1988, s. 170(2)
and Sch. 16 as from a day to be appointed.

CREDITOR'S PETITION

SEC. 267 Grounds of creditor's petition

267(1) **[Requirements]** A creditor's petition must be in respect of one or more debts owed by the debtor, and the petitioning creditor or each of the petitioning creditors must be a person to whom the debt or (as the case may be) at least one of the debts is owed.

267(2) **[Conditions for presentation of petition]** Subject to the next three sections, a creditor's petition may be presented to the court in respect of a debt or debts only if, at the time the petition is presented—

(a) the amount of the debt, or the aggregate amount of the debts, is equal to or exceeds the the bankruptcy level,

(b) the debt, or each of the debts, is for a liquidated sum payable to the petitioning creditor, or one or more of the petitioning creditors, either immediately or at some certain, future time, and is unsecured,

(c) the debt, or each of the debts, is a debt which the debtor appears either to be unable to pay or to have no reasonable prospect of being able to pay, and

(d) there is no outstanding application to set aside a statutory demand served (under section 268 below) is respect of the debt or any of the debts.

267(3) **[Interpretation]** A debt is not to be regarded for the purposes of subsection (2) as a debt for a liquidated sum by reason only that the amount of the debt is specified in a criminal bankruptcy order.

Note
S. 267(3) repealed by Criminal Justice Act 1988, s. 170(2)
and Sch. 16 as from a day to be appointed.

267(4) **["The bankruptcy level"]** "The bankruptcy level" is £750; but the Secretary of State may by order in a statutory instrument substitute any amount specified in the order for that amount or (as the case may be) for the amount which by virtue of such an order is for the time being the amount of the bankruptcy level.

267(5) **[Approval of order by Parliament]** An order shall not be made under subsection (4) unless a draft of it has been laid before, and approved by a resolution of, each House of Parliament.

SEC. 268 Definition of "inability to pay", etc.; the statutory demand

268(1) [Interpretation of sec. 267(2)(c)] For the purposes of section 267(2)(c), the debtor appears to be unable to pay a debt if, but only if, the debt is payable immediately and either—

(a) the petitioning creditor to whom the debt is owed has served on the debtor a demand (known as "the statutory demand") in the prescribed form requiring him to pay the debt or to secure or compound for it to the satisfaction of the creditor, at least 3 weeks have elapsed since the demand was served and the demand has been neither complied with nor set aside in accordance with the rules, or

(b) execution or other process issued in respect of the debt on a judgment or order of any court in favour of the petitioning creditor, or one or more of the petitioning creditors to whom the debt is owed, has been returned unsatisfied in whole or in part.

268(2) [Further interpretation] For the purposes of section 267(2)(c) the debtor appears to have no reasonable prospect of being able to pay a debt if, but only if, the debt is not immediately payable and—

(a) the petitioning creditor to whom it is owed has served on the debtor a demand (also known as "the statutory demand") in the prescribed form requiring him to establish to the satisfaction of the creditor that there is a reasonable prospect that the debtor will be able to pay the debt when it falls due,

(b) at least 3 weeks have elapsed since the demand was served, and

(c) the demand has been neither complied with nor set aside in accordance with the rules.

SEC. 269 Creditor with security

269(1) [Where debt not unsecured] A debt which is the debt, or one of the debts, in respect of which a creditor's petition is presented need not be unsecured if either—

(a) the petition contains a statement by the person having the right to enforce the security that he is willing, in the event of a bankruptcy order being made, to give up his security for the benefit of all the bankrupt's creditors, or

(b) the petition is expressed not to be made in respect of the secured part of the debt and contains a statement by that person of the estimated value at the date of the petition of the security for the secured part of the debt.

269(2) [Debt in sec. 269(1)(b)] In a case falling within subsection (1)(b) the secured and unsecured parts of the debt are to be treated for the purposes of sections 267 to 270 as separate debts.

SEC. 270 Expedited petition

270 In the case of a creditor's petition presented wholly or partly in respect of a debt which is the subject of a statutory demand under section 268, the petition may be presented before the end of the 3-week period there mentioned if there is a serious possibility that the debtor's property or the value of any of his property will be significantly diminished during that period and the petition contains a statement to that effect.

SEC. 271   Proceedings on creditor's petition

271(1)   **[Conditions for bankruptcy order]**   The court shall not make a bankruptcy order on a creditor's petition unless it is satisfied that the debt, or one of the debts, in respect of which the petition was presented is either—

    (a) a debt which, having been payable at the date of the petition or having since become payable, has been neither paid nor secured or compounded for, or

    (b) a debt which the debtor has no reasonable prospect of being able to pay when it falls due.

Note
Re s. 271(1)(a) see practice direction [1986] 3 All E.R. 864.

271(2)   **[Where petition contains sec. 270 statement]**   In a case in which the petition contains such a statement as is required by section 270, the court shall not make a bankruptcy order until at least 3 weeks have elapsed since the service of any statutory demand under section 268.

271(3)   **[Dismissal of petition]**   The court may dismiss the petition if it is satisfied that the debtor is able to pay all his debts or is satisfied—

    (a) that the debtor has made an offer to secure or compound for a debt in respect of which the petition is presented,

    (b) that the acceptance of that offer would have required the dismissal of the petition, and

    (c) that the offer has been unreasonably refused;

and, in determining for the purposes of this subsection whether the debtor is able to pay all his debts, the court shall take into account his contingent and prospective liabilities.

271(4)   **[Interpretation]**   In determining for the purposes of this section what constitutes a reasonable prospect that a debtor will be able to pay a debt when it falls due, it is to be assumed that the prospect given by the facts and other matters known to the creditor at the time he entered into the transaction resulting in the debt was a reasonable prospect.

271(5)   **[Powers of court to amend etc.]**   Nothing in sections 267 to 271 prejudices the power of the court, in accordance with the rules, to authorise a creditor's petition to be amended by the omission of any creditor or debt and to be proceeded with as if things done for the purposes of those sections had been done only by or in relation to the remaining creditors or debts.

DEBTOR'S PETITION

SEC. 272   Grounds of debtor's petition

272(1)   **[Presentation to court]**   A debtor's petition may be presented to the court only on the grounds that the debtor is unable to pay his debts.

272(2) **[Statement of debtor's affairs]** The petition shall be accompanied by a statement of the debtor's affairs containing—

(a) such particulars of the debtor's creditors and of his debts and other liabilities and of his assets as may be prescribed, and

(b) such other information as may be prescribed.

SEC. 273 Appointment of insolvency practitioner by the court

273(1) **[Where court not to make bankruptcy order]** Subject to the next section, on the hearing of a debtor's petition the court shall not make a bankruptcy order if it appears to the court—

(a) that if a bankruptcy order were made the aggregate amount of the bankruptcy debts, so far as unsecured, would be less than the small bankruptcies level,

(b) that if a bankruptcy order were made, the value of the bankrupt's estate would be equal to or more than the minimum amount,

(c) that within the period of 5 years ending with the presentation of the petition the debtor has neither been adjudged bankrupt nor made a composition with his creditors in satisfaction of his debts or a scheme of arrangement of his affairs, and

(d) that it would be appropriate to appoint a person to prepare a report under section 274.

"The minimum amount" and **"the small bankruptcies level"** mean such amounts as may for the time being be prescribed for the purposes of this section.

Note
The maximum level in s. 273(1)(a) is £20,000 and the minimum value in s. 273(1)(b) is £2,000 — see The Insolvency Proceedings (Monetary Limits) Order 1986 (S.I. 1986 No. 1996).

273(2) **[Appointment of person to prepare report]** Where on the hearing of the petition, it appears to the court as mentioned in subsection (1), the court shall appoint a person who is qualified to act as an insolvency practitioner in relation to the debtor—

(a) to prepare a report under the next section, and

(b) subject to section 258(3) in Part VIII, to act in relation to any voluntary arrangement to which the report relates either as trustee or otherwise for the purpose of supervising its implementation.

SEC. 274 Action on report of insolvency practitioner

274(1) **[Report to court]** A person appointed under section 273 shall inquire into the debtor's affairs and, within such period as the court may direct, shall submit a report to the court stating whether the debtor is willing, for the purposes of Part VIII, to make a proposal for a voluntary arrangement.

274(2) **[Contents of report]** A report which states that the debtor is willing as above mentioned shall also state—

(a) whether, in the opinion of the person making the report, a meeting of the debtor's creditors should be summoned to consider the proposal, and

(b) if in that person's opinion such a meeting should be summoned, the date on which, and time and place at which, he proposes the meetings should be held.

274(3)   [Powers of court]   On considering a report under this section the court may—

(a) without any application, make an interim order under section 252, if it thinks that it is appropriate to do so for the purpose of facilitating the consideration and implementation of the debtor's proposal, or

(b) if it thinks it would be inappropriate to make such an order, make a bankruptcy order.

274(4)   [Cessation of interim order]   An interim order by virtue of this section ceases to have effect at the end of such period as the court may specify for the purpose of enabling the debtor's proposal to be considered by his creditors in accordance with the applicable provisions of Part VIII.

274(5)   [Summoning of meeting]   Where it has been reported to the court under this section that a meeting of the debtor's creditors should be summoned, the person making the report shall, unless the court otherwise directs, summon that meeting for the time, date and place proposed in his report.

The meeting is then deemed to have been summoned under section 257 in Part VIII, and subsections (2) and (3) of that section, and sections 258 to 263 apply accordingly.

SEC. 275   Summary administration

275(1)   [Issue of certificate]   Where on the hearing of a debtor's petition the court makes a bankruptcy order and the case is as specified in the next subsection, the court shall, if it appears to it appropriate to do so, issue a certificate for the summary administration of the bankrupt's estate.

275(2)   [Case for issue of certificate]   That case is where it appears to the court—

(a) that if a bankruptcy order were made the aggregate amount of the bankruptcy debts so far as unsecured would be less than the small bankruptcies level (within the meaning given by section 273), and

(b) that within the period of 5 years ending with the presentation of the petition the debtor has neither been adjudged bankrupt nor made a composition with his creditors in satisfaction of his debts or a scheme of arrangement of his affairs,

whether the bankruptcy order is made because it does not appear to the court as mentioned in section 273(1)(b) or (d), or it is made beause the court thinks it would be inappropriate to make an interim order under section 252.

275(3)   [Revocation of certificate by court]   The court may at any time revoke a certificate issued under this section if it appears to it that, on any grounds existing at the time the certificate was issued, the certificate ought not to have been issued.

OTHER CASES FOR SPECIAL CONSIDERATION

SEC. 276 Default in connection with voluntary arrangement

276(1) **[Conditions for sec. 264(1)(c) bankruptcy order]** The court shall not make a bankruptcy order on a petition under section 264(1)(c) (supervisor of, or person bound by, voluntary arrangement proposed and approved) unless it is satisfied—

(a) that the debtor has failed to comply with his obligations under the voluntary arrangement, or

(b) that information which was false or misleading in any material particular or which contained material omissions—

(i) was contained in any statement of affairs or other document supplied by the debtor under Part VIII to any person, or

(ii) was otherwise made available by the debtor to his creditors at or in connection with a meeting summoned under that Part, or

(c) that the debtor has failed to do all such things as may for the purposes of the voluntary arrangement have been reasonably required of him by the supervisor of the arrangement.

276(2) **[Expenses]** Where a bankruptcy order is made on a petition under section 264(1)(c), any expenses properly incurred as expenses of the administration of the voluntary arrangement in question shall be a first charge on the bankrupt's estate.

SEC. 277 Petition based on criminal bankruptcy order

277(1) **[Duty of court]** Subject to section 266(3), the court shall make a bankruptcy order on a petition under section 264(1)(d) on production of a copy of the criminal bankruptcy order on which the petition is based.

This does not apply if it appears to the court that the criminal bankruptcy order has been rescinded on appeal.

277(2) **[Effect of appeal pending]** Subject to the provisions of this Part, the fact that an appeal is pending against any conviction by virtue of which a criminal bankruptcy order was made does not affect any proceedings on a petition under section 264(1)(d) based on that order.

277(3) **[When appeal is pending]** For the purposes of this section, an appeal against a conviction is pending—

(a) in any case, until the expiration of the period of 28 days beginning with the date of conviction;

(b) if notice of appeal to the Court of Appeal is given during that period and during that period the appellant notifies the official receiver of it, until the determination of the appeal and thereafter for so long as an appeal to the House of Lords is pending within the meaning of section 40(5) of the Powers of Criminal Courts Act 1973.

Note
S. 277 repealed by Criminal Justice Act 1988, s. 170(2) and
Sch. 16 as from a day to be appointed.

COMMENCEMENT AND DURATION OF BANKRUPTCY; DISCHARGE

SEC. 278 Commencement and continuance

278 The bankruptcy of an individual against whom a bankruptcy order has been made—

    (a) commences with the day on which the order is made, and

    (b) continues until the individual is discharged under the following provisions of this Chapter.

SEC. 279　Duration

279(1)　**[Discharge from bankruptcy]**　Subject as follows, a bankrupt is discharged from bankruptcy—

    (a) in the case of an individual who was adjudged bankrupt on a petition under section 264(1)(d) or who had been an undischarged bankrupt at any time in the period of 15 years ending with the commencement of the bankruptcy, by an order of the court under the section next following, and

    (b) in any other case, by the expiration of the relevant period under this section.

279(2)　**[Relevant period]**　That period is as follows—

    (a) where a certificate for the summary administration of the bankrupt's estate has been issued and is not revoked before the bankrupt's discharge, the period of 2 years beginning with the commencement of the bankruptcy, and

    (b) in any other case, the period of 3 years beginning with the commencement of the bankruptcy.

279(3)　**[Court order]**　Where the court is satisfied on the application of the official receiver that an undischarged bankrupt in relation to whom subsection (1)(b) applies has failed or is failing to comply with any of his obligations under this Part, the court may order that the relevant period under this section shall cease to run for such period, or until the fulfilment of such conditions (including a condition requiring the court to be satisfied as to any matter), as may be specified in the order.

279(4)　**[Power of annulment]**　This section is without prejudice to any power of the court to annul a bankruptcy order.

SEC. 280　Discharge by order of the court

280(1)　**[Application to court]**　An application for an order of the court discharging an individual from bankruptcy in a case falling within section 279(1)(a) may be made by the bankrupt at any time after the end of the period of 5 years beginning with the commencement of the bankruptcy.

280(2)　**[Powers of court]**　On an application under this section the court may—

    (a) refuse to discharge the bankrupt from bankruptcy,

    (b) make an order discharging him absolutely, or

    (c) make an order discharging him subject to such conditions with respect to any income which may subsequently become due to him, or with respect to property devolving upon him, or acquired by him, after his discharge, as may be specified in the order.

280(3)　**[Commencement of effect of order]**　The court may provide for an order falling within subsection (2)(b) or (c) to have immediate effect or to have its effect suspended for such period, or until the fulfilment of such conditions (including a condition requiring the court to be satisfied as to any matter), as may be specified in the order.

SEC. 281 Effect of discharge

281(1) [Discharge qualified release] Subject as follows, where a bankrupt is discharged, the discharge releases him from all the bankruptcy debts, but has no effect—

    (a) on the functions (so far as they remain to be carried out) of the trustee of his estate, or

    (b) on the operation, for the purposes of the carrying out of those functions, of the provisions of this Part;

and, in particular, discharge does not affect the right of any creditor of the bankrupt to prove in the bankruptcy for any debt from which the bankrupt is released.

281(2) [Enforcement of security] Discharge does not affect the right of any secured creditor of the bankrupt to enforce his security for the payment of a debt from which the bankrupt is released.

281(3) [Fraud etc.] Discharge does not release the bankrupt from any bankruptcy debt which he incurred in respect of, or forbearance in respect of which was secured by means of, any fraud or fraudulent breach of trust to which he was a party.

281(4) [Fines, other penalties] Discharge does not release the bankrupt from any liability in respect of a fine imposed for an offence or from any liability under a recognisance except, in the case of a penalty imposed for an offence under an enactment relating to the public revenue or of a recognisance, with the consent of the Treasury.

Note

S. 281(4) shall have effect as if the reference to a fine included a reference to a confiscation order, as from 3 April 1989 (see Criminal Justice Act 1988, s. 170(1) and Sch. 15, para. 110) (see also Criminal Justice Act 1988 (Commencement No. 7) Order 1989 (S.I. 1989 No. 264 (C. 8)), Appendix A).

281(5) [Debts re damages etc.] Discharge does not, except to such extent and on such conditions as the court may direct, release the bankrupt from any bankruptcy debt which—

    (a) consists in a liability to pay damages for negligence, nuisance or breach of a statutory, contractual or other duty, or to pay damages by virtue of Part I of the Consumer Protection Act 1987, being in either case damages in respect of personal injuries to any person, or

    (b) arises under any order made in family proceedings or in domestic proceedings.

History

In s. 281(5)(a) the words "or to pay damages by virtue of Part I of the Consumer Protection Act 1987, being in either case" substituted for the former word "being" by Consumer Protection Act 1987, s. 48 and Sch. 4, para. 12 as from 1 March 1988 (see S.I. 1988 No. 1680 (C. 51)).

281(6) [Other bankruptcy debts] Discharge does not release the bankrupt from such other bankruptcy debts, not being debts provable in his bankruptcy, as are prescribed.

281(7) [Liability as surety] Discharge does not release any person other than the bankrupt from any liability (whether as partner or co-trustee of the bankrupt or otherwise) from which the bankrupt is released by the discharge, or from any liability as surety for the bankrupt or as a person in the nature of such a surety.

281(8) [Definitions] In this section—

    "**domestic proceedings**" means domestic proceedings within the meaning of the Magistrates' Courts Act 1980 and any proceedings which would be such proceedings but for section 65(1)(ii) of that Act (proceedings for variation of order for periodical payments);

"**family proceedings**" means the same as in Part V of the Matrimonial and Family Proceedings Act 1984;

"**fine**" means the same as in the Magistrates' Courts Act 1980; and

"**personal injuries**" includes death and any disease or other impairment of a person's physical or mental condition.

SEC. 282   Court's power to annul bankruptcy order

282(1)   [Power of annulment]   The court may annul a bankruptcy order if it at any time appears to the court—

    (a) that, on any grounds existing at the time the order was made, the order ought not to have been made, or

    (b) that, to the extent required by the rules, the bankruptcy debts and the expenses of the bankruptcy have all, since the making of the order, been either paid or secured for to the satisfaction of the court.

282(2)   [Where petition under sec. 264(1)(a), (b), (c)]   The court may annul a bankruptcy order made against an individual on a petition under paragraph (a), (b) or (c) of section 264(1) if it at any time appears to the court, on an application by the Official Petitioner—

    (a) that the petition was pending at a time when a criminal bankruptcy order was made against the individual or was presented after such an order was so made, and

    (b) no appeal is pending (within the meaning of section 277) against the individual's conviction of any offence by virtue of which the criminal bankruptcy order was made;

and the court shall annul a bankruptcy order made on a petition under section 264(1)(d) if it at any time appears to the court that the criminal bankruptcy order on which the petition was based has been rescinded in consequence of an appeal.

Note
S. 282(2) repealed by Criminal Justice Act 1988, s. 170(2)
and Sch. 16 as from a day to be appointed.

282(3)   [Annulment whether or not discharged]   The court may annul a bankruptcy order whether or not the bankrupt has been discharged from the bankruptcy.

282(4)   [Effect of annulment]   Where the court annuls a bankruptcy order (whether under this section or under section 261 in Part VIII)—

    (a) any sale or other disposition of property, payment made or other thing duly done, under any provision in this Group of Parts, by or under the authority of the official receiver or a trustee of the bankrupt's estate or by the court is valid, but

    (b) if any of the bankrupt's estate is then vested, under any such provision, in such a trustee, it shall vest in such person as the court may appoint or, in default of any such appointment, revert to the bankrupt on such terms (if any) as the court may direct;

and the court may include in its order such supplemental provisions as may be authorised by the rules.

282(5)   [Undischarged bankrupt under sec. 279]   In determining for the purposes of section 279 whether a person was an undischarged bankrupt at any time, any time

[The next page is 53,801]

when he was a bankrupt by virtue of an order that was subsequently annulled is to be disregarded.

Chapter II — Protection of Bankrupt's Estate and Investigation of His Affairs

SEC. 283 Definition of bankrupt's estate

283(1) **[Bankrupt's estate]** Subject as follows, a bankrupt's estate for the purposes of any of this Group of Parts comprises—

    (a) all property belonging to or vested in the bankrupt at the commencement of the bankruptcy, and

    (b) any property which by virtue of any of the following provisions of this Part is comprised in that estate or is treated as falling within the preceding paragraph.

283(2) **[Non-application of sec. 283(1)]** Subsection (1) does not apply to—

    (a) such tools, books, vehicles and other items of equipment as are necessary to the bankrupt for use personally by him in his employment, business or vocation;

    (b) such clothing, bedding, furniture, household equipment and provisions as are necessary for satisfying the basic domestic needs of the bankrupt and his family.

This subsection is subject to section 308 in Chapter IV (certain excluded property reclaimable by trustee).

283(3) **[Further non-application of sec. 283(1)]** Subsection (1) does not apply to—

    (a) property held by the bankrupt on trust or any other person, or

    (b) the right of nomination to a vacant ecclesiastical benefice.

283(4) **[References to property]** References in any of this Group of Parts to property, in relation to a bankrupt, include references to any power exercisable by him over or in respect of property except in so far as the power is exercisable over or in respect of property not for the time being comprised in the bankrupt's estate and—

    (a) is so exercisable at a time after either the official receiver has had his release in respect of that estate under section 299(2) in Chapter III or a meeting summoned by the trustee of that estate under section 331 in Chapter IV has been held, or

    (b) cannot be so exercised for the benefit of the bankrupt;

and a power exercisable over or in respect of property is deemed for the purposes of any of this Group of Parts to vest in the person entitled to exercise it at the time of the transaction or event by virtue of which it is exercisable by that person (whether or not it becomes so exercisable at that time).

283(5) **[Property in bankrupt's estate]** For the purposes of any such provision in the Group of Parts, property comprised in a bankrupt's estate is so comprised subject to the rights of any person other than the bankrupt (whether as a secured creditor of the bankrupt or otherwise) in relation thereto, but disregarding—

   (a) any rights in relation to which a statement such as is required by section 269(1)(a) was made in the petition on which the bankrupt was adjudged bankrupt, and

   (b) any rights which have been otherwise given up in accordance with the rules.

283(6)   **[Other enactments]**   This section has effect subject to the provisions of any enactment not contained in this Act under which any property is to be excluded from a bankrupt's estate.

SEC. 284   Restrictions on dispositions of property

284(1)   **[Where person adjudged bankrupt]**   Where a person is adjudged bankrupt, any disposition of property made by that person in the period to which this section applies is void except to the extent that it is or was made with the consent of the court, or is or was subsequently ratified by the court.

284(2)   **[Application of sec. 284(1) to payment]**   Subsection (1) applies to a payment (whether in cash or otherwise) as it applies to a disposition of property and, accordingly, where any payment is void by virtue of that subsection, the person paid shall hold the sum paid for the bankrupt as part of his estate.

284(3)   **[Relevant period]**   This section applies to the period beginning with the day of the presentation of the petition for the bankruptcy order and ending with the vesting, under Chapter IV of this Part, of the bankrupt's estate in a trustee.

284(4)   **[Limit to effect of sec. 284(1)–(3)]**   The preceding provisions of this section do not give a remedy against any person—

   (a) in respect of any property or payment which he received before the commencement of the bankruptcy in good faith, for value and without notice that the petition had been presented, or

   (b) in respect of any interest in property which derives from an interest in respect of which there is, by virtue of this subsection, no remedy.

284(5)   **[Debt after commencement of bankruptcy]**   Where after the commencement of his bankruptcy the bankrupt has incurred a debt to a banker or other person by reason of the making of a payment which is void under this section, that debt is deemed for the purposes of any of this Group of Parts to have been incurred before the commencement of the bankruptcy unless—

   (a) that banker or person had notice of the bankruptcy before the debt was incurred, or

   (b) it is not reasonably practicable for the amount of the payment to be recovered from the person to whom it was made.

284(6)   **[Property not in bankrupt's estate]**   A disposition of property is void under this section notwithstanding that the property is not or, as the case may be, would not be comprised in the bankrupt's estate; but nothing in this section affects any disposition made by a person of property held by him on trust for any other person.

SEC. 285 Restriction on proceedings and remedies

285(1) [Court's power to stay] At any time when proceedings on a bankruptcy petition are pending or an individual has been adjudged bankrupt the court may stay an action, execution or other legal process against the property or person of the debtor or, as the case may be, of the bankrupt.

285(2) [Where proceedings pending against individual] Any court in which proceedings are pending against any individual may, on proof that a bankruptcy petition has been presented in respect of that individual or that he is an undischarged bankrupt, either stay the proceedings or allow them to continue on such terms as it thinks fit.

285(3) [Limit on creditors' actions] After the making of a bankruptcy order no person who is a creditor of the bankrupt in respect of a debt provable in the bankruptcy shall—

  (a) have any remedy against the property or person of the bankrupt in respect of that debt, or

  (b) before the discharge of the bankrupt, commence any action or other legal proceedings against the bankrupt except with leave of the court and on such terms as the court may impose.

This is subject to sections 346 (enforcement procedures) and 347 (limited right to distress).

285(4) [Right of secured creditor] Subject as follows, subsection (3) does not affect the right of a secured creditor of the bankrupt to enforce his security.

285(5) [Where goods of undischarged bankrupt held by pledge etc.] Where any goods of an undischarged bankrupt are held by any person by way of pledge, pawn or other security, the official receiver may, after giving notice in writing of his intention to do so, inspect the goods.

Where such a notice has been given to any person, that person is not entitled, without leave of the court, to realise his security unless he has given the trustee of the bankrupt's estate a reasonable opportunity of inspecting the goods and of exercising the bankrupt's right of redemption.

285(6) [Interpretation] References in this section to the property or goods of the bankrupt are to any of his property or goods, whether or not comprised in his estate.

SEC. 286 Power to appoint interim receiver

286(1) [Court's power] The court may, if it is shown to be necessary for the protection of the debtor's property, at any time after the presentation of a bankruptcy petition and before making a bankruptcy order, appoint the official receiver to be interim receiver of the debtor's property.

286(2) [Appointment of person instead of official receiver] Where the court has, on a debtor's petition, appointed an insolvency practitioner under section 273 and it is shown to the court as mentioned in subsection (1) of this section, the court may, without making a bankruptcy order, appoint that practitioner, instead of the official receiver, to be interim receiver of the debtor's property.

286(3) [Rights, powers etc. of interim receiver] The court may by an order appointing any person to be an interim receiver direct that his powers shall be limited or restricted in any respect; but, save as so directed, an interim receiver has, in relation to the debtor's property, all the rights, powers, duties and immunities of a receiver and manager under the next section.

286(4) [Contents of court order] An order of the court appointing any person to be an interim receiver shall require that person to take immediate possession of the debtor's property or, as the case may be, the part of it to which his powers as interim receiver are limited.

286(5) [Duties of debtor] Where an interim receiver has been appointed, the debtor shall give him such inventory of his property and such other information, and shall attend on the interim receiver at such times, as the latter may for the purpose of carrying out his functions under this section reasonably require.

286(6) [Application of sec. 285(3)] Where an interim receiver is appointed, section 285(3) applies for the period between the appointment and the making of a bankruptcy order on the petition, or the dismissal of the petition, as if the appointment were the making of such an order.

286(7) [Ceasing to be interim receiver] A person ceases to be interim receiver of a debtor's property if the bankruptcy petition relating to the debtor is dismissed, if a bankruptcy order is made on the petition or if the court by order otherwise terminates the appointment.

286(8) [Interpretation] References in this section to the debtor's property are to all his property, whether or not it would be comprised in his estate if he were adjudged bankrupt.

SEC. 287 Receivership pending appointment of trustee

287(1) [Official receiver, receiver and manager] Between the making of a bankruptcy order and the time at which the bankrupt's estate vests in a trustee under Chapter IV of this Part, the official receiver is the receiver and (subject to section 370 (special manager)) the manager of the bankrupt's estate and is under a duty to act as such.

287(2) [Function and powers of official receiver] The function of the official receiver while acting as receiver or manager of the bankrupt's estate under this section is to protect the estate; and for this purpose—

   (a) he has the same powers as if he were a receiver or manager appointed by the High Court, and

   (b) he is entitled to sell or otherwise dispose of any perishable goods comprised in the estate and any other goods so comprised the value of which is likely to diminish if they are not disposed of.

287(3) [Steps re protecting property] The official receiver while acting as receiver or manager of the estate under this section—

   (a) shall take all such steps as he thinks fit for protecting any property which may be claimed for the estate by the trustee of that estate,

   (b) is not, except in pursuance of directions given by the Secretary of State, required to do anything that involves his incurring expenditure,

IA 1986, sec. 286(4)   [The next page is 53,901]

(c) may, if he thinks fit (and shall, if so directed by the court) at any time summon a general meeting of the bankrupt's creditors.

287(4)   [Liability of official receiver]   Where—

(a) the official receiver acting as receiver or manager of the estate under this section seizes or disposes of any property which is not comprised in the estate, and

(b) at the time of the seizure or disposal the official receiver believes, and has reasonable grounds for believing, that he is entitled (whether in pursuance of an order of the court or otherwise) to seize or dispose of that property,

the official receiver is not liable to any person in respect of any loss or damage resulting from the seizure or disposal except in so far as that loss or damage is caused by his negligence; and he has a lien on the property, or the proceeds of its sale, for such of the expenses of the bankruptcy as were incurred in connection with the seizure or disposal.

287(5)   [Non-application]   This section does not apply where by virtue of section 297 (appointment of trustee; special cases) the bankrupt's estate vests in a trustee immediately on the making of the bankruptcy order.

SEC. 288   Statement of affairs

288(1)   [Submission of statement to official receiver]   Where a bankruptcy order has been made otherwise than on a debtor's petition, the bankrupt shall submit a statement of his affairs to the official receiver before the end of the period of 21 days beginning with the commencement of the bankruptcy.

288(2)   [Contents of statement]   The statement of affairs shall contain—

(a) such particulars of the bankrupt's creditors and of his debts and other liabilities and of his assets as may be prescribed, and

(b) such other information as may be prescribed.

Note
See also The Insolvency Rules 1986, r. 6.58–6.66.

288(3)   [Powers of official receiver]   The official receiver may, if he thinks fit—

(a) release the bankrupt from his duty under subsection (1), or

(b) extend the period specified in that subsection;

and where the official receiver has refused to exercise a power conferred by this section, the court, if it thinks fit, may exercise it.

288(4)   [Penalty for non-compliance]   A bankrupt who—

(a) without reasonable excuse fails to comply with the obligation imposed by this section, or

(b) without reasonable excuse submits a statement of affairs that does not comply with the prescribed requirements,

is guilty of a contempt of court and liable to be punished accordingly (in addition to any other punishment to which he may be subject).

SEC. 289   Investigatory duties of official receiver

289(1)   **[Investigation and report]**   Subject to subsection (5) below, it is the duty of the official receiver to investigate the conduct and affairs of every bankrupt and to make such report (if any) to the court as he thinks fit.

289(2)   **[Where application under sec. 280]**   Where an application is made by the bankrupt under section 280 for his discharge from bankruptcy, it is the duty of the official receiver to make a report to the court with respect to the prescribed matters; and the court shall consider that report before determining what order (if any) to make under that section.

Note
See also The Insolvency Rules 1986, r. 6.218.

289(3)   **[Report prima facie evidence]**   A report by the official receiver under this section shall, in any proceedings, be prima facie evidence of the facts stated in it.

289(4)   **[Interpretation of sec. 289(1)]**   In subsection (1) the reference to the conduct and affairs of a bankrupt includes his conduct and affairs before the making of the order by which he was adjudged bankrupt.

289(5)   **[Where certificate for administration]**   Where a certificate for the summary administration of the bankrupt's estate is for the time being in force, the official receiver shall carry out an investigation under subsection (1) only if he thinks fit.

SEC. 290   Public examination of bankrupt

290(1)   **[Application to court]**   Where a bankruptcy order has been made, the official receiver may at any time before the discharge of the bankrupt apply to the court for the public examination of the bankrupt.

290(2)   **[Duty of official receiver to make application]**   Unless the court otherwise orders, the official receiver shall make an application under subsection (1) if notice requiring him to do so is given to him, in accordance with the rules, by one of the bankrupt's creditors with the concurrence of not less than one-half, in value, of those creditors (including the creditor giving notice).

290(3)   **[Direction re public examination]**   On an application under subsection (1), the court shall direct that a public examination of the bankrupt shall be held on a day appointed by the court; and the bankrupt shall attend on that day and be publicly examined as to his affairs, dealings and property.

290(4)   **[Persons taking part in examination]**   The following may take part in the public examination of the bankrupt and may question him concerning his affairs, dealings and property and the causes of his failure, namely—

   (a)   the official receiver and, in the case of an individual adjudged bankrupt on a petition under section 264(1)(d), the Official Petitioner,

   (b)   the trustee of the bankrupt's estate, if his appointment has taken effect,

   (c)   any person who has been appointed as special manager of the bankrupt's estate or business.

   (d)   any creditor of the bankrupt who has tendered a proof in the bankruptcy.

290(5)   **[Penalty re non-attendance]**   If a bankrupt without reasonable excuse fails at any time to attend his public examination under this section he is guilty of a contempt of court and liable to be punished accordingly (in addition to any other punishment to which he may be subject).

SEC. 291　Duties of bankrupt in relation to official receiver

291(1)　[Duties where bankruptcy order made]　Where a bankruptcy order has been made, the bankrupt is under a duty—

   (a)　to deliver possession of his estate to the official receiver, and

   (b)　to deliver up to the official receiver all books, papers and other records of which he has possession or control and which relate to his estate and affairs (including any which would be privileged from disclosure in any proceedings).

291(2)　[Property not capable of delivery to official receiver]　In the case of any part of the bankrupt's estate which consists of things possession of which cannot be delivered to the official receiver, and in the case of any property that may be claimed for the bankrupt's estate by the trustee, it is the bankrupt's duty to do all things as may reasonably be required by the official receiver for the protection of those things or that property.

291(3)　[Non-application of sec. 291(1), (2)]　Subsections (1) and (2) do not apply where by virtue of section 297 below the bankrupt's estate vests in a trustee immediately on the making of the bankruptcy order.

291(4)　[Bankrupt to give information]　The bankrupt shall give the official receiver such inventory of his estate and such other information, and shall attend on the official receiver at such times, as the official receiver may for any of the purposes of this Chapter reasonably require.

291(5)　[Application of sec. 291(4)]　Subsection (4) applies to a bankrupt after his discharge.

291(6)　[Penalty for non-compliance]　If the bankrupt without reasonable excuse fails to comply with any obligation imposed by this section, he is guilty of a contempt of court and liable to be punished accordingly (in addition to any other punishment to which he may be subject).

Chapter III — Trustees In Bankruptcy

TENURE OF OFFICE AS TRUSTEE

SEC. 292　Power to make appointments

292(1)　[Exercise of power]　The power to appoint a person as trustee of a bankrupt's estate (whether the first such trustee or a trustee appointed to fill any vacancy) is exercisable—

   (a)　except at a time when a certificate for the summary administration of the bankrupt's estate is in force, by a general meeting of the bankrupt's creditors;

   (b)　under section 295(2), 296(2) or 300(6) below in this Chapter, by the Secretary of State; or

   (c)　under section 297, by the court.

292(2)　[Qualification for trustee]　No person may be appointed as trustee of a bankrupt's estate unless he is, at the time of the appointment, qualified to act as an insolvency practitioner in relation to the bankrupt.

292(3)　[Joint trustees]　Any power to appoint a person as trustee of a bankrupt's estate includes power to appoint two or more persons as joint trustees; but such an appointment must make provision as to the circumstances in which the trustees must act together and the circumstances in which one or more of them may act for the others.

292(4)　[Requirement of acceptance of appointment]　The appointment of any person as trustee takes effect only if that person accepts the appointment in accordance with the rules. Subject to this, the appointment of any person as trustee takes effect at the time specified in his certificate of appointment.

292(5)　[Effect]　This section is without prejudice to the provisions of this Chapter under which the official receiver is, in certain circumstances, to be trustee of the estate.

SEC. 293　Summoning of meeting to appoint first trustee

293(1)　[Duty of official receiver]　Where a bankruptcy order has been made and no certificate for the summary administration of the bankrupt's estate has been issued, it is the duty of the official receiver, as soon as practicable in the period of 12 weeks beginning with the day on which the order was made, to decide whether to summon a general meeting of the bankrupt's creditors for the purpose of appointing a trustee of the bankrupt's estate.

　　This section does not apply where the bankruptcy order was made on a petition under section 264(1)(d) (criminal bankruptcy); and it is subject to the provision made in sections 294(3) and 297(6) below.

Note
In s. 293(1) the words "does not apply where the bankruptcy order was made on a petition under section 264(1)(d) (criminal bankruptcy) and it" repealed by Criminal Justice Act 1988, s. 170(2) and Sch. 16 as from a day to be appointed.

293(2)　[Duty if no meeting summoned]　Subject to the next section, if the official receiver decides not to summon such a meeting, he shall, before the end of the period of 12 weeks above mentioned, give notice of his decision to the court and to every creditor of the bankrupt who is known to the official receiver or is identified in the bankrupt's statement of affairs.

293(3)　[Official receiver trustee from sec. 293(2) notice]　As from the giving to the court of a notice under subsection (2), the official receiver is the trustee of the bankrupt's estate.

SEC. 294　Power of creditors to requisition meeting

294(1)　[Request to official receiver]　Where in the case of any bankruptcy—

　　(a)　the official receiver has not yet summoned, or has decided not to summon, a general meeting of the bankrupt's creditors for the purpose of appointing the trustee, and

　　(b)　a certificate for the summary administration of the estate is not for the time being in force,

any creditor of the bankrupt may request the official receiver to summon such a meeting for that purpose.

294(2) **[Duty to summon meeting on request]** If such a request appears to the official receiver to be made with the concurrence of not less than one-quarter, in value, of the bankrupt's creditors (including the creditor making the request), it is the duty of the official receiver to summon the requested meeting.

294(3) **[Where sec. 294(2) duty has arisen]** Accordingly, where the duty imposed by subsection (2) has arisen, the official receiver is required neither to reach a decision for the purposes of section 293(1) nor (if he has reached one) to serve any notice under section 293(2).

SEC. 295   Failure of meeting to appoint trustee

295(1) **[Duty of official receiver]** If a meeting summoned under section 293 or 294 is held but no appointment of a person as trustee is made, it is the duty of the official receiver to decide whether to refer the need for an appointment to the Secretary of State.

295(2) **[Duty of Secretary of State]** On a reference made in pursuance of that decision, the Secretary of State shall either make an appointment or decline to make one.

295(3) **[Notice to court]** If—

   (a) the official receiver decides not to refer the need for an appointment to the Secretary of State, or

   (b) on such a reference the Secretary of State declines to make an appointment,

the official receiver shall give notice of his decision or, as the case may be, of the Secretary of State's decision to the court.

295(4) **[As from notice official receiver trustee]** As from the giving of notice under subsection (3) in a case in which no notice has been given under section 293(2), the official receiver shall be trustee of the bankrupt's estate.

SEC. 296   Appointment of trustee by Secretary of State

296(1) **[Application for appointment instead of official receiver]** At any time when the official receiver is the trustee of a bankrupt's estate by virtue of any provision of this Chapter (other than section 297(1) below) he may apply to the Secretary of State for the appointment of a person as trustee instead of the official receiver.

296(2) **[Duty of Secretary of State]** On an application under subsection (1) the Secretary of State shall either make an appointment or decline to make one.

296(3) **[Making of application]** Such an application may be made notwithstanding that the Secretary of State has declined to make an appointment either on a previous application under subsection (1) or on a reference under section 295 or under section 300(4) below.

296(4) **[Notice, etc., re appointment]** Where the trustee of a bankrupt's estate has been appointed by the Secretary of State (whether under this section or otherwise), the trustee shall give notice to the bankrupt's creditors of his appointment or, if the court so allows, shall advertise his appointment in accordance with the court's directions.

296(5)   **[Contents of notice]**   In that notice or advertisement the trustee shall—

(a) state whether he proposes to summon a general meeting of the bankrupt's creditors for the purpose of establishing a creditors' committee under section 301, and

(b) if he does not propose to summon such a meeting, set out the power of the creditors under this Part to require him to summon one.

SEC. 297   Special cases

297(1)   **[Where sec. 264(1)(d) bankruptcy order]**   Where a bankruptcy order is made on a petition under section 264(1)(d) (criminal bankruptcy), the official receiver shall be trustee of the bankrupt's estate.

Note
S. 297(1) repealed by Criminal Justice Act 1988, s. 170(2)
and Sch. 16 as from a day to be appointed.

297(2)   **[Where court issues certificate for summary administration]**   Subject to the next subsection, where the court issues a certificate for the summary administration of a bankrupt's estate, the official receiver shall, as from the issue of that certificate, be the trustee.

297(3)   **[Qualification to sec. 297(2)]**   Where such a certificate is issued or is in force, the court may, if it thinks fit, appoint a person other than the official receiver as trustee.

297(4)   **[Where no certificate for summary administration]**   Where a bankruptcy order is made in a case in which an insolvency practitioner's report has been submitted to the court under section 274 but no certificate for the summary administration of the estate is issued, the court, if it thinks fit, may on making the order appoint the person who made the report as trustee.

297(5)   **[Where there is supervisor]**   Where a bankruptcy order is made (whether or not on a petition under section 264(1)(c)) at a time when there is a supervisor of a voluntary arrangement approved in relation to the bankrupt under Part VIII, the court, if it thinks fit, may on making the order appoint the supervisor of the arrangement as trustee.

297(6)   **[Exception re sec. 293(1) duty]**   Where an appointment is made under subsection (4) or (5) of this section, the official receiver is not under the duty imposed by section 293(1) (to decide whether or not to summon a meeting of creditors).

297(7)   **[Notice where trustee appointed by court]**   Where the trustee of a bankrupt's estate has been appointed by the court, the trustee shall give notice to the bankrupt's creditors of his appointment or, if the court so allows, shall advertise his appointment in accordance with the directions of the court.

297(8)   **[Contents of notice]**   In that notice or advertisement he shall—

(a) state whether he proposes to summon a general meeting of the bankrupt's creditors for the purpose of establishing a creditors' committee under section 301 below, and

(b) if he does not propose to summon such a meeting, set out the power of the creditors under this Part to require him to summon one.

SEC. 298   Removal of trustee; vacation of office

298(1)   **[Removal by court order or creditors' meeting]**   Subject as follows, the trustee of a bankrupt's estate may be removed from office only by an order of the court or by a general meeting of the bankrupt's creditors summoned specially for that purpose in accordance with the rules.

298(2)   [Where official receiver trustee under sec. 297(1)]   Where the official receiver is trustee by virtue of section 297(1), he shall not be removed from office under this section.

298(3)   [Where certificate for summary administration]   A general meeting of the bankrupt's creditors shall not be held for the purpose of removing the trustee at any time when a certificate for the summary administration of the estate is in force.

298(4)   [Where official receiver trustee under sec. 293(3), 295(4)]   Where the official receiver is trustee by virtue of section 293(3) or 295(4) or a trustee is appointed by the Secretary of State or (otherwise than under section 297(5)) by the court, a general meeting of the bankrupt's creditors shall be summoned for the purpose of replacing the trustee only if—

(a)   the trustee thinks fit, or

(b)   the court so directs, or

(c)   the meeting is requested by one of the bankrupt's creditors with the concurrence of not less than one-quarter, in value, of the creditors (including the creditor making the request).

298(5)   [Where trustee appointed by Secretary of State]   If the trustee was appointed by the Secretary of State, he may be removed by a direction of the Secretary of State.

298(6)   [Vacation of office]   The trustee (not being the official receiver) shall vacate office if he ceases to be a person who is for the time being qualified to act as an insolvency practitioner in relation to the bankrupt.

298(7)   [Resignation]   The trustee may, in the prescribed circumstances, resign his office by giving notice of his resignation to the court.

298(8)   [Vacation on sec. 331 notice]   The trustee shall vacate office on giving notice to the court that a final meeting has been held under section 331 in Chapter IV and of the decision (if any) of that meeting.

298(9)   [When bankruptcy order annulled]   The trustee shall vacate office if the bankruptcy order is annulled.

SEC. 299   Release of trustee

299(1)   [Time of release for official receiver]   Where the official receiver has ceased to be the trustee of a bankrupt's estate and a person is appointed in his stead, the official receiver shall have his release with effect from the following time, that is to say—

(a)   where that person is appointed by a general meeting of the bankrupt's creditors or by the Secretary of State, the time at which the official receiver gives notice to the court that he has been replaced, and

(b)   where that person is appointed by the court, such time as the court may determine.

299(2)   [Time of release if notice given by official receiver]   If the official receiver while he is the trustee gives notice to the Secretary of State that the administration of the bankrupt's estate in accordance with Chapter IV of this Part is for practical purposes complete, he shall have his release with effect from such time as the Secretary of State may determine.

299(3)   **[Time of release for person not official receiver]**   A person other than the official receiver who has ceased to be the trustee shall have his release with effect from the following time, that is to say—

   (a) in the case of a person who has been removed from office by a general meeting of the bankrupt's creditors that has not resolved against his release or who has died, the time at which notice is given to the court in accordance with the rules that that person has ceased to hold office;

   (b) in the case of a person who has been removed from office by a general meeting of the bankrupt's creditors that has resolved against his release, or by the court, or by the Secretary of State, or who has vacated office under section 298(6), such time as the Secretary of State may, on an application by that person, determine;

   (c) in the case of a person who has resigned, such time as may be prescribed;

   (d) in the case of a person who has vacated office under section 298(8)—

      (i) if the final meeting referred to in that subsection has resolved against that person's release, such time as the Secretary of State may, on an application by that person, determine; and

      (ii) if that meeting has not so resolved, the time at which the person vacated office.

299(4)   **[Time of release where bankruptcy order annulled]**   Where a bankruptcy order is annulled, the trustee at the time of the annulment has his release with effect from such time as the court may determine.

299(5)   **[Effect of release]**   Where the official receiver or the trustee has his release under this section, he shall, with effect from the time specified in the preceding provisions of this section, be discharged from all liability both in respect of acts or omissions of his in the administration of the estate and otherwise in relation to his conduct as trustee.

But nothing in this section prevents the exercise, in relation to a person who has had his release under this section, of the court's powers under section 304.

SEC. 300   Vacancy in office of trustee

300(1)   **[Application]**   This section applies where the appointment of any person as trustee of a bankrupt's estate fails to take effect or, such an appointment having taken effect, there is otherwise a vacancy in the office of trustee.

300(2)   **[Official receiver trustee]**   The official receiver shall be trustee until the vacancy is filled.

300(3)   **[Summoning creditors' meeting]**   The official receiver may summon a general meeting of the bankrupt's creditors for the purpose of filling the vacancy and shall summon such a meeting if required to do so in pursuance of section 314(7) (creditors' requisition).

300(4)   **[If no meeting summoned within 28 days]**   If at the end of the period of 28 days beginning with the day on which the vacancy first came to the official receiver's attention he has not summoned, and is not proposing to summon, a general meeting of creditors for the purpose of filling the vacancy, he shall refer the need for an appointment to the Secretary of State.

300(5)   [Where certificate for summary administration]   Where a certificate for the summary administration of the estate is for the time being in force—

(a) the official receiver may refer the need to fill any vacancy to the court or, if the vacancy arises because a person appointed by the Secretary of State has ceased to hold office, to the court or the Secretary of State, and

(b) subsections (3) and (4) of this section do not apply.

300(6)   [Duty of Secretary of State re sec. 300(4), (5)]   On a reference to the Secretary of State under subsection (4) or (5) the Secretary of State shall either make an appointment or decline to make one.

300(7)   [If no appointment on sec. 300(4), (5) reference]   If on a reference under subsection (4) or (5) no appointment is made, the official receiver shall continue to be trustee of the bankrupt's estate, but without prejudice to his power to make a further reference.

300(8)   [Interpretation]   References in this section to a vacancy include a case where it is necessary, in relation to any property which is or may be comprised in a bankrupt's estate, to revive the trusteeship of that estate after holding of a final meeting summoned under section 331 or the giving by the official receiver of notice under section 299(2).

CONTROL OF TRUSTEE

SEC. 301   Creditors' committee

301(1)   [Meeting may establish committee]   Subject as follows, a general meeting of a bankrupt's creditors (whether summoned under the preceding provisions of this Chapter or otherwise) may, in accordance with the rules, establish a committee (known as "the creditors' committee") to exercise the functions conferred on it by or under this Act.

301(2)   [Exception]   A general meeting of the bankrupt's creditors shall not establish such a committee, or confer any functions on such a committee, at any time when the official receiver is the trustee of the bankrupt's estate, except in connection with an appointment made by that meeting of a person to be trustee instead of the official receiver.

SEC. 302   Exercise by Secretary of State of functions of creditors' committee

302(1)   [Where official receiver trustee]   The creditors' committee is not to be able or required to carry out its functions at any time when the official receiver is trustee of the bankrupt's estate; but at any such time the functions of the committee under this Act shall be vested in the Secretary of State, except to the extent that the rules otherwise provide.

302(2)   [Where no committee]   Where in the case of any bankruptcy there is for the time being no creditors' committee and the trustee of the bankrupt's estate is a person other than the official receiver, the functions of such a committee shall be vested in the Secretary of State, except to the extent that the rules otherwise provide.

SEC. 303   General control of trustee by the court

303(1)   **[Application to court]**   If a bankrupt or any of his creditors or any other person is dissatisfied by any act, omission or decision of a trustee of the bankrupt's estate, he may apply to the court; and on such an application the court may confirm, reverse or modify any act or decision of the trustee, may give him directions or may make such other order as it thinks fit.

303(2)   **[Application by trustee for directions]**   The trustee of a bankrupt's estate may apply to the court for directions in relation to any particular matter arising under the bankruptcy.

SEC. 304   Liability of trustee

304(1)   **[Powers of court on application]**   Where on an application under this section the court is satisfied—

   (a) that the trustee of a bankrupt's estate has misapplied or retained, or become accountable for, any money or other property comprised in the bankrupt's estate, or

   (b) that a bankrupt's estate has suffered any loss in consequence of any misfeasance or breach of fiduciary or other duty by a trustee of the estate in the carrying out of his functions,

the court may order the trustee, for the benefit of the estate, to repay, restore or account for money or other property (together with interest at such rate as the court thinks just) or, as the case may require, to pay such sum by way of compensation in respect of the misfeasance or breach of fiduciary or other duty as the court thinks just.

This is without prejudice to any liability arising apart from this section.

304(2)   **[Applicants]**   An application under this section may be made by the official receiver, the Secretary of State, a creditor of the bankrupt or (whether or not there is, or is likely to be, a surplus for the purposes of section 330(5) (final distribution)) the bankrupt himself.

But the leave of the court is required for the making of an application if it is to be made by the bankrupt or if it is to be made after the trustee has had his release under section 299.

304(3)   **[Limit on liability]**   Where—

   (a) the trustee seizes or disposes of any property which is not comprised in the bankrupt's estate, and

   (b) at the time of the seizure or disposal the trustee believes, and has reasonable grounds for believing, that he is entitled (whether in pursuance of an order of the court or otherwise) to seize or dispose of that property,

the trustee is not liable to any person (whether under this section or otherwise) in respect of any loss or damage resulting from the seizure or disposal except in so far as that loss or damage is caused by the negligence of the trustee; and he has a lien on the property, or the proceeds of its sale, for such of the expenses of the bankruptcy as were incurred in connection with the seizure or disposal.

Chapter IV — Administration by Trustee

PRELIMINARY

SEC. 305 General functions of trustee

305(1) [Application of Ch. IV] This Chapter applies in relation to any bankruptcy where either—

  (a) the appointment of a person as trustee of a bankrupt's estate takes effect, or

  (b) the official receiver becomes trustee of a bankrupt's estate.

305(2) [Function of trustee] The function of the trustee is to get in, realise and distribute the bankrupt's estate in accordance with the following provisions of this Chapter; and in the carrying out of that function and in the management of the bankrupt's estate the trustee is entitled, subject to those provisions, to use his own discretion.

305(3) [Duties of trustee] It is the duty of the trustee, if he is not the official receiver—

  (a) to furnish the official receiver with such information,

  (b) to produce to the official receiver, and permit inspection by the official receiver of, such books, papers and other records, and

  (c) to give the official receiver such other assistance,

as the official receiver may reasonably require for the purpose of enabling him to carry out his functions in relation to the bankruptcy.

305(4) [Official name of trustee] The official name of the trustee shall be "the trustee of the estate of . . . ., a bankrupt" (inserting the name of the bankrupt); but he may be referred to as "the trustee in bankruptcy" of the particular bankrupt.

ACQUISITION, CONTROL AND REALISATION OF BANKRUPT'S ESTATE

SEC. 306 Vesting of bankrupt's estate in trustee

306(1) [Time of vesting] The bankrupt's estate shall vest in the trustee immediately on his appointment taking effect or, in the case of the official receiver, on his becoming trustee.

306(2) [Mode of vesting] Where any property which is, or is to be, comprised in the bankrupt's estate vests in the trustee (whether under this section or under any other provision of this Part), it shall so vest without any conveyance, assignment or transfer.

SEC. 307   After-acquired property

307(1)   [Power of trustee]   Subject to this section and section 309, the trustee may by notice in writing claim for the bankrupt's estate any property which has been acquired by, or has devolved upon, the bankrupt since the commencement of the bankruptcy.

307(2)   [Limit on sec. 307(1) notice]   A notice under this section shall not be served in respect of—

   (a) any property falling within subsection (2) or (3) of section 283 in Chapter II.

   (b) any property which by virtue of any other enactment is excluded from the bankrupt's estate, or

   (c) without prejudice to section 280(2)(c) (order of court on application for discharge), any property which is acquired by, or devolves upon, the bankrupt after his discharge.

307(3)   [Vesting on service of notice]   Subject to the next subsection, upon the service on the bankrupt of a notice under this section the property to which the notice relates shall vest in the trustee as part of the bankrupt's estate; and the trustee's title to that property has relation back to the time at which the property was acquired by, or devolved upon, the bankrupt.

307(4)   [Outsiders]   Where, whether before or after service of a notice under this section—

   (a) a person acquires property in good faith, for value and without notice of the bankruptcy, or

   (b) a banker enters into a transaction in good faith and without such notice,

the trustee is not in respect of that property or transaction entitled by virtue of this section to any remedy against that person or banker, or any person whose title to any property derives from that person or banker.

307(5)   [Interpretation]   References in this section to property do not include any property which, as part of the bankrupt's income, may be the subject of an income payments order under section 310.

SEC. 308   Vesting in trustee of certain items of excess value

308(1)   [Claim by trustee in writing]   Subject to the next section, where—

   (a) property is excluded by virtue of section 283(2) (tools of trade, household effects, etc.) from the bankrupt's estate, and

   (b) it appears to the trustee that the realisable value of the whole or any part of that property exceeds the cost of a reasonable replacement for that property or that part of it,

the trustee may by notice in writing claim that property or, as the case may be, that part of it for the bankrupt's estate.

308(2)   [Vesting on service of sec. 308(1) notice]   Upon the service on the bankrupt of a notice under this section, the property to which the notice relates vests in the trustee as part of the bankrupt's estate; and, except against a purchaser in good faith, for value and without notice of the bankruptcy, the trustee's title to that property has relation back to the commencement of the bankruptcy.

308(3) **[Application of funds by trustee]** The trustee shall apply funds comprised in the estate to the purchase by or on behalf of the bankrupt of a reasonable replacement for any property vested in the trustee under this section; and the duty imposed by this subsection has priority over the obligation of the trustee to distribute the estate.

308(4) **[Reasonable replacement]** For the purposes of this section property is a reasonable replacement for other property if it is reasonably adequate for meeting the needs met by the other property.

SEC. 309 Time-limit for notice under sec. 307 or 308

309(1) **[Timing of notice]** Except with the leave of the court, a notice shall not be served—

- (a) under section 307, after the end of the period of 42 days beginning with the day on which it first came to the knowledge of the trustee that the property in question had been acquired by, or had devolved upon, the bankrupt;
- (b) under section 308, after the end of the period of 42 days beginning with the day on which the property in question first came to the knowledge of the trustee.

309(2) **[Deemed knowledge]** For the purposes of this section—

- (a) anything which comes to the knowledge of the trustee is deemed in relation to any successor of his as trustee to have come to the knowledge of the successor at the same time; and
- (b) anything which comes (otherwise than under paragraph (a)) to the knowledge of a person before he is the trustee is deemed to come to his knowledge on his appointment taking effect or, in the case of the official receiver, on his becoming trustee.

SEC. 310 Income payments orders

310(1) **[Order by court]** The court may, on the application of the trustee, make an order ("an income payments order") claiming for the bankrupt's estate so much of the income of the bankrupt during the period for which the order is in force as may be specified in the order.

310(2) **[Limit on order]** The court shall not make an income payments order the effect of which would be to reduce the income of the bankrupt below what appears to the court to be necessary for meeting the reasonable domestic needs of the bankrupt and his family.

310(3) **[Extent of order]** An income payments order shall, in respect of any payment of income to which it is to apply, either—

- (a) require the bankrupt to pay the trustee an amount equal to so much of that payment as is claimed by the order, or
- (b) require the person making the payment to pay so much of it as is so claimed to the trustee, instead of to the bankrupt.

310(4)   **[Power to discharge or vary attachment of earnings]**   Where the court makes an income payments order it may, if it thinks fit, discharge or vary any attachment of earnings order that is for the time being in force to secure payments by the bankrupt.

310(5)   **[Sums part of estate]**   Sums received by the trustee under an income payments order form part of the bankrupt's estate.

310(6)   **[After discharge of bankrupt]**   An income payments order shall not be made after the discharge of the bankrupt, and if made before, shall not have effect after his discharge except—

   (a) in the case of a discharge under section 279(1)(a) (order of court), by virtue of a condition imposed by the court under section 280(2)(c) (income, etc. after discharge), or

   (b) in the case of a discharge under section 279(1)(b) (expiration of relevant period), by virtue of a provision of the order requiring it to continue in force for a period ending after the discharge but no later than 3 years after the making of the order.

310(7)   **[Income of the bankrupt]**   For the purposes of this section the income of the bankrupt comprises every payment in the nature of income which is from time to time made to him or to which he from time to time becomes entitled, including any payment in respect of the carrying on of any business or in respect of any office or employment.

SEC. 311   Acquisition by trustee of control

311(1)   **[Trustee to take possession]**   The trustee shall take possession of all books, papers and other records which relate to the bankrupt's estate or affairs and which belong to him or are in his possession or under his control (including any which would be privileged from disclosure in any proceedings). .

311(2)   **[Trustee like receiver]**   In relation to, and for the purpose of acquiring or retaining possession of, the bankrupt's estate, the trustee is in the same position as if he were a receiver of property appointed by the High Court; and the court may, on his application, enforce such acquisition or retention accordingly.

311(3)   **[Where estate includes transferable property]**   Where any part of the bankrupt's estate consists of stock or shares in a company, shares in a ship or any other property transferable in the books of a company, office or person, the trustee may exercise the right to transfer the property to the same extent as the bankrupt might have exercised it if he had not become bankrupt.

311(4)   **[Where estate includes things in action]**   Where any part of the estate consists of things in action, they are deemed to have been assigned to the trustee; but notice of the deemed assignment need not be given except in so far as it is necessary, in a case where the deemed assignment is from the bankrupt himself, for protecting the priority of the trustee.

311(5)   **[Where goods held by pledge]**   Where any goods comprised in the estate are held by any person by way of pledge, pawn or other security and no notice has been served in respect of those goods by the official receiver under subsection (5) of section 285 (restriction on realising security), the trustee may serve such a notice in respect of the goods; and whether or not a notice has been served under this subsection or that subsection, the trustee may, if he thinks fit, exercise the bankrupt's right of redemption in respect of any such goods.

311(6) **[Effect of sec. 311(5) notice]** A notice served by the trustee under subsection (5) has the same effect as a notice served by the official receiver under section 285(5).

SEC. 312 Obligation to surrender control to trustee

312(1) **[Bankrupt to surrender property]** The bankrupt shall deliver up to the trustee possession of any property, books, papers or other records of which he has possession or control and of which the trustee is required to take possession.

This is without prejudice to the general duties of the bankrupt under section 333 in this Chapter.

312(2) **[Other persons in possession]** If any of the following is in possession of any property, books, papers or other records of which the trustee is required to take possession, namely—

(a) the official receiver,

(b) a person who has ceased to be trustee of the bankrupt's estate, or

(c) a person who has been the supervisor of a voluntary arrangement approved in relation to the bankrupt under Part VIII,

the official receiver or, as the case may be, that person shall deliver up possession of the property, books, papers or records to the trustee.

312(3) **[Bankers, agents et al. of bankrupt]** Any banker or agent of the bankrupt or any other person who holds any property to the account of, or for, the bankrupt shall pay or deliver to the trustee all property in his possession or under his control which forms part of the bankrupt's estate and which he is not by law entitled to retain as against the bankrupt or trustee.

312(4) **[Penalty for non-compliance]** If any person without reasonable excuse fails to comply with any obligation imposed by this section, he is guilty of a contempt of court and liable to be punished accordingly (in addition to any other punishment to which he may be subject).

SEC. 313 Charge on bankrupt's home

313(1) **[Application to court by trustee]** Where any property consisting of an interest in a dwelling house which is occupied by the bankrupt or by his spouse or former spouse is comprised in the bankrupt's estate and the trustee is, for any reason, unable for the time being to realise that property, the trustee may apply to the court for an order imposing a charge on the property for the benefit of the bankrupt's estate.

313(2) **[Benefit of charge]** If on an application under this section the court imposes a charge on any property, the benefit of that charge shall be comprised in the bankrupt's estate and is enforceable, up to the value from time to time of the property secured, for the payment of any amount which is payable otherwise than to the bankrupt out of the estate and of interest on that amount at the prescribed rate.

313(3) **[Provision in order]** An order under this section made in respect of property vested in the trustee shall provide, in accordance with the rules, for the property to cease to be comprised in the bankrupt's estate and, subject to the charge (and any prior charge), to vest in the bankrupt.

313(4) **[Effect of Charging Orders Act]** Subsections (1) and (2) and (4) to (6) of section 3 of the Charging Orders Act 1979 (supplemental provisions with respect to charging orders) have effect in relation to orders under this section as in relation to charging orders under that Act.

SEC. 314   Powers of trustee

314(1) **[Powers in Sch. 5, Pt. I and II]** The trustee may—

  (a) with the permission of the creditors' committee or the court, exercise any of the powers specified in Part I of Schedule 5 to this Act, and

  (b) without that permission, exercise any of the general powers specified in Part II of that Schedule.

314(2) **[Powers of appointment re bankrupt]** With the permission of the creditors' committee or the court, the trustee may appoint the bankrupt—

  (a) to superintend the management of his estate or any part of it,

  (b) to carry on his business (if any) for the benefit of his creditors, or

  (c) in any other respect to assist in administering the estate in such manner and on such terms as the trustee may direct.

314(3) **[Permission in sec. 314(1)(a), (2)]** A permission given for the purposes of subsection (1)(a) or (2) shall not be a general permission but shall relate to a particular proposed exercise of the power in question; and a person dealing with the trustee in good faith and for value is not to be concerned to enquire whether any permission required in either case has been given.

314(4) **[Where no permission under sec. 314(1)(a), (2)]** Where the trustee has done anything without the permission required by subsection (1)(a) or (2), the court or the creditors' committee may, for the purpose of enabling him to meet his expenses out of the bankrupt's estate, ratify what the trustee has done.

But the committee shall not do so unless it is satisfied that the trustee has acted in a case of urgency and has sought its ratification without undue delay.

314(5) **[Powers in Sch. 5, Pt. III]** Part III of Schedule 5 to this Act has effect with respect to the things which the trustee is able to do for the purposes of, or in connection with, the exercise of any of his powers under any of this Group of Parts.

314(6) **[Notice to committee]** Where the trustee (not being the official receiver) in exercise of the powers conferred on him by any provision in this Group of Parts—

  (a) disposes of any property comprised in the bankrupt's estate to an associate of the bankrupt, or

  (b) employs a solicitor,

he shall, if there is for the time being a creditors' committee, give notice to the committee of that exercise of his powers.

314(7) [Power to summon general meeting of creditors] Without prejudice to the generality of subsection (5) and Part III of Schedule 5, the trustee may, if he thinks fit, at any time summon a general meeting of the bankrupt's creditors.

Subject to the preceding provisions in this Group of Parts, he shall summon such a meeting if he is requested to do so by a creditor of the bankrupt and the request is made with the concurrence of not less than one-tenth, in value, of the bankrupt's creditors (including the creditor making the request).

314(8) [Capacity of trustee] Nothing in this Act is to be construed as restricting the capacity of the trustee to exercise any of his powers outside England and Wales.

DISCLAIMER OF ONEROUS PROPERTY

SEC. 315 Disclaimer (general power)

315(1) [Power of trustee to disclaim] Subject as follows, the trustee may, by the giving of the prescribed notice, disclaim any onerous property and may do so notwithstanding that he has taken possession of it, endeavoured to sell it or otherwise exercised rights of ownership in relation to it.

315(2) [Onerous property] The following is onerous property for the purposes of this section, that is to say—

(a) any unprofitable contract, and

(b) any other property comprised in the bankrupt's estate which is unsaleable or not readily saleable, or is such that it may give rise to a liability to pay money or perform any other onerous act.

315(3) [Effect of disclaimer] A disclaimer under this section—

(a) operates so as to determine, as from the date of the disclaimer, the rights, interests and liabilities of the bankrupt and his estate in or in respect of the property disclaimed, and

(b) discharges the trustee from all personal liability in respect of that property as from the commencement of his trusteeship,

but does not, except so far as is necessary for the purpose of releasing the bankrupt, the bankrupt's estate and the trustee from any liability, affect the rights or liabilities of any other person.

315(4) [Where notice of disclaimer not to be given] A notice of disclaimer shall not be given under this section in respect of any property that has been claimed for the estate under section 307 (after-acquired property) or 308 (personal property of bankrupt exceeding reasonable replacement value), except with the leave of the court.

315(5) [Persons sustaining loss or damage] Any person sustaining loss or damage in consequence of the operation of a disclaimer under this section is deemed to be a creditor of the bankrupt to the extent of the loss or damage and accordingly may prove for the loss or damage as a bankruptcy debt.

SEC. 316 Notice requiring trustee's decision

316(1) [Where notice not to be given] Notice of disclaimer shall not be given under section 315 in respect of any property if—

(a) a person interested in the property has applied in writing to the trustee or one of his predecessors as trustee requiring the trustee or that predecessor to decide whether he will disclaim or not, and

(b) the period of 28 days beginning with the day on which that application was made has expired without a notice of disclaimer having been given under section 315 in respect of that property.

316(2)　[Deemed adoption]　The trustee is deemed to have adopted any contract which by virtue of this section he is not entitled to disclaim.

SEC. 317　Disclaimer of leaseholds

317(1)　[Disclaimer of leasehold property]　The disclaimer of any property of a leasehold nature does not take effect unless a copy of the disclaimer has been served (so far as the trustee is aware of their addresses) on every person claiming under the bankrupt as underlessee or mortgagee and either—

(a) no application under section 320 below is made with respect to the property before the end of the period of 14 days beginning with the day on which the last notice served under this subsection was served, or

(b) where such an application has been made, the court directs that the disclaimer is to take effect.

317(2)　[Where court gives sec. 317(1)(b) direction]　Where the court gives a direction under subsection (1)(b) it may also, instead of or in addition to any order it makes under section 320, make such orders with respect to fixtures, tenant's improvements and other matters arising out of the lease as it thinks fit.

SEC. 318　Disclaimer of dwelling house

318　Without prejudice to section 317, the disclaimer of any property in a dwelling house does not take effect unless a copy of the disclaimer has been served (so far as the trustee is aware of their addresses) on every person in occupation of or claiming a right to occupy the dwelling house and either—

(a) no application under section 320 is made with respect to the property before the end of the period of 14 days beginning with the day on which the last notice served under this section was served, or

(b) where such an application has been made, the court directs that the disclaimer is to take effect.

SEC. 319　Disclaimer of land subject to rentcharge

319(1)　[Application]　The following applies where, in consequence of the disclaimer under section 315 of any land subject to a rentcharge, that land vests by operation of law in the Crown or any other person (referred to in the next subsection as "the proprietor").

319(2)　[Limit on liability]　The proprietor, and the successors in title of the proprietor, are not subject to any personal liability in respect of any sums becoming due under the rentcharge, except sums becoming due after the proprietor, or some person claiming under or through the proprietor, has taken possession or control of the land or has entered into occupation of it.

SEC. 320 Court order vesting disclaimed property

320(1) [Application] This section and the next apply where the trustee has disclaimed property under section 315.

320(2) [Application to court] An application may be made to the court under this section by—

(a) any person who claims an interest in the disclaimed property,

(b) any person who is under any liability in respect of the disclaimed property, not being a liability discharged by the disclaimer, or

(c) where the disclaimed property is property in a dwelling house, any person who at the time when the bankruptcy petition was presented was in occupation of or entitled to occupy the dwelling house.

320(3) [Order by court] Subject as follows in this section and the next, the court may, on an application under this section, make an order on such terms as it thinks fit for the vesting of the disclaimed property in, or for its delivery to—

(a) a person entitled to it or a trustee for such a person,

(b) a person subject to such a liability as is mentioned in subsection (2)(b) or a trustee for such a person, or

(c) where the disclaimed property is property in a dwelling house, any person who at the time when the bankruptcy petition was presented was in occupation of or entitled to occupy the dwelling house.

320(4) [Limit to sec. 320(3)(b)] The court shall not make an order by virtue of subsection (3)(b) except where it appears to the court that it would be just to do so for the purpose of compensating the person subject to the liability in respect of the disclaimer.

320(5) [Effect of order in sec. 315(5) assessment] The effect of any order under this section shall be taken into account in assessing for the purposes of section 315(5) the extent of any loss or damage sustained by any person in consequence of the disclaimer.

320(6) [Mode of vesting re order] An order under this section vesting property in any person need not be completed by any conveyance, assignment or transfer.

SEC. 321 Order under sec. 320 in respect of leaseholds

321(1) [Terms of order re leasehold property] The court shall not make an order under section 320 vesting property of a leasehold nature in any person, except on terms making that person—

(a) subject to the same liabilities and obligations as the bankrupt was subject to under the lease on the day the bankruptcy petition was presented, or

(b) if the court thinks fit, subject to the same liabilities and obligations as that person would be subject to if the lease had been assigned to him on that day.

321(2) [Where order re part of property in lease] For the purposes of an order under section 320 relating to only part of any property comprised in a lease, the requirements of subsection (1) apply as if the lease comprised only the property to which the order relates.

321(3)   **[Where no person accepts order in sec. 162(5) case]**   Where subsection (1) applies and no person is willing to accept an order under section 320 on the terms required by that subsection, the court may (by order under section 320) vest the estate or interest of the bankrupt in the property in any person who is liable (whether personally or in a representative capacity and whether alone or jointly with the bankrupt) to perform the lessee's covenants in the lease.

The court may by virtue of this subsection vest that estate and interest in such a person freed and discharged from all estates, incumbrances and interests created by the bankrupt.

321(4)   **[Exclusion from interest in property]**   Where subsection (1) applies and a person declines to accept any order under section 320, that person shall be excluded from all interest in the property.

DISTRIBUTION OF BANKRUPT'S ESTATE

SEC. 322   Proof of debts

322(1)   **[Proof in accordance with rules]**   Subject to this section and the next, the proof of any bankruptcy debt by a secured or unsecured creditor of the bankrupt and the admission or rejection of any proof shall take place in accordance with the rules.

322(2)   **[Where bankruptcy debt bears interest]**   Where a bankruptcy debt bears interest, that interest is provable as part of the debt except in so far as it is payable in respect of any period after the commencement of the bankruptcy.

322(3)   **[Estimation of debt]**   The trustee shall estimate the value of any bankruptcy debt which, by reason of its being subject to any contingency or contingencies or for any other reason, does not bear a certain value.

322(4)   **[Where estimate under sec. 303, 322(3)]**   Where the value of a bankruptcy debt is estimated by the trustee under subsection (3) or, by virtue of section 303 in Chapter III, by the court, the amount provable in the bankruptcy in respect of the debt is the amount of the estimate.

SEC. 323   Mutual credit and set-off

323(1)   **[Application]**   This section applies where before the commencement of the bankruptcy there have been mutual credits, mutual debts or other mutual dealings between the bankrupt and any creditor of the bankrupt proving or claiming to prove for a bankruptcy debt.

323(2)   **[Account to be taken]**   An account shall be taken of what is due from each party to the other in respect of the mutual dealings and the sums due from one party shall be set off against the sums due from the other.

323(3)   **[Qualification to sec. 323(2)]**   Sums due from the bankrupt to another party shall not be included in the account taken under subsection (2) if that other party had notice at the time they became due that a bankruptcy petition relating to the bankrupt was pending.

323(4)   [Balance to trustee]   Only the balance (if any) of the account taken under subsection (2) is provable as a bankruptcy debt or, as the case may be, to be paid to the trustee as part of the bankrupt's estate.

SEC. 324   Distribution by means of dividend

324(1)   [Duty to declare and distribute]   Whenever the trustee has sufficient funds in hand for the purpose he shall, subject to the retention of such sums as may be necessary for the expenses of the bankruptcy, declare and distribute dividends among the creditors in respect of the bankruptcy debts which they have respectively proved.

324(2)   [Notice of intention to declare and distribute]   The trustee shall give notice of his intention to declare and distribute a dividend.

324(3)   [Notice of dividend etc.]   Where the trustee has declared a dividend, he shall give notice of the dividend and of how it is proposed to distribute it; and a notice given under this subsection shall contain the prescribed particulars of the bankrupt's estate.

324(4)   [Calculation and distribution of dividend]   In the calculation and distribution of a dividend the trustee shall make provision—

(a) for any bankruptcy debts which appear to him to be due to persons who, by reason of the distance of their place of residence, may not have had sufficient time to tender and establish their proofs,

(b) for any bankruptcy debts which are the subject of claims which have not yet been determined, and

(c) for disputed proofs and claims.

SEC. 325   Claims by unsatisfied creditors

325(1)   [Entitlements of creditors]   A creditor who has not proved his debt before the declaration of any dividend is not entitled to disturb, by reason that he has not participated in it, the distribution of that dividend or any other dividend declared before his debt was proved, but—

(a) when he has proved that debt he is entitled to be paid, out of any money for the time being available for the payment of any further dividend, any dividend or dividends which he has failed to receive; and

(b) any dividend or dividends payable under paragraph (a) shall be paid before that money is applied to the payment of any such further dividend.

325(2)   [Order re payment of dividend]   No action lies against the trustee for a dividend, but if the trustee refuses to pay a dividend the court may, if it thinks fit, order him to pay it and also to pay, out of his own money—

(a) interest on the dividend, at the rate for the time being specified in section 17 of the Judgments Act 1838, from the time it was withheld, and

(b) the costs of the proceedings in which the order to pay is made.

SEC. 326   Distribution of property in specie

326(1)   [Division of unsaleable property]   Without prejudice to sections 315 to 319 (disclaimer), the trustee may, with the permission of the creditors' committee, divide in its existing form amongst the bankrupt's creditors, according to its estimated value, any property which from its peculiar nature or other special circumstances cannot be readily or advantageously sold.

326(2) **[Permission under sec. 326(1)]**   A permission given for the purposes of subsection (1) shall not be a general permission but shall relate to a particular proposed exercise of the power in question; and a person dealing with the trustee in good faith and for value is not to be concerned to enquire whether any permission required by subsection (1) has been given.

326(3) **[Where no permission under sec. 326(1)]**   Where the trustee has done anything without the permission required by subsection (1), the court or the creditors' committee may, for the purpose of enabling him to meet his expenses out of the bankrupt's estate, ratify what the trustee has done.

But the committee shall not do so unless it is satisfied that the trustee acted in a case of urgency and has sought its ratification without undue delay.

SEC. 327   Distribution in criminal bankruptcy

327   Where the bankruptcy order was made on a petition under section 264(1)(d) (criminal bankruptcy), no distribution shall be made under sections 324 to 326 so long as an appeal is pending (within the meaning of section 277) against the bankrupt's conviction of any offence by virtue of which the criminal bankruptcy order on which the petition was based was made.

Note
S. 327 repealed by Criminal Justice Act 1988, s. 170(2) and
Sch. 16 as from a day to be appointed.

SEC. 328   Priority of debts

328(1) **[Preferential debts to be paid first]**   In the distribution of the bankrupt's estate, his preferential debts (within the meaning given by section 386 in Part XII) shall be paid in priority to other debts.

328(2) **[Ranking of preferential debts]**   Preferential debts rank equally between themselves after the expenses of the bankruptcy and shall be paid in full unless the bankrupt's estate is insufficient for meeting them, in which case they abate in equal proportions between themselves.

328(3) **[Debts neither preferential nor under sec. 329]**   Debts which are neither preferential debts nor debts to which the next section applies also rank equally between themselves and, after the preferential debts, shall be paid in full unless the bankrupt's estate is insufficient for meeting them, in which case they abate in equal proportions between themselves.

328(4) **[Surplus after payment]**   Any surplus remaining after the payment of the debts that are preferential or rank equally under subsection (3) shall be applied in paying interest on those debts in respect of the periods during which they have been outstanding since the commencement of the bankruptcy; and interest on preferential debts ranks equally with interest on debts other than preferential debts.

328(5) **[Rate of interest under sec. 328(4)]**   The rate of interest payable under subsection (4) in respect of any debt is whichever is the greater of the following—

  (a) the rate specified in section 17 of the Judgments Act 1838 at the commencement of the bankruptcy, and

  (b) the rate applicable to that debt apart from the bankruptcy.

328(6) **[Other enactments]** This section and the next are without prejudice to any provision of this Act or any other Act under which the payment of any debt or the making of any other payment is, in the event of bankruptcy, to have a particular priority or to be postponed.

SEC. 329   Debts to spouse

329(1) **[Application]** This section applies to bankruptcy debts owed in respect of credit provided by a person who (whether or not the bankrupt's spouse at the time the credit was provided) was the bankrupt's spouse at the commencement of the bankruptcy.

329(2) **[Ranking, payment]** Such debts—

(a) rank in priority after the debts and interest required to be paid in pursuance of section 328(3) and (4), and

(b) are payable with interest at the rate specified in section 328(5) in respect of the period during which they have been outstanding since the commencement of the bankruptcy;

and the interest payable under paragraph (b) has the same priority as the debts on which it is payable.

SEC. 330   Final distribution

330(1) **[Notice re dividend, etc.]** When the trustee has realised all the bankrupt's estate or so much of it as can, in the trustee's opinion, be realised without needlessly protracting the trusteeship, he shall give notice in the prescribed manner either—

(a) of his intention to declare a final dividend, or

(b) that no dividend, or further dividend, will be declared.

330(2) **[Contents of notice]** The notice under subsection (1) shall contain the prescribed particulars and shall require claims against the bankrupt's estate to be established by a date ("the final date") specified in the notice.

330(3) **[Postponement of final date]** The court may, on the application of any person, postpone the final date.

330(4) **[Trustee's duties after final date]** After the final date, the trustee shall—

(a) defray any outstanding expenses of the bankruptcy out of the bankrupt's estate, and

(b) if he intends to declare a final dividend, declare and distribute that dividend without regard to the claim of any person in respect of a debt not already proved in the bankruptcy.

330(5) **[Where surplus]** If a surplus remains after payment in full and with interest of all the bankrupt's creditors and the payment of the expenses of the bankruptcy, the bankrupt is entitled to the surplus.

SEC. 331   Final meeting

331(1) **[Application]** Subject as follows in this section and the next, this section applies where—

(a) it appears to the trustee that the administration of the bankrupt's estate in accordance with this Chapter is for practical purposes complete, and

(b) the trustee is not the official receiver.

331(2) **[Duty of trustee]**   The trustee shall summon a final general meeting of the bankrupt's creditors which—

(a) shall receive the trustee's report of his administration of the bankrupt's estate, and

(b) shall determine whether the trustee should have his release under section 229 in Chapter III.

331(3) **[Time for notice]**   The trustee may, if he thinks fit, give the notice summoning the final general meeting at the same time as giving notice under section 330(1); but, if summoned for an earlier date, that meeting shall be adjourned (and, if necessary, further adjourned) until a date on which the trustee is able to report to the meeting that the administration of the bankrupt's estate is for practical purposes complete.

331(4) **[Expenses]**   In the administration of the estate it is the trustee's duty to retain sufficient sums from the estate to cover the expenses of summoning and holding the meeting required by this section.

SEC. 332   Saving for bankrupt's home

332(1) **[Application]**   This section applies where—

(a) there is comprised in the bankrupt's estate property consisting of an interest in a dwelling house which is occupied by the bankrupt or by his spouse or former spouse, and

(b) the trustee has been unable for any reason to realise that property.

332(2) **[Conditions for sec. 331 meeting]**   The trustee shall not summon a meeting under section 331 unless either—

(a) the court has made an order under section 313 imposing a charge on that property for the benefit of the bankrupt's estate, or

(b) the court has declined, on an application under that section, to make such an order, or

(c) the Secretary of State has issued a certificate to the trustee stating that it would be inappropriate or inexpedient for such an application to be made in the case in question.

SUPPLEMENTAL

SEC. 333   Duties of bankrupt in relation to trustee

333(1) **[Duties]**   The bankrupt shall—

(a) give to the trustee such information as to his affairs,

(b) attend on the trustee at such times, and

(c) do all such other things,

as the trustee may for the purposes of carrying out his functions under any of this Group of Parts reasonably require.

IA 1986, sec. 331(2)   [The next page is 54,501]   **CCH Editions Limited**

333(2) **[Notice re after-acquired property]** Where at any time after the commencement of the bankruptcy any property is acquired by, or devolves upon, the bankrupt or there is an increase of the bankrupt's income, the bankrupt shall, within the prescribed period, give the trustee notice of the property or, as the case may be, of the increase.

333(3) **[Application of sec. 333(1)]** Subsection (1) applies to a bankrupt after his discharge.

333(4) **[Penalty for non-compliance]** If the bankrupt without reasonable excuse fails to comply with any obligation imposed by this section, he is guilty of a contempt of court and liable to be punished accordingly (in addition to any other punishment to which he may be subject).

SEC. 334 Stay of distribution in case of second bankruptcy

334(1) **[Application, definitions]** This section and the next apply where a bankruptcy order is made against an undischarged bankrupt; and in both sections—

(a) **"the later bankruptcy"** means the bankruptcy arising from that order,

(b) **"the earlier bankruptcy"** means the bankruptcy (or, as the case may be, most recent bankruptcy) from which the bankrupt has not been discharged at the commencement of the later bankruptcy, and

(c) **"the existing trustee"** means the trustee (if any) of the bankrupt's estate for the purposes of the earlier bankruptcy.

334(2) **[Certain distributions void]** Where the existing trustee has been given the prescribed notice of the presentation of the petition for the later bankruptcy, any distribution or other disposition by him of anything to which the next subsection applies, if made after the giving of the notice, is void except to the extent that it was made with the consent of the court or is or was subsequently ratified by the court.

This is without prejudice to section 284 (restrictions on dispositions of property following bankruptcy order).

334(3) **[Application of sec. 334(2)]** This subsection applies to—

(a) any property which is vested in the existing trustee under section 307(3) (after-acquired property);

(b) any money paid to the existing trustee in pursuance of an income payments order under section 310; and

(c) any property or money which is, or in the hands of the existing trustee represents, the proceeds of sale or application of property or money falling within paragraph (a) or (b) of this subsection.

SEC. 335 Adjustment between earlier and later bankruptcy estates

335(1) **[Matters in bankrupt's estate]** With effect from the commencement of the later bankruptcy anything to which section 334(3) applies which, immediately before the commencement of that bankruptcy, is comprised in the bankrupt's estate for the purposes of the earlier bankruptcy is to be treated as comprised in the bankrupt's estate for the purposes of the later bankruptcy and, until there is a trustee of that estate, is to be dealt with by the existing trustee in accordance with the rules.

335(2) [Sums paid under sec. 310] Any sums which in pursuance of an income payments order under section 310 are payable after the commencement of the later bankruptcy to the existing trustee shall form part of the bankrupt's estate for the purposes of the later bankruptcy; and the court may give such consequential directions for the modification of the order as it thinks fit.

335(3) [Charge re bankruptcy expenses] Anything comprised in a bankrupt's estate by virtue of subsection (1) or (2) is so comprised subject to a first charge in favour of the existing trustee for any bankruptcy expenses incurred by him in relation thereto.

335(4) [Property not in estate] Except as provided above and in section 334, property which is, or by virtue of section 308 (personal property of bankrupt exceeding reasonable replacement value) is capable of being, comprised in the bankrupt's estate for the purposes of the earlier bankruptcy, or of any bankruptcy prior to it, shall not be comprised in his estate for the purposes of the later bankruptcy.

335(5) [Creditors of earlier bankruptcies] The creditors of the bankrupt in the earlier bankruptcy and the creditors of the bankrupt in any bankruptcy prior to the earlier one, are not to be creditors of his in the later bankruptcy in respect of the same debts; but the existing trustee may prove in the later bankruptcy for—

(a) the unsatisfied balance of the debts (including any debt under this subsection) ovable against the bankrupt's estate in the earlier bankruptcy;

(b) any interest payable on that balance; and

(c) any unpaid expenses of the earlier bankruptcy.

335(6) [Priority of amounts in sec. 335(5)] Any amount provable under subsection (5) ranks in priority after all the other debts provable in the later bankruptcy and after interest on those debts and, accordingly, shall not be paid unless those debts and that interest have first been paid in full.

Chapter V — Effect of Bankruptcy on Certain Rights, Transactions, Etc.

RIGHTS OF OCCUPATION

SEC. 336 Rights of occupation etc. of bankrupt's spouse

336(1) [Matrimonial Homes Act 1983] Nothing occurring in the initial period of the bankruptcy (that is to say, the period beginning with the day of the presentation of the petition for the bankruptcy order and ending with the vesting of the bankrupt's estate in a trustee) is to be taken as having given rise to any rights of occupation under the Matrimonial Homes Act 1983 in relation to a dwelling house comprised in the bankrupt's estate.

336(2) [Where spouse's rights of occupation charge on estate] Where a spouse's rights of occupation under the Act of 1983 are a charge on the estate or interest of the other spouse, or of trustees for the other spouse, and the other spouse is adjudged bankrupt—

(a) the charge continues to subsist notwithstanding the bankruptcy and, subject to the provisions of that Act, binds the trustee of the bankrupt's estate and persons deriving title under that trustee, and

(b) any application for an order under section 1 of that Act shall be made to the court having jurisdiction in relation to the bankruptcy.

336(3) **[Where bankrupt and spouse trustees for sale of dwelling house]** Where a person and his spouse or former spouse are trustees for sale of a dwelling house and that person is adjudged bankrupt, any application by the trustee of the bankrupt's estate for an order under section 30 of the Law of Property Act 1925 (powers of court where trustees for sale refuse to act) shall be made to the court having jurisdiction in relation to the bankruptcy.

336(4) **[Court orders]** On such an application as is mentioned in subsection (2) or (3) the court shall make such order under section 1 of the Act of 1983 or section 30 of the Act of 1925 as it thinks just and reasonable having regard to—

(a) the interests of the bankrupt's creditors,

(b) the conduct of the spouse or former spouse, so far as contributing to the bankruptcy,

(c) the needs and financial resources of the spouse or former spouse,

(d) the needs of any children, and

(e) all the circumstances of the case other than the needs of the bankrupt.

336(5) **[Assumption by court re interests of creditors]** Where such an application is made after the end of the period of one year beginning with the first vesting under Chapter IV of this Part of the bankrupt's estate in a trustee, the court shall assume, unless the circumstances of the case are exceptional, that the interests of the bankrupt's creditors outweigh all other considerations.

SEC. 337 Rights of occupation of bankrupt

337(1) **[Application]** This section applies where—

(a) a person who is entitled to occupy a dwelling house by virtue of a beneficial estate or interest is adjudged bankrupt, and

(b) any persons under the age of 18 with whom that person had at some time occupied that dwelling house had their home with that person at the time when the bankruptcy petition was presented and at the commencment of the bankruptcy.

337(2) **[Rights of occupation, etc.]** Whether or not the bankrupt's spouse (if any) has rights of occupation under the Matrimonial Homes Act 1983—

(a) the bankrupt has the following rights as against the trustee of his estate—

(i) if in occupation, right not to be evicted or excluded from the dwelling house or any part of it, except with the leave of the court,

(ii) if not in occupation, a right with the leave of the court to enter into and occupy the dwelling house, and

(b) the bankrupt's rights are a charge, having the like priority as an equitable interest created immediately before the commencement of the bankruptcy, on so much of his estate or interest in the dwelling house as vests in the trustee.

337(3) **[Application of Matrimonial Homes Act]**   The Act of 1983 has effect, with the necessary modifications, as if—

(a) the rights conferred by paragraph (a) of subsection (2) were rights of occupation under that Act,

(b) any application for leave such as is mentioned in that paragraph were an application for an order under section 1 of that Act, and

(c) any charge under paragraph (b) of that subsection on the estate or interest of the trustee were a charge under that Act on the estate or interest of a spouse.

337(4) **[Application to court]**   Any application for leave such as is mentioned in subsection (2)(a) or otherwise by virtue of this section for an order under section 1 of the Act of 1983 shall be made to the court having jurisdiction in relation to the bankruptcy.

337(5) **[Court order under sec. 337(4)]**   On such an application the court shall make such order under section 1 of the Act of 1983 as it thinks just and reasonable having regard to the interests of the creditors, to the bankrupt's financial resources, to the needs of the children and to all the circumstances of the case other than the needs of the bankrupt.

337(6) **[Assumption re interests of creditors]**   Where such an application is made after the end of the period of one year beginning with the first vesting (under Chapter IV of this Part) of the bankrupt's estate in a trustee, the court shall assume, unless the circumstances of the case are exceptional, that the interest of the bankrupt's creditors outweigh all other considerations.

SEC. 338   Payments in respect of premises occupied by bankrupt

338   Where any premises comprised in a bankrupt's estate are occupied by him (whether by virtue of the preceding section or otherwise) on condition that he makes payments towards satisfying any liability arising under a mortgage of the premises or otherwise towards the outgoings of the premises, the bankrupt does not, by virtue of those payments, acquire any interest in the premises.

ADJUSTMENT OF PRIOR TRANSACTIONS, ETC.

SEC. 339   Transactions at an undervalue

339(1) **[Application to court]**   Subject as follows in this section and sections 341 and 342, where an individual is adjudged bankrupt and he has at a relevant time (defined in section 341) entered into a transaction with any person at an undervalue, the trustee of the bankrupt's estate may apply to the court for an order under this section.

339(2) **[Order by court]**   The court shall, on such an application, make such order as it thinks fit for restoring the position to what it would have been if that individual had not entered into that transaction.

339(3) **[Where transaction is at undervalue]** For the purposes of this section and sections 341 and 342, an individual enters into a transaction with a person at an undervalue if—

(a) he makes a gift to that person or he otherwise enters into a transaction with that person on terms that provide for him to receive no consideration,

(b) he enters into a transaction with that person in consideration of marriage, or

(c) he enters into a transaction with that person for a consideration the value of which, in money or money's worth, is significantly less than the value, in money or money's worth, of the consideration provided by the individual.

SEC. 340   Preferences

340(1) **[Application to court]** Subject as follows in this and the next two sections, where an individual is adjudged bankrupt and he has at a relevant time (defined in section 341) given a preference to any person, the trustee of the bankrupt's estate may apply to the court for an order under this section.

340(2) **[Order by court]** The court shall, on such an application, make such order as it thinks fit for restoring the position to what it would have been if that individual had not given that preference.

340(3) **[Where preference given]** For the purposes of this and the next two sections, an individual gives a preference to a person if—

(a) that person is one of the individual's creditors or a surety or guarantor for any of his debts or other liabilities, and

(b) the individual does anything or suffers anything to be done which (in either case) has the effect of putting that person into a position which, in the event of the individual's bankruptcy, will be better than the position he would have been in if that thing had not been done.

340(4) **[Where court not to make order]** The court shall not make an order under this section in respect of a preference given to any person unless the individual who gave the preference was influenced in deciding to give it by a desire to produce in relation to that person the effect mentioned in subsection (3)(b) above.

340(5) **[Preference to associate]** An individual who has given a preference to a person who, at the time the preference was given, was an associate of his (otherwise than by reason only of being his employee) is presumed, unless the contrary is shown, to have been influenced in deciding to give it by such a desire as is mentioned in subsection (4).

340(6) **[Things done under court order]** The fact that something has been done in pursuance of the order of a court does not, without more, prevent the doing or suffering of that thing from constituting the giving of a preference.

SEC. 341   "Relevant time" under sec. 339, 340

341(1) **[Where relevant time]** Subject as follows, the time at which an individual enters into a transaction at an undervalue or gives a preference is a relevant time if the transaction is entered into or the preference given—

(a) in the case of a transaction at an undervalue, at a time in the period of 5 years ending with the day of the presentation of the bankruptcy petition on which the individual is adjudged bankrupt,

(b) in the case of a preference which is not a transaction at an undervalue and is given to a person who is an associate of the individual (otherwise than by reason only of being his employee), at a time in the period of 2 years ending with that day, and

(c) in any other case of a preference which is not a transaction at an undervalue, at a time in the period of 6 months ending with that day.

341(2) [Conditions for relevant time] Where an individual enters into a transaction at an undervalue or gives a preference at a time mentioned in paragraph (a), (b) or (c) of subsection (1) (not being, in the case of a transaction at an undervalue, a time less than 2 years before the end of the period mentioned in paragraph (a)), that time is not a relevant time for the purposes of sections 339 and 340 unless the individual—

(a) is insolvent at that time, or

(b) becomes insolvent in consequence of the transaction or preference;

but the requirements of this subsection are presumed to be satisfied, unless the contrary is shown, in relation to any transaction at an undervalue which is entered into by an individual with a person who is an associate of his (otherwise than by reason only of being his employee).

341(3) [Insolvent individual under sec. 341(2)] For the purposes of subsection (2), an individual is insolvent if—

(a) he is unable to pay his debts as they fall due, or

(b) the value of his assets is less than the amount of his liabilities, taking into account his contingent and prospective liabilities.

341(4) [Where person later bankrupt under sec. 264(1)(d)] A transaction entered into or preference given by a person who is subsequently adjudged bankrupt on a petition under section 264(1)(d) (criminal bankruptcy) is to be treated as having been entered into or given at a relevant time for the purposes of sections 339 and 340 if it was entered into or given at any time on or after the date specified for the purposes of this subsection in the criminal bankruptcy order on which the petition was based.

Note
See note to s. 341(5).

341(5) [Where appeal pending] No order shall be made under section 339 or 340 by virtue of subsection (4) of this section where an appeal is pending (within the meaning of section 277) against the individual's conviction of any offence by virtue of which the criminal bankruptcy order was made.

Note
S. 341(4) and (5) repealed by Criminal Justice Act 1988, s. 170(2) and Sch. 16 as from a day to be appointed.

SEC. 342   Orders under sec. 339, 340

342(1) [Extent of order] Without prejudice to the generality of section 339(2) or 340(2), an order under either of those sections with respect to a transaction or preference entered into or given by an individual who is subsequently adjudged bankrupt may (subject as follows)—

(a) require any property transferred as part of the transaction, or in connection with the giving of the preference, to be vested in the trustee of the bankrupt's estate as part of that estate;

(b) require any property to be so vested if it represents in any person's hands the application either of the proceeds of sale of property so transferred or of money so transferred;

(c) release or discharge (in whole or in part) any security given by the individual;

(d) require any person to pay, in respect of benefits received by him from the individual, such sums to the trustee of his estate as the court may direct;

(e) provide for any surety or guarantor whose obligations to any person were released or discharged (in whole or in part) under the transaction or by the giving of the preference to be under such new or revived obligations to that person as the court thinks appropriate;

(f) provide for security to be provided for the discharge of any obligation imposed by or arising under the order, for such an obligation to be charged on any property and for the security or charge to have the same priority as a security or charge released or discharged (in whole or in part) under the transaction or by the giving of the preference; and

(g) provide for the extent to which any person whose property is vested by the order in the trustee of the bankrupt's estate, or on whom obligations are imposed by the order, is to be able to prove in the bankruptcy for debts or other liabilities which arose from, or were released or discharged (in whole or in part) under or by, the transaction or the giving of the preference.

342(2) **[Effect of order]**   An order under section 339 or 340 may affect the property of, or impose any obligation on, any person whether or not he is the person with whom the individual in question entered into the transaction or, as the case may be, the person to whom the preference was given; but such an order—

(a) shall not prejudice any interest in property which was acquired from a person other than that individual and was acquired in good faith, for value and without notice of the relevant circumstances, or prejudice any interest deriving from such an interest, and

(b) shall not require a person who received a benefit from the transaction or preference in good faith, for value and without notice of the relevant circumstances to pay a sum to the trustee of the bankrupt's estate, except where he was a party to the transaction or the payment is to be in respect of a preference given to that person at a time when he was a creditor of that individual.

342(3) **[Sums to be paid to trustee]**   Any sums required to be paid to the trustee in accordance with an order under section 339 or 340 shall be comprised in the bankrupt's estate.

342(4) **[Relevant circumstances]**   For the purposes of this section the relevant circumstances, in relation to a transaction or preference, are—

(a) the circumstances by virtue of which an order under section 339 or 340 could be made in respect of the transaction or preference if the individual in question were adjudged bankrupt within a particular period after the transaction is entered into or the preference given, and

(b) if that period has expired, the fact that that individual has been adjudged bankrupt within that period.

SEC. 343   Extortionate credit transactions

343(1)   [Application]   This section applies where a person is adjudged bankrupt who is or has been a party to a transaction for, or involving, the provision to him of credit.

343(2)   [Order by court]   The court may, on the application of the trustee of the bankrupt's estate, make an order with respect to the transaction if the transaction is or was extortionate and was not entered into more than 3 years before the commencement of the bankruptcy.

343(3)   [Extortionate transaction]   For the purposes of this section a transaction is extortionate if, having regard to the risk accepted by the person providing the credit—

(a) the terms of it are or were such as to require grossly exorbitant payments to be made (whether unconditionally or in certain contingencies) in respect of the provision of the credit, or

(b) it otherwise grossly contravened ordinary principles of fair dealing;

and it shall be presumed, unless the contrary is proved, that a transaction with respect to which an application is made under this section is or, as the case may be, was extortionate.

343(4)   [Extent of order]   An order under this section with respect to any transaction may contain such one or more of the following as the court thinks fit, that is to say—

(a) provision setting aside the whole or part of any obligation created by the transaction;

(b) provision otherwise varying the terms of the transaction or varying the terms on which any security for the purposes of the transaction is held;

(c) provision requiring any person who is or was party to the transaction to pay to the trustee any sums paid to that person, by virtue of the transaction, by the bankrupt;

(d) provision requiring any person to surrender to the trustee any property held by him as security for the purposes of the transaction;

(e) provision directing accounts to be taken between any persons.

343(5)   [Sums to trustee]   Any sums or property required to be paid or surrendered to the trustee in accordance with an order under this section shall be comprised in the bankrupt's estate.

343(6)   [Application under Consumer Credit Act]   Neither the trustee of a bankrupt's estate nor an undischarged bankrupt is entitled to make an application under section 139(1)(a) of the Consumer Credit Act 1974 (re-opening of extortionate credit agreements) for any agreement by which credit is or has been provided to the bankrupt to be re-opened.

But the powers conferred by this section are exercisable in relation to any transaction concurrently with any powers exercisable under this Act in relation to that transaction as a transaction at an undervalue.

SEC. 344 Avoidance of general assignment of book debts

344(1) [Application] The following applies where a person engaged in any business makes a general assignment to another person of his existing or future book debts, or any class of them, and is subsequently adjudged bankrupt.

344(2) [Certain assignments void against trustee] The assignment is void against the trustee of the bankrupt's estate as regards book debts which were not paid before the presentation of the bankruptcy petition, unless the assignment has been registered under the Bills of Sale Act 1878.

344(3) [Definitions] For the purposes of subsections (1) and (2)—

(a) **"assignment"** includes an assignment by way of security or charge on book debts, and

(b) **"general assignment"** does not include—

(i) an assignment of book debts due at the date of the assignment from specified debtors or of debts becoming due under specified contracts, or

(ii) an assignment of book debts included either in a transfer of a business made in good faith and for value or in an assignment of assets for the benefit of creditors generally.

344(4) [Registration under Bills of Sales Act] For the purposes of registration under the Act of 1878 an assignment of book debts is to be treated as if it were a bill of sale given otherwise than by way of security for the payment of a sum of money; and the provisions of that Act with respect to the registration of bills of sale apply accordingly with such necessary modifications as may be made by rules under that Act.

SEC. 345 Contracts to which bankrupt is a party

345(1) [Application] The following applies where a contract has been made with a person who is subsequently adjudged bankrupt.

345(2) [Court order on application] The court may, on the application of any other party to the contract, make an order discharging obligations under the contract on such terms as to payment by the applicant or the bankrupt of damages for non-performance or otherwise as appear to the court to be equitable.

345(3) [Damages as bankruptcy debt] Any damages payable by the bankrupt by virtue of an order of the court under this section are provable as a bankruptcy debt.

345(4) [Where joint contract] Where an undischarged bankrupt is a contractor in respect of any contract jointly with any person, that person may sue or be sued in respect of the contract without the joinder of the bankrupt.

SEC. 346 Enforcement procedures

346(1) [Creditor's execution against bankrupt] Subject to section 285 in Chapter II (restrictions on proceedings and remedies) and to the following provisions of this section, where the creditor of any person who is adjudged bankrupt has, before the commencement of the bankruptcy—

(a) issued execution against the goods or land of that person, or

(b) attached a debt due to that person from another person,

that creditor is not entitled, as against the official receiver or trustee of the bankrupt's estate, to retain the benefit of the execution or attachment, or any sums paid to avoid it, unless the execution or attachment was completed, or the sums were paid, before the commencement of the bankruptcy.

346(2)   **[Where goods taken in execution]**   Subject as follows, where any goods of a person have been taken in execution, then, if before the completion of the execution notice is given to the sheriff or other officer charged with the execution that that person has been adjudged bankrupt—

(a) the sheriff or other officer shall on request deliver to the official receiver or trustee of the bankrupt's estate the goods and any money seized or recovered in part satisfaction of the execution, but

(b) the costs of the execution are a first charge on the goods or money so delivered and the official receiver or trustee may sell the goods or a sufficient part of them for the purpose of satisfying the charge.

346(3)   **[Balance of sale proceeds]**   Subject to subsection (6) below, where—

(a) under an execution in respect of a judgment for a sum exceeding such sum as may be prescribed for the purposes of this subsection, the goods of any person are sold or money is paid in order to avoid a sale, and

(b) before the end of the period of 14 days beginning with the day of the sale or payment the sheriff or other officer charged with the execution is given notice that a bankruptcy petition has been presented in relation to that person, and

(c) a bankruptcy order is or has been made on that petition,

the balance of the proceeds of sale or money paid, after deducting the costs of execution, shall (in priority to the claim of the execution creditor) be comprised in the bankrupt's estate.

Note
The minimum amount of judgment is £500 — see The
Insolvency Proceedings (Monetary Limits) Order 1986
(S.I. 1986 No. 1996).

346(4)   **[Duty of sheriff re sum in sec. 346(3)]**   Accordingly, in the case of an execution in respect of a judgment for a sum exceeding the sum prescribed for the purposes of subsection (3), the sheriff or other officer charged with the execution—

(a) shall not dispose of the balance mentioned in subsection (3) at any time within the period of 14 days so mentioned or while there is pending a bankruptcy petition of which he has been given notice under that subsection, and

(b) shall pay that balance, where by virtue of that subsection it is comprised in the bankrupt's estate, to the official receiver or (if there is one) to the trustee of that estate.

346(5)   **[Completion of execution or attachment]**   For the purposes of this section—

(a) an execution against goods is completed by seizure and sale or by the making of a charging order under section 1 of the Charging Orders Act 1979;

(b) an execution against land is completed by seizure, by the appointment of a receiver or by the making of a charging order under that section;

(c) an attachment of a debt is completed by the receipt of the debt.

346(6) **[Setting aside of sec. 346(1)–(3) rights by court]** The rights conferred by subsections (1) to (3) on the official receiver or the trustee may, to such extent and on such terms as it thinks fit, be set aside by the court in favour of the creditor who has issued the execution or attached the debt.

346(7) **[Acquisition in good faith]** Nothing in this section entitles the trustee of a bankrupt's estate to claim goods from a person who has acquired them in good faith under a sale by a sheriff or other officer charged with an execution.

346(8) **[Non-application of sec. 346(2), (3)]** Neither subsection (2) nor subsection (3) applies in relation to any execution against property which has been acquired by or has devolved upon the bankrupt since the commencement of the bankruptcy, unless, at the time the execution is issued or before it is completed—

(a) the property has been or is claimed for the bankrupt's estate under section 307 (after-acquired property), and

(b) a copy of the notice given under that section has been or is served on the sheriff or other officer charged with the execution.

SEC. 347 Distress, etc.

347(1) **[Limit on distraining goods]** The right of any landlord or other person to whom rent is payable to distrain upon the goods and effects of an undischarged bankrupt for rent due to him from the bankrupt is available (subject to subsection (5) below) against goods and effects comprised in the bankrupt's estate, but only for 6 months' rent accrued due before the commencement of the bankruptcy.

347(2) **[Distraining where order later made]** Where a landlord or other person to whom rent is payable has distrained for rent upon the goods and effects of an individual to whom a bankruptcy petition relates and a bankruptcy order is subsequently made on that petition, any amount recovered by way of that distress which—

(a) is in excess of the amount which by virtue of subsection (1) would have been recoverable after the commencement of the bankruptcy, or

(b) is in respect of rent for a period or part of a period after the distress was levied,

shall be held for the bankrupt as part of his estate.

347(3) **[Proceeds of sale re goods not held under sec. 347(2)]** Where any person (whether or not a landlord or person entitled to rent) has distrained upon the goods or effects of an individual who is adjudged bankrupt before the end of the period of 3 months beginning with the distraint, so much of those goods or effects, or of the proceeds of their sale, as is not held for the bankrupt under subsection (2) shall be charged for the benefit of the bankrupt's estate with the preferential debts of the bankrupt to the extent that the bankrupt's estate is for the time being insufficient for meeting those debts.

347(4)   **[Where surrender under sec. 347(3)]**   Where by virtue of any charge under subsection (3) any person surrenders any goods or effects to the trustee of a bankrupt's estate or makes a payment to such a trustee, that person ranks, in respect of the amount of the proceeds of the sale of those goods or effects by the trustee or, as the case may be, the amount of the payment, as a preferential creditor of the bankrupt, except as against so much of the bankrupt's estate as is available for the payment of preferential creditors by virtue of the surrender or payment.

347(5)   **[Rights of landlord after discharge]**   A landlord or other person to whom rent is payable is not at any time after the discharge of a bankrupt entitled to distrain upon any goods or effects comprised in the bankrupt's estate.

347(6)   **[Restriction of landlord's rights]**   Where in the case of any execution—

    (a) a landlord is (apart from this section) entitled under section 1 of the Landlord and Tenant Act 1709 or section 102 of the County Courts Act 1984 (claims for rent where goods seized in execution) to claim for an amount not exceeding one year's rent, and

    (b) the person against whom the execution is levied is adjudged bankrupt before the notice of claim is served on the sheriff or other officer charged with the execution,

the right of the landlord to claim under that section is restricted to a right to claim for an amount not exceeding 6 months' rent and does not extend to any rent payable in respect of a period after the notice of claim is so served.

347(7)   **[Limit to sec. 347(6)]**   Nothing in subsection (6) imposes any liability on a sheriff or other officer charged with an execution to account to the official receiver or the trustee of a bankrupt's estate for any sums paid by him to a landlord at any time before the sheriff or other officer was served with notice of the bankruptcy order in question.

But this section is without prejudice to the liability of the landlord.

347(8)   **[Rights to distrain other than for rent]**   Nothing in this Group of Parts affects any right to distrain otherwise than for rent; and any such right is at any time exercisable without restriction against property comprised in a bankrupt's estate, even if that right is expressed by any enactment to be exercisable in like manner as a right to distrain for rent.

347(9)   **[Exercise of right]**   Any right to distrain against property comprised in a bankrupt's estate is exercisable notwithstanding that the property has vested in the trustee.

347(10)   **[Landlord's right to prove]**   The provisions of this section are without prejudice to a landlord's right in a bankruptcy to prove for any bankruptcy debt in respect of rent.

SEC. 348   Apprenticeships, etc.

348(1)   **[Application]**   This section applies where—

(a) a bankruptcy order is made in respect of an individual to whom another individual was an apprentice or articled clerk at the time when the petition on which the order was made was presented, and

(b) the bankrupt or the apprentice or clerk gives notice to the trustee terminating the apprenticeship or articles.

348(2) **[Discharge etc.]** Subject to subsection (6) below, the indenture of apprenticeship or, as the case may be, the articles of agreement shall be discharged with effect from the commencement of the bankruptcy.

348(3) **[If money paid]** If any money has been paid by or on behalf of the apprentice or clerk to the bankrupt as a fee, the trustee may, on an application made by or on behalf of the apprentice or clerk pay such sum to the apprentice or clerk as the trustee thinks reasonable, having regard to—

(a) the amount of the fee,

(b) the proportion of the period in respect of which the fee was paid that has been served by the apprentice or clerk before the commencement of the bankruptcy, and

(c) the other circumstances of the case.

348(4) **[Priority of sec. 348(3) power]** The power of the trustee to make a payment under subsection (3) has priority over his obligation to distribute the bankrupt's estate.

348(5) **[Instead of sec. 348(3) payment]** Instead of making a payment under subsection (3), the trustee may, if it appears to him expedient to do so on an application made by or on behalf of the apprentice or clerk, transfer the indenture or articles to a person other than the bankrupt.

348(6) **[Where sec. 348(5) transfer]** Where a transfer is made under subsection (5), subsection (2) has effect only as between the apprentice or clerk and the bankrupt.

SEC. 349   Unenforceability of liens on books, etc.

349(1) **[Unenforceability]** Subject as follows, a lien or other right to retain possession of any of the books, papers or other records of a bankrupt is unenforceable to the extent that its enforcement would deny possession of any books, papers or other records to the official receiver or the trustee of the bankrupt's estate.

349(2) **[Non-application of sec. 349(1)]** Subsection (1) does not apply to a lien on documents which give a title to property and are held as such.

Chapter VI — Bankruptcy Offences

PRELIMINARY

SEC. 350   Scheme of this Chapter

350(1) **[Application]** Subject to section 360(3) below, this Chapter applies where the court has made a bankruptcy order on a bankruptcy petition.

350(2)   **[Effect of annulment of bankruptcy]**   This Chapter applies whether or not the bankruptcy order is annulled, but proceedings for an offence under this Chapter shall not be instituted after the annulment.

350(3)   **[Liability of bankrupt after discharge]**   Without prejudice to his liability in respect of a subsequent bankruptcy, the bankrupt is not guilty of an offence under this Chapter in respect of anything done after his discharge; but nothing in this Group of Parts prevents the institution of proceedings against a discharged bankrupt for an offence committed before his discharge.

350(4)   **[Where not defence]**   It is not a defence in proceedings for an offence under this Chapter that anything relied on, in whole or in part, as constituting that offence was done outside England and Wales.

350(5)   **[Institution of proceedings for offence]**   Proceedings for an offence under this Chapter or under the rules shall not be instituted except by the Secretary of State or by or with the consent of the Director of Public Prosecutions.

350(6)   **[Penalty]**   A person guilty of any offence under this Chapter is liable to imprisonment or a fine, or both.

SEC. 351   Definitions

351   In the following provisions of this Chapter—

   (a) references to property comprised in the bankrupt's estate or to property possession of which is required to be delivered up to the official receiver or the trustee of the bankrupt's estate include any property which would be such property if a notice in respect of it were given under section 307 (after-acquired property) or 308 (personal property and effects of bankrupt having more than replacement value);

   (b) "**the initial period**" means the period between the presentation of the bankruptcy petition and the commencement of the bankruptcy; and

   (c) a reference to a number of months or years before petition is to that period ending with the presentation of the bankruptcy petition.

SEC. 352   Defence of innocent intention

352   Where in the case of an offence under any provision of this Chapter it is stated that this section applies, a person is not guilty of the offence if he proves that, at the time of the conduct constituting the offence, he had no intent to defraud or to conceal the state of his affairs.

WRONGDOING BY THE BANKRUPT BEFORE AND AFTER BANKRUPTCY

SEC. 353   Non-disclosure

353(1)   **[Offence]**   The bankrupt is guilty of an offence if—

   (a) he does not to the best of his knowledge and belief disclose all the property comprised in his estate to the official receiver or the trustee, or

   (b) he does not inform the official receiver or the trustee of any disposal of any property which but for the disposal would be so comprised, stating how, when, to whom and for what consideration the property was disposed of.

353(2) **[Exception to sec. 353(1)(b)]** Subsection (1)(b) does not apply to any disposal in the ordinary course of a business carried on by the bankrupt or to any payment of the ordinary expenses of the bankrupt or his family.

353(3) **[Application of sec. 352]** Section 352 applies to this offence.

SEC. 354 Concealment of property

354(1) **[Offence of concealment etc.]** The bankrupt is guilty of an offence if—

(a) he does not deliver up possession to the official receiver or trustee, or as the official receiver or trustee may direct, of such part of the property comprised in his estate as is in his possession or under his control and possession of which he is required by law so to deliver up,

(b) he conceals any debt due to or from him or conceals any property the value of which is not less than the prescribed amount and possession of which he is required to deliver up to the official receiver or trustee, or

(c) in the 12 months before petition, or in the initial period, he did anything which would have been an offence under paragraph (b) above if the bankruptcy order had been made immediately before he did it.

Section 352 applies to this offence.

354(2) **[Offence re removal of property]** The bankrupt is guilty of an offence if he removes, or in the initial period removed, any property the value of which was not less than the prescribed amount and possession of which he has or would have been required to deliver up to the official receiver or the trustee.

Section 352 applies to this offence.

354(3) **[Offence re failure to account for loss]** The bankrupt is guilty of an offence if he without reasonable excuse fails, on being required to do so by the official receiver or the court—

(a) to account for the loss of any substantial part of his property incurred in the 12 months before petition or in the initial period, or

(b) to give a satisfactory explanation of the manner in which such a loss was incurred.

SEC. 355 Concealment of books and papers; falsification

355(1) **[Offence re non-delivery of books etc.]** The bankrupt is guilty of an offence if he does not deliver up possession to the official receiver or the trustee, or as the official receiver or trustee may direct, of all books, papers and other records of which he has possession or control and which relate to his estate or his affairs.

Section 352 applies to this offence.

355(2) **[Offence re destruction, concealment etc.]** The bankrupt is guilty of an offence if—

(a) he prevents, or in the initial period prevented, the production of any books, papers or records relating to his estate or affairs;

(b) he conceals, destroys, mutilates or falsifies, or causes or permits the concealment, destruction, mutilation or falsification of, any books, papers or other records relating to his estate or affairs;

    (c) he makes, or causes or permits the making of, any false entries in any book, document or record relating to his estate or affairs; or

    (d) in the 12 months before petition, or in the initial period, he did anything which would have been an offence under paragraph (b) or (c) above if the bankruptcy order had been made before he did it.

Section 352 applies to this offence.

355(3)   **[Offence re disposal, alteration etc.]**   The bankrupt is guilty of an offence if—

    (a) he disposes of, or alters or makes any omission in, or causes or permits the disposal, altering or making of any omission in, any book, document or record relating to his estate or affairs, or

    (b) in the 12 months before petition, or in the initial period, he did anything which would have been an offence under paragraph (a) if the bankruptcy order had been made before he did it.

Section 352 applies to this offence.

SEC. 356   False statements

356(1)   **[Offence re material omission]**   The bankrupt is guilty of an offence if he makes or has made any material omission in any statement made under any provision in this Group of Parts and relating to his affairs.

Section 352 applies to this offence.

356(2)   **[Offence re failing to inform etc.]**   The bankrupt is guilty of an offence if—

    (a) knowing or believing that a false debt has been proved by any person under the bankruptcy, he fails to inform the trustee as soon as practicable; or

    (b) he attempts to account for any part of his property by fictitious losses or expenses; or

    (c) at any meeting of his creditors in the 12 months before petition or (whether or not at such a meeting) at any time in the initial period, he did anything which would have been an offence under paragraph (b) if the bankruptcy order had been made before he did it; or

    (d) he is, or at any time has been, guilty of any false representation or other fraud for the purpose of obtaining the consent of his creditors, or any of them, to an agreement with reference to his affairs or to his bankruptcy.

SEC. 357   Fraudulent disposal of property

357(1)   **[Offence re transfer]**   The bankrupt is guilty of an offence if he makes or causes to be made, or has in the period of 5 years ending with the commencement of the bankruptcy made or caused to be made, any gift or transfer of, or any charge on, his property.

Section 352 applies to this offence.

357(2)   **[Interpretation]**   The reference to making a transfer of or charge on any property includes causing or conniving at the levying of any execution against that property.

357(3) **[Offence re concealment or removal of property]** The bankrupt is guilty of an offence if he conceals or removes, or has at any time before the commencement of the bankruptcy concealed or removed, any part of his property after, or within 2 months before, the date on which a judgment or order for the payment of money has been obtained against him, being a judgment or order which was not satisfied before the commencement of the bankruptcy.

Section 352 applies to this offence.

SEC. 358 Absconding

358 The bankrupt is guilty of an offence if—

(a) he leaves, or attempts or makes preparations to leave, England and Wales with any property the value of which is not less than the prescribed amount and possession of which he is required to deliver up to the official receiver or the trustee, or

(b) in the 6 months before petition, or in the initial period, he did anything which would have been an offence under paragraph (a) if the bankruptcy order had been made immediately before he did it.

Section 352 applies to this offence.

Note
The minimum value for s. 358(a) is £500 — see The
Insolvency Proceedings (Monetary Limits) Order 1986
(S.I. 1986 No. 1996).

SEC. 359 Fraudulent dealing with property obtained on credit

359(1) **[Offence re disposal of property obtained on credit]** The bankrupt is guilty of an offence if, in the 12 months before petition, or in the initial period, he disposed of any property which he had obtained on credit and, at the time he disposed of it, had not paid for.

Section 352 applies to this offence.

359(2) **[Offence re knowingly dealing with bankrupt]** A person is guilty of an offence if, in the 12 months before petition or in the initial period, he acquired or received property from the bankrupt knowing or believing—

(a) that the bankrupt owed money in respect of the property, and

(b) that the bankrupt did not intend, or was unlikely to be able, to pay the money he so owed.

359(3) **[Disposals etc. in ordinary course of business]** A person is not guilty of an offence under subsection (1) or (2) if the disposal, acquisition or receipt of the property was in the ordinary course of a business carried on by the bankrupt at the time of the disposal, acquisition or receipt.

359(4) **[Ordinary course of business]** In determining for the purposes of this section whether any property is disposed of, acquired or received in the ordinary course of a business carried on by the bankrupt, regard may be had, in particular, to the price paid for the property.

359(5) **[Interpretation]** In this section references to disposing of property include pawning or pledging it; and references to acquiring or receiving property shall be read accordingly.

SEC. 360   Obtaining credit; engaging in business

360(1)   **[Offence re credit, non-disclosure of bankruptcy]**   The bankrupt is guilty of an offence if—

(a) either alone or jointly with any other person, he obtains credit to the extent of the prescribed amount or more without giving the person from whom he obtains it the relevant information about his status; or

(b) he engages (whether directly or indirectly) in any business under a name other than that in which he was adjudged bankrupt without disclosing to all persons with whom he enters into any business transaction the name in which he was so adjudged.

Note
The figure from 29 December 1986 is £250 under The Insolvency Proceedings (Monetary Limits) Order 1986 (S.I. 1986 No. 1996) made under s. 418.

360(2)   **[Cases of bankrupt obtaining credit]**   The reference to the bankrupt obtaining credit includes the following cases—

(a) where goods are bailed to him under a hire-purchase agreement, or agreed to be sold to him under a conditional sale agreement, and

(b) where he is paid in advance (whether in money or otherwise) for the supply of goods or services.

360(3)   **[Scotland or Northern Ireland]**   A person whose estate has been sequestrated in Scotland, or who has been adjudged bankrupt in Northern Ireland, is guilty of an offence if, before his discharge, he does anything in England and Wales which would be an offence under subsection (1) if he were an undischarged bankrupt and the sequestration of his estate or the adjudication in Northern Ireland were an adjudication under this Part.

360(4)   **[Information for sec. 360(1)(a)]**   For the purposes of subsection (1)(a), the relevant information about the status of the person in question is the information that he is an undischarged bankrupt or, as the case may be, that his estate has been sequestrated in Scotland and that he has not been discharged.

SEC. 361   Failure to keep proper accounts of business

361(1)   **[Offence re no proper accounting records]**   Where the bankrupt has been engaged in any business for any of the period of 2 years before petition, he is guilty of an offence if he—

(a) has not kept proper accounting records throughout that period and throughout any part of the initial period in which he was so engaged, or

(b) has not preserved all the accounting records which he has kept.

361(2)   **[Exception to sec. 361(1)]**   The bankrupt is not guilty of an offence under subsection (1)—

(a) if his unsecured liabilities at the commencement of the bankruptcy did not exceed the prescribed amount, or

(b) if he proves that in the circumstances in which he carried on business the omission was honest and excusable.

Note
From 29 December 1986 the figure is £20,000 under The Insolvency Proceedings (Monetary Limits) Order 1986 (S.I. 1986 No. 1996).

361(3) [Interpretation] For the purposes of this section a person is deemed not to have kept proper accounting records if he has not kept such records as are necessary to show or explain his transactions and financial position in his business, including—

(a) records containing entries from day to day, in sufficient detail, of all cash paid and received,

(b) where the business involved dealings in goods, statements of annual stock-takings, and

(c) except in the case of goods sold by way of retail trade to the actual customer, records of all goods sold and purchased showing the buyers and sellers in sufficient detail to enable the goods and the buyers and sellers to be identified.

361(4) [Application of sec. 355(2)(d), (3)(b)] In relation to any such records as are mentioned in subsection (3), subsections (2)(d) and (3)(b) of section 355 apply with the substitution of 2 years for 12 months.

SEC. 362 Gambling

362(1) [Offence re gambling, rash and hazardous speculations] The bankrupt is guilty of an offence if he has—

(a) in the 2 years before petition, materially contributed to, or increased the extent of, his insolvency by gambling or by rash and hazardous speculations, or

(b) in the initial period, lost any part of his property by gambling or by rash and hazardous speculations.

362(2) [Rash and hazardous speculations] In determining for the purposes of this section whether any speculations were rash and hazardous, the financial position of the bankrupt at the time when he entered into them shall be taken into consideration.

Chapter VII — Powers of Court In Bankruptcy

SEC. 363 General control of court

363(1) [Power of court] Every bankruptcy is under the general control of the court and, subject to the provisions in this Group of Parts, the court has full power to decide all questions of priorities and all other questions, whether of law or fact, arising in any bankruptcy.

363(2) [Bankrupt to do as directed] Without prejudice to any other provision in this Group of Parts, an undischarged bankrupt or a discharged bankrupt whose estate is still being administered under Chapter IV of this Part shall do all such things as he may be directed to do by the court for the purposes of his bankruptcy or, as the case may be, the administration of that estate.

363(3) [Application for directions] The official receiver of the trustee of a bankrupt's estate may at any time apply to the court for a direction under subsection (2).

363(4) [Contempt of court] If any person without reasonable excuse fails to comply with any obligation imposed on him by subsection (2), he is guilty of a contempt of court and liable to be punished accordingly (in addition to any other punishment to which he may be subject).

SEC. 364   Power of arrest

364(1)   [Court's power re warrant]   In the cases specified in the next subsection the court may cause a warrant to be issued to a constable or prescribed officer of the court—

    (a)   for the arrest of a debtor to whom a bankruptcy petition relates or of an undischarged bankrupt, or of a discharged bankrupt whose estate is still being administered under Chapter IV of this Part, and

    (b)   for the seizure of any books, papers, records, money or goods in the possession of a person arrested under the warrant,

and may authorise a person arrested under such a warrant to be kept in custody, and anything seized under such a warrant to be held, in accordance with the rules, until such time as the court may order.

364(2)   [Where sec. 364(1) powers exercisable]   The powers conferred by subsection (1) are exercisable in relation to a debtor or undischarged bankrupt if, at any time after the presentation of the bankruptcy petition relating to him or the making of the bankruptcy order against him, it appears to the court—

    (a)   that there are reasonable grounds for believing that he has absconded, or is about to abscond, with a view to avoiding or delaying the payment of any of his debts or his appearance to a bankruptcy petition or to avoiding, delaying or disrupting any proceedings in bankruptcy against him or any examination of his affairs, or

    (b)   that he is about to remove his goods with a view to preventing or delaying possession being taken of them by the official receiver or the trustee of his estate, or

    (c)   that there are reasonable grounds for believing that he has concealed or destroyed, or is about to conceal or destroy, any of his goods or any books, papers or records which might be of use to his creditors in the course of his bankruptcy or in connection with the administration of his estate, or

    (d)   that he has, without the leave of the official receiver or the trustee of his estate, removed any goods in his possession which exceed in value such sum as may be prescribed for the purposes of this paragraph, or

    (e)   that he has failed, without reasonable excuse, to attend any examination ordered by the court.

Note
From 29 December 1986 the figure is £500 under The Insolvency Proceedings (Monetary Limits) Order 1986 (S.I. 1986 No. 1996).

SEC. 365   Seizure of bankrupt's property

365(1)   [Court's power re warrant]   At any time after a bankruptcy order has been made, the court may, on the application of the official receiver or the trustee of the bankrupt's estate, issue a warrant authorising the person to whom it is directed to seize any property comprised in the bankrupt's estate which is, or any books, papers or records relating to the bankrupt's estate or affairs which are, in the possession or under the control of the bankrupt or any other person who is required to deliver the property, books, papers or records to the official receiver or trustee.

365(2)   [Power to break open premises etc.]   Any person executing a warrant under this section may, for the purpose of seizing any property comprised in the bankrupt's estate or any books, papers or records relating to the bankrupt's estate or affairs, break open any premises where the bankrupt or anything that may be seized under the warrant is or is believed to be and any receptacle of the bankrupt which contains or is believed to contain anything that may be so seized.

365(3)   [Power of court re search]   If, after a bankruptcy order has been made, the court is satisfied that any property comprised in the bankrupt's estate is, or any books, papers or records relating to the bankrupt's estate or affairs are, concealed in any premises not belonging to him, it may issue a warrant authorising any constable or prescribed officer of the court to search those premises for the property, books, papers or records.

365(4)   [Execution of sec. 365(3) warrant]   A warrant under subsection (3) shall not be executed except in the prescribed manner and in accordance with its terms.

SEC. 366   Inquiry into bankrupt's dealings and property

366(1)   [Power of court to summon bankrupt to appear]   At any time after a bankruptcy order has been made the court may, on the application of the official receiver or the trustee of the bankrupt's estate, summon to appear before it—

   (a)   the bankrupt or the bankrupt's spouse or former spouse,

   (b)   any person known or believed to have any property comprised in the bankrupt's estate in his possession or to be indebted to the bankrupt,

   (c)   any person appearing to the court to be able to give information concerning the bankrupt or the bankrupt's dealings, affairs or property.

The court may require any such person as is mentioned in paragraph (b) or (c) to submit an affidavit to the court containing an account of his dealings with the bankrupt or to produce any documents in his possession or under his control relating to the bankrupt or the bankrupt's dealings, affairs or property.

366(2)   [Application of sec. 366(3)]   Without prejudice to section 364, the following applies in a case where—

   (a)   a person without reasonable excuse fails to appear before the court when he is summoned to do so under this section, or

   (b)   there are reasonable grounds for believing that a person has absconded, or is about to abscond, with a view to avoiding his appearance before the court under this section.

366(3)   [Issue of warrant re non-appearance]   The court may, for the purpose of bringing that person and anything in his possession before the court, cause a warrant to be issued to a constable or prescribed officer of the court—

   (a)   for the arrest of that person, and

   (b)   for the seizure of any books, papers, records, money or goods in that person's possession.

366(4)   **[Power re custody etc.]**   The court may authorise a person arrested under such a warrant to be kept in custody, and anything seized under such a warrant to be held, in accordance with the rules, until that person is brought before the court under the warrant or until such other time as the court may order.

SEC. 367   Court's enforcement powers under sec. 366

367(1)   **[Power to order delivery]**   If it appears to the court, on consideration of any evidence obtained under section 366 or this section, that any person has in his possession any property comprised in the bankrupt's estate, the court may, on the application of the official receiver or the trustee of the bankrupt's estate, order that person to deliver the whole or any part of the property to the official receiver or the trustee at such time, in such manner and on such terms as the court thinks fit.

367(2)   **[Power to order payment from bankrupt debtor]**   If it appears to the court, on consideration of any evidence obtained under section 366 or this section, that any person is indebted to the bankrupt, the court may, on the application of the official receiver or the trustee of the bankrupt's estate, order that person to pay to the official receiver or trustee, at such time and in such manner as the court may direct, the whole or part of the amount due, whether in full discharge of the debt or otherwise as the court thinks fit.

367(3)   **[Place of examination]**   The court may, if it thinks fit, order that any person who if within the jurisdiction of the court would be liable to be summoned to appear before it under section 366 shall be examined in any part of the United Kingdom where he may be for the time being, or in any place outside the United Kingdom.

367(4)   **[Examination on oath]**   Any person who appears or is brought before the court under section 366 or this section may be examined on oath, either orally or by interrogatories, concerning the bankrupt or the bankrupt's dealings, affairs and property.

SEC. 368   Provision corresponding to sec. 366, where interim receiver appointed

368   Sections 366 and 367 apply where an interim receiver has been appointed under section 286 as they apply where a bankruptcy order has been made, as if—

(a) references to the official receiver or the trustee were to the interim receiver, and

(b) references to the bankrupt and to his estate were (respectively) to the debtor and his property.

SEC. 369   Order for production of documents by inland revenue

369(1)   **[Power of court]**   For the purposes of an examination under section 290 (public examination of bankrupt) or proceedings under sections 366 to 368, the court may, on the application of the official receiver or the trustee of the bankrupt's estate, order an inland revenue official to produce to the court—

(a) any return, account or accounts submitted (whether before or after the commencement of the bankruptcy) by the bankrupt to any inland revenue official,

(b) any assessment or determination made (whether before or after the commencement of the bankruptcy) in relation to the bankrupt by any inland revenue official, or

(c) any correspondence (whether before or after the commencement of the bankruptcy) between the bankrupt and any inland revenue official.

369(2)   [Order re disclosure of document]   Where the court has made an order under subsection (1) for the purposes of any examination or proceedings, the court may, at any time after the document to which the order relates is produced to it, by order authorise the disclosure of the document, or of any part of its contents, to the official receiver, the trustee of the bankrupt's estate or the bankrupt's creditors.

369(3)   [Condition for sec. 369(1) order]   The court shall not address an order under subsection (1) to an inland revenue official unless it is satisfied that that official is dealing, or has dealt, with the affairs of the bankrupt.

369(4)   [Where sec. 369(1) document not in official's possession]   Where any document to which an order under subsection (1) relates is not in the possession of the official to whom the order is addressed, it is the duty of that official to take all reasonable steps to secure possession of it and, if he fails to do so, to report the reasons for his failure to the court.

369(5)   [Where document held by another official]   Where any document to which an order under subsection (1) relates is in the possession of an inland revenue official other than the one to whom the order is addressed, it is the duty of the official in possession of the document, at the request of the official to whom the order is addressed, to deliver it to the official making the request.

369(6)   ["Inland revenue official"]   In this section **"inland revenue official"** means any inspector or collector of taxes appointed by the Commissioners of Inland Revenue or any person appointed by the Commissioners to serve in any other capacity.

369(7)   [Non-application]   This section does not apply for the purposes of an examination under sections 366 and 367 which takes place by virtue of section 368 (interim receiver).

SEC. 370   Power to appoint special manager

370(1)   [Power of court]   The court may, on an application under this section, appoint any person to be the special manager—

(a) of a bankrupt's estate, or

(b) of the business of an undischarged bankrupt, or

(c) of the property or business of a debtor in whose case the official receiver has been appointed interim receiver under section 286.

370(2)   [Application to court]   An application under this section may be made by the official receiver or the trustee of the bankrupt's estate in any case where it appears to the official receiver or trustee that the nature of the estate, property or business, or the interests of the creditors generally, require the appointment of another person to manage the estate, property or business.

370(3)   [Powers of special manager]   A special manager appointed under this section has such powers as may be entrusted to him by the court.

370(4) [Powers included in sec. 370(3)] The power of the court under subsection (3) to entrust powers to a special manager include power to direct that any provision in this Group of Parts that has effect in relation to the official receiver, interim receiver or trustee shall have the like effect in relation to the special manager for the purposes of the carrying out by the special manager of any of the functions of the official receiver, interim receiver or trustee.

370(5) [Duties of special manager] A special manager appointed under this section shall—

  (a) give such security as may be prescribed,

  (b) prepare and keep such accounts as may be prescribed, and

  (c) produce those accounts in accordance with the rules to the Secretary of State or to such other persons as may be prescribed.

SEC. 371 Re-direction of bankrupt's letters, etc.

371(1) [Power of court] Where a bankruptcy order has been made, the court may from time to time, on the application of the official receiver or the trustee of the bankrupt's estate, order the Post Office to re-direct and send or deliver to the official receiver or trustee or otherwise any postal packet (within the meaning of the Post Office Act 1953) which would otherwise be sent or delivered by them to the bankrupt at such place or places as may be specified in the order.

371(2) [Duration of court order] An order under this section has effect for such period, not exceeding 3 months, as may be specified in the order.

PART X — INDIVIDUAL INSOLVENCY: GENERAL PROVISIONS

SEC. 372 Supplies of gas, water, electricity, etc.

372(1) [Application] This section applies where on any day ("**the relevant day**")—

  (a) a bankruptcy order is made against an individual or an interim receiver of an individual's property is appointed, or

  (b) a voluntary arrangement proposed by an individual is approved under Part VIII, or

  (c) a deed of arrangement is made for the benefit of an individual's creditors;

and in this section "**the office-holder**" means the official receiver, the trustee in bankruptcy, the interim receiver, the supervisor of the voluntary arrangement or the trustee under the deed of arrangement, as the case may be.

372(2) [Where sec. 372(3) request] If a request falling within the next subsection is made for the giving after the relevant day of any of the supplies mentioned in subsection (4), the supplier—

  (a) may make it a condition of the giving of the supply that the office-holder personally guarantees the payment of any charges in respect of the supply, but

(b) shall not make it a condition of the giving of the supply, or do anything which has the effect of making it a condition of the giving of the supply, that any outstanding charges in respect of a supply given to the individual before the relevant day are paid.

372(3) [Type of request] A request falls within this subsection if it is made—

(a) by or with the concurrence of the office-holder, and

(b) for the purposes of any business which is or has been carried on by the individual, by a firm or partnership of which the individual is or was a member, or by an agent or manager for the individual or for such a firm or partnership.

372(4) [Supplies in sec. 372(2)] The supplies referred to in subsection (2) are—

(a) a public supply of gas,

(b) a supply of electricity by an Electricity Board,

(c) a supply of water by a water undertaker,

(d) a supply of telecommunication services by a public telecommunications operator.

History
In s. 372(4)(c) the words "a water undertaker" substituted for the former words "statutory water undertakers" by Water Act 1989, s. 190(1) and Sch. 25, para. 78(1) as from 1 September 1989 (see Water Act 1989, s. 4, 194(4) and S.I. 1989 No. 1146 (C. 37) — see also S.I. 1989 No. 1530 (C. 51)).

372(5) [Definitions] The following applies to expressions used in subsection (4)—

(a) **"public supply of gas"** means a supply of gas by the British Gas Corporation as a public gas supplier within the meaning of Part I of the Gas Act 1986,

(b) **"Electricity Board"** means the same as in the Energy Act 1983; and

(c) **"telecommunication services"** and **"public telecommunications operator"** mean the same as in the Telecommunications Act 1984, except that the former does not include services consisting in the conveyance of programmes included in cable programme services (within the meaning of the Cable and Broadcasting Act 1984).

SEC. 373   Jurisdiction in relation to insolvent individuals

373(1) [High Court and county courts] The High Court and the county courts have jurisdiction throughout England and Wales for the purposes of the Parts in this Group.

373(2) [Powers of county court] For the purposes of those Parts, a county court has, in addition to its ordinary jurisdiction, all the powers and jurisdiction of the High Court; and the orders of the court may be enforced accordingly in the prescribed manner.

373(3) [Exercise of jurisdiction] Jurisdiction for the purposes of those Parts is exercised—

(a) by the High Court in relation to the proceedings which, in accordance with the rules, are allocated to the London insolvency district, and

(b) by each county court in relation to the proceedings which are so allocated to the insolvency district of that court.

373(4) **[Operation of sec. 373(3)]** Subsection (3) is without prejudice to the transfer of proceedings from one court to another in the manner prescribed by the rules; and nothing in that subsection invalidates any proceedings on the grounds that they were initiated or continued in the wrong court.

SEC. 374 Insolvency districts

374(1) **[Order by Lord Chancellor]** The Lord Chancellor may by order designate the areas which are for the time being to be comprised, for the purposes of the Parts in this Group, in the London insolvency district and the insolvency district of each county court; and an order under this section may—

    (a) exclude any county court from having jurisdiction for the purposes of those Parts, or

    (b) confer jurisdiction for those purposes on any county court which has not previously had that jurisdiction.

374(2) **[Incidental provisions etc.]** An order under this section may contain such incidental, supplemental and transitional provisions as may appear to the Lord Chancellor necessary or expedient.

374(3) **[Order by statutory instrument]** An order under this section shall be made by statutory instrument and, after being made, shall be laid before each House of Parliament.

374(4) **[Relevant districts]** Subject to any order under this section—

    (a) the district which, immediately before the appointed day, is the London bankruptcy district becomes, on that day, the London insolvency district;

    (b) any district which immediately before that day is the bankruptcy district of a county court becomes, on that day, the insolvency district of that court, and

    (c) any county court which immediately before that day is excluded from having jurisdiction in bankruptcy is excluded, on and after that day, from having jurisdiction for the purposes of the Parts in this Group.

SEC. 375 Appeals etc. from courts exercising insolvency jurisdiction

375(1) **[Review, rescission etc.]** Every court having jurisdiction for the purposes of the Parts in this Group may review, rescind or vary any order made by it in the exercise of that jurisdiction.

375(2) **[Appeals]** An appeal from a decision made in the exercise of jurisdiction for the purposes of those Parts by a county court or by a registrar in bankruptcy of the High Court lies to a single judge of the High Court; and an appeal from a decision of that judge on such an appeal lies, with the leave of the judge or of the Court of Appeal, to the Court of Appeal.

375(3) **[No other appeals]** A county court is not, in the exercise of its jurisdiction for the purposes of those Parts, to be subject to be restrained by the order of any other court, and no appeal lies from its decision in the exercise of that jurisdiction except as provided by this section.

SEC. 376 Time-limits

376 Where by any provision in this Group of Parts or by the rules the time for doing anything is limited, the court may extend the time, either before or after it has expired, on such terms, if any, as it thinks fit.

SEC. 377 Formal defects

377 The acts of a person as the trustee of a bankrupt's estate or as a special manager, and the acts of the creditors' committee established for any bankruptcy, are valid notwithstanding any defect in the appointment, election or qualifications of the trustee or manager or, as the case may be, of any member of the committee.

SEC. 378 Exemption from stamp duty

378 Stamp duty shall not be charged on—

 (a) any document, being a deed, conveyance, assignment, surrender, admission or other assurance relating solely to property which is comprised in a bankrupt's estate and which, after the execution of that document, is or remains at law or in equity the property of the bankrupt or of the trustee of that estate,

 (b) any writ, order, certificate or other instrument relating solely to the property of a bankrupt or to any bankruptcy proceedings.

SEC. 379 Annual report

379 As soon as practicable after the end of 1986 and each subsequent calendar year, the Secretary of State shall prepare and lay before each House of Parliament a report about the operation during that year of so much of this Act as is comprised in this Group of Parts, and about proceedings in the course of that year under the Deeds of Arrangement Act 1914.

PART XI — INTERPRETATION FOR SECOND GROUP OF PARTS

SEC. 380 Introductory

380 The next five sections have effect for the interpretation of the provisions of this Act which are comprised in this Group of Parts; and where a definition is provided for a particular expression, it applies except so far as the context otherwise requires.

SEC. 381 "Bankrupt" and associated terminology

381(1) ["**Bankrupt**"] "**Bankrupt**" means an individual who has been adjudged bankrupt and, in relation to a bankruptcy order, it means the individual adjudged bankrupt by that order.

381(2) ["**Bankruptcy order**"] "**Bankruptcy order**" means an order adjudging an individual bankrupt.

381(3) ["**Bankruptcy petition**"] "**Bankruptcy petition**" means a petition to the court for a bankruptcy order.

SEC. 382 "Bankruptcy debt", etc.

382(1) ["**Bankruptcy debt**"] "**Bankruptcy debt**", in relation to a bankrupt, means (subject to the next subsection) any of the following—

 (a) any debt or liability to which he is subject at the commencement of the bankruptcy,

(b) any debt or liability to which he may become subject after the commencement of the bankruptcy (including after his discharge from bankruptcy) by reason of any obligation incurred before the commencement of the bankruptcy,

(c) any amount specified in pursuance of section 39(3)(c) of the Powers of Criminal Courts Act 1973 in any criminal bankruptcy order made against him before the commencement of the bankruptcy, and

(d) any interest provable as mentioned in section 322(2) in Chapter IV of Part IX.

Note
S. 382(1)(c) repealed by Criminal Justice Act 1988,
s. 170(2) and Sch. 16 as from a day to be appointed.

382(2) [Liability in tort] In determining for the purposes of any provision in this Group of Parts whether any liability in tort is a bankruptcy debt, the bankrupt is deemed to become subject to that liability by reason of an obligation incurred at the time when the cause of action accrued.

382(3) [References to debtor liability] For the purposes of references in this Group of Parts to a debt or liability, it is immaterial whether the debt or liability is present or future, whether it is certain or contingent or whether its amount is fixed or liquidated, or is capable of being ascertained by fixed rules or as a matter of opinion; and references in this Group of Parts to owing a debt are to be read accordingly.

382(4) ["Liability"] In this Group of Parts, except in so far as the context otherwise requires, **"liability"** means (subject to subsection (3) above) a liability to pay money or money's worth, including any liability under an enactment, any liability for breach of trust, any liability in contract, tort or bailment and any liability arising out of an obligation to make restitution.

SEC. 383   "Creditor", "security", etc.

383(1) ["Creditor"]   "Creditor"—

(a) in relation to a bankrupt, means a person to whom any of the bankruptcy debts is owed (being, in the case of an amount falling within paragraph (c) of the definition in section 382(1) of **"bankruptcy debt"**, the person in respect of whom that amount is specified in the criminal bankruptcy order in question), and

(b) in relation to an individual to whom a bankruptcy petition relates, means a person who would be a creditor in the bankruptcy if a bankruptcy order were made on that petition.

Note
In s. 383(1)(a) the words from "(being," to "question)"
repealed by Criminal Justice Act 1988, s. 170(2) and Sch.
16 as from a day to be appointed.

383(2) [Securing of debt] Subject to the next two subsections and any provision of the rules requiring a creditor to give up his security for the purposes of proving a debt, a debt is secured for the purposes of this Group of Parts to the extent that the person to whom the debt is owed holds any security for the debt (whether a mortgage, charge, lien or other security) over any property of the person by whom the debt is owed.

383(3) [**Where sec. 269(1)(a) statement made**] Where a statement such as is mentioned in section 269(1)(a) in Chapter I of Part IX has been made by a secured creditor for the purposes of any bankruptcy petition and a bankruptcy order is subsequently made on that petition, the creditor is deemed for the purposes of the Parts in this Group to have given up the security specified in the statement.

383(4) [**Qualification to sec. 383(2)**] In subsection (2) the reference to a security does not include a lien on books, papers or other records, except to the extent that they consist of documents which give a title to property and are held as such.

SEC. 384 "Prescribed" and "the rules"

384(1) [**Definitions**] Subject to the next subsection, **"prescribed"** means prescribed by the rules; and **"the rules"** means rules made under section 412 in Part XV.

384(2) [**Interpretation**] References in this Group of Parts to the amount prescribed for the purposes of any of the following provisions—

> section 273;
> section 346(3);
> section 354(1) and (2);
> section 358;
> section 360(1);
> section 361(2); and
> section 364(2)(d),

and references in those provisions to the prescribed amount are to be read in accordance with section 418 in Part XV and orders made under that section.

SEC. 385 Miscellaneous definitions

385(1) [**Definitions**] The following definitions have effect—

"the court", in relation to any matter, means the court to which, in accordance with section 373 in Part X and the rules, proceedings with respect to that matter are allocated or transferred;

"creditor's petition" means a bankruptcy petition under section 264(1)(a);

"criminal bankruptcy order" means an order under section 39(1) of the Powers of Criminal Courts Act 1973;

"debt" is to be construed in accordance with section 382(3);

"the debtor"—

> (a) in relation to a proposal for the purposes of Part VIII, means the individual making or intending to make that proposal, and
>
> (b) in relation to a bankruptcy petition, means the individual to whom the petition relates;

"debtor's petition" means a bankruptcy petition presented by the debtor himself under section 264(1)(b);

"dwelling house" includes any building or part of a building which is occupied as a dwelling and any yard, garden, garage or outhouse belonging to the dwelling house and occupied with it;

"estate", in relation to a bankrupt is to be construed in accordance with section 283 in Chapter II of Part IX;

"**family**", in relation to a bankrupt, means the persons (if any) who are living with him and are dependent on him;

"**secured**" and related expressions are to be construed in accordance with section 383; and

"**the trustee**", in relation to a bankruptcy and the bankrupt, means the trustee of the bankrupt's estate.

Note
In s. 385(1) the definition of "criminal bankruptcy order" repealed by Criminal Justice Act 1988, s. 170(2) and Sch. 16 as from a day to be appointed.

385(2) **[Interpretation]** References in this Group of Parts to a person's affairs include his business, if any.

THE THIRD GROUP OF PARTS
MISCELLANEOUS MATTERS BEARING ON BOTH COMPANY AND INDIVIDUAL INSOLVENCY; GENERAL INTERPRETATION; FINAL PROVISIONS

PART XII — PREFERENTIAL DEBTS IN COMPANY AND INDIVIDUAL INSOLVENCY

SEC. 386   Categories of preferential debts

386(1) **[Debts listed in Sch. 6]** A reference in this Act to the preferential debts of a company or an individual is to the debts listed in Schedule 6 to this Act (money owed to the Inland Revenue for income tax deducted at source; VAT, car tax, betting and gaming duties; social security and pension scheme contributions; remuneration etc. of employees; levies on coal and steel production); and references to preferential creditors are to be read accordingly.

History
In s. 386(1) the words "; levies on coal and steel production"   1987 (S.I. 1987 No. 2093), reg. 2(2) as from 1 January inserted by The Insolvency (ECSC Levy Debts) Regulations   1988.

386(2) **["The debtor"]** In that Schedule "**the debtor**" means the company or the individual concerned.

386(3) **[Interpretation of Sch. 6]** Schedule 6 is to be read with Schedule 3 to the Social Security Pensions Act 1975 (occupational pension scheme contributions).

SEC. 387   "The relevant date"

387(1) **[Explanation of Sch. 6]** This section explains references in Schedule 6 to the relevant date (being the date which determines the existence and amount of a preferential debt).

387(2) **[Pt. I, sec. 4]** For the purposes of section 4 in Part I (meetings to consider company voluntary arrangement), the relevant date in relation to a company which is not being wound up is—

  (a) where an administration order is in force in relation to the company, the date of the making of that order, and

  (b) where no such order has been made, the date of the approval of the voluntary arrangement.

387(3) **[Company being wound up]** In relation to a company which is being wound up, the following applies—

(a) if the winding up is by the court, and the winding-up order was made immediately upon the discharge of an administration order, the relevant date is the date of the making of the administration order;

(b) if the case does not fall within paragraph (a) and the company—

 (i) is being wound up by the court, and

 (ii) had not commenced to be wound up voluntarily before the date of the making of the winding-up order,

 the relevant date is the date of the appointment (or first appointment) of a provisional liquidator or, if no such appointment has been made, the date of the winding-up order;

(c) if the case does not fall within either paragraph (a) or (b), the relevant date is the date of the passing of the resolution for the winding up of the company.

387(4) **[Company in receivership]** In relation to a company in receivership (where section 40 or, as the case may be, section 59 applies), the relevant date is—

(a) in England and Wales, the date of the appointment of the receiver by debenture-holders, and

(b) in Scotland, the date of the appointment of the receiver under section 53(6) or (as the case may be) 54(5).

387(5) **[Pt. VIII, sec. 258]** For the purposes of section 258 in Part VIII (individual voluntary arrangements), the relevant date is, in relation to a debtor who is not an undischarged bankrupt, the date of the interim order made under section 252 with respect to his proposal.

387(6) **[Bankrupt]** In relation to a bankrupt, the following applies—

(a) where at the time the bankruptcy order was made there was an interim receiver appointed under section 286, the relevant date is the date on which the interim receiver was first appointed after the presentation of the bankruptcy petition;

(b) otherwise, the relevant date is the date of the making of the bankruptcy order.

PART XIII — INSOLVENCY PRACTITIONERS AND THEIR QUALIFICATION

RESTRICTIONS ON UNQUALIFIED PERSONS ACTING AS LIQUIDATOR, TRUSTEE IN BANKRUPTCY, ETC.

SEC. 388 Meaning of "act as insolvency practitioner"

388(1) **[Acting as insolvency practitioner re company]** A person acts as an insolvency practitioner in relation to a company by acting—

(a) as its liquidator, provisional liquidator, administrator or administrative receiver, or

(b) as supervisor of a voluntary arrangement approved by it under Part I.

388(2) [Acting as insolvency practitioner re individual] A person acts as an insolvency practitioner in relation to an individual by acting—

(a) as his trustee in bankruptcy or interim receiver of his property or as permanent or interim trustee in the sequestration of his estate; or

(b) as trustee under a deed which is a deed of arrangement made for the benefit of his creditors or, in Scotland, a trust deed for his creditors; or

(c) as supervisor of a voluntary arrangement proposed by him and approved under Part VIII; or

(d) in the case of a deceased individual to the administration of whose estate this section applies by virtue of an order under section 421 (application of provisions of this Act to insolvent estates of deceased persons), as administrator of that estate.

388(3) [Interpretation] References in this section to an individual include, except in so far as the context otherwise requires, references to a partnership and to any debtor within the meaning of the Bankruptcy (Scotland) Act 1985.

388(4) [Definitions] In this section—

"**administrative receiver**" has the meaning given by section 251 in Part VII;

"**company**" means a company within the meaning given by section 735(1) of the Companies Act, a company which may be wound up under Part V of this Act or a building society within the meaning of the Building Societies Act 1986; and

"**interim trustee**" and "**permanent trustee**" mean the same as in the Bankruptcy (Scotland) Act 1985.

History
In s. 388(4) the definition of "company" substituted by Building Societies Act 1986, s. 120 and Sch. 18, para. 17(2) as from 1 January 1987 (see S.I. 1986 No. 1560 (C. 56)) in regard to the former provision, Insolvency Act 1985, s. 1(5). This definition included in this current provision as result of Sch. 11, para. 27, 29 of this Act and of Interpretation Act 1978, s. 17(2)(a). References to "1985 Act" and "Part XXI of that Act" replaced by CCH with references to "Companies Act" and "Part V of this Act".

388(5) [Non-application to official receiver] Nothing in this section applies to anything done by the official receiver.

SEC. 389   Acting without qualification an offence

389(1) [Penalty] A person who acts as an insolvency practitioner in relation to a company or an individual at a time when he is not qualified to do so is liable to imprisonment or a fine, or to both.

389(2) [Non-application to official receiver] This section does not apply to the official receiver.

THE REQUISITE QUALIFICATION,
AND THE MEANS OF OBTAINING IT

SEC. 390   Persons not qualified to act as insolvency practitioners

390(1) [Must be individual] A person who is not an individual is not qualified to act as an insolvency practitioner.

390(2) [Authorisation necessary] A person is not qualified to act as an insolvency practitioner at any time unless at that time—

(a) he is authorised so to act by virtue of membership of a professional body recognised under section 391 below, being permitted so to act by or under the rules of that body, or

    (b) he holds an authorisation granted by a competent authority under section 393.

390(3) **[Security as condition required]** A person is not qualified to act as an insolvency practitioner in relation to another person at any time unless—

    (a) there is in force at that time security or, in Scotland, caution for the proper performance of his functions, and (INDEMNITY INSURANCE)

    (b) that security or caution meets the prescribed requirements with respect to his so acting in relation to that other person.

390(4) **[Disqualification]** A person is not qualified to act as an insolvency practitioner at any time if at that time—

    (a) he has been adjudged bankrupt or sequestration of his estate has been awarded and (in either case) he has not been discharged,

    (b) he is subject to a disqualification order made under the Company Directors Disqualification Act 1986, or

    (c) he is a patient within the meaning of Part VII of the Mental Health Act 1983 or section 125(1) of the Mental Health (Scotland) Act 1984.

Note
Reference should be made to the Insolvency Practitioners
Regulations 1990 (S.I. 1990 No. 439).

SEC. 391 Recognised professional bodies

391(1) **[Order by Secretary of State]** The Secretary of State may by order declare a body which appears to him to fall within subsection (2) below to be a recognised professional body for the purposes of this section.

391(2) **[Bodies recognised]** A body may be recognised if it regulates the practice of a profession and maintains and enforces rules for securing that such of its members as are permitted by or under the rules to act as insolvency practitioners—

    (a) are fit and proper persons so to act, and

    (b) meet acceptable requirements as to education and practical training and experience.

391(3) **[Interpretation]** References to members of a recognised professional body are to persons who, whether members of that body or not, are subject to its rules in the practice of the profession in question.

    The reference in section 390(2) above to membership of a professional body recognised under this section is to be read accordingly.

391(4) **[Revocation of order]** An order made under subsection (1) in relation to a professional body may be revoked by a further order if it appears to the Secretary of State that the body no longer falls within subsection (2).

391(5) **[Effect of order]** An order of the Secretary of State under this section has effect from such date as is specified in the order; and any such order revoking a previous order may make provision whereby members of the body in question continue to be treated as authorised to act as insolvency practitioners for a specified period after the revocation takes effect.

Note
See the Insolvency Practitioners (Recognised Professional
Bodies) Order 1986 (S.I. 1986 No. 1764).

SEC. 392   Authorisation by competent authority

392(1)   [Application]   Application may be made to a competent authority for authorisation to act as an insolvency practitioner.

Note
See the Insolvency Practitioners Regulations 1990 (S.I. 1990 No. 439).

 392(2)   [Competent authorities]   The competent authorities for this purpose are—

   (a) in relation to a case of any description specified in directions given by the Secretary of State, the body or person so specified in relation to cases of that description, and

   (b) in relation to a case not falling within paragraph (a), the Secretary of State.

392(3)   [Application]   The application—

   (a) shall be made in such manner as the competent authority may direct,

   (b) shall contain or be accompanied by such information as that authority may reasonably require for the purpose of determining the application, and

   (c) shall be accompanied by the prescribed fee;

and the authority may direct that notice of the making of the application shall be published in such manner as may be specified in the direction.

392(4)   [Additional information]   At any time after receiving the application and before determining it the authority may require the applicant to furnish additional information.

392(5)   [Requirements may differ]   Directions and requirements given or imposed under subsection (3) or (4) may differ as between different applications.

392(6)   [Forms]   Any information to be furnished to the competent authority under this section shall, if it so requires, be in such form or verified in such manner as it may specify.

392(7)   [Withdrawal of application]   An application may be withdrawn before it is granted or refused.

392(8)   [Sums received]   Any sums received under this section by a competent authority other than the Secretary of State may be retained by the authority; and any sums so received by the Secretary of State shall be paid into the Consolidated Fund.

SEC. 393   Grant, refusal and withdrawal of authorisation

393(1)   [Power to grant, refuse application]   The competent authority may, on an application duly made in accordance with section 392 and after being furnished with all such information as it may require under that section, grant or refuse the application.

393(2)   [Granting application]   The authority shall grant the application if it appears to it from the information furnished by the applicant and having regard to such other information, if any, as it may have—

   (a) that the applicant is a fit and proper person to act as an insolvency practitioner, and

   (b) that the applicant meets the prescribed requirements with respect to education and practical training and experience.

393(3) **[Duration of authorisation]** An authorisation granted under this section, if not previously withdrawn, continues in force for such period not exceeding the prescribed maximum as may be specified in the authorisation.

393(4) **[Withdrawal of authorisation]** An authorisation so granted may be withdrawn by the competent authority if it appears to it—

    (a) that the holder of the authorisation is no longer a fit and proper person to act as an insolvency practitioner, or

    (b) without prejudice to paragraph (a), that the holder—

        (i) has failed to comply with any provision of this Part or of any regulations made under this Part or Part XV, or

        (ii) in purported compliance with any such provision, has furnished the competent authority with false, inaccurate or misleading information.

393(5) **[Withdrawal on request]** An authorisation granted under this section may be withdrawn by the competent authority at the request or with the consent of the holder of the authorisation.

Note
See the regulations referred to in the note to s. 392(1).

SEC. 394 Notices

394(1) **[Notice to applicant re grant]** Where a competent authority grants an authorisation under section 393, it shall give written notice of that fact to the applicant, specifying the date on which the authorisation takes effect.

394(2) **[Notice re proposed refusal, withdrawal]** Where the authority proposes to refuse an application, or to withdraw an authorisation under section 393(4), it shall give the applicant or holder of the authorisation written notice of its intention to do so, setting out particulars of the grounds on which is proposes to act.

394(3) **[Date to be stated re withdrawal]** In the case of a proposed withdrawal the notice shall state the date on which it is proposed that the withdrawal should take effect.

394(4) **[Notice to give details re rights]** A notice under subsection (2) shall give particulars of the rights exercisable under the next two sections by a person on whom the notice is served.

SEC. 395 Right to make representations

395(1) **[Right exercisable within 14 days]** A person on whom a notice is served under section 394(2) may within 14 days after the date of service make written representations to the competent authority.

395(2) **[Representations to be considered]** The competent authority shall have regard to any representations so made in determining whether to refuse the application or withdraw the authorisation, as the case may be.

SEC. 396 Reference to Tribunal

396(1) **[Application of Sch. 7]** The Insolvency Practitioners Tribunal ("**the Tribunal**") continues in being; and the provisions of Schedule 7 apply to it.

Note
See The Insolvency Practitioners Tribunal (Conduct of
Investigations) Rules 1986 (S.I. 1986 No. 952).

396(2)   **[Person served with notice]**   Where a person is served with a notice under section 394(2), he may—

    (a)   at any time within 28 days after the date of service of the notice, or

    (b)   at any time after the making by him of representations under section 395 and before the end of the period of 28 days after the date of the service on him of a notice by the competent authority that the authority does not propose to alter its decision in consequence of the representations,

give written notice to the authority requiring the case to be referred to the Tribunal.

396(3)   **[Reference]**   Where a requirement is made under subsection (2), then, unless the competent authority—

    (a)   has decided or decides to grant the application or, as the case may be, not to withdraw the authorisation, and

    (b)   within 7 days after the date of the making of the requirement, gives written notice of that decision to the person by whom the requirement was made,

it shall refer the case to the Tribunal.

SEC. 397   Action of Tribunal on reference

397(1)   **[Duties of Tribunal]**   On a reference under section 396 the Tribunal shall—

    (a)   investigate the case, and

    (b)   make a report to the competent authority stating what would in their opinion be the appropriate decision in the matter and the reasons for that opinion,

and it is the duty of the competent authority to decide the matter accordingly.

397(2)   **[Copy of report to applicant]**   The Tribunal shall send a copy of the report to the applicant or, as the case may be, the holder of the authorisation; and the competent authority shall serve him with a written notice of the decision made by it in accordance with the report.

397(3)   **[Publication of report]**   The competent authority may, if he thinks fit, publish the report of the Tribunal.

SEC. 398   Refusal or withdrawal without reference to Tribunal

398   Where in the case of any proposed refusal or withdrawal of an authorisation either—

    (a)   the period mentioned in section 396(2)(a) has expired without the making of any requirement under that subsection or of any representations under section 395, or

    (b)   the competent authority has given a notice such as is mentioned in section 396(2)(b) and the period so mentioned has expired without the making of any such requirement,

the competent authority may give written notice of the refusal or withdrawal to the person concerned in accordance with the proposal in the notice given under section 394(2).

PART XIV — PUBLIC ADMINISTRATION (ENGLAND AND WALES)

OFFICIAL RECEIVERS

SEC. 399 Appointment, etc. of official receivers

399(1) **[Official receiver]** For the purposes of this Act the official receiver, in relation to any bankruptcy or winding up, is any person who by virtue of the following provisions of this section or section 401 below is authorised to act as the official receiver in relation to that bankruptcy or winding up.

399(2) **[Power of appointment by Secretary of State]** The Secretary of State may (subject to the approval of the Treasury as to numbers) appoint persons to the office of official receiver, and a person appointed to that office (whether under this section or section 70 of the Bankruptcy Act 1914)—

(a) shall be paid out of money provided by Parliament such salary as the Secretary of State may with the concurrence of the Treasury direct,

(b) shall hold office on such other terms and conditions as the Secretary of State may with the concurrence of the Treasury direct, and

(c) may be removed from office by a direction of the Secretary of State.

399(3) **[Attachment to particular court]** Where a person holds the office of official receiver, the Secretary of State shall from time to time attach him either to the High Court or to a county court having jurisdiction for the purposes of the second Group of Parts of this Act.

399(4) **[Person authorised to act as official receiver]** Subject to any directions under subsection (6) below, an official receiver attached to a particular court is the person authorised to act as the official receiver in relation to every bankruptcy or winding up falling within the jurisdiction of that court.

399(5) **[Each court to have official receiver]** The Secretary of State shall ensure that there is, at all times, at least one official receiver attached to the High Court and at least one attached to each county court having jurisdiction for the purposes of the second Group of Parts; but he may attach the same official receiver to two or more different courts.

399(6) **[Directions by Secretary of State]** The Secretary of State may give directions with respect to the disposal of the business of official receivers, and such directions may, in particular—

(a) authorise an official receiver attached to one court to act as the official receiver in relation to any case or description of cases falling within the jurisdiction of another court;

(b) provide, where there is more than one official receiver authorised to act as the official receiver in relation to cases falling within the jurisdiction of any court, for the distribution of their business between or among themselves.

399(7) **[Continuation of official receiver]** A person who at the coming into force of section 222 of the Insolvency Act 1985 (replaced by this section) is an official receiver attached to a court shall continue in office after the coming into force of that section as an official receiver attached to that court under this section.

SEC. 400   Functions and status of official receivers

400(1)   **[Functions]**   In addition to any functions conferred on him by this Act, a person holding the office of official receiver shall carry out such other functions as may from time to time be conferred on him by the Secretary of State.

400(2)   **[Status]**   In the exercise of the functions of his office a person holding the office of official receiver shall act under the general directions of the Secretary of State and shall also be an officer of the court in relation to which he exercises those functions.

400(3)   **[Death or ceasing to hold office]**   Any property vested in his official capacity in a person holding the office of official receiver shall, on his dying, ceasing to hold office or being otherwise succeeded in relation to the bankruptcy or winding up in question by another official receiver, vest in his successor without any conveyance, assignment or transfer.

SEC. 401   Deputy official receivers and staff

401(1)   **[Deputy official receiver]**   The Secretary of State may, if he thinks it expedient to do so in order to facilitate the disposal of the business of the official receiver attached to any court, appoint an officer of his department to act as deputy to that official receiver.

401(2)   **[Same status and functions]**   Subject to any directions given by the Secretary of State under section 399 or 400, a person appointed to act as deputy to an official receiver has, on such conditions and for such period as may be specified in the terms of his appointment, the same status and functions as the official receiver to whom he is appointed deputy.

Accordingly, references in this Act (except section 399(1) to (5)) to an official receiver include a person appointed to act as his deputy.

401(3)   **[Termination of appointment]**   An appointment made under subsection (1) may be terminated at any time by the Secretary of State.

401(4)   **[Staff]**   The Secretary of State may, subject to the approval of the Treasury as to numbers and remuneration and as to the other terms and conditions of the appointments, appoint officers of his department to assist official receivers in the carrying out of their functions.

THE OFFICIAL PETITIONER

SEC. 402   Official Petitioner

402(1)   **[Continuation of officer]**   There continues to be an officer known as the Official Petitioner for the purpose of discharging, in relation to cases in which a criminal bankruptcy order is made, the functions assigned to him by or under this Act; and the Director of Public Prosecutions continues, by virtue of his office, to be the Official Petitioner.

402(2) **[Functions]** The functions of the Official Petitioner include the following—

(a) to consider whether, in a case in which a criminal bankruptcy order is made, it is in the public interest that he should himself present a petition under section 264(1)(d) of this Act;

(b) to present such a petition in any case where he determines that it is in the public interest for him to do so;

(c) to make payments, in such cases as he may determine, towards expenses incurred by other persons in connection with proceedings in pursuance of such a petition; and

(d) to exercise, so far as he considers it in the public interest to do so, any of the powers conferred on him by or under this Act.

402(3) **[Discharge of functions on authority]** Any functions of the Official Petitioner may be discharged on his behalf by any person acting with his authority.

402(4) **[Inability]** Neither the Official Petitioner nor any person acting with his authority is liable to any action or proceeding in respect of anything done or omitted to be done in the discharge, or purported discharge, of the functions of the Official Petitioner.

402(5) **["Criminal bankruptcy order"]** In this section **"criminal bankruptcy order"** means an order under section 39(1) of the Powers of Criminal Courts Act 1973.

Note
S. 402 repealed by Criminal Justice Act 1988, s. 170(2) and
Sch. 16 as from a day to be appointed.

INSOLVENCY SERVICE FINANCE, ACCOUNTING AND INVESTMENT

SEC. 403 Insolvency Services Account

403(1) **[Payment into Account]** All money received by the Secretary of State in respect of proceedings under this Act as it applies to England and Wales shall be paid into the Insolvency Services Account kept by the Secretary of State with the Bank of England; and all payments out of money standing to the credit of the Secretary of State in that account shall be made by the Bank of England in such manner as he may direct.

403(2) **[Where excess amount]** Whenever the cash balance standing to the credit of the Insolvency Services Account is in excess of the amount which in the opinion of the Secretary of State is required for the time being to answer demands in respect of bankrupts' estates or companies' estates, the Secretary of State shall—

(a) notify the excess to the National Debt Commissioners, and

(b) pay into the Insolvency Services Investment Account (**"the Investment Account"**) kept by the Commissioners with the Bank of England the whole or any part of the excess as the Commissioners may require for investment in accordance with the following provisions of this Part.

403(3) **[Where invested money required]** Whenever any part of the money so invested is, in the opinion of the Secretary of State, required to answer any demand in respect of bankrupts' estates or companies' estates, he shall notify to the National Debt Commissioners the amount so required and the Commissioners—

(a) shall thereupon repay to the Secretary of State such sum as may be required to the credit of the Insolvency Services Account, and

(b) for that purpose may direct the sale of such part of the securities in which the money has been invested as may be necessary.

Note
See The Insolvency Regulations 1986 (S.I. 1986 No. 1994).

SEC. 404   Investment Account

404   Any money standing to the credit of the Investment Account (including any money received by the National Debt Commissioners by way of interest on or proceeds of any investment under this section) may be invested by the Commissioners, in accordance with such directions as may be given by the Treasury, in any manner for the time being specified in Part II of Schedule 1 to the Trustee Investments Act 1961.

SEC. 405   Application of income in Investment Account; adjustment of balances

405(1)   [Payment of excess into Consolidated Fund]   Where the annual account to be kept by the National Debt Commissioners under section 409 below shows that in the year for which it is made up the gross amount of the interest accrued from the securities standing to the credit of the Investment Account exceeded the aggregate of—

(a) a sum, to be determined by the Treasury, to provide against the depreciation in the value of the securities, and

(b) the sums paid into the Insolvency Services Account in pursuance of the next section together with the sums paid in pursuance of that section to the Commissioners of Inland Revenue,

the National Debt Commissioners shall, within 3 months after the account is laid before Parliament, cause the amount of the excess to be paid out of the Investment Account into the Consolidated Fund in such manner as may from time to time be agreed between the Treasury and the Commissioners.

405(2)   [Deficiency into Investment Account]   Where the said annual account shows that in the year for which it is made up the gross amount of interest accrued from the securities standing to the credit of the Investment Account was less than the aggregate mentioned in subsection (1), an amount equal to the deficiency shall, at such times as the Treasury direct, be paid out of the Consolidated Fund into the Investment Account.

405(3)   [If funds in Investment Account insufficient]   If the Investment Account is insufficient to meet its liabilities the Treasury may, on being informed of the insufficiency by the National Debt Commissioners, issue the amount of the deficiency out of the Consolidated Fund and the Treasury shall certify the deficiency to Parliament.

SEC. 406   Interest on money received by liquidators and invested

406   Where under rules made by virtue of paragraph 16 of Schedule 8 to this Act (investment of money received by company liquidators) a company has become entitled to any sum by way of interest, the Secretary of State shall certify that sum and the amount of tax payable on it to the National Debt Commissioners; and the Commissioners shall pay, out of the Investment Account—

(a) into the Insolvency Services Account, the sum so certified less the amount of tax so certified, and

(b) to the Commissioners of Inland Revenue, the amount of tax so certified.

SEC. 407 Unclaimed dividends and undistributed balances

407(1) [Duty of Secretary of State] The Secretary of State shall from time to time pay into the Consolidated Fund out of the Insolvency Services Account so much of the sums standing to the credit of that Account as represents—

(a) dividends which were declared before such date as the Treasury may from time to time determine and have not been claimed, and

(b) balances ascertained before that date which are too small to be divided among the persons entitled to them.

407(2) [Sums to credit of Insolvency Services Account] For the purposes of this section the sums standing to the credit of the Insolvency Services Account are deemed to include any sums paid out of that Account and represented by any sums or securities standing to the credit of the Investment Account.

407(3) [Power of Secretary of State] The Secretary of State may require the National Debt Commissioners to pay out of the Investment Account into the Insolvency Services Account the whole or part of any sum which he is required to pay out of that account under subsection (1); and the Commissioners may direct the sale of such securities standing to the credit of the Investment Account as may be necessary for that purpose.

SEC. 408 Recourse to Consolidated Fund

408 If, after any repayment due to it from the Investment Account, the Insolvency Services Account is insufficient to meet its liabilities, the Treasury may, on being informed of it by the Secretary of State, issue the amount of the deficiency out of the Consolidated Fund, and the Treasury shall certify the deficiency to Parliament.

SEC. 409 Annual financial statement and audit

409(1) [Preparation of statement] The National Debt Commissioners shall for each year ending on 31st March prepare a statement of the sums credited and debited to the Investment Account in such form and manner as the Treasury may direct and shall transmit it to the Comptroller and Auditor General before the end of November next following the year.

409(2) [Duty of Secretary of State] The Secretary of State shall for each year ending 31st March prepare a statement of the sums received or paid by him under section 403 above in such form and manner as the Treasury may direct and shall transmit each statement to the Comptroller and Auditor General before the end of November next following the year.

409(3) [Additional information] Every such statement shall include such additional information as the Treasury may direct.

409(4)   **[Examination etc. of statement]**   The Comptroller and Auditor General shall examine, certify and report on every such statement and shall lay copies of it, and of his report, before Parliament.

SUPPLEMENTARY

SEC. 410   Extent of this Part

410   This Part of this Act extends to England and Wales only.

PART XV — SUBORDINATE LEGISLATION

GENERAL INSOLVENCY RULES

SEC. 411   Company insolvency rules

411(1)   **[Rules]**   Rules may be made—

    (a) in relation to England and Wales, by the Lord Chancellor with the concurrence of the Secretary of State, or

    (b) in relation to Scotland, by the Secretary of State,

for the purpose of giving effect to Parts I to VII of this Act.

411(2)   **[Contents of rules]**   Without prejudice to the generality of subsection (1), or to any provision of those Parts by virtue of which rules under this section may be made with respect to any matter, rules under this section may contain—

    (a) any such provision as is specified in Schedule 8 to this Act or corresponds to provision contained immediately before the coming into force of section 106 of the Insolvency Act 1985 in rules made, or having effect as if made, under section 663(1) or (2) of the Companies Act (old winding-up rules), and

    (b) such incidental, supplemental and transitional provisions as may appear to the Lord Chancellor or, as the case may be, the Secretary of State necessary or expedient.

Note
See the Insolvency Rules 1986 (S.I. 1986 No. 1925), the Insolvency (Scotland) Rules 1986 (S.I. 1986 No. 1915 (S. 139)). For insurance companies see the Insurance Companies (Winding-up) (Amendment) Rules 1986 (S.I. 1986 No. 2002) and the Insurance Companies (Winding Up) (Scotland) Rules 1986 (S.I. 1986 No. 1918 (S. 142)). There are also the Companies (Unfair Prejudice Applications) Proceedings Rules 1986 (S.I. 1986 No. 2000) and the two sets of rules on directors referred to in the note to Company Directors Disqualification Act 1986, s. 21(2) and the Insolvent Companies (Disqualification of Unfit Directors) Proceedings Rules 1987 (S.I. 1987 No. 2023).

411(3)   **[Interpretation of Sch. 8]**   In Schedule 8 to this Act "liquidator" includes a provisional liquidator; and references above in this section to Parts I to VII of this Act are to be read as including the Companies Act so far as relating to, and to matters connected with or arising out of, the insolvency or winding up of companies.

411(4)   **[Rules by statutory instrument etc.]**   Rules under this section shall be made by statutory instrument subject to annulment in pursuance of a resolution of either House of Parliament.

411(5) **[Regulations]** Regulations made by the Secretary of State under a power conferred by rules under this section shall be made by statutory instrument and, after being made, shall be laid before each House of Parliament.

Note
See the Insolvency Regulations 1986 (S.I. 1986 No. 1994).

411(6) **[Rules of court]** Nothing in this section prejudices any power to make rules of court.

SEC. 412 Individual insolvency rules (England and Wales)

412(1) **[Rules by Lord Chancellor]** The Lord Chancellor may, with the concurrence of the Secretary of State, make rules for the purpose of giving effect to Parts VIII to XI of this Act.

Note
See the Insolvency Rules 1986 (S.I. 1986 No. 1925).

412(2) **[Contents of rules]** Without prejudice to the generality of subsection (1), or to any provision of those Parts by virtue of which rules under this section may be made with respect to any matter, rules under this section may contain—

(a) any such provision as is specified in Schedule 9 to this Act or corresponds to provision contained immediately before the appointed day in rules made under section 132 of the Bankruptcy Act 1914; and

(b) such incidental, supplemental and transitional provisions as may appear to the Lord Chancellor necessary or expedient.

412(3) **[Rules to be made by statutory instrument]** Rules under this section shall be made by statutory instrument subject to annulment in pursuance of a resolution of either House of Parliament.

412(4) **[Regulations]** Regulations made by the Secretary of State under a power conferred by rules under this section shall be made by statutory instrument and, after being made, shall be laid before each House of Parliament.

Note
See the Insolvency Regulations 1986 (S.I. 1986 No. 1994).

412(5) **[Rules of court]** Nothing in this section prejudices any power to make rules of court.

SEC. 413 Insolvency Rules Committee

413(1) **[Continuation of committee]** The committee established under section 10 of the Insolvency Act 1976 (advisory committee on bankruptcy and winding-up rules) continues to exist for the purpose of being consulted under this section.

413(2) **[Consultation by Lord Chancellor]** The Lord Chancellor shall consult the committee before making any rules under section 411 or 412 other than rules which contain a statement that the only provision made by the rules is provision applying rules made under section 411, with or without modifications, for the purposes of provision made by section 23 or 24 of or Schedule 6 to the Water Act 1989.

History
In s. 413(2) the words "other than rules which contain" to the end inserted by Water Act 1989, s. 190(1) and Sch. 25, para. 78(2) as from 1 September 1989 (see Water Act 1989, s. 4, 194(4) and S.I. 1989 No. 1146 (C. 37) — see also S.I. 1989 No. 1530 (C. 51)).

413(3)   **[Members of committee]**   Subject to the next subsection, the committee shall consist of—

(a) a judge of the High Court attached to the Chancery Division;

(b) a circuit judge;

(c) a registrar in bankruptcy of the High Court;

(d) the registrar of a county court;

(e) a practising barrister;

(f) a practising solicitor; and

(g) a practising accountant;

and the appointment of any person as a member of the committee shall be made by the Lord Chancellor.

413(4)   **[Additional members]**   The Lord Chancellor may appoint as additional members of the committee any persons appearing to him to have qualifications or experience that would be of value to the committee in considering any matter with which it is concerned.

FEES ORDERS

SEC. 414   Fees orders (company insolvency proceedings)

414(1)   **[Fees]**   There shall be paid in respect of—

(a) proceedings under any of Parts I to VII of this Act, and

(b) the performance by the official receiver or the Secretary of State of functions under those Parts,

such fees as the competent authority may with the sanction of the Treasury by order direct.

Note
See the Insolvency Fees Order 1986 (S.I. 1986 No. 2030)
as amended, the County Court Fees (Amendment No. 2)
Order 1986 (S.I. 1986 No. 2143) and the Supreme
Court Fees (Amendment No. 2) Order 1986 (S.I. 1986 No.
2144).

414(2)   **[Security for fees]**   That authority is—

(a) in relation to England and Wales, the Lord Chancellor, and

(b) in relation to Scotland, the Secretary of State.

414(3)   **[Order by Treasury]**   The Treasury may by order direct by whom and in what manner the fees are to be collected and accounted for.

414(4)   **[Security for fees]**   The Lord Chancellor may, with the sanction of the Treasury, by order provide for sums to be deposited, by such persons, in such manner and in such circumstances as may be specified in the order, by way of security for fees payable by virtue of this section.

414(5)   **[Incidental matter under order]**   An order under this section may contain such incidental, supplemental and transitional provisions as may appear to the Lord Chancellor, the Secretary of State or (as the case may be) the Treasury necessary or expedient.

414(6) **[Order by statutory instrument etc.]** An order under this section shall be made by statutory instrument and, after being made, shall be laid before each House of Parliament.

414(7) **[Payment into Consolidated Fund]** Fees payable by virtue of this section shall be paid into the Consolidated Fund.

414(8) **[Interpretation]** References in subsection (1) to Parts I to VII of this Act are to be read as including the Companies Act so far as relating to, and to matters connected with or arising out of, the insolvency or winding up of companies.

414(9) **[Rules of court, Scotland]** Nothing in this section prejudices any power to make rules of court; and the application of this section to Scotland is without prejudice to section 2 of the Courts of Law Fees (Scotland) Act 1895.

SEC. 415 Fees orders (individual insolvency proceedings in England and Wales)

415(1) **[Payment of fees]** There shall be paid in respect of—

(a) proceedings under Parts VIII to XI of this Act, and

(b) the performance by the official receiver or the Secretary of State of functions under those Parts,

such fees as the Lord Chancellor may with the sanction of the Treasury by order direct.

415(2) **[Order by Treasury]** The Treasury may by order direct by whom and in what manner the fees are to be collected and accounted for.

415(3) **[Security for fees]** The Lord Chancellor may, with the sanction of the Treasury, by order provide for sums to be deposited, by such persons, in such manner and in such circumstances as may be specified in the order, by way of security for—

(a) fees payable by virtue of this section, and

(b) fees payable to any person who has prepared an insolvency practitioner's report under section 274 in Chapter I of Part IX.

415(4) **[Incidental provisions etc. of order]** An order under this section may contain such incidental, supplemental and transitional provisions as may appear to the Lord Chancellor or, as the case may be, the Treasury, necessary or expedient.

415(5) **[Order by statutory instrument etc.]** An order under this section shall be made by statutory instrument and, after being made, shall be laid before each House of Parliament.

415(6) **[Payment into Consolidated Fund]** Fees payable by virtue of this section shall be paid into the Consolidated Fund.

415(7) **[Rules of court]** Nothing in this section prejudices any power to make rules of court.

Note
See the note to s. 414(1).

SPECIFICATION, INCREASE AND REDUCTION OF MONEY SUMS
RELEVANT IN THE OPERATION OF THIS ACT

SEC. 416   Monetary limits (companies winding up)

416(1)   [Increase or reduction of certain provisions]   The Secretary of State may by order in a statutory instrument increase or reduce any of the money sums for the time being specified in the following provisions in the first Group of Parts—

section 117(2) (amount of company's share capital determining whether county court has jurisdiction to wind it up);

section 120(3) (the equivalent as respects sheriff court jurisdiction in Scotland);

section 123(1)(a) (minimum debt for service of demand on company by unpaid creditor);

section 184(3) (minimum value of judgment, affecting sheriff's duties on levying execution);

section 206(1)(a) and (b) (minimum value of company property concealed or fraudulently removed, affecting criminal liability of company's officer).

Note
See the Insolvency Proceedings (Monetary Limits) Order
1986 (S.I. 1986 No. 1996) in force from 29 December 1986
affecting s. 184(3) and 206(1)(a), (b).

416(2)   [Transitional provisions]   An order under this section may contain such transitional provisions as may appear to the Secretary of State necessary or expedient.

416(3)   [Approval by Parliament]   No order under this section increasing or reducing any of the money sums for the time being specified in section 117(2), 120(3) or 123(1)(a) shall be made unless a draft of the order has been laid before and approved by a resolution of each House of Parliament.

416(4)   [Annulment of statutory instrument]   A statutory instrument containing an order under this section, other than an order to which subsection (3) applies, is subject to annulment in pursuance of a resolution of either House of Parliament.

SEC. 417   Money sum in sec. 222

417   The Secretary of State may by regulations in a statutory instrument increase or reduce the money sum for the time being specified in section 222(1) (minimum debt for service of demand on unregistered company by unpaid creditor); but such regulations shall not be made unless a draft of the statutory instrument containing them has been approved by resolution of each House of Parliament.

SEC. 418   Monetary limits (bankruptcy)

418(1)   [Powers of Secretary of State]   The Secretary of State may by order prescribe amounts for the purposes of the following provisions in the second Group of Parts—

section 273 (minimum value of debtor's estate determining whether immediate bankruptcy order should be made; small bankruptcies level);

section 346(3) (minimum amount of judgment, determining whether amount recovered on sale of debtor's goods is to be treated as part of his estate in bankruptcy);

section 354(1) and (2) (minimum amount of concealed debt, or value of property concealed or removed, determining criminal liability under the section);

section 358 (minimum value of property taken by a bankrupt out of England and Wales, determining his criminal liability);

section 360(1) (maximum amount of credit which bankrupt may obtain without disclosure of his status);

section 361(2) (exemption of bankrupt from criminal liability for failure to keep proper accounts, if unsecured debts not more than the prescribed minimum);

section 364(2)(d) (minimum value of goods removed by the bankrupt, determining his liability to arrest);

and references in the second Group of Parts to the amount prescribed for the purposes of any of those provisions, and references in those provisions to the prescribed amount, are to be construed accordingly.

418(2) [Transitional provisions] An order under this section may contain such transitional provisions as may appear to the Secretary of State necessary or expedient.

418(3) [Order by statutory instrument etc.] An order under this section shall be made by statutory instrument subject to annulment in pursuance of a resolution of either House of Parliament.

Note
See the Insolvency Proceedings (Monetary Limits) Order
1986 (S.I. 1986 No. 1996) in force from 29 December 1986.

INSOLVENCY PRACTICE

SEC. 419   Regulations for purposes of Part XIII

419(1) [Power to make regulations] The Secretary of State may make regulations for the purpose of giving effect to Part XIII of this Act; and "**prescribed**" in that Part means prescribed by regulations made by the Secretary of State.

419(2) [Extent of regulations] Without prejudice to the generality of subsection (1) or to any provision of that Part by virtue of which regulations may be made with respect to any matter, regulations under this section may contain—

(a) provision as to the matters to be taken into account in determining whether a person is a fit and proper person to act as an insolvency practitioner;

(b) provision prohibiting a person from so acting in prescribed cases, being cases in which a conflict of interest will or may arise;

(c) provision imposing requirements with respect to—

   (i) the preparation and keeping by a person who acts as an insolvency practitioner of prescribed books, accounts and other records, and

   (ii) the production of those books, accounts and records to prescribed persons;

(d) provision conferring power on prescribed persons—

   (i) to require any person who acts or has acted as an insolvency practitioner to answer any inquiry in relation to a case in which he is so acting or has so acted, and

(ii) to apply to a court to examine such a person or any other person on oath concerning such a case;

(e) provision making non-compliance with any of the regulations a criminal offence; and

(f) such incidental, supplemental and transitional provisions as may appear to the Secretary of State necessary or expedient.

419(3)   [Power exercisable by statutory instrument etc.]   Any power conferred by Part XIII or this Part to make regulations, rules or orders is exercisable by statutory instrument subject to annulment by resolution of either House of Parliament.

419(4)   [Different provisions for different cases]   Any rule or regulation under Part XIII or this Part may make different provision with respect to different cases or descriptions of cases, including different provision for different areas.

Note
See the Insolvency Practitioners Regulations 1990 (S.I. 1990 No. 439).

OTHER ORDER-MAKING POWERS

SEC. 420   Insolvent partnerships

420(1)   [Application to insolvent partnerships]   The Lord Chancellor may, by order made with the concurrence of the Secretary of State, provide that such provisions of this Act as may be specified in the order shall apply in relation to insolvent partnerships with such modifications as may be so specified.

420(2)   [Incidental provisions etc.]   An order under this section may make different provision for different cases and may contain such incidental, supplemental and transitional provisions as may appear to the Lord Chancellor necessary or expedient.

420(3)   [Order by statutory instrument etc.]   An order under this section shall be made by statutory instrument subject to annulment in pursuance of a resolution of either House of Parliament.

Note
See the Insolvent Partnerships Order 1986 (S.I. 1986 No. 2142).

SEC. 421   Insolvent estates of deceased persons

421(1)   [Order by Lord Chancellor]   The Lord Chancellor may, by order made with the concurrence of the Secretary of State, provide that such provisions of this Act as may be specified in the order shall apply to the administration of the insolvent estates of deceased persons with such modifications as may be so specified.

421(2)   [Incidental provisions etc.]   An order under this section may make different provision for different cases and may contain such incidental, supplemental and transitional provisions as may appear to the Lord Chancellor necessary or expedient.

421(3)   [Order by statutory instrument]   An order under this section shall be made by statutory instrument subject to annulment in pursuance of a resolution of either House of Parliament.

421(4) **[Interpretation]** For the purposes of this section the estate of a deceased person is insolvent if, when realised, it will be insufficient to meet in full all the debts and other liabilities to which it is subject.

Note
See the Administration of Insolvent Estates of Deceased Persons Order (S.I. 1986 No. 1999).

SEC. 422   Recognised banks, etc.

422(1) **[Order by Secretary of State]** The Secretary of State may, by order made with the concurrence of the Treasury and after consultation with the Bank of England, provide that such provisions in the first Group of Parts as may be specified in the order shall apply in relation to authorised institutions and former authorised

[The next page is 55,701]

institutions within the meaning of the Banking Act 1987, with such modifications as may be so specified.

History

In s. 422(1) the words "authorised institutions and former authorised institutions within the meaning of the Banking Act 1987" substituted for the former para. (a) and (b) by Banking Act 1987, s. 108(1) and Sch. 6, para. 25(2) as from 1 October 1987 (see S.I. 1987 No. 1664 (C. 50)): the former para. (a) and (b) read as follows:

"(a) recognised banks and licensed institutions within the meaning of the Banking Act 1979, and

(b) institutions to which sections 16 and 18 of that Act apply as if they were licensed institutions,".

422(2)   [Incidental provisions etc.]   An order under this section may make different provision for different cases and may contain such incidental, supplemental and transitional provisions as may appear to the Secretary of State necessary or expedient.

422(3)   [Order by statutory instrument etc.]   An order under this section shall be made by statutory instrument subject to annulment in pursuance of a resolution of either House of Parliament.

Note

See the Banks (Administration Proceedings) Order 1989 (S.I. 1989 No. 1276).

PART XVI — PROVISIONS AGAINST DEBT AVOIDANCE (ENGLAND AND WALES ONLY)

SEC. 423   Transactions defrauding creditors

423(1)   [Transaction at undervalue]   This section relates to transactions entered into at an undervalue; and a person enters into such a transaction with another person if—

(a) he makes a gift to the other person or he otherwise enters into a transaction with the other on terms that provide for him to receive no consideration;

(b) he enters into a transaction with the other in consideration of marriage; or

(c) he enters into a transaction with the other for a consideration the value of which, in money or money's worth, is significantly less than the value, in money or money's worth, of the consideration provided by himself.

423(2)   [Order by court]   Where a person has entered into such a transaction, the court may, if satisfied under the next subsection, make such order as it thinks fit for—

(a) restoring the position to what it would have been if the transaction had not been entered into, and

(b) protecting the interests of persons who are victims of the transaction.

423(3)   [Conditions for court order]   In the case of a person entering into such a transaction, an order shall only be made if the court is satisfied that it was entered into by him for the purpose—

(a) of putting assets beyond the reach of a person who is making, or may at some time make, a claim against him, or

(b) of otherwise prejudicing the interests of such a person in relation to the claim which he is making or may make.

423(4)   ["The court"]   In this section **"the court"** means the High Court or—

(a) if the person entering into the transaction is an individual, any other court which would have jurisdiction in relation to a bankruptcy petition relating to him;

(b) if that person is a body capable of being wound up under Part IV or V of this Act, any other court having jurisdiction to wind it up.

423(5)   [Interpretation]   In relation to a transaction at an undervalue, references here and below to a victim of the transation are to a person who is, or is capable of being, prejudiced by it; and in the following two sections the person entering into the transaction is referred to as **"the debtor"**.

SEC. 424   Those who may apply for an order under sec. 423

424(1)   [Conditions for sec. 423 application]   An application for an order under section 423 shall not be made in relation to a transaction except—

(a) in a case where the debtor has been adjudged bankrupt or is a body corporate which is being wound up or in relation to which an administration order is in force, by the official receiver, by the trustee of the bankrupt's estate or the liquidator or administrator of the body corporate or (with the leave of the court) by a victim of the transaction;

(b) in a case where a victim of the transaction is bound by a voluntary arrangement approved under Part I or Part VIII of this Act, by the supervisor of the voluntary arrangement or by any person who (whether or not so bound) is such a victim; or

(c) in any other case, by a victim of the transaction.

424(2)   [Treatment of application]   An application made under any of the paragraphs of subsection (1) is to be treated as made on behalf of every victim of the transaction.

SEC. 425   Provision which may be made by order under sec. 423

425(1)   [Scope of order]   Without prejudice to the generality of section 423, an order made under that section with respect to a transaction may (subject as follows)—

(a) require any property transferred as part of the transaction to be vested in any person, either absolutely or for the benefit of all the persons on whose behalf the application for the order is treated as made;

(b) require any property to be so vested if it represents, in any person's hands, the application either of the proceeds of sale of property so transferred or of money so transferred;

(c) release or discharge (in whole or in part) any security given by the debtor;

(d) require any person to pay to any other person in respect of benefits received from the debtor such sums as the court may direct;

(e) provide for any surety or guarantor whose obligations to any person were released or discharged (in whole or in part) under the transaction to be under such new or revived obligations as the court thinks appropriate;

(f) provide for security to be provided for the discharge of any obligation imposed by or arising under the order, for such an obligation to be charged on any property and for such security or charge to have the same priority as a security or charge released or discharged (in whole or in part) under the transaction.

425(2) **[Limit to order]** An order under section 423 may affect the property of, or impose any obligation on, any person whether or not he is the person with whom the debtor entered into the transaction; but such an order—

(a) shall not prejudice any interest in property which was acquired from a person other than the debtor and was acquired in good faith, for value and without notice of the relevant circumstances, or prejudice any interest deriving from such an interest, and

(b) shall not require a person who received a benefit from the transaction in good faith, for value and without notice of the relevant circumstances to pay any sum unless he was a party to the transaction.

425(3) **[Relevant circumstances]** For the purposes of this section the relevant circumstances in relation to a transaction are the circumstances by virtue of which an order under section 423 may be made in respect of the transaction.

425(4) **["Security"]** In this section **"security"** means any mortgage, charge, lien or other security.

PART XVII — MISCELLANEOUS AND GENERAL

SEC. 426 Co-operation between courts exercising jurisdiction in relation to insolvency

426(1) **[Enforcement in other parts of UK]** An order made by a court in any part of the United Kingdom in the exercise of jurisdiction in relation to insolvency law shall be enforced in any other part of the United Kingdom as if it were made by a court exercising the corresponding jurisdiction in that other part.

426(2) **[Limit to sec. 426(1)]** However, without prejudice to the following provisions of this section, nothing in subsection (1) requires a court in any part of the United Kingdom to enforce, in relation to property situated in that part, any order made by a court in any other part of the United Kingdom.

426(3) **[Order by Secretary of State]** The Secretary of State, with the concurrence in relation to property situated in England and Wales of the Lord Chancellor, may by order make provision for securing that a trustee or assignee under the insolvency law of any part of the United Kingdom has, with such modifications as may be specified in the order, the same rights in relation to any property situated in another part of the United Kingdom as he would have in the corresponding circumstances if he were a trustee or assignee under the insolvency law of that other part.

426(4) **[Assistance between courts]** The courts having jurisdiction in relation to insolvency law in any part of the United Kingdom shall assist the courts having the corresponding jurisdiction in any other part of the United Kingdom or any relevant country or territory.

426(5) **[Request under sec. 426(4)]** For the purposes of subsection (4) a request made to a court in any part of the United Kingdom by a court in any other part of the United Kingdom or in a relevant country or territory is authority for the court to which the request is made to apply, in relation to any matters specified in the request, the insolvency law which is applicable by either court in relation to comparable matters falling within its jurisdiction.

In exercising its discretion under this subsection, a court shall have regard in particular to the rules of private international law.

426(6)   [Claim by trustee or assignee]   Where a person who is a trustee or assignee under the insolvency law of any part of the United Kingdom claims property situated in any other part of the United Kingdom (whether by virtue of an order under subsection (3) or otherwise), the submission of that claim to the court exercising jurisdiction in relation to insolvency law in that other part shall be treated in the same manner as a request made by a court for the purpose of subsection (4).

426(7)   [Application of Criminal Law Act]   Section 38 of the Criminal Law Act 1977 (execution of warrant of arrest throughout the United Kingdom) applies to a warrant which, in exercise of any jurisdiction in relation to insolvency law, is issued in any part of the United Kingdom for the arrest of a person as it applies to a warrant issued in that part of the United Kingdom for the arrest of a person charged with an offence.

426(8)   [Powers in subordinate legislation]   Without prejudice to any power to make rules of court, any power to make provision by subordinate legislation for the purpose of giving effect in relation to companies or individuals to the insolvency law of any part of the United Kingdom includes power to make provision for the purpose of giving effect in that part to any provision made by or under the preceding provisions of this section.

Note
See The Co-operation of Insolvency Courts (Designation
of Relevant Countries and Territories) Order 1986 (S.I.
1986 No. 2123).

426(9)   [Sec. 426(3) order by statutory instrument etc.]   An order under subsection (3) shall be made by statutory instrument subject to annulment in pursuance of a resolution of either House of Parliament.

426(10)   ["Insolvency law"]   In this section **"insolvency law"** means—

(a) in relation to England and Wales, provision made by or under this Act or sections 6 to 10, 12, 15, 19(c) and 20 (with Schedule 1) of the Company Directors Disqualification Act 1986 and extending to England and Wales;

(b) in relation to Scotland, provision extending to Scotland and made by or under this Act, sections 6 to 10, 12, 15, 19(c) and 20 (with Schedule 1) of the Company Directors Disqualification Act 1986, Part XVIII of the Companies Act or the Bankrupty (Scotland) Act 1985;

(c) in relation to Northern Ireland, provision made by or under the Bankruptcy Acts (Northern Ireland) 1857 to 1980, Part V, VI or IX of the Companies Act (Northern Ireland) 1960 or Part IV of the Companies (Northern Ireland) Order 1978;

(d) in relation to any relevant country or territory, so much of the law of that country or territory as corresponds to provisions falling within any of the foregoing paragraphs;

and references in this subsection to any enactment include, in relation to any time before the coming into force of that enactment the corresponding enactment in force at that time.

426(11) **["Relevant country or territory"]** In this section "relevant country or territory" means—

(a) any of the Channel Islands or the Isle of Man, or

(b) any country or territory designated for the purposes of this section by the Secretary of State by order made by statutory instrument.

Note
For s. 426(4), (5), (10) and (11) see the Insolvency Act
1986 (Guernsey) Order 1989 (S.I. 1989 No. 2409).

SEC. 427 Parliamentary disqualification

427(1) **[Disqualification of bankrupt]** Where a court in England and Wales or Northern Ireland adjudges an individual bankrupt or a court in Scotland awards sequestration of an individual's estate, the individual is disqualified—

(a) for sitting or voting in the House of Lords,

(b) for being elected to, or sitting or voting in, the House of Commons, and

(c) for sitting or voting in a committee of either House.

427(2) **[When disqualification ceases]** Where an individual is disqualified under this section, the disqualification ceases—

(a) except where the adjudication is annulled or the award recalled or reduced without the individual having been first discharged, on the discharge of the individual, and

(b) in the excepted case, on the annulment, recall or reduction, as the case may be.

427(3) **[Disqualified peer]** No writ of summons shall be issued to any lord of Parliament who is for the time being disqualified under this section for sitting and voting in the House of Lords.

427(4) **[Disqualified MP]** Where a member of the House of Commons who is disqualified under this section continues to be so disqualified until the end of the period of 6 months beginning with the day of the adjudication or award, his seat shall be vacated at the end of that period.

427(5) **[Certification of sec. 427(1) award etc.]** A court which makes an adjudication or award such as is mentioned in subsection (1) in relation to any lord of Parliament or member of the House of Commons shall forthwith certify the adjudication or award to the Speaker of the House of Lords or, as the case may be, to the Speaker of the House of Commons.

427(6) **[Further certification after sec. 427(5)]** Where a court has certified an adjudication or award to the Speaker of the House of Commons under subsection (5), then immediately after it becomes apparent which of the following certificates is applicable, the court shall certify to the Speaker of the House of Commons—

(a) that the period of 6 months beginning with the day of the adjudication or award has expired without the adjudication or award having been annulled, recalled or reduced, or

(b) that the adjudication or award has been annulled, recalled or reduced before the end of that period.

427(7) [Application of relevant law to peer or MP] Subject to the preceding provisions of this section, so much of this Act and any other enactment (whenever passed) and of any subordinate legislation (whenever made) as—

(a) makes provision for or in connection with bankruptcy in one or more parts of the United Kingdom, or

(b) makes provision conferring a power of arrest in connection with the winding up or insolvency of companies in one or more parts of the United Kingdom,

applies in relation to persons having privilege of Parliament or peerage as it applies in relation to persons not having such privilege.

SEC. 428 Exemptions from Restrictive Trade Practices Act

428(1) [No restrictions under Trade Practices Act] No restriction in respect of any of the matters specified in the next subsection shall, on or after the appointed day, be regarded as a restriction by virtue of which the Restrictive Trade Practices Act 1976 applies to any agreement (whenever made).

428(2) [Matters in sec. 428(1)] Those matters are—

(a) the charges to be made, quoted or paid for insolvency services supplied, offered or obtained;

(b) the terms or conditions on or subject to which insolvency services are to be supplied or obtained;

(c) the extent (if any) to which, or the scale (if any) on which, insolvency services are to be made available, supplied or obtained;

(d) the form or manner in which insolvency services are to be made available, supplied or obtained;

(e) the persons or classes of persons for whom or from whom, or the areas or places in or from which, insolvency services are to be made available or supplied or are to be obtained.

428(3) ["Insolvency services"] In this section **"insolvency services"** means the services of persons acting as insolvency practitioners or carrying out under the law of Northern Ireland functions corresponding to those mentioned in section 388(1) or (2) in Part XIII, in their capacity as such; and expressions which are also used in the Act of 1976 have the same meaning here as in that Act.

SEC. 429 Disabilities on revocation of administration order against an individual

429(1) [Application] The following applies where a person fails to make any payment which he is required to make by virtue of an administration order under Part VI of the County Courts Act 1984.

429(2) [Power of court] The court which is administering that person's estate under the order may, if it thinks fit—

(a) revoke the administration order, and

(b) make an order directing that this section and section 12 of the Company Directors Disqualification Act 1986 shall apply to the person for such period, not exceeding 2 years, as may be specified in the order.

429(3)   [Restrictions]   A person to whom this section so applies shall not—

(a) either alone or jointly with another person, obtain credit to the extent of the amount prescribed for the purposes of section 360(1)(a) or more, or

(b) enter into any transaction in the course of or for the purposes of any business in which he is directly or indirectly engaged,

without disclosing to the person from whom he obtains the credit, or (as the case may be) with whom the transaction is entered into, the fact that this section applies to him.

429(4)   [Person obtaining credit]   The reference in subsection (3) to a person obtaining credit includes—

(a) a case where goods are bailed or hired to him under a hire-purchase agreement or agreed to be sold to him under a conditional sale agreement, and

(b) a case where he is paid in advance (whether in money or otherwise) for the supply of goods or services.

429(5)   [Penalty]   A person who contravenes this section is guilty of an offence and liable to imprisonment or a fine, or both.

SEC. 430   Provision introducing Schedule of punishments

430(1)   [Sch. 10]   Schedule 10 to this Act has effect with respect to the way in which offences under this Act are punishable on conviction.

430(2)   [First, second and third columns of Schedule]   In relation to an offence under a provision of this Act specified in the first column of the Schedule (the general nature of the offence being described in the second column), the third column shows whether the offence is punishable on conviction on indictment, or on summary conviction, or either in the one way or the other.

430(3)   [Fourth column]   The fourth column of the Schedule shows, in relation to an offence, the maximum punishment by way of fine or imprisonment under this Act which may be imposed on a person convicted of the offence in the way specified in relation to it in the third column (that is to say, on indictment or summarily), a reference to a period of years or months being to a term of imprisonment of that duration.

430(4)   [Fifth column]   The fifth column shows (in relation to an offence for which there is an entry in that column) that a person convicted of the offence after continued contravention is liable to a daily default fine; that is to say, he is liable on a second or subsequent conviction of the offence to the fine specified in that column for each day on which the contravention is continued (instead of the penalty specified for the offence in the fourth column of the Schedule).

430(5)   ["Officer who is in default"]   For the purpose of any enactment in this Act whereby an officer of a company who is in default is liable to a fine or penalty, the expression **"officer who is in default"** means any officer of the company who knowingly and wilfully authorises or permits the default, refusal or contravention mentioned in the enactment.

SEC. 431   Summary proceedings

431(1)   **[Taking of summary proceedings]**   Summary proceedings for any offence under any of Parts I to VII of this Act may (without prejudice to any jurisdiction exercisable apart from this subsection) be taken against a body corporate at any place at which the body has a place of business, and against any other person at any place at which he is for the time being.

431(2)   **[Time for laying information]**   Notwithstanding anything in section 127(1) of the Magistrates' Courts Act 1980, an information relating to such an offence which is triable by a magistrates' court in England and Wales may be so tried if it is laid at any time within 3 years after the commission of the offence and within 12 months after the date on which evidence sufficient in the opinion of the Director of Public Prosecutions or the Secretary of State (as the case may be) to justify the proceedings comes to his knowledge.

431(3)   **[Time for commencement of summary proceedings in Scotland]**   Summary proceedings in Scotland for such an offence shall not be commenced after the expiration of 3 years from the commission of the offence.

Subject to this (and notwithstanding anything in section 331 of the Criminal Procedure (Scotland) Act 1975), such proceedings may (in Scotland) be commenced at any time within 12 months after the date on which evidence sufficient in the Lord Advocate's opinion to justify the proceedings came to his knowledge or, where such evidence was reported to him by the Secretary of State, within 12 months after the date on which it came to the knowledge of the latter; and subsection (3) of that section applies for the purpose of this subsection as it applies for the purpose of that section.

431(4)   **[Certificate by DPP et al. conclusive evidence]**   For the purposes of this section, a certificate of the Director of Public Prosecutions, the Lord Advocate or the Secretary of State (as the case may be) as to the date on which such evidence as is referred to above came to his knowledge is conclusive evidence.

SEC. 432   Offences by bodies corporate

432(1)   **[Application]**   This section applies to offences under this Act other than those excepted by subsection (4).

432(2)   **[Consent or connivance of various persons]**   Where a body corporate is guilty of an offence to which this section applies and the offence is proved to have been committed with the consent or connivance of, or to be attributable to any neglect on the part of, any director, manager, secretary or other similar officer of the body corporate or any person who was purporting to act in any such capacity he, as well as the body corporate, is guilty of the offence and liable to be proceeded against and punished accordingly.

432(3)   **[Where affairs managed by members]**   Where the affairs of a body corporate are managed by its members, subsection (2) applies in relation to the acts and defaults of a member in connection with his functions of management as if he were a director of the body corporate.

432(4) **[Offences excepted]** The offences excepted from this section are those under sections 30, 39, 51, 53, 54, 62, 64, 66, 85, 89, 164, 188, 201, 206, 207, 208, 209, 210 and 211.

SEC. 433 Admissibility in evidence of statements of affairs, etc.

433 In any proceedings (whether or not under this Act)—

(a) a statement of affairs prepared for the purposes of any provision of this Act which is derived from the Insolvency Act 1985, and

(b) any other statement made in pursuance of a requirement imposed by or under any such provision or by or under rules made under this Act,

may be used in evidence against any person making or concurring in making the statement.

SEC. 434 Crown application

434 For the avoidance of doubt it is hereby declared that provisions of this Act which derive from the Insolvency Act 1985 bind the Crown so far as affecting or relating to the following matters, namely—

(a) remedies against, or against the property of, companies or individuals;

(b) priorities of debts;

(c) transactions at an undervalue or preferences;

(d) voluntary arrangements approved under Part I or Part VIII, and

(e) discharge from bankruptcy.

PART XVIII — INTERPRETATION

SEC. 435 Meaning of "associate"

435(1) **[Determination of whether associate]** For the purposes of this Act any question whether a person is an associate of another person is to be determined in accordance with the following provisions of this section (any provision that a person is an associate of another person being taken to mean that they are associates of each other).

435(2) **[Associate of individual]** A person is an associate of an individual if that person is the individual's husband or wife, or is a relative, or the husband or wife of a relative, of the individual or of the individual's husband or wife.

435(3) **[Associate of partner]** A person is an associate of any person with whom he is in partership, and of the husband or wife or a relative of any individual with whom he is in partnership; and a Scottish firm is an associate of any person who is a member of the firm.

435(4) **[Associate of employee, employer]** A person is an associate of any person whom he employs or by whom he is employed.

435(5)   **[Associate of trustee]**   A person in his capacity as trustee of a trust other than—

    (a) a trust arising under any of the second Group of Parts or the Bankruptcy (Scotland) Act 1985, or

    (b) a pension scheme or an employees' share scheme (within the meaning of the Companies Act),

is an associate of another person if the beneficiaries of the trust include, or the terms of the trust confer a power that may be exercised for the benefit of, that other person or an associate of that other person.

435(6)   **[Company associate of another company]**   A company is an associate of another company—

    (a) if the same person has control of both, or a person has control of one and persons who are his associates, or he and persons who are his associates, have control of the other, or

    (b) if a group of two or more persons has control of each company, and the groups either consist of the same persons or could be regarded as consisting of the same persons by treating (in one or more cases) a member of either group as replaced by a person of whom he is an associate.

435(7)   **[Company associate of another person]**   A company is an associate of another person if that person has control of it or if that person and persons who are his associates together have control of it.

435(8)   **[Person relative of individual]**   For the purposes of this section a person is a relative of an individual if he is that individual's brother, sister, uncle, aunt, nephew, niece, lineal ancestor or lineal descendant, treating—

    (a) any relationship of the half blood as a relationship of the whole blood and the stepchild or adopted child of any person as his child, and

    (b) an illegitimate child as the legitimate child of his mother and reputed father;

and references in this section to a husband or wife include a former husband or wife and a reputed husband or wife.

435(9)   **[Director employee]**   For the purposes of this section any director or other officer of a company is to be treated as employed by that company.

435(10)   **[Person with control]**   For the purposes of this section a person is to be taken as having control of a company if—

    (a) the directors of the company or of another company which has control of it (or any of them) are accustomed to act in accordance with his directions or instructions, or

    (b) he is entitled to exercise, or control the exercise of, one third or more of the voting power at any general meeting of the company or of another company which has control of it;

and where two or more persons together satisfy either of the above conditions, they are to be taken as having control of the company.

435(11)   **["Company"]**   In this section **"company"** includes any body corporate (whether incorporated in Great Britain or elsewhere); and references to directors and other officers of a company and to voting power at any general meeting of a company have effect with any necessary modifications.

SEC. 436 Expressions used generally

436 In this Act, except in so far as the context otherwise requires (and subject to Parts VII and XI)—

"the appointed day" means the day on which this Act comes into force under section 443;

"associate" has the meaning given by section 435;

"business" includes a trade or profession;

"the Companies Act" means the Companies Act 1985;

"conditional sale agreement" and **"hire-purchase agreement"** have the same meanings as in the Consumer Credit Act 1974;

"modifications" includes additions, alterations and omissions and cognate expressions shall be construed accordingly;

"property" includes money, goods, things in action, land and every description of property wherever situated and also obligations and every description of interest, whether present or future or vested or contingent, arising out of, or incidental to, property;

"records" includes computer records and other non-documentary records;

"subordinate legislation" has the same meaning as in the Interpretation Act 1978; and

"transaction" includes a gift, agreement or arrangement, and references to entering into a transaction shall be contrued accordingly.

PART XIX — FINAL PROVISIONS

SEC. 437 Transitional provisions and savings

437 The transitional provisions and savings set out in Schedule 11 to this Act shall have effect, the Schedule comprising the following Parts—

Part I: company insolvency and winding up (matters arising before appointed day, and continuance of proceedings in certain cases as before that day);

Part II: individual insolvency (matters so arising, and continuance of bankruptcy proceedings in certain cases as before that day);

Part III: transactions entered into before the appointed day and capable of being affected by orders of the court under Part XVI of this Act;

Part IV: insolvency practitioners acting as such before the appointed day; and

Part V: general transitional provisions and savings required consequentially on, and in connection with, the repeal and replacement by this Act and the Company Directors Disqualification Act 1986 of provisions of the Companies Act, the greater part of the Insolvency Act 1985 and other enactments.

SEC. 438   Repeals

438   The enactments specified in the second column of Schedule 12 to this Act are repealed to the extent specified in the third column of that Schedule.

SEC. 439   Amendment of enactments

439(1)   **[Amendment of Companies Act]**   The Companies Act is amended as shown in Parts I and II of Schedule 13 to this Act, being amendments consequential on this Act and the Company Directors Disqualification Act 1986.

439(2)   **[Enactments in Sch. 14]**   The enactments specified in the first column of Schedule 14 to this Act (being enactments which refer, or otherwise relate, to those which are repealed and replaced by this Act or the Company Directors Disqualification Act 1986) are amended as shown in the second column of that Schedule.

439(3)   **[Consequential modifications of subordinate legislation]**   The Lord Chancellor may by order make such consequential modifications of any provision contained in any subordinate legislation made before the appointed day and such transitional provisions in connection with those modifications as appear to him necessary or expedient in respect of—

    (a)   any reference in that subordinate legislation to the Bankruptcy Act 1914;

    (b)   any reference in that subordinate legislation to any enactment repealed by Part III or IV of Schedule 10 to the Insolvency Act 1985; or

    (c)   any reference in that subordinate legislation to any matter provided for under the Act of 1914 or under any enactment so repealed.

439(4)   **[Order by statutory instrument etc.]**   An order under this section shall be made by statutory instrument subject to annulment in pursuance of a resolution of either House of Parliament.

Note
See The Insolvency (Amendment of Subordinate Legislation) Order 1986 (S.I. 1986 No. 2001) (and also The Insolvency (Land Registration Rules) Order 1986 (S.I. 1986 No. 2245)).

SEC. 440   Extent (Scotland)

440(1)   **[Extension to Scotland except where stated]**   Subject to the next subsection, provisions of this Act contained in the first Group of Parts extend to Scotland except where otherwise stated.

440(2)   **[Provisions not extending to Scotland]**   The following provisions of this Act do not extend to Scotland—

    (a)   in the first Groups of Parts—

             section 43;
             sections 238 to 241; and
             section 246;

    (b)   the second Group of Parts;

    (c)   in the third Group of Parts—

             sections 399 to 402,
             sections 412, 413, 415, 418, 420 and 421,
             sections 423 to 425, and
             section 429(1) and (2); and

(d) in the Schedules—

Parts II and III of Schedule 11; and

Schedules 12 and 14 so far as they repeal or amend enactments which extend to England and Wales only.

SEC. 441 Extent (Northern Ireland)

441(1) [Provisions extending to Northern Ireland] The following provisions of this Act extend to Northern Ireland—

(a) sections 197, 426, 427 and 428; and

(b) so much of section 439 and Schedule 14 as relates to enactments which extend to Northern Ireland.

441(2) [Most of provisions not extending to Northern Ireland] Subject as above, and to any provision expressly relating to companies incorporated elsewhere than in Great Britain, nothing in this Act extends to Northern Ireland or applies to or in relation to companies registered or incorporated in Northern Ireland.

SEC. 442 Extent (other territories)

442 Her Majesty may, by Order in Council, direct that such of the provisions of this Act as are specified in the Order, being provisions formerly contained in the Insolvency Act 1985, shall extend to any of the Channel Islands or any colony with such modifications as may be so specified.

Note
See the Insolvency Act 1986 (Guernsey) Order 1989 (S.I.
1989 No. 2409).

SEC. 443 Commencement

443 This Act comes into force on the day appointed under section 236(2) of the Insolvency Act 1985 for the coming into force of Part III of that Act (individual insolvency and bankruptcy), immediately after that part of that Act comes into force for England and Wales.

Note
The relevant date is 29 December 1986: see S.I. 1986
No. 1924 (C. 71).

SEC. 444 Citation

444 This Act may be cited as the Insolvency Act 1986.

SCHEDULES

Schedule 1 — Powers of Administrator or Administrative Receiver

Sections 14, 42

1   Power to take possession of, collect and get in the property of the company and, for that purpose, to take such proceedings as may seem to him expedient.

2   Power to sell or otherwise dispose of the property of the company by public auction or private auction or private contract or, in Scotland, to sell, feu, hire out or otherwise dispose of the property of the company by public roup or private bargain.

3   Power to raise or borrow money and grant security therefor over the property of the company.

4   Power to appoint a solicitor or accountant or other professionally qualified person to assist him in the performance of his functions.

5   Power to bring or defend any action or other legal proceedings in the name and on behalf of the company.

6   Power to refer to arbitration any question affecting the company.

7   Power to effect and maintain insurances in respect of the business and property of the company.

8   Power to use the company's seal.

9   Power to do all acts and to execute in the name and on behalf of the company any deed, receipt or other document.

10   Power to draw, accept, make and endorse any bill of exchange or promissory note in the name and on behalf of the company.

11   Power to appoint any agent to do any business which he is unable to do himself or which can more conveniently be done by an agent and power to employ and dismiss employees.

12   Power to do all such things (including the carrying out of works) as may be necessary for the realisation of the property of the company.

13   Power to make any payment which is necessary or incidental to the performance of his functions.

14   Power to carry on the business of the company.

15   Power to establish subsidiaries of the company.

16   Power to transfer to subsidiaries of the company the whole or any part of the business and property of the company.

17   Power to grant or accept a surrender of a lease or tenancy of any of the property of the company, and to take a lease or tenancy of any property required or convenient for the business of the company.

18   Power to make any arrangement or compromise on behalf of the company.

19   Power to call up any uncalled capital of the company.

20   Power to rank and claim in the bankruptcy, insolvency, sequestration or liquidation of any person indebted to the company and to receive dividends, and to accede to trust deeds for the creditors of any such person.

21   Power to present or defend a petition for the winding up of the company.

22   Power to change the situation of the company's registered office.

23   Power to do all other things incidental to the exercise of the foregoing powers.

Schedule 2 — Powers of a Scottish Receiver (Additional to Those Conferred on him by the Instrument of Charge)

Section 55

1   Power to take possession of, collect and get in the property from the company or a liquidator thereof or any other person, and for that purpose, to take such proceedings as may seem to him expedient.

2   Power to sell, feu, hire out or otherwise dispose of the property by public roup or private bargain and with or without advertisement.

3   Power to raise or borrow money and grant security therefor over the property.

4   Power to appoint a solicitor or accountant or other professionally qualified person to assist him in the performance of his functions.

5   Power to bring or defend any action or other legal proceedings in the name and on behalf of the company.

6   Power to refer to arbitration all questions affecting the company.

7   Power to effect and maintain insurances in respect of the business and property of the company.

8   Power to use the company's seal.

9   Power to do all acts and to execute in the name and on behalf of the company any deed, receipt or other document.

10   Power to draw, accept, make and endorse any bill of exchange or promissory note in the name and on behalf of the company.

11   Power to appoint any agent to do any business which he is unable to do himself or which can more conveniently be done by an agent, and power to employ and dismiss employees.

12   Power to do all such things (including the carrying out of works), as may be necessary for the realisation of the property.

13   Power to make any payment which is necessary or incidental to the performance of his functions.

14   Power to carry on the business of the company or any part of it.

15   Power to grant or accept a surrender of a lease or tenancy of any of the property, and to take a lease or tenancy of any property required or covenient for the business of the company.

16   Power to make any arrangement or compromise on behalf of the company.

17   Power to call up any uncalled capital of the company.

18   Power to establish subsidiaries of the company.

19   Power to transfer to subsidiaries of the company the business of the company or any part of it and any of the property.

20   Power to rank and claim in the bankruptcy, insolvency, sequestrian or liquidation of any person or company indebted to the company and to receive dividends, and to accede to trust deeds for creditors of any such person.

21   Power to present or defend a petition for the winding up of the company.

22   Power to change the situation of the company's registered office.

23   Power to do all other things incidental to the exercise of the powers mentioned in section 55(1) of this Act or above in this Schedule.

Schedule 3 — Orders in Course of Winding Up Pronounced in Vacation (Scotland)

Section 162

Part I — Orders Which are to be Final

Orders under section 153, as to the time for proving debts and claims.

Orders under section 195 as to meetings for ascertaining wishes of creditors or contributories.

Orders under section 198, as to the examination of witnesses in regard to the property or affairs of a company.

Part II — Orders Which are to take Effect until Matter Disposed of by Inner House

Orders under section 126(1), 130(2) or (3), 147, 227 or 228, restraining or permitting the commencement or the continuance of legal proceedings.

Orders under section 135(5), limiting the powers of provisional liquidators.

Orders under section 108, appointing a liquidator to fill a vacancy.

Orders under section 167 or 169, sanctioning the exercise of any powers by a liquidator, other than the powers specified in paragraphs 1, 2 and 3 of Schedule 4 to this Act.

Orders under section 158, as to the arrest and detention of an absconding contributory and his property.

Schedule 4 — Powers of Liquidator in a Winding Up

Sections 165, 167

Part I — Powers Exercisable with Sanction

1   Power to pay any class of creditors in full.

2   Power to make any compromise or arrangement with creditors or persons claiming to be creditors, or having or alleging themselves to have any claim (present or future, certain or contingent, ascertained or sounding only in damages) against the company, or whereby the company may be rendered liable.

3 Power to compromise, on such terms as may be agreed—

(a) all calls and liabilities to calls, all debts and liabilities capable of resulting in debts, and all claims (present or future, certain or contingent, ascertained or sounding only in damages) subsisting or supposed to subsist between the company and a contributory or alleged contributory or other debtor or person apprehending liability to the company, and

(b) all questions in any way relating to or affecting the assets or the winding up of the company,

and take any security for the discharge of any such call, debt, liability or claim and give a complete discharge in respect of it.

Part II — Powers Exercisable without Sanction in Voluntary Winding Up, with Sanction in Winding Up by the Court

4 Power to bring or defend any action or other legal proceeding in the name and on behalf of the company.

5 Power to carry on the business of the company so far as may be necessary for its beneficial winding up.

Part III — Powers Exercisable Without Sanction in any Winding Up

6 Power to sell any of the company's property by public auction or private contract, with power to transfer the whole of it to any person or to sell the same in parcels.

7 Power to do all acts and execute, in the name and on behalf of the company, all deeds, receipts and other documents and for that purpose to use, when necessary, the company's seal.

8 Power to prove, rank and claim in the bankruptcy, insolvency or sequestration of any contributory for any balance against his estate, and to receive dividends in the bankruptcy, insolvency or sequestration in respect of that balance, as a separate debt due from the bankrupt or insolvent, and rateably with the other separate creditors.

9 Power to draw, accept, make and indorse any bill of exchange or promissory note in the name and on behalf of the company, with the same effect with respect to the company's liability as if the bill or note had been drawn, accepted, made or indorsed by or on behalf of the company in the course of its business.

10 Power to raise on the security of the assets of the company any money requisite.

11 Power to take out in his official name letters of administration to any deceased contributory, and to do in his official name any other act necessary for obtaining payment of any money due from a contributory or his estate which cannot conveniently be done in the name of the company.

In all such cases the money due is deemed, for the purpose of enabling the liquidator to take out the letters of administration or recover the money, to be due to the liquidator himself.

12   Power to appoint an agent to do any business which the liquidator is unable to do himself.

13   Power to do all such other things as may be necessary for winding up the company's affairs and distributing its assets.

Schedule 5 — Powers of Trustee in Bankruptcy

Section 314

Part I — Powers Exercisable with Sanction

1   Power to carry on any business of the bankrupt so far as may be necessary for winding it up beneficially and so far as the trustee is able to do so without contravening any requirement imposed by or under any enactment.

2   Power to bring, institute or defend any action or legal proceedings relating to the property comprised in the bankrupt's estate.

3   Power to accept as the consideration for the sale of any property comprised in the bankrupt's estate a sum of money payable at a future time subject to such stipulations as to security or otherwise as the creditors' committee or the court thinks fit.

4   Power to mortgage or pledge any part of the property comprised in the bankrupt's estate for the purpose of raising money for the payment of his debts.

5   Power, where any right, option or other power forms part of the bankrupt's estate, to make payments or incur liabilities with a view to obtaining, for the benefit of the creditors, any property which is the subject of the right, option or power.

6   Power to refer to arbitration, or compromise on such terms as may be agreed on, any debts, claims or liabilities subsisting or supposed to subsist between the bankrupt and any person who may have incurred any liability to the bankrupt.

7   Power to make such compromise or other arrangement as may be thought expedient with creditors, or persons claiming to be creditors, in respect of bankruptcy debts.

8   Power to make such compromise or other arrangement as may be thought expedient with respect to any claim arising out of or incidental to the bankrupt's estate made or capable of being made on the trustee by any person or by the trustee on any person.

Part II — General Powers

9   Power to sell any part of the property for the time being comprised in the bankrupt's estate, including the goodwill and book debts of any business.

10   Power to give receipts for any money received by him, being receipts which effectually discharge the person paying the money from all responsibility in respect of its application.

11 Power to prove, rank, claim and draw a dividend in respect of such debts due to the bankrupt as are comprised in his estate.

12 Power to exercise in relation to any property comprised in the bankrupt's estate any powers the capacity to exercise which is vested in him under Parts VIII to XI of this Act.

13 Power to deal with any property comprised in the estate to which the bankrupt is beneficially entitled as tenant in tail in the same manner as the bankrupt might have dealt with it.

Part III — Ancillary Powers

14 For the purposes of, or in connection with, the exercise of any of his powers under Parts VIII to XI of this Act, the trustee may, by his official name—

   (a) hold property of every description,

   (b) make contracts,

   (c) sue and be sued,

   (d) enter into engagements binding on himself and, in respect of the bankrupt's estate, on his successors in office,

   (e) employ an agent,

   (f) execute any power of attorney, deed or other instrument;

and he may do any other act which is necessary or expedient for the purposes of or in connection with the exercise of those powers.

Schedule 6 — The Categories of Preferential Debts

Section 386

CATEGORY 1: DEBTS DUE TO INLAND REVENUE

1 Sums due at the relevant date from the debtor on account of deductions of income tax from emoluments paid during the period of 12 months next before that date.

   The deductions here referred to are those which the debtor was liable to make under section 203 of the Income and Corporation Taxes Act 1988 (pay as you earn), less the amount of the repayments of income tax which the debtor was liable to make during that period.

History
In para. 1 the words "203 of the Income and Corporation Taxes Act 1988" substituted for the former words "204 of the Income and Corporation Taxes Act 1970" by Income and Corporation Taxes Act 1988, s. 844 and Sch. 29, para. 32 for companies' accounting periods ending after 5 April 1988 (see s. 843(1)).

2 Sums due at the relevant date from the debtor in respect of such deductions as are required to be made by the debtor for that period under section 559 of the Income and Corporation Taxes Act 1988 (sub-contractors in the construction industry).

History
In para. 2 the words "559 of the Income and Corporation Taxes Act 1988" substituted for the former words "69 of the Finance (No. 2) Act 1975" by Income and Corporation Taxes Act 1988, s. 844 and Sch. 29, para. 32 for companies' accounting periods ending after 5 April 1988 (see s. 843(1)).

CATEGORY 2: DEBTS DUE TO CUSTOMS AND EXCISE

3 Any value added tax which is referable to the period of 6 months next before the relevant date (which period is referred to below as "the 6-month period").

For the purposes of this paragraph—

   (a) where the whole of the prescribed accounting period to which any value added tax is attributable falls within the 6-month period, the whole amount of that tax is referable to that period; and

   (b) in any other case the amount of any value added tax which is referable to the 6-month period is the proportion of the tax which is equal to such proportion (if any) of the accounting reference period in question as falls within the 6-month period;

and in sub-paragraph (a) **"prescribed"** means prescribed by regulations under the Value Added Tax Act 1983.

4   The amount of any car tax which is due at the relevant date from the debtor and which became due within a period of 12 months next before that date.

5   Any amount which is due—

   (a) by way of general betting duty or bingo duty, or

   (b) under section 12(1) of the Betting and Gaming Duties Act 1981 (general betting duty and pool betting duty recoverable from agent collecting stakes), or

   (c) under section 14 of, or Schedule 2 to, that Act (gaming licence duty),

from the debtor at the relevant date and which became due within the period of 12 months next before that date.

CATEGORY 3: SOCIAL SECURITY CONTRIBUTIONS

6   All sums which on the relevant date are due from the debtor on account of Class 1 or Class 2 contributions under the Social Security Act 1975 or the Social Security (Northern Ireland) Act 1975 and which became due from the debtor in the 12 months next before the relevant date.

7   All sums which on the relevant date have been assessed on and are due from the debtor on account of Class 4 contributions under either of those Acts of 1975, being sums which—

   (a) are due to the Commissioners of Inland Revenue (rather than to the Secretary of State or a Northern Ireland department), and

   (b) are assessed on the debtor up to 5th April next before the relevant date,

but not exceeding, in the whole, any one year's assessment.

CATEGORY 4: CONTRIBUTIONS TO OCCUPATIONAL PENSION SCHEMES, ETC.

8   Any sum which is owed by the debtor and is a sum to which Schedule 3 to the Social Security Pensions Act 1975 applies (contributions to occupational pension schemes and state scheme premiums).

CATEGORY 5: REMUNERATION, ETC., OF EMPLOYEES

9   So much of any amount which—

   (a) is owed by the debtor to a person who is or has been an employee of the debtor, and

(b) is payable by way of remuneration in respect of the whole or any part of the period of 4 months next before the relevant date,

as does not exceed so much as may be prescribed by order made by the Secretary of State.

Note
See Note after para. 12.

10 An amount owed by way of accrued holiday remuneration, in respect of any period of employment before the relevant date, to a person whose employment by the debtor has been terminated, whether before, on or after that date.

11 So much of any sum owed in respect of money advanced for the purpose as has been applied for the payment of a debt which, if it had not been paid, would have been a debt falling within paragraph 9 or 10.

12 So much of any amount which—

(a) is ordered (whether before or after the relevant date) to be paid by the debtor under the Reserve Forces (Safeguard of Employment) Act 1985, and

(b) is so ordered in respect of a default made by the debtor before that date in the discharge of his obligations under that Act.

as does not exceed such amount as may be prescribed by order made by the Secretary of State.

Note
The amount for para. 9, 12 is £800 — see The Insolvency Proceedings (Monetary Limits) Order 1986 (S.I. 1986 No. 1996), art. 4.

INTERPRETATION FOR CATEGORY 5

13(1) For the purposes of paragraphs 9 to 12, a sum is payable by the debtor to a person by way of remuneration in respect of any period if—

(a) it is paid as wages or salary (whether payable for time or for piece work or earned wholly or partly by way of commission) in respect of services rendered to the debtor in that period, or

(b) it is an amount falling within the following sub-paragraph and is payable by the debtor in respect of that period.

13(2) An amount falls within this sub-paragraph if it is—

(a) a guarantee payment under section 12(1) of the Employment Protection (Consolidation) Act 1978 (employee without work to do for a day or part of a day);

(b) remuneration on suspension on medical grounds under section 19 of that Act;

(c) any payment for time off under section 27(3) (trade union duties), 31(3) (looking for work, etc.) or 31A(4) (ante-natal care) of that Act; or

(d) remuneration under a protective award made by an industrial tribunal under section 101 of the Employment Protection Act 1975 (redundancy dismissal with compensation).

14(1)   This paragraph relates to a case in which a person's employment has been terminated by or in consequence of his employer going into liquidation or being adjudged bankrupt or (his employer being a company not in liquidation) by or in consequence of—

   (a)   a receiver being appointed as mentioned in section 40 of this Act (debenture-holders secured by floating charge), or

   (b)   the appointment of a receiver under section 53(6) or 54(5) of this Act (Scottish company with property subject to floating charge), or

   (c)   the taking of possession by debenture-holders (so secured), as mentioned in section 196 of the Companies Act.

14(2)   For the purposes of paragraphs 9 to 12, holiday remuneration is deemed to have accrued to that person in respect of any period of employment if, by virtue of his contract of employment or of any enactment, that remuneration would have accrued in respect of that period if his employment had continued until he became entitled to be allowed the holiday.

14(3)   The reference in sub-paragraph (2) to any enactment includes an order or direction made under an enactment.

15   Without prejudice to paragraphs 13 and 14—

   (a)   any remuneration payable by the debtor to a person in respect of a period of holiday or of absence from work through sickness or other good cause is deemed to be wages or (as the case may be) salary in respect of services rendered to the debtor in that period, and

   (b)   references here and in those paragraphs to remuneration in respect of a period of holiday include any sums which, if they had been paid, would have been treated for the purposes of the enactments relating to social security as earnings in repect of that period.

CATEGORY 6: LEVIES ON COAL AND STEEL PRODUCTION

15A   Any sums due at the relevant date from the debtor in respect of—

   (a)   the levies on the production of coal and steel referred to in Article 49 and 50 of the E.C.S.C. Treaty, or

   (b)   any surcharge for delay provided for in Article 50(3) of that Treaty and Article 6 of Decision 3/52 of the High Authority of the Coal and Steel Community.

History
Para. 15A inserted by The Insolvency (ECSC Levy Debts) Regulations 1987 (S.I. 1987 No. 2093), reg. 2(1) as from 1 January 1988.

Note
See The Insolvency (ECSC Levy Debts) Regulations 1987 (S.I. 1987 No. 2093), reg. 2(3) and 4 concerning the relevant date and preferential treatment under former law.

ORDERS

16   An order under paragraph 9 or 12—

   (a)   may contain such transitional provisions as may appear to the Secretary of State necessary or expedient;

   (b)   shall be made by statutory instrument subject to annulment in pursuance of a resolution of either House of Parliament.

Schedule 7 — Insolvency Practitioners Tribunal

Section 396

PANELS OF MEMBERS

1(1) The Secretary of State shall draw up and from time to time revise—

(a) a panel of persons who are barristers advocates or solicitors, in each case of not less than 7 years' standing, and are nominated for the purpose by the Lord Chancellor or the Lord President of the Court of Session, and

(b) a panel of persons who are experienced in insolvency matters;

and the members of the Tribunal shall be selected from those panels in accordance with this Schedule.

1(2) The power to revise the panels includes power to terminate a person's membership of either of them, and is accordingly to that extent subject to section 8 of the Tribunals and Inquiries Act 1971 (which makes it necessary to obtain the concurrence of the Lord Chancellor and the Lord President of the Court of Session to dismissals in certain cases).

REMUNERATION OF MEMBERS

2 The Secretary of State may out of money provided by Parliament pay to members of the Tribunal such remuneration as he may with the approval of the Treasury determine; and such expenses of the Tribunal as the Secretary of State and the Treasury may approve shall be defrayed by the Secretary of State out of money so provided.

SITTINGS OF TRIBUNAL

3(1) For the purposes of carrying out their functions in relation to any cases referred to them, the Tribunal may sit either as a single tribunal or in two or more divisions.

3(2) The functions of the Tribunal in relation to any case referred to them shall be exercised by three members consisting of—

(a) a chairman selected by the Secretary of State from the panel drawn up under paragraph 1(1)(a) above, and

(b) two other members selected by the Secretary of State from the panel drawn up under paragraph 1(1)(b).

PROCEDURE OF TRIBUNAL

4(1) Any investigation by the Tribunal shall be so conducted as to afford a reasonable opportunity for representations to be made to the Tribunal by or on behalf of the person whose case is the subject of the investigation.

4(2) For the purposes of any such investigation, the Tribunal—

(a) may by summons require any person to attend, at such time and place as is specified in the summons, to give evidence or to produce any books, papers and other records in his possession or under his control which the Tribunal consider it necessary for the purposes of the investigation to examine, and

(b) may take evidence on oath, and for the purpose administer oaths, or may, instead of administering an oath, require the person examined to make and subscribe a declaration of the truth of the matter respecting which he is examined;

but no person shall be required, in obedience to such a summons, to go more than ten miles from his place of residence, unless the necessary expenses of his attendance are paid or tendered to him.

4(3) Every person who—

(a) without reasonable excuse fails to attend in obedience to a summons issued under this paragraph, or refuses to give evidence, or

(b) intentionally alters, suppresses, conceals or destroys or refuses to produce any document which he may be required to produce for the purpose of an investigation by the Tribunal,

is liable to a fine.

4(4) Subject to the provisions of this paragraph, the Secretary of State may make rules for regulating the procedure on any investigation by the Tribunal.

4(5) In their application to Scotland, sub-paragraphs (2) and (3) above have effect as if for any reference to a summons there where substituted a reference to a notice in writing.

Note
See the note to s. 396(1).

Schedule 8 — Provisions Capable of Inclusion in Company Insolvency Rules

Section 411

COURTS

1 Provision for supplementing, in relation to the insolvency or winding up of companies, any provision made by or under section 117 of this Act (jurisdiction in relation to winding up).

2 Provision for regulating the practice and procedure of any court exercising jurisdiction for the purposes of Parts I to VII of this Act or the Companies Act so far as relating to, and to matters connected with or arising out of, the insolvency or winding up of companies, being any provision that could be made by rules of court.

NOTICES, ETC.

3 Provision requiring notice of any proceedings in connection with or arising out of the insolvency or winding up of a company to be given or published in the manner prescribed by the rules.

4 Provision with respect to the form, manner of serving, contents and proof of any petition, application, order, notice, statement or other document required to be presented, made, given, published or prepared under any enactment or subordinate legislation relating to, or to matters connected with or arising out of, the insolvency or winding up of companies.

5 Provision specifying the persons to whom any notice is to be given.

REGISTRATION OF VOLUNTARY ARRANGEMENTS

6 Provision for the registration of voluntary arrangements approved under Part I of this Act, including provision for the keeping and inspection of a register.

PROVISIONAL LIQUIDATOR

7 Provision as to the manner in which a provisional liquidator appointed under section 135 is to carry out his functions.

CONDUCT OF INSOLVENCY

8 Provision with respect to the certification of any person as, and as to the proof that a person is, the liquidator, administrator or administrative receiver of a company.

[The next page is 56,301]

9   The following provision with respect to meetings of a company's creditors, contributories or members—

(a)   provision as to the manner of summoning a meeting (including provision as to how any power to require a meeting is to be exercised, provision as to the manner of determining the value of any debt or contribution for the purposes of any such power and provision making the exercise of any such power subject to the deposit of a sum sufficient to cover the expenses likely to be incurred in summoning and holding a meeting);

(b)   provision specifying the time and place at which a meeting may be held and the period of notice required for a meeting;

(c)   provision as to the procedure to be followed at a meeting (including the manner in which decisions may be reached by a meeting and the manner in which the value of any vote at a meeting is to be determined);

(d)   provision for requiring a person who is or has been an officer of the company to attend a meeting;

(e)   provision creating, in the prescribed circumstances, a presumption that a meeting has been duly summoned and held;

(f)   provision as to the manner of proving the decisions of a meeting.

10(1)   Provision as to the functions, membership and proceedings of a committee established under section 26, 49, 68, 101, 141 or 142 of this Act.

10(2)   The following provision with respect to the establishment of a committee under section 101, 141 or 142 of this Act, that is to say—

(a)   provision for resolving differences between a meeting of the company's creditors and a meeting of its contributories or members;

(b)   provision authorising the establishment of the committee without a meeting of contributories in a case where a company is being wound up on grounds including its inability to pay its debts; and

(c)   provision modifying the requirements of this Act with respect to the establishment of the committee in a case where a winding-up order has been made immediately upon the discharge of an administration order.

11   Provision as to the manner in which any requirement that may be imposed on a person under any Parts I to VII of this Act by the official receiver, the liquidator, administrator or administrative receiver of a company or a special manager appointed under section 177 is to be so imposed.

12   Provision as to the debts that may be proved in a winding up, as to the manner and conditions of proving a debt and as to the manner and expenses of establishing the value of any debt or security.

13   Provision with respect to the manner of the distribution of the property of a company that is being wound up, including provision with respect to unclaimed funds and dividends.

14   Provision which, with or without modifications, applies in relation to the winding up of companies any enactment contained in Parts VIII to XI of this Act or in the Bankruptcy (Scotland) Act 1985.

FINANCIAL PROVISIONS

15 Provision as to the amount, or manner of determining the amount, payable to the liquidator, administrator or administrative receiver of a company or a special manager appointed under section 177, by way of remuneration for the carrying out of functions in connection with or arising out of the insolvency or winding up of a company.

16 Provision with respect to the manner in which moneys received by the liquidator of a company in the course of carrying out his functions as such are to be invested or otherwise handled and with respect to the payment of interest on sums which, in pursuance of rules made by virtue of this paragraph, have been paid into the Insolvency Services Account.

17 Provision as to the fees, costs, charges and other expenses that may be treated as the expenses of a winding up.

18 Provisions as to the fees, costs, charges and other expenses that may be treated as properly incurred by the administrator or administrative receiver of a company.

19 Provision as to the fees, costs, charges and other expenses that may be incurred for any of the purposes of Part I of this Act or in the administration of any voluntary arrangment approved under that Part.

INFORMATION AND RECORDS

20 Provision requiring registrars and other officers of courts having jurisdiction in England and Wales in relation to, or to matters connected with or arising out of, the insolvency or winding up of companies—

    (a) to keep books and other records with respect to the exercise of that jurisdiction, and

    (b) to make returns to the Secretary of State of the business of those courts.

21 Provision requiring a creditor, member or contributory, or such a committee as is mentioned in paragraph 10 above, to be supplied (on payment in precribed cases of the prescribed fee) with such information and with copies of such documents as may be prescribed.

22 Provision as to the manner in which public examinations under sections 133 and 134 of this Act and proceedings under sections 236 and 237 are to be conducted, as to the circumstances in which records of such examinations or proceedings are to be made available to prescribed persons and as to the costs of such examinations and proceedings.

23 Provision imposing requirements with respect to—

    (a) the preparation and keeping by the liquidator, administrator or administrative receiver of a company, or by the supervisor of a voluntary arrangement approved under Part I of this Act, of prescribed books, accounts and other records;

    (b) the production of those books, accounts and records for inspection by prescribed persons;

    (c) the auditing of accounts kept by the liquidator, administrator or administrative receiver of a company, or the supervisor of such a voluntary arrangement; and

(d) the issue by the administrator or administrative recever of a company of such a certificate as is mentioned in section 22(3)(b) of the Value Added Tax Act 1983 (refund of tax in cases of bad debts) and the supply of copies of the certificate to creditors of the company.

24 Provision requiring the person who is the supervisor of a voluntary arrangement approved under Part I, when it appears to him that the voluntary arrangement has been fully implemented and nothing remains to be done by him under the arrangement—

(a) to give notice to that fact to persons bound by the voluntary arrangement, and

(b) to report to those persons on the carrying out of the functions conferred on the supervisor of the arrangement.

25 Provision as to the manner in which the liquidator of a company is to act in relation to the books, papers and other records of the company, including provision authorising their disposal.

26 Provision imposing requirements in connection with the carrying out of functions under section 7(3) of the Company Directors Disqualification Act 1986 (including, in particular, requirements with respect to the making of periodic returns).

Note
For para. 26, see the rules referred to in the notes to Company Directors Disqualification Act 1986, s. 7.

For para. 27, see The Insolvency Regulations 1986 (S.I. 1986 No. 1994).

GENERAL

27 Provision conferring power on the Secretary of State to make regulations with respect to so much of any matter that may be provided for in the rules as relates to the carrying out of the functions of the liquidator, administrator or administrative receiver of a company.

28 Provision conferring a discretion on the court.

29 Provision conferring power on the court to make orders for the purpose of securing compliance with obligations imposed by or under section 22, 47, 66, 131, 143(2) or 235 of this Act or section 7(4) of the Company Directors Disqualification Act 1986.

30 Provision making non-compliance with any of the rules a criminal offence.

31 Provision making different provision for different cases or descriptions of cases, including different provisions for different areas.

Schedule 9 — Provisions Capable of Inclusion in Individual Insolvency Rules

Section 412

COURTS

1 Provision with respect to the arrangement and disposition of the business under Parts VIII to XI of this Act of courts having jurisdiction for the purpose of those Parts, including provision for the allocation of proceedings under those Parts to particular courts and for the transfer of such proceedings from one court to another.

2 Provision for enabling a registrar in bankruptcy of the High Court or a registrar of a county court having jurisdiction for the purposes of those Parts to exercise such of the jurisdiction conferred for those purposes on the High Court or, as the case may be, that county court as may be prescribed.

3 Provision for regulating the practice and procedure of any court exercising jurisdiction for the purposes of those Parts, being any provision that could be made by rules of court.

4 Provision conferring rights of audience, in courts exercising jurisdiction for the purposes of those Parts, on the official receiver and on solicitors.

NOTICES ETC.

5 Provision requiring notice of any proceedings under Parts VIII to XI of this Act or of any matter relating to or arising out of a proposal under Part VIII or a bankruptcy to be given or published in the prescribed manner.

6 Provision with respect to the form, manner of serving, contents and proof of any petition, application, order, notice, statement or other document required to be presented, made, given, published or prepared under any enactment contained in Parts VIII to XI or subordinate legislation under those Parts or Part XV (including provision requiring prescribed matters to be verified by affidavit).

7 Provision specifying the persons to whom any notice under Parts VIII to XI is to be given.

REGISTRATION OF VOLUNTARY ARRANGEMENTS

8 Provision for the registration of voluntary arrangements approved under Part VIII of this Act, including provision for the keeping and inspection of a register.

INTERIM RECEIVER

9 Provision as to the manner in which an interim receiver appointed under section 286 is to carry out his functions, including any such provision as is specified in relation to the trustee of a bankrupt's estate in paragraph 21 or 27 below.

RECEIVER OR MANAGER

10 Provision as to the manner in which the official receiver is to carry out his functions as receiver or manager of a bankrupt's estate under section 287, including any such provision as is specified in relation to the trustee of a bankrupt's estate in paragraph 21 or 27 below.

ADMINISTRATION OF INDIVIDUAL INSOLVENCY

11 Provision with respect to the certification of the appointment of any person as trustee of a bankrupt's estate and as to the proof of that appointment.

12 The following provision with respect to meetings of creditors—

    (a) provision as to the manner of summoning a meeting (including provision as to how any power to require a meeting is to be exercised, provision as to the manner of determining the value of any debt for the purposes of any such power and provision making the exercise of any such power subject to the deposit of a sum sufficient to cover the expenses likely to be incurred in summoning and holding a meeting);

(b) provision specifying the time and place at which a meeting may be held and the period of notice required for a meeting;

(c) provision as to the procedure to be followed at such a meeting (including the manner in which decisions may be reached by a meeting and the manner in which the value of any vote at a meeting is to be determined);

(d) provision for requiring a bankrupt or debtor to attend a meeting;

(e) provision creating, in the prescribed circumstances, a presumption that a meeting has been duly summoned and held; and

(f) provision as to the manner of proving the decisions of a meeting.

13 Provision as to the functions, membership and proceedings of a creditors' committee established under section 301.

14 Provision as to the manner in which any requirement that may be imposed on a person under Parts VIII to XI of this Act by the official receiver, the trustee of a bankrupt's estate or a special manager appointed under section 370 is to be imposed and, in the case of any requirement imposed under section 305(3) (information etc. to be given by the trustee to the official receiver), provision conferring power on the court to make orders for the purpose of securing compliance with that requirement.

15 Provision as to the manner in which any requirement imposed by virtue of section 310(3) (compliance with income payments order) is to take effect.

16 Provision as to the terms and conditions that may be included in a charge under section 313 (dwelling house forming part of bankrupt's estate).

17 Provision as to the debts that may be proved in any bankruptcy, as to the manner and conditions of proving a debt and as to the manner and expenses of establishing the value of any debt or security.

18 Provision with respect to the manner of the distribution of a bankrupt's estate, including provision with respect to unclaimed funds and dividends.

19 Provision modifying the application of Parts VIII to XI of this Act in relation to a debtor or bankrupt who has died.

FINANCIAL PROVISIONS

20 Provision as to the amount, or manner of determining the amount, payable to an interim receiver, the trustee of a bankrupt's estate or a special manager appointed under section 370 by way of remuneration for the performance of functions in connection with or arising out of the bankruptcy of any person.

21 Provision with respect to the manner in which moneys received by the trustee of a bankrupt's estate in the course of carrying out his functions as such are to be handled.

22 Provision as to the fees, costs, charges and other expenses that may be treated as the expenses of a bankruptcy.

23   Provision as to the fees, costs, charges and other expenses that may be incurred for any of the purposes of Part VIII of this Act or in the administration of any voluntary arrangement approved under that Part.

INFORMATION AND RECORDS

24   Provision requiring registrars and other officers of courts having jurisdiction for the purposes of Parts VIII to XI—

   (a) to keep books and other records with respect to the exercise of that jurisdiction and of jurisdiction under the Deeds of Arrangement Act 1914, and

   (b) to make returns to the Secretary of State of the business of those courts.

25   Provision requiring a creditor or a committee established under section 301 to be supplied (on payment in prescribed cases of the prescribed fee) with such information and with copies of such documents as may be prescribed.

26   Provision as to the manner in which public examinations under section 290 and proceedings under sections 366 to 368 are to be conducted, as to the circumstances in which records of such examinations and proceedings are to be made available to prescribed persons and as to the costs of such examinations and proceedings.

27   Provision imposing requirements with respect to—

   (a) the preparation and keeping by the trustee of a bankrupt's estate, or the supervisor of a voluntary arrangement approved under Part VIII, of prescribed books, accounts and other records;

   (b) the production of those books, accounts and records for inspection by prescribed persons; and

   (c) the auditing of accounts kept by the trustee of a bankrupt's estate or the supervisor of such a voluntary arrangement.

28   Provision requiring the person who is the supervisor of a voluntary arrangement approved under Part VIII, when it appears to him that the voluntary arrangement has been fully implemented and that nothing remains to be done by him under it—

   (a) to give notice of that fact to persons bound by the voluntary arrangement, and

   (b) to report to those persons on the carrying out of the functions conferred on the supervisor of it.

29   Provision as to the manner in which the trustee of a bankrupt's estate is to act in relation to the books, papers and other records of the bankrupt, including provision authorising their disposal.

GENERAL

30   Provision conferring power on the Secretary of State to make regulations with respect to so much of any matter that may be provided for in the rules as relates to the carrying out of the functions of an interim receiver appointed under section 286, of the official receiver while acting as a receiver or manager under section 287 or of a trustee of a bankrupt's estate.

Note
Re para. 30 see The Insolvency Regulations 1986 (S.I. 1986 No. 1994).

31 Provision conferring a discretion on the court.

32 Provision making non-compliance with any of the rules a criminal offence.

33 Provision making different provision for different cases, including different provision for different areas.

Schedule 10 — Punishment of Offences under this Act

Note: In the fourth and fifth columns of this Schedule, "the statutory maximum" means—
(a) in England and Wales, the prescribed sum under section 32 of the Magistrates' Courts Act 1980 (c. 43), and
(b) in Scotland, the prescribed sum under section 289B of the Criminal Procedure (Scotland) Act 1975 (c. 21).

Section of Act creating offence	General nature of offence	Mode of prosecution	Punishment	Daily default fine (where applicable)
12(2)	Company and others failing to state in correspondence etc. that administrator appointed.	Summary.	One-fifth of the statutory maximum.	
15(8)	Failure of administrator to register office copy of court order permitting disposal of charged property.	Summary.	One-fifth of the statutory maximum.	One fiftieth of the statutory maximum.
18(5)	Failure of administrator to register office copy of court order varying or discharging administration order.	Summary.	One-fifth of the statutory maximum.	One fiftieth of the statutory maximum.
21(3)	Administrator failing to register administration order and give notice of appointment.	Summary.	One-fifth of the statutory maximum.	One fiftieth of the statutory maximum.
22(6)	Failure to comply with provisions relating to statement of affairs, where administrator appointed.	1. On indictment. 2. Summary.	A fine. The statutory maximum.	One-tenth of the statutory maximum.
23(3)	Administrator failing to send out, register and lay before creditors statement of his proposals.	Summary.	One-fifth of the statutory maximum.	One-fiftieth of the statutory maximum.
24(7)	Administrator failing to file court order discharging administration order under sec. 24.	Summary.	One-fifth of the statutory maximum.	One-fiftieth of the statutory maximum.
27(6)	Administrator failing to file court order discharging administration order under sec. 27.	Summary.	One-fifth of the statutory maximum.	One-fiftieth of the statutory maximum.

Section of Act creating offence	General nature of offence	Mode of prosecution	Punishment	Daily default fine (where applicable)
30	Body corporate acting as receiver.	1. On indictment. 2. Summary.	A fine. The statutory maximum.	
31	Undischarged bankrupt acting as receiver or manager.	1. On indictment. 2. Summary.	2 years or a fine, or both. 6 months or the statutory maximum, or both.	
38(5) ...	Receiver failing to deliver accounts to registrar.	Summary.	One-fifth of the statutory maximum.	One-fiftieth of the statutory maximum.
39(2) ...	Company and others failing to state in correspondence that receiver appointed.	Summary.	One-fifth of the statutory maximum.	One-fiftieth of the statutory maximum.
43(6) ...	Administrative receiver failing to file office copy of order permitting disposal of charged property.	Summary.	One-fifth of the statutory maximum.	One-fiftieth of the statutory maximum.
45(5) ...	Administrative receiver failing to file notice of vacation of office.	Summary.	One-fifth of the statutory maximum.	One-fiftieth of the statutory maximum.
46(4) ...	Administrative receiver failing to give notice of his appointment.	Summary.	One-fifth of the statutory maximum.	One-fiftieth of the statutory maximum.
47(6) ...	Failure to comply with provisions relating to statement of affairs where administrative receiver appointed.	1. On indictment. 2. Summary.	A fine. The statutory maximum.	One-tenth of the statutory maximum.
48(8) ...	Administrative receiver failing to comply with requirements as to his report.	Summary.	One-fifth of the statutory maximum.	One-fiftieth of the statutory maximum.
51(4) ...	Body corporate or Scottish firm acting as receiver.	1. On indictment. 2. Summary.	A fine. The statutory maximum.	
51(5) ...	Undischarged bankrupt acting as receiver (Scotland).	1. On indictment. 2. Summary.	2 years or a fine, or both. 6 months or the statutory maximum, or both.	
53(2) ...	Failing to deliver to registrar copy of instrument of appointing of receiver.	Summary.	One-fifth of the statutory maximum.	One-fiftieth of the statutory maximum.

Section of Act creating offence	General nature of offence	Mode of prosecution	Punishment	Daily default fine (where applicable)
54(3) …	Failing to deliver to registrar the court's interlocutor appointing receiver.	Summary.	One-fifth of the statutory maximum.	One-fiftieth of the statutory maximum.
61(7) …	Receiver failing to send registrar certified copy of court order authorising disposal of charged property.	Summary.	One-fifth of the statutory maximum.	One-fiftieth of the statutory maximum.
62(5) …	Failing to give notice to registrar of cessation or removal of receiver.	Summary.	One-fifth of the statutory maximum.	One-fiftieth of the statutory maximum.
64(2) …	Company and others failing to state on correspondence etc. that receiver appointed.	Summary.	One-fifth of the statutory maximum.	
65(4) …	Receiver failing to send or publish notice of his appointment.	Summary.	One-fifth of the statutory maximum.	One-fiftieth of the statutory maximum.
66(6) …	Failing to comply with provisions concerning statement of affairs where receiver appointed.	1. On indictment. 2. Summary.	A fine. The statutory maximum.	One-tenth of the statutory maximum.
67(8) …	Receiver failing to comply with requirements as to his report.	Summary.	One-fifth of the statutory maximum.	One-fiftieth of the statutory maximum.
85(2) …	Company failing to give notice in Gazette of resolution for voluntary winding up.	Summary.	One-fifth of the statutory maximum.	One-fiftieth of the statutory maximum.
89(4) …	Director making statutory declaration of company's solvency without reasonable grounds for his opinion.	1. On indictment. 2. Summary.	2 years or a fine, or both. 6 months or the statutory maximum, or both.	
89(6) …	Declaration under section 89 not delivered to registrar within prescribed time.	Summary.	One-fifth of the statutory maximum.	One-fiftieth of the statutory maximum.
93(3) …	Liquidator failing to summon general meeting of company at each year's end.	Summary.	One-fifth of the statutory maximum.	One-fiftieth of the statutory maximum.
94(4) …	Liquidator failing to send to registrar a copy of account of winding up and return of final meeting.	Summary.	One-fifth of the statutory maximum.	One-fiftieth of the statutory maximum.

Section of Act creating offence	General nature of offence	Mode of prosecution	Punishment	Daily default fine (where applicable)
94(6) ...	Liquidator failing to call final meeting.	Summary.	One-fifth of the statutory maximum.	
95(8) ...	Liquidator failing to comply with sec. 95, where company insolvent	Summary.	The statutory maximum.	
98(6) ...	Company failing to comply with sec. 98 in respect of summoning and giving notice of creditors' meeting.	1. On indictment. 2. Summary.	A fine. The statutory maximum.	
99(3) ...	Directors failing to attend and lay statement in prescribed form before creditors' meeting.	1. On indictment. 2. Summary.	A fine. The statutory maximum.	
105(3) ...	Liquidator failing to summon company general meeting and creditors' meeting at each year's end.	Summary.	One-fifth of the statutory maximum.	
106(4) ...	Liquidator failing to send to registrar account of winding up and return of final meetings.	Summary.	One-fifth of the statutory maximum.	One-fiftieth of the statutory maximum.
106(6) ...	Liquidator failing to call final meeting of company or creditors.	Summary.	One-fifth of the statutory maximum.	
109(2) ...	Liquidator failing to publish notice of his appointment.	Summary.	One-fifth of the statutory maximum.	One-fiftieth of the statutory maximum.
114(4) ...	Directors exercising powers in breach of s. 114, where no liquidator.	Summary.	The statutory maximum.	
131(7) ...	Failing to comply with requirements as to statement of affairs, where liquidator appointed.	1. On indictment. 2. Summary.	A fine. The statutory maximum.	One-tenth of the statutory maximum.
164	Giving, offering etc. corrupt inducement affecting appointment of liquidator.	1. On indictment. 2. Summary.	A fine. The statutory maximum.	
166(7) ...	Liquidator failing to comply with requirements of sec. 166 in creditors' voluntary winding up.	Summary.	The statutory maximum.	

Section of Act creating offence	General nature of offence	Mode of prosecution	Punishment	Daily default fine (where applicable)
188(2)	Default in compliance with sec. 188 as to notification that company being wound up.	Summary.	One-fifth of the statutory maximum.	One-fiftieth of the statutory maximum.
192(2)	Liquidator failing to notify registrar as to progress of winding up.	Summary.	One-fifth of the statutory maximum.	One-fiftieth of the statutory maximum.
201(4)	Failing to deliver to registrar office copy of court order deferring dissolution.	Summary.	One-fifth of the statutory maximum.	One-fiftieth of the statutory maximum.
203(6)	Failing to deliver to registrar copy of directions or result of appeal under sec. 203.	Summary.	One-fifth of the statutory maximum.	One-fiftieth of the statutory maximum.
204(7)	Liquidator failing to deliver to registrar copy of court order for early dissolution.	Summary.	One-fifth of the statutory maximum.	One-fiftieth of the statutory maximum.
204(8)	Failing to deliver to registrar copy of court order deferring early dissolution.	Summary.	One-fifth of the statutory maximum.	One-fiftieth of the statutory maximum.
205(7)	Failing to deliver to registrar copy of Secretary of State's directions or court order deferring dissolution.	Summary.	One-fifth of the statutory maximum.	One-fiftieth of the statutory maximum.
206(1)	Fraud etc. in anticipation of winding up.	1. On indictment. 2. Summary.	7 years or a fine, or both. 6 months or the statutory maximum, or both.	
206(2)	Privity to fraud in anticipation of winding up; fraud or privity to fraud, after commencement of winding up.	1. On indictment. 2. Summary.	7 years or a fine, or both. 6 months or the statutory maximum, or both.	
206(5)	Knowingly taking in pawn or pledge, or otherwise receiving, company property.	1. On indictment. 2. Summary.	7 years or a fine, or both. 6 months or the statutory maximum, or both.	
207	Officer of company entering into transaction in fraud of company's creditors.	1. On indictment. 2. Summary.	2 years or a fine, or both. 6 months or the statutory maximum, or both.	

Section of Act creating offence	General nature of offence	Mode of prosecution	Punishment	Daily default fine (where applicable)
208 ...	Officer of company misconducting himself in course of winding up.	1. On indictment. 2. Summary.	7 years or a fine, or both. 6 months or the statutory maximum, or both.	
209 ...	Officer or contributory destroying, falsifying, etc. company' books.	1. On indictment. 2. Summary.	7 years or a fine, or both. 6 months or the statutory maximum, or both.	
210 ...	Officer of company making material omission from statement relating to company's affairs.	1. On indictment. 2. Summary.	7 years or a fine, or both. 6 months or the statutory maximum, or both.	
211 ...	False representation or fraud for purpose of obtaining creditors' consent to an agreement in connection with winding up.	1. On indictment. 2. Summary.	7 years or a fine, or both. 6 months or the statutory maximum, or both.	
216(4) ...	Contravening restrictions on re-use of name of company in insolvent liquidation	1. On indictment. 2. Summary.	2 years or a fine, or both. 6 months or the statutory maximum, or both.	
235(5) ...	Failing to co-operate with office-holder.	1. On indictment. 2. Summary.	A fine. The statutory maximum.	One-tenth of the statutory maximum.
353(1) ...	Bankrupt failing to disclose property or disposals to official receiver or trustee.	1. On indictment. 2. Summary.	7 years or a fine, or both. 6 months or the statutory maximum, or both.	
354(1) ...	Bankrupt failing to deliver property to, or concealing property from, official receiver or trustee.	1. On indictment. 2. Summary.	7 years or a fine, or both. 6 months or the statutory maximum, or both.	
354(2) ...	Bankrupt removing property which he is required to deliver to official receiver or trustee.	1. On indictment. 2. Summary.	7 years or a fine, or both. 6 months or the statutory maximum, or both.	

Section of Act creating offence	General nature of offence	Mode of prosecution	Punishment	Daily default fine (where applicable)
354(3) ...	Bankrupt failing to account for loss of substantial part of property.	1. On indictment. 2. Summary.	2 years or a fine, or both. 6 months or the statutory maximum, or both.	
355(1) ...	Bankrupt failing to deliver books, papers and records to official receiver or trustee.	1. On indictment. 2. Summary.	7 years or a fine, or both. 6 months or the statutory maximum, or both.	
355(2) ...	Bankrupt concealing, destroying etc. books, papers or records, or making false entries in them.	1. On indictment. 2. Summary.	7 years or a fine, or both. 6 months or the statutory maximum, or both.	
355(3) ...	Bankrupt disposing of, or altering, books, papers or records relating to his estate or affairs.	1. On indictment. 2. Summary.	7 years or a fine, or both. 6 months or the statutory maximum, or both.	
356(1) ...	Bankrupt making material omission in statement relating to his affairs.	1. On indictment. 2. Summary.	7 years or a fine, or both. 6 months or the statutory maximum, or both.	
356(2) ...	Bankrupt making false statement, or failing to inform trustee, where false debt proved.	1. On indictment. 2. Summary.	7 years or a fine, or both. 6 months or the statutory maximum, or both.	
357 ...	Bankrupt fraudulently disposing of property.	1. On indictment. 2. Summary.	2 years or a fine, or both. 6 months or the statutory maximum, or both.	
358 ...	Bankrupt absconding with property he is required to deliver to official receiver or trustee.	1. On indictment. 2. Summary.	2 years or a fine, or both. 6 months or the statutory maximum, or both.	
359(1) ...	Bankrupt disposing of property obtained on credit and not paid for.	1. On indictment. 2. Summary.	7 years or a fine, or both. 6 months or the statutory maximum, or both.	

Section of Act creating offence	General nature of offence	Mode of prosecution	Punishment	Daily default fine (where applicable)
359(2) …	Obtaining property in respect of which money is owed by a bankrupt.	1. On indictment. 2. Summary.	7 years or a fine, or both. 6 months or the statutory maximum, or both.	
360(1) …	Bankrupt obtaining credit or engaging in business without disclosing his status or name in which he was made bankrupt.	1. On indictment. 2. Summary.	2 years or a fine, or both. 6 months or the statutory maximum, or both.	
360(3) …	Person made bankrupt in Scotland or Northern Ireland obtaining credit, etc. in England and Wales.	1. On indictment. 2. Summary.	2 years or a fine, or both. 6 months or the statutory maximum, or both.	
361(1) …	Bankrupt failing to keep proper accounting records.	1. On indictment. 2. Summary.	2 years or a fine, or both. 6 months or the statutory maximum, or both.	
362 …	Bankrupt increasing extent of insolvency by gambling.	1. On indictment. 2. Summary.	2 years or a fine, or both. 6 months or the statutory maximum, or both.	
389 …	Acting as insolvency practitioner when not qualified.	1. On indictment. 2. Summary.	2 years or a fine, or both. 6 months or the statutory maximum, or both.	
429(5) …	Contravening sec. 429 in respect of disabilities imposed by county court on revocation of administration order.	1. On indictment. 2. Summary.	2 years or a fine, or both. 6 months or the statutory maximum, or both.	
Sch. 7, para. 4(3). …	Failure to attend and give evidence to Insolvency Practitioners Tribunal; suppressing, concealing, etc. relevant documents.	Summary.	Level 3 on the standard scale within the meaning given by section 75 of the Criminal Justice Act 1982.	

Note
The current statutory maximum is £2,000 (see S.I. 1984 No. 447).

Schedule 11 — Transitional Provisions and Savings

Section 437

Part I — Company Insolvency and Winding Up

ADMINISTRATION ORDERS

1(1) Where any right to appoint an administrative receiver of a company is conferred by any debentures or floating charge created before the appointed day, the conditions precedent to the exercise of that right are deemed to include the presentation of a petition applying for an administration order to be made in relation to the company.

1(2) "**Administrative receiver**" here has the meaning assigned by section 251.

RECEIVER AND MANAGERS (ENGLAND AND WALES)

2(1) In relation to any receiver or manager of a company's property who was appointed before the appointed day, the new law does not apply; and the relevant provisions of the former law continue to have effect.

2(2) "**The new law**" here means Chapter I of Part III, and Part VI, of this Act; and "**the former law**" means the Companies Act and so much of this Act as replaces provisions of that Act (without the amendments in paragraphs 15 to 17 of Schedule 6 to the Insolvency Act 1985, or the associated repeals made by that Act), and any provision of the Insolvency Act 1985 which was in force before the appointed day.

2(3) This paragraph is without prejudice to the power conferred by the Act under which rules under section 411 may make transitional provision in connection with the coming into force of those rules; and such provision may apply those rules in relation to the receiver or manager of a company's property notwithstanding that he was appointed before the coming into force of the rules or section 411.

RECEIVERS (SCOTLAND)

3(1) In relation to any receiver appointed under section 467 of the Companies Act before the appointed day, the new law does not apply and the relevant provisions of the former law continue to have effect.

3(2) "**The new law**" here means Chapter II of Part III, and Part VI, of this Act; and "**the former law**" means the Companies Act and so much of this Act as replaces provisions of that Act (without the amendments in paragraphs 18 to 22 of Schedule 6 to the Insolvency Act 1985 or the associated repeals made by that Act), and any provision of the Insolvency Act 1985 which was in force before the appointed day.

3(3) This paragraph is without prejudice to the power conferred by this Act under which rules under section 411 may make transitional provision in connection with the coming into force of those rules; and such provision may apply those rules in relation to a receiver appointed under section 467 notwithstanding that he was appointed before the coming into force of the rules or section 411.

WINDING UP ALREADY IN PROGRESS

4(1) In relation to any winding up which has commenced, or is treated as having commenced, before the appointed day, the new law does not apply, and the former law continues to have effect, subject to the following paragraphs.

4(2) "**The new law**" here means any provisions in the first Group of Parts of this Act which replace sections 66 to 87 and 89 to 105 of the Insolvency Act 1985; and "**the former law**" means Parts XX and XXI of the Companies Act (without the amendments in paragraphs 23 to 52 of Schedule 6 to the Insolvency Act 1985, or the associated repeals made by that Act).

STATEMENT OF AFFAIRS

5(1) Where a winding up by the court in England and Wales has commenced, or is treated as having commenced, before the appointed day, the official receiver or (on appeal from a refusal by him) the court may, at any time on or after that day—

(a) release a person from an obligation imposed on him by or under section 528 of the Companies Act (statement of affairs), or

(b) extend the period specified in subsection (6) of that section.

5(2) Accordingly, on and after the appointed day, section 528(6) has effect in relation to a winding up to which this paragraph applies with the omission of the words from "or within" onwards.

PROVISIONS RELATING TO LIQUIDATOR

6(1) This paragraph applies as regards the liquidator in the case of a winding up by the court in England and Wales commenced, or treated as having commenced, before the appointed day.

6(2) The official receiver may, at any time when he is liquidator of the company, apply to the Secretary of State for the appointment of a liquidator in his (the official receiver's) place; and on any such application the Secretary of State shall either make an appointment or decline to make one.

6(3) Where immediately before the appointed day the liquidator of the company has not made an application under section 545 of the Companies Act (release of liquidators), then—

(a) except where the Secretary of State otherwise directs, sections 146(1) and (2) and 172(8) of this Act apply, and section 545 does not apply, in relation to any liquidator of that company who holds office on or at any time after the appointed day and is not the official receiver;

(b) section 146(3) applies in relation to the carrying out at any time after that day by any liquidator of the company of any of his functions; and

(c) a liquidator in relation to whom section 172(8) has effect by virtue of this paragraph has his release with effect from the time specified in section 174(4)(d) of this Act.

6(4) Subsection (6) of section 174 of this Act has effect for the purposes of sub-paragraph (3)(c) above as it has for the purposes of that section, but as if the reference to section 212 were to section 631 of the Companies Act.

6(5) The liquidator may employ a solicitor to assist him in the carrying out of his functions without the permission of the committee of inspection; but if he does so employ a solicitor he shall inform the committee of inspection that he has done so.

WINDING UP UNDER SUPERVISION OF THE COURT

7 The repeals in Part II of Schedule 10 to the Insolvency Act 1985 of references (in the Companies Act and elsewhere) to a winding up under the supervision of the court do not affect the operation of the enactments in which the references are contained in relation to any case in which an order under section 606 of the Companies Act (power to order winding up under supervision) was made before the appointed day.

SAVING FOR POWER TO MAKE RULES

8(1) Paragraphs 4 to 7 are without prejudice to the power conferred by this Act under which rules made under section 411 may make transitional provision in connection with the coming into force of those rules.

8(2) Such provision may apply those rules in relation to a winding up notwithstanding that the winding up commenced, or is treated as having commenced, before the coming into force of the rules or section 411.

SETTING ASIDE OF PREFERENCES AND OTHER TRANSACTIONS

9(1) Where a provision in Part VI of this Act applies in relation to a winding up or in relation to a case in which an administration order has been made, a preference given, floating charge created or other transaction entered into before the appointed day shall not be set aside under that provision except to the extent that it could have been set aside under the law in force immediately before that day, assuming for this purpose that any relevant administration order had been a winding-up order.

9(2) The references above to setting aside a preference, floating charge or other transaction include the making of an order which varies or reverses any effect of a preference, floating charge or other transaction.

Part II — Individual Insolvency

BANKRUPTCY (GENERAL)

10(1) Subject to the following provisions of this Part of this Schedule, so much of this Act as replaces Part III of the Insolvency Act 1985 does not apply in relation to any case in which a petition in bankruptcy was presented, or a receiving order or adjudication in bankruptcy was made, before the appointed day.

10(2) In relation to any such case as is mentioned above, the enactments specified in Schedule 8 to that Act, so far as they relate to bankruptcy, and those specified in Parts III and IV of Schedule 10 to that Act, so far as they so relate, have effect without the amendments and repeals specified in those Schedules.

10(3) Where any subordinate legislation made under an enactment referred to in sub-paragraph (2) is in force immediately before the appointed day, that subordinate legislation continues to have effect on and after that day in relation to any such case as is mentioned in sub-paragraph (1).

11(1) In relation to any such case as is mentioned in paragraph 10(1) the references in any enactment or subordinate legislation to a petition, order or other matter which is provided for under the Bankruptcy Act 1914 and corresponds to a petition, order or other matter provided for under provisions of this Act replacing Part III of the

Insolvency Act 1985 continue on and after the appointed day to have effect as references to the petition, order or matter provided for by the Act of 1914; but otherwise those references have effect on and after that day as references to the petition, order or matter provided for by those provisions of this Act.

11(2) Without prejudice to sub-paragraph (1), in determining for the purposes of section 279 of this Act (period of bankruptcy) or paragraph 13 below whether any person was an undischarged bankrupt at a time before the appointed day, an adjudication in bankruptcy and an annulment of a bankruptcy under the Act of 1914 are to be taken into account in the same way, respectively, as a bankruptcy order under the provisions of this Act replacing Part III of the Insolvency Act 1985 and the annulment under section 282 of this Act of such an order.

12 Transactions entered into before the appointed day have effect on and after that day as if references to acts of bankruptcy in the provisions for giving effect to those transactions continued to be references to acts of bankruptcy within the meaning of the Bankruptcy Act 1914, but as if such acts included failure to comply with a statutory demand served under section 268 of this Act.

DISCHARGE FROM OLD BANKRUPTCY

13(1) Where a person—

    (a) was adjudged bankrupt before the appointed day or is adjudged on or after that day on a petition presented before that day, and

    (b) that person was not an undischarged bankrupt at any time in the period of 15 years ending with the adjudication,

that person is deemed (if not previously discharged) to be discharged from his bankruptcy for the purposes of the Bankruptcy Act 1914 at the end of the discharge period.

13(2) Subject to sub-paragraph (3) below, the discharge period for the purposes of this paragraph is—

    (a) in the case of a person adjudged bankrupt before the appointed day, the period of 3 years beginning with that day, and

    (b) in the case of a person who is adjudged bankrupt on or after that day on a petition presented before that day, the period of 3 years beginning with the date of the adjudication.

13(3) Where the court exercising jurisdiction in relation to a bankruptcy to which this paragraph applies is satisfied, on the application of the official receiver, that the bankrupt has failed, or is failing, to comply with any of his obligations under the Bankruptcy Act 1914, any rules made under that Act or any such rules as are mentioned in paragraph 19(1) below, the court may order that the discharge period shall cease to run for such period, or until the fulfilment of such conditions (including a condition requiring the court to be satisfied as to any matter) as may be specified in the order.

PROVISIONS RELATING TO TRUSTEE

14(1) This paragraph applies as regards the trustee in the case of a person adjudged bankrupt before the appointed day, or adjudged bankrupt on or after that day on a petition presented before that day.

14(2) The official receiver may at any time when he is trustee of the bankrupt's estate apply to the Secretary of State for the appointment of a person as trustee instead of the official receiver; and on any such application the Secretary of State shall either make an appointment or decline to make one.

14(3) Where on the appointed day the trustee of a bankrupt's estate has not made an application under section 93 of the Bankruptcy Act 1914 (release of trustee), then—

    (a) except where the Secretary of State otherwise directs, sections 298(8), 304 and 331(1) to (3) of this Act apply, and section 93 of the Act of 1914 does not apply, in relation to any trustee of the bankrupt's estate who holds office on or at any time after the appointed day and is not the official receiver;

    (b) section 331(4) of this Act applies in relation to the carrying out at any time on or after the appointed day by the trustee of the bankrupt's estate of any of his functions; and

    (c) a trustee in relation to whom section 298(8) of this Act has effect by virtue of this paragraph has his release with effect from the time specified in section 299(3)(d).

14(4) Subsection (5) of section 299 has effect for the purposes of sub-paragraph (3)(c) as it has for the purposes of that section.

14(5) In the application of subsection (3) of section 331 in relation to a case by virtue of this paragraph, the reference in that subsection to section 330(1) has effect as a reference to section 67 of the Bankruptcy Act 1914.

14(6) The trustee of the bankrupt's estate may employ a solicitor to assist him in the carrying out of his functions without the permission of the committee of inspection; but if he does so employ a solicitor, he shall inform the committee of inspection that he has done so.

COPYRIGHT

15 Where a person who is adjudged bankrupt on a petition presented on or after the appointed day is liable, by virtue of a transaction entered into before that day, to pay royalties or a share of the profits to any person in respect of any copyright or interest in copyright comprised in the bankrupt's estate, section 60 of the Bankruptcy Act 1914 (limitation on trustee's powers in relation to copyright) applies in relation to the trustee of that estate as it applies in relation to a trustee in bankruptcy under the Act of 1914.

SECOND BANKRUPTCY

16(1) Sections 334 and 335 of this Act apply with the following modifications where the earlier bankruptcy (within the meaning of section 334) is a bankruptcy in relation to which the Act of 1914 applies instead of the second Group of Parts in this Act, that is to say—

    (a) references to property vested in the existing trustee under section 307(3) of this Act have effect as references to such property vested in that trustee as was acquired by or devolved on the bankrupt after the commencement (within the meaning of the Act of 1914) of the earlier bankruptcy; and

(b) references to an order under section 310 of this Act have effect as references to an order under section 51 of the Act of 1914.

16(2) Section 39 of the Act of 1914 (second bankruptcy) does not apply where a person who is an undischarged bankrupt under that Act is adjudged bankrupt under this Act.

SETTING ASIDE OF PREFERENCES AND OTHER TRANSACTIONS

17(1) A preference given, assignment made or other transaction entered into before the appointed day shall not be set aside under any of sections 339 to 344 of this Act except to the extent that it could have been set aside under the law in force immediately before that day.

17(2) References in sub-paragraph (1) to setting aside a preference assignment or other transaction include the making of any order which varies or reverses any effect of a preference, assignment or other transaction.

BANKRUPTCY OFFENCES

18(1) Where a bankruptcy order is made under this Act on or after the appointed day, a person is not guilty of an offence under Chapter VI of Part IX in respect of anything done before that day; but, notwithstanding the repeal by the Insolvency Act 1985 of the Bankruptcy Act 1914, is guilty of an offence under the Act of 1914 in respect of anything done before the appointed day which would have been an offence under that Act if the making of the bankruptcy order had been the making of a receiving order under that Act.

18(2) Subsection (5) of section 350 of this Act applies (instead of sections 157(2), 158(2), 161 and 165 of the Act of 1914) in relation to proceedings for an offence under that Act which are instituted (whether by virtue of sub-paragraph (1) or otherwise) after the appointed day.

POWER TO MAKE RULES

19(1) The preceding provisions of this Part of this Schedule are without prejudice to the power conferred by this Act under which rules under section 412 may make transitional provision in connection with the coming into force of those rules; and such provision may apply those rules in relation to a bankruptcy notwithstanding that it arose from a petition presented before either the coming into force of the rules or the appointed day.

19(2) Rules under section 412 may provide for such notices served before the appointed day as may be prescribed to be treated for the purposes of this Act as statutory demands served under section 268.

Part III — Transitional Effect of Part XVI

20(1) A transaction entered into before the appointed day shall not be set aside under Part XVI of this Act except to the extent that it could have been set aside under the law in force immediately before that day.

20(2) References above to setting aside a transaction include the making of any order which varies or reverses any effect of a transaction.

Part IV — Insolvency Practitioners

21 Where an individual began to act as an insolvency practitioner in relation to any person before the appointed day, nothing in section 390(2) or (3) prevents that individual from being qualified to act as an insolvency practitioner in relation to that person.

Part V — General Transitional Provisions and Savings

INTERPRETATION FOR THIS PART

22 In this Part of this Schedule, **"the former enactments"** means so much of the Companies Act as is repealed and replaced by this Act, the Insolvency Act 1985 and the other enactments repealed by this Act.

GENERAL SAVING FOR PAST ACTS AND EVENTS

23 So far as anything done or treated as done under or for the purposes of any provision of the former enactments could have been done under or for the purposes of the corresponding provision of this Act, it is not invalidated by the repeal of that provision but has effect as if done under or for the purposes of the corresponding provision; and any order, regulation, rule or other instrument made or having effect under any provision of the former enactments shall, insofar as its effect is preserved by this paragraph, be treated for all purposes as made and having effect under the corresponding provision.

PERIODS OF TIME

24 Where any period of time specified in a provision of the former enactments is current immediately before the appointed day, this Act has effect as if the corresponding provision had been in force when the period began to run; and (without prejudice to the foregoing) any period of time so specified and current is deemed for the purposes of this Act—

    (a) to run from the date or event from which it was running immediately before the appointed day, and

    (b) to expire (subject to any provision of this Act for its extension) whenever it would have expired if this Act had not been passed;

and any rights, priorities, liabilities, reliefs, obligations, requirements, powers, duties or exemptions dependent on the beginning, duration or end of such a period as above mentioned shall be under this Act as they were or would have been under the former enactments.

INTERNAL CROSS-REFERENCES IN THIS ACT

25 Where in any provision of this Act there is a reference to another such provision, and the first-mentioned provision operates, or is capable of operating, in relation to things done or omitted, or events occurring or not occurring, in the past (including in particular past acts of compliance with any enactment, failures of compliance, contraventions, offences and convictions of offences), the reference to the other provision is to be read as including a reference to the corresponding provision of the former enactments.

PUNISHMENT OF OFFENCES

26(1) Offences committed before the appointed day under any provision of the former enactments may, notwithstanding any repeal by this Act, be prosecuted and punished after that day as if this Act had not passed.

26(2) A contravention of any provision of the former enactments committed before the appointed day shall not be visited with any severer punishment under or by virtue of this Act than would have been applicable under that provision at the time of the contravention; but where an offence for the continuance of which a penalty was provided has been committed under any provision of the former enactments, proceedings may be taken under this Act in respect of the continuance of the offence on and after the appointed day in the like manner as if the offence had been committed under the corresponding provision of this Act.

REFERENCES ELSEWHERE TO THE FORMER ENACTMENTS

27(1) A reference in any enactment, instrument or document (whether express or implied, and in whatever phraseology) to a provision of the former enactments (including the corresponding provision of any yet earlier enactment) is to be read, where necessary to retain for the enactment, instrument or document the same force and effect as it would have had but for the passing of this Act, as, or as including, a reference to the corresponding provision by which it is replaced in this Act.

27(2) The generality of the preceding sub-paragraph is not affected by any specific conversion of references made by this Act, nor by the inclusion in any provision of this Act of a reference (whether express or implied, and in whatever phraseology) to the provision of the former enactments corresponding to that provision, or to a provision of the former enactments which is replaced by a corresponding provision of this Act.

SAVING FOR POWER TO REPEAL PROVISIONS IN SECTION 51

28 The Secretary of State may by order in a statutory instrument repeal subsections (3) to (5) of section 51 of this Act and the entries in Schedule 10 relating to subsections (4) and (5) of that section.

SAVING FOR INTERPRETATION ACT 1978 SS. 16, 17

29 Nothing in this Schedule is to be taken as prejudicing sections 16 and 17 of the Interpretation Act 1978 (savings from, and effect of, repeals); and for the purposes of section 17(2) of that Act (construction of references to enactments repealed and replaced, etc.), so much of section 18 of the Insolvency Act 1985 as is replaced by a provision of this Act is deemed to have been repealed by this Act and not by the Company Directors Disqualification Act 1986.

Schedule 12 — Enactments Repealed

Section 438

Chapter	Short title	Extent of repeal
1970 c. 8.	The Insolvency Services (Accounting and Investment) Act 1970.	The whole Act.
1976 c. 60.	The Insolvency Act 1976.	Section 3.
1985 c. 6.	The Companies Act 1985.	In Section 463(4), the words "Subject to section 617".
		Sections 467 to 485.
		In section 486, in the definition of "company" the words "other than in Chapter II of this Part"; and the definitions of "instrument of appointment", "prescribed", "receiver" and "register of charges".
		Sections 488 to 650.
		Sections 659 to 664.
		Sections 665 to 674.
		Section 709(4).
		Section 710(4).
		Section 724.
		Schedule 16.
		In Schedule 24, the entries relating to the section 467; all entries thereafter up to and including section 641(2); and the entry relating to section 710(4).
1985 c. 65.	The Insolvency Act 1985.	Sections 1 to 11.
		Section 15.
		Section 17.
		Section 19.
		Sections 20 to 107.
		Section 108(1) and (3) to (7).
		Sections 109 to 211.
		Sections 212 to 214.
		Section 216.
		Section 217(1) to (3).

Chapter	Short title	Extent of repeal
		Sections 221 to 234.
		In section 235, subsections (2) to (5).
		In section 236, subsections (3) to (5).
		In Schedule 1, paragraphs 1 to 4, and sub-paragraph (4) of paragraph 5.
		Schedules 3 to 5.
		In Schedule 6, paragraphs 5, 6, 9, 15 to 17, 20 to 22, 25 to 44 and 48 to 52.
		Schedule 7.
		In Schedule 9, paragraphs 1 and 4 to 24.
		Schedule 10.
1985 c. 66.	The Bankruptcy (Scotland) Act 1985.	In Schedule 7, paragraphs 19 to 22.
1986 c. 44.	The Gas Act 1986.	In Schedule 7, paragraph 31.

Schedule 13 — Consequential Amendments of Companies Act 1985

Section 439(1)

Part I — Internal and Other Section References Amended or Re-amended

Section of Act	Consequential amendment or re-amendment
Section 13(4)	After "this Act", add "and the Insolvency Act".
Section 44(7)	In paragraph (a), for "section 582" substitute "section 110 of the Insolvency Act".
Section 103(7)	In paragraph (a), the same amendment.
Section 131(7)	The same amendment.
Section 140(2)	In paragraph (b), for "section 518" substitute "section 123 of the Insolvency Act".
Section 153(3)	In paragraph (f), for "section 582" substitute "section 110 of the Insolvency Act". In paragraph (g), for "Chapter II of Part II of the Insolvency Act 1985" substitute "Part I of the Insolvency Act".
Section 156(3)	For "section 517" substitute "section 122 of the Insolvency Act".
Section 173(4)	The same amendment.

Section of Act	Consequential amendment or re-amendment
Section 196	For this section substitute—
	"196.—(1) The following applies in the case of a company registered in England and Wales, where debentures of the company are secured by a charge which, as created, was a floating charge.
	(2) If possession is taken, by or on behalf of the holders of any of the debentures, of any property comprised in or subject to the charge, and the company is not at that time in course of being wound up, the company's preferential debts shall be paid out of assets coming to the hands of the person taking possession in priority to any claims for principal or interest in respect of the debentures.
	(3) "Preferential debts" means the categories of debts listed in Schedule 6 to the Insolvency Act; and for the purposes of that Schedule "the relevant date" is the date of possession being taken as above mentioned.
	(4) Payments made under this section shall be recouped, as far as may be, out of the assets of the company available for payment of general creditors."
Section 380(4)	In paragraph (j), for "section 572(1)(a)" substitute "section 84(1)(a) of the Insolvency Act".
Section 441(1)	For "section 13 of the Insolvency Act 1985" substitute "section 8 of the Company Directors Disqualification Act 1986".
Section 449(1)	In paragraph (ba), for "section 12 or 13 of the Insolvency Act 1985" substitute "section 6, 7 or 8 of the Company Directors Disqualification Act 1986".
Section 461(6)	For "section 106 of the Insolvency Act 1985" substitute "section 411 of the Insolvency Act".
Section 462(5)	After "this Part" insert "and Part III of the Insolvency Act 1986".
Section 463(2)	For "Part XX (except section 623(4))" substitute "Part IV of the Insolvency Act (except section 185)".
Section 463(3)	For this subsection substitute—
	"(3) Nothing in this section derogates from the provisions of sections 53(7) and 54(6) of the Insolvency Act (attachment of floating charge on appointment of receiver), or prejudices the operation of sections 175 and 176 of that Act (payment of preferential debts in winding up)".

Section of Act	Consequential amendment or re-amendment
Section 464(6)	For "section 89 of the Insolvency Act 1985" substitute "sections 175 and 176 of the Insolvency Act".
Section 657(2)	For "subsections (3) and (5) to (7) of section 91 of the Insolvency Act 1985 and section 92 of that Act" substitute "section 178(4) and sections 179 to 182 of the Insolvency Act".
Section 658(1)	For "Subsection (7) of section 91 of the Insolvency Act 1985" substitute "Section 180 of the Insolvency Act".
Section 711(2)	In paragraph (b), for "section 600" substitute "section 109 of the Insolvency Act".
Section 733	In subsection (1), omit "295(7)". In subsection (3), for "216(3) or 295(7)" substitute "or 216(3)".

History

In Pt. I entries relating to s. 222(4) and 225 repealed by CA 1989, s. 212 and Sch. 24 as from 1 April 1990 (see S.I. 1990 No. 355 (C. 13), art. 5(1)(d)); the entries formerly read as follows:

Section of Act	Consequential amendment or re-amendment
"Section 222(4)	For 'section 106 of the Insolvency Act 1985' substitute 'section 411 of the Insolvency Act'.
Section 225	At the end of the section add—
	'(8) At any time when an administration order under Part II of the Insolvency Act is in force, this section has effect as if subsections (3) and (5) to (7) were omitted'."

Part II — Amendment of Part XXVI (Interpretation)

In Part XXVI of the Companies Act, after section 735, insert the following section—

"Relationship of this Act to Insolvency Act

735A(1) In this Act **"the Insolvency Act"** means the Insolvency Act 1986; and in the following provisions of this Act, namely, sections 375(1)(b), 425(6)(a), 440, 449(1)(a) and (d), 460(2), 675, 676, 677, 699(1), 728 and Schedule 21, paragraph 6(1), the words "this Act" are to be read as including Parts I to VII of that Act, sections 411, 413, 414, 416 and 417 in Part XV of that Act, and also the Company Directors Disqualification Act 1986.

735A(2) In sections 704(5), 706(1), 707(1), 708(1)(a) and (4), 710(5), 713(1), 729 and 732(3) references to the Companies Acts include Parts I to VII of the Insolvency Act, sections 411, 413, 414, 416 and 417 in Part XV of that Act, and also the Company Directors Disqualification Act 1986.

735A(3) Subsections (1) and (2) apply unless the contrary intention appears."

Schedule 14 — Consequential Amendments of other Enactments

Enactment	Amendment
Deeds of Arrangement Act 1914 (c. 47):	
Section 3(1)	For "Part III of the Insolvency Act 1985" substitute "Parts VIII to XI of the Insolvency Act 1986".
Section 3(4)	The same amendment.
Section 11(1) and (2)	In each subsection, the same amendment.
Section 15(1)	For "section 207 of the Insolvency Act 1985" substitute "section 412 of the Insolvency Act 1986".
Section 16	The same amendment as of section 3(1).
Section 23	The same amendment.
Section 30(1)	For the definition of "property" substitute— "'property' has the meaning given by section 436 of the Insolvency Act 1986".
Law of Property Act 1925 (c. 20):	
Section 52(2)(b)	For "section 91 or 161 of the Insolvency Act 1985" substitute "sections 178 to 180 or sections 315 to 319 of the Insolvency Act 1986".
Land Registration Act 1925 (c. 21):	
Section 42(2)	For "section 161 of the Insolvency Act 1985" substitute "sections 315 to 319 of the Insolvency Act 1986".
Third Parties (Rights against Insurers) Act 1930 (c. 25):	
Section 1	In subsection (1)(b), for the words from "a composition" to "that Chapter" substitute "a voluntary arrangement proposed for the purposes of Part I of the Insolvency Act 1986 being approved under that Part".
	In subsection (2), for "228 of the Insolvency Act 1985" substitute "421 of the Insolvency Act 1986".
	In subsection (3), the same amendment.
Section 2	In subsection (1), the same amendment as of section 1(2).
	In subsection (1A), for the words from "composition or scheme" to the end of the subsection substitute "voluntary arrangement proposed for the purposes of, and approved under, Part I or Part VIII of the Insolvency Act 1986".
Section 4	In paragraph (b), the same amendment as of section 1(2).

Enactment	Amendment
Exchange Control Act 1947 (c. 14):	
Schedule 4	In paragraphs 6 and 8(4), for "section 120 of the Insolvency Act 1985" substitute "sections 267 to 270 of the Insolvency Act 1986".
Arbitration Act 1950 (c. 27):	
Section 3(2)	For "committee established under section 148 of the Insolvency Act 1985" substitute "creditors' committee established under section 301 of the Insolvency Act 1986".
Agricultural Marketing Act 1958 (c. 47):	
Schedule 2	For paragraph 4 substitute—
	"4.—(1) A scheme shall provide for the winding up of the board, and for that purpose may apply Part V of the Insolvency Act 1986 (winding up of unregistered companies), subject to the following modifications.
	(2) For the purposes of sections 221, 222 and 224 of the Act of 1986, the principal place of business of the board is deemed to be the office of the board the address of which is registered by the Minister under paragraph 3 above.
	(3) Section 223 does not apply.
	(4) Section 224 applies as if the words "or any member of it as such" were omitted.
	(5) A petition for winding up the board may be presented by the Minister as well as by any person authorised under Part IV of the Insolvency Act 1986 to present a petition for winding up a company".
Charities Act 1960 (c. 58):	
Section 30(1)	For "Companies Act 1985" substitute "Insolvency Act 1986".
Licensing Act 1964 (c. 26):	
Section 8(1)	In paragraph (c), for the words from "composition or scheme" to "Act 1985" substitute "voluntary arrangement proposed by the holder of the licence has been approved under Part VIII of the Insolvency Act 1986"; and for "composition or scheme" substitute "voluntary arrangement".
Section 10(5)	For the words from "composition or scheme" to "Act 1985" substitute "voluntary arrangement proposed by the holder of a justices' licence has been approved under Part VIII of the Insolvency Act 1986"; and for "composition or scheme" substitute "voluntary arrangement".
Industrial and Provident Societies Act 1965 (c. 12):	
Section 55	For "Companies Act 1985" substitute "Insolvency Act 1986".

Enactment	Amendment
Medicine Act 1968 (c. 67):	
Section 72(4)	For the words from "composition or scheme" to the end of the subsection substitute "voluntary arrangement proposed for the purposes of, and approved under, Part VIII of the Insolvency Act 1986".
Conveyancing and Feudal Reform (Scotland) Act 1970 (c. 35):	
Schedule 3	In Standard Condition 9(2)(b), for "228 of the Insolvency Act 1985" substitute "421 of the Insolvency Act 1986".
Tribunals and Inquiries Act 1971 (c. 62):	
Schedule 1	For paragraph 10A substitute—
	"10A. The Insolvency Practitioners Tribunal referred to in section 396 of the Insolvency Act 1986".
Superannuation Act 1972 (c. 11):	
Section 5(2)	For "156 of the Insolvency Act 1985" substitute "310 of the Insolvency Act 1986"; and for "the said section 156" substitute "the said section 310".
Road Traffic Act 1972 (c. 20):	
Section 150	In subsection (1)(b), for "228 of the Insolvency Act 1985" substitute "421 of the Insolvency Act 1986".
	In subsection (2), the same amendment.
Land Charges Act 1972 (c. 61):	
Section 16(2)	For "207 of the Insolvency Act 1985" substitute "412 of the Insolvency Act 1986"; and for "Part III" substitute "Parts VIII to XI".
Matrimonial Causes Act 1973 (c. 18):	
Section 39	For "section 174 of the Insolvency Act 1985" substitute "section 339 or 340 of the Insolvency Act 1986".
Powers of Criminal Courts Act 1973 (c. 62):	
Section 39(3):	In paragraph (d), for "174(10) of the Insolvency Act 1985" substitute "341(4) of the Insolvency Act 1986".
Friendly Societies Act 1974 (c. 46):	
Section 87(2)	For "Companies Act 1985" substitute "Insolvency Act 1986".

Enactment	Amendment
Social Security Pensions Act 1975 (c. 60):	
Section 58	The section is to have effect as originally enacted, and without the amendment made by paragraph 26(1) of Schedule 8 to the Insolvency Act 1985.
Schedule 3	At the end of paragraph 3(1) add—
	"or (in the case of a company not in liquidation)—
	(a) the appointment of a receiver as mentioned in section 40 of the Insolvency Act 1986 (debenture-holders secured by floating charge), or
	(b) the appointment of a receiver under section 53(6) or 54(5) of that Act (Scottish company with property subject to floating charge), or
	(c) the taking of possesion by debenture-holders (so secured) as mentioned in section 196 of the Companies Act 1985".
	In paragraph 4, for the words from the beginning to "Act 1985" substitute "Section 196(3) of the Companies Act 1985 and section 387 of the Insolvency Act 1986 apply as regards the meaning in this Schedule of the expression 'the relevant date'.".
Recess Elections Act 1975 (c. 66):	
Section 1(2)	In the definition of "certificate of vacancy", for "214(6)(a) of the Insolvency Act 1985" substitute "427(6)(a) of the Insolvency Act 1986".
Policyholders Protection Act 1975 (c. 75):	
Section 5(1)(a)	For "Companies Act 1985" substitute "Insolvency Act 1986".
Section 15(1)	For "532 of the Companies Act 1985" substitute "135 of the Insolvency Act 1986".
Section 16(1)(b)	The same amendment as of section 5(1)(a).
Development Land Tax Act 1976 (c. 24):	
Section 33(1)	For "538 of the Companies Act 1985" substitute "145 of the Insolvency Act 1986".
Restrictive Trade Practices Act 1976 (c. 34):	
Schedule 1	For paragraph 9A (inserted by Insolvency Act 1985, section 217(4)) substitute—
	"9A. Insolvency services within the meaning of section 428 of the Insolvency Act 1986".
Employment Protection (Consolidation) Act 1978 (c. 44):	
Section 106(5)	In paragraph (b), for "228 of the Insolvency Act 1985" substitute "421 of the Insolvency Act 1986".

Enactment	Amendment
	In paragraph (c), for the words from "a composition or" to the end of the paragraph substitute "a voluntary arrangement proposed for the purposes of Part I of the Insolvency Act 1986 is approved under that Part".
Section 106(6)	The same amendment as of section 106(5)(c).
Section 122	In subsection (7), for "181 of the Insolvency Act 1985" substitute "348 of the Insolvency Act 1986"; and for "section 106" substitute "section 411".
	In subsection (9), for the words from "composition or scheme" to "Act 1985" substitute "voluntary arrangement proposed for the purposes of, and approved under, Part I or VIII of the Insolvency Act 1986".
Section 123(6)	For the words from "composition or scheme" to "Act 1985" substitute "voluntary arrangement proposed for the purposes of, and approved under, Part I or VIII of the Insolvency Act 1986".
Section 127(1)	In paragraph (b), for "228 of the Insolvency Act 1985" substitute "421 of the Insolvency Act 1986".
	In paragraph (c), for the words from "composition or" to the end of the paragraph substitute "voluntary arrangement proposed for the purposes of Part I of the Insolvency Act 1986 is approved under that Part".
Section 127(2)	In paragraph (c), the same amendment as of section 127(1)(c).
Credit Unions Act 1979 (c. 34):	
Section 6(1)	For "517(1)(e) of the Companies Act 1985" substitute "122(1)(e) of the Insolvency Act 1986"; and for "517(1)(e) of the Act of 1985" substitute "122(1)(e) of the Act of 1986".
Banking Act 1979 (c. 37):	
Section 6(3)	In paragraph (b), for "Part XXI of the Companies Act 1985" substitute "Part V of the Insolvency Act 1986".
Section 18	In subsection (1), for "Companies Act 1985" substitute "Insolvency Act 1986"; and in paragraph (a) of the subsection for "518" substitute "123".
	In subsection (2), for "Companies Act 1985" substitute "Insolvency Act 1986"; and for "Part XXI" substitute "Part V".
	In subsection (4)—
	in paragraph (a), for "Companies Act 1985" substitute "Insolvency Act 1986";
	in paragraph (b), for "518 of the said Act of 1985" substitute "123 of the said Act of 1986"; and
	in paragraph (c), for "Part XXI of the said Act of 1985" substitute "Part V of the said Act of 1986".

Enactment	Amendment
Section 19	In subsection (2), for paragraph (ba) substitute—
	"(ba) in connection with any proceedings under any provision of—
	(i) Part XVIII or XX of the Companies Act 1985, or
	(ii) Parts I to VII of the Insolvency Act 1986 (other than sections 236 and 237)".
	In subsection (8), for paragraphs (a) and (aa) substitute—
	"(a) for the references in subsection (2) to Part XVIII or XX of the Companies Act 1985 and Parts I to VII of the Insolvency Act 1986, there shall be substituted references to Parts V, VI and IX of the Companies Act (Northern Ireland) 1960 (the reference to sections 236 and 237 of the Act of 1986 being disregarded)".
Section 28	In subsection (3), in paragraph (c), for "83 of the Insolvency Act 1985" substitute "95 of the Insolvency Act 1986".
	In subsection (4), in paragraph (a), for "Part XXI of the Companies Act 1985" substitute "Part V of the Insolvency Act 1986".
	In subsection (6)(b), for sub-paragraphs (ii) to (iv) substitute—
	"(ii) to be a member of a liquidation committee established under Part IV or V of the Insolvency Act 1986;
	(iii) to be a member of a creditors committee appointed under section 301 of that Act; and
	(iv) to be a commissioner under section 30 of the Bankruptcy (Scotland) Act 1985";
	(v) to be a member of a committee of inspection appointed for the purposes of Part V or Part IX of the Companies Act (Northern Ireland) 1960;
	and (in the passage following sub-paragraph (iv)) for "such a committee as is mentioned in paragraph (b)(ii) or (iv) above" substitute "a liquidation committee, creditors' committee or committee of inspection".
	In subsection (7), in paragraph (b), for the words from "section 116(4)" to the end of the paragraph substitute "section 261(1) of the Insolvency Act 1986 to any person in whom the property of the firm is vested under section 282(4) of that Act".
Section 31(7)	For paragraph (a) substitute—
	"(a) for England and Wales, under sections 411 and 412 of the Insolvency Act 1986";
	and in paragraph (b) for "the said section 106" substitute "section 411 of that Act".

Enactment	Amendment
British Aerospace Act 1980 (c. 26):	
Section 9(1)	In paragraph (a), for "Companies Act 1985" substitute "Insolvency Act 1986".
Public Passenger Vehicles Act 1981 (c. 14):	
Section 19(3)	In paragraph (a), for "Chapter III of Part II of the Insolvency Act 1985" substitute "Part II of the Insolvency Act 1986".
Supreme Court Act 1981 (c. 54):	
Section 40A(2)	For "section 179 of the Insolvency Act 1985" substitute "section 346 of the Insolvency Act 1986"; and for "621 of the Companies Act 1985" substitute "183 of the Insolvency Act 1986".
Trustee Savings Banks Act 1981 (c. 65):	
Section 31	In paragraph (b), for "666 to 669 of the Companies Act 1985" substitute "221 to 224 of the Insolvency Act 1986".
Section 54(2)	For "666(6) of the Companies Act 1985" substitute "221(6) of the Insolvency Act 1986".
Iron and Steel Act 1982 (c. 25):	
Schedule 4	In paragraph 3(3) after "Companies Act 1985" insert "or the Insolvency Act 1986".
Civil Jurisdiction and Judgments Act 1982 (c. 27):	
Section 18(3)	In paragraph (ba), for "213 of the Insolvency Act 1985" substitute "426 of the Insolvency Act 1986".
Schedule 5	In paragraph (1), for "Companies Act 1985" substitute "Insolvency Act 1986".
Insurance Companies Act 1982 (c. 50):	
Section 53	For "Companies Act" (the first time) substitute "Insolvency Act 1986"; and for "Companies Act" (the second time) substitute "that Act of 1986".
Section 54	In subsection (1), for "the Companies Act" (the first time) substitute "Part IV or V of the Insolvency Act 1986"; and in paragraph (a), for "518 or sections 667 to 669" substitute "123 or sections 222 to 224".
	In subsection (4) for "Companies Act" (the first time) substitute "Insolvency Act 1986".
Section 55	In subsection (5), for "subsection (3) of section 540 of the Companies Act" substitute "section 168(2) of the Insolvency Act 1986".
	In subsection (6), for "631 of the Companies Act" substitute "212 of the Insolvency Act 1986".

Enactment	Amendment
Section 56	In subsection (4), for "Section 90(5) of the Insolvency Act 1985" substitute "Section 177(5) of the Insolvency Act 1986"; and for "section 90 of the said Act of 1985" substitute "section 177 of the said Act of 1986".
	In subsection (7), for "section 539(1) of the Companies Act" substitute "section 167 of, and Schedule 4 to, the Insolvency Act 1986".
Section 59	In subsection (1), for "106 of the Insolvency Act 1985" substitute "411 of the Insolvency Act 1986".
	In subsection (2), for "106 of the Insolvency Act 1985" substitute "411 of the Insolvency Act 1986"; and for "section 89 of, and Schedule 4 to, the Insolvency Act 1985" substitute "sections 175 and 176 of, and Schedule 6 to, the Insolvency Act 1986".
Section 96(1)	In the definition of "insolvent", for "517 and 518 or section 666 of the Companies Act" substitute "122 and 123 or section 221 of the Insolvency Act 1986".
Telecommunications Act 1984 (c. 12):	
Section 68(1)	In paragraph (a), for "Companies Act 1985" substitute "Insolvency Act 1986".
County Courts Act 1984 (c. 28):	
Section 98	For subsection (3) substitute—
	"(3) The provisions of this section have effect subject to those of sections 183, 184 and 346 of the Insolvency Act 1986".
Section 102	For subsection (8) substitute—
	"(8) Nothing in this section affects section 346 of the Insolvency Act 1986".
Section 109(2)	For "179 of the Insolvency Act 1985" substitute "346 of the Insolvency Act 1986".
Finance Act 1985 (c. 54):	
Section 79	Omit the word "altogether"; and after "Companies Act 1985" insert "sections 110 and 111 of the Insolvency Act 1986".
Housing Act 1985 (c. 68):	
Schedule 18	In paragraphs 3(4) and 5(3), for "228 of the Insolvency Act 1985" substitute "421 of the Insolvency Act 1986".

History
(1) In Sch. 14 entries relating to the Income and Corporation Taxes Act 1970, the Finance Act 1972, the Finance Act 1981 and the Finance Act 1983 repealed by Income and Corporation Taxes Act 1988, s. 844 and Sch. 31 for

companies' accounting periods ending after 5 April 1988 (see s. 843(1)): the entries formerly read as follows:

Enactment	Amendment
"Income and Corporation Taxes Act 1970 (c. 10):	
Section 247(7)	For 'Companies Act 1985' substitute 'Insolvency Act 1986'.
Section 265(5)	For '538 of the Companies Act 1985' substitute '145 of the Insolvency Act 1986'.
Finance Act 1972 (c. 41):	
Schedule 16	In paragraph 13(5), for 'Companies Act 1985' substitute 'Insolvency Act 1986'.
Finance Act 1981 (c. 35):	
Section 55(4)	For 'Companies Act 1985' substitute 'Insolvency Act 1986'.
Finance Act 1983 (c. 28):	
Schedule 5	In paragraph 5(4), for 'Companies Act 1985' substitute 'Insolvency Act 1986'."

(2) In Sch. 14 entry relating to Land Registration Act 1925, s. 112AA(3)(a) repealed by Land Registration Act 1988, s. 2: the entry formerly read as follows:

Enactment	Amendment
"Section 112AA(3)(a)	For 'the Insolvency Act 1985 or the Companies Act 1985' substitute 'the Insolvency Act 1986'."

(3) In Sch. 14 entry relating to Employment Protection (Consolidation) Act 1978, s. 125(2) repealed by Employment Act 1989, s. 29(4) and Sch. 7 as from 16 November 1989: the entry formerly read as follows:

Enactment	Amendment
"Section 125(2)	For paragraph (a) substitute—
	'(a) the following provisions of the Insolvency Act 1986—
	(i) sections 175 and 176, 328 and 329, 348 and Schedule 6, and
	(ii) any rules under that Act applying section 348 of it to the winding up of a company; and'"

[The next page is 58,001]

TABLE OF DERIVATIONS

Note: The following abbreviations are used in this Table—

"INS 1970"	=	The Insolvency Services (Accounting and Investment) Act 1970 (c. 8).
"INS 1976"	=	The Insolvency Act 1976 (c. 60).
"CA"	=	The Companies Act 1985 (c. 6).
"IA"	=	The Insolvency Act 1985 (c. 65).
"B(Sc)"	=	The Bankruptcy (Scotland) Act 1985 (c. 66).

Provision	Derivation
1	IA s. 20.
2	IA s. 21.
3	IA s. 22.
4	IA s. 23(1)–(6), (7) (part).
5	IA s. 24.
6	IA s. 25.
7	IA s. 26.
8	IA s. 27.
9	IA s. 28.
10	IA s. 29.
11	IA s. 30.
12	IA s. 31.
13	IA s. 32.
14	IA s. 33.
15	IA s. 34(1)–(8), (12).
16	IA s. 34(9), (10).
17	IA s. 35.
18	IA s. 36.
19	IA s. 37(1)–(3).
20	IA s. 37(4), (5).
21	IA s. 38.
22	IA s. 39.
23	IA s. 40.
24	IA s. 41.
25	IA s. 42.
26	IA s. 43.
27	IA s. 34(11), 44.
28	CA s. 488; IA s. 45(1).
29	CA s. 500; IA s. 45(2).
30	CA s. 489.
31	CA s. 490.

Provision	Derivation
32	CA s. 491.
33	IA s. 46.
34	IA s. 47.
35	CA s. 492(1), (2); IA Sch. 6 para. 16(2).
36	CA s. 494.
37	CA s. 492(3); IA Sch. 6 para. 16(3), (4).
38	CA s. 498; IA Sch. 6 para. 17.
39	CA s. 493.
40	CA s. 196 (part); IA Sch. 6 para. 15(2), (3).
41	CA s. 499.
42	IA s. 48.
43	IA s. 49.
44	IA s. 50.
45	IA s. 51.
46	IA s. 52.
47	IA s. 53.
48	IA s. 54.
49	IA s. 55.
50	CA s. 487.
51	CA s. 467.
52	CA s. 468.
53	CA s. 469; IA s. 56 (part).
54	CA s. 470.
55	CA s. 471; IA s. 57.
56	CA s. 472.
57	CA s. 473; IA s. 58.
58	CA s. 474.
59	CA s. 475; IA Sch. 6 para. 20(2).
60	CA s. 476; IA Sch. 6 para. 21.
61	CA s. 477; IA s. 59.
62	CA s. 478; IA s. 60, Sch. 6 para. 13.
63	CA s. 479; IA s. 61.
64	CA s. 480.
65	CA s. 481; IA s. 62.
66	CA s. 482; IA s. 63.
67	CA s. 482A; IA s. 64.
68	CA s. 482B; IA s. 65.
69	CA s. 483.
70	CA s. 462(4), 484, 486 (part).

Provision	Derivation
71	CA s. 485.
72	CA s. 724.
73	CA s. 510.
74	CA s. 502.
75	CA s. 503.
76	CA s. 504.
77	CA s. 505.
78	CA s. 506.
79	CA s. 507; IA Sch. 6 para. 5.
80	CA s. 508.
81	CA s. 509.
82	CA s. 510
83	CA s. 511.
84	CA s. 572.
85	CA s. 573.
86	CA s. 574.
87	CA s. 575.
88	CA s. 576.
89	CA s. 577; IA Sch. 6 para. 35.
90	CA s. 578.
91	CA s. 580.
92	CA s. 581.
93	CA s. 584; IA Sch. 6 para. 36.
94	CA s. 585(1)–(4), (7).
95	IA s. 83(1)–(6), (9), (10).
96	IA s. 83(7) (part).
97	CA s. 587; IA s. 85(1).
98	IA s. 85(2), (3), (6)–(8), (9)(a), (10).
99	IA s. 85(4), (5), (9)(b), (c), (10).
100	CA s. 589; IA Sch. 6 para. 37(1), (2).
101	CA s. 590; IA Sch. 6 para. 38(2)–(4).
102	IA s. 83(7) (part).
103	CA s. 591; IA Sch. 6 para. 39.
104	CA s. 592.
105	CA s. 594; IA s. 83(8).
106	CA s. 595(1)–(5), (8).
107	CA s. 597.
108	CA s. 599.
109	CA s. 600.

Provision	Derivation
110	CA s. 582(1)–(4), (7), 593; IA Sch. 6 para. 40.
111	CA s. 582(5), (6), (8).
112	CA s. 602.
113	CA s. 603.
114	IA s. 82.
115	CA s. 604.
116	CA s. 605.
117	CA s. 512; IA Sch. 6 para. 25, 26.
118	CA s. 513.
119	CA s. 514.
120	CA s. 515; IA Sch. 6 para. 25.
121	CA s. 516.
122	CA s. 517.
123	CA s. 518; IA Sch. 6 para. 25, 27.
124	CA s. 519; IA Sch. 6 para. 28.
125	CA s. 520.
126	CA s. 521.
127	CA s. 522.
128	CA s. 523.
129	CA s. 524.
130	CA s. 525; IA Sch. 6 para. 29.
131	IA s. 66.
132	IA s. 67.
133	IA s. 68(1)–(4).
134	IA s. 68(5), (6).
135	CA s. 532; IA s. 69(3).
136	IA s. 70(1)–(3), (4)(a), (5), (6).
137	IA s. 70(4)(b), (7)–(9).
138	CA s. 535; IA s. 71, Sch. 6 para. 30.
139	IA s. 72.
140	IA s. 73.
141	IA s. 74.
142	IA s. 75.
143	IA s. 69(1), (2).
144	CA s. 537.
145	CA s. 538.
146	IA s. 78.
147	CA s. 549.
148	CA s. 550.

Provision	Derivation
149	CA s. 552; IA Sch. 6 para. 32.
150	CA s. 553.
151	CA s. 554.
152	CA s. 555.
153	CA s. 557.
154	CA s. 558.
155	CA s. 559.
156	CA s. 560.
157	CA s. 562; IA Sch. 6 para. 33.
158	CA s. 565.
159	CA s. 566.
160	CA s. 567; IA Sch. 6 para. 34.
161	CA s. 569.
162	CA s. 571.
163	IA s. 94.
164	CA s. 635.
165	CA s. 539(1)(d), (e), (f), 598; IA s. 84(1), Sch. 6 para. 41.
166	IA s. 84.
167	CA s. 539(1), (2), (2A), (3); IA Sch. 6 para. 31(2), (3).
168	CA s. 540(3)–(6).
169	CA s. 539(4), (5); IA Sch. 6 para. 31(4).
170	CA s. 636.
171	IA s. 86.
172	IA s. 79.
173	IA s. 87.
174	IA s. 80.
175	IA s. 89(1), (2).
176	IA s. 89(3), (4).
177	IA s. 90.
178	IA s. 91(1)–(4), (8).
179	IA s. 91(5), (6).
180	IA s. 91(7).
181	IA s. 92(1)–(4), (9), (10).
182	IA s. 92(5)–(8).
183	CA s. 621.
184	CA s. 622; IA Sch. 6 para. 25.
185	CA s. 623; B(Sc) Sch. 7 para. 21.
186	CA s. 619(4).
187	CA s. 659; IA Sch. 6 para. 48.

Provision	Derivation
188	CA s. 637.
189	IA s. 93.
190	CA s. 638.
191	CA s. 639.
192	CA s. 641.
193	CA s. 643; B(Sc) Sch. 7 para. 22.
194	CA s. 644.
195	CA s. 645.
196	CA s. 646.
197	CA s. 647.
198	CA s. 648.
199	CA s. 649.
200	CA s. 650.
201	CA s. 585(5), (6), 595(6), (7).
202	IA s. 76(1)–(3), (6).
203	IA s. 76(4), (5), (7)–(10).
204	IA s. 77.
205	IA s. 81.
206	CA s. 624; IA Sch. 6 para. 25.
207	CA s. 625; IA Sch. 6 para. 42.
208	CA s. 626; IA Sch. 6 para. 43.
209	CA s. 627.
210	CA s. 628.
211	CA s. 629.
212	IA s. 19.
213	CA s. 630(1), (2); IA Sch. 6 para. 6(1).
214	IA s. 12(9), 15(1)–(5), (7), Sch. 9 para. 4.
215	CA s. 630(3)–(6); IA s. 15(6), Sch. 6 para. 6(2), (3).
216	IA s. 17, Sch. 9 para. 5.
217	IA s. 18(1) (part), (2)–(6).
218	CA s. 632; IA Sch. 6 para. 44.
219	CA s. 633.
220	CA s. 665.
221	CA s. 666.
222	CA s. 667; IA Sch. 6 para. 50.
223	CA s. 668; IA Sch. 6 para. 51.
224	CA s. 669; IA Sch. 6 para. 52.
225	CA s. 670.
226	CA s. 671.

Provision	Derivation
227	CA s. 672.
228	CA s. 673.
229	CA s. 674.
230	IA s. 95(1), (2), 96(1).
231	IA s. 95(1), (2), 96(2).
232	IA s. 95(1), (2), 96(3).
233	IA s. 95, 97.
234	IA s. 95(1), (2), 98.
235	IA s. 95(1), (2), 99.
236	IA s. 95(1), (2), 100(1), (2), (6).
237	IA s. 100(3)–(5), (7).
238	IA s. 95(1)(a), (b), 101(1) (part)–(3).
239	IA s. 95(1)(a), (b), 101(1) (part), (4)–(7), (11).
240	IA s. 101(8)–(11).
241	IA s. 95(1), 102.
242	CA s. 615A; B(Sc) Sch. 7 para. 20.
243	CA s. 615B; B(Sc) Sch. 7 para. 20.
244	IA s. 95(1)(a), (b), 103.
245	IA s. 95(1)(a), (b), 104.
246	IA s. 95(1)(a), (b), (2), 105.
247	IA s. 108(3) (part), (4).
248	IA s. 108(3) (part).
249	IA s. 108(5).
250	IA s. 108(6).
251	IA s. 108(3) (part).
252	IA s. 112(1) (part), (3).
253	IA s. 110, 111(1), (2), (3) (part).
254	IA s. 111(4), (5).
255	IA s. 112(1) (part), (2), (4)–(7)(a).
256	IA s. 113.
257	IA s. 114(1) (part), (2), (3).
258	IA s. 115(1)–(6), (9), (10).
259	IA s. 115(7), (8).
260	IA s. 116(1)–(3), (6), (7).
261	IA s. 116(4), (5).
262	IA s. 117.
263	IA s. 118.
264	IA s. 119(1).
265	IA s. 119(2), (3).

Provision	Derivation
266	IA s. 119(4)–(7).
267	IA s. 120(1), (2), (7)–(9).
268	IA s. 120(3), (4).
269	IA s. 120(5).
270	IA s. 120(6).
271	IA s. 121.
272	IA s. 122.
273	IA s. 123(1), (2), (8).
274	IA s. 111(3) (part), 112(1) (part), (7)(b), 114(1) (part), 123(3)–(5).
275	IA s. 123(6), (7).
276	IA s. 124.
277	IA s. 125.
278	IA s. 126(1).
279	IA s. 126(2)–(5).
280	IA s. 127.
281	IA s. 128.
282	IA s. 129.
283	IA s. 130.
284	IA s. 131.
285	IA s. 132
286	IA s. 133.
287	IA s. 134.
288	IA s. 135.
289	IA s. 136.
290	IA s. 137.
291	IA s. 138.
292	IA s. 139.
293	IA s. 140.
294	IA s. 141.
295	IA s. 142.
296	IA s. 143.
297	IA s. 144.
298	IA s. 145.
299	IA s. 146.
300	IA s. 147.
301	IA s. 148.
302	IA s. 149.
303	IA s. 150.
304	IA s. 151.

[The next page is 58,041]

Provision	Derivation
305	IA s. 152.
306	IA s. 153.
307	IA s. 154(1)–(4), (7).
308	IA s. 155(1), (2), (4), (5).
309	IA s. 154(5), (6), 155(3).
310	IA s. 156.
311	IA s. 157.
312	IA s. 158.
313	IA s. 159.
314	IA s. 160.
315	IA s. 161(1)–(4), (10).
316	IA s. 161(5).
317	IA s. 161(6), (7).
318	IA s. 161(8).
319	IA s. 161(9).
320	IA s. 162(1)–(4), (9), (10).
321	IA s. 162(5)–(8).
322	IA s. 163.
323	IA s. 164.
324	IA s. 165(1)–(4).
325	IA s. 165(5), (6).
326	IA s. 165(7), (8).
327	IA s. 165(9).
328	IA s. 166(1)–(5), (7).
329	IA s. 166(6).
330	IA s. 167.
331	IA s. 168(1), (2), (4).
332	IA s. 168(3).
333	IA s. 169.
334	IA s. 170(1)–(3).
335	IA s. 170(4)–(9).
336	IA s. 171.
337	IA s. 172.
338	IA s. 173.
339	IA s. 174(1) (part), (2).
340	IA s. 174(1) (part), (3)–(6), (12) (part).
341	IA s. 174(7)–(11), (12) (part).
342	IA s. 175.
343	IA s. 176.

Provision	Derivation
344	IA s. 177.
345	IA s. 178.
346	IA s. 179.
347	IA s. 180.
348	IA s. 181.
349	IA s. 182.
350	IA s. 183(1)–(3), (5), (6), 192.
351	IA s. 184(5), 187(3)(a).
352	IA s. 183(4).
353	IA s. 183(4), 184(1).
354	IA s. 183(4), 184(2)–(4).
355	IA s. 183(4), 185.
356	IA s. 183(4), 186.
357	IA s. 183(4), 187(1), (3)(b).
358	IA s. 183(4), 187(2).
359	IA s. 183(4), 188.
360	IA s. 189.
361	IA s. 190.
362	IA s. 191.
363	IA s. 193.
364	IA s. 194.
365	IA s. 195.
366	IA s. 196(1), (2).
367	IA s. 196(3)–(6).
368	IA s. 196(7).
369	IA s. 197.
370	IA s. 198.
371	IA s. 199.
372	IA s. 200.
373	IA s. 201.
374	IA s. 202.
375	IA s. 203.
376	IA s. 204.
377	IA s. 205.
378	IA s. 206.
379	IA s. 210.
380	—
381	IA s. 211(1) (part).
382	IA s. 211(1) (part), (2), (3).

Provision	Derivation
383	IA s. 211(1) (part), (5)–(7).
384	IA s. 209(1) (part), 211(1) (part).
385	IA s. 211(1) (part), (4).
386	CA s. 196(2), 475(1); IA s. 23(7), 89(1), 108(3), 115(9), 166(1), Sch. 4 para. 1(1), Sch. 6 para. 15(3).
387	CA s. 196(2)–(4), 475(3), (4); IA s. 23(8), 115(10), Sch. 4, Pt. II, para. 1(2), (3), Sch. 6 para. 15(4), 20(3).
388	IA s. 1(2)–(6).
389	IA s. 1(1).
390	IA s. 2, 3(1).
391	IA s. 3(2)–(5).
392	IA s. 4, 11 (part).
393	IA s. 5.
394	IA s. 6.
395	IA s. 7.
396	IA s. 8(1), (2), (6), 11 (part).
397	IA s. 8(3)–(5).
398	IA s. 9.
399	IA s. 222.
400	IA s. 223.
401	IA s. 224.
402	IA s. 225.
403	INS 1970 s. 1; INS 1976 s. 3; IA Sch. 8 para. 28.
404	INS 1970 s. 2.
405	INS 1970 s. 3; INS 1976 Sch. 2 para. 5.
406	INS 1970 s. 4; INS 1976 Sch. 2 para. 6; IA Sch. 8 para. 17.
407	INS 1970 s. 5; INS 1976 Sch. 2 para. 7.
408	INS 1970 s. 6; INS 1976 Sch. 2 para. 8.
409	INS 1970 s. 7; INS 1976 Sch. 2 para. 9.
410	INS 1970 s. 9(3); INS 1976 s. 14(6); IA s. 236(3)(i).
411	IA s. 106.
412	IA s. 207.
413	IA s. 226.
414	IA s. 106(5), 107.
415	IA s. 207(5), 208(1)–(3), (5).
416	CA s. 664; IA Sch. 6 para. 49.
417	CA s. 667(2) (part).
418	IA s. 209(1) (part), (2), (3).
419	IA s. 10, 11 (part).

Provision	Derivation
420	IA s. 227.
421	IA s. 228.
422	IA s. 229.
423	IA s. 212(1), (3), (7) (part).
424	IA s. 212(2).
425	IA s. 212(4)–(6), (7) (part).
426	IA s. 213.
427	IA s. 214
428	IA s. 217(1)–(3).
429	IA s. 221(1), (3)–(5).
430	CA s. 730; IA passim.
431	CA s. 731; IA s. 108(1).
432	IA s. 230.
433	IA s. 231.
434	IA s. 234.
435	IA s. 233.
436	IA s. 232 (part).
437	—
438	—
439	—
440	IA s. 236(3).
441	CA s. 745; IA s. 236(4).
442	IA s. 236(5).
443	—
444	—
Sch. 1	IA Sch. 3.
Sch. 2	CA s. 471(1); IA s. 57.
Sch. 3	CA Sch. 16.
Sch. 4	
Pt I	CA s. 539(1)(d)–(f), 598(1).
Pt. II	CA s. 539(1)(a), (b), 598(2).
Pt. III	CA s. 539(2), 598(2).
Sch. 5	
Pt. I	IA s. 160(2).
Pt. II	IA s. 160(1).
Pt. III	IA s. 160(6).
Sch. 6	IA Sch. 4 Pt. I, Pt. II para. 2–4.
Sch. 7	IA Sch. 1.
Sch. 8	IA Sch. 5.
Sch. 9	IA Sch. 7.
Sch. 10	CA and IA passim.

[The next page is 58,061]
    CCH Editions Limited

Provision	Derivation
Sch. 11	
para. 1	IA Sch. 9 para. 6.
2	IA Sch. 9 para. 7.
3	IA Sch. 9 para. 8.
4	IA Sch. 9 para. 9(1).
5	IA Sch. 9 para. 9(2).
6	IA Sch. 9 para. 9(3)–(5), (8).
7	IA Sch. 9 para. 9(6).
8	IA Sch. 9 para. 9(7).
9	IA Sch. 9 para. 10.
10	IA Sch. 9 para. 11.
11	IA Sch. 9 para. 12.
12	IA Sch. 9 para. 13.
13	IA Sch. 9 para. 14.
14	IA Sch. 9 para. 15, 16, 17.
15	IA Sch. 9 para. 18.
16	IA Sch. 9 para. 19.
17	IA Sch. 9 para. 20.
18	IA Sch. 9 para. 21.
19	IA Sch. 9 para. 22.
20	IA Sch. 9 para. 24.
21	IA Sch. 9 para. 1.
22–28	—
Sch. 12–14	—

[The next page is 58,201]

TABLE OF DESTINATIONS

The table below, prepared by CCH editorial staff, relates the provisions of the former legislation (in the left-hand column) to the corresponding provisions of the consolidated legislation (in the right-hand column); namely:

Insolvency Act 1986
Company Directors Disqualification Act 1986

Note: References in the left-hand column are to sections unless otherwise stated.

The following abbreviations are used in this table:—

"IA 1985"	= Insolvency Act 1985.
"IA 1986"	= Insolvency Act 1986.
"CDDA 1986"	= Company Directors Disqualification Act 1986.

Provision of former Acts	Destination
Insolvency Services (Accounting and Investment) Act 1970	
1	see IA 1986, s. 403.
2	s. 404.
3	s. 405.
4 (as amended by IA 1985, Sch. 8, para. 17)	s. 406.
5	s. 407.
6	s. 408.
7	s. 409.
9(3)	s. 410.
Insolvency Act 1976	
3(3)–(5)	s. 403.
14(6)	see s. 410.
Companies Act 1985	
295(1) (as amended by IA 1985, Sch. 6, para. 1(2))	CDDA 1986, s. 1(1).
295(2) (as amended by IA 1985, Sch. 6, para. 1(3))	CDDA 1986, s. 1(2), 2(3), 3(5), 4(3), 5(5), 6(4), 8(4), 10(2).
295(3)	see s. 22(2)
295(4)	s. 1(4).
295(6) (as amended by IA 1985, Sch. 6, para. 1(4))	s. 16(1), 17(1), 19.
295(7)	s. 13(part).
296	s. 2(1), (2).
297	s. 3(1)–(4).
298	s. 4(1), (2).

Provision of former Acts	Destination
Companies Act 1985	
299	s. 5(1)–(4).
300	repealed by IA 1985, s. 235 and Sch. 10.
301 (301(1) as amended by IA 1985, Sch. 6, para. 2)	CDDA 1986, s. 18.
302(1) (words repealed by IA 1985, s. 235 and Sch. 10)	s. 11(1), 13.
302(2), (3)	s. 11(2), (3).
302(4)	s. 22(2)(a).
467 (467(3)–(5) repealed by IA 1985, Sch. 10)	IA 1986, s. 51 (see also Sch. 10).
468	s. 52.
469(1)–(5)	s. 53(1)–(5).
469(6) (as substituted by IA 1985, s. 56)	s. 53(6).
469(7)	s. 53(7).
469(8) (inserted by IA 1985, s. 56)	s. 251.
470 (470(2) as amended by IA 1985, Sch. 10)	s. 54 (see also Sch. 10).
471(1) (as amended by IA 1985, s. 57)	s. 55(1), (2), Sch. 2.
471(2), (3)	s. 55(3), (4).
472	s. 56.
473(1)–(4) (473(2) as amended by IA 1985, s. 58(2))	s. 57(1)–(4).
473(4A), (4B) (inserted by IA 1985, s. 58(3))	s. 57(5), (6).
473(5)	s. 57(7).
474(1), (2)	s. 58(1), (2).
474(3)	superseded by substitution of CA 1985, s. 481 by IA 1985, s. 62 (now IA 1986, s. 65).
474(4)	IA 1986, s. 58(3).
475(1), (2)	s. 59(1), (2) (see also s. 386).
475(3), (4)	(lapsed through other repeals etc.)
475(5)	IA 1986, s. 59(3).
476	s. 60.
477(1), (2) (477(2) as amended by by IA 1985, s. 59(2))	s. 61(1), (2).
477(2A)–(2E) (inserted by IA 1985, s. 59(3))	s. 61(3)–(7) (see also Sch. 10).
477(3), (4)	s. 61(8), (9).

Provision of former Acts	Destination
Companies Act 1985	
478(1), (2) (as substituted by IA 1985, s. 60(2))	s. 62(1), (2).
478(3)	s. 62(3).
478(4) (as substituted by IA 1985, s. 60(3))	s. 62(4).
478(5) (as amended by IA 1985, s. 60(4))	s. 62(5) (see also Sch. 10).
478(6)	s. 62(6).
479 (as substituted by IA 1985, s. 61)	s. 63.
480	s. 64 (see also Sch. 10).
481 (as substituted by IA 1985, s. 62)	s. 65 (see also Sch. 10).
482 (as substituted by IA 1985, s. 63)	s. 66 (see also Sch. 10).
482A (as inserted by IA 1985, s. 64)	s. 67 (see also Sch. 10).
482B (as inserted by IA 1985, s. 65)	s. 68.
483	s. 69.
484(1)	s. 70(1) (part).
484(2), (3)	s. 70(2), (3).
485	s. 71.
486 (part)	s. 70(1) (part).
487	s. 50.
488	s. 28.
489	s. 30 (see also Sch. 10).
490	s. 31 (see also Sch. 10).
491	s. 32.
492(1) (as substituted by IA 1985, Sch. 6, para. 16(2))	IA 1986, s. 35(1).
492(2)	s. 35(2).
492(3) (as amended by IA 1985, Sch. 6, para. 16(3)).	s. 37(1), (3).
492(4), (5) (inserted by IA 1985, Sch. 6, para. 16(4))	s. 37(2), (4).
493	s. 39 (see also Sch. 10).
494	s. 36.
495–497	repealed by IA 1985, s. 235 and Sch. 10.
498(1)–(3) (as amended by IA 1985, Sch. 6, para. 17)	s. 38(1)–(3).

Provision of former Acts	Destination
Companies Act 1985	
498(4)	s. 38(5), Sch. 10.
499	s. 41.
500	s. 29(1).
501(1) (para. (c) repealed by IA 1985, s. 235 and Sch. 10)	s. 73(1).
501(2)	s. 73(2).
502 (in 502(1) words repealed by IA 1985, s. 235 and Sch. 10)	s. 74.
503 (in 503(2)(c) words repealed by IA 1985, s. 235 and Sch. 10)	s. 75.
504 (in 504(1)(b) words repealed by IA 1985, s. 235 and Sch. 10)	s. 76.
505	s. 77.
506	s. 78.
507(1) (as amended by IA 1985, Sch. 6, para. 5)	s. 79(1).
507(2)	s. 79(3).
508	s. 80.
509	s. 81.
510	s. 82.
511 (in 511(2)(c) words repealed by IA 1985, s. 235 and Sch. 10)	s. 83.
512(1), (2)	s. 117(1), (2).
512(3), (4) (as amended by IA 1985, Sch. 6, para. 25, 26 and Sch. 10)	s. 117(3), (4).
512(5), (6)	s. 117(5), (6).
513	s. 118.
514	s. 119.
515(1)–(4)	IA 1986, s. 120(1)–(4)
515(5) as amended by IA 1985, Sch. 6, para. 25 and Sch. 10)	s. 120(5).
516	s. 121.
517	s. 122.
518(1) (as amended by IA 1985, Sch. 6, para. 27(2), (3))	s. 123(1).
518(1A) (as inserted by IA 1985, Sch. 6, para. 27(4))	s. 123(2).
518(2) (as amended by IA 1985, Sch. 6, para. 25 and Sch. 10)	s. 123(3).
519(1)(as amended by IA 1985, Sch. 6, para. 28)	s. 124(1).

Provision of former Acts	Destination
Companies Act 1985	
519(2), (3)	s. 124(2), (3).
519(4)	s. 124(4) (part).
519(5)	repealed by IA 1985, s. 235 and Sch. 10.
519(6)	IA 1986, s. 124(4) (part).
519(7) (some words repealed by IA 1985, s. 235 and Sch. 10)	s. 124(5).
520	s. 125.
521	s. 126.
522	s. 127.
523	s. 128.
524	s. 129.
525(1)	s. 130(1).
525(2), (3) (as amended by IA 1985, Sch. 6, para. 29)	s. 130(2), (3).
526–531	repealed by IA 1985, s. 235 and Sch. 10.
532(1)–(3)	IA 1986, s. 135(1)–(3).
532(4)	s. 135(5).
533, 534	repealed by IA 1985, s. 235 and Sch. 10.
535 (as substituted by IA 1985, Sch. 6, para. 30)	IA 1986, s. 138(1)
536	repealed by IA 1985, s. 235 and Sch. 10.
537	IA 1986, s. 144.
538	s. 145.
539(1) (as amended by IA 1985, Sch. 6, para. 31(2))	s. 165, 167(1).
(a), (b)	Sch. 4, para. 4, 5.
(c)	repealed by IA 1985, s. 235 and Sch. 10.
(d)–(f)	IA 1986, Sch. 4, para. 1–3.
539(2)	IA 1986, s. 167(1).
(a)–(h)	Sch. 4, para. 6–13.
539(2A) (as inserted by IA 1985, Sch. 6, para. 31(3))	s. 167(2).
539(3)	s. 167(3).
539(4) (as amended by IA 1985, Sch. 6, para. 31(4))	s. 169(1).
539(5)	s. 169(2).
540(1), (2)	repealed by IA 1985, s. 235 and Sch. 10.
540(3)–(6)	IA 1986, s. 168(2)–(5).
541–543	repealed by IA 1985, s. 235 and Sch. 10.
544	repealed by IA 1985, s. 235 and Sch. 10.

Provision of former Acts	Destination
Companies Act 1985	
545–548	repealed by IA 1986, s. 235 and Sch. 10.
549	IA 1986, s. 147.
550	s. 148.
551	repealed by IA 1985, s. 235 and Sch. 10.
552(1), (2)	IA 1986, 149(1), (2).
552(3) (as amended by IA 1985, Sch. 6, para. 32)	s. 149(3).
553	s. 150.
554	s. 151.
555	s. 152
556	repealed by IA 1985, s. 235 and Sch. 10.
557	IA 1986, s. 153.
558	s. 154.
559	s. 155.
560	s. 156.
561	repealed by IA 1985, s. 235 and Sch. 10.
562 (as amended by IA 1985, Sch. 6, para. 33)	IA 1986, s. 157.
563, 564	repealed by IA 1985, s. 235 and Sch. 10.
565 (words repealed by IA 1985, s. 235 and Sch. 10)	IA 1986, s. 158.
566	s. 159.
567(1)	s. 160(1).
567(2) (as amended by IA 1985, Sch. 6, para. 34)	s. 160(2).
568	repealed by IA 1985, s. 235 and Sch. 10.
569	IA 1986, s. 161.
570	repealed by IA 1985, s. 235 and Sch. 10.
571(1)–(4)	IA 1986, s. 162(1)–(4).
571(5) (words repealed by IA 1985, s. 235 and Sch. 10)	s. 162(5).
572	s. 84.
573	s. 85 (see also Sch. 10).
574	s. 86.
575	s. 87.
576	s. 88.
577(1) (as amended by IA 1985, Sch. 6, para. 35)	s. 89(1).
577(2), (3)	s. 89(2), (3).

Provision of former Acts	Destination
Companies Act 1985	
577(4), (5) (as amended by IA 1985, Sch. 6, para. 35)	s. 89(4), (5) (see also Sch. 10).
577(6)	s. 89(6) (see also Sch. 10).
578	s. 90.
580(1) (words repealed by IA 1985, s. 235 and Sch. 10)	s. 91(1).
580(2)	s. 91(2).
581	s. 92.
582(1)	s. 110(1).
582(2)	s. 110(2), (3)(a).
582(3), (4)	s. 110(4), (5).
582(5), (6)	s. 111(2), (3).
582(7) (words repealed by IA 1985, s. 235 and Sch. 10)	s. 110(6).
582(8)	s. 111(4).
583	repealed by IA 1985, s. 235 and Sch. 10.
584(1) (as amended by IA 1985, Sch. 6, para. 36)	IA 1986, s. 93(1), (2).
584(2)	s. 93(3) (see also Sch. 10).
585(1), (2)	s. 94(1), (2).
585(3)	s. 94(3), (4) (see also Sch. 10).
585(4)	s. 94(5).
585(5)	s. 201(2), (3).
585(6)	s. 201(4) (see also Sch. 10).
585(7)	s. 94(6).
586	repealed by IA 1985, s. 235 and Sch. 10.
587	IA 1986, s. 97(1).
588	repealed by IA 1985, s. 235 and Sch. 10.
589(1) (as amended by IA 1985, Sch. 6, para. 37(1))	IA 1986, s. 100(1).
589(2) (as substituted by IA 1985, Sch. 6, para. 37(2))	s. 100(2).
589(3)	s. 100(3).
590(1) (as substituted by IA 1985, Sch. 6, para. 38(2))	s. 101(1).
590(2)	s. 101(2).
590(3) (as amended by IA 1985, Sch. 6, para. 38(3))	s. 101(3).
590(4)	repealed by IA 1985, s. 235 and Sch. 10.
590(5) (as amended by IA 1985, Sch. 6, para. 38(4))	s. 101(4).

Provision of former Acts	Destination
Companies Act 1985	
591(1)	repealed by IA 1985, s. 235 and Sch. 10.
591(2) (as amended by IA 1985, Sch. 6, para. 39)	IA 1986, s. 103.
592	s. 104.
593 (as amended by IA 1985, Sch. 6, para. 40)	s. 110(3)(b).
594(1)	s. 105(1), (2).
594(2)	s. 105(3) (see also Sch. 10).
595(1)–(5)	s. 106(1)–(5).
595(6)	s. 201(2), (3).
595(7)	s. 201(4) (see also Sch. 10).
595(8)	s. 106(6) (see also Sch. 10).
597	s. 107.
598(1) (as amended by IA 1985, Sch. 6, para. 41(1)).	s. 165(2).
598(2)–(4)	s. 165(3)–(5).
598(4A) (inserted by IA 1985, Sch. 6, para. 41(2))	s. 165(6).
598(5)	repealed by IA 1985, s. 235 and Sch. 10.
599	IA 1986, s. 108.
600	s. 109 (see also Sch. 10).
601	repealed by IA 1985, s. 235 and Sch. 10.
602	IA 1986, s. 112.
603	s. 113.
604 (words repealed by IA 1985, s. 235 and Sch. 10)	s. 115.
605	s. 116.
606–610	repealed by IA 1985, s. 235 and Sch. 10.
611–615	repealed by IA 1985, s. 235 and Sch. 10.
615A(1)–(3)	IA 1986, s. 242(1)–(3).
615A(4), (5)	s. 242(4)–(7).
615A(6)	s. 242(8).
615B(1)	s. 243(1)–(6).
615B(2)	s. 243(7).
616–618	repealed by IA 1985, s. 235 and Sch. 10.
619(1)–(3)	repealed by IA 1985, s. 235 and Sch. 10.
619(4)	IA 1986, s. 186.
619(5)–(8)	repealed by IA 1985, s. 235 and Sch. 10.
620	repealed by IA 1985, s. 235 and Sch. 10.
621	IA 1986, s. 183.

Provision of former Acts	Destination
Companies Act 1985	
622(1)–(6)	s. 184(1)–(6).
622(7) (as amended by IA 1985, Sch. 6, para. 25 and Sch. 10)	s. 184(7).
622(8)	s. 184(8).
623(1)–(3)	s. 185(1)–(3).
623(6)	s. 185(4).
624(1)–(6)	s. 206(1)–(6) (see also Sch. 10).
624(7) (as amended by IA 1985, Sch. 6, para. 25)	s. 206(7).
625(1) (words repealed by IA 1985, s. 235 and Sch. 10)	s. 207(1).
625(1A) (inserted by IA 1985, Sch. 6, para. 42)	s. 207(2).
625(2)	s. 207(3) (see also Sch. 10).
626(1) (as amended by IA 1985, Sch. 6, para. 43 and Sch. 10)	s. 208(1).
626(2)–(5)	s. 208(2)–(5) (see also Sch. 10).
627	s. 209 (see also Sch. 10).
628 (words in 628(1) repealed by IA 1985, s. 235 and Sch. 10)	s. 210 (see also Sch. 10).
629 (words in 629(1) repealed by IA 1985, s. 235 and Sch. 10)	s. 211 (see also Sch. 10).
630(1)	s. 213(1).
630(2) (as substituted by IA 1985, Sch. 6, para. 6(1))	s. 213(2).
630(3) (as amended by IA 1985, Sch. 6, para. 6(2))	s. 215(1).
630(4), (5)	s. 215(2), (3).
630(5A) (as inserted by IA 1985, Sch. 6, para. 6(3))	IA 1986, s. 215(4).
630(6)	s. 215(5).
631	repealed by IA 1985, s. 235 and Sch. 10.
632(1) (words repealed by IA 1985, s. 235 and Sch. 10)	IA 1986, s. 218(1).
632(2)	s. 218(2).
632(2A) (inserted by IA 1985, Sch. 6, para. 44)	s. 218(3).
632(3)–(5)	s. 218(4)–(6).
633	s. 219.
634	repealed by IA 1985, s. 235 and Sch. 10.
635	IA 1986, s. 164 (see also Sch. 10).

Provision of former Acts	Destination
Companies Act 1985	
636	s. 170.
637 (words in s. 637(1) repealed by IA 1985, s. 235 and Sch. 10)	s. 188 (see also Sch. 10).
638	s. 190.
639	s. 191.
640	repealed by IA 1985, s. 235 and Sch. 10.
641	IA 1986, s. 192 (see also Sch. 10).
642	repealed by IA 1985, s. 235 and Sch. 10.
643	IA 1986, s. 193.
644	s. 194.
645	s. 195.
646	s. 196.
647	s. 197.
648	s. 198.
649	s. 199.
650	s. 200.
659(1)	IA 1986, s. 187(1).
659(2) (as amended by IA 1985, Sch. 6, para. 48)	s. 187(2).
659(3)–(5)	s. 187(3)–(5).
660–663	repealed by IA 1985, s. 235 and Sch. 10.
664(1) (as amended by IA 1985, Sch. 6, para. 49(1) and Sch. 10)	IA 1986, s. 416(1).
664(2)–(4) (as substituted by IA 1985, Sch. 6, para. 49(2))	s. 416(2)–(4).
665(a), (b)	s. 220(1).
665(c), (d)	repealed by IA 1985, s. 235 and Sch. 10.
666(1)–(3)	IA 1986, s. 221(1)–(3).
666(4) (words repealed by IA 1985, s. 235 and Sch. 10)	s. 221(4).
666(5), (6)	s. 221(5), (6).
666(7)	repealed by IA 1985, s. 235 and Sch. 10.
666(8)	IA 1986, s. 221(7).
667(1) (as amended by IA 1985, Sch. 6, para. 50)	s. 222(1).
667(2)	s. 222(2).
668 (as amended by IA 1985, Sch. 6, para. 51)	s. 223.
669(1) (as amended by IA 1985, Sch. 6, para. 52(1))	s. 224(1).

Provision of former Acts	Destination
Companies Act 1985	
669(2) (as inserted by IA 1985, Sch. 6, para. 52(2))	s. 224(2).
670	s. 225.
671(1) (words repealed by IA 1985, s. 235 and Sch. 10)	s. 226(1).
671(2)–(4)	s. 226(2)–(4).
672	s. 227.
673	s. 228.
674	s. 229.
724	s. 72.
730	s. 430.
731	s. 431.
745	s. 441.
Sch. 12	
para. 1–3	CCDA 1986, s. 16
para. 4 (as amended by IA 1985, Sch. 6, para. 14)	s. 17(1).
para. 5	s. 17(2).
para. 6–8	repealed by IA 1985, s. 235 and Sch. 10.
para. 9–14	CDDA 1986, Sch. 2.
para. 15, 16	repealed by IA 1985, s. 235.
Sch. 16	IA 1986, Sch. 3.
Sch. 24 (part)	CDDA 1986, s. 13 IA 1986, Sch. 10.
Insolvency Act 1985	
1(1)	IA 1986, s. 389(1), Sch. 10.
1(2)–(5)	IA 1986, s. 388(1)–(4).
1(6)	s. 388(5), 389(2).
2	s. 390.
3(1)	see s. 390(2)(a), 391(3) (part).
3(2)	s. 391(1), (4).
3(3)	s. 391(2).
3(4)	s. 391(5).
3(5)	s. 391(3) (part).
4	s. 392(3)–(8).
5	s. 393.
6	s. 394.
7	s. 395.

Provision of former Acts	Destination
Insolvency Act 1985	
8(1), (2)	s. 396(2), (3).
8(3)–(5)	s. 397.
8(6)	s. 396(1).
9	s. 398.
10	s. 419.
11	see s. 392, 396, 419.
12(1)	CDDA 1986, s. 6(1).
12(2)	s. 6(4) (part).
12(3)–(6)	s. 7.
12(7)	s. 6(2).
12(8), (9)	s. 6(3).
13	s. 8(1)–(3).
14	s. 9.
15(1)	IA 1986, s. 214(1).
15(2)	s. 214(2) (part).
15(3)–(5)	s. 214(3)–(5).
15(6)	s. 215.
15(7)	s. 214(6).
16	CDDA 1986, s. 10(1).
17(1)	IA 1986, s. 216(1), (2).
17(2)	s. 216(3).
17(3)	s. 216(4), Sch. 10.
17(4)–(7)	s. 216(5)–(8).
18	s. 217;
	CDDA 1986, s. 15.
19	IA 1986, s. 212.
20	s. 1.
21	IA 1986, s. 2(2)–(4).
22	s. 3.
23(1)–(6)	s. 4(1)–(6).
23(7)	s. 4(7), 386(3).
23(8)	see s. 387.
24	s. 5.
25	s. 6.
26	s. 7.
27(1)	s. 8(1), (2), (3) (part).
27(2)	s. 8(4).
27(3)	s. 8(3) (part).
27(4)	see s. 8(1)(a).

Provision of former Acts	Destination
Insolvency Act 1985	
28	s. 9.
29	s. 10.
30	s. 11.
31(1)	s. 12(1).
31(2)	s. 12(2), Sch. 10.
32	s. 13.
33	s. 14.
34(1)–(7)	s. 15(1)–(7).
34(8)	s. 15(8), Sch. 10.
34(9), (10)	s. 16.
34(11)	s. 27(5).
34(12)	s. 15(9).
35	s. 17.
36(1)–(4)	s. 18(1)–(4).
36(5)	s. 18(5), Sch. 10.
37(1), (2)	s. 19(1), (2).
37(3)	s. 19(3)–(5).
37(4)	s. 20(1).
37(5)	s. 20(2), (3).
38(1), (2)	s. 21(1), (2).
38(3)	s. 21(3), Sch. 10.
39(1)–(5)	s. 22(1)–(5).
39(6)	s. 22(6), Sch. 10.
40(1), (2)	s. 23(1), (2).
40(3)	s. 23(3), Sch. 10.
41(1)–(6)	s. 24(1)–(6).
41(7)	IA 1986, s. 24(7), Sch. 10.
42	s. 25.
43	s. 26.
44(1)–(4)	s. 27(1)–(4).
44(5), (6)	s. 27(6), Sch. 10.
45(1)	s. 28.
45(2)	s. 29(2).
46	s. 33.
47	s. 34.
48(1)	s. 42(1), (2).
48(2)	s. 42(3).
49(1)–(5)	s. 43(1)–(5).

Provision of former Acts		Destination
Insolvency Act 1985		
49(6)		s. 43(6), Sch. 10.
49(7)		s. 43(7).
50(1)		s. 44(1), (2).
50(2)		s. 44(3).
51(1)–(4)		s. 45(1)–(4).
51(5)		s. 45(5), Sch. 10.
52(1)–(3)		s. 46(1)–(3).
52(4)		s. 46(4), Sch. 10.
53(1)–(5)		s. 47(1)–(5).
53(6)		s. 47(6), Sch. 10.
54(1)–(6)		s. 47(1)–(6).
54(7)		s. 47(7), (8), Sch. 10.
55		s. 49.
56	see	s. 53.
57	see	s. 55.
58	see	s. 57.
59	see	s. 61.
60	see	s. 62.
61	see	s. 63.
62	see	s. 65.
63	see	s. 66.
64	see	s. 67.
65	see	s. 68.
66(1)–(6)		s. 131(1)–(6).
66(7)		s. 131(7), Sch. 10.
66(8)		s. 131(8).
67		s. 132.
68(1)–(4)		s. 133.
68(5)		s. 134(1).
68(6)		s. 134(2), (3).
69(1), (2)		s. 143.
69(3)		s. 135(4).
70(1)–(3)		s. 136(1)–(3).
70(4)(a)		s. 136(4).
70(4)(b)		s. 137(1).
70(5), (6)		s. 136(5), (6).
70(7), (8)		s. 137(2), (3).
70(9)		s. 137(4), (5).

Provision of former Acts	Destination
Insolvency Act 1985	
71	s. 138(2)–(6).
72	s. 139.
73	s. 140.
74	s. 141.
75	s. 142.
76(1)–(3)	s. 202(2)–(4).
76(4), (5)	s. 203(1), (2).
76(6)	s. 202(5).
76(7)–(9)	s. 203(3)–(5).
76(10)	s. 203(6), Sch. 10.
77(1)	s. 204(1), (2).
77(2)–(5)	s. 204(3)–(5).
77(6), (7)	s. 204(7), (8), Sch. 10.
78	s. 146.
79	s. 172.
80	s. 174.
81(1)	s. 205(1), (2).
81(2)–(5)	s. 205(3)–(6).
81(6)	s. 205(7), Sch. 10.
82(1)–(3)	s. 114(1)–(3).
82(4)	s. 114(4), Sch. 10.
83(1)–(6)	s. 95(1)–(6).
83(7)	s. 96, 102.
83(8)	s. 105(4).
83(9)	s. 95(7).
83(10)	s. 95(8), Sch. 10.
84(1)–(6)	IA 1986, s. 166(1)–(6).
84(7)	s. 166(7), Sch. 10.
85(1)	see s. 97(1).
85(2), (3)	s. 98(1), (2).
85(4), (5)	s. 99(1), (2).
85(6)–(8)	s. 98(3)–(5).
85(9)(a)	s. 98(6).
85(9)(b), (c)	s. 99(3).
85(10)	s. 98(6), 99(3), Sch. 10.
86	s. 171.
87	s. 173.
88	(repeal of CA 1985, Pt. XX, Ch. IV).

Provision of former Acts	Destination
Insolvency Act 1985	
89(1), (2)	IA 1986, s. 175.
89(3)	s. 176(1), (2).
89(4)	s. 176(3).
90	s. 177.
91(1)–(4)	s. 178(2)–(5).
91(5), (6)	s. 179.
91(7)	s. 180.
91(8)	s. 178(6).
92(1)–(4)	s. 181(1)–(4).
92(5)–(8)	s. 182.
92(9), (10)	s. 181(5), (6).
93	s. 189.
94	s. 163.
95(1), (2)	s. 230(1), 231(1), 233(1), 234(1), 235(1), 236(1), 238(1), 239(1), 241(1), 244(1), 245(1), 246(1).
95(2)	see s. 230, 231, 232, 234–236, 246.
95(3)	see s. 233.
96(1)	s. 230.
96(2)	s. 231.
96(3)	s. 232.
97(1), (2)	s. 233(2), (3).
97(3)	s. 233(5)(d).
97(4)	s. 233(4).
98(1)	s. 234(2).
98(2)	s. 234(3), (4).
99(1)	s. 235(2).
99(2)	IA 1986, s. 235(3).
99(3)	s. 235(3)(d), (4).
99(4)	s. 235(1).
99(5)	s. 235(5), Sch. 10.
100(1)	s. 236(2), (3).
100(2)	s. 236(3), (4).
100(3)	s. 237(4).
100(4), (5)	s. 237(1), (2).
100(6)	s. 236(1).
100(7)	s. 237(3).
101(1)	s. 238(2), 239(2), (3).
101(2), (3)	s. 238(4), (5).

Provision of former Acts	Destination
Insolvency Act 1985	
101(4)–(7)	s. 239(4)–(7).
101(8)–(10)	s. 240.
101(11)	s. 239(6) (part), 240(1)(a) (part).
102	s. 241.
103	s. 244.
104	s. 245(2)–(6).
105	s. 246(2), (3).
106(1)	s. 411(1).
106(2)	s. 411(2), 411(3) (part).
106(3)–(5)	s. 411(4)–(6).
107(1)	s. 414(1)–(3).
107(2)–(5)	s. 414(4)–(7).
107(6)	s. 414(9) (part).
108(1)	see s. 431, see CDDA 1986, s. 21, 22.
108(2)	see CDDA 1986, s. 18, 21, 22.
108(3)	see IA 1986, s. 247(1), 248, 251.
108(4)	s. 247(2).
108(5)	s. 249.
108(6)	s. 250.
108(7)	see s. 430(4).
109	see Sch. 13.
110	s. 253(1), (2).
111(1), (2)	s. 253(3), (4).
111(3)	s. 253(5), 274(3)(a) (part).
111(4), (5)	s. 254.
112(1)	s. 252(1), 255(2) (see s. 274).
112(2)	IA 1986, s. 255(1).
112(3)	s. 252(2).
112(4)–(6)	s. 255(3)–(5).
112(7)(a)	s. 255(6).
112(7)(b)	s. 274(4).
113(1), (2)	s. 256(1).
113(3)–(7)	s. 256(2)–(6).
114(1)	s. 257(1), 274(5).
114(2), (3)	s. 257(2), (3).
115(1)–(6)	s. 258(1)–(6).
115(7), (8)	s. 259.
115(9)	s. 258(7), see s. 386.

Provision of former Acts	Destination
Insolvency Act 1985	
115(10)	see s. 386.
116(1)–(3)	s. 260(1)–(3).
116(4), (5)	s. 261.
116(6), (7)	s. 260(4), (5).
117	s. 262.
118	s. 263.
119(1)	s. 264.
119(2), (3)	s. 265.
119(4)–(7)	s. 266.
120(1), (2)	s. 267(1), (2).
120(3), (4)	s. 268.
120(5)	s. 269.
120(6)	s. 270.
120(7)–(9)	s. 267(3)–(5).
121	s. 271.
122	s. 272.
123(1)	s. 273(1) (part).
123(2)	s. 273(2).
123(3)–(5)	s. 274(1)–(3).
123(6)	s. 275(1), (2).
123(7)	s. 275(3).
123(8)	s. 273(1) (part).
124	s. 276.
125	s. 277.
126(1)	s. 278.
126(2)–(5)	s. 279.
127(1)	IA 1986, s. 280(1).
127(2)	s. 280(2), (3).
128	s. 281.
129	s. 282.
130(1), (2)	s. 283(1), (2).
130(3), (4)	s. 283(3).
130(5)–(7)	s. 283(4)–(6).
131	s. 284.
132	s. 285.
133	s. 286.
134(1), (2)	s. 287(1), (2).
134(3), (4)	s. 287(3).

Provision of former Acts	Destination
Insolvency Act 1985	
134(5), (6)	s. 287(4), (5).
135	s. 288.
136	s. 289.
137	s. 290.
138	s. 291.
139	s. 292.
140	s. 293.
141	s. 294.
142	s. 295.
143(1)–(3)	s. 296(1)–(3).
143(4)	s. 296(4), (5).
144(1)–(6)	s. 297(1)–(6).
144(7)	s. 297(7), (8).
145	s. 298.
146	s. 299.
147	s. 300.
148	s. 301.
149	s. 302.
150	s. 303.
151	s. 304.
152	s. 305.
153	s. 306.
154(1)–(4)	s. 307(1)–(4).
154(5)	s. 309(1)(a).
154(6)	s. 309(2).
154(7)	s. 307(5).
155(1), (2)	IA 1986, s. 308(1), (2).
155(3)	s. 309(1)(b).
155(4), (5)	s. 308(3), (4).
156	s. 310.
157	s. 311.
158	s. 312.
159	s. 313.
160(1)	s. 314(1)(b), Sch. 5, Pt. II.
160(2)	s. 314(1)(a), Sch. 5, Pt. I.
160(3)–(5)	s. 314(2)–(4).
160(6)	s. 314(5), Sch. 5, Pt. II.
160(7)–(9)	s. 314(6)–(8).

British Companies Legislation

Provision of former Acts	Destination
Insolvency Act 1985	
161(1)–(4)	s. 315(1)–(4).
161(5)	s. 316.
161(6), (7)	s. 317.
161(8)	s. 318.
161(9)	s. 319.
161(10)	s. 315(5).
162(1)–(4)	s. 320(1)–(4).
162(5)–(8)	s. 321.
162(9)–(10)	s. 320(3), (6).
163	s. 322.
164	s. 323.
165(1)–(4)	s. 324.
165(5), (6)	s. 325.
165(7)	s. 326(1).
165(8)	s. 326(2), (3).
165(9)	s. 327.
166(1)–(5).	s. 328(1)–(5).
166(6)	s. 329.
166(7)	s. 328(6).
167	s. 330.
168(1), (2)	s. 331(2), (3).
168(3)	s. 332.
168(4)	s. 331(4).
169	s. 333.
170(1)–(3)	s. 334.
170(4)–(9)	s. 335.
171	IA 1986, s. 336.
172	s. 337.
173	s. 338.
174(1)	s. 339(1), (2), 340(1), (2).
174(2)	s. 339(3).
174(3)–(6)	s. 340(3)–(6).
174(7)–(11)	s. 341.
174(12)	s. 341(1)(b) (part), 341(2) (part).
175	s. 342.
176	s. 343.
177(1)	s. 344(1), (2).
177(2), (3)	s. 344(3), (4).

[The next page is 58,301]

Provision of former Acts	Destination
Insolvency Act 1985	
178(1)	s. 345(1), (2).
178(2), (3)	s. 345(3), (4).
179	s. 346.
180	s. 347.
181	s. 348.
182	s. 349.
183(1)–(3)	s. 350(1)–(3).
183(4)	s. 352, see s. 353–359.
183(5), (6)	s. 350(4), (5).
184(1)	s. 353(1).
184(2)–(4)	s. 354.
184(5)	s. 351(a).
185	s. 355.
186	s. 356.
187(1)	s. 357(1), (3).
187(2)	s. 358.
187(3)(a)	s. 351(a).
187(3)(b)	s. 357(2).
188	s. 359.
189	s. 360.
190	s. 361.
191	s. 362.
192	(see relevant entries in Sch. 10.)
193	IA 1986, s. 363.
194	s. 364.
195	s. 365.
196(1)	IA 1986, s. 366(1).
196(2)	s. 366(2)–(4).
196(3)	s. 367(4).
196(4)–(6)	s. 367(1)–(3).
196(7)	s. 368.
197	s. 369.
198	s. 370.
199	s. 371.
200(1)–(3)	s. 372(1)–(3).
200(4)	s. 372(4), 5(b), (c) (part).
200(5)	s. 372(5)(c) (part).
201	s. 373.

Provision of former Acts	Destination
Insolvency Act 1985	
202	s. 374.
203	s. 375.
204	s. 376.
205	s. 377.
206	s. 378.
207(1)–(4)	s. 412(1)–(4).
207(5)	s. 412(5), 415(7).
208(1)	s. 415(1), (2).
208(2)–(5)	s. 415(3)–(6).
209(1)	s. 384(2), 418(1).
209(2), (3)	s. 418(2), (3).
210	s. 379.
211(1)	s. 381, 382(1), 383(1), 384(1), 385(1).
211(2), (3)	s. 382(2), (3).
211(4)	s. 385(2).
211(5)–(7)	s. 383(2)–(4).
212(1)	s. 423(2), (3).
212(2)	s. 424.
212(3)	s. 423(1).
212(4)–(6)	s. 425(1)–(3).
212(7)	s. 423(4), 425(4).
213(1)	s. 426(1), (2).
213(2)–(10)	s. 426(3)–(11).
214	s. 427.
215, 216	(amending provisions).
217(1)–(3)	s. 428.
217(4), 218–220	(amending provisions).
221(1)	s. 429(1), (2).
221(2)	CDDA 1986, s. 12.
221(3), (4)	IA 1986, s. 429(3), (4).
221(5)	s. 429(5), Sch. 10.
222(1), (2)	s. 399(1), (2) see also CDDA 1986, s. 21.
222(3)	s. 399(3), (4).
222(4)–(6)	s. 399(5)–(7).
223	s. 400.
224	s. 401, see also CDDA 1986, s. 21.
225	s. 402.
226	s. 403.

Provision of former Acts	Destination
Insolvency Act 1985	
227	s. 420.
228	s. 421.
229	s. 422.
230	s. 432(2), (3).
231	s. 433, CDDA 1986, s. 20.
232	s. 436, Sch. 10 (note).
233	s. 435.
234	s. 434.
235	s. 437–439, CDDA 1986, s. 23.
236(1)	s. 444, CDDA 1986, s. 26.
236(2)	s. 443, CDDA 1986, s. 25.
236(3)–(5)	s. 440–442, CDDA 1986, s. 24.
Sch. 1	
para. 1–4	Sch. 7.
para. 5, 6	(amending provisions).
Sch. 2	CDDA 1986, Sch. 1.
Sch. 3	IA 1986, Sch. 1.
Sch. 4	
Pt. I	
para. 1	Sch. 6, para. 1, 2.
para. 2	para. 3 (part), 4, 5.
para. 3	para. 6, 7.
para. 4	para. 8.
para. 5	para. 9–11.
para. 6	para. 12.
Pt. II	
para. 1(1)	IA 1986, s. 386(2).
para. 1(2)	s. 387(3).
para. 1(3)	s. 387(6).
para. 2	Sch. 6, para. 3 (part).
para. 3(1), (2)	para. 13(1), (2).
para. 3(3)	para. 14(2).
para. 3(4)	para. 15.
para. 4	para. 16.
Sch. 5	Sch. 8.
Sch. 6	(amending provisions).
Sch. 7	IA 1986, Sch. 9.
Sch. 8	(amending provisions).

Provision of former Acts	Destination
Insolvency Act 1985	
Sch. 9	IA 1986, Sch. 11.
para. 1	Sch. 11, para. 21.
para. 2, 3	CDDA 1986, Sch. 2.
	para. 7, 8.
para. 4	IA 1986, s. 214(2) (part).
para. 5	s. 216(1) (part).
para. 6–8	Sch. 11, para. 1–3.
para. 9(1), (2)	para. 4, 5.
para. 9(3)–(5)	para. 6(1)–(4).
para. 9(6), (7)	para. 7, 8.
para. 9(8)	para. 6(5).
para. 10–14	para. 9–13.
para. 15	para. 14(1), (2).
para. 16(1)–(3)	para. 14(3)–(5).
para. 17	para. 14(6).
para. 18–22	para. 15–19.
para. 23	
para. 24	para. 20.
Sch. 10	see Sch. 12.

COMPANY DIRECTORS DISQUALIFICATION ACT 1986

Table of Contents

For a CCH Table of Destinations, indicating references in the former legislation (the *Insolvency Act* 1985 and certain provisions of the *Companies Act* 1985) and the corresponding references in the new legislation (the *Insolvency Act* 1986 and the *Company Directors Disqualification Act* 1986), see p. 58,201.

[The next page is 59,051]

COMPANY DIRECTORS DISQUALIFICATION ACT 1986

(1986 Chapter 46)

ARRANGEMENT OF SECTIONS

[The next page is 59,101]

COMPANY DIRECTORS DISQUALIFICATION ACT 1986

(1986 Chapter 46)

An Act to consolidate certain enactments relating to the disqualification of persons from being directors of companies, and from being otherwise concerned with a company's affairs.

[25th July 1986]

PRELIMINARY

SEC. 1 Disqualification orders: general

1(1) [Disqualification order] In the circumstances specified below in this Act a court may, and under section 6 shall, make against a person a disqualification order, that is to say an order that he shall not, without leave of the court—

- (a) be a director of a company, or
- (b) be a liquidator or administrator of a company, or
- (c) be a receiver or manager of a company's property, or
- (d) in any way, whether directly or indirectly, be concerned or take part in the promotion, formation or management of a company,

for a specified period beginning with the date of the order.

1(2) [Maximum, minimum periods] In each section of this Act which gives to a court power or, as the case may be, imposes on it the duty to make a disqualification order there is specified the maximum (and, in section 6, the minimum) period of disqualification which may or (as the case may be) must be imposed by means of the order.

1(3) [Where two orders] Where a disqualification order is made against a person who is already subject to such an order, the periods specified in those orders shall run concurrently.

1(4) [Criminal grounds] A disqualification order may be made on grounds which are or include matters other than criminal convictions, notwithstanding that the person in respect of whom it is to be made may be criminally liable in respect of those matters.

DISQUALIFICATION FOR GENERAL MISCONDUCT IN CONNECTION WITH COMPANIES

SEC. 2 Disqualification on conviction of indictable offence

2(1) [Court's power] The court may make a disqualification order against a person where he is convicted of an indictable offence (whether on indictment or summarily) in connection with the promotion, formation, management or liquidation of a company, or with the receivership or management of a company's property.

2(2) ["The court"] "The court" for this purpose means—

(a) any court having jurisdiction to wind up the company in relation to which the offence was committed, or

(b) the court by or before which the person is convicted of the offence, or

(c) in the case of a summary conviction in England and Wales, any other magistrates' court acting for the same petty sessions area;

and for the purposes of this section the definition of **"indictable offence"** in Schedule 1 to the Interpretation Act 1978 applies for Scotland as it does for England and Wales.

2(3)   **[Maximum period]**   The maximum period of disqualification under this section is—

(a) where the disqualification order is made by a court of summary jurisdiction, 5 years, and

(b) in any other case, 15 years.

SEC. 3   Disqualification for persistent breaches of companies legislation

3(1)   **[Court's power]**   The court may make a disqualification order against a person where it appears to it that he has been persistently in default in relation to provisions of the companies legislation requiring any return, account or other document to be filed with, delivered or sent, or notice of any matter to be given, to the registrar of companies.

3(2)   **[Conclusive proof of default]**   On an application to the court for an order to be made under this section, the fact that a person has been persistently in default in relation to such provisions as are mentioned above may (without prejudice to its proof in any other manner) be conclusively proved by showing that in the 5 years ending with the date of the application he has been adjudged guilty (whether or not on the same occasion) of three or more defaults in relation to those provisions.

3(3)   **[Guilty of default under sec. 3(2)]**   A person is to be treated under subsection (2) as being adjudged guilty of a default in relation to any provision of that legislation if—

(a) he is convicted (whether on indictment or summarily) of an offence consisting in a contravention of or failure to comply with that provision (whether on his own part or on the part of any company), or

(b) a default order is made against him, that is to say an order under any of the following provisions—

    (i) section 242(4) of the Companies Act (order requiring delivery of company accounts),

    (ii) section 713 of that Act (enforcement of company's duty to make returns),

    (iii) section 41 of the Insolvency Act (enforcement of receiver's or manager's duty to make returns), or

    (iv) section 170 of that Act (corresponding provision for liquidator in winding up),

    in respect of any such contravention of or failure to comply with that provision (whether on his own part or on the part of any company).

    CCH Editions Limited
BCL BCL13$135A

History
In s. 3(3)(b)(i) the words "section 242(4)" substituted for the former words "section 244" by CA 1989, s. 23 and Sch. 10, para. 35(1), (2)(a) as from 1 April 1990 subject to transitional and saving provisions (see S.I. 1990 No. 355 (C.13), art. 3, Sch. 1 and also art. 6–9).

Note
prospective insertion of new s. 3(3)(b)(ia) by CA 1989, s. 23 and Sch. 10, para. 35(1), (2)(b).

3(4) **["The court"]** In this section **"the court"** means any court having jurisdiction to wind up any of the companies in relation to which the offence or other default has been or is alleged to have been committed.

3(5) **[Maximum period]** The maximum period of disqualification under this section is 5 years.

SEC. 4 Disqualification for fraud, etc., in winding up

4(1) **[Court's power]** The court may make a disqualification order against a person if, in the course of the winding up of a company, it appears that he—

   (a) has been guilty of an offence for which he is liable (whether he has been convicted or not) under section 458 of the Companies Act (fraudulent trading), or

   (b) has otherwise been guilty, while an officer or liquidator of the company or receiver or manager of its property, of any fraud in relation to the company or of any breach of his duty as such officer, liquidator, receiver or manager.

4(2) **[Definitions]** In this section **"the court"** means any court having jurisdiction to wind up any of the companies in relation to which the offence or other default has been or is alleged to have been committed; and **"officer"** includes a shadow director.

4(3) **[Maximum period]** The maximum period of disqualification under this section is 15 years.

SEC. 5 Disqualification on summary conviction

5(1) **[Relevant offences]** An offence counting for the purposes of this section is one of which a person is convicted (either on indictment or summarily) in consequence of a contravention of, or failure to comply with, any provision of the companies legislation requiring a return, account or other document to be filed with, delivered or sent, or notice of any matter to be given, to the registrar of companies (whether the contravention or failure is on the person's own part or on the part of any company).

5(2) **[Court's power]** Where a person is convicted of a summary offence counting for those purposes, the court by which he is convicted (or, in England and Wales, any other magistrates' court acting for the same petty sessions area) may make a disqualification order against him if the circumstances specified in the next subsection are present.

5(3) **[Circumstances in sec. 5(2)]** Those circumstances are that, during the 5 years ending with the date of the conviction, the person has had made against him, or has been convicted of, in total not less than 3 default orders and offences counting for the purposes of this section; and those offences may include that of which he is convicted as mentioned in subsection (2) and any other offence of which he is convicted on the same occasion.

5(4) **[Definitions]** For the purposes of this section—

(a) the definition of **"summary offence"** in Schedule 1 to the Interpretation Act 1978 applies for Scotland as for England and Wales, and

(b) **"default order"** means the same as in section 3(3)(b).

5(5)   **[Maximum period]**   The maximum period of disqualification under this section is 5 years.

DISQUALIFICATION FOR UNFITNESS

SEC. 6   Duty of court to disqualify unfit directors of insolvent companies

6(1)   **[Court's duty]**   The court shall make a disqualification order against a person in any case where, on an application under this section, it is satisfied—

(a) that he is or has been a director of a company which has at any time become insolvent (whether while he was a director or subsequently), and

(b) that his conduct as a director of that company (either taken alone or taken together with his conduct as a director of any other company or companies) makes him unfit to be concerned in the management of a company.

6(2)   **[Interpretation]**   For the purposes of this section and the next, a company becomes insolvent if—

(a) the company goes into liquidation at a time when its assets are insufficient for the payment of its debts and other liabilities and the expenses of the winding up,

(b) an administration order is made in relation to the company, or

(c) an administrative receiver of the company is appointed;

and references to a person's conduct as a director of any company or companies include, where that company or any of those companies has become insolvent, that person's conduct in relation to any matter connected with or arising out of the insolvency of that company.

6(3)   **[Definitions]**   In this section and the next **"the court"** means—

(a) in the case of a person who is or has been a director of a company which is being wound up by the court, the court by which the company is being wound up,

(b) in the case of a person who is or has been a director of a company which is being wound up voluntarily, any court having jurisdiction to wind up the company,

(c) in the case of a person who is or has been a director of a company in relation to which an administration order is in force, the court by which that order was made, and

(d) in any other case, the High Court or, in Scotland, the Court of Session;

and in both sections **"director"** includes a shadow director.

6(4)   **[Minimum, maximum periods]**   Under this section the minimum period of disqualification is 2 years, and the maximum period is 15 years.

Note
See important CCH Note after s. 7.

SEC. 7 Applications to court under sec. 6; reporting provisions

7(1) [Application by Secretary of State, official receiver] If it appears to the Secretary of State that it is expedient in the public interest that a disqualification order under section 6 should be made against any person, an application for the making of such an order against that person may be made—

(a) by the Secretary of State, or

(b) if the Secretary of State so directs in the case of a person who is or has been a director of a company which is being wound up by the court in England and Wales, by the official receiver.

Note
For details, see the Insolvent Companies (Disqualification of Unfit Directors) Proceedings Rules 1986 (S.I. 1986 No. 612).

7(2) [Time for application] Except with the leave of the court, an application for the making under that section of a disqualification order against any person shall not be made after the end of the period of 2 years beginning with the day on which the company of which that person is or has been a director became insolvent.

7(3) [Report to Secretary of State] If it appears to the office-holder responsible under this section, that is to say—

(a) in the case of a company which is being wound up by the court in England and Wales, the official receiver,

(b) in the case of a company which is being wound up otherwise, the liquidator,

(c) in the case of a company in relation to which an administration order is in force, the administrator, or

(d) in the case of a company of which there is an administrative receiver, that receiver,

that the conditions mentioned in section 6(1) are satisfied as respects a person who is or has been a director of that company, the office-holder shall forthwith report the matter to the Secretary of State.

Note
See sets of rules referred to in the note to s. 21(2).

7(4) [Extra information etc.] The Secretary of State or the official receiver may require the liquidator, administrator or administrative receiver of a company, or the former liquidator, administrator or administrative receiver of a company—

(a) to furnish him with such information with respect to any person's conduct as a director of the company, and

(b) to produce and permit inspection of such books, papers and other records relevant to that person's conduct as such a director,

as the Secretary of State or the official receiver may reasonably require for the purpose of determining whether to exercise, or of exercising, any function of his under this section.

Important CCH Note for s. 6, 7
A further subsection inserted by Building Societies Act 1986, s. 120 and Sch. 18, para. 17(3) as from 1 January 1987 (see S.I. 1986 No. 1560 (C. 56)) in regard to the former provision, Insolvency Act 1985, s. 12 — the insertion was intended to be s. 12(10). The new subsection should appear in the current provisions (s. 6, 7) as a result of Sch. 3, para. 6 of this Act and Interpretation Act 1978, s. 17(2)(a). The new subsection, if inserted here as s. 7(5) and revised to

take into account other relevant current provisions, would read as follows:

"**7(5)** In this section and in sections 6, 9, 10 and 15 and in sections 212 and 214 to 217 of the Insolvency Act, a reference to a company or to a director (but not a shadow director) of a company includes a reference to a building society

within the meaning of the Building Societies Act 1986 or to a director of a building society."

Note that the first words of the subsection set out in the Building Societies Act read "(10) In this section and in sections 14 to 19 . . . "

SEC. 8   Disqualification after investigation of company

8(1)   [Application by Secretary of State]   If it appears to the Secretary of State from a report made by inspectors under section 437 of the Companies Act or section 94 or 177 of the Financial Services Act 1986, or from information or documents obtained under section 447 or 448 of the Companies Act or section 105 of the Financial Services Act 1986 or section 2 of the Criminal Justice Act 1987 or section 52 of the Criminal Justice (Scotland) Act 1987 or section 83 of the Companies Act 1989, that it is expedient in the public interest that a disqualification order should be made against any person who is or has been a director or shadow director of any company, he may apply to the court for such an order to be made against that person.

History

In s. 8(1) the words "or section 94 or 177 of the Financial Services Act 1986" inserted by Financial Services Act 1986, s. 198(2)(a) as from 15 November 1986 (see S.I. 1986 No. 1940 (C. 69)) and the words "the Companies Act or section 105 of the Financial Services Act 1986" substituted for the former words "that Act" by Financial Services Act 1986, s. 198(2)(b) as from 18 December 1986 (see S.I. 1986 No. 2246 (C. 88)). In addition the words "or section 52 of the Criminal Justice (Scotland) Act 1987" inserted

by Criminal Justice (Scotland) Act 1987, s. 55(b) as from 1 January 1988 (see S.I. 1987 No. 2119 (C. 62) (S. 143)). Also inserted are the words "or section 2 of the Criminal Justice Act 1987" after the words "the Financial Services Act 1986" in the second place where they occur, by Criminal Justice Act 1988, s. 145(b) as from 12 October 1988 (see S.I. 1988 No. 1676 (C.60)). The words "or section 83 of the Companies Act 1989" inserted by CA 1989, s. 79 as from 21 February 1990 (see S.I. 1990 No. 142 (C.5), art. 4).

8(2)   [Court's power]   The court may make a disqualification order against a person where, on an application under this section, it is satisfied that his conduct in relation to the company makes him unfit to be concerned in the management of a company.

8(3)   ["The court"]   In this section **"the court"** means the High Court or, in Scotland, the Court of Session.

8(4)   [Maximum period]   The maximum period of disqualification under this section is 15 years.

SEC. 9   Matters for determining unfitness of directors

9(1)   [Matters in Sch. 1]   Where it falls to a court to determine whether a person's conduct as a director or shadow director of any particular company or companies makes him unfit to be concerned in the management of a company, the court shall, as respects his conduct as a director of that company or, as the case may be, each of those companies, have regard in particular—

(a) to the matters mentioned in Part I of Schedule 1 to this Act, and

(b) where the company has become insolvent, to the matters mentioned in Part II of that Schedule;

and references in that Schedule to the director and the company are to be read accordingly.

9(2)   [Application of sec. 6(2)]   Section 6(2) applies for the purposes of this section and Schedule 1 as it applies for the purposes of sections 6 and 7.

9(3)   [Interpretation of Sch. 1]   Subject to the next subsection, any reference in Schedule 1 to an enactment contained in the Companies Act or the Insolvency Act includes, in relation to any time before the coming into force of that enactment, the corresponding enactment in force at that time.

9(4) **[Modification of Sch. 1]** The Secretary of State may by order modify any of the provisions of Schedule 1; and such an order may contain such transitional provisions as may appear to the Secretary of State necessary or expedient.

9(5) **[Power exercisable by statutory instrument etc.]** The power to make orders under this section is exercisable by statutory instrument subject to annulment in pursuance of a resolution of either House of Parliament.

OTHER CASES OF DISQUALIFICATION

SEC. 10 Participation in wrongful trading

10(1) **[Court's power]** Where the court makes a declaration under section 213 or 214 of the Insolvency Act that a person is liable to make a contribution to a company's assets, then, whether or not an application for such an order is made by any person, the court may, if it thinks fit, also make a disqualification order against the person to whom the declaration relates.

10(2) **[Maximum period]** The maximum period of disqualification under this section is 15 years.

SEC. 11 Undischarged bankrupts

11(1) **[Offence]** It is an offence for a person who is an undischarged bankrupt to act as director of, or directly or indirectly to take part in or be concerned in the promotion, formation or management of, a company, except with the leave of the court.

11(2) **["The court"]** "The court" for this purpose is the court by which the person was adjudged bankrupt or, in Scotland, sequestration of his estates was awarded.

11(3) **[Requirements for leave of court]** In England and Wales, the leave of the court shall not be given unless notice of intention to apply for it has been served on the official receiver; and it is the latter's duty, if he is of opinion that it is contrary to the public interest that the application should be granted, to attend on the hearing of the application and oppose it.

SEC. 12 Failure to pay under county court administration order

12(1) **[Effect of sec. 12(2)]** The following has effect where a court under section 429 of the Insolvency Act revokes an administration order under Part VI of the County Courts Act 1984.

12(2) **[Restriction on person]** A person to whom that section applies by virtue of the order under section 429(2)(b) shall not, except with the leave of the court which made the order, act as director or liquidator of, or directly or indirectly take part or be concerned in the promotion, formation or management of, a company.

CONSEQUENCES OF CONTRAVENTION

SEC. 13 Criminal penalties

13 If a person acts in contravention of a disqualification order or of section 12(2), or is guilty of an offence under section 11, he is liable—

(a) on conviction on indictment, to imprisonment for not more than 2 years or a fine or both; and

(b) on summary conviction, to imprisonment for not more than 6 months or a fine not exceeding the statutory maximum, or both.

SEC. 14　Offences by body corporate

14(1)　**[Offence re officer]**　Where a body corporate is guilty of an offence of acting in contravention of a disqualification order, and it is proved that the offence occurred with the consent or connivance of, or was attributable to any neglect on the part of any director, manager, secretary or other similar officer of the body corporate, or any person who was purporting to act in any such capacity he, as well as the body corporate, is guilty of the offence and liable to be proceeded against and punished accordingly.

14(2)　**[Where managers are members]**　Where the affairs of a body corporate are managed by its members, subsection (1) applies in relation to the acts and defaults of a member in connection with his functions of management as if he were a director of the body corporate.

SEC. 15　Personal liability for company's debts where person acts while disqualified

15(1)　**[Personal liability]**　A person is personally responsible for all the relevant debts of a company if at any time—

(a) in contravention of a disqualification order or of section 11 of this Act he is involved in the management of the company, or

(b) as a person who is involved in the management of the company, he acts or is willing to act on instructions given without the leave of the court by a person whom he knows at that time to be the subject of a disqualification order or to be an undischarged bankrupt.

15(2)　**[Joint and several liability]**　Where a person is personally responsible under this section for the relevant debts of a company, he is jointly and severally liable in respect of those debts with the company and any other person who, whether under this section or otherwise, is so liable.

15(3)　**[Relevant debts of company]**　For the purposes of this section the relevant debts of a company are—

(a) in relation to a person who is personally responsible under paragraph (a) of subsection (1), such debts and other liabilities of the company as are incurred at a time when that person was involved in the management of the company, and

(b) in relation to a person who is personally responsible under paragraph (b) of that subsection, such debts and other liabilities of the company as are incurred at a time when that person was acting or was willing to act on instructions given as mentioned in that paragraph.

15(4)　**[Person involved in management]**　For the purposes of this section, a person is involved in the management of a company if he is a director of the company or if he is concerned, whether directly or indirectly, or takes part, in the management of the company.

15(5) **[Interpretation]** For the purposes of this section a person who, as a person involved in the management of a company, has at any time acted on instructions given without the leave of the court by a person whom he knew at that time to be the subject of a disqualification order or to be an undischarged bankrupt is presumed, unless the contrary is shown, to have been willing at any time thereafter to act on any instructions given by that person.

SUPPLEMENTARY PROVISIONS

SEC. 16 Application for disqualification order

16(1) **[Notice, appearance, etc.]** A person intending to apply for the making of a disqualification order by the court having jurisdiction to wind up a company shall give not less than 10 days' notice of his intention to the person against whom the order is sought; and on the hearing of the application the last-mentioned person may appear and himself give evidence or call witnesses.

16(2) **[Applicants]** An application to a court with jurisdiction to wind up companies for the making against any person of a disqualification order under any of sections 2 to 5 may be made by the Secretary of State or the official receiver, or by the liquidator or any past or present member or creditor of any company in relation to which that person has committed or is alleged to have committed an offence or other default.

16(3) **[Appearance, etc. of applicant]** On the hearing of any application under this Act made by the Secretary of State or the official receiver or the liquidator the applicant shall appear and call the attention of the court to any matters which seem to him to be relevant, and may himself give evidence or call witnesses.

SEC. 17 Application for leave under an order

17(1) **[Court]** As regards the court to which application must be made for leave under a disqualification order, the following applies—

(a) where the application is for leave to promote or form a company, it is any court with jurisdiction to wind up companies, and

(b) where the application is for leave to be a liquidator, administrator or director of, or otherwise to take part in the management of a company, or to be a receiver or manager of a company's property, it is any court having jurisdiction to wind up that company.

17(2) **[Appearance, etc. of Secretary of State et al.]** On the hearing of an application for leave made by a person against whom a disqualification order has been made on the application of the Secretary of State, the official receiver or the liquidator, the Secretary of State, official receiver or liquidator shall appear and call the attention of the court to any matters which seem to him to be relevant, and may himself give evidence or call witnesses.

SEC. 18 Register of disqualification orders

18(1) **[Regulations re furnishing information]** The Secretary of State may make regulations requiring officers of courts to furnish him with such particulars as the regulations may specify of cases in which—

    (a) a disqualification order is made, or

    (b) any action is taken by a court in consequence of which such an order is varied or ceases to be in force, or

    (c) leave is granted by a court for a person subject to such an order to do any thing which otherwise the order prohibits him from doing;

and the regulations may specify the time within which, and the form and manner in which, such particulars are to be furnished.

Note
See the Companies (Disqualification Orders) Regulations
1986 (S.I. 1986 No. 2067).

18(2)   **[Register of orders]**   The Secretary of State shall, from the particulars so furnished, continue to maintain the register of orders, and of cases in which leave has been granted as mentioned in subsection (1)(c), which was set up by him under section 29 of the Companies Act 1976 and continued under section 301 of the Companies Act 1985.

18(3)   **[Deletion of orders no longer in force]**   When an order of which entry is made in the register ceases to be in force, the Secretary of State shall delete the entry from the register and all particulars relating to it which have been furnished to him under this section or any previous corresponding provision.

18(4)   **[Inspection of register]**   The register shall be open to inspection on payment of such fee as may be specified by the Secretary of State in regulations.

18(5)   **[Regulations by statutory instrument etc.]**   Regulations under this section shall be made by statutory instrument subject to annulment in pursuance of a resolution of either House of Parliament.

SEC. 19   Special savings from repealed enactments

19   Schedule 2 to this Act has effect—

    (a) in connection with certain transitional cases arising under sections 93 and 94 of the Companies Act 1981, so as to limit the power to make a disqualification order, or to restrict the duration of an order, by reference to events occurring or things done before those sections came into force,

    (b) to preserve orders made under section 28 of the Companies Act 1976 (repealed by the Act of 1981), and

    (c) to preclude any applications for a disqualification order under section 6 or 8, where the relevant company went into liquidation before 28th April 1986.

MISCELLANEOUS AND GENERAL

SEC. 20   Admissibility in evidence of statements

20   In any proceedings (whether or not under this Act), any statement made in pursuance of a requirement imposed by or under sections 6 to 10, 15 or 19(c) of, or Schedule 1 to, this Act, or by or under rules made for the purposes of this Act under the Insolvency Act, may be used in evidence against any person making or concurring in making the statement.

SEC. 21   Interaction with Insolvency Act

21(1)   [Reference to official receiver]   References in this Act to the official receiver, in relation to the winding up of a company or the bankruptcy of an individual, are to any person who, by virtue of section 399 of the Insolvency Act, is authorised to act as the official receiver in relation to that winding up or bankruptcy; and, in accordance with section 401(2) of that Act, references in this Act to an official receiver includes a person appointed as his deputy.

21(2)   [Pt. I to VII of IA]   Sections 6 to 10, 15, 19(c) and 20 of, and Schedule 1 to, this Act are deemed included in Parts I to VII of the Insolvency Act for the purposes of the following sections of that Act—

  section 411 (power to make insolvency rules);

  section 414 (fees orders);

  section 420 (orders extending provisions about insolvent companies to insolvent partnerships);

  section 422 (modification of such provisions in their application to recognised banks).

History
In s. 21(2) the words "and section 431 (summary proceedings) formerly appearing at the end" repealed by CA 1989, s. 212 and Sch. 24 as from 1 March 1990 (see S.I. 1990 No. 142 (C.5), art. 7(d)).
Note
In regard to the entry for s. 411 see the Insolvent Companies (Reports on Conduct of Directors) No. 2 Rules 1986 (S.I.

1986 No. 2134), the Insolvent Companies (Reports on Conduct of Directors) (No. 2) (Scotland) Rules 1986 (S.I. 1986 No. 1916 (S. 140)) and the Insolvent Companies (Disqualification of Unfit Directors) Proceedings Rules 1987 (S.I. 1987 No. 2023).
In regard to the entry for s. 420 see the Insolvent Partnerships Order 1986 (S.I. 1986 No. 2142).

21(3)   [Application of IA, sec. 434]   Section 434 of that Act (Crown application) applies to sections 6 to 10, 15, 19(c) and 20 of, and Schedule 1 to, this Act as it does to the provisions of that Act which are there mentioned.

21(4)   [Summary proceedings in Scotland]   For the purposes of summary proceedings in Scotland, section 431 of that Act applies to summary proceedings for an offence under section 11 or 13 of this Act as it applies to summary proceedings for an offence under Parts I to VII of that Act.

History
S. 21(4) added by CA 1989, s. 208 as from 1 March 1990 (see S.I. 1990 No. 142 (C.5), art. 7(a)).

SEC. 22   Interpretation

22(1)   [Effect]   This section has effect with respect to the meaning of expressions used in this Act, and applies unless the context otherwise requires.

22(2)   ["Company"]   The expression **"company"**—

  (a) in section 11, includes an unregistered company, a building society (within the meaning of the Building Societies Act 1986) and a company incorporated outside Great Britain which has an established place of business in Great Britain, and

  (b) elsewhere, includes any company which may be wound up under Part V of the Insolvency Act and a building society (within the meaning of the Building Societies Act 1986).

History
In s. 22(2) the words ", a building society (within the meaning of the Building Societies Act 1986)" in para. (a) and the words "and a building society (within the meaning of the Building Societies Act 1986)" in para. (b) inserted by Building Societies Act 1986, s. 120 and Sch. 18, para. 16 as from 1 January 1987 (see S.I. 1986 No. 1560 (C. 56)) in regard to the former provisions, s. 302(4) and s. 295(3) respectively of Companies Act 1985. These words included in the current provisions as result of Sch. 3, para. 6 of this Act and of Interpretation Act 1978, s. 17(2)(a).

22(3)   [Application of IA, sec. 247, 251]   Section 247 in Part VII of the Insolvency Act (interpretation for the first Group of Parts of that Act) applies as regards references to a company's insolvency and to its going into liquidation; and **"administrative receiver"** has the meaning given by section 251 of that Act.

22(4)   ["Director"]   **"Director"** includes any person occupying the position of director, by whatever name called, and in sections 6 to 9 includes a shadow director.

22(5)   ["Shadow director"]   **"Shadow director"**, in relation to a company, means a person in accordance with whose directions or instructions the directors of the company are accustomed to act (but so that a person is not deemed a shadow director by reason only that the directors act on advice given by him in a professional capacity).

22(6)   [Application of CA, sec. 740, 744]   Section 740 of the Companies Act applies as regards the meaning of **"body corporate"**; and **"officer"** has the meaning given by section 744 of that Act.

22(7)   [References to legislation]   In references to legislation other than this Act—

>   **"the Companies Act"** means the Companies Act 1985;

>   **"the Companies Acts"** has the meaning given by section 744 of that Act; and

>   **"the Insolvency Act"** means the Insolvency Act 1986;

and in sections 3(1) and 5(1) of this Act **"the companies legislation"** means the Companies Acts (except the Insider Dealing Act), Parts I to VII of the Insolvency Act and, in Part XV of that Act, sections 411, 413, 414, 416 and 417.

22(8)   [References to former legislation]   Any reference to provisions, or a particular provision, of the Companies Acts or the Insolvency Act includes the corresponding provisions or provision of the former Companies Acts (as defined by section 735(1)(c) of the Companies Act, but including also that Act itself) or, as the case may be, the Insolvency Act 1985.

22(9)   [Application of CA, Pt. XXVI]   Any expression for whose interpretation provision is made by Part XXVI of the Companies Act (and not by subsections (3) to (8) above) is to be construed in accordance with that provision.

SEC. 23   Transitional provisions, savings, repeals

23(1)   [Sch. 3]   The transitional provisions and savings in Schedule 3 to this Act have effect, and are without prejudice to anything in the Interpretation Act 1978 with regard to the effect of repeals.

23(2)   [Sch. 4]   The enactments specified in the second column of Schedule 4 to this Act are repealed to the extent specified in the third column of that Schedule.

SEC. 24   Extent

24(1)   [England, Wales, Scotland]   This Act extends to England and Wales and to Scotland.

24(2)   [Northern Ireland]   Nothing in this Act extends to Northern Ireland.

SEC. 25　Commencement

25　This Act comes into force simultaneously with the Insolvency Act 1986.

Note
The relevant date is 29 December 1986 — see Insolvency
Act 1986, s. 443 and S.I. 1986 No. 1924 (C. 71).

SEC. 26　Citation

26　This Act may be cited as the Company Directors Disqualification Act 1986.

SCHEDULES

Schedule 1 — Matters for Determining Unfitness of Directors

Section 9

Part I — Matters Applicable in all Cases

1　Any misfeasance or breach of any fiduciary or other duty by the director in relation to the company.

2　Any misapplication or retention by the director of, or any conduct by the director giving rise to an obligation to account for, any money or other property of the company.

3　The extent of the director's responsibility for the company entering into any transaction liable to be set aside under Part XVI of the Insolvency Act (provisions against debt avoidance).

4　The extent of the director's responsibility for any failure by the company to comply with any of the following provisions of the Companies Act, namely—

(a)　section 221 (companies to keep accounting records);

(b)　section 222 (where and for how long records to be kept);

(c)　section 288 (register of directors and secretaries);

(d)　section 352 (obligation to keep and enter up register of members);

(e)　section 353 (location of register of members);

(f)　sections 363 and 364 (company's duty to make annual return);

(g)　section 365 (time for completion of annual return); and

(h)　sections 399 and 415 (company's duty to register charges it creates).

5　The extent of the director's responsibility for any failure by the directors of the company to comply with—

(a)　section 226 or 227 of the Companies Act (duty to prepare annual accounts), or

(b)　section 233 of that Act (approval and signature of accounts).

History
Para. 5 substituted by CA 1989, s. 23 and Sch. 10, para. 35(1), (3) as from 1 April 1990 subject to transitional and saving provisions (see S.I. 1990 No. 355 (C.13), art. 3, Sch. 1 and also art. 6–9); para. 5 formerly read as follows:

"**5** The extent of the director's responsibility for any

failure by the directors of the company to comply with section 227 (directors' duty to prepare annual accounts) or section 238 (signing of balance sheet and documents to be annexed) of the Companies Act."

5A In the application of this Schedule to the directors of a building society, references to sections of the Insolvency Act or of the Companies Act other than sections which apply to building societies or their directors in any event, whether by virtue of the Insolvency Act or of the Building Societies Act 1986, shall be construed as references to the corresponding provisions (if any) of the Building Societies Act 1986.

History
Para. 5A inserted by Building Societies Act 1986, s. 120 and Sch. 18, para. 17(4) as from 1 January 1987 (see S.I. 1986 No. 1560 (C. 56)) in regard to the former Sch. 2 of Insolvency Act 1985. This paragraph included in the current schedule as result of Sch. 3, para. 6 of this Act and of

Interpretation Act 1978, s. 17(2)(a). Reference to "This Act or of the 1985 Act" and to "this Act" replaced by CCH with references to "the Insolvency Act or of the Companies Act" and to "the Insolvency Act".

Part II — Matters Applicable Where Company Has Become Insolvent

6 The extent of the director's responsibility for the causes of the company becoming insolvent.

7 The extent of the director's responsibility for any failure by the company to supply any goods or services which have been paid for (in whole or in part).

8 The extent of the director's responsibility for the company entering into any transaction or giving any preference, being a transaction or preference—

(a) liable to be set aside under section 127 or sections 238 to 240 of the Insolvency Act, or

(b) challengeable under section 242 or 243 of that Act or under any rule of law in Scotland.

9 The extent of the director's responsibility for any failure by the directors of the company to comply with section 98 of the Insolvency Act (duty to call creditors' meeting in creditors' voluntary winding up).

10 Any failure by the director to comply with any obligation imposed on him by or under any of the following provisions of the Insolvency Act—

(a) section 22 (company's statement of affairs in administration);

(b) section 47 (statement of affairs to administrative receiver);

(c) section 66 (statement of affairs in Scottish receivership);

(d) section 99 (directors' duty to attend meeting; statement of affairs in creditors' voluntary winding up);

(e) section 131 (statement of affairs in winding up by the court);

(f) section 234 (duty of any one with company property to deliver it up);

(g) section 235 (duty to co-operate with liquidator, etc.).

Schedule 2— Savings from Companies Act 1981 sec. 93, 94, and Insolvency Act 1985 Schedule 9

Section 19

1   Sections 2 and 4(1)(b) do not apply in relation to anything done before 15th June 1982 by a person in his capacity as liquidator of a company or as receiver or manager of a company's property.

2   Subject to paragraph 1—

(a)   section 2 applies in a case where a person is convicted on indictment of an offence which he committed (and, in the case of a continuing offence, has ceased to commit) before 15th June 1982; but in such a case a disqualification order under that section shall not be made for a period in excess of 5 years;

(b)   that section does not apply in a case where a person is convicted summarily—

(i)   in England and Wales, if he had consented so to be tried before that date, or

(ii)   in Scotland, if the summary proceedings commenced before that date.

3   Subject to paragraph 1, section 4 applies in relation to an offence committed or other thing done before 15th June 1982; but a disqualification order made on the grounds of such an offence or other thing done shall not be made for a period in excess of 5 years.

4   The powers of a court under section 5 are not exercisable in a case where a person is convicted of an offence which he committed (and, in the case of a continuing offence, had ceased to commit) before 15th June 1982.

5   For purposes of section 3(1) and section 5, no account is to be taken of any offence which was committed, or any default order which was made, before 1st June 1977.

6   An order made under section 28 of the Companies Act 1976 has effect as if made under section 3 of this Act; and an application made before 15th June 1982 for such an order is to be treated as an application for an order under the section last mentioned.

7   Where—

(a)   an application is made for a disqualification order under section 6 of this Act by virtue of paragraph (a) of subsection (2) of that section, and

(b)   the company in question went into liquidation before 28th April 1986 (the coming into force of the provision replaced by section 6),

the court shall not make an order under that section unless it could have made a disqualification order under section 300 of the Companies Act as it had effect immediately before the date specified in sub-paragraph (b) above.

8   An application shall not be made under section 8 of this Act in relation to a report made or information or documents obtained before 28th April 1986.

Schedule 3 — Transitional Provisions and Savings

Section 23(1)

1   In this Schedule, **"the former enactments"** means so much of the Companies Act, and so much of the Insolvency Act, as is repealed and replaced by this Act; and **"the appointed day"** means the day on which this Act comes into force.

2   So far as anything done or treated as done under or for the purposes of any provision of the former enactments could have been done under or for the purposes of the corresponding provision of this Act, it is not invalidated by the repeal of that provision but has effect as if done under or for the purposes of the corresponding provision; and any order, regulation, rule or other instrument made or having effect under any provision of the former enactments shall, insofar as its effect is preserved by this paragraph, be treated for all purposes as made and having effect under the corresponding provision.

3   Where any period of time specified in a provision of the former enactments is current immediately before the appointed day, this Act has effect as if the corresponding provision had been in force when the period began to run; and (without prejudice to the foregoing) any period of time so specified and current is deemed for the purposes of this Act—

(a) to run from the date or event from which it was running immediately before the appointed day, and

(b) to expire (subject to any provision of this Act for its extension) whenever it would have expired if this Act had not been passed;

and any rights, priorities, liabilities, reliefs, obligations, requirements, powers, duties or exemptions dependent on the beginning, duration or end of such a period as above mentioned shall be under this Act as they were or would have been under the former enactments.

4   Where in any provision of this Act there is a reference to another such provision, and the first-mentioned provision operates, or is capable of operating, in relation to things done or omitted, or events occurring or not occurring, in the past (including in particular past acts of compliance with any enactment, failures of compliance, contraventions, offences and convictions of offences) the reference to the other provision is to be read as including a reference to the corresponding provision of the former enactments.

5   Offences committed before the appointed day under any provision of the former enactments may, notwithstanding any repeal by this Act, be prosecuted and punished after that day as if this Act had not passed.

6   A reference in any enactment, instrument or document (whether express or implied, and in whatever phraseology) to a provision of the former enactments (including the corresponding provision of any yet earlier enactment) is to be read, where necessary to retain for the enactment, instrument or document the same force and effect as it would have had but for the passing of this Act, as, or as including, a reference to the corresponding provision by which it is replaced in this Act.

[The next page is 59,801]

Schedule 4 — Repeals

Section 23(2)

Chapter	Short title	Extent of repeal
1985 c. 6.	The Companies Act 1985.	Sections 295 to 299. Section 301. Section 302. Schedule 12. In Schedule 24, the entries relating to sections 295(7) and 302(1).
1985 c. 65.	The Insolvency Act 1985.	Sections 12 to 14. Section 16. Section 18. Section 108(2). Schedule 2. In Schedule 6, paragraphs 1, 2, 7 and 14. In Schedule 9, paragraphs 2 and 3.

TABLE OF DERIVATIONS

Note: The following abbreviations are used in this Table:—

"CA" = The Companies Act 1985 (c. 6).
"IA" = The Insolvency Act 1985 (c. 65).

Provision	Derivation
1	CA sec. 295(1), (2), (4); IA Sch. 6 para. 1(1)–(3).
2	CA ss. 295(2), 296.
3	CA ss. 295(2), 297.
4	CA ss. 295(2), 298.
5	CA ss. 295(2), 299.
6	CA sec. 295(2); IA ss. 12(1), (2), (7)–(9), 108(2).
7	IA sec. 12(3)–(6).
8	CA sec. 295(2); IA ss. 12(9), 13, 108(2).
9	IA ss. 12(9), 14.
10	CA sec. 295(2); IA ss. 16, 108(2).
11	CA sec. 302.
12	IA sec. 221(2).
13	CA ss. 295(7), 302(1), Sch. 24.
14	CA sec. 733(1)–(3); IA Sch. 6 para. 7.
15	IA sec. 18(1) (part), (2)–(6).
16	CA sec. 295(6) (part), Sch. 12 paras. 1–3; IA sec. 108(2), Sch. 6 para. 1(4).
17	CA sec. 295(6) (part), Sch. 12 paras. 4, 5; IA sec. 108(2), Sch. 6 paras. 1(4), 14.
18	CA sec. 301; IA sec. 108(2), Sch. 6 para. 2.
19	CA sec. 295(6); and see Sch. 2.
20	IA sec. 231 (part).
21	IA ss. 106, 107, 108(1), (2), 222(1), 224(2), 227, 229, 234.
22	IA sec. 108(1)–(4).
23	—
24	IA sec. 236(4)(*a*).
25	—
26	—
Sch. 1	IA Sch. 2.
Sch. 2	CA Sch. 12 Pt. III; IA Sch. 9 paras. 2, 3.
Sch. 3	—
Sch. 4	—

FINANCIAL SERVICES ACT 1986

Table of Contents

[The next page is 60,011]

FINANCIAL SERVICES ACT 1986

(1986 Chapter 60)

ARRANGEMENT OF SECTIONS

PART I — REGULATION OF INVESTMENT BUSINESS

CHAPTER I — PRELIMINARY

CHAPTER II — RESTRICTION ON CARRYING ON BUSINESS

CHAPTER III — AUTHORISED PERSONS

Members of recognised self-regulating organisations

Persons authorised by recognised professional bodies

Insurance companies

Friendly societies

SECTION

SCHEDULES

[The next page is 60,051]

FINANCIAL SERVICES ACT 1986

(1986 Chapter 60)

An Act to regulate the carrying on of investment business; to make related provision with respect to insurance business and business carried on by friendly societies; to make new provision with respect to the official listing of securities, offers of unlisted securities, takeover offers and insider dealing; to make provision as to the disclosure of information obtained under enactments relating to fair trading, banking, companies and insurance; to make provision for securing reciprocity with other countries in respect of facilities for the provision of financial services; and for connected purposes.

[*7th November 1986*]

PART I — REGULATION OF INVESTMENT BUSINESS

Chapter I — Preliminary

SEC. 1 Investments and investment business

1(1) **["Investment"]** In this Act, unless the context otherwise requires, **"investment"** means any asset, right or interest falling within any paragraph in Part I of Schedule 1 to this Act.

1(2) **["Investment business"]** In this Act **"investment business"** means the business of engaging in one or more of the activities which fall within the paragraphs in Part II of that Schedule and are not excluded by Part III of that Schedule.

1(3) **[Carrying an investment business in the UK]** For the purposes of this Act a person carries on investment business in the United Kingdom if he—

(a) carries on investment business from a permanent place of business maintained by him in the United Kingdom; or

(b) engages in the United Kingdom in one or more of the activities which fall within the paragraphs in Part II of that Schedule and are not excluded by Part III or IV of that Schedule and his doing so constitutes the carrying on by him of a business in the United Kingdom.

1(4) **[Construction of Sch. 1]** Parts I to IV of that Schedule shall be construed in accordance with Part V.

SEC. 2 Power to extend or restrict scope of Act

2(1) **[Power of Secretary of State]** The Secretary of State may by order amend Schedule 1 to this Act so as—

(a) to extend or restrict the meaning of investment for the purposes of all or any provisions of this Act; or

(b) to extend or restrict for the purposes of all or any of those provisions the activities that are to constitute the carrying on of investment business or the carrying on of such business in the United Kingdom.

2(2)   [Amendments for sec. 2(1)(b)]   The amendments that may be made for the purposes of subsection (1)(b) above include amendments conferring powers on the Secretary of State, whether by extending or modifying any provision of that Schedule which confers such powers or by adding further such provisions.

2(3)   [Approval of order by Parliament]   An order under this section which extends the meaning of investment or extends the activities that are to constitute the carrying on of investment business or the carrying on of such business in the United Kingdom shall be laid before Parliament after being made and shall cease to have effect at the end of the period of twenty-eight days beginning with the day on which it is made (but without prejudice to anything done under the order or to the making of a new order) unless before the end of that period the order is approved by a resolution of each House of Parliament.

2(4)   [Period in sec. 2(3)]   In reckoning the period mentioned in subsection (3) above no account shall be taken of any time during which Parliament is dissolved or prorogued or during which both Houses are adjourned for more than four days.

2(5)   [Annulment of order by Parliament]   Any order under this section to which subsection (3) above does not apply shall be subject to annulment in pursuance of a resolution of either House of Parliament.

2(6)   [Transitional provisions]   An order under this section may contain such transitional provisions as the Secretary of State thinks necessary or expedient.

Chapter II — Restriction on Carrying on Business

SEC. 3   Persons entitled to carry on investment business

3   No person shall carry on, or purport to carry on, investment business in the United Kingdom unless he is an authorised person under Chapter III or an exempted person under Chapter IV of this Part of this Act.

SEC. 4   Offences

4(1)   [Offence penalty]   Any person who carries on, or purports to carry on, investment business in contravention of section 3 above shall be guilty of an offence and liable—

(a) on conviction on indictment, to imprisonment for a term not exceeding two years or to a fine or to both;

(b) on summary conviction, to imprisonment for a term not exceeding six months or to a fine not exceeding the statutory maximum or to both.

4(2) **[Defence]** In proceedings brought against any person for an offence under this section it shall be a defence for him to prove that he took all reasonable precautions and exercised all due diligence to avoid the commission of the offence.

SEC. 5 Agreements made by or through unauthorised persons

5(1) **[Unenforceable investment agreements]** Subject to subsection (3) below, any agreement to which this subsection applies—

> (a) which is entered into by a person in the course of carrying on investment business in contravention of section 3 above; or
>
> (b) which is entered into—
>
>> (i) by a person who is an authorised person or an exempted person in respect of the investment business in the course of which he enters into the agreement; but
>>
>> (ii) in consequence of anything said or done by a person in the course of carrying on investment business in contravention of that section,

shall be unenforceable against the other party; and that party shall be entitled to recover any money or other property paid or transferred by him under the agreement, together with compensation for any loss sustained by him as a result of having parted with it.

5(2) **[Compensation under sec. 5(1)]** The compensation recoverable under subsection (1) above shall be such as the parties may agree or as the court may, on the application of either party, determine.

5(3) **[Condition for court allowing agreement]** A court may allow an agreement to which subsection (1) above applies to be enforced or money and property paid or transferred under it to be retained if it is satisfied—

> (a) in a case within paragraph (a) of that subsection, that the person mentioned in that paragraph reasonably believed that his entering into the agreement did not constitute a contravention of section 3 above;
>
> (b) in a case within paragraph (b) of that subsection, that the person mentioned in sub-paragraph (i) of that paragraph did not know that the agreement was entered into as mentioned in sub-paragraph (ii) of that paragraph; and
>
> (c) in either case, that it is just and equitable for the agreement to be enforced or, as the case may be, for the money or property paid or transferred under it to be retained.

5(4) **[Where agreement not performed]** Where a person elects not to perform an agreement which by virtue of this section is unenforceable against him or by virtue of this section recovers money paid or other property transferred by him under an agreement he shall repay any money and return any other property received by him under the agreement.

5(5) **[Where property has passed to third party]** Where any property transferred under an agreement to which this section applies has passed to a third party the references to that property in subsections (1), (3) and (4) above shall be construed as references to its value at the time of its transfer under the agreement.

5(6)   [Effect of contravention of sec. 3]   A contravention of section 3 above shall not make an agreement illegal or invalid to any greater extent than is provided in this section.

5(7)   [Application of sec. 5(1)]   Subsection (1) above applies to any agreement the making or performance of which by the person seeking to enforce it or from whom money or other property is recoverable under this section constitutes an activity which falls within any paragraph of Part II of Schedule 1 to this Act and is not excluded by Part III or IV of that Schedule.

SEC. 6   Injunctions and restitution orders

6(1)   [Power of court]   If, on the application of the Secretary of State, the court is satisfied—

  (a) that there is a reasonable likelihood that a person will contravene section 3 above; or

  (b) that any person has contravened that section and that there is a reasonable likelihood that the contravention will continue or be repeated,

the court may grant an injunction restraining the contravention or, in Scotland, an interdict prohibiting the contravention.

6(2)   [Power of court where sec. 3 contravened]   If, on the application of the Secretary of State, the court is satisfied that a person has entered into any transaction in contravention of section 3 above the court may order that person and any other person who appears to the court to have been knowingly concerned in the contravention to take such steps as the court may direct for restoring the parties to the position in which they were before the transaction was entered into.

6(3)   [Power of court to make sec. 6(4), (5) order]   The court may, on the application of the Secretary of State, make an order under subsection (4) below or, in relation to Scotland, under subsection (5) below if satisfied that a person has been carrying on investment business in contravention of section 3 above and—

  (a) that profits have accrued to that person as a result of carrying on that business; or

  (b) that one or more investors have suffered loss or been otherwise adversely affected as a result of his contravention of section 47 or 56 below or failure to act substantially in accordance with any of the rules or regulations made under Chapter V of this Part of this Act.

6(4)   [Order re payment into court, etc.]   The court may under this subsection order the person concerned to pay into court, or appoint a receiver to recover from him, such sum as appears to the court to be just having regard—

  (a) in a case within paragraph (a) of subsection (3) above, to the profits appearing to the court to have accrued;

  (b) in a case within paragraph (b) of that subsection, to the extent of the loss or other adverse effect; or

  (c) in a case within both paragraphs (a) and (b) of that subsection, to the profits and to the extent of the loss or other adverse effect.

6(5)　**[Order re payment to applicant]**　The court may under this subsection order the person concerned to pay to the applicant such sum as appears to the court to be just having regard to the considerations mentioned in paragraphs (a) to (c) of subsection (4) above.

6(6)　**[Payment of sums in sec. 6(4), (5)]**　Any amount paid into court by or recovered from a person in pursuance of an order under subsection (4) or (5) above shall be paid out to such person or distributed among such persons as the court may direct, being a person or persons appearing to the court to have entered into transactions with that person as a result of which the profits mentioned in paragraph (a) of subsection (3) above have accrued to him or the loss or other adverse effect mentioned in paragraph (b) of that subsection has been suffered.

6(7)　**[Information on sec. 6(3) application]**　On an application under subsection (3) above the court may require the person concerned to furnish it with such accounts or other information as it may require for establishing whether any and, if so, what profits have accrued to him as mentioned in paragraph (a) of that subsection and for determining how any amounts are to be paid or distributed under subsection (6) above; and the court may require any such accounts or other information to be verified in such manner as it may direct.

6(8)　**[Exercise of jurisdiction]**　The jurisdiction conferred by this section shall be exercisable by the High Court and the Court of Session.

6(9)　**[Other persons bringing proceedings]**　Nothing in this section affects the right of any person other than the Secretary of State to bring proceedings in respect of any of the matters to which this section applies.

Chapter III — Authorised Persons

MEMBERS OF RECOGNISED SELF-REGULATING ORGANISATIONS

SEC. 7　Authorisation by membership of recognised self-regulating organisation

7(1)　**[Authorised person if member]**　Subject to subsection (2) below, a member of a recognised self-regulating organisation is an authorised person by virtue of his membership of that organisation.

7(2)　**[Exception]**　This section does not apply to a member who is an authorised person by virtue of section 22 or 23 below or an insurance company which is an authorised person by virtue of section 31 below.

SEC. 8　Self-regulating organisations

8(1)　**["Self-regulating organisation"]**　In this Act a **"self-regulating organisation"** means a body (whether a body corporate or an unincorporated association) which regulates the carrying on of investment business of any kind by enforcing rules which are binding on persons carrying on business of that kind either because they are members of that body or because they are otherwise subject to its control.

8(2)　**[References to members]**　In this Act references to the members of a self-regulating organisation are references to the persons who, whether or not members of the organisation, are subject to its rules in carrying on the business in question.

8(3)   [References to the rules]   In this Act references to the rules of a self-regulating organisation are references to the rules (whether or not laid down by the organisation itself) which the organisation has power to enforce in relation to the carrying on of the business in question or which relate to the admission and expulsion of members of the organisation or otherwise to its constitution.

8(4)   [References to guidance]   In this Act reference to guidance issued by a self-regulating organisation are references to guidance issued or any recommendation made by it to all or any class of its members or persons seeking to become members which would, if it were a rule, fall within subsection (3) above.

SEC. 9   Applications for recognition

9(1)   [Application to Secretary of State]   A self-regulating organisation may apply to the Secretary of State for an order declaring it to be a recognised self-regulating organisation for the purposes of this Act.

9(2)   [Requirements for application]   Any such application—

    (a)   shall be made in such manner as the Secretary of State may direct; and

    (b)   shall be accompanied by such information as the Secretary of State may reasonably require for the purpose of determining the application.

9(3)   [Further information to be furnished]   At any time after receiving an application and before determining it the Secretary of State may require the applicant to furnish additional information.

9(4)   [Directions, requirements under sec. 9(2), (3)]   The directions and requirements given or imposed under subsections (2) and (3) above may differ as between different applications.

9(5)   [Form, verification of information]   Any information to be furnished to the Secretary of State under this section shall, if he so requires, be in such form or verified in such manner as he may specify.

9(6)   [Material to accompany application]   Every application shall be accompanied by a copy of the applicant's rules and of any guidance issued by the applicant which is intended to have continuing effect and is issued in writing or other legible form.

SEC. 10   Grant and refusal of recognition

10(1)   [Power of Secretary of State]   The Secretary of State may, on an application duly made in accordance with section 9 above and after being furnished with all such information as he may require under that section, make or refuse to make an order ("a recognition order") declaring the applicant to be a recognised self-regulating organisation.

10(2)   [Duty of Secretary of State if sec. 10(3), Sch. 2 requirements satisfied]   Subject to subsection (4) below and to Chapter XIV of this Part of this Act, the Secretary of State shall make a recognition order if it appears to him from the information furnished by the organisation making the application and having regard to any other information in his possession that the requirements of subsection (3) below and of Schedule 2 to this Act are satisfied as respects that organisation.

10(3)   [Where investment business with which sec. 20 not concerned]   Where there is a kind of investment business with which the organisation is not concerned, its rules must preclude a member from carrying on investment business of that kind unless he is an authorised person otherwise than by virtue of his membership of the organisation or an exempted person in respect of that business.

10(4)   [Where Secretary of State may refuse to make order]   The Secretary of State may refuse to make a recognition order in respect of an organisation if he considers that its recognition is unnecessary having regard to the existence of one or more other organisations which are concerned with investment business of a kind with which the applicant is concerned and which have been or are likely to be recognised under this section.

10(5)   [Notice re refusal]   Where the Secretary of State refuses an application for a recognition order he shall give the applicant a written notice to that effect specifying a requirement which in the opinion of the Secretary of State is not satisfied, stating that the application is refused on the ground mentioned in subsection (4) above or stating that it is refused by virtue of Chapter XIV.

10(6)   [Order to include date]   A recognition order shall state the date on which it takes effect.

SEC. 11   Revocation of recognition

11(1)   [Where recognition order may be revoked]   A recognition order may be revoked by a further order made by the Secretary of State if at any time it appears to him—

(a) that section 10(3) above or any requirement of Schedule 2 to this Act is not satisfied in the case of the organisation to which the recognition order relates ("the recognised organisation");

(b) that the recognised organisation has failed to comply with any obligation to which it is subject by virtue of this Act; or

(c) that the continued recognition of the organisation is undesirable having regard to the existence of one or more other organisations which have been or are to be recognised under section 10 above.

11(2)   [Revocation order to include date]   An order revoking a recognition order shall state the date on which it takes effect and that date shall not be earlier than three months after the day on which the revocation order is made.

11(3)   [Duties of Secretary of State before revocation]   Before revoking a recognition order the Secretary of State shall give written notice of his intention to do so to the recognised organisation, take such steps as he considers reasonably practicable for bringing the notice to the attention of members of the organisation and publish it in such manner as he thinks appropriate for bringing it to the attention of any other persons who are in his opinion likely to be affected.

11(4)   [Contents of sec. 11(3) notice]   A notice under subsection (3) above shall state the reasons for which the Secretary of State proposes to act and give particulars of the rights conferred by subsection (5) below.

11(5)   [Where sec. 11(3) notice written representations may be made]   An organisation on which a notice is served under subsection (3) above, any member of the organisation and any other person who appears to the Secretary of State to be affected may within three months after the date of service or publication, or within such longer time as the Secretary of State may allow, make written representations to the Secretary of State and, if desired, oral representations to a person appointed for that purpose by the Secretary of State; and the Secretary of State shall have regard to any representations made in accordance with this subsection in determining whether to revoke the recognition order.

11(6)   [Secretary of State may revoke recognition order in spite of sec. 11(2), (3)]   If in any case the Secretary of State considers it essential to do so in the interests of investors he may revoke a recognition order without regard to the restriction imposed by subsection (2) above and notwithstanding that no notice has been given or published under subsection (3) above or that the time for making representations in pursuance of such a notice has not expired.

11(7)   [Transitional provisions in order]   An order revoking a recognition order may contain such transitional provisions as the Secretary of State thinks necessary or expedient.

11(8)   [Revocation on request]   A recognition order may be revoked at the request or with the consent of the recognised organisation and any such revocation shall not be subject to the restrictions imposed by subsections (1) and (2) or the requirements of subsections (3) to (5) above.

11(9)   [Written notice etc. re revocation order]   On making an order revoking a recognition order the Secretary of State shall give the organisation written notice of the making of the order, take such steps as he considers reasonably practicable for bringing the making of the order to the attention of members of the organisation and publish a notice of the making of the order in such manner as he thinks appropriate for bringing it to the attention of any other persons who are in his opinion likely to be affected.

SEC. 12   Compliance orders

12(1)   [Application by Secretary of State]   If at any time it appears to the Secretary of State—

> (a) that subsection (3) of section 10 above or any requirement of Schedule 2 to this Act is not satisfied in the case of a recognised organisation; or
>
> (b) that a recognised organisation has failed to comply with any obligation to which it is subject by virtue of this Act,

he may, instead of revoking the recognition order under section 11 above, make an application to the court under this section.

12(2)   [Court may make compliance order]   If on any such application the court decides that subsection (3) of section 10 or the requirement in question is not satisfied or, as the case may be, that the organisation has failed to comply with the obligation in question it may order the organisation to take such steps as the court directs for securing that that subsection or requirement is satisfied or that that obligation is complied with.

12(3)   [Exercise of jurisdiction]   The jurisdiction conferred by this section shall be exercisable by the High Court and the Court of Session.

SEC. 13   Alteration of rules for protection of investors

13(1)   (Omitted by Companies Act 1989, sec. 206(1) and Sch. 23, para. 1(1), (2) as from 15 March 1990.)

History

In regard to the date of the above omission see S.I. 1990 No. 354(C. 12), art. 3; s. 13(1) formerly read as follows:

"**13(1)** If at any time it appears to the Secretary of State that the rules of a recognised organisation do not satisfy the requirements of paragraph 3(1) of Schedule 2 to this

Act he may, instead of revoking the recognition order or making an application under section 12 above, direct the organisation to alter, or himself alter, its rules in such manner as he considers necessary for securing that the rules satisfy those requirements."

13(2)   [Direction to alter if Sch. 2, para. 3(1) not satisfied]   If at any time it appears to the Secretary of State that—

(a)   a recognised self-regulating organisation is concerned with two or more kinds of investment business, and

(b)   the requirement in paragraph 3(1) of Schedule 2 to this Act is not satisfied in respect of investment business of one or more but not all of those kinds,

he may, instead of revoking the recognition order or making an application under section 12 above, direct the organisation to alter, or himself alter, its rules so that they preclude a member from carrying on investment business of a kind in respect of which that requirement is not satisfied, unless he is an authorised person otherwise than by virtue of membership of the organisation or is an exempted person in respect of that business.

History

S.13(2) substituted by CA 1989, s. 206(1) and Sch. 23, para. 1(1), (3) as from 15 March 1990 (see S.I. 1990 No. 354 (C. 12), art. 3); s. 13(2) formerly read as follows:

"**13(2)** If at any time it appears to the Secretary of State that the rules or practices of a recognised organisation which is concerned with two or more kinds of investment business do not satisfy any requirement of Schedule 2 to this Act in respect of investment business of any of those kinds he may, instead of revoking the recognition order or

making an application under section 12 above, direct the organisation to alter, or himself alter, its rules so that they preclude a member from carrying on investment business of that kind unless he is an authorised person otherwise than by virtue of membership of the organisation or an exempted person in respect of that business."

Note

For transitional provisions in relation to the amendment to s. 13(2) see S.I. 1990 No. 354(C. 12), art. 6.

13(3)   [Enforcement of direction]   A direction under this section is enforceable on the application of the Secretary of State by injunction or, in Scotland, by an order under section 45 of the Court of Session Act 1988.

History

S.13(3) substituted by CA 1989, s. 206(1) and Sch. 23, para. 1(1), (4) as from 15 March 1990 (see S.I. 1990 No. 354 (C. 12), art. 3); s. 13(3) formerly read as follows:

"**13(3)** Any direction given under this section shall, on the application of the Secretary of State, be enforceable by

mandamus or, in Scotland, by an order for specific performance under section 91 of the Court of Session Act 1868."

Note

For transitional provisions in relation to the amendment to s. 13(3) see S.I. 1990 No. 354 (C. 12), art. 6.

13(4)–(6)   (Omitted by Companies Act 1989, sec. 206(1) and Sch. 23, para. 1(1), (5) as from 15 March 1990.)

History

In regard to the date of the above omission see S.I. 1990 No. 354 (C. 12), art. 3; s. 13(4)–(6) formerly read as follows:

"**13(4)**   Before giving a direction or making any alteration under subsection (1) above the Secretary of State shall consult the organisation concerned.

(5)   A recognised organisation whose rules have been altered by or pursuant to a direction given by the Secretary of State under subsection (1) above may apply to the court and if the court is satisfied—

(a)   that the rules without the alteration satisfied the requirements mentioned in that subsection; or

(b)   that other alterations proposed by the organisation would result in the rules satisfying those requirements

the court may set aside the alteration made by or pursuant to the direction given by the Secretary of State and, in a case within paragraph (b) above, order the organisation to make the alterations proposed by it; but the setting aside of an alteration under this subsection shall not affect its previous operation.

(6)   The jurisdiction conferred by subsection (5) above shall be exercisable by the High Court and the Court of Session."

13(7)   [Application of sec. 11(2)–(7), (9)]   Section 11(2) to (7) and (9) above shall, with the necessary modifications, have effect in relation to any direction given or alteration made by the Secretary of State under subsection (2) above as they have effect in relation to an order revoking a recognition order.

13(8)   [Subsequent alteration, revocation by organisation]   The fact that the rules of a recognised organisation have been altered by or pursuant to a direction given by the Secretary of State or pursuant to an order made by the court under this section shall not preclude their subsequent alteration or revocation by that organisation.

SEC. 14   Notification requirements

14(1)   [Regulations re notification of certain events]   The Secretary of State may make regulations requiring a recognised organisation to give him forthwith notice of the occurrence of such events relating to the organisation or its members as are specified in the regulations and such information in respect of those events as is so specified.

14(2)   [Regulations re furnishing information]   The Secretary of State may make regulations requiring a recognised organisation to furnish him at such times or in respect of such periods as are specified in the regulations with such information relating to the organisation or its members as is so specified.

14(3)   [Extent of notices and information]   The notices and information required to be given or furnished under the foregoing provisions of this section shall be such as the Secretary of State may reasonably require for the exercise of his functions under this Act.

14(4)   [Regulations may require specified form, verification]   Regulations under the foregoing provisions of this section may require information to be given in a specified form and to be verified in a specified manner.

14(5)   [Manner of giving notice, information]   Any notice or information required to be given or furnished under the foregoing provisions of this section shall be given in writing or in such other manner as the Secretary of State may approve.

14(6)   [Notice where organisation amends rules, etc.]   Where a recognised organisation amends, revokes or adds to its rules or guidance it shall within seven days give the Secretary of State written notice of the amendment, revocation or addition; but notice need not be given of the revocation of guidance other than such as is mentioned in section 9(6) above or of any amendment of or addition to guidance which does not result in or consist of such guidance as is there mentioned.

14(7)   [Offence]   Contravention of, or of regulations under, this section shall not be an offence.

PERSONS AUTHORISED BY RECOGNISED PROFESSIONAL BODIES

SEC. 15   Authorisation by certification by recognised professional body

15(1)   [Authorised person]   A person holding a certificate issued for the purposes of this Part of this Act by a recognised professional body is an authorised person.

15(2) **[Issue of certificate]** Such a certificate may be issued by a recognised professional body to an individual, a body corporate, a partnership or an unincorporated association.

15(3) **[Certificate issued to partnership]** A certificate issued to a partnership—

(a) shall be issued in the partnership name; and

(b) shall authorise the carrying on of investment business in that name by the partnership to which the certificate is issued, by any partnership which succeeds to that business or by any person who succeeds to that business having previously carried it on in partnership;

and, in relation to a certificate issued to a partnership constituted under the law of England and Wales or Northern Ireland or the law of any other country or territory under which a partnership is not a legal person, references in this Act to the person who holds the certificate or is certified shall be construed as references to persons or person for the time being authorised by the certificate to carry on investment business as mentioned in paragraph (b) above.

SEC. 16 Professional bodies

16(1) **["Professional body"]** In this Act a **"professional body"** means a body which regulates the practice of a profession and references to the practice of a profession do not include references to carrying on a business consisting wholly or mainly of investment business.

16(2) **[References to members]** In this Act references to the members of a professional body are references to individuals who, whether or not members of the body, are entitled to practice the profession in question and, in practising it, are subject to the rules of that body.

16(3) **[References to notes]** In this Act references to the rules of a professional body are references to the rules (whether or not laid down by the body itself) which the body has power to enforce in relation to the practice of the profession in question and the carrying on of investment business by persons practising that profession or which relate to the grant, suspension or withdrawal of certificates under section 15 above, the admission and expulsion of members or otherwise to the constitution of the body.

16(4) **[Reference to guidance]** In this Act references to guidance issued by a professional body are references to guidance issued or any recommendation made by it to all or any class of its members or persons seeking to become members, or to persons or any class of persons who are or are seeking to be certified by the body, and which would, if it were a rule, fall within subsection (3) above.

SEC. 17 Applications for recognition

17(1) **[Application to Secretary of State]** A professional body may apply to the Secretary of State for an order declaring it to be a recognised professional body for the purposes of this Act.

17(2) **[Effect of sec. 9(2)–(6)]** Subsections (2) to (6) of section 9 above shall have effect in relation to an application under subsection (1) above as they have effect in relation to an application under subsection (1) of that section.

SEC. 18   Grant and refusal of recognition

18(1)   [Power of Secretary of State]   The Secretary of State may, on an application duly made in accordance with section 17 above and after being furnished with all such information as he may require under that section, make or refuse to make an order ("a recognition order") declaring the applicant to be a recognised professional body.

18(2)   [Conditions for recognition order]   The Secretary of State may make a recognition order if it appears to him from the information furnished by the body making the application and having regard to any other information in his possession that the requirements of subsection (3) below and of Schedule 3 to this Act are satisfied as respects that body.

18(3)   [Requirements for body's rules]   The body must have rules which impose acceptable limits on the kinds of investment business which may be carried on by persons certified by it and the circumstances in which they may carry on such business and which preclude a person certified by that body from carrying on any investment business outside those limits unless he is an authorised person otherwise than by virtue of the certification or an exempted person in respect of that business.

18(4)   [Written notice re refusal]   Where the Secretary of State refuses an application for a recognition order he shall give the applicant a written notice to that effect, stating the reasons for the refusal.

18(5)   [Order to include date]   A recognition order shall state the date on which it takes effect.

SEC. 19   Revocation of recognition

19(1)   [Where sec. 18 order may be revoked]   A recognition order under section 18 above may be revoked by a further order made by the Secretary of State if at any time it appears to him—

    (a) that section 18(3) above or any requirement of Schedule 3 to this Act is not satisfied in the case of the body to which the recognition order relates; or

    (b) that the body has failed to comply with any obligation to which it is subject by virtue of this Act.

19(2)   [Effect of sec. 11(2)–(9)]   Subsections (2) to (9) of section 11 above shall have effect in relation to the revocation of a recognition order under this section as they have effect in relation to the revocation of a recognition order under subsection (1) of that section.

SEC. 20   Compliance orders

20(1)   [Power of Secretary of State]   If at any time it appears to the Secretary of State—

    (a) that subsection (3) of section 18 above or any requirement of Schedule 3 to this Act is not satisfied in the case of a recognised professional body; or

    (b) that such a body has failed to comply with any obligation to which it is subject by virtue of this Act,

he may, instead of revoking the recognition order under section 19 above, make an application to the court under this section.

20(2) **[Order re non-compliance]** If on any such application the court decides that subsection (3) of section 18 above or the requirement in question is not satisfied or, as the case may be, that the body has failed to comply with the obligation in question it may order the body to take such steps as the court directs for securing that that subsection or requirement is satisfied or that that obligation is complied with.

20(3) **[Exercise of jurisdiction]** The jurisdiction conferred by this section shall be exercisable by the High Court and the Court of Session.

SEC. 21 Notification requirements

21(1) **[Regulations re notice]** The Secretary of State may make regulations requiring a recognised professional body to give him forthwith notice of the occurrence of such events relating to the body, its members or persons certified by it as are specified in the regulations and such information in respect of those events as is so specified.

21(2) **[Regulations re furnishing information]** The Secretary of State may make regulations requiring a recognised professional body to furnish him at such times or in respect of such periods as are specified in the regulations with such information relating to the body, its members and persons certified by it as is so specified.

21(3) **[Notices and information required]** The notices and information required to be given or furnished under the foregoing provisions of this section shall be such as the Secretary of State may reasonably require for the exercise of his functions under this Act.

21(4) **[Form and verification of information]** Regulations under the foregoing provisions of this section may require information to be given in a specified form and to be verified in a specified manner.

21(5) **[Manner of giving notices, information]** Any notice or information required to be given or furnished under the foregoing provisions of this section shall be given in writing or in such other manner as the Secretary of State may approve.

21(6) **[Notice re amendment etc. of rules or guidance]** Where a recognised professional body amends, revokes or adds to its rules or guidance it shall within seven days give the Secretary of State written notice of the amendment, revocation or addition; but—

    (a) notice need not be given of the revocation of guidance other than such as is mentioned in section 9(6) above or of any amendment of or addition to guidance which does not result in or consist of such guidance as is there mentioned; and

    (b) notice need not be given in respect of any rule or guidance, or rules or guidance of any description, in the case of which the Secretary of State has waived compliance with this subsection by notice in writing to the body concerned;

and any such waiver may be varied or revoked by a further notice in writing.

21(7) **[Offence]** Contravention of, or of regulations under, this section shall not be an offence.

INSURANCE COMPANIES

SEC. 22   Authorised insurers

22   A body which is authorised under section 3 or 4 of the Insurance Companies Act 1982 to carry on insurance business which is investment business and carries on such insurance business in the United Kingdom is an authorised person as respects—

(a) any insurance business which is investment business; and

(b) any other investment business which that body may carry on without contravening section 16 of that Act.

FRIENDLY SOCIETIES

SEC. 23   Registered friendly societies

23(1)   **[Certain societies authorised persons]**   A society which—

(a) is a friendly society within the meaning of section 7(1)(a) of the Friendly Societies Act 1974;

(b) is registered within the meaning of that Act as a society but not as a branch of a society;

(c) under its rules has its registered office at a place situated in Great Britain; and

(d) carries on investment business in the United Kingdom,

is an authorised person as respects any investment business which it carries on for or in connection with any of the purposes mentioned in Schedule 1 to that Act.

23(2)   **[Northern Ireland]**   A society which—

(a) is a friendly society within the meaning of section 1(1)(a) of the Friendly Societies Act (Northern Ireland) 1970;

(b) is registered or deemed to be registered as a society but not as a branch of a society under that Act;

(c) under its rules has its registered office at a place situated in Northern Ireland; and

(d) carries on investment business in the United Kingdom,

is an authorised person as respects any investment business which it carries on for or in connection with any of the purposes mentioned in Schedule 1 to that Act.

COLLECTIVE INVESTMENT SCHEMES

SEC. 24   Operators and trustees of recognised schemes

24   The operator or trustee of a scheme recognised under section 86 below is an authorised person as respects—

(a) investment business which consists in operating or acting as trustee in relation to that scheme; and

(b) any investment business which is carried on by him in connection with or for the purposes of that scheme.

PERSONS AUTHORISED BY THE SECRETARY OF STATE

SEC. 25   Authorisation by Secretary of State

25   A person holding an authorisation granted by the Secretary of State under the following provisions of this Chapter is an authorised person.

SEC. 26   Applications for authorisation

26(1)   [Applicants]   An application for authorisation by the Secretary of State may be made by—

(a) an individual;

(b) a body corporate;

(c) a partnership; or

(d) an unincorporated association.

26(2)   [Manner and contents of application]   Any such application—

(a) shall be made in such manner as the Secretary of State may direct;

(b) shall contain or be accompanied by—

(i) information as to the investment business which the applicant proposes to carry on and the services which he will hold himself out as able to provide in the carrying on of that business; and

(ii) such other information as the Secretary of State may reasonably require for the purpose of determining the application; and

(c) shall contain the address of a place in the United Kingdom for the service on the applicant of any notice or other document required or authorised to be served on him under this Act.

26(3)   [Additional information]   At any time after receiving an application and before determining it the Secretary of State may require the applicant to furnish additional information.

26(4)   [Differing requirements]   The directions and requirements given or imposed under subsections (2) and (3) above may differ as between different applications.

26(5)   [Form and verification of information]   Any information to be furnished to the Secretary of State under this section shall, if he so requires, be in such form or verified in such manner as he may specify.

SEC. 27   Grant and refusal of authorisation

27(1)   [Power of Secretary of State]   The Secretary of State may, on an application duly made in accordance with section 26 above and after being furnished with all such information as he may require under that section, grant or refuse the application.

27(2)   [Where application to be granted]   The Secretary of State shall grant the application if it appears to him from the information furnished by the applicant and having regard to any other information in his possession that the applicant is a fit and proper person to carry on the investment business and provide the services described in the application.

27(3)   [Matters to be considered re other persons]   In determining whether to grant or refuse an application the Secretary of State may take into account any matter relating to any person who is or will be employed by or associated with the applicant for the purposes of the business in question, to any person who is or will be acting as an appointed representative in relation to that business and—

    (a) if the applicant is a body corporate, to any director or controller of the body, to any other body corporate in the same group or to any director or controller of any such other body corporate;

    (b) if the applicant is a partnership, to any of the partners;

    (c) if the applicant is an unincorporated association, to any member of the governing body of the association or any officer or controller of the association.

27(4) **[Related business]** In determining whether to grant or refuse an application the Secretary of State may also have regard to any business which the applicant proposes to carry on in connection with his investment business.

27(5) **[Business in another member State]** In the case of an applicant who is authorised to carry on investment business in a member State other than the United Kingdom the Secretary of State shall have regard to that authorisation.

27(6) **[Authorisation to partnership]** An authorisation granted to a partnership—

    (a) shall be granted in the partnership name; and

    (b) shall authorise the carrying on of investment business in that name (or with the Secretary of State's consent in any other name) by the partnership to which the authorisation is granted, by any partnership which succeeds to that business or by any person who succeeds to that business or by any person who succeeds to that business having previously carried it on in partnership;

and, in relation to an authorisation granted to a partnership constituted under the law of England and Wales or Northern Ireland or the law of any other country or territory under which a partnership is not a legal person, references in this Act to the holder of the authorisation or the authorised person shall be construed as references to the persons or person for the time being authorised by the authorisation to carry on investment business as mentioned in paragraph (b) above.

27(7) **[Authorisation to unincorporated association]** An authorisation granted to an unincorporated association shall apply to the carrying on of investment business in the name of the association and in such manner as may be specified in the authorisation.

27(8) **[Notice re grant]** The Secretary of State shall give an applicant for authorisation written notice of the grant of authorisation specifying the date on which it takes effect.

SEC. 28   Withdrawal and suspension of authorisation

28(1) **[Power of Secretary of State]** The Secretary of State may at any time withdraw or suspend any authorisation granted by him if it appears to him—

    (a) that the holder of the authorisation is not a fit and proper person to carry on the investment business which he is carrying on or proposing to carry on; or

(b) without prejudice to paragraph (a) above, that the holder of the authorisation has contravened any provision of this Act or any rules or regulations made under it or, in purported compliance with any such provision, has furnished the Secretary of State with false, inaccurate or misleading information or has contravened any prohibition or requirement imposed under this Act.

28(2) **[Matters in sec. 27(3), (4)]** For the purposes of subsection (1)(a) above the Secretary of State may take into account any such matters as are mentioned in section 27(3) and (4) above.

28(3) **[Where holder of authorisation member of SRO]** Where the holder of the authorisation is a member of a recognised self-regulating organisation the rules, prohibitions and requirements referred to in paragraph (b) of subsection (1) above include the rules of that organisation and any prohibition or requirement imposed by virtue of those rules; and where he is a person certified by a recognised professional body the rules, prohibitions and requirements referred to in that paragraph include the rules of that body which regulate the carrying on by him of investment business and any prohibition or requirement imposed by virtue of those rules.

28(4) **[Suspension of authorisation]** The suspension of an authorisation shall be for a specified period or until the occurrence of a specified event or until specified conditions are complied with; and while an authorisation is suspended the holder shall not be an authorised person.

28(5) **[Variation of matters in sec. 28(4)]** Any period, event or conditions specified under subsection (4) above in the case of an authorisation may be varied by the Secretary of State on the application of the holder.

SEC. 29 Notice of proposed refusal, withdrawal or suspension

29(1) **[Written notice by Secretary of State]** Where the Secretary of State proposes—

(a) to refuse an application under section 26 or 28(5) above; or

(b) to withdraw or suspend an authorisation,

he shall give the applicant or the authorised person written notice of his intention to do so, stating the reasons for which he proposes to act.

29(2) **[Contents of notice]** In the case of a proposed withdrawal or suspension the notice shall state the date on which it is proposed that the withdrawal or suspension should take effect and, in the case of a proposed suspension, its proposed duration.

29(3) **[Copy of notice to other persons]** Where the reasons stated in a notice under this section relate specifically to matters which—

(a) refer to a person identified in the notice other than the applicant or the holder of the authorisation; and

(b) are in the opinion of the Secretary of State prejudicial to that person in any office or employment,

the Secretary of State shall, unless he considers it impracticable to do so, serve a copy of the notice on that person.

29(4)   [Notice to include reference to Tribunal]   A notice under this section shall give particulars of the right to require the case to be referred to the Tribunal under Chapter IX of this Part of this Act.

29(5)   [Where no right of reference to Tribunal]   Where a case is not required to be referred to the Tribunal by a person on whom a notice is served under this section the Secretary of State shall, at the expiration of the period within which such a requirement can be made—

    (a)   give that person written notice of the refusal, withdrawal or suspension; or

    (b)   give that person written notice of the grant of the application or, as the case may be, written notice that the authorisation is not to be withdrawn or suspended;

and the Secretary of State may give public notice of any decision notified by him under paragraph (a) or (b) above and the reasons for the decision except that he shall not do so in the case of a decision notified under paragraph (b) unless the person concerned consents to his doing so.

SEC. 30   Withdrawal of applications and authorisations by consent

30(1)   [Power to withdraw application]   An application under section 26 above may be withdrawn before it is granted or refused; and, subject to subsections (2) and (3) below, an authorisation granted under section 27 above may be withdrawn by the Secretary of State at the request or with the consent of the authorised person.

30(2)   [Power of Secretary of State to refuse withdrawal]   The Secretary of State may refuse to withdraw any such authorisation if he considers that the public interest requires any matter affecting the authorised person to be investigated as a preliminary to a decision on the question whether the Secretary of State should in respect of that person exercise his powers under section 28 above or under any other provision of this Part of this Act.

30(3)   [Further power of Secretary of State]   The Secretary of State may also refuse to withdraw an authorisation where in his opinion it is desirable that a prohibition or restriction should be imposed on the authorised person under Chapter VI of this Part of this Act or that a prohibition or restriction imposed on that person under that Chapter should continue in force.

30(4)   [Public notice of sec. 30(1) withdrawal]   The Secretary of State may give public notice of any withdrawal of authorisation under subsection (1) above.

PERSONS AUTHORISED IN OTHER MEMBER STATES

SEC. 31   Authorisation in other member State

31(1)   [Authorised person]   A person carrying on investment business in the United Kingdom is an authorised person if—

    (a)   he is established in a member State other than the United Kingdom;

    (b)   the law of that State recognises him as a national of that or another member State; and

(c) he is for the time being authorised under that law to carry on investment business or investment business of any particular kind.

31(2) [Establishment in another member State] For the purposes of this Act a person is established in a member State other than the United Kingdom if his head office is situated in that State and he does not transact investment business from a permanent place of business maintained by him in the United Kingdom.

31(3) [Conditions for application to persons in other member States] This section applies to a person only if the provisions of the law under which he is authorised to carry on the investment business in question—

(a) afford to investors in the United Kingdom protection, in relation to his carrying on of that business, which is at least equivalent to that provided for them by the provisions of this Chapter relating to members of recognised self-regulating organisations or to persons authorised by the Secretary of State; or

(b) satisfy the conditions laid down by a Community instrument for the co-ordination or approximation of the laws, regulations or administrative provisions of member States relating to the carrying on of investment business or investment business of the relevant kind.

31(4) [Certificate re sec. 31(3)(a)] A certificate issued by the Secretary of State and for the time being in force to the effect that the provisions of the law of a member State comply with the requirements of subsection (3)(a) above, either as respects all investment business or as respects investment business of a particular kind, shall be conclusive evidence of that matter but the absence or revocation of such a certificate shall not be regarded as indicating that those requirements are not complied with.

31(5) [Condition for sec. 31(3)(b)] This section shall not apply to a person by virtue of paragraph (b) of subsection (3) above unless the authority by which he is authorised to carry on the investment business in question certifies that he is authorised to do so under a law which complies with the requirements of that paragraph.

SEC. 32 Notice of commencement of business

32(1) [Written notice to be given offence] A person who is an authorised person by virtue of section 31 above shall be guilty of an offence unless, not less than seven days before beginning to carry on investment business in the United Kingdom, he has given notice of his intention to do so to the Secretary of State either in writing or in such other manner as the Secretary of State may approve.

32(2) [Contents of notice] The notice shall contain—

(a) information as to the investment business which that person proposes to carry on in the United Kingdom and the services which he will hold himself out as able to provide in the carrying on of that business;

(b) information as to the authorisation of that person in the member State in question;

(c) the address of a place (whether in the United Kingdom or elsewhere) for the service on that person of any notice or other document required or authorised to be served on him under this Act;

    (d) such other information as may be prescribed;

and the notice shall comply with such requirements as to the form in which any information is to be given and as to its verification as may be prescribed.

32(3)   **[Certificate re sec. 31]**   A notice by a person claiming to be authorised by virtue of subsection (3)(b) of section 31 above shall be accompanied by a copy of the certificate required by subsection (5) of that section.

32(4)   **[Penalty]**   A person guilty of an offence under subsection (1) above shall be liable—

    (a) on conviction on indictment, to a fine;

    (b) on summary conviction, to a fine not exceeding the statutory maximum.

32(5)   **[Defence]**   In proceedings brought against any person for an offence under subsection (1) above it shall be a defence for him to prove that he took all reasonable precautions and exercised all due diligence to avoid the commission of the offence.

SEC. 33   Termination and suspension of authorisation

33(1)   **[Power of Secretary of State]**   If it appears to the Secretary of State that a person who is an authorised person by virtue of section 31 above has contravened any provision of this Act or of any rules or regulations made under it or, in purported compliance with any such provision, has furnished the Secretary of State with false, inaccurate or misleading information or has contravened any prohibition or requirement imposed under this Act the Secretary of State may direct—

    (a) that he shall cease to be an authorised person by virtue of that section; or

    (b) that he shall not be an authorised person by virtue of that section for a specified period or until the occurrence of a specified event or until specified conditions are complied with.

33(2)   **[Rules in sec. 33(1) re member of SRO]**   In the case of a person who is a member of a recognised self-regulating organisation the rules, prohibitions and requirements referred to in subsection (1) above include the rules of that organisation and any prohibition or requirement imposed by virtue of those rules; and in the case of a person who is certified by a recognised professional body the rules, prohibitions and requirements referred to in that subsection include the rules of that body which regulate the carrying on by him of investment business and any prohibition or requirement imposed by virtue of those rules.

33(3)   **[Variation of matters in sec. 33(1)(b)]**   Any period, event or condition specified in a direction under subsection (1)(b) above may be varied by the Secretary of State on the application of the person to whom the direction relates.

33(4)   **[Consultation with relevant authority before direction]**   The Secretary of State shall consult the relevant supervisory authority before giving a direction under this section unless he considers it essential in the interests of investors that the direction should be given forthwith but in that case he shall consult the authority immediately after giving the direction and may then revoke or vary it if he considers it appropriate to do so.

33(5)   **[Revocation of direction]**   The Secretary of State shall revoke a direction under this section if he is satisfied, after consulting the relevant supervisory authority, that it will secure that the person concerned will comply with the provisions mentioned in subsection (1) above.

33(6) ["**The relevant supervisory authority**"] In this section "**the relevant supervisory authority**" means the authority of the member State where the person concerned is established which is responsible for supervising the carrying on of investment business of the kind which that person is or was carrying on.

SEC. 34 Notice of proposed termination or suspension

34(1) [Duty of Secretary of State to give written notice] Where the Secretary of State proposes—

(a) to give a direction under section 33 above; or

(b) to refuse an application under subsection (3) of that section,

he shall give the authorised person written notice of his intention to do so, stating the reasons for which he proposes to act.

34(2) [Where proposed direction under sec. 33] In the case of a proposed direction under section 33 above the notice shall state the date on which it is proposed that the direction should take effect and, in the case of a proposed direction under subsection (1)(b) of that section, its proposed duration.

34(3) [Copy of notice to other persons] Where the reasons stated in a notice under this section relate specifically to matters which—

(a) refer to a person identified in the notice other than the authorised person; and

(b) are in the opinion of the Secretary of State prejudicial to that person in any office or employment,

the Secretary of State shall, unless he considers it impracticable to do so, serve a copy of the notice on that other person.

34(4) [Notice to include reference to Tribunal] A notice under this section shall give particulars of the right to require the case to be referred to the Tribunal under Chapter IX of this Part of this Act.

34(5) [Where case not required to be referred to Tribunal] Where a case is not required to be referred to the Tribunal by a person on whom a notice is served under this section the Secretary of State shall, at the expiration of the period within which such a requirement can be made—

(a) give that person written notice of the direction or refusal; or

(b) give that person written notice that the direction is not to be given or, as the case may be, of the grant of the application;

and the Secretary of State may give public notice of any decision notified by him under paragraph (a) or (b) above and the reasons for the decision except that he shall not do so in the case of a decision within paragraph (b) unless the person concerned consents to his doing so.

Chapter IV — Exempted Persons

THE BANK OF ENGLAND

SEC. 35   The Bank of England

35   The Bank of England is an exempted person.

RECOGNISED INVESTMENT EXCHANGES AND CLEARING HOUSES

SEC. 36   Investment exchanges

36(1)   [Recognised investment exchange]   A recognised investment exchange is an exempted person as respects anything done in its capacity as such which constitutes investment business.

36(2)   [References to rules of investment exchange]   In this Act references to the rules of an investment exchange are references to the rules made or conditions imposed by it with respect to the matters dealt with in Schedule 4 to this Act, with respect to the admission of persons to or their exclusion from the use of its facilities or otherwise relating to its constitution.

36(3)   [References to guidance issued by investment exchange]   In this Act references to guidance issued by an investment exchange are references to guidance issued or any recommendation made by it to all or any class of its members or users or persons seeking to become members of the exchange or to use its facilities and which would, if it were a rule, fall within subsection (2) above.

SEC. 37   Grant and revocation of recognition

37(1)   [Application to Secretary of State]   Any body corporate or unincorporated association may apply to the Secretary of State for an order declaring it to be a recognised investment exchange for the purposes of this Act.

37(2)   [Effect of sec. 9(2)–(5)]   Subsections (2) to (5) of section 9 above shall have effect in relation to an application under subsection (1) above as they have effect in relation to an application under subsection (1) of that section; and every application under subsection (1) above shall be accompanied by—

    (a) a copy of the applicant's rules;

    (b) a copy of any guidance issued by the applicant which is intended to have continuing effect and is issued in writing or other legible form; and

    (c) particulars of any arrangements which the applicant has made or proposes to make for the provision of clearing services.

37(3)   [Power of Secretary of State to make order]   The Secretary of State may, on an application duly made in accordance with subsection (1) above and after being furnished with all such information as he may require in connection with the application, make or refuse to make an order ("a recognition order") declaring the applicant to be a recognised investment exchange for the purposes of this Act.

37(4)   [Where Sch. 4 requirements are satisfied]   Subject to Chapter XIV of this Part of this Act, the Secretary of State may make a recognition order if it appears to him from the information furnished by the exchange making the application and having regard to any other information in his possession that the requirements of Schedule 4 to this Act are satisfied as respects that exchange.

37(5) **[Notice to applicant re refusal]** Where the Secretary of State refuses an application for a recognition order he shall give the applicant a written notice to that effect stating the reasons for the refusal.

37(6) **[Date to be stated in order]** A recognition order shall state the date on which it takes effect.

37(7) **[Revocation of recognition order]** A recognition order may be revoked by a further order made by the Secretary of State if at any time it appears to him—

(a) that any requirement of Schedule 4 to this Act is not satisfied in the case of the exchange to which the recognition order relates; or

(b) that the exchange has failed to comply with any obligation to which it is subject by virtue of this Act;

and subsections (2) to (9) of section 11 above shall have effect in relation to the revocation of a recognition order under this subsection as they have effect in relation to the revocation of such an order under subsection (1) of that section.

37(8) **[Effect of sec. 12]** Section 12 above shall have effect in relation to a recognised investment exchange and the requirements and obligations referred to in subsection (7) above as it has effect in relation to the requirements and obligations there mentioned.

SEC. 38 Clearing houses

38(1) **[Recognised clearing house]** A recognised clearing house is an exempted person as respects anything done by it in its capacity as a person providing clearing services for the transaction of investment business.

38(2) **[References to rules of clearing house]** In this Act references to the rules of a clearing house are references to the rules made or conditions imposed by it with respect to the provision by it or its members of clearing services under clearing arrangements, that is to say, arrangements with a recognised investment exchange for the provision of clearing services in respect of transactions effected on the exchange.

38(3) **[References to guidance issued by clearing house]** In this Act references to guidance issued by a clearing house are references to guidance issued or any recommendation made by it to all or any class of its members or persons using or seeking to use its services and which would, if it were a rule, fall within subsection (2) above.

SEC. 39 Grant and revocation of recognition

39(1) **[Application to Secretary of State]** Any body corporate or unincorporated association may apply to the Secretary of State for an order declaring it to be a recognised clearing house for the purposes of this Act.

39(2) **[Effect of sec. 9(2)–(5)]** Subsections (2) to (5) of section 9 above shall have effect in relation to an application under subsection (1) above as they have effect in relation to an application under subsection (1) of that section; and any application under subsection (1) above shall be accompanied by—

    (a) a copy of the applicant's rules;

    (b) a copy of any guidance issued by the applicant which is intended to have continuing effect and is issued in writing or other legible form; and

    (c) particulars of any recognised investment exchange with which the applicant proposes to make clearing arrangements and of any other person (whether or not such an exchange) for whom the applicant provides clearing services.

39(3)   **[Power of Secretary of State to make order]**   The Secretary of State may, on an application duly made in accordance with subsection (1) above and after being furnished with all such information as he may require in connection with the application, make or refuse to make an order ("a recognition order") declaring the applicant to be a recognised clearing house for the purposes of this Act.

39(4)   **[Guidelines for making order]**   Subject to Chapter XIV of this Part of this Act, the Secretary of State may make a recognition order if it appears to him from the information furnished by the clearing house making the application and having regard to any other information in his possession that the clearing house—

    (a) has financial resources sufficient for the proper performance of its functions;

    (b) has adequate arrangements and resources for the effective monitoring and enforcement of compliance with its rules or, as respects monitoring, arrangements providing for that function to be performed on behalf of the clearing house (and without affecting its responsibility) by another body or person who is able and willing to perform it;

    (c) provides or is able to provide clearing services which would enable a recognised investment exchange to make arrangements with it that satisfy the requirements of Schedule 4 to this Act; and

    (d) is able and willing to comply with duties corresponding to those imposed in the case of a recognised investment exchange by paragraph 5 of that Schedule.

39(5)   **[Written notice to applicant re refusal]**   Where the Secretary of State refuses an application for a recognition order he shall give the applicant a written notice to that effect stating the reasons for the refusal.

39(6)   **[Order to state date]**   A recognition order shall state the date on which it takes effect.

39(7)   **[Revocation of recognition order]**   A recognition order may be revoked by a further order made by the Secretary of State if at any time it appears to him—

    (a) that any requirement of subsection (4) above is not satisfied in the case of the clearing house; or

    (b) that the clearing house has failed to comply with any obligation to which it is subject by virtue of this Act;

and subsections (2) to (9) of section 11 above shall have effect in relation to the revocation of a recognition order under this subsection as they have effect in relation to the revocation of such an order under subsection (1) of that section.

39(8) **[Effect of sec. 12]**   Section 12 above shall have effect in relation to a recognised clearing house and the requirements and obligations referred to in subsection (7) above as it has effect in relation to the requirements and obligations there mentioned.

SEC. 40   Overseas investment exchanges and clearing houses

40(1) **[Certain sec. 37(1), 39(1) applications]**   Any application under section 37(1) or 39(1) above by a body or association whose head office is situated in a country outside the United Kingdom shall contain the address of a place in the United Kingdom for the service on that body or association of notices or other documents required or authorised to be served on it under this Act.

40(2) **[Substitutions in sec. 37(4), 39(4)]**   In relation to any such body or association sections 37(4) and 39(4) above shall have effect with the substitution for the requirements there mentioned of the following requirements, that is to say—

   (a) that the body or association is, in the country in which its head office is situated, subject to supervision which, together with the rules and practices of that body or association, is such that investors in the United Kingdom are afforded protection in relation to that body or association at least equivalent to that provided by the provisions of this Act in relation to investment exchanges and clearing houses in respect of which recognition orders and made otherwise than by virtue of this subsection; and

   (b) that the body or association is able and willing to co-operate, by the sharing of information and otherwise, with the authorities, bodies and persons responsible in the United Kingdom for the supervision and regulation of investment business or other financial services; and

   (c) that adequate arrangements exist for such co-operation between those responsible for the supervision of the body or association in the country mentioned in paragraph (a) above and the authorities, bodies and persons mentioned in paragraph (b) above.

40(3) **[Matter for determining whether to make sec. 40(2) order]**   In determining whether to make a recognition order by virtue of subsection (2) above the Secretary of State may have regard to the extent to which persons in the United Kingdom and persons in the country mentioned in that subsection have access to the financial markets in each others' countries.

40(4) **[Further matters re sec. 40(2)]**   In relation to a body or association declared to be a recognised investment exchange or recognised clearing house by a recognition order made by virtue of subsection (2) above—

   (a) the reference in section 36(2) above to the matters dealt with in Schedule 4 to this Act shall be construed as a reference to corresponding matters;

   (b) sections 37(7) and (8) and 39(7) and (8) above shall have effect as if the requirements mentioned in section 37(7)(a) and in section 39(7)(a) were those of subsection (2)(a) and (b) above; and

   (c) the grounds on which the order may be revoked under section 37(7) or 39(7) above shall include the ground that it appears to the Secretary of State that revocation is desirable in the interests of investors and potential investors in the United Kingdom.

40(5)   **["Country"]**   In this section **"country"** includes any territory or any part of a country or territory.

40(6)   **["Overseas investment exchange", "overseas clearing house"]**   A body or association declared to be a recognised investment exchange or recognised clearing house by a recognition order made by virtue of subsection (2) above is in this Act referred to as an "overseas investment exchange" or an "overseas clearing house".

SEC. 41   Notification requirements

41(1)   **[Power of Secretary of State to make regulations re notice]**   The Secretary of State may make regulations requiring a recognised investment exchange or recognised clearing house to give him forthwith notice of the occurrence of such events relating to the exchange or clearing house as are specified in the regulations and such information in respect of those events as is so specified.

41(2)   **[Regulations re furnishing information]**   The Secretary of State may make regulations requiring a recognised investment exchange or recognised clearing house to furnish him at such times or in respect of such periods as are specified in the regulations with such information relating to the exchange or clearing house as is so specified.

41(3)   **[Extent of notices and information]**   The notices and information required to be given or furnished under the foregoing provisions of this section shall be such as the Secretary of State may reasonably require for the exercise of his functions under this Act.

41(4)   **[Form, verification of information]**   Regulations under the foregoing provisions of this section may require information to be given in a specified form and to be verified in a specified manner.

41(5)   **[Notice by recognised investment exchange]**   Where a recognised investment exchange—

    (a)   amends, revokes or adds to its rules or guidance; or

    (b)   makes, terminates or varies any clearing arrangements,

it shall within seven days give written notice to the Secretary of State of the amendment, revocation or addition or, as the case may be, of the matters mentioned in paragraph (b) above.

41(6)   **[Notice by recognised clearing house]**   Where a recognised clearing house—

    (a)   amends, revokes or adds to its rules or guidance; or

    (b)   makes a change in the persons for whom it provides clearing services,

it shall within seven days give written notice to the Secretary of State of the amendment, revocation or addition or, as the case may be, of the change.

41(7)   **[Limits on notice]**   Notice need not be given under subsection (5) or (6) above of the revocation of guidance other than such as is mentioned in section 37(2)(b) or 39(2)(b) above or of any amendment of or addition to guidance which does not result in or consist of such guidance as is there mentioned.

OTHER EXEMPTIONS

SEC. 42 Lloyd's

42 The Society of Lloyd's and persons permitted by the Council of Lloyd's to act as underwriting agents at Lloyd's are exempted persons as respects investment business carried on in connection with or for the purpose of insurance business at Lloyd's.

SEC. 43 Listed money market institutions

43(1) **["Listed institution"]** A person for the time being included in a list maintained by the Bank of England for the purposes of this section ("a listed institution") is an exempted person in respect of, and of anything done for the purposes of, any transaction to which Part I or Part II of Schedule 5 to this Act applies and in respect of any arrangements made by him with a view to other persons entering into a transaction to which Part III of that Schedule applies.

43(2) **[Admission to list etc.]** The conditions imposed by the Bank of England for admission to the list referred to in this section and the arrangements made by it for a person's admission to and removal from the list shall require the approval of the Treasury; and this section shall cease to have effect if that approval is withdrawn but without prejudice to its again having effect if approval is given for fresh conditions or arrangements.

43(3) **[Publication of list]** The Bank of England shall publish the list as for the time being in force and provide a certified copy of it at the request of any person wishing to refer to it in legal proceedings.

43(4) **[Certified copy of list]** Such a certified copy shall be evidence or, in Scotland, sufficient evidence of the contents of the list; and a copy purporting to be certified by or on behalf of the Bank shall be deemed to have been duly certified unless the contrary is shown.

SEC. 44 Appointed representatives

44(1) **[Exempted person]** An appointed representative is an exempted person as respects investment business carried on by him as such a representative.

44(2) **[Definition]** For the purposes of this Act an appointed representative is a person—

> (a) who is employed by an authorised person (his "principal") under a contract for services which—

>> (i) requires or permits him to carry on investment business to which this section applies; and

>> (ii) complies with subsections (4) and (5) below; and

> (b) for whose activities in carrying on the whole or part of that investment business his principal has accepted responsibility in writing;

and the investment business carried on by an appointed representative as such is the investment business for which his principal has accepted responsibility.

44(3) **[Application of section]** This section applies to investment business carried on by an appointed representative which consists of—

(a) procuring or endeavouring to procure the persons with whom he deals to enter into investment agreements with his principal or (if not prohibited by his contract) with other persons;

(b) giving advice to the persons with whom he deals about entering into investment agreements with his principal or (if not prohibited by his contract) with other persons; or

(c) giving advice as to the sale of investments issued by his principal or as to the exercise of rights conferred by an investment whether or not issued as aforesaid.

44(4)   [Contract between appointed representative and principal]   If the contract between an appointed representative and his principal does not prohibit the representative from procuring or endeavouring to procure persons to enter into investment agreements with persons other than his principal it must make provision for enabling the principal either to impose such a prohibition or to restrict the kinds of investment to which those agreements may relate or the other persons with whom they may be entered into.

44(5)   [Further matter re sec. 44(4) contract]   If the contract between an appointed representative and his principal does not prohibit the representative from giving advice about entering into investment agreements with persons other than his principal it must make provision for enabling the principal either to impose such a prohibition or to restrict the kinds of advice which the representative may give by reference to the kinds of investment in relation to which or the persons with whom the representative may advise that investment agreements should be made.

44(6)   [Responsibility of principal]   The principal of an appointed representative shall be responsible, to the same extent as if he had expressly authorised it, for anything said or done or omitted by the representative in carrying on the investment business for which he has accepted responsibility.

44(7)   [Determining compliance of authorised person]   In determining whether an authorised person has complied with—

(a) any provision contained in or made under this Act; or

(b) any rules of a recognised self-regulating organisation or recognised professional body,

anything which a person who at the material time is or was an appointed representative of the authorised person has said, done or omitted as respects investment business for which the authorised person has accepted responsibility shall be treated as having been said, done or omitted by the authorised person.

44(8)   [Limit on sec. 44(7)]   Nothing in subsection (7) above shall cause the knowledge or intentions of an appointed representative to be attributed to his principal for the purpose of determining whether the principal has committed a criminal offence unless in all the circumstances it is reasonable for them to be attributed to him.

44(9)   ["Investment agreement"]   In this Act "investment agreement" means any agreement the making or performance of which by either party constitutes an activity which falls within any paragraph of Part II of Schedule 1 to this Act or would do so apart from Parts III and IV of that Schedule.

FSA 1986, sec. 44(4)   [The next page is 60,451]   CCH Editions Limited

SEC. 45 Miscellaneous exemptions

45(1) **[Exempted persons]** Each of the following persons is an exempted person to the extent specified in relation to that person—

(a) the President of the Family Division of the High Court when acting in the exercise of his functions under section 9 of the Administration of Estates Act 1925;

(b) the Probate Judge of the High Court of Northern Ireland when acting in the exercise of his functions under section 3 of the Administration of Estates Act (Northern Ireland) 1955;

(c) the Accountant General of the Supreme Court when acting in the exercise of his functions under Part VI of the Administration of Justice Act 1982;

(d) the Accountant of Court when acting in the exercise of his functions in connection with the consignation or deposit of sums of money;

(e) the Public Trustee when acting in the exercise of his functions under the Public Trustee Act 1906;

(f) the Master of the Court of Protection when acting in the exercise of his functions under Part VII of the Mental Health Act 1983;

(g) the Official Solicitor to the Supreme Court when acting as judicial trustee under the Judicial Trustees Act 1896;

(h) a registrar of a county court when managing funds paid into court;

(i) a sheriff clerk when acting in the exercise of his functions in connection with the consignation or deposit of sums of money;

(j) a person acting in his capacity as manager of a fund established under section 22 of the Charities Act 1960, section 25 of the Charities Act (Northern Ireland) 1964, section 11 of the Trustee Investments Act 1961 or section 42 of the Administration of Justice Act 1982;

(k) the Central Board of Finance of the Church of England or a Diocesan Authority within the meaning of the Church Funds Investment Measure 1958 when acting in the exercise of its functions under that Measure;

(l) a person acting in his capacity as an official receiver within the meaning of section 399 of the Insolvency Act 1986 or in that capacity within the meaning of any corresponding provision in force in Northern Ireland.

45(2) **[Where bankruptcy order re authorised person etc.]** Where a bankruptcy order is made in respect of an authorised person or of a person whose authorisation is suspended under section 28 above or who is the subject of a direction under section 33(1)(b) above or a winding-up order is made in respect of a partnership which is such a person, the trustee in bankruptcy or liquidator acting in his capacity as such is an exempted person but—

(a) sections 48 to 71 below and, so far as relevant to any of those provisions, Chapter IX of this Part of this Act; and

(b) sections 104, 105 and 106 below.

shall apply to him to the same extent as they applied to the bankrupt or partnership and, if the bankrupt or partnership was subject to the rules of a recognised self-regulating organisation or recognised professional body, he shall himself also be subject to those rules.

45(3)   [Application of sec. 45(2) to Scotland]   In the application of subsection (2) above to Scotland—

(a)   for the reference to a bankruptcy order being made in respect of a person there shall be substituted a reference to the estate of that person being sequestrated;

(b)   the reference to a winding-up order in respect of a partnership is a reference to such an order made under section 72 below;

(c)   for the reference to the trustee in bankruptcy there shall be substituted a reference to the interim trustee or permanent trustee within the meaning of the Bankruptcy (Scotland) Act 1985; and

(d)   for the references to the bankrupt there shall be substituted references to the debtor.

45(4)   [Application of sec. 45(2) to Northern Ireland]   In the application of subsection (2) above to Northern Ireland for the reference to a bankruptcy order there shall be substituted a reference to an order of adjudication of bankruptcy and the reference to a trustee in bankruptcy shall include a reference to an assignee in bankruptcy.

SUPPLEMENTAL

SEC. 46   Power to extend or restrict exemptions

46(1)   [Order by Secretary of State]   The Secretary of State may by order provide—

(a)   for exemptions additional to those specified in the foregoing provisions of this Chapter; or

(b)   for removing or restricting any exemption conferred by section 42, 43 or 45 above;

and any such order may contain such transitional provisions as the Secretary of State thinks necessary or expedient.

46(2)   [Approval etc. by Parliament]   An order making such provision as is mentioned in paragraph (a) of subsection (1) above shall be subject to annulment in pursuance of a resolution of either House of Parliament; and no order making such provision as is mentioned in paragraph (b) of that subsection shall be made unless a draft of it has been laid before and approved by a resolution of each House of Parliament.

Chapter V — Conduct of Investment Business

SEC. 47   Misleading statements and practices

47(1)   [Offence re statements]   Any person who—

(a)   makes a statement, promise or forecast which he knows to be misleading, false or deceptive or dishonestly conceals any material facts; or

(b)   recklessly makes (dishonestly or otherwise) a statement, promise or forecast which is misleading, false or deceptive, is guilty of an offence if he makes the statement, promise or forecast or conceals the facts for the purpose of inducing, or is reckless as to whether it may induce, another person (whether or not the person to whom the statement, promise or forecast is made or from whom the facts are concealed) to enter or offer to enter into, or to refrain from entering or offering to enter into, an investment agreement or to exercise, or refrain from exercising, any rights conferred by an investment.

47(2) **[Offence re conduct]** Any person who does any act or engages in any course of conduct which creates a false or misleading impression as to the market in or the price or value of any investments is guilty of an offence if he does so for the purpose of creating that impression and of thereby inducing another person to acquire, dispose of, subscribe for or underwrite those investments or to refrain from doing so or to exercise, or refrain from exercising, any rights conferred by those investments.

47(3) **[Defence re sec. 47(2)]** In proceedings brought against any person for an offence under subsection (2) above it shall be a defence for him to prove that he reasonably believed that his act or conduct would not create an impression that was false or misleading as to the matters mentioned in that subsection.

47(4) **[Non-application of sec. 47(1)]** Subsection (1) above does not apply unless—

(a) the statement, promise or forecast is made in or from, or the facts are concealed in or from, the United Kingdom;

(b) the person on whom the inducement is intended to or may have effect is in the United Kingdom; or

(c) the agreement is or would be entered into or the rights are or would be exercised in the United Kingdom.

47(5) **[Non-application of sec. 47(2)]** Subsection (2) above does not apply unless—

(a) the act is done or the course of conduct is engaged in in the United Kingdom; or

(b) the false or misleading impression is created there.

47(6) **[Penalty]** A person guilty of an offence under this section shall be liable—

(a) on conviction on indictment, to imprisonment for a term not exceeding seven years or to a fine or to both;

(b) on summary conviction, to imprisonment for a term not exceeding six months or to a fine not exceeding the statutory maximum or to both.

SEC. **47A** Statements of principle

47A(1) **[Power of Secretary of State to issue statements of principle]** The Secretary of State may issue statements of principle with respect to the conduct and financial standing expected of persons authorised to carry on investment business.

47A(2) **[Conduct expected]** The conduct expected may include compliance with a code or standard issued by another person, as for the time being in force, and may allow for the exercise of discretion by any person pursuant to any such code or standard.

47A(3) **[Consequence of failure to comply]** Failure to comply with a statement of principle under this section is a ground for the taking of disciplinary action or the exercise of powers of intervention, but it does not of itself give rise to any right of action by investors or other persons affected or affect the validity of any transaction.

47A(4)   [Extent of disciplinary action]   The disciplinary action which may be taken by virtue of subsection (3) is—

(a) the withdrawal or suspension of authorisation under section 28 or the termination or suspension of authorisation under section 33,

(b) the giving of a disqualification direction under section 59,

(c) the making of a public statement under section 60, or

(d) the application by the Secretary of State for an injunction, interdict or other order under section 61(1);

and the reference in that subsection to powers of intervention is to the powers conferred by Chapter VI of this Part.

47A(5)   [Principles re compliance with code or standard]   Where a statement of principle relates to compliance with a code or standard issued by another person, the statement of principle may provide—

(a) that failure to comply with the code or standard shall be a ground for the taking of disciplinary action, or the exercise of powers of intervention, only in such cases and to such extent as may be specified; and

(b) that no such action shall be taken, or any such power exercised, except at the request of the person by whom the code or standard in question was issued.

47A(6)   [Manner of exercise of powers]   The Secretary of State shall exercise his powers in such manner as appears to him appropriate to secure compliance with statements of principle under this section.

History
S. 47A inserted by CA 1989, s. 192 as from 15 March 1990 (see S.I. 1990 No. 354 (C. 12), art. 3).

Note
For transfer of the Secretary of State's functions under s. 47A see S.I. 1990 No. 354 (C. 12), art. 4(3)(a)).

SEC. 48   Conduct of business rules

48(1)   [Power of Secretary of State to make rules]   The Secretary of State may make rules regulating the conduct of investment business by authorised persons but those rules shall not apply to persons certified by a recognised professional body in respect of investment business in the carrying on of which they are subject to the rules of the body.

History
In s. 48(1) the words "members of a recognised self-regulating organisation or" formerly appearing after the words "shall not apply to" and the words "organisation or" formerly appearing after the words "subject to the rules of the" omitted and repealed by CA 1989, s. 206(1), 212, Sch. 23, para. 2(1), (2), and Sch. 24 as from 15 March 1990 (see S.I. 1990 No. 354 (C. 12), art. 3).

48(2)   [Extent of rules]   Rules under this section may in particular make provision—

(a) prohibiting a person from carrying on, or holding himself out as carrying on—

(i) investment business of any kind specified in the rules; or

(ii) investment business of a kind or on a scale other than that notified by him to the Secretary of State in connection with an application for authorisation under Chapter III of this Part of this Act, in a notice under section 32 above or in accordance with any provision of the rules or regulations in that behalf;

(b) prohibiting a person from carrying on investment business in relation to persons other than those of a specified class or description;

(c) regulating the manner in which a person may hold himself out as carrying on investment business;

(d) regulating the manner in which a person makes a market in any investments;

(e) as to the form and content of advertisements in respect of investment business;

(f) requiring the principals of appointed representatives to impose restrictions on the investment business carried on by them;

(g) requiring the disclosure of the amount or value, or of arrangements for the payment or provision, of commissions or other inducements in connection with investment business and restricting the matters by reference to which or the manner in which their amount or value may be determined;

(h) enabling or requiring information obtained by an authorised person in the course of carrying on one part of his business to be withheld by him from persons with whom he deals in the course of carrying on another part and for that purpose enabling or requiring persons employed in one part of that business to withhold information from those employed in another part;

(i) as to the circumstances and manner in which and the time when or the period during which action may be taken for the purpose of stabilising the price of investments of any specified description;

(j) for arrangements for the settlement of disputes;

(k) requiring the keeping of accounts and other records, as to their form and content and for their inspection;

(l) requiring a person to whom the rules apply to make provision for the protection of investors in the event of the cessation of his investment business in consequence of his death, incapacity or otherwise.

48(3) **[Relationship between sec. 48(1) and (2)]** Subsection (2) above is without prejudice to the generality of subsection (1) above and accordingly rules under this section may make provision for matters other than those mentioned in subsection (2) or further provision as to any of the matters there mentioned except that they shall not impose limits on the amount or value of commissions or other inducements paid or provided in connection with investment business.

48(4) **[Related business]** Rules under this section may also regulate or prohibit the carrying on in connection with investment business of any other business or the carrying on of any other business which is held out as being for the purposes of investment.

48(5) **["Advertisement" in sec. 48(2)(e)]** In paragraph (e) of subsection (2) above **"advertisement"** does not include any advertisement which is subject to section 154 below or which is required or permitted to be published by listing rules under Part IV of this Act and relates to securities which have been admitted to listing under that

Part; and rules under that paragraph shall have effect subject to the provisions of Part V of this Act.

48(6)   [Matters done in conformity with sec. 48(2)(b)]   Nothing done in conformity with rules made under paragraph (h) of subsection (2) above shall be regarded as a contravention of section 47 above.

48(7)   [Contravention of sec. 47(2)]   Section 47(2) above shall not be regarded as contravened by anything done for the purpose of stabilising the price of investments if it is done in conformity with rules made under this section and—

(a) (i)   in respect of investments which fall within any of paragraphs 1 to 5 of Schedule 1 to this Act and are specified by the rules; and

(ii)   during such period before or after the issue of those investments as is specified by the rules,

or

(b) (i)   in respect of such investments as are mentioned in subparagraph (a)(i) above; and

(ii)   during a period starting with the date of the first public announcement of an offer of those investments which states the price or the minimum price at which the investments are to be sold and ending on the 30th day after the closing date specified in the announcement for acceptances of such offer.

History
In s. 48(7), "(i)" inserted after "(a)", (ii) substituted for "(b)" formerly appearing before the words "during such period", and the word "or" and para. (b)(i) and (ii) added by the Financial Services Act 1986 (Stabilisation) Order 1988 (S.I. 1988 No. 717), art. 2(a)–(c) as from 6 April 1988.

48(7A)   [Meaning of "an offer" in sec. 48(7)(b)(ii)]   For the purposes of subparagraph (b)(ii) of subsection (7) above **"an offer"** means an offer for cash (other than in relation to the issue of the investments in question) where either—

(a)   the investments have been admitted to dealing on a recognised investment exchange or any other exchange of repute outside the United Kingdom; or

(b)   the offer is on the occasion of such admission or conditional on such admission;

and the total cost of the investments subject to the offer at the price stated in the first public announcement mentioned in subsection (7) above is at least £15,000,000 (or the equivalent in the currency or unit of account in which the price is stated on the date of the announcement).

History
S. 48(7A) added by the Financial Services Act 1986 (Stabilisation) Order 1988 (S.I. 1988 No. 717), art. 2(d) as from 6 April 1988.

48(8)   [Power of Secretary of State to amend sec. 48(7)]   The Secretary of State may by order amend subsection (7) above—

(a)   by restricting or extending the kinds of investment to which it applies;

(b)   by restricting it so as to apply only in relation to the issue of investments in specified circumstances or by extending it, in respect of investments of any kind specified in the order, so as to apply to things done during a specified period before or after events other than the issue of those investments.

48(9) **[Approval by Parliament of sec. 48(4) order]** No order shall be made under subsection (8) above unless a draft of it has been laid before and approved by a resolution of each House of Parliament.

48(10) **[Incidental and transitional provisions]** Rules under this section may contain such incidental and transitional provisions as the Secretary of State thinks necessary or expedient.

48(11) **[Effect of sec. 63A]** Section 63A below (application of designated rules) has effect as regards the application of rules under this section to members of recognised self-regulating organisations in respect of investment business in the carrying on of which they are subject to the rules of the organisation.

History
S. 48(11) inserted by CA 1989, s. 206(1) and Sch. 23, para.
2(1), (3) as from 15 March 1990 (see S.I. 1990 No. 354
(C. 12), art. 3).

SEC. 49   Financial resources rules

49(1) **[Power of Secretary of State to make rules]** The Secretary of State may make rules requiring—

(a) a person authorised to carry on investment business by virtue of section 25 or 31 above, or

(b) a member of a recognised self-regulating organisation carrying on investment business in the carrying on of which he is subject to the rules of the organisation,

to have and maintain in respect of that business such financial resources as are required by the rules.

History
S. 49(1) substituted by CA 1989, s. 206(1) and Sch. 23, virtue of section 25 or 31 above to have and maintain in
para. 3(1), (2) as from 15 March 1990 (see S.I. 1990 respect of that business such financial resources as are
No. 354 (C. 12), art. 3); s. 49(1) formerly read as follows: required by the rules."
"**49(1)** The Secretary of State may make rules requiring
persons authorised to carry on investment business by

49(2) **[Extent of rules]** Without prejudice to the generality of subsection (1) above, rules under this section may—

(a) impose requirements which are absolute or which are to vary from time to time by reference to such factors as are specified in or determined in accordance with the rules;

(b) impose requirements which take account of any business (whether or not investment business) carried on by the person concerned in conjunction with or in addition to the business mentioned in subsection (1) above;

(c) make provision as to the assets, liabilities and other matters to be taken into account in determining a person's financial resources for the purposes of the rules and the extent to which and the manner in which they are to be taken into account for that purpose.

49(3) **[Effect of sec. 63A]** Section 63A below (application of designated rules) has effect as regards the application of rules under this section to members of recognised self-regulating organisations in respect of investment business in the carrying on of which they are subject to the rules of the organisation.

History
S. 49(3) inserted by CA 1989, s. 206(1) and Sch. 23, para. 3(1), (3) as from 15 March 1990 (see S.I. 1990 No. 354 (C. 12), art. 3).

SEC. 50   Modification of conduct of business and financial resources rules for particular cases

50(1)   [Power of Secretary of State]   The Secretary of State may, on the application of any person to whom any rules made under section 48 or 49 above apply, alter the requirements of the rules so as to adapt them to the circumstances of that person or to any particular kind of business carried on or to be carried on by him.

50(2)   [Conditions for sec. 50(1) power]   The Secretary of State shall not exercise the powers conferred by subsection (1) above in any case unless it appears to him that—

   (a)   compliance with the requirements in question would be unduly burdensome for the applicant having regard to the benefit which compliance would confer on investors; and

   (b)   the exercise of those powers will not result in any undue risk to investors.

50(3)   [Exercise of sec. 50(1) powers]   The powers conferred by subsection (1) above may be exercised unconditionally or subject to conditions.

50(4)   [Effect of sec. 63B powers exercisable]   The powers conferred by subsection (1) above shall not be exercised in a case where the powers conferred by section 63B below are exercisable (powers of recognised self-regulating organisation in relation to designated rules).

History
S. 50(4) inserted by CA 1989, s. 206(1) and Sch. 23, para. 4 as from 15 March 1990 (see S.I. 1990 No. 354 (C. 12), art. 3).

SEC. 51   Cancellation rules

51(1)   [Power of Secretary of State]   The Secretary of State may make rules for enabling a person who has entered or offered to enter into an investment agreement with an authorised person to rescind the agreement or withdraw the offer within such period and in such manner as may be prescribed.

51(2)   [Extent of rules]   Without prejudice to the generality of subsection (1) above, rules under this section may make provision—

   (a)   for requiring the service of notices with respect to the rights exercisable under the rules;

   (b)   for the restitution of property and the making or recovery of payments where those rights are exercised; and

   (c)   for such other incidental matters as the Secretary of State thinks necessary or expedient.

SEC. 52 Notification regulations

52(1) [Regulations re notice of certain events] The Secretary of State may make regulations requiring authorised persons to give him forthwith notice of the occurrence of such events as are specified in the regulations and such information in respect of those events as is so specified.

52(2) [Regulations re furnishing information] The Secretary of State may make regulations requiring authorised persons to furnish him at such times or in respect of such periods as are specified in the regulations with such information as is so specified.

52(3) [Exceptions to application of regulations] Regulations under this section shall not apply to a member of a recognised self-regulating organisation or a person certified by a recognised professional body unless he carries on investment business in the carrying on of which he is not subject to the rules of that organisation or body.

History
In s. 52(3) the words "not subject to the rules of that organisation or body" substituted for the words "subject to any of the rules made under section 48 above" by   CA 1989, s. 206(1) and Sch. 23, para. 5 as from 15 March 1990 (see S.I. 1990 No. 354 (C. 12), art. 3).

52(4) [Extent of regulations] Without prejudice to the generality of subsections (1) and (2) above, regulations under this section may relate to—

 (a) the nature of the investment business being carried on;

 (b) the nature of any other business carried on with or for the purposes of the investment business;

 (c) any proposal of an authorised person to alter the nature or extent of any business carried on by him;

 (d) any person becoming or ceasing to be a person of the kind to whom regard could be had by the Secretary of State under subsection (3) of section 27 above in deciding an application for authorisation under that section;

 (e) the financial position of an authorised person as respects his investment business or any other business carried on by him;

 (f) any property managed, and any property or money held, by an authorised person on behalf of other persons.

52(5) [Form, verification of information] Regulations under this section may require information to be given in a specified form and to be verified in a specified manner.

52(6) [Manner of giving notice of information] Any notice or information required to be given or furnished under this section shall be given in writing or in such other manner as the Secretary of State may approve.

SEC. 53 Indemnity rules

53(1) [Power of Secretary of State to make rules] The Secretary of State may make rules concerning indemnity against any claim in respect of any description of civil liability incurred by an authorised person in connection with his investment business.

53(2) [Exception to application of rules] Rules under this section shall not apply to a member of a recognised self-regulating organisation or a person certified by a recognised professional body in respect of investment business in the carrying on of which he is subject to the rules of the organisation or body unless that organisation or body has requested that rules under this section should apply to him; and any such request shall not be capable of being withdrawn after rules giving effect to it have been made but without prejudice to the power of the Secretary of State to revoke the rules if he thinks fit.

53(3)   **[Extent of rules providing indemnity]**   For the purpose of providing indemnity the rules—

  (a) may authorise the Secretary of State to establish and maintain a fund or funds;

  (b) may authorise the Secretary of State to take out and maintain insurance with insurers authorised to carry on insurance business under the law of the United Kingdom or any other member State;

  (c) may require any person to whom the rules apply to take out and maintain insurance with any such insurer.

53(4)   **[Further extent of rules]**   Without prejudice to the generality of the foregoing provisions, the rules may—

  (a) specify the terms and conditions on which, and the extent to which, indemnity is to be available and any circumstances in which the right to it is to be excluded or modified;

  (b) provide for the management, administration and protection of any fund maintained by virtue of subsection (3)(a) above and require persons to whom the rules apply to make payments to any such fund;

  (c) require persons to whom the rules apply to make payments by way of premium on any insurance policy maintained by the Secretary of State by virtue of subsection (3)(b) above;

  (d) prescribe the conditions which an insurance policy must satisfy for the purposes of subsection (3)(c) above;

  (e) authorise the Secretary of State to determine the amount which the rules require to be paid to him or an insurer, subject to such limits or in accordance with such provisions as may be prescribed by the rules;

  (f) specify circumstances in which, where sums are paid by the Secretary of State or an insurer in satisfaction of claims against a person subject to the rules, proceedings may be taken against that person by the Secretary of State or the insurer;

  (g) specify circumstances in which persons are exempt from the rules;

  (h) empower the Secretary of State to take such steps as he considers necessary or expedient to ascertain whether or not the rules are being complied with; and

  (i) contain incidental or supplementary provisions.

SEC. 54   Compensation fund

54(1)   **[Power of Secretary of State]**   The Secretary of State may by rules establish a scheme for compensating investors in cases where persons who are or have been authorised persons are unable, or likely to be unable, to satisfy claims in respect of any description of civil liability incurred by them in connection with their investment businesses.

54(2)   [Extent of rules]   Without prejudice to the generality of subsection (1) above, rules under this section may—

  (a) provide for the administration of the scheme and, subject to the rules, the determination and regulation of any matter relating to its operation by a body appearing to the Secretary of State to be representative of, or of any class of, authorised persons;

  (b) establish a fund out of which compensation is to be paid;

  (c) provide for the levying of contributions from, or from any class of, authorised persons and otherwise for financing the scheme and for the payment of contributions and other money into the fund;

  (d) specify the terms and conditions on which, and the extent to which, compensation is to be payable and any circumstances in which the right to compensation is to be excluded or modified;

  (e) provide for treating compensation payable under the scheme in respect of a claim against any person as extinguishing or reducing the liability of that person in respect of the claim and for conferring on the body administering the scheme a right of recovery against that person, being, in the event of his insolvency, a right not exceeding such right, if any, as the claimant would have had in that event; and

  (f) contain incidental and supplementary provisions.

54(3)   [Application of scheme to SRO members etc.]   A scheme under this section shall not be made so as to apply to persons who are members of a recognised self-regulating organisation except after consultation with that organisation or, except at the request of a recognised professionl body, to persons who are certified by it and subject to its rules in carrying on all the investment business carried on by them; and no scheme applying to such persons shall be made unless the Secretary of State is satisfied that the rules establishing it make sufficient provision—

  (a) for the administration of the scheme by a body on which the interests of those persons are adequately represented; and

  (b) for securing that the amounts which they are liable to contribute reflect, so far as practicable, the amount of the claims made or likely to be made or likely to be made in respect of those persons.

54(4)   [Where scheme applies to persons in sec. 54(3)]   Where a scheme applies to such persons as are mentioned in subsection (3) above the rules under this section may—

  (a) constitute the recognised self-regulating organisation or recognised professional body in question as the body administering the scheme in relation to those persons;

  (b) provide for the levying of contributions from that organisation or body instead of from those persons; and

  (c) establish a separate fund for the contributions and compensation payable in respect of those persons, with or without provision for payments and repayments in specified circumstances between that and any other fund established by the scheme.

54(5) [Request under sec. 54(3)] A request by a recognised professional body under subsection (3) above shall not be capable of being withdrawn after rules giving effect to it have been made but without prejudice to the power of the Secretary of State to revoke the rules if he thinks fit.

54(6) [Rules re procedure] Rules may be made—

    (a) for England and Wales, under sections 411 and 412 of the Insolvency Act 1986;

    (b) for Scotland—

        (i) under the said section 411; and

        (ii) in relation to the application of this section where the persons who are or have been authorised persons are persons whose estates may be sequestrated under the Bankruptcy (Scotland) Act 1985, by the Secretary of State under this section; and

    (c) for Northern Ireland, under Article 613 of the Companies (Northern Ireland) Order 1986 and section 65 of the Judicature (Northern Ireland) Act 1978,

for the purpose of integrating any procedure for which provision is made by virtue of subsection (2)(e) above into the general procedure on a winding-up, bankruptcy or sequestration.

SEC. 55   Clients' money

55(1) [Power of Secretary of State to make regulations] The Secretary of State may make regulations with respect to money (in this section referred to as "clients' money") which authorised persons, or authorised persons of any description, hold in such circumstances as are specified in the regulations.

55(2) [Extent of regulations] Without prejudice to the generality of subsection (1) above, regulations under this section may—

    (a) provide that clients' money held by an authorised person is held on trust;

    (b) require clients' money to be paid into an account the title of which contains the word "client" and which is with an institution of a kind specified in the regulations or, in the case of or a person certified by a recognised professional body, by the rules of that body;

    (c) make provision with respect to the opening and keeping of clients' accounts, including provision as to the circumstances in which money other than clients' money may be paid into such accounts and the circumstances in which and the persons to whom money held in such accounts may be paid out;

    (d) require the keeping of accounts and records in respect of clients' money;

(e) require any such accounts to be examined by an accountant having such qualifications as are specified in the regulations and require the accountant to report to the Secretary of State, or in the case of a person certified by a recognised professional body, to that body, whether in his opinion the provisions of the regulations have been complied with and on such other matters as may be specified in the regulations;

(f) authorise the retention, to such extent and in such cases as may be specified in regulations, of so much of clients' money as represents interest.

History

In s. 55(2)(b) and (e) the words "a member of a recognised self-regulating organisation or" formerly appearing in both instances after the words "in the case of" and the words "organisation or" formerly appearing after the words "by the rules of that" and the words "by a recognised professional body, to that" respectively, omitted and

repealed by CA 1989, s. 206(1), 212, Sch. 23, para. 6(1), (2) and Sch. 24 as from 15 March 1990 (see S.I. 1990 No. 354 (C. 12), art. 3).

Note

See note after s. 55(6).

55(3) [Where authorised person required to have auditor] Where an authorised person is required to have an auditor, whether by virtue of any provision contained in or made under any enactment (including this Act) or of the rules of any such body as is mentioned in paragraph (b) of subsection (2) above, the regulations may require the examination and report referred to in paragraph (e) of that subsection to be carried out and made by that auditor.

History

In s. 55(3) the words "organisation or" formerly appearing after the words "the rules of any such" omitted and repealed by CA 1989, s. 206(1), 212, Sch. 23, para. 6(1), (3) and Sch. 24 as from 15 March 1990 (see S.I. 1990 No. 354 (C. 12), art. 3).

Note

See note after s. 55(6).

55(4) [Liability of institution under regulations] An institution with which an account is kept in pursuance of regulations made under this section does not incur any liability as constructive trustee where money is wrongfully paid from the account unless the institution permits the payment with knowledge that it is wrongful or having deliberately failed to make enquiries in circumstances in which a reasonable and honest person would have done so.

55(5) [Application to Scotland] In the application of this section to Scotland for the reference to money being held on trust there shall be substituted a reference to its being held as agent for the person who is entitled to call for it to be paid over to him or to be paid on his direction or to have it otherwise credited to him.

55(6) [Effect of sec. 63A] Section 63A below (application of designated regulations) has effect as regards the application of regulations under this section to members of recognised self-regulating organisations in respect of investment business in the carrying on of which they are subject to the rules of the organisation.

History

S. 55(6) inserted by CA 1989, s. 206(1) and Sch. 23, para. 6(1), (4) as from 15 March 1990 (see S.I. 1990 No. 354 (C. 12), art. 3).

Note

For transitional provisions in relation to amendments to s. 55 effected by CA 1989, s. 206(1), 212, Sch. 23, para. 6 and Sch. 24 see S.I. 1990 No. 354 (C. 12) art. 6(4).

SEC. 56 Unsolicited calls

56(1) [Prohibition re unsolicited calls] Except so far as permitted by regulations made by the Secretary of State, no person shall in the course of or in consequence of an unsolicited call—

(a) made on a person in the United Kingdom; or

    (b) made from the United Kingdom on a person elsewhere,

by way of business enter into an investment agreement with the person on whom the call is made or procure or endeavour to procure that person to enter into such an agreement.

56(2) **[Qualification to sec. 56(1)]** A person shall not be guilty of an offence by reason only of contravening subsection (1) above, but subject to subsection (4) below—

    (a) any investment agreement which is entered into in the course of or in consequence of the unsolicited call shall not be enforceable against the person on whom the call was made; and

    (b) that person shall be entitled to recover any money or other property paid or transferred by him under the agreement, together with compensation for any loss sustained by him as a result of having parted with it.

56(3) **[Compensation under sec. 56(2)]** The compensation recoverable under subsection (2) above shall be such as the parties may agree or as a court may, on the application of either party, determine.

56(4) **[Power of court re sec. 56(2) agreements]** A court may allow an agreement to which subsection (2) above applies to be enforced or money and property paid or transferred under it to be retained if it is satisfied—

    (a) that the person on whom the call was made was not influenced, or not influenced to any material extent, by anything said or done in the course of or in consequence of the call;

    (b) without prejudice to paragraph (a) above, that the person on whom the call was made entered into the agreement—

        (i) following discussions between the parties of such a nature and over such a period that his entering into the agreement can fairly be regarded as a consequence of those discussions rather than the call; and

        (ii) was aware of the nature of the agreement and any risks involved in entering into it; or

    (c) that the call was not made by—

        (i) the person seeking to enforce the agreement or to retain the money or property or a person acting on his behalf or an appointed representative whose principal he was; or

        (ii) a person who has received or is to receive, or in the case of an appointed representative whose principal has received or is to receive, any commission or other inducement in respect of the agreement from a person mentioned in sub-paragraph (i) above.

56(5) **[Where agreement not performed or money recovered]** Where a person elects not to perform an agreement which by virtue of this section is unenforceable against him or by virtue of this section recovers money paid or other property transferred by him under an agreement he shall repay any money and return any other property received by him under the agreement.

56(6) **[Where property has passed to third party]** Where any property transferred under an agreement to which this section applies has passed to a third party the references to that property in this section shall be construed as references to its value at the time of its transfer under the agreement.

56(7) [Effect of sec. 63A] Section 63A below (application of designated regulations) has effect as regards the application of regulations under this section to members of recognised self-regulating organisations in respect of investment business in the carrying on of which they are subject to the rules of the organisation.

As it applies to such persons in respect of such business the reference in subsection (1) above to conduct permitted by regulations made by the Secretary of State shall be construed—

(a) where or to the extent that the regulations do not apply, as a reference to conduct permitted by the rules of the organisation; and

(b) where or to the extent that the regulations do apply but are expressed to have effect subject to the rules of the organisation, as a reference to conduct permitted by the regulations together with the rules of the organisation.

History
See history note after s. 56(7A).

56(7A) [Application to person certified by RPB] In the application of this section to anything done by a person certified by a recognised professional body in carrying on investment business in the carrying on of which he is subject to the rules of the body, the reference in subsection (1) above to conduct permitted by regulations made by the Secretary of State shall be construed as a reference to conduct permitted by the rules of the body.

History
S. 56(7), (7A) substituted for the former s. 56(7) by CA 1989, s. 206(1) and Sch. 23, para. 7 as from 15 March 1990; former s. 56(7) read as follows:

"**56(7)** In the application of this section to anything done by a member of a recognised self-regulating organisation or a person certified by a recognised professional body in carrying on investment business in the carrying on of which he is subject to the rules of the organisation or body the reference in subsection (1) above to regulations made by the Secretary of State shall be construed as references to the rules of the organisation or body."

56(8) ["Unsolicited call"] In this section "**unsolicited call**" means a personal visit or oral communication made without express invitation.

SEC. 57 Restrictions on advertising

57(1) [No advertising unless approved] Subject to section 58 below, no person other than an authorised person shall issue or cause to be issued an investment advertisement in the United Kingdom unless its contents have been approved by an authorised person.

57(2) ["An investment advertisement"] In this Act "**an investment advertisement**" means any advertisement inviting persons to enter or offer to enter into an investment agreement or to exercise any rights conferred by an investment to acquire, dispose of, underwrite or convert an investment or containing information calculated to lead directly or indirectly to persons doing so.

57(3) [Offence, penalty] Subject to subsection (4) below, any person who contravenes this section shall be guilty of an offence and liable—

(a) on conviction on indictment, to imprisonment for a term not exceeding two years or to a fine or to both;

(b) on summary conviction, to imprisonment for a term not exceeding six months or to a fine not exceeding the statutory maximum or to both.

57(4) **[Exception to sec. 57(3)]**   A person who in the ordinary course of a business other than investment business issues an advertisement to the order of another person shall not be guilty of an offence under this section if he proves that he believed on reasonable grounds that the person to whose order the advertisement was issued was an authorised person, that the contents of the advertisement were approved by an authorised person or that the advertisement was permitted by or under section 58 below.

57(5) **[Effect of contravention]**   If in contravention of this section a person issues or causes to be issued an advertisement inviting persons to enter or offer to enter into an investment agreement or containing information calculated to leads directly or indirectly to persons doing so, then, subject to subsection (8) below—

    (a) he shall not be entitled to enforce any agreement to which the advertisement related and which was entered into after the issue of the advertisement; and

    (b) the other party shall be entitled to recover any money or other property paid or transferred by him under the agreement, together with compensation for any loss sustained by him as a result of having parted with it.

57(6) **[Further effect of contravention]**   If in contravention of this section a person issues or causes to be issued an advertisement inviting persons to exercise any rights conferred by an investment or containing information calculated to lead directly or indirectly to persons doing so, then, subject to subsection (8) below—

    (a) he shall not be entitled to enforce any obligation to which a person is subject as a result of any exercise by him after the issue of the advertisement of any rights to which the advertisement related; and

    (b) that person shall be entitled to recover any money or other property paid or transferred by him under any such obligation, together with compensation for any loss sustained by him as a result of having parted with it.

57(7) **[Compensation under sec. 57(5), (6)]**   The compensation recoverable under subsection (5) or (6) above shall be such as the parties may agree or as a court may, on the application of either party, determine.

57(8) **[Power of court re enforcing sec. 57(5), (6) agreements]**   A court may allow any such agreement or obligation as is mentioned in subsection (5) or (6) above to be enforced or money or property paid or transferred under it to be retained if it is satisfied—

    (a) that the person against whom enforcement is sought or who is seeking to recover the money or property was not influenced, or not influenced to any material extent, by the advertisement in making his decision to enter into the agreement or as to the exercise of the rights in question; or

    (b) that the advertisement was not misleading as to the nature of the investment, the terms of the agreement or, as the case may be, the consequences of exercising the rights in question and fairly stated any risks involved in those matters.

57(9) **[Where agreement not performed or money recovered]**   Where a person elects not to perform an agreement or an obligation which by virtue of subsection (5) or (6) above is unenforceable against him or by virtue of either of those subsections recovers money paid or other property transferred by him under an agreement or obligation he shall repay any money and return any other property received by him under the agreement or, as the case may be, as a result of exercising the rights in question.

57(10) **[Where property has passed to third party]** Where any property transferred under an agreement or obligation to which subsection (5) or (6) above applies has passed to a third party the references to that property in this section shall be construed as references to its value at the time of its transfer under the agreement or obligation.

SEC. 58 Exceptions from restrictions on advertising

58(1) **[Non-application of sec. 57 — general]** Section 57 above does not apply to—

(a) any advertisement issued or caused to be issued by, and relating only to investments issued by—

  (i) the government of the United Kingdom, of Northern Ireland or of any country or territory outside the United Kingdom;

  (ii) a local authority in the United Kingdom or elsewhere;

  (iii) the Bank of England or the central bank of any country or territory outside the United Kingdom; or

  (iv) any international organisation the members of which include the United Kingdom or another member State;

(b) any advertisement issued or caused to be issued by a person who is exempt under section 36, 38, 42, 43, 44 or 45 above, or by virtue of an order under section 46 above, if the advertisement relates to a matter in respect of which he is exempt.

(c) any advertisement which is issued or caused to be issued by a national of a member State other than the United Kingdom in the course of investment business lawfully carried on by him in such a State and which conforms with any rules made under section 48(2)(e) above;

(d) any advertisement which—

  (i) is subject to section 154 below; or

  (ii) consists of or any part of listing particulars, supplementary listing particulars or any other document required or permitted to be published by listing rules under Part IV of this Act or by an approved exchange under Part V of this Act.

58(2) **[Non-application of sec. 57 re Pt. V]** Section 57 above does not apply to an advertisement inviting persons to subscribe in cash for any investments to which Part V of this Act applies if the advertisement is issued or caused to be issued by the person by whom the investments are to be issued and either the advertisement consists of a prospectus registered in accordance with that Part or the following matters (and no others that would make it an investment advertisement) are contained in the advertisement—

(a) the name of that person and his address or particulars of other means of communicating with him;

(b) the nature of the investments, the number offered for subscription and their nominal value and price;

(c) a statement that a prospectus for the purposes of that Part of this Act is or will be available and, if it is not yet available, when it will be; and

(d) instructions for obtaining a copy of the prospectus.

58(3) **[Non-application of sec. 57 re exempted advertisements]** Section 57 above does not apply to an advertisement issued in such circumstances as may be specified in an order made by the Secretary of State for the purpose of exempting from that section—

(a) advertisements appearing to him to have a private character, whether by reason of a connection between the person issuing them and those to whom they are issued or otherwise;

(b) advertisements appearing to him to deal with investment only incidentally;

(c) advertisements issued to persons appearing to him to be sufficiently expert to understand any risks involved; or

(d) such other classes of advertisement as he thinks fit.

58(4) **[Extent of sec. 58(3) order]** An order under subsection (3) above may require any person who by virtue of the order is authorised to issue an advertisement to comply with such requirements as are specified in the order.

58(5) **[Parliament approval etc. re sec. 58(3)]** An order made by virtue of paragraph (a), (b) or (c) of subsection (3) above shall be subject to annulment in pursuance of a resolution of either House of Parliament; and no order shall be made by virtue of paragraph (d) of that subsection unless a draft of it has been laid before and approved by a resolution of each House of Parliament.

58(6) **[Non-application of sec. 58(1)(c), (2)]** Subsections (1)(c) and (2) above do not apply to any advertisement relating to an investment falling within paragraph 5 of Schedule 1 to this Act.

SEC. 59   Employment of prohibited persons

59(1) **[Power of direction by Secretary of State]** If it appears to the Secretary of State that any individual is not a fit and proper person to be employed in connection with investment business or investment business of a particular kind he may direct that he shall not, without the written consent of the Secretary of State, be employed in connection with investment business or, as the case may be, investment business of that kind—

(a) by authorised persons or exempted persons; or

(b) by any specified person or persons, or by persons of any specified description, falling within paragraph (a) above.

59(2) **["A disqualification direction"]** A direction under this section ("a disqualification direction") shall specify the date on which it is to take effect and a copy of it shall be served on the person to whom it relates.

59(3) **[Consent by Secretary of State]** Any consent by the Secretary of State to the employment of a person who is the subject of a disqualification direction may relate to employment generally or to employment of a particular kind, may be given subject to conditions and restrictions and may be varied by him from time to time.

59(4) **[Notice by Secretary of State]** Where the Secretary of State proposes—

(a) to give a disqualification direction in respect of any person; or

(b) to refuse an application for his consent under this section or for the variation of such consent,

he shall give that person or the applicant written notice of his intention to do so, stating the reasons for which he proposes to act and giving particulars of the right to require the case to be referred to the Tribunal under Chapter IX of this Part of this Act.

59(5) **[Offence, penalty]** Any person who accepts or continues in any employment in contravention of a disqualification direction shall be guilty of an offence and liable on summary conviction to a fine not exceeding the fifth level on the standard scale.

59(6) **[Duty of authorised person, appointed representative]** It shall be the duty of an authorised person and an appointed representative to take reasonable care not to employ or continue to employ a person in contravention of a disqualification direction.

59(7) **[Revocation of disqualification direction]** The Secretary of State may revoke a disqualification direction.

59(8) **[Interpretation]** In this section references to employment include references to employment otherwise than under a contract of service.

SEC. 60 Public statement as to person's misconduct

60(1) **[Power of Secretary of State to publish statement]** If it appears to the Secretary of State that a person who is or was an authorised person by virtue of section 22, 24, 25 or 31 above has contravened—

(a) any provision of rules or regulations made under this Chapter or of section 56 or 59 above; or

(b) any condition imposed under section 50 above,

he may publish a statement to that effect.

60(2) **[Written notice to person concerned]** Before publishing a statement under subsection (1) above the Secretary of State shall give the person concerned written notice of the proposed statement and of the reasons for which he proposes to act.

60(3) **[Copy of notice to other persons]** Where the reasons stated in the notice relate specifically to matters which—

(a) refer to a person identified in the notice other than the person who is or was the authorised person; and

(b) are in the opinion of the Secretary of State prejudicial to that person in any office or employment,

the Secretary of State shall, unless he considers it impracticable to do so, serve a copy of the notice on that other person.

60(4) **[Notice to include reference to Tribunal]** A notice under this section shall give particulars of the right to have the case referred to the Tribunal under Chapter IX of this Part of this Act.

60(5) **[Where case not required to be referred to Tribunal]** Where a case is not required to be referred to the Tribunal by a person on whom a notice is served under this section the Secretary of State shall, at the expiration of the period within which such a requirement can be made, give that person written notice that the statement is or is not to be published; and if it is to be published the Secretary of State shall after publication send a copy of it to that person and to any person on whom a copy of the notice under subsection (2) above was served.

SEC. 61   Injunctions and restitution orders

61(1)   [Power of court on application by Secretary of State]   If on the application of the Secretary of State the court is satisfied—

(a) that there is a reasonable likelihood that any person will contravene any provision of—

  (i) rules or regulations made under this Chapter;

  (ii) sections 47, 56, 57, or 59 above;

  (iii) any requirements imposed by an order under section 58(3) above; or

  (iv) the rules of a recognised self-regulating organisation, recognised professional body, recognised investment exchange or recognised clearing house to which that person is subject and which regulate the carrying on by him of investment business,

or any condition imposed under section 50 above;

(b) that any person has contravened any such provision or condition and that there is a reasonable likelihood that the contravention will continue or be repeated; or

(c) that any person has contravened any such provision or condition and that there are steps that could be taken for remedying the contravention,

the court may grant an injunction restraining the contravention or, in Scotland, an interdict prohibiting the contravention or, as the case may be, make an order requiring that person and any other person who appears to the court to have been knowingly concerned in the contravention to take such steps as the court may direct to remedy it.

61(2)   [Restriction on sec. 61(1) application]   No application shall be made by the Secretary of State under subsection (1) above in respect of any such rules as are mentioned in subsection (1)(a)(iv) above unless it appears to him that the organisation, body, exchange or clearing house is unable or unwilling to take appropriate steps to restrain the contravention or to require the person concerned to take such steps as are mentioned in subsection (1) above.

61(3)   [Power of court to make sec. 61(4),(5) orders]   The court may, on the application of the Secretary of State, make an order under subsection (4) below or, in relation to Scotland, under subsection (5) below if satisfied—

(a) that profits have accrued to any person as a result of his contravention of any provision or condition mentioned in subsection (1)(a) above; or

(b) that one or more investors have suffered loss or been otherwise adversely affected as a result of that contravention.

61(4)   [Order re payment into court etc.]   The court may under this subsection order the person concerned to pay into court, or appoint a receiver to recover from him, such sum as appears to the court to be just having regard—

(a) in a case within paragraph (a) of subsection (3) above, to the profits appearing to the court to have accrued;

(b) in a case within paragraph (b) of that subsection, to the extent of the loss or other adverse effect; or

(c) in a case within both paragraphs (a) and (b) of that subsection, to the profits and to the extent of the loss or other adverse effect.

61(5) [Order re payment of sum] The court may under this subsection order the person concerned to pay to the applicant such sum as appears to the court to be just having regard to the considerations mentioned in paragraphs (a) to (c) of subsection (4) above.

61(6) [Payment of sums in sec. 61(4),(5)] Any amount paid into court by or recovered from a person in pursuance of an order under subsection (4) or (5) above shall be paid out to such person or distributed among such persons as the court may direct, being a person or persons appearing to the court to have entered into transactions with that person as a result of which the profits mentioned in paragraph (a) of subsection (3) above have accrued to him or the loss or adverse effect mentioned in paragraph (b) of that subsection has been suffered.

61(7) [Furnishing of accounts etc. re sec. 61(3)] On an application under subsection (3) above the court may require the person concerned to furnish it with such accounts or other information as it may require for establishing whether any and, if so, what profits have accrued to him as mentioned in paragraph (a) of that subsection and for determining how any amounts are to be paid or distributed under subsection (6) above; and the court may require any such accounts or other information to be verified in such manner as it may direct.

61(8) [Exercise of jurisdiction] The jurisdiction conferred by this section shall be exercisable by the High Court and the Court of Session.

61(9) [Effect on other rights] Nothing in this section affects the right of any person other than the Secretary of State to bring proceedings in respect of the matters to which this section applies.

SEC. 62 Actions for damages

62(1) [Certain contraventions actionable] Without prejudice to section 61 above, a contravention of—

(a) any rules or regulations made under this Chapter;

(b) any conditions imposed under section 50 above;

(c) any requirements imposed by an order under section 58(3) above;

(d) the duty imposed by section 59(6) above,

shall be actionable at the suit of a person who suffers loss as a result of the contravention subject to the defences and other incidents applying to actions for breach of statutory duty.

62(2) [Additional application of sec. 62(1)] Subsection (1) applies also to a contravention by a member of a recognised self-regulating organisation or a person certified by a recognised professional body of any rules of the organisation or body relating to a matter in respect of which rules or regulations have been or could be made under this Chapter in relation to an authorised person who is not such a member or so certified.

62(3)   [Non-application of sec. 62(1)]   Subsection (1) above does not apply—

(a) to a contravention of rules made under section 49 or conditions imposed under section 50 in connection with an alteration of the requirements of those rules; or

(b) by virtue of subsection (2) above to a contravention of rules relating to a matter in respect of which rules have been or could be made under section 49.

62(4)   [No offence re contraventions]   A person shall not be guilty of an offence by reason of any contravention to which subsection (1) above applies or of a contravention of rules made under section 49 above or such conditions as are mentioned in subsection (3)(a) above and no such contravention shall invalidate any transaction.

SEC. 62A   Restriction of right of action

62A(1)   [When sec. 62 action not to lie]   No action in respect of a contravention to which section 62 above applies shall lie at the suit of a person other than a private investor, except in such circumstances as may be specified by regulations made by the Secretary of State.

62A(2)   ["Private investor"]   The meaning of the expression **"private investor"** for the purposes of subsection (1) shall be defined by regulations made by the Secretary of State.

62A(3)   [Extent of sec. 62A(1) regulations]   Regulations under subsection (1) may make different provision with respect to different cases.

62A(4)   [Consultation before regulations]   The Secretary of State shall, before making any regulations affecting the right to bring an action in respect of a contravention of any rules or regulations made by a person other than himself, consult that person.

History
S.62A inserted by CA 1989, s. 193(1) as from 15 March 1990 (see S.I. 1990 No. 354 (C. 12), art. 3) insofar as is   necessary to enable regulations to be made under that section.

SEC. 63   Gaming contracts

63(1)   [Certain contracts not void]   No contract to which this section applies shall be void or unenforceable by reason of—

(a) section 18 of the Gaming Act 1845, section 1 of the Gaming Act 1892 or any corresponding provisions in force in Northern Ireland; or

(b) any rule of the law of Scotland whereby a contract by way of gaming or wagering is not legally enforceable.

63(2)   [Application of section]   This section applies to any contract entered into by either or each party by way of business and the making or performance of which by either party constitutes an activity which falls within paragraph 12 of Schedule 1 to this Act or would do so apart from Parts III and IV of that Schedule.

SEC. 63A   Application of designated rules and regulations to members of self-regulating organisations

63A(1)   [Power of Secretary of State to make rules and regulations]   The Secretary of State may in rules and regulations under—

(a)   section 48 (conduct of business rules),

(b)   section 49 (financial resources rules),

(c)   section 55 (clients' money regulations), or

(d)   section 56 (regulations as to unsolicited calls),

designate provisions which apply, to such extent as may be specified, to a member of a recognised self-regulating organisation in respect of investment business in the carrying on of which he is subject to the rules of the organisation.

63A(2)   [Qualification to designated rules]   It may be provided that the designated rules or regulations have effect, generally or to such extent as may be specified, subject to the rules of the organisation.

63A(3)   [Contravention]   A member of a recognised self-regulating organisation who contravenes a rule or regulation applying to him by virtue of this section shall be treated as having contravened the rules of the organisation.

63A(4)   [Modification or waiver]   It may be provided that, to such extent as may be specified, the designated rules or regulations may not be modified or waived (under section 63B below or section 50) in relation to a member of a recognised self-regulating organisation.

Where such provision is made any modification or waiver previously granted shall cease to have effect, subject to any transitional provision or saving contained in the rules or regulations.

63A(5)   [Extent of application of rules and regulations]   Except as mentioned in subsection (1), the rules and regulations referred to in that subsection do not apply to a member of a recognised self-regulating organisation in respect of investment business in the carrying on of which he is subject to the rules of the organisation.

History
See history note after s. 63B.

Note
For transfer of the Secretary of State's functions under s. 63A see S.I. 1990 No. 354 (C. 12), art. 4(2)(a).

SEC. 63B   Modification or waiver of designated rules and regulations

63B(1)   [Power of SRO on application of member]   A recognised self-regulating organisation may on the application of a member of the organisation—

(a)   modify a rule or regulation designated under section 63A so as to adapt it to his circumstances or to any particular kind of business carried on by him, or

(b)   dispense him from compliance with any such rule or regulation, generally or in relation to any particular kind of business carried on by him.

63B(2)   [When powers not exercisable]   The powers conferred by this section shall not be exercised unless it appears to the organisation—

(a) that compliance with the rule or regulation in question would be unduly burdensome for the applicant having regard to the benefit which compliance would confer on investors, and

(b) that the exercise of those powers will not result in any undue risk to investors.

63B(3)   [Extent of powers; contravention]   The powers conferred by this section may be exercised unconditionally or subject to conditions; and section 63A(3) applies in the case of a contravention of a condition as in the case of contravention of a designated rule or regulation.

63B(4)   [Monitoring and enforcement of compliance]   The reference in paragraph 4(1) of Schedule 2 (requirements for recognition of self-regulating organisations) to monitoring and enforcement of compliance with rules and regulations includes monitoring and enforcement of compliance with conditions imposed by the organisation under this section.

History
S. 63A and 63B inserted by CA 1989, s. 194 as from 15 March 1990 (see S.I. 1990 No. 354 (C. 12), art. 3).

SEC. 63C   Codes of practice

63C(1)   [Power of Secretary of State to issue]   The Secretary of State may issue codes of practice with respect to any matters dealt with by statements of principle issued under section 47A or by rules or regulations made under any provision of this Chapter.

63C(2)   [Determining failure to comply with statement of principle]   In determining whether a person has failed to comply with a statement of principle—

(a) a failure by him to comply with any relevant provision of a code of practice may be relied on as tending to establish failure to comply with the statement of principle, and

(b) compliance by him with the relevant provisions of a code of practice may be relied on as tending to negative any such failure.

63C(3)   [Effect of contravention]   A contravention of a code of practice with respect to a matter dealt with by rules or regulations shall not of itself give rise to any liability or invalidate any transaction; but in determining whether a person's conduct amounts to contravention of a rule or regulation—

(a) contravention by him of any relevant provision of a code of practice may be relied on as tending to establish liability, and

(b) compliance by him with the relevant provisions of a code of practice may be relied on as tending to negative liability.

63C(4)   [Limitation of rules and regulations]   Where by virtue of section 63A (application of designated rules and regulations to members of self-regulating organisations) rules or regulations—

(a) do not apply, to any extent, to a member of a recognised self-regulating organisation, or

(b) apply, to any extent, subject to the rules of the organisation,

FSA 1986, sec. 63B(3)   [The next page is 60,751]

a code of practice with respect to a matter dealt with by the rules or regulations may contain provision limiting its application to a corresponding extent.

History
S. 63C inserted by CA 1989, s. 195 as from 15 March 1990 (see S.I. 1990 No. 354 (C. 12), art. 3).

Note
For transfer of the Secretary of State's functions under s. 63C see S.I. 1990 No. 354 (C. 12), art. 4(3)(c).

Chapter VI — Powers of Intervention

SEC. 64 Scope of powers

64(1) **[Exercise of powers]** The powers conferred on the Secretary of State by this Chapter shall be exercisable in relation to any authorised person or, except in the case of the power conferred by section 65 below, any appointed representative of his if it appears to the Secretary of State—

(a) that the exercise of the powers is desirable for the protection of investors;

(b) that the authorised person is not fit to carry on investment business of a particular kind or to the extent to which he is carrying it on or proposing to carry it on; or

(c) that the authorised person has contravened any provision of this Act or of any rules or regulations made under it or, in purported compliance with any such provision, has furnished the Secretary of State with false, inaccurate or misleading information or has contravened any prohibition or requirement imposed under this Act.

64(2) **[Matter for sec. 64(1)(b)]** For the purposes of subsection (1)(b) above the Secretary of State may take into account any matters that could be taken into account in deciding whether to withdraw or suspend an authorisation under Chapter III of this Part of this Act.

64(3) **[Exercise of power re sec. 28, 33(1)(b) persons]** The powers conferred by this Chapter may be exercised in relation to a person whose authorisation is suspended under section 28 above or who is the subject of a direction under section 33(1)(b) above and references in this Chapter to an authorised person shall be construed accordingly.

64(4) **[Powers excluded]** The powers conferred by this Chapter shall not be exercisable in relation to—

(a) an authorised person who is a member of a recognised self-regulating organisation or a person certified by a recognised professional body and is subject to the rules of such an organisation or body in carrying on all the investment business carried on by him; or

(b) an appointed representative whose principal or, in the case of such a representative with more than one principal, each of whose principals is a member of such an organisation or body and is subject to the rules of such an organisation or body in carrying on the investment business in respect of which his principal or each of his principals has accepted responsibility for his activities;

except that the powers conferred by virtue of section 67(1)(b) below may on any of the grounds specified in subsection (1) above be exercised in relation to such a person at the request of any such organisation of which he or, in the case of an appointed representative, any of his principals is a member or any such body by which he or, as the case may be, any of his principals is certified.

SEC. 65   Restriction of business

65(1)   **[Power of Secretary of State to prohibit]**   The Secretary of State may prohibit an authorised person from—

    (a) entering into transactions of any specified kind or entering into them except in specified circumstances or to a specified extent;

    (b) soliciting business from persons of a specified kind or otherwise than from such persons or in a specified country or territory outside the United Kingdom;

    (c) carrying on business in a specified manner or otherwise than in a specified manner.

65(2)   **[Extent of prohibition]**   A prohibition under this section may relate to transactions entered into in connection with or for the purposes of investment business or to other business which is carried on in connection with or for the purposes of investment business.

SEC. 66   Restriction on dealing with assets

66(1)   **[Power of Secretary of State to prohibit]**   The Secretary of State may prohibit an authorised person or appointed representative from disposing of or otherwise dealing with any assets, or any specified assets, of that person or, as the case may be, representative in any specified manner or otherwise than in a specified manner.

66(2)   **[Assets outside UK]**   A prohibition under this section may relate to assets outside the United Kingdom.

SEC. 67   Vesting of assets in trustee

67(1)   **[Power of Secretary of State]**   The Secretary of State may impose a requirement that all assets, or all assets of any specified class or description, which at any time while the requirement is in force—

    (a) belong to an authorised person or appointed representative; or

    (b) belong to investors and are held by or to the order of an authorised person or appointed representative,

shall be transferred to and held by a trustee approved by the Secretary of State.

67(2)   **[Duty of authorised person]**   Where a requirement is imposed under this section it shall be the duty of the authorised person or, as the case may be, appointed representative to transfer the assets to the trustee and to give him all such other assistance as may be required to enable him to discharge his functions in accordance with the requirement.

67(3)   **[Release of assets etc. held by trustee]**   Assets held by a trustee in accordance with a requirement under this section shall not be released or dealt with except in accordance with directions given by the Secretary of State or in such circumstances as may be specified by him.

67(4) **[Assets outside UK]** A requirement under this section may relate to assets outside the United Kingdom.

SEC. 68 Maintenance of assets in United Kingdom

68(1) **[Power of Secretary of State]** The Secretary of State may require an authorised person or appointed representative to maintain in the United Kingdom assets of such value as appears to the Secretary of State to be desirable with a view to ensuring that the authorised person or, as the case may be, appointed representative will be able to meet his liabilities in respect of investment business carried on by him in the United Kingdom.

68(2) **[Assets to be taken into account]** The Secretary of State may direct that for the purposes of any requirement under this section assets of any specified class or description shall or shall not be taken into account.

SEC. 69 Rescission and variation

69 The Secretary of State may, either of his own motion or on the application of a person on whom a prohibition or requirement has been imposed under this Chapter, rescind or vary the prohibition or requirement if it appears to the Secretary of State that it is no longer necessary for the prohibition or requirement to take effect or continue in force or, as the case may be, that it should take effect or continue in force in a different form.

SEC. 70 Notices

70(1) **[Power to impose prohibitions etc., by written notice]** The power to impose, rescind or vary a prohibition or requirement under this Chapter shall be exercisable by written notice served by the Secretary of State on the person concerned; and any such notice shall take effect on such date as is specified in the notice.

70(2) **[Written notice re refusal to rescind etc.]** If the Secretary of State refuses to rescind or vary a prohibition or requirement on the application of the person to whom it applies he shall serve that person with a written notice of the refusal.

70(3) **[Notice to state reasons]** A notice imposing a prohibition or requirement, or varying a prohibition or requirement otherwise than on the application of the person to whom it applies, and a notice under subsection (2) above shall state the reasons for which the prohibition or requirement was imposed or varied or, as the case may be, why the application was refused.

70(4) **[Service of copy of notice on other persons]** Where the reasons stated in a notice to which subsection (3) above applies relate specifically to matters which—

(a) refer to a person identified in the notice other than the person to whom the prohibition or requirement applies; and

(b) are in the opinion of the Secretary of State prejudicial to that person in any office or employment,

the Secretary of State shall, unless he considers it impracticable to do so, serve a copy of the notice on that person.

70(5) **[Sec. 70(3) notice to refer to Tribunal]** A notice to which subsection (3) above applies shall give particulars of the right to have the case referred to the Tribunal under Chapter IX of this Part of this Act.

70(6) **[Public notice by Secretary of State]** The Secretary of State may give public notice of any prohibition or requirement imposed by him under this Chapter and of the rescission and variation of any such prohibition or requirement; and any such notice may, if the Secretary of State thinks fit, include a statement of the reasons for which the prohibition or requirement was imposed, rescinded or varied.

SEC. 71   Breach of prohibition or requirement

71(1) **[Effect of sec. 60, 61, 62]** Sections 60, 61, and 62 above shall have effect in relation to a contravention of a prohibition or requirement imposed under this Chapter as they have effect in relation to any such contravention as is mentioned in those sections.

71(2) **[Application of sec. 62(2)]** In its application by virtue of this section, section 62(2) shall have effect with the substitution—

    (a) for the reference to the rules of a recognised self-regulating organisation of a reference to any prohibition or requirement imposed by it in the exercise of powers for purposes corresponding to those of this Chapter; and

    (b) for the reference to the rules of a recognised professional body of a reference to any prohibition or requirement imposed in the exercise of powers for such purposes by that body or by any other body or person having functions in respect of the enforcement of the recognised professional body's rules relating to the carrying on of investment business.

71(3) **[Equitable remedies]** This section is without prejudice to any equitable remedy available in respect of property which by virtue of a requirement under section 67 above is subject to a trust.

Chapter VII — Winding up and Administration Orders

SEC. 72   Winding up orders

72(1) **[Power of court to wind up]** On a petition presented by the Secretary of State by virtue of this section, the court having jurisdiction under the Insolvency Act 1986 may wind up an authorised person or appointed representative to whom this subsection applies if—

    (a) the person is unable to pay his debts within the meaning of section 123 or, as the case may be, section 221 of that Act; or

    (b) the court is of the opinion that it is just and equitable that the person should be wound up.

72(2) **[Application of sec. 72(1)]** Subsection (1) above applies to any authorised person, any person whose authorisation is suspended under section 28 above or who is the subject of a direction under section 33(1)(b) above or any appointed representative who is—

(a) a company within the meaning of section 735 of the Companies Act 1985;

(b) an unregistered company within the meaning of section 220 of the Insolvency Act 1986;

(c) an oversea company within the meaning of section 744 of the Companies Act 1985; or

(d) a partnership.

72(3)   [Person unable to pay debts]   For the purposes of a petition under subsection (1) above a person who defaults in an obligation to pay any sum due and payable under any investment agreement shall be deemed to be unable to pay his debts.

72(4)   [Winding up of partnerships etc.]   Where a petition is presented under subsection (1) above for the winding up of a partnership on the ground mentioned in paragraph (b) of subsection (1) above or, in Scotland, on a ground mentioned in paragraph (a) or (b) of that subsection, the court shall have jurisdiction and the Insolvency Act 1986 shall have effect as if the partnership were an unregistered company within the meaning of section 220 of that Act.

72(5)   [Winding up re SROs etc.]   The Secretary of State shall not present a petition under subsection (1) above for the winding up of any person who is an authorised person by virtue of membership of a recognised self-regulating organisation or certification by a recognised professional body and is subject to the rules of the organisation or body in the carrying on of all investment business carried on by him, unless that organisation or body has consented to his doing so.

SEC. 73   Winding up orders: Northern Ireland

73(1)   [Power of High Court in Northern Ireland to wind up]   On a petition presented by the Secretary of State by virtue of this section, the High Court in Northern Ireland may wind up an authorised person or appointed representative to whom this subsection applies if—

(a) the person is unable to pay his debts within the meaning of Article 480 or, as the case may be, Article 616 of the Companies (Northern Ireland) Order 1986; or

(b) the court is of the opinion that it is just and equitable that the person should be wound up.

73(2)   [Application of sec. 73(1)]   Subsection (1) above applies to any authorised person, any person whose authorisation is suspended under section 28 above or who is the subject of a direction under section 33(1)(b) above or any appointed representative who is—

(a) a company within the meaning of Article 3 of the Companies (Northern Ireland) Order 1986;

(b) an unregistered company within the meaning of Article 615 of that Order; or

(c) a Part XXIII company within the meaning of Article 2 of that Order; or

(d) a partnership.

73(3)   [Person unable to pay debts]   For the purposes of a petition under subsection (1) above a person who defaults in an obligation to pay any sum due and payable under any investment agreement shall be deemed to be unable to pay his debts.

73(4) [Winding up of partnerships etc.] Where a petition is presented under subsection (1) above for the winding up of a partnership on the ground mentioned in paragraph (b) of subsection (1) above, the High Court in Northern Ireland shall have jurisdiction and the Companies (Northern Ireland) Order 1986 shall have effect as if the partnership were an unregistered company within the meaning of Article 615 of that Order.

73(5) [Winding up re SROs etc.] The Secretary of State shall not present a petition under subsection (1) above for the winding up of any person who is an authorised person by virtue of membership of a recognised self-regulating organisation or certification by a recognised professional body and is subject to the rules of the organisation or body in the carrying on of all investment business carried on by him, unless that organisation or body has consented to his doing so.

SEC. 74   Administration orders

74 A petition may be presented under section 9 of the Insolvency Act 1986 (applications for administration orders) in relation to a company to which section 8 of that Act applies which is an authorised person, a person whose authorisation is suspended under section 28 above or who is the subject of a direction under section 33(1)(b) above or an appointed representative—

  (a) in the case of an authorised person who is an authorised person by virtue of membership of a recognised self-regulating organisation or certification by a recognised professional body, by that organisation or body; and

  (b) in the case of an appointed representative or an authorised person who is not authorised as mentioned in paragraph (a) above or is so authorised but is not subject to the rules of the organisation or body in question in the carrying on of all investment business carried on by him, by the Secretary of State.

Chapter VIII — Collective Investment Schemes

PRELIMINARY

SEC. 75   Interpretation

75(1) ["A collective investment scheme"] In this Act **"a collective investment scheme"** means, subject to the provisions of this section, any arrangements with respect to property of any description, including money, the purpose or effect of which is to enable persons taking part in the arrangements (whether by becoming owners of the property or any part of it or otherwise) to participate in or receive profits or income arising from the acquisition, holding, management or disposal of the property or sums paid out of such profits or income.

75(2) [Arrangements for participants in sec. 75(1)] The arrangements must be such that the persons who are to participate as mentioned in subsection (1) above (in this Act referred to as **"participants"**) do not have day to day control over the management of the property in question, whether or not they have the right to be consulted or to give directions; and the arrangements must also have either or both of the characteristics mentioned in subsection (3) below.

75(3)   [Characteristics in sec. 75(2)]   Those characteristics are—

(a) that the contributions of the participants and the profits or income out of which payments are to be made to them are pooled;

(b) that the property in question is managed as a whole by or on behalf of the operator of the scheme.

75(4)   [Where pooling as in sec. 75(3)(a)]   Where any arrangements provide for such pooling as is mentioned in paragraph (a) of subsection (3) above in relation to separate parts of the property in question, the arrangements shall not be regarded as constituting a single collective investment scheme unless the participants are entitled to exchange rights in one part for rights in another.

75(5)   [Certain investments arrangements not a collective investment scheme]   Arrangements are not a collective investment scheme if—

(a) the property to which the arrangements relate (other than cash awaiting investment) consists of investments falling within any of paragraphs 1 to 5, 6 (so far as relating to units in authorised unit trust schemes and recognised schemes) and 10 of Schedule 1 to this Act;

(b) each participant is the owner of a part of that property and entitled to withdraw it at any time; and

(c) the arrangements do not have the characteristics mentioned in paragraph (a) of subsection (3) above and have those mentioned in paragraph (b) of that subsection only because the parts of the property belonging to different participants are not bought and sold separately except where a person becomes or ceases to be a participant.

75(5A), (5B)   (Repealed by Financial Services Act 1986 (Restriction of Scope of Act and Meaning of Collective Investment Scheme) Order 1990 (S.I. 1990 No. 349), art. 6(a) as from 26 March 1990.)

History
S. 75(5A), (5B) formerly read as follows:

"**75(5A)**   Arrangements are not a collective investment scheme if—

(a) the property to which the arrangements relate (other than cash awaiting investment) consists of shares;

(b) they constitute a complying fund;

(c) each participant is the owner of a part of the property to which the arrangements relate and, to the extent that his part of that property—

　(i) comprises relevant shares of a class which are admitted to the Official List of any member State or to dealings on a recognised investment exchange, he is entitled to withdraw it at any time after the end of the period of five years beginning with the date on which the shares in question were issued;

　(ii) comprises relevant shares which do not fall within (i) above, he is entitled to withdraw it at any time after the end of the period of two years beginning with the date upon which the period referred to in (i) above expired;

　(iii) comprises any other shares, he is entitled to withdraw it at any time after the end of the period of six months beginning with the date upon which the shares in question ceased to be relevant shares; and

　(iv) comprises cash which the operator has not agreed (conditionally or unconditionally) to apply in subscribing for shares, he is entitled to withdraw it at any time; and

(d) the arrangements would meet the conditions described in paragraph (c) of subsection (5) above were it not for the fact that the operator is entitled to exercise all or any of the rights conferred by shares included within the property to which the arrangements relate.

(5B)   For the purposes of subsection (5A) above—

(a) 'shares' means investments falling within paragraph 1 of Schedule 1 to this Act;

(b) shares shall be regarded as being relevant shares if and so long as they are shares in respect of which neither—

　(i) a claim for relief, made in accordance with section 306 of the Income and Corporation Taxes Act 1988 has been disallowed; nor

　(ii) an assessment has been made pursuant to section 307 of that Act withdrawing or refusing relief by reason of the body corporate in which the shares are held having ceased to be a body corporate which is a qualifying company for the purposes of section 293 of that Act; and

(c) arrangements shall be regarded as constituting a complying fund if they provide that—

(i) the operator will, so far as practicable, make investments each of which, subject to each participant's individual circumstances, qualify for relief by virtue of Chapter III of Part VII of the Income and Corporation Taxes Act 1988; and

(ii) the minimum subscription to the arrangements made by each participant must be not less than

£2000."

S. 75(5A) and (5B) formerly added by Financial Services Act 1986 (Restriction of Scope of Act and Meaning of Collective Investment Scheme) Order 1988 (S.I. 1988 No. 803), art. 5(a) as from 29 April 1988; art. 5 revoked by Financial Services Act 1986 (Restriction of Scope of Act and Meaning of Collective Investment Scheme) Order 1990 (S.I. 1990 No. 349), art. 8(c) as from 26 March 1990.

75(6)   **[Further arrangements etc. not collective investment schemes]**   The following are not collective investment schemes—

(a) arrangements operated by a person otherwise than by way of business;

(b) arrangements where each of the participants carries on a business other than investment business and enters into the arrangements for commercial purposes related to that business;

(c) arrangements where each of the participants is a body corporate in the same group as the operator;

(d) arrangements where—

   (i) each of the participants is a bona fide employee or former employee (or the wife, husband, widow, widower, child or step-child under the age of eighteen of such an employee or former employee) of a body corporate in the same group as the operator; and

   (ii) the property to which the arrangements relate consists of shares or debentures (as defined in paragraph 20(4) of Schedule 1 to this Act) in or of a member of that group;

(f) franchise arrangements, that is to say, arrangements under which a person earns profits or income by exploiting a right conferred by the arrangements to use a trade name or design or other intellectual property or the good-will attached to it;

(g) arrangements the predominant purpose of which is to enable persons participating in them to share in the use or enjoyment of a particular property or to make its use or enjoyment available gratuitously to other persons;

(h) arrangements under which the rights or interests of the participants are investments falling within paragraph 5 of Schedule 1 to this Act;

(i) arrangements the purpose of which is the provision of clearing services and which are operated by an authorised person, a recognised clearing house or a recognised investment exchange;

(j) contracts of insurance;

(k) occupational pension schemes;

(l) arrangements which by virtue of paragraph 34 or 35 of Schedule 1 to this Act are not collective investment schemes for the purposes of that Schedule.

History

S. 75(6)(e) repealed by Financial Services Act 1986 (Restriction of Scope of Act and Meaning of Collective Investment Scheme) Order 1990 (S.I. 1990 No. 349) art. 6(a) as from 26 March 1990; s. 75(6)(e) formerly read as follows:

"(e) arrangements where the entire contribution of each participant is a deposit within the meaning of section

5 of the Banking Act 1987 or a sum of a kind described in subsection (3) of that section."

Previously s. 75(6)(e) substituted by Financial Services Act 1986 (Extension of Scope of Act and Meaning of Collective Investment Scheme) Order 1988 (S.I. 1988 No. 496), art. 4 as from 25 March 1988; art 4 revoked by Financial Services Act 1986 (Restriction of Scope of Act and Meaning of Collective Investment Scheme) Order

1990 (S.I. 1990 No. 349), art. 8(b) as from 26 March 1990. The previous s. 75(6)(e) read as follows: "(e) arrangements where the receipt of the participants' contributions constitutes the acceptance of deposits in the course of a business which is a deposit-taking business for the purposes of the Banking Act 1987 and does not constitute a transaction prescribed for the purposes of section 4(4) of that Act by regulations made by the Treasury;".

In the previous s. 75(6)(e) the words "Banking Act1987", and "section 4(4)" previously substituted for the words "Banking Act 1979" and "section 2", respectively by Banking Act 1987, s. 108(1) and Sch. 6, para. 27(1) as from 1 October 1987 (see S.I. 1987 No. 1664 (C. 50)).

S. 75(6)(l) substituted for former s. 75(6)(l)–(n) by Financial Services Act 1986 (Restriction of Scope of Act and Meaning of Collective Investment Scheme) Order 1990 (S.I. 1990 No. 349), art. 6(b) as from 26 March 1990; s. 75(6)(l)–(n) formerly read as follows:

"(l) arrangements under which the rights or interests of the participants are represented by the following—

    (i) investments falling within paragraph 2 of Schedule 1 to this Act which are issued by a single body corporate which is not an open-ended investment company or which are issued by a single issuer which is not a body corporate and are guaranteed by the government of the United Kingdom, of Northern Ireland, or of any country or territory outside the United Kingdom; or

    (ii) investments falling within sub-paragraph (i) above which are convertible into or exchangeable for investments falling within paragraph 1 of Schedule 1 to this Act provided that those latter investments are issued by the same person as issued the investments falling within sub-paragraph (i) or are issued by a single other issuer; or

    (iii) investments falling within paragraph 3 of Schedule 1 to this Act issued by the same government, local authority or public authority; or

    (iv) investments falling within paragraph 4 of Schedule 1 to this Act which are issued otherwise than by an open-ended investment company and which confer rights in respect of investments, issued by the same issuer, falling within paragraph 1 of Schedule 1 to this Act or within sub-paragraph (i), (ii) or (iii) above;

(m) arrangements which would fall within paragraph (l) were it not for the fact that the rights or interests of a participant ('the counterparty') whose ordinary business involves him in engaging in activities which fall within Part II of Schedule 1 to this Act or would do so apart from Part III or Part IV of that Schedule are or include rights or interests under a swap arrangement, that is to say, an arrangement the purpose of which is to facilitate the making of payments to participants whether in a particular amount or currency or at a particular time or rate of interest or all or any combination of those things, being an arrangement under which—

    (i) the counterparty is entitled to receive amounts (whether representing principal or interest) payable in respect of any property subject to the scheme or sums determined by reference to such amounts; and

    (ii) the counterparty makes payments (whether or not of the same amount and whether or not in the same currency as those referred to in (i) above) which are calculated in accordance with an agreed formula by reference to the amounts or sums referred to in (i) above.

(n) arrangements under which the rights or interests of participants are rights to or interests in money held in a common account in circumstances in which the money so held is held on the understanding that an amount representing the contribution of each participant is to be applied either in making payments to him or in satisfaction of sums owed by him or in the acquisition of property or the provision of services for him."

S. 75(6)(l)–(n) formerly added by Financial Services Act 1986 (Restriction of Scope of Act and Meaning of Collective Investment Scheme) Order 1988 (S.I. 1988 No. 803), art. 5(b) as from 29 April 1988; art. 5 revoked by Financial Services Act 1986 (Restriction of Scope of Act and Meaning of Collective Investment Scheme) Order 1990 (S.I. 1990 No. 349), art. 8(c) as from 26 March 1990.

75(7) [Certain bodies corporate not collective investment schemes] No body incorporated under the law of, or of any part of, the United Kingdom relating to building societies or industrial and provident societies or registered under any such law relating to friendly societies, and no other body corporate other than an open-ended investment company, shall be regarded as constituting a collective investment scheme.

75(8) [Definitions] In this Act—

"a unit trust scheme" means a collective investment scheme under which the property in question is held on trust for the participants;

"an open-ended investment company" means a collective investment scheme under which—

(a) the property in question belongs beneficially to, and is managed by or on behalf of, a body corporate having as its purpose the investment of its funds with the aim of spreading investment risk and giving its members the benefit of the results of the management of those funds by or on behalf of that body; and

(b) the rights of the participants are represented by shares in or securities of that body which—

    (i) the participants are entitled to have redeemed or repurchased, or which (otherwise than under Chapter VII of Part V of the Companies Act 1985 or the corresponding Northern Ireland provision) are redeemed or repurchased from them by, or out of funds provided by, that body; or

    (ii) the body ensures can be sold by the participants on an investment exchange at a price related to the value of the property to which they relate;

"**trustee**", in relation to a unit trust scheme, means the person holding the property in question on trust for the participants and, in relation to a collective investment scheme constituted under the law of a country or territory outside the United Kingdom, means any person who (whether or not under a trust) is entrusted with the custody of the property in question;

"**units**" means the rights or interests (however described) of the participants in a collective investment scheme;

"**the operator**", in relation to a unit trust scheme with a separate trustee, means the manager and, in relation to an open-ended investment company, means that company.

75(9) [Amendment of sec. 2 order etc.]   If an order under section 2 above amends the references to a collective investment scheme in Schedule 1 to this Act it may also amend the provisions of this section.

PROMOTION OF SCHEMES

SEC. 76 Restrictions on promotion

76(1) [Restriction on authorised person] Subject to subsections (2), (3) and (4) below, an authorised person shall not—

(a) issue or cause to be issued in the United Kingdom any advertisement inviting persons to become or offer to become participants in a collective investment scheme or containing information calculated to lead directly or indirectly to persons becoming or offering to become participants in such a scheme; or

(b) advise or procure any person in the United Kingdom to become or offer to become a participant in such a scheme,

unless the scheme is an authorised unit trust scheme or a recognised scheme under the following provisions of this Chapter.

76(2) [Exception re advertisement to authorised person etc.] Subsection (1) above shall not apply if the advertisement is issued to or the person mentioned in paragraph (b) of that subsection is—

(a) an authorised person; or

(b) a person whose ordinary business involves the acquisition and disposal of property of the same kind as the property, or a substantial part of the property, to which the scheme relates.

FSA 1986, sec. 75(9)

76(3) **[Exception re things done under regulations]** Subsection (1) above shall not apply to anything done in accordance with regulations made by the Secretary of State for the purpose of exempting from that subsection the promotion otherwise than to the general public of schemes of such descriptions as are specified in the regulations.

76(4) **[Exempting single property schemes under sec. 76(1)]** The Secretary of State may by regulations make provision for exempting single property schemes from subsection (1) above.

76(5) **[Interpretation re sec. 76(4)]** For the purposes of subsection (4) above a single property scheme is a scheme which has the characteristics mentioned in subsection (6) below and satisfies such other requirements as are specified in the regulations conferring the exemption.

76(6) **[Characteristics in sec. 76(5)]** The characteristics referred to above are—

> (a) that the property subject to the scheme (apart from cash or other assets held for management purposes) consists of—
>
> > (i) a single building (or a single building with ancillary buildings) managed by or on behalf of the operator of the scheme; or
> >
> > (ii) a group of adjacent or contiguous buildings managed by him or on his behalf as a single enterprise,
>
> > with or without ancillary land and with or without furniture, fittings or other contents of the building or buildings in question; and
>
> (b) that the units of the participants in the scheme are either dealt in on a recognised investment exchange or offered on terms such that any agreement for their acquisition is conditional on their admission to dealings on such an exchange.

76(7) **[Extent of sec. 76(4) regulations]** Regulations under subsection (4) above may contain such supplementary and transitional provisions as the Secretary of State thinks necessary and may also contain provisions imposing obligations or liabilities on the operator and trustee (if any) of an exempted scheme, including, to such extent as he thinks appropriate, provisions for purposes corresponding to those for which provision can be made under section 85 below in relation to authorised unit trust schemes.

AUTHORISED UNIT TRUST SCHEMES

SEC. 77 Applications for authorisation

77(1) **[Applicants for order]** Any application for an order declaring a unit trust scheme to be an authorised unit trust scheme shall be made by the manager and trustee, or proposed manager and trustee, of the scheme and the manager and trustee shall be different persons.

77(2) **[Manner of application, other information]** Any such application—

> (a) shall be made in such manner as the Secretary of State may direct; and
>
> (b) shall contain or be accompanied by such information as he may reasonably require for the purpose of determining the application.

77(3) **[Additional information]** At any time after receiving an application and before determining it the Secretary of State may require the applicant to furnish additional information.

77(4) **[Differing directions and requirements]** The directions and requirements given or imposed under subsections (2) and (3) above may differ as between different applications.

77(5) **[Form and verification of information]** Any information to be furnished to the Secretary of State under this section shall, if he so requires, be in such form or verified in such manner as he may specify.

SEC. 78   Authorisation orders

78(1) **[Power of Secretary of State]** The Secretary of State may, on an application duly made in accordance with section 77 above and after being furnished with all such information as he may require under that section, make an order declaring a unit trust scheme to be an authorised unit trust scheme for the purposes of this Act if—

  (a) it appears to him that the scheme complies with the requirements of the regulations made under section 81 below and that the following provisions of this section are satisfied; and

  (b) he has been furnished with a copy of the trust deed and a certificate signed by a solicitor to the effect that it complies with such of those requirements as relate to its contents.

78(2) **[Manager and trustee independent]** The manager and the trustee must be persons who are independent of each other.

78(3) **[Manager and trustee member State bodies corporate]** The manager and the trustee must each be a body corporate incorporated in the United Kingdom or another member State, the affairs of each must be administered in the country in which it is incorporated, each must have a place of business in the United Kingdom and, if the manager is incorporated in another member State, the scheme must not be one which satisfies the requirements prescribed for the purposes of section 86 below.

78(4) **[Manager and trustee authorised persons]** The manager and the trustee must each be an authorised person and neither must be prohibited from acting as manager or trustee, as the case may be, by or under rules under section 48 above, by or under the rules of any recognised self-regulating organisation of which the manager or trustee is a member or by a prohibition imposed under section 65 above.

78(5) **[Name and purposes of scheme]** The name of the scheme must not be undesirable or misleading; and the purposes of the scheme must be reasonably capable of being successfully carried into effect.

78(6) **[Requirements re redemption of units etc.]** The participants must be entitled to have their units redeemed in accordance with the scheme at a price related to the net value of the property to which the units relate and determined in accordance with the scheme; but a scheme shall be treated as complying with this subsection if it requires the manager to ensure that a participant is able to sell his units on an investment exchange at a price not significantly different from that mentioned in this subsection.

78(7) **[Time for decision re application]** The Secretary of State shall inform the applicants of his decision on the application not later than six months after the date on which the application was received.

78(8) **[Certificate on making of order]** On making an order under this section the Secretary of State may issue a certificate to the effect that the scheme complies with the conditions necessary for it to enjoy the rights conferred by any relevant Community instrument.

SEC. 79 Revocation of authorisation

79(1) **[Power of Secretary of State]** The Secretary of State may revoke an order declaring a unit trust scheme to be an authorised unit trust scheme if it appears to him—

(a) that any of the requirements for the making of the order are no longer satisfied;

(b) that it is undesirable in the interests of the participants or potential participants that the scheme should continue to be authorised; or

(c) without prejudice to paragraph (b) above, that the manager or trustee of the scheme has contravened any provision of this Act or any rules or regulations made under it or, in purported compliance with any such provision, has furnished the Secretary of State with false, inaccurate or misleading information or has contravened any prohibition or requirement imposed under this Act.

79(2) **[Matter for sec. 79(1)(b)]** For the purposes of subsection (1)(b) above the Secretary of State may take into account any matter relating to the scheme, the manager or trustee, a director or controller of the manager or trustee or any person employed by or associated with the manager or trustee in connection with the scheme.

79(3) **[Rules in sec. 79(1)(c)]** In the case of a manager or trustee who is a member of a recognised self-regulating organisation the rules, prohibitions and requirements referred to in subsection (1)(c) above include the rules of that organisation and any prohibition or requirement imposed by virtue of those rules.

79(4) **[Revocation at request of manager or trustee etc.]** The Secretary of State may revoke an order declaring a unit trust scheme to be an authorised unit trust scheme at the request of the manager or trustee of the scheme; but he may refuse to do so if he considers that any matter concerning the scheme should be investigated as a preliminary to a decision on the question whether the order should be revoked or that revocation would not be in the interests of the participants or would be incompatible with a Community obligation.

SEC. 80 Representations against refusal or revocation

80(1) **[Written notice re refusal etc.]** Where the Secretary of State proposes—

(a) to refuse an application for an order under section 78 above; or

(b) to revoke such an order otherwise than at the request of the manager or trustee of the scheme,

he shall give the applicants or, as the case may be, the manager and trustee of the scheme written notice of his intention to do so, stating the reasons for which he proposes to act and giving particulars of the rights conferred by subsection (2) below.

80(2) [Written representations to Secretary of State]   A person on whom a notice is served under subsection (1) above may, within twenty-one days of the date of service, make written representations to the Secretary of State and, if desired, oral representations to a person appointed for that purpose by the Secretary of State.

80(3) [Secretary of State to have regard to representations]   The Secretary of State shall have regard to any representations made in accordance with subsection (2) above in determining whether to refuse the application or revoke the order, as the case may be.

SEC. 81   Constitution and management

81(1) [Power of Secretary of State to make regulations]   The Secretary of State may make regulations as to the constitution and management of authorised unit trust schemes, the powers and duties of the manager and trustee of any such scheme and the rights and obligations of the participants in any such scheme.

81(2) [Extent of regulations]   Without prejudice to the generality of subsection (1) above, regulations under this section may make provision—

    (a) as to the issue and redemption of the units under the scheme;

    (b) as to the expenses of the scheme and the means of meeting them;

    (c) for the appointment, removal, powers and duties of an auditor for the scheme;

    (d) for restricting or regulating the investment and borrowing powers exercisable in relation to the scheme;

    (e) requiring the keeping of records with respect to the transactions and financial position of the scheme and for the inspection of those records;

    (f) requiring the preparation of periodical reports with respect to the scheme and the furnishing of those reports to the participants and to the Secretary of State; and

    (g) with respect to the amendment of the scheme.

81(3) [Contents of trust deed etc.]   Regulations under this section may make provision as to the contents of the trust deed, including provision requiring any of the matters mentioned in subsection (2) above to be dealt with in the deed; but regulations under this section shall be binding on the manager, trustee and participants independently of the contents of the deed and, in the case of the participants, shall have effect as if contained in it.

81(4) [Remuneration to scheme manager]   Regulations under this section shall not impose limits on the remuneration payable to the manager of a scheme.

81(5) [Incidental and transitional provisions]   Regulations under this section may contain such incidental and transitional provisions as the Secretary of State thinks necessary or expedient.

SEC. 82   Alteration of schemes and changes of manager or trustee

82(1) [Manager to give written notice re alteration etc.]   The manager of an authorised unit trust scheme shall give written notice to the Secretary of State of—

    (a) any proposed alteration to the scheme; and

(b) any proposal to replace the trustee of the scheme;

and any notice given in respect of a proposed alteration involving a change in the trust deed shall be accompanied by a certificate signed by a solicitor to the effect that the change will not affect the compliance of the deed with the regulations made under section 81 above.

82(2)　[Trustee to give written notice re replacement]　The trustee of an authorised unit trust scheme shall give written notice to the Secretary of State of any proposal to replace the manager of the scheme.

82(3)　[Requirements for proposal to have effect]　Effect shall not be given to any such proposal unless—

(a) the Secretary of State has given his approval to the proposal; or

(b) one month has elapsed since the date on which the notice was given under subsection (1) or (2) above without the Secretary of State having notified the manager or trustee that the proposal is not approved.

82(4)　[Limit on replacements]　Neither the manager nor the trustee of an authorised unit trust scheme shall be replaced except by persons who satisfy the requirements of section 78(2) to (4) above.

SEC. 83　Restrictions on activities of manager

83(1)　[Only certain activities]　The manager of an authorised unit trust scheme shall not engage in any activities other than those mentioned in subsection (2) below.

83(2)　[Activities in sec. 83(1)]　Those activities are—

(a) acting as manager of—

(i) a unit trust scheme;

(ii) an open-ended investment company or any other body corporate whose business consists of investing its funds with the aim of spreading investment risk and giving its members the benefit of the results of the management of its funds by or on behalf of that body; or

(iii) any other collective investment scheme under which the contributions of the participants and the profits or income out of which payments are to be made to them are pooled;

(b) activities for the purposes of or in connection with those mentioned in paragraph (a) above.

83(3)　[Sec. 65 prohibition]　A prohibition under section 65 above may prohibit the manager of an authorised unit trust scheme from inviting persons in any specified country or territory outside the United Kingdom to become participants in the scheme.

SEC. 84　Avoidance of exclusion clauses

84　Any provision of the trust deed of an authorised unit trust scheme shall be void in so far as it would have the effect of exempting the manager or trustee from liability for any failure to exercise due care and diligence in the discharge of his functions in respect of the scheme.

SEC. 85   Publication of scheme particulars

85(1)   [Power of Secretary of State to make regulations]   The Secretary of State may make regulations requiring the manager of an authorised unit trust scheme to submit to him and publish or make available to the public on request a document ("scheme particulars") containing information about the scheme and complying with such requirements as are specified in the regulations.

85(2)   [Revised or further scheme particulars]   Regulations under this section may require the manager of an authorised unit trust scheme to submit and publish or make available revised or further scheme particulars if—

(a)   there is a significant change affecting any matter contained in such particulars previously published or made available whose inclusion was required by the regulations; or

(b)   a significant new matter arises the inclusion of information in respect of which would have been required in previous particulars if it had arisen when those particulars were prepared.

85(3)   [Payment of compensation]   Regulations under this section may provide for the payment, by the person or persons who in accordance with the regulations are treated as responsible for any scheme particulars, of compensation to any person who has become or agreed to become a participant in the scheme and suffered loss as a result of any untrue or misleading statement in the particulars or the omission from them of any matter required by the regulations to be included.

85(4)   [Liability apart from regulations]   Regulations under this section shall not affect any liability which any person may incur apart from the regulations.

RECOGNITION OF OVERSEAS SCHEMES

SEC. 86   Schemes constituted in other member States

86(1)   [Recognition on satisfying requirements]   Subject to subsection (2) below, a collective investment scheme constituted in a member State other than the United Kingdom is a recognised scheme if it satisfies such requirements as are prescribed for the purposes of this section.

86(2)   [Notice re invitation by scheme operator]   Not less than two months before inviting persons in the United Kingdom to become participants in the scheme the operator of the scheme shall give written notice to the Secretary of State of his intention to do so, specifying the manner in which the invitation is to be made; and the scheme shall not be a recognised scheme by virtue of this section if within two months of receiving the notice the Secretary of State notifies—

(a)   the operator of the scheme; and

(b)   the authorities of the State in question who are responsible for the authorisation of collective investment schemes,

that the manner in which the invitation is to be made does not comply with the law in force in the United Kingdom.

86(3)   [Requirements for sec. 86(2) notice]   The notice to be given to the Secretary of State under subsection (2) above—

FSA 1986, sec. 85(1)   [The next page is 60,951]

(a) shall be accompanied by a certificate from the authorities mentioned in subsection (2)(b) above to the effect that the scheme complies with the conditions necessary for it to enjoy the rights conferred by any relevant Community instrument;

(b) shall contain the address of a place in the United Kingdom for the service on the operator of notices or other documents required or authorised to be served on him under this Act; and

(c) shall contain or be accompanied by such other information and documents as may be prescribed.

86(4) **[Notice to contain reasons and sec. 86(5) rights]** A notice given by the Secretary of State under subsection (2) above shall give the reasons for which he considers that the law in force in the United Kingdom will not be complied with and give particulars of the rights conferred by subsection (5) below.

86(5) **[Rights re representations]** A person on whom a notice is served by the Secretary of State under subsection (2) above may, within twenty-one days of the date of service, make written representations to the Secretary of State and, if desired, oral representations to a person appointed for that purpose by the Secretary of State.

86(6) **[Withdrawal of notice after representations]** The Secretary of State may in the light of any representations made in accordance with subsection (5) above withdraw his notice and in that event the scheme shall be a recognised scheme from the date on which the notice is withdrawn.

86(7) **[Application of sec. 48 rules]** Rules under section 48 above shall not apply to investment business in respect of which the operator or trustee of a scheme recognised under this section is an authorised person by virtue of section 24 above except so far as they make provision as respects—

(a) procuring persons to become participants in the scheme and advising persons on the scheme and the exercise of the rights conferred by it;

(b) matters incidental to those mentioned in paragraph (a) above.

This subsection also applies to statements of principle under section 47A and codes of practice under section 63A so far as they relate to matters falling within the rule-making power in section 48.

History
In s. 86(7) the words "This subsection also applies" to the end added by CA 1989, s. 206(1) and Sch. 23, para. 8 as from 15 March 1990 (see S.I. 1990 No. 354 (C. 12), art. 3).

86(8) **[Interpretation]** For the purposes of this section a collective investment scheme is constituted in a member State if—

(a) it is constituted under the law of that State by a contract or under a trust and is managed by a body corporate incorporated under that law; or

(b) it takes the form of an open-ended investment company incorporated under that law.

86(9) **[Notice re cessation of recognition]** If the operator of a scheme recognised under this section gives written notice to the Secretary of State stating that he desires the scheme no longer to be recognised under this section it shall cease to be so recognised when the notice is given.

SEC. 87   Schemes authorised in designated countries or territories

87(1)   [Recognised scheme other than under sec. 86]   Subject to subsection (3) below, a collective investment scheme which is not a recognised scheme by virtue of section 86 above but is managed in and authorised under the law of a country or territory outside the United Kingdom is a recognised scheme if—

(a)   that country or territory is designated for the purposes of this section by an order made by the Secretary of State; and

(b)   the scheme is of a class specified by the order.

87(2)   [Requirements for Secretary of State's order]   The Secretary of State shall not make an order designating any country or territory for the purposes of this section unless he is satisfied that the law under which collective investment schemes of the class to be specified by the order are authorised and supervised in that country or territory affords to investors in the United Kingdom protection at least equivalent to that provided for them by this Chapter in the case of an authorised unit trust scheme.

87(3)   [Written notice by scheme operator]   A scheme shall not be recognised by virtue of this section unless the operator of the scheme gives written notice to the Secretary of State that he wishes it to be recognised; and the scheme shall not be recognised if within such period from receiving the notice as may be prescribed the Secretary of State notifies the operator that the scheme is not to be recognised.

87(4)   [Contents of sec. 87(3) notice]   The notice given by the operator under subsection (3) above—

(a)   shall contain the address of a place in the United Kingdom for the service on the operator of notices or other documents required or authorised to be served on him under this Act; and

(b)   shall contain or be accompanied by such information and documents as may be prescribed.

87(5)   [Effect of sec. 85]   Section 85 above shall have effect in relation to a scheme recognised under this section as it has effect in relation to an authorised unit trust scheme, taking references to the manager as references to the operator and, in the case of an operator who is not an authorised person, references to publishing particulars as references to causing them to be published; and regulations made by virtue of this subsection may make provision whereby compliance with any requirements imposed by or under the law of a country or territory designated under this section is treated as compliance with any requirement of the regulations.

87(6)   [Transitional provisions in order]   An order under subsection (1) above may contain such transitional provisions as the Secretary of State thinks necessary or expedient and shall be subject to annulment in pursuance of a resolution of either House of Parliament.

SEC. 88   Other overseas schemes

88(1)   [Power of Secretary of State to make order]   The Secretary of State may, on the application of the operator of a scheme which—

(a)   is managed in a country or territory outside the United Kingdom; but

(b)   does not satisfy the requirements mentioned in section 86(1) above and in relation to which there is no relevant order under section 87(1) above, make an order declaring the scheme to be a recognised scheme if it appears to him that it affords adequate protection to the participants, makes adequate provision for the matters dealt with by regulations under section 81 above and satisfies the following provisions of this section.

88(2) [General requirements] The operator must be a body corporate or the scheme must take the form of an open-ended investment company.

88(3) [Requirements re operator] Subject to subsection (4) below, the operator and the trustee, if any, must be fit and proper persons to act as operator or, as the case may be, as trustee; and for that purpose the Secretary of State may take into account any matter relating to—

(a) any person who is or will be employed by or associated with the operator or trustee for the purposes of the scheme;

(b) any director or controller of the operator or trustee;

(c) any other body corporate in the same group as the operator or trustee and any director or controller of any such other body.

88(4) [Non-application of sec. 88(3)] Subsection (3) above does not apply to an operator or trustee who is an authorised person and not prohibited from acting as operator or trustee, as the case may be, by or under rules under section 48 above, by or under the rules of any recognised self-regulating organisation of which he is a member or by any prohibition imposed under section 65 above.

88(5) [Authorised person as representative in UK] If the operator is not an authorised person he must have a representative in the United Kingdom who is an authorised person and has power to act generally for the operator and to accept service of notices and other documents on his behalf.

88(6) [Name and purposes of scheme] The name of the scheme must not be undesirable or misleading; and the purposes of the scheme must be reasonably capable of being successfully carried into effect.

88(7) [Redemption of units by participants] The participants must be entitled to have their units redeemed in accordance with the scheme at a price related to the net value of the property to which the units relate and determined in accordance with the scheme; but a scheme shall be treated as complying with this subsection if it requires the operator to ensure that a participant is able to sell his units on an investment exchange at a price not significantly different from that mentioned in this subsection.

88(8) [Application of sec. 77(2)–(5)] Subsections (2) to (5) of section 77 above shall apply also to an application under this section.

88(9) [Application of sec. 82] So much of section 82 above as applies to an alteration of the scheme shall apply also to a scheme recognised under this section, taking references to the manager as references to the operator and with the omission of the requirement relating to the solicitor's certificate; and if the operator or trustee of any such scheme is to be replaced the operator or, as the case may be, the trustee, or in either case the person who is to replace him, shall give at least one month's notice to the Secretary of State.

88(10) [Effect of sec. 85] Section 85 above shall have effect in relation to a scheme recognised under this section as it has effect in relation to an authorised unit trust scheme, taking references to the manager as references to the operator and, in the case of an operator who is not an authorised person, references to publishing particulars as references to causing them to be published.

SEC. 89   Refusal and revocation of recognition

89(1)   [Power of Secretary of State]   The Secretary of State may at any time direct that a scheme shall cease to be recognised by virtue of section 87 above or revoke an order under section 88 above if it appears to him—

  (a) that it is undesirable in the interests of the participants or potential participants in the United Kingdom that the scheme should continue to be recognised;

  (b) without prejudice to paragraph (a) above, that the operator or trustee of the scheme has contravened any provision of this Act or any rules or regulations made under it or, in purported compliance with any such provision, has furnished the Secretary of State with false, inaccurate or misleading information or has contravened any prohibition or requirement imposed under this Act; or

  (c) in the case of an order under section 88 that any of the requirements for the making of the order are no longer satisfied.

89(2)   [Matters for sec. 89(1)(a)]   For the purposes of subsection (1)(a) above the Secretary of State may take into account any matter relating to the scheme the operator or trustee, a director or controller of the operator or trustee or any person employed by or associated with the operator or trustee in connection with the scheme.

89(3)   [SRO member and sec. 89(1)(b)]   In the case of an operator or trustee who is a member of a recognised self-regulating organisation the rules, prohibitions and requirements referred to in subsection (1)(b) above include the rules of that organisation and any prohibition or requirement imposed by virtue of those rules.

89(4)   [Revocation at request of operator]   The Secretary of State may give such a direction or revoke such an order as is mentioned in subsection (1) above at the request of the operator or trustee of the scheme; but he may refuse to do so if he considers that any matter concerning the scheme should be investigated as a preliminary to a decision on the question whether the direction should be given or the order revoked or that the direction or revocation would not be in the interests of the participants.

89(5)   [Written notice to operator re sec. 87(3), 89(1)]   Where the Secretary of State proposes—

  (a) to notify the operator of a scheme under section 87(3) above; or

  (b) to give such a direction or to refuse to make or to revoke such an order as is mentioned in subsection (1) above,

he shall give the operator written notice of his intention to do so, stating the reasons for which he proposes to act and giving particulars of the rights conferred by subsection (6) below.

89(6) **[Written representations to Secretary of State]** A person on whom a notice is served under subsection (5) above may, within twenty-one days of the date of service, make written representations to the Secretary of State and, if desired, oral representations to a person appointed for that purpose by the Secretary of State.

89(7) **[Secretary of State to have regard to representations]** The Secretary of State shall have regard to any representations made in accordance with subsection (6) above in determining whether to notify the operator, give the direction or refuse to make or revoke the order, as the case may be.

SEC. 90 Facilities and information in the United Kingdom

90(1) **[Regulations by Secretary of State]** The Secretary of State may make regulations requiring operators of recognised schemes to maintain in the United Kingdom, or in such part or parts of it as may be specified in the regulations, such facilities as he thinks desirable in the interests of participants and as are specified in the regulations.

90(2) **[Operator to include certain information]** The Secretary of State may by notice in writing require the operator of any recognised scheme to include such explanatory information as is specified in the notice in any investment advertisement issued or caused to be issued by him in the United Kingdom in which the scheme is named.

POWERS OF INTERVENTION

SEC. 91 Directions

91(1) **[Power of Secretary of State]** If it appears to the Secretary of State—

(a) that any of the requirements for the making of an order declaring a scheme to be an authorised unit trust scheme are no longer satisfied;

(b) that the exercise of the power conferred by this subsection is desirable in the interest of participants or potential participants in the scheme; or

(c) without prejudice to paragraph (b) above, that the manager or trustee of such a scheme has contravened any provision of this Act or any rules or regulations made under it or, in purported compliance with any such provision, has furnished the Secretary of State with false, inaccurate or misleading information or has contravened any prohibition or requirement imposed under this Act,

he may give a direction under subsection (2) below.

91(2) **[Scope of directions]** A direction under this subsection may—

(a) require the manager of the scheme to cease the issue or redemption, or both the issue and redemption, of units under the scheme on a date specified in the direction until such further date as is specified in that or another direction;

(b) require the manager and trustee of the scheme to wind it up by such date as is specified in the direction or, if no date is specified, as soon as practicable.

91(3) **[Effect of revocation of order]** The revocation of the order declaring an authorised unit trust scheme to be such a scheme shall not affect the operation of any direction under subsection (2) above which is then in force; and a direction may be given under that subsection in relation to a scheme in the case of which the order declaring it to be an authorised unit trust scheme has been revoked if a direction under that subsection was already in force at the time of revocation.

91(4)   [Effect of sec. 60, 61, 62]   Sections 60, 61 and 62 above shall have effect in relation to a contravention of a direction under subsection (2) above as they have effect in relation to any such contravention as is mentioned in those sections.

91(5)   [Power to direct not to be scheme]   If it appears to the Secretary of State—

    (a) that the exercise of the power conferred by this subsection is desirable in the interests of participants or potential participants in a scheme recognised under section 87 or 88 above who are in the United Kingdom;

    (b) without prejudice to paragraph (a) above, that the operator of such a scheme has contravened any provision of this Act or any rules or regulations made under it or, in purported compliance with any such provision, has furnished the Secretary of State with false, inaccurate or misleading information or has contravened any prohibition or requirement imposed under this Act; or

    (c) that any of the requirements for the recognition of a scheme under section 88 above are no longer satisfied,

he may direct that the scheme shall not be a recognised scheme for a specified period or until the occurrence of a specified event or until specified conditions are complied with.

91(6)   [Matter for sec. 91(1)(b), (5)(a)]   For the purposes of subsections (1)(b) and (5)(a) above the Secretary of State may take into account any matter relating to the scheme, the manager, operator or trustee, a director or controller of the manager, operator or trustee or any person employed by or associated with the manager, operator or trustee in connection with the scheme.

91(7)   [Manager who is SRO member]   In the case of a manager, operator or trustee who is a member of a recognised self-regulating organisation the rules, prohibitions and requirements referred to in subsections (1)(c) and (5) (b) above include the rules of that organisation and any prohibition or requirement imposed by virtue of those rules.

91(8)   [Withdrawal or variation of directions]   The Secretary of State may, either of his own motion or on the application of the manager, trustee or operator of the scheme concerned, withdraw or vary a direction given under this section if it appears to the Secretary of State that it is no longer necessary for the direction to take effect or continue in force or, as the case may be, that it should take effect or continue in force in a different form.

SEC. 92   Notice of directions

92(1)   [Exercise of power to give direction]   The power to give a direction under section 91 above in relation to a scheme shall be exercisable by written notice served by the Secretary of State on the manager and trustee or, as the case may be, on the operator of the scheme and any such notice shall take effect on such date as is specified in the notice.

92(2) **[Written notice of refusal]** If the Secretary of State refuses to withdraw or vary a direction on the application of the manager, trustee or operator of the scheme concerned he shall serve that person with a written notice of refusal.

92(3) **[Notice to state reasons for refusal etc.]** A notice giving a direction, or varying it otherwise than on the application of the manager, trustee or operator concerned, or refusing to withdraw or vary a direction on the application of such a person shall state the reasons for which the direction was given or varied or, as the case may be, why the application was refused.

92(4) **[Public notice of sec. 91 direction]** The Secretary of State may give public notice of a direction given by him under section 91 above and of any withdrawal or variation of such a direction; and any such notice may, if the Secretary of State thinks fit, include a statement of the reasons for which the direction was given, withdrawn or varied.

SEC. 93 Applications to the court

93(1) **[Application by Secretary of State]** In any case in which the Secretary of State has power to give a direction under section 91(2) above in relation to an authorised unit trust scheme or, by virtue of subsection (3) of that section, in relation to a scheme which has been such a scheme, he may apply to the court—

  (a) for an order removing the manager or trustee, or both the manager and trustee, of the scheme and replacing either or both of them with a person or persons nominated by him and appearing to him to satisfy the requirements of section 78 above; or

  (b) if it appears to the Secretary of State that no, or no suitable, person satisfying those requirements is available, for an order removing the manager or trustee, or both the manager and trustee, and appointing an authorised person to wind the scheme up.

93(2) **[Power of court]** On an application under this section the court may make such order as it thinks fit; and the court may, on the application of the Secretary of State, rescind any such order as is mentioned in paragraph (b) of subsection (1) above and substitute such an order as is mentioned in paragraph (a) of that subsection.

93(3) **[Written notice to manager of making of application]** The Secretary of State shall give written notice of the making of an application under this section to the manager and trustee of the scheme concerned and take such steps as he considers appropriate for bringing the making of the application to the attention of the participants.

93(4) **[Exercise of jurisdiction]** The jurisdiction conferred by this section shall be exercisable by the High Court and the Court of Session.

93(5) **[Non-application of sec. 83]** Section 83 above shall not apply to a manager appointed by an order made on an application under subsection (1)(b) above.

SUPPLEMENTAL

SEC. 94 Investigations

94(1) **[Power of Secretary of State to appoint inspectors]** The Secretary of State may appoint one or more competent inspectors to investigate and report on—

(a) the affairs of, or of the manager or trustee of, any authorised unit trust scheme;

(b) the affairs of, or of the operator or trustee of, any recognised scheme so far as relating to activities carried on in the United Kingdom; or

(c) the affairs of, or of the operator or trustee of, any other collective investment scheme,

if it appears to the Secretary of State that it is in the interests of the participants to do so or that the matter is of public concern.

94(2)   **[Powers of inspector]**   An inspector appointed under subsection (1) above to investigate the affairs of, or of the manager, trustee or operator of, any scheme may also, if he thinks it necessary for the purposes of that investigation, investigate the affairs of, or of the manager, trustee or operator of, any other such scheme as is mentioned in that subsection whose manager, trustee or operator is the same person as the manager, trustee or operator of the first mentioned scheme.

94(3)   **[Application of Companies Act 1985]**   Sections 434 to 436 of the Companies Act 1985 (production of documents and evidence to inspectors), shall apply in relation to an inspector appointed under this section as they apply to an inspector appointed under section 431 of that Act but with the modifications specified in subsection (4) below.

History
In s. 94(3) the words "except section 435(1)(a) and (b) and (2)" formerly appearing after the words "evidence to inspectors)," repealed by CA 1989, s. 212 and Sch. 24 as from 21 February 1990 (see S.I. 1990 No. 142 (C. 5), art. 7(d)).

94(4)   **[Interpretation re sec. 94(1)–(3)]**   In the provisions applied by subsection (3) above for any reference to a company there shall be substituted a reference to the scheme under investigation by virtue of this section and any reference to an officer of the company shall include a reference to any director of the manager, trustee or operator of the scheme.

History
In s. 94(4) the words "or its affairs" formerly appearing after the words "reference to a company", the words "and the affairs mentioned in subsection (1) or (2) above" formerly appearing after the words "by virtue of this section" and the words "or director" formerly appearing after the words "reference to an officer" repealed by CA 1989, s. 212 and Sch. 24 as from 21 February 1990 (see S.I. 1990 No. 142 (C. 5), art. 7(d)).

94(5)   **[Non-disclosure re legal professional privilege]**   A person shall not under this section be required to disclose any information or produce any document which he would be entitled to refuse to disclose or produce on grounds of legal professional privilege in proceedings in the High Court or on grounds of confidentiality as between client and professional legal adviser in proceedings in the Court of Session except that a lawyer may be required to furnish the name and address of his client.

94(6)   **[Where lien claimed]**   Where a person claims a lien on a document its production under this section shall be without prejudice to the lien.

94(7)   **[Disclosure re bankers]**   Nothing in this section requires a person (except as mentioned in subsection (7A) below) to disclose any information or produce any document in respect of which he owes an obligation of confidence by virtue of carrying on the business of banking unless—

(a) the person to whom the obligation of confidence is owed consents to the disclosure or production, or

(b) the making of the requirement was authorised by the Secretary of State.

History
See history note after s. 94(7A).

94(7A) [Non-application of sec. 94(7)]   Subsection (7) does not apply where the person owing the obligation of confidence or the person to whom it is owed is—

(a) the manager, operator or trustee of the scheme under investigation, or

(b) a manager, operator or trustee whose own affairs are under investigation.

History
S. 94(7), (7A) substituted for the former s. 94(7) by CA 1989, s. 72(1), (2) as from 21 February 1990 (see S.I. 1990 No. 142 (C. 5), art. 4); the former s. 94(7) read as follows:

"**94(7)** Nothing in this section shall require a person carrying on the business of banking to disclose any information or produce any document relating to the affairs of a customer unless—

    (a) the customer is a person who the inspector has reason to believe may be able to give information relevant to the investigation; and

    (b) the Secretary of State is satisfied that the disclosure or production is necessary for the purposes of the investigation."

94(8) [Reports by inspector]   An inspector appointed under this section may, and if so directed by the Secretary of State shall, make interim reports to the Secretary of State and on the conclusion of his investigation shall make a final report to him.

94(8A) [Where suggestion re criminal offence]   If it appears to the Secretary of State that matters have come to light in the course of the inspectors' investigation which suggest that a criminal offence has been committed, and those matters have been referred to the appropriate prosecuting authority, he may direct the inspectors to take no further steps in the investigation or to take only such further steps as are specified in the direction.

History
See history note after s. 94(8B).

94(8B) [Where sec. 94(8A) direction]   Where an investigation is the subject of a direction under subsection (8A), the inspectors shall make a final report to the Secretary of State only where the Secretary of State directs them to do so.

History
S. 94(8A), (8B) inserted by CA 1989, s. 72(1), (3) as from 21 February 1990 (see S.I. 1990 No. 142 (C. 5), art. 4).

94(9) [Form, publication of report]   Any such report shall be written or printed as the Secretary of State may direct and the Secretary of State may, if he thinks fit—

(a) furnish a copy, on request and on payment of the prescribed fee, to the manager, trustee or operator or any participant in a scheme under investigation or any other person whose conduct is referred to in the report; and

(b) cause the report to be published.

94(10) [Order re expenses]   A person who is convicted on a prosecution instituted as a result of an investigation under this section may in the same proceedings be ordered to pay the expenses of the investigation to such extent as may be specified in the order.

There shall be treated as expenses of the investigation, in particular, such reasonable sums as the Secretary of State may determine in respect of general staff costs and overheads.

History
S. 94(10) added by CA 1989, s. 72(1), (4) as from 21 February 1990 (see S.I. 1990 No. 142 (C. 5), art. 4).

SEC. 95   Contraventions

95(1)   [Effect of contravention of Ch. VIII]   A person who contravenes any provision of this Chapter, a manager or trustee of an authorised unit trust scheme who contravenes any regulations made under section 81 above and a person who contravenes any other regulations made under this Chapter shall be treated as having contravened rules made under Chapter V of this Part of this Act or, in the case of a person who is an authorised person by virtue of his membership of a recognised self-regulating organisation or certification by a recognised professional body, the rules of that organisation or body.

95(2)   [Additional application of sec. 95(1)]   Subsection (1) above applies also to any contravention by the operator of a recognised scheme of a requirement imposed under section 90(2) above.

95(3)   [Action by virtue of sec. 47A]   The disciplinary action which may be taken by virtue of section 47A(3) (failure to comply with statement of principle) includes—

  (a) the giving of a direction under section 91(2), and

  (b) the application by the Secretary of State for an order under section 93;

and subsection (6) of section 47A (duty of the Secretary of State as to exercise of powers) has effect accordingly.

History
S. 95(3) added by CA 1989, s. 206(1) and Sch. 23, para. 9
as from 15 March 1990 (see S.I. 1990 No. 354 (C. 12),
art. 3).

Chapter IX — The Tribunal

SEC. 96   The Financial Services Tribunal

96(1)   ["The Tribunal"]   For the purposes of this Act shall be a Tribunal known as the Financial Services Tribunal (in this Act referred to as **"the Tribunal"**).

96(2)   [Panel of members]   There shall be a panel of not less than ten persons to serve as members of the Tribunal when nominated to do so in accordance with subsection (3) below; and that panel shall consist of—

  (a) persons with legal qualifications appointed by the Lord Chancellor after consultation with the Lord Advocate, including at least one person qualified in Scots law; and

  (b) persons appointed by the Secretary of State who appear to him to be qualified by experience or otherwise to deal with the cases that may be referred to the Tribunal.

96(3)   [Where case referred to Tribunal]   Where a case is referred to the Tribunal the Secretary of State shall nominate three persons from the panel to serve as members of the Tribunal in respect of that case and nominate one of them to be chairman.

96(4)   [Requirements re members]   The person nominated to be chairman of the Tribunal in respect of any case shall be a person with legal qualifications and, so far as practicable, at least one of the other members shall be a person with recent practical experience in business relevant to the case.

96(5) **[Where member unable to act]** If while a case is being dealt with by the Tribunal one of the three persons serving as members in respect of that case becomes unable to act the case may, with the consent of the Secretary of State and of the person or persons at whose request the case was referred to the Tribunal, be dealt with by the other two members.

96(6) **[Sch. 6]** Schedule 6 to this Act shall have effect as respects the Tribunal and its proceedings.

SEC. 97 References to the Tribunal

97(1) **[Requirement that Secretary of State make reference]** Any person—

    (a) on whom a notice is served under section 29, 34, 59(4), 60(2) or 70 above; or

    (b) on whom a copy of a notice under section 29, 34, 60(2) or 70 above is served or on whom the Secretary of State considers that a copy of such a notice would have been served if it had been practicable to do so,

may within twenty-eight days of the date of service of the notice require the Secretary of State to refer the matter to which the notice relates to the Tribunal and, subject to the provisions of this section, the Secretary of State shall refer that matter accordingly.

97(2) **[Where reference need not be made]** The Secretary of State need not refer a matter to the Tribunal at the request of the person on whom a notice was served under section 29, 34, 59(4) or 60(2) above if within the period mentioned in subsection (1) above he—

    (a) decides to grant the application or, as the case may be, decides not to withdraw or suspend the authorisation, give the direction or publish the statement to which the notice relates; and

    (b) gives written notice of his decision to that person.

97(3) **[Further non-reference situation]** The Secretary of State need not refer a matter to the Tribunal at the request of the person on whom a notice is served under section 70 above if—

    (a) that matter is the refusal of an application for the rescission or variation of a prohibition or requirement and within the period mentioned in subsection (1) above he—

        (i) decides to grant the application; and

        (ii) gives written notice of his decision to that person; or

    (b) that matter is the imposition or variation of a prohibition or requirement, being a prohibition, requirement or variation which has not yet taken effect, and within the period mentioned in subsection (1) above and before the prohibition, requirement or variation takes effect he—

        (i) decides to rescind the prohibition or requirement or decides not to make the variation; and

        (ii) gives written notice of his decision to that person.

97(4) **[Where new notice after suspension or withdrawal]** Where the notice served on a person under section 29 or 34 above—

    (a) proposed the withdrawal of an authorisation or the giving of a direction under section 33(1)(a) above; or

    (b) proposed the suspension of an authorisation or the giving of a direction under section 33(1)(b) above,

and at any time within the period mentioned in subsection (1) above the Secretary of State serves a new notice on that person in substitution for that previously served, then, if the substituted notice complies with subsection (5) below, subsection (1) above shall have effect in relation to the substituted notice instead of the original notice and as if the period there mentioned were twenty-eight days after the date of service of the original notice or fourteen days after the date of service of the substituted notice, whichever ends later.

97(5) **[Notices under sec. 97(4)]** A notice served in substitution for a notice within subsection (4)(a) above complies with this subsection if it proposes—

    (a) the suspension of an authorisation or the giving of a direction under section 33(1)(b) above; or

    (b) the exercise of the power conferred by section 60 above;

and a notice served in substitution for a notice within subsection (4)(b) above complies with this subsection if it proposes a less severe suspension or direction under section 33(1)(b) or the exercise of the power conferred by section 60 above.

97(6) **[Effective date of notice]** The reference of the imposition or variation of a prohibition or requirement under Chapter VI of this Part of this Act to the Tribunal shall not affect the date on which it comes into effect.

SEC. 98   Decisions on references by applicant or authorised person etc.

98(1) **[Where case referred to Tribunal]** Where a case is referred to the Tribunal at the request of a person within section 97(1)(a) above the Tribunal shall—

    (a) investigate the case; and

    (b) make a report to the Secretary of State stating what would in its opinion be the appropriate decision in the matter and the reasons for that opinion;

and it shall be the duty of the Secretary of State to decide the matter forthwith in accordance with the Tribunal's report.

98(2) **[Where matter referred is refusal of application]** Where the matter referred to the Tribunal is the refusal of an application the Tribunal may under this section report that the appropriate decision would be to grant or refuse the application or—

    (a) in the case of an application for the variation of a suspension, direction, consent, prohibition or requirement, to vary it in a specified manner;

    (b) in the case of an application for the rescission of a prohibition or requirement, to vary the prohibition or requirement in a specified manner.

98(3) **[Where matter referred is other action of Secretary of State]** Where the matter referred to the Tribunal is any action of the Secretary of State other than the refusal of an application the Tribunal may report that the appropriate decision would be—

(a) to take or not to take the action taken or proposed to be taken by the Secretary of State or to take any other action that he could take under the provision in question; or

(b) to take instead or in addition any action that he could take in the case of the person concerned under any one or more of the provisions mentioned in subsection (4) below other than that under which he was acting or proposing to act.

98(4) **[Provisions in sec. 98(1)(b)]** Those provisions are sections 28, 33 and 60 above and Chapter VI of this Part of this Act; and sections 29, 34, 60(2) and (3) and 70(2) and (4) above shall not apply to any action taken by the Secretary of State in accordance with the Tribunal's report.

98(5) **[Copy of report, notice of decision]** The Tribunal shall send a copy of its report under this section to the person at whose request the case was referred to it; and the Secretary of State shall serve him with a written notice of the decision made by him in accordance with the report.

SEC. 99 Decisions on references by third parties

99 Where a case is referred to the Tribunal at the request of a person within section 97(1)(b) above the Tribunal shall report to the Secretary of State whether the reasons stated in the notice in question which relate to that person are substantiated; and the Tribunal shall send a copy of the report to that person and to the person on whom the notice was served.

SEC. 100 Withdrawal of references

100(1) **[Person may withdraw reference]** A person who has required a case to be referred to the Tribunal may at any time before the conclusion of the proceedings before the Tribunal withdraw the reference.

100(2) **[Secretary of State may withdraw reference]** The Secretary of State may at any such time withdraw any reference made at the request of a person on whom a notice was served under any of the provisions mentioned in subsection (1)(a) of section 97 above if he—

(a) decides as mentioned in subsection (2)(a) or (3)(a)(i) or (b)(i) of that section; and

(b) gives such a notice as is mentioned in subsection (2)(b) or (3)(a)(ii) or (b)(ii) of that section;

but a reference shall not be withdrawn by virtue of such a decision and notice as are mentioned in paragraph (b) of subsection (3) unless the decision is made and the notice is given before the prohibition, requirement or variation has taken effect.

100(3) **[Where case withdrawn]** Where a case is withdrawn from the Tribunal under this section the Tribunal shall not further investigate the case or make a report under section 98 or 99 above; but where the reference is withdrawn otherwise than by the Secretary of State he may require the Tribunal to make a report to him on the results of its investigation up to the time when the reference was withdrawn.

100(4) **[Where withdrawal by one of two or more persons]** Where two or more persons have required a case to be referred to the Tribunal the withdrawal of the reference by one or more of them shall not affect the functions of the Tribunal as respects the case so far as relating to a person who has not withdrawn the reference.

100(5) [Where withdrawal by persons served with sec. 29, 34, 60 notice]   Where a person on whom a notice was served under section 29, 34 or 60 above withdraws a case from the Tribunal subsection (5) of each of those sections shall apply to him as if he had not required the case to be referred.

SEC. 101   Reports

101(1) [Exclusion re affairs of particular person]   In preparing its report on any case the Tribunal shall have regard to the need to exclude, so far as practicable, any matter which relates to the affairs of a particular person (not being a person who required or could have required the case to be referred to the Tribunal) where the publication of that matter would or might, in the opinion of the Tribunal, seriously and prejudicially affect the interests of that person.

101(2) [Publication and sale of reports]   The Secretary of State may, in such cases as he thinks fit, publish the report of the Tribunal and offer copies of any such report for sale.

101(3) [Copies to interested persons]   The Secretary of State may, on request and on payment of the prescribed fee, supply a copy of a report of the Tribunal to any person whose conduct is referred to in the report or whose interests as a client or creditor are affected by the conduct of a person to whom the proceedings before the Tribunal related.

101(4) [Parts of report omitted from publication]   If the Secretary of State is of opinion that there is good reason for not disclosing any part of a report he may cause that part to be omitted from the report as published under subsection (2) or from the copy of it supplied under subsection (3) above.

101(5) [Admissibility as evidence]   A copy of a report of the Tribunal endorsed with a certificate signed by or on behalf of the Secretary of State stating that it is a true copy shall be admissible as evidence of the opinion of the Tribunal as to any matter referred to in the report; and a certificate purporting to be signed as aforesaid shall be deemed to have been duly signed unless the contrary is shown.

Chapter X — Information

SEC. 102   Register of authorised persons and recognised organisations etc.

102(1) [Secretary of State to keep register]   The Secretary of State shall keep a register containing an entry in respect of—

(a) each person who is an authorised person by virtue of an authorisation granted by the Secretary of State;

(b) each other person who appears to him to be an authorised person by virtue of any provision of this Part of this Act;

(c) each recognised self-regulating organisation, recognised professional body, recognised investment exchange and recognised clearing house;

(d) each authorised unit trust scheme and recognised scheme;

(e) each person in respect of whom a direction under section 59 above is in force.

102(2) **[Entry re each authorised person]** The entry in respect of each authorised person shall consist of—

(a) a statement of the provision by virtue of which he is an authorised person;

(b) in the case of a person who is an authorised person by virtue of membership of a recognised self-regulating organisation or certification by a recognised professional body, the name and address of the organisation or body;

(c) in the case of a person who is an authorised person by virtue of section 25 or 31 above, information as to the services which that person holds himself out as able to provide;

(d) in the case of a person who is an authorised person by virtue of section 31 above, the address notified to the Secretary of State under section 32 above;

(e) in the case of a person who is an authorised person by virtue of any provision other than section 31 above, the date on which he became an authorised person by virtue of that provision; and

(f) such other information as the Secretary of State may determine.

102(3) **[Entry re sec. 102(1)(c) organisations etc.]** The entry in respect of each such organisation, body, exchange or clearing house as is mentioned in subsection (1)(c) above shall consist of its name and address and such other information as the Secretary of State may determine.

102(4) **[Entry re sec. 102(1)(d) schemes]** The entry in respect of each such scheme as is mentioned in subsection (1)(d) above shall consist of its name and, in the case of an authorised unit trust scheme, the name and address of the manager and trustee and, in the case of a recognised scheme, the name and address of the operator and of any representative of the operator in the United Kingdom and, in either case, such other information as the Secretary of State may determine.

102(5) **[Entry re sec. 102(1)(e) persons]** The entry in respect of each such person as is mentioned in subsection (1)(e) above shall include particulars of any consent for that person's employment given by the Secretary of State.

102(6) **[Where sec. 102 (1)(a), (b) person no longer authorised]** Where it appears to the Secretary of State that any person in respect of whom there is an entry in the register by virtue of subsection (1) (a) or (b) above has ceased to be an authorised person (whether by death, by withdrawal or other cessation of his authorisation, as a result of his ceasing to be a member of a recognised self-regulating organisation or otherwise) the Secretary of State shall make a note to that effect in the entry together with the reason why the person in question is no longer an authorised person.

102(7) **[Note re certain events]** Where—

(a) an organisation, body, exchange or clearing house in respect of which there is an entry in the register by virtue of paragraph (c) of subsection (1) above has ceased to be recognised or ceased to exist;

(b) an authorised unit trust scheme or recognised scheme in respect of which there is an entry in the register by virtue of paragraph (d) of that subsection has ceased to be authorised or recognised; or

(c) the direction applying to a person in respect of whom there is an entry in the register by virtue of paragraph (e) of that subsection has ceased to have effect,

the Secretary of State shall make a note to that effect in the entry.

102(8) [Removal of sec. 102(6), (7) note]   An entry in respect of which a note is made under subsection (6) or (7) above may be removed from the register at the end of such period as the Secretary of State thinks appropriate.

SEC. 103 Inspection of register

103(1) [Inspection and publication of information]   The information contained in the entries included in the register otherwise than by virtue of section 102(1)(e) above shall be open to inspection; and the Secretary of State may publish the information contained in those entries in any form he thinks appropriate and may offer copies of any such information for sale.

103(2) [Inspection re sec. 102(1)(e) entries]   A person shall be entitled to ascertain whether there is an entry in the register by virtue of subsection (1)(e) of section 102 above (not being an entry in respect of which there is a note under subsection (7) of that section) in respect of a particular person specified by him and, if there is such an entry, to inspect it.

103(3) [Limit on inspection re sec. 102(1)(e) entries]   Except as provided by subsection (2) above the information contained in the register by virtue of section 102(1)(e) above shall not be open to inspection by any person unless he satisfies the Secretary of State that he has a good reason for seeking the information.

103(4) [Limit on information available by sec. 103(3)]   A person to whom information is made available by the Secretary of State under subsection (3) above shall not, without the consent of the Secretary of State or of the person to whom the information relates, make use of it except for the purpose for which it was made available.

103(5) [Details re inspection]   Information which by virtue of this section is open to inspection shall be open to inspection free of charge but only at such times and places as the Secretary of State may appoint; and a person entitled to inspect any information may obtain a certified copy of it from the Secretary of State on payment of the prescribed fee.

103(6) [Form of register]   The register may be kept by the Secretary of State in such form as he thinks appropriate with a view to facilitating inspection of the information which it contains.

SEC. 104 Power to call for information

104(1) [Information from sec. 22, 24, 25, 31 persons]   The Secretary of State may by notice in writing require a person who is authorised to carry on investment business by virtue of section 22, 24, 25 or 31 above to furnish him with such information as he may reasonably require for the exercise of his functions under this Act.

104(2) **[Information from recognised bodies etc.]** The Secretary of State may by notice in writing require a recognised self-regulating organisation, recognised professional body, recognised investment exchange or recognised clearing house to furnish him with such information as he may reasonably require for the exercise of his functions under this Act.

104(3) **[Time, verification re information]** The Secretary of State may require any information which he requires under this section to be furnished within such reasonable time and verified in such manner as he may specify.

104(4) **[Effect of sec. 60, 61, 62]** Sections 60, 61 and 62 above shall have effect in relation to a contravention of a requirement imposed under subsection (1) above as they have effect in relation to a contravention of the provisions to which those sections apply.

SEC. 105 Investigation powers

105(1) **[Where Secretary of State's powers to be exercised]** The powers of the Secretary of State under this section shall be exercisable in any case in which it appears to him that there is good reason to do so for the purpose of investigating the affairs, or any aspect of the affairs, of any person so far as relevant to any investment business which he is or was carrying on or appears to the Secretary of State to be or to have been carrying on.

105(2) **[Limit on exercise of powers]** Those powers shall not be exercisable for the purpose of investigating the affairs of any exempted person unless he is an appointed representative or the investigation is in respect of investment business in respect of which he is not an exempted person and shall not be exercisable for the purpose of investigating the affairs of a member of a recognised self-regulating organisation or a person certified by a recognised professional body in respect of investment business in the carrying on of which he is subject to its rules unless—

(a) that organisation or body has requested the Secretary of State to investigate those affairs; or

(b) it appears to him that the organisation or body is unable or unwilling to investigate them in a satisfactory manner.

105(3) **[Power re attendance before Secretary of State]** The Secretary of State may require the person whose affairs are to be investigated ("the person under investigation") or any connected person to attend before the Secretary of State at a specified time and place and answer questions or otherwise furnish information with respect to any matter relevant to the investigation.

105(4) **[Power re production of documents]** The Secretary of State may require the person under investigation or any other person to produce at a specified time and place any specified documents which appear to the Secretary of State to relate to any matter relevant to the investigation; and—

(a) if any such documents are produced, the Secretary of State may take copies or extracts from them or require the person producing them or any connected person to provide an explanation of any of them;

(b) if any such documents are not produced, the Secretary of State may require the person who was required to produce them to state, to the best of his knowledge and belief, where they are.

105(5)   [Statement admissible in evidence]   A statement by person in compliance with a requirement imposed by virtue of this section may be used in evidence against him.

105(6)   [Legal professional privilege, confidentiality]   A person shall not under this section be required to disclose any information or produce any document which he would be entitled to refuse to disclose or produce on grounds of legal professional privilege in proceedings in the High Court or on grounds of confidentiality as between client and professional legal adviser in proceedings in the Court of Session except that a lawyer may be required to furnish the name and address of his client.

105(7)   (Omitted and repealed by Companies Act 1989, sec. 73(1), (2), 212 and Sch. 24 as from 21 February 1990.)

History

In regard to the date of the above omission and repeal see S.I. 1990 No. 142 (C. 5), art. 4, 7(d); s. 105(7) formerly read as follows:

"**105(7)**   The Secretary of State shall not require an institution authorised under the Banking Act 1987 to disclose any information or produce any document relating to the affairs of a customer unless the Secretary of State considers it necessary to do so for the purpose of investigating any investment business carried on, or appearing to the Secretary of State to be carried on or to

have been carried on, by the institution or customer or, if the customer is a related company of the person under investigation, by that person."

In that former s. 105(7) the words, "an institution authorised under the Banking Act 1987", and, "institution", substituted for the former words, "a recognised or licensed institution within the meaning of the Banking Act 1979", and "bank, institution", respectively, by Banking Act 1987, s. 108(1) and Sch. 6, para. 27(2) as from 1 October 1987 (see S.I. 1987 No. 1664 (C. 50)).

105(8)   [Where lien claimed]   Where a person claims a lien on a document its production under this section shall be without prejudice to the lien.

105(9)   [Definitions]   In this section—

"**connected person**", in relation to any other person means—

(a) any person who is or was that other person's partner, employee, agent, appointed representative, banker, auditor or solicitor; and

(b) where the other person is a body corporate, any person who is or was a director, secretary or controller of that body corporate or of another body corporate of which it is or was a subsidiary; and

(c) where the other person is an unincorporated association, any person who is or was a member of the governing body or an officer or controller of the association; and

(d) where the other person is an appointed representative, any person who is or was his principal; and

(e) where the other person is the person under investigation (being a body corporate), any related company of that body corporate and any person who is a connected person in relation to that company;

"**documents**" includes information recorded in any form and, in relation to information recorded otherwise than in legible form, the power to require its production includes power to require the production of a copy of the information in legible form;

"**related company**", in relation to a person under investigation (being a body corporate), means any other body corporate which is or at any material time was—

(a) a holding company or subsidiary of the person under investigation;

(b) a subsidiary of a holding company of that person; or

(c) a holding company of a subsidiary of that person,

and whose affairs it is in the Secretary of State's opinion necessary to investigate for the purpose of investigating the affairs of that person.

History
In s. 105(9) in the definition of "documents" the words "the power to require its productin includes power to require the production of" substituted for the former words "references to its production include references to producing" by CA 1989, s. 73(1), (3) as from 21 February 1990 (see S.I. 1990 No. 142 (C.5), art. 4).

105(10) **[Offence, penalty]** Any person who without reasonable excuse fails to comply with a requirement imposed on him under this section shall be guilty of an offence and liable on summary conviction to imprisonment for a term not exceeding six months or to a fine not exceeding the fifth level on the standard scale or to both.

105(11) **[Order re expenses]** A person who is convicted on a prosecution instituted as a result of an investigation under this section may in the same proceedings be ordered to pay the expenses of the investigation to such extent as may be specified in the order.

There shall be treated as expenses of the investigation, in particular, such reasonable sums as the Secretary of State may determine in respect of general staff costs and overheads.

History
S. 105(11) added by CA 1989, s. 73(1), (4) as from 21 February 1990 (see S.I. 1990 No. 142 (C.5), art. 4).

SEC. 106   Exercise of investigation powers by officer etc.

106(1) **[Secretary of State may authorise officer]** The Secretary of State may authorise any officer of his or any other competent person to exercise on his behalf all or any of the powers conferred by section 105 above but no such authority shall be granted except for the purpose of investigating the affairs, or any aspects of the affairs, of a person specified in the authority.

106(2) **[Compliance, production of evidence re authority]** No person shall be bound to comply with any requirement imposed by a person exercising powers by virtue of an authority granted under this section unless he has, if required to do so, produced evidence of his authority.

106(2A) **[Disclosure by bankers]** A person shall not by virtue of an authority under this section be required to disclose any information or produce any documents in respect of which he owes an obligation of confidence by virtue of carrying on the business of banking unless—

(a) he is the person under investigation or a related company,

(b) the person to whom the obligation of confidence is owed is the person under investigation or a related company,

(c) the person to whom the obligation of confidence is owed consents to the disclosure or production, or

(d) the imposing on him of a requirement with respect to such information or documents has been specifically authorised by the Secretary of State.

In this subsection **"documents"**, **"person under investigation"** and **"related company"** have the same meaning as in section 105.

History
S. 106(2A) inserted by CA 1989, s. 73(5) as from
21 February 1990 (see S.I. 1990 No. 142 (C.5), art. 4).

106(3) **[Report by officer re exercise of powers etc.]** Where the Secretary of State authorises a person other than one of his officers to exercise any powers by virtue of this section that person shall make a report to the Secretary of State in such manner as he may require on the exercise of those powers and the results of exercising them.

Chapter XI — Auditors

SEC. 107   Appointment of auditors

107(1) **[Power of Secretary of State to make rules]** The Secretary of State may make rules requiring—

    (a) a person authorised to carry on investment business by virture of section 25 or 31 above, or

    (b) a member of a recognised self-regulating organisation carrying on investment business in the carrying on of which he is subject to the rules of the organisation,

and who, apart from the rules, is not required by or under any enactment to appoint an auditor, to appoint as an auditor a person satisfying such conditions as to qualifications and otherwise as may be specified in or imposed under the rules.

History
S. 107(1) substituted by CA 1989, s. 206(1) and Sch. 23, para. 10(1), (2) as from 15 March 1990 (see S.I. 1990 No. 354 (C. 12), art. 3); s. 107(1) formerly read as follows: "**107(1)** The Secretary of State may make rules requiring a person who is authorised to carry on investment business by virtue of section 25 or 31 above and who, apart from the rules, is not required by or under any enactment to appoint an auditor to appoint as an auditor a person satisfying such conditions as to qualifications and otherwise as may be specified in or imposed under the rules."

107(2) **[Extent of rules]** Rules under this section may make provision—

    (a) specifying the manner in which and the time within which an auditor is to be appointed;

    (b) requiring the Secretary of State to be notified of any such appointment and enabling the Secretary of State to make an appointment if no appointment is made or notified as required by the rules;

    (c) with respect to the remuneration of an auditor appointed under the rules;

    (d) with respect to the term of office, removal and resignation of any such auditor;

    (e) requiring any such auditor who is removed, resigns or is not reappointed to notify the Secretary of State whether there are any circumstances connected with his ceasing to hold office which he considers should be brought to the Secretary of State's attention.

107(3) **[Duty of auditor]** An auditor appointed under the rules shall in accordance with the rules examine and report on the accounts of the authorised person in question and shall for that purpose have such duties and powers as are specified in the rules.

CCH Editions Limited
BCL BCLFS$$$16

107(4) **[Application to SRO members]** In its application to members of recognised self-regulating organisations, this section has effect subject to section 107A below.

History
S. 107(4) added by CA 1989, s.206(1) and Sch. 23, para.
10(1), (3) as from 15 March 1990 (see S.I. 1990 No. 354
(C.12), art. 3).

SEC. 107A Application of audit rules to members of self-regulating organisations

107A(1) **[Power of Secretary of State to make rules]** The Secretary of State may in rules under section 107 designate provisions which apply, to such extent as may be specified, to a member of a recognised self-regulating organisation in respect of investment business in the carrying on of which he is subject to the rules of the organisation.

107A(2) **[Extent of rules]** It may be provided that the designated rules have effect, generally or to such extent as may be specified, subject to the rules of the organisation.

107A(3) **[Contravention by SRO member]** A member of a recognised self-regulating organisation who contravenes a rule applying to him by virtue of that section shall be treated as having contravened the rules of the organisation.

107A(4) **[Application to SRO member]** Except as mentioned above, rules made under section 107 do not apply to members of recognised self-regulating organisations in respect of investment business in the carrying on of which they are subject to the rules of the organisation.

107A(5) **[Power of SRO to modify or dispense from rule]** A recognised self-regulating organisation may on the application of a member of the organisation—

    (a) modify a rule designated under this section so as to adapt it to his circumstances or to any particular kind of business carried on by him, or

    (b) dispense him from compliance with any such rule, generally or in relation to any particular kind of business carried on by him.

107A(6) **[Condition for sec. 107A(5) power]** The powers conferred by subsection (5) shall not be exercised unless it appears to the organisation—

    (a) that compliance with the rule in question would be unduly burdensome for the applicant having regard to the benefit which compliance would confer on investors, and

    (b) that the exercise of those powers will not result in any undue risk to investors.

107A(7) **[Exercise of sec. 107A(5) power may be conditional]** The powers conferred by subsection (5) may be exercised unconditionally or subject to conditions; and subsection (3) applies in the case of a contravention of a condition as in the case of contravention of a designated rule.

107A(8) **[Monitoring and enforcement of compliance]** The reference in paragraph 4(1) of Schedule 2 (requirements for recognition of self-regulating organisations) to monitoring and enforcement of compliance with rules includes monitoring and enforcement of compliance with conditions imposed by the organisation under subsection (7).

History
S. 107A inserted by CA 1989, s. 206(1) and Sch. 23, para.
11 as from 15 March 1990 (see S.I. 1990 No. 354 (C. 12),
art. 3).

Note
For transfer of the Secretary of State's functions under
s. 107A see S.I. 1990 No. 354 (C.12), art. 4(5).

SEC. 108   Power to require second audit

108(1)   **[Power of Secretary of State]**   If in any case it appears to the Secretary of State that there is good reason to do so he may direct any person who is authorised to carry on investment business by virtue of section 25 or 31 above to submit for further examination by a person approved by the Secretary of State—

(a) any accounts on which that person's auditor has reported or any information given under section 52 or 104 above which has been verified by that auditor; or

(b) such matters contained in any such accounts or information as are specified in the direction;

and the person making the further examination shall report his conclusions to the Secretary of State.

108(2)   **[Expense of further examination and report]**   Any further examination and report required by a direction under this section shall be at the expense of the authorised person concerned and shall be carried out and made within such time as is specified in the direction or within such further time as the Secretary of State may allow.

108(3)   **[Power of examiner]**   The person carrying out an examination under this section shall have all the powers that were available to the auditor; and it shall be the duty of the auditor to afford him all such assistance as he may require.

108(4)   **[Report being made available]**   Where a report made under this section relates to accounts which under any enactment are required to be sent to or made available for inspection by any person or to be delivered for registration, the report, or any part of it (or a note that such a report has been made) may be similarly sent, made available or delivered by the Secretary of State.

SEC. 109   Communication by auditor with supervisory authorities

109(1)   **[Communication with Secretary of State]**   No duty to which an auditor of an authorised person may be subject shall be regarded as contravened by reason of his communicating in good faith to the Secretary of State, whether or not in response to a request from him, any information or opinion on a matter of which the auditor has become aware in his capacity as auditor of that person and which is relevant to any functions of the Secretary of State under this Act.

109(2)   **[Power of Secretary of State to make rules]**   If it appears to the Secretary of State that any auditor or class of auditor to whom subsection (1) above applies is not subject to satisfactory rules made or guidance issued by a professional body specifying circumstances in which matters are to be communicated to the Secretary of State as mentioned in that subsection the Secretary of State may himself make rules applying to that auditor or that class of auditor and specifying such circumstances; and it shall be the duty of an auditor to whom the rules made by the Secretary of State apply to communicate a matter to the Secretary of State in the circumstances specified by the rules.

109(3)　**[Matters communicated]**　The matters to be communicated to the Secretary of State in accordance with any such rules or guidance may include matters relating to persons other than the authorised person.

109(4)　**[Approval etc. of sec. 109(2) rules]**　No such rules as are mentioned in subsection (2) above shall be made by the Secretary of State unless a draft of them has been laid before and approved by a resolution of each House of Parliament.

109(5)　**[Application of section]**　This section applies to—

(a) the communication by an auditor to a recognised self-regulating organisation or recognised professional body of matters relevant to its function of determining whether a person is a fit and proper person to carry on investment business; and

(b) the communication to such an organisation or body or any other authority or person of matters relevant to its or his function of determining whether a person is complying with the rules applicable to his conduct of investment business,

as it applies to the communication to the Secretary of State of matters relevant to his functions under this Act.

SEC. 110　Overseas business

110(1)　**[Auditor of overseas person]**　A person incorporated or having his head office outside the United Kingdom who is authorised as mentioned in subsection (1) of section 107 above may, whether or not he is required to appoint an auditor apart from the rules made under that subsection, appoint an auditor in accordance with those rules in respect of the investment business carried on by him in the United Kingdom and in that event that person shall be treated for the purposes of this Chapter as the auditor of that person.

110(2)　**[Conditions as to qualifications]**　In the case of a person to be appointed as auditor of a person incorporated or having his head office outside the United Kingdom the conditions as to qualifications imposed by or under the rules made under that section may be regarded as satisfied by qualifications obtained outside the United Kingdom which appear to the Secretary of State to be equivalent.

110(3)　**[Conditions to be fit and proper person under sec. 25]**　A person incorporated or having his head office outside the United Kingdom shall not be regarded for the purposes of section 25 above as a fit and proper person to carry on investment business unless—

(a) he has appointed an auditor in accordance with rules made under section 107 above in respect of the investment business carried on by him in the United Kingdom; or

(b) he has an auditor having qualifications, powers and duties appearing to the Secretary of State to be equivalent to those applying to an auditor appointed in accordance with those rules,

and, in either case, the auditor is able and willing to communicate with the Secretary of State and other bodies and persons as mentioned in section 109 above.

SEC. 111   Offences and enforcement

111(1)   **[Offence, penalty]**   Any authorised person and any officer, controller or manager of an authorised person, who knowingly or recklessly furnishes an auditor appointed under the rules made under section 107 or a person carrying out an examination under section 108 above with information which the auditor or that person requires or is entitled to require and which is false or misleading in a material particular shall be guilty of an offence and liable—

- (a) on conviction on indictment, to imprisonment for a term not exceeding two years or to a fine or to both;
- (b) on summary conviction, to imprisonment for a term not exceeding six months or to a fine not exceeding the statutory maximum or to both.

111(2)   **[Enforcement of auditor's duty]**   The duty of an auditor under section 108(3) above shall be enforceable by mandamus or, in Scotland, by an order for specific performance under section 91 of the Court of Session Act 1868.

111(3)   **[Secretary of State's disqualification power]**   If it appears to the Secretary of State that an auditor has failed to comply with the duty mentioned in section 109(2) above, the Secretary of State may disqualify him from being the auditor of an authorised person or any class of authorised person; but the Secretary of State may remove any disqualification imposed under this subsection if satisfied that the person in question will in future comply with that duty.

111(4)   **[Appointment of disqualified person]**   An authorised person shall not appoint as auditor a person disqualified under subsection (3) above; and a person who is an authorised person by virtue of membership of a recognised self-regulating organisation or certification by a recognised professional body who contravenes this subsection shall be treated as having contravened the rules of the organisation or body.

Chapter XII — Fees

SEC. 112   Application fees

112(1)   **[Applicant to pay required fees]**   An applicant for a recognition order under Chapter III or IV of this Part of this Act shall pay such fees in respect of his application as may be required by a scheme made and published by the Secretary of State; and no application for such an order shall be regarded as duly made unless this subsection is complied with.

112(2)   **[A scheme under sec. 112(1)]**   A scheme made for the purposes of subsection (1) above shall specify the time when the fees are to be paid and may—

- (a) provide for the determination of the fees in accordance with a specified scale or other specified factors;
- (b) provide for the return or abatement of any fees where an application is refused or withdrawn; and
- (c) make different provision for different cases.

112(3)   **[Date re sec. 112(1) scheme]**   Any scheme made for the purposes of subsection (1) above shall come into operation on such date as is specified in the scheme (not being earlier than the day on which it is first published) and shall apply to applications made on or after the date on which it comes into operation.

112(4) **[Power in sec. 112(1) includes variation, revocation]** The power to make a scheme for the purposes of subsection (1) above includes power to vary or revoke a previous scheme made under those provisions.

112(5) **[Fee with application and notices]** Every application under section 26, 77 or 88 above shall be accompanied by the prescribed fee and every notice given to the Secretary of State under section 32, 86(2) or 87(3) above shall be accompanied by such fee as may be prescribed; and no such application or notice shall be regarded as duly made or given unless this subsection is complied with.

SEC. 113 Periodical fees

113(1) **[Recognised bodies to pay]** Every recognised self-regulating organisation, recognised professional body, recognised investment exchange and recognised clearing house shall pay such periodical fees to the Secretary of State as may be prescribed.

113(2) **[Body authorised under sec. 22]** So long as a body is authorised under section 22 above to carry on insurance business which is investment business it shall pay to the Secretary of State such periodical fees as may be prescribed.

113(3) **[Society authorised under sec. 23]** So long as a society is authorised under section 23 above to carry on investment business it shall—

(a) if it is authorised by virtue of subsection (1) of that section, pay to the Chief Registrar of friendly societies such periodical fees as he may by regulations specify; and

(b) if it is authorised by virtue of subsection (2) of that section, pay to the Registrar of Friendly Societies for Northern Ireland such periodical fees as he may by regulations specify.

113(4) **[Person authorised under sec. 25, 31]** A person who is an authorised person by virtue of section 25 or 31 above shall pay such periodical fees to the Secretary of State as may be prescribed.

113(5) **[If person fails to pay sec. 113(4) fee]** If a person fails to pay any fee which is payable by him under subsection (4) above the Secretary of State may serve on him a written notice requiring him to pay the fee within twenty-eight days of service of the notice; and if the fee is not paid within that period that person's authorisation shall cease to have effect unless the Secretary of State otherwise directs.

113(6) **[Sec. 113(5) direction may be retrospective]** A direction under subsection (5) above may be given so as to have retrospective effect; and the Secretary of State may under that subsection direct that the person in question shall continue to be an authorised person only for such period as is specified in the direction.

113(7) **[Fees as debts due to Crown]** Subsection (5) above is without prejudice to the recovery of any fee as a debt due to the Crown.

113(8) **[Manager, operator to pay periodical fees]** The manager of each authorised unit trust scheme and the operator of each recognised scheme shall pay such periodical fees to the Secretary of State as may be prescribed.

Chapter XIII — Transfer of Functions to Designated Agency

SEC. 114   Power to transfer functions to designated agency

114(1)   [Power of Secretary of State]   If it appears to the Secretary of State—

(a) that a body corporate has been established which is able and willing to discharge all or any of the functions to which this section applies; and

(b) that the requirements of Schedule 7 to this Act are satisfied in the case of that body,

he may, subject to the provisions of this section and Chapter XIV of this Part of this Act, make an order transferring all or any of those functions to that body.

114(2)   [The Securities and Investments Board Limited]   The body to which functions are transferred by the first order made under subsection (1) above shall be the body known as The Securities and Investments Board Limited if it appears to the Secretary of State that it is able and willing to discharge them, that the requirements mentioned in paragraph (b) of that subsection are satisfied in the case of that body and that he is not precluded from making the order by the subsequent provisions of this section or Chapter XIV of this Part of this Act.

114(3)   ["A delegation order", "a designated agency"]   An order under subsection (1) above is in this Act referred to as "a delegation order" and a body to which functions are transferred by a delegation order is in this Act referred to as "a designated agency".

114(4)   [Application of section]   Subject to subsections (5) and (6) below, this section applies to any functions of the Secretary of State under Chapters II to XII of this Part of this Act and to his functions under paragraphs 23 and 25(2) of Schedule 1 and paragraphs 4, 5 and 15 of Schedule 15 to this Act.

114(5)   [Non-application of section]   This section does not apply to any functions under—

(a) section 31(4);

(b) section 46;

(c) section 48(8);

(d) section 58(3);

(e) section 86(1) or 87(1);

(f) section 96;

(g) section 109(2) above.

114(6)   [Overseas exchanges etc.]   This section does not apply to the making or revocation of a recognition order in respect of an overseas investment exchange or overseas clearing house or the making of an application to the court under section 12 above in respect of any such exchange or clearing house.

114(7)   [Transfer of functions]   Any function may be transferred by a delegation order either wholly or in part.

CCH Editions Limited
BCL BCLFS$$$16

114(8) **[Functions under sec. 6, 61, 72, 94, 105, 106]** In the case of a function under section 6 or 72 or a function under section 61 which is exercisable by virtue of subsection (1)(a)(ii) or (iii) of that section, the transfer may be subject to a reservation that it is to be exercisable by the Secretary of State concurrently with the designated agency and any transfer of a function under section 94, 105 or 106 shall be subject to such a reservation.

114(9) **[Conditions for transfer]** The Secretary of State shall not make a delegation order transferring any legislative functions unless—

(a) the agency has furnished him with a copy of the instruments it proposes to issue or make in the exercise of those functions, and

(b) he is satisfied that those instruments will afford investors an adequate level of protection and, in the case of such provisions as are mentioned in Schedule 8 to this Act, comply with the principles set out in that Schedule.

In this subsection **"legislative functions"** means the functions of issuing or making statements of principle, rules, regulations or codes of practice.

History
S. 114(9) substituted by CA 1989, s. 206(1) and Sch. 23, para. 12(1), (2) as from 15 March 1990 (see S.I. 1990 No. 354 (C. 12), art. 3); s. 114(9) formerly read as follows:

"**114(9)** The Secretary of State shall not make a delegation order transferring any function of making rules or regulations to a designated agency unless—

(a) the agency has furnished him with a copy of the

rules and regulations which it proposes to make in the exercise of those functions; and

(b) he is satisfied that those rules and regulations will afford investors an adequate level of protection and, in the case of such rules and regulations as are mentioned in Schedule 8 to this Act, comply with the principles set out in that Schedule."

114(10) **[Guidance to be furnished]** The Secretary of State shall also before making a delegation order transferring any functions to a designated agency require it to furnish him with a copy of any guidance intended to have continuing effect which it proposes to issue in writing or other legible form and the Secretary of State may take any such guidance into account in determining whether he is satisfied as mentioned in subsection (9)(b) above.

114(11) **[Approval of delegation order]** No delegation order shall be made unless a draft of it has been laid before and approved by a resolution of each House of Parliament.

114(12) **[Interpretation re guidance]** In this Act references to guidance issued by a designated agency are references to guidance issued or any recommendation made by it which is issued or made to persons generally or to any class of persons, being, in either case, persons who are or may be subject to statements of principle, rules, regulations or codes of practice issued or made by it, or who are or may be recognised or authorised by it, in the exercise of its functions under a delegation order.

History
In s. 114(12) the words "statements of principle, rules, regulations or codes of practice issued or made" substituted for the former words "rules or regulations made" by CA 1989, s. 206(1) and Sch. 23, para. 12(1), (3) as from 15 March 1990 (see S.I. 1990 No. 354 (C. 12), art. 3).

SEC. 115   Resumption of transferred functions

115(1) **[Power of Secretary of State]** The Secretary of State may at the request or with the consent of a designated agency make an order resuming all or any of the functions transferred to the agency by a delegation order.

115(2) **[Extent of resumption order]** The Secretary of State may, in the circumstances mentioned in subsection (3), (4) or (5) below, make an order resuming—

(a) all the functions transferred to a designated agency by a delegation order; or

(b) all, all legislative or all administrative functions transferred to a designated agency by a delegation order so far as relating to investments or investment business of any class.

115(3)   [Sec. 115(2) order if Sch. 7 not complied with]   An order may be made under subsection (2) above if at any time it appears to the Secretary of State that any of the requirements of Schedule 7 to this Act are not satisfied in the case of the agency.

115(4)   [Sec. 115(2) order if agency unable to discharge functions etc.]   An order may be made under subsection (2) above as respects functions relating to any class of investment or investment business if at any time it appears to the Secretary of State that the agency is unable or unwilling to discharge all or any of the transferred functions in respect of all or any investments or investment business falling within that class.

115(5)   [Sec. 115(2) order if agency rules do not satisfy sec. 114(9)(b)]   Where the transferred functions consist of or include any legislative functions, an order may be made under subsection (2) above if at any time it appears to the Secretary of State that the instruments issued or made by the agency do not satisfy the requirements of section 114(9)(b) above.

History
S. 115(5) substituted by CA 1989, s. 206(1) and Sch. 23, para. 13(1), (2) as from 15 March 1990 (see S.I. 1990 No. 354 (C. 12), art. 3); s. 115(5) formerly read as follows: "**115(5)** Where the transferred functions consist of or include any functions of making rules or regulations an order may be made under subsection (2) above if at any time it appears to the Secretary of State that the rules or regulations made by the agency do not satisfy the requirements of section 114(9)(b) above."

115(6)   [Approval of sec. 115(1) order by Parliament]   An order under subsection (1) above shall be subject to annulment in pursuance of a resolution of either House of Parliament; and no other order shall be made under this section unless a draft of it has been laid before and approved by a resolution of each House of Parliament.

115(7)   [Definitions]   In this section —

(a) "**legislative functions**" means functions of issuing or making statements of principle, rules, regulations or codes of practice;

(b) "**administrative functions**" means functions other than legislative functions;

but the resumption of legislative functions shall not deprive a designated agency of any function of prescribing fees to be paid or information to be furnished in connection with administrative functions retained by the agency; and the resumption of administrative functions shall extend to the function of prescribing fees to be paid and information to be furnished in connection with those administrative functions.

History
In s. 115(7) in the opening words the words "this section" substituted for the former words "subsection (2)(b) above" and in para. (a) the words "functions of issuing or making statements of principle, rules, regulations or codes of practice" substituted for the former words "functions of making rules or regulations" by CA 1989, s. 206(1) and Sch. 23, para. 13(1), (3)(a) and (b) respectively as from 15 March 1990 (see S.I. 1990 No. 354 (C. 12), art. 3).

SEC. 116   Status and exercise of transferred functions

116   Schedule 9 to this Act shall have effect as respects the status of a designated agency and the exercise of the functions transferred to it by a delegation order.

FSA 1986, sec. 115(3)   [The next page is 61,301]

CCH Editions Limited
BCL BCLFS$$$16

SEC. 117 Reports and accounts

117(1) [Annual report by agency] A designated agency shall at least once in each year for which the delegation order is in force make a report to the Secretary of State on the discharge of the functions transferred to it by the order and on such other matters as the order may require.

117(2) [Copies of report before Parliament] The Secretary of State shall lay before Parliament copies of each report received by him under this section.

117(3) [Directions re accounts of agency] The Secretary of State may give directions to a designated agency with respect to its accounts and the audit of its accounts; and it shall be the duty of the agency to comply with the directions.

117(4) [Qualification to sec. 117(3)] Subsection (3) above shall not apply to a designated agency which is a company to which section 226 of the Companies Act 1985 applies; but the Secretary of State may require any designated agency (whether or not such a company) to comply with any provisions of that Act which would not otherwise apply to it or direct that any provision of that Act shall apply to the agency with such modifications as are specified in the direction; and it shall be the duty of the agency to comply with any such requirement or direction.

History
See history note after s. 117(5).

117(5) [Northern Ireland] In subsection (4) above the references to the Companies Act 1985 and section 226 of that Act include references to the corresponding Northern Ireland provisions.

History
In s. 117(4), (5) the words "section 226" substituted for the former words "section 227" by CA 1989, s. 23 and Sch. 10, para. 36(1), (2) as from 1 April 1990 subject to transitional and saving provisions (see S.I. 1990 No. 355 (C. 13), art. 3, Sch. 1 and also art. 6–9).

SEC. 118 Transitional and supplementary provisions

118(1) [Things previously done] A delegation order shall not affect anything previously done in the exercise of a function which is transferred by the order; and any order resuming a function shall not affect anything previously done by the designated agency in the exercise of a function which is resumed.

118(2) [Transitional, supplementary provisions in delegation order] A delegation order and an order resuming any functions transferred by a delegation order may contain, or the Secretary of State may by a separate order under this section make, such transitional and other supplementary provisions as he thinks necessary or expedient in connection with the delegation order or the order resuming the functions in question.

118(3) [Scope of provisions under sec. 118(2)] The provisions that may be made under subsection (2) above in connection with a delegation order include, in particular, provisions—

   (a) for modifying or excluding any provision of this Act in its application to any function transferred by the order;

   (b) for applying to a designated agency, in connection with any such function, any provision applying to the Secretary of State which is contained in or made under any other enactment;

(c) for the transfer of any property, rights or liabilities from the Secretary of State to a designated agency;

(d) for the carrying on and completion by a designated agency of anything in process of being done by the Secretary of State when the order takes effect; and

(e) for the substitution of a designated agency for the Secretary of State in any instrument, contract or legal proceedings.

118(4)   [Scope of provisions under sec. 118(2) re resumption order]   The provisions that may be made under subsection (2) above in connection with an order resuming any functions include, in particular, provisions—

(a) for the transfer of any property, rights or liabilities from the agency to the Secretary of State;

(b) for the carrying on and completion by the Secretary of State of anything in process of being done by the agency when the order takes effect;

(c) for the substitution of the Secretary of State for the agency in any instrument, contract or legal proceedings; and

(d) in a case where some functions remain with the agency, for modifying or excluding any provision of this Act in its application to any such functions.

118(5)   [Scope of provisions under sec. 118(2) re designated agency]   In a case where any function of a designated agency is resumed and is to be immediately transferred by a delegation order to another designated agency, the provisions that may be made under subsection (2) above may include provisions for any of the matters mentioned in paragraphs (a) to (c) of subsection (4) above, taking references to the Secretary of State as references to that other agency.

118(6)   [Order may be annulled by Parliament]   Any order under this section shall be subject to annulment in pursuance of a resolution of either House of Parliament.

Chapter XIV — Prevention of Restrictive Practices

EXAMINATION OF RULES AND PRACTICES

SEC. 119   Recognised self-regulating organisations, investment exchanges and clearing houses

119(1)   [Conditions for making recognition order]   The Secretary of State shall not make a recognition order in respect of a self-regulating organisation, investment exchange or clearing house unless he is satisfied that—

(a) in the case of a self-regulating organisation, the rules and any guidance of which copies are furnished with the application for the order, together with any statements of principle, rules, regulations or codes of practice to which members of the organisation would be subject by virtue of Chapter V of this Part,

(b) in the case of an investment exchange, the rules and any guidance of which copies are furnished with the application for the order, together with any arrangements of which particulars are furnished with the application,

FSA 1986, sec. 118(4)

(c) in the case of a clearing house, the rules and any guidance of which copies are furnished with the application for the order,

do not have, and are not intended or likely to have, to any significant extent the effect of restricting, distorting or preventing competition or, if they have or are intended or likely to have that effect to any significant extent, that the effect is not greater than is necessary for the protection of investors.

History
S. 119(1)(a)–(c) substituted for former s. 119(1)(a),(b) by CA 1989, s. 206(1) and Sch. 23, para. 14(1), (b) as from 15 March 1990 (see S.I. 1990 No. 354 (C. 12), art. 3); former s. 119(1)(a), (b) read as follows:

"(a) the rules and any guidance of which copies are furnished with the application for the order; and
(b) in the case of an investment exchange, any arrangements of which particulars are furnished with the application.".

119(2) [Where sec. 119(3) powers to be exercised] The powers conferred by subsection (3) below shall be exercisable by the Secretary of State if at any time it appears to him that—

(a) in the case of a self-regulating organisation—

(i) any rules made or guidance issued by the organisation,

(ii) any practices of the organisation, or

(iii) any practices of persons who are members of, or otherwise subject to the rules made by, the organisation,

together with any statements of principle, rules, regulations or codes of practice to which members of the organisation are subject by virtue of Chapter V of this Part,

(b) in the case of a recognised investment exchange—

(i) any rules made or guidance issued by the exchange,

(ii) any practices of the exchange, or

(iii) any practices of persons who are members of, or otherwise subject to the rules made by, the exchange,

(c) in the case of a recognised clearing house —

(i) any rules made or guidance issued by the clearing house,

(ii) any practices of the clearing house, or

(iii) any practices of persons who are members of, or otherwise subject to the rules made by, the clearing house,

or any clearing arrangements made by the clearing house,

have, or are intended or likely to have, to a significant extent the effect of restricting, distorting or preventing competition and that that effect is greater than is necessary for the protection of investors.

History
S. 119(2)(a)–(c) substituted by CA 1989, s. 206(1) and Sch. 23, para. 14(1), (3) as from 15 March 1990 (see S.I. 1990 No. 354 (C. 12), art. 3); s. 119(2) (a)–(c) formerly read as follows:

"(a) any rules or guidance issued by a recognised self-regulating organisation, investment exchange

or clearing house or any clearing arrangements made by a recognised clearing house;
(b) any practices of any such organisation, exchange or clearing house; or
(c) any practices of persons who are members of, or otherwise subject to the rules made by, any such organisation, exchange or clearing house,".

119(3) [Powers re revocation etc.] The powers exercisable under this subsection are—

(a) to revoke the recognition order of the organisation, exchange or clearing house;

(b) to direct it to take specified steps for the purpose of securing that its rules, or the guidance, arrangements or practices in question do not have the effect mentioned in subsection (2) above;

(c) to make alterations in its rules for that purpose;

and subsections (2) to (5), (7) and (9) of section 11 above shall have effect in relation to the revocation of a recognition order under this subsection as they have effect in relation to the revocation of such an order under subsection (1) of that section.

History
In s. 119(3)(b) the words "its rules, or the" substituted for the former words "the rules" and in s. 119(3)(c) the words "its rules" substituted for the former words "the rules" by CA 1989, s. 206(1) and Sch. 23, para. 14(4)(a) and (b) respectively as from 15 March 1990 (see S.I. 1990 No. 354 (C. 12), art. 3).

119(4)   [Non-application of sec. 119(3)(c)]   Subsection (3)(c) above does not apply to an overseas investment exchange or overseas clearing house.

119(5)   [Practices in sec. 119(2)(b)]   The practices referred to in paragraph (a)(ii), (b)(ii) and (c)(ii) of subsection (2) above are practices of the organisation, exchange or clearing house in its capacity as such, being, in the case of a clearing house, practices in respect of its clearing arrangements.

History
In s. 119(5) the words "paragraph (a)(ii), (b)(ii) and (c)(ii) substituted for the former words "paragraph (b)" and the words "and the practices referred to in paragraph (c) of that subsection are practices in relation to business in respect of which the persons in question are subject to the rules of the organisation, exchange or clearing house and which are required or contemplated by its rules or guidance or otherwise attributable to its conduct in its capacity as such." formerly appearing at the end omitted and repealed by CA 1989, s. 206(1) and Sch. 23, para 14(1), (5)(a) and (b) respectively and s. 212 and Sch. 24 as from 15 March 1990 (see S.I. 1990 No. 354 (C.12), art. 3).

119(6)   [Practices in sec. 119(2)]   The practices referred to in paragraph (a)(iii), (b)(iii) and (c)(iii) of subsection (2) above are—

(a) in relation to a recognised self-regulating organisation, practices in relation to business in respect of which the persons in question are subject to—

(i) the rules of the organisation, or

(ii) statements of principle, rules, regulations or codes of practice to which its members are subject by virtue of Chapter V of this Part,

and which are required or contemplated by the rules of the organisation or by those statements, rules, regulations or codes, or by guidance issued by the organisation,

(b) in relation to a recognised investment exchange or clearing house, practices in relation to business in respect of which the persons in question are subject to the rules of the exchange or clearing house, and which are required or contemplated by its rules or guidance,

or which are otherwise attributable to the conduct of the organisation, exchange or clearing house as such.

History
S. 119(6) inserted by CA 1989, s. 206(1) and Sch. 23, para. 14(1), (6) as from 15 March 1990 (see S.I. 1990 No. 354 (C. 12), art. 3).

SEC. 120   Modification of sec. 119 where recognition function is transferred

120(1)   [Application]   This section applies instead of section 119 above where the function of making or revoking a recognition order in respect of a self-regulating organisation, investment exchange or clearing house is exercisable by a designated agency.

120(2)   [Duties of designated agency]   The designated agency—

    (a)   shall send to the Secretary of State a copy of the rules and of any guidance or arrangements of which copies or particulars are furnished with any application made to the agency for a recognition order together with any other information supplied with or in connection with the application; and

    (b)   shall not make the recognition order without the leave of the Secretary of State;

and he shall not give leave in any case in which he would (apart from the delegation order) have been precluded by section 119(1) above from making the recognition order.

120(3)   [Copy of notice to Secretary of State]   A designated agency shall send the Secretary of State a copy of any notice received by it under section 14(6) or 41(5) or (6) above.

120(4)   [Exercise of powers by Secretary of State]   If at any time it appears to the Secretary of State in the case of a recognised self-regulating organisation, recognised investment exchange or recognised clearing house that there are circumstances such that (apart from the delegation order) he would have been able to exercise any of the powers conferred by subsection (3) of section 119 above he may, notwithstanding the delegation order, himself exercise the power conferred by paragraph (a) of that subsection or direct the designated agency to exercise the power conferred by paragraph (b) or (c) of that subsection in such manner as he may specify.

SEC. 121   Designated agencies

121(1)   [Conditions re transferred functions]   The Secretary of State shall not make a delegation order transferring any function to a designated agency unless he is satisfied that any statements of principle, rules, regulations, codes of practice and guidance of which copies are furnished to him under section 114(9) or (10) above do not have, and are not intended or likely to have, to any significant extent the effect of restricting, distorting or preventing competition or, if they have or are intended or likely to have that effect to any significant extent, that the effect is not greater than is necessary for the protection of investors.

History

In s. 121(1) the words "statements of principle, rules, regulations, codes of practice" substituted for the former words "rules, regulations" by CA 1989, s. 206(1) and   Sch. 23, para. 15(1), (2) as from 15 March 1990 (see S.I. 1990 No. 354 (C. 12), art. 3).

121(2)   [Exercise of sec. 121(3) powers by Secretary of State]   The powers conferred by subsection (3) below shall be exercisable by the Secretary of State if at any time it appears to him that—

    (a)   any statements of principle, rules, regulations or codes of practice issued or made by a designated agency in the exercise of functions transferred to it by a delegation order or any guidance issued by a designated agency;

    (b)   any practices of a designated agency; or

    (c)   any practices of persons who are subject to statements of principle, rules, regulations or codes of practice issued or made by it in the exercise of those functions,

have, or are intended or are likely to have, to any significant extent the effect of restricting, distorting or preventing competition and that that effect is greater than is necessary for the protection of investors.

History
In s. 121(2)(a) and (c) the words "statements of principle, rules, regulations or codes of practice issued or made" substituted for the former words "rules or regulations"   made" by CA 1989, s. 206(1) and Sch. 23, para. 15(1), (3) as from 15 March 1990 (see S.I. 1990 No. 354 (C. 12), art. 3).

121(3)   [Powers in sec. 121(2)]   The powers exercisable under this subsection are—

(a) to make an order in respect of the agency under section 115(2) above as if the circumstances were such as are there mentioned; or

(b) to direct the agency to take specified steps for the purpose of securing that the statements of principle, rules, regulations, codes of practice, guidance or practices in question do not have the effect mentioned in subsection (2) above.

History
In s. 121(3)(b) the words "statements of principle, rules, regulations, codes of practice" substituted for the former words "rules, regulations" by CA 1989, s. 206(1) and   Sch. 23, para. 15(1), (4) as from 15 March 1990 (see S.I. 1990 No. 354 (C.12), art. 3).

121(4)   [Practices in sec. 121(2)]   The practices referred to in paragraph (b) of subsection (2) above are practices of the designated agency in its capacity as such; and the practices referred to in paragraph (c) of that subsection are practices in relation to business in respect of which the persons in question are subject to any such statements of principle, rules, regulations or codes of practice as are mentioned in paragraph (a) of that subsection and which are required or contemplated by those statements of principle, rules, regulations or codes of practice or by any such guidance as is there mentioned or are otherwise attributable to the conduct of the agency in its capacity as such.

History
In s. 121(4) the words "statements of principle, rules, regulations or codes of practice" substituted (twice) for the former words "rules or regulations" by CA 1989,   s. 206(1) and Sch. 23, para. 15(1), (5) as from 15 March 1990 (see S.I. 1990 No. 354 (C. 12), art. 3).

CONSULTATION WITH DIRECTOR GENERAL OF FAIR TRADING

SEC. 122   Reports by Director General of Fair Trading

122(1)   [Secretary of State to send copies of reports etc. to Director]   The Secretary of State shall before deciding—

(a) whether to refuse to make, or to refuse leave for the making of, a recognition order in pursuance of section 119(1) or 120(2) above; or

(b) whether he is precluded by section 121(1) above from making a delegation order,

send to the Director General of Fair Trading (in this Chapter referred to as "the Director") a copy of the rules, statements of principle, regulations and codes of practice and of any guidance or arrangements which the Secretary of State is required to consider in making that decision together with such other information as the Secretary of State considers will assist the Director in discharging his functions under subsection (2) below.

FSA 1986, sec. 121(3)

History
In s. 122(1) the words ", statements of principle, regulations and codes of practice" substituted for the former words "and regulations" by CA 1989, s. 206(1) and Sch. 23, para.

16(1), (2) as from 15 March 1990 (see S.I. 1990 No. 354 (C.12), art. 3).

122(2)   [Report to Secretary of State by Director]   The Director shall report to the Secretary of State whether, in his opinion, the rules, statements of principle, regulations, codes of practice, guidance or arrangements of which copies are sent to him under subsection (1) above have, or are intended or likely to have, to any significant extent the effect of restricting, distorting, or preventing competition and, if so, what that effect is likely to be; and in making any such decision as is mentioned in that subsection the Secretary of State shall have regard to the Director's report.

History
In s. 122(2) the words "statements of principle, regulations, codes of practice," substituted for the former word "regulations," by CA 1989, s. 206(1) and Sch. 23, para.

16(1), (3) as from 15 March 1990 (see S.I. 1990 No. 354 (C. 12), art. 3).

122(3)   [Secretary of State to send copies of notices etc. to Director]   The Secretary of State shall send the Director copies of any notice received by him under section 14(6), 41(5) or (6) or 120(3) above or under paragraph 4 of Schedule 9 to this Act together with such other information as the Secretary of State considers will assist the Director in discharging his functions under subsections (4) and (5) below.

122(4)   [Review and report by Director re sec. 119(2), 121(2), 122(3)]   The Director shall keep under review—

(a) the rules, statements of principle, regulations, codes of practice, guidance and arrangements mentioned in section 119(2) and 121(2) above; and

(b) the matters specified in the notices of which copies are sent to him under subsection (3) above;

and if at any time he is of the opinion that any such rules, statements of principle, regulations, codes of practice, guidance, arrangements or matters, or any such rules, statements of principle, regulations, codes of practice, guidance or arrangements taken together with any such matters, have, or are intended or likely to have, to any significant extent the effect mentioned in subsection (2) above, he shall make a report to the Secretary of State stating his opinion and what that effect is or is likely to be.

History
In s. 122(4):
- in para. (a) the words "rules, statements of principle, regulations, codes of practice, guidance and arrangements" substituted for the former words "rules, guidance, arrangements and regulations", and
- in the words following the paragraphs the words "rules, statements of principle, regulations, codes of practice, guidance, arrangements" substituted

for the former words "rules, guidance, arrangements, regulations" and the words "rules, statements of principle, regulations, codes of practice, guidance or arrangements" substituted for the former words "rules, guidance, arrangements or regulations" by CA 1989 s. 206(1) and Sch. 23, para. 16(1), (4)(a) and (b) respectively as from 15 March 1990 (see S.I. 1990 No. 354 (C. 12), art. 3).

122(5)   [Report re matter in sec. 122(4)(b)]   The Director may report to the Secretary of State his opinion that any such matter as is mentioned in subsection (4)(b) above does not in his opinion have, and is not intended or likely to have, to any significant extent the effect mentioned in subsection (2) above.

122(6)   [Report etc. re sec. 119(2), 121(2)]   The Director may from time to time consider whether any such practices as are mentioned in section 119(2) or 121(2) above have, or are intended or likely to have, to any significant extent the effect mentioned in subsection (2) above and, if so, what that effect is or is likely to be; and if he is of that opinion he shall make a report to the Secretary of State stating his opinion and what the effect is or is likely to be.

122(7)   **[Limit on exercise of power in sec. 119(3), 120(4), 121(3)]**   The Secretary of State shall not exercise his powers under section 119(3), 120(4) or 121(3) above except after receiving and considering a report from the Director under subsection (4) or (6) above.

122(8)   **[Publication of report by Director]**   The Director may, if he thinks fit, publish any report made by him under this section but shall exclude from a published report, so far as practicable, any matter which relates to the affairs of a particular person (other than the self-regulating organisation, investment exchange, clearing house or designated agency concerned) the publication of which would or might in his opinion seriously and prejudicially affect the interests of that person.

SEC. 123   Investigations by Director General of Fair Trading

123(1)   **[Powers of Director]**   For the purpose of investigating any matter with a view to its consideration under section 122 above the Director may by a notice in writing—

  (a) require any person to produce, at a time and place specified in the notice, to the Director or to any person appointed by him for the purpose, any documents which are specified or described in the notice and which are documents in his custody or under his control and relating to any matter relevant to the investigation; or

  (b) require any person carrying on any business to furnish to the Director such information as may be specified or described in the notice, and specify the time within which, and the manner and form in which, any such information is to be furnished.

123(2)   **[Legal professional privilege, confidentiality]**   A person shall not under this section be required to produce any document or disclose any information which he would be entitled to refuse to produce or disclose on grounds of legal professional privilege in proceedings in the High Court or on grounds of confidentiality as between client and professional legal adviser in proceedings in the Court of Session.

123(3)   **[Application of sec. 85(6)–(8) of Fair Trading Act]**   Subsections (6) to (8) of section 85 of the Fair Trading Act 1973 (enforcement provisions) shall apply in relation to a notice under this section as they apply in relation to a notice under subsection (1) of that section but as if, in subsection (7) of that section, for the words from "any one" to "the commission" there were substituted "the Director".

History
In s. 123(3) "(6)" substituted for the former "(5)" and the words from "but as if," to the end inserted by CA 1989,   s. 153 and Sch. 20, para. 26 as from 1 April 1990 (see S.I. 1990 No. 142 (C.5), art. 6(c)).

CONSEQUENTIAL EXEMPTIONS FROM COMPETITION LAW

SEC. 124   The Fair Trading Act 1973

124(1)   **[Consideration of whether monopoly situation]**   For the purpose of determining whether a monopoly situation within the meaning of the Fair Trading Act 1973 exists by reason of the circumstances mentioned in section 7(1)(c) of that Act, no account shall be taken of—

  (a) the rules made or guidance issued by a recognised self-regulating organisation, recognised investment exchange or recognised clearing house or any conduct constituting such a practice as is mentioned in section 119(2) above;

(b) any clearing arrangements or any conduct required or contemplated by any such arrangements; or

(c) the statements of principle, rules, regulations, codes of practice or guidance issued or made by a designated agency in the exercise of functions transferred to it by a delegation order or any conduct constituting such a practice as is mentioned in section 121(2) above.

History
In s. 124(1)(c) the words "statements of principle, rules, regulations, codes of practice or guidance issued or made" substituted for the former words "rules or regulations made or guidance issued" by CA 1989, s. 206(1) and Sch. 23, para. 17(1), (2) as from 15 March 1990 (see S.I. 1990 No. 354 (C. 12), art. 3).

124(2)   [Qualification to sec. 124(1)]   Where a recognition order is revoked there shall be disregarded for the purpose mentioned in subsection (1) above any such conduct as is mentioned in that subsection which occurred while the order was in force.

124(3)   [Where monopoly situation found to exist]   Where on a monopoly reference under section 50 or 51 of the said Act of 1973 falling within section 49 of that Act the Monopolies and Mergers Commission find that a monopoly situation within the meaning of that Act exists and—

(a) that the person (or, if more than one, any of the persons) in whose favour it exists is subject to the rules of a recognised self-regulating organisation, recognised investment exchange or recognised clearing house or to the statements of principle, rules, regulations or codes of practice issued or made by a designated agency in the exercise of functions transferred to it by a delegation order; or

(b) that any such person's conduct in carrying on any business to which those statements of principle, rules, regulations or codes of practice relate is the subject of guidance issued by such an organisation, exchange, clearing house or agency; or

(c) that any such person is a party to any clearing arrangements; or

(d) that the person (or, if more than one, any of the persons) in whose favour the monopoly situation exists is such an organisation, exchange or clearing house as is mentioned in paragraph (a) above or a designated agency,

the Commission, in making their report on that reference, shall exclude from their consideration the question whether the statements of principle, rules, regulations, codes of practice, guidance or clearing arrangements or any acts or omissions of such an organisation, exchange, clearing house or agency as is mentioned in paragraph (d) above in its capacity as such operate, or may be expected to operate, against the public interest; and section 54(3) of that Act shall have effect subject to the provisions of this subsection.

History
In s. 124(3):
- in para. (a) the words "statements of principle, rules, regulations or codes of practice issued or made" substituted for the former words "rules or regulations made",
- in para. (b) the words "statements of principle, rules, regulations or codes of practice" substituted for the former words "rules or regulations", and
- in the closing words the words "statements of principle, rules, regulations, codes of practice" substituted for the former words "rules, regulations"

by CA 1989, s. 206(1) and Sch. 23, para. 17(1), (3)(a)–(c) respectively as from 15 May 1990 (see S.I. 1990 No. 354 (C. 12), art. 3).

SEC. 125   The Restrictive Trade Practices Act 1976

125(1) **[Non-application to agreement re constitution of recognised bodies]** The Restrictive Trade Practices Act 1976 shall not apply to any agreement for the constitution of a recognised self-regulating organisation, recognised investment exchange or recognised clearing house, including any term deemed to be contained in it by virtue of section 8(2) or 16(3) of that Act.

125(2) **[Non-application to agreement where parties include sec. 125(1) body or person subject to rules]** The said Act of 1976 shall not apply to any agreement the parties to which consist of or include—

(a) any such organisation, exchange or clearing house as is mentioned in subsection (1) above; or

(b) a person who is subject to the rules of any such organisation, exchange or clearing house or to the rules or regulations made by a designated agency in the exercise of functions transferred to it by a delegation order,

by reason of any term the inclusion of which in the agreement is required or contemplated by the rules, regulations or guidance of that organisation, exchange, clearing house or agency.

125(3) **[Non-application to clearing arrangements etc.]** The said Act of 1976 shall not apply to any clearing arrangements or to any agreement between a recognised investment exchange and a recognised clearing house by reason of any term the inclusion of which in the agreement is required or contemplated by any clearing arrangements.

125(4) **[Where recognition order re body revoked]** Where the recognition order in respect of a self-regulating organisation, investment exchange or clearing house is revoked the foregoing provisions shall have effect as if the organisation, exchange or clearing house had continued to be recognised until the end of the period of six months beginning with the day on which the revocation takes effect.

125(5) **[Where agreement no longer registered, effect]** Where an agreement ceases by virtue of this section to be subject to registration—

(a) the Director shall remove from the register maintained by him under the said Act of 1976 any particulars which are entered or filed in that register in respect of the agreement; and

(b) any proceedings in respect of the agreement which are pending before the Restrictive Practices Court shall be discontinued.

125(6) **[Where agreement no longer exempt from registration]** Where an agreement which has been exempt from registration by virtue of this section ceases to be exempt in consequence of the revocation of a recognition order, the time within which particulars of the agreement are to be furnished in accordance with section 24 of and Schedule 2 to the said Act of 1976 shall be the period of one month beginning with the day on which the agreement ceased to be exempt from registration.

125(7) **[Where term ceases to be within sec. 125(2), (3)]** Where in the case of an agreement registered under the said Act of 1976 a term ceases to fall within subsection (2) or (3) above in consequence of the revocation of a recognition order and particulars of that term have not previously been furnished to the Director under section 24 of that Act, those particulars shall be furnished to him within the period of one month beginning with the day on which the term ceased to fall within that subsection.

125(8)   [Restrictive Trade Practices (Stock Exchange) Act]   The Restrictive Trade Practices (Stock Exchange) Act 1984 shall cease to have effect.

SEC. **126**   The Competition Act 1980

126(1)   [Sec. 119(2), 121(2) practices not anti-competitive]   No course of conduct constituting any such practice as is mentioned in section 119(2) or 121(2) above shall constitute an anti-competitive practice for the purposes of the Competition Act 1980.

126(2)   [Where recognition or delegation order revoked]   Where a recognition order or delegation order is revoked, there shall not be treated as an anti-competitive practice for the purposes of that Act any such course of conduct as is mentioned in subsection (1) above which occurred while the order was in force.

RECOGNISED PROFESSIONAL BODIES

SEC. **127**   Modification of Restrictive Trade Practices Act 1976 in relation to recognised professional bodies

127(1)   [Application]   This section applies to—

(a)   any agreement for the constitution of a recognised professional body, including any term deemed to be contained in it by virtue of section 16(3) of the Restrictive Trade Practices Act 1976; and

(b)   any other agreement—

  (i)   the parties to which consist of or include such a body, a person certified by such a body or a member of such a body; and

  (ii)   to which that Act applies by virtue of any term the inclusion of which in the agreement is required or contemplated by rules or guidance of that body relating to the carrying on of investment business by persons certified by it.

127(2)   [Powers of Secretary of State to give direction to Directors]   If it appears to the Secretary of State that the restrictions in an agreement to which this section applies—

(a)   do not have, and are not intended or likely to have, to any significant extent the effect of restricting, distorting or preventing competition; or

(b)   if all or any of them have, or are intended or likely to have, that effect to any significant extent, that the effect is not greater than is necessary for the protection of investors,

   he may give a direction to the Director requiring him not to make an application to the Restrictive Practices Court under Part I of the said Act of 1976 in respect of the agreement.

127(3)   [Declaration by Secretary of State]   If it appears to the Secretary of State that one or more (but not all) of the restrictions in an agreement to which this section applies—

   (a) do not have, and are not intended or likely to have, to any significant extent the effect mentioned in subsection (2) above; or

   (b) if they have, or are intended or likely to have, that effect to any significant extent that the effect is not greater than is necessary for the protection of investors,

he may make a declaration to that effect and give notice of it to the Director and the Restrictive Practices Court.

127(4)   [Limit re Restrictive Practices Court]   The Restrictive Practices Court shall not in any proceedings begun by an application made after notice has been given to it of a declaration under this section make any finding or exercise any power under Part I of the said Act of 1976 in relation to a restriction in respect of which the declaration has effect.

127(5)   [Limit on applications to Court by Director]   The Director shall not make any application to the Restrictive Practices Court under Part I of the said Act of 1976 in respect of any agreement to which this section applies unless—

   (a) he has notified the Secretary of State of his intention to do so; and

   (b) the Secretary of State has either notified him that he does not intend to give a direction or make a declaration under this section or has given him notice of a declaration in respect of it;

and where the Director proposes to make any such application he shall furnish the Secretary of State with particulars of the agreement and the restrictions by virtue of which the said Act of 1976 applies to it and such other information as he considers will assist the Secretary of State in deciding whether to exercise his powers under this section or as the Secretary of State may request.

127(6)   [Powers of Secretary of State re revocation, variation of declaration etc.]   The Secretary of State may—

   (a) revoke a direction or declaration under this section;

   (b) vary any such declaration; or

   (c) give a direction or make a declaration notwithstanding a previous notification to the Director that he did not intend to give a direction or make a declaration;

if he is satisfied that there has been a material change of circumstances such that the grounds for the direction or declaration have ceased to exist, that there are grounds for a different declaration or that there are grounds for giving a direction or making a declaration, as the case may be.

127(7)   [Notice to Director by Secretary of State]   The Secretary of State shall give notice to the Director of the revocation of a direction and to the Director and the Restrictive Practices Court of the revocation or variation of a declaration; and no such variation shall have effect so as to restrict the powers of the Court in any proceedings begun by an application already made by the Director.

127(8)   [Cesser of direction or declaration]   A direction or declaration under this section shall cease to have effect if the agreement in question ceases to be one to which this section applies.

127(9) **[Application]**   This section applies to information provisions as it applies to restrictions.

SUPPLEMENTAL

SEC. 128 Supplementary provisions

128(1) **[Duty of Secretary of State before exercising power]**   Before the Secretary of State exercises a power under section 119(3)(b) or (c) above, his power to refuse leave under section 120(2) above or his power to give a direction under section 120(4) above in respect of a self-regulating organisation, investment exchange or clearing house, or his power under section 121(3)(b) above in respect of a designated agency, he shall—

   (a) give written notice of his intention to do so to the organisation, exchange, clearing house or agency and take such steps (whether by publication or otherwise) as he thinks appropriate for bringing the notice to the attention of any other person who in his opinion is likely to be affected by the exercise of the power; and

   (b) have regard to any representation made within such time as he considers reasonable by the organisation, exchange, clearing house or agency or by any such other person.

128(2) **[Contents of sec. 128(1) notice]**   A notice under subsection (1) above shall give particulars of the manner in which the Secretary of State proposes to exercise the power in question and state the reasons for which he proposes to act; and the statement of reasons may include matters contained in any report received by him under section 122 above.

128(3) **[Enforcement of directions]**   Any direction given under this Chapter shall, on the application of the person by whom it was given, be enforceable by mandamus or, in Scotland, by an order for specific performance under section 91 of the Court of Session Act 1868.

128(4) **[Alteration of altered rules etc.]**   The fact that any rules or regulations made by a recognised self-regulating organisation, investment exchange or clearing house or by a designated agency have been altered by or pursuant to a direction given by the Secretary of State under this Chapter shall not preclude their subsequent alteration or revocation by that organisation, exchange, clearing house or agency.

128(5) **[Assumption re acting conforming to guidance]**   In determining under this Chapter whether any guidance has, or is likely to have, any particular effect the Secretary of State and the Director may assume that the persons to whom it is addressed will act in conformity with it.

Chapter XV — Relations with Other Regulatory Authorities

SEC. 128A Relevance of other controls

128A In determining—

   (a) in relation to a self-regulating organisation, whether the requirements of Schedule 2 are met, or

(b) in relation to a professional body, whether the requirements of Schedule 3 are met,

the Secretary of State shall take into account the effect of any other controls to which members of the organisation or body are subject.

History
See history note after s. 128C.

Note
For transfer of the Secretary of State's functions under s. 128A see S.I. 1990 No. 354(C. 12), art. 4(2)(b).

SEC. 128B   Relevance of information given and action taken by other regulatory authorities

128B(1)   [Application]   The following provisions apply in the case of—

(a) a person whose principal place of business is in a country or territory outside the United Kingdom, or

(b) a person whose principal business is other than investment business;

and in relation to such a person **"the relevant regulatory authority"** means the appropriate regulatory authority in that country or territory or, as the case may be, in relation to his principal business.

128B(2)   [When Secretary of State satisfied]   The Secretary of State may regard himself as satisfied with respect to any matter relevant for the purposes of this Part if—

(a) the relevant regulatory authority informs him that it is satisfied with respect to that matter, and

(b) he is satisfied as to the nature and scope of the supervision exercised by that authority.

128B(3)   [Matters taken into account]   In making any decision with respect to the exercise of his powers under this Part in relation to any such person, the Secretary of State may take into account whether the relevant regulatory authority has exercised, or proposes to exercise, its powers in relation to that person.

128B(4)   [Power of Secretary of State to enter arrangements]   The Secretary of State may enter into such arrangements with other regulatory authorities as he thinks fit for the purposes of this section.

128B(5)   [Community and international obligations]   Where any functions under this Part have been transferred to a designated agency, nothing in this section shall be construed as affecting the responsibility of the Secretary of State for the discharge of Community obligations or other international obligations of the United Kingdom.

History
See history note after s. 128C.

Note
For transfer of the Secretary of State's functions under s. 128B(1)–(4) see S.I. 1990 No. 354(C. 12), art. 4(3)(c).

SEC. 128C   Enforcement in support of overseas regulatory authority

128C(1)   [Powers of Secretary of State]   The Secretary of State may exercise his disciplinary powers or powers of intervention at the request of, or for the purpose of assisting, an overseas regulatory authority.

128C(2)   [Description of disciplinary powers]   The disciplinary powers of the Secretary of State means his powers—

(a) to withdraw or suspend authorisation under section 28 or to terminate or suspend authorisation under section 33,

(b) to give a disqualification direction under section 59,

(c) to make a public statement under section 60, or

(d) to apply for an injunction, interdict or other order under section 61(1);

and the reference to his powers of intervention is to the powers conferred by Chapter VI of this Part.

128C(3) [**"Overseas regulatory authority"**] An **"overseas regulatory authority"** means an authority in a country or territory outside the United Kingdom which exercises—

(a) any function corresponding to—

(i) a function of the Secretary of State under this Act, the Insurance Companies Act 1982 or the Companies Act 1985,

(ii) a function under this Act of a designated agency, transferee body or competent authority, or

(iii) a function of the Bank of England under the Banking Act 1987, or

(b) any functions in connection with the investigation of, or the enforcement of rules (whether or not having the force of law) relating to, conduct of the kind prohibited by the Company Securities (Insider Dealing) Act 1985, or

(c) any function prescribed for the purposes of this subsection, being a function which in the opinion of the Secretary of State relates to companies or financial services.

128C(4) [**Matters to be taken into account**] In deciding whether to exercise those powers the Secretary of State may take into account, in particular—

(a) whether corresponding assistance would be given in that country or territory to an authority exercising regulatory functions in the United Kingdom;

(b) whether the case concerns the breach of a law, or other requirement, which has no close parallel in the United Kingdom or involves the assertion of a jurisdiction not recognised by the United Kingdom;

(c) the seriousness of the case and its importance to persons in the United Kingdom;

(d) whether it is otherwise appropriate in the public interest to give the assistance sought.

128C(5) [**Undertaking from overseas regulatory authority**] The Secretary of State may decline to exercise those powers unless the overseas regulatory authority undertakes to make such contribution towards the cost of their exercise as the Secretary of State considers appropriate.

128C(6) [**"Financial Services" in sec. 128C(3)(c)**] The reference in subsection (3)(c) to financial services includes, in particular, investment business, insurance and banking.

History
S. 128A–128C inserted by CA 1989, s. 196 as from 15 March 1990 (see S.I. 1990 No. 354 (C. 12), art. 3).

Note
For transfer of the Secretary of State's functions under s. 128C see S.I. 1990 No. 354 (C. 12), art. 4(3)(d).

PART II — INSURANCE BUSINESS

SEC. 129 Application of investment business provisions to regulated insurance companies.

129 Schedule 10 to this Act shall have effect with respect to the application of the foregoing provisions of this Act to regulated insurance companies, that is to say—

(a) insurance companies to which Part II of the Insurance Companies Act 1982 applies; and

(b) insurance companies which are authorised persons by virtue of section 31 above.

SEC. 130 Restriction on promotion of contracts of insurance

130(1) [Limit on advertisements] Subject to subsections (2) and (3) below, no person shall—

(a) issue or cause to be issued in the United Kingdom an advertisement—

(i) inviting any person to enter or offer to enter into a contract of insurance rights under which constitute an investment for the purposes of this Act, or

(ii) containing information calculated to lead directly or indirectly to any person doing so; or

(b) in the course of a business, advise or procure any person in the United Kingdom to enter into such a contract.

130(2) [Non-application of sec. 130(1)] Subsection (1) above does not apply where the contract of insurance referred to in that subsection is to be with—

(a) a body authorised under section 3 or 4 of the Insurance Companies Act 1982 to effect and carry out such contracts of insurance;

(b) a body registered under the enactments relating to friendly societies;

(c) an insurance company the head office of which is in a member State other than the United Kingdom and which is entitled to carry on there insurance business of the relevant class;

(d) an insurance company which has a branch or agency in such a member State and is entitled under the law of that State to carry on there insurance business of the relevant class;

and in this subsection "the relevant class" means the class of insurance business specified in Schedule 1 or 2 to the Insurance Companies Act 1982 into which the effecting and carrying out of the contract in question falls.

130(3) [Additional non-application of sec. 130(1)] Subsection (1) above also does not apply where—

(a) the contract of insurance referred to in that subsection is to be with an insurance company authorised to effect or carry out such contracts of insurance in any country or territory which is for the time being designated for the purposes of this section by an order made by the Secretary of State; and

(b) any conditions imposed by the order designating the country or territory have been satisfied.

130(4) **[Limit on Secretary of State's power]** The Secretary of State shall not make an order designating any country or territory for the purposes of this section unless he is satisfied that the law under which insurance companies are authorised and supervised in that country or territory affords adequate protection to policy holders and potential policy holders against the risk that the companies may be unable to meet their liabilities; and, if at any time it appears to him that the law of a country or territory which has been designated under this section does not satisfy that requirement, he may by a further order revoke the order designating that country or territory.

130(5) **[Annulment of order by Parliament]** An order under this section shall be subject to annulment in pursuance of a resolution of either House of Parliament.

130(6) **[Offence, penalty]** Subject to subsections (7) and (8) below, any person who contravenes this section shall be guilty of an offence and liable—

(a) on conviction on indictment, to imprisonment for a term not exceeding two years or to a fine or to both;

(b) on summary conviction, to imprisonment for a term not exceeding six months or to a fine not exceeding the statutory maximum or to both.

130(7) **[Defence]** A person who in the ordinary course of a business other than investment business issues an advertisement to the order of another person shall not be guilty of an offence under this section if he proves that the matters contained in the advertisement were not (wholly or in part) devised or selected by him or by any person under his direction or control and that he believed on reasonable grounds after due enquiry that the person to whose order the advertisement was issued was an authorised person.

130(8) **[Further defence]** A person other than the insurance company with which the contract of insurance is to be made shall not be guilty of an offence under this section if he proves that he believed on reasonable grounds after due enquiry that subsection (2) or (3) above applied in the case of the contravention in question.

SEC. 131 Contracts made after contravention of sec. 130

131(1) **[Effect of contravention of sec. 130]** Where there has been a contravention of section 130 above, then, subject to subsections (3) and (4) below—

(a) the insurance company shall not be entitled to enforce any contract of insurance with which the advertisement, advice or procurement was concerned and which was entered into after the contravention occurred; and

(b) the other party shall be entitled to recover any money or other property paid or transferred by him under the contract, together with compensation for any loss sustained by him as a result of having parted with it.

131(2) **[Interest recoverable under sec. 131(1)]** The compensation recoverable under subsection (1) above shall be such as the parties may agree or as a court may, on the application of either party, determine.

131(3) **[Where contravention by insurance company]** In a case where the contravention referred to in subsection (1) above was a contravention by the insurance company with which the contract was made, the court may allow the contract to be enforced or money or property paid or transferred under it to be retained if it is satisfied—

   (a) that the person against whom enforcement is sought or who is seeking to recover the money or property was not influenced, or not influenced to any material extent, by the advertisement or, as the case may be, the advice in making his decision to enter into the contract; or

   (b) that the advertisement or, as the case may be, the advice was not misleading as to the nature of the company with which the contract was to be made or the terms of the contract and fairly stated any risks involved in entering into it.

131(4) **[Where contravention by person other than insurance company]** In a case where the contravention of section 130 above referred to in subsection (1) above was a contravention by a person other than the insurance company with which the contract was made the court may allow the contract to be enforced or money or property paid or transferred under it to be retained if it is satisfied that at the time the contract was made the company had no reason to believe that any contravention of section 130 above had taken place in relation to the contract.

131(5) **[Where election not to perform contract unenforceable by sec. 131(1)]** Where a person elects not to perform a contract which by virtue of subsection (1) above is unenforceable against him or by virtue of that subsection recovers money paid or other property transferred by him under a contract he shall not be entitled to any benefits under the contract and shall repay any money and return any other property received by him under the contract.

131(6) **[Where property has passed to third party]** Where any property transferred under a contract to which this section applies has passed to a third party the references to that property in this section shall be construed as references to its value at the time of its transfer under the contract.

131(7) **[Contravention of sec. 130]** A contravention of section 130 above by an authorised person shall be actionable at the suit of any person who suffers loss as a result of the contravention.

131(8) **[Effect of sec. 61 on sec. 130 contravention]** Section 61 above shall have effect in relation to a contravention or proposed contravention of section 130 above as it has effect in relation to a contravention or proposed contravention of section 57 above.

SEC. 132   Insurance contracts effected in contravention of sec. 2 of Insurance Companies Act 1982

132(1) **[Contracts unenforceable against other party]** Subject to subsection (3) below, a contract of insurance (not being an agreement to which section 5(1) above applies) which is entered into by a person in the course of carrying on insurance business in contravention of section 2 of the Insurance Companies Act 1982 shall be unenforceable against the other party; and that party shall be entitled to recover any money or other property paid or transferred by him under the contract, together with compensation for any loss sustained by him as a result of having parted with it.

132(2) **[Compensation recoverable under sec. 132(1)]** The compensation recoverable under subsection (1) above shall be such as the parties may agree or as a court may, on the application of either party, determine.

132(3) **[Court may allow enforcement of sec. 132(1) contract]** A court may allow a contract to which subsection (1) above applies to be enforced or money or property paid or transferred under it to be retained if it is satisfied—

> (a) that the person carrying on insurance business reasonably believed that his entering into the contract did not constitute a contravention of section 2 of the said Act of 1982; and

> (b) that it is just and equitable for the contract to be enforced or, as the case may be, for the money or property paid or transferred under it to be retained.

132(4) **[Where election not to perform unenforceable contract]** Where a person elects not to perform a contract which by virtue of this section is unenforceable against him or by virtue of this section recovers money or property paid or transferred under a contract he shall not be entitled to any benefits under the contract and shall repay any money and return any other property received by him under the contract.

132(5) **[Where property has passed to third party]** Where any property transferred under a contract to which this section applies has passed to a third party the references to that property in this section shall be construed as references to its value at the time of its transfer under the contract.

132(6) **[Effect of contravention of sec. 2 of 1982 Act]** A contravention of section 2 of the said Act of 1982 shall not make a contract of insurance illegal or invalid to any greater extent than is provided in this section; and a contravention of that section in respect of a contract of insurance shall not affect the validity of any re-insurance contract entered into in respect of that contract.

SEC. 133 Misleading statements as to insurance contracts

133(1) **[Offence]** Any person who—

> (a) makes a statement, promise or forecast which he knows to be misleading, false or deceptive or dishonestly conceals any material facts; or

> (b) recklessly makes (dishonestly or otherwise) a statement, promise or forecast which is misleading, false or deceptive,

is guilty of an offence if he makes the statement, promise or forecast or conceals the facts for the purpose of inducing, or is reckless as to whether it may induce, another person (whether or not the person to whom the statement, promise or forecast is made or from whom the facts are concealed) to enter into or offer to enter into, or to refrain from entering or offering to enter into, a contract of insurance with an insurance company (not being an investment agreement) or to exercise, or refrain from exercising, any rights conferred by such a contract.

133(2) **[Conditions for sec. 133(1)]** Subsection (1) above does not apply unless—

> (a) the statement, promise or forecast is made in or from, or the facts are concealed in or from, the United Kingdom;

(b) the person on whom the inducement is intended to or may have effect is in the United Kingdom; or

(c) the contract is or would be entered into or the rights are or would be exercisable in the United Kingdom.

133(3) **[Penalty]**   A person guilty of an offence under this section shall be liable—

(a) on conviction on indictment, to imprisonment for a term not exceeding seven years or to a fine or to both;

(b) on summary conviction, to imprisonment for a term not exceeding six months or to a fine not exceeding the statutory maximum or to both.

SEC. 134   Controllers of insurance companies

134 In section 7(4)(c) (ii) of the Insurance Companies Act 1982 (definition of controller by reference to exercise of not less than one-third of voting power) for the words "one-third" there shall be substituted the words "15 per cent".

SEC. 135   Communication by auditor with Secretary of State

135(1)   **[Insertion of sec. 21A of Insurance Companies Act 1982]**   After section 21 of the Insurance Companies Act 1982 there shall be inserted—

"Communication by auditor with Secretary of State

21A(1)   No duty to which an auditor of an insurance company to which this Part of this Act applies may be subject shall be regarded as contravened by reason of his communicating in good faith to the Secretary of State, whether or not in response to a request from him, any information or opinion on a matter of which the auditor has become aware in his capacity as auditor of that company and which is relevant to any functions of the Secretary of State under this Act.

21A(2)   If it appears to the Secretary of State that any auditor or class of auditor to whom subsection (1) above applies is not subject to satisfactory rules made or guidance issued by a professional body specifying circumstances in which matters are to be communicated to the Secretary of State as mentioned in that subsection the Secretary of State may make regulations applying to that auditor or class of auditor and specifying such circumstances; and it shall be the duty of an auditor to whom the regulations made by the Secretary of State apply to communicate a matter to the Secretary of State in the circumstances specified by the regulations.

21A(3)   The matters to be communicated to the Secretary of State in accordance with any such rules or guidance or regulations may include matters relating to persons other than the company.

21A(4)   No regulations shall be made under subsection (2) above unless a draft of them has been laid before and approved by a resolution of each House of Parliament.

21A(5)   If it appears to the Secretary of State that an auditor has failed to comply with duty mentioned in subsection (2) above, the Secretary of State may disqualify him from being the auditor of an insurance company or any class of insurance company to which Part II of this Act applies; but the Secretary of State may remove any disqualification imposed under this subsection if satisfied that the person in question will in future comply with that duty.

21A(6) An insurance company to which this Part of this Act applies shall not appoint as auditor a person disqualified under subsection (5) above.".

135(2) **[Insertion in sec. 71(7) of 1982 Act]** In section 71(7) of that Act (which lists the provisions of that Act default in complying with which is not an offence) after the words "section 16" there shall be inserted the word "21A", and in section 97(4) of that Act (which provides that regulations under that Act are to be subject to annulment) after the word "Act" there shall be inserted the words ", except regulations under section 21A(3),".

SEC. 136 Arrangements to avoid unfairness between separate insurance funds etc.

136(1) **[Insertion of sec. 31A of Insurance Companies Act 1982]** After section 31 of the Insurance Companies Act 1982 there shall be inserted—

"*Arrangements to avoid unfairness between separate insurance funds etc.*

31A(1) An insurance company to which this Part of this Act applies which carries on long term business in the United Kingdom shall secure that adequate arrangements are in force for securing that transactions affecting assets of the company (other than transactions outside its control) do not operate unfairly between the section 28 fund or funds and the other assets of the company or, in a case where the company has more than one identified fund, between those funds.

31A(2) In this section—

'**the section 28 fund or funds**' means the assets representing the fund or funds maintained by the company under section 28(1)(b) above; and

'**identified fund**', in relation to a company, means assets representing the company's receipts from a particular part of its long term business which can be identified as such by virtue of accounting or other records maintained by the company."

136(2) **[Insertion in sec. 71(7) of 1982 Act]** In section 71(7) of that Act (which lists the provisions of that Act default in complying with which is not an offence) before the word "or" there shall be inserted the word "31A".

SEC. 137 Regulations in respect of linked long term policies

137 In section 78(2) of the Insurance Companies Act 1982 (regulations in respect of linked long term policies) after paragraph (a) there shall be inserted—

"(aa) restricting the proportion of those benefits which may be determined by reference to property of a specified description or a specified index;".

SEC. 138   Insurance brokers

138(1)   **[Rules under sec. 8 of Insurance Brokers (Registration) Act 1977]**   Rules made under section 8 of the Insurance Brokers (Registration) Act 1977 may require an applicant for registration or enrolment to state whether he is an authorised person or exempted person under Part I of this Act and, if so, to give particulars of the authorisation or exemption; and an individual shall be treated as satisfying the requirements of section 3(2)(a) of that Act (applicant for registration to satisfy Council as to his character and suitability) if he is an authorised person or a member of a partnership or unincorporated association which is an authorised person.

138(2)   **[Statement, rules under sec. 10–12 of 1977 Act]**   In drawing up any statement under section 10 of that Act or making any rules under section 11 or 12 of that Act after the coming into force of this section the Insurance Brokers Registration Council shall take proper account of any provisions applicable to, and powers exercisable in relation to, registered insurance brokers or enrolled bodies corporate under this Act.

138(3)   **[Substitution in sec. 12(1), (2) of 1977 Act]**   In section 12(1) and (2) of that Act (which requires the Council to make professional indemnity rules) for the words "The Council shall" there shall be substituted the words "The Council may".

138(4)   **[Insertion of sec. 15(2A) of 1977 Act]**   In section 15 of that Act (erasure from register and list for unprofessional conduct etc.) after subsection (2) there shall be inserted—

> "**15(2A)**   The Disciplinary Committee may, if they think fit, direct that the name of a registered insurance broker or enrolled body corporate shall be erased from the register or list if it appears to the Committee that any responsible person has concluded that the broker (or a related person) or the body corporate has contravened or failed to comply with—
>
> (a) any provision of the Financial Services Act 1986 or any rule or regulation made under it to which he or it is or was subject at the time of the contravention or failure; or
>
> (b) any rule of any recognised self-regulating organisation or recognised professional body (within the meaning of that Act), to which he is or was subject at that time.
>
> **15(2B)**   In subsection (2A) above—
>
> (a) '**responsible person**' means a person responsible under the Financial Services Act 1986 or under the rules of any recognised self-regulating organisation or recognised professional body (within the meaning of that Act) for determining whether any contravention of any provision of that Act or rules or regulations made under it or any rules of that organisation or body has occurred; and
>
> (b) '**related person**' means a partnership or unincorporated association of which the broker in question is (or was at the time of the failure or contravention in question) a member or a body corporate of which he is (or was at that time) a director."

138(5)   **[Insurance Brokers Registration Council]**   The Insurance Brokers Registration Council shall co-operate, by the sharing of information and otherwise, with the Secretary of State and any other authority, body or person having responsibility for the supervision or regulation of investment business or other financial services.

138(6) [**"Authorised insurers"**] For the purposes of the said Act of 1977 **"authorised insurers"** shall include—

    (a) an insurance company the head office of which is in a member State other than the United Kingdom and which is entitled to carry on there insurance business corresponding to that mentioned in the definition of **"authorised insurers"** in that Act; and

    (b) an insurance company which has a branch or agency in such a member State and is entitled under the law of that State to carry on there insurance business corresponding to that mentioned in that definition.

SEC. 139　Industrial assurance

139(1) [**Interpretation of sec. 5 of Industrial Assurance Act 1923**] In section 5 of the Industrial Assurance Act 1923 (prohibition on issue of illegal policies) the references to policies which are illegal or not within the legal powers of a society or company shall not be construed as applying to any policy issued—

    (a) in the course of carrying on investment business in contravention of section 3 above; or

    (b) in the course of carrying on insurance business in contravention of section 2 of the Insurance Companies Act 1982.

139(2) [**Interpretation of sec. 20(4), 34 of 1923 Act**] In section 20(4) of the said Act of 1923 the reference to a person employed by a collecting society or industrial assurance company and in section 34 of that Act the references to a person in the regular employment of such a society or company shall include references to an appointed representative of such a society or company but as respects section 34 only if the contract in question is an investment agreement.

139(3) [**Reference of disputes to Industrial Assurance Commissioner**] Where it appears to the Industrial Assurance Commissioner that rules made by virtue of section 48(2)(j) (or corresponding rules made by a recognised self-regulating organisation) make arrangements for the settlement of a dispute referred to him under section 32 of the said Act of 1923 or that such rules relate to some of the matters in dispute he may, if he thinks fit, delegate his functions in respect of the dispute so as to enable it to be settled in accordance with the rules.

139(4) [**Power of Commissioner**] If such rules provide that any dispute may be referred to the Industrial Assurance Commissioner he may deal with any dispute referred to him in pursuance of those rules as if it were a dispute referred under section 77 of the Friendly Societies Act 1974 and may delegate his functions in respect of any such dispute to any other person.

139(5) [**Application to Northern Ireland**] The foregoing provisions of this section shall apply to Northern Ireland with the substitution for the references to sections 5, 20(4), 32 and 34 of the said Act of 1923 and section 77 of the said Act of 1974 of references to Articles 20, 27(2), 36 and 38 of the Industrial Assurance (Northern Ireland) Order 1979 and section 65 of the Friendly Societies Act (Northern Ireland)

1970 and for the references to the Industrial Assurance Commissioner of references to the Industrial Asssurance Commissioner for Northern Ireland.

PART III — FRIENDLY SOCIETIES

SEC. 140   Friendly societies

140   Schedule 11 to this Act shall have effect as respects the regulation of friendly societies.

SEC. 141   Indemnity schemes

141(1)   [Arrangement between Friendly Societies]   Any two or more registered friendly societies may, notwithstanding any provision to the contrary in their rules, enter into arrangements for the purpose of making funds available to meet losses incurred by any society which is a party to the arrangements or by the members of any such society by virtue of their membership of it.

141(2)   [Approval by Chief Registrar]   No such arrangements shall come into force unless they have been approved by the Chief Registrar of friendly societies or, as the case may be, the Registrar of Friendly Societies for Northern Ireland.

PART IV — OFFICIAL LISTING OF SECURITIES

SEC. 142   Official listing

142(1)   [Admission to official listing]   No investment to which this section applies shall be admitted to the Official List of The Stock Exchange except in accordance with the provisions of this Part of this Act.

142(2)   [Application to Sch. 1 investments]   Subject to subsections (3) and (4) below, this section applies to any investment falling within paragraph 1, 2, 4 or 5 of Schedule 1 to this Act.

142(3)   [Application of paragraphs in sec. 142(2)]   In the application of those paragraphs for the purposes of subsection (2) above—

(a) paragraphs 1, 4 and 5 shall have effect as if paragraph 1 did not contain the exclusion relating to building societies, industrial and provident societies or credit unions;

(b) paragraph 2 shall have effect as if it included any instrument falling within paragraph 3 issued otherwise than by the government of a member State or a local authority in a member State; and

(c) paragraphs 4 and 5 shall have effect as if they referred only to investments falling within paragraph 1.

142(4)   [Application to Sch. 1 para. 6 investments]   The Secretary of State may by order direct that this section shall apply also to investments falling within paragraph 6 of Schedule 1 to this Act or to such investments of any class or description.

142(5)   [Annulment of sec. 142(4) order]   An order under subsection (4) above shall be subject to annulment in pursuance of a resolution of either House of Parliament.

142(6) **["Competent authority"]** In this Part of this Act **"the competent authority"** means, subject to section 157 below, the Council of The Stock Exchange; and that authority may make rules (in this Act referred to as "listing rules") for the purposes of any of the following provisions.

142(7) **[Other definitions]** In this Part of this Act—

"**issuer**", in relation to any securities, means the person by whom they have been or are to be issued except that in relation to a certificate or other instrument falling within paragraph 5 of Schedule 1 to this Act it means the person who issued or is to issue the securities to which the certificate or instrument relates;

"**the Official List**" means the Official List of The Stock Exchange;

"**securities**" means investments to which this section applies;

and references to listing are references to inclusion in the Official List in pursuance of this Part of this Act.

142(8) **[Exercise of functions of competent authority]** Any functions of the competent authority under this Part of this Act may be exercised by any committee, sub-committee, officer or servant of the authority except that listing rules—

(a) shall be made only by the authority itself or by a committee or sub-committee of the authority; and

(b) if made by a committee or sub-committee, shall cease to have effect at the end of the period of twenty-eight days beginning with the day on which they are made (but without prejudice to anything done under them) unless before the end of that period they are confirmed by the authority.

142(9) **[Effect on powers of Council of The Stock Exchange]** Nothing in this Part of this Act affects the powers of the Council of The Stock Exchange in respect of investments to which this section does not apply and such investments may be admitted to the Official List otherwise than in accordance with this Part of this Act.

SEC. 143 Applications for listing

143(1) **[Manner of making application]** An application for listing shall be made to the competent authority in such manner as the listing rules may require.

143(2) **[Consent of issuer of securities]** No application for the listing of any securities shall be made except by or with the consent of the issuer of the securities.

143(3) **[Private companies, old public companies]** No application for listing shall be made in respect of securities to be issued by a private company or by an old public company within the meaning of section 1 of the Companies Consolidation (Consequential Provisions) Act 1985 or the corresponding Northern Ireland provision.

SEC. 144 Admission to list

144(1) **[Requirements for listings]** The competent authority shall not admit any securities to the Official List except on an application duly made in accordance with section 143 above and unless satisfied that—

(a) the requirements of the listing rules made by the authority for the purposes of this section and in force when the application is made; and

(b) any other requirements imposed by the authority in relation to that application,

are complied with.

144(2)   [Conditions in rules]   Without prejudice to the generality of the power of the competent authority to make listing rules for the purposes of this section, such rules may, in particular, require as a condition of the admission of any securities to the Official List—

(a) the submission to, and approval by, the authority of a document (in this Act referred to as "listing particulars") in such form and containing such information as may be specified in the rules; and

(b) the publication of that document;

or, in such cases as may be specified by the rules, the publication of a document other than listing particulars.

144(3)   [Possible grounds for refusing application]   The competent authority may refuse an application—

(a) if it considers that by reason of any matter relating to the issuer the admission of the securities would be detrimental to the interests of investors; or

(b) in the case of securities already officially listed in another member State, if the issuer has failed to comply with any obligations to which he is subject by virtue of that listing.

144(4)   [Notification to applicant of decision]   The competent authority shall notify the applicant or its decision on the application within six months from the date on which the application is received or, if within that period the authority has required the applicant to furnish further information in connection with the application, from the date on which that information is furnished.

144(5)   [If no application as in sec. 144(4)]   If the competent authority does not notify the applicant of its decision within the time required by subsection (4) above it shall be taken to have refused the application.

144(6)   [Once securities admitted]   When any securities have been admitted to the Official List their admission shall not be called in question on the ground that any requirement or condition for their admission has not been complied with.

SEC. 145   Discontinuance and suspension of listing

145(1)   [Power to discontinue listing]   The competent authority may, in accordance with the listing rules, discontinue the listing of any securities if satisfied that there are special circumstances which preclude normal regular dealings in the securities.

145(2)   [Power to suspend listing]   The competent authority may in accordance with the listing rules suspend the listing of any securities.

145(3)   [Suspended securities for sec. 153, 155]   Securities the listing of which is suspended under subsection (2) above shall nevertheless be regarded as listed for the purposes of sections 153 and 155 below.

145(4)   [Applications]   This section applies to securities included in the Official List at the coming into force of this Part of this Act as it applies to securities included by virtue of this Part.

SEC. 146   General duty of disclosure in listing particulars

146(1)   [Other information in listing particulars]   In addition to the information specified by listing rules or required by the competent authority as a condition of the admission of any securities to the Official List any listing particulars submitted to the competent authority under section 144 above shall contain all such information as investors and their professional advisers would reasonably require, and reasonably expect to find there, for the purpose of making an informed assessment of—

    (a) the assets and liabilities, financial position, profits and losses, and prospects of the issuer of the securities; and

    (b) the rights attaching to those securities.

146(2)   [Scope of information in sec. 146(1)]   The information to be included by virtue of this section shall be such information as is mentioned in subsection (1) above which is within the knowledge of any person responsible for the listing particulars or which it would be reasonable for him to obtain by making enquiries.

146(3)   [Relevant matters to be considered]   In determining what information is required to be included in listing particulars by virtue of this section regard shall be had—

    (a) to the nature of the securities and of the issuer of the securities;

    (b) to the nature of the persons likely to consider their acquisition;

    (c) to the fact that certain matters may reasonably be expected to be within the knowledge of professional advisers of any kind which those persons may reasonably be expected to consult; and

    (d) to any information available to investors or their professional advisers by virtue of requirements imposed under section 153 below or by or under any other enactment or by virtue of requirements imposed by a recognised investment exchange for the purpose of complying with paragraph 2(2)(b) of Schedule 4 to this Act.

SEC. 147   Supplementary listing particulars

147(1)   [Notification re significant changes, new matters]   If at any time after the preparation of listing particulars for submission to the competent authority under section 144 above and before the commencement of dealings in the securities following their admission to the Official List—

    (a) there is a significant change affecting any matter contained in those particulars whose inclusion was required by section 146 above or by listing rules or by the competent authority; or

    (b) a significant new matter arises the inclusion of information in respect of which would have been so required if it had arisen when the particulars were prepared,

the issuer of the securities shall, in accordance with listing rules made for the purposes of this section, submit to the competent authority for its approval and, if approved, publish supplementary listing particulars of the change or new matter.

147(2)   ["Significant" in sec. 147(1)]   In subsection (1) above **"significant"** means significant for the purpose of making an informed assessment of the matters mentioned in section 146(1) above.

147(3)   [Where issuer of securities not aware of change etc.]   Where the issuer of the securities is not aware of the change or new matter in question he shall not be under any duty to comply with subsection (1) above unless he is notified of it by a person responsible for the listing particulars; but it shall be the duty of any person responsible for those particulars who is aware of such a matter to give notice of it to the issuer.

147(4)   [Extended application of sec. 147(1)]   Subsection (1) above applies also as respects matters contained in any supplementary listing particulars previously published under this section in respect of the securities in question.

SEC. 148   Exemptions from disclosure

148(1)   [Grounds for omission of information]   The competent authority may authorise the omission from listing particulars or supplementary listing particulars of any information the inclusion of which would otherwise be required by section 146 above—

(a)   on the ground that its disclosure would be contrary to the public interest;

(b)   subject to subsection (2) below, on the ground that its disclosure would be seriously detrimental to the issuer of the securities; or

(c)   in the case of securities which fall within paragraph 2 of Schedule 1 to this Act as modified by section 142(3)(b) above and are of any class specified by listing rules, on the ground that its disclosure is unnecessary for persons of the kind who may be expected normally to buy or deal in the securities.

148(2)   [Qualification re sec. 148(1)(b)]   No authority shall be granted under subsection (1)(b) above in respect of, and no such authority shall be regarded as extending to, information the non-disclosure of which would be likely to mislead a person considering the acquisition of the securities as to any facts the knowledge of which it is essential for him to have in order to make an informed assessment.

148(3)   [Certificate re sec. 148(1)(a)]   The Secretary of State or the Treasury may issue a certificate to the effect that the disclosure of any information (including information that would otherwise have to be included in particulars for which they are themselves responsible) would be contrary to the public interest and the competent authority shall be entitled to act on any such certificate in exercising its powers under subsection (1)(a) above.

148(4)   [Rules under sec. 156(2)]   This section is without prejudice to any powers of the competent authority under rules made by virtue of section 156(2) below.

SEC. 149   Registration of listing particulars

149(1)   [Copy of particulars to registrar]   On or before the date on which listing particulars or supplementary listing particulars are published as required by listing rules a copy of the particulars shall be delivered for registration to the registrar of companies and a statement that a copy has been delivered to him shall be included in the particulars.

149(2) [**"The registrar of companies"**]   In subsection (1) above **"the registrar of companies"** means—

    (a) if the securities in question are or are to be issued by a company incorporated in Great Britain, the registrar of companies in England and Wales or the registrar of companies in Scotland according to whether the company's registered office is in England and Wales or in Scotland;

    (b) if the securities in question are or are to be issued by a company incorporated in Northern Ireland, the registrar of companies for Northern Ireland;

    (c) in any other case, any of those registrars.

149(3) [**Offence, penalty**]   If any particulars are published without a copy of them having been delivered as required by this section the issuer of the securities in question and any person who is knowingly a party to the publication shall be guilty of an offence and liable—

    (a) on conviction on indictment, to a fine;

    (b) on summary conviction, to a fine not exceeding the statutory maximum.

SEC. 150   Compensation for false or misleading particulars

150(1) [**Liability for compensation**]   Subject to section 151 below, the person or persons responsible for any listing particulars or supplementary listing particulars shall be liable to pay compensation to any person who has acquired any of the securities in question and suffered loss in respect of them as a result of any untrue or misleading statement in the particulars or the omission from them of any matter required to be included by section 146 or 147 above.

150(2) [**Omission of information from particulars**]   Where listing rules require listing particulars to include information as to any particular matter on the basis that the particulars must include a statement either as to that matter or, if such is the case, that there is no such matter, the omission from the particulars of the information shall be treated for the purposes of subsection (1) above as a statement that there is no such matter.

150(3) [**Non-compliance with sec. 147**]   Subject to section 151 below, a person who fails to comply with section 147 above shall be liable to pay compensation to any person who has acquired any of the securities in question and suffered loss in respect of them as a result of the failure.

150(4) [**Other liability**]   This section does not affect any liability which any person may incur apart from this section. (eg negligence claims)

150(5) [**Interpretation**]   References in this section to the acquisition by any person of securities include references to his contracting to acquire them or an interest in them.

150(6) [**Exclusion of liability as promoter etc.**]   No person shall by reason of being a promoter of a company or otherwise incur any liability for failing to disclose any information which he would not be required to disclose in listing particulars in respect of a company's securities if he were responsible for those particulars or, if he is responsible for them, which he is entitled to omit by virtue of section 148 above.

The reference above to a person incurring liability includes reference to any other person being entitled as against that person to be granted any civil remedy or to rescind or repudiate any agreement.

History
In s. 150(6) the words "The reference above to a person incurring liability" to the end inserted by CA 1989, s. 197(1) as from 15 March 1990 (see S.I. 1990 No. 354 (C. 12), art. 3).

SEC. 151   Exemption from liability to pay compensation

151(1) **[No liability if believed statement true etc.]** A person shall not incur any liability under section 150(1) above for any loss in respect of securities caused by any such statement or omission as is there mentioned if he satisfied the court that at the time when the particulars were submitted to the competent authority he reasonably believed, having made such enquiries (if any) as were reasonable, that the statement was true and not misleading or that the matter whose omission caused the loss was properly omitted and—

(a) that he continued in that belief until the time when the securities were acquired; or

(b) that they were acquired before it was reasonably practicable to bring a correction to the attention of persons likely to acquire the securities in question; or

(c) that before the securities were acquired he had taken all such steps as it was reasonable for him to have taken to secure that a correction was brought to the attention of those persons; or

(d) that he continued in that belief until after the commencement of dealings in the securities following their admission to the Official List and that the securities were acquired after such a lapse of time that he ought in the circumstances to be reasonably excused.

151(2) **[Where statement by expert]** A person shall not incur any liability under section 150(1) above for any loss in respect of securities caused by a statement purporting to be made by or on the authority of another person as an expert which is, and is stated to be, included in the particulars with that other person's consent if he satisfies the court that at the time when the particulars were submitted to the competent authority he believed on reasonable grounds that the other person was competent to make or authorise the statement and had consented to its inclusion in the form and context in which it was included and—

(a) that he continued in that belief until the time when the securities were acquired; or

(b) that they were acquired before it was reasonably practicable to bring the fact that the expert was not competent or had not consented to the attention of persons likely to acquire the securities in question; or

(c) that before the securities were acquired he had taken all such steps as it was reasonable for him to have taken to secure that that fact was brought to the attention of those persons; or

(d) that he continued in that belief until after the commencement of dealings in the securities following their admission to the Official List and that the securities were acquired after such a lapse of time that he ought in the circumstances to be reasonably excused.

151(3) **[Extra matters re sec. 150(1), 151(1), (2)]** Without prejudice to subsections (1) and (2) above, a person shall not incur any liability under section 150(1) above for any loss in respect of any securities caused by any such statement or omission as is there mentioned if he satisfies the court—

(a) that before the securities were acquired a correction, or where the statement was such as is mentioned in subsection (2), the fact that the expert was not competent or had not consented had been published in a manner calculated to bring it to the attention of persons likely to acquire the securities in question; or

(b) that he took all such steps as it was reasonable for him to take to secure such publication and reasonably believed that it had taken place before the securities were acquired.

151(4) **[Where statement by official]** A person shall not incur any liability under section 150(1) above for any loss resulting from a statement made by an official person or contained in a public official document which is included in the particulars if he satisfies the court that the statement is accurately and fairly reproduced.

151(5) **[Statement as in sec. 150(1), (3)]** A person shall not incur any liability under section 150(1) or (3) above if he satisfies the court that the person suffering the loss acquired the securities in question with knowledge that the statement was false or misleading, of the omitted matter or of the change or new matter, as the case may be.

151(6) **[Change etc. as in sec. 150(3)]** A person shall not incur any liability under section 150(3) above if he satisfies the court that he reasonably believed that the change or new matter in question was not such as to call for supplementary listing particulars.

151(7) **["Expert"]** In this section **"expert"** includes any engineer, valuer, accountant or other person whose profession, qualifications or experience give authority to a statement made by him; and references to the acquisition of securities include references to contracting to acquire them or an interest in them.

SEC. 152 Persons responsible for particulars

152(1) **[Persons responsible—interpretation]** For the purposes of this Part of this Act the persons responsible for listing particulars or supplementary listing particulars are—

(a) the issuer of the securities to which the particulars relate;

(b) where the issuer is a body corporate, each person who is a director of that body at the time when the particulars are submitted to the competent authority;

(c) where the issuer is a body corporate, each person who has authorised himself to be named, and is named, in the particulars as a director or as having agreed to become a director of that body either immediately or at a future time;

(d) each person who accepts, and is stated in the particulars as accepting, responsibility for, or for any part of, the particulars;

(e) each person not falling within any of the foregoing paragraphs who has authorised the contents of, or any part of, the particulars.

152(2) **[Where person not responsible under sec. 152(1)(b)]**   A person is not responsible for any particulars by virtue of subsection (1)(b) above if they are published without his knowledge or consent and on becoming aware of their publication he forthwith gives reasonable public notice that they were published without his knowledge or consent.

152(3) **[Where person only authorised part of particulars — sec. 152(1)(d), (e)]** Where a person has accepted responsibility for, or authorised, only part of the contents of any particulars, he is responsible under subsection (1)(d) or (e) above for only that part and only if it is included in (or substantially in) the form and context to which he has agreed.

152(4) **[Where particulars re offer by issuer etc.]**   Where the particulars relate to securities which are to be issued in connection with an offer by (or by a wholly-owned subsidiary of), the issuer for, or an agreement for the acquisition by (or by a wholly-owned subsidiary of) the issuer of, securities issued by another person or in connection with any arrangement whereby the whole of the undertaking of another person is to become the undertaking of the issuer (of a wholly-owned subsidiary of the issuer or of a body corporate which will become such a subsidiary by virtue of the arrangement) then if—

(a) that other person; and

(b) where that other person is a body corporate, each person who is a director of that body at the time when the particulars are submitted to the competent authority and each other person who has authorised himself to be named, and is named, in the particulars as a director of that body,

is responsible by virtue of paragraph (d) of subsection (1) above for any part of the particulars relating to that other person or to the securities or undertaking to which the offer, agreement or arrangement relates, no person shall be responsible for that part under paragraph (a), (b) or (c) of that subsection but without prejudice to his being responsible under paragraph (d).

152(5) **[Non-application of sec. 152(1)(b), (c) re international securities]**   Neither paragraph (b) nor paragraph (c) of subsection (1) above applies in the case of an issuer of international securities of a class specified by listing rules for the purposes of section 148(1)(c) above; and neither of those paragraphs nor paragraph (b) of subsection (4) above applies in the case of any director certified by the competent authority as a person to whom that paragraph should not apply by reason of his having an interest, or of any other circumstances, making it inappropriate for him to be responsible by virtue of that paragraph.

152(6) **["International securities"]** In subsection (5) above **"international securities"** means any investment falling within paragraph 2 of Schedule 1 to this Act as modified by section 142(3)(b) above which is of a kind likely to be dealt in by bodies incorporated in or persons resident in a country or territory outside the United Kingdom, is denominated in a currency other than sterling or is otherwise connected with such a country or territory.

FSA 1986, sec. 152(2)   [The next page is 61,701]   **CCH Editions Limited**
BCL BCLFS$$$20

152(7) [**"Wholly-owned subsidiary"**]   In this section **"wholly-owned subsidiary"**, in relation to a person other than a body corporate, means any body corporate that would be his wholly-owned subsidiary if he were a body corporate.

152(8) [**Advice given in professional capacity**]   Nothing in this section shall be construed as making a person responsible for any particulars by reason of giving advice as to their contents in a professional capacity.

152(9) [**Status of payment of compensation**]   Where by virtue of this section the issuer of any shares pays or is liable to pay compensation under section 150 above for loss suffered in respect of shares for which a person has subscribed no account shall be taken of that liability or payment in determining any question as to the amount paid on subscription for those shares or as to the amount paid up or deemed to be paid up on them.

SEC. 153   Obligations of issuers of listed securities

153(1) [**Listing rules may specify certain requirements**]   Listing rules may specify requirements to be complied with by issuers of listed securities and make provision with respect to the action that may be taken by the competent authority in the event of non-compliance, including provision—

(a)   authorising the authority to publish the fact that an issuer has contravened any provision of the rules; and

(b)   if the rules require an issuer to publish any information, authorising the authority to publish it in the event of his failure to do so.

153(2) [**Application**]   This section applies to the issuer of securities included in the Official List at the coming into force of this Part of this Act as it applies to the issuer of securities included by virtue of this Part.

SEC. 154   Advertisements etc. in connection with listing applications

154(1) [**Conditions re advertisement**]   Where listing particulars are or are to be published in connection with an application for the listing of any securities no advertisement or other information of a kind specified by listing rules shall be issued in the United Kingdom unless the contents of the advertisement or other information have been submitted to the competent authority and that authority has either—

(a)   approved those contents; or

(b)   authorised the issue of the advertisement or information without such approval.

154(2) [**Effect of contravention of section**]   An authorised person who contravenes this section shall be treated as having contravened rules made under Chapter V of Part I of this Act or, in the case of a person who is an authorised person by virtue of his membership of a recognised self-regulating organisation or certification by a recognised professional body, the rules of that organisation or body.

154(3) [**Offence, penalty**]   Subject to subsection (4) below, a person other than an authorised person, who contravenes this section shall be guilty of an offence and liable—

(a) on conviction on indictment, to imprisonment for a term not exceeding two years or to a fine or to both;

(b) on summary conviction, to a fine not exceeding the statutory maximum.

154(4) [Defence] A person who in the ordinary course of a business other than investment business issues an advertisement or other information to the order of another person shall not be guilty of an offence under this section if he proves that he believed on reasonable grounds that the advertisement or information had been approved or its issue authorised by the competent authority.

154(5) [Exclusion of liability for certain persons] Where information has been approved, or its issue has been authorised, under this section neither the person issuing it nor any person responsible for, or for any part of, the listing particulars shall incur any civil liability by reason of any statement in or omission from the information if that information and the listing particulars, taken together, would not be likely to mislead persons of the kind likely to consider the acquisition of the securities in question.

The reference above to a person incurring civil liability includes a reference to any other person being entitled as against that person to be granted any civil remedy or to rescind or repudiate any agreement.

History
In s. 154(5) the words "The reference above to a person incurring civil liability" to the end inserted by CA 1989, s. 197(2) as from 15 March 1990 (see S.I. 1990 No. 354 (C. 12), art. 3).

SEC. 155   Fees

155 Listing rules may require the payment of fees to the competent authority in respect of applications for listing and the retention of securities in the Official List.

SEC. 156   Listing rules: general provisions

156(1) [Different provisions] Listing rules may make different provision for different cases.

156(2) [Dispensing with or modifying rules] Listing rules may authorise the competent authority to dispense with or modify the application of the rules in particular cases and by reference to any circumstances.

156(3) [To be made by instrument in writing] Listing rules shall be made by an instrument in writing.

156(4) [Printing, publication] Immediately after an instrument containing listing rules is made it shall be printed and made available to the public with or without payment.

156(5) [Defence re contravention of rule] A person shall not be taken to have contravened any listing rule if he shows that at the time of the alleged contravention the instrument containing the rule had not been made available as required by subsection (4) above.

156(6) [Certificate on instrument] The production of a printed copy of an instrument purporting to be made by the competent authority on which is endorsed a certificate signed by an officer of the authority authorised by it for that purpose and stating—

(a) that the instrument was made by the authority;

(b) that the copy is a true copy of the instrument; and

(c) that on a specified date the instrument was made available to the public as required by subsection (4) above,

shall be prima facie evidence or, in Scotland, sufficient evidence of the facts stated in the certificate.

156(7) **[Deemed signing of certificate]** Any certificate purporting to be signed as mentioned in subsection (6) above shall be deemed to have been duly signed unless the contrary is shown.

156(8) **[Citation of instrument in legal proceedings]** Any person wishing in any legal proceedings to cite an instrument made by the competent authority may require the authority to cause a copy of it to be endorsed with such a certificate as is mentioned in subsection (6) above.

SEC. 157 Alteration of competent authority

157(1) **[Power of Secretary of State to transfer functions]** The Secretary of State may by order transfer the functions as competent authority of the Council of The Stock Exchange to another body or other bodies either at the request of the Council or if it appears to him—

(a) that the Council is exercising those functions in a manner which is unnecessary for the protection of investors and fails to take into account the proper interests of issuers and proposed issuers of securities; or

(b) that it is necessary to do so for the protection of investors.

157(2) **[Extent of power]** The Secretary of State may by order transfer all or any of the functions as competent authority from any body or bodies to which they have been previously transferred under this section to another body or bodies.

157(3) **[Annulment of sec. 157(1) order]** Any order made under subsection (1) above at the request of the Council shall be subject to annulment in pursuance of a resolution of either House of Parliament; and no other order shall be made under this section unless a draft of it has been laid before and approved by a resolution of each House of Parliament.

157(4) **[Effect and scope of order]** An order under this section shall not affect anything previously done by any body ("the previous authority") in the exercise of functions which are transferred by the order to another body ("the new authority") and may contain such supplementary provisions as the Secretary of State thinks necessary or expedient, including provisions—

(a) for modifying or excluding any provision of this Part of this Act in its application to any such functions;

(b) for the transfer of any property, rights or liabilities relating to any such functions from the previous authority to the new authority;

(c) for the carrying on and completion by the new authority of anything in process of being done by the previous authority when the order takes effect; and

(d) for the substitution of the new authority for the previous authority in any instrument, contract or legal proceedings.

157(5) **[Where certain functions exercisable other than by Council of Stock Exchange]**   If by virtue of this section the function of admission to or discontinuance or suspension of listing is exercisable otherwise than by the Council of The Stock Exchange, references in this Part of this Act to the competent authority admitting securities to the Official List or to discontinuing or suspending the listing of any securities shall be construed as references to the giving of directions to the Council of The Stock Exchange to admit the securities or to discontinue or suspend their listing; and it shall be the duty of the Council to comply with any such direction.

PART V — OFFERS OF UNLISTED SECURITIES

SEC. 158   Preliminary   LD INCLUDES USM

158(1) **[Application of Pt. V]**   This Part of this Act applies to any investment—

(a) which is not listed, or the subject of an application for listing, in accordance with Part IV of this Act; and

(b) falls within paragraph 1, 2, 4, or 5 of Schedule 1 to this Act.

158(2) **[Re application of paragraphs for sec. 158(1)]**   In the application of those paragraphs for the purposes of subsection (1) above—

(a) paragraphs 4 and 5 shall have effect with the omission of references to investments falling within paragraph 3; and

(b) paragraph 4 shall have effect as if it referred only to instruments issued by the person issuing the investment to be subscribed for.

158(3) **["Issues", "securities"]**   In this Part of this Act—

"**issuer**", in relation to any securities, means the person by whom they have been or are to be issued except that in relation to a certificate or other instrument falling within paragraph 5 of Schedule 1 to this Act it means the person who issued or is to issue the securities to which the certificate or instrument relates;

"**securities**" means investments to which this section applies.

158(4) **[Advertisement offering securities]**   For the purposes of this Part of this Act an advertisement offers securities if—

(a) it invites a person to enter into an agreement for or with a view to subscribing for or otherwise acquiring or underwriting any securities; or

(b) it contains information calculated to lead directly or indirectly to a person entering into such an agreement.

158(5) **["The registrar of companies"]**   In this Part of this Act "**the registrar of companies**", in relation to any securities, means—

(a) if the securities are or are to be issued by a company incorporated in Great Britain, the registrar of companies in England and Wales or the registrar of companies in Scotland according to whether the company's registered office is in England and Wales or in Scotland;

(b) if the securities are or are to be issued by a company incorporated in Northern Ireland, the registrar of companies for Northern Ireland;

(c) in any other case, any of those registrars.

158(6) **["Approved exchange"]** In this Part of this Act **"approved exchange"**, in relation to dealings in any securities, means a recognised investment exchange approved by the Secretary of State for the purposes of this Part of this Act either generally or in relation to such dealings, and the Secretary of State shall give notice in such manner as he thinks appropriate of the exchanges which are for the time being approved.

SEC. 159 Offers of securities on admission to approved exchange

159(1) **[Conditions for issue of advertisement in UK]** No person shall issue or cause to be issued in the United Kingdom an advertisement offering any securities on the occasion of their admission to dealings on an approved exchange or on terms that they will be issued if admitted to such dealings unless—

(a) a document (in this Part of this Act referred to as a "prospectus") containing information about the securities has been submitted to and approved by the exchange and delivered for registration to the registrar of companies; or

(b) the advertisement is such that no agreement can be entered into in pursuance of it until such a prospectus has been submitted, approved and delivered as aforesaid.

History
In s. 159(1) the words "Subject to subsection (2) and section 161 below," formerly appearing before the words "No person shall issue or cause to be issued" omitted and repealed by CA 1989, s. 198(3), s. 212 and Sch. 24 as from 15 March 1990 (see S.I. 1990 No. 354 (C. 12), art. 3).

159(2) **[Non-application of sec. 159(1)]** Subsection (1) above does not apply if a prospectus relating to the securities has been delivered for registration under this Part of this Act in the previous twelve months and the approved exchange certifies that it is satisfied that persons likely to consider acquiring the securities will have sufficient information to enable them to decide whether to do so from that prospectus and any information published in connection with the admission of the securities.

159(3) **[Sec. 159(1) subject to sec. 160A, 161]** Subsection (1) above has effect subject to section 160A (exemptions) and section 161 (exceptions).

History
S. 159(3) inserted by CA 1989, s. 198(3) as from 15 March 1990 (see S.I. 1990 No. 354 (C. 12), art. 3).

SEC. 160 Other offers of securities

160(1) **[Conditions for issue of advertisement re primary or secondary offer]** No person shall issue or cause to be issued in the United Kingdom an advertisement offering any securities which is a primary or secondary offer within the meaning of this section unless—

(a) he has delivered for registration to the registrar of companies a prospectus relating to the securities and expressed to be in respect of the offer; or

(b) the advertisement is such that no agreement can be entered into in pursuance of it until such a prospectus has been delivered by him as aforesaid.

History
In s. 160(1) the words "Subject to subsections (5) and (6) and section 161 below," formerly appearing before the words "No person shall issue or cause to be issued" omitted and repealed by CA 1989, s. 198(4), s. 212 and Sch. 24 as from 15 March 1990 (see S.I. 1990 No. 354 (C. 12), art. 3).

160(2)   **[Primary offer—interpretation]**   For the purposes of this section a primary offer is an advertisement issued otherwise than as mentioned in section 159(1) above inviting persons to enter into an agreement for or with a view to subscribing (whether or not in cash) for or underwriting the securities to which it relates or containing information calculated to lead directly or indirectly to their doing so.

160(3)   **[Secondary offer—interpretation]**   For the purposes of this section a secondary offer is any other advertisement issued otherwise than as mentioned in section 159(1) above inviting persons to enter into an agreement for or with a view to acquiring the securities to which it relates or containing information calculated to lead directly or indirectly to their doing so, being an advertisement issued or caused to be issued by—

(a) a person who has acquired the securities from the issuer with a view to issuing such an advertisement in respect of them;

(b) a person who, with a view to issuing such an advertisement in respect of them, has acquired the securities otherwise than from the issuer but without their having been admitted to dealings on an approved exchange or held by a person who acquired them as an investment and without any intention that such an advertisement should be issued in respect of them; or

(c) a person who is a controller of the issuer or has been such a controller in the previous twelve months and who is acting with the consent or participation of the issuer in issuing the advertisement.

160(4)   **[Interpretation re sec. 160(3)(a)]**   For the purposes of subsection (3)(a) above it shall be presumed in the absence of evidence to the contrary that a person has acquired securities with a view to issuing an advertisement offering the securities if he issues it or causes it to be issued—

(a) within six months after the issue of the securities; or

(b) before the consideration due from him for their acquisition is received by the person from whom he aquired them.

160(5)   **[Where sec. 160(1) does not apply to secondary offer]**   Subsection (1) above does not apply to a secondary offer if such a prospectus as is mentioned in that subsection has been delivered in accordance with that subsection in respect of an offer of the same securities made in the previous six months by a person making a primary offer or a previous secondary offer.

160(6)   **[Sec. 160(1) subject to sec. 160A, 161]**   Subsection (1) above has effect subject to section 160A (exemptions) and section 161 (exceptions).

History
S. 160(6) substituted for the former s. 160(6)–(9) by CA 1989, s. 198(4) as from 15 March 1990 (see S.I. 1990 No. 354 (C. 12), art. 3; s. 160(6)–(9) formerly read as follows:

"**160(6)** Subsection (1) above does not apply to an advertisement issued in such circumstances as may be specified by an order made by the Secretary of State for the purpose of exempting from that subsection—

(a) advertisements appearing to him to have a private character, whether by reason of a connection between the person issuing them and those to whom they are addressed or otherwise;

(b) advertisements appearing to him to deal with investments only incidentally;

(c) advertisements issued to persons appearing to him to be sufficiently expert to understand any risks involved; or

(d) such other classes of advertisement as he thinks fit.

(7) Without prejudice to subsection (6)(c) above an order made by the Secretary of State may exempt from subsection

CCH Editions Limited
BCL BCLFS$$$22

(1) above an advertisement issued in whatever circumstances if it relates to securities appearing to him to be of a kind that can be expected normally to be bought or dealt in only by persons sufficiently expert to understand any risks involved.

(8) An order under subsection (6) or (7) above may require any person who by virtue of the order is authorised to issue an advertisement to comply with such requirements as are specified in the order.

(9) An order made by virtue of subsection (6)(a), (b) or (c) or by virtue of subsection (7) above shall be subject to annulment in pursuance of a resolution of either House of Parliament; and no order shall be made by virtue of subsection (6)(d) above unless a draft of it has been laid before and approved by a resolution of each House of Parliament."

SEC. 160A Exemptions

160A(1) [Power of Secretary of State] The Secretary of State may by order exempt from sections 159 and 160 when issued in such circumstances as may be specified in the order—

- (a) advertisements appearing to him to have a private character, whether by reason of a connection between the person issuing them and those to whom they are addressed or otherwise;

- (b) advertisements appearing to him to deal with investments only incidentally;

- (c) advertisements issued to persons appearing to him to be sufficiently expert to understand any risks involved;

- (d) such other classes of advertisements as he thinks fit.

160A(2) [Securities dealt in by experts] The Secretary of State may by order exempt from sections 159 and 160 an advertisement issued in whatever circumstances which relates to securities appearing to him to be of a kind that can be expected normally to be bought or dealt in only by persons sufficiently expert to understand any risks involved.

160A(3) [Order conditional] An order under subsection (1) or (2) may require a person who by virtue of the order is authorised to issue an advertisement to comply with such requirements as are specified in the order.

160A(4) [Annulment of sec. 160(1)(a), (b), (c), (2) order] An order made by virtue of subsection (1)(a), (b) or (c) or subsection (2) shall be subject to annulment in pursuance of a resolution of either House of Parliament; and no order shall be made by virtue of subsection (1)(d) unless a draft of it has been laid before and approved by a resolution of each House of Parliament.

History
S. 160A inserted by CA 1989, s. 198(1) as from 15 March 1990 (see S.I. 1990 No. 354 (C.12), art. 3).

SEC. 161 Exceptions

161(1) [Where offer conditional on admission to listing etc.] Sections 159 and 160 above do not apply to any advertisement offering securities if the offer is conditional on their admission to listing in accordance with Part IV of this Act and section 159 above does not apply to any advertisement offering securities if they have been listed in accordance with that Part in the previous twelve months and the approved exchange in question certifies that persons likely to consider acquiring them will have sufficient information to enable them to decide whether to do so.

161(2) [Sec. 58(2) situation] Neither of those sections applies to any such advertisement as is mentioned in section 58(2) above.

161(3) **[Where other securities issued by same person already dealt on approved exchange etc.]** Neither of those sections applies if other securities issued by the same person (whether or not securities of the same class as those to which the offer relates) are already dealt in on an approved exchange and the exchange certifies that persons likely to consider acquiring the securities to which the offer relates will have sufficient information to enable them to decide whether to do so having regard to the steps that have been taken to comply in respect of those other securities with the requirements imposed by the exchange for the purpose of complying with paragraph 2(2)(b) of Schedule 4 to this Act, to the nature of the securities to which the offer relates, to the circumstances of their issue and to the information about the issuer which is available to investors by virtue of any enactment.

161(4) **[Order re certain advertisement]** If it appears to the Secretary of State that the law of a country or territory outside the United Kingdom provides investors in the United Kingdom with protection at least equivalent to that provided by Part IV of this Act or this Part of this Act in respect of securities dealt in on an exchange or exchanges in that country or territory he may by order specify circumstances in which those sections are not to apply to advertisements offering those securities.

161(5) **[Annulment of sec. 161(4) order]** An order under subsection (4) above shall be subject to annulment in pursuance of a resolution of either House of Parliament.

SEC. 162   Form and content of prospectus

162(1) **[Prospectus to comply with rules]** A prospectus shall contain such information and comply with such other requirements as may be prescribed by rules made by the Secretary of State for the purposes of this section.

162(2) **[Scope of rules]** Rules under this section may make provision whereby compliance with any requirements imposed by or under the law of a country or territory outside the United Kingdom is treated as compliance with any requirements of the rules.

162(3) **[Order by Secretary of State]** If it appears to the Secretary of State that an approved exchange has rules in respect of prospectuses relating to securities dealt in on the exchange, and practices in exercising any powers conferred by the rules, which provide investors with protection at least equivalent to that provided by rules under this section he may direct that any such prospectus shall be subject to the rules of the exchange instead of the rules made under this section.

SEC. 163   General duty of disclosure in prospectus

163(1) **[Additional contents of prospectus]** In addition to the information required to be included in a prospectus by virtue of rules applying to it by virtue of section 162 above a prospectus shall contain all such information as investors and their professional advisers would reasonably require, and reasonably expect to find there, for the purpose of making an informed assessment of—

(a) the assets and liabilities, financial position, profits and losses, and prospects of the issuer of the securities; and

(b) the rights attaching to those securities.

163(2) **[Information to be included]** The information to be included by virtue of this section shall be such information as is mentioned in subsection (1) above which is within the knowledge of any person responsible for the prospectus or which it would be reasonable for him to obtain by making enquiries.

163(3) **[Determining of what information to include]** In determining what information is required to be included in a prospectus by virtue of this section regard shall be had—

   (a) to the nature of the securities and of the issuer of the securities;

   (b) to the nature of the persons likely to consider their acquisition;

   (c) to the fact that certain matters may reasonably be expected to be within the knowledge of professional advisers of any kind which those persons may reasonably be expected to consult; and

   (d) to any information available to investors or their professional advisers by virtue of any enactment or by virtue of requirements imposed by a recognised investment exchange for the purpose of complying with paragraph 2(2)(b) of Schedule 4 to this Act.

SEC. 164 Supplementary prospectus

164(1) **[Where significant change, new matter]** Where a prospectus has been registered under this Part of this Act in respect of an offer of securities and at any time while an agreement in respect of those securities can be entered into in pursuance of that offer—

   (a) there is a significant change affecting any matter contained in the prospectus whose inclusion was required by rules applying to it by virtue of section 162 above or by section 163 above; or

   (b) a significant new matter arises the inclusion of information in respect of which would have been so required if it had arisen when the prospectus was prepared,

the person who delivered the prospectus for registration to the registrar of companies shall deliver to him for registration a supplementary prospectus containing particulars of the change or new matter.

164(2) **["Significant"]** In subsection (1) above **"significant"** means significant for the purpose of making an informed assessment of the matters mentioned in section 163(1) above.

164(3) **[Where person not aware of new matter etc.]** Where the person who delivered the prospectus for registration is not aware of the change or new matter in question he shall not be under any duty to comply with subsection (1) above unless he is notified of it by a person responsible for the prospectus; but any person responsible for the prospectus who is aware of such a matter shall be under a duty to give him notice of it.

164(4) **[Application of sec. 164(1)]** Subsection (1) above applies also as respects matters contained in a supplementary prospectus previously registered under this section in respect of the securities in question.

SEC. 165   Exemptions from disclosure

165(1)   [Power of approved exchange]   If in the case of any approved exchange the Secretary of State so directs, the exchange shall have power to authorise the omission from a prospectus or supplementary prospectus of any information the inclusion of which would otherwise be required by section 163 above—

    (a)   on the ground that its disclosure would be contrary to the public interest;

    (b)   subject to subsection (2) below, on the ground that its disclosure would be seriously detrimental to the issuer of the securities; or

    (c)   in the case of securities which fall within paragraph 2 of Schedule 1 to this Act and are of any class specified by the rules of the exchange, on the ground that its disclosure is unnecessary for persons of the kind who may be expected normally to buy or deal in the securities.

165(2)   [Limit on authority under sec. 165(1)(b)]   No authority shall be granted under subsection (1)(b) above in respect of, and no such authority shall be regarded as extending to, information the non-disclosure of which would be likely to mislead a person considering the acquisition of the securities as to any facts the knowledge of which it is essential for him to have in order to make an informed assessment.

165(3)   [Issue of certificate]   The Secretary of State or the Treasury may issue a certificate to the effect that the disclosure of any information (including information that would otherwise have to be included in a prospectus or supplementary prospectus for which they are themselves responsible) would be contrary to the public interest and the exchange shall be entitled to act on any such certificate in exercising its powers under subsection (1)(a) above.

SEC. 166   Compensation for false or misleading prospectus

166(1)   [Liability to pay compensation]   Subject to section 167 below, the person or persons responsible for a prospectus or supplementary prospectus shall be liable to pay compensation to any person who has acquired the securities to which the prospectus relates and suffered loss in respect of them as a result of any untrue or misleading statement in the prospectus or the omission from it of any matter required to be included by section 163 or 164 above.

166(2)   [Omission of certain information]   Where rules applicable to a prospectus by virtue of section 162 above require it to include information as to any particular matter on the basis that the prospectus must include a statement either as to that matter or, if such is the case, that there is no such matter, the omission from the prospectus of the information shall be treated for the purpose of subsection (1) above as a statement that there is no such matter.

166(3)   [Liability for failure to comply with sec. 164]   Subject to section 167 below, a person who fails to comply with section 164 above shall be liable to pay compensation to any person who has acquired any of the securities in question and suffered loss in respect of them as a result of the failure.

166(4)   [Other liability]   This section does not affect any liability which any person may incur apart from this section.

166(5)   [Interpretation]   References in this section to the acquisition by any person of securities include references to his contracting to acquire them or an interest in them.

SEC. 167   Exemption from liability to pay compensation

167(1)   **[Reasonable belief in truth of statement]**   A person shall not incur any liability under section 166(1) above for any loss in respect of securities caused by any such statement or omission as is there mentioned if he satisfies the court that at the time when the prospectus or supplementary prospectus was delivered for registration he reasonably believed, having made such enquiries (if any) as were reasonable, that the statement was true and not misleading or that the matter whose omission caused the loss was properly omitted and—

    (a) that he continued in that belief until the time when the securities were acquired; or

    (b) that they were acquired before it was reasonably practicable to bring a correction to the attention of persons likely to acquire the securities in question; or

    (c) that before the securities were acquired he had taken all such steps as it was reasonable for him to have taken to secure that a correction was brought to the attention of those persons; or

    (d) that the securities were acquired after such a lapse of time that he ought in the circumstances to be reasonably excused;

but paragraph (d) above does not apply where the securities are dealt in on an approved exchange unless he satisfies the court that he continued in that belief until after the commencement of dealings in the securities on that exchange.

167(2)   **[Reasonable belief in competence of expert etc.]**   A person shall not incur any liability under section 166(1) above for any loss in respect of securities caused by a statement purporting to be made by or on the authority of another person as an expert which is, and is stated to be, included in the prospectus or supplementary prospectus with that other person's consent if he satisfies the court that at the time when the prospectus or supplementary prospectus was delivered for registration he believed on reasonable grounds that the other person was competent to make or authorise the statement and had consented to its inclusion in the form and context in which it was included and—

    (a) that he continued in that belief until the time when the securities were acquired; or

    (b) that they were acquired before it was reasonably practicable to bring the fact that the expert was not competent or had not consented to the attention of persons likely to acquire the securities in question; or

    (c) that before the securities were acquired he had taken all such steps as it was reasonable for him to have taken to secure that that fact was brought to the attention of those persons; or

    (d) that the securities were acquired after such a lapse of time that he ought in the circumstances to be reasonably excused;

but paragraph (d) above does not apply where the securities are dealt in on an approved exchange unless he satisfies the court that he continued in that belief until after the commencement of dealings in the securities on that exchange.

167(3)   **[Attempt to publish correction etc. before securities acquired]**   Without prejudice to subsections (1) and (2) above, a person shall not incur any liability under section 166(1) above for any loss in respect of any securities caused by any such statement or omission as is there mentioned if he satisfies the court—

   (a) that before the securities were acquired a correction or, where the statement was such as is mentioned in subsection (2) above, the fact that the expert was not competent or had not consented had been published in a manner calculated to bring it to the attention of persons likely to acquire the securities in question; or

   (b) that he took all such steps as it was reasonable for him to take to secure such publication and reasonably believed that it had taken place before the securities were acquired.

167(4) **[Statement by official included in prospectus]** A person shall not incur any liability under section 166(1) above for any loss resulting from a statement made by an official person or contained in a public official document which is included in the prospectus or supplementary prospectus if he satisfies the court that the statement is accurately and fairly reproduced.

167(5) **[Person acquiring securities knew statement false]** A person shall not incur any liability under section 166(1) or (3) above if he satisfies the court that the person suffering the loss acquired the securities in question with knowledge that the statement was false or misleading, of the omitted matter or of the change or new matter, as the case may be.

167(6) **[Reasonable belief that change as new matter not warranting supplementary prospectus]** A person shall not incur any liability under section 166(3) above if he satisfies the court that he reasonably believed that the change or new matter in question was not such as to call for a supplementary prospectus.

167(7) **["Expert"]** In this section **"expert"** includes any engineer, valuer, accountant or other person whose profession, qualifications or experience give authority to a statement made by him; and references to the acquisition of securities include references to contracting to acquire them or an interest in them.

SEC. 168   Persons responsible for prospectus

168(1) **[Persons]** For the purposes of this Part of this Act the persons responsible for a prospectus or supplementary prospectus are—

   (a) the issuer of the securities to which the prospectus or supplementary prospectus relates;

   (b) where the issuer is a body corporate, each person who is a director of that body at the time when the prospectus or supplementary prospectus is delivered for registration;

   (c) where the issuer is a body corporate, each person who has authorised himself to be named, and is named, in the prospectus or supplementary prospectus as a director or as having agreed to become a director of that body either immediately or at a future time;

   (d) each person who accepts, and is stated in the prospectus or supplementary prospectus as accepting, responsibility for, or for any part of, the prospectus or supplementary prospectus;

(e) each person not falling within any of the foregoing paragraphs who has authorised the contents of, or of any part of, the prospectus or supplementary prospectus.

168(2)   [Conditions for responsibility under sec. 168(1)(a), (b), (c)]   A person is not responsible under subsection (1)(a), (b) or (c) above unless the issuer has made or authorised the offer in relation to which the prospectus or supplementary prospectus was delivered for registration; and a person is not responsible for a prospectus or supplementary prospectus by virtue of subsection (1)(b) above if it is delivered for registration without his knowledge or consent and on becoming aware of its delivery he forthwith gives reasonable public notice that it was delivered without his knowledge or consent.

168(3)   [Responsibility for part of prospectus under sec. 168(1)(d), (e)]   Where a person has accepted responsibility for, or authorised, only part of the contents of any prospectus or supplementary prospectus he is responsible under subsection (1)(d) or (e) above for only that part and only if it is included in (or substantially in) the form and context to which he has agreed.

168(4)   [Where prospectus re securities issued in connection with offer]   Where a prospectus or supplementary prospectus relates to securities which are to be issued in connection with an offer by (or by a wholly-owned subsidiary of) the issuer for, or an agreement for the acquisition by (or by a wholly-owned subsidiary of) the issuer of, securities issued by another person or in connection with any arrangement whereby the whole of the undertaking of another person is to become the undertaking of the issuer (of a wholly-owned subsidiary of the issuer or of a body corporate which will become such a subsidiary by virtue of the arrangement) then if—

(a) that other person; and

(b) where that other person is a body corporate, each person who is a director of that body at the time when the prospectus or supplementary prospectus is delivered for registration and each other person who has authorised himself to be named, and is named, in the prospectus or supplementary prospectus as a director of that body,

is responsible by virtue of paragraph (d) of subsection (1) above for any part of the prospectus or supplementary prospectus relating to that other person or to the securities or undertaking to which the offer, agreement or arrangement relates, no person shall be responsible for that part under paragraph (a), (b) or (c) of that subsection but without prejudice to his being responsible under paragraph (d).

168(5)   [Application of sec. 168(1)(b), (c), 4(b) to directors]   Neither paragraph (b) nor paragraph (c) of subsection (1) above nor paragraph (b) of subsection (4) above applies in the case of any director if the prospectus or supplementary prospectus is subject to the rules of an approved exchange by virtue of section 162(3) above and he is certified by the exchange as a person to whom that paragraph should not apply by reason of his having an interest, or of any other circumstances, making it inappropriate for him to be responsible by virtue of that paragraph.

168(6)   ["Wholly-owned subsidiary"]   In this section **"wholly-owned subsidiary"**, in relation to a person other than a body corporate, means any body corporate that would be his wholly-owned subsidiary if he was a body corporate.

168(7)　[Advice in professional capacity]　Nothing in the section shall be construed as making a person responsible for any prospectus or supplementary prospectus by reason only of giving advice as to its contents in a professional capacity.

168(8)　[Liability to pay compensation under sec. 166]　Where by virtue of this section the issuer of any shares pays or is liable to pay compensation under section 166 above for loss suffered in respect of shares for which a person has subscribed no account shall be taken of that liability or payment in determining any question as to the amount paid on subscription for those shares or as to the amount paid up or deemed to be paid up on them.

SEC. 169　Terms and implementation of offer

169(1)　[Power of Secretary of State]　The Secretary of State may make rules—

(a) regulating the terms on which a person may offer securities by an advertisement to which this Part of this Act applies; and

(b) otherwise regulating his conduct with a view to ensuring that the persons to whom the offer is addressed are treated equally and fairly.

169(2)　[Rules re priority]　Rules under this section may, in particular, make provision with respect to the giving of priority as between persons to whom an offer is made and with respect to the payment of commissions.

169(3)　[Application of sec. 162(2)]　Section 162(2) above shall apply also to rules made under this section.

SEC. 170　Advertisements by private companies and old public companies

170(1)　[Limit on advertisements]　No private company and no old public company shall issue or cause to be issued in the United Kingdom any advertisement offering securities to be issued by that company.

170(2)　[Power of Secretary of State to exempt from sec. 170(1)]　The Secretary of State may by order exempt from subsection (1) when issued in such circumstances as may be specified in the order—

(a) advertisements appearing to him to have a private character, whether by reason of a connection between the person issuing them and those to whom they are addressed or otherwise;

(b) advertisements appearing to him to deal with investments only incidentally;

(c) advertisements issued to persons appearing to him to be sufficiently expert to understand any risks involved;

(d) such other classes of advertisements as he thinks fit.

170(3)　[Securities dealt in by experts]　The Secretary of State may by order exempt from subsection (1) an advertisement issued in whatever circumstances which relates to securities appearing to him to be of a kind that can be expected normally to be bought or dealt in only by persons sufficiently expert to understand any risks involved.

170(4) **[Order conditional]** An order under subsection (2) or (3) may require a person who by virtue of the order is authorised to issue an advertisement to comply with such requirements as are specified in the order.

170(4A) **[Annulment of sec. 170(2)(a), (b), (c), (3) order]** An order made by virtue of subsection (2)(a), (b) or (c) or subsection (3) shall be subject to annulment in pursuance of a resolution of either House of Parliament; and no order shall be made by virtue of subsection (2)(d) unless a draft of it has been laid before and approved by a resolution of each House of Parliament.

History

S. 170(2)–4A substituted for the former s. 170(2)–(4) by CA 1989 s. 199 as from 15 March 1990 (see S.I. 1990 No. 354 (C. 12), art. 3); s. 170(2)–(4) formerly read as follows:

"**170(2)** Subsection (1) above shall not apply to an advertisement issued in such circumstances as may be specified by an order made by the Secretary of State for the purpose of exempting from that subsection such advertisements as are mentioned in section 160(6)(a), (b) or (c) above.

(3) An order under subsection (2) above may require any person who by virtue of the order is authorised to issue an advertisement to comply with such requirements as are specified in the order.

(4) An order under subsection (2) above shall be subject to annulment in pursuance of a resolution of either House of Parliament."

170(5) **["Old public company"]** In this section **"old public company"** has the meaning given in section 1 of the Companies Consolidation (Consequential Provisions) Act 1985 or the corresponding Northern Ireland provision.

SEC. 171 Contraventions

171(1) **[Effect of contraventions by authorised persons]** An authorised person who—

(a) contravenes section 159 or 160 above or rules made under section 169 above;

(b) contravenes any requirement imposed by an order under section 160A or 170 above; or

(c) on behalf of a company issues or causes to be issued an advertisement which that company is prohibited from issuing by section 170 above.

shall be treated as having contravened rules made under Chapter V of Part I of this Act or, in the case of a person who is an authorised person by virtue of his membership of a recognised self-regulating organisation or certification by a recognised professional body, the rules of that organisation or body.

History

See history note after s. 171(3).

171(2) **[Application of sec. 57]** Section 57 above shall apply to a company which issues or causes to be issued an advertisement in contravention of section 170 above as it applies to a person who issues an advertisement in contravention of that section.

171(3) **[Offence, penalty]** A person, other than an authorised person, who contravenes section 159 or 160, the rules made under section 169 or any requirement imposed by an order under section 160A or 170 above shall be guilty of an offence and liable—

(a) on conviction on indictment, to imprisonment for a term not exceeding two years or to a fine or to both;

(b) on summary conviction, to imprisonment for a term not exceeding six months or to a fine not exceeding the statutory maximum or to both.

History

In s. 171(1)(b) and (3) the words "section 160A" substituted for the former words "section 160(6) or (7)" as from 15 March 1990 (see S.I. 1990 No. 354 (C.12), art. 3).

171(4)   **[Ordinary course of business exception]**   A person who in the ordinary course of a business other than investment business issues an advertisement to the order of another person shall not be guilty of an offence under subsection (3) above in respect of a contravention of section 159 or 160 above if he proves that he believed on reasonable grounds that neither section 159 nor section 160 above applied to the advertisement or that one of those sections had been complied with in respect of the advertisement.

171(5)   **[Limit re contravention of sec. 166]**   Without prejudice to any liability under section 166 above, a person shall not be regarded as having contravened section 159 or 160 above by reason only of a prospectus not having fully complied with the requirements of this Part of this Act as to its form and content.

171(6)   **[Persons who may sue re contravention]**   Any contravention to which this section applies shall be actionable at the suit of a person who suffers loss as a result of the contravention subject to the defences and other incidents applying to actions for breach of statutory duty.

PART VI — TAKEOVER OFFERS

SEC. 172   Takeover offers

172(1)   **[Substitution of sec. 428–430 of Companies Act 1985]**   The provisions set out in Schedule 12 of this Act shall be substituted for sections 428, 429 and 430 of the Companies Act 1985.

172(2)   **[Exception re sec. 172(1)]**   Subsection (1) above does not affect any case in which the offer in respect of the scheme or contract mentioned in section 428(1) was made before the coming into force of this section.

PART VII — INSIDER DEALING

SEC. 173   Information obtained in official capacity: public bodies etc.

173(1)   **[Substitution in sec. 2 of Company Securities (Insider Dealing) Act 1985]**   In section 2 of the Company Securities (Insider Dealing) Act 1985 (abuse of information obtained by Crown servants in official capacity) for the word "Crown" wherever it occurs there shall be substituted the word "public".

173(2)   **[Addition of sec. 2(4)]**   At the end of that section there shall be added—

> "2(4)   **'Public servant'** means—

> (a)   a Crown servant;

(b) a member, officer or servant of a designated agency, competent authority or transferee body (within the meaning of the Financial Services Act 1986);

(c) an officer or servant of a recognised self-regulating organisation, recognised investment exchange or recognised clearing house (within the meaning of that Act);

(d) any person declared by an order for the time being in force under subsection (5) to be a public servant for the purposes of this section.

2(5) If it appears to the Secretary of State that the members, officers or employees of or persons otherwise connected with any body appearing to him to exercise public functions may have access to unpublished price sensitive information relating to securities, he may by order declare that those persons are to be public servants for the purposes of this section.

2(6) The power to make an order under subsection (5) shall be exercisable by statutory instrument and an instrument containing such an order shall be subject to annulment in pursuance of a resolution of either House of Parliament."

SEC. 174 Market makers, off-market dealers etc.

174(1) **[Insertion in sec. 3(1) of Company Securities (Insider Dealing) Act 1985]** In subsection (1) of section 3 of the Company Securities (Insider Dealing) Act 1985 (actions not prohibited by sections 1 and 2 of that Act) at the end of paragraph (c) there shall be inserted the words "; or

(d) doing any particular thing in relation to any particular securities if the information—

(i) was obtained by him in the course of a business of a market maker in those securities in which he was engaged or employed, and

(ii) was of a description which it would be reasonable to expect him to obtain in the ordinary course of that business.

and he does that thing in good faith in the course of that business".

174(2) **[Further insertion in sec. 3(1)]** At the end of that subsection there shall be inserted—

"'**Market maker**' means a person (whether an individual, partnership or company) who—

(a) holds himself out at all normal times in compliance with the rules of a recognised stock exchange as willing to buy and sell securities at prices specified by him; and

(b) is recognised as doing so by that recognised stock exchange.".

174(3) **[Insertion of sec. 4(2)]** The existing provisions of section 4 of that Act (off-market deals in advertised securities) shall become subsection (1) of that section and after that subsection there shall be inserted—

"**4(2)** In its application by virtue of this section the definition of 'market maker' in section 3(1) shall have effect as if the references to a recognised stock exchange were references to a recognised investment exchange (other than an overseas investment exchange) within the meaning of the Financial Services Act 1986.".

174(4)   [Amendments to sec. 13]   In section 13 of that Act—

(a) in subsection (1) (which defines dealing in securities and provides that references to dealing on a recognised stock exchange include dealing through an investment exchange) the words from "and references" onwards shall be omitted; and

(b) for subsection (3) (definition of off-market dealer) there shall be substituted—

> "**13(3)   'Off-market dealer'** means a person who is an authorised person within the meaning of the Financial Services Act 1986.".

SEC. 175   Price stabilisation

175   For section 6 of the Company Securities (Insider Dealing) Act 1985 (international bonds) there shall be substituted—

> "*Price stabilisation*

> **6(1)**   No provision of section 1, 2, 4 or 5 prohibits an individual from doing anything for the purpose of stabilising the price of securities if it is done in conformity with rules made under section 48 of the Financial Services Act 1986 and—

> (a) in respect of securities which fall within any of paragraphs 1 to 5 of Schedule 1 to that Act and are specified by the rules; and

> (b) during such period before or after the issue of those securities as is specified by the rules.

> **6(2)**   Any order under subsection (8) of section 48 of that Act shall apply also in relation to subsection (1) of this section.".

SEC. 176   Contracts for differences by reference to securities

176   After subsection (1) of section 13 of the Company Securities (Insider Dealing) Act 1985 (definition of dealing in securities), there shall be inserted—

> "**13(1A)**   For the purposes of this Act a person who (whether as principal or agent) buys or sells or agrees to buy or sell investments within paragraph 9 of Schedule 1 to the Financial Services Act 1986 (contracts for differences etc.) where the purpose or pretended purpose mentioned in that paragraph is to secure a profit or avoid a loss wholly or partly by reference to fluctuations in the value or price of securities shall be treated as if he were dealing in those securities.".

SEC. 177   Investigations into insider dealing

177(1)   [Power of Secretary of State to appoint inspectors]   If it appears to the Secretary of State that there are circumstances suggesting that there may have been a contravention of section 1, 2, 4 or 5 of the Company Securities (Insider Dealing) Act 1985, he may appoint one or more competent inspectors to carry out such investigations as are requisite to establish whether or not any such contravention has occurred and to report the results of their investigations to him.

177(2)   [Scope of appointment]   The appointment under this section of an inspector may limit the period during which he is to continue his investigation or confine it to particular matters.

177(2A)   [Variation of appointment]   At any time during the investigation the Secretary of State may vary the appointment by limiting or extending the period during which the inspector is to continue his investigation or by confining the investigation to particular matters.

History
S. 177(2A) inserted by CA 1989, s. 74(1), (2) as from
21 February 1990 (see S.I. 1990 No. 142 (C.5), art. 4).

177(3)   [Power of inspectors re production, attendance etc.]   If the inspectors consider that any person is or may be able to give information concerning any such contravention they may require that person—

   (a) to produce to them any documents in his possession or under his control relating to the company in relation to whose securities the contravention is suspected to have occurred or to its securities;

   (b) to attend before them; and

   (c) otherwise to give them all assistance in connection with the investigation which he is reasonably able to give;

and it shall be the duty of that person to comply with that requirement.

177(4)   [Power re examination under oath]   An inspector may examine on oath any person who he considers is or may be able to give information concerning any such contravention, and may administer an oath accordingly.

177(5)   [Reports to Secretary of State]   The inspectors shall make such interim reports to the Secretary of State as they think fit or he may direct and on the conclusion of the investigation they shall make a final report to him.

177(5A)   [Direction by Secretary of State]   If the Secretary of State thinks fit, he may direct the inspector to take no further steps in the investigation or to take only such further steps as are specified in the direction; and where an investigation is the subject of such a direction, the inspectors shall make a final report to the Secretary of State only where the Secretary of State directs them to do so.

History
S. 177(5A) inserted by CA 1989, s. 74(1), (3) as from
21 February 1990 (see S.I. 1990 No. 142 (C.5), art. 4).

177(6)   [Statement may be used in evidence]   A statement made by a person in compliance with a requirement imposed by virtue of this section may be used in evidence against him.

177(7)   [Legal professional privilege, confidentiality]   A person shall not under this section be required to disclose any information or produce any document which he would be entitled to refuse to disclose or produce on grounds of legal professional privilege in proceedings in the High Court or on grounds of confidentiality as between client and professional legal adviser in proceedings in the Court of Session.

177(8)   [Disclosure by bankers]   A person shall not under this section be required to disclose any information or produce any document in respect of which he owes an obligation of confidence by virtue of carrying on the business of banking unless—

   (a) the person to whom the obligation of confidence is owed consents to the disclosure or production, or

   (b) the making of the requirement was authorised by the Secretary of State.

History
S. 177(8) substituted by CA 1989, s. 74(1), (4) as from 21 February 1990 (see S.I. 1990 No. 142 (C. 5), art. 4); s. 177(8) formerly read as follows:

"**177(8)** Nothing in this section shall require a person carrying on the business of banking to disclose any information or produce any document relating to the affairs of a customer unless—

   (a) the customer is a person who the inspectors have reason to believe may be able to give information concerning a suspected contravention; and

   (b) the Secretary of State is satisfied that the disclosure or production is necessary for the purposes of the investigation."

177(9)   **[Where lien claimed]**   Where a person claims a lien on a document its production under this section shall be without prejudice to his lien.

177(10)   **["Document"]**   In this section **"document"** includes information recorded in any form; and in relation to information recorded otherwise than in legible form the power to require its production includes power to require the production of a copy of the information in legible form.

History
In s. 177(10) the words "the power to require its production includes power to require the production of" substituted for the former words "references to its production include references to producing" by CA 1989, s. 74(1), (5) as from 21 February 1990 (see S.I. 1990 No. 142 (C. 5), art. 4).

177(11)   **[Expenses]**   A person who is convicted on a prosecution instituted as a result of an investigation under this section my in the same proceedings be ordered to pay the expenses of the investigation to such extent as may be specified in the order.

    There shall be treated as expenses of the investigation, in particular, such reasonable sums as the Secretary of State may determine in respect of general staff costs and overheads.

History
S. 177(11) added by CA 1989, s. 74(1), (6) as from 21 February 1990 (see S.I. 1990 No. 142 (C. 5), art. 4).

SEC. 178   Penalties for failure to co-operate with sec. 177 investigations

178(1)   **[Certificate to court re refusal to co-operate]**   if any person—

   (a) refuses to comply with any request under subsection (3) of section 177 above; or

   (b) refuses to answer any question put to him by the inspectors appointed under that section with respect to any matter relevant for establishing whether or not any suspected contravention has occurred,

the inspectors may certify that fact in writing to the court and the court may inquire into the case.

178(2)   **[Power of court]**   If, after hearing any witness who may be produced against or on behalf of the alleged offender and any statement which may be offered in defence, the court is satisfied that he did without reasonable excuse refuse to comply with such a request or answer any such question, the court may—

   (a) punish him in like manner as if he had been guilty of contempt of the court; or

   (b) direct that the Secretary of State may exercise his powers under this section in respect of him;

and the court may give a direction under paragraph (b) above notwithstanding that the offender is not within the jurisdiction of the court if the court is satisfied that he was notified of his right to appear before the court and of the powers available under this section.

178(3) **[Power of Secretary of State re authorised person on sec. 178(2)(b) direction]** Where the court gives a direction under subsection (2)(b) above in respect of an authorised person the Secretary of State may serve a notice on him—

(a) cancelling any authorisation of his to carry on investment business after the expiry of a specified period after the service of the notice;

(b) disqualifying him from becoming authorised to carry on investment business after the expiry of a specified period;

(c) restricting any authorisation of his in respect of investment business during a specified period to the performance of contracts entered into before the notice comes into force;

(d) prohibiting him from entering into transactions of a specified kind or entering into them except in specified circumstances or to a specified extent;

(e) prohibiting him from soliciting business from persons of a specified kind or otherwise than from such persons; or

(f) prohibiting him from carrying on business in a specified manner or otherwise than in a specified manner.

178(4) **[Period in sec. 178(3)(a)–(c)]** The period mentioned in paragraphs (a) and (c) of subsection (3) above shall be such period as appears to the Secretary of State reasonable to enable the person on whom the notice is served to complete the performance of any contracts entered into before the notice comes into force and to terminate such of them as are of a continuing nature.

178(5) **[Power of Secretary of State re unauthorised person on sec. 178(2)(b) direction]** Where the court gives a direction under subsection (2)(b) above in the case of an unauthorised person the Secretary of State may direct that any authorised person who knowingly transacts investment business of a specified kind, or in specified circumstances or to a specified extent, with or on behalf of that unauthorised person shall be treated as having contravened rules made under Chapter V of Part I of this Act or, in the case of a person who is an authorised person by virtue of his membership of a recognised self-regulating organisation or certification by a recognised professional body, the rules of that organisation or body.

178(6) **[Interpretation re reasonable excuse in sec. 178(2)]** A person shall not be treated for the purposes of subsection (2) above as having a reasonable excuse for refusing to comply with a request or answer a question in a case where the contravention or suspected contravention being investigated relates to dealing by him on the instructions or for the account of another person, by reason that at the time of the refusal—

(a) he did not know the identity of that other person; or

(b) he was subject to the law of a country or territory outside the United Kingdom which prohibited him from disclosing information relating to the dealing without the consent of that other person, if he might have obtained that consent or obtained exemption from that law.

178(7) **[Revocation of sec. 178(3) above]** A notice served on a person under subsection (3) above may be revoked at any time by the Secretary of State by serving a revocation notice on him: and the Secretary of State shall revoke such a notice if it appears to him that he has agreed to comply with the relevant request or answer the relevant question.

178(8) **[Effect of revocation of sec. 178(3)(a) above]** The revocation of such a notice as is mentioned in subsection (3)(a) above shall not have the effect of reviving the authorisation cancelled by the notice except where the person would (apart from the notice) at the time of the revocation be an authorised person by virtue of his membership of a recognised self-regulating organisation or certification by a recognised professional body; but nothing in this subsection shall be construed as preventing any person who has been subject to such a notice from again becoming authorised after the revocation of the notice.

178(9) **[Service of notice on designated agency, recognised body]** If it appears to the Secretary of State—

(a) that a person on whom he serves a notice under subsection (3) above is an authorised person by virtue of an authorisation granted by a designated agency or by virtue of membership of a recognised self-regulating organisation or certificate by a recognised professional body; or

(b) that a person on whom he serves a revocation notice under subsection (7) above was such an authorised person at the time that the notice which is being revoked was served,

he shall serve a copy of the notice on that agency, organisation or body.

178(10) **[Functions for sec. 114]** The Functions to which section 114 above applies shall include the functions of the Secretary of State under this section but any transfer of those functions shall be subject to a reservation that they are to be exercisable by him concurrently with the designated agency and so as to be exercisable by the agency subject to such conditions or restrictions as the Secretary of State may from time to time impose.

PART VIII — RESTRICTIONS ON DISCLOSURE OF INFORMATION

SEC. 179 Restrictions on disclosure of information

179(1) **[No disclosure without consent]** Subject to section 180 below, information which is restricted information for the purposes of this section and relates to the business or other affairs of any person shall not be disclosed by a person mentioned in subsection (3) below ("the primary recipient") or any person obtaining the information directly or indirectly from him without the consent of the person from whom the primary recipient obtained the information and if different, the person to whom it relates.

179(2) **[Restricted information]** Subject to subsection (4) below, information is restricted information for the purposes of this section if it was obtained by the primary recipient for the purposes of, or in the discharge of his functions under, this

Act or any rules or regulations made under this Act (whether or not by virtue of any requirement to supply it made under those provisions).

179(3) **[Persons in sec. 179(1)]** The persons mentioned in subsection (1) above are—

(a) the Secretary of State;

(b) any designated agency, transferee body or body administering a scheme under section 54 above;

(c) the Director General of Fair Trading;

(d) the Chief Registrar of friendly societies;

(e) the Registrar of Friendly Societies for Northern Ireland;

(f) the Bank of England;

(g) any member of the Tribunal;

(h) any person appointed or authorised to exercise any powers under section 94, 106 or 177 above;

(i) any officer or servant of any such person as is mentioned in paragraphs (a) to (h) above;

(j) any constable or other person named in a warrant issued under this Act.

History
In s. 179(3) the word "and" formerly preceding para. (i) omitted and repealed by CA 1989, s. 75(1)(a), 212 and Sch. 24 and in para. (i) the words "as is mentioned in paragraphs (a) to (h) above" and para. (j) inserted by CA 1989, s. 75(1)(b), (c) as from 21 February 1990 (see S.I. 1990 No. 142 (C. 5), art. 4, 7(d)).

179(4) **[Information not to be treated as restricted]** Information shall not be treated as restricted information for the purposes of this section if it has been made available to the public by virtue of being disclosed in any circumstances in which or for any purpose for which disclosure is not precluded by this section.

179(5) **[Information obtained by competent authority]** Subject to section 180 below, information obtained by the competent authority in the exercise of its functions under Part IV of this Act or received by it pursuant to a Community obligation from any authority exercising corresponding functions in another member State shall not be disclosed without the consent of the person from whom the competent authority obtained the information and, if different, the person to whom it relates.

179(6) **[Offence, penalty]** Any person who contravenes this section shall be guilty of an offence and liable—

(a) on conviction on indictment, to imprisonment for a term not exceeding two years or to a fine or to both;

(b) on summary conviction, to imprisonment for a term not exceeding three months or to a fine not exceeding the statutory maximum or to both.

SEC. 180 Exceptions from restrictions on disclosure

180(1) **[Disclosures not precluded by sec. 179]** Section 179 above shall not preclude the disclosure of information—

(a) with a view to the institution of or otherwise for the purposes of criminal proceedings;

(b) with a view to the institution of or otherwise for the purposes of any civil proceedings arising under or by virtue of this Act or proceedings before the Tribunal;

(c) for the purpose of enabling or assisting the Secretary of State to exercise any powers conferred on him by this Act or by the enactments relating to companies, insurance companies or insolvency or by Part II, III or VII of the Companies Act 1989 or for the purpose of enabling or assisting any inspector appointed by him under the enactments relating to companies to discharge his functions;

(d) for the purpose of enabling or assisting the Department of Economic Development for Northern Ireland to exercise any powers conferred on it by the enactments relating to companies or insolvency or for the purpose of enabling or assisting any inspector appointed by it under the enactments relating to companies to discharge his functions;

(e) for the purpose—

   (i) of enabling or assisting a designated agency to discharge its functions under this Act or Part VII of the Companies Act 1989,

   (ii) of enabling or assisting a transferee body or the competent authority to discharge its functions under this Act, or

   (iii) of enabling or assisting the body administering a scheme under section 54 above to discharge its functions under the scheme;

(f) for the purpose of enabling or assisting the Bank of England to discharge its functions under the Banking Act 1987 or any other functions;

(g) for the purpose of enabling or assisting the Deposit Protection Board to discharge its functions under that Act;

(h) for the purpose of enabling or assisting the Chief Registrar of friendly societies or the Registrar of Friendly Societies for Northern Ireland to discharge his functions under this Act or under the enactments relating to friendly societies or building societies;

(hh) for the purpose of enabling or assisting a body established by order under section 46 of the Companies Act 1989 to discharge its functions under Part II of that Act, or of enabling or assisting a recognised supervisory or qualifying body within the meaning of that Part to discharge its functions as such;

(i) for the purpose of enabling or assisting the Industrial Assurance Commissioner or the Industrial Assurance Commissioner for Northern Ireland to discharge his functions under the enactments relating to industrial assurance;

(j) for the purpose of enabling or assisting the Insurance Brokers Registration Council to discharge its functions under the Insurance Brokers (Registration) Act 1977;

CCH Editions Limited
BCL BCLFS$$$24

(k) for the purpose of enabling or assisting an offical receiver to discharge his functions under the enactments relating to insolvency or for the purpose of enabling or assisting a body which is for the time being a recognised professional body for the purposes of section 391 of the Insolvency Act 1986 to discharge its functions as such;

(l) for the purpose of enabling or assisting the Building Societies Commission to discharge its functions under the Building Societies Act 1986;

(m) for the purpose of enabling or assisting the Director General of Fair Trading to discharge his functions under this Act;

(n) for the purpose of enabling or assisting a recognised self-regulating organisation, recognised investment exhange, recognised professional body, or recognised clearing house to discharge its functions as such;

(o) with a view to the institution of, or otherwise for the purposes of, any disciplinary proceedings relating to the exercise by a solicitor, auditor, accountant, valuer or actuary of his professional duties;

(oo) with a view to the institution of, or otherwise for the purposes of, any disciplinary proceedings relating to the discharge by a public servant of his duties;

(p) for the purpose of enabling or assisting any person appointed or authorised to exercise any powers under section 44 of the Insurance Companies Act 1982, section 447 of the Companies Act 1985, section 94, 106 or 177 above or section 84 of the Companies act 1989 to discharge his functions;

(q) for the purpose of enabling or assisting an auditor of an authorised person or a person approved under section 108 above to discharge his functions;

(qq) for the purpose of enabling or assisting an overseas regulatory authority to exercise its regulatory functions;

(r) if the information is or has been available to the public from other sources;

(s) in a summary or collection of information framed in such a way as not to enable the identity of any person to whom the information relates to be ascertained; or

(t) in pursuance of any Community obligation.

History

In s. 180(1)(c) the words "or by Part II, III or VII of the Companies Act 1989" inserted by CA 1989, s. 75(2), (3)(a) as from 21 February 1990 except in regard to the reference to Pt. VII (see S.I. 1990 No. 142 (C. 5), art. 4(b)).

S. 180(1)(e) substituted by CA 1989, s. 75(2), (3)(b) as from 21 February 1990 except in regard to the reference to Pt. VII (see S.I. 1990 No. 142 (C. 5), art. 4(b)); s. 180(1)(e) formerly read as follows:

"(e) for the purpose of enabling or assisting a designated agency or transferee body or the competent authority to discharge its functions under this Act or of enabling or assisting the body administering a scheme under section 54 above to discharge its functions under the scheme".

In s. 180(1)(f) the words "Banking Act 1987" substituted for the former words "Banking Act 1979" by Banking Act

1987, s. 108(1) and Sch. 6, para. 27(3) as from 1 October 1987 (see S.I. 1987 No. 1664 (C. 50)).

S. 180(1)(hh) inserted by CA 1989, s. 75(2), (3)(c) as from 21 February 1990 except in regard to the reference to a body established by an order under CA 1989, s. 46 (see S.I. 1990 No. 142 (C. 5), art. 4(a)).

S. 180(1)(oo) inserted by CA 1989, s. 75(2), (3)(d) as from 25 January 1990 (see S.I. 1990 No. 98 (C. 2), art. 2(a), (b)).

In s. 180(1)(p) the words "section 44 of the Insurance Companies Act 1982, section 447 of the Companies Act 1985," and "or section 84 of the Companies Act 1989" inserted by CA 1989, s. 75(2), (3)(e) as from 21 February 1990 (see S.I. 1990 No. 142 (C. 5), art. 4).

S. 180(1)(qq) inserted by CA 1989,s. 75(2), (3)(f) as from 21 February 1990 (see S.I. 1990 No. 142 (C. 5), art. 4).

180(1A)   [Definitions]   In subsection (1)—

(a) in paragraph (oo) **"public servant"** means an officer or servant of the Crown or of any public or other authority for the time being designated for the purposes of that paragraph by order of the Secretary of State; and

(b) in paragraph (qq) **"overseas regulatory authority"** and **"regulatory functions"** have the same meaning as in section 82 of the Companies Act 1989.

History
S. 180(1A) inserted by CA 1989, s. 75(2), (4) as from 25 January 1990 in regard to the "public servant" definition (see S.I. 1990 No. 98 (C. 2), art. 2(a), (b)) and as from 21 February 1990 in regard to the other definitions (see S.I. 1990 No. 142 (C. 5), art. 4).

180(2)   [Disclosure to Secretary of State or Treasury]   Section 179 above shall not preclude the disclosure of information to the Secretary of State or to the Treasury if the disclosure is made in the interests of investors or in the public interest.

180(3)   [Disclosures assisting public authorities etc.]   Subject to subsection (4) below, section 179 above shall not preclude the disclosure of information for the purpose of enabling or assisting any public or other authority for the time being designated for the purposes of this subsection by an order made by the Secretary of State to discharge any functions which are specified in the order.

History
In s. 180(3) the words "designated for the purposes of this subsection" substituted for the former words "designated for the purposes of this section" by CA 1989, s. 75(2), (5) as from 21 February 1990 (see S.I. 1990 No. 142 (C. 5), art. 4).

180(4)   [Scope of sec. 180(3) order]   An order under subsection (3) above designating an authority for the purposes of that subsection may—

(a) impose conditions subject to which the disclosure of information is permitted by that subsection; and

(b) otherwise restrict the circumstances in which that subsection permits disclosure.

180(5)   [Further disclosures not precluded by sec. 179]   Section 179 above shall not preclude the disclosure—

(a) of any information contained in an unpublished report of the Tribunal which has been made available to any person under this Act, by the person to whom it was made available or by any person obtaining the information directly or indirectly from him;

(b) of any information contained in any notice or copy of a notice served under this Act, notice of the contents of which has not been given to the public, by the person on whom it was served or any person obtaining the information directly or indirectly from him;

(c) of any information contained in the register kept under section 102 above by virtue of subsection (1)(e) of that section, by a person who has inspected the register under section 103(2) or (3) above or any person obtaining the information directly or indirectly from him.

180(6)   (Omitted and repealed by Companies Act 1989, sec. 75(2), (6), 212 and Sch. 24 as from 21 February 1990.)

FSA 1986, sec. 180(1A)

History
In regard to the date of the above omission and repeal see
S.I. 1990 No. 142 (C. 5), art. 4, 7(d); s. 180(6) formerly
read as follows:

"**180(6)** Section 179 above shall not preclude the disclosure
of information for the purpose of enabling or assisting an
authority in a country or territory outside the United
Kingdom to exercise functions corresponding to those of
the Secretary of State under this Act or the Insurance
Companies Act 1982 or to those of the Bank of England

under the Banking Act 1987 or to those of the competent
authority under this Act or any other functions in connection
with rules of law corresponding to the provisions of the
Company Securities (Insider Dealing) Act 1985 or Part VII
of this Act."

Previously the words "Banking Act 1987" substituted for
the former words "Banking Act 1979" by Banking Act
1987, s. 108(1) and Sch. 6, para. 27(3) as from 1 October
1987 (see S.I. 1987 No. 1664 (C. 50)).

180(7) **[Disclosures by Director General of Fair Trading]** Section 179 above shall
not preclude the disclosure of information by the Director General of Fair Trading
or any officer or servant of his or any person obtaining the information directly or
indirectly from the Director or any such officer or servant if the information was
obtained by the Director or any such officer or servant for the purposes of or in the
discharge of his functions under this Act (whether or not he was the primary recipient
of the information within the meaning of section 179 above) and the disclosure is
made—

(a) for the purpose of enabling or assisting the Director, the Secretary of State
or any other Minister, the Monopolies and Mergers Commission or any
Northern Ireland department to discharge any function conferred on him
or them by the Fair Trading Act 1973 (other than Part II or III of that Act),
the Restrictive Trade Practices Act 1976 or the Competition Act 1980; or

(b) for the purposes of any civil proceedings under any of those provisions;

and information shall not be treated as restricted information for the purposes of
section 179 above if it has been made available to the public by virtue of this
subsection.

180(8) **[Modification by Secretary of State]** The Secretary of State may by order
modify the application of any provision of this section so as—

(a) to prevent the disclosure by virtue of that provision; or

(b) to restrict the extent to which disclosure is permitted by virtue of that
provision,

of information received by a person specified in the order pursuant to a Community
obligation from a person exercising functions in relation to a collective investment
scheme who is also so specified.

180(9) **[Annulment of sec. 180(1A)(a), (3), (8) order by Parliament]** An order
under subsection (1A)(a), (3) or (8) above shall be subject to annulment in pursuance
of a resolution of either House of Parliament.

History
In s. 180(9) the words "subsection (1A)(a), (3) or (8)"
substituted for the former words "subsection (3) or (8)" by

CA 1989, s. 75(2), (7) as from 25 January 1990 (see S.I.
1990 No. 98 (C. 2), art. 2(a), (b)).

SEC. 181 Directions restricting disclosure of information overseas

181(1) **[Power of Secretary of State]** If it appears to the Secretary of State to be in
the public interest to do so, he may give a direction prohibiting the disclosure to any
person in a country or territory outside the United Kingdom which is specified in the
direction, or to such persons in such a country or territory as may be so specified, of
such information to which this section applies as may be so specified.

181(2)   **[Extent of sec. 181(1) direction]**   A direction under subsection (1) above—

(a)   may prohibit disclosure of the information to which it applies by all persons or only by such persons or classes of person as may be specified in it; and

(b)   may prohibit such disclosure absolutely or in such cases or subject to such conditions as to consent or otherwise as may be specified in it;

and a direction prohibiting disclosure by all persons shall be published by the Secretary of State in such manner as appears to him to be appropriate.

181(3)   **[Application of section]**   This section applies to any information relating to the business or other affairs of any person which was obtained (whether or not by virtue of any requirement to supply it) directly or indirectly—

(a)   by a designated agency, a transferee body, the competent authority or any person appointed or authorised to exercise any powers under section 94, 106 or 177 above (or any officer or servant of any such body or person) for the purposes or in the discharge of any functions of that body or person under this Act or any rules or regulations made under this Act or of any monitoring agency functions; or

(b)   by a recognised self-regulating organisation, a recognised professional body, a recognised investment exchange or a recognised clearing house other than an overseas investment exchange or clearing house (or any officer or servant of such an organisation, body, investment exchange or clearing house) for the purposes or in the discharge of any of its functions as such or of any monitoring agency functions.

181(4)   **["Monitoring agency functions" in sec. 181(3)]**   In subsection (3) above **"monitoring agency functions"** means any functions exercisable on behalf of another body by virtue of arrangements made pursuant to paragraph 4(2) of Schedule 2, paragraph 4(6) of Schedule 3, paragraph 3(2) of Schedule 4 or paragraph 3(2) of Schedule 7 to this Act or of such arrangements as are mentioned in section 39(4)(b) above.

181(5)   **[Disclosures not prohibited]**   A direction under this section shall not prohibit the disclosure by any person other than a person mentioned in subsection (3) above of—

(a)   information relating only to the affairs of that person; or

(b)   information obtained by that person otherwise than directly or indirectly from a person mentioned in subsection (3) above.

181(6)   **[Disclosures under Community obligations]**   A direction under this section shall not prohibit the disclosure of information in pursuance of any Community obligation.

181(7)   **[Offence, penalty]**   A person who knowingly discloses information in contravention of a direction under this section shall be guilty of an offence and liable—

(a)   on conviction on indictment, to imprisonment for a term not exceeding two years or to a fine or to both;

(b)   on summary conviction, to imprisonment for a term not exceeding three months or to a fine not exceeding the statutory maximum or to both.

181(8) **[Exception re offence]** A person shall not be guilty of an offence under this section by virtue of anything done or omitted to be done by him outside the United Kingdom unless he is a British citizen, a British Dependent Territories citizen, a British Overseas citizen or a body corporate incorporated in the United Kingdom.

SEC. 182 Disclosure of information under enactments relating to fair trading, banking, insurance and companies

182 The enactments mentioned in Schedule 13 to this Act shall have effect with the amendments there specified (which relate to the circumstances in which information obtained under those enactments may be disclosed).

PART IX — RECIPROCITY

SEC. 183 Reciprocal facilities for financial business

183(1) **[Power of Secretary of State, Treasury to serve notice]** If it appears to the Secretary of State or the Treasury that by reason of—

(a) the law of any country outside the United Kingdom; or

(b) any action taken by or the practices of the government or any other authority or body in that country,

persons connected with the United Kingdom are unable to carry on investment, insurance or banking business in, or in relation to, that country on terms as favourable as those on which persons connected with that country are able to carry on any such business in, or in relation to, the United Kingdom, the Secretary of State or, as the case may be, the Treasury may serve a notice under this subsection on any person connected with that country who is carrying on or appears to them to intend to carry on any such business in, or in relation to, the United Kingdom.

183(2) **[Conditions for service of sec. 183(1) notice]** No notice shall be served under subsection (1) above unless the Secretary of State or, as the case may be, the Treasury consider it in the national interest to serve it; and before doing so the Secretary of State or, as the case may be, the Treasury shall so far as they consider expedient consult such body or bodies as appear to them to represent the interests of persons likely to be affected.

183(3) **[Contents, date of notice]** A notice under subsection (1) above shall state the grounds on which it is given (identifying the country in relation to which those grounds are considered to exist); and any such notice shall come into force on such date as may be specified in it.

183(4) **[Connection with a country—interpretation]** For the purposes of this section a person is connected with a country if it appears to the Secretary of State or, as the case may be, the Treasury—

(a) in the case of an individual, that he is a national of or resident in that country or carries on investment, insurance or banking business from a principal place of business there;

(b) in the case of a body corporate, that it is incorporated or has a principal place of business in that country or is controlled by a person or persons connected with that country;

(c) in the case of a partnership, that it has a principal place of business in that country or that any partner is connected with that country;

(d) in the case of an unincorporated association which is not a partnership, that it is formed under the law of that country, has a principal place of business there or is controlled by a person or persons connected with that country.

183(5) **["Country"]** In this section **"country"** includes any territory or part of a country or territory; and where it appears to the Secretary of State or, as the case may be, the Treasury that there are such grounds as are mentioned in subsection (1) above in the case of any part of a country or territory their powers under that subsection shall also be exercisable in respect of any person who is connected with that country or territory or any other part of it.

SEC. 184   Investment and insurance business

184(1) **[Extent of sec. 183 notice]** A notice under section 183 above relating to the carrying on of investment business or insurance business shall be served by the Secretary of State and such a notice may be a disqualification notice, a restriction notice or a partial restriction notice and may relate to the carrying on of business of both kinds.

184(2) **[Effects of disqualification notice]** A disqualification notice as respects investment business or insurance business shall have the effect of—

(a) cancelling any authorisation of the person concerned to carry on that business after the expiry of such period after the service of the notice as may be specified in it;

(b) disqualifying him from becoming authorised to carry on that business after the expiry of that period; and

(c) restricting any authorisation of the person concerned in respect of that business during that period to the performance of contracts entered into before the notice comes into force;

and the period specified in such a notice shall be such period as appears to the Secretary of State to be reasonable to enable the person on whom it is served to complete the performance of those contracts and to terminate such of them as are of a continuing nature.

184(3) **[Effect of restriction notice]** A restriction notice as respects investment business or insurance business shall have the effect of restricting any authorisation of the person concerned in respect of that business to the performance of contracts entered into before the notice comes into force.

184(4) **[Effect of partial restriction notice]** A partial restriction notice as respects investment business may prohibit the person concerned from—

(a) entering into transactions of any specified kind or entering into them except in specified circumstances or to a specified extent;

(b) soliciting business from persons of a specified kind or otherwise than from such persons;

FSA 1986, sec. 183(5)

(c) carrying on business in a specified manner or otherwise than in a specified manner.

184(5)   [Effect of partial restriction notice re insurance business]   A partial restriction notice as respects insurance business may direct that the person concerned shall cease to be authorised under section 3 or 4 of the Insurance Companies Act 1982 to effect contracts of insurance of any description specified in the notice.

184(6)   [Copy of notice on designated agency, recognised body]   If it appears to the Secretary of State that a person on whom he serves a notice under section 183 above as respects investment business is an authorised person by virtue of an authorisation granted by a designated agency or by virtue of membership of a recognised self-regulating organisation or certification by a recognised professional body he shall serve a copy of the notice on that agency, organisation or body.

184(7)   [Power of Secretary of State re certain contraventions]   If it appears to the Secretary of State—

(a) that any person on whom a partial restriction notice has been served by him has contravened any provision of that notice or, in the case of a notice under subsection (5) above, effected a contract of insurance of a description specified in the notice; and

(b) that any such grounds as are mentioned in subsection (1) of section 183 above still exist in the case of the country concerned,

he may serve a disqualification notice or a restriction notice on him under that section.

184(8)   [Effect of sec. 28, 33, 60, 61, 62 re sec. 185(4) contravention]   Sections 28, 33, 60, 61 and 62 above shall have effect in relation to a contravention of such a notice as is mentioned in subsection (4) above as they have effect in relation to any such contravention as is mentioned in those sections.

SEC. 185   Banking business

185(1)   [Service of sec. 183 notice re banks]   A notice under section 183 above relating to the carrying on of a deposit-taking business as an authorised institution within the meaning of the Banking Act 1987 shall be served by the Treasury and may be either a disqualification notice or a partial restriction notice.

History
In s. 185(1) the words, "an authorised institution within the meaning of the Banking Act 1987", substituted for the former words, "a recognised bank or licensed institution within the meaning of the Banking Act 1979", by Banking Act 1987, s. 108(1) and Sch. 6, para. 27(4)(a) as from 1 October 1987 (see S.I. 1987 No. 1664 (C. 50)).

185(2)   [Effect of disqualification notice]   A disqualification notice relating to such business shall have the effect of—

(a) cancelling any authorisation granted to the person concerned under the Banking Act 1987; and

(b) disqualifying him from becoming an authorised institution within the meaning of that Act.

History
In s. 185(2) the words, "authorisation", "Banking Act 1987", and, "an authorised institution", substituted for the former words, "recognition or licence", "Banking Act 1979", and, "a recognised bank or licensed institution", by Banking Act 1987, s. 108(1) and Sch. 6, para. 27(4)(b) as from 1 October 1987 (see S.I. 1987 No. 1664 (C. 50)).

185(3)   [Effect of partial restriction notice]   A partial restriction notice relating to such business may—

(a) prohibit the person concerned from dealing with or disposing of his assets in any manner specified in the direction;

(b) impose limitations on the acceptance by him of deposits;

(c) prohibit him from soliciting deposits either generally or from persons who are not already depositors;

(d) prohibit him from entering into any other transaction or class of transactions;

(e) require him to take certain steps, to pursue or refrain from pursuing a particular course of activities or to restrict the scope of his business in a particular way.

185(4) [Copy of sec. 183 notice to Bank of England] The Treasury shall serve on the bank of England a copy of any notice served by them under section 183 above.

185(5) [Offence, penalty re partial restriction notice] Any person who contravenes any provision of a partial restriction notice served on him by the Treasury under this section shall be guilty of an offence and liable—

(a) on conviction on indictment, to a fine;

(b) on summary conviction, to a fine not exceeding the statutory maximum.

185(6) [Persons who may sue] Any such contravention shall be actionable at the suit of a person who suffers loss as a result of the contravention subject to the defences and other incidents applying to actions for breach of statutory duty, but no such contravention shall invalidate any transaction.

185(7) (Repealed by the Banking Act 1987, sec. 108(2) and Sch. 7, Pt. I as from 1 October 1987.)

History
In regard to the date of the above repeal, see S.I. 1987 No. 1664 (C. 50), art. 2 and Sch.

S. 185(7) formerly read as follows:

"**185(7)** At the end of subsection (1) of section 8 of the Banking Act 1979 (power to give directions in connection with termination of deposit-taking authority) there shall be inserted—

'(d) at any time after a disqualification notice has been served on the institution by the Treasury under section 183 of the Financial Services Act 1986.'."

SEC. 186　Variation and revocation of notices

186(1) [Power to vary restriction notice] The Secretary of State or the Treasury may vary a partial restriction notice served under section 183 above by a notice in writing served on the person concerned; and any such notice shall come into force on such date as is specified in the notice.

186(2) [Revocation of sec. 183 notice] A notice under section 183 above may be revoked at any time by the Secretary of State or, as the case may be, the Treasury by serving a revocation notice on the person concerned; and the Secretary of State or, as the case may be, the Treasury shall revoke a notice if it appears to them that there are no longer any such grounds as are mentioned in subsection (1) of that section in the case of the country concerned.

186(3) [Effect of revocation of disqualification notice re investment, insurance business] The revocation of a disqualification notice as respects investment business or insurance business shall not have the effect of reviving the authorisation which was cancelled by the notice except where the notice relates to investment business and the person concerned would (apart from the disqualification notice) at the time of the revocation be an authorised person as respects the investment business in question by virtue of his membership of a recognised self-regulating organisation or certification by a recognised professional body.

186(4)   [Effect of revocation of disqualification notice re banking business]   The revocation of a disqualification notice as respects banking business shall not have the effect of reviving the authorisation which was cancelled by the notice.

History
In s. 186(4) the word, "authorisation", substituted for the   1987, s. 108(1) and Sch. 6, para. 27(5)(a) as from 1 October
former words, "recognition or licence", by Banking Act   1987 (see S.I. 1987 No. 1664 (C. 50)).

186(5)   [Limit on effect of sec. 186(3), (4)]   Nothing in subsection (3) or (4) above shall be construed as preventing any person who has been subject to a disqualification notice as respects any business from again becoming authorised after the revocation of the notice.

History
In s. 186(5) the words, "or, as the case may be, becoming a   repealed by Banking Act 1987, s. 108(1) and Sch. 6, para.
recognised bank or licensed institution within the meaning   27(5)(b) and s. 108(2) and Sch. 7, Pt. I as from 1 October
of the Banking Act 1979", formerly appearing after the   1987 (S.I. 1988 No. 1664 (C. 50), art. 2 and Sch.).
words, "from again becoming authorised", omitted and

186(6)   [If person served notice is authorised designated agency, recognised body]   If it appears to the Secretary of State that a person on whom he serves a notice under this section as respects investment business was an authorised person by virtue of an authorisation granted by a designated agency or by virtue of membership of a recognised self-regulating organisation or certification by a recognised professional body at the time that the notice which is being varied or revoked was served, he shall serve a copy of the notice on that agency, organisation or body.

186(7)   [Copy of notice to Bank of England]   The Treasury shall serve on the Bank of England a copy of any notice served by them under this section.

PART X — MISCELLANEOUS AND SUPPLEMENTARY

SEC. 187   Exemption from liability for damages

187(1)   [Limit on liability re SROs and members]   Neither a recognised self-regulating organisation nor any of its officers or servants or members of its governing body shall be liable in damages for anything done or omitted in the discharge or purported discharge of any functions to which this subsection applies unless the act or omission is shown to have been in bad faith.

187(2)   [Functions for sec. 187(1)]   The functions to which subsection (1) above applies are the functions of the organisation so far as relating to, or to matters arising out of—

(a)   the rules, practices, powers and arrangements of the organisation to which the requirements in paragraphs 1 to 6 of Schedule 2 to this Act apply;

(b)   the obligations with which paragraph 7 of that Schedule requires the organisation to comply;

(c)   any guidance issued by the organisation;

(d)   the powers of the organisation under section 53(2), 64(4), 72(5), 73(5) or 105(2)(a) above; or

(e) the obligations to which the organisation is subject by virtue of this Act.

187(3) **[Limit on liability of designated agency and members et al.]** No designated agency or transferee body nor any member, officer or servant of a designated agency or transferee body shall be liable in damages for anything done or omitted in the discharge or purported discharge of the functions exercisable by the agency by virtue of a delegation order or, as the case may be, the functions exercisable by the body by virtue of a transfer order unless the act or omission is shown to have been in bad faith.

187(4) **[Limit on liability of competent authority and members et al.]** Neither the competent authority nor any member, officer, or servant of that authority shall be liable in damages for anything done or omitted in the discharge or purported discharge of any functions of the authority under Part IV of this Act unless the act or omission is shown to have been in bad faith.

187(5) **[Functions included in sec. 187(1), (3)]** The functions to which subsections (1) and (3) above apply also include any functions exercisable by a recognised self-regulating organisation, designated agency or transferee body on behalf of another body by virtue of arrangements made pursuant to paragraph 4(2) of Schedule 2, paragraph 4(6) of Schedule 3, paragraph 3(2) of Schedule 4 or paragraph 3(2) of Schedule 7 to this Act or of such arrangements as are mentioned in section 39(4)(b) above.

187(6) **[Condition in certificate by recognised professional body]** A recognised professional body may make it a condition of any certificate issued by it for the purposes of Part I of this Act that neither the body nor any of its officers or servants or members of its governing body is to be liable in damages for anything done or omitted in the discharge or purported discharge of any functions to which this subsection applies unless the act or omission is shown to have been in bad faith.

187(7) **[Functions for sec. 187(6)]** The functions to which subsection (6) above applies are the functions of the body so far as relating to, or to matters arising out of—

(a) the rules, practices and arrangements of the body to which the requirements in paragraphs 2 to 5 of Schedule 3 to this Act apply;

(b) the obligations with which paragraph 6 of that Schedule requires the body to comply;

(c) any guidance issued by the body in respect of any matters dealt with by such rules as are mentioned in paragraph (a) above;

(d) the powers of the body under the provisions mentioned in subsection (2)(d) above or under section 54(3) above; or

(e) the obligations to which the body is subject by virtue of this Act.

SEC. 188   Jurisdiction of High Court and Court of Session

188(1) **[Proceedings in High Court, Court of Session]** Proceedings arising out of any act or omission (or proposed act or omission) of—

(a) a recognised self-regulating organisation,

(b) a designated agency,

(c) a transferee body, or

(d) the competent authority,

in the discharge or purported discharge of any of its functions under this Act may be brought in the High Court or the Court of Session.

188(2)   [Sec. 188(1) jurisdiction additional]   The jurisdiction conferred by subsection (1) is in addition to any other jurisdiction exercisable by those courts.

History
S. 188 substituted by CA 1989, s. 200(1) as from 15 March 1990 (see S.I. 1990 No. 354 (C. 12), art. 3); s. 188 formerly read as follows:

"**SEC. 188   Jurisdiction as respects actions concerning designated agency etc.**

188(1)   Proceedings arising out of any act or omission (or proposed act or omission) of a designated agency, transferee body or the competent authority in the discharge or purported discharge of any of its functions under this Act may be brought in the High Court or the Court of Session.

(2)   At the end of Schedule 5 to the Civil Jurisdiction and Judgments Act 1982 (exclusion of certain proceedings from the provisions of Schedule 4 to that Act which determine whether the courts in each part of the United Kingdom have jurisdiction in proceedings) there shall be inserted—

'Proceedings concerning financial services agencies

  10   Such proceedings as are mentioned in section 188 of the Financial Services Act 1986.'."

SEC. 189   Restriction of Rehabilitation of Offenders Act 1974

189(1)   [Effect of 1974 Act]   The Rehabilitation of Offenders Act 1974 shall have effect subject to the provisions of this section in cases where the spent conviction is for—

(a) an offence involving fraud or other dishonesty; or

(b) an offence under legislation (whether or not of the United Kingdom) relating to companies (including insider dealing), building societies, industrial and provident societies, credit unions, friendly societies, insurance, banking or other financial services, insolvency, consumer credit or consumer protection.

189(2)   [Limit to sec. 4(1) of 1974 Act]   Nothing in section 4(1) (restriction on evidence as to spent convictions in proceedings) shall prevent the determination in any proceedings specified in Part I of Schedule 14 to this Act of any issue, or prevent the admission or requirement in any such proceedings of any evidence, relating to a person's previous convictions for any such offence as is mentioned in subsection (1) above or to circumstances ancillary thereto.

189(3)   [Qualification re sec. 4(2) of 1974 Act]   A conviction for any such offence as is mentioned in subsection (1) above shall not be regarded as spent for the purposes of section 4(2) (questions relating to an individual's previous convictions) if—

(a) the question is put by or on behalf of a person specified in the first column of Part II of that Schedule and relates to an individual (whether or not the person questioned) specified in relation to the person putting the question in the second column of that Part; and

(b) the person questioned is informed when the question is put that by virtue of this section convictions for any such offence are to be disclosed.

189(4)   [Limit on sec. 4(3)(b) of 1974 Act]   Section 4(3)(b) (spent conviction not to be ground for excluding person from office, occupation etc.) shall not prevent a person specified in the first column of Part III of that Schedule from taking such action as is specified in relation to that person in the second column of that Part by reason, or partly by reason, of a spent conviction for any such offence as is mentioned in subsection (1) above of an individual who is—

(a) the person in respect of whom the action is taken;

(b) as respects action within paragraph 1 or 4 of that Part, an associate of that person; or

(c) as respects action within paragraph 1 of that Part consisting of a decision to refuse or revoke an order declaring a collective investment scheme to be an authorised unit trust scheme or a recognised scheme, the operator or trustee of the scheme or an associate of his,

or of any circumstances ancillary to such a conviction or of a failure (whether or not by that individual) to disclose such a conviction or any such circumstances.

189(5) [Sch. 14] Parts I, II and III of that Schedule shall have effect subject to Part IV.

189(6) ["Associate"] In this section and that Schedule **"associate"** means—

(a) in relation to a body corporate, a director, manager or controller;

(b) in relation to a partnership, a partner or manager;

(c) in relation to a registered friendly society, a trustee, manager or member of the committee of the society;

(d) in relation to an unincorporated association, a member of its governing body or an officer, manager or controller;

(e) in relation to an individual, a manager.

189(7) [Application to Northern Ireland] This section and that Schedule shall apply to Northern Ireland with the substitution for the references to the said Act of 1974 and section 4(1), (2) and (3)(b) of that Act of references to the Rehabilitation of Offenders (Northern Ireland) Order 1978 and Articles 5(1), (2) and (3)(b) of that Order.

SEC. 190   Data protection

190 An order under section 30 of the Data Protection Act 1984 (exemption from subject access provisions of data held for the purpose of discharging designated functions conferred by or under enactments relating to the regulation of financial services etc.) may designate for the purposes of that section as if they were functions conferred by or under such an enactment as is there mentioned—

(a) any functions of a recognised self-regulating organisation in connection with the admission or expulsion of members, the suspension of a person's membership or the supervision or regulation of persons carrying on investment business by virtue of membership of the organisation;

(b) any functions of a recognised professional body in connection with the issue of certificates for the purposes of Part I of this Act, the withdrawal or suspension of such certificates or the supervision or regulation of persons carrying on investment business by virtue of certification by that body;

(c) any functions of a recognised self-regulating organisation for friendly societies in connection with the supervision or regulation of its member societies.

SEC. 191 Occupational pension schemes

191(1) **[Person carrying on investment business]** Subject to the provisions of this section, a person who apart from this section would not be regarded as carrying on investment business shall be treated as doing so if he engages in the activity of management falling within paragraph 14 of Schedule 1 to this Act in a case where the assets referred to in that paragraph are held for the purposes of an occupational pension scheme.

191(2) **[Non-application of sec. 191(1)]** Subsection (1) above does not apply where all decisions, or all day to day decisions, in the carrying on of that activity so far as relating to assets which are investments are taken on behalf of the person concerned by—

(a) an authorised person;

(b) an exempted person who in doing so is acting in the course of the business in respect of which he is exempt; or

(c) a person who does not require authorisation to manage the assets by virtue of Part IV of Schedule 1 to this Act.

191(3) **[Order by Secretary of State]** The Secretary of State may by order direct that a person of such description as is specified in the order shall not by virtue of this section be treated as carrying on investment business where the assets are held for the purposes of an occupational pension scheme of such description as is so specified, being a scheme in the case of which it appears to the Secretary of State that management by an authorised or exempted person is unnecessary having regard to the size of the scheme and the control exercisable over its affairs by the members.

191(4) **[Annulment of Order by Parliament]** An order under subsection (3) above shall be subject to annulment in pursuance of a resolution of either House of Parliament.

191(5) **[Sch. 1, para. 14]** For the purposes of subsection (1) above paragraph 14 of Schedule 1 to this Act shall be construed without reference to paragraph 22 of that Schedule.

SEC. 192 International obligations

192(1) **[Power of direction by Secretary of State]** If it appears to the Secretary of State—

(a) that any action proposed to be taken by a recognised self-regulating organisation, designated agency, transferee body or competent authority would be incompatible with Community obligations or any other international obligations of the United Kingdom; or

(b) that any action which that organisation, agency, body or authority has power to take is required for the purpose of implementing any such obligations,

he may direct the organisation, agency, body or authority not to take or, as the case may be, to take the action in question.

192(2)   [Application of sec. 192(1) to approved exchange]   Subsection (1) above applies also to an approved exchange within the meaning of Part V of this Act in respect of any action which it proposes to take or has power to take in respect of rules applying to a prospectus by virtue of a direction under section 162(3) above.

192(3)   [Supplementary or incidental requirements]   A direction under this section may include such supplementary or incidental requirements as the Secretary of State thinks necessary or expedient.

192(4)   [Where designated agency relevant]   Where the function of making or revoking a recognition order in respect of a self-regulating organisation is exercisable by a designated agency any direction under subsection (1) above in respect of that organisation shall be a direction requiring the agency to give the organisation such a direction as is specified in the direction given by the Secretary of State.

192(5)   [Enforcement of direction]   Any direction under this section shall, on the application of the person by whom it was given, be enforceable by mandamus or, in Scotland, by an order for specific performance under section 91 of the Court of Session Act 1868.

SEC. 193   Exemption from Banking Act 1979

193   (Repealed by the Banking Act 1987, sec. 108(2) and Sch. 7, Pt. I as from 29 April 1988.)

History
In regard to the date of the above repeal, see S.I. 1988 No. 644 (C. 20), art. 2. S. 193 formerly read as follows:

"**193(1)**   Section 1(1) of the Banking Act 1979 (control of deposit-taking) shall not apply to the acceptance of a deposit by an authorised or exempted person in the course or for the purpose of engaging in any activity falling within paragraph 12 of Schedule 1 to this Act with or on behalf of the person by whom or on whose behalf the deposit is made or any activity falling within paragraph 13, 14 or 16 of that Schedule on behalf of that person.

193(2)   Subsection (1) above applies to an exempted person only if the activity is one in respect of which he is exempt; and for the purposes of that subsection the paragraphs of Schedule 1 there mentioned shall be construed without reference to Parts III and IV of that Schedule.

193(3)   This section is without prejudice to any exemption from the said Act of 1979 which applies to an authorised or exempted person apart from this section."

SEC. 194   Transfers to or from recognised clearing houses

194(1)   [Amendments in sec. 5 of Stock Exchange (Completion of Bargains) Act 1976]   In section 5 of the Stock Exchange (Completion of Bargains) Act 1976 (protection of trustees etc. in case of transfer of shares etc. to or from a stock exchange nominee)—

(a) for the words "a stock exchange nominee", in the first place where they occur, there shall be substituted the words "a recognised clearing house or a nominee of a recognised clearing house or of a recognised investment exchange";

(b) for those words in the second place where they occur there shall be substituted the words "such a clearing house or nominee";

(c) at the end there shall be added the words "; but no person shall be a nominee for the purposes of this section unless he is a person designated for the purposes of this section in the rules of the recognised investment exchange in question."

194(2)   [Insertion of sec. 5(2) of 1976 Act]   The provisions of that section as amended by subsection (1) above shall become subsection (1) of that section and after that subsection there shall be inserted—

"**5(2)** In this section **'a recognised clearing house'** means a recognised clearing house within the meaning of the Financial Services Act 1986 acting in relation to a recognised investment exchange within the meaning of that Act and **'a recognised investment exchange'** has the same meaning as in that Act."

194(3) [Amendments in art. 7 of Stock Exchange (Completion of Bargains) (Northern Ireland) Order 1977] In Article 7 of the Stock Exchange (Completion of Bargains) (Northern Ireland) Order 1977 (protection of trustees etc. in case of transfer of shares etc. to or from a stock exchange nominee)—

(a) for the words "a stock exchange nominee", in the first place where they occur, there shall be substituted the words "a recognised clearing house or a nominee of a recognised clearing house or of a recognised investment exchange";

(b) for those words in the second place where they occur there shall be substituted the words "such a clearing house or nominee";

(c) at the end there shall be added the words "; but no person shall be a nominee for the purposes of this Article unless he is a person designated for the purposes of this Article in the rules of the recognised investment exchange in question".

194(4) [Insertion of art. 7(2) of 1977 Order] The provisions of that Article as amended by subsection (3) above shall become paragraph (1) of that Article and after that paragraph there shall be inserted—

"**(2)** In this Article **'a recognised clearing house'** means a recognised clearing house within the meaning of the Financial Services Act 1986 acting in relation to a recognised investment exchange within the meaning of that Act and 'a recognised investment exchange' has the same meaning as in that Act."

194(5) [Amendments in sec. 185(4) of Companies Act 1985] In subsection (4) of section 185 of the Companies Act 1985 (exemption from duty to issue certificates in respect of shares etc. in cases of allotment or transfer to a stock exchange nominee)—

(a) for the words "stock exchange nominee" in the first place where they occur there shall be substituted the words "a recognised clearing house or a nominee of a recognised clearing house or of a recognised investment exchange";

(b) for those words in the second place where they occur there shall be substituted the words "such a clearing house or nominee";

(c) at the end of the first paragraph in that subsection there shall be inserted the words "; but no person shall be a nominee for the purposes of this section unless he is a person designated for the purposes of this section in the rules of the recognised investment exchange in question"; and

(d) for the second paragraph in that subsection there shall be substituted—

"'**Recognised clearing house'** means a recognised clearing house within the meaning of the Financial Services Act 1986 acting in relation to a recognised investment exchange and 'recognised investment exchange' has the same meaning as in that Act".

194(6) **[Amendments in art. 195(4) of Companies (Northern Ireland) Order 1986]** In paragraph (4) of Article 195 of the Companies (Northern Ireland) Order 1986 (duty to issue certificates in respect of shares etc. in cases of allotment or transfer unless it is to a stock exchange nominee)—

(a) for the words "a stock exchange nominee" in the first place where they occur there shall be substituted the words "a recognised clearing house or a nominee of a recognised clearing house or of a recognised investment exchange";

(b) for those words in the second place where they occur there shall be substituted the words "such a clearing house or nominee";

(c) at the end of the first sub-paragraph in that paragraph there shall be inserted the words "; but no person shall be a nominee for the purposes of this Article unless he is a person designated for the purposes of this Article in the rules of the recognised investment exchange in question"; and

(d) for the second sub-paragraph in that paragraph there shall be substituted "'**recognised clearing house**' means a recognised clearing house within the meaning of the Financial Services Act 1986 acting in relation to a recognised investment exchange and 'recognised investment exchange' has the same meaning as in that Act.".

SEC. 195   Offers of short-dated debentures

195   As respects debentures which, under the terms of issue, must be repaid within five years of the date of issue—

(a) section 79(2) of the Companies Act 1985 (offer of debentures of oversea company deemed not to be an offer to the public if made to professional investor) shall apply for the purposes of Chapter I of Part III of that Act as well as for those of Chapter II of that Part; and

(b) Article 89(2) of the Companies (Northern Ireland) Order 1986 (corresponding provisions for Northern Ireland) shall apply for the purposes of Chapter I of Part IV of that Order as well as for those of Chapter II of that Part.

History
In s. 195 the words "repaid within five years of the date of issue" substituted for the former words "repaid within less than one year of the date of issue" by CA 1989, s. 202 as from 16 November 1989 (see CA 1989, s. 215(1)(c)).

SEC. 196   Financial assistance for employees' share schemes

196(1) **[Amendment of sec. 153 of Companies Act 1985]** Section 153 of the Companies Act 1985 (transactions not prohibited by section 151) shall be amended as follows.

196(2) **[Insertion of sec. 153(4)(bb) of 1985 Act]** After subsection (4)(b) there shall be inserted—

"(bb) without prejudice to paragraph (b), the provision of financial assistance by a company or any of its subsidiaries for the purposes of or in connection with anything done by the company (or a company connected with it) for the purpose of enabling or facilitating transactions in shares in the first-mentioned company between, and involving the acquisition of beneficial ownership of those shares by, any of the following persons—

    (i) the bona fide employees or former employees of that company or of another company in the same group; or

    (ii) the wives, husbands, widows, widowers, children or step-children under the age of eighteen of any such employees or former employees.".

196(3)   **[Insertion of sec. 153(5) of 1985 Act]**   After subsection (4) there shall be inserted—

    "**153(5)**   For the purposes of subsection (4)(bb) a company is connected with another company if—

      (a) they are in the same group; or

      (b) one is entitled, either alone or with any other company in the same group, to exercise or control the exercise of a majority of the voting rights attributable to the share capital which are exercisable in all circumstances at any general meeting of the other company or of its holding company;

    and in this section '**group**', in relation to a company, means that company, any other company which is its holding company or subsidiary and any other company which is a subsidiary of that holding company.".

196(4)   **[Amendment of art. 163 of Companies (Northern Ireland) Order 1986]**   Article 163 of the Companies (Northern Ireland) Order 1986 (transactions not prohibited by Article 161) shall be amended as follows.

196(5)   **[Insertion of art. 163 (4)(bb) of 1986 Order]**   After paragraph (4)(b) there shall be inserted—

    "(bb) without prejudice to sub-paragraph (b), the provision of financial assistance by a company or any of its subsidiaries for the purposes of or in connection with anything done by the company (or a company connected with it) for the purpose of enabling or facilitating transactions in shares in the first-mentioned company between, and involving the acquisition of beneficial ownership of those shares by, any of the following persons—

      (i) the bona fide employees or former employees of that company or of another company in the same group; or

      (ii) the wives, husbands, widows, widowers, children, step-children or adopted children under the age of eighteen of such employees of former employees."

196(6)   **[Insertion of art. 163(5) of 1986 Order]**   After paragraph (4) there shall be inserted—

    "**(5)**   For the purposes of paragraph (4)(bb) a company is connected with another company if—

      (a) they are in the same group; or

      (b) one is entitled, either alone or with any other company in the same group, to exercise or control the exercise of a majority of the voting rights attributable to the share capital which are exerciseable in all circumstances at any general meeting of the other company or of its holding company;

and in this Article **'group'**, in relation to a company, means that company, any other company which is its holding company or subsidiary and any other company which is a subsidiary of that holding company.".

SEC. 197   Disclosure of interests in shares: interest held by market maker

197(1)   [Insertions in sec. 209 of Companies Act 1985]   In section 209 of the Companies Act 1985 (interests to be disregarded for purposes of sections 198 to 202)—

(a) in subsection (1)(f) after the word "jobber" there shall be inserted the words "or market maker";

(b) after subsection (4) there shall be inserted—

"**209(4A)**   A person is a market maker for the purposes of subsection (1)(f) if—

(a) he holds himself out at all normal times in compliance with the rules of a recognised investment exchange other than an overseas investment exchange (within the meaning of the Financial Services Act 1986) as willing to buy and sell securities at prices specified by him; and

(b) is recognised as doing so by that investment exchange;

and an interest of such a person in shares is an exempt interest if he carries on business as a market maker in the United Kingdom, is subject to such rules in the carrying on of that business and holds the interest for the purposes of that business.".

197(2)   [Insertions in art. 217 of Companies (Northern Ireland) Order 1986]   In Article 217 of the Companies (Northern Ireland) Order 1986 (interests to be disregarded for purposes of Articles 206 to 210 (disclosure of interests in shares))—

(a) in paragraph (1)(d) after the word "jobber" there shall be inserted the words "or market maker";

(b) after paragraph (4) there shall be inserted—

"**(4A)**   A person is a market maker for the purposes of paragraph (1)(d) if—

(a) he holds himself out at all normal times in compliance with the rules of a recognised investment exchange other than an overseas investment exchange (within the meaning of the Financial Services Act 1986) as willing to buy and sell securities at prices specified by him; and

(b) is recognised as doing so by that investment exchange,

and an interest of such a person in shares is an exempt interest if he carries on business as a market maker in the United Kingdom, is subject to such rules in the carrying on of that business and holds the interest for the purposes of that business.".

SEC. 198 Power to petition for winding up etc. on information obtained under Act

198(1) (Repealed by Companies Act 1989, sec. 212 and Sch. 24 as from 21 February 1990.)

History
In regard to the date of the above repeal see S.I. 1990 No. 142 (C. 5), art. 7(d); s. 198(1) formerly read as follows:

"**198(1)** In section 440 of the Companies Act 1985—

  (a) after the words 'section 437' there shall be inserted the words 'above or section 94 of the Financial Services Act 1986'; and

  (b) after the words '448 below' there shall be inserted the words 'or section 105 of that Act'."

198(2) **[Amendments to sec. 8 of Company Directors Disqualification Act 1986]** In section 8 of the Company Directors Disqualification Act 1986—

  (a) after the words "the Companies Act" there shall be inserted the words "or section 94 or 177 of the Financial Services Act 1986"; and

  (b) for the words "that Act" there shall be substituted the words "the Companies Act or section 105 of the Financial Services Act 1986".

198(3) **[Insertions in art. 433 of Companies (Northern Ireland) Order 1986]** In Article 433 of the Companies (Northern Ireland) Order 1986—

  (a) after the words "Article 430" there shall be inserted the words "or section 94 of the Financial Services Act 1986"; and

  (b) after the word "441" there shall be inserted the words "or section 105 of that Act".

SEC. 199 Powers of entry

199(1) **[Power of JP to issue warrant]** A justice of the peace may issue a warrant under this section if satisfied on information on oath given by or on behalf of the Secretary of State that there are reasonable grounds for believing that an offence has been committed—

  (a) under section 4, 47, 57, 130, 133 or 171(2) or (3) above, or

  (b) section 1, 2, 4 or 5 of the Company Securities (Insider Dealing) Act 1985,

and that there are on any premises documents relevant to the question whether that offence has been committed.

History
See history note after s. 199(2).

199(2) **[Further powers of JP]** A justice of the peace may also issue a warrant under this section if satisfied on information on oath given by or on behalf of the Secretary of State, or by a person appointed or authorised to exercise powers under section 94, 106 or 177 above, that there are reasonable grounds for believing that there are on any premises documents whose production has been required under section 94, 105 or 177 above and which have not been produced in compliance with the requirement.

History

S. 199(1), (2) substituted by CA 1989, s. 76(1), (2) as from 21 February 1990 (see S.I. 1990 No. 142 (C. 5), art. 4); s. 199(1), (2) formerly read as follows:

"**199(1)**   A justice of the peace may issue a warrant under this section if satisfied on information on oath laid by or on behalf of the Secretary of State that there are reasonable grounds for believing—

(a) that an offence has been committed under section 4, 47, 57, 130, 133 or 171(2) or (3) above or section 1, 2, 4 or 5 of the Company Securities (Insider Dealing) Act 1985 and that there are on any premises documents relevant to the question whether that offence has been committed; or

(b) that there are on any premises owned or occupied by a person whose affairs, or any aspect of whose affairs, are being investigated under section 105 above documents whose production has been required under that section and which have not been produced in compliance with that requirement;

but paragraph (b) above applies only if the person there mentioned is an authorised person, a person whose authorisation has been suspended or who is the subject of a direction under section 33(1)(b) above or an appointed representative of an authorised person.

(2) A justice of the peace may issue a warrant under this section if satisfied on information on oath laid by an inspector appointed under section 94 above that there are reasonable grounds for believing that there are on any premises owned or occupied by—

(a) the manager, trustee or operator of any scheme the affairs of which are being investigated under subsection (1) of that section; or

(b) a manager, trustee or operator whose affairs are being investigated under that subsection,

any documents whose production has been required under that section and which have not been produced in compliance with that requirement."

199(3)   [Scope of warrant]   A warrant under this section shall authorise a constable, together with any other person named in it and any other constables—

(a) to enter the premises specified in the information, using such force as is reasonably necessary for the purpose;

(b) to search the premises and take possession of any documents appearing to be such documents as are mentioned in subsection (1) or, as the case may be, in subsection (2) above or to take, in relation to any such documents, any other steps which may appear to be necessary for preserving them or preventing interference with them;

(c) to take copies of any such documents; and

(d) to require any person named in the warrant to provide an explanation of them or to state where they may be found.

History

In s. 199(3)(b) the words "subsection (1)" substituted for the former words "subsection 1(a) or (b)" by CA 1989, s. 76(1), (3) as from 21 February 1990 (see S.I. 1990 No. 142 (C. 5), art. 4).

199(4)   [Duration of warrant]   A warrant under this section shall continue in force until the end of the period of one month beginning with the day on which it is issued.

199(5)   [Period for retention of documents]   Any documents of which possession is taken under this section may be retained—

(a) for a period of three months; or

(b) if within that period proceedings to which the documents are relevant are commenced against any person for any criminal offence, until the conclusion of those proceedings.

History

S. 199(5)(b) substituted by CA 1989, s. 76(1), (4) as from 21 February 1990 (see S.I. 1990 No. 142 (C. 5), art. 4); s. 199(5)(b) formerly read as follows:

"(b) if within that period proceedings to which the documents are relevant are commenced against any person for an offence under this Act or section 1, 2, 4 or 5 of the said Act of 1985, until the conclusion of those proceedings."

199(6)   [Offence, penalty]   Any person who intentionally obstructs the exercise of any rights conferred by a warrant issued under this section or fails without reasonable excuse to comply with any requirement imposed in accordance with subsection (3)(d) above shall be guilty of an offence and liable—

(a) on conviction on indictment, to a fine;

(b) on summary conviction, to a fine not exceeding the statutory maximum.

History
in s. 199(6) the word "intentionally" inserted by CA 1989,
s. 76(1), (5) as from 21 February 1990 (see S.I. 1990
No. 142 (C. 5), art 4).

199(7) **[Functions relevant for sec. 114]** The functions to which section 114 above applies shall include the functions of the Secretary of State under this section; but if any of those functions are transferred under that section the transfer may be subject to a reservation that they are to be exercisable by the Secretary of State concurrently with the designated agency and, in the case of functions exercisable by virtue of subsection (1) above, so as to be exercisable by the agency subject to such conditions or restrictions as the Secretary of State may from time to time impose.

History
In s. 199(7) the words "subsection (1) above" substituted
for the former words "subsection (1)(a) above" by CA
1989, s. 76(1), (6) as from 21 February 1990 (see S.I. 1990
No. 142 (C. 5), art. 4).

199(8) **[Scotland]** In the application of this section to Scotland for the references to a justice of the peace substitute references to a justice of the peace or a sheriff, and for the references to information on oath substitute references to evidence on oath.

History
S. 199(8) substituted by CA 1989, s. 76(1), (7) as from
21 February 1990 (see S.I. 1990 No. 142 (C. 5), art. 4);
s. 199(8) formerly read as follows:

"**199(8)** In the application of this section to Scotland the
references to a justice of the peace shall include references

to a sheriff and for references to the laying of information
on oath there shall be substituted references to furnishing
evidence on oath; and in the application of this section to
Northern Ireland for references to the laying of information
on oath there shall be substituted references to making a
complaint on oath."

199(9) **["Documents"]** In this section **"documents"** includes information recorded in any form.

History
In s. 199(9) the words "and, in relation to information
recorded otherwise than in legible form, references to its
production include references to producing a copy of the
information in legible form" formerly appearing at the end
omitted by CA 1989, s. 76(1), (8) as from 21 February 1990
(see S.I. 1990 No. 142 (C. 5), art. 4) and repealed by CA
1989, s. 212 and Sch. 24 as from 1 March 1990 (see S.I.
1990 No. 355 (C. 13), art. 5(1)).

CCH Note
The above omission and repeal were obviously intended to
coincide in S.I. 1990 No. 142 (C. 5), art. 7 purportedly
attempting to effect a non-existent repeal in FSA 1986,
s. 199(1) as from 21 February 1990; this clearly should have
referred to s. 199(9) and the incorrect reference to s. 199(1)
was revoked by S.I. 1990 No. 355 (C. 13), art. 16.

SEC. 200   False and misleading statements

200(1) **[Furnishing false information]** A person commits an offence if—

(a) for the purposes of or in connection with any application under this Act; or

(b) in purported compliance with any requirement imposed on him by or under this Act,

he furnishes information which he knows to be false or misleading in a material particular or recklessly furnishes information which is false or misleading in a material particular.

200(2) **[False description of person]** A person commits an offence if, not being an authorised person or exempted person, he—

(a) describes himself as such a person; or

(b) so holds himself out as to indicate or be reasonably understood to indicate that he is such a person.

200(3) **[False description of status]** A person commits an offence if, not having a status to which this subsection applies, he—

(a) describes himself as having that status, or

(b) so holds himself out as to indicate or be reasonably understood to indicate that he has that status.

200(4)   [Application of sec. 200(3)]   Subsection (3) above applies to the status of recognised self-regulating organisation, recognised professional body, recognised investment exchange or recognised clearing house.

200(5)   [Penalty for sec. 200(1) offence]   A person guilty of an offence under subsection (1) above shall be liable—

(a) on conviction on indictment, to imprisonment for a term not exceeding two years or to a fine or to both;

(b) on summary conviction, to imprisonment for a term not exceeding six months or to a fine not exceeding the statutory maximum or to both.

200(6)   [Penalty for sec. 200(2), (3) offences]   A person guilty of an offence under subsection (2) or (3) above shall be liable on summary conviction to imprisonment for a term not exceeding six months or to a fine not exceeding the fifth level on the standard scale or to both.

200(7)   [Maximum fine in sec. 200(6) if public display]   Where a contravention of subsection (2) or (3) above involves a public display of the offending description or other matter the maximum fine that may be imposed under subsection (6) above shall be an amount equal to the fifth level on the standard scale multiplied by the number of days for which the display has continued.

200(8)   [Defence re sec. 200(2), (3) offences]   In proceedings brought against any person for an offence under subsection (2) or (3) above it shall be a defence for him to prove that he took all reasonable precautions and exercised all due diligence to avoid the commission of the offence.

SEC. 201   Prosecutions

201(1)   [Proceedings other than under sec. 133, 185]   Proceedings in respect of an offence under any provision of this Act other than section 133 or 185 shall not be instituted—

(a) in England and Wales, except by or with the consent of the Secretary of State or the Director of Public Prosecutions; or

(b) in Northern Ireland, except by or with the consent of the Secretary of State or the Director of Public Prosecutions for Northern Ireland.

201(2)   [Sec. 133 proceedings]   Proceedings in respect of an offence under section 133 above shall not be instituted—

(a) in England and Wales, except by or with the consent of the Secretary of State, the Indusrial Assurance Commissioner or the Director of Public Prosecutions; or

(b) in Northern Ireland, except by or with the consent of the Secretary of State or the Director of Public Prosecutions for Northern Ireland.

201(3)   [Sec. 185 proceedings]   Proceedings in respect of an offence under section 185 above shall not be instituted—

(a) in England and Wales, except by or with the consent of the Treasury or the Director of Public Prosecutions; or

(b) in Northern Ireland, except by or with the consent of the Treasury or the Director of Public Prosecutions for Northern Ireland.

201(4) [Sec. 114 functions] The functions to which section 114 above applies shall include the function of the Secretary of State under subsection (1) above to institute proceedings but any transfer of that function shall be subject to a reservation that it is to be exercisable by him concurrently with the designated agency and so as to be exercisable by the agency subject to such conditions or restrictions as the Secretary of State may from time to time impose.

SEC. 202 Offences by bodies corporate, partnerships and unincorporated associations

202(1) [Offences by body corporate with connivance of offices] Where an offence under this Act committed by a body corporate is proved to have been committed with the consent or connivance of, or to be attributable to any neglect on the part of—

(a) any director, manager, secretary or other similar officer of the body corporate, or any person who was purporting to act in any such capacity; or

(b) a controller of the body corporate,

he, as well as the body corporate, shall be guilty of that offence and liable to be proceeded against and punished accordingly.

202(2) [Where affairs of body corporate managed by members] Where the affairs of a body corporate are managed by the members subsection (1) above shall apply in relation to the acts and defaults of a member in connection with his functions of management as if he were a director of the body corporate.

202(3) [Offence by partnership] Where a partnership is guilty of an offence under this Act every partner, other than a partner who is proved to have been ignorant of or to have attempted to prevent the commission of the offence, shall also be guilty of that offence and be liable to be proceeded against and punished accordingly.

202(4) [Offence by unincorporated association] Where an unincorporated association (other than a partnership) is guilty of an offence under this Act—

(a) every officer of the association who is bound to fulfil any duty of which the breach is the offence; or

(b) if there is no such officer, every member of the governing body other than a member who is proved to have been ignorant of or to have attempted to prevent the commission of the offence,

shall also be guilty of the offence and be liable to be proceeded against and punished accordingly.

SEC. 203 Jurisdiction and procedure in respect of offences

203(1) [Summary proceedings re place] Summary proceedings for an offence under this Act may, without prejudice to any jurisdiction exercisable apart from this section, be taken against any body corporate or unincorporated association at any place at which it has a place of business and against an individual at any place where he is for the time being.

203(2)　[Proceedings against unincorporated association]　Proceedings for an offence alleged to have been committed under this Act by an unincorporated association shall be brought in the name of the association (and not in that of any of its members) and for the purposes of any such proceedings any rules of court relating to the service of documents shall have effect as if the association were a corporation.

203(3)　[Procedure re unincorporated associations]　Section 33 of the Criminal Justice Act 1925 and Schedule 3 to the Magistrates' Courts Act 1980 (procedure on charge of offence against a corporation) shall have effect in a case in which an unincorporated association is charged in England and Wales with an offence under this Act in like manner as they have effect in the case of a corporation.

203(4)　[Procedure in Scotland re unincorporated associations]　In relation to any proceedings on indictment in Scotland for an offence alleged to have been committed under this Act by an unincorporated association, section 74 of the Criminal Procedure (Scotland) Act 1975 (proceedings on indictment against bodies corporate) shall have effect as if the association were a body corporate.

203(5)　[Procedure in Northern Ireland re unincorporated associations]　Section 18 of the Criminal Justice Act (Northern Ireland) 1945 and Schedule 4 to the Magistrates' Courts (Northern Ireland) Order 1981 (procedure on charge of offence against a corporation) shall have effect in a case in which an unincorporated association is charged in Northern Ireland with an offence under this Act in like manner as they have effect in the case of a corporation.

203(6)　[Fine to be paid by unincorporated association]　A fine imposed on an unincorporated association on its conviction of an offence under this Act shall be paid out of the funds of the association.

SEC. 204　Service of notices

204(1)　[Effect of section]　This section has effect in relation to any notice, direction or other document required or authorised by or under this Act to be given to or served on any person other than the Secretary of State, the Chief Registrar of friendly societies or the Registrar of Friendly Societies for Northern Ireland.

204(2)　[Service on person]　Any such document may be given to or served on the person in question—

(a) by delivering it to him;

(b) by leaving it at his proper address; or

(c) by sending it by post to him at that address.

204(3)　[Service on body corporate, partnership, unincorporated association, appointed representative]　Any such document may—

(a) in the case of a body corporate, be given to or served on the secretary or clerk of that body;

(b) in the case of a partnership, be given to or served on any partner;

(c) in the case of an unincorporated association other than a partnership, be given to or served on any member of the governing body of the association;

(d) in the case of an appointed representative, be given to or served on his principal.

204(4) **[Service by post]** For the purposes of this section and section 7 of the Interpretation Act 1978 (service of documents by post) in its application to this section, the proper address of any person is his last known address (whether of his residence or of a place where he carries on business or is employed) and also any address applicable in his case under the following provisions—

(a) in the case of a member of a recognised self-regulating organisation or a person certified by a recogniesed professional body who does not have a place of business in the United Kingdom, the address of that organisation or body;

(b) in the case of a body corporate, its secretary or its clerk, the address of its registered or principal office in the United Kingdom;

(c) in the case of an unincorporated association (other than a partnership) or a member of its governing body, its principal office in the United Kingdom.

204(5) **[Where new address notified re sec. 204(4)]** Where a person has notified the Secretary of State of an address or a new address at which documents may be given to or served on him under this Act that address shall also be his proper address for the purposes mentioned in subsection (4) above or, as the case may be, his proper address for those purposes in substitution for that previously notified.

SEC. 205 General power to make regulations

205 The Secretary of State may make regulations prescribing anything which by this Act is authorised or required to be prescribed.

History
See history note after s. 205A.

Note
For transfer of the Secretary of State's functions under s. 205 see S.I. 1990 No. 354 (C. 12), art. 4(5).

SEC. 205A Supplementary provisions with respect to subordinate legislation

205A(1) **[Application of power of Secretary of State]** The following provisions apply to any power of the Secretary of State under this Act—

(a) to issue statements of principle,

(b) to make rules or regulations,

(c) to make orders (other than such orders as are expected by subsection (4) below), or

(d) to issue codes of practice.

205A(2) **[Power exercisable by statutory instrument]** Any such power is exercisable by statutory instrument and includes power to make different provision for different cases.

205A(3) **[Annulment of statutory instrument]** Except as otherwise provided, a statutory instrument containing statements of principle, rules or regulations shall be subject to annulment in pursuance of a resolution of either House of Parliament.

205A(4) **[Non-application of sec. 205A(1)–(3)]** The above provisions do not apply to a recognition order, an order declaring a collective investment scheme to be an authorised unit trust scheme or a recognised scheme or to an order revoking any such order.

History

S. 205, 205A substituted for former s. 205 by CA 1989, s. 206(1) and Sch. 23, para. 18 as from 15 March 1990 (see S.I. 1990 No. 354 (C. 12), art. 3); former s. 205 read as follows:

"SEC. 205   Regulations, rules and orders

205(1) The Secretary of State may make regulations prescribing anything which by this Act is authorised or required to be prescribed.

(2) Subject to subsection (5) below, any power of the Secretary of State to make regulations, rules or orders under this Act shall be exercisable by statutory instrument.

(3) Subject to subsection (5) below, any regulations, rules or orders made under this Act by the Secretary of State may make different provision for different cases.

(4) Except as otherwise provided, a statutory instrument containing regulations or rules under this Act shall be subject to annulment in pursuance of a resolution of either House of Parliament.

(5) Subsections (2) and (3) above do not apply to a recognition order, an order declaring a collective investment scheme to be an authorised unit trust scheme or a recognised scheme or to an order revoking any such order."

SEC. 206   Publication of information and advice

206(1)   [Power of Secretary of State re information etc.]   The Secretary of State may publish information or give advice, or arrange for the publication of information or the giving of advice, in such form and manner as he considers appropriate with respect to—

(a) the operation of this Act and the statements of principle, rules, regulations and codes of pratice issued or made under it, including in particular the rights of investors, the duties of authorised persons and the steps to be taken for enforcing those rights or complying with those duties;

(b) any matters relating to the functions of the Secretary of State under this Act or any such statements of principle, rules, regulations or codes of practice;

(c) any other matters about which it appears to him to be desirable to publish information or give advice for the protection of investors or any class of investors.

History

In s. 206(1) in para. (a) the words "statements of principle, rules, regulations and codes of practice issued or made" substituted for the former words "rules and regulations made" and in para. (b) the words "statements of principle, rules, regulations or codes of practice" substituted for the former words "rules or regulations" by CA 1989, s. 206(1) and Sch. 23, para. 19(a) and (b) respectively as from 15 March 1990 (see S.I. 1990 No. 354 (C. 12), art. 3).

206(2)   [Sale of copies of information]   The Secretary of State may offer for sale copies of information published under this section and may, if he thinks fit, make a reasonable charge for advice given under this section at any person's request.

206(3)   [Sec. 179]   This section shall not be construed as authorising the disclosure of restricted information within the meaning of section 179 above in any case in which it could not be disclosed apart from the provisions of this section.

206(4)   [Functions under sec. 114]   The functions to which section 114 above applies shall include the functions of the Secretary of State under this section.

SEC. 207   Interpretation

207(1)   [Definitions]   In this Act, except where the context otherwise requires—

"**appointed representative**" has the meaning given in section 44 above;

"**authorised person**" means a person authorised under Chapter III of Part I of this Act;

"**authorised unit trust scheme**" means a unit trust scheme declared by an order of the Secretary of State for the time being in force to be an authorised unit trust scheme for the purposes of this Act;

"**body corporate**" includes a body corporate constituted under the law of a country or territory outside the United Kingdom;

"**certified**" and "**certification**" mean certified or certification by a recognised professional body for the purposes of Part I of this Act;

"**clearing arrangements**" has the meaning given in section 38(2) above;

"**competent authority**" means the competent authority for the purposes of Part IV of this Act;

"**collective investment scheme**" has the meaning given in section 75 above;

"**delegation order**" and "**designated agency**" have the meaning given in section 114(3) above;

"**director**", in relation to a body corporate, includes a person occupying in relation to it the position of a director (by whatever name called) and any person in accordance with whose directions or instructions (not being advice given in a professional capacity) the directors of that body are accustomed to act;

"**ensure**" and "**ensuring**", in relation to the performance of transactions on an investment exchange, have the meaning given in paragraph 6 of Schedule 4 to this Act;

"**exempted person**" means a person exempted under Chapter IV of Part I of this Act;

"**group**", in relation to a body corporate, means that body corporate, any other body corporate which is its holding company or subsidiary and any other body corporate which is a subsidiary of that holding company;

"**guidance**", in relation to a self-regulating organisation, professional body, investment exchange, clearing house or designated agency, has the meaning given in section 8(4), 16(4), 36(3), 38(3) or 114(12) above;

"**investment advertisement**" has the meaning given in section 57(2) above;

"**investment agreement**" has the meaning given in section 44(9) above;

"**listing particulars**" has the meaning given in section 144(2) above;

"**member**", in relation to a self-regulating organisation or professional body, has the meaning given in section 8(2) or 16(2) above;

"**occupational pension scheme**" means any scheme or arrangement which is comprised in one or more instruments or agreements and which has, or is capable of having, effect in relation to one or more descriptions or categories of employment so as to provide benefits, in the form of pensions or otherwise, payable on termination of service, or on death or retirement, to or in respect of earners with qualifying service in an employment of any such description or category;

"**operator**", in relation to a collective investment scheme, shall be construed in accordance with section 75(8) above;

"**open-ended investment company**" has the meaning given in section 75(8) above;

"**overseas investment exchange**" and "**overseas clearing house**" mean a recognised investment exchange or recognised clearing house in the case of which the recognition order was made by virtue of section 40 above;

"**participant**" has the meaning given in section 75(2) above;

"**partnership**" includes a partnership constituted under the law of a country or territory outside the United Kingdom;

"**prescribed**" means prescribed by regulations made by the Secretary of State;

"**principal**", in relation to an appointed representative, has the meaning given in section 44 above;

"**private company**" has the meaning given in section 1(3) of the Companies Act 1985 or the corresponding Northern Ireland provision;

"**recognised clearing house**" means a body declared by an order of the Secretary of State for the time being in force to be a recognised clearing house for the purposes of this Act;

"**recognised investment exchange**" means a body declared by an order of the Secretary of State for the time being in force to be a recognised investment exchange for the purposes of this Act;

"**recognised professional body**" means a body declared by an order of the Secretary of State for the time being in force to be a recognised professional body for the purposes of this Act;

"**recognised scheme**" means a scheme recognised under section 86, 87 or 88 above;

"**recognised self-regulating organisation**" means a body declared by an order of the Secretary of State for the time being in force to be a recognised self-regulating organisation for the purposes of this Act;

"**recognised self-regulating organisation for friendly societies**" has the meaning given in paragraph 1 of Schedule 11 to this Act;

"**recognition order**" means an order declaring a body to be a recognised self-regulating organisation, self-regulating organisation for friendly societies, professional body, investment exchange or clearing house;

"**registered friendly society**" means—

(a) a society which is a friendly society within the meaning of section 7(1)(a) of the Friendly Societies Act 1974 and is registered within the meaning of that Act; or

(b) a society which is a friendly society within the meaning of section 1(1)(a) of the Friendly Societies Act (Northern Ireland) 1970 and is registered or deemed to be registered under that Act;

"**rules**", in relation to a self-regulating organisation, professional body, investment exchange or clearing house, has the meaning given in section 8(3), 16(3), 36(2) or 38(2) above;

"**transfer order**" and "**transferee body**" have the meaning given in paragraph 28(4) of Schedule 11 to this Act;

"**the Tribunal**" means the Financial Services Tribunal;

"**trustee**", in relation to a collective investment scheme, has the meaning given in section 75(8) above;

"**unit trust scheme**" and "**units**" have the meaning given in section 75(8) above.

History
In s. 207(1) the definitions of "ensure" and "ensuring" inserted by CA 1989, s. 205(3) as from 15 March 1990 (see S.I. 1990 No. 354 (C. 12),art. 3).

207(2) **["Advertisement"]** In this Act "**advertisement**" includes every form of advertising, whether in a publication, by the display of notices, signs, labels or showcards, by means of circulars, catalogues, price lists or other documents, by an exhibition of pictures or photographic or cinematographic films, by way of sound broadcasting or television, by the distribution of recordings, or in any other manner; and references to the issue of an advertisement shall be construed accordingly.

207(3) **[Issue of advertisement in UK]** For the purposes of this Act an advertisement or other information issued outside the United Kingdom shall be treated as issued in the United Kingdom if it is directed to persons in the United Kingdom or is made available to them otherwise than in a newspaper, journal, magazine or other periodical publication published and circulating principally outside the United Kingdom or in a sound or television broadcast transmitted principally for reception outside the United Kingdom.

207(4) **[Independent Broadcasting Authority]** The Independent Broadcasting Authority shall not be regarded as contravening any provision of this Act by reason of broadcasting an advertisement in accordance with the provisions of the Broadcasting Act 1981.

207(5) **["Controller"]** In this Act "**controller**" means—

(a) in relation to a body corporate, a person who, either alone or with any associate or associates, is entitled to exercise, or control the exercise of, 15 per cent or more of the voting power at any general meeting of the body corporate or another body corporate of which it is a subsidiary; and

(b) in relation to an unincorporated association—

(i) any person in accordance with whose directions or instructions, either alone or with those of any associate or associates, the officers or members of the governing body of the association are accustomed to act (but disregarding advice given in a professional capacity); and

(ii) any person who, either alone or with any associate or associates, is entitled to exercise, or control the exercise of, 15 per cent or more of the voting power at any general meeting of the association;

and for the purposes of this subsection "**associate**", in relation to any person, means that person's wife, husband or minor child or step-child, any body corporate of which that person is a director, any person who is an employee or partner of that person and, if that person is a body corporate, any subsidiary of that body corporate and any employee of any such subsidiary.

207(6) ["**Manager**"] In this Act, except in relation to a unit trust scheme or a registered friendly society, "**manager**" means an employee who—

(a) under the immediate authority of his employer is responsible, either alone or jointly with one or more other persons, for the conduct of his employer's business; or

(b) under the immediate authority of his employer or of a person who is a manager by virtue of paragraph (a) above exercises managerial functions or is responsible for maintaining accounts or other records of his employer;

and, where the employer is not an individual, references in this subsection to the authority of the employer are references to the authority, in the case of a body corporate, of the directors, in the case of a partnership, of the partners and, in the case of an unincorporated association, of its officers or the members of its governing body.

207(7) ["**Insurance business**" etc.] In this Act "**insurance business**", "**insurance company**" and "**contract of insurance**" have the same meanings as in the Insurance Companies Act 1982.

207(8) [**Subsidiary, holding company**] Section 736 of the Companies Act 1985 (meaning of subsidiary and holding company) shall apply for the purposes of this Act.

207(9) [**Application to Scotland**] In the application of this Act to Scotland, references to a matter being actionable at the suit of a person shall be construed as references to the matter being actionable at the instance of that person.

207(10) [**Time limits**] For the purposes of any provision of this Act authorising or requiring a person to do anything within a specified number of days no account shall be taken of any day which is a public holiday in any part of the United Kingdom.

207(11) [**Investment business on behalf of Crown**] Nothing in Part I of this Act shall be construed as applying to investment business carried on by any person when acting as agent or otherwise on behalf of the Crown.

SEC. 208   Gibraltar

208(1) [**Application to Gibraltar**] Subject to the provisions of this section, section 31, 58(1)(c), 86 and 130(2)(c) and (d) above shall apply as if Gibraltar were a member State.

208(2) [**References to national of member State**] References in those provisions to a national of a member State shall, in relation to Gibraltar, be construed as references to a British Dependent Territories citizen or a body incorporated in Gibraltar.

208(3) [**Reference in sec. 86(3)(a) to relevant Community instrument**] In the case of a collective investment scheme constituted in Gibraltar the reference in subsection (3)(a) of section 86 above to a relevant Community instrument shall be taken as a reference to any Community instrument the object of which is the co-ordination or approximation of the laws, regulations or administrative provisions of member States relating to collective investment schemes of a kind which satisfy the requirements prescribed for the purposes of that section.

208(4) [**Power of Secretary of State to make regulations**] The Secretary of State may by regulations make such provision as appears to him to be necessary or expedient to secure—

(a) that he may give notice under subsection (2) of section 86 above on grounds relating to the law of Gibraltar; and

(b) that this Act applies as if a scheme which is constituted in a member State other than the United Kingdom and recognised in Gibraltar under provisions which appear to the Secretary of State to give effect to the provisions of a relevant Community instrument were a scheme recognised under that section.

SEC. 209 Northern Ireland

209(1) [Extent to Northern Ireland] This Act extends to Northern Ireland.

209(2) [Northern Ireland Constitution Act 1973] Subject to any Order made after the passing of this Act by virtue of subsection (1)(a) of section 3 of the Northern Ireland Constitution Act 1973 the regulation of investment business, the official listing of securities and offers off unlisted securities shall not be transferred matters for the purposes of that Act but shall for the purposes of subsection (2) of that section be treated as specified in Schedule 3 to that Act.

SEC. 210 Expenses and receipts

210(1) [Defraying of expenses] Any expenses incurred by the Secretary of State under this Act shall be defrayed out of moneys provided by Parliament.

210(2) [Payment of fees etc.] Any fees or other sums received by the Secretary of State under this Act shall be paid into the Consolidated Fund.

210(3) [Expenses, fees re Chief Registrar of Friendly Societies etc.] Subsections (1) and (2) above apply also to expenses incurred and fees received under this Act by the Chief Registrar of friendly societies; and any fees received under this Act by the Registrar of Friendly Societies for Northern Ireland shall be paid into the Consolidated Fund of Northern Ireland.

SEC. 211 Commencement and transitional provisions

211(1) [Commencement days by Order] This Act shall come into force on such day as the Secretary of State may by order appoint and different days may be appointed for different provisions or different purposes.

211(2) [Commencement of sec. 195] Subsection (1) above does not apply to section 195 which shall come into force when this Act is passed.

211(3) [Transitional matters] Schedule 15 to this Act shall have effect with respect to the transitional matters there mentioned.

SEC. 212 Short title, consequential amendments and repeals

212(1) [Citation] This Act may be cited as the Financial Services Act 1986.

212(2) [Consequential amendments] The enactments and instruments mentioned in Schedule 16 to this Act shall have effect with the amendments there specified, being amendments consequential on the provisions of this Act.

212(3) [Repeals] The enactments mentioned in Part I of Schedule 17 to this Act and the instruments mentioned in Part II of that Schedule are hereby repealed or revoked to the extent specified in the third column of those Parts.

SCHEDULES

Schedule 1 — Investments and Investment Business

Sections 1 and 2

Part I — Investments

SHARES ETC.

1   Shares and stock in the share capital of a company.

Note

In this paragraph **"company"** includes any body corporate and also any unincorporated body constituted under the law of a country or territory outside the United Kingdom but does not include an open-ended investment company or any body incorporated under the law of, or of any part of, the United Kingdom relating to building societies, industrial and provident societies or credit unions.

DEBENTURES

2   Debentures, including debenture stock, loan stock, bonds, certificates of deposit and other instruments creating or acknowledging indebtedness, not being instruments falling within paragraph 3 below.

Note

This paragraph shall not be construed as applying—

(a) to any instrument acknowledging or creating indebtedness for, or for money borrowed to defray, the consideration payable under a contract for the supply of goods or services;

(b) to a cheque or other bill of exchange, a banker's draft or a letter of credit; or

(c) to a banknote, a statement showing a balance in a current, deposit or savings account or (by reason of any financial obligation contained in it) to a lease or other disposition of property, a heritable security or an insurance policy.

GOVERNMENT AND PUBLIC SECURITIES

3   Loan stock, bonds and other instruments creating or acknowledging indebtedness issued by or on behalf of a government, local authority or public authority.

Notes

(1) In this paragraph **"government, local authority or public authority"** means—

(a) the government of the United Kingdom, of Northern Ireland, or of any country or territory outside the United Kingdom;

(b) a local authority in the United Kingdom or elsewhere;

(c) any international organisation the members of which include the United Kingdom or another member State.

(2) The Note to paragraph 2 above shall, so far as applicable, apply also to this paragraph.

(3) This paragraph does not apply to any instrument creating or acknowledging indebtedness in respect of money received by the Director of Savings as deposits or otherwise in connection with the business of the National Savings Bank or in respect of money raised under the National Loans Act 1968 under the auspices of the Director of Savings or in respect of money treated as having been so raised by virtue of section 11(3) of the National Debt Act 1972.

History
In para. 3, Note (3) added by Financial Services Act 1986 (Restriction of Scope of Act and Meaning of Collective Investment Scheme) Order 1990 (S.I. 1990 No. 349), art. 2(1) as from 26 March 1990.

INSTRUMENTS ENTITLING TO SHARES OR SECURITIES

4 Warrants or other instruments entitling the holder to subscribe for investments falling within paragraph 1, 2 or 3 above.

Notes

(1) It is immaterial whether the investments are for the time being in existence or identifiable.

(2) An investment falling within this paragraph shall not be regarded as falling within paragraph 7, 8 or 9 below.

CERTIFICATES REPRESENTING SECURITIES

5 Certificates or other instruments which confer—

(a) property rights in respect of any investment falling within paragraph 1, 2, 3 or 4 above;

(b) any right to acquire, dispose of, underwrite or convert an investment, being a right to which the holder would be entitled if he held any such investment to which the certificate or instrument relates; or

(c) a contractual right (other than an option) to acquire any such investment otherwise than by subscription.

Note

This paragraph does not apply to any instrument which confers rights in respect of two or more investments issued by different persons or in respect of two or more different investments falling within paragraph 3 above and issued by the same person.

UNITS IN COLLECTIVE INVESTMENT SCHEME

6 Units in a collective investment scheme, including shares in or securities of an open-ended investment company.

OPTIONS

7 Options to acquire or dispose of—

(a) an investment falling within any other paragraph of this Part of this Schedule;

(b) currency of the United Kingdom or of any other country or territory;

(c) gold, palladium, platinum or silver; or

(d) an option to acquire or dispose of an investment falling within this paragraph by virtue of (a), (b) or (c) above.

History
In para. 7(c) the words, ", palladium, platinum", inserted after the word, "gold", by the Financial Services Act 1986 (Extension of Scope of Act and Meaning of Collective Investment Scheme) Order 1988 (S.I. 1988 No. 496), art. 2 as from 25 March 1988.

FUTURES

8 Rights under a contract for the sale of a commodity or property of any other description under which delivery is to be made at a future date and at a price agreed upon when the contract is made.

Notes

(1) This paragraph does not apply if the contract is made for commercial and not investment purposes.

(2) A contract shall be regarded as made for investment purposes if it is made or traded on a recognised investment exchange or made otherwise than on a recognised investment exchange but expressed to be as traded on such an exchange or on the same terms as those on which an equivalent contract would be made on such an exchange.

(3) A contract not falling within Note (2) above shall be regarded as made for commercial purposes if under the terms of the contract delivery is to be made within seven days.

(4) The following are indications that any other contract is made for a commercial purpose and the absence of any of them is an indication that it is made for investment purposes—

   (a) either or each of the parties is a producer of the commodity or other property or uses it in his business;

   (b) the seller delivers or intends to deliver the property or the purchaser takes or intends to take delivery of it.

(5) It is an indication that a contract is made for commercial purposes that the price, the lot, the delivery date or the other terms are determined by the parties for the purposes of the particular contract and not by reference to regularly published prices, to standard lots or delivery dates or to standard terms.

(6) The following are also indications that a contract is made for investment purposes—

   (a) it is expressed to be as traded on a market or on an exchange;

   (b) performance of the contract is ensured by an investment exchange or a clearing house;

   (c) there are arrangements for the payment or provision of margin.

(7) A price shall be taken to have been agreed upon when a contract is made—

   (a) notwithstanding that it is left to be determined by reference to the price at which a contract is to be entered into on a market or exchange or could be entered into at a time and place specified in the contract; or

FSA 1986, Sch. 1, para. 8

(b) in a case where the contract is expressed to be by reference to a standard lot and quality, notwithstanding that provision is made for a variation in the price to take account of any variation in quantity or quality on delivery.

CONTRACTS FOR DIFFERENCES ETC.

9 Rights under a contract for differences or under any other contract the purpose or pretended purpose of which is to secure a profit or avoid a loss by reference to fluctuations in the value or price of property of any description or in an index or other factor designated for that purpose in the contract.

Notes

(1) This paragraph does not apply where the parties intend that the profit is to be obtained or the loss avoided by taking delivery of any property to which the contract relates.

(2) This paragraph does not apply to rights under any contract under which money is received by the Director of Savings as deposits or otherwise in connection with the business of the National Savings Bank or raised under the National Loans Act 1968 under the auspices of the Director of Savings or under which money raised is treated as having been so raised by virtue of section 11(3) of the National Debt Act 1972.

History
In para. 9 the word "Notes" substituted for the former word "Note", the previously unnumbered Note numbered (1) and Note (2) added by Financial Services Act 1986 (Restriction of Scope of Act and Meaning of Collective Investment Scheme) Order 1990 (S.I. 1990 No. 349), art. 2(2) as from 26 March 1990.

LONG TERM INSURANCE CONTRACTS

10 Rights under a contract the effecting and carrying out of which constitutes long term business within the meaning of the Insurance Companies Act 1982.

Notes

(1) This paragraph does not apply to rights under a contract of insurance if—

(a) the benefits under the contract are payable only on death or in respect of incapacity due to injury, sickness or infirmity;

(b) no benefits are payable under the contract on a death (other than a death due to accident) unless it occurs within ten years of the date on which the life of the person in question was first insured under the contract or before that person attains a specified age not exceeding seventy years;

(c) the contract has no surrender value or the consideration consists of a single premium and the surrender value does not exceed that premium; and

(d) the contract does not make provision for its conversion or extension in a manner that would result in its ceasing to comply with paragraphs (a), (b) and (c) above.

(2) Where the provisions of a contract of insurance are such that the effecting and carrying out of the contract—

(a) constitutes both long term business within the meaning of the Insurance Companies Act 1982 and general business within the meaning of that Act; or

(b) by virtue of section 1(3) of that Act constitutes long term business notwithstanding the inclusion of subsidiary general business provisions,

references in this paragraph to rights and benefits under the contract are references only to such rights and benefits as are attributable to the provisions of the contract relating to long term business.

(3) This paragraph does not apply to rights under a reinsurance contract.

(4) Rights falling within this paragraph shall not be regarded as falling within paragraph 9 above.

RIGHTS AND INTERESTS IN INVESTMENTS

11 Rights to and interests in anything which is an investment falling within any other paragraph of this Part of this Schedule.

Notes

(1) This paragraph does not apply to interests under the trusts of an occupational pension scheme.

(2) This paragraph does not apply to rights or interests which are investments by virtue of any other paragraph of this Part of this Schedule.

Part II — Activities Constituting Investment Business

DEALING IN INVESTMENTS

12 Buying, selling, subscribing for or underwriting investments or offering or agreeing to do so, either as principal or as an agent.

Notes

(1) This paragraph does not apply to a person by reason of his accepting, or offering or agreeing to accept, whether as principal or as agent, an instrument creating or acknowledging indebtedness in respect of any loan, credit, guarantee or other similar financial accommodation or assurance which he or his principal has made, granted or provided or which he or his principal has offered or agreed to make, grant or provide.

(2) The references in (1) above to a person accepting, or offering or agreeing to accept, an instrument include references to a person becoming, or offering or agreeing to become, a party to an instrument otherwise than as a debtor or a surety.

History
In para. 12 Notes (1) and (2) added by the Financial Services Act 1986 (Restriction of Scope of Act and Meaning of Collective Investment Scheme) Order 1988 (S.I. 1988 No. 803), art. 2 as from 29 April 1988.

ARRANGING DEALS IN INVESTMENTS

13 Making, or offering or agreeing to make—

(a) arrangements with a view to another person buying, selling, subscribing for or underwriting a particular investment; or

(b) arrangements with a view to a person who participates in the arrangements buying, selling, subscribing for or underwriting investments.

Notes

(1) This paragraph does not apply to a person by reason of his making, or offering or agreeing to make, arrangements with a view to a transaction to

which he will himself be a party as principal or which will be entered into by him as agent for one of the parties.

(2) The arrangements in (a) above are arrangements which bring about or would bring about the transaction in question.

(3) This paragraph does not apply to a person ("the relevant person") who is either a money-lending company within the meaning of section 338 of the Companies Act 1985 or a body corporate incorporated under the law of, or of any part of, the United Kingdom relating to building societies or a person whose ordinary business includes the making of loans or the giving of guarantees in connection with loans by reason of the relevant person making, or offering or agreeing to make, arrangements with a view to a person ("the authorised person") who is either authorised under section 22 or 23 of this Act or who is authorised under section 31 of this Act and carries on insurance business which is investment business selling an investment which falls within paragraph 10 above or, so far as relevant to that paragraph, paragraph 11 above if the arrangements are either—

(a) that the authorised person or a person on his behalf will introduce persons to whom the authorised person has sold or proposes to sell an investment of the kind described above, or will advise such persons to approach, the relevant person with a view to the relevant person lending money on the security of that investment; or

(b) that the authorised person gives an assurance to the relevant person as to the amount which will or may be received by the relevant person, should that person lend money to a person to whom the authorised person has sold or proposes to sell an investment of the kind described above, on the surrender or maturity of that investment if it is taken as security for the loan.

(4) This paragraph does not apply to a person by reason of his making, or offering or agreeing to make, arrangements with a view to a person accepting, whether as principal or as agent, an instrument creating or acknowledging indebtedness in respect of any loan, credit, guarantee or other similar financial accommodation or assurance which he or his principal has made, granted or provided or which he or his principal has offered or agreed to make, grant or provide.

(5) Arrangements do not fall within (b) above by reason of their having as their purpose the provision of finance to enable a person to buy, sell, subscribe for or underwrite investments.

(6) This paragraph does not apply to arrangements for the introduction of persons to another person if—

(a) the person to whom the introduction is made is an authorised or exempted person or is a person whose ordinary business involves him in engaging in activities which fall within this Part of this Schedule or would do apart from the provisions of Part III or Part IV and who is not unlawfully carrying on investment business in the United Kingdom; and

(b) the introduction is made with a view to the provision of independent advice or the independent exercise of discretion either—

   (i) in relation to investments generally; or

   (ii) in relation to any class of investments if the transaction or advice is or is to be with respect to an investment within that class.

(7) The references in (4) above to a person accepting an instrument include references to a person becoming a party to an instrument otherwise than as a debtor or a surety.

History

In para. 13 Note (3) added by the Financial Services Act 1986 (Restriction of Scope of Act) Order 1988 (S.I. 1988 No. 318), art. 2 as from 27 February 1988.

Notes (4)–(7) added by the Financial Services Act 1986 (Restriction of Scope of Act and Meaning of Collective Investment Scheme) Order 1988 (S.I. 1988 No. 803), art. 3 as from 29 April 1988.

MANAGING INVESTMENTS

14   Managing, or offering or agreeing to manage, assets belonging to another person if—

(a) those assets consist of or include investments; or

(b) the arrangements for their management are such that those assets may consist of or include investments at the discretion of the person managing or offering or agreeing to manage them and either they have at any time since the date of the coming into force of section 3 of this Act done so or the arrangements have at any time (whether before or after that date) been held out as arrangements under which they would do so.

INVESTMENT ADVICE

15   Giving, or offering or agreeing to give, to persons in their capacity as investors or potential investors advice on the merits of their purchasing, selling, subscribing for or underwriting an investment, or exercising any right conferred by an investment to acquire, dispose of, underwrite or convert an investment.

ESTABLISHING ETC. COLLECTIVE INVESTMENT SCHEMES

16   Establishing, operating or winding up a collective investment scheme, including acting as trustee of an authorised unit trust scheme.

Part III — Excluded Activities

DEALINGS AS PRINCIPAL

17(1)   Paragraph 12 above applies to a transaction which is or is to be entered into by a person as principal only if—

(a) he holds himself out as willing to enter into transactions of that kind at prices determined by him generally and continuously rather than in respect of each particular transaction; or

(b) he holds himself out as engaging in the business of buying investments with a view to selling them and those investments are or include investments of the kind to which the transaction relates; or

(c) he regularly solicits members of the public for the purpose of inducing them to enter as principals or agents into transactions to which that paragraph applies and the transaction is or is to be entered into as a result of his having solicited members of the public in that manner.

17(2) In sub-paragraph (1) above **"buying"** and **"selling"** means buying and selling by transactions to which paragraph 12 above applies and **"members of the public"**, in relation to the person soliciting them (**"the relevant person"**), means any other person except—

(a) authorised persons, exempted persons, or persons holding a permission under paragraph 23 below;

(b) members of the same group as the relevant person;

(c) persons who are, or propose to become, participators with the relevant person in a joint enterprise;

(d) any person who is solicited by the relevant person with a view to—

(i) the acquisition by the relevant person of 20 per cent, or more of the voting shares in a body corporate (that is to say, shares carrying not less than that percentage of the voting rights attributable to share capital which are exercisable in all circumstances at any general meeting of the body); or

(ii) if the relevant person (either alone or with other members of the same group as himself) holds 20 per cent, or more of the voting shares in a body corporate, the acquisition by him of further shares in the body or the disposal by him of shares in that body to the person solicited or to a member of the same group as that person; or

(iii) if the person solicited (either alone or with other members of the same group as himself) holds 20 per cent, or more of the voting shares in a body corporate, the disposal by the relevant person of further shares in that body to the person solicited or to a member of the same group as that person;

(e) any person whose head office is outside the United Kingdom, who is solicited by an approach made or directed to him at a place outside the United Kingdom and whose ordinary business involves him in engaging in activities which fall within Part II of this Schedule or would do so apart from this Part or Part IV.

17(3) Sub-paragraph (1) above applies only—

(a) if the investment to which the transaction relates or will relate falls within any of paragraphs 1 to 6 above or, so far as relevant to any of those paragraphs, paragraph 11 above; or

(b) if the transaction is the assignment (or, in Scotland, the assignation) of an investment falling within paragraph 10 above or is the assignment (or, in Scotland, the assignation) of an investment falling within paragraph 11 above which confers rights to or interests in an investment falling within paragraph 10 above.

History
Para. 17(3) substituted by the Financial Services Act 1986 (Restriction of Scope of Act) Order 1988 (S.I. 1988 No. 318), art. 3(1) as from 27 February 1988. The former para. 17(3) read as follows:

"**17(3)** Sub-paragraph (1) above applies only if the investment to which the transaction relates or will relate falls within any of paragraphs 1 to 6 above or, so far as relevant to any of those paragraphs, paragraph 11 above."

17(4) Paragraph 12 above does not apply to any transaction which relates or is to relate to an investment which falls within paragraph 10 above or, so far as relevant to that paragraph, paragraph 11 above nor does it apply to a transaction which relates or is to relate to an investment which falls within any of paragraphs 7 to 9 above or, so far as relevant to any of those paragraphs, paragraph 11 above being a transaction which, in either case, is or is to be entered into by a person as principal if he is not an authorised person and the transaction is or is to be entered into by him—

    (a) with or through an authorised person, an exempted person or a person holding a permission under paragraph 23 below; or

    (b) through an office outside the United Kingdom, maintained by a party to the transaction, and with or through a person whose head office is situated outside the United Kingdom and whose ordinary business is such as is mentioned in sub-paragraph (2)(e) above.

History
In para. 17(4) the words ", other than a transaction of a kind described in paragraph 3(a) or (b) above," formerly appearing after the words "does not apply to any transaction" deleted by Financial Services Act 1986 (Restriction of Scope of Act and Meaning of Collective Investment Scheme) Order 1990 (S.I. 1990 No. 349), art. 3 as from 26 March 1990.

Previously, in para. 17(4) the words, "any transaction, other than", to, "in either case,", substituted for the original words, "a transaction which relates or is to relate to any other investment and which", by Financial Services Act 1986 (Restriction of Scope of Act) Order 1988 (S.I. 1988 No. 318), art. 3(2) as from 27 February 1988.

GROUPS AND JOINT ENTERPRISES

18(1) Paragraph 12 above does not apply to any transaction which is or is to be entered into by a person as principal with another person if—

    (a) they are bodies corporate in the same group; or

    (b) they are, or propose to become, participators in a joint enterprise and the transaction is or is to be entered into for the purposes of, or in connection with, that enterprise.

18(2) Paragraph 12 above does not apply to any transaction which is or is to be entered into by any person as agent for another person in the circumstances mentioned in sub-paragraph (1)(a) or (b) above if—

    (a) where the investment falls within any of paragraphs 1 to 6 above or, so far as relevant to any of those paragraphs, paragraph 11 above, the agent does not—

        (i) hold himself out (otherwise than to other bodies corporate in the same group or persons who are or propose to become participators with him in a joint enterprise) as engaging in the business of buying investments with a view to selling them and those investments are or include investments of the kind to which the transaction relates; or

        (ii) regularly solicit members of the public for the purpose of inducing them to enter as principals or agents into transactions to which paragraph 12 above applies;

        and the transaction is not or is not to be entered into as a result of his having solicited members of the public in that manner;

(b) where the investment is not as mentioned in paragraph (a) above—

  (i) the agent enters into the transaction with or through an authorised person, an exempted person or a person holding a permission under paragraph 23 below; or

  (ii) the transaction is effected through an office outside the United Kingdom, maintained by a party to the transaction, and with or through a person whose head office is situated outside the United Kingdom and whose ordinary business involves him in engaging in activities which fall within Part II of this Schedule or would do so apart from this Part or Part IV.

18(3) Paragraph 13 above does not apply to arrangements which a person makes or offers or agrees to make if—

(a) that person is a body corporate and the arrangements are with a view to another body corporate in the same group entering into a transaction of the kind mentioned in that paragraph; or

(b) that person is or proposes to become a participator in a joint enterprise and the arrangements are with a view to another person who is or proposes to become a participator in the enterprise entering into such a transaction for the purposes of or in connection with that enterprise.

18(4) Paragraph 14 above does not apply to a person by reason of his managing or offering or agreeing to manage the investments of another person if—

(a) they are bodies corporate in the same group; or

(b) they are, or propose to become, participators in a joint enterprise and the investments are or are to be managed for the purposes of, or in connection with, that enterprise.

18(5) Paragraph 15 above does not apply to advice given by a person to another person if—

(a) they are bodies corporate in the same group; or

(b) they are, or propose to become, participators in a joint enterprise and the advice is given for the purposes of, or in connection with, that enterprise.

18(6) The definitions in paragraph 17(2) above shall apply also for the purposes of sub-paragraph (2)(a) above except that the relevant person referred to in paragraph 17(2)(d) shall be the person for whom the agent is acting.

SALE OF GOODS AND SUPPLY OF SERVICES

19(1) Subject to sub-paragraph (9) below, this paragraph has effect where a person ("the supplier") sells or offers or agrees to sell goods to another person ("the customer") or supplies or offers or agrees to supply him with services and the supplier's main business is to supply goods or services and not to engage in activities falling within Part II of this Schedule.

History
In para. 19(1) the words, "Subject to sub-paragraph (9) below,", inserted by the Financial Services Act 1986 (Extension of Scope of Act and Meaning of Collective Investment Scheme) Order 1988 (S.I. 1988 No. 496), art. 3(a) as from 25 March 1988.

19(2) Paragraph 12 above does not apply to any transaction which is or is to be entered into by the supplier as principal if it is or is to be entered into by him with the customer for the purposes of or in connection with the sale or supply or a related sale or supply (that is to say, a sale or supply to the customer otherwise than by the supplier but for or in connection with the same purpose as the first-mentioned sale or supply).

19(3)   Paragraph 12 above does not apply to any transaction which is or is to be entered into by the supplier as agent for the customer if it is or is to be entered into for the purposes of or in connection with the sale or supply or a related sale or supply and—

  (a) where the investment falls within any of paragraphs 1 to 6 above or, so far as relevant to any of those paragraphs, paragraph 11 above, the supplier does not—

    (i) hold himself out (otherwise than to the customer) as engaging in the business of buying investments with a view to selling them and those investments are or include investments of the kind to which the transaction relates; or

    (ii) regularly solicit members of the public for the purpose of inducing them to enter as principals or agents into transactions to which paragraph 12 above applies; and the transaction is not or is not to be entered into as a result of his having solicited members of the public in that manner;

  (b) where the investment is not as mentioned in paragraph (a) above, the supplier enters into the transaction—

    (i) with or through an authorised person, an exempted person or a person holding a permission under paragraph 23 below; or

    (ii) through an office outside the United Kingdom, maintained by a party to the transaction, and with or through a person whose head office is situated outside the United Kingdom and whose ordinary business involves him in engaging in activities which fall within Part II of this Schedule or would do so apart from this Part of Part IV.

Note
In para. 19(3)(a) the figure "5" to be substituted for "6" when a correction to Financial Services Act 1986 (Restriction of Scope of Act and Meaning of Collective Investment Scheme) Order 1990 (S.I. 1990 No. 349), art. 4 is published; art. 4 incorrectly purports to effect this amendment to para. 19(3)(b) as from 26 March 1990.

19(4)   Paragraph 13 above does not apply to arrangements which the supplier makes or offers or agrees to make with a view to the customer entering into a transaction for the purposes of or in connection with the sale or supply or a related sale or supply.

19(5)   Paragraph 14 above does not apply to the supplier by reason of his managing or offering or agreeing to manage the investments of the customer if they are or are to be managed for the purposes of or in connection with the sale or supply or a related sale or supply.

19(6)   Paragraph 15 above does not apply to advice given by the supplier to the customer for the purposes of or in connection with the sale or supply or a related sale or supply or to a person with whom the customer proposes to enter into a transaction for the purposes of or in connection with the sale or supply or a related sale or supply.

19(7)   Where the supplier is a body corporate and a member of a group sub-paragraphs (2) to (6) above shall apply to any other member of the group as they apply to the supplier; and where the customer is a body corporate and a member of a group references in those sub-paragraphs to the customer include references to any other member of the group.

19(8) The definitions in paragraph 17(2) above shall apply also for the purposes of sub-paragraph (3)(a) above.

19(9) This paragraph does not have effect where either—

(a) the customer is an individual; or

(b) the transaction in question is the purchase or sale of an investment which falls within paragraph 6 or 10 above or, so far as relevant to either of those paragraphs, paragraph 11 above; or

(c) the investments which the supplier manages or offers or agrees to manage consist of investments falling within paragraph 6 or 10 above or, so far as relevant to either of those paragraphs, paragraph 11 above; or

(d) the advice which the supplier gives is advice on an investment falling within the paragraph 6 or 10 above or, so far as relevant to either of those paragraphs, paragraph 11 above.

History
Para. 19(9) added by the Financial Services Act 1986 (Extension of Scope of Act and Meaning of Collective Investment Scheme) Order 1988 (S.I. 1988 No. 496), art. 3 as from 25 March 1988.

EMPLOYEES' SHARE SCHEMES

20(1) Paragraphs 12 and 13 above do not apply to anything done by a body corporate, a body corporate connected with it or a relevant trustee for the purpose of enabling or facilitating transactions in shares in or debentures of the first-mentioned body between or for the benefit of any of the persons mentioned in sub-paragraph (2) below or the holding of such shares or debentures by or for the benefit of any such persons.

20(2) The persons referred to in sub-paragraph (1) above are—

(a) the bona fide employees or former employees of the body corporate or of another body corporate in the same group; or

(b) the wives, husbands, widows, widowers, or children or step-children under the age of eighteen of such employees or former employees.

20(3) In this paragraph **"a relevant trustee"** means a person holding shares in or debentures of a body corporate as trustee in pursuance of arrangements made for the purpose mentioned in sub-paragraph (1) above by, or by a body corporate connected with, that body corporate.

20(4) In this paragraph "shares" and "debentures" include any investment falling within paragraph 1 or 2 above and also include any investment falling within paragraph 4 or 5 above so far as relating to those paragraphs or any investment falling within paragraph 11 above so far as relating to paragraph 1, 2, 4 or 5.

20(5) For the purposes of this paragraph a body corporate is connected with another body corporate if—

(a) they are in the same group; or

(b) one is entitled, either alone or with any other body corporate in the same group, to exercise or control the exercise of a majority of the voting rights attributable to the share capital which are exercisable in all circumstances at any general meeting of the other body corporate or of its holding company.

SALE OF BODY CORPORATE

21(1) Paragraphs 12 and 13 above do not apply to the acquisition or disposal of, or to anything done for the purposes of the acquisition or disposal of, shares in a body corporate other than an open-ended investment company, and paragraph 15 above does not apply to advice given in connection with the acquisition or disposal of such shares, if—

(a) the shares consist of or include shares carrying 75 per cent or more of the voting rights attributable to share capital which are exercisable in all circumstances at any general meeting of the body corporate; or

(b) the shares, together with any already held by the person acquiring them, carry not less than that percentage of those voting rights; and

(c) in either case, the acquisition and disposal is, or is to be between parties each of whom is a body corporate, a partnership, a single individual or a group of connected individuals.

History

The heading to para. 21 substituted by the Financial Services Act 1986 (Restriction of Scope of Act) Order 1988 (S.I. 1988 No. 318), art. 4(a) as from 27 February 1988. The former head read: "SALE OF PRIVATE COMPANY".

In para. 21(1) the words "body corporate other than an open-ended investment company" substituted for the former words "private company" by the Financial Services Act 1986 (Restriction of Scope of Act) Order 1988 (S.I. 1988 No. 318), art. 4(b) as from 27 February 1988.

In para. 21(1)(a) the words "body corporate" substituted for the former word "company" by the Financial Services Act 1986 (Restriction of Scope of Act) Order 1988 (S.I. 1988 No. 318), art. 4(d) as from 27 February 1988.

21(2) For the purposes of subsection (1)(c) above **"a group of connected individuals"**, in relation to the party disposing of the shares, means persons each of whom is, or is a close relative of, a director or manager of the body corporate and, in relation to the party acquiring the shares, means persons each of whom is, or is a close relative of, a person who is to be a director or manager of the body corporate.

History

In para. 21(2) the words "body corporate" substituted for the former word "company" where it appeared by the Financial Services Act 1986 (Restriction of Scope of Act) Order 1988 (S.I. 1988 No. 318), art. 4(d) as from 27 February 1988.

21(3) In this paragraph **"close relative"** means a person's spouse, his children and step-children, his parents and step-parents, his brothers and sisters and his step-brothers and step-sisters.

History

In para. 21(3) the words "'private company' means a private company within the meaning of section 1(3) of the Companies Act 1985 or the corresponding Northern Ireland provision and", formerly appearing after the words,

"In this paragraph", deleted by the Financial Services Act 1986 (Restriction of Scope of Act) Order 1988 (S.I. 1988 No. 318), art. 4(c) as from 27 February 1988.

TRUSTEES AND PERSONAL REPRESENTATIVES

22(1) Paragraph 12 above does not apply to a person by reason of his buying, selling or subscribing for an investment or offering or agreeing to do so if—

(a) the investment is or, as the case may be, is to be held by him as bare trustee or, in Scotland, as nominee for another person;

(b) he is acting on that person's instructions; and

(c) he does not hold himself out as providing a service of buying and selling investments.

22(2)   Paragraph 13 above does not apply to anything done by a person as trustee or personal representative with a view to—

(a) a fellow trustee or personal representative and himself engaging in their capacity as such in an activity falling within paragraph 12 above; or

(b) a beneficiary under the trust, will or intestacy engaging in any such activity,

unless that person is remunerated for what he does in addition to any remuneration he receives for discharging his duties as trustee or personal representative.

22(3)   Paragraph 14 above does not apply to anything done by a person as trustee or personal representative unless he holds himself out as offering investment management services or is remunerated for providing such services in addition to any remuneration he receives for discharging his duties as trustee or personal representative.

22(4)   Paragraph 15 above does not apply to advice given by a person as trustee or personal representative to—

(a) a fellow trustee or personal representative for the purposes of the trust or estate; or

(b) a beneficiary under the trust, will or intestacy concerning his interest in the trust fund or estate,

unless that person is remunerated for doing so in addition to any remuneration he receives for discharging his duties as trustee or personal representative.

22(5)   Sub-paragraph (1) above has effect to the exclusion of paragraph 17 above as respects any transaction in respect of which the conditions in sub-paragraph (1)(a) and (b) are satisfied.

DEALINGS IN COURSE OF NON-INVESTMENT BUSINESS

23(1)   Paragraph 12 above does not apply to anything done by a person—

(a) as principal;

(b) if that person is a body corporate in a group, as agent for another member of the group; or

(c) as agent for a person who is or proposes to become a participator with him in a joint enterprise and for the purposes of or in connection with that enterprise,

if it is done in accordance with the terms and conditions of a permission granted to him by the Secretary of State under this paragraph.

23(2)   Any application for permission under this paragraph shall be accompanied or supported by such information as the Secretary of State may require and shall not be regarded as duly made unless accompanied by the prescribed fee.

23(3)   The Secretary of State may grant a permission under this paragraph if it appears to him—

(a) that the applicant's main business, or if he is a member of a group the main business of the group, does not consist of activities for which a person is required to be authorised under this Act;

(b) that the applicant's business is likely to involve such activities which fall within paragraph 12 above; and

(c) that, having regard to the nature of the applicant's main business and, if he is a member of a group, the main business of the group taken as a whole, the manner in which, the persons with whom and the purposes for which the applicant proposes to engage in activities that would require him to be an authorised person and to any other relevant matters, it is inappropriate to require him to be subject to regulation as an authorised person.

23(4) Any permission under this paragraph shall be granted by a notice in writing; and the Secretary of State may by a further notice in writing withdraw any such permission if for any reason it appears to him that it is not appropriate for it to continue in force.

23(5) The Secretary of State may make regulations requiring persons holding permissions under this paragraph to furnish him with information for the purpose of enabling him to determine whether those permissions should continue in force; and such regulations may, in particular, require such persons—

(a) to give him notice forthwith of the occurrence of such events as are specified in the regulations and such information in respect of those events as is so specified;

(b) to furnish him at such times or in respect of such periods as are specified in the regulations with such information as is so specified.

23(6) Section 61 of this Act shall have effect in relation to a contravention of any condition imposed by a permission under this paragraph as it has effect in relation to any such contravention as is mentioned in subsection (1)(a) of that section.

23(7) Section 104 of this Act shall apply to a person holding a permission under this paragraph as if he were authorised to carry on investment business as there mentioned; and sections 105 and 106 of this Act shall have effect as if anything done by him in accordance with such permission constituted the carrying on of investment business.

ADVICE GIVEN OR ARRANGEMENTS MADE IN COURSE OF PROFESSION OR NON-INVESTMENT BUSINESS

24(1) Paragraph 15 above does not apply to advice—

(a) which is given in the course of the carrying on of any profession or of a business not otherwise constituting investment business; and

(b) the giving of which is a necessary part of other advice or services given in the course of carrying on that profession or business.

24(2) Paragraph 13 above does not apply to arrangements—

(a) which are made in the course of the carrying on of any profession or of a business not otherwise constituting investment business; and

(b) the making of which is a necessary part of other services provided in the course of carrying on that profession or business.

24(3) Advice shall not be regarded as falling within sub-paragraph (1)(b) above and the making of arrangements shall not be regarded as falling within sub-paragraph (2)(b) above if the giving of the advice or the making of the arrangements is remunerated separately from the other advice or services.

History
The words "OR ARRANGEMENTS MADE" in the heading to para. 24 inserted by the Financial Services Act 1986 (Restriction of Scope of Act and Meaning of Collective Investment Scheme) Order 1988 (S.I. 1988 No. 803), art. 4(1) as from 29 April 1988.

Para. 24(2) and (3) substituted for the former para. 24(2) by the Financial Services Act 1986 (Restriction of Scope of Act and Meaning of Collective Investment Scheme) Order 1988 (S.I. 1988 No. 803), art. 4(2) as from 29 April 1988. The former para. 24(2) read as follows:

"**24(2)** Advice shall not be regarded as falling within sub-paragraph (1)(b) above if it is remunerated separately from the other advice or services."

NEWSPAPERS

25(1)   Paragraph 15 above does not apply to advice given in a newspaper, journal, magazine or other periodical publication if the principal purpose of the publication, taken as a whole and including any advertisements contained in it, is not to lead persons to invest in any particular investment.

25(2)   The Secretary of State may, on the application of the proprietor of any periodical publication, certify that it is of the nature described in sub-paragraph (1) above and revoke any such certificate if he considers that it is no longer justified.

25(3)   A certificate given under sub-paragraph (2) above and not revoked shall be conclusive evidence of the matters certified.

ADVICE GIVEN IN SOUND, TELEVISION OR CABLE PROGRAMMES

25A(1)   Paragraph 15 above does not apply in respect of any advice given in any programme or teletext transmission—

(a) broadcast, or made for broadcasting, by the British Broadcasting Corporation or by the Independent Broadcasting Authority in accordance with the provisions of the Broadcasting Act 1981; or

(b) included, or made for inclusion, in a cable programme service which is, or does not require to be, licensed under the Cable and Broadcasting Act 1984; or

(c) broadcast, or made for broadcasting, by the Independent Broadcasting Authority in a DBS service.

25A(2)   In this paragraph—

(a) **"DBS service"** has the same meaning as in section 37(3) of the Cable and Broadcasting Act 1984;

(b) **"programme"**, in relation to a television or sound broadcasting service or a cable programme service, includes an advertisement and any other item included in that service; and

(c) **"teletext transmission"** has the same meaning as in section 14(6) of the Broadcasting Act 1981 and includes any such transmission broadcast in a DBS service or in a service which is an additional teletext service within the meaning of section 47(2) of the Cable and Broadcasting Act 1984.

History
Para. 25A substituted by Financial Services Act 1986 (Restriction of Scope of Act and Meaning of Collective Investment Scheme) Order 1990 (S.I. 1990 No. 349), art. 5 as from 26 March 1990; para. 25A formerly read as follows:

"**25A(1)**   Paragraph 15 above does not apply to any advice given in any programme or teletext transmission—

(a) broadcast, or made for broadcasting, by the British Broadcasting Corporation or by the Independent Broadcasting Authority in accordance with the provisions of the Broadcasting Act 1981; or

(b) included, or made for inclusion, in a cable programme service which is, or does not require to be, licensed under the Cable and Broadcasting Act 1984.

25A(2)   In this paragraph—

'**programme**', in relation to a television or sound broadcasting service or a cable programme service, includes an advertisement and any other item included in that service; and

'**teletext transmission**' has the same meaning as in section 14(6) of the Broadcasting Act 1981 and includes any such transmission broadcast by a service which is an additional teletext service within the meaning of section 47(2) of the Cable and Broadcasting Act 1984."

Previously, para. 25A inserted by Financial Services Act 1986 (Restriction of Scope of Act) Order 1988 (S.I. 1988 No. 318), art. 5 as from 27 February 1988; art. 5 revoked by Financial Services Act 1986 (Restriction of Scope of Act and Meaning of Collective Investment Scheme) Order 1990 (S.I. 1990 No. 349), art. 8(a) as from 26 March 1990.

INTERNATIONAL SECURITIES SELF-REGULATING ORGANISATIONS

25B(1)   An activity within paragraph 13 above engaged in for the purposes of carrying out the functions of a body or association which is approved under this paragraph as an international securities self-regulating organisation, whether by the organisation or by any person acting on its behalf, shall not constitute the carrying on of investment business in the United Kingdom for the purposes of Chapter II of Part I of this Act.

25B(2)   In this paragraph—

"**International securities business**" means the business of buying, selling, subscribing for or underwriting investments (or offering or agreeing to do so, either as principal or agent) which fall within any of the paragraphs in Part I above other than paragraph 10 and, so far as relevant to paragraph 10, paragraph 11 and which, by their nature, and the manner in which the business is conducted, may be expected normally to be bought or dealt in by persons sufficiently expert to understand any risks involved, where either the transaction is international or each of the parties may be expected to be indifferent to the location of the other, and, for the purposes of this definition, the fact that the investments may ultimately be bought otherwise than in the course of international securities business by persons not so expert shall be disregarded; and

"**international securities self-regulating organisation**" means a body corporate or unincorporated association which

(a) does not have its head office in the United Kingdom;

(b) is not eligible for recognition under section 37 or section 39 of this Act on the ground that (whether or not it has applied, and whether or not it would be eligible on other grounds) it is unable to satisfy the requirements of section 40(2)(a) or (c) of this Act;

(c) has a membership composed of persons falling within any of the following categories, that is to say, authorised persons, exempted persons, persons holding a permission under paragraph 23 above and persons whose head offices are outside the United Kingdom and whose ordinary business is such as is mentioned in paragraph 17(2)(e) above; and

(d) which facilitates and regulates the activity of its members in the conduct of international securities business.

25B(3) The Secretary of State may approve as an international securities self-regulating organisation any body or association appearing to him to fall within sub-paragraph (2) above if, having regard to such matters affecting international trade, overseas earnings and the balance of payments or otherwise as he considers relevant, it appears to him that to do so would be desirable and not result in any undue risk to investors.

25B(4) Any approval under this paragraph shall be given by notice in writing; and the Secretary of State may by a further notice in writing withdraw any such approval if for any reason it appears to him that it is not appropriate for it to continue in force.

History
Para. 25B inserted by the Financial Services Act 1986
(Restriction of Scope of Act) Order 1988 (S.I. 1988
No. 318), art. 6 as from 27 February 1988.

Part IV — Additional Exclusions for Persons Without Permanent Place of Business in United Kingdom

TRANSACTIONS WITH OR THROUGH AUTHORISED OR EXEMPTED PERSONS

26(1) Paragraph 12 above does not apply to any transaction by a person not falling within section 1(3)(a) of this Act ("an overseas person") with or through—

(a) an authorised person; or

(b) an exempted person acting in the course of business in respect of which he is exempt.

26(2) Paragraph 13 above does not apply if—

(a) the arrangements are made by an overseas person with, or the offer or agreement to make them is made by him to or with, an authorised person or an exempted person and, in the case of an exempted person, the arrangements are with a view to his entering into a transaction in respect of which he is exempt; or

(b) the transactions with a view to which the arrangements are made are, as respects transactions in the United Kingdom, confined to transactions by authorised persons and transactions by exempted persons in respect of which they are exempt.

UNSOLICITED OR LEGITIMATELY SOLICITED TRANSACTIONS ETC. WITH OR FOR OTHER PERSONS

27(1) Paragraph 12 above does not apply to any transaction entered into by an overseas person as principal with, or as agent for, a person in the United Kingdom, paragraphs 13, 14 and 15 above do not apply to any offer made by an overseas person to or agreement made by him with a person in the United Kingdom and paragraph 15 above does not apply to any advice given by an overseas person to a person in the United Kingdom if the transaction, offer, agreement or advice is the result of—

(a) an approach made to the overseas person by or on behalf of the person in the United Kingdom which either has not been in any way solicited by the overseas person or has been solicited by him in a way which has not contravened section 56 or 57 of this Act; or

(b)   an approach made by the overseas person which has not contravened either of those sections.

27(2)   Where the transaction is entered into by the overseas person as agent for a person in the United Kingdom, sub-paragraph (1) above applies only if—

(a)   the other party is outside the United Kingdom; or

(b)   the other party is in the United Kingdom and the transaction is the result of such an approach by the other party as is mentioned in sub-paragraph (1)(a) above or of such an approach as is mentioned in sub-paragraph (1)(b) above.

Part V — Interpretation

28(1)   In this Schedule—

(a)   "property" includes currency of the United Kingdom or any other country or territory;

(b)   references to an instrument include references to any record whether or not in the form of a document;

(c)   references to an offer include references to an invitation to treat;

(d)   references to buying and selling include references to any acquisition or disposal for valuable consideration.

28(2)   In sub-paragraph (1)(d) above "disposal" includes—

(a)   in the case of an investment consisting of rights under a contract or other arrangements, assuming the corresponding liabilities under the contract or arrangements;

(b)   in the case of any other investment, issuing or creating the investment or granting the rights or interests of which it consists;

(c)   in the case of an investment consisting of rights under a contract, surrendering, assigning or converting those rights.

28(3)   A company shall not by reason of issuing its own shares or share warrants, and a person shall not by reason of issuing his own debentures or debenture warrants, be regarded for the purpose of this Schedule as disposing of them or, by reason of anything done for the purpose of issuing them, be regarded as making arrangements with a view to a person subscribing for or otherwise acquiring them or underwriting them.

28(4)   In sub-paragraph (3) above **"company"** has the same meaning as in paragraph 1 above, "shares" and "debentures" include any investments falling within paragraph 1 or 2 above and **"share warrants"** and **"debenture warrants"** means any investment which falls within paragraph 4 above and relates to shares in the company concerned or, as the case may be, to debentures issued by the person concerned.

29   For the purposes of this Schedule a transaction is entered into through a person if he enters into it as agent or arranges for it to be entered into by another person as principal or agent.

30(1)   For the purposes of this Schedule a group shall be treated as including any body corporate in which a member of the group holds a qualifying capital interest.

30(2)   A qualifying capital interest means an interest in relevant shares of the body corporate which the member holds on a long-term basis for the purpose of securing a contribution to its own activities by the exercise of control or influence arising from that interest.

30(3)   Relevant shares means shares comprised in the equity share capital of the body corporate of a class carrying rights to vote in all circumstances at general meetings of the body.

30(4)   A holding of 20 per cent or more of the nominal value of the relevant shares of a body corporate shall be presumed to be a qualifying capital interest unless the contrary is shown.

30(5)   In this paragraph "equity share capital" has the same meaning as in the Companies Act 1985 and the Companies (Northern Ireland) Order 1986.

History
Para. 30 substituted by CA 1989, s. 23 and Sch. 10, para. 36(1), (3) as from 1 April 1990 subject to transitional and savings provisions (see S.I. 1990 No. 355 (C. 13), art. 3, Sch. 1 and also art. 6–9); former para. 30 read as follows:
"**30** For the purposes of this Schedule a group shall be treated as including any body corporate which is a related company within the meaning of paragraph 92 of Schedule 4 to the Companies Act 1985 of any member of the group or would be such a related company if the member of the group were a company within the meaning of that Act."

31   In this Schedule **"a joint enterprise"** means an enterprise into which two or more persons ("the participators") enter for commercial reasons related to a business or businesses (other than investment business) carried on by them; and where a participator is a body corporate and a member of a group each other member of the group shall also be regarded as a participator in the enterprise.

32   Where a person is an exempted person as respects only part of the investment business carried on by him anything done by him in carrying on that part shall be disregarded in determining whether any paragraph of Part III or IV of this Schedule applies to anything done by him in the course of business in respect of which he is not exempt.

33   In determining for the purposes of this Schedule whether anything constitutes an investment or the carrying on of investment business section 18 of the Gaming Act 1845, section 1 of the Gaming Act 1892, any corresponding provision in force in Northern Ireland and any rule of the law of Scotland whereby a contract by way of gaming or wagering is not legally enforceable shall be disregarded.

34(1)   For the purposes of this Schedule arrangements are not a collective investment scheme if—

> (a)   the property to which the arrangements relate (other than cash awaiting investment) consists of shares;

> (b)   they constitute a complying fund:

> (c)   each participant is the owner of a part of the property to which the arrangements relate and, to the extent that his part of that property—

>> (i)   comprises relevant shares of a class which are admitted to the Official List of any member State or to dealings on a recognised investment exchange, he is entitled to withdraw it at any time after the end of the

period of five years beginning with the date on which the shares in question were issued;

    (ii) comprises relevant shares which do not fall within sub-paragraph (i) above, he is entitled to withdraw it at any time after the end of the period of two years beginning with the date upon which the period referred to in sub-paragraph (i) above expired;

    (iii) comprises any other shares, he is entitled to withdraw it at any time after the end of the period of six months beginning with the date upon which the shares in question ceased to be relevant shares; and

    (iv) comprises cash which the operator has not agreed (conditionally or unconditionally) to apply in subscribing for shares, he is entitled to withdraw it at any time; and

  (d) the arrangements would meet the conditions described in section 75(5)(c) of this Act were it not for the fact that the operator is entitled to exercise all or any of the rights conferred by shares included in the property to which the arrangements relate.

34(2) For the purposes of this paragraph—

  (a) **"shares"** means investments falling within paragraph 1 of this Schedule;

  (b) shares shall be regarded as being relevant shares if and so long as they are shares in respect of which neither—

    (i) a claim for relief made in accordance with section 306 of the Income and Corporation Taxes Act 1988 has been disallowed; nor

    (ii) an assessment has been made pursuant to section 307 of that Act withdrawing or refusing relief by reason of the body corporate in which the shares are held having ceased to be a body corporate which is a qualifying company for the purposes of section 293 of that Act; and

  (c) arrangements shall be regarded as constituting a complying fund if they provide that—

    (i) the operator will, so far as practicable, make investments each of which, subject to each participant's individual circumstances, qualify for relief by virtue of Chapter III of Part VII of the Income and Corporation Taxes Act 1988; and

    (ii) the minimum subscription to the arrangements made by each participant must be not less than £2,000.

History
See history note after para. 35.

35 For the purposes of this Schedule the following are not collective investment schemes—

  (a) arrangements where the entire contribution of each participant is a deposit within the meaning of section 5 of the Banking Act 1987 or a sum of a kind described in subsection (3) of that section;

  (b) arrangements under which the rights or interests of the participants are represented by the following—

    (i) investments falling within paragraph 2 of this Schedule which are issued by a single body corporate which is not an open-ended investment company or which are issued by a single issuer which is not a body corporate and are guaranteed by the government of the United Kingdom, of Northern Ireland, or of any country or territory outside the United Kingdom; or

(ii) investments falling within sub-paragraph (i) above which are convertible into or exchangeable for investments falling within paragraph 1 of this Schedule provided that those latter investments are issued by the same person as issued the investments falling within sub-paragraph (i) above or are issued by a single other issuer; or

(iii) investments falling within paragraph 3 of this Schedule issued by the same government, local authority or public authority; or

(iv) investments falling within paragraph 4 of this Schedule which are issued otherwise than by an open-ended investment company and which confer rights in respect of investments, issued by the same issuer, falling within paragraph 1 of this Schedule or within sub-paragraph (i), (ii) or (iii) above;

(c) arrangements which would fall within paragraph (b) above were it not for the fact that the rights or interests of a participant ("the counterparty") whose ordinary business involves him in engaging in activities which fall within Part II of this Schedule or would do so apart from Part III or IV are or include rights or interests under a swap arrangement, that is to say, an arrangement the purpose of which is to facilitate the making of payments to participants whether in a particular amount or currency or at a particular time or rate of interest or all or any combination of those things, being an arrangement under which—

(i) the counterparty is entitled to receive amounts (whether representing principal or interest) payable in respect of any property subject to the scheme or sums determined by reference to such amounts; and

(ii) the counterparty makes payments (whether or not of the same amount and whether or not in the same currency as those referred to in sub-paragraph (i) above) which are calculated in accordance with an agreed formula by reference to the amounts or sums referred to in sub-paragraph (i) above;

(d) arrangements under which the rights or interests of participants are rights to or interests in money held in a common account in circumstances in which the money so held is held on the understanding that an amount representing the contribution of each participant is to be applied either in making payments to him or in satisfaction of sums owed by him or in the acquisition of property or the provision of services for him;

(e) arrangements under which the rights and interests of participants are rights and interests in a fund which is a trust fund within the meaning of section 42(1) of the Landlord and Tenant Act 1987.

History
Para. 34 and 35 added by Financial Services Act 1986 (Restriction of Scope of Act and Meaning of Collective Investment Scheme) Order 1990 (S.I. 1990 No. 349), art. 7 as from 26 March 1990.

Schedule 2 — Requirements for Recognition of Self-Regulating Organisation

Section 10

MEMBERS TO BE FIT AND PROPER PERSONS

1(1) The rules and practices of the organisation must be such as to secure that its members are fit and proper persons to carry on investment business of the kind with which the organisation is concerned.

1(2) Where the organisation is concerned with investment business of different kinds its rules and practices must be such as to secure that a member carrying on investment business of any of those kinds is a fit and proper person to carry on investment business of that kind.

1(3) The matters which may be taken into account under the rules in determining whether a person is a fit and proper person must include those that the Secretary of State may take into account under section 27 above.

1(4) This paragraph does not apply to a person who is not an authorised person by virtue of being a member of the organisation.

ADMISSION, EXPULSION AND DISCIPLINE

2 The rules and practices of the organisation relating to—

 (a) the admission and expulsion of members; and

 (b) the discipline it exercises over its members,

must be fair and reasonable and include adequate provision for appeals.

SAFEGUARDS FOR INVESTORS

3(1) The organisation must have rules governing the carrying on of investment business by its members which, together with the statements of principle, rules, regulations and codes of practice to which its members are subject under Chapter V of Part I of this Act, are such as to afford an adequate level of protection for investors.

3(2) In determining in any case whether an adequate level of protection is afforded for investors of any description, regard shall be had to the nature of the investment business carried on by members of the organisation, the kinds of investors involved and the effectiveness of the organisation's arrangements for enforcing compliance.

History
Para. 3(1), (2) substituted by CA 1989, s. 203(1) as from 15 March 1990 (see S.I. 1990 No. 354 (C. 12), art. 3); para. 3(1), (2) formerly read as follows:

"**3(1)** The rules of the organisation governing the carrying on of investment business of any kind by its members must afford investors protection at least equivalent to that afforded in respect of investment business of that kind by the rules and regulations for the time being in force under Chapter V of Part I of this Act.

(2) The rules under that Chapter to be taken into account for the purposes of sub-paragraph (1) above include the rules made under section 49 and under sections 53 and 54 so far as not themselves applying to the members of the organisation."

Note
For transitional provisions in relation to para. 3(1), (2) see CA 1989, s. 203(3) and S.I. 1990 No. 354 (C. 2), art. 6.

3(3) The organisation must, so far as practicable, have powers for purposes corresponding to those of Chapter VI of Part I of this Act.

3(4) The rules of the organisation must enable it to prevent a member resigning from the organisation if the organisation considers that any matter affecting him should be investigated as a preliminary to a decision on the question whether he should be expelled or otherwise disciplined or if it considers that it is desirable that a prohibition or requirement should be imposed on him under the powers mentioned in sub-paragraph (3) above or that any prohibition or requirement imposed on him under those powers should continue in force.

TAKING ACCOUNT OF COSTS OF COMPLIANCE

3A The organisation must have satisfactory arrangements for taking account, in framing its rules, of the cost to those to whom the rules would apply of complying with those rules and any other controls to which they are subject.

History
Para. 3A inserted by CA 1989, s. 204(1) as from 15 March 1990 (see S.I. 1990 No. 354 (C. 12), art. 3).

Note
See CA 1989, s. 204(2), (3).

MONITORING AND ENFORCEMENT

4(1) The organisation must have adequate arrangements and resources for the effective monitoring and enforcement of compliance with its rules and with any statements of principle, rules, regulations or codes of practice to which its members are subject under Chapter V of Part I of this Act in respect of investment business of a kind regulated by the organisation.

History
In para. 4(1) the words "statements of principle, rules, regulations or codes of practice" substituted for the former words "rules or regulations" by CA 1989, s. 206(1) and

Sch. 23, para. 20 as from 15 March 1990 (see S.I. 1990 No. 354 (C. 12), art. 3).

4(2) The arrangements for monitoring may make provision for that function to be performed on behalf of the organisation (and without affecting its responsibility) by any other body or person who is able and willing to perform it.

THE GOVERNING BODY

5(1) The arrangements of the organisation with respect to the appointment, removal from office and functions of the persons responsible for making or enforcing the rules of the organisation must be such as to secure a proper balance—

> (a) between the interests of the different members of the organisation; and

> (b) between the interests of the organisation or its members and the interests of the public.

5(2) The arrangements shall not be regarded as satisfying the requirements of this paragraph unless the persons responsible for those matters include a number of persons independent of the organisation and its members sufficient to secure the balance referred to in sub-paragraph (1)(b) above.

INVESTIGATION OF COMPLAINTS

6(1) The organisation must have effective arrangements for the investigation of complaints against the organisation or its members.

6(2) The arrangements may make provision for the whole or part of that function to be performed by and to be the responsibility of a body or person independent of the organisation.

PROMOTION AND MAINTENANCE OF STANDARDS

7 The organisation must be able and willing to promote and maintain high standards of integrity and fair dealing in the carrying on of investment business and to co-operate, by the sharing of information and otherwise, with the Secretary of State and any other authority, body or person having responsibility for the supervision or regulation of investment business or other financial services.

Schedule 3 — Requirements for Recognition of Professional Body

Section 18

STATUTORY STATUS

1 The body must—

    (a) regulate the practice of a profession in the exercise of statutory powers; or

    (b) be recognised (otherwise than under this Act) for a statutory purpose by a Minister of the Crown or by, or by the head of, a Northern Ireland department; or

    (c) be specified in a provision contained in or made under an enactment as a body whose members are qualified to exercise functions or hold offices specified in that provision.

CERTIFICATION

2(1) The body must have rules, practices and arrangements for securing that no person can be certified by the body for the purposes of Part I of this Act unless the following conditions are satisfied.

2(2) The certified person must be either—

    (a) an individual who is a member of the body; or

    (b) a person managed and controlled by one or more individuals each of whom is a member of a recognised professional body and at least one of whom is a member of the certifying body.

2(3) Where the certified person is an individual his main business must be the practice of the profession regulated by the certifying body and he must be practising that profession otherwise than in partnership; and where the certified person is not an individual that person's main business must be the practice of the profession or professions regulated by the recognised professional body or bodies of which the individual or individuals mentioned in sub-paragraph (2)(b) above are members.

2(4) In the application of sub-paragraphs (2) and (3) above to a certificate which is to be or has been issued to a partnership constituted under the law of England and Wales or Northern Ireland or the law of any other country or territory under which a partnership is not a legal person, references to the certified person shall be construed as references to the partnership.

SAFEGUARDS FOR INVESTORS

3(1) The body must have rules regulating the carrying on of investment business by persons certified by it which, together with the statements of principle, rules, regulations and codes of practice to which those persons are subject under Chapter V of Part I of this Act, afford an adequate level of protection for investors.

3(2) In determining in any case whether an adequate level of protection is afforded for investors of any description, regard shall be had to the nature of the investment business carried on by persons certified by the body, the kinds of investors involved and the effectiveness of the body's arrangements for enforcing compliance.

History
Para. 3 substituted by CA 1989, s. 203(2) as from 15 March 1990 (see S.I. 1990 No. 354 (C. 12), art. 3); para. 3 formerly read as follows:

"**3(1)** The body must have rules regulating the carrying on of investment business by persons certified by it; and those rules must in respect of investment business of any kind regulated by them afford to investors protection at least equivalent to that afforded in respect of investment business of that kind by the rules and regulations for the time being in force under Chapter V of Part I of this Act.

(2) The rules under that Chapter to be taken into account for the purposes of this paragraph include the rules made under section 49 and under sections 53 and 54 so far as not themselves applying to persons certified by the body."

Note
For transitional provisions in relation to para. 3 see CA 1989, s. 203(3) and S.I. 1990 No. 354 (C. 12), art. 6.

TAKING ACCOUNT OF COSTS OF COMPLIANCE

3A The organisation must have satisfactory arrangements for taking account, in framing its rules, of the cost to those to whom the rules would apply of complying with those rules and any other controls to which they are subject.

History
Para. 3A inserted by CA 1989, s. 204(1) as from 15 March 1990 (see S.I. 1990 No. 354 (C. 12), art. 3).

Note
See CA 1989, s. 204(2), (3).

MONITORING AND ENFORCEMENT

4(1) The body must have adequate arrangements and resources for the effective monitoring of the continued compliance by persons certified by it with the conditions mentioned in paragraph 2 above and rules, practices and arrangements for the withdrawal or suspension of certification (subject to appropriate transitional provisions) in the event of any of those conditions ceasing to be satisfied.

4(2) The body must have adequate arrangements and resources for the effective monitoring and enforcement of compliance by persons certified by it with the rules of the body relating to the carrying on of investment business and with any statements of principle, rules, regulations or codes of practice to which those persons are subject under Chapter V of Part I of this Act in respect of business of a kind regulated by the body.

History
In para. 4(2) the words "statements of principle, rules, regulations or codes of practice" substituted for the former words "rules or regulations" by CA 1989, s. 206(1) and

Sch. 23, para. 21 as from 15 March 1990 (see S.I. 1990 No. 354 (C. 12), art. 3).

4(3) The arrangements for enforcement must include provision for the withdrawal or suspension of certification and may include provision for disciplining members of the body who manage or control a certified person.

4(4) The arrangements for enforcement may make provision for the whole or part of that function to be performed by and to be the responsibility of a body or person independent of the professional body.

4(5) The arrangements for enforcement must be such as to secure a proper balance between the interests of persons certified by the body and the interests of the public; and the arrangements shall not be regarded as satisfying that requirement unless the persons responsible for enforcement include a sufficient number of persons who are independent of the body and its members and of persons certified by it.

4(6) The arrangements for monitoring may make provision for that function to be performed on behalf of the body (and without affecting its responsibility) by any other body or person who is able and willing to perform it.

INVESTIGATION OF COMPLAINTS

5(1) The body must have effective arrangements for the investigation of complaints relating to—

(a) the carrying on by persons certified by it of investment business in respect of which they are subject to its rules; and

(b) its regulation of investment business.

5(2) Paragraph 4(4) above applies also to arrangements made pursuant to this paragraph.

PROMOTION AND MAINTENANCE OF STANDARDS

6 The body must be able and willing to promote and maintain high standards of integrity and fair dealing in the carrying on of investment business and to co-operate, by the sharing of information and otherwise, with the Secretary of State and any other authority, body or person having responsibility for the supervision or regulation of investment business or other financial services.

Schedule 4 — Requirements for Recognition of Investment Exchange

Section 36 and 37

FINANCIAL RESOURCES

1 The exchange must have financial resources sufficient for the proper performance of its functions.

SAFEGUARDS FOR INVESTORS

2(1) The rules and practices of the exchange must ensure that business conducted by means of its facilities is conducted in an orderly manner and so as to afford proper protection to investors.

2(2) The exchange must—

(a) limit dealings on the exchange to investments in which there is a proper market; and

(b) where relevant, require issuers of investments dealt in on the exchange to comply with such obligations as will, so far as possible, afford to persons dealing in the investments proper information for determining their current value.

2(3) In the case of securities to which Part IV of this Act applies compliance by The Stock Exchange with the provisions of that Part shall be treated as compliance by it with sub-paragraph (2) above.

2(4) The exchange must either have its own arrangements for ensuring the performance of transactions effected on the exchange or ensure their performance by means of services provided under clearing arrangements made by it with a recognised clearing house.

2(5) The exchange must either itself have or secure the provision on its behalf of satisfactory arrangements for recording the transactions effected on the exchange.

2(6) Sub-paragraphs (2), (4) and (5) above are without prejudice to the generality of sub-paragraph (1) above.

MONITORING AND ENFORCEMENT

3(1) The exchange must have adequate arrangements and resources for the effective monitoring and enforcement of compliance with its rules and any clearing arrangements made by it.

3(2) The arrangements for monitoring may make provision for that function to be performed on behalf of the exchange (and without affecting its responsibility) by any other body or person who is able and willing to perform it.

INVESTIGATION OF COMPLAINTS

4 The exchange must have effective arrangements for the investigation of complaints in respect of business transacted by means of its facilities.

PROMOTION AND MAINTENANCE OF STANDARDS

5 The exchange must be able and willing to promote and maintain high standards of integrity and fair dealing in the carrying on of investement business and to co-operate, by the sharing of information and otherwise, with the Secretary of State and any other authority, body or person having responsibility for the supervision or regulation of investment business or other financial services.

SUPPLEMENTARY

6(1) The provisions of this Schedule relate to an exchange only so far as it provides facilities for the carrying on of investment business; and nothing in this Schedule shall be construed as requiring an exchange to limit dealings on the exchange to dealings in investments.

6(2) The references in this Schedule, and elsewhere in this Act, to ensuring the performance of transactions on an exchange are to providing satisfactory procedures (including default procedures) for the settlement of transactions on the exchange.

History
Para. 6 inserted by CA 1989, s. 205(1) as from 15 March 1990 (see S.I. 1990 No. 354 (C. 12), art. 3) but the amend-ment is deemed always to have had effect (see CA 1989, s. 205(2)).

Schedule 5 — Listed Money Market Institutions

Section 43

Part I — Transactions not Subject to Monetary Limit

1 This Part of this Schedule applies to any transaction entered into by the listed institution as principal (or as agent for another listed institution) with another listed institution or the Bank of England (whether acting as principal or agent) if the transaction falls within paragraph 2 or 3 below.

2(1) A transaction falls within this paragraph if it is in respect of an investment specified in sub-paragraph (2) below and—

(a) in the case of an investment within any of paragraphs (a) to (d) of that sub-paragraph, the transaction is not regulated by the rules of a recognised investment exchange; and

(b) in the case of any other investment specified in that sub-paragraph, the transaction is not made on such an exchange or expressed to be as so made.

2(2) The investments referred to above are—

(a) a debenture or other instrument falling within paragraph 2 of Schedule 1 to this Act which is issued—

   (i) by an authorised institution within the meaning of the Banking Act 1987 or a building society incorporated in, or in any part of, the United Kingdom; and

   (ii) on terms requiring repayment not later than five years from the date of issue;

(b) any other debenture or instrument falling within paragraph 2 of Schedule 1 to this Act which is issued on terms requiring repayment not later than one year from the date of issue;

(c) loan stock, or any other instrument, falling within paragraph 3 of Schedule 1 to this Act which is issued on terms requiring repayment not later than one year or, if issued by a local authority in the United Kingdom, five years from the date of issue;

(d) a warrant or other instrument falling within paragraph 4 of Schedule 1 to this Act which entitles the holder to subscribe for an investment within paragraph (a), (b) or (c) above;

(e) any certificate or other instrument falling within paragraph 5 or 11 of Schedule 1 to this Act and relating to an investment within paragraph (a), (b) or (c) above;

(f) an option falling within paragraph 7 of Schedule 1 to this Act and relating to—

   (i) an investment within paragraph (a), (b) or (c) above;

   (ii) currency of the United Kingdom or of any other country or territory; or

   (iii) gold or silver;

(g) rights under a contract falling within paragraph 8 of Schedule 1 to this Act for the sale of—

   (i) an investment within paragraph (a), (b) or (c) above;

   (ii) currency of the United Kingdom or of any other country or territory; or

   (iii) gold or silver;

(h) rights under a contract falling within paragraph 9 of Schedule 1 to this Act by reference to fluctuations in—

(i) the value or price of any investment falling within any of the foregoing paragraphs; or

(ii) currency of the United Kingdom or of any other country or territory; or

(iii) the rate of interest on loans in any such currency or any index of such rates;

(i) an option to aquire or dispose of an investment within paragraph (f), (g) or (h) above.

History
In para. 2(2) the words, "an authorised institution within the meaning of the Banking Act 1987", substituted for the former words, "a recognised bank or licensed institution within the meaning of the Banking Act 1979", by Banking Act 1987, s. 108(1) and Sch. 6, para. 27(6) as from 1 October 1987 (see S.I. 1987 No. 1664 (C. 50)).

3(1) A transaction falls within this paragraph if it is a transaction by which one of the parties agrees to sell or transfer an investment falling within paragraph 2 or 3 of Schedule 1 to this Act and by the same or a collateral agreement that party agrees, or acquires an option, to buy back or re-acquire that investment or an equivalent amount of a similar investment within twelve months of the sale or transfer.

3(2) For the purposes of this paragraph investments shall be regarded as similar if they entitle their holders to the same rights against the same persons as to capital and interest and the same remedies for the enforcement of those rights.

Part II — Transactions Subject to Monetary Limit

4(1) This Part of the Schedule applies to any transaction entered into by the listed institution—

(a) as principal (or as agent for another listed institution) with an unlisted person (whether acting as principal or agent);

(b) as agent for an unlisted person with a listed institution or the Bank of England (whether acting as principal or agent); or

(c) as agent for an unlisted person with another unlisted person (whether acting as principal or agent),

if the transaction falls within paragraph 2 or 3 above and the conditions in paragraph 5 or, as the case may be, paragraph 7 below are satisfied.

4(2) In this Part of this Schedule and in Part III below **"unlisted person"** means a person who is neither a listed institution nor the Bank of England.

5(1) In the case of a transaction falling within paragraph 2 above the conditions referred to above are as follows but subject to paragraph 6 below.

5(2) The consideration for a transaction in respect of an investment falling within paragraph 2(2)(a), (b), (c) or (e) above must be not less than £100,000.

5(3) The consideration payable on subscription in the case of an investment falling within paragraph 2(2)(d) must not be less than £500,000.

5(4) The value or price of the property in respect of which an option within paragraph 2(2)(f) above is granted must not be less than £500,000.

5(5) The price payable under a contract within paragraph 2(2)(g) above must be not less than £500,000.

5(6) The value or price the fluctuation in which, or the amount the fluctuation in the interest on which, is relevant for the purposes of a contract within paragraph 2(2)(h) above must not be less than £500,000.

5(7) In the case of an option falling within paragraph 2(2)(i) above the condition in sub-paragraph (4), (5) or (6) above, as the case may be, must be satisfied in respect of the investment to which the option relates.

6 The conditions in paragraph 5 above do not apply to a transaction entered into by the listed institution as mentioned in paragraph (a), (b) or (c) of paragraph 4(1) above if—

(a) the unlisted person mentioned in paragraph (a) or (b) or, as the case may be, each of the unlisted persons mentioned in paragraph (c) has in the previous eighteen months entered into another transaction in respect of an investment specified in paragraph 2(2) above;

(b) those conditions were satisfied in the case of that other transaction; and

(c) that other transaction was entered into by that person (whether acting as principal or agent) with the listed institution (whether acting as principal or agent) or was entered into by that person through the agency of that institution or was entered into by him (whether acting as principal or agent) as a result of arrangements made by that institution.

7 In the case of a transaction falling within paragraph 3 above the condition referred to in paragraph 4 above is that the consideration for the sale or transfer must be not less than £100,000.

8 The monetary limits mentioned in this Part of this Schedule refer to the time when the transaction is entered into; and where the consideration, value, price or amount referred to above is not in sterling it shall be converted at the rate of exchange prevailing at that time.

Part III — Transactions Arranged by Listed Institutions

9 Subject to paragraphs 10 and 11 below, this Part of this Schedule applies to any transaction arranged by the listed institution which—

(a) is entered into by another listed institution as principal (or as agent for another listed institution) with another listed institution or the Bank of England (whether acting as principal or agent);

(b) is entered into by another listed institution (whether acting as principal or agent) with an unlisted person (whether acting as principal or agent); or

(c) is entered into between unlisted persons (whether acting as principal or agent),

if the transaction falls within paragraph 2 or 3 above.

10 In the case of a transaction falling within paragraph 2 above paragraph 9(b) and (c) above do not apply unless either the conditions in paragraph 5 above are satisfied or—

(a) the unlisted person mentioned in paragraph (b) or, as the case may be, each of the unlisted persons mentioned in paragraph (c) has in the previous eighteen months entered into another transaction in respect of an investment specified in paragraph 2(2) above;

(b) those conditions were satisfied in the case of that other transaction; and

(c) that other transaction was entered into by that person (whether acting as principal or agent) with the listed institution making the arrangements (whether acting as principal or agent) or through the agency of that institution or was entered into by that person (whether acting as principal or agent) as a result of arrangments made by that institution.

11 In the case of a transaction falling within paragraph 3 above paragraph 9(b) and (c) above do not apply unless the condition in paragraph 7 above is satisfied.

Schedule 6 — The Financial Services Tribunal

Section 96(6)

TERM OF OFFICE OF MEMBERS

1(1) A person appointed to the panel mentioned in section 96(2) of this Act shall hold and vacate his office in accordance with the terms of his appointment and on ceasing to hold office shall be eligible for re-appointment.

1(2) A member of the panel appointed by the Lord Chancellor may resign his office by notice in writing to the Lord Chancellor; and a member of the panel appointed by the Secretary of State may resign his office by notice in writing to the Secretary of State.

EXPENSES

2 The Secretary of State shall pay to the persons serving as members of the Tribunal such remuneration and allowances as he may determine and shall defray such other expenses of the Tribunal as he may approve.

STAFF

3 The Secretary of State may provide the Tribunal with such officers and servants as he thinks necessary for the proper discharge of its functions.

PROCEDURE

4(1) The Secretary of State may make rules for regulating the procedure of the Tribunal, including provision for the holding of any proceedings in private, for the awarding of costs (or, in Scotland, expenses) and for the payment of expenses to persons required to attend before the Tribunal.

4(2) The Tribunal may appoint counsel or a solicitor to assist it in proceedings before the Tribunal.

EVIDENCE

5(1) The Tribunal may by summons require any person to attend, at such time and place as is specified in the summons, to give evidence or to produce any document in his custody or under his control which the Tribunal considers it necessary to examine.

5(2)   The Tribunal may take evidence on oath and for that purpose administer oaths or may, instead of administering an oath, require the person examined to make and subscribe a declaration of the truth of the matters in respect of which he is examined.

5(3)   Any person who without reasonable excuse—

(a)   refuses or fails to attend in obedience to a summons issued by the Tribunal or to give evidence; or

(b)   alters, suppresses, conceals or destroys or refuses to produce a document which he may be required to produce for the purposes of proceedings before the Tribunal,

shall be guilty of an offence.

5(4)   A person guilty of an offence under paragraph (a) of sub-paragraph (3) above shall be liable on summary conviction to a fine not exceeding the fifth level on the standard scale; and a person guilty of an offence under paragraph (b) of that sub-paragraph shall be liable—

(a)   on conviction on indictment, to imprisonment for a term not exceeding two years or to a fine or to both;

(b)   on summary conviction, to a fine not exceeding the statutory maximum.

5(5)   A person shall not under this paragraph be required to disclose any information or produce any document which he would be entitled to refuse to disclose or produce on grounds of legal professional privilege in proceedings in the High Court or on grounds of confidentiality as between client and professional legal adviser in proceedings in the Court of Session except that a lawyer may be required to furnish the name and address of his client.

5(6)   Any reference in this paragraph to the production of a document includes a reference to the production of a legible copy of information recorded otherwise than in legible form; and the reference to suppressing a document includes a reference to destroying the means of reproducing information recorded otherwise than in legible form.

APPEALS AND SUPERVISION BY COUNCIL ON TRIBUNALS

6   The Tribunals and Inquiries Act 1971 shall be amended as follows—

(a)   in section 8(2) after "6A" there shall be inserted "6B";

(b)   in section 13(1) after "6" there shall be inserted "6B";

(c)   in Schedule 1, after paragraph 6A there shall be inserted—

"Financial services

6B   The Financial Services Tribunal established by section 96 of the Financial Services Act 1986."

PARLIAMENTARY DISQUALIFICATION

7(1)   In Part III of Schedule 1 to the House of Commons Disqualification Act 1975 (disqualifying offices) there shall be inserted at the appropriate place "Any member of the Financial Services Tribunal in receipt of remuneration".

7(2)   A corresponding amendment shall be made in Part III of Schedule 1 to the Northern Ireland Assembly Disqualification Act 1975.

Schedule 7 — Qualifications of Designated Agency

Section 114

CONSTITUTION

1(1)   The constitution of the agency must provide for it to have—

(a) a chairman; and

(b) a governing body consisting of the chairman and other members;

and the provisions of the constitution relating to the chairman and the other members of the governing body must comply with the following provisions of this paragraph.

1(2)   The chairman and other members of the governing body must be persons appointed and liable to removal from office by the Secretary of State and the Governor of the Bank of England acting jointly.

1(3)   The members of the governing body must include—

(a) persons with experience of investment business of a kind relevant to the functions or proposed functions of the agency; and

(b) other persons, including regular users on their own account or on behalf of others of services provided by persons carrying on investment business of any such kind;

and the composition of that body must be such as to secure a proper balance between the interests of persons carrying on investment business and the interests of the public.

ARRANGEMENTS FOR DISCHARGE OF FUNCTIONS

2(1)   The agency's arrangements for the discharge of its functions must comply with the following provisions of this paragraph.

2(2)   Any statements of principle, rules, regulations and codes of practice must be issued or made by the governing body of the agency.

History
In para. 2(2) the words "statements of principle, rules, regulations and codes of practice must be issued or made" substituted for the former words "rules or regulations must be made" by CA 1989, s. 206(1) and Sch. 23, para. 22 as from 15 March 1990 (see S.I. No. 354 (C. 12), art. 3).

2(3)   Any decision taken in the exercise of other functions must be taken at a level appropriate to the importance of the decision.

2(4)   In the case of functions to be discharged by the governing body, the members falling respectively within paragraphs (a) and (b) of paragraph 1(3) above must, so far as practicable, have an opportunity to express their opinions.

2(5)   Subject to sub-paragraphs (2) to (4) above, the arrangements may enable any functions to be discharged by a committee, sub-committee, officer or servant of the agency.

TAKING ACCOUNT OF COSTS OF COMPLIANCE

2A(1)   The agency must have satisfactory arrangements for taking account, in framing any provisions which it proposes to make in the exercise of its legislative functions, of the cost to those to whom the provisions would apply of complying with those provisions and any other controls to which they are subject.

2A(2) In this paragraph **"legislative functions"** means the functions of issuing or making statements of principle, rules, regulations or codes of practice.

History
Para. 2A inserted by CA 1989, s. 204(4) as from 15 March 1990 (see S.I. 1990 No. 354 (C. 12), art. 3).

Note
See CA 1989, s. 204(5), (6).

MONITORING AND ENFORCEMENT

3(1) The agency must have a satisfactory system—

    (a) for enabling it to determine whether persons regulated by it are complying with the obligations which it is the responsibility of the agency to enforce; and

    (b) for the discharge of the agency's responsibility for the enforcement of those obligations.

3(2) The system may provide for the functions mentioned in sub-paragraph (1)(a) to be performed on its behalf (and without affecting its responsiblity) by any other body or person who is able and willing to perform them.

INVESTIGATION OF COMPLAINTS

4(1) The agency must have effective arrangements for the investigation of complaints arising out of the conduct of investment business by authorised persons or against any recognised self-regulating organisation, professional body, investment exchange or clearing house.

4(2) The arrangements must make provision for the investigation of complaints in respect of authorised persons to be carried out in appropriate cases independently of the agency and those persons.

PROMOTION AND MAINTENANCE OF STANDARDS

5 The agency must be able and willing to promote and maintain high standards of integrity and fair dealing in the carrying on of investment business and to co-operate, by the sharing of information and otherwise, with the Secretary of State and any other authority, body or person having responsibility for the supervision or regulation of investment business or other financial services.

RECORDS

6 The agency must have satisfactory arrangements for recording decisions made in the exercise of its functions and for the safe-keeping of those records which ought to be preserved.

Schedule 8 — Principles Applicable to Designated Agency's Legislative Provisions

Section 114

History
In the heading to Sch. 8 the words "Legislative Provisions" substituted for the former words "Rules and Regulations"   by CA 1989, s. 206(1) and Sch. 23, para. 23(1), (2) as from 15 March 1990 (see S.I. 1990 No. 354 (C. 12), art. 3).

INTRODUCTION

1(1) In this Schedule **"legislative provisions"** means the provisions of statements of principle, rules, regulations and codes of practice issued or made under Part I of this Act.

FSA 1986, Sch. 8, para. 1(1)

1(2) References in this Schedule to "conduct of business provisions" are to rules made under section 48 of this Act and statements of principle and codes of practice so far as they relate to matters falling within that rule-making power.

1(3) References in this Schedule to provisions made for the purposes of a specified section or Chapter are to rules or regulations made under that section or Chapter and statements of principle and codes of practice so far as they relate to matters falling within that power to make rules or regulations.

History
See history note after para. 1A.

STANDARDS

1A The conduct of business provisions and the other legislative provisions must promote high standards of integrity and fair dealing in the conduct of investment business.

History
Para. 1, 1A substituted for the former para. 1 and the cross-heading preceding it by CA 1989, s. 206(1) and Sch. 23, para. 23(1), (3) as from 15 March 1990 (see S.I. 1990 No. 354 (C. 12), art. 3); former para. 1 read as follows:
"STANDARDS
1 The rules made under section 48 of this Act (in this Schedule referred to as 'conduct of business rules') and the other rules and regulations made under Part I of this Act must promote high standards of integrity and fair dealing in the conduct of investment business."

2 The conduct of business provisions must make proper provision for requiring an authorised person to act with due skill, care and diligence in providing any service which he provides or holds himself out as willing to provide.

History
See history note after para. 6.

3 The conduct of business provisions must make proper provision for requiring an authorised person to subordinate his own interests to those of his clients and to act fairly between his clients.

History
See history note after para. 6.

4 The conduct of business provisions must make proper provision for requiring an authorised person to ensure that, in anything done by him for the persons with whom he deals, due regard is had to their circumstances.

History
See history note after para. 6.

DISCLOSURE

5 The conduct of business provisions must make proper provision for the disclosure by an authorised person of interests in, and facts material to, transactions which are entered into by him in the course of carrying on investment business or in respect of which he gives advice in the course of carrying on such business, including information as to any commissions or other inducements received or receivable from a third party in connection with any such transaction.

History
See history note after para. 6.

6 The conduct of business provisions must make proper provision for the disclosure by an authorised person of the capacity in which and the terms on which he enters into any such transaction.

History
In para. 2–6 the words "conduct of business provisions"   rules" by CA 1989, s. 206(1) and Sch. 23, para. 23(1), (4)
substituted for the former words "conduct of business   as from 15 March 1990 (see S.I. 1990 No. 354 (C. 12), art. 3).

7   The conduct of business provisions, or those provisions and provisions made for the purposes of section 51 of this Act, must make proper provision for requiring an authorised person who in the course of carrying on investment business enters or offers to enter into a transaction in respect of an investment with any person, or gives any person advice about such a transaction, to give that person such information as to the nature of the investment and the financial implications of the transaction as will enable him to make an informed decision.

History
In para. 7 the words "conduct of business provisions"   "those rules and rules under" by CA 1989, s. 206(1) and
substituted for the former words "conduct of business   Sch. 23, para. 23(1), (4), (5) as from 15 March 1990 (see
rules" and the words "those provisions and provisions   S.I. 1990 No. 354 (C. 12), art. 3).
made for the purposes of" substituted for the former words

8   Provisions made for the purposes of section 48 of this Act regulating action for the purpose of stabilising the price of investments must make proper provision for ensuring that where action is or is to be taken in conformity with the rules adequate arrangements exist for making known that the price of the investments in respect of which the action is or is to be taken (and, where relevant, of any other investments) may be affected by that action and the period during which it may be affected; and where a transaction is or is to be entered into during a period when it is known that the price of the investment to which it relates may be affected by any such action the information referred to in paragraph 7 above includes information to that effect.

History
In para. 8 the words "Provisions made for the purposes of"   CA 1989, s. 206(1) and Sch. 23, para. 23(1), (6) as from
substituted for the former words "Rules made under" by   15 March 1990 (see S.I. 1990 No. 354 (C. 12), art. 3).

PROTECTION

9   The conduct of business provisions and any provisions made for the purposes of section 55 of this Act must make proper provision for the protection of property for which an authorised person is liable to account to another person.

History
In para. 9 the words "conduct of business provisions"   under" by CA 1989, s. 206(1) and Sch. 23, para. 23(1), (4),
substituted for the former words "conduct of business   (7) as from 15 March 1990 (see S.I. 1990 No. 354 (C. 12),
rules" and the words "provisions made for the purposes   art. 3).
of" substituted for the former words "regulations made

10   Provisions made for the purposes of section 53 and 54 of this Act must make the best provision that can reasonably be made for the purposes of those sections.

History
In para. 10 the words "Provisions made for the purposes   by CA 1989, s. 206(1) and Sch. 23, para. 23, para. 23(1),
of" substituted for the former words "Rules made under"   (8) as from 15 March 1990 (see S.I. 1990 No. 354 (C. 12),
and the words "for the purposes of those sections"   art. 3).
substituted for the former words "under those sections"

RECORDS

11   The conduct of business provisions must require the keeping of proper records and make provision for their inspection in appropriate cases.

History
In para. 11 the words "conduct of business provisions"   1989, s. 206(1) and Sch. 23, para. 23, para. 23(1), (4) as
substituted for the words "conduct of business rule" by CA   from 15 March 1990 (see S.I. 1990 No. 354 (C. 12), art. 3).

CLASSES OF INVESTORS

12   The conduct of business provisions and the other provisions made for the purposes of Chapter V of Part I of this Act must take proper account of the fact that provisions that are appropriate for regulating the conduct of business in relation to some classes of investors may not (by reason of their knowledge, experience or otherwise) be appropriate in relation to others.

History
In para. 12 the words "conduct of business provisions" substituted for the former words "conduct of business rules" and the words "provisions made for the purposes of" substituted for the former words "rules and regulations made under" by CA 1989, s. 206(1), (4), (9) as from 15 March 1990 (see S.I. 1990 No. 354 (C. 12), art. 3).

Schedule 9— Designated Agencies: Status and Exercise of Transferred Functions

Section 116

STATUS

1(1) A designated agency shall not be regarded as acting on behalf of the Crown and its members, officers and servants shall not be regarded as Crown servants.

1(2) In Part III of Schedule 1 to the House of Commons Disqualification Act 1975 (disqualifying offices) there shall be inserted at the appropriate place—

> "Chairman of a designated agency within the meaning of the Financial Services Act 1986 if he is in receipt of remuneration".

1(3) An amendment corresponding to that in sub-paragraph (2) above shall be made in Part III of Schedule 1 to the Northern Ireland Assembly Disqualification Act 1975.

EXEMPTION FROM REQUIREMENT OF "LIMITED" IN NAME OF DESIGNATED AGENCY

2(1) A company is exempt from the requirements of the Companies Act 1985 relating to the use of "limited" as part of the company name if—

(a) it is a designated agency; and

(b) its memorandum or articles comply with the requirements specified in paragraph (b) of subsection (3) of section 30 of that Act.

2(2) In subsection (4) of that section (statutory declaration of compliance with requirements entitling company to exemption) the reference to the requirements of subsection (3) of that section shall include a reference to the requirements of sub-paragraph (1) above.

2(3) In section 31 of that Act (provisions applicable to exempted companies) the reference to a company which is exempt under section 30 of that Act shall include a reference to a company that is exempt under this paragraph and, in relation to such a company, the power conferred by subsection (2) of that section (direction to include "limited" in company name) shall be exercisable on the ground that the company has ceased to be a designated agency instead of the ground mentioned in paragraph (a) of that subsection.

2(4) In this paragraph references to the said Act of 1985 and sections 30 and 31 of that Act include references to the corresponding provisions in force in Northern Ireland.

THE TRIBUNAL

3(1)   Where a case is referred to the Tribunal by a designated agency the Tribunal shall send the Secretary of State a copy of any report made by it to the agency in respect of that case.

3(2)   Where the powers which the Tribunal could, apart from any delegation order, require the Secretary of State to exercise are by virtue of such an order or of an order resuming any function transferred by it, exercisable partly by the Secretary of State and partly by a designated agency or designated agencies the Tribunal may require any of them to exercise such of those powers as are exercisable by them respectively.

LEGISLATIVE FUNCTIONS

4(1)   A designated agency shall send the Secretary of State a copy of any statements of principle, rules, regulations or codes of practice issued or made by it by virtue of functions transferred to it by a delegation order and give him written notice of any amendment or revocation of or addition to any such rules or regulations.

History
In para. 4(1) the words "any statements of principle, rules, regulations or codes of practice issued or made" substituted for the former words "any rules or regulations made" by   CA 1989, s. 206(1) and Sch. 23, para. 24(1), (2) as from 15 March 1990 (see S.I. 1990 No. 354 (C. 12), art. 3).

4(2)   A designated agency shall—

    (a)   send the Secretary of State a copy of any guidance issued by the agency which is intended to have continuing effect and is issued in writing or other legible form; and

    (b)   give him written notice of any amendment, revocation of or addition to guidance issued by it;

but notice need not be given of the revocation of guidance other than such as is mentioned in paragraph (a) above or of any amendment or addition which does not result in or consist of such guidance as is there mentioned.

5   Paragraphs 6 to 9 below have effect instead of section 205A of this Act in relation to statements of principle, rules, regulations and codes of practice issued or made by a designated agency in the exercise of powers transferred to it by a delegation order.

History
See history note after para. 6.

6   Any such power is exercisable by instrument in writing and includes power to make different provision for different cases.

History
Para. 5 and 6 substituted by CA 1989, s. 206(1) and Sch. 23, para. 24(1), (3) as from 15 March 1990 (see S.I. 1990 No. 354 (C. 12), art. 3); former para. 5 and 6 read as follows:

"**5** Paragraphs 6 to 9 below shall have effect instead of section 205(2) and (4) of this Act in relation to rules and regulations made by a designated agency in the exercise of functions transferred to it by a delegation order.

6 The rules and regulations shall be made by an instrument in writing."

7   The instrument shall specify the provision of this Act under which is it made.

8(1)   Immediately after an instrument is issued or made it shall be printed and made available to the public with or without payment.

History
In para. 8(1) the words "is issued or made" substituted for the former words "is made" by CA 1984, s. 206(1) and   Sch. 23, para. 24(1), (4)(a) as from 15 March 1990 (see S.I. 1990 No. 354 (C. 12), art. 3).

8(2)   A person shall not be taken to have contravened any statement of principle,

FSA 1986, Sch. 9, para. 3(1)

rule, regulation or code of practice if he shows that at the time of the alleged contravention the instrument containing the statement of principle, rule, regulation or code of practice had not been made available as required by this paragraph.

History
In para. 8(2) the words "statement of principle, rule, regulation or code of practice" substituted (twice) for the words "rule or regulation" by CA 1989, s. 206(1) and Sch. 23, para. 24(1), (4)(b) as from 15 March 1990 (see S.I. 1990 No. 354 (C. 12), art. 3).

9(1) The production of a printed copy of an instrument purporting to be made or issued by the agency on which is endorsed a certificate signed by an officer of the agency authorised by it for that purpose and stating—

    (a) that the instrument was made or issued by the agency;

    (b) that the copy is a true copy of the instrument; and

    (c) that on a specified date the instrument was made available to the public as required by paragraph 8 above,

shall be prima facie evidence or, in Scotland, sufficient evidence of the facts stated in the certificate.

History
See history note after para. 9(3).

9(2) Any certificate purporting to be signed as mentioned in sub-paragraph (1) above shall be deemed to have been duly signed unless the contrary is shown.

9(3) Any person wishing in any legal proceedings to cite an instrument made or issued by the agency may require the agency to cause a copy of it to be endorsed with such a certificate as is mentioned in this paragraph.

History
In para. 9 the words "made or issued by the agency" substituted for the former words "made by the agency" by CA 1989, s. 206(1) and Sch. 23, para. 24(1), (5) as from 15 March 1990 (see S.I. 1990 No. 354 (C. 12), art. 3).

FEES

10(1) A designated agency may retain any fees payable to it by virtue of the delegation order.

10(2) Any such fees shall be applicable for meeting the expenses of the agency in discharging its functions under the order and for any purposes incidental thereto.

10(3) Any fees payable to a designated agency by virtue of a delegation order made before the coming into force of section 3 of this Act may also be applied for repaying the principal of, and paying interest on, any money borrowed by the agency (or by any other person whose liabilities in respect of the money are assumed by the agency) which has been used for the purpose of defraying expenses incurred before the making of the order (whether before or after the passing of this Act) in making preparations for the agency becoming a designated agency.

11 If the function of prescribing the amount of any fee, or of making a scheme under section 112 above, is exercisable by a designated agency it may prescribe or make provision for such fees as will enable it to defray any such expenses as are mentioned in paragraph 10 above.

CONSULTATION

12(1) Where a designated agency proposes, in the exercise of powers transferred to it by a delegation order, to issue or make any statements of principle, rules, regulations or codes of practice, it shall publish the proposed instrument in such manner as appears to it best calculated to bring the proposals to the attention of the public, together with a statement that representations about the proposals (and, in particular, representations as to the cost of complying with the proposed provisions) can be made to the agency within a specified time.

12(2) Before issuing or making the instrument the agency shall have regard to any representations duly made in accordance with that statement.

12(3) The above requirements do not apply—

    (a) where the agency considers that the delay involved in complying with them would be prejudicial to the interests of investors;

    (b) to the issuing or making of an instrument in the same, or substantially the same, terms as a proposed instrument which was furnished by the agency to the Secretary of State for the purposes of section 114(9) of this Act.

History
Para. 12 substituted by CA 1989, s. 206(1) and Sch. 23, para. 24(1), (6) as from 15 March 1990 (see S.I. 1990 No. 354 (C. 12), art. 3); former para. 12 read as follows:

"**12(1)** Before making any rules or regulations by virtue of functions transferred to it by a delegation order a designated agency shall, subject to sub-paragraphs (2) and (3) below, publish the proposed rules and regulations in such manner as appears to the agency to be best calculated to bring them to the attention of the public, together with a statement that representations in respect of the proposals can be made to the agency within a specified period; and before making the rules or regulations the agency shall have regard to any representations duly made in accordance with that statement.

(2) Sub-paragraph (1) above does not apply in any case in which the agency considers that the delay involved in complying with that sub-paragraph would be prejudicial to the interests of investors.

(3) Sub-paragraph (1) above does not apply to the making of any rule or regulation if it is in the same terms (or substantially the same terms) as a proposed rule or regulation which was furnished by the agency to the Secretary of State for the purposes of section 114(9) of this Act."

EXCHANGE OF INFORMATION

13(1) The Secretary of State may communicate to a designated agency any information in his possession of which he could have availed himself for the purpose of exercising any function which by virtue of a delegation order is for the time being exercisable by the agency.

13(2) A designated agency may in the exercise of any function which by virtue of a delegation order is for the time being exercisable by it communicate to any other person any information which has been communicated to the agency by the Secretary of State and which the Secretary of State could have communicated to that person in the exercise of that function.

13(3) No communication of information under sub-paragraph (1) above shall constitute publication for the purposes of the law of defamation.

Schedule 10 — Regulated Insurance Companies

Section 129

PRELIMINARY

1 In this Part of this Schedule **"a regulated insurance company"** means any such company as is mentioned in section 129 of this Act.

AUTHORISATIONS FOR INVESTMENT BUSINESS AND INSURANCE BUSINESS

2(1) An insurance company to which section 22 of this Act applies shall not be an authorised person except by virtue of that section.

2(2) If an insurance company to which Part II of the Insurance Companies Act 1982 applies but to which section 22 of this Act does not apply becomes an authorised person by virtue of any other provision of this Act it shall be an authorised person only as respects the management of the investments of any pension fund which is established solely for the benefit of the officers or employees and their dependants of that company or of any other body corporate in the same group as that company.

2(3) An insurance company to which section 31 of this Act applies shall not, so long as it is an authorised person by virtue of that section, be an authorised person by virtue of any other provision of this Act.

2(4) None of the provisions of Part I of this Act shall be construed as authorising any person to carry on insurance business in any case in which he could not lawfully do so apart from those provisions.

RECOGNITION OF SELF-REGULATING ORGANISATION WITH INSURANCE COMPANY MEMBERS

3(1) In the case of a self-regulating organisation whose members include or may include regulated insurance companies the requirements of Schedule 2 to this Act shall include a requirement that the rules of the organisation must take proper account of Part II of the Insurance Companies Act 1982 or, as the case may be, of the provisions for corresponding purposes in the law of any member State in which such companies are established.

3(2) Where the function of making or revoking a recognition order in respect of such a self-regulating organisation is exercisable by a designated agency it shall not regard that requirement as satisfied unless the Secretary of State has certified that he also regards it as satisfied.

3(3) A delegation order—

    (a) may reserve to the Secretary of State the function of revoking a recognition order in respect of such a self-regulating organisation as is mentioned in sub-paragraph (1) above on the ground that the requirement there mentioned is not satisfied; and

    (b) shall not transfer to a designated agency the function of revoking any such recognition order on the ground that the organisation has contravened sub-paragraphs (3) or (4) of paragraph 6 below as applied by sub-paragraph (5) of that paragraph.

3(4) In the case of such a self-regulating organisation as is mentioned in sub-paragraph (1) above the requirements of Schedule 2 to this Act referred to in section 187(2)(a) of this Act shall include the requirement mentioned in that sub-paragraph.

MODIFICATION OF PROVISIONS AS TO CONDUCT OF INVESTMENT BUSINESS

4(1) The rules under section 48 of this Act shall not apply to a regulated insurance company except so far as they make provision as respects the matters mentioned in sub-paragraph (2) below.

4(2) The matters referred to in sub-paragraph (1) above are—

    (a) procuring proposals for policies the rights under which constitute an investment for the purposes of this Act and advising persons on such policies and the exercise of the rights conferred by them;

(b) managing the investments of pension funds, procuring persons to enter into contracts for the management of such investments and advising persons on such contracts and the exercise of the rights conferred by them;

(c) matters incidental to those mentioned in paragraph (a) and (b) above.

4(2A) Sub-paragraphs (1) and (2) also apply to statements of principle under section 47A and codes of practice under section 63A so far as they relate to matters falling within the rule-making power in section 48.

History
Para. 4(2A) inserted by CA 1989, s. 206(1) and Sch. 23, para. 25(1), (2) as from 15 March 1990 (see S.I. 1990 No. 354 (C. 12), art. 3).

4(3) The rules under section 49 of this Act shall not apply to an insurance company which is an authorised person by virtue of section 31 of this Act.

4(4) The rules under sections 53 and 54 of this Act shall not apply to loss arising as a result of a regulated insurance company being unable to meet its liabilities under a contract of insurance.

4(5) A direction under section 59 of this Act shall not prohibit the employment of a person by a regulated insurance company except in connection with—

(a) the matters mentioned in sub-paragraph (2) above; or

(b) investment business carried on in connection with or for the purposes of those matters.

4(6) The Secretary of State shall not make a delegation order transferring any functions of making rules or regulations under Chapter V of Part I of this Act in relation to a regulated insurance company unless he is satisfied that those rules and regulations will take proper account of Part II of the Insurance Companies Act 1982 or, as the case may be, of the provisions for corresponding purposes in the law of the member State in which the company is established; and in section 115(5) of this Act the reference to the requirements of section 114(9)(b) shall include a reference to the requirements of this sub-paragraph.

RESTRICTION OF PROVISIONS AS TO CONDUCT OF INSURANCE BUSINESS

5(1) Regulations under section 72 of the Insurance Companies Act 1982 (insurance advertisements) shall not apply to so much of any advertisement issued by an authorised person as relates to a contract of insurance the rights under which constitute an investment for the purposes of this Act.

5(2) No requirement imposed under section 74 of that Act (intermediaries in insurance transactions) shall apply in respect of an invitation issued by, or by an appointed representative of, an authorised person in relation to a contract of insurance the rights under which constitute an investment for the purposes of this Act.

5(3) Subject to sub-paragraph (4) below, sections 75 to 77 of that Act (right to withdraw from long-term policies) shall not apply to a regulated insurance company in respect of a contract of insurance the rights under which constitute an investment for the purposes of this Act.

5(4) Sub-paragraph (3) above does not affect the operation of the said sections 75 to 77 in a case in which the statutory notice required by those sections has been or ought to have been served before the coming into force of that sub-paragraph.

EXERCISE OF POWERS OF INTERVENTION ETC.

6(1) The powers conferred by Chapter VI of Part I of this Act shall not be exercisable in relation to a regulated insurance company on the ground specified in section 64(1)(a) of this Act for reasons relating to the ability of the company to meet its liabilities to policy holders or potential policy holders.

6(2) The powers conferred by sections 66 and 68 of this Act, and those conferred by section 67 of this Act so far as applicable to assets belonging to the authorised person, shall not be exercisable in relation to a regulated insurance company.

6(3) A designated agency shall not in the case of a regulated insurance company impose any prohibition or requirement under section 65 or 67 of this Act, or vary any such prohibition or requirement, unless it has given reasonable notice of its intention to do so to the Secretary of State and informed him—

(a) of the manner in which and the date on or after which it intends to exercise that power; and

(b) in the case of a proposal to impose a prohibition or requirement, on which of the grounds specified in section 64(1) of this Act it proposes to act and its reasons for considering that the ground in question exists and that it is necessary to impose the prohibition or requirement.

6(4) A designated agency shall not exercise any power to which sub-paragraph (3) above applies if the Secretary of State has before the date specified in accordance with sub-paragraph (3), above served on it a notice in writing directing it not to do so; and the Secretary of State may serve such a notice if he considers it desirable for protecting policy holders or potential policy holders of the company against the risk that it may be unable to meet its liabilities or to fulfil the reasonable expectations of its policy holders or potential policy holders.

6(5) Sub-paragraphs (3) and (4) above shall, with the necessary modifications, apply also where a recognised self-regulating organisation proposes to exercise, in the case of a member who is a regulated insurance company, any powers of the organisation for purposes corresponding to those of Chapter VI of Part I of this Act.

6(6) The powers conferred by sections 72 and 73 of this Act shall not be exercisable in relation to a regulated insurance company.

WITHDRAWAL OF INSURANCE BUSINESS AUTHORISATION

7(1) At the end of section 11(2)(a) of the Insurance Companies Act 1982 (withdrawal of authorisation in respect of new business where insurance company has failed to satisfy an obligation to which it is subject by virtue of that Act) there shall be inserted the words "or the Financial Services Act 1986 or, if it is a member of a recognised self-regulating organisation within the meaning of that Act, an obligation to which it is subject by virtue of the rules of that organisation".

7(2)   After subsection (2) of section 13 of that Act (final withdrawal of authorisation) there shall be inserted—

> "**(2A)**   The Secretary of State may direct that an insurance company shall cease to be authorised to carry on business which is insurance business by virtue of section 95 (c)(ii) of this Act if it appears to him that the company has failed to satisfy an obligation to which it is subject by virtue of the Financial Services Act 1986 or, if it is a member of a recognised self-regulating organisation within the meaning of that Act, an obligation to which it is subject by virtue of the rules of that organisation.
>
> **(2B)**   Subsections (3), (5) and (6) of section 11 and subsections (1) and (5) to (8) of section 12 above shall apply to a direction under subsection (2A) above as they apply to a direction under section 11."

7(3)   The disciplinary action which may be taken by virtue of section 47A(3) of this Act (failure to comply with statement of principle) includes—

(a) the withdrawal of authorisation under section 11(2)(a) of the Insurance Companies Act 1982, and

(b) the giving of a direction under section 13(2A) of that Act; and subsection (6) of section 47A (duty of the Secretary of State as to exercise of powers) has effect accordingly.

History
Para. 7(3) inserted by CA 1989, s. 206(1) and Sch. 23, para. 25(1), (3) as from 15 March 1990 (see S.I. 1990 No. 354 (C. 12), art. 3).

TERMINATION OF INVESTMENT BUSINESS AUTHORISATION OF INSURER ESTABLISHED IN OTHER MEMBER STATE

8(1)   Sections 33(1)(b) and 34 of this Act shall not apply to a regulated insurance company.

8(2)   A direction under section 33(1)(a) of this Act in respect of such an insurance company may provide that the company shall cease to be an authorised person except as respects investment business of a kind specified in the direction and shall not make it unlawful for the company to effect a contract of insurance in pursuance of a subsisting contract of insurance.

8(3)   Where the Secretary of State proposes to give a direction under section 33(1)(a) of this Act in respect of such an insurance company he shall give it written notice of his intention to do so, giving particulars of the grounds on which he proposes to act and of the rights exercisable under sub-paragraph (4) below.

8(4)   An insurance company on which a notice is served under sub-paragraph (3) above may within fourteen days after the date of service make written representations to the Secretary of State and, if desired, oral representations to a person appointed for that purpose by the Secretary of State; and the Secretary of State shall have regard to any representations made in accordance with this sub-paragraph in determining whether to give the direction.

8(5)   After giving a direction under section 33(1)(a) of this Act in respect of a regulated insurance company the Secretary of State shall inform the company in writing of the reasons for giving the direction.

8(6) A delegation order shall not transfer to a designated agency the function of giving a direction under section 33(1)(a) of this Act in respect of a regulated insurance company.

POWERS OF TRIBUNAL

9 In the case of a regulated insurance company the provisions mentioned in section 98(4) of this Act shall include sections 11 and 13(2A) of the Insurance Companies Act 1982 but where the Tribunal reports that the appropriate decision would be to take action under either of those sections or under section 33(1)(a) of this Act the Secretary of State shall take the report into consideration but shall not be bound to act upon it.

CONSULTATION WITH DESIGNATED AGENCIES

10(1) Where any functions under this Act are for the time being exercisable by a designated agency in relation to regulated insurance companies the Secretary of State shall, before issuing an authorisation under section 3 of the Insurance Companies Act 1982 to a applicant who proposes to carry on in the United Kingdom insurance business which is investment business—

   (a) seek the advice of the designated agency with respect to any matters which are relevant to those functions of the agency and relate to the applicant, his proposed business or persons who will be associated with him in, or in connection with, that business; and

   (b) take into account any advice on those matters given to him by the agency before the end of the period within which the application is required to be decided.

10(2) The Secretary of State may for the purpose of obtaining the advice of a designated agency under sub-paragraph (1) above furnish it with any information obtained by him in connection with the application.

10(3) If a designated agency by which any functions under this Act are for the time being exercisable in relation to regulated insurance companies has reasonable grounds for believing that any such insurance company has failed to comply with an obligation to which it is subject by virtue of this Act it shall forthwith give notice of that fact to the Secretary of State so that he can take it into consideration in deciding whether to give a direction in respect of the company under section 11 or 13(2A) of the said Act of 1982 or section 33 of this Act.

10(4) A notice under sub-paragraph (3) above shall contain particulars of the obligation in question and of the agency's reasons for considering that the company has failed to satisfy that obligation.

10(5) A designated agency need not give a notice under sub-paragraph (3) above in respect of any matter unless it considers that that matter (either alone or in conjunction with other matters) would justify the withdrawal of authorisation under section 28 of this Act in the case of a person to whom that section applies.

Schedule 11 — Friendly Societies

Section 140

Part I — Preliminary

1   In this Schedule—

"**a regulated friendly society**" means a society which is an authorised person by virtue of section 23 of this Act as respects such investment business as is mentioned in that section;

"**regulated business**" in relation to a regulated friendly society, means investment business as respects which the society is authorised by virtue of that section;

"**a self-regulating organisation for friendly societies**" means a self-regulating organisation which is permitted under its rules to admit regulated friendly societies as members and to regulate the carrying on by such societies of regulated business;

"**a recognised self-regulating organisation for friendly societies**" means a body declared by an order of the Registrar for the time being in force to be a recognised self-regulating organisation for friendly societies for the purposes of this Schedule;

"**a member society**" means a regulated friendly society which is a member of an appropriate recognised self-regulating organisation for friendly societies and is subject to its rules in carrying on all its regulated business and, for the purposes of this definition, "**an appropriate recognised self-regulating organisation for friendly societies**" means—

(a)   in the case of any such society as is mentioned in section 23(1) of this Act, an organisation declared by an order of the Chief Registrar of friendly societies for the time being in force to be a recognised self-regulating organisation for friendly societies for the purposes of this Schedule; and

(b)   in the case of any such society as is mentioned in section 23(2) of this Act, an organisation declared by an order of the Registrar of Friendly Societies for Northern Ireland for the time being in force to be such an organisation;

"**the Registrar**" means—

(a)   in relation to any such society as is mentioned in section 23(1) of this Act, or to any self-regulating organisation for friendly societies which has applied for or been granted a recognition order made by him, the Chief Registrar of friendly societies; and

(b)   in relation to any such society as is mentioned in section 23(2) of this Act, or to any self-regulating organisation for friendly societies which has applied for or been granted a recognition order made by him, the Registrar of Friendly Societies for Northern Ireland.

Part II — Self-Regulating Organisations for Friendly Societies

RECOGNITION

2(1)   A self-regulating organisation for friendly societies may apply to the Chief Registrar of friendly societies or the Registrar of Friendly Societies for Northern

FSA 1986, Sch. 11, para. 1

Ireland for an order declaring it to be a recognised self-regulating organisation for friendly societies for the purposes of this Schedule.

2(2) An application under sub-paragraph (1) above—

(a) shall be made in such manner as the Registrar may direct; and

(b) shall be accompanied by such information as the Registrar may reasonably require for the purpose of determining the application.

2(3) At any time after receiving an application and before determining it the Registrar may require the applicant to furnish additional information.

2(4) The directions and requirements given or imposed under sub-paragraphs (2) and (3) above may differ as between different applications.

2(5) Any information to be furnished to the Registrar under this paragraph shall, if he so requires, be in such form or verified in such manner as he may specify.

2(6) Every application shall be accompanied by a copy of the applicant's rules and of any guidance issued by the applicant which is intended to have continuing effect and is issued in writing or other legible form.

3(1) If, on an application duly made in accordance with paragraph 2 above and after being furnished with all such information as he may require under that paragraph, it appears to the Registrar from that information and having regard to any other information in his possession that the requirements mentioned in paragraph 4 below are satisfied as respects that organisation, he may, with the consent of the Secretary of State and subject to sub-paragraph (2) below, make an order ("a recognition order") declaring the applicant to be a recognised self-regulating organisation for friendly societies.

3(2) Where the Registrar proposes to grant an application for a recognition order he shall send to the Secretary of State a copy of the application together with a copy of the rules and any guidance accompanying the application and the Secretary of State shall not consent to the making of the recognition order unless he is satisfied that the rules and guidance of which copies have been sent to him under this sub-paragraph, together with any statements of principle, rules, regulations or codes of practice to which members of the organisation would be subject by virtue of this Schedule, do not have, and are not intended or likely to have, to any significant extent the effect of restricting, distorting or preventing competition or, if they have or are intended or likely to have that effect to any significant extent, that the effect is not greater than is necessary for the protection of investors.

History
In para. 3(2) the words ", together with any statements of principle," to "by virtue of this Schedule," inserted by CA 1989, s. 206(1) and Sch. 23, para. 26, 27 as from 15 March 1990 (see S.I. 1990 No. 354 (C. 12), art. 3).

3(3) Section 122 of this Act shall apply in relation to the decision whether to consent to the making of a recognition order under this paragraph as it applies to the decisions mentioned in subsection (1) of that section.

3(4) Subsections (1) and (2) of section 128 of this Act shall apply for the purposes of this paragraph as if the powers there mentioned included the power of refusing consent to the making of a recognition order under this paragraph and subsection (5) of that section shall apply for that purpose as if the reference to Chapter XIV of Part I included a reference to this paragraph.

3(5) The Registrar may refuse to make a recognition order in respect of an organisation if he considers that its recognition is unnecessary having regard to the existence of one or more other organisations which are concerned with such investment business as is mentioned in section 23 of this Act and which have been or are likely to be recognised under this paragraph.

3(6) Where the Registrar refuses an application for a recognition order he shall give the applicant a written notice to that effect specifying a requirement which in the opinion of the Registrar is not satisfied, stating that the application is refused on the ground mentioned in sub-paragraph (5) above or stating that the Secretary of State has refused to consent to the making of the order.

3(7) A recognition order shall state the date on which it takes effect.

4(1) The requirements referred to in paragraph 3 above are that mentioned in sub-paragraph (2) below and those set out in paragraphs 2 to 7 of Schedule 2 to this Act as modified in sub-paragraphs (3) to (5) below.

4(2) The rules of the organisation must take proper account of the Friendly Societies Act 1974, or as the case may be, the Friendly Societies Act (Northern Ireland) 1970.

4(3) References in paragraphs 2, 3, 4 and 6 of Schedule 2 to members are to members who are regulated friendly societies.

4(4) In paragraph 3 of that Schedule—

    (a) in sub-paragraph (1) for the reference to Chapter V of Part I of this Act there shall be substituted a reference to paragraphs 14 to 22D below; and

    (c) in sub-paragraph (3) for the reference to Chapter VI of that Part there shall be substituted a reference to the powers exercisable by the Registrar by virtue of paragraph 23 below.

History
In para. 4(4):
- in (a) "22D" substituted for "22", and
- (b) omitted and repealed

by CA 1989, s. 206(1), 212, Sch. 23, para. 26, 28(1), (2) and Sch. 24 as from 15 March 1990 (see S.I. 1990 No. 354 (C. 12), art. 3); former para. 4(4)(b) read as follows:

"(b) in sub-paragraph (2) the reference to section 49 of this Act shall be omitted and for the reference to sections 53 and 54 there shall be substituted a reference to paragraphs 17 and 18 below; and"

4(5) In paragraph 4 of that Schedule for the reference to Chapter V of Part I of this Act there shall be substituted references to paragraphs 14 to 22D below.

History
In para. 4(5) "22D" substituted for "22" by CA 1989, s. 206(1) and Sch. 23, para. 26, 28(1), (3) as from 15 March 1990 (see S.I. 1990 No. 354 (C. 12), art. 3).

REVOCATION OF RECOGNITION

5(1) A recognition order may be revoked by a further order made by the Registrar if at any time it appears to him—

    (a) that any requirement mentioned in paragraph 4(1) above is not satisfied in the case of the organisation to which the recognition order relates ("the recognised organisation");

    (b) that the recognised organisation has failed to comply with any obligation to which it is subject by virtue of this Act; or

(c) that the continued recognition of the organisation is undesirable having regard to the existence of one or more other organisations which have been or are to be recognised under paragraph 3 above.

5(2) Subsections (2) to (9) of section 11 of this Act shall have effect in relation to the revocation of a recognition order under this paragraph as they have effect in relation to the revocation of a recognition order under subsection (1) of that section but with the substitution—

(a) for references to the Secretary of State of references to the Registrar;

(b) for the reference in subsection (3) to members of a reference to members of the organisation which are member societies in relation to it; and

(c) for the reference in subsection (6) to investors of a reference to members of the societies which are member societies in relation to the organisation.

COMPLIANCE ORDERS

6(1) If at any time it appears to the Registrar—

(a) that any requirement mentioned in paragraph 3 above is not satisfied in the case of a recognised self-regulating organisation for friendly societies; or

(b) that such an organisation has failed to comply with any obligation to which it is subject by virtue of this Act,

he may, instead of revoking the recognition order under paragraph 5 above, make an application to the court under this paragraph.

6(2) If on any such application the court decides that the requirement in question is not satisfied or, as the case may be, that the organisation has failed to comply with the obligation in question it may order the organisation concerned to take such steps as the court directs for securing that that requirement is satisfied or that that obligation is complied with.

6(3) The jurisdiction conferred by this paragraph shall be exercisable by the High Court and the Court of Session.

7 (Omitted by Companies Act 1989, sec. 206(1) and Sch. 23, para. 26, 29 as from 15 March 1990.)

History
In relation to the above date see S.I. 1990 No. 354 (C. 12), art. 3; former para. 7 read as follows:

"**7(1)** If at any time it appears to the Registrar that the rules of a recognised self-regulating organisation for friendly societies do not satisfy the requirements of paragraph 3(1) of Schedule 2 to this Act as modified by paragraph 4(4) above he may, instead of revoking the recognition order or making an application under paragraph 6 above, direct the organisation to alter, or himself alter, its rules in such manner as he considers necessary for securing that the rules satisfy those requirements.

(2) Before giving a direction or making any alteration under this paragraph the Registrar shall consult the organisation concerned.

(3) Any direction given under sub-paragraph (1) above shall, on the application of the Registrar, be enforceable by mandamus or, in Scotland, by an order for specific performance under section 91 of the Court of Session Act 1868.

(4) A recognised self-regulating organisation for friendly societies whose rules have been altered by or pursuant to a direction given by the Registrar under sub-paragraph (1) above may apply to the court and if the court is satisfied—

(a) that the rules without the alteration satisfied the

requirements mentioned in that sub-paragraph; or

(b) that other alterations proposed by the organisation would result in the rules satisfying those requirements,

the court may set aside the alteration made by or pursuant to the direction given by the Registrar and, in a case within paragraph (b) above, order the organisation to make the alterations proposed by it; but the setting aside of an alteration under this sub-paragraph shall not affect its previous operation.

(5) The jurisdiction conferred by sub-paragraph (4) above shall be exercisable by the High Court and the Court of Session.

(6) Subsections (2) to (7) and (9) of section 11 of this Act shall, with the modifications mentioned in paragraph 5(2) above and any other necessary modifications, have effect in relation to any direction given or alteration made by the Registrar under sub-paragraph (1) above as they have effect in relation to an order revoking a recognition order.

(7) The fact that the rules of an organisation have been altered by or pursuant to a direction given by the Registrar, or pursuant to an order made by the court, under this paragraph shall not preclude their subsequent alteration or revocation by that organisation."

8(1) The Registrar or the Secretary of State may make regulations requiring a recognised self-regulating organisation for friendly societies to give the Registrar or, as the case may be, the Secretary of State forthwith notice of the occurrence of such events relating to the organisation or its members as are specified in the regulations and such information in respect of those events as is so specified.

8(2) The Registrar or the Secretary of State may make regulations requiring a recognised self-regulating organisation for friendly societies to furnish the Registrar or, as the case may be, the Secretary of State at such times or in respect of such periods as are specified in the regulations with such information relating to the organisation or its members as is so specified.

8(3) The notices and information required to be given or furnished under the foregoing provisions of this paragraph shall be such as the Registrar or, as the case may be, the Secretary of State may reasonably require for the exercise of his functions under this Act.

8(4) Regulations under the foregoing provisions of this paragraph may require information to be given in a specified form and to be verified in a specified manner.

8(5) A notice or information required to be given or furnished under the foregoing provisions of this paragraph shall be given in writing or such other manner as the Registrar or, as the case may be, the Secretary of State may approve.

8(6) Where a recognised self-regulating organisation for friendly societies amends, revokes or adds to its rules or guidance it shall within seven days give the Registrar written notice of the amendment, revocation or addition; but notice need not be given of the revocation of guidance other than such as is mentioned in paragraph 2(6) above or of any amendment of or addition to guidance which does not result in or consist of such guidance as is there mentioned.

8(7) The Registrar shall send the Secretary of State a copy of any notice given to him under sub-paragraph (6) above.

8(8) Contravention of or of regulations under this paragraph shall not be an offence.

9(1) A recognised self-regulating organisation for friendly societies shall not exercise any powers for purposes corresponding to those of the powers exercisable by the Registrar by virtue of paragraph 23 below in relation to a regulated friendly society unless it has given reasonable notice of its intention to do so to the Registrar and informed him—

    (a) of the manner in which and the date on or after which it intends to exercise the power; and

    (b) in the case of a proposal to impose a prohibition or requirement, of the reason why it proposes to act and its reasons for considering that that reason exists and that it is necessary to impose the prohibition or requirement.

9(2) A recognised self-regulating organisation for friendly societies shall not exercise any power to which sub-paragraph (1)(a) above applies if before the date given in the notice in pursuance of that sub-paragraph the Registrar has served on it a notice in writing directing it not to do so; and the Registrar may serve such a notice if he considers it is desirable for protecting members or potential members of the society against the risk that it may be unable to meet its liabilities or to fulfil the reasonable expectations of its members or potential members.

PREVENTION OF RESTRICTIVE PRACTICES

10(1)   The powers conferred by sub-paragraph (2) below shall be exercisable by the Secretary of State if at any time it appears to him that—

    (a)   any rules made or guidance issued by a recognised self-regulating organisation for friendly societies;

    (b)   any practices of any such organisation; or

    (c)   any practices of persons who are members of, or otherwise subject to the rules made by, any such organisation,

together with any statements of principle, rules, regulations or codes of practice to which members of the organisation are subject by virtue of this Schedule, have, or are intended or likely to have, to a significant extent the effect of restricting, distorting or preventing competition and that that effect is greater than is necessary for the protection of investors.

History
In para. 10(1) the words "together with any statements" to "by virtue of this Schedule" inserted by CA 1989, s. 206(1) and Sch. 23, para. 26, 30(1), (2) as from 15 March 1990 (see S.I. 1990 No. 354 (C. 12), art. 3).

10(2)   The powers exercisable under this sub-paragraph are to direct the Registrar—

    (a)   to revoke the recognition order of the organisation;

    (b)   to direct the organisation to take specified steps for the purpose of securing that its rules, or the guidance or practices in question do not have the effect mentioned in sub-paragraph (1) above;

    (c)   to make alterations in its rules for that purpose;

and subsections (2) to (5), (7) and (9) of section 11 of this Act, as applied by sub-paragraph (2) of paragraph 5 above, shall have effect in relation to the revocation of a recognition order by virtue of a direction under this sub-paragraph as they have effect in relation to the revocation of such an order under sub-paragraph (1) of that paragraph.

History
In para. 10(2)(b) the words "its rules, or the" substituted for the former words "the rules"and in para. 10(2)(c) the words "its rules" substituted for the former words "the rules" by CA 1989, s. 206(1) and Sch. 23, para. 26, 30(1), (3) as from 15 March 1990 (see S.I. 1990 No. 354 (C. 12). art. 3).

10(3)   The practices referred to in paragraph (b) of sub-paragraph (1) above are practices of the organisation in its capacity as such.

History
In para. 10(3) the words "and the practices referred to in paragraph (c) of that sub-paragraph are practices in relation to business in respect of which the persons in question are subject to the rules of the organisation and which are required or contemplated by its rules or guidance or otherwise attributable to its conduct in its capacity as such." formerly appearing after the words "in its capacity as such" omitted and repealed by CA 1989, s. 206(1), 212, Sch. 23, para. 26, 30(1), (4) and Sch. 24 as from 15 March 1990 (see S.I. 1990 No. 354 (C.12), art. 3).

10(3A)   The practices referred to in paragraph (c) of sub-paragraph (1) above are practices in relation to business in respect of which the persons in question are subject to—

    (a)   the rules of the organisation, or

    (b)   statements of principle, rules, regulations or codes of practice to which its members are subject by virtue of this Schedule, and which are required or contemplated by the rules of the organisation or by those statements, rules, regulations or codes, or by guidance issued by the organisation, or which are otherwise attributable to the conduct of the organisation as such.

History
Para. 10(3A) inserted by CA 1989, s. 206(1) and Sch. 23,
para. 26, 30(1), (4) as from 15 March 1990 (see S.I. 1990
No. 354 (C. 12), art. 3).

10(4)   Subsections (3) to (8) of section 122 of this Act shall apply for the purposes of this paragraph as if—

    (a)   the reference to a notice in subsection (3) included a notice received under paragraph 8(7) above or 33(4) below;

    (b)   the references to rules and guidance in subsection (4) included such rules and guidance as are mentioned in sub-paragraph (1) above;

    (c)   the reference to practices in subsection (6) included such practices as are mentioned in sub-paragraph (1) above; and

    (d)   the reference to the Secretary of State's powers in subsection (7) included his powers under sub-paragraph (2) above.

10(5)   Section 128 of this Act shall apply for the purposes of this paragraph as if—

    (a)   the powers referred to in subsection (1) of that section included the powers conferred by sub-paragraph (2)(b) and (c) above;

    (b)   the references to Chapter XIV of Part I included references to this paragraph; and

    (c)   the reference to a recognised self-regulating organisation included a reference to a recognised self-regulating organisation for friendly societies.

FEES

11(1)   An applicant for a recognition order under paragraph 3 above shall pay such fees in respect of his application as may be required by a scheme made and published by the Registrar; and no application for such an order shall be regarded as duly made unless this sub-paragraph is complied with.

11(2)   Subsections (2) to (4) of section 112 of this Act apply to a scheme under sub-paragraph (1) above as they apply to a scheme under subsection (1) of that section.

11(3)   Every recognised self-regulating organisation for friendly societies shall pay such periodical fees to the Registrar as he may by regulations prescribe.

APPLICATION OF PROVISIONS OF THIS ACT

12(1)   Subject to the following provisions of this paragraph, sections 44(7), 102(1)(c), 124, 125, 126, 180(1)(n), 181, 187, 192 and 200(4) of this Act shall apply in relation to recognised self-regulating organisations for friendly societies as they apply in relation to recognised self-regulating organisations.

12(2)   In its application by virtue of sub-paragraph (1) above section 126(1) of this Act shall have effect as it the reference to section 119(2) were a reference to paragraph 10(1) above.

12(3)   In its application by virtue of sub-paragraph (1) above subsection (2) of section 187 of this Act shall have effect as if—

(a) the reference in paragraph (a) to paragraphs 1 to 6 of Schedule 2 were to paragraphs 2 to 6 of that Schedule (as they apply by virtue of paragraph 4 above) and to sub-paragraph (2) of paragraph 4 above; and

(b) paragraph (d) referred to the powers of the organisation under paragraph 23(4) below.

12(4) A direction under subsection (1) of section 192 of this Act as it applies by virtue of sub-paragraph (1) above shall direct the Registrar to direct the organisation not to take or, as the case may be, to take the action in question; and where the function of making or revoking a recognition order in respect of a self-regulating organisation for friendly societies is exercisable by a transferee body any direction under that subsection as it applies as aforesaid shall be a direction requiring the Registrar to direct the transferee body to give the organisation such a direction as is specified in the direction given by the Secretary of State.

12(5) Subsection (5) of that section shall not apply to a direction given to the Registrar by virtue of this paragraph.

Part III — Registrar's Powers in Relation to Regulated Friendly Societies

SPECIAL PROVISIONS FOR REGULATED FRIENDLY SOCIETIES

13 Paragraphs 13A to 25 below shall have effect in connection with the exercise of powers for the regulation of regulated friendly societies in relation to regulated business, but nothing in this Part of this Schedule shall affect the exercise of any power conferred by this Act in relation to a regulated friendly society which is an authorised person by virtue of section 25 of this Act to the extent that the power relates to other investment business.

History
In para. 13 the words "Paragraph 13A to 25" substituted for the former words "Paragraphs 14 to 25" by CA 1989, s. 206(1) and Sch. 23, para. 26, 31 as from 15 March 1990 (see S.I. 1990 No. 354 (C. 12), art. 3).

CONDUCT OF INVESTMENT BUSINESS

13A(1) The Registrar may issue statements of principle with respect to the conduct expected of regulated friendly societies.

13A(2) The conduct expected may include compliance with a code or standard issued by another person, as for the time being in force, and may allow for the exercise of discretion by any person pursuant to any such code or standard.

13A(3) Failure to comply with a statement of principle under this paragraph is a ground for the taking of disciplinary action or the exercise of powers of intervention, but it does not give rise to any right of action by investors or other persons affected or affect the validity of any transaction.

13A(4) The disciplinary action which may be taken by virtue of sub-paragraph (3) is—

(a) the making of a public statement under paragraph 21, or

(b) the application by the Registrar for an injunction, interdict or other order under paragraph 22(1), or

   (c) any action under paragraph 26 or 27 of this Schedule;

and the reference in that sub-paragraph to powers of intervention is to the powers conferred by Chapter VI of Part I of this Act.

13A(5) Where a statement of principle relates to compliance with a code or standard issued by another person, the statement of principle may provide—

   (a) that failure to comply with the code or standard shall be a ground for the taking of disciplinary action, or the exercise of powers of intervention, only in such cases and to such extent as may be specified; and

   (b) that no such action shall be taken, or any such power exercised, except at the request of the person by whom the code or standard in question was issued.

13A(6) The Registrar shall exercise his powers in such manner as appears to him appropriate to secure compliance with statements of principle under this paragraph.

History

Para. 13A inserted by CA 1989, s. 206(1) and Sch. 23, para. 26, 32 as from 15 March 1990 (see S.I. 1990 No. 354 (C. 12), art. 3).

Note

For transfer of the Registrar's functions under para. 13A see S.I. 1990 No. 354 (C. 12), art. 5(1).

14(1) The rules under section 48 of this Act shall not apply to a regulated friendly society but the Registrar may, with the consent of the Secretary of State, make such rules as may be made under that section regulating the conduct of any such society as respects the matters mentioned in sub-paragraph (2) below.

History

In para. 14(1) the words "other than a member society" formerly appearing after the words "the conduct of any such society" omitted and repealed by CA 1989, s. 206(1), 212, Sch. 23, para. 26, 33(1), (2) and Sch. 24 as from 15 March 1990 (see S.I. 1990 No. 354 (C. 12), art. 3).

14(2) The matters referred to in sub-paragraph (1) above are—

   (a) procuring persons to transact regulated business with it and advising persons as to the exercise of rights conferred by investments acquired from the society in the course of such business;

   (b) managing the investments of pension funds, procuring persons to enter into contracts for the management of such investments and advising persons on such contracts and the exercise of the rights conferred by them;

   (c) matters incidental to those mentioned in paragraphs (a) and (b) above.

14(2A) Paragraph 22B below has effect as regards the application of rules under this paragraph to member societies in respect of investment business in the carrying on of which they are subject to the rules of a recognised self-regulating organisation for friendly societies.

History

Para. 14(2A) inserted by CA 1989, s. 206(1) and Sch. 23, para. 26, 33(1), (3) as from 15 March 1990 (see S.I. 1990 No. 354 (C. 12), art. 3).

14(3) Section 50 of this Act shall apply in relation to rules under this paragraph as it applies in relation to rules under section 48 except that—

   (a) for the reference to the Secretary of State there shall be substituted a reference to the Registrar;

   (b) the Registrar shall not exercise the power under subsection (1) to alter the requirement of rules made under this paragraph without the consent of the Secretary of State; and

    (c) for the references in subsection (4) to section 63B and a recognised self-regulating organisation there shall be substituted references to paragraph 13B and a recognised self-regulating organisation for friendly societies.

History
In para. 14(3)(a) the word "and" formerly appearing at the end omitted and repealed and after para. 14(3)(b) the word "; and" and para. 14(3)(c) inserted by CA 1989,   s. 206(1), 212, Sch. 23, para. 26, 33(1), (4), Sch. 24 as from 15 March 1990 (see S.I. 1990 No. 354 (C. 12), art. 3).

15(1) The rules under section 51 of this Act shall not apply to any investment agreement which a person has entered or offered to enter into with a regulated friendly society if, as respects the society, entering into the agreement constitutes the carrying on of regulated business but the Registrar may, with the consent of the Secretary of State, make rules for enabling a person who has entered or offered to enter into such an agreement to rescind the agreement or withdraw the offer within such period and in such manner as may be specified in the rules.

15(2) Subsection (2) of section 51 of this Act shall apply in relation to rules under this paragraph as it applies in relation to rules under that section but with the substitution for the reference to the Secretary of State of a reference to the Registrar.

16(1) Regulations under section 52 of this Act shall not apply to any regulated friendly society but the Registrar may, with the consent of the Secretary of State, make such regulations as may be made under that section imposing requirements on regulated friendly societies other than member societies.

16(2) Any notice or information required to be given or furnished under this paragraph shall be given in writing or in such other manner as the Registrar may approve.

17(1) Rules under section 53 of this Act shall not apply to any regulated friendly society but the Registrar may, with the consent of the Secretary of State make rules concerning indemnity against any claim in respect of any description of civil liability incurred by a regulated friendly society in connection with any regulated business.

17(2) Such rules shall not apply to a member society of a recognised self-regulating organisation for friendly societies unless that organisation has requested that such rules should apply to it; and any such request shall not be capable of being withdrawn after rules giving effect to it have been made but without prejudice to the power of the Registrar to revoke the rules if he and the Secretary of State think fit.

17(3) Subsections (3) and (4) of section 53 of this Act shall apply in relation to such rules as they apply to rules under that section but with the substitution for references to the Secretary of State of references to the Registrar.

18(1) No scheme established by rules under section 54 shall apply in cases where persons who are or have been regulated friendly societies are unable, or likely to be unable, to satisfy claims in respect of any description of civil liability incurred by them in connection with any regulated business but the Registrar may, with the consent of the Secretary of State, by rules establish a scheme for compensating investors in such cases.

18(2) Subject to sub-paragraph (3) below, subsections (2) to (4) and (6) of that section shall apply in relation to such rules as they apply to rules under that section but with the substitution for the references to the Secretary of State, authorised persons, members and a recognised self-regulating organisation of references respectively to the Registrar, regulated friendly societies, member societies and a recognised self-regulating organisation for friendly societies.

18(3)   Subsection (3) of that section shall have effect with the substitution for the words "the Secretary of State is satisfied" of the words "the Registrar and the Secretary of State are satisfied".

18(4)   The references in section 179(3)(b) and 180(1)(e) of this Act to the body administering a scheme established under section 54 of this Act shall include the body administering a scheme established under this paragraph.

19(1)   Regulations under section 55 of this Act shall not apply to money held by regulated friendly societies but the Registrar may, with the consent of the Secretary of State, make regulations with respect to money held by a regulated friendly society in such circumstances as may be specified in the regulations.

19(2)   Regulations under this paragraph shall not provide that money held by a regulated friendly society shall be held as mentioned in paragraph (a) of subsection (2) of that section but paragraphs (b) to (f) of that subsection and subsections (3) and (4) of that section shall apply in relation to regulations made under this paragraph as they apply in relation to regulations under that section (but with the substitution for the reference in paragraph (e) of subsection (2) to the Secretary of State of a reference to the Registrar).

History
In para. 19(2) the words "(but with the substitution for the reference in paragraph (e)" to the end substituted for the former words "(but with the substitution for the reference in paragraphs (b) and (e) of subsection (2) to a member of a recognised self-regulating organisation of a reference to a member society of a recognised self-regulating organisation for friendly societies and for the reference in paragraph (e) of that subsection to the Secretary of State of a reference to the Registrar)." by CA 1989, s. 206(1) and Sch. 23, para. 26, 34(1), (2) as from 15 March 1990 (see S.I. 1990 No. 354 (C. 12), art. 3).

19(3)   Paragraph 22B below has effect as regards the application of regulations under this paragraph to member societies in respect of investment business in the carrying on of which they are subject to the rules of a recognised self-regulating organisation for friendly societies.

History
Para. 19(3) inserted by CA 1989, s. 206(1) and Sch. 23, para. 26, 34(1), (3) as from 15 March 1990 (see S.I. 1990 No. 354 (C. 12), art. 3).

20(1)   Regulations under section 56(1) of this Act shall not permit anything to be done by a regulated friendly society but that section shall not apply to anything done by such a society in the course of or in consequence of an unsolicited call which, as respects the society, constitutes the carrying on of regulated business, if it is permitted to be done by the society by regulations made by the Registrar with the consent of the Secretary of State.

20(2)   Paragraph 22B below has effect as regards the application of regulations under this paragraph to member societies in respect of investment business in the carrying on of which they are subject to the rules of a recognised self-regulating organisation for friendly societies.

20(3)   As it applies to such persons in respect of such business, the reference in sub-paragraph (1) above to conduct permitted by regulations made by the Registrar with the consent of the Secretary of State shall be construed—

    (a)   where or to the extent that the regulations do not apply, as a reference to conduct permitted by the rules of the organisation; and

FSA 1986, Sch. 11, para. 18(3)   [The next page is 63,101]

(b) where or to the extent that the regulations do not apply but are expressed to have effect subject to the rules of the organisation, as a reference to conduct permitted by the regulations together with the rules of the organisation.

History

Para. 20 substituted by CA 1989, s. 206(1) and Sch. 23, para. 26, 35 as from 15 March 1990 (see S.I. 1990 No. 354 (C. 12), art. 3); former para. 20 read as follows:

"**20** Regulations under section 56(1) of this Act shall not permit anything to be done by a regulated friendly society but that section shall not apply to anything done by such a society in the course of or in consequence of an unsolicited call which, as respects the society constitutes the carrying on of regulated business, if it is permitted to be done by the society in those circumstances—

(a) in the case of a member society, by the rules of the recognised self-regulating organisation for friendly societies of which it is a member; and

(b) in any other case, by regulations made by the Registrar with the consent of the Secretary of State."

21(1) If it appears to the Registrar that a regulated friendly society other than a member society has contravened—

(a) any provision of rules or regulations made under this Schedule or of section 56 or 59 of this Act;

(b) any condition imposed under section 50 of this Act as it applies by virtue of paragraph 14(3) above;

(c) any prohibition or requirement imposed under Chapter VI of Part I of this Act as it applies by virtue of paragraph 23 below; or

(d) any requirement imposed under paragraph 24 below;

he may publish a statement to that effect.

21(2) Subsections (2) to (5) of section 60 above shall apply in relation to the power under sub-paragraph (1) above as they apply in relation to the power in subsection (1) of that section but with the substitution for the references to the Secretary of State of references to the Registrar.

22(1) If on the application of the Registrar the court is satisfied—

(a) that there is a reasonable likelihood that any regulated friendly society will contravene any provision of—

(i) any prohibition or requirement imposed under Chapter VI of Part I of this Act as it applies by virtue of paragraph 23 below;

(ii) the rules or regulations made under this Schedule;

(iii) any requirement imposed under paragraph 24 below;

(iv) section 47, 56 or 59 of this Act;

(v) the rules of a recognised self-regulating organisation for friendly societies in relation to which it is a member society,

or any condition imposed under section 50 of this Act as it applies by virtue of paragraph 14(3) above;

(b) that any regulated friendly society has contravened any such provision or condition and that there is a reasonable likelihood that the contravention will continue or be repeated; or

(c) that any person has contravened any such provision or condition and that there are steps that could be taken for remedying the contravention,

the court may grant an injunction restraining the contravention or, in Scotland, an interdict prohibiting the contravention or, as the case may be, make an order requiring the society and any other person who appears to the court to have been knowingly concerned in the contravention to take steps to remedy it.

22(2)   No application shall be made by the Registrar under sub-paragraph (1) above in respect of any such rules as are mentioned in paragraph (a)(v) of that sub-paragraph unless it appears to him that the organisation is unable or unwilling to take appropriate steps to restrain the contravention or to require the society concerned to take such steps as are mentioned in sub-paragraph (1) above.

22(3)   Subsections (3) to (9) of section 61 of this Act apply to such a contravention as is mentioned in sub-paragraph (1)(a) above as they apply to such a contravention as is mentioned in subsection (3) of that section, but with the substitution for the references to the Secretary of State of references to the Registrar.

22(4)   Without prejudice to the preceding provisions of this paragraph—

    (a) a contravention of any rules or regulations made under this Schedule;

    (b) a contravention of any prohibition or requirement imposed under Chapter VI of Part I of this Act as it applies by virtue of paragraph 23 below;

    (c) a contravention of any requirement imposed under paragraph 24 below;

    (d) a contravention by a member society of any rules of the recognised self-regulating organisation for friendly societies of which it is a member relating to a matter in respect of which rules or regulations have been or could be made under this Schedule or of any requirement or prohibition imposed by the organisation in the exercise of powers for purposes corresponding to those of the said Chapter VI or paragraph 24;

shall be actionable at the suit of a person who suffers loss as a result of the contravention subject to the defences and other incidents applying to actions for breach of statutory duty, but no person shall be guilty of an offence by reason of any such contravention and no such contravention shall invalidate any transaction.

22(5)   This paragraph is without prejudice to any equitable remedy available in respect of property which by virtue of a requirement under section 67 of this Act as it applies by virtue of paragraph 23 below is subject to a trust.

22A(1)   No action in respect of a contravention to which paragraph 22(4) above applies shall lie at the suit of a person other than a private investor, except in such circumstances as may be specified by regulations made by the Registrar.

22A(2)   The meaning of the expression **"private investor"** for the purposes of sub-paragraph (1) shall be defined by regulations made by the Registrar.

22A(3)   Regulations under sub-paragraph (1) may make different provision with respect to different cases.

22A(4)   The Registrar shall, before making any regulations affecting the right to bring an action in respect of a contravention of any rules or regulations made by a person other than himself, consult that person.

History
Para. 22A inserted by CA 1989, s. 193(3) as from 15 March 1990 (see S.I. 1990 No. 354 (C. 12), art. 3) insofar as is necessary in order to enable regulations to be made under that paragraph.

22B(1)   The Registrar may in rules and regulations under—

    (a) paragraph 14 (conduct of business rules),

(b) paragraph 19 (clients' money regulations), or

(c) paragraph 20 (regulations as to unsolicited calls),

designate provisions which apply, to such extent as may be specified, to a member society in respect of investment business in the carrying on of which it is subject to the rules of a recognised self-regulating organisation for friendly societies.

22B(2) It may be provided that the designated rules or regulations have effect, generally or to such extent as may be specified, subject to the rules of the organisation.

22B(3) A member society which contravenes a rule or regulation applying to it by virtue of this paragraph shall be treated as having contravened the rules of the relevant recognised self-regulating organisation for friendly societies.

22B(4) It may be provided that, to such extent as may be specified, the designated rules or regulations may not be modified or waived (under paragraph 22C below or section 50) in relation to a member society.

Where such provision is made any modification or waiver previously granted shall cease to have effect, subject to any transitional provision or saving contained in the rules or regulations.

22B(5) Except as mentioned in sub-paragraph (1), the rules and regulations referred to in that sub-paragraph do not apply to a member society in respect of investment business in the carrying on of which it is subject to the rules of a recognised self-regulating organisation for friendly societies.

History
See history note after para. 22D.

Note
See note after para. 22D.

22C(1) A recognised self-regulating organisation for friendly societies may on the application of a society which is a member of the organisation—

(a) modify a rule or regulation designated under paragraph 22B so as to adapt it to the circumstances of the society or to any particular kind of business carried on by it, or

(b) dispense the society from compliance with any such rule or regulation, generally or in relation to any particular kind of business carried on by it.

22C(2) The powers conferred by this paragraph shall not be exercised unless it appears to the organisation—

(a) that compliance with the rule or regulation in question would be unduly burdensome for the applicant having regard to the benefit which compliance would confer on investors, and

(b) that the exercise of those powers will not result in any undue risk to investors.

22C(3) The powers conferred by this paragraph may be exercised unconditionally or subject to conditions; and paragraph 22B(3) applies in the case of a contravention of a condition as in the case of contravention of a designated rule or regulation.

22C(4) The reference in paragraph 4(1) of Schedule 2 as applied by paragraph 4 above (requirements for recognition of self-regulating organisation for friendly societies) to monitoring and enforcement of compliance with rules and regulations includes monitoring and enforcement of compliance with conditions imposed by the organisation under this paragraph.

History
See history note after para. 22D.

22D(1)   The Registrar may issue codes of practice with respect to any matters dealt with by statements of principle issued under paragraph 13A or by rules or regulations made under any provision of this Schedule.

22D(2)   In determining whether a society has failed to comply with a statement of principle—

     (a)   a failure by it to comply with any relevant provision of a code of practice may be relied on as tending to establish failure to comply with the statement of principle, and

     (b)   compliance by it with the relevant provisions of a code of practice may be relied on as tending to negative any such failure.

22D(3)   A contravention of a code of practice with respect to a matter dealt with by rules or regulations shall not of itself give rise to any liability or invalidate any transaction; but in determining whether a society's conduct amounts to contravention of a rule or regulation—

     (a)   contravention by it of any relevant provision of a code of practice may be relied on as tending to establish liability, and

     (b)   compliance by it with the relevant provisions of a code of practice may be relied on as tending to negative liability.

22D(4)   Where by virtue of paragraph 22B (application of designated rules and regulations to member societies) rules or regulations—

     (a)   do not apply, to any extent, to a member society of a recognised self-regulating organisation for friendly societies, or

     (b)   apply, to any extent, subject to the rules of the organisation,

a code of practice with respect to a matter dealt with by the rules or regulations may contain provision limiting its application to a corresponding extent.

History
Para. 22B–22D inserted by CA 1989, s. 206(1) and Sch. 23, para. 26, 36 as from 15 March 1990 (S.I. 1990 No. 354 (C. 12), art. 3).

Note
For transfer of the Registrar's functions under para. 22B, 22D see S.I. 1990 No. 354 (C. 12), art. 5(1).

INTERVENTION, INFORMATION AND INVESTIGATIONS

23(1) The powers conferred by Chapter VI of Part I of this Act shall not be exercisable in relation to a regulated friendly society or the appointed representative of such a society by the Secretary of State but instead shall be exercisable by the Registrar; and accordingly references in that Chapter to the Secretary of State shall as respects the exercise of powers in relation to a regulated friendly society or such a representative be taken as references to the Registrar.

23(2)   Section 64 of this Act shall not apply to the exercise of those powers by virtue of sub-paragraph (1) above but those powers shall only be exercisable by the Registrar if it appears to him—

     (a)   that the exercise of the powers is desirable in the interests of members or potential members of the regulated friendly society; or

     (b)   that the society is not a fit person to carry on regulated business of a particular kind or to the extent to which it is carrying it on or proposing to carry it on; or

(c) that the society has contravened any provision of this Act or of any rules or regulations made under it or in purported compliance with any such provision has furnished him with false, inaccurate or misleading information or has contravened any prohibition or requirement imposed under this Act.

23(3) For the purposes of sub-paragraph (2)(b) above the Registrar may take into account any matters that could be taken into account in deciding whether to withdraw or suspend an authorisation under Chapter III of Part I of this Act.

23(4) The powers conferred by this paragraph shall not be exercisable in relation—

(a) to a member society which is subject to the rules of a recognised self-regulating organisation for friendly societies in carrying on all the investment business carried on by it; or

(b) to an appointed representative of a member society if that member society, and each other member society which is his principal, is subject to the rules of such an organisation in carrying on the investment business in respect of which it has accepted responsibility for his activities;

except that the powers conferred by virtue of section 67(1)(b) of this Act may on any of the grounds mentioned in sub-paragraph (2) above be exercised in relation to a member society or appointed representative at the request of the organisation in relation to which the society or, as the case may be, the society which is the representative's principal is a member society.

24(1) The Registrar may by notice in writing require any regulated friendly society (other than a member society) or any self-regulating organisation for friendly societies to furnish him with such information as he may reasonably require for the exercise of his functions under this Act.

24(2) The Registrar may require any information which he requires under this paragraph to be furnished within such reasonable time and verified in such manner as he may specify.

25(1) Where a notice or copy of a notice is served on any person under section 60 or section 70 of this Act as they apply by virtue of paragraph 21(2) or 23 above, Chapter IX of Part I of this Act (other than section 96) shall, subject to sub-paragraph (2) below, have effect—

(a) with the substitution for the references to the Secretary of State of references to the Registrar; and

(b) as if for the references in section 98(4) to sections 28, 33 and 60 of this Act there were substituted references to paragraphs 21, 23, 24, 26 and 27 of this Schedule.

25(2) Where the friendly society in question is an authorised person by virtue of section 25 of this Act the provisions mentioned in sub-paragraph (1) above shall have effect as if the references substituted by that sub-paragraph had effect in addition to rather than in substitution for the references for which they are there substituted.

25(3) Where the Tribunal reports that the appropriate decision is to take action under paragraph 26 or 27 of this Schedule the Registrar shall take the report into account but shall not be bound to act on it.

EXERCISE OF POWERS UNDER ENACTMENTS RELATING TO FRIENDLY SOCIETIES

26(1) If it appears to the Chief Registrar of friendly societies that a regulated friendly society which is an authorised person by virtue of section 23(1) of this Act—

    (a) has contravened any provision of—

        (i) this Act or any rules or regulations made under it;

        (ii) any requirement imposed under paragraph 24 above;

        (iii) the rules of a recognised self-regulating organisation for friendly societies in relation to which it is a member society; or

    (b) in purported compliance with any such provision has furnished false, inaccurate or misleading information,

he may exercise any of the powers mentioned in sub-paragraph (2) below in relation to that society.

26(2) The powers mentioned in sub-paragraph (1) above are those under subsection (1) of section 87 (inspection and winding up of registered friendly societies), subsection (1) of section 88 (suspension of business of registered friendly societies), subsections (1) and (2) of section 89 (production of documents) and subsections (1) and (2) of section 91 (cancellation and suspension of registration) of the Friendly Societies Act 1974; and subject to sub-paragraph (3) below the remaining provisions of those sections shall apply in relation to the exercise of those powers by virtue of this paragraph as they do in relation to their exercise in the circumstances mentioned in those sections.

26(3) In its application by virtue of this paragraph—

    (a) section 88 of the said Act of 1974 shall have effect with the omission of subsections (3), (5) and (9); and

    (b) section 89 of that Act shall have effect with the omission of subsection (7).

27(1) If it appears to the Registrar of Friendly Societies for Northern Ireland that a regulated friendly society which is an authorised person by virtue of section 23(2) of this Act—

    (a) has contravened any provision of—

        (i) this Act or any rules or regulations made under it;

        (ii) any requirement imposed under paragraph 24 above;

        (iii) the rules of a recognised self-regulating organisation for friendly societies in relation to which it is a member society; or

    (b) in purported compliance with any such provision has furnished false, inaccurate or misleading information,

he may exercise any of the powers mentioned in sub-paragraph (2) below in relation to that society.

FSA 1986, Sch. 11, para. 25(3)

27(2)   The powers mentioned in sub-paragraph (1) above are those under subsection (1) of section 77 (inspection and winding up of registered friendly societies), subsection (1) of section 78 (suspension of business of registered friendly societies), subsections (1) and (2) of section 79 (production of documents) and subsections (1) and (2) of section 80 (cancellation and suspension of registration) of the Friendly Societies Act (Northern Ireland) 1970; and subject to sub-paragraph (3) below the remaining provisions of those sections shall apply in relation to the exercise of those powers by virtue of this paragraph as they do in relation to their exercise in the circumstances mentioned in those sections.

27(3)   In its application by virtue of this paragraph section 78 of the said Act of 1970 shall have effect with the omission in subsection (2) of the words from "and such notice" onwards and of subsection (4).

Part IV — Transfer of Registrar's Functions

28(1)   If it appears to the Registrar—

    (a) that a body corporate has been established which is able and willing to discharge all or any of the functions to which this paragraph applies; and

    (b) that the requirements of Schedule 7 to this Act (as it has effect by virtue of sub-paragraph (3) below) are satisfied in the case of that body,

he may, with the consent of the Secretary of State and subject to the following provisions of this paragraph and paragraphs 29 and 30 below, make an order transferring all or any of those functions to that body.

28(2)   The body to which functions are transferred by the first order made under sub-paragraph (1) above shall be the body known as The Securities and Investments Board Limited if the Secretary of State consents to the making of the order and it appears to the Registrar that that body is able and willing to discharge those functions, that the requirements mentioned in paragraph (b) of that sub-paragraph are satisfied in the case of that body and that he is not precluded from making the order by the following provisions of this paragraph or paragraph 29 or 30 below.

28(3)   For the purposes of sub-paragraph (1) above Schedule 7 shall have effect as if—

    (a) for references to a designated agency there were substituted references to a transferee body; and

    (b) for the reference to complaints in paragraph 4 there were substituted a reference to complaints arising out of the conduct by regulated friendly societies of regulated business.

28(4)   An order under sub-paragraph (1) above is in this Act referred to as a transfer order and a body to which functions are transferred by a transfer order is in this Act referred to as a transferee body.

28(5)   Subject to sub-paragraphs (6) and (8) below, this paragraph applies to the functions of the Registrar under section 113(3) of this Act and paragraph 38 below and any functions conferred on him by virtue of paragraphs 2 to 25 above other than the powers under sections 66 and 68 of this Act and, so far as applicable to assets belonging to a regulated friendly society, the power under section 67 of this Act.

28(6)   If the Registrar transfers his functions under Chapter VI of Part I of this Act they shall not be exercisable by the transferee body if the only reasons by virtue of which it appears to the body as mentioned in paragraph 23(2) above relate to the sufficiency of the funds of the society to meet existing claims or of the rates of contribution to cover benefits assured.

28(7)   Any function may be transferred by an order under this paragraph either wholly or in part and a function may be transferred in respect of all societies or only in respect of such societies as are specified in the order.

28(8)   A transfer order—

(a) may reserve to the Registrar the function of revoking a recognition order in respect of a self-regulating organisation for friendly societies on the ground that the requirement mentioned in paragraph 4(2) above is not satisfied; and

(b) shall not transfer to a transferee body the function of revoking any such recognition order on the ground that the organisation has contravened the provisions of paragraph 9 above.

28(9)   No transfer order shall be made unless a draft of it has been laid before and approved by a resolution of each House of Parliament.

29(1)   The Registrar shall not make a transfer order transferring any legislative functions to a transferee body unless—

(a) the body has furnished him and the Secretary of State with a copy of the instruments it proposes to issue or make in the exercise of those functions, and

(b) they are both satisfied that those instruments will—

(i) afford investors an adequate level of protection,

(ii) in the case of provisions corresponding to those mentioned in Schedule 8 to this Act, comply with the principles set out in that Schedule, and

(iii) take proper account of the supervision of friendly societies by the Registrar under the enactments relating to friendly societies.

29(2)   In this paragraph **"legislative functions"** means the functions of issuing or making statements of principle, rules, regulations or codes of practice.

History
Para. 29 substituted by CA 1989, s. 206(1) and Sch. 23, para. 26, 37 as from 15 March 1990 (see S.I. 1990 No. 354 (C. 12), art. 3); former para. 29 read as follows:

"**29**   The Registrar shall not make a transfer order transferring any function of making rules or regulations to a transferee body unless—

(a) the body has furnished him and the Secretary of State with a copy of the rules or regulations which it proposes to make in the exercise of those functions; and

(b) they are both satisfied that those rules or regulations will—

(i) afford investors an adequate level of protection,

(ii) in the case of rules and regulations corresponding to those mentioned in Schedule 8 to this Act, comply with the principles set out in that Schedule, and

(iii) take proper account of the supervision of the friendly societies by the Registrar under the enactments relating to friendly societies."

30(1)   The Registrar shall also before making a transfer order transferring any functions to a transferee body require it to furnish him and the Secretary of State with a copy of any guidance intended to have continuing effect which it proposes to issue in writing or other legible form and they may take such guidance into account in determining whether they are satisfied as mentioned in paragraph 29(b) above.

30(2) In this Act references to guidance issued by a transferee body are references to guidance issued or any recommendation made by it which is issued or made to regulated friendly societies or self-regulating organisations for friendly societies generally or to any class of regulated friendly societies or self-regulating organisations for friendly societies, being societies which are or may be subject to statements of principle, rules, regulations or codes of practice issued or made by it or organisations which are or may be recognised by it in the exercise of its functions under a transfer order.

History
In para. 30(2) the words "statements of principle, rules, regulations or codes of practice issued or made" substituted for the former words "rules or regulations made" by CA 1989, s. 206(1) and Sch. 23, para. 26, 38 as from 15 March 1990 (see S.I. 1990 No. 354 (C. 12), art. 3).

31(1) Subject to the provisions of this paragraph, sections 115, 116, 117(3) to (5) and 118 of this Act shall apply in relation to the transfer of functions under paragraph 28 above as they apply in relation to the transfer of functions under section 114 of this Act.

31(2) Subject to sub-paragraphs (5) and (6)(b) below, for references in those provisions to the Secretary of State, a designated agency and a delegation order there shall be substituted respectively references to the Registrar, a transferee body and a transfer order.

31(3) The Registrar may not exercise the powers conferred by subsections (1) and (2) of section 115 except with the consent of the Secretary of State.

31(4) In subsection (3) of section 115 for the reference to Schedule 7 to this Act there shall be substituted a reference to that Schedule as it has effect by virtue of paragraph 28(3) above and in subsection (5) of that section for the reference to section 114(9)(b) of this Act there shall be substituted a reference to paragraph 29(b) above.

31(5) Section 118(3)(b) shall have effect as if the reference to any provision applying to the Secretary of State were a reference to any provision applying to the Secretary of State or the Registrar.

31(6) In Schedule 9 to this Act—

    (a) paragraph 1(2) and (3) shall be omitted;

    (b) paragraph 4 shall have effect as if the references to the Secretary of State were references to the Secretary of State and the Registrar;

    (c) paragraph 5 shall have effect as if the reference to section 205A were a reference to paragraph 45(1) and (3) below;

    (d) paragraph 12(3) shall have effect as if the reference to section 114(9) were a reference to paragraph 29 above.

History
In para. 31(6)(c) the words "as if the reference to section 205A were a reference to paragraph 45(1) and (3) below" substituted for the former words "as if the reference to section 205(2) were a reference to paragraph 45(1) below" by CA 1989, s. 206(1) and Sch. 23, para. 26, 39 as from 15 March 1990 (see S.I. 1990 No. 354 (C. 12), art. 3).

31(7) The power mentioned in paragraph 2(3) of Schedule 9 to this Act shall not be exercisable on the ground that the company has ceased to be a designated agency or, as the case may be, a transferee body if the company remains a transferee body or, as the case may be, a designated agency.

32   A transferee body shall at least once in each year for which the transfer order is in force make a report to the Registrar on the discharge of the functions transferred to it by the order and on such other matters as the order may require and the Registrar shall send a copy of each report received by him under this paragraph to the Secretary of State who shall lay copies of the report before Parliament.

33(1)   This paragraph applies where the function of making or revoking a recognition order in respect of a self-regulating organisation for friendly societies is exercisable by a transferee body.

33(2)   Paragraph 3(2) above shall have effect as if the first reference to the Secretary of State included a reference to the Registrar.

33(3)   The transferee body shall not regard the requirement mentioned in paragraph 4(2) as satisfied unless the Registrar has certified that he also regards it as satisfied.

33(4)   A transferee body shall send the Registrar and the Secretary of State a copy of any notice received by it under paragraph 8(6) above.

33(5)   Where the Secretary of State exercises any of the powers conferred by paragraph 10(2) above in relation to an organisation the Registrar shall direct the transferee body to take the appropriate action in relation to that organisation and such a direction shall, on the application of the Registrar, be enforceable by mandamus or, in Scotland, by an order for specific performance under section 91 of the Court of Session Act 1868.

34(1)   A transferee body to which the Registrar has transferred any legislative functions may exercise those functions without the consent of the Secretary of State.

34(2)   In this paragraph **"legislative functions"** means the functions of issuing or making statements of principle, rules, regulations or codes of practice.

History
Para. 34 substituted by CA 1989, s. 206(1) and Sch. 23, para. 26, 40 as from 15 March 1990 (see S.I. 1990 No. 354 (C. 12), art. 3); former para. 34 read as follows:

"**34**   A transferee body to which the Registrar has transferred any function of making rules or regulations may make those rules or regulations without the consent of the Secretary of State." .

35(1)   A transferee body shall not impose any prohibition or requirement under section 65 or 67 of this Act on a regulated friendly society or vary any such prohibition or requirement unless it has given reasonable notice of its intention to do so to the Registrar and informed him—

    (a) of the manner in which and the date on or after which it intends to exercise the power; and

    (b) in the case of a proposal to impose a prohibition or requirement, on which of the grounds specified in paragraph 23(2) above it proposes to act and its reasons for considering that the ground in question exists and that it is necessary to impose the prohibition or requirement.

35(2)   A transferee body shall not exercise any power to which sub-paragraph (1) above applies if before the date given in the notice in pursuance of sub-paragraph (1)(a) above the Registrar has served on it a notice in writing directing it not to do so; and the Registrar may serve such a notice if he considers it is desirable for protecting members or potential members of the regulated friendly society against the risk that it may be unable to meet its liabilities or to fulfil the reasonable expectations of its members or potential members.

36(1) The Secretary of State shall not consent to the making of an order by the Registrar under paragraph 28 above transferring any functions to a transferee body unless he is satisfied that any statements of principle, rules, regulations, codes of practice, guidance and recommendations of which copies are furnished to him under paragraphs 29(a) and 30(1) above do not have, and are not intended or likely to have, to any significant extent the effect of restricting, distorting or preventing competition or, if they have or are intended or likely to have that effect to any significant extent, that the effect is not greater than is necessary for the protection of investors.

History
See history note after para. 36(3).

36(2) Section 121(2) and (4) and sections 122 to 128 above shall have effect in relation to transferee bodies and transfer orders as they have effect in relation to designated agencies and designation orders but subject to the following modifications.

36(3) Those provisions shall have effect as if the powers exercisable under section 121(3) were—

(a) to make an order transferring back to the Registrar all or any of the functions transferred to the transferee body by a transfer order; or

(b) to direct the Registrar to direct the transferee body to take specified steps for the purpose of securing that the statements of principle, rules, regulations, codes of practice, guidance or practices in question do not have the effect mentioned in sub-paragraph (1) above.

History
In para. 36(1) and (3)(b) the words "statements of principle, rules, regulations, codes of practice" substituted for the former words "rules, regulations" by CA 1989, s. 206(1) and Sch. 23, para. 26, 41 as from 15 March 1990 (see S.I. 1990 No. 354 (C. 12), art. 3).

36(4) No order shall be made by virtue of sub-paragraph (3) above unless a draft of it has been laid before and approved by a resolution of each House of Parliament.

36(5) For the decisions referred to in section 122(1) there shall be substituted a reference to the Secretary of State's decision whether he is precluded by sub-paragraph (1) above from giving his consent to the making of a transfer order.

36(6) Section 128 shall apply as if—

(a) the powers referred to in subsection (1) of that section included the power conferred by sub-paragraph (3)(b) above; and

(b) the references to Chapter XIV of Part I included references to this paragraph.

37(1) If a transferee body has reasonable grounds for believing that any regulated friendly society has failed to comply with an obligation to which it is subject by virtue of this Act it shall forthwith give notice of that fact to the Registrar so that he can take it into consideration in deciding whether to exercise in relation to the society any of the powers conferred on him by sections 87 to 89 and 91 of the Friendly Societies Act 1974 or, as the case may be, sections 77 to 80 of the Friendly Societies Act (Northern Ireland) 1970 (inspection, winding up, suspension of business and cancellation and suspension of registration).

37(2) A notice under sub-paragraph (1) above shall contain particulars of the obligation in question and of the transferee body's reasons for considering that the society has failed to satisfy that obligation.

37(3) A transferee body need not give a notice under sub-paragraph (1) above in respect of any matter unless it considers that that matter (either alone or in conjunction with other matters) would justify the withdrawal of authorisation under section 28 of this Act in the case of a person to whom that provision applies.

Part V — Miscellaneous and Supplemental

38(1) The Registrar may publish information or give advice, or arrange for the publication of information or the giving of advice, in such form and manner as he considers appropriate with respect to—

(a) the operation of this Schedule and the statements of principle, rules, regulations and codes of practice issued or made under it in relation to registered friendly societies, including in particular the rights of their members, the duties of such societies and the steps to be taken for enforcing those rights or complying with those duties;

(b) any matters relating to the functions of the Registrar under this Schedule or any such statements of principle, rules, regulations or codes of practice;

(c) any other matters about which it appears to him to be desirable to publish information or give advice for the protection of those members or any class of them.

History
In para. 38(1):

- in (a) the words "statements opf principle, rules, regulations and codes of practice issued or made" substituted for the former words "rules and regulations made", and

- in (b) the words "statements of principle, rules, regulations or codes of practice" substituted for the former words "rules or regulations"

by CA 1989, s. 206(1) and Sch. 23, para. 26, 42(a), (b) as from 15 March 1990 (see S.I. 1990 No. 354 (C. 12), art. 3).

38(2) The Registrar may offer for sale copies of information published under this paragraph and may, if he thinks fit, make reasonable charges for advice given under this paragraph at any person's request.

38(3) This paragraph shall not be construed as authorising the disclosure of restricted information within the meaning of section 179 of this Act in any case in which it could not be disclosed apart from the provisions of this paragraph.

39 In the case of an application for authorisation under section 26 of this Act made by a society which is registered under the Friendly Societies Act 1974 within the meaning of that Act or is registered or deemed to be registered under the Friendly Societies Act (Northern Ireland) 1970 ("a registered society"), section 27(3)(c) of this Act shall have effect as if it referred only to any person who is a trustee manager or member of the committee of the society.

40 Where the other person mentioned in paragraph (c) of the definition of "connected person" in section 105(9) of this Act is a registered society that paragraph shall have effect with the substitution for the words from "member" onwards of the words "trustee, manager or member of the committee of the society".

41 In relation to any such document as is mentioned in subsection (1) of section 204 of this Act which is required or authorised to be given to or served on a registered society—

(a) subsection (3)(c) of that section shall have effect with the substitution for the words from "member" onwards of the words "trustee, manager or member of the committee of the society"; and

(b) subsection (4)(c) of that section shall have effect as if for the words from "member" onwards there were substituted the words "trustee, manager or member of the committee of the society, the office which is its registered office in accordance with its rules".

42 Rules under paragraphs 14, 15, 17 and 18 above and regulations under paragraphs 16, 19 and 20 above shall apply notwithstanding any provision to the contrary in the rules of any regulated friendly society to which they apply.

43(1) Where it appears to the Registrar, the assistant registrar for Scotland, the Industrial Assurance Commissioner or the Industrial Assurance Commissioner for Northern Ireland that any such rules as are mentioned in section 48(2)(j) of this Act which are made by virtue of paragraph 14 above (or any corresponding rules made by a self-regulating organisation for friendly societies) make arrangements for the settlement of a dispute referred to him under section 77 of the Friendly Societies Act 1974, section 65 of the Friendly Societies Act (Northern Ireland) 1970, section 32 of the Industrial Assurance Act 1923 or Article 36 of the Industrial Assurance (Northern Ireland) Order 1979 or that such rules relate to some of the matters in dispute he may, if he thinks fit, delegate his functions in respect of the dispute so as to enable it to be settled in accordance with the rules.

43(2) If such rules provide that any dispute may be referred to such a person, that person may deal with any dispute referred to him in pursuance of those rules as if it were a dispute referred to him as aforesaid and may delegate his functions in respect of any such dispute to any other person.

44(1) In Part III of Schedule 1 to the House of Commons Disqualification Act 1975 (disqualifying offices) there shall be inserted at the appropriate place—

"Chairman of a transferee body within the meaning of Schedule 11 to the Financial Services Act 1986 if he is in receipt of remuneration."

44(2) A corresponding amendment shall be made in Part III of Schedule 1 to the Northern Ireland Assembly Disqualification Act 1975.

45(1) Any power of the Chief Registrar of friendly societies to issue or make statements of principle, rules, regulations, orders or codes of practice which is exercisable by virtue of this Act shall be exercisable by statutory instrument and the Statutory Instruments Act 1946 shall apply to any such power as if the Chief Registrar of friendly societies were a Minister of the Crown.

History

In para. 45(1) the words "issue or make statements of principle, rules, regulations, orders or codes of practice" substituted for the former words "make regulations, rules or orders" by CA 1989, s. 206(1) and Sch. 23, para. 26, 43(a) as from 15 March 1990 (see S.I. 1990 No. 354 (C. 12), art. 3).

45(2) Any such power of the Registrar of Friendly Societies for Northern Ireland shall be exercisable by statutory rule for the purposes of the Statutory Rules (Northern Ireland) Order 1979.

45(3) Any statements of principle, rules, regulations, orders or codes of practice made under this Schedule by the Registrar may make different provision for different cases.

History

In para. 45(3) the words "statements of principle, rules, regulations, orders or codes of practice" substituted for the former words "regulations, rules or orders" by CA 1989, s. 206(1) and Sch. 23, para. 26, 43(b) as from 15 March 1990 (see S.I. 1990 No. 354 (C. 12), art. 3).

Schedule 12 — Takeover Offers: Provisions Substituted for Sections 428, 429 and 430 of Companies Act 1985

Section 172

Part XIIIA — Takeover Offers

SEC. 428 "Takeover offers"

428(1) In this Part of this Act **"a takeover offer"** means an offer to acquire all the shares, or all the shares of any class or classes, in a company (other than shares which at the date of the offer are already held by the offeror), being an offer on terms which are the same in relation to all the shares to which the offer relates or, where those shares include shares of different classes, in relation to all the shares of each class.

428(2) In subsection (1) **"shares"** means shares which have been allotted on the date of the offer but a takeover offer may include among the shares to which it relates all or any shares that are subsequently allotted before a date specified in or determined in accordance with the terms of the offer.

428(3) The terms offered in relation to any shares shall for the purposes of this section be treated as being the same in relation to all the shares or, as the case may be, all the shares of a class to which the offer relates notwithstanding any variation permitted by subsection (4).

428(4) A variation is permitted by this subsection where—

    (a) the law of a country or territory outside the United Kingdom precludes an offer of consideration in the form or any of the forms specified in the terms in question or precludes it except after compliance by the offeror with conditions with which he is unable to comply or which he regards as unduly onerous; and

    (b) the variation is such that the persons to whom an offer of consideration in that form is precluded are able to receive consideration otherwise than in that form but of substantially equivalent value.

428(5) The reference in subsection (1) to shares already held by the offeror includes a reference to shares which he has contracted to acquire but that shall not be construed as including shares which are the subject of a contract binding the holder to accept the offer when it is made, being a contract entered into by the holder either for no consideration and under seal or for no consideration other than a promise by the offeror to make the offer.

428(6) In the application of subsection (5) to Scotland, the words "and under seal" shall be omitted.

428(7) Where the terms of an offer make provision for their revision and for acceptances on the previous terms to be treated as acceptances on the revised terms, the revision shall not be regarded for the purposes of this Part of this Act as the making of a fresh offer and references in this Part of this Act to the date of the offer shall accordingly be construed as references to the date on which the original offer was made.

428(8) In this Part of this Act **"the offeror"** means, subject to section 430D, the person making a takeover offer and "the company" means the company whose shares are the subject of the offer.

SEC. 429 Right of offeror to buy out minority shareholders

429(1) If, in a case in which a takeover offer does not relate to shares of different classes, the offeror has by virtue of acceptances of the offer acquired or contracted to acquire not less than nine-tenths in value of the shares to which the offer relates he may give notice to the holder of any shares to which the offer relates which the offeror has not acquired or contracted to acquire that he desires to acquire those shares.

429(2) If, in a case in which a takeover offer relates to shares of different classes, the offeror has by virtue of acceptances of the offer acquired or contracted to acquire not less than nine-tenths in value of the shares of any class to which the offer relates, he may give notice to the holder of any shares of that class which the offeror has not acquired or contracted to acquire that he desires to acquire those shares.

429(3) No notice shall be given under subsection (1) or (2) unless the offeror has acquired or contracted to acquire the shares necessary to satisfy the minimum specified in that subsection before the end of the period of four months beginning with the date of the offer; and no such notice shall be given after the end of the period of two months beginning with the date on which he has acquired or contracted to acquire shares which satisfy that minimum.

429(4) Any notice under this section shall be given in the prescribed manner; and when the offeror gives the first notice in relation to an offer he shall send a copy of it to the company together with a statutory declaration by him in the prescribed form stating that the conditions for the giving of the notice are satisfied.

429(5) Where the offeror is a company (whether or not a company within the meaning of this Act) the statutory declaration shall be signed by a director.

429(6) Any person who fails to send a copy of a notice or a statutory declaration as required by subsection (4) or makes such a declaration for the purposes of that subsection knowing it to be false or without having reasonable grounds for believing it to be true shall be liable to imprisonment or a fine, or both, and for continued failure to send the copy or declaration, to a daily default fine.

429(7) If any person is charged with an offence for failing to send a copy of a notice as required by subsection (4) it is a defence for him to prove that he took reasonable steps for securing compliance with that subsection.

429(8) Where during the period within which a takeover offer can be accepted the offeror acquires or contracts to acquire any of the shares to which the offer relates but otherwise than by virtue of acceptances of the offer, then, if—

  (a) the value of the consideration for which they are acquired or contracted to be acquired ("the acquisition consideration") does not at that time exceed the value of the consideration specified in the terms of the offer; or

  (b) those terms are subsequently revised so that when the revision is announced the value of the acquisition consideration, at the time mentioned in paragraph (a) above, no longer exceeds the value of the consideration specified in those terms, the offeror shall be treated for the purposes of this section as having acquired or contracted to acquire those shares by virtue of acceptances of the offer; but in any other case those shares shall be treated as excluded from those to which the offer relates.

SEC. 430　Effect of notice under sec. 429

430(1)　The following provisions shall, subject to section 430C, have effect where a notice is given in respect of any shares under section 429.

430(2)　The offeror shall be entitled and bound to acquire those shares on the terms of the offer.

430(3)　Where the terms of an offer are such as to give the holder of any shares a choice of consideration the notice shall give particulars of the choice and state—

(a) that the holder of the shares may within six weeks from the date of the notice indicate his choice by a written communication sent to the offeror at an address specified in the notice; and

(b) which consideration specified in the offer is to be taken as applying in default of his indicating a choice as aforesaid;

and the terms of the offer mentioned in subsection (2) shall be determined accordingly.

430(4)　Subsection (3) applies whether or not any time-limit or other conditions applicable to the choice under the terms of the offer can still be complied with; and if the consideration chosen by the holder of the shares—

(a) is not cash and the offeror is no longer able to provide it; or

(b) was to have been provided by a third party who is no longer bound or able to provide it,

the consideration shall be taken to consist of an amount of cash payable by the offeror which at the date of the notice is equivalent to the chosen consideration.

430(5)　At the end of six weeks from the date of the notice the offeror shall forthwith—

(a) send a copy of the notice to the company; and

(b) pay or transfer to the company the consideration for the shares to which the notice relates.

430(6)　If the shares to which the notice relates are registered the copy of the notice sent to the company under subsection (5)(a) shall be accompanied by an instrument of transfer executed on behalf of the shareholder by a person appointed by the offeror; and on receipt of that instrument the company shall register the offeror as the holder of those shares.

430(7)　If the shares to which the notice relates are transferable by the delivery of warrants or other instruments the copy of the notice sent to the company under subsection (5)(a) shall be accompanied by a statement to that effect; and the company shall on receipt of the statement issue the offeror with warrants or other instruments in respect of the shares and those already in issue in respect of the shares shall become void.

430(8)　Where the consideration referred to in paragraph (b) of subsection (5) consists of shares or securities to be allotted by the offeror the reference in that paragraph to the transfer of the consideration shall be construed as a reference to the allotment of the shares or securities to the company.

430(9)   Any sum received by a company under paragraph (b) of subsection (5) and any other consideration received under that paragraph shall be held by the company on trust for the person entitled to the shares in respect of which the sum or other consideration was received.

430(10)   Any sum received by a company under paragraph (b) of subsection (5), and any dividend or other sum accruing from any other consideration received by a company under that paragraph, shall be paid into a separate bank account, being an account the balance on which bears interest at an appropriate rate and can be withdrawn by such notice (if any) as is appropriate.

430(11)   Where after reasonable enquiry made at such intervals as are reasonable the person entitled to any consideration held on trust by virtue of subsection (9) cannot be found and twelve years have elapsed since the consideration was received or the company is wound up the consideration (together with any interest, dividend or other benefit that has accrued from it) shall be paid into court.

430(12)   In relation to a company registered in Scotland, subsections (13) and (14) shall apply in place of subsection (11).

430(13)   Where after reasonable enquiry made at such intervals as are reasonable the person entitled to any consideration held on trust by virtue of subsection (9) cannot be found and twelve years have elapsed since the consideration was received or the company is wound up—

> (a) the trust shall terminate;
>
> (b) the company or, as the case may be, the liquidator shall sell any consideration other than cash and any benefit other than cash that has accrued from the consideration; and
>
> (c) a sum representing—
>
>> (i) the consideration so far as it is cash;
>>
>> (ii) the proceeds of any sale under paragraph (b) above; and
>>
>> (iii) any interest, dividend or other benefit that has accrued from the consideration,
>
>> shall be deposited in the name of the Accountant of Court in a bank account such as is referred to in subsection (10) and the receipt for the deposit shall be transmitted to the Accountant of Court.

430(14)   Section 58 of the Bankruptcy (Scotland) Act 1985 (so far as consistent with this Act) shall apply with any necessary modifications to sums deposited under subsection (13) as that section applies to sums deposited under section 57(1)(a) of that Act.

430(15)   The expenses of any such enquiry as is mentioned in subsection (11) or (13) may be defrayed out of the money or other property held on trust for the person or persons to whom the enquiry relates.

SEC. 430A   Right of minority shareholder to be bought out by offeror

430A(1)   If a takeover offer relates to all the shares in a company and at any time before the end of the period within which the offer can be accepted—

(a) the offeror has by virtue of acceptances of the offer acquired or contracted to acquire some (but not all) of the shares to which the offer relates; and

(b) those shares, with or without any other shares in the company which he has acquired or contracted to acquire, amount to not less than nine-tenths in value of all the shares in the company,

the holder of any shares to which the offer relates who has not accepted the offer may by a written communication addressed to the offeror require him to acquire those shares.

430A(2)   If a takeover offer relates to shares of any class or classes and at any time before the end of the period within which the offer can be accepted—

(a) the offeror has by virtue of acceptances of the offer acquired or contracted to acquire some (but not all) of the shares of any class to which the offer relates; and

(b) those shares, with or without any other shares of that class which he has acquired or contracted to acquire, amount to not less than nine-tenths in value of all the shares of that class,

the holder of any shares of that class who has not accepted the offer may by a written communication addressed to the offeror require him to acquire those shares.

430A(3)   Within one month of the time specified in subsection (1) or, as the case may be, subsection (2) the offeror shall give any shareholder who has not accepted the offer notice in the prescribed manner of the rights that are exercisable by him under that subsection; and if the notice is given before the end of the period mentioned in that subsection it shall state that the offer is still open for acceptance.

430A(4)   A notice under subsection (3) may specify a period for the exercise of the rights conferred by this section and in that event the rights shall not be exercisable after the end of that period; but no such period shall end less than three months after the end of the period within which the offer can be accepted.

430A(5)   Subsection (3) does not apply if the offeror has given the shareholder a notice in respect of the shares in question under section 429.

430A(6)   If the offeror fails to comply with subsection (3) he and, if the offeror is a company, every officer of the company who is in default or to whose neglect the failure is attributable, shall be liable to a fine and, for continued contravention, to a daily default fine.

430A(7)   If an offeror other than a company is charged with an offence for failing to comply with subsection (3) it is a defence for him to prove that he took all reasonable steps for securing compliance with that subsection.

SEC. 430B   Effect of requirement under sec. 430A

430B(1)   The following provisions shall, subject to section 430C, have effect where a shareholder exercises his rights in respect of any shares under section 430A.

FSA 1986, Sch. 12

430B(2) The offeror shall be entitled and bound to acquire those shares on the terms of the offer or on such other terms as may be agreed.

430B(3) Where the terms of an offer are such as to give the holder of shares a choice of consideration the holder of the shares may indicate his choice when requiring the offeror to acquire them and the notice given to the holder under section 430A(3)—

    (a) shall give particulars of the choice and of the rights conferred by this subsection; and

    (b) may state which consideration specified in the offer is to be taken as applying in default of his indicating a choice;

and the terms of the offer mentioned in subsection (2) shall be determined accordingly.

430B(4) Subsection (3) applies whether or not any time-limit or other conditions applicable to the choice under the terms of the offer can still be complied with; and if the consideration chosen by the holder of the shares—

    (a) is not cash and the offeror is no longer able to provide it; or

    (b) was to have been provided by a third party who is no longer bound or able to provide it,

the consideration shall be taken to consist of an amount of cash payable by the offeror which at the date when the holder of the shares requires the offeror to acquire them is equivalent to the chosen consideration.

SEC. 430C Applications to the court

430C(1) Where a notice is given under section 429 to the holder of any shares the court may, on an application made by him within six weeks from the date on which the notice was given—

    (a) order that the offeror shall not be entitled and bound to acquire the shares; or

    (b) specify terms of acquisition different from those of the offer.

430C(2) If an application to the court under subsection (1) is pending at the end of the period mentioned in subsection (5) of section 430 that subsection shall not have effect until the application has been disposed of.

430C(3) Where the holder of any shares exercises his rights under section 430A the court may, on an application made by him or the offeror, order that the terms on which the offeror is entitled and bound to acquire the shares shall be such as the court thinks fit.

430C(4) No order for costs or expenses shall be made against a shareholder making an application under subsection (1) or (3) unless the court considers—

    (a) that the application was unnecessary, improper or vexatious; or

    (b) that there has been unreasonable delay in making the application or unreasonable conduct on his part in conducting the proceedings on the application.

430C(5) Where a takeover offer has not been accepted to the extent necessary for entitling the offeror to give notices under subsection (1) or (2) of section 429 the court may, on the application of the offeror, make an order authorising him to give notices under that subsection if satisfied—

(a) that the offeror has after reasonable enquiry been unable to trace one or more of the persons holding shares to which the offer relates;

(b) that the shares which the offeror has acquired or contracted to acquire by virtue of acceptances of the offer, together with the shares held by the person or persons mentioned in paragraph (a), amount to not less than the minimum specified in that subsection; and

(c) that the consideration offered is fair and reasonable;

but the court shall not make an order under this subsection unless it considers that it is just and equitable to do so having regard, in particular, to the number of shareholders who have been traced but who have not accepted the offer.

SEC. 430D   Joint offers

430D(1)   A takeover offer may be made by two or more persons jointly and in that event this Part of this Act has effect with the following modifications.

430D(2)   The conditions for the exercise of the rights conferred by sections 429 and 430A shall be satisfied by the joint offerors acquiring or contracting to acquire the necessary shares jointly (as respects acquisitions by virtue of acceptances of the offer) and either jointly or separately (in other cases); and, subject to the following provisions, the rights and obligations of the offeror under those sections and sections 430 and 430B shall be respectively joint rights and joint and several obligations of the joint offerors.

430D(3)   It shall be a sufficient compliance with any provision of those sections requiring or authorising a notice or other document to be given or sent by or to the joint offerors that it is given or sent by or to any of them; but the statutory declaration required by section 429(4) shall be made by all of them and, in the case of a joint offeror being a company, signed by a director of that company.

430D(4)   In sections 428, 430(8) and 430E references to the offeror shall be construed as references to the joint offerors or any of them.

430D(5)   In section 430(6) and (7) references to the offeror shall be construed as references to the joint offerors or such of them as they may determine.

430D(6)   In sections 430(4)(a) and 430B(4)(a) references to the offeror being no longer able to provide the relevant consideration shall be construed as references to none of the joint offerors being able to do so.

430D(7)   In section 430C references to the offeror shall be construed as references to the joint offerors except that any application under subsection (3) or (5) may be made by any of them and the reference in subsection (5)(a) to the offeror having been unable to trace one or more of the persons holding shares shall be construed as a reference to none of the offerors having been able to do so.

SEC. 430E   Associates

430E(1)   The requirement in section 428(1) that a takeover offer must extend to all the shares, or all the shares of any class or classes, in a company shall be regarded as satisfied notwithstanding that the offer does not extend to shares which associates of the offeror hold or have contracted to acquire; but, subject to subsection (2), shares which any such associate holds or has contracted to acquire, whether at the time when the offer is made or subsequently, shall be disregarded for the purposes of any reference in this Part of this Act to the shares to which a takeover offer relates.

430E(2)   Where during the period within which a takeover offer can be accepted any associate of the offeror acquires or contracts to acquire any of the shares to which the offer relates, then, if the condition specified in subsection (8)(a) or (b) of section 429 is satisfied as respects those shares they shall be treated for the purposes of that section as shares to which the offer relates.

430E(3)   In section 430A(1)(b) and (2)(b) the reference to shares which the offeror has acquired or contracted to acquire shall include a reference to shares which any associate of his has acquired or contracted to acquire.

430E(4)   In this section "**associate**", in relation to an offeror means—

 (a) a nominee of the offeror;

 (b) a holding company, subsidiary or fellow subsidiary of the offeror or a nominee of such a holding company, subsidiary or fellow subsidiary;

 (c) a body corporate in which the offeror is substantially interested; or

 (d) any person who is, or is a nominee of, a party to an agreement with the offeror for the acquisition of, or of an interest in, the shares which are the subject of the takeover offer, being an agreement which includes provisions imposing obligations or restrictions such as are mentioned in section 204(2)(a).

430E(5)   For the purposes of subsection (4)(b) a company is a fellow subsidiary of another body corporate if both are subsidiaries of the same body corporate but neither is a subsidiary of the other.

430E(6)   For the purposes of subsection (4)(c) an offeror has a substantial interest in a body corporate if—

 (a) that body or its directors are accustomed to act in accordance with his directions or instructions; or

 (b) he is entitled to exercise or control the exercise of one-third or more of the voting power at general meetings of that body.

430E(7)   Subsections (5) and (6) of section 204 shall apply to subsection (4)(d) above as they apply to that section and subsections (3) and (4) of section 203 shall apply for the purposes of subsection (6) above as they apply for the purposes of subsection (2)(b) of that section.

430E(8)   Where the offeror is an individual his associates shall also include his spouse and any minor child or step-child of his.

SEC. 430F   Convertible securities

430F(1)   For the purposes of this Part of this Act securities of a company shall be treated as shares in the company if they are convertible into or entitle the holder to subscribe for such shares; and references to the holder of shares or a shareholder shall be construed accordingly.

430F(2)   Subsection (1) shall not be construed as requiring any securities to be treated—

(a) as shares of the same class as those into which they are convertible or for which the holder is entitled to subscribe; or

(b) as shares of the same class as other securities by reason only that the shares into which they are convertible or for which the holder is entitled to subscribe are of the same class.

Schedule 13 — Disclosure of Information

Section 182

1 In section 133(2)(a) of the Fair Trading Act 1973 after the words "the Telecommunications Act 1984" there shall be inserted the words "or Chapter XIV of Part I of the Financial Services Act 1986".

2 In section 41(1)(a) of the Restrictive Trade Practices Act 1976 after the words "the Telecommunications Act 1984" there shall be inserted the words "or Chapter XIV of Part I of the Financial Services Act 1986".

3 (Repealed by the Banking Act 1987, sec. 108(2) and Sch. 7, Pt. I as from 1 October 1987.)

History
In regard to the above date see S.I. 1987 No. 1664 (C. 50), art. 2 and Sch. Para. 3 formerly read as follows:

"**3(1)** In section 19 of the Banking Act 1979 after subsection (2) there shall be inserted—

'**(2A)** Nothing in subsection (1) above prohibits the disclosure of information by the Bank to any person specified in the first column of the following Table if the Bank considers—

(a) that the disclosure would enable or assist the Bank to discharge its functions under this Act; or

(b) that it would enable or assist that person to discharge the functions specified in the second column of that Table.

TABLE

Person	Functions
The Secretary of State.	Functions under the Insurance Companies Act 1982 or the Financial Services Act 1986.
The Chief Registrar of friendly societies or the Registrar of Friendly Societies for Northern Ireland.	Functions under the Financial Services Act 1986 or under the enactments relating to friendly societies.
A designated agency or transferee body or the competent authority (within the meaning of the Financial Services Act 1986).	Functions under the Financial Services Act 1986.
A recognised self-regulating organisation, recognised professional body, recognised investment exchange, recognised clearing house or recognised self-regulating organisation for friendly societies (within the meaning of the Financial Services Act 1986).	Functions in its capacity as an organisation, body, exchange or clearing house recognised under the Financial Services Act 1986.
A person appointed or authorised to exercise any powers under section 94, 106 or 177 of the Financial Services Act 1986.	Functions arising from his appointment or authorisation under that section.
The body administering a scheme under section 54 of paragraph 18 of Schedule 11 to the Financial Services Act 1986.	Functions under the scheme.

(**2B**) Nothing in subsection (1) above prohibits the disclosure by a person specified in the first column of the Table in subsection (2A) above of information obtained by him by virtue of a disclosure authorised by that subsection if he makes the disclosure with the consent of the Bank and for the purpose of enabling or assisting himself to discharge any functions specified in relation to him in the second column of that Table; and before deciding whether to give its consent to such a disclosure by any person the Bank shall take account of any representations made by him as to the desirability of or the necessity for the disclosure.'.

3(2) For subsection (6) of that section there shall be substituted—

'(**6**) Nothing in subsection (1) above prohibits the disclosure of information by or with the consent of the Bank for the purpose of enabling or assisting an authority in a country or territory outside the United Kingdom to exercise functions corresponding to those of the Bank under this Act, or to those of the Secretary of State under the Insurance Companies Act 1982 or the Financial Services Act 1986 or to those of the competent authority under the said Act of 1986 or any other functions in connection with rules of law corresponding to the provisions of the Company Securities (Insider Dealing) Act 1985 or Part VII of the said Act of 1986.' "

4 (Repealed by the Banking Act 1987, sec. 108(2) and Sch. 7, Pt. I as from 15 July 1987.)

History
In regard to the above date see S.I. 1987 No. 1189 (C. 32); art. 2 and Sch. Para. 4 formerly read as follows:

"**4** In section 20(4) of that Act—

  (a) for the words 'in a country or territory outside the United Kingdom' there shall be substituted the

words 'in a member State other than the United Kingdom'; and

  (b) in paragraph (b) for the words 'subsections (4) to (6)' there shall be substituted the words 'subsections (2A), (2B) and (4) to (6)'."

5 At the end of section 19(3) of the Competition Act 1980 there shall be inserted—

> "(h) Chapter XIV of Part I of the Financial Services Act 1986".

6 For subsections (1) and (2) of section 47A of the Insurance Companies Act 1982 there shall be substituted—

> "**(1)** Subject to the following provisions of this section, no information relating to the business or other affairs of any person which has been obtained under section 44(2) to (4) above shall be disclosed without the consent of the person from whom the information was obtained and, if different, the person to whom it relates.
>
> **(2)** Subsection (1) above shall not preclude the disclosure of information to any person who is a competent authority for the purposes of section 449 of the Companies Act 1985.
>
> **(2A)** Subsection (1) above shall not preclude the disclosure of information as mentioned in any of the paragraphs except (m) of subsection (1) of section 180 of the Financial Services Act 1986 or in subsection (3) or (4) of that section or as mentioned in section 449(1) of the Companies Act 1985.
>
> **(2B)** Subsection (1) above shall not preclude the disclosure of any such information as is mentioned in section 180(5) of the Financial Services Act 1986 by any person who by virtue of that section is not precluded by section 179 of that Act from disclosing it."

7 After subsection (1) of section 437 of the Companies Act 1985 there shall be inserted—

> "**(1A)** Any persons who have been appointed under section 431 or 432 may at any time and, if the Secretary of State directs them to do so, shall inform him of any matters coming to their knowledge as a result of their investigations.";

and subsection (2) of section 433 of that Act shall be omitted.

8 In section 446 of that Act—

  (a) in subsection (3) for the words "to 436" there shall be substituted the words "to 437"; and

  (b) subsection (5) shall be omitted.

9(1) In subsection (1) of section 449 of that Act—

  (a) for paragraphs (a) and (b) there shall be substituted—

> "(a) with a view to the institution of or otherwise for the purposes of criminal proceedings;".

  (b) for paragraph (d) there shall be substituted—

> "(d) for the purpose of enabling or assisting the Secretary of State to

exercise any of his functions under this Act, the Insider Dealing Act, the Prevention of Fraud (Investments) Act 1958, the Insurance Companies Act 1982, the Insolvency Act 1986, the Company Directors Disqualification Act 1986 or the Financial Services Act 1986.

(dd) for the purpose of enabling or assisting the Department of Economic Development for Northern Ireland to exercise any powers conferred on it by the enactments relating to companies or insolvency or for the purpose of enabling or assisting any inspector appointed by it under the enactments relating to companies to discharge his functions";

(c) after paragraph (e) there shall be inserted—

"(f) for the purpose of enabling or assisting the Bank of England to discharge its functions under the Banking Act 1979 or any other functions,

(g) for the purpose of enabling or assisting the Deposit Protection Board to discharge its functions under that Act,

(h) for any purpose mentioned in section 180(1)(b), (e), (h), (n) or (p) of the Financial Services Act 1986,

(i) for the purpose of enabling or assisting the Industrial Assurance Commissioner or the Industrial Assurance Commissioner for Northern Ireland to discharge his functions under the enactments relating to industrial assurance,

(j) for the purpose of enabling or assisting the Insurance Brokers Registration Council to discharge its functions under the Insurance Brokers (Registration) Act 1977,

(k) for the purpose of enabling or assisting an official receiver to discharge his functions under the enactments relating to insolvency or for the purpose of enabling or assisting a body which is for the time being a recognised professional body for the purposes of section 391 of the Insolvency Act 1986 to discharge its functions as such,

(l) with a view to the institution of, or otherwise for the purposes of, any disciplinary proceedings relating to the exercise by a solicitor, auditor, accountant, valuer or actuary of his professional duties,

(m) for the purpose of enabling or assisting an authority in a country or territory outside the United Kingdom to exercise corresponding supervisory functions.".

9(2)   After subsection (1) of that section there shall be inserted—

"**(1A)**   In subsection (1) above **'corresponding supervisory functions'** means functions corresponding to those of the Secretary of State or the competent authority under the Financial Services Act 1986 or to those of the Secretary of State under the Insurance Companies Act 1982 or to those of the Bank of England under the Banking Act 1979 or any other functions in connection with rules of law corresponding to the provisions of the Insider Dealing Act or Part VII of the Financial Services Act 1986.

(1B)   Subject to subsection (1C), subsection (1) shall not preclude publication or disclosure for the purpose of enabling or assisting any public or other authority for the time being designated for the purposes of this section by the Secretary of State by an order in a statutory instrument to discharge any functions which are specified in the order.

(1C) An order under subsection (1B) designating an authority for the purpose of that subsection may—

(a) impose conditions subject to which the publication or disclosure of any information or document is permitted by that subsection; and

(b) otherwise restrict the circumstances in which that subsection permits publication or disclosure.

(1D) Subsection (1) shall not preclude the publication or disclosure of any such information as is mentioned in section 180(5) of the Financial Services Act 1986 by any person who by virtue of that section is not precluded by section 179 of that Act from disclosing it."

9(3) For subsection (3) of that section (competent authorities) there shall be substituted—

"**(3)** For the purposes of this section each of the following is a competent authority—

(a) the Secretary of State,

(b) the Department of Economic Development for Northern Ireland and any officer of that Department,

(c) an inspector appointed under this Part by the Secretary of State,

(d) the Treasury and any officer of the Treasury,

(e) the Bank of England and any officer or servant of the Bank,

(f) the Lord Advocate,

(g) the Director of Public Prosecutions, and the Director of Public Prosecutions for Northern Ireland,

(h) any designated agency or transferee body within the meaning of the Financial Services Act 1986 and any officer or servant of such an agency or body,

(i) any person appointed or authorised to exercise any powers under section 94, 106 or 177 of the Financial Services Act 1986 and any officer or servant of such a person,

(j) the body administering a scheme under section 54 of or paragraph 18 of Schedule 11 to that Act and any officer or servant of such a body,

(k) the chief Registrar of friendly societies and the Registrar of Friendly Societies for Northern Ireland and any officer or servant of either of them,

(l) the Industrial Assurance Commissioner and the Industrial Assurance Commissioner for Northern Ireland and any officer of either of them,

(m) any constable,

(n) any procurator fiscal.

(4) A statutory instrument containing an order under subsection (1B) is subject to annulment in pursuance of a resolution of either House of Parliament.".

10   After section 451 of that Act there shall be inserted—

    "Disclosure of information by Secretary of State

    451A   The Secretary of State may, if he thinks fit, disclose any information obtained under this Part of this Act—

    (a)   to any person who is a competent authority for the purposes of section 449, or

    (b)   in any circumstances in which or for any purpose for which that section does not preclude the disclosure of the information to which it applies."

11   After Article 430(1) of the Companies (Northern Ireland) Order 1986 there shall be inserted—

    "(1A)   Any persons who have been appointed under Article 424 or 425 may at any time and, if the Department directs them to do so shall, inform it of any matters coming to their knowledge as a result of their investigation.";

and Article 426(2) of that Order shall be omitted.

12   In Article 439 of that Order—

    (a)   in paragraph (3) for the words "to 429" there shall be substituted the words "to 430"; and

    (b)   paragraph (5) shall be omitted.

13(1)   In paragraph (1) of Article 442 of that Order—

    (a)   for sub-paragraphs (a) and (b) there shall be substituted—

    "(a)   with a view to the institution of or otherwise for the purposes of criminal proceedings;";

    (b)   for sub-paragraph (d) there shall be substituted—

    "(d)   for the purpose of enabling or assisting the Department to exercise any of its functions under this Order, the Insider Dealing Order or the Prevention of Fraud (Investments) Act (Northern Ireland) 1940;

    (dd)   for the purpose of enabling or assisting the Secretary of State to exercise any functions conferred on him by the enactments relating to companies or insolvency, the Prevention of Fraud (Investments) Act 1958, the Insurance Companies Act 1982, or the Financial Services Act 1986, or for the purpose of enabling or assisting any inspector appointed by him under the enactments relating to companies to discharge his functions";

    (c)   after sub-paragraph (e) there shall be inserted—

    "(f)   for the purposes of enabling or assisting the Bank of England to discharge its functions under the Banking Act 1979 or any other functions;

    (g)   for the purposes of enabling or assisting the Deposit Protection Board to discharge its functions under that Act;

    (h)   for any purpose mentioned in section 180(1)(b), (e), (h), (n) or (p) of the Financial Services Act 1986;

(i) for the purpose of enabling or assisting the Industrial Assurance Commissioner for Northern Ireland or the Industrial Assurance Commissioner in Great Britain to discharge his functions under the enactments relating to industrial assurance;

(j) for the purpose of enabling or assisting the Insurance Brokers Registration Council to discharge its functions under the Insurance Brokers (Registration) Act 1977;

(k) for the purpose of enabling or assisting the official assignee to discharge his functions under the enactments relating to companies or bankruptcy;

(l) with a view to the institution of, or otherwise for the purposes of, any disciplinary proceedings relating to the exercise by a solicitor, auditor, accountant, valuer or actuary of his professional duties;

(m) for the purpose of enabling or assisting an authority in a country or territory outside the United Kingdom to exercise corresponding supervisory functions.".

13(2) After paragraph (1) of that Article there shall be inserted—

"**(1A)** In paragraph (1) **'corresponding supervisory functions'** means functions corresponding to those of the Secretary of State or the competent authority under the Financial Services Act 1986 or to those of the Secretary of State under the Insurance Companies Act 1982 or to those of the Bank of England under the Banking Act 1979 or any other functions in connection with rules of law corresponding to the provisions of the Insider Dealing Order or Part VII of the Financial Services Act 1986.

(1B) Subject to paragraph (1C), paragraph (1) shall not preclude publication or disclosure for the purpose of enabling or assisting any public or other authority for the time being designated for the purposes of this Article by an order made by the Department to discharge any functions which are specified in the order.

(1C) An order under paragraph (1B) designating an authority for the purpose of that paragraph may—

(a) impose conditions subject to which the publication or disclosure of any information or document is permitted by that paragraph; and

(b) otherwise restrict the circumstances in which that paragraph permits publication or disclosure.

(1D) Paragraph (1) shall not preclude the publication or disclosure of any such information as is mentioned in section 180(5) of the Financial Services Act 1986 by any person who by virtue of that section is not precluded by section 179 of that Act from disclosing it."

13(3) For paragraph (3) of that Article (competent authorities) there shall be substituted—

"**(3)** For the purposes of this Article each of the following is a competent authority—

(a) the Department and any officer of the Department,

(b) the Secretary of State,

(c) an inspector appointed under this Part by the Department,

(d) the Department of Finance and Personnel and any officer of that Department;

(e) the Treasury and any officer of the Treasury,

(f) the Bank of England and any officer or servant of the Bank,

(g) the Lord Advocate,

(h) the Director of Public Prosecutions for Northern Ireland and the Director of Public Prosecutions in England and Wales,

(i) any designated agency or transferee body within the meaning of the Financial Services Act 1986 and any officer or servant of such an agency or body,

(j) any person appointed or authorised to exercise any powers under section 94, 106 or 177 of the Financial Services Act 1986 and any officer or servant of such a person,

(k) the body administering a scheme under section 54 of or paragraph 18 of Schedule 11 to that Act and any officer or servant of such a body,

(l) the Registrar of Friendly Societies and the Chief Registrar of friendly societies in Great Britain and any officer or servant of either of them,

(m) the Industrial Assurance Commissioner for Northern Ireland and the Industrial Assurance Commissioner in Great Britain and any officer of either of them,

(n) any constable,

(o) any procurator fiscal.

(4) An order under paragraph (1B) is subject to negative resolution."

14 After Article 444 of that order there shall be inserted—

"Disclosure of information by Department

444A The Department may, if it thinks fit, disclose any information obtained under this Part—

(a) to any person who is a competent authority for the purposes of Article 442, or

(b) in any circumstances in which or for any purpose for which that Article does not preclude the disclosure of the information to which it applies.".

Schedule 14—Restriction of Rehabilitation of Offenders Act 1974

Section 189

Part I — Exempted Proceedings

1 Any proceedings with respect to a decision or proposed decision of the Secretary of State or a designated agency—

(a) refusing, withdrawing or suspending an authorisation;

(b) refusing an application under section 28(5) of this Act;

(c) giving a direction under section 59 of this Act or refusing an application for consent or for the variation of a consent under that section;

(d) exercising a power under Chapter VI of Part I of this Act or refusing an application for the rescission or variation of a prohibition or requirement imposed under that Chapter;

(e) refusing to make or revoking an order declaring a collective investment scheme to be an authorised unit trust scheme or a recognised scheme.

2 Any proceedings with respect to a decision or proposed decision of a recognised self-regulating organisation—

(a) refusing or suspending a person's membership of the organisation;

(b) expelling a member of the organisation;

(c) exercising a power of the organisation for purposes corresponding to those of Chapter VI of Part I of this Act.

3(1) Any proceedings with respect to a decision or proposed decision of a recognised professional body—

(a) refusing or suspending a person's membership of the body;

(b) expelling a member of the body.

3(2) Any proceedings with respect to a decision or proposed decision of a recognised professional body or of any other body or person having functions in respect of the enforcement of the recognised professional body's rules relating to the carrying on of investment business—

(a) exercising a power for purposes corresponding to those of Chapter VI of Part I of this Act;

(b) refusing, suspending or withdrawing a certificate issued for the purposes of Part I of this Act.

4 Any proceedings with respect to a decision or proposed decision of the competent authority under Part IV of this Act refusing an application for listing or to discontinue or suspend the listing of any securities.

5 Any proceedings with respect to a decision or proposed decision of the Chief Registrar of friendly societies, the Registrar of Friendly Societies for Northern Ireland or a transferee body, exercising a power exercisable by virtue of paragraph 23 of Schedule 11 to this Act or refusing an application for the rescission or variation of a prohibition or requirement imposed in the exercise of such a power.

6 Any proceedings with respect to a decision or proposed decision of a recognised self-regulating organisation for friendly societies—

(a) refusing or suspending a society's membership of the organisation;

(b) expelling a member of the organisation;

(c) exercising a power of the organisation for purposes corresponding to those for which powers are exercisable by the Registrar by virtue of paragraph 23 of Schedule 11 to this Act.

Part II — Exempted Questions

Person putting question	*Individual to whom question relates*
1 The Secretary of State or a designated agency.	(a) An authorised person. (b) An applicant for authorisation under section 26 of this Act. (c) A person whose authorisation is suspended. (d) The operator or trustee of a recognised scheme or a collective investment scheme in respect of which a notice has been given by the operator under section 87(3) or an application made under section 88 of this Act. (e) An individual who is an associate of a person (whether or not an individual) described in paragraph (a), (b), (c) or (d) above.
2 A recognised self-regulating organisation or recognised professional body.	(a) A member of the organisation or body. (b) An applicant for membership of the organisation or body. (c) A person whose membership of the organisation or body is suspended. (d) An individual who is an associate of a person (whether or not an individual) described in paragraph (a), (b) or (c) above.
3 A recognised professional body.	(a) A person certified by the body. (b) An applicant for certification by the body. (c) A person whose certification by the body is suspended. (d) An individual who is an associate of a person (whether or not an individual) described in paragraph (a), (b) or (c) above.
4 A person (whether or not an individual) described in paragraph 1(a), (b), (c) or (d), paragraph 2(a), (b) or (c) or paragraph 3(a), (b) or (c) above.	An individual who is or is seeking to become an associate of the person in column 1.
5 The competent authority or any other person.	An individual from or in respect of whom information is sought in connection with an application for listing under Part IV of this Act.

6 The competent authority.

An individual who is or is seeking to become an associate of the issuer of securities listed under Part IV of this Act and from or in respect of whom information is sought which the issuer of the securities is required to furnish under listing rules.

7 The Chief Registrar of friendly societies, the Registrar of Friendly Societies for Northern Ireland or a transferee body.

An individual who is an associate of a society which is authorised under section 23 of this Act.

8 A recognised self-regulating organisation for friendly societies.

An individual who is an associate of a member or an applicant for membership of the organisation or of a society whose membership of the organisation is suspended.

Part III — Exempted Actions

Person taking action

Exempted action

1 The Secretary of State, a designated agency, a recognised self-regulating organisation, a recognised professional body, any other body or person mentioned in paragraph 3(2) of Part I of this Schedule or the competent authority.

Any such decision or proposed decision as is mentioned in Part I of this Schedule.

2 A person (whether or not an individual) described in paragraph 1(a), (b), (c) or (d), paragraph 2(a), (b) or (c) or paragraph 3(a), (b) or (c) of Part II of this Schedule.

Dismissing or excluding an individual from being or becoming an associate or the person in column 1.

3 The issuer of securities listed or subject to an application for listing under Part IV of this Act.

Dismissing or excluding an individual from being or becoming an associate of the issuer.

4 The Chief Registrar of friendly societies, the Registrar of Friendly Societies for Northern Ireland, a transferee body or a recognised self-regulating organisation for friendly societies.

Any such decision or proposed decision as is mentioned in Part I of this Schedule.

Part IV — Supplemental

1 In Part I of this Schedule "proceedings" includes any proceedings within the meaning of section 4 of the Rehabilitation of Offenders Act 1974.

2   In Parts II and III of this Schedule—

(a) references to an applicant for authorisation, membership or certification are references to an applicant who has not yet been informed of the decision on his application;

(b) references to an application for listing under Part IV of this Act are references to an application the decision on which has not yet been communicated to the applicant and which is not taken by virtue of section 144(5) of this Act to have been refused.

3   Paragraph 1(d) of Part II of this Schedule and so much of paragraph 1(e) as relates to it—

(a) apply only if the question is put to elicit information for the purpose of determining whether the operator or trustee is a fit and proper person to act as operator or trustee of the scheme in question;

(b) apply in the case of a scheme in respect of which a notice has been given under subsection (3) of section 87 only until the end of the period within which the operator may receive a notification from the Secretary of State under that subsection or, if earlier, the receipt by him of such a notification;

(c) apply in the case of a scheme in respect of which an application has been made under section 88 only until the applicant has been informed of the decision on the application.

Schedule 15 — Transitional Provisions

Section 211(3)

INTERIM AUTHORISATION

1(1)   If before such day as is appointed for the purposes of this paragraph by an order made by the Secretary of State a person has applied—

(a) for membership of any body which on that day is a recognised self-regulating organisation; or

(b) for authorisation by the Secretary of State,

and the application has not been determined before the day on which section 3 of this Act comes into force, that person shall, subject to sub-paragraphs (2), (3) and (4) below, be treated until the determination of the application as if he had been granted an authorisation by the Secretary of State.

1(2)   Sub-paragraph (1) above does not apply to a person who immediately before the day on which section 3 of this Act comes into force is prohibited by the Prevention of Fraud (Investments) Act 1958 (in this Schedule referred to as "the previous Act") from carrying on the business of dealing in securities—

(a) by reason of the refusal or revocation at any time before that day of a licence under that Act; or

(b) by reason of the revocation at any time before that day of an order declaring him to be an exempted dealer.

1(3)   If a person who has made any such application as is mentioned in sub-paragraph (1) above has before the day on which section 3 of this Act comes into

FSA 1986, Sch. 15, para. 1(1)   [The next page is 63,501]

force been served with a notice under section 6 or 16(3) of the previous Act (proposed refusal or revocation of licence or proposed revocation of exemption order) but the refusal or revocation to which the notice relates has not taken place before that day—

    (a) the provisions of that Act with respect to the refusal or revocation of a licence or the revocation of an order under section 16 of that Act shall continue to apply to him until the application mentioned in sub-paragraph (1) above is determined; and

    (b) that sub-paragraph shall cease to apply to him if before the determination of the application mentioned in that sub-paragraph his application for a licence under that Act is refused, his licence under that Act is revoked or the order declaring him to be an exempted dealer under that Act is revoked.

1(4) Notwithstanding sub-paragraph (1) above section 102(1)(a) of this Act shall not apply to a person entitled to carry on investment business by virtue of that sub-paragraph but the Secretary of State may make available for public inspection the information with respect to the holders of principal's licences mentioned in section 9 of the previous Act, any information in his possession by virtue of section 15(3) or (4) of that Act and the information mentioned in section 16(4) of that Act.

1(5) Notwithstanding subsection (2) of section 3 of the previous Act a licence granted under that section before the day on which section 3 of this Act comes into force shall, unless revoked under section 6 of that Act, continue in force until that day.

RETURN OF FEES ON PENDING APPLICATIONS

2 Any fee paid in respect of an application under section 3 of the previous Act which is pending on the day on which that Act is repealed shall be repaid to the applicant.

DEPOSITS AND UNDERTAKINGS

3 The repeal of section 4 of the previous Act shall not affect the operation of that section in a case where—

    (a) a sum deposited in accordance with that section has become payable as provided in subsection (2) of that section before the date on which the repeal takes effect; or

    (b) a sum has become payable before that date in pursuance of an undertaking given under subsection (4) of that section,

but, subject as aforesaid, any sum deposited under that section may be withdrawn by the depositor on application to the Accountant General of the Supreme Court and any undertaking given under that section shall be discharged.

INTERIM RECOGNITION OF PROFESSIONAL BODIES

4(1) If on an application made under section 17 of this Act it appears to the Secretary of State that any of the requirements of section 18(3) of this Act or paragraphs 2 to 6 of Schedule 3 to this Act are not satisfied he may in accordance with this paragraph make a recognition order under section 18 of this Act ("an interim recognition order") notwithstanding that all or any of those requirements are not satisfied.

4(2)   The Secretary of State may, subject to sub-paragraphs (3) and (4) below, make an interim recognition order if he is satisfied—

    (a) that the applicant proposes to adopt rules and practices and to make arrangements which will satisfy such of the requirements mentioned in sub-paragraph (1) above as are not satisfied;

    (b) that it is not practicable for those rules, practices and arrangements to be brought into effect before the date on which section 3 of this Act comes into force but that they will be brought into effect within a reasonable time thereafter; and

    (c) that in the meantime the applicant will enforce its existing rules in such a way, and issue such guidance, as will in respect of investment business of any kind carried on by persons certified by it (or by virtue of paragraph 5 below treated as certified by it) afford to investors protection as nearly as may be equivalent to that provided as respects investment business of that kind by the rules and regulations under Chapter V of Part I of this Act.

4(3)   Where the requirements which are not satisfied consist of or include those mentioned in paragraph 2 of Schedule 3 to this Act an application for an interim recognition order shall be accompanied by—

    (a) a list of the persons to whom the applicant proposes to issue certificates for the purposes of Part I of this Act; and

    (b) particulars of the criteria adopted for determining the persons included in the list;

and the Secretary of State shall not make the order unless it appears to him that those criteria conform as nearly as may be to the conditions mentioned in that paragraph and that the applicant will, until the requirements of that paragraph are satisfied, have arrangements for securing that no person is certified by it (or by virtue of paragraph 5 below treated as certified by it) except in accordance with those criteria and for the effective monitoring of continued compliance by those persons with those criteria.

4(4)   Where the requirements which are not satisfied consist of or include that mentioned in paragraph 6 of Schedule 3 to this Act, the Secretary of State shall not make an interim recognition order unless it appears to him that the applicant will, until that requirement is satisfied, take such steps for complying with it as are reasonably practicable.

4(5)   An application for an interim recognition order shall be accompanied by a copy of the rules and by particulars of the practices and arrangements referred to in sub-paragraph (2)(a) above.

4(6)   An interim recognition order shall not be revocable but shall cease to be in force at the end of such period as is specified in it; and that period shall be such as will in the opinion of the Secretary of State allow a reasonable time for the rules, practices and arrangements mentioned in sub-paragraph (5) above to be brought into effect.

4(7)   The Secretary of State may on the application of the body to which an interim recognition order relates extend the period specified in it if that body satisfies him—

(a) that there are sufficient reasons why the rules, practices and arrangements mentioned in sub-paragraph (5) above cannot be brought into effect by the end of that period; and

(b) that those rules, practices and arrangements, or other rules, practices and arrangements which satisfy the requirements mentioned in sub-paragraph (2)(a) above and of which copies or particulars are furnished to the Secretary of State, will be brought into effect within a reasonable time thereafter;

but not more than one application shall be made by a body under this sub-paragraph.

4(8) A recognition order under section 18 of this Act shall cease to be an interim recognition order if before it ceases to be in force—

(a) the rules, practices and arrangements of which copies or particulars were furnished to the Secretary of State under sub-paragraph (5) or (7)(b) above are brought into effect; or

(b) the Secretary of State certifies that other rules, practices and arrangements which have been brought into effect comply with the requirements mentioned in sub-paragraph (1) above.

4(9) In this paragraph references to the adoption of rules or the making of arrangements include references to taking such other steps as may be necessary for bringing them into effect.

INTERIM AUTHORISATION BY RECOGNISED PROFESSIONAL BODIES

5(1) If at the time when an interim recognition order is made in respect of a professional body that body is unable to issue certificates for the purposes of this Act, any person who at that time is included in the list furnished by that body to the Secretary of State in accordance with paragraph 4(3)(a) above shall be treated for the purposes of this Act as a person certified by that body.

5(2) If at any time while an interim recognition order is in force in respect of a professional body and before the body is able to issue certificates as mentioned in sub-paragraph (1) above the body notifies the Secretary of State that a person not included in that list satisfies the criteria of which particulars were furnished by the body in accordance with paragraph 4(3)(b) above, that person shall, on receipt of the notification by the Secretary of State, be treated for the purposes of this Act as a person certified by that body.

5(3) If at any time while an interim recognition order is in force in respect of a professional body it appears to the body—

(a) that a person treated by virtue of sub-paragraph (1) or (2) above as certified by it has ceased (after the expiration of such transitional period, if any, as appears to the body to be appropriate) to satisfy the criteria mentioned in sub-paragraph (2) above; or

(b) that any such person should for any other reason cease to be treated as certified by it,

it shall forthwith give notice of that fact to the Secretary of State and the person in question shall, on receipt of that notification by the Secretary of State, cease to be treated as certified by that body.

5(4)   Where by virtue of this paragraph a partnership is treated as certified by a recognised professional body section 15(3) of this Act shall apply as it applies where a certificate has in fact been issued to a partnership.

5(5)   Where by virtue of this paragraph any persons are treated as certified by a recognised professional body the requirements of paragraph 2 of Schedule 3 to this Act so far as relating to the retention by a person of a certificate issued by that body and the requirements of paragraph 4 of that Schedule shall apply to the body as if the references to persons certified by it included references to persons treated as certified.

POWER OF RECOGNISED PROFESSIONAL BODY TO MAKE RULES REQUIRED BY THIS ACT

6(1)   Where a recognised professional body regulates the practice of a profession in the exercise of statutory powers the matters in respect of which rules can be made in the exercise of those powers shall, if they would not otherwise do so, include any matter in respect of which rules are required to be made—

(a)   so that the recognition order in respect of that body can cease to be an interim recognition order; or

(b)   where the recognition order was not, or has ceased to be, an interim recognition order, so that the body can continue to be a recognised professional body.

6(2)   Rules made by virtue of this paragraph may in particular make provision for the issue, withdrawal and suspension of certificates for the purposes of this Act and the making of charges in respect of their issue and may accordingly apply to persons who are, or are to be, certified or treated as certified by the body in question whether or not they are persons in relation to whom rules could be made apart from this paragraph.

6(3)   Rules made by virtue of this paragraph may make different provision for different cases.

6(4)   The Secretary of State may at the request of a recognised professional body by order extend, modify or exclude any statutory provision relating to the regulation of the conduct, practice, or discipline of members of that body to such extent as he thinks necessary or expedient in consequence of the provisions of this paragraph; and any order made by virtue of this sub-paragraph shall be subject to annulment in pursuance of a resolution of either House of Parliament.

NOTICE OF COMMENCEMENT OF BUSINESS

7   In the case of a person who is carrying on investment business in the United Kingdom on the day on which section 31 of this Act comes into force, section 32 of this Act shall have effect as if it required him to give the notice referred to in that section forthwith.

ADVERTISEMENTS

8(1)   So long as Part III of the Companies Act 1985 remains in force section 57 of this Act shall not apply—

(a) in relation to any distribution of a prospectus to which section 56 of that Act applies or would apply if not excluded by subsection (5)(b) of that section or to which section 72 of that Act applies or would apply if not excluded by subsection (6)(b) of that section or by section 76 of that Act, or in relation to any distribution of a document relating to securities of a corporation incorporated in Great Britain which is not a registered company, being a document which—

    (i) would, if the corporation were a registered company, be a prospectus to which section 56 of that Act applies or would apply if not excluded as aforesaid, and

    (ii) contains all the matters and is issued with the consents which, by virtue of sections 72 to 75 of that Act, it would have to contain and be issued with if the corporation were a company incorporated outside Great Britain and the document were a prospectus issued by that company;

(b) in relation to any issue of a form of application for shares in, or debentures of, a corporation, together with—

    (i) a prospectus which complies with the requirements of section 56 of that Act or is not required to comply with them because excluded by subsection (5)(b) of that section, or complies with the requirements of Chapter II of Part III of that Act relating to prospectuses and is not issued in contravention of sections 74 and 75 of that Act, or

    (ii) in the case of a corporation incorporated in Great Britain which is not a registered company, a document containing all the matters and issued with the consents mentioned in sub-paragraph (a)(ii) of this paragraph, or in connection with a bona fide invitation to a person to enter into an underwriting agreement with respect to the shares or debentures.

8(2) The provisions of this paragraph shall apply to Northern Ireland with the substitution for the references to Part III and Chapter II of Part III of the Companies Act 1985 of references to Part IV and Chapter II of Part IV of the Companies (Northern Ireland) Order 1986, for the references to sections 56, 56(5)(b), 72, 72(6)(b), 74, 76 and 72 to 75 of the Companies Act 1985 of references to Articles 66, 66(5)(b), 82, 82(6)(b), 84, 86 and 82 to 85 of the Companies (Northern Ireland) Order 1986, for the references to a corporation incorporated in Great Britain of references to a corporation incorporated in Northern Ireland and for the reference to a company incorporated outside Great Britain of a reference to a company incorporated outside the United Kingdom.

AUTHORISED UNIT TRUST SCHEMES

9(1) Where an order under section 17 of the previous Act (authorisation of unit trust schemes) is in force in respect of a unit trust scheme immediately before the coming into force of Chapter VIII of Part I of this Act the scheme shall be treated as an authorised unit trust scheme under that Part and the order as an order under section 78 of this Act.

9(2) In relation to any such authorised unit trust scheme the reference in section 79(1)(a) of this Act to the requirements for the making of the order shall be construed as a reference to the requirements for the making of an order under section 78, but the scheme shall not be regarded as failing to comply with those requirements by reason of the manager or trustee not being an authorised person if he is treated as such a person by virtue of paragraph 1 above.

9(3)   If before the day on which Chapter VIII of Part I comes into force a notice in respect of a scheme has been served under subsection (2) of section 17 of the previous Act (proposed revocation of authorisation of unit trust scheme) but the revocation has not taken place before that day, the provisions of that subsection shall continue to apply in relation to the scheme and sub-paragraph (1) above shall cease to apply to it if the authorisation is revoked under that subsection.

RECOGNISED COLLECTIVE INVESTMENT SCHEMES

10(1)   If at any time before the coming into force of section 86 of this Act it appears to the Secretary of State that the law of a member State other than the United Kingdom confers rights on the managers and trustees of authorised unit trust schemes entitling them to carry on in that State on terms equivalent to those of that section—

(a) investment business which consists in operating or acting as trustee in relation to such schemes; and

(b) any investment business which is carried on by them in connection with or for the purposes of such schemes,

he may by order direct that schemes constituted in that State which satisfy such requirements as are specified in the order shall be recognised schemes for the purposes of this Act.

10(2)   Subsections (2) to (9) of section 86 of this Act shall have effect in relation to any scheme recognised by virtue of this paragraph; and the references in section 24 and 207(1) of this Act to a scheme recognised under section 86, and in section 76(1) of this Act to a scheme recognised under Chapter VIII of Part I of this Act, shall include references to any scheme recognised by virtue of this paragraph.

10(3)   In section 86(3)(a) as applied by sub-paragraph (2) above the reference to the rights conferred by any relevant Community instrument shall be construed as a reference to the rights conferred by virtue of an order made under this paragraph.

11(1)   Subsection (7) of section 88 of this Act shall not apply to a scheme which is in existence on the date on which this Act is passed if—

(a) the units under the scheme are included in the Official List of The Stock Exchange and have been so included throughout the period of five years ending on the date on which this paragraph comes into force;

(b) the law of the country or territory in which the scheme is established precludes the participants being entitled or the operator being required as mentioned in that subsection; and

(c) throughout the period of five years ending on the date on which the application is made under that section, units under the scheme have in fact been regularly redeemed as mentioned in that subsection or the operator has in fact regularly ensured that participants were able to sell their units as there mentioned.

11(2)   The grounds for revoking an order made under section 88 of this Act by virtue of this paragraph shall include the ground that it appears to the Secretary of State

FSA 1986, Sch. 15, para. 9(3)

that since the making of the order units under the scheme have ceased to be regularly redeemed or the operator has ceased regularly to ensure their sale as mentioned in sub-paragraph (1)(c) above.

DELEGATION ORDERS

12(1) A delegation order may transfer a function notwithstanding that the provision conferring it has not yet come into force but no such function shall be exercisable by virtue of the order until the coming into force of that provision.

12(2) Sub-paragraph (1) above applies also to a transfer order under paragraph 28(1) of Schedule 11 to this Act.

DISCLOSURE OF INFORMATION

13 In determining for the purposes of section 180(6) of this Act and the enactments amended by paragraphs 3(2), 9(2) and 13(2) of Schedule 13 to this Act whether the functions of an authority in a country or territory outside the United Kingdom correspond to functions conferred by any of the provisions of this Act regard shall be had to those provisions whether or not they have already come into force.

TEMPORARY EXEMPTIONS FOR FRIENDLY SOCIETIES

14(1) A registered friendly society which transacts no investment business after the date on which section 3 of this Act comes into force except for the purpose of making or carrying out relevant existing members' contracts shall be treated for the purposes of that section as if it were an exempted person under Chapter IV of Part I of this Act.

14(2) Subject to sub-paragraph (3) below, for the purposes of this paragraph **"relevant existing members' contracts"**, in relation to any society, means—

    (a) contracts made by the society before that date; and

    (b) in the case of a small income society—

        (i) during the period of three years beginning with that date, tax exempt investment agreements made by it with persons who were members of the society before that date; and

        (ii) after the expiry of that period, tax exempt investment agreements made by it with such persons before the expiry of that period.

14(3) Paragraph (b) of sub-paragraph (2) above shall not apply to a registered friendly society after the expiry of the period of two years beginning with that date unless before the expiry of that period it has by special resolution (within the meaning of the Friendly Societies Act 1974 or, as the case may be, the Friendly Societies Act (Northern Ireland) 1970) determined—

    (a) to transact no further investment business except for the purpose of carrying out contracts entered into before the expiry of the said period of three years; or

    (b) to take such action as is necessary to procure the transfer of its engagements to another such society or a company or the amalgamation of the society with another such society under section 82 of the said Act of 1974 or, as the case may be, section 70 of the said Act of 1970, and a copy of that resolution has been registered in accordance with section 86 of the said Act of 1974 or, as the case may be, section 75 of the said Act of 1970.

14(4)   For the purpose of sub-paragraph (2) above a society is a small income society if its income in 1985 from members' contributions did not exceed £50,000.

14(5)   For the purposes of sub-paragraph (2) above an investment agreement is a tax exempt investment agreement if the society by which it is made may obtain exemption from income and corporation tax on the profits from it under section 332 of the Income and Corporation Taxes Act 1970.

14(6)   A society to which sub-paragraph (1) or (2) above applies shall not be an authorised person for the purposes of this Act nor a regulated friendly society for the purposes of the provisions of Schedule 11 to this Act.

DEALINGS IN COURSE OF NON-INVESTMENT BUSINESS

15   If before the day on which section 3 of this Act comes into force a person has applied for permission under paragraph 23 of Schedule 1 to this Act and the application has not been determined before that day, that person shall, until the determination of the application and subject to his complying with such requirements as the Secretary of State may impose, be treated as if he had been granted a permission under that paragraph.

NORTHERN IRELAND

16   The foregoing provisions shall apply to Northern Ireland with the substitution for references to the previous Act or any provision of that Act of references to the Prevention of Fraud (Investments) Act (Northern Ireland) 1940 and the corresponding provision of that Act.

Schedule 16 — Consequential Amendments

Section 212(2)

1   In section 22 of the Charities Act 1960—

(a) subsection (10) shall be omitted; and

(b) in subsection (11) for the words "Subsections (9) and (10)" there shall be substituted the words "Subsection (9)".

2   In the Trustee Investments Act 1961—

(a) in section 11(3) for the words "the Prevention of Fraud (Investments) Act 1958 or the Prevention of Fraud (Investments) Act (Northern Ireland) 1940" there shall be substituted the words "the Financial Services Act 1986";

(b) for paragraph 3 of Part III of Schedule 1 there shall be substituted—

"**3.** In any units of an authorised unit trust scheme within the meaning of the Financial Services Act 1986";

(c) in paragraph 2(a) of Part IV of Schedule 1 for the words from "a recognised stock exchange" onwards there shall be substituted the words "a recognised investment exchange within the meaning of the Financial Services Act 1986";

(d) in the definition of "securities" in paragraph 4 of Part IV of that Schedule after the word "debentures" there shall be inserted the words "units within paragraph 3 of Part III of this Schedule".

3   In section 32 of the Clergy Pensions Measure 1961 No. 3—

(a) for paragraph (t) of subsection (1) there shall be substituted—

"(t) in any units in any authorised unit trust scheme or a recognised scheme within the meaning of the Financial Services Act 1986"; and

(b) in subsection (5)(a) for the words from "a recognised stock exchange" onwards there shall be substituted the words "a recognised investment exchange within the meaning of the Financial Services Act 1986.".

4   In the Stock Transfer Act 1963—

(a) for paragraph (e) of section 1(4) there shall be substituted—

"(e) units of an authorised unit trust scheme or a recognised scheme within the meaning of the Financial Services Act 1986"; and

(b) in the definition of "securities" in section 4(1) for the words from "unit trust scheme" to "scheme" there shall be substituted the words "collective investment scheme within the meaning of the Financial Services Act 1986".

5   In the Stock Transfer Act (Northern Ireland) 1963—

(a) for paragraph (e) of section 1(4) there shall be substituted—

"(e) units of an authorised unit trust scheme or a recognised scheme within the meaning of the Financial Services Act 1986"; and

(b) in the definition of "securities" in section 4(1) for the words from "unit trust scheme" to "scheme" there shall be substituted the words "collective investment scheme within the meaning of the Financial Services Act 1986".

6   In section 25 of the Charities Act (Northern Ireland) 1964—

(a) subsection (16) shall be omitted; and

(b) in subsection (17) for the words "Subsections (15) and (16)" there shall be substituted the words "Subsection (15)".

7   In the Local Authorities' Mutual Investment Trust Act 1968—

(a) in section 1(2) for the words "recognised stock exchange within the meaning of the Prevention of Fraud (Investments) Act 1958" there shall be substituted the words "recognised investment exchange within the meaning of the Financial Services Act 1986"; and

(b) in the definition of "unit trust scheme" in section 2 for the words "Prevention of Fraud (Investments) Act 1958" there shall be substituted the words "Financial Services Act 1986".

8   In the Local Government Act 1972—

(a) in section 98(1) for the words from "and" onwards there shall be substituted the words "means—

(a) investments falling within any of paragraphs 1 to 6 of Schedule 1 to the Financial Services Act 1986 or, so far as relevant to any of those paragraphs, paragraph 11 of that Schedule; or

(b) rights (whether actual or contingent) in respect of money lent to, or deposited with, any society registered under the Industrial and Provident Societies Act 1965 or any building society within the meaning of the Building Societies Act 1986."; and

(b) for the definition of "securities" in section 146(2) there shall be substituted—

"**'securities'** has the meaning given in section 98(1) above".

9   For subsection (1) of section 42 of the Local Government (Scotland) Act 1973 there shall be substituted—

"**(1)**   In sections 39 and 41 of this Act **'securities'** means—

(a) investments falling within any of paragraphs 1 to 6 of Schedule 1 to the Financial Services Act 1986 or, so far as relevant to any of those paragraphs, paragraph 11 of that Schedule; or

(b) rights (whether actual or contingent) in respect of money lent to, or deposited with, any society registered under the Industrial and Provident Societies Act 1965 or any building society within the meaning of the Building Societies Act 1986."

10   For paragraph 20 of Schedule 1 to the Industry Act 1975 there shall be substituted—

"**20**   Section 57 of the Financial Services Act 1986 (restrictions on advertising) shall not apply to any investment advertisement within the meaning of that section which the Board issue or cause to be issued in the discharge of their functions."

11   For paragraph 20 of Schedule 1 to the Scottish Development Agency Act 1975 there shall be substituted—

"**20**   Section 57 of the Financial Services Act 1986 (restrictions on advertising) shall not apply to any investment advertisement within the meaning of that section which the Agency issue or cause to be issued in the discharge of their functions."

12   For paragraph 21 of Schedule 1 to the Welsh Development Agency Act 1975 there shall be substituted—

"**21**   Section 57 of the Financial Services Act 1986 (restrictions on advertising) shall not apply to any investment advertisement within the meaning of that section which the Agency issue or cause to be issued in the discharge of their functions.".

13   In section 3(5) of the Aircraft and Shipbuilding Industries Act 1977 the words "Sections 428 to 430 of the Companies Act 1985 and" shall be omitted and for the words "those sections" there shall be substituted the words "that section".

14   In paragraph 10(1)(c) of Part II of Schedule 10 to the Finance Act 1980 for the words "sections 428 to 430" there shall be substituted the words "sections 428 to 430F".

15   For the definition of "securities" in section 3(6) of the Licensing (Alcohol Education and Research) Act 1981 there shall be substituted—

> "**'securities'** means any investments falling within any of paragraphs 1 to 6 of Schedule 1 to the Financial Services Act 1986 or, so far as relevant to any of those paragraphs, paragraph 11 of that Schedule".

16   In section 97 of the Companies Act 1985—

(a)   in subsection (1) after the word "conditions" there shall be inserted the words "and any conditions which apply in respect of any such payment by virtue of rules made under section 169(2) of the Financial Services Act 1986"; and

(b)   in subsection (2)(a) for the words from "10 per cent" onwards there shall be substituted the words—

> "(i)   any limit imposed on it by those rules or, if none is so imposed, 10 per cent, of the price at which the shares are issued; or

> (ii)   the amount or rate authorised by the articles, whichever is the less".

17   In section 163 of the Companies Act 1985—

(a)   for the words "a recognised stock exchange" in each place where they occur there shall be substituted the words "a recognised investment exchange";

(b)   for the words "that stock exchange" in subsection (1) there shall be substituted the words "that investment exchange";

(c)   in subsection (2) in paragraph (a) for the words "on that stock exchange" there shall be substituted the words "under Part IV of the Financial Services Act 1986" and in paragraph (b) for the words "that stock exchange" in both places where they occur there shall be substituted the words "that investment exchange";

(d)   after subsection (3) of that section there shall be inserted—

> "**(4)**   In this section 'recognised investment exchange' means a recognised investment exchange other than an overseas investment exchange within the meaning of the Financial Services Act 1986."

18   In section 209(1)(c) of the Companies Act 1985 for the words "the Prevention of Fraud (Investments) Act 1958" there shall be substituted the words "the Financial Services Act 1986".

19   In section 265(4)(a) of the Companies Act 1985 for the words "recognised stock exchange" there shall be substituted the words "recognised investment exchange other than an overseas investment exchange within the meaning of the Financial Services Act 1986".

20   In section 329(1) of the Companies Act 1985 for the words "recognised stock exchange", "that stock exchange" and "the stock exchange" there shall be substituted respectively the words "recognised investment exchange other than an overseas investment exchange within the meaning of the Financial Services Act 1986", "that investment exchange" and "the investment exchange".

21   For paragraphs (a) to (c) of section 446(4) of the Companies Act 1985 there shall be substituted—

"(a) to any individual who is an authorised person within the meaning of the Financial Services Act 1986;

(b) to any individual who holds a permission granted under paragraph 23 of Schedule 1 to that Act;

(c) to any officer (whether past or present) of a body corporate which is such an authorised person or holds such a permission;

(d) to any partner (whether past or present) in a partnership which is such an authorised person or holds such a permission;

(e) to any member of the governing body or officer (in either case whether past or present) of an unincorporated association which is such an authorised person or holds such a permission".

22   (Repealed by Companies Act 1989, sec. 212 and Sch. 24 as from 1 April 1990.)

History
In relation to the above date see S.I. 1990 No. 355 (C. 13), art. 5(1); former para. 22 read as follows:

"**22**   At the end of sections 716(2) and 717(1) of the Companies Act 1985 there shall be inserted the words—

'and in this subsection **"recognised stock exchange"** means The Stock Exchange and any other stock exchange which is declared to be a recognised stock exchange for the purposes of this section by an order in a statutory instrument made by the Secretary of State which is for the time being in force;'."

23   In Schedule 4 to the Companies Act 1985—

(a) in paragraph 45 for the words "recognised stock exchange" there shall be substituted the words "recognised investment exchange other than an overseas investment exchange within the meaning of the Financial Services Act 1986"; and

(b) in paragraph 84 for the words from "on a recognised stock exchange" onwards there shall be substituted the words "on a recognised investment exchange other than an overseas investment exchange within the meaning of the Financial Services Act 1986 or on any stock exchange of repute outside Great Britain".

24   In Schedule 9 to the Companies Act 1985 in paragraphs 10(3) and 33 for the words "recognised stock exchange" there shall be substituted the words "recognised investment exchange other than an overseas investment exchange within the meaning of the Financial Services Act 1986".

25   In paragraph 11 of Schedule 13 to the Companies Act 1985 for paragraph (a) there shall be substituted—

"(a) any unit trust scheme which is an authorised unit trust scheme within the meaning of the Financial Services Act 1986".

26   In Schedule 22 to the Companies Act 1985, in the second column of the entry relating to section 185(4) for the words "stock exchange" there shall be substituted the words "clearing house or".

27   In Schedule 24 to the Companies Act 1985—

(a) in the second column of the entry relating to section 329(3) for the words "stock exchange" there shall be substituted the words "investment exchange"; and

(b) after the entry relating to section 427(5) there shall be inserted—

"429(6)	Offeror failing to send copy of notice or making statutory declaration knowing it to be false, etc.	1. On indictment. 2. Summary.	2 years or a fine; or both. 6 months or the statutory maximum; or both.	One-fiftieth of the statutory maximum.
430A(6)	Offeror failing to give notice of rights to minority shareholder.	1. On indictment. 2. Summary.	A fine. The statutory maximum.	One-fiftieth of the statutory maximum."

28 In section 16 of the Company Securities (Insider Dealing) Act 1985—

(a) in subsection (1) for the definition of "recognised stock exchange" there shall be substituted—

"**'recognised stock exchange'** means The Stock Exchange and any other investment exchange which is declared by an order of the Secretary of State for the time being in force to be a recognised stock exchange for the purposes of this Act;"; and

(b) after that subsection there shall be inserted—

"**(1A)** The power to make an order under subsection (1) above shall be exercisable by statutory instrument.";

(c) in subsection (2) for the word "15" there shall be substituted the word "14".

29 For paragraph (c) of section 10(1) of the Bankruptcy (Scotland) Act 1985 there shall be substituted—

"(c) a petition is before a court for the winding up of the debtor under Part IV or V of the Insolvency Act 1986 or section 72 of the Financial Services Act 1986;".

30 In section 101 of the Building Societies Act 1986—

(a) for paragraph (1)(a) there shall be substituted—

"(a) offer for sale or invite subscription for any shares in or debentures of the company or allot or agree to allot any such shares or debentures with a view to their being offered for sale;";

(b) in subsection (1) after the words "the effect of the offer" there shall be inserted the words "the invitation"; and

(c) in subsection (2) for the words "the public" there shall be substituted the words ", invite subscription for,".

31 In Article 107 of the Companies (Northern Ireland) Order 1986—

(a) in paragraph (1) after the word "conditions" there shall be inserted the words "and any conditions which apply in respect of any such payment by virtue of rules made under section 169(2) of the Financial Services Act 1986"

(b) in sub-paragraph (2)(a) for the words from "10 per cent" onwards there shall be substituted the words—

"(i) any limit imposed on it by those rules or, if none is so imposed, 10 per cent of the price at which the shares are issued; or

(ii) the amount or rate authorised by the articles, whichever is the less".

32 In Article 173 of the Companies (Northern Ireland) Order 1986—

(a) for the words "a recognised stock exchange", in each place where they occur, there shall be substituted the words "a recognised investment exchange";

(b) for the words "that stock exchange" in paragraph (1) there shall be substituted the words "that investment exchange";

(c) in paragraph (2), in sub-paragraph (a) for the words "on that stock exchange" there shall be substituted the words "under Part IV of the Financial Services Act 1986" and in sub-paragraph (b) for the words "that stock exchange" in both places where they occur there shall be substituted the words "that investment exchange";

(d) after paragraph (3) there shall be inserted—

"**(4)** In this Article '**recognised investment exchange**' means a recognised investment exchange other than an overseas investment exchange within the meaning of the Financial Services Act 1986."

33 In Article 217(1)(b) of the Companies (Northern Ireland) Order 1986 for the words "the Prevention of Fraud (Investments) Act (Northern Ireland) 1940 or of the Prevention of Fraud (Investments) Act 1958" there shall be substituted the words "the Financial Services Act 1986".

34 In Article 273(4)(a) of the Companies (Northern Ireland) Order 1986 for the words "recognised stock exchange" there shall be substituted the words "recognised investment exchange other than an overseas investment exchange within the meaning of the Financial Services Act 1986".

35 In Article 337(1) of the Companies (Northern Ireland) Order 1986 for the words "recognised stock exchange", "that stock exchange" and "the stock exchange" there shall be substituted respectively the words "recognised investment exchange", "that investment exchange" and "the investment exchange".

36 For sub-paragraphs (a) to (c) of Article 439(4) of the Companies (Northern Ireland) Order 1986 there shall be substituted—

"(a) to any individual who is an authorised person within the meaning of the Financial Services Act 1986;

(b) to any individual who holds a permission granted under paragraph 23 of Schedule 1 to that Act;

(c) to an officer (whether past or present) of a body corporate which is such an authorised person or holds such a permission;

(d) to any partner (whether past or present) in a partnership which is such an authorised person or holds such a permission;

(e) to any member of the governing body or officer (in either case whether past or present) of an unincorporated association which is such an authorised person or holds such a permission".

37 At the end of Articles 665(2) and 666(1) of the Companies (Northern Ireland) Order 1986 there shall be inserted the words—

"and in this paragraph **'recognised stock exchange'** means The Stock Exchange and any other stock exchange which is declared by an order of the Department for the time being in force to be a recognised stock exchange for the purposes of this Article;".

38 In Schedule 4 to the Companies (Northern Ireland) Order 1986—

(a) in paragraph 45 for the words "recognised stock exchange" there shall be substituted the words "recognised investment exchange other than an overseas investment exchange within the meaning of the Financial Services Act 1986"

(b) in paragraph 83 for the words from "on a recognised stock exchange" onwards there shall be substituted the words "on a recognised investment exchange other than an overseas investment exchange within the meaning of the Financial Services Act 1986 or on any stock exchange of repute outside Northern Ireland".

39 In Schedule 9 to the Companies (Northern Ireland) Order 1986, in paragraph 10(3) and 33 for the words "recognised stock exchange" there shall be substituted the words "recognised investment exchange other than an overseas investment exchange within the meaning of the Financial Services Act 1986."

40 In paragraph 11 of Schedule 13 to the Companies (Northern Ireland) Order 1986 for paragraph (a) there shall be substituted—

"(a) any unit trust scheme which is an authorised unit trust scheme within the meaning of the Financial Services Act 1986".

41 In Schedule 21 to the Companies (Northern Ireland) Order 1986 in the second column of the entry relating to Article 195(4) for the words "stock exchange" there shall be substituted the words "clearing house or".

42 In Schedule 23 to the Companies (Northern Ireland) Order 1986 in the second column of the entry relating to Article 337(3) for the words "stock exchange" there shall be substituted the words "investment exchange".

43 In Article 2(1) of the Company Securities (Insider Dealing) (Northern Ireland) Order 1986, for the definition of "recognised stock exchange" there shall be substituted—

"'**recognised stock exchange'** means The Stock Exchange and any other investment exchange which is declared by an order of the Department for the time being in force to be a recognised stock exchange for the purposes of this Order;".

Schedule 17—Repeals and Revocations

Section 212(3)

Part I — Enactments

Chapter	Short title	Extent of repeal
4 & 5 Geo. 6. c. 9 (N.I.).	The Prevention of Fraud (Investments) Act (Northern Ireland) 1940.	The whole Act.
6 & 7 Eliz. 2. c. 45.	The Prevention of Fraud (Investments) Act 1958.	The whole Act.
8 & 9 Eliz. 2. c. 58.	The Charities Act 1960.	Section 22(10).
10 & 11 Eliz. 2. c. 23.	The South Africa Act 1962.	In Schedule 4, the entry relating to the Prevention of Fraud (Investments) Act 1958.
1964 c. 33 (N.I.).	The Charities Act (Northern Ireland) 1964.	Section 25(16).
1965 c. 2.	The Administration of Justice Act 1965.	Section 14(1)(e) and 5(e). In Schedule 1, the entry relating to the Prevention of Fraud (Investments) Act 1958.
1971 c. 62.	The Tribunals and Inquiries Act 1971.	In Part I of Schedule 1, the entry relating to the tribunal constituted under section 6 of the Prevention of Fraud (Investments) Act 1958.
1972 c. 71.	The Criminal Justice Act 1972.	In Schedule 5, the entry relating to the Prevention of Fraud (Investments) Act 1958.
1975 c. 24.	The House of Commons Disqualification Act 1975.	In Part II of Schedule 1 the words "The Tribunal established under the Prevention of Fraud (Investments) Act 1958."
1975 c. 68.	The Industry Act 1975.	In Schedule 1, paragraph 19.
1975 c. 69.	The Scottish Development Agency Act 1975.	In Schedule 1, paragraph 19.
1975 c. 70.	The Welsh Development Agency Act 1975.	In Schedule 1, paragraph 22.
1976 c. 47.	The Stock Exchange (Completion of Bargains) Act 1976.	Section 7(2).
1977 c. 3.	The Aircraft and Shipbuilding Industries Act 1977.	In section 3(5), the words "Sections 428 to 430 of the Companies Act 1985 and".
1978 c. 23.	The Judicature (Northern Ireland) Act 1978.	Section 84(3)(c).

[The next page is 63,701]

Chapter	Short title	Extent of repeal
1979 c. 37.	The Banking Act 1979.	Section 20(1) to (3). In Schedule 1, paragraph 9. In Schedule 6, paragraphs 4 and 5.
1982 c. 50.	The Insurance Companies Act 1982.	Section 73. Section 79.
1982 c. 53.	The Administration of Justice Act 1982.	Section 42(8).
1984 c. 2.	The Restrictive Trade Practices (Stock Exchange) Act 1984.	The whole Act.
1985 c. 6.	The Companies Act 1985.	Part III. Sections 81 to 83. In section 84(1) the words from "This" onwards. In section 85(1) the words "83 or". Sections 86 and 87. In section 97, subsection (2)(b) together with the word "and" immediately preceding it and subsections (3) and (4). Section 433(2). Section 446(5) and (6). In section 449(1)(d), the words "the Prevention of Fraud (Investments) Act 1958". In section 693, paragraph (a) and in paragraph (d) the words "in every such prospectus as above-mentioned and". Section 709(2) and (3). In section 744, the definitions of "recognised stock exchange" and "prospectus issued generally". Schedule 3. In Schedule 22, the entries relating to Parts III and IV. In Schedule 24, the entries relating to sections 56(4), 61, 64(5), 70(1), 78(1), 81(2), 82(5), 86(6), 87(4) and 97(4).
1985 c. 8.	The Company Securities (Insider Dealing) Act 1985.	In section 3(1), the word "or" immediately preceding paragraph (c). In section 13, in subsection (1), the words from "and references" onwards and subsection (2). Section 15.

Chapter	Short title	Extent of repeal
1985 c. 9.	The Companies Consolidation (Consequential Provisions) Act 1985.	Section 7. In Schedule 2, the entries relating to the Prevention of Fraud (Investments) Act 1958, paragraph 19 of Schedule 1 to the Scottish Development Agency Act 1975, paragraph 22 of Schedule 1 to the Welsh Development Agency Act 1975, the Stock Exchange (Completion of Bargains) Act 1976, section 3(5) of the Aircraft and Shipbuilding Industries Act 1977 and section 20 of the Banking Act 1979.
1986 c. 31.	The Airports Act 1986.	Section 10.
1986 c. 44.	The Gas Act 1986.	Section 58.
1986 c. 60.	The Financial Services Act 1986.	Section 195.

Part II — Instruments

Number	Title	Extent of revocation
S.I. 1977/1254 (6 N.I. 21).	The Stock Exchange (Completion of Bargains) (Northern Ireland) Order 1977.	Article 2(2).
S.I. 1986/1032 (N.I. 6).	The Companies (Northern Ireland) Order 1986.	Article 2(1), the definitions of "prospectus issued generally" and "recognised stock exchange". Part IV. Articles 91 to 93. In Article 94(1) the words from "This" onwards. In Article 95(1) the words "93 or". Articles 96 and 97. In Article 107, paragraph (2)(b) together with the word "and" immediately preceding it and paragraphs (3) and (4). Article 426(2). Article 439(5) and (6). In Article 442(1)(d), the words "the Prevention of Fraud (Investments) Act (Northern Ireland) 1940".

Number	Title	Extent of revocation
		In Article 643(1), sub-paragraph (a) and in sub-paragraph (d) the words "in every such prospectus as is mentioned in sub-paragraph (a) and". Article 658(2) and (3). Schedule 3. In Schedule 21, the entries relating to Parts IV and V. In Schedule 23, the entries relating to Articles 66(4), 71, 74(5), 80(1), 88(1), 91(2), 92(5), 96(6), 97(4) and 107(4).
S.I. 1986/1035 (N.I. 9).	The Companies (Consequential Provisions) (Northern Ireland) Order 1986.	In Schedule 2, the entries relating to the Prevention of Fraud (Investments) Act (Northern Ireland) 1940 and section 20 of the Banking Act 1979.
S.I. 1984/716.	The Stock Exchange (Listing) Regulations 1984.	The whole Regulations.

[The next page is 64,351]

THE FINANCIAL SERVICES ACT 1986
(COMMENCEMENT NO. 1) ORDER 1986

(S.I. 1986 No. 1940 (C. 69))

Made on 14 November 1986 by the Secretary of State under sec. 211(1) of the
Financial Services Act 1986.

1 This Order may be cited as the Financial Services Act 1986 (Commencement No. 1) Order 1986.

2 The provisions of the Financial Services Act 1986 specified in column 1 of the Schedule hereto shall come into operation for the purposes specified in column 2 of the Schedule hereto on 15th November 1986.

Schedule

Provisions	Purposes
Section 177 (Investigations into insider dealing)	All purposes
Section 178(1), (2)(a) and (6) (Penalties for failure to co-operate with s. 177 investigations)	All purposes
Section 179 (restrictions on disclosure of information)	For purposes of information obtained by a person mentioned in paragraph (h) of subsection (3) of the section so far as that paragraph applies to a person appointed or authorised to exercise any powers under section 177, or by a person mentioned in paragraph (i) of that subsection who is an officer or servant of any such person
Section 180 (exceptions from restrictions on disclosure)	All purposes
Section 182 and paragraphs 3, 4, 6, 7, 9, 10, 11, 13 and 14 of Schedule 13 (Disclosure of information under enactments relating to fair trading, banking, insurance and companies)	For purposes of anything done or which may be done under or by virtue of any provision brought into operation by this Order
Section 198(2)(a) (Disqualification of director after investigation)	For all purposes
Section 199(1)(a), (3) to (6), (8) and (9) (powers of entry)	For purposes relating to offences under section 1, 2, 4 or 5 of the Company Securities (Insider Dealing) Act 1985
Section 200(1)(b) and (5) (false and misleading statements)	For purposes of any requirement imposed by or under section 177
Sections 201(1), 202, 203, 205, 207, 209, 210 (Prosecution, offences, jurisdiction, miscellaneous and supplemental)	For purposes of any provision brought into operation by this Order.

EXPLANATORY NOTE
(*This Note is not part of the Order.*)

This Order brings into force on 15th November 1986 the provisions of the Financial Services Act 1986 specified in the Schedule to the Order. The provisions brought into force are the powers to investigate insider dealing, ancillary provisions relating to those powers, and related provisions restricting disclosure and the exceptions thereto, including consequential amendments of the Banking Act 1979 (c. 37), the Insurance Companies Act 1982 (c. 50), the Companies Act 1985 (c. 6), the Company Directors Disqualification Act 1986 (c. 46) and the Companies (Northern Ireland) Order 1986 (S.I. 1986/1032 (N.I. 6)).

THE FINANCIAL SERVICES ACT 1986
(COMMENCEMENT NO. 2) ORDER 1986

(S.I. 1986 No. 2031 (C. 76))

Made on 26 November 1986 by the Secretary of State under sec. 211(1) of the Financial Services Act 1986.

1 This Order may be cited as the Financial Services Act 1986 (Commencement No. 2) Order 1986.

2 The provisions of the Financial Services Act 1986 specified in the first column of the Schedule hereto shall come into force for the purposes specified in the second column on 27th November 1986.

Schedule
Article 2

Provisions of the Act	Purposes
Section 182 and paragraphs 7, 8, 9, 10, 11, 12, 13 and 14 of Schedule 13 (Disclosure of information under enactments relating to companies).	For all remaining purposes.
Section 211(3) insofar as it relates to paragraph 13 of Schedule 15	For all purposes.
Section 212(1) (citation)	For all purposes.
Section 212(3) and Schedule 17 insofar as they repeal sections	For all purposes.
(i) sections 20(1) to (3) of the Banking Act 1979 and the references to that Act in the Companies Consolidation (Consequential Provisions) Act 1985 and the Companies Consolidation (Consequential Provisions) (Northern Ireland) Order 1986	

Provisions	Purposes
(ii) sections 433(2) and 446(5) of the Companies Act 1985, and	
(iii) Articles 426(2) and 439(5) of the Companies (Northern Ireland) Order 1986.	

EXPLANATORY NOTE

(*This Note is not part of the Order.*)

This Order brings into force on 27th November 1986 the provisions of the Financial Services Act 1986 specified in the Schedule to the Order. The provisions brought into force concern the disclosure of information obtained under those provisions of the Companies Act 1985 and the Companies (Northern Ireland) Order 1986 which relate to the investigation of companies and their affairs and the requisition of documents. The Order also brings into force certain repeals which are consequential upon the other provisions brought into force.

NOTE AS TO EARLIER COMMENCEMENT ORDERS

(*This Note is not part of the Order.*)

The following provisions of the Financial Services Act 1986 have been brought into force by commencement order made before the date of this Order:—

Provision	Date of Commencement	S.I. No.
s. 177		
ss. 178 and 179 (partially)		
s. 180		
s. 182 (partially)		
ss. 198 to 203 (partially)	15.10.86	1986/1940
s. 205 (partially)		
s. 207 (partially)		
ss. 209 and 210 (partially)		
Schedule 13 (partially)		

The word ("partially") is used where the provision has been brought into force in part or for a limited area or for a limited purpose.

THE FINANCIAL SERVICES ACT 1986 (COMMENCEMENT NO. 3) ORDER 1986

(S.I. 1986 No. 2246 (C. 88))

Made on 17 December 1986 by the Secretary of State under sec. 211(1) of the Financial Services Act 1986.

1 This Order may be cited as the Financial Services Act 1986 (Commencement No. 3) Order 1986.

2 The provisions of the Financial Services Act 1986 specified in Schedule 1 hereto shall come into force on 18th December 1986.

3 The provisions of the Financial Services Act 1986 specified in Schedule 2 hereto shall come into force on 12th January 1987.

4 The provisions of the Financial Services Act 1986 specified in Schedule 3 hereto shall come into force on 30th April 1987.

5 The provisions of Part IV of the Financial Services Act 1986, other than section 154(2), (3) and (4), and the provisions specified in Schedule 4 hereto shall come into force:

(a) on 12th January 1987 for all purposes relating to the admission of securities offered by or on behalf of a Minister of the Crown or a body corporate controlled by a Minister of the Crown or a subsidiary of such a body corporate to the Official List in respect of which an application is made after that date;

(b) on 16th February 1987 for purposes relating to the admission of securities in respect of which an application is made after that date other than those referred to in the preceding paragraph and otherwise for all purposes.

Schedule 1 — Provisions coming into force on 18th December 1986

Article 2

Provisions of the Act	Subject matter of provisions
Section 1 and Schedule 1 except paragraphs 23 and 25(2) and (3) of that Schedule	Investments and investment business except dealings in the course of non-investment business and certification of periodical publications.
Section 2	Power to extend or restrict scope of the Act.
Sections 35, 42 and 45 insofar as they are relevant for the purposes of section 105	Certain exemptions.
Section 105	Investigation powers.
Section 106	Exercise of investigation powers by officer etc.
Section 174(1) and (2)	Market makers, off market dealers etc (insider dealing).
Section 179 insofar as not already in force	Restrictions on disclosure of information.
Section 182 and Schedule 13 insofar as not already in force	Disclosure of information under enactments relating to fair trading, banking insurance and companies.
Section 198(1)(b) and (2)(b)	Disqualification of director after investigation.
Section 200(1)(b) and (5) insofar as it relates to a requirement imposed by or under section 105	False and misleading statements.
Sections 201(1), 202 and 203 insofar as not already in force	Prosecution, offences and jurisdiction.
Sections 205, 207, 209 and 210 insofar as not already in force	Miscellaneous and supplemental.

Schedule 2 — Provisions coming into force on 12th January 1987

Article 3

Provisions of the Act	Subject matter of provisions
Section 5 insofar as is necessary in order to identify agreements to which section 5(1) applies for the purposes of section 132 insofar as that section has been brought into force by this Order	Agreements made by or through unauthorised persons.
Section 114 and Schedules 7 and 8	Power to transfer functions to designated agency, qualifications of agency and principles applicable to agency's rules.
Section 115	Resumption of transferred functions.
Section 116 and Schedule 9	Status of designated agency and exercise of transferred functions.
Section 117	Reports and accounts.
Section 118	Transitional and supplementary provisions.
Section 121	Designated agencies (prevention of restrictive trade practices).
Section 122 insofar as it is relevant for the purposes of section 121	Reports by Director General of Fair Trading.
Section 123 insofar as it is relevant for the purposes of any provisions brought into force by this Order	Investigations by Director General of Fair Trading.
Section 124	The Fair Trading Act 1973 (consequential exemption from competition law).
Section 126	The Competition Act 1980 (consequential exemption from competition law).
Section 128	Supplementary provisions (prevention of restrictive trade practices).
Section 129 insofar as is necessary to bring into force paragraphs 1, 3(3), 4(6), 8(6) and 10 of Schedule 10 and those paragraphs of that Schedule	Application of investment business provisions to regulated insurance companies (transfer of Secretary of State's functions).
Section 132(1) to (5)	Insurance contracts effected in contravention of Section 2 of the Insurance Companies Act 1982.
First part of section 132(6) (which provides that a contravention of section 2 of the Insurance Companies Act 1982 shall not make a contract of insurance illegal or invalid to any greater extent than is provided in section 132) for the purposes of any contract of insurance which is not an agreement to which section 5(1) of the Financial Services Act 1986 applies.	

Provisions of the Act	Subject matter of provisions
Second part of section 132(6) (which provides that a contravention of section 2 of the Insurance Companies Act 1982 in respect of a contract of insurance shall not affect the validity of any re-insurance contract entered into in respect of that contract) for the purposes of any re-insurance contract entered into in respect of a contract of insurance which is not an agreement to which section 5(1) of the Financial Services Act 1986 applies.	
Section 134, for the purpose of a person who on 12th January 1987 is not entitled (either alone or with any associate or associates) to exercise, or control the exercise of, 15% or more of the voting power at any general meeting of an applicant under section 3 of the Insurance Companies Act 1982 or of an insurance company in relation to which applicant or insurance company the question of who is its controller under that Act arises, or of a body corporate of which such an applicant or such an insurance company is a subsidiary. In this paragraph, "associate" has the meaning given in section 7(8) of the Insurance Companies Act 1982 and "body corporate" and "subsidiary" have the meanings which they have for the purposes of section 7(4)(c)(ii) of that Act as set out in section 96(1) of that Act.	Controllers of insurance companies.
Section 137	Regulations in respect of linked long term policies.
Section 138(3) and (5)	Insurance brokers.
Section 139(1)(b)	Industrial assurance.
Section 139(5) insofar as is necessary to bring into effect the substitution for the reference to section 5 of the Industrial Assurance Act 1923 of a reference to article 20 of the Industrial Assurance (Northern Ireland) Order 1979.	
Section 140 insofar as is necessary to bring into force Parts I and IV, and paragraphs 40, 41, 44 and 45, Schedule 11 and those Parts and those paragraphs of that Schedule.	Friendly societies (transfer of Registrar's functions).
Section 141	Indemnity schemes for friendly societies.
Section 173	Information obtained in official capacity, public bodies etc (insider dealing).

Provisions of the Act	Subject matter of provisions
Section 176	Contracts for differences by reference to securities (insider dealing).
Section 178(10)	Transferability of functions under section 178.
Section 181	Directions restricting disclosure of information overseas.
Section 187(3) and (4)	Exemption from liability for damages (designated agency, transferee body and competent authority).
Section 188	Jurisdiction as respects actions concerning designated agency etc.
Section 189 and Schedule 14 insofar as those provisions, that section and that Schedule make provision as to application of: (a) section 4(1) of the Rehabilitation of Offenders Act 1974 in relation to the determination of proceedings of the kind described in paragraph 4 of Part I of that Schedule; (b) section 4(2) of the Rehabilitation of Offenders Act 1974 to a question put by or on behalf of a person specified in paragraph 5 of the first column of Part II of that Schedule; and (c) section 4(3)(b) of the Rehabilitation of Offenders Act 1974 to action taken by the competent authority or by a person specified in paragraph 3 in the first column of Part III of that Schedule	Restriction of Rehabilitation of Offenders Act 1974 for the purposes of Part IV of the Financial Services Act 1986.
Section 192	International obligations.
Section 199(7)	Ability of Secretary of State to transfer functions under section 199 (powers of entry) and to make transfer subject to reservation, conditions and restrictions.
Section 200(1)(b) and (5) insofar as it relates to a requirement imposed by or under any provision brought into force by Article 3 of this Order	False and misleading statements.
Section 201(4)	Ability of Secretary of State to transfer functions under section 201 (Prosecutions) necessity for transfer to be subject to reservation and ability to impose conditions and restrictions on transfer.
Section 204	Service of notices.

Provisions of the Act	Subject matter of provisions
Section 211(3) insofar as is necessary to bring into force paragraph 12 of Schedule 15 and that paragraph of that Schedule	Transitional provisions (delegation orders).
Section 212(2) and paragraphs 17, 28(a) and (b) and 32 of Schedule 16 insofar as they provide for the amendment of the following provisions: (a) section 163(2)(a) of the Companies Act 1985; (b) section 16 of the Company Securities (Insider Dealing) Act 1985; (c) article 173(2)(a) of the Companies (Northern Ireland) Order 1986.	Consequential amendments.
Section 212(3) and Schedule 17 insofar as they provide for the repeal of, or of words in, the following provisions: (a) paragraph 9 of Schedule 1 to the Banking Act 1979; (b) section 3(1) of the Company Securities (Insider Dealing) Act 1985.	Repeals.

Schedule 3 — Provisions coming into force on 30th April 1987

Article 4

Provisions of the Act	Subject matter of provisions
Section 172	Takeover offers.
Section 212(2) and Schedule 16 insofar as they provide for the amendment of the following provisions: (a) section 3(5) of the Aircraft and Shipbuilding Industries Act 1977; (b) paragraph 10(1)(c) of Part II of Schedule 10 to the Finance Act 1980.	Consequential amendments.
Section 212(3) and Schedule 17 insofar as they provide for the repeal of, or of words in, the following provisions: (a) paragraph 19 of Schedule 1 to the Industry Act 1975; (b) paragraph 19 of Schedule 1 to the Scottish Development Agency Act 1975;	Repeals.

Provisions of the Act	Subject matter of provisions
(c) paragraph 22 of Schedule 1 to the Welsh Development Agency Act 1975; (d) section 3(5) of the Aircraft and Shipbuilding Industries Act 1977.	
Schedule 12	Takeover offers; provisions substituted for sections 428, 429 and 430 of Companies Act 1985.

Schedule 4 — Provisions coming into force on 12th January 1987 for the purposes specified in Article 5(a) and on 16th February 1987 for all other purposes

Article 5

Provisions	Subject matter of provisions
Section 212(3) and Schedule 17 insofar as they provide for the repeal of, or of words in, the following provisions: (a) the Stock Exchange (Listing) Regulations 1984; (b) Part III, sections 81 to 87, 97, 693 and 709 of, and Schedules 3, 22 and 24 to, the Companies Act 1985 and the corresponding provisions of the Companies (Northern Ireland) Order 1986 to the extent to which they would apply in relation to any investment which is listed or the subject of an application for listing in accordance with Part IV of the Act.	Repeals.

EXPLANATORY NOTE

(This Note is not part of the Order.)

This Order brings into force on 18th December 1986 those provisions of the Financial Services Act 1986 which enable the Secretary of State to investigate the affairs of a person who is or was or who appears to him to be or to have been carrying on investment business and certain ancillary provisions. It also brings into force on the same date those provisions of the Act not yet in force concerning disclosure of information obtained under certain other enactments and certain provisions concerning action which may be taken by a market maker in possession of unpublished price sensitive information.

The Order also brings certain provisions of the Act into force on 12th January 1987. In addition to the provisions of Part IV of the Act mentioned in the next paragraph, the provisions in question are:—

(a) the provisions necessary to enable the Secretary of State, the Chief Registrar of friendly societies and the Registrar of Friendly Societies for Northern Ireland to transfer functions under the Act;

(b) for certain purposes, those provisions of the Act which set out the consequences of entering into insurance contracts in the course of carrying on unauthorised insurance business or which amend the definition of a controller of an insurance company;

(c) provision enabling the Secretary of State to make further regulations in respect of linked long term insurance policies;

(d) an amendment relating to industrial assurance contracts and amendments to the Insurance Brokers (Registration) Act 1977 (c. 46) relating to the making of professional indemnity rules and co-operation with other bodies;

(e) provision enabling registered friendly societies to participate in approved indemnity schemes;

(f) provisions extending section 2 of the Company Securities (Insider Dealing) Act 1985 (abuse of information obtained by Crown Servant in official capacity) to certain other persons who exercise public functions and section 13 of that Act to dealings in contracts for differences by reference to securities; and

(g) certain related transitional and ancillary provisions and certain consequential amendments and repeals.

The Order also brings into force on 12th January 1987 most of the provisions of Part IV of the Financial Services Act 1986 which relate to the Official Listing of securities for the purposes of the admission to the Official List of securities offered by or on behalf of a Minister of the Crown or a body corporate controlled by a Minister of the Crown or a subsidiary of such a body corporate. The same provisions are brought into force for all remaining purposes on 16th February 1987.

The Order brings the provisions of section 172 of, and Schedule 12 to, the Act and certain consequential amendments and repeals into force on 30th April 1987. These provisions have effect in place of the provisions of sections 428, 429 and 430 of the Companies Act 1985.

NOTE AS TO EARLIER COMMENCEMENT ORDERS

(*This Note is not part of the Order.*)

The following provisions of the Financial Services Act 1986 have been brought into force by commencement order made before the date of this Order:—

Provision	Dated of Commencement	S.I. No.
s. 177	15.10.86	1986/1940
ss. 178 and 179 (partially)	15.10.86	1986/1940
s. 180	15.10.86	1986/1940
s. 182 (partially)	15.10.86	1986/1940
	27.10.86	1986/2031
ss. 198 to 203 (partially)	15.10.86	1986/1940
ss. 205, 207, 209 and 210 (partially)	15.10.86	1986/1940
ss. 211 and 212 (partially)	27.10.86	1986/2031
Schedule 13 (partially)	15.10.86	1986/1940
	27.10.86	1986/2031
Schedules 15 and 17 (partially)	27.10.86	1986/2031

The word ("partially") is used where the provision has been brought into force in part, or for a limited purpose or for a limited area.

THE FINANCIAL SERVICES ACT 1986 (COMMENCEMENT) (NO. 4) ORDER 1987

(S.I. 1987 No. 623 (C. 15))

Made on 2 April 1987 by the Secretary of State under sec. 211(1) of the Financial Services Act 1986.

1 This Order may be cited as the Financial Services Act 1986 (Commencement) (No. 4) Order 1987.

2 The provisions of the Financial Services Act 1986 specified in the first column of the Schedule hereto shall come into force on 23rd April 1987.

Schedule

Article 2

Provisions of Act	Subject matter of provisions
Section 63	Gaming contracts.
Section 183 insofar as it relates to notices relating to the carrying on of insurance business or of a deposit-taking business as a recognised bank or licensed institution within the meaning of the Banking Act 1979	Reciprocal facilities for financial business.
Section 184(1) to (3) insofar as it relates to notices relating to the carrying on of insurance business	Notices under section 183 relating to insurance business.
Section 184(5) and (7)	Partial restriction notices relating to insurance business and service of restriction or disqualification notice following such partial restriction notices.
Section 185	Banking business.
Section 186(1) to (5) and (7) for purposes relating to the provisions brought into force by this Order	Variation and revocation of notices.
Section 201(3)	Prosecution of offences under section 185.

EXPLANATORY NOTE

(*This Note is not part of the Order.*)

This Order brings into force on 23rd April 1987 provisions of the Financial Services Act 1986 enabling the Secretary of State or the Treasury to serve notices on a person connected with a country outside the United Kingdom preventing or restricting the ability of such a person to carry on insurance or deposit-taking business in or in relation to the United Kingdom. Such a notice may be served only if the Secretary of State or, as the case may be, the Treasury consider it in the national interest to do so for reasons related to the ability of persons connected with the United Kingdom to carry on business of the kinds covered by section 183 of the Act in or in relation to the country in question. The provisions brought into force also enable the Secretary of State or the Treasury, as the case may be, to vary or revoke notices served.

The Order also brings into force on the same date provisions of the Financial Services Act 1986 which prevent certain contracts for the purchase, sale, subscription for or underwriting of investments being avoided or rendered unenforceable by reason of the law relating to gaming or wagering.

NOTE AS TO EARLIER COMMENCEMENT ORDERS

(*This Note is not part of the Order.*)

The following provisions of the Financial Services Act 1986 have been brought into force by commencement orders made before the date of this Order:

Provision	S.I. No.
ss. 1 and 2	1986/2246
s. 5 (partially)	1986/2246
ss. 35, 42 and 45 (partially)	1986/2246
ss. 105 and 106	1986/2246
ss. 114 to 118	1986/2246
s. 121	1986/2246
s. 122 and 123 (partially)	1986/2246
ss. 124, 126 and 128	1986/2246
ss. 129, 132 and 134 (partially)	1986/2246
s. 137	1986/2246
ss. 138, 139 and 140 (partially)	1986/2246
s. 141	1986/2246
s. 142 to 153	1986/2246
s. 154 (partially)	1986/2246
ss. 155 to 157	1986/2246
s. 173	1986/2246
s. 174 (partially)	1986/2246
s. 176	1986/2246
s. 177	1986/1940
s. 178 (partially)	1986/1940
	1986/2246
s. 179	1986/2246
s. 180	1986/1940
s. 181	1986/2246
s. 182	1986/1940
	1986/2031
	1986/2246
s. 187 (partially)	1986/2246
s. 188	1986/2246
s. 189 (partially)	1986/2246
s. 192	1986/2246

Provision	S.I. No.
s. 198 (partially)	1986/1940
	1986/2246
s. 199 (partially)	1986/1940
	1986/2246
s. 200 (partially)	1986/1940
	1986/2246
s. 201 (partially)	1986/1940
	1986/2246
ss. 202 and 203	1986/1940
	1986/2246
s. 204	1986/2246
ss. 205, 207, 209 and 210	1986/1940
	1986/2246
s. 211 (partially)	1986/2031
	1986/2246
s. 212 (partially)	1986/2031
	1986/2246
Schedule 1 (partially)	1986/2246
Schedules 7, 8 and 9	1986/2246
Schedules 10 and 11 (partially)	1986/2246
Schedule 13	1986/1940
	1986/2031
	1986/2246
Schedule 14 (partially)	1986/2246
Schedule 15 (partially)	1986/2031
	1986/2246
Schedule 16 (partially)	1986/2246
Schedule 17 (partially)	1986/2031
	1986/2246

The following provisions of the Financial Services Act 1986 will come into force on 30th April 1987 by virtue of commencement order made before the date of this Order:

Provision	S.I. No.
s. 172	1986/2246
s. 212 (partially)	1986/2246
Schedule 12	1986/2246
Schedules 16 and 17 (partially)	1986/2246

The word ("partially") is used where the provision has been brought into force in part, or for a limited purpose or for a limited area.

THE FINANCIAL SERVICES ACT 1986
(COMMENCEMENT) (NO. 5) ORDER 1987

(S.I. 1987 No. 907 (C. 24))

Made on 14 May 1987 by the Secretary of State under sec. 211(1) of the Financial Services Act 1986.

1 This Order may be cited as the Financial Services Act 1986 (Commencement) (No. 5) Order 1987.

2 Section 206(4) of the Financial Services Act 1986 shall come into force on 15th May 1987.

3 The provisions of the Financial Services Act 1986 specified in the first column of the Schedule hereto shall come into force on 4th June 1987.

Schedule — Provisions of Financial Services Act 1986 coming into force on 4th June 1987

Article 3

Provisions of Act	Subject matter of provisions
Section 8	Self-regulating organisations.
Section 9	Applications for recognition by self-regulating organisations.
Section 10	Grant and refusal or recognition of self-regulating organisations.
Section 11	Revocation of recognition of self-regulating organisations.
Section 13	Alteration of rules of recognised self-regulating organisations for protection of investors.
Section 14	Notification requirements.
Section 15 except insofar as it has the effect of conferring authorisation	Certification by professional bodies.
Section 16	Professional bodies.
Section 17	Applications for recognition by professional bodies.
Section 18	Grant and refusal of recognition of professional bodies.
Section 19	Revocation of recognition of professional bodies.
Section 21	Notification requirements.
Section 36(2) and (3)	Investment exchanges.
Section 37 except insofar as it has effect in relation to a body or association of the kind described in section 40(1) of the Act	Grant and revocation of recognition of investment exchanges other than overseas investment exchanges.
Section 38(2) and (3)	Clearing houses.

Provisions of Act	Subject matter of provisions
Section 39 except insofar as it has effect in relation to a body or association of the kind described in section 40(1) of the Act	Grant and revocation of recognition of clearing houses other than overseas clearing houses.
Section 41	Notification requirements.
Section 46	Power to extend or restrict exemptions.
Section 48	Conduct of business rules.
Section 49	Financial resources rules.
Section 50	Modification of conduct of business and financial resources rules for particular cases.
Section 51	Cancellation rules.
Section 52	Notification regulations.
Section 54	Compensation Fund.
Section 55	Clients money.
Section 56 insofar as it is necessary in order to enable regulations to be made under section 56(1)	Unsolicited calls.
Section 102	Register of authorised persons and recognised organisations etc.
Section 103	Inspection of register.
Section 104(2) and (3)	Power to call for information.
Section 107	Appointment of auditors.
Section 110	Auditors for overseas business.
Section 112(1) to (4)	Application fees for recognition orders under Chapter III or IV of Part I of the Act.
Section 113(1)	Periodical fees — recognised self-regulating organisations, professional bodies, investment exchanges and clearing houses.
Section 119	Prevention of restrictive trade practices — recognised self-regulating organisations, investment exchanges, clearing houses.
Section 120	Modification of section 119 where recognition function is transferred.
Section 122	Reports by Director-General of Fair Trading.
Section 123	Investigations by Director-General of Fair Trading.
Section 125(1) to (7)	Consequential exemption from competition law — The Restrictive Trade Practices Act 1976.
Section 127	Modifications of Restrictive Trade Practices Act 1976 in relation to recognised professional bodies.

Provisions of Act	Subject matter of provisions
Section 129 insofar as is necessary to bring into force paragraphs 3(1), (2) and (4) and 4(1) to (4) of Schedule 10 to the Act, and those paragraphs of that Schedule	Application of investment business provisions to regulated insurance companies.
Section 138(1), (2) and (6)	Insurance brokers.
Section 140 insofar as is necessary to bring into force paragraphs 2 to 5, 7 to 16, 18 to 20, 24, 38 and 42 of Schedule 11 to the Act and those paragraphs of that Schedule	Friendly Societies.
Section 187 insofar as not yet in force	Exemption from liability in damages.
Section 190	Data Protection Act 1984.
Section 191	Occupational Pension Schemes.
Section 198(3)(b)	Power to petition for winding-up on information obtained under Act — Northern Ireland.
Section 200(1)(a) insofar as it has effect in relation to an application for a recognition order under Chapter III or IV of Part I of the Act	False and misleading statements in connection with applications.
Section 200(1)(b) insofar as it has effect in relation to a requirement imposed by or under any provision brought into force by this Order	False and misleading statements in purported compliance with requirements imposed by or under Act.
Section 200(3) and (4)	False and misleading statements as to recognised status.
Section 200(5) to (8) insofar as it has effect in relation to any provision brought into force by this Order	False and misleading statements — supplementary provisions.
Section 206(1) to (3)	Publication of information or advice.
Section 211(3) insofar as is necessary to bring into force paragraphs 4, 5, and 6 of Schedule 15 to the Act, and those paragraphs of that Schedule	Transitional provisions.
Section 212(2) insofar as is necessary to bring into force paragraph 27(b) of Schedule 16, and that paragraph of that Schedule	Consequential amendment.
Schedule 2	Requirements for recognition of self-regulating organisations.
Schedule 3	Requirements for recognition of recognised professional body.
Schedule 4	Requirements for recognition of recognised investment exchange.

[The next page is 64,391]

EXPLANATORY NOTE

(*This Note is not part of the Order.*)

This Order brings into force on 15th May 1987 those provisions of the Financial Services Act 1986 which enable the Secretary of State to transfer the function of publishing information and advice to a designated agency.

This Order brings into force on 4th June 1987 those provisions of the Financial Services Act 1986 which are necessary to enable recognition to be granted to self-regulating organisations (including self-regulating organisations for friendly societies), professional bodies and to investment exchanges and clearing houses whose head offices are situated in the United Kingdom. The Order also brings into force on the same date the provisions of the Act relating to withdrawal of recognition from organisations of the kind just described, to information to be supplied by them, to fees payable by them and to their position under competition law and the Data Protection Act 1984. Provisions of the Act concerning immunity from actions in damages and false and misleading statements made in connection with applications for recognition, recognised status and requirements imposed on recognised organisations are also brought into force on that date.

The Order also brings into force on the same date provisions which will enable rules and regulations to be made under Chapter V of Part I of and Schedule 11 to the Act.

The Order also brings into force on the same date the provisions of the Act relating to the maintenance and inspection of the register of authorised persons and recognised organisations etc., to the giving of information and advice, to the appointment of auditors by authorised persons and to communications by auditors with supervisory authorities.

The Order also brings into force on 4th June 1987 provisions concerning rules which may be made under the Insurance Brokers (Registration) Act 1977 (c. 46) and the meaning of the expression "authorised insurer" in that Act. Provisions concerning the position under the Act of managers of occupational pension schemes are also brought into force on that date.

NOTE AS TO EARLIER COMMENCEMENT ORDERS

(*This Note is not part of the Order.*)

The following provisions of the Financial Services Act 1986 have been brought into force by commencement orders made before the date of this Order;

Provision	S.I. No.
ss. 1 and 2	1986/2246
s. 5 (partially)	1986/2246
ss. 35, 42 and 45 (partially)	1986/2246
s. 63	1987/623
ss. 105 and 106	1986/2246
ss. 114 to 118	1986/2246
s. 121	1986/2246
s. 122 and 123 (partially)	1986/2246
ss. 124, 126 and 128	1986/2246
ss. 129, 132 and 134 (partially)	1986/2246
s. 137	1986/2246
s. 138, 139 and 140 (partially)	1986/2246

Provision	S.I. No.
s. 141	1986/2246
s. 142 to 153	1986/2246
s. 154 (partially)	1986/2246
ss. 155 to 157	1986/2246
s. 172	1986/2246
s. 173	1986/2246
s. 174 (partially)	1986/2246
s. 176	1986/2246
s. 177	1986/1940
s. 178 (partially)	1986/1940
	1986/2246
s. 179	1986/1940
	1986/2246
s. 180	1986/1940
s. 181	1986/2246
s. 182	1986/1940
	1986/2031
s. 183 (partially)	1987/623
s. 184 (partially)	1987/623
s. 185	1987/623
s. 186 (partially)	1987/623
s. 187 (partially)	1986/2246
s. 188	1986/2246
s. 189 (partially)	1986/2246
s. 192	1986/2246
s. 198 (partially)	1986/1940
	1986/2246
s. 199	1986/1940
	1986/2246
s. 200 (partially)	1986/1940
	1986/2246
s. 201 (partially)	1986/1940
	1986/2246
	1987/623
ss. 202 and 203	1986/1940
	1986/2246
s. 204	1986/2246
ss. 205, 207, 209 and 210	1986/1940
	1986/2246
s. 211 (partially)	1986/2031
	1986/2246

Provision	S.I. No.
s. 212	1986/2031
	1986/2246
Schedule 1 (partially)	1986/2246
Schedules 7, 8 and 9	1986/2246
Schedules 10 and 11 (partially)	1986/2246
Schedule 12	1986/2246
Schedule 13	1986/1940
	1986/2031
	1986/2246
Schedule 14 (partially)	1986/2246
Schedule 15 (partially)	1986/2031
	1986/2246
Schedule 16 (partially)	1986/2246
Schedule 17 (partially)	1986/2031
	1986/2246

The word ("partially") is used where the provision has been brought into force in part, or for a limited purpose or for a limited area.

THE FINANCIAL SERVICES ACT 1986
(COMMENCEMENT) (NO. 6) ORDER 1987
(S.I. 1987 No. 1997 (C. 59))

Made on 21 November 1987 by the Secretary of State, in exercise of his powers under sec. 211(1) of the Financial Services Act 1986.

1 This Order may be cited as the Financial Services Act 1986 (Commencement) (No. 6) Order 1987.

2 Section 62 of the Financial Services Act 1986 shall come into force on 1st December 1987 except for the purposes of the application of subsection (1) of that section to a contravention such as is mentioned in subsection (2) and in relation to any such contravention shall come into force on 3rd October 1988.

3 Subject to the provisions of Article 4 below, section 140 of the Financial Services Act 1986 shall come into force on 1st December 1987 insofar as it is necessary to bring paragraph 22(4) and (5) of Schedule 11 to that Act into force and, subject as aforesaid, paragraph 22(4) and (5) of that Schedule shall come into force on that date.

4 Section 140 of the Financial Services Act 1986 and paragraph 22(4) of Schedule 11 to that Act shall not come into force on 1st December 1987 for the purposes of making a contravention of the kind described in paragraph 22(4)(d) actionable at the suit of a person of the kind described in that paragraph; but that section and that paragraph shall come into force for that purpose on 3rd October 1988.

5 The provisions specified in Schedule 1 to this Order shall come into force on 23rd November 1987.

6 The provisions specified in Schedule 2 to this Order shall come into force on 1st December 1987.

Schedule 1 — Provisions Coming into Force on 23rd November 1987

Article 5

Provisions of Act	Subject matter of provisions
Section 37 insofar as not yet in force.	Investment exchanges — grant and revocation of recognition.
Section 39 insofar as not yet in force.	Clearing houses — grant and revocation of recognition.
Section 40	Overseas investment exchanges and clearing houses.

Schedule 2 — Provisions Coming into Force on 1st December 1987

Article 6

Provisions of Act	Subject matter of provisions
Section 1 insofar as is necessary to bring paragraph 23 of Schedule 1 into force and that paragraph of that Schedule.	Dealings in the course of non-investment business.
Section 12.	Compliance orders — recognised self-regulating organisations.
Section 20.	Compliance orders — recognised professional bodies.
Section 96 and Schedule 6.	The Financial Services Tribunal.
Section 140 insofar as it is necessary to bring into force paragraph 6 of Schedule 11 and that paragraph of that Schedule.	Compliance orders — recognised self-regulating organisations for friendly societies.
Section 189 and Schedule 14 insofar as that section and that Schedule make provision as to the application of—	Restriction of Rehabilitation of Offenders Act 1974.

[The next page is 64,401]

Provisions of Act	Subject matter of provisions

(a) section 4(1) of the Rehabilitation of Offenders Act 1974 in relation to the determination of proceedings of the kind described in paragraphs 2, 3 and 6 of Part I of that Schedule and Article 5(1) of the Rehabilitation of Offenders (Northern Ireland) Order 1978 in relation to the determination of proceedings of the kind described in those paragraphs and in paragraph 4 of that Part of that Schedule;

(b) section 4(2) of the Rehabilitation of Offenders Act 1974 to a question put by or on behalf of a person specified in paragraph 6 of the first column of Part II of that Schedule; and Article 5(2) of the Rehabilitation of Offenders (Northern Ireland) Order 1978 to a question put by or on behalf of a person specified in paragraph 5 or in paragraph 6 of the first column of Part II of that Schedule;

(c) section 4(2) of the Rehabilitation of Offenders Act 1974 and Article 5(2) of the Rehabilitation of Offenders (Northern Ireland) Order 1978 to a question put by or on behalf of a person specified in paragraph 2 or 3 of the first column of Part II of that Schedule or to a question put by or on behalf of a person specified in paragraph 4 of the first column of that Part of that Schedule insofar as it relates to persons described in paragraphs 2(a), (b) or (c) or 3(a), (b) or (c) or to a question put by or on behalf of a person specified in paragraph 8 of that column; and

Provisions of Act	Subject matter of provisions
(d) section 4(3)(b) of the Rehabilitation of Offenders Act 1974 to action taken by a person of a kind described in sub-paragraph (c) above and Article 5(3)(b) of the Rehabilitation of Offenders (Northern Ireland) Order 1978 to action taken by a person described in sub-paragraph (c) above or specified in paragraph 3 of the first column of Part III of that Schedule.	
Section 196	Financial assistance for employees' shares schemes.

EXPLANATORY NOTE

(This Note is not part of the Order.)

This Order brings into force on 23rd November 1987 those provisions of the Financial Services Act 1986 which will enable the Secretary of State to recognise and to revoke the recognition of investment exchanges and clearing houses which have their head office outside the United Kingdom.

The Order also brings into force on 1st December 1987 certain provisions of the Act concerning the Rehabilitation of Offenders Act 1974, and the Rehabilitation of Offenders (Northern Ireland) Order 1978, the establishment of the Financial Services Tribunal, the power to obtain compliance orders against recognised self-regulating organisations and recognised professional bodies and the provision of financial assistance for employees' share schemes.

The Order brings section 62 of and paragraphs 22(4) and (5) of Schedule 11 to the Financial Services Act 1986 into force on 1st December 1987 except insofar as those provisions would have the effect of making a breach of rules by a member of a recognised self-regulating organisation or recognised professional body actionable as a breach of statutory duty. Those provisions will come into force for that purpose on 3rd October 1988.

NOTE AS TO EARLIER COMMENCEMENT ORDERS

(This Note is not part of the Order.)

The following provisions of the Financial Services Act 1986 have been brought into force by commencement orders made before the date of this Order.

Provisions of Act	S.I. No.
s. 1 (partially	1986/2246
s. 2	1986/2246
s. 5 (partially)	1986/2246
ss. 8 to 11	1987/907
s. 13	1987/907
s. 14	1987/907

Financial Services Act 1986 (Commencement) (No. 6) Order 1987   **64,403**

Provisions of Act	S.I. No.
s. 15 (partially)	1987/907
ss. 16 to 19	1987/907
s. 21	1987/907
s. 35 (partially)	1986/2246
ss. 36 to 39 (partially)	1987/907
s. 41	1987/907
ss. 42 and 45 (partially)	1986/2246
s. 46	1987/907
ss. 49 to 52	1987/907
ss. 54 and 55	1987/907
s. 56 (partially)	1987/907
s. 63	1987/623
ss. 102 and 103	1987/907
s. 104 (partially)	1987/907
ss. 105 and 106	1986/2246
ss. 107 and 110	1987/907
ss. 112 and 113 (partially)	1987/907
ss. 114 to 118	1986/2246
ss. 119 and 120	1987/907
s. 121	1986/2246
ss. 122 and 123	1986/2246
	1987/907
s. 124	1986/2246
s. 125 (partially)	1987/907
s. 126	1986/2246
s. 127	1987/907
s. 128	1986/2246
s. 129 (partially)	1986/2246
	1987/907
s. 132 (partially)	1986/2246
s. 134	1986/2246
s. 137	1986/2246
s. 138 (partially)	1986/2246
	1987/907
s. 139 (partially)	1986/2246
s. 140 (partially)	1986/2246
	1987/907
s. 141 to 153	1986/2246
s. 154 (partially)	1986/2246
ss. 155 to 157	1986/2246

Provisions of Act	S.I. No.
ss. 172 and 173	1986/2246
s. 174 (partially)	1986/2246
s. 176	1986/2246
s. 177	1986/1940
s. 178 (partially)	1986/1940
	1986/2246
s. 179	1986/1940
	1986/2246
s. 180	1986/1940
s. 181	1986/2246
s. 182	1986/1940
	1986/2031
ss. 183 and 184 (partially)	1987/623
s. 185	1987/623
s. 186 (partially)	1987/623
s. 187	1986/2246
	1987/907
s. 188	1986/2246
s. 190	1987/907
s. 191	1987/907
s. 192	1986/2246
s. 198 (partially)	1986/1940
	1986/2246
	1987/907
s. 199 (partially)	1986/1940
	1986/2246
s. 200 (partially)	1986/1940
	1986/2246
	1987/907
s. 201 (partially)	1986/1940
	1986/2246
	1987/623
s. 202 and 203	1986/1940
	1986/2246
s. 204	1988/2246
s. 205	1986/1940
	1986/2246
s. 206	1987/907
ss. 207, 209 and 210	1986/1940
	1986/2246
s. 211 (partially)	1986/2031
	1986/2246
	1987/907

Provisions of Act	S.I. No.
s. 212 (partially)	1986/2031
	1986/2246
	1987/907
Schedule 1 (partially)	1987/907
Schedules 2 to 4	1986/2246
Schedules 7, 8 and 9	1986/2246
Schedule 10 and 11 (partially)	1986/2246
Schedule 12	1986/2246
Schedule 13	1986/1940
	1986/2031
	1986/2246
Schedule 14 (partially)	1986/2246
Schedule 15 (partially)	1986/2031
	1986/2246
	1987/907
Schedule 16 (partially)	1986/2246
Schedule 17 (partially)	1986/2031
	1986/2246
	1987/907

The word ("partially") is used where the provision has been brought into force in part, or for a limited purpose or for a limited area.

THE FINANCIAL SERVICES ACT 1986
(COMMENCEMENT) (NO. 7) ORDER 1987
(S.I. 1987 No. 2158 (C. 65))

Made on 14 December 1987 by the Secretary of State, in exercise of his powers under sec. 211(1) of the Financial Services Act 1986.

1   This Order may be cited as the Financial Services Act 1986 (Commencement) (No. 7) Order 1987.

2   The provisions of the Financial Services Act 1986 specified in the Schedule to this Order shall come into force on 1st January 1988.

3   The remaining provisions of section 1 of and Schedule 1 to the Financial Services Act 1986 shall come into force on 18th January 1988.

4   The provisions of section 211(3) of the Financial Services Act 1986 shall come into force on 27th February 1988 insofar as they relate to—

(a)   paragraph 1(1) to (3) and (5) of Schedule 15 to that Act, and

(b)   paragraph 16 of that Schedule insofar as it has effect in relation to the provisions of paragraph 1 of that Schedule referred to above

and those provisions of that Schedule shall also come into force on that date.

Schedule — Provisions of Financial Services Act 1986 Coming into Force on 1st January 1988

Article 2

Provisions of Act	Subject matter of provisions
Section 26.	Applications for authorisation.
Section 27.	Grant and refusal of authorisation.
Section 28.	Withdrawal and suspension of authorisation.
Section 29.	Notice of proposed refusal, withdrawal or suspension.
Section 30.	Withdrawal of application by consent.
Section 31(4) insofar as is necessary to enable the Secretary of State to issue and revoke certificates.	Authorisation in another member State-certification power.
Section 43 and Schedule 5.	Listed money market institutions.
Section 112(5) insofar as it has effect in relation to applications under section 26 of the Act.	Application Fees.
Section 140 insofar as is necessary to bring into force paragraph 39 of Schedule 11 to the Act and that paragraph of that Schedule.	Applications under section 26 — friendly societies.
Remaining provisions of section 189 and Schedule 14 except for the purposes of Article 1(2)(b) of the Rehabilitation of Offenders Act 1974 (Exceptions) (Amendment No. 2) Order 1986 and the Rehabilitation of Offenders (Exceptions) (Amendment) Order (Northern Ireland) 1987 respectively.	Rehabilitation of Offenders.
Section 200(1)(a) insofar as it has effect in relation to an application for authorisation under section 26 of the Act.	False and misleading statements in connection with applications for authorisation.
Section 200(1)(b) insofar as it has effect in relation to any requirement imposed by or under any provision brought into force by this Order.	False and misleading statements in purported compliance with requirements imposed by or under the Act.
Section 200(5) insofar as it has effect in relation to any provision brought into force by this Order.	False and misleading statements — supplementary provisions.

EXPLANATORY NOTE

(This Note is not part of the Order.)

This Order brings into force on 1st January 1988 provisions of the Financial Services Act 1986 which will enable The Securities and Investments Board to receive and grant applications for authorisation under the Act and which will enable the Secretary of State to certify that the law of another member State relating to authorisation to carry on investment business generally or of a particular kind confers protection equivalent to that afforded by the Act. The Order also brings into force on the same date provisions of the Financial Services Act 1986 conferring limited exemption from the requirement to obtain authorisation under the Act on a person who is for the time being included on a list maintained by the Bank of England.

The Order brings into force on 18th January 1988 provisions which will enable The Securities and Investments Board to certify whether the principal purpose of any particular newspaper or other periodical is to lead persons to invest in any particular investment.

The Order brings into force on 27th February 1988 transitional provisions concerning the position of persons who have applied for authorisation under the Act before a day to be appointed and of persons licensed or exempted or formerly licensed or exempted under the Prevention of Fraud (Investments) Act 1958 (c. 45).

NOTE AS TO EARLIER COMMENCEMENT ORDERS

(This Note is not part of the Order.)

The following provisions of the Financial Services Act 1986 have been brought into force by commencement orders made before the date of this Order.

Provisions of Act	S.I. No.
s. 1 (partially)	1986/2246
	1987/1997
s. 2	1986/2246
s. 5 (partially)	1986/2246
ss. 8 to 11	1987/907
s. 12	1987/1997
s. 13	1987/907
s. 14	1987/907
s. 15 (partially)	1987/907
ss. 16 to 19	1987/907
s. 20	1987/1997
s. 21	1987/907
s. 35 (partially)	1986/2246
s. 36 (partially)	1987/907
ss. 37 to 40	1987/907
	1987/1997
s. 41	1987/907
ss. 42 and 45 (partially)	1986/2246
s. 46	1987/907
ss. 49 to 52	1987/907
ss. 54 and 55	1987/907
s. 56 (partially)	1987/907
s. 62 (partially)	1987/1997
s. 63	1987/623

Provisions of Act	S.I. No.
s. 96	1987/1997
ss. 102 and 103	1987/907
s. 104 (partially)	1987/907
ss. 105 and 106	1986/2246
ss. 107 and 110	1987/907
ss. 112 and 113 (partially)	1987/907
ss. 114 to 118	1986/2246
ss. 119 and 120	1987/907
s. 121	1986/2246
ss. 122 and 123	1986/2246
	1987/907
s. 124	1986/2246
s. 125 (partially)	1987/907
s. 126	1986/2246
s. 127	1987/907
s. 128	1986/2246
s. 129 (partially)	1986/2246
	1987/907
s. 132 (partially)	1986/2246
s. 134	1986/2246
s. 137	1986/2246
s. 138 (partially)	1986/2246
	1987/907
s. 139 (partially)	1986/2246
s. 140 (partially)	1986/2246
	1987/907
	1987/1997
s. 141 to 153	1986/2246
s. 154 (partially)	1986/2246
ss. 155 to 157	1986/2246
ss. 172 and 173	1986/2246
s. 174 (partially)	1986/2246
s. 176	1986/2246
s. 177	1986/1940
s. 178 (partially)	1986/1940
	1986/2246
s. 179	1976/1940
	1986/2246
s. 180	1986/1940
s. 181	1986/2246

Provisions of Act	S.I. No.
s. 182	1986/1940
	1986/2031
ss. 183 and 184 (partially)	1987/623
s. 185	1987/623
s. 186 (partially)	1987/623
s. 187	1986/2246
	1987/907
s. 188	1986/2246
s. 189 (partially)	1986/2246
	1987/1997
s. 190	1987/907
s. 191	1987/907
s. 192	1986/2246
s. 196	1987/1997
s. 198 (partially)	1986/1940
	1986/2246
	1987/907
s. 199 (partially)	1986/1940
	1986/2246
s. 200 (partially)	1986/1940
	1986/2246
	1987/907
s. 201 (partially)	1986/1940
	1986/2246
	1987/623
s. 202 and 203	1986/1940
	1986/2246
s. 204	1988/2246
ss. 205	1986/1940
	1986/2246
s. 206	1987/907
ss. 207, 209 and 210	1986/1940
	1986/2246
s. 211 (partially)	1986/2031
	1986/2246
	1987/907
s. 212 (partially)	1986/2031
	1986/2246
	1987/907
Schedule 1 (partially)	1987/907
Schedules 2 to 4	1986/2246
Schedule 6	1987/1997
Schedules 7, 8 and 9	1986/2246

Provisions of Act	S.I. No.
Schedules 10 and 11 (partially)	1986/2246
	1987/1997
Schedule 12	1986/2246
Schedule 13	1986/1940
	1986/2031
	1986/2246
Schedule 14 (partially)	1986/2246
	1987/1997
Schedule 15 (partially)	1986/2031
	1986/2246
	1987/907
Schedule 16 (partially)	1986/2246
Schedule 17 (partially)	1986/2031
	1986/2246
	1987/907

The following provisions of the Financial Services Act 1986 will come into force on 3rd October 1988 by virtue of commencement order made before the date of this Order:

Provisions of Act	S.I. No.
s. 62 (insofar as not already in force)	1987/1997
s. 140 and Schedule 11 (partially)	1987/1997

The word ("partially") is used where the provision has been brought into force in part, or for a limited purpose or for a limited area.

THE FINANCIAL SERVICES ACT 1986 (COMMENCEMENT) (NO. 8) ORDER 1988

(S.I. 1988 No. 740 (C. 22))

Made on 8 April 1988 by the Secretary of State under sec. 211(1) of the Financial Services Act 1986.

1   This Order may be cited as the Financial Services Act 1986 (Commencement) (No. 8) Order 1988.

2   The provisions of the Financial Services Act 1986 specified in the Schedule to this Order shall come into force on 29th April 1988.

3   Except as provided in articles 4 and 5 of this Order, section 57 of the Financial Services Act 1986 shall come into force on 29th April 1988.

4   Except as provided in article 5 of this Order, section 57 of the Financial Services Act 1986 shall come into force on —
(a) 6th May 1988 insofar as it relates to an advertisement not falling within sub-

paragraph (b) or (c) below which is issued or caused to be issued by a person who is not an authorised person;

(b) 29th May 1988 insofar as it relates to an advertisement issued for valuable consideration in a newspaper, journal, magazine or other periodical publication which is published at intervals of less than 7 days; and

(c) 29th July 1988 insofar as it relates to an advertisement issued for valuable consideration either —

  (i) in any newspaper, journal, magazine or other publication which does not fall within sub-paragraph (b) above; or

  (ii) by way of sound broadcasting or television, by the exhibition of cinematographic films or by the distribution of recordings.

5 Section 57 of the Financial Services 1988 shall not come into force on whichever is applicable of the dates specified in article 3 or 4 of this Order insofar as it has effect in relation to an advertisement issued on or after whichever is applicable of those dates in an edition of a newspaper, magazine, journal or other publication first issued before the relevant date.

6(1) Section 76 of the Financial Services Act 1986 shall come into force on 29th April 1988 except insofar as it has effect in relation to —

(a) a collective investment scheme which takes the form of an open-ended investment company units in which are either included in the Official List of The International Stock Exchange of the United Kingdom and the Republic of Ireland Limited or are offered on terms such that any agreement for their acquisition is conditional upon their admission to that List; or

(b) any prospectus issued by or on behalf of an open-ended investment company which complies with Chapter II of Part III of the Companies Act 1985 or the corresponding provisions of the Companies (Northern Ireland) Order 1986 and the issue of which in the United Kingdom does not contravene section 74 or 75 of the Companies Act 1985 or the corresponding provisions of the Companies (Northern Ireland) Order 1986 as the case may be.

6(2) [Revoked by S.I. 1988 No. 1960 (C. 72), art. 2.]

History
Art. 6(2) formerly read as follows:

"**6(2)** Section 76 of the Financial Services Act 1986 shall come into force for all remaining purposes on 1st December 1988."

Previously the word "December" substituted for the original word "July" by S.I. 1988 No. 995 (C. 30).

7 [Revoked by S.I. 1988 No. 1960 (C. 72), art. 2.]

History
Art. 7 formerly read as follows:

"**7** Section 212(3) of and Schedule 17 to the Financial Services Act 1986 shall come into force on 1st December 1988 insofar as is necessary to have the effect that, to the extent that they do apply, the provisions of Part III and section 693 of and Schedule 3 to the Companies Act 1985 and the corresponding provisions of the Companies

(Northern Ireland) Order 1986 cease to apply to a prospectus offering for subscription, or to any application form for, units in a body corporate which is an open-ended investment company."

Previously the word "December" substituted for the original word "July" by S.I. 1988 No. 995 (C. 30).

Schedule — Provisions of Financial Services Act 1986 Coming into Force on 29th April 1988

Article 2

Provisions of Act	Subject matter of provisions
Section 3.	Persons entitled to carry on investment business.
Section 4.	Offences.
Section 5 insofar as not yet in force.	Agreements made by or through unauthorised persons.
Section 6.	Injunctions and restitution orders.
Section 7.	Authorisation by membership of recognised self-regulating organisations.
Section 15 insofar as not yet in force.	Authorisation by certification by recognised professional body.
Section 22.	Authorised insurers.
Section 23.	Registered friendly societies.
Section 24 insofar as is necessary for the purposes of paragraph 10 of Schedule 15 to the Act.	Operators and trustees of recognised collective investment schemes.
Section 25.	Authorisation by the Secretary of State.
Section 31 insofar as not yet in force.	Authorisation in another member State.
Section 32.	Notice of commencement of business by person authorised by virtue of section 31.
Section 33.	Termination and suspension of authorisation by virtue of section 31.
Section 34.	Notice of proposed termination or suspension of authorisation by virtue of section 31.
Section 35 insofar as not yet in force.	The Bank of England.
Section 36 insofar as not yet in force.	Investment exchanges.
Section 38 insofar as not yet in force.	Clearing houses.
Section 42 insofar as not yet in force.	Lloyd's.
Section 44 insofar as not yet in force.	Appointed representatives.
Section 45 insofar as not yet in force.	Miscellaneous exemptions.
Section 47.	Misleading statements and practices.
Section 56 insofar as not yet in force.	Unsolicited calls.
Section 58, except section 58(1)(d)(ii) insofar as it relates to an advertisement required or permitted to be published by an approved exchange under Part V of the Act, and except section 58(2).	Exceptions from restrictions on advertising.
Section 59.	Employment of prohibited persons.
Section 60.	Public statement as to person's misconduct.

Provisions of Act	Subject matter of provisions
Section 61.	Injunctions and restitution orders.
Section 64.	Powers of intervention — scope of powers.
Section 65.	Restriction of business.
Section 66.	Restriction on dealing with assets.
Section 67.	Vesting of assets in trustee.
Section 68.	Maintenance of assets in United Kingdom.
Section 69.	Rescission and variation.
Section 70.	Notices.
Section 71.	Breach of prohibition or requirement.
Section 72.	Winding up orders.
Section 73.	Winding up orders: Northern Ireland.
Section 74.	Administration orders.
Section 75.	Collective investment schemes: interpretation.
Section 77.	Applications for authorisation.
Section 78.	Authorisation orders.
Section 79.	Revocation of authorisation.
Section 80.	Representations against refusal or revocation.
Section 81.	Constitution and management.
Section 82.	Alteration of schemes and changes of manager or trustee.
Section 83.	Restrictions on activities of manager.
Section 84.	Avoidance of exclusion clauses.
Section 85.	Publication of scheme particulars.
Section 86 insofar as is necessary for the purposes of paragraph 10 of Schedule 15 to the Act.	Schemes constituted in other member States.
Section 87.	Schemes authorised in designated countries or territories.
Section 88.	Other overseas schemes.
Section 89.	Refusal and revocation of recognition.
Section 90.	Facilities and information in the United Kingdom.
Section 91.	Directions.
Section 92.	Notice of directions.
Section 93.	Applications to the court.
Section 94.	Investigations.
Section 95.	Contraventions.
Section 97.	References to the Tribunal.
Section 98.	Decisions on references by applicant or authorised person etc.

Provisions of Act	Subject matter of provisions
Section 99.	Decisions on references by third party.
Section 100.	Withdrawal of references.
Section 101.	Reports.
Section 104 insofar as not yet in force.	Power to call for information.
Section 108.	Power to call for second audit.
Section 109.	Communication by auditor with supervisory authorities.
Section 111.	Offences and enforcement.
Section 112 insofar as not yet in force.	Application fees.
Section 113 insofar as not yet in force.	Periodical fees.
Section 129 except insofar as it relates to paragraph 5(3) and (4) of Schedule 10 to the Act and, except as aforesaid, the provisions of that Schedule not yet in force.	Application of investment business provisions to regulated insurance companies.
Section 130.	Restriction on promotion of contracts of insurance.
Section 131.	Contracts made after contravention of section 130.
Section 132 insofar as not yet in force.	Insurance contracts effected in contravention of the Insurance Companies Act 1982.
Section 133.	Misleading statements as to insurance contracts.
Section 135.	Communication by auditor with Secretary of State.
Section 136.	Arrangements to avoid unfairness between separate insurance funds etc.
Section 138 insofar as not yet in force.	Insurance brokers.
Section 139 insofar as not yet in force.	Industrial assurance.
Section 140 insofar as not yet in force, but not insofar as it relates to paragraph 17 of Schedule 11 to the Act or to the provisions of Schedule 11 coming into force on 3rd October 1988 and, except as aforesaid, the provisions of that Schedule not yet in force.	Friendly societies.
Section 154 insofar as not yet in force.	Advertisements etc. issued in connection with listing particulars.
Section 160 insofar as is necessary to enable the Secretary of State to make an order under that section.	Other offers of securities.

Provisions of Act	Subject matter of provisions
Section 162 insofar as is necessary to enable the Secretary of State to make rules under that section and insofar as is necessary for the purposes of section 169.	Form and content of prospectus.
Section 169.	Terms and implementation of offer.
Section 170 insofar as is necessary to enable the Secretary of State to make an Order under that section.	Advertisements by private companies and old public companies.
The remaining provisions of section 174 except section 174(4)(a).	Market makers, off-market dealers etc.
Section 175.	Price stabilisation.
Section 178 insofar as not yet in force.	Penalties for failure to co-operate with section 177 investigations.
Section 183 insofar as not yet in force.	Reciprocal facilities for financial business.
Section 184 insofar as not yet in force.	Investment and insurance business.
Section 186 insofar as not yet in force.	Variation and revocation of notices.
Section 194.	Transfers to and from recognised clearing houses.
Section 197.	Disclosure of interests in shares: interest held by market maker.
Section 198 insofar as not yet in force.	Power to petition for winding up etc. on information obtained under the Act.
Section 199 insofar as not yet in force.	Powers of entry.
Section 200 insofar as not yet in force.	False and misleading statements.
Section 201 insofar as not yet in force.	Prosecutions.
Section 208 insofar as it has effect in relation to the application of section 130.	Gibraltar.
Section 211 of and Schedule 15 to the Act insofar as not yet in force.	Transitional provisions.
Section 212(2) except insofar as it relates to paragraphs 16 and 31 of Schedule 16 to the Act and, except as aforesaid, the provisions of that Schedule not yet in force.	Consequential amendments.
Section 212(3) of and Schedule 17 to the Act except insofar as they provide for the repeal of, or of words in, the following provisions:	
(a) such provisions of the Prevention of Fraud (Investments) Act (Northern Ireland) 1940 as are necessary for the purposes of paragraph 1(3) of Schedule 15 to the Act as it applies by virtue of paragraph 16 of that Schedule;	

Provisions of Act	*Subject matter of provisions*
(b) such provisions of the Prevention of Fraud (Investments) Act 1958 as are necessary for the purposes of paragraph 1(3) of Schedule 15 to the Act;	
(c) the Tribunals and Inquiries Act 1971;	
(d) The House of Commons Disqualification Act 1975;	
(e) The Restrictive Trade Practices (Stock Exchange) Act 1984;	
(f) section 13 of the Company Securities (Insider Dealing) Act 1985;	
(g) to the extent not yet repealed, and except insofar as is necessary to have the effect that those provisions cease to apply to a prospectus offering for subscription, or to any form of application for, units in a body corporate which is a recognised scheme, the provisions of Part III, sections 81 to 87, 97, 449(1)(d), 693, 709 and 744, insofar as it relates to the definition of "prospectus issued generally", of and Schedules 3, 22 and 24 to the Companies Act 1985 and the corresponding provisions of the Companies (Northern Ireland) Order 1986; and	
(h) Section 195 of the Act.	

EXPLANATORY NOTE

(*This Note is not part of the Order.*)

This Order brings into force on 29th April 1988 provisions of the Financial Services Act 1986 concerning the criminal and civil sanctions applicable if a person carries on investment business in the United Kingdom without authorisation or exemption under the Act. The Order also brings into force on the same date certain provisions of the Act concerning the regulation of investment business and of persons authorised to carry on that business.

Article 3 of the Order brings the provisions of the Act concerning the issue of certain investment advertisements into force on 29th April 1988 except insofar as those provisions concern certain advertisements which are contained in newspapers, journals, magazines and other periodical publications or are broadcast, televised or distributed through films or recordings. Depending upon the nature of the advertisement Article 4 brings the relevant provisions into force on either 6th May 1988, 29th May 1988 or 29th July 1988. Article 5 of the

Order contains provisions concerning advertisements contained in a publication first issued before whichever is relevant of the dates mentioned above.

Article 6 of the Order brings the provisions of the Financial Services Act 1986 concerning the promotion of collective investment schemes into force on 29th April 1988 except insofar as those provisions concern units which are listed or issued on terms conditional upon their being listed on The International Stock Exchange or are the subject of a prospectus which complies with relevant companies legislation. The relevant provisions come into force for all remaining purposes on 1st July 1988.

The Order brings into force on 29th April 1988 provisions of the Act concerning the authorisation and recognition of collective investment schemes and concerning the subsequent regulation of such schemes. Provisions concerning —

(a) the application of the provisions of the Act to insurance companies and friendly societies;

(b) the promotion of certain insurance contracts;

(c) the audit of investment businesses; and

(d) reciprocity.

are also brought into force on 29th April 1988.

The Order brings certain transitional and consequential provisions and repeals into force on 29th April 1988 including the repeal of the major part of the Prevention of Fraud (Investments) Act 1958 and the corresponding Northern Irish legislation.

NOTE AS TO EARLIER COMMENCEMENT ORDERS

(This Note is not part of the Order.)

The following provisions of the Financial Services Act 1986 have been brought into force by commencement orders made before the date of this Order.

Provisions of Act	S.I. No.
s. 1	1986/2246
	1987/1997
	1987/2158
s. 2	1986/2246
s. 5 (partially)	1986/2246
ss. 8 to 11	1987/907
s. 12	1987/1997
s. 13	1987/907
s. 14	1987/907
s. 15 (partially)	1987/907
ss. 16 to 19	1987/907
s. 20	1987/1997
s. 21	1987/907
ss. 26 to 30	1987/2158
s. 31 (partially)	1987/2158
s. 35 (partially)	1986/2246
s. 36 (partially)	1987/907

Provisions of Act	S.I. No.
s. 37	1987/907
	1987/1997
s. 38 (partially)	1987/907
s. 39	1987/907
	1987/1997
s. 40	1987/1997
s. 41	1987/907
s. 42 (partially)	1986/2246
s. 43	1987/2158
s. 45 (partially)	1986/2246
s. 46	1987/907
ss. 48 to 52	1987/907
ss. 54 and 55	1987/907
s. 56 (partially)	1987/907
s. 62 (partially)	1987/1997
s. 63	1987/623
s. 96	1987/1997
ss. 102 and 103	1987/907
s. 104 (partially)	1987/907
ss. 105 and 106	1986/2246
ss. 107 and 110	1987/907
s. 112 (partially)	1987/907
	1987/2158
s. 113 (partially)	1987/907
ss. 114 to 118	1986/2246
ss. 119 and 120	1987/907
s. 121	1986/2246
ss. 122 and 123	1986/2246
	1987/907
s. 124	1986/2246
s. 125 (partially)	1987/907
s. 126	1986/2246
s. 127	1987/907
s. 128	1986/2246
s. 129 (partially)	1986/2246
	1987/907
s. 132 (partially)	1986/2246
s. 134 (partially)	1986/2246
s. 137	1986/2246
s. 138 (partially)	1986/2246
	1987/907

Provisions of Act	S.I. No.
s. 139 (partially)	1986/2246
s. 140 (partially)	1986/2246
	1987/907
	1987/1997
	1987/2158
ss. 141 to 153	1986/2246
s. 154 (partially)	1986/2246
ss. 155 to 157	1986/2246
ss. 172 and 173	1986/2246
s. 174 (partially)	1986/2246
s. 176	1986/2246
s. 177	1986/1940
s. 178 (partially)	1986/1940
	1986/2246
s. 179	1986/1940
	1986/2246
s. 180	1986/1940
s. 181	1986/2246
s. 182	1986/1940
	1986/2031
	1986/2246
ss. 183 and 184 (partially)	1987/623
s. 185	1987/623
s. 186 (partially)	1987/623
s. 187	1986/2246
	1987/907
s. 188	1986/2246
s. 189 (partially)	1986/2246
	1987/1997
	1987/2158
s. 190	1987/907
s. 191	1987/907
s. 192	1986/2246
s. 195	Royal Assent
s. 196	1987/1997
s. 198 (partially)	1986/1940
	1986/2246
	1987/907
s. 199 (partially)	1986/1940
	1986/2246
s. 200 (partially)	1986/1940
	1986/2246
	1987/907
	1987/2158

Provisions of Act	S.I. No.
s. 201 (partially)	1986/1940
	1986/2246
	1987/623
ss. 202 and 203	1986/1940
	1986/2246
s. 204	1986/2246
s. 205	1986/1940
	1986/2246
s. 206	1987/907
ss. 207, 209 and 210	1986/1940
	1986/2246
s. 211 (partially)	1986/2031
	1986/2246
	1987/907
	1987/2158
s. 212 (partially)	1986/2031
	1986/2246
	1987/907
Schedule 1	1986/2246
	1987/1997
	1987/2158
Schedules 2 to 4	1987/907
Schedule 5	1987/2158
Schedule 6	1987/1997
Schedule 7, 8 and 9	1986/2246
Schedule 10 (partially)	1986/2246
	1987/907
Schedule 11 (partially)	1986/2246
	1987/907
	1987/1997
	1987/2158
Schedule 12	1986/2246
Schedule 13	1986/1940
	1986/2031
	1986/2246
Schedule 14 (partially)	1986/2246
	1987/1997
	1987/2158
Schedule 15 (partially)	1986/2031
	1986/2246
	1987/907
	1987/2158
Schedule 16 (partially)	1986/2246
	1987/907
Schedule 17 (partially)	1986/2031
	1986/2246

The following provisions of the Financial Services Act 1986 will come into force on 3rd October 1988 by virtue of commencement order made before the date of this Order:

Provisions of the Act	S.I. No.
s. 62 (insofar as not already in force)	1987/1997
s. 140 and Schedule 11 (partially)	1987/1997

The word ("partially") is used where the provision has been brought into force in part, or for a limited purpose or for a limited area.

THE FINANCIAL SERVICES ACT 1986 (COMMENCEMENT) (NO. 9) ORDER 1988

(S.I. 1988 No. 995 (C. 30))

Made on 6 June 1988 by the Secretary of State under sec. 211(1) of the Financial Services Act 1986.

1 This Order may be cited as the Financial Services Act 1986 (Commencement) (No. 9) Order 1988.

2 The provisions of section 125(8) of the Financial Services Act 1986 shall come into force on 1 July 1988 as shall the provisions of section 212(3) of and Schedule 17 to that Act insofar as they provide for the repeal of the Restrictive Trade Practices (Stock Exchange) Act 1984.

3 In articles 6(2) and 7 of The Financial Services Act 1986 (Commencement) (No. 8) Order 1988 for the word "July" there shall be substituted "December".

4 Section 129 of the Financial Services Act 1986 insofar as it relates to paragraph 5(3) and (4) of Schedule 10 to that Act and the provisions of that Schedule not yet in force shall come into force on 1 July.

EXPLANATORY NOTE

(This Note is not part of the Order.)

This Order brings into force on 1 July 1988 those provisions of the Financial Services Act 1986 which effect the repeal of the Restrictive Trade Practices (Stock Exchange) Act 1984.

It also amends the Financial Services Act 1986 (Commencement No. 8) Order 1988 so as to postpone the coming into force of the restriction on promotion of certain collective investment schemes, namely those included in the Official List or promoted by a compliant prospectus, from 1 July to 1 December.

It also brings into force on 1 July the provisions of the Financial Services Act 1986 which disapply sections 75 to 77 of the Insurance Companies Act 1982 (right to withdraw from long term policies) in respect of contracts which constitute an investment.

NOTE AS TO EARLIER COMMENCEMENT ORDERS

(*This Note is not part of the Order.*)

It is impracticable to follow the normal practice of setting out a table of commencement orders made before the date of this Order since to do so would result in unacceptable delay in preparation and printing. Such a table was appended to the Financial Services Act 1986 (Commencement) (No. 8) Order 1988 and the current position can be ascertained from that table, the body of the Order and this Order.

THE FINANCIAL SERVICES ACT 1986 (COMMENCEMENT) (NO. 10) ORDER 1988

(S.I. 1988 No. 1960 (C. 72))

Made on 9 November 1988 by the Secretary of State under sec. 211(1) of the Financial Services Act 1986.

1 This Order may be cited as the Financial Services Act 1986 (Commencement) (No. 10) Order 1988.

2 Articles 6(2) and 7 of the Financial Services Act 1986 (Commencement) (No. 8) Order 1988 shall be revoked.

3 Insofar as it is not yet in force, section 76 of the Financial Services Act 1986 shall come into force on 31st December 1988 except insofar as it has effect in relation to—

(a) an open-ended investment company units in which are either included in the Official List of The International Stock Exchange of the United Kingdom and the Republic of Ireland Limited or are offered on terms such that any agreement for their acquisition is conditional upon such listing being an open-ended investment company which either—

    (i) is managed in and authorised under the law of a country or territory in respect of which an order under section 87 of the Financial Services Act 1986 is in force on 31st December 1988 and which is of a class specified in that order; or

    (ii) is constituted in a member State in respect of which an order under paragraph 10 of Schedule 15 to the Financial Services Act 1986 is in force on 31st December 1988 and which meets the requirements specified in that order; or

(b) any prospectus issued by or on behalf of an open-ended investment company which fulfils the conditions described in paragraph (a)(i) of this article being a prospectus which complies with Chapter II of Part III of the Companies Act 1985 or the corresponding provisions of the Companies (Northern Ireland) Order 1986 and the issue of which in the United Kingdom does not contravene section 74 or 75 of the Companies Act 1985 or the corresponding provisions of the Companies (Northern Ireland) Order 1986 as the case may be, and

shall come into force on 1st March 1989 for all remaining purposes.

Note
See note after art. 4.

4 Section 212(3) of and Schedule 17 to the Financial Services Act 1986 shall come into force on 31st December 1988 insofar as is necessary to have the effect that, to the extent that they do apply, the provisions of Part III and section 693 of, and Schedule 3 to, the Companies Act 1985 and the corresponding provisions of the Companies (Northern Ireland) Order 1986 cease to apply to a prospectus offering for subscription, or to any application form for, units in an open-ended investment company which does not fulfil the conditions described in article 3(a)(i) of this Order and shall come into force on 1st March 1989 insofar as is necessary to have the effect described in this article with respect to a prospectus offering for subscription, or to any application form for, units in an open-ended investment company which does fulfil those conditions.

Note

Art. 3(b) and 4 have effect as if "or (a)(ii)" were inserted after "or (a)(i)" in each place in which it occurs: see S.I. 1988 No. 2285 (C. 85), art. 6. In regard to restriction of effect of art. 3 and 4 see also S.I. 1988 No. 2285 (C. 85), art. 2, 3.

EXPLANATORY NOTE

(*This Note is not part of the Order.*)

This Order revokes articles 6(2) and 7 of the Financial Services Act 1986 (Commencement) (No. 8) Order 1988 as amended by the Financial Services Act 1986 (Commencement) (No. 9) Order 1988. Those articles would have brought the provisions of the Financial Services Act 1986 restricting the promotion of certain collective investment schemes, namely those included in the Official List or promoted by a compliant prospectus, into force on 1st December 1988. This Order brings the relevant restrictions into force on—

(a) 31st December 1988 except in the cases described in Article 3 of the Order; and

(b) on 1st March 1989 in those cases.

NOTE AS TO EARLIER COMMENCEMENT

(*This Note is not part of the Order.*)

The following provisions of the Financial Services Act 1986 have been brought into force before the date of this Order in pursuance either of the Act or of previous commencement orders.

Provisions of the Act	S.I. No.
s. 1	1986/2246
	1987/1997
	1987/2158
s. 2	1986/2246
ss. 3 and 4	1988/740
s. 5	1986/2246
	1988/740
ss. 6 and 7	1988/740
ss. 8 to 11	1987/907
s. 12	1987/1997
s. 13 and 14	1987/907
s. 15	1987/907
	1988/740
ss. 16 to 19	1987/907
s. 20	1987/1997
s. 21	1987/907
ss. 22 and 23	1988/740

Provisions of the Act	S.I. No.
s. 24 (partially)	1988/740
s. 25	1988/740
ss. 26 to 30	1987/2158
s. 31	1987/2158
	1988/740
ss. 32 to 34	1988/740
s. 35	1986/2246
	1988/740
s. 36	1987/907
	1988/740
s. 37	1987/907
	1987/1997
s. 38	1987/907
	1988/740
s. 39	1987/907
	1987/1997
s. 40	1987/1997
s. 41	1987/907
s. 42	1986/2246
	1988/740
s. 43	1987/2158
s. 44	1988/740
s. 45	1986/2246
	1988/740
s. 46	1987/907
s. 47	1988/740
ss. 48 to 52	1987/907
ss. 54 and 55	1987/907
s. 56	1987/907
	1988/740
s. 57	1988/740
s. 58 (partially)	1988/740
ss. 59 to 61	1988/740
s. 62	1987/1997
s. 63	1987/623
ss. 64 to 75	1988/740
s. 76 (partially)	1988/740, Articles 6(2) and 7 of 1988/995) S.I. 1988/740 were amended by S.I. 1988/995 and revoked by this Order.
ss. 77 to 85	1988/740
s. 86 (partially)	1988/740

SI 1988/1960, Note   [The next page is 64,461]

Provisions of the Act	S.I. No.
ss. 87 to 95	1988/740
s. 96	1987/1997
ss. 97 to 101	1988/740
ss. 102 and 103	1987/907
s. 104	1987/907
	1988/740
ss. 105 and 106	1986/2246
s. 107	1987/907
ss. 108 and 109	1988/740
s. 110	1987/907
s. 111	1988/740
s. 112	1987/907
	1987/2158
	1988/740
s. 113	1987/907
	1988/740
ss. 114 to 118	1986/2246
ss. 119 and 120	1987/907
s. 121	1986/2246
s. 122 and 123	1986/2246
	1987/907
s. 124	1986/2246
s. 125	1987/907
	1988/995
s. 126	1986/2246
s. 127	1987/907
s. 128	1986/2246
s. 129	1986/2246
	1987/907
	1988/740
	1988/995
ss. 130 and 131	1988/740
s. 132	1986/2246
	1988/740
s. 133	1988/740
s. 134 (partially)	1986/2246
ss. 135 and 136	1988/740
s. 137	1986/2246
s. 138	1986/2246
	1987/907
	1988/740

Provisions of the Act	S.I. No.
s. 139	1986/2246
	1988/740
s. 140 (partially)	1986/2246
	1987/907
	1987/1997
	1987/2158
	1988/740
ss. 141 to 153	1986/2246
s. 154	1986/2246
	1988/740
ss. 155 to 157	1986/2246
s. 160 (partially)	1988/740
s. 162 (partially)	1988/740
s. 169	1988/740
s. 170 (partially)	1988/740
ss. 172 and 173	1986/2246
s. 174 (partially)	1986/2246
	1988/740
s. 175	1988/740
s. 176	1986/2246
s. 177	1986/1940
s. 178	1986/1940
	1986/2246
	1988/740
s. 179	1986/1940
	1986/2246
s. 180	1986/1940
s. 181	1986/2246
s. 182	1986/940
	1986/2031
	1986/2246
ss. 183 and 184	1987/623
	1988/740
s. 185	1987/623
s. 186	1987/623
	1988/740
s. 187	1986/2246
	1987/907
s. 188	1986/2246
s. 189 (partially)	1986/2246
	1987/1997
	1987/2158
ss. 190 and 191	1987/907

Provisions of the Act	S.I. No.
s. 192	1986/2246
s. 194	1988/740
s. 195	s. 211(2)
s. 196	1987/1997
s. 197	1988/740
s. 198	1986/1940
	1986//2246
	1987/907
	1988/740
s. 199	1986/1940
	1986/2246
	1988/740
s. 200	1986/1940
	1986/2246
	1987/907
	1987/2158
	1988/740
s. 201	1986/1940
	1986/2246
	1987/623
	1988/740
ss. 202 and 203	1986/1940
	1986/2246
s. 204	1986/2246
s. 205	1986/1940
	1986/2246
s.206	1987/1907
s. 207	1986/1940
	1986/2246
s. 208 (partially)	1988/740
ss. 209 and 210	1986/1940
	1986/2246
s. 211	1986/2031
	1986/2246
	1987/907
	1987/2158
	1988/740
s. 212 (partially)	1986/2031
	1986/2246
	1987/907
	1988/740
	1988/995
Schedule 1	1986/2246
	1987/1997
	1987/2158

Provisions of the Act	S.I. No.
Schedule 2 to 4	1987/907
Schedule 5	1987/2158
Schedule 6	1987/1997
Schedules 7 to 9	1986/2246
Schedule 10	1986/2246
	1987/907
	1988/740
	1988/995
Schedule 11 (partially)	1986/2246
	1987/907
	1987/1997
	1987/2158
	1988/740
Schedule 12	1986/2246
Schedule 13	1986/1940
	1986/2031
	1986/2246
Schedule 14 (partially)	1986/2246
	1987/1997
	1987/2158
Schedule 15	1986/2031
	1986/2246
	1987/907
	1987/2158
	1988/740
Schedule 16 (partially)	1986/2246
	1987/907
	1988/740
Schedule 17 (partially)	1986/2031
	1986/2246
	1988/740
	1988/995

[The next page is 64,471]

THE FINANCIAL SERVICES ACT 1986 (COMMENCEMENT) (No. 11) ORDER 1988

(S.I. 1988 No. 2285 (C. 85))

Made on 29 December 1988 by the Secretary of State under sec. 211(1) of the Financial Services Act 1986.

1   This Order may be cited as the Financial Services Act 1986 (Commencement) (No. 11) Order 1988.

2   Article 3 of the Financial Services Act 1986 (Commencement) (No. 10) Order 1988 shall not have effect in relation to—

(a)   an open-ended investment company managed in and authorised under the law of Bermuda units in which are, on 31st December 1988, included in the Official List of The International Stock Exchange of the United Kingdom and the Republic of Ireland Limited; or

(b)   any prospectus issued by or on behalf of an open-ended investment company which fulfils the conditions described in paragraph (a) of this article, being a prospectus which complies with Chapter II of Part III of the Companies Act 1985 or the corresponding provisions of the Companies (Northern Ireland) Order 1986 and the issue of which in the United Kingdom does not contravene section 74 or 75 of the Companies Act 1985 or the corresponding provisions of the Companies (Northern Ireland) Order 1986 as the case may be.

3   Article 4 of the Financial Services Act 1986 (Commencement) (No. 10) Order 1988 shall not have effect in relation to a prospectus offering for subscription, or to any application form for, units in an open-ended investment company which fulfils the conditions described in article 2(a) of this Order.

4   Section 76 of the Financial Services Act 1986 shall come into force on 1st May 1989 insofar as it has effect in relation to—

(a)   an open-ended investment company which fulfils the conditions described in article 2(a) of this Order and which is a scheme of a class specified in the Schedule to the Financial Services (Designated Countries and Territories) (Overseas Collective Investment Schemes) (Bermuda) Order; or

(b)   any prospectus issued by or on behalf of an open-ended investment company falling within paragraph (a) of this article, being a prospectus which fulfils the conditions described in article 2(b) of this Order,

and shall come into force on 28th February 1989 insofar as it has effect in relation to an open-ended investment company falling within article 2(a) of this Order but not falling within paragraph (a) of this article or to any prospectus which fulfils the conditions described in paragraph 2(b) of this Order issued by or on behalf of any such company.

5   Section 212(3) of and Schedule 17 to the Financial Services Act 1986 shall come into force on 1st May 1989 insofar as is necessary to have the effect that, to the extent that they do apply, the provisions of Part III and section 693 of, and Schedule 3 to, the Companies Act 1985 and the corresponding provisions of the Companies (Northern Ireland) Order 1986 cease to apply to a prospectus offering for subscription, or to any application form for, units in an open-ended investment company falling within article 4(a) of this Order and shall come into force on 28th February 1989 insofar as is necessary to have the effect described in this article with respect to a prospectus offering for subscription, or to any application form for, units in an open-ended investment company falling within article 2(a) of this order but not within article 4(a).

6   Articles 3(b) and 4 of the Financial Services Act 1986 (Commencement) (No. 10) Order 1988 shall have effect as if "or (a)(ii)" were inserted after "(a)(i)" in each place in which it occurs.

EXPLANATORY NOTE
(*This Note is not part of the Order.*)

This Order postpones, until 28th February 1989, the coming into force of the restriction on the promotion of certain collective investment schemes, namely open-ended invesment companies which are managed in and authorised under the law of Bermuda and units in which are included in the Official List on 31st December 1988 or are promoted by a complying prospectus. It also postpones, until 1st May 1989, the coming into force of that restriction with respect to schemes of the kind just described which are of a class specified in the Schedule to the Financial Services Act 1986 (Designated Countries and Territories) (Overseas Collective Investment Schemes) (Bermuda) Order 1988.

The Order also postpones, until 1st March 1989, the application of the restrictions which would otherwise be imposed, on 31st December 1988, by section 76 of the Financial Services Act 1986 on a prospectus issued by or on behalf of an open-ended investment company which meets the conditions described in article 3(a)(ii) of the Financial Services Act 1986 (Commencement) (No. 10) Order 1988.

NOTE AS TO EARLIER COMMENCEMENT
(*This Note is not part of the Order.*)

The following provisions of the Financial Services Act 1986 have been brought into force before the date of this Order in pursuance either of the Act or of previous commencement orders.

Provisions of the Act	S.I. No.
s.1	1986/2246
	1987/1997
	1987/2158
s.2	1986/2246
ss.3 and 4	1988/740
s.5	1986/2246
	1988/740
ss.6 and 7	1988/740
ss.8 to 11	1987/907
s.12	1987/1997
s.13 and 14	1987/907
s.15	1987/907
	1988/740
ss.16 to 19	1987/907
s.20	1987/1997
s.21	1987/907
ss.22 and 23	1988/740
s.24 (partially)	1988/740
s.25	1988/740
ss.26 to 30	1987/2158
s.31	1987/2158
	1988/740
ss.32 to 34	1988/740

Financial Services Act 1986 (Commencement) (No. 11) Order 1988

Provisions of the Act	S.I. No.	
s.35	1986/2246	
	1988/740	
s.36	1987/907	
	1988/740	
s.37	1987/907	
	1987/1997	
s.38	1987/907	
	1988/740	
s.39	1987/907	
	1987/1997	
s.40	1987/1997	
s.41	1987/907	
s.42	1986/2246	
	1988/740	
s.43	1987/2158	
s.44	1988/740	
s.45	1986/2246	
	1988/740	
s.46	1987/907	
s.47	1988/740	
ss.48 to 52	1987/907	
ss. 54 and 55	1987/907	
s.56	1987/907	
	1988/740	
s.57	1988/740	
s.58 (partially)	1988/740	
ss.59 to 61	1988/740	
s.62	1987/1997	
s.63	1987/623	
ss.64 to 75	1988/740	
s.76 (partially)	1988/740	articles 6(2) and 7
	1988/995	of S.I. 1988/740 were
	1988/1960	amended by S.I. 1988/995
		and revoked by
		S.I. 1988/1960
ss.77 to 85	1988/740	
s.86 (partially)	1988/740	
ss.87 to 95	1988/740	
s.96	1987/1997	
ss.97 to 101	1988/740	
ss.102 and 103	1987/907	
s.104	1987/907	
	1988/740	
ss.105 and 106	1986/2246	
s.107	1987/907	
ss.108 and 109	1988/740	
s.110	1987/907	
s.111	1988/740	
s.112	1987/907	
	1987/2158	
	1988/740	

Provisions of the Act	S.I. No.
s.113	1987/907
	1988/740
ss.114 to 118	1986/2246
ss.119 and 120	1987/907
s.121	1986/2246
ss.122 and 123	1986/2246
	1987/907
s.124	1986/2246
s.125	1987/907
	1988/995
s.126	1986/2246
s.127	1987/907
s.128	1986/2246
s.129	1986/2246
	1987/907
	1988/740
	1988/995
ss.130 and 131	1988/740
s.132	1986/2246
	1988/740
s.133	1988/740
s.134(partially)	1986/2246
ss.135 and 136	1988/740
s.137	1986/2246
s.138	1986/2246
	1987/907
	1988/740
s.139	1986/2246
	1988/740
s.140 (partially)	1986/2246
	1987/907
	1987/1997
	1987/2158
	1988/740
ss.141 to 153	1986/2246
s.154	1986/2246
	1988/740
ss.155 to 157	1986/2246
s.160 (partially)	1988/740
s.162 (partially)	1988/740
s.169	1988/740
s.170 (partially)	1988/740
ss.172 and 173	1986/2246
s.174 (partially)	1986/2246
	1988/740
s.175	1988/740
s.176	1986/2246
s.177	1986/1940
s.178	1986/1940
	1986/2246
	1988/740

Financial Services Act 1986 (Commencement) (No. 11) Order 1988

Provisions of the Act	S.I. No.
s.179	1986/1940
	1986/2246
s.180	1986/1940
s.181	1986/2246
s.182	1986/1940
	1986/2031
	1986/2246
ss.183 and 184	1987/623
	1988/740
s.185	1987/623
s.186	1987/623
	1988/740
s.187	1986/2246
	1987/907
s.188	1986/2246
s.189 (partially)	1986/2246
	1987/1997
	1987/2158
ss.190 and 191	1987/907
s.192	1986/2246
s.194	1988/740
s.195	s.211(2)
s.196	1987/1997
s.197	1988/740
s.198	1986/1940
	1986/2246
	1987/907
	1988/740
s.199	1986/1940
	1986/2246
	1988/740
s.200	1986/1940
	1986/2246
	1987/907
	1987/2158
	1988/740
s.201	1986/1940
	1986/2246
	1987/623
	1988/740
ss.202 and 203	1986/1940
	1986/2246
s.204	1986/2246
s.205	1986/1940
	1986/2246
s.206	1987/907
s.207	1986/1940
	1986/2246
s.208 (partially)	1988/740

Provisions of the Act	S.I. No.
ss.209 and 210	1986/1940
	1986/2246
s.211	1986/2031
	1986/2246
	1987/907
	1987/2158
	1988/740
s.212 (partially)	1986/2031
	1986/2246
	1987/907
	1988/740
	1988/995
	1988/1960
Schedule 1	1986/2246
	1987/1997
	1987/2158
Schedules 2 to 4	1987/907
Schedule 5	1987/2158
Schedule 6	1987/1997
Schedules 7 to 9	1986/2246
Schedule 10	1986/2246
	1987/907
	1988/740
	1988/995
Schedule 11 (partially)	1986/2246
	1987/907
	1987/1997
	1987/2158
	1988/740
Schedule 12	1986/2246
Schedule 13	1986/1940
	1986/2031
	1986/2246
Schedule 14 (partially)	1986/2246
	1987/1997
	1987/2158
Schedule 15	1986/2031
	1986/2246
	1987/907
	1987/2158
	1988/740
Schedule 16 (partially)	1986/2246
	1987/907
	1988/740
Schedule 17 (partially)	1986/2031
	1986/2246
	1988/740
	1988/995
	1988/1960

THE FINANCIAL SERVICES ACT 1986 (COMMENCEMENT) (NO. 12) ORDER 1989

(S.I. 1989 No. 1583 (C. 54))

Made on 31 August 1989 by the Secretary of State under sec. 211(1) of the Financial Services Act 1986. Operative from 1 October 1989.

CITATION AND INTERPRETATION

1(1) This Order may be cited as the Financial Services Act 1986 (Commencement) (No. 12) Order 1989.

1(2) In this Order **"the Act"** means the Financial Services Act 1986.

PROVISIONS BROUGHT INTO FORCE

2(1) Insofar as they are not yet in force, sections 24 and 86 of the Act shall come into force on 1st October 1989.

2(2) Section 212(3) of and Schedule 17 to the Act shall come into force on 1st October 1989—

(a) to the extent necessary to repeal the Prevention of Fraud (Investments) Act (Northern Ireland) 1940 and the Prevention of Fraud (Investments) Act 1958; for all remaining purposes and

(b) insofar as they provide for the repeal of words in the following enactments—

    (i) the Tribunal and Inquiries Act 1971; and

    (ii) The House of Commons Disqualification Act 1975.

EXPLANATORY NOTE

(*This Note is not part of the Order.*)

This Order brings sections 24 and 86 of the Financial Services Act 1986 into force on 1st October 1989. Those sections implement Community obligations arising by virtue of Council Directive No. 85/611/EEC (O.J. No. L375/3) as amended by Council Directive No. 88/220/EEC (O.J. No. L100/31). The relevant provisions concern the right of certain collective investment schemes constituted in other Member States to be recognised schemes for the purposes of the Financial Services Act 1986 and the right of the operators and trustees of such schemes to be authorised persons. The Order repeals the Prevention of Fraud (Investments) Act (Northern Ireland) 1940 and the Prevention of Fraud (Investments) Act 1958 for all remaining purposes with effect from 1st October 1989. It also brings certain related repeals into force.

NOTE AS TO EARLIER COMMENCEMENT ORDERS

(*This Note is not part of the Order.*)

The following provisions of the Financial Services Act 1986 have been brought into force by commencement orders made before the date of this Order.

Provisions of the Act	S.I. No.
s. 1	1986/2246
	1987/1997
	1987/2158

Provisions of the Act	S.I. No.
s. 2	1986/2246
ss. 3 and 4	1988/740
s. 5	1986/2246
	1988/740
ss. 6 and 7	1988/740
ss. 8 to 11	1987/907
s. 12	1987/1997
ss. 13 and 14	1987/907
s. 15	1987/907
	1988/740
ss. 16 to 19	1987/907
s. 20	1987/1997
s. 21	1987/907
ss. 22 and 23	1988/740
s. 24 (partially)	1988/740
s. 25	1988/740
ss. 26 to 30	1987/2158
s. 31	1987/2158
	1988/740
ss. 32 to 34	1988/740
s. 35	1986/2246
	1988/740
s. 36	1988/740
	1988/740
s. 37	1987/907
	1987/1997
s. 38	1987/907
	1988/740
s. 39	1987/907
	1987/1997
s. 40	1987/1997
s. 41	1987/907
s. 42	1986/2246
	1988/740
s. 43	1987/2158
s. 44	1988/740
s. 45	1986/2246
	1988/740
s. 46	1987/907
s. 47	1988/740
ss. 48 to 52	1987/907

Provisions of the Act	S.I. No.	
ss. 54 and 55	1987/907	
s. 56	1987/907 1988/740	
s. 57	1988/740	
s. 58 (partially)	1988/740	
ss. 59 to 61	1988/740	
s. 62	1987/1997	
s. 63	1987/623	
ss. 64 to 75	1988/740	
s. 76	1988/740 1988/995 1988/1960 1988/2285	Articles 6(2) and 7 of S.I. 1988/740 were amended by S.I. 1988/995 and revoked by S.I. 1988/1960. Articles 3 and 4 of S.I. 1988/1960 were amended by S.I. 1988/2285
ss. 77 to 85	1988/740	
s. 86 (partially)	1988/740	
ss. 87 to 95	1988/740	
s. 96	1987/1997	
ss. 97 to 101	1988/740	
ss. 102 and 103	1987/907	
s. 104	1987/907 1988/740	
ss. 105 and 106	1986/2246	
s. 107	1987/907	
ss. 108 and 109	1988/740	
s. 110	1987/907	
s. 111	1988/740	
s. 112	1987/907 1987/2158 1988/740	
s. 113	1987/907 1988/740	
ss. 114 to 118	1986/2246	
ss. 119 to 120	1987/907	
s. 121	1986/2246	
ss. 122 and 123	1986/2246 1987/907	
s. 124	1986/2246	
s. 125	1987/907 1988/995	
s. 126	1986/2246	
s. 127	1987/907	

Provisions of the Act	S.I. No.
s. 128	1986/2246
s. 129	1986/2246
	1987/907
	1988/740
	1988/995
ss. 130 and 131	1988/740
s. 132	1986/2246
	1988/740
s. 133	1988/740
s. 134 (partially)	1986/2246
ss. 135 and 136	1988/740
s. 137	1986/2246
s. 138	1986/2246
	1987/907
	1988/740
s. 139	1986/2246
	1988/740
s. 140 (partially)	1986/2246
	1987/907
	1987/1997
	1987/2158
	1988/740
ss. 141 to 153	1986/2246
s. 154	1986/2246
	1988/740
ss. 155 to 157	1986/2246
s. 160 (partially)	1988/740
s. 162 (partially)	1988/740
s. 169	1988/740
s. 170 (partially)	1988/740
ss. 172 and 173	1986/2246
s. 174	1986/2246
	1988/740
s. 175	1988/740
s. 176	1986/2246
s. 177	1986/1940
s. 178	1986/1940
	1988/740
	1986/2246
s. 179	1986/1940
	1986/2246
s.180	1986/1940
s. 181	1986/2246

Provisions of the Act	*S.I. No.*
s. 182	1986/1940
	1986/2031
	1986/2246
ss. 183 and 184	1987/623
	1988/740
s. 185	1987/623
s. 186	1987/623
	1988/740
s. 187	1986/2246
	1987/907
s. 188	1986/2246
s. 189 (partially)	1986/2246
	1987/1997
	1987/2158
ss. 190 and 191	1987/907
s. 192	1986/2246
s. 194	1988/740
s. 195	s. 211(2)
s. 196	1987/1997
s. 197	1988/740
s. 198	1986/1940
	1986/2246
	1987/907
	1988/740
s. 199	1986/1940
	1986/2246
	1988/740
s. 200	1986/1940
	1986/2246
	1987/907
	1987/2158
	1988/740
s. 201	1986/1940
	1986/2246
	1987/623
	1988/740
ss. 202 and 203	1986/1940
	1986/2246
s. 204	1986/2246
s. 205	1986/1940
	1986/2246
s. 206	1987/907
s. 207	1986/1940
	1986/2246

Provisions of the Act	S.I. No.
s. 208 (partially)	1988/740
ss. 209 and 210	1986/1940
	1986/2246
s. 211	1986/2031
	1986/2246
	1987/907
	1987/2158
	1988/740
s. 212 (partially)	1986/2031
	1986/2246
	1987/907
	1988/740
	1988/995
	1988/1960
	1988/2285
Schedule 1	1986/2246
	1987/1997
	1987/2158
Schedules 2 to 4	1987/907
Schedule 5	1987/2158
Schedule 6	1987/1997
Schedules 7 to 9	1986/2246
Schedule 10	1986/2246
	1987/907
	1988/740
	1988/995
Schedule 11	1986/2246
	1987/907
	1987/1997
	1987/2158
	1988/740
Schedule 12	1986/2246
Schedule 13	1986/1940
	1986/2031
	1986/2246
Schedule 14 (partially)	1986/2246
	1987/1997
	1987/2158
Schedule 15	1986/2031
	1986/2246
	1987/907
	1987/2158
	1988/740
Schedule 16 (partially)	1986/2246
	1987/907
	1988/740

Provisions of the Act	S.I. No.
Schedule 17 (partially)	1986/2031
	1986/2246
	1988/740
	1988/995
	1988/1960
	1988/2285

ANCILLARY ACTS

Table of Contents

[The next page is 65,051]

PARTNERSHIP ACT 1890

(53 & 54 Vict. c. 39)

ARRANGEMENT OF SECTIONS

PARTNERSHIP ACT 1890

An Act to declare and amend the Law of Partnership.

[14th August 1890]

NATURE OF PARTNERSHIP

SEC. 1 Definition of partnership

1(1) [Definition] Partnership is the relation which subsists between persons carrying on a business in common with a view of profit.

1(2) [Exclusion] But the relation between members of any company or association which is—

(a) Registered as a company under the Companies Act 1862, or any other Act of Parliament for the time being in force and relating to the registration of joint stock companies; or

(b) Formed or incorporated by or in pursuance of any other Act of Parliament or letters patent, or Royal Charter; or

(c) A company engaged in working mines within and subect to the jurisdiction of the Stannaries:

is not a partnership within the meaning of this Act.

SEC. 2   Rules for determining existence of partnership

2 In determining whether a partnership does or does not exist, regard shall be had to the following rules:

(1) Joint tenancy, tenancy in common, joint property, common property, or part ownership does not of itself create a partnership as to anything so held or owned, whether the tenants or owners do or do not share any profits made by the use thereof.

(2) The sharing of gross returns does not of itself create a partership, whether the persons sharing such returns have or have not a joint or common right or interest in any property from which or from the use of which the returns are derived.

(3) The receipt by a person of a share of the profits of a business is *primâ facie* evidence that he is a partner in the business, but the receipt of such a share, or of a payment contingent on or varying with the profits of a business, does not of itself make him a partner in the business; and in particular—

   (a) The receipt by a person of a debt or other liquidated amount by instalments or otherwise out of the accruing profits of a business does not of itself make him a partner in the business or liable as such:

   (b) A contract for the remuneration of a servant of agent of a person engaged in a business by a share of the profits of the business does not of itself make the servant or agent a partner in the business or liable as such:

   (c) A person being the widow or child of a deceased partner, and receiving by way of annuity a portion of the profits made in the business in which the deceased person was a partner, is not by reason only of such receipt a partner in the business or liable as such:

   (d) The advance of money by way of loan to a person engaged or about to engage in any business on a contract with that person that the lender shall receive a rate of interest varying with the profits, or shall receive a share of the profits arising from carrying on the business, does not of itself make the lender a partner with the person or persons carrying on the business or liable as such. Provided that the contract is in writing, and signed by or on behalf of all the parties thereto:

   (e) A person receiving by way of annuity or otherwise a portion of the profits of a business in consideration of the sale by him of the goodwill of the business is not by reason only of such receipt a partner in the business or liable as such.

SEC. 3   Postponement of rights of person lending or selling in consideration of share of profits in case of insolvency

3 In the event of any person to whom money has been advanced by way of loan upon such a contract as is mentioned in the last foregoing section, or of any buyer of a goodwill in consideration of a share of the profits of the business, being adjudged a bankrupt, entering into an arrangement to pay his creditors less than 100p in the pound, or dying in insolvent circumstances, the lender of the loan shall not be entitled to recover anything in respect of his loan, and the seller of the goodwill shall not be entitled to recover anything in respect of the share of profits contracted for, until the claims of the other creditors of the borrower or buyer for valuable consideration in money or money's worth have been satisfied.

History
S. 3 amended by Decimal Currency Act 1969, s. 10(1).

SEC. 4   Meaning of firm

4(1)   [Firm, firm-name]   Persons who have entered into partnership with one another are for the purposes of this Act called collectively a firm, and the name under which their business is carried on is called the firm-name.

4(2)   [Scotland]   In Scotland a firm is a legal person distinct from the partners of whom it is composed, but an individual partner may be charged on a decree or diligence directed against the firm, and on payment of the debts is entitled to relief *pro ratâ* from the firm and its other members.

Note
S. 4(2) excluded by Capital Transfer Act 1984, s. 119(2).

RELATIONS OF PARTNERS TO PERSONS DEALING WITH THEM

SEC. 5   Power of partner to bind the firm

5   Every partner is an agent of the firm and his other partners for the purpose of the business of the partnership; and the acts of every partner who does any act for carrying on in the usual way business of the kind carried on by the firm of which he is a member bind the firm and his partners, unless the partner so acting has in fact no authority to act for the firm in the particular matter, and the person with whom he is dealing either knows that he has no authority, or does not know or believe him to be a partner.

SEC. 6   Partners bound by acts on behalf of firm

6   An act or instrument relating to the business of the firm done or executed in the firm-name, or in any other manner showing an intention to bind the firm, by any person thereto authorised, whether a partner or not, is binding on the firm and all the partners.

> Provided that this section shall not affect any general rule of law relating to the execution of deeds or negotiable instruments.

SEC. 7   Partner using credit of firm for private purposes

7   Where one partner pledges the credit of the firm for a purpose apparently not connected with the firm's ordinary course of business, the firm is not bound, unless he is in fact specially authorised by the other partners; but this section does not affect any personal liability incurred by an individual partner.

SEC. 8 Effect of notice that firm will not be bound by acts of partner

8 If it has been agreed between the partners that any restriction shall be placed on the power of any one or more of them to bind the firm, no act done in contravention of the agreement is binding on the firm with respect to persons having notice of the agreement.

SEC. 9 Liability of partners

9 Every partner in a firm is liable jointly with the other partners, and in Scotland severally also, for all debts and obligations of the firm incurred while he is a partner; and after his death his estate is also severally liable in a due course of administration for such debts and obligations, so far as they remain unsatisfied, but subject in England or Ireland to the prior payment of his separate debts.

SEC. 10 Liability of the firm for wrongs

10 Where, by any wrongful act or omission of any partner acting in the ordinary course of the business of the firm, or with the authority of his co-partners, loss or injury is caused to any person not being a partner in the firm, or any penalty is incurred, the firm is liable therefor to the same extent as the partner so acting or omitting to act.

SEC. 11 Misapplication of money or property received for or in custody of the firm

11 In the following cases; namely—

(a) Where one partner acting within the scope of his apparent authority receives the money or property of a third person and misapplies it; and

(b) Where a firm in the course of its business receives money or property of a third person, and the money or property so received is misapplied by one or more of the partners while it is in the custody of the firm;

the firm is liable to make good the loss.

SEC. 12 Liability for wrongs joint and several

12 Every partner is liable jointly with his co-partners and also severally for everything for which the firm while he is a partner therein becomes liable under either of the two last preceding sections.

SEC. 13 Improper employment of trust-property for partnership purposes

13 If a partner, being a trustee, improperly employs trust-property in the business or on the account of the partnership, no other partner is liable for the trust property to the persons beneficially interested therein:

Provided as follows:—

(1) This section shall not affect any liability incurred by any partner by reason of his having notice of a breach of trust; and

(2) Nothing in this section shall prevent trust money from being followed and recovered from the firm if still in its possession or under its control.

SEC. 14   Persons liable by "holding out"

14(1) [Liability as partner] Every one who by words spoken or written or by conduct represents himself, or who knowingly suffers himself to be represented, as a partner in a particular firm, is liable as a partner to any one who has on the faith of any such representation given credit to the firm, whether the representation has or has not been made or communicated to the person so giving credit by or with the knowledge of the apparent partner making the representation or suffering it to be made.

14(2) [Exception for estate etc. after death] Provided that where after a partner's death the partnership business is continued in the old firm's name, the continued use of that name or of the deceased partner's name as part thereof shall not of itself make his executors or administrators estate or effects liable for any partnership debts contracted after his death.

SEC. 15   Admissions and representations of partners

15 An admission or representation made by any partner concerning the partnership affairs, and in the ordinary course of its business, is evidence against the firm.

SEC. 16   Notice to acting partner to be notice to the firm

16 Notice to any partner who habitually acts in the partnership business of any matter relating to partnership affairs operates as notice to the firm, except in the case of a fraud on the firm committed by or with the consent of that partner.

SEC. 17   Liabilities of incoming and outgoing partner

17(1) [Admitted partner] A person who is admitted as a partner into an existing firm does not thereby become liable to the creditors of the firm for anything done before he became a partner.

17(2) [Retiring partner] A partner who retires from a firm does not thereby cease to be liable for partnership debts or obligations incurred before his retirement.

17(3) [Discharge agreement re retiring partner] A retiring partner may be discharged from any existing liabilities, by an agreement to that effect between himself and the members of the firm as newly constituted and the creditors, and this agreement may be either expressed or inferred as a fact from the course of dealing between the creditors and the firm as newly constituted.

SEC. 18   Revocation of continuing guaranty by change in firm

18 A continuing guaranty or cautionary obligation given either to a firm or to a third person in respect of the transactions of a firm is, in the absence of agreement to the contrary, revoked as to future transactions by any change in the constitution of the firm to which, or of the firm in respect of the transactions of which, the guaranty or obligation was given.

RELATIONS OF PARTNERS TO ONE ANOTHER

SEC. 19 Variation by consent of terms of partnership

19 The mutual rights and duties of partners, whether ascertained by agreement or defined by this Act, may be varied by the consent of all the partners, and such consent may be either express or inferred from a course of dealing.

SEC. 20 Partnership property

20(1) [Property in partnership] All property and rights and interests in property originally brought into the partnership stock or acquired, whether by purchase or otherwise, on account of the firm, or for the purposes and in the course of the partnership business, are called in this Act partnership property, and must be held and applied by the partners exclusively for the purposes of the partnership and in accordance with the partnership agreement.

20(2) [Devolution of legal estate etc.] Provided that the legal estate or interest in any land, or in Scotland the title to and interest in any heritable estate, which belongs to the partnership shall devolve according to the nature and tenure thereof, and the general rules of law thereto applicable, but in trust so far as necessary, for the persons beneficially interested in the land under this section.

20(3) [Co-owners of land] Where co-owners of an estate or interest in any land, or in Scotland of any heritable estate, not being itself partnership property, are partners as to profits made by the use of that land or estate, and purchase other land or estate out of the profits to be used in like manner, the land or estate so purchased belongs to them, in the absence of an agreement to the contrary, not as partners, but as co-owners for the same respective estates and interests as are held by them in the land or estate first mentioned at the date of the purchase.

SEC. 21 Property bought with partnership money

21 Unless the contrary intention appears, property bought with money belonging to the firm is deemed to have been bought on account of the firm.

SEC. 22 Conversion into personal estate of land held as partnership property

22 Where land or any heritable interest therein has become partnership property, it shall, unless the contrary intention appears, be treated as between the partners (including the representatives of a deceased partner), and also as between the heirs of a deceased partner and his executors or administrators, as personal or moveable and not real or heritable estate.

SEC. 23 Procedure against partnership property for a partner's separate judgment debt

23(1) [Executions must be against firm] A writ of execution shall not issue against any partnership property except on a judgment against the firm.

23(2) [Order by court etc.] The High Court, or a judge thereof, a county court, may, on the application by summons of any judgment creditor of a partner, make an order charging that partner's interest in the partnership property and profits with payment of the amount of the judgment debt and interest thereon, and may by the same or a subsequent order appoint a receiver of that partner's share of profits (whether already declared or accruing), and of any other money which may be coming to him in respect of the partnership, and direct all accounts and inquiries, and give all other orders and directions which might have been directed or given if the charge had been made in favour of the judgment creditor by the partner, or which the circumstances of the case may require.

History
S. 23(2) amended by Courts Act 1971, Sch. 11, Pt. II.

23(3)   **[Right of redemption, purchase by other partner]**   The other partner or partners shall be at liberty at any time to redeem the interest charged, or in case of a sale being directed, to purchase the same.

23(4)   **[Cost-book companies]**   This section shall apply in the case of a cost-book company as if the company were a partnership within the meaning of this Act.

23(5)   **[Scotland]**   This section shall not apply to Scotland.

SEC. 24   Rules as to interests and duties of partners subject to special agreement

24   The interests of partners in the partnership property and their rights and duties in relation to the partnership shall be determined, subject to any agreement express or implied between the partners, by the following rules:—

(1) All the partners are entitled to share equally in the capital and profits of the business, and must contribute equally towards the losses whether of capital or otherwise sustained by the firm.

(2) The firm must indemnify every partner in respect of payments made and personal liabilities incurred by him—

     (a) In the ordinary and proper conduct of the business of the firm; or

     (b) In or about anything necessarily done for the preservation of the business or property of the firm.

(3) A partner making, for the purpose of the partnership, any actual payment or advance beyond the amount of capital which he has agreed to subscribe, is entitled to interest at the rate of five per cent per annum from the date of the payment or advance.

(4) A partner is not entitled, before the ascertainment of profits, to interest on the capital subscribed by him.

(5) Every partner may take part in the management of the partnership business.

(6) No partner shall be entitled to remuneration for acting in the partnership business.

(7) No person may be introduced as a partner without the consent of all existing partners.

(8) Any difference arising as to ordinary matters connected with the partnership business may be decided by a majority of the partners, but no change may

be made in the nature of the partnership business without the consent of all existing partners.

(9) The partnership books are to be kept at the place of business of the partnership (or the principal place, if there is more than one), and every partner may, when he thinks fit, have access to and inspect and copy any of them.

SEC. 25 Expulsion of partner

25 No majority of the partners can expel any partner unless a power to do so has been conferred by express agreement between the partners.

SEC. 26 Retirement from partnership at will

26(1) [Notice to all other partners] Where no fixed term has been agreed upon for the duration of the partnership, any partner may determine the partnership at any time on giving notice of his intention so to do to all the other partners.

26(2) [Partnership constituted by deed] Where the partnership has originally been constituted by deed, a notice in writing, signed by the partner giving it, shall be sufficient for this purpose.

SEC. 27 Where partnership for term is continued over, continuance on old terms presumed

27(1) [Where continuance] Where a partnership entered into for a fixed term is continued after the term has expired, and without any express new agreement, the rights and duties of the partners remain the same as they were at the expiration of the term, so far as is consistent with the incidents of a partnership at will.

27(2) [Presumed continuance] A continuance of the business by the partners or such of them as habitually acted therein during the term, without any settlement or liquidation of the partnership affairs, is presumed to be a continuance of the partnership.

SEC. 28 Duty of partners to render accounts, &c.

28 Partners are bound to render true accounts and full information of all things affecting the partnership to any partner or his legal representatives.

SEC. 29 Accountability of partners for private profits

29(1) [Every partner to account] Every partner must account to the firm for any benefit derived by him without the consent of the other partners from any transaction concerning the partnership, or from any use by him of the partnership property name or business connexion.

29(2) [Where partnership dissolved by death] This section applies also to transactions undertaken after a partnership has been dissolved by the death of a partner, and before the affairs thereof have been completely wound up, either by any surviving partner or by the representatives of the deceased partner.

SEC. 30 Duty of partner not to compete with firm

30 If a partner, without the consent of the other partners, carries on any business of the same nature as and competing with that of the firm, he must account for and pay over to the firm all profits made by him in that business.

SEC. 31 Rights of assignee of share in partnership

31(1) [Effect of assignment] An assignment by any partner of his share in the partnership, either absolute or by way of mortgage or redeemable charge, does not, as against the other partners, entitle the assignee, during the continuance of the partnership, to interfere in the management or administration of the partnership business or affairs, or to require any accounts of the partnership transactions, or to inspect the partnership books, but entitles the assignee only to receive the share of profits to which the assigning partner would otherwise be entitled, and the assignee must accept the account of profits agreed to by the partners.

31(2) [Where partnership dissolved] In case of a dissolution of the partnership, whether as respects all the partners or as respects the assigning partner, the assignee is entitled to receive the share of the partnership assets to which the assigning partner is entitled as between himself and the other partners, and, for the purpose of ascertaining that share, to an account as from the date of the dissolution.

DISSOLUTION OF PARTNERSHIP, AND ITS CONSEQUENCES

SEC. 32 Dissolution by expiration or notice

32 Subject to any agreement between the partners, a partnership is dissolved—

(a)   If entered into for a fixed term, by the expiration of that term:

(b)   If entered into for a single adventure or undertaking, by the termination of that adventure or undertaking:

(c)   If entered into for an undefined time, by any partner giving notice to the other or others of his intention to dissolve the partnership.

In the last-mentioned case the partnership is dissolved as from the date mentioned in the notice as the date of dissolution, or, if no date is so mentioned, as from the date of the communication of the notice.

SEC. 33 Dissolution by bankruptcy, death or charge

33(1) [Bankruptcy, death] Subject to any agreement between the partners, every partnership is dissolved as regards all the partners by the death or bankruptcy of any partner.

33(2) [Charge] A partnership may, at the option of the other partners, be dissolved if any partner suffers his share of the partnership property to be charged under this Act for his separate debt.

SEC. 34 Dissolution by illegality of partnership

34 A partnership is in every case dissolved by the happening of any event which makes it unlawful for the business of the firm to be carried on or for the members of the firm to carry it on in partnership.

SEC. 35 Dissolution by the Court

35 On application by a partner the Court may decree a dissolution of the partnership in any of the following cases:

(a) When a partner is found lunatic by inquisition, or in Scotland by cognition, or is shown to the satisfaction of the Court to be of permanently unsound mind, in either of which cases the application may be made as well on behalf of that partner by his committee or next friend or person having title to intervene as by any other partner:

(b) When a partner, other than the partner suing, becomes in any other way permanently incapable of performing his part of the partnership contract:

(c) When a partner, other than the partner suing, has been guilty of such conduct as, in the opinion of the Court, regard being had to the nature of the business, is calculated to prejudicially affect the carrying on of the business:

(d) When a partner, other than the partner suing, wilfully or persistently commits a breach of the partnership agreement, or otherwise so conducts himself in matters relating to the partnership business that it is not reasonably practicable for the other partner or partners to carry on the business in partnership with him:

(e) When the business of the partnership can only be carried on at a loss:

(f) Whenever in any case circumstances have arisen which, in the opinion of the Court, render it just and equitable that the partnership be dissolved.

History
S. 35(f) amended by National Health Service (Amendment) Act 1949, s. 714.

Note
S. 35(a) repealed for England and Wales by Mental Health Act 1959, Sch. 8, Pt. I.

SEC. 36 Rights of persons dealing with firm against apparent members of firm

36(1) **[After change]** Where a person deals with a firm after a change in its constitution he is entitled to treat all apparent members of the old firm as still being members of the firm until he has notice of the change.

36(2) **[Advertisement in Gazette]** An advertisement in the London Gazette as to a firm whose principal place of business is in England or Wales, in the Edinburgh Gazette as to a firm whose principal place of business is in Scotland, and in the Belfast Gazette as to a firm whose principal place of business is in Ireland, shall be notice as to persons who had not dealings with the firm before the date of the dissolution or change so advertised.

History
S. 36(2) amended by S.R. & O. 1921/1804, art. 7(a).

Note
Reference to Ireland to be construed as exclusive of Republic of Ireland: S.R. & O. 1923/405, art. 2.

36(3) **[Estate etc. not liable]** The estate of a partner who dies, or who becomes bankrupt, or of a partner who, not having been known to the person dealing with the firm to be a partner, retires from the firm, is not liable for partnership debts contracted after the date of the death, bankruptcy, or retirement respectively.

SEC. 37   Right of partners to notify dissolution

37   On the dissolution of a partnership or retirement of a partner any partner may publicly notify the same, and may require the other partner or partners to concur for that purpose in all necessary or proper acts, if any, which cannot be done without his or their concurrence.

SEC. 38   Continuing authority of partners for purposes of winding up

38   After the dissolution of a partnership the authority of each partner to bind the firm, and the other rights and obligations of the partners, continue notwithstanding the dissolution so far as may be necessary to wind up the affairs of the partnership, and to complete transactions begun but unfinished at the time of the dissolution, but not otherwise.

> Provided that the firm is in no case bound by the acts of a partner who has become bankrupt; but this proviso does not affect the liability of any person who has after the bankruptcy represented himself or knowingly suffered himself to be represented as a partner of the bankrupt.

SEC. 39   Rights of partners as to application of partnership property

39   On the dissolution of a partnership every partner is entitled, as against the other partners in the firm, and all persons claiming through them in respect of their interests as partners, to have the property of the partnership applied in payment of the debts and liabilities of the firm, and to have the surplus assets after such payment applied in payment of what may be due to the partner respectively after deducting what may be due from them as partners to the firm; and for that purpose any partner or his representatives may on the termination of the partnership apply to the Court to wind up the business and affairs of the firm.

SEC. 40   Apportionment of premium where partnership prematurely dissolved

40   Where one partner has paid a premium to another on entering into a partnership for a fixed term, and the partnership is dissolved before the expiration of that term otherwise than by the death of a partner, the Court may order the repayment of the premium, or of such part thereof as it thinks just, having regard to the terms of the partnership contract and to the length of time during which the partnership has continued; unless

(a) the dissolution is, in the judgment of the Court, wholly or chiefly due to the misconduct of the partner who paid the premium, or

(b) the partnership has been dissolved by an agreement containing no provision for a return of any part of the premium.

SEC. 41 Rights where partnership dissolved for fraud or misrepresentation

41 Where a partnership contract is rescinded on the ground of the fraud or misrepresentation of one of the parties thereto, the party entitled to rescind is, without prejudice to any other right, entitled—

(a) to a lien on, or right of retention of, the surplus of the partnership assets, after satisfying the partnership liabilities, for any sum of money paid by him for the purchase of a share in the partnership and for any capital contributed by him, and is

(b) to stand in the place of the creditors of the firm for any payments made by him in respect of the partnership liabilities, and

(c) to be indemnified by the person guilty of the fraud or making the representation against all the debts and liabilities of the firm.

SEC. 42 Right of outgoing partner in certain cases to share profits made after dissolution

42(1) **[Amount for outgoing partner or estate]** Where any member of a firm has died or otherwise ceased to be a partner, and the surviving or continuing partners carry on the business of the firm with its capital or assets without any final settlement of accounts as between the firm and the outgoing partner or his estate, then, in the absence of any agreement to the contrary, the outgoing partner or his estate is entitled at the option of himself or his repesentatives to such share of the profits made since the dissolution as the Court may find to be attributable to the use of his share of the partnership assets, or to interest at the rate of five per cent per annum on the amount of his share of the partnership assets.

42(2) **[Where option in partnership contract]** Provided that where by the partnership contract an option is given to surviving or continuing partners to purchase the interest of a deceased or outgoing partner, and that option is duly exercised, the estate of the deceased partner, or the outgoing partner or his estate, as the case may be, is not entitled to any further or other share of profits; but if any partner assuming to act in exercise of the option does not in all material respects comply with the terms thereof, he is liable to account under the foregoing provisions of this section.

SEC. 43 Retiring or deceased partner's share to be a debt

43 Subject to any agreement between the partners, the amount due from surviving or continuing partners to an outgoing partner or the representatives of a deceased partner in respect of the outgoing or deceased partner's share is a debt accruing at the date of the dissolution or death.

SEC. 44 Rule for distribution of assets on final settlement of accounts

44 In settling accounts between the partners after a dissolution of partnership, the following rules shall, subject to any agreement, be observed:

(a) Losses, including losses and deficiencies of capital, shall be paid first out of profits, next out of capital, and lastly, if necessary, by the partners individually in the proportion in which they were entitled to share profits:

(b) The assets of the firm including the sums, if any, contributed by the partners to make up losses or deficiencies of capital, shall be applied in the following manner and order:

(1) In paying the debts and liabilities of the firm to persons who are not partners therein:

(2) In paying to each partner rateably what is due from the firm to him for advances as distinguished from capital:

(3) In paying to each partner rateably what is due from the firm to him in respect of capital:

(4) The ultimate residue, if any, shall be divided among the partners in the proportion in which profits are divisible.

SUPPLEMENTAL

SEC. 45   Definitions of "court" and "business"

45   In this Act, unless the contrary intention appears,—

The expression **"court"** includes every court and judge having jurisdiction in the case:

The expression **"business"** includes every trade, occupation, or profession.

SEC. 46   Saving for rules of equity and common law

46   The rules of equity and of common law applicable to partnership shall continue in force except so far as they are inconsistent with the express provisions of this Act.

SEC. 47   Provision as to bankruptcy in Scotland

47(1)   [Bankruptcy to mean sequestration]   In the application of this Act to Scotland the bankruptcy of a firm or of an individual shall mean sequestration under the Bankruptcy (Scotland) Acts, and also in the case of an individual the issue against him of a decree of cessio bonorum.

47(2)   [Rules of law of Scotland]   Nothing in this Act shall alter the rules of the law of Scotland relating to the bankruptcy of a firm or of the individual partners thereof.

48, 49   (Repealed by Statute Law Revision Law Act 1908.)

SEC. 50   Short title

50   This Act may be cited as the Partnership Act 1890.

SCHEDULE

(Repealed by Statute Law Revision Act 1908.)

FORGED TRANSFERS ACT 1891

(54 & 55 Vict. c. 43)

An Act for preserving Purchasers of Stock from Losses by Forged Transfers

[*5th August 1891*]

SEC. 1 Power to make compensation for losses from forged transfer

1(1) **[Cash compensation]** Where a company or local authority issue or have issued shares, stock, or securities transferable by an instrument in writing or an exempt transfer, within the meaning of the Stock Transfer Act 1982 or by an entry, in any books or register kept by or on behalf of the company or local authority, they shall have power to make compensation by a cash payment out of their funds for any loss arising from a transfer of any such shares, stock, or securities, in pursuance of a forged instrument or of a transfer under a forged power of attorney, whether such loss arises, and whether the instrument or power of attorney was forged before or after the passing of this Act, and whether the person receiving such compensation, or any person through whom he claims, has or has not paid any fee or otherwise contributed to any fund out of which the compensation is paid.

1(1A) **["Instrument" in sec. 1(1)]** In subsection (1) above **"instrument"** has the same meaning as in Part I of the Forgery and Counterfeiting Act 1981.

History
S. 1(1) amended and s. 1(1A) added by Stock Transfer Act 1982, Sch. 2.

1(2) **[Fees for compensation fund]** Any company or local authority may, if they think fit, provide, either by fees not exceeding the rate of 5p on every one hundred pounds transferred with a minimum charge equal to that for twenty-five pounds to be paid by the transferee upon the entry of the transfer in the books of the company or local authority, or by insurance, reservation of capital, accumulation of income, or in any other manner which they may resolve upon, a fund to meet claims for such compensation.

History
S. 1(2) amended by Decimal Currency Act 1969, s. 10(1).

1(3) **[Borrowings to meet compensation]** For the purpose of providing such compensation any company may borrow on the security of their property, and any local authority may borrow with the like consent and on the like security and subject to the like conditions as to repayment by means of instalments or the provision of a sinking fund and otherwise as in the case of the securities in respect of which compensation is to be provided, but any money so borrowed by a local authority shall be repaid within a term not longer than five years. Any expenses incurred by a local authority in making compensation, or in the repayment of, or the payment of interest on, or otherwise in connexion with, any loan raised as aforesaid, shall, except so far as they may be met by such fees as aforesaid, be paid out of the fund or rate on which the security in respect of which compensation is to be made is charged.

1(4) **[Restrictions on transfers]** Any such company or local authority may impose such reasonable restrictions on the transfer of their shares, stock, or securities, or with respect to powers of attorney for the transfer thereof, as they may consider requisite for guarding against losses arising from forgery.

1(5) **[Remedies]** Where a company or local authority compensate a person under this Act for any loss arising from forgery, the company or local authority shall, without prejudice to any other rights or remedies, have the same rights and remedies against the person liable for the loss as the person compensated would have had.

SEC. 2 Definitions

2 For the purposes of this Act—

The expression "**company**" shall mean any company incorporated by or in pursuance of any Act of Parliament, or by royal charter.

The expression "**local authority**" shall mean the council of any county or municipal borough, and any authority having power to levy or require the levy of a rate the proceeds of which are applicable to public local purposes.

SEC. 3 Application to industrial societies, etc.

This Act shall apply to any industrial provident, friendly benefit, building, or loan society incorporated by or in pursuance of any Act of Parliament as if the society were a company.

SEC. 4 Application to habour and conservancy authorities

4(1) **[Application]** This act shall apply to any harbour authority or conservancy authority as if the authority were a company.

4(2) **["Harbour authority"]** For the purposes of this act the expression "**harbour authority**" includes all persons, being proprietors of, or entrusted with the duty or invested with power of constructing, improving, managing, regulating, maintaining, or lighting any harbour otherwise than for profit, and not being a joint stock company.

4(3) **["Conservancy authority"]** For the purposes of this Act the expression "**conservancy authority**" includes all persons entrusted with the duty or invested with the power of conserving, maintaining, or improving the navigation of any tidal water otherwise than for profit, and not being a joint stock company.

SEC. 5 Application to colonial stock

5 In the case of any colonial stock to which the Colonial Stock Act, 1877, applies, the Government of the colony of which the stock forms the whole or part of the public debt may, if they think fit, by declaration under their seal or under the signature of a person authorised by them in that behalf, and in either case deposited with the Commissioners of Inland Revenue, adopt this Act, and thereupon this Act shall apply to the colonial stock as if the registrar of the Government were a company and the stock were issued by him.

SEC. 6 Short title

6 This Act may be cited as the Forged Transfers Act, 1891.

FORGED TRANSFERS ACT 1892

An Act to remove doubts as to the meaning of the Forged Transfers Act, 1891

[*27th June 1892*]

[**CCH Note:** Only extant, non-amending provisions of this Act are reproduced here.]

SEC. 1   Short title

1   This Act may be cited as the Forged Transfers Act, 1892, and this Act and the Forged Transfers Act, 1891, may be cited together as the Forged Transfers Acts, 1891 and 1892.

SEC. 4   Provision where one company takes over shares, etc., of another company

4   Where the shares, stock, or securities of a company or local authority have by amalgamation or otherwise become the shares, stock, or securities of another company or local authority, the last-mentioned company and authority shall have the same power under the Forged Transfers Act, 1891, and this Act, as the original company or authority would have had if it had continued.

LIMITED PARTNERSHIPS ACT 1907

(7 Edw. 7 c. 24)

ARRANGEMENT OF SECTIONS

LIMITED PARTNERSHIPS ACT 1907

An Act to establish Limited Parterships.

[*28th August 1907*]

SEC. 1 Short title

1 This Act may be cited for all purposes as the Limited Partnerships Act 1907.

2 (Repealed by Statute Law Revision Act 1927.)

SEC. 3 Interpretation of terms

3 In the construction of this Act the following words and expressions shall have the meanings respectively assigned to them in this section, unless there be something in the subject or context repugnant to such construction:—

"**Firm**," "**firm name**," and "**business**" have the same meanings as in the Partnership Act 1890:

"**General partner**" shall mean any partner who is not a limited partner as defined by this Act.

SEC. 4 Definition and constitution of limited partnership

4(1) [Formation] Limited partnerships may be formed in the manner and subject to the conditions by this Act provided.

History
S. 4(1) amended by Statute Law Revision Act 1927.

4(2) [Constitution] A limited partnership shall not consist of more than twenty persons, and must consist of one or more persons called general partners, who shall be liable for all debts and obligations of the firm, and one or more persons to be called limited partners, who shall at the time of entering into such partnership contribute thereto a sum or sums as capital or property valued at a stated amount, and who shall not be liable for the debts or obligations of the firm beyond the amount so contributed.

History
S. 4(2) amended by Banking Act 1979, Sch. 7.

Note
S. 4(2) excluded by Companies Act 1985, s. 717(1), (2) and S.I. 1971 No. 782.

4(3) [Limitations] A limited partner shall not during the continuance of the partnership, either directly or indirectly, draw out or receive back any part of his contribution, and if he does so draw out or receive back any such part shall be liable for the debts and obligations of the firm up to the amount so drawn out or received back.

4(4) [Body corporate] A body corporate may be a limited partner.

SEC. 5 Registration of limited partnership required

5 Every limited partnership must be registered as such in accordance with the provisions of this Act, or in default thereof it shall be deemed to be a general partnership, and every limited partner shall be deemed to be a general partner.

SEC. 6 Modifications of general law in case of limited partnerships

6(1) **[Management, binding the firm]** A limited partner shall not take part in the management of the partnership business, and shall not have power to bind the firm:

Provided that a limited partner may by himself or his agent at any time inspect the books of the firm and examine into the state and prospects of the partnership business, and may advise with the partners thereon.

If a limited partner takes part in the management of the partnership business he shall be liable for all debts and obligations of the firm incurred while he so takes part in the management as though he were a general partner.

6(2) **[Limits on dissolution]** A limited partnership shall not be dissolved by the death or bankruptcy of a limited partner, and the lunacy of a limited partner shall not be a ground for dissolution of the partnership by the court unless the lunatic's share cannot be otherwise ascertained and realised.

Note
In s. 6(2) by Mental Treatment Act 1930, s. 20(5) reference
to "person of unsound mind" to be substituted for "lunatic".

6(3) **[Winding up of affairs]** In the event of the dissolution of a limited partnership its affairs shall be wound up by the general partners unless the court otherwise orders.

6(4) (Repealed by Statute Law Revision Act 1927.)

6(5) **[General]** Subject to any agreement expressed or implied between the partners—

(a) Any difference arising as to ordinary matters connected with the partnership business may be decided by a majority of the general partners;

(b) A limited partner may, with the consent of the general partners, assign his share in the partnership, and upon such an assignment the assignee shall become a limited partner with all the rights of the assignor;

(c) The other partners shall not be entitled to dissolve the partnership by reason of any limited partner suffering his share to be charged for his separate debt;

(d) A person may be introduced as a partner without the consent of the existing limited partners;

(e) A limited partner shall not be entitled to dissolve the partnership by notice.

SEC. 7 Law as to private partnerships to apply where not excluded by this Act

7 Subject to the provisions of this Act, the Partnership Act 1890, and the rules of equity and of common law applicable to partnerships, except so far as they are inconsistent with the express provisions of the last-mentioned Act, shall apply to limited partnerships.

SEC. 8 Manner and particulars of registration

8 The registration of a limited partnership shall be effected by sending by post or delivering to the registrar at the register office in that part of the United Kingdom in which the principal place of business of the limited partnership is situated or proposed to be situated a statement signed by the partners containing the following particulars:—

(a) The firm name;

(b) The general nature of the business;

(c) The principal place of business;

(d) The full name of each of the partners;

(e) The term, if any, for which the partnership is entered into, and the date of its commencement;

(f) A statement that the partnership is limited, and the description of every limited partner as such;

(g) The sum contributed by each limited partner, and whether paid in cash or how otherwise.

SEC. 9   Registration of changes in partnerships

9(1)   [Statement re changes to registrar]   If during the continuance of a limited partnership any change is made or occurs in—

(a) the firm name,

(b) the general nature of the business,

(c) the principal place of business,

(d) the partners or the name of any partner,

(e) the term of character of the partnership,

(f) the sum contributed by any limited partner,

(g) the liability of any partner by reason of his becoming a limited instead of a general partner or a general instead of a limited partner,

a statement, signed by the firm, specifying the nature of the change, shall within seven days be sent by post or delivered to the registrar at the register office in that part of the United Kingdom in which the partnership is registered.

9(2)   [Penalty on default]   If default is made in compliance with the requirements of this section each of the general partners shall, on conviction under the Magistrates' Courts Act 1952, be liable to a fine not exceeding one pound for each day during which the default continues.

History
S. 9(2) amended by Interpretation Act 1978, s. 17(2)(a).

SEC. 10   Advertisement in Gazette of statement of general partner becoming a limited partner and of assignment of share of limited partner

10(1)   [Notice]   Notice of any arrangement or transaction under which any person will cease to be a general partner in any firm, and will become a limited partner in that firm, or under which the share of a limited partner in a firm will be assigned to any person, shall be forthwith advertised in the Gazette, and until notice of the arrangement or transaction is so advertised the arrangement or transaction shall, for the purposes of this Act, be deemed to be of no effect.

10(2) ["**The Gazette**"] For the purposes of this section, the expression "**the Gazette**" means—

In the case of a limited partnership registered in England, the London Gazette;

In the case of a limited partnership registered in Scotland, the Edinburgh Gazette;

In the case of a limited partnership registered in Ireland, the Belfast Gazette.

History   Note
S. 10(2) amended by S.R. & O. 1921/1804, art. 7(a).   Reference to Ireland to be construed as exclusive of
                                                    Republic of Ireland: S.R. & O. 1923/405, art. 2.

11   (Repealed by Finance Act 1973, Sch. 22, Pt. V.)

12   (Repealed by Perjury Act 1911, Schedule and False Oaths (Scotland) Act 1933, Schedule.)

SEC. 13   Registrar to file statement and issue certificate of registration

13   On receiving any statement made in pursuance of this Act the registrar shall cause the same to be filed, and he shall send by post to the firm from whom such statement shall have been received a certificate of the registration thereof.

SEC. 14   Register and index to be kept

14   At each of the register offices herein-after referred to the registrar shall keep, in proper books to be provided for the purpose, a register and an index of all the limited partnerships registered as aforesaid, and of all the statements registered in relation to such partnerships.

SEC. 15   Registrar of joint stock companies to be registrar under Act

15   The registrar of joint stock companies shall be the registrar of limited partnerships, and the several offices for the registration of joint stock companies in London, Edinburgh, and Belfast shall be the offices for the registration of limited partnerships carrying on business within those parts of the United Kingdom in which they are respectively situated.

History
S. 15 amended by S.R. & O. 1921/1804, art. 7(b).

SEC. 16   Inspection of statements registered

16(1)   [**Inspection, certificates etc.**] Any person may inspect the statements filed by the registrar in the register offices aforesaid, and there shall be paid for such inspection such fees as may be appointed by the Board of Trade, not exceeding 5p for each inspection; and any person may require a certificate of the registration of any limited partnership, or a copy of or extract from any registered statement, to be certified by the registrar, and there shall be paid for such certificate of registration, certified copy, or extract such fees as the Board of Trade may appoint, not exceeding

10p for the certificate of registration, and not exceeding $2\frac{1}{2}$p for each folio of seventy-two words, or in Scotland for each sheet of two hundred words.

History
S. 16(1) amended by Decimal Currency Act 1969, s. 10(1).

Note
Re exercise of Functions by Secretary of State, see S.I. 1970 No. 1537, art. 2(1)(a).

16(2)   [Certificate to be received in evidence]   A certificate of registration, or a copy of or extract from any statement registered under this Act, if duly certified to be a true copy under the hand of the registrar or one of the assistant registrars (whom it shall not be necessary to prove to be the registrar or assistant registrar) shall, in all legal proceedings, civil or criminal, and in all cases whatsoever be received in evidence.

SEC. 17   Power to Board of Trade to make rules

17   The Board of Trade may make rules (but as to fees with the concurrence of the Treasury) concerning any of the following matters:—

  (a)   The fees to be paid to the registrar under this Act, so that they do not exceed in the case of the original registration of a limited partnership the sum of two pounds, and in any other case the sum of 25p;

  (b)   The duties or additional duties to be performed by the registrar for the purposes of this Act;

  (c)   The performance by assistant registrars and other officers of acts by this Act required to be done by the registrar;

  (d)   The forms to be used for the purposes of this Act;

  (e)   Generally the conduct and regulation of registration under this Act and any matters incidental thereto.

History
S. 17 amended by Decimal Currency Act 1969, s. 10(1).

Note
Re exercise of Functions by Secretary of State, see S.I. 1970 No. 1537, art. 2(1)(a).

FINANCE ACT 1930
(1930 Chapter 28)

[1st August 1930]

[CCH Note: Sec. 42 is the only extant provision of this Act with direct relevance to stamp duties.]

SEC. 42   Relief from transfer stamp duty in case of transfer of property as between associated companies

42(1)   [Transfer of property]   Stamp duty under the heading "Conveyance or Transfer on Sale" in the First Schedule to the Stamp Act 1891, shall not be chargeable on an instrument to which this section applies:

Provided that no such instrument shall be deemed to be duly stamped unless either it is stamped with the duty to which it would but for this section be liable, or it has in accordance with the provisions of section twelve of the said Act been stamped with a particular stamp denoting either that it is not chargeable with any duty or that it is duly stamped.

42(2) **[Beneficial interest from one body corporate to another]** This section applies to any instrument as respects which it is shown to the satisfaction of the Commissioners that the effect thereof is to convey or transfer a beneficial interest in property from one body corporate to another, and that the bodies in question are associated, that is to say, one is beneficial owner of not less than ninety per cent of the issued share capital of the other, or a third such body is beneficial owner of not less than ninety per cent of the issued share capital of each.

History
S. 42(2) substituted by Finance Act 1967, s. 27(2).

42(3) **[Ownership]** The ownership referred to in subsection (2) above is ownership either directly or through another body corporate or other bodies corporate, or partly directly and partly through another body corporate or other bodies corporate, and Part I of Schedule 4 to the Finance Act 1938 (determination of amount of capital held through other bodies corporate) shall apply for the purposes of this section with the substitution of references to issued share capital for references to ordinary share capital.

History
S. 42(3) substituted by Finance Act 1967, s. 27(2).

Note
S. 42 must be read in the light of Finance Act 1967, s. 27(3).

BORROWING (CONTROL AND GUARANTEES) ACT 1946

(9 & 10 Geo. 6 c. 58)

[12th July 1946]

SEC. 1 Treasury control of borrowing, etc.

1(1) **[Treasury orders]** The Treasury may make orders for regulating, subject to such exemptions as may be specified in the orders, all or any of the following transactions, that is to say—

    (a) the borrowing of money in Great Britain where the aggregate of the amount of money borrowed under the transaction and of any other amounts so borrowed by the same person in the previous twelve months (including any period before the passing of this Act) exceeds ten thousand pounds;

    (b) the raising of money in Great Britain by the issue, whether in Great Britain or elsewhere, by any body corporate, of any shares in that body corporate;

    (c) the issue for any purposes—

        (i) by any body corporate of any shares in or debentures or other securities of that body corporate, if either the body corporate is incorporated under the law of England or Scotland or the shares, debentures or other securities are or are to be registered in England or Scotland; or

(ii) by any Government, other than His Majesty's Government in the United Kingdom, of any securities of that Government which are or are to be registered in England or Scotland;

(d) the circulation in Great Britain of any offer for subscription, sale or exchange of—

(i) any shares in or debentures or other securities of any body corporate not incorporated under the law of England or Scotland; or

(ii) any securities of any Government other than His Majesty's Government in the United Kingdom:

Provided that paragraph (a) of this subsection shall not apply to the borrowing of money by any person in the ordinary course of his business from a person carrying on a banking undertaking.

1(2)   [Unit trust schemes]   The provisions of this section shall apply in relation to units under a unit trust scheme as they apply in relation to shares in a body corporate, but as if—

(a) any reference to the issue of shares in a body corporate by that body corporate were a reference to an issue of units for the purposes of the scheme; and

(b) any reference to shares in a body corporate incorporated, or not incorporated, under the law of England or Scotland were a reference to units issued under a scheme governed, or not governed, by the law of England or Scotland.

1(3)   [Effect of Schedule]   The provisions of the Schedule to this Act (which relate to enforcement and penalties) shall have effect in relation to orders made under this section but the rights of the persons concerned in any transaction shall not be affected by the fact that the transaction was in contravention of any such orders.

SEC. 3   Provisions as to orders

3(1)   [Annulment of orders]   Any order made under this Act shall be laid before Parliament as soon as may be after it is made, and if either House of Parliament within the period of forty days beginning with the day on which any such order is laid before it, resolves that the order be annulled, the order shall cease to have effect, but without prejudice to anything previously done thereunder or to the making of a new order.

3(2), (3)   (Repealed by Statute Law (Repeals) Act 1986, sec. 1(1) and Sch. 1 from 2 May 1986.)

History
S. 3(2), (3) formerly read as follows:

"**3(2)** In reckoning any such period of forty days, no account shall be taken of any time during which Parliament is dissolved or prorogued, or during which both Houses are adjourned for more than four days.

(3) Notwithstanding anything in subsection (4) of section one of the Rules Publication Act, 1893, an order made under this Act shall be deemed not to be, or to contain, a statutory rule to which that section applies."

3(4)   [Variation, revocation]   An order made under this Act may be varied or revoked by a subsequent order.

SEC. 4   Interpretation

4(1)   [Definitions]   In this Act, unless the context otherwise requires, the following expressions have the meanings hereby assigned to them, that is to say—

> "**issue**" includes reissue;
>
> "**local authority**" means any authority being within the meaning of the Local Loans Act, 1875, or the Local Authorities Loans (Scotland) Act, 1891, an authority having power to levy a rate;
>
> "**registered**", in relation to any security, includes inscribed, "**registered in England or Scotland**" means, in relation to securities, registered in a register in England or Scotland, and "**a register**", in relation to securities, includes any book in which securities are registered;
>
> "**security**" includes shares, bonds, notes, debentures, debenture stock and units under a unit trust scheme;
>
> "**share**" includes stock and any perpetual debenture or perpetual debenture stock;
>
> "**unit trust scheme**" means any arrangements made for the purpose, or having the effect, of providing facilities for the participation by persons, as beneficiaries under a trust, in profits or income arising from the acquisition, holding, management or disposal of securities or any other property whatsoever;
>
> "**unit**" means, in relation to a unit trust scheme, any right or interest, (described whether as a unit or otherwise) which may be acquired under the scheme, being a right or interest created or issued for the purpose of raising money for the purposes of the scheme or a right or interest created or issued in substitution (whether directly or indirectly) for any right or interest so created or issued.

4(2)   [Borrowing of money]   Any reference in this Act to the borrowing of money—

(a) includes a reference to the making of any arrangement by which a sum which would otherwise be payable at any date is payable at a later date, and includes in particular the making of any arrangement by which the whole or any part of the price of any property is allowed to remain unpaid either for a fixed period or indefinitely, but

(b) does not include a reference to the acceptance by a person carrying on a banking undertaking of moneys to be placed to the credit of a current or deposit account.

4(3)   [Person deemed borrower]   A person shall be deemed for the purposes of this Act to borrow or raise money in Great Britain if the money is made available in Great Britain, or, in any such case as is mentioned in subsection (2) of this section, if the money would, but for the arrangement in question, have been payable in Great Britain, and, without prejudice to the preceding provisions of this subsection, a person shall also be deemed for the purposes of this Act to borrow money in Great Britain if the money is borrowed on the security of property in Great Britain.

4(4)   [Guarantee arrangements]   An arrangement to provide any guarantee, or to mortgage or charge any property, to secure the repayment of any sum borrowed before the arrangement is made, being a sum which is already due when the arrangement is made or which is payable not later than six months, or such longer or shorter period as may be prescribed by order of the Treasury, after the arrangement is made, shall be deemed for the purposes of the two last preceding subsections to be an arrangement by which that sum is payable at a date later than it would otherwise have been payable.

4(5) [Sums payable] A sum which, at the time of, or by virtue of, the making of any arrangement, is payable on demand or on the expiration of a fixed period after demand shall be deemed for the purposes of the three last preceding subsections to be payable at the time of the making of the arrangement, or, as the case may be, on the expiration of the fixed period after the making of the arrangement, notwithstanding that no demand has been made.

SEC. 5 Expenses

5 Any expenses incurred by the Treasury in the administration of this Act shall be paid out of moneys provided by Parliament.

SEC. 6 Northern Ireland

6(1) [Northern Ireland] The provisions of this Act shall not extend to Northern Ireland.

6(2) (Repealed by Northern Ireland Constitution Act 1973, sec. 4, Sch. 6.)

SEC. 7 Short title

7 This Act may be cited as the Borrowing (Control and Guarantees) Act, 1946.

SCHEDULE

Section 1

PROVISIONS AS TO ENFORCEMENT AND PENALTIES

1 Any person who contravenes any provision of any order made under this Act shall be liable—

(a) on summary conviction to imprisonment for not more than three months or to a fine not exceeding the prescribed sum or to both such imprisonment and such fine; or

(b) on conviction on indictment to imprisonment for not more than two years or to a fine of any amount—

or to both such imprisonment and such fine.

2(1) The Treasury may give to any person directions requiring him, within such time and in such manner as may be specified in the directions, to furnish to them, or to any person designated in the directions as a person authorised to require it, any information in his possession or control which the Treasury or the person so authorised, as the case may be, may require for the purpose of securing compliance with, or detecting evasion of, any order made under this Act:

Provided that if a person required to give any information under this paragraph objects to the giving thereof on the ground that it might tend to incriminate that person or the husband or wife of that person, that person shall not be bound to give that information.

Nothing in this paragraph shall be taken to require any person who has acted as counsel or solicitor for any person to disclose any privileged communication made to him in that capacity.

2(2) The Treasury may give to any person directions requiring him, within such time and in such manner as may be specified in the directions, to produce such books, accounts or other documents (hereinafter referred to as "documents") in his possession or control as may be required for the purpose of securing compliance with, or detecting evasion of, any order made under this Act by the Treasury or by any person designated in the directions as a person authorised to require them and any documents produced by a person in compliance with any such requirements may be given in evidence against him notwithstanding that they may tend to incriminate him.

Nothing in this paragraph shall be taken to require any person who has acted as counsel or solicitor for any person to disclose any privileged communication made to him in that capacity.

2(3) If a justice of the peace is satisfied by information on oath given by an officer of the Treasury or with the authority of the Treasury that there is reasonable ground for suspecting that there are at any premises any documents which a person ought to have produced under the last preceding sub-paragraph but has failed or refused to produce, he may grant a search warrant authorising any constable, together with any other persons named in the warrant and any other constables, to enter the premises specified in the information (using such force as is reasonably necessary for the purpose) at any time within one month from the date of the warrant, and to search the premises and take possession of any documents appearing to be such documents as aforesaid or take in relation thereto any other steps which may appear necessary for preserving them and preventing interference therewith.

In this sub-paragraph the expression "a Justice of the Peace", in Scotland, includes the sheriff.

2(4) Any person who—

(a) fails or refuses to comply with any requirement to furnish information or produce documents imposed on him by or under this paragraph; or

(b) with intent to evade the provisions of this paragraph or of any order made under this Act destroys, mutilates, defaces, secretes or removes any documents; or

(c) obstructs any person exercising any powers conferred in him by or under this paragraph;

shall be liable, on summary conviction, to imprisonment for not more than three months or to a fine not exceeding level 3 on the standard scale or to both such imprisonment and such fine.

3(1) No proceedings for an offence under this Act shall be instituted in England except by or with the consent of the Director of Public Prosecutions.

3(2)   Any proceedings which may be taken against any person under this Act may be taken at any time not later than twelve months from the date of the commission of the alleged offence or within three months from the date on which evidence sufficient in the opinion of the Treasury to justify the proceedings comes to the knowledge of the Treasury, or, where the person in question was outside Great Britain at that date, within twelve months from the date on which he first lands in Great Britain thereafter whichever of the said periods last expires.

For the purposes of this sub-paragraph, a certificate of the Treasury as to the date on which such evidence as aforesaid came to the knowledge of the Treasury shall be conclusive evidence thereof.

This sub-paragraph shall, in its application to Scotland, have effect as if for the references to evidence sufficient to justify a prosecution there were substituted references to evidence sufficient to justify a report to the Lord Advocate with a view to consideration of the question of prosecution.

3(3)   Proceedings against any person in respect of an offence under this Act may be taken before the appropriate court in Great Britain having jurisdiction in the place where that person is for the time being.

3(4)   Where an offence under this Act has been committed by a body corporate (other than a local authority), every person who at the time of the commission of the offence was a director, general manager, secretary or similar officer of the body corporate, or was purporting to act in any such capacity, shall be deemed to be guilty of that offence, unless he proves that the offence was committed without his consent or connivance and that he exercised all such diligence to prevent the commission of the offence as he ought to have exercised having regard to the nature of his functions in that capacity and to all the circumstances.

History
Para. 1 amended by Magistrates' Courts Act 1980, s. 32(2) and Criminal Law Act 1977, s. 32(1); para. 2(1) amended by Civil Evidence Act 1968, s. 17(3), Sch. and para. 2(4) by Criminal Justice Act 1982, s. 37, 38, 46.

[The next page is 65,311]

STOCK TRANSFER ACT 1963

(1963 c. 18)

TABLE OF SECTIONS

SCHEDULES

An Act to amend the law with respect to the transfer of securities.

[*10th July 1963*]

SEC. 1 Simplified transfer of securities

1(1) [Transfer of certain securities] Registered securities to which this section applies may be transferred by means of an instrument under hand in the form set out in Schedule 1 to this Act (in this Act referred to as a stock transfer), executed by the transferor only and specifying (in addition to the particulars of the consideration, of the description and number or amount of the securities, and of the person by whom the transfer is made) the full name and address of the transferee.

1(2) [Execution, other particulars] The execution of a stock transfer need not be attested; and where such a transfer has been executed for the purpose of a stock exchange transaction, the particulars of the consideration and of the transferee may either be inserted in that transfer or, as the case may require, supplied by means of separate instruments in the form set out in Schedule 2 to this Act (in this Act referred to as brokers transfers), identifying the stock transfer and specifying the securities to which each such instrument relates and the consideration paid for those securities.

1(3) [Transfers apart from Act] Nothing in this section shall be construed as affecting the validity of any instrument which would be effective to transfer securities apart from this section; and any instrument purporting to be made in any form which was common or usual before the commencement of this Act, or in any other form authorised or required for that purpose apart from this section, shall be sufficient, whether or not it is completed in accordance with the form, if it complies with the requirements as to execution and contents which apply to a stock transfer.

Note
See Stock Transfer (Substitution of Forms) Order 1990
(S.I. 1990 No. 18), reg. 3, 4.

1(4) **[Application]** This section applies to fully paid up registered securities of any description, being—

  (a) securities issued by any company within the meaning of the Companies Act 1985 except a company limited by guarantee or an unlimited company;

  (b) securities issued by any body (other than a company within the meaning of the said Act) incorporated in Great Britain by or under any enactment or by Royal Charter except a building society within the meaning of the Building Societies Act 1986 or a society registered under the Industrial and Provident Societies Act 1893;

  (c) securities issued by the Government of the United Kingdom, except stock or bonds in the National Savings Stock Register and except national savings certificates;

  (d) securities issued by any local authority;

  (e) units of an authorised unit trust scheme or a recognised scheme within the meaning of the Financial Services Act 1986.

History

- S. 1 amended to facilitate the "Talisman" settlement system for transactions in securities on the Stock Exchange by the Stock Transfer (Addition of Forms) Order 1979, S.I. 1979 No. 277, effective from 4 April 1979. Rules 3 and 4 of that Order read as follows:

"**3(1)** Section 1 of the Stock Transfer Act 1963 shall have effect subject to the amendment that a sold transfer form, and a stock transfer form used to transfer securities to a stock exchange nominee, need not specify—

  (a) particulars of the consideration;

  (b) the address of the transferee.

(2) Section 1 of that Act shall have effect subject to the further amendment that a bought transfer form, and a stock transfer form used to transfer securities from a stock exchange nominee, need not, in the case of a transferor which is a body corporate, be executed under hand but shall be sufficiently executed by or on behalf of such transferor if they bear a facsimile of the corporate seal of the transferor, authenticated by the signature (whether actual or facsimile) of a director or the secretary of the transferor.

4 In this Order 'stock exchange nominee' has the same meaning as that given to it by section 7(2) of the Stock Exchange (Completion of Bargains) Act 1976."

- S. 1(4)(a) amended as from 1 July 1985 by Companies Consolidation (Consequential Provisions) Act 1985, Sch. 2.

- S. 1(4)(b) amended by Building Societies Act 1986, s. 120(1) and Sch. 18, Pt. I, para. 5 as from 1 January 1987 (see S.I. 1986 No. 1560 (C.56)).

- S. 1(4)(c) amended by Finance Act 1964, s. 24, 26(7), Sch. 8, para. 10, Sch. 10; Post Office Act 1969, s. 108(1)(f).

- S. 1(4)(e) substituted by Financial Services Act 1986, s. 212(2) and Sch. 16, para. 4(a) as from 29 April 1988 (see S.I. 1988 No. 740 (C. 22)): s. 1(4)(e) formerly read as follows:

"(e) units of a unit trust scheme, or other shares of the investments subject to the trusts of such a scheme, being a scheme in the case of which there is in force an order of the Board of Trade under section 17 of the Prevention of Fraud (Investments) Act 1958."

SEC. 2 Supplementary provisions as to simplified transfer

2(1) **[Application of sec. 1]** Section 1 of this Act shall have effect in relation to the transfer of any securities to which that section applies notwithstanding anything to the contrary in any enactment or instrument relating to the transfer of those securities; but nothing in that section affects—

  (a) any right to refuse to register a person as the holder of any securities on any ground other than the form in which those securities purport to be transferred to him: or

  (b) any enactment or rule of law regulating the execution of documents by companies or other bodies corporate, or any articles of association or other instrument regulating the execution of documents by any particular company or body corporate.

2(2) **[Application of other enactments and instruments]** Subject to the provisions of this section, any enactment or instrument relating to the transfer of securities to which section 1 of this Act applies shall, with any necessary modifications, apply in relation to an instrument of transfer authorised by that section as it applies in relation to an instrument of transfer to which it applies apart from this subsection; and without prejudice to the generality of the foregoing provision, the reference in section 184 of the Companies Act 1985 (certification of transfers) to any instrument of transfer shall be construed as including a reference to a brokers transfer.

History
S. 2(2) amended as from 1 July 1985 by Companies Consolidation (Consequential Provisions) Act 1985, Sch. 2.

2(3)   **[Interpretation]**   In relation to the transfer of securities by means of a stock transfer and a brokers transfer—

     (a)   any reference in any enactment or instrument (including in particular section 183(1) and (2) of the Companies Act 1985 and section 56(4) of the Finance Act 1946) to the delivery or lodging of an instrument (or proper instrument) of transfer shall be construed as a reference to the delivery or lodging of the stock transfer and the brokers transfer;

     (b)   any such reference to the date on which an instrument of transfer is delivered or lodged shall be construed as a reference to the date by which the later of those transfers to be delivered or lodged has been delivered or lodged; and

     (c)   subject to the foregoing provisions of this subsection, the brokers transfer (and not the stock transfer) shall be deemed to be the conveyance or transfer for the purposes of the enactments relating to stamp duty.

History
S. 2(3)(a) amended as from 1 July 1985 by Companies Consolidation (Consequential Provisions) Act 1985, Sch. 2.

2(4)   **[Application of sec. 1 to Scotland]**   Without prejudice to subsection (1) of this section, section 1 of this Act shall have effect, in its application to Scotland, notwithstanding anything to the contrary in any enactment relating to the execution of instruments or the validity of instruments delivered with particulars left blank; but so much of subsection (2) of that section as provides that the execution of a stock transfer need not be attested shall not apply to a transfer executed in accordance with section 18 of the Conveyancing (Scotland) Act 1924 on behalf of a person who is blind or unable to write.

SEC. 3   Additional provisions as to transfer forms

3(1)   **[Forms in Schedules]**   References in this Act to the forms set out in Schedule 1 and Schedule 2 include references to forms substantially corresponding to those forms respectively.

3(2)   **[Amendments to Schedules by order]**   The Treasury may by order amend the said Schedules either by altering the forms set out therein or by substituting different forms for those forms or by the addition of forms for use as alternatives to those forms; and references in this Act to the forms set out in those Schedules (including references in this section) shall be construed accordingly.

Note
See Stock Transfer (Substitution of Forms) Order 1990 (S.I. 1990 No. 18) — also S.I. 1974 No. 1214 and S.I. 1979 No. 277 — amendments included in Schedules.

3(3) [Direction in sec. 3(2) order] Any order under subsection (2) of this section which substitutes a different form for a form set out in Schedule 1 to this Act may direct that subsection (3) of section 1 of this Act shall apply, with any necessary modifications, in relation to the form for which that form is substituted as it applies to any form which was common or usual before the commencement of this Act.

3(4) [Order by statutory instrument] Any order of the Treasury under this section shall be made by statutory instrument, and may be varied or revoked by a subsequent order; and any statutory instrument made by virtue of this section shall be subject to annulment in pursuance of a resolution of either House of Parliament.

3(5) [Contents of sec. 3(2) order] An order under subsection (2) of this section may—

   (a) provide for forms on which some of the particulars mentioned in subsection (1) of section 1 of this Act are not required to be specified;

   (b) provide for that section to have effect, in relation to such forms as are mentioned in the preceding paragraph or other forms specified in the order, subject to such amendments as are so specified (which may include an amendment of the reference in subsection (1) of that section to an instrument under hand);

   (c) provide for all or any of the provisions of the order to have effect in such cases only as are specified in the order.

History
S. 3(5) inserted by Stock Exchange (Completion of Bargains) Act 1976, s. 6.

SEC. 4   Interpretation

4(1) [Definitions] In this Act the following expressions have the meanings hereby respectively assigned to them, that is to say—

   "**local authority**" means, in relation to England and Wales, any authority being, within the meaning of the Local Loans Act 1875, an authority having power to levy a rate and, in relation to Scotland, a county council, a town council and any statutory authority, commissioners or trustees to whom section 270 of the Local Government (Scotland) Act 1947 applies;

   "**registered securities**" means transferable securities the holders of which are entered in a register (whether maintained in Great Britain or not);

   "**securities**" means shares, stock, debentures, debenture stock, loan stock, bonds, units of a collective investment scheme within the meaning of the Financial Services Act 1986, and other securities of any description;

   "**stock exchange transaction**" means a sale and purchase of securities in which each of the parties is a member of a stock exchange acting in the ordinary course of his business as such or is acting through the agency of such a member;

   "**stock exchange**" means the Stock Exchange, London, and any other stock exchange (whether in Great Britain or not) which is declared by order of the Treasury to be a recognised stock exchange for the purposes of this Act.

History
In s. 4(1) in the definition of "securities" the words "collective investment scheme within the meaning of the Financial Services Act 1986" substituted for the former words "unit trust scheme, or other shares of the investments subject to the trusts of such a scheme" by Financial Services Act 1986, s. 212(2) and Sch. 16, para. 4(b) as from 29 April 1988 (see S.I. 1988 No. 740 (C. 22)).

4(2)   **[Order under section]**   Any order of the Treasury under this section shall be made by statutory instrument, and may be varied or revoked by a subsequent order.

SEC. 5   Application to Northern Ireland

5(1)   **[Limited application to Northern Ireland]**   This Act, so far as it applies to things done outside Great Britain, extends to Northern Ireland.

5(2)   **[Application of Act to securities in Northern Ireland register]**   Without prejudice to subsection (1) of this section, the provisions of this Act affecting securities issued by the Government of the United Kingdom shall apply to any such securities entered in a register maintained in Northern Ireland.

5(3)   (Repealed by Northern Ireland Constitution Act 1973, sec. 41(1), Sch. 6, Part I.)

5(4)   **[Extent]**   Except as provided by this section, this Act shall not extend to Northern Ireland.

SEC. 6   Short title and commencement

6(1)   **[Citation]**   This Act may be cited as the Stock Transfer Act 1963.

6(2)   **[Commencement]**   Subsection (3) of section 5 of this Act shall come into force on the passing of this Act, and the remaining provisions of this Act shall come into force on such date as the Treasury may by order made by statutory instrument direct.

[The next page is 65,351]

Stock Transfer Act 1963

SCHEDULES
Schedule 1 — Stock Transfer Form

Section 1

Certificate lodged with
the Registrar

(For completion by the
Registrar/Stock Exchange

Consideration Money	£ ....

Name of Undertaking.

Description of security.

Number or amount of Shares, Stock or other security and, in figures column only, number and denomination of units, if any.	Words	Figures
		(units of)

Name(s) of registered holder(s) should be given in full: the address should be given where there is only one holder.

in the name(s) of

If the transfer is not made by the registered holder(s) insert also the name(s) and capacity (e.g., Executor(s)), of the person(s) making the transfer.

Delete words in italics except for stock exchange transactions. Bodies corporate should execute under their common seal.

I/We hereby transfer the above security out of the name(s) aforesaid to the person(s) named below *or to the several persons named in Parts 2 of Brokers Transfer forms relating to the above security:*

Stamp of Selling Broker(s) or, for transactions which are not stock exchange transactions, of Agent(s), if any, acting for the Transferor(s).

Signature(s) of transferor(s)

1 ....   3 ....

2 ....   4 ....

Date ....

Full name(s), full postal address(es) (including County or, if applicable, Postal District number) of the person(s) to whom the security is transferred.

Please state title, if any, or whether Mr., Mrs., or Miss.

Please complete in typewriting or in Block Capitals.

I/We request that such entries be made in the register as are necessary to give effect to this transfer.

Stamp of Buying Broker(s) (if any).

Stamp or name and address of person lodging this form (if other than the Buying Broker(s)).

History
Stock transfer form amended by S.I. 1974 No. 1214.

Note
For exemption of stock transfers from stamp duty, see the Stamp Duty (Exempt Investments) Regulations 1987 (S.I. 1987 No. 516), reg. 2(1) and Sch.

TALISMAN
SOLD
TRANSFER

This transfer is exempt from Transfer Stamp Duty

Above this line for Registrar's use only

Bargain Reference No

Certificate lodged with Registrar

Name of Undertaking

Description of Security

(for completion by the Registrars/ Stock Exchange)

Amount of Stock or number of Stock units or shares or other security in words

Figures

In the name(s) of

Account Designation (if any)

Name(s) of registered holder(s) should be given in full; the address should be given where there is only one holder.

If the transfer is not made by the registered holder(s) insert also the name(s) and capacity (e.g. Executor(s)) of the person(s) making the transfer.

PLEASE SIGN HERE

I/We hereby transfer the above security out of the name(s) aforesaid into the name of   and request the necessary entries to be made in the register.

Balance Certificate Required for (amount or number in figures)

Bodies corporate should affix their common seal and each signatory should state his/her representative capacity (e.g. Company Secretary Director) agast his/her signature.

Stamp of Lodging Agent

1 _____

2 _____

3 _____

4 _____

Date

INSP Code (if applicable)

is lodging this transfer at the direction and on behalf of the Lodging Agent whose stamp appears herein ("the Original Lodging Agent") and does not in any manner or to any extent warrant or represent the validity, genuineness or correctness of the transfer instructions contained herein or the genuineness of the signature(s) of the transferor(s). The Original Lodging Agent be delivering this transfer to   authorises   to lodge this transfer for registration and agrees to be deemed for all purposes to be the person(s) actually lodging this transfer for registration

History

This sold transfer form substituted in Sch. 1 from 31 January 1990 by Stock Transfer (Substitution of Forms) Order 1990 (S.I. 1990 No.18), reg. 2 and Sch.: the former form was itself inserted from 4 April 1979, as an alternative to the stock transfer form preceding it, by Stock Transfer (Addition of Forms) Order 1979 (S.I. 1979 No. 277): for previous form see that 1979 Order set out in this tab division.

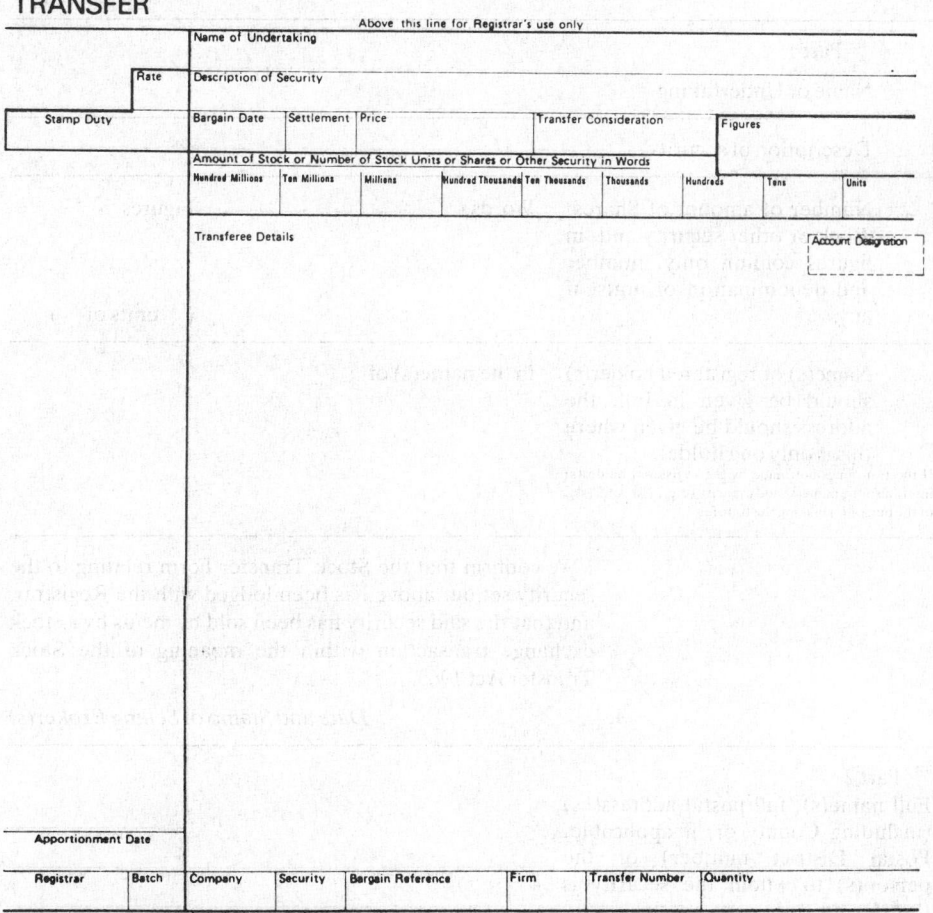

TALISMAN
BOUGHT
TRANSFER

Transfer Number

Above this line for Registrar's use only

		Name of Undertaking
	Rate	Description of Security
Stamp Duty		Bargain Date	Settlement	Price		Transfer Consideration	Figures

Amount of Stock or Number of Stock Units or Shares or Other Security in Words

Hundred Millions	Ten Millions	Millions	Hundred Thousands	Ten Thousands	Thousands	Hundreds	Tens	Units

Transferee Details

Account Designation

Apportionment Date

Registrar	Batch	Company	Security	Bargain Reference	Firm	Transfer Number	Quantity

hereby transfers the above security to the person(s) named under "Transferee Details" and requests the necessary entries to be made in the register. It confirms that the price and transfer consideration have been derived from information supplied by Member Firms.

is lodging this transfer at the direction and on behalf of the Member Firm whose code number appears herein ('the Original Lodging Agent') and does not in any manner or to any extent warrant or represent the validity or correctness of the transfer instructions contained herein. The Original Lodging Agent by instructing   to deliver this transfer for registration agrees to be deemed for all purposes to be the person(s) actually lodging this transfer for registration.

Dated

It is hereby certified on behalf of The Stock Exchange that the Stamp Duty indicated hereon has been or will be accounted for to the Commissioners of Inland Revenue pursuant to an agreement under Section 33 of the Finance Act 1970 as amended.

History
This bought transfer form, for use where registered securities to which s. 1 applies are transferred from a stock exchange nominee, inserted in Sch. 1 from 4 April 1979, as an alternative to the stock transfer form set out at the commencement of Sch. 1, by Stock Transfer (Addition of Forms) Order 1979, S.I. 1979, No. 277.

Schedule 2 — Brokers Transfer Form　　Section 1

Certificate lodged with the Registrar

Consideration Money	£................	(For completion by the Registrar/Stock Exchange)

Part 1

Name of Undertaking.

Description of security.

Number of amount of Shares, Stock or other security and, in figures column only, number and denomination of units, if any.	Words	Figures
		(units of)

Name(s) of registered holder(s) should be given in full: the address should be given where this is only one holder.

If the transfer is not made by the registered holder(s) insert also the name(s) and capacity (e.g., Executor(s)), of the person(s) making the transfer.

in the name(s) of

I/We confirm that the Stock Transfer Form relating to the security set out above has been lodged with the Registrar, and that the said security has been sold by me/us by a stock exchange transaction within the meaning of the Stock Transfer Act 1963.

Date and Stamp of Selling Broker(s)

Part 2

Full name(s), full postal address(es) (including County or, if applicable, Postal District number) of the person(s) to whom the security is transferred.

Please state title, if any, or whether Mr., Mrs. or Miss.

Please complete in typewriting or in Block Capitals.

I/We confirm that the security set out in Part 1 above has been purchased by a stock exchange transaction within the meaning of the Stock Transfer Act 1963, and I/we request that such entries be made in the register as are necessary to give effect to this transfer.

Stamp of Buying Broker(s).　　　　Stamp of Lodging Agent (if other than the Buying Broker(s)).

(Endorsement for use only in stock exchange transactions)

The security represented by the transfer overleaf has been sold as follows:

.... Shares/Stock   .... Shares/Stock

.... Shares/Stock   .... Shares/Stock

.... Shares/Stock   .... Shares/Stock

.... Shares/Stock   .... Shares/Stock

.... Shares/Stock   .... Shares/Stock

.... Shares/Stock   .... Shares/Stock

.... Shares/Stock   .... Shares/Stock

Balance (if any) due to Selling Broker(s) ....

Amount of Certificate(s)

Brokers Transfer forms for above amounts certified

Stamp of certifying Stock Exchange   *Stamp of Selling Broker(s)*

History
Brokers transfer form amended by S.I. 1974 No. 1214.

THEFT ACT 1968

(1968 Chapter 60)

[**CCH Note:** Only extant, non-amending provisions relevant to companies are reproduced here.]

SEC. 17   False accounting

17(1)   **[Penalty]**   Where a person dishonestly, with a view to gain for himself or another or with intent to cause loss to another,—

    (a) destroys, defaces, conceals or falsifies any account or any record or document made or required for any accounting purpose; or

    (b) in furnishing information for any purpose produces or makes use of any account, or any such record or document as aforesaid, which to his knowledge is or may be misleading, false or deceptive in a material particular;

he shall, on conviction on indictment, be liable to imprisonment for a term not exceeding seven years.

17(2)   **[Persons liable]**   For purposes of this section a person who makes or concurs in making in an account or other document an entry which is or may be misleading, false or deceptive in a material particular, or who omits or concurs in omitting a material particular from an account or other document, is to be treated as falsifying the account or document.

SEC. 18   Liability of company officers for certain offences by company

18(1)   **[Officers liable]**   Where an offence committed by a body corporate under section 15, 16 or 17 of this Act is proved to have been committed with the consent or connivance of any director, manager, secretary or other similar officer of the body corporate, or any person who was purporting to act in any such capacity, he as well as the body corporate shall be guilty of that offence, and shall be liable to be proceeded against and punished accordingly.

18(2)   **[Members liable]**   Where the affairs of a body corporate are managed by its members, this section shall apply in relation to the acts and defaults of a member in connection with his functions of management as if he were a director of the body corporate.

SEC. 19   False statements by company directors, etc.

19(1)   Where an officer of a body corporate or unincorporated association (or person purporting to act as such), with intent to deceive members or creditors of the body corporate or association about its affairs, publishes or concurs in publishing a written statement or account which to his knowledge is or may be misleading, false or deceptive in a material particular, he shall on conviction on indictment be liable to imprisonment for a term not exceeding seven years.

19(2)   For purposes of this section a person who has entered into a security for the benefit of a body corporate or association is to be treated as a creditor of it.

19(3)   Where the affairs of a body corporate or association are managed by its members, this section shall apply to any statement which a member publishes or concurs in publishing in connection with his functions of management as if he were an officer of the body corporate or association.

SEC. 20   Suppression, etc. of documents

20(1)   **[Penalty for destruction]**   A person who dishonestly, with a view to gain for himself or another or with intent to cause loss to another, destroys, defaces or conceals any valuable security, any will or other testamentary document or any original document of or belonging to, or filed or deposited in, any court of justice or any government department shall on conviction on indictment be liable to imprisonment for a term not exceeding seven years.

20(2)   **[Penalty for procuring execution of securities, etc.]**   A person who dishonestly, with a view to gain for himself or another or with intent to cause loss to another, by any deception procures the execution of a valuable security shall on conviction on indictment be liable to imprisonment for a term not exceeding seven years; and this subsection shall apply in relation to the making, acceptance, indorsement, alteration, cancellation or destruction in whole or in part of a valuable security, and in relation to the signing or sealing of any paper or other material in order that it may be made or converted into, or used or dealt with as, a valuable security, as if that were the execution of a valuable security.

20(3)   **[Definitions]**   For purposes of this section "**deception**" has the same meaning as in section 15 of this Act, and "**valuable security**" means any document creating, transferring, surrendering or releasing any right to, in or over property, or authorising the payment of money or delivery of any property, or evidencing the creation, transfer, surrender or release of any such right, or the payment of money or delivery of any property, or the satisfaction of any obligation.

FAIR TRADING ACT 1973

(1973 Chapter 41)

[CCH Note: Only certain provisions relating to merger control (other than that of newspapers) included.]

[25th July 1973]

PART V — MERGERS

OTHER MERGER REFERENCES

SEC. 63 Mergers references to which sec. 64 to 75 apply

63(1) [Construction]   Sections 64 to 75K of this Act shall not have effect in relation to newspaper merger references; and accordingly in those sections "**merger reference**" shall be construed—

(a) as not including a reference made under section 59 of this Act, but

(b) as including any merger reference relating to a transfer of a newspaper or of newspaper assets, if the reference is made under section 64 or section 75 of this Act in a case falling within section 59(2) of this Act.

History
In s. 63(1) the words "to 75K of this Act shall not have effect in relation to" substituted for the former words "to 75 of this Act shall have effect in relation to merger references other than" by CA 1989, s. 153 and Sch. 20, para. 3 as from 16 November 1989 (see CA 1989, s. 215(1)(b)(ii)).

63(2) [Definition]   In the following provisions of this Part of this Act "**enterprise**" means the activities, or part of the activities, of a business.

SEC. 64 Merger situation qualifying for investigation

64(1) [Merger references]   A merger reference may be made to the Commission by the Secretary of State where it appears to him that it is or may be the fact that two or more enterprises (in this section referred to as "the relevant enterprises"), of which one at least was carried on in the United Kingdom or by or under the control of a body corporate incorporated in the United Kingdom, have, at a time or in circumstances falling within subsection (4) of this section, ceased to be distinct enterprises, and that either—

(a) as a result, the condition specified in subsection (2) or in subsection (3) of this section prevails, or does so to a greater extent, with respect to the supply of goods or services of any description, or

(b) the value of the assets taken over exceeds £30 million.

History
S. 64(1)(b) figure increased by S.I. 1984 No. 932.

64(2) [Supply of goods]   The condition referred to in subsection (1)(a) of this section, in relation to the supply of goods of any description, is that at least one-quarter of all the goods of that description which are supplied in the United Kingdom, or in a substantial part of the United Kingdom, either—

(a) are supplied by one and the same person or are supplied to one and the same person, or

(b) are supplied by the persons by whom the relevant enterprises (so far as they continue to be carried on) are carried on, or are supplied to those persons.

64(3) **[Supply of services]** The condition referred to in subsection (1)(a) of this section, in relation to the supply of services of any description, is that the supply of services of that description in the United Kingdom, or in a substantial part of the United Kingdom, is, to the extent of at least one-quarter, either—

(a) supply by one and the same person, or supply for one and the same person, or

(b) supply by the persons by whom the relevant enterprises (so far as they continue to be carried on) are carried on, or supply for those persons.

64(4) **[Cessation of distinct enterprises]** For the purposes of subsection (1) of this section enterprises shall be taken to have ceased to be distinct enterprises at a time or in circumstances falling within this subsection if either—

(a) they did so not earlier than six months before the date on which the merger reference relating to them is to be made, or

(b) they did so under or in consequence of arrangements or transactions which were entered into without prior notice being given to the Secretary of State or to the Director of material facts about the proposed arrangements or transactions and in circumstances in which those facts had not been made public, and notice of those facts was not given to the Secretary of State or to the Director or made public more than six months before the date mentioned in the preceding paragraph.

64(5) **[Determination as soon as practicable]** In determining whether to make a merger reference to the Commission the Secretary of State shall have regard, with a view to the prevention or removal of uncertainty, to the need for making a determination as soon as is reasonably practicable.

64(6) **[Publication of reference]** On making a merger reference, the Secretary of State shall arrange for it to be published in such manner as he thinks most suitable for bringing it to the attention of persons who in his opinion would be affected by it.

64(7) **[Statutory instrument]** The Secretary of State may by order made by statutory instrument provide, subject to any transitional provisons contained in the order, that for the sum specified in subsection (1)(b) of this section (whether as originally enacted or as previously varied by an order under this subsection) there shall be substituted such other sum (not being less than £5 million) as is specified in the order.

64(8) **[Creation of merger situation]** The fact that two or more enterprises have ceased to be distinct enterprises in the circumstances described in subsection (1) of this section (including in those circumstances the result specified in paragraph (a), or fulfilment of the condition specified in paragraph (b), of that subsection) shall, for the purposes of this act, be regarded as creating a merger situation qualifying for investigation; and in this Act "**merger situation qualifying for investigation**" and any reference to the creation of such a situation shall be construed accordingly.

64(9)   [Definition]   In this section "**made public**" means so publicised as to be generally known or readily ascertainable.

SEC. 65   Enterprises ceasing to be distinct enterprises

65(1)   [Distinct enterprises]   For the purposes of this Part of this Act any two enterprises shall be regarded as ceasing to be distinct enterprises if either—

  (a) they are brought under common ownership or common control (whether or not the business to which either of them formerly belonged continues to be carried on under the same or different ownership or control), or

  (b) either of the enterprises ceases to be carried on at all and does so in consequence of any arrangements or transaction entered into to prevent competition between the enterprises.

65(2)   [Common control]   For the purposes of the preceding subsection enterprises shall (without prejudice to the generality of the words "common control" in that subsection) be regarded as being under common control if they are—

  (a) enterprises of interconnected bodies corporate, or

  (b) enterprises carried on by two or more bodies corporate of which one and the same person or group of persons has control, or

  (c) an enterprise carried on by a body corporate and an enterprise carried on by a person or group of persons having control of that body corporate.

65(3)   [Persons able to control policy]   A person or group of persons able, directly or indirectly, to control or materially to influence the policy of a body corporate, or the policy of any person in carrying on an enterprise, but without having a controlling interest in that body corporate or in that enterprise, may for the purposes of subsections (1) and (2) of this section be treated as having control of it.

65(4)   [Control of person carrying on enterprise]   For the purposes of subsection (1)(a) of this section, in so far as it relates to bringing two or more enterprises under common control, a person or group of persons may be treated as bringing an enterprise under his or their control if—

  (a) being already able to control or materially to influence the policy of the person carrying on the enterprise, that person or group of persons acquires a controlling interest in the enterprise, or, in the case of an enterprise carried on by a body corporate, acquires a controlling interest in that body corporate, or

  (b) being already able materially to influence the policy of the person carrying on the enterprise, that person or group of persons becomes able to control that policy.

SEC. 66   Time when enterprises cease to be distinct

66(1)   [Events treated as simultaneous]   Where under or in consequence of the same arrangements or transaction, or under or in consequence of successive arrangements or transactions between the same parties or interests, successive events to which this subsection applies occur within a period of two years, then for the purposes of a merger reference those events may, if the Secretary of State or the

Commission thinks fit, be treated as having occurred simultaneously on the date on which the latest of them occurred.

History

In s. 66(1) the words "or the Commission" inserted by CA 1989, s. 153 and Sch. 20, para. 4(a) as from 16 November 1989 (see CA 1989, s. 215(1)(b)(ii)).

66(2)   **[Applicable events]**   The preceding subsection applies to any event whereby, under or in consequence of the arrangements or the transaction or transactions in question, any enterprises cease as between themselves to be distinct enterprises.

66(3)   **[Arrangements between same interests]**   For the purposes of subsection (1) of this section any arrangements or transactions may be treated by the Secretary of State or the Commission as arrangements or transactions between the same interests if it appears to him to be appropriate that they should be so treated, having regard to the persons who are substantially concerned in them.

History

In s. 66(3) the words "or the Commission" inserted by CA 1989, s. 153 and Sch. 20, para. 4(a) as from 16 November 1989 (see CA 1989, s. 215(1)(b)(ii)).

66(4)   **[Time when enterprises cease to be distinct]**   Subject to the preceding provisions of this section and to section 66A of this Act, the time at which any two enterprises cease to be distinct enterprises, where they do so under or in consequence of any arrangements or transaction not having immediate effect, or having immediate effect in part only, shall be taken to be the time when the parties to the arrangements or transaction become bound to such extent as will result, on effect being given to their obligations, in the enterprises ceasing to be distinct enterprises.

History

In s. 66(4) the words "and to section 66A of this Act" inserted by CA 1989, s. 153 and Sch. 20, para. 4(b) as from 16 November 1989 (see CA 1989, s. 215(1)(b)(ii)).

66(5)   **[Options or conditional rights]**   In accordance with subsection (4) of this section (but without prejudice to the generality of that subsection) for the purpose of determining the time at which any two enterprises cease to be distinct enterprises no account shall be taken of any option or other conditional right until the option is exercised or the condition is satisfied.

SEC. 66A   Obtaining control by stages

66A(1)   **[Two sec. 66A(2) transactions on same day]**   Where an enterprise is brought under the control of a person or group of persons in the course of two or more transactions (referred to in this section as a "series of transactions") falling within subsection (2) of this section, those transactions may, if the Secretary of State or, as the case may be, the Commission thinks fit, be treated for the purposes of a merger reference as having occurred simultaneously on the date on which the latest of them occurred.

66A(2)   **["Series of transactions" by which control attained]**   The transactions falling within this subsection are—

     (a) any transaction which—

         (i) enables that person or group of persons directly or indirectly to control or materially to influence the policy of any person carrying on the enterprise,

(ii) enables that person or group of persons to do so to a greater degree, or

(iii) is a step (whether direct or indirect) towards enabling that person or group of persons to do so, and

(b) any transaction whereby that person or group of persons acquires a controlling interest in the enterprise or, where the enterprise is carried on by a body corporate, in that body corporate.

66A(3) [Any transaction after sec. 66A(2)(b) transaction] Where a series of transactions includes a transaction falling within subsection (2)(b) of this section, any transaction occurring after the occurrence of that transaction is to be diregarded for the purposes of subsection (1) of this section.

66A(4) [Where relevant period exceeds two years] Where the period within which a series of transactions occurs exceeds two years, the transactions that may be treated as mentioned in subsection (1) of this section are any of those transactions that occur within a period of two years.

66A(5) [Application of sec. 65(2)–(4), 77(1), (4)–(6)] Sections 65(2) to (4) and 77(1) and (4) to (6) of this Act apply for the purposes of this section to determine whether an enterprise is brought under the control of a person or group of persons and whether a transaction falls within subsection (2) of this section as they apply for the purposes of section 65 of this Act to determine whether enterprises are brought under common control.

66A(6) [Determination of time of transaction] In determining for the purposes of this section the time at which any transaction occurs, no account shall be taken of any option or other conditional right until the option is exercised or the condition is satisfied.

History
S. 66A inserted by CA 1989, s. 150(1) as from 16 November 1989 (see CA 1989, s. 215(1)(b)(i)).

Note
S. 66A does not apply in relation to any merger reference made before 16 November 1989 (see CA 1989, s. 150(2)).

SEC. 67   Valuation of assets taken over

67(1) [Effect] The provisions of this section shall have effect for the purposes of section 64(1)(b) of this Act.

67(2) [Value of assets] Subject to subsection (4) of this section, the value of the assets taken over—

(a) shall be determined by taking the total value of the assets employed in, or appropriated to, the enterprises which cease to be distinct enterprises, except

(i) any enterprise which remains under the same ownership and control, or

(ii) if none of the enterprises remains under the same ownership and control, the enterprise having the assets with the highest value, and

(b) shall be so determined by reference to the values at which, on the enterprises ceasing to be distinct enterprises or (if they have not then done so) on the making of the merger reference to the Commission, the assets stand in the books of the relevant business, less any relevant provisions for depreciation, renewals or diminution in value.

History
In s. 67(2)(a) para. (i) and (ii) substituted by CA 1989, s. 153 and Sch. 20, para. 5(1) as from 16 November 1989 (see CA 1989, s. 215(1)(b)(ii)); the former words read as follows:

"any enterprise which remains under the same ownership and control, or if none of the enterprises remains under the same ownership and control, then that one of the enterprises having the assets with the highest value, and".

67(3)   [Appropriation of assets]   For the purposes of subsection (2) of this section any assets of a body corporate which, on a change in the control of the body corporate or of any enterprise of it, are dealt with in the same way as assets appropriated to any such enterprise shall be treated as appropriated to that enterprise.

67(4)   [Events treated as simultaneous]   Where in accordance with subsection (1) of section 66 or subsection (1) of section 66A of this Act events to which either of those subsections applies are treated as having occurred simultaneously, subsection (2) of this section shall apply with such adjustments as appear to the Secretary of State or to the Commission to be appropriate.

History
In s. 67(4) the words "or subsection (1) of section 66A" inserted and the words "either of those subsections" substituted for the former words "that subsection" by CA
1989, s. 153 and Sch. 20, para. 5(2) as from 16 November 1989 (see CA 1989, s. 215(1)(b)(ii)).

SEC. 68   Supplementary provisions as to merger situations qualifying for investigation

68(1)   [Appropriate construction]   In relation to goods or services of any description which are the subject of different forms of supply—

(a) references in subsection (2) of section 64 of this Act to the supply of goods, or

(b) references in subsection (3) of that section to the supply of services,

shall be construed in whichever of the following ways appears to the Secretary of State or the Commission, as the case may be, to be appropriate in all the circumstances, that is to say, as references to any of those forms of supply taken separately, to all those forms of supply taken together, or to any of those forms of supply taken in groups.

68(2)   [Material differences]   For the purposes of the preceding subsection the Secretary of State or the Commission may treat goods or services as being the subject of different forms of supply whenever the transactions in question differ as to their nature, their parties, their terms or their surrounding circumstances, and the difference is one which, in the opinion of the Secretary of State or of the Commission, as the case may be, ought for the purposes of that subsection to be treated as a material difference.

68(3)   [Applicable criteria]   For the purpose of determining whether the proportion of one-quarter mentioned in subsection (2) or subsection (3) of section 64 of this Act is fulfilled with respect to goods or services of any description, the Secretary of State or the Commission, as the case may be, shall apply such criterion (whether it be value or cost or price or quantity or capacity or number of workers employed or some other criterion, of whatever nature) or such combination of criteria as may appear to the Secretary of State or the commission to be most suitable in all the circumstances.

68(4)   [Goods and services]   The criteria for determining when goods or services can be treated, for the purposes of section 64 of this Act, as goods or services of a separate description shall be such as in any particular case the Secretary of State or, as the case may be, the Commission thinks most suitable in the circumstances of that case.

History
In s. 68(4) the words "or, as the case may be, the Commission" inserted by CA 1989, s. 153 and Sch. 20, para. 6 as from 16 November 1989 (see CA 1989, s. 215(1)(b)(ii)).

SEC. 69   Different kinds of merger references

69(1)   [Investigation and report]   Subject to the following provisions of this Part of this Act, on a merger reference the Commission shall investigate and report on the questions—

(a) whether a merger situation qualifying for investigation has been created, and

(b) if so, whether the creation of that situation operates, or may be expected to operate, against the public interest.

69(2)   [Exclusions from consideration]   A merger reference may be so framed as to require the Commission, in relation to the question whether a merger situation qualifying for investigation has been created, to exclude from consideration paragraph (a) of subsection (1) of section 64 of this Act, or to exclude from consideration paragraph (b) of that subsection, or to exclude one of those paragraphs if the Commission find the other satisfied.

69(3)   [Confinement of investigation]   In relation to the question whether any such result as is mentioned in section 64(1)(a) of this Act has arisen, a merger reference may be so framed as to require the Commission to confine their investigation to the supply of goods or services in a specified part of the United Kingdom.

69(4)   [Limitation of investigation]   A merger reference may require the Commission, if they find that a merger situation qualifying for investigation has been created, to limit their consideration thereafter to such elements in, or possible consequences of, the creation of that situation as may be specified in the reference, and to consider whether, in respect only of those elements or possible consequences, the situation operates, or may be expected to operate, against the public interest.

SEC. 70   Time-limit for report on merger reference

70(1)   [Period for report to be made]   Every merger reference shall specify a period (not being longer than six months beginning with the date of the reference) within which a report on the reference is to be made; and a report of the Commission on a merger reference shall not have effect, and no action shall be taken in relation to it under this Act, unless the report is made before the end of that period or of such further period (if any) as may be allowed by the Secretary of State in accordance with the next following subsection.

70(2)   [Extension of time limit]   The Secretary of State shall not allow any further period for a report on a merger reference except on representations made by the Commission and on being satisfied that there are special reasons why the report cannot be made within the period specified in the reference; and the Secretary of State shall allow only one such further period on any one reference, and no such further period shall be longer than three months.

SEC. 71   Variation of certain merger references

71(1)   **[Variation]**   Subject to the following provisions of this section, the Secretary of State may at any time vary a merger reference.

History
In s. 71(1) the words "made under section 69(4) of this Act" formerly appearing at the end omitted by CA 1989, s. 153 and Sch. 20, para. 7(a) and repealed by CA 1989, s. 212 and Sch. 24 as from 16 November 1989 (see CA 1989, s. 215(1)(b)(ii), (d)).

71(2)   (Omitted by Companies Act 1989, sec. 153 and Sch. 20, para. 7(b) and repealed by Companies Act 1989, sec. 212 and Sch. 24 as from 16 November 1989.)

History
In regard to the omission and repeal of s. 71(2), see CA 1989, s. 215(b)(iii), (d); it formerly read as follows: "**71(2)**   A merger reference made under section 69(4) of this Act shall not be so varied that it ceases to be a reference limited in accordance with that subsection."

71(3)   **[Further restriction]**   Without prejudice to the powers of the Secretary of State under section 70 of this Act, a merger reference shall not be varied so as to specify a period within which a report on the reference is to be made which is different from the period specified in the reference in accordance with that section.

SEC. 72   Report of Commission on merger reference

72(1)   **[Matters to be in report]**   In making their report on a merger reference, the Commission shall include in it definite conclusions on the questions comprised in the reference, together with—

    (a)   such an account of their reasons for those conclusions, and

    (b)   such a survey of the general position with respect to the subject-matter of the reference, and of the developments which have led to that position,

as in their opinion are expedient for facilitating a proper understanding of those questions and of their conclusions.

72(2)   **[Effects adverse to public interest]**   Where on a merger reference the Commission find that a merger situation qualifying for investigation has been created and that the creation of that situation operates or may be expected to operate against the public interest (or, in a case falling within subsection (4) of section 69 of this Act, find that one or more elements in or consequences of that situation which were specified in the reference in accordance with that subsection so operate or may be expected so to operate) the Commission shall specify in their report the particular effects, adverse to the public interest, which in their opinion the creation of that situation (or, as the case may be, those elements in or consequences of it) have or may be expected to have; and the Commission—

    (a)   shall, as part of their investigations, consider what action (if any) should be taken for the purpose of remedying or preventing those adverse effects, and

    (b)   may, if they think fit, include in their report recommendations as to such action.

72(3)   **[Action to remedy adverse effect]**   In paragraph (a) of subsection (2) of this section the reference to action to be taken for the purpose mentioned in that paragraph is a reference to action to be taken for that purpose either—

    (a)   by one or more Ministers (including Ministers or departments of the Government of Northern Ireland) or other public authorities, or

FTA 1973, sec. 71(1)

(b) by one or more persons specified in the report as being persons carrying on, owning or controlling any of the enterprises which, in accordance with the conclusions of the Commission, have ceased to be distinct enterprises.

SEC. 73   Order of Secretary of State on report on merger reference

73(1) [Application]   The provisions of this section shall have effect where a report of the commission on a merger reference has been laid before Parliament in accordance with the provisions of Part VII of this act, and the conclusions of the commission set out in the report, as so laid,—

(a) include conclusions to the effect that a merger situation qualifying for investigation has been created and that its creation, or particular elements in or consequences of it specified in the report, operate or may be expected to operate against the public interest, and

(b) specify particular effects, adverse to the public interest, which in the opinion of the Commission the creation of that situation, or (as the case may be) those elements in or consequences of it, have or may be expected to have.

73(2) [Schedule 8 powers]   In the circumstances mentioned in the preceding subsection the Secretary of State may by order made by statutory instrument exercise such one or more of the powers specified in Parts I and II of Schedule 8 to this Act as he may consider it requisite to exercise for the purpose of remedying or preventing the adverse effects specified in the report as mentioned in the preceding subsection; and those powers may be so exercised to such extent and in such manner as the Secretary of State considers requisite for that purpose.

73(3) [Recommendations of Commission]   In determining whether, or to what extent or in what manner, to exercise any of those powers, the Secretary of State shall take into account any recommendations included in the report of the Commission in pursuance of section 72(2)(b) of this Act and any advice given by the Director under section 88 of this Act.

SEC. 74   Interim order in respect of merger reference

74(1) [Content of orders]   Where a merger reference has been made to the Commission, then, with a view to preventing action to which this subsection applies, the Secretary of State, subject to subsection (3) of this section, may by order made by statutory instrument—

(a) prohibit or restrict the doing of things which in his opinion would constitute action to which this subsection applies, or

(b) impose on any person concerned obligations as to the carrying on of any activities or the safeguarding of any assets, or

(c) provide for the carrying on of any activities or the safeguarding of any assets either by the appointment of a person to conduct or supervise the conduct of any activities (on such terms and with such powers as may be specified or described in the order) or in any other manner, or

(d) exercise any of the powers which, by virtue of paragraphs 12 and 12A of Schedule 8 to this Act, are exercisable by an order under section 73 of this Act.

History

In s. 74(1) the words "and does not impose on the Commission a limitation under section 69(4) of this Act" omitted by CA 1989, s. 153 and Sch. 20, para. 8(a) and repealed by CA 1989, s. 212 and Sch. 24; and in para. (d) the words "paragraphs 12 and 12A" substituted for the former words "paragraph 12" by CA 1989, s. 153 and Sch. 20, para. 8(b) as from 16 November 1989 (see CA 1989, s. 215(b)(iii), (d)).

74(2) [Application of sec. 74(1)] In relation to a merger reference the preceding subsection applies to any action which might prejudice the reference or impede the taking of any action under this Act which may be warranted by the Commission's report on the reference.

74(3) [Restriction on orders] No order shall be made under this section in respect of a merger reference after whichever of the following events first occurs, that is to say—

(a) the time (including any further period) allowed to the Commission for making a report on the reference expires without their having made such a report;

(b) the period for forty days beginning with the day on which a report of the Commission on the reference is laid before Parliament expires.

74(4) [Cessation of orders] An order under this section made in respect of a merger reference (if it has not previously ceased to have effect) shall cease to have effect on the occurrence of whichever of those events first occurs, but without prejudice to anything previously done under the order.

74(5) [Restricted application of sec. 74(4)] Subsection (4) of this section shall have effect without prejudice—

(a) to the operation, in relation to any such order, of section 134(1) of this Act, or

(b) to the operation of any order made under section 73 of this Act which exercises the same or similar powers to those exercised by the order under this section.

SEC. 75 Reference in anticipation of merger

75(1) [Merger references] A merger reference may be made to the Commission by the Secretary of State where it appears to him that it is or may be the fact that arrangements are in progress or in contemplation which, if carried into effect, will result in the creation of a merger situation qualifying for investigation.

75(2) [Procedure on reference] Subject to the following provisions of this section, on a merger reference under this section the Commission shall proceed in relation to the prospective and (if events so require) the actual results of the arrangements proposed or made as, in accordance with the preceding provisions of this Part of this Act, they could proceed if the arrangements in question had actually been made, and the results in question had followed immediately before the date of the reference under this section.

75(3) [Limitation of Commission's consideration] A merger reference under this section may require the Commission, if they find that a merger situation qualifying for investigation has been created, or will be created if the arrangements in question are carried into effect, to limit their consideration thereafter to such elements in, or possible consequences of, the creation of that situation as may be specified in the reference, and to consider whether, in respect only of those elements or possible consequences, the situation might be expected to operate against the public interest.

75(4) **[Application of other provisions]** In relation to a merger reference under this section, sections 66, 66A, 67, 69, 71, 72, 73 and 74 of this Act shall apply subject to the following modifications, that is to say—

(a) section 66 shall apply, where an event by which any enterprises cease as between themselves to be distinct enterprises will occur if the arrangements are carried into effect, as if the event had occurred immediately before the date of the reference;

(aa) section 66A shall apply, where a transaction falling within subsection (2) of that section will occur if the arrangements are carried into effect, as if the transaction had occurred immediately before the date of the reference;

(b) in section 67(4) the references to subsection (1) of section 66 and subsection (1) of section 66A shall be construed as references to those subsections as modified in accordance with paragraph (a) or (aa) of this subsection;

(c) in section 69, subsection (1) shall be construed as modified by subsection (2) of this section; in subsections (2) and (3) any reference to the question whether a merger situation qualifying for investigation has been created, or whether a result mentioned in section 64(1)(a) of this Act has arisen, shall be construed as including a reference to the question whether such a situation will be created or such a result will arise if the arrangements in question are carried into effect; and subsection (4) of that section shall not apply;

(d) in section 71, in section 72(2) and in section 74(1), the references to section 69(4) of this Act shall be construed as references to subsection (3) of this section; and

(e) in section 73(1), the reference to conclusions to the effect that a merger situation qualifying for investigation has been created shall be construed as including a reference to conclusions to the effect that such a situation will be created if the arrangements in question are carried into effect.

History
In s. 75(4) "66A" inserted and para. (a), (aa) and (b) substituted for the former para. (a) and (b) by CA 1989, s. 153 and Sch. 20, para. 9 as from 16 November 1989 (see CA 1989, s. 215(1)(b)(ii)); the former para. (a) and (b) read as follows:

"(a) section 66 shall apply with the necessary adaptations in relation to enterprises which will or may cease to be distinct enterprises under or in consequence of arrangements not yet carried into effect or not yet fully carried into effect;

(b) in section 67(4) the reference to subsection (1) of section 66 shall be construed as a reference to that subsection as modified in accordance with the preceding paragraph;".

75(4A) **[Effect of merger reference]** Where a merger reference is made under this section, it shall be unlawful, except with the consent of the Secretary of State under subsection (4C) of this section—

(a) for any person carrying on any enterprise to which the reference relates or having control of any such enterprise or for any subsidiary of his, or

(b) for any person associated with him or for any subsidiary of such a person, directly or indirectly to acquire, at any time during the period mentioned in subsection (4B) of this section, an interest in shares in a company if any enterprise to which the reference relates is carried on by or under the control of that company.

History
See history note after s. 75(4M).

75(4B) **[Period in sec. 75(4A)]** The period referred to in subsection (4A) of this section is the period beginning with the announcement by the Secretary of State of the making of the merger reference concerned and ending—

(a) where the reference is laid aside at any time, at that time,

(b) where the time (including any further period) allowed to the Commission for making a report on the reference expires without their having made such a report, on the expiration of that time,

(c) where a report of the Commission on the reference not including such conclusions as are referred to in section 73(1)(b) of this Act is laid before Parliament, at the end of the day on which the report is so laid,

(d) where a report of the Commission on the reference including such conclusions is laid before Parliament, at the end of the period of forty days beginning with the day on which the report is so laid,

and where such a report is laid before each House on different days, it is to be treated for the purposes of this subsection as laid on the earlier day.

History
See history note after s. 75(4M).

75(4C) **[Secretary of State's consent]** The consent of the Secretary of State—

(a) may be either general or special,

(b) may be revoked by the Secretary of State, and

(c) shall be published in such way as, in the opinion of the Secretary of State, to give any person entitled to the benefit of it an adequate opportunity of getting to know of it, unless in the Secretary of State's opinion publication is not necessary for that purpose.

History
See history note after s. 75(4M).

75(4D) **[Application of sec. 93]** Section 93 of this Act applies to any contravention or apprehended contravention of subsection (4A) of this section as it applies to a contravention or apprehended contravention of an order to which section 90 of this Act applies.

History
See history note after s. 75(4M).

75(4E) **[Interpretation of sec. 75(4A)]** Subsections (4F) to (4K) of this section apply for the interpretation of subsection (4A).

History
See history note after s. 75(4M).

75(4F) **[Circumstances where person acquires interest in shares]** The circumstances in which a person acquires an interest in shares include those where—

(a) he enters into a contract to acquire the shares (whether or not for cash),

(b) not being the registered holder, he acquires a right to exercise, or to control the exercise of, any right conferred by the holding of the shares, or

(c) he acquires a right to call for delivery of the shares to himself or to his order or to acquire an interest in the shares or assumes an obligation to acquire such an interest,

but does not include those where he acquires an interest in pursuance of an obligation assumed before the announcement by the Secretary of State of the making of the merger reference concerned.

History
See history note after s. 75(4M).

75(4G)　[Circumstances where sec. 75(4F) right acquired]　The circumstances in which a person acquires a right mentioned in subsection (4F) of this section—

(a) include those where he acquires a right or asumes an obligation the exercise or fulfilment of which would give him that right, but

(b) does not include those where he is appointed as proxy to vote at a specified meeting of a company or of any class of its members or at any adjournment of the meeting or he is appointed by a corporation to act as its representative at any meeting of the company or of any class of its members,

and references to rights and obligations in this subsection and subsection (4F) of this section include conditional rights and conditional obligations.

History
See history note after s. 75(4M).

75(4H)　[Person carrying on or having control of enterprise]　Any reference to a person carrying on or having control of any enterprise includes a group of persons carrying on or having control of an enterprise and any member of such a group.

History
See history note after s. 75(4M).

75(4J)　[Application of sec. 65(2)–(4), 77(1), (4)–(6)]　Sections 65(2) to (4) and 77(1) and (4) to (6) of this Act apply to determine whether any person or group of persons has control of any enterprise and whether persons are associated as they apply for the purposes of section 65 of this Act to determine whether enterprises are brought under common control.

History
See history note after s. 75(4M).

75(4K)　["Subsidiary"]　"Subsidiary" has the meaning given by section 736 of the Companies Act 1985, but that section and section 736A of that Act also apply to determine whether a company is a subsidiary of an individual or of a group of persons as they apply to determine whether it is a subsidiary of a company and references to a subsidiary in subsections (8) and (9) of section 736A as so applied are to be read accordingly.

History
See history note after s. 75(4M).

75(4L)　["Company", "share"]　In this section—

"**company**" includes any body corporate, and

"**share**" means share in the capital of a company, and includes stock.

History
See history note after s. 75(4M).

75(4M)　[Acts outside UK]　Nothing in subsection (4A) of this section makes anything done by a person outside the United Kingdom unlawful unless he is—

   (a) a British citizen, a British Dependent Territories citizen, a British Overseas citizen or a British National (Overseas),

   (b) a body corporate incorporated under the law of the United Kingdom or of a part of the United Kingdom, or

   (c) a person carrying on business in the United Kingdom, either alone or in partnership with one or more other persons.

History
S. 75(4A)–(4M) inserted by CA 1989, s. 149(1) as from 16 November 1989 (see CA 1989, s. 215(1)(b)(i)).

Note
S. 75(4A)–(4M) do not apply to any merger reference made before 16 November 1989 (see CA 1989, s. 149(2)).

75(5) [Abandonment of proposals] If, in the course of their investigations on a merger reference under this section, it appears to the Commission that the proposal to make arrangements such as are mentioned in the reference has been abandoned, the Commission—

   (a) shall, if the Secretary of State consents, lay the reference aside, but

   (b) shall in that case furnish to the Secretary of State such information as he may require as to the results until then of the investigations.

RESTRICTION ON POWER TO MAKE MERGER REFERENCE WHERE PRIOR NOTICE HAS BEEN GIVEN

SEC. 75A General rule where notice given by acquirer and no reference made within period for considering notice

75A(1) [Notice] Notice may be given to the Director by a person authorised by regulations to do so of proposed arrangements which might result in the creation of a merger situation qualifying for investigation.

Note
See the Merger (Prenotification) Regulations 1990 (S.I. 1990 No. 501).

75A(2) [Form of notice] The notice must be in the prescribed form and state that the existence of the proposal has been made public.

75A(3) [If period expires] If the period for considering the notice expires without any reference being made to the Commission with respect to the notified arrangements, no reference may be made under this Part of this Act to the Commission with respect to those arrangements or to the creation or possible creation of any merger situation qualifying for investigation which is created in consequence of carrying those arrangements into effect.

75A(4) [Qualification to sec. 75A(3)] Subsection (3) of this section is subject to sections 75B(5) and 75C of this Act.

75A(5) ["Merger notice"] A notice under subsection (1) of this section is referred to in sections 75B to 75F of this Act as a "merger notice".

History
See history note after s. 75F.

SEC. 75B The role of the Director

75B(1) [Duty of Director] The Director shall, when the period for considering any merger notice begins, take such action as he considers appropriate to bring the existence of the proposal, the fact that the merger notice has been given and the date on which the period for considering the notice may expire to the attention of those who in his opinion would be affected if the arrangements were carried into effect.

75B(2)   [Period for considering merger notice]   The period for considering a merger notice is the period of twenty days, determined in accordance with subsection (9) of this section, beginning with the first day after—

(a) the notice has been received by the Director, and

(b) any fee payable to the Director in respect of the notice has been paid.

75B(3)   [Extension of sec. 75B(2) period]   The Director may, and shall if required to do so by the Secretary of State, by notice to the person who gave the merger notice—

(a) extend the period mentioned in subsection (2) of this section by a further ten days, and

(b) extend that period as extended under paragraph (a) of this subsection by a further fifteen days.

75B(4)   [Request for information]   The Director may by notice to the person who gave the merger notice request him to provide the Director within such period as may be specified in the notice with such information as may be so specified.

75B(5)   [Where sec. 75G undertakings]   If the Director gives to the person who gave the merger notice (in this subsection referred to as "the relevant person") a notice stating that the Secretary of State is seeking undertakings under section 75G of this Act, section 75A(3) of this Act does not prevent a reference being made to the Commission unless—

(a) after the Director has given that notice, the relevant person has given a notice to the Director stating that he does not intend to give such undertakings, and

(b) the period of ten days beginning with the first day after the notice under paragraph (a) of this subsection was received by the Director has expired.

75B(6)   [Sec. 75B(3), (4), (5) notice]   A notice by the Director under subsection (3), (4) or (5) of this section must either be given to the person who gave the merger notice before the period for considering the merger notice expires or be sent in a properly addressed and pre-paid letter posted to him at such time that, in the ordinary course of post, it would be delivered to him before that period expires.

75B(7)   [Rejection of notice]   The Director may, at any time before the period for considering any merger notice expires, reject the notice if—

(a) he suspects that any information given in respect of the notified arrangements, whether in the merger notice or otherwise, by the person who gave the notice or any connected person is in any material respect false or misleading,

(b) he suspects that it is not proposed to carry the notified arrangements into effect, or

(c) any prescribed information is not given in the merger notice or any information requested by notice under subsection (4) of this section is not provided within the period specified in the notice.

75B(8)   [Where sec. 75B(3)(b) extension but no recommendation]   If—

(a) under subsection (3)(b) of this section the period for considering a merger notice has been extended by a further fifteen days, but

(b) the Director has not made any recommendation to the Secretary of State under section 76(b) of this Act as to whether or not it would in the Director's opinion be expedient for the Secretary of State to make a reference to the Commission with respect to the notified arrangements,

then, during the last five of those fifteen days, the power of the Secretary of State to make a reference to the Commission with respect to the notified arrangements is not affected by the absence of any such recommendation.

75B(9)   [Determining period for sec. 75B(2), (3), (5)]   In determining any period for the purposes of subsections (2), (3) and (5) of this section no account shall be taken of—

(a) Saturday, Sunday, Good Friday and Christmas Day, and

(b) any day which is a bank holiday in England and Wales.

History
See history note after s. 75F.

SEC. 75C   Cases where power to refer unaffected

75C(1)   [Effect of sec. 75A(3)]   Section 75A(3) of this Act does not prevent any reference being made to the Commission if—

(a) before the end of the period for considering the merger notice, it is rejected by the Director under section 75B(7) of this Act,

(b) before the end of that period, any of the enterprises to which the notified arrangements relate cease to be distinct from each other,

(c) any information (whether prescribed information or not) that—

  (i) is, or ought to be, known to the person who gave the merger notice or any connected person, and

  (ii) is material to the notified arrangements;

  is not disclosed to the Secretary of State or the Director by such time before the end of that period as may be specified in regulations,

(d) at any time after the merger notice is given but before the enterprises to which the notified arrangements relate cease to be distinct from each other, any of those enterprises ceases to be distinct from any enterprise other than an enterprise to which those arrangements relate,

(e) the six months beginning with the end of the period for considering the merger notice expires without the enterprises to which the notified arrangements relate ceasing to be distinct from each other,

(f) the merger notice is withdrawn, or

(g) any information given in respect of the notified arrangements, whether in the merger notice or otherwise, by the person who gave the notice or any connected person is in any material respect false or misleading.

Note
Re s. 75C(1)(C) see the Merger (Prenotification)
Regulations 1990 (S.I. 1990 No. 501).

75C(2) **[Further restriction re effect of sec. 75A(3)]** Where—

   (a) two or more transactions which have occurred or, if any arrangements are carried into effect, will occur may be treated for the purposes of a merger reference as having occurred simultaneously on a particular date, and

   (b) subsection (3) of section 75A of this Act does not prevent such a reference with respect to the last of those transactions,

that subsection does not prevent such a reference with respect to any of those transactions which actually occurred less than six months before—

   (i) that date, or

   (ii) the actual occurrence of another of those transactions with respect to which such a reference may be made (whether or not by virtue of this subsection).

75C(3) **[Determining time of transaction for sec. 75C(2)]** In determining for the purposes of subsection (2) of this section the time at which any transaction actually occurred, no account shall be taken of any option or other conditional right until the option is exercised or the condition is satisfied.

History
See history note after s. 75F.

SEC. 75D   Regulations

75D(1) **[Power of Secretary of State]** The Secretary of State may make regulations for the purposes of sections 75A to 75C of this Act.

75D(2) **[Scope of regulations]** The regulations may, in particular—

   (a) provide for section 75B(2) or (3) or section 75C(1)(e) of this Act to apply as if any reference to a period of days or months were a reference to a period specified in the regulations for the purposes of the provision in question,

   (b) provide for the manner in which any merger notice is authorised or required to be given, rejected or withdrawn, and the time at which any merger notice is to be treated as received or rejected,

   (c) provide for the manner in which any information requested by the Director or any other material information is authorised or required to be provided or disclosed, and the time at which such information is to be treated as provided or disclosed,

   (d) provide for the manner in which any notice under section 75B of this Act is authorised or required to be given,

   (e) provide for the time at which any notice under section 75B(5)(a) of this Act is to be treated as received,

   (f) provide for the address which is to be treated for the purposes of section 75B(6) of this Act and of the regulations as a person's proper address,

   (g) provide for the time at which any fee is to be treated as paid, and

   (h) provide that a person is, or is not, to be treated, in such circumstances as may be specified in the regulations, as acting on behalf of a person authorised by regulations to give a merger notice or a person who has given such a notice.

75D(3)   **[Different provisions]**   The regulations may make different provision for different cases.

75D(4)   **[By statutory instrument]**   Regulations under this section shall be made by statutory instrument.

History
See history note after s. 75F.

Note
See the Merger (Prenotification) Regulations 1990 (S.I. 1990 No. 501).

SEC. 75E   Interpretation of sec. 75A to 75D

75E   In this section and sections 75A to 75D of this Act—

"**connected person**", in relation to the person who gave a merger notice, means—

(a) any person who, for the purposes of section 77 of this Act, is associated with him, or

(b) any subsidiary of the person who gave the merger notice or of any person so associated with him,

"**merger notice**" is to be interpreted in accordance with section 75A(5) of this Act,

"**notified arrangements**" means the arrangements mentioned in the merger notice or arrangements not differing from them in any material respect,

"**prescribed**" means prescribed by the Director by notice having effect for the time being and published in the London, Edinburgh and Belfast Gazettes,

"**regulations**" means regulations under section 75D of this Act, and

"**subsidiary**" has the meaning given by section 75(4K) of this Act,

and references to the enterprises to which the notified arrangements relate are references to those enterprises that would have ceased to be distinct from one another if the arrangements mentioned in the merger notice in question had been carried into effect at the time when the notice was given.

History
See history note after s. 75F.

SEC. 75F   Power to amend sec. 75B to 75D

75F(1)   **[Power of Secretary of State]**   The Secretary of State may, for the purpose of determining the effect of giving a merger notice and the steps which may be or are to be taken by any person in connection with such a notice, by regulations made by statutory instrument amend sections 75B to 75D of this Act.

75F(2)   **[Different provisions]**   The regulations may make different provision for different cases and may contain such incidental and supplementary provisions as the Secretary of State thinks fit.

75F(3)   **[Approval by Parliament]**   No regulations shall be made under this section unless a draft of the regulations has been laid before and approved by resolution of each House of Parliament.

History
S. 75A to 75F inserted by CA 1989, s. 146 as from 1 April 1990 (see S.I. 1990 No. 142 (C. 5), art. 6(b)).

UNDERTAKINGS AS ALTERNATIVE TO MERGER REFERENCE

SEC. 75G   Acceptance of undertakings

75G(1)   [Powers of Secretary of State]   Where—

(a)   the Secretary of State has power to make a merger reference to the Commission under section 64 or 75 of this Act,

(b)   the Director has made a recommendation to the Seretary of State under section 76 of this Act that such a reference should be made, and

(c)   the Director has (in making that recommendation or subsequently) given advice to the Secretary of State specifying particular effects adverse to the public interest which in his opinion the creation of the merger situation qualifying for investigation may have or might be expected to have,

the Secretary of State may, instead of making a merger reference to the Commission, accept from such of the parties concerned as he considers appropriate undertakings complying with subsections (2) and (3) of this section to take specified action which the Secretary of State considers appropriate to remedy or prevent the effects adverse to the public interest specified in the advice.

75G(2)   [Contents of undertakings]   The undertakings must provide for one or more of the following—

(a)   the division of a business by the sale of any part of the undertaking or assets or otherwise (for which purpose all the activities carried on by way of business by any one person or by any two or more interconnected bodies corporate may be treated as a single business),

(b)   the division of a group of interconnected bodies corporate, and

(c)   the separation, by the sale of any part of the undertaking or assets concerned or other means, of enterprises which are under common control otherwise than by reason of their being enterprises of interconnected bodies corporate.

75G(3)   [Other provisions in undertakings]   The undertakings may also contain provision—

(a)   preventing or restricting the doing of things which might prevent or impede the division or separation,

(b)   as to the carrying on of any activities or the safeguarding of any assets until the division or separation is effected,

(c)   for any matters necessary to effect or take account of the division or separation, and

(d)   for enabling the Secretary of State to ascertain whether the undertakings are being fulfilled.

75G(4)   [Effect of acceptance of undertakings]   If the Secretary of State has accepted one or more undertakings under this section, no reference may be made to the Commission with respect to the creation or possible creation of the merger situation qualifying for investigation by reference to which the undertakings were accepted, except in a case falling within subsection (5) of this section.

75G(5)   [Qualification to sec. 75G(4)]   Subsection (4) of this section does not prevent a reference being made to the Commission if material facts about the arrangements or transactions, or proposed arrangements or transactions, in consequence of which the enterprises concerned ceased or may cease to be distinct enterprises were not—

(a) notified to the Secretary of State or the Director, or

(b) made public,

before the undertakings were accepted.

75G(6) **["Made public" in sec. 75G(5)]** In subsection (5) of this section **"made public"** has the same meaning as in section 64 of this Act.

History
See history note after s. 75K.

SEC. 75H   Publication of undertakings

75H(1) **[Duty of Secretary of State]** The Secretary of State shall arrange for—

(a) any undertaking accepted by him under section 75G of this Act,

(b) the advice given by the Director for the purposes of subsection (1)(c) of that section in any case where such an undertaking has been accepted, and

(c) any variation or release of such an undertaking,

to be published in such manner as he may consider appropriate.

75H(2) **[Giving advice for sec. 75G(1)(c) purposes]** In giving advice for the purposes of section 75G(1)(c) of this Act the Director shall have regard to the need for excluding, so far as practicable, any matter to which subsection (4) of this section applies.

75H(3) **[Duty of Secretary of State re exclusion]** The Secretary of State shall exclude from any such advice as published under this section—

(a) any matter to which subsection (4) of this section applies and in relation to which he is satisfied that its publication in the advice would not be in the public interest, and

(b) any other matter in relation to which he is satisfied that its publication in the advice would be against the public interest.

75H(4) **[Matters excluded from publication]** This subsection applies to—

(a) any matter which relates to the private affairs of an individual, where publication of that matter would or might, in the opinion of the Director or the Secretary of State, as the case may be, seriously and prejudicially affect the interests of that individual, and

(b) any matter which relates specifically to the affairs of a particular body of persons, whether corporate or incorporate, where publication of that matter would or might, in the opinion of the Director or the Secretary of State, as the case may be, seriously and prejudicially affect the interests of that body, unless in his opinion the inclusion of that matter relating specifically to that body is necesary for the purposes of the advice.

75H(5) **[Absolute privilege re sec. 75G(1)(c) matters]** For the purposes of the law relating to defamation, absolute privilege shall attach to any advice given by the Director for the purposes of section 75G(1)(c) of this Act.

History
See history note after s. 75K.

SEC. 75J Review of undertakings

75J Where an undertaking has been accepted by the Secretary of State under section 75G of this Act, it shall be the duty of the Director—

    (a) to keep under review the carrying out of that undertaking, and from time to time consider whether, by reason of any change of circumstances, the undertaking is no longer appropriate and either—

        (i) one or more of the parties to it can be released from it, or

        (ii) it needs to be varied or to be superseded by a new undertaking, and

    (b) if it appears to him that the undertaking has not been or is not being fulfilled, that any person can be so released or that the undertaking needs to be varied or superseded, to give such advice to the Secretary of State as he may think proper in the circumstances.

History
See history note after s. 75K.

SEC. 75K Order of Secretary of State where undertaking not fulfilled

75K(1) [Application] The provisions of this section shall have effect where it appears to the Secretary of State that an undertaking accepted by him under section 75G of this Act has not been, is not being or will not be fulfilled.

75K(2) [Power of Secretary of State to exercise Sch. 8 powers] The Secretary of State may by order made by statutory instrument exercise such one or more of the powers specified in paragraphs 9A and 12 to 12C and Part II of Schedule 8 to this Act as he may consider it requisite to exercise for the purpose of remedying or preventing the adverse effects specified in the advice given by the Director for the purposes of section 75G(1)(c) of this Act; and those powers may be so exercised to such extent and in such manner as the Secretary of State considers requisite for that purpose.

75K(3) [Sec. 75J(b) advice to be considered] In determining whether, or to what extent or in what manner, to exercise any of those powers, the Secretary of State shall take into account any advice given by the Director under section 75J(b) of this Act.

75K(4) [Order may differ from undertaking] The provision contained in an order under this section may be different from that contained in the undertaking.

75K(5) [Effect of order] On the making of an order under this section, the undertaking and any other undertaking accepted under section 75G of this Act by reference to the same merger situation qualifying for investigation are released by virtue of this section.

History
S. 75G–75K inserted by CA 1989, s. 147 as from 16 November 1989 (see CA 1989, s. 215(1)(b)(i)).

SUPPLEMENTARY

SEC. 76 Functions of Director in relation to merger situations

76(1) [Duty of Director] It shall be the duty of the Director—

    (a) to take all such steps as are reasonably practicable for keeping himself informed about actual or prospective arrangements or transactions which may constitute or result in the creation of merger situations qualifying for investigation, and

(b) to make recommendations to the Secretary of State as to any action under this Part of this Act which in the opinion of the Director it would be expedient for the Secretary of State to take in relation to any such arrangements or transactions.

76(2)   [Matters to be considered]   In exercising his duty under this section the Director shall take into consideration any representations made to him by persons appearing to him to have a substantial interest in any such arrangements or transactions or by bodies appearing to him to represent substantial numbers of persons who have such an interest.

History
S. 76(2) added by CA 1989, s. 153 and Sch. 20, para. 11 as
from 16 November 1989 (see CA 1989, s. 215(1)(b)(ii).

SEC. 77   Associated persons

77(1)   [Persons treated as one person]   For the following purposes, that is to say—

(a) for the purpose of determining under section 57(1) of this Act whether a person is a newspaper proprietor and, if so, which newspapers are his newspapers;

(b) for the purpose of determining under section 65 of this Act whether any two enterprises have been brought under common ownership or common control; and

(c) for the purpose of determining what activities are carried on by way of business by any one person, in so far as that question arises in the application, by virtue of an order under section 73 of this Act, of paragraph 14 of Schedule 8 to this Act,

associated persons, and any bodies corporate which they or any of them control, shall (subject to the next following subsection) be treated as one person.

77(2)   [Restriction on sec. 77(1)]   The preceding subsection shall not have effect—

(a) for the purpose mentioned in paragraph (a) of that subsection so as to exclude from section 58 of this Act any case which would otherwise fall within that section, or

(b) for the purpose mentioned in paragraph (b) of the preceding subsection so as to exclude from section 65 of this Act any case which would otherwise fall within that section.

77(3)   [Excluded matters]   A merger reference other than a newspaper merger reference (whether apart from this section the reference could be made or not) may be so framed as to exclude from consideration, either altogether or for any specified purpose or to any specified extent, any matter which, apart from this section, would not have been taken into account on that reference.

77(4)   [Associates]   For the purposes of this section the following persons shall be regarded as associated with one another, that is to say—

(a) any individual and that individual's husband or wife and any relative, or husband or wife of a relative, of that individual or of that individual's husband or wife;

(b) any person in his capacity as trustee of a settlement and the settlor or grantor and any person associated with the settlor or grantor;

(c) persons carrying on business in partnerhsip and the husband or wife and relatives of any of them;

(d) any two or more persons acting together to secure or exercise control of a body corporate or other association or to secure control of any enterprise or assets.

77(5) **["Control"]** The reference in subsection (1) of this section to bodies corporate which associated persons control shall be construed as follows, that is to say—

(a) in its application for the purpose mentioned in paragraph (a) of that subsection, "**control**" in that reference means having a controlling interest within the meaning of section 57(4) of this Act, and

(b) in its application for any other purpose mentioned in subsection (1) of this section, "**control**" in that reference shall be construed in accordance with section 65(3) and (4) of this Act.

77(6) **[Interpretation]** In this section "**relative**" means a brother, sister, uncle, aunt, nephew, niece, lineal ancestor or descendant (the stepchild or illegitimate child of any person, or anyone adopted by a person, whether legally or otherwise, as his child, being taken into account as a relative or to trace a relationship in the same way as that person's child); and references to a wife or husband shall include a former wife or husband and a reputed wife or husband.

PART VIII — ADDITIONAL PROVISIONS RELATING TO REFERENCES TO COMMISSION

SEC. 84   Public interest

84(1) **[Matters to be considered]** In determining for any purposes to which this section applies whether any particular matter operates, or may be expected to operate, against the public interest, the Commission shall take into account all matters which appear to them in the particular circumstances to be relevant and, among other things, shall have regard to the desirability—

(a) of maintaining and promoting effective competition between persons supplying goods and services in the United Kingdom;

(b) of promoting the interests of consumers, purchasers and other users of goods and services in the United Kingdom in respect of the prices charged for them and in respect of their quality and the variety of goods and services supplied;

(c) of promoting, through competition, the reduction of costs and the development and use of new techniques and new products, and of facilitating the entry of new competitors into existing markets;

   (d) of maintaining and promoting the balanced distribution of industry and employment in the United Kingdom; and

   (e) of maintaining and promoting competitive activity in markets outside the United Kingdom on the part of producers of goods, and of suppliers of goods and services, in the United Kingdom.

84(2)   **[Application]**   This section applies to the purposes of any functions of the Commission under this Act other than functions to which section 59(3) of this Act applies.

SEC. 93A   Enforcement of undertakings

93A(1)   **[Application]**   This section applies where a person (in this section referred to as "the responsible person") has given an undertaking which—

   (a) has been accepted by the Secretary of State under section 75G of this Act,

   (b) has been accepted by the appropriate Minister or Ministers under section 88 of this Act after the commencement of this section, or

   (c) has been accepted by the Director under section 4 or 9 of the Competition Act 1980 after that time.

93A(2)   **[Right to bring civil proceedings]**   Any person may bring civil proceedings in respect of any failure, or apprehended failure, of the responsible person to fulfil the undertaking, as if the obligations imposed by the undertaking on the responsible person had been imposed by an order to which section 90 of this Act applies.

History
S. 93A inserted by CA 1989, s. 148 as from 16 November
1989 (see CA 1989, s. 215(1)(b)(i)).

SEC. 93B   False or misleading information

93B(1)   **[Offence]**   If a person furnishes any information—

   (a) to the Secretary of State, the Director or the Commission in connection with any of their functions under Parts IV, V, VI or this Part of this Act or under the Competition Act 1980, or

   (b) to the Commission in connection with functions of the Commission under the Telecommunications Act 1984 or the Airports Act 1986,

and either he knows the information to be false or misleading in a material particular, or he furnishes the information recklessly and it is false or misleading in a material particular, he is guilty of an offence.

93B(2)   **[Further offence]**   A person who—

   (a) furnishes any information to another which he knows to be false or misleading in a material particular, or

   (b) recklessly furnishes any information to another which is false or misleading in a material particular,

knowing that the information is to be used for the purpose of furnishing information as mentioned in subsection (1)(a) or (b) of this section, is guilty of an offence.

93B(3)   **[Penalties]**   A person guilty of an offence under subsection (1) or (2) of this section is liable—

   (a) on summary conviction, to a fine not exceeding the statutory maximum, or

(b) on conviction on indictment, to imprisonment for a term not exceeding two years or to a fine or to both.

93B(4)   [Non-application of sec. 129(1)]   Section 129(1) of this Act does not apply to an offence under this section.

History
S. 93B inserted by CA 1989, s. 151 as from 1 April 1990
(see S.I. 1990 No. 142 (C. 5), art. 6(b)).

Schedule 8 — Powers Exercisable by Orders Under Sections 56 and 73

Sections 56, 73, 74,
77, 89, and 91

Part I — Powers Exercisable in All Cases

1   Subject to paragraph 3 of this Schedule, an order under section 56 or section 73 of this Act (in this Schedule referred to as an "order") may declare it to be unlawful, except to such extent and in such circumstances as may be provided by or under the order, to make or to carry out any such agreement as may be specified or described in the order.

2   Subject to the next following paragraph, an order may require any party to any such agreement as may be specified or described in the order to terminate the agreement within such time as may be so specified, either wholly or to such extent as may be so specified.

3(1)   An order shall not by virtue of paragraph 1 of this Schedule declare it to be unlawful to make any agreement in so far as, if made, it would be an agreement to which the Act of 1976 would apply.

3(2)   An order shall not by virtue of paragraph 1 or paragraph 2 of this Schedule declare it to be unlawful to carry out, or require any person to terminate, an agreement in so far as it is an agreement to which the Act of 1976 applies.

3(3)   An order shall not by virtue of either of those paragraphs declare it to be unlawful to make or to carry out, or require any person to terminate, an agreement in so far as, if made, it would relate, (or as the case may be) in so far as it relates, to the terms and conditions of employment of any workers, or to the physical conditions in which any workers are required to work.

3(4)   In this paragraph "**terms and conditions of employment**" has the meaning assigned to it by section 167(1) of the Industrial Relations Act 1971.

4   An order may declare it to be unlawful, except to such extent and in such circumstances as may be provided by or under the order, to withhold or to agree to withhold or to threaten to withhold, or to procure others to withhold or to agree to withhold or threaten to withhold, from any such persons as may be specified or described in the order, any supplies or services so specified or described or any orders for such supplies or services (whether the withholding is absolute or is to be effectual only in particular circumstances).

5   An order may declare it to be unlawful, except to such extent and in such circumstances as may be provided by or under the order, to require, as a condition of the supplying of goods or services to any person,—

   (a) the buying of any goods, or

   (b) the making of any payment in respect of services other than the goods or services supplied, or

   (c) the doing of any other such matter as may be specified or described in the order.

6 An order may declare it to be unlawful, except to such extent and in such circumstances as may be provided by or under the order,—

   (a) to discriminate in any manner specified or described in the order between any persons in the prices charged for goods or services so specified or described, or

   (b) to do anything so specified or described which appears to the appropriate Minister to amount to such discrimination,

or to procure others to do any of the things mentioned in sub-paragraph (a) or sub-paragraph (b) of this paragraph.

7 An order may declare it to be unlawful, except to such extent and in such circumstances as may be provided by or under the order,—

   (a) to give or agree to give in other ways any such preference in respect of the supply of goods or services, or the giving of orders for goods or services, as may be specified or described in the order, or

   (b) to do anything so specified or described which appears to the appropriate Minister to amount to giving such preference,

or to procure others to do any of the things mentioned in sub-paragraph (a) or sub-paragraph (b) of this paragraph.

8 An order may declare it to be unlawful, except to such extent and in such circumstances as may be provided by or under the order, to charge for goods or services supplied prices differing from those in any published list or notification, or to do anything specified or described in the order which appears to the appropriate Minister to amount to charging such prices.

9 An order may require a person supplying goods or services to publish a list of or otherwise notify prices, with or without such further information as may be specified or described in the order.

9A(1) An order may require a person supplying goods or services to publish—

   (a) any such accounting information in relation to the supply of the goods or services, and

   (b) any such information in relation to—

     (i) the quantities of goods or services supplied, or

     (ii) the geographical areas in which they are supplied,

as may be specified or described in the order.

9A(2) In this paragraph **"accounting information"**, in relation to a supply of goods or service, means information as to—

   (a) the costs of the supply, including fixed costs and overheads,

(b) the manner in which fixed costs and overheads are calculated and apportioned for accounting purposes of the supplier, and

(c) the income attributable to the supply.

History
Para. 9A inserted by CA 1989, s. 153 and Sch. 20,
para. 19(2) as from 16 November 1989 (see CA 1989,
s. 215(1)(b)(ii)).

10(1) Subject to the following provisions of this paragraph, an order may, to such extent and in such circumstances as may be provided by or under the order, regulate the prices to be charged for any goods or services specified or described in the order.

10(2) An order shall not exercise the power conferred by the preceding sub-paragraph in respect of goods or services of any description unless the matters specified in the relevant report as being those which in the opinion of the Commission operate, or may be expected to operate, against the public interest relate, or include matters relating, to the prices charged for goods or services of that description.

10(3) In this paragraph "**the relevant report**", in relation to an order, means the report of the Commission in consequence of which the order is made, in the form in which that report is laid before Parliament.

11 An order may declare it to be unlawful, except to such extent and in such circumstances as may be provided by or under the order, for any person, by publication or otherwise, to notify, to persons supplying goods or services, prices recommended or suggested as appropriate to be charged by those persons for those goods or services.

12(1) An order may prohibit or restrict the acquisition by any person of the whole or part of the undertaking or assets of another person's business, or the doing of anything which will or may have a result to which this paragraph applies, or may require that, if such an acquisition is made or anything is done which has such a result, the persons concerned or any of them shall thereafter observe any prohibitions or restrictions imposed by or under the order.

12(2) This paragraph applies to any result which consists in two or more bodies corporate becoming interconnected bodies corporate.

12(3) Where an order is made in consequence of a report of the Commission under section 72 of this Act, or is made under section 74 of this Act, this paragraph also applies to any result (other than that specified in sub-paragraph (2) of this paragraph) which, in accordance with section 65 of this Act, consists in two or more enterprises ceasing to be distinct enterprises.

12A An order may require any person to furnish any such information to the Director as may be specified or described in the order.

12B An order may require any activities to be carried on separately from any other activities.

12C An order may prohibit or restrict the exercise of any right to vote exercisable by virtue of the holding of any shares, stock or securities.

History
Para. 12A–12C inserted by CA 1989, s. 153 and Sch. 20,
para. 19(3) as from 16 November 1989 (see CA 1989,
s. 215(1)(b)(ii)).

13   In this Part of this schedule "**the appropriate Minister**", in relation to an order, means the Minister by whom the order is made.

Part II — Powers Exercisable Except in Cases Falling Within Section 56(6)

14   An order may provide for the division of any business by the sale of any part of the undertaking or assets or otherwise (for which purpose all the activities carried on by way of business by any one person or by any two or more interconnected bodies corporate may be treated as a single business), or for the division of any group of interconnected bodies corporate, and for all such matters as may be necessary to effect or take account of the division, including—

(a) the transfer or vesting of property, rights, liabilities or obligations;

(b) the adjustment of contracts, whether by discharge or reduction of any liability or obligation or otherwise;

(c) the creation, allotment, surrender or cancellation of any shares, stock or securities;

(d) the formation or winding up of a company or other association, corporate or unincorporate, or the amendment of the memorandum and articles or other instruments regulating any company or association;

(e) the extent to which, and the circumstances in which, provisions of the order affecting a company or association in its share, constitution or other matters may be altered by the company or association, and the registration under any enactment of the order by companies or associations so affected;

(f) the continuation, with any necessary change of parties, of any legal proceedings:

15   In relation to an order under section 73 of this Act, the reference in paragraph 14 of this Schedule to the division of a business as mentioned in that paragraph

[The next page is 65,701]

shall be construed as including a reference to the separation, by the sale of any part of any undertaking or assets concerned or other means, of enterprises which are under common control otherwise than by reason of their being enterprises of interconnected bodies corporate.

INDUSTRY ACT 1975

(1975 Chapter 68)

PART II — POWERS IN RELATION TO TRANSFERS OF CONTROL OF IMPORTANT MANUFACTURING UNDERTAKINGS TO NON-RESIDENTS

SEC. 11 General extent of powers in relation to control of important manufacturing undertakings

11(1) [Effect] The powers conferred by this Part of this Act shall have effect in relation to changes of control of important manufacturing undertakings.

11(2) [Definition] In this Part of this Act—

"**important manufacturing undertaking**" means an undertaking which, in so far as it is carried on in the United Kingdom, is wholly or mainly engaged in manufacturing industry and appears to the Secretary of State to be of special importance to the United Kingdom or to any substantial part of the United Kingdom.

SEC. 12 Meaning of "change of control"

12(1) [Change on relevant event] There is a change of control of an important manufacturing undertaking for the purposes of this Part of this Act only upon the happening of a relevant event.

12(2) ["Relevant event"] In subsection (1) above "**relevant event**" means any event as a result of which—

(a) the person carrying on the whole or part of the undertaking ceases to be resident in the United Kingdom;

(b) a person not resident in the United Kingdom acquires the whole or part of the undertaking;

(c) a body corporate resident in the United Kingdom but controlled by a person not so resident acquires the whole or part of the undertaking;

(d) a person not resident in the United Kingdom becomes able to exercise or control the exercise of the first, second or third qualifying percentage of votes in a body corporate carrying on the whole or part of the undertaking or in any other body corporate which is in control of such a body; or

(e) a person resident in the United Kingdom and able to exercise or control the exercise of the first, second or third qualifying percentage of votes in a body corporate carrying on the whole or part of the undertaking or in any other body corporate which is in control of such a body ceases to be resident in the United Kingdom.

12(3)   **[Control]**   For the purposes of subsection (2) above—

(a) a body corporate or individual entitled to cast 30 per cent or more of the votes that may be cast at any general meeting of a body corporate, is in control of that body; and

(b) control of a body corporate which has control of another body corporate gives control of the latter body.

12(4) **[Power to direct shareholders]** Any power to direct the holder of shares or stock in a body corporate as to the exercise of his votes at a general meeting of that body corporate is to be treated as entitlement to cast the votes in respect of the shares or stock in question.

12(5) **[Persons acting together]** Two or more persons acting together in concert may be treated as a single person for the purposes of any provision of this Part of this Act relating to change of control.

12(6) **[Qualifying percentages]** For the purposes of this Part of this Act—

(a) the first qualifying percentage of votes is 30 per cent;

(b) the second qualifying percentage is 40 per cent; and

(c) the third qualifying percentage is 50 per cent;

and the references to votes in this subsection are references to votes that may be cast at a general meeting.

SEC. 13 Power to make orders

13(1) **[Conditions for making orders]** If it appears to the Secretary of State—

(a) that there is a serious and immediate probability of a change of control of an important manufacturing undertaking; and

(b) that that change of control would be contrary to the interests of the United Kingdom, or contrary to the interest of any substantial part of the United Kingdom,

he may by order (in this Part of this Act referred to as a "prohibition order") specify the undertaking and

(i) prohibit that change of control; and

(ii) prohibit or restrict the doing of things which in his opinion would constitute or lead to it;

and may make such incidental or supplementary provision in the order as appears to him to be necessary or expedient.

13(2) **[Vesting orders]** Subject to subsection (3) below, if—

(a) the conditions specified in paragraphs (a) and (b) of subsection (1) above are satisfied, or

(b) a prohibition order has been made in relation to an important manufacturing undertaking, or

(c) the Secretary of State has learnt of circumstances which appear to him to constitute a change of control of an important manufacturing undertaking, occurring on or after 1st February 1975, and is satisfied that that change is contrary to the interests of the United Kingdom, or contrary to the interests of any substantial part of the United Kingdom,

the Secretary of State may by order made with the approval of the Treasury (in this Part of this Act referred to as a "vesting order") direct that on a day specified in the order—

(i) share capital and loan capital to which this subsection applies, or

(ii) any assets which are employed in the undertaking,

shall vest in the Board or in himself or in nominees for the Board or himself and may make such incidental or supplementary provision in the order as appears to him to be necessary or expedient.

13(3)   **[Vesting orders]**   A vesting order may only be made if the Secretary of State is satisfied that the order is necessary in the national interest and that, having regard to all the circumstances, that interest cannot, or cannot appropriately, be protected in any other way.

13(4)   **[Applicable share and loan capital]**   The share capital and loan capital to which subsection (2) above applies are—

    (a) in any case where the Secretary of State considers that the interests mentioned in subsection (2) (c) above cannot, or cannot appropriately, be protected unless all the share capital of any relevant body corporate vests by virtue of the order, the share capital of that body corporate, together with so much (if any) of the loan capital of that body as may be specified in the order,

    (b) in any other case, that part of the share capital of any relevant body corporate which, at the time that the draft of the order is laid before Parliament under section 15 (3) below, appears to the Secretary of State to be involved in the change of control.

13(5)   **[Definition]**   In this section "**relevant body corporate**" means—

    (a) a body corporate incorporated in the United Kingdom carrying on in the United Kingdom as the whole or the major part of its business there the whole or part of an important manufacturing undertaking, or

    (b) a body corporate incorporated in the United Kingdom—

       (i) which is the holding company of a group of companies carrying on in the United Kingdom as the whole or the major part of their business there the whole or part of an important manufacturing undertaking, and

      (ii) as to which one of the conditions specified in subsection (6) below is satisfied.

13(6)   **[Conditions]**   The conditions mentioned in subsection (5) above are—

    (a) that it appears to the Secretary of State that there is a serious and immediate probability of the happening of an event in relation to the company which would constitute a change of control of the undertaking, or

    (b) that the Secretary of State has learnt of circumstances relating to the company which appear to him to constitute a change of control of the undertaking on or after 1st February 1975.

SEC. 14   Notices to extend vesting orders to other holdings

14(1)   **[Notice to be served by Secretary of State]**   Where 30 per cent or more of the share capital of the body corporate vests in the Secretary of State or the Board by virtue of a vesting order, the Secretary of State shall serve on the holders of all the share capital that does not so vest, and on any other persons who to his knowledge have a present or prospective right to subscribe for share capital of the body corporate, within 28 days of the making of the order, a notice informing them of the making of the order and of the right of each of them to require the order to extend to the share capital or rights held by him.

14(2)　[Service of counter-notice]　The recipient of a notice under subsection (1) above may, within three months of the date of the notice, serve on the Secretary of State a counter-notice requiring the order to extend to the share capital or rights held by the recipient in the body corporate.

14(3)　[Vesting orders]　A vesting order shall have effect, from the date of a counter-notice, as if the share capital or rights specified in the notice had been specified in the vesting order.

14(4)　[Share capital vesting in nominees]　Subsections (1) to (3) above shall have the same effect in relation to share capital vesting in nominees for the Secretary of State or the Board as in relation to share capital vesting as mentioned in those subsections.

Note
"The Board" is the National Enterprise Board.

SEC. 15　Parliamentary control of orders

15(1)　[Approval of prohibition orders]　A prohibition order shall be laid before Parliament after being made, and the order shall cease to have effect at the end of the period of 28 days beginning on the day on which it was made (but without prejudice to anything previously done by virtue of the order or to the making of a new order) unless during that period it is approved by resolution of each House of Parliament.

15(2)　[Parliamentary term]　In reckoning the period mentioned in subsection (1) above no account shall be taken of any time during which Parliament is dissolved or prorogued or during which both Houses are adjourned for more than four days.

15(3)　[Draft orders]　A vesting order shall not be made unless a draft of the order has been laid before and approved by resolution of each House of Parliament.

15(4)　[Restriction on draft orders]　A draft of a vesting order shall not be laid before Parliament—

　　(a)　in a case such as is mentioned in paragraph (a) of section 13 (2) above, after the end of a period of three months from the service of a notice under section 16 (7) below of the Secretary of State's intention to lay the draft before Parliament;

　　(b)　in a case such as is mentioned in paragraph (b) of that subsection (2), after the end of a period of three months from the making of the prohibition order unless such circumstances as are mentioned in paragraph (a) or (c) of that subsection exist at the time when the draft of the order is laid before Parliament under subsection (3) above; and

　　(c)　in a case such as is mentioned in paragraph (c) of that subsection, after the end of a period of three months from the date on which the Secretary of State learnt of circumstances such as are mentioned in that paragraph.

15(5) [Parliamentary treatment of draft order] On the expiry of 28 days from the laying of the draft of a vesting order in a House of Parliament the order shall proceed in that House, whether or not it has been referred to a committee under Standing Orders of that House relating to Private Bills, as if its provisions would require to be enacted by a Public Bill which cannot be referred to such a Committee.

15(6) [Parliamentary term] In reckoning, for purposes of proceedings in either House of Parliament, the period mentioned in subsection (5) above, no account shall be taken of any time during which Parliament is dissolved or prorogued or during which that House is adjourned for more than four days.

SEC. 16   Contents of vesting order

16(1) [Provisions of orders] Without prejudice to the generality of section 13(2) above, a vesting order may contain provisions by virtue of which rights, liabilities or incumbrances to which assets or capital which will vest by virtue of the order are subject—

(a) will be extinguished in consideration of the payment of compensation as provided under section 19 below, or

(b) will be transferred to the Secretary of State or the Board, or

(c) will be charged on the compensation under section 19 below.

16(2) [Prohibitions in orders] A vesting order which provides for the vesting of assets employed in an undertaking may prohibit or set aside any transfer of assets so employed or of any right in respect of such assets.

16(3) [Safeguarding provisions] A vesting order may include such provisions as the Secretary of State considers necessary or expedient to safeguard—

(a) any capital which will vest by virtue of the order; and

(b) any assets—

(i) of a body corporate whose capital will so vest, or

(ii) of any subsidiary of such a body corporate;

and may in particular, but without prejudice to the generality of this subsection, prohibit or set aside the transfer of any such capital or assets or any right in respect of such capital or assets.

16(4) [Recovery of capital and assets] A vesting order setting aside a transfer of capital or a transfer of assets such as are mentioned in subsection (2) above shall entitle the Secretary of State or the Board to recover the capital or assets transferred.

16(5) [Recovery by body corporate] A vesting order setting aside a transfer of assets such as are mentioned in subsection (3) (b) above shall entitle the body corporate or subsidiary to recover the assets transferred.

16(6) [Compensation] Any vesting order setting aside a transfer shall give the person entitled to recover the capital or assets a right to be compensated in respect of the transfer.

16(7) [Transfers affected] The transfers to which this section applies include transfers made before the draft of the order is laid before Parliament but after the Secretary of State has served notice on the person concerned of his intention to lay a draft order.

16(8) **[Definition]** In subsection (7) above "**the person concerned**" means—

(a) in the case of an order such as is mentioned in paragraph (i) of section 13(2) above, the relevant body corporate, and

(b) in the case of an order such as is mentioned in paragraph (ii) of that subsection, the person carrying on the undertaking.

16(9) **[Publication in Gazette]** The Secretary of State shall publish a copy of any such notice in the London Gazette, the Edinburgh Gazette and the Belfast Gazette as soon as practicable after he has served it.

SEC. 17 Remedies for contravention of prohibition orders

17(1) **[No criminal proceedings]** No criminal proceedings shall lie against any person on the ground that he has committed, or aided, abetted, counselled or procured the commission of, or conspired or attempted to commit, or incited others to commit, any contravention of a prohibition order.

17(2) **[Civil proceedings]** Nothing in subsection (1) above shall limit any right of any person to bring civil proceedings in respect of any contravention or apprehended contravention of a prohibition order, and (without prejudice to the generality of the preceding words) compliance with any such order shall be enforceable by civil proceedings by the Crown for an injunction or interdict or for any other appropriate relief.

SEC. 18 Territorial scope of orders

18(1) **[Acts outside UK]** Nothing in a prohibition order shall have effect so as to apply to any person in relation to his conduct outside the United Kingdom unless he is—

(a) a citizen of the United Kingdom and Colonies or,

(b) a body corporate incorporated in the United Kingdom or,

(c) a person carrying on business in the United Kingdom either alone or in partnership with one or more other persons,

but in a case falling within paragraph (a), (b) or (c) above, any such order may extend to acts or omissions outside the United Kingdom.

18(2) **[Corporate residence]** For the purposes of this Part of this Act a body corporate shall be deemed not to be resident in the United Kingdom if it is not incorporated in the United Kingdom.

SEC. 19 Compensation orders

19(1) **[Order to be laid before Parliament]** No vesting order shall be made until there has also been laid before both Houses of Parliament an order (in this Part of this Act referred to as a "compensation order") providing for the payment of compensation for the acquisition of the capital or assets and for any extinguishment or transfer of rights, liabilities or encumbrances in question.

19(2) **[Special parliamentary procedure]** A compensation order shall be subject to special parliamentary procedure.

19(3)   [**Contents of orders**]   A compensation order—

  (a) shall identify the persons or descriptions of persons to be paid compensation and determine their rights and duties in relation to any compensation paid to them;

  (b) shall specify the manner in which compensation is to be paid;

  (c) shall provide for the payment of interest on compensation in respect of the relevant period;

  (d) may make different provision in relation to different descriptions of capital or assets and different rights, liabilities or incumbrances; and

  (e) may contain incidental and supplementary provisions;

and in paragraph (c) above "**the relevant period**" means—

  (i) in relation to capital or assets, the period commencing with the date on which the capital or assets vest in the board or the Secretary of State or their or his nominees and ending with the date of payment of compensation; and

  (ii) in relation to rights, liabilities and incumbrances, the period commencing with the date on which they are extinguished and ending on the date of payment.

19(4)   [**Funding of compensation**]   Compensation may be paid out—

  (a) out of moneys provided by Parliament, or

  (b) by the issue of government stock (that is to say, stock the principal whereof and the interest whereon is charged on the National Loans Fund with recourse to the Consolidated Fund),

and the power conferred by subsection (3) (b) above is a power to provide for compensation by one or both of the means specified in this subsection.

19(5)   [**Withdrawal or further consideration**]   The proviso to section 6(2) of the Statutory Orders (Special Procedure Act 1945 (power to withdraw an order or submit it to Parliament for further consideration by means of a Bill for its confirmation) shall have effect in relation to compensation orders as if for the words "may by notice given in the prescribed manner, withdraw the order or may" there were substituted the word "shall".

SEC. 20   Arbitration of disputes relating to vesting and compensation orders

20(1)   [**Determination of disputes**]   Any dispute to which this section applies shall be determined under Schedule 3 to this Act.

20(2)   [**Tribunal**]   Where any such dispute has been submitted to a tribunal constituted under that Schedule, any other dispute to which this section applies shall be determined by the same tribunal.

20(3)   [**Applicable disputes**]   This section applies to a dispute which arises out of a vesting order or a compensation order and to which one of the parties is the Secretary of State, the Board or a body corporate the whole or part of whose share capital has vested by virtue of the order in either of them or in nominees for either of them—

(a) if the provisions of the order require it to be submitted to arbitration; or

(b) if one of the parties wishes it to be so submitted;

and where this section applies to a dispute which arises out of an order, it also applies to any dispute which arises out of a related order.

20(4) **[Related orders]**   A vesting order and a compensation order are related for the purposes of this section if they relate to the same capital or assets.

PART V — GENERAL AND SUPPLEMENTARY

SEC. 35   Expenses

35   Any expenses of the Secretary of State or Minister of Agriculture, Fisheries and Food incurred in consequence of the provisions of this Act, including any increase attributable to those provisions in sums payable under any other Act, shall be defrayed out of money provided by Parliament.

SEC. 36   Service of documents

36(1) **[Method of service]**   Any notice or other document required or authorised by or by virtue of this Act to be served on any person may be served on him either by delivering it to him or by leaving it at his proper address or by sending it by post.

36(2) **[Service on firm's officer]**   Any notice or other document so required or authorised to be served on a body corporate or a firm shall be duly served if it is served on the secretary or clerk of that body or a partner of that firm.

36(3) **["Proper address"]**   For the purposes of this section, and of section 26 of the Interpretation Act 1889 in its application to this section, the proper address of a person, in the case of a secretary or clerk of a body corporate, shall be that of the registered or principal office of that body, in the case of a partner of a firm shall be that of the principal office of the firm, and in any other case shall be the last known address of the person to be served.

SEC. 37   Interpretation

37(1) **[Definitions]**   In this Act, unless the context otherwise requires—

"**accounting year**", in relation to the Board, means, subject to subsection (2) below, the period of twelve months ending with the 31st December in any year, except that the Board's first accounting year shall end on 31st December 1976;

"**enactment**" includes an enactment of the Parliament of Northern Ireland or the Northern Ireland Assembly;

"**holding company**" means a holding company as defined by section 736 of the Companies Act 1985 or Article 4 of the Companies (Northern Ireland) Order 1986;

"**industry**" includes any description of commercial activity, and any section of an industry, and "industrial" has a corresponding meaning;

"**manufacturing industry**" means, subject to subsection (3) below, activities which are described in any of the minimum list headings in Orders III to XIX (inclusive) of the Standard Industrial Classification;

"**Standard Industrial Classification**" means the revised edition published by Her Majesty's Stationery Office in 1968 of the publication of that name prepared by the Central Statistical Office;

"**subsidiary**" means a subsidiary as defined by section 736 of the Companies Act 1985 or Article 4 of the Companies (Northern Ireland) Order 1986;

"**wholly owned subsidiary**" has the meaning assigned to it by section 736(5)(b) of the Companies Act 1985 or Article 4(5)(b) of the Companies (Northern Ireland) Order 1986.

History
S. 37(1) amended by Industry Act 1980, Sch. 2 and as from 1 July 1985 by Companies Consolidation (Consequential Provisions) Act 1985, Sch. 2.

Also amendments by Co-operative Development Agency and Industrial Development Act 1984, s. 5, Sch. 1 and The Companies Consolidation (Consequential Provisions) (Northern Ireland) Order 1986 (S.I. 1986 No. 1035).

37(2)   **[Extension of accounting year]**   The Secretary of State may direct that any accounting year of the Board shall end on a date before or after that on which it would otherwise end.

37(3)   **[Manufacturing industry]**   In determining the extent to which an undertaking is engaged in manufacturing industry, the following activities shall be treated as manufacturing industry so far as they relate to products manufactured or to be manufactured by the undertaking—

research,
transport,
distribution,
repair and maintenance of machinery,
sales and marketing,
storage,
mining and quarrying,
production and distribution of energy and heating,
administration,
training of staff,
packaging.

37(4)   **[Public ownership of securities]**   Securities and other property are publicly owned for the purposes of this Act if they are held—

(a) by or on behalf of the Crown;

(b) by a company all of whose shares are held by or on behalf of the Crown or by a wholly owned subsidiary of such a company;

(c) by any corporation constituted by or under any enactment under which an industry or part of an industry is carried on by that corporation under national ownership or control; or

(d) by a wholly owned subsidiary of any such corporation.

37(5)   Except in so far as the context otherwise requires, any reference in this Act to an enactment shall be construed as a reference to that enactment as amended, applied or extended by or under any other enactment, including this Act.

SEC. 38 Orders

38(1) Any power to make an order conferred by this Act shall be exercisable by statutory instrument.

38(2) Any power to make an order conferred by any provision of this Act shall include power to make an order varying or revoking any order previously made under that provision.

38(3) It is hereby declared that any power of giving directions or making determinations conferred on the Secretary of State by any provision of this Act includes power to vary or revoke directions or determinations given or made under that provision.

SEC. 39 Citation etc.

39(1) **[Citation]** This Act may be cited as the Industry Act 1975.

39(2), (3) (Provisions not relevant to this service, and not reproduced here.)

39(4) **[Northern Ireland]** It is hereby declared that this Act extends to Northern Ireland.

39(5) **[Application to compensation order]** Notwithstanding the provisions—

(a) of section 12 (3) of the Statutory Orders (Special Procedure) Act 1945,

the former Act shall apply to any compensation order which extends to Northern Ireland.

History
S. 39(5) amended by Industry Act 1980, s. 21 and Sch. 2.

39(6) **[Commencement]** This Act shall come into force on such day as the Secretary of State may by order made by statutory instrument appoint.

39(7) **[Varying dates]** An order under subsection (6) above may appoint different days for different provisions and for different purposes.

Note
The Act came into force in full on 20 November 1975.

FINANCE ACT 1976

(1976 Chapter 40)

[29th July 1976]

SEC. 127 Stamp duty: stock exchange transfers

127(1) **[Exemption]** Stamp duty shall not be chargeable on any transfer to a stock exchange nominee.

History
In s. 127(1) the words "which is executed for the purposes of a stock exchange transaction" formerly appearing at the end omitted, as regards any transfer giving effect to such a transaction carried out on or after the day of The Stock Exchange reforms (i.e. the day on which the rule of the Stock Exchange that prohibits a person from conducting business both as broker and as jobber is abolished — 27 October 1986) by Finance Act 1986, s. 84(1) and repealed by Finance Act 1986, s. 114 and Sch. 23, Pt. IX(4) as from 20 March 1989 (see S.I. 1989 No. 291).

127(2), (3) (Repealed by Finance Act 1986, sec. 114 and Sch. 23, Pt IX(4) as from 20 March 1989.)

History

In regard to the date of the above repeals, see S.I. 1989 No. 291 — see also Finance Act 1986, s. 85(4) re s. 127(2); s. 127(2), (3) formerly read as follows:

"**127(2)** A transfer otherwise than on sale from a stock exchange nominee to a jobber or his nominee shall be regarded for the purposes of stamp duty as a transfer on sale for a consideration equal to the value of the stock or marketable securities thereby transferred.

(3) For the purposes of section 42 of the Finance Act 1920 (jobbers' transfers) a transfer by a jobber or his nominee to a stock exchange nominee shall be regarded as a transfer to a bona fide purchaser."

127(4) (Amends Finance Act 1970, sec. 33(1), not reproduced here.)

127(5) **[Construction]** This section shall be construed as one with the Stamp Act 1891 and in this section —

> "**stock exchange nominee**" means any person designated for the purposes of this section as a nominee of The Stock Exchange by an order made by the Secretary of State.

History

In s. 127(5) former definitions of "jobber" and "stock exchange transaction" repealed by Finance Act 1986, s. 114 and Sch. 23, Pt. IX(4) as from 20 March 1989 (see S.I. 1989 No. 291); the former definitions read as follows:

"**jobber**' means a member of The Stock Exchange who is recognised by the Council thereof as carrying on the business of a jobber and carries on that business in the United Kingdom;

'**stock exchange transaction**' has the meaning given in section 4 of the Stock Transfer Act 1963."

127(6) **[Making orders]** The power to make an order under subsection (5) above shall be exercisable by statutory instrument and includes power to vary or revoke a previous order.

127(7) **[Northern Ireland]** Section 33 of the Finance Act 1970 shall extend to Northern Ireland; and in the application of that section to Northern Ireland for any reference to the Stock Transfer Act 1963 there shall be substituted a reference to the Stock Transfer Act (Northern Ireland) 1963.

History

In s. 127(7) the words "and this section" formerly appearing after the words "of that section" repealed by Finance Act 1986, s. 114 and Sch. 23, Pt. IX(4) as from 20 March 1989 (see S.I. 1989 No. 291).

Note

Prospective repeal of s. 127(1), (4)–(7) by Finance Act 1990, s. 109(6)–(8), s. 132 and Sch. 19, Pt. VI as provided by Treasury Order.

ADMINISTRATION OF JUSTICE ACT 1977

(1977 Chapter 38)

[29th July 1977]

PART I — GENERAL

SEC. 7 Extent of powers of receivers and managers in respect of companies

7(1) **[Receivers' powers]** A receiver appointed under the law of any part of the United Kingdom in respect of the whole or part of any property or undertaking of a company and in consequence of the company having created a charge which, as created, was a floating charge may exercise his powers in any other part of the United Kingdom so far as their exercise is not inconsistent with the law applicable there.

7(2) **[Definition]** In subsection (1) above "**receiver**" includes a manager and a person who is appointed both receiver and manager.

Note
S. 7 effective from 29 August 1977.

EMPLOYMENT PROTECTION (CONSOLIDATION) ACT 1978

(1978 Chapter 44)

[CCH Note: Reproduced below are the remaining provisions of Pt. VII, that is sec. 122–127. Under sec. 160 of the Act, they came into force on 1 January 1979]

PART VII — INSOLVENCY OF EMPLOYER

SEC. 121 Priority of certain debts on insolvency

(Repealed by Insolvency Act 1985, sec. 235 and Sch. 10, Pt. IV as from 29 December 1986)

History
In regard to the date of the above repeal, see S.I. 1986 No. 1924 (C. 71).

Note
For current provisions, see Insolvency Act 1986, s. 386,387 and Sch. 6, para. 9–11, 13–16.

SEC. 122 Employee's rights on insolvency of employer

122(1) **[Power of Secretary of State to pay employee]** If on an application made to him in writing by an employee the Secretary of State is satisfied—

    (a) that the employer of that employee has become insolvent; and

    (aa) that the employment of the employee has been terminated; and

    (b) that on the relevant date the employee was entitled to be paid the whole or part of any debt to which this section applies,

the Secretary of State shall, subject to the provisions of this section, pay the employee out of the Redundancy Fund the amount to which in the opinion of the Secretary of State the employee is entitled in respect of that debt.

History
In s. 22(1) para. (aa) inserted by Insolvency Act 1985, s. 218(2) as from 29 December 1986 (see S.I. 1986 No. 1924 (C. 71)).

122(2) **["The relevant date"]** In this section **"the relevant date"**—

    (a) in relation to arrears of pay (not being remuneration under a protective award made under section 101 of the Employment Protection Act 1975) and to holiday pay, means the date on which the employer became insolvent;

    (b) in relation to such an award and to a basic award of compensation for unfair dismissal, means whichever is the latest of—

      (i) the date on which the employer became insolvent;

    (ii) the date of the termination of the employee's employment; and

   (iii) the date on which the award was made;

(c) in relation to any other debt to which this section applies, means whichever is the later of the dates mentioned in sub-paragraphs (i) and (ii) of paragraph (b).

History
S. 22(2) substituted by Insolvency Act 1985, s. 218(2) as from 29 December 1986 (see S.I. No. 1924 (C. 71)).

122(3) **[Application of section]** This section applies to the following debts:—

(a) any arrears of pay in respect of one or more (but not more than eight) weeks;

(b) any amount which the employer is liable to pay the employee for the period of notice required by section 49(1) or (2) or for any failure of the employer to give the period of notice required by section 49(1);

(c) any holiday pay—

      (i) in respect of a period or periods of holiday not exceeding six weeks in all; and

    (ii) to which all the employee became entitled during the twelve months ending with the relevant date;

(d) any basic award of compensation for unfair dismissal (within the meaning of section 72);

(e) any reasonable sum by way of reimbursement of the whole or part of any fee or premium paid by an apprentice or articled clerk.

History
In s. 122(3) para. (a), (b) and (c) substituted by Employment Act 1982, s. 21 and Sch. 3, para. 4 as from 1 December 1982.

122(4) **[Arrears of pay]** For the purposes of this section, the following amounts shall be treated as arrears of pay, namely—

(a) a guarantee payment;

(b) remuneration on suspension on medical grounds under section 19;

(c) any payment for time off under section 27(3) or 31(3) or 31A(4);

(d) remuneration under a protective award made under section 101 of the Employment Protection Act 1975;

(e) statutory sick pay, payable under Part I of the Social Security and Housing Benefits Act 1982.

History
S. 122(4) substituted by Insolvency Act 1985, s. 218(4) as from 29 December 1986 (see S.I. 1986 No. 1924 (C. 71)).

122(5) **[Total amount for sec. 122(3)]** The total amount payable to an employee in respect of any debt mentioned in subsection (3), where the amount of that debt is referable to a period of time, shall not exceed £172 in respect of any one week or, in

EP(C)A 1978, sec. 122(3)

respect of a shorter period, an amount bearing the same proportion to £172 as that shorter period bears to a week.

History
In s. 122(5) figure of "£172" substituted by S.I. 1989
No. 526 as from 1 April 1989. The previous figure was
£158 (S.I. 1986 No. 2283).

122(6) **[Variation of sec. 122(5) limit]** The Secretary of State may vary the limit referred to in subsection (5) after a review under section 148, by order made in accordance with that section.

122(7) **[Reasonable sum for sec. 122(3)(e)]** A sum shall be taken to be reasonable for the purposes of subsection (3)(e) in a case where a trustee in bankruptcy or liquidator has been or is required to be appointed if it is admitted to be reasonable by the trustee in bankruptcy or liquidator under section 348 of the Insolvency Act 1986 (effect of bankruptcy on apprenticeships, etc.) whether as originally enacted or as applied to the winding up of a company by rules under section 411 of that Act.

History
In s. 122(7) the words from "section 348" to the end
substituted by Insolvency Act 1985, s. 218(5) and Insolvency
Act 1986, s. 439 and Sch. 14 as from 29 December 1986
(see S.I. 1986 No. 1924 (C. 71)).

122(8) **[Reasonable sum for Scotland]** Subsection (7) shall not apply to Scotland, but in Scotland a sum shall be taken to be reasonable for the purposes of subsection (3)(e) in a case where a trustee in bankruptcy or liquidator has been or is required to be appointed if it is accepted by the trustee in bankruptcy or the liquidator for the purposes of the bankruptcy or winding-up.

History
S. 122(8) amended by Bankruptcy (Scotland) Act 1985,
s. 75 and Sch. 7, para. 14.

122(9) **[Application of sec. 122(10), (11)]** The provisions of subsections (10) and (11) shall apply in a case where one of the following officers (hereafter in this section referred to as the "relevant officer") has been or is required to be appointed in connection with the employer's insolvency, that is to say, a trustee in bankruptcy, a liquidator, an administrator, a receiver or manager, or a trustee under a composition or arrangement between the employer and his creditors or under a trust deed for his creditors executed by the employer; and in this subsection "trustee", in relation to a composition or arrangement, includes the supervisor of a voluntary arrangement proposed for the purposes of, and approved under, Part I or VIII of the Insolvency Act 1986.

History
In s. 122(9) the words ", an administrator" and the words   Act 1986, s. 439 and Sch. 14 as from 29 December 1986
from "'trustee', in relation" to the end inserted and   (see S.I. 1986 No. 1924 (C. 71)).
substituted by Insolvency Act 1985, s. 218(6) and Insolvency

122(10) **[Statement from relevant officer]** Subject to subsection (11), the Secretary of State shall not in such a case make any payment under this section in respect of any debt until he has received a statement from the relevant officer of the amount of that debt which appears to have been owed to the employee on the relevant date and to remain unpaid; and the relevant officer shall, on request by the Secretary of State, provide him, as soon as reasonably practicable, with such a statement.

122(11)   [Power of Secretary of State to make payment]   If the Secretary of State is satisfied that he does not require such a statement in order to determine the amount of the debt that was owed to the employee on the relevant date and remains unpaid, he may make a payment under this section in respect of the debt without having received such a statement.

History
S. 122(11) substituted by Employment Act 1989, s. 18(2), 30(3) as from 16 January 1990; s. 122(11) formerly read as follows:

"Where—

(a) the application for a payment under this section has been received by the Secretary of State, but no such payment has been made;

(b) the Secretary of State is satisfied that a payment under this section should be made; and

(c) it appears to the Secretary of State that there is likely to be unreasonable delay before he receives a statement about the debt in question,

then, the Secretary of State may, if the applicant so requests or, if the Secretary of State thinks fit, without such a request, make a payment under this section, notwithstanding that no such statement has been received."

Previously in former s. 122(11) para. (a) and (c) amended by Employment Act 1982, s. 21 and Sch. 3, para. 5 as from 1 December 1982.

SEC. 123   Payment of unpaid contributions to occupational pension scheme

123(1)   [Duty of Secretary of State]   If, on application made to him in writing by the person competent to act in respect of an occupational pension scheme or a personal pension scheme, the Secretary of State is satisfied that an employer has become insolvent and that at the time that he did so there remained unpaid relevant contributions falling to be paid by him to the scheme, the Secretary of State shall, subject to the provisions of this section, pay into the resources of the scheme out of the Redundancy Fund the sum which in his opinion is payable in respect of the unpaid relevant contributions.

History
In s. 123(1) the words "or a personal pension scheme" inserted by Social Security Act 1986, s. 86 and Sch. 10, para. 31.

123(2)   ["Relevant contributions"]   In this section **"relevant contributions"** means contributions falling to be paid by an employer to an occupational pension scheme or a personal pension scheme, either on his own account or on behalf of an employee; and for the purposes of this section a contribution of any amount shall not be treated as falling to be paid on behalf of an employee unless a sum equal to that amount has been deducted from the pay of the employee by way of a contribution from him.

History
In s. 123(2) the words "to an occupational pension scheme or a personal pension scheme" inserted by Social Security Act 1986, s. 86 and Sch. 10, para. 31.

123(3)   [Sum payable by employer re unpaid contributions]   The sum payable under this section in respect of unpaid contributions of an employer on his own account to an occupational pension scheme or a personal pension scheme shall be the least of the following amounts—

(a) the balance of relevant contributions remaining unpaid on the date when he became insolvent and payable by the employer on his own account to the scheme in respect of the twelve months immediately preceding that date;

(b) the amount certified by an actuary to be necessary for the purpose of meeting the liability of the scheme on dissolution to pay the benefits provided by the scheme to or in respect of the employees of the employer;

(c) an amount equal to ten per cent of the total amount of remuneration paid or payable to those employees in respect of the twelve months immediately preceeding the date on which the employer became insolvent.

History
In s. 123(3) the words "or a personal pension scheme" inserted by Social Security Act 1986, s. 86 and Sch. 10, para. 31.

123(4) ["Remuneration"] For the purposes of subsection (3)(c), "remuneration" includes holiday pay, statutory sick pay, statutory maternity pay under Part V of the Social Security Act 1986, maternity pay under Part III of this Act and any such payment as is referred to in section 122(4).

History
In s. 123(4) the words from "statutory sick pay" to "Part III of this Act" substituted by Social Security Act 1986, s. 86 and Sch. 10, para. 76 and the words "section 122(4)" substituted by Insolvency Act 1985, s. 235 and Sch. 8, para. 31(3)(a).

123(5) [Limit on payment of unpaid contributions] Any sum payable under this section in respect of unpaid contributions on behalf of an employee shall not exceed the amount deducted from the pay of the employee in respect of the employee's contributions to the scheme during the twelve months immediately preceding the date on which the employer became insolvent.

History
In s. 123(5) certain words repealed by Social Security Act 1986, s. 86 and Sch. 11.

123(6) [Application of sec. 123(7)–(9)] The provisions of subsections (7) to (9) shall apply in a case where one of the following officers (hereafter in this section referred to as the "relevant officer") has been or is required to be appointed in connection with the employer's insolvency, that is to say, a trustee in bankruptcy, a liquidator, an administrator, a receiver or manager, or a trustee under a composition or arrangement between the employer and his creditors or under a trust deed for his creditors executed by the employer; and in this subsection "trustee", in relation to a composition or arrangement, includes the supervisor of a voluntary arrangement proposed for the purposes of, and approved under, Part I or VIII of the Insolvency Act 1986.

History
In s. 123(6) the words "an administrator" and the words from "'trustee', in relation" to the end inserted and substituted by Insolvency Act 1985, s. 235 and Sch. 8, para. 31(3)(b) and Insolvency Act 1986, s. 439 and Sch. 14 as from 29 December 1986 (see S.I. 1906 No. 1924 (C. 71)).

123(7) [Statement from relevant officer] Subject to subsection (9), the Secretary of State shall not in such a case make any payment under this section in respect of unpaid relevant contributions until he has received a statement from the relevant officer of the amount of relevant contributions which appear to have been unpaid on the date on which the employer became insolvent and to remain unpaid: and the relevant officer shall, on request by the Secretary of State provide him, as soon as reasonably practicable, with such a statement.

123(8) [Certificate by relevant officer] Subject to subsection (9), an amount shall be taken to be payable, paid or deducted as mentioned in subsection (3)(a) or (c) or subsection (5), only if it is so certified by the relevant officer.

123(9)   [Power of Secretary of State to make payment]   If the Secretary of State is satisfied—

(a) that he does not require a statement under subsection (7) in order to determine the amount of relevant contributions that was unpaid on the date on which the employer became insolvent and remains unpaid, or

(b) that he does not require a certificate under subsection (8) in order to determine the amounts payable, paid or deducted as mentioned in subsections (3)(a) and (c) and (5),

he may make a payment under this section in respect of the contributions in question without having received a statement or (as the case may be) such a certificate.

History
S. 123(9) substituted by Employment Act 1989, s. 18(3), 30(3) as from 16 January 1990; s. 123(a) formerly read as follows:

"Where—

(a) the application for a payment under this section has been received by the Secretary of State, but no such payment has been made;

(b) the Secretary of State is satisfied that a payment under this section should be made; and

(c) it appears to the Secretary of State that there is likely to be unreasonable delay before he receives a statement or certificate about the contributions in question,

then, the Secretary of State may, if the applicants so request or, if the Secretary of State thinks fit, without such a request, make a payment under this section, notwithstanding that no such statement or certificate has been received."

Previously in former s. 123(9) the words "the application for a payment under this section has been" in para. (a) and the word "unreasonable" in para. (b) substituted by Employment Act 1982, s. 21 and Sch. 3, para. 5 as from 1 December 1982.

SEC. 124   Complaint to industrial tribunal

124(1)   [Entitlement to present complaint]   A person who has applied for a payment under section 122 may, within the period of three months beginning with the date on which the decision of the Secretary of State on that application was communicated to him or, if that is not reasonably practicable, within such further period as is reasonable, present a complaint to an industrial tribunal that—

(a) the Secretary of State has failed to make any such payment; or

(b) any such payment made by the Secretary of State is less than the amount which should have been paid.

124(2)   [Persons acting re pension schemes]   Any persons who are competent to act in respect of an occupational pension scheme or a personal pension scheme and who have applied for a payment to be made under section 123 into the resources of the scheme may, within the period of three months beginning with the date on which the decision of the Secretary of State on that application was communicated to them, or, if that is not reasonably practicable, within such further period as is reasonable, present a complaint to an industrial tribunal that—

(a) the Secretary of State has failed to make any such payment; or

(b) any such payment made by him is less than the amount which should have been paid.

History
In s. 124(2) the words "or a personal pension scheme" inserted by Social Security Act 1986, s. 26 and Sch. 10, para. 31.

124(3)   [Declaration by tribunal]   Where an industrial tribunal finds that the Secretary of State ought to make a payment under section 122 or 123, it shall make a declaration to that effect and shall also declare the amount of any such payment which it finds the Secretary of State ought to make.

SEC. 125 Transfer to Secretary of State of rights and remedies

125(1) **[Where Secretary of State makes sec. 122 payment to employee]** Where, in pursuance of section 122, the Secretary of State makes any payment to an employee in respect of any debt to which that section applies—

(a) any rights and remedies of the employee in respect of that debt (or, if the Secretary of State has paid only part of it, in respect of that part) shall, on the making of the payment, become rights and remedies of the Secretary of State; and

(b) any decision of an industrial tribunal requiring an employer to pay that debt to the employee shall have the effect that the debt or, as the case may be, that part of it which the Secretary of State has paid, is to be paid to the Secretary of State.

125(2) **[Extent of rights and remedies re sec. 122]** Where a debt or any part of a debt in respect of which the Secretary of State has made a payment in pursuance of section 122 constitutes—

(a) a preferential debt within the meaning of the Insolvency Act 1986 for the purposes of any provision of that Act (including any such provisions as applied by any order made under that Act) or any provision of the Companies Act 1985; or

(b) a preferred debt within the meaning of the Bankruptcy (Scotland) Act 1985 for the purposes of any provision of that Act (including any such provision as applied by section 11A of the Judicial Factors (Scotland) Act 1889),

then, without prejudice to the generality of subsection (1) above, there shall be included among the rights and remedies which become rights and remedies of the Secretary of State in accordance with that subsection any right arising under any such provision by reason of the status of the debt or that part of it as a preferential or preferred debt.

History
S. 125(2) substituted with s. 125(2A) — see below.

125(2A) **[Computation of debts in sec. 125(2)]** In computing for the purposes of any provision mentioned in subsection (2)(a) or (b) above the aggregate amount payable in priority to other creditors of the employer in respect of—

(a) any claim of the Secretary of State to be so paid by virtue of subsection (2) above; and

(b) any claim by the employee to be so paid made in his own right,

any claim falling within paragraph (a) above shall be treated as if it were a claim of the employee; but the Secretary of State shall be entitled, as against the employee, to be so paid in respect of any such claim of his (up to the full amount of the claim) before any payment is made to the employee in respect of any claim falling within paragraph (b) above.

History
S. 125(2), (2A) substituted for the former s. 125(2) by Employment Act 1989, s. 19(1), 30(3), as from 16 January 1990; see Employment Act 1989, Sch. 9, para. 5 for transitional provisions; the former s. 125(2) read as follows:

"There shall be included among the rights and remedies which become rights and remedies of the Secretary of State

in accordance with subsection (1)(a) any right to be paid in priority to other creditors of the employer in accordance with—

(a) the following provisions of the Insolvency Act 1986—

(i) sections 175 and 176, 328 and 329, 348 and Schedule 6, and

(ii) any rules under that Act applying section 348 of it to the winding up of a company; and

(b) section 51 of the Bankruptcy (Scotland) Act;

and the Secretary of State shall be entitled to be so paid in priority to any other unsatisfied claim of the employee; and in computing for the purposes of any of those provisions any limit on the amount of sums to be so paid any sums paid to the Secretary of State shall be treated as if they had been paid to the employee."

Previously in former s. 125(2), para. (a) substituted by Insolvency Act 1985, s. 235 and Sch. 8, para. 31(4) and Insolvency Act 1986, s. 439 and Sch. 14 as from 29 December 1986 (see S.I. 1986 No. 1924 (C. 71)); and para. (b) substituted by Bankruptcy (Scotland) Act 1985, s. 75 and Sch. 7, para. 14 and former para. (c) repealed by Insolvency Act 1986, s. 235 and Sch. 10 as from 29 December 1986 (see S.I. 1986 No. 1924 (C. 71)).

125(3)   [Where Secretary of State makes sec. 123 payment to pension scheme]   Where in pursuance of section 123 the Secretary of State makes any payment into the resources of an occupational pension scheme or a personal pension scheme in respect of those contributions to the scheme, any rights and remedies in respect of those contributions belonging to the persons competent to act in respect of the scheme shall, on the making of the payment, become rights and remedies of the Secretary of State.

History
In s. 125(3) the words "or a personal pension scheme" inserted by Social Security Act 1986, s. 86 and Sch. 10, para. 31.

125(3A)   [Extent of rights and remedies re sec. 125(3)]   Where the Secretary of State makes any such payment as is mentioned in subsection (3) above and the sum (or any part of the sum) falling to be paid by the employer on account of the contributions in respect of which the payment is made constitutes—

(a) a preferential debt within the meaning of the Insolvency Act 1986 for the purposes of any provision mentioned in subsection (2)(a) above; or

(b) a preferred debt within the meaning of the Bankruptcy (Scotland) Act 1985 for the purposes of any provision mentioned in subsection (2)(b) above,

then, without prejudice to the generality of subsection (3) above, there shall be included among the rights and remedies which become rights and remedies of the Secretary of State in accordance with that subsection any right arising under any such provision by reason of the status of that sum (or that part of it) as a preferential or preferred debt.

History
See history note after s. 125(3B).

125(3B)   [Computation of claims in sec. 125(3A)]   In computing for the purposes of any provision referred to in subsection (3A)(a) or (b) above the aggregate amount payable in priority to other creditors of the employer in respect of—

(a) any claim of the Secretary of State to be so paid by virtue of subsection (3A) above; and

(b) any claim by the persons competent to act in respect of the scheme,

any claim falling within paragraph (a) above shall be treated as if it were a claim of those persons; but the Secretary of State shall be entitled, as against those persons, to be so paid in respect of any such claim of his (up to the full amount of the claim) before any payment is made to them in respect of any claim falling within paragraph (b) above.

History
S. 125(3A), (3B) inserted by Employment Act 1989,
s. 19(2), 30(3) as from 16 January 1990; see Employment
Act 1989, Sch. 9, para. 5 for transitional provisions.

125(4)   [Sums recovered to Redundancy Fund]   Any sum recovered by the Secretary of State in exercising any right or pursuing any remedy which is his by virtue of this section shall be paid into the Redundancy Fund.

SEC. 126   Power of Secretary of State to obtain information in connection with applications

126(1)   [Power of Secretary of State on application]   Where an application is made to the Secretary of State under section 122 or 123 in respect of a debt owed, or contributions to an occupational pension scheme or a personal pension scheme falling to be made, by an employer, the Secretary of State may require—

(a)   the employer to provide him with such information as the Secretary of State may reasonably require for the purpose of determining whether the application is well-founded; and

(b)   any person having the custody or control of any relevant records or other documents to produce for examination on behalf of the Secretary of State any such document in that person's custody or under his control which is of such a description as the Secretary of State may require.

History
In s. 126(1) the words "or personal pension scheme" inserted
by Social Security Act 1986, s. 86 and Sch. 10, para. 31.

126(2)   [Requirement by notice etc.]   Any such requirement shall be made by notice in writing given to the person on whom the requirement is imposed and may be varied or revoked by a subsequent notice so given.

126(3)   [Penalty for refusal etc.]   If a person refuses or wilfully neglects to furnish any information or produce any document which he has been required to furnish or produce by a notice under this section he shall be liable on summary conviction to a fine not exceeding level 3 on the standard scale.

History
In s. 126(3) the words "level 3 on the standard scale"
substituted by Criminal Justice Act 1982, s. 38.

126(4)   [Penalty re false statement etc.]   If a person, in purporting to comply with a requirement of a notice under this section, knowingly or recklessly makes any false statement he shall be liable on summary conviction to a fine not exceeding level 5 on the standard scale.

History
In s. 126(4) the words "level 5 on the standard scale"
substituted by Criminal Justice Act 1982, s. 38.

SEC. 127   Interpretation of sec. 122 to 126

127(1)   [Employer insolvent in England and Wales]   For the purposes of sections 122 to 126, an employer shall be taken to be insolvent if, but only if, in England and Wales,—

(a)   he has been adjudged bankrupt or has made a composition or arrangement with his creditors;

(b) he has died and his estate falls to be administered in accordance with an order under section 421 of the Insolvency Act 1986; or

(c) where the employer is a company, a winding up order or an administration order is made or a resolution for voluntary winding up is passed with respect to it, or a receiver or manager of its undertaking is duly appointed, or possession is taken, by or on behalf of the holders of any debentures secured by a floating charge, of any property of the company comprised in or subject to the charge or a voluntary arrangement proposed for the purposes of Part I of the Insolvency Act 1986 is approved under that Part.

History
In s. 127(1), para. (a) and (b) and in para. (c) the words "or an administration order" and the words from "or a voluntary arrangement" to the end substituted and inserted by Insolvency Act 1985, s. 235 and Sch. 8, para. 31(5) and Insolvency Act 1986, s. 439 and Sch. 14 as from 29 December 1986 (see S.I. 1986 No. 1924 (C. 71)).

127(2) [Employer insolvent in Scotland] For the purposes of sections 122 to 126, an employer shall be taken to be insolvent if, but only if, in Scotland,—

(a) sequestration of his estate is awarded or he executes a trust deed for his creditors or enters into a composition contract;

(b) he has died and a judicial factor appointed under section 11A of the Judicial Factors (Scotland) Act 1889 is required by that section to divide his insolvent estate among his creditors; or

(c) where the employer is a company, a winding-up order or an administration order is made or a resolution for voluntary winding up is passed with respect to it or a receiver of its undertaking is duly appointed or a voluntary arrangement proposed for the purposes of Part I of the Insolvency Act 1986 is approved under that Part.

History
In s. 127(2), in para. (a) the words "sequestration of his estate is awarded" substituted for the former words "an award of sequestration is made on his estate" by Employment Act 1989, s. 29(3), 30(3), Sch. 6, para. 23 as from 16 January 1990, in para. (b) the words "11A of the Judicial Factors (Scotland) Act 1889" substituted by Bankruptcy (Scotland) Act 1985, s. 75 and Sch. 7, para. 14, and in para. (c) the words "or an administration order" and the words from "or a voluntary arrangement" to the end inserted and substituted by Insolvency Act 1985, s. 235 and Sch. 8, para. 31(5)(b) and Insolvency Act 1986, s. 439 and Sch. 14 as from 29 December 1986 (See S.I. 1986 No. 1924 (C. 71)).

127(3) [Definitions] In sections 122 to 126—

"**holiday pay**" means—

(a) pay in respect of a holiday actually taken; or

(b) any accrued holiday pay which under the employee's contract of employment would in the ordinary course have become payable to him in respect of the period of a holiday if his employment with the employer had continued until he became entitled to a holiday;

"**occupational pension scheme**" means any scheme or arrangement which provides or is capable of providing, in relation to employees in any description of employment, benefits (in the form of pensions or otherwise) payable to or in respect of any such employees on the termination of their employment or on their death or retirement;

"**personal pension scheme**" means any scheme or arrangement which is comprised in one or more instruments or agreements and which has, or is capable of having, effect so as to provide benefits, in the form of pension or otherwise, payable on death or retirement to or in respect of employees who have made arrangements with the trustees or managers of the scheme for them to become members of the scheme; and any reference in those sections to the resources of a scheme is a reference to the funds out of which the benefits provided by the scheme are from time to time payable.

History
In s. 127(3) definition of "personal pension scheme" inserted by Social Security Act 1986, s. 86 and Sch. 10, para. 31 and word repealed by Social Security Act 1986, s. 86 and Sch. 11.

STOCK TRANSFER ACT 1982
(1982 Chapter 41)

[**CCH Note:** Sections 4–6 commenced from 30 October 1982. The remaining provisions commenced on 23 July 1985 (S.I. 1985 No. 1137).]

TABLE OF SECTIONS

An Act to amend the law relating to the transfer, registration and redemption of securities, and for purposes connected therewith.

[*30th July 1982*]

SEC. 1 Transfer of certain securities through a computerised system

1(1) [Provision to permit transfer through computerised system] In the exercise of the appropriate power (as defined in subsection (3) below) provision may be made permitting a transfer in certain cases of specified securities to which the power extends through the medium of a computer-based system to be established by the Bank of England and The Stock Exchange.

1(2) [No requirement for instrument in writing] A transfer which (pursuant to any provision made under the appropriate power) is effected as mentioned in subsection (1) above is in this Act referred to as an "exempt transfer" and, notwithstanding anything in any enactment or in any prospectus or other document relating to the terms of issue, holding or transfer of specified securities, an exempt transfer shall be effective without the need for an instrument in writing.

1(3)   [Definition]   In this section "**the appropriate power**" means the power to make regulations or orders under—

(a)   section 47 of the Finance Act 1942 (Government stock) or section 11(1)(c) of the Exchequer and Financial Provisions Act (Northern Ireland) 1950 (Northern Ireland Exchequer stock); or

(b)   paragraph 4 of Schedule 13 to the Local Government Act 1972, paragraph 5 of Schedule 3 to the Local Government (Scotland) Act 1975 or section 70 of the Local Government Act (Northern Ireland) 1972 (local authority stocks); or

(c)   section 16(3) of the Electricity Act 1957 or Article 20 of the Electricity Supply (Northern Ireland) Order 1972 (electricity stock); or

(d)   (repealed by Gas Act 1986, Sch. 9, Pt. II as from 24 August 1986 (see S.I. 1986 No. 1318).)

(e)   subsection (4) below.

1(4)   [Treasury regulations]   Subject to subsection (5) below, with respect to any specified securities to which none of the provisions referred to in paragraphs (a) to (d) of subsection (3) above applies, the Treasury may by regulations under this subsection make the provision referred to in subsection (1) above; and any such regulations shall be made by statutory instrument which shall be subject to annulment in pursuance of a resolution of either House of Parliament.

1(5)   [Agreement of issuer required]   No provision shall be made, in the exercise of the appropriate power, for the application of the procedure of an exempt transfer to any securities or securities of any class except with the agreement of the person issuing the securities or, as the case may be, securities of that class or, if the liability for those securities or securities of that class has vested in another person, of that other person.

SEC. 2   Specified securities

2(1)   [Definition]   In this Act "**specified securities**" means, subject to subsection (2) below, securities for the time being specified in the list in Schedule 1 to this Act.

2(2)   [Stamp duty liability]   Notwithstanding that a security may at any time be specified as mentioned in subsection (1) above, it is not at that time a specified security for the purposes of this Act if, on a transfer of it at that time effected by a written instrument, that instrument would be liable to stamp duty.

2(3)   [Alterations in listed securities]   The Treasury may from time to time, after consultation with the Bank of England, by order—

(a)   add a security or class of securities to the list in Schedule 1 to this Act; or

(b)   remove a security or class of securities from that list (whether the security or class of securities was included in the list as originally enacted or was added by virtue of this subsection).

2(4) **[Statutory instruments]** The power to make an order under subsection (3) above shall be exercisable by statutory instrument which shall be laid before Parliament after being made.

SEC. 3 Regulations and amendments relating to the computerised system and exempt transfers

3(1) **[Related regulations]** The Treasury may by regulations made by statutory instrument make provision in connection with the operation of the system referred to in section 1(1) above.

3(2) **[Matters for which regulations may provide]** Without prejudice to the generality of subsection (1) above, but subject to any express provision made by or by virtue of any amendment contained in Schedule 2 to this Act, regulations under subsection (1) above may provide—

(a) that, for the purposes of any provision made by or under any enactment or contained in any prospectus or other document and requiring or relating to the lodging or deposit of any instrument of transfer, notification of an exempt transfer in the manner required by the regulations is to be regarded as lodging or depositing an instrument of the transfer concerned; and

(b) that, in such circumstances as may be specified in the regulations, certificates or other documents of or evidencing title to specified securities are or are not to be issued to persons who (by virtue of their participation in the system referred to in section 1(1) above) are or have been able to transfer such securities by exempt transfers.

3(3) **[Schedule 2 amendments]** The amendments specified in Schedule 2 to this Act shall have effect in consequence of the preceding provisions of this Act.

3(4) **[Alteration of other provisions]** The Secretary of State may by order made by statutory instrument repeal or amend any provision of—

(a) any local Act passed before or in the same session as this Act (including an Act confirming a provisional order), or

(b) any order or other instrument made under an Act so passed,

if it appears to him that the provision has become unnecessary or, requires alteration in consequence of any of the preceding provisions of this Act.

3(5) **[Orders subject to annulment]** A statutory instrument made in the exercise of the power conferred by subsection (1) or subsection (4) above shall be subject to annulment in pursuance of a resolution of either House of Parliament.

SEC. 4 Redemption of Government stock

4(1) **[Amendments to Finance Act 1921]** Schedule 3 to the Finance Act 1921 (provisions for carrying out redemption of Government stock) shall be amended in accordance with subsections (2) and (3) below.

4(2), (3)　(Amending provisions, not reproduced here.)

Note

S. 4 repealed by Finance Act 1989, s. 187(1) and Sch. 17, Pt. XII so far as relating to stock registered in the National Savings Stock Register on the coming into force of the first regulations made by virtue of National Debt Act 1972, s. 3(1)(bb) and so far as relating to other stock and bonds on the coming into force of the first regulations made by virtue of Finance Act 1942, s. 47(1)(bb).

SEC. 5　Custody and destruction of documents relating to local authority stocks and bonds

5(1), (2)　(Amendments to Local Government Act 1972 and Local Government (Scotland) Act 1975, not reproduced here.)

SEC. 6　Short title, commencement and extent

6(1)　**[Short title]**　This Act may be cited as the Stock Transfer Act 1982.

6(2)　**[Commencement]**　Sections 4 to 6 of this Act shall come into force at the expiry of the period of three months beginning on the day on which this Act is passed and the remaining provisions of this Act shall come into force on such later day as may be specified by the Treasury by order made by statutory instrument.

6(3)　**[Extent]**　This Act extends to Northern Ireland and, in so far as it amends the Exchange Control Act 1947, to the Channel Islands.

SCHEDULES

Schedule 1 — Specified Securities

Section 2

1(1)　Securities issued by Her Majesty's Government in the United Kingdom or the Government of Northern Ireland, not being excluded securities.

[The next page is 65,931]

1(2) In sub-paragraph (1) above "**excluded securities**" means—

   (a) securities in respect of which a stock certificate issued under Part V of the National Debt Act 1870 is for the time being outstanding;

   (b) any other bearer securities; and

   (c) any securities for the time being registered on the National Savings Stock Register.

2 Securities the payment of interest on which is guaranteed by Her Majesty's Government in the United Kingdom or the Government of Northern Ireland.

3 Securities issued in the United Kingdom by any public authority or nationalised industry or undertaking in the United Kingdom.

4(1) Securities issued in the United Kingdom by the government of any overseas territory, being securities registered in the United Kingdom.

4(2) The reference in sub-paragraph (1) above to the government of an overseas territory shall be construed as if it occurred in Part III of the Overseas Development and Co-operation Act 1980.

5 Securities issued in the United Kingdom by the International Bank for Reconstruction and Development, the Inter-American Development Bank, the European Investment Bank or the European Coal and Steel Community being, in each case, securities registered in the United Kingdom.

6(1) Debentures issued by the Agricultural Mortgage Corporation PLC, the Commonwealth Development Finance Company Limited, Finance for Industry Public Limited Company or the Scottish Agricultural Securities Corporation Limited.

6(2) In sub-paragraph (1) above "**debentures**" includes debenture stock and bonds, whether constituting a charge on assets or not, and loan stock or notes.

7(1) Securities issued by—

   (a) any local authority in the United Kingdom;

   (b) any authority all or the majority of the members of which are appointed or elected by one or more local authorities in the United Kingdom; or

   (c) the Receiver for the Metropolitan Police District.

7(2) In sub-paragraph (1) above "**local authority**" means—

   (a) any of the following authorities in England and Wales, namely, a county council, the Greater London Council, a district council, a London borough council, the Common Council of the City of London or the Council of the Isles of Scilly;

   (b) any of the following authorities in Scotland, namely, a regional council, an islands council or a district council; or

   (c) a council, within the meaning of the Local Government Act (Northern Ireland) 1972;

and any reference to a security issued by a local authority includes a reference to a security the liability for which is for the time being vested in a local authority (being a security issued by an authority which has ceased to exist).

8 Securities issued in the United Kingdom by the African Development Bank, the Asian Development Bank, Caisse Centrale de Coopération Economique, Crédit

Foncier de France, Electricité de France (E.D.F.) Service National or Hydro-Québec, being, in each case, securities registered in the United Kingdom.

History

The last type of securities in the list in Sch. 1 (allotted the number 8 by CCH) added by the Stock Transfer (Specified Securities) Order 1988 (S.I. 1988 No. 231), art. 2 and Sch. as from 17 March 1988.

Note

See also the Stock Transfer (Gilt-edged Securities) (CGO Service) Regulations 1985 (S.I. 1985 No. 1144), the Stock Transfer (Gilt-edged Securities) (Exempt Transfer) Regulations 1985 (S.I. 1985 No. 1145) as amended by the Stock Transfer (Gilt-edged Securities) (Exempt Transfer) (Amendment) Regulations 1990 (S.I. 1990 No. 1027), the Stock Transfer (Gilt-edged Securities) (Exempt Transfer) Regulations 1987 (S.I. 1987 No. 1294), the Stock Transfer (Gilt-edged Securities) (Exempt Transfer) Regulations 1988 (S.I. 1988 No. 232), the Stock Transfer (Gilt-edged Securities) (Exempt Transfer) Regulations 1989 (S.I. 1989 No. 880) and the Stock Transfer (Gilt-edged Securities) (Exempt Transfer) Regulations 1990 (S.I. 1990 No. 1211) in "Rules and Regulations" division.

Schedule 2 — Consequential Amendments

Section 3

(Amending provisions, not reproduced here.)

FINANCE ACT 1985

(1985 Chapter 54)

[*25th July 1985*]

SEC. 81   Renounceable letters of allotment etc.

81(1) [Application]   Subsection (2) below applies where there is an arrangement whereby—

(a) rights under an instrument are renounced in favour of a person (A),

(b) the rights are rights to shares in a company (company B), and

(c) A, or a person connected with A, or A and such a person together, has or have control of company B or will have such control in consequence of the arrangement.

81(2) [Instrument not exempt]   The instrument shall not be exempt by virtue of section 65(1) of the Finance Act 1963 (renounceable letters of allotment etc.) or section 14(1) of the Finance Act (Northern Ireland) 1963 (corresponding provision for Northern Ireland) from stamp duty under or by reference to the heading "Conveyance or Transfer on Sale" in Schedule 1 to the Stamp Act 1891.

81(3) [Shares in company B]   References in this section to shares in company B include references to its loan capital to which section 126(1) of the Finance Act 1976 does not apply by virtue of section 126(2) or (3) (convertible loan capital and excessive return capital).

Note

In construing s. 81(3) regard may still be had to Finance Act 1976, s. 126 — see Finance Act 1986, s. 78(1), (2), (10); s. 79.

81(4) [Shares]   In this section "**shares**" includes stock.

81(5) [Control]   For the purposes of this section a person has control of company B if he has power to control company B's affairs by virtue of holding shares in, or possessing voting power in relation to, company B or any other body corporate.

81(6) **[Connected persons]** For the purposes of this section one person is connected with another if he would be so connected for the purposes of the Capital Gains Tax Act 1979.

Note
See Capital Gains Tax Act 1979, s. 63(5).

81(7) **[Rights renounced]** This section applies to instruments if rights are renounced under them on or after 1st August 1985, except where the arrangement concerned includes an offer for the rights and on or before 27th June 1985 the offer became unconditional as to acceptances.

Note
Prospective repeal of s. 81 by Finance Act 1990, s. 132 and Sch. 19, Pt. VI in accordance with s. 107–111 of that Act.

FINANCE ACT 1986

(1986 Chapter 41)

[*25th July 1986*]

PART III — STAMP DUTY

SECURITIES

SEC. 66 Company's purchase of own shares

66(1) **[Application]** This section applies where a company purchases its own shares under section 162 of the Companies Act 1985 or Article 47 of the Companies (Northern Ireland) Order 1982.

Note
See now S.I. 1986 No. 1032 (N.I. 6) Companies (Northern Ireland) Order 1986.

66(2) **[Return treated as instrument of transfer]** The return which relates to the shares purchased and is delivered to the registrar of companies under section 169 of that Act or, as the case may be, Article 53 of that Order shall be charged with stamp duty, and treated for all purposes of the Stamp Act 1891, as if it were an instrument transferring the shares on sale to the company in pursuance of the contract (or contracts) of purchase concerned.

66(3) **[Effective date]** Subject to subsection (4) below, this section applies to any return under section 169 of the Companies Act 1985, or Article 53 of the Companies (Northern Ireland) Order 1982, which is delivered to the registrar of companies on or after the day of The Stock Exchange reforms.

66(4) **[Effective date — exception]** This section does not apply to any return to the extent that shares to which it relates were purchased under a contract entered into before the day of The Stock Exchange reforms.

66(5) **[Definition — day of Stock Exchange reforms]** In this section "**the day of The Stock Exchange reforms**" means the day on which the rule of The Stock Exchange that prohibits a person from carrying on business as both a broker and a jobber is abolished.

Note
Date of Stock Exchange Reforms ("Big Bang"): 27 October 1986.

Prospective repeal of s. 66 by Finance Act 1990, s. 132 and Sch. 19, Pt. VI in accordance with s. 107–111 of that Act.

SEC. 75　Acquisitions: reliefs

75(1)　[Application]　This section applies where a company (the acquiring company) acquires the whole or part of an undertaking of another company (the target company) in pursuance of a scheme for the reconstruction of the target company.

75(2)　[Conditional relief]　If the first and second conditions (as defined below) are fulfilled, stamp duty under the heading "Conveyance or Transfer on Sale" in Schedule 1 to the Stamp Act 1891 shall not be chargeable on an instrument executed for the purposes of or in connection with the transfer of the undertaking or part.

75(3)　[Instrument duly stamped]　An instrument on which stamp duty is not chargeable by virtue only of subsection (2) above shall not be taken to be duly stamped unless it is stamped with the duty to which it would be liable but for that subsection or it has, in accordance with section 12 of the Stamp Act 1891, been stamped with a particular stamp denoting that it is not chargeable with any duty.

75(4)　[Condition one — issue of shares by U.K. registered company]　The first condition is that the registered office of the acquiring company is in the United Kingdom and that the consideration for the acquisition—

(a) consists of or includes the issue of shares in the acquiring company to all the shareholders of the target company;

(b) includes nothing else (if anything) but the assumption or discharge by the acquiring company of liabilities of the target company.

75(5)　[Condition two — bona fide commercial arrangement]　The second condition is that—

(a) the acquisition is effected for bona fide commercial reasons and does not form part of a scheme or arrangement of which the main purpose, or one of the main purposes, is avoidance of liability to stamp duty, income tax, corporation tax or capital gains tax,

(b) after the acquisition has been made, each shareholder of each of the companies is a shareholder of the other, and

(c) after the acquisition has been made, the proportion of shares of one of the companies held by any shareholder is the same as the proprotion of shares of the other company held by that shareholder.

75(6)　[Effective date for instruments]　This section applies to any instrument which is executed after 24th March 1986 unless it is executed in pursuance of an unconditional contract made on or before 18th March 1986.

75(7)　[Deemed commencing date]　This section shall be deemed to have come into force on 25th March 1986.

SEC. 76　Acquisitions: further provisions about reliefs

76(1)　[Application]　This section applies where a company (the acquiring company) acquires the whole or part of an undertaking of another company (the target company).

76(2)　[Maximum rate of charge]　If the condition mentioned in subsection (3) below is fulfilled, and stamp duty under the heading "Conveyance or Transfer on

FA 1986, sec. 75(1)　　[The next page is 65,981]　　**CCH Editions Limited**

Sale" in Schedule 1 to the Stamp Act 1891 is chargeable on an instrument executed for the purposes of or in connection with—

    (a) the transfer of the undertaking or part, or

    (b) the assignment to the acquiring company by a creditor of the target company of any relevant debts (secured or unsecured) owed by the target company,

the rate at which the duty is charged under that heading shall not exceed that mentioned in subsection (4) below.

76(3) [Issue of shares by U.K. registered company] The condition is that the registered office of the acquiring company is in the United Kingdom and that the consideration for the acquisition—

    (a) consists of or includes the issue of shares in the acquiring company to the target company or to all or any of its shareholders;

    (b) includes nothing else (if anything) but cash not exceeding 10 per cent of the nominal value of those shares, or the assumption or discharge by the acquiring company of liabilities of the target company, or both.

76(4) [Rate of charge] The rate is the rate of 50p for every £100 or part of £100 of the amount or value of the consideration for the sale to which the instrument gives effect.

76(5) [Instrument duly stamped] An instrument on which, by virtue only of subsection (2) above, the rate at which stamp duty is charged is not to exceed that mentioned in subsection (4) above shall not be taken to be duly stamped unless it is stamped with the duty to which it would be liable but for subsection (2) above or it has, in accordance with section 12 of the Stamp Act 1891, been stamped with a particular stamp denoting that it is duly stamped.

76(6) [Definition — relevant debts] In subsection (2)(b) above **"relevant debts"** means—

    (a) any debt in the case of which the assignor is a bank or trade creditor, and

    (b) any other debt incurred not less than two years before the date on which the instrument is executed.

76(7) [Effective date] This section applies to any instrument executed on or after the day on which the rule of The Stock Exchange that prohibits a person from carrying on business as both a broker and a jobber is abolished.

Note
Date of Stock Exchange Reforms ("Big Bang"): 27 October 1986.

SEC. 77   Acquisition of target company's share capital

77(1) [Instrument transferring shares between companies] Stamp duty under the heading "Conveyance or Transfer on Sale" in Schedule 1 to the Stamp Act 1891 shall not be chargeable on an instrument transferring shares in one company (the target company) to another company (the acquiring company) if the conditions mentioned in subsection (3) below are fulfilled.

77(2) [Instrument duly stamped] An instrument on which stamp duty is not chargeable by virtue only of subsection (1) above shall not be taken to be duly stamped unless it is stamped with the duty to which it would be liable but for that subsection or it has, in accordance with section 12 of the Stamp Act 1891, been stamped with a particular stamp denoting that it is not chargeable with any duty.

77(3) [Conditions of exemption] The conditions are that—

(a) the registered office of the acquiring company is in the United Kingdom,

(b) the transfer forms part of an arrangement by which the acquiring company acquires the whole of the issued share capital of the target company,

(c) the acquisition is effected for bona fide commercial reasons and does not form part of a scheme or arrangement of which the main purpose, or one of the main purposes, is avoidance of liability to stamp duty, stamp duty reserve tax, income tax, corporation tax or capital gains tax,

(d) the consideration for the acquisition consists only of the issue of shares in the acquiring company to the shareholders of the target company,

(e) after the acquisition has been made, each person who immediately before it was made was a shareholder of the target company is a shareholder of the acquiring company,

(f) after the acquisition has been made, the shares in the acquiring company are of the same classes as were the shares in the target company immediately before the acquisition was made,

(g) after the acquisition has been made, the number of shares of any particular class in the acquiring company bears to all the shares in that company the same proportion as the number of shares of that class in the target company bore to all the shares in that company immediately before the acquisition was made, and

(h) after the acquisition has been made, the proportion of shares of any particular class in the acquiring company held by any particular shareholder is the same as the proportion of shares of that class in the target company held by him immediately before the acquisition was made.

77(4) [Inclusive reference to stock] In this section references to shares and to share capital include references to stock.

77(5) [Effective date] This section applies to any instrument executed on or after 1st August 1986.

Note
Prospective repeal of s. 77 by Finance Act 1990, s. 132 and
Sch. 19, Pt. VI in accordance with s. 107–111 of that Act.

LOAN CAPITAL, LETTERS OF ALLOTMENT ETC.

SEC. 79   Loan capital: new provisions

79(1) [Repeals] The following provisions shall cease to have effect—

(a) in section 62 of the Finance Act 1963, subsections (2) and (6) (commonwealth stock);

(b) in section 11 of the Finance Act (Northern Ireland) 1963, subsections (2) and (5) (commonwealth stock);

(c) section 29 of the Finance Act 1967 (local authority capital);

(d) section 6 of the Finance Act (Northern Ireland) 1967 (local authority capital);

(e) section 126 of the Finance Act 1976 (loan capital).

79(2)   [Inapplicability of Bearer Instrument heading]   Stamp duty under the heading "Bearer Instrument" in Schedule 1 to the Stamp Act 1891 shall not be chargeable on the issue of an instrument which relates to loan capital or on the transfer of the loan capital constituted by, or transferable by means of, such an instrument.

79(3)   [Issued or raised by specified organisations]   Stamp duty shall not be chargeable on an instrument which transfers loan capital issued or raised by—

(a) the financial support fund of the Organisation for Economic Co-operation and Development,

(b) the Inter-American Development Bank, or

(c) an organisation which was a designated international organisation at the time of the transfer (whether or not it was such an organisation at the time the loan capital was issued or raised).

79(4)   [Other loan capital]   Subject to subsections (5) and (6) below, stamp duty shall not be chargeable on an instrument which transfers any other loan capital.

79(5)   [Convertible loan capital]   Subsection (4) above does not apply to an instrument transferring loan capital which, at the time the instrument is executed, carries a right (exercisable then or later) of conversion into shares or other securities, or to the acquisition of shares or other securities, including loan capital of the same description.

79(6)   [Excessive interest or repayment]   Subject to subsection (7) below, subsection (4) above does not apply to an instrument transferring loan capital which, at the time the instrument is executed or any earlier time, carries or has carried—

(a) a right to interest the amount of which exceeds a reasonable commercial return on the nominal amount of the capital,

(b) a right to interest the amount of which falls or has fallen to be determined to any extent by reference to the results of, or of any part of, a business or to the value of any property, or

(c) a right on repayment to an amount which exceeds the nominal amount of the capital and is not reasonably comparable with what is generally repayable (in respect of a similar nominal amount of capital) under the terms of issue of loan capital listed in the Official List of The Stock Exchange.

79(7)   [Indexed interest or repayment]   Subsection (4) above shall not be prevented from applying to an instrument by virtue of subsection (6)(a) or (c) above by reason only that the loan capital concerned carries a right to interest, or (as the case may be) to an amount payable on repayment, determined to any extent by reference to an index showing changes in the general level of prices payable in the United Kingdom over a period substantially corresponding to the period between the issue or raising of the loan capital and its repayment.

79(8)   [Rate of charge]   Where stamp duty under the heading "Conveyance or Transfer on Sale" in Schedule 1 to the Stamp Act 1891 is chargeable on an instrument which transfers loan capital, the rate at which the duty is charged under that heading shall be the rate of 50p for every £100 or part of £100 of the amount or value of the consideration for the sale to which the instrument gives effect.

79(9)   **[Effective date — bearer instruments]**   This section applies to any instrument which falls within section 60(1) of the Finance Act 1963 and is issued after 31st July 1986.

79(10)   **[Effective date — stock transfer]**   This section applies to any instrument which falls within section 60(2) of that Act if the loan capital constituted by or transferable by means of it is transferred after 31st July 1986.

79(11)   **[Effective date — other instruments]**   This section applies, in the case of instruments not falling within section 60(1) or (2) of that Act, to any instrument which is executed after 31st July 1986.

79(12)   **[Inclusive references]**   Subsections (7), (9), (10) and (14) of section 78 above shall apply as if references to that section included references to this.

Note
Prospective repeal of s. 79(2)–(8) and reference in s. 79(12)
to s. 79(7), (9) by Finance Act 1990, s. 132 and Sch. 19,
Pt. VI in accordance with s. 107–111 of that Act.

SEC. 80   Bearer letters of allotment etc.

80(1)   **[Removal of exemption]**   In Schedule 1 to the Stamp Act 1891, in the heading "Bearer Instrument", paragraph 2 of the exemptions (bearer letter of allotment etc. required to be surrendered not later than six months after issue) shall be omitted.

80(2)   **[Application — bearer instruments]**   This section applies to any instrument which falls within section 60(1) of the Finance Act 1963 and is issued after 24th March 1986, unless it is issued by a company in pursuance of a general offer for its shares and the offer became unconditional as to acceptances on or before 18th March 1986.

80(3)   **[Application — stock transfer]**   This section applies to any instrument which falls within section 60(2) of that Act if the stock constituted by or transferable by means of it is transferred after 24th March 1986.

80(4)   **[Inclusive references — Northern Ireland]**   In this section the reference to section 60(1) of the Finance Act 1963 includes a reference to section 9(1)(a) of the Finance Act (Northern Ireland) 1963 and the reference to section 60(2) of the former Act includes a reference to section 9(1)(b) of the latter.

80(5)   **[Deemed effective date]**   This section shall be deemed to have come into force on 25th March 1986.

CHANGES IN FINANCIAL INSTITUTIONS

SEC. 81   Sales to market makers

81(1)   **[Exemption]**   Stamp duty shall not be chargeable on an instrument transferring stock on sale to a person or his nominee if it is shown to the satisfaction of the Commissioners that the transaction to which the instrument gives effect was carried out by the person in the ordinary course of his business as a market maker in stock of the kind transferred.

81(2)   **[Instrument duly stamped]**   An instrument on which stamp duty is not chargeable by virtue only of subsection (1) above shall not be deemed to be duly stamped unless it has been stamped with a stamp denoting that it is not chargeable with any duty; and notwithstanding anything in section 122(1) of the Stamp Act 1891, the stamp may be a stamp of such kind as the Commissioners may prescribe.

81(3) [Market maker] For the purposes of this section a person is a market maker in stock of a particular kind—

    (a) if he—

        (i) holds himself out at all normal items in compliance with the rules of The Stock Exchange as willing to buy and sell stock of that kind at a price specified by him, and

        (ii) is recognised as doing so by the Council of The Stock Exchange; or

    (b) if—

        (i) he is an authorised person under Chapter III of Part I of the Financial Services Act 1986,

        (ii) he carried out the transaction in the course of his business as a dealer in investments, within the meaning of paragraph 12 of Schedule 1 to the Financial Services Act 1986, as a principal and in circumstances where that paragraph was applicable for the purposes of that Act,

        (iii) he did not carry out the transaction in the course of any of the activities which fall within paragraph 14 or 16 of Schedule 1 to the Financial Services Act 1986, and

        (iv) the stock was not at the time the transaction was carried out dealt in on a recognised investment exchange.

History
S. 81(3) substituted in accordance with s. 81(5)–(7) by S.I. 1988 No. 654, reg. 1, 2 as from 29 April 1988; s. 81(3) formerly read as follows:

"For the purposes of this section a person is a market maker in stock of a particular kind if he—

    (a) holds himself out at all normal times in compliance with the rules of The Stock Exchange as willing to buy and sell stock of that kind at a price specified by him, and

    (b) is recognised as doing so by the Council of The Stock Exchange."

81(4) [Effective date] Subject to subsection (6) below, this section applies to any instrument giving effect to a transaction carried out on or after the day of The Stock Exchange reforms.

Note
Date of Stock Exchange Reforms: 27 October 1986.

81(5) [Power to substitute definition of market maker] The Treasury may by regulations provide that for subsection (3) above (as it has effect for the time being) there shall be substituted a subsection containing a different definition of a market maker for the purposes of this section.

81(6) [Effective date — regulations] Regulations under subsection (5) above shall apply in relation to any instrument giving effect to a transaction carried out on or after such day, after the day of The Stock Exchange reforms, as is specified in the regulations.

81(7) [Power to make regulations] The power to make regulations under subsection (5) above shall be exercisable by statutory instrument subject to annulment in pursuance of a resolution of the House of Commons.

Note
Prospective repeal of s. 81 by Finance Act 1990, s. 132 and Sch. 19, Pt. VI in accordance with s. 107–111 of that Act.

SEC. 82   Borrowing of stock by market makers

82(1) [Application — market makers] This section applies where a person (A) has contracted to sell stock in the ordinary course of his business as a market maker in stock of that kind and, to enable him to fulfil the contract, he enters into an arrangement under which—

(a) another person (B), who is not a market maker in stock of the kind concerned or a nominee of such a market maker, is to transfer stock to A or his nominee, and

(b) in return stock of the same kind and amount is to be transferred (whether or not by A or his nominee) to B or his nominee.

82(2) [Application — non-market makers] This section also applies where, to enable B to make the transfer to A or his nominee, B enters into an arrangement under which—

(a) another person (C), who is not a market maker in stock of the kind concerned or a nominee of such a market maker, is to transfer stock to B or his nominee, and

(b) in return stock of the same kind and amount is to be transferred (whether or not by B or his nominee) to C or his nominee.

82(3) [Fixed duty] The maximum stamp duty chargeable on an instrument effecting a transfer to B or his nominee or C or his nominee in pursuance of an arrangement mentioned in subsection (1) or (2) above shall be 50p.

82(4) [Definition — market maker] For the purposes of this section a person is a **market maker** in stock of a particular kind if he—

(a) holds himself out at all normal times in compliance with the rules of The Stock Exchange as willing to buy and sell stock of that kind at a price specified by him, and

(b) is recognised as doing so by the Council of The Stock Exchange.

82(5) [Effective date] Subject to subsection (7) below, this section applies to any instrument effecting a transfer in pursuance of an arrangement entered into on or after the day of The Stock Exchange reforms.

82(6) [Power to substitute definition of market maker] The Treasury may by regulations provide that for subsection (3) above (as it has effect for the time being) there shall be substituted a subsection containing a different definition of a market maker for the purposes of this section.

82(7) [Effective date — regulations] Regulations under subsection (6) above shall apply in relation to any instrument effecting a transfer in pursuance of an arrangement entered into on or after such day, after the day of The Stock Exchange reforms, as is specified in the regulations.

Note
In s. 82(4), (7) date of Stock Exchange Reforms: 27 October 1986.

82(8) [Power to make regulations] The power to make regulations under subsection (6) above shall be exercisable by statutory instrument subject to annulment in pursuance of a resolution of the House of Commons.

Note
Prospective repeal of s. 82 by Finance Act 1990, s. 132 and Sch. 19, Pt. VI in accordance with s. 107–111 of that Act.

SEC. **84** Miscellaneous exemptions

84(1) [Transfer to stock exchange nominee] In section 127(1) of the Finance Act 1976 (no stamp duty on transfer to stock exchange nominee executed for purposes of a stock exchange transaction) the words "which is executed for the purposes of a stock exchange transaction" shall be omitted.

84(2) [Transfer to recognised investment exchange or nominee] Stamp duty shall not be chargeable on an instrument effecting a transfer of stock if—

    (a) the transferee is a recognised investment exchange or a nominee of a recognised investment exchange, and

    (b) an agreement which relates to the stamp duty which would (apart from this subsection) be chargeable on the instrument, and was made between the Commissioners and the investment exchange under section 33 of the Finance Act 1970, is in force at the time of the transfer.

84(3) [Transfer to recognised clearing house or nominee] Stamp duty shall not be chargeable on an instrument effecting a transfer of stock if—

    (a) the transferee is a recognised clearing house or a nominee of a recognised clearing house, and

    (b) an agreement which relates to the stamp duty which would (apart from this subsection) be chargeable on the instrument, and was made between the Commissioners and the clearing house under section 33 of the Finance Act 1970, is in force at the time of the transfer.

84(4) [Effective date — stock exchange nominee] Subsection (1) above applies to any transfer giving effect to a transaction carried out on or after the day of The Stock Exchange reforms.

84(5) [Effective date — recognised investment exchange or nominee] Subsection (2) above applies to any instrument giving effect to a transaction carried out on or after such day as the Commissioners may appoint by order made by statutory instrument.

84(6) [Effective date — recognised clearing house or nominee] Subsection (3) above applies to any instrument giving effect to a transaction carried out on or after such day as the Commissioners may appoint by order made by statutory instrument.

Note
Prospective repeal of s. 84 by Finance Act 1990, s. 132 and Sch. 19, Pt. VI in accordance with s. 107–111 of that Act.

PART IV — STAMP DUTY RESERVE TAX

[CCH Note: Although imposed on transfers of chargeable securities, and so not technically a Stamp Duty, the Stamp Duty Reserve Tax provisions are included here for ease of reference.]

INTRODUCTION

SEC. **86** The tax: introduction

86(1) [Stamp duty reserve tax] A tax, to be known as stamp duty reserve tax, shall be charged in accordance with this Part of this Act.

86(2)   **[Administration]**   The tax shall be under the care and management of the Board.

86(3)   **[Provisional Collection of Taxes]**   Section 1 of the Provisional Collection of Taxes Act 1968 shall apply to the tax; and accordingly in subsection (1) of that section after the words "petroleum revenue tax" there shall be inserted the words "stamp duty reserve tax".

Note
Prospective repeal of s. 86 by Finance Act 1990, s. 132 and
Sch. 19, Pt. VII in relation to s. 87, 93 and 96 in accordance
with Finance Act 1990, s. 110, 111.

THE PRINCIPAL CHARGE

SEC. 87   The principal charge

87(1)   **[Application]**   This section applies where person (A) agrees with another person (B) to transfer chargeable securities (whether or not to B) for consideration in money or money's worth.

87(2)   **[Two months from relevant day]**   There shall be a charge to stamp duty reserve tax under this section on the expiry of the period of two months beginning with the relevant day, unless the agreement is to transfer the securities to B or his nominee and the first and second conditions mentioned below have been fulfilled by the time that period expires.

87(3)   **[Definition — relevant day]**   In subsection (2) above **"the relevant day"** means—

    (a)   in a case where the agreement is conditional, the day on which the condition is satisfied, and

    (b)   in any other case, the day on which the agreement is made.

87(4)   **[Transfer of all securities subject to the arrangement]**   The first condition is that an instrument is (or instruments are) executed in pursuance of the agreement and the instrument transfers (or the instruments between them transfer) to B or, as the case may be, to his nominee all the chargeable securities to which the agreement relates.

87(5)   **[Instrument to be duly stamped]**   The second condition is that the instrument (or each instrument) transferring the chargeable securities to which the agreement relates is duly stamped in accordance with the enactments relating to stamp duty if it is an instrument which, under those enactments, is chargeable with stamp duty or otherwise required to be stamped.

87(6)   **[Rate of charge]**   Tax under this section shall be charged at the rate of 50p for every £100 or part of £100 of the amount or value of the consideration mentioned in subsection (1) above.

87(7)   **[Non-monetary consideration]**   For the purposes of subsection (6) above the value of any consideration not consisting of money shall be taken to be the price it might reasonably be expected to fetch on a sale in the open market at the time the agreement mentioned in subsection (1) above is made.

87(7A)   **[Where no charge if separate agreements made]**   Where there would be no charge to tax under this section in relation to some of the chargeable securities to which the agreement between A and B relates if separate agreements had been made between them for the transfer of those securities and for the transfer of the remainder, this section shall have effect as if such separate agreements had been made.

87(7B)   [If transfer by way of security for loan to B]   This section shall have effect in relation to a person to whom the chargeable securities are transferred by way of security for a loan to B as it has effect in relation to a nominee of B.

History
S. 87(7A), (7B) inserted by Finance Act 1987, s. 56 and Sch. 7, para. 2 with retrospective effect.

87(8)   [Enactments relating to stamp duty]   In this section **"the enactments relating to stamp duty"** means the Stamp Act 1891 and any enactment which amends or is required to be construed together with that Act.

87(9)   [Effective date]   This section applies where the agreement to transfer is made on or after the day on which the rule of The Stock Exchange that prohibits a person from carrying on business as both a broker and a jobber is abolished.

Note
The day in s. 87(9) is 27 October 1986.

87(10)   [Exceptions and special cases]   This section has effect subject to sections 88 to 90 below.

Note
Prospective repeal of s. 87 by Finance Act 1990, s. 132 and Sch. 19, Pt. VII for agreements made or conditions satisfied (as appropriate) on or after a day to be appointed in accordance with Finance Act 1990, s. 110, 111.

SEC. 88   Section 87: special cases

88(1)   [Transfers of stock exempt from stamp duty]   An instrument on which stamp duty is not chargeable by virtue of—

  (a) section 127(1) of the Finance Act 1976 (transfer to stock exchange nominee), or

  (b) section 84(2) or (3) above,

shall be disregarded in construing section 87(4) and (5) above.

88(2)   [Inland bearer instruments exempt from stamp duty]   Subsection (3) below applies where the chargeable securities mentioned in section 87(1) above are constituted by or transferable by means of an inland bearer instrument, within the meaning of the heading "Bearer Instrument" in Schedule 1 to the Stamp Act 1891, which—

  (a) is exempt from stamp duty under that heading by virtue of exemption 3 in that heading, or

  (b) would be so exempt if it were otherwise chargeable under that heading.

88(3)   [Reserve duty on aforesaid inland bearer instruments]   In such a case section 87 above shall have effect as if the following were omitted—

  (a) in subsection (2) the words "the expiry of the period of two months beginning with" and the words from "unless" to the end;

  (b) subsections (4), (5) and (8).

History
In s. 88(3) "the words 'the expiry of the period of two months beginning with' and" inserted by Finance Act 1987, s. 56 and Sch. 7, para. 3 for agreements made after 31 July 1987.

Note
Prospective repeal of s. 88 by Finance Act 1990, s. 132 and Sch. 19, Pt. VII in relation to s. 87 in accordance with Finance Act 1990, s. 110, 111.

SEC. 89   Section 87: exceptions for market makers etc.

89(1)   **[B as market maker]**   Section 87 above shall not apply as regards an agreement to transfer securities if the agreement is made by B in the ordinary course of his business as a market maker in securities of the kind concerned.

89(1A)   **[Non-application of sec. 89(1)]**   Section 87 above shall not apply as regards an agreement to transfer securities to B or his nominee if the agreement is made by B in the ordinary course of his business as a market maker in securities consisting of related quoted options; and in this subsection—

     (a)   **"quoted options"** means options quoted on TheStock Exchange, and

     (b)   **"related quoted options"** means quoted options to buy or sell securities of the kind transferred.

History
S. 89(1A) inserted by Finance Act 1987, s. 56 and Sch. 7,
para. 4 with retrospective effect.

89(2)   **[B as broker and dealer]**   Section 87 above shall not apply as regards an agreement to transfer securities to B or his nominee if—

     (a)   the agreement is made by B as principal in the ordinary course of his business as a broker and dealer in relation to securities of the kind concerned, and

     (b)   before the end of the period of 7 days beginning with the day on which the agreement is made or (in a case where the agreement is conditional) the day on which the condition is satisfied, B enters into an unconditional agreement to sell the securities to another person.

89(3)   **[Market maker]**   For the purposes of this section a person is a market maker in securities of a particular kind—

     (a)   if he—

         (i)   holds himself out at all normal times in compliance with the rules of The Stock Exchange as willing to buy and sell securities of that kind at a price specified by him, and

         (ii)   is recognised as doing so by the Council of The Stock Exchange; or

     (b)   if—

         (i)   he is an authorised person under Chapter III of Part I of the Financial Services Act 1986,

         (ii)   he makes the agreement in the course of his business as a dealer in investments, within the meaning of paragraph 12 of Schedule 1 to the Financial Services Act 1986, as a principal and in circumstances where that paragraph is applicable for the purposes of that Act,

         (iii)   he does not make the agreement in the course of any activities which fall within paragraph 14 or 16 of Schedule 1 to the Financial Services Act 1986, and

(iv) the securities are not at the time the agreement is made dealt in on a recognised investment exchange within the meaning of the Financial Services Act 1986.

History
S. 89(3) substituted in accordance with s. 89(5), (9) by S.I. 1988 No. 654, reg. 1, 3 as from 29 April 1988; s. 89(3) formerly read as follows:

"**89(3)** For the purposes of this section, a person is a market maker in securities of a particular kind if he—

  (a) holds himself out at all normal times in compliance

with the rules of The Stock Exchange as willing to buy and sell securities of that kind at a price specified by him, and

  (b) is recognised as doing so by the Council of The Stock Exchange."

89(4) [Definition — broker and dealer]   For the purposes of this section, a person is a broker and dealer in relation to securities of a particular kind if he is a member of The Stock Exchange who carries on his business in the United Kingdom and is not a market maker in securities of that kind.

89(5) [Power to substitute definition — market maker]   The Treasury may by regulations provide that for subsection (3) above (as it has effect for the time being) there shall be substituted a subsection containing a different definition of a market maker for the purposes of this section.

89(6) [Power to substitute definition — broker and dealer]   The Treasury may by regulations provide that for subsection (4) above (as it has effect for the time being) there shall be substituted a subsection containing a different definition of a broker and dealer for the purposes of this section.

89(7) [Identification of securities]   For the purposes of subsection (2) above, if the securities which B sells cannot be identified (apart from this subsection) securities shall be taken as follows—

  (a) securities of the same kind acquired in the period of 7 days ending with the day of the sale (and not taken for the purposes of a previous sale by B) shall be taken before securities of that kind acquired outside that period;

  (b) securities of that kind acquired earlier in that period (and not taken for the purposes of a previous sale by B) shall be taken before securities of that kind acquired later in that period.

89(8) [Securities — acquisition and sale]   For the purposes of subsection (7) above—

  (a) securities are acquired when B enters into an agreement for them to be transferred to B or his nominee or (in a case where the agreement is conditional) when the condition is satisfied;

  (b) B sells securities when he enters into an unconditional agreement to sell them to another person.

89(9) [Power to make regulations]   The power to make regulations under this section shall be exercisable by statutory insltrument subject to annulment in pursuance of a resolution of the House of Commons.

SEC. **89A**   Section 87: exceptions for public issue

89A(1) [Certain units under unit trust scheme]   Section 87 above shall not apply as regards an agreement to transfer securities other than units under a unit trust scheme to B or B's nominee if—

(a) the agreement is part of an arrangement, entered into by B in the ordinary course of B's business as an issuing house, under which B (as principal) is to offer the securities for sale to the public,

(b) the agreement is conditional upon the admission of the securities to the Official List of The Stock Exchange,

(c) the consideration under the agreement for each security is the same as the price at which B is to offer the security for sale, and

(d) B sells the securities in accordance with the arrangements referred to in paragraph (a) above.

89A(2)   **[Certain newly subscribed securities]**   Section 87 above shall not apply as regards an agreement if the securities to which the agreement relates are newly subscribed securities other than units under a unit trust scheme and—

(a) the agreement is made in pursuance of an offer to the public made by A (as principal) under an arrangement entered into in the ordinary course of A's business as an issuing house,

(b) a right of allotment in respect of, or to subscribe for, the securities has been acquired by A under an agreement which is part of the arrangement,

(c) both those agreements are conditional upon the admission of the securities to the Official List of The Stock Exchange, and

(d) the consideration for each security is the same under both agreements;

and for the purposes of this subsection, "newly subscribed securities" are securities which, in pursuance of the arrangement referred to in paragraph (a) above, are issued wholly for new consideration.

89A(3)   **[Certain registered securities]**   Section 87 above shall not apply as regards an agreement if the securities to which the agreement relates are registered securities other than units under a unit trust scheme and—

(a) the agreement is made in pursuance of an offer to the public made by A,

(b) the agreement is conditional upon the admission of the securities to the Official List of The Stock Exchange, and

(c) under the agreement A issues to B or his nominee a renouncable letter of acceptance, or similar instrument, in respect of the securities.

89A(4)   **[Regulations]**   The Treasury may by regulations amend paragraph (b) of subsection (1) above, paragraph (c) of subsection (2) above, and paragraph (b) of subsection (3) above (as they have effect for the time being); and the power to make regulations under this section shall be exercisable by statutory instrument subject to annulment in pursuance of a resolution of the House of Commons.

History
S. 89A inserted by Finance (No. 2) Act 1987, s. 100(1) for agreements to transfer securities made after 7 May 1987.

Note
Prospective repeal of s. 89A by Finance Act 1990, s. 132 and Sch. 19, Pt. VII in relation to s. 87 in accordance with Finance Act 1990, s. 110, 111.

SEC. 90   Section 87: other exceptions

90(1)   **[Unit trusts]**   Section 87 above shall not apply as regards an agreement to transfer a unit under a unit trust scheme to the managers under the scheme.

90(2) **[Overseas unit trusts]** Section 87 above shall not apply as regards an agreement to transfer a unit under a unit trust scheme if at the time the agreement is made—

(a) all the trustees under the scheme are resident outside the United Kingdom, and

(b) the unit is not registered in a register kept in the United Kingdom by or on behalf of the trustees under the scheme.

90(3) **[Certain bearer instruments]** Section 87 above shall not apply as regards an agreement to transfer securities constituted by or transferable by means of—

(a) an overseas bearer instrument, within the meaning of the heading "Bearer Instrument" in Schedule 1 to the Stamp Act 1891;

(b) an inland bearer instrument, within the meaning of that heading, which does not fall within exemption 3 in that heading (renounceable letter of allotment etc. where rights are renounceable not later than six months after issue).

90(4) **[Sections 93(1) and 96(1)]** Section 87 above shall not apply as regards an agreement which forms part of an arrangement falling within section 93(1) or 96(1) below.

90(5) **[Securities held by sec. 90(6) person]** Section 87 above shall not apply as regards an agreement to transfer securities which the Board are satisfied are held, when the agreement is made, by a person within subsection (6) below.

90(6) **[Person for sec. 90(5)]** A person is within this subsection if his business is exclusively that of holding shares, stock or other marketable securities—

(a) as nominee or agent for a person whose business is or includes the provision of clearance services for the purchase and sale of shares, stock or other marketable securities, and

(b) for the purpose of such part of the business mentioned in paragraph (a) above as consists of the provision of such clearance services (in a case where the business does not consist exclusively of that);

and in this subsection, "marketable securities" shall be construed in accordance with section 122(1) of the Stamp Act 1891.

90(7) **[Agreements to certain bodies]** Section 87 above shall not apply as regards an agreement to transfer securities to—

(a) a body of persons established for charitable purposes only, or

(b) the trustees of a trust so established, or

(c) the Trustees of the National Heritage Memorial Fund, or

(d) the Historic Buildings and Monuments Commission for England.

History
S. 90(5), (6) substituted for the former s. 90(5) and s. 90(7) inserted by Finance Act 1987, s. 56 and Sch. 7, para. 5, 6 with retrospective effect; the former s. 90(5) read as follows:

"Section 87 above shall not apply as regards an agreement to transfer securities which the Board are satisfied are held, when the agreement is made, by a person whose business is exclusively that of holding chargeable securities—

(a)   as nominee or agent for a person whose business is or includes the provision of clearance services for the purchase and sale of chargeable securities, and

(b)   for the purposes of such part of the business mentioned in paragraph (a) above as consists of

the provision of such clearance services (in a case where the business does not consist exclusively of that)."

Note

Prospective repeal of s. 90 by Finance Act 1990, s. 132 and Sch. 19, Pt. VII in relation to s. 87 in accordance with Finance Act 1990, s. 110, 111.

SEC. 91   Liability to tax

91(1)   **[B liable to tax]**   Where tax is charged under section 87 above as regards an agreement, B shall be liable for the tax.

91(2)   (Repealed by Finance (No. 2) Act 1987, sec. 100(2) and Sch. 9, Pt. IV.)

History

S. 91(2) formerly read as follows:

"But where B is acting as nominee for another person, that other person shall be liable for the tax."

Note

Prospective repeal of s. 91 by Finance Act 1990, s. 132 and Sch. 19, Pt. VII in relation to s. 87 in accordance with Finance Act 1990, s. 110, 111.

SEC. 92   Repayment or cancellation of tax

92(1)   **[Application — conditions and timing]**   If, as regards an agreement to transfer securities to B or his nominee, tax is charged under section 87 above and it is proved to the Board's satisfaction that at a time after the expiry of the period of two months (beginning with the relevant day, as defined in section 87(3)) but before the expiry of the period of six years (so beginning) the conditions mentioned in section 87(4) and (5) have been fulfilled, the following provisions of this section shall apply.

92(2)   **[Repayment and interest]**   If any of the tax charged has been paid, and a claim for repayment is made within the period of six years mentioned in subsection (1) above, the tax paid shall be repaid; and where the tax paid is not less than £25 it shall be repaid with interest on it at the rate applicable under section 178 of the Finance Act 1989 from the date on which the payment was made until the order for repayment is issued.

History

In s. 92(2) the words "rate applicable under section 178 of the Finance Act 1989" substituted for the former words "appropriate rate" by Finance Act 1989, s. 179(1)(f), effective for any period for which Finance Act 1989, s. 178(1) has effect (period beginning on or after 18 August 1989: S.I. 1989 No. 1298) and the words "the date on which" to the end deemed always to have been substituted for the former words "the time it was paid" by Finance Act 1989, s. 180(5), (7).

92(3)   **[Cancellation of unpaid charge]**   To the extent that the tax charged has not been paid, the charge shall be cancelled by virtue of this subsection.

92(4)   (Repealed by Finance Act 1989, sec. 187 and Sch. 17, Pt. X for periods beginning on or after 18 August 1989.)

History

In regard to the above timing see S.I. 1989 No. 1298; s. 92(4) formerly read as follows:

"In subsection (2) above **'the appropriate rate'** means

11 per cent per annum or such other rate as the Treasury may from time to time specify by order."

The rate immediately before the repeal was 12.25 per cent (S.I. 1989 No. 1003).

92(4A)   **[Interest under sec. 92(2)]**   Interest paid under subsection (2) above shall not constitute income for any tax purposes.

History

S. 92(4A) inserted by Finance Act 1987, s. 56 and Sch. 7, para. 7 with retrospective effect.

92(5)   (Repealed by Finance Act 1989, sec. 187 and Sch. 17, Pt. X for periods beginning on or after 18 August 1989.)

History

In regard to the above timing see S.I. 1989 No. 1298; s. 92(5) formerly read as follows:

"The power to make an order under this section shall be exercisable by statutory instrument subject to annulment in pursuance of a resolution of the House of Commons."

Note

Prospective repeal of s. 92 by Finance Act 1990, s. 132 and Sch. 19, Pt. VII in relation to s. 87 in accordance with Finance Act 1990, s. 110, 111.

GENERAL

SEC. 99 Interpretation

99(1) **[Application]** This section applies for the purposes of this Part of this Act.

99(2) **["The Board"]** "**The Board**" means the Commissioners of Inland Revenue.

99(3) **["Chargeable securities"]** Subject to the following provisions of this section, "**chargeable securities**" means—

   (a) stocks, shares or loan capital,

   (b) interests in, or in dividends or other rights arising out of, stocks, shares or loan capital,

   (c) rights to allotments of or to subscribe for, or options to acquire, stocks, shares or loan capital, and

   (d) units under a unit trust scheme.

99(4) **[Overseas stocks etc.]** "Chargeable securities" does not include securities falling within paragraph (a), (b) or (c) of subsection (3) above which are issued or raised by a body corporate not incorporated in the United Kingdom unless—

   (a) they are registered in a register kept in the United Kingdom by or on behalf of the body corporate by which they are issued or raised, or

   (b) in the case of shares, they are paired with shares issued by a body corporate incorporated in the United Kingdom, or

   (c) in the case of securities falling within paragraph (b) or (c) of subsection (3) above, paragraph (a) or (b) above applies to the stocks, shares or loan capital to which they relate.

99(5) **[Securities exempt from stamp duty]** "Chargeable securities" does not include—

   (a) securities the transfer of which is exempt from all stamp duties, or

   (b) securities falling within paragraph (b) or (c) of subsection (3) above which relate to stocks, shares or loan capital the transfer of which is exempt from all stamp duties.

99(6) **[Interests in depositary receipts]** "Chargeable securities" does not include interests in depositary receipts for stocks or shares.

99(6A) **[Paired shares in sec. 99(4)(b)]** For the purposes of subsection (4) above, shares issued by a body corporate which is not incorporated in the United Kingdom ("the foreign company") are paired with shares issued by a body corporate which is so incorporated ("the UK company") where—

   (a) the articles of association of the UK company and the equivalent instruments governing the foreign company each provide that no share in the company to which they relate may be transferred otherwise than as part of a unit comprising one share in that company and one share in the other, and

   (b) such units have been offered for sale to the public in the United Kingdom and, at the same time, other such units have been offered for sale to the public at a broadly equivalent price in the country in which the foreign company is incorporated.

History

In s. 99(6A) the word "other" substituted for the former words "an equal number of" by Finance Act 1990, s. 113(1), (2) as from the date referred to in s. 113(5); previously s. 99(3)–(6A) substituted for the former s. 99(3)–(6) by Finance Act 1988, s. 144(2), (6) as from 9 December 1987: the former s. 99(3)–(6) read as follows:

"**99(3)** Subject to the following provisions of this section, **'chargeable securities'** means stocks, shares, loan capital and units under a unit trust scheme.

(4) 'Chargeable securities' does not include stocks, shares or loan capital which is (or are) issued or raised by a body corporate not incorporated in the United Kingdom unless the stocks, shares or loan capital is (or are) registered in a register kept in the United Kingdom by or on behalf of the body corporate.

(5) 'Chargeable securities' does not include stocks, shares or loan capital the transfer of which is exempt from all stamp duties.

(6) A reference to stocks, shares or loan capital includes a reference to—

    (a) an interest in, or in dividends or other rights arising out of, stocks, shares or loan capital the transfer of which is not exempt from all stamp duties;

    (b) a right to an allotment of or to subscribe for, or an option to acquire, stocks, shares or loan capital the transfer of which is not exempt from all stamp duties,

except that the reference does not include a reference to an interest in a depositary receipt for stocks or shares."

99(6B)   **[Interpretation of sec. 99(6A)]**   For the purposes of subsection (4) above, shares issued by a body corporate which is not incorporated in the United Kingdom ("the foreign company") are paired with shares issued by a body corporate which is so incorporated ("the UK company") where—

    (a) the articles of association of the UK company and the equivalent instruments governing the foreign company each provide that no share in the company to which they relate may be transferred otherwise than as part of a unit comprising one share in that company and one share in the other, and

    (b) the shares issued by the foreign company, and the shares issued by the UK company, are issued to give effect to an allotment of the shares (as part of such units) as fully or partly paid bonus shares.

History

S. 99(6B) inserted by Finance Act 1990, s. 113(1), (3) as from the date referred to in s. 113(6).

99(7)   **[Definition — depositary receipt for stocks or shares]**   A depositary receipt for stocks or shares is an instrument acknowledging—

    (a) that a person holds stocks or shares or evidence of the right to receive them, and

    (b) that another person is entitled to rights, whether expressed as units or otherwise, in or in relation to stocks or shares of the same kind, including the right to receive such stocks or shares (or evidence of the right to receive them) from the person mentioned in paragraph (a) above,

except that a depositary receipt for stocks or shares does not include an instrument acknowledging rights in or in relation to stocks or shares if they are issued or sold under terms providing for payment in instalments and for the issue of the instrument as evidence that an instalment has been paid.

99(8)   **[Power to substitute definition of depositary receipt]**   The Treasury may by regulations provide that for subsection (7) above (as it has effect for the time being) there shall be substituted a subsection containing a different definition of a depositary receipt; and the power to make regulations under this subsection shall be exerciseable by statutory instrument subject to annulment in pursuance of a resolution of the House of Commons.

99(9)   **["Unit", "unit trust schemes"]**   **"Unit"** (except in subsections (6A) and (6B) above) and **"unit trust scheme"** have the same meanings as in Part VII of the Finance Act 1946.

History
In s. 99(9) the words "subsections (6A) and (6B)" substituted for the former words "subsection (6A)" by Finance Act 1990, s. 113(1), (4) as from the date referred to in s. 113(6); previously the words "(except in subsection

(6A) above)" inserted by Finance Act 1988, s. 144(3), (6) as from 9 December 1987.

Note
See in particular Finance Act 1946, s. 57.

99(10) **[Definition — chargeable securities]** In interpreting "chargeable securities" in sections 93, 94 and 96 above—

    (a) paragraph (a) of subsection (4) above and the reference to that paragraph in paragraph (c) of that subsection shall be ignored, and

    (b) the effect of paragraph 8 of Schedule 14 to the Companies Act 1985 (share registered overseas) and of section 118 of the Companies Act (Northern Ireland) 1960 and paragraph 7 of Schedule 14 of the Companies (Northern Ireland) Order 1986 (equivalent provision for Northern Ireland) shall be ignored for the purposes of subsection (5) above.

History
In s. 99(10), para. (a) substituted by Finance Act 1988, s. 144(4), (6) as from 9 December 1987: the former para. (a) read as follows:

"(a) the words in subsection (4) above from "unless" to the end shall be ignored, and".

99(11) **["Chargeable securities" in sec. 93, 96]** In interpreting "chargeable securities" in section 93 or 96 above in a case where—

    (a) newly subscribed shares, or

    (b) securities falling within paragraph (b) or (c) of subsection (3) above which relate to newly subscribed shares,

are issued in pursuance of an arrangement such as is mentioned in that section (or an arrangement which would be such an arrangement if the securities issued were chargeable securities), paragraph (b) of subsection (4) above and the reference to that paragraph in paragraph (c) of that subsection shall be ignored.

99(12) **["Newly-subscribed shares" in sec. 99(11)]** In subsection (11) above, **"newly-subscribed shares"** means shares issued wholly for new consideration in pursuance of an offer for sale to the public.

History
S. 99(11) and (12) added by Finance Act 1988, s. 144(5), (6) as from 9 December 1987.

Note
Prospective repeal of s. 99 by Finance Act 1990, s. 132 and Sch. 19, Pt. VII in accordance with s. 110, 111 of that Act.

FINANCE ACT 1987
(1987 Chapter 16)

[*15th May 1987*]

SEC. 50   Warrants to purchase Government Stock etc.

50(1) **[Conveyances or transfers]** Where an interest in, a right to an allotment of or to subscribe for, or an option to acquire or to dispose of, exempt securities is transferred to or vested in any person by any instrument, no stamp duty shall be chargeable on the instrument by virtue of either of the following headings in Schedule 1 to the Stamp Act 1891—

    (a) "Conveyance or Transfer on Sale";

    (b) "Conveyance or Transfer of any kind not hereinbefore described".

History
In s. 50(1) the words "or to dispose of" inserted by Finance (No. 2) Act 1987, s. 99(1).

50(2) **[Certain bearer instruments]** No stamp duty under the heading "Bearer Instrument" in Schedule 1 to the Stamp Act 1891 shall be chargeable—

   (a) on the issue of an instrument which relates to such an interest, right or option as is mentioned in subsection (1) above, or

   (b) on the transfer of the interest, right or option constituted by, or transferable by means of, such an instrument.

50(3) **["Exempt securities", "securities"]** For the purposes of this section, **"exempt securities"** means—

   (a) securities the transfer of which is exempt from all stamp duties,

   (b) securities constituted by or transferable by means of an instrument the issue of which is by virtue of section 30 of the Finance Act 1967 or section 7 of the Finance Act (Northern Ireland) 1967 or section 79(2) of the Finance Act 1986 exempt from stamp duty under the heading "Bearer Instrument" in Schedule 1 to the Stamp Act 1891, or

   (c) securities the transfer of which is exempt by virtue of section 30 of the Finance Act 1967 or section 7 of the Finance Act (Northern Ireland) 1967 or section 79(2) of the Finance Act 1986 from stamp duty under that heading;

and **"securities"** means stock or marketable securities and includes loan capital as defined in section 78(7) of the Finance Act 1986.

History
In s. 50(3) the words "or section 79(2) of the Finance Act 1986" (appearing in para. (b) and (c)) inserted by Finance (No. 2) Act 1987, s. 99(2).

50(4) **[Application of sec. 50(1)]** Subsection (1) above applies to any instrument executed on or after 1st August 1987.

50(5) **[Application of sec. 50(2)]** Subsection (2) above applies—

   (a) to any instrument which falls within section 60(1) of the Finance Act 1963, or section 9(1)(a) of the Finance Act (Northern Ireland) 1963, and is issued on or after 1st August 1987, and

   (b) to any instrument which falls within section 60(2) of the Finance Act 1963, or section 9(1)(b) of the Finance Act (Northern Ireland) 1963, if the interest, right or option constituted by or transferable by means of it is transferred on or after 1st August 1987.

Note
Prospective repeal of s. 50 by Finance Act 1990, s. 132 and Sch. 19, Pt. VI in accordance with s. 107–111 of that Act.

CRIMINAL JUSTICE ACT 1987
(1987 Chapter 38)

[15th May 1987]

[CCH Note: Reproduced below are sec. 1–3, 12 and Sch. 1. Section 1 and Sch. 1 came into force on 20 July 1987 for the purpose of various appointments and the establishment of the office and sec. 12 on the same date (see S.I. 1987 No. 1061 (C. 27)); sec. 1 and Sch. 1 (as far as not already in force) and sec. 2 and 3 came into force on 6 April 1988 (see S.I. 1988 No. 397 (C. 10)); amendments by the Criminal Justice Act 1988 are included.]

SERIOUS FRAUD OFFICE

SEC. 1 The Serious Fraud Office

1(1) **[Constitution]** A Serious Fraud Office shall be constituted for England and Wales and Northern Ireland.

1(2) **[Appointment of Director]** The Attorney General shall appoint a person to be the Director of the Serious Fraud Office (referred to in this Part of this Act as "the Director"), and he shall discharge his functions under the superintendence of the Attorney General.

1(3) **[Power of investigation]** The Director may investigate any suspected offence which appears to him on reasonable grounds to involve serious or complex fraud.

1(4) **[Power re proper persons to join investigation]** The Director may, if he thinks fit, conduct any such investigation in conjunction either with the police or with any other person who is, in the opinion of the Director, a proper person to be concerned in it.

1(5) **[Power re criminal proceedings]** The Director may—

   (a) institute and have the conduct of any criminal proceedings which appear to him to relate to such fraud; and

   (b) take over the conduct of any such proceedings at any stage.

1(6) **[Discharge of functions]** The Director shall discharge such other functions in relation to fraud as may from time to time be assigned to him by the Attorney General.

1(7) **[Proper persons for sec. 1(5)]** The Director may designate for the purposes of subsection (5) above any member of the Serious Fraud Office who is—

   (a) a barrister in England and Wales or Northern Ireland;

   (b) a solicitor of the Supreme Court; or

   (c) a solicitor of the Supreme Court of Judicature of Northern Ireland.

1(8) **[Power of proper persons]** Any member so designated shall, without prejudice to any functions which may have been assigned to him in his capacity as a member of that Office, have all the powers of the Director as to the institution and conduct of proceedings but shall exercise those powers under the direction of the Director.

1(9) **[Rights of audience]** Any member so designated who is a barrister in England and Wales or a solicitor of the Supreme Court shall have, in any court, the rights of audience enjoyed by solicitors holding practising certificates and shall have such additional rights of audience in the Crown Court in England and Wales as may be given by virtue of subsection (11) below.

1(10) **[Interpretation re sec. 1(9)]** The reference in subsection (9) above to rights of audience enjoyed in any court by solicitors includes a reference to rights enjoyed in the Crown Court by virtue of any direction given by the Lord Chancellor under section 83 of the Supreme Court Act 1981.

1(11)   [Direction re sec. 1(10)]   For the purpose of giving members so designated who are barristers in England and Wales or solicitors of the Supreme Court additional rights of audience in the Crown Court in England and Wales, the Lord Chancellor may give any such direction as respects such members as he could give under the said section 83.

1(12)   [Rights of audience — Northern Ireland]   Any member so designated who is a barrister in Northern Ireland or a solicitor of the Supreme Court of Judicature of Northern Ireland shall have—

   (a)   in any court the rights of audience enjoyed by solicitors of the Supreme Court of Judicature of Northern Ireland and, in the Crown Court in Northern Ireland, such additional rights of audience as may be given by virtue of subsection (14) below; and

   (b)   in the Crown Court in Northern Ireland, the rights of audience enjoyed by barristers employed by the Director of Public Prosecutions for Northern Ireland.

1(13)   [Interpretation re sec. 1(12)(a)]   Subject to subsection (14) below, the reference in subsection (12)(a) above to rights of audience enjoyed by solicitors of the Supreme Court of Judicature of Northern Ireland is a reference to such rights enjoyed in the Crown Court in Northern Ireland as restricted by any direction given by the Lord Chief Justice of Northern Ireland under section 50 of the Judicature (Northern Ireland) Act 1978.

1(14)   [Direction re sec. 1(13)]   For the purpose of giving any member so designated who is a barrister in Northern Ireland or a solicitor of the Supreme Court of Judicature of Northern Ireland additional rights of audience in the Crown Court in Northern Ireland, the Lord Chief Justice of Northern Ireland may direct that any direction given by him under the said section 50 shall not apply to such members.

1(15)   [Sch. 1]   Schedule 1 to this Act shall have effect.

1(16)   [References to conduct of proceedings]   For the purposes of this section (including that Schedule) references to the conduct of any proceedings include references to the proceedings being discontinued and to the taking of any steps (including the bringing of appeals and making of representations in respect of applications for bail) which may be taken in relation to them.

1(17)   [Application to Northern Ireland]   In the application of this section (including that Schedule) to Northern Ireland references to the Attorney General are to be construed as references to him in his capacity as Attorney General for Northern Ireland.

SEC. 2   Director's investigation powers

2(1)   [Exercise of Director's powers]   The powers of the Director under this section shall be exercisable, but only for the purposes of an investigation under section 1 above or, on a request made by the Attorney General of the Isle of Man, Jersey or Guernsey, under legislation corresponding to that section and having effect in the Island whose Attorney General makes the request, in any case in which it appears to him that there is good reason to do so for the purpose of investigating the affairs, or any aspect of the affairs, of any person.

History
In s. 2(1) the words from "or, on a request made" to "whose Attorney General makes the request," inserted by   Criminal Justice Act 1988, s. 143 and 171(5) as from 29 July 1988.

2(2) [Notice to attend] The Director may by notice in writing require the person whose affairs are to be investigated ("the person under investigation") or any other person whom he has reason to believe has relevant information to answer questions or otherwise furnish information with respect to any matter relevant to the investigation at a specified place and either at a specified time or forthwith.

History
In s. 2(2) the words from "answer questions" to the end substituted for the former words "attend before the Director at a specified time and place and answer questions or otherwise furnish information with respect to any matter relevant to the investigation" by Criminal Justice Act 1988, s. 170(1), Sch. 15, para. 113(1) and s. 171(5) as from 29 July 1988.

2(3) [Notice to produce etc.] The Director may by notice in writing require the person under investigation or any other person to produce at such place as may be specified in the notice and either forthwith or at such time as may be so specified, any specified documents which appear to the Director to relate to any matter relevant to the investigation or any documents of a specified description which appear to him so to relate; and—

> (a) if any such documents are produced, the Director may—
>
>> (i) take copies or extracts from them;
>>
>> (ii) require the person producing them to provide an explanation of any of them;
>
> (b) if any such documents are not produced, the Director may require the person who was required to produce them to state, to the best of his knowledge and belief, where they are.

History
In s. 2(3) the words from "such place" to "as may be so specified" substituted for the former words "a specified time and place" and the word "description" substituted for the former word "class" by Criminal Justice Act 1988, s. 170(1), Sch. 15, para. 113(2) and s. 171(5) as from 29 July 1988.

2(4) [Issue of warrant] Where, on information on oath laid by a member of the Serious Fraud Office, a justice of the peace is satisfied, in relation to any documents, that there are reasonable grounds for believing—

> (a) that—
>
>> (i) a person has failed to comply with an obligation under this section to produce them;
>>
>> (ii) it is not practicable to serve a notice under subsection (3) above in relation to them; or
>>
>> (iii) the service of such a notice in relation to them might seriously prejudice the investigation; and
>
> (b) that they are on premises specified in the information,

he may issue such a warrant as is mentioned in subsection (5) below.

2(5) [Scope of warrant in sec. 2(4)] The warrant referred to above is a warrant authorising any constable—

> (a) to enter (using such force as is reasonably necessary for the purpose) and search the premises, and
>
> (b) to take possession of any documents appearing to be documents of the description specified in the information or to take in relation to any documents so appearing any other steps which may appear to be necessary for preserving them and preventing interference with them.

2(6)   **[Constable to be accompanied]**   Unless it is not practicable in the circumstances, a constable executing a warrant issued under subsection (4) above shall be accompanied by an appropriate person.

2(7)   **["Appropriate person" in sec. 2(6)]**   In subsection (6) above **"appropriate person"** means—

    (a)   a member of the Serious Fraud Office; or

    (b)   some person who is not a member of that Office but whom the Director has authorised to accompany the constable.

2(8)   **[Use of statement in evidence]**   A statement by a person in response to a requirement imposed by virtue of this section may only be used in evidence against him—

    (a)   on a prosecution for an offence under subsection (14) below; or

    (b)   on a prosecution for some other offence where in giving evidence he makes a statement inconsistent with it.

2(9)   **[Legal professional privilege]**   A person shall not under this section be required to disclose any information or produce any document which he would be entitled to refuse to disclose or produce on grounds of legal professional privilege in proceedings in the High Court except that a lawyer may be required to furnish the name and address of his client.

2(10)   **[Obligation of confidence re banking business]**   A person shall not under this section be required to disclose information or produce a document in respect of which he owes an obligation of confidence by virtue of carrying on any banking business unless—

    (a)   the person to whom the obligation of confidence is owed consents to the disclosure or production; or

    (b)   the Director has authorised the making of the requirement or, if it is impracticable for him to act personally, a member of the Serious Fraud Office designated by him for the purposes of this subsection has done so.

2(11)   **[Power to appoint outside investigator]**   Without prejudice to the powers of the Director to assign functions to members of the Serious Fraud Office, the Director may authorise any competent investigator (other than a constable) who is not a member of that Office to exercise on his behalf all or any of the powers conferred by this section, but no such authority shall be granted except for the purpose of investigating the affairs, or any aspect of the affairs, of a person specified in the authority.

2(12)   **[Compliance with requirement of person in sec. 2(11)]**   No person shall be bound to comply with any requirement imposed by a person exercising powers by virtue of any authority granted under subsection (11) above unless he has, if required to do so, produced evidence of his authority.

2(13)   **[Offence, penalty]**   Any person who without reasonable excuse fails to comply with a requirement imposed on him under this section shall be guilty of an offence and liable on summary conviction to imprisonment for a term not exceeding six months or to a fine not exceeding level 5 on the standard scale or to both.

2(14)   **[Offence re false or misleading statement]**   A person who, in purported compliance with a requirement under this section—

(a) makes a statement which he knows to be false or misleading in a material particular; or

(b) recklessly makes a statement which is false or misleading in a material particular,

shall be guilty of an offence.

2(15) **[Penalty re sec. 2(14)]** A person guilty of an offence under subsection (14) above shall—

(a) on conviction on indictment, be liable to imprisonment for a term not exceeding two years or a fine or to both; and

(b) on summary conviction, be liable to imprisonment for a term not exceeding six months or to a fine not exceeding the statutory maximum, or to both.

2(16) **[Offence re falsifying documents etc.]** Where any person—

(a) knows or suspects that an investigation by the police or the Serious Fraud Office into serious or complex fraud is being or is likely to be carried out; and

(b) falsifies, conceals, destroys or otherwise disposes of, or causes or permits the falsification, concealment, destruction or disposal of documents which he knows or suspects are or would be relevant to such an investigation,

he shall be guilty of an offence unless he proves that he had no intention of concealing the facts disclosed by the documents from persons carrying out such an investigation.

2(17) **[Penalty re sec. 2(16)]** A person guilty of an offence under subsection (16) above shall—

(a) on conviction on indictment, be liable to imprisonment for a term not exceeding 7 years or to a fine or to both; and

(b) on summary conviction, be liable to imprisonment for a term not exceeding 6 months or to a fine not exceeding the statutory maximum or to both.

2(18) **["Documents"]** In this section, **"documents"** includes information recorded in any form and, in relation to information recorded otherwise than in legible form, references to its production include references to producing a copy of the information in legible form.

2(19) **[Application to Scotland]** In the application of this section to Scotland, the reference to a justice of the peace is to be construed as a reference to the sheriff; and in the application of this section to Northern Ireland, subsection (4) above shall have effect as if for the references to information there were substituted references to a complaint.

Note
See CA 1989, s. 124A for petition for winding up on grounds of public interest on basis of information obtained under s. 2.

SEC. 3 Disclosure of information

3(1) **[Disclosure of information protected under Taxes Management Act]** Where any information subject to an obligation of secrecy under the Taxes Management Act 1970 had been disclosed by the Commissioners of Inland Revenue or an officer of those Commissioners to any member of the Serious Fraud Office for the purposes of any prosecution of an offence relating to inland revenue, that information may be disclosed by any member of the Serious Fraud Office—

    (a) for the purposes of any prosecution of which that Office has the conduct;

    (b) to any member of the Crown Prosecution Service for the purposes of any prosecution of an offence relating to inland revenue; and

    (c) to the Director of Public Prosecutions for Northern Ireland for the purposes of any prosecution of an offence relating to inland revenue,

but not otherwise.

3(2) **[Police and Criminal Evidence Act]**   Where the Serious Fraud Office has the conduct of any prosecution of an offence which does not relate to inland revenue, the court may not prevent the prosecution from relying on any evidence under section 78 of the Police and Criminal Evidence Act 1984 (discretion to exclude unfair evidence) by reason only of the fact that the information concerned was disclosed by the Commissioners of Inland Revenue or an officer of those Commissioners for the purposes of any prosecution of an offence relating to inland revenue.

3(3) **[Disclosure of information protected under other legislation]**   Where any information is subject to an obligation of secrecy imposed by or under any enactment other than an enactment contained in the Taxes Management Act 1970, the obligation shall not have effect to prohibit the disclosure of that information to any person in his capacity as a member of the Serious Fraud Office but any information disclosed by virtue of this subsection may only be disclosed by a member of the Serious Fraud Office for the purposes of any prosecution in England and Wales, Northern Ireland or elsewhere and may only be disclosed by such a member if he is designated by the Director for the purposes of this subsection.

3(4) **[Agreement re non-disclosure]**   Without prejudice to his power to enter into agreements apart from this subsection, the Director may enter into a written agreement for the supply of information to or by him subject, in either case, to an obligation not to disclose the information concerned otherwise than for a specified purpose.

3(5) **[Disclosure of information—general]**   Subject to subsections (1) and (3) above and to any provision of an agreement for the supply of information which restricts the disclosure of the information supplied, information obtained by any person in his capacity as a member of the Serious Fraud Office may be disclosed by any member of that office designated by the Director for the purposes of this subsection—

    (a) to any government department or Northern Ireland department or other authority or body discharging its functions on behalf of the Crown (including the Crown in right of Her Majesty's Government in Northern Ireland);

    (b) to any competent authority;

    (c) for the purposes of any prosecution in England and Wales, Northern Ireland or elsewhere; and

    (d) for the purposes of assisting any public or other authority for the time being designated for the purposes of this paragraph by an order made by the Secretary of State to discharge any functions which are specified in the order.

(6) **[Competent authorities for sec. 3(5)]**   The following are competent authorities for the purposes of subsection (5) above—

(a) an inspector appointed under Part XIV of the Companies Act 1985 or Part XV of the Companies (Northern Ireland) Order 1986;

(b) an Official Receiver;

(c) the Accountant in Bankruptcy;

(d) an Official Assignee;

(e) a person appointed to carry out an investigation under section 55 of the Building Societies Act 1986;

(f) a body administering a compensation scheme under section 54 of the Financial Services Act 1986;

(g) an inspector appointed under section 94 of that Act;

(h) a person exercising powers by virtue of section 106 of that Act;

(i) an inspector appointed under section 177 of that Act or any corresponding enactment having effect in Northern Ireland;

(j) a person appointed by the Bank of England under section 41 of the Banking Act 1987 to carry out an investigation and make a report;

(k) a person exercising powers by virtue of section 44(2) of the Insurance Companies Act 1982;

(l) any body having supervisory, regulatory or disciplinary functions in relation to any profession or any area of commercial activity; and

(m) any person or body having, under the law of any country or territory outside the United Kingdom, functions corresponding to any of the functions of any person or body mentioned in any of the foregoing paragraphs.

History
S. 3(6)(j) substituted by Criminal Justice Act 1988, s. 170(1), Sch. 15, para. 111 and s. 171(5) as from 29 July 1988: s. 3(6)(j) formerly read as follows:

"(j) an inspector appointed under section 38 of the Banking Act 1987;"

3(7) [Extent of sec. 3(5)(a) order] An order under subsection (5)(d) above may impose conditions subject to which, and otherwise restrict the circumstances in which, information may be disclosed under that paragraph.

CONSPIRACY TO DEFRAUD

SEC. 4 Charges of and penalty for conspiracy to defraud

4(1) [Possibility of charge being brought] If—

(a) a person agrees with any other person or persons that a course of conduct shall be pursued; and

(b) that course of conduct will necessarily amount to or involve the commission of any offence or offences by one or more of the parties to the agreement if the agreement is carried out in accordance with their intentions,

the fact that it will do so shall not preclude a charge of conspiracy to defraud being brought against any of them in respect of the agreement.

4(2) [Sec. 5(2) of Criminal Law Act] In section 5(2) of the Criminal Law Act 1977, the words from "and" to the end are hereby repealed.

4(3) [Penalty] A person guilty of conspiracy to defraud is liable on conviction on indictment to imprisonment for a term not exceeding 10 years or a fine or both.

Schedule 1 — The Serious Fraud Office

Section 1

GENERAL

1 There shall be paid to the Director of the Serious Fraud Office such remuneration as the Attorney General may, with the approval of the Treasury, determine.

2 The Director shall appoint such staff for the Serious Fraud Office as, with the approval of the Treasury as to numbers, remuneration and other terms and conditions of service, he considers necessary for the discharge of his functions.

3(1) As soon as practicable after 4th April in any year the Director shall make to the Attorney General a report on the discharge of his functions during the year ending with that date.

3(2) The Attorney General shall lay before Parliament a copy of every report received by him under sub-paragraph (1) above and shall cause every such report to be published.

PROCEDURE

4(1) Where any enactment (whenever passed) prohibits the taking of any step—

    (a) except by the Director of Public Prosecutions or except by him or another; or

    (b) without the consent of the Director of Public Prosecutions or without his consent or the consent of another,

it shall not prohibit the taking of any such step by the Director of the Serious Fraud Office.

4(2) In this paragraph references to the Director of Public Prosecutions include references to the Director of Public Prosecutions for Northern Ireland.

5(1) Where the Director has the conduct of any criminal proceedings in England and Wales, the Director of Public Prosecutions shall not in relation to those proceedings be subject to any duty by virtue of section 3(2) of the Prosecution of Offences Act 1985.

5(2) Where the Director has the conduct of any criminal proceedings in Northern Ireland, the Director of Public Prosecutions for Northern Ireland shall not in relation to those proceedings be required to exercise any function under Article 5 of the Prosecution of Offences (Northern Ireland) Order 1972.

6(1) Where the Director or any member of the Serious Fraud Office designated for the purposes of section 1(5) above ("designated official") gives notice to any justice of the peace that he has instituted, or is conducting, any criminal proceedings in England and Wales, the justice shall—

    (a) at the prescribed time and in the prescribed manner; or

    (b) in a particular case, at the time and in the manner directed by the Attorney General;

send him every recognizance, information, certificate, deposition, document and thing connected with those proceedings which the justice is required by law to deliver to the appropriate officer of the Crown Court.

History
In para. 6(1) in the reference to s. 1, "(5)" substituted for the former "(4)" by Criminal Justice Act 1988, s. 170(1), (5) and Sch. 15, para. 116 as from 29 July 1988.

6(2)   Where the Director of any designated official gives notice that he has instituted, or is conducting, any criminal proceedings in Northern Ireland—

(a) to a resident magistrate or a justice of the peace in Northern Ireland;

(b) to a clerk of petty sessions in Northern Ireland,

the person to whom the notice is given shall—

(i) at the prescribed time and in the prescribed manner; or

(ii) in a particular case, at the time and in the manner directed by the Attorney General,

send him every recognizance, complaint, certificate, deposition, document and thing connected with those proceedings which that person is required by law to deliver to the appropriate officer of the Crown Court.

6(3)   The Attorney General may make regulations for the purpose of supplementing this paragraph; and in this paragraph "prescribed" means prescribed by the regulations.

6(4)   The Director or, as the case may be, designated official shall—

(a) subject to the regulations, cause anything which is sent to him under this paragraph to be delivered to the appropriate officer of the Crown Court; and

(b) to be under the same obligation (on the same payment) to deliver to an applicant copies of anything so sent as that officer.

7(1)   The Attorney General may make regulations requiring the chief officer of any police force to which the regulations are expressed to apply to give to the Director information with respect to every offence of a kind prescribed by the regulations which is alleged to have been committed in his area and in respect of which it appears to him that there is a prima facie case for proceedings.

7(2)   The regulations may also require every such chief officer to give to the Director such information as the Director may require with respect to such cases or classes of case as he may from time to time specify.

8(1)   The Attorney General may, with the approval of the Treasury, by regulations make such provision as he considers appropriate in relation to—

(a) the fees of counsel briefed to appear on behalf of the Serious Fraud Office in any criminal proceedings; and

(b) the costs and expenses of witnesses attending to give evidence at the instance of the Serious Fraud Office and, subject to sub-paragraph (2) below, of any other person who in the opinion of that Office necessarily attends for the purpose of the case otherwise than to give evidence.

History
In para. 8(1)(b) the word "of" before the words "any other person" substituted for the former word "to" by Criminal   Justice Act 1988, s. 166(5)(a) and 171(5) as from 29 July 1988.

8(2) The power conferred on the Attorney General by sub-paragraph (1)(b) above only relates to the costs and expenses of an interpreter if he is required because of the lack of English of a person attending to give evidence at the instance of the Serious Fraud Office.

8(3) The regulations may, in particular—

    (a) prescribe scales or rates of fees, costs or expenses; and

    (b) specify conditions for the payment of fees, costs or expenses.

8(4) Regulations made under sub-paragraph (1)(b) above may provide that scales or rates of costs and expenses shall be determined by the Attorney General with the consent of the Treasury.

8(5) In sub-paragraph (1)(b) above **"attends"** means attends at the court or elsewhere.

History
Para. 8(5) inserted by Criminal Justice Act 1988, s. 166(5)(b)
and 171(5) as from 29 July 1988.

9(1) Any power to make regulations under this Schedule shall be exercisable by statutory instrument subject to annulment in pursuance of a resolution of either House of Parliament.

9(2) Any such regulations may make different provision with respect to different cases or classes of case.

FINANCE ACT 1988

(1988 Chapter 39)

[29th July 1988]

SEC. 143   Stamp duty: paired shares

143(1) **[Application]** This section applies where—

    (a) the articles of association of a company incorporated in the United Kingdom ("the UK company") and the equivalent instruments governing a company which is not so incorporated ("the foreign company") each provide that no share in the company to which they relate may be transferred otherwise than as part of a unit comprising one share in that company and one share in the other; and

    (b) such units are to be or have been offered for sale to the public in the United Kingdom and, at the same time, other such units are to be or, as the case may be, have been offered for sale to the public at a broadly equivalent price in the country in which the foreign company is incorporated ("the foreign country").

History
In s. 143(1)(b) the word "other" substituted for the former
words "an equal number of" by Finance Act 1990,
s. 112(1) as from the date referred to in s. 112(2).

143(2) **[Duty re sec. 143(3) instrument]** In relation to an instrument to which subsection (3) below applies, any duty chargeable on issue under the heading "Bearer Instrument" in Schedule 1 to the Stamp Act 1891 (which, apart from this subsection, would be payable by virtue of section 60 of the Finance Act 1963 or section 9 of the Finance Act (Northern Ireland) 1963) shall not be so payable; but nothing in this subsection shall be taken as affecting the other requirements of that section.

143(3) **[Bearer instrument re UK company]** This subsection applies to any bearer instrument issued on or after 1st November 1987 which represents shares in the UK company, or a right to an allotment of or to subscribe for such shares, if the purpose of the issue is—

(a) to make such shares available for sale (as part of such units as are referred to in subsection (1) above) in pursuance of either of the offers referred to in subsection (1)(b) above or of any other offer for sale of such units to the public made at the same time and at a broadly equivalent price in a country other than the United Kingdom or the foreign country; or

(b) to give effect to an allotment of such shares (as part of such units) as fully or partly paid bonus shares.

143(4) **[Duty re sec. 143(5) instrument]** In relation to an instrument to which subsection (5) below applies—

(a) the foreign company shall be treated—

(i) for the purposes of sections 59 and 60 of the Finance Act 1963 (which make provision in respect of stamp duty under the heading "Bearer Instrument" in Schedule 1 to the Stamp Act 1891) as a company formed or established in Great Britain; and

(ii) for the purposes of sections 8 and 9 of the Finance Act (Northern Ireland) 1963 (which make corresponding provision for Northern Ireland) as a company formed or established in Northern Ireland; and

(b) section 30 of the Finance Act 1967 and section 7 of the Finance Act (Northern Ireland) 1967 (exemption for bearer instruments relating to stock in foreign currencies) shall not apply.

143(5) **[Bearer instrument re foreign company]** This subsection applies to any bearer instrument issued on or after 9th December 1987 which represents shares in the foreign company, or a right to an allotment of or to subscribe for such shares; and is not issued for the purpose—

(a) of making shares in the foreign company available for sale (as part of such units as are referred to in subsection (1) above) in pursuance of either of the offers referred to in subsection (1)(b) above or of any other offer such as is mentioned in subsection (3)(a) above; or

(b) of giving effect to an allotment of such shares (as part of such units) as fully or partly paid bonus shares.

143(6) **[Certain foreign companies treated as UK companies]** In relation to any instrument which transfers such units as are referred to in subsection (1) above and is executed on or after the date of the passing of this Act, the foreign company shall be treated for the purposes of sections 67 and 68 (depositary receipts) and 70 and 71 (clearance services) of the Finance Act 1986 as a company incorporated in the United Kingdom.

143(7)   **[Non-application of Stamp Act 1891, sec. 3]**   Section 3 of the Stamp Act 1891 (which requires every instrument written upon the same piece of material as another instrument to be separately stamped) shall not apply in relation to any bearer instrument issued on or after 9th December 1987 which represents shares in the UK company or the foreign company, or a right to an allotment of or to subscribe for such shares.

143(8)   **[Construction]**   This section shall be construed as one with the Stamp Act 1891.

143(9)   **[Commencement]**   Subsections (2) and (3) above, together with subsection (1) above so far as relating to them, shall be deemed to have come into force on 1st November 1987, and subsections (4), (5) and (7) above, together with subsection (1) above so far as relating to them, shall be deemed to have come into force on 9th December 1987.

Note
Prospective repeal of s. 143 by Finance Act 1990, s. 132 and Sch. 19, Pt. VI in accordance with s. 107–111 of that Act.

FINANCE ACT 1989
(1989 Chapter 26)

[*27th July 1989*]

SEC. 175   Stamp duty: stock exchange nominees

175(1)   **[Regulations]**   The Treasury may by regulations provide that where—

   (a) circumstances would (apart from the regulations) give rise to a charge to stamp duty under the heading "Conveyance or Transfer on Sale" in Schedule 1 to the Stamp Act 1891 and to a charge to stamp duty reserve tax,

   (b) the circumstances involve a stock exchange nominee, and

   (c) the circumstances are such as are prescribed,

the charge to stamp duty shall be treated as not arising.

175(2)   **[Exercise of power]**   The power to make regulations under this section shall be exercisable by statutory instrument subject to annulment in pursuance of a resolution of the House of Commons.

175(3)   **[Definitions]**   In this section—

   (a) **"prescribed"** means prescribed by the regulations, and

   (b) **"stock exchange nominee"** means a person designated for the purposes of section 127 of the Finance Act 1976 as a nominee of The Stock Exchange by an order made by the Secretary of State under subsection (5) of that section.

Note
Prospective repeal of s. 175 by Finance Act 1990, s. 132 and Sch. 19, Pt. VI for instruments executed on or after a day to be appointed in accordance with s. 111.

        CCH Editions Limited
BCL BCL13$$151

SEC. 176 Stamp duty reserve tax: stock exchange nominees

176(1) **[Avoidance of double charge to SDRT]** The Treasury may by regulations provide that where—

(a) circumstances would (apart from the regulations) give rise to two charges to stamp duty reserve tax,

(b) the circumstances involve a stock exchange nominee, and

(c) the circumstances are such as are prescribed,

such one of the charges as may be prescribed shall be treated as not arising.

176(2) **[Avoidance of double charge to stamp duty, SDRT]** The Treasury may by regulations provide that where—

(a) circumstances would (apart from the regulations) give rise to a charge to stamp duty reserve tax and a charge to stamp duty,

(b) the circumstances involve a stock exchange nominee, and

(c) the circumstances are such as are prescribed,

the charge to stamp duty reserve tax shall be treated as not arising.

176(3) **[Relief for nominees]** The Treasury may by regulations provide that a provision of an Act by virtue of which there is no charge to stamp duty reserve tax shall also apply in circumstances which involve a stock exchange nominee and are such as are prescribed.

176(4) **[Further relief for nominees]** The Treasury may by regulations provide that a provision of an Act by virtue of which the rate at which stamp duty reserve tax is charged is less than it would be apart from the provision shall also apply in circumstances which involve a stock exchange nominee and are such as are prescribed.

176(5) **[Exercise of powers]** The power to make regulations under this section shall be exercisable by statutory instrument subject to annulment in pursuance of a resolution of the House of Commons.

176(6) **[Definitions]** In this section—

(a) "**prescribed**" means prescribed by the regulations, and

(b) "**stock exchange nominee**" means a person designated for the purposes of section 127 of the Finance Act 1976 as a nominee of The Stock Exchange by an order made by the Secretary of State under subsection (5) of that section.

Note
Prospective repeal of s. 176 by Finance Act 1990, s. 132
and Sch. 19, Pt. VI in accordance with s. 110, 111 of that
Act.

FINANCE ACT 1990
(1990 Chapter 29)

[26 July 1990]

PART III — STAMP DUTY AND STAMP DUTY RESERVE TAX

REPEALS

SEC. 107   Bearers: abolition of stamp duty

107(1)   [Stamp duty not chargeable]   Stamp duty shall not be chargeable under the heading "Bearer Instrument" in Schedule 1 to the Stamp Act 1891.

107(2)   [Instrument under Finance Act 1963, sec. 60(1)]   Subsection (1) above applies to an instrument which falls within section 60(1) of the Finance Act 1963 if it is issued on or after the abolition day.

107(3)   [Instrument under Finance Act 1963, sec. 60(2)]   Subsection (1) above applies to an instrument which falls within section 60(2) of that Act if the stock constituted by or transferable by means of it is transferred on or after the abolition day.

107(4)   [Interpretation of sec. 107(2)]   In subsection (2) above the reference to section 60(1) of the Finance Act 1963 includes a reference to section 9(1)(a) of the Finance Act (Northern Ireland) 1963 and in subsection (3) above the reference to section 60(2) of the former Act includes a reference to section 9(1)(b) of the latter.

SEC. 108   Transfer of securities: abolition of stamp duty

108(1)   [Stamp duty not chargeable]   Where defined securities are transferred to or vested in a person by an instrument, stamp duty shall not be chargeable on the instrument.

108(2)   ["Defined securities"]   In this section **"defined securities"** means—

(a) stocks, shares or loan capital,

(b) interests in, or in dividends or other rights arising out of, stocks, shares or loan capital,

(c) rights to allotments of or to subscribe for, or options to acquire or to dispose of, stocks, shares or loan capital, and

(d) units under a unit trust scheme.

108(3)   ["Loan capital"]   In this section **"loan capital"** means—

(a) any debenture stock, corporation stock or funded debt, by whatever name known, issued by a government or a body corporate or other body of persons (which here includes a local authority and any body whether formed or established in the United Kingdom or elsewhere);

(b) any capital raised by a government, or by such a body as is mentioned in paragraph (a) above, if the capital is borrowed or has the character of borrowed money, and whether it is in the form of stock or any other form;

(c) stock or marketable securities issued by a government.

108(4) **["Unit", "unit trust scheme"]** In this section **"unit"** and **"unit trust scheme"** have the same meanings as they had in Part VII of the Finance Act 1946 immediately before the abolition day.

108(5) **[Interpretation]** In this section references to a government include references to a government department, including a Northern Ireland department.

108(6) **["Government"]** In this section **"government"** means the government of the United Kingdom or of Northern Ireland or of any country or territory outside the United Kingdom.

108(7) **[Application]** Subject to subsection (8) below, this section applies if the instrument is executed in pursuance of a contract made on or after the abolition day.

108(8) **[Application to certain instruments]** In the case of an instrument—

    (a) which falls within section 67(1) or (9) of the Finance Act 1986 (depositary receipts) or section 70(1) or (9) of that Act (clearance services), or

    (b) which does not fall within section 67(1) or (9) or section 70(1) or (9) of that Act and is not executed in pursuance of a contract,

this section applies if the instrument is executed on or after the abolition day.

SEC. 109 Stamp duty: other repeals

109(1) **[Non-application of Stamp Act 1891, sec. 83]** Section 83 of the Stamp Act 1891 (fine for certain acts relating to securities) shall not apply where an instrument of assignment or transfer is executed, or a transfer or negotiation of the stock constituted by or transferable by means of a bearer instrument takes place, on or after the abolition day.

109(2) **[Non-application of certain provisions]** The following provisions (which relate to the cancellation of certain instruments) shall not apply where the stock certificate or other instrument is entered on or after the abolition day—

    (a) section 109(1) of the Stamp Act 1891,

    (b) section 5(2) of the Finance Act 1899,

    (c) section 56(2) of the Finance Act 1946, and

    (d) section 27(2) of the Finance (No. 2) Act (Northern Ireland) 1946.

109(3) **[Non-application of Finance Act 1963, sec. 67]** Section 67 of the Finance Act 1963 (prohibition of circulation of blank transfers) shall not apply where the sale is made on or after the abolition day; and section 16 of the Finance Act (Northern Ireland) 1963 (equivalent provision for Northern Ireland) shall not apply where the sale is made on or after the abolition day.

109(4) **[Revision of obligation in Finance Act 1986, sec. 68, 71]** No person shall be required to notify the Commissioners under section 68(1) or (2) or 71(1) or (2) of the Finance Act 1986 (depositary receipts and clearance services) if he first issues the receipts, provides the services or holds the securities as there mentioned on or after the abolition day.

109(5) **[Further revision of obligation]** No company shall be required to notify the Commissioners under section 68(3) or 71(3) of that Act if it first becomes aware as there mentioned on or after the abolition day.

109(6)   **[Cessation of certain provisions]**   The following provisions shall cease to have effect—

(a)   section 56(1), (3) and (4) and section 57(2) to (4) of the Finance Act 1946 (unit trusts),

(b)   section 27(1), (3) and (4) and section 28(2) to (4) of the Finance (No. 2) Act (Northern Ireland) 1946 (unit trusts),

(c)   section 33 of the Finance Act 1970 (composition by financial institutions in respect of stamp duty),

(d)   section 127(7) of the Finance Act 1976 (extension of composition provisions to Northern Ireland), and

(e)   section 85 of the Finance Act 1986 (provisions about stock, marketable securities, etc.).

109(7)   **[Treasury Order]**   The provisions mentioned in subsection (6) above shall cease to have effect as provided by the Treasury by order.

109(8)   **[Requirements for sec. 109(7) order]**   An order under subsection (7) above—

(a)   shall be made by statutory instrument;

(b)   may make different provision for different provisions or different purposes;

(c)   may include such supplementary, incidental, consequential or transitional provisions as appear to the Treasury to be necessary or expedient.

109(9)   **[Effect on other legislation]**   Nothing in this section shall affect the application of section 56 of the Finance Act 1946 or section 27 of the Finance (No. 2) Act (Northern Ireland) 1946 by section 259 of the Inheritance Tax Act 1984.

SEC. 110   Stamp duty reserve tax: abolition

110(1)   **[SDRT not chargeable]**   Stamp duty reserve tax shall cease to be chargeable.

110(2)   **[Finance Act 1986, sec. 87]**   In relation to the charge to tax under section 87 of the Finance Act 1986 subsection (1) above applies where—

(a)   the agreement to transfer is conditional and the condition is satisfied on or after the abolition day, or

(b)   the agreement is not conditional and is made on or after the abolition day.

110(3)   **[Finance Act 1986, sec. 93(1)]**   In relation to the charge to tax under section 93(1) of that Act subsection (1) above applies where securities are transferred, issued or appropriated on or after the abolition day (whenever the arrangement was made).

110(4)   **[Finance Act 1986, sec. 96(1)]**   In relation to the charge to tax under section 96(1) of that Act subsection (1) above applies where securities are transferred or issued on or after the abolition day (whenever the arrangement was made).

110(5)   **[Finance Act 1986, sec. 93(10)]**   In relation to the charge to tax under section 93(10) of that Act subsection (1) above applies where securities are issued or transferred on sale, under terms there mentioned, on or after the abolition day.

110(6)   **[Finance Act 1986, sec. 96(8)]**   In relation to the charge to tax under section 96(8) of that Act subsection (1) above applies where securities are issued or transferred on sale, under terms there mentioned, on or after the abolition day.

110(7) **[Finance Act 1986, sec. 93(10)]** Where before the abolition day securities are issued or transferred on sale under terms mentioned in section 93(10) of that Act, in construing section 93(10) the effect of subsections (1) and (3) above shall be ignored.

110(8) **[Finance Act 1986, sec. 96(8)]** Where before the abolition day securities are issued or transferred on sale under terms mentioned in section 96(8) of that Act, in construing section 96(8) the effect of subsections (1) and (4) above shall be ignored.

SEC. 111 General

111(1) **["The abolition day" in sec. 107–110]** In sections 106 to 109 above **"the abolition day"** means such day as may be appointed by the Treasury by order made by statutory instrument.

111(2) **[Construction of sec. 107–109]** Sections 106 to 108 above shall be construed as one with the Stamp Act 1891.

PAIRED SHARES

SEC. 112 Stamp duty

112(1) (Amendment of Finance Act 1988, sec. 143.)

112(2) **[Application of sec. 111(1)]** Subsection (1) above applies where—

  (a) the offers referred to in section 143(1) are made, or are to be made, on or after the day on which this Act is passed, and

  (b) before the offers are made, or are to be made, units comprising shares in the two companies concerned were offered (whether before or on or after the day on which this Act is passed) in circumstances where section 143 applied without the amendment made by subsection (1) above.

SEC. 113 Stamp duty reserve tax

113(1)–(4) (Substitution in Finance Act 1986, sec. 99(6A)(b), insertion of sec. 99(6B) and substitution in sec. 99(9).)

113(5) **[Application of sec. 113(2)]** Subsection (2) above applies where—

  (a) the offers referred to in section 99(6A) are made on or after the day on which this Act is passed, and

  (b) before the offers are made, units comprising shares in the two companies concerned were offered (whether before or on or after the day on which this Act is passed) in circumstances where section 99(6A) applied without the amendment made by subsection (2) above.

113(6) **[Application of sec. 113(3), (4)]** Subsections (3) and (4) above apply where—

  (a) the shares referred to in section 99(6B) are issued on or after the day on which this Act is passed, and

  (b) before they are issued, units comprising shares in the two companies concerned were offered (whether before or on or after the day on which this Act is passed) in circumstances where section 99(6A) applied without the amendment made by subsection (2) above.